NEWNES

COMPLETE

Word Game DICTIONARY

NEWNES

COMPLETE

Word Game DICTIONARY

Tom Pulliam & Gorton Carruth

NEWNES BOOKS

Scrabble® is a Registered Trade Mark owned in
the United Kingdom and most of the world by
J.W. Spear & Sons plc, Enfield, Middlesex.
Scrabble® is a Registered Trade Mark owned in the USA
and Canada by Selchow and Righter Co., New York.
Reference to Scrabble® is printed with the permission of
Murfett Pty Ltd, 7-13 Keys Rd (PO Box 152), Moorabbin,
Victoria SU. 3189, the Australian owners of Scrabble®.
Hangman® is a Registered Trade Mark owned in the USA by
Hangman Games.
Anagram® is a Registered Trade Mark owned in the USA by
Airtime Mfg. Inc.

Published 1985 by
Newnes Books, a Division of
The Hamlyn Publishing Group Limited
84-88 The Centre, Feltham, Middlesex,
TW13 4BH, England
and distributed for them by
Hamlyn Distribution Services Limited
Rushden, Northants, England

First published 1984 in the USA and the United Kingdom as
The Complete Word Game Dictionary
by Facts on File Publications, New York and Bicester

ISBN 0 600 33263 2

Printed in Finland

Contents

Preface

The *Newnes Complete Word Game Dictionary* is a unique dictionary. Its size and comprehensiveness put it in a class by itself. It is equally useful for tournament play and for family fun at home. It contains 230,000 words specially selected to help players of most word games, both those available in shops, and the kind that involve nothing more elaborate than a pencil and paper. It is designed to be used during play as the standard arbiter of the ever-present "challenge" which occurs in nearly every parlour word game: does your word exist or have you made it up? But the *Newnes Complete Word Game Dictionary* is also designed to be studied before and after play to increase one's knowledge of those words that help to make a player a winner.

Millions play word games. Of all parlour games, word games are perhaps the first that children develop an interest in. Whole families play word games together, not only because of their sharp competitiveness, but also because of their educational value. Even in the solitary activity of the inveterate crossword puzzler, there is something sharply competitive: can the puzzle be broken? And surely crossword puzzlers believe the new words they learn will prove useful. Nearly everyone would agree that, one way or another, a knowledge of words can help bring success in life.

Word games have been played in our own families for as long as we can remember. We were drawn to them as children and, with the passage of time, we have had neither the inclination nor the will-power to break away from their siren attraction.

The earliest in our memories – a game we still play now and then – has neither name nor title, to our knowledge. It consists of nothing more complex than selecting, in random fashion, a standard word from either dictionary or newspaper, which became the "base" word for all players. Any number of players can play. With the "base" word boldly lettered at the top of a sheet of paper and with an egg timer to hand, each player attempts to form new words from the letters contained in the "base" word. Each letter of the "base" word is taken in turn as the initial letter for the new words formed by the competitors.

Scoring, after time is called on each letter, is simplicity itself. For each word on our list we are awarded one point for each other competitor who does *not* have it on his list.

It is anything but a quiet game! chaotic is more like it. Debates are numerous and loud, and a dictionary is likely to be consulted every few moments in an attempt to decide arguments as to the acceptability of words. In our old family games, one of our grandfathers, who has long since departed, had a well-deserved reputation for being a wily, shrewd swindler, given to bluffing with charm and persuasion. Often, too, word games helped to wile away long hours in the family car, and our parents had to act as referees.

This is no place to indulge in personal memories. Suffice it to say that word games, be they simple or complex, are a flourishing activity. We know of no survey or indepth study that has been conducted on such matters, but we venture to say that in the average home of today, one or more of the following are played: crossword puzzles, hangman, word-squares, anagrams, ghost, the word games sold under the Scrabble® brand, and other similar commercially available games.

Of all modern word games, none can rival the acknowledged stature of the Scrabble® brand crossword games. Since it was first invented more than 40 years ago, it captured interest year by year until it has now become an international classic among today's gamesters. The Scrabble® set rests alongside the Monopoly® set in most family rooms. Because it challenges personal aptitudes ranging from structural visualisation to "knowing how to spell", Scrabble® contains some inherent complexities not present in most other word games. In recognition of this fact, the *Newnes Complete Word Game Dictionary* has been organised in such a way that its greatest value will be for the Scrabble® player, whether neophyte or of tournament calibre.

The number of commercial family word games available is growing by leaps and bounds, and practically all of them are absorbing. It is not our intention here to develop to any length the rules and conduct of these games. Each has its distinctive intricacies and individual traits. Some depend on using lettered cards to form words, with graduated rewards to the player for his skill in doing so. These games often require a good deal of guile and bluff as the player has to try to deduce the concealed words formed by his opponents.

Other games use a number of lettered dice. After the player has thrown these dice at random, there is a strictly measured time period during which bona-fide words must be formed from the letters that have been turned up. In some, the score depends on the number of words of different lengths that the player can construct; in others, the words formed must intersect, much in the style of crossword puzzles or the Scrabble® brand games.

Traditional word games have rules and procedures that are almost universally recognised and accepted, even though the games themselves have many forms and variations. We will briefly describe a few of our own favourites:

Anagrams is played with lettered cards or tiles. These are normally exposed one at a time in the centre of the playing area. Within a specified time any player may form acceptable words by withdrawing the required letters from the pile in the centre. Words formed by any player are liable to capture by any other player, to form a new word, incorporating the original word and adding on to it one or more other letters from the pile. Generally some basic change in the form and meaning of the word is a prerequisite for a capture.

In **Guggenheim**, or **Categories**, each player in turn names aloud one category (colour, country, tree, sport, etc.) and these categories are listed by each player in a vertical column on a piece of paper. Another word is then selected, either at random or by agreement. This word is not normally very long, contains no unusual letters and no repeated letters. Each player then writes the letters of this word by each vertical heading, and then attempts to find acceptable words for that category that begin with each letter in turn of the key-word. Thus, if the key-word is *table* and one of the categories is "colour", the player might enter the words *tan, azure, blue, lilac, emerald*.

In **Ghost**, each player in turn names a letter aloud. Letters thus announced are mentally visualised by all players as being written in the order in which they are announced. From the fourth letter onwards, each player attempts to continue the process by adding another letter while taking care not to form a complete word. He cannot, however, name any letter at random; he has to be prepared to face a challenge and state what word he has in mind that contains the letter-chain he has made. Thus, is the letters BEA are presented to a player, he obviously wishes to avoid ending a word by choosing D M N R T or U. Instead, he will perhaps add a G, forming BEAG, with the word *beagle* in mind. The succeeding players will look out for this and try somehow to avoid the trap.

Normally, a player ending a word or caught in a bluff becomes "one-third of a ghost" and begins a new word. The next time he falls into error he becomes "two-thirds of a ghost". After three such losses, the player is eliminated, while the game continues among the survivors until only one remains.

Superghost is an embellishment of Ghost. Here the player may add his letter before or after the letter-chain with which he has been faced. For example, if presented with STABL, he might choose to prefix N to form NSTABL, with the word *unstable* in mind. The trap may not work, however, as the next player then might prefix an O, thinking of the word *constable*. The game calls for an agile mind and an ample vocabulary, and no-one should be over-hasty in challenging without weighing the calibre of the opponent.

Hangman is relatively simple, and a game for two. One player thinks of a word and represents it on paper by a series of dashes, one for each letter. The other player simply tries to guess the word by naming letters of the alphabet. If he "hits" a letter in the concealed word, it is written into its appropriate position. If not, his opponent draws a piece of a gallows. The object is to guess the word before you have been "hanged" for your number of wrong guesses.

The *Newnes Complete Word Game Dictionary* has been developed as an aid and a wit-sharpener for the countless people who indulge in these and similar word games.

Part 1: The Comprehensive Word List

In practically all competitive word games there arises what is known as the "challenge". Most such games would be mild and placid were it not for this device. The word is self-explanatory: one player has made use of a word, another disagrees with its spelling or its validity, and issues a challenge to the first player to justify his word. Though the rules of many board games are not explicit about the steps to be taken after a challenge, most games agree in permitting the use of practically any word "found in a standard dictionary".

It sounds simple, but what happens in the heat of a hard-fought game, the outcome of which may depend on the resolution of the challenge? The opponents ought to have decided, before the contest, as to which edition of what dictionary will be used to settle any such differences. I may place great weight on my pet dictionary with which I am very familiar; but can I persuade you, my opponent, to accept it as the arbitrating medium – or do you prefer to use a different dictionary of your own?

Modern desk dictionaries, though valuable for normal day-to-day uses, are not adequate as mediators for word games, which are becoming increasingly complex. The home dictionary will usually contain something under 60,000 words. And it may well not include words of recent origin, especially technical or scientific terms, or the many words that are flooding into English from other languages. It may serve to clarify your game query to the satisfaction of all – or it may not.

Even after a dictionary has been selected, lesser questions still hinder the progress of the game. Are proper nouns permitted? How about foreign words? Abbreviations? Past tenses? Illogical plurals? Irregular endings? And so it goes on.

These problems lead us to the underlying premise and purpose of the *Newnes Complete Word Game Dictionary*. The greater part of it is devoted to a Comprehensive Word List, which serves, in the speediest way possible, to decide the acceptability of any word that arises during your game.

Does it have advantages over a dictionary that is mutually acceptable to all players? We believe it does.

In looking up any word in this Comprehensive Word List at the time of a challenge, you only have to skim through a single alphabetical list of 185,000 words to the exact word in question, be it commonplace or esoteric.

Not so with a normal dictionary. The major objective of a dictionary is to define and clarify the meaning of words, and the bulk of its space is occupied by definitive and descriptive text. Valuable though such information may be, the impatient player must wade through it to arrive at the word under challenge – all in the interests of a word game in which meanings play no role. So the Comprehensive Word List is, first of all, the easiest, quickest source for deciding on the acceptability of a questionable word.

Is it complete? The answer is an overwhelming Yes. The Comprehensive Word List is not based on any single dictionary. And, with its grand total of 185,000 words, it goes well beyond the scope of any desktop dictionary.

If a word is to be found in one dictionary but not in others, is it any less of a word? We think not. We will not launch into a philosophical discussion about what a word is; it remains largely a matter of editorial judgement. And we are relieving you, the player of word games, of becoming embroiled in this morass of judgement. When a challenge arises you have the simplest of all methods for resolving it – simply consult the Comprehensive Word List.

Let us further examine this Comprehensive Word List to discover what it does and does not contain.

Proper Names

Consider, for example, the use of proper nouns. It is up to you, the user, to determine whether your word game permits the use of proper names. Most do not. A certain game, for instance, specifies that "capitalised" words are not acceptable. This immediately throws us on the mercy of the "dictionary of your choice". If this should happen to be the *Oxford English Dictionary*, the whole game must immediately end – because *each* word listed therein is capitalised! At the other extreme, you may have agreed upon the *Merriam-Webster International Dictionary*, 3rd Edition, an equally reputable tome. You are now overwhelmed to find that "the sky's the limit": with very rare exceptions, no main entry is capitalised. You have to pore through the descriptive text to discover that a given word is "usually capitalised", "sometimes capitalised", etc.

So, to relieve you of this dilemma, we have established our own editorial criterion. Because most word games prohibit their use, we have excluded from the List all words that are always capitalised. You may find, on thumbing through the List, some words that seem to be proper names: Argentine, Inverness, Telamon, for example. But note that we have stated that we have omitted only words that are *always* capitalised. You will be well aware that "china" need not be capitalised when it is referring to porcelain; "argentine" is included here in its meaning of silvery, "inverness" is an overcoat, and "telamon" is an architectural figure.

To sum up, a word appears in the List only if we have found it as a common, or uncapitalised, word, in at least one source. As such, it deserves inclusion and warrants your using it freely in word games.

Foreign words

Most word games have some stated prohibition against the use of words "designated as foreign words". But one has only to scan representative dictionaries to see that they differ in their manner of designating foreign words. Some use special symbols antecedent to the main entry; others place the burden solely on the etymology to indicate the degree of "foreignness".

In the heat of a hotly contested word game you should not have to be concerned with such interpretations and decisions. The foreign word of yesterday is the English word of today. Such words as *confetti, junta, dirndl* and *houri* are commonplace to most game players now, without thought as to their being foreign in the recent past. So we have taken the view that the only foreign words are those that are *solely* foreign in their use. If a word appears in an authoritative English dictionary, regardless of foreign designation by either symbol or text, we have included it in the Comprehensive Word List and consider it acceptable for word play.

Variant and Archaic Forms

The same can be said for variant spellings, and archaic and obsolete words. Eventually many of these words will fade from current usage completely and will be, undoubtedly, dropped from reputable dictionaries. Until that time, we have included archaic and variant spellings. Indeed, in our experience they add spice to the game and often present an escape outlet just when we are being painted into a corner in a tight crossword game.

Long Words

You will quickly note many long words in the Comprehensive Word List. Remembering that in a game such as Scrabble® you have only seven letters to play with, you may doubt the value of, say, the twelve-letter words.

Yet, as top players know, the best scores are made by interconnecting with the letters already on the board, one or more. So while they are uncommon in normal social games, words of twelve letters or more are conceivable and actually occur in Scrabble® game patterns.

This does not mean we have included willy-nilly all long words that exist in reputable sources. We have exercised editorial prerogative here. If a long word is based upon an internal "root" word of common vintage, the chances are we have included it. The expert player closely inspects all existing words on the board to find a chance of adding letters to it fore or aft, or both. So we have chosen long words whose roots may easily be played in normal competition.

Verb Endings, Plurals and Adverbial Forms

These present a problem in all word games where the challenge is a factor. The rule of most word games are not sufficiently explicit to be certain of the permissibility of words in these categories. In Superghost, in particular, players are tempted to weasel out of a tight spot by means of a hastily contrived gerundive or participial form. In Scrabble®, the normal inflected forms are acceptable, whether or not they are specifically printed in standard dictionaries. These normal forms include past tense, past participle and present participle of verbs, and the plural of nouns. This gives free licence for the use of *-s, -es, -ed* and *-ing*. In most dictionaries such forms are entered only where there is an irregularity in spelling or form.

Comparative (*-er*) and superlative (*-est*) forms of adjectives are a somewhat different matter. One-syllable adjectives and their comparative and superlative forms (*strong, stronger, strongest*) are presumed to be acceptable, whether listed or not. Multisyllable adjectives are only permissible if the comparative and superlative forms actually appear in the agreed-upon authority.

The Comprehensive Word List frees you from the need for personal interpretation and judgement. It does not list *all* simple plurals that can be formed merely by adding *-s* or *-es*, though a great many are included. But it liberally includes inflected forms and unusual plurals, including those you might have trouble ferreting out of the dictionary. For instance, you might have trouble checking these plural forms in a normal dictionary: *feis* – plural *feiseanna*; *os* – *ora*; *drostdy* – *drostden*.

Definitions
One instantly apparent characteristic of the List is the absence of definitions. This is because we see no significant value or need for definitions in most word games. The basic consideration is simply whether the challenged word exists or not.

Some excellent books that serve as arbiters for word-game play do include definitions. But their users, in our experience, do not employ these definitions to edify the mind. The expressed purpose of the definitions is no more than to clarify the part of speech, and consequently the admissibility of plurals and inflected forms. The Comprehensive Word List already contains most inflected forms as well as unusual plurals. Including definitions as well would have been a labour of love without a corresponding benefit for the user.

Part 2: **The High-Scoring Word Lists**

In recognition of the more complex play found in Scrabble® over other word games, the *Newnes Complete Word Game Dictionary* contains a number of specialised lists. These are intended for the Scrabble® player, though their value extends to other word games as well.

Success in Scrabble® of course depends in large degree on the opportune placement of the high-scoring letters Z (ten points), Q (ten points), J (eight points) and X (eight points). Thus the high-scoring lists of Part 2 have been framed around words containing these four key letters. Each of these letters has a section, within which words are arranged first by word length, and then by type of list. There are three types of list: alphabetical, positional and scoring.

Alphabetical Lists
For any one of these key letters there first appear the Alphabetical Lists, arranged by word length, of acceptable words containing that letter. You should use these lists to become familiar with as many of the two- and three-letter words as you can. Most experts agree that familiarity with these words is a key factor in top-quality play, since they represent

the essential links in the interlocking process of forming new words in conjunction with those already appearing on the board.

Positional Lists
We have also prepared Positional Lists, by word length, for each of the key letters. These have a value far beyond the Scrabble® board; for instance for the crossword player who may be seeking a six-letter word with a Z in the fifth position.

Scoring Order Lists
Finally we have included for each of the key letters a Scoring Order List, in which the words are listed in order of the total Scrabble® score of all letters, arranged by word length.

This may require some clarification. We cannot, of course, allow for the variations in score brought about by double- or triple-letter scores. And you may come across some words, such as *jazz*, which seem to need more than the single Z tile that the Scrabble® set contains. In such cases we have assumed that the "extra" letter is formed by a blank or wild tile and its value has been computed as zero.

Perhaps you are a true logophile – one whose interest in words extends far beyond the confines of any single word game. You and others like you are blessed with a quarterly publication, *Word Ways: The Journal of Recreational Linguistics*. It deals with the appearance, spelling, derivation, sound, use and peculiarities of words and word forms. Information about it can be obtained from the editor: A. Ross Eckler, Spring Valley Road, Morristown, New Jersey 07960, USA. Many of the journal's readers are deeply involved in the gaming possibilities of high-scoring combinations and interesting patterns in Scrabble®. You and I, as average players, should not be unduly perturbed to learn that *Word Ways* contributors have constructed a theoretically possible Scrabble® crossword game with a combined score of 4,142 points for the two players! You might want to bear in mind, though, the single play that can bring you a score of 1,804 points (the word *benzoxycamphors*).

The *Newnes Complete Word Game Dictionary* is intended to be used. In any word game in which the challenge arises, it is meant to be a handy arbiter. If you familiarise yourself with the contents of this volume and actually use it for its intended purposes, it cannot help but promote your progress as a gamester – without diluting the fun!

Tom Pulliam
Gorton Carruth

PART I

Comprehensive Word List

AA
AABEC
AAL
AALII
AAM
AAR
AARDVARK
AARDWOLF
AASVOGEL
ABA
ABACA
ABACATE
ABACAXI
ABACAY
ABACI
ABACINATE
ABACINATION
ABACISCUS
ABACIST
ABACK
ABACOT
ABACTINAL
ABACTINALLY
ABACTION
ABACTOR
ABACULI
ABACULUS
ABACUS
ABACUSES
ABAD
ABADA
ABADEJO
ABADENGO
ABADI
ABADIA
ABAFF
ABAFT
ABAISANCE
ABAISER
ABAISSE
ABAISSED
ABAKA
ABALIENATE
ABALIENATED
ABALIENATION
ABALONE
ABAMPERE
ABAND
ABANDON
ABANDONED
ABANDONEDLY
ABANDONER
ABANDONMENT
ABANDUM
ABANGA
ABAPTISTON
ABAPTISTUM
ABARTICULAR
ABARTICULATION
ABAS
ABASE
ABASED
ABASEDLY
ABASEDNESS
ABASEMENT
ABASER
ABASH
ABASHED
ABASHEDLY
ABASHING
ABASHLESS
ABASHLESSLY
ABASHMENT
ABASIA
ABASING
ABASIO
ABASK
ABASSI
ABASTARDIZE
ABATA
ABATABLE
ABATE
ABATED
ABATEMENT
ABATER
ABATI
ABATING
ABATIS
ABATON
ABATOR
ABATTIS
ABATTISED
ABATTOIR
ABATTOIRS
ABATTU
ABATTUE
ABATURE
ABAVE
ABAWE
ABAXIAL
ABAXILE
ABAYAH
ABAZE
ABB
ABBA
ABBACIES
ABBACY
ABBAS
ABBASI
ABBASSI
ABBATE
ABBATIAL
ABBATICAL
ABBAYE
ABBE
ABBESS
ABBEST
ABBEY
ABBEYS
ABBEYSTEDE
ABBOGADA
ABBOT
ABBOTCIES
ABBOTCY
ABBOTSHIP
ABBOZZO
ABBREVIATE
ABBREVIATED
ABBREVIATELY
ABBREVIATING
ABBREVIATION
ABBREVIATOR
ABBREVIATORY
ABBREVIATURE
ABCOULOMB
ABDAL
ABDALI
ABDAT
ABDEST
ABDICABLE
ABDICANT
ABDICATE
ABDICATED
ABDICATING
ABDICATION
ABDICATIVE
ABDICATOR
ABDITIVE
ABDITORY
ABDOMEN
ABDOMINAL
ABDOMINALES
ABDOMINALIAN
ABDOMINALLY
ABDOMINALS
ABDOMINOUS
ABDUCE
ABDUCENS
ABDUCENT
ABDUCT
ABDUCTED
ABDUCTION
ABDUCTOR
ABE
ABEAM
ABEAR
ABEARANCE
ABECEDAIRE
ABECEDARIA
ABECEDARIAN
ABECEDARIES
ABECEDARIUM
ABECEDARIUS
ABECEDARY
ABED
ABEEN
ABEGGE
ABEIGH
ABELE
ABELITE
ABELMOSK
ABELMUSK
ABELTREE
ABENTERIC
ABEPITHYMIA
ABERDAVINE
ABERDEVINE
ABERDUVINE
ABERR
ABERRANCE
ABERRANCY
ABERRANT
ABERRATE
ABERRATED
ABERRATING
ABERRATION
ABERRATIONAL
ABERRATOR
ABERROMETER
ABERROSCOPE
ABESSIVE
ABET
ABETMENT
ABETO
ABETTAL
ABETTED
ABETTER
ABETTING
ABETTOR
ABEVACUATION
ABEY
ABEYANCE
ABEYANCY
ABEYANT
ABFARAD
ABHAL
ABHENRY
ABHINAYA
ABHISEKA
ABHOMINABLE
ABHOR
ABHORRED
ABHORRENCE
ABHORRENCY
ABHORRENT
ABHORRENTLY
ABHORRER
ABHORRIBLE
ABHORRING
ABIDAL
ABIDANCE
ABIDDEN
ABIDE
ABIDED
ABIDER
ABIDING
ABIDINGLY
ABIDINGNESS
ABIEGH
ABIENCE
ABIETATE
ABIETENE
ABIETIC
ABIETINEOUS
ABIETINIC
ABIGAIL
ABIGAILSHIP
ABIGEI
ABIGEUS
ABILAO
ABILITIES
ABILITY
ABILLA
ABILO
ABIME
ABINTESTATE
ABIOGENESIS
ABIOGENETIC
ABIOGENIST
ABIOLOGICAL
ABIOLOGY
ABIOSIS
ABIOTIC
ABIOTROPHIC
ABIOTROPHY
ABIR
ABIRRITANT
ABIRRITATE
ABIRRITATED
ABIRRITATING
ABIRRITATION
ABIRRITATIVE
ABISTON
ABIURET
ABJECT
ABJECTEDNESS
ABJECTION
ABJECTIVE
ABJECTLY
ABJECTNESS
ABJOINT
ABJUDGE
ABJUDICATE
ABJUDICATION
ABJUDICATOR
ABJUNCTIVE
ABJURATION
ABJURATORY
ABJURE
ABJURED
ABJUREMENT
ABJURER
ABJURING
ABKAR
ABKARI
ABKARY
ABLACH
ABLACTATE
ABLACTATION
ABLARE
ABLASTEMIC
ABLASTIN
ABLASTOUS
ABLATE
ABLATION
ABLATITIOUS
ABLATIVAL
ABLATIVE
ABLATOR
ABLAUT
ABLAZE
ABLE
ABLEEZE
ABLEGATE
ABLEGATION
ABLENESS
ABLEPHARIA
ABLEPHAROUS
ABLEPSIA
ABLEPSY
ABLEPTICAL
ABLEPTICALLY
ABLER
ABLEST
ABLEWHACKETS
ABLINGS
ABLINS
ABLOOM
ABLOW
ABLUDE
ABLUENT
ABLUSH
ABLUTION
ABLUTIONARY
ABLY
ABNEGATE
ABNEGATED
ABNEGATING
ABNEGATION
ABNEGATIVE
ABNEGATOR
ABNERVAL
ABNET
ABNEURAL
ABNORMAL
ABNORMALITIES
ABNORMALITY
ABNORMALIZE
ABNORMALLY
ABNORMALNESS
ABNORMITIES
ABNORMITY
ABNORMOUS
ABOARD
ABOCOCKET
ABODAH
ABODE
ABODED
ABODEMENT
ABODING
ABOGADO
ABOGADOS
ABOHM
ABOIDEAU
ABOIDEAUS
ABOIDEAUX
ABOIL
ABOITEAU
ABOLETE
ABOLISH
ABOLISHABLE
ABOLISHED
ABOLISHER
ABOLISHING
ABOLISHMENT

ABOLITION
ABOLITIONARY
ABOLITIONISM
ABOLITIONIST
ABOLITIONIZE
ABOLLA
ABOLLAE
ABOMA
ABOMASUM
ABOMASUS
ABOMINABLE
ABOMINABLY
ABOMINATE
ABOMINATED
ABOMINATING
ABOMINATION
ABOMINATOR
ABONDANCE
ABONNE
ABONNEMENT
ABOO
ABOON
ABORAD
ABORAL
ABORALLY
ABORD
ABORIGINAL
ABORIGINALLY
ABORIGINARY
ABORIGINE
ABORIGINES
ABORT
ABORTED
ABORTICIDE
ABORTIENT
ABORTIN
ABORTION
ABORTIONAL
ABORTIONIST
ABORTIVE
ABORTIVELY
ABORTIVENESS
ABORTUS
ABOUCHEMENT
ABOUGHT
ABOULIA
ABOULIC
ABOUND
ABOUNDING
ABOUNDINGLY
ABOUT
ABOUTS
ABOVE
ABOVEBOARD
ABOVEDECK
ABOVEGROUND
ABOVEPROOF
ABOVESTAIRS
ABOW
ABOX
ABRA
ABRACADABRA
ABRACHIA
ABRADANT
ABRADE
ABRADED
ABRADER
ABRADING
ABRAID
ABRANCHIAL
ABRANCHIAN
ABRANCHIATE
ABRANCHIOUS
ABRASAX
ABRASE
ABRASED
ABRASH
ABRASING
ABRASIOMETER
ABRASION
ABRASIVE
ABRASIVES
ABRASTOL
ABRAUM
ABRAXAS
ABRAZO
ABREACT
ABREACTION
ABREAST
ABREED
ABREGE
ABREID
ABRENOUNCE
ABRENUNCIATE
ABRET
ABREUVOIR
ABRI
ABRICO
ABRICOT
ABRIDGABLE
ABRIDGE
ABRIDGEABLE
ABRIDGED
ABRIDGEDLY
ABRIDGEMENT
ABRIDGER
ABRIDGING
ABRIDGMENT
ABRIM
ABRIN
ABRINE
ABRIS
ABRISTLE
ABROACH
ABROAD
ABROCOME
ABROGABLE
ABROGATE
ABROGATED
ABROGATING
ABROGATION
ABROGATIVE
ABROGATOR
ABRONIA
ABROOD
ABROOK
ABROTANUM
ABROTIN
ABROTINE
ABRUPT
ABRUPTEDLY
ABRUPTION
ABRUPTLY
ABRUPTNESS
ABSAROKITE
ABSCESS
ABSCESSED
ABSCESSES
ABSCESSION
ABSCESSROOT
ABSCIND
ABSCISE
ABSCISED
ABSCISING
ABSCISS
ABSCISSA
ABSCISSAE
ABSCISSAS
ABSCISSION
ABSCONCE
ABSCOND
ABSCONDED
ABSCONDEDLY
ABSCONDENCE
ABSCONDER
ABSEIL
ABSENCE
ABSENT
ABSENTATION
ABSENTEE
ABSENTEEISM
ABSENTER
ABSENTLY
ABSENTMENT
ABSENTMINDED
ABSENTMINDEDNESS
ABSENTNESS
ABSINTH
ABSINTHE
ABSINTHIAL
ABSINTHIAN
ABSINTHIATE
ABSINTHIATED
ABSINTHIATING
ABSINTHIC
ABSINTHIIN
ABSINTHIN
ABSINTHINE
ABSINTHISM
ABSINTHISMIC
ABSINTHIUM
ABSISTOS
ABSIT
ABSOLUTE
ABSOLUTELY
ABSOLUTENESS
ABSOLUTION
ABSOLUTISM
ABSOLUTIST
ABSOLUTISTA
ABSOLUTISTIC
ABSOLUTIVE
ABSOLUTORY
ABSOLVABLE
ABSOLVATORY
ABSOLVE
ABSOLVED
ABSOLVENT
ABSOLVER
ABSOLVING
ABSOLVITOR
ABSOLVITORY
ABSONANT
ABSORB
ABSORBABILITY
ABSORBABLE
ABSORBANCY
ABSORBED
ABSORBEDLY
ABSORBEDNESS
ABSORBENCY
ABSORBENT
ABSORBER
ABSORBING
ABSORBINGLY
ABSORBITION
ABSORPT
ABSORPTANCE
ABSORPTION
ABSORPTIVE
ABSORPTIVITY
ABSQUATULATE
ABSTAIN
ABSTAINER
ABSTAINMENT
ABSTEMIOUS
ABSTEMIOUSLY
ABSTENTION
ABSTENTIOUS
ABSTERGE
ABSTERGED
ABSTERGENT
ABSTERGING
ABSTERSION
ABSTERSIVE
ABSTINENCE
ABSTINENCY
ABSTINENT
ABSTINENTIAL
ABSTINENTLY
ABSTORT
ABSTRACT
ABSTRACTED
ABSTRACTEDLY
ABSTRACTEDNESS
ABSTRACTER
ABSTRACTION
ABSTRACTIVE
ABSTRACTIVELY
ABSTRACTIVENESS
ABSTRACTLY
ABSTRACTNESS
ABSTRACTS
ABSTRAHENT
ABSTRICT
ABSTRICTED
ABSTRICTION
ABSTRUDE
ABSTRUSE
ABSTRUSELY
ABSTRUSENESS
ABSTRUSION
ABSTRUSITIES
ABSTRUSITY
ABSUME
ABSUMPTION
ABSURD
ABSURDITIES
ABSURDITY
ABSURDLY
ABSURDNESS
ABSURDUM
ABTERMINAL
ABTHANAGE
ABU
ABUCCO
ABULEIA
ABULIA
ABULIC
ABULOMANIA
ABULYEIT
ABUNA
ABUNDANCE
ABUNDANCY
ABUNDANT
ABUNDANTLY
ABUNE
ABURA
ABURABOZU
ABURAGIRI
ABURST
ABURTON
ABUSABLE
ABUSAGE
ABUSE
ABUSED
ABUSEE
ABUSER
ABUSING
ABUSION
ABUSIOUS
ABUSIVE
ABUSIVELY
ABUSIVENESS
ABUT
ABUTTAL
ABUTTALS
ABUTTED
ABUTTER
ABUTTING
ABUZZ
ABVOLT
ABWAB
ABWATT
ABY
ABYE
ABYSM
ABYSMAL
ABYSMALLY
ABYSS
ABYSSAL
ACACATECHIN
ACACATECHOL
ACACETIN
ACACIA
ACACIIN
ACACIN
ACACINE
ACADEME
ACADEMIA
ACADEMIAL
ACADEMIAN
ACADEMIC
ACADEMICAL
ACADEMICALLY
ACADEMICALS
ACADEMICIAN
ACADEMICISM
ACADEMIE
ACADEMIES
ACADEMISM
ACADEMIST
ACADEMITE
ACADEMIZE
ACADEMIZED
ACADEMIZING
ACADEMY
ACADIALITE
ACAENA
ACAJOU
ACALE
ACALEPH
ACALEPHAN
ACALEPHE
ACALEPHOID
ACALYCAL
ACALYCINE
ACALYCINOUS
ACALYCULATE
ACALYPTRATE
ACAMPSIA
ACANA
ACANACEOUS
ACANTH
ACANTHA
ACANTHACEOUS
ACANTHAD
ACANTHI
ACANTHIAL
ACANTHIN
ACANTHINE
ACANTHION
ACANTHITE
ACANTHODEAN
ACANTHODIAN
ACANTHOLOGY
ACANTHOLYSIS
ACANTHOMA
ACANTHON
ACANTHOPOD
ACANTHOPORE
ACANTHOSIS
ACANTHOUS
ACANTHUS
ACANTHUSES

ACAPNIA
ACAPNIAL
ACAPSULAR
ACAPU
ACAPULCO
ACARA
ACARDIA
ACARDIAC
ACARDITE
ACARI
ACARIAN
ACARIASIS
ACARIATRE
ACARICIDAL
ACARICIDE
ACARID
ACARIDOMATIA
ACARIFORM
ACARINE
ACAROCECIDIA
ACAROID
ACAROL
ACAROLOGIST
ACAROLOGY
ACAROPHILOUS
ACAROPHOBIA
ACAROTOXIC
ACARPELLOUS
ACARPELOUS
ACARPOUS
ACATALECTIC
ACATALEPSIA
ACATALEPSY
ACATALEPTIC
ACATAPHASIA
ACATAPOSIS
ACATASTASIA
ACATASTATIC
ACATE
ACATER
ACATERY
ACATES
ACATHARSIA
ACATHARSY
ACATHOLIC
ACAUDAL
ACAUDATE
ACAULESCENCE
ACAULESCENT
ACAULINE
ACAULOSE
ACAULOUS
ACCA
ACCABLE
ACCADEMIA
ACCEDE
ACCEDED
ACCEDENCE
ACCEDER
ACCEDING
ACCELERABLE
ACCELERANDO
ACCELERANT
ACCELERATE
ACCELERATED
ACCELERATEDLY
ACCELERATING
ACCELERATION
ACCELERATIVE
ACCELERATOR
ACCELERATORY
ACCEND
ACCENDIBLE
ACCENSION
ACCENSOR
ACCENT
ACCENTED
ACCENTOR
ACCENTUABLE
ACCENTUAL
ACCENTUALITY
ACCENTUALLY
ACCENTUATE
ACCENTUATED
ACCENTUATING
ACCENTUATION
ACCENTUATOR
ACCENTUS
ACCEPT
ACCEPTABILITY
ACCEPTABLE
ACCEPTABLENESS
ACCEPTABLY
ACCEPTANCE
ACCEPTANCY
ACCEPTANT
ACCEPTATION
ACCEPTED
ACCEPTEDLY
ACCEPTER
ACCEPTILATE
ACCEPTILATED
ACCEPTILATING
ACCEPTILATION
ACCEPTION
ACCEPTIVE
ACCEPTOR
ACCERSE
ACCERSITION
ACCERSITOR
ACCESS
ACCESSARILY
ACCESSARY
ACCESSIBILITY
ACCESSIBLE
ACCESSIBLY
ACCESSION
ACCESSIONAL
ACCESSIONED
ACCESSIONING
ACCESSIT
ACCESSIVE
ACCESSIVELY
ACCESSLESS
ACCESSORIAL
ACCESSORIES
ACCESSORII
ACCESSORILY
ACCESSORIUS
ACCESSORY
ACCIACCATURA
ACCIDENCE
ACCIDENCIES
ACCIDENCY
ACCIDENT
ACCIDENTAL
ACCIDENTALITY
ACCIDENTALLY
ACCIDENTARILY
ACCIDENTARY
ACCIDENTED
ACCIDENTIAL
ACCIDENTLY
ACCIDIA
ACCIDIE
ACCINGE
ACCINGED
ACCINGING
ACCIPITER
ACCIPITRAL
ACCIPITRARY
ACCIPITRINE
ACCIPTER
ACCISMUS
ACCITE
ACCLAIM
ACCLAIMABLE
ACCLAIMER
ACCLAMATION
ACCLAMATOR
ACCLAMATORY
ACCLIMATABLE
ACCLIMATE
ACCLIMATED
ACCLIMATING
ACCLIMATION
ACCLIMATIZE
ACCLIMATIZED
ACCLIMATIZER
ACCLIMATIZING
ACCLIMATURE
ACCLINAL
ACCLINATE
ACCLIVITIES
ACCLIVITOUS
ACCLIVITY
ACCLIVOUS
ACCLOY
ACCOAST
ACCOIL
ACCOLADE
ACCOLADED
ACCOLENT
ACCOLL
ACCOLLE
ACCOLLEE
ACCOMBINATION
ACCOMMODABLE
ACCOMMODATE
ACCOMMODATED
ACCOMMODATING
ACCOMMODATION
ACCOMMODATIVE
ACCOMMODATOR
ACCOMPANIED
ACCOMPANIER
ACCOMPANIMENT
ACCOMPANIST
ACCOMPANY
ACCOMPANYING
ACCOMPANYIST
ACCOMPLETIVE
ACCOMPLICE
ACCOMPLICITY
ACCOMPLISH
ACCOMPLISHED
ACCOMPLISHER
ACCOMPLISHING
ACCOMPLISHMENT
ACCOMPT
ACCON
ACCORD
ACCORDABLE
ACCORDANCE
ACCORDANCY
ACCORDANT
ACCORDANTLY
ACCORDATURA
ACCORDER
ACCORDING
ACCORDINGLY
ACCORDION
ACCORDIONIST
ACCORPORATE
ACCOST
ACCOSTABLE
ACCOSTED
ACCOUCHE
ACCOUCHEMENT
ACCOUCHEUR
ACCOUCHEUSE
ACCOUNT
ACCOUNTABILITY
ACCOUNTABLE
ACCOUNTABLY
ACCOUNTANCY
ACCOUNTANT
ACCOUNTING
ACCOUNTS
ACCOUPLE
ACCOUTER
ACCOUTERED
ACCOUTERING
ACCOUTERMENT
ACCOUTERMENTS
ACCOUTRE
ACCOUTRED
ACCOUTREMENT
ACCOUTRING
ACCOY
ACCOYED
ACCOYING
ACCREDIT
ACCREDITATION
ACCREDITED
ACCREDITING
ACCRESCE
ACCRESCENCE
ACCRESCENT
ACCRETE
ACCRETED
ACCRETING
ACCRETION
ACCRETIONARY
ACCRETIVE
ACCROACH
ACCROACHED
ACCROACHING
ACCRUAL
ACCRUE
ACCRUED
ACCRUEMENT
ACCRUER
ACCRUING
ACCUBATION
ACCUBITA
ACCUBITUM
ACCUBITUS
ACCUEIL
ACCULTURAL
ACCULTURATE
ACCULTURATION
ACCULTURIZE
ACCUMB
ACCUMBENCY
ACCUMBENT
ACCUMBER
ACCUMULABLE
ACCUMULATE
ACCUMULATED
ACCUMULATING
ACCUMULATION
ACCUMULATIVE
ACCUMULATIVELY
ACCUMULATIVENESS
ACCUMULATOR
ACCURACY
ACCURATE
ACCURATELY
ACCURATENESS
ACCURRE
ACCURSE
ACCURSED
ACCURSEDLY
ACCURSEDNESS
ACCURSING
ACCURST
ACCUSABLE
ACCUSABLY
ACCUSAL
ACCUSANT
ACCUSATION
ACCUSATIVAL
ACCUSATIVE
ACCUSATIVELY
ACCUSATORIAL
ACCUSATORY
ACCUSATRIX
ACCUSE
ACCUSED
ACCUSER
ACCUSING
ACCUSINGLY
ACCUSIVE
ACCUSTOM
ACCUSTOMED
ACCUSTOMEDLY
ACCUSTOMING
ACCUSTOMIZE
ACCUSTOMIZED
ACCUSTOMIZING
ACE
ACEANTHRENE
ACECAFFIN
ACECAFFINE
ACECONITIC
ACED
ACEDIA
ACEDIAMIN
ACEDIAMINE
ACEDIAST
ACEITE
ACEITUNA
ACELDAMA
ACEMILA
ACENAPHTHENE
ACENSUADA
ACENSUADOR
ACENTRIC
ACENTROUS
ACEOLOGIC
ACEOLOGY
ACEPHAL
ACEPHALINE
ACEPHALIST
ACEPHALOCYST
ACEPHALOUS
ACEPHALUS
ACEPOTS
ACEQUIA
ACEQUIADOR
ACERACEOUS
ACERATE
ACERATED
ACERATHERE
ACERATOSIS
ACERB
ACERBATE
ACERBATED
ACERBATING
ACERBIC
ACERBITIES
ACERBITUDE
ACERBITY
ACERDOL
ACERIN
ACEROLA
ACEROSE
ACEROUS
ACERRA
ACERTANNIN
ACERVAL
ACERVATE
ACERVATELY
ACERVATIM

ACERVATION
ACERVATIVE
ACERVOSE
ACERVULI
ACERVULINE
ACERVULUS
ACES
ACESCENCE
ACESCENCY
ACESCENT
ACESODYNE
ACETA
ACETABLE
ACETABULA
ACETABULAR
ACETABULUM
ACETAL
ACETALDEHYDE
ACETALDOL
ACETALIZE
ACETAMID
ACETAMIDE
ACETAMIDINE
ACETAMIDO
ACETAMINOL
ACETANILID
ACETANILIDE
ACETANION
ACETANISIDE
ACETARIOUS
ACETARSONE
ACETATE
ACETATED
ACETATION
ACETENYL
ACETIAM
ACETIC
ACETIFICATION
ACETIFIED
ACETIFIER
ACETIFY
ACETIFYING
ACETIMETER
ACETIMETRY
ACETIN
ACETINE
ACETOACETATE
ACETOACETIC
ACETOBENZOIC
ACETOCHLORAL
ACETOIN
ACETOL
ACETOLYSIS
ACETOLYTIC
ACETOMETER
ACETOMETRY
ACETOMORPHIN
ACETONAEMIA
ACETONAEMIC
ACETONATE
ACETONATION
ACETONE
ACETONEMIA
ACETONEMIC
ACETONIC
ACETONITRILE
ACETONIZATION
ACETONIZE
ACETONURIA
ACETONYL
ACETOPHENIN
ACETOPHENINE
ACETOPHENONE
ACETOPYRIN
ACETOPYRINE
ACETOSE
ACETOSITY
ACETOSOLUBLE
ACETOTOLUID
ACETOTOLUIDE
ACETOUS
ACETOXIM
ACETOXIME
ACETOXYL
ACETRACT
ACETTOLUIDE
ACETUM
ACETURIC
ACETYL
ACETYLAMINE
ACETYLATE
ACETYLATED
ACETYLATING
ACETYLATION
ACETYLATOR
ACETYLBIURET
ACETYLENE
ACETYLENIC
ACETYLENYL
ACETYLGLYCIN
ACETYLIC
ACETYLID
ACETYLIDE
ACETYLIODIDE
ACETYLIZABLE
ACETYLIZATION
ACETYLIZE
ACETYLIZER
ACETYLSALOL
ACETYLTHYMOL
ACETYLUREA
ACH
ACHAETOUS
ACHAFE
ACHAGE
ACHALASIA
ACHAR
ACHARNE
ACHARNEMENT
ACHARYA
ACHATE
ACHATES
ACHATOUR
ACHE
ACHED
ACHEILIA
ACHEILOUS
ACHEIRIA
ACHEIROUS
ACHEIRUS
ACHENE
ACHENIA
ACHENIAL
ACHENIUM
ACHENOCARP
ACHENODIA
ACHENODIUM
ACHER
ACHETE
ACHEWEED
ACHIEVABLE
ACHIEVE
ACHIEVED
ACHIEVEMENT
ACHIEVEMENTS
ACHIEVER
ACHIEVING
ACHIGAN
ACHILARY
ACHILL
ACHILLEIN
ACHILLEINE
ACHILLODYNIA
ACHIME
ACHING
ACHINGLY
ACHIOTE
ACHIR
ACHIRA
ACHLAMYDATE
ACHLAMYDEOUS
ACHLORHYDRIA
ACHLOROPSIA
ACHOLIA
ACHOLIC
ACHOLOUS
ACHOLURIA
ACHOLURIC
ACHONDRITE
ACHONDRITIC
ACHOR
ACHORDAL
ACHORDATE
ACHRAS
ACHREE
ACHROACYTE
ACHROGLOBIN
ACHROITE
ACHROMA
ACHROMACYTE
ACHROMASIA
ACHROMAT
ACHROMATE
ACHROMATIC
ACHROMATIN
ACHROMATINIC
ACHROMATISM
ACHROMATIZE
ACHROMATIZED
ACHROMATOPE
ACHROMATOSIS
ACHROMATOUS
ACHROMATURIA
ACHROMIA
ACHROMIC
ACHROMOUS
ACHROOUS
ACHROPSIA
ACHT
ACHTEHALBER
ACHTEL
ACHTELTHALER
ACHTER
ACHTERVELD
ACHUETE
ACHY
ACHYLIA
ACHYLOUS
ACHYMIA
ACHYMOUS
ACICHLORID
ACICHLORIDE
ACICULA
ACICULAE
ACICULAR
ACICULARLY
ACICULATE
ACICULATED
ACICULUM
ACICULUMS
ACID
ACIDAEMIA
ACIDEMIA
ACIDER
ACIDIC
ACIDIFEROUS
ACIDIFIABLE
ACIDIFIANT
ACIDIFIC
ACIDIFIED
ACIDIFIER
ACIDIFY
ACIDIFYING
ACIDIMETER
ACIDIMETRIC
ACIDIMETRY
ACIDITE
ACIDITIES
ACIDITY
ACIDIZE
ACIDLY
ACIDNESS
ACIDOLOGY
ACIDOPHIL
ACIDOPHILE
ACIDOPHILIC
ACIDOPHILOUS
ACIDOPHILUS
ACIDOSIS
ACIDOTIC
ACIDPROOF
ACIDULATE
ACIDULATED
ACIDULATING
ACIDULATION
ACIDULENT
ACIDULOUS
ACIER
ACIERAGE
ACIERATE
ACIERATED
ACIERATING
ACIERATION
ACIES
ACIFORM
ACINACEOUS
ACINACES
ACINACIFORM
ACINARIOUS
ACINETAE
ACING
ACINI
ACINIC
ACINIFORM
ACINOSE
ACINOTUBULAR
ACINOUS
ACINUS
ACIPENSERID
ACIPENSERINE
ACIPENSEROID
ACIURGY
ACKEE
ACKER
ACKEY
ACKMAN
ACKMEN
ACKNEW
ACKNOW
ACKNOWING
ACKNOWLEDGE
ACKNOWLEDGEABLE
ACKNOWLEDGED
ACKNOWLEDGEMENT
ACKNOWLEDGER
ACKNOWLEDGING
ACKNOWLEDGMENT
ACKNOWN
ACLASTIC
ACLE
ACLEIDIAN
ACLEISTOUS
ACLIDIAN
ACLINAL
ACLINIC
ACLOUD
ACLYDES
ACMAESTHESIA
ACMATIC
ACME
ACMESTHESIA
ACMIC
ACMITE
ACNE
ACNEFORM
ACNEIFORM
ACNEMIA
ACNODAL
ACNODE
ACOASMA
ACOCANTHERIN
ACOCK
ACOCKBILL
ACOCOTL
ACOEL
ACOELOMATE
ACOELOUS
ACOIN
ACOINE
ACOLD
ACOLOGIC
ACOLOGY
ACOLOUS
ACOLUTHIC
ACOLYTE
ACOLYTH
ACOLYTHATE
ACOMIA
ACOMOUS
ACON
ACONDYLOSE
ACONDYLOUS
ACONE
ACONIC
ACONIN
ACONINE
ACONITAL
ACONITE
ACONITIA
ACONITIC
ACONITIN
ACONITINE
ACONITUM
ACONTIA
ACONTIUM
ACONURESIS
ACOPIC
ACOPON
ACOR
ACOREA
ACORIA
ACORN
ACORNED
ACOSMIC
ACOSMISM
ACOSMIST
ACOSMISTIC
ACOST
ACOTYLEDON
ACOUASM
ACOUCHI
ACOUCHY
ACOUMETER
ACOUMETRY
ACOUOPHONIA
ACOUP
ACOUPA
ACOUPE
ACOUSMA
ACOUSMATA
ACOUSMATIC
ACOUSTIC
ACOUSTICAL
ACOUSTICALLY
ACOUSTICIAN

ACOUSTICS
ACQUAINT
ACQUAINTANCE
ACQUAINTANT
ACQUAINTED
ACQUENT
ACQUEREUR
ACQUEST
ACQUIESCE
ACQUIESCED
ACQUIESCENCE
ACQUIESCENT
ACQUIESCER
ACQUIESCING
ACQUIRABLE
ACQUIRE
ACQUIRED
ACQUIREMENT
ACQUIRENDA
ACQUIRER
ACQUIRING
ACQUISIBLE
ACQUISITA
ACQUISITE
ACQUISITED
ACQUISITION
ACQUISITIVE
ACQUISITIVELY
ACQUISITIVENESS
ACQUISITOR
ACQUISITUM
ACQUIST
ACQUIT
ACQUITAL
ACQUITMENT
ACQUITTAL
ACQUITTANCE
ACQUITTED
ACQUITTER
ACQUITTING
ACRACY
ACRAEIN
ACRALDEHYDE
ACRANIA
ACRANIAL
ACRANIATE
ACRASIA
ACRASPEDOTE
ACRASY
ACRATIA
ACRATURESIS
ACRAWL
ACRAZE
ACRE
ACREABLE
ACREAGE
ACREAK
ACREAM
ACRED
ACREMAN
ACREMEN
ACRES
ACRESTAFF
ACRID
ACRIDAN
ACRIDANE
ACRIDIAN
ACRIDIC
ACRIDID
ACRIDIN
ACRIDINE
ACRIDINIC
ACRIDINIUM
ACRIDITY
ACRIDLY
ACRIDNESS
ACRIDONE
ACRIDONIUM
ACRIDOPHAGUS
ACRIDYL
ACRIFLAVIN
ACRIFLAVINE
ACRIMONIES
ACRIMONIOUS
ACRIMONIOUSLY
ACRIMONY
ACRINDOLIN
ACRINDOLINE
ACRINYL
ACRISIA
ACRISY
ACRITAN
ACRITE
ACRITICAL
ACRITOL
ACRITY
ACROAMA
ACROAMATA
ACROAMATIC
ACROAMATICS
ACROASPHYXIA
ACROATAXIA
ACROATIC
ACROBACY
ACROBAT
ACROBATIC
ACROBATICAL
ACROBATICALLY
ACROBATICS
ACROBATISM
ACROBLAST
ACROBRYOUS
ACROBYSTITIS
ACROCARPOUS
ACROCEPHALIA
ACROCEPHALIC
ACROCEPHALY
ACROCHORDON
ACROCONIDIUM
ACROCORACOID
ACROCYANOSIS
ACROCYST
ACRODACTYLA
ACRODACTYLUM
ACRODONT
ACRODONTISM
ACRODROME
ACRODROMOUS
ACRODYNIA
ACROESTHESIA
ACROGAMOUS
ACROGAMY
ACROGEN
ACROGENIC
ACROGENOUS
ACROGENOUSLY
ACROGRAPHY
ACROGYNOUS
ACROLEIN
ACROLITH
ACROLITHAN
ACROLITHIC
ACROLOGIC
ACROLOGISM
ACROLOGUE
ACROLOGY
ACROMANIA
ACROMEGALIA
ACROMEGALIC
ACROMEGALY
ACROMELALGIA
ACROMETER
ACROMIA
ACROMIAL
ACROMICRIA
ACROMION
ACROMPHALUS
ACROMYODIAN
ACROMYODIC
ACROMYODOUS
ACROMYOTONIA
ACROMYOTONUS
ACRON
ACRONARCOTIC
ACRONEUROSIS
ACRONIC
ACRONICAL
ACRONICALLY
ACRONICHAL
ACRONICHALLY
ACRONYC
ACRONYCAL
ACRONYCALLY
ACRONYCH
ACRONYCHAL
ACRONYCHALLY
ACRONYCTOUS
ACRONYM
ACRONYX
ACROOK
ACROPATHY
ACROPETAL
ACROPETALLY
ACROPHOBIA
ACROPHONETIC
ACROPHONIC
ACROPHONY
ACROPODIA
ACROPODIUM
ACROPOLIS
ACROPOLISES
ACROPOLITAN
ACROPORE
ACRORHAGUS
ACRORRHEUMA
ACROSARC
ACROSARCA
ACROSARCUM
ACROSCOPIC
ACROSE
ACROSOME
ACROSPIRE
ACROSPIRED
ACROSPIRING
ACROSPORE
ACROSPOROUS
ACROSS
ACROSTIC
ACROSTICAL
ACROSTICALLY
ACROSTICHAL
ACROSTICHIC
ACROSTICHOID
ACROSTICISM
ACROTARSIAL
ACROTARSIUM
ACROTELEUTIC
ACROTER
ACROTERIAL
ACROTERIC
ACROTERIUM
ACROTIC
ACROTISM
ACROTOMOUS
ACROTROPHIC
ACRYL
ACRYLATE
ACRYLIC
ACRYLYL
ACT
ACTA
ACTABILITY
ACTABLE
ACTED
ACTIFICATION
ACTIFIER
ACTIFY
ACTIN
ACTINAL
ACTINALLY
ACTINE
ACTINENCHYMA
ACTING
ACTINIA
ACTINIAN
ACTINIARIAN
ACTINIC
ACTINICAL
ACTINICALLY
ACTINIDE
ACTINIFEROUS
ACTINIFORM
ACTININE
ACTINISM
ACTINIUM
ACTINOBRANCH
ACTINOCARP
ACTINOCARPIC
ACTINOCRINID
ACTINODROME
ACTINOGRAM
ACTINOGRAPH
ACTINOGRAPHY
ACTINOID
ACTINOLITE
ACTINOLITIC
ACTINOLOGOUS
ACTINOLOGUE
ACTINOLOGY
ACTINOMERE
ACTINOMERIC
ACTINOMETER
ACTINOMETRIC
ACTINOMETRY
ACTINOMORPHIC
ACTINOMORPHY
ACTINOMYCETE
ACTINOMYCOMA
ACTINON
ACTINOPHONE
ACTINOPHONIC
ACTINOPHORE
ACTINOPHRYAN
ACTINOPRAXIS
ACTINOSCOPY
ACTINOSOMA
ACTINOSOME
ACTINOST
ACTINOSTOMAL
ACTINOSTOME
ACTINOTROCHA
ACTINOZOAL
ACTINOZOAN
ACTINULA
ACTINULAE
ACTIO
ACTION
ACTIONABLE
ACTIONABLY
ACTIONAL
ACTIONARY
ACTIONER
ACTIONES
ACTIONIZE
ACTIONIZED
ACTIONIZING
ACTIONS
ACTIOUS
ACTIVATE
ACTIVATED
ACTIVATING
ACTIVATION
ACTIVATOR
ACTIVE
ACTIVELY
ACTIVENESS
ACTIVISM
ACTIVIST
ACTIVITAL
ACTIVITIES
ACTIVITY
ACTIVIZE
ACTLESS
ACTO
ACTON
ACTOR
ACTORISH
ACTORS
ACTORY
ACTOS
ACTRESS
ACTRESSY
ACTS
ACTU
ACTUAL
ACTUALISM
ACTUALIST
ACTUALISTIC
ACTUALITIES
ACTUALITY
ACTUALIZATION
ACTUALIZE
ACTUALIZED
ACTUALIZING
ACTUALLY
ACTUALNESS
ACTUARIAL
ACTUARIALLY
ACTUARIAN
ACTUARIES
ACTUARY
ACTUATE
ACTUATED
ACTUATES
ACTUATING
ACTUATION
ACTUATOR
ACTURE
ACTURIENCE
ACTUS
ACUATE
ACUATING
ACUATION
ACUCHI
ACUCLOSURE
ACUDUCTOR
ACUERDO
ACUERDOS
ACUITY
ACULEA
ACULEAE
ACULEATE
ACULEATED
ACULEI
ACULEIFORM
ACULEOLATE
ACULEUS
ACUMEN
ACUMINATE
ACUMINATED
ACUMINATING
ACUMINATION
ACUMINOSE
ACUMINOUS
ACUMINULATE

ACUPRESS
ACUPRESSURE
ACUPUNCTUATE
ACUPUNCTURATOR
ACUPUNCTURE
ACUPUNCTURED
ACUS
ACUSHLA
ACUTA
ACUTANGULAR
ACUTATE
ACUTE
ACUTELY
ACUTENESS
ACUTIATOR
ACUTIFOLIATE
ACUTILINGUAL
ACUTILOBATE
ACUTIPLANTAR
ACUTOGRAVE
ACUTONODOSE
ACUTORSION
ACXOYATL
ACYANOPSIA
ACYCLIC
ACYESIS
ACYETIC
ACYL
ACYLAL
ACYLASE
ACYLATE
ACYLATION
ACYLOGEN
ACYLOIN
ACYROLOGICAL
ACYROLOGY
ACYSTIA
AD
ADACTYLIA
ADACTYLOUS
ADAD
ADAGA
ADAGE
ADAGIAL
ADAGIETTO
ADAGIO
ADAGIOS
ADALAT
ADALID
ADAMANCY
ADAMANT
ADAMANTEAN
ADAMANTINE
ADAMANTINOMA
ADAMANTOID
ADAMANTOMA
ADAMAS
ADAMELLITE
ADAMINE
ADAMITE
ADAMSITE
ADAN
ADANCE
ADANGLE
ADAPID
ADAPT
ADAPTABILITY
ADAPTABLE
ADAPTABLENESS
ADAPTATION
ADAPTATIONAL
ADAPTATIVE
ADAPTED
ADAPTEDNESS
ADAPTER
ADAPTION
ADAPTIONISM
ADAPTITUDE
ADAPTIVE
ADAPTIVELY
ADAPTIVENESS
ADAPTOMETER
ADAPTOR
ADAPTORIAL
ADARME
ADARO
ADAT
ADATI
ADATIS
ADATOM
ADATY
ADAUNT
ADAW
ADAWE
ADAWLUT
ADAWN
ADAXIAL
ADAY
ADAYS
ADAZZLE
ADCRAFT
ADD
ADDA
ADDABLE
ADDAX
ADDEBTED
ADDED
ADDEEM
ADDEND
ADDENDA
ADDENDUM
ADDER
ADDERBOLT
ADDERSPIT
ADDERWORT
ADDIBILITY
ADDIBLE
ADDICE
ADDICENT
ADDICT
ADDICTED
ADDICTEDNESS
ADDICTION
ADDICTIVE
ADDIMENT
ADDING
ADDIO
ADDIS
ADDITA
ADDITAMENT
ADDITIMENT
ADDITION
ADDITIONAL
ADDITIONALLY
ADDITIONARY
ADDITIONS
ADDITITIOUS
ADDITIVE
ADDITIVELY
ADDITIVITY
ADDITORY
ADDITUM
ADDLE
ADDLEBRAIN
ADDLEBRAINED
ADDLED
ADDLEHEAD
ADDLEHEADED
ADDLEHEADEDLY
ADDLEPATE
ADDLEPATED
ADDLEPLOT
ADDLING
ADDLINGS
ADDLINS
ADDORSED
ADDOSSED
ADDRESS
ADDRESSED
ADDRESSEE
ADDRESSER
ADDRESSFUL
ADDRESSING
ADDRESSOR
ADDREST
ADDUCE
ADDUCEABLE
ADDUCED
ADDUCENT
ADDUCER
ADDUCIBLE
ADDUCING
ADDUCT
ADDUCTION
ADDUCTIVE
ADDUCTOR
ADDULCE
ADE
ADEAD
ADEEM
ADEEP
ADELANTADO
ADELANTE
ADELING
ADELITE
ADELOCODONIC
ADELOMORPHIC
ADELOPOD
ADELPHOGAMY
ADELPHOLITE
ADELPHOPHAGY
ADEMONIST
ADEMPT
ADEMPTED
ADEMPTION
ADENALGY
ADENASE
ADENASTHENIA
ADENECTOMIES
ADENECTOMY
ADENECTOPIA
ADENECTOPIC
ADENIA
ADENIFORM
ADENIN
ADENINE
ADENITIS
ADENIZATION
ADENOBLAST
ADENOCELE
ADENOCHROME
ADENOCYST
ADENODERMIA
ADENODYNIA
ADENOFIBROMA
ADENOFIBROSIS
ADENOGENESIS
ADENOGENOUS
ADENOGRAPHY
ADENOID
ADENOIDAL
ADENOIDISM
ADENOLIPOMA
ADENOLOGICAL
ADENOLOGY
ADENOMA
ADENOMALACIA
ADENOMATA
ADENOMATOUS
ADENOMYCOSIS
ADENOMYOMA
ADENOMYXOMA
ADENONCUS
ADENONEURAL
ADENONEURE
ADENOPATHY
ADENOPHORE
ADENOPHOREUS
ADENOPHYLLOUS
ADENOPHYMA
ADENOPODOUS
ADENOSARCOMA
ADENOSE
ADENOSINE
ADENOSIS
ADENOTOME
ADENOTOMIC
ADENOTOMY
ADENOTYPHOID
ADENOTYPHUS
ADENOUS
ADENYLIC
ADEPHAGAN
ADEPHAGOUS
ADEPS
ADEPT
ADEPTION
ADEPTLY
ADEPTNESS
ADEQUACY
ADEQUATE
ADEQUATELY
ADEQUATENESS
ADEQUATION
ADEQUATIVE
ADERMIA
ADERMIN
ADESPOTA
ADESPOTON
ADEVISM
ADEW
ADFIX
ADHAKA
ADHAMANT
ADHARMA
ADHERE
ADHERED
ADHERENCE
ADHERENCY
ADHEREND
ADHERENT
ADHERENTLY
ADHERER
ADHERESCENCE
ADHERESCENT
ADHERING
ADHESION
ADHESIONAL
ADHESIVE
ADHESIVELY
ADHESIVENESS
ADHI
ADHIBIT
ADHIBITED
ADHIBITING
ADHIBITION
ADHORT
ADIABAT
ADIABATIC
ADIABOLIST
ADIACTINIC
ADIAGNOSTIC
ADIANTIFORM
ADIANTUM
ADIAPHON
ADIAPHONON
ADIAPHORA
ADIAPHORAL
ADIAPHORESIS
ADIAPHORETIC
ADIAPHORISM
ADIAPHORIST
ADIAPHORITE
ADIAPHORON
ADIAPHOROUS
ADIATE
ADIATED
ADIATHERMAL
ADIATHERMIC
ADIATHETIC
ADIATING
ADIATION
ADIBASI
ADICITY
ADIENCE
ADIEU
ADIEUS
ADIEUX
ADIGHE
ADIGHT
ADINIDAN
ADINOLE
ADION
ADIOS
ADIPATE
ADIPESCENT
ADIPIC
ADIPINIC
ADIPOCELE
ADIPOCERE
ADIPOCEROUS
ADIPOFIBROMA
ADIPOGENIC
ADIPOGENOUS
ADIPOID
ADIPOLYSIS
ADIPOLYTIC
ADIPOMA
ADIPOMATA
ADIPOMATOUS
ADIPOMETER
ADIPOPEXIA
ADIPOPEXIS
ADIPOSE
ADIPOSENESS
ADIPOSIS
ADIPOSITY
ADIPOSURIA
ADIPOUS
ADIPSIA
ADIPSIC
ADIPSOUS
ADIPYL
ADIT
ADITAL
ADITIO
ADITUS
ADIVE
ADJAB
ADJACENCY
ADJACENT
ADJACENTLY
ADJAG
ADJECT
ADJECTION
ADJECTIONAL
ADJECTIVAL
ADJECTIVALLY
ADJECTIVE
ADJECTIVELY
ADJIGA
ADJIGER
ADJOIN
ADJOINED
ADJOINEDLY

ADJOINING
ADJOINT
ADJOURN
ADJOURNAL
ADJOURNMENT
ADJOUST
ADJUDGE
ADJUDGED
ADJUDGER
ADJUDGING
ADJUDICATE
ADJUDICATED
ADJUDICATING
ADJUDICATION
ADJUDICATIVE
ADJUDICATOR
ADJUDICATURE
ADJUGATE
ADJUMENT
ADJUNCT
ADJUNCTION
ADJUNCTIVE
ADJUNCTIVELY
ADJUNCTLY
ADJURATION
ADJURATORY
ADJURE
ADJURED
ADJURER
ADJURING
ADJUROR
ADJUST
ADJUSTABLE
ADJUSTAGE
ADJUSTED
ADJUSTER
ADJUSTIVE
ADJUSTMENT
ADJUSTOR
ADJUTAGE
ADJUTANCIES
ADJUTANCY
ADJUTANT
ADJUTANTSHIP
ADJUTOR
ADJUTORIOUS
ADJUTORY
ADJUTRICE
ADJUTRIX
ADJUVANT
ADJUVATE
ADLAY
ADLUMIDIN
ADLUMIDINE
ADLUMIN
ADLUMINE
ADMAN
ADMARGINATE
ADMAXILLARY
ADMEASURE
ADMEASURED
ADMEASURER
ADMEASURING
ADMEDIAL
ADMEDIAN
ADMEN
ADMI
ADMINICLE
ADMINICULAR
ADMINICULARY
ADMINICULATE
ADMINICULUM
ADMINISTER
ADMINISTERED
ADMINISTERIAL
ADMINISTRABLE
ADMINISTRANT
ADMINISTRATE
ADMINISTRATED
ADMINISTRATING
ADMINISTRATION
ADMINISTRATIONAL
ADMINISTRATIVE
ADMINISTRATOR
ADMIRABLE
ADMIRABLY
ADMIRAL
ADMIRALSHIP
ADMIRALTIES
ADMIRALTY
ADMIRATION
ADMIRATIVE
ADMIRATOR
ADMIRE
ADMIRED
ADMIREDLY
ADMIRER
ADMIRING
ADMIRINGLY
ADMISSIBLE
ADMISSIBLY
ADMISSION
ADMISSIVE
ADMISSORY
ADMIT
ADMITTABLE
ADMITTANCE
ADMITTATUR
ADMITTED
ADMITTEDLY
ADMITTEE
ADMITTER
ADMITTING
ADMITTY
ADMIX
ADMIXED
ADMIXING
ADMIXT
ADMIXTION
ADMIXTURE
ADMONISH
ADMONISHER
ADMONISHMENT
ADMONITION
ADMONITIVE
ADMONITIVELY
ADMONITOR
ADMONITORIAL
ADMONITORILY
ADMONITORY
ADMOVE
ADNASCENCE
ADNATE
ADNATION
ADNERVAL
ADNESCENT
ADNEURAL
ADNEX
ADNEXA
ADNEXAL
ADNEXED
ADNEXITIS
ADNEXOPEXY
ADNOMINAL
ADNOMINALLY
ADNOMINATION
ADNOUN
ADNUL
ADNUMBER
ADO
ADOBE
ADOLESCE
ADOLESCED
ADOLESCENCE
ADOLESCENCY
ADOLESCENT
ADOLESCENTLY
ADOLESCING
ADON
ADONIDIN
ADONIN
ADONIS
ADONITE
ADONITOL
ADONIZE
ADONIZED
ADONIZING
ADOORS
ADOPERATE
ADOPERATION
ADOPT
ADOPTABLE
ADOPTANT
ADOPTATIVE
ADOPTED
ADOPTEDLY
ADOPTEE
ADOPTER
ADOPTIAN
ADOPTIANISM
ADOPTIANIST
ADOPTION
ADOPTIONAL
ADOPTIONISM
ADOPTIONIST
ADOPTIOUS
ADOPTIVE
ADOPTIVELY
ADOR
ADORABILITY
ADORABLE
ADORABLENESS
ADORABLY
ADORAL
ADORALLY
ADORANT
ADORATION
ADORATORY
ADORE
ADORED
ADORER
ADORING
ADORN
ADORNED
ADORNER
ADORNMENT
ADOSCULATION
ADOULIE
ADOWN
ADOXACEOUS
ADOXIES
ADOXOGRAPHY
ADOXY
ADOZE
ADPRESS
ADPROMISSION
ADRAD
ADRADIAL
ADRADIALLY
ADRADIUS
ADREAD
ADREAM
ADREAMED
ADREAMT
ADRECTAL
ADRENAL
ADRENALIN
ADRENALINE
ADRENALIZE
ADRENALONE
ADRENCH
ADRENIN
ADRENINE
ADRENT
ADRIFT
ADRIP
ADROGATE
ADROIT
ADROITLY
ADROITNESS
ADROOP
ADROP
ADROSTRAL
ADROWSE
ADRUE
ADRY
ADSBUD
ADSCITITIOUS
ADSCRIPT
ADSCRIPTION
ADSCRIPTIVE
ADSESSOR
ADSIGNIFY
ADSMITH
ADSMITHING
ADSORB
ADSORBABLE
ADSORBATE
ADSORBENT
ADSORPTION
ADSORPTIVE
ADSORPTIVELY
ADSTIPULATE
ADSTIPULATED
ADSTIPULATOR
ADSUM
ADTERMINAL
ADUANA
ADUB
ADULAR
ADULARIA
ADULATE
ADULATED
ADULATING
ADULATION
ADULATOR
ADULATORY
ADULATRESS
ADULCE
ADULT
ADULTER
ADULTERANT
ADULTERATE
ADULTERATED
ADULTERATING
ADULTERATION
ADULTERATOR
ADULTERER
ADULTERESS
ADULTERIES
ADULTERINE
ADULTERIZE
ADULTEROUS
ADULTEROUSLY
ADULTERY
ADULTHOOD
ADULTNESS
ADULTOID
ADULTRESS
ADUMBRAL
ADUMBRANT
ADUMBRATE
ADUMBRATED
ADUMBRATING
ADUMBRATION
ADUMBRATIVE
ADUNC
ADUNCATE
ADUNCITY
ADUNCOUS
ADURE
ADURENT
ADUSK
ADUST
ADUSTION
ADUSTIOSIS
ADUSTIVE
ADVANCE
ADVANCED
ADVANCEMENT
ADVANCER
ADVANCES
ADVANCING
ADVANCIVE
ADVANTAGE
ADVANTAGED
ADVANTAGEOUS
ADVANTAGEOUSLY
ADVANTAGEOUSNESS
ADVANTAGING
ADVECTION
ADVECTITIOUS
ADVECTIVE
ADVEHENT
ADVENE
ADVENIENCE
ADVENIENT
ADVENT
ADVENTIAL
ADVENTITIA
ADVENTITIOUS
ADVENTIVE
ADVENTUAL
ADVENTURE
ADVENTURED
ADVENTURER
ADVENTURESOME
ADVENTURESS
ADVENTURING
ADVENTUROUS
ADVENTUROUSLY
ADVENTUROUSNES
ADVERB
ADVERBIAL
ADVERBIALIZE
ADVERBIALLY
ADVERBIATION
ADVERSARIA
ADVERSARIES
ADVERSARY
ADVERSATIVE
ADVERSE
ADVERSED
ADVERSELY
ADVERSENESS
ADVERSING
ADVERSITIES
ADVERSITY
ADVERSUS
ADVERT
ADVERTENCE
ADVERTENCY
ADVERTENT
ADVERTENTLY
ADVERTISE
ADVERTISED
ADVERTISEMENT
ADVERTISER
ADVERTISING
ADVERTIZE
ADVERTIZEMENT
ADVERTIZING
ADVICE
ADVICEFUL
ADVISABILITY

ADVISABLE
ADVISABLENESS
ADVISABLY
ADVISAL
ADVISATORY
ADVISE
ADVISED
ADVISEDLY
ADVISEDNESS
ADVISEE
ADVISEMENT
ADVISER
ADVISING
ADVISIVE
ADVISIVENESS
ADVISO
ADVISOR
ADVISORILY
ADVISORY
ADVITANT
ADVOCAAT
ADVOCACY
ADVOCATE
ADVOCATED
ADVOCATES
ADVOCATING
ADVOCATION
ADVOCATOR
ADVOCATORY
ADVOCATRESS
ADVOKE
ADVOLUTION
ADVOWEE
ADVOWSON
ADY
ADYNAMIA
ADYNAMIC
ADYNAMY
ADYT
ADYTA
ADYTON
ADYTUM
ADZ
ADZE
ADZER
ADZES
AE
AEA
AECIA
AECIAL
AECIDIA
AECIDIUM
AECIOSPORE
AECIOSTAGE
AECIOTELIA
AECIOTELIUM
AECIUM
AEDEAGI
AEDEAGUS
AEDES
AEDICULA
AEDICULAE
AEDILE
AEDILESHIP
AEDILIAN
AEDILIC
AEDILITIAN
AEDILITIES
AEDILITY
AEDOEOLOGY
AEGAGRI
AEGAGROPILA
AEGAGROPILAE
AEGAGROPILE
AEGAGROPILES
AEGAGRUS
AEGER
AEGERIAN
AEGERIID
AEGICRANIA
AEGILOPS
AEGIRINE
AEGIRINOLITE
AEGIRITE
AEGIS
AEGROTANT
AEGROTAT
AEGYPTILLA
AEGYRITE
AELODICON
AELUROPHOBE
AELUROPHOBIA
AELUROPODOUS
AENACH
AENEAN
AENEOLITHIC
AENEOUS
AENIGMATITE
AEOLIAN
AEOLID
AEOLIGHT
AEOLINE
AEOLIPILE
AEOLIPYLE
AEOLISTIC
AEOLODICON
AEOLOTROPIC
AEOLOTROPISM
AEOLOTROPY
AEOLSKLAVIER
AEON
AEONIAL
AEONIAN
AEONIC
AEQUOR
AEQUOREAL
AER
AERAGE
AERARIAN
AERARIUM
AERATE
AERATED
AERATING
AERATION
AERATOR
AERENCHYMA
AERIAL
AERIALIST
AERIALITY
AERIALLY
AERIALNESS
AERIC
AERICAL
AERIDES
AERIE
AERIED
AERIFACTION
AERIFEROUS
AERIFICATION
AERIFIED
AERIFORM
AERIFY
AERIFYING
AERO
AEROBATE
AEROBATED
AEROBATICS
AEROBATING
AEROBE
AEROBIAN
AEROBIC
AEROBICALLY
AEROBIOLOGY
AEROBIOSCOPE
AEROBIOSIS
AEROBIOTIC
AEROBIOUS
AEROBIUM
AEROBOAT
AEROBUS
AEROCAMERA
AEROCOLPOS
AEROCURVE
AEROCYST
AERODONE
AERODONETIC
AERODONETICS
AERODROME
AERODROMICS
AERODUCT
AERODYNAMIC
AERODYNAMICS
AERODYNE
AEROEMBOLISM
AEROFOIL
AEROGEL
AEROGEN
AEROGENES
AEROGENIC
AEROGEOLOGY
AEROGNOSY
AEROGRAM
AEROGRAMME
AEROGRAPH
AEROGRAPHER
AEROGRAPHIC
AEROGRAPHICS
AEROGRAPHIES
AEROGRAPHY
AEROGUN
AEROHYDROUS
AEROIDES
AEROLITE
AEROLITH
AEROLITIC
AEROLITICS
AEROLOGIC
AEROLOGICAL
AEROLOGIES
AEROLOGIST
AEROLOGY
AEROMANCY
AEROMARINE
AEROMECHANIC
AEROMEDICAL
AEROMEDICINE
AEROMETER
AEROMETRIC
AEROMETRY
AEROMOTOR
AERONAT
AERONAUT
AERONAUTIC
AERONAUTICAL
AERONAUTICS
AERONAUTISM
AERONEF
AERONEUROSIS
AEROPATHY
AEROPAUSE
AEROPHAGIA
AEROPHAGIST
AEROPHANE
AEROPHILE
AEROPHILOUS
AEROPHOBIA
AEROPHOBIC
AEROPHONE
AEROPHOR
AEROPHORE
AEROPHYSICAL
AEROPHYSICS
AEROPHYTE
AEROPLANE
AEROPLANER
AEROPLANIST
AEROPLEUSTIC
AEROPOROTOMY
AEROSCEPSIS
AEROSCEPSY
AEROSCOPE
AEROSCOPIC
AEROSCOPY
AEROSE
AEROSIDERITE
AEROSOL
AEROSPACE
AEROSPHERE
AEROSTAT
AEROSTATIC
AEROSTATICAL
AEROSTATICS
AEROSTATION
AEROSTEAM
AEROTAXIS
AEROTHERAPY
AEROTROPIC
AEROTROPISM
AEROVIEW
AEROYACHT
AERUGINOUS
AERUGO
AERY
AES
AESC
AESCULACEOUS
AESTHESIA
AESTHESIS
AESTHETE
AESTHETIC
AESTHETICAL
AESTHETICALLY
AESTHETICIAN
AESTHETICISM
AESTHETICIZE
AESTHETICS
AESTIVAL
AESTIVATE
AESTIVATED
AESTIVATING
AESTIVATION
AESTIVATOR
AESTUATE
AESTUATION
AESTUOUS
AESTURE
AESTUS
AETHALIA
AETHALIUM
AETHELING
AETHEOGAM
AETHEOGAMIC
AETHEOGAMOUS
AETHER
AETHERED
AETHOGEN
AETHRIOSCOPE
AETIOGENIC
AETIOLOGICAL
AETIOLOGUE
AETIOLOGY
AETIOPHYLLIN
AETIOTROPIC
AETITES
AETOSAUR
AEVIA
AEVUM
AFACE
AFAINT
AFALD
AFAR
AFARA
AFEAR
AFEARD
AFEARED
AFERNAN
AFETAL
AFF
AFFA
AFFABILITY
AFFABLE
AFFABLENESS
AFFABLY
AFFABROUS
AFFAIR
AFFAIRE
AFFAIRS
AFFAITE
AFFAMISH
AFFECT
AFFECTATION
AFFECTED
AFFECTEDLY
AFFECTEDNESS
AFFECTER
AFFECTIBILITY
AFFECTIBLE
AFFECTING
AFFECTINGLY
AFFECTION
AFFECTIONAL
AFFECTIONALLY
AFFECTIONATE
AFFECTIONATELY
AFFECTIONATENESS
AFFECTIONED
AFFECTIVE
AFFECTIVELY
AFFECTIVITY
AFFEEBLE
AFFEER
AFFEERER
AFFEERMENT
AFFEEROR
AFFEIR
AFFERE
AFFERENT
AFFETTUOSO
AFFIANCE
AFFIANCED
AFFIANCER
AFFIANCING
AFFIANT
AFFICHE
AFFIDATION
AFFIDAVIT
AFFIDAVY
AFFIED
AFFILE
AFFILIABLE
AFFILIATE
AFFILIATED
AFFILIATING
AFFILIATION
AFFINAGE
AFFINAL
AFFINATION
AFFINE
AFFINED
AFFINELY
AFFINITATIVE
AFFINITATIVELY
AFFINITE
AFFINITIES
AFFINITION

AFFINITIVE
AFFINITY
AFFIRM
AFFIRMABLE
AFFIRMABLY
AFFIRMANCE
AFFIRMANT
AFFIRMATION
AFFIRMATIVE
AFFIRMATIVELY
AFFIRMATORY
AFFIRMER
AFFIX
AFFIXAL
AFFIXATION
AFFIXED
AFFIXER
AFFIXING
AFFIXION
AFFIXT
AFFIXTURE
AFFLATE
AFFLATED
AFFLATION
AFFLATUS
AFFLICT
AFFLICTED
AFFLICTER
AFFLICTING
AFFLICTINGLY
AFFLICTION
AFFLICTIVE
AFFLICTIVELY
AFFLOOF
AFFLUENCE
AFFLUENT
AFFLUENTLY
AFFLUENTNESS
AFFLUX
AFFLUXION
AFFODILL
AFFORCE
AFFORCED
AFFORCEMENT
AFFORCING
AFFORD
AFFORDABLE
AFFOREST
AFFORESTMENT
AFFORMATIVE
AFFRANCHISE
AFFRANCHISED
AFFRAP
AFFRAY
AFFRAYED
AFFRAYER
AFFRAYING
AFFREIGHT
AFFREIGHTER
AFFRET
AFFRETTANDO
AFFREUX
AFFRICATE
AFFRICATED
AFFRICATION
AFFRICATIVE
AFFRIGHT
AFFRIGHTED
AFFRIGHTEDLY
AFFRIGHTER
AFFRIGHTFUL
AFFRIGHTMENT
AFFRONT
AFFRONTE
AFFRONTED
AFFRONTEDLY
AFFRONTEE
AFFRONTER
AFFRONTIVE
AFFRONTY
AFFUSE
AFFUSED
AFFUSING
AFFUSION
AFFY
AFFYDAVY
AFFYING
AFGHAN
AFGHANI
AFGHANIS
AFICIONADO
AFIELD
AFIKOMEN
AFIND
AFINE
AFIRE
AFLAGELLAR
AFLAME
AFLARE
AFLAT
AFLAUNT
AFLEY
AFLICKER
AFLIGHT
AFLOAT
AFLOW
AFLOWER
AFLUKING
AFLUSH
AFLUTTER
AFOAM
AFONG
AFOOT
AFORE
AFOREHAND
AFOREMENTIONED
AFORENAMED
AFORESAID
AFORETHOUGHT
AFORETIME
AFOUL
AFOUNDE
AFRAID
AFREET
AFRESCA
AFRESH
AFRET
AFRETE
AFRIT
AFRITE
AFRONT
AFROWN
AFT
AFTABA
AFTEN
AFTER
AFTERBAY
AFTERBEAT
AFTERBIRTH
AFTERBODY
AFTERBRAIN
AFTERBREAST
AFTERBURNER
AFTERBURNING
AFTERCARE
AFTERCAST
AFTERCHROME
AFTERCLAP
AFTERCOME
AFTERCOMER
AFTERCOOLER
AFTERCROP
AFTERDAMP
AFTERDATE
AFTERDATED
AFTERDECK
AFTERDINNER
AFTEREFFECT
AFTEREYE
AFTERFEED
AFTERFORM
AFTERFUTURE
AFTERGAME
AFTERGAS
AFTERGLOW
AFTERGRASS
AFTERGROWTH
AFTERGUARD
AFTERHAND
AFTERHATCH
AFTERHEND
AFTERHOLD
AFTERIMAGE
AFTERINGS
AFTERLIFE
AFTERLIGHT
AFTERMAST
AFTERMATH
AFTERMILK
AFTERMOST
AFTERNIGHT
AFTERNOON
AFTERNOONS
AFTERNOTE
AFTERPAIN
AFTERPAINS
AFTERPART
AFTERPEAK
AFTERPIECE
AFTERPLAY
AFTERRAKE
AFTERRIDER
AFTERS
AFTERSHAFT
AFTERSHAFTED
AFTERSHINE
AFTERSHOCK
AFTERSONG
AFTERSOUND
AFTERSPRING
AFTERSTORM
AFTERSUPPER
AFTERSWARM
AFTERTASTE
AFTERTHOUGHT
AFTERTIME
AFTERTOUCH
AFTERTURN
AFTERVISION
AFTERWALE
AFTERWARD
AFTERWARDS
AFTERWASH
AFTERWHILE
AFTERWISE
AFTERWIT
AFTERWITTED
AFTERWORLD
AFTERWRIST
AFTERYEARS
AFTMOST
AFTOSA
AFTWARD
AFTWARDS
AFUNCTION
AFUNCTIONAL
AFWILLITE
AGA
AGABANEE
AGACANT
AGACANTE
AGACELLA
AGACERIE
AGAIN
AGAINBUY
AGAINSAY
AGAINST
AGAL
AGALACTIC
AGALACTOUS
AGALAXIA
AGALAXY
AGALITE
AGALLOCH
AGALLOCHUM
AGALMA
AGALMATOLITE
AGALWOOD
AGAMA
AGAME
AGAMETE
AGAMI
AGAMIAN
AGAMIC
AGAMICALLY
AGAMID
AGAMIS
AGAMIST
AGAMOBIA
AGAMOBIUM
AGAMOGENESIS
AGAMOGENETIC
AGAMOID
AGAMONT
AGAMOSPORE
AGAMOUS
AGAMY
AGANGLIONIC
AGAPAE
AGAPANTHUS
AGAPE
AGAPETAE
AGAPETI
AGAPETID
AGAR
AGARIC
AGARICACEOUS
AGARICIC
AGARICIFORM
AGARICIN
AGARICINE
AGARICINIC
AGARICOID
AGARITA
AGAROID
AGARWAL
AGASP
AGAST
AGASTRIC
AGATA
AGATE
AGATEWARE
AGATHIN
AGATHISM
AGATHIST
AGATHODAEMON
AGATHODEMON
AGATHOLOGY
AGATIFEROUS
AGATIFORM
AGATINE
AGATIZE
AGATIZED
AGATIZING
AGATOID
AGATY
AGAVE
AGAVOSE
AGAZE
AGAZED
AGBA
AGE
AGEABLE
AGED
AGEDLY
AGEDNESS
AGEE
AGEING
AGELESS
AGELONG
AGEN
AGENCIES
AGENCY
AGENDA
AGENDUM
AGENESIA
AGENESIC
AGENESIS
AGENIZE
AGENNESIS
AGENNETIC
AGENT
AGENTESS
AGENTIAL
AGENTING
AGENTIVAL
AGENTIVE
AGENTRY
AGEOMETRICAL
AGER
AGERASIA
AGERATUM
AGEUSIA
AGEUSIC
AGGER
AGGERATE
AGGEROSE
AGGEST
AGGLOMERANT
AGGLOMERATE
AGGLOMERATED
AGGLOMERATIC
AGGLOMERATING
AGGLOMERATION
AGGLOMERATIVE
AGGLOMERATOR
AGGLUTINABLE
AGGLUTINANT
AGGLUTINATE
AGGLUTINATED
AGGLUTINATION
AGGLUTINATIVE
AGGLUTINATOR
AGGLUTININ
AGGLUTINIZE
AGGLUTINOGEN
AGGLUTINOID
AGGRACE
AGGRADATION
AGGRADATIONAL
AGGRADE
AGGRADED
AGGRADING
AGGRANDIZE
AGGRANDIZED
AGGRANDIZEMENT
AGGRANDIZER
AGGRANDIZING
AGGRATE
AGGRAVATE
AGGRAVATED
AGGRAVATING
AGGRAVATINGLY
AGGRAVATION
AGGRAVATIVE

AGGRAVATOR
AGGREGABLE
AGGREGANT
AGGREGATE
AGGREGATED
AGGREGATELY
AGGREGATENESS
AGGREGATING
AGGREGATION
AGGREGATIVE
AGGREGATOR
AGGREGATORY
AGGREGE
AGGRESS
AGGRESSED
AGGRESSIN
AGGRESSING
AGGRESSION
AGGRESSIVE
AGGRESSIVELY
AGGRESSIVENESS
AGGRESSOR
AGGRI
AGGRIEVANCE
AGGRIEVE
AGGRIEVED
AGGRIEVEDLY
AGGRIEVING
AGGROUP
AGGRY
AGGUR
AGHA
AGHANEE
AGHAST
AGHASTNESS
AGIBLE
AGILAWOOD
AGILE
AGILELY
AGILENESS
AGILITY
AGIN
AGING
AGIO
AGIOS
AGIOTAGE
AGIST
AGISTER
AGISTMENT
AGISTOR
AGITABLE
AGITANT
AGITATE
AGITATED
AGITATEDLY
AGITATING
AGITATION
AGITATIONAL
AGITATIVE
AGITATO
AGITATOR
AGITATORIAL
AGITATRIX
AGITPROP
AGITPUNKT
AGLA
AGLANCE
AGLAOZONIA
AGLARE
AGLEAF
AGLEAM
AGLEE
AGLET
AGLETHEAD
AGLEY
AGLIMMER
AGLINT
AGLISTEN
AGLITTER
AGLOBULIA
AGLOBULISM
AGLOSSAL
AGLOSSATE
AGLOSSIA
AGLOW
AGLUCON
AGLUCONE
AGLUTITION
AGLYCON
AGLYCONE
AGLYPHOUS
AGMA
AGMATINE
AGMATOLOGY
AGMINATE
AGMINATED
AGNAIL
AGNAME
AGNAMED
AGNAT
AGNATE
AGNATHIA
AGNATHIC
AGNATHOUS
AGNATIC
AGNATICAL
AGNATICALLY
AGNATION
AGNEAU
AGNEAUX
AGNEL
AGNI
AGNIFICATION
AGNITION
AGNIZE
AGNIZED
AGNIZING
AGNOIOLOGY
AGNOMEN
AGNOMICAL
AGNOMINA
AGNOMINAL
AGNOMINATION
AGNOSIA
AGNOSTIC
AGNOSTICAL
AGNOSTICALLY
AGNOSTICISM
AGNOSY
AGNUS
AGNUSES
AGO
AGOG
AGOGE
AGOGIC
AGOGICS
AGOHO
AGOING
AGOJO
AGOMENSIN
AGOMPHIASIS
AGOMPHIOUS
AGON
AGONAL
AGONE
AGONES
AGONIA
AGONIADA
AGONIADIN
AGONIATITE
AGONIC
AGONIED
AGONIES
AGONIST
AGONISTARCH
AGONISTIC
AGONISTICAL
AGONISTICS
AGONIUM
AGONIZE
AGONIZED
AGONIZER
AGONIZING
AGONOTHETE
AGONOTHETIC
AGONY
AGOOD
AGORA
AGORAE
AGORAMANIA
AGORANOME
AGORANOMUS
AGORAPHOBIA
AGORAS
AGOS
AGOSTADERO
AGOUARA
AGOUTA
AGOUTI
AGOUTIES
AGOUTIS
AGOUTY
AGPAITE
AGPAITIC
AGRAFE
AGRAFFE
AGRAH
AGRAL
AGRAMED
AGRAMMATISM
AGRAPHA
AGRAPHIA
AGRAPHIC
AGRARIAN
AGRARIANISM
AGRARIANIZE
AGRARIANLY
AGREAT
AGREE
AGREEABILITY
AGREEABLE
AGREEABLENESS
AGREEABLY
AGREED
AGREEING
AGREEINGLY
AGREEMENT
AGREER
AGREGATION
AGREGE
AGREMENS
AGREMENT
AGREMENTS
AGREST
AGRESTAL
AGRESTIAL
AGRESTIAN
AGRESTIC
AGRESTICAL
AGRI
AGRIA
AGRICERE
AGRICOLE
AGRICOLIST
AGRICOLITE
AGRICOLOUS
AGRICULTOR
AGRICULTURAL
AGRICULTURALLY
AGRICULTURE
AGRICULTURER
AGRICULTURIST
AGRIEF
AGRIMONIES
AGRIMONY
AGRIMOTOR
AGRIN
AGRIOLOGIST
AGRIOLOGY
AGRIONID
AGRIOTYPE
AGRISE
AGRISED
AGRISING
AGRITO
AGRITOS
AGROAN
AGROBIOLOGIC
AGROBIOLOGY
AGRODOLCE
AGROGEOLOGY
AGROLOGIC
AGROLOGICAL
AGROLOGY
AGROM
AGROMYZID
AGRONOME
AGRONOMIC
AGRONOMICAL
AGRONOMICS
AGRONOMIST
AGRONOMY
AGROOF
AGROPE
AGROSTEROL
AGROSTOLOGIC
AGROSTOLOGY
AGROTE
AGROTECHNY
AGROTYPE
AGROUND
AGRUFE
AGRUIF
AGRYPNIA
AGRYPNIAI
AGRYPNOTIC
AGSAM
AGUA
AGUACATE
AGUADA
AGUADOR
AGUAJI
AGUAMAS
AGUAMIEL
AGUARA
AGUARDIENTE
AGUAVINA
AGUE
AGUEPROOF
AGUEWEED
AGUEY
AGUGLIA
AGUILARITE
AGUILT
AGUINALDO
AGUINALDOS
AGUIRAGE
AGUISE
AGUISH
AGUISHLY
AGUISHNESS
AGUJA
AGUJON
AGUNAH
AGUSH
AGUST
AGY
AGYE
AGYIOMANIA
AGYNARIOUS
AGYNARY
AGYNOUS
AGYRATE
AGYRIA
AH
AHA
AHAAINA
AHAMKARA
AHANKARA
AHARTALAV
AHAU
AHAUNCH
AHEAD
AHEAP
AHEIGHT
AHEM
AHEY
AHIGH
AHIMSA
AHIND
AHL
AHLUWALIA
AHM
AHMADI
AHMAR
AHMEDI
AHOLD
AHOLE
AHOLT
AHONG
AHOO
AHORSEBACK
AHOY
AHSAN
AHU
AHUACA
AHUATLE
AHUEHUETE
AHULL
AHUM
AHUNG
AHUNGERED
AHUNGRY
AHUNT
AHURA
AHUREWA
AHUSH
AHUULA
AHWAL
AHYPNIA
AI
AIBLINS
AICHMOPHOBIA
AID
AIDANCE
AIDANT
AIDE
AIDED
AIDER
AIDFUL
AIDING
AIDLESS
AIDMAN
AIE
AIEL
AIERY
AIGIALOSAUR
AIGLET
AIGREMORE
AIGRET
AIGRETTE
AIGUIERE
AIGUILLE
AIGUILLETTE
AIKANE

AIKEN
AIKINITE
AIL
AILANTERY
AILANTHIC
AILANTHUS
AILANTINE
AILANTO
AILD
AILE
AILED
AILERON
AILETTE
AILING
AILLT
AILMENT
AILSYTE
AILUROID
AILUROMANIA
AILWEED
AIM
AIMARA
AIMED
AIMER
AIMFUL
AIMFULLY
AIMING
AIMLESS
AIMLESSLY
AIMLESSNESS
AIN
AINALEH
AINCE
AINE
AINEE
AINHUM
AINI
AINOI
AINSELL
AION
AIPI
AIPIM
AIR
AIRABLE
AIRAMPO
AIRAN
AIRBOAT
AIRBORNE
AIRBOUND
AIRBRUSH
AIRBURST
AIRCRAFT
AIRCRAFTMAN
AIRCRAFTMEN
AIRCRAFTSMAN
AIRCREW
AIRCREWMAN
AIRDOCK
AIRDROME
AIRDROP
AIRDROPPED
AIRDROPPING
AIRE
AIRED
AIRER
AIRFIELD
AIRFLOW
AIRFOIL
AIRFRAME
AIRGLOW
AIRGRAPH
AIRHEAD
AIRIER
AIRIEST
AIRIFEROUS
AIRIFIED
AIRIG
AIRILY
AIRINESS
AIRING
AIRISH
AIRLESS
AIRLIFT
AIRLIKE
AIRLINE
AIRLINER
AIRLING
AIRMAIL
AIRMAN
AIRMANSHIP
AIRMARK
AIRMONGER
AIROHYDROGEN
AIROMETER
AIRPARK
AIRPLANE
AIRPLANED
AIRPLANING
AIRPLANIST
AIRPORT
AIRPROOF
AIRS
AIRSCAPE
AIRSCREW
AIRSHEET
AIRSHIP
AIRSICK
AIRSICKNESS
AIRSOME
AIRSPACE
AIRSPEED
AIRSTREAM
AIRSTRIP
AIRT
AIRTH
AIRTIGHT
AIRTIGHTLY
AIRTIGHTNESS
AIRVIEW
AIRWARD
AIRWARDS
AIRWAVE
AIRWAY
AIRWAYMAN
AIRWISE
AIRWOMAN
AIRWOMEN
AIRWORTHY
AIRY
AIS
AISEWEED
AISLE
AISLED
AISLING
AISTEOIR
AISTOPOD
AIT
AITCH
AITCHBONE
AITCHES
AITCHLESS
AITEN
AITESIS
AITHOCHROI
AITION
AITIOTROPIC
AITIS
AITS
AITU
AIVER
AIWAIN
AIWAN
AIZLE
AIZOACEOUS
AJAJA
AJANGLE
AJAR
AJARI
AJAVA
AJAX
AJEE
AJENJO
AJHAR
AJI
AJIMEZ
AJITTER
AJIVA
AJIVIKA
AJO
AJOG
AJOINT
AJONJOLI
AJOUR
AJOURE
AJOURISE
AJOWAN
AJUTMENT
AK
AKA
AKAAKAI
AKABO
AKALA
AKALIMBA
AKAMAI
AKAMATSU
AKAROA
AKASA
AKAZGA
AKAZGIN
AKAZGINE
AKCHA
AKCHEH
AKE
AKEAKE
AKEBI
AKED
AKEE
AKEKI
AKELA
AKELE
AKELEY
AKEMBOLL
AKENBOLD
AKENE
AKENOBEITE
AKEPIRO
AKEPIROS
AKER
AKERITE
AKEY
AKH
AKHOOND
AKHROT
AKHUN
AKHUND
AKHUNDZADA
AKIA
AKIMBO
AKIN
AKINDLE
AKINESIA
AKINESIC
AKINESIS
AKINETE
AKING
AKKUM
AKLE
AKMUDDAR
AKO
AKOLOUTHIA
AKOLUTHIA
AKONGE
AKORI
AKOV
AKPEK
AKRA
AKROCHORDITE
AKROTER
AKROTERIA
AKROTERIAL
AKROTERION
AKU
AKUA
AKUAMMIN
AKUAMMINE
AKULE
AKUND
AKVAVIT
AL
ALA
ALABAMIDE
ALABAMINE
ALABANDITE
ALABARCH
ALABASTER
ALABASTRA
ALABASTRIAN
ALABASTRINE
ALABASTRUM
ALACHA
ALACHAH
ALACK
ALACKADAY
ALACRAN
ALACREATINE
ALACREATININ
ALACRIFY
ALACRIOUS
ALACRIOUSLY
ALACRITOUS
ALACRITY
ALADA
ALAE
ALAGAO
ALAGARTO
ALAGAU
ALAHEE
ALAI
ALAIHI
ALAITE
ALAKE
ALAL
ALALA
ALALI
ALALIA
ALALITE
ALALOI
ALALONGA
ALALUNGA
ALALUS
ALAMBIQUE
ALAMEDA
ALAMIQUI
ALAMIRE
ALAMO
ALAMODALITY
ALAMODE
ALAMORT
ALAMOS
ALAMOSITE
ALAN
ALAND
ALANE
ALANG
ALANGE
ALANGIN
ALANGINE
ALANI
ALANIN
ALANINE
ALANNAH
ALANT
ALANTIC
ALANTIN
ALANTOL
ALANTOLIC
ALANYL
ALAR
ALARE
ALARES
ALARM
ALARMABLE
ALARMED
ALARMEDLY
ALARMING
ALARMINGLY
ALARMISM
ALARMIST
ALARUM
ALARY
ALAS
ALASAS
ALASKAITE
ALASKITE
ALASTRIM
ALATE
ALATED
ALATERN
ALATERNUS
ALATION
ALAUDINE
ALAUND
ALAUNT
ALAY
ALAZOR
ALB
ALBA
ALBACEA
ALBACORA
ALBACORE
ALBACORES
ALBAE
ALBAHACA
ALBAM
ALBAN
ALBANITE
ALBARCO
ALBARDINE
ALBARELLO
ALBARIUM
ALBASPIDIN
ALBATA
ALBATROSS
ALBATROSSES
ALBE
ALBEDO
ALBEDOGRAPH
ALBEE
ALBEIT
ALBERCA
ALBERGATRICE
ALBERGE
ALBERGO
ALBERTIN
ALBERTITE
ALBERTTYPE
ALBERTYPE
ALBESCENCE
ALBESCENT
ALBESPINE
ALBESTON
ALBETAD
ALBICANT
ALBICATION
ALBICORE

ALBICULI
ALBIFICATION
ALBIFICATIVE
ALBIFIED
ALBIFLOROUS
ALBIFY
ALBIFYING
ALBINAL
ALBINESS
ALBINIC
ALBINISM
ALBINISTIC
ALBINO
ALBINOISM
ALBINOS
ALBINOTIC
ALBINURIA
ALBITE
ALBITIC
ALBITICAL
ALBITITE
ALBITIZATION
ALBITOPHYRE
ALBIZZIA
ALBOCRACY
ALBOLITE
ALBOLITH
ALBOPANNIN
ALBOPRUINOSE
ALBORADA
ALBORANITE
ALBRICIAS
ALBRONZE
ALBUGINEOUS
ALBUGINES
ALBUGINITIS
ALBUGO
ALBUM
ALBUMEAN
ALBUMEN
ALBUMENIZE
ALBUMENIZED
ALBUMENIZER
ALBUMENIZING
ALBUMENOID
ALBUMIMETER
ALBUMIN
ALBUMINATE
ALBUMINIFORM
ALBUMINIZE
ALBUMINIZED
ALBUMINIZING
ALBUMINOID
ALBUMINOIDAL
ALBUMINOSE
ALBUMINOSIS
ALBUMINOUS
ALBUMINURIA
ALBUMINURIC
ALBUMOSCOPE
ALBUMOSE
ALBUMOSURIA
ALBURN
ALBURNOUS
ALBURNUM
ALBUS
ALBUTANNIN
ALCABALA
ALCADE
ALCAICERIA
ALCAIDE
ALCALDE
ALCALDIA
ALCALIZATE
ALCAMINE
ALCANNA
ALCANTARA
ALCARRAZA
ALCATRAS
ALCAVALA
ALCAYDE
ALCAZABA
ALCAZAR
ALCAZAVA
ALCE
ALCELAPHINE
ALCHEMIC
ALCHEMICAL
ALCHEMICALLY
ALCHEMIST
ALCHEMISTER
ALCHEMISTIC
ALCHEMISTRY
ALCHEMIZE
ALCHEMIZED
ALCHEMIZING
ALCHEMY
ALCHERA
ALCHERINGA
ALCHITRAN
ALCHOCHODEN
ALCHORNEA
ALCHYMY
ALCIDINE
ALCINE
ALCLAD
ALCO
ALCOGEL
ALCOGENE
ALCOHOL
ALCOHOLATE
ALCOHOLATURE
ALCOHOLIC
ALCOHOLICALLY
ALCOHOLICITY
ALCOHOLISM
ALCOHOLIST
ALCOHOLIZATION
ALCOHOLIZE
ALCOHOLIZED
ALCOHOLIZING
ALCOHOLOMETER
ALCOHOLURIA
ALCOHOLYSIS
ALCOHOLYTIC
ALCORNOQUE
ALCOSOL
ALCOVE
ALCUMY
ALCYON
ALCYONACEAN
ALCYONARIAN
ALCYONIC
ALCYONIFORM
ALCYONOID
ALD
ALDAMIN
ALDAMINE
ALDANE
ALDAY
ALDEA
ALDEAMENT
ALDEHOL
ALDEHYDASE
ALDEHYDE
ALDEHYDIC
ALDEHYDINE
ALDEIA
ALDER
ALDERFLY
ALDERLIEFEST
ALDERMAN
ALDERMANATE
ALDERMANCY
ALDERMANESS
ALDERMANIC
ALDERMANITY
ALDERMANLIKE
ALDERMANLY
ALDERMANRY
ALDERMANSHIP
ALDERMEN
ALDERN
ALDERS
ALDERWOMAN
ALDERWOMEN
ALDIMIN
ALDIMINE
ALDINE
ALDITOL
ALDOL
ALDOLIZATION
ALDOLIZE
ALDOLIZED
ALDOLIZING
ALDOSE
ALDOXIME
ALDRIN
ALE
ALEAK
ALEATORY
ALEBENCH
ALEBERRY
ALEBUSH
ALEC
ALECITHAL
ALECIZE
ALECONNER
ALECOST
ALECTORIA
ALECTORIAE
ALECTORIDINE
ALECTORIOID
ALECUP
ALEE
ALEF
ALEFNULL
ALEFT
ALEFZERO
ALEGAR
ALEGER
ALEHOOF
ALEHOUSE
ALEIKOUM
ALEIKUM
ALEIPTES
ALEKNIGHT
ALEM
ALEMBIC
ALEMBICATE
ALEMBROTH
ALEMITE
ALEMMAL
ALEMONGER
ALEN
ALENGE
ALENGTH
ALENU
ALEPH
ALEPHS
ALEPIDOTE
ALEPINE
ALEPOLE
ALEPOT
ALERCE
ALERSE
ALERT
ALERTA
ALERTLY
ALERTNESS
ALESAN
ALESE
ALESHOT
ALESTAKE
ALETAP
ALETHIC
ALETHIOLOGY
ALETHOSCOPE
ALETTE
ALEUCAEMIC
ALEUCEMIC
ALEUKAEMIC
ALEUKEMIC
ALEURITIC
ALEUROMANCY
ALEUROMETER
ALEURONAT
ALEURONE
ALEURONIC
ALEUROSCOPE
ALEUTITE
ALEVIN
ALEW
ALEWHAP
ALEWIFE
ALEWIVES
ALEXANDERS
ALEXANDRITE
ALEXIA
ALEXIN
ALEXINE
ALEXINIC
ALEXIPHARMIC
ALEXIPYRETIC
ALEXITERIC
ALEY
ALEYARD
ALEYRODID
ALEZAN
ALEZE
ALFA
ALFAJE
ALFAKI
ALFALFA
ALFAQUI
ALFAQUIN
ALFARGA
ALFENIDE
ALFEREZ
ALFET
ALFILARIA
ALFILERIA
ALFILERILLO
ALFIN
ALFIONA
ALFIONE
ALFONCINO
ALFONSIN
ALFONSO
ALFORGE
ALFORJA
ALFRESCO
ALFRIDARIC
ALFRIDARY
ALGA
ALGAE
ALGAECIDE
ALGAESTHESIS
ALGAL
ALGALIA
ALGAROBA
ALGARROBA
ALGARROBILLA
ALGARROBIN
ALGATE
ALGATES
ALGAZEL
ALGEBRA
ALGEBRAIC
ALGEBRAICAL
ALGEBRAIST
ALGEBRAIZE
ALGEBRAIZED
ALGEBRAIZING
ALGEBRIZATION
ALGEDO
ALGEDONIC
ALGEDONICS
ALGEFACIENT
ALGERINE
ALGESIA
ALGESIC
ALGESIS
ALGESTHESIS
ALGETIC
ALGIC
ALGICIDE
ALGID
ALGIDITY
ALGIDNESS
ALGIFIC
ALGIN
ALGINATE
ALGINE
ALGINIC
ALGINURESIS
ALGIST
ALGIVOROUS
ALGOCYAN
ALGODON
ALGODONITE
ALGOGENIC
ALGOID
ALGOLAGNIA
ALGOLAGNIC
ALGOLAGNIST
ALGOLAGNY
ALGOLOGICAL
ALGOLOGIST
ALGOLOGY
ALGOMETER
ALGOMETRIC
ALGOMETRICAL
ALGOMETRY
ALGOPHILIA
ALGOPHOBIA
ALGOR
ALGORISM
ALGORISMIC
ALGORIST
ALGORITHM
ALGORITHMIC
ALGOSIS
ALGOUS
ALGOVITE
ALGUACIL
ALGUAZIL
ALGUM
ALHACENA
ALHENNA
ALHET
ALIAS
ALIASES
ALIBANGBANG
ALIBI
ALIBIED
ALIBIING
ALIBILITY
ALIBIS
ALIBLE
ALICHEL
ALICOCHE
ALICTISAL
ALICULA
ALICULAE

ALICYCLIC
ALIDAD
ALIDADA
ALIDADE
ALIEN
ALIENABILITY
ALIENABLE
ALIENAGE
ALIENATE
ALIENATED
ALIENATING
ALIENATION
ALIENATOR
ALIENE
ALIENED
ALIENEE
ALIENER
ALIENICOLA
ALIENICOLAE
ALIENIGENATE
ALIENING
ALIENISM
ALIENIST
ALIENOR
ALIETHMOID
ALIETHMOIDAL
ALIF
ALIFE
ALIFEROUS
ALIFORM
ALIGEROUS
ALIGHT
ALIGHTED
ALIGHTEN
ALIGHTING
ALIGN
ALIGNED
ALIGNER
ALIGNING
ALIGNMENT
ALIGREEK
ALII
ALIIPOE
ALIKE
ALIKENESS
ALILA
ALILONGHI
ALIM
ALIMA
ALIMENT
ALIMENTAL
ALIMENTALLY
ALIMENTARY
ALIMENTATION
ALIMENTATIVE
ALIMENTER
ALIMENTIC
ALIMENTIVE
ALIMONIED
ALIMONY
ALIN
ALINASAL
ALINE
ALINEATION
ALINED
ALINEMENT
ALINER
ALINING
ALINIT
ALINOTUM
ALINTATAO
ALIOFAR
ALIPATA
ALIPED
ALIPHATIC
ALIPIN
ALIPTAE
ALIPTES
ALIPTIC
ALIQUANT
ALIQUID
ALIQUOT
ALISANDERS
ALISEPTAL
ALISH
ALISIER
ALISMA
ALISMACEOUS
ALISMAD
ALISMAL
ALISMOID
ALISO
ALISON
ALISONITE
ALISOS
ALISP
ALISPHENOID
ALIST
ALIT
ALITE
ALITER
ALITRUNK
ALITURGIC
ALITURGICAL
ALIUD
ALIUNDE
ALIVE
ALIVENESS
ALIVINCULAR
ALIYAH
ALIZARATE
ALIZARI
ALIZARIN
ALIZARINE
ALJAMA
ALJAMADO
ALJAMIA
ALJAMIADO
ALJAMIAH
ALJOFAINA
ALK
ALKAHEST
ALKAHESTIC
ALKAHESTICAL
ALKALAMIDE
ALKALEMIA
ALKALESCENCE
ALKALESCENCY
ALKALESCENT
ALKALI
ALKALIC
ALKALIES
ALKALIFIABLE
ALKALIFIED
ALKALIFY
ALKALIFYING
ALKALIGEN
ALKALIMETER
ALKALIMETRIC
ALKALIMETRY
ALKALINE
ALKALINITY
ALKALINIZE
ALKALINIZED
ALKALINIZING
ALKALINURIA
ALKALIS
ALKALIZABLE
ALKALIZATE
ALKALIZATION
ALKALIZE
ALKALIZER
ALKALOID
ALKALOIDAL
ALKALOIDS
ALKALOMETRY
ALKALOSIS
ALKANAL
ALKANET
ALKANNA
ALKANNIN
ALKANOL
ALKAPTON
ALKAPTONE
ALKAPTONURIA
ALKAPTONURIC
ALKARSIN
ALKARSINE
ALKEKENGI
ALKENE
ALKENYL
ALKERMES
ALKID
ALKIDE
ALKIN
ALKINE
ALKITRAN
ALKOOL
ALKOXID
ALKOXIDE
ALKOXY
ALKOXYL
ALKY
ALKYD
ALKYL
ALKYLAMINE
ALKYLAMINO
ALKYLATE
ALKYLATED
ALKYLATING
ALKYLATION
ALKYLENE
ALKYLIC
ALKYLIDENE
ALKYLIZE
ALKYLOGEN
ALKYLOL
ALKYNE
ALL
ALLA
ALLABUTA
ALLACTITE
ALLAEANTHUS
ALLAGITE
ALLALINITE
ALLAMONTI
ALLAMOTH
ALLAMOTTI
ALLAN
ALLANITE
ALLANITIC
ALLANTIASIS
ALLANTOIC
ALLANTOID
ALLANTOIDAL
ALLANTOIDEAN
ALLANTOIDIAN
ALLANTOIN
ALLANTOIS
ALLANTURIC
ALLARGANDO
ALLASSOTONIC
ALLATIVE
ALLATRATE
ALLAY
ALLAYED
ALLAYER
ALLAYING
ALLAYMENT
ALLBE
ALLBONE
ALLECRET
ALLECT
ALLEE
ALLEGATE
ALLEGATION
ALLEGATOR
ALLEGE
ALLEGEABLE
ALLEGED
ALLEGEDLY
ALLEGEMENT
ALLEGER
ALLEGIANCE
ALLEGIANT
ALLEGING
ALLEGORIC
ALLEGORICAL
ALLEGORICALLY
ALLEGORIES
ALLEGORISM
ALLEGORIST
ALLEGORISTER
ALLEGORISTIC
ALLEGORIZATION
ALLEGORIZE
ALLEGORIZED
ALLEGORIZER
ALLEGORIZING
ALLEGORY
ALLEGRESSE
ALLEGRETTO
ALLEGRETTOS
ALLEGRO
ALLEGROS
ALLEL
ALLELE
ALLELOMORPH
ALLELOTROPY
ALLELUIA
ALLELUIAH
ALLELUIATIC
ALLELUJA
ALLEMAND
ALLEMANDE
ALLEMONTITE
ALLENARLY
ALLENE
ALLENTANDO
ALLENTATO
ALLER
ALLERGEN
ALLERGENIC
ALLERGIC
ALLERGIES
ALLERGIN
ALLERGIST
ALLERGY
ALLERION
ALLEVIATE
ALLEVIATED
ALLEVIATING
ALLEVIATION
ALLEVIATIVE
ALLEVIATOR
ALLEVIATORY
ALLEY
ALLEYED
ALLEYITE
ALLEYS
ALLEYWAY
ALLGOOD
ALLGOVITE
ALLHEAL
ALLIABLE
ALLIABLY
ALLIACEOUS
ALLIANCE
ALLIANCED
ALLIANCER
ALLIANCING
ALLIANT
ALLICHOLLY
ALLICIENCY
ALLICIENT
ALLICIN
ALLIED
ALLIES
ALLIGATE
ALLIGATION
ALLIGATOR
ALLIGATORED
ALLIGATORING
ALLINEATE
ALLINEATION
ALLIS
ALLISION
ALLITERAL
ALLITERATE
ALLITERATED
ALLITERATING
ALLITERATION
ALLITERATIVE
ALLITERATOR
ALLIUM
ALLIVALITE
ALLMOUTH
ALLNESS
ALLO
ALLOBAR
ALLOBARIC
ALLOCABLE
ALLOCAFFEINE
ALLOCATABLE
ALLOCATE
ALLOCATED
ALLOCATING
ALLOCATION
ALLOCATUR
ALLOCHEIRIA
ALLOCHETITE
ALLOCHEZIA
ALLOCHIRAL
ALLOCHIRALLY
ALLOCHIRIA
ALLOCHROIC
ALLOCHROITE
ALLOCHROUS
ALLOCLASE
ALLOCLASITE
ALLOCOCHICK
ALLOCROTONIC
ALLOCRYPTIC
ALLOCTHONOUS
ALLOCUTE
ALLOCUTION
ALLOCUTIVE
ALLOCYANINE
ALLOD
ALLODELPHITE
ALLODESMISM
ALLODGE
ALLODIA
ALLODIAL
ALLODIALISM
ALLODIALIST
ALLODIALITY
ALLODIALLY
ALLODIAN
ALLODIARIES
ALLODIARY
ALLODIES
ALLODIUM
ALLODY
ALLOEOSIS

ALLOEOTIC
ALLOEROTIC
ALLOEROTISM
ALLOGAMOUS
ALLOGAMY
ALLOGENEITY
ALLOGENEOUS
ALLOGENIC
ALLOGRAPH
ALLOKINESIS
ALLOKINETIC
ALLOKURTIC
ALLOLALIA
ALLOLALIC
ALLOMERISM
ALLOMEROUS
ALLOMORPH
ALLOMORPHIC
ALLOMORPHISM
ALLOMORPHITE
ALLOMUCIC
ALLONGE
ALLONOMOUS
ALLONYM
ALLONYMOUS
ALLOPATH
ALLOPATHETIC
ALLOPATHIC
ALLOPATHIST
ALLOPATHY
ALLOPELAGIC
ALLOPHANAMID
ALLOPHANATES
ALLOPHANE
ALLOPHANIC
ALLOPHONE
ALLOPHORE
ALLOPHYLIAN
ALLOPHYTOID
ALLOPLASM
ALLOPLASMIC
ALLOPLAST
ALLOPLASTIC
ALLOPLASTY
ALLOPSYCHIC
ALLOQUIAL
ALLOQUIALISM
ALLOQUY
ALLOSAUR
ALLOSE
ALLOSEMATIC
ALLOSOME
ALLOT
ALLOTED
ALLOTELLURIC
ALLOTHEISM
ALLOTHIMORPH
ALLOTHOGENIC
ALLOTMENT
ALLOTRIURIA
ALLOTROPE
ALLOTROPIC
ALLOTROPICAL
ALLOTROPISM
ALLOTROPIZE
ALLOTROPOUS
ALLOTROPY
ALLOTRYLIC
ALLOTTED
ALLOTTEE
ALLOTTER
ALLOTTERY
ALLOTTING
ALLOTYPE
ALLOTYPICAL
ALLOVER
ALLOW
ALLOWABLE
ALLOWABLENESS
ALLOWABLY
ALLOWANCE
ALLOWANCED
ALLOWANCING
ALLOWED
ALLOWEDLY
ALLOWER
ALLOWING
ALLOXAN
ALLOXANATE
ALLOXANIC
ALLOXANTIN
ALLOXURIC
ALLOXY
ALLOY
ALLOYAGE
ALLOYED
ALLOYING
ALLOZOOID
ALLS
ALLSEED
ALLSPICE
ALLTHING
ALLTHORN
ALLTUD
ALLUDE
ALLUDED
ALLUDING
ALLUMETTE
ALLURE
ALLURED
ALLUREMENT
ALLURER
ALLURING
ALLURINGLY
ALLURINGNESS
ALLUSION
ALLUSIVE
ALLUSIVELY
ALLUSIVENESS
ALLUVIA
ALLUVIAL
ALLUVIATE
ALLUVIATION
ALLUVIO
ALLUVION
ALLUVIOUS
ALLUVIUM
ALLUVIUMS
ALLWHERE
ALLWHITHER
ALLWORK
ALLY
ALLYING
ALLYL
ALLYLAMINE
ALLYLATE
ALLYLATION
ALLYLENE
ALLYLIC
ALMA
ALMACEN
ALMACENISTA
ALMACIGA
ALMACIGO
ALMADIA
ALMADIE
ALMAGEST
ALMAGRA
ALMAH
ALMANAC
ALMANDER
ALMANDINE
ALMANDITE
ALME
ALMEH
ALMEIDINA
ALMEMAR
ALMEMOR
ALMENDRO
ALMENDRON
ALMERIITE
ALMICORE
ALMIGHTILY
ALMIGHTINESS
ALMIGHTY
ALMIQUE
ALMIRAH
ALMOCREBE
ALMOGAVAR
ALMOHAD
ALMOIGN
ALMOIN
ALMON
ALMOND
ALMONDY
ALMONER
ALMONING
ALMONRIES
ALMONRY
ALMOST
ALMOUS
ALMS
ALMSDEED
ALMSFOLK
ALMSGIVER
ALMSGIVING
ALMSHOUSE
ALMSMAN
ALMSMEN
ALMSMONEY
ALMSWOMAN
ALMSWOMEN
ALMUCANTAR
ALMUCE
ALMUD
ALMUDE
ALMUERZO
ALMUG
ALMURY
ALMUTEN
ALN
ALNAGE
ALNAGER
ALNAGERSHIP
ALNEIN
ALNICO
ALNIRESINOL
ALNOITE
ALNUIN
ALNUS
ALOCASIA
ALOCHIA
ALOD
ALODIAL
ALODIALISM
ALODIALIST
ALODIALITY
ALODIALLY
ALODIAN
ALODIARIES
ALODIARY
ALODIES
ALODIUM
ALODY
ALOE
ALOED
ALOEDARY
ALOEMODIN
ALOEROOT
ALOES
ALOESOL
ALOESWOOD
ALOETIC
ALOETICAL
ALOEWOOD
ALOFT
ALOGIA
ALOGICAL
ALOGICALLY
ALOGISM
ALOGY
ALOHA
ALOID
ALOIN
ALOISIITE
ALOJA
ALOMA
ALONE
ALONELY
ALONG
ALONGSHORE
ALONGSHOREMAN
ALONGSIDE
ALONGST
ALOOF
ALOOFE
ALOOFLY
ALOOFNESS
ALOOSE
ALOP
ALOPECIA
ALOPECIST
ALOPECOID
ALOPEKAI
ALOPEKE
ALOPHAS
ALOSE
ALOUATTE
ALOUD
ALOUT
ALOW
ALOWE
ALOYAU
ALOYSIA
ALP
ALPACA
ALPARGATA
ALPASOTES
ALPAX
ALPEEN
ALPENGLOW
ALPENHORN
ALPENSTOCK
ALPENSTOCKER
ALPESTRAL
ALPESTRIAN
ALPESTRINE
ALPHA
ALPHABET
ALPHABETARY
ALPHABETED
ALPHABETIC
ALPHABETICAL
ALPHABETICALLY
ALPHABETICS
ALPHABETIFORM
ALPHABETING
ALPHABETISM
ALPHABETIST
ALPHABETIZATION
ALPHABETIZE
ALPHABETIZED
ALPHABETIZER
ALPHABETIZING
ALPHATOLUIC
ALPHENIC
ALPHIN
ALPHOL
ALPHORN
ALPHOS
ALPHOSIS
ALPHYL
ALPHYN
ALPIEU
ALPIGENE
ALPINE
ALPINELY
ALPINERY
ALPINIA
ALPINISM
ALPINIST
ALPIST
ALPISTE
ALQUEIRE
ALQUIER
ALQUIFOU
ALRAUN
ALREADINESS
ALREADY
ALRIGHT
ALRIGHTY
ALROOT
ALRUNA
ALRUNE
ALS
ALSBACHITE
ALSIFILM
ALSIKE
ALSINACEOUS
ALSMEKILL
ALSO
ALSOON
ALSTONIDINE
ALSTONINE
ALSWEILL
ALSWITH
ALT
ALTAR
ALTARAGE
ALTARED
ALTARIST
ALTARLET
ALTARPIECE
ALTARWISE
ALTAZIMUTH
ALTEA
ALTER
ALTERABILITY
ALTERABLE
ALTERABLENESS
ALTERABLY
ALTERANT
ALTERATION
ALTERATIVE
ALTERCATE
ALTERCATED
ALTERCATING
ALTERCATION
ALTERCATIVE
ALTERED
ALTEREGOISM
ALTERER
ALTERING
ALTERITY
ALTERN
ALTERNACY
ALTERNAMENTE
ALTERNANCE
ALTERNANT
ALTERNARIOSE
ALTERNAT
ALTERNATE
ALTERNATED
ALTERNATELY
ALTERNATER

ALTERNATING
ALTERNATION
ALTERNATIVE
ALTERNATIVELY
ALTERNATIVENESS
ALTERNATIVITY
ALTERNATIVO
ALTERNATOR
ALTERNE
ALTERNIZE
ALTERUM
ALTESSE
ALTEZA
ALTEZZA
ALTHAEA
ALTHAEIN
ALTHEA
ALTHEIN
ALTHEINE
ALTHIONIC
ALTHO
ALTHORN
ALTHOUGH
ALTI
ALTIFY
ALTIGRAPH
ALTILIK
ALTILOQUENCE
ALTILOQUENT
ALTIMETER
ALTIMETRICAL
ALTIMETRY
ALTIN
ALTINCAR
ALTININCK
ALTIPLANICIE
ALTIPLANO
ALTISCOPE
ALTISONANT
ALTISSIMO
ALTITUDE
ALTITUDES
ALTITUDINAL
ALTO
ALTOCUMULUS
ALTOGETHER
ALTOIST
ALTOMETER
ALTOS
ALTOSTRATUS
ALTOUN
ALTRICES
ALTRICIAL
ALTROSE
ALTRUISM
ALTRUIST
ALTRUISTIC
ALTRUISTICALLY
ALTSCHIN
ALTUN
ALTURE
ALTUS
ALUDEL
ALULA
ALULAE
ALULAR
ALULET
ALUM
ALUMBLOOM
ALUMEN
ALUMETIZE
ALUMINA
ALUMINAPHONE
ALUMINATE
ALUMINE
ALUMINIC
ALUMINIDE
ALUMINIFORM
ALUMINITE
ALUMINIUM
ALUMINIZE
ALUMINIZED
ALUMINIZING
ALUMINOSE
ALUMINOSIS
ALUMINOSITY
ALUMINOTYPE
ALUMINOUS
ALUMINUM
ALUMINYL
ALUMITE
ALUMNA
ALUMNAE
ALUMNAL
ALUMNI
ALUMNIATE
ALUMNUS
ALUMROOT
ALUMSTONE
ALUNITE
ALUNOGEN
ALUPAG
ALURE
ALURGITE
ALUSHTITE
ALUTA
ALUTACEOUS
ALVAR
ALVEARIES
ALVEARIUM
ALVEARY
ALVEI
ALVELOS
ALVELOZ
ALVEOLA
ALVEOLAE
ALVEOLAR
ALVEOLARY
ALVEOLATE
ALVEOLATED
ALVEOLATION
ALVEOLE
ALVEOLI
ALVEOLIFORM
ALVEOLITE
ALVEOLONASAL
ALVEOLOTOMY
ALVEOLUS
ALVEUS
ALVIDUCOUS
ALVIN
ALVINE
ALVITE
ALVUS
ALWAY
ALWAYS
ALWISE
ALY
ALYMPHIA
ALYPIN
ALYPINE
ALYSSON
ALYSSUM
ALYTARCH
AM
AMA
AMAAS
AMABILE
AMABILITY
AMACRATIC
AMACRINAL
AMACRINE
AMADAVAT
AMADELPHOUS
AMADOU
AMAGA
AMAH
AMAIN
AMAINE
AMAIST
AMAISTER
AMAKEBE
AMALA
AMALAITA
AMALAKA
AMALETT
AMALGAM
AMALGAMABLE
AMALGAMATE
AMALGAMATED
AMALGAMATER
AMALGAMATING
AMALGAMATION
AMALGAMATIVE
AMALGAMATOR
AMALGAMIST
AMALGAMIZE
AMALTAS
AMAMAU
AMAND
AMANDIN
AMANG
AMANI
AMANIA
AMANITIN
AMANITINE
AMANORI
AMANOUS
AMANT
AMANTE
AMANUENSES
AMANUENSIS
AMAPA
AMAR
AMARANTH
AMARANTHINE
AMARANTHOID
AMARANTITE
AMARELLE
AMAREVOLE
AMARGOSA
AMARGOSO
AMARGOSOS
AMARILLO
AMARILLOS
AMARIN
AMARINE
AMARITY
AMAROID
AMAROIDAL
AMARTHRITIS
AMARYLLID
AMASESIS
AMASS
AMASSED
AMASSER
AMASSETTE
AMASSING
AMASSMENT
AMASTHENIC
AMASTIA
AMASTY
AMATE
AMATEUR
AMATEURISH
AMATEURISHLY
AMATEURISHNESS
AMATEURISM
AMATITO
AMATIVE
AMATIVELY
AMATIVENESS
AMATOL
AMATORIAL
AMATORIALLY
AMATORIAN
AMATORIES
AMATORIO
AMATORIOUS
AMATORY
AMATRICE
AMATUNGULA
AMAUROSIS
AMAUROTIC
AMAXOMANIA
AMAY
AMAZE
AMAZED
AMAZEFUL
AMAZEMENT
AMAZING
AMAZON
AMAZONITE
AMBA
AMBACH
AMBAGE
AMBAGES
AMBAGIOSITY
AMBAGIOUS
AMBAGIOUSLY
AMBAGITORY
AMBAK
AMBALAM
AMBAN
AMBAR
AMBAREE
AMBARELLA
AMBARI
AMBARY
AMBAS
AMBASH
AMBASSADE
AMBASSADOR
AMBASSADRESS
AMBASSY
AMBATCH
AMBAY
AMBE
AMBEER
AMBER
AMBERFISH
AMBERGRIS
AMBERIFEROUS
AMBERINA
AMBERITE
AMBERJACK
AMBEROID
AMBEROUS
AMBERY
AMBIANCE
AMBIDEXTER
AMBIDEXTERITY
AMBIDEXTRAL
AMBIDEXTROUS
AMBIENCE
AMBIENS
AMBIENT
AMBIER
AMBIGENOUS
AMBIGUITIES
AMBIGUITY
AMBIGUOUS
AMBIGUOUSLY
AMBIGUOUSNESS
AMBILATERAL
AMBILEVOUS
AMBILIAN
AMBIOPIA
AMBIPAROUS
AMBISINISTER
AMBIT
AMBITAL
AMBITENDENCY
AMBITION
AMBITIONIST
AMBITIONLESS
AMBITIOUS
AMBITIOUSLY
AMBITIOUSNESS
AMBITTY
AMBITUS
AMBIVALENCE
AMBIVALENCY
AMBIVALENT
AMBIVERSION
AMBIVERT
AMBLE
AMBLED
AMBLER
AMBLING
AMBLINGLY
AMBLOTIC
AMBLYGON
AMBLYGONITE
AMBLYOPE
AMBLYOPIA
AMBLYOPIC
AMBLYOSCOPE
AMBLYPOD
AMBLYSTEGITE
AMBO
AMBOCEPTOR
AMBOMALLEAL
AMBON
AMBONES
AMBONITE
AMBOS
AMBOSEXOUS
AMBRACAN
AMBRAIN
AMBRETTE
AMBRIES
AMBRITE
AMBROID
AMBROLOGY
AMBROSE
AMBROSIA
AMBROSIAC
AMBROSIAL
AMBROSIALLY
AMBROSIAN
AMBROSIATE
AMBROSIN
AMBROSINE
AMBROSTEROL
AMBROTYPE
AMBRY
AMBSACE
AMBULACRA
AMBULACRAL
AMBULACRUM
AMBULANCE
AMBULANCED
AMBULANCER
AMBULANCING
AMBULANT
AMBULATE
AMBULATED
AMBULATING
AMBULATION
AMBULATIVE
AMBULATOR
AMBULATORIA
AMBULATORIAL
AMBULATORIES

AMBULATORIUM
AMBULATORIUMS
AMBULATORY
AMBULIA
AMBULING
AMBULOMANCY
AMBURBIAL
AMBURY
AMBUSCADE
AMBUSCADED
AMBUSCADER
AMBUSCADING
AMBUSCADO
AMBUSCADOED
AMBUSH
AMBUSHER
AMBUSHMENT
AMCHOOR
AME
AMEBA
AMEBAE
AMEBAN
AMEBAS
AMEBIAN
AMEBIASIS
AMEBIC
AMEBICIDAL
AMEBICIDE
AMEBID
AMEBIFORM
AMEBOBACTER
AMEBOCYTE
AMEBOID
AMEBOIDISM
AMEBOUS
AMEBULA
AMEED
AMEEN
AMEER
AMEIOSIS
AMEL
AMELAND
AMELCORN
AMELET
AMELIORABLE
AMELIORANT
AMELIORATE
AMELIORATED
AMELIORATING
AMELIORATION
AMELIORATIVE
AMELIORATOR
AMELL
AMELLUS
AMELU
AMELUS
AMEN
AMENABILITY
AMENABLE
AMENABLENESS
AMENABLY
AMENAGE
AMENANCE
AMEND
AMENDABLE
AMENDATORY
AMENDE
AMENDER
AMENDING
AMENDMENT
AMENDS
AMENE
AMENITIES
AMENITY
AMENORRHEA
AMENORRHEAL
AMENORRHEIC
AMENORRHOEA
AMENORRHOEAL
AMENORRHOEIC
AMENT
AMENTA
AMENTACEOUS
AMENTAL
AMENTIA
AMENTIFEROUS
AMENTIFORM
AMENTULA
AMENTULUM
AMENTUM
AMENUSE
AMER
AMERCE
AMERCEABLE
AMERCED
AMERCEMENT
AMERCER
AMERCIAMENT
AMERCING
AMERICIUM
AMERIKANI
AMERISM
AMERISTIC
AMERVEIL
AMESACE
AMESE
AMESITE
AMETABOLE
AMETABOLIC
AMETABOLISM
AMETABOLOUS
AMETALLOUS
AMETHODICAL
AMETHYST
AMETHYSTINE
AMETRIA
AMETROMETER
AMETROPE
AMETROPIA
AMETROPIC
AMETROUS
AMGARN
AMHAR
AMHERSTITE
AMHRAN
AMI
AMIA
AMIABILITY
AMIABLE
AMIABLENESS
AMIABLY
AMIANTH
AMIANTHINE
AMIANTHOID
AMIANTHOIDAL
AMIANTHUS
AMIANTUS
AMIC
AMICABILITY
AMICABLE
AMICABLENESS
AMICABLY
AMICAL
AMICE
AMICED
AMICICIDE
AMICOUS
AMICROBIC
AMICRON
AMICTUS
AMID
AMIDASE
AMIDATE
AMIDATION
AMIDE
AMIDIC
AMIDIN
AMIDINE
AMIDO
AMIDOACETAL
AMIDOACETIC
AMIDOCAPRIC
AMIDOGEN
AMIDOHEXOSE
AMIDOKETONE
AMIDOL
AMIDOMYELIN
AMIDONE
AMIDOPHENOL
AMIDOPYRINE
AMIDOXIME
AMIDOXYL
AMIDRAZONE
AMIDSHIP
AMIDSHIPS
AMIDST
AMIDSTREAM
AMIDULIN
AMIE
AMIGA
AMIGO
AMIGOS
AMIL
AMIMIA
AMIN
AMINASE
AMINATE
AMINATION
AMINE
AMINI
AMINIC
AMINITY
AMINO
AMINOACETAL
AMINOACETONE
AMINOAZO
AMINOBENZENE
AMINOBENZOIC
AMINOCAPROIC
AMINOFORMIC
AMINOGEN
AMINOKETONE
AMINOLIPIN
AMINOLYSIS
AMINOLYTIC
AMINOMYELIN
AMINOPHENOL
AMINOPURINE
AMINOSIS
AMINOVALERIC
AMINOXYLOL
AMIR
AMIRAY
AMIS
AMISS
AMISSIBILITY
AMISSIBLE
AMISSION
AMIT
AMITATE
AMITIE
AMITIES
AMITOSIS
AMITOTIC
AMITOTICALLY
AMITY
AMIXIA
AMLA
AMLAH
AMLET
AMLI
AMLIKAR
AMLONG
AMMA
AMMAN
AMMELINE
AMMEOS
AMMER
AMMETER
AMMIACEOUS
AMMINE
AMMINOLYSIS
AMMINOLYTIC
AMMIOLITE
AMMO
AMMOBIUM
AMMOCETE
AMMOCHAETA
AMMOCHAETAE
AMMOCHRYSE
AMMOCOETE
AMMOCOETES
AMMOCOETID
AMMOCOETOID
AMMODYTE
AMMODYTOID
AMMONAL
AMMONATE
AMMONATION
AMMONIA
AMMONIAC
AMMONIACAL
AMMONIACUM
AMMONIAEMIA
AMMONIATE
AMMONIATED
AMMONIATING
AMMONIATION
AMMONIC
AMMONICAL
AMMONIEMIA
AMMONIFIER
AMMONIFY
AMMONION
AMMONITE
AMMONITIC
AMMONITOID
AMMONIUM
AMMONIURET
AMMONIURETED
AMMONIURIA
AMMONIZATION
AMMONOBASIC
AMMONOID
AMMONOIDEAN
AMMONOLYSIS
AMMONOLYTIC
AMMONOLYZE
AMMOPHILOUS
AMMORESLINOL
AMMOTHERAPY
AMMU
AMMUNITION
AMNEMONIC
AMNESIA
AMNESIC
AMNESTIC
AMNESTIES
AMNESTY
AMNIA
AMNIAC
AMNIC
AMNIOCHORIAL
AMNIOCLEPSIS
AMNIOMANCY
AMNION
AMNIONIC
AMNIONS
AMNIORRHEA
AMNIOS
AMNIOTE
AMNIOTIC
AMNIOTITIS
AMNIOTOME
AMOBARBITAL
AMOBER
AMOEBA
AMOEBAE
AMOEBAEA
AMOEBAEAN
AMOEBAEUM
AMOEBAN
AMOEBEAN
AMOEBEUM
AMOEBIAN
AMOEBIASIS
AMOEBIC
AMOEBICIDAL
AMOEBICIDE
AMOEBID
AMOEBIFORM
AMOEBOCYTE
AMOEBOID
AMOEBOIDISM
AMOEBOUS
AMOEBULA
AMOINDER
AMOK
AMOKE
AMOLE
AMOLILLA
AMOLISH
AMOLLISH
AMOMAL
AMOMUM
AMONG
AMONGST
AMONTILLADO
AMOR
AMORA
AMORADO
AMORAIC
AMORAIM
AMORAL
AMORALISM
AMORALITY
AMORALLY
AMORET
AMORETTI
AMORETTO
AMORINI
AMORINO
AMORISM
AMORIST
AMORISTIC
AMOROSA
AMOROSITY
AMOROSO
AMOROUS
AMOROUSLY
AMOROUSNESS
AMORPH
AMORPHA
AMORPHI
AMORPHIA
AMORPHIC
AMORPHINISM
AMORPHISM
AMORPHOPHYTE
AMORPHOTAE
AMORPHOUS
AMORPHOUSLY
AMORPHUS
AMORPHY
AMORT

AMORTISE
AMORTISSEUR
AMORTIZABLE
AMORTIZATION
AMORTIZE
AMORTIZED
AMORTIZEMENT
AMORTIZING
AMOSITE
AMOTION
AMOTUS
AMOULI
AMOUNT
AMOUR
AMOURET
AMOURETTE
AMOURIST
AMOVABILITY
AMOVABLE
AMOVE
AMOVED
AMOVING
AMPALAYA
AMPALEA
AMPANGABEITE
AMPARO
AMPASIMENITE
AMPASSY
AMPELITE
AMPELITIC
AMPELOGRAPHY
AMPELOPSIDIN
AMPELOPSIN
AMPELOPSIS
AMPER
AMPERAGE
AMPERE
AMPEREMETER
AMPEROMETER
AMPERSAND
AMPERY
AMPHANTHIA
AMPHANTHIUM
AMPHEROTOKY
AMPHETAMINE
AMPHIASTER
AMPHIB
AMPHIBALI
AMPHIBALUS
AMPHIBIA
AMPHIBIAL
AMPHIBIAN
AMPHIBIETY
AMPHIBIOLOGY
AMPHIBION
AMPHIBIOTIC
AMPHIBIOUS
AMPHIBIOUSLY
AMPHIBIUM
AMPHIBLASTIC
AMPHIBOLE
AMPHIBOLIA
AMPHIBOLIC
AMPHIBOLITE
AMPHIBOLITIC
AMPHIBOLOGY
AMPHIBOLOUS
AMPHIBOLY
AMPHIBRACH
AMPHIBRACHIC
AMPHIBRYOUS
AMPHICARPIA
AMPHICARPIC
AMPHICARPIUM
AMPHICENTRIC
AMPHICHROIC
AMPHICHROME
AMPHICHROMY
AMPHICOELOUS
AMPHICRANIA
AMPHICRIBRAL
AMPHICTYON
AMPHICTYONIC
AMPHICTYONY
AMPHICYRTIC
AMPHICYTULA
AMPHID
AMPHIDE
AMPHIDESMOUS
AMPHIDETIC
AMPHIDIPLOID
AMPHIDISC
AMPHIDISK
AMPHIEROTIC
AMPHIEROTISM
AMPHIGAEAN
AMPHIGAM
AMPHIGAMOUS
AMPHIGEAN
AMPHIGEN
AMPHIGENE
AMPHIGENESIS
AMPHIGENETIC
AMPHIGENOUS
AMPHIGONIA
AMPHIGONIC
AMPHIGONIUM
AMPHIGONOUS
AMPHIGONY
AMPHIGORIC
AMPHIGORIES
AMPHIGORY
AMPHIGOURI
AMPHIGOURIS
AMPHIKARYON
AMPHILOGISM
AMPHILOGY
AMPHIMACER
AMPHIMIXIS
AMPHIMORULA
AMPHIMORULAE
AMPHINEUROUS
AMPHINUCLEUS
AMPHIOXUS
AMPHIPHLOIC
AMPHIPLATYAN
AMPHIPNEUST
AMPHIPNEUSTIC
AMPHIPOD
AMPHIPODAL
AMPHIPODAN
AMPHIPODOUS
AMPHIPYRENIN
AMPHIRHINAL
AMPHIRHINE
AMPHISARCA
AMPHISBAENA
AMPHISBAENIC
AMPHISCIANS
AMPHISCII
AMPHISPORE
AMPHISTOME
AMPHISTOMOID
AMPHISTOMOUS
AMPHISTYLAR
AMPHISTYLIC
AMPHISTYLY
AMPHITENE
AMPHITHEATER
AMPHITHEATRE
AMPHITHECIA
AMPHITHECIAL
AMPHITHECIUM
AMPHITHECT
AMPHITHYRON
AMPHITOKAL
AMPHITOKOUS
AMPHITOKY
AMPHITRIAENE
AMPHITRICHA
AMPHITROPAL
AMPHITROPOUS
AMPHIVASAL
AMPHIVOROUS
AMPHODARCH
AMPHODELITE
AMPHOGENOUS
AMPHOLYTE
AMPHOPEPTONE
AMPHOPHILIC
AMPHOPHILOUS
AMPHORA
AMPHORAE
AMPHORAL
AMPHORE
AMPHORIC
AMPHORICITY
AMPHORILOQUY
AMPHOROPHONY
AMPHOROUS
AMPHOTERIC
AMPLE
AMPLECT
AMPLECTANT
AMPLENESS
AMPLEX
AMPLEXATION
AMPLEXICAUL
AMPLEXUS
AMPLIATE
AMPLIATION
AMPLIATIVE
AMPLICATIVE
AMPLIFICATE
AMPLIFICATION
AMPLIFICATIVE
AMPLIFICATOR
AMPLIFIED
AMPLIFIER
AMPLIFY
AMPLIFYING
AMPLITUDE
AMPLY
AMPOLLOSITY
AMPONGUE
AMPOULE
AMPTE
AMPUL
AMPULE
AMPULLA
AMPULLACEOUS
AMPULLAE
AMPULLAR
AMPULLARY
AMPULLATE
AMPULLATED
AMPULLIFORM
AMPULLITIS
AMPULLULA
AMPUTATE
AMPUTATED
AMPUTATING
AMPUTATION
AMPUTATIVE
AMPUTATOR
AMPUTEE
AMPYCES
AMPYX
AMPYXES
AMRA
AMREETA
AMREL
AMRELLE
AMRIT
AMRITA
AMSATH
AMSEL
AMSONIA
AMT
AMTER
AMTMAN
AMTMEN
AMTS
AMU
AMUCK
AMUGIS
AMUGUIS
AMULA
AMULAE
AMULAS
AMULET
AMULETIC
AMULLA
AMUNAM
AMURCA
AMURCOSITY
AMURCOUS
AMUSABLE
AMUSE
AMUSED
AMUSEDLY
AMUSEMENT
AMUSEMENTS
AMUSER
AMUSETTE
AMUSIA
AMUSING
AMUSINGLY
AMUSINGNESS
AMUSIVE
AMUSIVELY
AMUSIVENESS
AMUTTER
AMUYON
AMUYONG
AMUZE
AMVIS
AMY
AMYDON
AMYELIA
AMYELIC
AMYELINIC
AMYELONIC
AMYELOUS
AMYGDAL
AMYGDALA
AMYGDALAE
AMYGDALASE
AMYGDALATE
AMYGDALE
AMYGDALIC
AMYGDALIFORM
AMYGDALIN
AMYGDALINE
AMYGDALITIS
AMYGDALOID
AMYGDALOIDAL
AMYGDALOLITH
AMYGDALONCUS
AMYGDALOTOME
AMYGDALOTOMY
AMYGDOPHENIN
AMYGDULE
AMYL
AMYLACEOUS
AMYLAMINE
AMYLAN
AMYLASE
AMYLATE
AMYLEMIA
AMYLENE
AMYLIC
AMYLIDENE
AMYLIFEROUS
AMYLIN
AMYLO
AMYLOCLASTIC
AMYLODEXTRIN
AMYLOGEN
AMYLOGENESIS
AMYLOGENIC
AMYLOID
AMYLOIDAL
AMYLOIDOSIS
AMYLOLEUCITE
AMYLOLYSIS
AMYLOLYTIC
AMYLOM
AMYLOME
AMYLOMETER
AMYLON
AMYLOPECTIN
AMYLOPHAGIA
AMYLOPLAST
AMYLOPLASTIC
AMYLOPLASTID
AMYLOPSASE
AMYLOPSIN
AMYLOSE
AMYLOSIS
AMYLUM
AMYLURIA
AMYNODONT
AMYOSTHENIA
AMYOSTHENIC
AMYOTAXIA
AMYOTONIA
AMYOTROPHIA
AMYOTROPHIC
AMYOTROPHY
AMYOUS
AMYRIN
AMYROL
AMYROOT
AN
ANA
ANABAENA
ANABAENAS
ANABAPTIZED
ANABAPTIZING
ANABAS
ANABASES
ANABASIN
ANABASINE
ANABASIS
ANABASSE
ANABATA
ANABATHMOI
ANABATHMOS
ANABATIC
ANABEROGA
ANABIBAZON
ANABIOSIS
ANABIOTIC
ANABLEPS
ANABO
ANABOHITSITE
ANABOLIC
ANABOLIN
ANABOLISM
ANABOLITE
ANABOLIZE
ANABOLY
ANABONG
ANABRANCH

ANABROSIS
ANABROTIC
ANAC
ANACAHUITA
ANACAHUITE
ANACALYPSIS
ANACAMPSIS
ANACAMPTIC
ANACAMPTICS
ANACANTH
ANACANTHINE
ANACANTHOUS
ANACARA
ANACARD
ANACARDIC
ANACATHARSIS
ANACATHARTIC
ANACEPHALIZE
ANACHORISM
ANACHROMASIS
ANACHRONIC
ANACHRONICAL
ANACHRONICALLY
ANACHRONISM
ANACHRONIST
ANACHRONISTIC
ANACHRONIZE
ANACHRONOUS
ANACID
ANACIDITY
ANACK
ANACLASIS
ANACLASTIC
ANACLASTICS
ANACLETICA
ANACLETICUM
ANACLINAL
ANACLISIS
ANACLITIC
ANACOENOSIS
ANACOLUTHA
ANACOLUTHIC
ANACOLUTHON
ANACOLUTHONS
ANACONDA
ANACOUSTIC
ANACROGYNOUS
ANACROTIC
ANACROTISM
ANACRUSIS
ANACRUSTIC
ANACUSIA
ANACUSIC
ANACUSIS
ANADEM
ANADENIA
ANADICROTIC
ANADICROTISM
ANADIDYMUS
ANADIPLOSIS
ANADIPSIA
ANADIPSIC
ANADROM
ANADROMOUS
ANAEMATOSIS
ANAEMIA
ANAEMIC
ANAERETIC
ANAEROBATION
ANAEROBE
ANAEROBIA
ANAEROBIC
ANAEROBIOSIS
ANAEROBIOTIC
ANAEROBIUM
ANAEROPHYTE
ANAEROPLASTIC
ANAEROPLASTY
ANAESTHESIA
ANAESTHESIS
ANAESTHETIC
ANAESTHETIST
ANAESTHETIZE
ANAESTHETIZED
ANAESTHETIZER
ANAESTHETIZING
ANAESTHYL
ANAGALACTIC
ANAGAP
ANAGENESIS
ANAGENETIC
ANAGEP
ANAGLYPH
ANAGLYPHIC
ANAGLYPHICAL
ANAGLYPHY
ANAGLYPTIC
ANAGLYPTICS
ANAGLYPTON
ANAGNORISIS
ANAGNOST
ANAGNOSTES
ANAGOGE
ANAGOGIC
ANAGOGICAL
ANAGOGICALLY
ANAGOGICS
ANAGOGY
ANAGRAM
ANAGRAMMATIC
ANAGRAMS
ANAGRAPH
ANAGUA
ANAGYRINE
ANAHAO
ANAHAU
ANAI
ANAKINESIS
ANAKINETIC
ANAKTORON
ANAL
ANALABOS
ANALAV
ANALCIME
ANALCIMITE
ANALCITE
ANALCITITE
ANALECTA
ANALECTIC
ANALECTS
ANALEMMA
ANALEMMATIC
ANALEPSES
ANALEPSIS
ANALEPSY
ANALEPTIC
ANALGEN
ANALGENE
ANALGESIA
ANALGESIC
ANALGESIS
ANALGESIST
ANALGETIC
ANALGIA
ANALGIC
ANALGIZE
ANALLAGMATIC
ANALLANTOIC
ANALLERGIC
ANALLY
ANALOG
ANALOGA
ANALOGIC
ANALOGICAL
ANALOGICALLY
ANALOGICE
ANALOGIES
ANALOGION
ANALOGISM
ANALOGIST
ANALOGISTIC
ANALOGIZE
ANALOGIZED
ANALOGIZING
ANALOGON
ANALOGOUS
ANALOGOUSLY
ANALOGUE
ANALOGY
ANALPHABET
ANALPHABETE
ANALPHABETIC
ANALYSAND
ANALYSATION
ANALYSE
ANALYSED
ANALYSER
ANALYSES
ANALYSING
ANALYSIS
ANALYST
ANALYTIC
ANALYTICAL
ANALYTICALLY
ANALYTICS
ANALYZABLE
ANALYZATION
ANALYZE
ANALYZED
ANALYZER
ANALYZING
ANAM
ANAMA
ANAMESITE
ANAMIRTIN
ANAMMONIDE
ANAMNESIS
ANAMNESTIC
ANAMNIONIC
ANAMNIOTE
ANAMNIOTIC
ANAMORPHIC
ANAMORPHISM
ANAMORPHOSE
ANAMORPHOSES
ANAMORPHOSIS
ANAMORPHOTE
ANAMORPHOUS
ANAN
ANANA
ANANAS
ANANDA
ANANDRARIOUS
ANANDRIA
ANANDROUS
ANANEPIONIC
ANANGIOID
ANANKE
ANANTER
ANANTHERATE
ANANTHEROUS
ANANTHOUS
ANANYM
ANAPAEST
ANAPAESTIC
ANAPAESTICAL
ANAPAGANIZE
ANAPAITE
ANAPANAPA
ANAPEIRATIC
ANAPEST
ANAPESTIC
ANAPHASE
ANAPHIA
ANAPHORA
ANAPHORAL
ANAPHORIA
ANAPHORIC
ANAPHORICAL
ANAPHRODISIA
ANAPHRODITIC
ANAPHYLACTIC
ANAPHYLACTIN
ANAPHYLACTOID
ANAPHYLAXIS
ANAPHYTE
ANAPLASIA
ANAPLASIS
ANAPLASM
ANAPLASMOSIS
ANAPLASTIC
ANAPLASTY
ANAPLEROSIS
ANAPLEROTIC
ANAPNEA
ANAPNOGRAPH
ANAPNOIC
ANAPNOMETER
ANAPODEICTIC
ANAPOPHYSIAL
ANAPOPHYSIS
ANAPSID
ANAPSIDAN
ANAPTERYGOTE
ANAPTOTIC
ANAPTYCHI
ANAPTYCHUS
ANAPTYCTIC
ANAPTYCTICAL
ANAPTYXIS
ANAQUA
ANARCESTEAN
ANARCH
ANARCHIC
ANARCHICAL
ANARCHICALLY
ANARCHISM
ANARCHIST
ANARCHISTIC
ANARCHIZE
ANARCHY
ANARETA
ANARETIC
ANARETICAL
ANARGYROI
ANARGYROS
ANARTHRIA
ANARTHRIC
ANARTHROSIS
ANARTHROUS
ANARTHROUSLY
ANARTISMOS
ANARYA
ANASARCA
ANASARCOUS
ANASCHISTIC
ANASEISMIC
ANASPADIAS
ANASPALIN
ANASTALSIS
ANASTALTIC
ANASTASIMON
ANASTASIMOS
ANASTASIS
ANASTATE
ANASTATIC
ANASTIGMAT
ANASTIGMATIC
ANASTOMOSE
ANASTOMOSED
ANASTOMOSES
ANASTOMOSING
ANASTOMOSIS
ANASTOMOTIC
ANASTROPHE
ANASTROPHY
ANATASE
ANATEXIS
ANATHEMA
ANATHEMAS
ANATHEMATA
ANATHEMATIC
ANATHEMATISM
ANATHEMATIZE
ANATHEMIZE
ANATIFA
ANATIFAE
ANATIFER
ANATIFEROUS
ANATINE
ANATIRA
ANATMAN
ANATOCISM
ANATOMIC
ANATOMICAL
ANATOMICALLY
ANATOMIES
ANATOMISM
ANATOMIST
ANATOMIZE
ANATOMIZED
ANATOMIZER
ANATOMIZING
ANATOMY
ANATOPISM
ANATOXIN
ANATREPTIC
ANATRIPSIS
ANATRIPTIC
ANATRON
ANATROPAL
ANATROPOUS
ANATTA
ANATTO
ANAUDIA
ANAUNTER
ANAUNTERS
ANAUXITE
ANAXIAL
ANAXON
ANAXONE
ANAY
ANAZOTURIA
ANBA
ANBURY
ANCESTOR
ANCESTORIAL
ANCESTORS
ANCESTRAL
ANCESTRALLY
ANCESTRESS
ANCESTRIES
ANCESTRY
ANCHIETIN
ANCHIETINE
ANCHITHERE
ANCHITHERIOID
ANCHOR
ANCHORABLE
ANCHORAGE
ANCHORATE
ANCHORED
ANCHORER
ANCHORESS
ANCHORET

ANCHORETISM
ANCHORHOLD
ANCHORING
ANCHORITE
ANCHORITESS
ANCHORITIC
ANCHORITICAL
ANCHORITISM
ANCHORLESS
ANCHOVIES
ANCHOVY
ANCHUSA
ANCHUSIN
ANCHYLOSE
ANCHYLOSIS
ANCIENCE
ANCIENCY
ANCIENNETE
ANCIENT
ANCIENTISM
ANCIENTLY
ANCIENTNESS
ANCIENTRY
ANCIENTY
ANCILE
ANCILIA
ANCILLA
ANCILLARY
ANCIPITAL
ANCIPITOUS
ANCISTROID
ANCLE
ANCODONT
ANCOME
ANCON
ANCONA
ANCONAD
ANCONAGRA
ANCONAL
ANCONE
ANCONEAL
ANCONEI
ANCONES
ANCONEUS
ANCONITIS
ANCONOID
ANCONY
ANCORA
ANCYLOPOD
ANCYLOSE
ANCYLOSTOME
AND
ANDA
ANDABATA
ANDABATARIAN
ANDABATISM
ANDALUSITE
ANDANTE
ANDANTINO
ANDE
ANDERUN
ANDESINE
ANDESINITE
ANDESITE
ANDESITIC
ANDESYTE
ANDIRINE
ANDIROBA
ANDIRON
ANDORITE
ANDOUILLE
ANDOUILLET
ANDOUILLETTE
ANDRADITE
ANDRANATOMY
ANDRARCHY
ANDRENA
ANDRENID
ANDREWSITE
ANDRITE
ANDROCENTRIC
ANDROCLINIUM
ANDROCONIA
ANDROCONIUM
ANDROCRACY
ANDROCRATIC
ANDROCYTE
ANDROECIA
ANDROECIAL
ANDROECIUM
ANDROGEN
ANDROGENESIS
ANDROGENETIC
ANDROGENIC
ANDROGENOUS
ANDROGONIA
ANDROGONIAL
ANDROGYN
ANDROGYNAL
ANDROGYNARY
ANDROGYNE
ANDROGYNEITY
ANDROGYNIC
ANDROGYNISM
ANDROGYNOUS
ANDROGYNUS
ANDROGYNY
ANDROID
ANDROIDAL
ANDROIDES
ANDROKININ
ANDROL
ANDROLEPSIA
ANDROLEPSY
ANDROMANIA
ANDRON
ANDRONITIS
ANDROPETALAR
ANDROPHAGOUS
ANDROPHOBIA
ANDROPHORE
ANDROPHOROUS
ANDROPHORUM
ANDROPHYLL
ANDROSEME
ANDROSIN
ANDROSPHINX
ANDROSPORE
ANDROSTERONE
ANDROTAURIC
ANDS
ANE
ANEAR
ANEATH
ANECDOTA
ANECDOTAGE
ANECDOTAL
ANECDOTALISM
ANECDOTE
ANECDOTIC
ANECDOTICAL
ANECDOTIST
ANECHOIC
ANELE
ANELECTRIC
ANELED
ANELING
ANELYTROUS
ANEMATOSIS
ANEMI
ANEMIA
ANEMIC
ANEMOCHORD
ANEMOCHORE
ANEMOCLASTIC
ANEMOGRAM
ANEMOGRAPH
ANEMOGRAPHIC
ANEMOGRAPHY
ANEMOLOGIC
ANEMOLOGICAL
ANEMOLOGY
ANEMOMETER
ANEMOMETRIC
ANEMOMETRY
ANEMONAL
ANEMONE
ANEMONIN
ANEMONOL
ANEMOPATHY
ANEMOPHILE
ANEMOPHILOUS
ANEMOPHILY
ANEMOSCOPE
ANEMOSIS
ANEMOTAXIS
ANEMOTROPIC
ANEMOTROPISM
ANENCEPHALIA
ANENCEPHALIC
ANENCEPHALUS
ANENCEPHALY
ANEND
ANENERGIA
ANENST
ANENT
ANENTEROUS
ANEPIA
ANEPIGRAPHIC
ANEPIPLOIC
ANEPITHYMIA
ANERETHISIA
ANERETIC
ANERGIA
ANERGIC
ANERGY
ANERLY
ANEROID
ANEROTIC
ANESIS
ANESONE
ANESTHESIA
ANESTHESIANT
ANESTHESIOLOGIST
ANESTHESIOLOGY
ANESTHESIS
ANESTHETIC
ANESTHETIST
ANESTHETIZE
ANESTHETIZER
ANESTHYL
ANET
ANETH
ANETHOL
ANETHOLE
ANEUCH
ANEUPLOID
ANEUPLOIDY
ANEURIA
ANEURIC
ANEURILEMMIC
ANEURIN
ANEURISM
ANEURISMAL
ANEURISMALLY
ANEURISMATIC
ANEURYSM
ANEURYSMAL
ANEURYSMALLY
ANEURYSMATIC
ANEW
ANFEELD
ANFRACT
ANFRACTUOSE
ANFRACTUOUS
ANFRACTURE
ANGAKOK
ANGAKUT
ANGARALITE
ANGAREB
ANGAREEB
ANGAREP
ANGARIA
ANGARIATION
ANGARY
ANGEKKOK
ANGEKOK
ANGEKUT
ANGEL
ANGELATE
ANGELDOM
ANGELEEN
ANGELET
ANGELEYES
ANGELFISH
ANGELFISHES
ANGELHOOD
ANGELIC
ANGELICA
ANGELICAL
ANGELICALLY
ANGELICALNESS
ANGELICIZE
ANGELICO
ANGELIM
ANGELIN
ANGELINE
ANGELIQUE
ANGELITO
ANGELIZE
ANGELIZED
ANGELIZING
ANGELOCRACY
ANGELOGRAPHER
ANGELOLATER
ANGELOLATRY
ANGELOLOGIC
ANGELOLOGICAL
ANGELOLOGY
ANGELOMACHY
ANGELON
ANGELOPHANY
ANGELOT
ANGELS
ANGELUS
ANGER
ANGERED
ANGERING
ANGERLY
ANGERS
ANGEYOK
ANGIASTHENIA
ANGICO
ANGIECTASIS
ANGIECTOPIA
ANGIITIS
ANGILD
ANGILI
ANGINA
ANGINAL
ANGINIFORM
ANGINOID
ANGINOSE
ANGINOUS
ANGIOATAXIA
ANGIOBLAST
ANGIOBLASTIC
ANGIOCARP
ANGIOCARPIAN
ANGIOCARPIC
ANGIOCARPOUS
ANGIOCLAST
ANGIOCYST
ANGIOFIBROMA
ANGIOGENESIS
ANGIOGENIC
ANGIOGENY
ANGIOGLIOMA
ANGIOGRAPH
ANGIOGRAPHY
ANGIOID
ANGIOKINESIS
ANGIOKINETIC
ANGIOLIPOMA
ANGIOLITH
ANGIOLOGY
ANGIOMA
ANGIOMALACIA
ANGIOMAS
ANGIOMATA
ANGIOMATOSIS
ANGIOMATOUS
ANGIOMEGALY
ANGIOMETER
ANGIOMYOMA
ANGIONOMA
ANGIONOSIS
ANGIOPARESIS
ANGIOPATHY
ANGIOPHOROUS
ANGIOPLANY
ANGIOPLASTY
ANGIOPLEROSIS
ANGIOPOIETIC
ANGIORRHAGIA
ANGIORRHAPHY
ANGIORRHEA
ANGIORRHEXIS
ANGIOSARCOMA
ANGIOSCOPE
ANGIOSIS
ANGIOSPASM
ANGIOSPASTIC
ANGIOSPERM
ANGIOSPERMAL
ANGIOSPERMIC
ANGIOSPOROUS
ANGIOSTEOSIS
ANGIOSTOMIZE
ANGIOSTOMY
ANGIOSTROPHY
ANGIOTASIS
ANGIOTENOSIS
ANGIOTOME
ANGIOTOMY
ANGIOTONIC
ANGIOTRIBE
ANGIOTRIPSY
ANGIOTROPHIC
ANGKHAK
ANGLAISE
ANGLE
ANGLEBERRY
ANGLED
ANGLEDOG
ANGLEHOOK
ANGLEMETER
ANGLEPOD
ANGLER
ANGLES
ANGLESITE
ANGLESMITH
ANGLETOUCH
ANGLETWITCH
ANGLEWING

ANGLEWISE
ANGLEWORM
ANGLICIZE
ANGLICIZED
ANGLICIZING
ANGLIMANIAC
ANGLING
ANGO
ANGOISE
ANGOLAR
ANGOR
ANGOSTURA
ANGRIER
ANGRIEST
ANGRILY
ANGRINESS
ANGRITE
ANGRY
ANGST
ANGSTER
ANGSTROM
ANGUID
ANGUIFORM
ANGUILLIFORM
ANGUILLOID
ANGUINE
ANGUINEOUS
ANGUIPED
ANGUISH
ANGUISHED
ANGUISHOUS
ANGUISHOUSLY
ANGULA
ANGULAR
ANGULARE
ANGULARIA
ANGULARITIES
ANGULARITY
ANGULARIZATION
ANGULARIZE
ANGULARLY
ANGULARNESS
ANGULATE
ANGULATED
ANGULATELY
ANGULATENESS
ANGULATING
ANGULATION
ANGULE
ANGULIFEROUS
ANGULINERVED
ANGULOMETER
ANGULOSE
ANGULOSITY
ANGULOUS
ANGULUS
ANGURIA
ANGUS
ANGUST
ANGUSTATE
ANGUSTICLAVE
ANGWANTIBO
ANGWICH
ANHAEMATOSIS
ANHAEMOLYTIC
ANHALAMINE
ANHALINE
ANHALONIDINE
ANHALONIN
ANHALONINE
ANHANG
ANHARMONIC
ANHEDONIA
ANHEDRAL
ANHEDRON
ANHELATION
ANHELE
ANHELOSE
ANHELOUS
ANHEMATOSIS
ANHEMOLYTIC
ANHIDROSIS
ANHIDROTIC
ANHIMA
ANHINGA
ANHISTIC
ANHISTOUS
ANHUNGERED
ANHUNGRY
ANHYDRAEMIA
ANHYDRAEMIC
ANHYDRATE
ANHYDRATED
ANHYDRATING
ANHYDRATION
ANHYDREMIA
ANHYDREMIC
ANHYDRIDE
ANHYDRIDIZE
ANHYDRITE
ANHYDRIZE
ANHYDROUS
ANHYDROXIME
ANI
ANICCA
ANICONIC
ANICONISM
ANICULAR
ANICUT
ANIDIAN
ANIDROSIS
ANIENTE
ANIGH
ANIGHT
ANIGHTS
ANIL
ANILAO
ANILAU
ANILE
ANILENESS
ANILIC
ANILID
ANILIDE
ANILIDIC
ANILIDOXIME
ANILIID
ANILIN
ANILINE
ANILINISM
ANILINO
ANILITY
ANILLA
ANILOPYRIN
ANILOPYRINE
ANIMA
ANIMABILITY
ANIMABLE
ANIMABLENESS
ANIMADVERSION
ANIMADVERT
ANIMADVERTER
ANIMAL
ANIMALCULA
ANIMALCULAE
ANIMALCULAR
ANIMALCULE
ANIMALCULINE
ANIMALCULISM
ANIMALCULIST
ANIMALCULOUS
ANIMALCULUM
ANIMALIAN
ANIMALIC
ANIMALISH
ANIMALISM
ANIMALIST
ANIMALISTIC
ANIMALITY
ANIMALIZATION
ANIMALIZE
ANIMALIZED
ANIMALIZING
ANIMALLY
ANIMALS
ANIMANDO
ANIMASTIC
ANIMASTICAL
ANIMATE
ANIMATED
ANIMATEDLY
ANIMATELY
ANIMATENESS
ANIMATER
ANIMATING
ANIMATINGLY
ANIMATION
ANIMATISM
ANIMATISTIC
ANIMATIVE
ANIMATO
ANIMATOGRAPH
ANIMATOR
ANIME
ANIMETTA
ANIMIKITE
ANIMISM
ANIMIST
ANIMISTIC
ANIMIZE
ANIMO
ANIMOSE
ANIMOSENESS
ANIMOSITIES
ANIMOSITY
ANIMOSO
ANIMOUS
ANIMUS
ANION
ANIONIC
ANIRIDIA
ANIS
ANISADO
ANISAL
ANISALCOHOL
ANISALDEHYDE
ANISALDOXIME
ANISAMIDE
ANISANDROUS
ANISANILIDE
ANISATE
ANISE
ANISEED
ANISEIKONIA
ANISEIKONIC
ANISEROOT
ANISETTE
ANISIC
ANISIDINE
ANISIDINO
ANISIL
ANISILIC
ANISOCARPIC
ANISOCARPOUS
ANISOCERCAL
ANISOCHROMIA
ANISOCORIA
ANISOCOTYLY
ANISOCRATIC
ANISOCYCLE
ANISOCYTOSIS
ANISODACTYL
ANISODACTYLE
ANISODONT
ANISOGAMETE
ANISOGAMETES
ANISOGAMOUS
ANISOGAMY
ANISOGENOUS
ANISOGENY
ANISOGYNOUS
ANISOIN
ANISOL
ANISOLE
ANISOMELIA
ANISOMELUS
ANISOMERIC
ANISOMEROUS
ANISOMETRIC
ANISOMETROPE
ANISOMYARIAN
ANISOMYODIAN
ANISOMYODOUS
ANISOPHYLLY
ANISOPIA
ANISOPLEURAL
ANISOPTEROUS
ANISOSPORE
ANISOSTHENIC
ANISOSTOMOUS
ANISOTONIC
ANISOTROPAL
ANISOTROPE
ANISOTROPIC
ANISOTROPISM
ANISOTROPOUS
ANISOTROPY
ANISOYL
ANISUM
ANISURIA
ANISYL
ANISYLIDENE
ANITHER
ANITO
ANITOS
ANITROGENOUS
ANJAN
ANKARAMITE
ANKARATRITE
ANKEE
ANKER
ANKERHOLD
ANKERITE
ANKH
ANKLE
ANKLEBONE
ANKLEJACK
ANKLES
ANKLET
ANKLONG
ANKUS
ANKUSH
ANKUSHA
ANKYLENTERON
ANKYLODONTIA
ANKYLOMELE
ANKYLOMERISM
ANKYLOPHOBIA
ANKYLOPODIA
ANKYLOPOIETIC
ANKYLOSE
ANKYLOSED
ANKYLOSING
ANKYLOSIS
ANKYLOSTOMA
ANKYLOTIA
ANKYLOTIC
ANKYLOTOME
ANKYLOTOMY
ANKYROID
ANLACE
ANLAGE
ANLAGEN
ANLAGES
ANLAS
ANLAUT
ANLAUTE
ANLET
ANN
ANNA
ANNABERGITE
ANNAL
ANNALE
ANNALIA
ANNALINE
ANNALISM
ANNALIST
ANNALISTIC
ANNALIZE
ANNALS
ANNALY
ANNAT
ANNATES
ANNATTO
ANNEAL
ANNEALED
ANNEALER
ANNEALING
ANNECT
ANNECTANT
ANNECTENT
ANNELID
ANNELIDAN
ANNELIDIAN
ANNELIDOUS
ANNELISM
ANNELOID
ANNERODITE
ANNERRE
ANNET
ANNEX
ANNEXA
ANNEXABLE
ANNEXATION
ANNEXATIONAL
ANNEXATIONIST
ANNEXE
ANNEXED
ANNEXER
ANNEXING
ANNEXION
ANNEXIONIST
ANNEXIVE
ANNEXMENT
ANNEXURE
ANNICUT
ANNIDALIN
ANNIHILABLE
ANNIHILATE
ANNIHILATED
ANNIHILATING
ANNIHILATION
ANNIHILATIVE
ANNIHILATOR
ANNIHILATORY
ANNITE
ANNIVERSARIES
ANNIVERSARY
ANNIVERSE
ANNODATED
ANNONA
ANNONACEOUS
ANNONCE
ANNOTATE
ANNOTATED
ANNOTATING

ANNOTATION
ANNOTATIVE
ANNOTATOR
ANNOTATORY
ANNOTINE
ANNOTINOUS
ANNOTTO
ANNOUNCE
ANNOUNCED
ANNOUNCEMENT
ANNOUNCER
ANNOUNCING
ANNOY
ANNOYANCE
ANNOYANCER
ANNOYED
ANNOYER
ANNOYFUL
ANNOYING
ANNOYINGLY
ANNOYINGNESS
ANNOYMENT
ANNOYOUS
ANNOYOUSLY
ANNUAL
ANNUALIST
ANNUALIZE
ANNUALLY
ANNUARY
ANNUATION
ANNUELER
ANNUELLER
ANNUENT
ANNUITANT
ANNUITIES
ANNUITY
ANNUL
ANNULAR
ANNULARITY
ANNULARLY
ANNULARY
ANNULATE
ANNULATED
ANNULATION
ANNULE
ANNULET
ANNULETTEE
ANNULI
ANNULISM
ANNULLABLE
ANNULLATE
ANNULLATION
ANNULLED
ANNULLER
ANNULLING
ANNULMENT
ANNULOID
ANNULOSE
ANNULUS
ANNULUSES
ANNUNCIABLE
ANNUNCIATE
ANNUNCIATED
ANNUNCIATING
ANNUNCIATION
ANNUNCIATIVE
ANNUNCIATOR
ANNUNCIATORY
ANNUS
ANOA
ANOBING
ANOCARPOUS
ANOCIATION
ANOCOCCYGEAL
ANODAL
ANODE
ANODENDRON
ANODIC
ANODICALLY
ANODINE
ANODIZE
ANODIZED
ANODIZING
ANODONTIA
ANODOS
ANODYNE
ANODYNIA
ANODYNIC
ANODYNOUS
ANOEGENETIC
ANOESIA
ANOESIS
ANOESTROUS
ANOESTRUM
ANOESTRUS
ANOETIC
ANOGENIC
ANOGENITAL
ANOIA
ANOIL
ANOINE
ANOINT
ANOINTER
ANOINTMENT
ANOLE
ANOLI
ANOLIAN
ANOLYTE
ANOMALIES
ANOMALIPED
ANOMALIPOD
ANOMALISM
ANOMALIST
ANOMALISTIC
ANOMALONOMY
ANOMALOSCOPE
ANOMALOUS
ANOMALOUSLY
ANOMALURE
ANOMALY
ANOMER
ANOMIA
ANOMIC
ANOMIE
ANOMIES
ANOMITE
ANOMOCARPOUS
ANOMODONT
ANOMPHALOUS
ANOMURAL
ANOMURAN
ANOMUROUS
ANOMY
ANON
ANONANG
ANONCILLO
ANONOL
ANONYCHIA
ANONYM
ANONYMA
ANONYME
ANONYMITY
ANONYMOUS
ANONYMOUSLY
ANONYMOUSNESS
ANONYMUNCULE
ANOOPSIA
ANOPERINEAL
ANOPHELE
ANOPHELES
ANOPHELINE
ANOPHTHALMOS
ANOPHYTE
ANOPIA
ANOPLOTHERE
ANOPLOTHEROID
ANOPLURIFORM
ANOPSIA
ANOPUBIC
ANORAK
ANORCHI
ANORCHIA
ANORCHISM
ANORCHOUS
ANORCHUS
ANORECTAL
ANORECTIC
ANORECTOUS
ANOREXIA
ANOREXY
ANORGANA
ANORGANISM
ANORGANOLOGY
ANORMAL
ANORMALITY
ANORN
ANOROGENIC
ANORTH
ANORTHIC
ANORTHITE
ANORTHITIC
ANORTHITITE
ANORTHOCLASE
ANORTHOPHYRE
ANORTHOPIA
ANORTHOSCOPE
ANORTHOSE
ANORTHOSITE
ANOSCOPE
ANOSCOPY
ANOSMATIC
ANOSMIA
ANOSMIC
ANOSPHRASIA
ANOSPHRESIA
ANOSPINAL
ANOSTOSIS
ANOTERITE
ANOTHER
ANOTHERKINS
ANOTIA
ANOTUS
ANOUNOU
ANOVESICAL
ANOXAEMIA
ANOXAEMIC
ANOXEMIA
ANOXEMIC
ANOXIA
ANOXIC
ANOXIDATIVE
ANOXYBIOSIS
ANOXYBIOTIC
ANOXYSCOPE
ANQUERA
ANSA
ANSAE
ANSAR
ANSARIAN
ANSATE
ANSATED
ANSATION
ANSERATED
ANSERIN
ANSERINE
ANSEROUS
ANSU
ANSULATE
ANSWER
ANSWERABLE
ANSWERABLY
ANSWERED
ANSWERER
ANSWERINGLY
ANSWERLESS
ANSWERLESSLY
ANT
ANTA
ANTACID
ANTACRID
ANTADIFORM
ANTAE
ANTAGONISM
ANTAGONIST
ANTAGONISTIC
ANTAGONISTICAL
ANTAGONISTICALLY
ANTAGONIZATION
ANTAGONIZE
ANTAGONIZED
ANTAGONIZER
ANTAGONIZING
ANTAGONY
ANTAL
ANTALGESIC
ANTALGIC
ANTALGOL
ANTALKALI
ANTALKALIES
ANTALKALINE
ANTALKALIS
ANTANACLASIS
ANTANEMIC
ANTAPEX
ANTAPODOSIS
ANTAPOLOGY
ANTARCHISM
ANTARCHIST
ANTARCHISTIC
ANTARCHY
ANTARCTICA
ANTARCTICAL
ANTARCTICALLY
ANTARTHRITIC
ANTASPHYCTIC
ANTASTHENIC
ANTASTHMATIC
ANTATROPHIC
ANTBIRD
ANTE
ANTEAL
ANTEATER
ANTEBRACHIA
ANTEBRACHIAL
ANTEBRACHIUM
ANTECABINET
ANTECEDE
ANTECEDED
ANTECEDENCE
ANTECEDENCY
ANTECEDENT
ANTECEDENTAL
ANTECEDENTLY
ANTECEDING
ANTECESSOR
ANTECHAMBER
ANTECHAPEL
ANTECHOIR
ANTECHURCH
ANTECOLIC
ANTECORNU
ANTECOXAL
ANTED
ANTEDATE
ANTEDATED
ANTEDATING
ANTEDILUVIAL
ANTEDILUVIAN
ANTEDONIN
ANTEED
ANTEFIX
ANTEFIXA
ANTEFIXAL
ANTEFIXES
ANTEFLEXED
ANTEFLEXION
ANTEFURCA
ANTEFURCAE
ANTEFURCAL
ANTEGRADE
ANTEING
ANTELABIUM
ANTELOCATION
ANTELOPE
ANTELOPES
ANTELOPIAN
ANTELOPINE
ANTELUCAN
ANTELUDE
ANTEMARGINAL
ANTEMASK
ANTEMERIDIAN
ANTEMETIC
ANTEMINGENT
ANTEMUNDANE
ANTEMURAL
ANTENATAL
ANTENATI
ANTENATUS
ANTENAVE
ANTENNA
ANTENNAE
ANTENNAL
ANTENNARIID
ANTENNARY
ANTENNAS
ANTENNATE
ANTENNIFORM
ANTENNULA
ANTENNULAR
ANTENNULARY
ANTENNULE
ANTENUMBER
ANTENUPTIAL
ANTEOPERCLE
ANTEPAGMENTA
ANTEPAGMENTS
ANTEPALATAL
ANTEPASCHAL
ANTEPAST
ANTEPECTORAL
ANTEPECTUS
ANTEPENDIA
ANTEPENDIUM
ANTEPENUIT
ANTEPHIALTIC
ANTEPILEPTIC
ANTEPIRRHEMA
ANTEPONE
ANTEPORT
ANTEPOSITION
ANTER
ANTERETHIC
ANTERGIC
ANTERI
ANTERIAD
ANTERIN
ANTERIOR
ANTERIORITY
ANTERIORLY
ANTERIORNESS
ANTERODORSAL
ANTEROGRADE
ANTEROMEDIAL
ANTEROMEDIAN

ANTEROOM
ANTEROPYGAL
ANTEROSPINAL
ANTESCRIPT
ANTESIGNANI
ANTESTATURE
ANTESTERNAL
ANTESTERNUM
ANTETEMPLE
ANTETHEM
ANTETYPE
ANTEVENIENT
ANTEVERSION
ANTEVERT
ANTEVERTED
ANTEVERTING
ANTEVOCALIC
ANTEWAR
ANTHECOLOGY
ANTHELA
ANTHELAE
ANTHELIA
ANTHELICES
ANTHELION
ANTHELIONS
ANTHELIX
ANTHELMINTHIC
ANTHELMINTIC
ANTHEM
ANTHEMA
ANTHEMENE
ANTHEMIA
ANTHEMION
ANTHEMIS
ANTHEMWISE
ANTHEMY
ANTHER
ANTHERAL
ANTHERID
ANTHERIDIA
ANTHERIDIAL
ANTHERIDIUM
ANTHEROID
ANTHEROZOID
ANTHEROZOOID
ANTHESIS
ANTHESTERIN
ANTHESTEROL
ANTHEXIMETER
ANTHILL
ANTHINE
ANTHOBIOLOGY
ANTHOCARP
ANTHOCARPOUS
ANTHOCEROTE
ANTHOCHLOR
ANTHOCLINIUM
ANTHOCYAN
ANTHOCYANIN
ANTHODIA
ANTHODIUM
ANTHOECOLOGY
ANTHOGENESIS
ANTHOGENETIC
ANTHOGENOUS
ANTHOGRAPHY
ANTHOID
ANTHOLITE
ANTHOLOGICAL
ANTHOLOGIES
ANTHOLOGIST
ANTHOLOGIZE
ANTHOLOGIZED
ANTHOLOGIZING
ANTHOLOGY
ANTHOLYSIS
ANTHOMANIA
ANTHOMANIAC
ANTHOMEDUSAN
ANTHOMYIID
ANTHOPHAGOUS
ANTHOPHILE
ANTHOPHILIAN
ANTHOPHILOUS
ANTHOPHOBIA
ANTHOPHORE
ANTHOPHOROUS
ANTHOPHYTE
ANTHORINE
ANTHOTAXIS
ANTHOTAXY
ANTHOTROPIC
ANTHOTROPISM
ANTHOXANTHIN
ANTHOZOAN
ANTHOZOIC
ANTHOZOOID
ANTHOZOON
ANTHRACAEMIA
ANTHRACEMIA
ANTHRACENE
ANTHRACES
ANTHRACIA
ANTHRACIC
ANTHRACIN
ANTHRACITE
ANTHRACITIC
ANTHRACITISM
ANTHRACITOUS
ANTHRACNOSE
ANTHRACNOSIS
ANTHRACOCIDE
ANTHRACOID
ANTHRACONITE
ANTHRACOSIS
ANTHRACOTIC
ANTHRACYL
ANTHRADIOL
ANTHRAFLAVIC
ANTHRAGALLOL
ANTHRAMIN
ANTHRAMINE
ANTHRANIL
ANTHRANILATE
ANTHRANILIC
ANTHRANOL
ANTHRANONE
ANTHRANOYL
ANTHRANYL
ANTHRAQUINOL
ANTHRARUFIN
ANTHRATETROL
ANTHRATRIOL
ANTHRAX
ANTHRAXOLITE
ANTHRAXYLON
ANTHROIC
ANTHROL
ANTHRONE
ANTHROPIC
ANTHROPICAL
ANTHROPOGENY
ANTHROPOGLOT
ANTHROPOGONY
ANTHROPOID
ANTHROPOIDAL
ANTHROPOLITE
ANTHROPOLITH
ANTHROPOLOGIC
ANTHROPOLOGICAL
ANTHROPOLOGICALLY
ANTHROPOLOGIST
ANTHROPOLOGY
ANTHROPONOMY
ANTHROPOPHAGIT
ANTHROPOTOMY
ANTHROPOZOIC
ANTHROPURGIC
ANTHROXAN
ANTHROXANIC
ANTHRYL
ANTHRYLENE
ANTHURIUM
ANTI
ANTIABRIN
ANTIACID
ANTIADITIS
ANTIAE
ANTIAIRCRAFT
ANTIALBUMID
ANTIAR
ANTIARIN
ANTIBACCHIC
ANTIBACCHII
ANTIBACCHIUS
ANTIBACTERIAL
ANTIBARYON
ANTIBIONT
ANTIBIOSIS
ANTIBIOTIC
ANTIBLASTIC
ANTIBODIES
ANTIBODY
ANTIBROMIC
ANTIC
ANTICAL
ANTICARDIUM
ANTICATALASE
ANTICATALYST
ANTICATHODE
ANTICHANCE
ANTICHLOR
ANTICHLORINE
ANTICHRESES
ANTICHRESIS
ANTICHRETIC
ANTICHRIST
ANTICHTHON
ANTICIPANT
ANTICIPATE
ANTICIPATED
ANTICIPATING
ANTICIPATION
ANTICIPATIVE
ANTICIPATIVELY
ANTICIPATOR
ANTICIPATORY
ANTICIZE
ANTICK
ANTICKED
ANTICKER
ANTICKING
ANTICKT
ANTICLASTIC
ANTICLERICAL
ANTICLIMACTIC
ANTICLIMAX
ANTICLINAL
ANTICLINE
ANTICLINORIA
ANTICLY
ANTICNEMION
ANTICNESS
ANTICOAGULANT
ANTICOAGULIN
ANTICOR
ANTICOUS
ANTICREEP
ANTICREEPER
ANTICREEPING
ANTICROTALIC
ANTICRYPTIC
ANTICULARIA
ANTICUM
ANTICUS
ANTICYCLONE
ANTICYCLONIC
ANTIDACTYL
ANTIDETONANT
ANTIDORON
ANTIDOTAL
ANTIDOTALLY
ANTIDOTARY
ANTIDOTE
ANTIDOTED
ANTIDOTICAL
ANTIDOTING
ANTIDOTISM
ANTIDROMAL
ANTIDROMIC
ANTIDROMOUS
ANTIDROMY
ANTIENT
ANTIETHNIC
ANTIFEBRILE
ANTIFEDERAL
ANTIFOAM
ANTIFOGMATIC
ANTIFORMIN
ANTIFREEZE
ANTIFREEZING
ANTIFRICTION
ANTIGEN
ANTIGENE
ANTIGENIC
ANTIGLARE
ANTIGOD
ANTIGORITE
ANTIGRAPH
ANTIGRAVITY
ANTIGROPELOS
ANTIGUGGLER
ANTIHELICES
ANTIHELIX
ANTIHERO
ANTIHISTAMINE
ANTIHYDROPIN
ANTIKETOGEN
ANTIKETOGENIC
ANTIKNOCK
ANTILABORIST
ANTILEGALIST
ANTILEPSIS
ANTILEPTIC
ANTILIPOID
ANTILOBIUM
ANTILOG
ANTILOGIC
ANTILOGICAL
ANTILOGIES
ANTILOGISM
ANTILOGOUS
ANTILOGY
ANTILOQUY
ANTILUETIN
ANTILYSIN
ANTILYSIS
ANTILYSSIC
ANTILYTIC
ANTIMACASSAR
ANTIMASK
ANTIMASKER
ANTIMASQUE
ANTIMASQUER
ANTIMATTER
ANTIMELLIN
ANTIMENSIA
ANTIMENSION
ANTIMERE
ANTIMERIC
ANTIMERISM
ANTIMETABOLE
ANTIMETER
ANTIMINSIA
ANTIMINSION
ANTIMISSION
ANTIMNEMONIC
ANTIMONATE
ANTIMONIAL
ANTIMONIATED
ANTIMONIC
ANTIMONID
ANTIMONIDE
ANTIMONIOUS
ANTIMONITE
ANTIMONIUM
ANTIMONIURET
ANTIMONOUS
ANTIMONSOON
ANTIMONY
ANTIMONYL
ANTINEURITIC
ANTINEUTRINO
ANTINEUTRON
ANTINGANTING
ANTINIAL
ANTINION
ANTINODE
ANTINOME
ANTINOMIAN
ANTINOMIC
ANTINOMICAL
ANTINOMIES
ANTINOMIST
ANTINOMY
ANTIODONT
ANTIOPELMOUS
ANTIOXIDANT
ANTIOXYGEN
ANTIOXYGENIC
ANTIPARABEMA
ANTIPARALLEL
ANTIPART
ANTIPARTICLE
ANTIPASTIC
ANTIPASTO
ANTIPATHETIC
ANTIPATHIC
ANTIPATHIES
ANTIPATHIST
ANTIPATHIZE
ANTIPATHY
ANTIPEDAL
ANTIPEPSIN
ANTIPEPTONE
ANTIPERIODIC
ANTIPERTHITE
ANTIPETALOUS
ANTIPHARMIC
ANTIPHON
ANTIPHONA
ANTIPHONAL
ANTIPHONALLY
ANTIPHONARIES
ANTIPHONARY
ANTIPHONETIC
ANTIPHONIC
ANTIPHONICAL
ANTIPHONIES
ANTIPHONON
ANTIPHONY
ANTIPHRASES
ANTIPHRASIS
ANTIPHRASTIC
ANTIPLANET

ANTIPLASTIC
ANTIPLEION
ANTIPODAGRON
ANTIPODAL
ANTIPODE
ANTIPODEAN
ANTIPODES
ANTIPODIC
ANTIPODIST
ANTIPOINTS
ANTIPOLE
ANTIPOLEMIST
ANTIPOLO
ANTIPOPE
ANTIPRISM
ANTIPROTON
ANTIPTOSIS
ANTIPUDIC
ANTIPUTRID
ANTIPYIC
ANTIPYONIN
ANTIPYRESIS
ANTIPYRETIC
ANTIPYRIN
ANTIPYRINE
ANTIPYROTIC
ANTIPYRYL
ANTIQUA
ANTIQUARIAN
ANTIQUARIES
ANTIQUARISM
ANTIQUARY
ANTIQUATE
ANTIQUATED
ANTIQUATING
ANTIQUATION
ANTIQUE
ANTIQUED
ANTIQUELY
ANTIQUENESS
ANTIQUER
ANTIQUING
ANTIQUIST
ANTIQUITIES
ANTIQUITY
ANTIRACER
ANTIRACHITIC
ANTIRATTLER
ANTIRED
ANTIRENT
ANTIRENTER
ANTIRENTISM
ANTIRICIN
ANTIRRHINUM
ANTIS
ANTISALOON
ANTISCIA
ANTISCIANS
ANTISCII
ANTISCION
ANTISCOLIC
ANTISELENE
ANTISEPALOUS
ANTISEPSIS
ANTISEPTIC
ANTISEPTICAL
ANTISEPTICALLY
ANTISEPTICISM
ANTISEPTICIST
ANTISEPTICIZE
ANTISEPTION
ANTISERUM
ANTISIDERIC
ANTISIPHON
ANTISIPHONAL
ANTISLAVERY
ANTISNAPPER
ANTISOCIAL
ANTISOCIALIST
ANTISOCIALITY
ANTISOLAR
ANTISPACE
ANTISPADIX
ANTISPASMODIC
ANTISPAST
ANTISPASTIC
ANTISQUAMA
ANTISTES
ANTISTROPHAL
ANTISTROPHE
ANTISTROPHIC
ANTISTROPHON
ANTISUN
ANTITANK
ANTITHALIAN
ANTITHEFT
ANTITHEISM
ANTITHEIST
ANTITHEISTIC
ANTITHENAR
ANTITHERMIN
ANTITHESES
ANTITHESIS
ANTITHESISM
ANTITHESIZE
ANTITHET
ANTITHETIC
ANTITHETICAL
ANTITHETICS
ANTITOXIN
ANTITOXINE
ANTITRADE
ANTITRADES
ANTITRAGAL
ANTITRAGI
ANTITRAGIC
ANTITRAGICUS
ANTITRAGUS
ANTITROPE
ANTITROPIC
ANTITROPICAL
ANTITROPY
ANTITRUST
ANTITRYPSIN
ANTITRYPTIC
ANTITWILIGHT
ANTITYPAL
ANTITYPE
ANTITYPIC
ANTITYPICAL
ANTITYPY
ANTIVENENE
ANTIVENIN
ANTIVENINE
ANTIVIRAL
ANTIVIROTIC
ANTIWORLD
ANTIZOEA
ANTJAR
ANTLER
ANTLERED
ANTLERITE
ANTLERS
ANTLIA
ANTLIATE
ANTLING
ANTOECI
ANTOECIAN
ANTOECIANS
ANTONINIANI
ANTONINIANUS
ANTONOMASIA
ANTONOMASTIC
ANTONYM
ANTONYMOUS
ANTONYMY
ANTORBITAL
ANTRA
ANTRAL
ANTRALGIA
ANTRE
ANTRECTOMY
ANTRIN
ANTRITIS
ANTROCELE
ANTRONASAL
ANTROPHORE
ANTROPHOSE
ANTRORSE
ANTRORSELY
ANTROSCOPE
ANTROSCOPY
ANTROTOME
ANTROTOMY
ANTRUM
ANTRUSTION
ANTSHRIKE
ANTSY
ANUBIN
ANUBING
ANUKABIET
ANULOMA
ANUNDER
ANURAN
ANURESIS
ANURETIC
ANURIA
ANURIC
ANUROUS
ANURY
ANUS
ANUSIM
ANUSVARA
ANVIL
ANVILED
ANVILING
ANVILLED
ANVILLING
ANVILSMITH
ANVILTOP
ANXIETIES
ANXIETUDE
ANXIETY
ANXIOUS
ANXIOUSLY
ANXIOUSNESS
ANY
ANYBODIES
ANYBODY
ANYHOW
ANYMORE
ANYONE
ANYPLACE
ANYTHING
ANYWAY
ANYWAYS
ANYWHEN
ANYWHERE
ANYWHERENESS
ANYWHERES
ANYWHITHER
ANYWHY
ANYWISE
AO
AOGIRI
AONACH
AORIST
AORISTIC
AORISTICALLY
AORTA
AORTAE
AORTAL
AORTARCTIA
AORTAS
AORTECTASIA
AORTECTASIS
AORTIC
AORTICORENAL
AORTISM
AORTITIS
AORTOCLASIA
AORTOCLASIS
AORTOLITH
AORTOMALACIA
AORTOMALAXIS
AORTOPATHY
AORTOPTOSIA
AORTOPTOSIS
AORTORRHAPHY
AORTOTOMY
AOSMIC
AOUDAD
APA
APABHRAMSA
APACE
APACHE
APACHES
APACHISM
APACHITE
APADANA
APAESTHESIA
APAESTHETIC
APAESTHETIZE
APAESTICALLY
APAGOGE
APAGOGIC
APAGOGICAL
APAGOGICALLY
APAID
APALIT
APANAGE
APANAGED
APANAGING
APANDRY
APANG
APAR
APARA
APARAPHYSATE
APARDON
APAREJO
APAREJOS
APARITHMESIS
APART
APARTADO
APARTHEID
APARTHROSIS
APARTMENT
APARTMENTAL
APASOTE
APASS
APAST
APASTRON
APATAN
APATETIC
APATHETIC
APATHETICAL
APATHIA
APATHIC
APATHIES
APATHISM
APATHIST
APATHISTICAL
APATHOGENIC
APATHY
APATITE
APE
APEAK
APED
APEIRON
APELET
APELING
APELLOUS
APEPSIA
APEPSINIA
APEPSY
APEPTIC
APER
APERCH
APERCU
APERCUS
APEREA
APERIENT
APERIES
APERIODIC
APERISPERMIC
APERISTALSIS
APERITIF
APERITIVE
APERSEE
APERT
APERTION
APERTLY
APERTNESS
APERTOMETER
APERTURAL
APERTURE
APERTURED
APERULOSID
APERY
APESTHESIA
APESTHETIC
APESTHETIZE
APETALOID
APETALOSE
APETALOUS
APETALY
APEX
APEXED
APEXES
APEXING
APHAERESIS
APHAERETIC
APHAGIA
APHAKIA
APHAKIAL
APHAKIC
APHANESITE
APHANISIA
APHANISIS
APHANITE
APHANITIC
APHANITISM
APHANOPHYRE
APHASIA
APHASIAC
APHASIC
APHELIAN
APHELION
APHEMIA
APHEMIC
APHENGESCOPE
APHENGOSCOPE
APHENOSCOPE
APHERESIS
APHERETIC
APHESIS
APHETA
APHETIC
APHETICALLY
APHETISM
APHETIZE
APHID
APHIDES
APHIDIAN
APHIDICOLOUS

APHIDID
APHIDIOUS
APHIDIVOROUS
APHIDOLYSIN
APHIDOZER
APHIS
APHLEBIA
APHLOGISTIC
APHNOLOGY
APHODAL
APHODI
APHODIAN
APHODUS
APHONIA
APHONIC
APHONOUS
APHORIA
APHORISM
APHORISMATIC
APHORISMER
APHORISMIC
APHORISMICAL
APHORISMOS
APHORIST
APHORISTIC
APHORISTICAL
APHORIZE
APHORIZED
APHORIZER
APHORIZING
APHOTIC
APHOTOTACTIC
APHOTOTAXIS
APHOTOTROPIC
APHRASIA
APHRITE
APHRIZITE
APHRODISIA
APHRODISIAC
APHRODISIAN
APHRODITE
APHRODITIC
APHRODITOUS
APHROLITE
APHRONIA
APHTHA
APHTHAE
APHTHIC
APHTHITALITE
APHTHOID
APHTHONG
APHTHONGAL
APHTHONGIA
APHTHOUS
APHYLLOSE
APHYLLOUS
APHYLLY
APHYRIC
APIAN
APIARIAN
APIARIES
APIARIST
APIARY
APIATOR
APICAD
APICAL
APICALLY
APICES
APICIFIXED
APICILAR
APICILLARY
APICITIS
APICKABACK
APICKBACK
APICKPACK
APICOECTOMY
APICOLYSIS
APICULA
APICULATE
APICULATED
APICULATION
APICULI
APICULTURAL
APICULTURE
APICULTURIST
APICULUS
APIECE
APIECES
APIGENIN
APII
APIIN
APIKORES
APIKOROS
APIKORSIM
APILARY
APIMANIA
APINCH
APING
APINOID
APIO
APIOID
APIOIDAL
APIOL
APIOLE
APIOLIN
APIOLOGIST
APIOLOGY
APIONOL
APIOSE
APIPHOBIA
APISH
APISHAMORE
APISHLY
APISHNESS
APISM
APITONG
APITPAT
APIVOROUS
APJOHNITE
APLACENTAL
APLACOPHORAN
APLANAT
APLANATIC
APLANATISM
APLANOGAMETE
APLANOSPORE
APLASIA
APLASTIC
APLENTY
APLITE
APLITIC
APLOBASALT
APLODIORITE
APLOMB
APLOME
APLOTAXENE
APLOTOMY
APLUSTRA
APLUSTRE
APLUSTRIA
APNEA
APNEAL
APNEIC
APNEUMATIC
APNEUMATOSIS
APNEUMONOUS
APNEUSIS
APNEUSTIC
APNOEA
APNOEAL
APNOEIC
APOACONITINE
APOATROPINE
APOBIOTIC
APOBLAST
APOCAFFEINE
APOCALYPSE
APOCALYPST
APOCALYPT
APOCALYPTIC
APOCALYPTIST
APOCAMPHORIC
APOCARP
APOCARPOUS
APOCARPY
APOCATHARSIS
APOCENTER
APOCENTRE
APOCENTRIC
APOCHA
APOCHAE
APOCHOLIC
APOCHROMAT
APOCHROMATIC
APOCODEINE
APOCOPATE
APOCOPATED
APOCOPATING
APOCOPATION
APOCOPE
APOCOPIC
APOCRENIC
APOCRISIARY
APOCRUSTIC
APOCRYPH
APOCRYPHAL
APOCRYPHALLY
APOCRYPHATE
APOCYNACEOUS
APOCYNEOUS
APOCYTE
APOD
APODAN
APODE
APODEICTIC
APODEICTICAL
APODEIPNON
APODEMA
APODEMAL
APODEMATAL
APODEME
APODIA
APODICTIC
APODICTICAL
APODICTIVE
APODIXIS
APODOSES
APODOSIS
APODOUS
APODYTERIA
APODYTERIUM
APOEMBRYONY
APOFENCHENE
APOGAEIC
APOGAIC
APOGALACTEUM
APOGAMIC
APOGAMICALLY
APOGAMOUS
APOGAMOUSLY
APOGAMY
APOGEAL
APOGEAN
APOGEE
APOGENOUS
APOGENY
APOGEOTROPIC
APOGONID
APOGRAPH
APOGRAPHAL
APOHARMINE
APOHYAL
APOIKIA
APOISE
APOJOVE
APOKREA
APOKREOS
APOLAR
APOLARITY
APOLAUSTIC
APOLEGAMIC
APOLLONICON
APOLOG
APOLOGAL
APOLOGETE
APOLOGETIC
APOLOGETICAL
APOLOGETICALLY
APOLOGETICS
APOLOGIA
APOLOGIES
APOLOGIST
APOLOGIZE
APOLOGIZED
APOLOGIZER
APOLOGIZING
APOLOGUE
APOLOGY
APOLOUSIS
APOLUNE
APOLUSIS
APOLYSIS
APOLYTIKION
APOMECOMETER
APOMECOMETRY
APOMETABOLIC
APOMICT
APOMICTIC
APOMICTICAL
APOMIXIS
APOMORPHIA
APOMORPHIN
APOMORPHINE
APONEUROLOGY
APONEUROSES
APONEUROSIS
APONEUROTIC
APONEUROTOME
APONEUROTOMY
APONIA
APONIC
APOOP
APOPEMPTIC
APOPETALOUS
APOPHASIS
APOPHATIC
APOPHONIA
APOPHONIC
APOPHONY
APOPHTHEGM
APOPHYGE
APOPHYLACTIC
APOPHYLAXIS
APOPHYLLITE
APOPHYLLOUS
APOPHYSARY
APOPHYSATE
APOPHYSEAL
APOPHYSES
APOPHYSIAL
APOPHYSIS
APOPHYSITIS
APOPLECTIC
APOPLECTICAL
APOPLEX
APOPLEXIOUS
APOPLEXY
APOPYLE
APOQUININE
APORETIC
APORETICAL
APORHYOLITE
APORIA
APOROSE
APORPHIN
APORPHINE
APORRHAOID
APORRHEA
APORRHEGMA
APORT
APORTOISE
APOSAFRANINE
APOSATURN
APOSATURNIUM
APOSEMATIC
APOSEPALOUS
APOSIA
APOSIOPESIS
APOSIOPETIC
APOSITIA
APOSITIC
APOSORO
APOSPOROGONY
APOSPOROUS
APOSPORY
APOSTACY
APOSTASIES
APOSTASIS
APOSTASY
APOSTATE
APOSTATIC
APOSTATICAL
APOSTATISM
APOSTATIZE
APOSTATIZED
APOSTATIZING
APOSTAXIS
APOSTEMATE
APOSTEMATIC
APOSTEMATION
APOSTEMATOUS
APOSTEME
APOSTHIA
APOSTIL
APOSTILLE
APOSTLE
APOSTLES
APOSTLESHIP
APOSTOLATE
APOSTOLESS
APOSTOLI
APOSTOLIC
APOSTOLICAL
APOSTOLICISM
APOSTOLICITY
APOSTOLIZE
APOSTROPHAL
APOSTROPHE
APOSTROPHI
APOSTROPHIC
APOSTROPHIED
APOSTROPHIZE
APOSTROPHUS
APOTELESM
APOTHEC
APOTHECAL
APOTHECARIES
APOTHECARY
APOTHECE
APOTHECIA
APOTHECIAL
APOTHECIUM
APOTHEGM
APOTHEGMATIC
APOTHEM

APOTHEOSE
APOTHEOSES
APOTHEOSIS
APOTHEOSIZE
APOTHEOSIZED
APOTHESINE
APOTHESIS
APOTOME
APOTROPAIC
APOTROPAION
APOTROPAISM
APOTROPOUS
APOTURMERIC
APOTYPE
APOTYPIC
APOUT
APOXESIS
APOY
APOZEM
APOZEMA
APOZEMICAL
APPAIR
APPAL
APPALL
APPALLED
APPALLING
APPALLINGLY
APPALTO
APPANAGE
APPANAGED
APPANAGING
APPANAGIST
APPARATUS
APPARATUSES
APPAREL
APPARELED
APPARELING
APPARELLED
APPARELLING
APPARELMENT
APPARENCE
APPARENCY
APPARENT
APPARENTLY
APPARENTNESS
APPARITION
APPARITIONAL
APPARITOR
APPARTEMENT
APPASSIONATA
APPASSIONATO
APPAST
APPAUME
APPAUMEE
APPAY
APPEACH
APPEACHER
APPEACHMENT
APPEAL
APPEALABLE
APPEALED
APPEALER
APPEALING
APPEALINGLY
APPEALINGNESS
APPEAR
APPEARANCE
APPEARANCED
APPEARED
APPEARER
APPEARING
APPEASABLE
APPEASABLY
APPEASE
APPEASED
APPEASEMENT
APPEASER
APPEASING
APPEASINGLY
APPEASIVE
APPEL
APPELLABLE
APPELLANCY
APPELLANT
APPELLATION
APPELLATIVE
APPELLATIVED
APPELLATORY
APPELLEE
APPELLOR
APPENAGE
APPEND
APPENDAGE
APPENDAGED
APPENDALGIA
APPENDANCE
APPENDANCY
APPENDANT
APPENDECTOMIES
APPENDECTOMY
APPENDED
APPENDENT
APPENDICAL
APPENDICE
APPENDICEAL
APPENDICES
APPENDICITIS
APPENDICLE
APPENDICULAR
APPENDIX
APPENDIXED
APPENDIXES
APPENDIXING
APPENTICE
APPERCEIVE
APPERCEIVED
APPERCEIVING
APPERCEPTION
APPERCEPTIVE
APPERCIPIENT
APPERE
APPERIL
APPERT
APPERTAIN
APPERTISE
APPESTAT
APPET
APPETE
APPETENCE
APPETENCIES
APPETENCY
APPETENT
APPETENTLY
APPETIBILITY
APPETIBLE
APPETISER
APPETISING
APPETITE
APPETITION
APPETITIONAL
APPETITIOUS
APPETITIVE
APPETIZE
APPETIZED
APPETIZER
APPETIZING
APPETIZINGLY
APPINITE
APPLANATE
APPLANATION
APPLAUD
APPLAUDABLE
APPLAUDABLY
APPLAUDER
APPLAUDINGLY
APPLAUSE
APPLAUSIVE
APPLAUSIVELY
APPLE
APPLEBERRY
APPLEBLOSSOM
APPLECART
APPLED
APPLEDRANE
APPLEDRONE
APPLEGROWER
APPLEJACK
APPLEJOHN
APPLEMONGER
APPLENUT
APPLERINGIE
APPLERINGY
APPLEROOT
APPLES
APPLESAUCE
APPLEWIFE
APPLEWOMAN
APPLIABLE
APPLIABLENESS
APPLIABLY
APPLIANCE
APPLIANT
APPLICABLE
APPLICABLY
APPLICANCY
APPLICANT
APPLICATE
APPLICATION
APPLICATIVE
APPLICATOR
APPLICATORY
APPLIED
APPLIEDLY
APPLIER
APPLING
APPLIQUE
APPLIQUED
APPLIQUEING
APPLOSION
APPLOSIVE
APPLOT
APPLOTMENT
APPLY
APPLYING
APPLYINGLY
APPLYMENT
APPOGGIATURA
APPOGGIATURE
APPOINT
APPOINTE
APPOINTEE
APPOINTER
APPOINTIVE
APPOINTMENT
APPOINTOR
APPORT
APPORTION
APPORTIONER
APPORTIONMENT
APPOSABLE
APPOSE
APPOSED
APPOSER
APPOSING
APPOSITE
APPOSITELY
APPOSITENESS
APPOSITION
APPOSITIONAL
APPOSITIVE
APPOSITIVELY
APPRAISABLE
APPRAISAL
APPRAISE
APPRAISED
APPRAISEMENT
APPRAISER
APPRAISING
APPRAISIVE
APPRECIABLE
APPRECIABLY
APPRECIANT
APPRECIATE
APPRECIATED
APPRECIATING
APPRECIATION
APPRECIATIVE
APPRECIATIVELY
APPRECIATIVENESS
APPRECIATOR
APPRECIATORY
APPREHEND
APPREHENDED
APPREHENDER
APPREHENSIBLE
APPREHENSIBLY
APPREHENSION
APPREHENSIVE
APPREHENSIVELY
APPREHENSIVENESS
APPREND
APPRENTICE
APPRENTICED
APPRENTICESHIP
APPRENTICING
APPRESSED
APPRESSOR
APPRESSORIA
APPRESSORIAL
APPRESSORIUM
APPREST
APPRETEUR
APPRISE
APPRISED
APPRISING
APPRIZAL
APPRIZE
APPRIZEMENT
APPRIZER
APPRIZING
APPROACH
APPROACHABILITY
APPROACHABLE
APPROACHABLENESS
APPROACHER
APPROACHES
APPROACHING
APPROACHLESS
APPROACHMENT
APPROBATE
APPROBATED
APPROBATING
APPROBATION
APPROBATIVE
APPROBATOR
APPROBATORY
APPROOF
APPROPRE
APPROPRIABLE
APPROPRIATE
APPROPRIATED
APPROPRIATELY
APPROPRIATENES
APPROPRIATING
APPROPRIATION
APPROPRIATIVE
APPROPRIATOR
APPROVABLE
APPROVAL
APPROVANCE
APPROVE
APPROVED
APPROVEDLY
APPROVEMENT
APPROVER
APPROVING
APPROVINGLY
APPROXIMAL
APPROXIMATE
APPROXIMATED
APPROXIMATELY
APPROXIMATING
APPROXIMATION
APPROXIMATIVE
APPROXIMATOR
APPUI
APPULSE
APPULSION
APPULSIVE
APPULSIVELY
APPURTENANCE
APPURTENANT
APRAXIA
APRAXIC
APRENDIZ
APRES
APREYNTE
APRICATE
APRICATION
APRICKLE
APRICOT
APRIORISM
APRIORIST
APRIORISTIC
APRIORITY
APROCTIA
APROCTOUS
APRON
APRONEER
APRONLIKE
APROPOS
APROSEXIA
APROSOPIA
APROSOPOUS
APROTERODONT
APS
APSE
APSELAPHESIA
APSELAPHESIS
APSES
APSIDAL
APSIDALLY
APSIDES
APSIDIOLE
APSINTHION
APSIS
APSYCHIA
APSYCHICAL
APT
APTATE
APTERAL
APTERIA
APTERIAL
APTERIUM
APTEROID
APTEROUS
APTERYGIAL
APTERYGOTE
APTERYGOTOUS
APTERYLA
APTERYX
APTHA
APTITUDE
APTITUDINAL
APTITUDINALLY

APTLY
APTNESS
APTOTE
APTOTIC
APTYALIA
APTYALISM
APTYCHUS
APULMONIC
APULSE
APURPOSE
APUS
APYONIN
APYRASE
APYRENE
APYRETIC
APYREXIA
APYREXIAL
APYREXY
APYROTYPE
APYROUS
AQUA
AQUABIB
AQUACADE
AQUACULTURAL
AQUACULTURE
AQUAE
AQUAEMANALE
AQUAEMANALIA
AQUAFER
AQUAFORTIS
AQUAFORTIST
AQUAGE
AQUAGREEN
AQUALUNG
AQUAMARINE
AQUAMETER
AQUANAUT
AQUAPLANE
AQUAPLANED
AQUAPLANING
AQUAPUNCTURE
AQUARELLE
AQUARELLIST
AQUARIA
AQUARIAL
AQUARIAN
AQUARIIST
AQUARIST
AQUARIUM
AQUARIUMS
AQUARTER
AQUAS
AQUASCUTUM
AQUATE
AQUATIC
AQUATICAL
AQUATICALLY
AQUATICS
AQUATILE
AQUATINT
AQUATINTER
AQUATION
AQUATIVENESS
AQUATONE
AQUAVALENT
AQUAVIT
AQUEDUCT
AQUEITY
AQUEOGLACIAL
AQUEOIGNEOUS
AQUEOUS
AQUEOUSLY
AQUEOUSNESS
AQUICOLOUS
AQUICULTURAL
AQUICULTURE
AQUIFER
AQUIFEROUS
AQUIFORM
AQUIFUGE
AQUILA
AQUILAWOOD
AQUILEGE
AQUILEGIA
AQUILINE
AQUILINO
AQUIPAROUS
AQUIVER
AQUO
AQUOSE
AQUOSITY
AQUOTIZATION
AQUOTIZE
AR
ARA
ARABA
ARABAN
ARABESK
ARABESQUE
ARABESQUELY
ARABESQUERIE
ARABICA
ARABILITY
ARABIN
ARABINE
ARABINOSE
ARABINOSIC
ARABITE
ARABITOL
ARABLE
ARACA
ARACANGA
ARACARI
ARACE
ARACEOUS
ARACHE
ARACHIC
ARACHIDE
ARACHIDIC
ARACHIN
ARACHIS
ARACHNACTIS
ARACHNID
ARACHNIDAN
ARACHNIDIAL
ARACHNIDISM
ARACHNIDIUM
ARACHNISM
ARACHNITIS
ARACHNOID
ARACHNOIDAL
ARACHNOIDEA
ARACHNOIDEAN
ARACHNOLOGY
ARAD
ARADA
ARADID
ARADO
ARAGONITE
ARAGUANE
ARAGUATO
ARAH
ARAIN
ARAIRE
ARAK
ARAKE
ARAKI
ARALIA
ARALIACEOUS
ARALIAD
ARALIE
ARALKYL
ARALKYLATED
ARAMAYOITE
ARAMINA
ARANA
ARANEID
ARANEIDAN
ARANEIFORM
ARANEIN
ARANEOLOGIST
ARANEOLOGY
ARANEOSE
ARANEOUS
ARANGA
ARANGO
ARANGOES
ARANZADA
ARAPAHITE
ARAPAIMA
ARAPHOROSTIC
ARAPHOSTIC
ARAPONGA
ARAPUNGA
ARAR
ARARA
ARARAO
ARARAUNA
ARARIBA
ARAROBA
ARARU
ARAS
ARASE
ARATI
ARATINGA
ARATION
ARATORY
ARAUCARIA
ARAUCARIAN
ARAYNE
ARBA
ARBACIA
ARBACIN
ARBALEST
ARBALESTER
ARBALESTRE
ARBALIST
ARBALO
ARBALOS
ARBER
ARBITER
ARBITH
ARBITRABLE
ARBITRAGE
ARBITRAGER
ARBITRAGEUR
ARBITRAGIST
ARBITRAL
ARBITRAMENT
ARBITRARILY
ARBITRARINESS
ARBITRARY
ARBITRATE
ARBITRATED
ARBITRATING
ARBITRATION
ARBITRATIONAL
ARBITRATIVE
ARBITRATOR
ARBITREMENT
ARBITRER
ARBITRESS
ARBOLOCO
ARBOR
ARBORACEOUS
ARBORAL
ARBORARY
ARBORATOR
ARBOREAL
ARBOREALLY
ARBOREAN
ARBORED
ARBOREOUS
ARBORER
ARBORES
ARBORESCENCE
ARBORESCENT
ARBORESQUE
ARBORET
ARBORETA
ARBORETUM
ARBORETUMS
ARBORICAL
ARBORICOLE
ARBORICOLINE
ARBORICOLOUS
ARBORIFORM
ARBORISE
ARBORIST
ARBORIZATION
ARBORIZE
ARBORIZED
ARBORIZING
ARBOROID
ARBOROLATRY
ARBOROUS
ARBORS
ARBORVITAE
ARBORWAY
ARBOUR
ARBOURED
ARBUSCLE
ARBUSCULA
ARBUSCULAR
ARBUSCULE
ARBUSTA
ARBUSTERIN
ARBUSTEROL
ARBUSTUM
ARBUTE
ARBUTEAN
ARBUTIN
ARBUTUS
ARC
ARCA
ARCABUCERO
ARCADE
ARCADED
ARCADIAN
ARCADING
ARCAE
ARCANA
ARCANAL
ARCANE
ARCANUM
ARCATE
ARCATO
ARCATURE
ARCED
ARCELLA
ARCES
ARCH
ARCHA
ARCHAEOCYTE
ARCHAEOLATRY
ARCHAEOLOGER
ARCHAEOLOGIC
ARCHAEOLOGICAL
ARCHAEOLOGIST
ARCHAEOLOGY
ARCHAEUS
ARCHAI
ARCHAIC
ARCHAICAL
ARCHAICALLY
ARCHAICISM
ARCHAISE
ARCHAISM
ARCHAIST
ARCHAISTIC
ARCHAIZE
ARCHAIZED
ARCHAIZER
ARCHAIZING
ARCHANGEL
ARCHANGELIC
ARCHARIOS
ARCHBAND
ARCHBISHOP
ARCHBISHOPRIC
ARCHCHEMIC
ARCHDEACON
ARCHDEACONRY
ARCHDEAN
ARCHDIOCESAN
ARCHDIOCESE
ARCHDUCAL
ARCHDUCHESS
ARCHDUCHIES
ARCHDUCHY
ARCHDUKE
ARCHDUKEDOM
ARCHE
ARCHEAL
ARCHEBIOSIS
ARCHECENTRIC
ARCHED
ARCHEGONE
ARCHEGONIA
ARCHEGONIAL
ARCHEGONIATE
ARCHEGONIUM
ARCHEION
ARCHELOGY
ARCHENEMIES
ARCHENEMY
ARCHENTERIC
ARCHENTERON
ARCHEOCYTE
ARCHEOLITHIC
ARCHEOLOGIAN
ARCHEOLOGIC
ARCHEOLOGICAL
ARCHEOLOGIST
ARCHEOLOGY
ARCHEOPTERYX
ARCHEOSTOME
ARCHER
ARCHERFISH
ARCHERFISHES
ARCHERS
ARCHERY
ARCHES
ARCHESPORE
ARCHESPORIAL
ARCHESPORIUM
ARCHETYPAL
ARCHETYPALLY
ARCHETYPE
ARCHETYPIC
ARCHETYPICAL
ARCHETYPIST
ARCHEUS
ARCHFIEND
ARCHIATER
ARCHIBENTHAL
ARCHIBENTHIC
ARCHIBENTHOS
ARCHIBLAST
ARCHIBLASTIC
ARCHICAL
ARCHICARP
ARCHICEREBRA
ARCHICOELE
ARCHICYTE

ARCHICYTULA
ARCHIDOME
ARCHIE
ARCHIEREUS
ARCHIGENESIS
ARCHIKARYON
ARCHIL
ARCHILITHIC
ARCHILLA
ARCHILOWE
ARCHILUTE
ARCHIMAGE
ARCHIMAGUS
ARCHIMIME
ARCHIMORPHIC
ARCHIMORULA
ARCHIN
ARCHINE
ARCHINEURON
ARCHING
ARCHIPALLIAL
ARCHIPALLIUM
ARCHIPELAGIC
ARCHIPELAGO
ARCHIPELAGOES
ARCHIPELAGOS
ARCHIPHONEME
ARCHIPIN
ARCHIPLASM
ARCHIPLASMIC
ARCHISPERM
ARCHISPHERE
ARCHISPORE
ARCHISTOME
ARCHITECT
ARCHITECTIVE
ARCHITECTRESS
ARCHITECTURAL
ARCHITECTURALLY
ARCHITECTURE
ARCHITIS
ARCHITRAVAL
ARCHITRAVE
ARCHITRAVED
ARCHIVAL
ARCHIVAULT
ARCHIVE
ARCHIVED
ARCHIVES
ARCHIVING
ARCHIVIST
ARCHIVOLT
ARCHIZOIC
ARCHLUTE
ARCHLY
ARCHNESS
ARCHOCELE
ARCHOLOGY
ARCHON
ARCHONT
ARCHONTATE
ARCHONTIC
ARCHOPLASM
ARCHOPLASMA
ARCHOPLASMIC
ARCHOPTOMA
ARCHOPTOSIS
ARCHORRHAGIA
ARCHORRHEA
ARCHOSYRINX
ARCHPRIEST
ARCHPRIESTHOOD
ARCHPRIESTSHIP
ARCHSEE
ARCHWAY
ARCHWISE
ARCHY
ARCIFEROUS
ARCIFINIOUS
ARCIFORM
ARCING
ARCKED
ARCKING
ARCOCENTROUS
ARCOCENTRUM
ARCOGRAPH
ARCOSE
ARCOSOLIA
ARCOSOLIUM
ARCS
ARCT
ARCTATION
ARCTIAN
ARCTIC
ARCTICALLY
ARCTICIAN
ARCTICIZE
ARCTICIZED
ARCTICIZING
ARCTIID
ARCTOID
ARCTOIDEAN
ARCUAL
ARCUALE
ARCUALIA
ARCUATE
ARCUATED
ARCUATELY
ARCUATION
ARCULA
ARCULITE
ARCUS
ARD
ARDAB
ARDASSINE
ARDEB
ARDELIO
ARDELLA
ARDELLAE
ARDEN
ARDENCY
ARDENNITE
ARDENT
ARDENTLY
ARDENTNESS
ARDER
ARDILLA
ARDISH
ARDISIA
ARDITI
ARDITO
ARDOISE
ARDOO
ARDOR
ARDORS
ARDOUR
ARDRI
ARDRIGH
ARDU
ARDUINITE
ARDUOUS
ARDUOUSLY
ARDUOUSNESS
ARDURE
ARDUROUS
ARE
AREA
AREACH
AREAD
AREAE
AREAL
AREALITY
AREAR
AREAS
AREASON
AREAWAY
ARECA
ARECACEOUS
ARECHE
ARED
AREED
AREEK
AREEL
AREFACT
AREFACTION
AREFY
AREG
AREIC
AREITO
ARENA
ARENACEOUS
ARENAE
ARENARIAE
ARENARIOUS
ARENAS
ARENATION
AREND
ARENDALITE
ARENE
ARENG
ARENICOLITE
ARENICOLOUS
ARENILITIC
ARENITE
ARENOID
ARENOSE
ARENOSITY
AREOCENTRIC
AREOGRAPHER
AREOGRAPHIC
AREOGRAPHY
AREOLA
AREOLAE
AREOLAR
AREOLAS
AREOLATE
AREOLATED
AREOLATION
AREOLE
AREOLET
AREOLOGIC
AREOLOGICAL
AREOLOGIST
AREOLOGY
AREOMETER
AREOMETRIC
AREOMETRICAL
AREOMETRY
AREOPAGY
AREPA
ARERE
ARET
ARETAICS
ARETALOGY
ARETE
ARETHUSA
ARETTE
ARF
ARFVEDSONITE
ARGAL
ARGALA
ARGALI
ARGALIS
ARGASID
ARGEERS
ARGEL
ARGEMONE
ARGENOL
ARGENT
ARGENTAL
ARGENTAMID
ARGENTAMIDE
ARGENTAMIN
ARGENTAMINE
ARGENTARII
ARGENTARIUS
ARGENTATION
ARGENTEOUS
ARGENTER
ARGENTEUM
ARGENTIC
ARGENTIDE
ARGENTIN
ARGENTINE
ARGENTINO
ARGENTION
ARGENTITE
ARGENTOL
ARGENTOMETRY
ARGENTON
ARGENTOSE
ARGENTOUS
ARGENTUM
ARGH
ARGHAN
ARGHE
ARGHEL
ARGHOOL
ARGHOUL
ARGIFY
ARGIL
ARGILLACEOUS
ARGILLIC
ARGILLITE
ARGILLITIC
ARGILLOID
ARGILLOUS
ARGIN
ARGINASE
ARGINE
ARGININE
ARGLE
ARGO
ARGOL
ARGOLET
ARGOLETIER
ARGON
ARGONAUT
ARGONAUTIC
ARGONAUTID
ARGONAUTS
ARGOSIES
ARGOSY
ARGOT
ARGOTIC
ARGUABLE
ARGUE
ARGUED
ARGUENDO
ARGUER
ARGUFIED
ARGUFIER
ARGUFY
ARGUFYING
ARGUING
ARGUL
ARGUMENT
ARGUMENTA
ARGUMENTAL
ARGUMENTATION
ARGUMENTATIOUS
ARGUMENTATIVE
ARGUMENTATIVELY
ARGUMENTATIVENESS
ARGUMENTATOR
ARGUMENTATORY
ARGUMENTS
ARGUMENTUM
ARGUS
ARGUSFISH
ARGUSFISHES
ARGUTE
ARGUTELY
ARGUTENESS
ARGY
ARGYRANTHOUS
ARGYRIA
ARGYRIC
ARGYRITE
ARGYRODITE
ARGYROSE
ARGYRYTHROSE
ARHAR
ARHAT
ARIA
ARIBIN
ARIBINE
ARICIN
ARICINE
ARID
ARIDGE
ARIDIAN
ARIDITIES
ARIDITY
ARIDLY
ARIDNESS
ARIEGITE
ARIEL
ARIENZO
ARIES
ARIETATE
ARIETATION
ARIETINOUS
ARIETTA
ARIETTE
ARIGHT
ARIGHTLY
ARIGUE
ARIKI
ARIL
ARILED
ARILLARY
ARILLATE
ARILLATED
ARILLED
ARILLI
ARILLIFORM
ARILLODE
ARILLODIUM
ARILLOID
ARILLUS
ARIOLATE
ARIOLE
ARIOSE
ARIOSO
ARIOT
ARIPPLE
ARIS
ARISAID
ARISARD
ARISE
ARISEN
ARISING
ARISINGS
ARIST
ARISTA
ARISTAE
ARISTARCHIES
ARISTARCHY
ARISTATE
ARISTE
ARISTO
ARISTOCRACIES
ARISTOCRACY
ARISTOCRAT

ARISTOCRATIC
ARISTOCRATICAL
ARISTOCRATICALLY
ARISTOGENIC
ARISTOGENICS
ARISTOI
ARISTOLOGICAL
ARISTOLOGIST
ARISTOLOGY
ARISTOS
ARISTOTYPE
ARISTULATE
ARITE
ARITHMETIC
ARITHMETICAL
ARITHMETICALLY
ARITHMETICIAN
ARITHMETIZE
ARITHMOCRACY
ARITHMOGRAM
ARITHMOGRAPH
ARITHMOMANIA
ARITHMOMETER
ARITHROMANIA
ARIZONITE
ARJAN
ARJUN
ARK
ARKANSITE
ARKAR
ARKITE
ARKOSE
ARKOSIC
ARKSUTITE
ARLES
ARLING
ARLOUP
ARM
ARMADA
ARMADILLA
ARMADILLO
ARMADILLOS
ARMAGNAC
ARMAMENT
ARMAMENTARIA
ARMAMENTARY
ARMANGITE
ARMARIA
ARMARIUM
ARMATURE
ARMBAND
ARMBONE
ARMCHAIR
ARMCHAIRED
ARME
ARMED
ARMENIACEOUS
ARMENITE
ARMER
ARMET
ARMFUL
ARMFULS
ARMGAUNT
ARMGUARD
ARMHOLE
ARMHOOP
ARMIED
ARMIES
ARMIFEROUS
ARMIGER
ARMIGERAL
ARMIGERI
ARMIGEROUS
ARMIL
ARMILL
ARMILLA
ARMILLAE
ARMILLARY
ARMILLATE
ARMILLATED
ARMINE
ARMING
ARMIPOTENCE
ARMIPOTENT
ARMISONANT
ARMISONOUS
ARMISTICE
ARMITAS
ARMLET
ARMLOAD
ARMLOCK
ARMOIRE
ARMONICA
ARMOR
ARMORBEARER
ARMORED
ARMORER
ARMORIAL
ARMORIED
ARMORIES
ARMORIST
ARMORY
ARMOUR
ARMOURED
ARMOURER
ARMOURIES
ARMOURY
ARMOZEEN
ARMOZINE
ARMPIECE
ARMPIT
ARMPLATE
ARMRACK
ARMREST
ARMS
ARMSCYE
ARMSEYE
ARMSIZE
ARMURE
ARMY
ARMYWORM
ARN
ARNA
ARNATTA
ARNATTO
ARNBERRY
ARNEE
ARNEMENT
ARNI
ARNICA
ARNOTTO
ARNUT
AROAR
AROAST
AROCK
AROEIRA
AROID
AROIDEOUS
AROINT
AROLIA
AROLIUM
AROLLA
AROMA
AROMACITY
AROMADENDRIN
AROMAS
AROMATA
AROMATIC
AROMATICAL
AROMATICALLY
AROMATICITY
AROMATITAE
AROMATITE
AROMATITES
AROMATIZE
AROMATIZED
AROMATIZER
AROMATIZING
AROMATOUS
AROMO
AROOM
AROON
AROSE
AROUND
AROUSAL
AROUSE
AROUSED
AROUSER
AROUSING
AROW
AROXYL
AROYNT
ARPA
ARPEGGIANDO
ARPEGGIATION
ARPEGGIO
ARPEGGIOED
ARPEN
ARPENT
ARPENTEUR
ARQUEBUS
ARQUERITE
ARR
ARRA
ARRACACH
ARRACACHA
ARRACE
ARRACK
ARRAGE
ARRAH
ARRAIGN
ARRAIGNED
ARRAIGNER
ARRAIGNING
ARRAIGNMENT
ARRAME
ARRAND
ARRANGE
ARRANGED
ARRANGEMENT
ARRANGER
ARRANGING
ARRANT
ARRANTLY
ARRAS
ARRASED
ARRASENE
ARRASTRA
ARRASTRE
ARRATEL
ARRAU
ARRAY
ARRAYAL
ARRAYAN
ARRAYED
ARRAYER
ARRAYING
ARRAYMENT
ARREAR
ARREARAGE
ARREARS
ARRECT
ARRECTOR
ARRENT
ARRENTATION
ARREPTITIOUS
ARREST
ARRESTATION
ARRESTEE
ARRESTER
ARRESTING
ARRESTINGLY
ARRESTIVE
ARRESTMENT
ARRESTOR
ARRET
ARRHA
ARRHAL
ARRHENAL
ARRHENOTOKY
ARRHINIA
ARRHIZAL
ARRHIZOUS
ARRHYTHMIA
ARRHYTHMIC
ARRHYTHMICAL
ARRHYTHMICALLY
ARRHYTHMOUS
ARRHYTHMY
ARRIAGE
ARRIBA
ARRICCIO
ARRIDE
ARRIDGE
ARRIE
ARRIERE
ARRIERO
ARRIMBY
ARRIS
ARRISH
ARRISWAYS
ARRISWISE
ARRIVAGE
ARRIVAL
ARRIVE
ARRIVED
ARRIVER
ARRIVING
ARRIVISM
ARRIVIST
ARRIVISTE
ARROBA
ARRODE
ARROGANCE
ARROGANCY
ARROGANT
ARROGANTLY
ARROGANTNESS
ARROGATE
ARROGATED
ARROGATING
ARROGATION
ARROGATIVE
ARROGATOR
ARROJADITE
ARRONDI
ARROPE
ARROSION
ARROSIVE
ARROUND
ARROUSE
ARROW
ARROWBUSH
ARROWED
ARROWHEAD
ARROWHEADED
ARROWLEAF
ARROWLET
ARROWPLATE
ARROWROOT
ARROWS
ARROWSTONE
ARROWWEED
ARROWWOOD
ARROWWORM
ARROWY
ARROYA
ARROYO
ARROYOS
ARROYUELO
ARROZ
ARS
ARSANILIC
ARSE
ARSEDINE
ARSEFOOT
ARSENAL
ARSENATE
ARSENATION
ARSENETED
ARSENETTED
ARSENFAST
ARSENHEMOL
ARSENIASIS
ARSENIATE
ARSENIC
ARSENICAL
ARSENICALISM
ARSENICATE
ARSENICATED
ARSENICATING
ARSENICISM
ARSENICIZE
ARSENICKED
ARSENICKING
ARSENIDE
ARSENIDES
ARSENIFEROUS
ARSENILLO
ARSENIOUS
ARSENISM
ARSENITE
ARSENIUM
ARSENIURET
ARSENIURETED
ARSENIZATION
ARSENOFURAN
ARSENOLITE
ARSENOPHEN
ARSENOPHENOL
ARSENOPYRITE
ARSENOUS
ARSENOXIDE
ARSENYL
ARSES
ARSESMART
ARSHEEN
ARSHIN
ARSHINE
ARSHINS
ARSINE
ARSINIC
ARSINO
ARSIS
ARSLE
ARSNICKER
ARSOITE
ARSON
ARSONATE
ARSONATION
ARSONIC
ARSONIST
ARSONITE
ARSONIUM
ARSONO
ARSPHENAMINE
ARSYL
ARSYLENE
ART
ARTABA
ARTAL
ARTAR
ARTARIN
ARTARINE
ARTCRAFT

ARTEFAC
ARTEFACT
ARTEL
ARTEMIA
ARTEMISIA
ARTEMISIC
ARTEMISIN
ARTEMON
ARTER
ARTERIA
ARTERIAE
ARTERIAGRA
ARTERIAL
ARTERIALIZE
ARTERIALIZED
ARTERIALLY
ARTERIARCTIA
ARTERIASIS
ARTERIED
ARTERIES
ARTERIN
ARTERIOGRAM
ARTERIOGRAPH
ARTERIOLE
ARTERIOLITH
ARTERIOLOGY
ARTERIOMETER
ARTERIOMOTOR
ARTERIORENAL
ARTERIOSPASM
ARTERIOTOME
ARTERIOTOMY
ARTERIOUS
ARTERITIS
ARTERY
ARTERYING
ARTFUL
ARTFULLY
ARTFULNESS
ARTHA
ARTHEL
ARTHEMIS
ARTHRA
ARTHRAGRA
ARTHRAL
ARTHRALGIA
ARTHRALGIC
ARTHRECTOMY
ARTHREDEMA
ARTHRITIC
ARTHRITICAL
ARTHRITICINE
ARTHRITIDES
ARTHRITIS
ARTHRITISM
ARTHROBRANCH
ARTHROCACE
ARTHROCELE
ARTHROCLASIA
ARTHROCLISIS
ARTHRODERM
ARTHRODESIS
ARTHRODIA
ARTHRODIAE
ARTHRODIAL
ARTHRODIC
ARTHRODIRAN
ARTHRODIRE
ARTHRODIROUS
ARTHRODYMIC
ARTHRODYNIA
ARTHROGENOUS
ARTHROGRAPHY
ARTHROLITE
ARTHROLITH
ARTHROLOGY
ARTHROMERE
ARTHROMERIC
ARTHROMETER
ARTHROMETRY
ARTHRON
ARTHRONCUS
ARTHROPATHIC
ARTHROPATHY
ARTHROPHYMA
ARTHROPLASTY
ARTHROPLEURA
ARTHROPLEURE
ARTHROPOD
ARTHROPODAL
ARTHROPODAN
ARTHROPODOUS
ARTHROPYOSIS
ARTHROSES
ARTHROSIA
ARTHROSIS
ARTHROSPORE
ARTHROSPORIC
ARTHROSPOROUS
ARTHROSTOME
ARTHROSTOMY
ARTHROSYRINX
ARTHROTOME
ARTHROTOMIES
ARTHROTOMY
ARTHROTRAUMA
ARTHROTROPIC
ARTHROUS
ARTHROZOAN
ARTHROZOIC
ARTIAD
ARTICHOKE
ARTICLE
ARTICLED
ARTICLES
ARTICLING
ARTICULACY
ARTICULANT
ARTICULAR
ARTICULARE
ARTICULARLY
ARTICULARS
ARTICULATE
ARTICULATED
ARTICULATELY
ARTICULATENESS
ARTICULATING
ARTICULATION
ARTICULATIVE
ARTICULATOR
ARTICULATORY
ARTICULITE
ARTICULUS
ARTIFACT
ARTIFACTS
ARTIFEX
ARTIFICE
ARTIFICER
ARTIFICES
ARTIFICIAL
ARTIFICIALITIES
ARTIFICIALITY
ARTIFICIALLY
ARTIFICIALNESS
ARTILLER
ARTILLERIST
ARTILLERY
ARTILLERYMAN
ARTILLERYMEN
ARTILLERYSHIP
ARTINESS
ARTINITE
ARTIODACTYL
ARTIPHYLLOUS
ARTISAN
ARTISANRY
ARTISANSHIP
ARTIST
ARTISTE
ARTISTIC
ARTISTICAL
ARTISTICALLY
ARTISTRY
ARTLESS
ARTLESSLY
ARTLESSNESS
ARTLET
ARTLY
ARTOCARPAD
ARTOCARPEOUS
ARTOCARPOUS
ARTOLATER
ARTOPHAGOUS
ARTOPHORIA
ARTOPHORION
ARTOTYPE
ARTOTYPY
ARTS
ARTSMAN
ARTUS
ARTWARE
ARTWORK
ARTY
ARUI
ARUIN
ARUKE
ARUM
ARUMIN
ARUNDIFEROUS
ARUNDINEOUS
ARUPA
ARURA
ARUSA
ARUSHA
ARUSPEX
ARUSPICE
ARUSTLE
ARVAL
ARVEJON
ARVEL
ARVICOLE
ARVICOLINE
ARVICULTURE
ARX
ARY
ARYBALLOID
ARYBALLOS
ARYBALLUS
ARYL
ARYLAMINE
ARYLAMINO
ARYLATE
ARYLIDE
ARYTENOID
ARYTENOIDAL
ARZRUNITE
ARZUN
AS
ASADDLE
ASADO
ASAFETIDA
ASAFOETIDA
ASAK
ASAL
ASALE
ASAMBLEA
ASANA
ASAPHIA
ASAPHID
ASAR
ASARABACCA
ASARITE
ASARON
ASARONE
ASAROTUM
ASARUM
ASBEST
ASBESTIC
ASBESTIFORM
ASBESTINE
ASBESTINIZE
ASBESTOID
ASBESTOIDAL
ASBESTOS
ASBESTOSIS
ASBESTOUS
ASBESTUS
ASBOLAN
ASBOLANE
ASBOLIN
ASBOLITE
ASCAN
ASCARE
ASCARED
ASCARIASIS
ASCARICIDAL
ASCARICIDE
ASCARID
ASCARIDES
ASCARIDIASIS
ASCARIDOL
ASCARIDOLE
ASCARIS
ASCARON
ASCELLI
ASCELLUS
ASCEND
ASCENDABLE
ASCENDANCE
ASCENDANCY
ASCENDANT
ASCENDENCE
ASCENDENCY
ASCENDENT
ASCENDER
ASCENDIBLE
ASCENDING
ASCENDINGLY
ASCENSEUR
ASCENSION
ASCENSIONAL
ASCENSIVE
ASCENSOR
ASCENT
ASCERTAIN
ASCERTAINABLE
ASCERTAINABLY
ASCERTAINER
ASCERTAINMENT
ASCESIS
ASCETIC
ASCETICAL
ASCETICALLY
ASCETICISM
ASCHAFFITE
ASCHAM
ASCHER
ASCHISTIC
ASCI
ASCIAN
ASCIDIA
ASCIDIAN
ASCIDIATE
ASCIDICOLOUS
ASCIDIFEROUS
ASCIDIFORM
ASCIDIOID
ASCIDIOZOOID
ASCIDIUM
ASCIFEROUS
ASCIGEROUS
ASCII
ASCILL
ASCITES
ASCITIC
ASCITICAL
ASCITITIOUS
ASCLEPIAD
ASCLEPIDIN
ASCLEPIDOID
ASCLEPIN
ASCOCARP
ASCOCARPOUS
ASCOGENOUS
ASCOGONE
ASCOGONIAL
ASCOGONIDIA
ASCOGONIDIUM
ASCOGONIUM
ASCOLICHEN
ASCOMA
ASCOMATA
ASCOMYCETE
ASCOMYCETES
ASCOMYCETOUS
ASCON
ASCOPHORE
ASCOPHOROUS
ASCORBIC
ASCOSPORE
ASCOSPORIC
ASCOSPOROUS
ASCOT
ASCRIBABLE
ASCRIBE
ASCRIBED
ASCRIBING
ASCRIPT
ASCRIPTION
ASCRIPTITIOUS
ASCRIVE
ASCRY
ASCULA
ASCULAE
ASCUS
ASCYPHOUS
ASDIC
ASE
ASEA
ASEARCH
ASECRETORY
ASEETHE
ASEISMATIC
ASEISMIC
ASEISMICITY
ASEITAS
ASEITY
ASELAR
ASELGEIA
ASELLATE
ASELLUS
ASEM
ASEPSIS
ASEPTATE
ASEPTIC
ASEPTICALLY
ASEPTICISM
ASEPTICIZE
ASEPTICIZED
ASEPTICIZING
ASEPTIFY
ASEPTOL
ASEPTOLIN
ASEXUAL
ASEXUALITY

ASEXUALIZE
ASEXUALIZED
ASEXUALIZING
ASEXUALLY
ASH
ASHAKE
ASHAME
ASHAMED
ASHAMEDLY
ASHAMEDNESS
ASHAMNU
ASHBERRY
ASHCAKE
ASHCAN
ASHEN
ASHERAH
ASHERAHS
ASHERIES
ASHERIM
ASHERY
ASHES
ASHET
ASHFALL
ASHIER
ASHIEST
ASHILY
ASHIMMER
ASHINE
ASHINESS
ASHIPBOARD
ASHIVER
ASHKOKO
ASHLAR
ASHLARED
ASHLARING
ASHLER
ASHLERED
ASHLERING
ASHLING
ASHMAN
ASHMEN
ASHORE
ASHOT
ASHPAN
ASHPIT
ASHPLANT
ASHRAF
ASHRAFI
ASHRAM
ASHRAMA
ASHRE
ASHSTONE
ASHTRAY
ASHVAMEDHA
ASHWEED
ASHWORT
ASHY
ASIALIA
ASIDE
ASIDEHAND
ASIDEN
ASIENTO
ASIL
ASILID
ASIM
ASIMEN
ASIMMER
ASINEGO
ASINEGOES
ASININE
ASININELY
ASININITIES
ASININITY
ASIPHONATE
ASIS
ASITIA
ASK
ASKANCE
ASKANT
ASKAR
ASKAREL
ASKARI
ASKARIS
ASKER
ASKESIS
ASKEW
ASKI
ASKILE
ASKING
ASKINGLY
ASKIP
ASKOS
ASLAKE
ASLANT
ASLANTWISE
ASLAVER
ASLEEP
ASLOP
ASLOPE
ASLUMBER
ASMACK
ASMALTE
ASMEAR
ASMILE
ASMOKE
ASMOLDER
ASNIFFLE
ASNORT
ASOAK
ASOCIAL
ASOK
ASOKA
ASOMATOPHYTE
ASOMATOUS
ASONANT
ASONIA
ASOP
ASOR
ASOTE
ASOUTH
ASP
ASPACE
ASPALATHUS
ASPAR
ASPARAGIC
ASPARAGIN
ASPARAGINE
ASPARAGINIC
ASPARAGINOUS
ASPARAGUS
ASPARAGYL
ASPARKLE
ASPARTATE
ASPARTIC
ASPARTYL
ASPECT
ASPECTABLE
ASPECTANT
ASPECTION
ASPECTS
ASPEN
ASPER
ASPERATE
ASPERATED
ASPERATING
ASPERATION
ASPERGATION
ASPERGE
ASPERGER
ASPERGES
ASPERGILL
ASPERGILLA
ASPERGILLI
ASPERGILLIN
ASPERGILLUM
ASPERGILLUMS
ASPERGILLUS
ASPERITE
ASPERITIES
ASPERITY
ASPERMATIC
ASPERMATISM
ASPERMIA
ASPERMOUS
ASPEROUS
ASPEROUSLY
ASPERSE
ASPERSED
ASPERSER
ASPERSING
ASPERSION
ASPERSIONS
ASPERSIVE
ASPERSIVELY
ASPERSOR
ASPERSORIA
ASPERSORIUM
ASPERSORIUMS
ASPERSORY
ASPERULOSIDE
ASPERULOUS
ASPHALT
ASPHALTENE
ASPHALTER
ASPHALTIC
ASPHALTITE
ASPHALTUM
ASPHALTUS
ASPHETERISM
ASPHETERIZE
ASPHODEL
ASPHYCTIC
ASPHYCTOUS
ASPHYXIA
ASPHYXIAL
ASPHYXIANT
ASPHYXIATE
ASPHYXIATED
ASPHYXIATING
ASPHYXIATION
ASPHYXIATOR
ASPHYXIED
ASPHYXY
ASPIC
ASPIDATE
ASPIDE
ASPIDIARIA
ASPIDINOL
ASPIDISTRA
ASPIDIUM
ASPIDOMANCY
ASPIQUEE
ASPIRANT
ASPIRATA
ASPIRATAE
ASPIRATE
ASPIRATED
ASPIRATING
ASPIRATION
ASPIRATOR
ASPIRATORY
ASPIRE
ASPIRED
ASPIREE
ASPIRER
ASPIRIN
ASPIRING
ASPIRINGLY
ASPISH
ASPLANCHNIC
ASPLENIOID
ASPOROGENIC
ASPOROUS
ASPORT
ASPORTATION
ASPORULATE
ASPOUT
ASPRAWL
ASPREAD
ASPRING
ASPROUT
ASPY
ASQUARE
ASQUAT
ASQUEAL
ASQUINT
ASQUIRM
ASRAM
ASRAMA
ASS
ASSACU
ASSAFETIDA
ASSAFOETIDA
ASSAGAI
ASSAGAIED
ASSAGAIING
ASSAHY
ASSAI
ASSAIL
ASSAILABLE
ASSAILANT
ASSAILER
ASSAILMENT
ASSALTO
ASSAPAN
ASSAPANIC
ASSARION
ASSART
ASSARY
ASSASSIN
ASSASSINATE
ASSASSINATED
ASSASSINATING
ASSASSINATION
ASSASSINATIVE
ASSASSINATOR
ASSASSINATRESS
ASSASSINIST
ASSATE
ASSATION
ASSAULT
ASSAULTER
ASSAULTING
ASSAUT
ASSAY
ASSAYED
ASSAYER
ASSAYING
ASSBAA
ASSE
ASSEAL
ASSECURATION
ASSECURATOR
ASSEDAT
ASSEGAI
ASSEIZE
ASSELF
ASSEMBLABLE
ASSEMBLAGE
ASSEMBLE
ASSEMBLED
ASSEMBLEE
ASSEMBLER
ASSEMBLIES
ASSEMBLING
ASSEMBLY
ASSEMBLYMAN
ASSEMBLYMEN
ASSENT
ASSENTANEOUS
ASSENTATION
ASSENTATIOUS
ASSENTATORY
ASSENTED
ASSENTER
ASSENTIENT
ASSENTING
ASSENTIVE
ASSENTIVENESS
ASSENTOR
ASSERT
ASSERTA
ASSERTABLE
ASSERTATIVE
ASSERTER
ASSERTIBLE
ASSERTION
ASSERTIONAL
ASSERTIVE
ASSERTIVELY
ASSERTIVENESS
ASSERTOR
ASSERTORIAL
ASSERTORIC
ASSERTORICAL
ASSERTORILY
ASSERTORY
ASSERTRESS
ASSERTRIX
ASSERTUM
ASSERVE
ASSES
ASSESS
ASSESSABLE
ASSESSED
ASSESSEE
ASSESSING
ASSESSION
ASSESSIONARY
ASSESSMENT
ASSESSOR
ASSESSORIAL
ASSESSORY
ASSET
ASSETH
ASSETS
ASSEVER
ASSEVERATE
ASSEVERATED
ASSEVERATION
ASSEVERATIVE
ASSEVERATORY
ASSHEAD
ASSI
ASSIBILATE
ASSIBILATED
ASSIBILATING
ASSIBILATION
ASSIDENT
ASSIDUAL
ASSIDUALLY
ASSIDUITIES
ASSIDUITY
ASSIDUOUS
ASSIDUOUSLY
ASSIDUOUSNESS
ASSIEGE
ASSIENTIST
ASSIENTO
ASSIETTE
ASSIFY
ASSIGN
ASSIGNABLE
ASSIGNABLY
ASSIGNAT

ASSIGNATION
ASSIGNED
ASSIGNEE
ASSIGNER
ASSIGNMENT
ASSIGNOR
ASSILAG
ASSIMILABLE
ASSIMILATE
ASSIMILATED
ASSIMILATING
ASSIMILATION
ASSIMILATIVE
ASSIMILATOR
ASSIMILATORY
ASSIS
ASSISE
ASSISH
ASSISHLY
ASSISHNESS
ASSIST
ASSISTANCE
ASSISTANT
ASSISTANTED
ASSISTER
ASSISTFUL
ASSISTIVE
ASSISTLESS
ASSISTOR
ASSIZE
ASSIZED
ASSIZEMENT
ASSIZER
ASSIZES
ASSIZING
ASSMAN
ASSMANSHIP
ASSOCIABLE
ASSOCIATE
ASSOCIATED
ASSOCIATING
ASSOCIATION
ASSOCIATIVE
ASSOCIATIVELY
ASSOCIATIVENESS
ASSOCIATOR
ASSOCIE
ASSOIL
ASSOILMENT
ASSOILZIE
ASSOLUTO
ASSONANCE
ASSONANCED
ASSONANT
ASSONANTAL
ASSONANTIC
ASSONATE
ASSORT
ASSORTATIVE
ASSORTED
ASSORTER
ASSORTIVE
ASSORTMENT
ASSOT
ASSUADE
ASSUAGE
ASSUAGED
ASSUAGEMENT
ASSUAGER
ASSUAGING
ASSUASIVE
ASSUETUDE
ASSUMABLE
ASSUME
ASSUMED
ASSUMEDLY
ASSUMER
ASSUMING
ASSUMINGLY
ASSUMINGNESS
ASSUMMON
ASSUMPSIT
ASSUMPT
ASSUMPTION
ASSUMPTIOUS
ASSUMPTIVE
ASSUMPTIVELY
ASSURABLE
ASSURANCE
ASSURATE
ASSURD
ASSURE
ASSURED
ASSUREDLY
ASSUREDNESS
ASSURER
ASSURGE
ASSURGENCY
ASSURGENT
ASSURING
ASSURINGLY
ASSWAGE
ASSYNTITE
ASSYTH
ASSYTHMENT
ASTALK
ASTARBOARD
ASTARE
ASTART
ASTASIA
ASTATIC
ASTATICALLY
ASTATICISM
ASTATINE
ASTATIZE
ASTATIZED
ASTATIZER
ASTATIZING
ASTAY
ASTEAM
ASTEATOSIS
ASTEEP
ASTEER
ASTEISM
ASTELY
ASTER
ASTERACEOUS
ASTERIA
ASTERIAE
ASTERIAL
ASTERIATED
ASTERIN
ASTERION
ASTERISK
ASTERISKOS
ASTERISM
ASTERISMAL
ASTERN
ASTERNAL
ASTERNIA
ASTEROID
ASTEROIDAL
ASTEROIDEAN
ASTERT
ASTERWORT
ASTHENIA
ASTHENIC
ASTHENICAL
ASTHENOLOGY
ASTHENOPIA
ASTHENOPIC
ASTHENY
ASTHMA
ASTHMATIC
ASTHMATICAL
ASTHMATICALLY
ASTHMATOID
ASTHMOGENIC
ASTHORE
ASTHORIN
ASTICHOUS
ASTIGMATIC
ASTIGMATICAL
ASTIGMATISM
ASTIGMATIZER
ASTIGMIA
ASTIGMISM
ASTIGMOMETER
ASTIGMOMETRY
ASTILBE
ASTINT
ASTIPULATE
ASTIPULATION
ASTIR
ASTITE
ASTOGENY
ASTOMATAL
ASTOMATOUS
ASTOMIA
ASTOMOUS
ASTON
ASTOND
ASTONE
ASTONED
ASTONIED
ASTONISH
ASTONISHEDLY
ASTONISHER
ASTONISHING
ASTONISHINGLY
ASTONISHMENT
ASTONY
ASTONYING
ASTOOP
ASTORE
ASTOUND
ASTOUNDED
ASTOUNDING
ASTOUNDINGLY
ASTOUNDMENT
ASTRACHAN
ASTRADDLE
ASTRAEAN
ASTRAEID
ASTRAEIFORM
ASTRAGAL
ASTRAGALAR
ASTRAGALI
ASTRAGALUS
ASTRAIN
ASTRAKANITE
ASTRAKHAN
ASTRAL
ASTRALLY
ASTRAND
ASTRAPHOBIA
ASTRAY
ASTRE
ASTREAM
ASTRER
ASTRICT
ASTRICTION
ASTRICTIVE
ASTRICTIVELY
ASTRIDE
ASTRIER
ASTRIFEROUS
ASTRILD
ASTRINGE
ASTRINGED
ASTRINGENCY
ASTRINGENT
ASTRINGENTLY
ASTRINGER
ASTRINGING
ASTRION
ASTROBIOLOGY
ASTROBLAST
ASTROBOTANY
ASTROCHEMIST
ASTROCYTE
ASTROCYTOMA
ASTROCYTOMAS
ASTROCYTOMATA
ASTRODOME
ASTROFEL
ASTROFELL
ASTROGATE
ASTROGATED
ASTROGATING
ASTROGENY
ASTROGLIA
ASTROGNOSY
ASTROGONIC
ASTROGONY
ASTROGRAPH
ASTROGRAPHIC
ASTROGRAPHY
ASTROID
ASTROITE
ASTROLABE
ASTROLABICAL
ASTROLATER
ASTROLATRY
ASTROLOG
ASTROLOGE
ASTROLOGER
ASTROLOGIAN
ASTROLOGIC
ASTROLOGICAL
ASTROLOGICALLY
ASTROLOGISTIC
ASTROLOGIZE
ASTROLOGOUS
ASTROLOGY
ASTROMANCER
ASTROMANCY
ASTROMANTIC
ASTROMEDA
ASTROMETER
ASTROMETRY
ASTRONAUT
ASTRONAUTIC
ASTRONAUTICS
ASTRONOMER
ASTRONOMIC
ASTRONOMICAL
ASTRONOMICALLY
ASTRONOMICS
ASTRONOMIZE
ASTRONOMY
ASTROPHIL
ASTROPHOBIA
ASTROPHYSICS
ASTROSCOPE
ASTROSCOPY
ASTROSE
ASTROSPHERE
ASTRUT
ASTUCIOUS
ASTUCIOUSLY
ASTUCITY
ASTUTE
ASTUTELY
ASTUTENESS
ASTUTIOUS
ASTYLAR
ASUANG
ASUDDEN
ASUNDER
ASURA
ASWAIL
ASWARM
ASWASH
ASWAY
ASWEAT
ASWELL
ASWEVE
ASWIM
ASWING
ASWIRL
ASWOON
ASWOONED
ASYLA
ASYLLABIA
ASYLLABIC
ASYLLABICAL
ASYLUM
ASYLUMS
ASYMBOLIA
ASYMBOLIC
ASYMBOLICAL
ASYMMETRIC
ASYMMETRICAL
ASYMMETRICALLY
ASYMMETRY
ASYMPTOTE
ASYMPTOTIC
ASYMPTOTICAL
ASYNARTETE
ASYNARTETIC
ASYNCHRONISM
ASYNCHRONOUS
ASYNDETIC
ASYNDETON
ASYNERGIA
ASYNERGY
ASYNGAMIC
ASYNGAMY
ASYNTACTIC
ASYNTROPHY
ASYSTOLE
ASYSTOLIC
ASYSTOLISM
ASYZYGETIC
AT
ATA
ATABAL
ATABEG
ATABEK
ATABRINE
ATACAMITE
ATACTIC
ATACTIFORM
ATAGHAN
ATAJO
ATAKE
ATALAYA
ATAMAN
ATAMASCO
ATAME
ATANGLE
ATAP
ATAR
ATARACTIC
ATARAXIA
ATARAXIC
ATARAXY
ATATSCHITE
ATAUNT
ATAUNTO
ATAVI
ATAVIC
ATAVISM
ATAVIST

ATAVISTIC
ATAVUS
ATAXAPHASIA
ATAXIA
ATAXIAGRAM
ATAXIAGRAPH
ATAXIAMETER
ATAXIAPHASIA
ATAXIC
ATAXINOMIC
ATAXITE
ATAXONOMIC
ATAXOPHEMIA
ATAXY
ATAZIR
ATBASH
ATE
ATECHNIC
ATECHNICAL
ATECHNY
ATEES
ATEETER
ATEF
ATELECTASIS
ATELECTATIC
ATELESTITE
ATELIC
ATELIER
ATELIOSIS
ATELOCARDIA
ATELOGLOSSIA
ATELOGNATHIA
ATELOMITIC
ATELOMYELIA
ATELOPODIA
ATELOSTOMIA
ATEMOYA
ATEMPORAL
ATES
ATEUCHI
ATEUCHUS
ATHALAMOUS
ATHALLINE
ATHANASIA
ATHANASY
ATHANOR
ATHBASH
ATHECATE
ATHEISM
ATHEIST
ATHEISTIC
ATHEISTICAL
ATHEISTICALLY
ATHEIZE
ATHEIZER
ATHEL
ATHELIA
ATHELING
ATHEMATIC
ATHENAEUM
ATHENEUM
ATHENOR
ATHEOLOGICAL
ATHEOLOGY
ATHEOUS
ATHER
ATHERICERAN
ATHERICEROUS
ATHERINE
ATHERMANCY
ATHERMANOUS
ATHERMIC
ATHERMOUS
ATHEROMA
ATHEROMAS
ATHEROMASIA
ATHEROMATA
ATHEROMATOUS
ATHETESIS
ATHETIZE
ATHETIZED
ATHETIZING
ATHETOID
ATHETOSIC
ATHETOSIS
ATHIN
ATHING
ATHINK
ATHIRST
ATHLETE
ATHLETIC
ATHLETICAL
ATHLETICALLY
ATHLETICISM
ATHLETICS
ATHLETISM
ATHODYD
ATHOLD
ATHONITE
ATHREPSIA
ATHREPTIC
ATHRILL
ATHRIVE
ATHROB
ATHROGENIC
ATHRONG
ATHUMIA
ATHWART
ATHWARTHAWSE
ATHWARTSHIP
ATHWARTSHIPS
ATHWARTWISE
ATHYMIA
ATHYMIC
ATHYMY
ATHYREOSIS
ATHYRIA
ATHYRID
ATHYROID
ATHYROIDISM
ATI
ATILT
ATIMON
ATINGA
ATINGLE
ATINKLE
ATIP
ATIPTOE
ATIS
ATLANTAD
ATLANTAL
ATLANTES
ATLANTITE
ATLANTOAXIAL
ATLAS
ATLATL
ATLE
ATLEE
ATLOAXOID
ATLOID
ATLOIDEAN
ATLOIDOAXOID
ATMA
ATMAN
ATMIATRY
ATMID
ATMIDALBUMIN
ATMIDOMETER
ATMIDOMETRY
ATMOCAUSIS
ATMOCAUTERY
ATMOCLASTIC
ATMOGENIC
ATMOGRAPH
ATMOLOGIC
ATMOLOGICAL
ATMOLOGIST
ATMOLOGY
ATMOLYSIS
ATMOLYZATION
ATMOLYZE
ATMOLYZER
ATMOMETER
ATMOMETRIC
ATMOMETRY
ATMOSPHERE
ATMOSPHERIC
ATMOSPHERICAL
ATMOSPHERICALLY
ATMOSPHERICS
ATMOSTEA
ATMOSTEAL
ATMOSTEON
ATO
ATOCHA
ATOCIA
ATOKAL
ATOKE
ATOKOUS
ATOLE
ATOLL
ATOM
ATOMATIC
ATOMECHANICS
ATOMERG
ATOMIC
ATOMICAL
ATOMICALLY
ATOMICIAN
ATOMICISM
ATOMICITY
ATOMICS
ATOMIES
ATOMIFEROUS
ATOMISE
ATOMISM
ATOMIST
ATOMISTIC
ATOMISTICAL
ATOMISTICALLY
ATOMISTICS
ATOMITY
ATOMIZATION
ATOMIZE
ATOMIZED
ATOMIZER
ATOMIZING
ATOMOLOGY
ATOMS
ATOMY
ATONABLE
ATONAL
ATONALISM
ATONALISTIC
ATONALITY
ATONALLY
ATONE
ATONEABLE
ATONED
ATONEMENT
ATONENESS
ATONER
ATONIA
ATONIC
ATONICITY
ATONING
ATONINGLY
ATONY
ATOP
ATOPEN
ATOPIC
ATOPITE
ATOPY
ATOUR
ATRABILAIRE
ATRABILAR
ATRABILARIAN
ATRABILE
ATRABILIAR
ATRABILIARY
ATRABILIOUS
ATRACHEATE
ATRAGENE
ATRAIL
ATRAMENT
ATRAMENTAL
ATRAMENTARY
ATRAMENTOUS
ATRAUMATIC
ATREDE
ATREMATE
ATREMATOUS
ATREMBLE
ATRENNE
ATREPSY
ATREPTIC
ATRESIA
ATRESIC
ATRETIC
ATRIA
ATRIAL
ATRICHIA
ATRICHIC
ATRICHOUS
ATRICKLE
ATRIENSES
ATRIENSIS
ATRIO
ATRIOPORAL
ATRIOPORE
ATRIP
ATRIUM
ATROCE
ATROCHA
ATROCHAL
ATROCHOUS
ATROCIOUS
ATROCIOUSLY
ATROCIOUSNESS
ATROCITIES
ATROCITY
ATROLACTIC
ATROPACEOUS
ATROPAL
ATROPHIA
ATROPHIATED
ATROPHIC
ATROPHIED
ATROPHIES
ATROPHODERMA
ATROPHOUS
ATROPHY
ATROPHYING
ATROPIA
ATROPIC
ATROPIN
ATROPINE
ATROPINIZE
ATROPISM
ATROPOUS
ATRORUBENT
ATROUS
ATRY
ATRYPOID
ATSARA
ATT
ATTA
ATTABAL
ATTACCA
ATTACCO
ATTACH
ATTACHABLE
ATTACHE
ATTACHED
ATTACHEDLY
ATTACHER
ATTACHING
ATTACHMENT
ATTACK
ATTACKABLE
ATTACKER
ATTACKS
ATTACOLITE
ATTACUS
ATTAGEN
ATTAIN
ATTAINABILITY
ATTAINABLE
ATTAINABLENESS
ATTAINDER
ATTAINED
ATTAINER
ATTAINING
ATTAINMENT
ATTAINT
ATTAINTED
ATTAINTING
ATTAINTMENT
ATTAINTURE
ATTALEH
ATTAME
ATTAP
ATTAR
ATTARGUL
ATTASK
ATTASTE
ATTE
ATTEMPER
ATTEMPERANCE
ATTEMPERATE
ATTEMPERATOR
ATTEMPERED
ATTEMPERING
ATTEMPT
ATTEMPTABILITY
ATTEMPTABLE
ATTEMPTER
ATTEND
ATTENDANCE
ATTENDANCY
ATTENDANT
ATTENDANTLY
ATTENDANTS
ATTENDED
ATTENDEE
ATTENDING
ATTENDINGLY
ATTENDMENT
ATTENDRESS
ATTENSITY
ATTENT
ATTENTAT
ATTENTATE
ATTENTION
ATTENTIONAL
ATTENTIVE
ATTENTIVELY
ATTENTIVENESS
ATTENTLY
ATTENUABLE
ATTENUANT
ATTENUATE
ATTENUATED
ATTENUATING
ATTENUATION

ATTENUATOR
ATTER
ATTERCOP
ATTERMINE
ATTERN
ATTERR
ATTERY
ATTEST
ATTESTANT
ATTESTATION
ATTESTATIVE
ATTESTATOR
ATTESTED
ATTESTER
ATTESTIVE
ATTESTOR
ATTIC
ATTICE
ATTICISM
ATTICIST
ATTICIZE
ATTICIZED
ATTICIZING
ATTID
ATTIDAE
ATTINGE
ATTINGENCE
ATTINGENCY
ATTINGENT
ATTIRE
ATTIRED
ATTIREMENT
ATTIRER
ATTIRING
ATTITUDE
ATTITUDINAL
ATTITUDINISE
ATTITUDINIZE
ATTLE
ATTORN
ATTORNEY
ATTORNEYISM
ATTORNEYS
ATTORNEYSHIP
ATTORNMENT
ATTOUR
ATTOURNE
ATTRACT
ATTRACTABLE
ATTRACTANT
ATTRACTER
ATTRACTILE
ATTRACTINGLY
ATTRACTION
ATTRACTIVE
ATTRACTIVELY
ATTRACTIVENESS
ATTRACTIVITY
ATTRACTOR
ATTRAHENT
ATTRAP
ATTRIBUTABLE
ATTRIBUTAL
ATTRIBUTE
ATTRIBUTED
ATTRIBUTER
ATTRIBUTING
ATTRIBUTION
ATTRIBUTIVE
ATTRIBUTOR
ATTRIST
ATTRITE
ATTRITED
ATTRITION
ATTRITIVE
ATTRITUS
ATTRY
ATTUNE
ATTUNED
ATTUNELY
ATTUNEMENT
ATTUNING
ATTURN
ATU
ATUA
ATULE
ATUMBLE
ATUN
ATUNE
ATURN
ATWAIN
ATWEEL
ATWEEN
ATWIN
ATWIRL
ATWIST
ATWITCH
ATWITTER
ATWIXT
ATWO
ATYPIC
ATYPICAL
ATYPICALLY
ATYPY
AU
AUA
AUANTIC
AUBADE
AUBAIN
AUBAINE
AUBE
AUBERGE
AUBERGINE
AUBERGISTE
AUBIN
AUBRITE
AUBURN
AUCA
AUCHENIA
AUCHENIUM
AUCHLET
AUCHT
AUCTARY
AUCTION
AUCTIONARY
AUCTIONEER
AUCTIONING
AUCTOR
AUCTORIAL
AUCUBA
AUCUPATE
AUDACE
AUDACIOUS
AUDACIOUSLY
AUDACIOUSNESS
AUDACITY
AUDAD
AUDIBILITY
AUDIBLE
AUDIBLENESS
AUDIBLY
AUDIENCE
AUDIENCIA
AUDIENCIER
AUDIENT
AUDILE
AUDIO
AUDIOGRAM
AUDIOLOGICAL
AUDIOLOGY
AUDIOMETER
AUDIOMETRY
AUDION
AUDIOPHILE
AUDIPHONE
AUDIT
AUDITION
AUDITIVE
AUDITOR
AUDITORIA
AUDITORIAL
AUDITORIALLY
AUDITORILY
AUDITORIUM
AUDITORIUMS
AUDITORY
AUDITRESS
AUDITUAL
AUDIVISE
AUDIVISER
AUDIVISION
AUE
AUF
AUFAIT
AUFER
AUFGABE
AUFTAKT
AUGANITE
AUGE
AUGELITE
AUGEND
AUGER
AUGERER
AUGH
AUGHT
AUGHTLINS
AUGITE
AUGITIC
AUGITITE
AUGITOPHYRE
AUGMENT
AUGMENTABLE
AUGMENTATION
AUGMENTATIVE
AUGMENTED
AUGMENTEDLY
AUGMENTER
AUGMENTIVE
AUGRIM
AUGUR
AUGURAL
AUGURATE
AUGURATION
AUGURER
AUGURIES
AUGUROUS
AUGURY
AUGUST
AUGUSTAL
AUGUSTE
AUGUSTLY
AUGUSTNESS
AUH
AUHUHU
AUK
AUKLET
AUKSINAI
AUKSINAS
AUKSINU
AUL
AULA
AULARIAN
AULD
AULETE
AULETIC
AULETRIDES
AULETRIS
AULIC
AULICAL
AULICISM
AULLAY
AULOPHYTE
AULOS
AULOSTOMID
AULU
AUM
AUMAGA
AUMAIL
AUMAKUA
AUMIL
AUMILDAR
AUMONIERE
AUMOUS
AUMRIE
AUNCEL
AUNE
AUNT
AUNTER
AUNTERS
AUNTIE
AUNTRE
AUNTROUS
AUNTSARY
AUNTY
AUPAKA
AURA
AURAE
AURAL
AURALLY
AURAMIN
AURAMINE
AURANG
AURANTIA
AURANTIUM
AURAR
AURAS
AURATE
AURATED
AUREAL
AUREATE
AUREATELY
AUREATENESS
AUREATION
AUREI
AUREITY
AURELIA
AURELIAN
AURENE
AUREOLA
AUREOLE
AUREOLIN
AUREOLINE
AUREOMYCIN
AUREOUS
AUREOUSLY
AURES
AURESCA
AUREUS
AURIC
AURICHALCITE
AURICLE
AURICLED
AURICOMOUS
AURICULA
AURICULAE
AURICULAR
AURICULARE
AURICULARES
AURICULARIA
AURICULARIAE
AURICULARIAN
AURICULARIS
AURICULARLY
AURICULAS
AURICULATE
AURICULATED
AURICULATELY
AURIDE
AURIFEROUS
AURIFEX
AURIFIC
AURIFICATION
AURIFLAMME
AURIFORM
AURIFY
AURIGAL
AURIGATION
AURIGEROUS
AURIGO
AURILAVE
AURIN
AURINASAL
AURINE
AURIPHONE
AURIPHRYGIA
AURIPUNCTURE
AURIS
AURISCALP
AURISCOPE
AURISCOPY
AURIST
AURITE
AURIVOROUS
AUROAURIC
AUROBROMIDE
AUROCH
AUROCHS
AUROCYANIDE
AURODIAMINE
AUROPHOBIA
AUROPHORE
AURORA
AURORAL
AURORALLY
AURORE
AUROREAN
AURORIUM
AUROUS
AURRESCU
AURULENT
AURUM
AURUNG
AURURE
AURYL
AUSCULT
AUSCULTATE
AUSCULTATED
AUSCULTATING
AUSCULTATION
AUSCULTATOR
AUSCULTATORY
AUSLAUT
AUSPEX
AUSPICATE
AUSPICATED
AUSPICATING
AUSPICE
AUSPICES
AUSPICIAL
AUSPICIOUS
AUSPICIOUSLY
AUSPICIOUSNESS
AUSPICY
AUSTAUSCH
AUSTEMPER
AUSTENITE
AUSTENITIC
AUSTERE
AUSTERELY
AUSTERENESS
AUSTERITIES
AUSTERITY
AUSTRAL
AUSTRALENE
AUSTRALITE

AUSTRINE
AUSTRINGER
AUSTRIUM
AUSTROMANCY
AUSU
AUSUBO
AUTACOID
AUTACOIDAL
AUTANTITYPY
AUTARCH
AUTARCHIC
AUTARCHICAL
AUTARCHIES
AUTARCHY
AUTARKIC
AUTARKIK
AUTARKIKAL
AUTARKY
AUTE
AUTECHOSCOPE
AUTECOLOGY
AUTEM
AUTERE
AUTHENTIC
AUTHENTICAL
AUTHENTICALLY
AUTHENTICATE
AUTHENTICATED
AUTHENTICATING
AUTHENTICATION
AUTHENTICATOR
AUTHENTICITY
AUTHENTICLY
AUTHENTICNESS
AUTHIGENIC
AUTHIGENOUS
AUTHOR
AUTHORCRAFT
AUTHORESS
AUTHORIAL
AUTHORIALLY
AUTHORITARIAN
AUTHORITATIVE
AUTHORITATIVELY
AUTHORITATIVENESS
AUTHORITIES
AUTHORITY
AUTHORIZATION
AUTHORIZE
AUTHORIZED
AUTHORIZER
AUTHORIZING
AUTHORLESS
AUTHORLING
AUTHORLY
AUTHORS
AUTHORSHIP
AUTHOTYPE
AUTISM
AUTIST
AUTISTIC
AUTO
AUTOALARM
AUTOALLOGAMY
AUTOBAHN
AUTOBAHNEN
AUTOBAHNS
AUTOBASIDIA
AUTOBASIDIUM
AUTOBIOGRAPHAL
AUTOBIOGRAPHER
AUTOBIOGRAPHIC
AUTOBIOGRAPHICAL
AUTOBIOGRAPHICALLY
AUTOBIOGRAPHIES
AUTOBIOGRAPHIST
AUTOBIOGRAPHY

AUTOBLAST
AUTOBOAT
AUTOBOATING
AUTOBOLIDE
AUTOBUS
AUTOCAB
AUTOCAMP
AUTOCAMPER
AUTOCAMPING
AUTOCAR
AUTOCARIST
AUTOCARP
AUTOCARPIAN
AUTOCARPIC
AUTOCARPOUS
AUTOCATALYZE
AUTOCEPHALIA
AUTOCEPHALIC
AUTOCEPHALITY
AUTOCEPHALOUS
AUTOCEPHALY
AUTOCEPTIVE
AUTOCHROME
AUTOCHROMY
AUTOCHTHON
AUTOCHTHONAL
AUTOCHTHONES
AUTOCHTHONIC
AUTOCHTHONOUS
AUTOCHTHONS
AUTOCHTHONY
AUTOCIDE
AUTOCLASTIC
AUTOCLAVE
AUTOCOHERER
AUTOCOPIST
AUTOCOSM
AUTOCRACIES
AUTOCRACY
AUTOCRAT
AUTOCRATIC
AUTOCRATICAL
AUTOCRATICALLY
AUTOCRATOR
AUTOCRATORIC
AUTOCRATRIX
AUTODIDACT
AUTODIDACTIC
AUTODROME
AUTODYNAMIC
AUTODYNE
AUTOECIC
AUTOECIOUS
AUTOECIOUSLY
AUTOECISM
AUTOED
AUTOEROTIC
AUTOEROTISM
AUTOETTE
AUTOFRETTAGE
AUTOGAMIC
AUTOGAMOUS
AUTOGAMY
AUTOGAUGE
AUTOGENEAL
AUTOGENESIS
AUTOGENETIC
AUTOGENIC
AUTOGENOUS
AUTOGENOUSLY
AUTOGENY
AUTOGIRO
AUTOGIROS
AUTOGNOSIS
AUTOGNOSTIC
AUTOGRAFT
AUTOGRAFTING

AUTOGRAPH
AUTOGRAPHER
AUTOGRAPHIC
AUTOGRAPHICAL
AUTOGRAPHISM
AUTOGRAPHIST
AUTOGRAPHY
AUTOGRAVURE
AUTOGYRO
AUTOHEADER
AUTOHYPNOSIS
AUTOICOUS
AUTOIGNITION
AUTOING
AUTOIST
AUTOKINESIS
AUTOKINETIC
AUTOKRATOR
AUTOLITH
AUTOLOADING
AUTOLYSATE
AUTOLYSIN
AUTOLYSIS
AUTOLYTIC
AUTOLYZATE
AUTOLYZE
AUTOMA
AUTOMACY
AUTOMANIA
AUTOMANUAL
AUTOMAT
AUTOMATA
AUTOMATE
AUTOMATED
AUTOMATIC
AUTOMATICAL
AUTOMATICALLY
AUTOMATICITY
AUTOMATIN
AUTOMATING
AUTOMATISM
AUTOMATIST
AUTOMATIVE
AUTOMATIZATION
AUTOMATIZE
AUTOMATON
AUTOMATONS
AUTOMATOUS
AUTOMETRIC
AUTOMETRY
AUTOMOBILE
AUTOMOBILED
AUTOMOBILING
AUTOMOBILISM
AUTOMOBILIST
AUTOMOBILITY
AUTOMOLITE
AUTOMORPH
AUTOMORPHIC
AUTOMORPHISM
AUTOMOTIVE
AUTOMOWER
AUTOMPNE
AUTONOMIC
AUTONOMICAL
AUTONOMIES
AUTONOMIST
AUTONOMIZE
AUTONOMOUS
AUTONOMOUSLY
AUTONOMY
AUTONYM
AUTOPATHIC
AUTOPATHY
AUTOPELAGIC
AUTOPHAGI
AUTOPHAGIA

AUTOPHAGOUS
AUTOPHAGY
AUTOPHOBIA
AUTOPHOBY
AUTOPHON
AUTOPHONE
AUTOPHONOUS
AUTOPHONY
AUTOPHYTE
AUTOPHYTIC
AUTOPLASTIC
AUTOPLASTIES
AUTOPLASTY
AUTOPOLO
AUTOPOLOIST
AUTOPORE
AUTOPSIC
AUTOPSICAL
AUTOPSIES
AUTOPSY
AUTOPSYCHIC
AUTOPTIC
AUTOPTICAL
AUTOPTICALLY
AUTOPTICITY
AUTORAIL
AUTORISER
AUTOROTATION
AUTORRHAPHY
AUTOSCOPE
AUTOSCOPIC
AUTOSCOPY
AUTOSERUM
AUTOSIGHT
AUTOSITE
AUTOSITIC
AUTOSKELETON
AUTOSLED
AUTOSOMAL
AUTOSOME
AUTOSOTERIC
AUTOSOTERISM
AUTOSPORE
AUTOSPORIC
AUTOSPRAY
AUTOSTAGE
AUTOSTYLIC
AUTOSTYLISM
AUTOSTYLY
AUTOTELIC
AUTOTHEISM
AUTOTHEIST
AUTOTHERAPY
AUTOTOMIC
AUTOTOMIZE
AUTOTOMY
AUTOTOXAEMIA
AUTOTOXEMIA
AUTOTOXIC
AUTOTOXIN
AUTOTRACTOR
AUTOTROPHIC
AUTOTROPIC
AUTOTROPISM
AUTOTRUCK
AUTOTYPE
AUTOTYPIC
AUTOTYPY
AUTOVACCINE
AUTOVALVE
AUTOXIDATION
AUTOXIDATOR
AUTOXIDIZE
AUTOZOOID
AUTREFOIS
AUTUMN
AUTUMNAL

AUTUMNALLY
AUTUMNIAN
AUTUMNITY
AUTUNITE
AUWAI
AUX
AUXANOGRAM
AUXANOLOGY
AUXANOMETER
AUXESIS
AUXETIC
AUXETICAL
AUXETICALLY
AUXILIAR
AUXILIARIES
AUXILIARLY
AUXILIARY
AUXILIATE
AUXILIATION
AUXILIATOR
AUXILIATORY
AUXILIUM
AUXIMONE
AUXIN
AUXOACTION
AUXOAMYLASE
AUXOBLAST
AUXOBODY
AUXOCARDIA
AUXOCHROME
AUXOCHROMIC
AUXOCHROMISM
AUXOCHROMOUS
AUXOCYTE
AUXOFLORE
AUXOFLUOR
AUXOGRAPH
AUXOGRAPHIC
AUXOHORMONE
AUXOLOGY
AUXOMETER
AUXOSPORE
AUXOTONIC
AUXOTOX
AVA
AVADANA
AVADAVAT
AVADHUTA
AVAHI
AVAIL
AVAILABILITIES
AVAILABILITY
AVAILABLE
AVAILABLENESS
AVAILABLY
AVAILED
AVAILING
AVAILINGLY
AVAILS
AVAL
AVALANCHE
AVALANCHED
AVALANCHING
AVALE
AVALENT
AVALVULAR
AVANIA
AVANIOUS
AVANT
AVANTLAY
AVANYU
AVARAM
AVAREMOTEMO
AVARICE
AVARICIOUS
AVARICIOUSLY
AVAST

AVATAR
AVATARA
AVAUNT
AVE
AVEL
AVELL
AVELLAN
AVELLANE
AVELLANEOUS
AVELLANO
AVELONGE
AVELOZ
AVENACEOUS
AVENAGE
AVENALIN
AVENANT
AVENARY
AVENER
AVENERY
AVENGE
AVENGED
AVENGEFUL
AVENGEMENT
AVENGER
AVENGERESS
AVENGING
AVENGINGLY
AVENIDA
AVENIN
AVENINE
AVENOLITH
AVENOUS
AVENS
AVENTAIL
AVENTAYLE
AVENTRE
AVENTURIN
AVENTURINE
AVENUE
AVER
AVERA
AVERAGE
AVERAGED
AVERAGELY
AVERAGER
AVERAGING
AVERAH
AVERIL
AVERIN
AVERMENT
AVERRABLE
AVERRAL
AVERRED
AVERRING
AVERRUNCATE
AVERRUNCATOR
AVERSANT
AVERSATION
AVERSE
AVERSELY
AVERSENESS
AVERSION
AVERSIVE
AVERT
AVERTABLE
AVERTED
AVERTEDLY
AVERTER
AVERTIBLE
AVESTRUZ
AVEUGLE
AVGAS
AVIADOR
AVIAN
AVIANIZE
AVIARIST
AVIARY
AVIATE
AVIATED
AVIATIC
AVIATING
AVIATION
AVIATOR
AVIATORIAL
AVIATORY
AVIATRESS
AVIATRICE
AVIATRIX
AVICHI
AVICI
AVICIDE
AVICK
AVICOLOUS
AVICULAR
AVICULARIA
AVICULARIAN
AVICULARIUM
AVICULTURE
AVICULTURIST
AVID
AVIDIN
AVIDIOUS
AVIDIOUSLY
AVIDITY
AVIDLY
AVIDOUS
AVIDYA
AVIE
AVIEW
AVIFAUNA
AVIFAUNAL
AVIGATE
AVIGATION
AVIGATOR
AVIJJA
AVILE
AVILEMENT
AVINE
AVIOLITE
AVION
AVIONICS
AVIRULENCE
AVIRULENT
AVISION
AVISO
AVISOS
AVITAL
AVITAMINOSIS
AVITAMINOTIC
AVITIC
AVIVES
AVIZANDUM
AVO
AVOCADO
AVOCADOS
AVOCATE
AVOCATION
AVOCATIVE
AVOCATORY
AVOCET
AVODIRE
AVOGADRITE
AVOGRAM
AVOID
AVOIDABLE
AVOIDABLY
AVOIDANCE
AVOIDER
AVOIDLESS
AVOIDMENT
AVOIDS
AVOIRDUPOIS
AVOLATE
AVOLATION
AVONDBLOEM
AVOSET
AVOUCH
AVOUCHER
AVOUCHMENT
AVOUE
AVOURE
AVOURNEEN
AVOUTRY
AVOW
AVOWABLE
AVOWABLENESS
AVOWABLY
AVOWAL
AVOWANCE
AVOWANT
AVOWED
AVOWEDLY
AVOWEDNESS
AVOWER
AVOWRIES
AVOWRY
AVOY
AVOYER
AVOYERSHIP
AVULSE
AVULSION
AVUNCULAR
AVUNCULATE
AVYS
AVYSE
AW
AWA
AWABI
AWAFT
AWAG
AWAIT
AWAITER
AWAITING
AWAKE
AWAKED
AWAKEN
AWAKENER
AWAKENING
AWAKENINGLY
AWAKENMENT
AWAKING
AWALD
AWALE
AWALT
AWANE
AWANTING
AWANYU
AWAPUHI
AWARD
AWARDABLE
AWARDER
AWARDMENT
AWARE
AWARENESS
AWARP
AWARRANT
AWARUITE
AWASH
AWASTE
AWAT
AWATCH
AWATER
AWAVE
AWAY
AWAYNESS
AWBER
AWE
AWEARIED
AWEARY
AWEATHER
AWEBAND
AWED
AWEDE
AWEDNESS
AWEE
AWEEK
AWEEL
AWEIGH
AWEING
AWELESS
AWESOME
AWESOMELY
AWESOMENESS
AWEST
AWESTRUCK
AWETO
AWF
AWFUL
AWFULLY
AWFULNESS
AWHAPE
AWHEEL
AWHEFT
AWHET
AWHILE
AWHIR
AWHIRL
AWIDE
AWIGGLE
AWIKIWIKI
AWING
AWINK
AWIWI
AWK
AWKLY
AWKWARD
AWKWARDLY
AWKWARDNESS
AWL
AWLESS
AWLWORT
AWMER
AWMOUS
AWN
AWNED
AWNER
AWNIE
AWNING
AWNINGED
AWNLESS
AWNY
AWOKE
AWOKEN
AWONDER
AWORK
AWREAK
AWRIST
AWRONG
AWRY
AX
AXAL
AXAN
AXBREAKER
AXE
AXEBREAKER
AXED
AXEL
AXEMAN
AXEMASTER
AXENIC
AXES
AXHAMMER
AXHAMMERED
AXIAL
AXIALITY
AXIALLY
AXIATE
AXIFORM
AXIFUGAL
AXIL
AXILE
AXILEMMA
AXILEMMAS
AXILEMMATA
AXILLA
AXILLAE
AXILLANT
AXILLAR
AXILLARIES
AXILLARY
AXINE
AXINITE
AXINOMANCY
AXIOLITE
AXIOLITIC
AXIOLOGICAL
AXIOLOGIST
AXIOLOGY
AXIOM
AXIOMATIC
AXIOMATICAL
AXIOMATIZE
AXION
AXIOPISTY
AXIS
AXISYMMETRIC
AXITE
AXLE
AXLED
AXLESMITH
AXLETREE
AXLIKE
AXMAKER
AXMAKING
AXMAN
AXMANSHIP
AXMASTER
AXMEN
AXODENDRITE
AXOFUGAL
AXOGAMY
AXOID
AXOIDEAN
AXOLOTL
AXOLYSIS
AXOMETER
AXON
AXONAL
AXONE
AXONEME
AXONEURE
AXONEURON
AXONOLIPOUS
AXONOMETRIC
AXONOMETRY
AXONOPHOROUS
AXONOST
AXOPETAL
AXOPHYTE
AXOPLASM
AXOPODIUM
AXOSPERMOUS
AXOSTYLE
AXSEED
AXSTONE
AXTREE
AXUNGE
AXWEED
AY
AYA
AYACAHUITE
AYAH
AYAHAUSCA
AYAPANA
AYE

AYEGREEN
AYEL
AYELP
AYEN
AYENBITE
AYENS
AYENST
AYIN
AYLESS
AYLET
AYLLU
AYN
AYNE
AYOND
AYONT
AYOUS
AYRE
AYU
AYUDANTE
AYUNTAMIENTO
AYUNTAMIENTOS
AYUYU
AYWHERE
AZADIRACHTA
AZAFRAN
AZAFRIN
AZALEA
AZALEAMUM
AZAM
AZAN
AZAROLE
AZEDARACH
AZELAIC
AZELATE
AZEOTROPE
AZEOTROPIC
AZEOTROPISM
AZEOTROPY
AZEW
AZIDE
AZIETHANE
AZILUT
AZIMENE
AZIMETHYLENE
AZIMIN
AZIMINE
AZIMINO
AZIMUTH
AZIMUTHAL
AZIMUTHALLY
AZINE
AZIOLA
AZLACTONE
AZLON
AZO
AZOBENZENE
AZOBENZIL
AZOBENZOIC
AZOBENZOL
AZOBLACK
AZOCH
AZOCOCHINEAL
AZOCORALLINE
AZOCORINTH
AZOCYANIDE
AZOCYCLIC
AZODIPHENYL
AZOERYTHRIN
AZOFICATION
AZOFIER
AZOFORMIC
AZOFY
AZOGALLEIN
AZOGREEN
AZOHUMIC
AZOIC
AZOIMIDE
AZOLE
AZOLITMIN
AZOMETHINE
AZON
AZONAL
AZONIC
AZONIUM
AZOOSPERMIA
AZOPARAFFIN
AZOPHEN
AZOPHENETOLE
AZOPHENINE
AZOPHENOL
AZOPHENYL
AZOPHENYLENE
AZOPHOSPHIN
AZOPHOSPHORE
AZOPROTEIN
AZORITE
AZOSULPHINE
AZOSULPHONIC
AZOTATE
AZOTE
AZOTEA
AZOTED
AZOTEMIA
AZOTENESIS
AZOTETRAZOLE
AZOTH
AZOTHIONIUM
AZOTIC
AZOTIN
AZOTINE
AZOTITE
AZOTIZED
AZOTIZING
AZOTOBACTER
AZOTOLUENE
AZOTOMETER
AZOTORRHEA
AZOTORRHOEA
AZOTOUS
AZOTURIA
AZOVERNINE
AZOXINE
AZOXONIUM
AZOXY
AZOXYBENZENE
AZTECA
AZTHIONIUM
AZULEJO
AZULENE
AZULITE
AZUMBRE
AZURE
AZUREAN
AZURED
AZURINE
AZURITE
AZUROUS
AZURY
AZYGOMATOUS
AZYGOS
AZYGOSPERM
AZYGOSPORE
AZYGOTE
AZYGOUS
AZYM
AZYME
AZYMITE
AZYMOUS

BA
BAA
BAAED
BAAHLING
BAAING
BAAL
BAAN
BAAS
BABA
BABACOOTE
BABAI
BABAJAGA
BABAKOTO
BABASCO
BABASSU
BABAYLAN
BABAYLANES
BABBISHLY
BABBITT
BABBITTED
BABBITTER
BABBITTING
BABBLATIVE
BABBLE
BABBLED
BABBLEMENT
BABBLER
BABBLESOME
BABBLING
BABBLISH
BABBLY
BABBO
BABBY
BABE
BABERY
BABESHIP
BABESIASIS
BABICHE
BABIED
BABIES
BABIL
BABILLARD
BABINGTONITE
BABIROUSSA
BABIRUSA
BABIRUSSA
BABISH
BABISHED
BABISHLY
BABISHNESS
BABLAH
BABLOH
BABOEN
BABOO
BABOODOM
BABOOISM
BABOOL
BABOON
BABOONERY
BABOONROOT
BABOOS
BABOOSH
BABOUCHE
BABRACOT
BABROOT
BABU
BABUDOM
BABUINA
BABUISM
BABUL
BABURD
BABUS
BABUSHKA
BABY
BABYFIED
BABYHOOD
BABYHOUSE
BABYING
BABYISH
BABYISHLY
BABYISHNESS
BABYLIKE
BAC
BACABA
BACACH
BACALAO
BACALAOS
BACAO
BACAUAN
BACBAKIRI
BACCA
BACCACEOUS
BACCAE
BACCALAUREAN
BACCAR
BACCARA
BACCARAT
BACCARE
BACCATE
BACCATED
BACCHANAL
BACCHANALIA
BACCHANALIAN
BACCHANALIZE
BACCHANALS
BACCHANT
BACCHANTE
BACCHANTES
BACCHANTIC
BACCHANTS
BACCHAR
BACCHARIS
BACCHAROID
BACCHEION
BACCHIAC
BACCHIAN
BACCHIC
BACCHII
BACCHIUS
BACCIFEROUS
BACCIFORM
BACCIVOROUS
BACCO
BACCY
BACH
BACHE
BACHEL
BACHELOR
BACHELORHOOD
BACHELORIZE
BACHELORLY
BACHELORSHIP
BACHELORWISE
BACHELRY
BACILE
BACILLAR
BACILLARY
BACILLI
BACILLICIDAL
BACILLICIDE
BACILLICIDIC
BACILLIFORM
BACILLIGENIC
BACILLITE
BACILLOGENIC
BACILLOSIS
BACILLURIA
BACILLUS
BACK
BACKACHE
BACKACHY
BACKARE
BACKBAND
BACKBAR
BACKBEAR
BACKBEARING
BACKBENCHER
BACKBEND
BACKBERAND
BACKBEREND
BACKBIT
BACKBITE
BACKBITER
BACKBITING
BACKBITTEN
BACKBLOCKS
BACKBOARD
BACKBONE
BACKBONED
BACKBONELESS
BACKBRAND
BACKBREAKER
BACKBREAKING
BACKCAP
BACKCAST
BACKCHAIN
BACKCHAT
BACKCOUNTRY
BACKCOURT
BACKCROSS
BACKDOOR
BACKDOWN
BACKDROP
BACKED
BACKEN
BACKENED
BACKENING
BACKER
BACKET
BACKFALL
BACKFATTER
BACKFIELD
BACKFILL
BACKFILLER
BACKFILLING
BACKFIRE
BACKFIRED
BACKFIRING
BACKFLAP
BACKFLASH
BACKFLIP
BACKFLOW
BACKFOLD
BACKFRAME
BACKFRIEND
BACKFURROW
BACKGAME
BACKGAMMON
BACKGROUND
BACKHAND
BACKHANDED
BACKHANDEDLY
BACKHANDER
BACKHATCH
BACKHAUL
BACKHEEL
BACKHOE
BACKHOOKER
BACKHOUSE
BACKIE
BACKIEBIRD
BACKING
BACKINGS
BACKJAW
BACKJOINT
BACKLAND
BACKLANDS
BACKLASH
BACKLASHING
BACKLESS
BACKLET
BACKLIST
BACKLOG
BACKLOTTER
BACKMOST
BACKPACK
BACKPEDAL
BACKPIECE
BACKPLATE
BACKREST
BACKROPE
BACKRUN
BACKSAW
BACKSEAT
BACKSET
BACKSETTING
BACKSETTLER
BACKSEY
BACKSHEESH
BACKSHIFT
BACKSHISH
BACKSIDE
BACKSIGHT
BACKSLAP
BACKSLAPPER
BACKSLAPPING
BACKSLID
BACKSLIDDEN
BACKSLIDE
BACKSLIDER
BACKSLIDING
BACKSPACE
BACKSPACER
BACKSPANG
BACKSPEAR
BACKSPEER
BACKSPEIR
BACKSPIER
BACKSPIERER
BACKSPIN
BACKSPREAD
BACKSPRINGING
BACKSTAFF
BACKSTAGE
BACKSTAIR
BACKSTAIRS
BACKSTAMP
BACKSTAY
BACKSTER
BACKSTICK
BACKSTITCH
BACKSTOP
BACKSTRAP
BACKSTRETCH
BACKSTRING
BACKSTRIP
BACKSTROKE
BACKSTROKED
BACKSTROKING
BACKSTROMITE
BACKSWEPT
BACKSWING
BACKSWORD
BACKSWORDING
BACKSWORDMAN
BACKSWORDSMAN
BACKTACK
BACKTENTER
BACKTRACK
BACKTRACKER
BACKTRICK
BACKUP
BACKVELD
BACKVELDER
BACKWALL
BACKWARD
BACKWARDLY
BACKWARDNESS
BACKWARDS
BACKWASH
BACKWASHER
BACKWASHING
BACKWATER
BACKWATERED
BACKWAY
BACKWIND
BACKWOOD
BACKWOODS
BACKWOODSMAN
BACKWOODSY
BACKWORD
BACKWORM
BACKWORT
BACKY
BACKYARD
BACKYARDER
BACLIN
BACON
BACONER
BACONIZE
BACONWEED
BACONY
BACTERIA
BACTERIACEOUS
BACTERIAEMIA
BACTERIAL
BACTERIALLY
BACTERIAN
BACTERIC
BACTERICIDAL
BACTERICIDE
BACTERICIDIN
BACTERIEMIA
BACTERIFORM
BACTERIN
BACTERIOBLAST
BACTERIOCYTE
BACTERIOID
BACTERIOLOGIC
BACTERIOLOGICAL
BACTERIOLOGY
BACTERIOLYZE
BACTERIOSIS
BACTERIOSTAT
BACTERIOTOXIC
BACTERIOUS
BACTERITIC
BACTERIUM
BACTERIURIA
BACTERIZE
BACTERIZED
BACTERIZING
BACTEROID
BACTEROIDAL
BACTRITICONE
BACTRITOID
BACUBERT
BACULA
BACULE
BACULERE
BACULI
BACULIFEROUS
BACULIFORM
BACULINE
BACULITE

BACULITIC
BACULITICONE
BACULOID
BACULUS
BACURY
BAD
BADAK
BADAM
BADAN
BADAUD
BADAXE
BADCHAN
BADDELEYITE
BADDERLOCKS
BADDIE
BADDISH
BADDISHLY
BADDISHNESS
BADDOCK
BADDY
BADE
BADENITE
BADGE
BADGED
BADGEMAN
BADGEMEN
BADGER
BADGERER
BADGERLY
BADGERS
BADGERWEED
BADGING
BADGIR
BADHAN
BADIA
BADIAGA
BADIAN
BADIGEON
BADINAGE
BADINAGED
BADINAGING
BADINER
BADINERIE
BADINEUR
BADIOUS
BADJU
BADLAND
BADLANDS
BADLING
BADLY
BADMAN
BADMEN
BADMINTON
BADNESS
BADRANS
BAEL
BAETULI
BAETULUS
BAETYL
BAETYLIC
BAETYLUS
BAETZNER
BAFARO
BAFF
BAFFIES
BAFFLE
BAFFLED
BAFFLEPLATE
BAFFLER
BAFFLING
BAFFLINGLY
BAFFY
BAFT
BAFTA
BAFTAH
BAG
BAGA
BAGANI
BAGASS
BAGASSE
BAGATAWAY
BAGATELLE
BAGATINE
BAGATTINI
BAGATTINO
BAGEL
BAGFUL
BAGGAGE
BAGGAGEMAN
BAGGAGEMASTER
BAGGAGER
BAGGALA
BAGGE
BAGGED
BAGGER
BAGGIE
BAGGIER
BAGGIEST
BAGGILY
BAGGINESS
BAGGING
BAGGIT
BAGGY
BAGHOUSE
BAGLE
BAGLEAVES
BAGLIKE
BAGMAN
BAGMEN
BAGNE
BAGNES
BAGNET
BAGNIO
BAGNUT
BAGO
BAGONG
BAGOONG
BAGPIPE
BAGPIPER
BAGPIPES
BAGPOD
BAGRATIONITE
BAGRE
BAGREEF
BAGROOM
BAGS
BAGTIKAN
BAGUE
BAGUET
BAGUETTE
BAGUIO
BAGUIOS
BAGWIG
BAGWIGGED
BAGWORM
BAGWYN
BAH
BAHADA
BAHADUR
BAHAN
BAHAR
BAHAY
BAHERA
BAHI
BAHIA
BAHIAITE
BAHNUNG
BAHO
BAHOE
BAHR
BAHT
BAHTS
BAHU
BAHUR
BAHUT
BAHUVRIHI
BAIDAK
BAIDAR
BAIGNOIRE
BAIKALITE
BAIKERINITE
BAIKERITE
BAIKIE
BAIL
BAILABLE
BAILE
BAILEE
BAILER
BAILEY
BAILEYS
BAILIARIES
BAILIARY
BAILIE
BAILIERIES
BAILIERY
BAILIFF
BAILIFFRY
BAILIWICK
BAILLI
BAILLIAGE
BAILLONE
BAILMENT
BAILO
BAILOR
BAILOUT
BAILPIECE
BAILSMAN
BAILSMEN
BAILWOOD
BAIN
BAINITE
BAIOC
BAIOCCO
BAIRA
BAIRAGI
BAIRN
BAIRNIE
BAIRNISH
BAIRNISHNESS
BAIRNLINESS
BAIRNLY
BAIRNTEAM
BAIRNTEEM
BAIRNTIME
BAIT
BAITER
BAITFISH
BAITH
BAITING
BAITTLE
BAIZA
BAIZE
BAIZED
BAIZING
BAJADA
BAJOCCO
BAJOCHI
BAJOIRE
BAJONADO
BAJRA
BAJREE
BAJU
BAJULATE
BAK
BAKA
BAKAL
BAKE
BAKEAPPLE
BAKEBOARD
BAKED
BAKEHEAD
BAKEHOUSE
BAKELITE
BAKELIZE
BAKEMEAT
BAKEN
BAKEOUT
BAKEPAN
BAKER
BAKERIES
BAKERITE
BAKERLY
BAKERY
BAKESHOP
BAKESTONE
BAKEWARE
BAKIE
BAKING
BAKLAVA
BAKSHEESH
BAKSHI
BAKSHISH
BAKTUN
BAKU
BAKULA
BAKUPARI
BAL
BALABOS
BALACHAN
BALACHONG
BALADINE
BALAENID
BALAFO
BALAGAN
BALAGHAT
BALAGHAUT
BALAI
BALALAIKA
BALAM
BALANCE
BALANCEABLE
BALANCED
BALANCELLE
BALANCER
BALANCING
BALANDRA
BALANDRANA
BALANEUTICS
BALANGAY
BALANIC
BALANID
BALANIFEROUS
BALANISM
BALANITE
BALANITIS
BALANOCELE
BALANOID
BALANOPHORE
BALANOPHORIN
BALANOPLASTY
BALANOPS
BALANT
BALANTIDIAL
BALANTIDIC
BALAO
BALAPHON
BALARAO
BALAS
BALAT
BALATA
BALATE
BALATONG
BALATRON
BALATRONIC
BALATTE
BALAU
BALAUSTA
BALAUSTINE
BALAUSTRE
BALAYEUSE
BALBOA
BALBRIGGAN
BALBUSARD
BALBUTIATE
BALBUTIENT
BALBUTIES
BALCHE
BALCONE
BALCONET
BALCONETTE
BALCONIED
BALCONIES
BALCONY
BALD
BALDACCHINI
BALDACCHINO
BALDACHIN
BALDACHINED
BALDACHINO
BALDACHINOS
BALDAKIN
BALDAQUIN
BALDBERRY
BALDCROWN
BALDEN
BALDER
BALDERDASH
BALDFACED
BALDHEAD
BALDHEADED
BALDICOOT
BALDING
BALDISH
BALDLING
BALDLY
BALDMONEY
BALDMONEYS
BALDNESS
BALDPATE
BALDPATED
BALDRIB
BALDRIC
BALDRICK
BALDRICKED
BALDUCTA
BALDUCTUM
BALDY
BALE
BALEBOS
BALED
BALEEN
BALEFIRE
BALEFUL
BALEFULLY
BALEFULNESS
BALEI
BALEISE
BALER
BALESTRA
BALETE
BALEWORT
BALEYS
BALI
BALIAN
BALIBAGO
BALIMBING
BALINE
BALING
BALINGER
BALINGHASAY
BALISAUR
BALISIER
BALISTARII
BALISTARIUS
BALISTID

BALISTRARIA
BALITA
BALITAO
BALITI
BALK
BALKANIZE
BALKANIZED
BALKANIZING
BALKER
BALKIER
BALKIEST
BALKINGLY
BALKLINE
BALKY
BALL
BALLAD
BALLADE
BALLADEER
BALLADER
BALLADIC
BALLADICAL
BALLADIER
BALLADMONGER
BALLADROMIC
BALLADRY
BALLAHOO
BALLAHOU
BALLAM
BALLAN
BALLANT
BALLARAG
BALLARD
BALLAS
BALLAST
BALLASTAGE
BALLASTER
BALLASTING
BALLATA
BALLATOON
BALLCARRIER
BALLDRESS
BALLED
BALLER
BALLERINA
BALLERINAS
BALLERINE
BALLET
BALLETOMANE
BALLFLOWER
BALLHOOTER
BALLIAGE
BALLING
BALLISM
BALLIST
BALLISTA
BALLISTAE
BALLISTIC
BALLISTICALLY
BALLISTICIAN
BALLISTICS
BALLIUM
BALLMINE
BALLOCK
BALLOEN
BALLOGAN
BALLON
BALLONET
BALLONETTE
BALLONNE
BALLOON
BALLOONATION
BALLOONER
BALLOONERY
BALLOONET
BALLOONING
BALLOONIST
BALLOT
BALLOTADE
BALLOTAGE
BALLOTE
BALLOTED
BALLOTER
BALLOTING
BALLOTTEMENT
BALLOW
BALLPLAYER
BALLPROOF
BALLROOM
BALLS
BALLUP
BALLWEED
BALLY
BALLYHACK
BALLYHOO
BALLYHOOED
BALLYHOOER
BALLYHOOING
BALLYRAG
BALLYWACK
BALLYWRACK
BALM
BALMACAAN
BALMIER
BALMIEST
BALMILY
BALMINESS
BALMONIES
BALMONY
BALMORAL
BALMY
BALNEA
BALNEAE
BALNEAL
BALNEARY
BALNEATION
BALNEATORY
BALNEOGRAPHY
BALNEOLOGIC
BALNEOLOGY
BALNEUM
BALO
BALON
BALONEY
BALOO
BALOP
BALOTADE
BALOW
BALSA
BALSAM
BALSAMIC
BALSAMICAL
BALSAMICALLY
BALSAMINE
BALSAMITIC
BALSAMIZE
BALSAMO
BALSAMOUS
BALSAMROOT
BALSAMWEED
BALSAMY
BALSAS
BALTEI
BALTER
BALTEUS
BALTHEUS
BALTIMORITE
BALU
BALUSHAI
BALUSTER
BALUSTERED
BALUSTRADE
BALUSTRADED
BALUT
BALWARRA
BALZARINE
BAM
BAMAH
BAMBA
BAMBAN
BAMBINI
BAMBINO
BAMBINOS
BAMBOCCIADE
BAMBOCHE
BAMBOO
BAMBOOZLE
BAMBOOZLED
BAMBOOZLEMENT
BAMBOOZLER
BAMBOOZLING
BAMBOULA
BAMBUCO
BAMBUK
BAMIA
BAN
BANABA
BANAGO
BANAGOS
BANAK
BANAKITE
BANAL
BANALITIES
BANALITY
BANALLY
BANANA
BANANAS
BANANIST
BANANIVOROUS
BANAT
BANATE
BANATITE
BANAUSIC
BANC
BANCA
BANCAL
BANCALES
BANCHA
BANCO
BANCOS
BANCUS
BAND
BANDAGE
BANDAGED
BANDAGER
BANDAGING
BANDAGIST
BANDAITE
BANDAKA
BANDALA
BANDALORE
BANDANA
BANDANNA
BANDANNAED
BANDAR
BANDARLOG
BANDBOX
BANDBOXICAL
BANDBOXY
BANDCUTTER
BANDE
BANDEAU
BANDEAUX
BANDED
BANDELET
BANDELETTE
BANDENG
BANDER
BANDERILLA
BANDERILLAS
BANDERILLERO
BANDERILLEROS
BANDERLOG
BANDEROL
BANDEROLE
BANDEROLED
BANDEROLING
BANDERSNATCH
BANDFISH
BANDHAVA
BANDHOOK
BANDHU
BANDI
BANDICOOT
BANDICOY
BANDIDO
BANDIDOS
BANDIE
BANDIED
BANDIES
BANDIKAI
BANDING
BANDIT
BANDITRY
BANDITS
BANDITTI
BANDLE
BANDLEADER
BANDMAN
BANDMASTER
BANDO
BANDOG
BANDOLEER
BANDOLEERED
BANDOLERISMO
BANDOLERO
BANDOLEROS
BANDOLIER
BANDOLINE
BANDON
BANDONION
BANDORE
BANDOS
BANDS
BANDSMAN
BANDSMEN
BANDSTAND
BANDSTER
BANDSTRING
BANDURA
BANDURRIA
BANDURRIAS
BANDWAGON
BANDWORK
BANDWORM
BANDY
BANDYBALL
BANDYING
BANDYMAN
BANE
BANEBERRIES
BANEBERRY
BANED
BANEFUL
BANEFULLY
BANEFULNESS
BANEWORT
BANG
BANGA
BANGALAY
BANGALOW
BANGE
BANGER
BANGHY
BANGIACEOUS
BANGING
BANGKOK
BANGLE
BANGLED
BANGLING
BANGO
BANGOS
BANGS
BANGSTER
BANGTAIL
BANGTAILED
BANGY
BANI
BANIA
BANIAN
BANIG
BANILAD
BANING
BANISH
BANISHED
BANISHER
BANISHMENT
BANISTER
BANISTERINE
BANIYA
BANJARA
BANJO
BANJOES
BANJORE
BANJORINE
BANJOS
BANK
BANKABLE
BANKBOOK
BANKED
BANKER
BANKERA
BANKET
BANKFULL
BANKING
BANKMAN
BANKMEN
BANKRIDER
BANKROLL
BANKRUPT
BANKRUPTCIES
BANKRUPTCY
BANKRUPTISM
BANKRUPTLY
BANKRUPTURE
BANKS
BANKSHALL
BANKSIA
BANKSIDE
BANKSMAN
BANKSMEN
BANKWEED
BANKY
BANLIEU
BANLIEUE
BANNACK
BANNAT
BANNED
BANNER
BANNERED
BANNERER
BANNERET
BANNERETTE
BANNERFISH
BANNERMAN
BANNERMEN
BANNEROL
BANNEROLE
BANNET
BANNIMUS
BANNING
BANNISTER
BANNOCK
BANNS
BANNUT
BANOVINA

BANQUE
BANQUET
BANQUETED
BANQUETEER
BANQUETEERING
BANQUETER
BANQUETING
BANQUETTE
BANS
BANSALAGUE
BANSHEE
BANSHIE
BANSTICKLE
BANT
BANTAM
BANTAMIZE
BANTAMWEIGHT
BANTAY
BANTAYAN
BANTENG
BANTER
BANTERED
BANTERER
BANTERING
BANTERINGLY
BANTERY
BANTIN
BANTING
BANTINGIZE
BANTLING
BANTU
BANTY
BANUS
BANUYO
BANXRING
BANYA
BANYAN
BANZAI
BAOBAB
BAP
BAPISTERY
BAPTISIN
BAPTISM
BAPTISMAL
BAPTISMALLY
BAPTISTERIES
BAPTISTERY
BAPTISTIC
BAPTISTRIES
BAPTISTRY
BAPTIZE
BAPTIZED
BAPTIZEE
BAPTIZEMENT
BAPTIZER
BAPTIZING
BAPU
BAR
BARABARA
BARABORA
BARAD
BARADARI
BARAGNOSIS
BARAGOUIN
BARAITA
BARAJILLO
BARAMIN
BARANDOS
BARANGAY
BARANI
BARARITE
BARASINGHA
BARAT
BARATHEA
BARATHRA
BARATHRON
BARATHRUM
BARATO
BARATTE
BARB
BARBACOU
BARBAL
BARBARESQUE
BARBARIAN
BARBARIC
BARBARICAL
BARBARICALLY
BARBARIOUS
BARBARISM
BARBARITIES
BARBARITY
BARBARIZE
BARBARIZED
BARBARIZING
BARBAROUS
BARBAROUSLY
BARBARY
BARBAS
BARBASCO
BARBASTEL
BARBASTELLE
BARBATE
BARBATED
BARBATIMAO
BARBE
BARBEAU
BARBECUE
BARBECUED
BARBECUING
BARBED
BARBEIRO
BARBEL
BARBELL
BARBELLATE
BARBELLULA
BARBELLULAE
BARBELLULATE
BARBEQUE
BARBER
BARBERA
BARBERMONGER
BARBERO
BARBERRIES
BARBERRY
BARBERSHOP
BARBERY
BARBET
BARBETTE
BARBICAN
BARBICEL
BARBIGEROUS
BARBING
BARBION
BARBITA
BARBITAL
BARBITALISM
BARBITON
BARBITONE
BARBITURATE
BARBITURIC
BARBLESS
BARBLET
BARBOLA
BARBONE
BARBOTINE
BARBOTTE
BARBOY
BARBUDO
BARBUDOS
BARBULA
BARBULATE
BARBULE
BARBULYIE
BARBWIRE
BARCA
BARCAROLE
BARCAROLLE
BARCAS
BARCELLA
BARCELONA
BARCELONAS
BARCHAN
BARCHE
BARCOLONGO
BARD
BARDANE
BARDASH
BARDE
BARDEE
BARDEL
BARDELLE
BARDESS
BARDIC
BARDIE
BARDIGLIO
BARDILY
BARDINESS
BARDING
BARDINGS
BARDISH
BARDISM
BARDLET
BARDLING
BARDO
BARDS
BARDY
BARE
BAREBACK
BAREBACKED
BAREBONE
BARECA
BARED
BAREFACED
BAREFACEDLY
BAREFIT
BAREFOOT
BAREFOOTED
BAREGE
BAREHANDED
BAREHEAD
BAREHEADED
BAREKA
BARELEGGED
BARELY
BARENECKED
BARER
BARES
BARESARK
BARESMA
BARETTA
BARFF
BARFISH
BARFLIES
BARFLY
BARFUL
BARGAIN
BARGAINEE
BARGAINER
BARGAINING
BARGAINOR
BARGE
BARGEBOARD
BARGED
BARGEE
BARGEER
BARGEESE
BARGEHOUSE
BARGELIKE
BARGELLI
BARGELLO
BARGELOAD
BARGEMAN
BARGEMASTER
BARGEMEN
BARGER
BARGH
BARGHAM
BARGHEST
BARGING
BARGIR
BARGOOSE
BARHAL
BARHOP
BARI
BARIA
BARIC
BARID
BARIE
BARIL
BARILLA
BARIN
BARING
BARIOLAGE
BARIS
BARISH
BARIT
BARITE
BARITONE
BARIUM
BARK
BARKAN
BARKARY
BARKBOUND
BARKEEP
BARKEEPER
BARKEN
BARKENED
BARKENING
BARKENTINE
BARKER
BARKERY
BARKEVIKITE
BARKEVIKITIC
BARKEY
BARKHAN
BARKIER
BARKIEST
BARKING
BARKINGLY
BARKLE
BARKLYITE
BARKOMETER
BARKPEEL
BARKPEELER
BARKPEELING
BARKS
BARKSOME
BARKSTONE
BARKY
BARLA
BARLEY
BARLEYBIRD
BARLEYBRAKE
BARLEYBREAK
BARLEYCORN
BARLEYHOOD
BARLEYMOW
BARLEYSICK
BARLING
BARLOW
BARLY
BARM
BARMAID
BARMAN
BARMASTER
BARMBRACK
BARMCLOTH
BARMEN
BARMFEL
BARMIE
BARMIER
BARMIEST
BARMKIN
BARMOTE
BARMSKIN
BARMY
BARMYBRAINED
BARN
BARNACLE
BARNACLED
BARNACLING
BARNARD
BARNEY
BARNHARDTITE
BARNMAN
BARNMEN
BARNS
BARNSTORM
BARNSTORMER
BARNSTORMING
BARNY
BARNYARD
BARO
BAROCCO
BAROGNOSIS
BAROGRAM
BAROGRAPH
BAROGRAPHIC
BAROI
BAROLO
BAROLOGY
BAROMETER
BAROMETRIC
BAROMETRICAL
BAROMETRY
BAROMETZ
BAROMOTOR
BARON
BARONAGE
BARONESS
BARONET
BARONETAGE
BARONETCIES
BARONETCY
BARONETED
BARONETICAL
BARONETING
BARONG
BARONI
BARONIAL
BARONIES
BARONNE
BARONRIES
BARONRY
BARONY
BAROQUE
BAROSCOPE
BAROSCOPIC
BAROSCOPICAL
BAROSMIN
BAROSTAT
BAROTACTIC
BAROTAXIS
BAROTAXY
BAROTO
BAROUCHE
BAROUCHET
BAROUCHETTE
BAROXYTON
BARPOST
BARQUE
BARQUENTINE
BARQUEST
BARR
BARRA

BARRABLE
BARRABORA
BARRACAN
BARRACE
BARRACK
BARRACKER
BARRACKS
BARRACLADE
BARRACOON
BARRACOUTA
BARRACOUTAS
BARRACUDA
BARRACUDAS
BARRAD
BARRAGAN
BARRAGE
BARRAGED
BARRAGING
BARRAGON
BARRAMUNDA
BARRAMUNDAS
BARRAMUNDI
BARRAMUNDIES
BARRAMUNDIS
BARRANCA
BARRANCO
BARRANDITE
BARRAS
BARRAT
BARRATER
BARRATOR
BARRATRIES
BARRATROUS
BARRATROUSLY
BARRATRY
BARRE
BARRED
BARREL
BARRELAGE
BARRELED
BARRELER
BARRELET
BARRELFUL
BARRELFULS
BARRELHEAD
BARRELHOUSE
BARRELING
BARRELLED
BARRELLING
BARRELMAKER
BARRELMAKING
BARRELS
BARREN
BARRENER
BARRENLY
BARRENNESS
BARRENWORT
BARRER
BARRERA
BARRET
BARRETRY
BARRETTE
BARRETTER
BARRICADE
BARRICADED
BARRICADER
BARRICADING
BARRICO
BARRICOES
BARRICOS
BARRIER
BARRIERS
BARRIGUDA
BARRIGUDO
BARRIGUDOS
BARRIKIN
BARRING
BARRIO
BARRIOS
BARRISTER
BARRISTERIAL
BARRISTRESS
BARROOM
BARROW
BARROWCOAT
BARROWMAN
BARRULET
BARRULY
BARRY
BARS
BARSE
BARSOM
BARSPOON
BARSTOOL
BARTENDER
BARTENDING
BARTER
BARTERED
BARTERER
BARTERING
BARTH
BARTHITE
BARTHOLINITIS
BARTIZAN
BARTIZANED
BARTON
BARTREE
BARU
BARUKHZY
BARURIA
BARVEL
BARVELL
BARWAY
BARWAYS
BARWIN
BARWING
BARWISE
BARWOOD
BARYCENTER
BARYCENTRE
BARYCENTRIC
BARYE
BARYECOIA
BARYLITE
BARYON
BARYPHONIA
BARYPHONIC
BARYPHONY
BARYSILITE
BARYSPHERE
BARYTA
BARYTE
BARYTES
BARYTHYMIA
BARYTIC
BARYTINE
BARYTONE
BAS
BASAL
BASALE
BASALIA
BASALLY
BASALT
BASALTES
BASALTIC
BASALTIFORM
BASALTINE
BASALTOID
BASALTWARE
BASAN
BASANITE
BASAREE
BASCULE
BASCUNAN
BASE
BASEBALL
BASEBALLER
BASEBOARD
BASEBORN
BASEBRED
BASEBURNER
BASED
BASELARD
BASELESS
BASELESSLY
BASELESSNESS
BASELINER
BASELLACEOUS
BASELY
BASEMAN
BASEMEN
BASEMENT
BASENESS
BASENJI
BASEPLUG
BASER
BASES
BASEST
BASH
BASHA
BASHAW
BASHED
BASHER
BASHFUL
BASHFULLY
BASHFULNESS
BASHING
BASHLESS
BASHLIK
BASHLYK
BASI
BASIAL
BASIATE
BASIATION
BASIC
BASICALLY
BASICITY
BASICRANIAL
BASIDIA
BASIDIAL
BASIDIGITALE
BASIDIGITALIA
BASIDIOMYCETE
BASIDIOMYCETES
BASIDIOPHORE
BASIDIOSPORE
BASIDIUM
BASIDORSAL
BASIFACIAL
BASIFICATION
BASIFIED
BASIFIER
BASIFIXED
BASIFUGAL
BASIFY
BASIFYING
BASIG
BASIGAMOUS
BASIGAMY
BASIGENIC
BASIGENOUS
BASIHYAL
BASIL
BASILAR
BASILARY
BASILATERAL
BASILEIS
BASILEMMA
BASILEUS
BASILIC
BASILICA
BASILICAL
BASILICAN
BASILICAS
BASILICON
BASILINNA
BASILISCAN
BASILISCINE
BASILISK
BASILISSA
BASILWEED
BASILYSIS
BASILYST
BASIN
BASINASAL
BASINASIAL
BASINED
BASINET
BASING
BASION
BASIOPHITIC
BASIOTRIBE
BASIOTRIPSY
BASIPETAL
BASIPHOBIA
BASIPODITE
BASIPODITIC
BASIRADIAL
BASIRHINAL
BASIROSTRAL
BASIS
BASISCOPIC
BASISPHENOID
BASITEMPORAL
BASIVENTRAL
BASK
BASKER
BASKET
BASKETBALL
BASKETBALLER
BASKETING
BASKETMAKER
BASKETMAKING
BASKETRY
BASKETWARE
BASKETWOMAN
BASKETWOOD
BASKETWORK
BASOCYTE
BASON
BASOPHIL
BASOPHILE
BASOPHILIA
BASOPHILIC
BASOPHILOUS
BASOTE
BASOTHO
BASQUE
BASQUED
BASQUINE
BASS
BASSANELLO
BASSANITE
BASSARA
BASSARID
BASSARISK
BASSES
BASSET
BASSETED
BASSETING
BASSETITE
BASSETTA
BASSETTE
BASSI
BASSIE
BASSINE
BASSINET
BASSING
BASSIST
BASSO
BASSON
BASSOON
BASSOONIST
BASSORIN
BASSOS
BASSUS
BASSWOOD
BAST
BASTA
BASTANT
BASTARD
BASTARDA
BASTARDISM
BASTARDIZE
BASTARDIZED
BASTARDIZING
BASTARDLY
BASTARDY
BASTE
BASTED
BASTEN
BASTER
BASTIDE
BASTILE
BASTILLE
BASTINADE
BASTINADO
BASTINADOED
BASTINADOES
BASTINADOING
BASTING
BASTION
BASTIONARY
BASTIONED
BASTIONET
BASTITE
BASTNASITE
BASTO
BASTON
BASTONET
BASURAL
BASURALE
BAT
BATA
BATAAN
BATAD
BATAK
BATAKAN
BATALEUR
BATAMOTE
BATARA
BATARDE
BATARDEAU
BATATA
BATATILLA
BATCH
BATCHER
BATE
BATEA
BATEAU
BATEAUX
BATED
BATEFUL
BATEL
BATELEUR
BATEMAN
BATEMENT
BATER
BATES
BATETE
BATFISH
BATFOWL
BATFOWLER
BATFOWLING
BATFUL

BATH
BATHE
BATHEABLE
BATHED
BATHER
BATHETIC
BATHFLOWER
BATHHOUSE
BATHIC
BATHING
BATHKOL
BATHMAN
BATHMIC
BATHMISM
BATHMOTROPIC
BATHOCHROME
BATHOCHROMIC
BATHOCHROMY
BATHOFLORE
BATHOFLORIC
BATHOLITE
BATHOLITH
BATHOLITHIC
BATHOLITIC
BATHOMANIA
BATHOMETER
BATHOPHOBIA
BATHORSE
BATHOS
BATHQOL
BATHROBE
BATHROOM
BATHROOMED
BATHROOT
BATHS
BATHTUB
BATHUKOLPIAN
BATHVILLITE
BATHWORT
BATHYAL
BATHYBIAN
BATHYBIC
BATHYBIUS
BATHYCOLPIAN
BATHYCOLPIC
BATHYL
BATHYMETER
BATHYMETRIC
BATHYMETRY
BATHYPELAGIC
BATHYSCAPH
BATHYSCAPHE
BATHYSEISM
BATHYSMAL
BATHYSPHERE
BATIDACEOUS
BATIK
BATIKED
BATIKER
BATIKING
BATIKULIN
BATIKULING
BATING
BATINO
BATISTE
BATITINAN
BATLAN
BATLER
BATLET
BATLIKE
BATLING
BATLON
BATMAN
BATMEN
BATOID
BATON
BATONEER
BATONIST
BATONISTIC
BATONNE
BATONNIER
BATOPHOBIA
BATRACHIAN
BATRACHIATE
BATRACHITE
BATRACHOID
BATS
BATSMAN
BATSMANSHIP
BATSMEN
BATSWING
BATT
BATTA
BATTABLE
BATTAILOUS
BATTALIA
BATTALION
BATTE
BATTED
BATTEL
BATTELER
BATTEMENT
BATTEN
BATTENED
BATTENER
BATTENING
BATTENS
BATTER
BATTERCAKE
BATTERDOCK
BATTERED
BATTERER
BATTERFANG
BATTERIE
BATTERIES
BATTERING
BATTERMAN
BATTERY
BATTEUSE
BATTIER
BATTIES
BATTIEST
BATTIK
BATTING
BATTISH
BATTLE
BATTLED
BATTLEDORE
BATTLEDORED
BATTLEDORING
BATTLEFIELD
BATTLEFUL
BATTLEGROUND
BATTLEMENT
BATTLEMENTED
BATTLEPLANE
BATTLER
BATTLESHIP
BATTLESTEAD
BATTLEWAGON
BATTLING
BATTOLOGICAL
BATTOLOGIST
BATTOLOGIZE
BATTOLOGY
BATTON
BATTS
BATTU
BATTUE
BATTURE
BATTUTA
BATTY
BATTYCAKE
BATU
BATUKITE
BATULE
BATUQUE
BATWING
BATYPHONE
BATZ
BATZEN
BAUBEE
BAUBLE
BAUBLERY
BAUBLING
BAUCH
BAUCHLE
BAUCKIE
BAUD
BAUDEKIN
BAUDERY
BAUDRONS
BAUGH
BAUHINIA
BAUK
BAUL
BAULEA
BAULEAH
BAULK
BAULKY
BAUMHAUERITE
BAUMIER
BAUNO
BAUR
BAUSON
BAUSOND
BAUTA
BAUTTA
BAUXITE
BAUXITITE
BAVARDAGE
BAVAROISE
BAVAROY
BAVARY
BAVE
BAVENITE
BAVETTE
BAVIAN
BAVIN
BAVOSO
BAW
BAWARCHI
BAWBEE
BAWCOCK
BAWD
BAWDIER
BAWDIEST
BAWDILY
BAWDINESS
BAWDRIC
BAWDRICK
BAWDRY
BAWDSTROT
BAWDY
BAWDYHOUSE
BAWL
BAWLER
BAWLEY
BAWLING
BAWLY
BAWN
BAWNEEN
BAWREL
BAWSUNT
BAWTIE
BAWTY
BAXA
BAXTER
BAY
BAYA
BAYADEER
BAYADERE
BAYAL
BAYAMO
BAYAN
BAYANO
BAYARD
BAYARDLY
BAYBERRIES
BAYBERRY
BAYBOLT
BAYBUSH
BAYED
BAYETA
BAYETE
BAYGALL
BAYLET
BAYMAN
BAYMEN
BAYOG
BAYOK
BAYON
BAYONET
BAYONETED
BAYONETEER
BAYONETING
BAYONG
BAYOU
BAYOUS
BAYWOOD
BAZAAR
BAZAR
BAZE
BAZOO
BAZOOKA
BAZZITE
BB
BDELLID
BDELLIUM
BDELLOID
BDELLOTOMY
BE
BEACH
BEACHBOY
BEACHCOMB
BEACHCOMBER
BEACHCOMBING
BEACHDROPS
BEACHED
BEACHHEAD
BEACHIER
BEACHIEST
BEACHMAN
BEACHMASTER
BEACHMEN
BEACHY
BEACON
BEACONAGE
BEACONED
BEACONING
BEAD
BEADED
BEADER
BEADFLUSH
BEADHOUSE
BEADIER
BEADIEST
BEADILY
BEADINESS
BEADING
BEADLE
BEADLEDOM
BEADLERY
BEADMAN
BEADROLL
BEADROW
BEADS
BEADSMAN
BEADSWOMAN
BEADWORK
BEADY
BEAGLE
BEAGLING
BEAK
BEAKED
BEAKER
BEAKERMAN
BEAKERMEN
BEAKHEAD
BEAKIRON
BEAKLESS
BEAKLIKE
BEAKY
BEAL
BEALA
BEALACH
BEALING
BEALLACH
BEAM
BEAMAGE
BEAMBIRD
BEAMED
BEAMER
BEAMFILLING
BEAMFUL
BEAMHOUSE
BEAMIER
BEAMIEST
BEAMILY
BEAMINESS
BEAMING
BEAMINGLY
BEAMISH
BEAMLESS
BEAMLIKE
BEAMROOM
BEAMSMAN
BEAMSMEN
BEAMSTER
BEAMY
BEAN
BEANBAG
BEANBAGS
BEANBALL
BEANCOD
BEANERIES
BEANERY
BEANFEAST
BEANFEASTER
BEANFIELD
BEANIE
BEANIER
BEANIEST
BEANO
BEANPOLE
BEANS
BEANSETTER
BEANSHOOTER
BEANSTALK
BEANWEED
BEANY
BEAR
BEARABLE
BEARABLENESS
BEARABLY
BEARANCE
BEARBAITER
BEARBAITING
BEARBANE
BEARBERRIES
BEARBERRY
BEARBIND
BEARBINE
BEARCAT
BEARCOOT

BEARD
BEARDED
BEARDER
BEARDIE
BEARDING
BEARDLESS
BEARDLIKE
BEARDTONGUE
BEARDY
BEARER
BEARERS
BEARFOOT
BEARFOOTS
BEARHERD
BEARHOUND
BEARING
BEARINGS
BEARISH
BEARISHLY
BEARISHNESS
BEARLET
BEARM
BEARS
BEARSKIN
BEARWARD
BEARWOOD
BEARWORT
BEAST
BEASTIE
BEASTILY
BEASTLIER
BEASTLIEST
BEASTLIKE
BEASTLILY
BEASTLINESS
BEASTLINGS
BEASTLY
BEASTMAN
BEASTS
BEAT
BEATA
BEATAE
BEATEE
BEATEN
BEATER
BEATERMAN
BEATERMEN
BEATH
BEATI
BEATIFIC
BEATIFICAL
BEATIFICALLY
BEATIFICATE
BEATIFIED
BEATIFY
BEATIFYING
BEATILLE
BEATING
BEATITUDE
BEATNIK
BEATSTER
BEATUS
BEAU
BEAUED
BEAUETRY
BEAUFIN
BEAUING
BEAUISH
BEAUISM
BEAUPERE
BEAUS
BEAUSEANT
BEAUT
BEAUTEOUS
BEAUTEOUSLY
BEAUTEOUSNESS
BEAUTICIAN
BEAUTIED
BEAUTIES
BEAUTIFIED
BEAUTIFIER
BEAUTIFUL
BEAUTIFULLY
BEAUTIFY
BEAUTIFYING
BEAUTY
BEAUX
BEAVER
BEAVERBOARD
BEAVERED
BEAVERETTE
BEAVERIES
BEAVERITE
BEAVERIZE
BEAVERKIN
BEAVERPELT
BEAVERROOT
BEAVERTEEN
BEAVERWOOD
BEAVERY
BEBAY
BEBEERIN
BEBEERINE
BEBEERU
BEBILYA
BEBIZATION
BEBLED
BEBOG
BEBOP
BECAFICO
BECALL
BECALM
BECALMED
BECALMING
BECAME
BECARD
BECARVE
BECASSE
BECASSINE
BECAUSE
BECCAFICO
BECCAFICOS
BECCHI
BECCO
BECHAMEL
BECHANCE
BECHANCED
BECHANCING
BECHER
BECK
BECKELITE
BECKER
BECKET
BECKETT
BECKIRON
BECKON
BECKONED
BECKONER
BECKONING
BECKONINGLY
BECLAD
BECLAP
BECLIP
BECLOUD
BECLOUDED
BECLOUT
BECOME
BECOMED
BECOMES
BECOMING
BECOMINGLY
BECON
BECOOM
BECORESH
BECOUSINED
BECQUERELITE
BECREEP
BECROSS
BECRUSH
BECUIBA
BECUNA
BED
BEDA
BEDABBLE
BEDAD
BEDAFF
BEDAGGLE
BEDAMN
BEDANGLED
BEDASH
BEDAUB
BEDAWN
BEDAY
BEDAZE
BEDAZZLE
BEDAZZLED
BEDAZZLING
BEDAZZLINGLY
BEDBUG
BEDCHAIR
BEDCHAMBER
BEDCLOTHES
BEDCORD
BEDCOVER
BEDDED
BEDDER
BEDDING
BEDE
BEDECK
BEDECKED
BEDEEN
BEDEGAR
BEDEGUAR
BEDEHOUSE
BEDEL
BEDELL
BEDELVE
BEDEMAN
BEDEN
BEDENE
BEDESMAN
BEDESMEN
BEDEVIL
BEDEVILED
BEDEVILING
BEDEVILLED
BEDEVILLING
BEDEVILMENT
BEDEW
BEDEWED
BEDEWER
BEDFAST
BEDFELLOW
BEDFLOWER
BEDFRAME
BEDGERY
BEDGOWN
BEDIGHT
BEDIGHTED
BEDIGHTING
BEDIKAH
BEDIM
BEDIMMED
BEDIMMING
BEDIZEN
BEDIZENED
BEDIZENING
BEDIZENMENT
BEDKEY
BEDLAM
BEDLAMER
BEDLAMISM
BEDLAMITE
BEDLAMIZE
BEDLAR
BEDLIDS
BEDMAN
BEDMATE
BEDO
BEDOG
BEDOTE
BEDOWN
BEDOYO
BEDPAN
BEDPLATE
BEDPOST
BEDPOSTS
BEDQUILT
BEDRABBLE
BEDRAGGLE
BEDRAGGLED
BEDRAIL
BEDRAL
BEDRAPE
BEDREAD
BEDREL
BEDRESS
BEDRID
BEDRIDDEN
BEDRIGHT
BEDRIP
BEDRITE
BEDROCK
BEDROLL
BEDROOM
BEDROP
BEDS
BEDSIDE
BEDSITE
BEDSORE
BEDSPREAD
BEDSPRING
BEDSTAFF
BEDSTAND
BEDSTAVES
BEDSTEAD
BEDSTOCK
BEDSTRAW
BEDSWERVER
BEDTICK
BEDTIME
BEDU
BEDUB
BEDWARD
BEDWARDS
BEDWARMER
BEDWAY
BEDWELL
BEE
BEEBALL
BEEBEE
BEEBREAD
BEECH
BEECHDROPS
BEECHEN
BEECHES
BEECHNUT
BEECHNUTS
BEECHY
BEEF
BEEFCAKE
BEEFEATER
BEEFHEAD
BEEFHEADED
BEEFIER
BEEFIEST
BEEFILY
BEEFIN
BEEFINESS
BEEFISH
BEEFISHNESS
BEEFLESS
BEEFS
BEEFSTEAK
BEEFTONGUE
BEEFWOOD
BEEFY
BEEGERITE
BEEHEAD
BEEHEADED
BEEHERD
BEEHIVE
BEEHOUSE
BEEK
BEEKEEPER
BEEKEEPING
BEEKITE
BEELE
BEELINE
BEEMAN
BEEMASTER
BEEMEN
BEEN
BEENNUT
BEEP
BEEPER
BEER
BEERAGE
BEERBACHITE
BEERBIBBER
BEEREGAR
BEERHOUSE
BEERIER
BEERIEST
BEERILY
BEERINESS
BEERISH
BEERISHLY
BEERMAKER
BEERMAKING
BEERMONGER
BEEROCRACY
BEERPULL
BEERY
BEES
BEESTING
BEESTINGS
BEESWAX
BEESWING
BEET
BEETE
BEETEWK
BEETH
BEETIEST
BEETLE
BEETLED
BEETLEHEAD
BEETLEHEADED
BEETLER
BEETLESTOCK
BEETLESTONE
BEETLEWEED
BEETLING
BEETMISTER
BEETRAVE
BEETROOT
BEETROOTY
BEETS
BEETY
BEEVE
BEEVES
BEEVISH
BEEWARE
BEEWAY
BEEWEED

BEEWINGED
BEEWORT
BEEYARD
BEEZER
BEFALL
BEFALLEN
BEFALLING
BEFELL
BEFFROY
BEFILE
BEFIT
BEFITTED
BEFITTING
BEFITTINGLY
BEFLOUR
BEFLUM
BEFOG
BEFOGGED
BEFOGGING
BEFOOL
BEFOOLED
BEFOOLING
BEFORE
BEFOREHAND
BEFORETIME
BEFORTUNE
BEFOUL
BEFOULED
BEFOULER
BEFOULING
BEFOULMENT
BEFRET
BEFRIEND
BEFRIENDER
BEFUDDLE
BEFUDDLED
BEFUDDLEMENT
BEFUDDLER
BEFUDDLING
BEG
BEGA
BEGAD
BEGAN
BEGANI
BEGAR
BEGARI
BEGARIE
BEGARY
BEGASS
BEGAT
BEGATS
BEGATTAL
BEGEM
BEGEMMED
BEGEMMING
BEGET
BEGETTER
BEGETTING
BEGGAR
BEGGARDOM
BEGGARED
BEGGARER
BEGGARHOOD
BEGGARIES
BEGGARING
BEGGARLINESS
BEGGARLY
BEGGARMAN
BEGGARWEED
BEGGARWOMAN
BEGGARY
BEGGED
BEGGER
BEGGING
BEGILD
BEGIN
BEGINNER
BEGINNING
BEGIRD
BEGIRDED
BEGIRDING
BEGIRT
BEGLERBEG
BEGLERBEGLIC
BEGLERBEGLIK
BEGLERBEGLUC
BEGLEW
BEGNA
BEGNAW
BEGNAWED
BEGNAWN
BEGO
BEGOB
BEGOBS
BEGOD
BEGOHM
BEGONE
BEGONIA
BEGONIACEOUS
BEGORRA
BEGORRY
BEGOT
BEGOTTEN
BEGOWK
BEGRACE
BEGRIME
BEGRIMED
BEGRIMER
BEGRIMING
BEGRIPE
BEGRUDGE
BEGRUDGED
BEGRUDGING
BEGRUDGINGLY
BEGRUNTLE
BEGRUTTEN
BEGSTER
BEGTI
BEGUESS
BEGUILE
BEGUILED
BEGUILEMENT
BEGUILER
BEGUILING
BEGUIN
BEGUINE
BEGUM
BEGUMMED
BEGUN
BEGUNK
BEHALF
BEHALVES
BEHAR
BEHAVE
BEHAVED
BEHAVING
BEHAVIOR
BEHAVIORAL
BEHAVIORISM
BEHAVIORIST
BEHAVIOUR
BEHEAD
BEHEADAL
BEHEADED
BEHEADER
BEHEADING
BEHEAR
BEHEARS
BEHEIRA
BEHELD
BEHEMOTH
BEHEN
BEHENATE
BEHENIC
BEHEST
BEHEW
BEHIGHT
BEHIND
BEHINDHAND
BEHINDSIGHT
BEHN
BEHOLD
BEHOLDEN
BEHOLDER
BEHOLDING
BEHOOF
BEHOOVE
BEHOOVED
BEHOOVEFUL
BEHOOVEFULLY
BEHOOVES
BEHOOVING
BEHOVE
BEHOVED
BEHOVELY
BEHOVING
BEHOWL
BEHUNG
BEIGE
BEIGNET
BEIN
BEING
BEINGS
BEINLY
BEINNESS
BEIRA
BEISA
BEJABBERS
BEJABERS
BEJADE
BEJAN
BEJANT
BEJAPE
BEJEL
BEJESUS
BEJEWEL
BEJEWELED
BEJEWELING
BEJEWELLED
BEJEWELLING
BEJUCO
BEJUGGLE
BEKA
BEKAH
BEKEN
BEKING
BEKINKINITE
BEKISS
BEKKO
BEKNAVE
BEKNIGHT
BEKNOW
BEKNOWN
BEKRA
BEKTI
BEL
BELA
BELABOR
BELABOUR
BELACED
BELAGE
BELAH
BELAM
BELAMOUR
BELAMY
BELANDA
BELANDER
BELAR
BELAST
BELATE
BELATED
BELATEDLY
BELATEDNESS
BELATING
BELAUD
BELAY
BELAYED
BELAYING
BELCH
BELCHER
BELDAM
BELDAME
BELDER
BELDERROOT
BELDUQUE
BELE
BELEAGUER
BELEAGUERED
BELEAGUERER
BELEAGUERING
BELEAVE
BELEE
BELEED
BELEFT
BELEMNID
BELEMNITE
BELEMNITIC
BELEMNOID
BELETTER
BELEVE
BELFRIED
BELFRIES
BELFRY
BELGA
BELGARD
BELIBEL
BELIE
BELIED
BELIEF
BELIEFFUL
BELIEFFULNESS
BELIEFS
BELIER
BELIEVABLE
BELIEVE
BELIEVED
BELIEVER
BELIEVERS
BELIEVING
BELIEVINGLY
BELIGHT
BELIKE
BELIKELY
BELIME
BELITE
BELITTLE
BELITTLED
BELITTLER
BELITTLING
BELIVE
BELK
BELKNAP
BELL
BELLADONNA
BELLARMINE
BELLBIND
BELLBINDER
BELLBINE
BELLBIRD
BELLBOY
BELLE
BELLED
BELLEEK
BELLERIC
BELLETER
BELLETRIST
BELLETRISTIC
BELLFLOWER
BELLHANGING
BELLHOP
BELLHOUSE
BELLIC
BELLICAL
BELLICISM
BELLICOSE
BELLICOSELY
BELLICOSITY
BELLIED
BELLIES
BELLIFEROUS
BELLIGERENCE
BELLIGERENCY
BELLIGERENT
BELLING
BELLIPOTENT
BELLITE
BELLMAKER
BELLMAKING
BELLMAN
BELLMASTER
BELLMEN
BELLMOUTH
BELLMOUTHED
BELLONION
BELLOTA
BELLOTE
BELLOW
BELLOWER
BELLOWING
BELLOWS
BELLOWSMAKER
BELLOWSMAN
BELLPULL
BELLS
BELLTAIL
BELLTOPPER
BELLUINE
BELLUM
BELLWARE
BELLWAVER
BELLWEED
BELLWETHER
BELLWIND
BELLWINE
BELLWOOD
BELLWORT
BELLY
BELLYACHE
BELLYACHED
BELLYACHING
BELLYBAND
BELLYBUTTON
BELLYER
BELLYFISH
BELLYFUL
BELLYFULS
BELLYING
BELLYMAN
BELOEILITE
BELOID
BELOMANCY
BELONG
BELONGED
BELONGER
BELONGING
BELONGINGS
BELONID
BELONITE
BELONOID
BELOOK
BELORD
BELOTTE
BELOUKE
BELOVE
BELOVED

BELOW
BELOWSTAIRS
BELSIRE
BELT
BELTED
BELTER
BELTIE
BELTING
BELTMAKER
BELTMAKING
BELTMAN
BELTMEN
BELTON
BELTWAY
BELUE
BELUGA
BELUGITE
BELUTE
BELVE
BELVEDERE
BELVEDERED
BELY
BELYING
BELZEBUTH
BEMA
BEMASTER
BEMATA
BEMAUL
BEMAZED
BEME
BEMEAN
BEMEET
BEMENTITE
BEMETE
BEMIRE
BEMIRED
BEMIREMENT
BEMIRING
BEMIST
BEMOAN
BEMOANABLE
BEMOANER
BEMOCK
BEMOIL
BEMOL
BEMOON
BEMOURN
BEMOUTH
BEMUD
BEMUDDLE
BEMUDDLEMENT
BEMUSE
BEMUSED
BEMUSEDLY
BEMUSING
BEN
BENA
BENAB
BENADRYL
BENAME
BENAMED
BENAMEE
BENAMI
BENAMIDAR
BENAMING
BENASTY
BENBEN
BENCH
BENCHBOARD
BENCHER
BENCHES
BENCHFELLOW
BENCHING
BENCHLAND
BENCHMAN
BENCHMEN
BENCHWORK

BEND
BENDA
BENDAY
BENDED
BENDEE
BENDEL
BENDER
BENDERS
BENDING
BENDS
BENDSOME
BENDWAYS
BENDWISE
BENDY
BENE
BENEATH
BENECEPTION
BENECEPTIVE
BENECEPTOR
BENEDICITE
BENEDICK
BENEDICT
BENEDICTION
BENEDICTIVE
BENEDICTORY
BENEDIGHT
BENEFACTION
BENEFACTIVE
BENEFACTOR
BENEFACTORY
BENEFACTRESS
BENEFIC
BENEFICE
BENEFICED
BENEFICENCE
BENEFICENT
BENEFICENTLY
BENEFICIAIRE
BENEFICIAL
BENEFICIALLY
BENEFICIARIES
BENEFICIARY
BENEFICIATE
BENEFICING
BENEFICIUM
BENEFIT
BENEFITED
BENEFITER
BENEFITING
BENEGRO
BENEMPT
BENEMPTED
BENEPLACIT
BENEPLACITO
BENEPLACITY
BENET
BENETTED
BENETTING
BENEVOLENCE
BENEVOLENT
BENEVOLENTLY
BENEVOLIST
BENG
BENGALINE
BENIGHT
BENIGHTED
BENIGHTEDNESS
BENIGHTEN
BENIGHTER
BENIGHTING
BENIGN
BENIGNANCY
BENIGNANT
BENIGNANTLY
BENIGNITIES
BENIGNITY
BENIGNLY

BENISEED
BENISON
BENITIER
BENITOITE
BENJ
BENJAMIN
BENJAMINITE
BENJOIN
BENJY
BENK
BENMOST
BENN
BENNE
BENNEL
BENNET
BENNETWEED
BENNI
BENNIES
BENNISEED
BENNY
BENORTH
BENOTE
BENSAIL
BENSALL
BENSEL
BENSELL
BENSH
BENSIL
BENT
BENTANG
BENTHAL
BENTHIC
BENTHON
BENTHONIC
BENTHOS
BENTING
BENTLET
BENTONITE
BENTSTAR
BENTWOOD
BENTY
BENUMB
BENUMBED
BENUMBEDNESS
BENUMBING
BENUMBINGLY
BENUMBMENT
BENVENUTO
BENWARD
BENWEED
BENZAL
BENZALDEHYDE
BENZALDOXIME
BENZAMIDE
BENZAMIDO
BENZEDRINE
BENZEIN
BENZENE
BENZENOID
BENZENYL
BENZIDIN
BENZIDINE
BENZIDINO
BENZIL
BENZILIC
BENZIN
BENZINDULINE
BENZINE
BENZOATE
BENZOATED
BENZOBIS
BENZOCAINE
BENZOHYDROL
BENZOIC
BENZOIN
BENZOINATED
BENZOL

BENZOLATE
BENZOLE
BENZOLINE
BENZOLIZE
BENZONITRILE
BENZONITROL
BENZOPHENONE
BENZOPYRAN
BENZOXY
BENZOYL
BENZOYLATE
BENZOYLATION
BENZYL
BENZYLAMINE
BENZYLIC
BEO
BEPAINT
BEPAPER
BEPART
BEPRANKED
BEPRESS
BEPROSE
BEPUFFED
BEQAA
BEQUEATH
BEQUEATHAL
BEQUEATHER
BEQUEST
BEQUIRTLE
BER
BERAIN
BERAIROU
BERAKAH
BERAKOT
BERAKOTH
BERAT
BERATE
BERATED
BERATING
BERATTLE
BERAUNITE
BERAY
BERBAMINE
BERBE
BERBERID
BERBERIN
BERBERINE
BERBERRY
BERBERY
BERCEAU
BERCEUSE
BERCEUSES
BERDACHE
BERE
BEREAVE
BEREAVED
BEREAVEMENT
BEREAVEN
BEREAVER
BEREAVING
BEREDE
BEREFT
BERENDO
BERENGELITE
BERENGENA
BERESITE
BERG
BERGALITH
BERGAMIOL
BERGAMOT
BERGAPTENE
BERGER
BERGERE
BERGERETTE
BERGGYLT
BERGHAAN
BERGINIZATION

BERGINIZE
BERGSCHRUND
BERGUT
BERGY
BERGYLT
BERHYME
BERHYMED
BERHYMING
BERIBERI
BERIBERIC
BERIGORA
BERIME
BERIMED
BERIMING
BERINGITE
BERITH
BERKELIUM
BERLEY
BERLIN
BERLINE
BERLINITE
BERLOQUE
BERM
BERME
BERMUDITE
BERNICLE
BEROK
BERRENDO
BERRETTA
BERRETTINO
BERRI
BERRICHON
BERRICHONNE
BERRIED
BERRIES
BERRIGAN
BERRUGATE
BERRY
BERRYING
BERRYLIKE
BERSEEM
BERSERK
BERSERKER
BERSIM
BERTH
BERTHA
BERTHAGE
BERTHED
BERTHER
BERTHIERITE
BERTHING
BERTHS
BERTRANDITE
BERTRUM
BERUN
BERVIE
BERWICK
BERYCID
BERYCIFORM
BERYCINE
BERYCOID
BERYCOIDEAN
BERYL
BERYLLATE
BERYLLIA
BERYLLINE
BERYLLIUM
BERYLLOID
BERYLLONITE
BERYX
BERZELIANITE
BERZELIITE
BES
BESA
BESAGNE
BESAGUE
BESAIEL

BESAILE
BESAN
BESANT
BESAYLE
BESCREEN
BESEE
BESEECH
BESEECHED
BESEECHER
BESEECHING
BESEECHINGLY
BESEEM
BESEEMED
BESEEMING
BESEEMINGLY
BESEEMLINESS
BESEEMLY
BESEEN
BESEIGE
BESET
BESETMENT
BESETTER
BESETTING
BESHADE
BESHAG
BESHEAR
BESHINE
BESHLIK
BESHOW
BESHREW
BESICLOMETER
BESIDE
BESIDES
BESIEGE
BESIEGED
BESIEGEMENT
BESIEGER
BESIEGING
BESIEGINGLY
BESIN
BESING
BESIT
BESLAB
BESLAVER
BESLIME
BESLUBBER
BESLUIT
BESMEAR
BESMEARER
BESMIRCH
BESMIRCHER
BESMIRCHMENT
BESMOKE
BESMOTTERED
BESMUT
BESMUTTED
BESMUTTING
BESNOW
BESOIN
BESOM
BESOMER
BESOOTHE
BESOOTHEMENT
BESORT
BESOT
BESOTTED
BESOTTEDLY
BESOTTEDNESS
BESOTTING
BESOTTINGLY
BESOUGHT
BESPAKE
BESPANGLE
BESPANGLED
BESPANGLING
BESPATTER
BESPATTERED
BESPATTERER
BESPATTERING
BESPAWL
BESPEAK
BESPEAKER
BESPEAKING
BESPECKLE
BESPECTACLED
BESPELL
BESPETE
BESPIT
BESPOKE
BESPOKEN
BESPOT
BESPOTTED
BESPOTTING
BESPREAD
BESPREADING
BESPRENT
BESPRING
BESPRINKLE
BESPRINKLED
BESPRINKLER
BESPRINKLING
BESPRIZORNI
BESQUIRT
BESRA
BESSEMER
BESSEMERIZE
BESSEMERIZED
BESSEMERIZING
BESSES
BEST
BESTAIN
BESTAND
BESTEAD
BESTEAL
BESTED
BESTEER
BESTER
BESTIAL
BESTIALITIES
BESTIALITY
BESTIALIZE
BESTIALIZED
BESTIALIZING
BESTIALLY
BESTIALS
BESTIARIAN
BESTIARIES
BESTIARY
BESTICK
BESTICKING
BESTILL
BESTIR
BESTIRRED
BESTIRRING
BESTORM
BESTOW
BESTOWABLE
BESTOWAGE
BESTOWAL
BESTOWED
BESTOWER
BESTOWING
BESTOWMENT
BESTRADDLE
BESTRADDLED
BESTRADDLING
BESTRAUGHT
BESTREW
BESTREWED
BESTREWING
BESTREWN
BESTRID
BESTRIDDEN
BESTRIDE
BESTRIDING
BESTRODE
BESTRUT
BESTUCK
BESUGO
BESWINK
BET
BETA
BETACISM
BETACISMUS
BETAFITE
BETAINE
BETAINOGEN
BETAKE
BETAKEN
BETAKING
BETANAPHTHOL
BETEELA
BETEEM
BETEL
BETELNUT
BETERSCHAP
BETH
BETHABARA
BETHANKIT
BETHEL
BETHFLOWER
BETHINK
BETHINKING
BETHOUGHT
BETHROOT
BETHUMB
BETHUMP
BETHWACK
BETHYLID
BETID
BETIDE
BETIDED
BETIDING
BETIME
BETIMES
BETIS
BETISE
BETITLE
BETLE
BETOIL
BETOKEN
BETOKENED
BETOKENER
BETOKENING
BETON
BETONE
BETONGUE
BETONICA
BETONIES
BETONY
BETOOK
BETOSS
BETRAP
BETRAY
BETRAYAL
BETRAYED
BETRAYER
BETRAYING
BETRAYMENT
BETREND
BETRIM
BETROTH
BETROTHAL
BETROTHED
BETROTHING
BETROTHMENT
BETRUNK
BETRUST
BETS
BETSO
BETTED
BETTER
BETTERED
BETTERER
BETTERGATES
BETTERING
BETTERLY
BETTERMENT
BETTERMOST
BETTERNESS
BETTIES
BETTONG
BETTONGA
BETTOR
BETTY
BETULACEOUS
BETULIN
BETULINIC
BETULINOL
BETWEEN
BETWEENBRAIN
BETWEENITY
BETWEENMAID
BETWIXEN
BETWIXT
BEUDANITE
BEURRE
BEVARING
BEVATRON
BEVEL
BEVELED
BEVELER
BEVELING
BEVELLED
BEVELLER
BEVELLING
BEVER
BEVERAGE
BEVIES
BEVIL
BEVUE
BEVY
BEW
BEWAIL
BEWAILER
BEWAILING
BEWAILINGLY
BEWAKE
BEWARE
BEWARED
BEWARING
BEWED
BEWEEP
BEWEEPER
BEWEEPING
BEWEND
BEWEPT
BEWEST
BEWET
BEWHORE
BEWILDER
BEWILDERED
BEWILDEREDLY
BEWILDERING
BEWILDERMENT
BEWIT
BEWITCH
BEWITCHED
BEWITCHER
BEWITCHERY
BEWITCHING
BEWITCHINGLY
BEWITCHMENT
BEWITH
BEWONDER
BEWORK
BEWPERS
BEWRAP
BEWRAY
BEWRAYED
BEWRAYER
BEWRAYING
BEWRAYMENT
BEWREAK
BEY
BEYERITE
BEYLIC
BEYLICAL
BEYLIK
BEYOND
BEYRICHITE
BEZANT
BEZANTE
BEZANTEE
BEZANTY
BEZEL
BEZESTEEN
BEZETTA
BEZETTE
BEZIL
BEZIQUE
BEZOAR
BEZOARDIC
BEZONIAN
BEZZANT
BEZZLE
BEZZLED
BEZZLING
BEZZO
BHAGAT
BHAGAVAT
BHAGAVATA
BHAI
BHAIACHARA
BHAIYACHARA
BHAKTA
BHAKTI
BHALU
BHANDAR
BHANDARI
BHANG
BHANGI
BHARAL
BHARTI
BHAT
BHAVA
BHEESTIE
BHEESTY
BHIKSHU
BHISTI
BHISTIE
BHOKRA
BHOOSA
BHOY
BHUMIDAR
BHUNDER
BHUNGI
BHUNGINI
BHUSA
BHUT
BIABO
BIACETYL
BIACETYLENE
BIACUMINATE
BIACURU
BIAJAIBA
BIALATE
BIALLYL
BIALVEOLAR
BIALY
BIALYS
BIANCHITE
BIANCO
BIANGULAR
BIANGULATE

BIANGULATED
BIANGULOUS
BIANISIDINE
BIANNUAL
BIANNUALLY
BIARCHY
BIARCUATE
BIARCUATED
BIARTICULAR
BIARTICULATE
BIAS
BIASED
BIASES
BIASING
BIASSED
BIASSING
BIASTERIC
BIASWISE
BIATOMIC
BIAURICULAR
BIAURICULATE
BIAXAL
BIAXIAL
BIAXIALITY
BIAXIALLY
BIB
BIBACIOUS
BIBACITY
BIBASIC
BIBATION
BIBB
BIBBED
BIBBER
BIBBING
BIBBLE
BIBBLED
BIBBLER
BIBBLING
BIBBONS
BIBBY
BIBCOCK
BIBELOT
BIBENZYL
BIBERON
BIBI
BIBIONID
BIBIRI
BIBIRU
BIBITORY
BIBLE
BIBLICAL
BIBLIOCLASM
BIBLIOCLAST
BIBLIOFILM
BIBLIOGNOST
BIBLIOGONY
BIBLIOGRAPH
BIBLIOGRAPHIES
BIBLIOGRAPHY
BIBLIOKLEPT
BIBLIOLATER
BIBLIOLATRY
BIBLIOLOGIST
BIBLIOLOGY
BIBLIOMANCY
BIBLIOMANE
BIBLIOMANIA
BIBLIOMANIAC
BIBLIOMANIAN
BIBLIOPEGIC
BIBLIOPEGIST
BIBLIOPEGY
BIBLIOPHAGIC
BIBLIOPHIL
BIBLIOPHILE
BIBLIOPHILIC
BIBLIOPHOBIA
BIBLIOPOLAR
BIBLIOPOLE
BIBLIOPOLERY
BIBLIOPOLIC
BIBLIOPOLISM
BIBLIOPOLIST
BIBLIOPOLY
BIBLIOSOPH
BIBLIOTAPHIC
BIBLIOTHEC
BIBLIOTHECA
BIBLIOTHECAL
BIBLIOTHEKE
BIBLIOTHETIC
BIBLOS
BIBLUS
BIBULOSITY
BIBULOUS
BIBULOUSLY
BIBULOUSNESS
BICALCARATE
BICALVOUS
BICAMERAL
BICAMERIST
BICAPITATE
BICAPSULAR
BICARB
BICARBONATE
BICARBURETED
BICARBURETTED
BICARINATE
BICARPELLARY
BICARPELLATE
BICAUDAL
BICAUDATE
BICCHED
BICE
BICELLULAR
BICENTENARY
BICENTENNIAL
BICEPHALIC
BICEPHALOUS
BICEPS
BICEPSES
BICHLORIDE
BICHO
BICHORD
BICHOS
BICHROMATE
BICHROMATIC
BICHROME
BICHROMIC
BICHY
BICILIATE
BICILIATED
BICIPITAL
BICIPITOUS
BICIRCULAR
BICK
BICKER
BICKERED
BICKERER
BICKERING
BICKERN
BICKIRON
BICLINIA
BICLINIUM
BICOLLATERAL
BICOLLIGATE
BICOLOR
BICOLORED
BICOLOROUS
BICOLOUR
BICOLOURED
BICOLOUROUS
BICONCAVE
BICONCAVITY
BICONE
BICONIC
BICONICAL
BICONICALLY
BICONJUGATE
BICONVEX
BICORN
BICORNE
BICORNED
BICORNUATE
BICORNUOUS
BICORPORAL
BICORPORATE
BICORPOREAL
BICOSTATE
BICRENATE
BICROFARAD
BICRON
BICRURAL
BICULTURAL
BICURSAL
BICUSPID
BICUSPIDAL
BICUSPIDATE
BICYANIDE
BICYCLE
BICYCLED
BICYCLER
BICYCLIC
BICYCLICAL
BICYCLING
BICYCLISM
BICYCLIST
BICYCLO
BICYCULAR
BID
BIDAR
BIDARKA
BIDARKEE
BIDCOCK
BIDDABLE
BIDDABLENESS
BIDDABLY
BIDDANCE
BIDDEN
BIDDER
BIDDERY
BIDDIE
BIDDIES
BIDDING
BIDDY
BIDE
BIDED
BIDENE
BIDENT
BIDENTAL
BIDENTALIA
BIDENTATE
BIDER
BIDERY
BIDET
BIDI
BIDIGITATE
BIDING
BIDREE
BIDRI
BIDRY
BIDSTAND
BIDUOUS
BIEBERITE
BIEL
BIELBY
BIELD
BIELDY
BIELENITE
BIEN
BIENLY
BIENNE
BIENNESS
BIENNIA
BIENNIAL
BIENNIALLY
BIENNIUM
BIENSEANCE
BIENVENU
BIER
BIESTINGS
BIETLE
BIFACE
BIFACIAL
BIFANGED
BIFARA
BIFARIOUS
BIFARIOUSLY
BIFER
BIFEROUS
BIFF
BIFFIN
BIFFY
BIFID
BIFIDATE
BIFIDATED
BIFIDITY
BIFIDLY
BIFILAR
BIFILARLY
BIFISTULAR
BIFLABELLATE
BIFLAGELATE
BIFLECNODE
BIFLECTED
BIFLEX
BIFLORATE
BIFLOROUS
BIFLUORID
BIFLUORIDE
BIFOCAL
BIFOCALS
BIFOLD
BIFOLIA
BIFOLIATE
BIFOLIOLATE
BIFOLIUM
BIFOLLICULAR
BIFORATE
BIFORIN
BIFORINE
BIFORKED
BIFORM
BIFORMED
BIFORMITY
BIFRONT
BIFRONTAL
BIFRONTED
BIFURCAL
BIFURCATE
BIFURCATED
BIFURCATELY
BIFURCATING
BIFURCATION
BIFURCOUS
BIG
BIGA
BIGAMIC
BIGAMIST
BIGAMISTIC
BIGAMIZE
BIGAMOUS
BIGAMOUSLY
BIGAMY
BIGAN
BIGARADE
BIGAROON
BIGARREAU
BIGAS
BIGATE
BIGBLOOM
BIGBURY
BIGEMINAL
BIGEMINATE
BIGEMINATED
BIGENER
BIGENERIC
BIGENTIAL
BIGEYE
BIGG
BIGGED
BIGGEN
BIGGENED
BIGGENING
BIGGER
BIGGEST
BIGGETY
BIGGIE
BIGGIN
BIGGING
BIGGISH
BIGGITY
BIGGONET
BIGHA
BIGHEAD
BIGHEARTED
BIGHORN
BIGHORNS
BIGHT
BIGHTED
BIGHTING
BIGHTS
BIGLY
BIGMITT
BIGMOUTH
BIGMOUTHED
BIGNESS
BIGNONIA
BIGNONIAD
BIGNOU
BIGONIAC
BIGONIAL
BIGOT
BIGOTED
BIGOTEDLY
BIGOTHERO
BIGOTRIES
BIGOTRY
BIGOTTY
BIGRAM
BIGROOT
BIGTHATCH
BIGUANIDE
BIGUTTATE
BIGUTTULATE
BIGWIG
BIGWIGGED
BIGWIGGERY
BIGWIGGISM
BIHOURLY
BIJA
BIJASAL
BIJOU
BIJOUTERIE
BIJOUX
BIJUGATE
BIJUGOUS
BIJUGULAR
BIJWONER
BIKE
BIKER
BIKH
BIKIE
BIKINI
BIKKURIM

BILABE
BILABIAL
BILABIATE
BILALO
BILAMINAR
BILAMINATE
BILAMINATED
BILAN
BILAND
BILANDER
BILATERAL
BILATERALISM
BILATERALITY
BILATERALLY
BILBERRIES
BILBERRY
BILBI
BILBIE
BILBO
BILBOA
BILBOES
BILBOQUET
BILBY
BILCH
BILCOCK
BILDAR
BILDER
BILDERS
BILE
BILECTION
BILECTIONED
BILESTONE
BILEVE
BILGE
BILGED
BILGING
BILGY
BILHARZIAL
BILHARZIASIS
BILHARZIC
BILHARZIOSIS
BILIARY
BILIATE
BILIATION
BILIC
BILICYANIN
BILIFACTION
BILIFEROUS
BILIFICATION
BILIFUSCIN
BILIFY
BILIHUMIN
BILIMBI
BILIMBING
BILIMBIS
BILIMENT
BILINEAR
BILINGUAL
BILINGUALISM
BILINGUALLY
BILINGUIST
BILINIGRIN
BILINITE
BILIOUS
BILIOUSLY
BILIOUSNESS
BILIPRASIN
BILIPYRRHIN
BILIRUBIN
BILIRUBINIC
BILITERAL
BILITERALISM
BILITH
BILITHON
BILIVERDIN
BILK
BILKER
BILKIS
BILL
BILLABLE
BILLABONG
BILLAGE
BILLBACK
BILLBOARD
BILLBROKING
BILLBUG
BILLED
BILLER
BILLET
BILLETED
BILLETER
BILLETHEAD
BILLETING
BILLETTE
BILLETTY
BILLETY
BILLFISH
BILLFISHES
BILLFOLD
BILLHEAD
BILLHEADING
BILLHOLDER
BILLHOOK
BILLIAN
BILLIARD
BILLIARDIST
BILLIARDLY
BILLIARDS
BILLIE
BILLIES
BILLIKIN
BILLING
BILLINGS
BILLINGSGATE
BILLION
BILLIONAIRE
BILLIONISM
BILLIONTH
BILLMAN
BILLMEN
BILLON
BILLOT
BILLOW
BILLOWED
BILLOWIER
BILLOWIEST
BILLOWINESS
BILLOWING
BILLOWY
BILLPOSTER
BILLPOSTING
BILLS
BILLSTICKER
BILLSTICKING
BILLY
BILLYBOY
BILLYCAN
BILLYCOCK
BILLYER
BILLYHOOD
BILLYWIX
BILO
BILOBATE
BILOBATED
BILOBE
BILOBED
BILOBULAR
BILOCATION
BILOCELLATE
BILOCULAR
BILOCULATE
BILOCULINE
BILOPHODONT
BILOS
BILSH
BILSTED
BILTONG
BILTONGUE
BIMA
BIMACULATE
BIMACULATED
BIMAH
BIMANAL
BIMANE
BIMANOUS
BIMANUAL
BIMANUALLY
BIMARINE
BIMASTIC
BIMASTISM
BIMASTOID
BIMAXILLARY
BIMBASHI
BIMBIL
BIMBO
BIMEBY
BIMENSAL
BIMESTRIAL
BIMETAL
BIMETALISM
BIMETALLIC
BIMETALLIST
BIMILLENARY
BIMILLENIUM
BIMODAL
BIMODALITY
BIMOLECULAR
BIMONG
BIMONTHLY
BIMORPH
BIMOTORED
BIMOTORS
BIMUSCULAR
BIN
BINA
BINAL
BINAPTHYL
BINARIES
BINARY
BINATE
BINATELY
BINATION
BINAURAL
BINBASHI
BIND
BINDER
BINDERIES
BINDERY
BINDHEIMITE
BINDING
BINDINGLY
BINDINGNESS
BINDLE
BINDOREE
BINDWEB
BINDWEED
BINDWITH
BINDWOOD
BINE
BINERVATE
BINEWEED
BING
BINGE
BINGEE
BINGEY
BINGEYS
BINGHI
BINGIES
BINGLE
BINGO
BINGY
BINH
BINI
BINIOU
BINIT
BINK
BINMAN
BINMEN
BINNA
BINNACLE
BINNED
BINNING
BINNITE
BINNOGUE
BINNY
BINO
BINOCLE
BINOCULAR
BINOCULARITY
BINOCULARLY
BINOCULARS
BINOCULATE
BINODAL
BINODE
BINOMEN
BINOMIAL
BINOMIALISM
BINOMIALLY
BINOMINATED
BINOMINOUS
BINORMAL
BINOTIC
BINOTONOUS
BINOXALATE
BINOXIDE
BINT
BINTANGOR
BINTURONG
BINUCLEAR
BINUCLEATE
BINUCLEATED
BINUCLEOLATE
BINUKAU
BIOASSAY
BIOBLAST
BIOBLASTIC
BIOCATALYST
BIOCELLATE
BIOCENTRIC
BIOCHEMIC
BIOCHEMICAL
BIOCHEMICALLY
BIOCHEMICS
BIOCHEMIST
BIOCHEMISTRY
BIOCHEMY
BIOCHORE
BIOCHRON
BIOCIDE
BIOCOENOSE
BIOCOENOSES
BIOCOENOSIS
BIOCOENOTIC
BIOCYCLE
BIODYNAMIC
BIODYNAMICAL
BIODYNAMICS
BIOFLAVONOID
BIOGEN
BIOGENASE
BIOGENESIS
BIOGENESIST
BIOGENETIC
BIOGENETICAL
BIOGENOUS
BIOGENY
BIOGEOGRAPHY
BIOGNOSIS
BIOGRAPH
BIOGRAPHEE
BIOGRAPHER
BIOGRAPHIC
BIOGRAPHICAL
BIOGRAPHIES
BIOGRAPHIST
BIOGRAPHIZE
BIOGRAPHY
BIOHERM
BIOLITE
BIOLITH
BIOLOGIC
BIOLOGICAL
BIOLOGICALLY
BIOLOGIES
BIOLOGISM
BIOLOGIST
BIOLOGIZE
BIOLOGY
BIOLYSIS
BIOLYTIC
BIOME
BIOMETER
BIOMETRIC
BIOMETRICAL
BIOMETRICIAN
BIOMETRICIST
BIOMETRICS
BIOMETRY
BION
BIONERGY
BIONICS
BIONOMIC
BIONOMICAL
BIONOMICS
BIONOMIST
BIONOMY
BIONT
BIONTIC
BIOPHAGISM
BIOPHAGOUS
BIOPHAGY
BIOPHILOUS
BIOPHOR
BIOPHORE
BIOPHYSICAL
BIOPHYSICIST
BIOPHYSICS
BIOPHYTE
BIOPIC
BIOPLASM
BIOPLASMIC
BIOPLAST
BIOPLASTIC
BIOPOESIS
BIOPOTENTIAL
BIOPSIC
BIOPSIES
BIOPSY
BIOPSYCHIC
BIOPSYCHICAL
BIOPYRIBOLE
BIORDINAL
BIORGAN
BIOS
BIOSCOPE
BIOSCOPIC
BIOSCOPY
BIOSE
BIOSESTON
BIOSIS
BIOSOCIAL
BIOSOME
BIOSPHERE
BIOSTATIC
BIOSTATICAL

BIOSTATICS
BIOSTERIN
BIOSTEROL
BIOSTROME
BIOSYNTHESIS
BIOSYNTHETIC
BIOTA
BIOTAXY
BIOTIC
BIOTICAL
BIOTICS
BIOTIN
BIOTITE
BIOTITIC
BIOTOME
BIOTOMY
BIOTOPE
BIOTRON
BIOTYPE
BIOTYPIC
BIOZONE
BIPACK
BIPALEOLATE
BIPALMATE
BIPARASITIC
BIPARENTAL
BIPARIETAL
BIPAROUS
BIPARTED
BIPARTIBLE
BIPARTIENT
BIPARTILE
BIPARTISAN
BIPARTITE
BIPARTITELY
BIPARTITION
BIPECTINATE
BIPECTINATED
BIPED
BIPEDALITY
BIPELTATE
BIPENNIFORM
BIPETALOUS
BIPHASE
BIPHASIC
BIPHENOL
BIPHENYL
BIPHENYLENE
BIPINNARIA
BIPINNATE
BIPINNATED
BIPINNATELY
BIPLANAR
BIPLANE
BIPLICATE
BIPLICITY
BIPLOSION
BIPOD
BIPOLAR
BIPOLARITY
BIPOROSE
BIPOROUS
BIPRISM
BIPRONG
BIPROPELLANT
BIPUNCTAL
BIPUNCTATE
BIPUNCTUAL
BIPUPILLATE
BIPYRAMID
BIPYRAMIDAL
BIPYRIDINE
BIPYRIDYL
BIQUADRANTAL
BIQUADRATE
BIQUADRATIC
BIQUARTERLY
BIQUARTZ
BIQUINTILE
BIRADIAL
BIRADIATE
BIRADIATED
BIRAMOSE
BIRAMOUS
BIRATIONAL
BIRCH
BIRCHBARK
BIRCHEN
BIRCHES
BIRCHING
BIRCHMAN
BIRCHWOOD
BIRD
BIRDBANDER
BIRDBANDING
BIRDBATH
BIRDBERRY
BIRDBRAIN
BIRDCAGE
BIRDCALL
BIRDCLAPPER
BIRDEEN
BIRDER
BIRDEYE
BIRDGLUE
BIRDHOUSE
BIRDIE
BIRDIKIN
BIRDING
BIRDLIFE
BIRDLIME
BIRDLIMED
BIRDLIMING
BIRDLING
BIRDMAN
BIRDMEN
BIRDMOUTHED
BIRDNEST
BIRDS
BIRDSEED
BIRDSNEST
BIRDSONG
BIRDSTONE
BIRDWEED
BIRDWOMAN
BIRDY
BIREFRINGENT
BIREME
BIRETTA
BIRI
BIRIBA
BIRIMOSE
BIRK
BIRKEN
BIRKIE
BIRKREMITE
BIRKY
BIRL
BIRLE
BIRLER
BIRLING
BIRLINN
BIRMA
BIRN
BIRNE
BIRODO
BIROTATION
BIROTATORY
BIRR
BIRRED
BIRRING
BIRRUS
BIRSE
BIRSIT
BIRSLE
BIRSY
BIRTH
BIRTHBED
BIRTHDAY
BIRTHDOM
BIRTHING
BIRTHLAND
BIRTHLESS
BIRTHMARK
BIRTHMATE
BIRTHNIGHT
BIRTHPLACE
BIRTHRATE
BIRTHRIGHT
BIRTHROOT
BIRTHSTONE
BIRTHSTOOL
BIRTHWORT
BIRTHY
BIS
BISA
BISABOL
BISACROMIAL
BISAGRE
BISALT
BISAXILLARY
BISBEEITE
BISCAYEN
BISCHOFITE
BISCOTIN
BISCUIT
BISCUITING
BISCUITMAKER
BISCUITROOT
BISCUITS
BISE
BISECT
BISECTION
BISECTIONAL
BISECTOR
BISECTRICES
BISECTRIX
BISEGMENT
BISERIAL
BISERIALLY
BISERRATE
BISETOSE
BISETOUS
BISEXED
BISEXT
BISEXUAL
BISEXUALISM
BISEXUALITY
BISEXUALLY
BISEXUOUS
BISHOP
BISHOPDOM
BISHOPED
BISHOPESS
BISHOPING
BISHOPRIC
BISHOPSCAP
BISILIAC
BISILICATE
BISIMINE
BISINUATE
BISINUATION
BISISCHIADIC
BISISCHIATIC
BISK
BISKOP
BISMAR
BISMARINE
BISME
BISMER
BISMERPUND
BISMILLAH
BISMITE
BISMUTH
BISMUTHAL
BISMUTHATE
BISMUTHIC
BISMUTHIDE
BISMUTHINE
BISMUTHINITE
BISMUTHITE
BISMUTHOUS
BISMUTHYL
BISMUTITE
BISNAGA
BISON
BISONANT
BISONTINE
BISPINOSE
BISPINOUS
BISPORE
BISPOROUS
BISQUE
BISQUETTE
BISSABOL
BISSEXT
BISSEXTILE
BISSON
BIST
BISTER
BISTERED
BISTETRAZOLE
BISTI
BISTIPULAR
BISTIPULATE
BISTIPULED
BISTORT
BISTOURIES
BISTOURNAGE
BISTOURY
BISTRATAL
BISTRATOSE
BISTRE
BISTRED
BISTRIATE
BISTRIAZOLE
BISTRO
BISUBSTITUTED
BISULCATE
BISULCATED
BISULFATE
BISULFIDE
BISULFITE
BISULPHATE
BISULPHIDE
BISULPHITE
BISYLLABIC
BISYLLABISM
BISYMMETRIC
BISYMMETRY
BIT
BITABLE
BITANGENT
BITANGENTIAL
BITANHOL
BITARTRATE
BITBRACE
BITCH
BITCHERY
BITCHIER
BITCHIEST
BITCHY
BITE
BITEABLE
BITECHE
BITED
BITEMPORAL
BITEN
BITER
BITERNATE
BITERNATELY
BITEWING
BITHEISM
BITI
BITING
BITINGLY
BITINGNESS
BITO
BITOLYL
BITONALITY
BITORE
BITREADLE
BITRIPARTITE
BITRIPINNATIFID
BITRISEPTATE
BITS
BITSTALK
BITSTOCK
BITSY
BITT
BITTACLE
BITTE
BITTED
BITTEN
BITTER
BITTERBARK
BITTERBLAIN
BITTERBLOOM
BITTERBUR
BITTERBUSH
BITTERER
BITTEREST
BITTERHEAD
BITTERISH
BITTERISHNESS
BITTERLESS
BITTERLING
BITTERLY
BITTERN
BITTERNESS
BITTERNS
BITTERNUT
BITTERROOT
BITTERS
BITTERSWEET
BITTERWEED
BITTERWORM
BITTERWORT
BITTHEAD
BITTIE
BITTING
BITTOCK
BITTY
BITUBERCULAR
BITULITHIC
BITUME
BITUMED
BITUMEN
BITUMINIZE
BITUMINIZED
BITUMINIZING
BITUMINOID
BITUMINOUS
BITWISE
BITYITE
BITYPIC
BIUNE
BIUNIAL
BIUNITY
BIURATE
BIUREA
BIURET
BIVALENCE
BIVALENCY
BIVALENT

BIVALVE
BIVALVED
BIVALVES
BIVALVULAR
BIVARIANT
BIVASCULAR
BIVECTOR
BIVENTER
BIVENTRAL
BIVERBAL
BIVIOUS
BIVITTATE
BIVOCAL
BIVOCALIZED
BIVOLUMINOUS
BIVOUAC
BIVOUACKED
BIVOUACKING
BIWA
BIWEEKLY
BIXACEOUS
BIXBYITE
BIXIN
BIYEARLY
BIZ
BIZARDITE
BIZARRE
BIZARRELY
BIZARRENESS
BIZARRERIE
BIZE
BIZLE
BIZYGOMATIC
BIZZARRO
BLAA
BLAASOP
BLAB
BLABBED
BLABBER
BLABBERER
BLABBERMOUTH
BLABBING
BLACK
BLACKACRE
BLACKAMOOR
BLACKARM
BLACKBACK
BLACKBALL
BLACKBALLER
BLACKBERRIES
BLACKBERRY
BLACKBIRD
BLACKBIRDER
BLACKBIRDING
BLACKBOARD
BLACKBOY
BLACKBREAST
BLACKBRUSH
BLACKBUSH
BLACKBUTT
BLACKCAP
BLACKCOAT
BLACKCOCK
BLACKDAMP
BLACKEN
BLACKENED
BLACKENER
BLACKENING
BLACKER
BLACKEST
BLACKEY
BLACKEYE
BLACKEYES
BLACKFACE
BLACKFELLOW
BLACKFELLOWS
BLACKFIN
BLACKFIRE
BLACKFISH
BLACKFISHER
BLACKFISHES
BLACKFISHING
BLACKFLY
BLACKGUARD
BLACKGUARDISM
BLACKGUARDLY
BLACKGUARDRY
BLACKGUM
BLACKHEAD
BLACKHEADS
BLACKHEART
BLACKHEARTED
BLACKIE
BLACKIES
BLACKING
BLACKISH
BLACKISHLY
BLACKISHNESS
BLACKJACK
BLACKLAND
BLACKLEAD
BLACKLEG
BLACKLIST
BLACKLY
BLACKMAIL
BLACKMAILER
BLACKMAN
BLACKNEB
BLACKNECK
BLACKNESS
BLACKNOB
BLACKOUT
BLACKPOLL
BLACKPOT
BLACKPRINT
BLACKROOT
BLACKS
BLACKSHIRTED
BLACKSMITH
BLACKSNAKE
BLACKSTICK
BLACKSTRAP
BLACKTAIL
BLACKTHORN
BLACKTONGUE
BLACKTOP
BLACKTREE
BLACKWASH
BLACKWASHER
BLACKWATER
BLACKWEED
BLACKWOOD
BLACKWORK
BLACKWORT
BLACKY
BLAD
BLADDER
BLADDERET
BLADDERNOSE
BLADDERNUT
BLADDERSEED
BLADDERWEED
BLADDERWORT
BLADDERWRACK
BLADDERY
BLADE
BLADEBONE
BLADED
BLADELET
BLADER
BLADES
BLADESMITH
BLADING
BLADY
BLADYGRASS
BLAE
BLAEBERRY
BLAEWORT
BLAFF
BLAFFERT
BLAFLUM
BLAGGARD
BLAGUE
BLAH
BLAHLAUT
BLAIK
BLAIN
BLAIR
BLAIRMORITE
BLAKE
BLAKEBERYED
BLAKEITE
BLAMABLE
BLAMABLENESS
BLAMABLY
BLAME
BLAMEABLE
BLAMED
BLAMEFUL
BLAMEFULLY
BLAMEFULNESS
BLAMELESS
BLAMELESSLY
BLAMER
BLAMEWORTHY
BLAMING
BLAMINGLY
BLANC
BLANCA
BLANCARD
BLANCH
BLANCHED
BLANCHER
BLANCHING
BLANCHINGLY
BLANCMANGE
BLANCMANGER
BLANCO
BLAND
BLANDA
BLANDISH
BLANDISHER
BLANDISHING
BLANDISHMENT
BLANDLY
BLANDNESS
BLANK
BLANKBOOK
BLANKED
BLANKEEL
BLANKET
BLANKETED
BLANKETEER
BLANKETING
BLANKETRY
BLANKETY
BLANKING
BLANKISH
BLANKLY
BLANKNESS
BLANKS
BLANKY
BLANQUETTE
BLANQUILLO
BLARE
BLARED
BLARING
BLARNEY
BLARNEYER
BLART
BLAS
BLASE
BLASH
BLASHY
BLASPHEME
BLASPHEMED
BLASPHEMER
BLASPHEMIES
BLASPHEMING
BLASPHEMOUS
BLASPHEMY
BLAST
BLASTAEA
BLASTED
BLASTEMA
BLASTEMAL
BLASTEMATA
BLASTEMATIC
BLASTEMIC
BLASTER
BLASTHOLE
BLASTID
BLASTIE
BLASTING
BLASTMAN
BLASTMENT
BLASTOCELE
BLASTOCHEME
BLASTOCHYLE
BLASTOCOLLA
BLASTOCYST
BLASTOCYTE
BLASTODERM
BLASTODERMIC
BLASTODISC
BLASTODISK
BLASTOFF
BLASTOGENIC
BLASTOGENY
BLASTOID
BLASTOMA
BLASTOMATA
BLASTOMERE
BLASTOMERIC
BLASTOMYCETE
BLASTOPHITIC
BLASTOPHORAL
BLASTOPHORE
BLASTOPHORIC
BLASTOPORAL
BLASTOPORE
BLASTOPORIC
BLASTOSPHERE
BLASTOSTYLAR
BLASTOSTYLE
BLASTOZOOID
BLASTPLATE
BLASTULA
BLASTULAE
BLASTULAR
BLASTULATION
BLASTULE
BLASTY
BLAT
BLATANCY
BLATANT
BLATANTLY
BLATCH
BLATCHANG
BLATE
BLATELY
BLATENESS
BLATEROON
BLATHER
BLATHERER
BLATHERSKITE
BLATHERY
BLATIFORM
BLATJANG
BLATTA
BLATTED
BLATTER
BLATTERED
BLATTERER
BLATTERING
BLATTI
BLATTID
BLATTING
BLATTOID
BLAUBOK
BLAUBOKS
BLAVER
BLAW
BLAWORT
BLAY
BLAZE
BLAZED
BLAZER
BLAZES
BLAZING
BLAZON
BLAZONED
BLAZONER
BLAZONING
BLAZONMENT
BLAZONRY
BLAZY
BLEA
BLEACH
BLEACHED
BLEACHER
BLEACHERIES
BLEACHERITE
BLEACHERMAN
BLEACHERS
BLEACHERY
BLEACHFIELD
BLEACHHOUSE
BLEACHING
BLEACHMAN
BLEACHWORKS
BLEACHYARD
BLEAK
BLEAKISH
BLEAKLY
BLEAKNESS
BLEAKS
BLEAKY
BLEAR
BLEARED
BLEAREDNESS
BLEAREYE
BLEARIER
BLEARIEST
BLEARILY
BLEARINESS
BLEARY
BLEAT
BLEATER
BLEATING
BLEATINGLY
BLEAUNT
BLEB
BLEBBY
BLECHNOID
BLECK
BLED
BLEE
BLEED
BLEEDER
BLEEDING
BLEEKBOK
BLEERY
BLEEZE
BLEEZY

BLEIR
BLELLUM
BLEMISH
BLEMISHED
BLEMISHER
BLENCH
BLENCHER
BLENCHING
BLENCHINGLY
BLEND
BLENDCORN
BLENDE
BLENDED
BLENDER
BLENDING
BLENDURE
BLENK
BLENNIES
BLENNIID
BLENNIIFORM
BLENNIOID
BLENNORRHEA
BLENNORRHOEA
BLENNY
BLENS
BLENT
BLEO
BLEPHARA
BLEPHARAL
BLEPHARISM
BLEPHARITIS
BLEPHAROPLAST
BLESBOK
BLESBOKS
BLESBUCK
BLESMOL
BLESS
BLESSE
BLESSED
BLESSEDLY
BLESSEDNESS
BLESSER
BLESSING
BLESSINGLY
BLEST
BLET
BLETHE
BLETHER
BLETHERATION
BLETHERS
BLETTED
BLETTING
BLEU
BLEW
BLEWITS
BLIAUT
BLIBE
BLICK
BLICKEY
BLICKEYS
BLICKIE
BLICKIES
BLICKY
BLIGHT
BLIGHTBIRD
BLIGHTED
BLIGHTER
BLIGHTING
BLIGHTINGLY
BLIGHTY
BLIJVER
BLIMBING
BLIMP
BLIMY
BLIN
BLIND
BLINDAGE
BLINDBALL
BLINDED
BLINDEDLY
BLINDER
BLINDEST
BLINDEYES
BLINDFAST
BLINDFISH
BLINDFOLD
BLINDFOLDED
BLINDFOLDER
BLINDFOLDLY
BLINDING
BLINDINGLY
BLINDISM
BLINDLY
BLINDNESS
BLINDSTITCH
BLINDSTORIES
BLINDSTORY
BLINDWEED
BLINDWORM
BLINE
BLINGER
BLINK
BLINKARD
BLINKED
BLINKER
BLINKING
BLINKINGLY
BLINKS
BLINKY
BLINTER
BLINTZ
BLINTZE
BLIP
BLISS
BLISSFUL
BLISSFULLY
BLISSFULNESS
BLISSOM
BLIST
BLISTER
BLISTERED
BLISTERING
BLISTEROUS
BLISTERS
BLISTERWEED
BLISTERWORT
BLISTERY
BLITE
BLITHE
BLITHEFUL
BLITHEFULLY
BLITHELY
BLITHEMEAT
BLITHEN
BLITHENESS
BLITHER
BLITHERED
BLITHERING
BLITHESOME
BLITHESOMELY
BLITTER
BLITZ
BLIZZ
BLIZZARD
BLIZZARDLY
BLIZZARDOUS
BLIZZARDY
BLO
BLOAK
BLOAT
BLOATED
BLOATEDNESS
BLOATER
BLOATING
BLOB
BLOBBED
BLOBBER
BLOBBIER
BLOBBIEST
BLOBBING
BLOBBY
BLOC
BLOCAGE
BLOCK
BLOCKADE
BLOCKADED
BLOCKADER
BLOCKADING
BLOCKAGE
BLOCKBUSTER
BLOCKED
BLOCKER
BLOCKHEAD
BLOCKHEADED
BLOCKHEADISM
BLOCKHOLE
BLOCKHOLER
BLOCKHOUSE
BLOCKIER
BLOCKIEST
BLOCKING
BLOCKISH
BLOCKISHLY
BLOCKISHNESS
BLOCKLAYER
BLOCKLIKE
BLOCKLINE
BLOCKMAKER
BLOCKMAKING
BLOCKMAN
BLOCKOUT
BLOCKPATE
BLOCKS
BLOCKSHIP
BLOCKY
BLODE
BLODITE
BLOEDITE
BLOKE
BLOLLY
BLOND
BLONDE
BLONDENESS
BLONDINE
BLONDNESS
BLOO
BLOOD
BLOODALP
BLOODBERRY
BLOODBIRD
BLOODCURDLER
BLOODCURDLING
BLOODED
BLOODFIN
BLOODFLOWER
BLOODGUILT
BLOODGUILTY
BLOODHOUND
BLOODIED
BLOODIER
BLOODIEST
BLOODILY
BLOODINESS
BLOODING
BLOODLEAF
BLOODLESS
BLOODLESSLY
BLOODLETTER
BLOODLETTING
BLOODLINE
BLOODMOBILE
BLOODMONGER
BLOODNOUN
BLOODRIPE
BLOODROOT
BLOODSHED
BLOODSHEDDER
BLOODSHOT
BLOODSHOTTEN
BLOODSPILLER
BLOODSPILLING
BLOODSTAIN
BLOODSTAINED
BLOODSTANCH
BLOODSTOCK
BLOODSTONE
BLOODSUCK
BLOODSUCKER
BLOODSUCKING
BLOODTHIRST
BLOODTHIRSTER
BLOODTHIRSTY
BLOODWEED
BLOODWIT
BLOODWITE
BLOODWOOD
BLOODWORM
BLOODWORT
BLOODY
BLOODYBONES
BLOODYING
BLOOEY
BLOOIE
BLOOM
BLOOMAGE
BLOOMER
BLOOMERIES
BLOOMERS
BLOOMERY
BLOOMFELL
BLOOMING
BLOOMINGLY
BLOOMINGNESS
BLOOMY
BLOOP
BLOOPER
BLOOPING
BLOOTH
BLORE
BLOSMY
BLOSSOM
BLOSSOMBILL
BLOSSOMED
BLOSSOMING
BLOSSOMLESS
BLOSSOMRY
BLOSSOMS
BLOSSOMY
BLOT
BLOTCH
BLOTCHED
BLOTCHIER
BLOTCHIEST
BLOTCHINESS
BLOTCHING
BLOTCHY
BLOTE
BLOTLESS
BLOTTED
BLOTTER
BLOTTESQUE
BLOTTESQUELY
BLOTTING
BLOTTO
BLOTTY
BLOUSE
BLOUSED
BLOUSELIKE
BLOUSING
BLOUSY
BLOUT
BLOVIATE
BLOW
BLOWBACK
BLOWBALL
BLOWBY
BLOWBYS
BLOWCASE
BLOWDOWN
BLOWEN
BLOWER
BLOWFISH
BLOWFLIES
BLOWFLY
BLOWGUN
BLOWHARD
BLOWHOLE
BLOWIER
BLOWIEST
BLOWINESS
BLOWING
BLOWIRON
BLOWLAMP
BLOWLINE
BLOWN
BLOWOFF
BLOWOUT
BLOWPIPE
BLOWPIT
BLOWPOINT
BLOWPROOF
BLOWS
BLOWSPRAY
BLOWSY
BLOWTH
BLOWTORCH
BLOWTUBE
BLOWUP
BLOWY
BLOWZE
BLOWZED
BLOWZIER
BLOWZIEST
BLOWZING
BLOWZY
BLUB
BLUBBED
BLUBBER
BLUBBERED
BLUBBERER
BLUBBERING
BLUBBERMAN
BLUBBERY
BLUBBING
BLUCHER
BLUDE
BLUDGE
BLUDGEON
BLUDGEONED
BLUDGEONEER
BLUDGEONER
BLUDGER
BLUE
BLUEBACK
BLUEBALL
BLUEBEAD
BLUEBELL
BLUEBELLED
BLUEBERRIES
BLUEBERRY
BLUEBILL
BLUEBIRD
BLUEBLAW
BLUEBLOOD
BLUEBLOSSOM

BLUEBONNET
BLUEBOOK
BLUEBOTTLE
BLUEBREAST
BLUEBUCK
BLUEBUSH
BLUEBUTTON
BLUECAP
BLUECOAT
BLUECUP
BLUECURLS
BLUED
BLUEFIN
BLUEFISH
BLUEFISHES
BLUEGILL
BLUEGOWN
BLUEGRASS
BLUEGUM
BLUEHEARTS
BLUEING
BLUEISH
BLUEJACK
BLUEJACKET
BLUEJOINT
BLUELEGS
BLUELINE
BLUENESS
BLUENOSE
BLUENOSED
BLUEPOINT
BLUEPRINT
BLUEPRINTER
BLUER
BLUES
BLUESIDES
BLUEST
BLUESTEM
BLUESTOCKING
BLUESTONE
BLUESTONER
BLUET
BLUETICK
BLUETONGUE
BLUETOP
BLUETOPS
BLUEWEED
BLUEWING
BLUEWOOD
BLUEY
BLUEYS
BLUFF
BLUFFED
BLUFFER
BLUFFING
BLUFFLY
BLUFFNESS
BLUFFY
BLUFTER
BLUGGY
BLUID
BLUING
BLUISH
BLUISHNESS
BLUISNESS
BLUME
BLUMED
BLUMING
BLUNDER
BLUNDERBUSS
BLUNDERED
BLUNDERER
BLUNDERHEAD
BLUNDERING
BLUNDERINGLY
BLUNGE
BLUNGED
BLUNGER
BLUNGING
BLUNK
BLUNKER
BLUNKET
BLUNKS
BLUNT
BLUNTED
BLUNTER
BLUNTIE
BLUNTISH
BLUNTISHNESS
BLUNTLY
BLUNTNESS
BLUP
BLUR
BLURB
BLURBIST
BLURRED
BLURREDNESS
BLURRER
BLURRING
BLURRY
BLURT
BLUSH
BLUSHED
BLUSHER
BLUSHET
BLUSHFUL
BLUSHFULLY
BLUSHFULNESS
BLUSHINESS
BLUSHING
BLUSHINGLY
BLUSHT
BLUSHWORT
BLUSHY
BLUSTER
BLUSTERATION
BLUSTERED
BLUSTERER
BLUSTERING
BLUSTERINGLY
BLUSTEROUS
BLUSTEROUSLY
BLUSTERY
BLY
BLYPE
BO
BOA
BOAR
BOARD
BOARDED
BOARDER
BOARDING
BOARDINGHOUSE
BOARDLY
BOARDMAN
BOARDS
BOARDWALK
BOARDY
BOARFISH
BOARFISHES
BOARHOUND
BOARISH
BOARISHLY
BOARISHNESS
BOARS
BOART
BOARWOOD
BOAS
BOAST
BOASTER
BOASTFUL
BOASTFULLY
BOASTFULNESS
BOASTING
BOASTINGLY
BOAT
BOATABLE
BOATAGE
BOATBILL
BOATBUILDER
BOATBUILDING
BOATER
BOATHOOK
BOATHOUSE
BOATING
BOATION
BOATKEEPER
BOATLIP
BOATLOAD
BOATLOADER
BOATLOADING
BOATMAN
BOATMASTER
BOATMEN
BOATOWNER
BOATS
BOATSETTER
BOATSHOP
BOATSIDE
BOATSWAIN
BOATTAIL
BOATWRIGHT
BOB
BOBA
BOBAC
BOBACHE
BOBACHEE
BOBANCE
BOBBED
BOBBEJAAN
BOBBER
BOBBERIES
BOBBERY
BOBBIE
BOBBIES
BOBBIN
BOBBINER
BOBBINET
BOBBING
BOBBINS
BOBBISH
BOBBISHLY
BOBBLE
BOBBLED
BOBBLING
BOBBY
BOBBYSOXER
BOBCAT
BOBCATS
BOBCOAT
BOBECHE
BOBFLIES
BOBFLY
BOBIERRITE
BOBIZATION
BOBJEROM
BOBLET
BOBO
BOBOLINK
BOBOOTI
BOBOTEE
BOBOTIE
BOBSLED
BOBSLEDDED
BOBSLEDDING
BOBSLEIGH
BOBSTAY
BOBTAIL
BOBTAILED
BOBWHITE
BOBWOOD
BOCA
BOCACCIO
BOCAGE
BOCAL
BOCAN
BOCARDO
BOCASINE
BOCCA
BOCCALE
BOCCARELLA
BOCCARO
BOCCE
BOCCIE
BOCCONIA
BOCE
BOCHE
BOCHER
BOCHISM
BOCHUR
BOCK
BOCKEREL
BOCKERET
BOCKING
BOCO
BOCON
BOCOR
BOCOY
BOD
BODACH
BODACIOUS
BODACIOUSLY
BODAI
BODDAGH
BODDLE
BODE
BODED
BODEFUL
BODEGA
BODEGON
BODEMENT
BODEN
BODER
BODEWASH
BODEWORD
BODGE
BODGER
BODGERY
BODHI
BODHISAT
BODHISATTVA
BODHISATTWA
BODICE
BODICED
BODIED
BODIER
BODIERON
BODIES
BODIKIN
BODILESS
BODILESSNESS
BODILY
BODIMENT
BODING
BODINGLY
BODKIN
BODLE
BODOCK
BODONID
BODRAGE
BODSTICK
BODWORD
BODY
BODYBUILDER
BODYCHECK
BODYGUARD
BODYING
BODYKINS
BODYMAKER
BODYMAKING
BODYPLATE
BODYSHIRT
BODYWOOD
BODYWORK
BOE
BOEA
BOEG
BOEOTARCH
BOES
BOFF
BOFFIN
BOFFOLA
BOG
BOGA
BOGACH
BOGAN
BOGATYR
BOGBEAN
BOGBERRIES
BOGBERRY
BOGET
BOGEY
BOGEYMAN
BOGEYS
BOGFERN
BOGGARD
BOGGART
BOGGED
BOGGIER
BOGGIEST
BOGGIN
BOGGINESS
BOGGING
BOGGISH
BOGGISHNESS
BOGGLE
BOGGLEBO
BOGGLED
BOGGLER
BOGGLING
BOGGLISH
BOGGY
BOGHOLE
BOGIE
BOGIEMAN
BOGIER
BOGIES
BOGLAND
BOGLANDER
BOGLE
BOGLET
BOGMAN
BOGMIRE
BOGO
BOGONG
BOGOTANA
BOGSUCKER
BOGTROT
BOGTROTTER
BOGTROTTING
BOGUE
BOGUM
BOGUS
BOGWAY
BOGWOOD
BOGWORT
BOGY
BOH
BOHAWN
BOHEA
BOHIO
BOHMITE
BOHO
BOHOR
BOHORA

BOHUNK
BOID
BOIGID
BOIL
BOILDOWN
BOILED
BOILER
BOILERMAKER
BOILERY
BOILING
BOILOVER
BOILY
BOINA
BOIS
BOISSEAU
BOISSEAUX
BOIST
BOISTEROUS
BOISTEROUSLY
BOISTOUS
BOISTOUSLY
BOISTOUSNESS
BOITE
BOITHRIN
BOJITE
BOKADAM
BOKARD
BOKARK
BOKE
BOKO
BOKOM
BOLA
BOLAR
BOLAS
BOLBONAC
BOLD
BOLDEN
BOLDER
BOLDEST
BOLDFACE
BOLDHEARTED
BOLDIN
BOLDINE
BOLDLY
BOLDNESS
BOLDO
BOLDOINE
BOLE
BOLECTION
BOLECTIONED
BOLED
BOLEITE
BOLERO
BOLEROS
BOLETACEOUS
BOLETE
BOLETIC
BOLETUS
BOLEWEED
BOLEWORT
BOLIA
BOLICHE
BOLIDE
BOLIMBA
BOLIS
BOLITA
BOLIVAR
BOLIVARES
BOLIVARS
BOLIVIA
BOLIVIANO
BOLIVIANOS
BOLK
BOLL
BOLLARD
BOLLED
BOLLEN
BOLLER
BOLLIES
BOLLING
BOLLIX
BOLLIXED
BOLLIXING
BOLLO
BOLLOCK
BOLLWORM
BOLLY
BOLNE
BOLO
BOLOED
BOLOGNA
BOLOGRAPH
BOLOGRAPHIC
BOLOGRAPHY
BOLOING
BOLOISM
BOLOMAN
BOLOMEN
BOLOMETER
BOLOMETRIC
BOLONEY
BOLOROOT
BOLOS
BOLSA
BOLSHEVIK
BOLSHEVISM
BOLSHEVIST
BOLSHEVIZE
BOLSHEVIZED
BOLSHEVIZING
BOLSHIE
BOLSON
BOLSTER
BOLSTERED
BOLSTERER
BOLSTERING
BOLSTERWORK
BOLT
BOLTAGE
BOLTANT
BOLTEL
BOLTER
BOLTHEAD
BOLTHEADER
BOLTHEADING
BOLTI
BOLTIN
BOLTING
BOLTINGS
BOLTONIA
BOLTONITE
BOLTROPE
BOLTSTRAKE
BOLTY
BOLUS
BOLUSES
BOM
BOMA
BOMB
BOMBARD
BOMBARDE
BOMBARDELLE
BOMBARDER
BOMBARDIER
BOMBARDMAN
BOMBARDMEN
BOMBARDMENT
BOMBARDON
BOMBARDS
BOMBASINE
BOMBAST
BOMBASTER
BOMBASTIC
BOMBASTICAL
BOMBASTICALLY
BOMBASTRY
BOMBAZET
BOMBAZETTE
BOMBAZINE
BOMBE
BOMBED
BOMBER
BOMBERNICKEL
BOMBICCITE
BOMBILATE
BOMBILATION
BOMBILLA
BOMBINATE
BOMBINATION
BOMBLE
BOMBLINE
BOMBO
BOMBOLA
BOMBONNE
BOMBOUS
BOMBPROOF
BOMBS
BOMBSHELL
BOMBSIGHT
BOMBYCID
BOMBYCIFORM
BOMBYCINE
BOMBYX
BOMOS
BON
BONA
BONACE
BONACI
BONAGH
BONAGHT
BONAILIE
BONAIR
BONAIRE
BONAIRLY
BONAIRNESS
BONALLY
BONAMANO
BONANG
BONANZA
BONAO
BONASSUS
BONASUS
BONAUGHT
BONAV
BONAVIST
BONBON
BONBONNIERE
BONCE
BONCHIEF
BOND
BONDAGE
BONDAGER
BONDAR
BONDED
BONDER
BONDERMAN
BONDFOLK
BONDHOLDER
BONDHOLDING
BONDIEUSERIE
BONDING
BONDLAND
BONDMAID
BONDMAN
BONDMEN
BONDMINDER
BONDOC
BONDON
BONDSERVANT
BONDSHIP
BONDSLAVE
BONDSMAN
BONDSMEN
BONDSTONE
BONDSWOMAN
BONDUC
BONDUCNUT
BONDWOMAN
BONDWOMEN
BONE
BONEACHE
BONEBLACK
BONEBREAKER
BONED
BONEDOG
BONEEN
BONEFISH
BONEHEAD
BONEHEADED
BONELESS
BONELESSLY
BONELESSNESS
BONELET
BONER
BONES
BONESET
BONESETTER
BONESETTING
BONESHAKER
BONESHAVE
BONESHAW
BONETAIL
BONETE
BONEWOOD
BONEWORK
BONEWORT
BONEYARD
BONFIRE
BONG
BONGA
BONGAR
BONGO
BONGOS
BONGRACE
BONHOMIE
BONHOMMIE
BONIATA
BONIER
BONIEST
BONIFACE
BONIFICATION
BONIFORM
BONIFY
BONINESS
BONING
BONINITE
BONITA
BONITARIAN
BONITARY
BONITO
BONITOES
BONITOS
BONITY
BONK
BONKA
BONNAZ
BONNE
BONNET
BONNETED
BONNETING
BONNETMAN
BONNETMEN
BONNETS
BONNIBEL
BONNIE
BONNIER
BONNIEST
BONNILY
BONNINESS
BONNIVE
BONNOCK
BONNY
BONNYCLABBER
BONNYVIS
BONSAI
BONSER
BONSPELL
BONSPIEL
BONTE
BONTEBOK
BONTEBOKS
BONTEE
BONUM
BONUS
BONUSES
BONXIE
BONY
BONYFISH
BONYTAIL
BONZA
BONZE
BONZER
BONZERY
BONZIAN
BOO
BOOB
BOOBERY
BOOBIES
BOOBILY
BOOBOO
BOOBOOK
BOOBOOS
BOOBY
BOOBYALLA
BOOD
BOODIE
BOODLE
BOODLED
BOODLER
BOODLING
BOODY
BOOED
BOOER
BOOF
BOOGER
BOOGERMAN
BOOGEYMAN
BOOGIE
BOOGUM
BOOH
BOOHOO
BOOHOOED
BOOHOOING
BOOHOOS
BOOING
BOOJUM
BOOK
BOOKBINDER
BOOKBINDERIES
BOOKBINDERY
BOOKBINDING
BOOKBOARD
BOOKCASE
BOOKCASES
BOOKCRAFT
BOOKDEALER
BOOKED
BOOKEND
BOOKER
BOOKERY
BOOKFAIR
BOOKFOLD
BOOKHOLDER
BOOKIE
BOOKING

BOOKISH
BOOKISHLY
BOOKISHNESS
BOOKIT
BOOKKEEPER
BOOKKEEPING
BOOKLAND
BOOKLEAR
BOOKLESS
BOOKLET
BOOKLIFT
BOOKLORE
BOOKLOVER
BOOKMAKER
BOOKMAKING
BOOKMAN
BOOKMARK
BOOKMARKER
BOOKMATE
BOOKMEN
BOOKMOBILE
BOOKMONGER
BOOKPLATE
BOOKPRESS
BOOKRACK
BOOKREST
BOOKROOM
BOOKS
BOOKSELLER
BOOKSELLERISH
BOOKSELLERISM
BOOKSELLING
BOOKSHELF
BOOKSHELVES
BOOKSHOP
BOOKSTACK
BOOKSTALL
BOOKSTAND
BOOKSTORE
BOOKSY
BOOKWORK
BOOKWORM
BOOKWRIGHT
BOOKY
BOOL
BOOLEY
BOOLEYS
BOOLIES
BOOLY
BOOLYA
BOOM
BOOMAGE
BOOMAH
BOOMBOAT
BOOMDAS
BOOMER
BOOMERANG
BOOMINESS
BOOMING
BOOMINGLY
BOOMKIN
BOOMLET
BOOMORAH
BOOMSLANG
BOOMSLANGE
BOOMSTER
BOOMTOWN
BOOMY
BOON
BOONDOCK
BOONDOCKS
BOONDOGGLE
BOONDOGGLED
BOONDOGGLER
BOONDOGGLING
BOONG
BOONGARY
BOONK
BOOPIS
BOOR
BOORDLY
BOORISH
BOORISHLY
BOORISHNESS
BOORT
BOOS
BOOSE
BOOSIES
BOOST
BOOSTER
BOOSY
BOOT
BOOTBLACK
BOOTBOY
BOOTED
BOOTEE
BOOTER
BOOTERIES
BOOTERY
BOOTH
BOOTHAGE
BOOTHALE
BOOTHEEL
BOOTHER
BOOTHITE
BOOTHOLDER
BOOTHOSE
BOOTHS
BOOTIE
BOOTIED
BOOTIES
BOOTIKIN
BOOTING
BOOTJACK
BOOTJACKS
BOOTLACE
BOOTLE
BOOTLEG
BOOTLEGGED
BOOTLEGGER
BOOTLEGGING
BOOTLESS
BOOTLESSLY
BOOTLESSNESS
BOOTLICK
BOOTLICKER
BOOTMAKER
BOOTMAKING
BOOTMAN
BOOTS
BOOTSTRAP
BOOTY
BOOZE
BOOZED
BOOZER
BOOZILY
BOOZINESS
BOOZING
BOOZY
BOP
BOPEEP
BOPPED
BOPPER
BOPPING
BOPPIST
BOPSTER
BOPYRID
BOPYRIDIAN
BOR
BORA
BORACHIO
BORACIC
BORACIFEROUS
BORACITE
BORACOUS
BORAGE
BORAK
BORAL
BORANE
BORASCA
BORASCO
BORASQUE
BORATE
BORATED
BORAX
BORAZON
BORD
BORDAGE
BORDAR
BORDEL
BORDELLO
BORDER
BORDEREAU
BORDEREAUX
BORDERED
BORDERER
BORDERING
BORDERISM
BORDERLAND
BORDERLANDER
BORDERLINE
BORDRAG
BORDROOM
BORDUN
BORDURE
BORDURED
BORE
BOREAD
BOREAL
BOREALIS
BOREAN
BORECOLE
BORED
BOREDOM
BOREE
BOREEN
BOREGAT
BOREHOLE
BORELE
BORER
BORESOME
BORG
BORGH
BORGHI
BORGO
BORIC
BORICKITE
BORIDE
BORINE
BORING
BORINGLY
BORINGNESS
BORISH
BORISM
BORITH
BORITIES
BORITY
BORIZE
BORLASE
BORLEY
BORN
BORNANE
BORNE
BORNEOL
BORNING
BORNITE
BORNITIC
BORNYL
BORO
BOROCALCITE
BOROLANITE
BORON
BORONIC
BOROPHENOL
BOROSILICATE
BOROTUNGSTIC
BOROUGH
BORRACHA
BORRASCA
BORREL
BORRELIA
BORROW
BORROWED
BORROWER
BORROWING
BORSCH
BORSCHT
BORSHOLDER
BORSHT
BORSTAL
BORSTALL
BORT
BORTSCH
BORTZ
BORUN
BORWORT
BORYL
BORZOI
BOS
BOSA
BOSAL
BOSC
BOSCAGE
BOSCH
BOSCHBOK
BOSCHVARK
BOSCHVELD
BOSE
BOSER
BOSEY
BOSH
BOSHBOK
BOSHER
BOSHES
BOSHVARK
BOSK
BOSKAGE
BOSKER
BOSKET
BOSKINESS
BOSKY
BOSOM
BOSOMED
BOSOMER
BOSOMY
BOSON
BOSPORUS
BOSQUE
BOSQUET
BOSS
BOSSAGE
BOSSDOM
BOSSE
BOSSED
BOSSELATED
BOSSELATION
BOSSER
BOSSET
BOSSIER
BOSSIES
BOSSIEST
BOSSING
BOSSISM
BOSSY
BOST
BOSTAL
BOSTANGI
BOSTANJI
BOSTHOON
BOSTON
BOSTONITE
BOSTRYCHID
BOSTRYCHOID
BOSTRYX
BOSUN
BOT
BOTA
BOTANIC
BOTANICAL
BOTANICALLY
BOTANICS
BOTANIES
BOTANIST
BOTANIZE
BOTANIZED
BOTANIZER
BOTANIZING
BOTANY
BOTARGO
BOTARGOS
BOTCH
BOTCHED
BOTCHEDLY
BOTCHER
BOTCHERLY
BOTCHERY
BOTCHES
BOTCHIER
BOTCHIEST
BOTCHILY
BOTCHINESS
BOTCHING
BOTCHKA
BOTCHY
BOTE
BOTELER
BOTELLA
BOTEN
BOTEROL
BOTEROLL
BOTETE
BOTFLIES
BOTFLY
BOTH
BOTHER
BOTHERATION
BOTHERED
BOTHERER
BOTHERHEADED
BOTHERING
BOTHERMENT
BOTHERSOME
BOTHIE
BOTHIES
BOTHRENCHYMA
BOTHRIA
BOTHRIUM
BOTHROI
BOTHROPIC
BOTHROS
BOTHSIDED
BOTHWAY
BOTHY
BOTONE
BOTONEE
BOTONG
BOTONY
BOTOYAN
BOTRY
BOTRYOGEN
BOTRYOID
BOTRYOIDAL
BOTRYOIDALLY
BOTRYOLITE
BOTRYOMYCOMA

BOTRYOPTERID
BOTRYOSE
BOTS
BOTT
BOTTEGA
BOTTEGHE
BOTTEKIN
BOTTIER
BOTTINE
BOTTLE
BOTTLEBIRD
BOTTLED
BOTTLEFLOWER
BOTTLEHEAD
BOTTLEHOLDER
BOTTLEMAKER
BOTTLEMAKING
BOTTLEMAN
BOTTLENECK
BOTTLENEST
BOTTLENOSE
BOTTLER
BOTTLESTONE
BOTTLING
BOTTOM
BOTTOMED
BOTTOMER
BOTTOMING
BOTTOMLAND
BOTTOMLESS
BOTTOMLESSLY
BOTTOMMOST
BOTTOMRIED
BOTTOMRY
BOTTOMRYING
BOTTOMS
BOTTSTICK
BOTTU
BOTULIFORM
BOTULIN
BOTULINUS
BOTULISM
BOTULISMUS
BOUBA
BOUBAS
BOUBOU
BOUCAN
BOUCH
BOUCHAL
BOUCHALEEN
BOUCHARDE
BOUCHE
BOUCHEE
BOUCHER
BOUCHERISM
BOUCHERIZE
BOUCHETTE
BOUCHON
BOUCHONS
BOUCLE
BOUD
BOUDERIE
BOUDIN
BOUDOIR
BOUDOIRESQUE
BOUET
BOUFFANCY
BOUFFANT
BOUFFANTE
BOUFFE
BOUFFON
BOUGAR
BOUGE
BOUGEE
BOUGERON
BOUGET
BOUGH
BOUGHED
BOUGHPOT
BOUGHT
BOUGHTEN
BOUGHY
BOUGIE
BOUILLI
BOUILLON
BOUILLONE
BOUK
BOUKIT
BOUL
BOULANGERITE
BOULDER
BOULDERHEAD
BOULDERING
BOULDERS
BOULDERY
BOULE
BOULEUTERIA
BOULEUTERION
BOULEVARD
BOULEVARDIER
BOULIMIA
BOULLE
BOULT
BOULTEL
BOULTER
BOULTERER
BOUN
BOUNCE
BOUNCEABLE
BOUNCEABLY
BOUNCED
BOUNCER
BOUNCIER
BOUNCIEST
BOUNCILY
BOUNCING
BOUNCINGLY
BOUNCY
BOUND
BOUNDARIES
BOUNDARY
BOUNDED
BOUNDEN
BOUNDER
BOUNDING
BOUNDINGLY
BOUNDLESS
BOUNDLESSLY
BOUNDLY
BOUNDS
BOUNTEOUS
BOUNTEOUSLY
BOUNTIED
BOUNTIES
BOUNTIFUL
BOUNTIFULLY
BOUNTITH
BOUNTREE
BOUNTY
BOUQUET
BOUQUETIERE
BOUQUINISTE
BOURASQUE
BOURBON
BOURBONIZE
BOURD
BOURDER
BOURDON
BOURETTE
BOURG
BOURGADE
BOURGEOIS
BOURGEOISE
BOURGEOISIE
BOURGEON
BOURI
BOURN
BOURNE
BOURNONITE
BOUROCK
BOURRAN
BOURRE
BOURREAU
BOURREE
BOURRELET
BOURSE
BOURTREE
BOUSE
BOUSED
BOUSER
BOUSING
BOUSY
BOUT
BOUTADE
BOUTEFEU
BOUTELL
BOUTIQUE
BOUTO
BOUTON
BOUTONNIERE
BOUTRE
BOUTYLKA
BOUW
BOVARISM
BOVARYSM
BOVATE
BOVENLAND
BOVICIDE
BOVICULTURE
BOVID
BOVIFORM
BOVINE
BOVINELY
BOVINITY
BOVO
BOVOID
BOVOVACCINE
BOW
BOWABLE
BOWBACK
BOWBELLS
BOWBENT
BOWBOY
BOWDEN
BOWDITCH
BOWDLERISM
BOWDLERIZE
BOWDLERIZED
BOWDLERIZING
BOWED
BOWEL
BOWELED
BOWELING
BOWELLED
BOWELLING
BOWELS
BOWENITE
BOWER
BOWERBIRD
BOWERIES
BOWERLY
BOWERMAIDEN
BOWERMAY
BOWERWOMAN
BOWERY
BOWET
BOWFIN
BOWGRACE
BOWHEAD
BOWIE
BOWIEFUL
BOWING
BOWINGLY
BOWK
BOWKAIL
BOWKNOT
BOWL
BOWLA
BOWLDER
BOWLDERHEAD
BOWLDERING
BOWLDERY
BOWLED
BOWLEG
BOWLEGGED
BOWLER
BOWLIN
BOWLINE
BOWLING
BOWLMAKER
BOWLS
BOWLY
BOWMAKER
BOWMAKING
BOWMAN
BOWMEN
BOWN
BOWPIN
BOWPOT
BOWRALITE
BOWS
BOWSE
BOWSER
BOWSERY
BOWSHOT
BOWSIE
BOWSMAN
BOWSPRIT
BOWSSEN
BOWSTAVE
BOWSTRING
BOWSTRINGED
BOWSTRINGING
BOWSTRUNG
BOWTELL
BOWWOMAN
BOWWOOD
BOWWORT
BOWWOW
BOWWOWS
BOWYANG
BOWYER
BOX
BOXBERRIES
BOXBERRY
BOXBOARD
BOXBUSH
BOXCAR
BOXCARS
BOXEN
BOXER
BOXES
BOXFISH
BOXHAUL
BOXHEAD
BOXHOLDER
BOXING
BOXINGS
BOXKEEPER
BOXLIKE
BOXMAN
BOXROOM
BOXTHORN
BOXTREE
BOXTY
BOXWALLAH
BOXWOOD
BOXWORK
BOXY
BOY
BOYANG
BOYAR
BOYARD
BOYARDISM
BOYARISM
BOYAU
BOYAUS
BOYAUX
BOYCOTT
BOYCOTTAGE
BOYCOTTER
BOYER
BOYFRIEND
BOYHOOD
BOYISH
BOYISHLY
BOYISHNESS
BOYISM
BOYLA
BOYO
BOYSENBERRIES
BOYSENBERRY
BOZA
BOZAH
BOZAL
BOZINE
BOZO
BOZZE
BOZZETTO
BRA
BRAB
BRABAGIOUS
BRABANT
BRABBLE
BRABBLED
BRABBLEMENT
BRABBLER
BRABBLING
BRACA
BRACAE
BRACCAE
BRACCATE
BRACCIALE
BRACCIANITE
BRACCIO
BRACE
BRACED
BRACELET
BRACELETED
BRACER
BRACERO
BRACEROS
BRACES
BRACH
BRACHE
BRACHELYTROUS
BRACHERER
BRACHERING
BRACHET
BRACHIA
BRACHIAL
BRACHIALIS
BRACHIATE
BRACHIATED
BRACHIATING
BRACHIATION
BRACHIATOR
BRACHIOLARIA
BRACHIOPOD
BRACHIOSAUR
BRACHIUM
BRACHYAXIS
BRACHYCEPHAL
BRACHYCEPHALES
BRACHYCEPHALI

BRACHYCEROUS
BRACHYCRANIC
BRACHYDACTYL
BRACHYDONT
BRACHYGRAPHY
BRACHYLOGY
BRACHYPODINE
BRACHYPODOUS
BRACHYSKELIC
BRACHYSM
BRACHYTIC
BRACHYTMEMA
BRACHYTYPOUS
BRACHYURAL
BRACHYURAN
BRACHYURE
BRACHYUROUS
BRACING
BRACINGLY
BRACINGNESS
BRACK
BRACKED
BRACKEN
BRACKENED
BRACKER
BRACKET
BRACKETING
BRACKING
BRACKISH
BRACKISHNESS
BRACKMARD
BRACKY
BRACONID
BRACONNIERE
BRACOZZO
BRACT
BRACTEA
BRACTEAL
BRACTEATE
BRACTED
BRACTEIFORM
BRACTEOLATE
BRACTEOLE
BRACTEOSE
BRACTLET
BRAD
BRADAWL
BRADDED
BRADDING
BRADENHEAD
BRADOON
BRADSOT
BRADYCARDIA
BRADYCARDIC
BRADYCROTIC
BRADYPOD
BRADYPODE
BRADYPODOID
BRADYSEISM
BRADYSEISMAL
BRADYSEISMIC
BRADYTELY
BRAE
BRAEFACE
BRAEHEAD
BRAEMAN
BRAES
BRAESIDE
BRAG
BRAGAS
BRAGER
BRAGGADOCIAN
BRAGGADOCIO
BRAGGADOCIOS
BRAGGART
BRAGGARTISM
BRAGGARTLY
BRAGGARTRY
BRAGGED
BRAGGER
BRAGGERY
BRAGGET
BRAGGING
BRAGGINGLY
BRAGGISH
BRAGGISHLY
BRAGGITE
BRAGGLE
BRAGGY
BRAGITE
BRAGLY
BRAGOZZO
BRAGUETTE
BRAGWORT
BRAHMA
BRAHMACHARI
BRAID
BRAIDED
BRAIDER
BRAIDING
BRAIES
BRAIL
BRAILLE
BRAILLER
BRAILS
BRAIN
BRAINER
BRAINFAG
BRAINGE
BRAINIER
BRAINIEST
BRAINILY
BRAININESS
BRAINISH
BRAINLESS
BRAINLESSLY
BRAINPAN
BRAINPOWER
BRAINS
BRAINSICK
BRAINSICKLY
BRAINSTEM
BRAINSTORM
BRAINWASH
BRAINWASHING
BRAINWOOD
BRAINWORK
BRAINWORKER
BRAINY
BRAIRD
BRAIRDED
BRAIRDING
BRAIREAU
BRAIRO
BRAISE
BRAISED
BRAISING
BRAIZE
BRAK
BRAKE
BRAKEAGE
BRAKED
BRAKEHAND
BRAKEHEAD
BRAKELESS
BRAKEMAKER
BRAKEMAN
BRAKEMEN
BRAKER
BRAKESMAN
BRAKIE
BRAKIER
BRAKIEST
BRAKING
BRAKY
BRAMBLE
BRAMBLEBERRIES
BRAMBLEBERRY
BRAMBLEBUSH
BRAMBLED
BRAMBLIER
BRAMBLIEST
BRAMBLING
BRAMBLY
BRAME
BRAN
BRANCARD
BRANCARDIER
BRANCH
BRANCHAGE
BRANCHED
BRANCHER
BRANCHERY
BRANCHES
BRANCHIA
BRANCHIAE
BRANCHIAL
BRANCHIATE
BRANCHIER
BRANCHIER
BRANCHIEST
BRANCHIFORM
BRANCHIHYAL
BRANCHING
BRANCHIOMERE
BRANCHIOPOD
BRANCHIOSAUR
BRANCHIREME
BRANCHIUROUS
BRANCHLET
BRANCHLING
BRANCHMAN
BRANCHSTAND
BRANCHWAY
BRANCHY
BRAND
BRANDED
BRANDER
BRANDERING
BRANDIED
BRANDIES
BRANDING
BRANDISE
BRANDISH
BRANDISHER
BRANDISITE
BRANDLE
BRANDLIN
BRANDLING
BRANDRETH
BRANDS
BRANDSOLDER
BRANDY
BRANDYBALL
BRANDYING
BRANDYMAN
BRANDYWINE
BRANGLE
BRANGLED
BRANGLEMENT
BRANGLER
BRANGLING
BRANIAL
BRANK
BRANKIE
BRANKS
BRANKURSINE
BRANKY
BRANLE
BRANNER
BRANNERITE
BRANNIGAN
BRANNY
BRANSLE
BRANT
BRANTAIL
BRANTNESS
BRAROW
BRAS
BRASERO
BRASEROS
BRASH
BRASHIER
BRASHIEST
BRASHINESS
BRASHLY
BRASHNESS
BRASHY
BRASIER
BRASILETE
BRASILETTO
BRASQUE
BRASQUED
BRASQUING
BRASS
BRASSAGE
BRASSARD
BRASSART
BRASSBOUND
BRASSBOUNDER
BRASSE
BRASSER
BRASSERIE
BRASSES
BRASSEY
BRASSIDIC
BRASSIE
BRASSIER
BRASSIERE
BRASSIES
BRASSIEST
BRASSILY
BRASSINESS
BRASSY
BRAT
BRATCHET
BRATLING
BRATSTVA
BRATTACH
BRATTICE
BRATTICED
BRATTICER
BRATTICING
BRATTISH
BRATTLE
BRATTLED
BRATTLING
BRATWURST
BRAUL
BRAULA
BRAUNA
BRAUNITE
BRAVA
BRAVADE
BRAVADO
BRAVADOED
BRAVADOES
BRAVADOING
BRAVADOS
BRAVE
BRAVEHEARTED
BRAVELY
BRAVENESS
BRAVER
BRAVERIES
BRAVERY
BRAVEST
BRAVING
BRAVISSIMO
BRAVO
BRAVOES
BRAVOITE
BRAVOS
BRAVURA
BRAW
BRAWL
BRAWLER
BRAWLING
BRAWLINGLY
BRAWLY
BRAWN
BRAWNED
BRAWNEDNESS
BRAWNER
BRAWNIER
BRAWNIEST
BRAWNINESS
BRAWNY
BRAWS
BRAXIES
BRAXY
BRAY
BRAYED
BRAYER
BRAYERA
BRAYERIN
BRAYING
BRAYSTONE
BRAZA
BRAZE
BRAZED
BRAZEN
BRAZENED
BRAZENFACE
BRAZENFACED
BRAZENING
BRAZENLY
BRAZENNESS
BRAZER
BRAZERA
BRAZIER
BRAZIERY
BRAZIL
BRAZILEIN
BRAZILETTE
BRAZILITE
BRAZILWOOD
BRAZING
BREA
BREACH
BREACHER
BREACHY
BREAD
BREADBASKET
BREADBERRY
BREADBOARD
BREADBOX
BREADEARNER
BREADEARNING
BREADED
BREADEN
BREADFRUIT
BREADMAKER
BREADMAKING
BREADMAN
BREADNUT
BREADROOT
BREADS
BREADSELLER
BREADSTITCH
BREADSTUFF
BREADTH
BREADTHRIDERS
BREADTHWAYS
BREADTHWISE

BREADWINNER
BREADWINNING
BREAGHE
BREAK
BREAKABLE
BREAKABLY
BREAKAGE
BREAKAWAY
BREAKAX
BREAKAXE
BREAKBACK
BREAKBONE
BREAKBONES
BREAKDOWN
BREAKER
BREAKERMAN
BREAKERMEN
BREAKFAST
BREAKFASTER
BREAKFRONT
BREAKING
BREAKNECK
BREAKOFF
BREAKOUT
BREAKOVER
BREAKS
BREAKSTONE
BREAKTHROUGH
BREAKUP
BREAKWATER
BREAM
BREAMS
BREAN
BREARDS
BREAST
BREASTBAND
BREASTBEAM
BREASTBONE
BREASTED
BREASTER
BREASTHOOK
BREASTING
BREASTMARK
BREASTPIECE
BREASTPIN
BREASTPLATE
BREASTPLOUGH
BREASTPLOW
BREASTRAIL
BREASTROPE
BREASTS
BREASTSUMMER
BREASTWEED
BREASTWISE
BREASTWOOD
BREASTWORK
BREATH
BREATHABLE
BREATHE
BREATHED
BREATHER
BREATHIER
BREATHIEST
BREATHING
BREATHLESS
BREATHLESSLY
BREATHLESSNESS
BREATHSELLER
BREATHTAKING
BREATHY
BREBA
BRECCIA
BRECCIAL
BRECCIATED
BRECCIATION
BRECHAM
BRECHAN
BRECK
BRED
BREDBERGITE
BREDE
BREDESTITCH
BREDI
BREDSTITCH
BREE
BREECH
BREECHBLOCK
BREECHCLOTH
BREECHCLOUT
BREECHED
BREECHES
BREECHING
BREECHLOADER
BREECHLOADING
BREED
BREEDBATE
BREEDER
BREEDING
BREEDY
BREEKS
BREEKUMS
BREEM
BREENGE
BREER
BREEZE
BREEZED
BREEZEWAY
BREEZIER
BREEZIEST
BREEZILY
BREEZINESS
BREEZING
BREEZY
BREGMA
BREGMATA
BREGMATE
BREGMATIC
BREHON
BREI
BREIRD
BREISLAKITE
BREITHAUPTITE
BRELAN
BRELOQUE
BREME
BREMELY
BREMENESS
BREN
BRENNAGE
BRENNSCHLUSS
BRENT
BREPHIC
BRER
BREST
BRET
BRETELLE
BRETESSE
BRETH
BRETHEL
BRETHREN
BRETT
BREVA
BREVE
BREVET
BREVETCIES
BREVETCY
BREVETE
BREVETED
BREVETING
BREVETTED
BREVETTING
BREVIARIES
BREVIARY
BREVIATE
BREVIATURE
BREVICAUDATE
BREVICIPITID
BREVIER
BREVIFOLIATE
BREVIGER
BREVILINGUAL
BREVILOQUENT
BREVIPED
BREVIPEN
BREVIPENNATE
BREVIRADIATE
BREVIROSTRAL
BREVIT
BREVITIES
BREVITY
BREW
BREWAGE
BREWED
BREWER
BREWERIES
BREWERY
BREWHOUSE
BREWING
BREWIS
BREWMASTER
BREWSTER
BREWSTERITE
BREY
BRIAR
BRIARBERRY
BRIARED
BRIARROOT
BRIARWOOD
BRIARY
BRIBABLE
BRIBE
BRIBED
BRIBEE
BRIBEGIVER
BRIBEGIVING
BRIBEMONGER
BRIBER
BRIBERIES
BRIBERY
BRIBETAKER
BRIBETAKING
BRIBEWORTHY
BRIBING
BRICHETTE
BRICK
BRICKBAT
BRICKBATTED
BRICKBATTING
BRICKED
BRICKEN
BRICKFIELDER
BRICKIER
BRICKIEST
BRICKING
BRICKKILN
BRICKLAYING
BRICKLE
BRICKLENESS
BRICKLINER
BRICKLINING
BRICKLY
BRICKMAKER
BRICKMAKING
BRICKS
BRICKSET
BRICKSETTER
BRICKTIMBER
BRICKWORK
BRICKY
BRICKYARD
BRICOLE
BRIDAL
BRIDALE
BRIDALER
BRIDALLY
BRIDALTY
BRIDE
BRIDEBED
BRIDEBOWL
BRIDECAKE
BRIDECHAMBER
BRIDECUP
BRIDEGOD
BRIDEGROOM
BRIDEKNOT
BRIDELACE
BRIDELY
BRIDEMAIDEN
BRIDEMAN
BRIDESMAID
BRIDESMAIDING
BRIDESMAN
BRIDESMEN
BRIDESTAKE
BRIDEWAIN
BRIDEWEED
BRIDEWELL
BRIDEWORT
BRIDGE
BRIDGEABLE
BRIDGEBOARD
BRIDGEBUILDER
BRIDGEBUILDING
BRIDGED
BRIDGEHEAD
BRIDGEKEEPER
BRIDGEMAKER
BRIDGEMAKING
BRIDGEMAN
BRIDGEMASTER
BRIDGEMEN
BRIDGEPOT
BRIDGER
BRIDGETREE
BRIDGEWARD
BRIDGEWAY
BRIDGEWORK
BRIDGING
BRIDLE
BRIDLED
BRIDLEMAN
BRIDLER
BRIDLING
BRIDOON
BRIE
BRIEF
BRIEFCASE
BRIEFED
BRIEFING
BRIEFLESS
BRIEFLESSLY
BRIEFLY
BRIEFNESS
BRIEFS
BRIER
BRIERBERRY
BRIERED
BRIERROOT
BRIERS
BRIERWOOD
BRIERY
BRIEVE
BRIG
BRIGADE
BRIGADED
BRIGADIER
BRIGADING
BRIGALOW
BRIGAND
BRIGANDAGE
BRIGANDER
BRIGANDINE
BRIGANDISH
BRIGANDISHLY
BRIGANDISM
BRIGANTINE
BRIGBOTE
BRIGE
BRIGHT
BRIGHTEN
BRIGHTENER
BRIGHTER
BRIGHTEST
BRIGHTEYES
BRIGHTLY
BRIGHTNESS
BRIGHTS
BRIGHTSMITH
BRIGHTSOME
BRIGHTWORK
BRIGUE
BRIGUED
BRIGUER
BRIGUING
BRIKE
BRILL
BRILLANTE
BRILLIANCE
BRILLIANCY
BRILLIANDEER
BRILLIANT
BRILLIANTINE
BRILLIANTLY
BRILLS
BRIM
BRIMBORION
BRIMBORIUM
BRIMFUL
BRIMFULLY
BRIMFULNESS
BRIMING
BRIMLY
BRIMMED
BRIMMER
BRIMMERED
BRIMMERING
BRIMMING
BRIMMINGLY
BRIMSTONE
BRIMSTONY
BRIN
BRINCE
BRINDED
BRINDISI
BRINDLE
BRINDLED
BRINE
BRINED
BRINER
BRING
BRINGELA
BRINGER
BRINGING
BRINGS
BRINGSEL
BRINIE
BRINIER
BRINIEST
BRININESS
BRINING
BRINISH
BRINJAL
BRINJAREE
BRINJARRIES
BRINJARRY

BRINJAUL
BRINK
BRINKMANSHIP
BRINSELL
BRINSTON
BRINY
BRIO
BRIOCHE
BRIOLET
BRIOLETTE
BRIQUE
BRIQUET
BRIQUETTE
BRIS
BRISANCE
BRISANT
BRISCOLA
BRISE
BRISEMENT
BRISK
BRISKED
BRISKEN
BRISKENED
BRISKENING
BRISKET
BRISKING
BRISKLY
BRISKNESS
BRISKY
BRISLING
BRISQUE
BRISS
BRIST
BRISTLE
BRISTLEBIRD
BRISTLECONE
BRISTLED
BRISTLELIKE
BRISTLER
BRISTLES
BRISTLETAIL
BRISTLEWORT
BRISTLIER
BRISTLIEST
BRISTLINESS
BRISTLING
BRISTLY
BRISURE
BRIT
BRITANNIA
BRITCHEL
BRITCHES
BRITE
BRITH
BRITSKA
BRITT
BRITTEN
BRITTLE
BRITTLEBUSH
BRITTLELY
BRITTLENESS
BRITTLESTEM
BRITTLEWOOD
BRITTLEWORT
BRITTLING
BRITZKA
BRITZSKA
BRIZE
BRIZZ
BROACH
BROACHED
BROACHER
BROACHING
BROAD
BROADACRE
BROADAX
BROADAXE
BROADBILL
BROADBRIM
BROADCAST
BROADCASTED
BROADCASTER
BROADCASTING
BROADCLOTH
BROADEN
BROADENED
BROADENING
BROADEST
BROADGAGE
BROADHEAD
BROADHEARTED
BROADHORN
BROADLEAF
BROADLING
BROADLINGS
BROADLOOM
BROADLY
BROADNESS
BROADPIECE
BROADSHARE
BROADSHEET
BROADSIDE
BROADSWORD
BROADTAIL
BROADWAY
BROADWAYS
BROADWISE
BROB
BROCADE
BROCADED
BROCADING
BROCARD
BROCATEL
BROCATELLE
BROCCOLI
BROCH
BROCHAN
BROCHANT
BROCHANTITE
BROCHE
BROCHETTE
BROCHO
BROCHOPHONY
BROCHT
BROCHURE
BROCK
BROCKAGE
BROCKED
BROCKET
BROCKLE
BROD
BRODDER
BRODE
BRODEE
BRODEKIN
BRODEQUIN
BRODERER
BRODERIE
BRODIE
BRODYAGA
BRODYAGI
BROG
BROGAN
BROGGER
BROGGERITE
BROGGLE
BROGUE
BROGUED
BROGUENEER
BROGUER
BROGUES
BROGUING
BROH
BROIDER
BROIDERED
BROIDERER
BROIDERIES
BROIDERING
BROIDERY
BROIGNE
BROIL
BROILED
BROILER
BROILERY
BROILING
BROKAGE
BROKE
BROKEN
BROKENHEARTED
BROKENLY
BROKENNESS
BROKER
BROKERAGE
BROKERY
BROKES
BROKING
BROLETTI
BROLETTO
BROLGA
BROLL
BROLLIES
BROLLY
BROMA
BROMAL
BROMAMIDE
BROMARGYRITE
BROMATE
BROMATIUM
BROME
BROMEGRASS
BROMELIAD
BROMELIN
BROMELLITE
BROMHIDROSIS
BROMHYDRATE
BROMHYDRIC
BROMIC
BROMID
BROMIDE
BROMIDIC
BROMIDROSIS
BROMIN
BROMINATE
BROMINATED
BROMINATING
BROMINATION
BROMINE
BROMINISM
BROMISM
BROMITE
BROMIZATION
BROMIZE
BROMIZER
BROMLITE
BROMOACETONE
BROMOAURATES
BROMOBENZENE
BROMOCYANID
BROMOCYANIDE
BROMOFORM
BROMOHYDRATE
BROMOHYDRIN
BROMOIL
BROMOIODID
BROMOIODIDE
BROMOIODISM
BROMOIODIZED
BROMOL
BROMOMANIA
BROMOMETRIC
BROMOMETRY
BROMOPICRIN
BROMOPIKRIN
BROMOPROTEIN
BROMOTHYMOL
BROMOUS
BROMPICRIN
BROMTHYMOL
BROMURET
BROMVOEL
BROMVOGEL
BROMYRITE
BRON
BRONC
BRONCHI
BRONCHIA
BRONCHIAL
BRONCHIALLY
BRONCHILOQUY
BRONCHIOCELE
BRONCHIOLAR
BRONCHIOLE
BRONCHITIC
BRONCHITIS
BRONCHO
BRONCHOBUSTER
BRONCHOGENIC
BRONCHOS
BRONCHOSCOPE
BRONCHOSCOPY
BRONCHOTOMY
BRONCHUS
BRONCO
BRONCOBUSTER
BRONCOS
BRONGNIARDITE
BRONTEON
BRONTEPHOBIA
BRONTEUM
BRONTIDE
BRONTIDES
BRONTOGRAM
BRONTOGRAPH
BRONTOLITE
BRONTOLITH
BRONTOLOGY
BRONTOMETER
BRONTOPHOBIA
BRONTOSAUR
BRONTOSAURUS
BRONTOSAURUSES
BRONTOSCOPY
BRONZE
BRONZED
BRONZEN
BRONZER
BRONZESMITH
BRONZEWING
BRONZIFY
BRONZINE
BRONZING
BRONZITE
BRONZITITE
BRONZY
BROO
BROOCH
BROOCHED
BROOCHING
BROOD
BROODED
BROODER
BROODIER
BROODIEST
BROODING
BROODSAC
BROODY
BROOK
BROOKED
BROOKFLOWER
BROOKIE
BROOKIER
BROOKIEST
BROOKING
BROOKITE
BROOKLET
BROOKLIME
BROOKS
BROOKSIDE
BROOKWEED
BROOKY
BROOL
BROOM
BROOMBUSH
BROOMCORN
BROOMER
BROOMMAKER
BROOMMAKING
BROOMRAPE
BROOMROOT
BROOMSHANK
BROOMSTAFF
BROOMSTICK
BROOMSTRAW
BROOMTAIL
BROOMWEED
BROOMWOOD
BROOMWORT
BROOMY
BROON
BROOZLED
BROQUERY
BROQUINEER
BROSE
BROSOT
BROSSE
BROSY
BROT
BROTCHEN
BROTEL
BROTH
BROTHE
BROTHEL
BROTHER
BROTHERED
BROTHERHOOD
BROTHERING
BROTHERLY
BROTHERS
BROTHERWORT
BROTHY
BROTOCRYSTAL
BROTT
BROTULID
BROTULIFORM
BROUD
BROUETTE
BROUGH
BROUGHAM
BROUGHT
BROUHAHA
BROUILLON
BROUZE
BROW
BROWACHE
BROWBAND
BROWBEAT
BROWBEATEN
BROWBEATER
BROWBEATING
BROWBOUND
BROWDEN
BROWED
BROWET
BROWIS
BROWLESS

BROWMAN
BROWN
BROWNBACK
BROWNED
BROWNER
BROWNEST
BROWNIE
BROWNING
BROWNISH
BROWNNESS
BROWNNOSE
BROWNOUT
BROWNPRINT
BROWNSTONE
BROWNTAIL
BROWNTOP
BROWNWEED
BROWNWORT
BROWNY
BROWPIECE
BROWPOST
BROWSE
BROWSED
BROWSER
BROWSING
BROWST
BROWZER
BRUANG
BRUBRU
BRUCELLOSIS
BRUCHID
BRUCIA
BRUCIN
BRUCINA
BRUCINE
BRUCITE
BRUCKLE
BRUCKLED
BRUCKLENESS
BRUET
BRUGH
BRUH
BRUIN
BRUISE
BRUISED
BRUISER
BRUISEWORT
BRUISING
BRUIT
BRUITER
BRUJERIA
BRUJO
BRUKE
BRULEE
BRULOT
BRULYIE
BRULYIEMENT
BRULZIE
BRUM
BRUMAL
BRUMBEE
BRUMBIE
BRUMBIES
BRUMBY
BRUME
BRUMMAGEM
BRUMMER
BRUMMY
BRUMOUS
BRUNCH
BRUNE
BRUNET
BRUNETNESS
BRUNETTE
BRUNETTENESS
BRUNISSURE
BRUNIZEM
BRUNNEOUS
BRUNT
BRUSCUS
BRUSH
BRUSHBALL
BRUSHBIRD
BRUSHBUSH
BRUSHED
BRUSHER
BRUSHES
BRUSHET
BRUSHIER
BRUSHIEST
BRUSHING
BRUSHITE
BRUSHLAND
BRUSHMAKER
BRUSHMAKING
BRUSHMAN
BRUSHMEN
BRUSHOFF
BRUSHUP
BRUSHWOOD
BRUSHWORK
BRUSHY
BRUSK
BRUSQUE
BRUSQUELY
BRUSQUENESS
BRUSQUERIE
BRUSSEL
BRUSTLE
BRUSTLED
BRUSTLING
BRUT
BRUTAL
BRUTALITIES
BRUTALITY
BRUTALIZE
BRUTALIZED
BRUTALIZING
BRUTALLY
BRUTE
BRUTIFIED
BRUTIFY
BRUTIFYING
BRUTING
BRUTISH
BRUTISHLY
BRUTISHNESS
BRUTISM
BRUTTER
BRUXISM
BRUYERE
BRUZZ
BRYACEOUS
BRYNZA
BRYOGENIN
BRYOLOGICAL
BRYOLOGIST
BRYOLOGY
BRYONIA
BRYONIDIN
BRYONIES
BRYONIN
BRYONY
BRYOPHYTE
BRYOPHYTIC
BRYOZOAN
BRYOZOON
BRYOZOUM
BU
BUAL
BUAT
BUAZE
BUB
BUBA
BUBAL
BUBALE
BUBALINE
BUBALIS
BUBAS
BUBBER
BUBBIES
BUBBLE
BUBBLEBOW
BUBBLED
BUBBLER
BUBBLES
BUBBLIER
BUBBLIEST
BUBBLING
BUBBLINGLY
BUBBLY
BUBBY
BUBBYBUSH
BUBINGA
BUBO
BUBOED
BUBOES
BUBONALGIA
BUBONIC
BUBONOCELE
BUBU
BUBUD
BUBUKLE
BUCAN
BUCARE
BUCAYO
BUCCA
BUCCAL
BUCCAN
BUCCANED
BUCCANEER
BUCCANING
BUCCANNED
BUCCANNING
BUCCATE
BUCCHERO
BUCCIN
BUCCINA
BUCCINAE
BUCCINAL
BUCCINATOR
BUCCINATORY
BUCCINIFORM
BUCCINOID
BUCCO
BUCCOLINGUAL
BUCCULA
BUCCULAE
BUCENTAUR
BUCHITE
BUCHNERITE
BUCHONITE
BUCHU
BUCK
BUCKAROO
BUCKASS
BUCKAYRO
BUCKBEAN
BUCKBERRY
BUCKBOARD
BUCKBRUSH
BUCKBUSH
BUCKED
BUCKEEN
BUCKER
BUCKET
BUCKETED
BUCKETEER
BUCKETER
BUCKETING
BUCKETMAKER
BUCKETMAKING
BUCKETMAN
BUCKETY
BUCKEYE
BUCKEYED
BUCKHORN
BUCKHOUND
BUCKIE
BUCKING
BUCKISH
BUCKISHLY
BUCKISHNESS
BUCKISM
BUCKJUMP
BUCKLE
BUCKLED
BUCKLER
BUCKLING
BUCKLUM
BUCKO
BUCKOES
BUCKONE
BUCKPLATE
BUCKPOT
BUCKRA
BUCKRAM
BUCKRAMED
BUCKRAMING
BUCKS
BUCKSAW
BUCKSHEE
BUCKSHOT
BUCKSKIN
BUCKSKINNED
BUCKSTALL
BUCKSTAY
BUCKSTONE
BUCKTAIL
BUCKTHORN
BUCKTOOTH
BUCKTOOTHED
BUCKU
BUCKWAGON
BUCKWASH
BUCKWASHER
BUCKWASHING
BUCKWHEAT
BUCKWHEATER
BUCKY
BUCOLIAST
BUCOLIC
BUCOLICAL
BUCOLICALLY
BUCRANE
BUCRANIA
BUCRANIUM
BUD
BUDA
BUDBREAK
BUDDAGE
BUDDAH
BUDDED
BUDDER
BUDDHI
BUDDIE
BUDDIES
BUDDING
BUDDLE
BUDDLEIA
BUDDLER
BUDDY
BUDGE
BUDGED
BUDGER
BUDGEREE
BUDGEREEGAH
BUDGERIGAH
BUDGERIGAR
BUDGERO
BUDGEROW
BUDGERYGAH
BUDGET
BUDGETARY
BUDGETED
BUDGETEER
BUDGETER
BUDGETING
BUDGIE
BUDGING
BUDLET
BUDLING
BUDMASH
BUDTIME
BUDWOOD
BUDWORM
BUDZART
BUDZAT
BUF
BUFAGIN
BUFF
BUFFA
BUFFABLE
BUFFALO
BUFFALOBACK
BUFFALOED
BUFFALOES
BUFFALOING
BUFFALOS
BUFFBALL
BUFFBAR
BUFFCOAT
BUFFED
BUFFER
BUFFET
BUFFETED
BUFFETER
BUFFETING
BUFFI
BUFFIN
BUFFING
BUFFLE
BUFFLEHEAD
BUFFLEHORN
BUFFO
BUFFONE
BUFFONT
BUFFOON
BUFFOONERIES
BUFFOONERY
BUFFOONISH
BUFFOONISM
BUFFWARE
BUFFY
BUFIDIN
BUFO
BUFONID
BUFONITE
BUFOTALIN
BUG
BUGA
BUGABOO
BUGALA
BUGAN
BUGARA
BUGBANE
BUGBEAR
BUGBITE
BUGEYE
BUGFISH
BUGGANE
BUGGED
BUGGER
BUGGERY
BUGGIER

BUGGIES
BUGGIEST
BUGGINESS
BUGGING
BUGGY
BUGGYMAN
BUGGYMEN
BUGHEAD
BUGHOUSE
BUGHT
BUGHT
BUGIA
BUGLE
BUGLED
BUGLER
BUGLET
BUGLEWEED
BUGLING
BUGLOSS
BUGLOSSES
BUGOLOGIST
BUGOLOGY
BUGOR
BUGOUT
BUGRE
BUGS
BUGSEED
BUGWEED
BUGWORT
BUHL
BUHLBUHL
BUHLWORK
BUHR
BUHRMILL
BUHRSTONE
BUILD
BUILDER
BUILDING
BUILDINGS
BUILDRESS
BUILDUP
BUILT
BUIRD
BUIRDLY
BUIRE
BUISSON
BUIST
BUKE
BUKH
BUKID
BUKK
BUKSHEE
BUKSHI
BULAK
BULAQ
BULB
BULBACEOUS
BULBAR
BULBED
BULBI
BULBIER
BULBIEST
BULBIFEROUS
BULBIFORM
BULBIL
BULBILLA
BULBLET
BULBLIKE
BULBOSE
BULBOTUBER
BULBOUS
BULBS
BULBUL
BULBULE
BULBUS
BULBY
BULCH
BULCHIN
BULDER
BULE
BULGE
BULGED
BULGER
BULGIER
BULGIEST
BULGINESS
BULGING
BULGUR
BULGY
BULIES
BULIMIA
BULIMIAC
BULIMIC
BULIMIFORM
BULIMOID
BULIMY
BULK
BULKED
BULKER
BULKHEAD
BULKHEADED
BULKIER
BULKIEST
BULKILY
BULKINESS
BULKING
BULKY
BULL
BULLA
BULLACE
BULLAE
BULLAMACOW
BULLAN
BULLARIES
BULLARY
BULLATE
BULLATED
BULLATION
BULLBAITING
BULLBAT
BULLBEGGAR
BULLBERRY
BULLBIRD
BULLBOAT
BULLCOMBER
BULLDOG
BULLDOGGED
BULLDOGGER
BULLDOGGING
BULLDOGGY
BULLDOZE
BULLDOZED
BULLDOZER
BULLDOZING
BULLDUST
BULLED
BULLER
BULLET
BULLETED
BULLETHEAD
BULLETIN
BULLETINED
BULLETINING
BULLETMAKER
BULLETMAKING
BULLETPROOF
BULLETS
BULLETWOOD
BULLETY
BULLFICE
BULLFIGHT
BULLFIGHTER
BULLFIGHTING
BULLFINCH
BULLFIST
BULLFLOWER
BULLFOOT
BULLFROG
BULLGINE
BULLHEAD
BULLHEADED
BULLHEADEDLY
BULLHOOF
BULLHORN
BULLIED
BULLIES
BULLIFORM
BULLIMONG
BULLING
BULLION
BULLISH
BULLISHLY
BULLISHNESS
BULLISM
BULLNECK
BULLNECKED
BULLNOSE
BULLNUT
BULLOCK
BULLOCKER
BULLOCKMAN
BULLOCKY
BULLOSE
BULLOUS
BULLPATES
BULLPEN
BULLPOUT
BULLPUP
BULLRING
BULLROARER
BULLS
BULLSTICKER
BULLSUCKER
BULLTOAD
BULLULE
BULLWEED
BULLWHACK
BULLWHACKER
BULLWHIP
BULLWHIPPED
BULLWHIPPING
BULLWORK
BULLWORT
BULLY
BULLYBOY
BULLYHUFF
BULLYING
BULLYINGLY
BULLYRAG
BULLYRAGGED
BULLYRAGGER
BULLYRAGGING
BULLYROCK
BULLYROOK
BULREEDY
BULRUSH
BULSE
BULT
BULTEN
BULTER
BULTEY
BULTI
BULTO
BULTONG
BULTOW
BULWAND
BULWARK
BULWARKED
BULWARKING
BULWARKS
BUM
BUMAREE
BUMBAILIFF
BUMBARD
BUMBARGE
BUMBASS
BUMBASTE
BUMBAZE
BUMBEE
BUMBERSHOOT
BUMBLE
BUMBLEBEE
BUMBLEBERRY
BUMBLED
BUMBLEFOOT
BUMBLEKITE
BUMBLEPUPPY
BUMBLER
BUMBLING
BUMBO
BUMBOAT
BUMBOATMAN
BUMBOATWOMAN
BUMCLOCK
BUMF
BUMFEG
BUMICKY
BUMKIN
BUMMACK
BUMMALO
BUMMALOS
BUMMAREE
BUMMED
BUMMEL
BUMMER
BUMMERY
BUMMIL
BUMMING
BUMMLE
BUMMLER
BUMMOCK
BUMP
BUMPER
BUMPERED
BUMPERING
BUMPIER
BUMPIEST
BUMPILY
BUMPINESS
BUMPING
BUMPINGLY
BUMPITY
BUMPKIN
BUMPOLOGY
BUMPSY
BUMPTIOUS
BUMPTIOUSLY
BUMPY
BUMTRAP
BUMWOOD
BUN
BUNA
BUNCAL
BUNCE
BUNCH
BUNCHBERRIES
BUNCHBERRY
BUNCHED
BUNCHER
BUNCHFLOWER
BUNCHIER
BUNCHIEST
BUNCHILY
BUNCHINESS
BUNCHING
BUNCHY
BUNCO
BUNCOED
BUNCOING
BUNCOMBE
BUNCOS
BUND
BUNDER
BUNDIES
BUNDLE
BUNDLER
BUNDLET
BUNDOBUST
BUNDOC
BUNDOCKS
BUNDOOK
BUNDWEED
BUNDY
BUNEMOST
BUNG
BUNGALOID
BUNGALOW
BUNGARUM
BUNGED
BUNGEE
BUNGERLY
BUNGEY
BUNGFU
BUNGFULL
BUNGHOLE
BUNGING
BUNGLE
BUNGLED
BUNGLER
BUNGLING
BUNGLINGLY
BUNGMAKER
BUNGO
BUNGOS
BUNGS
BUNGTOWN
BUNGWALL
BUNGY
BUNION
BUNK
BUNKED
BUNKER
BUNKERMAN
BUNKERMEN
BUNKHOUSE
BUNKIE
BUNKING
BUNKLOAD
BUNKMATE
BUNKO
BUNKOED
BUNKOING
BUNKOS
BUNKS
BUNKUM
BUNN
BUNNELL
BUNNIA
BUNNIES
BUNNING
BUNNY
BUNNYMOUTH
BUNODONT
BUNSENITE
BUNT
BUNTAL
BUNTED
BUNTER
BUNTINE
BUNTING
BUNTLINE
BUNTON
BUNTS
BUNTY
BUNUELO

BUNYA
BUNYAH
BUNYIP
BUONAMANI
BUONAMANO
BUOY
BUOYAGE
BUOYANCE
BUOYANCIES
BUOYANCY
BUOYANT
BUOYANTLY
BUOYANTNESS
BUOYED
BUOYING
BUPHTHALMIA
BUPHTHALMIC
BUPHTHALMOS
BUPLEUROL
BUPLEVER
BUPRESTID
BUPRESTIDAN
BUR
BURA
BURAN
BURAO
BURBANKIAN
BURBARK
BURBLER
BURBLY
BURBOLT
BURBOT
BURBOTS
BURD
BURDASH
BURDEN
BURDENABLE
BURDENED
BURDENER
BURDENING
BURDENOUS
BURDENSOME
BURDENSOMELY
BURDIE
BURDOCK
BURDON
BURE
BUREAU
BUREAUCRACIES
BUREAUCRACY
BUREAUCRAT
BUREAUCRATIC
BUREAUS
BUREAUX
BUREL
BURELAGE
BURELE
BURELY
BUREO
BURET
BURETTE
BURFISH
BURG
BURGAGE
BURGALITY
BURGALL
BURGAMOT
BURGEE
BURGENSIC
BURGEON
BURGEONED
BURGEONING
BURGER
BURGESS
BURGH
BURGHAL
BURGHALPENNY
BURGHBOTE
BURGHER
BURGHMASTER
BURGHMOOT
BURGHMOTE
BURGI
BURGLAR
BURGLARIES
BURGLARIOUS
BURGLARIZE
BURGLARIZED
BURGLARIZING
BURGLARPROOF
BURGLARY
BURGLE
BURGLED
BURGLING
BURGOMASTER
BURGONET
BURGOO
BURGOOS
BURGOUT
BURGOYNE
BURGRAVE
BURGRAVIATE
BURGUL
BURGULLIAN
BURGUS
BURGWARE
BURGWERE
BURH
BURHEAD
BURHMOOT
BURI
BURIAL
BURIAN
BURIED
BURIER
BURIN
BURINIST
BURION
BURITI
BURK
BURKA
BURKE
BURKED
BURKER
BURKHA
BURKING
BURKITE
BURKUNDAUZE
BURKUNDAZ
BURL
BURLA
BURLAP
BURLAPS
BURLE
BURLED
BURLER
BURLESK
BURLESQUE
BURLESQUED
BURLESQUELY
BURLESQUER
BURLESQUING
BURLET
BURLETTA
BURLEY
BURLEYS
BURLIER
BURLIES
BURLIEST
BURLILY
BURLINESS
BURLING
BURLY
BURMITE
BURN
BURNABLE
BURNBEAT
BURNED
BURNER
BURNET
BURNETTIZE
BURNETTIZED
BURNETTIZING
BURNEWIN
BURNFIRE
BURNIE
BURNIEBEE
BURNING
BURNINGLY
BURNISH
BURNISHER
BURNISHING
BURNISHMENT
BURNOOSE
BURNOOSED
BURNOUS
BURNOUT
BURNOVER
BURNSIDE
BURNSIDES
BURNT
BURNUP
BURNUT
BURNWEED
BURNWOOD
BURNY
BURO
BURP
BURR
BURRA
BURRAH
BURRAWANG
BURRBARK
BURRED
BURREL
BURRER
BURRHEL
BURRIER
BURRIEST
BURRIO
BURRITO
BURRITOS
BURRKNOT
BURRO
BURROS
BURROW
BURROWED
BURROWEED
BURROWER
BURROWING
BURROWS
BURROWSTOWN
BURRSTONE
BURRY
BURSA
BURSAE
BURSAL
BURSAR
BURSARIAL
BURSARIES
BURSARY
BURSAS
BURSATE
BURSATI
BURSATTEE
BURSAUTEE
BURSE
BURSEED
BURSERACEOUS
BURSICLE
BURSICULATE
BURSIFORM
BURSITIS
BURST
BURSTED
BURSTER
BURSTING
BURSTONE
BURSTWORT
BURSULA
BURT
BURTHEN
BURTHENMAN
BURTON
BURTONIZATION
BURTONIZE
BURTREE
BURUCHA
BURWEED
BURY
BURYING
BUS
BUSBIES
BUSBOY
BUSBY
BUSCARL
BUSCARLE
BUSE
BUSED
BUSES
BUSH
BUSHBEATER
BUSHBOY
BUSHBUCK
BUSHED
BUSHEL
BUSHELED
BUSHELER
BUSHELING
BUSHELLED
BUSHELLER
BUSHELLING
BUSHELMAN
BUSHELS
BUSHELWOMAN
BUSHER
BUSHES
BUSHET
BUSHFIGHTER
BUSHFIGHTING
BUSHGOAT
BUSHGRASS
BUSHHAMMER
BUSHI
BUSHIDO
BUSHIER
BUSHIEST
BUSHILY
BUSHINESS
BUSHING
BUSHLAND
BUSHMAKER
BUSHMAKING
BUSHMASTER
BUSHMENT
BUSHPIG
BUSHRANGER
BUSHRANGING
BUSHROPE
BUSHTIT
BUSHVELD
BUSHWA
BUSHWACK
BUSHWAH
BUSHWHACK
BUSHWHACKER
BUSHWHACKING
BUSHWIFE
BUSHWOMAN
BUSHWOOD
BUSIED
BUSIER
BUSIEST
BUSILY
BUSINE
BUSINESS
BUSINESSES
BUSINESSLIKE
BUSINESSMAN
BUSINESSMEN
BUSINESSWOMAN
BUSING
BUSK
BUSKED
BUSKER
BUSKET
BUSKIN
BUSKINED
BUSKINS
BUSKLE
BUSMAN
BUSMEN
BUSS
BUSSE
BUSSED
BUSSER
BUSSES
BUSSING
BUSSOCK
BUSSU
BUSSY
BUST
BUSTARD
BUSTED
BUSTEE
BUSTER
BUSTHEAD
BUSTI
BUSTIAN
BUSTIC
BUSTICATE
BUSTING
BUSTLE
BUSTLED
BUSTLER
BUSTLING
BUSTLINGLY
BUSTO
BUSWAY
BUSY
BUSYBODIES
BUSYBODY
BUSYING
BUSYNESS
BUSYWORK
BUT
BUTADIENE
BUTANE
BUTANOL
BUTANONE
BUTCH
BUTCHA
BUTCHER
BUTCHERBIRD
BUTCHERBROOM
BUTCHERER
BUTCHERESS
BUTCHERIES
BUTCHERING
BUTCHERLY
BUTCHEROUS
BUTCHERY
BUTEIN
BUTENYL
BUTEONINE

BUTIN
BUTINE
BUTLER
BUTLERAGE
BUTLERIES
BUTLERY
BUTMENT
BUTOMACEOUS
BUTOR
BUTOXY
BUTOXYL
BUTS
BUTSUDAN
BUTT
BUTTAL
BUTTE
BUTTED
BUTTER
BUTTERACEOUS
BUTTERBACK
BUTTERBALL
BUTTERBILL
BUTTERBIRD
BUTTERBOUGH
BUTTERBOX
BUTTERBUMP
BUTTERBUR
BUTTERBURR
BUTTERBUSH
BUTTERCUP
BUTTERED
BUTTERFAT
BUTTERFISH
BUTTERFISHES
BUTTERFLIES
BUTTERFLOWER
BUTTERFLY
BUTTERHEAD
BUTTERIES
BUTTERINE
BUTTERIS
BUTTERJAGS
BUTTERMAN
BUTTERMILK
BUTTERMONGER
BUTTERNOSE
BUTTERNUT
BUTTERSCOTCH
BUTTERWEED
BUTTERWORKER
BUTTERWORT
BUTTERY
BUTTING
BUTTINSKY
BUTTLE
BUTTOCK
BUTTOCKED
BUTTOCKER
BUTTOCKS
BUTTON
BUTTONBALL
BUTTONBUR
BUTTONBUSH
BUTTONED
BUTTONER
BUTTONHOLD
BUTTONHOLDER
BUTTONHOLE
BUTTONHOLED
BUTTONHOLER
BUTTONHOLING
BUTTONHOOK
BUTTONING
BUTTONLIKE
BUTTONMOLD
BUTTONMOULD
BUTTONS
BUTTONWEED
BUTTONWOOD
BUTTONY
BUTTRESS
BUTTRESSED
BUTTRESSING
BUTTS
BUTTSTOCK
BUTTWOMAN
BUTTWOMEN
BUTTY
BUTTYMAN
BUTYL
BUTYLAMINE
BUTYLATION
BUTYLENE
BUTYLIC
BUTYNE
BUTYRACEOUS
BUTYRATE
BUTYRIC
BUTYRICALLY
BUTYRIN
BUTYRINASE
BUTYROMETER
BUTYROMETRIC
BUTYRONE
BUTYROUS
BUTYRYL
BUVETTE
BUXACEOUS
BUXERRIES
BUXERRY
BUXOM
BUXOMLY
BUXOMNESS
BUY
BUYABLE
BUYER
BUYING
BUYO
BUZANE
BUZZ
BUZZARD
BUZZARDLY
BUZZED
BUZZER
BUZZERPHONE
BUZZGLOAK
BUZZIER
BUZZIES
BUZZIEST
BUZZING
BUZZLE
BUZZWIG
BUZZY
BWANA
BWAZI
BY
BYARD
BYCOCKET
BYCOKET
BYE
BYEE
BYELAW
BYEMAN
BYERITE
BYERLITE
BYGO
BYGOING
BYGONE
BYHAND
BYLAND
BYLAW
BYLINA
BYLINER
BYLINY
BYNAME
BYNEDESTIN
BYON
BYOUS
BYOUSLY
BYPASS
BYPASSED
BYPASSER
BYPASSING
BYPAST
BYPATH
BYPLAY
BYRE
BYREMAN
BYREWOMAN
BYRL
BYRLADY
BYRLAW
BYRLAWMAN
BYRLAWMEN
BYRNIE
BYROAD
BYRRUS
BYRTHYNSAK
BYSEN
BYSMALITH
BYSPELL
BYSSACEOUS
BYSSAL
BYSSI
BYSSIFEROUS
BYSSIN
BYSSINE
BYSSOGENOUS
BYSSOID
BYSSOLITE
BYSSUS
BYSSUSES
BYSTANDER
BYSTREET
BYTH
BYTOWNITE
BYTOWNITITE
BYWALK
BYWALKER
BYWALKING
BYWAY
BYWONER
BYWORD
BYWORK
BYZANT
BYZEN

CAAM
CAAMA
CAAMING
CAAPEBA
CAAPI
CAATINGA
CAB
CABA
CABAAN
CABACK
CABAHO
CABAL
CABALA
CABALASSOU
CABALETTA
CABALIC
CABALISM
CABALIST
CABALISTIC
CABALISTICAL
CABALISTICALLY
CABALL
CABALLED
CABALLER
CABALLERIA
CABALLERO
CABALLEROS
CABALLINE
CABALLING
CABALLO
CABAN
CABANA
CABANE
CABARET
CABARETIER
CABAS
CABASA
CABASSET
CABASSOU
CABBAGE
CABBAGED
CABBAGEHEAD
CABBAGEWOOD
CABBAGING
CABBAGY
CABBALAH
CABBED
CABBER
CABBIES
CABBING
CABBLE
CABBLER
CABBY
CABDA
CABDRIVER
CABDRIVING
CABECERA
CABECUDO
CABELIAU
CABELLEROTE
CABER
CABERNET
CABESTRO
CABEZON
CABIE
CABILDO
CABILLIAU
CABIN
CABINED
CABINET
CABINETED
CABINETING
CABINETMAKER
CABINETMAKING
CABINETRY
CABINETTED
CABINETWORK
CABINETWORKER
CABINETWORKING
CABINING
CABINLIKE
CABIO
CABLE
CABLED
CABLEGRAM
CABLEMAN
CABLEMEN
CABLER
CABLES
CABLESE
CABLET
CABLEWAY
CABLING
CABMAN
CABOB
CABOCEER
CABOCHED
CABOCHON
CABOCLE
CABOCLO
CABOODLE
CABOOK
CABOOSE
CABOSHED
CABOT
CABOTAGE
CABOTIN
CABOTINAGE
CABOUCA
CABREE
CABRERITE
CABRESTA
CABRESTO
CABRET
CABRETTA
CABREUVA
CABRIE
CABRILLA
CABRIOLE
CABRIOLET
CABRIT
CABRITO
CABSTAND
CABUJA
CABULLA
CABURN
CABUYA
CACAESTHESIA
CACAFUEGO
CACAFUGO
CACAM
CACAO
CACAOS
CACAXTE
CACESTHESIA
CACESTHESIS
CACHACA
CACHAEMIA
CACHAEMIC
CACHALOT
CACHAZA
CACHE
CACHECTICAL
CACHED
CACHEMIA
CACHEMIC
CACHEPOT
CACHES
CACHET
CACHETIC
CACHEXIA
CACHEXIC
CACHEXY
CACHIBOU
CACHILA
CACHIMILLA
CACHINA
CACHING
CACHINNATE
CACHINNATION
CACHINNATOR
CACHINNATORY
CACHOEIRA
CACHOLONG
CACHOT
CACHOU
CACHRYS
CACHUA
CACHUCHA
CACHUCHO
CACHUNDE
CACIDROSIS
CACIOCAVALLO
CACIQUE
CACIQUISM
CACK
CACKEREL
CACKLE
CACKLED
CACKLER
CACKLING
CACO
CACOCHOLIA
CACOCHROIA
CACOCHYLIA
CACOCHYMIA
CACOCHYMIC
CACOCHYMICAL
CACOCHYMY
CACODAEMON
CACODEMON
CACODEMONIA
CACODEMONIAC
CACODEMONIAL
CACODEMONIC
CACODOXIAN
CACODOXICAL
CACODOXY
CACODYL
CACODYLIC
CACOECONOMY
CACOEPIST
CACOEPISTIC
CACOEPY
CACOETHES
CACOETHIC
CACOGALACTIA
CACOGASTRIC
CACOGENESIS
CACOGENIC
CACOGENICS
CACOGEUSIA
CACOGLOSSIA
CACOGRAPHER
CACOGRAPHIC
CACOGRAPHY
CACOLET
CACOLOGY
CACOMELIA
CACOMISTLE
CACOMIXL
CACOMIXLE
CACOMORPHIA
CACONYM
CACOON
CACOPATHY
CACOPHARYNGIA
CACOPHONIA
CACOPHONIC
CACOPHONICAL
CACOPHONICALLY
CACOPHONIST
CACOPHONIZE
CACOPHONOUS
CACOPHONOUSLY
CACOPHONY
CACOPLASIA
CACOPLASTIC
CACOPROCTIA
CACORHYTHMIC
CACORRHACHIS
CACORRHINIA
CACOSPERMIA
CACOSTOMIA
CACOTHELIN
CACOTHELINE
CACOTHYMIA
CACOTRICHIA
CACOTROPHIA
CACOTROPHY
CACOTYPE
CACOXENE
CACOXENITE
CACOZEAL
CACOZEALOUS
CACOZYME
CACTACEOUS
CACTAL
CACTI
CACTIFORM
CACTOID
CACTUS
CACTUSES
CACUMEN
CACUMINAL
CACUMINATE
CACUMINATION
CACUMINOUS
CACUR
CAD
CADALENE
CADAMBA
CADAR
CADASTER
CADASTRAL
CADASTRATION
CADASTRE
CADAVER
CADAVERIC
CADAVERIN
CADAVERINE
CADAVEROUS
CADAVEROUSLY
CADBAIT
CADBIT
CADBOTE
CADDED
CADDI
CADDICE
CADDICED
CADDIE
CADDIED
CADDIES
CADDING
CADDIS
CADDISED
CADDISH
CADDISHLY
CADDISHNESS
CADDLE
CADDOW
CADDY
CADDYING
CADE
CADEAU
CADELLE
CADENCE
CADENCED
CADENCIES
CADENCY
CADENETTE
CADENT
CADENTIAL
CADENZA
CADER
CADESSE
CADET
CADETCY
CADETSHIP
CADETTE
CADEW
CADGE
CADGED
CADGER
CADGILY
CADGINESS
CADGING
CADGY
CADI
CADIE
CADILESKER
CADILLO
CADINENE
CADIS
CADISH
CADJAN
CADLOCK
CADMIA
CADMIC
CADMIDE
CADMIFEROUS
CADMIUM
CADRANS
CADRE
CADUA
CADUAC
CADUCA
CADUCARY
CADUCE
CADUCEAN
CADUCEUS
CADUCIARY
CADUCIBRANCH
CADUCICORN
CADUCITY
CADUKE
CADUS
CADWEED
CADY
CAECA
CAECALLY
CAECECTOMY
CAECIFORM
CAECILIAN
CAECITIS
CAECOCOLIC
CAECOSTOMY
CAECOTOMY
CAECUM
CAELOMETER
CAENOSTYLIC
CAENOSTYLY
CAEOMA
CAESAREAN
CAESARIAN

CAESIOUS
CAESIUM
CAESPITOSE
CAESTUS
CAESURA
CAESURAE
CAESURAL
CAESURAS
CAESURIC
CAFARD
CAFARDISE
CAFE
CAFENEH
CAFENET
CAFETAL
CAFETERIA
CAFETIERE
CAFF
CAFFA
CAFFE
CAFFEATE
CAFFEIC
CAFFEIN
CAFFEINE
CAFFEINIC
CAFFEINISM
CAFFEISM
CAFFEOL
CAFFEONE
CAFFETANNIN
CAFFISO
CAFFLE
CAFFLED
CAFFLING
CAFFOLINE
CAFFOY
CAFILA
CAFIZ
CAFOY
CAFTA
CAFTAN
CAFTANED
CAFUSO
CAG
CAGE
CAGED
CAGELING
CAGEMAN
CAGEOT
CAGER
CAGESTER
CAGEWORK
CAGEY
CAGGY
CAGIER
CAGIEST
CAGIT
CAGMAG
CAHAR
CAHIER
CAHINCIC
CAHIZ
CAHOOT
CAHOOTS
CAHOT
CAHOW
CAHUITA
CAHUY
CAIARARA
CAID
CAILCEDRA
CAILLE
CAILLEACH
CAILLIACH
CAIMACAM
CAIMAKAM
CAIMAN
CAIMITILLO
CAIMITO
CAIN
CAINGIN
CAIQUE
CAIQUEJEE
CAIRD
CAIRN
CAIRNED
CAIRNGORM
CAIRNGORUM
CAIRNY
CAISSE
CAISSON
CAISSONED
CAITIF
CAITIFF
CAIXINHA
CAJA
CAJANG
CAJAPUT
CAJAVA
CAJEPUT
CAJETA
CAJI
CAJOLE
CAJOLED
CAJOLEMENT
CAJOLER
CAJOLERIES
CAJOLERY
CAJOLING
CAJOLINGLY
CAJON
CAJOO
CAJOU
CAJU
CAJUELA
CAJUN
CAJUPUT
CAJUPUTENE
CAJUPUTOL
CAKE
CAKEBOX
CAKEBREAD
CAKED
CAKEHOUSE
CAKEMAKER
CAKEMAKING
CAKER
CAKES
CAKETTE
CAKEWALK
CAKEY
CAKIER
CAKIEST
CAKING
CAKRA
CAKY
CAL
CALABA
CALABAR
CALABASH
CALABAZA
CALABAZILLA
CALABER
CALABOOSE
CALABOZO
CALABRASELLA
CALABRESE
CALABUR
CALADE
CALADIUM
CALAHAN
CALAITE
CALALU
CALAMANCOES
CALAMANCOS
CALAMANSI
CALAMARIAN
CALAMARIES
CALAMARIOID
CALAMAROID
CALAMARY
CALAMBAC
CALAMBOUR
CALAMI
CALAMIFORM
CALAMINE
CALAMINED
CALAMINING
CALAMINT
CALAMISTRAL
CALAMISTRUM
CALAMITE
CALAMITEAN
CALAMITIES
CALAMITOID
CALAMITOUS
CALAMITOUSLY
CALAMITY
CALAMONDIN
CALAMUS
CALAN
CALANDER
CALANDO
CALANDRE
CALANDRIA
CALANGAY
CALANID
CALANQUE
CALANTAS
CALANTHE
CALAO
CALAPITE
CALAPITTE
CALASCIONE
CALASH
CALATHEA
CALATHI
CALATHIDIA
CALATHIDIUM
CALATHISCI
CALATHISCUS
CALATHOS
CALATHUS
CALAVERITE
CALCAEMIA
CALCANEAL
CALCANEAN
CALCANEI
CALCANEUM
CALCANEUS
CALCAR
CALCARATE
CALCARATED
CALCAREOUS
CALCAREOUSLY
CALCARIA
CALCARIFORM
CALCARINE
CALCARIUM
CALCEATE
CALCED
CALCEDONY
CALCEIFORM
CALCEMIA
CALCEOLATE
CALCES
CALCEUS
CALCIC
CALCICLASE
CALCICOLOUS
CALCICOSIS
CALCIFEROL
CALCIFEROUS
CALCIFIC
CALCIFICATION
CALCIFIED
CALCIFORM
CALCIFUGAL
CALCIFUGE
CALCIFUGOUS
CALCIFY
CALCIFYING
CALCIGENOUS
CALCIGEROUS
CALCIMETER
CALCIMINE
CALCIMINED
CALCIMINER
CALCIMINING
CALCINATION
CALCINATORY
CALCINE
CALCINED
CALCINER
CALCINING
CALCINO
CALCIPEXY
CALCIPHILE
CALCIPHILIA
CALCIPHILOUS
CALCIPHYRE
CALCIPRIVIC
CALCITE
CALCITRANT
CALCITRATE
CALCITRATION
CALCIUM
CALCIVOROUS
CALCOGRAPHER
CALCOGRAPHIC
CALCOGRAPHY
CALCRETE
CALCSINTER
CALCSPAR
CALCTUFA
CALCTUFF
CALCULABLE
CALCULABLY
CALCULARY
CALCULATE
CALCULATED
CALCULATING
CALCULATION
CALCULATIONAL
CALCULATIVE
CALCULATOR
CALCULATORY
CALCULER
CALCULIFORM
CALCULIST
CALCULOUS
CALCULUS
CALCULUSES
CALDARIA
CALDARIUM
CALDEN
CALDERA
CALDRON
CALE
CALEAN
CALECHE
CALEDONITE
CALEFACIENT
CALEFACTION
CALEFACTIVE
CALEFACTOR
CALEFACTORY
CALELECTRIC
CALEMBOUR
CALENDAL
CALENDAR
CALENDARIAL
CALENDARIAN
CALENDARIC
CALENDER
CALENDERED
CALENDERER
CALENDERING
CALENDRIC
CALENDRICAL
CALENDRY
CALENDS
CALENDULA
CALENDULIN
CALENTURAL
CALENTURE
CALENTURED
CALENTURING
CALENTURIST
CALEPIN
CALESA
CALESCENCE
CALESCENT
CALESERO
CALESIN
CALF
CALFBOUND
CALFKILL
CALFLING
CALFSKIN
CALIBER
CALIBERED
CALIBOGUS
CALIBRATE
CALIBRATED
CALIBRATION
CALIBRATOR
CALIBRE
CALIBRED
CALICHE
CALICIFORM
CALICLE
CALICO
CALICOBACK
CALICOED
CALICOES
CALICOS
CALICULAR
CALID
CALIDITY
CALIDUCT
CALIF
CALIFORNITE
CALIFORNIUM
CALIGA
CALIGATED
CALIGINOSITY
CALIGINOUS
CALIGINOUSLY
CALIGO
CALIGRAPHY
CALIMANCO
CALIN
CALINDA
CALINE
CALINUT
CALIOLOGICAL
CALIOLOGIST
CALIOLOGY
CALIPASH
CALIPEE
CALIPER
CALIPERER
CALIPERS
CALIPH

CALIPHAL
CALIPHATE
CALISAYA
CALISTHENEUM
CALISTHENIC
CALISTHENICS
CALIVER
CALIX
CALK
CALKAGE
CALKER
CALKING
CALL
CALLA
CALLABLE
CALLAINITE
CALLAIS
CALLAN
CALLANT
CALLATE
CALLBOY
CALLE
CALLED
CALLER
CALLES
CALLET
CALLI
CALLID
CALLIDITY
CALLIDNESS
CALLIGRAPH
CALLIGRAPHER
CALLIGRAPHIC
CALLIGRAPHY
CALLING
CALLIOPE
CALLIOPHONE
CALLIOPSIS
CALLIPASH
CALLIPEE
CALLIPER
CALLIPERER
CALLIPHORID
CALLIPHORINE
CALLIPYGIAN
CALLIPYGOUS
CALLISECTION
CALLISTEIA
CALLISTHENIC
CALLISTHENICS
CALLITHUMP
CALLITYPE
CALLITYPED
CALLITYPING
CALLOP
CALLOSAL
CALLOSE
CALLOSITY
CALLOSUM
CALLOUS
CALLOUSED
CALLOUSING
CALLOUSLY
CALLOUSNESS
CALLOW
CALLOWER
CALLOWMAN
CALLUS
CALLUSES
CALM
CALMANT
CALMATIVE
CALMATO
CALMECAC
CALMER
CALMEST
CALMIERER
CALMLY
CALMNESS
CALMY
CALO
CALODAEMON
CALODEMON
CALODEMONIAL
CALOMBA
CALOMBIGAS
CALOMBO
CALOMEL
CALOOL
CALOR
CALORESCENCE
CALORESCENT
CALORIC
CALORICITY
CALORIE
CALORIFIC
CALORIFICAL
CALORIFICS
CALORIFIER
CALORIFY
CALORIGENIC
CALORIMETER
CALORIMETRIC
CALORIMETRY
CALORIMOTOR
CALORIS
CALORISATOR
CALORIST
CALORIZE
CALORIZER
CALOSOMA
CALOTIN
CALOTTE
CALOTYPE
CALOTYPIC
CALOTYPIST
CALOYER
CALP
CALPAC
CALPACK
CALPACKED
CALPOLLI
CALPUL
CALPULLI
CALQUE
CALSOUNS
CALTHROP
CALTRAP
CALTROP
CALTROPS
CALUMBA
CALUMET
CALUMNIATE
CALUMNIATED
CALUMNIATION
CALUMNIATIVE
CALUMNIATOR
CALUMNIATORY
CALUMNIES
CALUMNIOUS
CALUMNIOUSLY
CALUMNY
CALUSAR
CALVA
CALVAIRE
CALVARIA
CALVARIAL
CALVARIES
CALVARIUM
CALVARY
CALVE
CALVED
CALVER
CALVES
CALVING
CALVISH
CALVITIES
CALVITY
CALVOUS
CALX
CALXES
CALYCANTH
CALYCANTHEMY
CALYCANTHIN
CALYCANTHINE
CALYCATE
CALYCES
CALYCIFEROUS
CALYCIFLORAL
CALYCIFORM
CALYCINE
CALYCLE
CALYCLED
CALYCOID
CALYCOIDEOUS
CALYCOPHORAN
CALYCULAR
CALYCULATE
CALYCULATED
CALYCULE
CALYCULUS
CALYMMA
CALYPHYOMY
CALYPSO
CALYPTER
CALYPTRA
CALYPTRATE
CALYPTRIFORM
CALYPTROGEN
CALYX
CALZADA
CALZONERAS
CALZOONS
CAM
CAMACA
CAMACEY
CAMACHILE
CAMAGON
CAMAIEU
CAMAIL
CAMAILE
CAMAILED
CAMALIG
CAMALOTE
CAMAN
CAMANAY
CAMANSI
CAMARA
CAMARADA
CAMARADE
CAMARADERIE
CAMARERA
CAMARILLA
CAMARIN
CAMARON
CAMAS
CAMASS
CAMATA
CAMATINA
CAMAURO
CAMAY
CAMBAYE
CAMBER
CAMBERED
CAMBERING
CAMBIAL
CAMBIATA
CAMBIFORM
CAMBIO
CAMBISM
CAMBIST
CAMBISTRY
CAMBIUM
CAMBLET
CAMBOGIA
CAMBOOSE
CAMBOUIS
CAMBRESINE
CAMBRIC
CAMBUCA
CAME
CAMEIST
CAMEL
CAMELEER
CAMELHAIR
CAMELINE
CAMELISH
CAMELISHNESS
CAMELKEEPER
CAMELLIA
CAMELLIN
CAMELMAN
CAMELOID
CAMELOPARD
CAMELOT
CAMELRY
CAMEO
CAMEOGRAPH
CAMEOGRAPHY
CAMEOS
CAMERA
CAMERAE
CAMERAL
CAMERALISM
CAMERALIST
CAMERALISTIC
CAMERALISTICS
CAMERAMAN
CAMERAS
CAMERATE
CAMERATED
CAMERATION
CAMERIER
CAMERIERA
CAMERIERI
CAMERIST
CAMERLENGO
CAMERLINGO
CAMIAS
CAMILLA
CAMINO
CAMION
CAMIS
CAMISA
CAMISADE
CAMISADO
CAMISCIA
CAMISE
CAMISIA
CAMISOLE
CAMLET
CAMLETED
CAMLETEEN
CAMLETINE
CAMLETING
CAMMED
CAMMOCK
CAMMOCKY
CAMOGIE
CAMOIS
CAMOMILE
CAMOOCH
CAMOODI
CAMOODIE
CAMOTE
CAMOUDIE
CAMOUFLAGE
CAMOUFLAGED
CAMOUFLAGER
CAMOUFLAGING
CAMOUFLET
CAMOUFLEUR
CAMP
CAMPAGNA
CAMPAGNOL
CAMPAIGN
CAMPAIGNER
CAMPANA
CAMPANE
CAMPANELLA
CAMPANERO
CAMPANIFORM
CAMPANILE
CAMPANILES
CAMPANILLA
CAMPANINI
CAMPANIST
CAMPANISTIC
CAMPANOLOGER
CAMPANOLOGY
CAMPANULAR
CAMPANULATE
CAMPANULOUS
CAMPBELLITE
CAMPCRAFT
CAMPECHE
CAMPED
CAMPEPHAGINE
CAMPER
CAMPESINO
CAMPESTRAL
CAMPFIGHT
CAMPFIRE
CAMPGROUND
CAMPHANE
CAMPHANIC
CAMPHANONE
CAMPHANYL
CAMPHENE
CAMPHINE
CAMPHIRE
CAMPHOID
CAMPHOL
CAMPHOLIDE
CAMPHOR
CAMPHORATE
CAMPHORATED
CAMPHORATING
CAMPHORIC
CAMPHOROYL
CAMPHORWOOD
CAMPHORYL
CAMPHYLENE
CAMPIER
CAMPIEST
CAMPILAN
CAMPIMETER
CAMPIMETRY
CAMPING
CAMPIT
CAMPLE
CAMPMAN
CAMPMASTER
CAMPO
CAMPODEID
CAMPODEIFORM
CAMPODEOID
CAMPODY
CAMPONG
CAMPOO
CAMPOODY
CAMPOREE
CAMPSHED
CAMPSHEDDING
CAMPSHEETING

CAMPSHOT
CAMPSITE
CAMPSTOOL
CAMPTODROME
CAMPTONITE
CAMPUS
CAMPUSES
CAMPWARD
CAMPY
CAMPYLITE
CAMPYLODROME
CAMPYLOMETER
CAMSHACH
CAMSHACHLE
CAMSHAFT
CAMSTANE
CAMSTEARY
CAMSTEERY
CAMSTONE
CAMSTRARY
CAMUNING
CAMUS
CAMUSE
CAMUSED
CAMWOOD
CAN
CANABA
CANABAE
CANACUAS
CANADA
CANADITE
CANADOL
CANAFISTOLO
CANAFISTULA
CANAFISTULO
CANAGLIA
CANAIGRE
CANAILLE
CANAJONG
CANAKIN
CANAL
CANALBOAT
CANALE
CANALER
CANALETE
CANALI
CANALICULAR
CANALICULATE
CANALICULI
CANALICULUS
CANALIFEROUS
CANALIFORM
CANALING
CANALIS
CANALIZATION
CANALIZE
CANALIZED
CANALIZING
CANALLA
CANALLER
CANALLING
CANAMO
CANAO
CANAPE
CANAPINA
CANARD
CANARI
CANARIES
CANARIN
CANARINE
CANARY
CANASTER
CANAUT
CANAVALIN
CANCAN
CANCEL
CANCELABLE
CANCELATION
CANCELED
CANCELEER
CANCELER
CANCELIER
CANCELING
CANCELLARIAN
CANCELLARIUS
CANCELLATE
CANCELLATED
CANCELLATION
CANCELLED
CANCELLER
CANCELLI
CANCELLING
CANCELLOUS
CANCELS
CANCER
CANCERATE
CANCERATED
CANCERATING
CANCERATION
CANCERDROPS
CANCERED
CANCERIGENIC
CANCERISM
CANCERITE
CANCEROPHOBE
CANCEROUS
CANCEROUSLY
CANCERROOT
CANCERWEED
CANCERWORT
CANCH
CANCHA
CANCHALAGUA
CANCHITO
CANCION
CANCIONERO
CANCIONES
CANCRID
CANCRIFORM
CANCRINITE
CANCRISOCIAL
CANCRIVOROUS
CANCRIZANS
CANCROID
CANCRUM
CANCRUMS
CAND
CANDAREEN
CANDELABRA
CANDELABRAS
CANDELABRUM
CANDELABRUMS
CANDELILLA
CANDENCY
CANDENT
CANDESCENCE
CANDESCENT
CANDESCENTLY
CANDI
CANDID
CANDIDACIES
CANDIDACY
CANDIDATE
CANDIDATED
CANDIDATES
CANDIDATING
CANDIDATURE
CANDIDLY
CANDIDNESS
CANDIED
CANDIEL
CANDIER
CANDIES
CANDIFY
CANDIL
CANDIRU
CANDITE
CANDLE
CANDLEBALL
CANDLEBEAM
CANDLEBERRY
CANDLEBOMB
CANDLEBOX
CANDLED
CANDLEFISH
CANDLEHOLDER
CANDLELIGHT
CANDLELIGHTING
CANDLELIT
CANDLEMAKER
CANDLEMAKING
CANDLENUT
CANDLEPIN
CANDLEPOWER
CANDLER
CANDLERENT
CANDLES
CANDLESHINE
CANDLESHRIFT
CANDLESNUFFER
CANDLESTAND
CANDLESTICK
CANDLEWASTER
CANDLEWICK
CANDLEWICKING
CANDLEWOOD
CANDLEWRIGHT
CANDLING
CANDOCK
CANDOR
CANDOUR
CANDROY
CANDROYS
CANDUC
CANDY
CANDYING
CANDYMAKER
CANDYS
CANDYSTICK
CANDYTUFT
CANDYWEED
CANE
CANEBRAKE
CANED
CANEL
CANELA
CANELL
CANELLA
CANELLACEOUS
CANELLE
CANELO
CANEOLOGY
CANEPHOR
CANEPHORA
CANEPHORAE
CANEPHORI
CANEPHOROE
CANEPHOROI
CANEPHOROS
CANEPHORUS
CANEPIN
CANER
CANESCENT
CANETON
CANETTE
CANEWARE
CANEWORK
CANEZOU
CANFIELDITE
CANG
CANGAN
CANGIA
CANGLE
CANGUE
CANGY
CANHOOP
CANI
CANICULE
CANID
CANILLE
CANIN
CANINAL
CANINE
CANING
CANINIFORM
CANINITY
CANINUS
CANIONED
CANIONS
CANISTEL
CANISTER
CANITIES
CANK
CANKER
CANKERBERRY
CANKERBIRD
CANKEREAT
CANKERED
CANKEREDLY
CANKEREDNESS
CANKERFLOWER
CANKERFRET
CANKEROUS
CANKERROOT
CANKERWEED
CANKERWORM
CANKERWORT
CANKERY
CANMAN
CANN
CANNA
CANNABIC
CANNABIN
CANNABINE
CANNABIS
CANNABISM
CANNACEOUS
CANNACH
CANNAT
CANNE
CANNED
CANNEL
CANNELE
CANNELLATE
CANNELLATED
CANNELLE
CANNELLONI
CANNELON
CANNELURE
CANNELURED
CANNEQUIN
CANNER
CANNERIES
CANNERY
CANNET
CANNETILLE
CANNIBAL
CANNIBALIC
CANNIBALISM
CANNIBALISTIC
CANNIBALITY
CANNIBALIZE
CANNIBALIZED
CANNIBALIZING
CANNIBALLY
CANNIER
CANNIEST
CANNIKIN
CANNILY
CANNINESS
CANNING
CANNON
CANNONADE
CANNONADED
CANNONADING
CANNONED
CANNONEER
CANNONEERING
CANNONIER
CANNONPROOF
CANNONRY
CANNOPHORI
CANNOT
CANNULA
CANNULAR
CANNULATE
CANNULATED
CANNY
CANOE
CANOEING
CANOEIST
CANOELOAD
CANOEMAN
CANOES
CANOEWOOD
CANON
CANONCITO
CANONESS
CANONIC
CANONICAL
CANONICALLY
CANONICALS
CANONICATE
CANONICITY
CANONICS
CANONIST
CANONISTIC
CANONISTICAL
CANONIZANT
CANONIZATION
CANONIZE
CANONIZED
CANONIZER
CANONIZING
CANONRY
CANONS
CANONSHIP
CANOODLE
CANOPID
CANOPIED
CANOPIES
CANOPY
CANOPYING
CANOR
CANOROUS
CANOROUSLY
CANOROUSNESS
CANOS
CANOTIER
CANROY
CANROYER
CANSH
CANSO
CANSOS
CANST
CANT
CANTABANK
CANTABILE
CANTADOR
CANTALA
CANTALEVER
CANTALITE
CANTALOUP
CANTALOUPE
CANTANKEROUS

CANTAR
CANTARA
CANTARE
CANTARO
CANTATA
CANTATION
CANTATIVE
CANTATORY
CANTATRICE
CANTED
CANTEEN
CANTER
CANTERED
CANTERER
CANTERING
CANTHAL
CANTHARI
CANTHARIDAL
CANTHARIDATE
CANTHARIDEAN
CANTHARIDES
CANTHARIDIAN
CANTHARIDIN
CANTHARIDISM
CANTHARIDIZE
CANTHARIS
CANTHARUS
CANTHECTOMY
CANTHI
CANTHITIS
CANTHOLYSIS
CANTHOPLASTY
CANTHOTOMY
CANTHUS
CANTIC
CANTICLE
CANTICLES
CANTICO
CANTIGA
CANTIL
CANTILATED
CANTILATING
CANTILENA
CANTILENE
CANTILENES
CANTILEVER
CANTILLATE
CANTILLATION
CANTILY
CANTINA
CANTING
CANTINGLY
CANTINGNESS
CANTINO
CANTION
CANTLE
CANTLET
CANTLINE
CANTO
CANTON
CANTONAL
CANTONED
CANTONER
CANTONMENT
CANTOON
CANTOR
CANTORAL
CANTORIA
CANTORIAL
CANTORIS
CANTOROUS
CANTOS
CANTRAIP
CANTRAP
CANTRED
CANTREF
CANTRIP
CANTUS
CANTUT
CANTUTA
CANTY
CANULA
CANULATE
CANUN
CANVAS
CANVASBACK
CANVASBACKS
CANVASMAN
CANVASS
CANVASSED
CANVASSER
CANVASSING
CANY
CANYON
CANZON
CANZONA
CANZONE
CANZONET
CANZONI
CAOBA
CAOINE
CAOUTCHOUC
CAP
CAPA
CAPABILITIES
CAPABILITY
CAPABLE
CAPABLENESS
CAPABLY
CAPACIOUS
CAPACIOUSLY
CAPACITANCE
CAPACITATE
CAPACITATED
CAPACITATING
CAPACITATION
CAPACITATIVE
CAPACITIES
CAPACITIVE
CAPACITOR
CAPACITY
CAPANNA
CAPANNE
CAPARISON
CAPARISONED
CAPARISONING
CAPATAZ
CAPAX
CAPCASE
CAPE
CAPEADOR
CAPEL
CAPELET
CAPELIN
CAPELINE
CAPELLET
CAPER
CAPERBUSH
CAPERCAILLIE
CAPERCAILZIE
CAPERCUT
CAPERED
CAPERER
CAPERING
CAPERNOITED
CAPERNOITIE
CAPERNOITY
CAPERNUTIE
CAPERS
CAPERSOME
CAPERWORT
CAPES
CAPESKIN
CAPETTE
CAPEWEED
CAPFUL
CAPH
CAPHAR
CAPHITE
CAPIAS
CAPIASES
CAPIBARA
CAPICHA
CAPILACEOUS
CAPILLAIRE
CAPILLAMENT
CAPILLARIES
CAPILLARITIES
CAPILLARITY
CAPILLARY
CAPILLATION
CAPILLI
CAPILLIFORM
CAPILLITIA
CAPILLITIAL
CAPILLITIUM
CAPILLOSE
CAPILLUS
CAPILOTADE
CAPISTRATE
CAPITA
CAPITAL
CAPITALED
CAPITALING
CAPITALISM
CAPITALIST
CAPITALISTIC
CAPITALIZE
CAPITALIZED
CAPITALIZING
CAPITALLY
CAPITAN
CAPITANA
CAPITANO
CAPITATE
CAPITATED
CAPITATIM
CAPITATION
CAPITATIVE
CAPITATUM
CAPITE
CAPITELLA
CAPITELLAR
CAPITELLATE
CAPITELLUM
CAPITOL
CAPITOUL
CAPITOULATE
CAPITULANT
CAPITULAR
CAPITULARIES
CAPITULARY
CAPITULATE
CAPITULATED
CAPITULATING
CAPITULATION
CAPITULATOR
CAPITULATORY
CAPITULIFORM
CAPITULUM
CAPLE
CAPLIN
CAPLING
CAPLOCK
CAPMAKER
CAPMAKING
CAPMAN
CAPMINT
CAPNOMANCY
CAPOCCHIA
CAPOMO
CAPON
CAPONIER
CAPONIERE
CAPONIZE
CAPONIZER
CAPONNIERE
CAPORAL
CAPOT
CAPOTASTO
CAPOTE
CAPOUCH
CAPPA
CAPPADINE
CAPPAE
CAPPED
CAPPELENITE
CAPPER
CAPPIE
CAPPING
CAPPLE
CAPPO
CAPPY
CAPRATE
CAPRELLINE
CAPREOL
CAPREOLATE
CAPREOLINE
CAPRETTO
CAPRIC
CAPRICCETTO
CAPRICCETTOS
CAPRICCIO
CAPRICCIOS
CAPRICCIOSO
CAPRICE
CAPRICIOUS
CAPRICIOUSLY
CAPRICIOUSNESS
CAPRID
CAPRIFICATE
CAPRIFICATOR
CAPRIFIG
CAPRIFOIL
CAPRIFOLE
CAPRIFORM
CAPRIGENOUS
CAPRIMULGINE
CAPRIN
CAPRINE
CAPRINIC
CAPRIOLE
CAPRIOLED
CAPRIOLING
CAPRIPED
CAPRIPEDE
CAPRIZANT
CAPROATE
CAPROIC
CAPROIN
CAPRONE
CAPRONIC
CAPRONYL
CAPROYL
CAPRYL
CAPRYLATE
CAPRYLIC
CAPRYLIN
CAPRYLONE
CAPRYLYL
CAPS
CAPSA
CAPSAICIN
CAPSHEAF
CAPSHORE
CAPSICIN
CAPSICUM
CAPSID
CAPSIZAL
CAPSIZE
CAPSIZED
CAPSIZING
CAPSTAN
CAPSTONE
CAPSULA
CAPSULAR
CAPSULATE
CAPSULATED
CAPSULATION
CAPSULE
CAPSULECTOMY
CAPSULED
CAPSULER
CAPSULING
CAPSULITIS
CAPSULOTOME
CAPSULOTOMY
CAPSUMIN
CAPTACULA
CAPTACULUM
CAPTAIN
CAPTAINCIES
CAPTAINCY
CAPTAINESS
CAPTAINRIES
CAPTAINRY
CAPTAINSHIP
CAPTATION
CAPTION
CAPTIOUS
CAPTIOUSLY
CAPTIOUSNESS
CAPTIVATE
CAPTIVATED
CAPTIVATELY
CAPTIVATING
CAPTIVATION
CAPTIVATIVE
CAPTIVATOR
CAPTIVE
CAPTIVED
CAPTIVING
CAPTIVITIES
CAPTIVITY
CAPTOR
CAPTURE
CAPTURED
CAPTURER
CAPTURING
CAPUCHE
CAPUCHIN
CAPUCINE
CAPUL
CAPULI
CAPULIN
CAPUT
CAPUTIUM
CAPYBARA
CAR
CARA
CARABAO
CARABAOS
CARABEEN
CARABID
CARABIDAN
CARABIDEOUS
CARABIDOID
CARABIN
CARABINE
CARABINEER
CARABINERO
CARABINIER
CARABINIERE
CARABINIERI
CARABOID

CARABUS
CARAC
CARACAL
CARACARA
CARACK
CARACO
CARACOA
CARACOL
CARACOLE
CARACOLED
CARACOLER
CARACOLI
CARACOLING
CARACOLITE
CARACOLLER
CARACORA
CARACORE
CARACT
CARACTER
CARACUL
CARAFE
CARAFON
CARAGHEEN
CARAGUATA
CARAIBE
CARAIPE
CARAIPI
CARAJO
CARAJURA
CARAMBA
CARAMBOLA
CARAMBOLE
CARAMBOLED
CARAMBOLING
CARAMEL
CARAMELAN
CARAMELEN
CARAMELIN
CARAMELIZE
CARAMELIZED
CARAMELIZING
CARANCHA
CARANCHO
CARANDA
CARANDAY
CARANE
CARANGID
CARANGIN
CARANGOID
CARANNA
CARANX
CARAP
CARAPA
CARAPACE
CARAPACED
CARAPACIC
CARAPATO
CARAPAX
CARAPINE
CARAPO
CARAT
CARATCH
CARATS
CARAUNA
CARAUNDA
CARAVAN
CARAVANEER
CARAVANIST
CARAVANNER
CARAVANSARY
CARAVANSERAI
CARAVEL
CARAVELLE
CARAWAY
CARBAMATE
CARBAMIC
CARBAMIDE
CARBAMINE
CARBAMINO
CARBAMYL
CARBANIL
CARBANILIC
CARBANILID
CARBANILIDE
CARBARN
CARBASUS
CARBAZIC
CARBAZIDE
CARBAZIN
CARBAZINE
CARBAZOLE
CARBAZYLIC
CARBEEN
CARBENE
CARBERRY
CARBETHOXYL
CARBIDE
CARBIMIDE
CARBIN
CARBINE
CARBINEER
CARBINOL
CARBINYL
CARBO
CARBOAZOTINE
CARBOCER
CARBODIIMIDE
CARBOGELATIN
CARBOHYDRASE
CARBOHYDRATE
CARBOHYDRIDE
CARBOLATE
CARBOLATED
CARBOLIC
CARBOLINEATE
CARBOLIZE
CARBOLIZED
CARBOLIZING
CARBOLXYLOL
CARBON
CARBONA
CARBONACEOUS
CARBONADO
CARBONADOED
CARBONADOES
CARBONADOS
CARBONATE
CARBONATED
CARBONATING
CARBONATION
CARBONATOR
CARBONE
CARBONEMIA
CARBONERO
CARBONIC
CARBONIDE
CARBONIMETER
CARBONIMIDE
CARBONITE
CARBONITRIDE
CARBONIUM
CARBONIZE
CARBONIZED
CARBONIZER
CARBONIZING
CARBONOMETRY
CARBONOUS
CARBONURIA
CARBONYL
CARBONYLENE
CARBONYLIC
CARBOPHILOUS
CARBORA
CARBORUNDUM
CARBOSTYRIL
CARBOXIDE
CARBOXYL
CARBOXYLASE
CARBOXYLATE
CARBOXYLATED
CARBOXYLIC
CARBOY
CARBOYED
CARBOYS
CARBRO
CARBROMAL
CARBUNCLE
CARBUNCLED
CARBUNCULAR
CARBUNGI
CARBURAN
CARBURANT
CARBURATE
CARBURATED
CARBURATING
CARBURET
CARBURETANT
CARBURETED
CARBURETING
CARBURETION
CARBURETOR
CARBURETTED
CARBURETTER
CARBURETTING
CARBURETTOR
CARBURISE
CARBURIZE
CARBURIZED
CARBURIZER
CARBURIZING
CARBUROMETER
CARBYL
CARBYLAMINE
CARCAJOU
CARCAKE
CARCAN
CARCANET
CARCANETED
CARCANETTED
CARCASE
CARCASS
CARCASSED
CARCASSES
CARCASSING
CARCEAG
CARCEL
CARCER
CARCERAL
CARCERATE
CARCERATED
CARCERATING
CARCERATION
CARCHARIID
CARCHARIOID
CARCHARODONT
CARCINOGEN
CARCINOGENIC
CARCINOID
CARCINOLOGY
CARCINOLYSIN
CARCINOLYTIC
CARCINOMA
CARCINOMAS
CARCINOSIS
CARCINUS
CARCOON
CARD
CARDAISSIN
CARDAMOM
CARDAMUM
CARDANOL
CARDBOARD
CARDCASE
CARDE
CARDECU
CARDED
CARDEL
CARDER
CARDIA
CARDIAC
CARDIACAL
CARDIACEAN
CARDIAGRA
CARDIAGRAM
CARDIAGRAPH
CARDIAGRAPHY
CARDIAL
CARDIALGIA
CARDIALGIC
CARDIALGY
CARDIAMETER
CARDIANEURIA
CARDIANT
CARDIAPLEGIA
CARDIARCTIA
CARDIASTHMA
CARDIATAXIA
CARDIATOMY
CARDIAUXE
CARDIECTASIS
CARDIECTOMY
CARDIELCOSIS
CARDIFORM
CARDIN
CARDINAL
CARDINALATE
CARDINALATED
CARDINALIC
CARDINALIST
CARDINALLY
CARDINALS
CARDINES
CARDING
CARDIOBLAST
CARDIOCARPUM
CARDIOCELE
CARDIOCLASIA
CARDIODYNIA
CARDIOGENIC
CARDIOGRAM
CARDIOGRAPH
CARDIOGRAPHY
CARDIOID
CARDIOLITH
CARDIOLOGIST
CARDIOLOGY
CARDIOLYSIS
CARDIOMEGALY
CARDIOMETER
CARDIOMETRIC
CARDIOMETRY
CARDIONCUS
CARDIONEURAL
CARDIONOSUS
CARDIOPATHIC
CARDIOPATHY
CARDIOPHOBE
CARDIOPHOBIA
CARDIOPLASTY
CARDIOPLEGIA
CARDIOPTOSIS
CARDIORENAL
CARDIOSCOPE
CARDIOSPASM
CARDIOTOMY
CARDIOTONIC
CARDIOTOXIC
CARDITA
CARDITIC
CARDITIS
CARDMAKER
CARDMAKING
CARDO
CARDOL
CARDON
CARDONA
CARDONCILLO
CARDOOER
CARDOON
CARDOPHAGUS
CARDOSANTO
CARDPLAYER
CARDPLAYING
CARDS
CARDSHARP
CARDSHARPER
CARDSHARPING
CARDUACEOUS
CARE
CARECLOTH
CARED
CAREEN
CAREENAGE
CAREENED
CAREENER
CAREENING
CAREER
CAREERED
CAREERER
CAREERING
CAREERISM
CAREERIST
CAREFOX
CAREFREE
CAREFUL
CAREFULLY
CAREFULNESS
CARELESS
CARELESSLY
CARELESSNESS
CAREME
CARENE
CARER
CARESS
CARESSANT
CARESSED
CARESSER
CARESSING
CARESSINGLY
CARESSIVE
CARESSIVELY
CAREST
CARET
CARETAKER
CAREWORN
CAREX
CARF
CARFARE
CARFAX
CARFOUR
CARFUFFLE
CARFUFFLED
CARFUFFLING
CARGA
CARGADOR
CARGADORES
CARGASON
CARGO
CARGOES
CARGOOSE
CARGOS
CARHOP
CARHOUSE
CARIBE
CARIBOU

CARIBOUS
CARICACEOUS
CARICATURAL
CARICATURE
CARICATURED
CARICATURING
CARICATURIST
CARICETUM
CARICOGRAPHY
CARICOLOGIST
CARICOUS
CARID
CARIDEAN
CARIDEER
CARIDOID
CARIE
CARIEN
CARIES
CARILLON
CARILLONNED
CARILLONNEUR
CARILLONNING
CARINA
CARINAE
CARINAL
CARINATE
CARINATED
CARINATION
CARING
CARINIFORM
CARIOCA
CARIOLE
CARIOLING
CARIOSITY
CARIOUS
CARIOUSNESS
CARITAS
CARITATIVE
CARITIVE
CARK
CARKING
CARKINGLY
CARKLED
CARL
CARLAGE
CARLE
CARLET
CARLEY
CARLIN
CARLINA
CARLINE
CARLING
CARLINGS
CARLINO
CARLINS
CARLOAD
CARLOADING
CARLOADINGS
CARLOT
CARLS
CARMAGNOLE
CARMALUM
CARMAN
CARMELE
CARMELOITE
CARMEN
CARMETTA
CARMINATIVE
CARMINE
CARMINETTE
CARMINIC
CARMINITE
CARMOT
CARN
CARNAGE
CARNAL
CARNALITE
CARNALITIES
CARNALITY
CARNALIZE
CARNALIZED
CARNALIZING
CARNALLITE
CARNALLY
CARNAPTIOUS
CARNASSIAL
CARNATE
CARNATION
CARNATIONED
CARNATIONIST
CARNAUBA
CARNAUBYL
CARNEAU
CARNEL
CARNELIAN
CARNEOL
CARNEOUS
CARNET
CARNEY
CARNEYED
CARNIC
CARNIED
CARNIFEROUS
CARNIFERRIN
CARNIFEX
CARNIFEXES
CARNIFICES
CARNIFICIAL
CARNIFIED
CARNIFORM
CARNIFY
CARNIFYING
CARNIVAL
CARNIVALER
CARNIVALLER
CARNIVORAL
CARNIVORE
CARNIVORISM
CARNIVOROUS
CARNOSE
CARNOSIN
CARNOSINE
CARNOSITIES
CARNOSITY
CARNOTITE
CARNOUS
CARNY
CAROA
CAROACH
CAROB
CAROBA
CAROCH
CAROCHE
CAROL
CAROLE
CAROLED
CAROLER
CAROLIN
CAROLINE
CAROLING
CAROLLED
CAROLLER
CAROLLING
CAROLS
CAROLUS
CAROM
CAROMBOLETTE
CAROMS
CARONE
CAROOME
CAROON
CAROSELLA
CAROT
CAROTENE
CAROTENOID
CAROTIC
CAROTID
CAROTIDAL
CAROTIN
CAROTINAEMIA
CAROTINEMIA
CAROTINOID
CAROTOL
CAROTTE
CAROUBIER
CAROUSAL
CAROUSE
CAROUSED
CAROUSEL
CAROUSER
CAROUSING
CAROUSINGLY
CARP
CARPAINE
CARPAL
CARPALE
CARPALIA
CARPED
CARPEL
CARPELLARY
CARPELLATE
CARPELLUM
CARPELS
CARPENT
CARPENTER
CARPENTERING
CARPENTRY
CARPER
CARPET
CARPETBAG
CARPETBAGGER
CARPETBAGISM
CARPETBEATER
CARPETING
CARPETMAKING
CARPETMONGER
CARPETWEB
CARPETWEED
CARPETWORK
CARPETWOVEN
CARPHOLITE
CARPI
CARPID
CARPIDIUM
CARPINCHO
CARPING
CARPINGLY
CARPINTERO
CARPITIS
CARPOCACE
CARPOCARPAL
CARPOCERITE
CARPOGAM
CARPOGAMY
CARPOGENIC
CARPOGONE
CARPOGONIA
CARPOGONIUM
CARPOLITE
CARPOLITH
CARPOLOGICAL
CARPOLOGIST
CARPOLOGY
CARPOMANIA
CARPOPEDAL
CARPOPHORE
CARPOPHYL
CARPOPHYTE
CARPOPODITE
CARPOPTOSIS
CARPOS
CARPOSPERM
CARPOSPORE
CARPOSPORIC
CARPOSPOROUS
CARPOSTOME
CARPS
CARPSUCKER
CARPUS
CARQUAISE
CARR
CARRACK
CARRAGEEN
CARRAGEENIN
CARRAGHEEN
CARRE
CARREAU
CARREE
CARREFOUR
CARREL
CARRELL
CARRETA
CARRETELA
CARRETERA
CARRETON
CARRETTA
CARRIABLE
CARRIAGE
CARRIAGEABLE
CARRIAGEWAY
CARRICK
CARRIED
CARRIER
CARRIES
CARRIGEEN
CARRIOLE
CARRION
CARRITCH
CARRITCHES
CARRIWITCHET
CARRIZO
CARROCCI
CARROCCIO
CARROCH
CARROLLITE
CARROM
CARROMATA
CARRONADE
CARROON
CARROSSERIE
CARROT
CARROTAGE
CARROTER
CARROTIEST
CARROTIN
CARROTINESS
CARROTING
CARROTTOP
CARROTY
CARROUSEL
CARROW
CARROZZA
CARRY
CARRYABLE
CARRYALL
CARRYING
CARS
CARSE
CARSHOP
CARSICK
CARSMITH
CARSTONE
CART
CARTAGE
CARTE
CARTEL
CARTELISM
CARTELIST
CARTELIZE
CARTELLIST
CARTERLY
CARTHAME
CARTHAMIN
CARTIER
CARTIEST
CARTILAGE
CARTILAGINEAN
CARTILAGINEOUS
CARTILAGINOID
CARTILAGINOUS
CARTISANE
CARTLOAD
CARTMAKER
CARTMAKING
CARTMAN
CARTOGRAM
CARTOGRAPH
CARTOGRAPHER
CARTOGRAPHIC
CARTOGRAPHICAL
CARTOGRAPHY
CARTOMANCY
CARTON
CARTONER
CARTONNAGE
CARTOON
CARTOONED
CARTOONING
CARTOONIST
CARTOUCH
CARTOUCHE
CARTRIDGE
CARTSALE
CARTULARIES
CARTULARY
CARTWARE
CARTWAY
CARTWHEEL
CARTWHIP
CARTWRIGHT
CARTY
CARUAGE
CARUCAGE
CARUCAL
CARUCARIUS
CARUCATE
CARUCATED
CARUE
CARUNCLE
CARUNCULA
CARUNCULAR
CARUNCULATE
CARUNCULATED
CARUNCULOUS
CARUS
CARVACROL
CARVACRYL
CARVAL
CARVE
CARVED
CARVEL
CARVEN
CARVENE
CARVES
CARVESTRENE
CARVING
CARVOEIRA
CARVOL
CARVONE
CARVY
CARVYL
CARWITCHET
CARYATIC
CARYATID
CARYATIDAL

CARYATIDEAN
CARYL
CARYOPHYLLIN
CARYOPILITE
CARYOPSIS
CARYOTIN
CASA
CASABA
CASAL
CASALTY
CASAQUE
CASAQUIN
CASATE
CASAUN
CASCABEL
CASCABLE
CASCADE
CASCADED
CASCADING
CASCADITE
CASCADO
CASCALHO
CASCALOTE
CASCAN
CASCARA
CASCARILLA
CASCARON
CASCAVEL
CASCHROM
CASCO
CASCOL
CASCROM
CASCROME
CASE
CASEASE
CASEATE
CASEATED
CASEATING
CASEATION
CASEBOOK
CASEBOX
CASED
CASEFIED
CASEFY
CASEFYING
CASEHARDEN
CASEHARDENED
CASEIC
CASEIN
CASEINATE
CASEINE
CASEINOGEN
CASEKEEPER
CASELTY
CASEMAKER
CASEMAKING
CASEMATE
CASEMATED
CASEMENT
CASEMENTED
CASEOLYSIS
CASEOSE
CASEOUS
CASER
CASERIO
CASERIOS
CASERN
CASERNE
CASES
CASEWEED
CASEWOOD
CASEWORK
CASEWORKER
CASEWORM
CASH
CASHABLE
CASHAW
CASHBOOK
CASHBOX
CASHBOY
CASHED
CASHEL
CASHEW
CASHGIRL
CASHIER
CASHIERED
CASHIERER
CASHING
CASHKEEPER
CASHMERE
CASHMERETTE
CASHOO
CASIMERE
CASIMIRE
CASINA
CASINET
CASING
CASINO
CASINOS
CASIRI
CASITA
CASK
CASKET
CASKING
CASKS
CASQUE
CASQUED
CASQUET
CASQUETEL
CASQUETTE
CASS
CASSABA
CASSABANANA
CASSABULLY
CASSADA
CASSALTY
CASSAN
CASSARE
CASSAREEP
CASSATE
CASSATION
CASSAVA
CASSE
CASSELTY
CASSENA
CASSEROLE
CASSETTE
CASSIA
CASSICAN
CASSIDEOUS
CASSIDID
CASSIDONY
CASSIDULOID
CASSIE
CASSIMERE
CASSINA
CASSINE
CASSINETTE
CASSINO
CASSINOID
CASSIOBERRY
CASSIRI
CASSIS
CASSITERITE
CASSITES
CASSOCK
CASSOCKED
CASSOLETTE
CASSON
CASSONADE
CASSONE
CASSONS
CASSOON
CASSOWARIES
CASSOWARY
CASSUMUNAR
CASSUMUNIAR
CASSY
CAST
CASTAGNOLE
CASTANA
CASTANEAN
CASTANEOUS
CASTANET
CASTANIAN
CASTANO
CASTAWAY
CASTE
CASTELET
CASTELLAN
CASTELLANIES
CASTELLANO
CASTELLANY
CASTELLAR
CASTELLATE
CASTELLATED
CASTELLATION
CASTELLET
CASTEN
CASTER
CASTHOUSE
CASTICE
CASTIGABLE
CASTIGATE
CASTIGATED
CASTIGATING
CASTIGATION
CASTIGATIVE
CASTIGATOR
CASTIGATORIES
CASTIGATORY
CASTILE
CASTILIAN
CASTILLO
CASTING
CASTINGS
CASTLE
CASTLED
CASTLERY
CASTLET
CASTOCK
CASTOFF
CASTOR
CASTOREUM
CASTORIAL
CASTORIN
CASTORITE
CASTORIZED
CASTORY
CASTRAL
CASTRATE
CASTRATED
CASTRATER
CASTRATING
CASTRATION
CASTRATO
CASTRATOR
CASTRENSIAN
CASTRUM
CASTULI
CASUAL
CASUALISM
CASUALIST
CASUALLY
CASUALNESS
CASUALTY
CASUIST
CASUISTIC
CASUISTICAL
CASUISTICALLY
CASUISTRIES
CASUISTRY
CASULA
CASUS
CASWELLITE
CAT
CATABAPTIST
CATABASES
CATABASIS
CATABATIC
CATABIBAZON
CATABIOTIC
CATABOLIC
CATABOLICALLY
CATABOLIN
CATABOLISM
CATABOLITE
CATABOLIZE
CATABOLIZED
CATABOLIZING
CATACAUSTIC
CATACHRESES
CATACHRESIS
CATACHRESTIC
CATACHTHONIAN
CATACHTHONIC
CATACLASM
CATACLASMIC
CATACLASTIC
CATACLINAL
CATACLYSM
CATACLYSMAL
CATACLYSMIC
CATACLYSMIST
CATACOMB
CATACOROLLA
CATACOUSTICS
CATACROTIC
CATACUMBAL
CATADICROTIC
CATADIOPTRIC
CATADROMOUS
CATADUPE
CATAFALQUE
CATAGENESIS
CATAGENETIC
CATAGMATIC
CATAKINESIS
CATALASE
CATALECTA
CATALECTIC
CATALEPSY
CATALEPTIZE
CATALEXIS
CATALIN
CATALINA
CATALINETA
CATALINITE
CATALLACTIC
CATALLACTICS
CATALLUM
CATALO
CATALOES
CATALOG
CATALOGED
CATALOGER
CATALOGIC
CATALOGICAL
CATALOGING
CATALOGIST
CATALOGISTIC
CATALOGUE
CATALOGUED
CATALOGUER
CATALOGUING
CATALOGUIST
CATALOGUIZE
CATALOON
CATALOS
CATALOWNE
CATALPA
CATALUFA
CATALYSES
CATALYSIS
CATALYST
CATALYTE
CATALYTIC
CATALYZATOR
CATALYZE
CATALYZED
CATALYZER
CATALYZING
CATAMARAN
CATAMENIA
CATAMENIAL
CATAMITE
CATAMNESIS
CATAMOUNT
CATAMOUNTAIN
CATAN
CATAPAN
CATAPASM
CATAPETALOUS
CATAPHATIC
CATAPHORA
CATAPHORESIS
CATAPHORIA
CATAPHRACT
CATAPHRENIC
CATAPHYLL
CATAPHYLLARY
CATAPLASIA
CATAPLASIS
CATAPLASM
CATAPLEIITE
CATAPLEXY
CATAPULT
CATAPULTIC
CATAPULTIER
CATARACT
CATARACTAL
CATARACTED
CATARACTINE
CATARACTOUS
CATARIA
CATARINITE
CATARRH
CATARRHAL
CATARRHED
CATARRHINE
CATARRHINIAN
CATARRHOUS
CATASARKA
CATASTA
CATASTALTIC
CATASTASES
CATASTASIS
CATASTATE
CATASTATIC
CATASTERISM
CATASTROPHAL
CATASTROPHE
CATASTROPHIC
CATATHYMIC
CATATONIA
CATATONIAC
CATATONIC
CATAWAMPUS
CATBERRY
CATBIRD
CATBOAT
CATBRIER
CATCALL
CATCH
CATCHALL

CATCHCRY
CATCHED
CATCHER
CATCHFLY
CATCHIER
CATCHIEST
CATCHING
CATCHINGLY
CATCHINGNESS
CATCHLAND
CATCHMENT
CATCHPENNY
CATCHPLATE
CATCHPOLE
CATCHPOLED
CATCHPOLERY
CATCHPOLING
CATCHPOLL
CATCHPOLLED
CATCHPOLLERY
CATCHPOLLING
CATCHUP
CATCHWEED
CATCHWEIGHT
CATCHWORD
CATCHWORK
CATCHY
CATE
CATECHESES
CATECHESIS
CATECHETIC
CATECHETICAL
CATECHIN
CATECHISE
CATECHISED
CATECHISER
CATECHISING
CATECHISM
CATECHISMAL
CATECHIST
CATECHISTIC
CATECHISTICAL
CATECHIZATION
CATECHIZE
CATECHIZED
CATECHIZER
CATECHIZING
CATECHOL
CATECHU
CATECHUMEN
CATECHUMENAL
CATEGOREM
CATEGORIAL
CATEGORIC
CATEGORICAL
CATEGORIES
CATEGORIST
CATEGORIZE
CATEGORIZED
CATEGORIZING
CATEGORY
CATELLA
CATENA
CATENAE
CATENARIAN
CATENARIES
CATENARY
CATENATE
CATENATED
CATENATING
CATENATION
CATENOID
CATENULATE
CATEPUCE
CATER
CATERAN
CATERCAP
CATERCOUSIN
CATERED
CATERER
CATERESS
CATERING
CATERPILLAR
CATERPILLARS
CATERS
CATERVA
CATERWAUL
CATERWAULER
CATERWAULING
CATES
CATFACE
CATFACED
CATFALL
CATFIGHT
CATFISH
CATFISHES
CATFOOT
CATFOOTED
CATGUT
CATHARIZE
CATHARIZED
CATHARIZING
CATHARPING
CATHARSIS
CATHARTIC
CATHARTICAL
CATHEAD
CATHECTIC
CATHEDRA
CATHEDRAL
CATHEDRALIC
CATHEDRATIC
CATHEPSIN
CATHETER
CATHETERISM
CATHETERIZE
CATHETERIZED
CATHETOMETER
CATHETUS
CATHEXIS
CATHISMA
CATHODE
CATHODEGRAPH
CATHODIC
CATHODICAL
CATHODICALLY
CATHODOGRAPH
CATHOLE
CATHOLIC
CATHOLICAL
CATHOLICALLY
CATHOLICATE
CATHOLICISM
CATHOLICITY
CATHOLICIZE
CATHOLICIZED
CATHOLICIZING
CATHOLICLY
CATHOLICNESS
CATHOLICON
CATHOLICOS
CATHOLICUS
CATHOLYTE
CATHOP
CATHOUSE
CATION
CATIVO
CATJANG
CATKIN
CATKINATE
CATLA
CATLAP
CATLIKE
CATLIN
CATLINE
CATLING
CATLINITE
CATMALISON
CATMINT
CATNACHE
CATNEP
CATNIP
CATOBLEPAS
CATOCALID
CATOCTIN
CATODONT
CATOGENE
CATOGENIC
CATOPTRIC
CATOPTRICAL
CATOPTRICS
CATOPTRITE
CATOSTOMID
CATOSTOMOID
CATOUSE
CATPIECE
CATPIPE
CATS
CATSKIN
CATSKINNER
CATSLIDE
CATSO
CATSOS
CATSTANE
CATSTEP
CATSTICK
CATSTITCH
CATSTITCHER
CATSTONE
CATSUP
CATTABU
CATTAIL
CATTALO
CATTAN
CATTED
CATTER
CATTERIES
CATTERY
CATTIER
CATTIES
CATTIEST
CATTILY
CATTIMANDOO
CATTINESS
CATTISH
CATTISHLY
CATTISHNESS
CATTLE
CATTLEBUSH
CATTLEHIDE
CATTLEMAN
CATTLEYA
CATTLEYAK
CATTY
CATTYMAN
CATUR
CATVINE
CATWALK
CATWORT
CATYDID
CATZERIE
CAUBEEN
CAUBOGE
CAUCH
CAUCHEMAR
CAUCHILLO
CAUCHO
CAUCUS
CAUCUSED
CAUCUSING
CAUCUSSED
CAUCUSSING
CAUDA
CAUDAD
CAUDAL
CAUDALLY
CAUDATE
CAUDATED
CAUDATION
CAUDATORY
CAUDATUM
CAUDEX
CAUDEXES
CAUDICES
CAUDICLE
CAUDIFORM
CAUDILLO
CAUDLE
CAUDODORSAL
CAUDOFEMORAL
CAUDOLATERAL
CAUDOTIBIAL
CAUFLE
CAUGHT
CAUK
CAUKED
CAUKING
CAUL
CAULD
CAULDRIFE
CAULES
CAULESCENT
CAULICLE
CAULICOLOUS
CAULICULI
CAULICULUS
CAULIFLOROUS
CAULIFLORY
CAULIFLOWER
CAULIFORM
CAULIGENOUS
CAULINE
CAULIS
CAULOCARPIC
CAULOCARPOUS
CAULOME
CAULOMER
CAULOMIC
CAULOTAXY
CAULOTE
CAULP
CAUM
CAUMA
CAUMATIC
CAUP
CAUPONATE
CAUPONATION
CAUPONES
CAUPONIZE
CAUR
CAURALE
CAURE
CAUSA
CAUSABILITY
CAUSABLE
CAUSAE
CAUSAL
CAUSALGIA
CAUSALITIES
CAUSALITY
CAUSALLY
CAUSATA
CAUSATE
CAUSATION
CAUSATIONAL
CAUSATIONIST
CAUSATIVE
CAUSATIVELY
CAUSATUM
CAUSE
CAUSED
CAUSER
CAUSERIE
CAUSES
CAUSEUR
CAUSEUSE
CAUSEWAY
CAUSEWAYED
CAUSEWAYING
CAUSEWAYMAN
CAUSEY
CAUSEYS
CAUSIDICAL
CAUSING
CAUSINGNESS
CAUSSE
CAUSSON
CAUSTIC
CAUSTICAL
CAUSTICALLY
CAUSTICISER
CAUSTICISM
CAUSTICITY
CAUSTICIZE
CAUSTICIZED
CAUSTICIZER
CAUSTICIZING
CAUSTICLY
CAUSTICNESS
CAUSTIFIED
CAUSTIFY
CAUSTIFYING
CAUTEL
CAUTELA
CAUTELOUS
CAUTER
CAUTERANT
CAUTERIES
CAUTERIZATION
CAUTERIZE
CAUTERIZED
CAUTERIZING
CAUTERY
CAUTIO
CAUTION
CAUTIONARIES
CAUTIONARY
CAUTIONER
CAUTIONES
CAUTIONRY
CAUTIOUS
CAUTIOUSLY
CAUTIOUSNESS
CAVAL
CAVALCADE
CAVALCADED
CAVALCADING
CAVALIER
CAVALIERE
CAVALIERED
CAVALIERING
CAVALIERISM
CAVALIERLY
CAVALIERO
CAVALLA
CAVALRIES
CAVALRY
CAVALRYMAN
CAVASCOPE
CAVATE
CAVATINA
CAVAYARD
CAVE
CAVEA
CAVEAT

CAVEATEE
CAVEATOR
CAVEFISH
CAVEFISHES
CAVEKEEPER
CAVEL
CAVENDISH
CAVER
CAVERN
CAVERNAL
CAVERNED
CAVERNITIS
CAVERNOMA
CAVERNOUS
CAVERNOUSLY
CAVERNULOUS
CAVESON
CAVESSON
CAVETTO
CAVEY
CAVIAR
CAVIARE
CAVICORN
CAVIE
CAVIES
CAVIL
CAVILED
CAVILER
CAVILING
CAVILINGLY
CAVILINGNESS
CAVILLATION
CAVILLED
CAVILLINGLY
CAVING
CAVINGS
CAVITARY
CAVITATE
CAVITATED
CAVITATING
CAVITATION
CAVITENO
CAVITIED
CAVITIES
CAVITY
CAVIYA
CAVORT
CAVORTED
CAVORTING
CAVUM
CAVY
CAVYYARD
CAW
CAWF
CAWK
CAWKY
CAWL
CAWNEY
CAWNIE
CAWNY
CAWQUAW
CAXI
CAXIRI
CAXON
CAY
CAYAR
CAYENNE
CAYENNED
CAYMAN
CAYMANS
CAYNARD
CAYO
CAYOS
CAYUCA
CAYUCO
CAYUSE
CAZA
CAZIBI
CAZIMI
CAZIQUE
CAZY
CE
CEARIN
CEASE
CEASED
CEASELESS
CEASELESSLY
CEASING
CEASMIC
CEBELL
CEBID
CEBIL
CEBINE
CEBOID
CEBOLLITE
CEBUR
CECA
CECCHINE
CECIDIOLOGY
CECIDIUM
CECILITE
CECILS
CECITIS
CECITY
CECOGRAPH
CECOMORPHIC
CECOTOMY
CECUTIENCY
CEDAR
CEDARBIRD
CEDARED
CEDARN
CEDARWARE
CEDARWOOD
CEDE
CEDED
CEDENS
CEDENT
CEDILLA
CEDILLAS
CEDING
CEDOR
CEDRA
CEDRAT
CEDRATE
CEDRE
CEDRENE
CEDRIN
CEDRINE
CEDRIRET
CEDRIUM
CEDROL
CEDRON
CEDRY
CEDULA
CEDUOUS
CEE
CEEL
CEIBA
CEIBO
CEIL
CEILE
CEILED
CEILER
CEILIDH
CEILIDHE
CEILING
CEILINGED
CEILOMETER
CEINT
CEINTURE
CEL
CELADONITE
CELANDINE
CELARENT
CELATION
CELATIVE
CELATURE
CELEB
CELEBE
CELEBRANT
CELEBRATE
CELEBRATED
CELEBRATER
CELEBRATING
CELEBRATION
CELEBRATIVE
CELEBRATOR
CELEBRATORY
CELEBRIOUS
CELEBRIOUSLY
CELEBRITIES
CELEBRITY
CELEMIN
CELEMINES
CELEOMORPH
CELEOMORPHIC
CELER
CELERIAC
CELERITY
CELERY
CELESTA
CELESTE
CELESTIAL
CELESTIALITY
CELESTIALIZE
CELESTIALIZED
CELESTINA
CELESTINE
CELESTITE
CELIADELPHUS
CELIAGRA
CELIBACY
CELIBATAIRE
CELIBATARIAN
CELIBATE
CELIBATIC
CELIBATIST
CELIBATORY
CELIDOGRAPHY
CELIOCELE
CELIOCYESIS
CELIODYNIA
CELIOLYMPH
CELIOMYALGIA
CELIORRHAPHY
CELIORRHEA
CELIOSCHISIS
CELIOSCOPE
CELIOSCOPY
CELIOTOMY
CELITE
CELL
CELLA
CELLAE
CELLAR
CELLARAGE
CELLARED
CELLARER
CELLARESS
CELLARET
CELLARING
CELLARMAN
CELLAROUS
CELLARWAY
CELLARWOMAN
CELLATED
CELLED
CELLI
CELLIFORM
CELLIPETAL
CELLIST
CELLO
CELLOBIOSE
CELLOCUT
CELLOID
CELLOIDIN
CELLOIST
CELLOPHANE
CELLOS
CELLOSE
CELLS
CELLULAR
CELLULARITY
CELLULARLY
CELLULASE
CELLULATE
CELLULATED
CELLULATION
CELLULE
CELLULIFUGAL
CELLULIN
CELLULIPETAL
CELLULITIS
CELLULOID
CELLULOIDED
CELLULOSE
CELLULOSED
CELLULOSIC
CELLULOSING
CELLULOSITIES
CELLULOSITY
CELLULOUS
CELOM
CELOTOMIES
CELOTOMY
CELSIAN
CELSITUDE
CELT
CELTIFORM
CELTIUM
CELTUCE
CELURE
CEMBALIST
CEMBALO
CEMBALON
CEMBALOS
CEMENT
CEMENTAL
CEMENTATION
CEMENTATORY
CEMENTER
CEMENTIN
CEMENTITE
CEMENTITIOUS
CEMENTMAKER
CEMENTMAKING
CEMENTOBLAST
CEMENTOMA
CEMENTUM
CEMETERIAL
CEMETERIES
CEMETERY
CENA
CENACLE
CENACULUM
CENANTHOUS
CENANTHY
CENATION
CENATORY
CENCERRO
CENCERROS
CENESTHESIA
CENESTHESIS
CENESTHETIC
CENIZO
CENOBE
CENOBIAN
CENOBIES
CENOBITE
CENOBITIC
CENOBITICAL
CENOBITISM
CENOBIUM
CENOBY
CENOGENESIS
CENOGENETIC
CENOGONOUS
CENOSITE
CENOSITY
CENOTAPH
CENOTAPHIC
CENOTAPHIES
CENOTAPHY
CENOTE
CENOZOOLOGY
CENS
CENSE
CENSED
CENSER
CENSING
CENSITAIRE
CENSIVE
CENSO
CENSOR
CENSORATE
CENSORED
CENSORIAL
CENSORIAN
CENSORING
CENSORIOUS
CENSORIOUSLY
CENSORSHIP
CENSUAL
CENSURABLE
CENSURABLY
CENSURE
CENSURED
CENSURER
CENSURESHIP
CENSURING
CENSUS
CENSUSES
CENT
CENTAGE
CENTAL
CENTAS
CENTAUR
CENTAURIAL
CENTAURIAN
CENTAURIC
CENTAURIES
CENTAURY
CENTAVO
CENTAVOS
CENTENA
CENTENAR
CENTENARIAN
CENTENARIES
CENTENARY
CENTENIER
CENTENNIAL
CENTENNIUM
CENTER
CENTERBOARD
CENTERED
CENTEREDNESS
CENTERER
CENTERING
CENTERLESS
CENTERMOST
CENTERPIECE
CENTESIMAL
CENTESIMALLY
CENTESIMATE

CENTESIMI
CENTESIMO
CENTESIMOS
CENTESIS
CENTESM
CENTETID
CENTGENER
CENTIARE
CENTIBAR
CENTIDAY
CENTIFOLIOUS
CENTIGRADE
CENTIGRAM
CENTIGRAMME
CENTILE
CENTILITER
CENTILITRE
CENTILLION
CENTILLIONTH
CENTIME
CENTIMETER
CENTIMETRE
CENTIMOLAR
CENTINORMAL
CENTIPEDAL
CENTIPEDE
CENTIPLUME
CENTIPOISE
CENTISTERE
CENTISTOKE
CENTNER
CENTO
CENTON
CENTONICAL
CENTONISM
CENTOS
CENTRA
CENTRAD
CENTRAL
CENTRALISM
CENTRALIST
CENTRALISTIC
CENTRALITY
CENTRALIZE
CENTRALIZED
CENTRALIZER
CENTRALIZING
CENTRANTH
CENTRARCHOID
CENTRE
CENTREBOARD
CENTRED
CENTRELESS
CENTREMOST
CENTREPIECE
CENTRER
CENTRIC
CENTRICAL
CENTRICALITY
CENTRICALLY
CENTRICIPUT
CENTRICITY
CENTRIFFED
CENTRIFUGAL
CENTRIFUGATE
CENTRIFUGE
CENTRIFUGED
CENTRIFUGING
CENTRING
CENTRIOLE
CENTRIPETAL
CENTRISCID
CENTRIST
CENTRO
CENTROACINAR
CENTROBARIC
CENTROCLINAL
CENTRODE
CENTRODORSAL
CENTROID
CENTROIDAL
CENTROLINEAD
CENTROLINEAL
CENTROPLASM
CENTROSOME
CENTROSOMIC
CENTROSPHERE
CENTRUM
CENTRUMS
CENTRY
CENTS
CENTUM
CENTUMVIR
CENTUMVIRAL
CENTUMVIRATE
CENTUPLE
CENTUPLICATE
CENTUPLY
CENTURE
CENTURIAL
CENTURIATE
CENTURIATION
CENTURIATOR
CENTURIED
CENTURIES
CENTURION
CENTURY
CEORL
CEP
CEPA
CEPACEOUS
CEPE
CEPHAELINE
CEPHALAD
CEPHALAGRA
CEPHALALGIA
CEPHALALGIC
CEPHALALGY
CEPHALATE
CEPHALEMIA
CEPHALETRON
CEPHALIC
CEPHALIN
CEPHALINE
CEPHALISM
CEPHALITIS
CEPHALOB
CEPHALOCELE
CEPHALOCHORD
CEPHALOCLAST
CEPHALOCONE
CEPHALOCONIC
CEPHALOCYST
CEPHALOGRAM
CEPHALOGRAPH
CEPHALOID
CEPHALOLOGY
CEPHALOMANCY
CEPHALOMANT
CEPHALOMELUS
CEPHALOMENIA
CEPHALOMERE
CEPHALOMETER
CEPHALOMETRIC
CEPHALOMETRY
CEPHALOMOTOR
CEPHALON
CEPHALONASAL
CEPHALOPAGUS
CEPHALOPATHY
CEPHALOPHINE
CEPHALOPHYMA
CEPHALOPOD
CEPHALOPODAN
CEPHALOPODIC
CEPHALOSOME
CEPHALOSTYLE
CEPHALOTHECA
CEPHALOTOME
CEPHALOTOMY
CEPHALOTRIBE
CEPHALOUS
CEPHID
CEPTER
CEPTOR
CEQUI
CERACEOUS
CERAGO
CERAL
CERAMAL
CERAMBYCID
CERAMIACEOUS
CERAMIC
CERAMICITE
CERAMICS
CERAMIDIUM
CERAMIST
CERAMOGRAPHY
CERARGYRITE
CERAS
CERASEIN
CERASIN
CERASTES
CERATA
CERATE
CERATECTOMY
CERATED
CERATIASIS
CERATIID
CERATIOID
CERATION
CERATITE
CERATITIC
CERATITOID
CERATOBRANCHIA
CERATOHYAL
CERATOID
CERATOMANIA
CERATOPHYTE
CERATOPSIAN
CERATOPSID
CERATORHINE
CERATOTHECA
CERATOTHECAE
CERATOTHECAL
CERAUNIA
CERAUNICS
CERAUNOGRAM
CERAUNOGRAPH
CERAUNOMANCY
CERAUNOPHONE
CERAUNOSCOPE
CERAUNOSCOPY
CERCAL
CERCARIA
CERCARIAE
CERCARIAL
CERCARIAN
CERCARIFORM
CERCIS
CERCLE
CERCOMONAD
CERCOPID
CERCOPOD
CERCUS
CERE
CEREAL
CEREALIAN
CEREALISM
CEREALIST
CEREALS
CEREBELLA
CEREBELLAR
CEREBELLUM
CEREBELLUMS
CEREBRAL
CEREBRALGIA
CEREBRALISM
CEREBRALIST
CEREBRATE
CEREBRATED
CEREBRATING
CEREBRATION
CEREBRIC
CEREBRICITY
CEREBRIFORM
CEREBRIFUGAL
CEREBRIN
CEREBRIPETAL
CEREBRITIS
CEREBRIZE
CEREBROID
CEREBROLOGY
CEREBROMA
CEREBROMETER
CEREBRON
CEREBRONIC
CEREBROPATHY
CEREBROPEDAL
CEREBROSCOPE
CEREBROSCOPY
CEREBROSE
CEREBROSIDE
CEREBROSIS
CEREBROSURIA
CEREBROTOMY
CEREBRUM
CERECLOTH
CERED
CEREMENT
CEREMONIAL
CEREMONIALLY
CEREMONIES
CEREMONIOUS
CEREMONY
CEREOUS
CERER
CERESIN
CERESINE
CEREUS
CEREVIS
CEREZA
CERFOIL
CERIA
CERIANTHID
CERIANTHOID
CERIC
CERID
CERIDE
CERIFEROUS
CERILLO
CERIMAN
CERIN
CERINE
CERING
CERIOPS
CERIPH
CERISE
CERITE
CERITHIOID
CERIUM
CERN
CERNED
CERNING
CERNITURE
CERNUOUS
CERO
CEROGRAPH
CEROGRAPHIC
CEROGRAPHICAL
CEROGRAPHIES
CEROGRAPHIST
CEROGRAPHY
CEROID
CEROLINE
CEROLITE
CEROMA
CEROMANCY
CEROPHILOUS
CEROPLAST
CEROPLASTIC
CEROPLASTICS
CEROS
CEROTATE
CEROTE
CEROTENE
CEROTIC
CEROTIN
CEROTYPE
CEROUS
CEROXYLE
CERRERO
CERRIAL
CERRIS
CERRO
CERT
CERTAIN
CERTAINLY
CERTAINTIES
CERTAINTY
CERTES
CERTIE
CERTIFIABLE
CERTIFICATE
CERTIFICATED
CERTIFICATING
CERTIFICATION
CERTIFICATIVE
CERTIFICATOR
CERTIFICATORY
CERTIFIED
CERTIFIER
CERTIFY
CERTIFYING
CERTIORARI
CERTIORATE
CERTIORATING
CERTITUDE
CERTOSA
CERTOSE
CERTOSINA
CERTOSINO
CERTY
CERULE
CERULEAN
CERULEITE
CERULEOUS
CERULEUM
CERULIGNOL
CERULIGNONE
CERUMEN
CERUMINOUS
CERUSE
CERUSITE
CERUSSITE
CERVALET
CERVANTITE
CERVELAT
CERVELIERE
CERVICAL
CERVICECTOMY
CERVICES
CERVICITIS
CERVICONASAL
CERVICORN

CERVID
CERVINE
CERVISIA
CERVISIAL
CERVIX
CERVIXES
CERVOID
CERYL
CESAREAN
CESAREVITCH
CESARIAN
CESAROLITE
CESIOUS
CESIUM
CESPITITIOUS
CESPITOSE
CESPITOSELY
CESS
CESSANT
CESSATION
CESSATIVE
CESSAVIT
CESSE
CESSED
CESSER
CESSING
CESSIO
CESSION
CESSIONAIRE
CESSIONARIES
CESSIONARY
CESSOR
CESSPIPE
CESSPIT
CESSPOOL
CEST
CESTA
CESTODE
CESTODES
CESTOID
CESTON
CESTRUM
CESTUI
CESTUS
CESTUY
CETACEAN
CETACEOUS
CETACEUM
CETE
CETENE
CETERACH
CETIC
CETICIDE
CETIN
CETIOSAURIAN
CETOLOGICAL
CETOLOGIST
CETOLOGY
CETONIAN
CETORHINID
CETORHINOID
CETOTOLITE
CETRARIN
CETYL
CETYLENE
CETYLIC
CEVADILLA
CEVIAN
CEVICHE
CEVIN
CEVINE
CEYLANITE
CEYLONITE
CHA
CHAA
CHAAC
CHAB
CHABASIE
CHABASITE
CHABAZITE
CHABER
CHABO
CHABOT
CHABOUK
CHABUK
CHABUTRA
CHACATE
CHACCON
CHACE
CHACK
CHACKER
CHACKLE
CHACMA
CHACOLI
CHACONA
CHACONNE
CHACRA
CHACTE
CHADACRYST
CHADELLE
CHADLOCK
CHADOR
CHAETA
CHAETAE
CHAETIFEROUS
CHAETOGNATH
CHAETOPOD
CHAETOPODAN
CHAETOPTERIN
CHAETOSEMA
CHAETOTAXY
CHAFE
CHAFED
CHAFER
CHAFERY
CHAFEWAX
CHAFEWEED
CHAFF
CHAFFCUTTER
CHAFFED
CHAFFER
CHAFFERED
CHAFFERER
CHAFFERING
CHAFFERY
CHAFFIER
CHAFFIEST
CHAFFINCH
CHAFFING
CHAFFMAN
CHAFFSEED
CHAFFWAX
CHAFFWEED
CHAFFY
CHAFING
CHAFT
CHAGIGAH
CHAGOMA
CHAGRIN
CHAGRINED
CHAGRINING
CHAGRINS
CHAGUAR
CHAGUL
CHAHAR
CHAI
CHAIN
CHAINAGE
CHAINBEARER
CHAINED
CHAINER
CHAINETTE
CHAINING
CHAINLESS
CHAINLET
CHAINMAKER
CHAINMAKING
CHAINMAN
CHAINMEN
CHAINON
CHAINS
CHAINWORK
CHAIR
CHAIRER
CHAIRMAKER
CHAIRMAKING
CHAIRMAN
CHAIRMEN
CHAIRMENDER
CHAIRMENDING
CHAIRWARMER
CHAIRWAY
CHAIRWOMAN
CHAIRWOMEN
CHAIS
CHAISE
CHAITRA
CHAITYA
CHAITYAS
CHAJA
CHAK
CHAKAR
CHAKARI
CHAKAZI
CHAKDAR
CHAKOBU
CHAKRA
CHAKRAVARTIN
CHAKSI
CHAL
CHALACO
CHALANA
CHALASTIC
CHALAZA
CHALAZAE
CHALAZAL
CHALAZAS
CHALAZE
CHALAZIAN
CHALAZION
CHALAZIUM
CHALAZOGAM
CHALAZOGAMIC
CHALAZOGAMY
CHALAZOIDITE
CHALCANTHITE
CHALCEDONIC
CHALCEDONIES
CHALCEDONOUS
CHALCEDONY
CHALCEDONYX
CHALCHIHUITL
CHALCHUITE
CHALCID
CHALCIDICUM
CHALCIDID
CHALCIDIFORM
CHALCITES
CHALCOCITE
CHALCOGRAPH
CHALCOGRAPHY
CHALCOLITE
CHALCOLITHIC
CHALCOMANCY
CHALCOMENITE
CHALCON
CHALCONE
CHALCOPYRITE
CHALCOSINE
CHALCOTRIPT
CHALCUS
CHALDER
CHALDESE
CHALDRON
CHALET
CHALICE
CHALICED
CHALICOSIS
CHALICOTHERE
CHALININE
CHALK
CHALKBOARD
CHALKCUTTER
CHALKED
CHALKER
CHALKIER
CHALKIEST
CHALKINESS
CHALKING
CHALKOGRAPHY
CHALKONE
CHALKOS
CHALKOTHEKE
CHALKSTONE
CHALKWORKER
CHALKY
CHALLAH
CHALLENGE
CHALLENGED
CHALLENGEE
CHALLENGER
CHALLENGING
CHALLIS
CHALLOTE
CHALMER
CHALON
CHALONE
CHALOUPE
CHALQUE
CHALTA
CHALUKA
CHALUMEAU
CHALUMEAUX
CHALYBEATE
CHALYBEOUS
CHALYBITE
CHAM
CHAMADE
CHAMAERRHINE
CHAMAL
CHAMAR
CHAMBELLAN
CHAMBER
CHAMBERED
CHAMBERER
CHAMBERING
CHAMBERLAIN
CHAMBERLET
CHAMBERLETED
CHAMBERLETTED
CHAMBERMAID
CHAMBERWOMAN
CHAMBRANLE
CHAMBRAY
CHAMBUL
CHAMECEPHALY
CHAMELEON
CHAMELEONIC
CHAMELEONIZE
CHAMETZ
CHAMFER
CHAMFERER
CHAMFRAIN
CHAMFRON
CHAMISAL
CHAMISE
CHAMISO
CHAMITE
CHAMM
CHAMMA
CHAMMY
CHAMOIS
CHAMOISITE
CHAMOLINE
CHAMOTTE
CHAMP
CHAMPAC
CHAMPACA
CHAMPAGNE
CHAMPAGNED
CHAMPAGNING
CHAMPAGNIZE
CHAMPAGNIZED
CHAMPAGNIZING
CHAMPAIGN
CHAMPAIN
CHAMPAK
CHAMPART
CHAMPE
CHAMPED
CHAMPER
CHAMPERTIES
CHAMPERTOR
CHAMPERTOUS
CHAMPERTY
CHAMPIAN
CHAMPIGNON
CHAMPION
CHAMPIONED
CHAMPIONESS
CHAMPIONING
CHAMPIONSHIP
CHAMPLEVE
CHAMPY
CHAMSIN
CHAN
CHANCE
CHANCEABLE
CHANCEABLY
CHANCED
CHANCEFUL
CHANCEFULLY
CHANCEL
CHANCELED
CHANCELLED
CHANCELLERY
CHANCELLOR
CHANCELOR
CHANCELRY
CHANCER
CHANCERIES
CHANCERY
CHANCEY
CHANCHE
CHANCIER
CHANCIEST
CHANCILY
CHANCING
CHANCITO
CHANCO
CHANCRE
CHANCRIFORM
CHANCROID
CHANCROIDAL
CHANCROUS
CHANCY
CHANDALA
CHANDAM
CHANDELIER
CHANDI
CHANDLER
CHANDLERIES
CHANDLERING
CHANDLERLY
CHANDLERY

CHANDOO
CHANDRAKANTA
CHANDRAKHI
CHANDU
CHANDUL
CHANFRIN
CHANG
CHANGA
CHANGAR
CHANGE
CHANGEABLE
CHANGEABLENESS
CHANGEABLY
CHANGED
CHANGEFUL
CHANGEFULLY
CHANGELESS
CHANGELESSLY
CHANGELING
CHANGEOVER
CHANGER
CHANGES
CHANGING
CHANK
CHANKINGS
CHANNEL
CHANNELBILL
CHANNELED
CHANNELING
CHANNELIZE
CHANNELIZED
CHANNELIZING
CHANNELLED
CHANNELLING
CHANNELS
CHANNER
CHANOYU
CHANSON
CHANSONNETTE
CHANSONNIER
CHANT
CHANTAGE
CHANTANT
CHANTECLER
CHANTEFABLE
CHANTEPLEURE
CHANTER
CHANTERELLE
CHANTEUR
CHANTEUSE
CHANTEY
CHANTEYMAN
CHANTICLEER
CHANTIER
CHANTING
CHANTINGLY
CHANTLATE
CHANTMENT
CHANTOR
CHANTRESS
CHANTRY
CHANTY
CHAOGENOUS
CHAOLOGY
CHAOS
CHAOTIC
CHAOTICAL
CHAOTICALLY
CHAOUA
CHAOUSH
CHAP
CHAPAH
CHAPAPOTE
CHAPARAJOS
CHAPAREJOS
CHAPARRAL
CHAPARRO
CHAPATTI
CHAPATTIES
CHAPATTY
CHAPBOOK
CHAPE
CHAPEAU
CHAPEAUS
CHAPEAUX
CHAPEL
CHAPELED
CHAPELET
CHAPELGOER
CHAPELGOING
CHAPELING
CHAPELLANY
CHAPELLED
CHAPELLING
CHAPELMAN
CHAPELMASTER
CHAPELRIES
CHAPELRY
CHAPERNO
CHAPERON
CHAPERONAGE
CHAPERONED
CHAPERONING
CHAPFALLEN
CHAPFALLENLY
CHAPIN
CHAPITER
CHAPITRAL
CHAPLAIN
CHAPLAINCIES
CHAPLAINCY
CHAPLAINRY
CHAPLAINSHIP
CHAPLANRY
CHAPLESS
CHAPLET
CHAPLETED
CHAPMAN
CHAPON
CHAPOTE
CHAPOURNET
CHAPOURNETTED
CHAPPAUL
CHAPPE
CHAPPED
CHAPPER
CHAPPIE
CHAPPIES
CHAPPING
CHAPPOW
CHAPPY
CHAPRASI
CHAPS
CHAPT
CHAPTER
CHAPTERAL
CHAPTERED
CHAPTERING
CHAPTREL
CHAQUETA
CHAR
CHARABANC
CHARABANCER
CHARABANCS
CHARACEOUS
CHARACETUM
CHARACIN
CHARACINE
CHARACINID
CHARACINOID
CHARACT
CHARACTER
CHARACTERED
CHARACTERIAL
CHARACTERICAL
CHARACTERIES
CHARACTERING
CHARACTERISM
CHARACTERIST
CHARACTERISTIC
CHARACTERISTICALLY
CHARACTERIZATION
CHARACTERIZE
CHARACTERIZED
CHARACTERIZER
CHARACTERIZING
CHARACTERLESS
CHARACTERS
CHARACTERY
CHARADE
CHARADES
CHARADRINE
CHARADRIOID
CHARANGO
CHARAS
CHARBOCLE
CHARBON
CHARBONNIER
CHARCO
CHARCOAL
CHARCOALY
CHARCUTERIE
CHARCUTIER
CHARD
CHARDOCK
CHARE
CHARED
CHARELY
CHARER
CHARET
CHARETER
CHARETTE
CHARGE
CHARGEABLE
CHARGEABLY
CHARGED
CHARGEE
CHARGEFUL
CHARGEHOUSE
CHARGELING
CHARGEMAN
CHARGER
CHARGING
CHARIER
CHARIEST
CHARILY
CHARINESS
CHARIOT
CHARIOTED
CHARIOTEE
CHARIOTEER
CHARIOTEERS
CHARIOTMAN
CHARIOTRY
CHARISM
CHARISMATIC
CHARISTICARY
CHARITABLE
CHARITABLENESS
CHARITABLY
CHARITATIVE
CHARITIES
CHARITY
CHARIVARI
CHARIVARIS
CHARK
CHARKA
CHARKED
CHARKHA
CHARKHANA
CHARKING
CHARLADY
CHARLATAN
CHARLATANIC
CHARLATANISH
CHARLATANISM
CHARLATANRIES
CHARLATANRY
CHARLET
CHARLOCK
CHARLOTTE
CHARM
CHARMED
CHARMEDLY
CHARMER
CHARMEUSE
CHARMFUL
CHARMFULLY
CHARMING
CHARMINGLY
CHARNECO
CHARNEL
CHAROSES
CHARPIE
CHARPIT
CHARPOY
CHARQUE
CHARQUI
CHARR
CHARRE
CHARRED
CHARRIER
CHARRIEST
CHARRING
CHARRO
CHARRY
CHARS
CHARSHAF
CHART
CHARTA
CHARTACEOUS
CHARTER
CHARTERED
CHARTERER
CHARTERHOUSE
CHARTERING
CHARTERMASTER
CHARTHOUSE
CHARTLESS
CHARTOGRAPHY
CHARTOLOGY
CHARTOMETER
CHARTOPHYLAX
CHARTREUSE
CHARTROOM
CHARTS
CHARTULA
CHARTULAE
CHARTULARIES
CHARTULARY
CHARTULAS
CHARUK
CHARWOMAN
CHARWOMEN
CHARY
CHASE
CHASED
CHASER
CHASING
CHASM
CHASMA
CHASMAL
CHASMED
CHASMIC
CHASMOGAMIC
CHASMOGAMOUS
CHASMOGAMY
CHASMOPHYTE
CHASMY
CHASSE
CHASSED
CHASSEING
CHASSEPOT
CHASSEUR
CHASSIGNITE
CHASSIS
CHASTE
CHASTELY
CHASTEN
CHASTENER
CHASTENESS
CHASTISABLE
CHASTISE
CHASTISED
CHASTISEMENT
CHASTISER
CHASTISING
CHASTITY
CHASUBLE
CHASUBLED
CHAT
CHATAKA
CHATEAU
CHATEAUGRAY
CHATEAUX
CHATELAIN
CHATELAINE
CHATELAINRY
CHATHAMITE
CHATI
CHATON
CHATOYANCY
CHATOYANT
CHATS
CHATSOME
CHATTA
CHATTABLE
CHATTACK
CHATTAH
CHATTATION
CHATTED
CHATTEL
CHATTELISM
CHATTELIZE
CHATTELS
CHATTER
CHATTERATION
CHATTERBAG
CHATTERBOX
CHATTERED
CHATTERER
CHATTERING
CHATTERMAG
CHATTERY
CHATTIER
CHATTIES
CHATTIEST
CHATTILY
CHATTINESS
CHATTING
CHATTY
CHATWOOD
CHAUDRON
CHAUFER
CHAUFFAGE
CHAUFFER
CHAUFFEUR
CHAUFFEUSE
CHAUK
CHAUKIDARI
CHAULE
CHAULMAUGRA
CHAULMOOGRA
CHAULMOOGRIC
CHAULMUGRA

CHAUM
CHAUMER
CHAUMIERE
CHAUN
CHAURI
CHAUS
CHAUSSEE
CHAUSSEES
CHAUSSES
CHAUSSURE
CHAUTAUQUA
CHAUTE
CHAUTH
CHAUVE
CHAUVIN
CHAUVINISM
CHAUVINIST
CHAUVINISTIC
CHAVEL
CHAVENDER
CHAVER
CHAVIBETOL
CHAVICIN
CHAVICINE
CHAVICOL
CHAVISH
CHAVO
CHAW
CHAWAN
CHAWBACON
CHAWBONE
CHAWBUCK
CHAWDRON
CHAWER
CHAWK
CHAWL
CHAWLE
CHAWN
CHAWSTICK
CHAY
CHAYOTE
CHAZAN
CHAZANUT
CHAZZAN
CHAZZANUT
CHEAP
CHEAPEN
CHEAPENED
CHEAPENER
CHEAPENING
CHEAPER
CHEAPERY
CHEAPEST
CHEAPIE
CHEAPING
CHEAPISH
CHEAPLY
CHEAPNESS
CHEAPSKATE
CHEAT
CHEATED
CHEATEE
CHEATER
CHEATERS
CHEATERY
CHEATING
CHEATRIE
CHEATRY
CHEATS
CHEBEC
CHEBECK
CHEBEL
CHEBOG
CHEBULE
CHEBULIC
CHEBULINIC
CHECHAKO
CHECHEM
CHECHIA
CHECK
CHECKABLE
CHECKAGE
CHECKBIRD
CHECKBITE
CHECKBOOK
CHECKE
CHECKED
CHECKER
CHECKERBELLIES
CHECKERBELLY
CHECKERBERRIES
CHECKERBERRY
CHECKERBLOOM
CHECKERBOARD
CHECKERBREAST
CHECKERED
CHECKERING
CHECKERIST
CHECKERS
CHECKERWISE
CHECKERWORK
CHECKHOOK
CHECKING
CHECKLE
CHECKLESS
CHECKLINE
CHECKMAN
CHECKMATE
CHECKMATED
CHECKMATING
CHECKOFF
CHECKOUT
CHECKRACK
CHECKREIN
CHECKROLL
CHECKROOM
CHECKROPE
CHECKROW
CHECKROWER
CHECKS
CHECKSTONE
CHECKSTRAP
CHECKSTRING
CHECKWEIGHER
CHECKWORK
CHECKY
CHEDDAR
CHEDDARING
CHEDDITE
CHEDER
CHEDITE
CHEDLOCK
CHEE
CHEECHA
CHEECHACO
CHEECHAKO
CHEEK
CHEEKBONE
CHEEKER
CHEEKIER
CHEEKIEST
CHEEKILY
CHEEKINESS
CHEEKY
CHEENEY
CHEEP
CHEEPER
CHEEPIER
CHEEPIEST
CHEEPILY
CHEEPINESS
CHEER
CHEERED
CHEERER
CHEERFUL
CHEERFULIZE
CHEERFULLY
CHEERFULNESS
CHEERFULSOME
CHEERIER
CHEERIEST
CHEERILY
CHEERINESS
CHEERING
CHEERINGLY
CHEERIO
CHEERIOS
CHEERLEADER
CHEERLESS
CHEERLESSLY
CHEERLESSNESS
CHEERLY
CHEERO
CHEERS
CHEERY
CHEESE
CHEESEBURGER
CHEESECAKE
CHEESECLOTH
CHEESECURD
CHEESECUTTER
CHEESED
CHEESEFLOWER
CHEESELEP
CHEESELIP
CHEESEMONGER
CHEESEPARER
CHEESEPARING
CHEESER
CHEESERY
CHEESEWOOD
CHEESIER
CHEESIEST
CHEESINESS
CHEESING
CHEESY
CHEET
CHEETAH
CHEETAL
CHEETER
CHEEWINK
CHEF
CHEFE
CHEGOE
CHEGRE
CHEICERAL
CHEILION
CHEILITIS
CHEILOPLASTY
CHEIR
CHEIRAGRA
CHEIROGNOMY
CHEIROGRAPHY
CHEIROLIN
CHEIROLINE
CHEIROLOGY
CHEIROMANCY
CHEIROMEGALY
CHEIROPODIST
CHEIROPODY
CHEIROSOPHY
CHEIROSPASM
CHEK
CHEKAN
CHEKE
CHEKEN
CHEKI
CHEKKER
CHEKMAK
CHELA
CHELAE
CHELASHIP
CHELATE
CHELATED
CHELATION
CHELE
CHELEM
CHELERYTHRIN
CHELICERA
CHELICERATE
CHELIDON
CHELIDONATE
CHELIDONIAN
CHELIDONIC
CHELIDONIN
CHELIDONINE
CHELIFEROUS
CHELIFORM
CHELINGA
CHELINGAS
CHELINGO
CHELINGOS
CHELIPED
CHELODINE
CHELONE
CHELONIAN
CHELONID
CHELONIN
CHELOPHORE
CHELP
CHELYDROID
CHELYS
CHEMASTHENIA
CHEMAWINITE
CHEMESTHESIS
CHEMIATRIST
CHEMIATRY
CHEMIC
CHEMICAL
CHEMICALIZE
CHEMICALLY
CHEMICALS
CHEMICK
CHEMICKED
CHEMICKER
CHEMICKING
CHEMIGRAPH
CHEMIGRAPHIC
CHEMIGRAPHY
CHEMILOON
CHEMIN
CHEMINEE
CHEMIOTACTIC
CHEMIOTAXIC
CHEMIOTAXIS
CHEMIOTROPIC
CHEMIPHOTIC
CHEMIS
CHEMISE
CHEMISETTE
CHEMISM
CHEMIST
CHEMISTRIES
CHEMISTRY
CHEMITYPE
CHEMITYPIES
CHEMITYPY
CHEMIZO
CHEMMY
CHEMOCEPTOR
CHEMOKINESIS
CHEMOKINETIC
CHEMOLYSIS
CHEMOLYTIC
CHEMOLYZE
CHEMOREFLEX
CHEMOSES
CHEMOSIS
CHEMOSMOSES
CHEMOSMOSIS
CHEMOSMOTIC
CHEMOSPHERE
CHEMOSPHERIC
CHEMOSTAT
CHEMOTACTIC
CHEMOTAXIS
CHEMOTAXY
CHEMOTHERAPY
CHEMOTIC
CHEMOTROPIC
CHEMOTROPISM
CHEMURGIC
CHEMURGICAL
CHEMURGY
CHENA
CHENDE
CHENEAU
CHENET
CHENEVIXITE
CHENFISH
CHENG
CHENGAL
CHENICA
CHENIER
CHENILLE
CHENOPOD
CHEOPLASTIC
CHEPSTER
CHEQUE
CHEQUEEN
CHEQUER
CHEQUERBOARD
CHEQUERED
CHEQUERING
CHEQUERS
CHEQUERWISE
CHEQUERWORK
CHEQUIN
CHERCOCK
CHERE
CHERELY
CHERI
CHERIE
CHERIMOYA
CHERIMOYER
CHERISH
CHERISHED
CHERISHER
CHERISHING
CHERISHINGLY
CHERISHMENT
CHERMES
CHERNA
CHERNOZEM
CHEROGRIL
CHEROOT
CHERRIED
CHERRIES
CHERRY
CHERRYING
CHERRYSTONE
CHERSONESE
CHERT
CHERTE
CHERTY
CHERUB
CHERUBIC
CHERUBICAL
CHERUBICALLY
CHERUBIM
CHERUBIMIC
CHERUBIN
CHERUBS
CHERVIL
CHERVONETS

CHERVONETZ
CHERVONTSI
CHESBOLL
CHESIL
CHESON
CHESOUN
CHESS
CHESSART
CHESSBOARD
CHESSEL
CHESSER
CHESSET
CHESSMAN
CHESSMEN
CHESSNER
CHESSOM
CHESSTREE
CHESSYLITE
CHEST
CHESTER
CHESTERBED
CHESTERFIELD
CHESTERLITE
CHESTIER
CHESTIEST
CHESTILY
CHESTINESS
CHESTNUT
CHESTS
CHESTY
CHETAH
CHETH
CHETIF
CHETIVE
CHETOPOD
CHETTIK
CHETTY
CHETVERT
CHEUNG
CHEVACHIE
CHEVAGE
CHEVAL
CHEVALET
CHEVALINE
CHEVANCE
CHEVE
CHEVEE
CHEVELURE
CHEVENER
CHEVEREL
CHEVERIL
CHEVESAILE
CHEVESNE
CHEVET
CHEVEYS
CHEVIED
CHEVIES
CHEVILLE
CHEVIN
CHEVIOT
CHEVISANCE
CHEVISE
CHEVON
CHEVRET
CHEVRETTE
CHEVREUIL
CHEVRON
CHEVRONE
CHEVRONEL
CHEVRONELLY
CHEVRONWISE
CHEVRONY
CHEVROTAIN
CHEVVY
CHEVY
CHEVYING
CHEW
CHEWBARK
CHEWED
CHEWELER
CHEWER
CHEWET
CHEWIER
CHEWIEST
CHEWING
CHEWINK
CHEWSTICK
CHEWY
CHEYNEY
CHEYNEYS
CHEZ
CHHATRI
CHI
CHIA
CHIACK
CHIAROSCURIST
CHIAROSCURO
CHIAROSCUROS
CHIASM
CHIASMA
CHIASMAL
CHIASMATA
CHIASMATYPE
CHIASMATYPY
CHIASMIC
CHIASMUS
CHIASTIC
CHIASTOLITE
CHIASTONEURY
CHIAUS
CHIAVE
CHIAVETTA
CHIB
CHIBINITE
CHIBOUK
CHIBOUQUE
CHIBRIT
CHIC
CHICA
CHICADEE
CHICALOTE
CHICANE
CHICANED
CHICANER
CHICANERIES
CHICANERY
CHICANING
CHICARIC
CHICAYOTE
CHICH
CHICHA
CHICHARRA
CHICHICASTE
CHICHIMECAN
CHICHIPATE
CHICHIPE
CHICHITUNA
CHICK
CHICKABIDDY
CHICKADEE
CHICKAREE
CHICKASAW
CHICKEE
CHICKELL
CHICKEN
CHICKENBERRY
CHICKENBILL
CHICKENS
CHICKENWEED
CHICKENWORT
CHICKER
CHICKERY
CHICKIES
CHICKPEA
CHICKSTONE
CHICKWEED
CHICKWIT
CHICKY
CHICLE
CHICLERO
CHICNESS
CHICO
CHICORIES
CHICORY
CHICOS
CHICOT
CHICOTE
CHICQUED
CHICQUER
CHICQUING
CHID
CHIDDEN
CHIDE
CHIDED
CHIDER
CHIDING
CHIDINGLY
CHIDINGNESS
CHIDRA
CHIEF
CHIEFDOM
CHIEFERY
CHIEFLY
CHIEFRY
CHIEFTAIN
CHIEFTAINCY
CHIEFTAINESS
CHIEFTAINRIES
CHIEFTAINRY
CHIEFTAINSHIP
CHIEFTESS
CHIEFTY
CHIEL
CHIELD
CHIEN
CHIEVANCE
CHIEVE
CHIFFCHAFF
CHIFFER
CHIFFON
CHIFFONADE
CHIFFONIER
CHIFFONNIER
CHIFFOROBE
CHIFFRE
CHIGETAI
CHIGGA
CHIGGER
CHIGNON
CHIGOE
CHIH
CHIKARA
CHIKEE
CHIL
CHILACAYOTE
CHILALGIA
CHILARIA
CHILARIUM
CHILBLAIN
CHILD
CHILDAGE
CHILDBEARING
CHILDBED
CHILDBIRTH
CHILDCROWING
CHILDE
CHILDED
CHILDHOOD
CHILDING
CHILDISH
CHILDISHLY
CHILDISHNESS
CHILDKIND
CHILDLESS
CHILDLIER
CHILDLIEST
CHILDLIKE
CHILDLIKENESS
CHILDLY
CHILDNESS
CHILDREN
CHILDRENITE
CHILDRIDDEN
CHILDSHIP
CHILDWIFE
CHILE
CHILENITE
CHILI
CHILIAD
CHILIADAL
CHILIADIC
CHILIAEDRON
CHILIAGON
CHILIAHEDRON
CHILIARCH
CHILIARCHIA
CHILIARCHY
CHILIASM
CHILIAST
CHILIASTIC
CHILICOTE
CHILICOTHE
CHILIES
CHILIOMB
CHILITIS
CHILL
CHILLA
CHILLAGITE
CHILLED
CHILLER
CHILLI
CHILLIER
CHILLIEST
CHILLILY
CHILLINESS
CHILLING
CHILLINGLY
CHILLNESS
CHILLO
CHILLOES
CHILLROOM
CHILLSOME
CHILLUM
CHILLUMCHEE
CHILLY
CHILODON
CHILOGNATH
CHILOGNATHAN
CHILOMA
CHILOMATA
CHILONCUS
CHILOPLASTY
CHILOPOD
CHILOPODAN
CHILOPODOUS
CHILOTOMY
CHILTE
CHILVER
CHIMACHIMA
CHIMAERA
CHIMAERID
CHIMAEROID
CHIMANGO
CHIMB
CHIMBLE
CHIME
CHIMED
CHIMER
CHIMERA
CHIMERAL
CHIMERAS
CHIMERIC
CHIMERICAL
CHIMERICALLY
CHIMES
CHIMINAGE
CHIMING
CHIMLA
CHIMLEY
CHIMNEY
CHIMNEYLESS
CHIMO
CHIMOPELAGIC
CHIMP
CHIMPANZEE
CHIN
CHINA
CHINABERRIES
CHINABERRY
CHINAFISH
CHINAFY
CHINAMANIA
CHINAMANIAC
CHINAMPA
CHINANTA
CHINAPHTHOL
CHINAR
CHINAROOT
CHINAWARE
CHINCAPIN
CHINCH
CHINCHA
CHINCHAYOTE
CHINCHE
CHINCHER
CHINCHILLA
CHINCHY
CHINCOF
CHINCONA
CHINCOUGH
CHINDEE
CHINDI
CHINE
CHINED
CHINELA
CHINFEST
CHING
CHINGMA
CHINIK
CHINIKS
CHININ
CHINING
CHINIOFON
CHINK
CHINKARA
CHINKED
CHINKER
CHINKERS
CHINKING
CHINKLE
CHINKS
CHINKY
CHINNED
CHINNIER
CHINNIEST
CHINNING
CHINNY
CHINOA
CHINOISERIE
CHINOL
CHINOOK
CHINOS
CHINOTTI
CHINOTTO
CHINOVNIK

CHINPIECE
CHINQUAPIN
CHINSE
CHINTS
CHINTZ
CHINTZE
CHINTZES
CHINTZIER
CHINTZIEST
CHINTZY
CHINWOOD
CHIOCOCCINE
CHIOLITE
CHIONABLEPSIA
CHIP
CHIPCHOP
CHIPLET
CHIPLING
CHIPMUNK
CHIPOLATA
CHIPPABLE
CHIPPAGE
CHIPPED
CHIPPER
CHIPPERED
CHIPPERING
CHIPPIER
CHIPPIES
CHIPPIEST
CHIPPING
CHIPPINGS
CHIPPY
CHIPS
CHIPWOOD
CHIPYARD
CHIQUERO
CHIQUEST
CHIR
CHIRAGRA
CHIRAL
CHIRALGIA
CHIRALITY
CHIRAPSIA
CHIRATA
CHIRIMEN
CHIRIMIA
CHIRIMOYA
CHIRIMOYER
CHIRIPA
CHIRIVITA
CHIRK
CHIRKED
CHIRKING
CHIRL
CHIRM
CHIRO
CHIROGALE
CHIROGNOMIC
CHIROGNOMY
CHIROGNOSTIC
CHIROGRAPH
CHIROGRAPHER
CHIROGRAPHIC
CHIROGRAPHICAL
CHIROGRAPHY
CHIROGYMNAST
CHIROLOGICAL
CHIROLOGIST
CHIROLOGY
CHIROMANCE
CHIROMANCER
CHIROMANCIST
CHIROMANCY
CHIROMANT
CHIROMANTIC
CHIROMEGALY
CHIROMETER
CHIRONOMIC
CHIRONOMID
CHIRONOMY
CHIRONYM
CHIROPLASTY
CHIROPOD
CHIROPODIAL
CHIROPODIC
CHIROPODICAL
CHIROPODIST
CHIROPODISTRY
CHIROPODOUS
CHIROPODY
CHIROPRACTIC
CHIROPRACTOR
CHIROPRAXIS
CHIROPTER
CHIROPTERAN
CHIROPTERITE
CHIROS
CHIROSOPHIST
CHIROTHERIAN
CHIROTHESIA
CHIROTONSOR
CHIROTONSORY
CHIROTONY
CHIROTYPE
CHIRP
CHIRPED
CHIRPER
CHIRPIER
CHIRPIEST
CHIRPILY
CHIRPING
CHIRPINGLY
CHIRPLING
CHIRPY
CHIRR
CHIRRE
CHIRRED
CHIRRING
CHIRRUP
CHIRRUPED
CHIRRUPER
CHIRRUPING
CHIRRUPY
CHIRT
CHIRU
CHIRURGEON
CHIRURGEONLY
CHIRURGERY
CHIRURGIC
CHIRURGICAL
CHISEL
CHISELED
CHISELER
CHISELING
CHISELLED
CHISELLER
CHISELLING
CHISELLY
CHISELMOUTH
CHISTERA
CHISTKA
CHIT
CHITAL
CHITARRA
CHITARRINO
CHITARRONE
CHITCHAT
CHITCHATTY
CHITI
CHITIN
CHITINIZATION
CHITINIZED
CHITINOID
CHITINOUS
CHITLIN
CHITLING
CHITLINS
CHITON
CHITOSAMINE
CHITOSAN
CHITOSE
CHITRA
CHITS
CHITTACK
CHITTAK
CHITTAMWOOD
CHITTED
CHITTER
CHITTERLING
CHITTING
CHITTY
CHIURM
CHIV
CHIVAGE
CHIVALRESQUE
CHIVALRIC
CHIVALROUS
CHIVALROUSLY
CHIVALRY
CHIVARI
CHIVARRA
CHIVARRO
CHIVE
CHIVER
CHIVERET
CHIVEY
CHIVIATITE
CHIVIED
CHIVVY
CHIVY
CHIVYING
CHIZZ
CHIZZEL
CHKALIK
CHLADNITE
CHLAMYDATE
CHLAMYDEOUS
CHLAMYDOZOAN
CHLAMYPHORE
CHLAMYS
CHLAMYSES
CHLOANTHITE
CHLOASMA
CHLORAEMIA
CHLORAGEN
CHLORAGOGEN
CHLORAGOGUE
CHLORAL
CHLORALIDE
CHLORALISM
CHLORALIZATION
CHLORALIZE
CHLORALIZED
CHLORALIZING
CHLORALOSE
CHLORALUM
CHLORAMIDE
CHLORAMIN
CHLORAMINE
CHLORANAEMIA
CHLORANEMIA
CHLORANEMIC
CHLORANIL
CHLORANTHY
CHLORAPATITE
CHLORASTROLITE
CHLORATE
CHLORAZIDE
CHLORCOSANE
CHLORDANE
CHLORE
CHLORED
CHLORELLA
CHLOREMIA
CHLORENCHYMA
CHLORIC
CHLORIDATE
CHLORIDATED
CHLORIDE
CHLORIDIC
CHLORIDIZE
CHLORIDIZED
CHLORIDIZING
CHLORIN
CHLORINATE
CHLORINATED
CHLORINATING
CHLORINATION
CHLORINATOR
CHLORINE
CHLORINITY
CHLORINOUS
CHLORIODIDE
CHLORITE
CHLORITIC
CHLORITIZE
CHLORITOID
CHLOROACETIC
CHLOROAMIDE
CHLOROAMINE
CHLOROAURATE
CHLOROAURIC
CHLOROAURITE
CHLOROCHROUS
CHLOROCRESOL
CHLORODIZE
CHLORODIZED
CHLORODIZING
CHLOROFORM
CHLOROFORMED
CHLOROFORMIC
CHLOROGENIC
CHLOROGENINE
CHLOROHYDRIN
CHLOROIODIDE
CHLOROMA
CHLOROMATA
CHLOROMETER
CHLOROMETRIC
CHLOROMETRY
CHLOROPAL
CHLOROPHANE
CHLOROPHENOL
CHLOROPHYL
CHLOROPHYLL
CHLOROPICRIN
CHLOROPLAST
CHLOROPRENE
CHLOROPSIA
CHLOROSIS
CHLOROSPINEL
CHLOROTIC
CHLOROUS
CHLORPIKRIN
CHLORSALOL
CHLORYL
CHO
CHOACHYTE
CHOANA
CHOANATE
CHOANOCYTAL
CHOANOCYTE
CHOANOID
CHOANOSOME
CHOAR
CHOATE
CHOATY
CHOB
CHOBDAR
CHOBIE
CHOCA
CHOCALHO
CHOCARD
CHOCHO
CHOCHOS
CHOCK
CHOCKABLOCK
CHOCKER
CHOCKFUL
CHOCKS
CHOCOLATE
CHOCOLATIER
CHOCOLATIERE
CHOCOLATY
CHOEL
CHOENIX
CHOFFER
CHOGA
CHOGAK
CHOGSET
CHOICE
CHOICEFUL
CHOICELY
CHOICENESS
CHOICIER
CHOICIEST
CHOICY
CHOIL
CHOILE
CHOILER
CHOIR
CHOIRBOY
CHOIRMAN
CHOIRMASTER
CHOIRWISE
CHOKAGE
CHOKE
CHOKEBERRIES
CHOKEBERRY
CHOKEBORE
CHOKECHERRIES
CHOKECHERRY
CHOKED
CHOKEDAMP
CHOKER
CHOKERED
CHOKERMAN
CHOKES
CHOKEWEED
CHOKEY
CHOKIDAR
CHOKIER
CHOKIEST
CHOKING
CHOKINGLY
CHOKRA
CHOKY
CHOL
CHOLAEMIA
CHOLAGOGIC
CHOLAGOGUE
CHOLAM
CHOLANE
CHOLANGITIS
CHOLATE
CHOLD
CHOLEATE
CHOLECYANIN
CHOLECYANINE
CHOLECYST
CHOLECYSTIC
CHOLECYSTIS
CHOLEDOCH
CHOLEINE
CHOLELITH

CHOLELITHIC
CHOLEMIA
CHOLENT
CHOLEOKINASE
CHOLEPOIETIC
CHOLER
CHOLERA
CHOLERAIC
CHOLERIC
CHOLERICLY
CHOLERICNESS
CHOLERINE
CHOLEROID
CHOLERRHAGIA
CHOLESTANE
CHOLESTANOL
CHOLESTENE
CHOLESTERATE
CHOLESTERIC
CHOLESTERIN
CHOLESTEROL
CHOLESTERYL
CHOLETELIN
CHOLETHERAPY
CHOLI
CHOLIAMB
CHOLIAMBIC
CHOLIAMBIST
CHOLIC
CHOLICK
CHOLINE
CHOLINIC
CHOLLA
CHOLLER
CHOLLERS
CHOLO
CHOLOCHROME
CHOLOGENETIC
CHOLOLITH
CHOLOLITHIC
CHOLOPHAEIN
CHOLOPHEIN
CHOLORRHEA
CHOLOSCOPY
CHOLUM
CHOLURIA
CHOMAGE
CHOMER
CHOMP
CHON
CHONDRAL
CHONDRALGIA
CHONDRECTOMY
CHONDRIC
CHONDRIFIED
CHONDRIFY
CHONDRIGEN
CHONDRIN
CHONDRINOUS
CHONDRIOCONT
CHONDRIOMA
CHONDRIOME
CHONDRIOMITE
CHONDRIOSOME
CHONDRIOSOMES
CHONDRITE
CHONDRITIC
CHONDRITIS
CHONDROBLAST
CHONDROCELE
CHONDROCLAST
CHONDROCYTE
CHONDRODITE
CHONDRODITIC
CHONDRODYNIA
CHONDROFETAL
CHONDROGENY
CHONDROID
CHONDROITIN
CHONDROLOGY
CHONDROMA
CHONDROMAS
CHONDROMATA
CHONDROMYOMA
CHONDROPHORE
CHONDROPHYTE
CHONDROSIN
CHONDROSIS
CHONDROSTEAN
CHONDROTOME
CHONDROTOMY
CHONDRULE
CHONDRUS
CHONK
CHONOLITH
CHONTA
CHOOCHOO
CHOOK
CHOOKIE
CHOOP
CHOOSABLE
CHOOSE
CHOOSEABLE
CHOOSER
CHOOSEY
CHOOSIER
CHOOSIEST
CHOOSING
CHOOSINGLY
CHOOSY
CHOP
CHOPA
CHOPBOAT
CHOPDAR
CHOPFALLEN
CHOPHOUSE
CHOPIN
CHOPINE
CHOPLOGIC
CHOPPED
CHOPPER
CHOPPERS
CHOPPIER
CHOPPIEST
CHOPPIN
CHOPPINESS
CHOPPING
CHOPPY
CHOPS
CHOPSTICK
CHOPSTICKS
CHOR
CHORAGI
CHORAGIC
CHORAGION
CHORAGIUM
CHORAGUS
CHORAGY
CHORAL
CHORALCELO
CHORALE
CHORALIST
CHORALLY
CHORD
CHORDA
CHORDACEOUS
CHORDAL
CHORDATE
CHORDED
CHORDEE
CHORDITIS
CHORDOID
CHORDOTOMY
CHORDOTONAL
CHORDS
CHORE
CHOREA
CHOREAL
CHORED
CHOREE
CHOREGRAPHY
CHOREI
CHOREIC
CHOREIFORM
CHOREOGRAPHY
CHOREOID
CHOREOMANIA
CHOREUS
CHOREUTIC
CHORIAL
CHORIAMB
CHORIAMBI
CHORIAMBIC
CHORIAMBIZE
CHORIAMBUS
CHORIAMBUSES
CHORIC
CHORINE
CHORING
CHORIOCELE
CHORIOID
CHORIOMA
CHORION
CHORIONIC
CHORIOPTIC
CHORISIS
CHORISM
CHORIST
CHORISTATE
CHORISTER
CHORISTIC
CHORISTOMA
CHORISTRY
CHORIZATION
CHORIZONT
CHORIZONTES
CHORIZONTIC
CHORIZONTIST
CHOROGI
CHOROGRAPH
CHOROGRAPHER
CHOROGRAPHIC
CHOROGRAPHIES
CHOROGRAPHY
CHOROID
CHOROIDITIS
CHOROLOGICAL
CHOROLOGIST
CHOROLOGY
CHOROMANIA
CHOROMANIC
CHOROMETRY
CHOROOK
CHOROUS
CHORT
CHORTEN
CHORTLE
CHORTLED
CHORTLER
CHORTLING
CHORTOSTEROL
CHORUS
CHORUSED
CHORUSING
CHORUSSED
CHORUSSING
CHORYOS
CHOSE
CHOSEN
CHOTT
CHOU
CHOUCROUTE
CHOUETTE
CHOUFLEUR
CHOUGH
CHOUKA
CHOULTRY
CHOUNCE
CHOUP
CHOUPIC
CHOUQUETTE
CHOUS
CHOUSE
CHOUSED
CHOUSH
CHOUSING
CHOUT
CHOUX
CHOW
CHOWCHOW
CHOWDER
CHOWK
CHOWRIES
CHOWRY
CHOY
CHOZA
CHREMATIST
CHREMATISTIC
CHREOTECHNICS
CHRESARD
CHRESMOLOGY
CHRESTOMATHY
CHRIA
CHRIMSEL
CHRISM
CHRISMA
CHRISMAL
CHRISMALE
CHRISMARY
CHRISMATINE
CHRISMATION
CHRISMATITE
CHRISMATORY
CHRISMON
CHRISOM
CHRISROOT
CHRISTCROSS
CHRISTEN
CHRISTENER
CHRISTENING
CHRISTIANITE
CHROATOL
CHROMA
CHROMAFFIN
CHROMAFFINIC
CHROMAMAMIN
CHROMAMMINE
CHROMATE
CHROMATIC
CHROMATICALLY
CHROMATICIAN
CHROMATICISM
CHROMATICITY
CHROMATICS
CHROMATID
CHROMATIN
CHROMATINIC
CHROMATISM
CHROMATIST
CHROMATIZE
CHROMATOCYTE
CHROMATOID
CHROMATOLOGIES
CHROMATOLOGY
CHROMATOPHORE
CHROMATOPSIA
CHROMATOSIS
CHROMATROPE
CHROMATYPE
CHROME
CHROMED
CHROMIC
CHROMICIZE
CHROMICIZING
CHROMID
CHROMIDE
CHROMIDIAL
CHROMIDIUM
CHROMIDROSIS
CHROMIFEROUS
CHROMING
CHROMIOLE
CHROMITE
CHROMITITE
CHROMIUM
CHROMO
CHROMOBLAST
CHROMOCTYE
CHROMOGEN
CHROMOGENIC
CHROMOGENOUS
CHROMOGRAM
CHROMOGRAPH
CHROMOISOMER
CHROMOLIPOID
CHROMOLITH
CHROMOLITHIC
CHROMOMERE
CHROMOMETER
CHROMONE
CHROMOPAROUS
CHROMOPHANE
CHROMOPHIL
CHROMOPHILE
CHROMOPHILIC
CHROMOPHOBE
CHROMOPHOBIC
CHROMOPHOR
CHROMOPHORE
CHROMOPHORIC
CHROMOPHYL
CHROMOPHYLL
CHROMOPLASM
CHROMOPLAST
CHROMOPSIA
CHROMOS
CHROMOSCOPE
CHROMOSCOPIC
CHROMOSCOPY
CHROMOSOME
CHROMOSPHERE
CHROMOSPHERIC
CHROMOTROPE
CHROMOTROPIC
CHROMOTROPY
CHROMOTYPE
CHROMOTYPIC
CHROMOTYPY
CHROMOUS
CHROMY
CHROMYL
CHRONAL
CHRONANAGRAM
CHRONAXIA
CHRONAXIE
CHRONAXIES
CHRONAXY
CHRONIC
CHRONICA
CHRONICAL
CHRONICALLY
CHRONICITY
CHRONICLE
CHRONICLED
CHRONICLER

CHRONICLING
CHRONICON
CHRONIST
CHRONOCRATOR
CHRONODEIK
CHRONOGRAM
CHRONOGRAPH
CHRONOGRAPHIC
CHRONOGRAPHY
CHRONOLOGER
CHRONOLOGIC
CHRONOLOGICAL
CHRONOLOGIES
CHRONOLOGIST
CHRONOLOGIZE
CHRONOLOGIZED
CHRONOLOGIZING
CHRONOLOGY
CHRONOMANCY
CHRONOMANTIC
CHRONOMETER
CHRONOMETRIC
CHRONOMETRY
CHRONONOMY
CHRONOPHER
CHRONOSCOPIC
CHRONOSCOPY
CHRONOSEMIC
CHRONOTROPIC
CHROOCOCCOID
CHROTTA
CHRYSALID
CHRYSALIDAL
CHRYSALIDES
CHRYSALIDIAN
CHRYSALINE
CHRYSALIS
CHRYSALISES
CHRYSALOID
CHRYSAMMIC
CHRYSANILIN
CHRYSANILINE
CHRYSANISIC
CHRYSANTHEMUM
CHRYSANTHOUS
CHRYSAROBIN
CHRYSAZIN
CHRYSAZOL
CHRYSENE
CHRYSIN
CHRYSOBERYL
CHRYSOBULL
CHRYSOCHLORE
CHRYSOCHROUS
CHRYSOCOLLA
CHRYSOCRACY
CHRYSOERIOL
CHRYSOGEN
CHRYSOGRAPH
CHRYSOGRAPHY
CHRYSOIDINE
CHRYSOLITE
CHRYSOLITIC
CHRYSOLOGY
CHRYSOME
CHRYSOMELID
CHRYSOMONAD
CHRYSOPAL
CHRYSOPEE
CHRYSOPHAN
CHRYSOPHANE
CHRYSOPHANIC
CHRYSOPOEIA
CHRYSOPOETIC
CHRYSOPRASE
CHRYSOPRASUS
CHRYSORIN
CHRYSOSPERM
CHRYSOTILE
CHRYSTOCRENE
CHTHONIAN
CHUANA
CHUB
CHUBA
CHUBBED
CHUBBEDNESS
CHUBBIER
CHUBBIEST
CHUBBILY
CHUBBINESS
CHUBBY
CHUBS
CHUCHO
CHUCK
CHUCKAWALLA
CHUCKED
CHUCKER
CHUCKHOLE
CHUCKIE
CHUCKIES
CHUCKING
CHUCKINGLY
CHUCKLE
CHUCKLED
CHUCKLEHEAD
CHUCKLEHEADED
CHUCKLER
CHUCKLING
CHUCKLINGLY
CHUCKRAM
CHUCKSTONE
CHUCKWALLA
CHUCKY
CHUD
CHUDDAH
CHUDDAR
CHUDDER
CHUET
CHUFA
CHUFF
CHUFFIER
CHUFFIEST
CHUG
CHUGGED
CHUGGER
CHUGGING
CHUGHOLE
CHUHRA
CHUKAR
CHUKKA
CHUKKAR
CHUKKER
CHUKOR
CHULAN
CHULHA
CHULLO
CHULLPA
CHULO
CHULPA
CHULTUN
CHUM
CHUMAR
CHUMBLE
CHUMMAGE
CHUMMER
CHUMMERY
CHUMMIER
CHUMMIES
CHUMMIEST
CHUMMILY
CHUMMY
CHUMP
CHUMPA
CHUMPISH
CHUMPY
CHUNAM
CHUNARI
CHUNDARI
CHUNGA
CHUNK
CHUNKED
CHUNKHEAD
CHUNKIER
CHUNKIEST
CHUNKINESS
CHUNKING
CHUNKY
CHUNNER
CHUNO
CHUNTER
CHUPA
CHUPAK
CHUPON
CHUPRASSIE
CHUPRASSY
CHURCH
CHURCHANITY
CHURCHCRAFT
CHURCHGOER
CHURCHGOING
CHURCHIANITY
CHURCHIER
CHURCHIEST
CHURCHIFIED
CHURCHING
CHURCHITE
CHURCHLESS
CHURCHLIKE
CHURCHLINESS
CHURCHLY
CHURCHMAN
CHURCHMANLY
CHURCHMANSHIP
CHURCHMASTER
CHURCHMEN
CHURCHREEVE
CHURCHSCOT
CHURCHSHOT
CHURCHWARD
CHURCHWARDEN
CHURCHWARDS
CHURCHWAY
CHURCHWOMAN
CHURCHWOMEN
CHURCHY
CHURCHYARD
CHUREL
CHURINGA
CHURL
CHURLED
CHURLIER
CHURLIEST
CHURLISH
CHURLISHLY
CHURLISHNESS
CHURLY
CHURN
CHURNABILITY
CHURNED
CHURNING
CHURNMILK
CHURNSTAFF
CHURR
CHURRASCO
CHURRED
CHURRING
CHURRO
CHURRUCK
CHURRUS
CHURRWORM
CHUSE
CHUSER
CHUT
CHUTE
CHUTER
CHUTNEE
CHUTNEY
CHUTNEYS
CHUTZPAH
CHUZWI
CHWAS
CHYACK
CHYAK
CHYLACEOUS
CHYLE
CHYLIFACTION
CHYLIFACTIVE
CHYLIFACTORY
CHYLIFEROUS
CHYLIFIC
CHYLIFIED
CHYLIFORM
CHYLIFY
CHYLIFYING
CHYLOCAULOUS
CHYLOCAULY
CHYLOCELE
CHYLOMICRON
CHYLOPHYLLY
CHYLOPOETIC
CHYLOPOIESIS
CHYLOPOIETIC
CHYLOTHORAX
CHYLOUS
CHYLURIA
CHYMAQUEOUS
CHYME
CHYMIA
CHYMIC
CHYMIFEROUS
CHYMIFIED
CHYMIFY
CHYMIFYING
CHYMIST
CHYMOSIN
CHYMOUS
CHYPRE
CHYTRA
CHYTRID
CHYTRIDIAL
CHYTRIDIOSE
CHYTRIDIOSIS
CIBARIAL
CIBARIAN
CIBARIOUS
CIBATION
CIBOL
CIBOLERO
CIBOPHOBIA
CIBORIA
CIBORIUM
CIBOULE
CICAD
CICADA
CICADAE
CICADAS
CICADID
CICALA
CICATRICE
CICATRICES
CICATRICIAL
CICATRICLE
CICATRICOSE
CICATRICULA
CICATRICULAE
CICATRISATE
CICATRISIVE
CICATRIX
CICATRIXES
CICATRIZANT
CICATRIZATE
CICATRIZE
CICATRIZED
CICATRIZER
CICATRIZING
CICATROSE
CICELIES
CICELY
CICER
CICERO
CICERONAGE
CICERONE
CICERONES
CICERONI
CICERONING
CICERONISM
CICERONIZE
CICHAR
CICHLID
CICHLIDAE
CICHLIDS
CICHLOID
CICINDELID
CICISBEISM
CICISBEO
CICLATOUN
CICONIFORM
CICONIID
CICONINE
CICOREE
CICURATE
CICUTOXIN
CIDARID
CIDARIS
CIDER
CIDERIST
CIEL
CIENAGA
CIERGE
CIG
CIGALA
CIGALE
CIGAR
CIGARESQUE
CIGARET
CIGARETTE
CIGARETTES
CIGARFISH
CIGARILLO
CIGARILLOS
CIGARITO
CIGARITOS
CIGUA
CIGUATERA
CILERY
CILIA
CILIARY
CILIATE
CILIATED
CILIATELY
CILIATION
CILICE
CILICIOUS
CILIECTOMY
CILIELLA
CILIFEROUS
CILIFORM
CILIIFORM
CILIOGRADE
CILIOLA
CILIOLATE
CILIOLUM
CILIORETINAL
CILIOSCLERAL
CILIOSPINAL

CILIUM
CILLOSIS
CIMA
CIMAROON
CIMBAL
CIMBALOM
CIMBIA
CIMBORIO
CIMELIA
CIMETER
CIMEX
CIMICID
CIMICIDE
CIMICIFORM
CIMICIFUGIN
CIMICOID
CIMIER
CIMINITE
CIMLINE
CIMMARON
CIMOLITE
CINCH
CINCHA
CINCHER
CINCHOLOIPON
CINCHONA
CINCHONAMIN
CINCHONAMINE
CINCHONATE
CINCHONIA
CINCHONIC
CINCHONICIN
CINCHONICINE
CINCHONIDIA
CINCHONIN
CINCHONINE
CINCHONISM
CINCHONIZE
CINCHONIZED
CINCHONIZING
CINCHONOLOGY
CINCHOTINE
CINCINNAL
CINCINNI
CINCINNUS
CINCLIDES
CINCLIS
CINCT
CINCTURE
CINCTURED
CINCTURING
CINDER
CINDERED
CINDERING
CINDERMAN
CINDERS
CINDERY
CINEAST
CINEFACTION
CINEL
CINEMA
CINEMATIC
CINEMATICAL
CINEMATOGRAPH
CINEMIZE
CINEMOGRAPH
CINENCHYMA
CINENE
CINENEGATIVE
CINEOL
CINEOLE
CINEPHONE
CINERACEOUS
CINERARIA
CINERARIUM
CINERARY
CINERATION
CINERATOR
CINEREA
CINEREAL
CINEREOUS
CINERIN
CINERITIOUS
CINEROUS
CINEVARIETY
CINGLE
CINGULA
CINGULAR
CINGULATE
CINGULATED
CINGULUM
CINNABAR
CINNABARIC
CINNABARINE
CINNAMAL
CINNAMATE
CINNAMEIN
CINNAMIC
CINNAMOL
CINNAMON
CINNAMONED
CINNAMONIC
CINNAMONROOT
CINNAMONWOOD
CINNAMYL
CINNOLIN
CINNOLINE
CINQ
CINQFOIL
CINQUAIN
CINQUE
CINQUECENTO
CINQUEFOIL
CINQUEPACE
CINQUES
CINTER
CINTRE
CINURAN
CINUROUS
CION
CIONECTOMY
CIONITIS
CIONOCRANIAL
CIONOCRANIAN
CIONOPTOSIS
CIONOTOME
CIONOTOMY
CIOPPINO
CIPAYE
CIPHER
CIPHERED
CIPHERING
CIPO
CIPOLIN
CIPPI
CIPPUS
CIRC
CIRCA
CIRCADIAN
CIRCAR
CIRCINAL
CIRCINATE
CIRCINATELY
CIRCINATION
CIRCITER
CIRCLE
CIRCLED
CIRCLER
CIRCLES
CIRCLET
CIRCLETING
CIRCLINE
CIRCLING
CIRCOVARIAN
CIRCS
CIRCUE
CIRCUIT
CIRCUITAL
CIRCUITEER
CIRCUITER
CIRCUITIES
CIRCUITION
CIRCUITMAN
CIRCUITMEN
CIRCUITOR
CIRCUITOUS
CIRCUITOUSLY
CIRCUITRY
CIRCUITY
CIRCULABLE
CIRCULANT
CIRCULAR
CIRCULARITIES
CIRCULARITY
CIRCULARIZE
CIRCULARIZED
CIRCULARIZING
CIRCULARLY
CIRCULARNESS
CIRCULATE
CIRCULATED
CIRCULATING
CIRCULATION
CIRCULATIVE
CIRCULATOR
CIRCULATORIES
CIRCULATORY
CIRCULIN
CIRCULUS
CIRCUMANAL
CIRCUMARCTIC
CIRCUMAVIATE
CIRCUMAXIAL
CIRCUMAXILE
CIRCUMAXILLARY
CIRCUMBASAL
CIRCUMBOREAL
CIRCUMBUCCAL
CIRCUMBULBAR
CIRCUMCENTER
CIRCUMCINCT
CIRCUMCIRCLE
CIRCUMCISE
CIRCUMCISED
CIRCUMCISER
CIRCUMCISING
CIRCUMCISION
CIRCUMCLUDE
CIRCUMCLUSION
CIRCUMCONE
CIRCUMCONIC
CIRCUMCORNEAL
CIRCUMDUCE
CIRCUMDUCING
CIRCUMDUCT
CIRCUMDUCTED
CIRCUMFER
CIRCUMFERENCE
CIRCUMFERENT
CIRCUMFERENTOR
CIRCUMFLECT
CIRCUMFLEX
CIRCUMFLUENT
CIRCUMFLUOUS
CIRCUMFUSE
CIRCUMFUSILE
CIRCUMFUSING
CIRCUMFUSION
CIRCUMGYRATE
CIRCUMJACENT
CIRCUMLENTAL
CIRCUMLITIO
CIRCUMLOCUTE
CIRCUMLOCUTION
CIRCUMMURE
CIRCUMMURED
CIRCUMMURING
CIRCUMNATANT
CIRCUMNUTATE
CIRCUMOCULAR
CIRCUMORAL
CIRCUMORBITAL
CIRCUMPOLAR
CIRCUMPOSE
CIRCUMRENAL
CIRCUMROTATE
CIRCUMSAIL
CIRCUMSCRIBE
CIRCUMSCRIBED
CIRCUMSCRIBER
CIRCUMSCRIPT
CIRCUMSOLAR
CIRCUMSPECT
CIRCUMSPECTION
CIRCUMSPECTLY
CIRCUMSTANCE
CIRCUMSTANCED
CIRCUMSTANCES
CIRCUMSTANTIAL
CIRCUMSTANTIALLY
CIRCUMSTANTIATE
CIRCUMSTANTIATED
CIRCUMSTANTIATING
CIRCUMVENT
CIRCUMVENTED
CIRCUMVENTER
CIRCUMVENTING
CIRCUMVENTION
CIRCUMVIATE
CIRCUMVOLANT
CIRCUMVOLUTE
CIRCUMVOLVE
CIRCUMVOLVED
CIRCUMVOLVING
CIRCUS
CIRE
CIRL
CIRQUE
CIRRATE
CIRRATED
CIRRHOSED
CIRRHOSIS
CIRRHOTIC
CIRRHOUS
CIRRHUS
CIRRI
CIRRIBRANCH
CIRRIFEROUS
CIRRIFORM
CIRRIGEROUS
CIRRIPED
CIRRIPEDIAL
CIRROCUMULUS
CIRROLITE
CIRROPODOUS
CIRROSE
CIRROSTOME
CIRROSTRATUS
CIRROUS
CIRRUS
CIRSECTOMY
CIRSOID
CIRSOMPHALOS
CIRSOTOME
CIRSOTOMIES
CIRSOTOMY
CIRUELA
CISALPINE
CISANDINE
CISATLANTIC
CISCO
CISCOES
CISCOS
CISE
CISEAUX
CISELE
CISELEUR
CISELURE
CISGANGETIC
CISIUM
CISJURANE
CISLEITHAN
CISLUNAR
CISMARINE
CISMONTANE
CISOCEANIC
CISPADANE
CISPLATINE
CISPONTINE
CISRHENANE
CISSA
CISSING
CISSOID
CISSOIDAL
CIST
CISTACEOUS
CISTED
CISTERN
CISTERNA
CISTERNAL
CISTIC
CISTOPHORIC
CISTOPHORUS
CISTUS
CISTVAEN
CIT
CITABLE
CITADEL
CITAL
CITATION
CITATOR
CITATORY
CITE
CITEABLE
CITED
CITEE
CITER
CITHARA
CITHARIST
CITHAROEDIC
CITHAROEDUS
CITHER
CITHERN
CITIED
CITIES
CITIFICATION
CITIFIED
CITIFY
CITIGRADE
CITIZEN
CITIZENESS
CITIZENISM
CITIZENIZE
CITIZENIZED
CITIZENIZING
CITIZENLY
CITIZENRIES
CITIZENRY
CITIZENSHIP
CITO
CITOLA
CITOLE
CITOLER
CITOYEN
CITOYENNE

CITRACONATE
CITRACONIC
CITRAL
CITRAMIDE
CITRANGE
CITRANGEADE
CITRATE
CITRATED
CITREAN
CITRENE
CITREOUS
CITRIC
CITRICULTURE
CITRIL
CITRIN
CITRINATION
CITRINE
CITRININ
CITROCOLA
CITROMETER
CITRON
CITRONADE
CITRONELLA
CITRONELLAL
CITRONELLE
CITRONELLOL
CITRONIN
CITRONIZE
CITRONWOOD
CITROUS
CITRUL
CITRULLIN
CITRUS
CITTERN
CITTERNHEAD
CITUA
CITY
CITYCISM
CITYFIED
CITYSCAPE
CITYWARD
CIUDAD
CIVE
CIVET
CIVETONE
CIVIC
CIVICAL
CIVICALLY
CIVICISM
CIVICS
CIVIES
CIVIL
CIVILIAN
CIVILISE
CIVILIST
CIVILITE
CIVILITIES
CIVILITY
CIVILIZABLE
CIVILIZATION
CIVILIZATORY
CIVILIZE
CIVILIZED
CIVILIZEE
CIVILIZER
CIVILIZING
CIVISM
CIVITAS
CIVITE
CIVORY
CIVVIES
CIVVY
CIXIID
CLABBER
CLABBERY
CLACH
CLACHAN
CLACK
CLACKDISH
CLACKED
CLACKER
CLACKET
CLACKETY
CLACKING
CLACO
CLAD
CLADANTHOUS
CLADAUTOICOUS
CLADDING
CLADI
CLADINE
CLADOCARPOUS
CLADOCERAN
CLADOCEROUS
CLADODE
CLADODIAL
CLADODONT
CLADODONTID
CLADOGENOUS
CLADONIOID
CLADOPHYLL
CLADOPHYLLUM
CLADOPTOSIS
CLADOSE
CLADUS
CLAG
CLAGGUM
CLAGGY
CLAIK
CLAIM
CLAIMABLE
CLAIMANT
CLAIMER
CLAIMS
CLAIRAUDIENT
CLAIRÇE
CLAIRÉ
CLAIRSCHACH
CLAIRVOYANCE
CLAIRVOYANT
CLAITH
CLAIVER
CLAM
CLAMANT
CLAMAROO
CLAMATORIAL
CLAMATORY
CLAMBAKE
CLAMBER
CLAMBERER
CLAMCRACKER
CLAME
CLAMEHEWIT
CLAMFLAT
CLAMJAMFERY
CLAMJAMFRY
CLAMJAMPHRIE
CLAMMED
CLAMMER
CLAMMERSOME
CLAMMIER
CLAMMIEST
CLAMMILY
CLAMMINESS
CLAMMING
CLAMMISH
CLAMMY
CLAMOR
CLAMORED
CLAMORER
CLAMORING
CLAMORIST
CLAMOROUS
CLAMOROUSLY
CLAMOROUSNESS
CLAMORSOME
CLAMOUR
CLAMOURED
CLAMOURER
CLAMOURING
CLAMOURIST
CLAMOUROUS
CLAMOURSOME
CLAMP
CLAMPED
CLAMPER
CLAMPING
CLAMSHELL
CLAMWORM
CLAN
CLANCULAR
CLANCULARLY
CLANDESTINE
CLANDESTINELY
CLANFELLOW
CLANG
CLANGOR
CLANGOROUS
CLANGOROUSLY
CLANGOUR
CLANK
CLANKED
CLANKETY
CLANKING
CLANKINGLY
CLANKINGNESS
CLANKUM
CLANNISH
CLANNISHLY
CLANNISHNESS
CLANSHIP
CLANSMAN
CLANSMEN
CLANSWOMAN
CLANSWOMEN
CLAP
CLAPBOARD
CLAPBOARDING
CLAPBREAD
CLAPCAKE
CLAPDISH
CLAPHOLT
CLAPMATCH
CLAPNEST
CLAPNET
CLAPPE
CLAPPED
CLAPPER
CLAPPERCLAW
CLAPPERED
CLAPPERING
CLAPPERS
CLAPPING
CLAPTRAP
CLAPWORT
CLAQUE
CLAQUEUR
CLARABELLA
CLARAIN
CLARENCE
CLARENDON
CLARET
CLARIBELLA
CLARIES
CLARIFIANT
CLARIFICATION
CLARIFIED
CLARIFIER
CLARIFY
CLARIFYING
CLARIGATION
CLARIGOLD
CLARIN
CLARINA
CLARINET
CLARINETIST
CLARINETTIST
CLARINO
CLARION
CLARIONET
CLARISSIMO
CLARITY
CLARO
CLAROS
CLARSACH
CLART
CLARTIER
CLARTIEST
CLARTY
CLARY
CLASH
CLASHED
CLASHEE
CLASHER
CLASHES
CLASHING
CLASHY
CLASMATOCYTE
CLASMATOSIS
CLASP
CLASPED
CLASPER
CLASPING
CLASPT
CLASS
CLASSBOOK
CLASSER
CLASSES
CLASSFELLOW
CLASSIC
CLASSICAL
CLASSICALISM
CLASSICALIST
CLASSICALITIES
CLASSICALITY
CLASSICALLY
CLASSICISM
CLASSICIST
CLASSICISTIC
CLASSICIZE
CLASSICIZED
CLASSICIZING
CLASSICS
CLASSIER
CLASSIEST
CLASSIFIABLE
CLASSIFIC
CLASSIFICATION
CLASSIFIED
CLASSIFIER
CLASSIFY
CLASSIFYING
CLASSIS
CLASSMAN
CLASSMATE
CLASSMEN
CLASSROOM
CLASSWORK
CLASSY
CLASTIC
CLAT
CLATCH
CLATCHY
CLATHRACEOUS
CLATHRARIAN
CLATHRATE
CLATHROID
CLATHROSE
CLATHRULATE
CLATTER
CLATTERED
CLATTERER
CLATTERING
CLATTERINGLY
CLATTERTRAPS
CLATTERY
CLATTY
CLAUBER
CLAUCHT
CLAUD
CLAUDENT
CLAUDETITE
CLAUDICANT
CLAUDICATE
CLAUDICATION
CLAUGHT
CLAUSAL
CLAUSE
CLAUSTHALITE
CLAUSTRA
CLAUSTRAL
CLAUSTRATION
CLAUSTRUM
CLAUSULA
CLAUSULAR
CLAUSULE
CLAUSURE
CLAUT
CLAVA
CLAVACIN
CLAVAE
CLAVAL
CLAVATE
CLAVATED
CLAVATELY
CLAVATIN
CLAVATION
CLAVE
CLAVECIN
CLAVECINIST
CLAVEL
CLAVELIZE
CLAVELLATED
CLAVER
CLAVES
CLAVIAL
CLAVIATURE
CLAVICEMBALO
CLAVICHORD
CLAVICITHERN
CLAVICLE
CLAVICOR
CLAVICORN
CLAVICORNATE
CLAVICOTOMY
CLAVICULAR
CLAVICULATE
CLAVICYMBAL
CLAVIER
CLAVIERIST
CLAVIFORM
CLAVIGER
CLAVIHARP
CLAVILUX
CLAVIOL
CLAVIOLE
CLAVIS
CLAVISES
CLAVODELTOID
CLAVUS
CLAVY
CLAW
CLAWBACK
CLAWED
CLAWER

CLAWK
CLAWKER
CLAWS
CLAWSICK
CLAY
CLAYBANK
CLAYBRAINED
CLAYED
CLAYEN
CLAYER
CLAYEY
CLAYIER
CLAYIEST
CLAYING
CLAYISH
CLAYMAN
CLAYMORE
CLAYPAN
CLAYTONIA
CLAYWARE
CLAYWEED
CLEACH
CLEAD
CLEADED
CLEADING
CLEAM
CLEAMER
CLEAN
CLEANABLE
CLEANED
CLEANER
CLEANEST
CLEANHANDED
CLEANING
CLEANLIER
CLEANLIEST
CLEANLILY
CLEANLINESS
CLEANLY
CLEANNESS
CLEANOUT
CLEANSE
CLEANSED
CLEANSER
CLEANSING
CLEANUP
CLEAR
CLEARABLE
CLEARAGE
CLEARANCE
CLEARCOLE
CLEARCOLED
CLEARCOLING
CLEARED
CLEAREDNESS
CLEARER
CLEAREST
CLEARHEADED
CLEARING
CLEARINGHOUSE
CLEARLY
CLEARNESS
CLEARS
CLEARSKINS
CLEARSTARCH
CLEARSTORIED
CLEARSTORY
CLEARWEED
CLEARWING
CLEAT
CLEATED
CLEATING
CLEATS
CLEAVABILITY
CLEAVABLE
CLEAVAGE
CLEAVE
CLEAVED
CLEAVER
CLEAVERS
CLEAVERWORT
CLEAVING
CLEAVINGLY
CLECHE
CLECHEE
CLECHY
CLECK
CLEDDE
CLEDGE
CLEDGY
CLEDONISM
CLEE
CLEECH
CLEED
CLEEK
CLEEKED
CLEEKING
CLEEKS
CLEEKY
CLEEVE
CLEF
CLEFT
CLEFTED
CLEG
CLEGG
CLEIDAGRA
CLEIDOCOSTAL
CLEIDOHYOID
CLEIDOIC
CLEIDOMANCY
CLEIDOTOMY
CLEIDOTRIPSY
CLEISTOCARP
CLEISTOGAMIC
CLEISTOGAMY
CLEISTOGENE
CLEITHRA
CLEITHRAL
CLEITHRUM
CLEM
CLEMATIS
CLEMATITE
CLEMENCE
CLEMENCIES
CLEMENCY
CLEMENT
CLEMENTLY
CLENCH
CLENCHED
CLENCHING
CLENK
CLEOID
CLEOME
CLEP
CLEPE
CLEPED
CLEPING
CLEPSYDRA
CLEPSYDRAE
CLEPSYDRAS
CLEPTOBIOSIS
CLEPTOBIOTIC
CLEPTOMANIA
CLERESTOREY
CLERESTORIED
CLERESTORIES
CLERESTORY
CLERGEON
CLERGESS
CLERGIAL
CLERGIES
CLERGION
CLERGY
CLERGYABLE
CLERGYMAN
CLERGYMEN
CLERGYWOMAN
CLERGYWOMEN
CLERIC
CLERICAL
CLERICALISM
CLERICALIST
CLERICALITY
CLERICALLY
CLERICATE
CLERICATURE
CLERICISM
CLERICITY
CLERID
CLERIHEW
CLERISY
CLERK
CLERKAGE
CLERKED
CLERKERY
CLERKESS
CLERKING
CLERKISH
CLERKLESS
CLERKLIER
CLERKLIEST
CLERKLIKE
CLERKLINESS
CLERKLY
CLERKSHIP
CLEROMANCY
CLERONOMY
CLERUCH
CLERUCHIAL
CLERUCHIC
CLERUCHIES
CLERUCHY
CLETCH
CLEUCH
CLEUGH
CLEUK
CLEVE
CLEVEITE
CLEVER
CLEVERALITY
CLEVERER
CLEVEREST
CLEVERISH
CLEVERISHLY
CLEVERLY
CLEVERNESS
CLEVIS
CLEVY
CLEW
CLEWED
CLEWING
CLIACK
CLIANTHUS
CLICHE
CLICK
CLICKED
CLICKER
CLICKET
CLICKING
CLICKY
CLIENCY
CLIENT
CLIENTAGE
CLIENTAL
CLIENTED
CLIENTELE
CLIENTRY
CLIER
CLIFF
CLIFFED
CLIFFHANGER
CLIFFHANGING
CLIFFING
CLIFFS
CLIFFSIDE
CLIFFSMAN
CLIFFY
CLIFT
CLIFTONITE
CLIFTY
CLIMACTER
CLIMACTERIC
CLIMACTERICAL
CLIMACTIC
CLIMACUS
CLIMATAL
CLIMATE
CLIMATH
CLIMATIC
CLIMATICAL
CLIMATICALLY
CLIMATIZE
CLIMATOLOGIC
CLIMATOLOGY
CLIMATOMETER
CLIMATURE
CLIMAX
CLIMAXED
CLIMAXING
CLIMB
CLIMBABLE
CLIMBED
CLIMBER
CLIMBERS
CLIMBING
CLIME
CLIMOGRAPH
CLINAMEN
CLINANDRIA
CLINANDRIUM
CLINANTHIA
CLINANTHIUM
CLINCH
CLINCHER
CLINE
CLINER
CLING
CLINGER
CLINGFISH
CLINGFISHES
CLINGING
CLINGINGLY
CLINGINGNESS
CLINGSTONE
CLINGY
CLINIA
CLINIC
CLINICAL
CLINICIAN
CLINIQUE
CLINIUM
CLINK
CLINKED
CLINKER
CLINKERER
CLINKERMAN
CLINKING
CLINKSTONE
CLINKUM
CLINOCEPHALY
CLINOCHLORE
CLINOCLASE
CLINOCLASITE
CLINODOMATIC
CLINODOME
CLINOEDRITE
CLINOGRAPH
CLINOGRAPHIC
CLINOHEDRAL
CLINOHEDRITE
CLINOHUMITE
CLINOID
CLINOLOGIC
CLINOLOGY
CLINOMETER
CLINOMETRIC
CLINOMETRY
CLINOSTAT
CLINQUANT
CLINT
CLINTONIA
CLINTONITE
CLINTY
CLIP
CLIPBOARD
CLIPEUS
CLIPPABLE
CLIPPED
CLIPPER
CLIPPING
CLIPS
CLIPSE
CLIPSHEET
CLIPSOME
CLIQUE
CLIQUED
CLIQUIER
CLIQUIEST
CLIQUING
CLIQUISH
CLIQUISHLY
CLIQUISHNESS
CLIQUISM
CLIQUY
CLISEOMETER
CLISTOCARP
CLISTOGAMIC
CLISTOGAMOUS
CLISTOGAMY
CLISTOGENE
CLIT
CLITCH
CLITE
CLITELLAR
CLITELLINE
CLITELLUM
CLITELLUS
CLITES
CLITHE
CLITHRIDIATE
CLITION
CLITORAL
CLITORIDAUXE
CLITORIDEAN
CLITORIDITIS
CLITORIS
CLITORISM
CLITORITIS
CLITTER
CLIVAL
CLIVE
CLIVERS
CLIVIS
CLIVOSE
CLIVUS
CLOACA
CLOACAE
CLOACAL
CLOACITIS
CLOAK
CLOAKAGE
CLOAKED
CLOAKEDLY
CLOAKING
CLOAKMAKER

CLOAKMAKING
CLOAKROOM
CLOAM
CLOAMEN
CLOAMER
CLOBBER
CLOBBERER
CLOCHAN
CLOCHE
CLOCHER
CLOCHETTE
CLOCK
CLOCKBIRD
CLOCKCASE
CLOCKED
CLOCKER
CLOCKFACE
CLOCKHOUSE
CLOCKING
CLOCKKEEPER
CLOCKMAKER
CLOCKMAKING
CLOCKMUTCH
CLOCKROOM
CLOCKSMITH
CLOCKWISE
CLOCKWORK
CLOCKWORKED
CLOD
CLODBREAKER
CLODDED
CLODDER
CLODDIER
CLODDIEST
CLODDILY
CLODDINESS
CLODDING
CLODDISH
CLODDISHLY
CLODDISHNESS
CLODDY
CLODHEAD
CLODHOPPER
CLODHOPPING
CLODPATE
CLODPATED
CLODPOLE
CLODPOLL
CLODS
CLOES
CLOFF
CLOG
CLOGDOGDO
CLOGGED
CLOGGER
CLOGGIER
CLOGGIEST
CLOGGILY
CLOGGINESS
CLOGGING
CLOGGY
CLOGHAD
CLOGHAUN
CLOGHEAD
CLOGMAKER
CLOGMAKING
CLOGWHEEL
CLOGWOOD
CLOGWYN
CLOINE
CLOISON
CLOISONNE
CLOISTER
CLOISTERAL
CLOISTERED
CLOISTERER
CLOISTERING
CLOISTERLY
CLOISTRAL
CLOISTRESS
CLOIT
CLOKY
CLOMB
CLONAL
CLONE
CLONIC
CLONICITY
CLONICOTONIC
CLONISM
CLONK
CLONOS
CLONUS
CLOOF
CLOOK
CLOOP
CLOOT
CLOOTIE
CLOP
CLOPPED
CLOPPING
CLOQUE
CLOS
CLOSE
CLOSED
CLOSEFISTED
CLOSEHANDED
CLOSELY
CLOSEMOUTH
CLOSEMOUTHED
CLOSEN
CLOSENESS
CLOSER
CLOSEST
CLOSESTOOL
CLOSET
CLOSEUP
CLOSH
CLOSING
CLOSISH
CLOSTER
CLOSTRIDIA
CLOSTRIDIAL
CLOSTRIDIUM
CLOSURE
CLOSURED
CLOSURING
CLOT
CLOTBUR
CLOTE
CLOTH
CLOTHE
CLOTHED
CLOTHES
CLOTHESBAG
CLOTHESBRUSH
CLOTHESHORSE
CLOTHESLINE
CLOTHESMAN
CLOTHESPIN
CLOTHESPRESS
CLOTHESYARD
CLOTHIER
CLOTHIFY
CLOTHING
CLOTHMAKER
CLOTHMAKING
CLOTHS
CLOTHWORKER
CLOTHY
CLOTS
CLOTTAGE
CLOTTED
CLOTTER
CLOTTY
CLOTURE
CLOTWEED
CLOU
CLOUD
CLOUDAGE
CLOUDBERRIES
CLOUDBERRY
CLOUDBURST
CLOUDCAP
CLOUDED
CLOUDIER
CLOUDIEST
CLOUDILY
CLOUDINESS
CLOUDING
CLOUDLAND
CLOUDLESSLY
CLOUDS
CLOUDY
CLOUE
CLOUEE
CLOUGH
CLOUR
CLOUT
CLOUTED
CLOUTER
CLOUTERLY
CLOUTY
CLOVE
CLOVEN
CLOVENE
CLOVER
CLOVERLAY
CLOVERLEAF
CLOVERLEAFS
CLOVERLEY
CLOVEROOT
CLOVERY
CLOVES
CLOVEWORT
CLOW
CLOWDER
CLOWE
CLOWER
CLOWN
CLOWNADE
CLOWNAGE
CLOWNERIES
CLOWNERY
CLOWNHEAL
CLOWNISH
CLOWNISHLY
CLOWNISHNESS
CLOWRE
CLOWRING
CLOY
CLOYED
CLOYEDNESS
CLOYER
CLOYING
CLOYINGLY
CLOYINGNESS
CLOYMENT
CLOYSOME
CLUB
CLUBABLE
CLUBBABILITY
CLUBBED
CLUBBER
CLUBBIER
CLUBBIEST
CLUBBILY
CLUBBING
CLUBBISH
CLUBBIST
CLUBBY
CLUBFEET
CLUBFELLOW
CLUBFIST
CLUBFISTED
CLUBFOOT
CLUBFOOTED
CLUBHAUL
CLUBHOUSE
CLUBIONID
CLUBLAND
CLUBMAN
CLUBMATE
CLUBMEN
CLUBMONGER
CLUBRIDDEN
CLUBROOM
CLUBROOT
CLUBS
CLUBSTART
CLUBSTER
CLUBWEED
CLUBWOMAN
CLUBWOMEN
CLUBWOOD
CLUCK
CLUCKED
CLUCKING
CLUE
CLUED
CLUF
CLUFE
CLUFF
CLUING
CLUM
CLUMBER
CLUMP
CLUMPER
CLUMPISH
CLUMPS
CLUMPST
CLUMPY
CLUMSE
CLUMSIER
CLUMSIEST
CLUMSILY
CLUMSINESS
CLUMSY
CLUNCH
CLUNG
CLUNK
CLUNTER
CLUPEID
CLUPEIFORM
CLUPEIN
CLUPEINE
CLUPEOID
CLUPIEN
CLUPPE
CLURICAUNE
CLUSE
CLUSIACEOUS
CLUSTER
CLUSTERBERRY
CLUSTERED
CLUSTERFIST
CLUSTERING
CLUSTERS
CLUSTERY
CLUTCH
CLUTCHED
CLUTCHING
CLUTHER
CLUTTER
CLUTTERED
CLUTTERER
CLUTTERING
CLUTTERY
CLY
CLYER
CLYERS
CLYFAKER
CLYPE
CLYPEAL
CLYPEASTROID
CLYPEATE
CLYPEATED
CLYPEI
CLYPEIFORM
CLYPEOLA
CLYPEOLAR
CLYPEOLATE
CLYPEOLE
CLYPEUS
CLYSIS
CLYSMA
CLYSMIAN
CLYSMIC
CLYSSUS
CLYSTER
CLYTE
CNAFE
CNEMIAL
CNEMIDIUM
CNEMIS
CNICIN
CNIDA
CNIDARIAN
CNIDOCELL
CNIDOCIL
CNIDOPHORE
CNIDOPOD
CNIDOSAC
CNIDOSIS
CO
COACERVATE
COACERVATION
COACH
COACHABILITY
COACHABLE
COACHBUILDER
COACHED
COACHEE
COACHER
COACHFELLOW
COACHING
COACHMAKER
COACHMAKING
COACHMAN
COACHMASTER
COACHMEN
COACHSMITH
COACHWAY
COACHWHIP
COACHWOMAN
COACHWORK
COACHWRIGHT
COACHY
COACT
COACTED
COACTING
COACTION
COACTIVE
COACTIVELY
COACTIVITY
COACTOR
COADAMITE
COADAPT
COADJACENCE
COADJACENT
COADJACENTLY
COADJUMENT
COADJUST
COADJUTANT
COADJUTATOR
COADJUTE

COADJUTEMENT
COADJUTIVE
COADJUTOR
COADJUTRESS
COADJUTRICE
COADJUTRICES
COADJUTRIX
COADJUVANT
COADMIT
COADSORBENT
COADUNATE
COADUNATED
COADUNATING
COADUNATION
COADUNATIVE
COADUNATIVELY
COADVENTURE
COADVENTURER
COAEVAL
COAGED
COAGEL
COAGMENT
COAGULA
COAGULABLE
COAGULANT
COAGULASE
COAGULATE
COAGULATED
COAGULATING
COAGULATION
COAGULATIVE
COAGULATOR
COAGULATORY
COAGULIN
COAGULOMETER
COAGULUM
COAITA
COAK
COAKUM
COAL
COALBAG
COALBAGGER
COALBIN
COALBOX
COALDEALER
COALED
COALER
COALESCE
COALESCED
COALESCENCE
COALESCENCY
COALESCENT
COALESCING
COALFIELD
COALFISH
COALFISHES
COALHEUGH
COALHOLE
COALIFY
COALING
COALITE
COALITION
COALITIONAL
COALITIONER
COALITIONIST
COALIZE
COALIZED
COALIZING
COALMONGER
COALMOUSE
COALPIT
COALRAKE
COALS
COALSACK
COALSHED
COALTERNATE
COALTITUDE
COALY
COALYARD
COAMING
COAPT
COAPTATE
COAPTATION
COAPTED
COAPTING
COARB
COARCT
COARCTATE
COARCTATION
COARCTED
COARCTING
COARSE
COARSELY
COARSEN
COARSENESS
COARSER
COARSEST
COART
COAST
COASTAL
COASTER
COASTING
COASTLAND
COASTLINE
COASTMAN
COASTMEN
COASTSIDE
COASTWAITER
COASTWARD
COASTWAYS
COASTWISE
COAT
COATED
COATEE
COATER
COATH
COATI
COATING
COATIS
COATLESS
COATRACK
COATROOM
COATS
COATTAIL
COATTAILED
COAX
COAXAL
COAXATION
COAXED
COAXER
COAXIAL
COAXIALLY
COAXING
COAXINGLY
COAXY
COAZERVATE
COAZERVATION
COB
COBAEA
COBALAMIN
COBALT
COBALTAMINE
COBALTAMMINE
COBALTIC
COBALTOUS
COBANG
COBB
COBBE
COBBER
COBBERER
COBBIN
COBBLE
COBBLED
COBBLER
COBBLERFISH
COBBLERY
COBBLES
COBBLESTONE
COBBLING
COBBLY
COBBRA
COBBY
COBCAB
COBEGO
COBERGER
COBHEAD
COBHOUSE
COBIA
COBIRON
COBISHOP
COBLE
COBLEMAN
COBLOAF
COBNUT
COBOLA
COBOSS
COBRA
COBRIDGEHEAD
COBRIFORM
COBROTHER
COBS
COBSTONE
COBURG
COBWEB
COBWEBBED
COBWEBBERY
COBWEBBING
COBWEBBY
COBWEBS
COBWORK
COCA
COCAIN
COCAINE
COCAINISM
COCAINIZE
COCAINIZED
COCAINIZING
COCAINOMANIA
COCASH
COCASHWEED
COCCACEOUS
COCCAGEE
COCCAL
COCCERIN
COCCI
COCCID
COCCIDIA
COCCIDIAL
COCCIDIAN
COCCIDIOIDAL
COCCIDIOSIS
COCCIDIUM
COCCIDOLOGY
COCCIFEROUS
COCCIFORM
COCCIGENIC
COCCINELLA
COCCIONELLA
COCCO
COCCOGONE
COCCOGONIUM
COCCOID
COCCOLITE
COCCOLITH
COCCOSPHERE
COCCOSTEAN
COCCOSTEID
COCCOUS
COCCYGALGIA
COCCYGEAL
COCCYGEAN
COCCYGECTOMY
COCCYGES
COCCYGEUS
COCCYGINE
COCCYGODYNIA
COCCYGOMORPH
COCCYGOTOMY
COCCYX
COCHAL
COCHER
COCHERO
COCHINEAL
COCHLEA
COCHLEAE
COCHLEAR
COCHLEARE
COCHLEATE
COCHLEATED
COCHLEIFORM
COCHLEITIS
COCHLEOUS
COCHLIODONT
COCHLITIS
COCHON
COCHYLIS
COCILLANA
COCINERA
COCINERO
COCIRCULAR
COCK
COCKADE
COCKADED
COCKAL
COCKALAN
COCKALEEKIE
COCKALORUM
COCKAMAMIE
COCKAMAMY
COCKANDY
COCKARD
COCKAROUSE
COCKATEEL
COCKATIEL
COCKATOO
COCKATOOS
COCKATRICE
COCKAWEE
COCKBELL
COCKBILL
COCKBIRD
COCKBOAT
COCKBRAIN
COCKCHAFER
COCKCROW
COCKCROWER
COCKCROWING
COCKED
COCKER
COCKEREL
COCKERIE
COCKERING
COCKERNONNIE
COCKERNONY
COCKEROUSE
COCKET
COCKETED
COCKETING
COCKEYE
COCKEYED
COCKEYES
COCKFIGHT
COCKFIGHTING
COCKHEAD
COCKHORSE
COCKIE
COCKIELEEKIE
COCKIER
COCKIES
COCKIEST
COCKILY
COCKINESS
COCKING
COCKISH
COCKISHLY
COCKISHNESS
COCKLE
COCKLEBOAT
COCKLEBUR
COCKLED
COCKLER
COCKLESHELL
COCKLEWIFE
COCKLIGHT
COCKLING
COCKLOCHE
COCKLOFT
COCKLY
COCKMASTER
COCKMATCH
COCKMATE
COCKNEIAN
COCKNEITY
COCKNEY
COCKNEYBRED
COCKNEYDOM
COCKNEYESE
COCKNEYESS
COCKNEYFY
COCKNEYFYING
COCKNEYISH
COCKNEYISM
COCKNEYIZE
COCKNEYLAND
COCKPADDLE
COCKPIT
COCKROACH
COCKSCOMB
COCKSCOMBED
COCKSFOOT
COCKSHEAD
COCKSHIES
COCKSHOOT
COCKSHOT
COCKSHUT
COCKSHY
COCKSHYING
COCKSPUR
COCKSURE
COCKSURENESS
COCKSURETY
COCKSWAIN
COCKSY
COCKTAIL
COCKTHROWING
COCKUP
COCKWEED
COCKY
COCLEA
COCO
COCOA
COCOANUT
COCOAWOOD
COCOBOLO
COCOMAT
COCONA
COCONSCIOUS
COCONUT
COCOON
COCOONERIES
COCOONERY
COCOONS
COCOPAN
COCORICO
COCOROOT

COCOTTE
COCOWOOD
COCOWORT
COCOYAM
COCT
COCTILE
COCTION
COCTO
COCTOANTIGEN
COCUISA
COCUIZA
COCULLO
COCUM
COCUSWOOD
COCUYO
COD
CODA
CODAMIN
CODAMINE
CODBANK
CODDED
CODDER
CODDING
CODDLE
CODDLED
CODDLER
CODDLING
CODDY
CODE
CODED
CODEIA
CODEIN
CODEINE
CODEN
CODER
CODETTA
CODEX
CODFISH
CODFISHER
CODFISHERIES
CODFISHERY
CODFISHES
CODFISHING
CODGER
CODHEAD
CODHEADED
CODIACEOUS
CODICAL
CODICES
CODICIL
CODICILIC
CODIFICATION
CODIFIED
CODIFIER
CODIFY
CODIFYING
CODILLA
CODING
CODINIAC
CODIST
CODLIN
CODLING
CODLINGS
CODMAN
CODOL
CODOMINANT
CODON
CODPIECE
CODPITCHINGS
CODS
CODSHEAD
CODWORM
COE
COED
COEDUCATION
COEDUCATIONAL
COEFFECT
COEFFICIENT
COEHORN
COELACANTH
COELACANTHID
COELAR
COELARIUM
COELELMINTH
COELENTERATE
COELENTERIC
COELENTERON
COELESTINE
COELHO
COELIA
COELIAC
COELIALGIA
COELIGENOUS
COELIN
COELIORRHEA
COELIORRHOEA
COELIOSCOPY
COELIOTOMY
COELOBLASTIC
COELODONT
COELOM
COELOMA
COELOMATA
COELOMATE
COELOMATIC
COELOMATOUS
COELOME
COELOMIC
COELOMOPORE
COELOPLANULA
COELOSPERM
COELOSTAT
COELOZOIC
COEMPT
COEMPTIO
COEMPTION
COEMPTIONAL
COEMPTIVE
COEMPTOR
COENA
COENACULOUS
COENANTHIUM
COENENCHYMA
COENENCHYMAL
COENENCHYMATA
COENENCHYME
COENESTHESIA
COENESTHESIS
COENOBE
COENOBIAR
COENOBIC
COENOBIOD
COENOBITE
COENOBIUM
COENOBLAST
COENOBLASTIC
COENOBY
COENOCENTRUM
COENOCYTE
COENOCYTIC
COENOECIAL
COENOECIC
COENOECIUM
COENOGAMETE
COENOGENESIS
COENOSARC
COENOSARCAL
COENOSARCOUS
COENOSTEAL
COENOSTEUM
COENOTROPE
COENOTYPE
COENURE
COENURUS
COENZYME
COEQUAL
COEQUALITY
COEQUALLY
COEQUALNESS
COEQUATE
COEQUATED
COEQUATION
COERCE
COERCED
COERCER
COERCIBILITY
COERCIBLE
COERCIBLY
COERCING
COERCION
COERCIONARY
COERCIONIST
COERCITIVE
COERCIVE
COERCIVELY
COERCIVENESS
COERCIVITY
COESSENTIAL
COESTATE
COETANEITY
COETANEOUS
COETANEOUSLY
COETERNALLY
COETERNITY
COETUS
COEVAL
COEVALLY
COEXIST
COEXISTENCE
COEXISTENCY
COEXISTENT
COEXTEND
COEXTENSION
COEXTENSIVE
COFACTOR
COFEOFFEE
COFF
COFFE
COFFEE
COFFEEBERRIES
COFFEEBERRY
COFFEEBUSH
COFFEECAKE
COFFEEGROWER
COFFEEHOUSE
COFFEELEAF
COFFEEMAN
COFFEEPOT
COFFEEROOM
COFFEEWEED
COFFEEWOOD
COFFER
COFFERDAM
COFFERED
COFFERER
COFFERING
COFFERWORK
COFFIN
COFFINED
COFFING
COFFINING
COFFINMAKER
COFFINMAKING
COFFLE
COFFLED
COFFLING
COFFRET
COFT
COG
COGBOAT
COGENCE
COGENCY
COGENER
COGENT
COGGED
COGGER
COGGERS
COGGIE
COGGING
COGGLE
COGGLEDY
COGGLETY
COGGLY
COGHLE
COGIDA
COGITABILITY
COGITABLE
COGITABUND
COGITABUNDLY
COGITANT
COGITATE
COGITATED
COGITATING
COGITATION
COGITATIVE
COGITATIVELY
COGITATIVITY
COGITATOR
COGITO
COGMAN
COGNAC
COGNATE
COGNATIC
COGNATION
COGNATUS
COGNISE
COGNITION
COGNITIONAL
COGNITIVE
COGNITIVELY
COGNITUM
COGNIZABLE
COGNIZABLY
COGNIZANCE
COGNIZANT
COGNIZE
COGNIZED
COGNIZEE
COGNIZER
COGNIZING
COGNIZOR
COGNOMEN
COGNOMENS
COGNOMINA
COGNOMINAL
COGNOMINALLY
COGNOMINATE
COGNOMINATED
COGNOSCE
COGNOSCENTE
COGNOSCIBLE
COGNOSCITIVE
COGON
COGONAL
COGRAIL
COGREDIENCY
COGREDIENT
COGROAD
COGUE
COGWAY
COGWHEEL
COGWOOD
COHAB
COHABIT
COHABITANCY
COHABITANT
COHABITATION
COHABITED
COHABITER
COHABITING
COHEIR
COHEIRESS
COHENITE
COHERE
COHERED
COHERENCE
COHERENCY
COHERENT
COHERENTLY
COHERER
COHERING
COHERITAGE
COHERITOR
COHERT
COHESIBILITY
COHESIBLE
COHESION
COHESIVE
COHESIVELY
COHESIVENESS
COHIBIT
COHIBITION
COHIBITIVE
COHIBITOR
COHITRE
COHO
COHOBA
COHOBATE
COHOBATED
COHOBATING
COHOBATION
COHOBATOR
COHOE
COHOL
COHORT
COHORTATION
COHORTATIVE
COHOSH
COHOW
COHU
COHUE
COHUNE
COIF
COIFED
COIFFE
COIFFEUR
COIFFEUSE
COIFFURE
COIFFURED
COIFFURING
COIFING
COIGN
COIGNE
COIGNY
COIGUE
COIL
COILED
COILER
COILING
COILS
COILSMITH
COILYEAR
COIMPLICANT
COIN
COINABLE
COINAGE
COINCIDE
COINCIDENCE
COINCIDENCY
COINCIDENT
COINCIDENTAL
COINCIDENTALLY
COINCIDENTLY
COINCIDER
COINCIDING

COINDICANT
COINDICATE
COINDICATION
COINED
COINER
COINHABIT
COINHABITOR
COINHERITOR
COINING
COINMAKER
COINMAKING
COINS
COINSURANCE
COINSURE
COINSURED
COINSURER
COINSURING
COINTENSE
COINTENSITY
COINTISE
COIR
COISTREL
COISTRIL
COITION
COITURE
COITUS
COIX
COJONES
COJUROR
COKE
COKEMAN
COKENEY
COKER
COKERNUT
COKERY
COKES
COKEWOLD
COKEY
COKIE
COL
COLA
COLAGE
COLALGIA
COLANDER
COLANE
COLATE
COLATION
COLATITUDE
COLATORIUM
COLATORY
COLATURE
COLAUXE
COLAZIONE
COLBERTER
COLBERTINE
COLCANNON
COLCHICIA
COLCHICIN
COLCHICINE
COLCHICUM
COLCOTHAR
COLD
COLDCOCK
COLDER
COLDFINCH
COLDHEARTED
COLDHEARTEDLY
COLDISH
COLDLY
COLDONG
COLE
COLECTOMIES
COLECTOMY
COLEGATEE
COLEMANITE
COLEOPTER
COLEOPTERA
COLEOPTERAL
COLEOPTERAN
COLEOPTERIST
COLEOPTEROID
COLEOPTERON
COLEOPTEROUS
COLEOPTILE
COLEOPTILUM
COLEORHIZA
COLESEED
COLESLAW
COLETIT
COLEUR
COLEUS
COLEWORT
COLF
COLFOX
COLI
COLIBERT
COLIBRI
COLIC
COLICAL
COLICHEMARDE
COLICIN
COLICKER
COLICKY
COLICROOT
COLICWEED
COLICWORT
COLIES
COLIFORM
COLIMA
COLIN
COLINEAR
COLING
COLISEUM
COLITIC
COLITIS
COLK
COLL
COLLABENT
COLLABORATE
COLLABORATED
COLLABORATING
COLLABORATOR
COLLAGEN
COLLAGENIC
COLLAGENOUS
COLLAPSABLE
COLLAPSE
COLLAPSED
COLLAPSIBLE
COLLAPSING
COLLAR
COLLARBAND
COLLARBIRD
COLLARBONE
COLLARD
COLLARED
COLLARET
COLLARETTE
COLLARMAN
COLLATE
COLLATED
COLLATEE
COLLATERAL
COLLATERALLY
COLLATING
COLLATION
COLLATIONER
COLLATITIOUS
COLLATIVE
COLLATOR
COLLATRESS
COLLAUD
COLLAUDATION
COLLEAGUE
COLLEAGUED
COLLEAGUING
COLLECT
COLLECTABLE
COLLECTANEA
COLLECTARIUM
COLLECTED
COLLECTEDLY
COLLECTIBLE
COLLECTION
COLLECTIONAL
COLLECTIONER
COLLECTIVE
COLLECTIVELY
COLLECTIVISM
COLLECTIVIST
COLLECTIVITY
COLLECTIVIZE
COLLECTIVIZED
COLLECTIVIZING
COLLECTOR
COLLECTORATE
COLLECTORSHIP
COLLEEN
COLLEGATARY
COLLEGE
COLLEGER
COLLEGIA
COLLEGIAL
COLLEGIALISM
COLLEGIALITY
COLLEGIAN
COLLEGIANER
COLLEGIATE
COLLEGIATELY
COLLEGIATION
COLLEGIUM
COLLEMBOLAN
COLLEMBOLE
COLLEMBOLIC
COLLEMBOLOUS
COLLEN
COLLENCHYMA
COLLENCHYME
COLLENCYTAL
COLLENCYTE
COLLERY
COLLET
COLLETER
COLLETERIA
COLLETERIAL
COLLETERIUM
COLLETIC
COLLETIN
COLLEY
COLLIBERT
COLLICLE
COLLICULATE
COLLICULUS
COLLIDE
COLLIDED
COLLIDIN
COLLIDINE
COLLIDING
COLLIE
COLLIED
COLLIER
COLLIERY
COLLIFORM
COLLIGATE
COLLIGATED
COLLIGATING
COLLIGATION
COLLIGATIVE
COLLIGIBLE
COLLIMATE
COLLIMATED
COLLIMATING
COLLIMATION
COLLIN
COLLINAL
COLLINE
COLLINEARITY
COLLINEARLY
COLLINEATE
COLLINEATION
COLLING
COLLINGUAL
COLLINSIA
COLLINSITE
COLLIQUATE
COLLIQUATION
COLLIQUATIVE
COLLIS
COLLISION
COLLISIONAL
COLLISIVE
COLLOBLAST
COLLOCAL
COLLOCATE
COLLOCATED
COLLOCATING
COLLOCATION
COLLOCK
COLLOCUTION
COLLOCUTOR
COLLOCUTORY
COLLODION
COLLODIONIZE
COLLODIOTYPE
COLLODIUM
COLLOGEN
COLLOGUE
COLLOGUED
COLLOGUING
COLLOID
COLLOIDAL
COLLOIDALITY
COLLOMIA
COLLOP
COLLOPED
COLLOPHANITE
COLLOPHORE
COLLOQUE
COLLOQUIAL
COLLOQUIALLY
COLLOQUIST
COLLOQUIUM
COLLOQUIZE
COLLOQUIZED
COLLOQUIZING
COLLOQUY
COLLOTYPE
COLLOTYPIC
COLLOTYPY
COLLOXYLIN
COLLUDE
COLLUDED
COLLUDER
COLLUDING
COLLUM
COLLUSION
COLLUSIVE
COLLUSIVELY
COLLUSORY
COLLUTORIES
COLLUTORIUM
COLLUTORY
COLLUVIAL
COLLUVIES
COLLY
COLLYBA
COLLYING
COLLYRIA
COLLYRIE
COLLYRITE
COLLYRIUM
COLLYRIUMS
COLLYWEST
COLLYWESTON
COLLYWOBBLES
COLMAR
COLMOSE
COLOBIN
COLOBIUM
COLOBOMA
COLOCENTESIS
COLOCLYSIS
COLOCOLA
COLOCOLIC
COLOCOLO
COLOCYNTH
COLOCYNTHIN
COLOGARITHM
COLOGNE
COLOLITE
COLOMBIER
COLOMBIN
COLOMETRIC
COLOMETRY
COLON
COLONATE
COLONEL
COLONELCIES
COLONELCY
COLONGITUDE
COLONIAL
COLONIALISM
COLONIC
COLONIES
COLONISE
COLONIST
COLONITIS
COLONIZATION
COLONIZE
COLONIZED
COLONIZER
COLONIZING
COLONNADE
COLONNADED
COLONNETTE
COLONOPATHY
COLONOPEXY
COLONOSCOPE
COLONOSCOPY
COLONS
COLONUS
COLONY
COLOPEXIA
COLOPEXOTOMY
COLOPEXY
COLOPHAN
COLOPHANE
COLOPHENE
COLOPHON
COLOPHONATE
COLOPHONIST
COLOPHONITE
COLOPHONY
COLOPLICATION
COLOPPE
COLOQUIES
COLOQUINTIDA
COLOR
COLORABILITY
COLORABLE
COLORABLY
COLORADO
COLORANT
COLORATE
COLORATION

COLORATIONAL
COLORATIVE
COLORATURA
COLORCAST
COLORED
COLORER
COLORFAST
COLORFUL
COLORIFIC
COLORIFICS
COLORIMETER
COLORIMETRIC
COLORIMETRY
COLORIN
COLORING
COLORISM
COLORIST
COLORISTIC
COLORIZATION
COLORIZE
COLORLESS
COLORMAKER
COLORMAKING
COLORMAN
COLOROTO
COLORRHAPHY
COLORS
COLORTYPE
COLORY
COLOSSAL
COLOSSALITY
COLOSSALLY
COLOSSEAN
COLOSSEUM
COLOSSO
COLOSSUS
COLOSTOMIES
COLOSTOMY
COLOSTRAL
COLOSTRIC
COLOSTROUS
COLOSTRUM
COLOTOMIES
COLOTOMY
COLOTYPHOID
COLOUR
COLOURABILITY
COLOURABLE
COLOURABLY
COLOURATION
COLOURATIVE
COLOURED
COLOURER
COLOURFUL
COLOURFULLY
COLOURFULNESS
COLOURIFIC
COLOURIFICS
COLOURING
COLOURIST
COLOURISTIC
COLOURIZE
COLOURLESS
COLOURLESSLY
COLOURMAN
COLOURTYPE
COLOURY
COLPENCHYMA
COLPEO
COLPEURYNTER
COLPEURYSIS
COLPHEG
COLPINDACH
COLPITIS
COLPOCELE
COLPOPLASTIC
COLPOPLASTY
COLPOPTOSIS
COLPORRHAGIA
COLPORRHAPHY
COLPORRHEA
COLPORRHEXIS
COLPORT
COLPORTAGE
COLPORTER
COLPORTEUR
COLPOSCOPE
COLPOSCOPY
COLPOSTAT
COLPOTOMY
COLT
COLTER
COLTISH
COLTPIXY
COLTS
COLTSFOOT
COLTSKIN
COLUBRID
COLUBRIFORM
COLUBRINE
COLUBROID
COLUGO
COLUGOS
COLUMBACEOUS
COLUMBARIA
COLUMBARIUM
COLUMBARY
COLUMBATE
COLUMBEION
COLUMBIAD
COLUMBIC
COLUMBIER
COLUMBIN
COLUMBINE
COLUMBITE
COLUMBIUM
COLUMBO
COLUMBOID
COLUMEL
COLUMELLA
COLUMELLAE
COLUMELLAR
COLUMELLATE
COLUMN
COLUMNAL
COLUMNAR
COLUMNATED
COLUMNEA
COLUMNED
COLUMNER
COLUMNIATION
COLUMNIFORM
COLUMNING
COLUMNIST
COLUMNS
COLUNAR
COLURE
COLUSITE
COLY
COLYBA
COLYMBIFORM
COLYMBION
COLYTIC
COLYUM
COLYUMIST
COLZA
COMA
COMACINE
COMAE
COMAL
COMALES
COMAMIE
COMARCA
COMART
COMAS
COMATE
COMATIC
COMATOSE
COMATOSELY
COMATOSENESS
COMATOSITY
COMATOUS
COMATULA
COMATULID
COMB
COMBARON
COMBASOU
COMBAT
COMBATABLE
COMBATANT
COMBATANTS
COMBATED
COMBATING
COMBATIVE
COMBATIVELY
COMBATIVITY
COMBATTED
COMBATTER
COMBATTING
COMBED
COMBER
COMBFISH
COMBFLOWER
COMBINABLE
COMBINANT
COMBINANTIVE
COMBINATE
COMBINATION
COMBINATIONS
COMBINATIVE
COMBINE
COMBINED
COMBINEDLY
COMBINEDNESS
COMBINEMENT
COMBINER
COMBING
COMBINGS
COMBINING
COMBITE
COMBLE
COMBMAKER
COMBMAKING
COMBO
COMBOLOIO
COMBOY
COMBURE
COMBURENT
COMBURGESS
COMBURIMETER
COMBURIMETRY
COMBUST
COMBUSTIBLE
COMBUSTIBLY
COMBUSTION
COMBUSTIOUS
COMBUSTIVE
COMBUSTOR
COMBWISE
COMBWRIGHT
COMBY
COME
COMEBACK
COMEDDLE
COMEDIA
COMEDIAL
COMEDIAN
COMEDIANT
COMEDIC
COMEDICAL
COMEDICALLY
COMEDIENNE
COMEDIES
COMEDIST
COMEDO
COMEDONES
COMEDOS
COMEDOWN
COMEDY
COMELIER
COMELIEST
COMELILY
COMELINESS
COMELING
COMELY
COMENDITE
COMEPHOROUS
COMER
COMES
COMESSATION
COMESTIBLE
COMESTION
COMET
COMETARIA
COMETARIUM
COMETARY
COMETHER
COMETIC
COMEUPANCE
COMEUPPANCE
COMFIT
COMFITURE
COMFORT
COMFORTABLE
COMFORTABLY
COMFORTED
COMFORTER
COMFORTING
COMFORTINGLY
COMFORTLESS
COMFREY
COMFREYS
COMFY
COMIC
COMICAL
COMICALITY
COMICALLY
COMICALNESS
COMICOCRATIC
COMICOGRAPHY
COMICRY
COMIDA
COMIFEROUS
COMING
COMINO
COMIQUE
COMISM
COMITAL
COMITANT
COMITATIVE
COMITATUS
COMITE
COMITES
COMITIA
COMITIAL
COMITIES
COMITIVA
COMITJE
COMITRAGEDY
COMITY
COMMA
COMMAES
COMMAING
COMMAND
COMMANDANT
COMMANDED
COMMANDEER
COMMANDER
COMMANDERY
COMMANDING
COMMANDINGLY
COMMANDMENT
COMMANDMENTS
COMMANDO
COMMANDOES
COMMANDOS
COMMANDRIES
COMMANDRY
COMMAS
COMMASSATION
COMMASSEE
COMMATA
COMMATIC
COMMATION
COMMATISM
COMMEASURE
COMMEASURED
COMMEASURING
COMMEM
COMMEMORABLE
COMMEMORATE
COMMEMORATED
COMMEMORATING
COMMEMORATION
COMMEMORATIVE
COMMEMORATOR
COMMEMORIZE
COMMEMORIZED
COMMEMORIZING
COMMENCE
COMMENCED
COMMENCEMENT
COMMENCER
COMMENCING
COMMEND
COMMENDA
COMMENDABLE
COMMENDABLY
COMMENDADOR
COMMENDAM
COMMENDATARY
COMMENDATION
COMMENDATOR
COMMENDATORIES
COMMENDATORY
COMMENDED
COMMENDER
COMMENDING
COMMENSAL
COMMENSALISM
COMMENSALIST
COMMENSALISTIC
COMMENSALITY
COMMENSALLY
COMMENSURABLE
COMMENSURABLY
COMMENSURATE
COMMENSURATED
COMMENSURATING
COMMENT
COMMENTARIAL
COMMENTARIES
COMMENTARY
COMMENTATE
COMMENTATION
COMMENTATOR
COMMENTER
COMMERCE
COMMERCED
COMMERCER
COMMERCIA
COMMERCIABLE
COMMERCIAL
COMMERCIALISM
COMMERCIALITY

COMMERCIALIZE
COMMERCIALIZED
COMMERCIALIZING
COMMERCIALLY
COMMERCING
COMMERCIUM
COMMERGE
COMMERS
COMMESSO
COMMINATE
COMMINATED
COMMINATING
COMMINATION
COMMINATIVE
COMMINATOR
COMMINATORY
COMMINGLE
COMMINGLER
COMMINISTER
COMMINUATE
COMMINUTE
COMMINUTED
COMMINUTING
COMMINUTION
COMMINUTOR
COMMIS
COMMISE
COMMISERABLE
COMMISERATE
COMMISERATED
COMMISERATING
COMMISERATION
COMMISERATIVE
COMMISERATOR
COMMISSAR
COMMISSARIAL
COMMISSARIAT
COMMISSARIES
COMMISSARY
COMMISSION
COMMISSIONAIRE
COMMISSIONAL
COMMISSIONARY
COMMISSIONATE
COMMISSIONATED
COMMISSIONATING
COMMISSIONER
COMMISSIVE
COMMISSIVELY
COMMISSURAL
COMMISSURE
COMMIT
COMMITMENT
COMMITTABLE
COMMITTAL
COMMITTED
COMMITTEE
COMMITTEEMAN
COMMITTEEMEN
COMMITTENT
COMMITTER
COMMITTIBLE
COMMITTING
COMMITTOR
COMMIX
COMMIXED
COMMIXING
COMMIXT
COMMIXTION
COMMIXTURE
COMMODATA
COMMODATARY
COMMODATE
COMMODATION
COMMODATUM
COMMODE
COMMODIOUS
COMMODIOUSLY
COMMODITIES
COMMODITY
COMMODORE
COMMON
COMMONABLE
COMMONAGE
COMMONALITIES
COMMONALITY
COMMONALTY
COMMONED
COMMONER
COMMONEY
COMMONING
COMMONLY
COMMONNESS
COMMONPLACE
COMMONPLACELY
COMMONPLACENES
COMMONS
COMMONTY
COMMONWEAL
COMMONWEALTH
COMMORANCY
COMMORANT
COMMORIENT
COMMORTH
COMMOS
COMMOT
COMMOTE
COMMOTION
COMMOTIONAL
COMMOVE
COMMOVED
COMMOVING
COMMUNAL
COMMUNALISM
COMMUNALIST
COMMUNALISTIC
COMMUNALITY
COMMUNALIZE
COMMUNALIZED
COMMUNALIZER
COMMUNALLY
COMMUNARD
COMMUNE
COMMUNED
COMMUNER
COMMUNICABLE
COMMUNICABLY
COMMUNICANT
COMMUNICATE
COMMUNICATED
COMMUNICATING
COMMUNICATION
COMMUNICATIVE
COMMUNICATOR
COMMUNICATORY
COMMUNING
COMMUNION
COMMUNIONABLE
COMMUNIONAL
COMMUNIONIST
COMMUNIQUE
COMMUNISM
COMMUNIST
COMMUNISTERIES
COMMUNISTERY
COMMUNISTIC
COMMUNISTICAL
COMMUNITAL
COMMUNITARIAN
COMMUNITARY
COMMUNITIES
COMMUNITIVE
COMMUNITY
COMMUNIZATION
COMMUNIZE
COMMUNIZED
COMMUNIZING
COMMUTABLE
COMMUTANT
COMMUTATE
COMMUTATED
COMMUTATING
COMMUTATION
COMMUTATIVE
COMMUTATOR
COMMUTE
COMMUTED
COMMUTER
COMMUTING
COMMUTUAL
COMMUTUALITY
COMMY
COMODATO
COMODO
COMOEDIA
COMOEDUS
COMOID
COMOLECULE
COMONTE
COMOQUER
COMORADO
COMOSE
COMOUS
COMP
COMPACT
COMPACTED
COMPACTEDLY
COMPACTER
COMPACTING
COMPACTION
COMPACTLY
COMPACTNESS
COMPACTURE
COMPADRE
COMPAGE
COMPAGES
COMPAGINATE
COMPANIED
COMPANIES
COMPANION
COMPANIONABLE
COMPANIONABLY
COMPANIONAGE
COMPANIONATE
COMPANIONED
COMPANIONING
COMPANIONIZE
COMPANIONIZED
COMPANIONIZING
COMPANIONSHIP
COMPANIONWAY
COMPANY
COMPANYING
COMPARABLE
COMPARABLY
COMPARATE
COMPARATIVAL
COMPARATIVE
COMPARATIVELY
COMPARATOR
COMPARE
COMPARED
COMPARER
COMPARING
COMPARISON
COMPAROGRAPH
COMPARSA
COMPART
COMPARTED
COMPARTING
COMPARTITION
COMPARTMENT
COMPARTMENTS
COMPASS
COMPASSABLE
COMPASSED
COMPASSER
COMPASSES
COMPASSING
COMPASSION
COMPASSIONATE
COMPASSIONATED
COMPASSIONATING
COMPASSIVE
COMPASSIVITY
COMPATERNITY
COMPATIBLE
COMPATIBLY
COMPATIENCE
COMPATIENT
COMPATRIOT
COMPATRIOTIC
COMPEAR
COMPEARANCE
COMPEARANT
COMPEER
COMPEL
COMPELLABLE
COMPELLABLY
COMPELLATION
COMPELLATIVE
COMPELLED
COMPELLENT
COMPELLER
COMPELLING
COMPELLINGLY
COMPEND
COMPENDENCY
COMPENDENT
COMPENDIA
COMPENDIARY
COMPENDIATE
COMPENDIOUS
COMPENDIUM
COMPENDIUMS
COMPENETRATE
COMPENSABLE
COMPENSATE
COMPENSATED
COMPENSATING
COMPENSATION
COMPENSATIVE
COMPENSATOR
COMPENSATORY
COMPENSE
COMPENSER
COMPERE
COMPERT
COMPESCE
COMPETE
COMPETED
COMPETENCE
COMPETENCY
COMPETENT
COMPETENTLY
COMPETIBLE
COMPETING
COMPETITION
COMPETITIVE
COMPETITIVELY
COMPETITOR
COMPETITORY
COMPETITRESS
COMPETITRIX
COMPILATION
COMPILATOR
COMPILATORY
COMPILE
COMPILED
COMPILEMENT
COMPILER
COMPILING
COMPITAL
COMPITUM
COMPLACENCE
COMPLACENCIES
COMPLACENCY
COMPLACENT
COMPLACENTLY
COMPLAIN
COMPLAINANT
COMPLAINED
COMPLAINER
COMPLAINING
COMPLAINT
COMPLAINTIVE
COMPLAISANCE
COMPLAISANT
COMPLAISANTLY
COMPLANATE
COMPLANATION
COMPLANT
COMPLECT
COMPLECTED
COMPLEMENT
COMPLEMENTAL
COMPLETE
COMPLETED
COMPLETELY
COMPLETENESS
COMPLETER
COMPLETING
COMPLETION
COMPLETIVE
COMPLETIVELY
COMPLETORIES
COMPLETORY
COMPLEX
COMPLEXIFY
COMPLEXION
COMPLEXIONAL
COMPLEXIONARY
COMPLEXIONED
COMPLEXITIES
COMPLEXITY
COMPLEXLY
COMPLEXNESS
COMPLEXUS
COMPLIABLE
COMPLIABLY
COMPLIANCE
COMPLIANCY
COMPLIANT
COMPLIANTLY
COMPLICACIES
COMPLICACY
COMPLICANT
COMPLICATE
COMPLICATED
COMPLICATING
COMPLICATION
COMPLICATIVE
COMPLICE
COMPLICITIES
COMPLICITOUS
COMPLICITY
COMPLIER
COMPLIMENT
COMPLIMENTAL
COMPLIMENTARY
COMPLIMENTER
COMPLIMENTS
COMPLIN
COMPLINE
COMPLINES

COMPLINS
COMPLISH
COMPLOT
COMPLOTTED
COMPLOTTER
COMPLOTTING
COMPLUVIUM
COMPLY
COMPLYING
COMPO
COMPOED
COMPOER
COMPOING
COMPONE
COMPONED
COMPONENCY
COMPONENDO
COMPONENT
COMPONENTAL
COMPONENTED
COMPONENTS
COMPONY
COMPORT
COMPORTABLE
COMPORTANCE
COMPORTMENT
COMPOS
COMPOSE
COMPOSED
COMPOSEDLY
COMPOSEDNESS
COMPOSER
COMPOSING
COMPOSIT
COMPOSITA
COMPOSITE
COMPOSITED
COMPOSITELY
COMPOSITING
COMPOSITION
COMPOSITIVE
COMPOSITOR
COMPOSITURE
COMPOSOGRAPH
COMPOSSIBLE
COMPOST
COMPOSTED
COMPOSTING
COMPOSTURE
COMPOSURE
COMPOT
COMPOTATION
COMPOTATOR
COMPOTATORY
COMPOTE
COMPOTOR
COMPOUND
COMPOUNDED
COMPOUNDER
COMPOUNDING
COMPRACHICO
COMPRACHICOS
COMPRADOR
COMPRADORE
COMPRECATION
COMPREHEND
COMPREHENDER
COMPREHENSE
COMPREHENSIBLE
COMPREHENSION
COMPREHENSIVE
COMPREHENSIVELY
COMPREHENSIVENESS
COMPREHENSOR
COMPRESBYTER
COMPRESENCE
COMPRESENT
COMPRESS
COMPRESSED
COMPRESSIBLE
COMPRESSING
COMPRESSION
COMPRESSIVE
COMPRESSIVELY
COMPRESSOR
COMPRESSURE
COMPREST
COMPRIEST
COMPRISABLE
COMPRISAL
COMPRISE
COMPRISED
COMPRISING
COMPRIZAL
COMPRIZE
COMPRIZED
COMPRIZING
COMPROBATE
COMPROBATION
COMPRODUCE
COMPROMISE
COMPROMISED
COMPROMISER
COMPROMISING
COMPROMIT
COMPROMITTED
COMPROMITTING
COMPT
COMPTER
COMPTIBLE
COMPTIE
COMPTLY
COMPTNESS
COMPTOIR
COMPTOMETER
COMPTROLLER
COMPULSATIVE
COMPULSATORY
COMPULSED
COMPULSION
COMPULSITOR
COMPULSIVE
COMPULSIVELY
COMPULSORILY
COMPULSORY
COMPUNCT
COMPUNCTION
COMPUNCTIOUS
COMPUNCTIVE
COMPURGATION
COMPURGATOR
COMPURGATORY
COMPURSION
COMPUTABLE
COMPUTABLY
COMPUTATION
COMPUTATIVE
COMPUTE
COMPUTED
COMPUTER
COMPUTING
COMPUTIST
COMPUTUS
COMRADE
COMRADELY
COMRADERY
COMRADESHIP
COMROGUE
COMSTOCKERIES
COMSTOCKERY
COMTE
COMTESSE
COMUNIDAD
CON
CONACASTE
CONACRE
CONAL
CONAMED
CONAND
CONARIAL
CONARIUM
CONATION
CONATIONAL
CONATIVE
CONATURAL
CONATUS
CONCAMERATE
CONCAMERATED
CONCANAVALIN
CONCAPTIVE
CONCASSATION
CONCATENARY
CONCATENATE
CONCATENATED
CONCATENATING
CONCATENATOR
CONCAUSE
CONCAVATION
CONCAVE
CONCAVED
CONCAVELY
CONCAVENESS
CONCAVER
CONCAVING
CONCAVITIES
CONCAVITY
CONCEAL
CONCEALED
CONCEALEDLY
CONCEALER
CONCEALING
CONCEALMENT
CONCEDE
CONCEDED
CONCEDEDLY
CONCEDER
CONCEDING
CONCEIT
CONCEITED
CONCEITEDLY
CONCEITING
CONCEITLESS
CONCEITY
CONCEIVABLE
CONCEIVABLY
CONCEIVE
CONCEIVED
CONCEIVER
CONCEIVING
CONCELEBRATE
CONCENT
CONCENTER
CONCENTERED
CONCENTERING
CONCENTIVE
CONCENTRATE
CONCENTRATED
CONCENTRATING
CONCENTRATION
CONCENTRATOR
CONCENTRE
CONCENTRED
CONCENTRIC
CONCENTRICAL
CONCENTRING
CONCENTUAL
CONCENTUS
CONCEPT
CONCEPTACLE
CONCEPTION
CONCEPTIONAL
CONCEPTISM
CONCEPTIVE
CONCEPTUAL
CONCEPTUALISM
CONCEPTUALITY
CONCEPTUALLY
CONCERN
CONCERNED
CONCERNEDLY
CONCERNING
CONCERNINGLY
CONCERNMENT
CONCERT
CONCERTATION
CONCERTED
CONCERTEDLY
CONCERTGOER
CONCERTI
CONCERTINA
CONCERTING
CONCERTINI
CONCERTINIST
CONCERTINO
CONCERTINOS
CONCERTION
CONCERTIST
CONCERTIZE
CONCERTIZED
CONCERTIZER
CONCERTIZING
CONCERTMASTER
CONCERTMEISTER
CONCERTO
CONCERTOS
CONCESSIBLE
CONCESSION
CONCESSIONAIRE
CONCESSIONAL
CONCESSIONER
CONCESSIVE
CONCESSIVELY
CONCESSOR
CONCESSORY
CONCETTI
CONCETTISM
CONCETTIST
CONCETTO
CONCH
CONCHA
CONCHAE
CONCHAL
CONCHATE
CONCHE
CONCHED
CONCHER
CONCHES
CONCHIES
CONCHIFEROUS
CONCHIFORM
CONCHININ
CONCHININE
CONCHIOLIN
CONCHITE
CONCHITIC
CONCHITIS
CONCHO
CONCHOID
CONCHOIDAL
CONCHOIDALLY
CONCHOLOGIST
CONCHOLOGIZE
CONCHOLOGY
CONCHOMETER
CONCHOMETRY
CONCHOTOME
CONCHS
CONCHY
CONCHYLIATED
CONCHYLIUM
CONCIERGE
CONCILE
CONCILIABLE
CONCILIABULE
CONCILIAR
CONCILIATE
CONCILIATED
CONCILIATING
CONCILIATION
CONCILIATIVE
CONCILIATOR
CONCILIATORY
CONCILIUM
CONCINNATE
CONCINNITIES
CONCINNITY
CONCINNOUS
CONCIO
CONCION
CONCIONAL
CONCIONARY
CONCIONATE
CONCIONATOR
CONCIONATORY
CONCIPIENCY
CONCIPIENT
CONCISE
CONCISELY
CONCISENESS
CONCISION
CONCITATION
CONCLAVE
CONCLAVIST
CONCLUDE
CONCLUDED
CONCLUDENCE
CONCLUDENCY
CONCLUDENT
CONCLUDENTLY
CONCLUDER
CONCLUDING
CONCLUDINGLY
CONCLUSION
CONCLUSIONAL
CONCLUSIVE
CONCLUSIVELY
CONCLUSORY
CONCOAGULATE
CONCOCT
CONCOCTER
CONCOCTION
CONCOCTIVE
CONCOCTOR
CONCOLOR
CONCOLOROUS
CONCOLOUR
CONCOMITANCE
CONCOMITANCY
CONCOMITANT
CONCOMITATE
CONCORD
CONCORDABLE
CONCORDABLY
CONCORDAL
CONCORDANCE
CONCORDANCER
CONCORDANCY
CONCORDANT
CONCORDANTLY
CONCORDAT
CONCORDATORY
CONCORDER
CONCORDIAL
CONCORDIST
CONCORDITY

CONCORDLY
CONCORPORATE
CONCORPORATED
CONCORPORATING
CONCOURS
CONCOURSE
CONCREATE
CONCREDIT
CONCREMATION
CONCREMENT
CONCRESCE
CONCRESCENCE
CONCRESCIBLE
CONCRESCIVE
CONCRETE
CONCRETED
CONCRETELY
CONCRETENESS
CONCRETER
CONCRETING
CONCRETION
CONCRETIONAL
CONCRETISM
CONCRETIVE
CONCRETIVELY
CONCRETIZE
CONCRETIZED
CONCRETIZING
CONCRETOR
CONCREW
CONCUBINAGE
CONCUBINAL
CONCUBINARY
CONCUBINE
CONCUBITANCY
CONCUBITANT
CONCUBITOUS
CONCUBITUS
CONCULCATE
CONCULCATION
CONCUMBENCY
CONCUPISCENCE
CONCUPISCENT
CONCUPY
CONCUR
CONCURRED
CONCURRENCE
CONCURRENCY
CONCURRENT
CONCURRENTLY
CONCURRING
CONCURRINGLY
CONCURSION
CONCURSO
CONCURSUS
CONCUSS
CONCUSSATION
CONCUSSED
CONCUSSING
CONCUSSION
CONCUSSIONAL
CONCUSSIVE
CONCUTIENT
CONCYCLIC
COND
CONDECENT
CONDEMN
CONDEMNATE
CONDEMNATION
CONDEMNATORY
CONDEMNED
CONDEMNER
CONDEMNING
CONDEMNINGLY
CONDEMNS
CONDENSABLE
CONDENSATE
CONDENSATION
CONDENSATIVE
CONDENSATOR
CONDENSE
CONDENSED
CONDENSER
CONDENSERY
CONDENSIBLE
CONDENSING
CONDENSITY
CONDER
CONDESCEND
CONDESCENDER
CONDESCENDING
CONDESCENSION
CONDESCENT
CONDICTION
CONDICTIOUS
CONDIDDLE
CONDIDDLED
CONDIDDLING
CONDIGN
CONDIGNITY
CONDIGNLY
CONDIGNNESS
CONDIMENT
CONDIMENTAL
CONDIMENTARY
CONDIMENTS
CONDISCIPLE
CONDITE
CONDITION
CONDITIONAL
CONDITIONALLY
CONDITIONATE
CONDITIONED
CONDITIONER
CONDITIONING
CONDIVISION
CONDOG
CONDOLATORY
CONDOLE
CONDOLED
CONDOLEMENT
CONDOLENCE
CONDOLENT
CONDOLER
CONDOLING
CONDOLINGLY
CONDOMINATE
CONDOMINIUM
CONDONANCE
CONDONATION
CONDONATIVE
CONDONE
CONDONED
CONDONER
CONDONING
CONDOR
CONDOTTIERE
CONDOTTIERI
CONDUCE
CONDUCED
CONDUCEMENT
CONDUCENT
CONDUCER
CONDUCIBLE
CONDUCIBLY
CONDUCING
CONDUCIVE
CONDUCT
CONDUCTA
CONDUCTANCE
CONDUCTED
CONDUCTIBLE
CONDUCTILITY
CONDUCTING
CONDUCTIO
CONDUCTION
CONDUCTIONAL
CONDUCTIVE
CONDUCTIVELY
CONDUCTIVITY
CONDUCTOR
CONDUCTORS
CONDUCTORY
CONDUCTRESS
CONDUCTUS
CONDUIT
CONDUPLICATE
CONDURANGIN
CONDYLAR
CONDYLARTH
CONDYLE
CONDYLION
CONDYLOID
CONDYLOMA
CONDYLOMATA
CONDYLOPOD
CONDYLOS
CONDYLURE
CONE
CONED
CONEEN
CONEFLOWER
CONEHEAD
CONEINE
CONELET
CONELRAD
CONEMAKER
CONEMAKING
CONENOSE
CONEPATE
CONEPATL
CONER
CONES
CONESSINE
CONEY
CONEYS
CONFAB
CONFABBED
CONFABBING
CONFABULAR
CONFABULATE
CONFABULATED
CONFABULATING
CONFACT
CONFARREATE
CONFARREATED
CONFATED
CONFECT
CONFECTION
CONFECTIONARIES
CONFECTIONARY
CONFECTIONER
CONFECTIONERIES
CONFECTIONERY
CONFECTORY
CONFECTURE
CONFEDER
CONFEDERACIES
CONFEDERACY
CONFEDERAL
CONFEDERALIST
CONFEDERATE
CONFEDERATED
CONFEDERATING
CONFEDERATIO
CONFEDERATION
CONFEDERATOR
CONFER
CONFEREE
CONFERENCE
CONFERENTIAL
CONFERMENT
CONFERRABLE
CONFERRED
CONFERREE
CONFERRER
CONFERRING
CONFERTED
CONFERVA
CONFERVAE
CONFERVAL
CONFERVAS
CONFERVOID
CONFERVOUS
CONFESS
CONFESSANT
CONFESSARIUS
CONFESSARY
CONFESSED
CONFESSEDLY
CONFESSER
CONFESSING
CONFESSION
CONFESSIONAL
CONFESSOR
CONFESSORY
CONFETTI
CONFIDANT
CONFIDANTE
CONFIDE
CONFIDED
CONFIDENCE
CONFIDENCES
CONFIDENCY
CONFIDENT
CONFIDENTIAL
CONFIDENTIALLY
CONFIDENTLY
CONFIDER
CONFIDING
CONFIDINGLY
CONFIGURAL
CONFIGURATE
CONFIGURATED
CONFIGURATING
CONFIGURATION
CONFIGURE
CONFIGURED
CONFIGURING
CONFINABLE
CONFINE
CONFINEABLE
CONFINED
CONFINEDLY
CONFINEDNESS
CONFINELESS
CONFINEMENT
CONFINER
CONFINES
CONFINING
CONFINITY
CONFIRM
CONFIRMABLE
CONFIRMAND
CONFIRMATION
CONFIRMATIVE
CONFIRMATORY
CONFIRMED
CONFIRMEDLY
CONFIRMEE
CONFIRMER
CONFIRMING
CONFIRMINGLY
CONFIRMITY
CONFIRMMENT
CONFIRMOR
CONFISCABLE
CONFISCATE
CONFISCATED
CONFISCATION
CONFISCATOR
CONFISCATORY
CONFISERIE
CONFISK
CONFISTICATING
CONFITENT
CONFITEOR
CONFITURE
CONFIX
CONFIXED
CONFIXING
CONFLAB
CONFLAGRANT
CONFLAGRATE
CONFLAGRATED
CONFLAGRATING
CONFLAGRATION
CONFLAGRATIVE
CONFLAGRATOR
CONFLATE
CONFLATED
CONFLATING
CONFLATION
CONFLICT
CONFLICTED
CONFLICTING
CONFLICTION
CONFLICTIVE
CONFLICTORY
CONFLICTS
CONFLOW
CONFLUENCE
CONFLUENT
CONFLUX
CONFLUXIBLE
CONFOCAL
CONFORM
CONFORMABLE
CONFORMABLY
CONFORMAL
CONFORMANCE
CONFORMANT
CONFORMATE
CONFORMATION
CONFORMATOR
CONFORMED
CONFORMER
CONFORMING
CONFORMIST
CONFORMITIES
CONFORMITY
CONFOUND
CONFOUNDED
CONFOUNDEDLY
CONFOUNDER
CONFOUNDING
CONFRATER
CONFRATERNAL
CONFRATERNITIES
CONFRATERNITY
CONFRERE
CONFRONT
CONFRONTAL
CONFRONTED
CONFRONTER
CONFRONTING
CONFRONTMENT
CONFUSABLE
CONFUSABLY
CONFUSE
CONFUSED
CONFUSEDLY
CONFUSEDNESS
CONFUSING
CONFUSINGLY

CONFUSION
CONFUSIONAL
CONFUSTICATE
CONFUTATION
CONFUTATIVE
CONFUTE
CONFUTED
CONFUTER
CONFUTING
CONGE
CONGEABLE
CONGEAL
CONGEALABLE
CONGEALED
CONGEALER
CONGEALING
CONGEALMENT
CONGED
CONGEE
CONGEING
CONGELATION
CONGENER
CONGENERACY
CONGENERIC
CONGENERICAL
CONGENEROUS
CONGENETIC
CONGENIAL
CONGENIALITY
CONGENIALIZE
CONGENIALLY
CONGENITAL
CONGENITALLY
CONGEON
CONGER
CONGEREE
CONGERIE
CONGERIES
CONGERY
CONGESSION
CONGEST
CONGESTED
CONGESTION
CONGESTIVE
CONGIARIES
CONGIARY
CONGIUS
CONGLACIATE
CONGLOBATE
CONGLOBATED
CONGLOBATELY
CONGLOBATING
CONGLOBATION
CONGLOBE
CONGLOBED
CONGLOBING
CONGLOBULATE
CONGLOMERATE
CONGLOMERATED
CONGLOMERATIC
CONGLOMERATING
CONGLOMERATION
CONGLUTIN
CONGLUTINANT
CONGLUTINATE
CONGLUTINATED
CONGLUTINATING
CONGO
CONGONI
CONGOU
CONGRATULANT
CONGRATULATE
CONGRATULATED
CONGRATULATING
CONGRATULATION
CONGREE
CONGREET
CONGREGABLE
CONGREGANIST
CONGREGANT
CONGREGATE
CONGREGATED
CONGREGATING
CONGREGATION
CONGREGATIVE
CONGREGATOR
CONGRESS
CONGRESSER
CONGRESSIONAL
CONGRESSIST
CONGRESSIVE
CONGRESSMAN
CONGRESSMEN
CONGRESSWOMAN
CONGRESSWOMEN
CONGRIO
CONGROID
CONGRUE
CONGRUENCE
CONGRUENCIES
CONGRUENCY
CONGRUENT
CONGRUENTIAL
CONGRUENTLY
CONGRUISM
CONGRUIST
CONGRUISTIC
CONGRUITIES
CONGRUITY
CONGRUOUS
CONGRUOUSLY
CONHYDRIN
CONHYDRINE
CONIC
CONICAL
CONICALITY
CONICALLY
CONICALNESS
CONICEIN
CONICEINE
CONICHALCITE
CONICINE
CONICITY
CONICLE
CONICOID
CONICOPOLY
CONICS
CONIDIA
CONIDIAL
CONIDIAN
CONIDIOID
CONIDIOPHORE
CONIDIOSPORE
CONIDIUM
CONIES
CONIFER
CONIFERIN
CONIFEROUS
CONIFERS
CONIFICATION
CONIFORM
CONIINE
CONIMA
CONIMENE
CONIN
CONING
CONIOLOGY
CONIROSTER
CONIROSTRAL
CONIUM
CONJECT
CONJECTIVE
CONJECTURAL
CONJECTURALLY
CONJECTURE
CONJECTURED
CONJECTURER
CONJECTURING
CONJEE
CONJOBBLE
CONJOIN
CONJOINED
CONJOINER
CONJOINING
CONJOINT
CONJOINTLY
CONJOINTNESS
CONJON
CONJUBILANT
CONJUGABLE
CONJUGACY
CONJUGAL
CONJUGALITY
CONJUGALLY
CONJUGANT
CONJUGATA
CONJUGATE
CONJUGATED
CONJUGATING
CONJUGATION
CONJUGATIVE
CONJUGATOR
CONJUGIAL
CONJUGIUM
CONJUNCT
CONJUNCTION
CONJUNCTIVAE
CONJUNCTIVAL
CONJUNCTIVAS
CONJUNCTIVE
CONJUNCTIVELY
CONJUNCTLY
CONJUNCTUR
CONJUNCTURAL
CONJUNCTURE
CONJURATION
CONJURATOR
CONJURE
CONJURED
CONJURER
CONJURING
CONJUROR
CONJURY
CONK
CONKER
CONKERS
CONKY
CONN
CONNACH
CONNARACEOUS
CONNARITE
CONNASCENCY
CONNASCENT
CONNATAL
CONNATE
CONNATELY
CONNATENESS
CONNATION
CONNATURAL
CONNATURALLY
CONNATURE
CONNECT
CONNECTED
CONNECTER
CONNECTING
CONNECTION
CONNECTIONAL
CONNECTIVAL
CONNECTIVE
CONNECTIVELY
CONNECTIVITY
CONNECTOR
CONNED
CONNELLITE
CONNER
CONNEX
CONNEXES
CONNEXION
CONNEXITIES
CONNEXITY
CONNEXIVA
CONNEXIVE
CONNEXIVUM
CONNEXUS
CONNING
CONNIPTION
CONNIVANCE
CONNIVANCY
CONNIVANT
CONNIVE
CONNIVED
CONNIVENCE
CONNIVENT
CONNIVER
CONNIVING
CONNOISSANCE
CONNOISSEUR
CONNOTATE
CONNOTATION
CONNOTATIVE
CONNOTE
CONNOTED
CONNOTING
CONNOTIVE
CONNOTIVELY
CONNU
CONNUBIAL
CONNUBIALITY
CONNUBIALLY
CONNUBIATE
CONNUBIUM
CONNUMERATE
CONOCLINIUM
CONOCUNEUS
CONODONT
CONOID
CONOIDAL
CONOIDALLY
CONOIDIC
CONOIDICAL
CONOIDICALLY
CONOPID
CONOPLAIN
CONOPODIUM
CONORMAL
CONOSCENTE
CONOSCENTI
CONOSCOPE
CONOURISH
CONPLANE
CONQUASSATE
CONQUEDLE
CONQUER
CONQUERABLE
CONQUERED
CONQUERING
CONQUERINGLY
CONQUEROR
CONQUEST
CONQUIAN
CONQUINAMINE
CONQUININE
CONQUISTADOR
CONQUISTADORES
CONRECTOR
CONRED
CONREY
CONS
CONSACRE
CONSANGUINE
CONSANGUINEOUS
CONSANGUINITY
CONSARCINATE
CONSARN
CONSARNED
CONSCIENCE
CONSCIENT
CONSCIENTIOUS
CONSCIENTIOUSLY
CONSCIENTIOUSNESS
CONSCIONABLE
CONSCIONABLY
CONSCIOUS
CONSCIOUSLY
CONSCIOUSNESS
CONSCIVE
CONSCRIBE
CONSCRIPT
CONSCRIPTION
CONSECRATE
CONSECRATED
CONSECRATER
CONSECRATING
CONSECRATION
CONSECRATIVE
CONSECRATOR
CONSECRATORY
CONSECTARY
CONSECUTE
CONSECUTION
CONSECUTIVE
CONSECUTIVELY
CONSECUTIVENESS
CONSECUTIVES
CONSENSION
CONSENSUAL
CONSENSUALLY
CONSENSUS
CONSENSUSES
CONSENT
CONSENTABLE
CONSENTANT
CONSENTED
CONSENTER
CONSENTFUL
CONSENTFULLY
CONSENTIENCE
CONSENTIENT
CONSENTIENTLY
CONSENTING
CONSENTINGLY
CONSENTIVE
CONSENTMENT
CONSEQUENCE
CONSEQUENT
CONSEQUENTIAL
CONSEQUENTLY
CONSERTAL
CONSERVABLE
CONSERVACY
CONSERVANCIES
CONSERVANCY
CONSERVANT
CONSERVATE
CONSERVATION
CONSERVATIONAL
CONSERVATISM
CONSERVATIST
CONSERVATIVE
CONSERVATIZE
CONSERVATOR
CONSERVATORIES
CONSERVATORY
CONSERVE
CONSERVED

CONSERVER
CONSERVING
CONSIDER
CONSIDERABLE
CONSIDERABLY
CONSIDERANCE
CONSIDERATE
CONSIDERATELY
CONSIDERATENESS
CONSIDERATION
CONSIDERATOR
CONSIDERED
CONSIDERER
CONSIDERING
CONSIGN
CONSIGNABLE
CONSIGNATARY
CONSIGNATION
CONSIGNED
CONSIGNEE
CONSIGNER
CONSIGNIFIED
CONSIGNIFY
CONSIGNIFYING
CONSIGNING
CONSIGNMENT
CONSIGNOR
CONSILIARY
CONSILIENCE
CONSILIENT
CONSIMILAR
CONSIMILATE
CONSIMILATED
CONSIMILATING
CONSIST
CONSISTENCE
CONSISTENCIES
CONSISTENCY
CONSISTENT
CONSISTENTLY
CONSISTORIAL
CONSISTORIAN
CONSISTORY
CONSOCIATE
CONSOCIATED
CONSOCIATING
CONSOCIATION
CONSOCIATIVE
CONSOCIES
CONSOL
CONSOLABLE
CONSOLATE
CONSOLATION
CONSOLATORY
CONSOLATRIX
CONSOLE
CONSOLED
CONSOLER
CONSOLIDANT
CONSOLIDATE
CONSOLIDATED
CONSOLIDATING
CONSOLIDATOR
CONSOLING
CONSOLS
CONSOLUTE
CONSOMME
CONSONANCE
CONSONANCY
CONSONANT
CONSONANTAL
CONSONANTIC
CONSONANTISM
CONSONANTIZE
CONSONANTLY
CONSONATE
CONSONOUS
CONSORT
CONSORTABLE
CONSORTED
CONSORTER
CONSORTIA
CONSORTIAL
CONSORTING
CONSORTION
CONSORTISM
CONSORTIUM
CONSOUND
CONSPECIES
CONSPECIFIC
CONSPECT
CONSPECTUS
CONSPECTUSES
CONSPERSE
CONSPERSION
CONSPICUITY
CONSPICUOUS
CONSPICUOUSLY
CONSPIRACIES
CONSPIRACY
CONSPIRANT
CONSPIRATIVE
CONSPIRATOR
CONSPIRE
CONSPIRED
CONSPIRER
CONSPIRING
CONSPIRINGLY
CONSPUE
CONSTABLE
CONSTABULAR
CONSTABULARIES
CONSTABULARY
CONSTANCE
CONSTANCY
CONSTANT
CONSTANTAN
CONSTANTLY
CONSTAT
CONSTATATION
CONSTATE
CONSTATORY
CONSTELLATE
CONSTELLATED
CONSTELLATING
CONSTELLATION
CONSTELLATORY
CONSTER
CONSTERNATE
CONSTERNATED
CONSTERNATING
CONSTERNATION
CONSTIPATE
CONSTIPATED
CONSTIPATING
CONSTIPATION
CONSTITUENCIES
CONSTITUENCY
CONSTITUENT
CONSTITUTE
CONSTITUTED
CONSTITUTER
CONSTITUTING
CONSTITUTION
CONSTITUTIONAL
CONSTITUTIVE
CONSTITUTIVELY
CONSTITUTOR
CONSTRAIN
CONSTRAINED
CONSTRAINER
CONSTRAINING
CONSTRAINT
CONSTRICT
CONSTRICTED
CONSTRICTING
CONSTRICTION
CONSTRICTIVE
CONSTRICTOR
CONSTRINGE
CONSTRINGED
CONSTRINGENT
CONSTRINGING
CONSTRUABLE
CONSTRUCT
CONSTRUCTED
CONSTRUCTER
CONSTRUCTION
CONSTRUCTIVE
CONSTRUCTIVELY
CONSTRUCTIVENESS
CONSTRUCTOR
CONSTRUE
CONSTRUED
CONSTRUER
CONSTRUING
CONSTUPRATE
CONSUETE
CONSUETUDE
CONSUL
CONSULAGE
CONSULAR
CONSULARITY
CONSULARY
CONSULATE
CONSULSHIP
CONSULT
CONSULTANT
CONSULTARY
CONSULTATION
CONSULTATIVE
CONSULTATORY
CONSULTEE
CONSULTER
CONSULTING
CONSULTIVE
CONSULTOR
CONSULTORY
CONSUMABLE
CONSUME
CONSUMED
CONSUMEDLY
CONSUMELESS
CONSUMER
CONSUMERS
CONSUMING
CONSUMINGLY
CONSUMMATE
CONSUMMATED
CONSUMMATELY
CONSUMMATING
CONSUMMATION
CONSUMMATIVE
CONSUMMATOR
CONSUMMATORY
CONSUMPT
CONSUMPTED
CONSUMPTIBLE
CONSUMPTION
CONSUMPTIVE
CONSUTE
CONTABESCENT
CONTACT
CONTACTOR
CONTACTUAL
CONTACTUALLY
CONTAGIA
CONTAGION
CONTAGIONED
CONTAGIONIST
CONTAGIOSITY
CONTAGIOUS
CONTAGIOUSLY
CONTAGIOUSNESS
CONTAGIUM
CONTAIN
CONTAINABLE
CONTAINED
CONTAINER
CONTAINING
CONTAINMENT
CONTAMINABLE
CONTAMINANT
CONTAMINATE
CONTAMINATED
CONTAMINATING
CONTAMINATION
CONTAMINATIVE
CONTAMINATOR
CONTAMINOUS
CONTANGO
CONTE
CONTECK
CONTECT
CONTECTION
CONTEK
CONTEKE
CONTEMN
CONTEMNED
CONTEMNER
CONTEMNING
CONTEMNINGLY
CONTEMNOR
CONTEMPER
CONTEMPERATE
CONTEMPLABLE
CONTEMPLAMEN
CONTEMPLANCE
CONTEMPLANT
CONTEMPLATE
CONTEMPLATED
CONTEMPLATING
CONTEMPLATION
CONTEMPLATIST
CONTEMPLATIVE
CONTEMPLATIVELY
CONTEMPLATOR
CONTEMPORANEOUS
CONTEMPORARY
CONTEMPORIZE
CONTEMPORIZED
CONTEMPORIZING
CONTEMPT
CONTEMPTFUL
CONTEMPTIBLE
CONTEMPTIBLENESS
CONTEMPTIBLY
CONTEMPTUOUS
CONTEMPTUOUSLY
CONTEND
CONTENDED
CONTENDER
CONTENDING
CONTENDINGLY
CONTENT
CONTENTATION
CONTENTED
CONTENTEDLY
CONTENTFUL
CONTENTING
CONTENTION
CONTENTIONAL
CONTENTIOUS
CONTENTLESS
CONTENTLY
CONTENTMENT
CONTENTNESS
CONTENTS
CONTENU
CONTERMINAL
CONTERMINANT
CONTERMINATE
CONTERMINE
CONTERMINOUS
CONTESSA
CONTEST
CONTESTABLE
CONTESTANT
CONTESTANTS
CONTESTATION
CONTESTER
CONTEUR
CONTEXT
CONTEXTUAL
CONTEXTUALLY
CONTEXTURAL
CONTEXTURE
CONTEXTURED
CONTICENT
CONTIGNATION
CONTIGUITIES
CONTIGUITY
CONTIGUOUS
CONTIGUOUSLY
CONTINENCE
CONTINENCY
CONTINENT
CONTINENTAL
CONTINENTLY
CONTINEU
CONTINGENCY
CONTINGENT
CONTINGENTLY
CONTINUABLE
CONTINUAL
CONTINUALITY
CONTINUALLY
CONTINUANCE
CONTINUANDO
CONTINUANT
CONTINUANTLY
CONTINUATE
CONTINUATELY
CONTINUATION
CONTINUATIVE
CONTINUATOR
CONTINUE
CONTINUED
CONTINUEDLY
CONTINUER
CONTINUING
CONTINUIST
CONTINUITY
CONTINUO
CONTINUOUS
CONTINUOUSLY
CONTINUUM
CONTISE
CONTLINE
CONTO
CONTOISE
CONTORNIATE
CONTORNIATES
CONTORNO
CONTORSIVE
CONTORT
CONTORTED
CONTORTEDLY
CONTORTING
CONTORTION
CONTORTIONAL
CONTORTIONED
CONTORTIONIST
CONTORTIVE
CONTOS

CONTOUR
CONTOURED
CONTOURING
CONTRABAND
CONTRABASS
CONTRABASSO
CONTRACIVIL
CONTRACT
CONTRACTANT
CONTRACTED
CONTRACTEDLY
CONTRACTER
CONTRACTIBLE
CONTRACTILE
CONTRACTILITY
CONTRACTING
CONTRACTION
CONTRACTIVE
CONTRACTOR
CONTRACTUAL
CONTRACTURE
CONTRACTURED
CONTRADA
CONTRADANCE
CONTRADE
CONTRADICT
CONTRADICTER
CONTRADICTION
CONTRADICTIVE
CONTRADICTOR
CONTRADICTORIES
CONTRADICTORY
CONTRADIVIDE
CONTRAFLOW
CONTRAFOCAL
CONTRAHENT
CONTRAIR
CONTRALTI
CONTRALTO
CONTRALTOS
CONTRAMARQUE
CONTRAOCTAVE
CONTRAPLEX
CONTRAPONEND
CONTRAPOSE
CONTRAPOSITA
CONTRAPTION
CONTRAPTIOUS
CONTRAPUNTAL
CONTRARIANT
CONTRARIES
CONTRARIETY
CONTRARILY
CONTRARINESS
CONTRARIOUS
CONTRARIOUSLY
CONTRARIWISE
CONTRARY
CONTRAST
CONTRASTABLE
CONTRASTED
CONTRASTING
CONTRASTIVE
CONTRASTY
CONTRATE
CONTRAVENE
CONTRAVENED
CONTRAVENER
CONTRAVENING
CONTRAVENTION
CONTRAYERVA
CONTREDANSE
CONTRETEMPS
CONTRIBUTE
CONTRIBUTED
CONTRIBUTING
CONTRIBUTION
CONTRIBUTIVE
CONTRIBUTOR
CONTRIBUTORIES
CONTRIBUTORY
CONTRIST
CONTRITE
CONTRITELY
CONTRITENESS
CONTRITION
CONTRITURATE
CONTRIVABLE
CONTRIVANCE
CONTRIVANCY
CONTRIVE
CONTRIVED
CONTRIVER
CONTRIVING
CONTROL
CONTROLLABLE
CONTROLLED
CONTROLLER
CONTROLLING
CONTROVERSIAL
CONTROVERSIALIST
CONTROVERSIALLY
CONTROVERSIES
CONTROVERSY
CONTROVERT
CONTROVERTED
CONTROVERTER
CONTRUDE
CONTUBERNAL
CONTUBERNIAL
CONTUBERNIUM
CONTUMACIES
CONTUMACIOUS
CONTUMACITIES
CONTUMACITY
CONTUMACY
CONTUMAX
CONTUMELIES
CONTUMELIOUS
CONTUMELY
CONTUND
CONTUNE
CONTURB
CONTURBATION
CONTUSE
CONTUSED
CONTUSING
CONTUSION
CONTUSIONED
CONTUSIVE
CONUBIUM
CONULE
CONUNDRUM
CONURBATION
CONURE
CONUS
CONUSES
CONVALESCE
CONVALESCED
CONVALESCENT
CONVALESCING
CONVALLARIN
CONVECT
CONVECTION
CONVECTIONAL
CONVECTIVE
CONVECTIVELY
CONVECTOR
CONVELL
CONVENABLE
CONVENABLY
CONVENANCE
CONVENE
CONVENED
CONVENER
CONVENERIES
CONVENERY
CONVENIENCE
CONVENIENCED
CONVENIENCY
CONVENIENT
CONVENIENTLY
CONVENING
CONVENT
CONVENTICAL
CONVENTICLE
CONVENTICLER
CONVENTION
CONVENTIONAL
CONVENTIONALIST
CONVENTIONALITY
CONVENTIONALIZE
CONVENTIONALIZED
CONVENTIONALIZING
CONVENTIONALLY
CONVENTIONER
CONVENTO
CONVENTUAL
CONVERGE
CONVERGED
CONVERGENCE
CONVERGENCY
CONVERGENT
CONVERGING
CONVERSABLE
CONVERSABLY
CONVERSANCE
CONVERSANCY
CONVERSANT
CONVERSANTLY
CONVERSATION
CONVERSATIONAL
CONVERSATIONALIST
CONVERSATIONALLY
CONVERSATIONIST
CONVERSATIVE
CONVERSE
CONVERSED
CONVERSELY
CONVERSER
CONVERSIBLE
CONVERSING
CONVERSION
CONVERSIONAL
CONVERSIVE
CONVERSO
CONVERT
CONVERTED
CONVERTEND
CONVERTER
CONVERTIBLE
CONVERTIBLY
CONVERTING
CONVERTISE
CONVERTITE
CONVERTIVE
CONVERTOR
CONVETH
CONVEX
CONVEXED
CONVEXEDLY
CONVEXEDNESS
CONVEXITIES
CONVEXITY
CONVEXLY
CONVEXNESS
CONVEY
CONVEYABLE
CONVEYAL
CONVEYANCE
CONVEYANCER
CONVEYANCING
CONVEYED
CONVEYER
CONVEYING
CONVEYOR
CONVICINITY
CONVICT
CONVICTABLE
CONVICTED
CONVICTIBLE
CONVICTING
CONVICTION
CONVICTIONAL
CONVICTISM
CONVICTIVE
CONVICTIVELY
CONVICTOR
CONVINCE
CONVINCED
CONVINCEMENT
CONVINCER
CONVINCIBLE
CONVINCING
CONVINCINGLY
CONVITE
CONVITO
CONVIVAL
CONVIVE
CONVIVIAL
CONVIVIALIST
CONVIVIALITY
CONVIVIALLY
CONVIVIO
CONVOCANT
CONVOCATE
CONVOCATED
CONVOCATING
CONVOCATION
CONVOCATIVE
CONVOCATOR
CONVOKE
CONVOKED
CONVOKER
CONVOKING
CONVOLUTE
CONVOLUTED
CONVOLUTELY
CONVOLUTING
CONVOLUTION
CONVOLUTIVE
CONVOLVE
CONVOLVED
CONVOLVING
CONVOLVULAD
CONVOLVULIN
CONVOLVULUS
CONVOY
CONVOYED
CONVOYING
CONVULSANT
CONVULSE
CONVULSED
CONVULSEDLY
CONVULSING
CONVULSION
CONVULSIONAL
CONVULSIVE
CONVULSIVELY
CONVULSIVENESS
CONY
CONYCATCHER
CONYGER
CONYNGE
CONYRIN
CONYRINE
COO
COOB
COOBA
COOBAH
COOCH
COODLE
COOED
COOEE
COOEED
COOEEING
COOER
COOEY
COOEYED
COOEYING
COOF
COOING
COOINGLY
COOJA
COOK
COOKABLE
COOKBOOK
COOKED
COOKEE
COOKEITE
COOKER
COOKERIES
COOKERY
COOKEY
COOKHOUSE
COOKIE
COOKIES
COOKING
COOKMAID
COOKROOM
COOKSHACK
COOKSHOP
COOKSTOVE
COOKY
COOL
COOLABAH
COOLAMAN
COOLANT
COOLED
COOLEN
COOLER
COOLEST
COOLEY
COOLHEADED
COOLHEADEDLY
COOLHOUSE
COOLIBAH
COOLIE
COOLIES
COOLIMAN
COOLING
COOLINGLY
COOLINGNESS
COOLISH
COOLLY
COOLNESS
COOLTH
COOLUNG
COOLWEED
COOLWORT
COOLY
COOM
COOMB
COOMBE
COOMY
COON
COONCAN
COONER
COONIER
COONIEST
COONILY
COONJINE
COONROOT
COONSKIN
COONTAIL

COONTIE
COONY
COOP
COOPED
COOPER
COOPERAGE
COOPERANCY
COOPERANT
COOPERATE
COOPERATED
COOPERATING
COOPERATION
COOPERATIVE
COOPERATIVELY
COOPERATOR
COOPERED
COOPERIES
COOPERING
COOPERY
COOPING
COOPT
COOPTATE
COOPTATION
COOPTATIVE
COOPTION
COOPTIVE
COORDAIN
COORDINAL
COORDINATE
COORDINATED
COORDINATELY
COORDINATING
COORDINATION
COORDINATIVE
COORDINATOR
COORDINATORY
COOREE
COORIE
COOSE
COOSER
COOSIFY
COOST
COOT
COOTCH
COOTER
COOTFOOT
COOTHAY
COOTIE
COOTY
COP
COPA
COPACETIC
COPAENE
COPAIBA
COPAIBIC
COPAIN
COPAIVA
COPAL
COPALCHE
COPALCHI
COPALCOCOTE
COPALINE
COPALITE
COPALJOCOTE
COPALM
COPARCENARY
COPARCENER
COPARCENY
COPART
COPARTNER
COPARTNERY
COPASETIC
COPATAIN
COPE
COPECK
COPED
COPEI
COPELIDINE
COPEMAN
COPEMATE
COPEN
COPEPOD
COPEPODAN
COPEPODOUS
COPER
COPEROSE
COPERTA
COPESETIC
COPESETTIC
COPESMATE
COPESTONE
COPHASAL
COPHOSIS
COPIA
COPIAPITE
COPIER
COPIHUE
COPING
COPIOSITY
COPIOUS
COPIOUSLY
COPIOUSNESS
COPIS
COPIST
COPLA
COPLANAR
COPLANARITY
COPOLYMER
COPOLYMERIZE
COPOLYMERIZED
COPOLYMERIZING
COPPA
COPPAELITE
COPPE
COPPED
COPPER
COPPERAH
COPPERAS
COPPERBOTTOM
COPPERED
COPPERHEAD
COPPERING
COPPERIZATION
COPPERIZE
COPPERLEAF
COPPERNOSE
COPPERNOSED
COPPERPLATE
COPPERPROOF
COPPERSKIN
COPPERSMITH
COPPERWING
COPPERWORKS
COPPERY
COPPET
COPPICE
COPPICED
COPPICING
COPPIN
COPPING
COPPLE
COPPLED
COPPRA
COPPY
COPRA
COPRAEMIA
COPRAEMIC
COPRAH
COPREMIA
COPREMIC
COPRODAEUM
COPROLAGNIA
COPROLAGNIST
COPROLALIA
COPROLALIAC
COPROLITE
COPROLITH
COPROLITIC
COPROLOGY
COPROPHAGAN
COPROPHAGIA
COPROPHAGIST
COPROPHAGOUS
COPROPHAGY
COPROPHILIA
COPROPHILIAC
COPROPHILIC
COPROPHILISM
COPROPHILOUS
COPROPHYTE
COPROSE
COPROSMA
COPROSTASIA
COPROSTASIS
COPROSTEROL
COPROZOIC
COPS
COPSE
COPSEWOOD
COPSEWOODED
COPSING
COPSY
COPTER
COPULA
COPULABLE
COPULAE
COPULAR
COPULARIUM
COPULAS
COPULATE
COPULATED
COPULATING
COPULATION
COPULATIVE
COPULATIVELY
COPULATORY
COPUNCTAL
COPUS
COPY
COPYBOOK
COPYCAT
COPYDESK
COPYGRAPH
COPYGRAPHED
COPYHOLD
COPYHOLDER
COPYHOLDING
COPYING
COPYIST
COPYMAN
COPYREAD
COPYREADER
COPYRIGHT
COPYRIGHTER
COPYWRITER
COQUE
COQUECIGRUE
COQUELICOT
COQUELUCHE
COQUET
COQUETOON
COQUETRIES
COQUETRY
COQUETTE
COQUETTED
COQUETTING
COQUETTISH
COQUETTISHLY
COQUILLE
COQUIMBITE
COQUIN
COQUINA
COQUITA
COQUITO
COR
CORACIIFORM
CORACINE
CORACLE
CORACLER
CORACOCOSTAL
CORACOHYOID
CORACOID
CORACOIDAL
CORADICATE
CORAGIO
CORAH
CORAL
CORALBERRY
CORALFLOWER
CORALIST
CORALITA
CORALLA
CORALLIC
CORALLIFORM
CORALLIN
CORALLINE
CORALLITE
CORALLOID
CORALLOIDAL
CORALLUM
CORALROOT
CORALWORT
CORAM
CORANCE
CORAVECA
CORB
CORBAN
CORBE
CORBEAU
CORBEIL
CORBEL
CORBELED
CORBELING
CORBELLED
CORBELLING
CORBET
CORBICULA
CORBICULAE
CORBICULATE
CORBIE
CORBINA
CORBLEU
CORBOVINUM
CORBULA
CORCASS
CORCHAT
CORCHORUS
CORCIR
CORCOPALI
CORD
CORDAGE
CORDAITALEAN
CORDAITEAN
CORDATE
CORDATELY
CORDAX
CORDE
CORDED
CORDEL
CORDELIERE
CORDELLE
CORDELLED
CORDELLING
CORDER
CORDIAL
CORDIALITIES
CORDIALITY
CORDIALLY
CORDIALNESS
CORDICEPS
CORDICOLE
CORDIFORM
CORDIGERI
CORDILLERA
CORDILLERAN
CORDING
CORDITE
CORDITIS
CORDLEAF
CORDMAKER
CORDOBA
CORDOBAN
CORDON
CORDONNET
CORDOVAN
CORDS
CORDUROY
CORDUROYED
CORDUROYING
CORDWAIN
CORDWAINER
CORDWAINERY
CORDWOOD
CORDY
CORE
COREBOX
CORED
COREDUCTASE
COREGONID
COREGONINE
COREGONOID
COREID
COREIGN
COREIGNER
CORELATION
CORELATIVE
CORELATIVELY
CORELESS
CORELIGIONIST
CORELLA
CORELYSIS
COREMAKER
COREMAKING
COREMIUM
COREOMETER
COREOPSIS
COREPLASTIC
COREPLASTY
CORER
CORESIDUAL
CORESPONDENT
CORETOMY
CORF
CORGE
CORIA
CORIACEOUS
CORIAL
CORIAMYRTIN
CORIANDER
CORIAUS
CORIIN
CORINDON
CORING
CORINNE
CORINTH
CORIUM
CORK
CORKAGE
CORKBOARD
CORKE
CORKED
CORKER
CORKIER
CORKIEST
CORKINESS

CORKING
CORKIR
CORKITE
CORKLINE
CORKMAKER
CORKSCREW
CORKSCREWY
CORKWING
CORKWOOD
CORKY
CORM
CORMEL
CORMI
CORMIDIUM
CORMOID
CORMOPHYTE
CORMOPHYTIC
CORMORANT
CORMOUS
CORMUS
CORN
CORNACEOUS
CORNADA
CORNAGE
CORNAMUTE
CORNBALL
CORNBELL
CORNBERRY
CORNBIN
CORNBIND
CORNBINKS
CORNBIRD
CORNBOLE
CORNBOTTLE
CORNBRASH
CORNCOB
CORNCOCKLE
CORNCRACKER
CORNCRAKE
CORNCRIB
CORNCRUSHER
CORNCUTTER
CORNCUTTING
CORNDODGER
CORNEA
CORNEAGEN
CORNEAL
CORNEAS
CORNED
CORNEIN
CORNEL
CORNELIAN
CORNEMUSE
CORNEOUS
CORNER
CORNERBIND
CORNERCAP
CORNERED
CORNERER
CORNERING
CORNERPIECE
CORNERS
CORNERSTONE
CORNERWAYS
CORNERWISE
CORNET
CORNETCIES
CORNETCY
CORNETER
CORNETFISH
CORNETIST
CORNETTER
CORNETTINO
CORNETTIST
CORNETTO
CORNEULE
CORNFIELD
CORNFLOOR
CORNFLOWER
CORNGROWER
CORNHUSK
CORNHUSKER
CORNHUSKING
CORNIC
CORNICE
CORNICED
CORNICING
CORNICLE
CORNICULATE
CORNICULER
CORNICULUM
CORNIER
CORNIEST
CORNIFIC
CORNIFIED
CORNIFORM
CORNIGEROUS
CORNIN
CORNING
CORNIPLUME
CORNLAND
CORNLOFT
CORNMASTER
CORNMEAL
CORNMONGER
CORNO
CORNOPEAN
CORNPIPE
CORNRICK
CORNROOT
CORNSACK
CORNSTALK
CORNSTALKS
CORNSTARCH
CORNSTOOK
CORNU
CORNUA
CORNUAL
CORNUATE
CORNUATED
CORNUBIANITE
CORNUCOPIA
CORNUCOPIAN
CORNUCOPIATE
CORNULE
CORNULITE
CORNUPETE
CORNUS
CORNUTE
CORNUTED
CORNUTIN
CORNUTINE
CORNUTO
CORNUTOS
CORNWALLIS
CORNWALLITE
CORNY
COROA
COROCLEISIS
CORODIARY
CORODIASTOLE
CORODIES
CORODY
COROJO
COROL
COROLLA
COROLLACEOUS
COROLLARIAL
COROLLARIES
COROLLARY
COROLLATE
COROLLATED
COROLLIFORM
COROLLINE
COROLLITIC
CORONA
CORONACH
CORONAD
CORONADITE
CORONAE
CORONAGRAPH
CORONAL
CORONALE
CORONALED
CORONALLED
CORONALLY
CORONAMEN
CORONARY
CORONAS
CORONATE
CORONATED
CORONATION
CORONATORIAL
CORONENE
CORONER
CORONERSHIP
CORONET
CORONETED
CORONETTED
CORONETTEE
CORONETTY
CORONIFORM
CORONILLIN
CORONILLO
CORONION
CORONITIS
CORONIUM
CORONIZE
CORONOFACIAL
CORONOID
CORONULE
COROPLAST
COROPLASTAE
COROPLASTIC
COROSCOPY
COROTOMY
COROZO
COROZOS
CORPORA
CORPORAL
CORPORALE
CORPORALISM
CORPORALITIES
CORPORALITY
CORPORALLY
CORPORALSHIP
CORPORAS
CORPORATE
CORPORATELY
CORPORATION
CORPORATIVE
CORPORATIVELY
CORPORATOR
CORPORATURE
CORPOREAL
CORPOREALIST
CORPOREALITY
CORPOREALIZE
CORPOREITY
CORPORIFY
CORPOROSITY
CORPOSANT
CORPS
CORPSBRUDER
CORPSE
CORPSMEN
CORPULENCE
CORPULENCY
CORPULENT
CORPULENTLY
CORPUS
CORPUSCLE
CORPUSCULAR
CORPUSCULE
CORRADE
CORRADED
CORRADIAL
CORRADIATE
CORRADIATED
CORRADIATING
CORRADIATION
CORRADING
CORRAL
CORRALLED
CORRALLING
CORRASION
CORRASIVE
CORREAL
CORREALITY
CORRECT
CORRECTABLE
CORRECTANT
CORRECTED
CORRECTEDNESS
CORRECTIBLE
CORRECTIFY
CORRECTING
CORRECTINGLY
CORRECTION
CORRECTIONAL
CORRECTIONER
CORRECTITUDE
CORRECTIVE
CORRECTIVELY
CORRECTLY
CORRECTNESS
CORRECTOR
CORRECTRESS
CORRECTRICE
CORREGIDOR
CORRELATE
CORRELATED
CORRELATING
CORRELATION
CORRELATIVE
CORREO
CORREPTION
CORRESOL
CORRESPOND
CORRESPONDED
CORRESPONDENCE
CORRESPONDENT
CORRESPONDER
CORRESPONDING
CORRESPONDINGLY
CORRIDA
CORRIDO
CORRIDOR
CORRIDORED
CORRIE
CORRIGE
CORRIGENDUM
CORRIGENT
CORRIGIBLE
CORRIGIBLY
CORRIVAL
CORRIVALITY
CORRIVALRY
CORRIVATE
CORRIVATION
CORRIVE
CORROBBOREE
CORROBER
CORROBORANT
CORROBORATE
CORROBORATED
CORROBORATING
CORROBORATOR
CORROBOREE
CORROBOREED
CORROBOREEING
CORROBORI
CORRODE
CORRODED
CORRODENT
CORRODER
CORRODIARY
CORRODIBLE
CORRODING
CORROSIBLE
CORROSION
CORROSIONAL
CORROSIVE
CORROSIVED
CORROSIVELY
CORROSIVING
CORROSIVITY
CORRUGATE
CORRUGATED
CORRUGATING
CORRUGATION
CORRUGATOR
CORRUMP
CORRUMPABLE
CORRUP
CORRUPABLE
CORRUPT
CORRUPTED
CORRUPTEDLY
CORRUPTER
CORRUPTFUL
CORRUPTIBLE
CORRUPTIBLY
CORRUPTING
CORRUPTINGLY
CORRUPTION
CORRUPTIVE
CORRUPTIVELY
CORRUPTLESS
CORRUPTLY
CORRUPTNESS
CORRUPTOR
CORRUPTRESS
CORSAC
CORSAGE
CORSAINT
CORSAIR
CORSAK
CORSE
CORSELET
CORSELETED
CORSELETING
CORSEQUE
CORSER
CORSET
CORSETIER
CORSETIERE
CORSETRY
CORSETS
CORSIE
CORSITE
CORSLET
CORSO
CORTA
CORTARO
CORTEGE
CORTEISE
CORTEX
CORTICAL
CORTICALLY
CORTICATE
CORTICATED
CORTICATING
CORTICATION
CORTICES

CORTICIFORM
CORTICIFUGAL
CORTICIPETAL
CORTICOLE
CORTICOLINE
CORTICOLOUS
CORTICOSE
CORTICOUS
CORTILE
CORTIN
CORTINA
CORTINAE
CORTINARIOUS
CORTINATE
CORTINE
CORTLANDTITE
CORUCO
CORUNDUM
CORUSCANT
CORUSCATE
CORUSCATED
CORUSCATING
CORUSCATION
CORVEE
CORVER
CORVES
CORVET
CORVETTE
CORVETTO
CORVIFORM
CORVILLOSUM
CORVINA
CORVINE
CORVISER
CORVISOR
CORVOID
CORVUS
CORYBANTIASM
CORYBANTIC
CORYDALIN
CORYDALINE
CORYDALIS
CORYDORA
CORYL
CORYLACEOUS
CORYLET
CORYLIN
CORYMB
CORYMBED
CORYMBIATE
CORYMBIATED
CORYMBIFORM
CORYMBOSE
CORYMBOSELY
CORYMBOUS
CORYPHAEI
CORYPHAENID
CORYPHAENOID
CORYPHAEUS
CORYPHEE
CORYPHENE
CORYPHODONT
CORYPHYLLY
CORYZA
COSALITE
COSAQUE
COSCET
COSCINOMANCY
COSCOROBA
COSEC
COSECANT
COSEISM
COSEISMAL
COSEISMIC
COSESSION
COSET
COSEY
COSH
COSHER
COSHERED
COSHERER
COSHERIES
COSHERING
COSHERY
COSIE
COSIER
COSIEST
COSIGNATORIES
COSIGNATORY
COSIGNER
COSILY
COSINAGE
COSINE
COSINESS
COSINGULAR
COSMECOLOGY
COSMESIS
COSMETIC
COSMETICAL
COSMETICALLY
COSMETICIAN
COSMETICS
COSMETISTE
COSMETOLOGY
COSMIC
COSMICAL
COSMICALITY
COSMICALLY
COSMINE
COSMISM
COSMIST
COSMOCRACY
COSMOCRAT
COSMOCRATIC
COSMOGENESIS
COSMOGENETIC
COSMOGONAL
COSMOGONIC
COSMOGONICAL
COSMOGONIES
COSMOGONIST
COSMOGONIZE
COSMOGONY
COSMOGRAPHER
COSMOGRAPHIC
COSMOGRAPHIES
COSMOGRAPHY
COSMOLABE
COSMOLATRY
COSMOLINE
COSMOLOGIC
COSMOLOGICAL
COSMOLOGICALLY
COSMOLOGIES
COSMOLOGIST
COSMOLOGY
COSMOMETRY
COSMONAUT
COSMOPATHIC
COSMOPLASTIC
COSMOPOIETIC
COSMOPOLICY
COSMOPOLIS
COSMOPOLITAN
COSMOPOLITE
COSMOPOLITIC
COSMORAMA
COSMORAMIC
COSMORGANIC
COSMOS
COSMOSCOPE
COSMOSOPHY
COSMOSPHERE
COSMOTHEISM
COSMOTHEIST
COSMOTHETIC
COSMOTRON
COSMOZOANS
COSMOZOIC
COSMOZOISM
COSO
COSPECIFIC
COSS
COSSAS
COSSET
COSSETTE
COSSETTED
COSSETTING
COSSHEN
COSSIC
COSSID
COSSNENT
COSSYRITE
COST
COSTA
COSTAE
COSTAGE
COSTAL
COSTALGIA
COSTALLY
COSTANDER
COSTAR
COSTARD
COSTARRED
COSTARRING
COSTATE
COSTATED
COSTEAN
COSTEANING
COSTECTOMY
COSTED
COSTEEN
COSTELLATE
COSTER
COSTERMONGER
COSTFUL
COSTIFEROUS
COSTIFORM
COSTING
COSTIVE
COSTIVELY
COSTIVENESS
COSTLESS
COSTLESSNESS
COSTLEW
COSTLIER
COSTLIEST
COSTLINESS
COSTLY
COSTMARY
COSTOAPICAL
COSTOCENTRAL
COSTOCHONDRAL
COSTOCOLIC
COSTOGENIC
COSTOINFERIOR
COSTOPHRENIC
COSTOPLEURAL
COSTOSTERNAL
COSTOTOME
COSTOTOMIES
COSTOTOMY
COSTOXIPHOID
COSTRAIGHT
COSTREL
COSTS
COSTULA
COSTULATION
COSTUME
COSTUMED
COSTUMER
COSTUMERY
COSTUMIC
COSTUMIER
COSTUMIERE
COSTUMING
COSTUMIST
COSTUSROOT
COSWEARER
COSY
COSYMMEDIAN
COT
COTANGENT
COTANGENTIAL
COTARIUS
COTARNIN
COTARNINE
COTBETTY
COTCH
COTE
COTEAU
COTED
COTEEN
COTELE
COTELINE
COTELLER
COTEMPORARY
COTENANCY
COTENANT
COTENURE
COTERELL
COTERIE
COTERMINOUS
COTH
COTHAMORE
COTHE
COTHISH
COTHON
COTHOUSE
COTHURN
COTHURNAL
COTHURNATE
COTHURNED
COTHURNI
COTHURNIAN
COTHURNUS
COTHY
COTICE
COTIDAL
COTILLAGE
COTILLION
COTILLON
COTING
COTINGA
COTINGID
COTINGOID
COTISE
COTISED
COTISING
COTITULAR
COTLAND
COTMAN
COTO
COTOIN
COTONIA
COTONIER
COTORO
COTOROS
COTQUEAN
COTRINE
COTRUSTEE
COTS
COTSET
COTSETLAND
COTSETLE
COTT
COTTA
COTTABUS
COTTAE
COTTAGE
COTTAGED
COTTAGER
COTTAGERS
COTTAR
COTTAS
COTTE
COTTED
COTTER
COTTERED
COTTEREL
COTTERING
COTTERITE
COTTERWAY
COTTID
COTTIER
COTTIFORM
COTTISE
COTTOID
COTTON
COTTONADE
COTTONED
COTTONEE
COTTONEER
COTTONER
COTTONING
COTTONIZE
COTTONMOUTH
COTTONOCRACY
COTTONSEED
COTTONTAIL
COTTONWEED
COTTONWOOD
COTTONY
COTTREL
COTTY
COTUIT
COTULA
COTUNNITE
COTYLA
COTYLAR
COTYLE
COTYLEDON
COTYLEDONAL
COTYLEDONAR
COTYLEDONARY
COTYLEDONOUS
COTYLIGEROUS
COTYLISCUS
COTYLOID
COTYLOIDAL
COTYLOPUBIC
COTYLOSACRAL
COTYLOSAUR
COTYLOSAURIAN
COTYPE
COUAC
COUCAL
COUCH
COUCHANCY
COUCHANT
COUCHE
COUCHED
COUCHEE
COUCHER
COUCHING
COUCHMAKER
COUCHMAKING
COUCHMATE
COUCHY
COUDE
COUDEE
COUGAR
COUGH
COUGHED
COUGHER

COUGHING
COUGHROOT
COUGHWEED
COUGNAR
COUHAGE
COUL
COULAGE
COULD
COULDNA
COULDST
COULE
COULEE
COULEUR
COULIE
COULIER
COULIS
COULISSE
COULOIR
COULOMB
COULOMETER
COULTER
COULTERNEB
COUMA
COUMALIN
COUMARAN
COUMARANE
COUMARATE
COUMARIC
COUMARIN
COUMARONE
COUMAROU
COUMBITE
COUNCIL
COUNCILLOR
COUNCILMAN
COUNCILMEN
COUNCILOR
COUNITE
COUNSEL
COUNSELED
COUNSELEE
COUNSELING
COUNSELLED
COUNSELLING
COUNSELLOR
COUNSELOR
COUNT
COUNTABLE
COUNTABLY
COUNTDOWN
COUNTED
COUNTENANCE
COUNTENANCED
COUNTENANCING
COUNTER
COUNTERACT
COUNTERACTANT
COUNTERACTED
COUNTERACTER
COUNTERACTING
COUNTERACTION
COUNTERACTIVE
COUNTERACTOR
COUNTERAPSE
COUNTERARCH
COUNTERBALANCE
COUNTERBALANCING
COUNTERBLAST
COUNTERBORE
COUNTERBRACE
COUNTERBRAND
COUNTERBUFF
COUNTERCHANGE
COUNTERCHANGED
COUNTERCHARGE
COUNTERCHARGED
COUNTERCHARGING
COUNTERCHECK
COUNTERCLAIM
COUNTERCLAIMING
COUNTERCLOCKWISE
COUNTERCOUPE
COUNTERCURRENT
COUNTERDIKE
COUNTERDRAIN
COUNTEREARTH
COUNTERFEIT
COUNTERFEITER
COUNTERFEITING
COUNTERFLORY
COUNTERFOIL
COUNTERFORT
COUNTERFUGUE
COUNTERGAGE
COUNTERGAGER
COUNTERGAUGE
COUNTERGLOW
COUNTERION
COUNTERIRRITANT
COUNTERLATH
COUNTERLATHED
COUNTERLODE
COUNTERMAN
COUNTERMAND
COUNTERMANDED
COUNTERMARCH
COUNTERMARK
COUNTERMINE
COUNTERMINED
COUNTERMINING
COUNTERMOVED
COUNTERMOVEMEN
COUNTERMOVING
COUNTERMURE
COUNTERPALY
COUNTERPANE
COUNTERPANED
COUNTERPART
COUNTERPLEA
COUNTERPLOT
COUNTERPLOTTED
COUNTERPLOTTING
COUNTERPOINT
COUNTERPOISE
COUNTERPOISED
COUNTERPOISING
COUNTERPOISON
COUNTERPOLE
COUNTERPROOF
COUNTERPROVE
COUNTERPUNCH
COUNTERRATE
COUNTERROLL
COUNTERROUND
COUNTERS
COUNTERSANK
COUNTERSCALE
COUNTERSEA
COUNTERSEAL
COUNTERSENSE
COUNTERSHADE
COUNTERSHAFT
COUNTERSIGN
COUNTERSIGNED
COUNTERSINK
COUNTERSINKING
COUNTERSLOPE
COUNTERSPY
COUNTERSTAIN
COUNTERSTAND
COUNTERSTOCK
COUNTERSTROKE
COUNTERSUN
COUNTERSUNK
COUNTERSUNKEN
COUNTERTAIL
COUNTERTALLY
COUNTERTENOR
COUNTERTERM
COUNTERTIME
COUNTERTURN
COUNTERTYPE
COUNTERVAIL
COUNTERVAILED
COUNTERVAILING
COUNTERVAIR
COUNTERVENE
COUNTERVIEW
COUNTERVOTE
COUNTERWALL
COUNTERWEIGH
COUNTERWEIGHED
COUNTERWEIGHING
COUNTERWEIGHT
COUNTERWHEEL
COUNTERWORD
COUNTERWORK
COUNTESS
COUNTIES
COUNTING
COUNTLESS
COUNTOR
COUNTOUR
COUNTRIES
COUNTRIFIED
COUNTRY
COUNTRYFIED
COUNTRYFOLK
COUNTRYMAN
COUNTRYMEN
COUNTRYSEAT
COUNTRYSIDE
COUNTRYWOMAN
COUNTRYWOMEN
COUNTS
COUNTY
COUP
COUPAGE
COUPE
COUPED
COUPEE
COUPELET
COUPER
COUPLE
COUPLED
COUPLER
COUPLERESS
COUPLET
COUPLETEER
COUPLING
COUPON
COUPS
COUPSTICK
COUPURE
COUR
COURAGE
COURAGEOUS
COURAGEOUSLY
COURAGER
COURANT
COURANTE
COURANTO
COURAP
COURATARI
COURB
COURBARIL
COURBE
COURE
COURGE
COURIDA
COURIE
COURIER
COURIL
COURLAN
COURONNE
COURSE
COURSED
COURSER
COURSES
COURSING
COURT
COURTAL
COURTBRED
COURTBY
COURTCRAFT
COURTEOUS
COURTEOUSLY
COURTEPY
COURTER
COURTESAN
COURTESIES
COURTESY
COURTEZAN
COURTHOUSE
COURTIER
COURTIERLY
COURTIERY
COURTIN
COURTING
COURTLET
COURTLIER
COURTLIEST
COURTLIKE
COURTLINESS
COURTLING
COURTLY
COURTMAN
COURTROOM
COURTS
COURTSHIP
COURTY
COURTYARD
COUS
COUSCOUS
COUSERANITE
COUSIN
COUSINAGE
COUSINHOOD
COUSINLY
COUSINRIES
COUSINRY
COUSINS
COUSINSHIP
COUSINY
COUTEAU
COUTEAUX
COUTEL
COUTELLE
COUTER
COUTH
COUTHE
COUTHIE
COUTHILY
COUTHINESS
COUTHLESS
COUTHLY
COUTHY
COUTIL
COUTILLE
COUTURE
COUTURIER
COUTURIERE
COUVADE
COUVERT
COUVERTE
COUVEUSE
COUXIA
COUXIO
COVADO
COVALENCE
COVALENCY
COVALENT
COVARIANT
COVARIATION
COVE
COVED
COVELLINE
COVELLITE
COVEN
COVENABLE
COVENABLY
COVENANT
COVENANTAL
COVENANTALLY
COVENANTED
COVENANTEE
COVENANTER
COVENANTING
COVENANTOR
COVENT
COVER
COVERAGE
COVERALLS
COVERCHIEF
COVERCLE
COVERED
COVERER
COVERING
COVERLET
COVERLID
COVERSINE
COVERSLUT
COVERT
COVERTICAL
COVERTLY
COVERTNESS
COVERTURE
COVET
COVETABLE
COVETED
COVETER
COVETING
COVETINGLY
COVETISE
COVETIVENESS
COVETOUS
COVETOUSLY
COVETOUSNESS
COVEY
COVEYS
COVID
COVIDO
COVIN
COVINE
COVING
COVINOUS
COVITE
COVOLUME
COW
COWAGE
COWAL
COWAN
COWARD
COWARDICE
COWARDISH
COWARDLINESS
COWARDLY
COWARDNESS
COWARDY
COWBANE
COWBELL
COWBERRIES
COWBERRY
COWBIND
COWBIRD

COWBOY
COWBRUTE
COWCATCHER
COWD
COWDIE
COWED
COWEEN
COWER
COWFISH
COWFISHES
COWGATE
COWGIRL
COWGRAM
COWGRASS
COWHAGE
COWHEART
COWHEARTED
COWHEEL
COWHERB
COWHERD
COWHIDE
COWHIDED
COWHIDING
COWHOUSE
COWISH
COWITCH
COWKEEPER
COWL
COWLE
COWLED
COWLEECH
COWLEECHING
COWLICK
COWLICKS
COWLIKE
COWLING
COWLSTAFF
COWMAN
COWMEN
COWP
COWPATH
COWPEA
COWPEN
COWPER
COWPERITIS
COWPOX
COWPUNCHER
COWQUAKE
COWR
COWRIE
COWRIES
COWROID
COWRY
COWS
COWSHARD
COWSHARN
COWSHED
COWSHOT
COWSHUT
COWSKIN
COWSLIP
COWSLIPPED
COWSON
COWSUCKER
COWTAIL
COWTHWORT
COWTONGUE
COWWEED
COWWHEAT
COWY
COWYARD
COX
COXA
COXAE
COXAL
COXALGIA
COXALGIC
COXALGY
COXARTHRITIS
COXBONES
COXCOMB
COXCOMBESS
COXCOMBICAL
COXCOMBRY
COXCOMBY
COXCOMICAL
COXIER
COXIEST
COXITE
COXITIS
COXOCERITE
COXOCERITIC
COXODYNIA
COXOFEMORAL
COXOPODITE
COXSWAIN
COXY
COY
COYAN
COYDOG
COYISH
COYLY
COYNE
COYNESS
COYNYE
COYO
COYOL
COYOS
COYOTE
COYOTES
COYOTING
COYPOU
COYPU
COYPUS
COYSTREL
COYURE
COZ
COZE
COZED
COZEN
COZENAGE
COZENER
COZENING
COZENINGLY
COZEY
COZIE
COZIER
COZIEST
COZILY
COZINESS
COZING
COZY
CRAAL
CRAB
CRABBED
CRABBEDLY
CRABBEDNESS
CRABBER
CRABBERY
CRABBIER
CRABBIEST
CRABBING
CRABBISH
CRABBIT
CRABBY
CRABCATCHER
CRABEATER
CRABER
CRABFISH
CRABHOLE
CRABMILL
CRABS
CRABSIDLE
CRABSTICK
CRABWEED
CRABWOOD
CRACCUS
CRACHOIR
CRACK
CRACKAJACK
CRACKBRAIN
CRACKBRAINED
CRACKDOWN
CRACKED
CRACKER
CRACKERBERRY
CRACKERS
CRACKHEMP
CRACKING
CRACKJAW
CRACKLE
CRACKLED
CRACKLEWARE
CRACKLING
CRACKLY
CRACKNEL
CRACKPOT
CRACKROPE
CRACKS
CRACKSMAN
CRACKSMEN
CRACKUP
CRACKY
CRACOVIENNE
CRACOWE
CRADDY
CRADGE
CRADLE
CRADLEBOARD
CRADLECHILD
CRADLED
CRADLEFELLOW
CRADLELAND
CRADLELIKE
CRADLEMAKER
CRADLEMAKING
CRADLEMAN
CRADLEMATE
CRADLEMEN
CRADLER
CRADLESIDE
CRADLESONG
CRADLETIME
CRADLING
CRAER
CRAFT
CRAFTIER
CRAFTIEST
CRAFTILY
CRAFTINESS
CRAFTLY
CRAFTSMAN
CRAFTSMANSHIP
CRAFTSMASTER
CRAFTSMEN
CRAFTSWOMAN
CRAFTWORK
CRAFTWORKER
CRAFTY
CRAG
CRAGGAN
CRAGGED
CRAGGEDNESS
CRAGGIER
CRAGGIEST
CRAGGINESS
CRAGGY
CRAGSMAN
CRAGSMEN
CRAICHY
CRAIGHLE
CRAIGMONTITE
CRAIN
CRAISEY
CRAIZEY
CRAKE
CRAKED
CRAKEFEET
CRAKING
CRAKOW
CRAL
CRAM
CRAMASIE
CRAMBAMBULEE
CRAMBAMBULI
CRAMBE
CRAMBID
CRAMBLE
CRAMBLY
CRAMBO
CRAME
CRAMMED
CRAMMEL
CRAMMER
CRAMMING
CRAMOISIE
CRAMOISY
CRAMP
CRAMPBIT
CRAMPED
CRAMPER
CRAMPET
CRAMPETTE
CRAMPFISH
CRAMPING
CRAMPIT
CRAMPON
CRAMPONNEE
CRAMPOON
CRAMPS
CRAMPY
CRAN
CRANAGE
CRANBERRIES
CRANBERRY
CRANCE
CRANCH
CRANDALL
CRANE
CRANEBILL
CRANED
CRANEMAN
CRANER
CRANES
CRANESBILL
CRANET
CRANEWAY
CRANEY
CRANG
CRANIA
CRANIAD
CRANIAL
CRANIALLY
CRANIAN
CRANIATE
CRANIC
CRANING
CRANIOCELE
CRANIOCLASIS
CRANIOCLASM
CRANIOCLAST
CRANIOFACIAL
CRANIOGNOMIC
CRANIOGNOMY
CRANIOGNOSY
CRANIOGRAPH
CRANIOGRAPHY
CRANIOLOGICAL
CRANIOLOGIST
CRANIOLOGY
CRANIOMETER
CRANIOMETRIC
CRANIOMETRY
CRANIOPAGUS
CRANIOPATHIC
CRANIOPATHY
CRANIOPHORE
CRANIOPLASTY
CRANIOSACRAL
CRANIOSCOPY
CRANIOSPINAL
CRANIOSTOSIS
CRANIOTABES
CRANIOTOME
CRANIOTOMIES
CRANIOTOMY
CRANIUM
CRANIUMS
CRANK
CRANKBIRD
CRANKCASE
CRANKED
CRANKER
CRANKERY
CRANKIER
CRANKIEST
CRANKILY
CRANKINESS
CRANKING
CRANKISH
CRANKLE
CRANKLED
CRANKLING
CRANKMAN
CRANKOUS
CRANKPIN
CRANKS
CRANKSHAFT
CRANKUM
CRANKY
CRANNAGE
CRANNEL
CRANNIED
CRANNIES
CRANNOCK
CRANNOG
CRANNOGE
CRANNOGER
CRANNY
CRANNYING
CRANREUCH
CRANSIER
CRANTARA
CRANTS
CRANY
CRAP
CRAPAUD
CRAPAUDINE
CRAPE
CRAPEFISH
CRAPEHANGER
CRAPETTE
CRAPON
CRAPPER
CRAPPIE
CRAPPIES
CRAPPIN
CRAPPLE
CRAPPO
CRAPPY
CRAPS
CRAPSHOOTER
CRAPULATE
CRAPULENCE
CRAPULENCY

CRAPULENT
CRAPULOUS
CRAPULOUSLY
CRAPWA
CRAPY
CRAQUELURE
CRARE
CRASES
CRASH
CRASHED
CRASHER
CRASHING
CRASIS
CRASPEDAL
CRASPEDON
CRASPEDOTAL
CRASPEDOTE
CRASPEDUM
CRASS
CRASSAMENTUM
CRASSIER
CRASSITUDE
CRASSLY
CRASSNESS
CRASSULACEOUS
CRATCH
CRATCHENS
CRATCHES
CRATCHINS
CRATE
CRATED
CRATEMAN
CRATEMEN
CRATER
CRATERAL
CRATERIFORM
CRATERKIN
CRATERLET
CRATEROUS
CRATICULAR
CRATING
CRATOMETER
CRATOMETRIC
CRATOMETRY
CRAUNCH
CRAVAT
CRAVATTED
CRAVATTING
CRAVE
CRAVED
CRAVEN
CRAVENETTE
CRAVENLY
CRAVENNESS
CRAVER
CRAVING
CRAVINGLY
CRAVINGNESS
CRAVO
CRAW
CRAWDAD
CRAWFISH
CRAWFISHES
CRAWFOOT
CRAWFOOTS
CRAWK
CRAWL
CRAWLED
CRAWLER
CRAWLIE
CRAWLIER
CRAWLIEST
CRAWLING
CRAWLINGLY
CRAWLY
CRAWM
CRAY
CRAYER
CRAYFISH
CRAYFISHES
CRAYLET
CRAYON
CRAYTHUR
CRAZE
CRAZED
CRAZEDLY
CRAZEDNESS
CRAZIER
CRAZIES
CRAZIEST
CRAZILY
CRAZINESS
CRAZING
CRAZY
CRAZYCAT
CRAZYWEED
CREA
CREACH
CREACHY
CREAGH
CREAGHT
CREAK
CREAKER
CREAKIER
CREAKIEST
CREAKILY
CREAKINESS
CREAKING
CREAKY
CREAM
CREAMCUPS
CREAMED
CREAMER
CREAMERIES
CREAMERY
CREAMERYMAN
CREAMERYMEN
CREAMFRUIT
CREAMIER
CREAMIEST
CREAMILY
CREAMINESS
CREAMING
CREAMMAKER
CREAMMAKING
CREAMOMETER
CREAMSACS
CREAMWARE
CREAMY
CREANCE
CREANCER
CREANT
CREASE
CREASED
CREASER
CREASHAKS
CREASIER
CREASIEST
CREASING
CREASOL
CREASY
CREAT
CREATE
CREATED
CREATIC
CREATIN
CREATINE
CREATING
CREATININ
CREATININE
CREATION
CREATIONAL
CREATIONARY
CREATIONISM
CREATIONIST
CREATIVE
CREATIVELY
CREATIVENESS
CREATIVITY
CREATOR
CREATORRHEA
CREATORSHIP
CREATOTOXISM
CREATURAL
CREATURE
CREATURELY
CREBRITY
CREBROUS
CRECHE
CREDDOCK
CREDENCE
CREDENCIVE
CREDENDA
CREDENDUM
CREDENS
CREDENSIVE
CREDENT
CREDENTIAL
CREDENZA
CREDIBILITY
CREDIBLE
CREDIBLENESS
CREDIBLY
CREDIT
CREDITABLE
CREDITABLY
CREDITED
CREDITIVE
CREDITOR
CREDNERITE
CREDO
CREDOS
CREDULITIES
CREDULITY
CREDULOUS
CREDULOUSLY
CREE
CREED
CREEDAL
CREEDALISM
CREEDALIST
CREEDED
CREEDITE
CREEDMORE
CREEDSMAN
CREEK
CREEKER
CREEKFISH
CREEKFISHES
CREEKS
CREEKSIDE
CREEKY
CREEL
CREELED
CREELER
CREELING
CREEM
CREEN
CREEP
CREEPAGE
CREEPER
CREEPERS
CREEPHOLE
CREEPIE
CREEPIER
CREEPIEST
CREEPILY
CREEPINESS
CREEPING
CREEPMOUSE
CREEPS
CREEPY
CREESE
CREESH
CREESHIE
CREESHY
CREIRGIST
CREMANT
CREMASTER
CREMASTERIAL
CREMASTERIC
CREMATE
CREMATED
CREMATING
CREMATION
CREMATIONISM
CREMATIONIST
CREMATOR
CREMATORIAL
CREMATORIES
CREMATORIUM
CREMATORY
CREMBALUM
CREME
CREMERIE
CREMNOPHOBIA
CREMOCARP
CREMOMETER
CREMOR
CREMULE
CRENA
CRENAE
CRENATE
CRENATED
CRENATELY
CRENATION
CRENATURE
CRENEL
CRENELATE
CRENELATED
CRENELATING
CRENELATION
CRENELE
CRENELED
CRENELEE
CRENELET
CRENELING
CRENELLATE
CRENELLATED
CRENELLATING
CRENELLATION
CRENELLE
CRENELLED
CRENELLING
CRENIC
CRENITIC
CRENOLOGY
CRENOTHERAPY
CRENULA
CRENULATE
CRENULATED
CRENULATION
CREODONT
CREOLE
CREOLEIZE
CREOLISM
CREOLITE
CREOLIZATION
CREOLIZE
CREOLIZED
CREOLIZING
CREOPHAGIA
CREOPHAGISM
CREOPHAGIST
CREOPHAGOUS
CREOPHAGY
CREOSOL
CREOSOTE
CREOSOTED
CREOSOTER
CREOSOTIC
CREOSOTING
CREPANCE
CREPE
CREPED
CREPEY
CREPINE
CREPINESS
CREPING
CREPITACULA
CREPITACULUM
CREPITANT
CREPITATE
CREPITATED
CREPITATING
CREPITATION
CREPITOUS
CREPITUS
CREPON
CREPT
CREPUSCLE
CREPUSCULAR
CREPUSCULINE
CREPUSCULUM
CREPY
CRESAMINE
CRESCENDO
CRESCENDOED
CRESCENDOING
CRESCENDOS
CRESCENT
CRESCENTADE
CRESCENTED
CRESCENTIC
CRESCENTING
CRESCENTLIKE
CRESCENTOID
CRESCIVE
CRESCOGRAPH
CRESOLIN
CRESOLINE
CRESORCIN
CRESORCINOL
CRESOTATE
CRESOTIC
CRESOTINATE
CRESOTINIC
CRESOXID
CRESOXIDE
CRESS
CRESSED
CRESSES
CRESSET
CRESSWEED
CRESSWORT
CRESSY
CREST
CRESTED
CRESTFALLEN
CRESTING
CRESTLESS
CRESTLINE
CRESTMOREITE
CRESYL
CRESYLATE
CRESYLENE
CRESYLIC
CRESYLITE
CRETA
CRETACEOUS
CRETACEOUSLY
CRETEFACTION
CRETIC
CRETIFY
CRETIN

CRETINIC
CRETINISM
CRETINOID
CRETINOUS
CRETION
CRETIONARY
CRETONNE
CREVALLE
CREVASS
CREVASSE
CREVASSED
CREVASSING
CREVET
CREVETTE
CREVICE
CREVICED
CREVICES
CREW
CREWE
CREWEL
CREWELIST
CREWELLERY
CREWELWORK
CREWER
CREWET
CREWMAN
CRIANCE
CRIANT
CRIB
CRIBBAGE
CRIBBED
CRIBBER
CRIBBING
CRIBBLE
CRIBBLED
CRIBELLA
CRIBELLUM
CRIBO
CRIBRAL
CRIBRATE
CRIBRATELY
CRIBRATION
CRIBRIFORM
CRIBROSE
CRIBWORK
CRIC
CRICETID
CRICETINE
CRICK
CRICKE
CRICKET
CRICKETER
CRICKETERS
CRICKETING
CRICKETINGS
CRICKETY
CRICKEY
CRICKLE
CRICOID
CRICOTHYROID
CRICOTOMY
CRIDDLE
CRIED
CRIER
CRIERS
CRIES
CRIEY
CRIG
CRIKE
CRIKEY
CRILE
CRIMBLE
CRIME
CRIMEFUL
CRIMES
CRIMINAL
CRIMINALISM
CRIMINALIST
CRIMINALITIES
CRIMINALITY
CRIMINALLY
CRIMINALOID
CRIMINALS
CRIMINATE
CRIMINATED
CRIMINATING
CRIMINATION
CRIMINATIVE
CRIMINATOR
CRIMINATORY
CRIMINE
CRIMINI
CRIMINOGENIC
CRIMINOLOGIC
CRIMINOLOGY
CRIMINOUS
CRIMINOUSLY
CRIMMY
CRIMOGENIC
CRIMP
CRIMPAGE
CRIMPED
CRIMPER
CRIMPIER
CRIMPIEST
CRIMPING
CRIMPLE
CRIMPLED
CRIMPLING
CRIMPNESS
CRIMPY
CRIMSON
CRIMSONLY
CRIMSONNESS
CRIN
CRINAL
CRINANITE
CRINATED
CRINATORY
CRINCH
CRINE
CRINED
CRINET
CRINGE
CRINGED
CRINGELING
CRINGER
CRINGING
CRINGINGLY
CRINGINGNESS
CRINGLE
CRINICULTURE
CRINIERE
CRINIFEROUS
CRINIGEROUS
CRINION
CRINIPAROUS
CRINITE
CRINITORY
CRINIVOROUS
CRINK
CRINKLE
CRINKLED
CRINKLEROOT
CRINKLIER
CRINKLIEST
CRINKLING
CRINKLY
CRINKUM
CRINOID
CRINOIDAL
CRINOIDEAN
CRINOLINE
CRINOSE
CRINOSITY
CRINULA
CRINUM
CRIOBOLIUM
CRIOBOLY
CRIOCERATITE
CRIOLLA
CRIOLLO
CRIOPHORE
CRIOSPHINX
CRIP
CRIPES
CRIPPLE
CRIPPLED
CRIPPLER
CRIPPLES
CRIPPLING
CRIPPLY
CRIPS
CRISE
CRISES
CRISIC
CRISIS
CRISLE
CRISP
CRISPATE
CRISPATED
CRISPATION
CRISPATURE
CRISPED
CRISPER
CRISPEST
CRISPIER
CRISPIEST
CRISPILY
CRISPINESS
CRISPING
CRISPLY
CRISPNESS
CRISPY
CRISS
CRISSA
CRISSAL
CRISSCROSS
CRISSCROSSED
CRISSET
CRISSUM
CRISTA
CRISTAE
CRISTATE
CRISTATED
CRISTIFORM
CRISTOBALITE
CRISTY
CRITCH
CRITERIA
CRITERIOLOGY
CRITERION
CRITERIONAL
CRITERIONS
CRITH
CRITHMENE
CRITHOMANCY
CRITIC
CRITICAL
CRITICALITY
CRITICALLY
CRITICALNESS
CRITICASTER
CRITICASTRY
CRITICISED
CRITICISER
CRITICISING
CRITICISM
CRITICIZABLE
CRITICIZE
CRITICIZED
CRITICIZER
CRITICIZING
CRITICKIN
CRITICULE
CRITIQUE
CRITIZE
CRITLING
CRITTER
CRIZZEL
CRIZZLE
CRO
CROAK
CROAKED
CROAKER
CROAKIER
CROAKIEST
CROAKILY
CROAKINESS
CROAKING
CROAKS
CROAKY
CROAPE
CROC
CROCARD
CROCEIN
CROCEINE
CROCEOUS
CROCETIN
CROCEUS
CROCHE
CROCHET
CROCHETED
CROCHETING
CROCI
CROCIARY
CROCIATE
CROCIDOLITE
CROCIN
CROCINE
CROCK
CROCKARD
CROCKED
CROCKER
CROCKERY
CROCKERYWARE
CROCKET
CROCKETED
CROCKETING
CROCKING
CROCKY
CROCODILE
CROCODILEAN
CROCODILIAN
CROCODILINE
CROCODILITY
CROCODILOID
CROCOISITE
CROCOITE
CROCONATE
CROCONIC
CROCUS
CROCUSED
CROCUSES
CROCUTA
CROFT
CROFTER
CROFTERIZE
CROFTING
CROFTLAND
CROIGHLE
CROISADE
CROISE
CROISEE
CROISES
CROISSANT
CROISSANTE
CROJIK
CROMA
CROMALTITE
CROMB
CROMBEC
CROME
CROMFORDITE
CROMLECH
CROMME
CROMMEL
CROMORNA
CROMORNE
CROMSTER
CRONE
CRONEBERRY
CRONET
CRONIED
CRONIES
CRONISH
CRONK
CRONKNESS
CRONSTEDTITE
CRONY
CRONYING
CROO
CROOCH
CROOD
CROODLE
CROOK
CROOKBACK
CROOKBACKED
CROOKBILLED
CROOKED
CROOKEDLY
CROOKEDNESS
CROOKEN
CROOKESITE
CROOKFINGERED
CROOKHEADED
CROOKING
CROOKKNEED
CROOKLE
CROOKLEGGED
CROOKNECK
CROOKNECKED
CROOKNOSED
CROOKS
CROOKSIDED
CROOKSTERNED
CROOKTOOTHED
CROOL
CROOM
CROON
CROONED
CROONER
CROONING
CROOSE
CROP
CROPE
CROPHEAD
CROPLAND
CROPMAN
CROPPA
CROPPED
CROPPER
CROPPIE
CROPPING
CROPPY
CROPS
CROPSHIN
CROPSICK
CROPSICKNESS
CROPWEED
CROQUET
CROQUETED
CROQUETING
CROQUETTE
CROQUIGNOLE

CROQUIS
CRORE
CROSA
CROSET
CROSHABELL
CROSIER
CROSIERED
CROSNE
CROSNES
CROSS
CROSSABILITY
CROSSABLE
CROSSARM
CROSSBAND
CROSSBAR
CROSSBARRED
CROSSBARRING
CROSSBEAK
CROSSBEAM
CROSSBELT
CROSSBILL
CROSSBIRTH
CROSSBITE
CROSSBONES
CROSSBOW
CROSSBOWMAN
CROSSBOWMEN
CROSSBRED
CROSSBREED
CROSSBREEDING
CROSSCHECK
CROSSCURRENT
CROSSCUT
CROSSCUTTER
CROSSCUTTING
CROSSE
CROSSED
CROSSER
CROSSES
CROSSETTE
CROSSFALL
CROSSFIRE
CROSSFIRED
CROSSFIRING
CROSSFISH
CROSSFLOWER
CROSSFOOT
CROSSHACKLE
CROSSHAND
CROSSHATCH
CROSSHATCHED
CROSSHATCHER
CROSSHATCHING
CROSSHAUL
CROSSHEAD
CROSSING
CROSSITE
CROSSJACK
CROSSLEGS
CROSSLET
CROSSLETED
CROSSLIGHT
CROSSLIGHTED
CROSSLINE
CROSSLY
CROSSNESS
CROSSOPODIA
CROSSOPT
CROSSOVER
CROSSPATCH
CROSSPIECE
CROSSPOINT
CROSSPOST
CROSSRAIL
CROSSROAD
CROSSROW
CROSSRUFF
CROSSTALK
CROSSTIE
CROSSTIED
CROSSTOES
CROSSTREE
CROSSWALK
CROSSWAY
CROSSWAYS
CROSSWEB
CROSSWEED
CROSSWIND
CROSSWISE
CROSSWORD
CROSSWORDER
CROSSWORT
CROST
CROSTARIE
CROT
CROTAL
CROTALIC
CROTALID
CROTALIFORM
CROTALIN
CROTALINE
CROTALISM
CROTALO
CROTALOID
CROTALUM
CROTAPHIC
CROTAPHION
CROTAPHITE
CROTAPHITIC
CROTCH
CROTCHED
CROTCHET
CROTCHETED
CROTCHETEER
CROTCHETINESS
CROTCHETING
CROTCHETY
CROTCHING
CROTCHY
CROTESCO
CROTIN
CROTON
CROTONATE
CROTONIC
CROTONYL
CROTTAL
CROTTELS
CROTTLE
CROTYL
CROUCH
CROUCHANT
CROUCHE
CROUCHED
CROUCHER
CROUCHIE
CROUCHING
CROUD
CROUKE
CROUP
CROUPADE
CROUPAL
CROUPE
CROUPERBUSH
CROUPIER
CROUPIEST
CROUPILY
CROUPINESS
CROUPON
CROUPOUS
CROUPY
CROUSE
CROUSELY
CROUSTADE
CROUT
CROUTE
CROUTH
CROUTON
CROW
CROWBAIT
CROWBAR
CROWBELL
CROWBERRIES
CROWBERRY
CROWBILL
CROWD
CROWDED
CROWDEDLY
CROWDEDNESS
CROWDER
CROWDING
CROWDLE
CROWDWEED
CROWDY
CROWED
CROWER
CROWFEET
CROWFLOWER
CROWFOOT
CROWFOOTED
CROWHOP
CROWING
CROWKEEPER
CROWL
CROWN
CROWNAL
CROWNBEARD
CROWNED
CROWNER
CROWNET
CROWNING
CROWNLAND
CROWNLESS
CROWNLET
CROWNLING
CROWNMENT
CROWNPIECE
CROWNWORK
CROWNWORT
CROWSTEP
CROWSTONE
CROWTOE
CROY
CROYDON
CROZE
CROZED
CROZER
CROZIER
CROZING
CROZLE
CROZZLE
CROZZLY
CRU
CRUB
CRUBEEN
CRUCE
CRUCES
CRUCETHOUSE
CRUCHE
CRUCIAL
CRUCIALITY
CRUCIALLY
CRUCIAN
CRUCIATE
CRUCIATED
CRUCIATELY
CRUCIATING
CRUCIATION
CRUCIBLE
CRUCIFER
CRUCIFEROUS
CRUCIFICIAL
CRUCIFIED
CRUCIFIER
CRUCIFIX
CRUCIFIXION
CRUCIFORM
CRUCIFORMITY
CRUCIFORMLY
CRUCIFY
CRUCIFYING
CRUCIGEROUS
CRUCIS
CRUCK
CRUDDLE
CRUDE
CRUDELY
CRUDENESS
CRUDER
CRUDEST
CRUDITIES
CRUDITY
CRUDWORT
CRUDY
CRUE
CRUEL
CRUELER
CRUELEST
CRUELIZE
CRUELLY
CRUELNESS
CRUELS
CRUELTIES
CRUELTY
CRUENT
CRUENTOUS
CRUET
CRUETY
CRUISE
CRUISED
CRUISER
CRUISING
CRUISKEEN
CRUISKEN
CRUIVE
CRUL
CRULL
CRULLER
CRUM
CRUMB
CRUMBABLE
CRUMBCLOTH
CRUMBED
CRUMBER
CRUMBIER
CRUMBIEST
CRUMBING
CRUMBLE
CRUMBLED
CRUMBLIER
CRUMBLIEST
CRUMBLINESS
CRUMBLING
CRUMBLINGS
CRUMBLY
CRUMBS
CRUMBY
CRUMEN
CRUMENA
CRUMENAL
CRUMMABLE
CRUMMER
CRUMMIE
CRUMMIER
CRUMMIEST
CRUMMOCK
CRUMMY
CRUMP
CRUMPER
CRUMPET
CRUMPLE
CRUMPLED
CRUMPLER
CRUMPLING
CRUMPLY
CRUMPY
CRUMSTER
CRUNCH
CRUNCHED
CRUNCHILY
CRUNCHINESS
CRUNCHING
CRUNCHINGLY
CRUNCHWEED
CRUNCHY
CRUNK
CRUNKLE
CRUNODAL
CRUNODE
CRUNT
CRUOR
CRUP
CRUPPEN
CRUPPER
CRUPPERED
CRUPPERING
CRURA
CRURAL
CRUROGENITAL
CRUROTARSAL
CRUS
CRUSADE
CRUSADED
CRUSADER
CRUSADERS
CRUSADING
CRUSADO
CRUSADOES
CRUSADOS
CRUSE
CRUSET
CRUSH
CRUSHABILITY
CRUSHABLE
CRUSHED
CRUSHER
CRUSHING
CRUSIE
CRUSILE
CRUSILEE
CRUSILY
CRUST
CRUSTA
CRUSTACEAN
CRUSTACEOUS
CRUSTADE
CRUSTAL
CRUSTALOGIST
CRUSTALOGY
CRUSTATE
CRUSTATED
CRUSTATION
CRUSTED
CRUSTEDLY
CRUSTER
CRUSTIER
CRUSTIEST
CRUSTIFIC
CRUSTILY
CRUSTINESS
CRUSTING
CRUSTOSE
CRUSTOSIS
CRUSTS
CRUSTY
CRUT

CRUTCH
CRUTCHED
CRUTCHER
CRUTCHING
CRUTCHLIKE
CRUTH
CRUTTER
CRUX
CRUXES
CRUZADO
CRUZEIRO
CRWTH
CRY
CRYABLE
CRYBABIES
CRYBABY
CRYER
CRYING
CRYINGLY
CRYMODYNIA
CRYMOTHERAPY
CRYOCHORE
CRYOCHORIC
CRYOCONITE
CRYOGEN
CRYOGENIC
CRYOGENY
CRYOHYDRATE
CRYOHYDRIC
CRYOLITE
CRYOLOGY
CRYOMETER
CRYOPHORIC
CRYOPHORUS
CRYOPHYLLITE
CRYOPLANKTON
CRYOSCOPE
CRYOSCOPIC
CRYOSCOPY
CRYOSEL
CRYOSTASE
CRYOSTAT
CRYOTHERAPY
CRYPT
CRYPTAL
CRYPTAMNESIC
CRYPTANALYST
CRYPTARCH
CRYPTARCHY
CRYPTED
CRYPTIC
CRYPTICAL
CRYPTICALLY
CRYPTOBRANCH
CRYPTOCARP
CRYPTOCARPIC
CRYPTOCARPOUS
CRYPTOCEROUS
CRYPTOCOCCI
CRYPTOCOCCIC
CRYPTODEIST
CRYPTODIRAN
CRYPTODIRE
CRYPTODIROUS
CRYPTODOUBLE
CRYPTOGAM
CRYPTOGAMIAN
CRYPTOGAMIC
CRYPTOGAMIST
CRYPTOGAMOUS
CRYPTOGAMY
CRYPTOGENIC
CRYPTOGENOUS
CRYPTOGLIOMA
CRYPTOGRAM
CRYPTOGRAPH
CRYPTOGRAPHER
CRYPTOGRAPHY
CRYPTOHERESY
CRYPTOLOGY
CRYPTOMERE
CRYPTOMEROUS
CRYPTOMNESIA
CRYPTOMNESIC
CRYPTOMONAD
CRYPTONEMA
CRYPTONYM
CRYPTONYMOUS
CRYPTOPAPIST
CRYPTOPHYTE
CRYPTOPIN
CRYPTOPINE
CRYPTORCHID
CRYPTOSCOPE
CRYPTOSCOPY
CRYPTOSTOMA
CRYPTOSTOME
CRYPTOUS
CRYPTOZOIC
CRYPTOZONATE
CRYPTOZYGOUS
CRYSTAL
CRYSTALED
CRYSTALING
CRYSTALITIC
CRYSTALLED
CRYSTALLIC
CRYSTALLIKE
CRYSTALLIN
CRYSTALLINE
CRYSTALLING
CRYSTALLITE
CRYSTALLIZE
CRYSTALLIZED
CRYSTALLIZER
CRYSTALLIZING
CRYSTALLOGRAPH
CRYSTALLOID
CRYSTALS
CRYSTALWORT
CRYSTE
CRYSTIC
CRYSTOGRAPH
CRYSTOLEUM
CRYSTOSPHENE
CSARDAS
CTENE
CTENIDIA
CTENIDIAL
CTENIDIUM
CTENIFORM
CTENII
CTENIZID
CTENOCYST
CTENODACTYL
CTENODONT
CTENOID
CTENOIDEAN
CTENOIDIAN
CTENOLIUM
CTENOPHORAL
CTENOPHORAN
CTENOPHORE
CTENOPHOROUS
CTENOSTOME
CTETOLOGY
CUADRA
CUADRILLA
CUAPINOLE
CUARENTA
CUARTA
CUARTEL
CUARTERON
CUARTILLA
CUARTILLO
CUARTINO
CUARTO
CUB
CUBA
CUBAGE
CUBALAYA
CUBANGLE
CUBANITE
CUBATION
CUBATORY
CUBATURE
CUBBIES
CUBBING
CUBBISH
CUBBISHLY
CUBBISHNESS
CUBBY
CUBBYHOLE
CUBBYHOUSE
CUBBYYEW
CUBE
CUBEB
CUBED
CUBELET
CUBER
CUBERA
CUBIC
CUBICA
CUBICAL
CUBICALLY
CUBICALNESS
CUBICITY
CUBICLE
CUBICONE
CUBICULA
CUBICULAR
CUBICULARY
CUBICULO
CUBICULUM
CUBIFORM
CUBING
CUBISM
CUBIST
CUBIT
CUBITAL
CUBITALE
CUBITALIA
CUBITED
CUBITIERE
CUBITO
CUBITOCARPAL
CUBITOPALMAR
CUBITORADIAL
CUBITUS
CUBMASTER
CUBOID
CUBOIDAL
CUBOIDES
CUBOMEDUSAN
CUCHIA
CUCK
CUCKHOLD
CUCKING
CUCKOLD
CUCKOLDED
CUCKOLDIZE
CUCKOLDLY
CUCKOLDOM
CUCKOLDRY
CUCKOO
CUCKOOFLOWER
CUCKOOMAID
CUCKOOMAIDEN
CUCKOOMATE
CUCKOOPINT
CUCKOOPINTLE
CUCKQUEAN
CUCKSTOOL
CUCOLINE
CUCULARIS
CUCULE
CUCULIFORM
CUCULINE
CUCULLA
CUCULLATE
CUCULLATED
CUCULLATELY
CUCULLIFORM
CUCULLUS
CUCULOID
CUCUMBER
CUCUMIFORM
CUCURB
CUCURBIT
CUCURBITE
CUCURBITINE
CUCUYO
CUD
CUDA
CUDAVA
CUDBEAR
CUDDEN
CUDDIE
CUDDIES
CUDDLE
CUDDLED
CUDDLESOME
CUDDLING
CUDDLY
CUDDY
CUDDYHOLE
CUDEIGH
CUDGEL
CUDGELED
CUDGELER
CUDGELING
CUDGELLED
CUDGELLER
CUDGELLING
CUDGERIE
CUDWEED
CUE
CUEBALL
CUECA
CUED
CUEIST
CUEMAN
CUEMANSHIP
CUEMEN
CUENA
CUER
CUERDA
CUERPO
CUESTA
CUFF
CUFFED
CUFFER
CUFFIN
CUFFING
CUFFLE
CUFFY
CUFFYISM
CUGGERMUGGER
CUICA
CUIDADO
CUIEJO
CUIF
CUINAGE
CUING
CUIR
CUIRASS
CUIRASSED
CUIRASSES
CUIRASSIER
CUISH
CUISINARY
CUISINE
CUISINIER
CUISSE
CUIT
CUITLE
CUITTLE
CUKE
CUL
CULBERT
CULBUT
CULCH
CULEBRA
CULERAGE
CULET
CULETT
CULGEE
CULICID
CULICIDE
CULICIFORM
CULICIFUGAL
CULICIFUGE
CULICINE
CULILAWAN
CULINARILY
CULINARY
CULL
CULLA
CULLAGE
CULLAS
CULLAY
CULLE
CULLED
CULLENDER
CULLER
CULLET
CULLIBLE
CULLIED
CULLIES
CULLING
CULLION
CULLIONLY
CULLIONRY
CULLIONS
CULLIS
CULLY
CULLYING
CULM
CULMEN
CULMICOLOUS
CULMIFEROUS
CULMINAL
CULMINANT
CULMINATE
CULMINATED
CULMINATING
CULMINATION
CULMS
CULMY
CULOT
CULOTTE
CULOTTES
CULOTTIC
CULOTTISM
CULP
CULPA
CULPABILITY
CULPABLE
CULPABLENESS
CULPABLY
CULPATE
CULPATORY
CULPEO
CULPON
CULPOSE

CULPRIT
CULT
CULTCH
CULTELLATION
CULTELLUS
CULTI
CULTIC
CULTIGEN
CULTIROSTRAL
CULTISM
CULTIST
CULTIVABLE
CULTIVABLY
CULTIVAR
CULTIVATABLE
CULTIVATE
CULTIVATED
CULTIVATING
CULTIVATION
CULTIVATOR
CULTIVE
CULTRATE
CULTRATED
CULTURABLE
CULTURAL
CULTURALIST
CULTURALLY
CULTURE
CULTURED
CULTURINE
CULTURIST
CULTUS
CULTUSES
CULVER
CULVERFOOT
CULVERHOUSE
CULVERIN
CULVERINEER
CULVERINER
CULVERKEY
CULVERS
CULVERT
CULVERTAGE
CULVERWORT
CUM
CUMACEAN
CUMACEOUS
CUMAL
CUMALDEHYDE
CUMALIN
CUMAPHYTE
CUMAPHYTIC
CUMAPHYTISM
CUMARU
CUMAY
CUMBENT
CUMBER
CUMBERED
CUMBERING
CUMBERSOME
CUMBERSOMELY
CUMBERWORLD
CUMBHA
CUMBLE
CUMBLY
CUMBRAITE
CUMBRANCE
CUMBRE
CUMBROUS
CUMBROUSLY
CUMBROUSNESS
CUMBU
CUMENE
CUMENGITE
CUMENYL
CUMFLUTTER
CUMHAL
CUMIC
CUMIDIN
CUMIDINE
CUMIN
CUMINOIN
CUMINSEED
CUMLY
CUMMER
CUMMERBUND
CUMMIN
CUMMOCK
CUMOL
CUMQUAT
CUMSHA
CUMSHAW
CUMULANT
CUMULAR
CUMULATE
CUMULATED
CUMULATELY
CUMULATING
CUMULATION
CUMULATIST
CUMULATIVE
CUMULATIVELY
CUMULENE
CUMULI
CUMULIFORM
CUMULITE
CUMULOCIRRUS
CUMULONIMBUS
CUMULOSE
CUMULOUS
CUMULUS
CUMYL
CUNABULA
CUNABULAR
CUNCTATION
CUNCTATIOUS
CUNCTATIVE
CUNCTATOR
CUNCTATORY
CUNCTIPOTENT
CUNDITE
CUNDUM
CUNDY
CUNEAL
CUNEATE
CUNEATED
CUNEATELY
CUNEATIC
CUNEATOR
CUNEI
CUNEIFORM
CUNEIFORMIST
CUNEOCUBOID
CUNETTE
CUNEUS
CUNGEBOI
CUNGEVOI
CUNIC
CUNICULAR
CUNICULI
CUNICULUS
CUNIFORM
CUNIT
CUNJAH
CUNJER
CUNJEVOI
CUNNE
CUNNER
CUNNING
CUNNINGLY
CUNNINGNESS
CUNNY
CUNONIACEOUS
CUNYE
CUNYIE
CUNZIE
CUORIN
CUP
CUPAY
CUPBEARER
CUPBOARD
CUPCAKE
CUPEL
CUPELED
CUPELER
CUPELING
CUPELLATION
CUPELLED
CUPELLER
CUPELLING
CUPFLOWER
CUPFUL
CUPHEAD
CUPHOLDER
CUPIDINOUS
CUPIDITY
CUPIDON
CUPIDONE
CUPIUBA
CUPMAKER
CUPMAKING
CUPMAN
CUPMATE
CUPOLA
CUPOLAED
CUPOLAING
CUPOLAMAN
CUPOLAR
CUPOLAS
CUPOLATED
CUPPED
CUPPEN
CUPPER
CUPPIER
CUPPIEST
CUPPIN
CUPPING
CUPPY
CUPRAMMONIUM
CUPREIN
CUPREINE
CUPRENE
CUPREOUS
CUPRIC
CUPRIDE
CUPRIFEROUS
CUPRITE
CUPROCYANIDE
CUPROID
CUPRONICKEL
CUPROSILICON
CUPROUS
CUPRUM
CUPS
CUPSEED
CUPSTONE
CUPULA
CUPULAR
CUPULATE
CUPULE
CUPULIFEROUS
CUPULIFORM
CUR
CURA
CURABILITY
CURABLE
CURABLENESS
CURABLY
CURACAO
CURACE
CURACIES
CURACY
CURARE
CURARI
CURARINE
CURARIZATION
CURARIZE
CURARIZED
CURARIZING
CURASSOW
CURATAGE
CURATE
CURATEL
CURATESS
CURATIAL
CURATIC
CURATICAL
CURATION
CURATIVE
CURATIVELY
CURATIVENESS
CURATOLATRY
CURATOR
CURATORIAL
CURATORIUM
CURATORSHIP
CURATORY
CURB
CURBASH
CURBING
CURBLINE
CURBSTONE
CURBSTONER
CURBY
CURCAS
CURCH
CURCHY
CURCUDDOCH
CURCULIO
CURCULIONID
CURCULIONIST
CURCULIOS
CURCUMA
CURCUMIN
CURD
CURDED
CURDINESS
CURDING
CURDLE
CURDLED
CURDLER
CURDLING
CURDLY
CURDOO
CURDWORT
CURDY
CURE
CURED
CURELESS
CUREMASTER
CURER
CURET
CURETTAGE
CURETTE
CURETTED
CURETTEMENT
CURETTING
CURFEW
CURIA
CURIAE
CURIAL
CURIALISM
CURIALIST
CURIALISTIC
CURIALITIES
CURIALITY
CURIARA
CURIATE
CURIBOCA
CURIE
CURIEGRAM
CURIESCOPY
CURIET
CURIETHERAPY
CURINE
CURING
CURIO
CURIOLOGIC
CURIOLOGICAL
CURIOLOGICS
CURIOLOGY
CURIOMANIAC
CURIOS
CURIOSA
CURIOSI
CURIOSITIES
CURIOSITY
CURIOSO
CURIOSOS
CURIOUS
CURIOUSLY
CURIOUSNESS
CURIOUSNESSES
CURITE
CURIUM
CURL
CURLED
CURLEDLY
CURLEDNESS
CURLER
CURLEW
CURLEWS
CURLICUE
CURLIER
CURLIEST
CURLIEWURLIE
CURLIEWURLY
CURLINESS
CURLING
CURLINGLY
CURLPAPER
CURLS
CURLY
CURLYCUE
CURLYHEAD
CURLYLOCKS
CURMUDGEON
CURMUDGEONLY
CURMURGING
CURMURRING
CURN
CURNEY
CURNEYS
CURNIE
CURNIES
CURPEL
CURPIN
CURPLE
CURR
CURRACH
CURRACK
CURRAGH
CURRAJONG
CURRAN
CURRANCE
CURRANE
CURRANT
CURRATOW
CURRAWANG
CURRAWONG
CURRENCIES
CURRENCY
CURRENT
CURRENTLY
CURRENTNESS

CURRENTWISE
CURRICLE
CURRICLED
CURRICLING
CURRICULA
CURRICULAR
CURRICULUM
CURRICULUMS
CURRIED
CURRIER
CURRIERIES
CURRIERY
CURRIES
CURRISH
CURRISHLY
CURRISHNESS
CURROCK
CURRY
CURRYCOMB
CURRYFAVEL
CURRYFAVOUR
CURRYING
CURSAL
CURSARO
CURSE
CURSED
CURSEDLY
CURSEDNESS
CURSER
CURSING
CURSITOR
CURSIVE
CURSIVELY
CURSIVENESS
CURSOR
CURSORARY
CURSORIAL
CURSORILY
CURSORINESS
CURSORIOUS
CURSORY
CURST
CURSTFUL
CURSTFULLY
CURSTLY
CURSTNESS
CURSUS
CURT
CURTAIL
CURTAILED
CURTAILEDLY
CURTAILER
CURTAILING
CURTAILMENT
CURTAIN
CURTAINED
CURTAINING
CURTAL
CURTATE
CURTATION
CURTAXE
CURTED
CURTESIES
CURTESY
CURTILAGE
CURTLAX
CURTLY
CURTNESS
CURTSEY
CURTSEYED
CURTSEYING
CURTSEYS
CURTSIED
CURTSIES
CURTSY
CURTSYING
CURUA
CURUBA
CURUCUCU
CURULE
CURUPAY
CURUPAYS
CURUPEY
CURURO
CURUROS
CURVACEOUS
CURVANT
CURVATE
CURVATED
CURVATION
CURVATURE
CURVE
CURVED
CURVEDLY
CURVEDNESS
CURVER
CURVES
CURVET
CURVETED
CURVETING
CURVETTED
CURVETTING
CURVEY
CURVICAUDATE
CURVICOSTATE
CURVIDENTATE
CURVIFOLIATE
CURVIFORM
CURVILINEAL
CURVILINEAR
CURVINERVATE
CURVINERVED
CURVING
CURVIROSTRAL
CURVISERIAL
CURVITAL
CURVITIES
CURVITY
CURVOGRAPH
CURVOMETER
CURVOUS
CURVULATE
CURVY
CURWHIBBLE
CURY
CUSCOHYGRIN
CUSCOHYGRINE
CUSCONIN
CUSCONINE
CUSCUTACEOUS
CUSEC
CUSELITE
CUSH
CUSHA
CUSHAG
CUSHAT
CUSHAW
CUSHIE
CUSHIER
CUSHIEST
CUSHION
CUSHIONED
CUSHIONING
CUSHIONLIKE
CUSHIONY
CUSHY
CUSIE
CUSINERO
CUSK
CUSKS
CUSP
CUSPAL
CUSPATE
CUSPATED
CUSPED
CUSPID
CUSPIDAL
CUSPIDATE
CUSPIDATED
CUSPIDATION
CUSPIDES
CUSPIDOR
CUSPING
CUSPIS
CUSPULE
CUSS
CUSSED
CUSSEDLY
CUSSEDNESS
CUSSER
CUSTARD
CUSTERITE
CUSTODEE
CUSTODIA
CUSTODIAL
CUSTODIAN
CUSTODIER
CUSTODIES
CUSTODY
CUSTOM
CUSTOMABLE
CUSTOMABLY
CUSTOMANCE
CUSTOMARIES
CUSTOMARILY
CUSTOMARY
CUSTOMED
CUSTOMER
CUSTOMHOUSE
CUSTOMING
CUSTOMLY
CUSTOMS
CUSTOS
CUSTREL
CUSTRON
CUSTROUN
CUSTUMAL
CUT
CUTANEAL
CUTANEOUS
CUTAWAY
CUTBACK
CUTBANK
CUTCH
CUTCHA
CUTCHER
CUTCHERIES
CUTCHERRIES
CUTCHERRY
CUTCHERY
CUTDOWN
CUTE
CUTELY
CUTENESS
CUTER
CUTEST
CUTGRASS
CUTHEAL
CUTICLE
CUTICOLOR
CUTICULA
CUTICULAR
CUTICULARIZE
CUTICULATE
CUTIDURE
CUTIDURIS
CUTIE
CUTIES
CUTIFICATION
CUTIGERAL
CUTIKIN
CUTIN
CUTINIZATION
CUTINIZE
CUTINIZED
CUTINIZING
CUTIREACTION
CUTIS
CUTISECTOR
CUTITIS
CUTIZATION
CUTLAS
CUTLASH
CUTLASS
CUTLER
CUTLERESS
CUTLERY
CUTLET
CUTLING
CUTLINGS
CUTLIPS
CUTOFF
CUTOUT
CUTOVER
CUTPURSE
CUTS
CUTTABLE
CUTTAGE
CUTTAIL
CUTTANEE
CUTTED
CUTTER
CUTTERHEAD
CUTTHROAT
CUTTIES
CUTTIKIN
CUTTING
CUTTINGLY
CUTTINGNESS
CUTTINGS
CUTTLE
CUTTLEBONE
CUTTLEFISH
CUTTLEFISHES
CUTTLER
CUTTOO
CUTTOOS
CUTTY
CUTTYHUNK
CUTUP
CUTUPS
CUTWATER
CUTWEED
CUTWORK
CUTWORM
CUVAGE
CUVEE
CUVETTE
CUVIES
CUVY
CUYA
CUYAS
CUZCENO
CWIERC
CWM
CYAMELID
CYAMELIDE
CYANACETIC
CYANAMID
CYANAMIDE
CYANATE
CYANAURATE
CYANAURIC
CYANBENZYL
CYANEAN
CYANEMIA
CYANEOUS
CYANFORMATE
CYANFORMIC
CYANHYDRATE
CYANHYDRIC
CYANHYDRIN
CYANICIDE
CYANID
CYANIDATION
CYANIDE
CYANIDED
CYANIDIN
CYANIDINE
CYANIDING
CYANIDROSIS
CYANIMIDE
CYANIN
CYANINE
CYANITE
CYANIZE
CYANIZED
CYANIZING
CYANOACETATE
CYANOACETIC
CYANOAURATE
CYANOAURIC
CYANOBENZENE
CYANOCHROIA
CYANOCHROIC
CYANODERMA
CYANOGEN
CYANOGENESIS
CYANOGENETIC
CYANOHYDRIN
CYANOMETER
CYANOMETRIC
CYANOMETRIES
CYANOMETRY
CYANOPATHIC
CYANOPATHY
CYANOPHIL
CYANOPHILE
CYANOPHILOUS
CYANOPHORIC
CYANOPHOSE
CYANOPHYCEAN
CYANOPIA
CYANOPLASTID
CYANOPSIA
CYANOSE
CYANOSIS
CYANOSITE
CYANOTIC
CYANOTYPE
CYANURAMIDE
CYANURET
CYANURIC
CYANUS
CYAPHENINE
CYATH
CYATHIFORM
CYATHIUM
CYATHOLITH
CYATHOS
CYATHOZOOID
CYATHUS
CYBERNETIC
CYBERNETICS
CYCAD
CYCADACEOUS
CYCADEAN
CYCADEOID
CYCADEOUS
CYCADIFORM
CYCADITE
CYCLADES
CYCLAMEN
CYCLAMIN
CYCLAMINE

CYCLANE
CYCLAR
CYCLAS
CYCLE
CYCLECAR
CYCLED
CYCLENE
CYCLER
CYCLESMITH
CYCLIAN
CYCLIC
CYCLICAL
CYCLICALLY
CYCLIDE
CYCLINDROID
CYCLING
CYCLIST
CYCLISTIC
CYCLITIS
CYCLIZATION
CYCLIZE
CYCLOALKANE
CYCLOCOELIC
CYCLOCOELOUS
CYCLODIOLEFIN
CYCLODIOLEFINE
CYCLOGANOID
CYCLOGRAM
CYCLOGRAPH
CYCLOGRAPHER
CYCLOHEPTANE
CYCLOHEXANE
CYCLOHEXANOL
CYCLOHEXENE
CYCLOHEXYL
CYCLOID
CYCLOIDAL
CYCLOIDALLY
CYCLOIDEAN
CYCLOIDIAN
CYCLOLITH
CYCLOMANIA
CYCLOMETER
CYCLOMETRIC
CYCLOMETRIES
CYCLOMETRY
CYCLOMYARIAN
CYCLONAL
CYCLONE
CYCLONIC
CYCLONICAL
CYCLONICALLY
CYCLONIST
CYCLONOLOGY
CYCLONOMETER
CYCLONOSCOPE
CYCLOOLEFIN
CYCLOOLEFINE
CYCLOPAEDIA
CYCLOPAEDIAS
CYCLOPAEDIC
CYCLOPAEDIST
CYCLOPE
CYCLOPEAN
CYCLOPEDIA
CYCLOPEDIAS
CYCLOPEDIC
CYCLOPEDICAL
CYCLOPEDIST
CYCLOPENTANE
CYCLOPENTENE
CYCLOPHORIA
CYCLOPHORIC
CYCLOPIA
CYCLOPISM
CYCLOPITE
CYCLOPLEGIA
CYCLOPLEGIC
CYCLOPOID
CYCLOPROPANE
CYCLOPTEROID
CYCLOPY
CYCLORAMA
CYCLORAMAS
CYCLORAMIC
CYCLOSCOPE
CYCLOSE
CYCLOSIS
CYCLOSPOROUS
CYCLOSTOMATE
CYCLOSTOME
CYCLOSTYLE
CYCLOTHEM
CYCLOTHYME
CYCLOTHYMIA
CYCLOTHYMIAC
CYCLOTHYMIC
CYCLOTOME
CYCLOTOMIC
CYCLOTOMY
CYCLOTRON
CYCLUS
CYDIPPIAN
CYDIPPID
CYDONIUM
CYESIOLOGY
CYESIS
CYGNEOUS
CYGNET
CYGNINE
CYKE
CYLICES
CYLINDER
CYLINDERED
CYLINDERER
CYLINDERING
CYLINDERS
CYLINDRIC
CYLINDRICAL
CYLINDRICULE
CYLINDRIFORM
CYLINDRITE
CYLINDROID
CYLINDROIDAL
CYLINDROMA
CYLINDROMATA
CYLINDRURIA
CYLIX
CYLLOSES
CYLLOSIS
CYMA
CYMAE
CYMAPHEN
CYMAR
CYMARIN
CYMAROSE
CYMATIA
CYMATION
CYMATIUM
CYMBA
CYMBAL
CYMBALED
CYMBALEER
CYMBALIST
CYMBALLED
CYMBALLING
CYMBALOM
CYMBALS
CYMBATE
CYMBID
CYMBIFORM
CYMBLIN
CYMBLING
CYMBOCEPHALY
CYME
CYMENE
CYMIFEROUS
CYMLIN
CYMLING
CYMOGENE
CYMOGRAPH
CYMOGRAPHIC
CYMOID
CYMOMETER
CYMOPHANE
CYMOPHANOUS
CYMOPHENOL
CYMOSCOPE
CYMOSE
CYMOSELY
CYMOTRICHY
CYMOUS
CYMRITE
CYMULE
CYMULOSE
CYNANCHE
CYNANTHROPY
CYNARACEOUS
CYNAREOUS
CYNAROID
CYNEBOT
CYNEGETIC
CYNEGETICS
CYNEGILD
CYNHYENA
CYNIATRIA
CYNIATRICS
CYNIC
CYNICAL
CYNICALLY
CYNICALNESS
CYNICISM
CYNICIST
CYNIPID
CYNIPIDOUS
CYNIPOID
CYNISM
CYNOCEPHALIC
CYNOCEPHALUS
CYNOCLEPT
CYNODON
CYNODONT
CYNOID
CYNOLOGY
CYNOMORPHIC
CYNOMORPHOUS
CYNOPHILE
CYNOPHILIC
CYNOPHILIST
CYNOPHOBE
CYNOPHOBIA
CYNOPODOUS
CYNORRHODA
CYNORRHODON
CYNOSURAL
CYNOSURE
CYNOTHERAPY
CYP
CYPERACEOUS
CYPHELLA
CYPHELLAE
CYPHELLATE
CYPHER
CYPHONAUTES
CYPHONISM
CYPRAEA
CYPRAEID
CYPRAEIFORM
CYPRE
CYPRES
CYPRESS
CYPRESSED
CYPRESSES
CYPRESSROOT
CYPRID
CYPRIDINOID
CYPRINE
CYPRINID
CYPRINIFORM
CYPRININ
CYPRININE
CYPRINODONT
CYPRINODONTOID
CYPRINOID
CYPRINOIDEAN
CYPRIPEDIUM
CYPSELA
CYPSELAE
CYPSELINE
CYPSELOID
CYPSELOMORPH
CYPSELOUS
CYRTOLITE
CYRTOMETER
CYRTOPIA
CYRTOSIS
CYRTOSTYLE
CYRUS
CYST
CYSTADENOMA
CYSTAL
CYSTALGIA
CYSTATROPHIA
CYSTATROPHY
CYSTECTASIA
CYSTECTASY
CYSTECTOMIES
CYSTECTOMY
CYSTED
CYSTEIN
CYSTEINE
CYSTEINIC
CYSTELCOSIS
CYSTENCHYMA
CYSTENCHYME
CYSTENCYTE
CYSTERETHISM
CYSTIC
CYSTICARPIC
CYSTICARPIUM
CYSTICERCI
CYSTICERCOID
CYSTICERCUS
CYSTICOLOUS
CYSTID
CYSTIDIA
CYSTIDIUM
CYSTIDIUMS
CYSTIFEROUS
CYSTIFORM
CYSTIGEROUS
CYSTIN
CYSTINE
CYSTINURIA
CYSTIRRHEA
CYSTIS
CYSTITIS
CYSTITOME
CYSTOADENOMA
CYSTOCARP
CYSTOCARPIC
CYSTOCELE
CYSTOCYTE
CYSTODYNIA
CYSTOFIBROMA
CYSTOGENESIS
CYSTOGRAM
CYSTOID
CYSTOIDEAN
CYSTOLITH
CYSTOLITHIC
CYSTOMA
CYSTOMATA
CYSTOMYOMA
CYSTOMYXOMA
CYSTONECTOUS
CYSTOPHORE
CYSTOPLASTY
CYSTOPLEGIA
CYSTOPTOSIS
CYSTORRHAGIA
CYSTORRHAPHY
CYSTORRHEA
CYSTOSARCOMA
CYSTOSCHISIS
CYSTOSCOPE
CYSTOSCOPIC
CYSTOSCOPY
CYSTOSE
CYSTOSPASM
CYSTOSPASTIC
CYSTOSTOMIES
CYSTOSTOMY
CYSTOSYRINX
CYSTOTOME
CYSTOTOMY
CYSTOUS
CYTASE
CYTASIC
CYTASTER
CYTE
CYTHERA
CYTIDINE
CYTIODERM
CYTIODERMA
CYTISINE
CYTITIS
CYTOBLAST
CYTOBLASTEMA
CYTOCHROME
CYTOCHYLEMA
CYTOCIDE
CYTOCLASIS
CYTOCLASTIC
CYTOCOCCI
CYTOCOCCUS
CYTOCYST
CYTODE
CYTODENDRITE
CYTODERM
CYTODIERESIS
CYTOGAMY
CYTOGENE
CYTOGENESIS
CYTOGENETIC
CYTOGENETICS
CYTOGENIC
CYTOGENOUS
CYTOGENY
CYTOGLOBIN
CYTOID
CYTOKINESIS
CYTOLIST
CYTOLOGIC
CYTOLOGICAL
CYTOLOGICALLY
CYTOLOGIES
CYTOLOGIST
CYTOLOGY
CYTOLYMPH
CYTOLYSIN
CYTOLYSIS
CYTOLYTIC
CYTOME
CYTOMERE

CYTOMETER
CYTON
CYTONE
CYTOPHAGOUS
CYTOPHARYNX
CYTOPHIL
CYTOPHYSICS
CYTOPHYSIOLOGY
CYTOPLASM
CYTOPLASMIC
CYTOPLAST
CYTOPLASTIC
CYTOPROCT
CYTOPYGE
CYTORYCTES
CYTOSIN
CYTOSINE
CYTOSOME
CYTOST
CYTOSTOMAL
CYTOSTOME
CYTOSTROMA
CYTOSTROMATIC
CYTOTACTIC
CYTOTAXIS
CYTOTOXIC
CYTOTOXIN
CYTOTROPHY
CYTOTROPIC
CYTOTROPISM
CYTOZOIC
CYTOZOON
CYTOZYMASE
CYTOZYME
CYTULA
CYTULAE
CYWYDD
CZAR
CZARDOM
CZAREVITCH
CZAREVNA
CZARINA
CZARINIAN
CZARISH
CZARISM
CZARIST
CZARISTIC
CZARITZA
CZIGANY

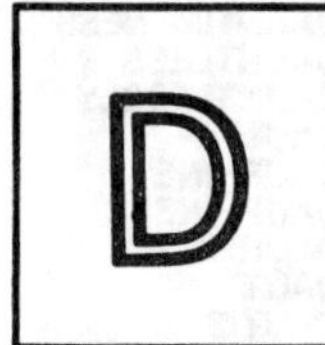

DA
DAALDER
DAB
DABB
DABBA
DABBED
DABBER
DABBING
DABBLE
DABBLED
DABBLER
DABBLING
DABBLINGLY
DABBLINGNESS
DABBY
DABCHICK
DABOIA
DABOYA
DABSTER
DABUH
DACE
DACELONINE
DACES
DACHA
DACHS
DACHSHUND
DACITE
DACITIC
DACKER
DACOIT
DACOITAGE
DACOITED
DACOITIES
DACOITING
DACOITS
DACOITY
DACRYOCYST
DACRYOLITE
DACRYOLITH
DACRYOMA
DACRYON
DACRYOPS
DACTYLAR
DACTYLATE
DACTYLIC
DACTYLICALLY
DACTYLIOLOGY
DACTYLION
DACTYLIST
DACTYLITIC
DACTYLITIS
DACTYLOGRAM
DACTYLOGRAPH
DACTYLOID
DACTYLOLOGY
DACTYLONOMY
DACTYLOPORE
DACTYLORHIZA
DACTYLOSCOPY
DACTYLOSE
DACTYLOTHECA
DACTYLOUS
DACTYLOZOOID
DACTYLUS
DAD
DADA
DADAISM
DADAIST
DADAISTIC
DADAP
DADDER
DADDING
DADDLE
DADDLED
DADDLING
DADDOCK
DADDOCKY
DADDY
DADDYNUT
DADE
DADED
DADENHUDD
DADING
DADO
DADOED
DADOES
DADOING
DADOUCHOS
DADUCHUS
DAEDAL
DAEDALOID
DAEKON
DAEMON
DAEMONES
DAEMONIC
DAEMONIES
DAEMONS
DAEMONURGIST
DAEMONURGY
DAEMONY
DAENA
DAER
DAEVA
DAFF
DAFFADILLY
DAFFED
DAFFERY
DAFFIER
DAFFIEST
DAFFING
DAFFISH
DAFFLE
DAFFLED
DAFFLING
DAFFODIL
DAFFODILLY
DAFFY
DAFT
DAFTAR
DAFTARDAR
DAFTBERRY
DAFTLY
DAFTNESS
DAG
DAGABA
DAGAME
DAGASSA
DAGESH
DAGG
DAGGA
DAGGAR
DAGGE
DAGGED
DAGGER
DAGGERBUSH
DAGGERED
DAGGERING
DAGGERS
DAGGING
DAGGLE
DAGGLED
DAGGLETAIL
DAGGLETAILED
DAGGLING
DAGGLY
DAGGY
DAGH
DAGHESH
DAGLOCK
DAGO
DAGOBA
DAGOES
DAGON
DAGOS
DAGS
DAGSWAIN
DAGUE
DAGUILLA
DAH
DAHABEAH
DAHABEEYAH
DAHABIAH
DAHABIEH
DAHABIYEH
DAHI
DAHIL
DAHLIA
DAHOMEY
DAHOON
DAIDLE
DAIDLED
DAIDLIE
DAIDLING
DAIDLY
DAIGH
DAIKER
DAIKON
DAILIES
DAILINESS
DAILY
DAIM
DAIMEN
DAIMIATE
DAIMIEL
DAIMIO
DAIMIOATE
DAIMIOS
DAIMIOTE
DAIMON
DAIMONIC
DAIMONION
DAIMONISTIC
DAIMYO
DAIN
DAINCHA
DAINCHAS
DAINFUL
DAINT
DAINTETH
DAINTIER
DAINTIES
DAINTIEST
DAINTIFIED
DAINTIFY
DAINTIFYING
DAINTILY
DAINTINESS
DAINTITH
DAINTREL
DAINTY
DAIQUIRI
DAIRA
DAIRI
DAIRIES
DAIROUS
DAIRT
DAIRY
DAIRYING
DAIRYMAID
DAIRYMAN
DAIRYMEN
DAIRYWOMAN
DAIRYWOMEN
DAIS
DAISED
DAISEE
DAISES
DAISIED
DAISIES
DAISING
DAISY
DAISYBUSH
DAITYA
DAIVA
DAK
DAKER
DAKHMA
DAKOIT
DAKOO
DAKTYLOS
DAKU
DAL
DALAG
DALAGA
DALAR
DALE
DALER
DALES
DALESFOLK
DALESMAN
DALESMEN
DALESPEOPLE
DALESWOMAN
DALETH
DALIS
DALK
DALLACK
DALLE
DALLES
DALLI
DALLIANCE
DALLIED
DALLIER
DALLIS
DALLOP
DALLY
DALLYING
DALLYINGLY
DALLYMAN
DALMATIC
DALO
DALT
DALTEEN
DAM
DAMA
DAMAGE
DAMAGEABLE
DAMAGEABLY
DAMAGED
DAMAGEOUS
DAMAGER
DAMAGES
DAMAGING
DAMAN
DAMAR
DAMAS
DAMASCENE
DAMASCENED
DAMASCENER
DAMASCENINE
DAMASCENING
DAMASK
DAMASKEEN
DAMASKIN
DAMASKINE
DAMASSE
DAMASSIN
DAMBO
DAMBOARD
DAMBONITOL
DAMBOSE
DAMBROD
DAME
DAMENIZATION
DAMEWORT
DAMFOOL
DAMIANA
DAMIE
DAMIER
DAMINE
DAMKJERNITE
DAMMAR
DAMMARET
DAMME
DAMMED
DAMMER
DAMMING
DAMMISH
DAMMIT
DAMN
DAMNABILITY
DAMNABLE
DAMNABLENESS
DAMNABLY
DAMNATION
DAMNATORY
DAMNDEST
DAMNED
DAMNEDEST
DAMNER
DAMNIFIED
DAMNIFY
DAMNIFYING
DAMNING
DAMNINGLY
DAMNINGNESS
DAMNOUS
DAMNOUSLY
DAMNUM
DAMOISEAU
DAMOISELLE
DAMONICO
DAMOSEL
DAMOURITE
DAMOZEL
DAMP
DAMPANG
DAMPED
DAMPEN
DAMPENED
DAMPENER
DAMPENING
DAMPER
DAMPEST
DAMPING
DAMPISH
DAMPLY
DAMPNESS
DAMPPROOF
DAMPPROOFING
DAMSEL
DAMSELFISH
DAMSITE
DAMSON
DAMYANKEE
DAN
DANAIDE
DANAINE
DANAITE
DANALITE
DANARO
DANBURITE
DANCALITE
DANCE
DANCED

DANCER
DANCERESS
DANCERS
DANCERY
DANCES
DANCETTE
DANCETTEE
DANCETTY
DANCING
DAND
DANDA
DANDELION
DANDER
DANDI
DANDIACAL
DANDIACALLY
DANDIE
DANDIER
DANDIES
DANDIEST
DANDIFIED
DANDIFY
DANDIFYING
DANDILLY
DANDILY
DANDIPRAT
DANDIS
DANDISETTE
DANDIZETTE
DANDLE
DANDLED
DANDLER
DANDLING
DANDRUFF
DANDRUFFY
DANDY
DANDYISH
DANDYISM
DANDYIZE
DANDYPRAT
DANEWORT
DANG
DANGER
DANGEROUS
DANGEROUSLY
DANGERSOME
DANGLE
DANGLEBERRY
DANGLED
DANGLER
DANGLIN
DANGLING
DANGLINGLY
DANICISM
DANIO
DANK
DANKER
DANKEST
DANKISH
DANKISHNESS
DANKLY
DANKNESS
DANLI
DANNEMORITE
DANNER
DANNOCK
DANSANT
DANSEUR
DANSEUSE
DANSEUSES
DANSY
DANTA
DANTON
DANZA
DANZON
DAO
DAOINE
DAP
DAPHNE
DAPHNETIN
DAPHNI
DAPHNID
DAPHNIN
DAPHNITE
DAPICHO
DAPICO
DAPIFER
DAPPED
DAPPER
DAPPERLING
DAPPERLY
DAPPERNESS
DAPPING
DAPPLE
DAPPLED
DAPPLING
DAPS
DAR
DARABUKKA
DARAC
DARAF
DARAK
DARAT
DARB
DARBHA
DARBIES
DARBUKKA
DARBY
DARCY
DARDANARIUS
DARDANIUM
DARDAOL
DARE
DAREALL
DARED
DAREDEVIL
DAREDEVILRY
DAREDEVILTRY
DAREFUL
DARER
DARES
DARESAY
DARG
DARGAH
DARGER
DARGSMAN
DARGUE
DARI
DARIBAH
DARIC
DARING
DARINGLY
DARINGNESS
DARIOLE
DARK
DARKED
DARKEN
DARKENED
DARKENER
DARKENING
DARKER
DARKEST
DARKEY
DARKEYS
DARKFUL
DARKIE
DARKIES
DARKING
DARKISH
DARKISHNESS
DARKLE
DARKLED
DARKLING
DARKLINGS
DARKLY
DARKMANS
DARKNESS
DARKROOM
DARKS
DARKSKIN
DARKSOME
DARKSOMENESS
DARKSUM
DARKY
DARLING
DARLINGLY
DARLINGNESS
DARN
DARNDEST
DARNED
DARNEDEST
DARNEL
DARNER
DARNEX
DARNING
DAROGA
DAROGAH
DAROGHA
DAROO
DARR
DARREIN
DARSHAN
DARSHANA
DARSO
DARST
DART
DARTARS
DARTED
DARTER
DARTING
DARTINGLY
DARTINGNESS
DARTLE
DARTLIKE
DARTMAN
DARTOS
DARTRE
DARTROSE
DARTS
DARWAN
DARWESH
DARZEE
DARZI
DAS
DASEIN
DASH
DASHBOARD
DASHED
DASHEDLY
DASHEE
DASHEEN
DASHEL
DASHER
DASHIER
DASHIEST
DASHING
DASHINGLY
DASHMAKER
DASHPLATE
DASHPOT
DASHT
DASHWHEEL
DASHY
DASI
DASS
DASSENT
DASSIE
DASSY
DAST
DASTARD
DASTARDIZE
DASTARDLY
DASTARDY
DASTUR
DASTURI
DASWEN
DASYMETER
DASYPAEDAL
DASYPAEDES
DASYURE
DASYURID
DASYURINE
DASYUROID
DATA
DATABLE
DATANA
DATARIA
DATARIES
DATARY
DATCH
DATCHA
DATE
DATED
DATELESS
DATELINE
DATEMARK
DATER
DATIL
DATING
DATIO
DATION
DATISCETIN
DATISCIN
DATISCOSID
DATISCOSIDE
DATIVAL
DATIVE
DATIVELY
DATO
DATOLITE
DATOLITIC
DATTO
DATTOCK
DATTOS
DATU
DATUM
DATURISM
DAUB
DAUBE
DAUBED
DAUBER
DAUBERY
DAUBING
DAUBREEITE
DAUBREELITE
DAUBREITE
DAUBRY
DAUBSTER
DAUBY
DAUD
DAUDED
DAUDING
DAUDIT
DAUERLAUF
DAUGHTER
DAUGHTERLY
DAUGHTERS
DAUKIN
DAULT
DAUNCH
DAUNCY
DAUNDER
DAUNER
DAUNT
DAUNTED
DAUNTER
DAUNTING
DAUNTINGLY
DAUNTINGNESS
DAUNTLESS
DAUNTLESSLY
DAUPHIN
DAUPHINE
DAUPHINESS
DAURNA
DAUT
DAUTIE
DAUW
DAVACH
DAVAINEA
DAVEN
DAVENPORT
DAVER
DAVERDY
DAVIDSONITE
DAVIELY
DAVIES
DAVIESITE
DAVIT
DAVOCH
DAVY
DAVYNE
DAW
DAWCOCK
DAWDLE
DAWDLED
DAWDLER
DAWDLING
DAWISH
DAWK
DAWKIN
DAWN
DAWNED
DAWNING
DAWNY
DAWPATE
DAWSONITE
DAWT
DAWTIE
DAWUT
DAY
DAYABHAGA
DAYAL
DAYAN
DAYBEAM
DAYBED
DAYBERRY
DAYBLUSH
DAYBOOK
DAYBREAK
DAYDAWN
DAYDREAM
DAYDREAMED
DAYDREAMER
DAYDREAMY
DAYDRUDGE
DAYFLOWER
DAYFLY
DAYLIGHT
DAYLIGHTED
DAYLIGHTING
DAYLIGHTS
DAYLILIES
DAYLILY
DAYLIT
DAYLONG
DAYMAN
DAYMARE
DAYMARK
DAYMEN
DAYMENT
DAYNET
DAYROOM
DAYS
DAYSHINE

DAYSIDE
DAYSMAN
DAYSPRING
DAYSTAR
DAYSTREAK
DAYTALE
DAYTIDE
DAYTIME
DAYTIMES
DAYWORK
DAYWORKER
DAYWRIT
DAZE
DAZED
DAZEDLY
DAZEDNESS
DAZING
DAZY
DAZZLE
DAZZLED
DAZZLER
DAZZLING
DAZZLINGLY
DE
DEACETYLATE
DEACON
DEACONAL
DEACONATE
DEACONESS
DEACONRIES
DEACONRY
DEACONSHIP
DEACTIVATE
DEACTIVATED
DEACTIVATING
DEACTIVATION
DEAD
DEADBEAT
DEADBORN
DEADEN
DEADENED
DEADENER
DEADENING
DEADER
DEADEYE
DEADFALL
DEADHEAD
DEADHEARTED
DEADHOUSE
DEADING
DEADISH
DEADISHLY
DEADISHNESS
DEADLATCH
DEADLIER
DEADLIEST
DEADLIGHT
DEADLINE
DEADLINESS
DEADLOCK
DEADLY
DEADMAN
DEADMELT
DEADNESS
DEADPAN
DEADPANNED
DEADPANNING
DEADPAY
DEADS
DEADTONGUE
DEADWOOD
DEADWORKS
DEADWORT
DEAERATE
DEAERATION
DEAERATOR
DEAF
DEAFEN
DEAFENED
DEAFENING
DEAFENINGLY
DEAFISH
DEAFLY
DEAFNESS
DEAL
DEALATE
DEALATED
DEALATION
DEALBATE
DEALBATION
DEALER
DEALERS
DEALFISH
DEALFISHES
DEALING
DEALKALIZE
DEALKYLATE
DEALKYLATION
DEALT
DEAMBULATION
DEAMBULATORY
DEAMIDASE
DEAMIDATE
DEAMINASE
DEAMINATE
DEAMINATION
DEAN
DEANER
DEANERIES
DEANERY
DEANESS
DEANSHIP
DEAR
DEARBORN
DEARER
DEAREST
DEARIE
DEARIES
DEARLING
DEARLY
DEARN
DEARNESS
DEARSENICATE
DEARTH
DEARTHFU
DEARWORTH
DEARWORTHILY
DEARY
DEAS
DEASIL
DEASPIRATE
DEASPIRATION
DEATH
DEATHBED
DEATHBLOW
DEATHCUP
DEATHDAY
DEATHFUL
DEATHIFY
DEATHIN
DEATHINESS
DEATHLESS
DEATHLESSLY
DEATHLIKE
DEATHLINESS
DEATHLY
DEATHROOT
DEATHSMAN
DEATHSMEN
DEATHTRAP
DEATHWATCH
DEATHWEED
DEATHWORM
DEATHY
DEAURATE
DEAVE
DEAVED
DEAVELY
DEAVING
DEBACLE
DEBAG
DEBAR
DEBARK
DEBARKATION
DEBARKMENT
DEBARMENT
DEBARRANCE
DEBARRASS
DEBARRATION
DEBARRED
DEBARRING
DEBASE
DEBASED
DEBASEMENT
DEBASER
DEBASING
DEBAT
DEBATABLE
DEBATE
DEBATEFUL
DEBATEFULLY
DEBATEMENT
DEBATER
DEBATING
DEBATINGLY
DEBATTER
DEBAUCH
DEBAUCHED
DEBAUCHEDLY
DEBAUCHEDNESS
DEBAUCHEE
DEBAUCHER
DEBAUCHERIES
DEBAUCHERY
DEBAUCHING
DEBAUCHMENT
DEBBIES
DEBEL
DEBELL
DEBELLATE
DEBELLATION
DEBELLATOR
DEBEN
DEBENTURE
DEBENTURED
DEBENZOLIZE
DEBILE
DEBILISSIMA
DEBILITANT
DEBILITATE
DEBILITATED
DEBILITATING
DEBILITATION
DEBILITATIVE
DEBILITY
DEBIND
DEBIT
DEBITED
DEBITEUSE
DEBITING
DEBITOR
DEBITUM
DEBLAI
DEBLATERATE
DEBLOCK
DEBOISE
DEBOIST
DEBONAIR
DEBONAIRE
DEBONAIRITY
DEBONAIRLY
DEBONAIRNESS
DEBONNAIRE
DEBORD
DEBORDMENT
DEBOSH
DEBOSHED
DEBOSS
DEBOUCH
DEBOUCHE
DEBOUCHMENT
DEBOUCHURE
DEBOUT
DEBOWEL
DEBRIDE
DEBRIDEMENT
DEBRIEF
DEBRIS
DEBRUISE
DEBT
DEBTED
DEBTEE
DEBTFUL
DEBTOR
DEBTS
DEBUG
DEBUGGED
DEBUGGING
DEBUNK
DEBUNKER
DEBUNKMENT
DEBURSE
DEBUS
DEBUT
DEBUTANT
DEBUTANTE
DEBUTED
DEBUTING
DEBYE
DECACHORD
DECAD
DECADAL
DECADALLY
DECADARY
DECADATION
DECADE
DECADENCE
DECADENCY
DECADENT
DECADENZA
DECADESCENT
DECADIANOME
DECADIC
DECADIST
DECADRACHMA
DECADRACHMAE
DECAEDRON
DECAFFEINIZE
DECAFID
DECAGON
DECAGONAL
DECAGONALLY
DECAGRAM
DECAGRAMME
DECAHEDRA
DECAHEDRAL
DECAHEDRON
DECAHEDRONS
DECAHYDRATE
DECAHYDRATED
DECAL
DECALAGE
DECALCIFIED
DECALCIFIER
DECALCIFY
DECALCIFYING
DECALCOMANIA
DECALESCENCE
DECALESCENT
DECALITER
DECALITRE
DECALOBATE
DECALVANT
DECALVATION
DECAMERAL
DECAMEROUS
DECAMETER
DECAMETER
DECAMETRE
DECAMP
DECAMPED
DECAMPING
DECAMPMENT
DECAN
DECANAL
DECANALLY
DECANATE
DECANDENTLY
DECANDROUS
DECANE
DECANI
DECANICALLY
DECANOL
DECANOYL
DECANT
DECANTATE
DECANTATION
DECANTER
DECANTIST
DECAPITABLE
DECAPITATE
DECAPITATED
DECAPITATING
DECAPITATION
DECAPITATOR
DECAPOD
DECAPODAL
DECAPODAN
DECAPODIFORM
DECAPODOUS
DECAPPER
DECAPSULATE
DECARBONATE
DECARBONATED
DECARBONATING
DECARBONATOR
DECARBONIZE
DECARBONIZED
DECARBONIZER
DECARBURIZE
DECARBURIZED
DECARCH
DECARCHIES
DECARCHY
DECARD
DECARE
DECARHINUS
DECARNATE
DECARNATED
DECASEMIC
DECAST
DECASTELLATE
DECASTERE
DECASTICH
DECASUALIZE
DECASYLLABIC
DECASYLLABLE
DECATE
DECATHLON
DECATING
DECATIZE
DECATIZER
DECATOIC
DECATYL
DECAUDATE

DECAUDATION
DECAY
DECAYED
DECAYEDNESS
DECAYER
DECAYING
DECEASE
DECEASED
DECEASING
DECEDE
DECEDENT
DECEIT
DECEITFUL
DECEITFULLY
DECEITFULNESS
DECEIVABLE
DECEIVABLY
DECEIVE
DECEIVED
DECEIVER
DECEIVING
DECEIVINGLY
DECELERATE
DECELERATED
DECELERATING
DECELERATION
DECELERATOR
DECEMVIR
DECEMVIRAL
DECEMVIRATE
DECEMVIRI
DECEMVIRS
DECENARY
DECENCE
DECENCIES
DECENCY
DECENE
DECENNAL
DECENNARY
DECENNIA
DECENNIAL
DECENNIALLY
DECENNIUM
DECENNIUMS
DECENT
DECENTER
DECENTERED
DECENTERING
DECENTLY
DECENTNESS
DECENTRALISM
DECENTRALIST
DECENTRALIZE
DECENTRATION
DECENTRE
DECENTRED
DECENTRING
DECENYL
DECEPTIBLE
DECEPTION
DECEPTIOUS
DECEPTIOUSLY
DECEPTITIOUS
DECEPTIVE
DECEPTIVELY
DECEPTIVENESS
DECEPTIVITY
DECEREBRATE
DECEREBRATED
DECEREBRATING
DECEREBRIZE
DECERN
DECERNITURE
DECERP
DECESS
DECESSION
DECHENITE
DECHORALIZE
DECIARE
DECIBEL
DECICERONIZE
DECIDABLE
DECIDE
DECIDED
DECIDEDLY
DECIDEDNESS
DECIDER
DECIDING
DECIDINGLY
DECIDUA
DECIDUAL
DECIDUARY
DECIDUATE
DECIDUITIS
DECIDUOMA
DECIDUOUS
DECIDUOUSLY
DECIGRAM
DECIGRAMME
DECIL
DECILE
DECILITER
DECILITRE
DECILLION
DECILLIONTH
DECIMA
DECIMAL
DECIMALISM
DECIMALIST
DECIMALIZE
DECIMALIZED
DECIMALIZING
DECIMALLY
DECIMATE
DECIMATED
DECIMATING
DECIMATION
DECIMATOR
DECIME
DECIMESTRIAL
DECIMETER
DECIMETRE
DECIMOLAR
DECIMOLE
DECIMOSEXTO
DECINE
DECINORMAL
DECIPHER
DECIPHERED
DECIPHERER
DECIPHERING
DECIPHERMENT
DECIPIUM
DECIPOLAR
DECISE
DECISION
DECISIONAL
DECISIVE
DECISIVELY
DECISIVENESS
DECISTERE
DECIVILIZE
DECK
DECKE
DECKED
DECKEL
DECKEN
DECKER
DECKHAND
DECKHEAD
DECKHOUSE
DECKIE
DECKING
DECKLE
DECKLOAD
DECKMAN
DECKS
DECLAIM
DECLAIMANT
DECLAIMED
DECLAIMER
DECLAIMING
DECLAMANDO
DECLAMATION
DECLAMATORY
DECLARANT
DECLARATION
DECLARATIVE
DECLARATOR
DECLARATORY
DECLARE
DECLARED
DECLAREDLY
DECLAREDNESS
DECLARER
DECLARING
DECLASS
DECLASSE
DECLASSED
DECLASSEE
DECLASSING
DECLENSION
DECLENSIONAL
DECLINABLE
DECLINAL
DECLINATE
DECLINATION
DECLINATIONS
DECLINATORY
DECLINATURE
DECLINE
DECLINED
DECLINER
DECLINING
DECLINOGRAPH
DECLINOMETER
DECLIVATE
DECLIVE
DECLIVITIES
DECLIVITOUS
DECLIVITY
DECLIVOUS
DECLUTCH
DECOCT
DECOCTION
DECOCTIVE
DECOCTUM
DECODE
DECODED
DECODER
DECODING
DECOHERE
DECOHERER
DECOIC
DECOKE
DECOLL
DECOLLATE
DECOLLATED
DECOLLATING
DECOLLATION
DECOLLATOR
DECOLLETAGE
DECOLLETE
DECOLOR
DECOLORANT
DECOLORATE
DECOLORATION
DECOLORIZE
DECOLORIZED
DECOLORIZER
DECOLORIZING
DECOLOUR
DECOLOURISE
DECOLOURIZE
DECOMMISSION
DECOMPENSATE
DECOMPLEX
DECOMPONIBLE
DECOMPOSABLE
DECOMPOSE
DECOMPOSED
DECOMPOSER
DECOMPOSING
DECOMPOSITE
DECOMPOSITION
DECOMPOSURE
DECOMPOUND
DECOMPRESS
DECONGESTIVE
DECONSIDER
DECONTROL
DECONTROLLED
DECOPED
DECOR
DECORAMENT
DECORATE
DECORATED
DECORATING
DECORATION
DECORATIVE
DECORATOR
DECORATORY
DECORE
DECOREMENT
DECORIST
DECOROUS
DECOROUSLY
DECOROUSNESS
DECORTICATE
DECORTICATED
DECORUM
DECOUPAGE
DECOY
DECOYED
DECOYER
DECOYING
DECOYMAN
DECOYMEN
DECOYS
DECRASSIFIED
DECRASSIFY
DECREASE
DECREASED
DECREASELESS
DECREASING
DECREASINGLY
DECREATION
DECREATIVE
DECREE
DECREED
DECREEING
DECREEMENT
DECREER
DECREET
DECREMENT
DECREMETER
DECREPID
DECREPIT
DECREPITATE
DECREPITATED
DECREPITLY
DECREPITNESS
DECREPITUDE
DECREPITY
DECRESCENCE
DECRESCENDO
DECRESCENT
DECRETAL
DECRETALIST
DECRETE
DECRETIST
DECRETIVE
DECRETIVELY
DECRETORIAL
DECRETORILY
DECRETORY
DECRETUM
DECREW
DECRIAL
DECRIED
DECRIER
DECROWN
DECRUSTATION
DECRY
DECRYING
DECRYPT
DECUBITAL
DECUBITUS
DECULTURATE
DECULTURATED
DECUMAN
DECUMANA
DECUMANI
DECUMANUS
DECUMARY
DECUMBENCE
DECUMBENCY
DECUMBENT
DECUMBITURE
DECUPLE
DECUPLED
DECUPLET
DECUPLING
DECURIA
DECURIES
DECURION
DECURIONATE
DECURRENCE
DECURRENCES
DECURRENCIES
DECURRENCY
DECURRENT
DECURRENTLY
DECURSION
DECURSIVE
DECURSIVELY
DECURT
DECURTATE
DECURVATION
DECURVE
DECURVED
DECURVING
DECURY
DECUS
DECUSSATE
DECUSSATED
DECUSSATELY
DECUSSATING
DECUSSATION
DECUSSION
DECUSSIS
DECUSSORIA
DECUSSORIUM
DECYL
DECYLENE
DECYLENIC
DECYLIC
DECYNE
DED
DEDAL
DEDANS
DEDDY
DEDE
DEDECORATE
DEDECORATION

DEDECOROUS
DEDENDA
DEDENDUM
DEDENTITION
DEDICATE
DEDICATED
DEDICATEE
DEDICATING
DEDICATION
DEDICATIONAL
DEDICATIVE
DEDICATOR
DEDICATORIAL
DEDICATORILY
DEDICATORY
DEDICATURE
DEDIMUS
DEDIT
DEDITICIAN
DEDITION
DEDO
DEDOLATION
DEDOLENCE
DEDOLENCY
DEDOLENT
DEDUCE
DEDUCED
DEDUCEMENT
DEDUCIBILITY
DEDUCIBLE
DEDUCIBLY
DEDUCING
DEDUCIVE
DEDUCT
DEDUCTED
DEDUCTIBLE
DEDUCTILE
DEDUCTING
DEDUCTIO
DEDUCTION
DEDUCTIONS
DEDUCTIVE
DEDUCTIVELY
DEDUCTORY
DEDUIT
DEE
DEECE
DEED
DEEDBOX
DEEDED
DEEDEED
DEEDFUL
DEEDFULLY
DEEDILY
DEEDINESS
DEEDING
DEEDLESS
DEEDS
DEEDY
DEEJAY
DEEL
DEEM
DEEMED
DEEMER
DEEMIE
DEEMING
DEEMSTER
DEEMSTERSHIP
DEEN
DEENER
DEENY
DEEP
DEEPEN
DEEPENER
DEEPENING
DEEPER
DEEPEST
DEEPFREEZE
DEEPFREEZED
DEEPFREEZING
DEEPFROZE
DEEPFROZEN
DEEPING
DEEPLY
DEEPMOST
DEEPMOUTHED
DEEPNESS
DEEPSOME
DEEPWATER
DEEPWATERMAN
DEEPWATERMEN
DEER
DEERBERRY
DEERDOG
DEERDRIVE
DEERFLY
DEERFOOD
DEERGRASS
DEERHAIR
DEERHERD
DEERHORN
DEERHOUND
DEERKILL
DEERLET
DEERSKIN
DEERSTALKER
DEERSTALKING
DEERSTAND
DEERTONGUE
DEERVETCH
DEERWEED
DEERWOOD
DEERYARD
DEES
DEESCALATE
DEESCALATED
DEESCALATING
DEESCALATION
DEESE
DEESIS
DEESS
DEEVE
DEEVEY
DEEVILICK
DEEWAN
DEFACE
DEFACED
DEFACEMENT
DEFACER
DEFACING
DEFACINGLY
DEFADE
DEFAIL
DEFAILANCE
DEFAILLANCE
DEFAILMENT
DEFAITISME
DEFAITISTE
DEFALCATE
DEFALCATED
DEFALCATING
DEFALCATION
DEFALCATOR
DEFALK
DEFAMATION
DEFAMATORY
DEFAME
DEFAMED
DEFAMER
DEFAMING
DEFAMINGLY
DEFAMOUS
DEFAMY
DEFASSA
DEFAT
DEFATIGABLE
DEFATIGATE
DEFATIGATED
DEFATIGATION
DEFATTED
DEFATTING
DEFAULT
DEFAULTANT
DEFAULTER
DEFAULTURE
DEFEASANCE
DEFEASANCED
DEFEASE
DEFEASIBLE
DEFEAT
DEFEATED
DEFEATER
DEFEATISM
DEFEATIST
DEFEATMENT
DEFEATURE
DEFECANT
DEFECATE
DEFECATED
DEFECATING
DEFECATION
DEFECATOR
DEFECT
DEFECTIBLE
DEFECTION
DEFECTIONIST
DEFECTIOUS
DEFECTIVE
DEFECTIVELY
DEFECTOR
DEFECTOSCOPE
DEFECTS
DEFEDATION
DEFEISE
DEFEIT
DEFEMINIZE
DEFENCE
DEFENCELESS
DEFEND
DEFENDABLE
DEFENDANT
DEFENDED
DEFENDER
DEFENDRESS
DEFENSATIVE
DEFENSE
DEFENSELESS
DEFENSER
DEFENSIBLE
DEFENSIBLY
DEFENSION
DEFENSIVE
DEFENSIVELY
DEFENSOR
DEFENSORY
DEFER
DEFERENCE
DEFERENT
DEFERENTIAL
DEFERENTITIS
DEFERMENT
DEFERRABLE
DEFERRAL
DEFERRED
DEFERRER
DEFERRING
DEFERRIZE
DEFERRIZED
DEFERRIZING
DEFERVESCE
DEFERVESCENT
DEFET
DEFI
DEFIABLE
DEFIAL
DEFIANCE
DEFIANT
DEFIANTLY
DEFIANTNESS
DEFIBER
DEFIBRINATE
DEFIBRINIZE
DEFICIENCE
DEFICIENCY
DEFICIENT
DEFICIENTLY
DEFICIT
DEFIED
DEFIER
DEFIES
DEFIGURATION
DEFIGURE
DEFILADE
DEFILADED
DEFILADING
DEFILE
DEFILED
DEFILEMENT
DEFILER
DEFILIATION
DEFILING
DEFILINGLY
DEFINABILITY
DEFINABLE
DEFINABLY
DEFINE
DEFINED
DEFINEDLY
DEFINEMENT
DEFINER
DEFINING
DEFINITE
DEFINITELY
DEFINITENESS
DEFINITION
DEFINITIONAL
DEFINITIVE
DEFINITIVELY
DEFINITIZE
DEFINITIZED
DEFINITIZING
DEFINITOR
DEFINITUDE
DEFIX
DEFLAGRABLE
DEFLAGRATE
DEFLAGRATED
DEFLAGRATING
DEFLAGRATION
DEFLAGRATOR
DEFLATE
DEFLATED
DEFLATING
DEFLATION
DEFLATIONARY
DEFLATIONIST
DEFLATOR
DEFLECT
DEFLECTED
DEFLECTING
DEFLECTION
DEFLECTIVE
DEFLECTOR
DEFLEX
DEFLEXED
DEFLEXING
DEFLEXION
DEFLEXURE
DEFLOCCULANT
DEFLOCCULATE
DEFLOCCULENT
DEFLORATE
DEFLORATION
DEFLORE
DEFLOWER
DEFLOWERER
DEFLUENT
DEFLUVIUM
DEFLUX
DEFLUXION
DEFOIL
DEFOLIATE
DEFOLIATED
DEFOLIATING
DEFOLIATION
DEFOLIATOR
DEFORCE
DEFORCED
DEFORCEMENT
DEFORCER
DEFORCIANT
DEFORCING
DEFOREST
DEFORESTER
DEFORM
DEFORMABLE
DEFORMATION
DEFORMATIVE
DEFORMED
DEFORMEDLY
DEFORMEDNESS
DEFORMER
DEFORMETER
DEFORMING
DEFORMISM
DEFORMITIES
DEFORMITY
DEFOUL
DEFRAUD
DEFRAUDATION
DEFRAUDED
DEFRAUDER
DEFRAUDING
DEFRAUDMENT
DEFRAY
DEFRAYAL
DEFRAYED
DEFRAYER
DEFRAYING
DEFRAYMENT
DEFROCK
DEFROST
DEFROSTER
DEFT
DEFTER
DEFTERDAR
DEFTEST
DEFTLY
DEFTNESS
DEFUNCT
DEFUNCTION
DEFUSE
DEFUSION
DEFY
DEFYING
DEG
DEGAGE
DEGAME
DEGAS
DEGASES
DEGASSED
DEGASSER
DEGASSES
DEGASSING
DEGAUSS

DEGELATION
DEGEN
DEGENDER
DEGENER
DEGENERACY
DEGENERATE
DEGENERATED
DEGENERATELY
DEGENERATING
DEGENERATION
DEGENERATIVE
DEGERM
DEGERMINATE
DEGGED
DEGGER
DEGGING
DEGLAZE
DEGLAZED
DEGLAZING
DEGLUTINATE
DEGLUTINATED
DEGLUTITION
DEGLUTITIVE
DEGLUTITORY
DEGOMME
DEGRADAND
DEGRADATION
DEGRADATIVE
DEGRADE
DEGRADED
DEGRADEDLY
DEGRADEDNESS
DEGRADEMENT
DEGRADER
DEGRADING
DEGRADINGLY
DEGRAIN
DEGRAS
DEGREASE
DEGREASED
DEGREASER
DEGREASING
DEGREE
DEGREED
DEGREEING
DEGREES
DEGREEWISE
DEGRESSION
DEGRESSIVE
DEGRESSIVELY
DEGRINGOLADE
DEGU
DEGUELIN
DEGUM
DEGUMMED
DEGUMMING
DEGUST
DEGUSTATE
DEGUSTATION
DEHA
DEHAIR
DEHAIRER
DEHEMATIZE
DEHEPATIZE
DEHISCE
DEHISCED
DEHISCENCE
DEHISCENT
DEHISCING
DEHNSTUFE
DEHORN
DEHORNER
DEHORS
DEHORT
DEHORTATION
DEHORTATIVE
DEHORTATORY
DEHORTED
DEHORTER
DEHORTING
DEHULL
DEHUMANIZE
DEHUMANIZED
DEHUMANIZING
DEHUMIDIFIED
DEHUMIDIFIER
DEHUMIDIFY
DEHUSK
DEHYDRANT
DEHYDRATE
DEHYDRATED
DEHYDRATING
DEHYDRATION
DEHYDRATOR
DEHYPNOTIZE
DEHYPNOTIZED
DEI
DEICE
DEICED
DEICER
DEICIDAL
DEICIDE
DEICING
DEICTIC
DEICTICALLY
DEIFIC
DEIFICAL
DEIFICATION
DEIFICATORY
DEIFIED
DEIFIER
DEIFORM
DEIFORMITY
DEIFY
DEIFYING
DEIGN
DEIGNED
DEIGNING
DEIGNOUS
DEIL
DEIN
DEINCRUSTANT
DEINOS
DEIONIZE
DEIPOTENT
DEIRID
DEISEAL
DEISM
DEIST
DEISTIC
DEISTICAL
DEISTICALLY
DEITIES
DEITY
DEJECT
DEJECTA
DEJECTED
DEJECTEDLY
DEJECTEDNESS
DEJECTILE
DEJECTION
DEJECTORY
DEJECTURE
DEJERATE
DEJEUNE
DEJEUNER
DEJUNKERIZE
DEKADRACHM
DEKAGRAM
DEKALITER
DEKALITRE
DEKAMETER
DEKAMETRE
DEKAN
DEKAPARSEC
DEKAPODE
DEKARCH
DEKASTERE
DEKE
DEKED
DEKING
DEKKO
DEL
DELACTATION
DELAINE
DELAMINATE
DELAMINATED
DELAMINATING
DELAMINATION
DELAPSE
DELAPSION
DELASSEMENT
DELATE
DELATED
DELATER
DELATING
DELATION
DELATOR
DELATORIAN
DELAVY
DELAWN
DELAY
DELAYAGE
DELAYED
DELAYER
DELAYING
DELAYINGLY
DELE
DELEAD
DELEATUR
DELECTABLE
DELECTABLY
DELECTATE
DELECTATED
DELECTATING
DELECTATION
DELECTUS
DELED
DELEERIT
DELEGABLE
DELEGACIES
DELEGACY
DELEGALIZE
DELEGANT
DELEGATE
DELEGATED
DELEGATEE
DELEGATING
DELEGATION
DELEGATIVE
DELEGATORY
DELEING
DELENDA
DELETE
DELETED
DELETERIOUS
DELETERY
DELETING
DELETION
DELETIVE
DELETORY
DELF
DELFT
DELFTWARE
DELIBATE
DELIBER
DELIBERANT
DELIBERATE
DELIBERATED
DELIBERATELY
DELIBERATENESS
DELIBERATING
DELIBERATION
DELIBERATIVE
DELIBERATOR
DELIBLE
DELICACIES
DELICACY
DELICATE
DELICATELY
DELICATENESS
DELICATESSEN
DELICE
DELICIAE
DELICIOSO
DELICIOUS
DELICIOUSLY
DELICIOUSNESS
DELICT
DELICTUM
DELIE
DELIERET
DELIGATED
DELIGATION
DELIGHT
DELIGHTABLE
DELIGHTED
DELIGHTEDLY
DELIGHTEDNESS
DELIGHTER
DELIGHTFUL
DELIGHTFULLY
DELIGHTFULNESS
DELIGHTING
DELIGHTINGLY
DELIGHTSOME
DELIGHTSOMELY
DELIGHTSOMENESS
DELIGNATE
DELIGNATED
DELIME
DELIMER
DELIMIT
DELIMITATE
DELIMITATED
DELIMITATING
DELIMITATION
DELIMITATIVE
DELIMITED
DELIMITER
DELIMITIZE
DELIMITIZED
DELIMITIZING
DELINE
DELINEABLE
DELINEATE
DELINEATED
DELINEATING
DELINEATION
DELINEATIVE
DELINEATOR
DELINEATORY
DELINEAVIT
DELINQUENCIES
DELINQUENCY
DELINQUENT
DELINQUENTLY
DELIQUESCE
DELIQUESCED
DELIQUESCENT
DELIQUESCING
DELIQUIUM
DELIRACY
DELIRAMENT
DELIRANT
DELIRATION
DELIRE
DELIRIA
DELIRIOUS
DELIRIOUSLY
DELIRIUM
DELIRIUMS
DELISK
DELITESCENCE
DELITESCENT
DELITOUS
DELIVER
DELIVERABLE
DELIVERANCE
DELIVERED
DELIVERER
DELIVERIES
DELIVERING
DELIVERLY
DELIVEROR
DELIVERY
DELIVERYMAN
DELIVERYMEN
DELK
DELL
DELLA
DELLENITE
DELLS
DELOCALIZE
DELOCALIZED
DELOCALIZING
DELOMORPHIC
DELOMORPHOUS
DELOUL
DELOUSE
DELOUSED
DELOUSING
DELPH
DELPHIN
DELPHINE
DELPHINIC
DELPHININ
DELPHININE
DELPHINITE
DELPHINIUM
DELPHINOID
DELT
DELTA
DELTAHEDRA
DELTAHEDRON
DELTAIC
DELTAITE
DELTAL
DELTATION
DELTHYRIA
DELTHYRIAL
DELTHYRIUM
DELTIC
DELTIDIA
DELTIDIAL
DELTIDIUM
DELTOHEDRA
DELTOHEDRON
DELTOID
DELTOIDAL
DELUBRUM
DELUDE
DELUDED
DELUDER
DELUDHER
DELUDING
DELUDINGLY
DELUGE
DELUGED
DELUGING
DELUL
DELUMINIZE
DELUNDUNG
DELUSION
DELUSIONAL

DELUSIONIST
DELUSIVE
DELUSIVELY
DELUSIVENESS
DELUSORY
DELUSTER
DELUXE
DELVE
DELVED
DELVER
DELVING
DEM
DEMAGNETIZE
DEMAGNETIZED
DEMAGNETIZER
DEMAGOG
DEMAGOGIC
DEMAGOGICAL
DEMAGOGISM
DEMAGOGUE
DEMAGOGUERY
DEMAGOGUISM
DEMAGOGY
DEMAIN
DEMAL
DEMAND
DEMANDABLE
DEMANDANT
DEMANDED
DEMANDER
DEMANDING
DEMANGANIZE
DEMANTOID
DEMARCATE
DEMARCATED
DEMARCATING
DEMARCATION
DEMARCH
DEMARCHE
DEMARCHY
DEMAREE
DEMARK
DEMARKATION
DEMARKED
DEMARKING
DEMAST
DEMATIACEOUS
DEME
DEMEAN
DEMEANED
DEMEANING
DEMEANOR
DEMEANOUR
DEMEGORIC
DEMELE
DEMEMBRATION
DEMENCY
DEMENT
DEMENTATE
DEMENTATION
DEMENTED
DEMENTEDLY
DEMENTEDNESS
DEMENTHOLIZE
DEMENTI
DEMENTIA
DEMEORE
DEMEPHITIZE
DEMERGE
DEMERIT
DEMEROL
DEMERSAL
DEMERSE
DEMERSED
DEMERSION
DEMESMAN
DEMESNE
DEMESNIAL
DEMETHYLATE
DEMI
DEMIBASTION
DEMIBATH
DEMIBRIGADE
DEMICADENCE
DEMICANNON
DEMICANTON
DEMICAPONIER
DEMICHAMFRON
DEMICIRCLE
DEMICIRCULAR
DEMICIVILIZED
DEMICUIRASS
DEMICULVERIN
DEMIDITONE
DEMIDOLMEN
DEMIES
DEMIGAUNTLET
DEMIGOD
DEMIGODDESS
DEMIGORGE
DEMIHAG
DEMIHAGBUT
DEMIHAGUE
DEMIHAKE
DEMIHAQUE
DEMIJAMBE
DEMIJOHN
DEMILANCE
DEMILANCER
DEMILEGATO
DEMILITARIZE
DEMILITARIZED
DEMILUNE
DEMIMARK
DEMIMETOPE
DEMIMONDAIN
DEMIMONDAINE
DEMIMONDE
DEMINERALIZE
DEMIOURGOI
DEMIPARALLEL
DEMIPAULDRON
DEMIPIKE
DEMIPIQUE
DEMIQUAVER
DEMIRACLE
DEMIRELIEF
DEMIREP
DEMIRHUMB
DEMIRILIEVO
DEMISABLE
DEMISANG
DEMISE
DEMISEASON
DEMISED
DEMISEMITONE
DEMISING
DEMISOLDE
DEMISPHERE
DEMISS
DEMISSION
DEMISSIONARY
DEMISSLY
DEMISSNESS
DEMISUIT
DEMIT
DEMITASSE
DEMITINT
DEMITOILET
DEMITONE
DEMITTED
DEMITTING
DEMIURGE
DEMIURGEOUS
DEMIURGIC
DEMIURGICAL
DEMIURGISM
DEMIURGOS
DEMIURGUS
DEMIVIERGE
DEMIVOL
DEMIVOLT
DEMIVOLTE
DEMIWOLF
DEMOB
DEMOBBED
DEMOBBING
DEMOBILIZE
DEMOBILIZED
DEMOBILIZING
DEMOCRACIES
DEMOCRACY
DEMOCRAT
DEMOCRATIAN
DEMOCRATIC
DEMOCRATICAL
DEMOCRATISM
DEMOCRATIZE
DEMOCRATIZED
DEMOCRAW
DEMODE
DEMODED
DEMODULATE
DEMODULATED
DEMODULATING
DEMODULATION
DEMODULATOR
DEMOGENIC
DEMOGRAPHER
DEMOGRAPHIC
DEMOGRAPHICAL
DEMOGRAPHIST
DEMOGRAPHY
DEMOID
DEMOISELLE
DEMOLISH
DEMOLISHER
DEMOLISHMENT
DEMOLITION
DEMOLOGICAL
DEMOLOGY
DEMON
DEMONASTERY
DEMONETIZE
DEMONETIZED
DEMONETIZING
DEMONIAC
DEMONIACAL
DEMONIACALLY
DEMONIACISM
DEMONIAL
DEMONIAN
DEMONIANISM
DEMONIAST
DEMONIC
DEMONICAL
DEMONIFUGE
DEMONIO
DEMONISM
DEMONIST
DEMONIZE
DEMONIZED
DEMONIZING
DEMONOLATER
DEMONOLATRY
DEMONOLOGER
DEMONOLOGIC
DEMONOLOGIST
DEMONOLOGY
DEMONRY
DEMONS
DEMONSTRABLE
DEMONSTRABLY
DEMONSTRANCE
DEMONSTRANT
DEMONSTRATE
DEMONSTRATED
DEMONSTRATION
DEMONSTRATIVE
DEMONSTRATOR
DEMOPHIL
DEMOPHILE
DEMOPHILISM
DEMOPHOBE
DEMORALIZE
DEMORALIZED
DEMORALIZER
DEMORALIZING
DEMORPHISM
DEMOS
DEMOTE
DEMOTED
DEMOTIC
DEMOTICS
DEMOTING
DEMOTION
DEMOTIST
DEMOUNT
DEMOUNTABLE
DEMPNE
DEMPSTER
DEMULCE
DEMULCEATE
DEMULCENT
DEMULSIFY
DEMULSION
DEMUR
DEMURE
DEMURELY
DEMURENESS
DEMUREST
DEMURITY
DEMURRABLE
DEMURRAGE
DEMURRAL
DEMURRANT
DEMURRED
DEMURRER
DEMURRING
DEMURRINGLY
DEMUTIZATION
DEMY
DEMYSHIP
DEN
DENAR
DENARI
DENARIES
DENARII
DENARIUS
DENARO
DENARY
DENAT
DENATURALIZE
DENATURANT
DENATURATE
DENATURATION
DENATURE
DENATURED
DENATURING
DENATURIZE
DENATURIZER
DENAY
DENAZIFIED
DENAZIFY
DENAZIFYING
DENDA
DENDRACHATE
DENDRAL
DENDRAXON
DENDRIC
DENDRIFORM
DENDRITE
DENDRITIC
DENDRITICAL
DENDRITIFORM
DENDROBE
DENDROCOELE
DENDRODONT
DENDROGRAPH
DENDROGRAPHY
DENDROID
DENDROIDAL
DENDROLITE
DENDROLOGIC
DENDROLOGIST
DENDROLOGY
DENDROMETER
DENDRON
DENE
DENEGATE
DENEGATION
DENEHOLE
DENERVATE
DENERVATION
DENGUE
DENIABLE
DENIABLY
DENIAL
DENICOTINE
DENICOTINIZE
DENIED
DENIER
DENIERAGE
DENIERER
DENIGRATE
DENIGRATED
DENIGRATING
DENIGRATION
DENIGRATOR
DENIM
DENIMS
DENITRATE
DENITRATED
DENITRATING
DENITRATION
DENITRATOR
DENITRIFIED
DENITRIFIER
DENITRIFY
DENITRIFYING
DENITRIZE
DENIZATE
DENIZATION
DENIZE
DENIZEN
DENIZENATION
DENIZENIZE
DENNED
DENNET
DENNING
DENOMINABLE
DENOMINATE
DENOMINATED
DENOMINATING
DENOMINATION
DENOMINATIONAL
DENOMINATIVE
DENOMINATOR
DENOTABLE
DENOTATE
DENOTATION
DENOTATIVE
DENOTATIVELY
DENOTE
DENOTED

DENOTEMENT
DENOTING
DENOTIVE
DENOUEMENT
DENOUNCE
DENOUNCED
DENOUNCEMENT
DENOUNCER
DENOUNCING
DENS
DENSATE
DENSATION
DENSE
DENSELY
DENSEN
DENSENESS
DENSER
DENSEST
DENSIFIED
DENSIFIER
DENSIFY
DENSIMETER
DENSIMETRIC
DENSIMETRY
DENSITIES
DENSITOMETER
DENSITY
DENT
DENTAGRA
DENTAL
DENTALE
DENTALISM
DENTALITY
DENTALIZE
DENTAPHONE
DENTARY
DENTATA
DENTATE
DENTATED
DENTATELY
DENTATION
DENTEL
DENTELATED
DENTELLATED
DENTELLE
DENTELLIERE
DENTELLO
DENTELURE
DENTEX
DENTICAL
DENTICATE
DENTICLE
DENTICULAR
DENTICULATE
DENTICULATED
DENTICULE
DENTIFORM
DENTIFRICE
DENTIGEROUS
DENTIL
DENTILABIAL
DENTILATED
DENTILATION
DENTILE
DENTILINGUAL
DENTILOGUY
DENTILOQUIST
DENTIMETER
DENTIN
DENTINAL
DENTINALGIA
DENTINASAL
DENTINE
DENTINITIS
DENTINOBLAST
DENTINOID
DENTINOMA
DENTIPAROUS
DENTIPHONE
DENTIROSTER
DENTIROSTRAL
DENTISCALP
DENTIST
DENTISTIC
DENTISTICAL
DENTISTRY
DENTITION
DENTOID
DENTOLOLABIAL
DENTONASAL
DENTURAL
DENTURE
DENTY
DENUDANT
DENUDATE
DENUDATED
DENUDATING
DENUDATION
DENUDATIVE
DENUDE
DENUDED
DENUDER
DENUDING
DENUM
DENUMERABLE
DENUMERABLY
DENUMERAL
DENUMERANT
DENUMERATION
DENUMERATIVE
DENUNCIABLE
DENUNCIANT
DENUNCIATE
DENUNCIATED
DENUNCIATING
DENUNCIATION
DENUNCIATIVE
DENUNCIATOR
DENUNCIATORY
DENUTRITION
DENY
DENYING
DEOBSTRUENT
DEOCULATE
DEODAND
DEODAR
DEODATE
DEODORANT
DEODORIZE
DEODORIZED
DEODORIZER
DEODORIZING
DEONTOLOGIST
DEONTOLOGY
DEOPERCULATE
DEOPPILANT
DEOPPILATE
DEOPPILATION
DEOPPILATIVE
DEORDINATION
DEORSUM
DEOTA
DEOXIDIZE
DEOXIDIZED
DEOXIDIZER
DEOXIDIZING
DEOXYGENATE
DEOXYGENATED
DEOXYGENIZE
DEOZONIZE
DEOZONIZER
DEPA
DEPAINT
DEPAINTED
DEPAINTING
DEPAIR
DEPARLIAMENT
DEPART
DEPARTED
DEPARTEMENT
DEPARTER
DEPARTING
DEPARTITION
DEPARTMENT
DEPARTMENTAL
DEPARTURE
DEPAS
DEPASCENT
DEPASS
DEPASTURABLE
DEPASTURAGE
DEPASTURE
DEPASTURED
DEPASTURING
DEPATRIATE
DEPAUPERATE
DEPAUPERIZE
DEPAUPERIZED
DEPAYSE
DEPAYSEE
DEPE
DEPECHE
DEPEL
DEPENCIL
DEPEND
DEPENDABILITY
DEPENDABLE
DEPENDABLY
DEPENDANCY
DEPENDANT
DEPENDED
DEPENDENCE
DEPENDENCIES
DEPENDENCY
DEPENDENT
DEPENDER
DEPENDING
DEPENDINGLY
DEPEOPLE
DEPERDITE
DEPERDITELY
DEPERDITION
DEPERITION
DEPERM
DEPERSONIZE
DEPETALIZE
DEPETER
DEPETTICOAT
DEPHASE
DEPHASED
DEPHASING
DEPHLEGMATE
DEPHLEGMATED
DEPHLEGMATOR
DEPICT
DEPICTED
DEPICTER
DEPICTING
DEPICTION
DEPICTIVE
DEPICTOR
DEPICTURE
DEPICTURED
DEPICTURING
DEPIGMENT
DEPIGMENTATE
DEPIGMENTIZE
DEPILATE
DEPILATED
DEPILATING
DEPILATION
DEPILATOR
DEPILATORY
DEPILITANT
DEPILOUS
DEPIT
DEPLACE
DEPLANE
DEPLANED
DEPLANING
DEPLANT
DEPLANTATION
DEPLENISH
DEPLETE
DEPLETED
DEPLETHORIC
DEPLETING
DEPLETION
DEPLETIVE
DEPLETORY
DEPLORABILIA
DEPLORABLE
DEPLORABLY
DEPLORATION
DEPLORE
DEPLORED
DEPLORER
DEPLORING
DEPLOY
DEPLOYMENT
DEPLUMATE
DEPLUMATED
DEPLUMATION
DEPLUME
DEPLUMED
DEPLUMING
DEPOH
DEPOLARIZE
DEPOLARIZED
DEPOLARIZER
DEPOLARIZING
DEPOLISH
DEPOLISHING
DEPOLYMERIZE
DEPONE
DEPONED
DEPONENT
DEPONER
DEPONING
DEPOPULATE
DEPOPULATED
DEPOPULATING
DEPOPULATION
DEPOPULATIVE
DEPOPULATOR
DEPORT
DEPORTATION
DEPORTE
DEPORTED
DEPORTEE
DEPORTER
DEPORTING
DEPORTMENT
DEPOSABLE
DEPOSAL
DEPOSE
DEPOSED
DEPOSER
DEPOSING
DEPOSIT
DEPOSITA
DEPOSITARIES
DEPOSITARY
DEPOSITATION
DEPOSITED
DEPOSITEE
DEPOSITING
DEPOSITION
DEPOSITIONAL
DEPOSITIVE
DEPOSITO
DEPOSITOR
DEPOSITORIES
DEPOSITORY
DEPOSITS
DEPOSITUM
DEPOSITURE
DEPOSURE
DEPOT
DEPOTENTIATE
DEPRAVATE
DEPRAVATION
DEPRAVE
DEPRAVED
DEPRAVEDLY
DEPRAVEDNESS
DEPRAVER
DEPRAVING
DEPRAVITIES
DEPRAVITY
DEPRECABLE
DEPRECATE
DEPRECATED
DEPRECATING
DEPRECATION
DEPRECATIVE
DEPRECATOR
DEPRECATORY
DEPRECIABLE
DEPRECIANT
DEPRECIATE
DEPRECIATED
DEPRECIATING
DEPRECIATION
DEPRECIATIVE
DEPRECIATOR
DEPRECIATORY
DEPREDATE
DEPREDATED
DEPREDATING
DEPREDATION
DEPREDATOR
DEPREDATORY
DEPREHEND
DEPREHENSION
DEPRESS
DEPRESSANT
DEPRESSED
DEPRESSING
DEPRESSINGLY
DEPRESSION
DEPRESSIVE
DEPRESSIVELY
DEPRESSOR
DEPREST
DEPRETER
DEPRINT
DEPRIORIZE
DEPRIVABLE
DEPRIVAL
DEPRIVATE
DEPRIVATION
DEPRIVATIVE
DEPRIVE
DEPRIVED
DEPRIVEMENT
DEPRIVER
DEPRIVING
DEPROME
DEPSID
DEPSIDE
DEPTH
DEPTHEN
DEPTHING
DEPTHLESS

DEPTHOMETER
DEPTHS
DEPULSE
DEPURANT
DEPURATE
DEPURATED
DEPURATING
DEPURATIVE
DEPURATOR
DEPUTATION
DEPUTATIVE
DEPUTATOR
DEPUTE
DEPUTED
DEPUTIES
DEPUTING
DEPUTIZE
DEPUTIZED
DEPUTIZING
DEPUTY
DEQUEEN
DER
DERACIALIZE
DERACINATE
DERACINATED
DERACINATING
DERACINATION
DERADELPHUS
DERADENITIS
DERADENONCUS
DERAH
DERAIGN
DERAIGNMENT
DERAIL
DERAILED
DERAILER
DERAILING
DERAILMENT
DERANGE
DERANGED
DERANGEMENT
DERANGER
DERANGING
DERAT
DERATE
DERATED
DERATER
DERATING
DERATIZATION
DERAY
DERBUKKA
DERBY
DERBYLITE
DERE
DERECHO
DERELICT
DERELICTION
DERELICTLY
DERELICTNESS
DERELIGION
DERERE
DERESINATE
DERESINIFY
DERESINIZE
DERF
DERFLY
DERFNESS
DERHAM
DERIC
DERIDE
DERIDED
DERIDER
DERIDING
DERIDINGLY
DERINGER
DERISIBLE
DERISION
DERISIVE
DERISIVELY
DERISIVENESS
DERISORY
DERIVABILITY
DERIVABLE
DERIVABLY
DERIVAL
DERIVANT
DERIVATE
DERIVATELY
DERIVATION
DERIVATIONAL
DERIVATIST
DERIVATIVE
DERIVE
DERIVED
DERIVEDLY
DERIVEDNESS
DERIVER
DERIVING
DERK
DERM
DERMA
DERMAD
DERMAHEMIA
DERMAL
DERMALITH
DERMAMYIASIS
DERMAPTERAN
DERMAPTEROUS
DERMASURGERY
DERMATALGIA
DERMATAUXE
DERMATHEMIA
DERMATIC
DERMATINE
DERMATITIS
DERMATOCELE
DERMATOCYST
DERMATODYNIA
DERMATOGEN
DERMATOGRAPH
DERMATOID
DERMATOLOGY
DERMATOLYSIS
DERMATOMA
DERMATOME
DERMATOMIC
DERMATOMYOMA
DERMATONOSUS
DERMATOPHONE
DERMATOPHONY
DERMATOPHYTE
DERMATOPLASM
DERMATOPLAST
DERMATOPSY
DERMATORRHEA
DERMATOSCOPY
DERMATOSIS
DERMATOTHERAPY
DERMATOTOMY
DERMATOZOON
DERMIC
DERMIS
DERMOBLAST
DERMOCHROME
DERMOCOCCUS
DERMOGASTRIC
DERMOGRAPHIA
DERMOGRAPHIC
DERMOHEMAL
DERMOHEMIA
DERMOID
DERMOIDAL
DERMOL
DERMOLYSIS
DERMONEURAL
DERMOOSSEOUS
DERMOPATHIC
DERMOPATHY
DERMOPHOBE
DERMOPHYTE
DERMOPHYTIC
DERMOPLASTY
DERMOPTERAN
DERMOPTEROUS
DERMOSTOSIS
DERMOTROPIC
DERMOVACCINE
DERMUTATION
DERN
DERNE
DERNED
DERNER
DERNFUL
DERNIER
DERNING
DERNLY
DERODIDYMUS
DEROGATE
DEROGATED
DEROGATELY
DEROGATING
DEROGATION
DEROGATIVE
DEROGATIVELY
DEROGATOR
DEROGATORILY
DEROGATORY
DEROUT
DERRICK
DERRICKING
DERRICKMAN
DERRICKMEN
DERRID
DERRIDE
DERRIERE
DERRIES
DERRINGER
DERRY
DERTRA
DERTROTHECA
DERTRUM
DERVISH
DERVISHHOOD
DERVISHISM
DERVISHLIKE
DESA
DESACRALIZE
DESALT
DESAND
DESATURATE
DESAURIN
DESAURINE
DESCALE
DESCAMISADO
DESCAMISADOS
DESCANT
DESCANTED
DESCANTER
DESCANTING
DESCEND
DESCENDABLE
DESCENDANCE
DESCENDANT
DESCENDED
DESCENDENCE
DESCENDENT
DESCENDENTAL
DESCENDER
DESCENDIBLE
DESCENDING
DESCENDINGLY
DESCENSION
DESCENSIONAL
DESCENSIVE
DESCENT
DESCLOIZITE
DESCORT
DESCRIAL
DESCRIBABLE
DESCRIBABLY
DESCRIBE
DESCRIBED
DESCRIBER
DESCRIBING
DESCRIED
DESCRIER
DESCRIPT
DESCRIPTION
DESCRIPTIVE
DESCRIPTORY
DESCRIVE
DESCRY
DESCRYING
DESCURE
DESEAM
DESECATE
DESECRATE
DESECRATED
DESECRATER
DESECRATING
DESECRATION
DESECRATOR
DESEED
DESEGREGATE
DESEGREGATED
DESEMER
DESENSITIZE
DESENSITIZER
DESERET
DESERT
DESERTED
DESERTEDLY
DESERTEDNESS
DESERTER
DESERTFUL
DESERTFULLY
DESERTIC
DESERTION
DESERTLESS
DESERTLESSLY
DESERTNESS
DESERTS
DESERVE
DESERVED
DESERVEDLY
DESERVEDNESS
DESERVER
DESERVING
DESERVINGLY
DESEX
DESEXUALIZE
DESEXUALIZED
DESH
DESHABILLE
DESI
DESIATIN
DESICCANT
DESICCATE
DESICCATED
DESICCATING
DESICCATION
DESICCATIVE
DESICCATOR
DESICCATORY
DESIDERANT
DESIDERATE
DESIDERATED
DESIDERATING
DESIDERATION
DESIDERATIVE
DESIDERATUM
DESIDERIUM
DESIGHT
DESIGHTMENT
DESIGN
DESIGNABLE
DESIGNADO
DESIGNATE
DESIGNATED
DESIGNATING
DESIGNATION
DESIGNATIVE
DESIGNATOR
DESIGNATORY
DESIGNED
DESIGNEDLY
DESIGNEDNESS
DESIGNEE
DESIGNER
DESIGNFUL
DESIGNFULLY
DESIGNING
DESIGNINGLY
DESILICATE
DESILICATED
DESILICATING
DESILICIFIED
DESILICIFY
DESILICONIZE
DESILVER
DESILVERIZE
DESILVERIZER
DESINENCE
DESINENT
DESINENTIAL
DESIPIENCE
DESIPIENCY
DESIPIENT
DESIRABILITY
DESIRABLE
DESIRABLY
DESIRE
DESIRED
DESIREDLY
DESIREDNESS
DESIREFUL
DESIRER
DESIRING
DESIROUS
DESIROUSLY
DESIROUSNESS
DESIST
DESISTANCE
DESISTENCE
DESISTIVE
DESITION
DESITIVE
DESIZE
DESK
DESKILL
DESKMAN
DESLIME
DESMA
DESMACHYME
DESMACYTE
DESMAN
DESMECTASIA
DESMIC
DESMID
DESMIDIAN
DESMIDIOLOGY
DESMINE
DESMITIS
DESMODONT
DESMODYNIA

DESMOGEN
DESMOID
DESMOLOGY
DESMOMA
DESMON
DESMONEME
DESMOPELMOUS
DESMOSE
DESMOSIS
DESMOSITE
DESMOTOMY
DESMOTROPE
DESMOTROPIC
DESMOTROPISM
DESMOTROPY
DESOEUVRE
DESOLATE
DESOLATED
DESOLATELY
DESOLATENESS
DESOLATER
DESOLATING
DESOLATINGLY
DESOLATION
DESOLATIVE
DESOLATOR
DESONATION
DESORPTION
DESOXALATE
DESPAIR
DESPAIRED
DESPAIRER
DESPAIRFUL
DESPAIRFULLY
DESPAIRING
DESPAIRINGLY
DESPATCH
DESPATCHER
DESPECT
DESPERACY
DESPERADO
DESPERADOES
DESPERADOS
DESPERATE
DESPERATELY
DESPERATION
DESPERT
DESPICABLE
DESPICABLY
DESPISAL
DESPISE
DESPISED
DESPISEMENT
DESPISER
DESPISING
DESPITE
DESPITED
DESPITEFUL
DESPITEFULLY
DESPITEOUS
DESPITEOUSLY
DESPITING
DESPOIL
DESPOILER
DESPOILMENT
DESPOLIATION
DESPOND
DESPONDENCE
DESPONDENCY
DESPONDENT
DESPONDENTLY
DESPONDER
DESPONDING
DESPONDINGLY
DESPOT
DESPOTIC
DESPOTICAL
DESPOTICALLY
DESPOTISM
DESPOTIST
DESPOTIZE
DESPOUSE
DESPUMATE
DESPUMATED
DESPUMATING
DESPUMATION
DESPUME
DESQUAMATE
DESQUAMATED
DESQUAMATING
DESQUAMATION
DESQUAMATIVE
DESQUAMATORY
DESRAY
DESS
DESSA
DESSE
DESSERT
DESSERTSPOON
DESSIATINE
DESSIL
DESSOUS
DESSUS
DESTERILIZE
DESTINATE
DESTINATION
DESTINE
DESTINED
DESTINEZITE
DESTINIES
DESTINING
DESTINISM
DESTINIST
DESTINY
DESTITUTE
DESTITUTELY
DESTITUTION
DESTO
DESTOOL
DESTOUR
DESTRER
DESTRIER
DESTROY
DESTROYED
DESTROYER
DESTROYING
DESTRUCT
DESTRUCTIBLE
DESTRUCTION
DESTRUCTIVE
DESTRUCTOR
DESTRUDO
DESUCRATION
DESUETE
DESUETUDE
DESUGAR
DESUGARIZE
DESULFURATE
DESULFURIZE
DESULFURIZED
DESULFURIZER
DESULPHUR
DESULPHURATE
DESULPHURIZE
DESULTOR
DESULTORILY
DESULTORY
DESUME
DESYL
DESYNONYMIZE
DETACH
DETACHABLE
DETACHE
DETACHED
DETACHEDLY
DETACHEDNESS
DETACHER
DETACHING
DETACHMENT
DETAIL
DETAILED
DETAILEDLY
DETAILEDNESS
DETAILER
DETAILING
DETAIN
DETAINAL
DETAINED
DETAINEE
DETAINER
DETAINING
DETAINMENT
DETASSEL
DETECT
DETECTABLE
DETECTAPHONE
DETECTER
DETECTIBLE
DETECTING
DETECTION
DETECTIVE
DETECTIVES
DETECTOR
DETENT
DETENTE
DETENTION
DETENTIVE
DETENU
DETER
DETERGE
DETERGED
DETERGENCE
DETERGENCY
DETERGENT
DETERGING
DETERIORATE
DETERIORATED
DETERIORATING
DETERIORATION
DETERIORATOR
DETERIORISM
DETERIORITY
DETERM
DETERMA
DETERMENT
DETERMINABLE
DETERMINABLY
DETERMINACY
DETERMINANT
DETERMINANTS
DETERMINATE
DETERMINATION
DETERMINATIVE
DETERMINE
DETERMINED
DETERMINEDLY
DETERMINER
DETERMINING
DETERMINISM
DETERMINIST
DETERMINOID
DETERRED
DETERRENCE
DETERRENT
DETERRING
DETERSION
DETERSIVE
DETERSIVELY
DETEST
DETESTABLE
DETESTABLY
DETESTATION
DETESTED
DETESTER
DETESTING
DETHRONE
DETHRONED
DETHRONEMENT
DETHRONER
DETHRONING
DETHYROIDISM
DETIN
DETINET
DETINUE
DETINUIT
DETONABLE
DETONATE
DETONATED
DETONATING
DETONATION
DETONATIVE
DETONATOR
DETONIZE
DETORSION
DETORT
DETOUR
DETOXICANT
DETOXICATE
DETOXICATED
DETOXICATING
DETOXICATION
DETOXICATOR
DETOXIFY
DETRACT
DETRACTED
DETRACTER
DETRACTING
DETRACTION
DETRACTIVE
DETRACTIVELY
DETRACTOR
DETRACTORY
DETRAIN
DETRAINMENT
DETRAQUE
DETRAY
DETRECT
DETRIBALIZE
DETRIMENT
DETRIMENTAL
DETRITAL
DETRITED
DETRITION
DETRITUS
DETRUCK
DETRUDE
DETRUDED
DETRUDING
DETRUNCATE
DETRUNCATED
DETRUNCATING
DETRUNCATION
DETRUSION
DETRUSIVE
DETRUSOR
DETUBATION
DETUMESCENCE
DETUNE
DETUNED
DETUNING
DETUR
DETURB
DETURN
DEUCE
DEUCED
DEUCEDLY
DEUL
DEUNAM
DEURWAARDER
DEUS
DEUSAN
DEUTERANOMAL
DEUTERIC
DEUTERIDE
DEUTERIUM
DEUTEROCONE
DEUTEROCONID
DEUTERODOME
DEUTEROGAMY
DEUTEROGENIC
DEUTERON
DEUTEROPATHY
DEUTEROPLASM
DEUTEROSCOPY
DEUTEROSTOMA
DEUTEROTOKY
DEUTEROTYPE
DEUTEROZOOID
DEUTOBROMIDE
DEUTOMALA
DEUTOMALAL
DEUTOMALAR
DEUTOMERITE
DEUTON
DEUTONYMPH
DEUTONYMPHAL
DEUTOPLASM
DEUTOPLASMIC
DEUTOPLASTIC
DEUTOVUM
DEUTSCHEMARK
DEUZAN
DEVA
DEVACHAN
DEVADASI
DEVAL
DEVALL
DEVALOKA
DEVALUATE
DEVALUATED
DEVALUATING
DEVALUATION
DEVALUE
DEVANCE
DEVANT
DEVAPORATE
DEVAPORATION
DEVARAJA
DEVARSHI
DEVAST
DEVASTATE
DEVASTATED
DEVASTATING
DEVASTATION
DEVASTATIVE
DEVASTATOR
DEVASTAVIT
DEVASTER
DEVATA
DEVAUL
DEVAUNT
DEVEIN
DEVEL
DEVELIN
DEVELOP
DEVELOPABLE
DEVELOPE
DEVELOPED
DEVELOPEMENT
DEVELOPER
DEVELOPING
DEVELOPMENT
DEVELOPMENTAL
DEVELOPOID
DEVELOPS

DEVER
DEVEST
DEVEX
DEVIABILITY
DEVIABLE
DEVIANT
DEVIATE
DEVIATED
DEVIATING
DEVIATION
DEVIATIONISM
DEVIATIONIST
DEVIATIVE
DEVIATOR
DEVIATORY
DEVICE
DEVICEFUL
DEVICEFULLY
DEVIL
DEVILBIRD
DEVILDOM
DEVILED
DEVILER
DEVILET
DEVILFISH
DEVILFISHES
DEVILING
DEVILISH
DEVILISHLY
DEVILISHNESS
DEVILISM
DEVILIZE
DEVILIZED
DEVILIZING
DEVILKIN
DEVILLED
DEVILMENT
DEVILRIES
DEVILRY
DEVILS
DEVILTRY
DEVILWOOD
DEVILY
DEVIOUS
DEVIOUSLY
DEVIOUSNESS
DEVIRGINATE
DEVIRGINATOR
DEVIRILIZE
DEVISABLE
DEVISAL
DEVISE
DEVISED
DEVISEE
DEVISER
DEVISING
DEVISOR
DEVITALIZE
DEVITALIZED
DEVITALIZING
DEVITAMINIZE
DEVITRIFIED
DEVITRIFY
DEVITRIFYING
DEVOCALIZE
DEVOCALIZED
DEVOCALIZING
DEVOCATE
DEVOCATION
DEVOICED
DEVOID
DEVOIR
DEVOIRS
DEVOLUTE
DEVOLUTION
DEVOLVE
DEVOLVED
DEVOLVEMENT
DEVOLVING
DEVONITE
DEVORATIVE
DEVOT
DEVOTARY
DEVOTE
DEVOTED
DEVOTEDLY
DEVOTEDNESS
DEVOTEE
DEVOTEEISM
DEVOTEMENT
DEVOTER
DEVOTING
DEVOTION
DEVOTIONAL
DEVOTIONALLY
DEVOTIONARY
DEVOTIONATE
DEVOTIONIST
DEVOTIONS
DEVOTO
DEVOUR
DEVOURED
DEVOURER
DEVOURING
DEVOURINGLY
DEVOUT
DEVOUTLY
DEVOUTNESS
DEVOVE
DEVOW
DEVULGARIZE
DEW
DEWA
DEWAN
DEWANEE
DEWANNY
DEWAR
DEWATA
DEWATER
DEWATERER
DEWAX
DEWBEAM
DEWBERRIES
DEWBERRY
DEWCAP
DEWCLAW
DEWCLAWED
DEWCUP
DEWDROP
DEWDROPPER
DEWER
DEWEYLITE
DEWFALL
DEWFLOWER
DEWIER
DEWIEST
DEWILY
DEWINESS
DEWLAP
DEWLAPPED
DEWOOL
DEWORM
DEWRET
DEWROT
DEWTRY
DEWY
DEXIOTROPE
DEXIOTROPIC
DEXIOTROPISM
DEXIOTROPOUS
DEXTER
DEXTERICAL
DEXTERITY
DEXTEROUS
DEXTEROUSLY
DEXTRAD
DEXTRAL
DEXTRALITY
DEXTRALLY
DEXTRAN
DEXTRANE
DEXTRAURAL
DEXTRIN
DEXTRINASE
DEXTRINATE
DEXTRINE
DEXTRINIZE
DEXTRINOUS
DEXTRO
DEXTROCARDIA
DEXTROCULAR
DEXTROGYRATE
DEXTROGYRE
DEXTRORSAL
DEXTRORSE
DEXTROSAZONE
DEXTROSE
DEXTROSURIA
DEXTROUS
DEXTROUSLY
DEXTROUSNESS
DEY
DEYHOUSE
DEYS
DEYWOMAN
DEZINC
DEZINCATION
DEZINCIFIED
DEZINCIFY
DEZINCIFYING
DEZINKIFY
DEZYMOTIZE
DGHAISA
DHA
DHABB
DHAI
DHAK
DHAL
DHAMAN
DHAMNOO
DHAN
DHANGAR
DHANUK
DHANUSH
DHAO
DHARANA
DHARANI
DHARMA
DHARMSALA
DHARNA
DHAURA
DHAURI
DHAVA
DHAW
DHER
DHERI
DHIKR
DHOBEE
DHOBEY
DHOBI
DHOBIE
DHOBIES
DHOBIS
DHOBY
DHOLE
DHOLES
DHOLL
DHONI
DHOON
DHOOTIE
DHOTEE
DHOTI
DHOTIS
DHOTY
DHOUL
DHOURRA
DHOW
DHU
DHURNA
DHURRA
DHURRIE
DHURRY
DHYAL
DHYANA
DI
DIA
DIABASE
DIABASIC
DIABETES
DIABETIC
DIABETICAL
DIABETOGENIC
DIABETOMETER
DIABLE
DIABLERIE
DIABLERY
DIABLO
DIABLOTIN
DIABOLARCH
DIABOLEPSY
DIABOLEPTIC
DIABOLIC
DIABOLICAL
DIABOLICALLY
DIABOLIFY
DIABOLISM
DIABOLIST
DIABOLIZE
DIABOLIZED
DIABOLIZING
DIABOLO
DIABOLOLOGY
DIABOLUS
DIABROSIS
DIABROTIC
DIACAUSTIC
DIACETATE
DIACETIC
DIACETURIA
DIACETYL
DIACETYLENE
DIACHORETIC
DIACHRONIC
DIACHYLON
DIACHYLUM
DIACID
DIACLASE
DIACLASIS
DIACLE
DIACLINAL
DIACODION
DIACODIUM
DIACOELE
DIACOELIA
DIACONAL
DIACONATE
DIACONIA
DIACONICON
DIACOPE
DIACRANTERIC
DIACRISIS
DIACRITIC
DIACRITICAL
DIACT
DIACTIN
DIACTINAL
DIACTINE
DIACTINIC
DIACTINISM
DIACULUM
DIAD
DIADELPHIAN
DIADELPHOUS
DIADEM
DIADERM
DIADERMIC
DIADOCHE
DIADOCHITE
DIADOUMENOS
DIADROME
DIADROMOUS
DIADUMENUS
DIAENE
DIAERESIS
DIAERETIC
DIAETETAE
DIAGENESIS
DIAGENETIC
DIAGEOTROPIC
DIAGLYPH
DIAGLYPHIC
DIAGLYPTIC
DIAGNOSE
DIAGNOSED
DIAGNOSES
DIAGNOSING
DIAGNOSIS
DIAGNOSTIC
DIAGNOSTICS
DIAGOMETER
DIAGONAL
DIAGONALITY
DIAGONALIZE
DIAGONALLY
DIAGONIC
DIAGRAM
DIAGRAMED
DIAGRAMING
DIAGRAMMATIC
DIAGRAMMED
DIAGRAMMETER
DIAGRAMMING
DIAGRAPH
DIAGRAPHIC
DIAGRAPHICAL
DIAGRAPHICS
DIAGREDIUM
DIAGRYDIUM
DIAKINESIS
DIAL
DIALCOHOL
DIALDEHYDE
DIALECT
DIALECTAL
DIALECTALIZE
DIALECTALLY
DIALECTIC
DIALECTICAL
DIALECTICALLY
DIALECTICIAN
DIALECTICISM
DIALECTICIZE
DIALECTICS
DIALECTOLOGY
DIALECTOR
DIALECTS
DIALED
DIALER
DIALIN
DIALING
DIALIST
DIALKYL
DIALKYLAMINE
DIALKYLIC
DIALLAGE

DIALLAGIC
DIALLAGITE
DIALLAGOID
DIALLED
DIALLEL
DIALLELA
DIALLELI
DIALLELON
DIALLELUS
DIALLER
DIALLING
DIALLIST
DIALOG
DIALOGER
DIALOGIC
DIALOGICAL
DIALOGICALLY
DIALOGISM
DIALOGIST
DIALOGISTIC
DIALOGITE
DIALOGIZE
DIALOGIZED
DIALOGIZING
DIALOGUE
DIALOGUED
DIALOGUER
DIALOGUING
DIALURIC
DIALYCARPOUS
DIALYSE
DIALYSES
DIALYSIS
DIALYSTELIC
DIALYTIC
DIALYTICALLY
DIALYZABLE
DIALYZATE
DIALYZATION
DIALYZATOR
DIALYZE
DIALYZED
DIALYZER
DIALYZING
DIAMAGNETIC
DIAMANTE
DIAMANTINE
DIAMANTOID
DIAMAT
DIAMB
DIAMBER
DIAMBIC
DIAMETER
DIAMETRAL
DIAMETRALLY
DIAMETRIC
DIAMETRICAL
DIAMICTON
DIAMIDE
DIAMIDO
DIAMIDOGEN
DIAMIN
DIAMINE
DIAMMONIUM
DIAMOND
DIAMONDBACK
DIAMONDED
DIAMONDING
DIAMONDIZE
DIAMONDIZED
DIAMONDIZING
DIAMONDS
DIAMORPHINE
DIAMYLOSE
DIAN
DIANDROUS
DIANITE
DIANODAL
DIANOETIC
DIANOETICAL
DIANOIA
DIANTRE
DIAPALMA
DIAPASE
DIAPASM
DIAPASON
DIAPASONAL
DIAPAUSE
DIAPEDESIS
DIAPEDETIC
DIAPENTE
DIAPER
DIAPERED
DIAPERING
DIAPERY
DIAPHANE
DIAPHANEITY
DIAPHANIE
DIAPHANOTYPE
DIAPHANOUS
DIAPHANOUSLY
DIAPHONE
DIAPHONIC
DIAPHONICAL
DIAPHONIES
DIAPHONY
DIAPHORESIS
DIAPHORETIC
DIAPHORITE
DIAPHOTE
DIAPHRAGM
DIAPHRAGMAL
DIAPHRAGMATIC
DIAPHRAGMED
DIAPHRAGMING
DIAPHTHERIN
DIAPHYSES
DIAPHYSIAL
DIAPHYSIS
DIAPIR
DIAPLASMA
DIAPLEXUS
DIAPNOIC
DIAPOPHYSES
DIAPOPHYSIS
DIAPOSITIVE
DIAPSID
DIAPSIDAN
DIAPYESIS
DIAPYETIC
DIARCH
DIARCHIAL
DIARCHIC
DIARCHIES
DIARCHY
DIARIAL
DIARIAN
DIARIST
DIARISTIC
DIARIZE
DIARRHEA
DIARRHEAL
DIARRHEIC
DIARRHETIC
DIARRHOEA
DIARRHOEAL
DIARRHOEIC
DIARRHOETIC
DIARSENIDE
DIARTHRODIAL
DIARTHROSIS
DIARTICULAR
DIARY
DIASCHISIS
DIASCHISMA
DIASCHISTIC
DIASCOPE
DIASCORD
DIASCORDIUM
DIASENE
DIASKEUASIS
DIASKEUAST
DIASPER
DIASPIDINE
DIASPIRIN
DIASPORE
DIASTALSES
DIASTALTIC
DIASTASE
DIASTASIC
DIASTASIS
DIASTATAXIC
DIASTATAXY
DIASTATIC
DIASTEM
DIASTEMA
DIASTEMATA
DIASTEMATIC
DIASTER
DIASTIMETER
DIASTOLE
DIASTOLIC
DIASTOMATIC
DIASTRAL
DIASTROPHE
DIASTROPHIC
DIASTROPHISM
DIASTYLE
DIASYNTHESIS
DIASYRM
DIATESSARON
DIATHERMACY
DIATHERMANCE
DIATHERMANCY
DIATHERMIA
DIATHERMIC
DIATHERMIES
DIATHERMY
DIATHESES
DIATHESIS
DIATHETIC
DIATOM
DIATOMACEAN
DIATOMACEOID
DIATOMACEOUS
DIATOMIC
DIATOMICITY
DIATOMIN
DIATOMINE
DIATOMITE
DIATOMOUS
DIATONIC
DIATONICAL
DIATONICALLY
DIATONICISM
DIATONOUS
DIATORIC
DIATREME
DIATRIBE
DIATROPIC
DIATROPISM
DIAULI
DIAULIC
DIAULOS
DIAVOLO
DIAXIAL
DIAXON
DIAXONE
DIAXONIC
DIAZENITHAL
DIAZEUTIC
DIAZEUXIS
DIAZID
DIAZIDE
DIAZIN
DIAZINE
DIAZO
DIAZOAMIN
DIAZOAMINE
DIAZOATE
DIAZOBENZENE
DIAZOIC
DIAZOIMIDE
DIAZOLE
DIAZOMA
DIAZOMETHANE
DIAZONIUM
DIAZOTATE
DIAZOTIC
DIAZOTIZE
DIAZOTIZED
DIAZOTIZING
DIAZOTYPE
DIB
DIBASE
DIBASIC
DIBASICITY
DIBATAG
DIBBED
DIBBER
DIBBING
DIBBLE
DIBBLED
DIBBLER
DIBBLING
DIBBUK
DIBENZOYL
DIBENZYL
DIBHOLE
DIBLASTULA
DIBRACH
DIBRANCH
DIBRANCHIATE
DIBROMID
DIBROMIDE
DIBS
DIBSTONE
DICACITY
DICAEOLOGY
DICARBONATE
DICARBOXYLIC
DICAST
DICASTERY
DICASTIC
DICATALECTIC
DICATALEXIS
DICE
DICEBOARD
DICEBOX
DICECUP
DICED
DICELLATE
DICEMAN
DICENTRIN
DICENTRINE
DICEPHALISM
DICEPHALOUS
DICEPHALUS
DICEPLAY
DICER
DICERION
DICEROUS
DICETYL
DICH
DICHAS
DICHASIA
DICHASIAL
DICHASIUM
DICHASTIC
DICHLONE
DICHLORAMIN
DICHLORAMINE
DICHLORIDE
DICHOCARPOUS
DICHOGAMIC
DICHOGAMOUS
DICHOGAMY
DICHONDRA
DICHOPTIC
DICHORD
DICHOREE
DICHOTIC
DICHOTOMAL
DICHOTOMIC
DICHOTOMIES
DICHOTOMIST
DICHOTOMIZE
DICHOTOMIZED
DICHOTOMOUS
DICHOTOMY
DICHROIC
DICHROISM
DICHROITE
DICHROITIC
DICHROMASIA
DICHROMASY
DICHROMAT
DICHROMATE
DICHROMATIC
DICHROMATISM
DICHROMIC
DICHROMISM
DICHRONOUS
DICHROOSCOPE
DICHROOUS
DICHROSCOPE
DICHROSCOPIC
DICHT
DICING
DICK
DICKCISSEL
DICKENS
DICKER
DICKERED
DICKERING
DICKEY
DICKEYBIRD
DICKEYS
DICKIES
DICKINSONITE
DICKTY
DICKY
DICKYBIRD
DICLINIC
DICLINISM
DICLINOUS
DICLINY
DICOCCOUS
DICODEINE
DICOELIOUS
DICOELOUS
DICOLIC
DICOLON
DICONDYLIAN
DICOPHANE
DICOT
DICOTYL
DICOTYLEDON
DICROTAL
DICROTIC
DICROTISM
DICROTOUS
DICT
DICTA
DICTAMEN

DICTAMINA
DICTAPHONE
DICTATE
DICTATED
DICTATING
DICTATINGLY
DICTATION
DICTATIONAL
DICTATIVE
DICTATOR
DICTATORIAL
DICTATORSHIP
DICTATORY
DICTATRESS
DICTATRIX
DICTATURE
DICTERY
DICTIC
DICTION
DICTIONARIES
DICTIONARY
DICTOGRAPH
DICTUM
DICTUMS
DICTY
DICTYNID
DICTYOGEN
DICTYOSOME
DICTYOSTELE
DICTYOSTELIC
DICTYOTIC
DICYANID
DICYANIDE
DICYANIN
DICYANINE
DICYCLE
DICYCLIC
DICYCLIST
DICYEMID
DID
DIDACTIC
DIDACTICAL
DIDACTICALLY
DIDACTICIAN
DIDACTICISM
DIDACTICITY
DIDACTICS
DIDACTIVE
DIDACTYL
DIDACTYLISM
DIDACTYLOUS
DIDAPPER
DIDASCALAR
DIDASCALIAE
DIDASCALIC
DIDASCALOS
DIDASCALY
DIDDER
DIDDERED
DIDDERING
DIDDEST
DIDDIES
DIDDLE
DIDDLED
DIDDLER
DIDDLING
DIDDY
DIDELPH
DIDELPHIAN
DIDELPHIC
DIDELPHID
DIDELPHINE
DIDELPHOUS
DIDEST
DIDIE
DIDINE
DIDLE
DIDLER
DIDNA
DIDRACHM
DIDRACHMA
DIDRACHMAL
DIDRACHMAS
DIDRIC
DIDROMIES
DIDROMY
DIDST
DIDUCE
DIDUCED
DIDUCING
DIDUCTION
DIDUCTOR
DIDY
DIDYM
DIDYMATE
DIDYMIA
DIDYMIUM
DIDYMOID
DIDYMOLITE
DIDYMOUS
DIDYMUS
DIDYNAMOUS
DIDYNAMY
DIE
DIEB
DIEBACK
DIECASE
DIECIOUS
DIECTASIS
DIED
DIEDRIC
DIEHARD
DIEING
DIELDRIN
DIELECTRIC
DIELECTRICAL
DIEM
DIEMAKING
DIENCEPHALIC
DIENCEPHALON
DIENE
DIENER
DIER
DIERESES
DIERESIS
DIERETIC
DIES
DIESEL
DIESELIZE
DIESES
DIESINKER
DIESINKING
DIESIS
DIESTOCK
DIESTRUM
DIESTRUS
DIET
DIETAL
DIETARIAN
DIETARIES
DIETARY
DIETER
DIETETIC
DIETETICAL
DIETETICALLY
DIETETICS
DIETETIST
DIETHER
DIETHYL
DIETHYLAMINE
DIETIC
DIETICAL
DIETICIAN
DIETICS
DIETINE
DIETING
DIETIST
DIETITIAN
DIETOTHERAPY
DIETOTOXIC
DIETRICHITE
DIETTED
DIETZEITE
DIEU
DIEUGARD
DIEWISE
DIEZEUGMENON
DIFERRION
DIFFA
DIFFAME
DIFFER
DIFFERED
DIFFERENCE
DIFFERENCED
DIFFERENCING
DIFFERENCY
DIFFERENT
DIFFERENTIA
DIFFERENTIAE
DIFFERENTIAL
DIFFERENTIATE
DIFFERENTIATION
DIFFERENTLY
DIFFERING
DIFFERINGLY
DIFFICILE
DIFFICULT
DIFFICULTIES
DIFFICULTY
DIFFIDATION
DIFFIDE
DIFFIDED
DIFFIDENCE
DIFFIDENT
DIFFIDENTLY
DIFFIDING
DIFFINITY
DIFFLUENCE
DIFFLUENT
DIFFORM
DIFFORME
DIFFORMED
DIFFORMITY
DIFFRACT
DIFFRACTED
DIFFRACTING
DIFFRACTION
DIFFRACTIVE
DIFFRANGIBLE
DIFFUGIENT
DIFFUND
DIFFUSATE
DIFFUSE
DIFFUSED
DIFFUSEDLY
DIFFUSEDNESS
DIFFUSELY
DIFFUSENESS
DIFFUSER
DIFFUSIBLE
DIFFUSIBLY
DIFFUSING
DIFFUSION
DIFFUSIONISM
DIFFUSIONIST
DIFFUSIVE
DIFFUSIVELY
DIFFUSIVITY
DIFFUSOR
DIG
DIGALLATE
DIGALLIC
DIGAMETIC
DIGAMIST
DIGAMMA
DIGAMMATE
DIGAMMATED
DIGAMOUS
DIGAMY
DIGASTRIC
DIGENESIS
DIGENETIC
DIGENITE
DIGENOUS
DIGENY
DIGERENT
DIGEST
DIGESTANT
DIGESTED
DIGESTEDLY
DIGESTEDNESS
DIGESTER
DIGESTIBLE
DIGESTIBLY
DIGESTING
DIGESTION
DIGESTIVE
DIGESTIVELY
DIGESTOR
DIGGED
DIGGER
DIGGING
DIGGINGS
DIGHT
DIGHTED
DIGHTER
DIGHTING
DIGIT
DIGITAL
DIGITALEIN
DIGITALIN
DIGITALIS
DIGITALISM
DIGITALIZE
DIGITALLY
DIGITATE
DIGITATED
DIGITATELY
DIGITATION
DIGITIFORM
DIGITIGRADE
DIGITIZE
DIGITIZED
DIGITIZER
DIGITIZING
DIGITOGENIN
DIGITONIN
DIGITORIUM
DIGITOXIN
DIGITOXOSE
DIGITULE
DIGITUS
DIGLADIATE
DIGLADIATED
DIGLADIATING
DIGLADIATION
DIGLADIATOR
DIGLOSSIA
DIGLOT
DIGLOTTIC
DIGLOTTISM
DIGLOTTIST
DIGLUCOSIDE
DIGLYPH
DIGLYPHIC
DIGMEAT
DIGNATION
DIGNE
DIGNIFIED
DIGNIFIEDLY
DIGNIFY
DIGNIFYING
DIGNITARIAL
DIGNITARIAN
DIGNITARIES
DIGNITARY
DIGNITAS
DIGNITIES
DIGNITY
DIGNOSCE
DIGONAL
DIGONEUTIC
DIGONEUTISM
DIGONOPOROUS
DIGONOUS
DIGOXIN
DIGRAM
DIGRAPH
DIGRAPHIC
DIGREDIENCY
DIGREDIENT
DIGRESS
DIGRESSED
DIGRESSING
DIGRESSION
DIGRESSIONAL
DIGRESSIVE
DIGRESSIVELY
DIGRESSORY
DIGS
DIGUE
DIHALID
DIHALIDE
DIHALO
DIHALOGEN
DIHEDRAL
DIHEDRON
DIHELIOS
DIHELIUM
DIHELY
DIHEXAGONAL
DIHEXAHEDRAL
DIHEXAHEDRON
DIHYBRID
DIHYBRIDISM
DIHYDRATE
DIHYDRATED
DIHYDRIC
DIHYDRIDE
DIHYDRITE
DIHYDROGEN
DIHYDROXY
DII
DIIAMB
DIIODID
DIIODIDE
DIIODO
DIIODOFORM
DIISATOGEN
DIJUDICATE
DIJUDICATION
DIK
DIKA
DIKAGE
DIKAMALI
DIKAMALLI
DIKARYON
DIKDIK
DIKE
DIKED
DIKEGRAVE
DIKELET
DIKER
DIKEREEVE
DIKERIA

DIKERION
DIKETENE
DIKETO
DIKETONE
DIKING
DIKKOP
DIKSHA
DIKTAT
DIKTYONITE
DILACERATE
DILACERATED
DILACERATING
DILACERATION
DILACTONE
DILAMBDODONT
DILAPIDATE
DILAPIDATED
DILAPIDATING
DILAPIDATION
DILAPIDATOR
DILATABILITY
DILATABLY
DILATANCY
DILATANT
DILATATE
DILATATION
DILATATIVE
DILATATOR
DILATE
DILATED
DILATEDLY
DILATEDNESS
DILATEMENT
DILATER
DILATING
DILATION
DILATIVE
DILATOMETER
DILATOMETRIC
DILATOMETRY
DILATOR
DILATORILY
DILATORINESS
DILATORY
DILDO
DILDOES
DILDOS
DILECTION
DILEMMA
DILEMMATIC
DILEMMIC
DILETANT
DILETTANIST
DILETTANTE
DILETTANTES
DILETTANTI
DILETTANTISH
DILETTANTISM
DILIGENCE
DILIGENT
DILIGENTIA
DILIGENTLY
DILIGENTNESS
DILIS
DILKER
DILL
DILLENIAD
DILLESK
DILLI
DILLIER
DILLIES
DILLIGROUT
DILLING
DILLIS
DILLISK
DILLSEED
DILLUE
DILLUER
DILLWEED
DILLY
DILLYDALLIED
DILLYDALLIER
DILLYDALLY
DILLYMAN
DILLYMEN
DILO
DILOGY
DILOS
DILUCID
DILUENDO
DILUENT
DILUTE
DILUTED
DILUTEDLY
DILUTEDNESS
DILUTEE
DILUTELY
DILUTENESS
DILUTENT
DILUTER
DILUTING
DILUTION
DILUTIVE
DILUVIA
DILUVIAL
DILUVIALIST
DILUVIAN
DILUVIANISM
DILUVIUM
DILUVIUMS
DILUVY
DILVE
DIM
DIMANGANION
DIMASTIGATE
DIMBER
DIMBLE
DIME
DIMEDON
DIMEDONE
DIMENSIBLE
DIMENSION
DIMENSIONAL
DIMENSIONED
DIMENSIONING
DIMENSIVE
DIMENSUM
DIMER
DIMERAN
DIMERCAPROL
DIMERCURION
DIMERIC
DIMERISM
DIMERIZATION
DIMEROUS
DIMES
DIMETALLIC
DIMETER
DIMETHOXY
DIMETHYL
DIMETRIA
DIMETRIC
DIMICATION
DIMIDIATE
DIMIDIATED
DIMIDIATING
DIMIDIATION
DIMINISH
DIMINISHED
DIMINISHER
DIMINISHING
DIMINISHMENT
DIMINUE
DIMINUENDO
DIMINUENDOED
DIMINUTAL
DIMINUTE
DIMINUTED
DIMINUTELY
DIMINUTING
DIMINUTION
DIMINUTIVAL
DIMINUTIVE
DIMINUTIVELY
DIMISS
DIMISSION
DIMISSORY
DIMIT
DIMITIES
DIMITTED
DIMITTING
DIMITY
DIMLY
DIMMED
DIMMER
DIMMERS
DIMMEST
DIMMET
DIMMING
DIMMISH
DIMMIT
DIMMY
DIMNESS
DIMOLECULAR
DIMORIC
DIMORPH
DIMORPHIC
DIMORPHISM
DIMORPHOUS
DIMPLE
DIMPLED
DIMPLEMENT
DIMPLIER
DIMPLIEST
DIMPLING
DIMPLY
DIMPS
DIMPSY
DIMWIT
DIMWITTED
DIMWITTEDLY
DIMYARIAN
DIN
DINAMODE
DINANDERIE
DINAPHTHYL
DINAR
DINDER
DINDLE
DINDLED
DINDLING
DINE
DINED
DINER
DINERGATE
DINERIC
DINERO
DINEROS
DINES
DINETTE
DINEURIC
DINEUTRON
DING
DINGAR
DINGBAT
DINGDONG
DINGE
DINGED
DINGEING
DINGER
DINGEY
DINGEYS
DINGHIES
DINGHY
DINGIER
DINGIES
DINGIEST
DINGILY
DINGINESS
DINGLE
DINGLEBERRY
DINGLED
DINGLEDANGLE
DINGLING
DINGLY
DINGMAN
DINGMAUL
DINGO
DINGOES
DINGTHRIFT
DINGUS
DINGWALL
DINGY
DINHEIRO
DINIC
DINICAL
DINING
DINITRATE
DINK
DINKED
DINKEY
DINKEYS
DINKIER
DINKIES
DINKIEST
DINKING
DINKUM
DINKY
DINMAN
DINMONT
DINNA
DINNED
DINNER
DINNERLY
DINNERTIME
DINNERWARE
DINNERY
DINNING
DINOCERAS
DINOMIC
DINOS
DINOSAUR
DINOSAURIAN
DINOTHERE
DINSOME
DINT
DINTED
DINTING
DINUS
DIOBELY
DIOBOL
DIOBOLON
DIOCESAN
DIOCESE
DIOCOEL
DIOCTAHEDRAL
DIODE
DIODONT
DIOECIAN
DIOECIOUS
DIOECIOUSLY
DIOECISM
DIOESTROUS
DIOESTRUM
DIOESTRUS
DIOGENITE
DIOICOUS
DIOL
DIOLEFIN
DIOLEFINE
DIOLEFINIC
DIOMATE
DIONISE
DIONYM
DIONYMAL
DIOPSIDE
DIOPTASE
DIOPTER
DIOPTOGRAPH
DIOPTOMETER
DIOPTOMETRY
DIOPTRA
DIOPTRAL
DIOPTRATE
DIOPTRE
DIOPTRIC
DIOPTRICAL
DIOPTRICALLY
DIOPTRICS
DIOPTROSCOPY
DIOPTRY
DIORAMA
DIORAMIC
DIORDINAL
DIORITE
DIORITIC
DIORTHOSIS
DIORTHOTIC
DIOSCOREIN
DIOSCORINE
DIOSE
DIOSMIN
DIOSMOSE
DIOSPHENOL
DIOTA
DIOTIC
DIOVULAR
DIOXAN
DIOXANE
DIOXIDE
DIOXIME
DIOXY
DIP
DIPARTITE
DIPARTITION
DIPASCHAL
DIPCOAT
DIPENTENE
DIPENTINE
DIPETALOUS
DIPHASE
DIPHASER
DIPHASIC
DIPHEAD
DIPHENAN
DIPHENOL
DIPHENYL
DIPHENYLENE
DIPHOSGENE
DIPHOSPHATE
DIPHOSPHID
DIPHOSPHIDE
DIPHOSPHORIC
DIPHRELATIC
DIPHTHERIA
DIPHTHERIAL
DIPHTHERIAN
DIPHTHERIC
DIPHTHERITIC
DIPHTHERITIS
DIPHTHEROID
DIPHTHONG
DIPHTHONGAL
DIPHTHONGED
DIPHTHONGIC

DIPHTHONGING
DIPHTHONGIZE
DIPHTHONGIZED
DIPHYCERCAL
DIPHYCERCY
DIPHYGENIC
DIPHYLETIC
DIPHYLLOUS
DIPHYODONT
DIPHYOZOOID
DIPLACUSIS
DIPLANETIC
DIPLANETISM
DIPLANTIDIAN
DIPLARTHRISM
DIPLARTHROUS
DIPLASIASMUS
DIPLASIC
DIPLASION
DIPLEGIA
DIPLEURA
DIPLEURAL
DIPLEURIC
DIPLEX
DIPLEXER
DIPLOBLASTIC
DIPLOCARDIA
DIPLOCARDIAC
DIPLOCEPHALY
DIPLOCOCCAL
DIPLOCOCCI
DIPLOCOCCIC
DIPLOCOCCUS
DIPLOCONICAL
DIPLOCORIA
DIPLODOCUS
DIPLOE
DIPLOETIC
DIPLOGENESIS
DIPLOGENETIC
DIPLOGENIC
DIPLOGRAPH
DIPLOGRAPHY
DIPLOHEDRAL
DIPLOHEDRON
DIPLOIC
DIPLOID
DIPLOIDIC
DIPLOIDION
DIPLOIDIZE
DIPLOIDY
DIPLOIS
DIPLOKARYON
DIPLOMA
DIPLOMACIES
DIPLOMACY
DIPLOMAED
DIPLOMAING
DIPLOMAT
DIPLOMATE
DIPLOMATIC
DIPLOMATICAL
DIPLOMATICS
DIPLOMATISM
DIPLOMATIST
DIPLOMATIZE
DIPLOMATIZED
DIPLOMYELIA
DIPLONEMA
DIPLONEURAL
DIPLONT
DIPLOPHASE
DIPLOPHYTE
DIPLOPIA
DIPLOPIAS
DIPLOPIC
DIPLOPLACULA
DIPLOPOD
DIPLOPODIC
DIPLOPODOUS
DIPLOSIS
DIPLOSOME
DIPLOSPHENAL
DIPLOTEGIA
DIPLOTENE
DIPLUMBIC
DIPMETER
DIPNEUST
DIPNOAN
DIPNOID
DIPNOOUS
DIPODE
DIPODIC
DIPODID
DIPODIES
DIPODY
DIPOLAR
DIPOLARIZE
DIPOLE
DIPOLSPHENE
DIPORPA
DIPPED
DIPPER
DIPPIER
DIPPIEST
DIPPING
DIPPY
DIPRIMARY
DIPRISMATIC
DIPROPYL
DIPSADES
DIPSAS
DIPSETIC
DIPSEY
DIPSIE
DIPSO
DIPSOMANIA
DIPSOMANIAC
DIPSOSIS
DIPSTICK
DIPSY
DIPT
DIPTER
DIPTERAL
DIPTERAN
DIPTERIST
DIPTEROCARP
DIPTEROLOGY
DIPTERON
DIPTEROS
DIPTEROUS
DIPTOTE
DIPTYCA
DIPTYCH
DIPTYCHON
DIPWARE
DIPYGI
DIPYGUS
DIPYLON
DIPYRE
DIPYRENOUS
DIRD
DIRDUM
DIRE
DIRECT
DIRECTABLE
DIRECTED
DIRECTER
DIRECTING
DIRECTION
DIRECTIONAL
DIRECTIONS
DIRECTITUDE
DIRECTIVE
DIRECTIVELY
DIRECTIVITY
DIRECTLY
DIRECTNESS
DIRECTOR
DIRECTORAL
DIRECTORATE
DIRECTORIAL
DIRECTORIES
DIRECTORSHIP
DIRECTORY
DIRECTRESS
DIRECTRICES
DIRECTRIX
DIRECTRIXES
DIREFUL
DIREFULLY
DIREFULNESS
DIRELY
DIREMPT
DIREMPTION
DIRENESS
DIREPTION
DIRER
DIREST
DIRGE
DIRGED
DIRGEFUL
DIRGELIKE
DIRGEMAN
DIRGIE
DIRGING
DIRGLER
DIRGY
DIRHAM
DIRHEM
DIRIGENT
DIRIGIBILITY
DIRIGIBLE
DIRIGO
DIRIGOMOTOR
DIRIMENT
DIRK
DIRKED
DIRKING
DIRL
DIRNDL
DIRT
DIRTBIRD
DIRTBOARD
DIRTEN
DIRTIED
DIRTIER
DIRTIEST
DIRTILY
DIRTINESS
DIRTPLATE
DIRTY
DIRTYING
DIS
DISABILITIES
DISABILITY
DISABLE
DISABLED
DISABLEMENT
DISABLENESS
DISABLING
DISABUSAL
DISABUSE
DISABUSED
DISABUSING
DISACCHARID
DISACCHARIDE
DISACCORD
DISACCORDANT
DISACCUSTOM
DISACCUSTOMED
DISACIDIFIED
DISACIDIFY
DISACKNOWLEDGE
DISACQUAINT
DISADJUST
DISADVANCE
DISADVANCED
DISADVANCING
DISADVANTAGE
DISADVANTAGEOUS
DISADVENTURE
DISADVISE
DISADVISED
DISADVISING
DISAFFECT
DISAFFECTED
DISAFFECTING
DISAFFECTION
DISAFFILIATE
DISAFFIRM
DISAFFOREST
DISAGIO
DISAGREE
DISAGREEABLE
DISAGREEABLENESS
DISAGREEABLY
DISAGREED
DISAGREEING
DISAGREEMENT
DISAGREER
DISALIGN
DISALIGNED
DISALIGNING
DISALIGNMENT
DISALLIEGE
DISALLOW
DISALLOWABLE
DISALLOWANCE
DISALLOWED
DISALLOWING
DISALLY
DISANCHOR
DISANIMATE
DISANIMATED
DISANIMATING
DISANIMATION
DISANNEX
DISANNUL
DISANNULLER
DISANOINT
DISAPPAREL
DISAPPEAR
DISAPPEARANCE
DISAPPEARED
DISAPPEARER
DISAPPEARING
DISAPPOINT
DISAPPOINTED
DISAPPOINTER
DISAPPOINTING
DISAPPOINTMENT
DISAPPROBATION
DISAPPROVAL
DISAPPROVE
DISAPPROVED
DISAPPROVER
DISAPPROVING
DISAPPROVINGLY
DISARD
DISARM
DISARMAMENT
DISARMATURE
DISARMED
DISARMER
DISARMING
DISARMINGLY
DISARRANGE
DISARRANGED
DISARRANGEMENT
DISARRANGING
DISARRAY
DISARRAYED
DISASINIZE
DISASSEMBLE
DISASSEMBLED
DISASSEMBLY
DISASSENT
DISASSIDUITY
DISASSOCIATE
DISASTER
DISASTERLY
DISASTROUS
DISASTROUSLY
DISATTAINT
DISATTIRE
DISAVAIL
DISAVOUCH
DISAVOW
DISAVOWAL
DISAVOWANCE
DISAVOWER
DISAVOWMENT
DISAWA
DISBALANCE
DISBAND
DISBANDED
DISBANDING
DISBANDMENT
DISBAR
DISBARK
DISBARMENT
DISBARRED
DISBARRING
DISBASE
DISBECOME
DISBELIEF
DISBELIEVE
DISBELIEVED
DISBELIEVER
DISBELIEVING
DISBENCH
DISBENCHED
DISBENCHING
DISBEND
DISBLAME
DISBOARD
DISBODIED
DISBODY
DISBOSOM
DISBOWEL
DISBRANCH
DISBRANCHED
DISBRANCHING
DISBUD
DISBUDDED
DISBUDDER
DISBUDDING
DISBURDEN
DISBURDENED
DISBURDENING
DISBURSABLE
DISBURSE
DISBURSED
DISBURSEMENT
DISBURSER
DISBURSING
DISBURTHEN
DISBURY
DISBUTTON
DISC
DISCAL
DISCALCEATE
DISCALCED
DISCAMP

DISCANDY
DISCANONIZE
DISCANONIZED
DISCANT
DISCARD
DISCARDED
DISCARDER
DISCARDING
DISCARNATE
DISCARNATION
DISCASE
DISCEDE
DISCEPT
DISCEPTATION
DISCEPTATOR
DISCERN
DISCERNED
DISCERNER
DISCERNIBLE
DISCERNIBLY
DISCERNING
DISCERNINGLY
DISCERNMENT
DISCERP
DISCERPED
DISCERPING
DISCERPTIBLE
DISCERPTION
DISCHARGE
DISCHARGED
DISCHARGER
DISCHARGING
DISCHARM
DISCHASE
DISCHURCH
DISCI
DISCIDE
DISCIFLORAL
DISCIFLOROUS
DISCINCT
DISCIND
DISCIPLE
DISCIPLED
DISCIPLESHIP
DISCIPLINAL
DISCIPLINANT
DISCIPLINARIAN
DISCIPLINARY
DISCIPLINE
DISCIPLINED
DISCIPLINER
DISCIPLING
DISCIPLINING
DISCIPULAR
DISCISSION
DISCITIS
DISCLAIM
DISCLAIMANT
DISCLAIMED
DISCLAIMER
DISCLAIMING
DISCLAMATION
DISCLAMATORY
DISCLOISTER
DISCLOSE
DISCLOSED
DISCLOSER
DISCLOSING
DISCLOSIVE
DISCLOSURE
DISCLOUD
DISCOAST
DISCOBLASTIC
DISCOBOLOS
DISCOBOLUS
DISCODACTYL
DISCOGRAPHY
DISCOID
DISCOIDAL
DISCOLICHEN
DISCOLITH
DISCOLOR
DISCOLORATE
DISCOLORATED
DISCOLORATION
DISCOLORED
DISCOLORING
DISCOLORMENT
DISCOLOUR
DISCOLOURED
DISCOLOURING
DISCOMEDUSAN
DISCOMFIT
DISCOMFITER
DISCOMFITURE
DISCOMFORT
DISCOMFORTED
DISCOMMEND
DISCOMMENDER
DISCOMMODE
DISCOMMODED
DISCOMMODING
DISCOMMODITY
DISCOMMON
DISCOMMONED
DISCOMMONING
DISCOMMUNITY
DISCOMORULA
DISCOMPOSE
DISCOMPOSED
DISCOMPOSING
DISCOMPOSURE
DISCOMPT
DISCOMYCETE
DISCONCERT
DISCONCERTED
DISCONGRUITY
DISCONNECT
DISCONNECTED
DISCONNECTER
DISCONNECTOR
DISCONSIDER
DISCONSOLATE
DISCONTENT
DISCONTENTED
DISCONTINUANCE
DISCONTINUE
DISCONTINUED
DISCONTINUEE
DISCONTINUER
DISCONTINUITY
DISCONTINUOR
DISCONTINUOUS
DISCONULA
DISCOPHILE
DISCOPHOROUS
DISCOPLASM
DISCOPODOUS
DISCORD
DISCORDANCE
DISCORDANCY
DISCORDANT
DISCORDANTLY
DISCORDER
DISCORDING
DISCORPORATE
DISCOTHEQUE
DISCOUNT
DISCOUNTABLE
DISCOUNTED
DISCOUNTER
DISCOUNTING
DISCOURAGE
DISCOURAGED
DISCOURAGEMENT
DISCOURAGER
DISCOURAGING
DISCOURSE
DISCOURSED
DISCOURSER
DISCOURSING
DISCOURSIVE
DISCOURTEOUS
DISCOURTEOUSLY
DISCOURTESY
DISCOUS
DISCOVER
DISCOVERABLE
DISCOVERED
DISCOVERER
DISCOVERIES
DISCOVERING
DISCOVERT
DISCOVERTURE
DISCOVERY
DISCREATE
DISCREATION
DISCREDIT
DISCREDITABLE
DISCREDITED
DISCREDITING
DISCREET
DISCREETER
DISCREETEST
DISCREETLY
DISCREETNESS
DISCREPANCE
DISCREPANCY
DISCREPANT
DISCREPANTLY
DISCREPATE
DISCREPATED
DISCREPATING
DISCRETE
DISCRETELY
DISCRETENESS
DISCRETION
DISCRETIONAL
DISCRETIVE
DISCRIMINAL
DISCRIMINANT
DISCRIMINATE
DISCRIMINATED
DISCRIMINATING
DISCRIMINATINGLY
DISCRIMINATION
DISCROWN
DISCULPATE
DISCULPATION
DISCULPATORY
DISCUMB
DISCUMBER
DISCURE
DISCUREN
DISCURRE
DISCURSATIVE
DISCURSIFY
DISCURSION
DISCURSIVE
DISCURSIVELY
DISCURSORY
DISCURSUS
DISCURTAIN
DISCUS
DISCUSES
DISCUSS
DISCUSSANT
DISCUSSED
DISCUSSER
DISCUSSIBLE
DISCUSSING
DISCUSSION
DISCUSSIONAL
DISCUSSIVE
DISCUTABLE
DISCUTE
DISDAIN
DISDAINED
DISDAINER
DISDAINFUL
DISDAINFULLY
DISDAINING
DISDAINLY
DISDAINOUS
DISDAR
DISDECEIVE
DISDIACLAST
DISDIAPASON
DISDIAZO
DISEASE
DISEASED
DISEASEDLY
DISEASEDNESS
DISEASEFUL
DISEASES
DISEASING
DISEASY
DISECONDARY
DISEDGE
DISEDIFY
DISELENID
DISELENIDE
DISEMATISM
DISEMBARK
DISEMBARKED
DISEMBARKING
DISEMBARRASS
DISEMBODIED
DISEMBODIMENT
DISEMBODY
DISEMBODYING
DISEMBOGUE
DISEMBOGUED
DISEMBOGUING
DISEMBOSOM
DISEMBOWEL
DISEMBOWELED
DISEMBURDEN
DISEME
DISEMIC
DISEMPLANE
DISEMPLANED
DISEMPLOY
DISENABLE
DISENABLED
DISENABLING
DISENACT
DISENCHANT
DISENCHANTED
DISENCHANTER
DISENCUMBER
DISENCUMBER
DISENDOW
DISENDOWER
DISENDOWMENT
DISENGAGE
DISENGAGED
DISENGAGING
DISENSOUL
DISENTAIL
DISENTANGLE
DISENTANGLED
DISENTANGLEMENT
DISENTANGLER
DISENTANGLING
DISENTHRALL
DISENTHRALLED
DISENTHRONE
DISENTHRONED
DISENTITLE
DISENTITLED
DISENTITLING
DISENTOMB
DISENTRACED
DISENTRAIN
DISENTRAINMENT
DISENTRANCE
DISENTWINE
DISENTWINED
DISEPALOUS
DISEQUALIZE
DISERT
DISESTABLISH
DISESTEEM
DISESTEEMED
DISESTEEMER
DISESTEEMING
DISEUR
DISEUSE
DISFAITH
DISFAME
DISFASHION
DISFAVOR
DISFAVORED
DISFAVORER
DISFAVORING
DISFAVOUR
DISFAVOURED
DISFAVOURER
DISFAVOURING
DISFEATURE
DISFEATURED
DISFEATURING
DISFEN
DISFIGURE
DISFIGURED
DISFIGUREMENT
DISFIGURER
DISFIGURING
DISFLESH
DISFOREST
DISFORM
DISFRANCHISE
DISFROCK
DISFURNISH
DISFURNISHED
DISFURNITURE
DISGAGE
DISGARNISH
DISGAVEL
DISGAVELED
DISGAVELING
DISGAVELLED
DISGAVELLING
DISGENERIC
DISGENIC
DISGLORY
DISGOOD
DISGORGE
DISGORGED
DISGORGER
DISGORGING
DISGOSPELIZE
DISGOWN
DISGRACE
DISGRACED
DISGRACEFUL
DISGRACER
DISGRACING
DISGRACIOUS
DISGRADE
DISGRADED
DISGRADING
DISGREGATE
DISGREGATION

DISGRESS
DISGRUNTLE
DISGRUNTLED
DISGRUNTLING
DISGUISAL
DISGUISE
DISGUISED
DISGUISEDLY
DISGUISER
DISGUISING
DISGULF
DISGUST
DISGUSTED
DISGUSTEDLY
DISGUSTER
DISGUSTFUL
DISGUSTFULLY
DISGUSTING
DISGUSTINGLY
DISH
DISHABILLE
DISHABIT
DISHABITUATE
DISHALLOW
DISHARMONIC
DISHARMONIES
DISHARMONIZE
DISHARMONY
DISHBOARD
DISHCLOTH
DISHCLOUT
DISHEART
DISHEARTEN
DISHEARTENED
DISHEARTENER
DISHEARTENING
DISHEATHING
DISHED
DISHEIR
DISHELM
DISHER
DISHERENT
DISHERISON
DISHERIT
DISHERITMENT
DISHES
DISHEVEL
DISHEVELED
DISHEVELING
DISHEVELLED
DISHEVELLING
DISHFUL
DISHING
DISHLIKE
DISHMAKER
DISHMAKING
DISHMONGER
DISHMOP
DISHONEST
DISHONESTIES
DISHONESTLY
DISHONESTY
DISHONOR
DISHONORABLE
DISHONORARY
DISHONORED
DISHONORER
DISHONORING
DISHONOUR
DISHONOURARY
DISHONOURED
DISHONOURER
DISHONOURING
DISHORSE
DISHPAN
DISHRAG
DISHTOWEL
DISHUMOR
DISHWASH
DISHWASHER
DISHWASHINGS
DISHWATER
DISHWATERY
DISHWIPER
DISIDENTIFY
DISILICID
DISILICIDE
DISILLUDE
DISILLUDED
DISILLUSION
DISILLUSIVE
DISIMAGINE
DISIMITATE
DISIMITATION
DISIMPRISON
DISINCLINATION
DISINCLINE
DISINCLINED
DISINCLINING
DISINFECT
DISINFECTANT
DISINFECTED
DISINFECTING
DISINFECTION
DISINFECTIVE
DISINFECTOR
DISINFEST
DISINFLATION
DISINGENUITY
DISINGENUOUS
DISINHERISON
DISINHERIT
DISINHUME
DISINTEGRANT
DISINTEGRATE
DISINTEGRATING
DISINTEGRATION
DISINTEGROUS
DISINTER
DISINTEREST
DISINTERESTED
DISINTERMENT
DISINTERRED
DISINTERRING
DISINTRENCH
DISINVEST
DISINVITE
DISINVOLVE
DISJASKED
DISJASKIT
DISJECT
DISJECTED
DISJECTING
DISJECTION
DISJEUNE
DISJOIN
DISJOINED
DISJOINING
DISJOINT
DISJOINTED
DISJOINTEDLY
DISJOINTING
DISJOINTLY
DISJOINTURE
DISJUNCT
DISJUNCTION
DISJUNCTIVE
DISJUNCTIVELY
DISJUNCTOR
DISJUNCTURE
DISJUNE
DISK
DISKELION
DISKER
DISKERY
DISKLESS
DISKLIKE
DISKOS
DISKS
DISLEAF
DISLEAFED
DISLEAFING
DISLEAL
DISLEAVE
DISLEAVED
DISLEAVING
DISLEVELMENT
DISLIKABLE
DISLIKE
DISLIKED
DISLIKEFUL
DISLIKEN
DISLIKER
DISLIKING
DISLIMB
DISLIMN
DISLINK
DISLOAD
DISLOCATE
DISLOCATED
DISLOCATING
DISLOCATION
DISLOCATOR
DISLOCATORY
DISLOCK
DISLODGE
DISLODGED
DISLODGEMENT
DISLODGING
DISLODGMENT
DISLOYAL
DISLOYALIST
DISLOYALLY
DISLOYALTIES
DISLOYALTY
DISLUSTER
DISLUSTERED
DISLUSTERING
DISLUSTRE
DISLUSTRED
DISLUSTRING
DISMAIL
DISMAIN
DISMAL
DISMALITIES
DISMALITY
DISMALLY
DISMALNESS
DISMALS
DISMANTLE
DISMANTLED
DISMANTLER
DISMANTLING
DISMARBLE
DISMARCH
DISMARK
DISMARKET
DISMARKETED
DISMARKETING
DISMASK
DISMAST
DISMASTED
DISMASTING
DISMAY
DISMAYED
DISMAYEDNESS
DISMAYFUL
DISMAYFULLY
DISMAYING
DISME
DISMEMBER
DISMEMBERED
DISMEMBERER
DISMEMBERING
DISMEMBRATE
DISMEMBRATED
DISMEMBRATOR
DISMISS
DISMISSAL
DISMISSED
DISMISSIBLE
DISMISSING
DISMISSION
DISMISSIVE
DISMIT
DISMODED
DISMOUNT
DISMOUNTABLE
DISMUTATION
DISNA
DISNATURE
DISNATURED
DISNATURING
DISOBEDIENCE
DISOBEDIENT
DISOBEY
DISOBEYAL
DISOBEYED
DISOBEYER
DISOBEYING
DISOBLIGE
DISOBLIGED
DISOBLIGER
DISOBLIGING
DISOCCUPIED
DISOCCUPY
DISOCCUPYING
DISOMATIC
DISOMATOUS
DISOMATY
DISOMUS
DISORB
DISORDER
DISORDERED
DISORDEREDLY
DISORDERING
DISORDERLY
DISORDERS
DISORDINATE
DISORDINATED
DISORGANIC
DISORGANIZE
DISORGANIZED
DISORGANIZER
DISORIENT
DISORIENTATE
DISOUR
DISOWN
DISOXYGENATE
DISPACE
DISPAIR
DISPAND
DISPAR
DISPARAGE
DISPARAGED
DISPARAGEMENT
DISPARAGER
DISPARAGING
DISPARATE
DISPARATELY
DISPARATION
DISPARATUM
DISPARISH
DISPARITIES
DISPARITY
DISPARK
DISPARPLE
DISPARPLED
DISPARPLING
DISPART
DISPARTMENT
DISPASSION
DISPASSIONATE
DISPASSIONED
DISPATCH
DISPATCHED
DISPATCHER
DISPATCHFUL
DISPATCHING
DISPATRIATED
DISPAUPER
DISPAUPERIZE
DISPEACE
DISPEACEFUL
DISPEED
DISPEL
DISPELLED
DISPELLER
DISPELLING
DISPEND
DISPENDER
DISPENDIOUS
DISPENDITURE
DISPENSABLE
DISPENSARIES
DISPENSARY
DISPENSATE
DISPENSATED
DISPENSATING
DISPENSATION
DISPENSATIVE
DISPENSATOR
DISPENSATORY
DISPENSATRIX
DISPENSE
DISPENSED
DISPENSER
DISPENSING
DISPEOPLE
DISPEOPLED
DISPEOPLER
DISPEOPLING
DISPERATO
DISPERGATE
DISPERGATED
DISPERGATING
DISPERGATION
DISPERGATOR
DISPERMIC
DISPERMOUS
DISPERSAL
DISPERSE
DISPERSED
DISPERSEDLY
DISPERSER
DISPERSIBLE
DISPERSING
DISPERSION
DISPERSITY
DISPERSIVE
DISPERSIVELY
DISPERSOID
DISPHENOID
DISPIECE
DISPIREM
DISPIREME
DISPIRIT
DISPIRITED
DISPIRITEDLY
DISPIRITING
DISPITEOUS
DISPITEOUSLY
DISPLACE
DISPLACED
DISPLACEMENT

DISPLACENCY
DISPLACER
DISPLACING
DISPLANT
DISPLAY
DISPLAYED
DISPLAYER
DISPLAYING
DISPLAYS
DISPLE
DISPLEASE
DISPLEASED
DISPLEASER
DISPLEASING
DISPLEASURE
DISPLENISH
DISPLICENCY
DISPLODE
DISPLODED
DISPLODING
DISPLUME
DISPLUMED
DISPLUMING
DISPLUVIATE
DISPOINT
DISPONDAIC
DISPONDEE
DISPONE
DISPONENT
DISPOROUS
DISPORT
DISPORTIVE
DISPORTMENT
DISPOSABLE
DISPOSAL
DISPOSE
DISPOSED
DISPOSEDLY
DISPOSEDNESS
DISPOSER
DISPOSING
DISPOSITION
DISPOSITIVE
DISPOSSESS
DISPOSSESSED
DISPOSSESSOR
DISPOST
DISPOSURE
DISPRAISE
DISPRAISED
DISPRAISER
DISPRAISING
DISPREAD
DISPREADER
DISPREADING
DISPREPARE
DISPRIVACIED
DISPRIZE
DISPRIZED
DISPRIZING
DISPROBATIVE
DISPROFIT
DISPROOF
DISPROPORTIONATE
DISPROVABLE
DISPROVAL
DISPROVE
DISPROVED
DISPROVEMENT
DISPROVEN
DISPROVER
DISPROVING
DISPUNCT
DISPUNGE
DISPUTABLE
DISPUTABLY
DISPUTANT
DISPUTATION
DISPUTATIOUS
DISPUTATIVE
DISPUTATOR
DISPUTE
DISPUTED
DISPUTER
DISPUTING
DISQUALIFIED
DISQUALIFY
DISQUIET
DISQUIETED
DISQUIETEDLY
DISQUIETER
DISQUIETING
DISQUIETLY
DISQUIETUDE
DISQUIPARANT
DISQUISIT
DISQUISITE
DISQUISITED
DISQUISITING
DISQUISITION
DISQUISITIVE
DISQUISITOR
DISQUISITORY
DISQUIXOTE
DISRANK
DISRATE
DISRATED
DISRATING
DISRAY
DISREALIZE
DISREGARD
DISREGARDED
DISREGARDER
DISREGARDFUL
DISREGARDING
DISRELATED
DISRELATION
DISRELISH
DISREMEMBER
DISREPAIR
DISREPUTABLE
DISREPUTABLENESS
DISREPUTABLY
DISREPUTE
DISRESPECT
DISRESPECTFUL
DISREST
DISROBE
DISROBED
DISROBEMENT
DISROBER
DISROBING
DISROOF
DISROOT
DISRUMP
DISRUPT
DISRUPTED
DISRUPTER
DISRUPTION
DISRUPTIVE
DISRUPTIVELY
DISRUPTMENT
DISRUPTOR
DISRUPTURE
DISS
DISSAIT
DISSATISFACTION
DISSATISFIED
DISSATISFY
DISSATURATE
DISSAVA
DISSCEPTER
DISSCEPTERED
DISSCEPTRE
DISSCEPTRED
DISSCEPTRING
DISSEAT
DISSECT
DISSECTED
DISSECTING
DISSECTION
DISSECTIONAL
DISSECTIVE
DISSECTOR
DISSEISE
DISSEISED
DISSEISEE
DISSEISIN
DISSEISOR
DISSEISORESS
DISSEIZE
DISSEIZED
DISSEIZEE
DISSEIZIN
DISSEIZING
DISSEIZOR
DISSEIZORESS
DISSEIZURE
DISSELBOOM
DISSEMBLANCE
DISSEMBLE
DISSEMBLED
DISSEMBLER
DISSEMBLIES
DISSEMBLING
DISSEMBLY
DISSEMINATE
DISSEMINATED
DISSEMINATOR
DISSEMINULE
DISSENSION
DISSENT
DISSENTED
DISSENTER
DISSENTIENCE
DISSENTIENT
DISSENTING
DISSENTINGLY
DISSENTIOUS
DISSENTIVE
DISSEPIMENT
DISSERT
DISSERTATE
DISSERTATED
DISSERTATING
DISSERTATION
DISSERTATIVE
DISSERTATOR
DISSERVE
DISSERVED
DISSERVICE
DISSERVING
DISSEVER
DISSEVERANCE
DISSEVERED
DISSEVERING
DISSHEATHE
DISSHEATHED
DISSIDENCE
DISSIDENT
DISSIDENTLY
DISSIGHT
DISSIGHTLY
DISSILIENCY
DISSILIENT
DISSIMILAR
DISSIMILARLY
DISSIMILARS
DISSIMILATE
DISSIMULATE
DISSIMULATED
DISSIMULATION
DISSIMULATOR
DISSIMULE
DISSIPABLE
DISSIPATE
DISSIPATED
DISSIPATEDLY
DISSIPATER
DISSIPATING
DISSIPATION
DISSIPATIVE
DISSIPATOR
DISSITE
DISSOCIABLE
DISSOCIABLY
DISSOCIAL
DISSOCIALITY
DISSOCIALIZE
DISSOCIANT
DISSOCIATE
DISSOCIATED
DISSOCIATING
DISSOCIATION
DISSOCIATIVE
DISSOCONCH
DISSOGENY
DISSOLUBLE
DISSOLUTE
DISSOLUTELY
DISSOLUTION
DISSOLUTIVE
DISSOLVABLE
DISSOLVE
DISSOLVED
DISSOLVENT
DISSOLVER
DISSOLVING
DISSONANCE
DISSONANCY
DISSONANT
DISSONANTLY
DISSONATE
DISSONOUS
DISSOUR
DISSPREAD
DISSUADE
DISSUADED
DISSUADER
DISSUADING
DISSUASION
DISSUASIVE
DISSUASIVELY
DISSUASORY
DISSUIT
DISSUITABLE
DISSUITED
DISSYLLABIC
DISSYLLABIFY
DISSYLLABISM
DISSYLLABIZE
DISSYLLABLE
DISSYMMETRIC
DISSYMMETRY
DISTAD
DISTAFF
DISTAFFS
DISTAIN
DISTAL
DISTALE
DISTALIA
DISTALLY
DISTANCE
DISTANCED
DISTANCING
DISTANCY
DISTANT
DISTANTLY
DISTANTNESS
DISTASTE
DISTASTED
DISTASTEFUL
DISTASTING
DISTAVES
DISTELFINK
DISTEMPER
DISTEMPERED
DISTEMPERING
DISTEND
DISTENDED
DISTENDER
DISTENDING
DISTENSIBLE
DISTENSION
DISTENSIVE
DISTENT
DISTENTION
DISTER
DISTHENE
DISTHRONE
DISTHRONED
DISTHRONING
DISTICH
DISTICHOUS
DISTICHOUSLY
DISTICHS
DISTIL
DISTILL
DISTILLABLE
DISTILLAGE
DISTILLATE
DISTILLATION
DISTILLATORY
DISTILLED
DISTILLER
DISTILLERY
DISTILLING
DISTILLMENT
DISTILMENT
DISTINCT
DISTINCTIFY
DISTINCTIO
DISTINCTION
DISTINCTIONAL
DISTINCTITY
DISTINCTIVE
DISTINCTIVENESS
DISTINCTLY
DISTINCTNESS
DISTINGUE
DISTINGUEE
DISTINGUISH
DISTINGUISHED
DISTINGUISHING
DISTOCLUSION
DISTOMATOUS
DISTOME
DISTOMIASIS
DISTORT
DISTORTED
DISTORTEDLY
DISTORTER
DISTORTING
DISTORTION
DISTORTIONAL
DISTORTIVE
DISTRACT
DISTRACTED
DISTRACTEDLY
DISTRACTER
DISTRACTIBLE
DISTRACTING
DISTRACTION
DISTRACTIVE
DISTRAIN

DISTRAINABLE
DISTRAINED
DISTRAINEE
DISTRAINER
DISTRAINING
DISTRAINMENT
DISTRAINOR
DISTRAINT
DISTRAIT
DISTRAITE
DISTRAUGHT
DISTRAUGHTED
DISTRESS
DISTRESSED
DISTRESSEDLY
DISTRESSFUL
DISTRESSING
DISTREST
DISTRIBUTARY
DISTRIBUTE
DISTRIBUTED
DISTRIBUTEE
DISTRIBUTER
DISTRIBUTING
DISTRIBUTION
DISTRIBUTIVE
DISTRIBUTIVELY
DISTRIBUTOR
DISTRICT
DISTRICTLY
DISTRICTS
DISTRINGAS
DISTRITO
DISTRITOS
DISTRUSS
DISTRUST
DISTRUSTED
DISTRUSTER
DISTRUSTFUL
DISTRUSTING
DISTURB
DISTURBANCE
DISTURBANT
DISTURBATIVE
DISTURBED
DISTURBER
DISTURBING
DISTURN
DISULFATE
DISULFID
DISULFIDE
DISULFOXID
DISULFOXIDE
DISULFURET
DISULPHATE
DISULPHID
DISULPHIDE
DISULPHONATE
DISULPHOXID
DISULPHOXIDE
DISULPHURET
DISUNIFORM
DISUNIFY
DISUNION
DISUNIONISM
DISUNIONIST
DISUNITE
DISUNITED
DISUNITER
DISUNITIES
DISUNITING
DISUNITY
DISUSAGE
DISUSE
DISUSED
DISUSING
DISUTILITY
DISVALUE
DISVALUED
DISVALUING
DISVELOP
DISVISAGE
DISVOUCH
DISWARREN
DISWARRENED
DISWARRENING
DISWASHING
DISWORSHIP
DISYLLABLE
DISYOKE
DISYOKED
DISYOKING
DIT
DITA
DITAL
DITALI
DITALINI
DITATION
DITCH
DITCHBANK
DITCHBUR
DITCHDIGGER
DITCHDOWN
DITCHED
DITCHER
DITCHING
DITCHSIDE
DITE
DITED
DITER
DITERTIARY
DITHECAL
DITHECOUS
DITHEISM
DITHEIST
DITHEISTIC
DITHEISTICAL
DITHER
DITHERED
DITHERING
DITHERY
DITHION
DITHIONATE
DITHIONIC
DITHYRAMB
DITHYRAMBIC
DITING
DITION
DITOKOUS
DITOLYL
DITONE
DITREMATOUS
DITREMID
DITRIGLYPH
DITRIGLYPHIC
DITRIGONAL
DITRIGONALLY
DITROCHEAN
DITROCHEE
DITROCHOUS
DITROITE
DITT
DITTAMY
DITTANDER
DITTANIES
DITTANY
DITTAY
DITTED
DITTIED
DITTIES
DITTING
DITTO
DITTOED
DITTOGRAM
DITTOGRAPH
DITTOGRAPHIC
DITTOGRAPHY
DITTOING
DITTOLOGIES
DITTOLOGY
DITTON
DITTOS
DITTY
DITTYING
DIURANATE
DIURESIS
DIURETIC
DIURETICAL
DIURETICALLY
DIURN
DIURNAL
DIURNALLY
DIURNALNESS
DIURNATION
DIURNE
DIURNULE
DIUTURNAL
DIUTURNITY
DIV
DIVA
DIVAGATE
DIVAGATED
DIVAGATING
DIVAGATION
DIVALENCE
DIVALENT
DIVAN
DIVARICATE
DIVARICATED
DIVARICATELY
DIVARICATING
DIVARICATION
DIVARICATOR
DIVAS
DIVATA
DIVE
DIVED
DIVEKEEPER
DIVEL
DIVELLED
DIVELLENT
DIVELLICATE
DIVELLING
DIVER
DIVERB
DIVERGE
DIVERGED
DIVERGENCE
DIVERGENCES
DIVERGENCIES
DIVERGENCY
DIVERGENT
DIVERGENTLY
DIVERGING
DIVERGINGLY
DIVERS
DIVERSE
DIVERSELY
DIVERSENESS
DIVERSIFIED
DIVERSIFIER
DIVERSIFORM
DIVERSIFY
DIVERSIFYING
DIVERSION
DIVERSIONAL
DIVERSIONARY
DIVERSITIES
DIVERSITY
DIVERSLY
DIVERSORY
DIVERT
DIVERTED
DIVERTEDLY
DIVERTER
DIVERTICLE
DIVERTICULAR
DIVERTICULUM
DIVERTIMENTO
DIVERTING
DIVERTINGLY
DIVERTISE
DIVERTISSANT
DIVERTIVE
DIVERTOR
DIVES
DIVEST
DIVESTED
DIVESTING
DIVESTITIVE
DIVESTITURE
DIVESTMENT
DIVESTURE
DIVI
DIVIDABLE
DIVIDANT
DIVIDE
DIVIDED
DIVIDEDLY
DIVIDEDNESS
DIVIDEND
DIVIDER
DIVIDERS
DIVIDING
DIVIDINGLY
DIVIDUAL
DIVIDUALLY
DIVIDUITY
DIVIDUOUS
DIVINAIL
DIVINATION
DIVINATOR
DIVINATORY
DIVINE
DIVINED
DIVINELY
DIVINENESS
DIVINER
DIVINERESS
DIVINESSE
DIVINEST
DIVING
DIVINIFIED
DIVINIFY
DIVINIFYING
DIVINING
DIVININGLY
DIVINISTRE
DIVINITIES
DIVINITY
DIVINIZATION
DIVINIZE
DIVINIZED
DIVINIZING
DIVINYL
DIVISA
DIVISI
DIVISIBILITY
DIVISIBLE
DIVISIBLENESS
DIVISIBLY
DIVISION
DIVISIONAL
DIVISIONALLY
DIVISIONARY
DIVISIONISM
DIVISIONIST
DIVISIVE
DIVISIVELY
DIVISIVENESS
DIVISOR
DIVISORIAL
DIVISORY
DIVISURAL
DIVORCE
DIVORCED
DIVORCEE
DIVORCEMENT
DIVORCER
DIVORCEUSE
DIVORCING
DIVORCIVE
DIVORT
DIVOT
DIVOTO
DIVULGATE
DIVULGATED
DIVULGATER
DIVULGATING
DIVULGATION
DIVULGATORY
DIVULGE
DIVULGED
DIVULGEMENT
DIVULGENCE
DIVULGER
DIVULGING
DIVULSE
DIVULSED
DIVULSING
DIVULSION
DIVULSIVE
DIVULSOR
DIVUS
DIVVIED
DIVVIES
DIVVY
DIVVYING
DIWAN
DIWANI
DIWATA
DIX
DIXAIN
DIXENITE
DIXI
DIXIE
DIXIT
DIXY
DIZAIN
DIZAINE
DIZDAR
DIZEN
DIZENED
DIZENING
DIZENMENT
DIZYGOTIC
DIZZARD
DIZZARDLY
DIZZEN
DIZZIED
DIZZIER
DIZZIEST
DIZZILY
DIZZINESS
DIZZY
DIZZYING
DJAGOONG
DJALMAITE
DJATI
DJEBEL
DJELFA
DJERIB
DJERSA
DJIBBAH
DJIN

DJINN
DJINNI
DJO
DO
DOAB
DOABLE
DOACH
DOARIUM
DOAT
DOATED
DOATER
DOATISH
DOATY
DOB
DOBBER
DOBBIE
DOBBIES
DOBBIN
DOBBY
DOBE
DOBIE
DOBLA
DOBLON
DOBLONES
DOBOS
DOBRA
DOBRAO
DOBRAS
DOBROES
DOBSON
DOBY
DOC
DOCENT
DOCENTSHIP
DOCETISM
DOCHMIAC
DOCHMIACAL
DOCHMIASIS
DOCHMII
DOCHMIUS
DOCHTER
DOCIBILITY
DOCIBLE
DOCIBLENESS
DOCILE
DOCILELY
DOCILITY
DOCIMASIES
DOCIMASTIC
DOCIMASTICAL
DOCIMASY
DOCIMOLOGY
DOCIOUS
DOCITY
DOCK
DOCKAGE
DOCKED
DOCKEN
DOCKER
DOCKET
DOCKHAND
DOCKHEAD
DOCKHOUSE
DOCKING
DOCKIZATION
DOCKIZE
DOCKMACKIE
DOCKMAN
DOCKMASTER
DOCKSIDE
DOCKYARD
DOCMAC
DOCOSANE
DOCTOR
DOCTORAL
DOCTORALLY
DOCTORATE
DOCTORBIRD
DOCTORED
DOCTORESS
DOCTORFISH
DOCTORIAL
DOCTORIALLY
DOCTORING
DOCTORIZE
DOCTORLY
DOCTORS
DOCTORSHIP
DOCTRESS
DOCTRINABLE
DOCTRINAIRE
DOCTRINAL
DOCTRINALISM
DOCTRINALIST
DOCTRINALITY
DOCTRINALLY
DOCTRINARIAN
DOCTRINARILY
DOCTRINARITY
DOCTRINARY
DOCTRINATE
DOCTRINE
DOCTRINES
DOCTRINISM
DOCTRINIST
DOCTRINIZE
DOCTRINIZED
DOCTRINIZING
DOCTUS
DOCUMENT
DOCUMENTAL
DOCUMENTARY
DOCUMENTIZE
DOD
DODA
DODAD
DODD
DODDARD
DODDART
DODDED
DODDER
DODDERED
DODDERER
DODDERING
DODDERY
DODDIE
DODDLE
DODDY
DODDYPOLL
DODECADE
DODECADRACHM
DODECAFID
DODECAGON
DODECAGONAL
DODECAHEDRA
DODECAHEDRAL
DODECAHEDRON
DODECAMEROUS
DODECANE
DODECANT
DODECAPHONIC
DODECARCH
DODECARCHY
DODECASEMIC
DODECASTYLE
DODECASTYLOS
DODECATEMORY
DODECATYL
DODECATYLIC
DODECUPLET
DODECYL
DODECYLENE
DODECYLIC
DODGASTED
DODGE
DODGED
DODGER
DODGERY
DODGILY
DODGINESS
DODGING
DODGY
DODKIN
DODLET
DODMAN
DODO
DODOES
DODOISM
DODOMA
DODOS
DODS
DODUNK
DOE
DOEBIRD
DOEGLING
DOELING
DOER
DOES
DOESKIN
DOEST
DOETH
DOFF
DOFFED
DOFFER
DOFFING
DOFTBERRY
DOFUNNY
DOG
DOGAL
DOGANA
DOGARESSA
DOGATE
DOGBANE
DOGBERRIES
DOGBERRY
DOGBITE
DOGBLOW
DOGBOAT
DOGBODY
DOGBOLT
DOGBUSH
DOGCART
DOGCATCHER
DOGDOM
DOGE
DOGEDOM
DOGELESS
DOGES
DOGESHIP
DOGFACE
DOGFALL
DOGFENNEL
DOGFIGHT
DOGFISH
DOGFISHES
DOGFOOT
DOGGED
DOGGEDLY
DOGGEDNESS
DOGGER
DOGGEREL
DOGGERELED
DOGGERELER
DOGGERELIZE
DOGGERELIZER
DOGGERELIZING
DOGGERELLED
DOGGERELLING
DOGGERIES
DOGGERY
DOGGESS
DOGGIE
DOGGIER
DOGGIES
DOGGIEST
DOGGING
DOGGISH
DOGGISHLY
DOGGISHNESS
DOGGLE
DOGGO
DOGGONE
DOGGONED
DOGGONING
DOGGREL
DOGGRELIZE
DOGGY
DOGHEAD
DOGHOLE
DOGHOUSE
DOGIE
DOGLEG
DOGLIKE
DOGLY
DOGMA
DOGMAN
DOGMAS
DOGMATA
DOGMATIC
DOGMATICAL
DOGMATICALLY
DOGMATICIAN
DOGMATICS
DOGMATISM
DOGMATIST
DOGMATIZE
DOGMATIZED
DOGMATIZER
DOGMATIZING
DOGMEAT
DOGMEN
DOGMOUTH
DOGPLATE
DOGS
DOGSHORE
DOGSKIN
DOGSLED
DOGSLEEP
DOGSTAIL
DOGSTONE
DOGTAIL
DOGTIE
DOGTOOTH
DOGTRICK
DOGTROT
DOGVANE
DOGWATCH
DOGWOOD
DOGY
DOH
DOHL
DOIGT
DOIGTE
DOILED
DOILIES
DOILY
DOINA
DOINE
DOING
DOINGS
DOIT
DOITED
DOITRIFIED
DOJO
DOKE
DOKHMA
DOL
DOLABRA
DOLABRATE
DOLABRIFORM
DOLCAN
DOLCE
DOLCIAN
DOLCINO
DOLCISSIMO
DOLD
DOLDRUM
DOLDRUMS
DOLE
DOLEANCE
DOLED
DOLEFISH
DOLEFUL
DOLEFULLY
DOLEFULNESS
DOLEFULS
DOLENT
DOLENTE
DOLENTISSIMO
DOLERITE
DOLERITIC
DOLESMAN
DOLESOME
DOLESS
DOLEY
DOLICHOBLOND
DOLICHURIC
DOLICHURUS
DOLINA
DOLINE
DOLING
DOLIOFORM
DOLISIE
DOLITE
DOLITTLE
DOLIUM
DOLL
DOLLAR
DOLLARBIRD
DOLLARDEE
DOLLARFISH
DOLLARFISHES
DOLLARLEAF
DOLLARS
DOLLBEER
DOLLEY
DOLLFACE
DOLLFISH
DOLLHOUSE
DOLLIE
DOLLIED
DOLLIER
DOLLIES
DOLLIN
DOLLINESS
DOLLISH
DOLLISHLY
DOLLISHNESS
DOLLMAKER
DOLLMAKING
DOLLOP
DOLLS
DOLLY
DOLLYING
DOLLYMAN
DOLLYWAY
DOLMAN
DOLMEN
DOLOMITE
DOLOMITIC
DOLOMITIZE
DOLOR
DOLORIFEROUS
DOLORIFIC
DOLORIFUGE

DOLORIMETRY
DOLOROSO
DOLOROUS
DOLOROUSLY
DOLOROUSNESS
DOLOS
DOLOSE
DOLOUR
DOLPHIN
DOLT
DOLTHEAD
DOLTISH
DOLTISHLY
DOLTISHNESS
DOLUS
DOM
DOMAIN
DOMAL
DOMANIAL
DOMATIUM
DOMBA
DOME
DOMED
DOMENT
DOMER
DOMESDAY
DOMESTIC
DOMESTICABLE
DOMESTICALLY
DOMESTICATE
DOMESTICATED
DOMESTICATOR
DOMESTICITY
DOMESTICIZE
DOMESTICIZED
DOMESTICS
DOMETT
DOMEYKITE
DOMIC
DOMICAL
DOMICALLY
DOMICIL
DOMICILE
DOMICILED
DOMICILIAR
DOMICILIARY
DOMICILIATE
DOMICILIATED
DOMICILING
DOMIFICATION
DOMIFY
DOMINA
DOMINAE
DOMINANCE
DOMINANCY
DOMINANT
DOMINANTLY
DOMINATE
DOMINATED
DOMINATING
DOMINATION
DOMINATIVE
DOMINATOR
DOMINE
DOMINEER
DOMINEERED
DOMINEERER
DOMINEERING
DOMING
DOMINI
DOMINIAL
DOMINICAL
DOMINIE
DOMINION
DOMINIONISM
DOMINIONIST
DOMINIONS
DOMINIUM
DOMINO
DOMINOES
DOMINOS
DOMINULE
DOMINUS
DOMITE
DOMITIC
DOMN
DOMNEI
DOMOID
DOMPT
DOMPTEUSE
DOMRA
DOMUS
DOMY
DON
DONA
DONABLE
DONACIFORM
DONACK
DONAH
DONARIES
DONARY
DONATARIES
DONATARY
DONATE
DONATED
DONATEE
DONATING
DONATIO
DONATION
DONATIVE
DONATIVELY
DONATOR
DONATORIES
DONATORY
DONATRESS
DONAX
DONCELLA
DONCY
DONDAINE
DONDINE
DONE
DONEE
DONEY
DONG
DONGA
DONGOLA
DONGON
DONI
DONICKER
DONJON
DONK
DONKEY
DONKEYBACK
DONKEYMAN
DONKEYMEN
DONKEYS
DONKEYWORK
DONNA
DONNE
DONNED
DONNEE
DONNERED
DONNERT
DONNICK
DONNING
DONNISH
DONNISHNESS
DONNISM
DONNOCK
DONNOT
DONNY
DONNYBROOK
DONOR
DONOUGHT
DONSHIP
DONSIE
DONSKY
DONSY
DONUM
DONUT
DONZEL
DONZELLA
DOO
DOOB
DOOCOT
DOODAB
DOODAD
DOODAH
DOODLE
DOODLEBUG
DOODLED
DOODLESACK
DOODLING
DOODSKOP
DOOHICKEY
DOOHICKEYS
DOOHICKUS
DOOHINKEY
DOOHINKUS
DOOK
DOOKET
DOOL
DOOLEE
DOOLEY
DOOLFU
DOOLI
DOOLIE
DOOLIES
DOOLY
DOOM
DOOMAGE
DOOMBOOK
DOOMED
DOOMER
DOOMFUL
DOOMING
DOOMLIKE
DOOMS
DOOMSDAY
DOOMSMAN
DOOMSTEAD
DOOMSTER
DOON
DOOPUTTY
DOOR
DOORBELL
DOORBOY
DOORBRAND
DOORCASE
DOORCHEEK
DOORED
DOORFRAME
DOORHAWK
DOORHEAD
DOORJAMB
DOORKEEPER
DOORKNOB
DOORMAID
DOORMAKER
DOORMAKING
DOORMAN
DOORMAT
DOORNAIL
DOORNBOOM
DOORPLATE
DOORPOST
DOORS
DOORSILL
DOORSTEAD
DOORSTEP
DOORSTONE
DOORSTOP
DOORWARD
DOORWAY
DOORWEED
DOORYARD
DOOSE
DOOZY
DOP
DOPA
DOPAMELANIN
DOPAOXIDASE
DOPATTA
DOPCHICK
DOPE
DOPEBOOK
DOPED
DOPEHEAD
DOPER
DOPESHEET
DOPESTER
DOPEY
DOPIER
DOPIEST
DOPING
DOPP
DOPPED
DOPPER
DOPPERBIRD
DOPPIA
DOPPING
DOPPIO
DOPPLERITE
DOPSTER
DOPY
DOR
DORAB
DORAD
DORADILLA
DORADO
DORALIUM
DORAY
DORBEETLE
DORBEL
DORBIE
DORBUG
DORCASTRY
DORE
DOREA
DOREE
DOREY
DORHAWK
DORIA
DORIES
DORIPPID
DORJE
DORLACH
DORLOT
DORM
DORMANCY
DORMANT
DORME
DORMER
DORMERED
DORMETTE
DORMEUSE
DORMICE
DORMIE
DORMIENT
DORMILONA
DORMITARY
DORMITION
DORMITIVE
DORMITORIES
DORMITORY
DORMOUSE
DORMY
DORN
DORNECK
DORNIC
DORNICK
DORNOCK
DORON
DOROSACRAL
DOROSCENTRAL
DOROSTERNAL
DORP
DORPER
DORR
DORRBEETLE
DORRE
DORSA
DORSAD
DORSAL
DORSALIS
DORSALLY
DORSALMOST
DORSE
DORSEL
DORSER
DORSICOLLAR
DORSICOLUMN
DORSICORNU
DORSIDUCT
DORSIFEROUS
DORSIFIXED
DORSIFLEX
DORSIFLEXION
DORSIFLEXOR
DORSIGRADE
DORSILATERAL
DORSILUMBAR
DORSIMEDIAN
DORSIMESAL
DORSIPAROUS
DORSIPINAL
DORSIVENTRAL
DORSO
DORSOCAUDAD
DORSOLATERAL
DORSOMEDIAL
DORSOMESAL
DORSONASAL
DORSONUCHAL
DORSOPLEURAL
DORSORADIAL
DORSOVENTRAD
DORSOVENTRAL
DORSULA
DORSULUM
DORSUM
DORSUMBONAL
DORT
DORTER
DORTINESS
DORTISHIP
DORTOUR
DORTS
DORTY
DORUCK
DORY
DORYLINE
DORYMAN
DORYPHOROS
DORYPHORUS
DOS
DOSA
DOSADH
DOSAGE
DOSAIN
DOSE
DOSED
DOSER
DOSES
DOSIMETER

DOSIMETRIC
DOSIMETRIST
DOSIMETRY
DOSING
DOSIOLOGY
DOSIS
DOSOLOGY
DOSS
DOSSAL
DOSSED
DOSSEL
DOSSENNUS
DOSSER
DOSSERET
DOSSETY
DOSSIER
DOSSIERE
DOSSIL
DOSSING
DOSSMAN
DOSSMEN
DOSSY
DOST
DOT
DOTAGE
DOTAL
DOTANT
DOTARD
DOTARDISM
DOTARDLY
DOTARDY
DOTATE
DOTATION
DOTCHIN
DOTE
DOTED
DOTER
DOTES
DOTH
DOTHER
DOTIER
DOTIEST
DOTINESS
DOTING
DOTINGLY
DOTINGNESS
DOTISH
DOTISHNESS
DOTKIN
DOTLET
DOTS
DOTTED
DOTTEL
DOTTER
DOTTEREL
DOTTERELS
DOTTI
DOTTIER
DOTTIEST
DOTTILY
DOTTINESS
DOTTING
DOTTLE
DOTTLED
DOTTLER
DOTTLING
DOTTREL
DOTTY
DOTY
DOUANE
DOUANIER
DOUAR
DOUBLE
DOUBLED
DOUBLEDAMN
DOUBLEGANGER
DOUBLELEAF
DOUBLENESS
DOUBLER
DOUBLES
DOUBLET
DOUBLETED
DOUBLETHINK
DOUBLETON
DOUBLETONE
DOUBLETREE
DOUBLETS
DOUBLETTE
DOUBLEYOU
DOUBLING
DOUBLOON
DOUBLURE
DOUBLY
DOUBT
DOUBTABLE
DOUBTANCE
DOUBTED
DOUBTEDLY
DOUBTER
DOUBTFUL
DOUBTFULLY
DOUBTFULNESS
DOUBTING
DOUBTINGLY
DOUBTINGNESS
DOUBTLESS
DOUBTLESSLY
DOUBTMONGER
DOUBTOUS
DOUBTSOME
DOUBTY
DOUC
DOUCE
DOUCELY
DOUCENESS
DOUCET
DOUCEUR
DOUCHE
DOUCHED
DOUCHING
DOUCIN
DOUCINE
DOUDLE
DOUF
DOUGH
DOUGHBOY
DOUGHFACE
DOUGHHEAD
DOUGHINESS
DOUGHMAKER
DOUGHMAKING
DOUGHMAN
DOUGHMEN
DOUGHNUT
DOUGHT
DOUGHTIER
DOUGHTIEST
DOUGHTILY
DOUGHTINESS
DOUGHTY
DOUGHY
DOULCE
DOULOCRACY
DOUM
DOUMA
DOUMAIST
DOUNDAKE
DOUP
DOUPER
DOUPING
DOUPION
DOUPIONI
DOUR
DOURA
DOURADE
DOURE
DOURICOULI
DOURINE
DOURLY
DOURNESS
DOUSE
DOUSED
DOUSER
DOUSING
DOUT
DOUTER
DOUTOUS
DOUX
DOUZAINE
DOUZAINIER
DOUZEPER
DOUZEPERS
DOVAP
DOVE
DOVECOT
DOVECOTE
DOVEFLOWER
DOVEFOOT
DOVEHOUSE
DOVEKEY
DOVEKIE
DOVELET
DOVELIKE
DOVELING
DOVER
DOVES
DOVETAIL
DOVETAILED
DOVETAILER
DOVETAILING
DOVEWEED
DOVEWOOD
DOVISH
DOW
DOWABLE
DOWAGE
DOWAGER
DOWCET
DOWCOTE
DOWD
DOWDIER
DOWDIES
DOWDIEST
DOWDILY
DOWDINESS
DOWDY
DOWDYISH
DOWDYISM
DOWED
DOWEL
DOWELED
DOWELING
DOWELLED
DOWELLING
DOWER
DOWERAL
DOWERED
DOWERESS
DOWERING
DOWERY
DOWF
DOWFART
DOWFF
DOWIE
DOWILY
DOWINESS
DOWING
DOWITCH
DOWITCHER
DOWITCHERS
DOWL
DOWLAS
DOWLE
DOWLESS
DOWLY
DOWN
DOWNA
DOWNBEAR
DOWNBEARD
DOWNBEAT
DOWNBEND
DOWNBENT
DOWNBY
DOWNBYE
DOWNCAST
DOWNCASTLY
DOWNCASTNESS
DOWNCOME
DOWNCOMER
DOWNCOMING
DOWNCRIED
DOWNCRY
DOWNCRYING
DOWNCURVED
DOWNCUT
DOWNDALE
DOWNDRAFT
DOWNDRAUGHT
DOWNED
DOWNER
DOWNFACE
DOWNFALL
DOWNFALLEN
DOWNFALLING
DOWNFEED
DOWNFLOW
DOWNFOLD
DOWNFOLDED
DOWNGATE
DOWNGONE
DOWNGRADE
DOWNGRADED
DOWNGRADING
DOWNGROWTH
DOWNGYVED
DOWNHANGING
DOWNHAUL
DOWNHEADED
DOWNHEARTED
DOWNHILL
DOWNIER
DOWNIEST
DOWNINESS
DOWNING
DOWNLAND
DOWNLIE
DOWNLIER
DOWNLIGGING
DOWNLINE
DOWNLOOKED
DOWNLOOKER
DOWNLYING
DOWNMOST
DOWNPIPE
DOWNPOUR
DOWNPOURING
DOWNRIGHT
DOWNRIGHTLY
DOWNRUSH
DOWNRUSHING
DOWNS
DOWNSET
DOWNSHORE
DOWNSIDE
DOWNSINKING
DOWNSITTING
DOWNSLIDING
DOWNSLIP
DOWNSLOPE
DOWNSMAN
DOWNSOME
DOWNSPOUT
DOWNSTAGE
DOWNSTAIR
DOWNSTAIRS
DOWNSTATE
DOWNSTATER
DOWNSTREAM
DOWNSTREET
DOWNSTROKE
DOWNSWING
DOWNTAKE
DOWNTHROW
DOWNTHROWN
DOWNTHRUST
DOWNTOWN
DOWNTREADING
DOWNTROD
DOWNTRODDEN
DOWNTURN
DOWNWARD
DOWNWARDLY
DOWNWARDNESS
DOWNWARDS
DOWNWARP
DOWNWASH
DOWNWAY
DOWNWEED
DOWNWEIGH
DOWNWEIGHT
DOWNWEIGHTED
DOWNWIND
DOWNWITH
DOWNY
DOWP
DOWRY
DOWSABEL
DOWSE
DOWSED
DOWSER
DOWSET
DOWSETS
DOWSING
DOWVE
DOWY
DOXASTIC
DOXASTICON
DOXIE
DOXIES
DOXOGRAPHER
DOXOGRAPHY
DOXOLOGICAL
DOXOLOGIES
DOXOLOGIZE
DOXOLOGIZED
DOXOLOGIZING
DOXOLOGY
DOXY
DOYEN
DOYENNE
DOYLEY
DOYLT
DOYLY
DOYST
DOZE
DOZED
DOZEN
DOZENED
DOZENER
DOZENS
DOZENT
DOZENTH
DOZER
DOZIER
DOZIEST

DOZILY
DOZINESS
DOZING
DOZY
DOZZLE
DOZZLED
DRA
DRAA
DRAB
DRABANT
DRABBED
DRABBER
DRABBEST
DRABBET
DRABBING
DRABBISH
DRABBLE
DRABBLED
DRABBLER
DRABBLETAIL
DRABBLING
DRABBY
DRABI
DRABLER
DRABLY
DRABNESS
DRACHEN
DRACHM
DRACHMA
DRACHMAE
DRACHMAI
DRACHMAL
DRACHMAS
DRACMA
DRACONIAN
DRACONITES
DRACONITIC
DRACONTIAN
DRACONTIASIS
DRACONTIC
DRACONTINE
DRACONTITES
DRACUNCULUS
DRAD
DRAFF
DRAFFISH
DRAFFMAN
DRAFFSACK
DRAFFY
DRAFT
DRAFTAGE
DRAFTED
DRAFTEE
DRAFTER
DRAFTIER
DRAFTILY
DRAFTINESS
DRAFTING
DRAFTS
DRAFTSMAN
DRAFTY
DRAG
DRAGADE
DRAGADED
DRAGADING
DRAGBAR
DRAGBOAT
DRAGBOLT
DRAGEE
DRAGEOIR
DRAGGED
DRAGGER
DRAGGIER
DRAGGIEST
DRAGGILY
DRAGGINESS
DRAGGING
DRAGGLE
DRAGGLED
DRAGGLETAIL
DRAGGLING
DRAGGLY
DRAGGY
DRAGHOUND
DRAGLINE
DRAGMAN
DRAGNET
DRAGO
DRAGOMAN
DRAGOMANATE
DRAGOMANIC
DRAGOMANISH
DRAGOMANS
DRAGOMEN
DRAGON
DRAGONESS
DRAGONET
DRAGONFISH
DRAGONFISHES
DRAGONFLIES
DRAGONFLY
DRAGONHEAD
DRAGONISM
DRAGONIZE
DRAGONKIND
DRAGONNADE
DRAGONNE
DRAGONROOT
DRAGONTAIL
DRAGONWORT
DRAGOON
DRAGOONAGE
DRAGOONED
DRAGOONER
DRAGOONING
DRAGROPE
DRAGSAW
DRAGSHOE
DRAGSMAN
DRAGSMEN
DRAGSTAFF
DRAGSTER
DRAIL
DRAILED
DRAILING
DRAIN
DRAINAGE
DRAINAGEWAY
DRAINBOARD
DRAINE
DRAINED
DRAINER
DRAINERMAN
DRAINERMEN
DRAINING
DRAINLESS
DRAINMAN
DRAINPIPE
DRAINS
DRAINTILE
DRAISENE
DRAISINE
DRAKE
DRAKELET
DRAKESTONE
DRAKONITE
DRAM
DRAMA
DRAMALOGUE
DRAMAMINE
DRAMATIC
DRAMATICAL
DRAMATICALLY
DRAMATICISM
DRAMATICS
DRAMATICULE
DRAMATISE
DRAMATISM
DRAMATIST
DRAMATIZATION
DRAMATIZE
DRAMATIZED
DRAMATIZER
DRAMATIZING
DRAMATURGE
DRAMATURGIC
DRAMATURGIST
DRAMATURGY
DRAME
DRAMM
DRAMMAGE
DRAMME
DRAMMED
DRAMMER
DRAMMING
DRAMMOCK
DRAMSELLER
DRAMSHOP
DRANE
DRANG
DRANK
DRANT
DRAP
DRAPE
DRAPEAU
DRAPED
DRAPER
DRAPERESS
DRAPERIED
DRAPERIES
DRAPERY
DRAPET
DRAPING
DRAPPIE
DRAPPY
DRASH
DRASHEL
DRASS
DRASSID
DRAST
DRASTIC
DRASTICALLY
DRASTY
DRAT
DRATCHELL
DRATE
DRATTED
DRATTING
DRAUGHT
DRAUGHTAGE
DRAUGHTBOARD
DRAUGHTED
DRAUGHTER
DRAUGHTHOUSE
DRAUGHTIER
DRAUGHTIEST
DRAUGHTILY
DRAUGHTINESS
DRAUGHTING
DRAUGHTS
DRAUGHTSMAN
DRAUGHTSMEN
DRAUGHTY
DRAUNT
DRAVE
DRAVITE
DRAW
DRAWABLE
DRAWARM
DRAWBACK
DRAWBAND
DRAWBAR
DRAWBEAM
DRAWBENCH
DRAWBOARD
DRAWBOLT
DRAWBORE
DRAWBORED
DRAWBORING
DRAWBOY
DRAWBRIDGE
DRAWCARD
DRAWCORD
DRAWCUT
DRAWCUTTING
DRAWDOWN
DRAWEE
DRAWER
DRAWERS
DRAWFILE
DRAWFILED
DRAWFILING
DRAWGATE
DRAWGEAR
DRAWGLOVE
DRAWGLOVES
DRAWHEAD
DRAWHORSE
DRAWING
DRAWK
DRAWKNIFE
DRAWKNIVES
DRAWKNOT
DRAWL
DRAWLATCH
DRAWLED
DRAWLER
DRAWLIER
DRAWLIEST
DRAWLING
DRAWLINGLY
DRAWLINGNESS
DRAWLINK
DRAWLOOM
DRAWLY
DRAWN
DRAWNET
DRAWOFF
DRAWOUT
DRAWPLATE
DRAWPOINT
DRAWROD
DRAWSHAVE
DRAWSHEET
DRAWSPAN
DRAWSPRING
DRAWSTOP
DRAWSTRING
DRAWTONGS
DRAWTUBE
DRAY
DRAYAGE
DRAYED
DRAYING
DRAYMAN
DRAYMEN
DRAZEL
DRAZIL
DREAD
DREADABLE
DREADED
DREADER
DREADFUL
DREADFULLY
DREADFULNESS
DREADING
DREADINGLY
DREADLESS
DREADLESSLY
DREADLY
DREADNAUGHT
DREADNESS
DREADNOUGHT
DREAM
DREAMED
DREAMER
DREAMERIES
DREAMERY
DREAMFUL
DREAMFULLY
DREAMFULNESS
DREAMHOLE
DREAMIER
DREAMIEST
DREAMILY
DREAMINESS
DREAMING
DREAMINGLY
DREAMLAND
DREAMLESS
DREAMLESSLY
DREAMLIKE
DREAMLIT
DREAMLORE
DREAMS
DREAMSILY
DREAMSINESS
DREAMSY
DREAMT
DREAMTIDE
DREAMTIME
DREAMWHILE
DREAMWORLD
DREAMY
DREAR
DREARIER
DREARIEST
DREARIHEAD
DREARIHOOD
DREARILY
DREARIMENT
DREARINESS
DREARING
DREARLY
DREARNESS
DREARY
DRECK
DREDDOUR
DREDGE
DREDGED
DREDGEMAN
DREDGER
DREDGIE
DREDGING
DREE
DREECH
DREED
DREEING
DREEL
DREELY
DREEN
DREEP
DREEPINESS
DREEPY
DREG
DREGGIER
DREGGIEST
DREGGILY
DREGGINESS
DREGGISH
DREGGY
DREGS
DREICH
DREIDEL
DREIE

DREIGH
DREILING
DRENCH
DRENCHED
DRENCHER
DRENCHING
DRENCHINGLY
DRENG
DRENGAGE
DRENGH
DREPANE
DREPANIA
DREPANID
DREPANIFORM
DREPANIUM
DREPANOID
DREPE
DRESS
DRESSAGE
DRESSED
DRESSER
DRESSES
DRESSIER
DRESSIEST
DRESSILY
DRESSINESS
DRESSING
DRESSMAKER
DRESSMAKERY
DRESSMAKING
DRESSY
DREST
DRETCH
DREW
DREWITE
DREY
DRIAS
DRIB
DRIBBED
DRIBBER
DRIBBING
DRIBBLE
DRIBBLED
DRIBBLER
DRIBBLET
DRIBBLING
DRIBLET
DRIDDER
DRIDDLE
DRIECH
DRIED
DRIEGH
DRIER
DRIERMAN
DRIES
DRIEST
DRIFT
DRIFTAGE
DRIFTBOLT
DRIFTED
DRIFTER
DRIFTIER
DRIFTIEST
DRIFTING
DRIFTINGLY
DRIFTLAND
DRIFTLESS
DRIFTLET
DRIFTMAN
DRIFTPIECE
DRIFTPIN
DRIFTWAY
DRIFTWEED
DRIFTWIND
DRIFTWOOD
DRIFTY
DRIGHTEN
DRIGHTIN
DRIKI
DRILL
DRILLED
DRILLER
DRILLET
DRILLING
DRILLMAN
DRILLMASTER
DRILLSTOCK
DRILVIS
DRILY
DRING
DRINGLE
DRINK
DRINKABILITY
DRINKABLE
DRINKABLY
DRINKER
DRINKERY
DRINKING
DRINKLESS
DRINKS
DRINKY
DRINN
DRIP
DRIPOLATOR
DRIPPED
DRIPPER
DRIPPIER
DRIPPIEST
DRIPPING
DRIPPLE
DRIPPY
DRIPSTICK
DRIPSTONE
DRIPT
DRISHEEN
DRISK
DRISSEL
DRIVABLE
DRIVAGE
DRIVE
DRIVEABLE
DRIVEAWAY
DRIVEBOAT
DRIVEBOLT
DRIVECAP
DRIVEHEAD
DRIVEL
DRIVELED
DRIVELER
DRIVELING
DRIVELINGLY
DRIVELLED
DRIVELLER
DRIVELLING
DRIVEN
DRIVEPIPE
DRIVER
DRIVESCREW
DRIVEWAY
DRIVING
DRIVINGLY
DRIZZLE
DRIZZLED
DRIZZLING
DRIZZLY
DROB
DROCHUIL
DRODDUM
DROFLAND
DROGER
DROGERMAN
DROGERMEN
DROGH
DROGHER
DROGHERMAN
DROGHLIN
DROGUE
DROGUET
DROICH
DROIL
DROIT
DROITS
DROITURAL
DROKE
DROLE
DROLERIE
DROLL
DROLLED
DROLLER
DROLLERIES
DROLLERY
DROLLEST
DROLLING
DROLLISH
DROLLISHNESS
DROLLIST
DROLLY
DROME
DROMED
DROMEDARIAN
DROMEDARIES
DROMEDARIST
DROMEDARY
DROMETER
DROMI
DROMIC
DROMICAL
DROMOGRAPH
DROMOMANIA
DROMOMETER
DROMON
DROMOND
DROMOS
DROMOTROPIC
DRONA
DRONAGE
DRONE
DRONED
DRONEL
DRONER
DRONET
DRONG
DRONGO
DRONGOS
DRONING
DRONISH
DRONISHLY
DRONISHNESS
DRONKGRASS
DRONY
DROOK
DROOL
DROOLED
DROOP
DROOPED
DROOPER
DROOPIER
DROOPIEST
DROOPILY
DROOPINESS
DROOPING
DROOPINGLY
DROOPINGNESS
DROOPT
DROOPY
DROP
DROPCLOTH
DROPFORGE
DROPFORGED
DROPFORGING
DROPHEAD
DROPKICK
DROPLET
DROPLIGHT
DROPLINE
DROPLING
DROPMAN
DROPMEAL
DROPOUT
DROPPED
DROPPER
DROPPING
DROPPY
DROPS
DROPSEED
DROPSICAL
DROPSICALLY
DROPSIED
DROPSIES
DROPSY
DROPT
DROPVIE
DROPWISE
DROPWORM
DROPWORT
DROSHKIES
DROSHKY
DROSKY
DROSOGRAPH
DROSOMETER
DROSOPHILA
DROSS
DROSSED
DROSSEL
DROSSER
DROSSIER
DROSSIEST
DROSSINESS
DROSSING
DROSSY
DROSTDEN
DROSTDY
DROUD
DROUGHERMEN
DROUGHT
DROUGHTINESS
DROUGHTY
DROUK
DROUKAN
DROUKED
DROUKET
DROUKING
DROUKIT
DROUMY
DROUTH
DROUTHY
DROVE
DROVED
DROVER
DROVING
DROVY
DROW
DROWK
DROWN
DROWNED
DROWNER
DROWNING
DROWSE
DROWSED
DROWSIER
DROWSIEST
DROWSIHEAD
DROWSIHOOD
DROWSILY
DROWSINESS
DROWSING
DROWSY
DROY
DROZE
DRUB
DRUBBED
DRUBBER
DRUBBING
DRUBBLE
DRUBLY
DRUCKEN
DRUDGE
DRUDGED
DRUDGER
DRUDGERIES
DRUDGERY
DRUDGING
DRUDGINGLY
DRUDGISM
DRUERY
DRUG
DRUGGE
DRUGGED
DRUGGER
DRUGGERIES
DRUGGERY
DRUGGET
DRUGGIER
DRUGGIEST
DRUGGING
DRUGGIST
DRUGGY
DRUGLESS
DRUGMAN
DRUGS
DRUGSHOP
DRUGSTORE
DRUID
DRUIDESS
DRUIDIC
DRUIDICAL
DRUIDISM
DRUIDRY
DRUK
DRUM
DRUMBEAT
DRUMBLE
DRUMBLED
DRUMBLEDORE
DRUMBLER
DRUMBLING
DRUMFIRE
DRUMFISH
DRUMFISHES
DRUMHEAD
DRUMHEADS
DRUMLER
DRUMLIN
DRUMLINE
DRUMLINOID
DRUMLOID
DRUMLOIDAL
DRUMLY
DRUMMED
DRUMMER
DRUMMING
DRUMMOCK
DRUMMY
DRUMS
DRUMSKIN
DRUMSLER
DRUMSTICK
DRUMWOOD
DRUN
DRUNG
DRUNGAR
DRUNK
DRUNKARD
DRUNKELEW
DRUNKEN

DRUNKENLY
DRUNKENNESS
DRUNKER
DRUNKERIES
DRUNKERY
DRUNKOMETER
DRUNT
DRUPACEOUS
DRUPAL
DRUPE
DRUPEL
DRUPELET
DRUPEOLE
DRUPETUM
DRUPIFEROUS
DRURY
DRUSE
DRUSED
DRUSH
DRUSY
DRUTHER
DRUTHERS
DRUTTLE
DRUVE
DRUVY
DRUXEY
DRUXINESS
DRUXY
DRY
DRYAD
DRYADES
DRYADIC
DRYAS
DRYASDUST
DRYBEARD
DRYER
DRYERMAN
DRYERMEN
DRYEST
DRYFIST
DRYFOOT
DRYGOODSMAN
DRYHOUSE
DRYING
DRYINID
DRYISH
DRYLOT
DRYLY
DRYNESS
DRYOPTEROID
DRYPOINT
DRYS
DRYSALTER
DRYSALTERIES
DRYSALTERY
DRYSNE
DRYSTER
DRYTH
DRYWORKER
DU
DUAB
DUAD
DUADIC
DUAL
DUALI
DUALIN
DUALISM
DUALIST
DUALISTIC
DUALITY
DUALIZATION
DUALIZE
DUALIZED
DUALIZING
DUAN
DUANT
DUAR
DUARCH
DUARCHY
DUB
DUBASH
DUBB
DUBBA
DUBBAH
DUBBED
DUBBEH
DUBBELTJE
DUBBER
DUBBIN
DUBBING
DUBBY
DUBIETIES
DUBIETY
DUBIOSITIES
DUBIOSITY
DUBIOUS
DUBIOUSLY
DUBIOUSNESS
DUBITABLE
DUBITABLY
DUBITANT
DUBITANTE
DUBITATE
DUBITATION
DUBITATIVE
DUBITATIVELY
DUBS
DUC
DUCAL
DUCALLY
DUCAPE
DUCAT
DUCATO
DUCATON
DUCATOON
DUCATUS
DUCDAME
DUCE
DUCES
DUCHAN
DUCHERY
DUCHESS
DUCHESSE
DUCHIES
DUCHN
DUCHY
DUCK
DUCKBILL
DUCKBLIND
DUCKBOARD
DUCKBOAT
DUCKED
DUCKER
DUCKERIES
DUCKERY
DUCKFOOT
DUCKHEARTED
DUCKHOUSE
DUCKHUNTING
DUCKIE
DUCKIER
DUCKIEST
DUCKING
DUCKISH
DUCKLAR
DUCKLET
DUCKLING
DUCKMEAT
DUCKMOLE
DUCKPIN
DUCKPINS
DUCKPOND
DUCKS
DUCKSTONE
DUCKTAIL
DUCKWEED
DUCKWIFE
DUCKWING
DUCKY
DUCT
DUCTIBILITY
DUCTIBLE
DUCTILE
DUCTILELY
DUCTILENESS
DUCTILIMETER
DUCTILITY
DUCTILIZE
DUCTILIZED
DUCTILIZING
DUCTION
DUCTOR
DUCTULE
DUCTURE
DUCTUS
DUD
DUDAIM
DUDDER
DUDDERY
DUDDIE
DUDDLE
DUDDY
DUDE
DUDEEN
DUDGEN
DUDGEON
DUDINE
DUDISH
DUDLER
DUDLEY
DUDLEYITE
DUDMAN
DUDS
DUE
DUEFUL
DUEL
DUELED
DUELER
DUELING
DUELIST
DUELISTIC
DUELLED
DUELLER
DUELLING
DUELLIST
DUELLISTIC
DUELLIZE
DUELLO
DUELLOS
DUENA
DUENAS
DUENNA
DUENNAS
DUES
DUET
DUETTED
DUETTING
DUETTINO
DUETTIST
DUETTO
DUFF
DUFFADAR
DUFFED
DUFFEL
DUFFER
DUFFIES
DUFFING
DUFFLE
DUFFY
DUFOIL
DUFRENITE
DUFRENOYSITE
DUFTER
DUFTERDAR
DUFTERY
DUFTITE
DUFTRY
DUG
DUGAL
DUGDUG
DUGGLER
DUGON
DUGONG
DUGOUT
DUGWAY
DUHAT
DUI
DUIKER
DUIKERBOK
DUIKERBOKS
DUIKERBUCK
DUIM
DUIME
DUINHEWASSEL
DUIT
DUJAN
DUKAN
DUKE
DUKEDOM
DUKELING
DUKELY
DUKERY
DUKES
DUKHN
DUKKER
DUKKERIPEN
DUKU
DUKUMA
DULBERT
DULCAMARA
DULCARNON
DULCE
DULCELY
DULCENESS
DULCET
DULCETLY
DULCETNESS
DULCIAN
DULCIANA
DULCID
DULCIFIED
DULCIFLUOUS
DULCIFY
DULCIFYING
DULCILOQUENT
DULCILOQUY
DULCIMER
DULCITE
DULCITOL
DULCITUDE
DULCITY
DULCOR
DULEDGE
DULER
DULIA
DULL
DULLARD
DULLARDISM
DULLARDNESS
DULLBRAINED
DULLED
DULLER
DULLERY
DULLEST
DULLHEAD
DULLHEARTED
DULLIFY
DULLING
DULLISH
DULLITY
DULLNESS
DULLPATE
DULLSOME
DULLY
DULNESS
DULOCRACY
DULOSIS
DULOTIC
DULSE
DULT
DULTIE
DULWILLY
DULY
DUMA
DUMAIST
DUMAL
DUMB
DUMBA
DUMBBELL
DUMBBELLER
DUMBCOW
DUMBFISH
DUMBFOUND
DUMBFOUNDED
DUMBHEAD
DUMBLE
DUMBLEDORE
DUMBLY
DUMBNESS
DUMBWAITER
DUMBY
DUMDUM
DUMFOUND
DUMFOUNDED
DUMKA
DUMKY
DUMMEL
DUMMERED
DUMMERER
DUMMIES
DUMMKOPF
DUMMY
DUMONTITE
DUMORTIERITE
DUMOSE
DUMOSITY
DUMOUS
DUMP
DUMPAGE
DUMPCART
DUMPED
DUMPER
DUMPIER
DUMPIES
DUMPIEST
DUMPILY
DUMPING
DUMPISH
DUMPISHLY
DUMPISHNESS
DUMPLE
DUMPLED
DUMPLER
DUMPLING
DUMPOKE
DUMPS
DUMPTY
DUMPY
DUN
DUNAIR
DUNAL
DUNAM
DUNAMIS
DUNBIRD
DUNCE

DUNCERY
DUNCH
DUNCICAL
DUNCIFY
DUNCIFYING
DUNCISH
DUNCISHLY
DUNCISHNESS
DUNDASITE
DUNDER
DUNDERFUNK
DUNDERHEAD
DUNDERHEADED
DUNDERPATE
DUNE
DUNES
DUNFISH
DUNG
DUNGA
DUNGANNONITE
DUNGAREE
DUNGARI
DUNGBECK
DUNGBIRD
DUNGED
DUNGEON
DUNGEONER
DUNGER
DUNGHILL
DUNGHILLY
DUNGING
DUNGON
DUNGY
DUNIEWASSAL
DUNITE
DUNK
DUNKADOO
DUNKER
DUNKING
DUNKLE
DUNKLED
DUNKLING
DUNLIN
DUNLINS
DUNNAGE
DUNNAGED
DUNNAGING
DUNNE
DUNNED
DUNNER
DUNNESS
DUNNIEWASSEL
DUNNING
DUNNISH
DUNNITE
DUNNOCK
DUNNY
DUNST
DUNSTABLE
DUNSTER
DUNT
DUNTED
DUNTING
DUNTLE
DUNUM
DUNY
DUNZIEKTE
DUO
DUOCOSANE
DUODECANE
DUODECENNIAL
DUODECILLION
DUODECIMAL
DUODECIMALITY
DUODECIMALLY
DUODECIMO
DUODECIMOLE
DUODECIMOS
DUODECUPLE
DUODENA
DUODENAL
DUODENARY
DUODENATE
DUODENATION
DUODENE
DUODENITIS
DUODENUM
DUODRAMA
DUOGRAPH
DUOLE
DUOLITERAL
DUOLOG
DUOLOGUE
DUOMACHY
DUOMI
DUOMO
DUOPOD
DUOS
DUOSECANT
DUOTONED
DUOTYPE
DUOVIRI
DUP
DUPABILITY
DUPABLE
DUPE
DUPED
DUPER
DUPERIES
DUPERY
DUPING
DUPION
DUPLATION
DUPLE
DUPLET
DUPLEX
DUPLEXED
DUPLEXER
DUPLEXES
DUPLEXING
DUPLEXITY
DUPLICABLE
DUPLICAND
DUPLICANDO
DUPLICATE
DUPLICATED
DUPLICATELY
DUPLICATING
DUPLICATION
DUPLICATIVE
DUPLICATOR
DUPLICATURE
DUPLICIDENT
DUPLICITAS
DUPLICITIES
DUPLICITY
DUPLIFIED
DUPLIFY
DUPLIFYING
DUPLONE
DUPLY
DUPONDIUS
DUPPER
DUPPIES
DUPPY
DUR
DURA
DURABILITIES
DURABILITY
DURABLE
DURABLENESS
DURABLY
DURACINE
DURAIN
DURAL
DURAMEN
DURANCE
DURANGITE
DURANT
DURANTE
DURAPLASTY
DURAQUARA
DURATION
DURATIONAL
DURATIVE
DURAX
DURBACHITE
DURBAR
DURDENITE
DURDUM
DURE
DUREE
DUREFUL
DURENOL
DURESS
DURESSOR
DUREZZA
DURGAH
DURGAN
DURGEN
DURIAN
DURICRUST
DURIDINE
DURING
DURINGLY
DURION
DURITY
DURMAST
DURN
DURNED
DURO
DUROMETER
DUROQUINONE
DUROS
DUROY
DURR
DURRA
DURRIE
DURRIES
DURRIN
DURRY
DURST
DURUKULI
DURUM
DURWAN
DURWAUN
DURYL
DURZEE
DUSACK
DUSCLE
DUSE
DUSH
DUSIO
DUSK
DUSKEN
DUSKIER
DUSKIEST
DUSKILY
DUSKINESS
DUSKINGTIDE
DUSKISH
DUSKLY
DUSKNESS
DUSKY
DUST
DUSTBAND
DUSTBIN
DUSTBLU
DUSTBOX
DUSTCLOTH
DUSTCOAT
DUSTED
DUSTEE
DUSTER
DUSTERMAN
DUSTERMEN
DUSTFALL
DUSTHEAP
DUSTIER
DUSTIEST
DUSTILY
DUSTINESS
DUSTING
DUSTLESS
DUSTLIKE
DUSTMAN
DUSTOOR
DUSTOORI
DUSTOUR
DUSTPAN
DUSTPOINT
DUSTPROOF
DUSTRAG
DUSTUCK
DUSTUK
DUSTUP
DUSTY
DUSTYFOOT
DUTCH
DUTCHED
DUTCHESS
DUTCHING
DUTCHMAN
DUTCHMEN
DUTEOUS
DUTEOUSLY
DUTEOUSNESS
DUTIABILITY
DUTIABLE
DUTIED
DUTIES
DUTIFUL
DUTIFULLY
DUTIFULNESS
DUTRA
DUTUBURI
DUTY
DUUMVIR
DUUMVIRAL
DUUMVIRATE
DUUMVIRI
DUUMVIRS
DUVEL
DUVET
DUVETINE
DUVETYN
DUVETYNE
DUX
DUXELLES
DUXES
DUYKER
DVAITA
DVANDVA
DVORNIK
DWAIBLE
DWAIBLY
DWAIN
DWALE
DWALL
DWALM
DWAM
DWANG
DWARF
DWARFED
DWARFING
DWARFISH
DWARFISHLY
DWARFISHNESS
DWARFISM
DWARFLING
DWARFNESS
DWARFS
DWARFY
DWARVES
DWAYBERRY
DWEEBLE
DWELL
DWELLED
DWELLER
DWELLING
DWELT
DWERE
DWINDLE
DWINDLED
DWINDLING
DWINE
DWINED
DWINING
DYAD
DYADIC
DYARCHIC
DYARCHICAL
DYARCHY
DYBBUK
DYCE
DYDE
DYE
DYEABLE
DYEBECK
DYED
DYEHOUSE
DYEING
DYELEAVES
DYER
DYESTER
DYESTUFF
DYEWARE
DYEWEED
DYEWOOD
DYGOGRAM
DYING
DYKAGE
DYKE
DYKEHOPPER
DYKER
DYKEREEVE
DYNAGRAPH
DYNAM
DYNAMETER
DYNAMETRIC
DYNAMETRICAL
DYNAMIC
DYNAMICAL
DYNAMICALLY
DYNAMICS
DYNAMIS
DYNAMISM
DYNAMIST
DYNAMISTIC
DYNAMITARD
DYNAMITE
DYNAMITED
DYNAMITER
DYNAMITIC
DYNAMITICAL
DYNAMITING
DYNAMITISM
DYNAMITIST
DYNAMIZATION
DYNAMIZE
DYNAMO
DYNAMOGENIC
DYNAMOGENOUS
DYNAMOMETER
DYNAMOMETRIC

DYNAMOMETRY
DYNAMONEURE
DYNAMOPHONE
DYNAMOSTATIC
DYNAMOTOR
DYNAST
DYNASTIC
DYNASTICAL
DYNASTICALLY
DYNASTID
DYNASTIDAN
DYNASTIES
DYNASTY
DYNATRON
DYNE
DYNODE
DYOPHONE
DYOTHEISM
DYPHONE
DYPNONE
DYSACOUSIA
DYSACOUSIS
DYSAESTHESIA
DYSANALYTE
DYSAPHIA
DYSARTHRIA
DYSARTHRIC
DYSARTHROSIS
DYSBULIA
DYSBULIC
DYSCHIRIA
DYSCHROA
DYSCHROIA
DYSCHRONOUS
DYSCRASE
DYSCRASED
DYSCRASIA
DYSCRASIC
DYSCRASING
DYSCRASITE
DYSCRATIC
DYSENTERIC
DYSENTERY
DYSERGASIA
DYSERGIA
DYSESTHESIA
DYSFUNCTION
DYSGENESIC
DYSGENESIS
DYSGENIC
DYSGENICS
DYSGEOGENOUS
DYSGNOSIA
DYSGRAPHIA
DYSIDROSIS
DYSKINESIA
DYSKINETIC
DYSLOGIA
DYSLOGISTIC
DYSLOGY
DYSLUITE
DYSLYSIN
DYSMENORRHEA
DYSMERISM
DYSMERISTIC
DYSMEROMORPH
DYSMNESIA
DYSMORPHISM
DYSNEURIA
DYSNOMY
DYSODILE
DYSOREXY
DYSOXIDATION
DYSOXIDIZE
DYSPATHETIC
DYSPATHY
DYSPEPSIA
DYSPEPSY
DYSPEPTIC
DYSPEPTICAL
DYSPHAGIA
DYSPHAGIC
DYSPHASIA
DYSPHASIC
DYSPHONIA
DYSPHONIC
DYSPHORIA
DYSPHORIC
DYSPHOTIC
DYSPHRASIA
DYSPHRENIA
DYSPNEA
DYSPNEAL
DYSPNEIC
DYSPNOEA
DYSPNOEAL
DYSPROSIA
DYSPROSIUM
DYSSNITE
DYSSYNERGIA
DYSSYNERGY
DYSSYSTOLE
DYSTAXIA
DYSTECTIC
DYSTELEOLOGY
DYSTHYMIA
DYSTOCIA
DYSTOCIAL
DYSTOME
DYSTOMIC
DYSTOMOUS
DYSTONIA
DYSTOPIA
DYSTROPHIA
DYSTROPHIC
DYSTROPHY
DYSURIA
DYSURIC
DYSYNTRIBITE
DYTE
DYTISCID
DYVOUR
DZEREN
DZERIN
DZERON
DZIGGETAI
DZO

EA
EACEWORM
EACH
EACHWHERE
EAGER
EAGERLY
EAGERNESS
EAGLE
EAGLESS
EAGLESTONE
EAGLET
EAGLEWOOD
EAGRASS
EAGRE
EALDERMAN
EALDORMAN
EAN
EANED
EANING
EANLING
EAR
EARABLE
EARACHE
EARBASH
EARBOB
EARCAP
EARCLIP
EARCOCKLE
EARD
EARDROP
EARDROPPER
EARDROPS
EARDRUM
EARED
EARFLAP
EARFLOWER
EARFUL
EARHEAD
EARHOLE
EARING
EARJEWEL
EARL
EARLAP
EARLDOM
EARLDUCK
EARLET
EARLIER
EARLIEST
EARLIKE
EARLINESS
EARLOBE
EARLOCK
EARLSHIP
EARLY
EARLYISH
EARMARK
EARMARKED
EARMARKING
EARMUFF
EARN
EARNED
EARNER
EARNEST
EARNESTLY
EARNESTNESS
EARNFUL
EARNING
EARNINGS
EAROCK
EARPHONE
EARPICK
EARPIECE
EARPLUG
EARREACH
EARRING
EARRINGED
EARS
EARSCREW
EARSHOT
EARSORE
EARSPLITTING
EARSPOOL
EARSTONE
EARTAB
EARTAG
EARTH
EARTHBOARD
EARTHBORN
EARTHBRED
EARTHDRAKE
EARTHED
EARTHEN
EARTHENHEARTED
EARTHENWARE
EARTHFALL
EARTHFAST
EARTHGALL
EARTHGRUBBER
EARTHIAN
EARTHIER
EARTHIEST
EARTHINESS
EARTHING
EARTHKIN
EARTHLESS
EARTHLIGHT
EARTHLIKE
EARTHLINESS
EARTHLING
EARTHLY
EARTHMAKER
EARTHMAKING
EARTHNUT
EARTHPEA
EARTHQUAKE
EARTHQUAKED
EARTHQUAKEN
EARTHQUAKING
EARTHQUAVE
EARTHS
EARTHSET
EARTHSHINE
EARTHSHOCK
EARTHSLIDE
EARTHSMOKE
EARTHSTAR
EARTHTONGUE
EARTHWARD
EARTHWARDS
EARTHWORK
EARTHWORM
EARTHY
EARWAX
EARWIG
EARWIGGED
EARWIGGINESS
EARWIGGING
EARWIGGY
EARWITNESS
EARWORM
EARWORT
EASE
EASED
EASEFUL
EASEFULLY
EASEFULNESS
EASEL
EASELED
EASELESS
EASEMENT
EASER
EASIER
EASIEST
EASILY
EASINESS
EASING
EASSEL
EAST
EASTABOUT
EASTBOUND
EASTED
EASTER
EASTERLING
EASTERLY
EASTERMOST
EASTERN
EASTERNER
EASTERNLY
EASTERNMOST
EASTING
EASTLAND
EASTLIN
EASTLING
EASTLINGS
EASTLINS
EASTMOST
EASTWARD
EASTWARDLY
EASTWARDS
EASY
EASYGOING
EASYLIKE
EAT
EATABILITY
EATABLE
EATABLENESS
EATABLES
EATAGE
EATBERRY
EATCHE
EATEN
EATER
EATERY
EATH
EATHLY
EATING
EATS
EAU
EAUX
EAVE
EAVEDROP
EAVEDROPPER
EAVEDROPPING
EAVER
EAVES
EAVESDRIP
EAVESDROP
EAVESDROPPER
EAVESING
EAWT
EBANO
EBAUCHE
EBB
EBBED
EBBET
EBBING
EBBMAN
EBENEOUS
EBO
EBOE
EBON
EBONIST
EBONITE
EBONIZE
EBONIZED
EBONIZING
EBONY
EBRACTEATE
EBRACTEOLATE
EBRIATE
EBRIATED
EBRIETY
EBRILLADE
EBRIOSE
EBRIOSITY
EBRIOUS
EBRIOUSLY
EBULLATE
EBULLIATE
EBULLIENCE
EBULLIENCY
EBULLIENT
EBULLIENTLY
EBULLIOMETER
EBULLIOSCOPE
EBULLIOSCOPIC
EBULLITION
EBULLITIVE
EBULUS
EBURATED
EBURE
EBURINE
EBURNATED
EBURNATION
EBURNEAN
EBURNEOID
EBURNEOUS
ECAD
ECALCARATE
ECANDA
ECARDINAL
ECARINATE
ECARTE
ECAUDATE
ECBASIS
ECBATIC
ECBLASTESIS
ECBOLE
ECBOLIC
ECCALEOBION
ECCE
ECCENTRATE
ECCENTRIC
ECCENTRICAL
ECCENTRICALLY
ECCENTRICITIES
ECCENTRICITY
ECCENTRING
ECCHONDROMA
ECCHYMOMA
ECCHYMOSE
ECCHYMOSES
ECCHYMOSIS
ECCHYMOTIC
ECCLE
ECCLESIA
ECCLESIAL
ECCLESIARCH
ECCLESIARCHY
ECCLESIAST
ECCLESIASTIC
ECCLESIASTICAL
ECCLESIASTICALLY
ECCLESIASTICIS
ECCLESIASTICS
ECCLESIASTRY
ECCLESIOLATER
ECCLESIOLOGIC
ECCOPROTIC
ECCRINOLOGY
ECCRISIS
ECCRITIC
ECCYCLEMA
ECCYESIS
ECDEMIC
ECDEMITE
ECDERON
ECDERONIC
ECDYSES
ECDYSIAST
ECDYSIS
ECE
ECESIC
ECESIS
ECGONIN
ECGONINE
ECHAPPE
ECHAPPEE
ECHARD
ECHE
ECHEA
ECHELETTE
ECHELLE
ECHELON
ECHENEID
ECHENEIDID
ECHEVIN
ECHIDNA
ECHIDNAE
ECHINACEA
ECHINAL
ECHINATE
ECHINATED
ECHINID
ECHINIDAN
ECHINIFORM
ECHINITAL
ECHINITE
ECHINOCHROME
ECHINOCOCCUS
ECHINODERM
ECHINODERMAL
ECHINODERMIC
ECHINOID
ECHINOLOGIST
ECHINOLOGY
ECHINOPSINE
ECHINULATE
ECHINULATION
ECHINULIFORM
ECHINUS
ECHITAMINE
ECHIUROID
ECHO
ECHOER
ECHOES
ECHOIC
ECHOISM
ECHOIZE
ECHOIZED
ECHOIZING
ECHOLALIA
ECHOLALIC
ECHOLOCATION
ECHOPRACTIC
ECHOPRAXIA
ECILIATE
ECIZE
ECKLE
ECLAIR
ECLAMPSIA
ECLAMPTIC
ECLAT
ECLATED
ECLATING

ECLECTIC
ECLECTICAL
ECLECTICALLY
ECLECTICISM
ECLEGM
ECLEGMA
ECLIPSAREON
ECLIPSE
ECLIPSED
ECLIPSER
ECLIPSING
ECLIPSIS
ECLIPTIC
ECLIPTICAL
ECLIPTICALLY
ECLOGITE
ECLOGUE
ECLOSION
ECMNESIA
ECOD
ECOID
ECOLE
ECOLOGIC
ECOLOGICAL
ECOLOGICALLY
ECOLOGIST
ECOLOGY
ECONOMETER
ECONOMETRIC
ECONOMETRICAL
ECONOMETRICS
ECONOMIC
ECONOMICAL
ECONOMICALLY
ECONOMICS
ECONOMIES
ECONOMISM
ECONOMIST
ECONOMIZATION
ECONOMIZE
ECONOMIZED
ECONOMIZER
ECONOMIZING
ECONOMY
ECOPHENE
ECOPHOBIA
ECORCHE
ECORTICATE
ECOSPECIES
ECOSTATE
ECOTIPICALLY
ECOTONE
ECOTYPE
ECOTYPIC
ECPHONESIS
ECPHORIA
ECPHORIAE
ECPHORIAS
ECPHORIZE
ECPHORY
ECPHRASIS
ECRASE
ECRASEUR
ECRASITE
ECRU
ECRUSTACEOUS
ECSTASIES
ECSTASY
ECSTATIC
ECSTATICA
ECSTATICAL
ECSTATICALLY
ECTAD
ECTAL
ECTALLY
ECTASIA
ECTASIS
ECTENE
ECTENTAL
ECTETHMOID
ECTETHMOIDAL
ECTHETICALLY
ECTHLIPSIS
ECTHYMA
ECTHYMATA
ECTIRIS
ECTOBATIC
ECTOBLAST
ECTOCARDIA
ECTOCARPOUS
ECTOCELIC
ECTOCINEREA
ECTOCINEREAL
ECTOCOELIC
ECTOCONDYLE
ECTOCONDYLOID
ECTOCORNEA
ECTOCRANIAL
ECTOCYST
ECTODERM
ECTODERMAL
ECTODERMIC
ECTODERMOSIS
ECTOENTAD
ECTOENZYM
ECTOENZYME
ECTOETHMOID
ECTOGENESIS
ECTOGENIC
ECTOGENOUS
ECTOGLIA
ECTOLECITHAL
ECTOLOPH
ECTOMERE
ECTOMERIC
ECTOMORPHIC
ECTOMORPHY
ECTOPARASITE
ECTOPATAGIA
ECTOPATAGIUM
ECTOPHLOIC
ECTOPHYTE
ECTOPHYTIC
ECTOPIA
ECTOPIC
ECTOPLACENTA
ECTOPLASM
ECTOPLASMIC
ECTOPLASY
ECTOPROCTAN
ECTOPROCTOUS
ECTORETINA
ECTORHINAL
ECTOSARC
ECTOSARCOUS
ECTOSKELETON
ECTOSOMAL
ECTOSOME
ECTOSPHERE
ECTOSTEAL
ECTOSTOSIS
ECTOTHECA
ECTOTHERM
ECTOTROPHIC
ECTOZOA
ECTOZOAN
ECTOZOIC
ECTRODACTYLY
ECTROGENIC
ECTROGENY
ECTROMELIA
ECTROMELIAN
ECTROMELIC
ECTROPION
ECTYPAL
ECTYPE
ECTYPOGRAPHY
ECU
ECUELLE
ECUELLING
ECUMENE
ECUMENIC
ECUMENICAL
ECUMENICALLY
ECUMENICITY
ECUMENISM
ECYPHELLATE
ECZEMA
ECZEMATOID
ECZEMATOSIS
ECZEMATOUS
EDACIOUS
EDACIOUSLY
EDACIOUSNESS
EDACITY
EDAPHIC
EDAPHOLOGY
EDAPHON
EDDER
EDDIED
EDDIES
EDDISH
EDDO
EDDY
EDDYING
EDDYROOT
EDEA
EDEAGRA
EDELWEISS
EDEMA
EDEMATA
EDEMATOUS
EDEMIC
EDENITE
EDENTAL
EDENTATE
EDENTULATE
EDENTULOUS
EDEODYNIA
EDEOLOGY
EDEOMANIA
EDEOSCOPY
EDEOTOMY
EDESTAN
EDESTIN
EDGE
EDGEBONE
EDGED
EDGELESS
EDGEMAKER
EDGEMAKING
EDGEMAN
EDGER
EDGERMAN
EDGES
EDGESHOT
EDGESTONE
EDGEWAYS
EDGEWEED
EDGEWISE
EDGINESS
EDGING
EDGINGLY
EDGREW
EDGROW
EDGY
EDH
EDI
EDIBILITY
EDIBLE
EDIBLENESS
EDICT
EDICTAL
EDICTALLY
EDICULE
EDIFICABLE
EDIFICATE
EDIFICATION
EDIFICATOR
EDIFICATORY
EDIFICE
EDIFICED
EDIFICES
EDIFICING
EDIFIED
EDIFY
EDIFYING
EDIFYINGLY
EDILE
EDILITY
EDINGTONITE
EDIT
EDITAL
EDITION
EDITOR
EDITORIAL
EDITORIALIZE
EDITORIALIZED
EDITORIALIZING
EDITORIALLY
EDITORSHIP
EDUCABILIAN
EDUCABILITY
EDUCABLE
EDUCAND
EDUCATABLE
EDUCATE
EDUCATED
EDUCATEE
EDUCATING
EDUCATION
EDUCATIONAL
EDUCATIONALLY
EDUCATIONARY
EDUCATIONIST
EDUCATIVE
EDUCATOR
EDUCATORY
EDUCE
EDUCED
EDUCIBLE
EDUCING
EDUCT
EDUCTION
EDUCTIVE
EDUCTOR
EDULCORATE
EDULCORATED
EDULCORATING
EDULCORATION
EDULCORATIVE
EDULCORATOR
EDULE
EE
EEBREE
EED
EEGRASS
EEL
EELBOAT
EELBOB
EELBOBBER
EELCAKE
EELCATCHER
EELED
EELER
EELERY
EELFARE
EELFISH
EELGRASS
EELING
EELPOT
EELPOUT
EELS
EELSHOP
EELSKIN
EELSPEAR
EELWARE
EELWORM
EELY
EEM
EEMIS
EEN
EENCE
EER
EERIE
EERILY
EERINESS
EERISOME
EEROCK
EERY
EES
EESOME
EF
EFECKS
EFF
EFFABLE
EFFACE
EFFACEABLE
EFFACED
EFFACEMENT
EFFACER
EFFACING
EFFATE
EFFATUM
EFFECT
EFFECTER
EFFECTFUL
EFFECTIBLE
EFFECTIVE
EFFECTIVELY
EFFECTIVENESS
EFFECTIVITY
EFFECTOR
EFFECTS
EFFECTUAL
EFFECTUALITY
EFFECTUALIZE
EFFECTUALLY
EFFECTUALNESS
EFFECTUATE
EFFECTUATED
EFFECTUATING
EFFECTUATION
EFFEIR
EFFEMINACY
EFFEMINATE
EFFEMINATED
EFFEMINATELY
EFFEMINATING
EFFEMINATION
EFFEMINATIZE
EFFEMINIZE
EFFEMINIZED
EFFEMINIZING
EFFENDI
EFFENDIS
EFFERENT
EFFERVESCE
EFFERVESCED
EFFERVESCENCE
EFFERVESCENCY
EFFERVESCENT
EFFERVESCENTLY
EFFERVESCING
EFFERVESCIVE

EFFET
EFFETE
EFFETMAN
EFFETMEN
EFFICACIES
EFFICACIOUS
EFFICACITY
EFFICACY
EFFICIENCE
EFFICIENCIES
EFFICIENCY
EFFICIENT
EFFICIENTLY
EFFIGIAL
EFFIGIATE
EFFIGIATION
EFFIGIES
EFFIGURATE
EFFIGURATION
EFFIGY
EFFLATE
EFFLATION
EFFLORESCE
EFFLORESCED
EFFLORESCENCE
EFFLORESCENCY
EFFLORESCENT
EFFLORESCING
EFFLOWER
EFFLUENCE
EFFLUENCY
EFFLUENT
EFFLUVE
EFFLUVIA
EFFLUVIAL
EFFLUVIOUS
EFFLUVIUM
EFFLUX
EFFLUXES
EFFODIENT
EFFORM
EFFORMATION
EFFORT
EFFORTLESS
EFFORTLESSLY
EFFORTLESSNESS
EFFOSSION
EFFRACTION
EFFRANCHISE
EFFRAY
EFFRONT
EFFRONTERIES
EFFRONTERY
EFFULGE
EFFULGED
EFFULGENCE
EFFULGENT
EFFULGENTLY
EFFULGING
EFFUME
EFFUND
EFFUSE
EFFUSED
EFFUSING
EFFUSION
EFFUSIVE
EFFUSIVENESS
EFFUVIATE
EFOVEOLATE
EFREET
EFT
EFTER
EFTEST
EFTSOON
EFTSOONS
EGAD
EGADI
EGAL
EGALITARIAN
EGALITARIANISM
EGALITE
EGALITY
EGALLY
EGENCE
EGENCY
EGER
EGERAN
EGEST
EGESTA
EGESTED
EGESTING
EGESTION
EGESTIVE
EGG
EGGAR
EGGBERRIES
EGGBERRY
EGGCUP
EGGCUPFUL
EGGEATER
EGGED
EGGER
EGGFISH
EGGFRUIT
EGGHEAD
EGGHOT
EGGING
EGGLER
EGGMENT
EGGNOG
EGGPLANT
EGGS
EGGSHELL
EGGY
EGILOPS
EGIS
EGLANDULAR
EGLANDULOSE
EGLANDULOUS
EGLANTINE
EGLATERE
EGLESTONITE
EGLING
EGMA
EGO
EGOCENTRIC
EGOCENTRICITY
EGOCENTRISM
EGOISM
EGOIST
EGOISTIC
EGOISTICAL
EGOISTICALLY
EGOITY
EGOIZE
EGOL
EGOLATROUS
EGOMANIA
EGOMANIAC
EGOMANIACAL
EGOPHONIC
EGOPHONY
EGOS
EGOSYNTONIC
EGOTHEISM
EGOTISM
EGOTIST
EGOTISTIC
EGOTISTICAL
EGOTISTICALLY
EGOTIZE
EGOTIZED
EGOTIZING
EGREGIOUS
EGREGIOUSLY
EGREGIOUSNESS
EGRESS
EGRESSES
EGRESSION
EGRESSOR
EGRET
EGRETS
EGRIMONY
EGROMANCY
EGUALMENTE
EGUEIITE
EGURGITATE
EGURGITATED
EGURGITATING
EH
EHEU
EHLITE
EHRWALDITE
EHTANETHIAL
EHUAWA
EICHBERGITE
EICOSANE
EIDE
EIDENT
EIDENTLY
EIDER
EIDERDOWN
EIDETIC
EIDOGRAPH
EIDOLIC
EIDOLISM
EIDOLOLOGY
EIDOLON
EIDOPTOMETRY
EIDOS
EIDOURANION
EIE
EIGHE
EIGHT
EIGHTEEN
EIGHTEENMO
EIGHTEENTH
EIGHTFOIL
EIGHTFOLD
EIGHTH
EIGHTHLY
EIGHTIETH
EIGHTLING
EIGHTS
EIGHTSCORE
EIGHTSMAN
EIGHTSMEN
EIGHTSOME
EIGHTVO
EIGHTY
EIGNE
EIK
EIKON
EILD
EILE
EIMER
EIMERIA
EINKORN
EIRACK
EIRE
EIRESIONE
EISEGESIS
EISEL
EISELL
EISTEDDFOD
EISTEDDFODAU
EISTEDDFODIC
EISTEDDFODS
EITH
EITHER
EJACULATE
EJACULATED
EJACULATING
EJACULATION
EJACULATIVE
EJACULATOR
EJACULATORY
EJECT
EJECTA
EJECTAMENTA
EJECTED
EJECTING
EJECTION
EJECTIVE
EJECTIVELY
EJECTIVITY
EJECTMENT
EJECTOR
EJICIENT
EJIDAL
EJIDO
EJOO
EJULATE
EJURATE
EKABORON
EKACAESIUM
EKAHA
EKAMANGANESE
EKASILICON
EKATANTALUM
EKE
EKEBERGITE
EKED
EKENAME
EKER
EKERITE
EKHIMI
EKING
EKKA
EKKI
EKPHORE
EKPHORIA
EKPHORIAS
EKPHORIZE
EKPHORY
EKTENE
EL
ELABOR
ELABORATE
ELABORATED
ELABORATELY
ELABORATENESS
ELABORATING
ELABORATION
ELABORATIVE
ELABORATOR
ELABORATORY
ELABRATE
ELAENIA
ELAEOBLAST
ELAEOBLASTIC
ELAEODOCHON
ELAEOPTEN
ELAEOPTENE
ELAEOTHESIUM
ELAIDATE
ELAIDIC
ELAIDIN
ELAIOLEUCITE
ELAIOPLAST
ELAIOSOME
ELAN
ELANCE
ELAND
ELANDS
ELANET
ELAPHINE
ELAPHURE
ELAPHURINE
ELAPID
ELAPINE
ELAPOID
ELAPSE
ELAPSED
ELAPSING
ELASMOBRANCH
ELASMOTHERE
ELASTANCE
ELASTASE
ELASTIC
ELASTICA
ELASTICALLY
ELASTICIAN
ELASTICIN
ELASTICITY
ELASTICIZE
ELASTICIZER
ELASTIN
ELASTIVITY
ELASTOMER
ELASTOMETER
ELASTOMETRY
ELASTOSE
ELATE
ELATED
ELATEDLY
ELATEDNESS
ELATER
ELATERID
ELATERIN
ELATERITE
ELATERIUM
ELATINACEOUS
ELATING
ELATION
ELATIVE
ELATOR
ELATROMETER
ELAYL
ELB
ELBOIC
ELBOW
ELBOWBOARD
ELBOWBUSH
ELBOWCHAIR
ELBOWED
ELBOWER
ELBOWPIECE
ELBOWROOM
ELBOWS
ELBOWY
ELBUCK
ELCAJA
ELCHEE
ELCHI
ELD
ELDER
ELDERBERRY
ELDERBUSH
ELDERLIES
ELDERLY
ELDERMAN
ELDERMEN
ELDERN
ELDERSHIP
ELDERWOMAN
ELDERWOMEN
ELDERWOOD
ELDERWORT
ELDEST
ELDIN
ELDING
ELDMOTHER
ELDRICH
ELDRITCH

ELE
ELEAN
ELECAMPANE
ELECT
ELECTANT
ELECTED
ELECTING
ELECTION
ELECTIONEER
ELECTIONEERER
ELECTIVE
ELECTIVELY
ELECTIVENESS
ELECTIVITY
ELECTO
ELECTOR
ELECTORATE
ELECTORIAL
ELECTRAGIST
ELECTRAL
ELECTRALIZE
ELECTRE
ELECTREPETER
ELECTRESS
ELECTRET
ELECTRIC
ELECTRICAL
ELECTRICALIZE
ELECTRICALLY
ELECTRICIAN
ELECTRICITY
ELECTRICIZE
ELECTRIFIED
ELECTRIFIER
ELECTRIFY
ELECTRIFYING
ELECTRIZE
ELECTRIZED
ELECTRIZER
ELECTRIZING
ELECTRO
ELECTROBATH
ELECTROBUS
ELECTROCUTE
ELECTROCUTED
ELECTROCUTING
ELECTROCUTION
ELECTRODE
ELECTRODEPOSIT
ELECTRODES
ELECTROED
ELECTROFORM
ELECTROFUSED
ELECTROGILT
ELECTROGRAPH
ELECTROING
ELECTROIONIC
ELECTROLIER
ELECTROLYSIS
ELECTROLYTE
ELECTROLYTIC
ELECTROLYZE
ELECTROLYZED
ELECTROLYZER
ELECTROLYZING
ELECTROMAGNET
ELECTROMAGNETIC
ELECTROMER
ELECTROMETER
ELECTROMETRY
ELECTROMOBILE
ELECTROMOTOR
ELECTRON
ELECTRONIC
ELECTRONICS
ELECTROPATHY
ELECTROPHONE
ELECTROPISM
ELECTROPLATE
ELECTROPLATED
ELECTROPLATING
ELECTROPOION
ELECTROPOLAR
ELECTROPOWER
ELECTROS
ELECTROSCOPE
ELECTROSHOCK
ELECTROSTATIC
ELECTROSTATICS
ELECTROSTEEL
ELECTROTAXIS
ELECTROTEST
ELECTROTONIC
ELECTROTONIZE
ELECTROTONUS
ELECTROTYPE
ELECTROTYPED
ELECTROTYPER
ELECTROTYPY
ELECTROVITAL
ELECTROWIN
ELECTRUM
ELECTUARY
ELEEMOSINAR
ELEEMOSYNAR
ELEEMOSYNARY
ELEGANCE
ELEGANCIES
ELEGANCY
ELEGANT
ELEGANTE
ELEGANTLY
ELEGIAC
ELEGIACAL
ELEGIAMBIC
ELEGIAMBUS
ELEGIAST
ELEGIES
ELEGIOUS
ELEGIST
ELEGIT
ELEGIZE
ELEGIZED
ELEGIZING
ELEGY
ELEIDIN
ELEME
ELEMENT
ELEMENTAL
ELEMENTALISM
ELEMENTALIST
ELEMENTALITY
ELEMENTARILY
ELEMENTARINESS
ELEMENTARITY
ELEMENTARY
ELEMENTOID
ELEMENTS
ELEMI
ELEMICIN
ELEMIN
ELEMOL
ELENCH
ELENCHI
ELENCHIZE
ELENCHUS
ELENCTIC
ELENCTICAL
ELENGE
ELENGELY
ELENGENESS
ELEOLITE
ELEOMARGARIC
ELEONORITE
ELEOPLAST
ELEOPTENE
ELEOTRID
ELEPAIO
ELEPHANT
ELEPHANTA
ELEPHANTIAC
ELEPHANTIASIS
ELEPHANTIC
ELEPHANTINE
ELEPHANTOID
ELEPHANTOIDAL
ELEPHANTOUS
ELEPHANTS
ELEUTHERISM
ELEVATE
ELEVATED
ELEVATEDLY
ELEVATEDNESS
ELEVATING
ELEVATINGLY
ELEVATIO
ELEVATION
ELEVATIONAL
ELEVATO
ELEVATOR
ELEVE
ELEVEN
ELEVENER
ELEVENS
ELEVENTH
ELEVON
ELF
ELFENFOLK
ELFIC
ELFIN
ELFISH
ELFISHLY
ELFISHNESS
ELFKIN
ELFLAND
ELFLIKE
ELFLOCK
ELFS
ELFT
ELFWORT
ELGER
ELIAD
ELIASITE
ELICIT
ELICITABLE
ELICITATE
ELICITATION
ELICITED
ELICITING
ELICITOR
ELICITORY
ELIDE
ELIDED
ELIDIBLE
ELIDING
ELIGENT
ELIGIBILITIES
ELIGIBILITY
ELIGIBLE
ELIMINABLE
ELIMINAND
ELIMINANT
ELIMINATE
ELIMINATED
ELIMINATING
ELIMINATION
ELIMINATIVE
ELIMINATOR
ELIMINATORY
ELIQUATE
ELIQUATED
ELIQUATING
ELIQUATION
ELISION
ELISOR
ELITE
ELIX
ELIXATE
ELIXATION
ELIXIR
ELK
ELKHOUND
ELKS
ELKSLIP
ELKWOOD
ELL
ELLACHICK
ELLAGATE
ELLAGIC
ELLAGITANNIN
ELLE
ELLECK
ELLER
ELLFISH
ELLIPSE
ELLIPSES
ELLIPSIS
ELLIPSOGRAPH
ELLIPSOID
ELLIPSOIDAL
ELLIPSONE
ELLIPTIC
ELLIPTICAL
ELLIPTICALLY
ELLIPTICALNESS
ELLIPTICITY
ELLIPTOID
ELLOPS
ELLWAND
ELM
ELMEN
ELMY
ELOCULAR
ELOCUTE
ELOCUTION
ELOCUTIONARY
ELOCUTIONER
ELOCUTIONIST
ELOD
ELOGE
ELOGIUM
ELOGY
ELOIGN
ELOIGNER
ELOIGNMENT
ELOINE
ELON
ELONG
ELONGATE
ELONGATED
ELONGATING
ELONGATION
ELONGATIVE
ELOPE
ELOPED
ELOPEMENT
ELOPER
ELOPING
ELOPS
ELOQUENCE
ELOQUENT
ELOQUENTIAL
ELOTILLO
ELPASOLITE
ELPIDITE
ELRITCH
ELS
ELSE
ELSEHOW
ELSEN
ELSEWARDS
ELSEWAYS
ELSEWHAT
ELSEWHEN
ELSEWHERE
ELSEWHERES
ELSEWHITHER
ELSEWISE
ELSHIN
ELSIN
ELSON
ELT
ELTROT
ELUATE
ELUCIDATE
ELUCIDATED
ELUCIDATING
ELUCIDATION
ELUCIDATIVE
ELUCIDATOR
ELUCIDATORY
ELUCTATE
ELUCUBRATE
ELUDE
ELUDED
ELUDER
ELUDING
ELUENT
ELUSION
ELUSIVE
ELUSIVELY
ELUSIVENESS
ELUSORINESS
ELUSORY
ELUTE
ELUTION
ELUTOR
ELUTRIATE
ELUTRIATED
ELUTRIATING
ELUTRIATION
ELUTRIATOR
ELUVIAL
ELUVIATION
ELUVIUM
ELVAN
ELVANITE
ELVANITIC
ELVEN
ELVER
ELVES
ELVISH
ELVISHLY
ELY
ELYDORIC
ELYNG
ELYTRA
ELYTRAL
ELYTRIFEROUS
ELYTRIFORM
ELYTRIGEROUS
ELYTRIN
ELYTROCELE
ELYTROCLASIA
ELYTROID
ELYTRON
ELYTROPLASTIC
ELYTROPTOSIS
ELYTRORHAGIA
ELYTROTOMY
ELYTROUS
ELYTRUM
EM
EMACIATE
EMACIATED

EMACIATING
EMACIATION
EMAGRAM
EMAIL
EMAJAGUA
EMANANT
EMANATE
EMANATED
EMANATING
EMANATION
EMANATIONAL
EMANATIONISM
EMANATIONIST
EMANATIVE
EMANATIVELY
EMANATOR
EMANATORY
EMANCIPATE
EMANCIPATED
EMANCIPATING
EMANCIPATIO
EMANCIPATION
EMANCIPATIONIST
EMANCIPATIVE
EMANCIPATOR
EMANCIPATORY
EMANCIPATRESS
EMANCIPIST
EMANDIBULATE
EMANE
EMANIUM
EMARCID
EMARGINATE
EMARGINATED
EMARGINATING
EMARGINATION
EMASCULATE
EMASCULATED
EMASCULATING
EMASCULATION
EMASCULATIVE
EMASCULATOR
EMASCULATORY
EMBAIN
EMBALE
EMBALL
EMBALM
EMBALMED
EMBALMER
EMBALMING
EMBALMMENT
EMBANK
EMBANKMENT
EMBAR
EMBARCATION
EMBARGO
EMBARGOED
EMBARGOES
EMBARGOING
EMBARK
EMBARKATION
EMBARKED
EMBARKING
EMBARKMENT
EMBARMENT
EMBARRAS
EMBARRASS
EMBARRASSED
EMBARRASSING
EMBARRASSINGLY
EMBARRASSMENT
EMBARRED
EMBARRING
EMBASE
EMBASSADOR
EMBASSAGE
EMBASSY
EMBATHE
EMBATTLE
EMBATTLED
EMBATTLING
EMBAY
EMBAYED
EMBAYING
EMBAYMENT
EMBED
EMBEDDED
EMBEDDING
EMBEDMENT
EMBELIF
EMBELIN
EMBELLISH
EMBELLISHED
EMBELLISHER
EMBELLISHING
EMBELLISHMENT
EMBER
EMBERGEESE
EMBERGOOSE
EMBERS
EMBEZZLE
EMBEZZLED
EMBEZZLEMENT
EMBEZZLER
EMBEZZLING
EMBIID
EMBIND
EMBIOTOCID
EMBIOTOCOID
EMBIRA
EMBITTER
EMBITTERED
EMBITTERER
EMBITTERING
EMBITTERMENT
EMBLANCH
EMBLAZE
EMBLAZED
EMBLAZER
EMBLAZING
EMBLAZON
EMBLAZONED
EMBLAZONER
EMBLAZONMENT
EMBLAZONRY
EMBLEM
EMBLEMA
EMBLEMATIC
EMBLEMATICAL
EMBLEMATICIZE
EMBLEMATIST
EMBLEMATIZE
EMBLEMATIZED
EMBLEMATIZING
EMBLEMENT
EMBLEMENTS
EMBLEMIST
EMBLEMIZE
EMBLEMIZED
EMBLEMIZING
EMBLIC
EMBLISS
EMBLOSSOM
EMBODIED
EMBODIER
EMBODIMENT
EMBODY
EMBODYING
EMBOG
EMBOITE
EMBOITEMENT
EMBOLDEN
EMBOLDENER
EMBOLE
EMBOLECTOMIES
EMBOLECTOMY
EMBOLEMIA
EMBOLIC
EMBOLIFORM
EMBOLISM
EMBOLISMIC
EMBOLITE
EMBOLIUM
EMBOLIZE
EMBOLO
EMBOLOLALIA
EMBOLOMERISM
EMBOLOMEROUS
EMBOLOMYCOTIC
EMBOLON
EMBOLUM
EMBOLUS
EMBOLY
EMBONPOINT
EMBORDER
EMBOSK
EMBOSOM
EMBOSS
EMBOSSED
EMBOSSER
EMBOSSING
EMBOSSMAN
EMBOSSMEN
EMBOSSMENT
EMBOST
EMBOUCHURE
EMBOUND
EMBOW
EMBOWED
EMBOWEL
EMBOWELED
EMBOWELER
EMBOWELING
EMBOWELLED
EMBOWELLER
EMBOWELLING
EMBOWER
EMBOWERED
EMBOWERING
EMBOWING
EMBOWMENT
EMBOX
EMBRACE
EMBRACED
EMBRACEMENT
EMBRACEOR
EMBRACER
EMBRACERY
EMBRACING
EMBRACIVE
EMBRAID
EMBRAKE
EMBRANCHMENT
EMBRANGLE
EMBRANGLED
EMBRANGLEMENT
EMBRANGLING
EMBRASE
EMBRASURE
EMBRASURED
EMBRASURING
EMBRAVE
EMBRAWN
EMBREATHE
EMBREW
EMBRIGHT
EMBRIGHTEN
EMBRITTLE
EMBRITTLEMENT
EMBROADEN
EMBROCATE
EMBROCATED
EMBROCATING
EMBROCATION
EMBROCHE
EMBROIDER
EMBROIDERED
EMBROIDERER
EMBROIDERESS
EMBROIDERIES
EMBROIDERING
EMBROIDERY
EMBROIL
EMBROILED
EMBROILER
EMBROILING
EMBROILMENT
EMBRONZE
EMBROSCOPIC
EMBROWN
EMBRUE
EMBRYECTOMY
EMBRYO
EMBRYOCARDIA
EMBRYOCTONY
EMBRYOFEROUS
EMBRYOGENIC
EMBRYOGENY
EMBRYOGONY
EMBRYOGRAPHY
EMBRYOID
EMBRYOLOGIC
EMBRYOLOGICAL
EMBRYOLOGICALLY
EMBRYOLOGIST
EMBRYOLOGY
EMBRYOMA
EMBRYOMAS
EMBRYOMATA
EMBRYON
EMBRYONAL
EMBRYONARY
EMBRYONATE
EMBRYONATED
EMBRYONIC
EMBRYONICALLY
EMBRYONIFORM
EMBRYONY
EMBRYOPHAGOUS
EMBRYOPHORE
EMBRYOPLASTIC
EMBRYOS
EMBRYOSCOPE
EMBRYOTEGA
EMBRYOTEGAE
EMBRYOTIC
EMBRYOTOME
EMBRYOTOMY
EMBRYOTROPHY
EMBRYOUS
EMBUE
EMBUIA
EMBUS
EMBUSK
EMBUSQUE
EMBUSSED
EMBUSSING
EMCEE
EMCUMBERING
EME
EMEER
EMEND
EMENDABLE
EMENDATE
EMENDATED
EMENDATELY
EMENDATING
EMENDATION
EMENDATOR
EMENDATORY
EMENDER
EMERALD
EMERANT
EMERAUDE
EMERGE
EMERGED
EMERGENCE
EMERGENCIES
EMERGENCY
EMERGENT
EMERGENTLY
EMERGENTNESS
EMERGING
EMERIED
EMERIL
EMERITED
EMERITI
EMERITUS
EMERIZE
EMEROD
EMERODS
EMEROID
EMERSED
EMERSION
EMERY
EMERYING
EMESIS
EMETIC
EMETICAL
EMETIN
EMETINE
EMETOLOGY
EMEU
EMEUTE
EMFORTH
EMGALLA
EMICTION
EMICTORY
EMIGRANT
EMIGRATE
EMIGRATED
EMIGRATING
EMIGRATION
EMIGRATIONAL
EMIGRATIVE
EMIGRATOR
EMIGRATORY
EMIGRE
EMIGREE
EMIGRES
EMINENCE
EMINENCIES
EMINENCY
EMINENT
EMINENTLY
EMIR
EMIRATE
EMISSARIA
EMISSARIUM
EMISSARY
EMISSILE
EMISSION
EMISSIVE
EMISSIVITY
EMIT
EMITTED
EMITTENT
EMITTER
EMITTING
EMMA
EMMARBLE
EMMARVEL
EMMELEIA
EMMENAGOGUE
EMMENIC

EMMENIOPATHY
EMMENOLOGY
EMMENSITE
EMMER
EMMET
EMMETROPE
EMMETROPIA
EMMETROPIC
EMODIN
EMOL
EMOLLESCENCE
EMOLLIATE
EMOLLIENT
EMOLOA
EMOLUMENT
EMOLUMENTAL
EMONY
EMORY
EMOTE
EMOTION
EMOTIONABLE
EMOTIONAL
EMOTIONALISM
EMOTIONALIST
EMOTIONALITY
EMOTIONALIZE
EMOTIONALIZED
EMOTIONED
EMOTIONIZE
EMOTIONLESS
EMOTIONS
EMOTIVE
EMOTIVELY
EMOTIVENESS
EMOTIVITY
EMPACKET
EMPAESTIC
EMPAISTIC
EMPALE
EMPANADA
EMPANEL
EMPANELMENT
EMPANOPLY
EMPAPER
EMPARADISE
EMPARK
EMPARL
EMPASM
EMPASMA
EMPATHIC
EMPATHICALLY
EMPATHIZE
EMPATHIZED
EMPATHIZING
EMPATHY
EMPATRON
EMPEARL
EMPEINE
EMPEIREMA
EMPENNAGE
EMPERESS
EMPERIES
EMPERIL
EMPEROR
EMPERORSHIP
EMPERY
EMPEST
EMPETRACEOUS
EMPEXA
EMPHASES
EMPHASIS
EMPHASIZE
EMPHASIZED
EMPHASIZING
EMPHATIC
EMPHATICAL
EMPHATICALLY
EMPHATICALNESS
EMPHEMERALNESS
EMPHLYSIS
EMPHRACTIC
EMPHRAXIS
EMPHYSEMA
EMPHYTEUSIS
EMPHYTEUTA
EMPHYTEUTIC
EMPICTURE
EMPID
EMPIECEMENT
EMPIGHT
EMPIRE
EMPIREMA
EMPIRIC
EMPIRICAL
EMPIRICALLY
EMPIRICALNESS
EMPIRICISM
EMPIRICIST
EMPIRICS
EMPIRISM
EMPIRISTIC
EMPIRY
EMPLACE
EMPLACEMENT
EMPLANE
EMPLANED
EMPLANING
EMPLASTIC
EMPLASTRA
EMPLASTRATION
EMPLASTRUM
EMPLECTITE
EMPLEOMANIA
EMPLOY
EMPLOYE
EMPLOYED
EMPLOYEE
EMPLOYER
EMPLOYING
EMPLOYMENT
EMPODIA
EMPODIUM
EMPOISON
EMPOISONED
EMPOISONER
EMPOISONING
EMPOISONMENT
EMPOLDER
EMPORETIC
EMPOREUTIC
EMPORIA
EMPORIAL
EMPORIUM
EMPORIUMS
EMPORTE
EMPORY
EMPOVER
EMPOVERISH
EMPOWER
EMPRESA
EMPRESARIO
EMPRESS
EMPRESSE
EMPRESSEMENT
EMPRISE
EMPRIZE
EMPT
EMPTIED
EMPTIER
EMPTIES
EMPTIEST
EMPTILY
EMPTINESS
EMPTINGS
EMPTINS
EMPTIO
EMPTION
EMPTOR
EMPTY
EMPTYHEARTED
EMPTYING
EMPTYSIS
EMPURPLE
EMPURPLED
EMPURPLING
EMPYEMA
EMPYEMATA
EMPYEMIC
EMPYESIS
EMPYOCELE
EMPYREAL
EMPYREAN
EMPYREUM
EMPYREUMA
EMPYREUMATA
EMPYREUMATIC
EMPYROMANCY
EMRAUD
EMU
EMULABLE
EMULANT
EMULATE
EMULATED
EMULATING
EMULATION
EMULATIVE
EMULATOR
EMULATORY
EMULATRESS
EMULE
EMULGE
EMULGENCE
EMULGENT
EMULOUS
EMULOUSLY
EMULOUSNESS
EMULSIBILITY
EMULSIBLE
EMULSIFIABILITY
EMULSIFIABLE
EMULSIFIED
EMULSIFIER
EMULSIFY
EMULSIFYING
EMULSIN
EMULSION
EMULSIONIZE
EMULSIVE
EMULSOID
EMULSOR
EMUNCTORY
EMUNDATION
EMUNGE
EMURE
EMYD
EMYDIAN
EN
ENABLE
ENABLED
ENABLER
ENABLING
ENACH
ENACT
ENACTION
ENACTIVE
ENACTMENT
ENACTOR
ENACTORY
ENACTURE
ENAENA
ENAGE
ENALID
ENALIOSAUR
ENALIOSAURIAN
ENALITE
ENALLAGE
ENALURON
ENALYRON
ENAM
ENAMDAR
ENAMEL
ENAMELED
ENAMELER
ENAMELING
ENAMELIST
ENAMELLED
ENAMELLER
ENAMELLING
ENAMELLIST
ENAMELOMA
ENAMELWARE
ENAMOR
ENAMORATO
ENAMORED
ENAMOREDNESS
ENAMORING
ENAMOUR
ENAMOURED
ENAMOUREDNESS
ENAMOURING
ENANTHEM
ENANTHEMA
ENANTHEMATOUS
ENANTHESIS
ENANTIOMORPH
ENANTIOPATHY
ENANTIOSIS
ENANTIOTROPY
ENARCHED
ENARGITE
ENARM
ENARME
ENARRATION
ENARTHRODIA
ENARTHRODIAL
ENARTHROSIS
ENATE
ENATIC
ENATION
ENBUSSHE
ENCAENIA
ENCAGE
ENCAGED
ENCAGING
ENCAMP
ENCAMPMENT
ENCANTHIS
ENCAPSULATE
ENCAPSULATED
ENCAPSULATING
ENCAPSULATION
ENCARNALIZE
ENCARNALIZED
ENCARNALIZING
ENCARPIUM
ENCARPUS
ENCASE
ENCASED
ENCASEMENT
ENCASH
ENCASHABLE
ENCASHMENT
ENCASTAGE
ENCASTRE
ENCASTREMENT
ENCAUMA
ENCAUSTES
ENCAUSTIC
ENCAUSTICALLY
ENCAVE
ENCEINT
ENCEINTE
ENCEPHALA
ENCEPHALIC
ENCEPHALIN
ENCEPHALITIC
ENCEPHALITIS
ENCEPHALOGRAM
ENCEPHALOGRAPH
ENCEPHALOID
ENCEPHALOLOGY
ENCEPHALOMA
ENCEPHALOMAS
ENCEPHALOMATA
ENCEPHALON
ENCEPHALOUS
ENCHAFE
ENCHAIN
ENCHAINED
ENCHAINING
ENCHAINMENT
ENCHANNEL
ENCHANT
ENCHANTED
ENCHANTER
ENCHANTING
ENCHANTINGLY
ENCHANTINGNESS
ENCHANTMENT
ENCHANTRESS
ENCHARGE
ENCHARGED
ENCHARGING
ENCHASE
ENCHASED
ENCHASER
ENCHASING
ENCHASTEN
ENCHEASON
ENCHEER
ENCHEQUER
ENCHESON
ENCHILADA
ENCHILADAS
ENCHIRIDION
ENCHODONTID
ENCHODONTOID
ENCHONDROMA
ENCHONDROMAS
ENCHONDROMATA
ENCHONDROSIS
ENCHORIAL
ENCHORIC
ENCHURCH
ENCHYLEMA
ENCHYMATOUS
ENCHYTRAE
ENCHYTRAEID
ENCINA
ENCINAL
ENCINCTURE
ENCINILLO
ENCIPHER
ENCIPHERED
ENCIPHERING
ENCIRCLE
ENCIRCLED
ENCIRCLEMENT
ENCIRCLER
ENCIRCLING
ENCLARET
ENCLASP
ENCLASPED
ENCLASPING
ENCLAVE

ENCLAVED
ENCLAVEMENT
ENCLAVING
ENCLEAR
ENCLISIS
ENCLITIC
ENCLITICAL
ENCLITICALLY
ENCLOAK
ENCLOG
ENCLOISTER
ENCLOSE
ENCLOSED
ENCLOSER
ENCLOSING
ENCLOSURE
ENCLOTHE
ENCLOUD
ENCODE
ENCODED
ENCODER
ENCODING
ENCOIGNURE
ENCOLLAR
ENCOLOR
ENCOLOUR
ENCOLPIA
ENCOLPION
ENCOLURE
ENCOMENDERO
ENCOMIA
ENCOMIAST
ENCOMIASTIC
ENCOMIC
ENCOMIENDA
ENCOMIOLOGIC
ENCOMIUM
ENCOMIUMS
ENCOMPASS
ENCOMPASSED
ENCOMPASSER
ENCOMPASSING
ENCOMY
ENCORBELMENT
ENCORE
ENCORED
ENCORING
ENCOUNTER
ENCOUNTERABLE
ENCOUNTERED
ENCOUNTERER
ENCOUNTERING
ENCOUNTERS
ENCOURAGE
ENCOURAGED
ENCOURAGEMENT
ENCOURAGER
ENCOURAGING
ENCOURAGINGLY
ENCRANIAL
ENCRATIC
ENCRATY
ENCRIMSON
ENCRINAL
ENCRINIC
ENCRINITAL
ENCRINITE
ENCRINITIC
ENCRINITICAL
ENCRINOID
ENCRISP
ENCROACH
ENCROACHED
ENCROACHER
ENCROACHING
ENCROACHMENT
ENCROTCHET
ENCRUST
ENCRUSTED
ENCRUSTMENT
ENCRYPT
ENCULTURATION
ENCUMBER
ENCUMBERED
ENCUMBERMENT
ENCUMBRANCE
ENCUMBRANCER
ENCURTAIN
ENCYCLIC
ENCYCLICAL
ENCYCLOPAEDIA
ENCYCLOPAEDIAC
ENCYCLOPAEDIAL
ENCYCLOPAEDIAN
ENCYCLOPAEDIC
ENCYCLOPAEDICAL
ENCYCLOPAEDICALLY
ENCYCLOPAEDISM
ENCYCLOPAEDIST
ENCYCLOPAEDIZE
ENCYCLOPEDIA
ENCYCLOPEDIAC
ENCYCLOPEDIACAL
ENCYCLOPEDIAL
ENCYCLOPEDIAN
ENCYCLOPEDIAST
ENCYCLOPEDIC
ENCYCLOPEDICAL
ENCYCLOPEDICALLY
ENCYCLOPEDISM
ENCYCLOPEDIST
ENCYCLOPEDIZE
ENCYRTID
ENCYST
ENCYSTATION
ENCYSTED
ENCYSTING
ENCYSTMENT
END
ENDAMAGE
ENDAMAGEABLE
ENDAMAGED
ENDAMAGEMENT
ENDAMAGING
ENDAMASK
ENDAMEBA
ENDAMEBIASIS
ENDAMEBIC
ENDAMOEBIASIS
ENDAMOEBIC
ENDANGER
ENDANGERED
ENDANGERER
ENDANGERING
ENDANGERMENT
ENDANGIUM
ENDAORTIC
ENDAORTITIS
ENDARCH
ENDARCHY
ENDARK
ENDARTERIAL
ENDARTERITIS
ENDARTERIUM
ENDASEH
ENDASPIDEAN
ENDAZE
ENDBALL
ENDBOARD
ENDBRAIN
ENDEAR
ENDEARANCE
ENDEARED
ENDEAREDLY
ENDEARING
ENDEARINGLY
ENDEARINGNESS
ENDEARMENT
ENDEAVOR
ENDEAVORED
ENDEAVORER
ENDEAVORING
ENDEAVOUR
ENDEAVOURED
ENDEAVOURER
ENDEAVOURING
ENDECHA
ENDED
ENDEICTIC
ENDELLIONITE
ENDEMIC
ENDEMICAL
ENDEMICALLY
ENDEMICITY
ENDEMIOLOGICAL
ENDEMIOLOGY
ENDEMISM
ENDENIZEN
ENDER
ENDERMATIC
ENDERMIC
ENDERON
ENDEW
ENDGATE
ENDIMANCHE
ENDING
ENDITE
ENDIVE
ENDLESS
ENDLESSLY
ENDLESSNESS
ENDLONG
ENDMOST
ENDOBLAST
ENDOBLASTIC
ENDOCARDIAC
ENDOCARDIAL
ENDOCARDITIC
ENDOCARDITIS
ENDOCARDIUM
ENDOCARP
ENDOCARPAL
ENDOCARPIC
ENDOCARPOID
ENDOCENTRIC
ENDOCHROME
ENDOCHYLOUS
ENDOCLINAL
ENDOCLINE
ENDOCOELAR
ENDOCOELE
ENDOCONE
ENDOCONIDIA
ENDOCONIDIUM
ENDOCRANIAL
ENDOCRANIUM
ENDOCRIN
ENDOCRINAL
ENDOCRINE
ENDOCRINIC
ENDOCRINISM
ENDOCRINOLOGY
ENDOCRINOUS
ENDOCRITIC
ENDOCYCLE
ENDOCYCLIC
ENDOCYEMATE
ENDOCYST
ENDODERM
ENDODERMAL
ENDODERMIC
ENDODERMIS
ENDODONTIA
ENDODONTICS
ENDOENZYME
ENDOGAMIC
ENDOGAMOUS
ENDOGAMY
ENDOGASTRIC
ENDOGEN
ENDOGENESIS
ENDOGENETIC
ENDOGENIC
ENDOGENOUS
ENDOGENOUSLY
ENDOGENY
ENDOGLOBULAR
ENDOGNATH
ENDOGNATHAL
ENDOGNATHION
ENDOLEMMA
ENDOLYMPH
ENDOLYMPHIC
ENDOLYSIN
ENDOMETRIAL
ENDOMETRITIS
ENDOMETRIUM
ENDOMETRY
ENDOMIXIS
ENDOMORPH
ENDOMORPHIC
ENDOMORPHISM
ENDOMORPHY
ENDOMYSIAL
ENDOMYSIUM
ENDONEURIUM
ENDONUCLEOLUS
ENDOPARASITE
ENDOPATHIC
ENDOPERIDIAL
ENDOPERIDIUM
ENDOPHAGOUS
ENDOPHAGY
ENDOPHRAGM
ENDOPHRAGMAL
ENDOPHYTAL
ENDOPHYTE
ENDOPHYTOUS
ENDOPLASM
ENDOPLASMA
ENDOPLASMIC
ENDOPLAST
ENDOPLASTULAR
ENDOPLASTULE
ENDOPLEURA
ENDOPLEURAL
ENDOPLEURITE
ENDOPLEURITIC
ENDOPOD
ENDOPODITE
ENDOPODITIC
ENDOPROCT
ENDOPROCTOUS
ENDOPSYCHIC
ENDORACHIS
ENDORAL
ENDORE
ENDORSABLE
ENDORSATION
ENDORSE
ENDORSED
ENDORSEE
ENDORSEMENT
ENDORSER
ENDORSING
ENDORSOR
ENDOSARC
ENDOSARCOUS
ENDOSCLERITE
ENDOSCOPE
ENDOSCOPY
ENDOSEPSIS
ENDOSKELETAL
ENDOSKELETON
ENDOSMOMETER
ENDOSMOSIC
ENDOSMOSIS
ENDOSMOTIC
ENDOSMOTICALLY
ENDOSOME
ENDOSPERM
ENDOSPERMIC
ENDOSPORE
ENDOSPORIUM
ENDOSPOROUS
ENDOSS
ENDOSTEAL
ENDOSTEALLY
ENDOSTEITIS
ENDOSTEOMA
ENDOSTEOMAS
ENDOSTEOMATA
ENDOSTERNITE
ENDOSTEUM
ENDOSTITIS
ENDOSTOMA
ENDOSTOMATA
ENDOSTOME
ENDOSTOSIS
ENDOSTRACAL
ENDOSTRACUM
ENDOSTYLAR
ENDOSTYLE
ENDOSTYLIC
ENDOTHECA
ENDOTHECAL
ENDOTHECIA
ENDOTHECIAL
ENDOTHECIUM
ENDOTHELIA
ENDOTHELIAL
ENDOTHELIOMA
ENDOTHELIUM
ENDOTHELOID
ENDOTHERM
ENDOTHERMAL
ENDOTHERMIC
ENDOTHERMOUS
ENDOTHERMY
ENDOTHORAX
ENDOTHYS
ENDOTOXIC
ENDOTOXIN
ENDOTROPHIC
ENDOTYS
ENDOUTE
ENDOW
ENDOWED
ENDOWER
ENDOWING
ENDOWMENT
ENDPAPERS
ENDPIECE
ENDPLATE
ENDRIN
ENDRUMPF
ENDS
ENDSEAL
ENDSHIP
ENDUE
ENDUED
ENDUING
ENDUNGEON
ENDURA
ENDURABILITY

ENDURABLE
ENDURABLENESS
ENDURABLY
ENDURANCE
ENDURANT
ENDURE
ENDURED
ENDURER
ENDURING
ENDURINGLY
ENDURINGNESS
ENDWAYS
ENDWISE
ENDYSIS
ENECATE
ENEMA
ENEMAS
ENEMATA
ENEMIED
ENEMIES
ENEMY
ENEMYING
ENEPIDERMIC
ENERGEIA
ENERGESIS
ENERGETIC
ENERGETICALLY
ENERGETICIST
ENERGETICS
ENERGETISTIC
ENERGIC
ENERGICO
ENERGID
ENERGIES
ENERGISM
ENERGIST
ENERGIZE
ENERGIZED
ENERGIZER
ENERGIZING
ENERGUMEN
ENERGY
ENERVATE
ENERVATED
ENERVATING
ENERVATION
ENERVATIVE
ENERVATOR
ENEW
ENFACE
ENFACED
ENFACEMENT
ENFACING
ENFAMISH
ENFANT
ENFARCE
ENFATICO
ENFAVOR
ENFEEBLE
ENFEEBLED
ENFEEBLEMENT
ENFEEBLER
ENFEEBLING
ENFELON
ENFEOFF
ENFEOFFED
ENFEOFFING
ENFEOFFMENT
ENFETTER
ENFILADE
ENFILADED
ENFILADING
ENFILE
ENFILED
ENFIN
ENFIRE
ENFIRM
ENFLAGELLATE
ENFLAGELLATION
ENFLAME
ENFLESH
ENFLEURAGE
ENFLOWER
ENFLOWERED
ENFLOWERING
ENFOLD
ENFOLDED
ENFOLDEN
ENFOLDING
ENFONCE
ENFONCED
ENFONCEE
ENFORCE
ENFORCEABLE
ENFORCED
ENFORCEDLY
ENFORCEMENT
ENFORCER
ENFORCING
ENFORCIVE
ENFORCIVELY
ENFORT
ENFORTH
ENFRAI
ENFRAME
ENFRAMED
ENFRAMEMENT
ENFRAMING
ENFRANCHISED
ENFRANCHISEMENT
ENFRANCHISER
ENFRANCHISING
ENFRENZY
ENFUME
ENG
ENGAGE
ENGAGED
ENGAGEDLY
ENGAGEDNESS
ENGAGEMENT
ENGAGER
ENGAGING
ENGAGINGLY
ENGAGINGNESS
ENGARDE
ENGARLAND
ENGARRISON
ENGASTRIMYTH
ENGASTRIMYTHIC
ENGAZE
ENGENDER
ENGENDERED
ENGENDERER
ENGENDERING
ENGENDERMENT
ENGENDRURE
ENGENDURE
ENGHLE
ENGHOSTED
ENGI
ENGILD
ENGINE
ENGINED
ENGINEER
ENGINEERED
ENGINEERING
ENGINEMAN
ENGINEMEN
ENGINERY
ENGINING
ENGINOUS
ENGIRD
ENGIRDED
ENGIRDING
ENGIRDLE
ENGIRDLED
ENGIRT
ENGLACIAL
ENGLEIM
ENGLISH
ENGLISHER
ENGLOBE
ENGLUE
ENGLUT
ENGLUTE
ENGLYN
ENGLYNS
ENGOBE
ENGORE
ENGORGE
ENGORGED
ENGORGEMENT
ENGORGING
ENGOUE
ENGOUEE
ENGOUEMENT
ENGOULED
ENGOUMENT
ENGRACE
ENGRACED
ENGRACING
ENGRAFF
ENGRAFFED
ENGRAFFING
ENGRAFT
ENGRAFTATION
ENGRAFTED
ENGRAFTER
ENGRAFTING
ENGRAFTMENT
ENGRAIL
ENGRAILED
ENGRAILING
ENGRAILMENT
ENGRAIN
ENGRAINED
ENGRAINEDLY
ENGRAINER
ENGRAINING
ENGRAM
ENGRAMMA
ENGRAMMATIC
ENGRAMME
ENGRAMMIC
ENGRANDIZE
ENGRAPHIA
ENGRAPHIC
ENGRAPHICALLY
ENGRAPHY
ENGRAVE
ENGRAVED
ENGRAVEMENT
ENGRAVER
ENGRAVING
ENGREGGE
ENGRIEVE
ENGROSS
ENGROSSED
ENGROSSEDLY
ENGROSSER
ENGROSSING
ENGROSSINGLY
ENGROSSINGNESS
ENGROSSMENT
ENGULF
ENGYSCOPE
ENHAEMOSPORE
ENHALO
ENHANCE
ENHANCED
ENHANCEMENT
ENHANCER
ENHANCING
ENHANCIVE
ENHARBOR
ENHARDEN
ENHARDY
ENHARMONIC
ENHARMONICAL
ENHARMONICALLY
ENHAUNT
ENHEART
ENHEARTEN
ENHEDGE
ENHEMOSPORE
ENHORROR
ENHYDRITE
ENHYDRITIC
ENHYDROUS
ENHYPOSTASIA
ENHYPOSTASIS
ENHYPOSTATIC
ENHYPOSTATIZE
ENIAC
ENIGMA
ENIGMAS
ENIGMATIC
ENIGMATICAL
ENIGMATICALLY
ENIGMATIST
ENIGMATIZE
ENIGMATIZED
ENIGMATIZING
ENIGMATOGRAPHER
ENIGMATOGRAPHY
ENIGUA
ENISLE
ENISLED
ENISLING
ENIUN
ENJAIL
ENJAMB
ENJAMBED
ENJAMBEMENT
ENJAMBMENT
ENJEOPARD
ENJEOPARDY
ENJEWEL
ENJOIN
ENJOINDER
ENJOINED
ENJOINER
ENJOINING
ENJOINMENT
ENJOY
ENJOYABLE
ENJOYABLENESS
ENJOYABLY
ENJOYED
ENJOYER
ENJOYING
ENJOYMENT
ENKINDLE
ENKINDLED
ENKINDLER
ENKINDLING
ENKO
ENLACE
ENLACED
ENLACEMENT
ENLACING
ENLARD
ENLARGE
ENLARGED
ENLARGEDLY
ENLARGEDNESS
ENLARGEMENT
ENLARGER
ENLARGING
ENLARGINGLY
ENLIGHT
ENLIGHTEN
ENLIGHTENED
ENLIGHTENER
ENLIGHTENING
ENLIGHTENMENT
ENLIMN
ENLINK
ENLINKED
ENLINKING
ENLINKMENT
ENLIST
ENLISTED
ENLISTER
ENLISTING
ENLISTMENT
ENLIVEN
ENLIVENED
ENLIVENER
ENLIVENING
ENLIVENINGLY
ENLIVENMENT
ENLOCK
ENLURE
ENLUTE
ENMESH
ENMESHED
ENMESHING
ENMESHMENT
ENMITIES
ENMITY
ENMOVE
ENMUFFLE
ENNEAD
ENNEADIC
ENNEAGON
ENNEAGONAL
ENNEAGYNOUS
ENNEAHEDRA
ENNEAHEDRAL
ENNEAHEDRIA
ENNEAHEDRON
ENNEAHEDRONS
ENNEASEMIC
ENNEASTYLE
ENNEASTYLOS
ENNEASYLLABIC
ENNEATIC
ENNOBLE
ENNOBLED
ENNOBLEMENT
ENNOBLER
ENNOBLING
ENNOMIC
ENNUE
ENNUI
ENNUIED
ENNUIS
ENNUYANT
ENNUYE
ENNUYEE
ENNUYING
ENODAL
ENODALLY
ENODATE
ENODATION
ENODE
ENOIL
ENOL
ENOLASE
ENOLATE
ENOLIC
ENOLIZABLE
ENOLIZATION
ENOLIZE

ENOLOGY
ENOMANIA
ENOMOTARCH
ENOMOTY
ENOPHTHALMOS
ENOPHTHALMUS
ENOPLAN
ENOPLION
ENOPTROMANCY
ENORGANIC
ENORM
ENORMITIES
ENORMITY
ENORMOUS
ENORMOUSLY
ENORMOUSNESS
ENOSIS
ENOSTOSIS
ENOUGH
ENOUNCE
ENOUNCED
ENOUNCEMENT
ENOUNCING
ENOW
ENPHYTOTIC
ENPLANE
ENPLANED
ENPLANING
ENQUIRE
ENQUIRER
ENQUIRY
ENRACE
ENRAGE
ENRAGED
ENRAGEDLY
ENRAGEDNESS
ENRAGING
ENRAMADA
ENRANGE
ENRANK
ENRAPT
ENRAPTURE
ENRAPTURED
ENRAPTURER
ENRAPTURING
ENRAVISH
ENRAVISHED
ENRAVISHING
ENRAVISHINGLY
ENREGIMENT
ENREGISTER
ENREGISTERED
ENREGISTERING
ENREGISTRATION
ENREGISTRY
ENRICH
ENRICHED
ENRICHER
ENRICHING
ENRICHINGLY
ENRICHMENT
ENRIDGED
ENRIGHT
ENRING
ENRINGED
ENRINGING
ENROBE
ENROBED
ENROBEMENT
ENROBER
ENROBING
ENROCKMENT
ENROL
ENROLL
ENROLLED
ENROLLER
ENROLLING
ENROLLMENT
ENROLMENT
ENROOT
ENROOTED
ENROOTING
ENROUGH
ENROUND
ENS
ENSAINT
ENSALADA
ENSAMPLE
ENSAMPLER
ENSANGUINE
ENSANGUINED
ENSANGUINING
ENSATE
ENSCENE
ENSCONCE
ENSCONCED
ENSCONCING
ENSCROLL
ENSE
ENSEAL
ENSEALED
ENSEALING
ENSEAM
ENSEAR
ENSEARCH
ENSEARCHER
ENSEAT
ENSEATED
ENSEATING
ENSELLURE
ENSEMBLE
ENSEPULCHER
ENSEPULCHERED
ENSEPULCHERING
ENSEPULCHRE
ENSETE
ENSHEATHE
ENSHIELD
ENSHIELDED
ENSHIELDING
ENSHRINE
ENSHRINED
ENSHRINEMENT
ENSHRINING
ENSHROUD
ENSIFORM
ENSIGN
ENSIGNCY
ENSIGNED
ENSIGNING
ENSIGNMENT
ENSIGNRY
ENSIGNSHIP
ENSILAGE
ENSILATE
ENSILATION
ENSILE
ENSILIST
ENSISTERNUM
ENSKIED
ENSKY
ENSKYED
ENSLAVE
ENSLAVED
ENSLAVEDNESS
ENSLAVEMENT
ENSLAVER
ENSLAVING
ENSLUMBER
ENSMALL
ENSNARE
ENSNARED
ENSNAREMENT
ENSNARER
ENSNARING
ENSNARINGLY
ENSNARL
ENSNOW
ENSORCEL
ENSORCELIZE
ENSORCELL
ENSORCERIZE
ENSOUL
ENSPHERE
ENSPHERED
ENSPHERING
ENSTAMP
ENSTAR
ENSTATE
ENSTATITE
ENSTATITIC
ENSTATITITE
ENSTATOLITE
ENSTEEP
ENSTOOL
ENSTORE
ENSTRANGED
ENSTYLE
ENSUABLE
ENSUANCE
ENSUANT
ENSUE
ENSUED
ENSUER
ENSUING
ENSURE
ENSURED
ENSURER
ENSURING
ENSWATHE
ENSWATHED
ENSWATHEMENT
ENSWATHING
ENSWEEP
ENTABLATURE
ENTABLATURED
ENTABLEMENT
ENTACH
ENTAD
ENTAIL
ENTAILED
ENTAILING
ENTAILMENT
ENTAL
ENTALENT
ENTAME
ENTAMEBIC
ENTAMOEBA
ENTAMOEBIC
ENTANGLE
ENTANGLED
ENTANGLEDLY
ENTANGLEDNESS
ENTANGLEMENT
ENTANGLER
ENTANGLING
ENTAPOPHYSIAL
ENTAPOPHYSIS
ENTARTHROTIC
ENTASIA
ENTASIS
ENTASTIC
ENTE
ENTELAM
ENTELECHIES
ENTELECHY
ENTELLUS
ENTELODONT
ENTEMPLE
ENTENTE
ENTER
ENTERA
ENTERADEN
ENTERAL
ENTERALGIA
ENTERATE
ENTERAUXE
ENTERCLOSE
ENTERECTOMY
ENTERED
ENTERER
ENTERGOGENIC
ENTERIC
ENTERICOID
ENTERING
ENTERITIDIS
ENTERITIS
ENTERMETE
ENTEROCELE
ENTEROCEPTOR
ENTEROCOELE
ENTEROCOELIC
ENTEROCOELOUS
ENTEROCYST
ENTERODYNIA
ENTEROGENOUS
ENTEROGRAM
ENTEROGRAPH
ENTEROGRAPHY
ENTEROID
ENTEROKINASE
ENTEROLITH
ENTEROLOGY
ENTEROLYSIS
ENTEROMERE
ENTERON
ENTEROPATHY
ENTEROPEXIA
ENTEROPLASTY
ENTEROPLEGIA
ENTEROPTOSIS
ENTEROPTOTIC
ENTERORRHEA
ENTEROSCOPE
ENTEROSCOPY
ENTEROSEPSIS
ENTEROSPASM
ENTEROSTASIS
ENTEROSTOMY
ENTEROTOMY
ENTEROTOXEMIA
ENTERPILLAR
ENTERPRISE
ENTERPRISED
ENTERPRISER
ENTERPRISING
ENTERPRISINGLY
ENTERTAIN
ENTERTAINED
ENTERTAINER
ENTERTAINING
ENTERTAININGLY
ENTERTAININGNESS
ENTERTAINMENT
ENTHALPY
ENTHEATE
ENTHELMINTHA
ENTHELMINTHES
ENTHEOS
ENTHETIC
ENTHRAL
ENTHRALL
ENTHRALLED
ENTHRALLER
ENTHRALLING
ENTHRALLINGLY
ENTHRALLMENT
ENTHRALMENT
ENTHRILL
ENTHRONE
ENTHRONED
ENTHRONG
ENTHRONING
ENTHRONIZATION
ENTHRONIZE
ENTHRONIZED
ENTHRONIZING
ENTHUSE
ENTHUSIASM
ENTHUSIAST
ENTHUSIASTIC
ENTHUSIASTICAL
ENTHUSIASTICALLY
ENTHUSIASTLY
ENTHYMEMATIC
ENTHYMEME
ENTIA
ENTICE
ENTICED
ENTICEMENT
ENTICER
ENTICING
ENTICINGLY
ENTICINGNESS
ENTIFICAL
ENTIFICATION
ENTIFY
ENTIRE
ENTIRELY
ENTIRENESS
ENTIRETY
ENTIRIS
ENTITATIVE
ENTITATIVELY
ENTITLE
ENTITLED
ENTITLING
ENTITY
ENTOBLAST
ENTOBLASTIC
ENTOCAROTID
ENTOCELE
ENTOCNEMIAL
ENTOCOELE
ENTOCOELIC
ENTOCONDYLE
ENTOCONE
ENTOCONID
ENTOCRANIAL
ENTOCYEMATE
ENTODERM
ENTODERMAL
ENTODERMIC
ENTOGASTRIC
ENTOGENOUS
ENTOGLOSSAL
ENTOIL
ENTOILED
ENTOILING
ENTOIRE
ENTOMB
ENTOMBED
ENTOMBING
ENTOMBMENT
ENTOMERE
ENTOMERIC
ENTOMICAL
ENTOMION
ENTOMOGENOUS
ENTOMOID
ENTOMOLITE
ENTOMOLOGIC
ENTOMOLOGICAL
ENTOMOLOGICALL
ENTOMOLOGIES

ENTOMOLOGIZE
ENTOMOLOGIZED
ENTOMOLOGIZING
ENTOMOLOGY
ENTOMOPHAGAN
ENTOMOPHILY
ENTOMOTAXY
ENTOMOTOMIST
ENTOMOTOMY
ENTOOLITIC
ENTOPHYTAL
ENTOPHYTE
ENTOPHYTIC
ENTOPHYTICALLY
ENTOPHYTOUS
ENTOPIC
ENTOPICAL
ENTOPLASM
ENTOPLASTIC
ENTOPLASTRAL
ENTOPLASTRON
ENTOPTICAL
ENTOPTICALLY
ENTOPTICS
ENTOPTOSCOPE
ENTOPTOSCOPIC
ENTOPTOSCOPY
ENTORETINA
ENTORGANISM
ENTOSPHERE
ENTOSTERNA
ENTOSTERNAL
ENTOSTERNITE
ENTOSTERNUM
ENTOTIC
ENTOTYMPANIC
ENTOURAGE
ENTOZOA
ENTOZOAL
ENTOZOAN
ENTOZOIC
ENTOZOOLOGY
ENTOZOON
ENTRADA
ENTRAIL
ENTRAILS
ENTRAIN
ENTRAINED
ENTRAINER
ENTRAINING
ENTRANCE
ENTRANCED
ENTRANCEMENT
ENTRANCEWAY
ENTRANCING
ENTRANCINGLY
ENTRANT
ENTRAP
ENTRAPMENT
ENTRAPPED
ENTRAPPER
ENTRAPPING
ENTREASURE
ENTREAT
ENTREATABLE
ENTREATED
ENTREATER
ENTREATFUL
ENTREATIES
ENTREATING
ENTREATMENT
ENTREATY
ENTRECHAT
ENTRECOTE
ENTREDEUX
ENTREE
ENTREFER
ENTREMES
ENTREMESS
ENTREMETS
ENTRENCH
ENTRENCHMENT
ENTREPAS
ENTREPOT
ENTREPRENANT
ENTREPRENEUR
ENTREPRENEUSE
ENTRER
ENTRESALLE
ENTRESOL
ENTRESSE
ENTREZ
ENTRIES
ENTRIKE
ENTROCHITE
ENTROPIES
ENTROPION
ENTROPY
ENTRUST
ENTRY
ENTRYMAN
ENTRYMEN
ENTRYWAY
ENTUM
ENTUNE
ENTWINE
ENTWINED
ENTWINING
ENTWIST
ENTWISTED
ENTWISTING
ENUCLEATE
ENUCLEATED
ENUCLEATING
ENUCLEATION
ENUCLEATOR
ENUMERABLE
ENUMERATE
ENUMERATED
ENUMERATING
ENUMERATION
ENUMERATIVE
ENUMERATOR
ENUNCIABILITY
ENUNCIABLE
ENUNCIATE
ENUNCIATED
ENUNCIATING
ENUNCIATION
ENUNCIATIVE
ENUNCIATIVELY
ENUNCIATOR
ENUNCIATORY
ENURE
ENURESIS
ENURNY
ENVASSAL
ENVASSALAGE
ENVAYE
ENVEIL
ENVELOP
ENVELOPE
ENVELOPED
ENVELOPER
ENVELOPING
ENVELOPMENT
ENVENOM
ENVENOMATION
ENVENOMED
ENVENOMING
ENVERGURE
ENVERMEIL
ENVIABLE
ENVIABLENESS
ENVIABLY
ENVIED
ENVIER
ENVIES
ENVINE
ENVIOUS
ENVIOUSLY
ENVIOUSNESS
ENVIRE
ENVIRON
ENVIRONAL
ENVIRONED
ENVIRONIC
ENVIRONING
ENVIRONMENT
ENVIRONMENTAL
ENVIRONMENTALI
ENVIRONMENTALI
ENVIRONS
ENVISAGE
ENVISAGED
ENVISAGEMENT
ENVISAGING
ENVISION
ENVOI
ENVOLUME
ENVOY
ENVY
ENVYING
ENVYINGLY
ENWHEEL
ENWIND
ENWOMB
ENWOMBED
ENWOMBING
ENWORTHY
ENWRAP
ENWRAPPED
ENWRAPPING
ENWRAPT
ENWREATHE
ENWROUGHT
ENZOOTIC
ENZYM
ENZYMATIC
ENZYME
ENZYMICALLY
ENZYMOLOGY
ENZYMOLYSIS
ENZYMOLYTIC
ENZYMOSIS
ENZYMOTIC
EOAN
EOBIONT
EODISCID
EOHIPPUS
EOLATION
EOLIAN
EOLIENNE
EOLIPILE
EOLITH
EOLITHIC
EOLOTROPIC
EON
EONIAN
EONISM
EOPHYTE
EOPHYTIC
EORHYOLITE
EORL
EOSATE
EOSIN
EOSINE
EOSINIC
EOSINOBLAST
EOSINOPHIL
EOSINOPHILE
EOSINOPHILIA
EOSINOPHILIC
EOSINOPHILOUS
EOSPHORITE
EOZOON
EOZOONAL
EP
EPACMAIC
EPACME
EPACRID
EPACRIDACEOUS
EPACT
EPACTAL
EPAGOGE
EPAGOGIC
EPAGOMENAE
EPAGOMENAL
EPAGOMENIC
EPAGOMENOUS
EPALPATE
EPANADIPLOSIS
EPANALEPSIS
EPANALEPTIC
EPANAPHORA
EPANAPHORAL
EPANASTROPHE
EPANODOS
EPANODY
EPANORTHOSIS
EPANTHOUS
EPAPILLATE
EPAPOPHYSIAL
EPAPOPHYSIS
EPAPPOSE
EPARC
EPARCH
EPARCHATE
EPARCHIAL
EPARCHIES
EPARCHY
EPARCUALE
EPARTERIAL
EPAULE
EPAULEMENT
EPAULET
EPAULETED
EPAULETTE
EPAULETTED
EPAULIERE
EPAXIAL
EPAXIALLY
EPEDAPHIC
EPEE
EPEEIST
EPEIRIC
EPEIROGENETIC
EPEIROGENIC
EPEIROGENY
EPEISODION
EPEMBRYONIC
EPENCEPHAL
EPENCEPHALIC
EPENCEPHALON
EPENDYMA
EPENDYMAL
EPENDYMOMA
EPENDYTES
EPENETIC
EPENTHESES
EPENTHESIS
EPENTHESIZE
EPENTHETIC
EPERGNE
EPERLAN
EPEROTESIS
EPERVA
EPEUS
EPEXEGESIS
EPEXEGETIC
EPEXEGETICAL
EPEXEGETICALLY
EPHA
EPHAH
EPHAPSE
EPHARMONIC
EPHARMONY
EPHEBE
EPHEBEION
EPHEBEUM
EPHEBIC
EPHEBOS
EPHEBUS
EPHECTIC
EPHEDRIN
EPHEDRINE
EPHELCYSTIC
EPHELIS
EPHEMERA
EPHEMERAE
EPHEMERAL
EPHEMERALITY
EPHEMERALLY
EPHEMERAN
EPHEMERAS
EPHEMERID
EPHEMERIDES
EPHEMERIS
EPHEMEROMORPHIC
EPHEMERON
EPHEMERONS
EPHEMEROUS
EPHERERIST
EPHESTIA
EPHETAE
EPHETE
EPHETIC
EPHIDROSIS
EPHIPPIA
EPHIPPIAL
EPHIPPIUM
EPHOD
EPHOR
EPHORAL
EPHORALTY
EPHORATE
EPHORI
EPHORIC
EPHORS
EPHORUS
EPHPHATHA
EPHTHIANURE
EPHYDRIAD
EPHYDRID
EPHYMNIUM
EPHYRA
EPHYRAE
EPHYRULA
EPI
EPIBASAL
EPIBATUS
EPIBENTHIC
EPIBENTHOS
EPIBIOTIC
EPIBLAST
EPIBLASTIC
EPIBLEMA
EPIBLEMATA
EPIBOLE
EPIBOLISM
EPIBOLY
EPIBRANCHIAL
EPIC
EPICAL
EPICALLY

EPICALYCES
EPICALYX
EPICALYXES
EPICANTHIC
EPICANTHUS
EPICARDIA
EPICARDIAC
EPICARDIAL
EPICARDIUM
EPICARID
EPICARIDAN
EPICARP
EPICE
EPICEDE
EPICEDIAL
EPICEDIUM
EPICENE
EPICENISM
EPICENITY
EPICENTER
EPICENTRA
EPICENTRAL
EPICENTRE
EPICENTRUM
EPICHEIREMA
EPICHEIREMATA
EPICHILE
EPICHILIA
EPICHILIUM
EPICHIREMA
EPICHONDROSIS
EPICHONDROTIC
EPICHORDAL
EPICHORIAL
EPICHORIC
EPICHORION
EPICHORISTIC
EPICIER
EPICISM
EPICIST
EPICLASTIC
EPICLEIDIAN
EPICLEIDIUM
EPICLESIS
EPICLY
EPICNEMIAL
EPICOELAR
EPICOELE
EPICOELIA
EPICOELIAC
EPICOELIAN
EPICOELOMA
EPICOELOUS
EPICOLIC
EPICONDYLE
EPICONDYLIAN
EPICONDYLIC
EPICONTINENTAL
EPICORACOID
EPICORACOIDAL
EPICORMIC
EPICOTYL
EPICRANIAL
EPICRANIUM
EPICRISES
EPICRISIS
EPICRITIC
EPICRYSTALLINE
EPICURE
EPICUREAN
EPICUREANISM
EPICYCLE
EPICYCLIC
EPICYCLICAL
EPICYCLOID
EPICYCLOIDAL
EPICYEMATE
EPICYESIS
EPICYSTOTOMY
EPICYTE
EPIDEICTIC
EPIDEICTICAL
EPIDEISTIC
EPIDEMIC
EPIDEMICAL
EPIDEMICALLY
EPIDEMICALNESS
EPIDEMICITY
EPIDEMIOGRAPHY
EPIDEMIOLOGY
EPIDEMY
EPIDENDRAL
EPIDENDRIC
EPIDERM
EPIDERMA
EPIDERMAL
EPIDERMATIC
EPIDERMATOID
EPIDERMIC
EPIDERMICAL
EPIDERMICALLY
EPIDERMIS
EPIDERMIZATION
EPIDERMOID
EPIDERMOIDAL
EPIDERMOLYSIS
EPIDERMOSE
EPIDERMOUS
EPIDESMINE
EPIDIALOGUE
EPIDIASCOPE
EPIDIDYMAL
EPIDIDYMIDES
EPIDIDYMIS
EPIDIDYMITE
EPIDIDYMITIS
EPIDIORITE
EPIDOSITE
EPIDOTE
EPIDOTIC
EPIDOTIZATION
EPIDURAL
EPIFOCAL
EPIGAMIC
EPIGASTER
EPIGASTRAL
EPIGASTRIA
EPIGASTRIAL
EPIGASTRIC
EPIGASTRICAL
EPIGASTRIUM
EPIGASTROCELE
EPIGEAL
EPIGEAN
EPIGEE
EPIGEIC
EPIGENE
EPIGENESIS
EPIGENESIST
EPIGENETIC
EPIGENETICALLY
EPIGENIC
EPIGENIST
EPIGENOUS
EPIGEOUS
EPIGEUM
EPIGLOTTAL
EPIGLOTTIDEAN
EPIGLOTTIDITIS
EPIGLOTTIS
EPIGLOTTITIS
EPIGNATHOUS
EPIGNE
EPIGONAL
EPIGONATION
EPIGONE
EPIGONIC
EPIGONIUM
EPIGONOUS
EPIGRAM
EPIGRAMMATIC
EPIGRAMMATICAL
EPIGRAMMATISM
EPIGRAMMATIST
EPIGRAMMATIZE
EPIGRAMMATIZED
EPIGRAMME
EPIGRAPH
EPIGRAPHER
EPIGRAPHIC
EPIGRAPHICAL
EPIGRAPHICALLY
EPIGRAPHIST
EPIGRAPHY
EPIGUANINE
EPIGYNE
EPIGYNOUS
EPIGYNUM
EPIGYNY
EPIHYAL
EPIKEIA
EPIKIA
EPIKLESIS
EPIKY
EPILABRA
EPILABRUM
EPILAMELLAR
EPILARYNGEAL
EPILATE
EPILATED
EPILATING
EPILATION
EPILATOR
EPILEGOMENON
EPILEMMA
EPILEMMAL
EPILEPSY
EPILEPTIC
EPILEPTICAL
EPILEPTICALLY
EPILEPTIFORM
EPILEPTOID
EPILIMNION
EPILOBE
EPILOG
EPILOGATION
EPILOGIC
EPILOGICAL
EPILOGISM
EPILOGIST
EPILOGIZE
EPILOGIZED
EPILOGIZING
EPILOGUE
EPILOIA
EPIMACUS
EPIMANDIBULAR
EPIMANIKIA
EPIMANIKION
EPIMER
EPIMERAL
EPIMERE
EPIMERITE
EPIMERITIC
EPIMERON
EPIMORPHA
EPIMORPHIC
EPIMORPHOSIS
EPIMYSIUM
EPIMYTH
EPINAOI
EPINAOS
EPINARD
EPINASTIC
EPINASTICALLY
EPINASTY
EPINEPHRIN
EPINEPHRINE
EPINETTE
EPINEURAL
EPINEURIAL
EPINEURIUM
EPINGLE
EPINGLETTE
EPINICIA
EPINICIAN
EPINICION
EPINIKIA
EPINIKIAN
EPINIKION
EPININE
EPIOPTICON
EPIOTIC
EPIPALEOLITHIC
EPIPARODOS
EPIPASTIC
EPIPERIPHERAL
EPIPETALOUS
EPIPHANOUS
EPIPHANY
EPIPHARYNGEAL
EPIPHARYNX
EPIPHLOEDAL
EPIPHLOEDIC
EPIPHONEMA
EPIPHORA
EPIPHRAGM
EPIPHRAGMAL
EPIPHYLL
EPIPHYLLINE
EPIPHYSARY
EPIPHYSEAL
EPIPHYSES
EPIPHYSIAL
EPIPHYSIS
EPIPHYSITIS
EPIPHYTAL
EPIPHYTE
EPIPHYTIC
EPIPHYTICAL
EPIPHYTICALLY
EPIPHYTOTIC
EPIPHYTOUS
EPIPIAL
EPIPLANKTON
EPIPLASM
EPIPLASMIC
EPIPLASTRAL
EPIPLASTRON
EPIPLECTIC
EPIPLEURA
EPIPLEURAE
EPIPLEURAL
EPIPLEXIS
EPIPLOCE
EPIPLOCELE
EPIPLOIC
EPIPLOITIS
EPIPLOON
EPIPLOPEXY
EPIPODIA
EPIPODIAL
EPIPODIALE
EPIPODIALIA
EPIPODITE
EPIPODIUM
EPIPOLISM
EPIPOLIZE
EPIPROCT
EPIPTERIC
EPIPTEROUS
EPIPTERYGOID
EPIPUBES
EPIPUBIC
EPIPUBIS
EPIRHIZOUS
EPIROGENIC
EPIROGENY
EPIROTULIAN
EPIRRHEMA
EPIRRHEMATIC
EPIRRHEME
EPISARCINE
EPISARKINE
EPISCENIA
EPISCENIUM
EPISCIA
EPISCLERA
EPISCLERAL
EPISCLERITIS
EPISCOPABLE
EPISCOPACIES
EPISCOPACY
EPISCOPAL
EPISCOPALIAN
EPISCOPALISM
EPISCOPALITY
EPISCOPALLY
EPISCOPATE
EPISCOPATION
EPISCOPATURE
EPISCOPE
EPISCOPICIDE
EPISCOPIZATION
EPISCOPIZE
EPISCOPIZED
EPISCOPIZING
EPISCOPOLATRY
EPISCOPY
EPISCOTISTER
EPISEMATIC
EPISEPALOUS
EPISIOCELE
EPISIOPLASTY
EPISIOTOMY
EPISKELETAL
EPISODAL
EPISODE
EPISODIC
EPISODICAL
EPISODICALLY
EPISPADIA
EPISPADIAC
EPISPADIAS
EPISPASTIC
EPISPERM
EPISPLENITIS
EPISPORE
EPISTAPEDIAL
EPISTASIS
EPISTATIC
EPISTAXIS
EPISTEME
EPISTEMIC
EPISTEMOLOG
EPISTEMOLOGY
EPISTEMONIC
EPISTEMONICAL
EPISTERNA
EPISTERNAL
EPISTERNALIA
EPISTERNITE
EPISTERNUM
EPISTILBITE
EPISTLE

EPISTLER
EPISTOLARIAN
EPISTOLARILY
EPISTOLATORY
EPISTOLER
EPISTOLET
EPISTOLIC
EPISTOLICAL
EPISTOLIST
EPISTOLIZABLE
EPISTOLIZATION
EPISTOLIZE
EPISTOLOGRAPHER
EPISTOLOGRAPHIST
EPISTOLOGRAPHY
EPISTOMA
EPISTOMAL
EPISTOMATA
EPISTOME
EPISTOMIAN
EPISTROPHE
EPISTROPHEAL
EPISTROPHEUS
EPISTROPHIC
EPISTROPHY
EPISTYLAR
EPISTYLE
EPISYLLOGISM
EPISYNALOEPHE
EPISYNTHETON
EPITACTIC
EPITAPH
EPITAPHER
EPITAPHIAL
EPITAPHIAN
EPITAPHIC
EPITAPHICAL
EPITAPHIZE
EPITASIS
EPITELA
EPITENDINEUM
EPITHALAMIA
EPITHALAMIC
EPITHALAMION
EPITHALAMIUM
EPITHALAMIUMS
EPITHALAMIZE
EPITHALAMUS
EPITHALAMY
EPITHALLINE
EPITHECA
EPITHECAL
EPITHECATE
EPITHECIA
EPITHECIUM
EPITHELIA
EPITHELIAL
EPITHELIOID
EPITHELIOMA
EPITHELIOMAS
EPITHELIOMATA
EPITHELIOSIS
EPITHELIUM
EPITHELIUMS
EPITHELIZATION
EPITHELIZE
EPITHELOID
EPITHEM
EPITHEMA
EPITHEME
EPITHESIS
EPITHET
EPITHETIC
EPITHETICAL
EPITHETICIAN
EPITHETON
EPITHYME
EPITHYMETIC
EPITIMESIS
EPITOKE
EPITOMATOR
EPITOMATORY
EPITOME
EPITOMES
EPITOMIC
EPITOMICAL
EPITOMICALLY
EPITOMISE
EPITOMIST
EPITOMIZATION
EPITOMIZE
EPITOMIZED
EPITOMIZER
EPITOMIZING
EPITONIC
EPITONION
EPITOXOID
EPITRICHIAL
EPITRICHIUM
EPITRITE
EPITRITIC
EPITROCHLEA
EPITROCHLEAR
EPITROCHOID
EPITROCHOIDAL
EPITROPE
EPITROPHIC
EPITROPHY
EPITYMPANIC
EPITYMPANUM
EPITYPHLITIS
EPITYPHLON
EPIURAL
EPIVALVE
EPIZEUXIS
EPIZOA
EPIZOAL
EPIZOAN
EPIZOIC
EPIZOON
EPIZOOTIC
EPIZOOTIOLOGY
EPIZOOTY
EPOCH
EPOCHA
EPOCHAL
EPOCHALLY
EPOCHE
EPOCHISM
EPOCHIST
EPODE
EPODIC
EPOLLICATE
EPONGE
EPONYCHIUM
EPONYM
EPONYMIC
EPONYMOUS
EPONYMY
EPOOPHORON
EPOPEE
EPOPOEAN
EPOPOEIA
EPOPOEIST
EPOPT
EPOPTAE
EPOPTIC
EPORNITIC
EPORNITICALLY
EPOS
EPOTE
EPOXIDE
EPOXY
EPRIS
EPRISE
EPRUINOSE
EPSILON
EPSOMITE
EPULARY
EPULATION
EPULIS
EPULO
EPULOID
EPULOSIS
EPULOTIC
EPUPILLATE
EPURAL
EPURATE
EPURATION
EPURE
EPYLLIA
EPYLLION
EQUABILITY
EQUABLE
EQUABLENESS
EQUABLY
EQUAEVAL
EQUAL
EQUALED
EQUALING
EQUALISE
EQUALIST
EQUALITARIAN
EQUALITARIANISM
EQUALITIES
EQUALITY
EQUALIZATION
EQUALIZE
EQUALIZED
EQUALIZER
EQUALIZING
EQUALLED
EQUALLING
EQUALLY
EQUALNESS
EQUANGULAR
EQUANIMITY
EQUANIMOUS
EQUANIMOUSLY
EQUANT
EQUATE
EQUATED
EQUATING
EQUATION
EQUATIONAL
EQUATIONALLY
EQUATIONISM
EQUATIONIST
EQUATIVE
EQUATOR
EQUATOREAL
EQUATORIAL
EQUATORIALLY
EQUERRIES
EQUERRY
EQUES
EQUESTRIAN
EQUESTRIENNE
EQUIANGULAR
EQUIAXED
EQUID
EQUIDISTANCE
EQUIDISTANT
EQUIDISTANTIAL
EQUIDISTANTLY
EQUIDIURNAL
EQUIFORM
EQUIFORMAL
EQUIFORMITY
EQUIGRANULAR
EQUIJACENT
EQUILATERAL
EQUILIBRANT
EQUILIBRATE
EQUILIBRATED
EQUILIBRATING
EQUILIBRATION
EQUILIBRATIVE
EQUILIBRATOR
EQUILIBRATORY
EQUILIBRIA
EQUILIBRIAL
EQUILIBRIATE
EQUILIBRIOUS
EQUILIBRIST
EQUILIBRISTAT
EQUILIBRISTIC
EQUILIBRITY
EQUILIBRIUM
EQUILIBRIUMS
EQUILIBRIZE
EQUILIN
EQUIMODAL
EQUIMOLAR
EQUIMOLECULAR
EQUIMOMENTAL
EQUIMULTIPLE
EQUINAL
EQUINATE
EQUINE
EQUINIA
EQUINITY
EQUINOCTIAL
EQUINOCTIALLY
EQUINOVARUS
EQUINOX
EQUINUS
EQUIP
EQUIPAGA
EQUIPAGE
EQUIPARANT
EQUIPARATE
EQUIPARATION
EQUIPARTILE
EQUIPARTITION
EQUIPEDAL
EQUIPLUVE
EQUIPMENT
EQUIPOISE
EQUIPOISED
EQUIPOISING
EQUIPOLLENCE
EQUIPOLLENCY
EQUIPOLLENT
EQUIPOLLENTLY
EQUIPONDERANT
EQUIPONDERATE
EQUIPONDERATED
EQUIPONDERATING
EQUIPOSTILE
EQUIPOTENTIAL
EQUIPPED
EQUIPPER
EQUIPPING
EQUIPROBABLE
EQUIPT
EQUISETA
EQUISETACEOUS
EQUISETIC
EQUISETUM
EQUISETUMS
EQUISIGNAL
EQUISON
EQUISONANCE
EQUISONANT
EQUITABLE
EQUITABLY
EQUITANT
EQUITATION
EQUITATIVE
EQUITES
EQUITIES
EQUITIST
EQUITY
EQUIVALENCE
EQUIVALENCED
EQUIVALENCY
EQUIVALENT
EQUIVALENTLY
EQUIVALVE
EQUIVOCACY
EQUIVOCAL
EQUIVOCALITY
EQUIVOCATE
EQUIVOCATED
EQUIVOCATING
EQUIVOCATION
EQUIVOCATOR
EQUIVOCATORY
EQUIVOKE
EQUIVOLUMINAL
EQUIVOQUE
EQUIVOROUS
EQUOID
EQUULEI
EQUULEUS
ER
ERA
ERADE
ERADIATE
ERADIATED
ERADIATING
ERADIATION
ERADICABLE
ERADICATE
ERADICATED
ERADICATING
ERADICATION
ERADICATIVE
ERADICATOR
ERADICATORY
ERADICULOSE
ERAL
ERANIST
ERASABLE
ERASE
ERASED
ERASER
ERASING
ERASION
ERASURE
ERBER
ERBIA
ERBIUM
ERD
ERDVARK
ERE
EREB
ERECT
ERECTED
ERECTER
ERECTILE
ERECTILITY
ERECTING
ERECTION
ERECTIVE
ERECTLY
ERECTNESS
ERECTOPATENT
ERECTOR
ERELONG
EREMACAUSIS
EREMIC
EREMITAL
EREMITE

EREMITIC
EREMITICAL
EREMITISH
EREMOLOGY
EREMOPHYTE
ERENACH
ERENOW
EREPSIN
EREPT
EREPTASE
EREPTIC
ERER
ERETHIC
ERETHISIA
ERETHISM
ERETHISMIC
ERETHISTIC
ERETHITIC
EREV
EREWHILE
ERF
ERG
ERGAL
ERGAMINE
ERGASIA
ERGASTERION
ERGASTIC
ERGASTOPLASM
ERGASTOPLASMIC
ERGASTULUM
ERGATANDROUS
ERGATANDRY
ERGATE
ERGATES
ERGATIVE
ERGATOCRACY
ERGATOGYNE
ERGATOGYNOUS
ERGATOGYNY
ERGATOID
ERGATOMORPH
ERGATOMORPHIC
ERGATOMORPHISM
ERGMETER
ERGO
ERGODIC
ERGOGRAM
ERGOGRAPH
ERGOISM
ERGOLOGY
ERGOMANIAC
ERGOMETER
ERGON
ERGOPHILE
ERGOPHOBIA
ERGOPHOBIAC
ERGOPLASM
ERGOSTAT
ERGOSTEROL
ERGOT
ERGOTAMINE
ERGOTAMININE
ERGOTED
ERGOTIC
ERGOTIN
ERGOTINE
ERGOTININE
ERGOTISM
ERGOTIST
ERGOTIZATION
ERGOTIZE
ERGOTIZED
ERGOTIZING
ERGOTOXINE
ERGUSIA
ERIA
ERIC
ERICACEOUS
ERICAD
ERICAL
ERICETAL
ERICHTHOID
ERICHTHUS
ERICINEOUS
ERICIUS
ERICOID
ERICOLIN
ERICOPHYTE
ERIGERON
ERIGIBLE
ERIGLOSSATE
ERIKA
ERIKITE
ERINACEOUS
ERINEUM
ERINGO
ERINITE
ERINOSE
ERIOMETER
ERIONITE
ERIOPHORUM
ERIOPHYLLOUS
ERISTIC
ERISTICAL
ERISTICALLY
ERIZO
ERK
ERLICHE
ERLKING
ERME
ERMELIN
ERMILINE
ERMIN
ERMINE
ERMINED
ERMINEE
ERMINES
ERMINING
ERMINITES
ERMINOIS
ERN
ERNE
ERODE
ERODED
ERODENT
ERODING
EROGATE
EROGENEITY
EROGENESIS
EROGENETIC
EROGENIC
EROGENOUS
EROSE
EROSIBLE
EROSION
EROSIONAL
EROSIONIST
EROSIVE
EROSTRATE
EROTEMA
EROTEME
EROTESIS
EROTETIC
EROTIC
EROTICA
EROTICAL
EROTICALLY
EROTICISM
EROTICOMANIA
EROTISM
EROTOGENIC
EROTOMANIA
EROTOMANIAC
EROTOPATH
EROTOPATHY
EROTYLID
ERR
ERRABILITY
ERRABLE
ERRABLENESS
ERRABUND
ERRANCY
ERRAND
ERRANT
ERRANTLY
ERRANTNESS
ERRANTRIES
ERRANTRY
ERRATA
ERRATIC
ERRATICAL
ERRATICALLY
ERRATICALNESS
ERRATUM
ERRED
ERRHINE
ERRING
ERRINGLY
ERRITE
ERRONEOUS
ERRONEOUSLY
ERRONEOUSNESS
ERROR
ERRORIST
ERS
ERSATZ
ERST
ERSTWHILE
ERSTWHILES
ERT
ERUB
ERUBESCENCE
ERUBESCENT
ERUC
ERUCA
ERUCIN
ERUCT
ERUCTATE
ERUCTATION
ERUCTATIVE
ERUDIT
ERUDITE
ERUDITELY
ERUDITENESS
ERUDITICAL
ERUDITION
ERUDITIONAL
ERUDITIONIST
ERUGATE
ERUGATION
ERUGATORY
ERUMPENT
ERUPT
ERUPTED
ERUPTING
ERUPTION
ERUPTIONAL
ERUPTIVE
ERUPTIVELY
ERUPTIVENESS
ERUPTIVITY
ERUPTURIENT
ERUV
ERVEN
ERVENHOLDER
ERVIL
ERYNGO
ERYOPID
ERYSIPELAS
ERYSIPELATOID
ERYSIPELOID
ERYTHEMA
ERYTHEMATIC
ERYTHEMATOUS
ERYTHEMIC
ERYTHRAEAN
ERYTHRAEMIA
ERYTHRASMA
ERYTHREAN
ERYTHREMIA
ERYTHRIN
ERYTHRINE
ERYTHRISM
ERYTHRISMAL
ERYTHRISTIC
ERYTHRITE
ERYTHRITIC
ERYTHRITOL
ERYTHROBLAST
ERYTHROCARPOUS
ERYTHROCYTOSIS
ERYTHRODERMIA
ERYTHROGENIC
ERYTHROGLUCIN
ERYTHROID
ERYTHROL
ERYTHROLEIN
ERYTHROLYSIN
ERYTHROLYSIS
ERYTHROLYTIC
ERYTHROMANIA
ERYTHRONIUM
ERYTHROPENIA
ERYTHROPHOBIA
ERYTHROPHORE
ERYTHROPHYLL
ERYTHROPIA
ERYTHROPSIA
ERYTHROPSIN
ERYTHROSCOPE
ERYTHROSE
ERYTHROSIN
ERYTHROSIS
ERYTHROZYME
ERYTHRULOSE
ERZAHLER
ES
ESAN
ESBAY
ESCA
ESCADRILLE
ESCALADE
ESCALADED
ESCALADER
ESCALADING
ESCALADO
ESCALAN
ESCALATE
ESCALATED
ESCALATING
ESCALATION
ESCALATOR
ESCALIER
ESCALLOP
ESCALLOPED
ESCALOP
ESCALOPED
ESCAMBIO
ESCAMBRON
ESCAMOTAGE
ESCAPABLE
ESCAPADE
ESCAPAGE
ESCAPE
ESCAPED
ESCAPEE
ESCAPEMENT
ESCAPER
ESCAPING
ESCAPISM
ESCAPIST
ESCARBUNCLE
ESCARGOT
ESCAROLE
ESCARP
ESCARPMENT
ESCHALOT
ESCHAR
ESCHARA
ESCHARINE
ESCHAROID
ESCHAROTIC
ESCHATOCOL
ESCHATOLOGY
ESCHAUFE
ESCHEAT
ESCHEATABLE
ESCHEATAGE
ESCHEATED
ESCHEATING
ESCHEATOR
ESCHEL
ESCHEW
ESCHEWAL
ESCHEWANCE
ESCHEWED
ESCHEWER
ESCHEWING
ESCHYNITE
ESCLANDRE
ESCLAVAGE
ESCOBA
ESCOBADURA
ESCOBILLA
ESCOBITA
ESCOLAR
ESCOLARS
ESCONSON
ESCOPET
ESCOPETA
ESCOPETTE
ESCORT
ESCORTED
ESCORTING
ESCOT
ESCRIBANO
ESCRIBE
ESCRIBED
ESCRIBIENTE
ESCRIBIENTES
ESCRIBING
ESCRIME
ESCRIPT
ESCRITOIRE
ESCRITORIAL
ESCROD
ESCROL
ESCROLL
ESCROW
ESCROWEE
ESCRY
ESCUAGE
ESCUDERO
ESCUDO
ESCUDOS
ESCULENT
ESCULETIN
ESCULIN
ESCUTCHEON
ESCUTCHEONED
ESCUTELLATE
ESEMPLASTIC
ESEMPLASY
ESEPTATE
ESERE

ESERIN
ESERINE
ESEXUAL
ESGUARD
ESHIN
ESILL
ESIPHONAL
ESK
ESKAR
ESKER
ESLABON
ESMERALDA
ESMERALDITE
ESNE
ESNECY
ESOANHYDRIDE
ESOCIFORM
ESODIC
ESOENTERITIS
ESOGASTRITIS
ESONARTHEX
ESONEURAL
ESOPHAGAL
ESOPHAGEAL
ESOPHAGEAN
ESOPHAGISM
ESOPHAGITIS
ESOPHAGOCELE
ESOPHAGOTOME
ESOPHAGOTOMY
ESOPHAGUS
ESOPHORIA
ESOTERIC
ESOTERICA
ESOTERICAL
ESOTERICALLY
ESOTERICISM
ESOTERICS
ESOTERISM
ESOTERIST
ESOTERIZE
ESOTERY
ESOTHYROPEXY
ESOTROPE
ESOTROPIA
ESOTROPIC
ESOX
ESP
ESPACEMENT
ESPADA
ESPADON
ESPADRILLE
ESPAGNOLETTE
ESPALIER
ESPALIERED
ESPALIERING
ESPANTOON
ESPARCET
ESPARTO
ESPATHATE
ESPAVE
ESPAVEL
ESPECE
ESPECIAL
ESPECIALLY
ESPECIALNESS
ESPEIRE
ESPERANCE
ESPHRESIS
ESPIAL
ESPIED
ESPIEGLE
ESPIEGLERIE
ESPIER
ESPINAL
ESPINEL
ESPINGOLE
ESPINO
ESPINOS
ESPIONAGE
ESPLANADE
ESPLEES
ESPOUSAL
ESPOUSE
ESPOUSED
ESPOUSER
ESPOUSING
ESPRESSIVO
ESPRESSOS
ESPRINGAL
ESPRISE
ESPRIT
ESPROVE
ESPUNDIA
ESPY
ESPYING
ESQUAMATE
ESQUAMULOSE
ESQUIRE
ESQUIRED
ESQUIRING
ESQUISSE
ESS
ESSANG
ESSART
ESSAY
ESSAYED
ESSAYER
ESSAYETTE
ESSAYICAL
ESSAYING
ESSAYIST
ESSAYISTIC
ESSAYISTICAL
ESSE
ESSED
ESSEDA
ESSEDE
ESSENCE
ESSENCED
ESSENCING
ESSENHOUT
ESSENTIA
ESSENTIAL
ESSENTIALITIES
ESSENTIALITY
ESSENTIALLY
ESSENTIATE
ESSENWOOD
ESSES
ESSEXITE
ESSIVE
ESSLING
ESSOIGN
ESSOIN
ESSOINED
ESSOINEE
ESSOINER
ESSOINING
ESSONITE
ESSORANT
EST
ESTABLISH
ESTABLISHED
ESTABLISHER
ESTABLISHING
ESTABLISHMENT
ESTACADE
ESTADAL
ESTADEL
ESTADIO
ESTADO
ESTAFA
ESTAFET
ESTAFETTE
ESTAFETTED
ESTAMENE
ESTAMIN
ESTAMINET
ESTAMP
ESTAMPAGE
ESTAMPEDE
ESTAMPEDERO
ESTAMPIE
ESTANCIA
ESTANCIERO
ESTANTION
ESTATE
ESTATED
ESTATES
ESTATESMAN
ESTATESMEN
ESTATING
ESTATS
ESTEEM
ESTEEMABLE
ESTEEMED
ESTEEMER
ESTEEMING
ESTER
ESTERASE
ESTERELLITE
ESTERIFEROUS
ESTERIFICATION
ESTERIFIED
ESTERIFY
ESTERIFYING
ESTERIZATION
ESTERIZE
ESTERIZING
ESTERLIN
ESTERO
ESTEROS
ESTEVIN
ESTHEMATOLOGY
ESTHERIAN
ESTHESIA
ESTHESIOGEN
ESTHESIOLOGY
ESTHESIS
ESTHETE
ESTHETIC
ESTHETICAL
ESTHETICALLY
ESTHETICIAN
ESTHETICISM
ESTHETICS
ESTHETOLOGY
ESTHETOPHORE
ESTHIOMENE
ESTHIOMENUS
ESTIMABLE
ESTIMABLY
ESTIMATE
ESTIMATED
ESTIMATING
ESTIMATINGLY
ESTIMATION
ESTIMATIVE
ESTIMATOR
ESTIPULATE
ESTIVAGE
ESTIVAL
ESTIVATE
ESTIVATED
ESTIVATING
ESTIVATION
ESTIVATOR
ESTIVE
ESTMARK
ESTOC
ESTOCADA
ESTOILE
ESTOLIDE
ESTOP
ESTOPPAGE
ESTOPPED
ESTOPPEL
ESTOPPING
ESTOQUE
ESTOVERS
ESTRADA
ESTRADAS
ESTRADE
ESTRADIOL
ESTRAGOL
ESTRAGOLE
ESTRAGON
ESTRANGE
ESTRANGED
ESTRANGEDNESS
ESTRANGEMENT
ESTRANGER
ESTRANGING
ESTRAPADE
ESTRAY
ESTRAYED
ESTRAYING
ESTRE
ESTREAT
ESTREATED
ESTREATING
ESTREPE
ESTREPEMENT
ESTRIATE
ESTRICHE
ESTRIF
ESTRIOL
ESTRO
ESTROGEN
ESTROGENIC
ESTRONE
ESTROUS
ESTRUAL
ESTRUM
ESTRUS
ESTUARIAL
ESTUARIAN
ESTUARIES
ESTUARINE
ESTUARY
ESTUATE
ESTUDY
ESTUFA
ESTUOUS
ESTURE
ESTUS
ESURIENCE
ESURIENCY
ESURIENT
ESURIENTLY
ESURINE
ET
ETA
ETAAC
ETABALLI
ETABELLI
ETACISM
ETAERIO
ETAGE
ETAGERE
ETALAGE
ETALON
ETAMINE
ETAPE
ETAS
ETATISM
ETATISME
ETCETERA
ETCETERAS
ETCH
ETCHANT
ETCHED
ETCHEMIN
ETCHER
ETCHING
ETEN
ETERN
ETERNAL
ETERNALIST
ETERNALIZATION
ETERNALIZE
ETERNALLY
ETERNALNESS
ETERNE
ETERNISH
ETERNITIES
ETERNITY
ETERNIZATION
ETERNIZE
ETERNIZED
ETERNIZING
ETESIAN
ETH
ETHAL
ETHALDEHYDE
ETHANAL
ETHANAMIDE
ETHANE
ETHANETHIOL
ETHANOL
ETHANOYL
ETHEL
ETHELING
ETHENE
ETHENOID
ETHENOIDAL
ETHENOL
ETHENYL
ETHEOSTOMOID
ETHER
ETHERATE
ETHEREAL
ETHEREALISM
ETHEREALITY
ETHEREALIZE
ETHEREALIZED
ETHEREALIZING
ETHEREALLY
ETHEREALNESS
ETHERED
ETHEREOUS
ETHERIC
ETHERICAL
ETHERIFIED
ETHERIFORM
ETHERIFY
ETHERIFYING
ETHERIN
ETHERION
ETHERISM
ETHERIZATION
ETHERIZE
ETHERIZED
ETHERIZER
ETHERIZING
ETHEROLATE
ETHEROUS
ETHIC
ETHICAL
ETHICALITY
ETHICALLY
ETHICALNESS
ETHICIAN
ETHICIST

ETHICIZE
ETHICIZED
ETHICIZING
ETHICS
ETHIDE
ETHIDENE
ETHINE
ETHINYL
ETHIODIDE
ETHIOPS
ETHIZE
ETHMOID
ETHMOIDAL
ETHMOIDITIS
ETHMOLITH
ETHMYPHITIS
ETHNARCH
ETHNARCHIES
ETHNARCHY
ETHNIC
ETHNICAL
ETHNICALLY
ETHNICISM
ETHNICIST
ETHNOBOTANY
ETHNOCENTRIC
ETHNOCENTRISM
ETHNOCRACY
ETHNODICY
ETHNOFLORA
ETHNOGENIC
ETHNOGENIES
ETHNOGENY
ETHNOGRAPHER
ETHNOGRAPHIC
ETHNOGRAPHIES
ETHNOGRAPHIST
ETHNOGRAPHY
ETHNOLOGER
ETHNOLOGIC
ETHNOLOGICAL
ETHNOLOGIST
ETHNOLOGY
ETHNOMANIAC
ETHNOPSYCHIC
ETHNOS
ETHNOZOOLOGY
ETHOGRAPHY
ETHOLIDE
ETHOLOGIC
ETHOLOGICAL
ETHOLOGY
ETHONOMIC
ETHONOMICS
ETHOPOEIA
ETHOS
ETHOXIDE
ETHOXYL
ETHROG
ETHYL
ETHYLAMIDE
ETHYLAMIME
ETHYLAMIN
ETHYLATE
ETHYLATED
ETHYLATING
ETHYLATION
ETHYLENE
ETHYLENIC
ETHYLIC
ETHYLIDENE
ETHYLIN
ETHYNE
ETHYNYL
ETHYSULPHURIC
ETIK
ETIOLATE
ETIOLATED
ETIOLATING
ETIOLATION
ETIOLIN
ETIOLIZE
ETIOLOGICAL
ETIOLOGICALLY
ETIOLOGIST
ETIOLOGUE
ETIOLOGY
ETIOPHYLLIN
ETIOTROPIC
ETIQUET
ETIQUETTE
ETIQUETTICAL
ETNA
ETOILE
ETOUFFE
ETOURDERIE
ETRENNE
ETROG
ETTERCAP
ETTLE
ETTLED
ETTLING
ETUDE
ETUI
ETWEE
ETWITE
ETYM
ETYMA
ETYMIC
ETYMOGRAPHY
ETYMOLOGER
ETYMOLOGIC
ETYMOLOGICAL
ETYMOLOGICON
ETYMOLOGIST
ETYMOLOGIZE
ETYMOLOGIZED
ETYMOLOGIZING
ETYMOLOGY
ETYMON
ETYMONS
ETYPIC
ETYPICAL
ETYPICALLY
EUANGIOTIC
EUASTER
EUBACTERIUM
EUCAINE
EUCAIRITE
EUCALYPT
EUCALYPTEOL
EUCALYPTI
EUCALYPTIAN
EUCALYPTIC
EUCALYPTOL
EUCALYPTOLE
EUCALYPTUS
EUCALYPTUSES
EUCATROPINE
EUCEPHALOUS
EUCHARIS
EUCHARIST
EUCHARISTIAL
EUCHARISTIC
EUCHARISTICAL
EUCHARISTIZE
EUCHARISTIZED
EUCHARISTIZING
EUCHLORHYDRIA
EUCHLORINE
EUCHOLOGION
EUCHOLOGY
EUCHRE
EUCHRED
EUCHRING
EUCHROITE
EUCHROME
EUCHROMOSOME
EUCLASE
EUCLEID
EUCOLITE
EUCONE
EUCONIC
EUCOSMID
EUCRASIA
EUCRASITE
EUCRASY
EUCRITE
EUCRYPTITE
EUCRYSTALLINE
EUCTICAL
EUCYCLIC
EUDAEMON
EUDAEMONIA
EUDAEMONIC
EUDAEMONICAL
EUDAEMONICS
EUDAEMONISM
EUDAEMONIST
EUDAEMONIZE
EUDAEMONY
EUDALENE
EUDEMON
EUDESMOL
EUDIAGNOSTIC
EUDIALYTE
EUDIDYMITE
EUDIOMETER
EUDIOMETRY
EUDIPLEURAL
EUGE
EUGENESIC
EUGENESIS
EUGENETIC
EUGENIC
EUGENICAL
EUGENICALLY
EUGENICIST
EUGENICS
EUGENISM
EUGENIST
EUGENOL
EUGENOLATE
EUGENY
EUGLENOID
EUGLOBULIN
EUGRANITIC
EUHARMONIC
EUHEDRAL
EUHEMERISM
EUHEMERIST
EUHEMERISTIC
EUHEMERIZE
EUHEMERIZED
EUHEMERIZING
EUHYOSTYLIC
EUHYOSTYLY
EUKTOLITE
EULACHAN
EULACHANS
EULACHON
EULACHONS
EULALIA
EULOGIA
EULOGIC
EULOGICAL
EULOGICALLY
EULOGIES
EULOGIOUS
EULOGISM
EULOGIST
EULOGISTIC
EULOGISTICAL
EULOGIUM
EULOGIUMS
EULOGIZATION
EULOGIZE
EULOGIZED
EULOGIZER
EULOGIZING
EULOGY
EULOPHID
EULYSITE
EULYTINE
EULYTITE
EUMEMORRHEA
EUMENID
EUMERISM
EUMERISTIC
EUMEROMORPH
EUMITOSIS
EUMITOTIC
EUMOIROUS
EUMOLPIQUE
EUMORPHOUS
EUMYCETE
EUMYCETIC
EUNICID
EUNOMY
EUNUCH
EUNUCHAL
EUNUCHOID
EUNUCHOIDISM
EUNUCHRY
EUOMPHALID
EUONYM
EUONYMIN
EUONYMOUS
EUONYMUS
EUONYMY
EUOSMITE
EUOUAE
EUPAD
EUPATHY
EUPATORIN
EUPATORIUM
EUPATORY
EUPATRID
EUPATRIDAE
EUPATRIDS
EUPEPSIA
EUPEPSY
EUPEPTIC
EUPEPTICISM
EUPEPTICITY
EUPHAUSID
EUPHEMIAN
EUPHEMIOUS
EUPHEMIOUSLY
EUPHEMISM
EUPHEMIST
EUPHEMISTIC
EUPHEMIZE
EUPHEMIZED
EUPHEMIZER
EUPHEMIZING
EUPHEMOUS
EUPHEMY
EUPHON
EUPHONE
EUPHONETIC
EUPHONETICS
EUPHONIA
EUPHONIC
EUPHONICAL
EUPHONICALLY
EUPHONIES
EUPHONIOUS
EUPHONIOUSLY
EUPHONISM
EUPHONIUM
EUPHONIZE
EUPHONIZED
EUPHONIZING
EUPHONON
EUPHONOUS
EUPHONY
EUPHONYM
EUPHORBIA
EUPHORBIAL
EUPHORBIUM
EUPHORIA
EUPHORIC
EUPHORY
EUPHRASY
EUPHROE
EUPHUISM
EUPHUIST
EUPHUISTIC
EUPHUISTICALLY
EUPHUIZE
EUPHUIZED
EUPHUIZING
EUPION
EUPIONE
EUPITTONE
EUPLASTIC
EUPLOID
EUPLOIDY
EUPNEA
EUPNOEA
EUPOLYZOAN
EUPRACTIC
EUPRAXIA
EUPSYCHICS
EUPYRCHROITE
EUPYRENE
EUPYRION
EURE
EUREKA
EURHODINE
EURHODOL
EURHYTHMIC
EURHYTHMICAL
EURHYTHMICS
EURHYTHMY
EURIPUS
EURITE
EURO
EUROBIN
EUROPIUM
EUROUS
EURYALIDAN
EURYBENTHIC
EURYCEPHALIC
EURYGNATHIC
EURYGNATHISM
EURYGNATHOUS
EURYHALINE
EURYLAIMOID
EURYON
EURYPROSOPIC
EURYPTERID
EURYPTEROID
EURYPYLOUS
EURYSCOPE
EURYTE
EURYTHERMAL
EURYTHERMIC
EURYTHMIC
EURYTHMICAL
EURYTHMICS
EURYTHMY
EURYTOMID
EURYZYGOUS

EUSOL
EUSTACY
EUSTATIC
EUSTELE
EUSTOMATOUS
EUSTYLE
EUSUCHIAN
EUSYNCHITE
EUTAXIC
EUTAXIE
EUTAXITE
EUTAXITIC
EUTAXY
EUTECHNIC
EUTECHNICS
EUTECTIC
EUTECTOID
EUTELEGENIC
EUTEXIA
EUTHANASIA
EUTHANASY
EUTHENICS
EUTHENIST
EUTHERMIC
EUTHYTROPIC
EUTOCIA
EUTOMOUS
EUTROPHIC
EUTROPHY
EUTROPIC
EUTROPOUS
EUXANTHATE
EUXANTHONE
EUXENITE
EVACUANT
EVACUATE
EVACUATED
EVACUATING
EVACUATION
EVACUATOR
EVACUE
EVACUEE
EVADABLE
EVADE
EVADED
EVADER
EVADIBLE
EVADING
EVAGATION
EVAGINABLE
EVAGINATE
EVAGINATED
EVAGINATING
EVAGINATION
EVALUABLE
EVALUATE
EVALUATED
EVALUATING
EVALUATION
EVALUATIVE
EVALUE
EVANESCE
EVANESCED
EVANESCENCE
EVANESCENCY
EVANESCENT
EVANESCENTLY
EVANESCIBLE
EVANESCING
EVANGEL
EVANGELIAN
EVANGELIC
EVANGELICAL
EVANGELICALLY
EVANGELICITY
EVANGELION
EVANGELISM
EVANGELIST
EVANGELISTARIES
EVANGELISTARY
EVANGELISTIC
EVANGELIUM
EVANGELIZE
EVANGELIZED
EVANGELIZER
EVANGELIZING
EVANID
EVANISH
EVANISHED
EVANISHING
EVANISHMENT
EVANSITE
EVAPORABLE
EVAPORATE
EVAPORATED
EVAPORATING
EVAPORATION
EVAPORATIVE
EVAPORATIVITY
EVAPORATOR
EVAPORIMETER
EVAPORIZE
EVASE
EVASIBLE
EVASION
EVASIONAL
EVASIVE
EVASIVELY
EVASIVENESS
EVE
EVECHURR
EVECK
EVECTION
EVECTIONAL
EVEJAR
EVEL
EVELIGHT
EVELONG
EVEN
EVENDOWN
EVENE
EVENED
EVENER
EVENFALL
EVENGLOME
EVENGLOW
EVENHAND
EVENHANDED
EVENHANDEDLY
EVENING
EVENK
EVENLONG
EVENLY
EVENMETE
EVENMINDED
EVENNESS
EVENOO
EVENS
EVENSONG
EVENT
EVENTAIL
EVENTFUL
EVENTFULLY
EVENTFULNESS
EVENTIDE
EVENTLESS
EVENTLESSLY
EVENTOGNATH
EVENTRATION
EVENTS
EVENTUAL
EVENTUALITIES
EVENTUALITY
EVENTUALIZE
EVENTUALLY
EVENTUATE
EVENTUATED
EVENTUATING
EVENWISE
EVEQUE
EVER
EVERBEARER
EVERBEARING
EVERBLOOMING
EVERDURING
EVERGLADE
EVERGLADES
EVERGREEN
EVERGREENERY
EVERGREENITE
EVERICH
EVERLASTING
EVERLASTINGLY
EVERLIVING
EVERLY
EVERMO
EVERMORE
EVERNIOID
EVERSE
EVERSIBLE
EVERSION
EVERSIVE
EVERSPORTING
EVERT
EVERTEBRAL
EVERTEBRATE
EVERTED
EVERTILE
EVERTING
EVERTOR
EVERWHICH
EVERWHO
EVERY
EVERYBODY
EVERYDAY
EVERYHOW
EVERYLIKE
EVERYONE
EVERYTHING
EVERYWHERE
EVERYWHERES
EVERYWHITHER
EVESTAR
EVET
EVETIDE
EVEWEED
EVIBRATE
EVICKE
EVICT
EVICTED
EVICTING
EVICTION
EVICTOR
EVIDENCE
EVIDENCED
EVIDENCING
EVIDENCIVE
EVIDENT
EVIDENTIAL
EVIDENTIALLY
EVIDENTIARY
EVIDENTLY
EVIL
EVILDOER
EVILHEARTED
EVILLY
EVILNESS
EVILSAYER
EVILSPEAKER
EVILSPEAKING
EVILWISHING
EVINCE
EVINCED
EVINCEMENT
EVINCIBLE
EVINCING
EVINCIVE
EVIRATE
EVIRATO
EVISCERATE
EVISCERATED
EVISCERATING
EVISCERATION
EVISITE
EVITABLE
EVITATE
EVITATION
EVITE
EVITTATE
EVOCABLE
EVOCATE
EVOCATED
EVOCATING
EVOCATION
EVOCATIVE
EVOCATOR
EVOCATORY
EVOE
EVOHE
EVOID
EVOKE
EVOKED
EVOKER
EVOKING
EVOLUTE
EVOLUTION
EVOLUTIONAL
EVOLUTIONARY
EVOLUTIONISM
EVOLUTIONIST
EVOLUTIONIZE
EVOLUTIVE
EVOLVABLE
EVOLVE
EVOLVEMENT
EVOLVENT
EVOME
EVOMIT
EVONYMUS
EVOVAE
EVULGATE
EVULGATION
EVULGE
EVULSE
EVULSION
EVZONE
EVZONES
EWAGE
EWDER
EWE
EWELEASE
EWER
EWERER
EWERIES
EWERY
EWEST
EWHOW
EWK
EWRY
EX
EXACERBATE
EXACERBATED
EXACERBATING
EXACERBATION
EXACT
EXACTA
EXACTABLE
EXACTED
EXACTER
EXACTING
EXACTINGLY
EXACTINGNESS
EXACTION
EXACTITUDE
EXACTIVE
EXACTIVENESS
EXACTLY
EXACTMENT
EXACTNESS
EXACTOR
EXACUATE
EXADVERSO
EXADVERSUM
EXAGGERATE
EXAGGERATED
EXAGGERATING
EXAGGERATION
EXAGGERATIVE
EXAGGERATOR
EXAGGERATORY
EXAGITATE
EXAIRESIS
EXALATE
EXALBUMINOSE
EXALBUMINOUS
EXALLOTRIOTE
EXALT
EXALTATE
EXALTATION
EXALTATIVE
EXALTE
EXALTED
EXALTEDLY
EXALTEDNESS
EXALTEE
EXALTER
EXALTING
EXAM
EXAMEN
EXAMINABLE
EXAMINANT
EXAMINATE
EXAMINATION
EXAMINATIONAL
EXAMINATIVE
EXAMINATOR
EXAMINATORY
EXAMINE
EXAMINED
EXAMINEE
EXAMINER
EXAMINING
EXAMPLE
EXAMPLED
EXAMPLING
EXANIMATE
EXANIMATION
EXANTHEM
EXANTHEMA
EXANTHEMAS
EXANTHEMATA
EXANTHEMATIC
EXANTLATE
EXANTLATION
EXARATE
EXARATION
EXARCH
EXARCHAL
EXARCHATE
EXARCHIST
EXARCHY
EXARTERITIS
EXARTICULATE
EXASPER
EXASPERATE

EXASPERATED
EXASPERATER
EXASPERATING
EXASPERATION
EXASPERATIVE
EXASPIDEAN
EXAUCTORATE
EXAUGURATE
EXAUGURATION
EXAUTHORIZE
EXCALATE
EXCALATION
EXCALCARATE
EXCALCEATE
EXCAMB
EXCAMBER
EXCAMBION
EXCANDESCENT
EXCANTATION
EXCARNATE
EXCARNATION
EXCATHEDRAL
EXCAUDATE
EXCAVATE
EXCAVATED
EXCAVATING
EXCAVATION
EXCAVATIONS
EXCAVATOR
EXCAVE
EXCECATE
EXCECATION
EXCEDENT
EXCEED
EXCEEDED
EXCEEDING
EXCEEDINGLY
EXCEL
EXCELENTE
EXCELLED
EXCELLENCE
EXCELLENCIES
EXCELLENCY
EXCELLENT
EXCELLENTLY
EXCELLING
EXCELS
EXCELSE
EXCELSIN
EXCELSIOR
EXCENTRAL
EXCENTRIC
EXCEPT
EXCEPTANT
EXCEPTED
EXCEPTER
EXCEPTING
EXCEPTIO
EXCEPTION
EXCEPTIONAL
EXCEPTIONALLY
EXCEPTIONARY
EXCEPTIONER
EXCEPTIOUS
EXCEPTIVE
EXCEPTIVELY
EXCERN
EXCERPT
EXCERPTA
EXCERPTED
EXCERPTIBLE
EXCERPTING
EXCERPTION
EXCERPTIVE
EXCERPTOR
EXCESS
EXCESSIVE
EXCESSIVELY
EXCESSIVENESS
EXCESSMAN
EXCESSMEN
EXCHANGE
EXCHANGEABLE
EXCHANGEABLY
EXCHANGED
EXCHANGER
EXCHANGING
EXCHEAT
EXCHEQUER
EXCIDE
EXCIDED
EXCIDING
EXCIPIENT
EXCIPLE
EXCIPULAR
EXCIPULE
EXCIPULIFORM
EXCIPULUM
EXCIRCLE
EXCISABLE
EXCISE
EXCISED
EXCISEMAN
EXCISEMEN
EXCISING
EXCISION
EXCISOR
EXCITABILITIES
EXCITABILITY
EXCITABLE
EXCITABLENESS
EXCITABLY
EXCITANCY
EXCITANT
EXCITATE
EXCITATION
EXCITATIVE
EXCITATOR
EXCITATORY
EXCITE
EXCITED
EXCITEDLY
EXCITEDNESS
EXCITEMENT
EXCITER
EXCITING
EXCITINGLY
EXCITIVE
EXCITOMOTOR
EXCITOMOTORY
EXCITON
EXCITOR
EXCITORY
EXCITRON
EXCLAIM
EXCLAIMED
EXCLAIMER
EXCLAIMING
EXCLAMATION
EXCLAMATIONAL
EXCLAMATIVE
EXCLAMATIVELY
EXCLAMATORILY
EXCLAMATORY
EXCLAVE
EXCLUDE
EXCLUDED
EXCLUDER
EXCLUDING
EXCLUSION
EXCLUSIONARY
EXCLUSIONER
EXCLUSIONISM
EXCLUSIONIST
EXCLUSIVE
EXCLUSIVELY
EXCLUSIVENESS
EXCLUSIVISM
EXCLUSIVITY
EXCLUSORY
EXCOCT
EXCOCTION
EXCOGITABLE
EXCOGITATE
EXCOGITATED
EXCOGITATING
EXCOGITATION
EXCOGITATIVE
EXCOGITATOR
EXCOMMUNICABLE
EXCOMMUNICANT
EXCOMMUNICATE
EXCOMMUNICATED
EXCOMMUNICATING
EXCOMMUNICATION
EXCOMMUNICATIVE
EXCOMMUNICATOR
EXCOMMUNICATORY
EXCOMMUNION
EXCONJUGANT
EXCORIABLE
EXCORIATE
EXCORIATED
EXCORIATING
EXCORIATION
EXCORIATOR
EXCORTICATE
EXCORTICATED
EXCORTICATING
EXCORTICATION
EXCREMENT
EXCREMENTAL
EXCREMENTARY
EXCREMENTIVE
EXCRESCE
EXCRESCENCE
EXCRESCENCES
EXCRESCENCIES
EXCRESCENCY
EXCRESCENT
EXCRESCENTIAL
EXCRETA
EXCRETAL
EXCRETE
EXCRETED
EXCRETER
EXCRETES
EXCRETING
EXCRETION
EXCRETIONARY
EXCRETIVE
EXCRETORY
EXCRIMINATE
EXCRUCIABLE
EXCRUCIATE
EXCRUCIATED
EXCRUCIATING
EXCRUCIATINGLY
EXCRUCIATION
EXCRUCIATOR
EXCUBANT
EXCUDATE
EXCUDERUNT
EXCUDIT
EXCULPABLE
EXCULPATE
EXCULPATED
EXCULPATING
EXCULPATION
EXCULPATIVE
EXCULPATORY
EXCUR
EXCURRENT
EXCURSE
EXCURSED
EXCURSING
EXCURSION
EXCURSIONAL
EXCURSIONARY
EXCURSIONER
EXCURSIONISM
EXCURSIONIST
EXCURSIONIZE
EXCURSIVE
EXCURSIVELY
EXCURSUS
EXCURVATE
EXCURVATED
EXCURVATURE
EXCURVED
EXCUSABILITY
EXCUSABLE
EXCUSABLENESS
EXCUSABLY
EXCUSAL
EXCUSATIVE
EXCUSATOR
EXCUSATORY
EXCUSE
EXCUSED
EXCUSER
EXCUSING
EXCUSIVE
EXCUSS
EXCUSSED
EXCUSSING
EXCYST
EXCYSTATION
EXCYSTED
EXCYSTMENT
EXEAT
EXEC
EXECRABLE
EXECRABLENESS
EXECRABLY
EXECRATE
EXECRATED
EXECRATING
EXECRATION
EXECRATIVE
EXECRATOR
EXECRATORY
EXECUTABLE
EXECUTANCY
EXECUTANT
EXECUTE
EXECUTED
EXECUTER
EXECUTING
EXECUTION
EXECUTIONAL
EXECUTIONEERING
EXECUTIONER
EXECUTIONERESS
EXECUTIONS
EXECUTIVE
EXECUTIVELY
EXECUTIVENESS
EXECUTOR
EXECUTORIAL
EXECUTORY
EXECUTRESS
EXECUTRICES
EXECUTRIX
EXECUTRIXES
EXECUTRY
EXEDE
EXEDENT
EXEDRA
EXEEM
EXEGESES
EXEGESIS
EXEGETE
EXEGETIC
EXEGETICAL
EXEGETICALLY
EXEGETICS
EXEGETIST
EXEME
EXEMPLA
EXEMPLAR
EXEMPLARIC
EXEMPLARILY
EXEMPLARINESS
EXEMPLARISM
EXEMPLARITY
EXEMPLARY
EXEMPLIFICATION
EXEMPLIFIED
EXEMPLIFIER
EXEMPLIFY
EXEMPLIFYING
EXEMPLUM
EXEMPT
EXEMPTIBLE
EXEMPTILE
EXEMPTION
EXEMPTIVE
EXENCEPHALIA
EXENCEPHALIC
EXENCEPHALUS
EXENTERATE
EXENTERATED
EXENTERATING
EXENTERATION
EXEQUATUR
EXEQUIAL
EXEQUIES
EXEQUY
EXERCE
EXERCENT
EXERCISABLE
EXERCISE
EXERCISED
EXERCISER
EXERCISES
EXERCISING
EXERCITANT
EXERCITATION
EXERCITOR
EXERCITORIAL
EXERESIS
EXERGUAL
EXERGUE
EXERT
EXERTED
EXERTING
EXERTION
EXERTIVE
EXES
EXESION
EXEUNT
EXFIGURATION
EXFIGURE
EXFILTRATION
EXFLAGELLATE
EXFLECT
EXFODIATE
EXFODIATION
EXFOLIATE
EXFOLIATED
EXFOLIATING
EXFOLIATION
EXFOLIATIVE
EXFOLIATORY

EXHALABLE
EXHALANT
EXHALATE
EXHALATION
EXHALATORY
EXHALE
EXHALED
EXHALING
EXHANCE
EXHAUST
EXHAUSTED
EXHAUSTEDLY
EXHAUSTEDNESS
EXHAUSTER
EXHAUSTIBLE
EXHAUSTING
EXHAUSTINGLY
EXHAUSTION
EXHAUSTIVE
EXHAUSTIVELY
EXHAUSTIVENESS
EXHAUSTLESS
EXHAUSTLESSLY
EXHEDRA
EXHIBIT
EXHIBITANT
EXHIBITED
EXHIBITING
EXHIBITION
EXHIBITIONAL
EXHIBITIONER
EXHIBITIONISM
EXHIBITIONIST
EXHIBITIONISTIC
EXHIBITIVE
EXHIBITIVELY
EXHIBITOR
EXHIBITORSHIP
EXHIBITORY
EXHIBITS
EXHILARANT
EXHILARATE
EXHILARATED
EXHILARATING
EXHILARATINGLY
EXHILARATION
EXHILARATIVE
EXHILARATOR
EXHILARATORY
EXHORT
EXHORTATION
EXHORTATIVE
EXHORTATIVELY
EXHORTATORY
EXHORTED
EXHORTER
EXHORTING
EXHUMATE
EXHUMATED
EXHUMATING
EXHUMATION
EXHUMATOR
EXHUMATORY
EXHUME
EXHUMED
EXHUMER
EXHUMING
EXIDO
EXIES
EXIGEANT
EXIGEANTE
EXIGENCE
EXIGENCIES
EXIGENCY
EXIGENT
EXIGENTER
EXIGENTLY
EXIGIBLE
EXIGUITY
EXIGUOUS
EXIGUOUSLY
EXIGUOUSNESS
EXILARCH
EXILARCHATE
EXILE
EXILED
EXILER
EXILIAN
EXILIC
EXILING
EXILITY
EXIMIOUS
EXIMIOUSLY
EXIMIOUSNESS
EXINANITE
EXINANITION
EXINE
EXINGUINAL
EXINITE
EXIST
EXISTED
EXISTENCE
EXISTENT
EXISTENTIAL
EXISTENTIALISM
EXISTENTIALIST
EXISTENTIALLY
EXISTENTLY
EXISTER
EXISTING
EXISTLESSNESS
EXIT
EXITE
EXITIAL
EXITION
EXITIOUS
EXITURE
EXITUS
EXLEX
EXOARTERITIS
EXOCARDIA
EXOCARDIAC
EXOCARDIAL
EXOCARP
EXOCCIPITAL
EXOCENTRIC
EXOCHORION
EXOCLINAL
EXOCLINE
EXOCOELAR
EXOCOELE
EXOCOELIC
EXOCOELOM
EXOCOELUM
EXOCOLITIS
EXOCONE
EXOCULATE
EXOCULATED
EXOCULATING
EXOCYCLIC
EXODE
EXODERM
EXODERMIS
EXODIC
EXODIST
EXODIUM
EXODONTIA
EXODROMIC
EXODROMY
EXODUS
EXODY
EXOENZYME
EXOGAMIC
EXOGAMOUS
EXOGAMY
EXOGASTRIC
EXOGASTRICALLY
EXOGASTRITIS
EXOGEN
EXOGENETIC
EXOGENIC
EXOGENOUS
EXOGENOUSLY
EXOGNATHION
EXOGNATHITE
EXOGRAPH
EXOLEMMA
EXOLETE
EXOLVE
EXOMETRITIS
EXOMION
EXOMIS
EXOMOLOGESIS
EXOMORPHIC
EXOMORPHISM
EXOMPHALOS
EXOMPHALOUS
EXOMPHALUS
EXON
EXONARTHEX
EXONER
EXONERATE
EXONERATED
EXONERATING
EXONERATION
EXONERATIVE
EXONERATOR
EXONERETUR
EXONEURAL
EXOPATHIC
EXOPERIDIUM
EXOPHAGOUS
EXOPHAGY
EXOPHORIA
EXOPHORIC
EXOPHTHALMIA
EXOPHTHALMIC
EXOPHTHALMOS
EXOPHTHALMUS
EXOPOD
EXOPODITE
EXOPODITIC
EXORABILITY
EXORABLE
EXORABLENESS
EXORATE
EXORBITAL
EXORBITANCE
EXORBITANCY
EXORBITANT
EXORBITANTLY
EXORBITATE
EXORBITATION
EXORCISATION
EXORCISE
EXORCISED
EXORCISEMENT
EXORCISER
EXORCISING
EXORCISM
EXORCISMAL
EXORCISORY
EXORCIST
EXORCISTIC
EXORCISTICAL
EXORCIZATION
EXORCIZE
EXORCIZED
EXORCIZEMENT
EXORCIZER
EXORCIZING
EXORDIAL
EXORDIUM
EXORDIUMS
EXORDIZE
EXORGANIC
EXORMIA
EXORN
EXORNATION
EXOSEPSIS
EXOSKELETAL
EXOSKELETON
EXOSMIC
EXOSMOSIS
EXOSMOTIC
EXOSPERM
EXOSPHERE
EXOSPHERIC
EXOSPORAL
EXOSPORE
EXOSPORIUM
EXOSPOROUS
EXOSTOME
EXOSTOSED
EXOSTOSES
EXOSTOSIS
EXOSTOTIC
EXOSTRA
EXOSTRACISM
EXOSTRACIZE
EXOSTRAE
EXOTERIC
EXOTERICAL
EXOTERICALLY
EXOTERICISM
EXOTERICS
EXOTHECA
EXOTHECAL
EXOTHECATE
EXOTHECIUM
EXOTHERMAL
EXOTHERMIC
EXOTHERMOUS
EXOTIC
EXOTICALLY
EXOTICALNESS
EXOTICISM
EXOTICIST
EXOTICITY
EXOTICNESS
EXOTISM
EXOTOSPORE
EXOTOXIC
EXOTOXIN
EXOTROPIA
EXOTROPISM
EXPALPATE
EXPAND
EXPANDED
EXPANDEDLY
EXPANDEDNESS
EXPANDER
EXPANDING
EXPANDINGLY
EXPANSE
EXPANSIBILITY
EXPANSIBLE
EXPANSIBLENESS
EXPANSIBLY
EXPANSILE
EXPANSION
EXPANSIONAL
EXPANSIONISM
EXPANSIONIST
EXPANSIVE
EXPANSIVELY
EXPANSIVENESS
EXPANSIVITY
EXPANSUM
EXPANSURE
EXPATIATE
EXPATIATED
EXPATIATER
EXPATIATING
EXPATIATION
EXPATIATIVE
EXPATIATOR
EXPATIATORY
EXPATRIATE
EXPATRIATED
EXPATRIATING
EXPATRIATION
EXPECT
EXPECTABLE
EXPECTANCE
EXPECTANCIES
EXPECTANCY
EXPECTANT
EXPECTANTLY
EXPECTATION
EXPECTATIVE
EXPECTED
EXPECTER
EXPECTING
EXPECTIVE
EXPECTORANT
EXPECTORATE
EXPECTORATED
EXPECTORATING
EXPECTORATION
EXPECTORATOR
EXPEDE
EXPEDED
EXPEDIATE
EXPEDIENCE
EXPEDIENCIES
EXPEDIENCY
EXPEDIENT
EXPEDIENTE
EXPEDIENTIAL
EXPEDIENTIALLY
EXPEDIENTIST
EXPEDIENTLY
EXPEDING
EXPEDITATE
EXPEDITATED
EXPEDITATING
EXPEDITATION
EXPEDITE
EXPEDITED
EXPEDITELY
EXPEDITENESS
EXPEDITER
EXPEDITING
EXPEDITION
EXPEDITIONARY
EXPEDITIONIST
EXPEDITIOUS
EXPEDITIOUSLY
EXPEDITIOUSNESS
EXPEDITOR
EXPEL
EXPELLABLE
EXPELLANT
EXPELLED
EXPELLEE
EXPELLENT
EXPELLER
EXPELLING
EXPEND
EXPENDABILITY
EXPENDABLE
EXPENDED
EXPENDER
EXPENDING

EXPENDITOR
EXPENDITRIX
EXPENDITURE
EXPENSE
EXPENSEFUL
EXPENSEFULNESS
EXPENSES
EXPENSILATION
EXPENSIVE
EXPENSIVELY
EXPENSIVENESS
EXPENTHESIS
EXPERIENCE
EXPERIENCED
EXPERIENCER
EXPERIENCES
EXPERIENCING
EXPERIENT
EXPERIENTIAL
EXPERIENTIALLY
EXPERIMENT
EXPERIMENTAL
EXPERIMENTALISM
EXPERIMENTALIST
EXPERIMENTALIZE
EXPERIMENTALLY
EXPERIMENTARIAN
EXPERIMENTATION
EXPERIMENTATIVE
EXPERIMENTATOR
EXPERIMENTED
EXPERIMENTEE
EXPERIMENTER
EXPERIMENTING
EXPERIMENTIST
EXPERIMENTIZE
EXPERIMENTLY
EXPERMENTIZED
EXPERT
EXPERTISE
EXPERTLY
EXPERTNESS
EXPIABLE
EXPIATE
EXPIATED
EXPIATING
EXPIATION
EXPIATIONAL
EXPIATIST
EXPIATIVE
EXPIATOR
EXPIATORINESS
EXPIATORY
EXPILATE
EXPILATION
EXPILATOR
EXPIRANT
EXPIRATE
EXPIRATION
EXPIRATOR
EXPIRATORY
EXPIRE
EXPIRED
EXPIREE
EXPIRER
EXPIRIES
EXPIRING
EXPIRY
EXPISCATE
EXPISCATED
EXPISCATING
EXPISCATION
EXPISCATOR
EXPISCATORY
EXPLAIN
EXPLAINABLE
EXPLAINED
EXPLAINER
EXPLAINING
EXPLANATE
EXPLANATION
EXPLANATIVE
EXPLANATIVELY
EXPLANATOR
EXPLANATORILY
EXPLANATORINES
EXPLANATORY
EXPLANT
EXPLANTATION
EXPLAT
EXPLEMENT
EXPLEMENTAL
EXPLETE
EXPLETIVE
EXPLETIVELY
EXPLETIVENESS
EXPLETORY
EXPLICABLE
EXPLICATE
EXPLICATED
EXPLICATING
EXPLICATION
EXPLICATIVE
EXPLICATOR
EXPLICATORY
EXPLICIT
EXPLICITLY
EXPLICITNESS
EXPLODE
EXPLODED
EXPLODENT
EXPLODER
EXPLODING
EXPLOIT
EXPLOITABLE
EXPLOITAGE
EXPLOITATION
EXPLOITATIONIST
EXPLOITATIVE
EXPLOITED
EXPLOITER
EXPLOITING
EXPLOITIVE
EXPLOITURE
EXPLORATION
EXPLORATIONAL
EXPLORATIVE
EXPLORATIVELY
EXPLORATIVENESS
EXPLORATOR
EXPLORATORY
EXPLORE
EXPLORED
EXPLOREMENT
EXPLORER
EXPLORING
EXPLOSIBILITY
EXPLOSIBLE
EXPLOSION
EXPLOSIONIST
EXPLOSIVE
EXPLOSIVELY
EXPLOSIVENESS
EXPLOSIVES
EXPONE
EXPONENCE
EXPONENT
EXPONENTIAL
EXPONENTIALLY
EXPONENTS
EXPONIBLE
EXPORT
EXPORTABILITY
EXPORTABLE
EXPORTATION
EXPORTED
EXPORTER
EXPORTING
EXPOSAL
EXPOSE
EXPOSED
EXPOSER
EXPOSING
EXPOSIT
EXPOSITION
EXPOSITIONAL
EXPOSITIONARY
EXPOSITIVE
EXPOSITIVELY
EXPOSITOR
EXPOSITORIAL
EXPOSITORIALLY
EXPOSITORILY
EXPOSITORINESS
EXPOSITORY
EXPOSTULATE
EXPOSTULATED
EXPOSTULATING
EXPOSTULATION
EXPOSTULATIVE
EXPOSTULATIVELY
EXPOSTULATOR
EXPOSTULATORY
EXPOSURE
EXPOUND
EXPOUNDED
EXPOUNDER
EXPOUNDING
EXPREME
EXPRESS
EXPRESSAGE
EXPRESSED
EXPRESSER
EXPRESSIBLE
EXPRESSING
EXPRESSION
EXPRESSIONAL
EXPRESSIONISM
EXPRESSIONIST
EXPRESSIONISTIC
EXPRESSIONLESS
EXPRESSIONLESSLY
EXPRESSIVE
EXPRESSIVELY
EXPRESSIVENESS
EXPRESSLESS
EXPRESSLY
EXPRESSMAN
EXPRESSWAY
EXPROBATE
EXPROBRATORY
EXPROMISSION
EXPROPRIATE
EXPROPRIATED
EXPROPRIATING
EXPROPRIATION
EXPROPRIATOR
EXPUGN
EXPUGNABLE
EXPUITION
EXPULSATORY
EXPULSE
EXPULSER
EXPULSION
EXPULSIVE
EXPULSORY
EXPUNCTION
EXPUNGE
EXPUNGED
EXPUNGER
EXPUNGING
EXPURGATE
EXPURGATED
EXPURGATING
EXPURGATION
EXPURGATIVE
EXPURGATOR
EXPURGATORIAL
EXPURGATORY
EXPURGE
EXQUIRE
EXQUISITE
EXQUISITELY
EXQUISITENESS
EXQUISITISM
EXQUISITIVELY
EXQUISITIVENES
EXRADIO
EXRADIUS
EXRUPEAL
EXSANGUINATE
EXSANGUINE
EXSANGUINOUS
EXSANGUIOUS
EXSCIND
EXSCINDED
EXSCINDING
EXSCRIBE
EXSCRIPT
EXSCRIPTURAL
EXSCULPTATE
EXSCUTELLATE
EXSECANT
EXSECT
EXSECTILE
EXSECTION
EXSECTOR
EXSERT
EXSERTED
EXSERTILE
EXSERTING
EXSERTION
EXSHEATH
EXSIBILATE
EXSICCATAE
EXSICCATE
EXSICCATED
EXSICCATING
EXSICCATION
EXSICCATIVE
EXSILIENCY
EXSOLVE
EXSOMATIC
EXSPUITION
EXSPUTORY
EXSTIPULATE
EXSTROPHY
EXSUCCOUS
EXSUCTION
EXSUFFLATE
EXSUFFLATION
EXSUFFLICATE
EXSURGE
EXSURGENT
EXTANCY
EXTANT
EXTEMPORAL
EXTEMPORALLY
EXTEMPORALNESS
EXTEMPORANEOUS
EXTEMPORANEOUSLY
EXTEMPORANEOUSNESS
EXTEMPORARILY
EXTEMPORARINESS
EXTEMPORARY
EXTEMPORE
EXTEMPORIZE
EXTEMPORIZED
EXTEMPORIZER
EXTEMPORIZING
EXTEND
EXTENDED
EXTENDEDLY
EXTENDEDNESS
EXTENDER
EXTENDIBILITY
EXTENDIBLE
EXTENDING
EXTENSE
EXTENSIBILITY
EXTENSIBLE
EXTENSIBLENESS
EXTENSILE
EXTENSIMETER
EXTENSION
EXTENSIONAL
EXTENSIONIST
EXTENSITY
EXTENSIVE
EXTENSIVELY
EXTENSIVENESS
EXTENSOMETER
EXTENSOR
EXTENSUM
EXTENT
EXTENUATE
EXTENUATED
EXTENUATING
EXTENUATINGLY
EXTENUATION
EXTENUATIVE
EXTENUATOR
EXTENUATORY
EXTER
EXTERIOR
EXTERIORATE
EXTERIORATION
EXTERIORITY
EXTERIORIZATION
EXTERIORIZE
EXTERIORIZED
EXTERIORIZING
EXTERIORLY
EXTERIORNESS
EXTERMINATE
EXTERMINATED
EXTERMINATING
EXTERMINATION
EXTERMINATIVE
EXTERMINATOR
EXTERMINATORY
EXTERMINE
EXTERN
EXTERNA
EXTERNAL
EXTERNALISM
EXTERNALIST
EXTERNALISTIC
EXTERNALITIES
EXTERNALITY
EXTERNALIZATION
EXTERNALIZE
EXTERNALLY
EXTERNAT
EXTERNATE
EXTERNATION
EXTERNE
EXTERNIZATION
EXTERNIZE
EXTERNUM
EXTEROCEPTIST
EXTEROCEPTIVE
EXTEROCEPTOR
EXTERRANEOUS
EXTERRESTRIAL

EXTERRITORIAL
EXTILL
EXTIMA
EXTIME
EXTINCT
EXTINCTEUR
EXTINCTION
EXTINCTIVE
EXTINCTOR
EXTINE
EXTINGUISH
EXTINGUISHED
EXTINGUISHER
EXTIRP
EXTIRPATE
EXTIRPATED
EXTIRPATING
EXTIRPATION
EXTIRPATIVE
EXTIRPATOR
EXTIRPATORY
EXTISPEX
EXTISPICES
EXTISPICIOUS
EXTISPICY
EXTOGENOUS
EXTOL
EXTOLL
EXTOLLATION
EXTOLLED
EXTOLLER
EXTOLLING
EXTOLLMENT
EXTOLMENT
EXTOOLITIC
EXTORSIVE
EXTORSIVELY
EXTORT
EXTORTED
EXTORTER
EXTORTING
EXTORTION
EXTORTIONARY
EXTORTIONATE
EXTORTIONER
EXTORTIONIST
EXTORTIVE
EXTRA
EXTRABOLD
EXTRABULBAR
EXTRACAPSULAR
EXTRACARPAL
EXTRACOSTAL
EXTRACT
EXTRACTABLE
EXTRACTED
EXTRACTIBLE
EXTRACTIFORM
EXTRACTING
EXTRACTION
EXTRACTIVE
EXTRACTOR
EXTRACTS
EXTRACURRICULAR
EXTRACYSTIC
EXTRADITABLE
EXTRADITE
EXTRADITED
EXTRADITING
EXTRADITION
EXTRADOS
EXTRADOSED
EXTRADOTAL
EXTRADUCTION
EXTRAENTERIC
EXTRAFORMAL
EXTRAGALACTIC
EXTRAJUDICIAL
EXTRALATERAL
EXTRALITE
EXTRALITY
EXTRAMUNDANE
EXTRAMURAL
EXTRAMURALLY
EXTRANEAN
EXTRANEITY
EXTRANEOUS
EXTRANEOUSLY
EXTRANEOUSNESS
EXTRAORDINARIES
EXTRAORDINARILY
EXTRAORDINARY
EXTRAPHYSICAL
EXTRAPOLAR
EXTRAPOLATE
EXTRAPOLATED
EXTRAPOLATING
EXTRAPOLATION
EXTRAPOLATIVE
EXTRAPOLATOR
EXTRARED
EXTRAREGULAR
EXTRARETINAL
EXTRASENSORY
EXTRASEROUS
EXTRASOLAR
EXTRASTAPEDIAL
EXTRASYSTOLE
EXTRATARSAL
EXTRATERRESTRIAL
EXTRATRIBAL
EXTRATUBAL
EXTRAUTERINE
EXTRAVAGANCE
EXTRAVAGANCIES
EXTRAVAGANCY
EXTRAVAGANT
EXTRAVAGANTLY
EXTRAVAGANTNESS
EXTRAVAGANZA
EXTRAVAGATE
EXTRAVAGATED
EXTRAVAGATING
EXTRAVAGATION
EXTRAVAGINAL
EXTRAVASATE
EXTRAVASATED
EXTRAVASATING
EXTRAVASATION
EXTRAVASCULAR
EXTRAVENTRICULAR
EXTRAVERSION
EXTRAVERT
EXTRAVIOLET
EXTRE
EXTREAT
EXTREME
EXTREMELY
EXTREMENESS
EXTREMER
EXTREMES
EXTREMEST
EXTREMISM
EXTREMIST
EXTREMISTIC
EXTREMITAL
EXTREMITIES
EXTREMITY
EXTREMUM
EXTRICABLE
EXTRICABLY
EXTRICATE
EXTRICATED
EXTRICATING
EXTRICATION
EXTRINSIC
EXTRINSICAL
EXTRINSICALLY
EXTRINSICATE
EXTROITIVE
EXTROPICAL
EXTRORSAL
EXTRORSE
EXTRORSELY
EXTROSPECT
EXTROSPECTION
EXTROSPECTIVE
EXTROVERSION
EXTROVERSIVE
EXTROVERT
EXTRUCT
EXTRUDE
EXTRUDED
EXTRUDER
EXTRUDING
EXTRUSILE
EXTRUSION
EXTRUSIVE
EXTRUSORY
EXTUBATE
EXTUBATION
EXTUMESCENCE
EXTUND
EXTURB
EXTUSION
EXUBERANCE
EXUBERANCY
EXUBERANT
EXUBERANTLY
EXUBERANTNESS
EXUBERATE
EXUBERATED
EXUBERATING
EXUBERATION
EXUDATE
EXUDATION
EXUDATIVE
EXUDATORY
EXUDE
EXUDED
EXUDENCE
EXUDING
EXUL
EXULATE
EXULCERATE
EXULCERATED
EXULCERATING
EXULCERATION
EXULCERATIVE
EXULCERATORY
EXULT
EXULTANCY
EXULTANT
EXULTANTLY
EXULTATION
EXULTED
EXULTET
EXULTING
EXULTINGLY
EXULULATE
EXUMBRAL
EXUMBRELLA
EXUMBRELLAR
EXUNDATE
EXUNDATION
EXURB
EXURBANITE
EXURBIA
EXUST
EXUTE
EXUVIABILITY
EXUVIABLE
EXUVIAE
EXUVIAL
EXUVIATE
EXUVIATED
EXUVIATING
EXUVIATION
EXZODIACAL
EY
EYAH
EYALET
EYAS
EYDENT
EYE
EYEABLE
EYEBALL
EYEBALM
EYEBAR
EYEBEAM
EYEBERRY
EYEBLINK
EYEBOLT
EYEBREE
EYEBRIDLED
EYEBRIGHT
EYEBROW
EYECUP
EYED
EYEDNESS
EYEDOT
EYEDROP
EYEFLAP
EYEFUL
EYEGLANCE
EYEGLASS
EYEGLASSES
EYEGROUND
EYEHOLE
EYEHOOK
EYEING
EYELASH
EYELAST
EYELESS
EYELET
EYELETED
EYELETEER
EYELETING
EYELETTER
EYELID
EYELIDS
EYELIGHT
EYELINE
EYEMARK
EYEN
EYEPIECE
EYEPIT
EYEPOINT
EYER
EYEREACH
EYEROOT
EYES
EYESALVE
EYESEED
EYESERVANT
EYESERVER
EYESERVICE
EYESHADE
EYESHIELD
EYESHINE
EYESHOT
EYESIGHT
EYESOME
EYESORE
EYESPOT
EYESS
EYESTALK
EYESTONE
EYESTRAIN
EYESTRING
EYETEETH
EYETOOTH
EYEWAITER
EYEWASH
EYEWATER
EYEWEAR
EYEWINK
EYEWINKER
EYEWITNESS
EYEWORT
EYEY
EYING
EYLE
EYLIAD
EYNE
EYOT
EYRA
EYRE
EYREN
EYRIE
EYRIR
EYRY
EYSOGE
EZBA

FA
FABA
FABACEOUS
FABE
FABELLA
FABES
FABIFORM
FABLE
FABLED
FABLEDOM
FABLEIST
FABLELAND
FABLEMAKER
FABLEMONGER
FABLER
FABLIAU
FABLIAUX
FABLING
FABRIC
FABRICANT
FABRICATE
FABRICATED
FABRICATES
FABRICATING
FABRICATION
FABRICATIVE
FABRICATOR
FABRICATURE
FABRICS
FABRIKOID
FABRILE
FABRIQUE
FABULA
FABULAR
FABULIST
FABULIZE
FABULOSITY
FABULOUS
FABULOUSLY
FABULOUSNESS
FABURDEN
FAC
FACADAL
FACADE
FACE
FACEABLE
FACEBOW
FACED
FACELESS
FACEMAKER
FACEMAKING
FACEMAN
FACEMARK
FACEPIECE
FACEPLATE
FACER
FACES
FACET
FACETE
FACETED
FACETELY
FACETENESS
FACETIAE
FACETIATION
FACETING
FACETIOUS
FACETIOUSLY
FACETIOUSNESS
FACETTE
FACEWORK
FACIA
FACIAL
FACIEND
FACIENT
FACIER
FACIES
FACIEST
FACILE
FACILELY
FACILENESS
FACILITATE
FACILITATED
FACILITATING
FACILITATION
FACILITATIVE
FACILITATOR
FACILITIES
FACILITY
FACING
FACINGLY
FACINOROUS
FACIOCERVICAL
FACIOPLEGIA
FACK
FACKELTANZ
FACKINS
FACON
FACONNE
FACSIMILE
FACSIMILED
FACSIMILEING
FACSIMILES
FACSIMILIST
FACSIMILIZE
FACT
FACTA
FACTABLE
FACTICE
FACTICIDE
FACTION
FACTIONAL
FACTIONALISM
FACTIONARIES
FACTIONARY
FACTIONATE
FACTIONEER
FACTIONISM
FACTIONIST
FACTIOUS
FACTIOUSLY
FACTIOUSNESS
FACTISH
FACTITIAL
FACTITIOUS
FACTITIOUSLY
FACTITIOUSNESS
FACTITIVE
FACTITIVELY
FACTITUDE
FACTIVE
FACTO
FACTOR
FACTORABILITY
FACTORABLE
FACTORAGE
FACTORED
FACTORIAL
FACTORIALLY
FACTORIES
FACTORING
FACTORIST
FACTORIZATION
FACTORIZE
FACTORIZED
FACTORIZING
FACTORS
FACTORSHIP
FACTORY
FACTORYSHIP
FACTOTUM
FACTRIX
FACTS
FACTUAL
FACTUALITY
FACTUALLY
FACTUALNESS
FACTUM
FACTURE
FACTY
FACULA
FACULAE
FACULAR
FACULOUS
FACULTATE
FACULTATIVE
FACULTATIVELY
FACULTIED
FACULTIES
FACULTIZE
FACULTY
FACUND
FACUNDITY
FACY
FAD
FADAISE
FADDINESS
FADDING
FADDISH
FADDISHNESS
FADDISM
FADDIST
FADDLE
FADDY
FADE
FADEAWAY
FADED
FADEDLY
FADEDNESS
FADELESS
FADELESSLY
FADER
FADGE
FADGED
FADGING
FADING
FADINGLY
FADINGNESS
FADME
FADO
FADS
FADY
FAE
FAECAL
FAECALITH
FAECES
FAECULA
FAENA
FAENUS
FAERIE
FAERY
FAEX
FAFF
FAFFLE
FAFFY
FAG
FAGACEOUS
FAGALD
FAGARA
FAGE
FAGER
FAGGED
FAGGER
FAGGERY
FAGGING
FAGGOT
FAGGOTED
FAGGOTY
FAGGY
FAGINE
FAGOPYRISM
FAGOT
FAGOTED
FAGOTER
FAGOTING
FAGOTT
FAGOTTE
FAGOTTINO
FAGOTTIST
FAGOTTO
FAGOTTONE
FAGOTY
FAHAM
FAHLBAND
FAHLERZ
FAHLORE
FAHLUNITE
FAIENCE
FAIK
FAIL
FAILANCE
FAILED
FAILING
FAILINGLY
FAILINGNESS
FAILLE
FAILURE
FAIN
FAINAIGUE
FAINAIGUED
FAINAIGUER
FAINAIGUING
FAINEANCE
FAINEANCY
FAINEANT
FAINEANTISE
FAINLY
FAINNESS
FAINS
FAINT
FAINTED
FAINTER
FAINTEST
FAINTFUL
FAINTHEART
FAINTHEARTED
FAINTHEARTEDLY
FAINTHEARTEDNESS
FAINTING
FAINTINGLY
FAINTISH
FAINTLING
FAINTLY
FAINTNESS
FAINTS
FAINTY
FAIPULE
FAIR
FAIRD
FAIRED
FAIRER
FAIREST
FAIRFIELDITE
FAIRGROUND
FAIRHEAD
FAIRIES
FAIRILY
FAIRING
FAIRISH
FAIRISHLY
FAIRLY
FAIRNESS
FAIRSHIP
FAIRSOME
FAIRWATER
FAIRWAY
FAIRY
FAIRYDOM
FAIRYFOLK
FAIRYHOOD
FAIRYISM
FAIRYLAND
FAIRYLIKE
FAIRYOLOGY
FAISCEAU
FAIT
FAITERY
FAITH
FAITHBREACH
FAITHBREAKER
FAITHFUL
FAITHFULLY
FAITHFULNESS
FAITHLESS
FAITHLESSLY
FAITHLESSNESS
FAITHWORTHINESS
FAITHWORTHY
FAITOR
FAITOUR
FAIZE
FAJA
FAKE
FAKED
FAKEER
FAKEMENT
FAKER
FAKERY
FAKING
FAKIR
FAKY
FALANAKA
FALBALA
FALBELO
FALCADE
FALCATE
FALCATED
FALCATION
FALCES
FALCHION
FALCIAL
FALCIFORM
FALCON
FALCONBILL
FALCONER
FALCONET
FALCONINE
FALCONOID
FALCONRY
FALCOPERN
FALCULA
FALCULAR
FALCULATE
FALDA
FALDAGE
FALDERAL
FALDEROL
FALDETTA
FALDFEE
FALDING
FALDISTORY
FALDSTOOL
FALDWORTH
FALK
FALL
FALLACIA

FALLACIES
FALLACIOUS
FALLACIOUSLY
FALLACIOUSNESS
FALLACY
FALLAGE
FALLAL
FALLALERY
FALLATION
FALLAWAY
FALLBACK
FALLECTOMY
FALLEN
FALLENCY
FALLER
FALLFISH
FALLFISHES
FALLIBILITY
FALLIBLE
FALLIBLENESS
FALLIBLY
FALLING
FALLOFF
FALLOSTOMY
FALLOUT
FALLOW
FALLOWED
FALLOWING
FALLOWNESS
FALLS
FALLTIME
FALLWAY
FALLY
FALSARY
FALSE
FALSEDAD
FALSEHEARTED
FALSEHEARTEDLY
FALSEHEARTEDNESS
FALSEHOOD
FALSEHOODS
FALSELY
FALSEN
FALSENESS
FALSER
FALSEST
FALSETTIST
FALSETTO
FALSETTOS
FALSEWORK
FALSIDICAL
FALSIE
FALSIES
FALSIFICATE
FALSIFICATION
FALSIFICATOR
FALSIFIED
FALSIFIER
FALSIFY
FALSIFYING
FALSISM
FALSITEIT
FALSITIES
FALSITY
FALSUM
FALTBOAT
FALTER
FALTERED
FALTERER
FALTERING
FALTERINGLY
FALUN
FALUS
FALX
FAM
FAMATINITE
FAMBLE
FAME
FAMED
FAMEFLOWER
FAMELESS
FAMELIC
FAMILIA
FAMILIAL
FAMILIAR
FAMILIARISM
FAMILIARITY
FAMILIARIZATION
FAMILIARIZE
FAMILIARIZED
FAMILIARIZER
FAMILIARIZING
FAMILIARIZINGLY
FAMILIARLY
FAMILIES
FAMILISM
FAMILIST
FAMILISTERE
FAMILISTIC
FAMILISTICAL
FAMILY
FAMINE
FAMING
FAMISH
FAMISHED
FAMISHING
FAMISHMENT
FAMOSE
FAMOUS
FAMOUSLY
FAMOUSNESS
FAMULAR
FAMULARY
FAMULI
FAMULUS
FAN
FANA
FANAKALO
FANAL
FANALOKA
FANAM
FANATIC
FANATICAL
FANATICALLY
FANATICALNESS
FANATICISM
FANATICIZE
FANATICIZED
FANATICIZING
FANATICS
FANBACK
FANBEARER
FANCICAL
FANCIED
FANCIER
FANCIES
FANCIEST
FANCIFUL
FANCIFULLY
FANCIFULNESS
FANCIFY
FANCILESS
FANCILY
FANCY
FANCYING
FANCYMONGER
FANCYWORK
FAND
FANDANGLE
FANDANGO
FANE
FANEGA
FANEGADA
FANFARE
FANFARON
FANFARONADE
FANFARONADING
FANFLOWER
FANFOLD
FANFOOT
FANG
FANGA
FANGED
FANGER
FANGING
FANGLE
FANGLED
FANGLESS
FANGLIKE
FANGLOMERATE
FANGO
FANGOT
FANGS
FANGY
FANHOUSE
FANIENTE
FANION
FANIONED
FANIT
FANJET
FANK
FANKLE
FANLIGHT
FANLIKE
FANMAKER
FANMAKING
FANMAN
FANNED
FANNEL
FANNELING
FANNER
FANNIER
FANNIES
FANNING
FANNINGS
FANNON
FANO
FANON
FANS
FANTAD
FANTADDISH
FANTAIL
FANTAISIE
FANTASIA
FANTASIED
FANTASIST
FANTASIZE
FANTASIZED
FANTASIZING
FANTASM
FANTASMAL
FANTASQUE
FANTASSIN
FANTAST
FANTASTIC
FANTASTICAL
FANTASTICALITY
FANTASTICALLY
FANTASTICALNESS
FANTASTICATE
FANTASTICATION
FANTASTICLY
FANTASTICNESS
FANTASTICO
FANTASTRY
FANTASY
FANTASYING
FANTEAGUE
FANTEEG
FANTIGUE
FANTOCCINI
FANTOCINE
FANTOD
FANTODDISH
FANTOM
FANUM
FANWEED
FANWORK
FANWORT
FANWRIGHT
FANZINE
FAON
FAP
FAPE
FAPESMO
FAQIH
FAQUIR
FAR
FARAD
FARADAIC
FARADAY
FARADIC
FARADISM
FARADIZATION
FARADIZE
FARADIZED
FARADIZER
FARADMETER
FARAND
FARANDINE
FARANDMAN
FARANDMEN
FARANDOLA
FARANDOLE
FARAON
FARASULA
FARAWAY
FARAWAYNESS
FARCE
FARCED
FARCER
FARCETTA
FARCEUR
FARCEUSE
FARCI
FARCIALIZE
FARCICAL
FARCICALITY
FARCICALLY
FARCICALNESS
FARCIE
FARCIED
FARCIFY
FARCIN
FARCING
FARCIST
FARCTATE
FARCY
FARD
FARDA
FARDAGE
FARDEL
FARDELS
FARDH
FARDO
FARE
FARED
FARER
FAREWELL
FARFARA
FARFEL
FARFET
FARFETCH
FARFETCHED
FARFETCHEDNESS
FARGOING
FARGOOD
FARINA
FARINACEOUS
FARINE
FARING
FARINHA
FARINOMETER
FARINOSE
FARINOSELY
FARINULENT
FARISH
FARKLEBERRY
FARL
FARLE
FARLEU
FARLEY
FARM
FARMAGE
FARMED
FARMER
FARMERESS
FARMERETTE
FARMERLY
FARMERY
FARMHAND
FARMHOLD
FARMHOUSE
FARMING
FARMLAND
FARMOST
FARMOUT
FARMPLACE
FARMSTEAD
FARMSTEADING
FARMTOWN
FARMWIFE
FARMY
FARMYARD
FARMYARDY
FARNESOL
FARNESS
FARO
FAROEISH
FAROL
FAROLITO
FAROUCHE
FARRAGE
FARRAGINOUS
FARRAGO
FARRAGOES
FARRAND
FARRANDLY
FARRANT
FARRANTLY
FARREL
FARRIER
FARRIERIES
FARRIERY
FARRISITE
FARROW
FARRUCA
FARSAKH
FARSANG
FARSE
FARSEEING
FARSEEINGNESS
FARSEER
FARSET
FARSIGHTED
FARSIGHTEDLY
FARSIGHTEDNESS
FARSTEPPED
FART
FARTHER
FARTHERMOST
FARTHEST
FARTHING
FARTHINGALE
FARTHINGS

FARWELTERED
FASCES
FASCET
FASCIA
FASCIAL
FASCIATE
FASCIATED
FASCIATELY
FASCIATION
FASCICLE
FASCICLED
FASCICULAR
FASCICULARLY
FASCICULATE
FASCICULATED
FASCICULATELY
FASCICULATION
FASCICULE
FASCICULI
FASCICULUS
FASCINATE
FASCINATED
FASCINATING
FASCINATINGLY
FASCINATION
FASCINATIVE
FASCINATOR
FASCINATRESS
FASCINE
FASCINERY
FASCINES
FASCIOLA
FASCIOLAE
FASCIOLAR
FASCIOLE
FASCIOLET
FASCIOLIASIS
FASCIOLOID
FASCIS
FASCISM
FASCIST
FASCISTIC
FASCISTICIZE
FASCISTIZE
FASELS
FASH
FASHER
FASHERIE
FASHERY
FASHION
FASHIONABILITY
FASHIONABLE
FASHIONABLENESS
FASHIONABLY
FASHIONATIVE
FASHIONED
FASHIONER
FASHIONING
FASHIONIST
FASHIONIZE
FASHIONMONGER
FASHIOUS
FASHIOUSNESS
FASIBITIKITE
FASINITE
FASNACHT
FASOLA
FASSAITE
FAST
FASTEN
FASTENED
FASTENER
FASTENING
FASTENINGS
FASTENS
FASTER
FASTEST
FASTHOLD
FASTI
FASTIDIOSITY
FASTIDIOUS
FASTIDIOUSLY
FASTIDIOUSNESS
FASTIDIUM
FASTIGATE
FASTIGIA
FASTIGIATE
FASTIGIATED
FASTIGIUM
FASTING
FASTINGLY
FASTLAND
FASTLY
FASTNESS
FASTUOUS
FASTUOUSLY
FASTUOUSNESS
FAT
FATAL
FATALISM
FATALIST
FATALISTIC
FATALISTICALLY
FATALITY
FATALIZE
FATALLY
FATBACK
FATBIRD
FATCAKE
FATE
FATED
FATEFUL
FATEFULLY
FATEFULNESS
FATES
FATHEAD
FATHEADED
FATHEADEDNESS
FATHEARTED
FATHER
FATHERED
FATHERHOOD
FATHERING
FATHERLAND
FATHERLESS
FATHERLESSNESS
FATHERLINESS
FATHERLY
FATHOM
FATHOMABLE
FATHOMAGE
FATHOMED
FATHOMER
FATHOMING
FATHOMLESS
FATHOMLESSLY
FATHOMLESSNESS
FATHOMS
FATIDIC
FATIDICAL
FATIDICALLY
FATIFEROUS
FATIGABILITY
FATIGABLE
FATIGABLENESS
FATIGATE
FATIGATION
FATIGUE
FATIGUED
FATIGUES
FATIGUESOME
FATIGUING
FATIHA
FATIHAH
FATILOQUENT
FATING
FATISCENCE
FATISCENT
FATLESS
FATLIKE
FATLING
FATLY
FATNESS
FATSIA
FATSO
FATSTOCK
FATTED
FATTEN
FATTENED
FATTENER
FATTENING
FATTER
FATTEST
FATTIER
FATTIEST
FATTILY
FATTINESS
FATTING
FATTISH
FATTISHNESS
FATTRELS
FATTY
FATUITIES
FATUITOUS
FATUITY
FATUOID
FATUOUS
FATUOUSLY
FATUOUSNESS
FATWOOD
FAUBOURG
FAUCAL
FAUCALIZE
FAUCES
FAUCET
FAUCHARD
FAUCIAL
FAUCITIS
FAUCONNIER
FAUCRE
FAUD
FAUGH
FAUJASITE
FAUJDAR
FAULD
FAULT
FAULTAGE
FAULTED
FAULTER
FAULTFIND
FAULTFINDER
FAULTFINDING
FAULTFUL
FAULTIER
FAULTIEST
FAULTILY
FAULTINESS
FAULTING
FAULTLESS
FAULTLESSLY
FAULTLESSNESS
FAULTSMAN
FAULTY
FAULX
FAUN
FAUNA
FAUNAE
FAUNAL
FAUNALLY
FAUNAS
FAUNCH
FAUNIST
FAUNISTIC
FAUNISTICAL
FAUNOLOGICAL
FAUNOLOGY
FAUNULA
FAUNULE
FAUR
FAURD
FAURED
FAUS
FAUSANT
FAUSE
FAUSEN
FAUSSEBRAIE
FAUSSEBRAYE
FAUSSEBRAYED
FAUST
FAUSTER
FAUTERER
FAUTEUIL
FAUTOR
FAUTORSHIP
FAUVE
FAUVETTE
FAUX
FAVA
FAVAGINOUS
FAVEL
FAVELIDIUM
FAVELLA
FAVELLOID
FAVEOLATE
FAVEOLUS
FAVI
FAVIFORM
FAVILLA
FAVILLAE
FAVILLOUS
FAVISM
FAVISSA
FAVISSAE
FAVONIAN
FAVOR
FAVORABLE
FAVORABLY
FAVORED
FAVOREDLY
FAVOREDNESS
FAVORER
FAVORESS
FAVORING
FAVORINGLY
FAVORITE
FAVORITISM
FAVORLESS
FAVORS
FAVOSE
FAVOSELY
FAVOSITE
FAVOSITOID
FAVOUR
FAVOURABLE
FAVOURABLENESS
FAVOURED
FAVOUREDLY
FAVOUREDNESS
FAVOURER
FAVOURESS
FAVOURING
FAVOURINGLY
FAVOURITE
FAVOURITISM
FAVOURLESS
FAVOUS
FAVUS
FAW
FAWN
FAWNED
FAWNER
FAWNERY
FAWNING
FAWNINGLY
FAWNINGNESS
FAWNY
FAX
FAXED
FAY
FAYALITE
FAYED
FAYING
FAYLES
FAZE
FAZED
FAZENDA
FAZENDEIRO
FAZING
FEABERRY
FEAGUE
FEAK
FEAKED
FEAKING
FEAL
FEALTIES
FEALTY
FEAR
FEARBABE
FEARED
FEAREDLY
FEAREDNESS
FEARER
FEARFUL
FEARFULLY
FEARFULNESS
FEARING
FEARINGLY
FEARLESS
FEARLESSLY
FEARLESSNESS
FEARNAUGHT
FEARNOUGHT
FEARSOME
FEARSOMELY
FEARSOMENESS
FEASANCE
FEASE
FEASIBILITY
FEASIBLE
FEASIBLENESS
FEASIBLY
FEASOR
FEAST
FEASTED
FEASTEN
FEASTER
FEASTFUL
FEASTFULLY
FEASTING
FEASTLY
FEAT
FEATER
FEATEST
FEATHER
FEATHERBACK
FEATHERBEDDED
FEATHERBEDDING
FEATHERBIRD
FEATHERBONE
FEATHERBRAIN
FEATHERBRAINED
FEATHERCUT
FEATHERDOM
FEATHERED
FEATHEREDGE

FEATHEREDGED
FEATHERER
FEATHERFEW
FEATHERFOIL
FEATHERHEAD
FEATHERHEADED
FEATHERINESS
FEATHERING
FEATHERLEAF
FEATHERMAN
FEATHERMONGER
FEATHERS
FEATHERSTITCH
FEATHERTOP
FEATHERWAY
FEATHERWEED
FEATHERWEIGHT
FEATHERWING
FEATHERWOOD
FEATHERWORK
FEATHERWORKER
FEATHERY
FEATISH
FEATISHLY
FEATISHNESS
FEATLESS
FEATLINESS
FEATLY
FEATOUS
FEATURAL
FEATURALLY
FEATURE
FEATURED
FEATUREFUL
FEATURELESS
FEATURELINESS
FEATURELY
FEATURES
FEATURING
FEATY
FEAZE
FEAZED
FEAZING
FEAZINGS
FEBRICANT
FEBRICIDE
FEBRICITY
FEBRICULA
FEBRIFACIENT
FEBRIFIC
FEBRIFUGAL
FEBRIFUGE
FEBRILE
FEBRILITY
FEBRIS
FEBRUATION
FECAL
FECALITH
FECALOID
FECCHE
FECES
FECIAL
FECIT
FECK
FECKET
FECKFUL
FECKFULLY
FECKLESS
FECKLESSLY
FECKLESSNESS
FECKLY
FECULA
FECULAE
FECULENCE
FECULENCY
FECULENT
FECUND
FECUNDATE
FECUNDATED
FECUNDATING
FECUNDATION
FECUNDATIVE
FECUNDATOR
FECUNDATORY
FECUNDIFY
FECUNDITY
FECUNDIZE
FED
FEDAI
FEDARIE
FEDAYEE
FEDDAN
FEDELINI
FEDERACIES
FEDERACY
FEDERAL
FEDERALISM
FEDERALIST
FEDERALISTIC
FEDERALIZATION
FEDERALIZE
FEDERALIZED
FEDERALIZING
FEDERALLY
FEDERALNESS
FEDERARY
FEDERATE
FEDERATED
FEDERATING
FEDERATION
FEDERATIVE
FEDERATIVELY
FEDERATOR
FEDIFRAGOUS
FEDITY
FEDORA
FEE
FEEB
FEEBLE
FEEBLEBRAINED
FEEBLEHEARTED
FEEBLEHEARTEDLY
FEEBLEHEARTEDNESS
FEEBLEMINDED
FEEBLENESS
FEEBLER
FEEBLEST
FEEBLISH
FEEBLY
FEED
FEEDBACK
FEEDBAG
FEEDBIN
FEEDBOARD
FEEDBOX
FEEDER
FEEDHEAD
FEEDING
FEEDLOT
FEEDMAN
FEEDS
FEEDSMAN
FEEDSTUFF
FEEDWAY
FEEDY
FEEING
FEEK
FEEL
FEELABLE
FEELER
FEELING
FEELINGLY
FEELINGNESS
FEELINGS
FEER
FEERE
FEERIE
FEERING
FEES
FEEST
FEET
FEEZE
FEFNICUTE
FEGARY
FEGS
FEHME
FEI
FEID
FEIGH
FEIGHER
FEIGN
FEIGNED
FEIGNEDLY
FEIGNEDNESS
FEIGNER
FEIGNING
FEIL
FEINT
FEINTER
FEIRIE
FEIS
FEISEANNA
FEIST
FEISTIER
FEISTIEST
FEISTY
FEKE
FELAPTON
FELD
FELDSHER
FELDSPAR
FELDSPARPHYRE
FELDSPATH
FELDSPATHIC
FELDSPATHOID
FELDSPATHOSE
FELF
FELICIDE
FELICIFIC
FELICIFY
FELICITATE
FELICITATED
FELICITATING
FELICITATION
FELICITATOR
FELICITIES
FELICITOUS
FELICITOUSLY
FELICITOUSNESS
FELICITY
FELID
FELIFORM
FELINE
FELINELY
FELINENESS
FELINITY
FELINOPHILE
FELINOPHOBE
FELIS
FELL
FELLABLE
FELLAGE
FELLAGHA
FELLAH
FELLAHEEN
FELLAHIN
FELLAHS
FELLATA
FELLED
FELLEN
FELLER
FELLFARE
FELLIC
FELLIES
FELLIFLUOUS
FELLING
FELLMONGER
FELLNESS
FELLOE
FELLOW
FELLOWCRAFT
FELLOWED
FELLOWING
FELLOWLIKE
FELLOWLY
FELLOWMAN
FELLOWS
FELLOWSHIP
FELLOWSHIPED
FELLOWSHIPING
FELLOWSHIPPED
FELLOWSHIPPING
FELLSIDE
FELLY
FELO
FELOID
FELON
FELONIES
FELONIOUS
FELONIOUSLY
FELONIOUSNESS
FELONOUS
FELONRY
FELONSETTER
FELONWEED
FELONWOOD
FELONWORT
FELONY
FELS
FELSITE
FELSITIC
FELSOBANYITE
FELSOPHYRE
FELSOPHYRIC
FELSPAR
FELSPATH
FELSTONE
FELT
FELTED
FELTER
FELTING
FELTLIKE
FELTMAKER
FELTMAKING
FELTMAN
FELTMONGER
FELTWORK
FELTWORT
FELTY
FELTYFARE
FELTYFLIER
FELUCCA
FELWORT
FELZE
FEMALE
FEMALELY
FEMALENESS
FEMALIST
FEMALITY
FEMCEE
FEME
FEMEREIL
FEMERELL
FEMIC
FEMICIDE
FEMINACY
FEMINAL
FEMINALITY
FEMINATE
FEMINEITY
FEMINIE
FEMINILITY
FEMININ
FEMININE
FEMININELY
FEMININENESS
FEMININITY
FEMINISM
FEMINIST
FEMINISTIC
FEMINITY
FEMINIZATION
FEMINIZE
FEMME
FEMORA
FEMORAL
FEMUR
FEMURS
FEN
FENAGLE
FENBANK
FENBERRY
FENCE
FENCED
FENCEFUL
FENCELESS
FENCELESSNESS
FENCEPLAY
FENCER
FENCHENE
FENCHOL
FENCHONE
FENCHYL
FENCIBLE
FENCING
FEND
FENDABLE
FENDED
FENDER
FENDERING
FENDING
FENDY
FENERATION
FENESTELLA
FENESTER
FENESTRA
FENESTRAE
FENESTRAL
FENESTRATE
FENESTRATED
FENESTRATION
FENESTRATO
FENESTRONE
FENESTRULE
FENETRE
FENITE
FENKS
FENLAND
FENLANDER
FENMAN
FENMAN
FENNEC
FENNEL
FENNELFLOWER
FENNER
FENNIG
FENNISH
FENNY
FENOUILLET
FENOUILLETTE
FENS
FENSTER
FENT
FENTER
FENUGREEK

FEOD
FEODAL
FEODALITY
FEODARY
FEODATORY
FEODUM
FEOFF
FEOFFED
FEOFFEE
FEOFFEESHIP
FEOFFER
FEOFFING
FEOFFMENT
FEOFFOR
FER
FERACIOUS
FERACITY
FERAL
FERASH
FERBAM
FERBERITE
FERDWIT
FERE
FERETORIES
FERETORY
FERETRA
FERETRUM
FERFEL
FERGANITE
FERGUSITE
FERGUSONITE
FERIA
FERIAE
FERIAL
FERIDJEE
FERIDJI
FERIE
FERIGEE
FERIJEE
FERINE
FERINELY
FERINENESS
FERIO
FERISON
FERITY
FERK
FERLIE
FERLIED
FERLIES
FERLING
FERLY
FERLYING
FERM
FERMAIL
FERMATA
FERME
FERMENT
FERMENTABILITY
FERMENTABLE
FERMENTARIAN
FERMENTATION
FERMENTATIVE
FERMENTATIVELY
FERMENTATIVENESS
FERMENTATORY
FERMENTED
FERMENTER
FERMENTING
FERMENTIVE
FERMENTOLOGY
FERMENTOR
FERMENTUM
FERMERER
FERMERY
FERMI
FERMION
FERMIUM
FERMORITE
FERN
FERNBIRD
FERNBRAKE
FERNED
FERNENT
FERNERIES
FERNERY
FERNGALE
FERNGROWER
FERNINST
FERNLAND
FERNLEAF
FERNLIKE
FERNSHAW
FERNSICK
FERNTICKLE
FERNTICKLED
FERNWORT
FERNY
FERNYEAR
FEROCE
FEROCIOUS
FEROCIOUSLY
FEROCIOUSNESS
FEROCITIES
FEROCITY
FEROHER
FERRAMENT
FERRASH
FERRATE
FERRATED
FERRATIN
FERRE
FERREIRO
FERREL
FERREOUS
FERRER
FERRET
FERRETED
FERRETER
FERRETING
FERRETTO
FERRETY
FERRI
FERRIAGE
FERRIC
FERRICYANIC
FERRICYANIDE
FERRIED
FERRIER
FERRIES
FERRIFEROUS
FERRING
FERRITE
FERRITIN
FERRIVOROUS
FERROALLOY
FERROBORON
FERROCALCITE
FERROCERIUM
FERROCHROME
FERROCONCRETE
FERROCYANIC
FERROCYANIDE
FERROINCLAVE
FERROMAGNETIC
FERROMAGNETISM
FERRONATRITE
FERRONICKEL
FERROPRINT
FERROSILICON
FERROTYPE
FERROTYPER
FERROUS
FERRUGINATE
FERRUGINATED
FERRUGINATING
FERRUGINEAN
FERRUGINEOUS
FERRUGINOUS
FERRUGO
FERRULE
FERRULED
FERRULER
FERRULING
FERRUM
FERRUMINATE
FERRUMINATED
FERRUMINATING
FERRY
FERRYAGE
FERRYBOAT
FERRYHOUSE
FERRYING
FERRYMAN
FERRYMEN
FERRYWAY
FERS
FERSMITE
FERTILE
FERTILELY
FERTILENESS
FERTILITIES
FERTILITY
FERTILIZABLE
FERTILIZATION
FERTILIZATIONAL
FERTILIZE
FERTILIZED
FERTILIZER
FERTILIZIN
FERTILIZING
FERU
FERULA
FERULACEOUS
FERULAE
FERULAS
FERULE
FERULED
FERULIC
FERULING
FERVANITE
FERVENCIES
FERVENCY
FERVENT
FERVENTLY
FERVENTNESS
FERVESCENCE
FERVESCENT
FERVID
FERVIDITY
FERVIDLY
FERVIDNESS
FERVOR
FERVOROUS
FERVOUR
FESAPO
FESCENNINITY
FESCUE
FESH
FESS
FESSE
FESSEWISE
FESSWAYS
FESSWISE
FEST
FESTA
FESTAL
FESTALLY
FESTER
FESTERED
FESTERING
FESTERMENT
FESTILOGIES
FESTILOGY
FESTINATE
FESTINATED
FESTINATELY
FESTINATING
FESTINATION
FESTINE
FESTINO
FESTIVAL
FESTIVALLY
FESTIVE
FESTIVELY
FESTIVENESS
FESTIVITIES
FESTIVITY
FESTIVOUS
FESTOLOGY
FESTON
FESTOON
FESTOONED
FESTOONERIES
FESTOONERY
FESTOONING
FESTOONY
FESTUCA
FESTUCINE
FESTY
FET
FETA
FETAL
FETALISM
FETATION
FETCH
FETCHED
FETCHER
FETCHING
FETCHINGLY
FETE
FETED
FETERITA
FETIAL
FETIALES
FETIALIS
FETICH
FETICHIC
FETICHISM
FETICHIST
FETICHISTIC
FETICHIZE
FETICHRY
FETICIDAL
FETICIDE
FETID
FETIDLY
FETIDNESS
FETIFEROUS
FETII
FETING
FETIPAROUS
FETIS
FETISH
FETISHEER
FETISHER
FETISHIC
FETISHISM
FETISHIST
FETISHISTIC
FETISHIZE
FETISHRY
FETLOCK
FETLOCKED
FETLOW
FETOGRAPHY
FETOMETRY
FETOR
FETTED
FETTER
FETTERBUSH
FETTERED
FETTERER
FETTERING
FETTERLOCK
FETTERS
FETTICUS
FETTING
FETTLE
FETTLED
FETTLER
FETTLING
FETTUCINI
FETURE
FETUS
FETUSES
FEU
FEUAGE
FEUAR
FEUCHT
FEUD
FEUDAL
FEUDALISM
FEUDALIST
FEUDALISTIC
FEUDALITY
FEUDALIZATION
FEUDALIZE
FEUDALIZED
FEUDALIZING
FEUDALLY
FEUDARIES
FEUDARY
FEUDATORIAL
FEUDATORIES
FEUDATORY
FEUDEE
FEUDIST
FEUDUM
FEUED
FEUILLAGE
FEUILLE
FEUILLETON
FEUING
FEUTE
FEUTER
FEVER
FEVERBERRIES
FEVERBERRY
FEVERBUSH
FEVERCUP
FEVERED
FEVERET
FEVERFEW
FEVERGUM
FEVERING
FEVERISH
FEVERISHLY
FEVERISHNESS
FEVERLESS
FEVEROUS
FEVEROUSLY
FEVERROOT
FEVERTRAP
FEVERTWIG
FEVERWEED
FEVERWORT
FEVERY
FEW
FEWER
FEWEST
FEWMAND
FEWMET
FEWNESS
FEWSOME
FEWTER

FEWTERER
FEWTRILS
FEY
FEZ
FEZZED
FEZZES
FEZZY
FIACRE
FIADOR
FIANCAILLES
FIANCE
FIANCED
FIANCEE
FIANCHETTI
FIANCHETTO
FIANCING
FIANT
FIANTS
FIAR
FIARD
FIASCO
FIASCOES
FIASCOS
FIAT
FIB
FIBBED
FIBBER
FIBBERY
FIBBING
FIBER
FIBERBOARD
FIBERED
FIBERIZE
FIBERIZER
FIBERS
FIBRA
FIBRATION
FIBRE
FIBREBOARD
FIBRED
FIBRIFORM
FIBRIL
FIBRILLA
FIBRILLAE
FIBRILLAR
FIBRILLARY
FIBRILLATE
FIBRILLATED
FIBRILLATION
FIBRILLED
FIBRILLIFORM
FIBRILLOSE
FIBRILLOUS
FIBRILS
FIBRIN
FIBRINATE
FIBRINATION
FIBRINE
FIBRINOGEN
FIBRINOGENIC
FIBRINOLYSIN
FIBRINOLYSIS
FIBRINOLYTIC
FIBRINOSE
FIBRINOSIS
FIBRINOUS
FIBROADENIA
FIBROADENOMA
FIBROADIPOSE
FIBROAREOLAR
FIBROBLAST
FIBROBLASTIC
FIBROCARTILAGE
FIBROCASEOSE
FIBROCELLULAR
FIBROCYST
FIBROCYSTIC
FIBROCYSTOMA
FIBROCYTE
FIBROELASTIC
FIBROFATTY
FIBROFERRITE
FIBROGLIA
FIBROGLIOMA
FIBROID
FIBROIN
FIBROLIPOMA
FIBROLITIC
FIBROMA
FIBROMAS
FIBROMATA
FIBROMATOID
FIBROMATOSIS
FIBROMATOUS
FIBROMUCOUS
FIBROMYITIS
FIBROMYOMA
FIBROMYOTOMY
FIBROMYXOMA
FIBRONEUROMA
FIBRONUCLEAR
FIBROPLASIA
FIBROPLASTIC
FIBROPOLYPUS
FIBROSARCOMA
FIBROSE
FIBROSEROUS
FIBROSIS
FIBROSITIS
FIBROTIC
FIBROUS
FIBROUSLY
FIBROUSNESS
FIBROVASAL
FIBRY
FIBSTER
FIBULA
FIBULAE
FIBULAR
FIBULARE
FIBULARIA
FIBULAS
FICARIES
FICARY
FICCHE
FICE
FICELLE
FICHAT
FICHE
FICHTELITE
FICHU
FICIFORM
FICK
FICKLE
FICKLEHEARTED
FICKLENESS
FICKLETY
FICKLY
FICO
FICOES
FICOID
FICOIDAL
FICTATION
FICTIL
FICTILE
FICTILENESS
FICTILITY
FICTION
FICTIONAL
FICTIONALIZATION
FICTIONALIZED
FICTIONALIZING
FICTIONALLY
FICTIONARY
FICTIONEER
FICTIONER
FICTIONIST
FICTIONISTIC
FICTIONIZE
FICTIONIZED
FICTIONIZING
FICTIOUS
FICTITIOUS
FICTITIOUSLY
FICTITIOUSNESS
FICTIVE
FICTIVELY
FICTOR
FID
FIDAI
FIDALGO
FIDATE
FIDATION
FIDAWI
FIDDED
FIDDING
FIDDLE
FIDDLEBACK
FIDDLECOME
FIDDLED
FIDDLEDEEDEE
FIDDLEFACED
FIDDLEHEAD
FIDDLEHEADED
FIDDLENECK
FIDDLER
FIDDLERFISH
FIDDLERFISHES
FIDDLERY
FIDDLESTICK
FIDDLESTICKS
FIDDLESTRING
FIDDLEWOOD
FIDDLEY
FIDDLEYS
FIDDLIES
FIDDLING
FIDE
FIDEICOMMISS
FIDEISM
FIDEIST
FIDEJUSSION
FIDEJUSSOR
FIDEJUSSORY
FIDELITIES
FIDELITY
FIDEOS
FIDFAD
FIDGE
FIDGED
FIDGET
FIDGETATION
FIDGETED
FIDGETER
FIDGETILY
FIDGETINESS
FIDGETING
FIDGETINGLY
FIDGETY
FIDGING
FIDICINAL
FIDICINALES
FIDICULA
FIDICULAE
FIDUCIA
FIDUCIAL
FIDUCIALLY
FIDUCIARIES
FIDUCIARILY
FIDUCIARY
FIE
FIEDLERITE
FIEF
FIELD
FIELDBIRD
FIELDED
FIELDEN
FIELDER
FIELDFARE
FIELDFIGHT
FIELDIE
FIELDING
FIELDMAN
FIELDMEN
FIELDPIECE
FIELDS
FIELDSMAN
FIELDSMEN
FIELDSTONE
FIELDWORK
FIELDWORKER
FIELDWORT
FIELDY
FIEND
FIENDFUL
FIENDFULLY
FIENDHEAD
FIENDISH
FIENDISHLY
FIENDISHNESS
FIENDLIKE
FIENDLINESS
FIENDLY
FIENDSHIP
FIENT
FIER
FIERASFEROID
FIERCE
FIERCEHEARTED
FIERCELY
FIERCEN
FIERCENED
FIERCENESS
FIERCENING
FIERCER
FIERCEST
FIERDING
FIERIER
FIERIEST
FIERILY
FIERINESS
FIERY
FIESTA
FIFE
FIFED
FIFER
FIFIE
FIFING
FIFISH
FIFTEEN
FIFTEENER
FIFTEENTH
FIFTEENTHLY
FIFTH
FIFTHLY
FIFTIES
FIFTIETH
FIFTY
FIG
FIGARY
FIGBIRD
FIGBOY
FIGEATER
FIGENT
FIGGED
FIGGERY
FIGGING
FIGGLE
FIGGY
FIGHT
FIGHTABLE
FIGHTER
FIGHTING
FIGHTINGLY
FIGHTWITE
FIGMENT
FIGMENTAL
FIGO
FIGPECKER
FIGS
FIGSHELL
FIGULATE
FIGULATED
FIGULINE
FIGURA
FIGURABILITY
FIGURABLE
FIGURAE
FIGURAL
FIGURANT
FIGURANTE
FIGURATE
FIGURATELY
FIGURATION
FIGURATIVE
FIGURATIVELY
FIGURATIVENESS
FIGURATO
FIGURE
FIGURED
FIGUREDLY
FIGUREHEAD
FIGURER
FIGURES
FIGURESOME
FIGURETTE
FIGURIAL
FIGURINE
FIGURING
FIGURISM
FIGURIST
FIGURIZE
FIGURY
FIGWORM
FIGWORT
FIKE
FIKERY
FIKEY
FIKIE
FIKY
FIL
FILA
FILACE
FILACEOUS
FILACER
FILAGREE
FILAMENT
FILAMENTAR
FILAMENTARY
FILAMENTED
FILAMENTOID
FILAMENTOSE
FILAMENTOUS
FILAMENTS
FILAMENTULE
FILANDER
FILANDERS
FILAO
FILAR
FILAREE
FILARIA
FILARIAE
FILARIAL
FILARIAN
FILARIASIS

FILARICIDAL
FILARIFORM
FILARIID
FILARIOUS
FILASSE
FILATE
FILATOR
FILATURE
FILAZER
FILBERT
FILCH
FILCHED
FILCHER
FILCHERY
FILCHING
FILCHINGLY
FILE
FILED
FILEFISH
FILEFISHES
FILEMAKER
FILEMAKING
FILEMOT
FILER
FILET
FILETED
FILETING
FILI
FILIAL
FILIALITY
FILIALLY
FILIALNESS
FILIATE
FILIATED
FILIATING
FILIATION
FILIBEG
FILIBRANCH
FILIBRANCHIATE
FILIBUSTER
FILIBUSTERED
FILIBUSTERER
FILIBUSTERING
FILIBUSTERISM
FILIBUSTEROUS
FILIBUSTROUS
FILICAL
FILICAULINE
FILICIDAL
FILICIDE
FILICIFORM
FILICIN
FILICINEAN
FILICINIAN
FILICITE
FILICOID
FILID
FILIETY
FILIFEROUS
FILIFORM
FILIFORMED
FILIGEROUS
FILIGRAIN
FILIGRAINED
FILIGRANE
FILIGRANED
FILIGREE
FILIGREED
FILIGREEING
FILII
FILING
FILINGS
FILIONYMIC
FILIOQUE
FILIP
FILIPPI
FILIPPIC
FILIPPO
FILIPUNCTURE
FILITE
FILIUS
FILL
FILLAGREE
FILLE
FILLED
FILLER
FILLERCAP
FILLET
FILLETED
FILLETER
FILLETING
FILLETS
FILLIES
FILLING
FILLINGLY
FILLINGNESS
FILLIP
FILLIPED
FILLIPEEN
FILLIPING
FILLISTER
FILLMASS
FILLOCK
FILLOWITE
FILLY
FILM
FILMED
FILMGOER
FILMGOING
FILMIC
FILMIER
FILMIEST
FILMIFORM
FILMILY
FILMINESS
FILMING
FILMISH
FILMIST
FILMIZE
FILMIZED
FILMIZING
FILMLAND
FILMLIKE
FILMOGEN
FILMS
FILMSLIDE
FILMY
FILO
FILOPLUME
FILOPODIA
FILOPODIUM
FILOSE
FILOSELLE
FILS
FILTER
FILTERABILITY
FILTERABLE
FILTERABLENESS
FILTERED
FILTERER
FILTERING
FILTERMAN
FILTERMEN
FILTH
FILTHIER
FILTHIEST
FILTHIFIED
FILTHIFY
FILTHIFYING
FILTHILY
FILTHINESS
FILTHY
FILTRABILITY
FILTRABLE
FILTRATABLE
FILTRATE
FILTRATED
FILTRATING
FILTRATION
FILUM
FIMBLE
FIMBRIA
FIMBRIAE
FIMBRIAL
FIMBRIATE
FIMBRIATED
FIMBRIATING
FIMBRIATION
FIMBRICATE
FIMBRICATED
FIMBRILLA
FIMBRILLAE
FIMBRILLATE
FIMBRILLOSE
FIME
FIMETIC
FIMICOLOUS
FIN
FINABLE
FINABLENESS
FINAGLE
FINAGLED
FINAGLER
FINAGLING
FINAL
FINALE
FINALIS
FINALISM
FINALIST
FINALITIES
FINALITY
FINALIZE
FINALIZED
FINALIZING
FINALLY
FINANCE
FINANCED
FINANCIAL
FINANCIALIST
FINANCIALLY
FINANCIER
FINANCIERED
FINANCIERING
FINANCIERY
FINANCING
FINANCIST
FINBACK
FINBONE
FINCA
FINCAS
FINCH
FINCHBACKED
FINCHED
FINCHERY
FINCHES
FIND
FINDAL
FINDER
FINDFAULT
FINDING
FINDJAN
FINE
FINEABLE
FINEBENT
FINECOMB
FINED
FINELEAF
FINELESS
FINELY
FINEMENT
FINENESS
FINER
FINERIES
FINERY
FINES
FINESPUN
FINESSE
FINESSED
FINESSER
FINESSING
FINEST
FINESTILL
FINESTILLER
FINETOP
FINEW
FINEWED
FINFISH
FINFOOTS
FINGAN
FINGENT
FINGER
FINGERBERRY
FINGERBOARD
FINGERED
FINGERER
FINGERFISH
FINGERFISHES
FINGERFLOWER
FINGERHOLD
FINGERHOOK
FINGERING
FINGERLEAF
FINGERLING
FINGERNAIL
FINGERNAILS
FINGERPARTED
FINGERPRINT
FINGERPRINTING
FINGERROOT
FINGERS
FINGERSMITH
FINGERSPIN
FINGERSTALL
FINGERSTONE
FINGERTIP
FINGERWORK
FINGERY
FINGIAN
FINGRIGO
FINIAL
FINIALED
FINICAL
FINICALITY
FINICALLY
FINICALNESS
FINICISM
FINICK
FINICKILY
FINICKING
FINICKINGLY
FINICKY
FINIFIC
FINIFY
FINIKIN
FINIKING
FINING
FINIS
FINISES
FINISH
FINISHED
FINISHER
FINISHES
FINISHING
FINITE
FINITELY
FINITENESS
FINITESIMAL
FINITISM
FINITIVE
FINITUDE
FINITY
FINJAN
FINK
FINKEL
FINLAND
FINLESS
FINLET
FINNAC
FINNACK
FINNED
FINNER
FINNESKO
FINNICK
FINNICKING
FINNICKY
FINNING
FINNIP
FINNOC
FINNY
FINO
FINOCHIO
FINTA
FINTADORES
FIORD
FIORDED
FIORIN
FIORITE
FIORITURA
FIORITURE
FIP
FIPENNY
FIPPLE
FIQUE
FIR
FIRCA
FIRE
FIREARM
FIREBACK
FIREBALL
FIREBED
FIREBIRD
FIREBLENDE
FIREBOARD
FIREBOAT
FIREBOLT
FIREBOLTED
FIREBOOT
FIREBOTE
FIREBOX
FIREBOY
FIREBRAND
FIREBRAT
FIREBREAK
FIREBRICK
FIREBUG
FIRECLAY
FIRECOAT
FIRECRACKER
FIRECREST
FIRED
FIREDAMP
FIREDOG
FIREDRAGON
FIREDRAKE
FIREFALL
FIREFANG
FIREFANGED
FIREFANGING
FIREFIGHTER
FIREFLAUGHT
FIREFLIES
FIREFLIRT
FIREFLOWER
FIREFLY
FIREGUARD

FIREHALL
FIREHOUSE
FIRELESS
FIRELIGHT
FIRELIT
FIRELOCK
FIREMAN
FIREMASTER
FIREMEN
FIREPAN
FIREPINK
FIREPLACE
FIREPLOUGH
FIREPLOW
FIREPLUG
FIREPOT
FIREPOWER
FIREPROOF
FIREPROOFED
FIREPROOFING
FIREPROOFNESS
FIRER
FIREROOM
FIRESAFE
FIRESAFENESS
FIRESAFETY
FIRESHINE
FIRESIDE
FIRESIDER
FIRESIDESHIP
FIRESPOUT
FIRESTONE
FIRESTOPPING
FIRETAIL
FIRETHORN
FIRETOP
FIRETRAP
FIREWARD
FIREWARDEN
FIREWATER
FIREWEED
FIREWOOD
FIREWORK
FIREWORKLESS
FIREWORKS
FIREWORKY
FIREWORM
FIRING
FIRK
FIRKED
FIRKER
FIRKIN
FIRKING
FIRLOT
FIRM
FIRMA
FIRMAMENT
FIRMAMENTAL
FIRMAN
FIRMANS
FIRMARII
FIRMARIUS
FIRMED
FIRMER
FIRMEST
FIRMHEARTED
FIRMING
FIRMISTERNAL
FIRMISTERNIAL
FIRMISTERNOUS
FIRMLAND
FIRMLY
FIRMNESS
FIRMS
FIRN
FIRRY
FIRS
FIRST
FIRSTBORN
FIRSTCOMER
FIRSTER
FIRSTLING
FIRSTLY
FIRTH
FISC
FISCAL
FISCALITY
FISCALIZATION
FISCALIZE
FISCALIZED
FISCALIZING
FISCHERITE
FISCUS
FISETIN
FISH
FISHABLE
FISHBACK
FISHBED
FISHBERRIES
FISHBERRY
FISHBOLT
FISHBONE
FISHBOWL
FISHEATER
FISHED
FISHER
FISHERBOAT
FISHERBOY
FISHERFOLK
FISHERGIRL
FISHERIES
FISHERMAN
FISHERMEN
FISHERPEOPLE
FISHERS
FISHERWOMAN
FISHERY
FISHES
FISHET
FISHEYE
FISHFALL
FISHGARTH
FISHGIG
FISHGRASS
FISHHOLD
FISHHOOK
FISHHOOKS
FISHHOUSE
FISHIER
FISHIEST
FISHIFIED
FISHIFY
FISHIFYING
FISHILY
FISHINESS
FISHING
FISHLIKE
FISHLINE
FISHMAN
FISHMEAL
FISHMEN
FISHMONGER
FISHMOUTH
FISHNET
FISHPLATE
FISHPOLE
FISHPOND
FISHPOOL
FISHPOT
FISHPOTTER
FISHPOUND
FISHSKIN
FISHSPEAR
FISHTAIL
FISHTAILS
FISHWAY
FISHWEED
FISHWEIR
FISHWIFE
FISHWIVES
FISHWOMAN
FISHWOOD
FISHWORKER
FISHWORKS
FISHWORM
FISHY
FISHYARD
FISK
FISNOGA
FISSATE
FISSILE
FISSILINGUAL
FISSILITY
FISSION
FISSIONABLE
FISSIPALMATE
FISSIPARISM
FISSIPARITY
FISSIPAROUS
FISSIPED
FISSIPEDAL
FISSIPEDATE
FISSIPEDIAL
FISSIROSTRAL
FISSIVE
FISSLE
FISSURA
FISSURAL
FISSURATION
FISSURE
FISSURED
FISSURIFORM
FISSURING
FISSURY
FIST
FISTED
FISTER
FISTFIGHT
FISTFUL
FISTFULS
FISTIANA
FISTIC
FISTICAL
FISTICUFF
FISTICUFFED
FISTICUFFER
FISTICUFFERY
FISTICUFFING
FISTIFY
FISTINESS
FISTING
FISTLE
FISTMELE
FISTNOTE
FISTUCA
FISTULA
FISTULAE
FISTULAR
FISTULAS
FISTULATOME
FISTULATOUS
FISTULIFORM
FISTULIZE
FISTULOSE
FISTULOUS
FISTY
FIT
FITCH
FITCHE
FITCHEE
FITCHER
FITCHERED
FITCHERING
FITCHERY
FITCHES
FITCHET
FITCHEW
FITE
FITFUL
FITFULLY
FITFULNESS
FITIFIED
FITLY
FITMENT
FITMENTS
FITNESS
FITOUT
FITROOT
FITS
FITTABLE
FITTAGE
FITTED
FITTEDNESS
FITTEN
FITTER
FITTERS
FITTEST
FITTIER
FITTIEST
FITTILY
FITTINESS
FITTING
FITTINGLY
FITTINGNESS
FITTIT
FITTY
FITTYFIED
FITTYWAYS
FITTYWISE
FITWEED
FIVE
FIVEBAR
FIVEFOLD
FIVELING
FIVEPENCE
FIVEPENNY
FIVEPINS
FIVER
FIVES
FIVESCORE
FIVESOME
FIVESTONES
FIX
FIXABLE
FIXAGE
FIXATE
FIXATED
FIXATIF
FIXATING
FIXATION
FIXATIVE
FIXATOR
FIXATURE
FIXED
FIXEDLY
FIXEDNESS
FIXER
FIXIDITY
FIXING
FIXINGS
FIXITIES
FIXITY
FIXT
FIXTURE
FIXURE
FIXY
FIZ
FIZELYITE
FIZGIG
FIZZ
FIZZED
FIZZER
FIZZIER
FIZZIEST
FIZZING
FIZZLE
FIZZLED
FIZZLING
FIZZY
FJALL
FJELD
FJORD
FJORDED
FLAB
FLABBERGAST
FLABBERGASTED
FLABBERGASTING
FLABBIER
FLABBIEST
FLABBILY
FLABBINESS
FLABBY
FLABEL
FLABELLA
FLABELLATE
FLABELLATION
FLABELLIFORM
FLABELLUM
FLABRA
FLABRUM
FLACCID
FLACCIDITY
FLACCIDLY
FLACCIDNESS
FLACHERIE
FLACHERY
FLACK
FLACKED
FLACKER
FLACKET
FLACON
FLAE
FLAFF
FLAFFER
FLAG
FLAGARIE
FLAGBOAT
FLAGELLA
FLAGELLANT
FLAGELLAR
FLAGELLATE
FLAGELLATED
FLAGELLATING
FLAGELLATION
FLAGELLATIVE
FLAGELLATOR
FLAGELLATORY
FLAGELLIFORM
FLAGELLIST
FLAGELLOSIS
FLAGELLULA
FLAGELLULAE
FLAGELLUM
FLAGELLUMS
FLAGEOLET
FLAGFALL
FLAGFISH
FLAGGED
FLAGGER
FLAGGERY
FLAGGIER
FLAGGIEST
FLAGGILY
FLAGGINESS
FLAGGING

FLAGGINGLY
FLAGGISH
FLAGGY
FLAGITATE
FLAGITATION
FLAGITIOUS
FLAGITIOUSLY
FLAGLEAF
FLAGLESS
FLAGLIKE
FLAGMAKER
FLAGMAKING
FLAGMAN
FLAGON
FLAGONET
FLAGPOLE
FLAGRANCE
FLAGRANCY
FLAGRANT
FLAGRANTLY
FLAGRANTNESS
FLAGROOT
FLAGS
FLAGSHIP
FLAGSTAFF
FLAGSTAFFS
FLAGSTAVES
FLAGSTICK
FLAGSTONE
FLAGWORM
FLAIL
FLAILED
FLAILING
FLAIR
FLAITE
FLAITH
FLAITHSHIP
FLAJOLOTITE
FLAK
FLAKAGE
FLAKE
FLAKED
FLAKER
FLAKIER
FLAKIEST
FLAKILY
FLAKINESS
FLAKING
FLAKY
FLAM
FLAMANT
FLAMB
FLAMBAGE
FLAMBANT
FLAMBE
FLAMBEAU
FLAMBEAUS
FLAMBEAUX
FLAMBEE
FLAMBERG
FLAMBERGE
FLAMBOYANCE
FLAMBOYANCY
FLAMBOYANT
FLAMBOYANTISM
FLAMBOYANTIZE
FLAMBOYANTLY
FLAME
FLAMED
FLAMELET
FLAMEN
FLAMENCO
FLAMENS
FLAMEOUT
FLAMEPROOF
FLAMER
FLAMFEW
FLAMIER
FLAMIEST
FLAMINEOUS
FLAMINES
FLAMING
FLAMINGLY
FLAMINGO
FLAMINGOES
FLAMINGOS
FLAMINICA
FLAMINICAL
FLAMMABILITY
FLAMMABLE
FLAMMANT
FLAMMED
FLAMMEOUS
FLAMMING
FLAMMULATED
FLAMMULATION
FLAMMULE
FLAMY
FLAN
FLANCARD
FLANCH
FLANCHARD
FLANCHE
FLANCHED
FLANCONADE
FLANCONNADE
FLANDAN
FLANERIE
FLANEUR
FLANG
FLANGE
FLANGED
FLANGER
FLANGEWAY
FLANGING
FLANK
FLANKARD
FLANKED
FLANKER
FLANKING
FLANNED
FLANNEL
FLANNELBUSH
FLANNELED
FLANNELET
FLANNELETTE
FLANNELFLOWER
FLANNELLEAF
FLANNELLED
FLANNELLY
FLANNELMOUTH
FLANNELMOUTHED
FLANNELS
FLANNING
FLAP
FLAPCAKE
FLAPDOCK
FLAPDOODLE
FLAPDRAGON
FLAPJACK
FLAPMOUTHED
FLAPPED
FLAPPER
FLAPPERDOM
FLAPPERED
FLAPPERHOOD
FLAPPERING
FLAPPERISH
FLAPPERISM
FLAPPET
FLAPPING
FLAPPY
FLAPS
FLARE
FLAREBACK
FLAREBOARD
FLARED
FLARER
FLARING
FLARINGLY
FLARY
FLASER
FLASH
FLASHBACK
FLASHBOARD
FLASHED
FLASHER
FLASHET
FLASHGUN
FLASHIER
FLASHIEST
FLASHILY
FLASHINESS
FLASHING
FLASHINGLY
FLASHLIGHT
FLASHLIKE
FLASHLY
FLASHNESS
FLASHOVER
FLASHPAN
FLASHPROOF
FLASHTESTER
FLASHY
FLASK
FLASKER
FLASKET
FLASKLET
FLASQUE
FLAT
FLATBED
FLATBOAT
FLATBOTTOM
FLATBROD
FLATCAP
FLATCAR
FLATDOM
FLATED
FLATFISH
FLATFISHES
FLATFOOT
FLATH
FLATHE
FLATHEAD
FLATIRON
FLATLAND
FLATLET
FLATLING
FLATLINGS
FLATLONG
FLATLY
FLATMAN
FLATMEN
FLATNESS
FLATNOSE
FLATS
FLATTEN
FLATTENED
FLATTENER
FLATTENING
FLATTER
FLATTERABLE
FLATTERCAP
FLATTERDOCK
FLATTERED
FLATTERER
FLATTERESS
FLATTERIES
FLATTERING
FLATTERINGLY
FLATTERINGNESS
FLATTEROUS
FLATTERY
FLATTEST
FLATTIE
FLATTING
FLATTISH
FLATTOP
FLATTY
FLATULENCE
FLATULENCY
FLATULENT
FLATULENTLY
FLATULENTNESS
FLATUOUS
FLATUS
FLATUSES
FLATWARE
FLATWAY
FLATWAYS
FLATWEED
FLATWISE
FLATWOODS
FLATWORK
FLATWORM
FLAUCHT
FLAUGHT
FLAUGHTBRED
FLAUGHTER
FLAUGHTS
FLAUNT
FLAUNTED
FLAUNTER
FLAUNTIER
FLAUNTIEST
FLAUNTILY
FLAUNTINESS
FLAUNTING
FLAUNTINGLY
FLAUNTY
FLAUTATO
FLAUTINO
FLAUTIST
FLAUTO
FLAVANILIN
FLAVANILINE
FLAVANTHRENE
FLAVANTHRONE
FLAVE
FLAVEDO
FLAVESCENCE
FLAVESCENT
FLAVIC
FLAVICANT
FLAVID
FLAVIN
FLAVINE
FLAVONE
FLAVONOL
FLAVOPROTEIN
FLAVOR
FLAVORED
FLAVORER
FLAVORFUL
FLAVORING
FLAVORLESS
FLAVOROUS
FLAVORSOME
FLAVORY
FLAVOUR
FLAVOURED
FLAVOURER
FLAVOURING
FLAVOUROUS
FLAVOURSOME
FLAVOURY
FLAW
FLAWED
FLAWFLOWER
FLAWIER
FLAWIEST
FLAWING
FLAWLESS
FLAWLESSLY
FLAWLESSNESS
FLAWN
FLAWS
FLAWY
FLAX
FLAXBIRD
FLAXBOARD
FLAXBUSH
FLAXDROP
FLAXEN
FLAXIER
FLAXIEST
FLAXMAN
FLAXSEED
FLAXTAIL
FLAXWEED
FLAXWENCH
FLAXWIFE
FLAXWOMAN
FLAXWORT
FLAXY
FLAY
FLAYER
FLAYFLINT
FLEA
FLEABAG
FLEABANE
FLEABITE
FLEABITING
FLEADOCK
FLEAK
FLEAM
FLEAS
FLEASEED
FLEAWEED
FLEAWOOD
FLEAWORT
FLEAY
FLEBILE
FLECH
FLECHE
FLECHETTE
FLECHETTES
FLECK
FLECKED
FLECKER
FLECKERED
FLECKERING
FLECKIER
FLECKIEST
FLECKINESS
FLECKING
FLECKLED
FLECKY
FLECNODE
FLECTION
FLECTIONAL
FLECTOR
FLED
FLEDGE
FLEDGED
FLEDGELESS
FLEDGELING
FLEDGING
FLEDGLING
FLEDGY
FLEE
FLEECE
FLEECED
FLEECEFLOWER
FLEECER

FLEECH
FLEECHMENT
FLEECIER
FLEECIEST
FLEECILY
FLEECINESS
FLEECING
FLEECY
FLEEING
FLEEM
FLEER
FLEERED
FLEERER
FLEERING
FLEERINGLY
FLEERISH
FLEET
FLEETER
FLEETEST
FLEETING
FLEETINGLY
FLEETINGNESS
FLEETINGS
FLEETLY
FLEETNESS
FLEETWING
FLEG
FLEME
FLEMER
FLEMISH
FLENCH
FLENSE
FLENSED
FLENSER
FLENSING
FLENTES
FLERRIED
FLERRY
FLERRYING
FLESH
FLESHBRUSH
FLESHED
FLESHEN
FLESHER
FLESHFUL
FLESHHOOK
FLESHIER
FLESHIEST
FLESHINESS
FLESHING
FLESHINGS
FLESHLESS
FLESHLILY
FLESHLINESS
FLESHLY
FLESHMENT
FLESHPOT
FLESHQUAKE
FLESHY
FLET
FLETCH
FLETCHED
FLETCHER
FLETCHING
FLETHER
FLETTON
FLEUR
FLEURET
FLEURETTEE
FLEURETTY
FLEURON
FLEURONEE
FLEURONNE
FLEURONNEE
FLEURY
FLEW
FLEWED
FLEWIT
FLEWS
FLEX
FLEXANIMOUS
FLEXED
FLEXIBILITY
FLEXIBLE
FLEXIBLENESS
FLEXIBLY
FLEXILE
FLEXILITY
FLEXING
FLEXION
FLEXIONAL
FLEXIVE
FLEXOR
FLEXUOSE
FLEXUOSITIES
FLEXUOSITY
FLEXUOUS
FLEXUOUSLY
FLEXUOUSNESS
FLEXURA
FLEXURAL
FLEXURE
FLEXURED
FLEY
FLEYEDLY
FLEYEDNESS
FLEYLAND
FLEYSOME
FLIC
FLICFLAC
FLICHTER
FLICHTERED
FLICK
FLICKED
FLICKER
FLICKERED
FLICKERING
FLICKERS
FLICKERTAIL
FLICKERY
FLICKING
FLICKS
FLICKY
FLIDDER
FLIED
FLIER
FLIERS
FLIES
FLIEST
FLIFFUS
FLIGGED
FLIGGER
FLIGHT
FLIGHTED
FLIGHTER
FLIGHTFUL
FLIGHTHEAD
FLIGHTIER
FLIGHTIEST
FLIGHTILY
FLIGHTINESS
FLIGHTING
FLIGHTLESS
FLIGHTS
FLIGHTSHOT
FLIGHTWORTHY
FLIGHTY
FLIMFLAM
FLIMFLAMMED
FLIMFLAMMER
FLIMFLAMMERY
FLIMFLAMMING
FLIMMER
FLIMP
FLIMSIER
FLIMSIES
FLIMSIEST
FLIMSILY
FLIMSINESS
FLIMSY
FLINCH
FLINCHED
FLINCHER
FLINCHING
FLINCHINGLY
FLINDER
FLINDERS
FLINDOSA
FLINDOSY
FLING
FLINGDUST
FLINGER
FLINGING
FLINGY
FLINKITE
FLINT
FLINTED
FLINTER
FLINTHEAD
FLINTHEARTED
FLINTIER
FLINTIEST
FLINTIFIED
FLINTIFY
FLINTIFYING
FLINTILY
FLINTINESS
FLINTING
FLINTLOCK
FLINTS
FLINTWOOD
FLINTWORK
FLINTWORKER
FLINTY
FLIOMA
FLIP
FLIPE
FLIPED
FLIPING
FLIPJACK
FLIPPANCE
FLIPPANCIES
FLIPPANCY
FLIPPANT
FLIPPANTLY
FLIPPANTNESS
FLIPPED
FLIPPER
FLIPPERLING
FLIPPERY
FLIPPING
FLIRD
FLIRE
FLIRT
FLIRTABLE
FLIRTATION
FLIRTATIONAL
FLIRTATIOUS
FLIRTATIOUSLY
FLIRTATIOUSNESS
FLIRTED
FLIRTER
FLIRTIER
FLIRTIEST
FLIRTIGIG
FLIRTING
FLIRTISH
FLIRTISHNESS
FLIRTY
FLISK
FLISKED
FLISKIER
FLISKIEST
FLISKING
FLISKMAHOY
FLISKY
FLIT
FLITCH
FLITCHED
FLITCHEN
FLITCHING
FLITE
FLITED
FLITFOLD
FLITING
FLITTED
FLITTER
FLITTERBAT
FLITTERED
FLITTERING
FLITTERMICE
FLITTERMOUSE
FLITTERN
FLITTERS
FLITTINESS
FLITTING
FLITTINGLY
FLITTY
FLITWITE
FLIVVER
FLIX
FLIXWEED
FLO
FLOAT
FLOATABILITY
FLOATABLE
FLOATAGE
FLOATATION
FLOATATIVE
FLOATBOARD
FLOATED
FLOATER
FLOATERS
FLOATIER
FLOATIEST
FLOATINESS
FLOATING
FLOATINGLY
FLOATIVE
FLOATS
FLOATSMAN
FLOATSMEN
FLOATSTONE
FLOATY
FLOB
FLOC
FLOCCI
FLOCCILATION
FLOCCIPEND
FLOCCOSE
FLOCCOSELY
FLOCCULABLE
FLOCCULAR
FLOCCULATE
FLOCCULATED
FLOCCULATING
FLOCCULATION
FLOCCULATOR
FLOCCULE
FLOCCULENCE
FLOCCULENCY
FLOCCULENT
FLOCCULENTLY
FLOCCULI
FLOCCULOSE
FLOCCULOUS
FLOCCULUS
FLOCCUS
FLOCK
FLOCKED
FLOCKER
FLOCKET
FLOCKIER
FLOCKIEST
FLOCKING
FLOCKLING
FLOCKMAN
FLOCKMASTER
FLOCKMEAL
FLOCKMEN
FLOCKOWNER
FLOCKS
FLOCKWISE
FLOCKY
FLOCOON
FLODGE
FLOE
FLOEBERG
FLOG
FLOGGABLE
FLOGGED
FLOGGER
FLOGGING
FLOGMASTER
FLOGSTER
FLOIT
FLOKITE
FLONG
FLOOD
FLOODAGE
FLOODBOARD
FLOODCOCK
FLOODED
FLOODER
FLOODGATE
FLOODING
FLOODLIGHT
FLOODLIGHTED
FLOODLIGHTING
FLOODLIT
FLOODMARK
FLOODOMETER
FLOODPLAIN
FLOODTIME
FLOODWATER
FLOODWAY
FLOODWOOD
FLOODY
FLOOEY
FLOOKAN
FLOOR
FLOORAGE
FLOORBOARD
FLOORCLOTH
FLOORED
FLOORER
FLOORHEAD
FLOORING
FLOORMAN
FLOORMEN
FLOORS
FLOORWALKER
FLOORWAY
FLOOSY
FLOOZIES
FLOOZY
FLOP
FLOPEROO
FLOPHOUSE
FLOPOVER
FLOPPED
FLOPPER
FLOPPERS
FLOPPIER
FLOPPIEST

FLOPPILY
FLOPPINESS
FLOPPING
FLOPPY
FLOPWING
FLOR
FLORA
FLORAE
FLORAISON
FLORAL
FLORALIZE
FLORALLY
FLORAMOR
FLORAMOUR
FLORAN
FLORAS
FLORATE
FLOREAL
FLOREATE
FLOREATED
FLOREATING
FLORENCE
FLORENT
FLORENTIUM
FLORES
FLORESCENCE
FLORESCENT
FLORESSENCE
FLORET
FLORETA
FLORETED
FLORETTY
FLORETUM
FLORIATE
FLORIATED
FLORIATION
FLORIBUNDA
FLORICAN
FLORICIN
FLORICULTURE
FLORID
FLORIDEAN
FLORIDEOUS
FLORIDITIES
FLORIDITY
FLORIDLY
FLORIDNESS
FLORIFEROUS
FLORIFEROUSLY
FLORIFEROUSNESS
FLORIFICATION
FLORIFORM
FLORIGEN
FLORIGRAPHY
FLORILEGE
FLORILEGIA
FLORILEGIUM
FLORIMANIA
FLORIMANIST
FLORIN
FLORIPAROUS
FLORIPONDIO
FLORISCOPE
FLORIST
FLORISTIC
FLORISTICALLY
FLORISTICS
FLORISTRY
FLORISUGENT
FLORIZINE
FLOROON
FLOROSCOPE
FLORUIT
FLORULA
FLORULAE
FLORULAS
FLORULENT
FLORY
FLOSCULAR
FLOSCULARIAN
FLOSCULE
FLOSCULOSE
FLOSCULOUS
FLOSH
FLOSS
FLOSSA
FLOSSER
FLOSSFLOWER
FLOSSIE
FLOSSIER
FLOSSIES
FLOSSIEST
FLOSSING
FLOSSY
FLOT
FLOTA
FLOTAGE
FLOTANT
FLOTATION
FLOTATIVE
FLOTE
FLOTILLA
FLOTS
FLOTSAM
FLOTSAN
FLOTSEN
FLOTSON
FLOTTER
FLOUNCE
FLOUNCED
FLOUNCING
FLOUNCY
FLOUNDER
FLOUNDERED
FLOUNDERING
FLOUNDERINGLY
FLOUNDERS
FLOUR
FLOURED
FLOURING
FLOURISH
FLOURISHED
FLOURISHER
FLOURISHES
FLOURISHING
FLOURISHINGLY
FLOURISHY
FLOURY
FLOUSE
FLOUSH
FLOUT
FLOUTED
FLOUTER
FLOUTING
FLOUTINGLY
FLOW
FLOWAGE
FLOWED
FLOWER
FLOWERAGE
FLOWERED
FLOWERER
FLOWERET
FLOWERFENCE
FLOWERFLY
FLOWERIER
FLOWERIEST
FLOWERILY
FLOWERINESS
FLOWERING
FLOWERIST
FLOWERLET
FLOWERPECKER
FLOWERPOT
FLOWERS
FLOWERWORK
FLOWERY
FLOWING
FLOWINGLY
FLOWINGNESS
FLOWMETER
FLOWN
FLOWOFF
FLU
FLUATE
FLUAVIL
FLUAVILE
FLUB
FLUBBED
FLUBBING
FLUBDUB
FLUBDUBBERIES
FLUBDUBBERY
FLUCAN
FLUCTUABILITY
FLUCTUABLE
FLUCTUANT
FLUCTUATE
FLUCTUATED
FLUCTUATING
FLUCTUATION
FLUCTUOSITY
FLUCTUOUS
FLUE
FLUED
FLUELLEN
FLUELLIN
FLUELLITE
FLUEMAN
FLUEMEN
FLUENCE
FLUENCIES
FLUENCY
FLUENT
FLUENTLY
FLUENTNESS
FLUER
FLUEWORK
FLUEY
FLUFF
FLUFFED
FLUFFER
FLUFFIER
FLUFFIEST
FLUFFILY
FLUFFINESS
FLUFFING
FLUFFY
FLUGEL
FLUGELHORN
FLUGELMAN
FLUGELMEN
FLUIBLE
FLUID
FLUIDAL
FLUIDALLY
FLUIDEXTRACT
FLUIDIC
FLUIDICS
FLUIDIFICATION
FLUIDIFIED
FLUIDIFIER
FLUIDIFY
FLUIDIFYING
FLUIDIMETER
FLUIDISM
FLUIDIST
FLUIDITY
FLUIDIZATION
FLUIDIZE
FLUIDIZED
FLUIDIZING
FLUIDLY
FLUIDNESS
FLUIDRACHM
FLUIDRAM
FLUIGRAM
FLUIGRAMME
FLUING
FLUITANT
FLUKE
FLUKED
FLUKES
FLUKEWORT
FLUKEY
FLUKIER
FLUKIEST
FLUKILY
FLUKINESS
FLUKING
FLUKY
FLUM
FLUMDIDDLE
FLUME
FLUMED
FLUMERIN
FLUMING
FLUMINOSE
FLUMINOUS
FLUMMER
FLUMMERIES
FLUMMERY
FLUMMOX
FLUMMOXED
FLUMMOXING
FLUMP
FLUMPED
FLUMPING
FLUNG
FLUNK
FLUNKED
FLUNKER
FLUNKEY
FLUNKEYISM
FLUNKEYISTIC
FLUNKEYITE
FLUNKEYS
FLUNKIES
FLUNKING
FLUNKY
FLUNKYISM
FLUNKYISTIC
FLUNKYITE
FLUOARSENATE
FLUOBORATE
FLUOBORIC
FLUOBORITE
FLUOCERINE
FLUOCERITE
FLUOHYDRIC
FLUOR
FLUORAN
FLUORANE
FLUORANTHENE
FLUORAPATITE
FLUORATE
FLUORENE
FLUORESAGE
FLUORESCE
FLUORESCED
FLUORESCEIN
FLUORESCEINE
FLUORESCENCE
FLUORESCENT
FLUORESCIN
FLUORESCING
FLUORHYDRIC
FLUORIC
FLUORID
FLUORIDATE
FLUORIDATED
FLUORIDATING
FLUORIDATION
FLUORIDE
FLUORIN
FLUORINATE
FLUORINATION
FLUORINDIN
FLUORINE
FLUORITE
FLUORMETER
FLUOROBORATE
FLUOROCARBON
FLUOROFORM
FLUOROFORMOL
FLUOROGEN
FLUOROGENIC
FLUOROGRAPHY
FLUOROID
FLUOROMETER
FLUOROSCOPE
FLUOROSCOPIC
FLUOROSCOPY
FLUOROTYPE
FLUORSPAR
FLUORYL
FLUOSILICATE
FLUOSILICIC
FLUOTANTALIC
FLURN
FLURR
FLURRIED
FLURRIEDLY
FLURRIES
FLURRIMENT
FLURRY
FLURRYING
FLUSH
FLUSHBOARD
FLUSHED
FLUSHER
FLUSHERMAN
FLUSHERMEN
FLUSHEST
FLUSHGATE
FLUSHING
FLUSHINGLY
FLUSHNESS
FLUSHY
FLUSK
FLUSKER
FLUSTER
FLUSTERATE
FLUSTERATION
FLUSTERED
FLUSTERER
FLUSTERING
FLUSTERY
FLUSTRATE
FLUSTRATION
FLUSTRINE
FLUSTROID
FLUSTRUM
FLUTE
FLUTEBIRD
FLUTED
FLUTEMOUTH
FLUTER
FLUTES
FLUTEWORK
FLUTHER
FLUTIER
FLUTIEST
FLUTINA
FLUTING

FLUTINGS
FLUTIST
FLUTTER
FLUTTERATION
FLUTTERED
FLUTTERER
FLUTTERING
FLUTTERINGLY
FLUTTERSOME
FLUTTERY
FLUTY
FLUVANNA
FLUVIAL
FLUVIALIST
FLUVIATIC
FLUVIATILE
FLUVICOLINE
FLUVIOGRAPH
FLUVIOLOGY
FLUVIOMARINE
FLUVIOSE
FLUVIOUS
FLUX
FLUXATION
FLUXED
FLUXER
FLUXIBILITY
FLUXIBLE
FLUXIBLENESS
FLUXIBLY
FLUXILE
FLUXILITY
FLUXING
FLUXION
FLUXIONAL
FLUXIONALLY
FLUXIONARY
FLUXIONIST
FLUXIVE
FLUXMETER
FLUXROOT
FLUXURE
FLUXWEED
FLY
FLYABLE
FLYAWAY
FLYBACK
FLYBALL
FLYBANE
FLYBELT
FLYBLEW
FLYBLOW
FLYBLOWN
FLYBOAT
FLYBOY
FLYBRUSH
FLYBY
FLYCATCHER
FLYEATER
FLYER
FLYFLAP
FLYFLAPPER
FLYFLOWER
FLYING
FLYINGLY
FLYINGS
FLYLEAF
FLYLEAVES
FLYMAN
FLYMEN
FLYNESS
FLYOVER
FLYPAPER
FLYPE
FLYPROOF
FLYSPECK
FLYSWAT
FLYTAIL
FLYTE
FLYTED
FLYTIER
FLYTIME
FLYTING
FLYTRAP
FLYWAY
FLYWEIGHT
FLYWHEEL
FLYWINCH
FLYWIRE
FLYWORT
FNESE
FOAL
FOALED
FOALFOOT
FOALFOOTS
FOALING
FOALY
FOAM
FOAMBOW
FOAMED
FOAMER
FOAMFLOWER
FOAMIER
FOAMIEST
FOAMILY
FOAMINESS
FOAMING
FOAMY
FOB
FOBBED
FOBBING
FOCAL
FOCALIZATION
FOCALIZE
FOCALIZED
FOCALIZING
FOCALLY
FOCALOID
FOCI
FOCIMETER
FOCIMETRY
FOCKLE
FOCOIDS
FOCOMETER
FOCOMETRY
FOCSLE
FOCUS
FOCUSED
FOCUSER
FOCUSES
FOCUSING
FOCUSSED
FOCUSSING
FODDA
FODDER
FODDERED
FODDERER
FODDERING
FODE
FODGE
FODGEL
FODIENT
FOE
FOEDERATI
FOEDERATUS
FOEHN
FOEHOOD
FOEMAN
FOEMANSHIP
FOEMEN
FOETAL
FOETALISM
FOETATION
FOETICIDAL
FOETICIDE
FOETIFEROUS
FOETIPAROUS
FOETOR
FOETURE
FOETUS
FOETUSES
FOFARRAW
FOG
FOGAS
FOGBOUND
FOGBOW
FOGDOG
FOGE
FOGEATER
FOGEY
FOGFRUIT
FOGGAGE
FOGGARA
FOGGED
FOGGER
FOGGIER
FOGGIEST
FOGGILY
FOGGINESS
FOGGING
FOGGY
FOGHORN
FOGIE
FOGIES
FOGLE
FOGLIETTO
FOGMAN
FOGMEN
FOGO
FOGON
FOGOU
FOGRAM
FOGRAMITE
FOGRAMITY
FOGRUM
FOGSCOFFER
FOGUS
FOGY
FOGYDOM
FOGYISH
FOGYISM
FOH
FOHAT
FOHN
FOIBLE
FOIE
FOIL
FOILED
FOILER
FOILING
FOILSMAN
FOILSMEN
FOIN
FOINED
FOINING
FOISON
FOISONLESS
FOISONS
FOIST
FOISTED
FOISTER
FOISTINESS
FOISTING
FOISTY
FOITER
FOLCGEMOT
FOLD
FOLDAGE
FOLDBOAT
FOLDCOURSE
FOLDED
FOLDEDLY
FOLDEN
FOLDER
FOLDEROL
FOLDING
FOLDOUT
FOLDS
FOLDSKIRT
FOLDURE
FOLDY
FOLEYE
FOLIA
FOLIACEOUS
FOLIAGE
FOLIAGED
FOLIAGEOUS
FOLIAGING
FOLIAL
FOLIAR
FOLIARY
FOLIATE
FOLIATED
FOLIATING
FOLIATION
FOLIATURE
FOLIE
FOLIICOLOUS
FOLIIFEROUS
FOLIIFORM
FOLIO
FOLIOBRANCH
FOLIOED
FOLIOING
FOLIOLATE
FOLIOLE
FOLIOLOSE
FOLIOS
FOLIOSE
FOLIOSITY
FOLIOT
FOLIOUS
FOLIOUSLY
FOLIUM
FOLIUMS
FOLK
FOLKCRAFT
FOLKFREE
FOLKLAND
FOLKLORE
FOLKLORIC
FOLKLORISH
FOLKLORISM
FOLKLORIST
FOLKLORISTIC
FOLKMOOT
FOLKMOOTER
FOLKMOT
FOLKMOTE
FOLKMOTER
FOLKRIGHT
FOLKS
FOLKSEY
FOLKSIER
FOLKSIEST
FOLKSINESS
FOLKSY
FOLKWAY
FOLKWAYS
FOLKY
FOLLE
FOLLER
FOLLES
FOLLETTI
FOLLETTO
FOLLICLE
FOLLICULAR
FOLLICULATE
FOLLICULATED
FOLLICULE
FOLLICULITIS
FOLLICULOSE
FOLLICULOSIS
FOLLICULOUS
FOLLIED
FOLLIES
FOLLIFUL
FOLLILY
FOLLIS
FOLLOW
FOLLOWED
FOLLOWER
FOLLOWERSHIP
FOLLOWING
FOLLOWS
FOLLY
FOLLYER
FOLLYING
FOLO
FOMENT
FOMENTATION
FOMENTED
FOMENTER
FOMENTING
FOMENTO
FOMES
FOMITES
FON
FOND
FONDA
FONDACO
FONDANT
FONDATEUR
FONDER
FONDEST
FONDISH
FONDLE
FONDLED
FONDLER
FONDLING
FONDLY
FONDNESS
FONDOUK
FONDU
FONDUE
FONDUK
FONIO
FONO
FONS
FONT
FONTAL
FONTALLY
FONTANEL
FONTANELLE
FONTANGE
FONTED
FONTES
FONTICULUS
FONTINA
FONTINAL
FOO
FOOD
FOODER
FOODLESS
FOODS
FOODSTUFF
FOODY
FOOFARAW
FOOL
FOOLED
FOOLER
FOOLERIES
FOOLERY
FOOLESS
FOOLFISH

FOOLFISHES
FOOLHARDIER
FOOLHARDIEST
FOOLHARDIHOOD
FOOLHARDILY
FOOLHARDINESS
FOOLHARDY
FOOLHEAD
FOOLIFY
FOOLING
FOOLISH
FOOLISHLY
FOOLISHNESS
FOOLMONGER
FOOLOCRACY
FOOLPROOF
FOOLPROOFNESS
FOOLSCAP
FOONER
FOOSTER
FOOSTERER
FOOT
FOOTAGE
FOOTBACK
FOOTBALL
FOOTBALLER
FOOTBALLIST
FOOTBAND
FOOTBEAT
FOOTBLOWER
FOOTBOARD
FOOTBOARDS
FOOTBOY
FOOTBREADTH
FOOTBRIDGE
FOOTCLOTH
FOOTCLOTHS
FOOTED
FOOTEITE
FOOTER
FOOTFALL
FOOTFARER
FOOTFAULT
FOOTFEED
FOOTFOLK
FOOTFUL
FOOTGANGER
FOOTGEAR
FOOTGELD
FOOTGLOVE
FOOTGRIP
FOOTH
FOOTHALT
FOOTHILL
FOOTHOLD
FOOTHOOK
FOOTHOT
FOOTIER
FOOTIEST
FOOTING
FOOTINGLY
FOOTINGS
FOOTLE
FOOTLED
FOOTLER
FOOTLESS
FOOTLICKER
FOOTLIGHT
FOOTLIGHTS
FOOTLIKE
FOOTLING
FOOTLINING
FOOTLOCK
FOOTLOCKER
FOOTLOG
FOOTLOOSE
FOOTMAKER
FOOTMAN
FOOTMANHOOD
FOOTMANRY
FOOTMANSHIP
FOOTMARK
FOOTMEN
FOOTNOTE
FOOTNOTED
FOOTNOTING
FOOTPACE
FOOTPAD
FOOTPADDERY
FOOTPATH
FOOTPICK
FOOTPLATE
FOOTPRINT
FOOTRAIL
FOOTREST
FOOTRILL
FOOTROOM
FOOTROPE
FOOTS
FOOTSCALD
FOOTSLOG
FOOTSLOGGER
FOOTSORE
FOOTSORENESS
FOOTSTALK
FOOTSTALL
FOOTSTEP
FOOTSTICK
FOOTSTOCK
FOOTSTONE
FOOTSTOOL
FOOTWALK
FOOTWALL
FOOTWAY
FOOTWEAR
FOOTWORK
FOOTWORN
FOOTY
FOOYOUNG
FOOYUNG
FOOZLE
FOOZLED
FOOZLER
FOOZLING
FOP
FOPDOODLE
FOPLING
FOPPERIES
FOPPERLY
FOPPERY
FOPPISH
FOPPISHLY
FOPPISHNESS
FOPPY
FOPSHIP
FOR
FORA
FORAGE
FORAGED
FORAGEMENT
FORAGER
FORAGERS
FORAGING
FORALITE
FORAM
FORAMEN
FORAMENS
FORAMINA
FORAMINATE
FORAMINATED
FORAMINATION
FORAMINIFER
FORAMINOSE
FORAMINOUS
FORAMINULATE
FORAMINULE
FORAMINULOSE
FORAMINULOUS
FORANE
FORANEOUS
FORASTERO
FORAY
FORAYED
FORAYER
FORAYING
FORB
FORBAD
FORBADE
FORBAR
FORBARE
FORBARRED
FORBEAR
FORBEARABLE
FORBEARANCE
FORBEARANT
FORBEARANTLY
FORBEARER
FORBEARING
FORBESITE
FORBID
FORBIDDAL
FORBIDDANCE
FORBIDDEN
FORBIDDENLY
FORBIDDENNESS
FORBIDDER
FORBIDDING
FORBIDDINGLY
FORBIDDINGNESS
FORBITE
FORBLED
FORBLOW
FORBODE
FORBORE
FORBORNE
FORBREAK
FORBY
FORBYE
FORBYSEN
FORBYSENING
FORCAT
FORCE
FORCEABLE
FORCED
FORCEDLY
FORCEDNESS
FORCEFUL
FORCEFULLY
FORCEFULNESS
FORCELET
FORCEMEAT
FORCEMENT
FORCENE
FORCEPS
FORCEPSES
FORCEPUT
FORCER
FORCET
FORCHASE
FORCHES
FORCIBILITY
FORCIBLE
FORCIBLENESS
FORCIBLY
FORCING
FORCIPATE
FORCIPATED
FORCIPES
FORCIPIFORM
FORCIPRESSURE
FORCIPULATE
FORCIVE
FORCUT
FORCY
FORD
FORDABLE
FORDEAL
FORDID
FORDING
FORDO
FORDOING
FORDONE
FORDULL
FORDWINE
FORDY
FORE
FOREARM
FOREBACKWARDLY
FOREBAR
FOREBAY
FOREBEAR
FOREBITT
FOREBITTER
FOREBOARD
FOREBODE
FOREBODED
FOREBODER
FOREBODING
FOREBODINGLY
FOREBODINGNESS
FOREBODY
FOREBOOM
FOREBOOT
FOREBOW
FOREBOWELS
FOREBOWS
FOREBRACE
FOREBRAIN
FOREBREAST
FOREBROADS
FOREBUSH
FOREBY
FOREBYE
FORECABIN
FORECAR
FORECARRIAGE
FORECAST
FORECASTED
FORECASTER
FORECASTING
FORECASTLE
FORECASTLEHEAD
FORECASTLEMAN
FORECASTLEMEN
FORECHASE
FORECHURCH
FORECLOSABLE
FORECLOSE
FORECLOSED
FORECLOSING
FORECLOSURE
FORECOME
FORECOMINGNESS
FORECOOL
FORECOOLER
FORECOURSE
FORECOURT
FOREDATE
FOREDATED
FOREDATING
FOREDAWN
FOREDAY
FOREDAYS
FOREDECK
FOREDEEM
FOREDEEP
FOREDESTINE
FOREDESTINED
FOREDESTINING
FOREDESTINY
FOREDO
FOREDONE
FOREDOOM
FOREDOOMED
FOREDOOMER
FOREDOOMING
FOREDOOR
FOREDUNE
FOREFACE
FOREFATHER
FOREFATHERLY
FOREFEEL
FOREFEELING
FOREFEELINGLY
FOREFEET
FOREFELT
FOREFEND
FOREFIELD
FOREFINGER
FOREFOOT
FOREFRONT
FOREGAME
FOREGANGER
FOREGATE
FOREGATHER
FOREGIFT
FOREGIRTH
FOREGLANCE
FOREGLEAM
FOREGLIMPSE
FOREGO
FOREGOER
FOREGOING
FOREGONE
FOREGONENESS
FOREGROUND
FOREGUT
FOREHALL
FOREHAMMER
FOREHAND
FOREHANDED
FOREHANDEDNESS
FOREHARD
FOREHEAD
FOREHEADED
FOREHEARTH
FOREHEATER
FOREHENT
FOREHOLD
FOREHOOF
FOREHOOK
FOREIGN
FOREIGNEERING
FOREIGNER
FOREIGNISM
FOREIGNNESS
FOREIRON
FOREJUDGE
FOREJUDGED
FOREJUDGER
FOREJUDGING
FOREKNEW
FOREKNOW
FOREKNOWER
FOREKNOWING
FOREKNOWLEDGE
FOREKNOWN
FOREL
FORELADIES
FORELADY
FORELAID
FORELAND
FORELAY
FORELAYING
FORELEECH

FORELEG
FORELIMB
FORELOCK
FORELOOK
FORELOOP
FORELOOPER
FORELOPER
FORELOUPER
FOREMAN
FOREMANSHIP
FOREMARCH
FOREMAST
FOREMASTHAND
FOREMASTMAN
FOREMASTMEN
FOREMEN
FOREMILK
FOREMIND
FOREMISTRESS
FOREMOST
FOREMOTHER
FORENAME
FORENAMED
FORENENT
FORENIGHT
FORENOON
FORENOTE
FORENSAL
FORENSIC
FORENSICAL
FORENSICALITY
FORENSICALLY
FOREORDAIN
FOREORDAINMENT
FOREORDINATE
FOREORDINATED
FOREORDINATING
FOREORDINATION
FOREPALE
FOREPALED
FOREPALING
FOREPARENT
FOREPARENTS
FOREPART
FOREPASS
FOREPASSED
FOREPAST
FOREPEAK
FOREPIECE
FOREPLOT
FOREPOINT
FOREPOINTER
FOREPOLE
FOREPOLED
FOREPOLING
FOREPOST
FOREPRISE
FOREPRIZE
FOREQUARTER
FORERAN
FORERANK
FOREREACH
FOREREACHING
FORERIBS
FORERIGHT
FOREROOM
FORERUN
FORERUNNER
FORERUNNING
FORERUNNINGS
FORES
FORESADDLE
FORESAID
FORESAIL
FORESAW
FORESAY
FORESAYING
FORESCENT
FORESCRIPT
FORESEE
FORESEEING
FORESEEINGLY
FORESEEN
FORESEER
FORESET
FORESEY
FORESHADOW
FORESHADOWER
FORESHAFT
FORESHEET
FORESHIFT
FORESHIP
FORESHOCK
FORESHORE
FORESHORTEN
FORESHORTENING
FORESHOT
FORESHOW
FORESHOWED
FORESHOWER
FORESHOWING
FORESHOWN
FORESIDE
FORESIGHT
FORESIGHTED
FORESIGHTEDLY
FORESIGHTEDNESS
FORESIGHTFUL
FORESIGN
FORESIGNIFY
FORESINGER
FORESKIN
FORESLEEVE
FORESLOW
FORESOUND
FORESPAKE
FORESPEAK
FORESPEAKER
FORESPEAKING
FORESPEECH
FORESPEED
FORESPOKE
FORESPOKEN
FOREST
FORESTAFF
FORESTAGE
FORESTAIR
FORESTAL
FORESTALL
FORESTALLED
FORESTALLER
FORESTALLING
FORESTARLING
FORESTATION
FORESTAY
FORESTAYSAIL
FORESTCRAFT
FORESTED
FORESTEM
FORESTEP
FORESTER
FORESTIAL
FORESTICK
FORESTINE
FORESTING
FORESTLESS
FORESTOLOGY
FORESTRAL
FORESTRESS
FORESTRY
FORESTS
FORESTSIDE
FORESTY
FORESWEAT
FORETACK
FORETACKLE
FORETAKE
FORETALK
FORETALKING
FORETASTE
FORETASTED
FORETASTER
FORETASTING
FORETEETH
FORETELL
FORETELLER
FORETELLING
FORETHINK
FORETHINKER
FORETHINKING
FORETHOUGHT
FORETHOUGHTED
FORETHOUGHTFUL
FORETHOUGHTFULLY
FORETHOUGHTFULNESS
FORETIME
FORETOKEN
FORETOKENED
FORETOKENING
FORETOLD
FORETOOTH
FORETOP
FORETOPMAN
FORETOPMAST
FORETOPMEN
FORETOPSAIL
FORETURN
FORETYPE
FOREVER
FOREVERMORE
FOREWARD
FOREWARM
FOREWARMER
FOREWARN
FOREWARNED
FOREWARNER
FOREWARNING
FOREWATERS
FOREWENT
FOREWING
FOREWINNING
FOREWISDOM
FOREWIT
FOREWOMAN
FOREWOMEN
FOREWORD
FOREWORLD
FOREWORN
FOREYARD
FORFAIRN
FORFAR
FORFARE
FORFARS
FORFAULT
FORFAULTURE
FORFEIT
FORFEITABLE
FORFEITED
FORFEITER
FORFEITING
FORFEITS
FORFEITURE
FORFEND
FORFENDED
FORFENDING
FORFEX
FORFICATE
FORFICATED
FORFICATION
FORFICIFORM
FORFICULATE
FORFOUCHTEN
FORFOUGHEN
FORFOUGHTEN
FORGAB
FORGAINST
FORGAT
FORGATHER
FORGATHERED
FORGATHERING
FORGAVE
FORGE
FORGED
FORGEFUL
FORGEMAN
FORGEMEN
FORGER
FORGERIES
FORGERY
FORGET
FORGETFUL
FORGETFULLY
FORGETFULNESS
FORGETIVE
FORGETNESS
FORGETT
FORGETTABLE
FORGETTE
FORGETTER
FORGETTING
FORGETTINGLY
FORGIFT
FORGING
FORGIVABLE
FORGIVE
FORGIVELESS
FORGIVEN
FORGIVENESS
FORGIVER
FORGIVING
FORGIVINGLY
FORGIVINGNESS
FORGO
FORGOER
FORGOING
FORGONE
FORGOT
FORGOTTEN
FORGROW
FORGROWN
FORHAILE
FORHEED
FORHOO
FORHOOIE
FORHOOY
FORHOW
FORINSEC
FORINT
FORJASKIT
FORJESKET
FORJUDGE
FORJUDGED
FORJUDGER
FORJUDGING
FORK
FORKBEARD
FORKED
FORKEDLY
FORKEDNESS
FORKER
FORKHEAD
FORKINESS
FORKING
FORKLIFT
FORKMAN
FORKMEN
FORKSMITH
FORKTAIL
FORKY
FORLAIN
FORLANA
FORLAY
FORLEAVE
FORLEAVING
FORLEFT
FORLEIT
FORLESE
FORLET
FORLETTING
FORLIE
FORLIVE
FORLOIN
FORLORN
FORLORNITY
FORLORNLY
FORLORNNESS
FORM
FORMA
FORMAL
FORMALAZINE
FORMALDEHYD
FORMALDEHYDE
FORMALDOXIME
FORMALESQUE
FORMALISM
FORMALIST
FORMALISTIC
FORMALITER
FORMALITH
FORMALITIES
FORMALITY
FORMALIZATION
FORMALIZE
FORMALIZED
FORMALIZER
FORMALIZING
FORMALLY
FORMAMIDE
FORMAMIDINE
FORMANILIDE
FORMANT
FORMAT
FORMATE
FORMATION
FORMATIONAL
FORMATIVE
FORMATIVELY
FORMATIVENESS
FORMATURE
FORMAZAN
FORMAZYL
FORMBY
FORME
FORMED
FORMEDON
FORMEE
FORMEL
FORMELT
FORMENE
FORMENIC
FORMER
FORMERET
FORMERLY
FORMFUL
FORMIATE
FORMIC
FORMICA
FORMICARIAN
FORMICARIES
FORMICARY
FORMICATE
FORMICATED
FORMICATING
FORMICATION
FORMICATIVE

FORMICID
FORMICIDE
FORMICINE
FORMIDABILITY
FORMIDABLE
FORMIDABLENESS
FORMIDABLY
FORMIN
FORMING
FORMISM
FORMITY
FORMLESS
FORMLESSLY
FORMLESSNESS
FORMLY
FORMOLIT
FORMOLITE
FORMONITRILE
FORMOSE
FORMOSITY
FORMOUS
FORMS
FORMULA
FORMULABLE
FORMULAE
FORMULAIC
FORMULAR
FORMULARIES
FORMULARISM
FORMULARIST
FORMULARIZATION
FORMULARIZE
FORMULARIZED
FORMULARIZING
FORMULARY
FORMULAS
FORMULATE
FORMULATED
FORMULATING
FORMULATION
FORMULATOR
FORMULATORY
FORMULE
FORMULISM
FORMULIST
FORMULISTIC
FORMULIZATION
FORMULIZE
FORMULIZED
FORMULIZER
FORMULIZING
FORMWORK
FORMY
FORMYL
FORMYLATE
FORMYLATED
FORMYLATING
FORMYLATION
FORNACIC
FORNAXID
FORNCAST
FORNE
FORNENST
FORNENT
FORNICAL
FORNICATE
FORNICATED
FORNICATING
FORNICATION
FORNICATOR
FORNICATRICES
FORNICATRIX
FORNINST
FORNIX
FOROLD
FORPASS
FORPET
FORPINE
FORPINED
FORPINING
FORPIT
FORPRISE
FORREL
FORRIL
FORRIT
FORRITSOME
FORSADO
FORSAKE
FORSAKEN
FORSAKENLY
FORSAKENNESS
FORSAKER
FORSAKES
FORSAKING
FORSAR
FORSAY
FORSEEK
FORSET
FORSHAPE
FORSLACK
FORSLAKE
FORSLOW
FORSOOK
FORSOOTH
FORSPEAK
FORSPEAKING
FORSPEND
FORSPENT
FORSPOKE
FORSPOKEN
FORSTAND
FORSTEAL
FORSTERITE
FORSUNG
FORSWEAR
FORSWEARER
FORSWEARING
FORSWORE
FORSWORN
FORSWORNNESS
FORT
FORTAKE
FORTALICE
FORTE
FORTEMENTE
FORTEPIANO
FORTES
FORTESCUE
FORTESCURE
FORTH
FORTHBRING
FORTHBRINGER
FORTHBRINGING
FORTHBROUGHT
FORTHBY
FORTHCALL
FORTHCAME
FORTHCOME
FORTHCOMER
FORTHCOMING
FORTHFARE
FORTHGAZE
FORTHGO
FORTHGOING
FORTHINK
FORTHINKING
FORTHON
FORTHOUGHT
FORTHPUTTING
FORTHRIGHT
FORTHRIGHTLY
FORTHRIGHTNESS
FORTHRIGHTS
FORTHSET
FORTHTELL
FORTHTELLER
FORTHWARD
FORTHWITH
FORTHY
FORTIES
FORTIETH
FORTIFIABLE
FORTIFICATION
FORTIFICATIONS
FORTIFIED
FORTIFIER
FORTIFY
FORTIFYING
FORTIFYINGLY
FORTIN
FORTIS
FORTISSIMI
FORTISSIMO
FORTISSIMOS
FORTITUDE
FORTITUDINOUS
FORTLET
FORTNIGHT
FORTNIGHTLY
FORTO
FORTRAVAIL
FORTREAD
FORTRESS
FORTRESSED
FORTRESSING
FORTUITIES
FORTUITISM
FORTUITIST
FORTUITOUS
FORTUITOUSLY
FORTUITOUSNESS
FORTUITY
FORTUNATE
FORTUNATELY
FORTUNATENESS
FORTUNATION
FORTUNE
FORTUNED
FORTUNEL
FORTUNETELL
FORTUNETELLER
FORTUNETELLING
FORTUNING
FORTUNITE
FORTY
FORUM
FORUMIZE
FORUMS
FORVAY
FORWAKE
FORWAKED
FORWALK
FORWANDER
FORWARD
FORWARDAL
FORWARDATION
FORWARDED
FORWARDER
FORWARDING
FORWARDLY
FORWARDNESS
FORWARDS
FORWARN
FORWASTE
FORWEAN
FORWEAR
FORWEARIED
FORWEARY
FORWEARYING
FORWEEND
FORWELK
FORWENT
FORWHY
FORWODEN
FORWORDEN
FORWORE
FORWORK
FORWORN
FORWRAP
FORYIELD
FORZANDO
FORZATO
FOSH
FOSS
FOSSA
FOSSAE
FOSSAGE
FOSSANE
FOSSARIAN
FOSSE
FOSSES
FOSSETTE
FOSSICK
FOSSICKED
FOSSICKER
FOSSICKING
FOSSIFIED
FOSSIFORM
FOSSIL
FOSSILAGE
FOSSILATED
FOSSILATION
FOSSILED
FOSSILFYING
FOSSILIFEROUS
FOSSILIFICATION
FOSSILIFY
FOSSILIST
FOSSILIZATION
FOSSILIZE
FOSSILIZED
FOSSILIZING
FOSSILOGIST
FOSSILOGY
FOSSILOLOGIST
FOSSILOLOGY
FOSSILS
FOSSOR
FOSSORES
FOSSORIAL
FOSSORIOUS
FOSSORS
FOSSULA
FOSSULAE
FOSSULATE
FOSSULE
FOSSULET
FOSTELL
FOSTER
FOSTERAGE
FOSTERED
FOSTERER
FOSTERING
FOSTERINGLY
FOSTERITE
FOSTERLAND
FOSTERLING
FOSTRESS
FOT
FOTCH
FOTCHED
FOTHER
FOTHERED
FOTHERING
FOTMAL
FOTUI
FOU
FOUCH
FOUD
FOUDROYANT
FOUETTE
FOUETTEE
FOUGADE
FOUGASSE
FOUGHT
FOUGHTEN
FOUGHTY
FOUGUE
FOUJDAR
FOUJDARRY
FOUJDARY
FOUL
FOULAGE
FOULARD
FOULDRE
FOULE
FOULED
FOULER
FOULEST
FOULING
FOULLY
FOULMART
FOULMOUTHED
FOULMOUTHEDLY
FOULMOUTHEDNESS
FOULNESS
FOULSOME
FOUMART
FOUN
FOUNCE
FOUND
FOUNDATION
FOUNDATIONAL
FOUNDATIONALLY
FOUNDATIONARY
FOUNDATIONER
FOUNDED
FOUNDER
FOUNDERED
FOUNDERING
FOUNDEROUS
FOUNDING
FOUNDLING
FOUNDRIES
FOUNDRY
FOUNDRYMAN
FOUNDRYMEN
FOUNT
FOUNTAIN
FOUNTAINED
FOUNTAINEER
FOUNTAINHEAD
FOUNTAINOUS
FOUNTAINOUSLY
FOUNTE
FOUNTFUL
FOUR
FOURB
FOURBE
FOURBLE
FOURCHE
FOURCHEE
FOURCHER
FOURCHET
FOURCHETTE
FOURCHITE
FOURER
FOURFLUSHER
FOURFOLD
FOURGON
FOURHANDED
FOURLING
FOURPENCE
FOURPENNY
FOURPOUNDER

FOURQUINE
FOURRAGERE
FOURRE
FOURRIER
FOURS
FOURSCORE
FOURSCORTH
FOURSOME
FOURSQUARE
FOURSQUARELY
FOURSQUARENESS
FOURSTRAND
FOURTEEN
FOURTEENER
FOURTEENTH
FOURTEENTHLY
FOURTH
FOURTHER
FOURTHLY
FOUSSA
FOUTE
FOUTER
FOUTH
FOUTRA
FOUTRE
FOUTY
FOVEA
FOVEAE
FOVEAL
FOVEATE
FOVEATED
FOVEATION
FOVEIFORM
FOVENT
FOVEOLA
FOVEOLAE
FOVEOLARIOUS
FOVEOLATE
FOVEOLATED
FOVEOLE
FOVEOLET
FOW
FOWD
FOWL
FOWLED
FOWLER
FOWLERITE
FOWLERY
FOWLFOOT
FOWLING
FOWLS
FOX
FOXBANE
FOXBERRIES
FOXBERRY
FOXCHOP
FOXED
FOXER
FOXERY
FOXES
FOXFEET
FOXFIRE
FOXFISH
FOXGLOVE
FOXHOLE
FOXHOUND
FOXIER
FOXIEST
FOXILY
FOXINESS
FOXING
FOXISH
FOXLIKE
FOXSKIN
FOXTAIL
FOXTAILED
FOXTROT
FOXY
FOY
FOYAITE
FOYAITIC
FOYBOAT
FOYER
FOYLE
FOZE
FOZINESS
FOZY
FRA
FRAB
FRABBIT
FRABJOUS
FRABJOUSLY
FRABOUS
FRACAS
FRACASES
FRACEDINOUS
FRACHE
FRACID
FRACK
FRACT
FRACTABLE
FRACTABLING
FRACTED
FRACTILE
FRACTION
FRACTIONAL
FRACTIONALISM
FRACTIONALIZE
FRACTIONALLY
FRACTIONARY
FRACTIONATE
FRACTIONATED
FRACTIONATING
FRACTIONATION
FRACTIONATOR
FRACTIONED
FRACTIONING
FRACTIONIZATION
FRACTIONIZE
FRACTIONIZED
FRACTIONIZING
FRACTIOUS
FRACTIOUSLY
FRACTIOUSNESS
FRACTUOSITY
FRACTUR
FRACTURAL
FRACTURE
FRACTURED
FRACTURING
FRADICIN
FRAE
FRAENA
FRAENULAR
FRAENULUM
FRAENUM
FRAENUMS
FRAG
FRAGE
FRAGGING
FRAGHAN
FRAGILE
FRAGILELY
FRAGILENESS
FRAGILITIES
FRAGILITY
FRAGMENT
FRAGMENTAL
FRAGMENTALLY
FRAGMENTARILY
FRAGMENTARINESS
FRAGMENTARY
FRAGMENTATION
FRAGMENTED
FRAGMENTIST
FRAGMENTITIOUS
FRAGMENTIZE
FRAGMENTS
FRAGOR
FRAGRANCE
FRAGRANCIES
FRAGRANCY
FRAGRANT
FRAGRANTLY
FRAGRANTNESS
FRAICHEUR
FRAID
FRAIK
FRAIL
FRAILE
FRAILEJON
FRAILER
FRAILES
FRAILEST
FRAILLY
FRAILNESS
FRAILTIES
FRAILTY
FRAIM
FRAIN
FRAISE
FRAISED
FRAISING
FRAIST
FRAKE
FRAM
FRAMBESIA
FRAMBOESIA
FRAME
FRAMEA
FRAMEAE
FRAMED
FRAMER
FRAMES
FRAMESMITH
FRAMEWORK
FRAMING
FRAMMIT
FRAMPLER
FRAMPOLD
FRANC
FRANCHISE
FRANCHISEMENT
FRANCHISER
FRANCISC
FRANCISCA
FRANCIUM
FRANCO
FRANCOLIN
FRANCOLITE
FRANGENT
FRANGIBILITY
FRANGIBLE
FRANGIBLENESS
FRANGIPANE
FRANGIPANI
FRANGULA
FRANGULIC
FRANGULIN
FRANGULINIC
FRANION
FRANK
FRANKALMOIGN
FRANKALMOIGNE
FRANKALMOIN
FRANKED
FRANKENIACEOUS
FRANKER
FRANKEST
FRANKFORT
FRANKFORTER
FRANKFURT
FRANKFURTER
FRANKHEARTED
FRANKHEARTEDLY
FRANKHEARTNESS
FRANKINCENSE
FRANKINCENSED
FRANKING
FRANKLANDITE
FRANKLIN
FRANKLINITE
FRANKLY
FRANKMARRIAGE
FRANKNESS
FRANKPLEDGE
FRANSERIA
FRANTIC
FRANTICALLY
FRANTICLY
FRANTICNESS
FRAP
FRAPE
FRAPLE
FRAPLER
FRAPPE
FRAPPED
FRAPPEED
FRAPPEING
FRAPPING
FRARY
FRASE
FRASER
FRASIER
FRASS
FRAT
FRATCH
FRATCHED
FRATCHEOUS
FRATCHER
FRATCHETY
FRATCHY
FRATE
FRATER
FRATERIES
FRATERNAL
FRATERNALISM
FRATERNALIST
FRATERNALITY
FRATERNALLY
FRATERNATE
FRATERNATION
FRATERNISM
FRATERNITIES
FRATERNITY
FRATERNIZATION
FRATERNIZE
FRATERNIZED
FRATERNIZER
FRATERNIZING
FRATERY
FRATI
FRATRICIDAL
FRATRICIDE
FRATRIES
FRATRY
FRAUD
FRAUDER
FRAUDFUL
FRAUDFULLY
FRAUDLESS
FRAUDLESSLY
FRAUDLESSNESS
FRAUDULENCE
FRAUDULENCY
FRAUDULENT
FRAUDULENTLY
FRAUDULENTNESS
FRAUEN
FRAUGHT
FRAUGHTED
FRAUGHTING
FRAUNCH
FRAVASHI
FRAWN
FRAXETIN
FRAXIN
FRAXINELLA
FRAY
FRAYED
FRAYING
FRAYN
FRAYNE
FRAZE
FRAZER
FRAZIL
FRAZZLE
FRAZZLED
FRAZZLING
FREAK
FREAKED
FREAKERY
FREAKFUL
FREAKIER
FREAKIEST
FREAKILY
FREAKINESS
FREAKING
FREAKISH
FREAKISHLY
FREAKISHNESS
FREAKPOT
FREAKY
FREAM
FREATH
FRECK
FRECKEN
FRECKET
FRECKLE
FRECKLED
FRECKLEDNESS
FRECKLING
FRECKLY
FREDAINE
FREDDO
FREDERIK
FREDRICITE
FREE
FREEBOARD
FREEBOOT
FREEBOOTED
FREEBOOTER
FREEBOOTERY
FREEBOOTING
FREEBOOTY
FREEBORN
FREED
FREEDMAN
FREEDMEN
FREEDOM
FREEDWOMAN
FREEDWOMEN
FREEHAND
FREEHANDED
FREEHANDEDLY
FREEHANDEDNESS
FREEHEARTED
FREEHOLD
FREEHOLDER
FREEHOLDING
FREEING
FREELAGE
FREELOAD
FREELOADER
FREELY

FREEMAN
FREEMARTIN
FREEMASON
FREEMASONIC
FREEMASONICAL
FREEMASONISM
FREEMASONS
FREEMEN
FREENESS
FREER
FREESIA
FREEST
FREESTANDING
FREESTONE
FREESTYLE
FREESTYLER
FREET
FREETHINKER
FREETHINKING
FREETRADER
FREETY
FREEWARD
FREEWAY
FREEWHEEL
FREEWHEELER
FREEWHEELING
FREEWILL
FREEWOMAN
FREEWOMEN
FREEZABLE
FREEZE
FREEZER
FREEZING
FREEZY
FREIBERGITE
FREIGHT
FREIGHTAGE
FREIGHTED
FREIGHTER
FREIGHTING
FREIJO
FREINAGE
FREIT
FREITH
FREITY
FREKE
FREM
FREMD
FREMDLY
FREMDNESS
FREMESCENCE
FREMESCENT
FREMITUS
FREMT
FRENA
FRENAL
FRENATE
FRENCHED
FRENCHEN
FRENCHIFY
FRENCHING
FRENETIC
FRENETICAL
FRENETICALLY
FRENNE
FRENULA
FRENULAR
FRENULUM
FRENUM
FRENUMS
FRENZIED
FRENZIEDLY
FRENZIES
FRENZILY
FRENZY
FRENZYING
FREQUENCE
FREQUENCIES
FREQUENCY
FREQUENT
FREQUENTABLE
FREQUENTAGE
FREQUENTATION
FREQUENTATIVE
FREQUENTED
FREQUENTER
FREQUENTING
FREQUENTLY
FREQUENTNESS
FRERE
FRERES
FRESCADE
FRESCO
FRESCOED
FRESCOER
FRESCOES
FRESCOING
FRESCOIST
FRESCOS
FRESE
FRESH
FRESHEN
FRESHENER
FRESHER
FRESHEST
FRESHET
FRESHHEARTED
FRESHING
FRESHLY
FRESHMAN
FRESHMANIC
FRESHMEN
FRESHNESS
FRESNE
FRESNEL
FRET
FRETA
FRETFUL
FRETFULLY
FRETFULNESS
FRETISH
FRETIZE
FRETSAW
FRETSOME
FRETT
FRETTAGE
FRETTATION
FRETTE
FRETTED
FRETTEN
FRETTER
FRETTIER
FRETTIEST
FRETTING
FRETTINGLY
FRETTY
FRETUM
FRETWORK
FRETWORKED
FREYALITE
FRIABILITY
FRIABLE
FRIABLENESS
FRIAND
FRIANDISE
FRIAR
FRIARBIRD
FRIARIES
FRIARLY
FRIARY
FRIATION
FRIB
FRIBBLE
FRIBBLED
FRIBBLER
FRIBBLERY
FRIBBLING
FRIBBY
FRIBORG
FRIBOURG
FRICACE
FRICANDEAU
FRICANDEAUX
FRICANDEL
FRICANDELLE
FRICANDO
FRICASSEE
FRICASSEED
FRICASSEEING
FRICATION
FRICATIVE
FRICATRICE
FRICK
FRICTION
FRICTIONAL
FRICTIONALLY
FRICTIONIZE
FRICTIONIZED
FRICTIONIZING
FRICTIONLESS
FRIDGE
FRIDSTOOL
FRIE
FRIED
FRIEDCAKE
FRIEDELITE
FRIEND
FRIENDED
FRIENDING
FRIENDLESS
FRIENDLESSNESS
FRIENDLIER
FRIENDLIES
FRIENDLIEST
FRIENDLILY
FRIENDLINESS
FRIENDLY
FRIENDS
FRIENDSHIP
FRIER
FRIESEITE
FRIEZE
FRIEZED
FRIEZER
FRIEZING
FRIEZY
FRIG
FRIGATE
FRIGATOON
FRIGGLE
FRIGHT
FRIGHTED
FRIGHTEN
FRIGHTENED
FRIGHTENEDLY
FRIGHTENEDNESS
FRIGHTENER
FRIGHTENING
FRIGHTENINGLY
FRIGHTER
FRIGHTFUL
FRIGHTFULLY
FRIGHTFULNESS
FRIGHTING
FRIGHTSOME
FRIGHTY
FRIGID
FRIGIDARIA
FRIGIDARIUM
FRIGIDITIES
FRIGIDITY
FRIGIDLY
FRIGIDNESS
FRIGIFEROUS
FRIGO
FRIGOLABILE
FRIGOR
FRIGORIC
FRIGORIFIC
FRIGORIFICAL
FRIGORIFICO
FRIGORIFY
FRIGORIMETER
FRIGOSTABLE
FRIGOTHERAPY
FRIJOL
FRIJOLE
FRIJOLES
FRIJOLILLO
FRIKE
FRILAL
FRILL
FRILLBACK
FRILLED
FRILLER
FRILLERY
FRILLIER
FRILLIES
FRILLIEST
FRILLILY
FRILLINESS
FRILLING
FRILLY
FRIM
FRIMITTS
FRINGE
FRINGED
FRINGEFLOWER
FRINGEFOOT
FRINGENT
FRINGEPOD
FRINGES
FRINGIER
FRINGIEST
FRINGILLACEOUS
FRINGILLINE
FRINGILLOID
FRINGING
FRINGY
FRIPPER
FRIPPERER
FRIPPERIES
FRIPPERY
FRISADO
FRISCA
FRISCAL
FRISCH
FRISCO
FRISE
FRISETTE
FRISEUR
FRISK
FRISKER
FRISKEST
FRISKET
FRISKFUL
FRISKIER
FRISKIEST
FRISKILY
FRISKIN
FRISKINESS
FRISKING
FRISKINGLY
FRISKLE
FRISKY
FRISOLEE
FRISON
FRISS
FRISSON
FRIST
FRISURE
FRISZKA
FRIT
FRITH
FRITHBORGH
FRITHBORH
FRITHBOT
FRITHLES
FRITHSOKEN
FRITHSTOOL
FRITHWORK
FRITHY
FRITILLARIES
FRITILLARY
FRITT
FRITTATA
FRITTED
FRITTER
FRITTERED
FRITTERER
FRITTERING
FRITTERS
FRITTING
FRIVOL
FRIVOLED
FRIVOLER
FRIVOLISM
FRIVOLITIES
FRIVOLITY
FRIVOLIZE
FRIVOLIZED
FRIVOLIZING
FRIVOLLED
FRIVOLLER
FRIVOLOUS
FRIVOLOUSLY
FRIVOLOUSNESS
FRIZ
FRIZADO
FRIZE
FRIZEL
FRIZER
FRIZETTE
FRIZZ
FRIZZED
FRIZZEN
FRIZZER
FRIZZES
FRIZZIER
FRIZZIEST
FRIZZILY
FRIZZINESS
FRIZZING
FRIZZLE
FRIZZLED
FRIZZLER
FRIZZLING
FRIZZLY
FRIZZY
FRO
FROCK
FROCKING
FROCKMAKER
FROE
FROEMAN
FROG
FROGBIT
FROGEATER
FROGEYE
FROGFACE
FROGFISH
FROGFISHES
FROGFLOWER
FROGFOOT
FROGGED

FROGGER
FROGGERY
FROGGIER
FROGGIES
FROGGIEST
FROGGINESS
FROGGING
FROGGISH
FROGGY
FROGHOPPER
FROGLAND
FROGLEAF
FROGLET
FROGMAN
FROGMEN
FROGMOUTH
FROGNOSE
FROGS
FROGSKIN
FROGSTOOL
FROGTONGUE
FROGWORT
FROHLICH
FROIDEUR
FROISE
FROISSE
FROKIN
FROLIC
FROLICFUL
FROLICKED
FROLICKER
FROLICKING
FROLICKY
FROLICLY
FROLICNESS
FROLICSOME
FROLICSOMELY
FROLICSOMENESS
FROM
FROMAGE
FROMENTY
FROMWARD
FROMWARDS
FROND
FRONDAGE
FRONDED
FRONDENT
FRONDESCE
FRONDESCED
FRONDESCENCE
FRONDESCENT
FRONDESCING
FRONDIFEROUS
FRONDIFORM
FRONDIGEROUS
FRONDIVOROUS
FRONDLET
FRONDOSE
FRONDOSELY
FRONDOUS
FRONS
FRONT
FRONTAD
FRONTAGE
FRONTAGER
FRONTAL
FRONTALIS
FRONTALITY
FRONTED
FRONTER
FRONTES
FRONTIER
FRONTIERMAN
FRONTIERSMAN
FRONTIERSMEN
FRONTING
FRONTIS
FRONTISPIECE
FRONTISPIECED
FRONTISPIECING
FRONTLESS
FRONTLESSLY
FRONTLESSNESS
FRONTLET
FRONTOLYSIS
FRONTOMALAR
FRONTOMENTAL
FRONTON
FRONTONASAL
FRONTPIECE
FRONTSMAN
FRONTSTALL
FRONTURE
FROOM
FROPPISH
FRORE
FROREN
FRORY
FROSH
FROSK
FROST
FROSTATION
FROSTBIRD
FROSTBIT
FROSTBITE
FROSTBITING
FROSTBITTEN
FROSTBOW
FROSTED
FROSTER
FROSTFISH
FROSTFISHES
FROSTFLOWER
FROSTIER
FROSTIEST
FROSTILY
FROSTINESS
FROSTING
FROSTLESS
FROSTPROOFING
FROSTROOT
FROSTWEED
FROSTWORK
FROSTY
FROT
FROTH
FROTHED
FROTHER
FROTHIER
FROTHIEST
FROTHILY
FROTHINESS
FROTHING
FROTHY
FROTTAGE
FROTTED
FROTTING
FROTTOLA
FROTTON
FROUD
FROUFROU
FROUGH
FROUGHY
FROUNCE
FROUNCED
FROUNCING
FROUST
FROUSTY
FROUZE
FROUZY
FROW
FROWARD
FROWARDLY
FROWARDNESS
FROWER
FROWL
FROWN
FROWNED
FROWNER
FROWNING
FROWNY
FROWST
FROWSTIER
FROWSTIEST
FROWSTY
FROWSY
FROWY
FROWZE
FROWZIER
FROWZIEST
FROWZILY
FROWZINESS
FROWZLED
FROWZY
FROZE
FROZEN
FROZENLY
FROZENNESS
FRUB
FRUBBISH
FRUCTED
FRUCTESCENCE
FRUCTESCENT
FRUCTICULTURAL
FRUCTIFEROUS
FRUCTIFIED
FRUCTIFIER
FRUCTIFORM
FRUCTIFY
FRUCTIFYING
FRUCTIPAROUS
FRUCTIVOROUS
FRUCTOSE
FRUCTOSIDE
FRUCTUARIUS
FRUCTUOSE
FRUCTUOSITY
FRUCTUOUS
FRUCTUOUSLY
FRUCTUOUSNESS
FRUGAL
FRUGALISM
FRUGALIST
FRUGALITIES
FRUGALITY
FRUGALLY
FRUGALNESS
FRUGGAN
FRUGGIN
FRUGIFEROUS
FRUGIFEROUSNESS
FRUGIVOROUS
FRUIT
FRUITADE
FRUITAGE
FRUITARIAN
FRUITARIANISM
FRUITCAKE
FRUITED
FRUITER
FRUITERER
FRUITERESS
FRUITERIES
FRUITERY
FRUITFUL
FRUITFULLY
FRUITFULNESS
FRUITGROWER
FRUITGROWING
FRUITIER
FRUITIEST
FRUITINESS
FRUITING
FRUITION
FRUITIST
FRUITIVE
FRUITLESS
FRUITLESSLY
FRUITLESSNESS
FRUITLET
FRUITS
FRUITSTALK
FRUITTIME
FRUITWISE
FRUITWOMAN
FRUITWOMEN
FRUITWORM
FRUITY
FRUM
FRUMARYL
FRUMENT
FRUMENTATION
FRUMENTUM
FRUMENTY
FRUMETY
FRUMP
FRUMPERIES
FRUMPERY
FRUMPIER
FRUMPIEST
FRUMPILY
FRUMPINESS
FRUMPISH
FRUMPISHLY
FRUMPISHNESS
FRUMPLE
FRUMPLED
FRUMPLING
FRUMPS
FRUMPY
FRUNDEL
FRUSH
FRUST
FRUSTA
FRUSTRANEOUS
FRUSTRATE
FRUSTRATED
FRUSTRATELY
FRUSTRATER
FRUSTRATES
FRUSTRATING
FRUSTRATION
FRUSTRATIVE
FRUSTRATORY
FRUSTULE
FRUSTULENT
FRUSTULOSE
FRUSTUM
FRUSTUMS
FRUTESCENCE
FRUTESCENT
FRUTEX
FRUTICES
FRUTICETA
FRUTICETUM
FRUTICOSE
FRUTICOUS
FRUTICULOSE
FRUTICULTURE
FRUTIFY
FRUTILLA
FRY
FRYER
FRYING
FRYPAN
FU
FUANG
FUB
FUBBERY
FUBBY
FUBSIER
FUBSIEST
FUBSY
FUCACEOUS
FUCATE
FUCATION
FUCATIOUS
FUCHSIA
FUCHSIN
FUCHSINE
FUCHSINOPHIL
FUCHSITE
FUCHSONE
FUCI
FUCINITA
FUCIPHAGOUS
FUCIVOROUS
FUCOID
FUCOIDAL
FUCOIDIN
FUCOSAN
FUCOSE
FUCOUS
FUCOXANTHIN
FUCUS
FUCUSED
FUCUSES
FUD
FUDDLE
FUDDLED
FUDDLER
FUDDLING
FUDER
FUDGE
FUDGED
FUDGER
FUDGING
FUDGY
FUEL
FUELED
FUELER
FUELING
FUELIZER
FUELLED
FUELLER
FUELLING
FUERO
FUERTE
FUFF
FUFFIT
FUFFLE
FUFFY
FUG
FUGA
FUGACIOUS
FUGACIOUSLY
FUGACIOUSNESS
FUGACITIES
FUGACITY
FUGACY
FUGAL
FUGALLY
FUGARA
FUGATO
FUGGY
FUGI
FUGIE
FUGIENT
FUGITATE
FUGITATED
FUGITATING
FUGITATION
FUGITIVE
FUGITIVELY
FUGITIVENESS

FUGITIVITY
FUGLE
FUGLED
FUGLEMAN
FUGLEMEN
FUGLER
FUGLING
FUGU
FUGUE
FUGUIST
FUIDHIR
FUIRDAYS
FUJI
FULCIFORM
FULCRA
FULCRAL
FULCRATE
FULCRUM
FULCRUMAGE
FULCRUMED
FULCRUMING
FULCRUMS
FULFIL
FULFILL
FULFILLED
FULFILLER
FULFILLING
FULFILLMENT
FULFILMENT
FULGENCE
FULGENCY
FULGENT
FULGENTLY
FULGENTNESS
FULGID
FULGIDE
FULGIDITY
FULGOR
FULGORID
FULGOROUS
FULGOUR
FULGOUROUS
FULGURAL
FULGURANT
FULGURANTLY
FULGURATA
FULGURATE
FULGURATED
FULGURATING
FULGURATION
FULGURITE
FULGUROUS
FULHAM
FULICINE
FULIGINOSITY
FULIGINOUS
FULIGINOUSLY
FULIGINOUSNESS
FULIGULINE
FULK
FULL
FULLAM
FULLBACK
FULLDO
FULLED
FULLER
FULLERBOARD
FULLERED
FULLERIES
FULLERING
FULLERY
FULLFACE
FULLHEARTED
FULLING
FULLMOUTH
FULLMOUTHED
FULLMOUTHEDLY
FULLNESS
FULLOM
FULLY
FULMAR
FULMEN
FULMINA
FULMINANCY
FULMINANT
FULMINATE
FULMINATED
FULMINATING
FULMINATION
FULMINATOR
FULMINATORY
FULMINE
FULMINED
FULMINEOUS
FULMINING
FULMINOUS
FULMINURATE
FULMINURIC
FULNESS
FULSOME
FULSOMELY
FULSOMENESS
FULTH
FULTZ
FULVENE
FULVESCENT
FULVID
FULVIDNESS
FULVOUS
FULWA
FULYIE
FULZIE
FUM
FUMACIOUS
FUMADO
FUMADOS
FUMAGE
FUMAGINE
FUMARASE
FUMARATE
FUMARIA
FUMARIC
FUMARINE
FUMARIUM
FUMAROID
FUMAROIDAL
FUMAROLE
FUMAROLIC
FUMATORIA
FUMATORIES
FUMATORIUM
FUMATORIUMS
FUMATORY
FUMBA
FUMBLE
FUMBLED
FUMBLER
FUMBLING
FUMBULATOR
FUME
FUMED
FUMER
FUMEROOT
FUMET
FUMETTE
FUMEWORT
FUMID
FUMIDITY
FUMIDUCT
FUMIER
FUMIEST
FUMIFEROUS
FUMIGANT
FUMIGATE
FUMIGATED
FUMIGATING
FUMIGATION
FUMIGATOR
FUMIGATORIES
FUMIGATORY
FUMILY
FUMINESS
FUMING
FUMINGLY
FUMISH
FUMISHLY
FUMISHNESS
FUMISTERY
FUMITORIES
FUMITORY
FUMMEL
FUMMLE
FUMOSE
FUMOSITY
FUMOUS
FUMOUSLY
FUMULI
FUMULUS
FUMY
FUN
FUNA
FUNAMBULATE
FUNAMBULATED
FUNAMBULATING
FUNAMBULATION
FUNAMBULATORY
FUNAMBULIC
FUNAMBULISM
FUNAMBULIST
FUNAMBULO
FUNAMBULOES
FUNCTION
FUNCTIONAL
FUNCTIONALISM
FUNCTIONALIST
FUNCTIONALITY
FUNCTIONALIZE
FUNCTIONALIZED
FUNCTIONALIZIN
FUNCTIONALLY
FUNCTIONARIES
FUNCTIONARISM
FUNCTIONARY
FUNCTIONATE
FUNCTIONATED
FUNCTIONATING
FUNCTIONATION
FUNCTIONED
FUNCTIONING
FUNCTIONIZE
FUNCTIONLESS
FUNCTOR
FUND
FUNDA
FUNDAL
FUNDAMENT
FUNDAMENTAL
FUNDAMENTALISM
FUNDAMENTALIST
FUNDAMENTALITY
FUNDAMENTALLY
FUNDATORIAL
FUNDATRICES
FUNDATRIX
FUNDED
FUNDER
FUNDHOLDER
FUNDI
FUNDIC
FUNDIFORM
FUNDING
FUNDITOR
FUNDITORES
FUNDMONGER
FUNDMONGERING
FUNDO
FUNDS
FUNDUCK
FUNDULINE
FUNDUS
FUNEBRE
FUNEBRIAL
FUNEBRIOUS
FUNEBROUS
FUNERAL
FUNERALIZE
FUNERALLY
FUNERALS
FUNERARY
FUNERATE
FUNERATION
FUNEREAL
FUNEREALLY
FUNEST
FUNESTAL
FUNFEST
FUNGACEOUS
FUNGAL
FUNGATE
FUNGATED
FUNGATING
FUNGE
FUNGI
FUNGIAN
FUNGIBILITY
FUNGIBLE
FUNGIC
FUNGICIDAL
FUNGICIDE
FUNGID
FUNGIFORM
FUNGIFY
FUNGILLIFORM
FUNGIN
FUNGISTAT
FUNGISTATIC
FUNGO
FUNGOES
FUNGOID
FUNGOIDAL
FUNGOLOGICAL
FUNGOLOGIST
FUNGOLOGY
FUNGOSE
FUNGOSITY
FUNGOUS
FUNGUS
FUNGUSED
FUNGUSES
FUNGUSY
FUNICLE
FUNICULAR
FUNICULATE
FUNICULI
FUNICULITIS
FUNICULUS
FUNIFORM
FUNIS
FUNK
FUNKED
FUNKER
FUNKIER
FUNKIEST
FUNKINESS
FUNKING
FUNKY
FUNMAKER
FUNNED
FUNNEL
FUNNELED
FUNNELFORM
FUNNELING
FUNNELLED
FUNNELLIKE
FUNNELLING
FUNNIER
FUNNIES
FUNNIEST
FUNNILY
FUNNIMENT
FUNNINESS
FUNNING
FUNNY
FUNNYMAN
FUNNYMEN
FUNORI
FUNORIN
FUNSTER
FUNT
FUR
FURACANA
FURACIOUS
FURACIOUSNESS
FURACITY
FURAL
FURAN
FURANE
FURANOSE
FURBEARER
FURBELOW
FURBELOWED
FURBELOWING
FURBISH
FURBISHED
FURBISHER
FURBISHING
FURCA
FURCAE
FURCAL
FURCATE
FURCATED
FURCATELY
FURCATING
FURCATION
FURCELLATE
FURCIFERINE
FURCIFEROUS
FURCIFORM
FURCILIA
FURCRAEA
FURCULA
FURCULAE
FURCULAR
FURCULE
FURCULUM
FURDEL
FURDLE
FURE
FURFUR
FURFURACEOUS
FURFURAL
FURFURAMID
FURFURAMIDE
FURFURAN
FURFURATION
FURFURES
FURFURINE
FURFUROID
FURFUROL
FURFUROLE
FURFUROUS
FURFURYL
FURIAL
FURIANT
FURIBUND

FURICANE
FURIED
FURIES
FURIFY
FURIL
FURILE
FURILIC
FURIOSO
FURIOUS
FURIOUSITY
FURIOUSLY
FURIOUSNESS
FURISON
FURL
FURLANA
FURLED
FURLER
FURLING
FURLONG
FURLOUGH
FURLOUGHED
FURLOUGHING
FURMENTY
FURMETY
FURMITY
FURNACE
FURNACED
FURNACEMAN
FURNACEMEN
FURNACER
FURNACING
FURNACITE
FURNAGE
FURNER
FURNISH
FURNISHED
FURNISHER
FURNISHING
FURNISHINGS
FURNISHMENT
FURNISHNESS
FURNITURE
FUROATE
FUROID
FUROIN
FUROL
FUROLE
FUROMONAZOLE
FUROR
FURORE
FURPHY
FURR
FURRED
FURRIER
FURRIERED
FURRIERIES
FURRIERY
FURRIEST
FURRILY
FURRINESS
FURRING
FURROW
FURROWED
FURROWER
FURROWING
FURROWS
FURROWY
FURRURE
FURRY
FURS
FURTHER
FURTHERANCE
FURTHERED
FURTHERER
FURTHERING
FURTHERLY
FURTHERMORE
FURTHERMOST
FURTHERSOME
FURTHEST
FURTHY
FURTIVE
FURTIVELY
FURTIVENESS
FURTUM
FURUNCLE
FURUNCULAR
FURUNCULOID
FURUNCULOSIS
FURUNCULOUS
FURWA
FURY
FURYL
FURZE
FURZECHAT
FURZED
FURZERY
FURZETOP
FURZY
FUSAIN
FUSARIAL
FUSARIOSE
FUSARIOSIS
FUSAROLE
FUSATE
FUSC
FUSCESCENT
FUSCIN
FUSCOHYALINE
FUSCOUS
FUSE
FUSEAU
FUSEBOARD
FUSED
FUSEE
FUSEL
FUSELAGE
FUSEPLUG
FUSIBILITY
FUSIBLE
FUSIBLENESS
FUSIBLY
FUSIFORM
FUSIL
FUSILADED
FUSILADING
FUSILE
FUSILEER
FUSILIER
FUSILLADE
FUSILLY
FUSING
FUSINIST
FUSINITE
FUSION
FUSIONAL
FUSIONISM
FUSIONIST
FUSIONLESS
FUSOID
FUSS
FUSSED
FUSSER
FUSSIER
FUSSIEST
FUSSIFICATION
FUSSIFY
FUSSILY
FUSSINESS
FUSSING
FUSSLE
FUSSOCK
FUSSY
FUST
FUSTANELLA
FUSTANELLE
FUSTEE
FUSTER
FUSTERIC
FUSTET
FUSTIAN
FUSTIANIST
FUSTIC
FUSTIE
FUSTIER
FUSTIEST
FUSTIGATE
FUSTIGATED
FUSTIGATING
FUSTIGATION
FUSTIGATOR
FUSTIGATORY
FUSTILUGS
FUSTILY
FUSTIN
FUSTINESS
FUSTLE
FUSTOC
FUSTY
FUSULA
FUSUMA
FUSURE
FUT
FUTCHEL
FUTCHELL
FUTE
FUTHARC
FUTHARK
FUTHORC
FUTHORK
FUTILE
FUTILELY
FUTILENESS
FUTILITARIAN
FUTILITIES
FUTILITY
FUTILOUS
FUTTAH
FUTTER
FUTTERET
FUTTOCK
FUTURAL
FUTURAMA
FUTURE
FUTURELESS
FUTURELY
FUTURISM
FUTURIST
FUTURISTIC
FUTURITIES
FUTURITION
FUTURITY
FUTWA
FUYE
FUZE
FUZEE
FUZIL
FUZZ
FUZZBALL
FUZZIER
FUZZIEST
FUZZILY
FUZZINESS
FUZZLE
FUZZTAIL
FUZZY
FYCE
FYKE
FYLE
FYLFOT
FYLGJA
FYLGJUR
FYLKE
FYLKER
FYND
FYRD
FYRDUNG

GA
GAAL
GAATCH
GAB
GABARDINE
GABARI
GABARIT
GABBACK
GABBAI
GABBARD
GABBART
GABBED
GABBER
GABBIER
GABBIEST
GABBING
GABBLE
GABBLED
GABBLEMENT
GABBLER
GABBLING
GABBRO
GABBROIC
GABBROID
GABBROITIC
GABBROS
GABBY
GABE
GABELER
GABELLE
GABELLED
GABELLEMAN
GABELLER
GABERDINE
GABERLUNZIE
GABGAB
GABI
GABION
GABIONADE
GABIONAGE
GABIONED
GABLATORES
GABLE
GABLEBOARD
GABLET
GABLEWISE
GABLOCK
GABY
GACHUPIN
GAD
GADABOUT
GADBEE
GADBUSH
GADDED
GADDER
GADDI
GADDING
GADDINGLY
GADDISH
GADDISHNESS
GADE
GADES
GADFLY
GADGE
GADGER
GADGET
GADGETRY
GADHI
GADID
GADININE
GADLING
GADMAN
GADOID
GADOLINIA
GADOLINIC
GADOLINITE
GADOLINIUM
GADROON
GADROONAGE
GADSMAN
GADUIN
GADWALL
GADWELL
GAE
GAED
GAEDOWN
GAET
GAFF
GAFFE
GAFFED
GAFFER
GAFFING
GAFFLE
GAFFLET
GAFFSAIL
GAFFSMAN
GAG
GAGA
GAGATE
GAGE
GAGED
GAGEE
GAGEITE
GAGEL
GAGER
GAGES
GAGGED
GAGGER
GAGGERY
GAGGING
GAGGLE
GAGGLED
GAGGLER
GAGGLING
GAGING
GAGMAN
GAGOR
GAGROOT
GAGTOOTH
GAHE
GAHNITE
GAIAC
GAIASSA
GAIETY
GAIG
GAIL
GAILLARD
GAILY
GAIN
GAINAGE
GAINBIRTH
GAINCALL
GAINCOME
GAINCOPE
GAINE
GAINED
GAINER
GAINFUL
GAINFULLY
GAINFULNESS
GAINGIVING
GAINING
GAINLESS
GAINLINESS
GAINLY
GAINOR
GAINPAIN
GAINS
GAINSAY
GAINSAYER
GAINSET
GAINSOME
GAINSPEAKER
GAINSPEAKING
GAINST
GAINSTAND
GAINSTRIVE
GAINTURN
GAINTWIST
GAINWARD
GAINYIELD
GAIR
GAIRFISH
GAIRFOWL
GAIST
GAIT
GAITED
GAITER
GAITING
GAITT
GAIZE
GAJO
GAL
GALA
GALABEAH
GALABIA
GALABIEH
GALACTAGOG
GALACTAGOGUE
GALACTAN
GALACTASE
GALACTEMIA
GALACTIC
GALACTIN
GALACTITE
GALACTOCELE
GALACTOGOGUE
GALACTOHEMIA
GALACTOID
GALACTOLYSIS
GALACTOLYTIC
GALACTOMETER
GALACTONIC
GALACTOPATHY
GALACTOPHORE
GALACTOPYRA
GALACTOSCOPE
GALACTOSE
GALACTOSIDE
GALACTOSIS
GALACTOSURIA
GALACTURIA
GALAGALA
GALAH
GALANAS
GALANGAL
GALANGIN
GALANT
GALANTE
GALANTINE
GALAPAGO
GALATEA
GALAVANT
GALAXIAN
GALAXY
GALBAN
GALBANUM
GALBE
GALBULUS
GALD
GALE
GALEA
GALEAE
GALEAGE
GALEATE
GALEATED
GALECHE
GALEE
GALEENY
GALEGINE
GALEID
GALEIFORM
GALEMPONG
GALENA
GALENIC
GALENICAL
GALENITE
GALENOID
GALEOID
GALERA
GALERICULATE
GALERIE
GALERUM
GALERUS
GALESAUR
GALET
GALETTE
GALEWORT
GALGAL
GALI
GALIANES
GALILEE
GALIMATIAS
GALINGALE
GALIONGEE
GALIONJI
GALIOT
GALIPOT
GALIVANT
GALJOEN
GALL
GALLA
GALLACH
GALLAH
GALLANILIDE
GALLANT
GALLANTLY
GALLANTNESS
GALLANTRY
GALLATE
GALLATURE
GALLBERRY
GALLBUSH
GALLEASS
GALLED
GALLEIN
GALLEINE
GALLEON
GALLER
GALLERA
GALLERIAN
GALLERIES
GALLERY
GALLET
GALLETA
GALLEY
GALLEYMAN
GALLEYS
GALLEYWORM
GALLFLOWER
GALLFLY
GALLIAMBIC
GALLIAMBUS
GALLIARD
GALLIARDISE
GALLIARDLY
GALLIARDNESS
GALLIASS
GALLIC
GALLICIZER
GALLICOLA
GALLICOLOUS
GALLIFEROUS
GALLIFORM
GALLIGASKIN
GALLIGASKINS
GALLIMAUFRY
GALLINACEAN
GALLINACEOUS
GALLINAZO
GALLINE
GALLINEY
GALLING
GALLINGLY
GALLINGNESS
GALLINIPPER
GALLINULE
GALLINULINE
GALLIOT
GALLIPOT
GALLISH
GALLIUM
GALLIVANT
GALLIVANTER
GALLIVAT
GALLIVOROUS
GALLIWASP
GALLIZE
GALLNUT
GALLOFLAVIN
GALLOFLAVINE
GALLOGLASS
GALLON
GALLONAGE
GALLOON
GALLOONED
GALLOOT
GALLOP
GALLOPADE
GALLOPED
GALLOPER
GALLOPING
GALLOPTIOUS
GALLOTANNATE
GALLOTANNIN
GALLOUS
GALLOW
GALLOWAY
GALLOWGLASS
GALLOWS
GALLOWSNESS
GALLSTONE
GALLUSES
GALLWEED
GALLWORT
GALLY
GALLYBAGGER
GALLYBEGGAR
GALLYCROW
GALLYGASKINS
GALLYWASP
GALON
GALOOT
GALOP
GALOPADE
GALOPED
GALOPIN
GALOPING
GALORE
GALOSH
GALOSHE
GALOUBET
GALP
GALRAVAGE
GALRAVITCH

GALT
GALTRAP
GALUCHAT
GALUMPH
GALUMPTIOUS
GALUT
GALUTH
GALVANIC
GALVANICAL
GALVANICALLY
GALVANISE
GALVANISM
GALVANIST
GALVANIZATION
GALVANIZE
GALVANIZED
GALVANIZER
GALVANIZING
GALVANOGRAPH
GALVANOLOGY
GALVANOMETER
GALVANOMETRY
GALVANOSCOPE
GALVANOSCOPY
GALVANOTAXIS
GALVAYNE
GALVAYNED
GALVAYNING
GALYAC
GALYAK
GAM
GAMAHE
GAMARI
GAMASHES
GAMB
GAMBA
GAMBADE
GAMBADO
GAMBANG
GAMBE
GAMBEER
GAMBEERED
GAMBEERING
GAMBESON
GAMBET
GAMBETTE
GAMBIAE
GAMBIER
GAMBIR
GAMBIST
GAMBIT
GAMBLE
GAMBLED
GAMBLER
GAMBLERS
GAMBLING
GAMBO
GAMBOGE
GAMBOGIAN
GAMBOISED
GAMBOL
GAMBOLED
GAMBOLING
GAMBOLLED
GAMBOLLING
GAMBONE
GAMBREL
GAMBRELED
GAMBRELLED
GAMBROON
GAMDEBOO
GAME
GAMEBAG
GAMEBALL
GAMECOCK
GAMECRAFT
GAMED
GAMEFUL
GAMEKEEPER
GAMEKEEPING
GAMELAN
GAMELANG
GAMELIN
GAMELOTE
GAMELOTTE
GAMELY
GAMENE
GAMENESS
GAMER
GAMES
GAMESOME
GAMESOMELY
GAMESOMENESS
GAMEST
GAMESTER
GAMETAL
GAMETANGIUM
GAMETE
GAMETIC
GAMETICALLY
GAMETOCYST
GAMETOCYTE
GAMETOGENIC
GAMETOGENOUS
GAMETOGENY
GAMETOGONIUM
GAMETOID
GAMETOPHORE
GAMETOPHYLL
GAMETOPHYTE
GAMEY
GAMIC
GAMIE
GAMIER
GAMIEST
GAMILY
GAMIN
GAMINE
GAMINESS
GAMING
GAMLA
GAMMA
GAMMACISM
GAMMADION
GAMMARID
GAMMAROID
GAMMATION
GAMME
GAMMELOST
GAMMER
GAMMERSTANG
GAMMICK
GAMMOCK
GAMMON
GAMMONER
GAMMONING
GAMMY
GAMOBIUM
GAMODEME
GAMODESMIC
GAMODESMY
GAMOGAMY
GAMOGENESIS
GAMOGENETIC
GAMOGENY
GAMOND
GAMONT
GAMOPETALOUS
GAMOPHAGIA
GAMOPHYLLOUS
GAMORI
GAMOSEPALOUS
GAMOSTELE
GAMOSTELIC
GAMOSTELY
GAMP
GAMPHREL
GAMUT
GAMY
GAN
GANAM
GANANCIAL
GANANCIALES
GANANCIAS
GANCH
GANCHED
GANCHING
GANDER
GANDERESS
GANDERGOOSE
GANDERMOONER
GANDERTEETH
GANDI
GANDOURA
GANDUL
GANDUM
GANDURAH
GANE
GANEF
GANG
GANGA
GANGAVA
GANGBOARD
GANGE
GANGED
GANGER
GANGEREL
GANGFLOWER
GANGGANG
GANGING
GANGION
GANGLAND
GANGLANDER
GANGLIA
GANGLIAC
GANGLIAL
GANGLIAR
GANGLIATE
GANGLIATED
GANGLIFORM
GANGLING
GANGLIOBLAST
GANGLIOCYTE
GANGLIOFORM
GANGLIOMA
GANGLIOMAS
GANGLIOMATA
GANGLION
GANGLIONARY
GANGLIONATE
GANGLIONATED
GANGLIONIC
GANGLIONITIS
GANGLIONS
GANGLY
GANGMAN
GANGMASTER
GANGPLANK
GANGPLOW
GANGREL
GANGRENATE
GANGRENE
GANGRENED
GANGRENING
GANGRENOUS
GANGSA
GANGSMAN
GANGSTER
GANGSTERISM
GANGTIDE
GANGUE
GANGWA
GANGWAY
GANGWAYMAN
GANGWAYMEN
GANISTER
GANJA
GANNER
GANNET
GANNETRY
GANNETS
GANOF
GANOID
GANOIDAL
GANOIDEAN
GANOIDIAN
GANOIN
GANOMALITE
GANOPHYLLITE
GANOSIS
GANSEL
GANSEY
GANSH
GANSY
GANT
GANTA
GANTANG
GANTANGS
GANTLET
GANTLETED
GANTLETING
GANTLINE
GANTLOPE
GANTRIES
GANTRY
GANTRYMAN
GANYIE
GANZA
GANZIE
GAOL
GAOLAGE
GAOLBIRD
GAOLER
GAOLERING
GAOLERNESS
GAOLORING
GAP
GAPE
GAPED
GAPER
GAPES
GAPESEED
GAPEWORM
GAPING
GAPINGSTOCK
GAPO
GAPPED
GAPPER
GAPPIER
GAPPIEST
GAPPING
GAPPY
GAPS
GAPY
GAR
GARABATO
GARAD
GARAGE
GARAGED
GARAGEMAN
GARAGING
GARANCE
GARANCIN
GARAPATA
GARAPATO
GARAU
GARAVA
GARAVANCE
GARAWI
GARB
GARBAGE
GARBANZO
GARBILL
GARBLE
GARBLED
GARBLER
GARBLING
GARBLINGS
GARBOARD
GARBOIL
GARBURE
GARCE
GARCON
GARD
GARDANT
GARDE
GARDEBRAS
GARDEEN
GARDEN
GARDENED
GARDENER
GARDENIN
GARDENING
GARDENIZE
GARDENS
GARDENY
GARDEROBE
GARDEVIANCE
GARDEVIN
GARDEVISURE
GARDINOL
GARDNAP
GARDON
GARDY
GARDYLOO
GARE
GAREFOWL
GAREH
GARETTA
GAREWAITE
GARFISH
GARFISHES
GARGANEY
GARGET
GARGETY
GARGIL
GARGLE
GARGLED
GARGLING
GARGOYLE
GARGOYLEY
GARIAL
GARIBA
GARIBALDI
GARIGUE
GARISH
GARISHLY
GARISHNESS
GARLAND
GARLANDAGE
GARLANDED
GARLANDING
GARLANDRY
GARLE
GARLIC
GARLICKY
GARLION
GARLOPA
GARMENT
GARMENTED
GARMENTING
GARMENTMAKER
GARMENTS
GARMENTURE
GARN

GARNEL
GARNER
GARNERED
GARNERING
GARNET
GARNETBERRY
GARNETER
GARNETT
GARNETWORK
GARNETZ
GARNI
GARNIEC
GARNIERITE
GARNISH
GARNISHED
GARNISHEE
GARNISHEED
GARNISHEEING
GARNISHER
GARNISHING
GARNISHMENT
GARNISHRY
GARNITURE
GAROO
GAROOKUH
GAROTE
GAROTTE
GAROTTED
GAROTTER
GARPIKE
GARR
GARRAFA
GARRAN
GARRAT
GARRE
GARRETEER
GARRICK
GARRIDGE
GARRIGUE
GARRISON
GARRON
GARROO
GARROT
GARROTE
GARROTED
GARROTER
GARROTING
GARROTTE
GARROTTING
GARRULINE
GARRULITY
GARRULOUS
GARRULOUSLY
GARRUPA
GARSE
GARSIL
GARSTON
GARTEN
GARTER
GARTERED
GARTERING
GARTERS
GARTH
GARTHMAN
GARUM
GARVANCE
GARVANZO
GARVEY
GARVIE
GARVOCK
GAS
GASALIER
GASBAG
GASBOAT
GASCHECK
GASCON
GASCONADE
GASCONADED
GASCONADER
GASCONADING
GASCONISM
GASEITY
GASELIER
GASEOSITY
GASEOUS
GASEOUSNESS
GASH
GASHED
GASHES
GASHFUL
GASHING
GASHLINESS
GASHLY
GASHOLDER
GASHOUSE
GASHY
GASIFIABLE
GASIFICATION
GASIFIED
GASIFIER
GASIFORM
GASIFY
GASIFYING
GASKET
GASKIN
GASKING
GASKINS
GASLIGHT
GASLIGHTED
GASLIGHTING
GASLIT
GASLOCK
GASMAN
GASMEN
GASOGEN
GASOGENE
GASOLIER
GASOLIERY
GASOLINE
GASOLINER
GASOMETER
GASOMETRIC
GASOMETRICAL
GASOMETRY
GASP
GASPARILLO
GASPER
GASPEREAU
GASPERGOU
GASPING
GASPY
GASSER
GASSES
GASSING
GASSY
GAST
GASTALDITE
GASTALDO
GASTER
GASTERALGIA
GASTERIA
GASTEROPOD
GASTEROSTEID
GASTEROTHECA
GASTEROZOOID
GASTFUL
GASTIGHT
GASTIGHTNESS
GASTNESS
GASTRAEA
GASTRAEAL
GASTRAEUM
GASTRAL
GASTRALGIA
GASTRALGIC
GASTRECTOMY
GASTRELCOSIS
GASTRIC
GASTRICISM
GASTRIMARGY
GASTRIN
GASTRITIC
GASTRITIS
GASTROATONIA
GASTROCELE
GASTROCOEL
GASTROCOELE
GASTROCOLIC
GASTROCYSTIS
GASTRODISK
GASTRODYNIA
GASTROGRAPH
GASTROID
GASTROLATER
GASTROLIENAL
GASTROLITH
GASTROLOGER
GASTROLOGIST
GASTROLOGY
GASTROLYSIS
GASTROMANCY
GASTROMELUS
GASTROMENIA
GASTROMYCES
GASTRONOME
GASTRONOMER
GASTRONOMIC
GASTRONOMIST
GASTRONOMY
GASTRONOSUS
GASTROPEXY
GASTROPHILE
GASTROPLASTY
GASTROPOD
GASTROPODAN
GASTROPORE
GASTROPTOSIS
GASTRORRHEA
GASTROSCOPE
GASTROSCOPIC
GASTROSCOPY
GASTROSOPH
GASTROSOPHER
GASTROSOPHY
GASTROSPASM
GASTROSTEGAL
GASTROSTEGE
GASTROSTOMY
GASTROTAXIS
GASTROTHECA
GASTROTHECAL
GASTROTOME
GASTROTOMIC
GASTROTOMY
GASTROXYNSIS
GASTROZOOID
GASTRULA
GASTRULATE
GASTRULATION
GASWORKER
GASWORKS
GAT
GATA
GATCH
GATCHWORK
GATE
GATEADO
GATEAGE
GATEAU
GATED
GATEFOLD
GATEHOUSE
GATEKEEPER
GATEMAKER
GATEMAN
GATEPOST
GATER
GATES
GATETENDER
GATEWARD
GATEWAY
GATEWAYMAN
GATEWAYMEN
GATEWOMAN
GATEWORKS
GATEWRIGHT
GATHER
GATHERED
GATHERER
GATHERING
GATHERUM
GATING
GATO
GATOR
GATTER
GATTINE
GAU
GAUB
GAUCHE
GAUCHELY
GAUCHENESS
GAUCHERIE
GAUCIE
GAUCY
GAUD
GAUDEAMUS
GAUDERY
GAUDFUL
GAUDIER
GAUDIES
GAUDIEST
GAUDILY
GAUDINESS
GAUDISH
GAUDSMAN
GAUDY
GAUE
GAUFFER
GAUFFERED
GAUFFERER
GAUFFERING
GAUFFRE
GAUFFRED
GAUFRE
GAUFRETTE
GAUFRETTES
GAUG
GAUGE
GAUGEABLE
GAUGED
GAUGER
GAUGING
GAULDING
GAULE
GAULIN
GAULOISERIE
GAULSH
GAULT
GAULTER
GAULTHERASE
GAULTHERIA
GAULTHERIN
GAULTHERINE
GAUM
GAUMISH
GAUMLESS
GAUMLIKE
GAUMY
GAUN
GAUNCH
GAUNT
GAUNTED
GAUNTER
GAUNTEST
GAUNTLET
GAUNTLETED
GAUNTLY
GAUNTNESS
GAUNTRY
GAUNTY
GAUP
GAUPUS
GAUR
GAURIC
GAURIE
GAUS
GAUSS
GAUSSAGE
GAUSSBERGITE
GAUSTER
GAUSTERER
GAUT
GAUTEITE
GAUZE
GAUZELIKE
GAUZEWING
GAUZIER
GAUZIEST
GAUZILY
GAUZINESS
GAUZY
GAV
GAVAGE
GAVALL
GAVE
GAVEL
GAVELAGE
GAVELER
GAVELKIND
GAVELKINDER
GAVELLER
GAVELMAN
GAVELMEN
GAVELOCK
GAVIAL
GAVIALOID
GAVOT
GAVOTTE
GAVYUTI
GAW
GAWCEY
GAWD
GAWISH
GAWK
GAWKHAMMER
GAWKIER
GAWKIEST
GAWKILY
GAWKINESS
GAWKISH
GAWKY
GAWN
GAWNEY
GAWP
GAWSIE
GAWSY
GAY
GAYAL
GAYALS
GAYATRI
GAYBINE
GAYCAT
GAYDIANG
GAYER
GAYEST

GAYETY
GAYLIES
GAYLUSSITE
GAYLY
GAYMENT
GAYNESS
GAYSOME
GAYWAY
GAYWINGS
GAYYOU
GAZ
GAZABO
GAZABOES
GAZABOS
GAZANGABIN
GAZE
GAZEBO
GAZEBOES
GAZEBOS
GAZED
GAZEHOUND
GAZEL
GAZELESS
GAZELLE
GAZELLES
GAZEMENT
GAZER
GAZET
GAZETTAL
GAZETTE
GAZETTED
GAZETTEER
GAZETTEERAGE
GAZETTING
GAZI
GAZING
GAZINGLY
GAZINGSTOCK
GAZOGENE
GAZON
GAZOO
GAZOOK
GAZOZ
GAZPACHO
GAZY
GAZZETTA
GBO
GEAL
GEAN
GEANTICLINAL
GEANTICLINE
GEAR
GEARBOX
GEARCASE
GEARE
GEARED
GEARING
GEARKSUTITE
GEARLESS
GEARMAN
GEARS
GEARSET
GEARSHIFT
GEARWHEEL
GEASON
GEAST
GEBANG
GEBANGA
GEBBIE
GEBUR
GECK
GECKO
GECKOES
GECKOS
GED
GEDACT
GEDANITE
GEDD
GEDDA
GEDDER
GEDECKT
GEDECKTWORK
GEDRITE
GEDUNK
GEE
GEEBUNG
GEED
GEEING
GEEK
GEELBEC
GEELBECK
GEELBEK
GEELHOUT
GEEPOUND
GEERAH
GEES
GEESE
GEEST
GEET
GEEZER
GEFULLTEFISH
GEG
GEGENION
GEGENSCHEIN
GEGG
GEGGEE
GEGGER
GEGGERY
GEHLENITE
GEIG
GEIGE
GEIGER
GEIKIELITE
GEIN
GEIR
GEIRA
GEISHA
GEISHAS
GEISON
GEISOTHERM
GEISOTHERMAL
GEISTLICH
GEITJIE
GEITONOGAMY
GEKKONID
GEKKONOID
GEL
GELABLE
GELADA
GELANDESPRUNG
GELASTIC
GELATE
GELATIA
GELATIN
GELATINATE
GELATINATED
GELATINATING
GELATINATION
GELATINE
GELATINED
GELATINITY
GELATINIZE
GELATINIZED
GELATINIZER
GELATINIZING
GELATINOID
GELATINOTYPE
GELATINOUS
GELATINOUSLY
GELATION
GELATOSE
GELD
GELDANT
GELDED
GELDER
GELDING
GELEE
GELEEM
GELID
GELIDITY
GELIDLY
GELIDNESS
GELIGNITE
GELILAH
GELINOTTE
GELL
GELLED
GELLING
GELLY
GELOFER
GELOFRE
GELOGENIC
GELONG
GELOSCOPY
GELOSE
GELOSIN
GELOSINE
GELOTHERAPY
GELOTOSCOPY
GELSEMIN
GELSEMINE
GELSEMININE
GELSEMIUM
GELT
GEM
GEMATRIA
GEMATRICAL
GEMATRIOT
GEMAUVE
GEMEINDE
GEMEL
GEMELED
GEMELLED
GEMELLION
GEMELLUS
GEMELS
GEMINATE
GEMINATED
GEMINATELY
GEMINATING
GEMINATION
GEMINATIVE
GEMINIFORM
GEMINOUS
GEMLIKE
GEMMA
GEMMACEOUS
GEMMAE
GEMMAN
GEMMARY
GEMMATE
GEMMATED
GEMMATING
GEMMATION
GEMMATIVE
GEMMED
GEMMEL
GEMMEOUS
GEMMER
GEMMIFEROUS
GEMMIFORM
GEMMILY
GEMMINESS
GEMMING
GEMMIPARA
GEMMIPARES
GEMMIPARITY
GEMMIPAROUS
GEMMOID
GEMMOLOGY
GEMMULA
GEMMULATION
GEMMULE
GEMMY
GEMOLOGY
GEMOT
GEMOTE
GEMSBOK
GEMSBUCK
GEMSHORN
GEMSTONE
GEMUL
GEMUTLICH
GEMWORK
GEN
GENA
GENAE
GENAL
GENAPP
GENAPPE
GENAPPER
GENARCH
GENARCHA
GENDARME
GENDARMERIE
GENDARMERY
GENDERED
GENDERER
GENDERING
GENDERLESS
GENE
GENEAL
GENEALOGIC
GENEALOGICAL
GENEALOGIES
GENEALOGIST
GENEALOGIZE
GENEALOGIZER
GENEALOGY
GENEAT
GENEKI
GENEPI
GENER
GENERA
GENERABILITY
GENERABLE
GENERAL
GENERALATE
GENERALCIES
GENERALCY
GENERALE
GENERALIA
GENERALIFIC
GENERALISM
GENERALIST
GENERALISTIC
GENERALITER
GENERALITY
GENERALIZABLE
GENERALIZATION
GENERALIZE
GENERALIZED
GENERALIZER
GENERALL
GENERALLY
GENERALNESS
GENERALSHIP
GENERALTY
GENERANT
GENERATE
GENERATED
GENERATING
GENERATION
GENERATIONAL
GENERATIVE
GENERATOR
GENERATRICES
GENERATRIX
GENERIC
GENERICAL
GENERICALLY
GENEROSITIES
GENEROSITY
GENEROUS
GENEROUSLY
GENEROUSNESS
GENESERIN
GENESERINE
GENESES
GENESIAL
GENESIC
GENESIOLOGY
GENESIS
GENESIURGIC
GENET
GENETHLIAC
GENETHLIC
GENETIC
GENETICAL
GENETICALLY
GENETICISM
GENETICIST
GENETICS
GENETOR
GENETOUS
GENETRIX
GENETTE
GENEVOISE
GENIAL
GENIALITY
GENIALIZE
GENIALLY
GENIC
GENICULATE
GENICULATED
GENICULATELY
GENICULUM
GENIE
GENII
GENIN
GENIO
GENIOGLOSSAL
GENIOGLOSSUS
GENIOHYOID
GENIOLATRY
GENION
GENIOPLASTY
GENIP
GENIPAP
GENIPAPADA
GENISARO
GENISTEIN
GENISTIN
GENITAL
GENITALIA
GENITALS
GENITIVAL
GENITIVALLY
GENITIVE
GENITOCRURAL
GENITOR
GENITORIAL
GENITORY
GENITURE
GENIUS
GENIUSES
GENIZAH
GENOBLAST
GENOBLASTIC
GENOCIDE
GENOME
GENOS
GENOTYPE
GENOTYPIC
GENOTYPICAL

GENOUILLERE
GENOVINO
GENRE
GENRO
GENROS
GENS
GENSON
GENT
GENTE
GENTEEL
GENTEELISM
GENTEELLY
GENTEELNESS
GENTES
GENTHITE
GENTIAN
GENTIANELLA
GENTIANOSE
GENTIANWORT
GENTIL
GENTILE
GENTILES
GENTILESSE
GENTILIC
GENTILISH
GENTILISM
GENTILITIAL
GENTILITIAN
GENTILITIES
GENTILITIOUS
GENTILITY
GENTILIZE
GENTIOBIOSE
GENTIOPICRIN
GENTISEIN
GENTISIN
GENTLE
GENTLED
GENTLEFOLK
GENTLEFOLKS
GENTLEHOOD
GENTLEMAN
GENTLEMANLY
GENTLEMEN
GENTLENESS
GENTLER
GENTLESHIP
GENTLEST
GENTLEWOMAN
GENTLEWOMEN
GENTLING
GENTLY
GENTMAN
GENTRICE
GENTRY
GENTY
GENU
GENUA
GENUAL
GENUCLAST
GENUFLECT
GENUFLECTED
GENUFLECTING
GENUFLECTION
GENUFLECTOR
GENUFLECTORY
GENUFLEXION
GENUFLEXUOUS
GENUINE
GENUINELY
GENUINENESS
GENUS
GENUSES
GEO
GEOBIOLOGIC
GEOBIOLOGY
GEOBIONT
GEOBIOS
GEOBLAST
GEOBOTANY
GEOCARPIC
GEOCENTRIC
GEOCENTRICAL
GEOCERITE
GEOCHEMICAL
GEOCHEMIST
GEOCHEMISTRY
GEOCHRONIC
GEOCHRONY
GEOCLINE
GEOCORONIUM
GEOCRATIC
GEOCRONITE
GEOCYCLIC
GEODAESIA
GEODE
GEODESIA
GEODESIC
GEODESICAL
GEODESIST
GEODESY
GEODETE
GEODETIC
GEODETICAL
GEODETICALLY
GEODETICS
GEODIC
GEODIFEROUS
GEODIST
GEODUCK
GEODYNAMIC
GEODYNAMICAL
GEODYNAMICS
GEOETHNIC
GEOFORM
GEOGEN
GEOGENESIS
GEOGENETIC
GEOGENIC
GEOGENOUS
GEOGENY
GEOGLYPHIC
GEOGNOSIS
GEOGNOSIST
GEOGNOST
GEOGNOSTIC
GEOGNOSTICAL
GEOGNOSY
GEOGONIC
GEOGONICAL
GEOGONY
GEOGRAPHER
GEOGRAPHIC
GEOGRAPHICAL
GEOGRAPHICS
GEOGRAPHIES
GEOGRAPHIZED
GEOGRAPHY
GEOHYDROLOGY
GEOID
GEOIDAL
GEOLATRY
GEOLOGER
GEOLOGIAN
GEOLOGIC
GEOLOGICAL
GEOLOGICALLY
GEOLOGIES
GEOLOGIST
GEOLOGIZE
GEOLOGIZED
GEOLOGIZING
GEOLOGY
GEOM
GEOMAGNETIC
GEOMAGNETICS
GEOMAGNETISM
GEOMALIC
GEOMALISM
GEOMANCE
GEOMANCER
GEOMANCY
GEOMANT
GEOMANTIC
GEOMANTICAL
GEOMEDICINE
GEOMETER
GEOMETRIC
GEOMETRICAL
GEOMETRICIAN
GEOMETRICIZE
GEOMETRID
GEOMETRIES
GEOMETRIZE
GEOMETRIZED
GEOMETRIZING
GEOMETRY
GEOMOROI
GEOMORPHIC
GEOMORPHIST
GEOMORPHY
GEOMYID
GEONEGATIVE
GEOPHAGIA
GEOPHAGISM
GEOPHAGIST
GEOPHAGOUS
GEOPHAGY
GEOPHILID
GEOPHILOUS
GEOPHYSICAL
GEOPHYSICIST
GEOPHYSICS
GEOPHYTE
GEOPHYTIC
GEOPOLAR
GEOPOLITIC
GEOPOLITICAL
GEOPOLITICS
GEOPONIC
GEOPONICAL
GEOPONICS
GEOPONY
GEOPOSITIVE
GEORAMA
GEORG
GEORGIC
GEORGICAL
GEOSCOPIC
GEOSCOPY
GEOSELENIC
GEOSPHERE
GEOSTATIC
GEOSTATICS
GEOSTROPHIC
GEOSYNCLINAL
GEOSYNCLINE
GEOTACTIC
GEOTAXIS
GEOTAXY
GEOTECHNICS
GEOTECTOLOGY
GEOTECTONIC
GEOTHERM
GEOTHERMAL
GEOTHERMIC
GEOTONIC
GEOTONUS
GEOTROPIC
GEOTROPISM
GEOTROPY
GEPHYREAN
GER
GERA
GERAERA
GERAH
GERANIACEOUS
GERANIAL
GERANIOL
GERANIUM
GERANYL
GERARA
GERARDIA
GERASTIAN
GERATE
GERATED
GERATELY
GERATIC
GERATOLOGY
GERB
GERBE
GERBIL
GERBILLE
GERCROW
GERE
GEREAGLE
GEREFA
GERENDUM
GERENT
GERENUK
GERFALCON
GERFUL
GERHARDTITE
GERIATRIC
GERIATRICIAN
GERIATRICS
GERIATRIST
GERIP
GERKIN
GERM
GERMAL
GERMAN
GERMANDER
GERMANE
GERMANIC
GERMANITE
GERMANITY
GERMANIUM
GERMANIZE
GERMANOUS
GERMANYL
GERMARIUM
GERMEN
GERMENS
GERMFREE
GERMICIDAL
GERMICIDE
GERMIFUGE
GERMIN
GERMINABLE
GERMINAL
GERMINALLY
GERMINANCE
GERMINANCY
GERMINANT
GERMINATE
GERMINATED
GERMINATING
GERMINATION
GERMINATIVE
GERMINATOR
GERMING
GERMINOGONY
GERMIPARITY
GERMLING
GERMON
GERMPROOF
GERMS
GERMULE
GEROCOMIA
GEROCOMICAL
GEROCOMY
GERODERMA
GERODERMIA
GEROMORPHISM
GERONTAL
GERONTES
GERONTIC
GERONTINE
GERONTISM
GERONTOCRACY
GERONTOGEOUS
GERONTOLOGY
GERONTOXON
GEROUSIA
GERRYMANDER
GERS
GERSDORFFITE
GERSUM
GERTRUDE
GERUND
GERUNDIAL
GERUNDIALLY
GERUNDIVAL
GERUNDIVE
GERUNDIVELY
GERUSIA
GERVAO
GERY
GERYONID
GESITH
GESITHCUND
GESNERAD
GESSERON
GESSO
GEST
GESTALT
GESTALTEN
GESTALTER
GESTALTIST
GESTALTS
GESTANT
GESTATE
GESTATED
GESTATING
GESTATION
GESTATIONAL
GESTATIVE
GESTATORIAL
GESTATORIUM
GESTATORY
GESTE
GESTED
GESTEN
GESTENING
GESTER
GESTIC
GESTICAL
GESTICULANT
GESTICULAR
GESTICULATE
GESTICULATED
GESTICULATOR
GESTIO
GESTION
GESTNING
GESTONIE
GESTURAL
GESTURE
GESTURED
GESTURER
GESTURES
GESTURING
GESWARP
GET

GETA
GETAN
GETAS
GETAWAY
GETHSEMANE
GETLING
GETPENNY
GETT
GETTABLE
GETTER
GETTING
GETUP
GEULAH
GEVE
GEWGAW
GEWGAWED
GEWGAWISH
GEWGAWRY
GEY
GEYAN
GEYERITE
GEYLIES
GEYSER
GEYSERAL
GEYSERIC
GEYSERINE
GEYSERITE
GEYZE
GEZ
GEZERAH
GHAFFIR
GHAFIR
GHALVA
GHARIAL
GHARNAO
GHARRI
GHARRIES
GHARRY
GHAST
GHASTFUL
GHASTFULLY
GHASTFULNESS
GHASTILY
GHASTLIER
GHASTLIEST
GHASTLILY
GHASTLINESS
GHASTLY
GHAT
GHATS
GHATWAL
GHAUT
GHAWAZEE
GHAWAZI
GHAZAL
GHAZEL
GHAZI
GHAZIES
GHEBETA
GHEE
GHELD
GHENTING
GHERKIN
GHETCHOO
GHETTO
GHI
GHILLIE
GHIZITE
GHOL
GHOOM
GHOR
GHORKHAR
GHOST
GHOSTCRAFT
GHOSTDOM
GHOSTED
GHOSTER
GHOSTFISH
GHOSTFLOWER
GHOSTIFIED
GHOSTILY
GHOSTING
GHOSTISM
GHOSTLAND
GHOSTLIER
GHOSTLIEST
GHOSTLIFY
GHOSTLIKE
GHOSTLY
GHOSTMONGER
GHOSTOLOGY
GHOSTS
GHOSTSHIP
GHOSTWEED
GHOSTWRITE
GHOSTWRITER
GHOSTWRITING
GHOSTWRITTEN
GHOSTWROTE
GHOSTY
GHOUL
GHOULIE
GHOULISH
GHOULISHLY
GHOULISHNESS
GHURRY
GHYLL
GI
GIALLOLINO
GIANSAR
GIANT
GIANTESS
GIANTISM
GIANTIZE
GIANTKIND
GIANTLY
GIANTRY
GIANTS
GIAOUR
GIARDIASIS
GIB
GIBARO
GIBBALS
GIBBAR
GIBBARTAS
GIBBED
GIBBER
GIBBERED
GIBBERELLIN
GIBBERGUNYAH
GIBBERING
GIBBERISH
GIBBEROSE
GIBBEROSITY
GIBBERT
GIBBET
GIBBETED
GIBBETING
GIBBLEGABLE
GIBBLES
GIBBOL
GIBBON
GIBBOSE
GIBBOSITIES
GIBBOSITY
GIBBOUS
GIBBOUSLY
GIBBOUSNESS
GIBBSITE
GIBBUS
GIBBY
GIBE
GIBED
GIBEL
GIBELITE
GIBER
GIBETTING
GIBING
GIBINGLY
GIBLEH
GIBLET
GIBLETS
GIBOIA
GIBSTAFF
GIBUS
GID
GIDDAP
GIDDIED
GIDDIER
GIDDIEST
GIDDIFY
GIDDILY
GIDDINESS
GIDDY
GIDDYBERRY
GIDDYBRAIN
GIDDYHEAD
GIDDYING
GIDE
GIDGEA
GIDGEE
GIDIA
GIDJEE
GIDYA
GIDYEA
GIE
GIER
GIESECKITE
GIF
GIFBLAAR
GIFFGAFF
GIFT
GIFTBOOK
GIFTED
GIFTEDLY
GIFTEDNESS
GIFTIE
GIFTING
GIFTS
GIFTURE
GIFTWARE
GIG
GIGA
GIGACYCLE
GIGANT
GIGANTAL
GIGANTEAN
GIGANTESQUE
GIGANTIC
GIGANTICAL
GIGANTICALLY
GIGANTICIDAL
GIGANTICIDE
GIGANTICNESS
GIGANTISM
GIGANTIZE
GIGANTOBLAST
GIGANTOCYTE
GIGANTOLITE
GIGANTOLOGY
GIGATON
GIGBACK
GIGELIRA
GIGERIUM
GIGGE
GIGGED
GIGGER
GIGGING
GIGGISH
GIGGIT
GIGGLE
GIGGLED
GIGGLER
GIGGLIER
GIGGLIEST
GIGGLING
GIGGLY
GIGLET
GIGLIATO
GIGLIO
GIGLOT
GIGMAN
GIGMANESS
GIGMANHOOD
GIGMANIA
GIGMANIC
GIGMANICALLY
GIGMANISM
GIGMANITY
GIGNATE
GIGNITIVE
GIGOLO
GIGOT
GIGSMAN
GIGSMEN
GIGSTER
GIGTREE
GIGUE
GIGUNU
GIKE
GIL
GILBERT
GILBERTAGE
GILBERTITE
GILD
GILDABLE
GILDED
GILDEN
GILDER
GILDING
GILDSHIP
GILDSMAN
GILENYER
GILENYIE
GILET
GILGAI
GILGAMES
GILGAMESH
GILGUL
GILGUY
GILIAK
GILL
GILLAR
GILLAROO
GILLED
GILLER
GILLFLIRT
GILLHOOTER
GILLIE
GILLIED
GILLIES
GILLING
GILLIVER
GILLNET
GILLOT
GILLOTAGE
GILLOTYPE
GILLS
GILLSTOUP
GILLY
GILLYFLOWER
GILLYGAUPUS
GILLYING
GILO
GILOE
GILP
GILPEY
GILPY
GILRAVAGE
GILRAVAGER
GILSONITE
GILT
GILTCUP
GILTEN
GILTHEAD
GILTTAIL
GILVER
GIM
GIMBAL
GIMBALED
GIMBALJAWED
GIMBALS
GIMBERJAWED
GIMBLE
GIMBRI
GIMCRACK
GIMCRACKERY
GIMCRACKY
GIME
GIMEL
GIMLET
GIMLETEYED
GIMLETY
GIMMAL
GIMMALED
GIMME
GIMMER
GIMMERINGLY
GIMMICK
GIMMICKRY
GIMMICKY
GIMMOR
GIMP
GIMPER
GIMPIER
GIMPIEST
GIMPING
GIMPY
GIN
GINEP
GINETE
GING
GINGAL
GINGALL
GINGE
GINGELEY
GINGELI
GINGELLY
GINGELY
GINGER
GINGERADE
GINGERBERRY
GINGERBREAD
GINGERBREADY
GINGERIN
GINGERLEAF
GINGERLINE
GINGERLY
GINGERNUT
GINGEROL
GINGEROUS
GINGERROOT
GINGERSNAP
GINGERSPICE
GINGERWORK
GINGERWORT
GINGERY
GINGHAM
GINGHAMED
GINGILI
GINGIVA
GINGIVAL
GINGIVALGIA
GINGIVECTOMY
GINGIVITIS

GINGKO
GINGLYFORM
GINGLYMOID
GINGLYMUS
GINGRAS
GINHOUSE
GINK
GINNED
GINNEL
GINNER
GINNERIES
GINNERS
GINNERY
GINNING
GINNLE
GINNY
GINORITE
GINSENG
GIO
GIOCOSO
GIOJOSO
GIORNATA
GIP
GIPON
GIPPED
GIPPER
GIPPING
GIPPO
GIPSEIAN
GIPSER
GIPSIES
GIPSIOLOGIST
GIPSIRE
GIPSOLOGY
GIPSY
GIPSYDOM
GIPSYFY
GIPSYHEAD
GIPSYRY
GIPSYWEED
GIPSYWORT
GIR
GIRAFFE
GIRAFFES
GIRAFFINE
GIRAFFOID
GIRANDOLE
GIRASOL
GIRASOLE
GIRBA
GIRD
GIRDED
GIRDER
GIRDERAGE
GIRDING
GIRDLE
GIRDLECAKE
GIRDLED
GIRDLER
GIRDLESTEAD
GIRDLING
GIRDLINGLY
GIREH
GIRG
GIRL
GIRLEEN
GIRLERY
GIRLFULLY
GIRLHOOD
GIRLIE
GIRLING
GIRLISH
GIRLISHLY
GIRLISHNESS
GIRLY
GIRN
GIRNAL

GIRNEL
GIRNIE
GIRNY
GIRO
GIRON
GIROSOL
GIROUETTE
GIROUETTISM
GIRR
GIRRIT
GIRSE
GIRSH
GIRT
GIRTED
GIRTH
GIRTING
GIRTLINE
GISANT
GISARME
GISE
GISH
GISLER
GISMO
GISMONDITE
GISMOS
GISPIN
GIST
GISTS
GIT
GITALIGENIN
GITALIN
GITANA
GITANEMUK
GITANO
GITANOS
GITE
GITERNE
GITH
GITONIN
GITOXIGENIN
GITOXIN
GITTER
GITTERN
GITTITH
GIULIO
GIUSTAMENTE
GIUSTINA
GIUSTO
GIVE
GIVEAWAY
GIVEN
GIVER
GIVEY
GIVING
GIZMO
GIZZ
GIZZARD
GIZZEN
GIZZENED
GIZZERN
GJEDOST
GJOLL
GLABELLA
GLABELLAE
GLABELLAR
GLABELLOUS
GLABRATE
GLABRESCENT
GLABROUS
GLACE
GLACIABLE
GLACIAL
GLACIALISM
GLACIALIST
GLACIALLY
GLACIARIUM
GLACIATE

GLACIATION
GLACIER
GLACIERED
GLACIERET
GLACIERIST
GLACIOLOGIC
GLACIOLOGIST
GLACIOLOGY
GLACIOMARINE
GLACIOMETER
GLACIONATANT
GLACIS
GLACK
GLACON
GLAD
GLADDED
GLADDEN
GLADDENED
GLADDENER
GLADDENING
GLADDER
GLADDEST
GLADDING
GLADDON
GLADDY
GLADE
GLADEN
GLADES
GLADEYE
GLADFUL
GLADFULLY
GLADFULNESS
GLADHEARTED
GLADIATE
GLADIATOR
GLADIATORIAL
GLADIFY
GLADIOLA
GLADIOLAR
GLADIOLI
GLADIOLUS
GLADIOLUSES
GLADITE
GLADIUS
GLADKAITE
GLADLESS
GLADLY
GLADNESS
GLADSHIP
GLADSOME
GLADSOMELY
GLADSOMENESS
GLADY
GLAGA
GLAGAH
GLAIEUL
GLAIK
GLAIKET
GLAIKETNESS
GLAIKIT
GLAIKITNESS
GLAIKS
GLAIR
GLAIRED
GLAIREOUS
GLAIRIER
GLAIRIEST
GLAIRINESS
GLAIRING
GLAIRY
GLAISTER
GLAISTIG
GLAIVE
GLAIZIE
GLAKED
GLAKY
GLAM

GLAMBERRY
GLAME
GLAMOR
GLAMORIZE
GLAMORIZED
GLAMORIZING
GLAMOROUS
GLAMOROUSLY
GLAMOUR
GLAMOURED
GLAMOURIE
GLAMOURING
GLAMOUROUS
GLAMOUROUS
GLAMOUROUSLY
GLAMOURY
GLAMP
GLANCE
GLANCED
GLANCER
GLANCING
GLANCINGLY
GLAND
GLANDACEOUS
GLANDERED
GLANDEROUS
GLANDERS
GLANDES
GLANDIFEROUS
GLANDIFORM
GLANDULA
GLANDULAR
GLANDULE
GLANDULOSE
GLANDULOUS
GLANIS
GLANS
GLAR
GLARE
GLAREOLE
GLAREOUS
GLAREWORM
GLARIER
GLARIEST
GLARILY
GLARINESS
GLARING
GLARINGLY
GLARINGNESS
GLARRY
GLARY
GLASHAN
GLASS
GLASSBLOWER
GLASSBLOWING
GLASSED
GLASSEN
GLASSER
GLASSES
GLASSEYE
GLASSFUL
GLASSHOUSE
GLASSIE
GLASSIER
GLASSIEST
GLASSILY
GLASSIN
GLASSINE
GLASSINESS
GLASSING
GLASSMAKER
GLASSMAKING
GLASSMAN
GLASSMEN
GLASSTEEL
GLASSWARE
GLASSWEED

GLASSWORK
GLASSWORKER
GLASSWORKERS
GLASSWORKING
GLASSWORKS
GLASSWORM
GLASSWORT
GLASSY
GLAUBERITE
GLAUCESCENCE
GLAUCESCENT
GLAUCINE
GLAUCODOT
GLAUCOLITE
GLAUCOMA
GLAUCOMATOUS
GLAUCONITE
GLAUCONITIC
GLAUCOPHANE
GLAUCOUS
GLAUM
GLAUMRIE
GLAUR
GLAVE
GLAVER
GLAVERED
GLAVERING
GLAZE
GLAZED
GLAZEN
GLAZER
GLAZEWORK
GLAZIER
GLAZIERS
GLAZIERY
GLAZIEST
GLAZILY
GLAZINESS
GLAZING
GLAZY
GLEAD
GLEAM
GLEAMED
GLEAMIER
GLEAMIEST
GLEAMILY
GLEAMINESS
GLEAMING
GLEAMY
GLEAN
GLEANER
GLEANING
GLEARY
GLEAVE
GLEBA
GLEBE
GLEBOUS
GLEBY
GLED
GLEDE
GLEDGE
GLEDY
GLEE
GLEED
GLEEDS
GLEEFUL
GLEEFULLY
GLEEFULNESS
GLEEK
GLEEMAIDEN
GLEEMAN
GLEEMEN
GLEEN
GLEESOME
GLEESOMELY
GLEESOMENESS
GLEET

GLEETY
GLEG
GLEGLY
GLEGNESS
GLEIT
GLEN
GLENE
GLENOHUMERAL
GLENOID
GLENOIDAL
GLENT
GLESSITE
GLET
GLETTY
GLEW
GLEY
GLEYD
GLEYDE
GLIA
GLIADIN
GLIAL
GLIB
GLIBBER
GLIBBERY
GLIBBEST
GLIBLY
GLIBNESS
GLIDDER
GLIDDERY
GLIDE
GLIDED
GLIDELESS
GLIDENESS
GLIDER
GLIDERPORT
GLIDEWORT
GLIDING
GLIDINGLY
GLIFF
GLIFFING
GLIFFY
GLIM
GLIMA
GLIME
GLIMMER
GLIMMERED
GLIMMERING
GLIMMERITE
GLIMMEROUS
GLIMMERS
GLIMMERY
GLIMPSE
GLIMPSED
GLIMPSER
GLIMPSING
GLIMS
GLIN
GLINK
GLINSE
GLINT
GLINTED
GLINTING
GLIOCYTE
GLIOMA
GLIOMAS
GLIOMATA
GLIOMATOUS
GLIOSA
GLIOSIS
GLIRIFORM
GLIRINE
GLISK
GLISKY
GLISS
GLISSADE
GLISSADED
GLISSADER
GLISSADING
GLISSANDO
GLISSETTE
GLIST
GLISTEN
GLISTENED
GLISTENING
GLISTER
GLISTERED
GLISTERING
GLIT
GLITTER
GLITTERANCE
GLITTERED
GLITTERING
GLITTERINGLY
GLITTERY
GLOAM
GLOAMING
GLOAT
GLOATED
GLOATER
GLOATING
GLOATINGLY
GLOB
GLOBAL
GLOBALLY
GLOBATE
GLOBATED
GLOBE
GLOBED
GLOBEFISH
GLOBEFLOWER
GLOBEHOLDER
GLOBETROTTER
GLOBICAL
GLOBIFEROUS
GLOBIGERINA
GLOBIN
GLOBING
GLOBOID
GLOBOSE
GLOBOSELY
GLOBOSENESS
GLOBOSITE
GLOBOSITY
GLOBOUS
GLOBOUSLY
GLOBOUSNESS
GLOBULAR
GLOBULARITY
GLOBULARLY
GLOBULARNESS
GLOBULE
GLOBULET
GLOBULICIDE
GLOBULIN
GLOBULITE
GLOBULITIC
GLOBULOID
GLOBULOSE
GLOBULOUS
GLOBULYSIS
GLOBY
GLOCHID
GLOCHIDEOUS
GLOCHIDIAL
GLOCHIDIATE
GLOCHIDIUM
GLOCHIS
GLOCK
GLOCKENSPIEL
GLODE
GLOEA
GLOEAL
GLOEOCAPSOID
GLOFF
GLOGG
GLOM
GLOME
GLOMERA
GLOMERATE
GLOMERATION
GLOMERULAR
GLOMERULATE
GLOMERULE
GLOMERULOSE
GLOMERULUS
GLOMMOX
GLOMUS
GLONOIN
GLONOINE
GLOOM
GLOOMED
GLOOMFUL
GLOOMFULLY
GLOOMIER
GLOOMIEST
GLOOMILY
GLOOMINESS
GLOOMING
GLOOMINGLY
GLOOMS
GLOOMTH
GLOOMY
GLOP
GLOPNEN
GLOPPEN
GLOR
GLORE
GLORIATION
GLORIED
GLORIETTE
GLORIFICATION
GLORIFIED
GLORIFIER
GLORIFY
GLORIFYING
GLORIOLE
GLORIOSO
GLORIOUS
GLORIOUSLY
GLORIOUSNESS
GLORY
GLORYFUL
GLORYLESS
GLOSE
GLOSS
GLOSSA
GLOSSAGRA
GLOSSAL
GLOSSALGIA
GLOSSALGY
GLOSSARIAL
GLOSSARIALLY
GLOSSARIAN
GLOSSARIES
GLOSSARIST
GLOSSARY
GLOSSATE
GLOSSATOR
GLOSSATORIAL
GLOSSECTOMY
GLOSSED
GLOSSER
GLOSSIC
GLOSSIER
GLOSSIEST
GLOSSILY
GLOSSINESS
GLOSSING
GLOSSIST
GLOSSITIC
GLOSSITIS
GLOSSMETER
GLOSSOCELE
GLOSSOCOMA
GLOSSOCOMON
GLOSSODYNIA
GLOSSOGRAPH
GLOSSOGRAPHER
GLOSSOGRAPHY
GLOSSOHYAL
GLOSSOID
GLOSSOLABIAL
GLOSSOLALIA
GLOSSOLALIST
GLOSSOLALY
GLOSSOLOGIST
GLOSSOLOGY
GLOSSOPATHY
GLOSSOPETRA
GLOSSOPHYTIA
GLOSSOPLASTY
GLOSSOPLEGIA
GLOSSOPODIUM
GLOSSOPTOSIS
GLOSSOSCOPIA
GLOSSOSCOPY
GLOSSOSPASM
GLOSSOTOMY
GLOSSOTYPE
GLOSSY
GLOST
GLOTTAL
GLOTTALITE
GLOTTALIZE
GLOTTIC
GLOTTID
GLOTTIDEAN
GLOTTIDES
GLOTTIS
GLOTTISCOPE
GLOTTISES
GLOTTOGONIC
GLOTTOGONIST
GLOTTOGONY
GLOTTOLOGIC
GLOTTOLOGICAL
GLOTTOLOGIST
GLOTTOLOGY
GLOTUM
GLOUP
GLOUT
GLOVE
GLOVEMAKER
GLOVEMAKING
GLOVEMAN
GLOVER
GLOVERESS
GLOVING
GLOW
GLOWBIRD
GLOWED
GLOWER
GLOWERER
GLOWERING
GLOWERINGLY
GLOWFLIES
GLOWFLY
GLOWING
GLOWINGLY
GLOWWORM
GLOX
GLOY
GLOZE
GLOZED
GLOZER
GLOZING
GLUB
GLUCAEMIA
GLUCASE
GLUCEMIA
GLUCIDE
GLUCINA
GLUCINE
GLUCINIC
GLUCINIUM
GLUCINUM
GLUCK
GLUCKE
GLUCOKININ
GLUCOSAMIN
GLUCOSAMINE
GLUCOSAN
GLUCOSAZONE
GLUCOSE
GLUCOSIC
GLUCOSIDAL
GLUCOSIDE
GLUCOSIDIC
GLUCOSINE
GLUCOSONE
GLUCOSURIA
GLUCURONIC
GLUE
GLUED
GLUEMAKER
GLUEMAKING
GLUEMAN
GLUEPOT
GLUER
GLUEY
GLUEYNESS
GLUG
GLUGGLUG
GLUHWEIN
GLUING
GLUISH
GLUISHNESS
GLUM
GLUMA
GLUMACEOUS
GLUMAL
GLUME
GLUMES
GLUMIFEROUS
GLUMLY
GLUMMER
GLUMMEST
GLUMMY
GLUMNESS
GLUMOSE
GLUMOSITY
GLUMOUS
GLUMP
GLUMPIER
GLUMPIEST
GLUMPILY
GLUMPINESS
GLUMPISH
GLUMPY
GLUNCH
GLUSIDE
GLUT
GLUTAMIC
GLUTAMINE
GLUTAMINIC
GLUTARIC
GLUTATHIONE
GLUTCH
GLUTEAL
GLUTELIN
GLUTEN
GLUTENIN
GLUTENOUS
GLUTEUS
GLUTIN

GLUTINATE
GLUTINATION
GLUTINATIVE
GLUTINIZE
GLUTINOSE
GLUTINOSITY
GLUTINOUS
GLUTINOUSLY
GLUTITION
GLUTOID
GLUTOSE
GLUTTED
GLUTTER
GLUTTERY
GLUTTING
GLUTTON
GLUTTONIES
GLUTTONIZE
GLUTTONIZED
GLUTTONIZING
GLUTTONOUS
GLUTTONOUSLY
GLUTTONY
GLY
GLYCAN
GLYCERATE
GLYCERIC
GLYCERIDE
GLYCERIN
GLYCERINATE
GLYCERINE
GLYCERINIZE
GLYCERITE
GLYCERIZE
GLYCEROGEL
GLYCEROL
GLYCEROLATE
GLYCEROSE
GLYCERYL
GLYCID
GLYCIDE
GLYCIDIC
GLYCIDOL
GLYCIN
GLYCININ
GLYCOCHOLATE
GLYCOCHOLIC
GLYCOCIN
GLYCOCOLL
GLYCOGELATIN
GLYCOGEN
GLYCOGENESIS
GLYCOGENETIC
GLYCOGENIC
GLYCOGENOUS
GLYCOGENY
GLYCOL
GLYCOLATE
GLYCOLIC
GLYCOLIDE
GLYCOLIPID
GLYCOLIPIDE
GLYCOLIPIN
GLYCOLIPINE
GLYCOLURIL
GLYCOLYL
GLYCOLYSIS
GLYCOLYTIC
GLYCOLYTICALLY
GLYCONIC
GLYCONIN
GLYCOPROTEIN
GLYCOSE
GLYCOSIDE
GLYCOSIN
GLYCOSINE
GLYCOSURIA
GLYCOSURIC
GLYCURESIS
GLYCYL
GLYCYPHYLLIN
GLYCYRRHIZIN
GLYDE
GLYN
GLYOXAL
GLYOXALASE
GLYOXALIC
GLYOXALINE
GLYOXIME
GLYOXYL
GLYOXYLIC
GLYPH
GLYPHIC
GLYPHOGRAPH
GLYPHOGRAPHY
GLYPTIC
GLYPTICAL
GLYPTICIAN
GLYPTICS
GLYPTODONT
GLYPTOGRAPH
GLYPTOGRAPHY
GLYPTOLOGY
GLYPTOTHECA
GMELINITE
GNABBLE
GNAP
GNAR
GNARE
GNARL
GNARLED
GNARLIER
GNARLIEST
GNARLINESS
GNARLING
GNARLY
GNARR
GNARRED
GNARRING
GNASH
GNASHED
GNASHING
GNAT
GNATCATCHER
GNATFLOWER
GNATHAL
GNATHIC
GNATHIDIUM
GNATHION
GNATHISM
GNATHITE
GNATHOBASE
GNATHOBASIC
GNATHOMETER
GNATHONIC
GNATHONICAL
GNATHONIZE
GNATHOPOD
GNATHOPODITE
GNATHOSTOME
GNATHOTHECA
GNATLING
GNATSNAP
GNATSNAPPER
GNATTER
GNATTY
GNATWORM
GNAW
GNAWED
GNAWER
GNAWING
GNAWINGLY
GNAWINGS
GNAWN
GNEDE
GNEDELY
GNEISS
GNEISSIC
GNEISSITIC
GNEISSOID
GNEISSOSE
GNEISSY
GNIB
GNOCCHETTI
GNOCCHI
GNOF
GNOFF
GNOME
GNOMED
GNOMIC
GNOMICAL
GNOMICALLY
GNOMIDE
GNOMISH
GNOMIST
GNOMOLOGIC
GNOMOLOGICAL
GNOMOLOGIST
GNOMOLOGY
GNOMON
GNOMONIC
GNOMONICS
GNOMONOLOGY
GNOSIOLOGY
GNOSIS
GNOSTIC
GNOSTICAL
GNOSTICALLY
GNOSTICITY
GNU
GO
GOA
GOAD
GOADED
GOADING
GOADMAN
GOADSMAN
GOADSTER
GOAF
GOAI
GOAL
GOALAGE
GOALEE
GOALIE
GOALKEEPER
GOALKEEPING
GOALLESS
GOALMOUTH
GOALTENDER
GOAM
GOANA
GOANNA
GOAT
GOATBEARD
GOATBRUSH
GOATBUSH
GOATEE
GOATEED
GOATFISH
GOATFISHES
GOATHERD
GOATHERDESS
GOATISH
GOATISHLY
GOATISHNESS
GOATLAND
GOATLING
GOATLY
GOATROOT
GOATSBANE
GOATSBEARD
GOATSFOOT
GOATSFOOTS
GOATSKIN
GOATSTONE
GOATSUCKER
GOATWEED
GOATY
GOAVE
GOB
GOBACK
GOBAN
GOBANG
GOBBE
GOBBER
GOBBET
GOBBIN
GOBBING
GOBBLE
GOBBLED
GOBBLEDYGOOK
GOBBLER
GOBBLING
GOBBO
GOBBY
GOBELIN
GOBERNADOR
GOBERNADORA
GOBIERNO
GOBIES
GOBIID
GOBIIFORM
GOBIOID
GOBLET
GOBLETED
GOBLIN
GOBLINE
GOBLINRY
GOBMOUTHED
GOBO
GOBONATED
GOBONE
GOBONY
GOBOS
GOBSTICK
GOBURRA
GOBY
GOCART
GOD
GODCHILD
GODDAM
GODDAMN
GODDAMNED
GODDARD
GODDAUGHTER
GODDESS
GODDIZE
GODE
GODET
GODFATHER
GODFORSAKEN
GODHEAD
GODHOOD
GODIVEAU
GODKIN
GODLESS
GODLESSLY
GODLESSNESS
GODLET
GODLIER
GODLIEST
GODLIKE
GODLIKENESS
GODLILY
GODLINESS
GODLING
GODLY
GODMAMMA
GODMOTHER
GODOWN
GODPAPA
GODPARENT
GODPHERE
GODROON
GODS
GODSEND
GODSHIP
GODSON
GODSONSHIP
GODWIT
GOEL
GOELAND
GOELISM
GOER
GOES
GOETHITE
GOETIC
GOETY
GOFE
GOFER
GOFF
GOFFER
GOFFERED
GOFFERER
GOFFERING
GOFFLE
GOG
GOGA
GOGGA
GOGGAN
GOGGANS
GOGGLE
GOGGLED
GOGGLER
GOGGLES
GOGGLING
GOGGLY
GOGLET
GOGO
GOH
GOI
GOIABADA
GOING
GOINGS
GOITCHO
GOITER
GOITERED
GOITRE
GOITRED
GOITROUS
GOL
GOLA
GOLACH
GOLADAR
GOLAH
GOLANDAAS
GOLANDAUSE
GOLANDAUZE
GOLD
GOLDARN
GOLDBACK
GOLDBEATER
GOLDBEATING
GOLDBRICK
GOLDBUG
GOLDCREST
GOLDCUP
GOLDE
GOLDEN
GOLDENBACK
GOLDENEYE
GOLDENEYES
GOLDENFLEECE
GOLDENLOCKS
GOLDENLY

GOLDENNESS
GOLDENPERT
GOLDENROD
GOLDENSEAL
GOLDENTOP
GOLDENWING
GOLDER
GOLDEYE
GOLDFIELDER
GOLDFINCH
GOLDFINNIES
GOLDFINNY
GOLDFISH
GOLDFISHES
GOLDFLOWER
GOLDHAMMER
GOLDHEAD
GOLDIE
GOLDILOCKS
GOLDIN
GOLDING
GOLDMIST
GOLDNEY
GOLDSMITH
GOLDSMITHERY
GOLDSMITHING
GOLDSMITHRY
GOLDSPINK
GOLDSTONE
GOLDTAIL
GOLDTHREAD
GOLDTIT
GOLDURN
GOLDWATER
GOLDWEED
GOLDWORK
GOLDWORKER
GOLDY
GOLE
GOLEE
GOLEM
GOLES
GOLF
GOLFER
GOLFING
GOLI
GOLIAD
GOLIARD
GOLIARDERY
GOLIARDIC
GOLILLA
GOLKAKRA
GOLL
GOLLAND
GOLLAR
GOLLER
GOLLIWOG
GOLLIWOGG
GOLLOP
GOLLY
GOLOCH
GOLOE
GOLOKA
GOLOSH
GOLP
GOLPE
GOLUNDAUZE
GOM
GOMARI
GOMART
GOMASHTA
GOMASTA
GOMAVEL
GOMBAY
GOMBEEN
GOMBO
GOMBROON
GOME
GOMER
GOMERAL
GOMEREL
GOMERIL
GOMLAH
GOMMIER
GOMPHODONT
GOMPHOSIS
GOMUKHI
GOMUTI
GON
GONAD
GONADAL
GONADIAL
GONADIC
GONADUCT
GONAGRA
GONAKE
GONAKIE
GONAL
GONALGIA
GONAPOD
GONAPOPHYSAL
GONAPOPHYSIS
GONARTHRITIS
GONCALO
GONDANG
GONDITE
GONDOLA
GONDOLET
GONDOLIER
GONE
GONENESS
GONEOCLINIC
GONEPOIESIS
GONEPOIETIC
GONER
GONESOME
GONEY
GONFALON
GONFALONIER
GONFANON
GONG
GONGMAN
GONGORISTIC
GONIAC
GONIAL
GONIALE
GONID
GONIDANGIUM
GONIDIA
GONIDIAL
GONIDIOSE
GONIDIOSPORE
GONIDIUM
GONIMIC
GONIMOBLAST
GONIMOLOBE
GONIMOUS
GONIOMETER
GONIOMETRIC
GONIOMETRY
GONION
GONIOSTAT
GONIOTHECA
GONIOTROPOUS
GONITIS
GONIUM
GONNARDITE
GONOBLAST
GONOBLASTIC
GONOCALYX
GONOCHORISM
GONOCOCCI
GONOCOCCUS
GONOCOEL
GONOCOELE
GONOCYTE
GONOECIUM
GONOF
GONOMERE
GONOMERY
GONOPH
GONOPHORE
GONOPHORIC
GONOPHOROUS
GONOPLASM
GONOPOD
GONOPOIETIC
GONORRHEA
GONORRHEAL
GONORRHEIC
GONORRHOEA
GONORRHOEAL
GONORRHOEIC
GONOSOMAL
GONOSOME
GONOSPHERE
GONOSTYLE
GONOTHECA
GONOTHECAL
GONOTOCONT
GONOTOKONT
GONOTOME
GONOTYL
GONOTYPE
GONOZOOID
GONY
GONYALGIA
GONYDEAL
GONYDIAL
GONYOCELE
GONYONCUS
GONYS
GONYTHECA
GONZALO
GOO
GOOBER
GOOD
GOODHAP
GOODHEARTED
GOODIES
GOODING
GOODISH
GOODISHNESS
GOODLIER
GOODLIEST
GOODLIHEAD
GOODLIKE
GOODLINESS
GOODLY
GOODMAN
GOODNESS
GOODS
GOODSIRE
GOODWIFE
GOODWILL
GOODWILLIT
GOODWILLY
GOODWIVES
GOODY
GOODYEAR
GOOEY
GOOF
GOOFA
GOOFAH
GOOFBALL
GOOFER
GOOFIER
GOOFIEST
GOOFILY
GOOFINESS
GOOFY
GOOG
GOOGLY
GOOGOL
GOOGOLPLEX
GOOGUL
GOOIER
GOOIEST
GOOK
GOOL
GOOLAH
GOOLDE
GOOLS
GOOM
GOOMA
GOOMBAY
GOON
GOONCH
GOONDA
GOONDIE
GOONEY
GOONIE
GOONY
GOOR
GOORAL
GOORANUT
GOOSANDER
GOOSE
GOOSEBEAK
GOOSEBERRY
GOOSEBILL
GOOSEBIRD
GOOSEBONE
GOOSEBOY
GOOSECAP
GOOSED
GOOSEFLESH
GOOSEFLOWER
GOOSEFOOT
GOOSEGIRL
GOOSEGOG
GOOSEGRASS
GOOSEHERD
GOOSEHOUSE
GOOSEMOUTH
GOOSENECK
GOOSERIES
GOOSERUMPED
GOOSERY
GOOSES
GOOSESKIN
GOOSETONGUE
GOOSEWEED
GOOSEWING
GOOSEWINGED
GOOSEY
GOOSIER
GOOSIEST
GOOSING
GOOSISH
GOOSISHLY
GOOSISHNESS
GOOSY
GOOTE
GOOTEE
GOOZLE
GOPAK
GOPE
GOPHER
GOPHERBERRY
GOPHERMAN
GOPHERROOT
GOPHERWOOD
GOPURA
GOR
GORA
GORACCO
GORAH
GORAL
GORALOG
GORALS
GORAN
GORB
GORBELLIES
GORBELLY
GORBET
GORBIT
GORBLE
GORBLIMY
GORBLIN
GORCE
GORCOCK
GORCROW
GORDIID
GORDIOID
GORDOLOBO
GORDUNITE
GORE
GORED
GOREFISH
GORER
GOREVAN
GORFLY
GORGE
GORGED
GORGEDLY
GORGELET
GORGEOUS
GORGEOUSLY
GORGEOUSNESS
GORGER
GORGERIN
GORGES
GORGET
GORGETED
GORGIA
GORGING
GORGIO
GORGON
GORGONACEAN
GORGONESQUE
GORGONEUM
GORGONIAN
GORGONIN
GORGONIZE
GORGONIZED
GORHEN
GORIC
GORILLA
GORILLAS
GORILLIAN
GORILLOID
GORILY
GORINESS
GORING
GORKUN
GORLIN
GORLING
GORM
GORMA
GORMAND
GORMANDIZE
GORMANDIZER
GORMAW
GORMED
GORRAF
GORREL
GORSE
GORSEBIRD
GORSECHAT
GORSEDD
GORSEHATCH
GORSIER
GORSIEST
GORST

GORSY
GORY
GOS
GOSAIN
GOSCHENS
GOSH
GOSHAWK
GOSHENITE
GOSLARITE
GOSLET
GOSLING
GOSMORE
GOSPEL
GOSPELER
GOSPELIZE
GOSPELLER
GOSPELLIKE
GOSPELLY
GOSPODAR
GOSPODIN
GOSPORT
GOSSAMER
GOSSAMERED
GOSSAMERY
GOSSAMPINE
GOSSAN
GOSSARD
GOSSIP
GOSSIPED
GOSSIPER
GOSSIPHOOD
GOSSIPINESS
GOSSIPING
GOSSIPINGLY
GOSSIPMONGER
GOSSIPPED
GOSSIPPING
GOSSIPRED
GOSSIPRY
GOSSIPY
GOSSOON
GOSSY
GOSSYPIN
GOSSYPINE
GOSSYPOL
GOSTER
GOSTHER
GOT
GOTA
GOTCH
GOTCHED
GOTCHY
GOTE
GOTHIC
GOTHITE
GOTHS
GOTRA
GOTRAJA
GOTTEN
GOUACHE
GOUAREE
GOUFF
GOUGE
GOUGED
GOUGER
GOUGING
GOUJAT
GOUJON
GOUK
GOUL
GOULASH
GOULDIAN
GOUM
GOUMI
GOUMIER
GOUNAU
GOUND
GOUNDOU
GOUPEN
GOUPIN
GOUR
GOURA
GOURAMI
GOURD
GOURDE
GOURDED
GOURDHEAD
GOURDINESS
GOURDING
GOURDY
GOURMAND
GOURMANDER
GOURMANDERIE
GOURMANDISE
GOURMET
GOUROUNUT
GOURY
GOUSTIE
GOUSTROUS
GOUSTY
GOUT
GOUTER
GOUTIER
GOUTIEST
GOUTIFY
GOUTILY
GOUTINESS
GOUTISH
GOUTTE
GOUTWEED
GOUTWORT
GOUTY
GOUVERNANTE
GOVE
GOVERN
GOVERNABLE
GOVERNAIL
GOVERNANCE
GOVERNED
GOVERNESS
GOVERNING
GOVERNMENT
GOVERNMENTAL
GOVERNOR
GOVERNORATE
GOVERNORS
GOVERNORSHIP
GOW
GOWAN
GOWANED
GOWANY
GOWD
GOWDIE
GOWDNIE
GOWDNOOK
GOWDY
GOWF
GOWFF
GOWIDDIE
GOWK
GOWKED
GOWKEDLY
GOWKEDNESS
GOWKIT
GOWL
GOWLAN
GOWLAND
GOWN
GOWNED
GOWNING
GOWNSMAN
GOWP
GOWPEN
GOWPIN
GOWT
GOY
GOYAL
GOYAZITE
GOYIM
GOYIN
GOYISH
GOYLE
GOZELL
GOZILL
GOZZAN
GOZZARD
GRA
GRAAL
GRAAP
GRAB
GRABBED
GRABBER
GRABBING
GRABBLE
GRABBLER
GRABBLING
GRABBOTS
GRABBY
GRABEN
GRABHOOK
GRABMAN
GRABOUCHE
GRACE
GRACED
GRACEFUL
GRACEFULLY
GRACEFULNESS
GRACELESS
GRACELESSLY
GRACER
GRACES
GRACILARIID
GRACILE
GRACILENESS
GRACILESCENT
GRACILIS
GRACILITY
GRACING
GRACIOSITY
GRACIOSO
GRACIOUS
GRACIOUSLY
GRACIOUSNESS
GRACKLE
GRACY
GRAD
GRADAL
GRADATE
GRADATED
GRADATIM
GRADATING
GRADATION
GRADATIONAL
GRADATIVE
GRADATORY
GRADDAN
GRADE
GRADED
GRADEFINDER
GRADELY
GRADER
GRADES
GRADGRIND
GRADIENT
GRADIENTER
GRADIN
GRADINE
GRADING
GRADINO
GRADIOMETER
GRADIOMETRIC
GRADO
GRADOMETER
GRADUAL
GRADUALE
GRADUALISM
GRADUALIST
GRADUALISTIC
GRADUALITY
GRADUALLY
GRADUALNESS
GRADUAND
GRADUATE
GRADUATED
GRADUATICAL
GRADUATING
GRADUATION
GRADUS
GRAFF
GRAFFAGE
GRAFFER
GRAFFITO
GRAFT
GRAFTAGE
GRAFTED
GRAFTER
GRAFTING
GRAFTONITE
GRAGER
GRAHAM
GRAHAMITE
GRAIL
GRAILER
GRAILING
GRAILLE
GRAIN
GRAINAGE
GRAINE
GRAINED
GRAINER
GRAINERING
GRAINERY
GRAINFIELD
GRAINIER
GRAINIEST
GRAININESS
GRAINING
GRAINLAND
GRAINLESS
GRAINMAN
GRAINS
GRAINSICK
GRAINSICKNESS
GRAINSMAN
GRAINSMEN
GRAINY
GRAIP
GRAISSE
GRAITH
GRAITHLY
GRALLATORIAL
GRALLATORY
GRALLIC
GRALLINE
GRALLOCH
GRAM
GRAMA
GRAMARY
GRAMARYE
GRAME
GRAMENITE
GRAMERCY
GRAMINEAL
GRAMINEOUS
GRAMINIFORM
GRAMININ
GRAMINIVORE
GRAMINOLOGY
GRAMINOUS
GRAMMA
GRAMMALOGUE
GRAMMAR
GRAMMARIAN
GRAMMATES
GRAMMATICAL
GRAMMATICALLY
GRAMMATICISM
GRAMMATICIZE
GRAMMATICS
GRAMMATIST
GRAMME
GRAMMEL
GRAMOCHES
GRAMOPHONE
GRAMOPHONIC
GRAMP
GRAMPS
GRAMPUS
GRAMY
GRAN
GRANA
GRANADILLA
GRANADILLO
GRANAGE
GRANAM
GRANARY
GRANAT
GRANATE
GRANATUM
GRANCH
GRAND
GRANDAD
GRANDADA
GRANDADDY
GRANDAM
GRANDAME
GRANDAUNT
GRANDCHILD
GRANDDAD
GRANDDADA
GRANDDADDY
GRANDDAM
GRANDDAUGHTER
GRANDE
GRANDEE
GRANDER
GRANDESQUE
GRANDEST
GRANDEUR
GRANDEVAL
GRANDEVITY
GRANDEZA
GRANDFATHER
GRANDFER
GRANDFILIAL
GRANDGORE
GRANDILOQUENT
GRANDIOSE
GRANDIOSELY
GRANDIOSITY
GRANDIOSO
GRANDISONANT
GRANDISONOUS
GRANDITY
GRANDLY
GRANDMA
GRANDMAMA
GRANDMAMMA
GRANDMATERNAL
GRANDMOTHER
GRANDNEPHEW
GRANDNESS
GRANDNIECE
GRANDO
GRANDPA

GRANDPAPA
GRANDPARENT
GRANDPARENTS
GRANDPATERNAL
GRANDSIR
GRANDSIRE
GRANDSON
GRANDSTAND
GRANDSTANDER
GRANDUNCLE
GRANE
GRANES
GRANET
GRANGE
GRANGER
GRANGERISM
GRANGERITE
GRANGERIZE
GRANI
GRANIFEROUS
GRANIFORM
GRANILLA
GRANITA
GRANITE
GRANITEWARE
GRANITIC
GRANITICAL
GRANITITE
GRANITIZE
GRANITOID
GRANITOIDAL
GRANIVORE
GRANIVOROUS
GRANJENO
GRANK
GRANNAM
GRANNIE
GRANNOM
GRANNY
GRANNYBUSH
GRANNYKNOT
GRANO
GRANOBLASTIC
GRANODIORITE
GRANOGABBRO
GRANOLITH
GRANOLITHIC
GRANOMERITE
GRANOPHYRE
GRANOPHYRIC
GRANOSE
GRANOSPHERITE
GRANT
GRANTABLE
GRANTED
GRANTEE
GRANTER
GRANTHI
GRANTING
GRANTOR
GRANTS
GRANULA
GRANULAR
GRANULARITY
GRANULARLY
GRANULARY
GRANULATE
GRANULATED
GRANULATER
GRANULATING
GRANULATION
GRANULATIVE
GRANULATOR
GRANULE
GRANULET
GRANULITE
GRANULITIC
GRANULITIS
GRANULITIZE
GRANULIZE
GRANULOCYTE
GRANULOMA
GRANULOMAS
GRANULOMATA
GRANULOSE
GRANUM
GRANZA
GRAO
GRAPE
GRAPED
GRAPEFLOWER
GRAPEFRUIT
GRAPEFRUITS
GRAPELET
GRAPELIKE
GRAPENUTS
GRAPEROOT
GRAPERY
GRAPES
GRAPESHOT
GRAPESKIN
GRAPESTALK
GRAPESTONE
GRAPEVINE
GRAPEWORT
GRAPH
GRAPHALLOY
GRAPHIC
GRAPHICAL
GRAPHICALLY
GRAPHICLY
GRAPHICNESS
GRAPHICS
GRAPHIOLOGY
GRAPHITE
GRAPHITER
GRAPHITIC
GRAPHITIZE
GRAPHITIZED
GRAPHITOID
GRAPHITOIDAL
GRAPHOLOGIC
GRAPHOLOGIST
GRAPHOLOGY
GRAPHOMETER
GRAPHOMETRIC
GRAPHOMETRY
GRAPHOMOTOR
GRAPHOPHONE
GRAPHOPHONIC
GRAPHORRHEA
GRAPHOSCOPE
GRAPHOSPASM
GRAPHOSTATIC
GRAPHOTYPE
GRAPHY
GRAPIER
GRAPIEST
GRAPING
GRAPLIN
GRAPLINE
GRAPNEL
GRAPPA
GRAPPLE
GRAPPLED
GRAPPLER
GRAPPLING
GRAPSOID
GRAPTOLITE
GRAPTOLITIC
GRAPTOMANCY
GRAPY
GRASH
GRASNI
GRASO
GRASP
GRASPABLE
GRASPED
GRASPER
GRASPING
GRASPINGLY
GRASPINGNESS
GRASPLESS
GRASS
GRASSANT
GRASSATION
GRASSBIRD
GRASSCHAT
GRASSCUT
GRASSCUTTER
GRASSED
GRASSER
GRASSERIE
GRASSET
GRASSEYE
GRASSFLAT
GRASSFLOWER
GRASSHOP
GRASSHOPPER
GRASSHOUSE
GRASSIE
GRASSIER
GRASSIEST
GRASSILY
GRASSINESS
GRASSING
GRASSLAND
GRASSLESS
GRASSLIKE
GRASSMAN
GRASSMEN
GRASSNUT
GRASSPLAT
GRASSPLOT
GRASSQUIT
GRASSROOTS
GRASSWEED
GRASSWIDOW
GRASSWORK
GRASSWORM
GRASSY
GRAT
GRATE
GRATED
GRATEFUL
GRATEFULLY
GRATEFULNESS
GRATEMAN
GRATER
GRATHER
GRATICULATE
GRATICULE
GRATIFICATION
GRATIFIED
GRATIFIEDLY
GRATIFIER
GRATIFY
GRATIFYING
GRATIFYINGLY
GRATILITY
GRATILLITY
GRATIN
GRATINATE
GRATINATED
GRATINATING
GRATING
GRATINGLY
GRATINGS
GRATIOLIN
GRATIOSOLIN
GRATIS
GRATITUDE
GRATTEN
GRATTERS
GRATTOIR
GRATTON
GRATUITANT
GRATUITIES
GRATUITO
GRATUITOUS
GRATUITOUSLY
GRATUITY
GRATULANT
GRATULATE
GRATULATED
GRATULATION
GRATULATORY
GRAUPEL
GRAVAMEN
GRAVAMINA
GRAVAMINOUS
GRAVAT
GRAVATA
GRAVE
GRAVECLOD
GRAVECLOTH
GRAVECLOTHES
GRAVED
GRAVEDIGGER
GRAVEDO
GRAVEGARTH
GRAVEL
GRAVELED
GRAVELING
GRAVELLED
GRAVELLINESS
GRAVELLING
GRAVELLY
GRAVELSTONE
GRAVELWEED
GRAVELY
GRAVEMAKER
GRAVEMAKING
GRAVEMAN
GRAVEMASTER
GRAVEN
GRAVENESS
GRAVEOLENCE
GRAVEOLENCY
GRAVEOLENT
GRAVER
GRAVERY
GRAVES
GRAVESHIP
GRAVESIDE
GRAVEST
GRAVESTEAD
GRAVESTONE
GRAVETTE
GRAVEWARD
GRAVEWARDS
GRAVEYARD
GRAVIC
GRAVID
GRAVIDA
GRAVIDATE
GRAVIDATION
GRAVIDITY
GRAVIDLY
GRAVIDNESS
GRAVIERS
GRAVIFIC
GRAVIGRADE
GRAVILEA
GRAVIMETER
GRAVIMETRIC
GRAVIMETRY
GRAVING
GRAVIPAUSE
GRAVISPHERIC
GRAVITATE
GRAVITATED
GRAVITATER
GRAVITATING
GRAVITATION
GRAVITATIONAL
GRAVITATIVE
GRAVITIES
GRAVITY
GRAVURE
GRAVY
GRAWLS
GRAY
GRAYBACK
GRAYBEARD
GRAYCOAT
GRAYED
GRAYER
GRAYEST
GRAYFISH
GRAYFLY
GRAYHEAD
GRAYHOUND
GRAYISH
GRAYLAG
GRAYLAGS
GRAYLING
GRAYLINGS
GRAYLY
GRAYMILL
GRAYNESS
GRAYOUT
GRAYPATE
GRAYS
GRAYSBY
GRAYWACKE
GRAYWALL
GRAYWARE
GRAYWETHER
GRAZE
GRAZED
GRAZIER
GRAZIERY
GRAZING
GRAZINGLY
GRAZIOSO
GREABLE
GREABLY
GREASE
GREASEBUSH
GREASED
GREASEHORN
GREASER
GREASEWOOD
GREASIER
GREASIEST
GREASILY
GREASINESS
GREASING
GREASY
GREAT
GREATCOAT
GREATCOATED
GREATEN
GREATER
GREATEST
GREATHEAD
GREATHEART
GREATHEARTED
GREATLY
GREATMOUTHED
GREATNESS
GREAVE
GREAVES
GREBE

GREBES
GRECE
GRECQUE
GREDE
GREE
GREED
GREEDIER
GREEDIEST
GREEDILY
GREEDINESS
GREEDLESS
GREEDSOME
GREEDY
GREEDYGUT
GREEDYGUTS
GREEGREE
GREEN
GREENALITE
GREENBACK
GREENBELT
GREENBOARD
GREENBONE
GREENBRIER
GREENBUL
GREENCOAT
GREENED
GREENER
GREENERIES
GREENERY
GREENEY
GREENFINCH
GREENFISH
GREENFLY
GREENGAGE
GREENGILL
GREENGROCER
GREENGROCERY
GREENHEAD
GREENHEADED
GREENHEART
GREENHEW
GREENHIDE
GREENHORN
GREENHOUSE
GREENIER
GREENIEST
GREENING
GREENISH
GREENISHNESS
GREENKEEPER
GREENKEEPING
GREENLANDITE
GREENLEEK
GREENLET
GREENLING
GREENLY
GREENNESS
GREENOCKITE
GREENOVITE
GREENROOM
GREENS
GREENSAND
GREENSAUCE
GREENSHANK
GREENSICK
GREENSICKNESS
GREENSIDE
GREENSTONE
GREENSWARD
GREENSWARDED
GREENTH
GREENUK
GREENWAX
GREENWEED
GREENWING
GREENWITHE
GREENWOOD
GREENY
GREENYARD
GREESAGH
GREESE
GREESHOCH
GREET
GREETED
GREETER
GREETING
GREETINGLY
GREFFE
GREFFIER
GREFFOTOME
GREGAL
GREGALE
GREGALOID
GREGARIAN
GREGARIANISM
GREGARINE
GREGARINIDAL
GREGARINOSIS
GREGARINOUS
GREGARIOUS
GREGARIOUSLY
GREGARITIC
GREGATIM
GREGE
GREGGLE
GREGO
GREIGE
GREILLADE
GREIN
GREISEN
GREKING
GRELOT
GREMIAL
GREMIALE
GREMIO
GREMLIN
GRENADE
GRENADES
GRENADIER
GRENADIERIAL
GRENADIERLY
GRENADIN
GRENADINE
GRENADO
GRENAT
GRENIER
GRES
GRESIL
GRESSORIAL
GRESSORIOUS
GRETH
GREUND
GREW
GREWHOUND
GREWSOME
GREWSOMELY
GREWSOMENESS
GREWT
GREX
GREY
GREYBACK
GREYBEARD
GREYCOAT
GREYER
GREYEST
GREYFISH
GREYFLIES
GREYFLY
GREYHOUND
GREYHOUNDS
GREYLAG
GREYLY
GREYNESS
GREYPATE
GREYS
GREYSKIN
GREYWACKE
GREYWARE
GREYWETHER
GRI
GRIBANE
GRIBBLE
GRICE
GRID
GRIDDER
GRIDDLE
GRIDDLECAKE
GRIDDLED
GRIDDLER
GRIDDLING
GRIDE
GRIDELIN
GRIDING
GRIDIRON
GRIEBEN
GRIECE
GRIECED
GRIEF
GRIEFFUL
GRIEGE
GRIEKO
GRIEN
GRIESHOCH
GRIESHUCKLE
GRIEVANCE
GRIEVE
GRIEVED
GRIEVER
GRIEVESHIP
GRIEVING
GRIEVINGLY
GRIEVOUS
GRIEVOUSLY
GRIEVOUSNESS
GRIFF
GRIFFADE
GRIFFADO
GRIFFAUN
GRIFFE
GRIFFIN
GRIFFINAGE
GRIFFITHITE
GRIFFON
GRIFFONAGE
GRIFT
GRIFTER
GRIG
GRIGGLES
GRIGNET
GRIGRI
GRIGS
GRIHYASUTRA
GRIKE
GRIL
GRILL
GRILLADE
GRILLAGE
GRILLE
GRILLED
GRILLEE
GRILLER
GRILLING
GRILLROOM
GRILLWORK
GRILLY
GRILSE
GRILSES
GRIM
GRIMACE
GRIMACED
GRIMACER
GRIMACING
GRIMACINGLY
GRIMALKIN
GRIME
GRIMED
GRIMFUL
GRIMGRIBBER
GRIMIER
GRIMIEST
GRIMILY
GRIMINESS
GRIMING
GRIMLY
GRIMME
GRIMMER
GRIMMEST
GRIMNESS
GRIMOIRE
GRIMP
GRIMSIR
GRIMSIRE
GRIMY
GRIN
GRINAGOG
GRINCH
GRINCOME
GRIND
GRINDAL
GRINDED
GRINDER
GRINDERMAN
GRINDERS
GRINDERY
GRINDING
GRINDLE
GRINDSTONE
GRINGO
GRINGOLE
GRINGOLEE
GRINNED
GRINNER
GRINNIE
GRINNING
GRINNINGLY
GRINNY
GRINT
GRINTER
GRINTERN
GRIOTTE
GRIP
GRIPE
GRIPED
GRIPEFUL
GRIPER
GRIPES
GRIPGRASS
GRIPH
GRIPHE
GRIPHITE
GRIPHUS
GRIPIER
GRIPIEST
GRIPING
GRIPINGLY
GRIPLESS
GRIPMAN
GRIPPAL
GRIPPE
GRIPPED
GRIPPER
GRIPPERS
GRIPPING
GRIPPINGLY
GRIPPINGNESS
GRIPPIT
GRIPPLE
GRIPPLENESS
GRIPPOTOXIN
GRIPPY
GRIPS
GRIPSACK
GRIPT
GRIPY
GRIQUAITE
GRIS
GRISAILLE
GRISARD
GRISBET
GRISE
GRISEOUS
GRISETTE
GRISETTISH
GRISKIN
GRISLIER
GRISLIEST
GRISLINESS
GRISLY
GRISON
GRISONS
GRISOUNITE
GRISOUTINE
GRISP
GRISPING
GRISSEN
GRISSET
GRIST
GRISTBITE
GRISTER
GRISTLE
GRISTLINESS
GRISTLY
GRISTMILL
GRISTMILLER
GRISTMILLING
GRISTY
GRIT
GRITH
GRITHBREACH
GRITHMAN
GRITROCK
GRITS
GRITTED
GRITTEN
GRITTER
GRITTIE
GRITTIER
GRITTIEST
GRITTILY
GRITTINESS
GRITTING
GRITTLE
GRITTY
GRIVE
GRIVET
GRIVNA
GRIVOIS
GRIVOISE
GRIZARD
GRIZZLE
GRIZZLED
GRIZZLER
GRIZZLIER
GRIZZLIES
GRIZZLIEST
GRIZZLING
GRIZZLY
GRIZZLYMAN
GROAK
GROAN
GROANED
GROANER
GROANFUL
GROANING
GROANINGLY

GROAT
GROATS
GROATSWORTH
GROBIAN
GROBIANISM
GROCER
GROCERIES
GROCERLY
GROCERY
GROFF
GROG
GROGGED
GROGGER
GROGGERIES
GROGGERY
GROGGIER
GROGGIEST
GROGGILY
GROGGINESS
GROGGING
GROGGY
GROGNARD
GROGRAM
GROGSHOP
GROIN
GROINED
GROINERY
GROINING
GROM
GROMATIC
GROMATICAL
GROMATICS
GROMET
GROMMET
GROMWELL
GROMYL
GRONDWET
GRONT
GROOF
GROOM
GROOMED
GROOMER
GROOMING
GROOMLET
GROOMSMAN
GROOMSMEN
GROOMY
GROOP
GROOSE
GROOT
GROOTY
GROOVE
GROOVED
GROOVER
GROOVERHEAD
GROOVIER
GROOVIEST
GROOVING
GROOVY
GROPE
GROPED
GROPER
GROPING
GROPINGLY
GROPPLE
GRORUDITE
GROS
GROSBEAK
GROSCHEN
GROSER
GROSET
GROSGRAIN
GROSGRAINED
GROSS
GROSSEN
GROSSER
GROSSES
GROSSEST
GROSSIERETE
GROSSIFY
GROSSLY
GROSSO
GROSSULAR
GROSSULARITE
GROSZ
GROSZY
GROT
GROTE
GROTEN
GROTESCO
GROTESQUE
GROTESQUELY
GROTESQUERIE
GROTESQUERY
GROTHINE
GROTHITE
GROTTO
GROTTOED
GROTTOWORK
GROTZEN
GROUCH
GROUCHIER
GROUCHIEST
GROUCHILY
GROUCHINESS
GROUCHY
GROUF
GROUGH
GROUND
GROUNDABLE
GROUNDAGE
GROUNDBERRY
GROUNDBIRD
GROUNDED
GROUNDEDLY
GROUNDEDNESS
GROUNDEN
GROUNDENELL
GROUNDER
GROUNDHOG
GROUNDING
GROUNDLESS
GROUNDLESSLY
GROUNDLINE
GROUNDLINESS
GROUNDLING
GROUNDLY
GROUNDMAN
GROUNDMASS
GROUNDNEEDLE
GROUNDNUT
GROUNDS
GROUNDSEL
GROUNDSILL
GROUNDSMAN
GROUNDWALL
GROUNDWARD
GROUNDWARDS
GROUNDWOOD
GROUNDWORK
GROUNDY
GROUP
GROUPAGE
GROUPED
GROUPER
GROUPIE
GROUPING
GROUPMENT
GROUPS
GROUSE
GROUSED
GROUSER
GROUSING
GROUSY
GROUT
GROUTED
GROUTER
GROUTHEAD
GROUTIER
GROUTIEST
GROUTING
GROUTITE
GROUTS
GROUTY
GROUZE
GROVE
GROVED
GROVEL
GROVELED
GROVELER
GROVELING
GROVELINGLY
GROVELINGS
GROVELLED
GROVELLER
GROVELLING
GROVELLINGLY
GROVELLINGS
GROVET
GROVY
GROW
GROWAN
GROWER
GROWING
GROWL
GROWLED
GROWLER
GROWLERIES
GROWLERY
GROWLING
GROWLY
GROWN
GROWNUP
GROWS
GROWSE
GROWSOME
GROWTH
GROWTHINESS
GROWTHY
GROWZE
GROYNE
GROZART
GROZER
GRU
GRUB
GRUBBED
GRUBBER
GRUBBERIES
GRUBBERY
GRUBBIER
GRUBBIEST
GRUBBILY
GRUBBINESS
GRUBBING
GRUBBLE
GRUBBY
GRUBROOT
GRUBS
GRUBSTAKE
GRUBSTAKER
GRUBSTREET
GRUBWORM
GRUDGE
GRUDGED
GRUDGER
GRUDGERY
GRUDGING
GRUDGINGLY
GRUE
GRUEL
GRUELED
GRUELER
GRUELING
GRUELLED
GRUELLER
GRUELLING
GRUELLY
GRUESOME
GRUESOMELY
GRUESOMENESS
GRUF
GRUFF
GRUFFER
GRUFFEST
GRUFFILY
GRUFFINESS
GRUFFLY
GRUFFNESS
GRUFFS
GRUFFY
GRUFT
GRUFTED
GRUG
GRUGOUS
GRUGRU
GRUIFORM
GRUINE
GRULLA
GRUM
GRUMBLE
GRUMBLED
GRUMBLER
GRUMBLING
GRUMBLINGLY
GRUMBLY
GRUME
GRUMLY
GRUMMEL
GRUMMELS
GRUMMER
GRUMMEST
GRUMMET
GRUMMETER
GRUMNESS
GRUMOSE
GRUMOUS
GRUMOUSNESS
GRUMP
GRUMPH
GRUMPHIE
GRUMPHY
GRUMPIER
GRUMPIEST
GRUMPILY
GRUMPINESS
GRUMPISH
GRUMPS
GRUMPY
GRUN
GRUNCH
GRUNDY
GRUNERITE
GRUNION
GRUNT
GRUNTER
GRUNTING
GRUNTLE
GRUNTLED
GRUNTLING
GRUNZIE
GRUP
GRUPPETTO
GRUPPO
GRUSH
GRUSHIE
GRUSS
GRUTCH
GRY
GRYLLE
GRYLLI
GRYLLID
GRYLLOS
GRYLLUS
GRYPANIAN
GRYPHON
GRYPOSIS
GRYS
GRYSBOK
GUACA
GUACACOA
GUACHAMACA
GUACHARO
GUACHIPILIN
GUACIMO
GUACIN
GUACO
GUACONIZE
GUADUA
GUAGUANCHE
GUAHIVO
GUAIAC
GUAIACOL
GUAIACUM
GUAIASANOL
GUAICAN
GUAIOCUM
GUAIOL
GUAJILLO
GUAJIRA
GUAKO
GUALE
GUAMA
GUAN
GUANA
GUANABANA
GUANABANO
GUANACO
GUANAJUATITE
GUANAMINE
GUANARE
GUANASE
GUANAY
GUANEIDE
GUANGO
GUANIDINE
GUANIFEROUS
GUANINE
GUANIZE
GUANO
GUANOPHORE
GUANOSINE
GUANYL
GUAO
GUAPENA
GUAPILLA
GUAPINOL
GUAR
GUARA
GUARABU
GUARACHA
GUARACHE
GUARAGUAO
GUARANA
GUARAND
GUARANINE
GUARANTEE
GUARANTEED
GUARANTEES
GUARANTIED
GUARANTIES
GUARANTOR
GUARANTY
GUARANTYING
GUARAPO
GUARAPUCU

GUARD
GUARDAGE
GUARDANT
GUARDED
GUARDEDLY
GUARDEDNESS
GUARDEE
GUARDER
GUARDFUL
GUARDFULLY
GUARDHOUSE
GUARDIAN
GUARDIANCY
GUARDIANLY
GUARDIANSHIP
GUARDING
GUARDO
GUARDRAIL
GUARDROOM
GUARDS
GUARDSMAN
GUARDSMEN
GUARDSTONE
GUARIBA
GUARICO
GUARINITE
GUARISH
GUARRI
GUARY
GUASA
GUASO
GUATAMBU
GUATIBERO
GUATIVERE
GUAVA
GUAVABERRY
GUAVINA
GUAXIMA
GUAYABA
GUAYABI
GUAYABO
GUAYACAN
GUAYROTO
GUAYULE
GUAZA
GUAZUTI
GUB
GUBAT
GUBBERTUSH
GUBBIN
GUBBINGS
GUBBINS
GUBBO
GUBERNATION
GUBERNATIVE
GUBERNATOR
GUBERNATRIX
GUBERNIA
GUBERNIYA
GUCK
GUCKED
GUDAME
GUDDA
GUDDLE
GUDE
GUDEMOTHER
GUDESIRE
GUDEWIFE
GUDGE
GUDGEON
GUDGET
GUDOK
GUE
GUEBUCU
GUEJARITE
GUEMAL
GUEMUL
GUENON
GUEPARD
GUEPARDE
GUERDON
GUERDONER
GUEREBA
GUEREZA
GUERIDON
GUERILLA
GUERISON
GUERITE
GUERNSEYED
GUERNSEYS
GUERRILLA
GUESS
GUESSED
GUESSER
GUESSING
GUESSTIMATE
GUESSWORK
GUESSWORKER
GUEST
GUESTCHAMBER
GUESTED
GUESTEN
GUESTER
GUESTHOUSE
GUESTING
GUESTIVE
GUESTMASTER
GUETRE
GUF
GUFA
GUFF
GUFFAW
GUFFER
GUFFIN
GUFFY
GUGAL
GUGGLE
GUGGLET
GUGLET
GUGLIA
GUGLIO
GUGU
GUGUL
GUHR
GUIB
GUIBA
GUICHET
GUID
GUIDA
GUIDABLE
GUIDAGE
GUIDANCE
GUIDE
GUIDEBOARD
GUIDEBOOK
GUIDECRAFT
GUIDED
GUIDELINE
GUIDEPOST
GUIDER
GUIDERESS
GUIDESHIP
GUIDEWAY
GUIDING
GUIDMAN
GUIDON
GUIDSIRE
GUIDWIFE
GUIGE
GUIGNE
GUIJO
GUILD
GUILDER
GUILDHALL
GUILDIC
GUILDITE
GUILDRY
GUILDSHIP
GUILDSMAN
GUILDSMEN
GUILE
GUILEFUL
GUILEFULLY
GUILEFULNESS
GUILELESS
GUILELESSLY
GUILER
GUILERY
GUILLEMET
GUILLEMOT
GUILLEVAT
GUILLOCHE
GUILLOCHEE
GUILLOTINADE
GUILLOTINE
GUILLOTINED
GUILLOTINER
GUILLOTINING
GUILLOTINISM
GUILLOTINIST
GUILT
GUILTFUL
GUILTIER
GUILTIEST
GUILTILY
GUILTINESS
GUILTLESS
GUILTLESSLY
GUILTSICK
GUILTY
GUILY
GUIMBARD
GUIMPE
GUINEA
GUIPURE
GUIRO
GUISE
GUISED
GUISER
GUISING
GUITAR
GUITARFISH
GUITARIST
GUITERMANITE
GUITGUIT
GUJERAT
GUL
GULA
GULAMAN
GULANCHA
GULAR
GULARIS
GULASH
GULCH
GULDEN
GULE
GULES
GULF
GULFWEED
GULFY
GULGUL
GULINULA
GULINULAR
GULIX
GULL
GULLAGE
GULLED
GULLER
GULLERIES
GULLERY
GULLET
GULLEY
GULLIBILITY
GULLIBLE
GULLIBLY
GULLIED
GULLIES
GULLING
GULLION
GULLISH
GULLISHLY
GULLISHNESS
GULLY
GULLYGUT
GULLYHOLE
GULLYING
GULMOHAR
GULOC
GULOSE
GULOSITY
GULP
GULPED
GULPER
GULPH
GULPIN
GULPING
GULPINGLY
GULPS
GULPY
GULSACH
GULY
GUM
GUMBE
GUMBO
GUMBOIL
GUMBOTIL
GUMBY
GUMCHEWER
GUMDIGGER
GUMDIGGING
GUMDROP
GUME
GUMFIELD
GUMFLOWER
GUMHAR
GUMIHAN
GUMLAH
GUMLY
GUMMA
GUMMAGE
GUMMAKER
GUMMAS
GUMMATA
GUMMATOUS
GUMMED
GUMMER
GUMMIER
GUMMIEST
GUMMIFEROUS
GUMMINESS
GUMMING
GUMMITE
GUMMOSE
GUMMOSIS
GUMMOSITY
GUMMOUS
GUMMY
GUMP
GUMPHEON
GUMPHION
GUMPTION
GUMPUS
GUMS
GUMSHOE
GUMSHOED
GUMSHOEING
GUMTREE
GUMWEED
GUMWOOD
GUN
GUNA
GUNATE
GUNATED
GUNATING
GUNATION
GUNBOAT
GUNBOATS
GUNBUILDER
GUNCOTTON
GUNDA
GUNDALOW
GUNDECK
GUNDELOW
GUNDI
GUNDIE
GUNDOG
GUNDY
GUNDYGUT
GUNFIGHT
GUNFIRE
GUNFLINT
GUNGE
GUNHOUSE
GUNITER
GUNJ
GUNJA
GUNJAH
GUNK
GUNKHOLE
GUNLAYER
GUNLAYING
GUNLINE
GUNLOCK
GUNMAKER
GUNMAKING
GUNMAN
GUNMEN
GUNMETAL
GUNNAGE
GUNNED
GUNNEL
GUNNELS
GUNNER
GUNNERY
GUNNIES
GUNNING
GUNNUNG
GUNNY
GUNNYSACK
GUNOCRACY
GUNONG
GUNPAPER
GUNPLAY
GUNPORT
GUNPOWDER
GUNPOWDEROUS
GUNPOWER
GUNRACK
GUNREACH
GUNRUNNER
GUNRUNNING
GUNS
GUNSEL
GUNSHIP
GUNSHOP
GUNSHOT
GUNSMAN
GUNSMITH
GUNSMITHERY
GUNSMITHING
GUNSTER
GUNSTICK
GUNSTOCK
GUNSTOCKER
GUNSTOCKING

GUNSTONE
GUNTER
GUNTUB
GUNUNG
GUNWALE
GUNYAH
GUNYANG
GUNYEH
GUP
GUPPIES
GUPPY
GUPTAVIDYA
GUR
GURDFISH
GURDWARA
GURDY
GURGE
GURGEONS
GURGES
GURGITATION
GURGLE
GURGLED
GURGLET
GURGLING
GURGLINGLY
GURGLY
GURGULATION
GURGULIO
GURJAN
GURJUN
GURK
GURL
GURLET
GURLY
GURNARD
GURNARDS
GURNEY
GURR
GURRAH
GURRY
GURT
GURU
GUSAIN
GUSH
GUSHED
GUSHER
GUSHET
GUSHIER
GUSHIEST
GUSHILY
GUSHINESS
GUSHING
GUSHINGLY
GUSHINGNESS
GUSHY
GUSLA
GUSLE
GUSLEE
GUSLI
GUSS
GUSSET
GUSSIE
GUST
GUSTABLE
GUSTATION
GUSTATIVE
GUSTATORY
GUSTFUL
GUSTFULLY
GUSTFULNESS
GUSTIER
GUSTIEST
GUSTILY
GUSTINESS
GUSTO
GUSTOSO
GUSTY
GUT
GUTBUCKET
GUTLESS
GUTLING
GUTS
GUTSIER
GUTSIEST
GUTSY
GUTT
GUTTA
GUTTAE
GUTTATE
GUTTATED
GUTTATIM
GUTTE
GUTTED
GUTTEE
GUTTER
GUTTERAL
GUTTERBLOOD
GUTTERED
GUTTERING
GUTTERLING
GUTTERMAN
GUTTERS
GUTTERSNIPE
GUTTERY
GUTTIDE
GUTTIE
GUTTIFEROUS
GUTTIFORM
GUTTING
GUTTLE
GUTTLED
GUTTLER
GUTTLING
GUTTULA
GUTTULAR
GUTTULATE
GUTTULE
GUTTULOUS
GUTTUR
GUTTURAL
GUTTURALISM
GUTTURALITY
GUTTURALIZE
GUTTURALIZING
GUTTURALLY
GUTTURALNESS
GUTTUS
GUTTY
GUTWEED
GUTWORT
GUV
GUY
GUYED
GUYER
GUYING
GUYO
GUYOT
GUYTRASH
GUYVER
GUZ
GUZE
GUZERAT
GUZZLE
GUZZLED
GUZZLER
GUZZLING
GWAG
GWANTUS
GWEDUC
GWEDUCK
GWEED
GWEEON
GWELY
GWERZIOU
GWINIAD
GWYNIAD
GYANI
GYASCUTUS
GYASSA
GYBE
GYLE
GYM
GYMEL
GYMKHANA
GYMNANTHOUS
GYMNASIA
GYMNASIAL
GYMNASIARCH
GYMNASIARCHY
GYMNASIAST
GYMNASIC
GYMNASIUM
GYMNAST
GYMNASTIC
GYMNASTICAL
GYMNASTICS
GYMNETROUS
GYMNIC
GYMNICAL
GYMNICS
GYMNITE
GYMNOBLASTIC
GYMNOCARPIC
GYMNOCARPOUS
GYMNOCIDIUM
GYMNODONT
GYMNOGENOUS
GYMNOGLOSSATE
GYMNOGYNOUS
GYMNOPAEDIC
GYMNOPLAST
GYMNORHINAL
GYMNOSOPH
GYMNOSOPHIST
GYMNOSOPHY
GYMNOSPERM
GYMNOSPERMY
GYMNOSPORE
GYMNOSPOROUS
GYMNOSTOMOUS
GYMNOTID
GYMNOTOKOUS
GYMNURE
GYMNURINE
GYMPIE
GYN
GYNAECEUM
GYNAECIUM
GYNAECOCRACY
GYNAECOCRAT
GYNAECOLOGIC
GYNAECOLOGY
GYNAECONITIS
GYNAEOCRACY
GYNAEOLATER
GYNAEOLATRY
GYNANDER
GYNANDRARCHY
GYNANDRIA
GYNANDRIAN
GYNANDRISM
GYNANDROID
GYNANDROUS
GYNANDRY
GYNANTHEROUS
GYNARCHIC
GYNARCHIES
GYNARCHY
GYNE
GYNECIC
GYNECIDAL
GYNECIDE
GYNECIUM
GYNECOCRACY
GYNECOCRAT
GYNECOCRATIC
GYNECOID
GYNECOLATRY
GYNECOLOGIC
GYNECOLOGIST
GYNECOLOGY
GYNECOMASTIA
GYNECOMASTY
GYNECOMAZIA
GYNECONITIS
GYNECOPATHIC
GYNECOPATHY
GYNECOTELIC
GYNECRATIC
GYNEE
GYNEOCRACY
GYNEOLATER
GYNEOLATRY
GYNETHUSIA
GYNETYPE
GYNIATRICS
GYNICS
GYNOBASE
GYNOBASEOUS
GYNOBASIC
GYNOCARDIC
GYNOCRACY
GYNOCRATIC
GYNOECIUM
GYNOGENESIS
GYNOPARA
GYNOPHAGITE
GYNOPHORE
GYNOPHORIC
GYNOSTEGIUM
GYOKURO
GYP
GYPE
GYPPED
GYPPERY
GYPPING
GYPS
GYPSEIAN
GYPSIED
GYPSIES
GYPSIFEROUS
GYPSINE
GYPSIOLOGIST
GYPSITE
GYPSOGRAPHY
GYPSOLOGIST
GYPSOLOGY
GYPSOPLAST
GYPSOUS
GYPSUM
GYPSUMED
GYPSUMING
GYPSY
GYPSYFY
GYPSYHEAD
GYPSYING
GYPSYRY
GYPSYWEED
GYPSYWORT
GYRAL
GYRALLY
GYRANT
GYRATE
GYRATED
GYRATING
GYRATION
GYRATIONAL
GYRATOR
GYRATORY
GYRE
GYRED
GYRENE
GYRFALCON
GYRING
GYRINID
GYRO
GYROCAR
GYROCERACONE
GYROCERAN
GYROCHROME
GYROCOMPASS
GYRODYNE
GYROGONITE
GYROGRAPH
GYROHORIZON
GYROIDAL
GYROIDALLY
GYROLITE
GYROLITH
GYROMA
GYROMAGNETIC
GYROMANCY
GYROMELE
GYROMETER
GYRON
GYRONNY
GYROPIGEON
GYROPLANE
GYROSCOPE
GYROSCOPIC
GYROSE
GYROSTAT
GYROSTATIC
GYROSTATICS
GYROUS
GYROVAGUES
GYROWHEEL
GYRTH
GYRUS
GYTE
GYTLING
GYTRASH
GYTTJA
GYVE
GYVED
GYVING

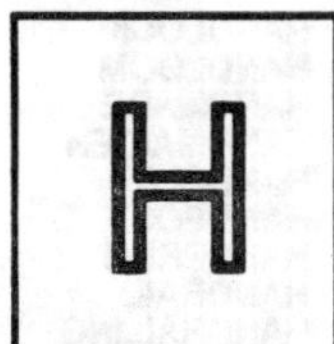

HA
HAAB
HAAF
HAAK
HAAR
HABBLE
HABDALAH
HABEAS
HABENA
HABENAL
HABENAR
HABENDUM
HABENULA
HABENULAR
HABERDASH
HABERDASHER
HABERDASHERY
HABERDINE
HABERGEON
HABI
HABIL
HABILABLE
HABILE
HABILIMENT
HABILIMENTAL
HABILIMENTARY
HABILIMENTATIO
HABILIMENTED
HABILITATE
HABILITATION
HABILITATOR
HABILITY
HABILLE
HABIT
HABITABLE
HABITABLY
HABITACLE
HABITACULE
HABITALLY
HABITAN
HABITANCE
HABITANT
HABITAT
HABITATAL
HABITATE
HABITATIO
HABITATION
HABITATIVE
HABITUAL
HABITUALITY
HABITUALLY
HABITUALNESS
HABITUATE
HABITUATED
HABITUATION
HABITUDE
HABITUE
HABITUS
HABNAB
HABOOB
HABRO
HABRONEMIC
HABROWNE
HABU
HABUKA
HABUTAI
HABUTAYE
HACCUCAL
HACEK
HACHE
HACHIS
HACHMENT
HACHT
HACHURE
HACIENDA
HACK
HACKAMORE
HACKBARROW
HACKBERRY
HACKBOLT
HACKBUSH
HACKBUT
HACKBUTEER
HACKBUTTER
HACKED
HACKEE
HACKEEM
HACKER
HACKERY
HACKEYMAL
HACKIA
HACKIE
HACKIN
HACKING
HACKINGLY
HACKLE
HACKLEBACK
HACKLER
HACKLES
HACKLET
HACKLOG
HACKLY
HACKMACK
HACKMALL
HACKMAN
HACKMATACK
HACKNEY
HACKNEYED
HACKNEYER
HACKNEYMAN
HACKSAW
HACKSILBER
HACKSTER
HACKTHORN
HACKTREE
HACKWOOD
HACKY
HAD
HADADA
HADBOT
HADBOTE
HADDEN
HADDER
HADDIE
HADDIN
HADDO
HADDOCK
HADDOCKER
HADE
HADES
HADING
HADIT
HADJ
HADJI
HADLAND
HADNA
HADROM
HADROME
HADROSAUR
HAE
HAEC
HAECCEITY
HAEM
HAEMAD
HAEMATHERM
HAEMATHERMAL
HAEMATHERMOUS
HAEMATID
HAEMATITE
HAEMONY
HAEMOPHILE
HAEMOPOD
HAEMOSTAT
HAEN
HAEREMAI
HAERES
HAET
HAFF
HAFFET
HAFFIT
HAFFLE
HAFFLINS
HAFIZ
HAFLIN
HAFNIUM
HAFNYL
HAFT
HAFTARAH
HAFTER
HAG
HAGADA
HAGADIST
HAGBERRY
HAGBOAT
HAGBOLT
HAGBORN
HAGBUSH
HAGBUT
HAGDEN
HAGDIN
HAGDON
HAGDOWN
HAGEEN
HAGEIN
HAGFISH
HAGG
HAGGADAL
HAGGADAY
HAGGADIC
HAGGADIST
HAGGARD
HAGGARDLY
HAGGARDNESS
HAGGED
HAGGEIS
HAGGIOGRAPHAL
HAGGIS
HAGGISH
HAGGISHLY
HAGGISHNESS
HAGGLE
HAGGLER
HAGGLING
HAGGLY
HAGGY
HAGI
HAGIA
HAGIARCHY
HAGIGAH
HAGIOCRACY
HAGIOGRAPHER
HAGIOGRAPHIC
HAGIOGRAPHIST
HAGIOGRAPHY
HAGIOLATER
HAGIOLATROUS
HAGIOLATRY
HAGIOLITH
HAGIOLOGIC
HAGIOLOGIST
HAGIOLOGY
HAGIOSCOPE
HAGLET
HAGLIKE
HAGLIN
HAGMALL
HAGMENA
HAGRIDDEN
HAGRIDE
HAGROPE
HAGSEED
HAGSTONE
HAGTAPER
HAGWEED
HAGWORM
HAH
HAHAM
HAHR
HAI
HAIARI
HAICK
HAIK
HAIKAI
HAIKAL
HAIKU
HAIKUN
HAIKWAN
HAIL
HAILER
HAILL
HAILPROOF
HAILSE
HAILSHOT
HAILSTONE
HAILSTORM
HAILWEED
HAIM
HAIMSUCKEN
HAIN
HAINBERRY
HAINCH
HAINE
HAINED
HAIR
HAIRBALL
HAIRBAND
HAIRBEARD
HAIRBELL
HAIRBIRD
HAIRBRAIN
HAIRBRAINED
HAIRBREADTH
HAIRBRUSH
HAIRCAP
HAIRCLOTH
HAIRCUT
HAIRDO
HAIRDRESS
HAIRDRESSER
HAIRDRESSING
HAIRE
HAIRED
HAIREN
HAIRHOOF
HAIRHOUND
HAIRIF
HAIRINESS
HAIRLACE
HAIRLESS
HAIRLIKE
HAIRLINE
HAIRLOCK
HAIRMONEERING
HAIRMONGER
HAIRN
HAIROF
HAIRPIECE
HAIRPIN
HAIRS
HAIRSBREADTH
HAIRSE
HAIRSPLITTER
HAIRSPLITTING
HAIRSPRING
HAIRST
HAIRSTANE
HAIRSTONE
HAIRSTREAK
HAIRTAIL
HAIRUP
HAIRWEAVE
HAIRWEAVING
HAIRWEED
HAIRWORK
HAIRWORM
HAIRY
HAIT
HAITH
HAITSAI
HAIVER
HAJ
HAJE
HAJI
HAJIB
HAJILIJ
HAJJ
HAJJI
HAK
HAKA
HAKAFOTH
HAKAM
HAKAMIM
HAKDAR
HAKE
HAKED
HAKEEM
HAKH
HAKIM
HAKO
HAKU
HAL
HALA
HALACHA
HALACHAH
HALACHIST
HALAKA
HALAKAH
HALAKIC
HALAKIST
HALAL
HALALCOR
HALAPEPE
HALAS
HALATION
HALAZONE
HALBE
HALBERD
HALBERDIER
HALBERDMAN
HALBERDS
HALBERT
HALCH
HALCYON
HALDI
HALDU
HALE
HALEBI
HALECRET
HALEDAY
HALELY
HALENESS
HALER
HALERZ
HALES
HALESOME

HALEWEED
HALF
HALFA
HALFBACK
HALFBEAK
HALFCOCK
HALFCOCKED
HALFEN
HALFHEADED
HALFHEARTED
HALFHEARTEDLY
HALFHEARTEDNESS
HALFLANG
HALFLIN
HALFLING
HALFLINGS
HALFLY
HALFMAN
HALFNESS
HALFPACE
HALFPACED
HALFPENCE
HALFPENNIES
HALFPENNY
HALFWAY
HALFWISE
HALFY
HALIBIOS
HALIBIU
HALIBUT
HALIBUTER
HALID
HALIDE
HALIDOM
HALIDOME
HALIEUTIC
HALIEUTICAL
HALIEUTICALLY
HALIEUTICS
HALIMOT
HALIMOUS
HALINOUS
HALIOTOID
HALIPLID
HALITE
HALITOSIS
HALITUOUS
HALITUS
HALK
HALKE
HALL
HALLAGE
HALLAH
HALLALCOR
HALLALI
HALLAN
HALLBOY
HALLCIST
HALLE
HALLEBARDIER
HALLECRET
HALLEL
HALLELUIAH
HALLIARD
HALLICET
HALLIDOME
HALLING
HALLION
HALLMAN
HALLMARK
HALLMARKER
HALLMOOT
HALLMOTE
HALLO
HALLOA
HALLOCK
HALLOO
HALLOW
HALLOWD
HALLOWED
HALLOWEDLY
HALLOWEDNESS
HALLOWER
HALLUCES
HALLUCINATE
HALLUCINATION
HALLUCINED
HALLUX
HALLWAY
HALM
HALMA
HALMALILLE
HALO
HALOBIOS
HALOBIOTIC
HALOESQUE
HALOGEN
HALOGENATION
HALOID
HALOLIKE
HALOMETER
HALOPHILE
HALOPHYTE
HALOPHYTIC
HALOSCOPE
HALOSERE
HALPACE
HALPER
HALS
HALSE
HALSEN
HALSFANG
HALSH
HALT
HALTER
HALTERBREAK
HALTERE
HALTERES
HALTING
HALTINGLY
HALTINGNESS
HALTLESS
HALUCKET
HALUKKAH
HALURGIST
HALURGY
HALUTZ
HALUTZIM
HALVANER
HALVANS
HALVE
HALVED
HALVELINGS
HALVER
HALVERS
HALVES
HALVING
HALWE
HALY
HALYARD
HAM
HAMADA
HAMADRYAD
HAMAL
HAMALD
HAMAMELIN
HAMARTIA
HAMARTITE
HAMATE
HAMATED
HAMATUM
HAMAUL
HAMBER
HAMBLE
HAMBO
HAMBONE
HAMBURGER
HAMDMAID
HAME
HAMEIL
HAMEL
HAMELT
HAMESOKEN
HAMESUCKEN
HAMETZ
HAMEWITH
HAMFARE
HAMFAT
HAMFATTER
HAMHUNG
HAMI
HAMIFORM
HAMILT
HAMINGJA
HAMINOEA
HAMLAH
HAMLET
HAMLETED
HAMLETEER
HAMLETIZE
HAMLINE
HAMLINITE
HAMMAID
HAMMAL
HAMMER
HAMMERABLE
HAMMERBIRD
HAMMERCLOTH
HAMMERDRESS
HAMMERED
HAMMERER
HAMMERFISH
HAMMERHEAD
HAMMERHEADED
HAMMERING
HAMMERKOP
HAMMERLESS
HAMMERLIKE
HAMMERMAN
HAMMERSMITH
HAMMERSTONE
HAMMERTOE
HAMMERWORT
HAMMOCK
HAMMY
HAMOSE
HAMOTZI
HAMOUS
HAMP
HAMPER
HAMPERED
HAMPERER
HAMPERING
HAMPERMAN
HAMRONGITE
HAMSA
HAMSHACKLE
HAMSTER
HAMSTRING
HAMULAR
HAMULATE
HAMULE
HAMULOSE
HAMULOUS
HAMULUS
HAMUS
HAMZA
HAMZAH
HAN
HANAHILL
HANAP
HANAPER
HANASTER
HANCE
HANCED
HANCH
HANCOCKITE
HAND
HANDARM
HANDBAG
HANDBALL
HANDBALLER
HANDBANK
HANDBANKER
HANDBARROW
HANDBELL
HANDBILL
HANDBLOW
HANDBOLT
HANDBOOK
HANDBOW
HANDBREADTH
HANDBREED
HANDCAR
HANDCART
HANDCLAP
HANDCLASP
HANDCLOTH
HANDCRAFT
HANDCUFF
HANDED
HANDEDNESS
HANDER
HANDERSOME
HANDFAST
HANDFASTING
HANDFASTLY
HANDFASTNESS
HANDFISH
HANDFLAG
HANDFLOWER
HANDFUL
HANDGRAVURE
HANDGRIP
HANDGRIPING
HANDGUN
HANDHAVING
HANDHOLD
HANDHOLE
HANDICAP
HANDICAPPED
HANDICAPPER
HANDICRAFT
HANDICRAFTSMAN
HANDICRAFTSWOMAN
HANDICUFF
HANDIER
HANDIEST
HANDILY
HANDINESS
HANDING
HANDIRON
HANDISTROKE
HANDIWORK
HANDJAR
HANDKERCHER
HANDLAID
HANDLE
HANDLEABLE
HANDLEBAR
HANDLED
HANDLER
HANDLES
HANDLESS
HANDLIKE
HANDLING
HANDLOAD
HANDLOADING
HANDLOCK
HANDLOOM
HANDMADE
HANDMAIDEN
HANDOUT
HANDPOST
HANDPRINT
HANDRAIL
HANDRAILING
HANDREADER
HANDREADING
HANDREST
HANDS
HANDSALE
HANDSAW
HANDSCRAPE
HANDSEL
HANDSELLER
HANDSET
HANDSHAKE
HANDSHAKER
HANDSHAKING
HANDSLED
HANDSMOOTH
HANDSOME
HANDSOMELY
HANDSOMENESS
HANDSPADE
HANDSPAN
HANDSPEC
HANDSPIKE
HANDSPOKE
HANDSPRING
HANDSTAFF
HANDSTAND
HANDSTONE
HANDSTROKE
HANDTRAP
HANDWALED
HANDWHEEL
HANDWHILE
HANDWORK
HANDWORKMAN
HANDWORM
HANDWRIST
HANDWRIT
HANDWRITE
HANDWRITING
HANDY
HANDYBLOW
HANDYBOOK
HANDYCUFF
HANDYFIGHT
HANDYFRAME
HANDYGRIP
HANDYGRIPE
HANDYMAN
HANG
HANGABLE
HANGALAI
HANGAR
HANGBIRD
HANGBY
HANGDOG
HANGE
HANGEE
HANGER
HANGFIRE
HANGI
HANGIE
HANGING
HANGKANG
HANGLE
HANGMAN
HANGMENT
HANGNAIL
HANGNEST

HANGOUT
HANGOVER
HANGTAG
HANGUL
HANGUP
HANGWORM
HANGWORTHY
HANIF
HANIFISM
HANIFITE
HANIFIYA
HANK
HANKER
HANKERER
HANKERING
HANKERINGLY
HANKIE
HANKING
HANKLE
HANKS
HANKSITE
HANKT
HANKUL
HANKY
HANNA
HANNAYITE
HANOLOGATE
HANSA
HANSE
HANSEL
HANSELIN
HANSGRAVE
HANSOM
HANT
HANTLE
HANUM
HANUMAN
HAO
HAOLE
HAOMA
HAP
HAPALOTE
HAPHAZARD
HAPHAZARDLY
HAPHAZARDNESS
HAPHTARAH
HAPITON
HAPLESS
HAPLESSLY
HAPLESSNESS
HAPLITE
HAPLITIC
HAPLODONT
HAPLODONTY
HAPLOID
HAPLOIDIC
HAPLOIDY
HAPLOLALY
HAPLOLOGIC
HAPLOLOGY
HAPLOMA
HAPLOME
HAPLOMID
HAPLONT
HAPLOPHASE
HAPLOSCOPE
HAPLOSIS
HAPLOTYPE
HAPLY
HAPPEN
HAPPENING
HAPPER
HAPPIER
HAPPIEST
HAPPIFY
HAPPILESS
HAPPILY
HAPPINESS
HAPPING
HAPPY
HAPS
HAPT
HAPTERA
HAPTERE
HAPTERON
HAPTIC
HAPTICS
HAPTOMETER
HAPTOR
HAPTOTROPIC
HAPU
HAPUKU
HAQUETON
HAR
HARACE
HARAKEKE
HARANG
HARANGUE
HARANGUEFUL
HARANGUER
HARAS
HARASS
HARASSED
HARASSEDLY
HARASSER
HARASSING
HARASSINGLY
HARASSMENT
HARAST
HARATCH
HARATEEN
HARAUCANA
HARBERGAGE
HARBI
HARBINGE
HARBINGER
HARBORAGE
HARBORER
HARBORLESS
HARBORMASTER
HARBORSIDE
HARBOUR
HARBOURAGE
HARBOURER
HARBOURSIDE
HARD
HARDANGER
HARDBACK
HARDBAKE
HARDBALL
HARDBEAM
HARDBERRY
HARDCASE
HARDEN
HARDENED
HARDENER
HARDENING
HARDENITE
HARDER
HARDEST
HARDFERN
HARDFIST
HARDFISTED
HARDHACK
HARDHANDED
HARDHEAD
HARDHEADED
HARDHEADEDLY
HARDHEADEDNESS
HARDHEARTED
HARDHEARTEDLY
HARDHEARTEDNESS
HARDHEWER
HARDIE
HARDIER
HARDIES
HARDIESSE
HARDIEST
HARDIHEAD
HARDIHOOD
HARDILY
HARDIM
HARDIMENT
HARDINESS
HARDISH
HARDLY
HARDMOUTH
HARDMOUTHED
HARDNESS
HARDOCK
HARDPAN
HARDS
HARDSALT
HARDSET
HARDSHIP
HARDSTAND
HARDTACK
HARDTAIL
HARDTOP
HARDWARE
HARDWAY
HARDWEED
HARDWOOD
HARDWORKING
HARDY
HARDYHEAD
HARE
HAREBELL
HAREBOTTLE
HAREBRAIN
HAREBRAINED
HAREBUR
HAREEM
HAREFOOT
HAREFOOTED
HAREHEARTED
HAREHOUND
HARELIKE
HARELIP
HARELIPPED
HAREM
HAREMISM
HAREMLIK
HARENUT
HARES
HAREWOOD
HARFANG
HARIANA
HARICO
HARICOT
HARIER
HARIF
HARIFFE
HARIGALDS
HARIOLATE
HARIOLATION
HARISH
HARK
HARKA
HARKEN
HARKENER
HARL
HARLE
HARLEQUIN
HARLEQUINA
HARLEQUINADE
HARLEQUINESQUE
HARLEQUINIC
HARLEQUINIZE
HARLING
HARLOCK
HARLOT
HARLOTRIES
HARLOTRY
HARM
HARMAL
HARMALA
HARMALIN
HARMALINE
HARMAN
HARMATTAN
HARMEL
HARMER
HARMFUL
HARMFULLY
HARMFULNESS
HARMIN
HARMINE
HARMLESS
HARMLESSLY
HARMLESSNESS
HARMONIA
HARMONIACAL
HARMONIC
HARMONICA
HARMONICAL
HARMONICALLY
HARMONICI
HARMONICON
HARMONICS
HARMONIES
HARMONIOUS
HARMONIOUSLY
HARMONIOUSNESS
HARMONIST
HARMONISTIC
HARMONISTICALLY
HARMONIUM
HARMONIZE
HARMONIZER
HARMONIZING
HARMONY
HARMOOT
HARMOST
HARMOTOME
HARMOUT
HARN
HARNESS
HARNESSED
HARNESSER
HARNESSRY
HARNPAN
HARO
HAROSET
HARP
HARPAGO
HARPAGON
HARPE
HARPER
HARPIER
HARPIES
HARPIN
HARPINGS
HARPINS
HARPIST
HARPLESS
HARPLIKE
HARPOON
HARPOONED
HARPOONEER
HARPOONER
HARPSICAL
HARPSICHON
HARPSICHORD
HARPULA
HARPWISE
HARPY
HARQUEBUS
HARQUEBUSS
HARR
HARRAGE
HARRATEEN
HARRID
HARRIDAN
HARRIED
HARRIER
HARRISITE
HARROW
HARROWED
HARROWER
HARROWING
HARROWINGLY
HARROWINGNESS
HARROWMENT
HARROWTRY
HARRUMPH
HARRY
HARRYCANE
HARSH
HARSHISH
HARSHLY
HARSHNESS
HARSK
HARSLET
HARST
HARSTIGITE
HARSTRANG
HARSTRONG
HART
HARTAIL
HARTAKE
HARTAL
HARTALL
HARTBERRY
HARTEBEEST
HARTEN
HARTH
HARTIN
HARTITE
HARTLY
HARTSHORN
HARTSTONGUE
HARTTITE
HARUSPEX
HARUSPICAL
HARUSPICE
HARUSPICES
HARVEST
HARVESTER
HARVESTING
HARVESTLESS
HARVESTMAN
HARVESTRY
HARVESTTIME
HARZBURGITE
HAS
HASAN
HASARD
HASEL
HASH
HASHAB
HASHABI
HASHEESH
HASHER
HASHISH
HASHT
HASHY
HASK
HASKARD
HASKNESS
HASKWORT
HASKY
HASLET
HASLOCK
HASP

HASPICOL
HASS
HASSAR
HASSEL
HASSING
HASSLE
HASSLET
HASSOCK
HASSOCKY
HASTA
HASTATE
HASTATED
HASTATELY
HASTATI
HASTE
HASTEFUL
HASTEFULLY
HASTEN
HASTENER
HASTER
HASTIER
HASTIEST
HASTIF
HASTIFLY
HASTIFNESS
HASTILUDE
HASTILY
HASTINESS
HASTINGS
HASTINGSITE
HASTISH
HASTIVE
HASTLER
HASTULA
HASTY
HAT
HATABLE
HATBAND
HATBOX
HATCH
HATCHABLE
HATCHED
HATCHEL
HATCHELER
HATCHELLER
HATCHER
HATCHERIES
HATCHERY
HATCHERYMAN
HATCHET
HATCHETBACK
HATCHETLIKE
HATCHETTINE
HATCHETTITE
HATCHETY
HATCHGATE
HATCHING
HATCHITE
HATCHLING
HATCHMAN
HATCHMENT
HATCHWAY
HATCHWAYMAN
HATE
HATEABLE
HATEFUL
HATEFULLY
HATEFULNESS
HATEL
HATEN
HATER
HATFUL
HATH
HATHERLITE
HATHI
HATLESS
HATLIKE
HATMAKER
HATMAKING
HATPIN
HATRACK
HATRAIL
HATRED
HATRESS
HATS
HATSTAND
HATT
HATTE
HATTED
HATTER
HATTERIA
HATTERY
HATTING
HATTOCK
HATTY
HAU
HAUBERGEON
HAUBERGET
HAUBERK
HAUD
HAUERITE
HAUF
HAUFLIN
HAUGH
HAUGHLAND
HAUGHT
HAUGHTILY
HAUGHTINESS
HAUGHTONITE
HAUGHTY
HAUL
HAULABOUT
HAULAGE
HAULAGEWAY
HAULAWAY
HAULBACK
HAULD
HAULE
HAULER
HAULIER
HAULING
HAULM
HAULMY
HAULSTER
HAULT
HAULYARD
HAUN
HAUNCH
HAUNCHED
HAUNCHER
HAUNCHES
HAUNCHING
HAUNCHLESS
HAUNCHY
HAUNT
HAUNTED
HAUNTER
HAUNTING
HAUNTINGLY
HAUNTY
HAUPIA
HAURIANT
HAURIENT
HAURN
HAUSE
HAUSEN
HAUSSE
HAUSTELLA
HAUSTELLATE
HAUSTELLATED
HAUSTELLUM
HAUSTORIUM
HAUSTRAL
HAUSTRUM
HAUSTUS
HAUT
HAUTAIN
HAUTBOIS
HAUTBOY
HAUTBOYIST
HAUTESSE
HAUTEUR
HAUYNE
HAUYNITE
HAVAGE
HAVANCE
HAVE
HAVEAGE
HAVEL
HAVELESS
HAVELOCK
HAVEN
HAVENAGE
HAVENER
HAVENET
HAVER
HAVERAL
HAVERCAKE
HAVEREL
HAVERER
HAVERGRASS
HAVERING
HAVERMEAL
HAVERS
HAVERSACK
HAVERSINE
HAVIER
HAVILDAR
HAVING
HAVINGNESS
HAVINGS
HAVIOR
HAVIORED
HAVIOUR
HAVIOURED
HAVLAGAH
HAVOC
HAVOCKER
HAW
HAWAIITE
HAWBUCK
HAWCUBITE
HAWEBAKE
HAWER
HAWFINCH
HAWK
HAWKBILL
HAWKBIT
HAWKED
HAWKER
HAWKERY
HAWKEY
HAWKIE
HAWKING
HAWKINS
HAWKISH
HAWKNOSE
HAWKNOSED
HAWKNUT
HAWKS
HAWKSBILL
HAWKSHAW
HAWKWEED
HAWKY
HAWM
HAWN
HAWOK
HAWSE
HAWSEHOLE
HAWSEMAN
HAWSEPIECE
HAWSEPIPE
HAWSER
HAWTHORN
HAWTHORNY
HAY
HAYA
HAYBAND
HAYBIRD
HAYBOTE
HAYBURNER
HAYCAP
HAYCOCK
HAYDENITE
HAYE
HAYEY
HAYFIELD
HAYFORK
HAYING
HAYLOFT
HAYMAKER
HAYMAKING
HAYMARKET
HAYMOW
HAYNE
HAYRACK
HAYRICK
HAYRIDE
HAYS
HAYSEED
HAYSEL
HAYSHOCK
HAYSTACK
HAYSUCK
HAYWARD
HAYWEED
HAYWIRE
HAYZ
HAZAN
HAZANUT
HAZARD
HAZARDER
HAZARDOUS
HAZARDOUSLY
HAZARDOUSNESS
HAZARDRY
HAZE
HAZEL
HAZELED
HAZELLY
HAZELNUT
HAZEN
HAZER
HAZIER
HAZIEST
HAZILY
HAZINESS
HAZING
HAZLE
HAZNADAR
HAZY
HAZZAN
HAZZANUT
HE
HEAD
HEADACHE
HEADACHY
HEADBAND
HEADBANDER
HEADBOARD
HEADBOROUGH
HEADBOX
HEADCAP
HEADCHAIR
HEADCHEESE
HEADCHUTE
HEADCLOTH
HEADDRESS
HEADED
HEADENDER
HEADER
HEADFAST
HEADFIRST
HEADFISH
HEADFOREMOST
HEADFRAME
HEADFUL
HEADGEAR
HEADHUNT
HEADHUNTER
HEADIER
HEADIEST
HEADILY
HEADINESS
HEADING
HEADINGS
HEADLAND
HEADLE
HEADLEDGE
HEADLESS
HEADLIGHT
HEADLIGHTING
HEADLINE
HEADLINER
HEADLING
HEADLOAD
HEADLOCK
HEADLONG
HEADLONGLY
HEADLONGNESS
HEADLY
HEADMAN
HEADMARK
HEADMASTER
HEADMASTERLY
HEADMISTRESS
HEADMOLD
HEADMOST
HEADMOULD
HEADNOTE
HEADPENNY
HEADPHONE
HEADPIECE
HEADPIN
HEADPLATE
HEADPOST
HEADQUARTER
HEADQUARTERS
HEADRAIL
HEADREACH
HEADRENT
HEADREST
HEADRIG
HEADRIGHT
HEADRING
HEADROOM
HEADROPE
HEADS
HEADSAIL
HEADSAW
HEADSET
HEADSHAKE
HEADSHIP
HEADSILL
HEADSKIN
HEADSMAN
HEADSPACE
HEADSPRING
HEADSTALL
HEADSTAND
HEADSTICK
HEADSTOCK
HEADSTONE
HEADSTREAM
HEADSTRONG

HEADSTRONGLY
HEADSTRONGNESS
HEADTIRE
HEADWAITER
HEADWALL
HEADWARD
HEADWARDS
HEADWARK
HEADWATER
HEADWATERS
HEADWAY
HEADWEAR
HEADWORK
HEADWORKER
HEADWORKING
HEADY
HEAF
HEAL
HEALD
HEALDER
HEALED
HEALER
HEALFUL
HEALING
HEALINGLY
HEALLESS
HEALSOME
HEALSOMENESS
HEALTH
HEALTHCRAFT
HEALTHFUL
HEALTHFULLY
HEALTHFULNESS
HEALTHGUARD
HEALTHIER
HEALTHIEST
HEALTHLESS
HEALTHSOME
HEALTHY
HEAM
HEAP
HEAPED
HEAPER
HEAPING
HEAPS
HEAPSTEAD
HEAPY
HEAR
HEARD
HEARER
HEARING
HEARKEN
HEARKENER
HEARSAY
HEARSE
HEARSECLOTH
HEARST
HEART
HEARTACHE
HEARTACHING
HEARTBEAT
HEARTBIRD
HEARTBLOCK
HEARTBLOOD
HEARTBREAK
HEARTBREAKER
HEARTBREAKING
HEARTBROKEN
HEARTBROKENLY
HEARTBROKENNESS
HEARTBURN
HEARTBURNING
HEARTDEEP
HEARTEASE
HEARTED
HEARTEDLY
HEARTEN
HEARTENER
HEARTENING
HEARTFELT
HEARTFUL
HEARTFULLY
HEARTFULNESS
HEARTGRIEF
HEARTH
HEARTHMAN
HEARTHPENNY
HEARTHRUG
HEARTHS
HEARTHSTONE
HEARTHWARD
HEARTHWARMING
HEARTIER
HEARTIES
HEARTIEST
HEARTIKIN
HEARTILY
HEARTINESS
HEARTING
HEARTLEAF
HEARTLESS
HEARTLESSLY
HEARTLESSNESS
HEARTLY
HEARTNUT
HEARTPEA
HEARTQUAKE
HEARTROOT
HEARTROT
HEARTS
HEARTSCALD
HEARTSEASE
HEARTSEED
HEARTSETTE
HEARTSICK
HEARTSOME
HEARTSOMELY
HEARTSORE
HEARTSTRING
HEARTSTRINGS
HEARTTHROB
HEARTWATER
HEARTWEED
HEARTWOOD
HEARTWORM
HEARTWORT
HEARTY
HEAT
HEATDROPS
HEATED
HEATEDLY
HEATEN
HEATER
HEATERMAN
HEATH
HEATHBERRY
HEATHBIRD
HEATHEN
HEATHENDOM
HEATHENESSE
HEATHENISH
HEATHENISHLY
HEATHENISHNESS
HEATHENISM
HEATHENIST
HEATHENIZE
HEATHENLY
HEATHENRY
HEATHER
HEATHERED
HEATHERINESS
HEATHERY
HEATHIER
HEATHIEST
HEATHLIKE
HEATHWORT
HEATHY
HEATING
HEATINGLY
HEATLESS
HEATSMAN
HEATSTROKE
HEAUME
HEAUMER
HEAUTARIT
HEAVE
HEAVEN
HEAVENLY
HEAVENS
HEAVENWARD
HEAVENWARDLY
HEAVENWARDNESS
HEAVENWARDS
HEAVER
HEAVES
HEAVIER
HEAVIES
HEAVIEST
HEAVILY
HEAVINESS
HEAVING
HEAVISOME
HEAVITY
HEAVY
HEAVYBACK
HEAVYSET
HEAVYWEIGHT
HEAZY
HEBAMIC
HEBDOMAD
HEBDOMADAL
HEBDOMADALLY
HEBDOMADARY
HEBDOMADER
HEBEANTHOUS
HEBECARPOUS
HEBECLADOUS
HEBENON
HEBEPHRENIC
HEBETATE
HEBETATION
HEBETATIVE
HEBETE
HEBETIC
HEBETUDE
HECATOMB
HECATOMPED
HECCEITY
HECCO
HECH
HECHIMA
HECHSHER
HECK
HECKIMAL
HECKLE
HECKLER
HECTARE
HECTE
HECTIC
HECTICAL
HECTICALLY
HECTIVE
HECTOGRAM
HECTOGRAMME
HECTOGRAPH
HECTOGRAPHIC
HECTOLITER
HECTOLITRE
HECTOR
HECTORED
HECTORING
HECTORLY
HECTOSTERE
HECTOWATT
HED
HEDDE
HEDDLE
HEDDLER
HEDDLES
HEDEBO
HEDER
HEDERACEOUS
HEDERATED
HEDERIC
HEDERIN
HEDEROSE
HEDGE
HEDGEBERRY
HEDGEBETTY
HEDGEBOTE
HEDGEHOG
HEDGEHOGGY
HEDGEHOP
HEDGEPIG
HEDGER
HEDGEROW
HEDGES
HEDGESMITH
HEDGESTRAW
HEDGETAPER
HEDGING
HEDGINGLY
HEDGY
HEDONIC
HEDONICAL
HEDONICALLY
HEDONICS
HEDONISM
HEDONIST
HEDONISTIC
HEDONISTICALLY
HEDROCELE
HEDRUMITE
HEDYPHANE
HEE
HEED
HEEDER
HEEDFUL
HEEDFULLY
HEEDFULNESS
HEEDILY
HEEDINESS
HEEDLESS
HEEDLESSLY
HEEDLESSNESS
HEEDY
HEEHAW
HEEL
HEELBALL
HEELCAP
HEELD
HEELED
HEELER
HEELING
HEELPATH
HEELPIECE
HEELPLATE
HEELPOST
HEELS
HEELSTRAP
HEELTAP
HEELTREE
HEELWORK
HEEMRAAD
HEEMRAAT
HEER
HEEZE
HEFT
HEFTER
HEFTIER
HEFTIEST
HEFTILY
HEFTINESS
HEFTY
HEG
HEGEMON
HEGEMONIC
HEGEMONICAL
HEGEMONIST
HEGEMONY
HEGIRA
HEGUMEN
HEGUMENESS
HEGUMENOS
HEGUMENY
HEIAU
HEIFER
HEIGH
HEIGHT
HEIGHTEN
HEIGHTENER
HEIGHTH
HEII
HEIL
HEIMIN
HEIMLICH
HEIN
HEINOUS
HEINOUSLY
HEINOUSNESS
HEIR
HEIRDOM
HEIRESS
HEIRLOOM
HEIRMOS
HEIRSHIP
HEIST
HEISTER
HEITIKI
HEJIRA
HEKTEUS
HEL
HELAS
HELBEH
HELCOID
HELCOLOGY
HELCOPLASTY
HELCOSIS
HELCOTIC
HELD
HELDER
HELENIN
HELEPOLE
HELER
HELIAC
HELIACAL
HELIACALLY
HELIANTHUS
HELIAST
HELIASTIC
HELICAL
HELICALLY
HELICED
HELICINE
HELICITIC
HELICLINE
HELICOGRAPH
HELICOGYRE
HELICOID
HELICOIDAL
HELICOIDALLY
HELICOMETRY
HELICON
HELICONIST
HELICOPROTEIN

HELICOPTER
HELICORUBIN
HELICOTREMA
HELICTITE
HELID
HELIDE
HELIO
HELIOCENTRIC
HELIOCENTRICAL
HELIOCENTRICITY
HELIOCHROME
HELIOCHROMIC
HELIOCHROMY
HELIOCULTURE
HELIODON
HELIODOR
HELIOELECTRIC
HELIOFUGAL
HELIOGRAM
HELIOGRAPH
HELIOGRAPHER
HELIOGRAPHIC
HELIOGRAPHY
HELIOGRAVURE
HELIOID
HELIOLATER
HELIOLATOR
HELIOLATROUS
HELIOLATRY
HELIOLITE
HELIOMETER
HELIOMETRIC
HELIOMETRY
HELIOSCOPE
HELIOSIS
HELIOSTAT
HELIOTACTIC
HELIOTAXIS
HELIOTHERAPY
HELIOTROPE
HELIOTROPIC
HELIOTROPISM
HELIOTROPY
HELIOTYPE
HELIOZOAN
HELIPORT
HELIUM
HELIX
HELIXIN
HELL
HELLBENDER
HELLBOX
HELLBROTH
HELLCAT
HELLDOG
HELLEBORE
HELLEBOREIN
HELLEBORIC
HELLEBORIN
HELLER
HELLERI
HELLERY
HELLFIRE
HELLGRAMMITE
HELLHAG
HELLHOLE
HELLHOUND
HELLICAT
HELLICATE
HELLIER
HELLIM
HELLION
HELLISH
HELLISHLY
HELLISHNESS
HELLKITE
HELLO
HELLROOT
HELLSHIP
HELLUO
HELLVINE
HELLWEED
HELLY
HELM
HELMAGE
HELMED
HELMET
HELMETED
HELMETFLOWER
HELMETLIKE
HELMETPOD
HELMINTH
HELMINTHIC
HELMINTHISM
HELMSMAN
HELO
HELOBIOUS
HELODES
HELOE
HELOMA
HELONIN
HELOSIS
HELOT
HELOTISM
HELOTOMY
HELOTRY
HELP
HELPER
HELPFUL
HELPFULLY
HELPFULNESS
HELPING
HELPLESS
HELPLESSLY
HELPLESSNESS
HELPLY
HELPMATE
HELPMEET
HELPSOME
HELPWORTHY
HELVE
HELVELL
HELVELLIC
HELVIN
HELVINE
HELVITE
HELZEL
HEM
HEMACHATE
HEMACHROME
HEMACITE
HEMAD
HEMAGOG
HEMAGOGIC
HEMAGOGUE
HEMAL
HEMAMEBA
HEMAPOD
HEMATAL
HEMATEIN
HEMATIC
HEMATID
HEMATIN
HEMATINE
HEMATINIC
HEMATITE
HEMATITIC
HEMATOCELE
HEMATOID
HEMATOLIN
HEMATOMA
HEMATOMETER
HEMATOSCOPE
HEMATOSE
HEMATOSIN
HEMATOSIS
HEMATOZOON
HEMATURIA
HEME
HEMEL
HEMEN
HEMERA
HEMERALOPE
HEMERALOPIA
HEMERALOPIC
HEMIACETAL
HEMIALGIA
HEMIAMB
HEMIAUXIN
HEMIBRANCH
HEMIC
HEMICARDIA
HEMICARP
HEMICENTRUM
HEMICHORDATE
HEMICOLLIN
HEMICRANE
HEMICRANIA
HEMICYCLE
HEMICYCLIC
HEMIDITONE
HEMIDOME
HEMIEPES
HEMIFACIAL
HEMIFORM
HEMIGLYPH
HEMIHEDRAL
HEMIHEDRIC
HEMIKARYON
HEMIMELLITIC
HEMIMELUS
HEMIMORPH
HEMIMORPHIC
HEMIMORPHITE
HEMIN
HEMINA
HEMINE
HEMINEE
HEMIOLA
HEMIOLIA
HEMIOLIC
HEMIONUS
HEMIOPE
HEMIOPIA
HEMIOPIC
HEMIOPSIA
HEMIPENIS
HEMIPHRASE
HEMIPIC
HEMIPLEGIA
HEMIPLEGIC
HEMIPLEGY
HEMIPOD
HEMIPODE
HEMIPPE
HEMIPRISM
HEMIPROTEIN
HEMIPTER
HEMIPTERAL
HEMIPTERAN
HEMIPTERON
HEMIPTEROUS
HEMISECT
HEMISPHERAL
HEMISPHERE
HEMISPHERED
HEMISTATER
HEMISTICH
HEMITERATA
HEMITERIA
HEMITERY
HEMITONE
HEMITROPAL
HEMITROPE
HEMITROPIC
HEMITYPE
HEMITYPIC
HEML
HEMLOCK
HEMMEL
HEMMER
HEMMING
HEMOBLAST
HEMOCHROME
HEMOCONIA
HEMOCYTE
HEMOFUSCIN
HEMOGASTRIC
HEMOGLOBIN
HEMOGRAM
HEMOID
HEMOL
HEMOLYSIN
HEMOLYSIS
HEMOLYZE
HEMOPHILE
HEMOPHILIA
HEMOPHILIAC
HEMOPHILIC
HEMOPTOE
HEMORRHAGE
HEMORRHOID
HEMOSCOPE
HEMOSCOPY
HEMOSTASIA
HEMOSTASIS
HEMOSTAT
HEMOSTATIC
HEMOTHORAX
HEMOTOXIC
HEMOTOXIN
HEMOTROPHE
HEMOTROPIC
HEMOZOON
HEMP
HEMPBUSH
HEMPEN
HEMPHERDS
HEMPIE
HEMPIER
HEMPIEST
HEMPSEED
HEMPSTRING
HEMPWEED
HEMPWORT
HEMPY
HEMSELF
HEMSTITCH
HEMSTITCHER
HEN
HENAD
HENBANE
HENBILL
HENBIT
HENCE
HENCEFORTH
HENCEFORWARDS
HENCH
HENCHBOY
HENCHMAN
HENCOOP
HEND
HENDE
HENDECAGON
HENDECANE
HENDECOIC
HENDECYL
HENDIADYS
HENEQUEN
HENFISH
HENHEARTED
HENHUSSIES
HENHUSSY
HENISM
HENNA
HENNERIES
HENNERY
HENNIN
HENNISH
HENNY
HENOTIC
HENPECK
HENPECKED
HENPEN
HENRIES
HENRYS
HENS
HENT
HENWARE
HENWILE
HENWOODITE
HEO
HEP
HEPAR
HEPARIN
HEPATIC
HEPATICAE
HEPATICAL
HEPATITE
HEPATITIS
HEPATIZE
HEPATOID
HEPATOMA
HEPPEN
HEPPER
HEPTACHORD
HEPTACOLIC
HEPTAD
HEPTAGLOT
HEPTAGON
HEPTAGONAL
HEPTAHEDRAL
HEPTAHEDRON
HEPTAL
HEPTAMETER
HEPTANE
HEPTANGULAR
HEPTANONE
HEPTAPLOID
HEPTAPODY
HEPTARCH
HEPTARCHAL
HEPTARCHIC
HEPTARCHIES
HEPTARCHIST
HEPTARCHY
HEPTASTICH
HEPTENE
HEPTERIS
HEPTITE
HEPTITOL
HEPTOIC
HEPTORITE
HEPTOSE
HEPTOXIDE
HEPTYL
HEPTYLENE
HEPTYLIC
HEPTYNE
HER
HERALD
HERALDIC
HERALDICAL
HERALDIST
HERALDIZE

HERALDRIES
HERALDRY
HERB
HERBACEOUS
HERBAGE
HERBAGED
HERBAGER
HERBAGIOUS
HERBAL
HERBALIST
HERBALIZE
HERBARISM
HERBARIZE
HERBARY
HERBBANE
HERBER
HERBESCENT
HERBICIDE
HERBIFEROUS
HERBIVORE
HERBLET
HERBMAN
HERBORIST
HERBORIZE
HERBOSE
HERBS
HERBWIFE
HERBWOMAN
HERBY
HERCULEAN
HERCYNITE
HERD
HERDBOOK
HERDBOY
HERDER
HERDERITE
HERDIC
HERDING
HERDSMAN
HERDSMEN
HERDSWOMAN
HERDWICK
HERE
HEREABOUT
HEREABOUTS
HEREADAYS
HEREAFTER
HEREAFTERWARD
HEREAGAIN
HEREAGAINST
HEREAMONG
HEREANENT
HEREAT
HEREAWAY
HEREBEFORE
HEREBY
HEREDIA
HEREDITABLE
HEREDITAL
HEREDITAMENT
HEREDITARY
HEREDITAS
HEREDITIES
HEREDITISM
HEREDITIST
HEREDITY
HEREDOLUES
HEREFORE
HEREFROM
HEREGELD
HEREGILD
HEREHENCE
HEREIN
HEREINABOVE
HEREINAFTER
HEREINBEFORE
HEREINTO
HEREM
HERENACH
HERENIGING
HEREOF
HEREON
HEREOUT
HERERIGHT
HERES
HERESIARCH
HERESIES
HERESIMACH
HERESIOLOGER
HERESIOLOGY
HERESY
HERETIC
HERETICAL
HERETICALLY
HERETICALNESS
HERETICATE
HERETICATED
HERETICATION
HERETICATOR
HERETICIDE
HERETICIZE
HERETO
HERETOFORE
HERETOGA
HEREUNDER
HEREUNTO
HEREUPON
HEREWITH
HEREWITHAL
HEREZELD
HERIF
HERILE
HERIOT
HERIOTABLE
HERISSON
HERITABLE
HERITABLY
HERITAGE
HERITANCE
HERITOR
HERITRIX
HERL
HERLING
HERM
HERMA
HERMAE
HERMAEAN
HERMAI
HERMAIC
HERMANDAD
HERMAPHRODITE
HERMAPHRODITIC
HERMAPHRODITISM
HERME
HERMELE
HERMENEUT
HERMENEUTIC
HERMETIC
HERMETICAL
HERMIDIN
HERMIT
HERMITAGE
HERMITARY
HERMITIC
HERMITICAL
HERMITRY
HERN
HERNE
HERNIA
HERNIAE
HERNIAL
HERNIARIN
HERNIARY
HERNIATE
HERNIATED
HERNIATION
HERO
HERODIAN
HEROES
HEROESS
HEROIC
HEROICAL
HEROICITY
HEROICOMIC
HEROICS
HEROID
HEROIFY
HEROIN
HEROINE
HEROISM
HEROISTIC
HEROLA
HERON
HERONBILL
HERONER
HERONITE
HERONRY
HERONS
HERONSEW
HEROOGONY
HEROOLOGY
HERPES
HERPESTINE
HERPETIC
HERRING
HERRINGBONE
HERRINGER
HERRINGS
HERRY
HERS
HERSALL
HERSCHELITE
HERSE
HERSED
HERSELF
HERSHIP
HERSIR
HERTZ
HERTZIAN
HERY
HESH
HESITANCE
HESITANCY
HESITANT
HESITANTLY
HESITATE
HESITATER
HESITATING
HESITATION
HESITATIVE
HESITATOR
HESPED
HESPEL
HESPERIDATE
HESPERIDENE
HESPERIDIN
HESSITE
HESSONITE
HEST
HET
HETAERA
HETAERIA
HETAERIO
HETAERISM
HETAERIST
HETAERY
HETAIRIA
HETAIRY
HETE
HETERAKID
HETERIC
HETERISM
HETERIZE
HETEROCENTRIC
HETEROCERC
HETEROCERCAL
HETEROCHIRAL
HETEROCHROME
HETEROCLINE
HETEROCLITE
HETEROCLITIC
HETEROCYCLE
HETEROCYCLIC
HETEROCYST
HETERODONT
HETERODOX
HETERODOXIES
HETERODOXY
HETERODYNE
HETEROECY
HETEROEROTISM
HETEROGAMETE
HETEROGAMIC
HETEROGAMY
HETEROGENE
HETEROGENEOUS
HETEROGONY
HETEROGRAFT
HETEROGRAPHIES
HETEROGRAPHY
HETEROGYNAL
HETEROLATERAL
HETEROLITH
HETEROLOGICAL
HETEROLOGIES
HETEROLOGY
HETEROLYSIS
HETEROLYTIC
HETEROMORPHIC
HETERONOMOUS
HETERONOMY
HETERONUCLEAR
HETERONYM
HETERONYMOUS
HETEROPATHIC
HETEROPATHY
HETEROPLASM
HETEROPLASTIC
HETEROPLASTIES
HETEROPLASTY
HETEROPOLAR
HETEROPTICS
HETEROSCOPE
HETEROSEXUAL
HETEROSIS
HETEROSPHERE
HETEROSTATIC
HETEROTACTIC
HETEROTAXIA
HETEROTAXIC
HETEROTAXIS
HETEROTELIC
HETEROTOPIA
HETEROTOPIC
HETEROTOPY
HETEROTROPAL
HETEROTROPHIC
HETEROTYPIC
HETEROXENOUS
HETEROZYGOTE
HETEROZYGOUS
HETHEN
HETHING
HETMAN
HETTER
HEU
HEUCH
HEUGH
HEURETIC
HEURT
HEUVEL
HEVEN
HEVER
HEVI
HEW
HEWE
HEWEL
HEWER
HEWGAG
HEWHALL
HEWHOLE
HEWN
HEWT
HEX
HEXABASIC
HEXABIOSE
HEXABROMID
HEXABROMIDE
HEXACHORD
HEXACID
HEXACOLIC
HEXACOSANE
HEXACTINAL
HEXACYCLIC
HEXAD
HEXADE
HEXADECANE
HEXADECYL
HEXADIC
HEXADIENE
HEXADIINE
HEXADIYNE
HEXAEMERIC
HEXAEMERON
HEXAFOIL
HEXAFOOS
HEXAGLOT
HEXAGON
HEXAGONAL
HEXAGONALLY
HEXAGRAM
HEXAGYN
HEXAGYNOUS
HEXAHEDRA
HEXAHEDRAL
HEXAHEDRON
HEXAHYDRIC
HEXAMER
HEXAMERAL
HEXAMERISM
HEXAMERON
HEXAMEROUS
HEXAMETER
HEXAMETRAL
HEXAMETRIC
HEXAMINE
HEXAMMIN
HEXAMMINE
HEXANAL
HEXANDRIC
HEXANDROUS
HEXANDRY
HEXANE
HEXANGULAR
HEXAPED
HEXAPLA
HEXAPLAR
HEXAPLARIC
HEXAPLOID
HEXAPOD
HEXAPODIES
HEXAPODY
HEXARADIAL
HEXARCHIES
HEXARCHY

HEXASEME
HEXASEMIC
HEXASTER
HEXASTICH
HEXASTICHIC
HEXASTICHY
HEXASTIGM
HEXASTYLOS
HEXATHLON
HEXATOMIC
HEXATRIOSE
HEXAVALENT
HEXAXON
HEXENE
HEXER
HEXEREI
HEXERIS
HEXINE
HEXIS
HEXITOL
HEXOBARBITAL
HEXODE
HEXOIC
HEXONE
HEXONIC
HEXOSAN
HEXOSE
HEXPARTITE
HEXT
HEXYL
HEXYLENE
HEXYLIC
HEXYNE
HEY
HEYDAY
HEYDEGUY
HEYDEY
HEYRAT
HEYT
HI
HIA
HIANT
HIATAL
HIATE
HIATION
HIATUS
HIBACHI
HIBBIN
HIBERNAL
HIBERNATE
HIBERNATING
HIBERNATION
HIC
HICACO
HICAN
HICATEE
HICCAN
HICCOUGH
HICCUP
HICHT
HICHU
HICK
HICKEY
HICKORY
HICKWALL
HICKWAY
HICKY
HID
HIDAGE
HIDALGO
HIDATED
HIDATION
HIDDELS
HIDDEN
HIDDENITE
HIDE
HIDEAWAY
HIDEBIND
HIDEBOUND
HIDEBOUNDNESS
HIDED
HIDEL
HIDELAND
HIDELING
HIDEOSITY
HIDEOUS
HIDEOUSLY
HIDEOUSNESS
HIDEOUT
HIDER
HIDES
HIDING
HIDLING
HIDLINGS
HIDLINS
HIDROSIS
HIDROTIC
HIE
HIEDER
HIELAMAN
HIELAMEN
HIELD
HIELMITE
HIEMAL
HIEMATION
HIEMS
HIEN
HIER
HIERA
HIERAPICRA
HIERARCH
HIERARCHAL
HIERARCHIC
HIERARCHICAL
HIERARCHICALLY
HIERARCHISM
HIERARCHIST
HIERARCHIZE
HIERARCHY
HIERATIC
HIERATICAL
HIERATICALLY
HIERATITE
HIEROCRACIES
HIEROCRACY
HIEROCRATIC
HIEROCRATICAL
HIERODULE
HIEROGAMY
HIEROGLYPH
HIEROGLYPHER
HIEROGLYPHIC
HIEROGRAM
HIEROGRAPH
HIEROGRAPHER
HIEROGRAPHIC
HIEROGRAPHY
HIEROLATRY
HIEROLOGIC
HIEROLOGIST
HIEROLOGY
HIEROMACHY
HIEROMANCY
HIEROMNEMON
HIEROMONACH
HIERON
HIEROPATHIC
HIEROPHANCY
HIEROPHANT
HIEROS
HIEROSCOPY
HIERURGY
HIFALUTIN
HIGDON
HIGGAION
HIGGLE
HIGGLEHAGGLE
HIGGLER
HIGGLERY
HIGH
HIGHBALL
HIGHBINDER
HIGHBORN
HIGHBOY
HIGHBRED
HIGHBROW
HIGHBROWED
HIGHBROWISM
HIGHCHAIR
HIGHDAY
HIGHER
HIGHERMOST
HIGHEST
HIGHFALUTIN
HIGHFALUTING
HIGHFLIER
HIGHFLYER
HIGHFLYING
HIGHHANDED
HIGHHEARTED
HIGHHOLE
HIGHJACK
HIGHJACKER
HIGHLAND
HIGHLANDER
HIGHLIGHT
HIGHLINE
HIGHLOW
HIGHLY
HIGHMAN
HIGHMOOR
HIGHMOST
HIGHNESS
HIGHROAD
HIGHT
HIGHTAIL
HIGHTIDE
HIGHTOBY
HIGHTOP
HIGHVELD
HIGHWAY
HIGHWAYMAN
HIGRE
HIGUERO
HIJACK
HIJACKER
HIJINKS
HIKE
HIKER
HIKU
HIKULI
HILARIOUS
HILARIOUSLY
HILARIOUSNESS
HILARITY
HILASMIC
HILCH
HILDING
HILL
HILLBILLIES
HILLBILLY
HILLBIRD
HILLER
HILLET
HILLMAN
HILLO
HILLOA
HILLOCK
HILLOCKED
HILLOCKY
HILLS
HILLSALE
HILLSALESMAN
HILLSIDE
HILLSMAN
HILLTOP
HILLTROT
HILLWORT
HILLY
HILSA
HILSAH
HILT
HILUM
HILUS
HIM
HIMATIA
HIMATION
HIMENE
HIMMING
HIMP
HIMPLE
HIMSELF
HIN
HINAU
HINCH
HIND
HINDBERRY
HINDBRAIN
HINDCAST
HINDDECK
HINDER
HINDERANCE
HINDERED
HINDERER
HINDEREST
HINDERFUL
HINDERFULLY
HINDERLY
HINDERMENT
HINDERMOST
HINDERSOME
HINDGUT
HINDHAND
HINDHEAD
HINDMOST
HINDQUARTER
HINDQUARTERS
HINDRANCE
HINDS
HINDSADDLE
HINDSIGHT
HINE
HING
HINGE
HINGECORNER
HINGED
HINGEFLOWER
HINGLE
HINK
HINNA
HINNER
HINNIBLE
HINNIES
HINNY
HINOID
HINOIDEOUS
HINOKI
HINSDALITE
HINT
HINTERLAND
HIODONT
HIP
HIPBERRY
HIPBONE
HIPE
HIPHALT
HIPHAPE
HIPLINE
HIPMOLD
HIPPARCH
HIPPED
HIPPEN
HIPPIAN
HIPPIATER
HIPPIATRIC
HIPPIATRY
HIPPIC
HIPPIE
HIPPING
HIPPISH
HIPPLE
HIPPO
HIPPOBOSCID
HIPPOCAMPAL
HIPPOCAMPUS
HIPPOCAUST
HIPPOCERF
HIPPOCRAS
HIPPODROME
HIPPOGRIFF
HIPPOGRYPH
HIPPOID
HIPPOLITH
HIPPOLOGY
HIPPOMANES
HIPPONOUS
HIPPOPHILE
HIPPOPOD
HIPPOPOTAMIC
HIPPOPOTAMUS
HIPPOTOMY
HIPPURATE
HIPPURIC
HIPPURID
HIPPURITE
HIPPUS
HIPPY
HIPS
HIPSHOT
HIPSTER
HIRABLE
HIRAGANA
HIRCARRA
HIRCH
HIRCINE
HIRCINOUS
HIRCUS
HIRE
HIRED
HIRELING
HIRER
HIRING
HIRLING
HIRMOS
HIRO
HIRONDELLE
HIRPLE
HIRR
HIRRIENT
HIRSE
HIRSEL
HIRSELED
HIRSELING
HIRSELLED
HIRSELLING
HIRSH
HIRSLE
HIRST
HIRSUTE
HIRSUTENESS
HIRSUTIES
HIRSUTISM
HIRTCH
HIRUDINEAN
HIRUDINOID

HIRUNDINE
HIS
HISH
HISINGERITE
HISLOPITE
HISN
HISPID
HISPIDITY
HISPIDULATE
HISPIDULOUS
HISS
HISSEL
HISSELF
HISSER
HISSING
HISSY
HIST
HISTAMINE
HISTAMINIC
HISTER
HISTIDINE
HISTIE
HISTOBLAST
HISTOCHEMIC
HISTOCHEMICAL
HISTOCLASTIC
HISTOGEN
HISTOGENESIS
HISTOGENETIC
HISTOGENIC
HISTOGENOUS
HISTOGENY
HISTOGRAM
HISTOGRAPHIC
HISTOGRAPHY
HISTOID
HISTOLOGIC
HISTOLOGICAL
HISTOLOGIES
HISTOLOGIST
HISTOLOGY
HISTOLYSIS
HISTON
HISTONAL
HISTONE
HISTONOMY
HISTORIAL
HISTORIAN
HISTORIC
HISTORICAL
HISTORICALNESS
HISTORICS
HISTORIED
HISTORIER
HISTORIES
HISTORIETTE
HISTORIFY
HISTORIOGRAPH
HISTORIOGRAPHER
HISTORIOUS
HISTORISM
HISTORIZE
HISTORY
HISTOTOME
HISTOTOMY
HISTOTROPHIC
HISTOTROPHY
HISTOTROPIC
HISTRIO
HISTRION
HISTRIONIC
HISTRIONICAL
HISTRIONICALLY
HISTRIONICS
HIT
HITCH
HITCHER
HITCHHIKE
HITCHHIKER
HITCHILY
HITCHING
HITCHY
HITHE
HITHER
HITHERMOST
HITHERTILLS
HITHERTO
HITHERTOWARD
HITHERUNTO
HITHERWARD
HITTABLE
HITTER
HIVE
HIVER
HIVES
HIYA
HIYAKKIN
HIZ
HIZZ
HIZZIE
HO
HOACTZIN
HOAR
HOARD
HOARDED
HOARDER
HOARDING
HOARDWARD
HOARFROST
HOARHEAD
HOARHEADED
HOARHOUND
HOARINESS
HOARISH
HOARSE
HOARSELY
HOARSEN
HOARSENESS
HOARSTONE
HOARWORT
HOARY
HOAST
HOASTMAN
HOATZIN
HOAX
HOAXEE
HOAXER
HOAXPROOF
HOB
HOBB
HOBBER
HOBBET
HOBBIL
HOBBINOLL
HOBBIT
HOBBLE
HOBBLEBUSH
HOBBLEDEHOY
HOBBLER
HOBBLES
HOBBLING
HOBBLY
HOBBY
HOBBYHORSE
HOBBYISM
HOBBYIST
HOBGOBLIN
HOBHOUCHIN
HOBLIKE
HOBLOB
HOBNAIL
HOBNAILED
HOBNAILER
HOBNOB
HOBO
HOBOISM
HOBTHRUSH
HOC
HOCCO
HOCH
HOCK
HOCKELTY
HOCKER
HOCKET
HOCKEY
HOCKING
HOCKSHIN
HOCKY
HOCUS
HOD
HODAG
HODDEN
HODDER
HODDLE
HODDY
HODENING
HODFUL
HODGEPODGE
HODIERNAL
HODJA
HODMAN
HODMANDOD
HODOGRAPH
HODOMETER
HODOMETRICAL
HODOSCOPE
HODURE
HOE
HOECAKE
HOEDOWN
HOER
HOERNESITE
HOG
HOGA
HOGAN
HOGBACK
HOGBUSH
HOGCHOKER
HOGCOTE
HOGFISH
HOGFRAME
HOGG
HOGGASTER
HOGGED
HOGGEE
HOGGER
HOGGEREL
HOGGERY
HOGGET
HOGGIE
HOGGIN
HOGGING
HOGGINS
HOGGISH
HOGGISHLY
HOGGISHNESS
HOGGLER
HOGGY
HOGHEAD
HOGHERD
HOGLING
HOGMACE
HOGMANAY
HOGNOSE
HOGNUT
HOGO
HOGREEVE
HOGS
HOGSHEAD
HOGSHOUTHER
HOGSKIN
HOGSTEER
HOGSUCKER
HOGTON
HOGWARD
HOGWASH
HOGWEED
HOGWORT
HOI
HOICK
HOICKS
HOIDEN
HOIGH
HOIHERE
HOIN
HOISE
HOIST
HOISTAWAY
HOISTED
HOISTER
HOISTING
HOISTMAN
HOISTWAY
HOIT
HOJA
HOJU
HOK
HOKE
HOKER
HOKERER
HOKERLY
HOKEY
HOKKU
HOKUM
HOL
HOLA
HOLARCTIC
HOLARD
HOLCAD
HOLCODONT
HOLD
HOLDALL
HOLDBACK
HOLDE
HOLDENITE
HOLDER
HOLDFAST
HOLDING
HOLDINGS
HOLDMAN
HOLDOUT
HOLDOVER
HOLDSMAN
HOLDUP
HOLE
HOLEABLE
HOLEMAN
HOLER
HOLES
HOLEWORT
HOLEY
HOLIA
HOLIDAY
HOLIDAYER
HOLIES
HOLILY
HOLINESS
HOLING
HOLISHKES
HOLISM
HOLISTIC
HOLISTICALLY
HOLL
HOLLA
HOLLAITE
HOLLANDAISE
HOLLEKE
HOLLER
HOLLIN
HOLLIPER
HOLLO
HOLLOA
HOLLOCK
HOLLONG
HOLLOW
HOLLOWED
HOLLOWER
HOLLOWFACED
HOLLOWFOOT
HOLLOWHEARTED
HOLLOWLY
HOLLOWNESS
HOLLOWROOT
HOLLUSCHICK
HOLLY
HOLLYHOCK
HOLLYLEAF
HOLM
HOLMBERRY
HOLMES
HOLMGANG
HOLMIA
HOLMIC
HOLMIUM
HOLMOS
HOLOBAPTIST
HOLOBENTHIC
HOLOBLASTIC
HOLOBRANCH
HOLOCAINE
HOLOCARPIC
HOLOCAUST
HOLOCAUSTAL
HOLOCAUSTIC
HOLOCHORDATE
HOLOCHROAL
HOLOCLASTIC
HOLOGAMOUS
HOLOGAMY
HOLOGRAM
HOLOGRAPH
HOLOGRAPHIC
HOLOGRAPHY
HOLOHEDRAL
HOLOHEDRIC
HOLOHEDRON
HOLOKU
HOLOMETER
HOLOMORPH
HOLOMORPHIC
HOLOMORPHISM
HOLOMORPHY
HOLOPARASITE
HOLOPHOTAL
HOLOPHOTE
HOLOPHRASE
HOLOPHRASM
HOLOPHRASTIC
HOLOPHYTE
HOLOPHYTIC
HOLOPLEXIA
HOLOPTIC
HOLORHINAL
HOLOSIDE
HOLOSIDERITE
HOLOSTEAN
HOLOSTERIC
HOLOSTOME
HOLOSTYLIC
HOLOTHURIAN
HOLOTONY
HOLOTYPE
HOLOTYPIC
HOLOUR
HOLOZOIC

HOLP
HOLSOM
HOLSTER
HOLSTERED
HOLSTERS
HOLT
HOLY
HOLYDAY
HOLYSTONE
HOLYTIDE
HOMA
HOMAGE
HOMAGEABLE
HOMAGER
HOMALOID
HOMARD
HOMATOMIC
HOMAXIAL
HOME
HOMEBODY
HOMEBORN
HOMEBOUND
HOMEBRED
HOMECOMING
HOMECRAFT
HOMECROFT
HOMEFELT
HOMEKEEPER
HOMEKEEPING
HOMELAND
HOMELESS
HOMELIFE
HOMELIKE
HOMELIKENESS
HOMELILY
HOMELINESS
HOMELING
HOMELY
HOMELYN
HOMEMADE
HOMEMAKER
HOMEMAKING
HOMEOID
HOMEOIDAL
HOMEOPATH
HOMEOPOLAR
HOMEOSIS
HOMEOSTASIS
HOMEOSTATIC
HOMEOTIC
HOMEOTYPE
HOMEOTYPIC
HOMEOWNER
HOMER
HOMEROOM
HOMESEEKER
HOMESICK
HOMESICKLY
HOMESICKNESS
HOMESITE
HOMESOME
HOMESPUN
HOMESTALL
HOMESTEAD
HOMESTEADER
HOMESTER
HOMESTRETCH
HOMETOWN
HOMEWARD
HOMEWARDLY
HOMEWARDS
HOMEWORK
HOMEWORKER
HOMEWORT
HOMEY
HOMEYNESS
HOMICIDAL
HOMICIDALLY
HOMICIDE
HOMICULTURE
HOMILETE
HOMILETIC
HOMILETICAL
HOMILETICS
HOMILIST
HOMILITE
HOMILIZE
HOMILY
HOMINAL
HOMINESS
HOMING
HOMINID
HOMININE
HOMINOID
HOMINY
HOMISH
HOMISHNESS
HOMME
HOMO
HOMOBARIC
HOMOBLASTIC
HOMOBLASTY
HOMOCENTRIC
HOMOCENTRICAL
HOMOCERC
HOMOCERCAL
HOMOCERCY
HOMOCEREBRIN
HOMOCHIRAL
HOMOCHROME
HOMOCHROMIC
HOMOCHRONOUS
HOMOCLINE
HOMOCYCLIC
HOMODERMIC
HOMODERMY
HOMODONT
HOMODOX
HOMODROMAL
HOMODROME
HOMODROMY
HOMODYNAMIC
HOMODYNE
HOMOEOMERIC
HOMOEOMERY
HOMOGAMY
HOMOGEN
HOMOGENE
HOMOGENEAL
HOMOGENEITY
HOMOGENEOUS
HOMOGENESIS
HOMOGENETIC
HOMOGENIZE
HOMOGENIZER
HOMOGENOUS
HOMOGENY
HOMOGLOT
HOMOGONE
HOMOGONY
HOMOGRAPH
HOMOGRAPHIC
HOMOGRAPHY
HOMOHEDRAL
HOMOLATERAL
HOMOLOG
HOMOLOGATE
HOMOLOGIC
HOMOLOGICAL
HOMOLOGIES
HOMOLOGIZE
HOMOLOGON
HOMOLOGOUS
HOMOLOGUE
HOMOLOGY
HOMOLOSINE
HOMOMERAL
HOMOMEROUS
HOMOMORPH
HOMOMORPHIC
HOMOMORPHISM
HOMOMORPHY
HOMONID
HOMONYM
HOMONYMIC
HOMONYMOUS
HOMONYMY
HOMOPATHY
HOMOPHENE
HOMOPHONE
HOMOPHONIC
HOMOPHONY
HOMOPHYLIC
HOMOPHYLY
HOMOPLASIS
HOMOPLASMIC
HOMOPLASMY
HOMOPLASSY
HOMOPLAST
HOMOPLASTIC
HOMOPLASY
HOMOPOLAR
HOMOPOLIC
HOMOPTER
HOMORGANIC
HOMOSEXUAL
HOMOSEXUALITY
HOMOSTYLED
HOMOSTYLIC
HOMOSTYLY
HOMOTACTIC
HOMOTATIC
HOMOTAXIS
HOMOTAXY
HOMOTHALLIC
HOMOTHETIC
HOMOTHETY
HOMOTONIC
HOMOTONY
HOMOTOPIC
HOMOTROPAL
HOMOTYPAL
HOMOTYPE
HOMOTYPIC
HOMOTYPY
HOMOZYGOTE
HOMOZYGOUS
HOMUNCIO
HOMUNCLE
HOMY
HON
HONAN
HONDA
HONDO
HONE
HONEST
HONESTLY
HONESTONE
HONESTY
HONEWORT
HONEY
HONEYBALLS
HONEYBEE
HONEYBEES
HONEYBERRY
HONEYBIND
HONEYBLOB
HONEYBLOOM
HONEYBUN
HONEYCOMB
HONEYCOMBED
HONEYCOMBING
HONEYCUP
HONEYDEW
HONEYDEWED
HONEYED
HONEYEDNESS
HONEYFALL
HONEYFLOWER
HONEYFOGLE
HONEYFUGLE
HONEYLIPPED
HONEYMONTH
HONEYMOON
HONEYMOONY
HONEYMOUTHED
HONEYPOD
HONEYPOT
HONEYS
HONEYSUCK
HONEYSUCKER
HONEYSUCKLE
HONEYSUCKLED
HONEYSWEET
HONEYWARE
HONEYWOOD
HONEYWORT
HONG
HONIED
HONK
HONKER
HONKIE
HONKIES
HONKY
HONOR
HONORABILITY
HONORABLE
HONORABLENESS
HONORABLY
HONORANCE
HONORARIUM
HONORARY
HONORED
HONORER
HONORIFIC
HONORIFICALLY
HONORS
HONOUR
HONOURABILITY
HONOURABLE
HONOURABLY
HONOURER
HONOURS
HONTISH
HONTOUS
HOO
HOOCH
HOOD
HOODCAP
HOODED
HOODIE
HOODING
HOODLUM
HOODMAN
HOODMOLD
HOODOO
HOODSHY
HOODSHYNESS
HOODWINK
HOODWINKER
HOODWORT
HOODY
HOOEY
HOOF
HOOFBEAT
HOOFBOUND
HOOFED
HOOFER
HOOFLET
HOOFPRINT
HOOFS
HOOFWORM
HOOGAARS
HOOK
HOOKA
HOOKAH
HOOKAROON
HOOKED
HOOKEDNESS
HOOKER
HOOKERS
HOOKHEAL
HOOKLAND
HOOKLET
HOOKLIKE
HOOKMAN
HOOKNOSE
HOOKS
HOOKSHOP
HOOKTIP
HOOKUM
HOOKUP
HOOKUPU
HOOKWEED
HOOKWORM
HOOKWORMER
HOOKWORMY
HOOKY
HOOLAKIN
HOOLAULEA
HOOLEY
HOOLIE
HOOLIGAN
HOOLIHAN
HOOLOCK
HOOLY
HOON
HOONDEE
HOONDI
HOOP
HOOPED
HOOPER
HOOPING
HOOPLA
HOOPLE
HOOPLIKE
HOOPMAKER
HOOPMAN
HOOPOE
HOOPS
HOOPSKIRT
HOOPSTER
HOOPSTICK
HOOPWOOD
HOORAH
HOORAY
HOOROOSH
HOOSE
HOOSEGOW
HOOSH
HOOT
HOOTAY
HOOTER
HOOTS
HOOVE
HOOVEY
HOOZE
HOP
HOPBIND
HOPBINE
HOPBUSH
HOPCALITE
HOPCREASE
HOPE
HOPED

HOPEFUL
HOPEFULLY
HOPEFULNESS
HOPEITE
HOPELESS
HOPELESSLY
HOPELESSNESS
HOPER
HOPHEAD
HOPLITE
HOPLITIC
HOPLOLOGY
HOPLOMACHIC
HOPLOMACHY
HOPO
HOPOFF
HOPPE
HOPPED
HOPPER
HOPPERBURN
HOPPERDOZER
HOPPERETTE
HOPPERINGS
HOPPERMAN
HOPPERS
HOPPESTERE
HOPPET
HOPPING
HOPPITY
HOPPLE
HOPPO
HOPPY
HOPS
HOPSACK
HOPSACKING
HOPSAGE
HOPSCOTCH
HOPTOAD
HOPVINE
HOPYARD
HORA
HORAL
HORARY
HORBACHITE
HORDARIAN
HORDARY
HORDE
HORDEACEOUS
HORDEATE
HORDEIFORM
HORDEIN
HORDENINE
HORDEOLUM
HORDOCK
HORE
HOREHOUND
HORISMOLOGY
HORIZOMETER
HORIZON
HORIZONTAL
HORIZONTALITY
HORIZONTALIZE
HORIZONTALLY
HORIZONTIC
HORIZONTICAL
HORIZONTICALLY
HORKEY
HORME
HORMIC
HORMIGO
HORMION
HORMISM
HORMIST
HORMONE
HORMONES
HORMOS
HORN
HORNADA
HORNBEAM
HORNBILL
HORNBLENDE
HORNBLOWER
HORNBOOK
HORNED
HORNER
HORNERAH
HORNERO
HORNET
HORNETY
HORNFAIR
HORNFELS
HORNFISH
HORNGELD
HORNIFY
HORNING
HORNIST
HORNITO
HORNKECK
HORNLESS
HORNLIKE
HORNOTINE
HORNPIE
HORNPIPE
HORNPLANT
HORNS
HORNSLATE
HORNSMAN
HORNSTAY
HORNSTONE
HORNSWOGGLE
HORNTAIL
HORNTHUMB
HORNTIP
HORNWEED
HORNWOOD
HORNWORK
HORNWORM
HORNWORT
HORNY
HORNYHANDED
HORNYHEAD
HOROGRAPH
HOROGRAPHER
HOROGRAPHY
HOROKAKA
HOROLOGE
HOROLOGER
HOROLOGIC
HOROLOGICAL
HOROLOGICALLY
HOROLOGIST
HOROLOGIUM
HOROLOGUE
HOROLOGY
HOROMETRY
HOROPITO
HOROPTER
HOROPTERIC
HOROPTERY
HOROSCOPAL
HOROSCOPE
HOROSCOPER
HOROSCOPICAL
HOROSCOPIST
HOROSCOPY
HOROTELY
HORRAL
HORRENDOUS
HORRENDOUSLY
HORRENT
HORRESCENT
HORREUM
HORRIBLE
HORRIBLENESS
HORRIBLES
HORRIBLY
HORRID
HORRIDITY
HORRIDLY
HORRIFIC
HORRIFICATION
HORRIFIED
HORRIFY
HORRIFYING
HORRIPILANT
HORRIPILATE
HORRISONANT
HORROR
HORROROUS
HORRORS
HORRORSOME
HORRY
HORS
HORSE
HORSEBACK
HORSEBACKER
HORSEBANE
HORSEBLOCK
HORSEBOY
HORSEBREAKER
HORSEBUSH
HORSECAR
HORSECLOTH
HORSEDRAWING
HORSEFAIR
HORSEFIGHT
HORSEFISH
HORSEFLESH
HORSEFLIES
HORSEFLOWER
HORSEFLY
HORSEFOOT
HORSEGATE
HORSEHAIR
HORSEHAIRED
HORSEHEAD
HORSEHEAL
HORSEHEEL
HORSEHIDE
HORSEHOOF
HORSEKEEPER
HORSEKEEPING
HORSELAUGH
HORSELAUGHTER
HORSELEACH
HORSELEECH
HORSELESS
HORSELOAD
HORSELOCK
HORSELY
HORSEMAN
HORSEMANSHIP
HORSEMEN
HORSEMINT
HORSENAIL
HORSEPIPE
HORSEPOND
HORSEPOWER
HORSEPOX
HORSER
HORSERADISH
HORSES
HORSESHOE
HORSESHOER
HORSETAIL
HORSETONGUE
HORSETREE
HORSEWAY
HORSEWEED
HORSEWHIP
HORSEWHIPPER
HORSEWOMAN
HORSEWOMANSHIP
HORSEWOOD
HORSFORDITE
HORSIFY
HORSINESS
HORSING
HORST
HORSTE
HORSY
HORSYISM
HORTATION
HORTATIVE
HORTATOR
HORTATORILY
HORTATORY
HORTENSIAL
HORTESIAN
HORTICULTURAL
HORTICULTURALLY
HORTICULTURE
HORTITE
HORTONOLITE
HORTULAN
HORTYARD
HORY
HOSANNA
HOSE
HOSEBIRD
HOSED
HOSEL
HOSEMAN
HOSEN
HOSEPIPE
HOSIER
HOSIERY
HOSIOMARTYR
HOSPICE
HOSPITABLE
HOSPITABLENESS
HOSPITABLY
HOSPITAGE
HOSPITAL
HOSPITALARY
HOSPITALER
HOSPITALISM
HOSPITALITY
HOSPITALIZATION
HOSPITALIZE
HOSPITALLER
HOSPITANT
HOSPITATE
HOSPITIUM
HOSPODAR
HOSPODARIAT
HOSPODARIATE
HOSS
HOST
HOSTAGE
HOSTAGER
HOSTEL
HOSTELER
HOSTELRY
HOSTER
HOSTESS
HOSTILE
HOSTILELY
HOSTILENESS
HOSTILITIES
HOSTILITY
HOSTING
HOSTLE
HOSTLER
HOSTLERWIFE
HOSTLY
HOSTRY
HOT
HOTBED
HOTBLOOD
HOTBOX
HOTCH
HOTCHA
HOTCHPOT
HOTCHPOTCH
HOTCHPOTCHLY
HOTE
HOTEL
HOTELIER
HOTELKEEPER
HOTFOOT
HOTHEAD
HOTHEADED
HOTHEADEDLY
HOTHEADEDNESS
HOTHOUSE
HOTI
HOTLY
HOTMELT
HOTMOUTHED
HOTNESS
HOTPRESS
HOTSPUR
HOTSPURRED
HOTT
HOTTER
HOTTERY
HOTTLE
HOUBARA
HOUGH
HOUGHER
HOUGHITE
HOUGHMAGANDY
HOUGHSINEW
HOUHERE
HOUNCE
HOUND
HOUNDER
HOUNDFISH
HOUNDING
HOUNDMAN
HOUNDS
HOUNDSBANE
HOUNDSBERRY
HOUNDSHARK
HOUNDY
HOUPPELANDE
HOUR
HOURGLASS
HOURI
HOURLY
HOUSAGE
HOUSAL
HOUSE
HOUSEBALL
HOUSEBOAT
HOUSEBOATING
HOUSEBOTE
HOUSEBOUND
HOUSEBOY
HOUSEBREAK
HOUSEBREAKER
HOUSEBROKE
HOUSEBROKEN
HOUSEBUG
HOUSEBUILDER
HOUSECARL
HOUSECOAT
HOUSEDRESS
HOUSEFAST
HOUSEFATHER
HOUSEFLY
HOUSEFUL
HOUSEHOLD
HOUSEHOLDER

HOUSEHOLDING
HOUSEHOLDRY
HOUSEKEEP
HOUSEKEEPER
HOUSEKEEPERLY
HOUSEKEEPING
HOUSEL
HOUSELEEK
HOUSELESS
HOUSELINE
HOUSELING
HOUSEMAID
HOUSEMAIDENLY
HOUSEMAIDY
HOUSEMAN
HOUSEMASTER
HOUSEMATE
HOUSEMINDER
HOUSEMISTRESS
HOUSEMOTHER
HOUSER
HOUSERIDDEN
HOUSEROOM
HOUSES
HOUSESMITH
HOUSETOP
HOUSEWARES
HOUSEWARM
HOUSEWARMING
HOUSEWIFE
HOUSEWIFELY
HOUSEWIFERY
HOUSEWIVES
HOUSEWORK
HOUSEWRIGHT
HOUSING
HOUSINGS
HOUSTONIA
HOUSTY
HOUSY
HOUTING
HOUTOU
HOUVARI
HOUVE
HOVEDANCE
HOVEL
HOVELER
HOVELLER
HOVEN
HOVER
HOVERCRAFT
HOVERER
HOVERING
HOVERINGLY
HOVERLY
HOW
HOWADJI
HOWARDITE
HOWBEIT
HOWD
HOWDAH
HOWDER
HOWDIE
HOWDY
HOWE
HOWEL
HOWEVER
HOWF
HOWFF
HOWFING
HOWGATES
HOWISH
HOWITZ
HOWITZER
HOWK
HOWKIT
HOWL
HOWLER
HOWLET
HOWLING
HOWLINGLY
HOWLITE
HOWSO
HOWSOEVER
HOWSOMEVER
HOWSOUR
HOX
HOY
HOYDEN
HOYMAN
HSIEN
HSIN
HU
HUACA
HUACO
HUAJILLO
HUAMUCHIL
HUAPANGO
HUARACHE
HUARACHO
HUARIZO
HUB
HUBAM
HUBB
HUBBA
HUBBABOO
HUBBER
HUBBLE
HUBBLY
HUBBUB
HUBBUBOO
HUBBY
HUBCAP
HUBNERITE
HUBRIS
HUBRISTIC
HUBSHI
HUCCATOON
HUCH
HUCHEN
HUCHO
HUCK
HUCKABACK
HUCKLE
HUCKLEBACK
HUCKLEBACKED
HUCKLEBERRIES
HUCKLEBERRY
HUCKLEBONE
HUCKMUCK
HUCKSTER
HUCKSTERER
HUCKSTERISM
HUCKSTERY
HUD
HUDDERON
HUDDLE
HUDDLER
HUDDLING
HUDDOCK
HUDDROUN
HUDDUP
HUDE
HUDGE
HUDSONIA
HUE
HUED
HUEFUL
HUEHUETL
HUEL
HUELESS
HUELESSNESS
HUEMUL
HUER
HUERTA
HUFFCAP
HUFFER
HUFFILY
HUFFINESS
HUFFINGLY
HUFFISH
HUFFISHLY
HUFFISHNESS
HUFFLE
HUFFLER
HUFFY
HUG
HUGE
HUGELITE
HUGELY
HUGENESS
HUGEOUS
HUGEOUSLY
HUGEOUSNESS
HUGGABLE
HUGGER
HUGGING
HUGGLE
HUGMATEE
HUGONIS
HUH
HUHU
HUI
HUIA
HUILA
HUIPIL
HUIPILLA
HUISACHE
HUISCOYOL
HUISHER
HUISQUIL
HUISSIER
HUITAIN
HUITRE
HUKE
HULA
HULCH
HULCHY
HULDEE
HULDI
HULK
HULKAGE
HULKING
HULKY
HULL
HULLABALOO
HULLED
HULLER
HULLING
HULLO
HULLOCK
HULLOO
HULLS
HULSITE
HULSTER
HULU
HULVER
HULVERHEAD
HULVERHEADED
HULWORT
HUM
HUMAN
HUMANE
HUMANELY
HUMANENESS
HUMANIFY
HUMANISM
HUMANIST
HUMANISTIC
HUMANITARIAN
HUMANITARY
HUMANITIES
HUMANITY
HUMANIZE
HUMANIZER
HUMANKIND
HUMANLY
HUMANOID
HUMATE
HUMATION
HUMBIRD
HUMBLE
HUMBLEBEE
HUMBLED
HUMBLENESS
HUMBLER
HUMBLESSO
HUMBLIE
HUMBLING
HUMBLY
HUMBO
HUMBOLDTITE
HUMBUG
HUMBUGGER
HUMBUZZ
HUMDINGER
HUMDRUM
HUMECT
HUMECTANT
HUMECTATE
HUMERAL
HUMERUS
HUMET
HUMETTEE
HUMETTY
HUMHUM
HUMIC
HUMID
HUMIDATE
HUMIDIFIER
HUMIDIFY
HUMIDITY
HUMIDLY
HUMIDNESS
HUMIDOR
HUMIFIC
HUMIFUSE
HUMIFY
HUMILIANT
HUMILIATE
HUMILIATED
HUMILIATION
HUMILITIES
HUMILITY
HUMIN
HUMIT
HUMITE
HUMLIE
HUMMAUL
HUMMEL
HUMMELER
HUMMER
HUMMIE
HUMMING
HUMMINGBIRD
HUMMINGLY
HUMMOCK
HUMMOCKY
HUMMUM
HUMOR
HUMORAL
HUMORALISM
HUMORALIST
HUMORED
HUMORESQUE
HUMORISM
HUMORIST
HUMORISTIC
HUMORIZE
HUMOROUS
HUMOROUSLY
HUMOROUSNESS
HUMORS
HUMOUR
HUMOURAL
HUMOURIST
HUMOURIZE
HUMOURS
HUMOUS
HUMP
HUMPBACK
HUMPBACKED
HUMPED
HUMPH
HUMPINESS
HUMPTY
HUMPY
HUMSTRUM
HUMULENE
HUMULON
HUMULONE
HUMUS
HUNCH
HUNCHBACK
HUNCHBACKED
HUNCHET
HUNCHY
HUNDER
HUNDI
HUNDRED
HUNDREDAL
HUNDREDER
HUNDREDFOLD
HUNDREDPENNY
HUNDREDTH
HUNDREDWEIGHT
HUNDREDWORK
HUNFYSH
HUNG
HUNGARITE
HUNGER
HUNGERINGLY
HUNGERLY
HUNGERROOT
HUNGERWEED
HUNGRIER
HUNGRIEST
HUNGRIFY
HUNGRILY
HUNGRINESS
HUNGRY
HUNH
HUNIA
HUNK
HUNKER
HUNKEROUS
HUNKERS
HUNKIES
HUNKS
HUNKY
HUNNER
HUNT
HUNTER
HUNTILITE
HUNTING
HUNTRESS
HUNTSMAN
HUNTSWOMAN
HUP
HUPP
HURA
HURCHEON
HURDIES
HURDIS
HURDLE

HURDLEMAN
HURDLER
HURDLES
HURDS
HURE
HUREAULITE
HUREEK
HURGILA
HURKLE
HURL
HURLBARROW
HURLBAT
HURLED
HURLEMENT
HURLER
HURLEY
HURLEYHACKET
HURLEYHOUSE
HURLIES
HURLING
HURLOCK
HURLY
HURON
HURR
HURRAH
HURRAY
HURRER
HURRICANE
HURRICANIZE
HURRICANO
HURRIED
HURRIEDLY
HURRIEDNESS
HURRIER
HURRIES
HURRISOME
HURROCK
HURROO
HURROOSH
HURRY
HURSE
HURST
HURT
HURTER
HURTFUL
HURTFULLY
HURTFULNESS
HURTING
HURTINGEST
HURTLE
HURTLEBERRY
HURTLESS
HURTLESSLY
HURTLESSNESS
HURTLING
HURTSOME
HURTY
HUSBAND
HUSBANDAGE
HUSBANDED
HUSBANDER
HUSBANDFIELD
HUSBANDLAND
HUSBANDLY
HUSBANDMAN
HUSBANDRESS
HUSBANDRY
HUSCARL
HUSE
HUSH
HUSHABY
HUSHCLOTH
HUSHED
HUSHEEN
HUSHEL
HUSHER
HUSHFUL
HUSHING
HUSHION
HUSHPUPPIES
HUSHPUPPY
HUSI
HUSK
HUSKANAW
HUSKED
HUSKENED
HUSKER
HUSKIER
HUSKIEST
HUSKING
HUSKROOT
HUSKS
HUSKWORT
HUSKY
HUSO
HUSPEL
HUSPIL
HUSS
HUSSAR
HUSSIES
HUSSY
HUST
HUSTING
HUSTINGS
HUSTLE
HUSTLECAP
HUSTLEMENT
HUSTLER
HUSTLING
HUT
HUTCH
HUTCHER
HUTCHET
HUTHOLD
HUTIA
HUTKEEPER
HUTMENT
HUTS
HUTTONING
HUTTONWEED
HUTUKHTU
HUTUKTU
HUTUNG
HUTZPAH
HUURDER
HUVELYK
HUXEN
HUZ
HUZOOR
HUZZ
HUZZA
HUZZAH
HUZZARD
HUZZY
HWAN
HY
HYACINTH
HYACINTHINE
HYAENA
HYAENID
HYAHYA
HYALESCENCE
HYALESCENT
HYALIN
HYALINE
HYALINIZE
HYALITE
HYALITHE
HYALITIS
HYALOGEN
HYALOGRAPH
HYALOGRAPHER
HYALOGRAPHY
HYALOID
HYALOLIPARITE
HYALOLITH
HYALOMUCOID
HYALOPLASM
HYALOPLASMA
HYALOPLASMIC
HYALOPSITE
HYALOSIDERITE
HYALOTEKITE
HYALOTYPE
HYBODONT
HYBOSIS
HYBRID
HYBRIDAL
HYBRIDATION
HYBRIDISM
HYBRIDITY
HYBRIDIZABLE
HYBRIDIZATION
HYBRIDIZE
HYBRIDIZER
HYBRIDOUS
HYBRIS
HYDANTOIC
HYDANTOIN
HYDATHODE
HYDATID
HYDATIFORM
HYDATOGENESIS
HYDATOGENIC
HYDATOID
HYDATOMORPHIC
HYDNOID
HYDRA
HYDRACID
HYDRACORAL
HYDRACRYLATE
HYDRACRYLIC
HYDRAE
HYDRAGOG
HYDRAGOGUE
HYDRAGOGY
HYDRAMINE
HYDRANGEA
HYDRANT
HYDRANTH
HYDRARCH
HYDRASE
HYDRASTINE
HYDRATE
HYDRATED
HYDRATION
HYDRATOR
HYDRAULIC
HYDRAULICS
HYDRAZIN
HYDRAZINE
HYDRAZOATE
HYDRAZOIC
HYDRAZONE
HYDRIA
HYDRIC
HYDRIDE
HYDRIFORM
HYDRIODIC
HYDRION
HYDRO
HYDROA
HYDROAERIC
HYDROAROMATIC
HYDROBENZOIN
HYDROBIOLOGY
HYDROBIOSIS
HYDROBIPLANE
HYDROBROMATE
HYDROBROMIC
HYDROBROMID
HYDROBROMIDE
HYDROCARBON
HYDROCARBONATE
HYDROCARBONIC
HYDROCAULINE
HYDROCAULUS
HYDROCELE
HYDROCEPHALIC
HYDROCEPHALY
HYDROCERAMIC
HYDROCHLORATE
HYDROCHLORIC
HYDROCHLORID
HYDROCHLORIDE
HYDROCLADIUM
HYDROCLASTIC
HYDROCOELE
HYDROCONION
HYDROCYANIC
HYDROCYANIDE
HYDROCYCLE
HYDROCYCLIC
HYDROCYCLIST
HYDROCYST
HYDROCYSTIC
HYDRODYNAMIC
HYDRODYNAMICS
HYDROELECTRIC
HYDROEXTRACT
HYDROEXTRACTOR
HYDROFLUATE
HYDROFLUORIC
HYDROFOIL
HYDROFUGE
HYDROGEL
HYDROGEN
HYDROGENASE
HYDROGENATE
HYDROGENATOR
HYDROGENIC
HYDROGENIZE
HYDROGEOLOGY
HYDROGLIDER
HYDROGNOSY
HYDROGODE
HYDROGRAPH
HYDROGRAPHER
HYDROGRAPHIC
HYDROGRAPHY
HYDROHALID
HYDROHALIDE
HYDROHEMATITE
HYDROID
HYDROKINETIC
HYDROL
HYDROLASE
HYDROLATRY
HYDROLOGIC
HYDROLOGICAL
HYDROLOGICALLY
HYDROLOGIST
HYDROLYSIS
HYDROLYST
HYDROLYTE
HYDROLYTIC
HYDROLYZATE
HYDROLYZE
HYDROMANIA
HYDROMANIAC
HYDROMANTIC
HYDROME
HYDROMEL
HYDROMETER
HYDROMETRA
HYDROMETRIC
HYDROMETRID
HYDROMETRY
HYDROMICA
HYDROMOTOR
HYDROMYOMA
HYDRONE
HYDRONITRIC
HYDRONIUM
HYDROPATH
HYDROPATHIC
HYDROPATHY
HYDROPERIOD
HYDROPHANE
HYDROPHANOUS
HYDROPHID
HYDROPHIL
HYDROPHILE
HYDROPHILIC
HYDROPHILID
HYDROPHILY
HYDROPHOBE
HYDROPHOBIA
HYDROPHOBIC
HYDROPHOBICAL
HYDROPHOBIST
HYDROPHOBOUS
HYDROPHONE
HYDROPHORIA
HYDROPHYLL
HYDROPHYLLIUM
HYDROPHYTE
HYDROPHYTIC
HYDROPHYTON
HYDROPIC
HYDROPICAL
HYDROPLANE
HYDROPOLYP
HYDROPONIC
HYDROPONICS
HYDROPOT
HYDROPS
HYDROPSY
HYDROPTIC
HYDROPULT
HYDROQUININE
HYDROQUINONE
HYDRORHIZA
HYDRORHIZAL
HYDRORRHEA
HYDRORRHOEA
HYDRORUBBER
HYDROSALT
HYDROSCOPE
HYDROSCOPIC
HYDROSELENIDE
HYDROSOL
HYDROSOLE
HYDROSOMA
HYDROSOME
HYDROSORBIC
HYDROSPHERE
HYDROSPIRE
HYDROSPIRIC
HYDROSTAT
HYDROSTATIC
HYDROSTATICS
HYDROSTOME
HYDROSULFATE
HYDROTALCITE
HYDROTAXIS
HYDROTECHNIC
HYDROTECHNY
HYDROTERPENE
HYDROTHECA
HYDROTHECAL
HYDROTHERAPY
HYDROTHERMAL
HYDROTHORAX
HYDROTYPE

HYDROUS
HYDROVANE
HYDROXIDE
HYDROZINCITE
HYDROZOAL
HYDROZOAN
HYDROZOIC
HYDROZOON
HYDRULA
HYE
HYENA
HYENIA
HYENIC
HYENINE
HYENOID
HYETAL
HYETOGRAPH
HYETOGRAPHIC
HYETOGRAPHY
HYGEEN
HYGEIST
HYGEISTIC
HYGIEIST
HYGIENE
HYGIENIC
HYGIENICS
HYGIENIST
HYGIENIZE
HYGRE
HYGRIC
HYGRIN
HYGRINE
HYGRODEIK
HYGROGRAPH
HYGROMA
HYGROMETER
HYGROMETRIC
HYGROMETRY
HYGROPHOBIA
HYGROPHYTE
HYGROPLASM
HYGROSCOPE
HYGROSCOPIC
HYGROSCOPY
HYGROSTAT
HYGROSTATICS
HYGROSTOMIA
HYGROTHERMAL
HYINGLY
HYKE
HYLA
HYLACTIC
HYLE
HYLEAN
HYLEG
HYLEGIACAL
HYLIC
HYLICIST
HYLID
HYLISM
HYLOID
HYLOLOGY
HYLOTHEISM
HYLOTHEIST
HYLOZOIC
HYLOZOISM
HYLOZOIST
HYMEN
HYMENAL
HYMENEAL
HYMENEALS
HYMENEAN
HYMENIAL
HYMENIC
HYMENIUM
HYMENOID
HYMN
HYMNAL
HYMNARY
HYMNBOOK
HYMNER
HYMNIC
HYMNIST
HYMNODE
HYMNODIST
HYMNODY
HYMNOLOGY
HYNDE
HYNE
HYOID
HYOIDES
HYOMENTAL
HYOPLASTRAL
HYOPLASTRON
HYOSCINE
HYOSTERNAL
HYOSTERNUM
HYOSTYLIC
HYOSTYLY
HYOTHERE
HYP
HYPALGIA
HYPALLAGE
HYPANTRUM
HYPASPIST
HYPATE
HYPATON
HYPAXIAL
HYPE
HYPER
HYPERABELIAN
HYPERACUSIA
HYPERALGESIA
HYPERALGESIC
HYPERALGESIS
HYPERAPHIA
HYPERAPHIC
HYPERBARIC
HYPERBARISM
HYPERBATIC
HYPERBATON
HYPERBOLA
HYPERBOLAS
HYPERBOLE
HYPERBOLIC
HYPERBOLISM
HYPERBOLIZE
HYPERBOLIZED
HYPERBOLIZING
HYPERBOREAL
HYPERBOREAN
HYPERBULIA
HYPERCONE
HYPERCORACOID
HYPERCORRECT
HYPERCRITIC
HYPERCRITICAL
HYPERCUBE
HYPERCYCLE
HYPERCYLINDER
HYPERDACTYL
HYPERDIAPASON
HYPERDIAPENTE
HYPERDITONE
HYPERDULIA
HYPERDULIC
HYPERELLIPTIC
HYPEREMESIS
HYPEREMIA
HYPEREMIC
HYPERESSENCE
HYPERESTHESIA
HYPERESTHETIC
HYPEREUTECTIC
HYPERFOCAL
HYPERGAMY
HYPERGEOMETRY
HYPERGOLIC
HYPERIN
HYPERKINESIA
HYPERKINESIS
HYPERKINETIC
HYPERMETER
HYPERMETRIC
HYPERMETRICAL
HYPERMORPH
HYPERNIC
HYPERON
HYPEROON
HYPEROPIC
HYPEROSMIA
HYPEROSMIC
HYPEROSTOSIS
HYPEROSTOTIC
HYPEROTRETAN
HYPEROXIDE
HYPERPENCIL
HYPERPER
HYPERPHORIA
HYPERPHORIC
HYPERPIESIA
HYPERPIESIS
HYPERPIETIC
HYPERPLANE
HYPERPLASIA
HYPERPLASTIC
HYPERPLOID
HYPERPLOIDY
HYPERPNEA
HYPERPRISM
HYPERPYRAMID
HYPERPYRETIC
HYPERSOLID
HYPERSONIC
HYPERSONICS
HYPERSPACE
HYPERSPHERE
HYPERTELY
HYPERTHESIS
HYPERTHETIC
HYPERTHYROID
HYPERTONIA
HYPERTONIC
HYPERTONUS
HYPERTROPHY
HYPERTROPIA
HYPERTYPE
HYPERTYPIC
HYPERTYPICAL
HYPETHRAL
HYPHA
HYPHAE
HYPHAL
HYPHEMA
HYPHEMIA
HYPHEN
HYPHENATE
HYPHENATED
HYPHENED
HYPHO
HYPHODROME
HYPNALE
HYPNOBATE
HYPNOCYST
HYPNODY
HYPNOETIC
HYPNOID
HYPNOIDAL
HYPNOIDIZE
HYPNOLOGIC
HYPNOLOGY
HYPNOSIS
HYPNOSPORE
HYPNOSPORIC
HYPNOTIC
HYPNOTISM
HYPNOTIST
HYPNOTIZE
HYPNOTOID
HYPO
HYPOADENIA
HYPOADRENIA
HYPOBARIC
HYPOBARISM
HYPOBASAL
HYPOBLAST
HYPOBLASTIC
HYPOBOLE
HYPOBROMITES
HYPOBROMOUS
HYPOBULIA
HYPOBULIC
HYPOCARP
HYPOCAUST
HYPOCENTER
HYPOCENTRUM
HYPOCHIL
HYPOCHNOSE
HYPOCHONDRIA
HYPOCHONDRIAC
HYPOCHORDAL
HYPOCHROMIA
HYPOCHROSIS
HYPOCIST
HYPOCONE
HYPOCORISTIC
HYPOCOTYL
HYPOCRATER
HYPOCRISIS
HYPOCRISY
HYPOCRITAL
HYPOCRITE
HYPOCRITIC
HYPOCRITICAL
HYPOCRITICALLY
HYPOCRIZE
HYPOCYCLOID
HYPOCYTOSIS
HYPODERM
HYPODERMA
HYPODERMAL
HYPODERMIC
HYPODERMIS
HYPODITONE
HYPOEUTECTIC
HYPOGAMY
HYPOGASTRIC
HYPOGEAL
HYPOGEAN
HYPOGEE
HYPOGEIC
HYPOGENE
HYPOGENESIS
HYPOGENIC
HYPOGEOUS
HYPOGEUM
HYPOGLOSSAL
HYPOGLOSSUS
HYPOGLOTTIS
HYPOGYNIC
HYPOGYNIUM
HYPOHALOUS
HYPOHEMIA
HYPOHIDROSIS
HYPOHYAL
HYPOID
HYPOMANIA
HYPOMANIC
HYPOMERAL
HYPOMERE
HYPOMORPH
HYPONASTIC
HYPONASTY
HYPONITRITE
HYPONOIA
HYPONOME
HYPONYM
HYPOPHARE
HYPOPHARYNX
HYPOPHONIC
HYPOPHORA
HYPOPHORIA
HYPOPHRENIA
HYPOPHYGE
HYPOPHYLL
HYPOPHYSE
HYPOPLASIA
HYPOPLASTIC
HYPOPLASTRAL
HYPOPLASTRON
HYPOPLOID
HYPOPNEA
HYPOPODIUM
HYPOPRAXIA
HYPOPTERAL
HYPOPTERON
HYPOPTILUM
HYPOPUS
HYPOPYON
HYPORADIAL
HYPORADIUS
HYPORHINED
HYPORIT
HYPOSCLERAL
HYPOSCOPE
HYPOSKELETAL
HYPOSMIA
HYPOSPADIAC
HYPOSPADIAS
HYPOSPHENE
HYPOSTASIS
HYPOSTATIC
HYPOSTATICAL
HYPOSTATIZE
HYPOSTHENIA
HYPOSTIGMA
HYPOSTILBITE
HYPOSTOMA
HYPOSTOME
HYPOSTYLE
HYPOSTYPSIS
HYPOSTYPTIC
HYPOTARSAL
HYPOTARSUS
HYPOTAXIA
HYPOTAXIC
HYPOTAXIS
HYPOTENSION
HYPOTENSIVE
HYPOTENSOR
HYPOTENUSE
HYPOTHEC
HYPOTHECA
HYPOTHECARY
HYPOTHECATE
HYPOTHECIAL
HYPOTHENAL
HYPOTHENAR
HYPOTHENIC
HYPOTHERMAL
HYPOTHERMIA
HYPOTHERMIC
HYPOTHESIS
HYPOTHETICAL
HYPOTONIC

HYPOTOXICITY
HYPOTRACHELIUM
HYPOTROPHY
HYPOTYPE
HYPOTYPIC
HYPOVALVE
HYPOVANADATE
HYPOVANADIC
HYPOXANTHIC
HYPOXANTHINE
HYPOZEUGMA
HYPOZEUXIS
HYPOZOAN
HYPOZOIC
HYPPISH
HYPSIPYLE
HYPSOMETER
HYPSOMETRIC
HYPSOMETRY
HYPSOPHOBIA
HYPSOPHYLL
HYPURAL
HYRACEUM
HYRACID
HYRAX
HYRST
HYSON
HYSSOP
HYSTERIA
HYSTERIAC
HYSTERIC
HYSTERICAL
HYSTERICALLY
HYSTERICS
HYSTERIFORM
HYSTEROGEN
HYSTEROGENETIC
HYSTEROGENIC
HYSTEROID
HYSTEROLITH
HYSTEROLOGY
HYSTEROMANIA
HYSTEROMETER
HYSTEROMETRY
HYSTEROPATHY
HYSTEROSCOPE
HYSTEROTOME
HYTE

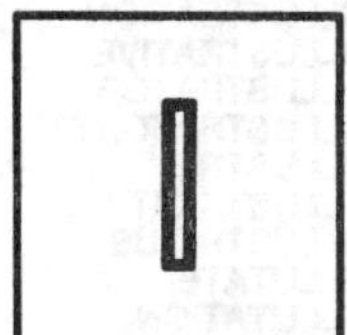

IAMATOLOGY
IAMB
IAMBELEGUS
IAMBIC
IAMBICAL
IAMBICALLY
IAMBIST
IAMBIZE
IAMBOGRAPHER
IAMBUS
IANTHINE
IANTHINITE
IAO
IATRALIPTIC
IATRALIPTICS
IATRIC
IATRICAL
IATROCHEMICAL
IATROCHEMISTRY
IATROGENIC
IATROLOGICAL
IATROLOGY
IATROPHYSICS
IATROTECHNICS
IBA
IBE
IBERITE
IBEX
IBEXES
IBICES
IBID
IBIDEM
IBIS
IBISBILL
IBISES
IBIT
IBOLIUM
IBOTA
ICACINACEOUS
ICACO
ICE
ICEBERG
ICEBLINK
ICEBOAT
ICEBONE
ICEBOUND
ICEBOX
ICEBREAKER
ICECAP
ICECRAFT
ICED
ICEFALL
ICEFISH
ICEFISHES
ICEHOUSE
ICELAND
ICELEAF
ICEMAN
ICEMEN
ICEQUAKE
ICER
ICEROOT
ICEWORK
ICH
ICHAM
ICHEBU
ICHIBU
ICHNEUMON
ICHNEUMONED
ICHNEUMOUS
ICHNEUTIC
ICHNITE
ICHNOGRAPHIC
ICHNOGRAPHY
ICHNOLITE
ICHNOLITIC
ICHNOLOGICAL
ICHNOLOGY
ICHNOMANCY
ICHO
ICHOGLAN
ICHOR
ICHOROUS
ICHORRHAEMIA
ICHORRHEA
ICHORRHEMIA
ICHORRHOEA
ICHTHULIN
ICHTHULINIC
ICHTHUS
ICHTHYAL
ICHTHYIC
ICHTHYISM
ICHTHYISMUS
ICHTHYIZATION
ICHTHYIZED
ICHTHYOCOL
ICHTHYOCOLLA
ICHTHYODIAN
ICHTHYODONT
ICHTHYOFAUNA
ICHTHYOID
ICHTHYOIDAL
ICHTHYOLATRY
ICHTHYOLITE
ICHTHYOLOGIC
ICHTHYOLOGY
ICHTHYOMANIA
ICHTHYOPHAGI
ICHTHYOPHAGY
ICHTHYOPSID
ICHTHYOSAUR
ICHTHYOSIS
ICHTHYOSISM
ICHTHYOTOMY
ICHTHYOTOXIN
ICHTHYS
ICHU
ICHULLE
ICICA
ICICLE
ICICLED
ICIER
ICIEST
ICILY
ICINESS
ICING
ICK
ICKER
ICKLE
ICKY
ICON
ICONES
ICONIC
ICONICAL
ICONISM
ICONOCLASM
ICONOCLAST
ICONOCLASTIC
ICONODULE
ICONODULIC
ICONODULIST
ICONODULY
ICONOGRAPH
ICONOGRAPHER
ICONOGRAPHIC
ICONOGRAPHIST
ICONOGRAPHY
ICONOLATER
ICONOLATROUS
ICONOLATRY
ICONOLOGICAL
ICONOLOGIST
ICONOLOGY
ICONOMACHAL
ICONOMACHIST
ICONOMACHY
ICONOMANIA
ICONOMATIC
ICONOMATICISM
ICONOMETER
ICONOMETRIC
ICONOMETRICAL
ICONOMETRY
ICONOPHILE
ICONOPHILISM
ICONOPHILIST
ICONOPHILY
ICONOPLAST
ICONOSCOPE
ICONOSTAS
ICONOSTASES
ICONOSTASION
ICONOSTASIS
ICONOTYPE
ICONS
ICOSAHEDRA
ICOSAHEDRAL
ICOSAHEDRON
ICOSASEMIC
ICOSIAN
ICOSTEID
ICOSTEINE
ICOTYPE
ICRE
ICTERIC
ICTERICAL
ICTERINE
ICTERITIOUS
ICTERITOUS
ICTERODE
ICTEROGENIC
ICTEROHEMATURIA
ICTEROID
ICTERUS
ICTIC
ICTUATE
ICTUS
ICTUSES
ICY
ID
IDAEIN
IDALIA
IDANT
IDDAT
IDE
IDEA
IDEAED
IDEAGENOUS
IDEAL
IDEALISM
IDEALIST
IDEALISTIC
IDEALISTICAL
IDEALISTICALLY
IDEALITIES
IDEALITY
IDEALIZATION
IDEALIZE
IDEALIZED
IDEALIZER
IDEALIZING
IDEALLY
IDEAS
IDEATE
IDEATED
IDEATING
IDEATION
IDEATIONAL
IDEATIONALLY
IDEATIVE
IDEATUM
IDEE
IDEIN
IDEIST
IDEM
IDEMPOTENT
IDENT
IDENTIC
IDENTICAL
IDENTICALISM
IDENTICALLY
IDENTIFICATION
IDENTIFIED
IDENTIFIER
IDENTIFY
IDENTIFYING
IDENTISM
IDENTITIES
IDENTITY
IDEOGENICAL
IDEOGENY
IDEOGLYPH
IDEOGRAM
IDEOGRAMMIC
IDEOGRAPH
IDEOGRAPHIC
IDEOGRAPHY
IDEOLOGIC
IDEOLOGICAL
IDEOLOGICALLY
IDEOLOGIES
IDEOLOGIST
IDEOLOGY
IDEOMANIA
IDEOMOTION
IDEOMOTOR
IDEOPHONE
IDEOPHONOUS
IDEOPLASTIA
IDEOPLASTIC
IDEOPLASTICS
IDEOPLASTY
IDEOPRAXIST
IDEOTYPE
IDES
IDESIA
IDGAH
IDIASM
IDIGBO
IDIOBLAST
IDIOBLASTIC
IDIOCRASIES
IDIOCRASIS
IDIOCRASY
IDIOCRATIC
IDIOCRATICAL
IDIOCY
IDIOELECTRIC
IDIOGENOUS
IDIOGLOSSIA
IDIOGLOTTIC
IDIOGRAM
IDIOGRAPH
IDIOGRAPHIC
IDIOGRAPHICAL
IDIOLATRY
IDIOLECT
IDIOLOGISM
IDIOM
IDIOMATIC
IDIOMATICAL
IDIOMATICALLY
IDIOMATICALNESS
IDIOMELON
IDIOMETER
IDIOMOGRAPHY
IDIOMOLOGY
IDIOMORPHIC
IDIOMORPHOUS
IDIOMUSCULAR
IDIOPATHETIC
IDIOPATHIC
IDIOPATHICAL
IDIOPATHICALLY
IDIOPATHIES
IDIOPATHY
IDIOPHANISM
IDIOPHANOUS
IDIOPHONE
IDIOPHONIC
IDIOPLASM
IDIOPLASMATIC
IDIOPLASMIC
IDIORETINAL
IDIOSOME
IDIOSPASM
IDIOSPASTIC
IDIOSTATIC
IDIOSYNCRASIES
IDIOSYNCRASY
IDIOSYNCRATIC
IDIOSYNCRATICA
IDIOT
IDIOTCIES
IDIOTCY
IDIOTHERMIC
IDIOTHERMOUS
IDIOTHERMY
IDIOTIC
IDIOTICAL
IDIOTICALLY
IDIOTICON
IDIOTISM
IDIOTROPIAN
IDIOTRY
IDIOTYPE
IDIOTYPIC
IDIOZOME
IDITE
IDITOL
IDLE
IDLEBY
IDLED
IDLEFUL
IDLEHEADED
IDLEHOOD
IDLEMAN
IDLEMEN
IDLENESS
IDLER
IDLESET
IDLESHIP
IDLESSE
IDLEST
IDLING
IDLY
IDOCRASE
IDOL
IDOLA
IDOLASTER
IDOLASTRE
IDOLATER
IDOLATRIC
IDOLATRICAL

IDOLATRIES
IDOLATRIZE
IDOLATRIZED
IDOLATRIZER
IDOLATRIZING
IDOLATROUS
IDOLATROUSLY
IDOLATRY
IDOLET
IDOLIFY
IDOLISH
IDOLISM
IDOLIST
IDOLISTIC
IDOLIZATION
IDOLIZE
IDOLIZED
IDOLIZER
IDOLIZING
IDOLOCLAST
IDOLOCLASTIC
IDOLODULIA
IDOLOMANCY
IDOLOMANIA
IDOLON
IDOLOTHYTE
IDOLOTHYTIC
IDOLOUS
IDOLUM
IDONEAL
IDONEITY
IDONEOUS
IDONEOUSNESS
IDORGAN
IDOSACCHARIC
IDOSE
IDRIALIN
IDRIALINE
IDRIALITE
IDROSIS
IDRYL
IDYL
IDYLER
IDYLIAN
IDYLIST
IDYLL
IDYLLER
IDYLLIA
IDYLLIAN
IDYLLIC
IDYLLICAL
IDYLLICALLY
IDYLLICISM
IDYLLION
IDYLLIST
IDYLLIUM
IE
IEROE
IF
IFE
IFFEN
IFFY
IFIL
IFRIT
IGAD
IGARAPE
IGELSTROMITE
IGITUR
IGLESIA
IGLOO
IGLU
IGNAME
IGNARO
IGNATIA
IGNAVIA
IGNAVY
IGNEOUS
IGNESCENT
IGNICOLIST
IGNIFEROUS
IGNIFIED
IGNIFORM
IGNIFUGE
IGNIFY
IGNIFYING
IGNIGENOUS
IGNIPOTENT
IGNIPUNCTURE
IGNITE
IGNITED
IGNITER
IGNITING
IGNITION
IGNITIVE
IGNITOR
IGNITRON
IGNIVOMOUS
IGNOBILITY
IGNOBLE
IGNOBLESSE
IGNOBLY
IGNOMINIES
IGNOMINIOUS
IGNOMINIOUSLY
IGNOMINY
IGNOMIOUS
IGNORAMUS
IGNORAMUSES
IGNORANCE
IGNORANT
IGNORANTISM
IGNORANTIST
IGNORANTLY
IGNORATION
IGNORE
IGNORED
IGNORER
IGNORING
IGNOTE
IGUANA
IGUANODONT
IGUANOID
IHI
IHLEITE
IHRAM
IIWI
IJMA
IJMAA
IJOLITE
IJUSSITE
IKARY
IKAT
IKBAL
IKEY
IKEYNESS
IKMO
IKON
IKONA
IL
ILD
ILE
ILEAC
ILEECTOMY
ILEITIS
ILEOCAECAL
ILEOCECAL
ILEOCOLIC
ILEOCOLITIS
ILEOSTOMIES
ILEOSTOMY
ILEOTOMY
ILESITE
ILEUM
ILEUS
ILEX
ILEXES
ILIAC
ILIACUS
ILIAHI
ILIAL
ILIAU
ILICACEOUS
ILICIC
ILICIN
ILIMA
ILIOCAUDALIS
ILION
ILIOPSOAS
ILIOPSOATIC
ILK
ILKA
ILKANE
ILL
ILLABORATE
ILLAPSABLE
ILLAPSE
ILLAPSED
ILLAPSING
ILLAPSIVE
ILLAQUEATE
ILLATION
ILLATIVE
ILLATIVELY
ILLAUDABLE
ILLAUDABLY
ILLAUDATION
ILLAUDATORY
ILLBRED
ILLE
ILLECEBROUS
ILLECK
ILLEGAL
ILLEGALITIES
ILLEGALITY
ILLEGALIZE
ILLEGALIZED
ILLEGALIZING
ILLEGALLY
ILLEGALNESS
ILLEGIBILITY
ILLEGIBLE
ILLEGIBLY
ILLEGITIMACIES
ILLEGITIMACY
ILLEGITIMATE
ILLEGITIMATED
ILLEGITIMATING
ILLEISM
ILLEIST
ILLER
ILLFARE
ILLGUIDE
ILLGUIDED
ILLGUIDING
ILLIBERAL
ILLIBERALITY
ILLIBERALLY
ILLICIT
ILLICITLY
ILLICITNESS
ILLIMITABLE
ILLIMITABLY
ILLIMITATE
ILLIMITATION
ILLIMITED
ILLINITION
ILLINIUM
ILLIPENE
ILLIQUATION
ILLIQUID
ILLIQUIDLY
ILLISH
ILLISION
ILLITE
ILLITERACIES
ILLITERACY
ILLITERAL
ILLITERATE
ILLITERATELY
ILLITERATURE
ILLIUM
ILLNESS
ILLOCAL
ILLOCALITY
ILLOCALLY
ILLOGIC
ILLOGICAL
ILLOGICALITY
ILLOGICIAN
ILLOGICITY
ILLORICATE
ILLOYAL
ILLTH
ILLUCIDATE
ILLUCIDATION
ILLUCIDATIVE
ILLUDE
ILLUDED
ILLUDER
ILLUDING
ILLUK
ILLUME
ILLUMED
ILLUMER
ILLUMINANCE
ILLUMINANT
ILLUMINATE
ILLUMINATED
ILLUMINATI
ILLUMINATING
ILLUMINATION
ILLUMINATISM
ILLUMINATIVE
ILLUMINATO
ILLUMINATOR
ILLUMINATORY
ILLUMINATUS
ILLUMINE
ILLUMINED
ILLUMINEE
ILLUMINER
ILLUMING
ILLUMINING
ILLUMINIST
ILLUMINOMETER
ILLUMINOUS
ILLUPI
ILLURE
ILLUREMENT
ILLUSIBLE
ILLUSION
ILLUSIONABLE
ILLUSIONAL
ILLUSIONARY
ILLUSIONED
ILLUSIONISM
ILLUSIONIST
ILLUSIVE
ILLUSIVELY
ILLUSIVENESS
ILLUSOR
ILLUSORILY
ILLUSORINESS
ILLUSORY
ILLUSTRABLE
ILLUSTRATE
ILLUSTRATED
ILLUSTRATING
ILLUSTRATION
ILLUSTRATIVE
ILLUSTRATOR
ILLUSTRATORY
ILLUSTRE
ILLUSTRICITY
ILLUSTRIOUS
ILLUTATE
ILLUTATION
ILLUVIAL
ILLUVIATION
ILLY
ILMENITE
ILMENORUTILE
ILOT
ILVAITE
ILYSIOID
IMAGE
IMAGED
IMAGER
IMAGERIAL
IMAGERIALLY
IMAGERY
IMAGES
IMAGINABLE
IMAGINAL
IMAGINANT
IMAGINARILY
IMAGINARY
IMAGINATE
IMAGINATED
IMAGINATING
IMAGINATION
IMAGINATIONAL
IMAGINATIVE
IMAGINATOR
IMAGINE
IMAGINED
IMAGINER
IMAGINES
IMAGING
IMAGINING
IMAGINIST
IMAGINOUS
IMAGISM
IMAGIST
IMAGISTIC
IMAGO
IMAGOES
IMAMAH
IMAMATE
IMAMBARA
IMAMBARAH
IMAMBARRA
IMAMIC
IMANLAUT
IMARET
IMAUM
IMAUMBARAH
IMBALANCE
IMBALM
IMBAN
IMBAND
IMBANNERED
IMBARGE
IMBARK
IMBARKATION
IMBARN
IMBASED
IMBASTARDIZE
IMBAT
IMBAUBA
IMBE
IMBECILE
IMBECILELY
IMBECILITATE
IMBECILITATED

IMBECILITIES
IMBECILITY
IMBED
IMBEDDED
IMBEDDING
IMBELLIC
IMBELLIOUS
IMBER
IMBERBE
IMBIBE
IMBIBED
IMBIBER
IMBIBING
IMBIBITION
IMBIBITIONAL
IMBIBITORY
IMBIRUSSU
IMBITTER
IMBLAZE
IMBODY
IMBOLDEN
IMBOLISH
IMBONDO
IMBONITY
IMBORDURE
IMBORSATION
IMBOSCATA
IMBOSK
IMBOSOM
IMBOST
IMBOWER
IMBREATHE
IMBREVIATE
IMBREVIATED
IMBREVIATING
IMBREX
IMBRICATE
IMBRICATED
IMBRICATELY
IMBRICATING
IMBRICATION
IMBRICATIVE
IMBRICES
IMBRIER
IMBROGLIO
IMBROGLIOS
IMBROIN
IMBROWN
IMBRUE
IMBRUED
IMBRUING
IMBRUTE
IMBRUTED
IMBRUTING
IMBUE
IMBUED
IMBUIA
IMBUING
IMBURSE
IMBURSED
IMBURSING
IMELLE
IMI
IMID
IMIDAZOL
IMIDAZOLE
IMIDAZOLYL
IMIDE
IMIDIC
IMIDO
IMIDOGEN
IMIN
IMINE
IMINO
IMITABILITY
IMITABLE
IMITANCY
IMITANT
IMITATE
IMITATED
IMITATEE
IMITATING
IMITATION
IMITATIONAL
IMITATIONIST
IMITATIVE
IMITATIVELY
IMITATOR
IMMACULACY
IMMACULANCE
IMMACULATE
IMMACULATELY
IMMALLEABLE
IMMANACLE
IMMANACLED
IMMANACLING
IMMANATION
IMMANE
IMMANELY
IMMANENCE
IMMANENCY
IMMANENESS
IMMANENT
IMMANENTAL
IMMANENTISM
IMMANENTIST
IMMANENTLY
IMMANIFEST
IMMANITY
IMMANTLE
IMMANTLED
IMMANTLING
IMMARBLE
IMMARGINATE
IMMASK
IMMATCHABLE
IMMATCHLESS
IMMATERIAL
IMMATERIALISM
IMMATERIALIST
IMMATERIALITIES
IMMATERIALITY
IMMATERIALIZE
IMMATERIALS
IMMATERIATE
IMMATRICULATE
IMMATURE
IMMATURED
IMMATURELY
IMMATURENESS
IMMATURITIES
IMMATURITY
IMMEABILITY
IMMEASURABLE
IMMEASURABLY
IMMEASURED
IMMECHANICAL
IMMEDIACY
IMMEDIAL
IMMEDIATE
IMMEDIATELY
IMMEDIATENESS
IMMEDIATISM
IMMEDIATIST
IMMEDICABLE
IMMEDICABLY
IMMELODIOUS
IMMEMBER
IMMEMORABLE
IMMEMORIAL
IMMENSE
IMMENSELY
IMMENSENESS
IMMENSIBLE
IMMENSITIES
IMMENSITY
IMMENSIVE
IMMENSURABLE
IMMENSURATE
IMMERD
IMMERGE
IMMERGED
IMMERGENCE
IMMERGENT
IMMERGING
IMMERIT
IMMERITED
IMMERITORIOUS
IMMERSE
IMMERSED
IMMERSIBLE
IMMERSING
IMMERSION
IMMERSIONISM
IMMERSIONIST
IMMERSIVE
IMMESH
IMMETHODIC
IMMETHODIZE
IMMEW
IMMI
IMMIE
IMMIGRANT
IMMIGRANTS
IMMIGRATE
IMMIGRATED
IMMIGRATING
IMMIGRATION
IMMIGRATOR
IMMIGRATORY
IMMIND
IMMINENCE
IMMINENCY
IMMINENT
IMMINENTLY
IMMINGLE
IMMINUTION
IMMIS
IMMISCIBLE
IMMISCIBLY
IMMISS
IMMISSION
IMMIT
IMMITIGABLE
IMMITIGABLY
IMMITTED
IMMITTING
IMMIX
IMMIXT
IMMIXTURE
IMMOBILE
IMMOBILITY
IMMOBILIZATION
IMMOBILIZE
IMMOBILIZED
IMMOBILIZING
IMMODERACY
IMMODERATE
IMMODERATENESS
IMMODERATION
IMMODEST
IMMODESTY
IMMOLATE
IMMOLATED
IMMOLATING
IMMOLATION
IMMOLATOR
IMMOMENT
IMMONASTERED
IMMORAL
IMMORALISM
IMMORALIST
IMMORALITIES
IMMORALITY
IMMORIGEROUS
IMMORTABLE
IMMORTAL
IMMORTALISM
IMMORTALIST
IMMORTALITY
IMMORTALIZE
IMMORTALIZED
IMMORTALIZER
IMMORTALIZING
IMMORTALLY
IMMORTELLE
IMMORTIFIED
IMMOTE
IMMOTILE
IMMOTIONED
IMMOTIVE
IMMOUND
IMMOVABILITY
IMMOVABLE
IMMOVABLY
IMMOVED
IMMUND
IMMUNDITY
IMMUNE
IMMUNIST
IMMUNITIES
IMMUNITY
IMMUNIZATION
IMMUNIZE
IMMUNIZED
IMMUNOGENIC
IMMUNOLOGY
IMMUNOREACTION
IMMUNOTOXIN
IMMURATION
IMMURE
IMMURED
IMMURING
IMMUSICAL
IMMUSICALLY
IMMUTABILITY
IMMUTABLE
IMMUTABLY
IMMUTATION
IMMUTE
IMMUTILATE
IMMUTUAL
IMO
IMONIUM
IMP
IMPACABLE
IMPACK
IMPACT
IMPACTED
IMPACTER
IMPACTING
IMPACTION
IMPACTIONIZE
IMPACTMENT
IMPACTOR
IMPACTUAL
IMPAGES
IMPAINT
IMPAIR
IMPAIRED
IMPAIRER
IMPAIRING
IMPAIRMENT
IMPALA
IMPALACE
IMPALE
IMPALED
IMPALEMENT
IMPALER
IMPALING
IMPALM
IMPALPABLE
IMPALPABLY
IMPALSY
IMPALUDISM
IMPANATE
IMPANATED
IMPANATION
IMPANATOR
IMPANE
IMPANEL
IMPANELED
IMPANELING
IMPANELLED
IMPANELLING
IMPAPYRATE
IMPAPYRATED
IMPAR
IMPARADISE
IMPARALLELED
IMPARASITIC
IMPARDONABLE
IMPARITY
IMPARK
IMPARKATION
IMPARKED
IMPARKING
IMPARL
IMPARLANCE
IMPARLED
IMPARLING
IMPARSONEE
IMPART
IMPARTABLE
IMPARTANCE
IMPARTATION
IMPARTED
IMPARTER
IMPARTIAL
IMPARTIALITY
IMPARTIALLY
IMPARTIBLE
IMPARTIBLY
IMPARTICIPABLE
IMPARTING
IMPARTITE
IMPARTIVE
IMPARTIVITY
IMPARTMENT
IMPASSABLE
IMPASSABLY
IMPASSE
IMPASSES
IMPASSIBLE
IMPASSIBLY
IMPASSION
IMPASSIONATE
IMPASSIONED
IMPASSIONING
IMPASSIVE
IMPASSIVELY
IMPASSIVENESS
IMPASTATION
IMPASTE
IMPASTED
IMPASTING
IMPASTO
IMPASTURE
IMPATERNATE
IMPATIBLE
IMPATIENCE
IMPATIENCY
IMPATIENS
IMPATIENT
IMPATIENTLY

IMPATRONIZE
IMPAVE
IMPAVID
IMPAVIDITY
IMPAVIDLY
IMPAWN
IMPAWNED
IMPAWNING
IMPAYABLE
IMPEACH
IMPEACHABLE
IMPEACHED
IMPEACHER
IMPEACHING
IMPEACHMENT
IMPEARL
IMPEARLED
IMPEARLING
IMPECCABLE
IMPECCABLY
IMPECCANCE
IMPECCANCY
IMPECCANT
IMPECTINATE
IMPECUNIARY
IMPECUNIOUS
IMPEDANCE
IMPEDE
IMPEDED
IMPEDER
IMPEDIBILITY
IMPEDIBLE
IMPEDIENT
IMPEDIMENT
IMPEDIMENTA
IMPEDIMENTAL
IMPEDIMENTARY
IMPEDING
IMPEDINGLY
IMPEDITE
IMPEDITION
IMPEDITIVE
IMPEDOMETER
IMPEDOR
IMPEEVISH
IMPEL
IMPELLED
IMPELLENT
IMPELLER
IMPELLING
IMPEN
IMPEND
IMPENDED
IMPENDENCE
IMPENDENCY
IMPENDENT
IMPENDING
IMPENETRABILITY
IMPENETRABLE
IMPENETRABLY
IMPENETRATE
IMPENITENCE
IMPENITENCY
IMPENITENT
IMPENITENTLY
IMPENITIBLE
IMPENNATE
IMPENT
IMPERANCE
IMPERANT
IMPERATE
IMPERATION
IMPERATIVE
IMPERATIVELY
IMPERATOR
IMPERATORIAL
IMPERATORY
IMPERATRICE
IMPERATRIX
IMPERCEIVED
IMPERCEPTIBLE
IMPERCEPTION
IMPERCEPTIVE
IMPERCIPIENT
IMPERENT
IMPERFECT
IMPERFECTED
IMPERFECTIBLE
IMPERFECTION
IMPERFECTIOUS
IMPERFECTIVE
IMPERFECTLY
IMPERFORABLE
IMPERFORATE
IMPERFORATED
IMPERFORATION
IMPERIA
IMPERIAL
IMPERIALIN
IMPERIALINE
IMPERIALISM
IMPERIALIST
IMPERIALISTIC
IMPERIALITIES
IMPERIALITY
IMPERIALIZE
IMPERIALIZED
IMPERIALIZING
IMPERIALTY
IMPERIL
IMPERILED
IMPERILING
IMPERILLED
IMPERILLING
IMPERIOUS
IMPERIOUSLY
IMPERISH
IMPERISHABLE
IMPERITE
IMPERIUM
IMPERMANENCE
IMPERMANENT
IMPERMEABLE
IMPERMEABLY
IMPERMEATOR
IMPERMISSIBLE
IMPERMIXT
IMPERMUTABLE
IMPERSONABLE
IMPERSONAL
IMPERSONALITIES
IMPERSONALITY
IMPERSONALIZE
IMPERSONALIZED
IMPERSONALIZING
IMPERSONATE
IMPERSONATED
IMPERSONATING
IMPERSONATION
IMPERSONATIVE
IMPERSONATOR
IMPERSUADABLE
IMPERSUASIBLE
IMPERTINACY
IMPERTINENCE
IMPERTINENCES
IMPERTINENCIES
IMPERTINENCY
IMPERTINENT
IMPERTRANSIBLE
IMPERTURBABILITY
IMPERTURBABLE
IMPERTURBABLY
IMPERTURBED
IMPERVERSE
IMPERVERTIBLE
IMPERVIABLE
IMPERVIAL
IMPERVIOUS
IMPERVIOUSLY
IMPEST
IMPESTATION
IMPESTER
IMPETICOS
IMPETIGINOUS
IMPETIGO
IMPETITION
IMPETRATE
IMPETRATED
IMPETRATING
IMPETRATION
IMPETRATIVE
IMPETRATOR
IMPETRATORY
IMPETRE
IMPETULANT
IMPETUOSITY
IMPETUOSO
IMPETUOUS
IMPETUOUSLY
IMPETUS
IMPETUSES
IMPHEE
IMPI
IMPICTURE
IMPIERCEABLE
IMPIETIES
IMPIETY
IMPIGNORATE
IMPIGNORATED
IMPIGNORATING
IMPING
IMPINGE
IMPINGED
IMPINGEMENT
IMPINGENCE
IMPINGENT
IMPINGER
IMPINGING
IMPINGUATE
IMPIOUS
IMPIOUSLY
IMPIOUSNESS
IMPISH
IMPISHLY
IMPISHNESS
IMPITEOUS
IMPITIABLY
IMPLACABLE
IMPLACABLY
IMPLACEMENT
IMPLACENTAL
IMPLACENTATE
IMPLANT
IMPLANTATION
IMPLANTED
IMPLANTER
IMPLANTING
IMPLASTIC
IMPLATE
IMPLAUSIBILITY
IMPLAUSIBLE
IMPLEACH
IMPLEAD
IMPLEADABLE
IMPLEADER
IMPLEDGE
IMPLEMENT
IMPLEMENTAL
IMPLETE
IMPLETION
IMPLETIVE
IMPLEX
IMPLIABLE
IMPLIAL
IMPLICANT
IMPLICATE
IMPLICATED
IMPLICATELY
IMPLICATING
IMPLICATION
IMPLICATIONAL
IMPLICATIVE
IMPLICATORY
IMPLICIT
IMPLICITLY
IMPLICITNESS
IMPLIED
IMPLIEDLY
IMPLODE
IMPLODED
IMPLODENT
IMPLODING
IMPLORATION
IMPLORATOR
IMPLORATORY
IMPLORE
IMPLORED
IMPLORER
IMPLORING
IMPLORINGLY
IMPLOSION
IMPLOSIVE
IMPLOSIVELY
IMPLUME
IMPLUNGE
IMPLUVIA
IMPLUVIUM
IMPLY
IMPLYING
IMPOCKET
IMPOFO
IMPOLICY
IMPOLISHED
IMPOLITE
IMPOLITELY
IMPOLITENESS
IMPOLITIC
IMPOLITICAL
IMPOLITICLY
IMPOLLUTE
IMPONDERABILIA
IMPONDERABLE
IMPONDERABLY
IMPONDEROUS
IMPONE
IMPONENT
IMPOOR
IMPOROSITY
IMPOROUS
IMPORT
IMPORTABLE
IMPORTABLY
IMPORTANCE
IMPORTANT
IMPORTATION
IMPORTED
IMPORTER
IMPORTING
IMPORTLESS
IMPORTMENT
IMPORTRAITURE
IMPORTRAY
IMPORTUNACY
IMPORTUNANCE
IMPORTUNATE
IMPORTUNATELY
IMPORTUNATOR
IMPORTUNE
IMPORTUNED
IMPORTUNELY
IMPORTUNEMENT
IMPORTUNER
IMPORTUNING
IMPORTUNITIES
IMPORTUNITY
IMPOSAL
IMPOSE
IMPOSED
IMPOSEMENT
IMPOSER
IMPOSING
IMPOSINGLY
IMPOSINGNESS
IMPOSITION
IMPOSITIONAL
IMPOSSIBILIST
IMPOSSIBILITIES
IMPOSSIBILITY
IMPOSSIBLE
IMPOSSIBLY
IMPOST
IMPOSTED
IMPOSTER
IMPOSTEROUS
IMPOSTHUMATE
IMPOSTHUME
IMPOSTING
IMPOSTOR
IMPOSTRIX
IMPOSTROUS
IMPOSTUMATE
IMPOSTUME
IMPOSTURE
IMPOSTUROUS
IMPOSURE
IMPOT
IMPOTENCE
IMPOTENCY
IMPOTENT
IMPOTENTLY
IMPOTENTNESS
IMPOUND
IMPOUNDAGE
IMPOUNDED
IMPOUNDER
IMPOUNDING
IMPOUNDMENT
IMPOVERISH
IMPOVERISHED
IMPOVERISHER
IMPOVERISHING
IMPOWER
IMPRACTICABLE
IMPRACTICAL
IMPRECANT
IMPRECATE
IMPRECATED
IMPRECATING
IMPRECATION
IMPRECATOR
IMPRECATORY
IMPRECISE
IMPRECISELY
IMPRECISION
IMPREDICABLE
IMPREGN
IMPREGNABILITY
IMPREGNABLE
IMPREGNABLY
IMPREGNANT
IMPREGNATE
IMPREGNATED
IMPREGNATING
IMPREGNATION

IMPREGNATIVE
IMPREGNATOR
IMPREGNATORY
IMPREJUDICE
IMPREMEDITATE
IMPREPARATION
IMPRESA
IMPRESARI
IMPRESARIO
IMPRESARIOS
IMPRESCIENCE
IMPRESE
IMPRESS
IMPRESSED
IMPRESSEDLY
IMPRESSER
IMPRESSIBLE
IMPRESSIBLY
IMPRESSING
IMPRESSION
IMPRESSIONABLE
IMPRESSIONARY
IMPRESSIONISM
IMPRESSIONIST
IMPRESSIONISTIC
IMPRESSIVE
IMPRESSIVELY
IMPRESSMENT
IMPRESSOR
IMPRESSURE
IMPREST
IMPRESTED
IMPRESTING
IMPREVISION
IMPREVU
IMPRIMATUR
IMPRIME
IMPRIMENT
IMPRIMERIE
IMPRIMERY
IMPRIMIS
IMPRIMITIVE
IMPRINT
IMPRINTED
IMPRINTER
IMPRINTING
IMPRISON
IMPRISONED
IMPRISONER
IMPRISONING
IMPRISONMENT
IMPROBABILITIES
IMPROBABILITY
IMPROBABILIZE
IMPROBABLE
IMPROBABLY
IMPROBATION
IMPROBATIVE
IMPROBATORY
IMPROBITY
IMPROCREANT
IMPRODUCIBLE
IMPROFICIENCY
IMPROMPT
IMPROMPTITUDE
IMPROMPTU
IMPROOF
IMPROPER
IMPROPERATION
IMPROPERLY
IMPROPRIATE
IMPROPRIATED
IMPROPRIATING
IMPROPRIATION
IMPROPRIATOR
IMPROPRIATRICE
IMPROPRIATRIX
IMPROPRIETIES
IMPROPRIETY
IMPROVABLE
IMPROVABLY
IMPROVE
IMPROVED
IMPROVEMENT
IMPROVER
IMPROVIDENCE
IMPROVIDENT
IMPROVING
IMPROVINGLY
IMPROVISATE
IMPROVISATION
IMPROVISATOR
IMPROVISATORY
IMPROVISE
IMPROVISED
IMPROVISER
IMPROVISING
IMPROVISO
IMPRUDENCE
IMPRUDENT
IMPRUDENTIAL
IMPRUDENTLY
IMPUBERAL
IMPUBERATE
IMPUBERTY
IMPUBIC
IMPUDENCE
IMPUDENCIES
IMPUDENCY
IMPUDENT
IMPUDENTLY
IMPUDENTNESS
IMPUDICITY
IMPUGN
IMPUGNABLE
IMPUGNATION
IMPUGNED
IMPUGNER
IMPUGNING
IMPUISSANCE
IMPUISSANT
IMPULSE
IMPULSES
IMPULSION
IMPULSIVE
IMPULSIVELY
IMPULSIVITY
IMPULSOR
IMPULSORY
IMPUNIBLE
IMPUNITY
IMPURE
IMPURELY
IMPURENESS
IMPURIFY
IMPURITAN
IMPURITIES
IMPURITY
IMPUT
IMPUTABILITY
IMPUTABLE
IMPUTABLY
IMPUTATION
IMPUTATIVE
IMPUTATIVELY
IMPUTE
IMPUTED
IMPUTER
IMPUTING
IMPUTRESCENCE
IMPY
IMSHI
IMSONIC
IMU
IN
INA
INABILITY
INABORDABLE
INACCEPTABLE
INACCESSIBILITY
INACCESSIBLE
INACCESSIBLY
INACCURACIES
INACCURACY
INACCURATE
INACCURATELY
INACHID
INACHOID
INACTION
INACTIONIST
INACTIVATE
INACTIVATION
INACTIVE
INACTIVELY
INACTIVENESS
INACTIVITY
INACTUATE
INACTUATION
INADAPTABLE
INADAPTATION
INADEQUACY
INADEQUATE
INADEQUATELY
INADEQUATION
INADMISSIBLE
INADVERTENCE
INADVERTENCES
INADVERTENCY
INADVERTENT
INADVERTENTLY
INADVISABLE
INADVISEDLY
INAESTHETIC
INAFFABILITY
INAFFABLE
INAFFABLY
INAGGLUTINABLE
INAJA
INALACRITY
INALIENABLE
INALIENABLY
INALTERABLE
INALTERABLY
INAM
INAMIA
INAMISSIBLE
INAMORATA
INAMORATE
INAMORATION
INAMORATO
INAMORATOS
INAMOVABLE
INANE
INANELY
INANGA
INANIMATE
INANIMATED
INANIMATELY
INANIMATION
INANITIES
INANITION
INANITY
INANTHERATE
INAPPEASABLE
INAPPETENCE
INAPPETENCY
INAPPETENT
INAPPLICABLE
INAPPLICABLY
INAPPLICATION
INAPPOSITE
INAPPOSITELY
INAPPRECIABLE
INAPPROPRIATE
INAPT
INAPTITUDE
INAPTLY
INAPTNESS
INARCH
INARCHING
INARCULUM
INARM
INARTICULACY
INARTICULATE
INARTICULATED
INARTICULATELY
INARTICULATION
INARTIFICIAL
INARTISTIC
INASMUCH
INASSIMILATION
INATTENTION
INATTENTIVE
INAUDIBILITY
INAUDIBLE
INAUDIBLY
INAUGUR
INAUGURAL
INAUGURATE
INAUGURATED
INAUGURATING
INAUGURATION
INAUGURATIVE
INAUGURATOR
INAUGURATORY
INAUGURER
INAURATE
INAURATION
INAUSPICIOUS
INAUTHENTIC
INAXON
INBASSAT
INBE
INBEAMING
INBEARING
INBEING
INBENDING
INBENT
INBIRTH
INBLOW
INBLOWING
INBLOWN
INBOARD
INBODY
INBOND
INBORN
INBOUND
INBOW
INBREAD
INBREAK
INBREAKING
INBREATHE
INBREATHED
INBREATHER
INBREATHING
INBRED
INBREED
INBREEDING
INBRING
INBRINGER
INBRINGING
INBROUGHT
INBUILT
INBURNING
INBURNT
INBURST
INBUSH
INBY
INBYE
INCAGE
INCALCULABLE
INCALCULABLY
INCALESCENT
INCALICULATE
INCALVER
INCALVING
INCAMERATION
INCAMP
INCANDENT
INCANDESCE
INCANDESCED
INCANDESCENCE
INCANDESCENT
INCANDESCING
INCANOUS
INCANT
INCANTATION
INCANTATOR
INCANTATORY
INCANTON
INCAPABILITY
INCAPABLE
INCAPABLY
INCAPACIOUS
INCAPACITATE
INCAPACITATED
INCAPACITATING
INCAPACITATION
INCAPACITIES
INCAPACITY
INCAPSULATE
INCAPSULATED
INCAPSULATING
INCAPSULATION
INCAPTIVATE
INCARCERATE
INCARCERATED
INCARCERATING
INCARCERATOR
INCARDINATE
INCARMINED
INCARN
INCARNADINE
INCARNADINED
INCARNADINING
INCARNANT
INCARNATE
INCARNATED
INCARNATING
INCARNATION
INCARNATIONAL
INCARNATIONIST
INCARNATIVE
INCASE
INCASED
INCASEMENT
INCASING
INCASK
INCAST
INCASTELLATE
INCATENATE
INCATENATION
INCAUTION
INCAUTIOUS
INCAUTIOUSLY
INCAVATE
INCAVATED
INCAVATION
INCAVERN
INCAVO
INCEDE
INCEDINGLY
INCELEBRITY
INCEND
INCENDIARIES

INCENDIARISM
INCENDIARY
INCENDIUM
INCENDIVITY
INCENSATION
INCENSE
INCENSED
INCENSER
INCENSING
INCENSION
INCENSOR
INCENSORIES
INCENSORY
INCENTER
INCENTIVE
INCENTIVELY
INCENTOR
INCENTRE
INCEPT
INCEPTED
INCEPTING
INCEPTION
INCEPTIVE
INCEPTIVELY
INCEPTOR
INCERATE
INCERATION
INCERTITUDE
INCESSABLE
INCESSABLY
INCESSANCY
INCESSANT
INCESSANTLY
INCESSION
INCEST
INCESTUOUS
INCESTUOUSLY
INCH
INCHAIN
INCHED
INCHER
INCHES
INCHLING
INCHMEAL
INCHOACY
INCHOANT
INCHOATE
INCHOATED
INCHOATELY
INCHOATENESS
INCHOATING
INCHOATION
INCHOATIVE
INCHPIN
INCHWORM
INCIDE
INCIDENCE
INCIDENT
INCIDENTAL
INCIDENTALLY
INCIENSO
INCINERABLE
INCINERATE
INCINERATED
INCINERATING
INCINERATION
INCINERATOR
INCIPIENCE
INCIPIENCY
INCIPIENT
INCIPIENTLY
INCIPIT
INCIRCLET
INCISAL
INCISE
INCISED
INCISELY
INCISIFORM
INCISING
INCISION
INCISIVE
INCISIVELY
INCISIVENESS
INCISOR
INCISORIAL
INCISORY
INCISURA
INCISURE
INCITABILITY
INCITABLE
INCITAMENTUM
INCITANT
INCITATE
INCITATION
INCITE
INCITED
INCITEMENT
INCITER
INCITING
INCITIVE
INCIVIL
INCIVILITIES
INCIVILITY
INCIVILIZATION
INCIVILLY
INCIVISM
INCLASP
INCLASPED
INCLASPING
INCLE
INCLEMENCIES
INCLEMENCY
INCLEMENT
INCLEMENTLY
INCLINABLE
INCLINABLENESS
INCLINATION
INCLINATOR
INCLINATORY
INCLINE
INCLINED
INCLINER
INCLINING
INCLINOGRAPH
INCLINOMETER
INCLIP
INCLOSE
INCLOSURE
INCLUDE
INCLUDED
INCLUDER
INCLUDING
INCLUSA
INCLUSE
INCLUSION
INCLUSIVE
INCLUSIVELY
INCLUSORY
INCLUSUS
INCOALESCENCE
INCOERCIBLE
INCOG
INCOGITABLE
INCOGITANCY
INCOGITANT
INCOGITANTLY
INCOGITATIVE
INCOGNITA
INCOGNITE
INCOGNITO
INCOGNITOS
INCOGNIZABLE
INCOGNIZANCE
INCOGNIZANT
INCOGNOSCENT
INCOGNOSCIBILITY
INCOHERENCE
INCOHERENCES
INCOHERENCIES
INCOHERENCY
INCOHERENT
INCOHERENTIFIC
INCOHERENTLY
INCOHERENTNESS
INCOHERING
INCOLANT
INCOMBUSTIBLE
INCOME
INCOMER
INCOMING
INCOMMENSURABILITY
INCOMMENSURABLE
INCOMMENSURABLENESS
INCOMMENSURABLY
INCOMMENSURATE
INCOMMISCIBLE
INCOMMODATE
INCOMMODATION
INCOMMODE
INCOMMODED
INCOMMODING
INCOMMODIOUS
INCOMMODITIES
INCOMMODITY
INCOMMUNICABLE
INCOMMUTABILITY
INCOMMUTABLE
INCOMPACT
INCOMPACTLY
INCOMPARABILITY
INCOMPARABLE
INCOMPARABLY
INCOMPARED
INCOMPATIBILITY
INCOMPATIBLE
INCOMPATIBLY
INCOMPENSATION
INCOMPETENCE
INCOMPETENCY
INCOMPETENT
INCOMPLETABLE
INCOMPLETE
INCOMPLETED
INCOMPLETELY
INCOMPLETENESS
INCOMPLETION
INCOMPLEX
INCOMPLIANCE
INCOMPLIANCY
INCOMPLIANT
INCOMPLIANTLY
INCOMPOSED
INCOMPOSEDLY
INCOMPOSEDNESS
INCOMPOSITE
INCOMPOSSIBLE
INCOMPREHENSIBLE
INCOMPREHENSIBLY
INCOMPRESSIBLE
INCOMPT
INCOMPUTABLE
INCONCEIVABILITY
INCONCEIVABLE
INCONCINNATE
INCONCINNITY
INCONCINNOUS
INCONCLUDENT
INCONCLUDING
INCONCLUSION
INCONCLUSIVE
INCONDENSABLE
INCONDENSIBLE
INCONDITE
INCONFORMITY
INCONFUSED
INCONFUSEDLY
INCONFUSION
INCONGEALABLE
INCONGRUENCE
INCONGRUENT
INCONGRUENTLY
INCONGRUITIES
INCONGRUITY
INCONGRUOUS
INCONJOINABLE
INCONJUNCT
INCONNU
INCONSCIENCE
INCONSCIENT
INCONSCIENTLY
INCONSCIOUS
INCONSEQUENCE
INCONSEQUENT
INCONSEQUENTIAL
INCONSEQUENTLY
INCONSEQUENTNESS
INCONSIDERABLE
INCONSIDERABLY
INCONSIDERATE
INCONSIDERATELY
INCONSIDERATION
INCONSIDERED
INCONSISTENCE
INCONSISTENCIES
INCONSISTENCY
INCONSISTENT
INCONSISTENTLY
INCONSOLABLE
INCONSOLABLY
INCONSOLATE
INCONSONANCE
INCONSONANT
INCONSPICUOUS
INCONSPICUOUSLY
INCONSPICUOUSNESS
INCONSTANCY
INCONSTANT
INCONSTANTLY
INCONSTANTNESS
INCONSUMABLE
INCONSUMABLY
INCONTAMINATE
INCONTESTABLE
INCONTESTABLY
INCONTINENCE
INCONTINENCY
INCONTINENT
INCONTINENTLY
INCONTINUITY
INCONTINUOUS
INCONTRACTILE
INCONTRACTION
INCONTROLLABLE
INCONTROLLABLY
INCONTROVERTIBLE
INCONVENIENCE
INCONVENIENCY
INCONVENIENT
INCONVERSABLE
INCONVERTIBLE
INCONVINCIBLE
INCONY
INCOORDINATION
INCORONATE
INCORONATED
INCORONATION
INCORPORABLE
INCORPORAL
INCORPORALITY
INCORPORALLY
INCORPORALNESS
INCORPORATE
INCORPORATED
INCORPORATING
INCORPORATION
INCORPORATIVE
INCORPORATOR
INCORPOREAL
INCORPOREITIES
INCORPOREITY
INCORPOREOUS
INCORPSE
INCORRECT
INCORRECTION
INCORRECTLY
INCORRECTNESS
INCORRIGIBLE
INCORRIGIBLENESS
INCORRIGIBLY
INCORRUPT
INCORRUPTED
INCORRUPTIBILITY
INCORRUPTIBLE
INCORRUPTION
INCORRUPTLY
INCOUP
INCOURSE
INCOURTEOUS
INCOURTEOUSLY
INCRASH
INCRASSATE
INCRASSATED
INCRASSATING
INCRASSATION
INCREASE
INCREASED
INCREASEMENT
INCREASER
INCREASING
INCREASINGLY
INCREATE
INCREATELY
INCREATIVE
INCREDIBILITIES
INCREDIBILITY
INCREDIBLE
INCREDIBLENESS
INCREDIBLY
INCREDULITY
INCREDULOUS
INCREDULOUSLY
INCREEP
INCREEPING
INCREMATE
INCREMATED
INCREMATING
INCREMATION
INCREMENT
INCREMENTAL
INCREPATION
INCREPT
INCRESCENCE
INCRESCENT
INCREST
INCRETION
INCRETIONARY
INCRETORY
INCRIMINATE
INCRIMINATED
INCRIMINATING
INCRIMINATION
INCRIMINATOR
INCRIMINATORY
INCROSS
INCROSSING

INCROTCHET
INCROYABLE
INCRUENT
INCRUENTAL
INCRUENTOUS
INCRUST
INCRUSTANT
INCRUSTATE
INCRUSTATED
INCRUSTATING
INCRUSTATION
INCRUSTATOR
INCRUSTED
INCRUSTING
INCRUSTIVE
INCRUSTMENT
INCRYSTAL
INCUBATE
INCUBATED
INCUBATING
INCUBATION
INCUBATIONAL
INCUBATIVE
INCUBATOR
INCUBATORIUM
INCUBATORY
INCUBE
INCUBI
INCUBOUS
INCUBUS
INCUBUSES
INCUDAL
INCUDATE
INCUDECTOMY
INCUDES
INCULCATE
INCULCATED
INCULCATING
INCULCATION
INCULCATIVE
INCULCATOR
INCULCATORY
INCULK
INCULPABLE
INCULPABLY
INCULPATE
INCULPATED
INCULPATING
INCULPATION
INCULPATIVE
INCULPATORY
INCULT
INCULTURE
INCUMBENCE
INCUMBENCIES
INCUMBENCY
INCUMBENT
INCUMBENTLY
INCUMBER
INCUMBRANCE
INCUNABLE
INCUNABULA
INCUNABULAR
INCUNABULIST
INCUNABULUM
INCUNEATION
INCUR
INCURABILITY
INCURABLE
INCURABLENESS
INCURABLY
INCURIOSITY
INCURIOUS
INCURIOUSLY
INCURRED
INCURRENCE
INCURRENT
INCURRING
INCURSE
INCURSION
INCURSIONIST
INCURSIVE
INCURVATE
INCURVATED
INCURVATING
INCURVATION
INCURVATURE
INCURVE
INCURVED
INCUS
INCUSE
INCUSED
INCUSING
INCUSS
INCUTE
INCUTTING
INDABA
INDACONITIN
INDACONITINE
INDAGATE
INDAGATION
INDAGATIVE
INDAGATOR
INDAGATORY
INDAMIN
INDAMINE
INDAN
INDANE
INDART
INDAZOL
INDAZOLE
INDEBT
INDEBTED
INDEBTEDNESS
INDEBTING
INDEBTMENT
INDECENCE
INDECENCIES
INDECENCY
INDECENT
INDECENTLY
INDECENTNESS
INDECIDUATE
INDECIDUOUS
INDECISION
INDECISIVE
INDECISIVELY
INDECISIVENESS
INDECLINABLE
INDECLINABLY
INDECOROUS
INDECOROUSLY
INDECORUM
INDEED
INDEFATIGABLE
INDEFEASIBLE
INDEFEASIBLY
INDEFECTIBLE
INDEFECTIBLY
INDEFECTIVE
INDEFENSIBLE
INDEFICIENCY
INDEFICIENT
INDEFICIENTLY
INDEFINABLE
INDEFINABLY
INDEFINITE
INDEFINITELY
INDEFINITY
INDEFLECTIBLE
INDEHISCENCE
INDEHISCENT
INDELECTABLE
INDELIBERATE
INDELIBILITY
INDELIBLE
INDELIBLY
INDELICACIES
INDELICACY
INDELICATE
INDELICATELY
INDEMNIFICATION
INDEMNIFIED
INDEMNIFIER
INDEMNIFY
INDEMNIFYING
INDEMNITEE
INDEMNITIES
INDEMNITOR
INDEMNITY
INDEMONIATE
INDEMONSTRABLE
INDENE
INDENIZE
INDENT
INDENTATION
INDENTED
INDENTEDLY
INDENTEE
INDENTER
INDENTING
INDENTION
INDENTMENT
INDENTOR
INDENTURE
INDENTURED
INDENTURING
INDENTWISE
INDEPENDENCE
INDEPENDENCIES
INDEPENDENCY
INDEPENDENT
INDEPENDENTLY
INDERITE
INDESCRIBABLE
INDESCRIPT
INDESERT
INDESIGNATE
INDESTRUCTIBLE
INDETERMINACY
INDETERMINATE
INDEVOTION
INDEX
INDEXED
INDEXER
INDEXES
INDEXICAL
INDEXICALLY
INDEXING
INDEXTERITY
INDIANAITE
INDICAN
INDICANT
INDICANURIA
INDICATE
INDICATED
INDICATING
INDICATION
INDICATIVE
INDICATIVELY
INDICATOR
INDICATORY
INDICATRIX
INDICAVIT
INDICE
INDICES
INDICIA
INDICIAL
INDICIBLE
INDICO
INDICOLITE
INDICT
INDICTABLE
INDICTABLY
INDICTED
INDICTEE
INDICTER
INDICTING
INDICTION
INDICTIONAL
INDICTIVE
INDICTMENT
INDICTOR
INDIENNE
INDIFEROUS
INDIFFERENCE
INDIFFERENCIES
INDIFFERENCY
INDIFFERENT
INDIFFERENTIAL
INDIFFERENTISM
INDIFFERENTIST
INDIFFERENTLY
INDIGENA
INDIGENAE
INDIGENAL
INDIGENATE
INDIGENCE
INDIGENCY
INDIGENE
INDIGENEITY
INDIGENITY
INDIGENOUS
INDIGENT
INDIGENTLY
INDIGEST
INDIGESTED
INDIGESTIBLE
INDIGESTIBLY
INDIGESTION
INDIGESTIVE
INDIGITATE
INDIGITATION
INDIGN
INDIGNANCE
INDIGNANCY
INDIGNANT
INDIGNANTLY
INDIGNATION
INDIGNATORY
INDIGNIFIED
INDIGNIFY
INDIGNIFYING
INDIGNITIES
INDIGNITY
INDIGNLY
INDIGO
INDIGOES
INDIGOFEROUS
INDIGOID
INDIGOS
INDIGOTIC
INDIGOTIN
INDIGOTINE
INDIMENSIBLE
INDIMPLE
INDIO
INDIRECT
INDIRECTION
INDIRECTLY
INDIRECTNESS
INDIRUBIN
INDIRUBINE
INDISCERNIBLE
INDISCERNIBLY
INDISCIPLINE
INDISCREET
INDISCREETLY
INDISCRETE
INDISCRETELY
INDISCRETION
INDISCRIMINATE
INDISCRIMINATED
INDISCRIMINATELY
INDISCRIMINATING
INDISCRIMINATION
INDISCRIMINATIVE
INDISPENSABLE
INDISPOSE
INDISPOSED
INDISPOSING
INDISPOSITION
INDISPUTABLE
INDISPUTABLY
INDISSOLUBLE
INDISSOLUBLY
INDISSOLUTE
INDISSOLVABLE
INDISTINCT
INDISTINCTION
INDISTINCTIVE
INDISTINCTLY
INDISTINCTNESS
INDISTORTABLE
INDISTURBANCE
INDITE
INDITED
INDITEMENT
INDITER
INDITING
INDIUM
INDIVERTIBLE
INDIVERTIBLY
INDIVIDUA
INDIVIDUAL
INDIVIDUALISM
INDIVIDUALIST
INDIVIDUALITIES
INDIVIDUALITY
INDIVIDUALIZE
INDIVIDUALIZED
INDIVIDUALIZING
INDIVIDUALLY
INDIVIDUATE
INDIVIDUATED
INDIVIDUATING
INDIVIDUATION
INDIVIDUATOR
INDIVIDUITY
INDIVIDUUM
INDIVIDUUMS
INDIVINABLE
INDIVISIBLE
INDIVISIBLY
INDIVISIM
INDIVISION
INDOCIBLE
INDOCILE
INDOCILITY
INDOCTRINATE
INDOCTRINATED
INDOCTRINATING
INDOCTRINE
INDOCTRINIZE
INDOGEN
INDOGENIDE
INDOL
INDOLE
INDOLENCE
INDOLENT
INDOLENTLY
INDOLES
INDOLIN
INDOLINE
INDOLOID

INDOMITABLE
INDONE
INDOOR
INDOORS
INDOPHENIN
INDOPHENOL
INDORSATION
INDORSE
INDORSED
INDORSING
INDOXYL
INDOXYLIC
INDRAFT
INDRAPE
INDRAUGHT
INDRAWAL
INDRAWING
INDRAWN
INDRENCH
INDRI
INDUBIOUS
INDUBIOUSLY
INDUBITABLE
INDUBITABLY
INDUCE
INDUCED
INDUCEMENT
INDUCER
INDUCIAE
INDUCIBLE
INDUCING
INDUCIVE
INDUCT
INDUCTANCE
INDUCTED
INDUCTEE
INDUCTEOUS
INDUCTILE
INDUCTILITY
INDUCTING
INDUCTION
INDUCTIONAL
INDUCTIVE
INDUCTIVELY
INDUCTIVITY
INDUCTOMETER
INDUCTOPHONE
INDUCTOR
INDUCTORY
INDUCTOSCOPE
INDUE
INDUED
INDUING
INDULGE
INDULGED
INDULGENCE
INDULGENCED
INDULGENCY
INDULGENT
INDULGENTIAL
INDULGENTLY
INDULGENTNESS
INDULGER
INDULGING
INDULGINGLY
INDULIN
INDULINE
INDULT
INDULTO
INDULTS
INDUMENT
INDUMENTUM
INDUNA
INDUPLICATE
INDUPLICATION
INDUPLICATIVE
INDURATE
INDURATED
INDURATING
INDURATION
INDURATIVE
INDURE
INDURITE
INDUSIA
INDUSIAL
INDUSIATE
INDUSIATED
INDUSIFORM
INDUSIOID
INDUSIUM
INDUSTRIAL
INDUSTRIALLY
INDUSTRIES
INDUSTRIOUS
INDUSTRY
INDUVIAE
INDUVIAL
INDUVIATE
INDWELL
INDWELLER
INDWELLING
INDWELT
INDYL
INDYLIC
INEARTH
INEBRIACY
INEBRIANT
INEBRIATE
INEBRIATED
INEBRIATING
INEBRIATION
INEBRIATIVE
INEBRIETY
INEBRIOUS
INEDIBILITY
INEDIBLE
INEDITA
INEDITED
INEDUCATION
INEE
INEFFABILITY
INEFFABLE
INEFFABLY
INEFFACEABLE
INEFFACEABLY
INEFFECTIBLE
INEFFECTIBLY
INEFFECTIVE
INEFFECTIVELY
INEFFECTUAL
INEFFICACITY
INEFFICACY
INEFFICIENCE
INEFFICIENCY
INEFFICIENT
INELASTIC
INELASTICATE
INELASTICITY
INELEGANCE
INELEGANCES
INELEGANCIES
INELEGANCY
INELEGANT
INELEGANTLY
INELIGIBLE
INELIGIBLY
INELOQUENCE
INELOQUENT
INELUCTABLE
INELUCTABLY
INELUDIBLE
INENARRABLE
INENUBILABLE
INEPT
INEPTITUDE
INEPTLY
INEPTNESS
INEQUAL
INEQUALITARIAN
INEQUALITIES
INEQUALITY
INEQUALLY
INEQUALNESS
INEQUATION
INEQUITABLE
INEQUITABLY
INEQUITIES
INEQUITY
INEQUIVALVE
INERADICABLE
INERASABLE
INERASABLY
INERM
INERMOUS
INERRABLE
INERRANCY
INERRANT
INERRANTLY
INERRATIC
INERRING
INERRINGLY
INERT
INERTIA
INERTION
INERTLY
INERTNESS
INERUDITE
INERUDITELY
INERUDITION
INESCAPABLE
INESCATE
INESCATION
INESCULENT
INESCUTCHEON
INESITE
INESSENTIAL
INESTHETIC
INESTIMABLE
INESTIMABLY
INEUNT
INEVAPORABLE
INEVASIBLE
INEVIDENCE
INEVIDENT
INEVITABILITY
INEVITABLE
INEVITABLY
INEXACT
INEXACTITUDE
INEXACTLY
INEXACTNESS
INEXCUSABLE
INEXCUSABLY
INEXECUTION
INEXERTION
INEXHAUSTIBLE
INEXHAUSTIVE
INEXIST
INEXISTENCE
INEXISTENCY
INEXISTENT
INEXORABLE
INEXORABLY
INEXPECTED
INEXPECTEDLY
INEXPEDIENCY
INEXPEDIENT
INEXPENSIVE
INEXPERIENCE
INEXPERIENCED
INEXPERT
INEXPERTLY
INEXPERTNESS
INEXPIABLE
INEXPIABLENESS
INEXPIABLY
INEXPIATE
INEXPLICABLE
INEXPLICABLES
INEXPLICABLY
INEXPLICIT
INEXPLICITLY
INEXPRESS
INEXPRESSIBLE
INEXPRESSIVE
INEXPUGNABLE
INEXTENSIVE
INEXTERMINABLE
INEXTIRPABLE
INEXTRICABLE
INEXTRICABLY
INEYE
INFACE
INFAIR
INFALL
INFALLIBILIST
INFALLIBILITY
INFALLIBLE
INFALLIBLY
INFALLID
INFALLING
INFAME
INFAMED
INFAMIES
INFAMIZE
INFAMIZED
INFAMIZING
INFAMONIZE
INFAMOUS
INFAMOUSLY
INFAMOUSNESS
INFAMY
INFANCIES
INFANCY
INFAND
INFANDOUS
INFANG
INFANGLEMENT
INFANGTHEF
INFANGTHIEF
INFANS
INFANT
INFANTA
INFANTADO
INFANTE
INFANTICIDAL
INFANTICIDE
INFANTILE
INFANTILISM
INFANTILITY
INFANTINE
INFANTRIES
INFANTRY
INFANTRYMAN
INFANTS
INFARCT
INFARCTATE
INFARCTED
INFARCTION
INFARE
INFATUATE
INFATUATED
INFATUATEDLY
INFATUATING
INFATUATION
INFATUATOR
INFAUST
INFAUSTING
INFEASIBLE
INFECT
INFECTANT
INFECTED
INFECTEDNESS
INFECTING
INFECTION
INFECTIOUS
INFECTIVE
INFECTIVENESS
INFECTIVITY
INFECTOR
INFECTUM
INFECTUOUS
INFECUND
INFEED
INFEFT
INFEFTING
INFEFTMENT
INFELICIFIC
INFELICITIES
INFELICITOUS
INFELICITY
INFELT
INFEOFF
INFEOFFMENT
INFER
INFERABLE
INFERENCE
INFERENT
INFERENTIAL
INFERENTIALISM
INFERENTIALLY
INFERI
INFERIAE
INFERIAL
INFERIOR
INFERIORITY
INFERN
INFERNAL
INFERNALITY
INFERNALLY
INFERNALRY
INFERNO
INFERNOS
INFERRED
INFERRER
INFERRIBLE
INFERRING
INFERTILE
INFERTILELY
INFERTILITY
INFEST
INFESTANT
INFESTATION
INFESTED
INFESTER
INFESTING
INFESTIOUS
INFESTIVE
INFESTIVITY
INFESTMENT
INFEUDATION
INFIBULATE
INFIBULATION
INFICETE
INFIDEL
INFIDELIC
INFIDELICAL
INFIDELITIES
INFIDELITY
INFIELD
INFIELDER
INFIGHTER
INFIGHTING
INFILE
INFILL

INFILLING
INFILM
INFILTER
INFILTERED
INFILTERING
INFILTRATE
INFILTRATED
INFILTRATING
INFILTRATION
INFILTRATIVE
INFINITANT
INFINITARILY
INFINITARY
INFINITATE
INFINITATED
INFINITATING
INFINITATION
INFINITE
INFINITELY
INFINITENESS
INFINITESIMAL
INFINITETH
INFINITIES
INFINITIETH
INFINITIVAL
INFINITIVE
INFINITIVELY
INFINITO
INFINITUDE
INFINITUM
INFINITUPLE
INFINITY
INFIRM
INFIRMARER
INFIRMARESS
INFIRMARIAN
INFIRMARIES
INFIRMARY
INFIRMATE
INFIRMATION
INFIRMATIVE
INFIRMED
INFIRMING
INFIRMITIES
INFIRMITY
INFIT
INFITTER
INFIX
INFIXED
INFIXES
INFIXING
INFIXION
INFLAME
INFLAMED
INFLAMEDLY
INFLAMEDNESS
INFLAMER
INFLAMING
INFLAMINGLY
INFLAMMABILITY
INFLAMMABLE
INFLAMMABLENESS
INFLAMMABLY
INFLAMMATION
INFLAMMATIVE
INFLAMMATORY
INFLATE
INFLATED
INFLATEDLY
INFLATEDNESS
INFLATER
INFLATILE
INFLATING
INFLATION
INFLATIONARY
INFLATIONISM
INFLATIONIST
INFLATIVE
INFLATUS
INFLECT
INFLECTED
INFLECTING
INFLECTION
INFLECTIONAL
INFLECTIVE
INFLECTOR
INFLEX
INFLEXED
INFLEXIBILITY
INFLEXIBLE
INFLEXIBLY
INFLEXION
INFLEXIVE
INFLICT
INFLICTED
INFLICTER
INFLICTING
INFLICTION
INFLICTIVE
INFLOOD
INFLORESCENCE
INFLORESCENT
INFLOW
INFLUENCE
INFLUENCED
INFLUENCER
INFLUENCES
INFLUENCING
INFLUENCIVE
INFLUENT
INFLUENTIAL
INFLUENZA
INFLUENZAL
INFLUENZIC
INFLUX
INFLUXION
INFLUXIONISM
INFLUXIVE
INFO
INFOLD
INFOLDED
INFOLDER
INFOLDING
INFOLIATE
INFORM
INFORMAL
INFORMALITIES
INFORMALITY
INFORMALIZE
INFORMALLY
INFORMANT
INFORMATION
INFORMATIONAL
INFORMATIVE
INFORMATIVELY
INFORMATORY
INFORMED
INFORMEDLY
INFORMER
INFORMIDABLE
INFORMING
INFORMITY
INFORTIATE
INFORTITUDE
INFORTUNATE
INFORTUNE
INFOUND
INFRA
INFRABASAL
INFRACENTRAL
INFRACLUSION
INFRACOSTAL
INFRACT
INFRACTED
INFRACTING
INFRACTION
INFRACTOR
INFRADENTARY
INFRAGLACIAL
INFRAGLENOID
INFRAGULAR
INFRAHUMAN
INFRAHYOID
INFRALABIAL
INFRALITTORAL
INFRAMEDIAN
INFRANATURAL
INFRANGIBLE
INFRAPOSE
INFRAPOSED
INFRAPOSING
INFRAPROTEIN
INFRARED
INFRASONIC
INFRASPINAL
INFRASPINATUS
INFRASPINOUS
INFRATEMPORAL
INFRAVENTRAL
INFREQUENCE
INFREQUENCY
INFREQUENT
INFRIGIDATE
INFRINGE
INFRINGED
INFRINGEMENT
INFRINGER
INFRINGIBLE
INFRINGING
INFRUCTUOSE
INFRUCTUOUS
INFRUNITE
INFULA
INFULAE
INFUMATE
INFUMATED
INFUND
INFUNDIBULAR
INFUNDIBULUM
INFURIATE
INFURIATED
INFURIATELY
INFURIATING
INFURIATION
INFUSCATE
INFUSCATED
INFUSCATION
INFUSE
INFUSED
INFUSER
INFUSIBILITY
INFUSIBLE
INFUSING
INFUSION
INFUSIONISM
INFUSIONIST
INFUSIVE
INFUSORIAL
INFUSORIAN
INFUSORIES
INFUSORY
INGALLANTRY
INGANG
INGANGS
INGATE
INGATES
INGATHER
INGATHERED
INGATHERER
INGATHERING
INGE
INGEMINATE
INGEMINATED
INGEMINATING
INGENDER
INGENE
INGENERABLE
INGENERABLY
INGENERATE
INGENERATED
INGENERATING
INGENERATION
INGENIER
INGENIOSITY
INGENIOUS
INGENIOUSLY
INGENIT
INGENITAL
INGENITE
INGENT
INGENUE
INGENUITIES
INGENUITY
INGENUOUS
INGENUOUSLY
INGENUOUSNESS
INGENY
INGERMINATE
INGEST
INGESTA
INGESTED
INGESTER
INGESTIBLE
INGESTING
INGESTION
INGESTIVE
INGINE
INGIVER
INGIVING
INGLE
INGLENOOK
INGLES
INGLESA
INGLESIDE
INGLOBATE
INGLOBE
INGLOBED
INGLOBING
INGLORIOUS
INGLORIOUSLY
INGLORIOUSNESS
INGLUTITION
INGLUVIAL
INGLUVIES
INGLUVIITIS
INGOING
INGOT
INGOTED
INGOTING
INGOTMAN
INGOTMEN
INGOTS
INGRAFT
INGRAIN
INGRAINED
INGRAINEDLY
INGRAINING
INGRAMNESS
INGRANDIZE
INGRATE
INGRATEFUL
INGRATEFULNESS
INGRATELY
INGRATIATE
INGRATIATED
INGRATIATING
INGRATIATION
INGRATIATORY
INGRATITUDE
INGRAVESCENT
INGRAVIDATE
INGREAT
INGREDIENCE
INGREDIENT
INGRESS
INGRESSION
INGRESSIVE
INGROSS
INGROUP
INGROW
INGROWING
INGROWN
INGROWTH
INGRUENT
INGUEN
INGUINAL
INGULF
INGULFMENT
INGURGITATE
INGURGITATED
INGURGITATING
INGUSTABLE
INGYRE
INHABILE
INHABIT
INHABITABILITY
INHABITABLE
INHABITANCE
INHABITANCY
INHABITANT
INHABITATE
INHABITATION
INHABITATIVE
INHABITED
INHABITER
INHABITING
INHABITRESS
INHALANT
INHALATION
INHALE
INHALED
INHALENT
INHALER
INHALING
INHAME
INHARMONIC
INHARMONIOUS
INHARMONY
INHAUL
INHAULER
INHAUST
INHAUSTION
INHEARSE
INHEAVEN
INHELDE
INHERE
INHERED
INHERENCE
INHERENCIES
INHERENCY
INHERENT
INHERENTLY
INHERING
INHERIT
INHERITABLE
INHERITABLY
INHERITAGE
INHERITANCE
INHERITED
INHERITING
INHERITOR
INHESION
INHIATE
INHIBIT
INHIBITABLE

INHIBITED
INHIBITER
INHIBITION
INHIBITIONIST
INHIBITIONS
INHIBITIVE
INHIBITOR
INHIBITORY
INHOLDER
INHONEST
INHOOP
INHOSPITABLE
INHOSPITABLY
INHOSPITALITY
INHUMAN
INHUMANE
INHUMANELY
INHUMANITIES
INHUMANITY
INHUMANLY
INHUMANNESS
INHUMATE
INHUMATION
INHUMATIONIST
INHUME
INHUMED
INHUMER
INHUMING
INIAL
INIMICABLE
INIMICAL
INIMICALITY
INIMICALLY
INIMICALNESS
INIMICITIOUS
INIMICOUS
INIMITABILITY
INIMITABLE
INIMITABLY
INIOME
INIOMOUS
INION
INIQUITABLE
INIQUITIES
INIQUITOUS
INIQUITOUSLY
INIQUITY
INIRRITABILITY
INIRRITABLE
INISSUABLE
INITIAL
INITIALED
INITIALER
INITIALING
INITIALIST
INITIALLED
INITIALLY
INITIANT
INITIARY
INITIATE
INITIATED
INITIATING
INITIATION
INITIATIVE
INITIATIVELY
INITIATOR
INITIATORILY
INITIATORY
INITION
INJECT
INJECTED
INJECTING
INJECTION
INJECTOR
INJELLY
INJOINT
INJUDICIAL
INJUDICIALLY
INJUDICIOUS
INJUDICIOUSLY
INJUDICIOUSNESS
INJUNCT
INJUNCTION
INJUNCTIVE
INJUNCTIVELY
INJURE
INJURED
INJUREDLY
INJUREDNESS
INJURER
INJURIA
INJURIES
INJURING
INJURIOUS
INJURIOUSLY
INJURY
INJUST
INJUSTICE
INJUSTLY
INK
INKBERRIES
INKBERRY
INKBLOT
INKED
INKEN
INKER
INKET
INKFISH
INKHOLDER
INKHORN
INKHORNISM
INKHORNIST
INKHORNIZE
INKHORNIZER
INKIER
INKIEST
INKINDLE
INKING
INKLE
INKLING
INKMAN
INKNIT
INKNOT
INKOS
INKOSI
INKPOT
INKROOT
INKS
INKSHED
INKSLINGER
INKSLINGING
INKSTAND
INKSTANDISH
INKSTONE
INKWEED
INKWELL
INKWOOD
INKWRITER
INKY
INLAGATION
INLAID
INLAIK
INLAKE
INLAND
INLANDER
INLANDISH
INLAPIDATE
INLARD
INLAUT
INLAW
INLAWRY
INLAY
INLAYER
INLAYING
INLEAGUE
INLEAGUED
INLEAGUING
INLEAK
INLEAKAGE
INLESS
INLET
INLETTING
INLIER
INLIKE
INLOOK
INLOOKER
INLOOKING
INLY
INLYING
INMATE
INMEATS
INMESH
INMIXTURE
INMORE
INMOST
INN
INNAM
INNARDS
INNASCIBLE
INNATE
INNATELY
INNATENESS
INNATISM
INNATIVE
INNATURAL
INNATURALITY
INNATURALLY
INNEITY
INNER
INNERLY
INNERMORE
INNERMOST
INNERVATE
INNERVATED
INNERVATING
INNERVATION
INNERVATIONAL
INNERVE
INNERVED
INNERVING
INNESS
INNEST
INNET
INNHOLDER
INNING
INNINGS
INNINMORITE
INNITENCY
INNKEEPER
INNOCENCE
INNOCENCIES
INNOCENCY
INNOCENT
INNOCENTLY
INNOCENTNESS
INNOCUITY
INNOCUOUS
INNOCUOUSLY
INNOCUOUSNESS
INNODATE
INNOMINABLE
INNOMINABLES
INNOMINATA
INNOMINATE
INNOMINATUM
INNOVANT
INNOVATE
INNOVATED
INNOVATING
INNOVATION
INNOVATIVE
INNOVATOR
INNOVATORY
INNOXIOUS
INNOXIOUSLY
INNUATE
INNUENDO
INNUENDOED
INNUENDOES
INNUENDOING
INNUMERABLE
INNUMERABLY
INNUMEROUS
INNUTRIENT
INNUTRITION
INNUTRITIOUS
INNYARD
INOBEDIENCE
INOBEDIENT
INOBNOXIOUS
INOBSCURABLE
INOBSERVANCE
INOBSERVANCY
INOBSERVANT
INOBSERVANTLY
INOBSERVATION
INOBTAINABLE
INOBTRUSIVE
INOCCUPATION
INOCULABILITY
INOCULABLE
INOCULANT
INOCULAR
INOCULATE
INOCULATED
INOCULATING
INOCULATION
INOCULATIVE
INOCULATOR
INOCULUM
INODIATE
INODOROUS
INODOROUSLY
INODOROUSNESS
INOFFENSIVE
INOFFICIOSITY
INOFFICIOUS
INOFFICIOUSNESS
INOGEN
INOMA
INOMINOUS
INONE
INOPERABLE
INOPERATIVE
INOPERCULAR
INOPERCULATE
INOPINABLE
INOPINATE
INOPINATELY
INOPINE
INOPPORTUNE
INOPPORTUNELY
INOPPORTUNIST
INOPPORTUNITY
INOPULENT
INORB
INORDINACY
INORDINATE
INORDINATELY
INORDINATENESS
INORDINATION
INORGANIC
INORGANIZATION
INORIGINATE
INORNATE
INOSCULATED
INOSCULATING
INOSINE
INOSITE
INOSITOL
INOTROPIC
INOWER
INOXIDIZE
INOXIDIZED
INOXIDIZING
INPARFIT
INPATIENT
INPAYMENT
INPENSIONER
INPHASE
INPORT
INPOUR
INPOURING
INPUSH
INPUT
INQUAINTANCE
INQUARTATION
INQUEST
INQUESTUAL
INQUIET
INQUIETLY
INQUIETNESS
INQUIETUDE
INQUILINE
INQUILINISM
INQUILINITY
INQUILINOUS
INQUINATE
INQUINATED
INQUINATING
INQUINATION
INQUIRABLE
INQUIRATION
INQUIRE
INQUIRED
INQUIRENDO
INQUIRENT
INQUIRER
INQUIRIES
INQUIRING
INQUIRINGLY
INQUIRY
INQUISIT
INQUISITE
INQUISITION
INQUISITIONAL
INQUISITIONIST
INQUISITIVE
INQUISITOR
INQUISITORIAL
INQUISITORY
INRADIUS
INRIGGED
INRIGGER
INRIGHTED
INRING
INRO
INROAD
INROADER
INROLL
INROOTED
INRUB
INRUN
INRUNNING
INRUPTION
INRUSH
INS
INSACK
INSAGACITY
INSALIVATE
INSALIVATED
INSALIVATING
INSALIVATION
INSALUBRIOUS
INSALUBRITY

INSAME
INSANE
INSANELY
INSANENESS
INSANIFY
INSANITARY
INSANITATION
INSANITY
INSATIABLE
INSATIABLY
INSATIATE
INSATIATED
INSATIATELY
INSATIETY
INSATISFACTION
INSATURABLE
INSCENATION
INSCIENCE
INSCIENT
INSCIOUS
INSCRIBABLE
INSCRIBE
INSCRIBED
INSCRIBER
INSCRIBING
INSCRIPT
INSCRIPTIBLE
INSCRIPTION
INSCRIPTIONED
INSCRIPTIVE
INSCRIPTURED
INSCROLL
INSCROLLED
INSCROLLING
INSCRUTABLE
INSCRUTABLES
INSCRUTABLY
INSCULP
INSCULPTURE
INSEA
INSEAM
INSEAMER
INSECT
INSECTAN
INSECTARIA
INSECTARIES
INSECTARIUM
INSECTARIUMS
INSECTARY
INSECTEAN
INSECTED
INSECTICIDAL
INSECTICIDE
INSECTILE
INSECTION
INSECTIVAL
INSECTIVORE
INSECTIVOROUS
INSECTMONGER
INSECTOLOGER
INSECTOLOGY
INSECTS
INSECURE
INSECURELY
INSECURENESS
INSECURITIES
INSECURITY
INSEE
INSEEING
INSEER
INSELBERG
INSELBERGE
INSEMINATE
INSEMINATED
INSEMINATING
INSEMINATION
INSENESCIBLE
INSENSATE
INSENSATELY
INSENSE
INSENSED
INSENSIBILITY
INSENSIBILIZE
INSENSIBLE
INSENSIBLY
INSENSING
INSENSITIVE
INSENSUOUS
INSENTIENCE
INSENTIENCY
INSENTIENT
INSEPARABLE
INSEPARABLY
INSEPARATE
INSEPARATELY
INSEQUENT
INSERT
INSERTED
INSERTER
INSERTING
INSERTION
INSERTIONAL
INSERTIVE
INSERVIENT
INSESSION
INSESSOR
INSESSORIAL
INSET
INSETTER
INSEVERABLE
INSEVERABLY
INSHAVE
INSHEATHE
INSHEATHED
INSHEATHING
INSHELL
INSHINING
INSHIP
INSHOE
INSHOOT
INSHORE
INSHRINE
INSIDE
INSIDENT
INSIDER
INSIDES
INSIDIATE
INSIDIATION
INSIDIATOR
INSIDIOSITY
INSIDIOUS
INSIDIOUSLY
INSIGHT
INSIGHTED
INSIGHTFUL
INSIGNE
INSIGNIA
INSIGNIFICANCE
INSIGNIFICANCIES
INSIGNIFICANCY
INSIGNIFICANT
INSIGNIFICANTLY
INSIMPLICITY
INSINCERE
INSINCERELY
INSINCERITIES
INSINCERITY
INSINEW
INSINKING
INSINUANT
INSINUATE
INSINUATED
INSINUATING
INSINUATION
INSINUATIVE
INSINUATOR
INSINUATORY
INSINUENDO
INSIPID
INSIPIDITIES
INSIPIDITY
INSIPIDLY
INSIPIDNESS
INSIPIENCE
INSIPIENT
INSIPIENTLY
INSIST
INSISTED
INSISTENCE
INSISTENCY
INSISTENT
INSISTENTLY
INSISTER
INSISTING
INSISTIVE
INSISTURE
INSITE
INSITION
INSITITIOUS
INSNARE
INSNAREMENT
INSNARER
INSOBRIETY
INSOCIABILITY
INSOCIABLE
INSOCIABLY
INSOCIAL
INSOCIALLY
INSOLATE
INSOLATED
INSOLATING
INSOLATION
INSOLE
INSOLENCE
INSOLENCY
INSOLENT
INSOLENTLY
INSOLENTNESS
INSOLID
INSOLIDITY
INSOLITE
INSOLUBILITY
INSOLUBLE
INSOLUBLY
INSOLVABLE
INSOLVABLY
INSOLVENCE
INSOLVENCIES
INSOLVENCY
INSOLVENT
INSOMNIA
INSOMNIAC
INSOMNIOUS
INSOMNOLENCE
INSOMNOLENCY
INSOMNOLENT
INSOMUCH
INSOOTH
INSORB
INSORDID
INSOUCIANCE
INSOUCIANT
INSOUCIANTLY
INSOUL
INSPAKE
INSPAN
INSPANNED
INSPANNING
INSPEAK
INSPEAKING
INSPECT
INSPECTED
INSPECTING
INSPECTION
INSPECTIONAL
INSPECTIONEER
INSPECTIVE
INSPECTOR
INSPECTORAL
INSPECTORATE
INSPECTORIAL
INSPECTRESS
INSPECTRIX
INSPEXIMUS
INSPHERATION
INSPHERE
INSPIRABILITY
INSPIRABLE
INSPIRANT
INSPIRATION
INSPIRATIONAL
INSPIRATIVE
INSPIRATOR
INSPIRATORY
INSPIRE
INSPIRED
INSPIREDLY
INSPIRER
INSPIRING
INSPIRINGLY
INSPIRIT
INSPIRITED
INSPIRITER
INSPIRITING
INSPIRITINGLY
INSPIROMETER
INSPISSANT
INSPISSATE
INSPISSATED
INSPISSATING
INSPISSATION
INSPISSATOR
INSPISSOSIS
INSPOKE
INSPOKEN
INSPREITH
INSTABILITIES
INSTABILITY
INSTABLE
INSTAL
INSTALL
INSTALLANT
INSTALLATION
INSTALLED
INSTALLER
INSTALLING
INSTALLMENT
INSTANCE
INSTANCED
INSTANCING
INSTANCY
INSTANDING
INSTANT
INSTANTANEITY
INSTANTANEOUS
INSTANTER
INSTANTIAL
INSTANTLY
INSTAR
INSTARRED
INSTARRING
INSTATE
INSTATED
INSTATING
INSTAURATE
INSTAURATION
INSTAURATOR
INSTEAD
INSTEALING
INSTEAM
INSTEEP
INSTELLATION
INSTEP
INSTIGANT
INSTIGATE
INSTIGATED
INSTIGATING
INSTIGATION
INSTIGATIVE
INSTIGATOR
INSTIL
INSTILL
INSTILLATION
INSTILLATOR
INSTILLATORY
INSTILLED
INSTILLER
INSTILLING
INSTINCT
INSTINCTION
INSTINCTIVE
INSTINCTIVELY
INSTINCTIVIST
INSTINCTIVITY
INSTINCTUAL
INSTIPULATE
INSTITOR
INSTITORIAL
INSTITORY
INSTITUE
INSTITUTE
INSTITUTED
INSTITUTING
INSTITUTION
INSTITUTIONAL
INSTITUTIVE
INSTITUTOR
INSTONEMENT
INSTOP
INSTORE
INSTRATIFIED
INSTRENGTHEN
INSTRESSED
INSTROKE
INSTRUCT
INSTRUCTED
INSTRUCTING
INSTRUCTION
INSTRUCTIONAL
INSTRUCTIVE
INSTRUCTOR
INSTRUMENT
INSTRUMENTAL
INSTRUMENTALIST
INSTRUMENTALITIES
INSTRUMENTALITY
INSTRUMENTATE
INSTRUMENTED
INSTRUMENTS
INSTYLE
INSUAVITY
INSUBJECTION
INSUBMISSION
INSUBORDINATE
INSUBORDINATION
INSUBSTANTIAL
INSUBSTANTIALITY
INSUBSTANTIATE
INSUCCATION
INSUCCESS
INSUCCESSFUL
INSUCKEN
INSUETUDE
INSUFFERABLE
INSUFFERABLY

INSUFFICIENCE
INSUFFICIENCY
INSUFFICIENT
INSUFFICIENTLY
INSUFFLATE
INSUFFLATED
INSUFFLATION
INSUFFLATOR
INSULA
INSULAE
INSULANCE
INSULANT
INSULAR
INSULARITY
INSULARY
INSULATE
INSULATED
INSULATING
INSULATION
INSULATOR
INSULIN
INSULIZE
INSULPHURED
INSULSE
INSULSITY
INSULT
INSULTANT
INSULTATION
INSULTED
INSULTER
INSULTING
INSULTINGLY
INSUME
INSUNK
INSUPER
INSUPERABLE
INSUPERABLY
INSUPPORTABLE
INSUPPRESSIVE
INSURABILITY
INSURABLE
INSURANCE
INSURANT
INSURE
INSURED
INSUREDS
INSURER
INSURGE
INSURGENCE
INSURGENCY
INSURGENT
INSURGESCENCE
INSURING
INSURMOUNTABLE
INSURRECT
INSURRECTION
INSURRECTO
INSURRECTORY
INSUSCEPTIBLE
INSWARMING
INSWATHE
INSWATHEMENT
INSWEEPING
INSWELL
INSWEPT
INSWING
INSWINGER
INTABULATE
INTACT
INTACTILE
INTACTLY
INTACTNESS
INTAGLI
INTAGLIATED
INTAGLIO
INTAGLIOED
INTAGLIOING
INTAGLIOS
INTAKE
INTAKER
INTANGIBLE
INTANGIBLY
INTARISSABLE
INTARSIA
INTARSIATE
INTARSIST
INTEGER
INTEGERS
INTEGRABLE
INTEGRAL
INTEGRALITY
INTEGRANT
INTEGRAPH
INTEGRATE
INTEGRATED
INTEGRATING
INTEGRATION
INTEGRATIVE
INTEGRATOR
INTEGRIOUS
INTEGRIOUSLY
INTEGRITY
INTEGUMENT
INTEGUMENTAL
INTEIND
INTELLECT
INTELLECTATION
INTELLECTED
INTELLECTIBLE
INTELLECTION
INTELLECTIVE
INTELLECTUAL
INTELLIGENCE
INTELLIGENCY
INTELLIGENT
INTELLIGENTLY
INTELLIGENTSIA
INTELLIGIBLE
INTELLIGIBLY
INTELLIGIZE
INTEMERATE
INTEMERATELY
INTEMERATION
INTEMPERANCE
INTEMPERANCY
INTEMPERATE
INTEMPERATURE
INTEMPESTIVE
INTEMPORAL
INTEMPORALLY
INTEND
INTENDANCE
INTENDANCIES
INTENDANCY
INTENDANT
INTENDED
INTENDEDLY
INTENDEDNESS
INTENDENCE
INTENDENCIA
INTENDENTE
INTENDER
INTENDIBLE
INTENDING
INTENDINGLY
INTENDIT
INTENDMENT
INTENERATE
INTENERATED
INTENERATING
INTENERATION
INTENIBLE
INTENSATE
INTENSATION
INTENSATIVE
INTENSE
INTENSELY
INTENSIFIED
INTENSIFIER
INTENSIFY
INTENSIFYING
INTENSION
INTENSIONAL
INTENSIONALLY
INTENSITIES
INTENSITIVE
INTENSITY
INTENSIVE
INTENSIVELY
INTENSIVENESS
INTENT
INTENTED
INTENTION
INTENTIONAL
INTENTIONALITY
INTENTIONED
INTENTIVE
INTENTIVELY
INTENTLY
INTER
INTERACINOUS
INTERACT
INTERACTION
INTERACTIONISM
INTERACTIVE
INTERADDITIVE
INTERAGENT
INTERALLIED
INTERAMNIAN
INTERATOMIC
INTERAXAL
INTERAXIAL
INTERAXIS
INTERBANDED
INTERBED
INTERBEDDED
INTERBLEND
INTERBLENDED
INTERBLENDING
INTERBLENT
INTERBONDING
INTERBOROUGH
INTERBOURSE
INTERBRAIN
INTERBREED
INTERBREEDING
INTERCADENCE
INTERCADENT
INTERCALARE
INTERCALARIUM
INTERCALARY
INTERCALATE
INTERCALATED
INTERCALATING
INTERCALATION
INTERCANAL
INTERCARDINAL
INTERCAROTID
INTERCARPAL
INTERCEDE
INTERCEDED
INTERCEDER
INTERCEDING
INTERCENSAL
INTERCENTRA
INTERCENTRAL
INTERCENTRUM
INTERCEPT
INTERCEPTED
INTERCEPTER
INTERCEPTING
INTERCEPTION
INTERCEPTIVE
INTERCEPTOR
INTERCESS
INTERCESSION
INTERCESSIVE
INTERCESSOR
INTERCESSORY
INTERCHANGE
INTERCHANGEABLE
INTERCHANGED
INTERCHANGER
INTERCHANGING
INTERCHURCH
INTERCILIARY
INTERCILIUM
INTERCISION
INTERCIVIC
INTERCLAVICLE
INTERCLOUD
INTERCLUDE
INTERCLUSION
INTERCOASTAL
INTERCOLLEGE
INTERCOLLINE
INTERCOLONIAL
INTERCOLUMNIATION
INTERCOM
INTERCOMMON
INTERCOMMONED
INTERCOMMONING
INTERCOMMUNE
INTERCOMMUNED
INTERCOMMUNICATION
INTERCOMMUNING
INTERCONNECTED
INTERCONNECTING
INTERCONNECTION
INTERCOOLER
INTERCOOLING
INTERCOSMIC
INTERCOSTAL
INTERCOURSE
INTERCROP
INTERCROPPED
INTERCROPPING
INTERCROSS
INTERCROSSED
INTERCROSSING
INTERCUR
INTERCURRENT
INTERCUT
INTERDEAL
INTERDEALER
INTERDENTAL
INTERDENTIL
INTERDEPEND
INTERDEPENDENT
INTERDICT
INTERDICTION
INTERDICTIVE
INTERDICTOR
INTERDICTORY
INTERDIGITATE
INTERDIGITATED
INTERDIGITATING
INTERDOME
INTERESS
INTERESSE
INTERESSEE
INTEREST
INTERESTED
INTERESTER
INTERESTING
INTERESTINGLY
INTERESTS
INTERFACE
INTERFACIAL
INTERFECTOR
INTERFERANT
INTERFERE
INTERFERED
INTERFERENCE
INTERFERENT
INTERFERER
INTERFERING
INTERFEROMETER
INTERFERON
INTERFERRIC
INTERFERTILE
INTERFILAR
INTERFINGER
INTERFLANGE
INTERFLOW
INTERFLUENCE
INTERFLUENT
INTERFLUOUS
INTERFLUVE
INTERFLUVIAL
INTERFOLD
INTERFOLIATE
INTERFRET
INTERFRETTED
INTERFRONTAL
INTERFUSE
INTERFUSED
INTERFUSING
INTERFUSION
INTERGLACIAL
INTERGLYPH
INTERGRADE
INTERGRADED
INTERGRADING
INTERGRAFT
INTERGRAVE
INTERGROW
INTERGROWN
INTERGROWTH
INTERGULAR
INTERHAEMAL
INTERHEMAL
INTERHYAL
INTERIEUR
INTERIM
INTERIMIST
INTERIMISTIC
INTERIONIC
INTERIOR
INTERIORITY
INTERJACENCE
INTERJACENT
INTERJECT
INTERJECTED
INTERJECTING
INTERJECTION
INTERJECTOR
INTERJECTORY
INTERJOIN
INTERJOIST
INTERJUNCTION
INTERKINESIS
INTERKINETIC
INTERKNIT
INTERKNOT
INTERKNOW
INTERLACE
INTERLACED
INTERLACEDLY
INTERLACEMENT
INTERLACERY
INTERLACING
INTERLAID
INTERLAMINATE
INTERLAMINATED

INTERLAMINATING
INTERLAP
INTERLAPSE
INTERLARD
INTERLARDED
INTERLARDING
INTERLAY
INTERLAYING
INTERLEAF
INTERLEAGUE
INTERLEAVE
INTERLEAVED
INTERLEAVER
INTERLEAVES
INTERLEAVING
INTERLIBEL
INTERLINE
INTERLINEAL
INTERLINEAR
INTERLINEARLY
INTERLINEARY
INTERLINEATE
INTERLINED
INTERLINER
INTERLINGUAL
INTERLINING
INTERLINK
INTERLINKED
INTERLOCAL
INTERLOCATE
INTERLOCK
INTERLOCKED
INTERLOCKER
INTERLOCKING
INTERLOCULUS
INTERLOCUTION
INTERLOCUTIVE
INTERLOCUTOR
INTERLOCUTORY
INTERLOPE
INTERLOPED
INTERLOPER
INTERLOPING
INTERLOT
INTERLUCENT
INTERLUDE
INTERLUDER
INTERLUDIAL
INTERLUNAR
INTERLUNARY
INTERLUNATION
INTERMARRIED
INTERMARRY
INTERMARRYING
INTERMASTOID
INTERMEDDLE
INTERMEDDLED
INTERMEDDLER
INTERMEDDLING
INTERMEDE
INTERMEDIA
INTERMEDIACY
INTERMEDIAE
INTERMEDIAL
INTERMEDIARIES
INTERMEDIARY
INTERMEDIATE
INTERMEDIATED
INTERMEDIATING
INTERMEDIATOR
INTERMEDIUM
INTERMEDIUS
INTERMEMBRAL
INTERMENT
INTERMENTION
INTERMESH
INTERMESSAGE
INTERMEW
INTERMEWED
INTERMEWER
INTERMEZZI
INTERMEZZO
INTERMEZZOS
INTERMINABLE
INTERMINANT
INTERMINATE
INTERMINATED
INTERMINE
INTERMINED
INTERMINGLE
INTERMINGLED
INTERMINGLING
INTERMINING
INTERMISSION
INTERMISSIVE
INTERMIT
INTERMITTED
INTERMITTENT
INTERMITTENTLY
INTERMITTING
INTERMIX
INTERMIXED
INTERMIXEDLY
INTERMIXING
INTERMIXT
INTERMIXTLY
INTERMIXTURE
INTERMURAL
INTERMUTATION
INTERMUTUAL
INTERN
INTERNAL
INTERNALITIES
INTERNALITY
INTERNALIZE
INTERNALLY
INTERNALNESS
INTERNARIAL
INTERNASAL
INTERNATION
INTERNATIONAL
INTERNE
INTERNECINE
INTERNECION
INTERNECIVE
INTERNECT
INTERNECTION
INTERNED
INTERNEE
INTERNETTED
INTERNEURAL
INTERNEURON
INTERNING
INTERNIST
INTERNMENT
INTERNOBASAL
INTERNODAL
INTERNODE
INTERNODIA
INTERNODIAL
INTERNODIAN
INTERNODIUM
INTERNSHIP
INTERNUCLEAR
INTERNUNCIAL
INTERNUNCIO
INTERNUNCIOS
INTERNUPTIAL
INTERNUPTIALS
INTEROCEPTOR
INTEROCULAR
INTEROLIVARY
INTEROPERCLE
INTEROPTIC
INTEROSCULANT
INTEROSCULATE
INTEROSCULATED
INTEROSCULATING
INTEROSSEAL
INTEROSSEI
INTEROSSEOUS
INTEROSSEUS
INTERPAGE
INTERPASS
INTERPAUSE
INTERPEAL
INTERPEL
INTERPELLANT
INTERPELLATE
INTERPELLATED
INTERPELLATING
INTERPELLATION
INTERPELLED
INTERPELLING
INTERPENDENT
INTERPENETRATE
INTERPENETRATE
INTERPHASE
INTERPIECE
INTERPLACE
INTERPLAIT
INTERPLAY
INTERPLEA
INTERPLEAD
INTERPLEADER
INTERPLEURAL
INTERPLICATE
INTERPOINT
INTERPOLABLE
INTERPOLAR
INTERPOLARY
INTERPOLATE
INTERPOLATED
INTERPOLATER
INTERPOLATING
INTERPOLATION
INTERPOLATOR
INTERPOLE
INTERPOLISH
INTERPOLITY
INTERPONE
INTERPORTAL
INTERPOSAL
INTERPOSE
INTERPOSED
INTERPOSER
INTERPOSING
INTERPOSURE
INTERPRET
INTERPRETABLE
INTERPRETATE
INTERPRETATION
INTERPRETED
INTERPRETER
INTERPRETING
INTERPRETIVE
INTERPUBIC
INTERRACIAL
INTERRADIAL
INTERRADII
INTERRADIUM
INTERRADIUS
INTERRAMAL
INTERRED
INTERREGAL
INTERREGES
INTERREGNA
INTERREGNAL
INTERREGNUM
INTERREIGN
INTERRELATE
INTERRELATED
INTERRELATING
INTERRELATION
INTERRELATIONS
INTERRENAL
INTERRER
INTERREX
INTERRIGHT
INTERRING
INTERROGANT
INTERROGATE
INTERROGATED
INTERROGATEE
INTERROGATING
INTERROGATION
INTERROGATOR
INTERROGEE
INTERRUPT
INTERRUPTED
INTERRUPTER
INTERRUPTING
INTERRUPTION
INTERRUPTIVE
INTERRUPTOR
INTERSCRIBE
INTERSEAMED
INTERSECT
INTERSECTANT
INTERSECTED
INTERSECTING
INTERSECTION
INTERSEPTAL
INTERSERTAL
INTERSESSION
INTERSEX
INTERSEXUAL
INTERSEXUALITY
INTERSHOCK
INTERSHOOT
INTERSOCIAL
INTERSOMNIAL
INTERSOW
INTERSPACE
INTERSPATIAL
INTERSPEAKER
INTERSPERSAL
INTERSPERSE
INTERSPERSED
INTERSPERSING
INTERSPHERE
INTERSPINAL
INTERSPINOUS
INTERSPORAL
INTERSTADIAL
INTERSTAGE
INTERSTATE
INTERSTELLAR
INTERSTERILE
INTERSTERNAL
INTERSTICE
INTERSTICED
INTERSTICES
INTERSTITIAL
INTERSTRATIFY
INTERSTRIAL
INTERTALK
INTERTANGLE
INTERTEAR
INTERTERGAL
INTERTEX
INTERTEXTURE
INTERTIDAL
INTERTIE
INTERTILL
INTERTILLAGE
INTERTISSUED
INTERTONE
INTERTONGUE
INTERTONIC
INTERTRAGIAN
INTERTRIBAL
INTERTRIGO
INTERTROPIC
INTERTROPICS
INTERTRUDE
INTERTWINE
INTERTWINED
INTERTWINING
INTERTWIST
INTERTWISTED
INTERTWISTING
INTERURBAN
INTERVAL
INTERVALE
INTERVALED
INTERVALING
INTERVALLED
INTERVALLIC
INTERVALLING
INTERVALS
INTERVEIN
INTERVEINAL
INTERVEINED
INTERVEINING
INTERVENANT
INTERVENE
INTERVENED
INTERVENER
INTERVENIENT
INTERVENING
INTERVENIUM
INTERVENOR
INTERVENT
INTERVENTION
INTERVENTIVE
INTERVENTOR
INTERVENULAR
INTERVERBAL
INTERVERSION
INTERVERT
INTERVERTED
INTERVERTING
INTERVIEW
INTERVIEWED
INTERVIEWEE
INTERVIEWER
INTERVIEWING
INTERVILLOUS
INTERVISIT
INTERVITAL
INTERVOCAL
INTERVOCALIC
INTERVOLVE
INTERVOLVED
INTERVOLVING
INTERWEAVE
INTERWEAVED
INTERWEAVER
INTERWEAVING
INTERWED
INTERWIND
INTERWINDING
INTERWORK
INTERWORKED
INTERWORKING
INTERWOUND
INTERWOVE
INTERWOVEN
INTERWREATHE
INTERWREATHED
INTERWREATHING
INTERWROUGHT
INTERXYLARY
INTERZONAL

INTESTABLE
INTESTACIES
INTESTACY
INTESTATE
INTESTATION
INTESTINAL
INTESTINE
INTESTINES
INTEXINE
INTEXT
INTEXTINE
INTEXTURE
INTHRAL
INTHRALL
INTHRALLMENT
INTHRALMENT
INTHRONE
INTHRONG
INTHRONISTIC
INTHRONIZATE
INTHRONIZE
INTHROW
INTHRUST
INTIL
INTILL
INTIMA
INTIMACIES
INTIMACY
INTIMADO
INTIMADOS
INTIMAE
INTIMAL
INTIMATE
INTIMATED
INTIMATELY
INTIMATENESS
INTIMATER
INTIMATING
INTIMATION
INTIME
INTIMIDATE
INTIMIDATED
INTIMIDATING
INTIMIDATION
INTIMIDATOR
INTIMISM
INTIMITY
INTINCT
INTINCTION
INTINE
INTISY
INTITLE
INTITULE
INTITULED
INTITULING
INTO
INTOED
INTOLERABLE
INTOLERABLY
INTOLERANCE
INTOLERANCY
INTOLERANT
INTOLERANTLY
INTOLERATING
INTOLERATION
INTOMB
INTONABLE
INTONACO
INTONATE
INTONATED
INTONATING
INTONATION
INTONATOR
INTONE
INTONED
INTONER
INTONING
INTOOTHED
INTORSION
INTORT
INTORTED
INTORTILLAGE
INTORTING
INTOWER
INTOWN
INTOXATION
INTOXICABLE
INTOXICANT
INTOXICATE
INTOXICATED
INTOXICATING
INTOXICATION
INTOXICATIVE
INTOXICATOR
INTRA
INTRABIONTIC
INTRABRED
INTRACARDIAC
INTRACHORDAL
INTRACISTERN
INTRACOASTAL
INTRACTABLE
INTRACTABLY
INTRACTILE
INTRADA
INTRADO
INTRADOS
INTRADURAL
INTRAFUSAL
INTRAGANTES
INTRAGLACIAL
INTRAGROUP
INTRAGROUPAL
INTRAIL
INTRAIT
INTRALOGICAL
INTRAMENTAL
INTRAMONTANE
INTRAMUNDANE
INTRAMURAL
INTRAMURALLY
INTRANATAL
INTRANEOUS
INTRANSIENT
INTRANSIGENT
INTRANSITABLE
INTRANSITIVE
INTRANT
INTRAPIAL
INTRAPOLAR
INTRAPSYCHIC
INTRASTATE
INTRATE
INTRATHECAL
INTRATHYROID
INTRAUTERINE
INTRAVAGINAL
INTRAVENOUS
INTRAVITAL
INTRAXYLARY
INTREAT
INTRENCH
INTRENCHANT
INTRENCHED
INTRENCHER
INTRENCHING
INTREPID
INTREPIDITY
INTREPIDLY
INTREPIDNESS
INTRICACIES
INTRICACY
INTRICATE
INTRICATELY
INTRIGANT
INTRIGANTE
INTRIGANTS
INTRIGO
INTRIGUE
INTRIGUED
INTRIGUER
INTRIGUERY
INTRIGUING
INTRIGUINGLY
INTRINE
INTRINSE
INTRINSIC
INTRINSICAL
INTRINSICALLY
INTRINSICATE
INTRO
INTROCEPTIVE
INTRODDEN
INTRODUCE
INTRODUCED
INTRODUCEE
INTRODUCER
INTRODUCING
INTRODUCTION
INTRODUCTIVE
INTRODUCTOR
INTRODUCTORY
INTROFACTION
INTROFIED
INTROFIER
INTROFLEX
INTROFLEXION
INTROFY
INTROFYING
INTROIT
INTROITUS
INTROJECTION
INTROMISSION
INTROMISSIVE
INTROMIT
INTROMITTED
INTROMITTENT
INTROMITTER
INTROMITTING
INTROPULSIVE
INTRORSE
INTRORSELY
INTROSPECT
INTROSPECTED
INTROSPECTING
INTROSPECTION
INTROSPECTOR
INTROSUSCEPT
INTROVENIENT
INTROVERSE
INTROVERSION
INTROVERSIVE
INTROVERT
INTROVERTED
INTROVERTING
INTROVERTIVE
INTRUDANCE
INTRUDE
INTRUDED
INTRUDER
INTRUDING
INTRUDINGLY
INTRUS
INTRUSE
INTRUSION
INTRUSIONAL
INTRUSIONIST
INTRUSIVE
INTRUSIVELY
INTRUSO
INTRUST
INTUBATE
INTUBATION
INTUBATOR
INTUBE
INTUE
INTUENT
INTUICITY
INTUIT
INTUITABLE
INTUITION
INTUITIONAL
INTUITIONISM
INTUITIONIST
INTUITIVE
INTUITIVELY
INTUITIVISM
INTUITIVIST
INTUMESCE
INTUMESCED
INTUMESCENCE
INTUMESCENT
INTUMESCING
INTURBIDATE
INTURN
INTURNED
INTURNING
INTUSE
INTUSSUSCEPT
INTWINE
INTWIST
INUKSHUK
INULA
INULACEOUS
INULASE
INULIN
INULOID
INUMBRATE
INUNCT
INUNCTION
INUNCTUM
INUND
INUNDABLE
INUNDANT
INUNDATE
INUNDATED
INUNDATING
INUNDATION
INUNDATOR
INUNDATORY
INURBANE
INURBANITY
INURE
INURED
INUREDNESS
INURING
INURN
INURNED
INURNING
INUSITATE
INUSITATION
INUSTION
INUTILE
INUTILELY
INUTILITIES
INUTILITY
INUTTERABLE
INVACCINATE
INVADE
INVADED
INVADER
INVADERS
INVADING
INVAGINABLE
INVAGINATE
INVAGINATED
INVAGINATING
INVAGINATION
INVALESCENCE
INVALID
INVALIDATE
INVALIDATED
INVALIDATING
INVALIDATOR
INVALIDED
INVALIDING
INVALIDISM
INVALIDITY
INVALUABLE
INVALUABLY
INVALUED
INVARIABLE
INVARIABLENESS
INVARIABLY
INVARIANCE
INVARIANCY
INVARIANT
INVARIANTIVE
INVARIANTLY
INVARIED
INVASION
INVASIVE
INVECT
INVECTED
INVECTION
INVECTIVE
INVECTIVELY
INVEIGH
INVEIGHED
INVEIGHER
INVEIGHING
INVEIGLE
INVEIGLED
INVEIGLER
INVEIGLING
INVEIL
INVENIENT
INVENIT
INVENT
INVENTARY
INVENTED
INVENTER
INVENTIBLE
INVENTING
INVENTION
INVENTIONAL
INVENTIVE
INVENTIVELY
INVENTIVENESS
INVENTOR
INVENTORIAL
INVENTORIED
INVENTORIES
INVENTORY
INVENTORYING
INVERACITY
INVERITY
INVERMINATE
INVERSE
INVERSED
INVERSEDLY
INVERSELY
INVERSION
INVERSIVE
INVERT
INVERTASE
INVERTEBRAL
INVERTEBRATE
INVERTED
INVERTEDLY
INVERTEND
INVERTER
INVERTIBLE
INVERTILE
INVERTIN

INVERTING
INVERTOR
INVEST
INVESTED
INVESTIENT
INVESTIGABLE
INVESTIGATE
INVESTIGATED
INVESTIGATING
INVESTIGATION
INVESTIGATOR
INVESTING
INVESTITIVE
INVESTITOR
INVESTITURE
INVESTMENT
INVESTOR
INVETERACY
INVETERATE
INVETERATELY
INVIABLE
INVIABLY
INVICT
INVICTED
INVICTIVE
INVIDIOUS
INVIDIOUSLY
INVIGILATE
INVIGILATION
INVIGILATOR
INVIGORANT
INVIGORATE
INVIGORATED
INVIGORATING
INVIGORATION
INVIGORATIVE
INVIGORATOR
INVINATE
INVINATION
INVINCIBLE
INVINCIBLY
INVIOLABILITY
INVIOLABLE
INVIOLABLY
INVIOLACY
INVIOLATE
INVIOLATELY
INVIOUS
INVIOUSNESS
INVIRTUATE
INVISCATE
INVISED
INVISIBILITY
INVISIBLE
INVISIBLY
INVITANT
INVITATION
INVITATIONAL
INVITATORY
INVITE
INVITED
INVITEE
INVITER
INVITING
INVITINGLY
INVITINGNESS
INVIVID
INVOCABLE
INVOCANT
INVOCATE
INVOCATION
INVOCATIVE
INVOCATOR
INVOCATORY
INVOICE
INVOICED
INVOICING
INVOKE
INVOKED
INVOKER
INVOKING
INVOLUCEL
INVOLUCRA
INVOLUCRAL
INVOLUCRATE
INVOLUCRE
INVOLUCRED
INVOLUCRUM
INVOLUNTARY
INVOLUTE
INVOLUTED
INVOLUTEDLY
INVOLUTION
INVOLUTIONAL
INVOLUTORIAL
INVOLUTORY
INVOLVE
INVOLVED
INVOLVEMENT
INVOLVENT
INVOLVER
INVOLVING
INVULNERABLE
INVULNERABLY
INVULTUATION
INWALE
INWALL
INWANDERING
INWARD
INWARDLY
INWARDNESS
INWARDS
INWEAVE
INWEDGED
INWEED
INWEIGHT
INWICK
INWIND
INWINDING
INWIT
INWITH
INWORK
INWORKS
INWORN
INWOUND
INWOVEN
INWRAP
INWRAPPED
INWRAPPING
INWRAPT
INWREATHE
INWRIT
INWRITTEN
INWROUGHT
INYALA
INYOITE
INYOKE
IOA
IOD
IODATE
IODATED
IODATING
IODATION
IODIC
IODID
IODIDE
IODIN
IODINATE
IODINATION
IODINE
IODINOPHIL
IODINOPHILE
IODINOPHILIC
IODISM
IODIZATION
IODIZE
IODIZED
IODIZER
IODIZING
IODO
IODOBEHENATE
IODOBENZENE
IODOBROMITE
IODOCASEIN
IODOCHLORID
IODOCHLORIDE
IODOCRESOL
IODODERMA
IODOETHANE
IODOFORM
IODOGALLICIN
IODOHYDRIN
IODOL
IODOMETHANE
IODOMETRIC
IODOMETRY
IODONIUM
IODOSO
IODOSPONGIN
IODOTHERAPY
IODOTHYRIN
IODOUS
IODOXY
IODYRITE
IOLITE
ION
IONIC
IONICAL
IONIUM
IONIZABLE
IONIZATION
IONIZE
IONIZER
IONOGEN
IONOGENIC
IONONE
IONOPAUSE
IONOSPHERE
IOTA
IOTACISM
IOTACISMUS
IOTACIST
IOTAS
IOTIZATION
IOTIZE
IOTIZED
IOTIZING
IPECAC
IPECACUANHA
IPECACUANHIC
IPETE
IPI
IPID
IPIL
IPILIPIL
IPITI
IPO
IPOMEA
IPOMOEIN
IPSE
IPSEAND
IPSEITY
IR
IRACUND
IRACUNDITY
IRACUNDULOUS
IRADE
IRASCENT
IRASCIBILITY
IRASCIBLE
IRASCIBLY
IRATE
IRATELY
IRBIS
IRCHIN
IRE
IREFUL
IREFULLY
IREFULNESS
IRENARCH
IRENIC
IRENICA
IRENICAL
IRENICALLY
IRENICISM
IRENICIST
IRENICON
IRENICS
IREOS
IRIAN
IRID
IRIDACEOUS
IRIDAL
IRIDATE
IRIDECTOMIES
IRIDECTOMY
IRIDEOUS
IRIDES
IRIDESCE
IRIDESCENCE
IRIDESCENCY
IRIDESCENT
IRIDESCENTLY
IRIDIATE
IRIDIC
IRIDICAL
IRIDIN
IRIDINE
IRIDIOUS
IRIDITE
IRIDIUM
IRIDIZATION
IRIDIZE
IRIDIZED
IRIDIZING
IRIDOCYTE
IRIDODESIS
IRIDODONESIS
IRIDOPHORE
IRIDOPLEGIA
IRIDOSMINE
IRIDOTASIS
IRIDOTOMIES
IRIDOTOMY
IRIRI
IRIS
IRISATED
IRISATION
IRISCOPE
IRISED
IRISES
IRISIN
IRISING
IRISROOT
IRITIC
IRITIS
IRK
IRKED
IRKING
IRKSOME
IRKSOMELY
IRKSOMENESS
IRNE
IROK
IROKO
IRON
IRONBACK
IRONBARK
IRONBOUND
IRONBUSH
IRONCLAD
IRONE
IRONED
IRONER
IRONFISTED
IRONFLOWER
IRONHANDED
IRONHARD
IRONHEAD
IRONHEADED
IRONHEARTED
IRONIC
IRONICAL
IRONICALLY
IRONICALNESS
IRONICE
IRONIES
IRONING
IRONIOUSLY
IRONISH
IRONISM
IRONIST
IRONIZE
IRONLESS
IRONLIKE
IRONLY
IRONMAN
IRONMASTER
IRONMEN
IRONMONGER
IRONMONGERY
IRONNESS
IRONS
IRONSHOD
IRONSHOT
IRONSIDE
IRONSIDED
IRONSIDES
IRONSMITH
IRONSTONE
IRONWARE
IRONWEED
IRONWOOD
IRONWORK
IRONWORKED
IRONWORKER
IRONWORKING
IRONWORKS
IRONWORT
IRONY
IROUS
IRPE
IRRADIANCE
IRRADIANCY
IRRADIANT
IRRADIATE
IRRADIATED
IRRADIATING
IRRADIATION
IRRADIATIVE
IRRADIATOR
IRRADICABLE
IRRADICATE
IRRAREFIABLE
IRRATIONABLE
IRRATIONAL
IRRATIONALLY
IRREALITY
IRREALIZABLE
IRREBUTTABLE
IRRECEPTIVE
IRRECIPROCAL
IRRECLAIMED
IRRECONCILE
IRRECORDABLE

IRRECUSABLE
IRREDEEMABLE
IRREDEEMABLY
IRREDENTA
IRREDENTIAL
IRREDRESSIBLE
IRREDUCIBLE
IRREDUCIBLY
IRREDUCTIBLE
IRREDUCTION
IRREFERABLE
IRREFLECTION
IRREFLECTIVE
IRREFLEXIVE
IRREFORMABLE
IRREFRAGABLE
IRREFRANGIBLE
IRREFUSABLE
IRREFUTABLE
IRREGARDLESS
IRREGENERACY
IRREGENERATE
IRREGULAR
IRREGULARIST
IRREGULARITIES
IRREGULARITY
IRREGULARIZE
IRREGULARLY
IRREGULATE
IRREGULATED
IRREGULOUS
IRRELATE
IRRELATED
IRRELATION
IRRELATIVE
IRRELATIVELY
IRRELEVANCE
IRRELEVANCIES
IRRELEVANCY
IRRELEVANT
IRRELEVANTLY
IRRELIEVABLE
IRRELIGION
IRRELIGIOUS
IRRELUCTANT
IRREMEABLE
IRREMEABLY
IRREMEDIABLE
IRREMEDIABLY
IRREMEDILESS
IRREMISSIBLE
IRREMISSIBLY
IRREMISSIVE
IRREMOVABLE
IRREMOVABLY
IRRENDERABLE
IRRENEWABLE
IRREPAIR
IRREPAIRABLE
IRREPARABLE
IRREPARABLY
IRREPASSABLE
IRREPEALABLE
IRREPEALABLY
IRREPENTANCE
IRREPENTANT
IRREPORTABLE
IRREPRESSIVE
IRREPROACHABLE
IRREPROVABLE
IRREPROVABLY
IRREPTITIOUS
IRRESILIENT
IRRESISTANCE
IRRESISTIBLE
IRRESISTIBLY
IRRESOLUBLE
IRRESOLUTE
IRRESOLUTELY
IRRESOLUTION
IRRESOLVABLE
IRRESOLVED
IRRESOLVEDLY
IRRESONANCE
IRRESONANT
IRRESPECTABLE
IRRESPECTFUL
IRRESPECTIVE
IRRESPIRABLE
IRRESPONSIBLE
IRRESPONSIVE
IRRESTRICTIVE
IRRESULTIVE
IRRETENTION
IRRETENTIVE
IRRETICENCE
IRRETICENT
IRRETRACEABLE
IRRETRACTABLE
IRRETRACTILE
IRRETRIEVABLE
IRRETURNABLE
IRREVEALABLE
IRREVEALABLY
IRREVERENCE
IRREVEREND
IRREVERENDLY
IRREVERENT
IRREVERENTLY
IRREVERSIBLE
IRREVERSIBLY
IRREVERTIBLE
IRREVISABLE
IRREVOCABLE
IRREVOCABLY
IRREVOLUBLE
IRRIDE
IRRIGABLE
IRRIGABLY
IRRIGANT
IRRIGATE
IRRIGATED
IRRIGATING
IRRIGATION
IRRIGATIONAL
IRRIGATIVE
IRRIGATOR
IRRIGATORY
IRRIGUOUS
IRRISION
IRRISOR
IRRISORY
IRRITABILITIES
IRRITABILITY
IRRITABLE
IRRITABLY
IRRITAMENT
IRRITANCIES
IRRITANCY
IRRITANT
IRRITATE
IRRITATED
IRRITATING
IRRITATINGLY
IRRITATION
IRRITATIVE
IRRITATOR
IRRITATORY
IRRITE
IRRITOMOTILE
IRROGATE
IRRORATE
IRRORATION
IRROTATIONAL
IRRUBRICAL
IRRUGATE
IRRUPT
IRRUPTED
IRRUPTIBLE
IRRUPTING
IRRUPTION
IRRUPTIVE
IRRUPTIVELY
IRUL
IRY
IS
ISABELINA
ISABELITA
ISABELITE
ISABNORMAL
ISACOUSTIC
ISADELPHOUS
ISAGOGE
ISAGOGIC
ISAGOGICAL
ISAGOGICALLY
ISAGOGICS
ISAGON
ISALLOBAR
ISALLOTHERM
ISAMIN
ISAMINE
ISANDROUS
ISANEMONE
ISANOMAL
ISANOMALOUS
ISANTHOUS
ISAPOSTOLIC
ISARIOID
ISATATE
ISATIC
ISATID
ISATIDE
ISATIN
ISATINE
ISATOGEN
ISATOGENIC
ISBA
ISCHAR
ISCHEMIA
ISCHIA
ISCHIAC
ISCHIADIC
ISCHIALGIA
ISCHIALGIC
ISCHIATIC
ISCHIDROSIS
ISCHIOCERITE
ISCHIOPODITE
ISCHIOPUBIS
ISCHIUM
ISCHOCHOLIA
ISCHURETIC
ISCHURIA
ISCHURY
ISE
ISEL
ISENERGIC
ISENTROPIC
ISEPIPTESIAL
ISEPIPTESIS
ISERINE
ISERITE
ISETHIONATE
ISH
ISHPINGO
ISIDIA
ISIDIOID
ISIDIOSE
ISIDIUM
ISING
ISINGLASS
ISLAND
ISLANDED
ISLANDER
ISLANDIC
ISLANDING
ISLANDMAN
ISLANDMEN
ISLANDRY
ISLANDS
ISLANDY
ISLAY
ISLE
ISLED
ISLEMAN
ISLESMEN
ISLET
ISLETED
ISLING
ISLOT
ISM
ISMAL
ISMATIC
ISMATICAL
ISMY
ISNAD
ISO
ISOAMID
ISOAMIDE
ISOAMYL
ISOBAR
ISOBARE
ISOBARIC
ISOBARISM
ISOBASE
ISOBATH
ISOBATHIC
ISOBORNEOL
ISOBRONT
ISOBRONTON
ISOBUTYRIC
ISOCARPIC
ISOCARPOUS
ISOCELLULAR
ISOCEPHALIC
ISOCEPHALISM
ISOCEPHALY
ISOCERCAL
ISOCERCY
ISOCHASM
ISOCHASMIC
ISOCHEIM
ISOCHEIMAL
ISOCHEIMENAL
ISOCHEIMIC
ISOCHELA
ISOCHLOR
ISOCHOR
ISOCHORE
ISOCHORIC
ISOCHROMATIC
ISOCHRONAL
ISOCHRONALLY
ISOCHRONE
ISOCHRONIC
ISOCHRONISM
ISOCHRONIZE
ISOCHRONIZED
ISOCHRONIZING
ISOCHRONON
ISOCHRONOUS
ISOCHROOUS
ISOCLASITE
ISOCLINAL
ISOCLINE
ISOCLINIC
ISOCOLA
ISOCOLIC
ISOCOLON
ISOCORIA
ISOCRACY
ISOCRAT
ISOCRATIC
ISOCRYMAL
ISOCRYME
ISOCRYMIC
ISOCYANATE
ISOCYANIC
ISOCYANID
ISOCYANIDE
ISOCYANIN
ISOCYANINE
ISOCYANO
ISOCYTIC
ISODACTYLOUS
ISODIABATIC
ISODIAMETRIC
ISODOMON
ISODOMOUS
ISODOMUM
ISODONT
ISODONTOUS
ISODRIN
ISODROME
ISODYNAMIA
ISODYNAMIC
ISOELECTRIC
ISOENERGETIC
ISOEUGENOL
ISOGAM
ISOGAMETE
ISOGAMETIC
ISOGAMETISM
ISOGAMIC
ISOGAMOUS
ISOGAMY
ISOGEN
ISOGENESIS
ISOGENETIC
ISOGENIC
ISOGENOTYPE
ISOGENOUS
ISOGENY
ISOGEOTHERM
ISOGLOSS
ISOGLOSSAL
ISOGLOSSES
ISOGNATHISM
ISOGNATHOUS
ISOGON
ISOGONAL
ISOGONALITY
ISOGONALLY
ISOGONIC
ISOGONIOSTAT
ISOGONISM
ISOGRAFT
ISOGRAM
ISOGRAPH
ISOGRAPHIC
ISOGRAPHY
ISOGRIV
ISOGYNOUS
ISOGYRE
ISOHALSINE
ISOHEL
ISOHYDRIC
ISOHYET
ISOHYETAL
ISOKERAUNIC
ISOKONTAN
ISOLABILITY
ISOLABLE
ISOLATE

ISOLATED
ISOLATING
ISOLATION
ISOLATIONISM
ISOLATIONIST
ISOLATIVE
ISOLATOR
ISOLEAD
ISOLETTE
ISOLEUCINE
ISOLICHENIN
ISOLINE
ISOLOG
ISOLOGOUS
ISOLOGUE
ISOLOGY
ISOLYSIN
ISOLYSIS
ISOMAGNETIC
ISOMALTOSE
ISOMASTIGATE
ISOMER
ISOMERE
ISOMERIC
ISOMERICAL
ISOMERICALLY
ISOMERIDE
ISOMERISM
ISOMERIZE
ISOMEROUS
ISOMERY
ISOMETRIC
ISOMETRICAL
ISOMETROGRAPH
ISOMETROPIA
ISOMETRY
ISOMORPH
ISOMORPHIC
ISOMORPHISM
ISOMORPHOUS
ISOMYARIAN
ISONEPH
ISONEPHELIC
ISONIAZID
ISONITRIL
ISONITRILE
ISONITRO
ISONITROSO
ISONOMIC
ISONOMOUS
ISONOMY
ISONUCLEAR
ISONYM
ISONYMIC
ISONYMY
ISOOCTANE
ISOPACHOUS
ISOPAG
ISOPARAFFIN
ISOPERIMETER
ISOPERIMETRY
ISOPETALOUS
ISOPHANAL
ISOPHANE
ISOPHASAL
ISOPHENE
ISOPHORIA
ISOPHOTE
ISOPHTHALIC
ISOPHTHALYL
ISOPHYLLOUS
ISOPHYLLY
ISOPIESTIC
ISOPLERE
ISOPLETH
ISOPOD
ISOPODAN
ISOPODIFORM
ISOPODOUS
ISOPOGONOUS
ISOPOLITE
ISOPOLITICAL
ISOPOLITY
ISOPOLY
ISOPRENE
ISOPROPENYL
ISOPROPYL
ISOPSEPHIC
ISOPSEPHISM
ISOPTEROUS
ISOPTIC
ISOPYCNIC
ISOPYRE
ISOQUINOLINE
ISORHYTHM
ISORITHM
ISORRHYTHMIC
ISORROPIC
ISOSCELE
ISOSCELES
ISOSCOPE
ISOSEISMAL
ISOSEISMIC
ISOSMOTIC
ISOSPORE
ISOSPORIC
ISOSPOROUS
ISOSPORY
ISOSTASIST
ISOSTASY
ISOSTATIC
ISOSTATICAL
ISOSTEMONY
ISOSTER
ISOSTERE
ISOSTERIC
ISOSTERISM
ISOTAC
ISOTACH
ISOTE
ISOTELES
ISOTELY
ISOTHERAL
ISOTHERE
ISOTHERM
ISOTHERMAL
ISOTHERMIC
ISOTHERMICAL
ISOTHERMOUS
ISOTHIOCYANO
ISOTOME
ISOTOMOUS
ISOTONE
ISOTONIA
ISOTONIC
ISOTONICITY
ISOTOPE
ISOTOPIC
ISOTOPISM
ISOTOPY
ISOTRON
ISOTROPE
ISOTROPIC
ISOTROPISM
ISOTROPOUS
ISOTROPY
ISOTYPE
ISOTYPIC
ISOTYPICAL
ISOVALERATE
ISOXAZOLE
ISOZOOID
ISPAGHUL
ISPRAYNIK
ISSITE
ISSUABLE
ISSUANCE
ISSUANT
ISSUE
ISSUED
ISSUER
ISSUING
IST
ISTHMI
ISTHMIAN
ISTHMIATE
ISTHMIC
ISTHMOID
ISTHMUS
ISTHMUSES
ISTLE
ISURETINE
ISUROID
IT
ITABIRITE
ITAC
ITACISM
ITACIST
ITACISTIC
ITACOLUMITE
ITACONIC
ITALIC
ITALICIZE
ITALICIZED
ITALICIZING
ITALICS
ITALITE
ITAUBA
ITCH
ITCHED
ITCHEOGLAN
ITCHIER
ITCHIEST
ITCHING
ITCHINGLY
ITCHLESS
ITCHREED
ITCHWEED
ITCHWOOD
ITCHY
ITCZE
ITEM
ITEMING
ITEMIZATION
ITEMIZE
ITEMIZED
ITEMIZER
ITEMIZING
ITEMS
ITEMY
ITER
ITERABLE
ITERANCE
ITERANCY
ITERANT
ITERATE
ITERATED
ITERATELY
ITERATING
ITERATION
ITERATIVE
ITERATIVELY
ITERS
ITERUM
ITHAGINE
ITHAND
ITHER
ITHOMIID
ITHYPHALLIC
ITINERACY
ITINERANCY
ITINERANT
ITINERANTLY
ITINERARIAN
ITINERARIES
ITINERARY
ITINERATE
ITINERATED
ITINERATING
ITINERATION
ITMO
ITOUBOU
ITR
ITS
ITSELF
ITZEBU
IUS
IVA
IVIED
IVIES
IVIN
IVORIED
IVORIES
IVORINE
IVORINESS
IVORIST
IVORY
IVORYTYPE
IVRAY
IVRESSE
IVY
IVYBELLS
IVYBERRY
IVYFLOWER
IVYING
IVYWOOD
IVYWORT
IWA
IWAIWA
IWAN
IWEARTH
IWIS
IWORTH
IWURCHE
IWURTHEN
IXODIAN
IXODIC
IXODID
IXTLE
IYA
IYO
IZAFAT
IZAR
IZARD
IZBA
IZLE
IZOTE
IZTLE
IZTLI
IZVOZCHIK
IZZARD
IZZAT

JA
JAB
JABBED
JABBER
JABBERED
JABBERER
JABBERING
JABBERINGLY
JABBERMENT
JABBING
JABBLE
JABERS
JABIA
JABIRU
JABORANDI
JABORIN
JABORINE
JABOT
JABOTICABA
JABOTS
JABUL
JABULES
JACA
JACAL
JACALES
JACAMAR
JACAMEROPINE
JACAMIN
JACANA
JACARANDA
JACARE
JACATE
JACATOO
JACCHUS
JACCONET
JACCONOT
JACENT
JACINTH
JACINTHE
JACITARA
JACK
JACKAL
JACKALS
JACKANAPES
JACKAROO
JACKASH
JACKASS
JACKASSERY
JACKBIRD
JACKBOOT
JACKBOX
JACKBOY
JACKDAW
JACKED
JACKEEN
JACKER
JACKEROO
JACKEROOS
JACKET
JACKETED
JACKETING
JACKETY
JACKFISH
JACKFISHES
JACKFRUIT
JACKHAMMER
JACKHEAD
JACKING
JACKKNIFE
JACKKNIVES
JACKLEG
JACKLIGHT
JACKMAN
JACKMEN
JACKO
JACKPLANE
JACKPOT
JACKPOTS
JACKPUDDING
JACKROD
JACKROLL
JACKS
JACKSAW
JACKSCREW
JACKSHAFT
JACKSHAY
JACKSHEA
JACKSLAVE
JACKSMELT
JACKSMITH
JACKSNIPE
JACKSNIPES
JACKSTAY
JACKSTOCK
JACKSTONE
JACKSTRAW
JACKTAN
JACKWEED
JACKWOOD
JACKY
JACOBAEA
JACOBIN
JACOBSITE
JACOBUS
JACOBY
JACOLATT
JACONET
JACOUNCE
JACQUARD
JACQUERIE
JACTANCE
JACTANCY
JACTANT
JACTATION
JACTITATE
JACTITATED
JACTITATING
JACTITATION
JACTURE
JACU
JACUARU
JACULATE
JACULATED
JACULATING
JACULATION
JACULATIVE
JACULATOR
JACULATORIAL
JACULATORY
JACULIFEROUS
JACUTINGA
JAD
JADDED
JADDER
JADDING
JADE
JADED
JADEDLY
JADEDNESS
JADEITE
JADERY
JADING
JADISH
JADISHLY
JADISHNESS
JADOO
JADU
JADY
JAEGER
JAELA
JAG
JAGAT
JAGEER
JAGER
JAGG
JAGGAR
JAGGARY
JAGGED
JAGGEDLY
JAGGEDNESS
JAGGER
JAGGERY
JAGGHERY
JAGGIER
JAGGIEST
JAGGING
JAGGY
JAGHEER
JAGHEERDAR
JAGHIR
JAGHIRDAR
JAGHIRE
JAGHIREDAR
JAGIR
JAGIRDAR
JAGLA
JAGONG
JAGRA
JAGRATA
JAGS
JAGUA
JAGUAR
JAGUARETE
JAGUARONDI
JAGUARS
JAGUARUNDI
JAGUEY
JAIL
JAILAGE
JAILBIRD
JAILED
JAILER
JAILERESS
JAILERING
JAILHOUSE
JAILKEEPER
JAILMATE
JAILOR
JAILORING
JAILYARD
JAK
JAKE
JAKES
JAKEY
JAKFRUIT
JAKO
JAKOS
JALAP
JALAPA
JALAPENO
JALAPIC
JALAPIN
JALEO
JALET
JALKAR
JALLOPED
JALOP
JALOPIES
JALOPPY
JALOPY
JALOUSE
JALOUSED
JALOUSIE
JALOUSIED
JALOUSING
JALPAITE
JAM
JAMA
JAMAH
JAMAN
JAMB
JAMBA
JAMBALAYA
JAMBE
JAMBEAU
JAMBEAUX
JAMBEE
JAMBER
JAMBO
JAMBOLAN
JAMBOLANA
JAMBON
JAMBONE
JAMBOOL
JAMBOREE
JAMBOSA
JAMBSTONE
JAMBUL
JAMDANEE
JAMDANI
JAMESONITE
JAMI
JAMMED
JAMMER
JAMMING
JAMMY
JAMNUT
JAMOKE
JAMON
JAMPAN
JAMPANEE
JAMPANI
JAMROSADE
JAMTLAND
JAMWOOD
JAN
JANAPA
JANAPAN
JANAPUM
JANDERS
JANE
JANG
JANGADA
JANGAR
JANGKAR
JANGLE
JANGLED
JANGLER
JANGLING
JANGLY
JANICEPS
JANISARY
JANISSARY
JANITOR
JANITORIAL
JANITRESS
JANITRIX
JANIZARIES
JANIZARY
JANK
JANKER
JANKERS
JANN
JANNER
JANNOCK
JANTEE
JANTU
JANTY
JANUA
JAOB
JAOUR
JAP
JAPACONIN
JAPACONINE
JAPACONITIN
JAPACONITINE
JAPAN
JAPANNED
JAPANNER
JAPANNERY
JAPANNING
JAPE
JAPED
JAPER
JAPERIES
JAPERY
JAPING
JAPISH
JAPISHLY
JAPISHNESS
JAPONICA
JAPYGID
JAPYGOID
JAQUETTE
JAQUIMA
JAR
JARA
JARABE
JARAGUA
JARANA
JARARACA
JARARACUSSU
JARBIRD
JARBLE
JARBOT
JARDE
JARDINIERE
JAREED
JARFLY
JARFUL
JARG
JARGON
JARGONAL
JARGONED
JARGONEL
JARGONELLE
JARGONER
JARGONIC
JARGONING
JARGONISH
JARGONIST
JARGONIUM
JARGONIZE
JARGONIZED
JARGONIZING
JARGONNELLE
JARGOON
JARHEAD
JARINA
JARK
JARKMAN
JARL
JARLESS
JARLITE
JARNUT
JAROOL
JAROSITE
JAROVIZATION
JAROVIZE
JAROVIZED
JAROVIZING
JARRA
JARRAH
JARRED
JARRET

JARRING
JARRY
JARVEY
JARVEYS
JASEY
JASEYED
JASEYS
JASK
JASM
JASMIN
JASMINE
JASMINED
JASMINEWOOD
JASMONE
JASPACHATE
JASPAGATE
JASPE
JASPER
JASPERATED
JASPERED
JASPERITE
JASPERIZE
JASPERIZED
JASPERIZING
JASPEROID
JASPERY
JASPIDEAN
JASPIDEOUS
JASPILITE
JASPILYTE
JASPIS
JASPOID
JASPONYX
JASPOPAL
JASS
JASSID
JATACO
JATAMANSI
JATEORHIZIN
JATEORHIZINE
JATHA
JATI
JATO
JATOBA
JATROPHIC
JAUD
JAUDIE
JAUG
JAUK
JAUN
JAUNCE
JAUNDER
JAUNDERS
JAUNDICE
JAUNDICED
JAUNDICEROOT
JAUNDICING
JAUNE
JAUNER
JAUNT
JAUNTED
JAUNTIE
JAUNTIER
JAUNTIEST
JAUNTILY
JAUNTINESS
JAUNTING
JAUNTY
JAUP
JAUPS
JAVA
JAVALI
JAVEL
JAVELIN
JAVELINA
JAVELINEER
JAVELOT
JAVER
JAVVER
JAW
JAWAB
JAWBATION
JAWBONE
JAWBREAKER
JAWBREAKING
JAWBREAKINGLY
JAWCRUSHER
JAWED
JAWFALL
JAWFALLEN
JAWFEET
JAWFISH
JAWFISHES
JAWFOOT
JAWFOOTED
JAWHOLE
JAWING
JAWS
JAWSMITH
JAWY
JAY
JAYGEE
JAYHAWK
JAYHAWKER
JAYPIE
JAYPIET
JAYVEE
JAYWALK
JAYWALKER
JAYWALKING
JAZEL
JAZERAN
JAZERANT
JAZZ
JAZZBOW
JAZZER
JAZZIER
JAZZIEST
JAZZILY
JAZZINESS
JAZZY
JEALOUS
JEALOUSE
JEALOUSIES
JEALOUSLY
JEALOUSNESS
JEALOUSY
JEAN
JEANS
JEBAT
JEBEL
JECORAL
JECORIN
JECORIZE
JED
JEDCOCK
JEDDOCK
JEDGE
JEE
JEEL
JEEP
JEEPERS
JEEPNEY
JEER
JEERED
JEERER
JEERING
JEERINGLY
JEERS
JEERY
JEETEE
JEEZ
JEFE
JEFF
JEFFERISITE
JEFFERSONITE
JEHAD
JEHUP
JEJUNA
JEJUNAL
JEJUNATOR
JEJUNE
JEJUNELY
JEJUNENESS
JEJUNITIS
JEJUNITY
JEJUNOSTOMY
JEJUNOTOMY
JEJUNUM
JELAB
JELERANG
JELICK
JELL
JELLAB
JELLICA
JELLICO
JELLIED
JELLIEDNESS
JELLIES
JELLIFICATION
JELLIFIED
JELLIFY
JELLIFYING
JELLILY
JELLO
JELLOID
JELLY
JELLYBEAN
JELLYFISH
JELLYFISHES
JELLYING
JELLYLEAF
JELLYLIKE
JELOTONG
JELUTONG
JEMADAR
JEMBLE
JEMIDAR
JEMMIES
JEMMILY
JEMMINESS
JEMMY
JEN
JENKIN
JENNA
JENNERIZE
JENNET
JENNETING
JENNIER
JENNIES
JENNY
JENOAR
JENTACULAR
JEOFAIL
JEOPARD
JEOPARDED
JEOPARDER
JEOPARDIED
JEOPARDING
JEOPARDIOUS
JEOPARDIZE
JEOPARDIZED
JEOPARDIZING
JEOPARDOUS
JEOPARDOUSLY
JEOPARDY
JEOPARDYING
JEQUERITY
JEQUIRITIES
JEQUIRITY
JERBOA
JEREED
JEREMIAD
JEREZ
JERIB
JERICAN
JERK
JERKED
JERKER
JERKIER
JERKIEST
JERKILY
JERKIN
JERKINED
JERKINESS
JERKING
JERKISH
JERKS
JERKSOME
JERKWATER
JERKY
JERL
JERM
JERMONAL
JERMOONAL
JERNIE
JEROBOAM
JERQUE
JERQUED
JERQUER
JERQUING
JERRICAN
JERRID
JERRIES
JERRY
JERRYBUILD
JERRYBUILDING
JERRYBUILT
JERRYISM
JERSEY
JERSEYED
JERSEYS
JERT
JERVIA
JERVIN
JERVINA
JERVINE
JES
JESS
JESSAKEED
JESSAMIES
JESSAMINE
JESSAMY
JESSANT
JESSED
JESSING
JESSUR
JEST
JESTBOOK
JESTED
JESTEE
JESTER
JESTING
JESTINGLY
JESTINGSTOCK
JESTWORD
JET
JETBEAD
JETE
JETEE
JETLINER
JETON
JETPORT
JETSAM
JETTAGE
JETTATORE
JETTATURA
JETTEAU
JETTED
JETTER
JETTIED
JETTIES
JETTINESS
JETTING
JETTISON
JETTO
JETTON
JETTRU
JETTY
JETTYHEAD
JETWARE
JEU
JEUNESSE
JEUX
JEW
JEWBIRD
JEWBUSH
JEWEL
JEWELED
JEWELER
JEWELHOUSE
JEWELING
JEWELLED
JEWELLER
JEWELLERY
JEWELLING
JEWELLY
JEWELRY
JEWELS
JEWELSMITH
JEWELWEED
JEWELY
JEWFISH
JEWFISHES
JEWING
JEZAIL
JEZEKITE
JEZIA
JEZIAH
JHANA
JHARAL
JHEEL
JHIL
JHOOL
JHOOM
JHOW
JHUM
JIB
JIBBA
JIBBAH
JIBBED
JIBBEH
JIBBER
JIBBING
JIBBINGS
JIBBOOM
JIBE
JIBED
JIBER
JIBHEAD
JIBI
JIBING
JIBMAN
JIBMEN
JIBOA
JIBOYA
JIBSTAY
JICAMA
JICARA
JIFF
JIFFIES
JIFFLE
JIFFY
JIG
JIGAMAREE

JIGGED
JIGGER
JIGGERED
JIGGERER
JIGGERMAN
JIGGERS
JIGGET
JIGGETY
JIGGINESS
JIGGING
JIGGISH
JIGGIT
JIGGLE
JIGGLED
JIGGLING
JIGGLY
JIGGUMBOB
JIGGY
JIGMAN
JIGMEN
JIGOTE
JIGSAW
JIGUA
JIHAD
JIKUNGU
JILL
JILLET
JILLFLIRT
JILLING
JILLION
JILT
JILTED
JILTEE
JILTER
JILTING
JIMBANG
JIMBERJAW
JIMBERJAWED
JIMCRACK
JIMJAM
JIMJAMS
JIMMER
JIMMIED
JIMMIES
JIMMY
JIMMYING
JIMMYWEED
JIMP
JIMPLY
JIMPNESS
JIMPRICUTE
JIMPY
JIMSEDGE
JIMSON
JINA
JINETE
JING
JINGAL
JINGALL
JINGBANG
JINGLE
JINGLEBOB
JINGLED
JINGLEJANGLE
JINGLER
JINGLET
JINGLING
JINGLINGLY
JINGLY
JINGO
JINGOED
JINGOES
JINGOING
JINGOISH
JINGOISM
JINGOIST
JINGOISTIC
JINJA
JINJILI
JINK
JINKED
JINKER
JINKET
JINKING
JINKLE
JINKS
JINN
JINNEE
JINNESTAN
JINNI
JINNIES
JINNIWINK
JINNIYEH
JINNY
JINNYWINK
JINRICKSHA
JINRIKI
JINRIKIMAN
JINRIKIMEN
JINRIKISHA
JINSHA
JINSHANG
JINSING
JINX
JIPIJAPA
JIPPER
JIPPO
JIQUE
JIQUI
JIRBLE
JIRD
JIRGA
JIRGAH
JIRKINET
JIRT
JITI
JITNEUR
JITNEUSE
JITNEY
JITNEYMAN
JITNEYS
JITTER
JITTERBUG
JITTERS
JITTERY
JIUJITSU
JIUJUTSU
JIVA
JIVATMA
JIVE
JIXIE
JIZ
JIZYA
JIZYAH
JIZZEN
JNANA
JNANAMARGA
JNANASHAKTI
JNANAYOGA
JNANENDRIYA
JNANI
JO
JOANNES
JOAQUINITE
JOB
JOBADE
JOBARBE
JOBATION
JOBBED
JOBBER
JOBBERIES
JOBBERNOWL
JOBBERY
JOBBING
JOBBISH
JOBBLE
JOBE
JOBHOLDER
JOBLESS
JOBLESSNESS
JOBMAN
JOBMASTER
JOBMEN
JOBMISTRESS
JOBMONGER
JOBO
JOBS
JOBSITE
JOBSMITH
JOBSON
JOCANT
JOCATORY
JOCH
JOCK
JOCKER
JOCKEY
JOCKEYED
JOCKEYING
JOCKEYISM
JOCKEYS
JOCKO
JOCKOS
JOCKS
JOCKSTRAP
JOCKTELEG
JOCO
JOCOQUE
JOCOQUI
JOCOSE
JOCOSELY
JOCOSENESS
JOCOSERIOUS
JOCOSITIES
JOCOSITY
JOCOTE
JOCTELEG
JOCU
JOCULAR
JOCULARITY
JOCULARLY
JOCULARNESS
JOCULATOR
JOCULATORY
JOCUM
JOCUMA
JOCUND
JOCUNDITIES
JOCUNDITY
JOCUNDLY
JOCUNDNESS
JOCUNDRY
JOD
JODEL
JODHPURS
JOE
JOEBUSH
JOES
JOEWOOD
JOEY
JOG
JOGGED
JOGGER
JOGGING
JOGGLE
JOGGLED
JOGGLER
JOGGLETY
JOGGLEWORK
JOGGLING
JOGGLY
JOGI
JOGTROTTISM
JOHANNES
JOHANNITE
JOHN
JOHNBOAT
JOHNIN
JOHNNYCAKE
JOHNSTRUPITE
JOIN
JOINANT
JOINDER
JOINED
JOINER
JOINERED
JOINERING
JOINERY
JOINHAND
JOINING
JOININGLY
JOINT
JOINTAGE
JOINTED
JOINTEDLY
JOINTEDNESS
JOINTER
JOINTING
JOINTIST
JOINTLY
JOINTRESS
JOINTS
JOINTURE
JOINTURED
JOINTURESS
JOINTURING
JOINTWEED
JOINTWOOD
JOINTWORM
JOINTY
JOISE
JOIST
JOISTED
JOISTING
JOJOBA
JOKE
JOKED
JOKELET
JOKER
JOKESMITH
JOKESOME
JOKESOMENESS
JOKESTER
JOKEY
JOKIER
JOKIEST
JOKING
JOKINGLY
JOKISH
JOKIST
JOKUL
JOKY
JOLE
JOLI
JOLIE
JOLL
JOLLIED
JOLLIER
JOLLIES
JOLLIEST
JOLLIFICATION
JOLLIFIED
JOLLIFY
JOLLIFYING
JOLLILY
JOLLIMENT
JOLLINESS
JOLLITIES
JOLLITRY
JOLLITY
JOLLOP
JOLLOPED
JOLLY
JOLLYHEAD
JOLLYING
JOLT
JOLTED
JOLTER
JOLTERHEAD
JOLTERHEADED
JOLTHEAD
JOLTHEADED
JOLTINESS
JOLTING
JOLTY
JONDLA
JONG
JONGLERY
JONGLEUR
JONK
JONQUIL
JONQUILLE
JOOKERIE
JOOLA
JOOM
JOPY
JORAM
JORDAN
JORDANITE
JORDANON
JORDEN
JOREE
JORNADA
JOROPO
JORRAM
JORUM
JOSEF
JOSEFITE
JOSEITE
JOSEPH
JOSEPHINITE
JOSEY
JOSH
JOSHER
JOSHI
JOSIE
JOSKIN
JOSS
JOSSA
JOSSER
JOSTLE
JOSTLED
JOSTLEMENT
JOSTLER
JOSTLING
JOSUP
JOT
JOTA
JOTATION
JOTI
JOTISARU
JOTISI
JOTTED
JOTTER
JOTTING
JOTTY
JOUBARB
JOUG
JOUGH
JOUGS
JOUISSANCE
JOUK
JOUKERY
JOULE
JOULEAN
JOULEMETER

JOUNCE
JOUNCED
JOUNCING
JOURNAL
JOURNALED
JOURNALESE
JOURNALING
JOURNALISE
JOURNALISM
JOURNALIST
JOURNALISTIC
JOURNALIZE
JOURNALIZED
JOURNALIZER
JOURNALIZING
JOURNALLED
JOURNALLING
JOURNEY
JOURNEYCAKE
JOURNEYED
JOURNEYER
JOURNEYING
JOURNEYMAN
JOURNEYMEN
JOURNEYS
JOURNEYWOMAN
JOURNEYWOMEN
JOURNEYWORK
JOURS
JOUST
JOUSTER
JOUSTING
JOUSTS
JOUTES
JOVIAL
JOVIALIST
JOVIALISTIC
JOVIALITY
JOVIALIZE
JOVIALIZED
JOVIALIZING
JOVIALLY
JOVIALNESS
JOVIALTY
JOVILABE
JOVY
JOW
JOWAR
JOWARI
JOWEL
JOWER
JOWERY
JOWL
JOWLER
JOWLOP
JOWLY
JOWPY
JOWSER
JOWTER
JOY
JOYANCE
JOYANCY
JOYANT
JOYED
JOYFUL
JOYFULLY
JOYFULNESS
JOYHOP
JOYHOUSE
JOYING
JOYLEAF
JOYLESS
JOYLESSLY
JOYLESSNESS
JOYOUS
JOYOUSLY
JOYOUSNESS
JOYPOPPER
JOYRIDE
JOYSOME
JOYWEED
JUAMAVE
JUB
JUBA
JUBARB
JUBARTAS
JUBARTES
JUBATE
JUBBAH
JUBBE
JUBE
JUBEROUS
JUBHAH
JUBILANCE
JUBILANCY
JUBILANT
JUBILANTLY
JUBILARIAN
JUBILATE
JUBILATED
JUBILATING
JUBILATIO
JUBILATION
JUBILATORY
JUBILE
JUBILEAN
JUBILEE
JUBILIST
JUBILIZATION
JUBILIZE
JUBILUS
JUBO
JUBUS
JUCHART
JUCK
JUCKIES
JUCUNDITY
JUD
JUDAIZER
JUDCOCK
JUDD
JUDDER
JUDDOCK
JUDEX
JUDGE
JUDGED
JUDGEMENT
JUDGER
JUDGING
JUDGMATIC
JUDGMATICAL
JUDGMENT
JUDGMENTS
JUDICABLE
JUDICATE
JUDICATION
JUDICATIVE
JUDICATOR
JUDICATORIAL
JUDICATORIES
JUDICATORY
JUDICATURE
JUDICES
JUDICIABLE
JUDICIAL
JUDICIALITY
JUDICIALIZE
JUDICIALLY
JUDICIARIES
JUDICIARILY
JUDICIARY
JUDICIOUS
JUDICIOUSLY
JUDICIOUSNESS
JUDICIUM
JUDKA
JUDO
JUDOPHOBIA
JUECES
JUEY
JUEZ
JUFFER
JUFTI
JUFTS
JUG
JUGA
JUGAL
JUGALE
JUGATE
JUGATED
JUGATION
JUGER
JUGFUL
JUGGED
JUGGER
JUGGERNAUT
JUGGING
JUGGINS
JUGGLE
JUGGLED
JUGGLEMENT
JUGGLER
JUGGLERIES
JUGGLERY
JUGGLING
JUGGLINGLY
JUGHEAD
JUGLANDIN
JUGLAR
JUGLONE
JUGULA
JUGULAR
JUGULATE
JUGULATED
JUGULATING
JUGULATION
JUGULUM
JUGUM
JUGUMS
JUICE
JUICER
JUICIER
JUICIEST
JUICILY
JUICINESS
JUICY
JUISE
JUJITSU
JUJU
JUJUBE
JUJUISM
JUJUIST
JUJUTSU
JUKE
JUKEBOX
JUKES
JULEP
JULID
JULIDAN
JULIENITE
JULIENNE
JULIETT
JULIO
JULOID
JULOIDIAN
JULOL
JULOLE
JULOLIDIN
JULOLIDINE
JULOLIN
JULOLINE
JUM
JUMART
JUMBA
JUMBIE
JUMBLE
JUMBLED
JUMBLEMENT
JUMBLER
JUMBLING
JUMBLY
JUMBO
JUMBOISM
JUMBOS
JUMBUCK
JUMBY
JUMELLE
JUMENT
JUMENTOUS
JUMFRU
JUMILLITE
JUMMA
JUMP
JUMPED
JUMPER
JUMPERS
JUMPIER
JUMPIEST
JUMPINESS
JUMPING
JUMPOFF
JUMPROCK
JUMPROCKS
JUMPS
JUMPSCRAPE
JUMPSEED
JUMPSOME
JUMPY
JUNCACEOUS
JUNCIFORM
JUNCITE
JUNCO
JUNCOS
JUNCOUS
JUNCTION
JUNCTIONAL
JUNCTIVE
JUNCTLY
JUNCTURE
JUNCUS
JUNDIE
JUNDY
JUNE
JUNECTOMY
JUNEFISH
JUNGLE
JUNGLED
JUNGLESIDE
JUNGLEWOOD
JUNGLI
JUNGLIER
JUNGLIEST
JUNGLY
JUNIATA
JUNIOR
JUNIORATE
JUNIORITY
JUNIPER
JUNK
JUNKBOARD
JUNKDEALER
JUNKER
JUNKERDOM
JUNKERISM
JUNKET
JUNKETED
JUNKETER
JUNKETING
JUNKIE
JUNKING
JUNKMAN
JUNKMEN
JUNKY
JUNKYARD
JUNT
JUNTA
JUNTAS
JUNTO
JUNTOS
JUPATI
JUPE
JUPES
JUPON
JUR
JURA
JURAL
JURALLY
JURAMENT
JURAMENTA
JURAMENTADO
JURAMENTAL
JURAMENTALLY
JURAMENTUM
JURANT
JURARA
JURAT
JURATA
JURATION
JURATIVE
JURATOR
JURATORIAL
JURATORY
JURE
JUREL
JURIDIC
JURIDICAL
JURIDICALLY
JURIDICIAL
JURIES
JURING
JURISCONSULT
JURISDICTION
JURISDICTIVE
JURISPRUDENCE
JURISPRUDENT
JURIST
JURISTIC
JURISTICAL
JURISTICALLY
JURM
JUROR
JURORS
JURR
JURT
JURUPAITE
JURY
JURYMAN
JURYMEN
JURYWOMAN
JUS
JUSI
JUSLIK
JUSSAL
JUSSEL
JUSSHELL
JUSSION
JUSSIVE
JUSSORY
JUST
JUSTAUCORPS
JUSTEN
JUSTER
JUSTICE
JUSTICED
JUSTICEHOOD

JUSTICER
JUSTICESHIP
JUSTICEWEED
JUSTICIABLE
JUSTICIAL
JUSTICIAR
JUSTICIARY
JUSTICIER
JUSTICIES
JUSTICING
JUSTICO
JUSTIFIABLE
JUSTIFIABLY
JUSTIFICATION
JUSTIFICATIVE
JUSTIFICATOR
JUSTIFIED
JUSTIFIER
JUSTIFY
JUSTIFYING
JUSTIFYINGLY
JUSTITIA
JUSTLE
JUSTLER
JUSTLY
JUSTMENT
JUSTMENTS
JUSTNESS
JUSTO
JUT
JUTE
JUTES
JUTIA
JUTKA
JUTTED
JUTTIES
JUTTING
JUTTINGLY
JUTTY
JUVENAL
JUVENATE
JUVENESCENCE
JUVENESCENT
JUVENILE
JUVENILELY
JUVENILENESS
JUVENILIA
JUVENILIFY
JUVENILISM
JUVENILITIES
JUVENILITY
JUVENT
JUVENTUDE
JUVIA
JUVITE
JUWISE
JUXTA
JUXTAMARINE
JUXTAPOSE
JUXTAPOSED
JUXTAPOSING
JUXTAPOSIT
JUXTAPOSITION
JUXTAPYLORIC
JUXTASPINAL
JUZAIL
JYNGINE
JYNX

KA
KAAMA
KAAS
KAB
KABAKA
KABALA
KABAR
KABAYA
KABBALA
KABEL
KABELJOU
KABERU
KABIET
KABOB
KABUKI
KACHIN
KACHINA
KADDER
KADE
KADEIN
KADI
KADIKANE
KADINE
KADISCHI
KADOS
KADSURA
KADY
KAE
KAEMPFEROL
KAFERITA
KAFFIR
KAFFIRS
KAFFIYEH
KAFIR
KAFIRIN
KAFIZ
KAFTAN
KAGO
KAGU
KAGURA
KAHA
KAHAL
KAHALA
KAHAR
KAHAU
KAHAWAI
KAHIKATEA
KAHILI
KAHU
KAHUNA
KAI
KAIAK
KAID
KAIF
KAIK
KAIKA
KAIKARA
KAIKAWAKA
KAIL
KAILS
KAILYARD
KAILYARDER
KAILYARDISM
KAIN
KAINGA
KAINGIN
KAINIT
KAINITE
KAINSI
KAIO
KAIR
KAIRI
KAIRIN
KAIRINE
KAIROLIN
KAIROLINE
KAIROS
KAISER
KAISERDOM
KAISERISM
KAITAKA
KAIVALYA
KAIWHIRIA
KAIWI
KAJAWAH
KAJEPUT
KAJUGARU
KAKA
KAKAPO
KAKAR
KAKARALI
KAKARALLI
KAKARIKI
KAKAWAHIE
KAKEL
KAKEMONO
KAKI
KAKIDROSIS
KAKISTOCRACY
KAKKAK
KAKKE
KAKORTOKITE
KAKU
KAKUR
KAL
KALA
KALAC
KALACH
KALADANA
KALAM
KALAMANSANAI
KALAMKARI
KALAN
KALASIE
KALE
KALEIDOPHON
KALEIDOPHONE
KALEIDOSCOPE
KALEMA
KALENDS
KALEWIFE
KALEWIVES
KALEYARD
KALI
KALIAN
KALIDIUM
KALIF
KALIFORM
KALIGENOUS
KALIJ
KALINITE
KALIOPHILITE
KALIPAYA
KALIPH
KALIUM
KALKVIS
KALLAH
KALLEGE
KALLILITE
KALLITYPE
KALMIA
KALMUCK
KALMUK
KALO
KALOKAGATHIA
KALON
KALONG
KALPAK
KALPIS
KALSOMINE
KALUA
KALUMPANG
KALUMPIT
KALUNTI
KALYMMOCYTE
KALYPTRA
KAM
KAMAAINA
KAMACHI
KAMACHILE
KAMACITE
KAMAHI
KAMALA
KAMALOKA
KAMANCHILE
KAMANI
KAMAO
KAMAREZITE
KAMARUPA
KAMARUPIC
KAMAS
KAMASS
KAMASSI
KAMAVACHARA
KAMBAL
KAMBOH
KAMBOU
KAME
KAMEEL
KAMEELDOORN
KAMEELTHORN
KAMELA
KAMELAUKION
KAMERAD
KAMI
KAMIAN
KAMIAS
KAMICHI
KAMIK
KAMIKA
KAMIKAZE
KAMIKS
KAMIS
KAMLEIKA
KAMMALAN
KAMMERERITE
KAMMEU
KAMPERITE
KAMPONG
KAMPTOMORPH
KAMSEEN
KAMSIN
KAN
KANA
KANAE
KANAF
KANAFF
KANAGI
KANAIMA
KANARA
KANARI
KANAT
KANCHIL
KANDE
KANDH
KANDJAR
KANE
KANEH
KANGA
KANGANI
KANGANY
KANGAROO
KANGAROOER
KANGAROOS
KANGAYAM
KANGLA
KANGRI
KANIN
KANKEDORT
KANKIE
KANKREJ
KANNA
KANNE
KANNEN
KANNU
KANNUME
KANONE
KANOON
KANS
KANT
KANTAR
KANTELA
KANTELE
KANTELETAR
KANTEN
KANTIARA
KANUKA
KANYAW
KANZU
KAOLIANG
KAOLIN
KAOLINATE
KAOLINE
KAOLINIC
KAOLINITE
KAOLINIZE
KAORI
KAPA
KAPAI
KAPEIKA
KAPH
KAPOK
KAPOR
KAPOTE
KAPP
KAPPA
KAPPARAH
KAPPE
KAPPIE
KAPPLAND
KAPU
KAPUKA
KAPUR
KAPUT
KAPUTT
KARABINER
KARAGAN
KARAKA
KARAKUL
KARAKULE
KARAKURT
KARAMU
KARAO
KARAT
KARATAS
KARATE
KARATTO
KARAYA
KARBI
KARCH
KAREAO
KAREAU
KAREETA
KARELA
KAREWA
KAREZ
KARI
KARINGHOTA
KARITE
KARITI
KARMA
KARMADHARAYA
KARMIC
KARMOUTH
KARN
KARO
KAROO
KAROOS
KAROSS
KAROU
KARPAS
KARREE
KARREN
KARRI
KARROO
KARROOS
KARRUSEL
KARSHA
KARST
KARSTIC
KARTEL
KARTOS
KARUNA
KARVAR
KARWAR
KARYOCHROME
KARYOGAMIC
KARYOGAMY
KARYOKINESIS
KARYOKINETIC
KARYOLYMPH
KARYOLYSIS
KARYOLYTIC
KARYOMERE
KARYOMERITE
KARYOMITOIC
KARYOMITOME
KARYOMITOSIS
KARYOMITOTIC
KARYON
KARYOPLASM
KARYOPLASMA
KARYOPLASMIC
KARYORRHEXIS
KARYOSOMA
KARYOSOME
KARYOTIN
KAS
KASA
KASBA
KASBEKE
KASCAMIOL
KASHA
KASHER
KASHGA
KASHI
KASHIM
KASHIMA
KASHMIR
KASHRUTH
KASIDA
KASM
KASOLITE
KASSABAH
KASSU
KASTURA
KASWA
KAT
KATA
KATABASES
KATABASIS
KATABATIC
KATABELLA
KATABOLIC
KATABOLISM

KATABOLITE
KATABOLIZE
KATABOTHRA
KATABOTHRON
KATACROTIC
KATACROTISM
KATAGENESIS
KATAGENETIC
KATAKANA
KATAKINESIS
KATAKINETIC
KATAKIRIBORI
KATALASE
KATALYSIS
KATALYST
KATALYTIC
KATALYZE
KATAMORPHISM
KATANA
KATAPHORESIS
KATAPHORETIC
KATAPHORIC
KATAPHRENIA
KATAPLASIA
KATAPLECTIC
KATAPLEXY
KATAR
KATASTATE
KATASTATIC
KATATONIA
KATATONIC
KATATYPE
KATCHUNG
KATCINA
KATE
KATEL
KATH
KATHA
KATHAK
KATHAKALI
KATHAL
KATHAROMETER
KATHARSIS
KATHARTIC
KATHODE
KATI
KATIN
KATION
KATIPO
KATJEPIERING
KATMON
KATOGLE
KATONKEL
KATSU
KATUKA
KATUN
KATURAI
KATYDID
KATZENJAMMER
KAURI
KAURY
KAVA
KAVAKAVA
KAVASS
KAVIKA
KAVVANAH
KAVYA
KAW
KAWA
KAWAKA
KAWAKAWA
KAY
KAYA
KAYAK
KAYAKER
KAYLE
KAYLES
KAYO
KAYS
KAZAK
KAZI
KAZOO
KAZY
KEA
KEACH
KEACORN
KEAWE
KEBAR
KEBBIE
KEBBOCK
KEBBUCK
KEBBY
KEBOB
KEBYAR
KECHEL
KECHIL
KECK
KECKLE
KECKLING
KECKSY
KECKY
KED
KEDDAH
KEDGE
KEDGER
KEDGEREE
KEDGY
KEDIRI
KEDJAVE
KEDLOCK
KEDUSHAH
KEECH
KEEF
KEEK
KEEKER
KEEKERS
KEEL
KEELAGE
KEELBACK
KEELBILL
KEELBIRD
KEELBLOCK
KEELBOAT
KEELBOATMAN
KEELED
KEELER
KEELFAT
KEELHALE
KEELHAUL
KEELIE
KEELING
KEELIVINE
KEELMAN
KEELS
KEELSON
KEELVAT
KEEN
KEENA
KEENED
KEENER
KEENLY
KEENNESS
KEEP
KEEPER
KEEPERING
KEEPING
KEEPS
KEEPSAKE
KEEPSAKY
KEEPWORTHY
KEEROGUE
KEESH
KEESHOND
KEESHONDEN
KEESLIP
KEEST
KEESTER
KEET
KEETH
KEEVE
KEF
KEFFEL
KEFIR
KEFIRIC
KEG
KEGLER
KEGLING
KEGMEG
KEHAYA
KEHILLAH
KEHILLOTH
KEHOEITE
KEIKI
KEILHAUITE
KEIR
KEIRI
KEIST
KEISTER
KEITLOA
KELCHIN
KELCHYN
KELD
KELDER
KELE
KELEBE
KELECTOME
KELEH
KELEK
KELEP
KELK
KELL
KELLA
KELLECK
KELLEG
KELLIN
KELLION
KELLUPWEED
KELLY
KELOID
KELP
KELPER
KELPFISH
KELPIE
KELPWARE
KELPWORT
KELPY
KELSON
KELT
KELTER
KELTIE
KELTY
KELVIN
KELYPHITE
KEM
KEMANCHA
KEMB
KEMIRI
KEMP
KEMPAS
KEMPER
KEMPERYMAN
KEMPITE
KEMPLE
KEMPSTER
KEMPT
KEMPY
KEN
KENAF
KENCH
KENDIR
KENDNA
KENDO
KENDYR
KENEMA
KENLORE
KENMARK
KENNA
KENNEBUNKER
KENNED
KENNEL
KENNELED
KENNELING
KENNELLED
KENNELLING
KENNELLY
KENNELMAN
KENNELMEN
KENNER
KENNET
KENNING
KENNINGWORT
KENNO
KENO
KENOGENESIS
KENOSIS
KENOTIC
KENOTICISM
KENOTICIST
KENOTISM
KENOTIST
KENOTOXIN
KENOTRON
KENSCOFF
KENSINGTON
KENSPECK
KENSPECKLE
KENT
KENTALLENITE
KENTIA
KENTLEDGE
KENTROGON
KENTROLITE
KENYTE
KEOUT
KEP
KEPE
KEPHIR
KEPI
KEPT
KERALITE
KERAMIC
KERAMICS
KERANA
KERAPHYLLOUS
KERASIN
KERASINE
KERAT
KERATALGIA
KERATECTASIA
KERATECTOMY
KERATIN
KERATINIZE
KERATINOSE
KERATINOUS
KERATITIS
KERATOCELE
KERATOCONUS
KERATODE
KERATODERMIA
KERATOGENIC
KERATOGENOUS
KERATOGLOBUS
KERATOHYAL
KERATOID
KERATOIRITIS
KERATOL
KERATOLYSIS
KERATOLYTIC
KERATOMA
KERATOME
KERATOMETER
KERATOMETRY
KERATONCUS
KERATONOSUS
KERATONYXIS
KERATOPHYRE
KERATOPLASTY
KERATOSCOPE
KERATOSCOPY
KERATOSE
KERATOSES
KERATOSIS
KERATOTOME
KERATOTOMY
KERATTO
KERAULOPHON
KERAULOPHONE
KERAUNIA
KERAUNION
KERAUNOGRAPH
KERAUNOPHONE
KERB
KERBAU
KERBSTONE
KERCHER
KERCHIEF
KERCHIEFED
KERCHIEFT
KERCHOO
KERCHUG
KERCHUNK
KERE
KEREL
KERF
KERFLAP
KERFLOP
KERFLUMMOX
KERI
KERIAH
KERION
KERITE
KERLOCK
KERMES
KERMESITE
KERMESS
KERMIS
KERN
KERNE
KERNEL
KERNELED
KERNELLATE
KERNELLED
KERNELLY
KERNER
KERNETTY
KERNISH
KERNITE
KERNOI
KERNOS
KEROGEN
KEROSENE
KEROSINE
KERPLUNK
KERRANA
KERRIL
KERRITE
KERRY
KERS
KERSANNE
KERSANTITE
KERSE
KERSENNEH
KERSEY
KERSEYMERE
KERSEYS

KERSLAM
KERSLOSH
KERSMASH
KERUGMA
KERUING
KERWHAM
KERYGMA
KERYGMATIC
KERYKEION
KERYSTIC
KESSLERMAN
KESTREL
KET
KETA
KETAL
KETAPANG
KETATE
KETCH
KETCHCRAFT
KETCHUP
KETCHY
KETEMBILLA
KETEN
KETENE
KETHIB
KETHIBH
KETIB
KETIMID
KETIMIDE
KETIMIN
KETIMINE
KETIPATE
KETIPIC
KETMIE
KETOGEN
KETOGENESIS
KETOGENIC
KETOHEPTOSE
KETOL
KETOLE
KETOLYSIS
KETOLYTIC
KETONAEMIA
KETONE
KETONEMIA
KETONIC
KETONIZATION
KETONIZE
KETONURIA
KETOSE
KETOSIDE
KETOSIS
KETOXIME
KETTE
KETTLE
KETTLECASE
KETTLEDRUM
KETTLER
KETTRIN
KETTY
KETUBA
KETUBAH
KETUPA
KETYL
KEUP
KEURBOOM
KEVALIN
KEVAZINGO
KEVEL
KEVELHEAD
KEVUTZAH
KEVUTZOTH
KEWEENAWITE
KEWPIE
KEX
KEXY
KEY
KEYAKI
KEYBOARD
KEYED
KEYER
KEYHOLE
KEYLOCK
KEYMAN
KEYMOVE
KEYNOTE
KEYNOTER
KEYSEAT
KEYSEATER
KEYSERLICK
KEYSLOT
KEYSMITH
KEYSTER
KEYSTONE
KEYSTONED
KEYWAY
KHADDAR
KHADI
KHAGIARITE
KHAIKI
KHAIR
KHAJA
KHAJUR
KHAKAN
KHAKHAM
KHAKI
KHAKIED
KHAKIS
KHAL
KHALAL
KHALAT
KHALIF
KHALIFA
KHALIFAT
KHALSA
KHALSAH
KHAMAL
KHAMSEEN
KHAMSIN
KHAN
KHANATE
KHANDA
KHANDAIT
KHANJAR
KHANJEE
KHANKAH
KHANSAMA
KHANSAMAH
KHANSAMAN
KHANUM
KHAR
KHARAJ
KHARIF
KHAROUBA
KHARUA
KHARWA
KHAS
KHASS
KHAT
KHATIB
KHATIN
KHATRI
KHAUR
KHAYA
KHAZEN
KHEDAH
KHEDIVE
KHEDIVIAH
KHEDIVIAL
KHEDIVIATE
KHELLA
KHELLIN
KHEPESH
KHESARI
KHET
KHIDMATGAR
KHIDMUTGAR
KHILAT
KHIR
KHIRKA
KHIRKAH
KHOA
KHODJA
KHOJA
KHOJAH
KHOKA
KHOR
KHOT
KHUBBER
KHUD
KHULA
KHUR
KHUSKHUS
KHUTBA
KHUTBAH
KHVAT
KI
KIABOOCA
KIACK
KIAK
KIAKI
KIALEE
KIANG
KIAUGH
KIBBE
KIBBEH
KIBBER
KIBBLE
KIBBLER
KIBBLERMAN
KIBBUTZ
KIBBUTZIM
KIBE
KIBITKA
KIBITZ
KIBITZER
KIBLA
KIBLAH
KIBOSH
KIBSEY
KIBY
KICHEL
KICK
KICKBACK
KICKBALL
KICKDOWN
KICKER
KICKING
KICKISH
KICKOFF
KICKOUT
KICKS
KICKSEYS
KICKSHAW
KICKSIES
KICKUP
KICKXIA
KICKY
KID
KIDANG
KIDCOTE
KIDDED
KIDDER
KIDDIE
KIDDIER
KIDDIES
KIDDING
KIDDISH
KIDDLE
KIDDUSH
KIDDUSHIN
KIDDY
KIDLET
KIDNAP
KIDNAPER
KIDNAPING
KIDNAPPER
KIDNEY
KIDNEYLIPPED
KIDNEYROOT
KIDNEYS
KIDNEYWORT
KIDSKIN
KIDSMAN
KIEF
KIEFEKIL
KIEKIE
KIELBASA
KIER
KIESELGUHR
KIESELGUR
KIESERITE
KIESTER
KIESTLESS
KIEVE
KIF
KIKAR
KIKE
KIKEPA
KIKI
KIKORI
KIKU
KIKUEL
KIKUMON
KIL
KILADJA
KILAH
KILDEE
KILDERKIN
KILE
KILEH
KILERG
KILEY
KILHIG
KILIARE
KILIM
KILL
KILLABLE
KILLADAR
KILLAS
KILLBUCK
KILLCALF
KILLCROP
KILLCU
KILLDEE
KILLDEER
KILLED
KILLEEKILLEE
KILLEEN
KILLER
KILLICK
KILLIFISH
KILLIG
KILLIKINICK
KILLING
KILLINGLY
KILLINGNESS
KILLINITE
KILLJOY
KILLOCK
KILLOGIE
KILLOW
KILLWEED
KILLWORT
KILLY
KILN
KILNEYE
KILNHOLE
KILNRIB
KILNSTICK
KILNTREE
KILO
KILOAMPERE
KILOBAR
KILOCALORIE
KILOCYCLE
KILODYNE
KILOGAUSS
KILOGRAM
KILOGRAMME
KILOJOULE
KILOLITER
KILOLITRE
KILOLUMEN
KILOMETER
KILOMETRE
KILOMETRIC
KILOMETRICAL
KILOPARSEC
KILOS
KILOTON
KILOVAR
KILOVOLT
KILOWARE
KILOWATT
KILP
KILT
KILTED
KILTER
KILTIE
KILTIES
KILTING
KILTY
KIM
KIMBERLIN
KIMBERLITE
KIMBO
KIMCHI
KIMIGAYO
KIMMER
KIMNEL
KIMONO
KIMONOED
KIMRI
KIN
KINA
KINAESTHESIA
KINAESTHESIS
KINAH
KINASE
KINBOOT
KINBOT
KINBOTE
KINCH
KINCHIN
KINCHINMORT
KINCOB
KIND
KINDAL
KINDERGARTEN
KINDHEART
KINDHEARTED
KINDLE
KINDLER
KINDLESOME
KINDLESS
KINDLESSLY
KINDLIER
KINDLIEST
KINDLINESS
KINDLING
KINDLY
KINDNESS
KINDRED
KINDREDLY

KINDREDNESS
KINE
KINEMATIC
KINEMATICAL
KINEMATICS
KINEMOMETER
KINEPLASTY
KINEPOX
KINESALGIA
KINESCOPE
KINESIATRIC
KINESIATRICS
KINESIC
KINESIMETER
KINESIOMETER
KINESIS
KINESODIC
KINESTHESIA
KINESTHESIS
KINESTHETIC
KINETIC
KINETICAL
KINETICALLY
KINETICS
KINETOGENESIS
KINETOGENIC
KINETOGRAM
KINETOGRAPH
KINETOPHONE
KINETOSCOPE
KINETOSCOPIC
KINETOSIS
KINFOLK
KING
KINGBIRD
KINGBOLT
KINGCOB
KINGCRAFT
KINGCUP
KINGDOM
KINGDOMED
KINGDOMSHIP
KINGFISH
KINGFISHER
KINGHEAD
KINGHOOD
KINGHUNTER
KINGKLIP
KINGLESS
KINGLESSNESS
KINGLET
KINGLIER
KINGLIEST
KINGLIHOOD
KINGLIKE
KINGLILY
KINGLINESS
KINGLING
KINGLY
KINGMAKER
KINGMAKING
KINGPIECE
KINGPIN
KINGSHIP
KINGSMAN
KINGWEED
KINGWOOD
KINIC
KININ
KINK
KINKAJOU
KINKCOUGH
KINKER
KINKHAB
KINKHAUST
KINKHOST
KINKIER
KINKIEST
KINKILY
KINKINESS
KINKING
KINKLE
KINKLED
KINKSBUSH
KINKY
KINNERY
KINNIKINIC
KINNIKINNICK
KINNOR
KINO
KINOFLUOUS
KINOLOGY
KINOPLASM
KINOPLASMIC
KINOSPORE
KINOT
KINOTANNIC
KINSEN
KINSFOLK
KINSHIP
KINSMAN
KINSMANLY
KINSMEN
KINSPEOPLE
KINSWOMAN
KINTAR
KINTRA
KINTRY
KINURA
KIO
KIOEA
KIORE
KIOSK
KIOTOME
KIP
KIPE
KIPFEL
KIPP
KIPPAGE
KIPPEEN
KIPPER
KIPPERER
KIPPIN
KIPPY
KIPSEY
KIPSKIN
KIPUKA
KIRBY
KIRI
KIRIMON
KIRK
KIRKER
KIRKIFY
KIRKMAN
KIRKTON
KIRKTOWN
KIRKYARD
KIRMESS
KIRMEW
KIRN
KIROMBO
KIRPAN
KIRSCH
KIRSCHWASSER
KIRSEN
KIRTLE
KIRTLED
KIRVE
KIRVER
KIRVI
KISAENG
KISAN
KISANG
KISH
KISHEN
KISHKE
KISI
KISKADEE
KISKATOM
KISKATOMAS
KISKITOM
KISKITOMAS
KISM
KISMET
KISRA
KISS
KISSAGE
KISSAR
KISSER
KISSES
KISSING
KISSINGLY
KIST
KISTFUL
KISTVAEN
KISWA
KISWAH
KIT
KITAB
KITABI
KITAR
KITCAT
KITCHEN
KITCHENER
KITCHENET
KITCHENETTE
KITCHENMAID
KITCHENMAN
KITCHENRY
KITCHENWARE
KITCHENY
KITCHIE
KITE
KITEFLIER
KITEFLYING
KITES
KITH
KITHARA
KITHE
KITHOGUE
KITISH
KITLING
KITMAN
KITMUDGAR
KITT
KITTAR
KITTE
KITTEL
KITTEN
KITTENISH
KITTENISHLY
KITTER
KITTEREEN
KITTHOGE
KITTIE
KITTIWAKE
KITTLE
KITTLEPINS
KITTLES
KITTLISH
KITTLY
KITTOCK
KITTOOL
KITTUL
KITTY
KITTYSOL
KITUL
KIUTLE
KIVA
KIVER
KIVIKIVI
KIVU
KIVVER
KIWACH
KIWI
KIYAS
KIYI
KJELDAHLIZE
KLAFTER
KLAM
KLATSCH
KLAVERN
KLAXON
KLEENEBOC
KLEENEX
KLEG
KLEINITE
KLEPHT
KLEPHTIC
KLEPHTISM
KLEPTIC
KLEPTISTIC
KLEPTOMANIA
KLEPTOMANIAC
KLEPTOMANIST
KLEPTOPHOBIA
KLEZMER
KLICKET
KLINK
KLIP
KLIPBOK
KLIPDAS
KLIPFISH
KLIPHAAS
KLIPPE
KLIPPEN
KLIPSPRINGER
KLISMOS
KLISTER
KLOCKMANNITE
KLOM
KLOMP
KLONG
KLOOCH
KLOOF
KLOOTCHMAN
KLOP
KLOPS
KLOSH
KLOWET
KLUCKER
KLYSTRON
KMET
KNAB
KNABBLE
KNACK
KNACKAWAY
KNACKEBROD
KNACKER
KNACKERY
KNACKIER
KNACKIEST
KNACKWURST
KNACKY
KNAG
KNAGGED
KNAGGIER
KNAGGIEST
KNAGGY
KNAIDEL
KNAP
KNAPE
KNAPPAN
KNAPPE
KNAPPER
KNAPPISH
KNAPPISHLY
KNAPPLE
KNAPSACK
KNAPSACKED
KNAPSACKING
KNAPSCAP
KNAPSCULL
KNAPWEED
KNAR
KNARK
KNARL
KNARRED
KNARRY
KNASH
KNATCH
KNATTE
KNAUR
KNAVE
KNAVERY
KNAVESHIP
KNAVISH
KNAVISHLY
KNAVISHNESS
KNAW
KNAWEL
KNEAD
KNEADER
KNEADING
KNEADINGLY
KNEBELITE
KNECK
KNEE
KNEEBRUSH
KNEECAP
KNEED
KNEEHOLE
KNEEL
KNEELER
KNEELET
KNEELING
KNEELINGLY
KNEEPAD
KNEEPAN
KNEEPIECE
KNEESTONE
KNELL
KNELT
KNETCH
KNEVEL
KNEW
KNEZ
KNEZI
KNIAZ
KNICK
KNICKER
KNICKERED
KNICKERS
KNICKKNACK
KNICKKNACKED
KNICKKNACKET
KNICKKNACKY
KNICKPOINT
KNIFE
KNIFEBOARD
KNIFEFUL
KNIFELIKE
KNIFEMAN
KNIFER
KNIFESMITH
KNIFEWAY
KNIGHT
KNIGHTAGE
KNIGHTESS
KNIGHTHEAD
KNIGHTHOOD
KNIGHTLESS
KNIGHTLIKE
KNIGHTLINESS
KNIGHTLY

KNIP
KNISH
KNIT
KNITBACK
KNITCH
KNITTED
KNITTER
KNITTING
KNITTLE
KNITWEAR
KNITWEED
KNITWORK
KNIVE
KNIVED
KNIVES
KNIVEY
KNOB
KNOBBED
KNOBBER
KNOBBIER
KNOBBIEST
KNOBBLE
KNOBBLER
KNOBBLIER
KNOBBLIEST
KNOBBLY
KNOBBY
KNOBKERRY
KNOBLIKE
KNOBSTICK
KNOBSTONE
KNOBULAR
KNOBWEED
KNOBWOOD
KNOCK
KNOCKABOUT
KNOCKAWAY
KNOCKDOWN
KNOCKEMDOWN
KNOCKER
KNOCKING
KNOCKOFF
KNOCKOUT
KNOCKSTONE
KNOCKUP
KNOCKWURST
KNOIT
KNOLL
KNOLLER
KNOLLY
KNOP
KNOPITE
KNOPPED
KNOPPER
KNOPPIE
KNOPPY
KNORHAAN
KNOSP
KNOSPED
KNOT
KNOTBERRY
KNOTGRASS
KNOTHEAD
KNOTHOLE
KNOTHORN
KNOTROOT
KNOTS
KNOTTED
KNOTTER
KNOTTIER
KNOTTIEST
KNOTTINESS
KNOTTING
KNOTTY
KNOTWEED
KNOTWORK
KNOTWORT
KNOUT
KNOW
KNOWABILITY
KNOWABLE
KNOWABLENESS
KNOWE
KNOWER
KNOWING
KNOWINGLY
KNOWINGNESS
KNOWLEDGE
KNOWLEDGEABLE
KNOWLEDGED
KNOWLEDGEMENT
KNOWLEDGING
KNOWN
KNUB
KNUBBIER
KNUBBIEST
KNUBBLY
KNUBBY
KNUCK
KNUCKLE
KNUCKLEBONE
KNUCKLED
KNUCKLER
KNUCKLESOME
KNUCKLING
KNUCKLY
KNUCKS
KNULLING
KNUR
KNURL
KNURLED
KNURLIER
KNURLIEST
KNURLIN
KNURLING
KNURLY
KNURR
KNURRY
KNUT
KNYAZ
KNYSNA
KO
KOA
KOAE
KOALA
KOALI
KOAN
KOB
KOBA
KOBAN
KOBANG
KOBELLITE
KOBIL
KOBIRD
KOBOLD
KOBONG
KOBU
KOCHIA
KODA
KODAK
KODAKED
KODAKER
KODAKING
KODAKIST
KODAKKED
KODAKKING
KODAKRY
KODKOD
KODRA
KODURITE
KOECHLINITE
KOEL
KOENENITE
KOFF
KOFT
KOFTGAR
KOFTGARI
KOGASIN
KOGON
KOHEKOHE
KOHEMP
KOHL
KOHLRABI
KOHLRABIES
KOHUA
KOI
KOIL
KOILON
KOIMESIS
KOINE
KOINON
KOINONIA
KOJI
KOK
KOKAKO
KOKAM
KOKAMA
KOKAN
KOKANEE
KOKERBOOM
KOKIL
KOKILA
KOKIO
KOKKO
KOKLA
KOKLAS
KOKO
KOKOON
KOKOONA
KOKOPU
KOKOWAI
KOKRA
KOKSTAD
KOKTAITE
KOKU
KOKUM
KOKUMIN
KOLA
KOLACH
KOLAMI
KOLATTAM
KOLEA
KOLEK
KOLEL
KOLEROGA
KOLINSKI
KOLINSKY
KOLKHOS
KOLKHOZ
KOLKOZ
KOLLER
KOLLERGANG
KOLM
KOLO
KOLOBIA
KOLOBION
KOLOKOLO
KOLS
KOLSKITE
KOLSUN
KOLTUNNA
KOM
KOMARCH
KOMATIK
KOMBO
KOMBU
KOMINUTER
KOMITADJI
KOMITAJI
KOMMETJE
KOMMOS
KOMONDOR
KOMPENI
KOMPOW
KOMTOK
KON
KONA
KONAK
KONFYT
KONG
KONGONI
KONGSBERGITE
KONGU
KONIMETER
KONINCKITE
KONINI
KONIOLOGY
KONISCOPE
KONJAK
KONK
KONOHIKI
KONSEAL
KONZE
KOODOO
KOODOOS
KOOKA
KOOKABURRA
KOOKIE
KOOKIER
KOOKIEST
KOOKINESS
KOOKY
KOOLAH
KOOLAU
KOOLETAH
KOOLIMAN
KOOLOKAMBA
KOOMBAR
KOOMKIE
KOONTI
KOOP
KOOPBRIEF
KOORAJONG
KOORHAAN
KOORKA
KOOSIN
KOOTCHA
KOOTCHAR
KOP
KOPECK
KOPEK
KOPH
KOPI
KOPJE
KOPPA
KOPPEN
KOPPIE
KOPPITE
KOR
KORA
KORADJI
KORAIT
KORAKAN
KORARI
KORDAX
KORE
KOREC
KORERO
KORHAAN
KORI
KORIMAKO
KORIN
KORNERUPINE
KORO
KOROMIKA
KOROMIKO
KORONA
KOROVA
KORREL
KORRIGAN
KORRIGUM
KORUMBURRA
KORUN
KORUNA
KORUNY
KORZEC
KOS
KOSAM
KOSHARE
KOSHER
KOSIN
KOSMOKRATOR
KOSO
KOSONG
KOSOTOXIN
KOSS
KOSSO
KOSWITE
KOTAL
KOTO
KOTOITE
KOTSCHUBEITE
KOTTIGITE
KOTUKU
KOTUKUTUKU
KOTWAL
KOTWALEE
KOTYLE
KOU
KOUBA
KOULAN
KOUMISS
KOUMYS
KOUPREY
KOUPROH
KOURBASH
KOUROS
KOUS
KOUSE
KOUSIN
KOUSSIN
KOUSSO
KOUZA
KOVIL
KOWBIRD
KOWHAI
KOWL
KOWTOW
KOWTOWER
KOY
KOYEMSHI
KOZO
KRA
KRAAL
KRAFT
KRAGEROITE
KRAIT
KRAKEN
KRAKOWIAK
KRAL
KRAN
KRANG
KRANS
KRANTZ
KRANTZITE
KRAPFEN
KRAS
KRASIS
KRATER
KRATOGEN
KRATOGENIC
KRAUSEN
KRAUSITE
KRAUT
KRAUTHEAD

KRAUTWEED
KRAVERS
KREEF
KREESE
KREIS
KREISTLE
KREITONITE
KRELOS
KREMERSITE
KREMLIN
KREMS
KRENG
KRENNERITE
KREPLACH
KREPLECH
KREUTZER
KREUZER
KREX
KRIEGSPIEL
KRIEKER
KRIGIA
KRILL
KRIMMER
KRIS
KRISS
KRITARCHY
KRITRIMA
KROBYLOI
KROBYLOS
KROCKET
KROHNKITE
KROMESKI
KROMESKY
KROMOGRAM
KROMSKOP
KRONA
KRONE
KRONEN
KRONER
KRONOR
KRONOS
KRONUR
KROON
KROONI
KROONS
KROSA
KROUCHKA
KROUSHKA
KRUBI
KRUBUT
KRULLER
KRUMHORN
KRUMMHORN
KRYOKONITE
KRYOLITE
KRYOLITH
KRYPSIS
KRYPTIC
KRYPTICISM
KRYPTOL
KRYPTON
KTHIB
KTHIBH
KUAN
KUBA
KUBBA
KUBONG
KUBUKLION
KUCHEN
KUDIZE
KUDOS
KUDU
KUDZU
KUE
KUEI
KUERR
KUFA
KUGE
KUGEL
KUGELHOF
KUICHUA
KUJAWIAK
KUKERI
KUKRI
KUKU
KUKUI
KUKUPA
KULA
KULAH
KULAITE
KULAK
KULAKISM
KULAN
KULANG
KULKARNI
KULLAITE
KULM
KULMET
KULP
KUMARA
KUMBI
KUMBUK
KUMHAR
KUMISS
KUMKUM
KUMMEL
KUMMERBUND
KUMQUAT
KUMRAH
KUMYS
KUNAI
KUNG
KUNK
KUNKUR
KUNMIUT
KUNZITE
KUPFERNICKEL
KUPFFERITE
KUPHAR
KUPPER
KURBASH
KURCHICINE
KURCHINE
KURGAN
KURI
KURK
KURRAJONG
KURSI
KURTOSIS
KURUMA
KURUMAYA
KURUNG
KURUNJ
KURVEY
KURVEYOR
KUSA
KUSAM
KUSHA
KUSIMANSE
KUSIMANSEL
KUSKITE
KUSKUS
KUSSO
KUSTI
KUSU
KUSUM
KUTAI
KUTCH
KUTCHA
KUTTAB
KUTTAR
KUVASZ
KVARNER
KVAS
KVASS
KVINT
KVUTZA
KVUTZAH
KWAN
KWARTA
KWASHIORKOR
KWATUMA
KWAZOKU
KWEEK
KWEI
KWIEN
KWINTRA
KYAAK
KYACK
KYAH
KYANG
KYANISE
KYANITE
KYANIZATION
KYANIZE
KYAR
KYAT
KYATHOS
KYAUNG
KYE
KYKE
KYL
KYLE
KYLIE
KYLIKES
KYLIN
KYLITE
KYLIX
KYMATOLOGY
KYMBALON
KYMOGRAM
KYMOGRAPH
KYMOGRAPHIC
KYNURENIC
KYNURIN
KYNURINE
KYOODLE
KYPHOSIS
KYPHOTIC
KYPOO
KYRIAL
KYRIALE
KYRIELLE
KYRIN
KYRINE
KYRIOS
KYSCHTYMITE
KYTE
KYTHE

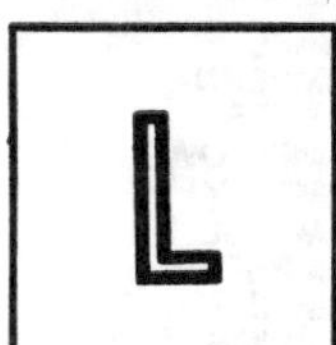

LA
LAAGER
LAAGTE
LAANG
LAAP
LAARP
LAB
LABARA
LABARIA
LABARUM
LABBA
LABBER
LABDACISM
LABDACISMUS
LABDANUM
LABEFACT
LABEFACTION
LABEFIED
LABEFY
LABEFYING
LABEL
LABELED
LABELER
LABELING
LABELLATE
LABELLED
LABELLER
LABELLING
LABELLOID
LABELLUM
LABIA
LABIAL
LABIALISM
LABIALISMUS
LABIALITY
LABIALIZE
LABIALIZED
LABIALIZING
LABIALLY
LABIATE
LABIATED
LABIE
LABIELLA
LABILE
LABILITY
LABILIZATION
LABILIZE
LABIODENTAL
LABIOGLOSSAL
LABIOGRAPH
LABIOLINGUAL
LABIOMANCY
LABIOMENTAL
LABIONASAL
LABIOPALATAL
LABIOPLASTY
LABIOSE
LABIOVELAR
LABIOVERSION
LABIS
LABITE
LABIUM
LABLAB
LABOR
LABORAGE
LABORANT
LABORATORIAL
LABORATORIAN
LABORATORIES
LABORATORY
LABORED
LABOREDLY
LABOREDNESS
LABORER
LABORES
LABORESS
LABORING
LABORINGLY
LABORIOUS
LABORIOUSLY
LABORIOUSNESS
LABORISM
LABORIST
LABORITE
LABOROUS
LABORSAVING
LABORSOME
LABORSOMELY
LABOUR
LABOURAGE
LABOURED
LABOUREDLY
LABOUREDNESS
LABOURER
LABOURESS
LABOURING
LABOURINGLY
LABOURISM
LABOURIST
LABOURITE
LABOURSAVING
LABOURSOME
LABOURSOMELY
LABRA
LABRADORITE
LABRADORITIC
LABRAL
LABRAS
LABRET
LABRETIFERY
LABRID
LABROID
LABROSAURID
LABROSAUROID
LABROSE
LABRUM
LABRUSCA
LABRYS
LABURNUM
LABYRINTH
LABYRINTHAL
LABYRINTHALLY
LABYRINTHED
LABYRINTHIAN
LABYRINTHIC
LABYRINTHICAL
LABYRINTHICALLY
LABYRINTHINE
LAC
LACATAN
LACCA
LACCASE
LACCOL
LACCOLITE
LACCOLITH
LACCOLITHIC
LACCOLITIC
LACE
LACEBARK
LACED
LACEFLOWER
LACELEAF
LACEMAKER
LACEMAKING
LACEMAN
LACEMEN
LACEPIECE
LACEPOD
LACER
LACERABILITY
LACERABLE
LACERANT
LACERATE
LACERATED
LACERATELY
LACERATING
LACERATION
LACERATIVE
LACERT
LACERTIAN
LACERTIFORM
LACERTILIAN
LACERTILOID
LACERTINE
LACERTOID
LACERY
LACET
LACEWING
LACEWOMAN
LACEWOMEN
LACEWOOD
LACEWORK
LACEWORKER
LACHE
LACHES
LACHRYMA
LACHRYMAL
LACHRYMALLY
LACHRYMARY
LACHRYMATION
LACHRYMATOR
LACHRYMATORY
LACHRYMIFORM
LACHRYMIST
LACHRYMOSAL
LACHRYMOSE
LACHRYMOSELY
LACHRYMOSITY
LACHRYMOUS
LACHSA
LACIER
LACIEST
LACILY
LACINESS
LACING
LACINIA
LACINIATE
LACINIATED
LACINIATION
LACINIFORM
LACINIOSE
LACINIOUS
LACINULA
LACINULAS
LACINULATE
LACINULOSE
LACIS
LACK
LACKADAISICAL
LACKADAISY
LACKADAY
LACKED
LACKER
LACKERER
LACKERING
LACKEY
LACKEYED
LACKEYING
LACKEYS
LACKIES
LACKING
LACKLAND
LACKLUSTER
LACKLUSTRE
LACKLUSTROUS
LACKWIT
LACKWITTEDLY
LACKWITTEDNESS
LACMOID
LACMUS
LACONIC
LACONICAL
LACONICALLY
LACONICISM
LACONICS
LACONICUM
LACONISM
LACONIZE
LACONIZED
LACONIZER
LACONIZING
LACQUER
LACQUERED
LACQUERER
LACQUERING
LACQUERIST
LACQUERWORK
LACQUEY
LACRIMAL
LACRIMATOR
LACROIXITE
LACROSSE
LACROSSER
LACTALBUMIN
LACTAM
LACTAMIDE
LACTANT
LACTARENE
LACTARINE
LACTARIUM
LACTARY
LACTASE
LACTATE
LACTATED
LACTATING
LACTATION
LACTEAL
LACTEAN
LACTENIN
LACTEOUS
LACTESCE
LACTESCENCE
LACTESCENCY
LACTESCENT
LACTIC
LACTICINIA
LACTID
LACTIDE
LACTIFEROUS
LACTIFIC
LACTIFICAL
LACTIFIED
LACTIFLOROUS
LACTIFLUOUS
LACTIFORM
LACTIFUGE
LACTIFY
LACTIFYING
LACTIGENIC
LACTIGENOUS
LACTIGEROUS
LACTIM
LACTIMIDE
LACTINATE
LACTIVOROUS
LACTO
LACTOCHROME
LACTOCITRATE
LACTOFLAVIN
LACTOGEN
LACTOGENIC
LACTOID
LACTOL
LACTOMETER
LACTONE
LACTONIC
LACTONIZE
LACTOPROTEID
LACTOPROTEIN
LACTOSCOPE
LACTOSE
LACTOSID
LACTOSIDE
LACTOSURIA
LACTOTOXIN
LACTUCARIUM
LACTUCERIN
LACTUCIN
LACTUCOL
LACTUCON
LACTYL
LACUNA
LACUNAE
LACUNAL
LACUNAR
LACUNARIA
LACUNARS
LACUNARY
LACUNAS
LACUNE
LACUNOME
LACUNOSE
LACUNOSITY
LACUNULE
LACUNULOSE
LACUSCULAR
LACUSTRAL
LACUSTRIAN
LACUSTRINE
LACWORK
LACY
LAD
LADANG
LADANIGEROUS
LADANUM
LADDER
LADDERED
LADDERING
LADDERWAY
LADDERY
LADDESS
LADDIE
LADDIKIE
LADDISH
LADDOCK
LADE
LADED
LADEMAN
LADEN
LADENED
LADENING
LADER
LADIES
LADIFIED
LADIFY
LADIFYING
LADING
LADKIN
LADLE
LADLED
LADLEFUL
LADLER
LADLEWOOD
LADLING
LADRONE

LADRONISM
LADRONIZE
LADY
LADYBIRD
LADYBUG
LADYCLOCK
LADYFINGER
LADYFISH
LADYFLIES
LADYFLY
LADYFY
LADYHOOD
LADYKIN
LADYKIND
LADYLIKE
LADYLIKELY
LADYLING
LADYLOVE
LADYPALM
LADYSFINGER
LADYSHIP
LADYSLIPPER
LAEMODIPOD
LAEMODIPODAN
LAEN
LAENDER
LAEOTROPIC
LAEOTROPISM
LAEOTROPOUS
LAET
LAETATION
LAETI
LAETIC
LAEVO
LAEVODUCTION
LAEVOGYRATE
LAEVOGYRE
LAEVOVERSION
LAFAYETTE
LAFE
LAFT
LAG
LAGAN
LAGE
LAGEN
LAGENA
LAGENAE
LAGEND
LAGER
LAGERED
LAGERING
LAGETTO
LAGGAR
LAGGARD
LAGGARDLY
LAGGARDNESS
LAGGED
LAGGEN
LAGGER
LAGGIN
LAGGING
LAGLAST
LAGNA
LAGNAPPE
LAGNIAPPE
LAGO
LAGOMORPH
LAGOMORPHIC
LAGOMORPHOUS
LAGONITE
LAGOON
LAGOONAL
LAGOPODE
LAGOPODOUS
LAGOPOUS
LAGOSTOMA
LAGS
LAGUNA
LAGUNE
LAGWORT
LAHAR
LAHN
LAI
LAIC
LAICAL
LAICALITY
LAICALLY
LAICH
LAICISM
LAICITY
LAICIZATION
LAICIZE
LAICIZED
LAICIZER
LAICIZING
LAID
LAIDE
LAIDLY
LAIGH
LAIN
LAINAGE
LAINE
LAINER
LAIOSE
LAIR
LAIRAGE
LAIRD
LAIRDESS
LAIRDIE
LAIRDLY
LAIRDOCRACY
LAIRDSHIP
LAIRED
LAIRING
LAIRMAN
LAIRMEN
LAIRSTONE
LAIRY
LAISSE
LAIT
LAITANCE
LAITH
LAITHE
LAITHLY
LAITIES
LAITY
LAK
LAKARPITE
LAKATAN
LAKATOI
LAKE
LAKED
LAKELAND
LAKELANDER
LAKELET
LAKEMANSHIP
LAKER
LAKES
LAKESHORE
LAKEWEED
LAKEY
LAKH
LAKIE
LAKIER
LAKIEST
LAKIN
LAKING
LAKISH
LAKISHNESS
LAKISM
LAKIST
LAKMUS
LAKY
LALA
LALANG
LALAPALOOZA
LALAQUI
LALI
LALLAPALOOZA
LALLATION
LALLING
LALLYGAG
LALO
LALONEUROSIS
LALOPATHY
LALOPHOBIA
LALOPLEGIA
LAM
LAMA
LAMAIC
LAMANTIN
LAMANY
LAMASERIES
LAMASERY
LAMB
LAMBA
LAMBACK
LAMBALE
LAMBAST
LAMBASTE
LAMBASTED
LAMBASTING
LAMBDA
LAMBDACISM
LAMBDOID
LAMBDOIDAL
LAMBEAU
LAMBENCIES
LAMBENCY
LAMBENT
LAMBENTLY
LAMBER
LAMBERT
LAMBIE
LAMBINESS
LAMBISH
LAMBITIVE
LAMBKILL
LAMBKIN
LAMBLIASIS
LAMBLIKE
LAMBLING
LAMBOYS
LAMBREQUIN
LAMBS
LAMBSDOWN
LAMBSKIN
LAMDAN
LAMDEN
LAME
LAMED
LAMEDH
LAMEL
LAMELLA
LAMELLAE
LAMELLAR
LAMELLARY
LAMELLAS
LAMELLATE
LAMELLATED
LAMELLATELY
LAMELLATION
LAMELLICORN
LAMELLIFORM
LAMELLOID
LAMELLOSE
LAMELLOSITY
LAMELLULE
LAMELY
LAMENESS
LAMENT
LAMENTABLE
LAMENTABLY
LAMENTATION
LAMENTATORY
LAMENTED
LAMENTEDLY
LAMENTER
LAMENTFUL
LAMENTING
LAMENTINGLY
LAMENTIVE
LAMENTORY
LAMER
LAMEST
LAMESTER
LAMETER
LAMETTA
LAMIA
LAMIACEOUS
LAMIAE
LAMIAS
LAMIGER
LAMIID
LAMIN
LAMINA
LAMINABILITY
LAMINABLE
LAMINAE
LAMINAL
LAMINAR
LAMINARIAN
LAMINARIN
LAMINARIOID
LAMINARITE
LAMINARY
LAMINAS
LAMINATE
LAMINATED
LAMINATING
LAMINATION
LAMINBOARD
LAMINECTOMY
LAMING
LAMINIFEROUS
LAMINIFORM
LAMINITIS
LAMINOSE
LAMINOUS
LAMISH
LAMITER
LAMM
LAMMAS
LAMMED
LAMMER
LAMMERGEIER
LAMMERGEIR
LAMMERGEYER
LAMMIE
LAMMING
LAMMOCK
LAMMY
LAMNID
LAMNOID
LAMP
LAMPAD
LAMPADARIES
LAMPADARY
LAMPADEDROMY
LAMPADEPHORE
LAMPADITE
LAMPARA
LAMPAS
LAMPATIA
LAMPBLACK
LAMPBLACKED
LAMPBLACKING
LAMPED
LAMPER
LAMPERN
LAMPERS
LAMPFLOWER
LAMPFLY
LAMPFUL
LAMPHOLE
LAMPING
LAMPION
LAMPIST
LAMPISTRY
LAMPLESS
LAMPLET
LAMPLIGHT
LAMPLIGHTED
LAMPLIGHTER
LAMPLIT
LAMPMAKER
LAMPMAKING
LAMPMAN
LAMPMEN
LAMPOON
LAMPOONED
LAMPOONER
LAMPOONERY
LAMPOONING
LAMPOONIST
LAMPPOST
LAMPREL
LAMPRET
LAMPREY
LAMPREYS
LAMPROPHONY
LAMPROPHYRE
LAMPROPHYRIC
LAMPROTYPE
LAMPS
LAMPSHADE
LAMPSTAND
LAMPWICK
LAMPYRID
LAMPYRINE
LAMSIEKTE
LAMSTER
LAMZIEKTE
LAN
LANA
LANAC
LANAI
LANAMETER
LANARKITE
LANAS
LANATE
LANATED
LANAZ
LANCE
LANCED
LANCEGAY
LANCEGAYE
LANCELET
LANCELY
LANCEMAN
LANCEMEN
LANCEOLATE
LANCEOLATED
LANCEOLATELY
LANCEOLATION
LANCEPESADE
LANCEPOD
LANCEPRISADO
LANCER
LANCERS
LANCES
LANCET
LANCETED
LANCETEER
LANCEWOOD

LANCHA
LANCHARA
LANCIERS
LANCIFEROUS
LANCIFORM
LANCINATE
LANCINATED
LANCINATING
LANCINATION
LANCING
LAND
LANDAGE
LANDAMMAN
LANDAU
LANDAULET
LANDAULETTE
LANDBLINK
LANDBOC
LANDBOOK
LANDDROST
LANDDROSTEN
LANDE
LANDED
LANDER
LANDESITE
LANDFALL
LANDFANG
LANDFAST
LANDFLOOD
LANDFOLK
LANDFORM
LANDGAFOL
LANDGATE
LANDGATES
LANDGRAVE
LANDGRAVESS
LANDGRAVIATE
LANDGRAVINE
LANDHOLDER
LANDHOLDING
LANDIMERE
LANDING
LANDIRON
LANDLADIES
LANDLADY
LANDLEAPER
LANDLER
LANDLESS
LANDLESSNESS
LANDLINE
LANDLOCK
LANDLOCKED
LANDLOOK
LANDLOOKER
LANDLOPER
LANDLOPING
LANDLORD
LANDLORDISM
LANDLORDLY
LANDLORDRY
LANDLORDSHIP
LANDLOUPER
LANDLOUPING
LANDLUBBER
LANDLUBBERISH
LANDLUBBERLY
LANDLUBBING
LANDMAN
LANDMARK
LANDMASS
LANDMEN
LANDOCRACY
LANDOCRAT
LANDOWNER
LANDOWNERSHIP
LANDOWNING
LANDPLANE
LANDRACE
LANDRAKER
LANDREEVE
LANDRIGHT
LANDS
LANDSALE
LANDSCAPE
LANDSCAPED
LANDSCAPING
LANDSCAPIST
LANDSHARD
LANDSHIP
LANDSICK
LANDSIDE
LANDSKIP
LANDSLIDE
LANDSLIP
LANDSMAN
LANDSMEN
LANDSPOUT
LANDSPRINGY
LANDSTORM
LANDTROST
LANDWAITER
LANDWARD
LANDWARDS
LANDWASH
LANDWAY
LANDWAYS
LANDWHIN
LANDWIRE
LANDWRACK
LANDWRECK
LANDYARD
LANE
LANELY
LANER
LANESOME
LANETE
LANEWAY
LANEY
LANG
LANGAHA
LANGARAI
LANGBANITE
LANGBEINITE
LANGCA
LANGEL
LANGI
LANGITE
LANGKA
LANGLAUF
LANGLAUFER
LANGLE
LANGOON
LANGOOTY
LANGOSTA
LANGOUSTE
LANGRAGE
LANGREL
LANGRET
LANGRIDGE
LANGSETTLE
LANGSHAN
LANGSPIEL
LANGSPIL
LANGSYNE
LANGUAGE
LANGUAGED
LANGUAGES
LANGUAGING
LANGUE
LANGUENT
LANGUESCENT
LANGUET
LANGUETTE
LANGUID
LANGUIDLY
LANGUIDNESS
LANGUISH
LANGUISHED
LANGUISHER
LANGUISHING
LANGUISHINGLY
LANGUISHMENT
LANGUOR
LANGUORMENT
LANGUOROUS
LANGUOROUSLY
LANGUR
LANIA
LANIARD
LANIARIES
LANIARIFORM
LANIARY
LANIATE
LANIFEROUS
LANIFIC
LANIFICE
LANIFLOROUS
LANIFORM
LANIGEROUS
LANIIFORM
LANISTA
LANISTAE
LANITAL
LANK
LANKER
LANKEST
LANKET
LANKIER
LANKIEST
LANKILY
LANKINESS
LANKLY
LANKNESS
LANKY
LANNER
LANNERET
LANOLIN
LANOLINE
LANOSE
LANOSITY
LANSA
LANSAT
LANSDOWNE
LANSEH
LANSFORDITE
LANSQUENET
LANT
LANTACA
LANTAKA
LANTANA
LANTCHA
LANTERLOO
LANTERN
LANTERNED
LANTERNING
LANTERNLEAF
LANTERNMAN
LANTERNS
LANTHANA
LANTHANIA
LANTHANID
LANTHANIDE
LANTHANITE
LANTHANON
LANTHANUM
LANTHOPIN
LANTHOPINE
LANTHORN
LANTUM
LANUGINOSE
LANUGINOUS
LANUGO
LANUGOS
LANUM
LANX
LANYARD
LANZON
LAODAH
LAP
LAPACHO
LAPACHOL
LAPACTIC
LAPAN
LAPARECTOMY
LAPAROCELE
LAPAROMYITIS
LAPAROSCOPY
LAPAROSTICT
LAPAROTOME
LAPAROTOMIST
LAPAROTOMIZE
LAPAROTOMY
LAPBOARD
LAPCOCK
LAPDOG
LAPEL
LAPELER
LAPELLED
LAPFUL
LAPFULS
LAPICIDE
LAPIDARIAN
LAPIDARIES
LAPIDARIST
LAPIDARY
LAPIDATE
LAPIDATED
LAPIDATING
LAPIDATION
LAPIDATOR
LAPIDEON
LAPIDEOUS
LAPIDES
LAPIDESCENCE
LAPIDESCENT
LAPIDICOLOUS
LAPIDIFIC
LAPIDIFICAL
LAPIDIFIED
LAPIDIFY
LAPIDIFYING
LAPIDIST
LAPIDITY
LAPIDOSE
LAPIES
LAPILLI
LAPILLIFORM
LAPILLO
LAPILLUS
LAPIN
LAPIS
LAPLING
LAPON
LAPPACEOUS
LAPPAGE
LAPPED
LAPPER
LAPPET
LAPPETED
LAPPETHEAD
LAPPING
LAPPISH
LAPSABILITY
LAPSABLE
LAPSATION
LAPSE
LAPSED
LAPSER
LAPSI
LAPSIBILITY
LAPSIBLE
LAPSING
LAPSINGLY
LAPSTONE
LAPSTRAKE
LAPSTREAK
LAPSTREAKED
LAPSTREAKER
LAPSUS
LAPULAPU
LAPWING
LAPWORK
LAQUEAR
LAQUEARIA
LAQUEARIAN
LAQUEUS
LAR
LARARIUM
LARB
LARBOARD
LARBOLINS
LARBOWLINES
LARCENER
LARCENIC
LARCENIES
LARCENISH
LARCENIST
LARCENOUS
LARCENOUSLY
LARCENY
LARCH
LARCIN
LARCINRY
LARD
LARDACEIN
LARDACEOUS
LARDED
LARDER
LARDERELLITE
LARDERER
LARDIFORM
LARDINER
LARDING
LARDITE
LARDON
LARDOON
LARDRY
LARDY
LAREABELL
LARES
LARGAMENTE
LARGANDO
LARGE
LARGEBRAINED
LARGEHEARTED
LARGEHEARTEDNESS
LARGELY
LARGEMOUTHED
LARGEN
LARGENESS
LARGEOUR
LARGEOUS
LARGER
LARGESS
LARGESSE
LARGEST
LARGHETTO
LARGHETTOS
LARGHISSIMO
LARGHISSIMOS
LARGIFICAL
LARGISH
LARGITION
LARGITIONAL
LARGO

LARGY
LARI
LARIAT
LARIATED
LARIATING
LARICK
LARID
LARIDINE
LARIGO
LARIGOT
LARIID
LARIN
LARINE
LARIOT
LARIX
LARIXIN
LARK
LARKED
LARKER
LARKING
LARKINGLY
LARKISH
LARKISHNESS
LARKS
LARKSOME
LARKSPUR
LARKY
LARM
LARME
LARMIER
LARMOYANT
LARNAKES
LARNAX
LAROID
LARON
LARREE
LARRIES
LARRIGAN
LARRIKIN
LARRIKINESS
LARRIKINISM
LARRIMAN
LARRUP
LARRUPED
LARRUPING
LARRY
LARS
LARSENITE
LARUM
LARVA
LARVAE
LARVAL
LARVARIA
LARVARIUM
LARVARIUMS
LARVATE
LARVATED
LARVE
LARVICIDAL
LARVICIDE
LARVICOLOUS
LARVIFORM
LARVIGEROUS
LARVIPAROUS
LARVIPOSIT
LARVIPOSITION
LARVIVOROUS
LARVULE
LARY
LARYNGAL
LARYNGALGIA
LARYNGEAL
LARYNGEAN
LARYNGEATING
LARYNGECTOMY
LARYNGES
LARYNGIC
LARYNGISMAL
LARYNGISMUS
LARYNGITIC
LARYNGITIS
LARYNGOCELE
LARYNGOGRAPH
LARYNGOLOGY
LARYNGOMETRY
LARYNGOPATHY
LARYNGOPHONY
LARYNGORRHEA
LARYNGOSCOPE
LARYNGOSCOPY
LARYNGOSTOMY
LARYNGOTOME
LARYNGOTOMY
LARYNX
LARYNXES
LAS
LASAGNA
LASAGNE
LASCAR
LASCHETY
LASCIVIENT
LASCIVIENTLY
LASCIVIOUS
LASCIVIOUSLY
LASCIVIOUSNESS
LASER
LASERWORT
LASH
LASHED
LASHER
LASHES
LASHING
LASHINGS
LASHINS
LASHLESS
LASHLIGHT
LASHLITE
LASHNESS
LASHORN
LASIOCAMPID
LASIOCARPOUS
LASK
LASKE
LASKET
LASKING
LASPRING
LASQUE
LASS
LASSET
LASSIE
LASSIKY
LASSITUDE
LASSLORN
LASSO
LASSOCK
LASSOCKIE
LASSOED
LASSOER
LASSOES
LASSOING
LASSOS
LASSU
LAST
LASTAGE
LASTER
LASTEX
LASTING
LASTINGLY
LASTINGNESS
LASTLY
LASTRE
LASTY
LASYA
LAT
LATA
LATAH
LATANIER
LATCH
LATCHED
LATCHER
LATCHET
LATCHING
LATCHKEY
LATCHMAN
LATCHMEN
LATCHSTRING
LATE
LATEBRA
LATEBRICOLE
LATECOMER
LATECOMING
LATED
LATEEN
LATEENER
LATELINESS
LATELY
LATEMOST
LATEN
LATENCE
LATENCIES
LATENCY
LATENESS
LATENT
LATENTLY
LATER
LATERA
LATERAD
LATERAL
LATERALITY
LATERALIZE
LATERALIZED
LATERALIZING
LATERALLY
LATERAN
LATERIFLORAL
LATERIGRADE
LATERITE
LATERITIC
LATERIZATION
LATEROCAUDAL
LATERODORSAL
LATERONUCHAL
LATESCENCE
LATESCENT
LATESOME
LATEST
LATEWARD
LATEWHILE
LATEWHILES
LATEWOOD
LATEX
LATEXES
LATEXOSIS
LATH
LATHE
LATHED
LATHEE
LATHEMAN
LATHEN
LATHER
LATHERED
LATHEREEVE
LATHERER
LATHERIN
LATHERING
LATHERWORT
LATHERY
LATHESMAN
LATHESMEN
LATHI
LATHIE
LATHIER
LATHIEST
LATHING
LATHREEVE
LATHS
LATHWORK
LATHY
LATHYRIC
LATHYRISM
LATI
LATIBULIZE
LATICES
LATICIFEROUS
LATICLAVE
LATICOSTATE
LATIDENTATE
LATIFOLIATE
LATIFOLIOUS
LATIFUNDIA
LATIFUNDIAN
LATIFUNDIUM
LATIGO
LATINISM
LATINIZE
LATION
LATIPENNATE
LATIPENNINE
LATIPLANTAR
LATIROSTRAL
LATIROSTROUS
LATISEPT
LATISEPTAL
LATISEPTATE
LATISH
LATISTERNAL
LATITANCY
LATITANT
LATITAT
LATITE
LATITUDE
LATITUDINAL
LATITUDINALLY
LATITUDINARIAN
LATITUDINARY
LATITUDINOUS
LATIVE
LATKE
LATOMIA
LATOMY
LATOSOL
LATRANT
LATRATION
LATREDE
LATREUTIC
LATREUTICAL
LATRIA
LATRIAL
LATRIALLY
LATRIAN
LATRINE
LATRO
LATROBE
LATROBITE
LATROCINIUM
LATROCINY
LATRON
LATS
LATTEN
LATTENER
LATTENS
LATTER
LATTERLY
LATTERMATH
LATTERMOST
LATTICE
LATTICED
LATTICELEAF
LATTICEWORK
LATTICING
LATTICINIO
LATTIN
LATU
LATUS
LAUAN
LAUBANITE
LAUD
LAUDABILITY
LAUDABLE
LAUDABLENESS
LAUDABLY
LAUDANIDINE
LAUDANIN
LAUDANINE
LAUDANOSINE
LAUDANUM
LAUDATION
LAUDATIVE
LAUDATORILY
LAUDATORY
LAUDED
LAUDER
LAUDIFICATION
LAUDING
LAUDIST
LAUDS
LAUGH
LAUGHABLE
LAUGHABLENESS
LAUGHABLY
LAUGHED
LAUGHEE
LAUGHER
LAUGHFUL
LAUGHING
LAUGHINGLY
LAUGHINGSTOCK
LAUGHS
LAUGHSOME
LAUGHTER
LAUGHWORTHY
LAUGHY
LAUHALA
LAUIA
LAUK
LAULAU
LAUMONITE
LAUMONTITE
LAUN
LAUNCE
LAUNCH
LAUNCHED
LAUNCHER
LAUNCHING
LAUND
LAUNDER
LAUNDERED
LAUNDERER
LAUNDERETTE
LAUNDERING
LAUNDRESS
LAUNDRIES
LAUNDROMAT
LAUNDRY
LAUNDRYMAID
LAUNDRYMAN
LAUNDRYMEN
LAUNDRYOWNER
LAUNDRYWOMAN
LAUNDRYWOMEN
LAUNEDDAS
LAURA
LAURACEOUS
LAURAE
LAURALDEHYDE

LAURAS
LAURATE
LAURDALITE
LAURE
LAUREATE
LAUREATED
LAUREATESHIP
LAUREATING
LAUREATION
LAUREL
LAURELED
LAURELING
LAURELLED
LAURELLING
LAURELS
LAURELSHIP
LAURELWOOD
LAUREOLE
LAURIC
LAURIN
LAURINOXYLON
LAURIONITE
LAURITE
LAURONE
LAURUSTINE
LAURUSTINUS
LAURVIKITE
LAURY
LAURYL
LAUTARITE
LAUTER
LAUTITE
LAUTITIOUS
LAUTU
LAUWINE
LAVA
LAVABO
LAVABOES
LAVACRE
LAVADERO
LAVAGE
LAVALIER
LAVALIERE
LAVAMENT
LAVANDERA
LAVANDERAS
LAVANDERO
LAVANDEROS
LAVANDIN
LAVANGA
LAVANT
LAVARET
LAVASH
LAVATIC
LAVATION
LAVATIONAL
LAVATORIES
LAVATORY
LAVE
LAVED
LAVEER
LAVEMENT
LAVENDER
LAVENDERED
LAVENDERING
LAVENITE
LAVER
LAVEROCK
LAVETTE
LAVIALITE
LAVING
LAVISH
LAVISHED
LAVISHER
LAVISHING
LAVISHINGLY
LAVISHLY
LAVISHNESS
LAVOLTA
LAVROCK
LAVROFFITE
LAVROVITE
LAVY
LAW
LAWBOOK
LAWBREAKER
LAWBREAKERS
LAWBREAKING
LAWFUL
LAWFULLY
LAWFULNESS
LAWGIVER
LAWGIVING
LAWINE
LAWING
LAWISH
LAWK
LAWKS
LAWLANTS
LAWLESS
LAWLESSLY
LAWLESSNESS
LAWLIKE
LAWMAKER
LAWMAKING
LAWMAN
LAWMEN
LAWMONGER
LAWN
LAWNED
LAWNER
LAWNLEAF
LAWNLET
LAWNLIKE
LAWNY
LAWPROOF
LAWRENCITE
LAWRENCIUM
LAWRIGHTMAN
LAWRIGHTMEN
LAWS
LAWSONE
LAWSONITE
LAWSUIT
LAWSUITING
LAWTER
LAWYER
LAWYERLIKE
LAWYERLY
LAWYERY
LAX
LAXATE
LAXATION
LAXATIVE
LAXATIVELY
LAXATIVENESS
LAXER
LAXEST
LAXIFLOROUS
LAXIFOLIATE
LAXIFOLIOUS
LAXISM
LAXIST
LAXITY
LAXLY
LAXNESS
LAY
LAYAWAY
LAYBACK
LAYBOY
LAYER
LAYERAGE
LAYERED
LAYERING
LAYERS
LAYERY
LAYETTE
LAYFOLK
LAYING
LAYLAND
LAYLIGHT
LAYLOCK
LAYMAN
LAYMANSHIP
LAYMEN
LAYNE
LAYOFF
LAYOUT
LAYOVER
LAYROCK
LAYSTALL
LAYSTOW
LAYWOMAN
LAYWOMEN
LAZAR
LAZARET
LAZARETTE
LAZARETTO
LAZARETTOS
LAZARLY
LAZAROLE
LAZARONE
LAZAROUS
LAZARY
LAZE
LAZED
LAZIER
LAZIEST
LAZILY
LAZINESS
LAZING
LAZO
LAZULE
LAZULI
LAZULITE
LAZULITIC
LAZURITE
LAZY
LAZYBACK
LAZYBED
LAZYBIRD
LAZYBONE
LAZYBONES
LAZYBOOTS
LAZYLEGS
LAZZARONE
LAZZARONI
LAZZO
LE
LEA
LEACH
LEACHATE
LEACHED
LEACHER
LEACHIER
LEACHIEST
LEACHING
LEACHMAN
LEACHMEN
LEACHY
LEAD
LEADAGE
LEADBACK
LEADED
LEADEN
LEADENLY
LEADENNESS
LEADER
LEADERETTE
LEADERS
LEADERSHIP
LEADHILLITE
LEADIN
LEADING
LEADMAN
LEADOFF
LEADOFFS
LEADOUT
LEADPLANT
LEADS
LEADSMAN
LEADSMEN
LEADWAY
LEADWOOD
LEADWORK
LEADWORT
LEADY
LEAF
LEAFAGE
LEAFBIRD
LEAFBOY
LEAFCUP
LEAFDOM
LEAFED
LEAFEN
LEAFER
LEAFERY
LEAFGIRL
LEAFHOPPER
LEAFIER
LEAFIEST
LEAFINESS
LEAFING
LEAFIT
LEAFLESS
LEAFLET
LEAFLETEER
LEAFLIKE
LEAFMOLD
LEAFSTALK
LEAFWOOD
LEAFWORK
LEAFWORM
LEAFY
LEAG
LEAGUE
LEAGUED
LEAGUER
LEAGUERER
LEAGUING
LEAK
LEAKAGE
LEAKANCE
LEAKED
LEAKER
LEAKIER
LEAKIEST
LEAKINESS
LEAKING
LEAKY
LEAL
LEALAND
LEALLY
LEALNESS
LEALTY
LEAM
LEAMER
LEAN
LEANED
LEANER
LEANING
LEANLY
LEANNESS
LEANT
LEANY
LEAP
LEAPED
LEAPER
LEAPFROG
LEAPFROGGER
LEAPFROGGING
LEAPING
LEAPINGLY
LEAPS
LEAPT
LEAR
LEARN
LEARNED
LEARNEDLY
LEARNEDNESS
LEARNER
LEARNING
LEARNT
LEARY
LEASE
LEASEBACK
LEASED
LEASEHOLD
LEASEHOLDER
LEASEHOLDING
LEASEMONGER
LEASER
LEASH
LEASING
LEASOW
LEAST
LEASTWAYS
LEASTWISE
LEAT
LEATH
LEATHER
LEATHERBACK
LEATHERBARK
LEATHERBOARD
LEATHERCOAT
LEATHERER
LEATHERETTE
LEATHERFISH
LEATHERFISHES
LEATHERFLOWER
LEATHERHEAD
LEATHERINE
LEATHERINESS
LEATHERING
LEATHERIZE
LEATHERJACKET
LEATHERLEAF
LEATHERN
LEATHERNECK
LEATHEROID
LEATHERS
LEATHERSIDE
LEATHERWARE
LEATHERWING
LEATHERWOOD
LEATHERWORK
LEATHERWORKER
LEATHERWORKING
LEATHERY
LEATHWAKE
LEATMAN
LEATMEN
LEAVE
LEAVED
LEAVELESS
LEAVELOOKER
LEAVEN
LEAVENED
LEAVENING
LEAVENOUS
LEAVER
LEAVES
LEAVIER
LEAVIEST
LEAVING

LEAVINGS
LEAVY
LEAWILL
LEAZE
LEBAN
LEBBAN
LEBBEK
LEBEN
LEBHAFT
LEBO
LEBRANCHO
LEBU
LECAMA
LECANIID
LECANINE
LECANOMANCER
LECANOMANCY
LECANOMANTIC
LECANORINE
LECANOROID
LECANOSCOPIC
LECANOSCOPY
LECCE
LECH
LECHER
LECHERER
LECHERIES
LECHEROUS
LECHEROUSLY
LECHEROUSNESS
LECHERY
LECHOSA
LECHRIODONT
LECHUGUILLA
LECHWE
LECIDEIFORM
LECIDEINE
LECIDIOID
LECITHAL
LECITHALITY
LECITHIN
LECITHOBLAST
LECK
LECKER
LECONTITE
LECOTROPAL
LECTERN
LECTION
LECTIONARIES
LECTIONARY
LECTOR
LECTORATE
LECTORIAL
LECTOTYPE
LECTRESS
LECTRICE
LECTUAL
LECTUARY
LECTURE
LECTURED
LECTURER
LECTURESHIP
LECTURETTE
LECTURING
LECYTH
LECYTHI
LECYTHID
LECYTHOI
LECYTHOID
LECYTHUS
LED
LEDE
LEDEN
LEDERHOSEN
LEDERITE
LEDGE
LEDGED
LEDGEMAN
LEDGEMENT
LEDGER
LEDGERED
LEDGERING
LEDGES
LEDGIER
LEDGIEST
LEDGING
LEDGMENT
LEDGY
LEDOL
LEE
LEEANGLE
LEEBOARD
LEECH
LEECHCRAFT
LEECHDOM
LEECHEATER
LEECHED
LEECHER
LEECHERY
LEECHES
LEECHING
LEECHMAN
LEECHWORT
LEED
LEEFANG
LEEFANGE
LEEFTAIL
LEEFUL
LEEFULLY
LEEFULNESS
LEEGTE
LEEK
LEEKY
LEELANE
LEELANG
LEEM
LEEN
LEEP
LEEPIT
LEER
LEERED
LEERFISH
LEERIER
LEERIEST
LEERING
LEERISH
LEERNESS
LEERY
LEES
LEESE
LEESER
LEESING
LEESOME
LEESOMELY
LEET
LEETLE
LEETMAN
LEETMEN
LEEVE
LEEWAN
LEEWARD
LEEWARDLY
LEEWARDMOST
LEEWAY
LEEWILL
LEFSE
LEFSEL
LEFSEN
LEFT
LEFTISM
LEFTIST
LEFTMENTS
LEFTOVER
LEFTWARD
LEFTWARDLY
LEFTWARDS
LEFTY
LEG
LEGACIES
LEGACY
LEGAL
LEGALESE
LEGALISE
LEGALISM
LEGALIST
LEGALISTIC
LEGALISTICALLY
LEGALITIES
LEGALITY
LEGALIZATION
LEGALIZE
LEGALIZED
LEGALIZING
LEGALLY
LEGANTINE
LEGATARY
LEGATE
LEGATEE
LEGATESHIP
LEGATI
LEGATINE
LEGATION
LEGATIONARY
LEGATIVE
LEGATO
LEGATOR
LEGATORIAL
LEGATOS
LEGATUS
LEGBAR
LEGEND
LEGENDA
LEGENDARIAN
LEGENDARY
LEGENDIC
LEGENDRY
LEGENDS
LEGER
LEGERDEMAIN
LEGERDEMAINIST
LEGERETE
LEGERITY
LEGES
LEGGE
LEGGED
LEGGER
LEGGIER
LEGGIERO
LEGGIEST
LEGGINESS
LEGGING
LEGGINGED
LEGGINGS
LEGGY
LEGHORN
LEGIBILITY
LEGIBLE
LEGIBLENESS
LEGIBLY
LEGIFER
LEGIFIC
LEGION
LEGIONARIES
LEGIONARY
LEGIONED
LEGIONER
LEGIONNAIRE
LEGIONRY
LEGISLATE
LEGISLATED
LEGISLATING
LEGISLATION
LEGISLATIONAL
LEGISLATIVE
LEGISLATIVELY
LEGISLATOR
LEGISLATORIAL
LEGISLATRESS
LEGISLATRIX
LEGISLATURE
LEGIST
LEGISTER
LEGIT
LEGITIM
LEGITIMACY
LEGITIMATE
LEGITIMATED
LEGITIMATELY
LEGITIMATENESS
LEGITIMATING
LEGITIMATION
LEGITIMATIST
LEGITIMATIZE
LEGITIMATIZED
LEGITIMATIZING
LEGITIME
LEGITIMISM
LEGITIMIST
LEGITIMISTIC
LEGITIMITY
LEGITIMIZATION
LEGITIMIZE
LEGITIMIZED
LEGITIMIZING
LEGLEN
LEGLESS
LEGLET
LEGMAN
LEGOA
LEGONG
LEGPIECE
LEGPULL
LEGPULLER
LEGPULLING
LEGROOM
LEGS
LEGUA
LEGUAN
LEGULEIAN
LEGULEIOUS
LEGUME
LEGUMELIN
LEGUMEN
LEGUMIN
LEGUMINIFORM
LEGUMINOSE
LEGUMINOUS
LEGWORK
LEHAYIM
LEHIITE
LEHR
LEHRBACHITE
LEHRMAN
LEHRMEN
LEHRSMAN
LEHRSMEN
LEHUA
LEI
LEIE
LEIF
LEIFITE
LEIGHTON
LEIMTYPE
LEIOCOME
LEIOMYOMA
LEIOMYOMATA
LEIOTRICHINE
LEIOTRICHOUS
LEIOTRICHY
LEIOTROPIC
LEIR
LEIS
LEISHMANIA
LEISHMANIASIS
LEISS
LEISTER
LEISTERER
LEISURABLE
LEISURABLY
LEISURE
LEISURED
LEISURELINESS
LEISURELY
LEITMOTIF
LEITMOTIV
LEK
LEKACH
LEKANAI
LEKANE
LEKIN
LEKYTHOS
LELWEL
LEMAN
LEMANRY
LEMANS
LEMEL
LEMMA
LEMMAS
LEMMATA
LEMMING
LEMMINGS
LEMMOBLASTIC
LEMMOCYTE
LEMMON
LEMNACEOUS
LEMNAD
LEMNISCATA
LEMNISCATE
LEMNISCATIC
LEMNISCI
LEMNISCUS
LEMOGRAPHY
LEMOLOGY
LEMON
LEMONADE
LEMONADO
LEMONGRASS
LEMONWEED
LEMONWOOD
LEMONY
LEMPIRA
LEMUR
LEMURES
LEMURIFORM
LEMURINE
LEMUROID
LEMURS
LENA
LENAD
LENARD
LENCH
LENCHEON
LEND
LENDE
LENDER
LENDING
LENE
LENES
LENG
LENGTH
LENGTHEN
LENGTHENED
LENGTHENING
LENGTHER
LENGTHIER

LENGTHIEST
LENGTHILY
LENGTHINESS
LENGTHS
LENGTHSMAN
LENGTHSMEN
LENGTHWAYS
LENGTHWISE
LENGTHY
LENIATE
LENIENCE
LENIENCY
LENIENT
LENIENTLY
LENIFY
LENIS
LENITIC
LENITIES
LENITION
LENITIVE
LENITIVELY
LENITIVENESS
LENITUDE
LENITY
LENNILITE
LENNOACEOUS
LENNOW
LENO
LENOS
LENS
LENSED
LENSES
LENSLESS
LENSMAN
LENT
LENTAMENTE
LENTANDO
LENTEN
LENTICEL
LENTICELLATE
LENTICLE
LENTICONUS
LENTICULA
LENTICULAE
LENTICULAR
LENTICULARE
LENTICULARIS
LENTICULARLY
LENTICULAS
LENTICULATE
LENTICULE
LENTIFORM
LENTIGEROUS
LENTIGINES
LENTIGINOSE
LENTIGINOUS
LENTIGO
LENTIL
LENTILE
LENTINER
LENTISCINE
LENTISCUS
LENTISSIMO
LENTITUDE
LENTNER
LENTO
LENTOID
LENTOR
LENTOUS
LENVOY
LEODICID
LEONCITO
LEONHARDITE
LEONINE
LEONINELY
LEONINES
LEONITE
LEONTIASIS
LEOPARD
LEOPARDE
LEOPARDESS
LEOPARDITE
LEOTARD
LEOTARDS
LEP
LEPADID
LEPADOID
LEPER
LEPERED
LEPERO
LEPID
LEPIDIN
LEPIDINE
LEPIDITY
LEPIDLY
LEPIDOBLASTIC
LEPIDOID
LEPIDOLITE
LEPIDOMELANE
LEPIDOPHYTE
LEPIDOPHYTIC
LEPIDOPTER
LEPIDOPTERA
LEPIDOPTERAL
LEPIDOPTERAN
LEPIDOPTERID
LEPIDOPTERIST
LEPIDOPTERON
LEPIDOPTEROUS
LEPIDOSIREN
LEPIDOSIS
LEPIDOSTEOID
LEPIDOTE
LEPOCYTA
LEPOCYTE
LEPORID
LEPORIDE
LEPORIFORM
LEPORINE
LEPOTHRIX
LEPPER
LEPPY
LEPRA
LEPRECHAUN
LEPRIC
LEPRID
LEPROID
LEPROLOGIC
LEPROLOGIST
LEPROLOGY
LEPROMA
LEPROMATOUS
LEPROSARIA
LEPROSARIUM
LEPROSARIUMS
LEPROSE
LEPROSED
LEPROSERIES
LEPROSERY
LEPROSIED
LEPROSIS
LEPROSITY
LEPROSY
LEPROUS
LEPROUSLY
LEPROUSNESS
LEPRY
LEPTA
LEPTANDRIN
LEPTENE
LEPTID
LEPTINOLITE
LEPTITE
LEPTOBOS
LEPTOCARDIAN
LEPTOCENTRIC
LEPTOCERCAL
LEPTOCHROA
LEPTOCHROUS
LEPTOCLASE
LEPTODACTYL
LEPTODERMOUS
LEPTOFORM
LEPTOLOGY
LEPTOMATIC
LEPTOME
LEPTOMEDUSAN
LEPTOMETER
LEPTOMONAD
LEPTON
LEPTONEMA
LEPTONS
LEPTOPELLIC
LEPTOPROSOPE
LEPTOPROSOPY
LEPTORRHIN
LEPTORRHINE
LEPTOSOME
LEPTOSPERM
LEPTOSPIROSIS
LEPTOSTRACAN
LEPTOTENE
LEPTUS
LEPTYNITE
LERE
LERED
LERER
LERNAEAN
LEROT
LERP
LERRET
LES
LESBIAN
LESBIANISM
LESCHE
LESE
LESED
LESHEY
LESHY
LESION
LESIY
LESKEACEOUS
LESS
LESSE
LESSEE
LESSEN
LESSENED
LESSENER
LESSENING
LESSER
LESSES
LESSEST
LESSIVE
LESSNESS
LESSON
LESSONED
LESSONING
LESSOR
LEST
LESTIWARITE
LESTOBIOSIS
LESTOBIOTIC
LESTRAD
LET
LETCH
LETCHY
LETDOWN
LETGAME
LETHAL
LETHALITY
LETHARGIC
LETHARGICAL
LETHARGICALLY
LETHARGIZE
LETHARGIZED
LETHARGIZING
LETHARGUS
LETHARGY
LETHIED
LETHIFEROUS
LETHOLOGICA
LETOFF
LETON
LETTED
LETTEN
LETTER
LETTERED
LETTERER
LETTERET
LETTERGAE
LETTERGRAM
LETTERHEAD
LETTERING
LETTERLEAF
LETTERMAN
LETTERMEN
LETTERPRESS
LETTERS
LETTERSPACE
LETTERWEIGHT
LETTICE
LETTIGA
LETTING
LETTRURE
LETTUCE
LETUP
LEU
LEUCAETHIOP
LEUCAETHIOPES
LEUCAETHIOPIC
LEUCANILINE
LEUCANTHOUS
LEUCAUGITE
LEUCAURIN
LEUCIN
LEUCINE
LEUCITE
LEUCITIC
LEUCITIS
LEUCITITE
LEUCITOID
LEUCITOPHYRE
LEUCO
LEUCOBASALT
LEUCOBLAST
LEUCOBLASTIC
LEUCOCARPOUS
LEUCOCHOLIC
LEUCOCHOLY
LEUCOCHROIC
LEUCOCIDIC
LEUCOCIDIN
LEUCOCRATE
LEUCOCRATIC
LEUCOCYAN
LEUCOCYTE
LEUCOCYTIC
LEUCOCYTOID
LEUCOCYTOSIS
LEUCOCYTOTIC
LEUCODERMA
LEUCODERMIA
LEUCODERMIC
LEUCOGENIC
LEUCOID
LEUCOMA
LEUCOMAINE
LEUCOMATOUS
LEUCOMELANIC
LEUCON
LEUCONES
LEUCOPENIA
LEUCOPENIC
LEUCOPHANE
LEUCOPHANITE
LEUCOPHORE
LEUCOPHYRE
LEUCOPLAKIA
LEUCOPLAKIAL
LEUCOPLAST
LEUCOPLASTID
LEUCOPOIESIS
LEUCOPYRITE
LEUCORRHEA
LEUCORRHEAL
LEUCORRHOEA
LEUCORRHOEAL
LEUCORYX
LEUCOSPHERE
LEUCOSPHERIC
LEUCOSTASIS
LEUCOSYENITE
LEUCOTOME
LEUCOTOXIC
LEUCOUS
LEUCOXENE
LEUCYL
LEUD
LEUDES
LEUDS
LEUGH
LEUKAEMIA
LEUKAEMIC
LEUKEMIA
LEUKEMIC
LEUKEMID
LEUKOCIDIC
LEUKOCIDIN
LEUKOCYTE
LEUKOCYTOSIS
LEUKOCYTOTIC
LEUKODERMA
LEUKODERMIC
LEUKOMA
LEUKOPENIA
LEUKOPENIC
LEUKORRHEA
LEUKOSIS
LEUMA
LEV
LEVA
LEVADE
LEVAN
LEVANCE
LEVANCY
LEVANT
LEVANTER
LEVANTINE
LEVATION
LEVATOR
LEVATORES
LEVATORS
LEVE
LEVEE
LEVEED
LEVEEING
LEVEL
LEVELED
LEVELER
LEVELHEADED
LEVELHEADEDLY
LEVELHEADEDNESS
LEVELING
LEVELISM
LEVELLED

LEVELLER
LEVELLING
LEVELLY
LEVELMAN
LEVELNESS
LEVER
LEVERAGE
LEVERED
LEVERER
LEVERET
LEVERING
LEVERMAN
LEVERS
LEVESEL
LEVET
LEVIABLE
LEVIATHAN
LEVIED
LEVIER
LEVIES
LEVIGABLE
LEVIGATE
LEVIGATION
LEVIGATOR
LEVIN
LEVINING
LEVIR
LEVIRATE
LEVIRATIC
LEVIRATICAL
LEVIRATION
LEVITANT
LEVITATE
LEVITATED
LEVITATING
LEVITATION
LEVITATIONAL
LEVITATIVE
LEVITATOR
LEVITIES
LEVITY
LEVODUCTION
LEVOGYRATE
LEVOGYRE
LEVOROTATION
LEVOROTATORY
LEVOVERSION
LEVULIN
LEVULINIC
LEVULOSE
LEVULOSURIA
LEVY
LEVYING
LEVYIST
LEVYNE
LEVYNITE
LEW
LEWAN
LEWD
LEWDER
LEWDEST
LEWDLY
LEWDNESS
LEWIS
LEWISITE
LEWISSON
LEWTH
LEWTY
LEX
LEXIA
LEXIC
LEXICAL
LEXICALIC
LEXICALITY
LEXICOGRAPHY
LEXICOLOGIC
LEXICOLOGICAL
LEXICOLOGIST
LEXICOLOGY
LEXICON
LEXICONIST
LEXICONIZE
LEXIGRAPHIC
LEXIGRAPHICAL
LEXIGRAPHY
LEXIPHANIC
LEY
LEYE
LEYLAND
LEYSING
LEZA
LHERZITE
LI
LIABILITIES
LIABILITY
LIABLE
LIABLENESS
LIAISON
LIAMBA
LIANA
LIANE
LIANG
LIANGLE
LIAR
LIARD
LIB
LIBAMENT
LIBANIFEROUS
LIBANT
LIBATE
LIBATED
LIBATING
LIBATION
LIBATIONARY
LIBATIONER
LIBATORY
LIBBARD
LIBBER
LIBBET
LIBBRA
LIBECCIO
LIBEL
LIBELANT
LIBELED
LIBELEE
LIBELER
LIBELING
LIBELIST
LIBELLANT
LIBELLARY
LIBELLATE
LIBELLED
LIBELLEE
LIBELLER
LIBELLING
LIBELLIST
LIBELLOUS
LIBELLOUSLY
LIBELLULID
LIBELLULOID
LIBELOUS
LIBELOUSLY
LIBER
LIBERAL
LIBERALISM
LIBERALIST
LIBERALISTIC
LIBERALITES
LIBERALITY
LIBERALIZATION
LIBERALIZE
LIBERALIZED
LIBERALIZER
LIBERALIZING
LIBERALLY
LIBERALNESS
LIBERATE
LIBERATED
LIBERATING
LIBERATION
LIBERATIONISM
LIBERATIONIST
LIBERATIVE
LIBERATOR
LIBERATORY
LIBERATRESS
LIBERATRICE
LIBERATRIX
LIBEROMOTOR
LIBERTARIAN
LIBERTARIANISM
LIBERTICIDAL
LIBERTICIDE
LIBERTIES
LIBERTINAGE
LIBERTINE
LIBERTINISM
LIBERTY
LIBETHENITE
LIBIDIBI
LIBIDINAL
LIBIDINALLY
LIBIDINOSITY
LIBIDINOUS
LIBIDINOUSLY
LIBIDINOUSNESS
LIBIDO
LIBKEN
LIBKIN
LIBRA
LIBRAE
LIBRAL
LIBRARIAN
LIBRARIANESS
LIBRARIANSHIP
LIBRARIES
LIBRARII
LIBRARIOUS
LIBRARIUS
LIBRARY
LIBRAS
LIBRATE
LIBRATED
LIBRATING
LIBRATION
LIBRATORY
LIBRETTI
LIBRETTIST
LIBRETTO
LIBRETTOS
LIBRIFORM
LIBROPLAST
LICAREOL
LICCA
LICE
LICENCE
LICENCED
LICENCEE
LICENCER
LICENSABLE
LICENSE
LICENSED
LICENSEE
LICENSER
LICENSING
LICENSOR
LICENSURE
LICENTIATE
LICENTIATION
LICENTIOUS
LICENTIOUSLY
LICENTIOUSNESS
LICET
LICH
LICHAM
LICHANOS
LICHEE
LICHEN
LICHENACEOUS
LICHENED
LICHENIAN
LICHENIASIS
LICHENIC
LICHENIFORM
LICHENIN
LICHENISM
LICHENIST
LICHENIZATION
LICHENIZE
LICHENOID
LICHENOLOGY
LICHENOSE
LICHENOUS
LICHENS
LICHI
LICHT
LICHWAKE
LICIT
LICITATION
LICITLY
LICITNESS
LICK
LICKED
LICKER
LICKERISH
LICKERISHLY
LICKERISHNESS
LICKING
LICKPENNY
LICKSPIT
LICKSPITTLE
LICORICE
LICORN
LICORNE
LICTOR
LICTORIAN
LICURI
LICURY
LID
LIDDED
LIDDER
LIDDERON
LIDFLOWER
LIDGATE
LIDLESS
LIE
LIEBENERITE
LIEBIGITE
LIEBLICH
LIED
LIEDER
LIEDERKRANZ
LIEF
LIEFER
LIEFEST
LIEFLY
LIEFSOME
LIEGE
LIEGEFUL
LIEGEFULLY
LIEGELESS
LIEGELY
LIEGEMAN
LIEGEMEN
LIEGER
LIEGEWOMAN
LIEN
LIENAL
LIENCULI
LIENCULUS
LIENEE
LIENIC
LIENITIS
LIENOCELE
LIENOGASTRIC
LIENOR
LIENORENAL
LIENOTOXIN
LIENTERIC
LIENTERY
LIEPOT
LIER
LIERNE
LIERRE
LIES
LIESPFUND
LIEU
LIEUE
LIEUTENANCY
LIEUTENANT
LIEVE
LIEVER
LIEVEST
LIEVRITE
LIFE
LIFEBLOOD
LIFEBOAT
LIFEBOATMAN
LIFEBOATMEN
LIFEDAY
LIFEDROP
LIFEFUL
LIFEFULLY
LIFEFULNESS
LIFEGUARD
LIFEHOLD
LIFEHOLDER
LIFEHOOD
LIFELEAF
LIFELESS
LIFELESSLY
LIFELESSNESS
LIFELET
LIFELIKE
LIFELIKENESS
LIFELINE
LIFELONG
LIFER
LIFERENT
LIFERENTED
LIFERENTER
LIFERENTING
LIFERENTRIX
LIFEROOT
LIFESAVER
LIFESAVING
LIFESOME
LIFESOMELY
LIFESOMENESS
LIFESPRING
LIFETIME
LIFEWAY
LIFEWORK
LIFEY
LIFT
LIFTED
LIFTER
LIFTING
LIFTMAN
LIFTMEN
LIFTOFF
LIG
LIGABLE
LIGAMENT
LIGAMENTA

LIGAMENTAL
LIGAMENTARY
LIGAMENTOUS
LIGAMENTOUSLY
LIGAMENTS
LIGAMENTUM
LIGAN
LIGAND
LIGAS
LIGATE
LIGATED
LIGATING
LIGATION
LIGATIVE
LIGATOR
LIGATORY
LIGATURE
LIGATURED
LIGATURING
LIGE
LIGEANCE
LIGER
LIGG
LIGGAT
LIGGER
LIGHT
LIGHTBOAT
LIGHTED
LIGHTEN
LIGHTENED
LIGHTENER
LIGHTENING
LIGHTER
LIGHTERAGE
LIGHTERMAN
LIGHTERMEN
LIGHTEST
LIGHTFACE
LIGHTFOOT
LIGHTFUL
LIGHTHEADED
LIGHTHEADEDLY
LIGHTHEADEDNESS
LIGHTHEARTEDLY
LIGHTHEARTEDNESS
LIGHTHOUSE
LIGHTHOUSES
LIGHTING
LIGHTISH
LIGHTKEEPER
LIGHTLESS
LIGHTLY
LIGHTMAN
LIGHTMANSHIP
LIGHTMEN
LIGHTMOUTHED
LIGHTNESS
LIGHTNING
LIGHTPROOF
LIGHTROOM
LIGHTS
LIGHTSCOT
LIGHTSHIP
LIGHTSMAN
LIGHTSMEN
LIGHTSOME
LIGHTSOMELY
LIGHTSOMENESS
LIGHTWEIGHT
LIGHTWOOD
LIGNALOES
LIGNE
LIGNEOUS
LIGNESCENT
LIGNICOLE
LIGNICOLINE
LIGNICOLOUS
LIGNIFEROUS
LIGNIFICATION
LIGNIFIED
LIGNIFORM
LIGNIFY
LIGNIFYING
LIGNIN
LIGNIPERDOUS
LIGNITE
LIGNITIC
LIGNITIZE
LIGNIVOROUS
LIGNOCERIC
LIGNOGRAPHY
LIGNONE
LIGNOSE
LIGNOSITY
LIGNOUS
LIGNUM
LIGROIN
LIGROINE
LIGULA
LIGULAE
LIGULAR
LIGULAS
LIGULATE
LIGULE
LIGULIFORM
LIGULIN
LIGULOID
LIGURE
LIGURITE
LIGURITION
LIGURRITION
LIIN
LIJA
LIKABILITY
LIKABLE
LIKABLENESS
LIKE
LIKEABILITY
LIKEABLE
LIKEABLENESS
LIKED
LIKEFUL
LIKELIER
LIKELIEST
LIKELIHEAD
LIKELIHOOD
LIKELY
LIKEN
LIKENED
LIKENESS
LIKENING
LIKER
LIKEROUS
LIKES
LIKESOME
LIKEST
LIKEWAYS
LIKEWISE
LIKEWISELY
LIKEWISENESS
LIKIN
LIKING
LIKINGLY
LIKNA
LIKNON
LIL
LILAC
LILACEOUS
LILACIN
LILACKY
LILACTHROAT
LILACTIDE
LILAS
LILBURNE
LILE
LILES
LILIACEOUS
LILIAL
LILIATED
LILIED
LILIES
LILIFORM
LILIUM
LILL
LILLIANITE
LILLIBULLERO
LILT
LILTED
LILTING
LILY
LILYFY
LILYWORT
LIM
LIMA
LIMACEL
LIMACELLE
LIMACEOUS
LIMACIFORM
LIMACINE
LIMACINID
LIMACOID
LIMACON
LIMAIL
LIMAILLE
LIMAN
LIMATION
LIMB
LIMBA
LIMBATE
LIMBATION
LIMBEC
LIMBECK
LIMBED
LIMBER
LIMBERED
LIMBERER
LIMBEREST
LIMBERHAM
LIMBERING
LIMBERLY
LIMBERNESS
LIMBERS
LIMBIC
LIMBIFEROUS
LIMBING
LIMBMEAL
LIMBO
LIMBOS
LIMBOUS
LIMBURGER
LIMBURGITE
LIMBUS
LIMBY
LIME
LIMEADE
LIMEBERRIES
LIMEBERRY
LIMEBUSH
LIMED
LIMEHOUSE
LIMEKILN
LIMELIGHT
LIMELIGHTER
LIMEMAN
LIMEN
LIMENS
LIMEQUAT
LIMER
LIMERICK
LIMES
LIMESTONE
LIMETTIN
LIMEWASH
LIMEWATER
LIMEWORT
LIMEY
LIMEYS
LIMICOLINE
LIMICOLOUS
LIMIER
LIMIEST
LIMINA
LIMINAL
LIMINARY
LIMING
LIMIT
LIMITABLE
LIMITAL
LIMITARIAN
LIMITARIES
LIMITARY
LIMITATE
LIMITATION
LIMITATIVE
LIMITATIVELY
LIMITED
LIMITEDLY
LIMITEDNESS
LIMITER
LIMITES
LIMITING
LIMITIVE
LIMITLESS
LIMITLESSLY
LIMITLESSNESS
LIMITROPHE
LIMITS
LIMITY
LIMIVOROUS
LIMMA
LIMMATA
LIMMER
LIMMOCK
LIMMU
LIMN
LIMNAL
LIMNANTH
LIMNED
LIMNER
LIMNERY
LIMNETIC
LIMNIAD
LIMNIMETER
LIMNIMETRIC
LIMNING
LIMNITE
LIMNOBIOLOGY
LIMNOBIOS
LIMNOGRAPH
LIMNOLOGIC
LIMNOLOGICAL
LIMNOLOGIST
LIMNOLOGY
LIMNOMETER
LIMNOPHIL
LIMNOPHILE
LIMNOPHILID
LIMNOPHILOUS
LIMNORIOID
LIMON
LIMONCILLO
LIMONCITO
LIMONENE
LIMONIAD
LIMONIN
LIMONITE
LIMONITIC
LIMONIUM
LIMOSE
LIMOUS
LIMOUSINE
LIMP
LIMPA
LIMPED
LIMPER
LIMPEST
LIMPET
LIMPHAULT
LIMPID
LIMPIDITY
LIMPIDLY
LIMPIDNESS
LIMPIN
LIMPING
LIMPINGLY
LIMPINGNESS
LIMPKIN
LIMPLY
LIMPNESS
LIMPSY
LIMPY
LIMSY
LIMU
LIMULID
LIMULOID
LIMULUS
LIMURITE
LIMY
LIN
LINA
LINABLE
LINACEOUS
LINAGA
LINAGE
LINALOA
LINALOE
LINALOOL
LINALYL
LINAMARIN
LINARITE
LINCH
LINCHBOLT
LINCHET
LINCHPIN
LINCHPINNED
LINCLOTH
LINCTUS
LIND
LINDACKERITE
LINDANE
LINDEN
LINDER
LINDO
LINDOITE
LINDWORM
LINE
LINEA
LINEABLE
LINEAGE
LINEAGED
LINEAL
LINEALITY
LINEALLY
LINEAMENT
LINEAMENTAL
LINEAMETER
LINEAR
LINEARITY
LINEARIZATION
LINEARIZE
LINEARLY
LINEARY
LINEAS
LINEATE
LINEATED

LINEATION
LINEATURE
LINEBACKER
LINEBACKING
LINECUT
LINED
LINEIFORM
LINELESS
LINELET
LINEMAN
LINEMEN
LINEN
LINENER
LINENETTE
LINENIZE
LINENIZER
LINENMAN
LINENS
LINEOGRAPH
LINEOLATE
LINEOLATED
LINER
LINES
LINESIDES
LINESMAN
LINESMEN
LINEUP
LINEWALKER
LINEWORK
LINEY
LING
LINGA
LINGAM
LINGBERRIES
LINGBERRY
LINGBIRD
LINGCOD
LINGE
LINGEL
LINGENBERRY
LINGER
LINGERED
LINGERER
LINGERIE
LINGERING
LINGERINGLY
LINGET
LINGLE
LINGO
LINGOE
LINGOES
LINGONBERRIES
LINGONBERRY
LINGOT
LINGS
LINGSTER
LINGTOW
LINGTOWMAN
LINGUA
LINGUACIOUS
LINGUADENTAL
LINGUAE
LINGUAL
LINGUALE
LINGUALIS
LINGUALITY
LINGUALIZE
LINGUANASAL
LINGUATULOID
LINGUET
LINGUIDENTAL
LINGUIFORM
LINGUISHED
LINGUIST
LINGUISTER
LINGUISTIC
LINGUISTICAL
LINGUISTICALLY
LINGUISTICIAN
LINGUISTICS
LINGUISTRY
LINGULA
LINGULAE
LINGULATE
LINGULATED
LINGULID
LINGULIFORM
LINGULOID
LINGUODENTAL
LINGUODISTAL
LINGWORT
LINGY
LINHA
LINHAY
LINIE
LINIER
LINIEST
LINIMENT
LININ
LINING
LININGS
LINITIS
LINIYA
LINJA
LINJE
LINK
LINKAGE
LINKBOY
LINKED
LINKER
LINKIER
LINKIEST
LINKING
LINKMAN
LINKMEN
LINKS
LINKSMITH
LINKSTER
LINKWORK
LINKY
LINN
LINNAEITE
LINNEON
LINNET
LINO
LINOLATE
LINOLEATE
LINOLEIC
LINOLEIN
LINOLENATE
LINOLENIC
LINOLENIN
LINOLEUM
LINOMETER
LINON
LINOTYPE
LINOTYPED
LINOTYPER
LINOTYPING
LINOTYPIST
LINQUISH
LINS
LINSANG
LINSEED
LINSEY
LINSTOCK
LINT
LINTEL
LINTELED
LINTELING
LINTELLED
LINTELLING
LINTEN
LINTER
LINTERN
LINTERS
LINTIE
LINTIER
LINTIEST
LINTONITE
LINTSEED
LINTWHITE
LINTY
LINWOOD
LINY
LIODERMIA
LIOMYOMA
LION
LIONCEL
LIONESS
LIONET
LIONHEART
LIONHEARTED
LIONHEARTEDNESS
LIONISM
LIONIZABLE
LIONIZATION
LIONIZE
LIONIZED
LIONIZER
LIONIZING
LIONLIKE
LIONLY
LIONS
LIOS
LIP
LIPA
LIPARIAN
LIPAROCELE
LIPAROID
LIPAROUS
LIPASE
LIPE
LIPID
LIPIDE
LIPIN
LIPOBLAST
LIPOBLASTOMA
LIPOCELE
LIPOCERATOUS
LIPOCERE
LIPOCHROME
LIPOCLASIS
LIPOCLASTIC
LIPOCYTE
LIPOFEROUS
LIPOFIBROMA
LIPOGENESIS
LIPOGENETIC
LIPOGENIC
LIPOGENOUS
LIPOGRAM
LIPOGRAPHY
LIPOHEMIA
LIPOID
LIPOIDAEMIA
LIPOIDAL
LIPOIDEMIA
LIPOIDIC
LIPOLYSIS
LIPOLYTIC
LIPOMA
LIPOMAS
LIPOMATA
LIPOMATOSIS
LIPOMATOUS
LIPOMYOMA
LIPOMYXOMA
LIPOPEXIA
LIPOPHAGIC
LIPOPHORE
LIPOPOD
LIPOPROTEIN
LIPOSARCOMA
LIPOSIS
LIPOSOME
LIPOSTOMY
LIPOTHYMIA
LIPOTHYMIAL
LIPOTHYMIC
LIPOTHYMY
LIPOTROPHIC
LIPOTROPHY
LIPOTROPIC
LIPOTROPY
LIPOTYPE
LIPOVACCINE
LIPOXENOUS
LIPOXENY
LIPPED
LIPPEN
LIPPER
LIPPIE
LIPPIER
LIPPIEST
LIPPINESS
LIPPING
LIPPITUDE
LIPPITUDO
LIPPY
LIPS
LIPSANOTHECA
LIPSTICK
LIPURIA
LIPWORK
LIQUABLE
LIQUAMEN
LIQUATE
LIQUATED
LIQUATING
LIQUATION
LIQUEFACIENT
LIQUEFACTION
LIQUEFACTIVE
LIQUEFIABLE
LIQUEFIED
LIQUEFIER
LIQUEFY
LIQUEFYING
LIQUESCE
LIQUESCENCE
LIQUESCENCY
LIQUESCENT
LIQUET
LIQUEUR
LIQUEURED
LIQUEURING
LIQUID
LIQUIDABLE
LIQUIDAMBAR
LIQUIDAMBER
LIQUIDATE
LIQUIDATED
LIQUIDATING
LIQUIDATION
LIQUIDATOR
LIQUIDITY
LIQUIDIZE
LIQUIDIZED
LIQUIDIZING
LIQUIDLY
LIQUIDNESS
LIQUIDOGENIC
LIQUIDS
LIQUIDUS
LIQUIDY
LIQUIFORM
LIQUIFY
LIQUOR
LIQUORED
LIQUORER
LIQUORICE
LIQUORING
LIQUORISH
LIQUORISHLY
LIQUORISHNESS
LIQUORIST
LIQUORS
LIQUORY
LIRA
LIRAS
LIRATE
LIRATION
LIRE
LIRELLA
LIRELLATE
LIRELLIFORM
LIRELLINE
LIRELLOUS
LIRIODENDRON
LIRIPIPE
LIRIPOOP
LIRK
LIROCONITE
LIRP
LIS
LISERE
LISETTE
LISH
LISI
LISIERE
LISK
LISLE
LISP
LISPED
LISPER
LISPING
LISPOUND
LISPUND
LISS
LISSE
LISSES
LISSOM
LISSOME
LISSOMELY
LISSOMENESS
LISSOTRICHAN
LISSOTRICHY
LIST
LISTABLE
LISTED
LISTEDNESS
LISTEL
LISTEN
LISTENED
LISTENER
LISTENERS
LISTENING
LISTER
LISTERIA
LISTFUL
LISTING
LISTLESS
LISTLESSLY
LISTLESSNESS
LISTRED
LISTS
LISTWORK
LISTY
LIT
LITAI
LITANEUTICAL
LITANIES
LITANY
LITAS

LITATION
LITCH
LITCHI
LITE
LITER
LITERACY
LITERAL
LITERALISM
LITERALIST
LITERALISTIC
LITERALITIES
LITERALITY
LITERALIZATION
LITERALIZE
LITERALIZED
LITERALIZER
LITERALIZING
LITERALLY
LITERALNESS
LITERARIAN
LITERARILY
LITERARINESS
LITERARY
LITERATE
LITERATED
LITERATI
LITERATIM
LITERATION
LITERATIST
LITERATO
LITERATOR
LITERATOS
LITERATURE
LITERATURED
LITERATUS
LITEROSE
LITEROSITY
LITH
LITHAEMIA
LITHAEMIC
LITHAGOGUE
LITHANGIURIA
LITHANTHRAX
LITHARGE
LITHATE
LITHATIC
LITHE
LITHECTASY
LITHECTOMY
LITHELY
LITHEMIA
LITHEMIC
LITHENESS
LITHER
LITHERLY
LITHERNESS
LITHESOME
LITHESOMENESS
LITHEST
LITHI
LITHIA
LITHIASIS
LITHIASTIC
LITHIATE
LITHIC
LITHIFICATION
LITHIFIED
LITHIFY
LITHIFYING
LITHITE
LITHIUM
LITHLESS
LITHO
LITHOBIID
LITHOBIOID
LITHOCENOSIS
LITHOCHROMIC
LITHOCHROMY
LITHOCLASE
LITHOCLAST
LITHOCULTURE
LITHOCYST
LITHODESMA
LITHODID
LITHODOMOUS
LITHOFELLIC
LITHOFELLINIC
LITHOFRACTEUR
LITHOFRACTOR
LITHOGENESIS
LITHOGENESY
LITHOGENETIC
LITHOGENOUS
LITHOGENY
LITHOGLYPH
LITHOGLYPHER
LITHOGLYPHIC
LITHOGLYPTIC
LITHOGLYPTICS
LITHOGRAPH
LITHOGRAPHED
LITHOGRAPHER
LITHOGRAPHIC
LITHOGRAPHING
LITHOGRAPHY
LITHOGRAVURE
LITHOID
LITHOIDAL
LITHOIDITE
LITHOLABE
LITHOLAPAXY
LITHOLATROUS
LITHOLATRY
LITHOLOGIC
LITHOLOGICAL
LITHOLOGIST
LITHOLOGY
LITHOLYSIS
LITHOLYTE
LITHOLYTIC
LITHOMANCY
LITHOMARGE
LITHOMETER
LITHONEPHRIA
LITHONTRIPTIC
LITHOPAEDION
LITHOPAEDIUM
LITHOPEDION
LITHOPEDIUM
LITHOPHAGOUS
LITHOPHANE
LITHOPHANIC
LITHOPHANY
LITHOPHILOUS
LITHOPHONE
LITHOPHYL
LITHOPHYLL
LITHOPHYSA
LITHOPHYSAE
LITHOPHYSAL
LITHOPHYTE
LITHOPHYTIC
LITHOPHYTOUS
LITHOPONE
LITHOSCOPE
LITHOSIAN
LITHOSIID
LITHOSIS
LITHOSPERM
LITHOSPERMON
LITHOSPHERE
LITHOTINT
LITHOTOME
LITHOTOMIC
LITHOTOMICAL
LITHOTOMIES
LITHOTOMIST
LITHOTOMIZE
LITHOTOMOUS
LITHOTOMY
LITHOTONY
LITHOTRESIS
LITHOTRIPSY
LITHOTRITE
LITHOTRITIC
LITHOTRITIES
LITHOTRITIST
LITHOTRITOR
LITHOTRITY
LITHOTYPE
LITHOTYPED
LITHOTYPIC
LITHOTYPING
LITHOTYPY
LITHOUS
LITHOXYL
LITHOXYLE
LITHOXYLITE
LITHSMAN
LITHURESIS
LITHURIA
LITHY
LITI
LITIGABLE
LITIGANT
LITIGATE
LITIGATED
LITIGATING
LITIGATION
LITIGATOR
LITIGATORY
LITIGIOSITY
LITIGIOUS
LITIGIOUSLY
LITIGIOUSNESS
LITISCONTEST
LITMUS
LITORINOID
LITOTES
LITRA
LITRE
LITRO
LITS
LITTEN
LITTER
LITTERATEUR
LITTERATIM
LITTERBUG
LITTERED
LITTERER
LITTERING
LITTERY
LITTLE
LITTLENECK
LITTLENESS
LITTLER
LITTLEST
LITTLEWALE
LITTLIN
LITTLING
LITTORAL
LITTRESS
LITU
LITUATE
LITUI
LITUIFORM
LITUITE
LITUITOID
LITUOLINE
LITUOLOID
LITURATE
LITURGIC
LITURGICAL
LITURGICALLY
LITURGICIAN
LITURGICS
LITURGIES
LITURGIOLOGY
LITURGISM
LITURGIST
LITURGIZE
LITURGY
LITUS
LITUUS
LITZ
LIVABILITY
LIVABLE
LIVABLENESS
LIVE
LIVEABLE
LIVED
LIVEDO
LIVELIER
LIVELIEST
LIVELIHOOD
LIVELINESS
LIVELONG
LIVELY
LIVEN
LIVENER
LIVER
LIVERANCE
LIVERBERRY
LIVERED
LIVERIED
LIVERIES
LIVERING
LIVERISH
LIVERISHNESS
LIVERLEAF
LIVERWORT
LIVERWURST
LIVERY
LIVERYMAN
LIVERYMEN
LIVES
LIVESTOCK
LIVETIN
LIVEYER
LIVID
LIVIDITY
LIVIDLY
LIVIDNESS
LIVIER
LIVING
LIVINGS
LIVISH
LIVISHLY
LIVOR
LIVRE
LIVRES
LIVYER
LIWA
LIWAN
LIXIVIAL
LIXIVIATE
LIXIVIATED
LIXIVIATING
LIXIVIATION
LIXIVIATOR
LIXIVIOUS
LIXIVIUM
LIZA
LIZARD
LIZARDTAIL
LIZARY
LLAMA
LLAMAS
LLANERO
LLANO
LLANOS
LLARETA
LLAUTU
LLYN
LO
LOA
LOACH
LOACHES
LOAD
LOADED
LOADEN
LOADER
LOADING
LOADPENNY
LOADS
LOADSOME
LOADSTAR
LOADSTONE
LOADUM
LOAF
LOAFER
LOAFING
LOAFINGLY
LOAGHTAN
LOAIASIS
LOAM
LOAMIER
LOAMIEST
LOAMILY
LOAMINESS
LOAMING
LOAMY
LOAN
LOANABLE
LOANBLEND
LOANED
LOANER
LOANGE
LOANIN
LOANING
LOANMONGER
LOANSHIFT
LOANWORD
LOASACEOUS
LOATH
LOATHE
LOATHED
LOATHER
LOATHFUL
LOATHFULLY
LOATHFULNESS
LOATHING
LOATHINGLY
LOATHLINESS
LOATHLY
LOATHSOME
LOATHSOMELY
LOATHSOMENESS
LOATHY
LOAVE
LOAVES
LOB
LOBA
LOBAL
LOBAR
LOBATE
LOBATED
LOBATION
LOBBED
LOBBER
LOBBIED
LOBBIES
LOBBING
LOBBISH
LOBBY

LOBBYER
LOBBYGOW
LOBBYING
LOBBYISM
LOBBYIST
LOBBYMAN
LOBBYMEN
LOBCOCK
LOBCOKT
LOBE
LOBECTOMY
LOBED
LOBEFOOT
LOBEFOOTED
LOBEFOOTS
LOBELIA
LOBELIACEOUS
LOBELIN
LOBELINE
LOBELLATED
LOBFIG
LOBI
LOBIFORM
LOBIGEROUS
LOBING
LOBIPED
LOBLOLLIES
LOBLOLLY
LOBO
LOBOLA
LOBOPODIUM
LOBOS
LOBOSE
LOBOTOMIES
LOBOTOMY
LOBSCOURSE
LOBSCOUSE
LOBSCOUSER
LOBSTER
LOBSTERING
LOBSTERPROOF
LOBSTERS
LOBSTICK
LOBTAIL
LOBULAR
LOBULARLY
LOBULATE
LOBULATED
LOBULATION
LOBULE
LOBULETTE
LOBULI
LOBULOSE
LOBULOUS
LOBULUS
LOBUS
LOBWORM
LOCA
LOCABLE
LOCAL
LOCALE
LOCALED
LOCALING
LOCALISM
LOCALIST
LOCALISTIC
LOCALITIES
LOCALITY
LOCALIZABLE
LOCALIZATION
LOCALIZE
LOCALIZED
LOCALIZER
LOCALIZING
LOCALLED
LOCALLING
LOCALLY
LOCALNESS
LOCANDA
LOCATABLE
LOCATE
LOCATED
LOCATER
LOCATING
LOCATIO
LOCATION
LOCATIONAL
LOCATIONS
LOCATIVE
LOCATOR
LOCELLATE
LOCELLUS
LOCH
LOCHAGUS
LOCHAN
LOCHE
LOCHETIC
LOCHI
LOCHIA
LOCHIAL
LOCHIOCOLPOS
LOCHIOCYTE
LOCHIOMETRA
LOCHIOPYRA
LOCHIORRHEA
LOCHOPYRA
LOCHUS
LOCHY
LOCI
LOCK
LOCKABLE
LOCKAGE
LOCKBOX
LOCKED
LOCKER
LOCKERMAN
LOCKERMEN
LOCKET
LOCKFAST
LOCKFUL
LOCKHOLE
LOCKING
LOCKJAW
LOCKLESS
LOCKLET
LOCKMAKER
LOCKMAN
LOCKNUT
LOCKOUT
LOCKPIN
LOCKRAM
LOCKRUM
LOCKSMAN
LOCKSMITH
LOCKSMITHERY
LOCKSMITHING
LOCKSPIT
LOCKUP
LOCKWORK
LOCKY
LOCKYER
LOCO
LOCOED
LOCOFOCO
LOCOFOCOS
LOCOING
LOCOISM
LOCOMOBILE
LOCOMOBILITY
LOCOMOTE
LOCOMOTILITY
LOCOMOTION
LOCOMOTIVE
LOCOMOTIVELY
LOCOMOTIVEMAN
LOCOMOTIVEMEN
LOCOMOTIVITY
LOCOMOTOR
LOCOMOTORY
LOCOMUTATION
LOCOS
LOCOWEED
LOCULAMENT
LOCULAR
LOCULATE
LOCULATED
LOCULATION
LOCULE
LOCULI
LOCULICIDAL
LOCULOSE
LOCULOUS
LOCULUS
LOCUM
LOCUPLETE
LOCUPLETELY
LOCUS
LOCUST
LOCUSTA
LOCUSTBERRY
LOCUSTELLE
LOCUSTID
LOCUSTING
LOCUTION
LOCUTOR
LOCUTORIES
LOCUTORSHIP
LOCUTORY
LOD
LODE
LODEMAN
LODEMANAGE
LODEN
LODESMAN
LODESMEN
LODESTAR
LODESTONE
LODESTUFF
LODGE
LODGED
LODGEMAN
LODGEMENT
LODGEPOLE
LODGER
LODGING
LODGINGHOUSE
LODGMENT
LODICULA
LODICULE
LOESS
LOESSAL
LOESSIAL
LOESSIC
LOESSLAND
LOESSOID
LOF
LOFT
LOFTED
LOFTER
LOFTIER
LOFTIEST
LOFTILY
LOFTINESS
LOFTING
LOFTMAN
LOFTMEN
LOFTSMAN
LOFTSMEN
LOFTY
LOG
LOGAN
LOGANBERRIES
LOGANBERRY
LOGANIACEOUS
LOGANIN
LOGAOEDIC
LOGARITHM
LOGARITHMAL
LOGARITHMIC
LOGARITHMICAL
LOGARITHMICALLY
LOGBOOK
LOGCOCK
LOGE
LOGEIA
LOGEION
LOGGAT
LOGGATS
LOGGED
LOGGER
LOGGERHEAD
LOGGERHEADED
LOGGERHEADS
LOGGET
LOGGIA
LOGGIAS
LOGGIN
LOGGING
LOGGY
LOGHE
LOGHEAD
LOGHEADED
LOGIA
LOGIC
LOGICAL
LOGICALIST
LOGICALITY
LOGICALIZATION
LOGICALIZE
LOGICALLY
LOGICALNESS
LOGICASTER
LOGICIAN
LOGICIANER
LOGICISM
LOGICITY
LOGICIZE
LOGICS
LOGIE
LOGIER
LOGIEST
LOGIN
LOGION
LOGIS
LOGISTIC
LOGISTICAL
LOGISTICIAN
LOGISTICS
LOGJAM
LOGMAN
LOGOCRACY
LOGODAEDALY
LOGOGOGUE
LOGOGRAM
LOGOGRAPH
LOGOGRAPHER
LOGOGRAPHIC
LOGOGRAPHICAL
LOGOGRAPHY
LOGOGRIPH
LOGOGRIPHIC
LOGOLATRY
LOGOLOGY
LOGOMACH
LOGOMACHER
LOGOMACHIC
LOGOMACHICAL
LOGOMACHIES
LOGOMACHIST
LOGOMACHIZE
LOGOMACHY
LOGOMANCY
LOGOMANIAC
LOGOMETER
LOGOMETRIC
LOGOMETRICAL
LOGOPEDIA
LOGOPEDICS
LOGORRHEA
LOGORRHOEA
LOGOS
LOGOTHETE
LOGOTYPE
LOGOTYPY
LOGROLL
LOGROLLER
LOGROLLING
LOGS
LOGWAY
LOGWOOD
LOGWORK
LOGY
LOHAN
LOHOCH
LOHOCK
LOI
LOIMIC
LOIMOGRAPHY
LOIMOLOGY
LOIN
LOINCLOTH
LOINED
LOINS
LOIR
LOITER
LOITERED
LOITERER
LOITERING
LOKA
LOKAO
LOKAPALA
LOKE
LOKELANI
LOKIEC
LOKSHEN
LOLL
LOLLAPALOOSA
LOLLAPALOOZA
LOLLED
LOLLER
LOLLIES
LOLLING
LOLLINGITE
LOLLIPOP
LOLLOP
LOLLOPY
LOLLUP
LOLLY
LOLLYGAG
LOLLYPOP
LOMA
LOMASTOME
LOMATA
LOMATINE
LOMATINOUS
LOMBOY
LOMENT
LOMENTACEOUS
LOMENTUM
LOMILOMI
LOMITA
LOMONITE
LONE
LONEFUL
LONELIER

LONELIEST
LONELIHOOD
LONELILY
LONELINESS
LONELY
LONENESS
LONER
LONESOME
LONESOMELY
LONESOMENESS
LONG
LONGA
LONGACRE
LONGAN
LONGANIMITIES
LONGANIMITY
LONGANIMOUS
LONGBEAK
LONGBEARD
LONGBILL
LONGBOAT
LONGBOW
LONGCLOTH
LONGE
LONGEAR
LONGED
LONGER
LONGERON
LONGEST
LONGEVAL
LONGEVE
LONGEVITY
LONGEVOUS
LONGFIN
LONGFUL
LONGHAIR
LONGHAND
LONGHEAD
LONGHEADED
LONGHEADEDLY
LONGHEADEDNESS
LONGHORN
LONGICAUDAL
LONGICAUDATE
LONGICONE
LONGICORN
LONGILATERAL
LONGILINGUAL
LONGIMANOUS
LONGIMETRIC
LONGIMETRY
LONGING
LONGINGLY
LONGINQUITY
LONGIPENNATE
LONGIPENNINE
LONGIROSTRAL
LONGIROSTRATE
LONGISH
LONGITUDE
LONGITUDINAL
LONGITUDINALLY
LONGJAW
LONGJAWS
LONGLEAF
LONGLEGS
LONGLICK
LONGLINE
LONGLINER
LONGLINERMAN
LONGLINERMEN
LONGNECK
LONGNOSE
LONGPOD
LONGROOT
LONGS
LONGSHANKS
LONGSHORE
LONGSHOREMAN
LONGSHOREMEN
LONGSHUCKS
LONGSOME
LONGSOMELY
LONGSOMENESS
LONGSPUR
LONGTAIL
LONGTIMER
LONGUE
LONGUEUR
LONGULITE
LONGUS
LONGWALL
LONGWAYS
LONGWISE
LONGWOOD
LONGWOOL
LONGWORK
LONGYI
LONQUHARD
LONTAR
LOO
LOOBIES
LOOBILY
LOOBY
LOOCH
LOOD
LOOED
LOOF
LOOFA
LOOFAH
LOOFIE
LOOING
LOOK
LOOKED
LOOKER
LOOKING
LOOKOUT
LOOKOUTS
LOOKUM
LOOL
LOOM
LOOMED
LOOMER
LOOMERY
LOOMFIXER
LOOMING
LOOMS
LOON
LOONERY
LOONEY
LOONIER
LOONIES
LOONIEST
LOONY
LOOP
LOOPED
LOOPER
LOOPFUL
LOOPHOLE
LOOPHOLED
LOOPHOLING
LOOPIER
LOOPIEST
LOOPING
LOOPIST
LOOPS
LOOPY
LOORY
LOOS
LOOSE
LOOSED
LOOSELY
LOOSEN
LOOSENED
LOOSENER
LOOSENESS
LOOSENING
LOOSER
LOOSEST
LOOSESTRIFE
LOOSING
LOOT
LOOTED
LOOTER
LOOTIE
LOOTIEWALLAH
LOOTING
LOOTSMAN
LOOTSMANS
LOP
LOPE
LOPED
LOPER
LOPESKONCE
LOPHEAVY
LOPHIID
LOPHIN
LOPHINE
LOPHIODONT
LOPHOBRANCH
LOPHOCERCAL
LOPHODONT
LOPHOPHORAL
LOPHOPHORE
LOPHOPHORINE
LOPHOSTEA
LOPHOSTEON
LOPHOSTEONS
LOPHOTRIAENE
LOPING
LOPOLITH
LOPPARD
LOPPE
LOPPED
LOPPER
LOPPET
LOPPIER
LOPPIEST
LOPPING
LOPPY
LOPSEED
LOPSIDED
LOPSIDEDLY
LOPSIDEDNESS
LOPSTICK
LOQUACIOUS
LOQUACIOUSLY
LOQUACIOUSNESS
LOQUACITY
LOQUAT
LOQUENCE
LOQUENCY
LOQUENT
LOQUENTLY
LOQUITUR
LOR
LORA
LORAE
LORAL
LORAN
LORANDITE
LORANSKITE
LORARII
LORARIUS
LORATE
LORCHA
LORD
LORDAN
LORDED
LORDING
LORDINGS
LORDLESS
LORDLIER
LORDLIEST
LORDLIKE
LORDLINESS
LORDLING
LORDLY
LORDOLATRY
LORDOMA
LORDOSIS
LORDOTIC
LORDSHIP
LORDSWIKE
LORDWOOD
LORE
LOREAL
LORED
LOREL
LORENZENITE
LORETIN
LORETTOITE
LORGNETTE
LORGNON
LORIC
LORICA
LORICAE
LORICARIAN
LORICARIOID
LORICATE
LORICATED
LORICATING
LORICATION
LORICOID
LORIES
LORIKEET
LORILET
LORIMER
LORINER
LORING
LORIOT
LORIS
LORISES
LORMERY
LORN
LORO
LOROS
LORRE
LORRIES
LORRIKER
LORRY
LORS
LORUM
LORY
LOSABLE
LOSE
LOSEL
LOSELRY
LOSENGER
LOSER
LOSH
LOSING
LOSINGLY
LOSS
LOSSE
LOSSENITE
LOSSER
LOSSFUL
LOST
LOT
LOTA
LOTAH
LOTASE
LOTE
LOTEBUSH
LOTEWOOD
LOTH
LOTHE
LOTIC
LOTIFORM
LOTION
LOTIUM
LOTMENT
LOTONG
LOTOPHAGOUS
LOTOS
LOTRITE
LOTS
LOTTED
LOTTER
LOTTERIES
LOTTERY
LOTTING
LOTTO
LOTUS
LOTUSIN
LOUCH
LOUCHE
LOUCHETTES
LOUD
LOUDEN
LOUDERING
LOUDISH
LOUDLY
LOUDMOUTHED
LOUDNESS
LOUDSPEAKER
LOUEY
LOUGH
LOUGHEEN
LOUIS
LOUISINE
LOUK
LOUKE
LOUKOUM
LOUKOUMI
LOULU
LOUN
LOUND
LOUNDER
LOUNDERER
LOUNGE
LOUNGED
LOUNGER
LOUNGING
LOUNGY
LOUP
LOUPE
LOUR
LOURD
LOURDISH
LOURDY
LOURE
LOURED
LOURIE
LOURING
LOURINGLY
LOURINGNESS
LOURY
LOUSE
LOUSEBERRIES
LOUSEBERRY
LOUSED
LOUSEWORT
LOUSIER
LOUSIEST
LOUSILY
LOUSINESS
LOUSING
LOUSTER
LOUSY
LOUT
LOUTER
LOUTHER
LOUTISH

LOUTISHLY
LOUTISHNESS
LOUTRE
LOUTROPHOROS
LOUTY
LOUVAR
LOUVER
LOUVERED
LOUVERWORK
LOVABILITY
LOVABLE
LOVABLENESS
LOVABLY
LOVAGE
LOVANENTY
LOVAT
LOVE
LOVEABLE
LOVEBIRD
LOVED
LOVEFLOWER
LOVEHOOD
LOVELASS
LOVELESS
LOVELESSLY
LOVELESSNESS
LOVELIER
LOVELIEST
LOVELIHEAD
LOVELILY
LOVELINESS
LOVELING
LOVELOCK
LOVELORN
LOVELORNNESS
LOVELY
LOVEMAKING
LOVEMAN
LOVEMANS
LOVEMATE
LOVEMONGER
LOVER
LOVERED
LOVERING
LOVERLINESS
LOVERLY
LOVESICK
LOVESICKNESS
LOVESOME
LOVESOMELY
LOVESOMENESS
LOVEVINE
LOVING
LOVINGLY
LOVINGNESS
LOW
LOWA
LOWABLE
LOWAN
LOWANCE
LOWBALL
LOWBELL
LOWBORN
LOWBOY
LOWBRED
LOWBROW
LOWBROWISM
LOWDAH
LOWDER
LOWDOWN
LOWE
LOWED
LOWEITE
LOWER
LOWERCLASSMAN
LOWERCLASSMEN
LOWERED
LOWERER
LOWERING
LOWERINGLY
LOWERINGNESS
LOWERMOST
LOWERY
LOWEST
LOWIGITE
LOWING
LOWLAND
LOWLANDER
LOWLIER
LOWLIEST
LOWLIHEAD
LOWLY
LOWMEN
LOWMOST
LOWN
LOWNESS
LOWRIE
LOWRY
LOWSE
LOWSIN
LOWTH
LOWWOOD
LOWY
LOX
LOXIA
LOXOCLASE
LOXOCOSM
LOXODOGRAPH
LOXODONT
LOXODROME
LOXODROMIC
LOXODROMICS
LOXODROMISM
LOXODROMY
LOXOSOMA
LOXOTIC
LOXOTOMY
LOY
LOYAL
LOYALISM
LOYALIST
LOYALLY
LOYALNESS
LOYALTIES
LOYALTY
LOYN
LOZEN
LOZENGE
LOZENGED
LOZENGER
LOZENGY
LUAU
LUBBER
LUBBERCOCK
LUBBERLINESS
LUBBERLY
LUBRA
LUBRIC
LUBRICAL
LUBRICANT
LUBRICATE
LUBRICATED
LUBRICATING
LUBRICATION
LUBRICATIONAL
LUBRICATIVE
LUBRICATOR
LUBRICATORY
LUBRICIOUS
LUBRICITIES
LUBRICITY
LUBRICOUS
LUBRIFY
LUBRITORIAN
LUBRITORIUM
LUBRITORY
LUCANID
LUCARNE
LUCBAN
LUCE
LUCENCE
LUCENCY
LUCENT
LUCENTLY
LUCERN
LUCERNAL
LUCERNE
LUCES
LUCET
LUCIBLE
LUCID
LUCIDA
LUCIDITY
LUCIDLY
LUCIDNESS
LUCIFER
LUCIFERASE
LUCIFERIN
LUCIFEROID
LUCIFEROUS
LUCIFEROUSLY
LUCIFIC
LUCIFORM
LUCIFUGAL
LUCIFUGOUS
LUCIGEN
LUCIMETER
LUCINOID
LUCIVEE
LUCK
LUCKEN
LUCKFUL
LUCKIE
LUCKIER
LUCKIES
LUCKIEST
LUCKILY
LUCKINESS
LUCKLESS
LUCKLESSLY
LUCKLESSNESS
LUCKLY
LUCKY
LUCOMBE
LUCRATION
LUCRATIVE
LUCRATIVELY
LUCRATIVENESS
LUCRE
LUCRIFEROUS
LUCRIFIC
LUCRIFY
LUCROUS
LUCTATION
LUCTIFEROUS
LUCTUAL
LUCUBRATE
LUCUBRATED
LUCUBRATING
LUCUBRATION
LUCUBRATOR
LUCUBRATORY
LUCULE
LUCULENT
LUCULENTLY
LUCULLITE
LUCUMIA
LUCUMONY
LUCY
LUD
LUDDEN
LUDDY
LUDI
LUDIBRIOUS
LUDIBRY
LUDICROSITIES
LUDICROSITY
LUDICROUS
LUDICROUSLY
LUDICROUSNESS
LUDIFICATION
LUDLAMITE
LUDO
LUDWIGITE
LUE
LUES
LUETIC
LUETICALLY
LUFF
LUFFA
LUFFED
LUFFER
LUFFING
LUG
LUGE
LUGER
LUGGAGE
LUGGAR
LUGGARD
LUGGED
LUGGER
LUGGIE
LUGGING
LUGHDOAN
LUGMARK
LUGS
LUGSAIL
LUGSOME
LUGUBRIOSITY
LUGUBRIOUS
LUGUBRIOUSLY
LUGUBRIOUSNESS
LUGUBROUS
LUGWORM
LUHINGA
LUIGINI
LUIGINO
LUJAURITE
LUJAVRITE
LUJULA
LUKE
LUKET
LUKEWARD
LUKEWARM
LUKEWARMLY
LUKEWARMNESS
LUKEWARMTH
LULAB
LULL
LULLABIES
LULLABY
LULLAY
LULLED
LULLER
LULLILOO
LULLILOOED
LULLILOOING
LULLING
LULLY
LULU
LULUAI
LUM
LUMACHEL
LUMACHELLA
LUMACHELLE
LUMBAGINOUS
LUMBAGO
LUMBANG
LUMBAR
LUMBAYAO
LUMBER
LUMBERDAR
LUMBERED
LUMBERER
LUMBERING
LUMBERINGLY
LUMBERJACK
LUMBERJACKET
LUMBERLY
LUMBERMAN
LUMBERMEN
LUMBERYARD
LUMBODYNIA
LUMBOSACRAL
LUMBRICAL
LUMBRICALES
LUMBRICALIS
LUMBRICID
LUMBRICIFORM
LUMBRICINE
LUMBRICOID
LUMBRICOSIS
LUMBROUS
LUMEN
LUMENS
LUMINA
LUMINAIRE
LUMINAL
LUMINANCE
LUMINANT
LUMINARIES
LUMINARIOUS
LUMINARISM
LUMINARIST
LUMINARY
LUMINATE
LUMINATION
LUMINATIVE
LUMINATOR
LUMINE
LUMINESCE
LUMINESCED
LUMINESCENCE
LUMINESCENT
LUMINESCING
LUMINIFEROUS
LUMINIFICENT
LUMINISM
LUMINIST
LUMINISTE
LUMINOSITIES
LUMINOSITY
LUMINOUS
LUMINOUSLY
LUMINOUSNESS
LUMM
LUMMOX
LUMMY
LUMP
LUMPED
LUMPEN
LUMPER
LUMPET
LUMPFISH
LUMPFISHES
LUMPIER
LUMPIEST
LUMPILY
LUMPINESS
LUMPING
LUMPINGLY
LUMPISH
LUMPISHLY
LUMPISHNESS
LUMPKIN

LUMPMAN
LUMPMEN
LUMPS
LUMPSUCKER
LUMPY
LUMUT
LUNA
LUNACIES
LUNACY
LUNAMBULISM
LUNAR
LUNARE
LUNARIA
LUNARIAN
LUNARIST
LUNARIUM
LUNARY
LUNATA
LUNATE
LUNATED
LUNATELLUS
LUNATELY
LUNATIC
LUNATICAL
LUNATICALLY
LUNATION
LUNATIZE
LUNATUM
LUNCH
LUNCHEON
LUNCHEONER
LUNCHEONETTE
LUNCHER
LUNCHROOM
LUNDYFOOT
LUNE
LUNES
LUNET
LUNETS
LUNETTE
LUNETTES
LUNG
LUNGE
LUNGED
LUNGEE
LUNGEOUS
LUNGER
LUNGFISH
LUNGFISHES
LUNGFLOWER
LUNGI
LUNGIE
LUNGING
LUNGIS
LUNGMOTOR
LUNGOOR
LUNGS
LUNGSICK
LUNGWORM
LUNGWORT
LUNGY
LUNICURRENT
LUNIES
LUNIFORM
LUNISOLAR
LUNISTICE
LUNISTITIAL
LUNITIDAL
LUNKER
LUNKHEAD
LUNKHEADED
LUNN
LUNOID
LUNT
LUNULA
LUNULAE
LUNULAR
LUNULATE
LUNULATED
LUNULE
LUNULET
LUNULITE
LUNY
LUNYIE
LUPANAR
LUPANARIAN
LUPANIN
LUPANINE
LUPE
LUPEOL
LUPEOSE
LUPETIDIN
LUPETIDINE
LUPICIDE
LUPIFORM
LUPIN
LUPINASTER
LUPINE
LUPININ
LUPININE
LUPINOSIS
LUPINOUS
LUPIS
LUPOID
LUPOUS
LUPULIN
LUPULINE
LUPULINIC
LUPULINOUS
LUPULUS
LUPUS
LUR
LURA
LURACAN
LURCH
LURCHER
LURCHING
LURDAN
LURDANE
LURE
LURED
LUREMENT
LURER
LURG
LURGWORM
LURID
LURIDITY
LURIDLY
LURIDNESS
LURING
LURK
LURKED
LURKER
LURKING
LURKINGLY
LURKY
LURRIER
LURRIES
LURRY
LUSCIOUS
LUSCIOUSLY
LUSCIOUSNESS
LUSH
LUSHBURG
LUSHER
LUSHLY
LUSHNESS
LUSHY
LUSK
LUSKISH
LUSKY
LUSORY
LUST
LUSTED
LUSTER
LUSTERED
LUSTERER
LUSTERING
LUSTERLESS
LUSTERWARE
LUSTFUL
LUSTFULLY
LUSTFULNESS
LUSTICK
LUSTIER
LUSTIEST
LUSTIHOOD
LUSTILY
LUSTING
LUSTLESS
LUSTLY
LUSTRA
LUSTRAL
LUSTRANT
LUSTRATE
LUSTRATED
LUSTRATING
LUSTRATION
LUSTRATIVE
LUSTRATORY
LUSTRE
LUSTRED
LUSTREWARE
LUSTRICAL
LUSTRIFY
LUSTRINE
LUSTRING
LUSTROUS
LUSTROUSLY
LUSTROUSNESS
LUSTRUM
LUSTRUMS
LUSTY
LUSUS
LUTACEOUS
LUTANIST
LUTANY
LUTATION
LUTE
LUTEAL
LUTECIA
LUTECIUM
LUTED
LUTEIN
LUTENIST
LUTEOFULVOUS
LUTEOFUSCOUS
LUTEOLIN
LUTEOLOUS
LUTEOMA
LUTEOUS
LUTER
LUTESCENT
LUTETIUM
LUTEUM
LUTFISK
LUTH
LUTHERN
LUTHIER
LUTIANID
LUTIANOID
LUTIDIN
LUTIDINE
LUTIDINIC
LUTING
LUTIST
LUTJANID
LUTONG
LUTOSE
LUTRIN
LUTRINE
LUTULENCE
LUTULENT
LUTZ
LUX
LUXATE
LUXATED
LUXATING
LUXATION
LUXE
LUXES
LUXIVE
LUXULLIANITE
LUXUR
LUXURIANCE
LUXURIANCY
LUXURIANT
LUXURIANTLY
LUXURIANTNESS
LUXURIATE
LUXURIATED
LUXURIATING
LUXURIATION
LUXURIES
LUXURIOUS
LUXURIOUSLY
LUXURIOUSNESS
LUXURIST
LUXURITY
LUXURY
LUXUS
LY
LYAM
LYANCE
LYARD
LYART
LYCAENID
LYCANTHROPE
LYCANTHROPIC
LYCANTHROPY
LYCEA
LYCEAL
LYCEE
LYCEUM
LYCEUMS
LYCHEE
LYCHNIS
LYCHNOMANCY
LYCHNOSCOPE
LYCHNOSCOPIC
LYCID
LYCODOID
LYCOPENE
LYCOPERDOID
LYCOPIN
LYCOPOD
LYCOPODE
LYCOPODIUM
LYCORINE
LYCOSID
LYCTID
LYDDITE
LYDITE
LYE
LYED
LYERY
LYFKIE
LYGAEID
LYGUS
LYING
LYINGLY
LYKEWAKE
LYM
LYMANTRIID
LYME
LYMNAEAN
LYMNAEID
LYMPH
LYMPHAD
LYMPHADENIA
LYMPHADENOID
LYMPHADENOMA
LYMPHAEMIA
LYMPHAGOGUE
LYMPHANGIAL
LYMPHANGIOMA
LYMPHANGIOMATA
LYMPHANGITIC
LYMPHANGITIS
LYMPHATIC
LYMPHATICAL
LYMPHATION
LYMPHATISM
LYMPHATITIS
LYMPHECTASIA
LYMPHEDEMA
LYMPHEMIA
LYMPHOBLAST
LYMPHOBLASTIC
LYMPHOCELE
LYMPHOCYST
LYMPHOCYTE
LYMPHOCYTIC
LYMPHOCYTOSIS
LYMPHOCYTOTIC
LYMPHODERMIA
LYMPHODUCT
LYMPHOEDEMA
LYMPHOGENIC
LYMPHOID
LYMPHOLOGY
LYMPHOMA
LYMPHOMATOUS
LYMPHOPATHY
LYMPHOPENIAL
LYMPHORRHAGE
LYMPHORRHEA
LYMPHOSTASIS
LYMPHOTOME
LYMPHOTOMY
LYMPHOTOXIN
LYMPHOTROPHY
LYMPHOUS
LYMPHURIA
LYMPHY
LYN
LYNCEAN
LYNCH
LYNCHED
LYNCHER
LYNCHET
LYNCHING
LYNCINE
LYNE
LYNNHAVEN
LYNX
LYNXES
LYOMEROUS
LYONETIID
LYONNAISE
LYOPHIL
LYOPHILE
LYOPHILIC
LYOPHOBE
LYOPHOBIC
LYOTROPE
LYOTROPIC
LYPEMANIA
LYPOTHYMIA
LYRA
LYRATE
LYRATED
LYRATELY
LYRAWAY
LYRE

LYREBIRD
LYREMAN
LYRETAIL
LYRIC
LYRICAL
LYRICALLY
LYRICALNESS
LYRICHORD
LYRICISM
LYRICIST
LYRICKED
LYRICKING
LYRIFORM
LYRISM
LYRIST
LYSATE
LYSE
LYSED
LYSIDIN
LYSIDINE
LYSIGENIC
LYSIGENOUS
LYSIGENOUSLY
LYSIMETER
LYSIN
LYSINE
LYSING
LYSIS
LYSOGEN
LYSOGENESIS
LYSOGENETIC
LYSOGENIC
LYSSA
LYSSIC
LYTERIAN
LYTHE
LYTHRACEOUS
LYTIC
LYTTA
LYTTAE
LYXOSE

MA
MAA
MAABARA
MAAL
MAAR
MAARAD
MAARIB
MAASS
MAATJE
MAB
MABE
MABI
MABOLO
MABUTI
MABYER
MAC
MACAASIM
MACABER
MACABI
MACABRE
MACAC
MACACO
MACACOS
MACADAM
MACADAMER
MACADAMIA
MACADAMITE
MACADAMIZE
MACADAMIZED
MACADAMIZER
MACADAMIZING
MACAN
MACANA
MACAO
MACAQUE
MACARISM
MACARIZE
MACARIZED
MACARIZING
MACARON
MACARONI
MACARONIC
MACARONICAL
MACARONICALLY
MACARONICISM
MACARONIES
MACARONIS
MACARONISM
MACAROON
MACAW
MACCABOY
MACCHIA
MACCHIE
MACCO
MACCOBOY
MACCUS
MACE
MACEBEARER
MACEDOINE
MACEHEAD
MACELLUM
MACEMAN
MACER
MACERABLE
MACERAL
MACERATE
MACERATED
MACERATER
MACERATING
MACERATION
MACERATOR
MACH
MACHAIR
MACHAIRODONT
MACHAN
MACHAON
MACHAR
MACHEER
MACHETE
MACHI
MACHICOLATE
MACHICOLATED
MACHILA
MACHIN
MACHINA
MACHINABLE
MACHINAL
MACHINAMENT
MACHINATE
MACHINATED
MACHINATING
MACHINATION
MACHINATOR
MACHINE
MACHINED
MACHINELY
MACHINEMAN
MACHINEMEN
MACHINER
MACHINERY
MACHINING
MACHINISM
MACHINIST
MACHINULE
MACHISMO
MACHMETER
MACHOPOLYP
MACHREE
MACIES
MACILENCE
MACILENCY
MACILENT
MACINTOSH
MACK
MACKALLOW
MACKAYBEAN
MACKENBOY
MACKEREL
MACKERELER
MACKERELING
MACKERELS
MACKINAW
MACKINBOY
MACKINS
MACKINTOSH
MACKINTOSHITE
MACKLE
MACKLED
MACKLIKE
MACKLING
MACLE
MACLED
MACLURIN
MACO
MACONITE
MACONNE
MACRADENOUS
MACRAME
MACRANDER
MACRANDRE
MACRANDROUS
MACRIO
MACROANALYST
MACROBIAN
MACROBIOSIS
MACROBIOTE
MACROBIOTICS
MACROCEPHALY
MACROCHAETA
MACROCHAETAE
MACROCHIRAN
MACROCLIMATE
MACROCOSM
MACROCOSMIC
MACROCOSMOS
MACROCYST
MACROCYTE
MACROCYTIC
MACROCYTOSIS
MACRODONT
MACRODONTIA
MACRODONTISM
MACROGAMETE
MACROGAMY
MACROGRAPH
MACROGRAPHIC
MACROGRAPHY
MACROLOGY
MACROMANIA
MACROMERAL
MACROMERE
MACROMERIC
MACROMERITE
MACROMERITIC
MACROMETER
MACROMETHOD
MACROMYELON
MACRON
MACRONUCLEAR
MACRONUCLEUS
MACROPHAGE
MACROPHAGUS
MACROPHYSICS
MACROPODIAN
MACROPODINE
MACROPODOUS
MACROPSIA
MACROPSY
MACROPTEROUS
MACROSCIAN
MACROSCOPIC
MACROSEISM
MACROSEISMIC
MACROSMATIC
MACROSPECIES
MACROSPORE
MACROSPORIC
MACROSTRUCTURE
MACROSTYLE
MACROSTYLOUS
MACROTHERE
MACROTHERM
MACROTIA
MACROTIN
MACROTOME
MACROTOUS
MACROURID
MACRURAL
MACRURAN
MACRUROID
MACRUROUS
MACTATION
MACTROID
MACUCA
MACULA
MACULAE
MACULAR
MACULATE
MACULATED
MACULATING
MACULATION
MACULE
MACULED
MACULICOLE
MACULICOLOUS
MACULIFEROUS
MACULING
MACULOSE
MACUPA
MACUPI
MACUSHLA
MACUTA
MACUTE
MAD
MADAM
MADAME
MADAMS
MADAPOLAM
MADAPOLAN
MADAPOLLAM
MADAR
MADAROSIS
MADAROTIC
MADBRAIN
MADBRAINED
MADCAP
MADDED
MADDEN
MADDENED
MADDENING
MADDENINGLY
MADDER
MADDERISH
MADDERWORT
MADDEST
MADDING
MADDINGLY
MADDISH
MADDLE
MADDOCK
MADE
MADEFACTION
MADEFY
MADELEINE
MADELINE
MADEMOISELLE
MADESCENT
MADHAB
MADHOUSE
MADHUCA
MADID
MADIDANS
MADISTERIUM
MADLING
MADLY
MADMAN
MADMEN
MADNEP
MADNESS
MADO
MADONNA
MADOQUA
MADOR
MADRAGUE
MADRAS
MADRASA
MADRASAH
MADRASSAH
MADRASSEH
MADRE
MADREPERL
MADREPORAL
MADREPORE
MADREPORIAN
MADREPORIC
MADREPORITE
MADREPORITIC
MADRIER
MADRIGAL
MADRIGALER
MADRIGALETTO
MADRIGALIAN
MADRIGALIST
MADRIH
MADRILENE
MADRONA
MADRONO
MADSTONE
MADURO
MADWEED
MADWOMAN
MADWOMEN
MADWORT
MAE
MAEANDER
MAEANDRINE
MAEANDRINOID
MAEANDROID
MAEGBOT
MAEGBOTE
MAELSTROM
MAENAD
MAENADES
MAENADIC
MAENADICALLY
MAENADISM
MAENADS
MAENAITE
MAESTIVE
MAESTOSO
MAESTRA
MAESTRO
MAESTROS
MAFEY
MAFFIA
MAFFICK
MAFFICKED
MAFFICKER
MAFFICKING
MAFFIOSO
MAFFLE
MAFFLER
MAFFLIN
MAFIA
MAFIC
MAFIOSO
MAFOO
MAFTIR
MAFU
MAFURA
MAFURRA
MAG
MAGADIS
MAGADIZE
MAGANI
MAGAS
MAGAZINABLE
MAGAZINAGE
MAGAZINE
MAGAZINED
MAGAZINER
MAGAZINING
MAGAZINISM
MAGAZINIST
MAGAZINY
MAGBOTE
MAGDALEN
MAGE
MAGENTA
MAGERFUL
MAGG
MAGGED
MAGGID
MAGGIORE
MAGGLE

MAGGOT
MAGGOTINESS
MAGGOTPIE
MAGGOTRY
MAGGOTY
MAGHZEN
MAGI
MAGIC
MAGICAL
MAGICALLY
MAGICIAN
MAGICKED
MAGICKING
MAGILP
MAGIRIC
MAGIRICS
MAGIRIST
MAGIRISTIC
MAGIROLOGIST
MAGIROLOGY
MAGISTER
MAGISTERIAL
MAGISTERIES
MAGISTERIUM
MAGISTERY
MAGISTRACIES
MAGISTRACY
MAGISTRAL
MAGISTRALITY
MAGISTRALLY
MAGISTRAND
MAGISTRANT
MAGISTRATE
MAGISTRATIVE
MAGISTRATURE
MAGMA
MAGMAS
MAGMATA
MAGMATIC
MAGNA
MAGNALE
MAGNANERIE
MAGNANIME
MAGNANIMITY
MAGNANIMOUS
MAGNANIMOUSLY
MAGNASCOPE
MAGNASCOPIC
MAGNATE
MAGNELECTRIC
MAGNEOPTIC
MAGNES
MAGNESIA
MAGNESIAL
MAGNESIAN
MAGNESIC
MAGNESITE
MAGNESIUM
MAGNET
MAGNETA
MAGNETIC
MAGNETICAL
MAGNETICALLY
MAGNETICIAN
MAGNETICS
MAGNETIFY
MAGNETIMETER
MAGNETISM
MAGNETIST
MAGNETITE
MAGNETITIC
MAGNETIZABLE
MAGNETIZATION
MAGNETIZE
MAGNETIZED
MAGNETIZER
MAGNETIZING
MAGNETO
MAGNETOBELL
MAGNETOGRAM
MAGNETOGRAPH
MAGNETOID
MAGNETOLYSIS
MAGNETOMETER
MAGNETOMETRY
MAGNETOMOTOR
MAGNETON
MAGNETOOPTIC
MAGNETOPHONE
MAGNETOS
MAGNETOSCOPE
MAGNETRON
MAGNETS
MAGNICAUDATE
MAGNIFIABLE
MAGNIFIC
MAGNIFICAL
MAGNIFICALLY
MAGNIFICATE
MAGNIFICATION
MAGNIFICE
MAGNIFICENCE
MAGNIFICENT
MAGNIFICENTLY
MAGNIFICO
MAGNIFICOES
MAGNIFIED
MAGNIFIER
MAGNIFIQUE
MAGNIFY
MAGNIFYING
MAGNILOQUENT
MAGNIPOTENCE
MAGNIPOTENT
MAGNISONANT
MAGNITUDE
MAGNITUDES
MAGNITUDINOUS
MAGNOLIA
MAGNUM
MAGOT
MAGPIE
MAGPIED
MAGRIM
MAGSMAN
MAGUARI
MAGUEY
MAHA
MAHAJAN
MAHAJUN
MAHAL
MAHALA
MAHALAMAT
MAHALEB
MAHALLA
MAHALY
MAHAN
MAHANT
MAHAR
MAHARAJA
MAHARAJAH
MAHARAJRANA
MAHARANA
MAHARANEE
MAHARANI
MAHARAO
MAHARAWAL
MAHARAWAT
MAHARMAH
MAHARSHI
MAHAT
MAHATMA
MAHATMAISM
MAHBUB
MAHIMAHI
MAHJONG
MAHJONGG
MAHLSTICK
MAHMAL
MAHMUDI
MAHO
MAHOE
MAHOGANIES
MAHOGANIZE
MAHOGANY
MAHOITRE
MAHOLI
MAHOLTINE
MAHONE
MAHOUT
MAHR
MAHSEER
MAHSIR
MAHSUR
MAHUA
MAHUANG
MAHWA
MAHZOR
MAI
MAIAN
MAID
MAIDAN
MAIDCHILD
MAIDEN
MAIDENCHILD
MAIDENHAIR
MAIDENHEAD
MAIDENHOOD
MAIDENLINESS
MAIDENLY
MAIDENWEED
MAIDHEAD
MAIDHOOD
MAIDIN
MAIDISM
MAIDKIN
MAIDLY
MAIDSERVANT
MAIDY
MAIEUTIC
MAIEUTICAL
MAIEUTICS
MAIG
MAIGRE
MAIHEM
MAIID
MAIL
MAILABLE
MAILBAG
MAILBOX
MAILCATCHER
MAILCLAD
MAILE
MAILED
MAILER
MAILGUARD
MAILIE
MAILING
MAILL
MAILLE
MAILLECHORT
MAILLOT
MAILMAN
MAILMEN
MAILPLANE
MAILPOUCH
MAIM
MAIMED
MAIMEDLY
MAIMEDNESS
MAIMER
MAIMING
MAIMON
MAIMUL
MAIN
MAINE
MAINFERRE
MAINLAND
MAINLANDER
MAINLINE
MAINLINED
MAINLINER
MAINLINING
MAINLY
MAINMAST
MAINMORTABLE
MAINOR
MAINOUR
MAINPAST
MAINPERNABLE
MAINPERNOR
MAINPIN
MAINPORT
MAINPOST
MAINPRISE
MAINPRIZE
MAINPRIZER
MAINS
MAINSAIL
MAINSHEET
MAINSPRING
MAINSTAY
MAINSTREAM
MAINT
MAINTAIN
MAINTAINED
MAINTAINER
MAINTAINING
MAINTAINOR
MAINTENANCE
MAINTOP
MAINTOPMAN
MAINTOPMAST
MAINTOPMEN
MAINTOPSAIL
MAINWARD
MAIOLICA
MAIPO
MAIRATOUR
MAIRE
MAIRIE
MAISON
MAISONETTE
MAIST
MAISTRY
MAITLANDITE
MAITRE
MAITRESSE
MAITRISE
MAIZE
MAIZEBIRD
MAIZER
MAJA
MAJAGUA
MAJAS
MAJESTIC
MAJESTICAL
MAJESTICALLY
MAJESTIES
MAJESTIOUS
MAJESTY
MAJID
MAJIDIEH
MAJO
MAJOE
MAJOLICA
MAJOLIST
MAJOON
MAJOR
MAJORAT
MAJORATE
MAJORATION
MAJORDOMO
MAJORETTE
MAJORITIES
MAJORITY
MAJORIZE
MAJOS
MAJUSCULAE
MAJUSCULAR
MAJUSCULE
MAK
MAKADOO
MAKAHIKI
MAKAI
MAKALE
MAKAR
MAKARA
MAKATEA
MAKE
MAKEBATE
MAKEDOM
MAKEFAST
MAKELESS
MAKER
MAKEREADY
MAKERESS
MAKERS
MAKES
MAKESHIFT
MAKESHIFTY
MAKEWEIGHT
MAKHORKA
MAKHZAN
MAKHZEN
MAKI
MAKIMONO
MAKIN
MAKING
MAKINGS
MAKLUK
MAKO
MAKOMAKO
MAKOPA
MAKOUA
MAKRAN
MAKROSKELIC
MAKUK
MAKUTU
MAL
MALA
MALAANONANG
MALABATHRUM
MALACANTHID
MALACEOUS
MALACHITE
MALACIA
MALACODERM
MALACOID
MALACOLITE
MALACOLOGIST
MALACOLOGY
MALACON
MALACONE
MALACTIC
MALADAPTATION
MALADDRESS
MALADE
MALADIES
MALADIVE
MALADJUSTED
MALADJUSTMENT
MALADROIT
MALADROITLY
MALADVENTURE

MALADY
MALAGMA
MALAHACK
MALAISE
MALAKIN
MALAKON
MALAMBO
MALAMUTE
MALANDERED
MALANDERS
MALANDROUS
MALANGA
MALAPAHO
MALAPERT
MALAPERTLY
MALAPERTNESS
MALAPROP
MALAPROPIAN
MALAPROPISM
MALAPROPOS
MALAR
MALARIA
MALARIAL
MALARIAN
MALARIN
MALARIOID
MALARIOLOGY
MALARIOUS
MALARKEY
MALARKY
MALATE
MALATI
MALAX
MALAXABLE
MALAXAGE
MALAXATE
MALAXATION
MALAXATOR
MALAXED
MALAXERMAN
MALAXERMEN
MALAXING
MALBROUCK
MALCHITE
MALCONDUCT
MALCONTENT
MALCONTENTED
MALCONTENTEDLY
MALCONTENTISM
MALCONTENTLY
MALCONTENTMENT
MALDOCCHIO
MALDONITE
MALDUCK
MALE
MALEABILITY
MALEASE
MALEATE
MALEDICENT
MALEDICT
MALEDICTION
MALEDICTIVE
MALEDICTORY
MALEFACTION
MALEFACTOR
MALEFACTORY
MALEFACTRESS
MALEFIC
MALEFICAL
MALEFICALLY
MALEFICE
MALEFICENCE
MALEFICENT
MALEFICIAL
MALEFICIATE
MALEIC
MALEINOID
MALEINOIDAL
MALELLA
MALELLAE
MALEMIUT
MALEMUTE
MALENESS
MALENGINE
MALENTENDU
MALEO
MALEOS
MALETOTE
MALEVOLENCE
MALEVOLENCY
MALEVOLENT
MALEVOLENTLY
MALEVOLOUS
MALFEASANCE
MALFEASANT
MALFEASOR
MALFORMATION
MALFORMED
MALFUNCTION
MALGRACE
MALGRADO
MALGRE
MALGUZAR
MALGUZARI
MALHEUR
MALI
MALIC
MALICE
MALICEFUL
MALICIOUS
MALICIOUSLY
MALICORIUM
MALIFEROUS
MALIFORM
MALIGN
MALIGNANCE
MALIGNANCIES
MALIGNANCY
MALIGNANT
MALIGNANTLY
MALIGNATION
MALIGNED
MALIGNER
MALIGNIFIED
MALIGNIFY
MALIGNIFYING
MALIGNING
MALIGNITIES
MALIGNITY
MALIGNLY
MALIGNMENT
MALIHINI
MALIK
MALIKANA
MALINCHE
MALINE
MALINES
MALINGER
MALINGERED
MALINGERER
MALINGERING
MALINGERY
MALINOWSKITE
MALINTENT
MALISM
MALISON
MALIST
MALISTIC
MALKIN
MALL
MALLADRITE
MALLANGONG
MALLARD
MALLARDITE
MALLARDS
MALLEABLE
MALLEABLEIZE
MALLEABLEIZED
MALLEABLEIZING
MALLEABLIZE
MALLEABLY
MALLEAL
MALLEATE
MALLEATED
MALLEATING
MALLEATION
MALLED
MALLEE
MALLEI
MALLEIFEROUS
MALLEIFORM
MALLEIN
MALLEINIZE
MALLEMUCK
MALLENDERS
MALLEOINCUDAL
MALLEOLABLE
MALLEOLAR
MALLEOLI
MALLEOLUS
MALLET
MALLETED
MALLETING
MALLEUS
MALLING
MALLOPHAGAN
MALLOPHAGOUS
MALLOSEISMIC
MALLOW
MALLOWWORT
MALLUM
MALLUS
MALM
MALMARSH
MALMED
MALMIGNATTE
MALMING
MALMOCK
MALMSEY
MALMSEYS
MALMSTONE
MALMY
MALNUTRITE
MALNUTRITION
MALO
MALOCA
MALOCCHIO
MALOCCLUDED
MALOCCLUSION
MALODOR
MALODOROUS
MALODOROUSLY
MALODOUR
MALONATE
MALONIC
MALONYL
MALONYLUREA
MALOUAH
MALPAIS
MALPOSED
MALPOSITION
MALPRACTICE
MALPRACTITIONER
MALPRAXIS
MALPROPRIETY
MALT
MALTASE
MALTED
MALTER
MALTHA
MALTHOUSE
MALTIER
MALTIEST
MALTING
MALTMAN
MALTOLTE
MALTOSE
MALTREAT
MALTREATED
MALTREATING
MALTREATMENT
MALTREATOR
MALTSTER
MALTWORM
MALTY
MALUM
MALURINE
MALVACEOUS
MALVASIA
MALVASIAN
MALVERSATION
MALVERSE
MALVIN
MALVOISIE
MAMA
MAMALOI
MAMAMU
MAMBA
MAMBO
MAMBOS
MAMBU
MAMELIERE
MAMELON
MAMELUCO
MAMEYES
MAMEYS
MAMILLA
MAMLATDAR
MAMLUTDAR
MAMMA
MAMMAE
MAMMAL
MAMMALGIA
MAMMALIAN
MAMMALITY
MAMMALOGICAL
MAMMALOGIST
MAMMALOGY
MAMMARY
MAMMATE
MAMMATUS
MAMME
MAMMEE
MAMMER
MAMMET
MAMMEY
MAMMIE
MAMMIES
MAMMIFER
MAMMIFEROUS
MAMMIFORM
MAMMILATE
MAMMILATED
MAMMILLA
MAMMILLAE
MAMMILLAR
MAMMILLARY
MAMMILLATION
MAMMILLIFORM
MAMMILLOID
MAMMITIS
MAMMOCK
MAMMOCKED
MAMMOCKING
MAMMON
MAMMONI
MAMMONIACAL
MAMMONISH
MAMMONISM
MAMMONIST
MAMMONISTIC
MAMMONITE
MAMMONITISH
MAMMONIZATION
MAMMONIZE
MAMMONOLATRY
MAMMOSE
MAMMOTH
MAMMOTHREPT
MAMMULA
MAMMULAE
MAMMULAR
MAMMY
MAMO
MAMONA
MAMOTY
MAMPALON
MAMPUS
MAMRY
MAMUSHI
MAMZER
MAN
MANA
MANACLE
MANACLED
MANACLES
MANACLING
MANADA
MANAGE
MANAGEABILITY
MANAGEABLE
MANAGEABLENESS
MANAGEABLY
MANAGED
MANAGELESS
MANAGEMENT
MANAGEMENTAL
MANAGER
MANAGERESS
MANAGERIAL
MANAGERIALLY
MANAGERSHIP
MANAGERY
MANAGES
MANAGING
MANAI
MANAKIN
MANAL
MANANA
MANARVEL
MANAS
MANATEE
MANATI
MANATINE
MANATION
MANATOID
MANAVEL
MANAVELINS
MANAVILINS
MANBARKLAK
MANBIRD
MANBOT
MANBOTE
MANCALA
MANCANDO
MANCHE
MANCHET
MANCHINEEL
MANCINISM
MANCIPABLE
MANCIPANT
MANCIPATE
MANCIPATION
MANCIPATIVE
MANCIPATORY

MANCIPEE
MANCIPIA
MANCIPIUM
MANCIPLE
MANCIPULAR
MANCO
MANCONO
MANCUS
MAND
MANDALA
MANDAMENT
MANDAMUS
MANDAMUSED
MANDAMUSING
MANDAPA
MANDAR
MANDARAH
MANDARIN
MANDARINATE
MANDARINED
MANDARINESS
MANDARINIC
MANDARINING
MANDARINISM
MANDAT
MANDATARIES
MANDATARY
MANDATE
MANDATED
MANDATEE
MANDATING
MANDATION
MANDATIVE
MANDATOR
MANDATORIES
MANDATORILY
MANDATORY
MANDATS
MANDATUM
MANDELATE
MANDELIC
MANDIBLE
MANDIBULAR
MANDIBULARY
MANDIBULATE
MANDIBULATED
MANDIL
MANDILION
MANDIR
MANDLEN
MANDOER
MANDOLA
MANDOLIN
MANDOLINIST
MANDOLUTE
MANDORA
MANDORE
MANDORLA
MANDORLE
MANDRA
MANDRAGON
MANDRAGORA
MANDRAKE
MANDREL
MANDRIARCH
MANDRIL
MANDRILL
MANDRIN
MANDRITTA
MANDRUKA
MANDS
MANDUA
MANDUCABLE
MANDUCATE
MANDUCATED
MANDUCATING
MANDUCATION
MANDUCATORY
MANDYAS
MANE
MANED
MANEGE
MANEH
MANEI
MANELESS
MANENT
MANERIAL
MANES
MANESHEET
MANESS
MANET
MANEUVER
MANEUVERABLE
MANEUVERED
MANEUVERER
MANEUVERING
MANEUVRABLE
MANEUVRE
MANEUVRED
MANEUVRING
MANEY
MANFISH
MANFUL
MANFULLY
MANFULNESS
MANG
MANGA
MANGABEIRA
MANGABEY
MANGABY
MANGANA
MANGANATE
MANGANBLENDE
MANGANEISEN
MANGANESE
MANGANESIAN
MANGANESIC
MANGANETIC
MANGANIC
MANGANITE
MANGANIUM
MANGANIZE
MANGANOSITE
MANGANOUS
MANGE
MANGEAO
MANGEL
MANGELIN
MANGER
MANGERITE
MANGERY
MANGI
MANGIER
MANGIEST
MANGILY
MANGINESS
MANGLE
MANGLED
MANGLEMAN
MANGLER
MANGLING
MANGLINGLY
MANGO
MANGOES
MANGOLD
MANGONA
MANGONEL
MANGONISM
MANGONIZE
MANGORO
MANGOS
MANGOSTEEN
MANGOUR
MANGRASS
MANGRATE
MANGROVE
MANGUE
MANGWE
MANGY
MANHANDLE
MANHANDLED
MANHANDLING
MANHEAD
MANHOLE
MANHOOD
MANHUNT
MANHUNTER
MANHUNTING
MANI
MANIA
MANIABLE
MANIAC
MANIACAL
MANIACALLY
MANIC
MANICATE
MANICHORDON
MANICOLE
MANICON
MANICORD
MANICURE
MANICURED
MANICURING
MANICURIST
MANID
MANIFEST
MANIFESTABLE
MANIFESTANT
MANIFESTATION
MANIFESTED
MANIFESTER
MANIFESTING
MANIFESTIVE
MANIFESTLY
MANIFESTO
MANIFESTOES
MANIFESTOS
MANIFOLD
MANIFOLDED
MANIFOLDER
MANIFOLDING
MANIFOLDLY
MANIFOLDNESS
MANIFORM
MANIFY
MANIHOT
MANIKIN
MANIKINISM
MANILA
MANILLA
MANILLE
MANINI
MANIOC
MANIPLE
MANIPULABLE
MANIPULAR
MANIPULARY
MANIPULATE
MANIPULATED
MANIPULATING
MANIPULATION
MANIPULATIVE
MANIPULATOR
MANIPULATORY
MANISM
MANIST
MANISTIC
MANITO
MANITOU
MANITRUNK
MANITU
MANIU
MANJACK
MANJAK
MANJEET
MANJEL
MANK
MANKEEPER
MANKIE
MANKILLER
MANKILLING
MANKIN
MANKIND
MANKINDLY
MANKY
MANLESS
MANLESSLY
MANLESSNESS
MANLIER
MANLIEST
MANLIHOOD
MANLIKE
MANLIKELY
MANLIKENESS
MANLILY
MANLINESS
MANLY
MANMADE
MANNA
MANNAIA
MANNAN
MANNED
MANNEQUIN
MANNER
MANNERABLE
MANNERED
MANNERING
MANNERISM
MANNERIST
MANNERISTIC
MANNERIZE
MANNERLESS
MANNERLINESS
MANNERLY
MANNERS
MANNERSOME
MANNESS
MANNET
MANNIE
MANNIFEROUS
MANNIFY
MANNIKIN
MANNIKINISM
MANNING
MANNISH
MANNISHLY
MANNISHNESS
MANNITAN
MANNITE
MANNITIC
MANNITOL
MANNITOSE
MANNOHEPTITE
MANNOHEPTITOL
MANNOHEPTOSE
MANNONIC
MANNOSAN
MANNOSE
MANNY
MANO
MANOC
MANOEUVER
MANOEUVRE
MANOEUVRER
MANOGRAPH
MANOIR
MANOMETER
MANOMETRIC
MANOMETRICAL
MANOMETRY
MANOMIN
MANOR
MANORIAL
MANORIALISM
MANORIALIZE
MANOSCOPE
MANPOWER
MANQUE
MANQUEE
MANRED
MANRENT
MANROOT
MANROPE
MANSARD
MANSARDED
MANSE
MANSERVANT
MANSHIP
MANSION
MANSIONAL
MANSIONARY
MANSIONED
MANSIONRY
MANSLAUGHTER
MANSLAUGHTERER
MANSLAUGHTERING
MANSLAYER
MANSLAYING
MANSO
MANSTEALER
MANSTEALING
MANSTOPPER
MANSTOPPING
MANSUETE
MANSUETELY
MANSUETUDE
MANSWEAR
MANSWORN
MANT
MANTA
MANTAL
MANTEAU
MANTEAUS
MANTEAUX
MANTEEL
MANTEGAR
MANTEL
MANTELET
MANTELLETTA
MANTELLONE
MANTELPIECE
MANTELSHELF
MANTELTREE
MANTER
MANTES
MANTEVIL
MANTIC
MANTICISM
MANTICORA
MANTICORE
MANTID
MANTILLA
MANTIS
MANTISES
MANTISPID
MANTISSA
MANTISTIC
MANTLE
MANTLED
MANTLEROCK
MANTLET
MANTLING
MANTO
MANTOID
MANTOLOGIST

MANTOLOGY
MANTRA
MANTRAM
MANTRAP
MANTUA
MANTUAMAKER
MANTUAMAKING
MANTY
MANU
MANUAL
MANUALII
MANUALIST
MANUALITER
MANUALLY
MANUAO
MANUARY
MANUBALISTE
MANUBRIA
MANUBRIAL
MANUBRIATED
MANUBRIUM
MANUBRIUMS
MANUCAPTION
MANUCAPTOR
MANUCAPTURE
MANUCODE
MANUCODIATA
MANUDUCE
MANUDUCT
MANUDUCTION
MANUDUCTIVE
MANUDUCTOR
MANUDUCTORY
MANUFACT
MANUFACTION
MANUFACTOR
MANUFACTORY
MANUFACTURAL
MANUFACTURE
MANUFACTURED
MANUFACTURER
MANUFACTURING
MANUKA
MANUL
MANUMA
MANUMEA
MANUMISABLE
MANUMISE
MANUMISSION
MANUMISSIVE
MANUMIT
MANUMITTED
MANUMITTER
MANUMITTING
MANUMOTIVE
MANUPRISOR
MANURABLE
MANURAGE
MANURANCE
MANURE
MANURED
MANUREMENT
MANURER
MANURIAL
MANURIALLY
MANURING
MANUS
MANUSCRIPT
MANUSCRIPTAL
MANUSCRIPTION
MANUSINA
MANUTAGI
MANUTERGIUM
MANWARD
MANWARDS
MANWAY
MANWEED
MANWISE
MANY
MANYATTA
MANYBERRY
MANYFOLD
MANYPLIES
MANYROOT
MANYWHERE
MANZANA
MANZANILLA
MANZANILLO
MANZANITA
MANZIL
MAO
MAOMAO
MAORMOR
MAP
MAPACH
MAPACHE
MAPAU
MAPLAND
MAPLE
MAPLEFACE
MAPLES
MAPO
MAPPED
MAPPEMONDE
MAPPEN
MAPPER
MAPPING
MAPPIST
MAPPY
MAPS
MAPWISE
MAQUAHUITL
MAQUETTE
MAQUI
MAQUIS
MAR
MARABOTIN
MARABOU
MARABOUT
MARABUTO
MARACA
MARACAN
MARACOCK
MARAE
MARAI
MARAKAPAS
MARAL
MARAN
MARANAO
MARANG
MARANON
MARANTACEOUS
MARANTIC
MARARA
MARARIE
MARAS
MARASCA
MARASCHINO
MARASMIC
MARASMOID
MARASMOUS
MARASMUS
MARATHON
MARATHONER
MARAUD
MARAUDED
MARAUDER
MARAUDING
MARAVEDI
MARAY
MARBELIZE
MARBLE
MARBLED
MARBLEHEAD
MARBLEHEADER
MARBLEIZE
MARBLEIZED
MARBLEIZER
MARBLEIZING
MARBLER
MARBLES
MARBLEWOOD
MARBLING
MARBLY
MARBRINUS
MARC
MARCANDO
MARCANTANT
MARCASITE
MARCASITIC
MARCASITICAL
MARCATISSIMO
MARCATO
MARCEL
MARCELINE
MARCELLA
MARCELLED
MARCELLER
MARCELLING
MARCELLO
MARCESCENCE
MARCESCENT
MARCH
MARCHAND
MARCHED
MARCHER
MARCHESA
MARCHESE
MARCHESI
MARCHET
MARCHETTI
MARCHETTO
MARCHING
MARCHIONESS
MARCHITE
MARCHLAND
MARCHMAN
MARCHMEN
MARCHPANE
MARCID
MARCO
MARCONI
MARCONIGRAM
MARCONIGRAPH
MARCOR
MARCOT
MARCOTTAGE
MARDY
MARE
MAREBLOB
MARECHAL
MARECHALE
MAREKANITE
MAREMMA
MAREMMATIC
MAREMME
MAREMMESE
MARENGO
MARENNIN
MARES
MARFIRE
MARGA
MARGARATE
MARGARIC
MARGARIN
MARGARINE
MARGARITA
MARGARITAE
MARGARITE
MARGARITIC
MARGARODITE
MARGAY
MARGE
MARGELINE
MARGENT
MARGIN
MARGINAL
MARGINALIA
MARGINALITY
MARGINALIZE
MARGINALLY
MARGINATE
MARGINATED
MARGINATING
MARGINATION
MARGINED
MARGINIFORM
MARGINING
MARGINOPLASTY
MARGINS
MARGOSA
MARGRAVATE
MARGRAVE
MARGRAVELY
MARGRAVIAL
MARGRAVIATE
MARGRAVINE
MARGUERITE
MARGULLIE
MARHALA
MARIA
MARIACHI
MARIALITE
MARIANA
MARIANNA
MARIANNE
MARICA
MARICOLOUS
MARID
MARIGENOUS
MARIGOLD
MARIGRAM
MARIGRAPH
MARIGRAPHIC
MARIHUANA
MARIJUANA
MARIKINA
MARIMBA
MARIMONDA
MARINA
MARINADE
MARINADED
MARINADING
MARINAL
MARINATE
MARINATED
MARINATING
MARINE
MARINER
MARINERSHIP
MARINHEIRO
MARINIST
MARINORAMA
MARIONET
MARIONETTE
MARIPOSITE
MARIS
MARISH
MARISHNESS
MARISHY
MARITA
MARITAGE
MARITAGIUM
MARITAL
MARITALITY
MARITALLY
MARITICIDAL
MARITICIDE
MARITIMAL
MARITIMATE
MARITIME
MARITIMES
MARITORIOUS
MARIUPOLITE
MARJORAM
MARK
MARKA
MARKABLE
MARKAZ
MARKAZES
MARKDOWN
MARKED
MARKEDLY
MARKEDNESS
MARKER
MARKERY
MARKET
MARKETABILITY
MARKETABLE
MARKETABLY
MARKETED
MARKETEER
MARKETER
MARKETING
MARKETMAN
MARKETPLACE
MARKETSTEAD
MARKFIELDITE
MARKHOOR
MARKHOR
MARKING
MARKINGLY
MARKINGS
MARKKA
MARKKAA
MARKLAND
MARKMAN
MARKMEN
MARKMOOT
MARKMOTE
MARKS
MARKSHOT
MARKSMAN
MARKSMANLY
MARKSMANSHIP
MARKSMEN
MARKSTONE
MARKSWOMAN
MARKSWOMEN
MARKUP
MARKWEED
MARKWORTHY
MARL
MARLACEOUS
MARLBERRY
MARLED
MARLER
MARLET
MARLI
MARLIN
MARLINE
MARLINESPIKE
MARLING
MARLINGSPIKE
MARLINSPIKE
MARLITE
MARLITIC
MARLOCK
MARLPIT
MARLY
MARM
MARMALADE
MARMALADY
MARMARITIN
MARMARIZE

MARMARIZED
MARMARIZING
MARMAROSIS
MARMATITE
MARMELOS
MARMENNILL
MARMION
MARMIT
MARMITE
MARMOLITE
MARMOR
MARMORACEOUS
MARMORATE
MARMOREAL
MARMOREALLY
MARMOREAN
MARMORIC
MARMOSE
MARMOSET
MARMOT
MARO
MAROCAIN
MAROK
MAROON
MAROONED
MAROONER
MAROONING
MAROQUIN
MAROR
MAROS
MAROTTE
MARPLOT
MARPLOTRY
MARQUE
MARQUEE
MARQUESS
MARQUETERIE
MARQUETRY
MARQUIS
MARQUISAL
MARQUISATE
MARQUISDOM
MARQUISE
MARQUISESS
MARQUISETTE
MARQUISINA
MARQUISOTTE
MARQUITO
MARRAINE
MARRAM
MARRANISM
MARRANIZE
MARRANO
MARRED
MARREE
MARRER
MARRIABLE
MARRIAGE
MARRIAGEABLE
MARRIED
MARRIER
MARRING
MARROCK
MARRON
MARROT
MARROW
MARROWBONE
MARROWED
MARROWFAT
MARROWING
MARROWSKY
MARROWSKYER
MARROWY
MARRUBE
MARRY
MARRYER
MARRYING
MARRYMUFFE
MARSE
MARSEILLE
MARSEILLES
MARSH
MARSHAL
MARSHALATE
MARSHALCY
MARSHALED
MARSHALER
MARSHALESS
MARSHALING
MARSHALLED
MARSHALLER
MARSHALLING
MARSHALMAN
MARSHALSHIP
MARSHBERRIES
MARSHBERRY
MARSHBUCK
MARSHFIRE
MARSHFLOWER
MARSHIER
MARSHIEST
MARSHINESS
MARSHITE
MARSHLAND
MARSHLANDER
MARSHLOCKS
MARSHMALLOW
MARSHMAN
MARSHMEN
MARSHWORT
MARSHY
MARSOON
MARSUPIA
MARSUPIAL
MARSUPIALIAN
MARSUPIALIZE
MARSUPIAN
MARSUPIATE
MARSUPIUM
MART
MARTAGON
MARTEL
MARTELINE
MARTELLATE
MARTELLATO
MARTELLEMENT
MARTELLO
MARTEN
MARTENIKO
MARTENOT
MARTENS
MARTENSITE
MARTENSITIC
MARTEXT
MARTIAL
MARTIALISM
MARTIALIST
MARTIALITY
MARTIALIZE
MARTIALLY
MARTIALNESS
MARTILOGE
MARTIN
MARTINET
MARTINETA
MARTINETISM
MARTINGAL
MARTINGALE
MARTINI
MARTINICO
MARTINIS
MARTINOE
MARTITE
MARTLET
MARTRIX
MARTYR
MARTYRDOM
MARTYRED
MARTYRER
MARTYRESS
MARTYRIES
MARTYRING
MARTYRIUM
MARTYRIZE
MARTYRIZED
MARTYRIZER
MARTYRIZING
MARTYRLY
MARTYROLATRY
MARTYROLOGE
MARTYROLOGIC
MARTYROLOGICAL
MARTYROLOGY
MARTYRY
MARU
MARUA
MARUM
MARVEL
MARVELED
MARVELING
MARVELLED
MARVELLING
MARVELLOUS
MARVELLOUSLY
MARVELOUS
MARVELOUSLY
MARVELRY
MARVER
MARY
MARYBUD
MARYSOLE
MARZIPAN
MAS
MASA
MASARID
MASARIDID
MASCAGNINE
MASCAGNITE
MASCALLY
MASCARA
MASCARON
MASCLE
MASCLED
MASCON
MASCOT
MASCOTISM
MASCOTRY
MASCOTTE
MASCULARITY
MASCULATE
MASCULATION
MASCULINE
MASCULINELY
MASCULINENESS
MASCULINISM
MASCULINIST
MASCULINITY
MASCULY
MASDEU
MASER
MASH
MASHA
MASHAK
MASHAL
MASHALLAH
MASHAM
MASHED
MASHELTON
MASHER
MASHGIAH
MASHIE
MASHIER
MASHIES
MASHIEST
MASHING
MASHLOCH
MASHLUM
MASHMAN
MASHMEN
MASHRU
MASHY
MASI
MASJID
MASK
MASKALONGE
MASKED
MASKEG
MASKELYNITE
MASKER
MASKERY
MASKETTE
MASKFLOWER
MASKING
MASKINONGE
MASKOID
MASLIN
MASOCHISM
MASOCHIST
MASOCHISTIC
MASON
MASONED
MASONER
MASONIC
MASONING
MASONITE
MASONRIED
MASONRIES
MASONRY
MASONRYING
MASONS
MASONWORK
MASOOKA
MASOOLA
MASQUE
MASQUER
MASQUERADE
MASQUERADED
MASQUERADER
MASQUERADING
MASS
MASSA
MASSACRE
MASSACRED
MASSACRER
MASSACRING
MASSACROUS
MASSAGE
MASSAGED
MASSAGER
MASSAGEUSE
MASSAGING
MASSAGIST
MASSARANDUBA
MASSASAUGA
MASSE
MASSEBAH
MASSECUITE
MASSED
MASSEL
MASSELGEM
MASSER
MASSES
MASSETER
MASSETERIC
MASSETERINE
MASSEUR
MASSEURS
MASSEUSE
MASSEUSES
MASSICOT
MASSIER
MASSIEST
MASSIF
MASSIG
MASSINESS
MASSIVE
MASSIVELY
MASSIVENESS
MASSIVITY
MASSOTHERAPY
MASSOY
MASSULA
MASSY
MASSYMORE
MAST
MASTABA
MASTABAH
MASTADENITIS
MASTADENOMA
MASTAGE
MASTALGIA
MASTATROPHIA
MASTATROPHY
MASTAUXE
MASTAX
MASTECTOMIES
MASTECTOMY
MASTED
MASTER
MASTERATE
MASTERDOM
MASTERED
MASTERER
MASTERFAST
MASTERFUL
MASTERFULLY
MASTERFULNESS
MASTERHOOD
MASTERIES
MASTERING
MASTERLESS
MASTERLILY
MASTERLINESS
MASTERLY
MASTERMAN
MASTERMEN
MASTERMIND
MASTEROUS
MASTERPIECE
MASTERSHIP
MASTERSINGER
MASTERSINGERS
MASTERSTROKE
MASTERWORK
MASTERWORT
MASTERY
MASTFUL
MASTHEAD
MASTIC
MASTICABLE
MASTICATE
MASTICATED
MASTICATING
MASTICATION
MASTICATOR
MASTICATORIES
MASTICATORY
MASTICIC
MASTICUROUS
MASTIFF
MASTIGATE
MASTIGIA
MASTIGIUM
MASTIGONEME
MASTIGOPOD

MASTIGOTE
MASTIGURE
MASTING
MASTITIS
MASTMAN
MASTMEN
MASTODON
MASTODONT
MASTODONTIC
MASTODONTINE
MASTODONTOID
MASTODYNIA
MASTOID
MASTOIDALE
MASTOIDITIS
MASTOIDOTOMY
MASTOLOGICAL
MASTOLOGIST
MASTOLOGY
MASTOMENIA
MASTOPATHY
MASTOPEXY
MASTOPLASTIA
MASTORRHAGIA
MASTOTOMY
MASTS
MASTURBATE
MASTURBATED
MASTURBATING
MASTURBATION
MASTURBATOR
MASTURBATORY
MASTWOOD
MASTY
MASU
MASURIUM
MAT
MATA
MATACHIN
MATACHINA
MATACHINAS
MATACO
MATADERO
MATADOR
MATAEOLOGUE
MATAEOLOGY
MATAEOTECHNY
MATAGASSE
MATAGORY
MATAI
MATAJUELO
MATALAN
MATAMATA
MATAMORO
MATANZA
MATAPAN
MATAPI
MATARA
MATASANO
MATAX
MATBOARD
MATCH
MATCHABLE
MATCHABLY
MATCHBOARD
MATCHBOARDING
MATCHBOOK
MATCHBOX
MATCHCLOTH
MATCHCOAT
MATCHED
MATCHER
MATCHING
MATCHLESS
MATCHLESSLY
MATCHLESSNESS
MATCHLOCK
MATCHMAKER
MATCHMAKING
MATCHMARK
MATCHSAFE
MATCHSTALK
MATCHSTICK
MATCHWOOD
MATCHY
MATE
MATED
MATEE
MATEGRIFFON
MATELASSE
MATELEY
MATELOT
MATELOTAGE
MATELOTE
MATELOTTE
MATER
MATERFAMILIAS
MATERIA
MATERIABLE
MATERIAL
MATERIALISM
MATERIALIST
MATERIALISTIC
MATERIALITY
MATERIALIZATION
MATERIALIZE
MATERIALIZED
MATERIALIZER
MATERIALIZING
MATERIALLY
MATERIALMAN
MATERIALMEN
MATERIALNESS
MATERIALS
MATERIATE
MATERIATION
MATERIEL
MATERNAL
MATERNALITY
MATERNALIZE
MATERNALLY
MATERNALNESS
MATERNITIES
MATERNITY
MATERNOLOGY
MATEY
MATEZITE
MATFELLON
MATFELON
MATGRASS
MATH
MATHE
MATHEMATIC
MATHEMATICAL
MATHEMATICALLY
MATHEMATICALS
MATHEMATICIAN
MATHEMATICS
MATHEMATIZE
MATHEMEG
MATHER
MATHES
MATHESIS
MATHETIC
MATHS
MATICO
MATIE
MATIES
MATILDITE
MATIN
MATINA
MATINAL
MATINEE
MATING
MATINS
MATIPO
MATKA
MATKAH
MATLOCKITE
MATLOW
MATMAKER
MATMAKING
MATMAN
MATRA
MATRACE
MATRAH
MATRAL
MATRANEE
MATRASS
MATREED
MATRIARCH
MATRIARCHAL
MATRIARCHATE
MATRIARCHIC
MATRIARCHIES
MATRIARCHIST
MATRIARCHY
MATRIC
MATRICAL
MATRICE
MATRICES
MATRICIDAL
MATRICIDE
MATRICULA
MATRICULABLE
MATRICULAE
MATRICULANT
MATRICULAR
MATRICULATE
MATRICULATED
MATRICULATING
MATRICULATION
MATRICULATOR
MATRICULATORY
MATRIHERITAGE
MATRIHERITAL
MATRILINEAL
MATRILINEAR
MATRILINY
MATRILOCAL
MATRIMONIAL
MATRIMONIES
MATRIMONIOUS
MATRIMONY
MATRIOTISM
MATRIS
MATRIX
MATRIXES
MATROCLINAL
MATROCLINIC
MATROCLINOUS
MATROCLINY
MATRON
MATRONAGE
MATRONAL
MATRONIZE
MATRONIZED
MATRONIZING
MATRONLIKE
MATRONLINESS
MATRONLY
MATRONYMIC
MATROSS
MATSTER
MATSU
MATSUE
MATSURI
MATTA
MATTAMORE
MATTARO
MATTE
MATTED
MATTEDLY
MATTEDNESS
MATTER
MATTERED
MATTERING
MATTERS
MATTERY
MATTI
MATTIN
MATTING
MATTO
MATTOCK
MATTOID
MATTOIR
MATTRASS
MATTRESS
MATTULLA
MATURABLE
MATURATE
MATURATED
MATURATING
MATURATION
MATURATIVE
MATURE
MATURED
MATURELY
MATURENESS
MATURER
MATURESCENCE
MATURESCENT
MATUREST
MATURING
MATURITY
MATUTINAL
MATUTINALLY
MATUTINARY
MATUTINE
MATUTINELY
MATWEED
MATY
MATZO
MATZOH
MATZOON
MATZOS
MATZOT
MATZOTH
MAU
MAUCACO
MAUCHERITE
MAUD
MAUDELINE
MAUDLE
MAUDLIN
MAUDLINISM
MAUDLINLY
MAUGER
MAUGH
MAUGHT
MAUGRE
MAUKA
MAUKIN
MAUL
MAULA
MAULANA
MAULED
MAULER
MAULEY
MAULING
MAULSTICK
MAULVI
MAUM
MAUMET
MAUMETRY
MAUN
MAUNA
MAUNCHE
MAUND
MAUNDER
MAUNDERED
MAUNDERER
MAUNDERING
MAUNDFUL
MAUNDY
MAUNGE
MAUNNA
MAURICIO
MAUSOLE
MAUSOLEA
MAUSOLEAL
MAUSOLEAN
MAUSOLEUM
MAUSOLEUMS
MAUT
MAUTHER
MAUVE
MAUVEIN
MAUVETTE
MAUVINE
MAUX
MAVERICK
MAVIE
MAVIS
MAVOURNEEN
MAVOURNIN
MAVRODAPHNE
MAW
MAWALI
MAWBOUND
MAWK
MAWKIN
MAWKISH
MAWKISHLY
MAWKISHNESS
MAWKS
MAWKY
MAWMISH
MAWP
MAWTHER
MAWWORM
MAX
MAXILLA
MAXILLAE
MAXILLARIES
MAXILLARY
MAXILLIFORM
MAXILLIPED
MAXILLIPEDARY
MAXILLIPEDE
MAXILLOJUGAL
MAXILLOLABIAL
MAXIM
MAXIMA
MAXIMAL
MAXIMALLY
MAXIMATE
MAXIMATION
MAXIMED
MAXIMIST
MAXIMISTIC
MAXIMITE
MAXIMIZATION
MAXIMIZE
MAXIMIZED
MAXIMIZER
MAXIMIZING
MAXIMUM
MAXIMUMS
MAXIMUS
MAXIXE
MAXWELL
MAY
MAYA
MAYACACEOUS

MAYAPIS
MAYAPPLE
MAYBE
MAYBERRY
MAYBUSH
MAYCOCK
MAYDAY
MAYDUKE
MAYENCE
MAYEST
MAYFISH
MAYFISHES
MAYFLOWER
MAYFLY
MAYHAP
MAYHAPPEN
MAYHAPS
MAYHEM
MAYNE
MAYONNAISE
MAYOR
MAYORAL
MAYORALTY
MAYORESS
MAYORSHIP
MAYPOLE
MAYPOP
MAYSIN
MAYST
MAYTEN
MAYTHE
MAYTHES
MAYWEED
MAZA
MAZAGRAN
MAZALGIA
MAZAME
MAZAPILITE
MAZAR
MAZARD
MAZARINE
MAZDOOR
MAZE
MAZED
MAZEDLY
MAZEDNESS
MAZEFUL
MAZER
MAZIC
MAZIER
MAZIEST
MAZILY
MAZINESS
MAZING
MAZODYNIA
MAZOLYSIS
MAZOLYTIC
MAZOPATHIA
MAZOPATHIC
MAZOPEXY
MAZOURKA
MAZUCA
MAZUMA
MAZURKA
MAZUT
MAZY
MAZZARD
MBORI
ME
MEABLE
MEACHING
MEACOCK
MEAD
MEADER
MEADOW
MEADOWED
MEADOWER
MEADOWING
MEADOWINK
MEADOWLAND
MEADOWLARK
MEADOWS
MEADOWSWEET
MEADOWY
MEADSMAN
MEADWORT
MEAGER
MEAGERLY
MEAGERNESS
MEAGRE
MEAGRELY
MEAGRENESS
MEAK
MEAL
MEALABLE
MEALED
MEALER
MEALIE
MEALIER
MEALIES
MEALIEST
MEALILY
MEALINESS
MEALING
MEALMAN
MEALMEN
MEALMONGER
MEALMOUTH
MEALMOUTHED
MEALOCK
MEALS
MEALTIDE
MEALTIME
MEALY
MEALYBUG
MEALYMOUTH
MEALYMOUTHED
MEALYWING
MEAN
MEANDER
MEANDERED
MEANDERER
MEANDERING
MEANDRITE
MEANDROUS
MEANED
MEANER
MEANEST
MEANIE
MEANING
MEANINGFUL
MEANINGFULLY
MEANINGFULNESS
MEANINGLESS
MEANINGLY
MEANINGNESS
MEANLESS
MEANLY
MEANNESS
MEANS
MEANT
MEANTIME
MEANTONE
MEANWHILE
MEANY
MEAR
MEARE
MEARSTONE
MEASE
MEASLE
MEASLED
MEASLEDNESS
MEASLES
MEASLIER
MEASLIEST
MEASLY
MEASONDUE
MEASURABILITY
MEASURABLE
MEASURABLY
MEASURAGE
MEASURATION
MEASURE
MEASURED
MEASUREDLY
MEASUREDNESS
MEASURELESS
MEASURELY
MEASUREMENT
MEASURER
MEASURES
MEASURING
MEAT
MEATAL
MEATBALL
MEATBIRD
MEATCUTTER
MEATED
MEATH
MEATHE
MEATHOOK
MEATIC
MEATIER
MEATIEST
MEATINESS
MEATLESS
MEATMAN
MEATMEN
MEATOMETER
MEATORRHAPHY
MEATOSCOPE
MEATOSCOPY
MEATOTOME
MEATOTOMY
MEATURE
MEATUS
MEATUSES
MEATWORKS
MEATY
MEBBE
MEBOS
MECATE
MECCA
MECHANALITY
MECHANALIZE
MECHANIC
MECHANICAL
MECHANICALLY
MECHANICIAN
MECHANICS
MECHANISM
MECHANIST
MECHANISTIC
MECHANIZATION
MECHANIZE
MECHANIZER
MECHANOLATER
MECHANOLOGY
MECHOACAN
MECKELECTOMY
MECODONT
MECOMETER
MECOMETRY
MECON
MECONIC
MECONIDIUM
MECONIN
MECONIOID
MECONIUM
MECONOLOGY
MECOPTERAN
MECOPTERON
MECOPTEROUS
MEDA
MEDAL
MEDALED
MEDALET
MEDALING
MEDALIST
MEDALIZE
MEDALLARY
MEDALLED
MEDALLIC
MEDALLICALLY
MEDALLING
MEDALLION
MEDALLIONED
MEDALLIONING
MEDALLIONIST
MEDDLE
MEDDLECOME
MEDDLED
MEDDLER
MEDDLESOME
MEDDLESOMELY
MEDDLING
MEDENAGAN
MEDIA
MEDIACID
MEDIACY
MEDIAD
MEDIAE
MEDIAEVAL
MEDIAEVALISM
MEDIAEVALIST
MEDIAL
MEDIALIZE
MEDIALKALINE
MEDIALLY
MEDIAN
MEDIANIC
MEDIANIMIC
MEDIANIMITY
MEDIANISM
MEDIANITY
MEDIANLY
MEDIANT
MEDIASTINA
MEDIASTINAL
MEDIASTINE
MEDIASTINUM
MEDIATE
MEDIATED
MEDIATELY
MEDIATING
MEDIATINGLY
MEDIATION
MEDIATIVE
MEDIATIZE
MEDIATIZED
MEDIATIZING
MEDIATOR
MEDIATORIAL
MEDIATORIOUS
MEDIATORY
MEDIATRESS
MEDIATRICE
MEDIATRIX
MEDIC
MEDICABLE
MEDICAL
MEDICALLY
MEDICAMENT
MEDICAMENTAL
MEDICARE
MEDICASTER
MEDICATE
MEDICATED
MEDICATING
MEDICATION
MEDICATIVE
MEDICATOR
MEDICATORY
MEDICINABLE
MEDICINAL
MEDICINARY
MEDICINE
MEDICINED
MEDICINER
MEDICINING
MEDICK
MEDICO
MEDICODENTAL
MEDICOLEGAL
MEDICOMORAL
MEDICOS
MEDIETY
MEDIEVAL
MEDIEVALISM
MEDIEVALIST
MEDIEVALLY
MEDIFIXED
MEDIGLACIAL
MEDILLE
MEDIMNO
MEDIMNOS
MEDIMNUS
MEDIN
MEDINE
MEDINO
MEDIO
MEDIOCARPAL
MEDIOCRAL
MEDIOCRE
MEDIOCRITIES
MEDIOCRITY
MEDIOCUBITAL
MEDIODIGITAL
MEDIODORSAL
MEDIOFRONTAL
MEDIOLATERAL
MEDIOPALATAL
MEDIOPASSIVE
MEDIOPONTINE
MEDIOSILICIC
MEDIOTARSAL
MEDIOVENTRAL
MEDISANCE
MEDISECT
MEDISECTION
MEDITABUND
MEDITANCE
MEDITANT
MEDITATE
MEDITATED
MEDITATER
MEDITATING
MEDITATION
MEDITATIST
MEDITATIVE
MEDITATIVELY
MEDITATOR
MEDITERRANE
MEDITERRANEAN
MEDITHORAX
MEDITULLIUM
MEDIUM
MEDIUMISTIC
MEDIUMIZE
MEDIUMS
MEDIUS
MEDJIDIE
MEDJIDIEH
MEDLAR
MEDLEY

MEDLEYED
MEDLEYING
MEDLEYS
MEDLIED
MEDREGAL
MEDRICK
MEDRINACKS
MEDRINACLES
MEDRINAQUE
MEDULLA
MEDULLAE
MEDULLAR
MEDULLARY
MEDULLAS
MEDULLATE
MEDULLATED
MEDULLATION
MEDULLITIS
MEDULLOSE
MEDULLOUS
MEDUSA
MEDUSAE
MEDUSAL
MEDUSAN
MEDUSAS
MEDUSIFEROUS
MEDUSIFORM
MEDUSOID
MEEBOS
MEECH
MEECHER
MEECHING
MEED
MEEDLESS
MEEK
MEEKEN
MEEKER
MEEKEST
MEEKHEARTED
MEEKLY
MEEKNESS
MEER
MEERED
MEERKAT
MEERSCHAUM
MEES
MEESE
MEET
MEETEN
MEETER
MEETERLY
MEETHELP
MEETHELPER
MEETING
MEETINGER
MEETINGHOUSE
MEETINGS
MEETLY
MEG
MEGABAR
MEGACEPHALIA
MEGACEPHALIC
MEGACEPHALY
MEGACERINE
MEGACEROTINE
MEGACHILID
MEGACOLON
MEGACURIE
MEGACYCLE
MEGADONT
MEGADYNAMICS
MEGADYNE
MEGAFARAD
MEGAFOG
MEGAGAMETE
MEGALEME
MEGALESTHETE
MEGALITH
MEGALITHIC
MEGALOBLAST
MEGALOBLASTIC
MEGALOCARDIA
MEGALOCORNEA
MEGALOCYTE
MEGALOGRAPH
MEGALOGRAPHY
MEGALOMANIA
MEGALOMANIAC
MEGALOMELIA
MEGALOPENIS
MEGALOPHONIC
MEGALOPIC
MEGALOPINE
MEGALOPOLIS
MEGALOPORE
MEGALOPS
MEGALOPSYCHY
MEGALOSAUR
MEGALOSCOPE
MEGALOSCOPY
MEGALOSPHERE
MEGAMETER
MEGAMETRE
MEGAMPERE
MEGAPHONE
MEGAPHONED
MEGAPHONIC
MEGAPHONING
MEGAPOD
MEGAPODE
MEGAPOLIS
MEGAPROSOPOUS
MEGAPTERINE
MEGARON
MEGASCLERE
MEGASCLERIC
MEGASCLEROUS
MEGASCLERUM
MEGASCOPE
MEGASCOPIC
MEGASCOPICAL
MEGASEISM
MEGASEISMIC
MEGASPORANGE
MEGASPORE
MEGASPORIC
MEGASS
MEGASSE
MEGATHERE
MEGATHERIAN
MEGATHERINE
MEGATHERIOID
MEGATHERIUM
MEGATHERM
MEGATHERMIC
MEGATHEROID
MEGATON
MEGATYPE
MEGATYPY
MEGAVOLT
MEGAZOOID
MEGAZOOSPORE
MEGILP
MEGILPH
MEGOHM
MEGOHMIT
MEGOHMMETER
MEGOMIT
MEGOTALC
MEGRIM
MEGRIMS
MEGUILP
MEHALLA
MEHARI
MEHARIS
MEHARIST
MEHMANDAR
MEHTAR
MEHTARSHIP
MEILE
MEILER
MEIN
MEINIE
MEINIES
MEINY
MEIO
MEIOBAR
MEIONITE
MEIOPHYLLY
MEIOSIS
MEIOTAXY
MEIOTIC
MEISJE
MEITH
MEIZOSEISMAL
MEIZOSEISMIC
MEJORANA
MEKE
MEKIL
MEKILTA
MEKOMETER
MEL
MELA
MELACONITE
MELADA
MELADIORITE
MELAENA
MELAENIC
MELAGABBRO
MELAGRA
MELAGRANITE
MELALGIA
MELAM
MELAMED
MELAMIN
MELAMINE
MELAMMED
MELAMPOD
MELAMPODE
MELAMPODIUM
MELAMPYRIN
MELAMPYRITE
MELAMPYRITOL
MELANAEMIA
MELANAEMIC
MELANAGOGAL
MELANAGOGUE
MELANCHOLIA
MELANCHOLIAC
MELANCHOLIC
MELANCHOLIES
MELANCHOLIOUS
MELANCHOLIST
MELANCHOLIZE
MELANCHOLY
MELANEMIA
MELANEMIC
MELANGE
MELANGER
MELANGES
MELANGEUR
MELANIAN
MELANIC
MELANIFEROUS
MELANIN
MELANISM
MELANISTIC
MELANITE
MELANITIC
MELANIZE
MELANO
MELANOBLAST
MELANOCERITE
MELANOCHROIC
MELANOCOMOUS
MELANOCRATE
MELANOCRATIC
MELANODERMA
MELANODERMIA
MELANODERMIC
MELANOGEN
MELANOID
MELANOMA
MELANOMAS
MELANOMATA
MELANOPATHIA
MELANOPATHY
MELANOPHORE
MELANOPLAKIA
MELANORRHEA
MELANOSCOPE
MELANOSE
MELANOSED
MELANOSITY
MELANOTEKITE
MELANOTIC
MELANOUS
MELANTERITE
MELANTHY
MELANURE
MELANURENIC
MELANURESIS
MELANURIA
MELANURIC
MELAPHYRE
MELASMA
MELASMIC
MELASSIGENIC
MELASTOMAD
MELASTOME
MELATOPE
MELAXUMA
MELCH
MELD
MELDER
MELDOMETER
MELDROP
MELE
MELEAGRINE
MELEE
MELENA
MELENE
MELENIC
MELEZITASE
MELEZITOSE
MELIACEOUS
MELIATIN
MELIBIOSE
MELIC
MELICERA
MELICERIC
MELICERIS
MELICEROUS
MELICHROUS
MELICITOSE
MELICRATE
MELICRATON
MELICRATORY
MELICRATUM
MELILITE
MELILITITE
MELILOT
MELINE
MELINITE
MELIORABILITY
MELIORABLE
MELIORANT
MELIORATE
MELIORATED
MELIORATER
MELIORATING
MELIORATION
MELIORATIVE
MELIORATOR
MELIORISM
MELIORIST
MELIORISTIC
MELIORITY
MELIPHAGOUS
MELIPHANITE
MELIPONINE
MELIS
MELISMA
MELISMATA
MELISMATIC
MELISMATICS
MELITAEMIA
MELITEMIA
MELITHAEMIA
MELITHEMIA
MELITIS
MELITTOLOGIST
MELITTOLOGY
MELITURIA
MELITURIC
MELKHOUT
MELL
MELLAGINOUS
MELLAH
MELLATE
MELLAY
MELLEOUS
MELLER
MELLIFEROUS
MELLIFICATE
MELLIFICATION
MELLIFLUATE
MELLIFLUENCE
MELLIFLUENT
MELLIFLUENTLY
MELLIFLUOUS
MELLILOT
MELLISONANT
MELLISUGENT
MELLIT
MELLITATE
MELLITE
MELLITIC
MELLIVOROUS
MELLON
MELLONE
MELLONIDES
MELLOPHONE
MELLOW
MELLOWED
MELLOWER
MELLOWEST
MELLOWING
MELLOWLY
MELLOWNESS
MELLOWY
MELLSMAN
MELOCOTON
MELOCOTOON
MELODEON
MELODIA
MELODIAL
MELODIALLY
MELODIC
MELODICA
MELODICAL
MELODICALLY
MELODICS
MELODIED
MELODIES

MELODION
MELODIOUS
MELODIOUSLY
MELODIOUSNESS
MELODISM
MELODIST
MELODIZE
MELODIZED
MELODIZER
MELODIZING
MELODRAMA
MELODRAMATIC
MELODRAMATICAL
MELODRACTICALLY
MELODRAMATICS
MELODRAMATIST
MELODRAMATIZE
MELODY
MELODYING
MELOE
MELOGRAM
MELOGRAPH
MELOGRAPHIC
MELOID
MELOLOGUE
MELOLONTHINE
MELOMAME
MELOMANIA
MELOMANIAC
MELOMANIC
MELON
MELONCUS
MELONGENA
MELONGROWER
MELONIST
MELONITE
MELONLIKE
MELONMONGER
MELONRY
MELOPHONE
MELOPHONIC
MELOPHONIST
MELOPIANO
MELOPIANOS
MELOPLAST
MELOPLASTIC
MELOPLASTY
MELOPOEIA
MELOPOEIC
MELOS
MELOTE
MELOTRAGEDY
MELOTRAGIC
MELOTROPE
MELPELL
MELSH
MELT
MELTABILITY
MELTABLE
MELTAGE
MELTED
MELTEIGITE
MELTER
MELTERS
MELTETH
MELTING
MELTINGLY
MELTINGNESS
MELTITH
MELTON
MELTWATER
MELVIE
MEM
MEMBER
MEMBERED
MEMBERS
MEMBERSHIP
MEMBRACID
MEMBRACINE
MEMBRAL
MEMBRALLY
MEMBRANA
MEMBRANATE
MEMBRANE
MEMBRANED
MEMBRANELLA
MEMBRANELLE
MEMBRANIFORM
MEMBRANIN
MEMBRANOID
MEMBRANOLOGY
MEMBRANOSIS
MEMBRANOUS
MEMBRANOUSLY
MEMBRANULA
MEMBRANULE
MEMBRETTE
MEMBRETTO
MEMEL
MEMENTO
MEMENTOES
MEMENTOS
MEMINNA
MEMO
MEMOIR
MEMOIRISM
MEMOIRIST
MEMOIRS
MEMORABILE
MEMORABILIA
MEMORABILITY
MEMORABLE
MEMORABLY
MEMORANDA
MEMORANDIST
MEMORANDIZE
MEMORANDUM
MEMORANDUMS
MEMORATE
MEMORATION
MEMORATIVE
MEMORIA
MEMORIAL
MEMORIALIST
MEMORIALIZE
MEMORIALIZED
MEMORIALIZER
MEMORIALIZING
MEMORIALLY
MEMORIED
MEMORIES
MEMORIOUS
MEMORIST
MEMORITER
MEMORIZATION
MEMORIZE
MEMORIZED
MEMORIZER
MEMORIZING
MEMORY
MEMOS
MEN
MENACE
MENACED
MENACER
MENACING
MENACINGLY
MENACME
MENAGE
MENAGERIE
MENAGERIST
MENALD
MENARCHE
MENAT
MEND
MENDACIOUS
MENDACIOUSLY
MENDACITIES
MENDACITY
MENDED
MENDEE
MENDELEVIUM
MENDER
MENDICANCY
MENDICANT
MENDICATE
MENDICATED
MENDICATING
MENDICATION
MENDICITY
MENDIGO
MENDING
MENDINGS
MENDIPITE
MENDOLE
MENDOZITE
MENDY
MENE
MENEGHINITE
MENEHUNE
MENEL
MENFOLK
MENFOLKS
MENG
MENHADEN
MENHADENS
MENHIR
MENIAL
MENIALISM
MENIALITY
MENIALLY
MENIALTY
MENILITE
MENINGEAL
MENINGES
MENINGIC
MENINGINA
MENINGISM
MENINGISMUS
MENINGITIC
MENINGITIDES
MENINGITIS
MENINGOCELE
MENINGORRHEA
MENINGOSIS
MENINTING
MENINX
MENISCAL
MENISCATE
MENISCI
MENISCIFORM
MENISCITIS
MENISCOID
MENISCOIDAL
MENISCUS
MENISCUSES
MENISE
MENISON
MENISPERM
MENISPERMIN
MENISPERMINE
MENKIND
MENNOM
MENNON
MENNUET
MENO
MENOGNATH
MENOGNATHOUS
MENOLOGIES
MENOLOGY
MENOMINEE
MENOPAUSE
MENOPAUSIC
MENOPHANIA
MENOPLANIA
MENORRHAGIA
MENORRHAGIC
MENORRHAGY
MENORRHEA
MENORRHEIC
MENORRHOEA
MENORRHOEIC
MENOSCHESIS
MENOSCHETIC
MENOSEPSIS
MENOSTASIA
MENOSTASIS
MENOSTATIC
MENOSTAXIS
MENOTYPHLIC
MENOXENIA
MENSA
MENSAE
MENSAL
MENSALIZE
MENSE
MENSEFUL
MENSELESS
MENSERVANTS
MENSES
MENSHEVIK
MENSK
MENSTRUA
MENSTRUAL
MENSTRUANT
MENSTRUATE
MENSTRUATED
MENSTRUATING
MENSTRUATION
MENSTRUOSITY
MENSTRUOUS
MENSTRUUM
MENSTRUUMS
MENSUAL
MENSURABLE
MENSURABLY
MENSURAL
MENSURALIST
MENSURATE
MENSURATION
MENSURATIVE
MENT
MENTA
MENTAGRA
MENTAL
MENTALIS
MENTALISM
MENTALIST
MENTALISTIC
MENTALITIES
MENTALITY
MENTALLY
MENTATION
MENTERY
MENTHACEOUS
MENTHADIENE
MENTHAN
MENTHANE
MENTHE
MENTHENE
MENTHENOL
MENTHENONE
MENTHOL
MENTHOLATED
MENTHONE
MENTHYL
MENTICULTURE
MENTIFEROUS
MENTIFORM
MENTIGEROUS
MENTIMETER
MENTION
MENTIONABLE
MENTIONED
MENTIONER
MENTIONING
MENTOHYOID
MENTOLABIAL
MENTONIERE
MENTONNIERE
MENTOR
MENTORIAL
MENTUM
MENU
MENUS
MEOW
MEPHITIC
MEPHITICAL
MEPHITINE
MEPHITIS
MEPHITISM
MEPROBAMATE
MER
MERAI
MERALGIA
MERALINE
MERBABY
MERCANTILE
MERCANTILELY
MERCANTILISM
MERCANTILIST
MERCANTILISTIC
MERCANTILITY
MERCAPTAL
MERCAPTAN
MERCAPTIDES
MERCAPTIDS
MERCAPTO
MERCAPTOL
MERCAPTOLE
MERCATORIAL
MERCATURE
MERCE
MERCEMENT
MERCENARIAN
MERCENARIES
MERCENARILY
MERCENARY
MERCER
MERCERESS
MERCERIES
MERCERIZE
MERCERIZED
MERCERIZER
MERCERIZING
MERCERY
MERCH
MERCHANDISABLE
MERCHANDISE
MERCHANDISED
MERCHANDISER
MERCHANDIZE
MERCHANDRISE
MERCHANDRY
MERCHANDY
MERCHANT
MERCHANTABLE
MERCHANTEER
MERCHANTER
MERCHANTLIKE
MERCHANTLY
MERCHANTMAN
MERCHANTMEN
MERCHANTRY
MERCHANTSHIP

MERCHET
MERCI
MERCIABLE
MERCIABLELY
MERCIABLY
MERCIES
MERCIFUL
MERCIFULLY
MERCIFULNESS
MERCIFY
MERCILESS
MERCILESSLY
MERCILESSNESS
MERCIMENT
MERCURATE
MERCURATION
MERCURIAL
MERCURIALISM
MERCURIALIST
MERCURIALITY
MERCURIALIZE
MERCURIALLY
MERCURIATE
MERCURIC
MERCURID
MERCURIDE
MERCURIES
MERCURIFIED
MERCURIFY
MERCURIFYING
MERCURIZE
MERCURIZED
MERCURIZING
MERCUROUS
MERCURY
MERCY
MERD
MERDA
MERDIVOROUS
MERDURINOUS
MERE
MERED
MEREL
MERELS
MERELY
MERENCHYMA
MERESMAN
MERESMEN
MEREST
MERESTONE
MERESWINE
MERETRICES
MERETRICIOUS
MERETRIX
MERFOLD
MERFOLK
MERGANSER
MERGE
MERGED
MERGENCE
MERGER
MERGH
MERGING
MERIAH
MERICARP
MERICE
MERIDIAN
MERIDIONAL
MERIDIONALLY
MERINGUE
MERINGUED
MERINO
MERINOS
MERIQUINONE
MERIQUINONIC
MERISM
MERISMATIC
MERISMOID
MERIST
MERISTELE
MERISTEM
MERISTEMATIC
MERISTIC
MERISTICALLY
MERIT
MERITABLE
MERITED
MERITEDLY
MERITER
MERITING
MERITMONGER
MERITMONGERY
MERITORIOUS
MERITORY
MERKHET
MERKIN
MERL
MERLE
MERLETTE
MERLIGO
MERLIN
MERLON
MERMAID
MERMAIDEN
MERMAN
MERMEN
MERMITHANER
MERMITHIZED
MERMITHOGYNE
MERMOTHER
MERO
MEROBLASTIC
MEROCELE
MEROCELIC
MEROCERITE
MEROCERITIC
MEROCYTE
MEROGAMY
MEROGASTRULA
MEROGENESIS
MEROGENETIC
MEROGENIC
MEROGNATHITE
MEROGONIC
MEROGONY
MEROHEDRAL
MEROHEDRIC
MEROHEDRISM
MEROISTIC
MEROMORPHIC
MEROP
MEROPIA
MEROPIC
MEROPIDAN
MEROPLANKTON
MEROPODITE
MEROPODITIC
MERORGANIZE
MEROS
MEROSOMAL
MEROSOMATOUS
MEROSOME
MEROSTHENIC
MEROSTOME
MEROTOMIZE
MEROTOMY
MEROTROPISM
MEROTROPY
MEROXENE
MEROZOITE
MERPEOPLE
MERRIER
MERRIEST
MERRILESS
MERRILY
MERRIMENT
MERRINESS
MERROW
MERROWES
MERRY
MERRYMAKE
MERRYMAKER
MERRYMAKING
MERRYMAN
MERRYMEETING
MERRYMEN
MERRYTHOUGHT
MERRYTROTTER
MERRYWING
MERSE
MERSION
MERULIOID
MERVEILLEUX
MERWINITE
MERWOMAN
MERYCISM
MES
MESA
MESABITE
MESACONATE
MESACONIC
MESADENIA
MESAIL
MESAL
MESALLIANCE
MESALLY
MESAMEBOID
MESANGE
MESAORTITIS
MESARAIC
MESARAICAL
MESARCH
MESARTERITIC
MESARTERITIS
MESATICEPHAL
MESATISKELIC
MESAXONIC
MESCAL
MESCALISM
MESCHANT
MESCHANTLY
MESDAMES
MESE
MESECTODERM
MESEEMS
MESEL
MESELED
MESELEDNESS
MESELRY
MESELY
MESEM
MESEMBRYO
MESEMBRYONIC
MESENCHYMA
MESENCHYMAL
MESENCHYME
MESENDODERM
MESENNA
MESENTERA
MESENTERIAL
MESENTERIC
MESENTERICAL
MESENTERIES
MESENTERITIC
MESENTERITIS
MESENTERIUM
MESENTERON
MESENTERONIC
MESENTERY
MESEPIMERAL
MESEPIMERON
MESETHMOID
MESETHMOIDAL
MESH
MESHED
MESHING
MESHRABIYEH
MESHREBEEYEH
MESHUGGA
MESHUMMAD
MESHWORK
MESHY
MESIAD
MESIAL
MESIALLY
MESIAN
MESIC
MESILLA
MESIODISTAL
MESIOINCISAL
MESIOLABIAL
MESIOLINGUAL
MESIOPULPAL
MESITINE
MESITITE
MESITYL
MESITYLENE
MESKED
MESMERIAN
MESMERIC
MESMERICAL
MESMERICALLY
MESMERISE
MESMERISM
MESMERIST
MESMERITE
MESMERIZATION
MESMERIZE
MESMERIZED
MESMERIZEE
MESMERIZER
MESMERIZING
MESNALITY
MESNALTIES
MESNALTY
MESNE
MESO
MESOAPPENDIX
MESOARIAL
MESOARIUM
MESOBAR
MESOBENTHOS
MESOBLAST
MESOBLASTEM
MESOBLASTEMA
MESOBLASTIC
MESOBREGMATE
MESOCAECAL
MESOCAECUM
MESOCARDIA
MESOCARDIUM
MESOCARP
MESOCENTROUS
MESOCEPHAL
MESOCEPHALIC
MESOCEPHALON
MESOCEPHALOUS
MESOCEPHALY
MESOCHILIUM
MESOCHROIC
MESOCOELE
MESOCOELIA
MESOCOELIAN
MESOCOELIC
MESOCOLIC
MESOCOLON
MESOCORACOID
MESOCRANIAL
MESOCRATIC
MESODE
MESODERM
MESODERMAL
MESODERMIC
MESODIC
MESODONT
MESOFURCA
MESOFURCAL
MESOGASTER
MESOGASTRAL
MESOGASTRIC
MESOGASTRIUM
MESOGLOEA
MESOGLOEAL
MESOGNATHIC
MESOGNATHION
MESOGNATHISM
MESOGNATHOUS
MESOGNATHY
MESOGYRATE
MESOHEPAR
MESOLABE
MESOLE
MESOLECITHAL
MESOLIMNION
MESOLITE
MESOLITHIC
MESOLOGIC
MESOLOGY
MESOMERE
MESOMETRAL
MESOMETRIC
MESOMETRIUM
MESOMORPH
MESOMORPHIC
MESOMORPHOUS
MESOMORPHY
MESOMYODIAN
MESOMYODOUS
MESON
MESONASAL
MESONEPHRIC
MESONEPHROS
MESONOTAL
MESONOTUM
MESOPAUSE
MESOPETALUM
MESOPHIL
MESOPHILE
MESOPHILIC
MESOPHILOUS
MESOPHRAGMA
MESOPHRAGMAL
MESOPHRYON
MESOPHYL
MESOPHYLL
MESOPHYLLUM
MESOPHYTE
MESOPHYTIC
MESOPHYTISM
MESOPIC
MESOPLANKTON
MESOPLAST
MESOPLASTIC
MESOPLASTRA
MESOPLASTRAL
MESOPLASTRON
MESOPLEURA
MESOPLEURAL
MESOPLEURON
MESOPLODONT
MESOPODIA
MESOPODIAL
MESOPODIALE
MESOPODIALIA
MESOPODIUM

MESOPOTAMIA
MESOPROSOPIC
MESORCHIAL
MESORCHIUM
MESORECTAL
MESORECTUM
MESORHIN
MESORHINAL
MESORHINE
MESORHINIAN
MESORHINISM
MESORHINIUM
MESORHINY
MESORRHIN
MESORRHINAL
MESORRHINIAN
MESORRHINISM
MESORRHINIUM
MESORRHINY
MESOSALPINX
MESOSAUR
MESOSCAPULA
MESOSCAPULAR
MESOSCUTAL
MESOSCUTUM
MESOSEISMAL
MESOSEME
MESOSIGMOID
MESOSOMA
MESOSOMATA
MESOSOMATIC
MESOSPERM
MESOSPHERE
MESOSPHERIC
MESOSPORE
MESOSPORIC
MESOSTASIS
MESOSTERNA
MESOSTERNAL
MESOSTERNUM
MESOSTETHIUM
MESOSTOMID
MESOSTYLOUS
MESOSUCHIAN
MESOTARSAL
MESOTHELIAL
MESOTHELIUM
MESOTHERM
MESOTHERMAL
MESOTHESIS
MESOTHETIC
MESOTHETICAL
MESOTHORACIC
MESOTHORAX
MESOTHORIUM
MESOTONIC
MESOTROCH
MESOTROCHA
MESOTROCHAL
MESOTROCHOUS
MESOTRON
MESOTROPIC
MESOTYPE
MESOVARIA
MESOVARIAN
MESOVARIUM
MESOVENTRAL
MESOVENTRALLY
MESOXALATE
MESOXALIC
MESOXALYL
MESOZOAN
MESPIL
MESQUIN
MESQUITA
MESQUITE
MESS
MESSAGE
MESSAGED
MESSAGERY
MESSAGING
MESSALINE
MESSAN
MESSE
MESSED
MESSELITE
MESSENGER
MESSER
MESSET
MESSIER
MESSIEST
MESSIEURS
MESSILY
MESSIN
MESSINESS
MESSING
MESSIRE
MESSMAN
MESSMATE
MESSMEN
MESSOR
MESSROOM
MESSTIN
MESSUAGE
MESSY
MESTA
MESTEE
MESTENO
MESTESO
MESTFULL
MESTINO
MESTIZA
MESTIZO
MESTIZOES
MESTIZOS
MESTLEN
MESTO
MESTOME
MESYMNION
MET
META
METABASES
METABASIS
METABASITE
METABATIC
METABIOLOGICAL
METABIOLOGY
METABIOSIS
METABIOTIC
METABLETIC
METABOLE
METABOLIAN
METABOLIC
METABOLICAL
METABOLISM
METABOLITE
METABOLIZE
METABOLIZED
METABOLIZING
METABOLON
METABOLOUS
METABOLY
METABORATE
METABORIC
METABRANCHIAL
METABRUSHITE
METABULAR
METACARPAL
METACARPALE
METACARPUS
METACENTER
METACENTRAL
METACENTRE
METACENTRIC
METACHEMIC
METACHEMICAL
METACHEMISTRY
METACHROME
METACHRONISM
METACHROSIS
METACISM
METACLASE
METACNEME
METACOELE
METACONAL
METACONE
METACONID
METACONULE
METACORACOID
METACRASIS
METACROMIAL
METACROMION
METACRYST
METACYCLIC
METAD
METADROMOUS
METAE
METAFLUIDAL
METAGALACTIC
METAGALAXIES
METAGALAXY
METAGASTER
METAGASTRIC
METAGASTRULA
METAGE
METAGELATIN
METAGELATINE
METAGENESIS
METAGENETIC
METAGENIC
METAGEOMETER
METAGEOMETRY
METAGNATH
METAGNATHISM
METAGNATHOUS
METAGNOMY
METAGNOSTIC
METAGRAM
METAGRAPHIC
METAGRAPHY
METAIGNEOUS
METAIRIE
METAKINESIS
METAKINETIC
METAL
METALCRAFT
METALDEHYDE
METALED
METALEPSES
METALEPSIS
METALEPTIC
METALEPTICAL
METALER
METALINE
METALINED
METALING
METALISE
METALIST
METALIZATION
METALIZE
METALIZED
METALIZING
METALLARY
METALLED
METALLEITY
METALLER
METALLIC
METALLICAL
METALLICALLY
METALLICITY
METALLICLY
METALLICS
METALLIDE
METALLIFORM
METALLIFY
METALLIK
METALLINE
METALLING
METALLISH
METALLIST
METALLIZATION
METALLIZE
METALLOGENIC
METALLOGENY
METALLOGRAPH
METALLOID
METALLOIDAL
METALLOMETER
METALLOPHONE
METALLURGIC
METALLURGICAL
METALLURGIST
METALLURGY
METALOGIC
METALOGICAL
METALOPH
METALORGANIC
METALOSCOPE
METALOSCOPY
METALS
METALUMINATE
METALWARE
METALWORK
METALWORKER
METALWORKING
METALWORKS
METAMER
METAMERAL
METAMERE
METAMERIC
METAMERIDE
METAMERISM
METAMERIZED
METAMEROUS
METAMERY
METAMORPHIC
METAMORPHISM
METAMORPHIZE
METAMORPHOSE
METAMORPHOSED
METAMORPHOSING
METAMORPHOSIS
METAMORPHOSY
METAMORPHOUS
METAMORPHY
METANALYSIS
METANAUPLIUS
METANEPHRIC
METANEPHRITIC
METANEPHRON
METANEPHROS
METANEPIONIC
METANILINE
METANOMEN
METANOTAL
METANOTUM
METANYM
METAPEPTONE
METAPHASE
METAPHLOEM
METAPHONICAL
METAPHONIZE
METAPHONY
METAPHOR
METAPHORIC
METAPHORICAL
METAPHORICALLY
METAPHORIST
METAPHRAGM
METAPHRAGMA
METAPHRAGMAL
METAPHRASE
METAPHRASED
METAPHRASING
METAPHRAST
METAPHRASTIC
METAPHYSEAL
METAPHYSIC
METAPHYSICAL
METAPHYSICALLY
METAPHYSICIAN
METAPHYSICIST
METAPHYSICS
METAPHYSIS
METAPHYTE
METAPLASIA
METAPLASIS
METAPLASM
METAPLASMIC
METAPLAST
METAPLASTIC
METAPLEUR
METAPLEURA
METAPLEURAL
METAPLEURE
METAPLEURON
METAPNEUSTIC
METAPODIA
METAPODIAL
METAPODIALE
METAPODIUM
METAPOLITIC
METAPOLITICAL
METAPOLITICIAN
METAPOLITICS
METAPOPHYSIS
METAPORE
METAPROTEIN
METAPSYCHIC
METAPSYCHICAL
METAPSYCHICS
METAPSYCHISM
METAPSYCHIST
METAPSYCHOLOGY
METAROSSITE
METASCUTUM
METASOMA
METASOMASIS
METASOMATA
METASOMATIC
METASOMATISM
METASPERM
METASPERMIC
METASPERMOUS
METASTABLE
METASTANNATE
METASTASES
METASTASIS
METASTASIZE
METASTASIZED
METASTATIC
METASTATICAL
METASTATICALLY
METASTERNAL
METASTERNUM
METASTHENIC
METASTIBNITE
METASTOMA
METASTOMATA
METASTROPHE
METASTROPHIC
METATARSAL
METATARSALE
METATARSE
METATARSI

METATARSUS
METATATIC
METATATICAL
METATAXIC
METATAXIS
METATE
METATHALAMUS
METATHESES
METATHESIS
METATHETIC
METATHETICAL
METATHORACIC
METATHORAX
METATHORAXES
METATITANATE
METATROPHIC
METATYPE
METATYPIC
METAVANADATE
METAVAUXITE
METAVOLTINE
METAXITE
METAXYLEM
METAYAGE
METAYER
METAZOAL
METAZOAN
METAZOEA
METAZOIC
METAZOON
METE
METED
METEL
METEMPIRIC
METEMPIRICAL
METEMPIRICS
METEMPSYCHIC
METEMPSYCHOSIS
METEMPTOSIS
METENTERON
METENTERONIC
METEOR
METEORGRAPH
METEORIC
METEORICAL
METEORICALLY
METEORISM
METEORIST
METEORISTIC
METEORITAL
METEORITE
METEORITICS
METEORIZE
METEORLIKE
METEOROGRAM
METEOROGRAPH
METEOROID
METEOROIDAL
METEOROLITE
METEOROLITIC
METEOROLOGIC
METEOROLOGICAL
METEOROLOGICALLY
METEOROLOGIST
METEOROLOGY
METEOROMETER
METEOROSCOPY
METEOROUS
METEORSCOPE
METEPIMERON
METER
METERAGE
METERED
METERER
METERGRAM
METERING
METERMAN
METESTICK
METEWAND
METEYARD
METHACRYLATE
METHACRYLIC
METHADONE
METHANAL
METHANATE
METHANATED
METHANATING
METHANE
METHANOIC
METHANOL
METHANOMETER
METHE
METHEGLIN
METHENAMINE
METHENE
METHENYL
METHER
METHIDE
METHINE
METHINKS
METHIODIDE
METHIONIC
METHIONINE
METHOD
METHODIC
METHODICAL
METHODICALLY
METHODICALNESS
METHODICS
METHODISM
METHODIST
METHODIZE
METHODIZED
METHODIZER
METHODIZING
METHODLESS
METHODOLOGICAL
METHODOLOGICALLY
METHODOLOGIST
METHODOLOGY
METHODS
METHONE
METHOUGHT
METHOXY
METHOXYL
METHRONIC
METHYL
METHYLAL
METHYLAMINE
METHYLATE
METHYLATED
METHYLATING
METHYLATION
METHYLATOR
METHYLENE
METHYLENITAN
METHYLIC
METHYLOSIS
METHYLOTIC
METIC
METICULOSITY
METICULOUS
METICULOUSLY
METIER
METIF
METING
METIS
METISSE
METOCHOUS
METOCHY
METOESTROUS
METOESTRUM
METONYM
METONYMIC
METONYMICAL
METONYMOUS
METONYMOUSLY
METONYMY
METOPE
METOPIC
METOPION
METOPISM
METOPOMANCY
METOPON
METOPOSCOPIC
METOPOSCOPY
METORGANISM
METOSTEAL
METOSTEON
METRA
METRALGIA
METRAN
METRANEMIA
METRATONIA
METRAZOL
METRE
METRECTASIA
METRECTATIC
METRECTOMY
METRECTOPIA
METRECTOPIC
METRECTOPY
METREGRAM
METREME
METRETA
METRETES
METREZA
METRIA
METRIC
METRICAL
METRICALLY
METRICIAN
METRICISM
METRICIST
METRICIZE
METRICS
METRIFIED
METRIFIER
METRIFY
METRIFYING
METRIST
METRITIS
METRO
METROLOGICAL
METROLOGIST
METROLOGUE
METROLOGY
METROMANIA
METROMANIAC
METRONOME
METRONOMIC
METRONOMICAL
METRONYM
METRONYMIC
METRONYMY
METROPOLE
METROPOLEIS
METROPOLIC
METROPOLIS
METROPOLISES
METROPOLITAN
METROPOLITE
METRORRHAGIA
METRORRHAGIC
METRORTHOSIS
METROSTYLE
METTAR
METTLE
METTLED
METTLESOME
METTLESOMELY
METUMP
METUSIA
METWAND
METZE
MEUBLES
MEUM
MEURE
MEUSE
MEUTE
MEW
MEWED
MEWER
MEWING
MEWL
MEWLED
MEWLER
MEWLING
MEWS
MEXICAL
MEZCAL
MEZCALINE
MEZEREON
MEZEREUM
MEZQUIT
MEZQUITE
MEZUZA
MEZUZAH
MEZUZAHS
MEZUZOTH
MEZZA
MEZZANINE
MEZZO
MEZZOGRAPH
MEZZOS
MEZZOTINT
MEZZOTINTED
MEZZOTINTER
MEZZOTINTING
MEZZOTINTO
MHO
MHOMETER
MHORR
MI
MIAMIA
MIAN
MIANG
MIAOU
MIAOW
MIAOWER
MIARGYRITE
MIAROLITIC
MIAS
MIASCITE
MIASKITE
MIASM
MIASMA
MIASMAL
MIASMAS
MIASMATA
MIASMATIC
MIASMATICAL
MIASMATOLOGY
MIASMATOUS
MIASMIC
MIASMOLOGY
MIASMOUS
MIAUER
MIAUL
MIAULED
MIAULER
MIAULING
MIAUW
MIB
MICA
MICACEOUS
MICACIOUS
MICACITE
MICASIZATION
MICASIZE
MICATE
MICATION
MICE
MICELL
MICELLA
MICELLAR
MICELLE
MICH
MICHE
MICHED
MICHER
MICHERY
MICHING
MICK
MICKERY
MICKEY
MICKEYS
MICKLE
MICKLENESS
MICO
MICONCAVE
MICRA
MICRACOUSTIC
MICRAESTHETE
MICRAMOCK
MICRANDER
MICRANDROUS
MICRANER
MICRESTHETE
MICRIFIED
MICRIFY
MICRIFYING
MICRO
MICROAMMETER
MICROANALYSIS
MICROANALYST
MICROBAL
MICROBALANCE
MICROBATTERY
MICROBE
MICROBEPROOF
MICROBIAL
MICROBIAN
MICROBIC
MICROBICIDE
MICROBIOSIS
MICROBIOTA
MICROBIOTIC
MICROBIOUS
MICROBISM
MICROBOTANY
MICROBURNER
MICROCARPOUS
MICROCENTRUM
MICROCEPHAL
MICROCEPHALI
MICROCEPHALY
MICROCHAETA
MICROCHAETAE
MICROCIRCUIT
MICROCLASTIC
MICROCLIMATE
MICROCLINE
MICROCOAT
MICROCOCCAL
MICROCOCCI
MICROCOCCUS
MICROCOPIED
MICROCOPIES
MICROCOPY
MICROCOPYING
MICROCOSM
MICROCOSMAL
MICROCOSMIAN
MICROCOSMIC

MICROCOSMOS
MICROCRANOUS
MICROCRITH
MICROCYST
MICROCYTE
MICROCYTOSIS
MICRODONT
MICRODONTISM
MICRODONTOUS
MICRODRAWING
MICRODRIVE
MICROFELSITE
MICROFICHE
MICROFILARIA
MICROFILM
MICROFLUIDAL
MICROFORM
MICROGAMETE
MICROGAMY
MICROGLIA
MICROGRAM
MICROGRAMME
MICROGRANITE
MICROGRAPH
MICROGRAPHER
MICROGRAPHIC
MICROGRAPHY
MICROGRAVER
MICROGROOVE
MICROHMMETER
MICROINCH
MICROLEVEL
MICROLITE
MICROLITH
MICROLITHIC
MICROLITIC
MICROLOGIC
MICROLOGICAL
MICROLOGUE
MICROLOGY
MICROMANIA
MICROMANIAC
MICROMELIA
MICROMELIC
MICROMELUS
MICROMERAL
MICROMERE
MICROMERIC
MICROMERISM
MICROMERITIC
MICROMETER
MICROMETHOD
MICROMETRIC
MICROMETRY
MICROMHO
MICROMICRON
MICROMODULE
MICROMOTION
MICRON
MICRONOMETER
MICRONUCLEAR
MICRONUCLEI
MICRONUCLEUS
MICROORGANIC
MICROORGANISM
MICROORGANISMS
MICROPHAGE
MICROPHAGOUS
MICROPHAGY
MICROPHONE
MICROPHONIC
MICROPHONICS
MICROPHYSICS
MICROPHYTAL
MICROPHYTE
MICROPHYTIC
MICROPIN
MICROPIPET
MICROPIPETTE
MICROPLAKITE
MICROPODAL
MICROPODOUS
MICROPORE
MICROPRINT
MICROPSIA
MICROPSY
MICROPTERISM
MICROPTEROUS
MICROPYLAR
MICROPYLE
MICRORHABDUS
MICROSAURIAN
MICROSCLERE
MICROSCLEROUS
MICROSCLERUM
MICROSCOPE
MICROSCOPIC
MICROSCOPICAL
MICROSCOPICS
MICROSCOPIST
MICROSCOPIZE
MICROSCOPY
MICROSECOND
MICROSEISM
MICROSEISMIC
MICROSEPTUM
MICROSMATIC
MICROSMATISM
MICROSOMA
MICROSOME
MICROSOMMITE
MICROSPECIES
MICROSPHERE
MICROSPHERIC
MICROSPORE
MICROSPORIC
MICROSPOROUS
MICROSTAT
MICROSTHENE
MICROSTOME
MICROSTOMOUS
MICROSTYLOUS
MICROTECHNIC
MICROTHEOS
MICROTHERM
MICROTHERMIC
MICROTHORAX
MICROTIA
MICROTOME
MICROTOMIC
MICROTOMICAL
MICROTOMIST
MICROTOMY
MICROTONE
MICROTYPAL
MICROTYPE
MICROTYPICAL
MICROVOLUME
MICROWATT
MICROWAVE
MICROZOA
MICROZOAL
MICROZOAN
MICROZOARIA
MICROZOARIAN
MICROZOARY
MICROZOIC
MICROZONE
MICROZOOID
MICROZOON
MICROZYMA
MICROZYME
MICROZYMIAN
MICRURGIC
MICRURGICAL
MICRURGIST
MICRURGY
MICTION
MICTURATE
MICTURATED
MICTURATING
MICTURITION
MID
MIDAFTERNOON
MIDAIR
MIDBRAIN
MIDCARPAL
MIDDAY
MIDDEN
MIDDENSTEAD
MIDDES
MIDDIES
MIDDLE
MIDDLEBROW
MIDDLECLASS
MIDDLED
MIDDLELAND
MIDDLEMAN
MIDDLEMEN
MIDDLEMOST
MIDDLER
MIDDLES
MIDDLETONE
MIDDLEWAY
MIDDLEWEIGHT
MIDDLEWOMAN
MIDDLEWOMEN
MIDDLING
MIDDLINGLY
MIDDLINGNESS
MIDDY
MIDE
MIDEWIN
MIDEWIWIN
MIDGE
MIDGET
MIDGETY
MIDGUT
MIDGY
MIDHEAVEN
MIDINETTE
MIDIRON
MIDLAND
MIDMAIN
MIDMORN
MIDMOST
MIDNIGHT
MIDNIGHTLY
MIDNOON
MIDPARENT
MIDPARENTAGE
MIDPARENTAL
MIDPOINT
MIDRASH
MIDRASHIC
MIDRASHIM
MIDRASHOTH
MIDRIB
MIDRIBBED
MIDRIFF
MIDS
MIDSHIP
MIDSHIPMAN
MIDSHIPMEN
MIDSHIPMITE
MIDSHIPS
MIDST
MIDSTEAD
MIDSTYLED
MIDSUMMER
MIDSUMMERY
MIDTARSAL
MIDTERM
MIDTOWN
MIDVEIN
MIDVENTRAL
MIDWARD
MIDWATCH
MIDWAY
MIDWEEK
MIDWEEKLY
MIDWIFE
MIDWIFED
MIDWIFERY
MIDWIFING
MIDWINTER
MIDWINTERLY
MIDWINTRY
MIDWISE
MIDWIVED
MIDWIVES
MIDWIVING
MIDYEAR
MIEN
MIERSITE
MIFF
MIFFED
MIFFIER
MIFFIEST
MIFFINESS
MIFFY
MIG
MIGALE
MIGGLE
MIGGLES
MIGHT
MIGHTED
MIGHTFUL
MIGHTFULLY
MIGHTFULNESS
MIGHTIER
MIGHTIEST
MIGHTILY
MIGHTINESS
MIGHTLESS
MIGHTLY
MIGHTS
MIGHTY
MIGLIO
MIGMATITE
MIGNIARD
MIGNIARDISE
MIGNIARDIZE
MIGNON
MIGNONETTE
MIGNONNE
MIGRAINE
MIGRAINOID
MIGRAINOUS
MIGRANS
MIGRANT
MIGRATE
MIGRATED
MIGRATING
MIGRATION
MIGRATIONAL
MIGRATIONIST
MIGRATIVE
MIGRATOR
MIGRATORIAL
MIGRATORY
MIHARAITE
MIHRAB
MIJAKITE
MIJNHEER
MIKADO
MIKADOATE
MIKADOS
MIKE
MIKER
MIKRA
MIKRON
MIKVAH
MIL
MILA
MILACRE
MILADI
MILADIES
MILADY
MILAGE
MILAN
MILARITE
MILCH
MILCHER
MILCHIGS
MILCHY
MILD
MILDEN
MILDENED
MILDENING
MILDER
MILDEST
MILDEW
MILDEWER
MILDEWY
MILDFUL
MILDFULNESS
MILDHEARTED
MILDLY
MILDNESS
MILE
MILEAGE
MILEPOST
MILER
MILES
MILESIMA
MILESTONE
MILEWAY
MILFOIL
MILHA
MILIA
MILIACEOUS
MILIARENSES
MILIARENSIS
MILIARIA
MILIARIUM
MILIARY
MILICE
MILIEU
MILIOLIFORM
MILIOLINE
MILIOLITE
MILIOLITIC
MILITANCY
MILITANT
MILITANTLY
MILITANTNESS
MILITAR
MILITARILY
MILITARISM
MILITARIST
MILITARISTIC
MILITARISTICAL
MILITARIZATION
MILITARIZE
MILITARIZED
MILITARIZING
MILITARY
MILITARYISM
MILITARYMENT
MILITASTER
MILITATE
MILITATED
MILITATING
MILITATION

MILITIA
MILITIAMAN
MILITIAMEN
MILITIATE
MILIUM
MILJEE
MILK
MILKBUSH
MILKED
MILKEN
MILKER
MILKERESS
MILKFISH
MILKFISHES
MILKGRASS
MILKIER
MILKIEST
MILKILY
MILKINESS
MILKING
MILKLESS
MILKMAID
MILKMAN
MILKMEN
MILKNESS
MILKSHED
MILKSICK
MILKSOP
MILKSOPPING
MILKSOPPISH
MILKSOPPY
MILKSTONE
MILKTOAST
MILKWEED
MILKWOOD
MILKWORT
MILKY
MILL
MILLA
MILLAGE
MILLANARE
MILLBOARD
MILLCLAPPER
MILLCOURSE
MILLDAM
MILLDOLL
MILLE
MILLED
MILLEFIORE
MILLEFIORI
MILLEFLEURS
MILLEFLOROUS
MILLEFOLIATE
MILLENARIAN
MILLENARIES
MILLENARIST
MILLENARY
MILLENIUM
MILLENNIA
MILLENNIAL
MILLENNIALLY
MILLENNIAN
MILLENNIARY
MILLENNIUMS
MILLEPED
MILLEPEDE
MILLEPORE
MILLEPORINE
MILLEPORITE
MILLEPOROUS
MILLER
MILLERESS
MILLERING
MILLERITE
MILLESIMAL
MILLET
MILLFEED
MILLHOUSE
MILLIAD
MILLIAMMETER
MILLIAMPERE
MILLIARD
MILLIARDAIRE
MILLIARY
MILLIBAR
MILLICRON
MILLICURIE
MILLIEME
MILLIER
MILLIFARAD
MILLIFOLD
MILLIFORM
MILLIGRADE
MILLIGRAM
MILLIGRAMAGE
MILLIGRAMME
MILLIHENRY
MILLILAMBERT
MILLILE
MILLILITER
MILLILITRE
MILLILUX
MILLIMETER
MILLIMETRE
MILLIMICRON
MILLIMOL
MILLIMOLAR
MILLIMOLE
MILLINCOST
MILLINE
MILLINER
MILLINERIAL
MILLINERING
MILLINERY
MILLING
MILLINORMAL
MILLIOCTAVE
MILLIOERSTED
MILLION
MILLIONAIRE
MILLIONAIRESS
MILLIONARY
MILLIONED
MILLIONER
MILLIONFOLD
MILLIONISM
MILLIONIST
MILLIONIZE
MILLIONNAIRE
MILLIONS
MILLIONTH
MILLIPED
MILLIPEDE
MILLIPHOT
MILLIPOISE
MILLISECOND
MILLISTERE
MILLITHRUM
MILLIVOLT
MILLIWATT
MILLIWEBER
MILLKEN
MILLMAN
MILLMEN
MILLOCRACY
MILLOCRAT
MILLOCRATISM
MILLOWNER
MILLPOND
MILLPOOL
MILLPOST
MILLRACE
MILLRIND
MILLRYND
MILLS
MILLSITE
MILLSTOCK
MILLSTONE
MILLSTONES
MILLSTREAM
MILLTAIL
MILLWARD
MILLWORK
MILLWORKER
MILLWRIGHT
MILLY
MILN
MILNER
MILO
MILORD
MILPA
MILQUETOAST
MILREIS
MILRIND
MILSEY
MILSIE
MILT
MILTED
MILTER
MILTING
MILTSICK
MILTY
MILVINE
MILVINOUS
MILWELL
MIM
MIMA
MIMAE
MIMAMSA
MIMBAR
MIMBLE
MIME
MIMED
MIMEOGRAPH
MIMEOGRAPHED
MIMEOGRAPHIC
MIMEOGRAPHING
MIMER
MIMESIS
MIMESTER
MIMETENE
MIMETESITE
MIMETIC
MIMETICALLY
MIMETISM
MIMETITE
MIMIAMBI
MIMIAMBIC
MIMIAMBICS
MIMIC
MIMICAL
MIMICALLY
MIMICISM
MIMICKED
MIMICKER
MIMICKING
MIMICRIES
MIMICRY
MIMINE
MIMING
MIMINYPIMINY
MIMMATION
MIMMED
MIMMING
MIMMOCK
MIMMOCKING
MIMMOCKY
MIMMOUTHED
MIMODRAMA
MIMOGRAPHER
MIMOGRAPHY
MIMOLOGIST
MIMOSA
MIMOSACEOUS
MIMOSITE
MIMOTYPE
MIMOTYPIC
MIMP
MIMSEY
MIMZY
MIN
MINA
MINACIOUS
MINACIOUSLY
MINACIOUSNESS
MINACITY
MINAE
MINAL
MINAR
MINARET
MINARETED
MINARGENT
MINAS
MINASRAGRITE
MINATORIAL
MINATORIALLY
MINATORIES
MINATORILY
MINATORY
MINAUDERIE
MINAWAY
MINBAR
MINBU
MINCE
MINCED
MINCEMEAT
MINCER
MINCHAH
MINCHEN
MINCHERY
MINCHIATE
MINCING
MINCINGLY
MINCINGNESS
MINCIO
MIND
MINDED
MINDEDNESS
MINDER
MINDFUL
MINDFULLY
MINDFULNESS
MINDING
MINDLESS
MINDLESSLY
MINDLESSNESS
MINDLY
MINDSIGHT
MINE
MINED
MINEFIELD
MINELAYER
MINEOWNER
MINER
MINERAL
MINERALIZATION
MINERALIZE
MINERALIZED
MINERALIZER
MINERALIZING
MINERALOGIC
MINERALOGIES
MINERALOGIST
MINERALOGIZE
MINERALOGY
MINERALS
MINERS
MINERVAL
MINERY
MINES
MINESTRA
MINESTRONE
MINESWEEPER
MINETTE
MINEWORKER
MING
MINGE
MINGIE
MINGLE
MINGLED
MINGLER
MINGLING
MINGUETITE
MINGWORT
MINGY
MINHAG
MINHAH
MINIACEOUS
MINIATE
MINIATED
MINIATING
MINIATOR
MINIATOUS
MINIATURE
MINIATURED
MINIATURING
MINIATURIST
MINIATURIZE
MINIATURIZED
MINIBUS
MINICAM
MINIFICATION
MINIFIED
MINIFY
MINIFYING
MINIKEN
MINIKIN
MINIKINLY
MINIM
MINIMA
MINIMACID
MINIMAL
MINIMALIST
MINIMALLY
MINIMETRIC
MINIMI
MINIMIFIDIAN
MINIMISE
MINIMISM
MINIMISTIC
MINIMIZATION
MINIMIZE
MINIMIZED
MINIMIZER
MINIMIZING
MINIMUM
MINIMUMS
MINIMUS
MINIMUSCULAR
MINING
MINION
MINIONETTE
MINIONLY
MINISH
MINISHED
MINISHER
MINISHING
MINISHMENT
MINISKIRT
MINISTER
MINISTERED
MINISTERIAL
MINISTERING
MINISTERIUM
MINISTERSHIP

MINISTRABLE
MINISTRANT
MINISTRATE
MINISTRATION
MINISTRATIVE
MINISTRATOR
MINISTRER
MINISTRIES
MINISTRY
MINITANT
MINITRACK
MINIUM
MINIVER
MINIVET
MINK
MINKERY
MINKS
MINNESINGER
MINNESONG
MINNIE
MINNIEBUSH
MINNING
MINNOW
MINNOWS
MINNY
MINO
MINOIZE
MINOR
MINORAGE
MINORATE
MINORATION
MINORESS
MINORITY
MINOT
MINSITIVE
MINSTER
MINSTERYARD
MINSTREL
MINSTRELESS
MINSTRELSY
MINT
MINTAGE
MINTBUSH
MINTED
MINTER
MINTING
MINTMAN
MINTMASTER
MINTWEED
MINTY
MINUEND
MINUET
MINUETIC
MINUETISH
MINUS
MINUSCULAR
MINUSCULE
MINUTARY
MINUTATION
MINUTE
MINUTED
MINUTELY
MINUTEMAN
MINUTEMEN
MINUTENESS
MINUTER
MINUTES
MINUTHESIS
MINUTIA
MINUTIAE
MINUTIAL
MINUTING
MINUTIOSE
MINUTIOUS
MINUTIOUSLY
MINUTISSIMIC
MINVERITE
MINX
MINXES
MINY
MINYAN
MIOCARDIA
MIOMBO
MIOPLASMIA
MIOSIS
MIOTHERMIC
MIOTIC
MIQRA
MIQUELET
MIR
MIRABILIA
MIRABILIARY
MIRABILITE
MIRABLE
MIRAC
MIRACH
MIRACIDIUM
MIRACLE
MIRACLED
MIRACLING
MIRACLIST
MIRACULAR
MIRACULIST
MIRACULIZE
MIRACULOSITY
MIRACULOUS
MIRACULOUSLY
MIRADOR
MIRAGE
MIRAGY
MIRANDOUS
MIRATE
MIRCROBICIDAL
MIRD
MIRDAHA
MIRDHA
MIRE
MIRED
MIREPOIS
MIREPOIX
MIRESNIPE
MIRID
MIRIER
MIRIEST
MIRIFIC
MIRIFICAL
MIRIKI
MIRING
MIRISH
MIRK
MIRKILY
MIRKINESS
MIRKISH
MIRKLY
MIRKNESS
MIRKSOME
MIRKY
MIRLED
MIRLIGO
MIRLITON
MIRLY
MIRO
MIRROR
MIRRORED
MIRRORING
MIRRORSCOPE
MIRRORY
MIRTH
MIRTHFUL
MIRTHFULLY
MIRTHFULNESS
MIRTHLESS
MIRTHLESSLY
MIRY
MIRYACHIT
MIRZA
MIS
MISACCEPT
MISACCEPTION
MISADVENTURE
MISADVISE
MISADVISED
MISADVISEDLY
MISADVISING
MISAFFECT
MISALLIANCE
MISALLIED
MISALLY
MISALLYING
MISANDRY
MISANTHROPE
MISANTHROPI
MISANTHROPIC
MISANTHROPOS
MISANTHROPY
MISAPPLIED
MISAPPLIER
MISAPPLY
MISAPPLYING
MISAPPREHEND
MISAPPREHENSION
MISAPPREHENSIVE
MISARCHISM
MISARCHIST
MISARRANGE
MISARRANGED
MISARRANGEMENT
MISARRANGING
MISATTEND
MISAUNTER
MISBAPTIZE
MISBEAR
MISBECAME
MISBECOME
MISBECOMING
MISBEDE
MISBEFALL
MISBEFALLEN
MISBEGET
MISBEGOT
MISBEGOTTEN
MISBEHAVE
MISBEHAVED
MISBEHAVING
MISBEHAVIOR
MISBEHAVIOUR
MISBEHOLDEN
MISBELIEF
MISBELIEVE
MISBELIEVED
MISBELIEVER
MISBELIEVING
MISBIRTH
MISBODE
MISBORN
MISBRAND
MISCAL
MISCALCULATE
MISCALCULATED
MISCALCULATING
MISCALCULATION
MISCALCULATOR
MISCALL
MISCALLED
MISCALLER
MISCALLING
MISCARRIAGE
MISCARRIED
MISCARRY
MISCARRYING
MISCAST
MISCASTING
MISCASUALTY
MISCE
MISCEABILITY
MISCEGENATE
MISCEGENATION
MISCEGENATOR
MISCEGENETIC
MISCEGENIST
MISCEGINE
MISCELLANE
MISCELLANEA
MISCELLANEAL
MISCELLANEOUS
MISCELLANIES
MISCELLANIST
MISCELLANY
MISCHANCE
MISCHANCY
MISCHIEF
MISCHIEFFUL
MISCHIEVE
MISCHIEVOUS
MISCHIEVOUSLY
MISCHIEVOUSNESS
MISCHIO
MISCHOICE
MISCHOOSE
MISCHOOSING
MISCHOSE
MISCHOSEN
MISCIBILITY
MISCIBLE
MISCOGNIZANT
MISCOLOR
MISCOLOUR
MISCONCEIVE
MISCONCEIVED
MISCONCEIVER
MISCONCEIVING
MISCONCEPTION
MISCONDUCT
MISCONDUCTED
MISCONDUCTING
MISCONSTRUCT
MISCONSTRUCTIO
MISCONSTRUE
MISCONSTRUED
MISCONSTRUER
MISCONVEY
MISCORRECT
MISCORRECTED
MISCORRECTING
MISCOUNSEL
MISCOUNSELED
MISCOUNSELING
MISCOUNSELLED
MISCOUNSELLING
MISCOUNT
MISCREANCE
MISCREANCY
MISCREANT
MISCREATE
MISCREATED
MISCREATING
MISCREATION
MISCREATIVE
MISCREATOR
MISCREED
MISCROP
MISCUE
MISCUED
MISCUING
MISDATE
MISDATED
MISDATEFUL
MISDATING
MISDEAL
MISDEALER
MISDEALING
MISDEALT
MISDEED
MISDEEM
MISDEEMED
MISDEEMFUL
MISDEEMING
MISDEMEAN
MISDEMEANANT
MISDEMEANED
MISDEMEANING
MISDEMEANIST
MISDEMEANOR
MISDEMEANOUR
MISDERIVE
MISDERIVED
MISDERIVING
MISDESCRIBE
MISDESCRIBED
MISDESCRIBER
MISDESERT
MISDESERVE
MISDID
MISDIRECT
MISDIRECTED
MISDIRECTING
MISDIRECTION
MISDIVISION
MISDO
MISDOER
MISDOING
MISDONE
MISDOUBT
MISDOUBTED
MISDOUBTING
MISDREAD
MISE
MISEASE
MISEASED
MISEMPHASIS
MISEMPHASIZE
MISEMPLOY
MISEMPLOYED
MISEMPLOYING
MISENITE
MISENTREAT
MISER
MISERABILISM
MISERABILIST
MISERABILITY
MISERABLE
MISERABLY
MISERE
MISERERE
MISERICORD
MISERICORDE
MISERICORDIA
MISERIES
MISERISM
MISERLINESS
MISERLY
MISERY
MISES
MISESTEEM
MISESTEEMED
MISESTEEMING
MISESTIMATE
MISESTIMATED
MISFAITH
MISFALL
MISFARE
MISFATE
MISFEASANCE
MISFEASOR
MISFEATURE

MISFEIGN
MISFIELD
MISFIGURE
MISFIRE
MISFIRED
MISFIRING
MISFIT
MISFITTED
MISFITTING
MISFORGIVE
MISFORTUNATE
MISFORTUNE
MISFORTUNED
MISFORTUNER
MISGAVE
MISGIVE
MISGIVEN
MISGIVING
MISGIVINGLY
MISGO
MISGOTTEN
MISGOVERN
MISGOVERNED
MISGOVERNING
MISGOVERNOR
MISGRAFF
MISGROWTH
MISGUGGLE
MISGUIDANCE
MISGUIDE
MISGUIDED
MISGUIDEDLY
MISGUIDER
MISGUIDING
MISGUIDINGLY
MISGUISE
MISHANDLE
MISHANDLED
MISHANDLING
MISHANTER
MISHAP
MISHAPPEN
MISHARA
MISHAVE
MISHEAR
MISHEARD
MISHEARING
MISHIT
MISHMASH
MISHMEE
MISHMI
MISIMPROVE
MISIMPROVED
MISIMPROVING
MISINFORM
MISINFORMANT
MISINFORMED
MISINFORMER
MISINFORMING
MISINTERPRET
MISINTERPRETATION
MISIONES
MISJOINDER
MISJUDGE
MISJUDGED
MISJUDGEMENT
MISJUDGER
MISJUDGING
MISJUDGINGLY
MISJUDGMENT
MISKAL
MISKEN
MISKENNING
MISKNEW
MISKNOW
MISKNOWLEDGE
MISKNOWN
MISKY
MISLAID
MISLAY
MISLAYER
MISLAYING
MISLE
MISLEAD
MISLEADER
MISLEADING
MISLEADINGLY
MISLEAR
MISLEARED
MISLED
MISLEERED
MISLEST
MISLIKE
MISLIKED
MISLIKEN
MISLIKER
MISLIKING
MISLIKINGLY
MISLIPPEN
MISLUCK
MISMADE
MISMAKE
MISMANAGE
MISMANAGEABLE
MISMANAGED
MISMANAGEMENT
MISMANAGER
MISMANAGING
MISMANNERED
MISMANNERS
MISMARRIAGE
MISMARRY
MISMATCH
MISMATCHMENT
MISMATE
MISMATED
MISMATING
MISMAZE
MISMEAN
MISMOVE
MISNAME
MISNAMED
MISNAMING
MISNOMED
MISNOMER
MISO
MISOCAPNIC
MISOCAPNIST
MISOGALLIC
MISOGAMIC
MISOGAMIST
MISOGAMY
MISOGYNE
MISOGYNIC
MISOGYNICAL
MISOGYNISM
MISOGYNIST
MISOGYNISTIC
MISOGYNOUS
MISOGYNY
MISOHELLENE
MISOLOGIST
MISOLOGY
MISOMATH
MISONEISM
MISONEIST
MISONEISTIC
MISOPAEDIA
MISOPAEDISM
MISOPAEDIST
MISOPATERIST
MISOPEDIA
MISOPEDISM
MISOPEDIST
MISORDER
MISOSCOPIST
MISOSOPHER
MISOSOPHIST
MISOSOPHY
MISOTHEISM
MISOTHEIST
MISOTHEISTIC
MISOTYRANNY
MISOXENE
MISOXENY
MISPAID
MISPAY
MISPAYING
MISPICK
MISPICKEL
MISPLACE
MISPLACED
MISPLACEMENT
MISPLACING
MISPLANT
MISPLAY
MISPLEAD
MISPLEADED
MISPLEADING
MISPLED
MISPRAISE
MISPRINT
MISPRISAL
MISPRISE
MISPRISION
MISPRIZE
MISPRIZED
MISPRIZER
MISPRIZING
MISPROFESS
MISPRONOUNCE
MISPRONOUNCED
MISPRONUNCIATI
MISPROUD
MISPUT
MISQUOTATION
MISQUOTE
MISQUOTED
MISQUOTER
MISQUOTING
MISREAD
MISREADER
MISREADING
MISRECKON
MISRECKONED
MISRECKONING
MISREMEMBER
MISREPORT
MISREPORTER
MISREPRESENT
MISREPRESENTATION
MISRULE
MISRULED
MISRULING
MISRUN
MISS
MISSAID
MISSAL
MISSARY
MISSATICAL
MISSAY
MISSAYING
MISSCRIPT
MISSED
MISSEEM
MISSEL
MISSERVE
MISSERVICE
MISSES
MISSET
MISSETTING
MISSHAPE
MISSHAPED
MISSHAPEN
MISSHAPENLY
MISSHAPING
MISSI
MISSIBLE
MISSIES
MISSILE
MISSILEMAN
MISSILEMEN
MISSILERY
MISSILES
MISSILRY
MISSING
MISSINGLY
MISSION
MISSIONAL
MISSIONARIES
MISSIONARIZE
MISSIONARY
MISSIONER
MISSIONIZER
MISSIS
MISSISH
MISSIT
MISSIVE
MISSMARK
MISSMENT
MISSOURITE
MISSOUT
MISSPEAK
MISSPEAKING
MISSPEECH
MISSPEED
MISSPELL
MISSPELLED
MISSPELLING
MISSPEND
MISSPENDER
MISSPENDING
MISSPENT
MISSPOKE
MISSTATE
MISSTATED
MISSTATEMENT
MISSTATER
MISSTATING
MISSTAY
MISSTEP
MISSUADE
MISSUS
MISSY
MIST
MISTAKABLE
MISTAKABLY
MISTAKE
MISTAKEN
MISTAKENLY
MISTAKENNESS
MISTAKER
MISTAKING
MISTAKINGLY
MISTAL
MISTASSINI
MISTASTE
MISTAUGHT
MISTBOW
MISTEACH
MISTEACHER
MISTED
MISTELL
MISTELLING
MISTEMPER
MISTEMPERED
MISTER
MISTERED
MISTERING
MISTERS
MISTETCH
MISTEUK
MISTFALL
MISTFLOWER
MISTHINK
MISTHINKING
MISTHOUGHT
MISTIC
MISTICO
MISTIDE
MISTIER
MISTIEST
MISTIFY
MISTIGRI
MISTIGRIS
MISTILY
MISTIME
MISTIMED
MISTIMING
MISTINESS
MISTING
MISTION
MISTLE
MISTLETOE
MISTOLD
MISTONE
MISTONUSK
MISTOOK
MISTRADITION
MISTRAIN
MISTRAL
MISTRANSLATE
MISTREAT
MISTREATMENT
MISTRESS
MISTRESSLY
MISTRIAL
MISTRIST
MISTROW
MISTRUST
MISTRUSTER
MISTRUSTFUL
MISTRUSTFULLY
MISTRUSTFULNESS
MISTRUSTING
MISTRUSTINGLY
MISTRY
MISTRYST
MISTURE
MISTURN
MISTY
MISUNDERSTAND
MISUNDERSTANDI
MISUNDERSTOOD
MISURA
MISUSAGE
MISUSE
MISUSED
MISUSING
MISVALUATION
MISVALUE
MISVALUED
MISVALUING
MISVENTURE
MISVENTUROUS
MISVOUCH
MISWED
MISWEND
MISWERN
MISWISH
MISWOMAN
MISWORD
MISWORDED
MISWORDING
MISWORSHIP

MISWORSHIPER
MISWREST
MISWRITE
MISWRITING
MISWRITTEN
MISWROTE
MISY
MISZEALOUS
MIT
MITAPSIS
MITCHBOARD
MITE
MITER
MITERED
MITERER
MITERFLOWER
MITERING
MITERWORT
MITHAN
MITHER
MITHRIDATE
MITHRIDATIC
MITHRIDATISM
MITHRIDATIZE
MITIGABLE
MITIGANT
MITIGATE
MITIGATED
MITIGATING
MITIGATION
MITIGATIVE
MITIGATOR
MITIGATORY
MITING
MITIS
MITOCHONDRIA
MITOGENETIC
MITOME
MITOSIS
MITOSOME
MITOTIC
MITOTICALLY
MITRA
MITRAILLE
MITRAILLEUR
MITRAILLEUSE
MITRAL
MITRATE
MITRE
MITRED
MITREFLOWER
MITRER
MITREWORT
MITRIFORM
MITRING
MITSUMATA
MITSVAH
MITSVOTH
MITT
MITTELHAND
MITTEN
MITTENED
MITTIMUS
MITTLE
MITTY
MITY
MITZVAH
MITZVAHS
MITZVOTH
MIURUS
MIX
MIXABLE
MIXBLOOD
MIXED
MIXEN
MIXER
MIXERESS
MIXHILL
MIXIBLE
MIXILINEAL
MIXING
MIXITE
MIXOBARBARIC
MIXOTROPHIC
MIXT
MIXTIFORM
MIXTILINEAR
MIXTION
MIXTURE
MIXUP
MIXY
MIZENMAST
MIZMAZE
MIZRACH
MIZZEN
MIZZENMAST
MIZZENTOPMAN
MIZZENTOPMEN
MIZZLE
MIZZLED
MIZZLING
MIZZLY
MIZZONITE
MIZZY
MKS
MLECHCHHA
MNEME
MNEMONIC
MNEMONICAL
MNEMONICALLY
MNEMONICON
MNEMONICS
MNEMONISM
MNEMONIST
MNEMONIZE
MNEMONIZED
MNEMONIZING
MNEMOTECHNY
MNESIC
MNESTIC
MNIACEOUS
MNIOID
MO
MOA
MOAB
MOALA
MOAN
MOANED
MOANFUL
MOANFULLY
MOANING
MOANO
MOAT
MOATHILL
MOB
MOBBED
MOBBER
MOBBIE
MOBBING
MOBBISH
MOBBISHLY
MOBBISHNESS
MOBBISM
MOBBIST
MOBBY
MOBCAP
MOBED
MOBILE
MOBILIANER
MOBILIARY
MOBILISE
MOBILITIES
MOBILITY
MOBILIZATION
MOBILIZE
MOBILIZED
MOBILIZING
MOBILOMETER
MOBLE
MOBOCRACIES
MOBOCRACY
MOBOCRAT
MOBOCRATIC
MOBOCRATICAL
MOBOLATRY
MOBSMAN
MOBSMEN
MOBSTER
MOCCASIN
MOCCENIGO
MOCH
MOCHA
MOCHILA
MOCHRAS
MOCHUDI
MOCHY
MOCK
MOCKADO
MOCKAGE
MOCKBIRD
MOCKED
MOCKER
MOCKERIES
MOCKERNUT
MOCKERY
MOCKETER
MOCKGROUND
MOCKING
MOCKINGBIRD
MOCKINGLY
MOCKINGSTOCK
MOCKISH
MOCKUP
MOCMAIN
MOCO
MOCOCK
MOCOMOCO
MOCUCK
MODAL
MODALIST
MODALISTIC
MODALITIES
MODALITY
MODALIZE
MODALLY
MODDER
MODE
MODEL
MODELED
MODELER
MODELESS
MODELESSNESS
MODELING
MODELIST
MODELIZE
MODELLED
MODELLER
MODELLING
MODELMAKER
MODELMAKING
MODENA
MODER
MODERANT
MODERANTISM
MODERANTIST
MODERATE
MODERATED
MODERATELY
MODERATENESS
MODERATING
MODERATION
MODERATISM
MODERATIST
MODERATO
MODERATOR
MODERN
MODERNER
MODERNISM
MODERNIST
MODERNISTIC
MODERNITIES
MODERNITY
MODERNIZATION
MODERNIZE
MODERNIZED
MODERNIZER
MODERNIZING
MODERNLY
MODERNNESS
MODEST
MODESTIES
MODESTLY
MODESTNESS
MODESTY
MODIATION
MODICA
MODICITY
MODICUM
MODICUMS
MODIFIABLE
MODIFIABLY
MODIFICABLE
MODIFICATION
MODIFICATIVE
MODIFICATOR
MODIFICATORY
MODIFIED
MODIFIER
MODIFY
MODIFYING
MODILLION
MODIOLAR
MODIOLI
MODIOLUS
MODISH
MODISHLY
MODISHNESS
MODIST
MODISTE
MODISTRY
MODS
MODULABILITY
MODULANT
MODULAR
MODULATE
MODULATED
MODULATING
MODULATION
MODULATIVE
MODULATOR
MODULATORY
MODULE
MODULET
MODULI
MODULIZE
MODULO
MODULUS
MODUR
MODUS
MODY
MOE
MOELLON
MOERITHERE
MOERITHERIAN
MOEURS
MOFETTE
MOFF
MOFFETTE
MOFFLE
MOFUSSIL
MOFUSSILITE
MOG
MOGADORE
MOGGAN
MOGGED
MOGGI
MOGGIES
MOGGING
MOGGIO
MOGGY
MOGIGRAPHIC
MOGIGRAPHY
MOGILALIA
MOGILALISM
MOGIPHONIA
MOGITOCIA
MOGO
MOGOTE
MOGUEY
MOGUL
MOHA
MOHABAT
MOHAIR
MOHAR
MOHATRA
MOHAWKITE
MOHEL
MOHNSEED
MOHO
MOHOE
MOHOS
MOHR
MOHUR
MOHWA
MOIDER
MOIDORE
MOIETER
MOIETIES
MOIETY
MOIL
MOILED
MOILER
MOILES
MOILING
MOILINGLY
MOILSOME
MOINE
MOINEAU
MOIO
MOIRE
MOIREED
MOIREING
MOIRETTE
MOISE
MOISON
MOISSANITE
MOIST
MOISTEN
MOISTENED
MOISTENER
MOISTENING
MOISTFUL
MOISTIFY
MOISTLESS
MOISTLY
MOISTNESS
MOISTURE
MOISTY
MOIT
MOITY
MOJARRA
MOJO
MOJOS
MOKADDAM
MOKAMOKA

MOKE
MOKI
MOKIHANA
MOKIHI
MOKO
MOKSHA
MOKUM
MOKY
MOL
MOLA
MOLAL
MOLALITY
MOLAR
MOLARIFORM
MOLARIMETER
MOLARITY
MOLARY
MOLASSES
MOLASSIED
MOLASSY
MOLAVE
MOLD
MOLDABLE
MOLDAVITE
MOLDBOARD
MOLDED
MOLDER
MOLDERED
MOLDERING
MOLDERY
MOLDINESS
MOLDING
MOLDINGS
MOLDMADE
MOLDWARP
MOLDY
MOLE
MOLECAST
MOLECULA
MOLECULAR
MOLECULARIST
MOLECULARITY
MOLECULE
MOLED
MOLEHEAD
MOLEHEAP
MOLEHILL
MOLEHILLISH
MOLEHILLY
MOLEISM
MOLENDINAR
MOLENDINARY
MOLESKIN
MOLEST
MOLESTATION
MOLESTED
MOLESTER
MOLESTFUL
MOLESTFULLY
MOLESTIE
MOLESTING
MOLESTIOUS
MOLET
MOLIES
MOLIMEN
MOLIMINOUS
MOLINARY
MOLINE
MOLINET
MOLING
MOLITION
MOLKA
MOLLA
MOLLAH
MOLLAND
MOLLE
MOLLES
MOLLESCENCE
MOLLESCENT
MOLLETON
MOLLICHOP
MOLLICRUSH
MOLLIE
MOLLIENISIA
MOLLIENT
MOLLIFIABLE
MOLLIFIED
MOLLIFIER
MOLLIFY
MOLLIFYING
MOLLIFYINGLY
MOLLIGRANT
MOLLIPILOSE
MOLLISIOSE
MOLLISOL
MOLLITIES
MOLLITIOUS
MOLLITUDE
MOLLUSC
MOLLUSCAN
MOLLUSCOID
MOLLUSCOIDAL
MOLLUSCOUS
MOLLUSCUM
MOLLUSK
MOLLY
MOLLYCODDLE
MOLLYCODDLED
MOLLYCODDLER
MOLLYCOSSET
MOLLYCOT
MOLMAN
MOLMEN
MOLOCH
MOLOCKER
MOLOID
MOLOKER
MOLOMPI
MOLOSSIC
MOLOSSINE
MOLOSSOID
MOLOSSUS
MOLPE
MOLROOKEN
MOLT
MOLTED
MOLTEN
MOLTENLY
MOLTER
MOLTING
MOLTO
MOLY
MOLYBDATE
MOLYBDENA
MOLYBDENIC
MOLYBDENITE
MOLYBDENOUS
MOLYBDENUM
MOLYBDIC
MOLYBDITE
MOLYBDOCOLIC
MOLYBDOMANCY
MOLYBDONOSUS
MOLYBDOSIS
MOLYBDOUS
MOLYSITE
MOM
MOMBIN
MOMBLE
MOME
MOMENT
MOMENTA
MOMENTAL
MOMENTALLY
MOMENTANEITY
MOMENTANEOUS
MOMENTANEOUSLY
MOMENTARILY
MOMENTARY
MOMENTLY
MOMENTOUS
MOMENTOUSLY
MOMENTOUSNESS
MOMENTUM
MOMENTUMS
MOMI
MOMIOLOGY
MOMISH
MOMISM
MOMIST
MOMMA
MOMME
MOMMY
MOMO
MOMUS
MOMUSES
MON
MONA
MONACANTHID
MONACANTHINE
MONACANTHOUS
MONACH
MONACHAL
MONACHATE
MONACHISM
MONACHIST
MONACHIZE
MONACID
MONACT
MONACTIN
MONACTINAL
MONACTINE
MONAD
MONADELPH
MONADELPHIAN
MONADELPHOUS
MONADES
MONADIC
MONADICAL
MONADICALLY
MONADIFORM
MONADIGEROUS
MONADISM
MONADISTIC
MONADNOCK
MONADOLOGY
MONAL
MONAMNIOTIC
MONANDER
MONANDRIAN
MONANDRIC
MONANDROUS
MONANDRY
MONANTHOUS
MONAPHASE
MONAPSAL
MONARCH
MONARCHAL
MONARCHALLY
MONARCHIAN
MONARCHIC
MONARCHICAL
MONARCHIES
MONARCHISM
MONARCHIST
MONARCHISTIC
MONARCHIZE
MONARCHIZED
MONARCHIZER
MONARCHIZING
MONARCHY
MONARDA
MONARTICULAR
MONAS
MONASCIDIAN
MONASE
MONASTER
MONASTERIAL
MONASTERIES
MONASTERY
MONASTIC
MONASTICAL
MONASTICALLY
MONASTICISM
MONATOMIC
MONATOMICITY
MONATOMISM
MONAUL
MONAULI
MONAULOS
MONAURAL
MONAX
MONAXIAL
MONAXON
MONAXONIAL
MONAXONIC
MONAZITE
MONCHIQUITE
MONDAINE
MONDE
MONDEGO
MONDIAL
MONDO
MONDSEE
MONE
MONECIOUS
MONEMBRYONIC
MONEMBRYONY
MONEPIC
MONEPISCOPAL
MONEPISCOPUS
MONER
MONERA
MONERAL
MONERAN
MONERGIC
MONERGISM
MONERGIST
MONERGISTIC
MONERIC
MONERON
MONERONS
MONERULA
MONESIA
MONETARILY
MONETARY
MONETITE
MONETIZATION
MONETIZE
MONETIZED
MONETIZING
MONEY
MONEYAGE
MONEYBAG
MONEYBAGS
MONEYCHANGER
MONEYED
MONEYER
MONEYGRUB
MONEYGRUBBER
MONEYING
MONEYLENDER
MONEYLENDING
MONEYMAKER
MONEYMAKING
MONEYMAN
MONEYMONGER
MONEYS
MONEYSAVING
MONEYWORT
MONG
MONGER
MONGERING
MONGERY
MONGLER
MONGO
MONGOE
MONGOOSE
MONGOOSES
MONGREL
MONGRELDOM
MONGRELISH
MONGRELISM
MONGRELITY
MONGRELIZE
MONGRELLY
MONGRELNESS
MONHEIMITE
MONIAL
MONICA
MONICKER
MONIE
MONIER
MONIES
MONIKER
MONILATED
MONILETHRIX
MONILIACEOUS
MONILICORN
MONILIFORM
MONILIFORMLY
MONILIOID
MONIMENT
MONIMIACEOUS
MONIMOLITE
MONIMOSTYLIC
MONISH
MONISHER
MONISHMENT
MONISM
MONIST
MONISTIC
MONISTICAL
MONISTICALLY
MONITION
MONITIVE
MONITOR
MONITORIAL
MONITORIALLY
MONITORSHIP
MONITORY
MONITRESS
MONK
MONKBIRD
MONKCRAFT
MONKERIES
MONKERY
MONKESS
MONKEY
MONKEYBOARD
MONKEYFIED
MONKEYFY
MONKEYFYING
MONKEYING
MONKEYNUT
MONKEYPOD
MONKEYPOT
MONKEYRY
MONKEYS
MONKEYSHINE
MONKEYTAIL
MONKFISH
MONKFISHES
MONKFLOWER
MONKHOOD

MONKISH
MONKISHLY
MONKISHNESS
MONKISM
MONKLINESS
MONKLY
MONKMONGER
MONKS
MONKSHOOD
MONMOUTHITE
MONNIKER
MONO
MONOACETATE
MONOACID
MONOACIDIC
MONOAMID
MONOAMIDE
MONOAMIN
MONOAMINE
MONOAMINO
MONOAZO
MONOBASE
MONOBASIC
MONOBASICITY
MONOBLASTIC
MONOBLEPSIA
MONOBLEPSIS
MONOBLOC
MONOBROMATED
MONOBROMIDE
MONOCARBONIC
MONOCARDIAN
MONOCARP
MONOCARPAL
MONOCARPELLARY
MONOCARPIAN
MONOCARPIC
MONOCARPOUS
MONOCELLULAR
MONOCENTRIC
MONOCERCOUS
MONOCEROS
MONOCEROUS
MONOCHASIAL
MONOCHASIUM
MONOCHLOR
MONOCHLORIDE
MONOCHLORO
MONOCHORD
MONOCHORDIST
MONOCHORDIZE
MONOCHROIC
MONOCHROMASY
MONOCHROMAT
MONOCHROMATE
MONOCHROME
MONOCHROMIC
MONOCHROMIST
MONOCHROMOUS
MONOCHROMY
MONOCHRONIC
MONOCILIATED
MONOCLE
MONOCLED
MONOCLEID
MONOCLEIDE
MONOCLINAL
MONOCLINALLY
MONOCLINE
MONOCLINIAN
MONOCLINIC
MONOCLINISM
MONOCLINOUS
MONOCONDYLAR
MONOCOQUE
MONOCORMIC
MONOCOT
MONOCOTYL
MONOCRACY
MONOCRAT
MONOCRATIC
MONOCROTIC
MONOCROTISM
MONOCULAR
MONOCULARITY
MONOCULARLY
MONOCULE
MONOCULOUS
MONOCULTURE
MONOCULUS
MONOCYCLE
MONOCYCLIC
MONOCYSTIC
MONOCYTE
MONOCYTIC
MONODACTYL
MONODACTYLE
MONODACTYLY
MONODELPHIAN
MONODELPHIC
MONODELPHOUS
MONODERMIC
MONODIC
MONODICAL
MONODICALLY
MONODIES
MONODIMETRIC
MONODIST
MONODIZE
MONODOMOUS
MONODONT
MONODONTAL
MONODRAM
MONODRAMA
MONODRAME
MONODROMIC
MONODROMY
MONODY
MONODYNAMIC
MONODYNAMISM
MONOECIAN
MONOECIOUS
MONOECIOUSLY
MONOECISM
MONOEIDIC
MONOESTROUS
MONOGAMIAN
MONOGAMIC
MONOGAMIST
MONOGAMISTIC
MONOGAMOUS
MONOGAMOUSLY
MONOGAMY
MONOGASTRIC
MONOGENE
MONOGENEITY
MONOGENEOUS
MONOGENESIS
MONOGENESIST
MONOGENESY
MONOGENETIC
MONOGENIC
MONOGENISM
MONOGENIST
MONOGENISTIC
MONOGENOUS
MONOGENY
MONOGLOT
MONOGONEUTIC
MONOGONY
MONOGRAM
MONOGRAMING
MONOGRAMMED
MONOGRAMMIC
MONOGRAMMING
MONOGRAPH
MONOGRAPHED
MONOGRAPHER
MONOGRAPHIC
MONOGRAPHING
MONOGRAPHIST
MONOGRAPHY
MONOGRAPTID
MONOGYNIC
MONOGYNIOUS
MONOGYNIST
MONOGYNOUS
MONOGYNY
MONOHYBRID
MONOHYDRATE
MONOHYDRATED
MONOHYDRIC
MONOHYDROGEN
MONOICOUS
MONOID
MONOLATER
MONOLATRIST
MONOLATROUS
MONOLATRY
MONOLAYER
MONOLINE
MONOLINGUAL
MONOLINGUIST
MONOLITERAL
MONOLITH
MONOLITHIC
MONOLITHS
MONOLOBULAR
MONOLOCULAR
MONOLOG
MONOLOGIAN
MONOLOGIC
MONOLOGICAL
MONOLOGIST
MONOLOGIZE
MONOLOGIZED
MONOLOGIZING
MONOLOGUE
MONOLOGUIST
MONOLOGY
MONOMACHIST
MONOMACHY
MONOMANIA
MONOMANIAC
MONOMANIACAL
MONOMER
MONOMERIC
MONOMEROUS
MONOMETALISM
MONOMETALIST
MONOMETALLIC
MONOMETER
MONOMETHYL
MONOMETHYLIC
MONOMETRIC
MONOMETRICAL
MONOMIAL
MONOMICT
MONOMINERAL
MONOMORPHIC
MONOMORPHISM
MONOMORPHOUS
MONOMYARIAN
MONONCH
MONONEURAL
MONONITRATE
MONONITRATED
MONONOMIAL
MONONOMIAN
MONONT
MONONUCLEAR
MONONYCHOUS
MONONYM
MONONYMIC
MONONYMIZE
MONONYMY
MONOOUSIAN
MONOOUSIOUS
MONOPARENTAL
MONOPARESIS
MONOPERSONAL
MONOPETALOUS
MONOPHAGIA
MONOPHAGISM
MONOPHAGOUS
MONOPHAGY
MONOPHASIC
MONOPHOBIA
MONOPHONE
MONOPHONIC
MONOPHONOUS
MONOPHOTAL
MONOPHOTE
MONOPHTHONG
MONOPHTHONGAL
MONOPHTHONGIZE
MONOPHYLETIC
MONOPHYLITE
MONOPHYLLOUS
MONOPHYODONT
MONOPLACULA
MONOPLACULAR
MONOPLANE
MONOPLANIST
MONOPLAST
MONOPLASTIC
MONOPLEGIA
MONOPLEGIC
MONOPODE
MONOPODIA
MONOPODIAL
MONOPODIALLY
MONOPODIC
MONOPODIES
MONOPODIUM
MONOPODOUS
MONOPODY
MONOPOLAR
MONOPOLARIC
MONOPOLARITY
MONOPOLE
MONOPOLIES
MONOPOLISE
MONOPOLISM
MONOPOLIST
MONOPOLISTIC
MONOPOLIZE
MONOPOLIZED
MONOPOLIZER
MONOPOLIZING
MONOPOLOUS
MONOPOLY
MONOPRIONID
MONOPSYCHISM
MONOPTERAL
MONOPTEROUS
MONOPTIC
MONOPTICAL
MONOPTOTE
MONOPTOTIC
MONOPYRENOUS
MONORAIL
MONORAILROAD
MONORAILWAY
MONORCHID
MONORCHIDISM
MONORCHIS
MONORCHISM
MONORGANIC
MONORHYME
MONORHYMED
MONORHYTHMIC
MONOSACCHARIDE
MONOSCHEMIC
MONOSE
MONOSEMIC
MONOSEPALOUS
MONOSERVICE
MONOSILANE
MONOSIPHONIC
MONOSKI
MONOSPERM
MONOSPERMAL
MONOSPERMIC
MONOSPERMOUS
MONOSPORE
MONOSPORED
MONOSPOROUS
MONOSTELE
MONOSTELIC
MONOSTELOUS
MONOSTELY
MONOSTICH
MONOSTICHOUS
MONOSTOME
MONOSTOMOUS
MONOSTROPHE
MONOSTROPHIC
MONOSTYLOUS
MONOSULPHIDE
MONOSYLLABIC
MONOSYLLABLE
MONOSYMMETRY
MONOTHALAMAN
MONOTHECAL
MONOTHEISM
MONOTHEIST
MONOTHEISTIC
MONOTHELIOUS
MONOTHETIC
MONOTIC
MONOTINT
MONOTOCOUS
MONOTOMOUS
MONOTONE
MONOTONIC
MONOTONICAL
MONOTONIST
MONOTONIZE
MONOTONOUS
MONOTONOUSLY
MONOTONY
MONOTREMAL
MONOTREMATE
MONOTREME
MONOTREMOUS
MONOTRICHIC
MONOTRICHOUS
MONOTRIGLYPH
MONOTROCHAL
MONOTROCHIAN
MONOTROCHOUS
MONOTROPHIC
MONOTROPIC
MONOTROPY
MONOTYPAL
MONOTYPE
MONOTYPIC
MONOTYPICAL
MONOTYPOUS
MONOVALENCE
MONOVALENCY
MONOVALENT
MONOVARIANT
MONOVOLTINE

MONOVULAR
MONOXENOUS
MONOXIDE
MONOXYLA
MONOXYLE
MONOXYLIC
MONOXYLON
MONOXYLOUS
MONOZOAN
MONOZOIC
MONOZYGOTIC
MONROLITE
MONS
MONSEIGNEUR
MONSIEUR
MONSIGNOR
MONSIGNORE
MONSIGNORIAL
MONSOON
MONSOONAL
MONSPERMY
MONSTER
MONSTRANCE
MONSTRICIDE
MONSTRIFY
MONSTROSITIES
MONSTROSITY
MONSTROUS
MONSTROUSLY
MONT
MONTABYN
MONTAGE
MONTANAS
MONTANE
MONTANITE
MONTANT
MONTANTO
MONTBRETIA
MONTE
MONTEGRE
MONTEITH
MONTEM
MONTERA
MONTERO
MONTEROS
MONTES
MONTGOLFIER
MONTH
MONTHLIES
MONTHLY
MONTHON
MONTHS
MONTICELLITE
MONTICLE
MONTICOLINE
MONTICULATE
MONTICULE
MONTICULOSE
MONTICULOUS
MONTICULUS
MONTIFORM
MONTIGENEOUS
MONTILLA
MONTJOY
MONTJOYE
MONTMARTRITE
MONTON
MONTRE
MONTROYDITE
MONTURE
MONTUVIO
MONUMENT
MONUMENTAL
MONUMENTALLY
MONUMENTARY
MONUMENTED
MONUMENTING
MONY
MONZODIORITE
MONZOGABBRO
MONZONITE
MONZONITIC
MOO
MOOCAH
MOOCH
MOOCHA
MOOCHER
MOOD
MOODER
MOODIER
MOODIEST
MOODILY
MOODINESS
MOODIR
MOODISH
MOODISHLY
MOODISHNESS
MOODS
MOODY
MOOED
MOOING
MOOKHTAR
MOOKTAR
MOOL
MOOLAH
MOOLEY
MOOLINGS
MOOLS
MOOLUM
MOON
MOONACK
MOONAL
MOONBEAM
MOONBILL
MOONBLIND
MOONBLINK
MOONCALF
MOONCREEPER
MOONDOG
MOONDOWN
MOONDROP
MOONED
MOONER
MOONERY
MOONET
MOONEYE
MOONFACE
MOONFACED
MOONFALL
MOONFISH
MOONFISHES
MOONFLOWER
MOONGLADE
MOONGLOW
MOONHEAD
MOONIE
MOONIER
MOONIEST
MOONING
MOONISH
MOONITE
MOONJA
MOONLET
MOONLIGHT
MOONLIGHTED
MOONLIGHTER
MOONLIGHTING
MOONLING
MOONLIT
MOONLITTEN
MOONMAN
MOONMEN
MOONPATH
MOONPENNY
MOONRAKER
MOONRAKING
MOONRAT
MOONRISE
MOONSAIL
MOONSEED
MOONSET
MOONSHADE
MOONSHEE
MOONSHINE
MOONSHINER
MOONSHINING
MOONSHINY
MOONSHOT
MOONSICK
MOONSICKNESS
MOONSTONE
MOONSTRICKEN
MOONSTRUCK
MOONTIDE
MOONWORT
MOONY
MOOP
MOOR
MOORAGE
MOORBALL
MOORBAND
MOORBERRIES
MOORBERRY
MOORBIRD
MOORBURN
MOORBURNER
MOORBURNING
MOORED
MOORFLOWER
MOORFOWL
MOORHEN
MOORIER
MOORIEST
MOORING
MOORISH
MOORLAND
MOORLANDER
MOORMAN
MOORMEN
MOORPAN
MOORPUNKY
MOORS
MOORSTONE
MOORTETTER
MOORUP
MOORWORT
MOORY
MOOS
MOOSA
MOOSE
MOOSEBERRIES
MOOSEBERRY
MOOSEBIRD
MOOSEBUSH
MOOSECALL
MOOSEFLOWER
MOOSEMILK
MOOSETONGUE
MOOSEWOOD
MOOSEY
MOOST
MOOT
MOOTCH
MOOTED
MOOTER
MOOTH
MOOTING
MOOTMAN
MOOTMEN
MOOTSTEAD
MOOTSUDDY
MOOTWORTHY
MOP
MOPANE
MOPANI
MOPBOARD
MOPE
MOPED
MOPEHAWK
MOPER
MOPERY
MOPES
MOPH
MOPHEAD
MOPHEADED
MOPING
MOPISH
MOPISHLY
MOPISHNESS
MOPLA
MOPLAH
MOPOKE
MOPPED
MOPPER
MOPPET
MOPPY
MOPS
MOPSEY
MOPSTICK
MOPSY
MOPUS
MOPUSES
MOPUSSES
MOQUETTE
MORA
MORABIT
MORACEOUS
MORADA
MORAE
MORAINAL
MORAINE
MORAINIC
MORAL
MORALE
MORALER
MORALISE
MORALISM
MORALIST
MORALISTIC
MORALITIES
MORALITY
MORALIZATION
MORALIZE
MORALIZED
MORALIZER
MORALIZING
MORALLER
MORALLY
MORALS
MORAS
MORASS
MORASSIC
MORASSWEED
MORASSY
MORAT
MORATE
MORATION
MORATORIA
MORATORIUM
MORATORY
MORAVITE
MORAY
MORB
MORBID
MORBIDEZZA
MORBIDITIES
MORBIDITY
MORBIDLY
MORBIDNESS
MORBIFERAL
MORBIFEROUS
MORBIFIC
MORBIFICAL
MORBIFICALLY
MORBIFY
MORBILLARY
MORBILLI
MORBILLIFORM
MORBILLOUS
MORBLEU
MORBOSE
MORBUS
MORCEAU
MORCEAUX
MORCELLATE
MORCELLATED
MORCELLATING
MORCELLATION
MORDACIOUS
MORDACIOUSLY
MORDACITY
MORDANCY
MORDANT
MORDANTED
MORDANTING
MORDELLID
MORDELLOID
MORDENITE
MORDENT
MORDICATE
MORDICATION
MORDICATIVE
MORDIEU
MORDISHEEN
MORDORE
MORDU
MORE
MOREEN
MOREISH
MOREL
MORELLA
MORELLE
MORELLO
MORENA
MORENCITE
MORENDO
MORENESS
MORENITA
MORENOSITE
MOREOVER
MOREPEON
MOREPORK
MORES
MORFOND
MORFOUND
MORFOUNDER
MORFREY
MORG
MORGA
MORGANATIC
MORGANATICAL
MORGANIC
MORGANITE
MORGANIZE
MORGAY
MORGEN
MORGENS
MORGLAY
MORGUE
MORIBUND
MORIBUNDITY
MORIBUNDLY
MORICHE
MORIFORM
MORIGERATE

MORIGERATION
MORIGEROUS
MORIGEROUSLY
MORIGLIO
MORILLON
MORIN
MORINDIN
MORINDONE
MORINEL
MORINGACEOUS
MORINGAD
MORINGUID
MORINGUOID
MORION
MORKIN
MORLING
MORLOP
MORMAER
MORMAL
MORMAOR
MORMAORDOM
MORMAORSHIP
MORMO
MORMON
MORMORANDO
MORMYR
MORMYRE
MORMYRIAN
MORMYRID
MORMYROID
MORN
MORNE
MORNED
MORNETTE
MORNING
MORNINGLY
MORNINGS
MORNINGTIDE
MORNTIME
MORO
MOROC
MOROCAIN
MOROCCO
MOROCOTA
MOROLOGICAL
MOROLOGIST
MOROLOGY
MOROMANCY
MORON
MORONCY
MORONES
MORONG
MORONIC
MORONICALLY
MORONISM
MORONITY
MORONRY
MOROR
MOROSAURIAN
MOROSAUROID
MOROSE
MOROSELY
MOROSENESS
MOROSIS
MOROSITY
MOROSOPH
MOROXITE
MORPH
MORPHALLAXIS
MORPHEA
MORPHEME
MORPHEMES
MORPHEMIC
MORPHETIC
MORPHEW
MORPHIA
MORPHIATE
MORPHIC
MORPHICALLY
MORPHIN
MORPHINE
MORPHINIC
MORPHINISM
MORPHINIST
MORPHINIZE
MORPHIOMANIA
MORPHOGENIC
MORPHOGENY
MORPHOGRAPHY
MORPHOLIN
MORPHOLINE
MORPHOLOGIC
MORPHOLOGICAL
MORPHOLOGIES
MORPHOLOGIST
MORPHOLOGY
MORPHOMETRY
MORPHON
MORPHONOMIC
MORPHONOMY
MORPHOPHYLY
MORPHOPLASM
MORPHOSIS
MORPHOTIC
MORPHOTROPIC
MORPHOTROPY
MORPHOUS
MORPHREY
MORPION
MORPUNKEE
MORRAL
MORRHUATE
MORRHUIN
MORRICER
MORRION
MORRIS
MORRO
MORROS
MORROW
MORROWING
MORROWMASS
MORROWSPEECH
MORSAL
MORSE
MORSEL
MORSELED
MORSELING
MORSELIZE
MORSELLED
MORSELLING
MORSING
MORSURE
MORT
MORTACIOUS
MORTAL
MORTALISM
MORTALIST
MORTALITIES
MORTALITY
MORTALIZE
MORTALIZED
MORTALIZING
MORTALLY
MORTAR
MORTARBOARD
MORTARED
MORTARING
MORTARWARE
MORTARY
MORTBELL
MORTCLOTH
MORTERSHEEN
MORTGAGE
MORTGAGED
MORTGAGEE
MORTGAGER
MORTGAGING
MORTGAGOR
MORTH
MORTHWYRTHA
MORTICE
MORTICED
MORTICER
MORTICIAN
MORTICING
MORTIER
MORTIFEROUS
MORTIFIC
MORTIFICATION
MORTIFIED
MORTIFIEDLY
MORTIFY
MORTIFYING
MORTIFYINGLY
MORTISE
MORTISED
MORTISER
MORTISING
MORTLAKE
MORTLING
MORTMAIN
MORTMAINER
MORTORIO
MORTREUX
MORTREWES
MORTUARIES
MORTUARY
MORTUOUS
MORULA
MORULAE
MORULAR
MORULATION
MORULOID
MORVIN
MORWONG
MOS
MOSAIC
MOSAICAL
MOSAICALLY
MOSAICIST
MOSAICKED
MOSAICKING
MOSAIST
MOSANDRITE
MOSASAUR
MOSASAURIAN
MOSASAURID
MOSASAUROID
MOSCH
MOSCHATE
MOSCHATEL
MOSCHIFEROUS
MOSCHINE
MOSE
MOSESITE
MOSEY
MOSEYED
MOSEYING
MOSHAV
MOSK
MOSKENEER
MOSKER
MOSLINGS
MOSQUE
MOSQUITAL
MOSQUITO
MOSQUITOBILL
MOSQUITOES
MOSQUITOEY
MOSQUITOS
MOSS
MOSSBACK
MOSSBACKED
MOSSBANKER
MOSSBERRY
MOSSBUNKER
MOSSED
MOSSER
MOSSERY
MOSSES
MOSSHEAD
MOSSHORN
MOSSIER
MOSSIEST
MOSSINESS
MOSSING
MOSSO
MOSSTROOPER
MOSSTROOPERY
MOSSWORT
MOSSY
MOST
MOSTDEAL
MOSTLIKE
MOSTLINGS
MOSTLY
MOSTRA
MOSTWHAT
MOT
MOTACIL
MOTACILLID
MOTACILLINE
MOTATORIOUS
MOTATORY
MOTE
MOTED
MOTEL
MOTER
MOTET
MOTETTIST
MOTETUS
MOTEY
MOTH
MOTHBALL
MOTHED
MOTHER
MOTHERED
MOTHERER
MOTHERGATE
MOTHERHOOD
MOTHERING
MOTHERLAND
MOTHERLESS
MOTHERLINESS
MOTHERLY
MOTHERWORT
MOTHERY
MOTHIER
MOTHIEST
MOTHPROOF
MOTHPROOFED
MOTHPROOFING
MOTHS
MOTHWORM
MOTHY
MOTIF
MOTIFIC
MOTILE
MOTILITY
MOTION
MOTIONABLE
MOTIONAL
MOTIONED
MOTIONER
MOTIONING
MOTIONIST
MOTIONLESS
MOTIONLESSLY
MOTIONS
MOTITATION
MOTIVATE
MOTIVATED
MOTIVATING
MOTIVATION
MOTIVATIONAL
MOTIVE
MOTIVED
MOTIVENESS
MOTIVING
MOTIVITY
MOTLEY
MOTLEYER
MOTLEYEST
MOTLEYNESS
MOTMOT
MOTO
MOTOFACIENT
MOTOGRAPH
MOTOGRAPHIC
MOTOMAGNETIC
MOTONEURON
MOTOPHONE
MOTOR
MOTORABLE
MOTORBIKE
MOTORBOAT
MOTORBOATMAN
MOTORBUS
MOTORCAB
MOTORCADE
MOTORCAR
MOTORCYCLE
MOTORCYCLED
MOTORCYCLING
MOTORCYCLIST
MOTORDROME
MOTORED
MOTORING
MOTORISM
MOTORIST
MOTORIUM
MOTORIZATION
MOTORIZE
MOTORIZED
MOTORIZING
MOTORMAN
MOTORMEN
MOTORNEER
MOTORPHOBE
MOTORPHOBIA
MOTORPHOBIAC
MOTORSHIP
MOTORTRUCK
MOTORWAY
MOTRE
MOTRICITY
MOTT
MOTTE
MOTTLE
MOTTLED
MOTTLEDNESS
MOTTLEMENT
MOTTLER
MOTTLING
MOTTO
MOTTOED
MOTTOES
MOTTOS
MOTTRAMITE
MOTTY
MOTU
MOTYKA
MOU
MOUCH
MOUCHARABIES

MOUCHARABY
MOUCHARD
MOUCHARDISM
MOUCHE
MOUCHOIR
MOUDIE
MOUDIEMAN
MOUDY
MOUE
MOUFFLON
MOUFLON
MOUFLONS
MOUILLATION
MOUILLE
MOUILLURE
MOUJIK
MOUL
MOULAGE
MOULD
MOULDBOARD
MOULDED
MOULDER
MOULDERED
MOULDERING
MOULDERY
MOULDIER
MOULDIEST
MOULDING
MOULDMADE
MOULDWARP
MOULDY
MOULE
MOULIN
MOULINAGE
MOULINET
MOULLEEN
MOULRUSH
MOULS
MOULT
MOULTED
MOULTER
MOULTING
MOULY
MOUND
MOUNDED
MOUNDING
MOUNDSMAN
MOUNDWORK
MOUNT
MOUNTABLE
MOUNTAIN
MOUNTAINED
MOUNTAINEER
MOUNTAINEERING
MOUNTAINET
MOUNTAINETTE
MOUNTAINOUS
MOUNTAINS
MOUNTAINSIDE
MOUNTAINTOP
MOUNTAINY
MOUNTANCE
MOUNTANT
MOUNTEBANK
MOUNTEBANKED
MOUNTEBANKLY
MOUNTED
MOUNTEE
MOUNTER
MOUNTIE
MOUNTING
MOUNTINGLY
MOUNTS
MOUNTURE
MOUNTY
MOUP
MOURN
MOURNE
MOURNED
MOURNER
MOURNFUL
MOURNFULLY
MOURNFULNESS
MOURNING
MOURNINGLY
MOURNIVAL
MOUSE
MOUSEBANE
MOUSEBIRD
MOUSED
MOUSEFISH
MOUSEFISHES
MOUSEHAWK
MOUSEHOLE
MOUSEHOUND
MOUSELET
MOUSELING
MOUSEMILL
MOUSEPROOF
MOUSER
MOUSERIES
MOUSERY
MOUSETAIL
MOUSETRAP
MOUSETRAPPED
MOUSEWEB
MOUSEY
MOUSIER
MOUSIEST
MOUSILY
MOUSINESS
MOUSING
MOUSLE
MOUSLINGLY
MOUSME
MOUSMEE
MOUSQUETAIRE
MOUSSE
MOUSSELINE
MOUSSEUX
MOUSTACHE
MOUSTACHED
MOUSTACHIAL
MOUSTACHIO
MOUSTOC
MOUSY
MOUTAN
MOUTH
MOUTHABLE
MOUTHBREEDER
MOUTHED
MOUTHER
MOUTHFUL
MOUTHFULS
MOUTHIER
MOUTHIEST
MOUTHILY
MOUTHINESS
MOUTHING
MOUTHISHLY
MOUTHLIKE
MOUTHPART
MOUTHPIECE
MOUTHPIPE
MOUTHS
MOUTHWASH
MOUTHY
MOUTON
MOUTONEED
MOUTONNEE
MOUZAH
MOUZOUNA
MOVABILITY
MOVABLE
MOVABLENESS
MOVABLY
MOVANT
MOVE
MOVEABILITY
MOVEABLE
MOVEABLENESS
MOVEABLY
MOVED
MOVELESS
MOVELESSLY
MOVELESSNESS
MOVEMENT
MOVEMENTS
MOVENT
MOVER
MOVES
MOVIE
MOVIEGOER
MOVIEGOING
MOVIELAND
MOVING
MOVINGLY
MOW
MOWABLE
MOWANA
MOWBURN
MOWBURNT
MOWE
MOWED
MOWER
MOWHA
MOWHAY
MOWIE
MOWING
MOWLAND
MOWN
MOWRA
MOWS
MOWSTEAD
MOWTH
MOXA
MOXIE
MOXIEBERRY
MOY
MOYEN
MOYENANT
MOYENER
MOYENNE
MOYITE
MOYLE
MOYO
MOZAMBIQUE
MOZEMIZE
MOZETTA
MOZING
MOZO
MOZZARELLA
MOZZETTA
MPRET
MU
MUABLE
MUANCE
MUANG
MUBARAT
MUCAGO
MUCARO
MUCEDIN
MUCEDINE
MUCEDINEOUS
MUCEDINOUS
MUCH
MUCHACHA
MUCHACHO
MUCHACHOS
MUCHLY
MUCHNESS
MUCHWHAT
MUCID
MUCIDITY
MUCIDNESS
MUCIFEROUS
MUCIFIC
MUCIFORM
MUCIGEN
MUCIGENOUS
MUCILAGE
MUCILAGINOUS
MUCIN
MUCINOGEN
MUCINOID
MUCINOUS
MUCIPAROUS
MUCIVORE
MUCIVOROUS
MUCK
MUCKAMUCK
MUCKED
MUCKENDER
MUCKER
MUCKERER
MUCKET
MUCKHILL
MUCKIBUS
MUCKIER
MUCKIEST
MUCKILY
MUCKINESS
MUCKING
MUCKITE
MUCKLE
MUCKMAN
MUCKMENT
MUCKMIDDEN
MUCKNA
MUCKRAKE
MUCKRAKED
MUCKRAKER
MUCKRAKING
MUCKSWEAT
MUCKSY
MUCKTHRIFT
MUCKWEED
MUCKWORM
MUCKY
MUCOCELE
MUCODERMAL
MUCOFIBROUS
MUCOID
MUCOIDAL
MUCOPROTEIN
MUCOPURULENT
MUCOPUS
MUCOR
MUCORACEOUS
MUCORINE
MUCORIOID
MUCORMYCOSIS
MUCORRHEA
MUCORRHOEA
MUCOSA
MUCOSAL
MUCOSE
MUCOSEROUS
MUCOSITY
MUCOUS
MUCRO
MUCRONATE
MUCRONATED
MUCRONATELY
MUCRONATION
MUCRONES
MUCRONIFORM
MUCRONULATE
MUCULENT
MUCUS
MUCUSIN
MUD
MUDAR
MUDBANK
MUDCAP
MUDCAPPED
MUDCAPPING
MUDCAT
MUDDEN
MUDDER
MUDDIED
MUDDIER
MUDDIEST
MUDDIFY
MUDDILY
MUDDINESS
MUDDISH
MUDDLE
MUDDLED
MUDDLEDOM
MUDDLEHEAD
MUDDLEHEADED
MUDDLER
MUDDLESOME
MUDDLING
MUDDY
MUDDYBRAINED
MUDDYBREAST
MUDDYHEADED
MUDDYING
MUDFISH
MUDFISHES
MUDFLOW
MUDGE
MUDGUARD
MUDHEAD
MUDHOLE
MUDHOOK
MUDIR
MUDIRIA
MUDIRIEH
MUDLAND
MUDLARK
MUDLARKER
MUDRA
MUDROCK
MUDSILL
MUDSKIPPER
MUDSLINGER
MUDSLINGING
MUDSPATE
MUDSTAIN
MUDSTONE
MUDSUCKER
MUDTRACK
MUDWEED
MUDWORT
MUEDDIN
MUERMO
MUET
MUETTE
MUEZZIN
MUFASAL
MUFF
MUFFED
MUFFET
MUFFETEE
MUFFIN
MUFFINEER
MUFFING
MUFFLE
MUFFLED
MUFFLEMAN
MUFFLEMEN
MUFFLER

MUFFLIN
MUFFLING
MUFFY
MUFTI
MUFTIS
MUFTY
MUG
MUGA
MUGEARITE
MUGG
MUGGA
MUGGAR
MUGGED
MUGGER
MUGGET
MUGGIER
MUGGIEST
MUGGINESS
MUGGING
MUGGINS
MUGGISH
MUGGLES
MUGGS
MUGGUR
MUGGY
MUGHOPINE
MUGHOUSE
MUGIENCE
MUGIENCY
MUGIENT
MUGILIFORM
MUGILOID
MUGS
MUGUET
MUGWEED
MUGWET
MUGWORT
MUGWUMP
MUGWUMPERY
MUGWUMPIAN
MUGWUMPISM
MUHAMMADI
MUHLIES
MUHLY
MUID
MUIR
MUIRBURN
MUIRCOCK
MUIRFOWL
MUISHOND
MUJER
MUJERES
MUJIK
MUJTAHID
MUKHTAR
MUKLUK
MUKTAR
MUKTATMA
MUKTEAR
MUKTI
MUKTUK
MULADA
MULADI
MULAPRAKRITI
MULATTO
MULATTOES
MULBERRIES
MULBERRY
MULCH
MULCHED
MULCHING
MULCT
MULCTABLE
MULCTARY
MULCTATION
MULCTATIVE
MULCTATORY
MULCTED
MULCTUARY
MULE
MULEBACK
MULEFOOT
MULEFOOTED
MULEMAN
MULEMEN
MULES
MULET
MULETA
MULETEER
MULETRESS
MULETTA
MULEWORT
MULEY
MULGA
MULIEBRAL
MULIEBRIA
MULIEBRILE
MULIEBRITY
MULIEBROUS
MULIER
MULIERINE
MULIERLY
MULIEROSE
MULIEROSITY
MULISH
MULISHLY
MULISHNESS
MULITA
MULK
MULL
MULLA
MULLAH
MULLAR
MULLED
MULLEIN
MULLEN
MULLENIZE
MULLER
MULLET
MULLETRY
MULLETS
MULLEY
MULLID
MULLIGAN
MULLIGATAWNY
MULLIGRUBS
MULLING
MULLION
MULLIONED
MULLIONING
MULLOCK
MULLOCKER
MULLOCKY
MULLOID
MULLOWAY
MULM
MULMUL
MULSE
MULT
MULTANGLE
MULTANGULAR
MULTANGULOUS
MULTANGULUM
MULTANIMOUS
MULTEITY
MULTIBREAK
MULTICOLORED
MULTICYCLE
MULTIFARIOUS
MULTIFARIOUSNE
MULTIFEROUS
MULTIFID
MULTIFIDLY
MULTIFIDOUS
MULTIFIDUS
MULTIFLOW
MULTIFOIL
MULTIFOILED
MULTIFOLD
MULTIFORM
MULTIFORMED
MULTIFORMITY
MULTIGAP
MULTIGRAPH
MULTIGRAPHER
MULTILATERAL
MULTILINGUAL
MULTILITERAL
MULTILITH
MULTILOCATION
MULTILOQUENT
MULTILOQUOUS
MULTILOQUY
MULTIMARBLE
MULTIMEDIA
MULTIMODAL
MULTINOMIAL
MULTIPARA
MULTIPARAE
MULTIPARITY
MULTIPAROUS
MULTIPARTITE
MULTIPED
MULTIPEDE
MULTIPHASE
MULTIPHASER
MULTIPLANE
MULTIPLE
MULTIPLET
MULTIPLEX
MULTIPLIABLE
MULTIPLICAND
MULTIPLICATE
MULTIPLICATION
MULTIPLICITY
MULTIPLIED
MULTIPLIER
MULTIPLY
MULTIPLYING
MULTIPOLAR
MULTIPOLE
MULTIPOTENT
MULTIPRESENT
MULTISCIENCE
MULTISECT
MULTISECTOR
MULTISENSUAL
MULTISONANT
MULTISONOUS
MULTISTAGE
MULTITARIAN
MULTITHEISM
MULTITUBE
MULTITUDE
MULTITUDINAL
MULTITUDINOUS
MULTITURN
MULTIVAGANT
MULTIVALENCE
MULTIVALENCY
MULTIVALENT
MULTIVALVE
MULTIVARIANT
MULTIVARIOUS
MULTIVERSANT
MULTIVERSE
MULTIVIOUS
MULTIVOCAL
MULTIVOLENT
MULTIVOLTINE
MULTIWALL
MULTOCULAR
MULTUM
MULTUNGULATE
MULTURE
MULTURER
MULVEL
MUM
MUMBLE
MUMBLEBEE
MUMBLED
MUMBLEMENT
MUMBLER
MUMBLING
MUMBLINGLY
MUMBUDGET
MUMCHANCE
MUME
MUMHOUSE
MUMJUMA
MUMM
MUMMED
MUMMER
MUMMERIES
MUMMERY
MUMMIA
MUMMICHOG
MUMMICK
MUMMIED
MUMMIES
MUMMIFIED
MUMMIFORM
MUMMIFY
MUMMIFYING
MUMMING
MUMMY
MUMMYING
MUMMYLIKE
MUMP
MUMPED
MUMPER
MUMPHEAD
MUMPING
MUMPISH
MUMPISHLY
MUMPISHNESS
MUMPS
MUMPSIMUS
MUMRUFFIN
MUMU
MUN
MUNA
MUNCH
MUNCHED
MUNCHEE
MUNCHEEL
MUNCHER
MUNCHET
MUNCHING
MUND
MUNDAL
MUNDANE
MUNDANELY
MUNDANENESS
MUNDANISM
MUNDANITY
MUNDATORY
MUNDIC
MUNDIFICANT
MUNDIFIER
MUNDIFY
MUNDIL
MUNDIVAGANT
MUNDLE
MUNDUNGO
MUNDUNGUS
MUNG
MUNGA
MUNGCORN
MUNGE
MUNGER
MUNGEY
MUNGO
MUNGOFA
MUNGOOSE
MUNGOOSES
MUNGUBA
MUNGY
MUNI
MUNICIPAL
MUNICIPALISM
MUNICIPALIST
MUNICIPALITIES
MUNICIPALITY
MUNICIPALIZE
MUNICIPALIZED
MUNICIPALIZING
MUNICIPALLY
MUNICIPIA
MUNICIPIUM
MUNIFIC
MUNIFICENCE
MUNIFICENCY
MUNIFICENT
MUNIFICENTLY
MUNIFY
MUNIMENT
MUNIMENTS
MUNITE
MUNITION
MUNITIONARY
MUNITIONEER
MUNITIONER
MUNITY
MUNJ
MUNJEET
MUNJISTIN
MUNK
MUNNION
MUNSHI
MUNSIFF
MUNTIN
MUNTING
MUNTJAC
MUNTJAK
MUON
MUR
MURA
MURAENOID
MURAGE
MURAL
MURALED
MURALIST
MURARIUM
MURASAKITE
MURCHY
MURCIANA
MURDER
MURDERED
MURDERER
MURDERESS
MURDERING
MURDERINGLY
MURDEROUS
MURDEROUSLY
MURDRUM
MURE
MURED
MURENGER
MURES
MUREX
MUREXAN
MUREXES
MUREXID
MUREXIDE

MURGEON
MURIATE
MURIATED
MURIATIC
MURICATE
MURICATED
MURICES
MURICID
MURICIFORM
MURICINE
MURICOID
MURICULATE
MURID
MURIE
MURIFORM
MURIFORMLY
MURINE
MURING
MURINUS
MURIONITRIC
MURIUM
MURK
MURKIER
MURKIEST
MURKILY
MURKINESS
MURKISH
MURKLY
MURKNESS
MURKSOME
MURKY
MURL
MURLACK
MURLAIN
MURLEMEWES
MURLIN
MURLOCK
MURLY
MURMUR
MURMURATION
MURMURATOR
MURMURED
MURMURER
MURMURING
MURMURINGLY
MURMURISH
MURMUROUS
MURMUROUSLY
MURNIVAL
MUROID
MUROMONTITE
MURON
MURPHIES
MURPHY
MURR
MURRA
MURRAH
MURRAIN
MURRAL
MURRAY
MURRE
MURRELET
MURRES
MURREY
MURRHA
MURRHINE
MURRHUINE
MURRINA
MURRNONG
MURRY
MURSHID
MURTHER
MURTHERER
MURUMURU
MURUP
MURVA
MURZA
MUSACEOUS
MUSAF
MUSAL
MUSANG
MUSAR
MUSARD
MUSARDRY
MUSCA
MUSCADE
MUSCADEL
MUSCADIN
MUSCADINE
MUSCAE
MUSCARDINE
MUSCARIFORM
MUSCARINE
MUSCAT
MUSCATEL
MUSCAVADA
MUSCICAPINE
MUSCICIDE
MUSCICOLE
MUSCICOLINE
MUSCICOLOUS
MUSCID
MUSCIFORM
MUSCLE
MUSCLED
MUSCLEMAN
MUSCLES
MUSCLING
MUSCLY
MUSCOID
MUSCOLOGIC
MUSCOLOGIST
MUSCOLOGY
MUSCONE
MUSCOSE
MUSCOSENESS
MUSCOSITY
MUSCOVADE
MUSCOVADITE
MUSCOVADO
MUSCOVITE
MUSCOVITIZE
MUSCOVITIZED
MUSCOVY
MUSCULAR
MUSCULARITY
MUSCULARIZE
MUSCULARLY
MUSCULATION
MUSCULATURE
MUSCULE
MUSCULI
MUSCULIN
MUSCULUS
MUSE
MUSED
MUSEE
MUSEFUL
MUSEFULLY
MUSELESS
MUSELESSNESS
MUSEOGRAPHER
MUSEOGRAPHY
MUSEOLOGIST
MUSEOLOGY
MUSER
MUSERY
MUSES
MUSET
MUSETTE
MUSEUM
MUSH
MUSHA
MUSHAA
MUSHED
MUSHER
MUSHHEAD
MUSHHEADED
MUSHIER
MUSHIEST
MUSHILY
MUSHINESS
MUSHING
MUSHLA
MUSHMELON
MUSHROOM
MUSHROOMER
MUSHROOMIC
MUSHROOMING
MUSHROOMY
MUSHRU
MUSHRUMP
MUSHY
MUSIC
MUSICA
MUSICAL
MUSICALE
MUSICALITY
MUSICALIZE
MUSICALLY
MUSICALNESS
MUSICATE
MUSICIAN
MUSICIANER
MUSICIANLY
MUSICIANS
MUSICIANSHIP
MUSICKER
MUSICLESS
MUSICMONGER
MUSICO
MUSICOGRAPHY
MUSICOLOGIES
MUSICOLOGIST
MUSICOLOGY
MUSICOMANIA
MUSICOPHOBIA
MUSICOPOETIC
MUSICRY
MUSIMON
MUSING
MUSINGLY
MUSION
MUSIVE
MUSJID
MUSK
MUSKALLUNGE
MUSKEG
MUSKEGGY
MUSKELLUNGE
MUSKELLUNGES
MUSKET
MUSKETADE
MUSKETEER
MUSKETOON
MUSKETRY
MUSKGRASS
MUSKIE
MUSKIER
MUSKIEST
MUSKIFIED
MUSKILY
MUSKINESS
MUSKISH
MUSKIT
MUSKMELON
MUSKRAT
MUSKRATS
MUSKROOT
MUSKWOOD
MUSKY
MUSLIN
MUSLINED
MUSLINET
MUSLINETTE
MUSNUD
MUSOPHAGINE
MUSPIKE
MUSQUASH
MUSQUASHROOT
MUSQUASHWEED
MUSQUASPEN
MUSQUAW
MUSROL
MUSROOMED
MUSS
MUSSACK
MUSSAL
MUSSALCHEE
MUSSED
MUSSEL
MUSSELCRACKER
MUSSELED
MUSSELER
MUSSICK
MUSSIER
MUSSIEST
MUSSILY
MUSSINESS
MUSSING
MUSSITATE
MUSSITATION
MUSSUCK
MUSSUK
MUSSURANA
MUSSY
MUST
MUSTACHE
MUSTACHED
MUSTACHIAL
MUSTACHIO
MUSTACHIOED
MUSTAFINA
MUSTAFUZ
MUSTANG
MUSTANGER
MUSTARD
MUSTARDER
MUSTED
MUSTEE
MUSTELID
MUSTELIN
MUSTELINE
MUSTELINOUS
MUSTELOID
MUSTER
MUSTERED
MUSTERER
MUSTERING
MUSTERMASTER
MUSTERS
MUSTH
MUSTIER
MUSTIEST
MUSTIFY
MUSTILY
MUSTINESS
MUSTING
MUSTULENT
MUSTY
MUSUMEE
MUT
MUTA
MUTABILITY
MUTABLE
MUTABLENESS
MUTABLY
MUTAGE
MUTAGEN
MUTANT
MUTAROTATE
MUTAROTATION
MUTASE
MUTATE
MUTATED
MUTATING
MUTATION
MUTATIONAL
MUTATIONALLY
MUTATIONISM
MUTATIONIST
MUTATIVE
MUTATORY
MUTAWALLI
MUTAWALLIS
MUTCH
MUTCHKIN
MUTE
MUTED
MUTELY
MUTENESS
MUTER
MUTESCENCE
MUTESSARIF
MUTESSARIFAT
MUTH
MUTHMANNITE
MUTI
MUTIC
MUTICOUS
MUTILATE
MUTILATED
MUTILATING
MUTILATION
MUTILATIVE
MUTILATOR
MUTILATORY
MUTILLID
MUTILOUS
MUTINADO
MUTINE
MUTINEER
MUTINEERS
MUTING
MUTINIED
MUTINIES
MUTINOUS
MUTINOUSLY
MUTINOUSNESS
MUTINY
MUTINYING
MUTISM
MUTIST
MUTISTIC
MUTIVE
MUTIVITY
MUTOSCOPE
MUTOSCOPIC
MUTSJE
MUTSUDDY
MUTT
MUTTER
MUTTERED
MUTTERER
MUTTERING
MUTTERINGLY
MUTTON
MUTTONBIRD
MUTTONCHOP
MUTTONCHOPS
MUTTONFISH
MUTTONFISHES
MUTTONHEAD
MUTTONHEADED
MUTTONMONGER

MUTTONWOOD
MUTUA
MUTUAL
MUTUALISM
MUTUALIST
MUTUALISTIC
MUTUALITY
MUTUALIZE
MUTUALIZED
MUTUALIZING
MUTUALLY
MUTUARY
MUTUATE
MUTUATITIOUS
MUTUEL
MUTULE
MUTUUM
MUTWALLI
MUUMUU
MUVULE
MUX
MUY
MUYUSA
MUZHIK
MUZJIK
MUZOONA
MUZZ
MUZZIER
MUZZIEST
MUZZLE
MUZZLED
MUZZLELOADER
MUZZLELOADING
MUZZLER
MUZZLEWOOD
MUZZLING
MUZZY
MWAMI
MY
MYAL
MYALGIA
MYALGIC
MYALISM
MYALL
MYARIAN
MYASTHENIA
MYASTHENIC
MYATONIA
MYATONIC
MYATONY
MYATROPHY
MYCELE
MYCELIAL
MYCELIAN
MYCELIOID
MYCELIUM
MYCELOID
MYCETISM
MYCETOCYTE
MYCETOGENIC
MYCETOGENOUS
MYCETOID
MYCETOLOGY
MYCETOMA
MYCETOMATA
MYCETOMATOUS
MYCETOME
MYCETOUS
MYCETOZOAN
MYCETOZOON
MYCOCECIDIUM
MYCODERM
MYCODERMA
MYCODERMIC
MYCODOMATIUM
MYCOID
MYCOLOGIC
MYCOLOGICAL
MYCOLOGIES
MYCOLOGIST
MYCOLOGIZE
MYCOLOGY
MYCOMYCETE
MYCOMYCETOUS
MYCOPHAGIST
MYCOPHAGOUS
MYCOPHAGY
MYCOPLASM
MYCOPLASMA
MYCORHIZA
MYCORHIZAL
MYCORRHIZA
MYCORRHIZAL
MYCORRHIZIC
MYCOSE
MYCOSIN
MYCOSIS
MYCOSTEROL
MYCOTIC
MYCOTROPHIC
MYCTERIC
MYCTERISM
MYCTOPHID
MYDALEINE
MYDATOXINE
MYDINE
MYDRIASINE
MYDRIASIS
MYDRIATIC
MYDRIATINE
MYECTOMIZE
MYECTOMY
MYECTOPIA
MYECTOPY
MYELALGIA
MYELAPOPLEXY
MYELASTHENIA
MYELATROPHY
MYELAUXE
MYELEMIA
MYELIC
MYELIN
MYELINATE
MYELINATED
MYELINATION
MYELINE
MYELINIC
MYELINOGENY
MYELITIC
MYELITIS
MYELOBLAST
MYELOBLASTIC
MYELOCELE
MYELOCOELE
MYELOCYST
MYELOCYSTIC
MYELOCYTE
MYELOCYTIC
MYELOCYTOSIS
MYELOGENESIS
MYELOGENETIC
MYELOGENOUS
MYELOGONIUM
MYELOIC
MYELOID
MYELOMA
MYELOMALACIA
MYELOMAS
MYELOMATA
MYELOMATOID
MYELOMATOSIS
MYELOMENIA
MYELON
MYELONAL
MYELONIC
MYELOPATHIC
MYELOPATHY
MYELOPETAL
MYELOPLAST
MYELOPLASTIC
MYELOPLAX
MYELOPLAXES
MYELOPLEGIA
MYELOPOIESIS
MYELOPOIETIC
MYELORRHAGIA
MYELORRHAPHY
MYELOSARCOMA
MYELOSPASM
MYELOTHERAPY
MYENTASIS
MYENTERIC
MYENTERON
MYGALE
MYGALID
MYGALOID
MYIASIS
MYIODESOPSIA
MYKISS
MYLODONT
MYLOHYOID
MYLOHYOIDEAN
MYLONITE
MYLONITIC
MYMARID
MYNA
MYNAH
MYNHEER
MYNPACHT
MYOALBUMIN
MYOALBUMOSE
MYOATROPHY
MYOBLAST
MYOBLASTIC
MYOCARDIAC
MYOCARDIAL
MYOCARDITIC
MYOCARDITIS
MYOCARDIUM
MYOCLONIC
MYOCLONUS
MYOCOEL
MYOCOELE
MYOCOELOM
MYOCOLPITIS
MYOCOMMA
MYOCOMMATA
MYOCYTE
MYODIASTASIS
MYODYNAMIA
MYODYNAMIC
MYODYNAMICS
MYOEDEMA
MYOELECTRIC
MYOENOTOMY
MYOFIBRIL
MYOFIBRILLA
MYOFIBROMA
MYOGEN
MYOGENESIS
MYOGENETIC
MYOGENIC
MYOGENOUS
MYOGLOBIN
MYOGLOBULIN
MYOGRAM
MYOGRAPH
MYOGRAPHER
MYOGRAPHIC
MYOGRAPHICAL
MYOGRAPHIST
MYOGRAPHY
MYOHAEMATIN
MYOHEMATIN
MYOID
MYOKINESIS
MYOLEMMA
MYOLIPOMA
MYOLIPOSIS
MYOLOGIC
MYOLOGICAL
MYOLOGIST
MYOLOGY
MYOLYSIS
MYOMA
MYOMALACIA
MYOMANCY
MYOMANTIC
MYOMATA
MYOMATOUS
MYOMECTOMIES
MYOMECTOMY
MYOMELANOSIS
MYOMERE
MYOMETRITIS
MYOMETRIUM
MYOMORPH
MYOMORPHIC
MYOMOTOMY
MYONEMA
MYONEME
MYONEURAL
MYONEURALGIA
MYONEURE
MYONEUROMA
MYONEUROSIS
MYONOSUS
MYOPACHYNSIS
MYOPARALYSIS
MYOPARESIS
MYOPATHIA
MYOPATHIC
MYOPATHY
MYOPE
MYOPHAN
MYOPHORE
MYOPHOROUS
MYOPHYSICAL
MYOPHYSICS
MYOPIA
MYOPIC
MYOPICAL
MYOPICALLY
MYOPLASM
MYOPLASTIC
MYOPLASTY
MYOPOLAR
MYOPORACEOUS
MYOPORAD
MYOPROTEID
MYOPROTEIN
MYOPROTEOSE
MYOPS
MYOPY
MYORRHAPHY
MYORRHEXIS
MYOSARCOMA
MYOSCLEROSIS
MYOSCOPE
MYOSEPTUM
MYOSIN
MYOSIS
MYOSITIC
MYOSITIS
MYOSOTE
MYOSOTIS
MYOSPASM
MYOSPASMIA
MYOSUTURE
MYOSYNIZESIS
MYOTASIS
MYOTHERMIC
MYOTIC
MYOTOME
MYOTOMIC
MYOTOMY
MYOTONIA
MYOTROPHY
MYOWUN
MYOXINE
MYRCENE
MYRIACOULOMB
MYRIAD
MYRIADED
MYRIADLY
MYRIAGRAM
MYRIAGRAMME
MYRIALITER
MYRIALITRE
MYRIAMETER
MYRIAMETRE
MYRIAPOD
MYRIAPODAN
MYRIAPODOUS
MYRIARCH
MYRIARCHY
MYRIARE
MYRICA
MYRICACEOUS
MYRICETIN
MYRICIN
MYRICYL
MYRICYLIC
MYRINGA
MYRINGECTOMY
MYRINGITIS
MYRINGOTOME
MYRINGOTOMY
MYRIOLOGIST
MYRIOLOGUE
MYRIORAMA
MYRIOSCOPE
MYRIOSPOROUS
MYRIOTHEISM
MYRISTATE
MYRISTIC
MYRISTIN
MYRISTONE
MYRMECOBIINE
MYRMECOCHORY
MYRMECOID
MYRMECOIDY
MYRMECOLOGY
MYRMECOPHILE
MYRMECOPHILY
MYRMECOPHYTE
MYRMEKITE
MYRMICID
MYRMICINE
MYRMICOID
MYRMIDON
MYRMOTHERINE
MYROBALAN
MYRONATE
MYROPOLIST
MYROSIN
MYRRH
MYRRHED
MYRRHIC
MYRRHINE
MYRRHOL
MYRRHOPHORE
MYRRHY
MYRSINACEOUS
MYRSINAD

MYRT
MYRTACEOUS
MYRTAL
MYRTIFORM
MYRTLE
MYRTLEBERRY
MYRTOL
MYSELF
MYSEN
MYSID
MYSIDEAN
MYSOID
MYSOPHOBIA
MYSOST
MYST
MYSTACAL
MYSTACIAL
MYSTACINE
MYSTACINOUS
MYSTAGOG
MYSTAGOGIC
MYSTAGOGICAL
MYSTAGOGUE
MYSTAGOGY
MYSTAX
MYSTERIAL
MYSTERIARCH
MYSTERIES
MYSTERIOUS
MYSTERIOUSLY
MYSTERIZE
MYSTERY
MYSTES
MYSTIC
MYSTICAL
MYSTICALITY
MYSTICALLY
MYSTICALNESS
MYSTICETE
MYSTICISM
MYSTICITY
MYSTIFICALLY
MYSTIFICATOR
MYSTIFIED
MYSTIFIER
MYSTIFY
MYSTIFYING
MYSTIFYINGLY
MYSTIQUE
MYTACISM
MYTH
MYTHE
MYTHIC
MYTHICAL
MYTHICALISM
MYTHICALITY
MYTHICALLY
MYTHICALNESS
MYTHICISM
MYTHICIST
MYTHICIZE
MYTHICIZED
MYTHICIZER
MYTHICIZING
MYTHIFY
MYTHIST
MYTHOCLAST
MYTHOCLASTIC
MYTHOGENESIS
MYTHOGENY
MYTHOGONIC
MYTHOGONY
MYTHOGRAPHER
MYTHOGRAPHY
MYTHOGREEN
MYTHOHEROIC
MYTHOLOGEMA
MYTHOLOGER
MYTHOLOGIAN
MYTHOLOGIC
MYTHOLOGICAL
MYTHOLOGIES
MYTHOLOGISE
MYTHOLOGIST
MYTHOLOGIZE
MYTHOLOGIZED
MYTHOLOGIZER
MYTHOLOGIZING
MYTHOLOGUE
MYTHOLOGY
MYTHOMANIA
MYTHOMANIAC
MYTHOMETER
MYTHONOMY
MYTHOPEIC
MYTHOPEIST
MYTHOPOEIA
MYTHOPOEIC
MYTHOPOEISM
MYTHOPOEIST
MYTHOPOEM
MYTHOPOESIS
MYTHOPOESY
MYTHOPOET
MYTHOPOETIC
MYTHOPOETIZE
MYTHOPOETRY
MYTHOS
MYTILACEAN
MYTILACEOUS
MYTILID
MYTILIFORM
MYTILOID
MYTILOTOXINE
MYXA
MYXADENITIS
MYXADENOMA
MYXAEMIA
MYXAMOEBA
MYXANGITIS
MYXASTHENIA
MYXEDEMA
MYXEDEMATOUS
MYXEDEMIC
MYXEMIA
MYXINOID
MYXO
MYXOBLASTOMA
MYXOCYSTOMA
MYXOCYTE
MYXOEDEMA
MYXOEDEMIC
MYXOFIBROMA
MYXOGASTER
MYXOGLIOMA
MYXOID
MYXOINOMA
MYXOLIPOMA
MYXOMA
MYXOMAS
MYXOMATA
MYXOMATOSIS
MYXOMATOUS
MYXOMYCETE
MYXOMYCETOUS
MYXOMYOMA
MYXONEUROMA
MYXOPODIA
MYXOPODIUM
MYXORRHEA
MYXOSARCOMA
MYXOSPORE
MYXOSPOROUS
MYXOTHECA
MYZONT
MYZOSTOMID
MYZOSTOMIDAN
MYZOSTOMOUS

NA
NAAM
NAARTJE
NAB
NABAK
NABAM
NABBED
NABBER
NABBING
NABBUK
NABBY
NABCHEAT
NABEE
NABK
NABLA
NABLE
NABLUS
NABO
NABOB
NABOBERY
NABOBESS
NABOBICAL
NABOBISH
NABOBISHLY
NABOBISM
NABOBRY
NABS
NACARAT
NACARINE
NACE
NACELLE
NACHTMAAL
NACK
NACKET
NACRE
NACRED
NACREOUS
NACRINE
NACROUS
NACRY
NADA
NADDER
NADIR
NADIRAL
NADORITE
NAE
NAEGAIT
NAEGATE
NAEGATES
NAEL
NAEVE
NAEVOID
NAEVUS
NAG
NAGA
NAGAIKA
NAGAMI
NAGANA
NAGARA
NAGATELITE
NAGGAR
NAGGED
NAGGER
NAGGIN
NAGGING
NAGGINGLY
NAGGINGNESS
NAGGISH
NAGGLE
NAGGLY
NAGGY
NAGHT
NAGID
NAGKASSAR
NAGMAAL
NAGMAN
NAGOR
NAGSMAN
NAGSTER
NAGUAL
NAGUALISM
NAGUALIST
NAGYAGITE
NAHIE
NAHOOR
NAIAD
NAIANT
NAIB
NAID
NAIF
NAIFLY
NAIG
NAIGUE
NAIK
NAIL
NAILED
NAILER
NAILERY
NAILHEAD
NAILING
NAILLESS
NAILROD
NAILS
NAILSICK
NAILWORT
NAILY
NAINSEL
NAINSELL
NAINSOOK
NAIO
NAIQUE
NAIRY
NAIS
NAISH
NAISSANCE
NAISSANT
NAIT
NAITLY
NAIVE
NAIVELY
NAIVENESS
NAIVETE
NAIVETY
NAK
NAKE
NAKED
NAKEDIZE
NAKEDLY
NAKEDNESS
NAKEDWOOD
NAKER
NAKHLITE
NAKHOD
NAKHODA
NAKONG
NAKOO
NAL
NALL
NALLAH
NALLE
NAMABILITY
NAMABLE
NAMAQUA
NAMAYCUSH
NAMAZ
NAMAZLIK
NAMBY
NAMDA
NAME
NAMEABILITY
NAMEABLE
NAMEBOARD
NAMED
NAMELESS
NAMELESSLY
NAMELESSNESS
NAMELING
NAMELY
NAMEPLATE
NAMER
NAMESAKE
NAMING
NAMMAD
NAN
NANA
NANANDER
NANAWOOD
NANCA
NANCY
NANDIN
NANDINE
NANDOW
NANDU
NANDUTI
NANE
NANES
NANGA
NANGCA
NANGER
NANGKA
NANIGO
NANISM
NANITIC
NANIZATION
NANKEEN
NANKEENS
NANKIN
NANKINS
NANMU
NANNANDER
NANNIE
NANNIES
NANNINOSE
NANNY
NANOCEPHALIA
NANOCEPHALIC
NANOCEPHALUS
NANOCEPHALY
NANOID
NANOMELIA
NANOMELOUS
NANOMELUS
NANOPLANKTON
NANOSOMA
NANOSOMUS
NANPIE
NANSOMIA
NANT
NANTLE
NANTOKITE
NANTS
NAO
NAOLOGICAL
NAOLOGY
NAOMETRY
NAOS
NAP
NAPA
NAPAL
NAPALM
NAPE
NAPEAD
NAPECREST
NAPELLUS
NAPERER
NAPERIES
NAPERY
NAPHTHA
NAPHTHACENE
NAPHTHALATE
NAPHTHALENE
NAPHTHALENIC
NAPHTHALIC
NAPHTHALIZE
NAPHTHAMINE
NAPHTHENE
NAPHTHENIC
NAPHTHIONATE
NAPHTHOIC
NAPHTHOL
NAPHTHOLATE
NAPHTHOUS
NAPHTHYL
NAPHTHYLENE
NAPHTHYLIC
NAPIFORM
NAPKIN
NAPKINED
NAPKINING
NAPKINS
NAPLESS
NAPLESSNESS
NAPOLEON
NAPOO
NAPOOH
NAPPE
NAPPED
NAPPER
NAPPIE
NAPPINESS
NAPPING
NAPPISHNESS
NAPPY
NAPRAPATHY
NAPRON
NAPU
NAR
NARCEIN
NARCEINE
NARCISM
NARCISSISM
NARCISSIST
NARCISSISTIC
NARCISSUS
NARCIST
NARCISTIC
NARCOHYPNIA
NARCOLEPSY
NARCOLEPTIC
NARCOMA
NARCOMANIA
NARCOMANIAC
NARCOMANIACAL
NARCOMAS
NARCOMATA
NARCOMEDUSAN
NARCOSE
NARCOSIS
NARCOTIA
NARCOTIC
NARCOTICAL
NARCOTICALLY
NARCOTICISM
NARCOTICS
NARCOTIN
NARCOTINA
NARCOTINE
NARCOTINIC
NARCOTISM
NARCOTIST
NARCOTIZE
NARCOTIZED
NARCOTIZING
NARD
NARDINE
NARDO
NARDOO
NARDU
NARE
NARES
NARGHILE
NARGIL
NARGILE
NARGILEH
NARIAL
NARICA
NARICORN
NARIFORM
NARINE
NARINGENIN
NARINGIN
NARIS
NARK
NARKY
NARR
NARRA
NARRANTE
NARRAS
NARRATABLE
NARRATE
NARRATION
NARRATIONAL
NARRATIVE
NARRATIVELY
NARRATOR
NARRATORY
NARRATRESS
NARRAWOOD
NARROW
NARROWED
NARROWER
NARROWEST
NARROWING
NARROWLY
NARROWNESS
NARROWY
NARSARSUKITE
NARSINGA
NARTHECAL
NARTHEX
NARWAL
NARWHAL
NARWHALE
NARY
NAS
NASAB
NASAL
NASALIS
NASALISM
NASALITY
NASALIZATION
NASALIZE
NASALIZED
NASALIZING
NASALLY
NASARD
NASAT
NASAUMP
NASCENCE
NASCENCY
NASCENT
NASCH
NASE
NASEBERRY
NASETHMOID

NASH
NASHGAB
NASHGOB
NASI
NASIAL
NASICORN
NASICORNOUS
NASIFORM
NASILABIAL
NASILLATE
NASILLATION
NASION
NASITIS
NASOANTRAL
NASOBASILAR
NASOBUCCAL
NASOCILIARY
NASOFRONTAL
NASOLABIAL
NASOLOGICAL
NASOLOGIST
NASOLOGY
NASOMALAR
NASONITE
NASOORBITAL
NASOPALATAL
NASOPALATINE
NASOPHARYNX
NASOROSTRAL
NASOSCOPE
NASOSEPTAL
NASOSINUITIS
NASOSUBNASAL
NASROL
NASSOLOGY
NAST
NASTALIQ
NASTIC
NASTIER
NASTIEST
NASTIKA
NASTILY
NASTINESS
NASTURTIUM
NASTY
NASUS
NASUTE
NASUTENESS
NASUTIFORM
NAT
NATA
NATABILITY
NATAKA
NATAL
NATALITIAL
NATALITY
NATANT
NATANTLY
NATATION
NATATOR
NATATORIAL
NATATORIOUS
NATATORIUM
NATATORY
NATCH
NATCHBONE
NATCHNEE
NATE
NATED
NATES
NATHE
NATHER
NATHLESS
NATICIFORM
NATICINE
NATICOID
NATIFORM
NATION
NATIONAL
NATIONALISM
NATIONALIST
NATIONALISTIC
NATIONALISTICALLY
NATIONALITY
NATIONALIZATION
NATIONALIZE
NATIONALIZED
NATIONALIZER
NATIONALIZING
NATIONALLY
NATIONALNESS
NATIONS
NATIVE
NATIVELY
NATIVISM
NATIVIST
NATIVISTIC
NATIVITIES
NATIVITY
NATR
NATRIUM
NATROCHALCITE
NATROJAROSITE
NATROLITE
NATRON
NATTE
NATTER
NATTERED
NATTEREDNESS
NATTERJACK
NATTIER
NATTIEST
NATTILY
NATTLE
NATTOCK
NATTY
NATUARY
NATURA
NATURAL
NATURALESQUE
NATURALIA
NATURALISE
NATURALISM
NATURALIST
NATURALISTIC
NATURALITY
NATURALIZE
NATURALIZED
NATURALIZER
NATURALIZING
NATURALLY
NATURALNESS
NATURATA
NATURE
NATURECRAFT
NATURED
NATURING
NATURISM
NATURIST
NATURISTIC
NATURIZE
NATUROPATH
NATUROPATHIC
NATUROPATHY
NATYA
NAU
NAUCORID
NAUCRAR
NAUCRARY
NAUFRAGE
NAUFRAGOUS
NAUGER
NAUGHT
NAUGHTIER
NAUGHTIEST
NAUGHTILY
NAUGHTINESS
NAUGHTY
NAUJAITE
NAUKRAR
NAULUM
NAUMACHIA
NAUMACHIAE
NAUMACHIAS
NAUMACHIES
NAUMACHY
NAUMANNITE
NAUMK
NAUMKEAG
NAUMKEAGER
NAUNT
NAUNTLE
NAUPATHIA
NAUPLIAL
NAUPLIIFORM
NAUPLIOID
NAUPLIUS
NAUROPOMETER
NAUSCOPY
NAUSEA
NAUSEANT
NAUSEATE
NAUSEATED
NAUSEATING
NAUSEATION
NAUSEOUS
NAUSEOUSLY
NAUSEOUSNESS
NAUSITY
NAUT
NAUTCH
NAUTHER
NAUTIC
NAUTICAL
NAUTICALITY
NAUTICALLY
NAUTICS
NAUTIFORM
NAUTILACEAN
NAUTILI
NAUTILICONE
NAUTILIFORM
NAUTILITE
NAUTILOID
NAUTILOIDEAN
NAUTILUS
NAUTILUSES
NAVAL
NAVALISM
NAVALIST
NAVALISTIC
NAVARCH
NAVARCHY
NAVARHO
NAVARIN
NAVE
NAVEL
NAVELED
NAVELWORT
NAVET
NAVETA
NAVETTE
NAVEW
NAVIA
NAVICELLA
NAVICERT
NAVICULA
NAVICULAR
NAVICULARE
NAVICULOID
NAVIES
NAVIFORM
NAVIGABILITY
NAVIGABLE
NAVIGABLENESS
NAVIGABLY
NAVIGANT
NAVIGATE
NAVIGATED
NAVIGATING
NAVIGATION
NAVIGATIONAL
NAVIGATOR
NAVIGEROUS
NAVIPENDULAR
NAVIPENDULUM
NAVITE
NAVVIE
NAVVIES
NAVVY
NAVY
NAW
NAWAB
NAWOB
NAWT
NAY
NAYAK
NAYAUR
NAYSAY
NAYWARD
NAYWORD
NAZARD
NAZE
NAZI
NAZIFICATION
NAZIFIED
NAZIFY
NAZIFYING
NAZIM
NAZIR
NAZIS
NE
NEAKES
NEAL
NEALLOTYPE
NEANIC
NEAP
NEAPED
NEAR
NEARABOUT
NEARABOUTS
NEARAWAY
NEARAWAYS
NEARBY
NEARED
NEARER
NEAREST
NEARING
NEARISH
NEARLIER
NEARLIEST
NEARLY
NEARMOST
NEARNESS
NEARSIGHT
NEARSIGHTED
NEARSIGHTEDLY
NEARSIGHTEDNESS
NEARTHROSIS
NEASCUS
NEAT
NEATEN
NEATER
NEATEST
NEATH
NEATHERD
NEATHERDESS
NEATHMOST
NEATIFY
NEATLY
NEATNESS
NEAVIL
NEB
NEBACK
NEBALIOID
NEBBED
NEBBUCK
NEBBUK
NEBBY
NEBENKERN
NEBRIS
NEBRODI
NEBUK
NEBULA
NEBULAE
NEBULAR
NEBULARIZATION
NEBULARIZE
NEBULAS
NEBULATED
NEBULATION
NEBULE
NEBULESCENT
NEBULIFEROUS
NEBULITE
NEBULIUM
NEBULIZATION
NEBULIZE
NEBULIZED
NEBULIZER
NEBULIZING
NEBULON
NEBULOSE
NEBULOSITY
NEBULOUS
NEBULOUSLY
NEBULOUSNESS
NECESSAR
NECESSARIES
NECESSARILY
NECESSARY
NECESSE
NECESSISM
NECESSIST
NECESSITARIAN
NECESSITATE
NECESSITATED
NECESSITATING
NECESSITATIVE
NECESSITIES
NECESSITOUS
NECESSITUDE
NECESSITY
NECK
NECKAR
NECKATEE
NECKBAND
NECKCLOTH
NECKED
NECKENGER
NECKER
NECKERCHER
NECKERCHIEF
NECKGUARD
NECKING
NECKINGER
NECKLACE
NECKLACED
NECKLACEWEED
NECKLET
NECKLINE
NECKMOLD
NECKMOULD
NECKPIECE
NECKTIE

NECKWEAR
NECKWEED
NECRAEMIA
NECRECTOMY
NECREMIA
NECROBIOSIS
NECROBIOTIC
NECROGENIC
NECROGENOUS
NECROLATRY
NECROLOGICAL
NECROLOGIST
NECROLOGUE
NECROLOGY
NECROMANCER
NECROMANCING
NECROMANCY
NECROMANIA
NECROMANTIC
NECRONITE
NECROPATHY
NECROPHAGOUS
NECROPHIL
NECROPHILE
NECROPHILIA
NECROPHILIC
NECROPHILOUS
NECROPHOBIA
NECROPHOBIC
NECROPOLEIS
NECROPOLIS
NECROPOLISES
NECROPOLITAN
NECROPSIES
NECROPSY
NECROSCOPIC
NECROSCOPY
NECROSE
NECROSED
NECROSES
NECROSING
NECROSIS
NECROTIC
NECROTIZE
NECROTOMIC
NECROTOMIES
NECROTOMIST
NECROTOMY
NECROTYPE
NECROTYPIC
NECTAR
NECTAREAL
NECTAREAN
NECTARED
NECTAREOUS
NECTAREOUSLY
NECTARIAL
NECTARIAN
NECTARIED
NECTARIES
NECTARIFEROUS
NECTARIN
NECTARINE
NECTARIOUS
NECTARIUM
NECTARIZE
NECTAROUS
NECTARY
NECTIFEROUS
NECTOCALYCES
NECTOCALYCINE
NECTOCALYX
NECTON
NECTOPHORE
NECTOPOD
NECTRON
NEDDER
NEDDIES
NEDDY
NEE
NEED
NEEDER
NEEDFIRE
NEEDFUL
NEEDFULLY
NEEDFULNESS
NEEDGATES
NEEDIER
NEEDIEST
NEEDINESS
NEEDING
NEEDLE
NEEDLEBILL
NEEDLEBOOK
NEEDLEBUSH
NEEDLECASE
NEEDLED
NEEDLEFISH
NEEDLEFISHES
NEEDLEFUL
NEEDLELIKE
NEEDLEMAKER
NEEDLEMAKING
NEEDLEMAN
NEEDLEMEN
NEEDLEMONGER
NEEDLEPOINT
NEEDLEPROOF
NEEDLER
NEEDLES
NEEDLESS
NEEDLESSLY
NEEDLESSNESS
NEEDLESTONE
NEEDLEWOMAN
NEEDLEWOOD
NEEDLEWORK
NEEDLEWORKER
NEEDLING
NEEDLY
NEEDMENTS
NEEDS
NEEDSOME
NEEDY
NEELE
NEEM
NEEMBA
NEEN
NEENCEPHALIC
NEENCEPHALON
NEEP
NEER
NEESE
NEEZE
NEF
NEFANDOUS
NEFARIOUS
NEFARIOUSLY
NEFAS
NEFAST
NEFFY
NEFTE
NEFTGIL
NEGARA
NEGATE
NEGATED
NEGATING
NEGATION
NEGATIONAL
NEGATIONIST
NEGATIVE
NEGATIVED
NEGATIVELY
NEGATIVENESS
NEGATIVER
NEGATIVING
NEGATIVISM
NEGATIVIST
NEGATIVISTIC
NEGATIVITY
NEGATOR
NEGATORY
NEGER
NEGINOTH
NEGLECT
NEGLECTABLE
NEGLECTED
NEGLECTER
NEGLECTFUL
NEGLECTFULLY
NEGLECTFULNESS
NEGLECTING
NEGLECTION
NEGLECTIVE
NEGLECTOR
NEGLIGEE
NEGLIGENCE
NEGLIGENCY
NEGLIGENT
NEGLIGENTLY
NEGLIGIBILITY
NEGLIGIBLE
NEGLIGIBLY
NEGOCE
NEGOTIABLE
NEGOTIANT
NEGOTIATE
NEGOTIATED
NEGOTIATING
NEGOTIATION
NEGOTIATOR
NEGOTIATORY
NEGOTIATRESS
NEGOTIATRIX
NEGRILLO
NEGRINE
NEGRITA
NEGRITUDE
NEGRO
NEGROHEAD
NEGROS
NEGUS
NEHILOTH
NEHU
NEI
NEIF
NEIFE
NEIGH
NEIGHBOR
NEIGHBORED
NEIGHBORER
NEIGHBORESS
NEIGHBORHOOD
NEIGHBORHOODS
NEIGHBORING
NEIGHBORLY
NEIGHBORS
NEIGHBOUR
NEIGHBOURED
NEIGHBOURER
NEIGHBOURESS
NEIGHBOURHOOD
NEIGHBOURING
NEIGHBOURLY
NEIGHED
NEIGHER
NEIGHING
NEILAH
NEIPER
NEIST
NEITHER
NEKTON
NELLY
NELMA
NELSONITE
NELUMBIAN
NELUMBO
NEMA
NEMALINE
NEMALITE
NEMATHECE
NEMATHECIAL
NEMATHECIUM
NEMATOBLAST
NEMATOCERAN
NEMATOCIDE
NEMATOCYST
NEMATOCYSTIC
NEMATODE
NEMATODIASIS
NEMATOGEN
NEMATOGENE
NEMATOGENIC
NEMATOGONE
NEMATOIDEAN
NEMATOLOGIST
NEMATOLOGY
NEMATOPHYTON
NEMATOZOOID
NEMBUTSU
NEMEA
NEMERTEAN
NEMERTIAN
NEMERTINE
NEMERTINEAN
NEMERTOID
NEMESIC
NEMESIS
NEMME
NEMN
NEMOPHILIST
NEMOPHILOUS
NEMOPHILY
NEMORAL
NEMORICOLE
NEMORICOLINE
NEMORICOLOUS
NEMPNE
NENE
NENTA
NENUPHAR
NEO
NEOBLASTIC
NEOCEROTIC
NEOCLASSIC
NEOCLASSICISM
NEOCOSMIC
NEOCRACY
NEOCRITICISM
NEOCYANINE
NEOCYTE
NEOCYTOSIS
NEODAMODE
NEODIDYMIUM
NEODYMIUM
NEOFETAL
NEOFETUS
NEOFORMATION
NEOFORMATIVE
NEOGAMOUS
NEOGAMY
NEOGENESIS
NEOGENETIC
NEOGNATHIC
NEOGNATHOUS
NEOGRAPHIC
NEOIMPRESSIONISM
NEOLATER
NEOLATRY
NEOLITH
NEOLITHIC
NEOLOGIAN
NEOLOGIC
NEOLOGICAL
NEOLOGICALLY
NEOLOGISM
NEOLOGIST
NEOLOGISTIC
NEOLOGISTICAL
NEOLOGIZE
NEOLOGIZED
NEOLOGIZING
NEOLOGY
NEOMENIA
NEOMENIAN
NEOMIRACLE
NEOMODAL
NEOMORPH
NEOMORPHIC
NEOMORPHISM
NEOMYCIN
NEON
NEONATAL
NEONATUS
NEONOMIAN
NEONOMIANISM
NEONYCHIUM
NEOORTHODOXY
NEOPAGAN
NEOPAGANISM
NEOPAGANIZE
NEOPALLIAL
NEOPALLIUM
NEOPHILISM
NEOPHOBIA
NEOPHOBIC
NEOPHRASTIC
NEOPHYTE
NEOPHYTIC
NEOPHYTISH
NEOPHYTISM
NEOPINE
NEOPLASIA
NEOPLASM
NEOPLASMS
NEOPLASTIC
NEOPLASTIES
NEOPLASTY
NEOPRENE
NEORAMA
NEOSSIN
NEOSSOLOGY
NEOSSOPTILE
NEOSTRIATUM
NEOSTYLE
NEOTEINIA
NEOTENIA
NEOTENY
NEOTERIC
NEOTERICAL
NEOTERICALLY
NEOTERISM
NEOTERIST
NEOTERISTIC
NEOTERIZE
NEOTHALAMUS
NEOTYPE
NEOVITALISM
NEOVOLCANIC
NEOYTTERBIUM
NEP
NEPAL
NEPE
NEPENTHE
NEPENTHEAN

NEPENTHES
NEPER
NEPHALISM
NEPHALIST
NEPHELINE
NEPHELINIC
NEPHELINITE
NEPHELINITIC
NEPHELITE
NEPHELOGNOSY
NEPHELOID
NEPHELOMETER
NEPHELOSCOPE
NEPHESH
NEPHEW
NEPHIONIC
NEPHOGRAM
NEPHOGRAPH
NEPHOLOGICAL
NEPHOLOGIST
NEPHOLOGY
NEPHOSCOPE
NEPHRALGIA
NEPHRALGIC
NEPHRATONIA
NEPHRAUXE
NEPHRECTASIA
NEPHRECTASIS
NEPHRECTOMIES
NEPHRECTOMY
NEPHRELCOSIS
NEPHREMIA
NEPHRIA
NEPHRIC
NEPHRIDIA
NEPHRIDIAL
NEPHRIDIUM
NEPHRISM
NEPHRITE
NEPHRITIC
NEPHRITICAL
NEPHRITIS
NEPHROCELE
NEPHROCOELE
NEPHROCOLIC
NEPHROCYTE
NEPHRODINIC
NEPHROGENIC
NEPHROGENOUS
NEPHROID
NEPHROLITH
NEPHROLITHIC
NEPHROLOGY
NEPHROLYSIN
NEPHROLYSIS
NEPHROLYTIC
NEPHROMERE
NEPHRON
NEPHRONCUS
NEPHROPATHY
NEPHROPEXY
NEPHROPORE
NEPHROPTOSIA
NEPHROPTOSIS
NEPHROPYOSIS
NEPHROS
NEPHROSIS
NEPHROSTOME
NEPHROTIC
NEPHROTOME
NEPHROTOMY
NEPHROTOXIC
NEPHROTOXIN
NEPHROTYPHUS
NEPID
NEPIONIC
NEPMAN
NEPMEN
NEPOTAL
NEPOTE
NEPOTIC
NEPOTIOUS
NEPOTISM
NEPOTIST
NEPOTISTICAL
NEPOUITE
NEPTUNISM
NEPTUNIUM
NER
NERAL
NERE
NEREITE
NERITE
NERITIC
NERITOID
NERKA
NEROL
NEROLI
NERTEROLOGY
NERVAL
NERVATE
NERVATION
NERVATURE
NERVE
NERVED
NERVELESS
NERVELESSLY
NERVELESSNESS
NERVELET
NERVER
NERVEROOT
NERVES
NERVI
NERVID
NERVIDUCT
NERVIER
NERVIEST
NERVIMOTION
NERVIMOTOR
NERVINE
NERVING
NERVISH
NERVISM
NERVOSE
NERVOSISM
NERVOSITY
NERVOUS
NERVOUSLY
NERVOUSNESS
NERVULAR
NERVULE
NERVULET
NERVULOSE
NERVURATION
NERVURE
NERVUS
NERVY
NESCIENCE
NESCIENT
NESE
NESH
NESIOTE
NESLAVE
NESLE
NESLIA
NESQUEHONITE
NESS
NESSBERRY
NESSLERIZE
NESSLERIZED
NEST
NESTABLE
NESTAGE
NESTED
NESTER
NESTIATRIA
NESTING
NESTITHERAPY
NESTLE
NESTLED
NESTLER
NESTLING
NESTORINE
NESTY
NET
NETBALL
NETBRAIDER
NETBUSH
NETCHA
NETER
NETHE
NETHEIST
NETHER
NETHERMORE
NETHERMOST
NETHERSTOCK
NETHERSTONE
NETHERWARD
NETHERWORLD
NETI
NETLEAF
NETLIKE
NETMAKER
NETMAKING
NETMAN
NETMONGER
NETOP
NETS
NETSMAN
NETSUKE
NETTABLE
NETTED
NETTER
NETTING
NETTLE
NETTLEBIRD
NETTLED
NETTLEFIRE
NETTLEFOOT
NETTLEMONGER
NETTLER
NETTLESOME
NETTLEWORT
NETTLING
NETTLY
NETTY
NETWORK
NEU
NEUCK
NEUGROSCHEN
NEUM
NEUMATIC
NEUMATIZE
NEUME
NEUMIC
NEURAD
NEURAL
NEURALGIA
NEURALGIAC
NEURALGIC
NEURALGIFORM
NEURALGY
NEURALIST
NEURASTHENIA
NEURASTHENIC
NEURASTHENICAL
NEURATAXIA
NEURATAXY
NEURATION
NEURATROPHIA
NEURATROPHIC
NEURATROPHY
NEURAXIS
NEURAXON
NEURAXONE
NEURECTASIA
NEURECTASIS
NEURECTASY
NEURECTOME
NEURECTOMIC
NEURECTOMY
NEURECTOPIA
NEURECTOPY
NEURENTERIC
NEURERGIC
NEURHYPNOTIST
NEURIC
NEURILEMMA
NEURILEMMAL
NEURILITY
NEURIN
NEURINE
NEURINOMA
NEURINOMAS
NEURINOMATA
NEURISM
NEURITE
NEURITIC
NEURITIDES
NEURITIS
NEUROBLAST
NEUROCANAL
NEUROCARDIAC
NEUROCENTRAL
NEUROCENTRUM
NEUROCHITIN
NEUROCHORD
NEUROCITY
NEUROCLONIC
NEUROCOELE
NEUROCYTE
NEUROCYTOMA
NEURODYNIA
NEUROFIBRIL
NEUROFIBROMA
NEUROFIL
NEUROGASTRIC
NEUROGENESIS
NEUROGENETIC
NEUROGENIC
NEUROGENOUS
NEUROGLIA
NEUROGLIAC
NEUROGLIAL
NEUROGLIAR
NEUROGLIOMA
NEUROGLIOSIS
NEUROGRAM
NEUROGRAPHY
NEUROID
NEUROKERATIN
NEUROKYME
NEUROLOGICAL
NEUROLOGIST
NEUROLOGIZE
NEUROLOGY
NEUROLYMPH
NEUROLYSIS
NEUROMA
NEUROMALACIA
NEUROMALAKIA
NEUROMATOSIS
NEUROMATOUS
NEUROMERE
NEUROMERISM
NEUROMEROUS
NEUROMOTOR
NEURON
NEURONIC
NEURONISM
NEURONYM
NEURONYMY
NEUROPATH
NEUROPATHIC
NEUROPATHIST
NEUROPATHY
NEUROPHILE
NEUROPHILIC
NEUROPIL
NEUROPILE
NEUROPILEM
NEUROPLASM
NEUROPLASMIC
NEUROPLASTY
NEUROPLEXUS
NEUROPODIUM
NEUROPODOUS
NEUROPORE
NEUROPSYCHIC
NEUROPTERIST
NEUROPTEROID
NEUROPTERON
NEUROSAL
NEUROSES
NEUROSIS
NEUROSKELETAL
NEUROSOME
NEUROSPASM
NEUROSPAST
NEUROSTHENIA
NEUROSURGEON
NEUROSURGERY
NEUROSUTURE
NEUROSYNAPSE
NEUROTENSION
NEUROTHERAPY
NEUROTIC
NEUROTICALLY
NEUROTICISM
NEUROTOME
NEUROTOMICAL
NEUROTOMIST
NEUROTOMIZE
NEUROTOMY
NEUROTONIC
NEUROTOXIA
NEUROTOXIC
NEUROTOXIN
NEUROTRIPSY
NEUROTROPHIC
NEUROTROPHY
NEUROTROPIC
NEUROTROPISM
NEUROTROPY
NEUROVACCINE
NEURULA
NEURYPNOLOGY
NEUSTON
NEUTER
NEUTERDOM
NEUTERED
NEUTERING
NEUTERLY
NEUTERNESS
NEUTRAL
NEUTRALISE
NEUTRALISM
NEUTRALIST
NEUTRALITIES
NEUTRALITY
NEUTRALIZE
NEUTRALIZED
NEUTRALIZER
NEUTRALIZING
NEUTRALLY

NEUTRALNESS
NEUTRIA
NEUTRINO
NEUTRON
NEUTROPHIL
NEUTROPHILE
NEUTROPHILIA
NEVADITE
NEVAT
NEVE
NEVEL
NEVELL
NEVEN
NEVER
NEVERMASS
NEVERMORE
NEVERTHELESS
NEVES
NEVOID
NEVOY
NEVUS
NEVYANSKITE
NEW
NEWBERYITE
NEWBORN
NEWCAL
NEWCOME
NEWCOMER
NEWEL
NEWELTY
NEWER
NEWEST
NEWFANGLE
NEWFANGLED
NEWFISH
NEWING
NEWISH
NEWLANDITE
NEWLIGHT
NEWLINGS
NEWLINS
NEWLY
NEWLYWED
NEWMARKET
NEWMOWN
NEWNESS
NEWS
NEWSAGENT
NEWSBILL
NEWSBOARD
NEWSBOAT
NEWSBOY
NEWSCAST
NEWSCASTER
NEWSDEALER
NEWSIER
NEWSIEST
NEWSINESS
NEWSLETTER
NEWSMAGAZINE
NEWSMAN
NEWSMEN
NEWSMONGER
NEWSMONGERING
NEWSMONGERY
NEWSPAPER
NEWSPAPERMAN
NEWSPAPERMEN
NEWSPAPERWOMAN
NEWSPAPERWOMEN
NEWSPAPERY
NEWSPRINT
NEWSREADER
NEWSREEL
NEWSROOM
NEWSSHEET
NEWSSTAND
NEWSTELLER
NEWSWORTHY
NEWSY
NEWT
NEWTAKE
NEWTON
NEWTONITE
NEXAL
NEXT
NEXTLY
NEXTNESS
NEXUM
NEXUS
NEXUSES
NEY
NEYANDA
NGAI
NGAIO
NGAN
NGAPI
NGU
NI
NIACIN
NIATA
NIB
NIBBED
NIBBER
NIBBLE
NIBBLED
NIBBLER
NIBBLING
NIBBY
NIBLIC
NIBLICK
NIBONG
NIBS
NIBSOME
NIBUNG
NICCOLIC
NICCOLITE
NICCOLO
NICCOLOUS
NICE
NICELING
NICELY
NICENESS
NICER
NICEST
NICETIES
NICETISH
NICETY
NICHE
NICHED
NICHELINO
NICHEVO
NICHIL
NICHING
NICHT
NICK
NICKED
NICKEL
NICKELBLOOM
NICKELIC
NICKELIFEROUS
NICKELINE
NICKELIZE
NICKELODEON
NICKELOUS
NICKELTYPE
NICKER
NICKERPECKER
NICKERY
NICKEY
NICKING
NICKLE
NICKNACK
NICKNAME
NICKNAMED
NICKNAMEE
NICKNAMER
NICKNAMING
NICKPOT
NICKSTICK
NICKUM
NICKY
NICOLAYITE
NICOLO
NICOTIA
NICOTIAN
NICOTIANIN
NICOTIN
NICOTINA
NICOTINE
NICOTINEAN
NICOTINED
NICOTINIAN
NICOTINIC
NICOTINISM
NICOTINIZE
NICOTISM
NICOTIZE
NICTATE
NICTATED
NICTATING
NICTATION
NICTITANT
NICTITATE
NICTITATED
NICTITATING
NICTITATION
NID
NIDAL
NIDAMENTAL
NIDANA
NIDARY
NIDATION
NIDATORY
NIDDER
NIDDERING
NIDDICK
NIDDICOCK
NIDDLE
NIDE
NIDERING
NIDGE
NIDGET
NIDGETY
NIDI
NIDICOLOUS
NIDIFICANT
NIDIFICATE
NIDIFICATED
NIDIFICATING
NIDIFICATION
NIDIFICATIONAL
NIDIFIED
NIDIFUGOUS
NIDIFY
NIDIFYING
NIDING
NIDIOT
NIDOLOGIST
NIDOLOGY
NIDOR
NIDOROSE
NIDOROSITY
NIDOROUS
NIDORULENT
NIDULANT
NIDULATE
NIDULATION
NIDULI
NIDULUS
NIDUS
NIDUSES
NIE
NIECE
NIEF
NIELLATED
NIELLED
NIELLI
NIELLIST
NIELLO
NIELLOED
NIELLOING
NIELLOS
NIEPA
NIESHOUT
NIEVE
NIEVETA
NIEVLING
NIF
NIFE
NIFESIMA
NIFFER
NIFIC
NIFLE
NIFLING
NIFTIER
NIFTIEST
NIFTY
NIG
NIGGARD
NIGGARDLY
NIGGER
NIGGERED
NIGGERFISH
NIGGERFISHES
NIGGERGOOSE
NIGGERHEAD
NIGGERISH
NIGGERISM
NIGGERLING
NIGGERTOE
NIGGERWEED
NIGGERY
NIGGET
NIGGLE
NIGGLED
NIGGLER
NIGGLING
NIGGLINGLY
NIGGLY
NIGGOT
NIGGUN
NIGH
NIGHED
NIGHER
NIGHEST
NIGHING
NIGHLY
NIGHT
NIGHTCAP
NIGHTCAPPED
NIGHTCAPS
NIGHTCLOTHES
NIGHTCLUB
NIGHTDRESS
NIGHTED
NIGHTERY
NIGHTFALL
NIGHTFISH
NIGHTFLIT
NIGHTFOWL
NIGHTGALE
NIGHTGLASS
NIGHTGOWN
NIGHTHAWK
NIGHTIE
NIGHTIES
NIGHTING
NIGHTINGALE
NIGHTINGALIZE
NIGHTISH
NIGHTJAR
NIGHTLONG
NIGHTLY
NIGHTMAN
NIGHTMARE
NIGHTMARISH
NIGHTMARISHLY
NIGHTMARY
NIGHTMEN
NIGHTRIDER
NIGHTS
NIGHTSHADE
NIGHTSHIRT
NIGHTSPOT
NIGHTSTICK
NIGHTTIDE
NIGHTTIME
NIGHTWAKE
NIGHTWALKER
NIGHTWALKING
NIGHTWARD
NIGHTWEAR
NIGHTWORK
NIGHTWORKER
NIGHTY
NIGNAY
NIGNYE
NIGON
NIGORI
NIGRE
NIGRESCENCE
NIGRESCENT
NIGRESCITE
NIGRICANT
NIGRIFICATION
NIGRIFIED
NIGRIFY
NIGRIFYING
NIGRINE
NIGRITIES
NIGRITUDE
NIGROSIN
NIGROSINE
NIGROUS
NIGS
NIGUA
NIGUN
NIHIL
NIHILIANISM
NIHILIFICATION
NIHILIFY
NIHILISM
NIHILIST
NIHILISTIC
NIHILITIC
NIHILITIES
NIHILITY
NIHILOBSTAT
NIHILUM
NIKAU
NIKENO
NIKLESITE
NIL
NILGAI
NILGAIS
NILGAU
NILL
NILPOTENT
NIM
NIMB
NIMBATED
NIMBI
NIMBIFEROUS
NIMBIFICATION

NIMBLE
NIMBLEBRAINED
NIMBLENESS
NIMBLER
NIMBLEST
NIMBLY
NIMBOSE
NIMBOSTRATUS
NIMBUS
NIMBUSED
NIMBUSES
NIMIETY
NIMINY
NIMIOUS
NIMMED
NIMMER
NIMMING
NIMSHI
NINCOM
NINCOMPOOP
NINCOMPOOPERY
NINCOMPOOPHOOD
NINCOMPOOPISH
NINCUM
NINE
NINEBARK
NINEFOLD
NINEHOLES
NINEPEGS
NINEPENCE
NINEPENCES
NINEPENNIES
NINEPENNY
NINEPIN
NINEPINS
NINESCORE
NINETED
NINETEEN
NINETEENTH
NINETEENTHLY
NINETIETH
NINETY
NINGLE
NINNIES
NINNY
NINNYHAMMER
NINNYISH
NINNYISM
NINNYSHIP
NINNYWATCH
NINO
NINOS
NINTH
NINTHLY
NINTU
NINUT
NIOBATE
NIOBIC
NIOBITE
NIOBIUM
NIOBOUS
NIOG
NIOTA
NIP
NIPA
NIPCHEESE
NIPE
NIPER
NIPMUCK
NIPPED
NIPPER
NIPPERKIN
NIPPERS
NIPPIER
NIPPIEST
NIPPING
NIPPINGLY
NIPPITATE
NIPPITATO
NIPPITATUM
NIPPITATY
NIPPLE
NIPPLED
NIPPLEWORT
NIPPLING
NIPPONIUM
NIPPY
NIPS
NIPTER
NIRIS
NIRLES
NIRLS
NIRMANAKAYA
NIRVANA
NIRVANIC
NIS
NISBERRY
NISHIKI
NISI
NISNAS
NISPERO
NISSE
NISUS
NIT
NITCH
NITCHEVO
NITCHIE
NITE
NITENCY
NITENT
NITER
NITERED
NITERING
NITHER
NITHING
NITID
NITIDOUS
NITO
NITON
NITOR
NITOS
NITRAMIN
NITRAMINE
NITRANILIC
NITRATE
NITRATED
NITRATINE
NITRATING
NITRATION
NITRATOR
NITRE
NITRED
NITRIARIES
NITRIARY
NITRIC
NITRID
NITRIDATION
NITRIDE
NITRIDING
NITRIDIZATION
NITRIDIZE
NITRIFACTION
NITRIFEROUS
NITRIFIABLE
NITRIFICATION
NITRIFIED
NITRIFIER
NITRIFY
NITRIFYING
NITRIL
NITRILE
NITRITE
NITRO
NITROAMINE
NITROANILIN
NITROANILINE
NITROBACTERIA
NITROBARITE
NITROBENZENE
NITROCALCITE
NITROCOTTON
NITROFORM
NITROGELATIN
NITROGELATINE
NITROGEN
NITROGENATE
NITROGENATION
NITROGENIZATION
NITROGENIZE
NITROGENIZED
NITROGENIZING
NITROGENOUS
NITROGLYCERIN
NITROGLYCERINE
NITROLAMINE
NITROLIC
NITROMAGNESITE
NITROMETER
NITROMURIATE
NITROPARAFFIN
NITROPHENOL
NITROPHILOUS
NITROPHYTE
NITROPHYTIC
NITROPRUSSIC
NITROSAMIN
NITROSAMINE
NITROSATE
NITROSIFY
NITROSITE
NITROSTARCH
NITROSULPHATE
NITROSYL
NITROTOLUENE
NITROTOLUOL
NITROUS
NITROXYL
NITRYL
NITTE
NITTER
NITTY
NITWIT
NIVAL
NIVATION
NIVEAU
NIVELLATE
NIVELLATION
NIVELLATOR
NIVELLIZATION
NIVENITE
NIVEOUS
NIVER
NIVERNAISE
NIVICOLOUS
NIVOSITY
NIX
NIXE
NIXEN
NIXES
NIXIE
NIXTAMAL
NIXY
NIYANDA
NIYO
NIYOGA
NIZ
NIZAMAT
NIZAMATE
NIZAMUT
NIZEY
NIZY
NJAVE
NO
NOA
NOANCE
NOB
NOBBER
NOBBIER
NOBBIEST
NOBBLE
NOBBLED
NOBBLER
NOBBLING
NOBBUT
NOBBY
NOBELIUM
NOBILIARY
NOBILITATE
NOBILITIES
NOBILITY
NOBLE
NOBLED
NOBLEHEARTED
NOBLEMAN
NOBLEMANLY
NOBLEMEN
NOBLENESS
NOBLER
NOBLESSE
NOBLEST
NOBLEWOMAN
NOBLEWOMEN
NOBLEY
NOBLIFY
NOBLING
NOBLY
NOBOB
NOBODIES
NOBODY
NOBODYNESS
NOBS
NOBUT
NOCAKE
NOCENCE
NOCENT
NOCERITE
NOCHT
NOCICEPTIVE
NOCICEPTOR
NOCIVE
NOCK
NOCKED
NOCKERL
NOCKET
NOCKING
NOCKTAT
NOCTAMBULANT
NOCTAMBULE
NOCTIDIAL
NOCTIDIURNAL
NOCTILUCA
NOCTILUCAN
NOCTILUCENCE
NOCTILUCENT
NOCTILUCIN
NOCTILUCINE
NOCTILUCOUS
NOCTIMANIA
NOCTIVAGANT
NOCTIVAGATION
NOCTIVAGOUS
NOCTOGRAPH
NOCTOVISION
NOCTUID
NOCTUIDEOUS
NOCTUIDOUS
NOCTUIFORM
NOCTULE
NOCTUOID
NOCTURIA
NOCTURN
NOCTURNAL
NOCTURNALLY
NOCTURNE
NOCUMENT
NOCUOUS
NOCUOUSLY
NOCUOUSNESS
NOD
NODAL
NODALITY
NODALLY
NODATED
NODDED
NODDER
NODDIES
NODDING
NODDLE
NODDLEBONE
NODDLED
NODDLING
NODDY
NODE
NODED
NODIAK
NODICAL
NODICORN
NODIFEROUS
NODIFLOROUS
NODIFORM
NODOSARIAN
NODOSARIFORM
NODOSARINE
NODOSAUR
NODOSE
NODOSITIES
NODOSITY
NODOUS
NODULAR
NODULATE
NODULATED
NODULATION
NODULE
NODULED
NODULES
NODULIZE
NODULIZED
NODULIZING
NODULOSE
NODUS
NOED
NOEGENESIS
NOEGENETIC
NOEL
NOEMATICAL
NOESIS
NOETIC
NOETICS
NOEUD
NOG
NOGADA
NOGAI
NOGAKU
NOGAL
NOGG
NOGGED
NOGGEN
NOGGIN
NOGGING
NOGHEAD
NOGHEADED
NOH
NOHOW
NOI
NOIBWOOD

NOIL
NOILAGE
NOILER
NOILY
NOING
NOINT
NOIO
NOIR
NOISANCE
NOISE
NOISED
NOISEFUL
NOISEFULLY
NOISELESS
NOISELESSLY
NOISELESSNESS
NOISEMAKER
NOISEMAKING
NOISES
NOISETTE
NOISIER
NOISIEST
NOISILY
NOISINESS
NOISING
NOISOME
NOISOMELY
NOISOMENESS
NOISY
NOIT
NOIX
NOKI
NOKIN
NOKTA
NOLA
NOLD
NOLITION
NOLL
NOLLEITY
NOLO
NOM
NOMA
NOMAD
NOMADE
NOMADIAN
NOMADIC
NOMADICAL
NOMADICALLY
NOMADISM
NOMAN
NOMANCY
NOMARCH
NOMARCHIES
NOMARCHY
NOMARTHRAL
NOMBLES
NOMBRIL
NOME
NOMEN
NOMENCLATE
NOMENCLATIVE
NOMENCLATOR
NOMENCLATORIAL
NOMENCLATORY
NOMENCLATURAL
NOMENCLATURE
NOMENCLATURIST
NOMEUS
NOMIAL
NOMIC
NOMINA
NOMINABLE
NOMINAL
NOMINALISM
NOMINALIST
NOMINALISTIC
NOMINALITY
NOMINALLY
NOMINATE
NOMINATED
NOMINATELY
NOMINATING
NOMINATION
NOMINATIVE
NOMINATOR
NOMINATRIX
NOMINATURE
NOMINEE
NOMINEEISM
NOMINY
NOMISM
NOMISMA
NOMISMATA
NOMISTIC
NOMOCANON
NOMOCRACY
NOMOGENIST
NOMOGENOUS
NOMOGENY
NOMOGRAM
NOMOGRAPH
NOMOGRAPHER
NOMOGRAPHIC
NOMOGRAPHICAL
NOMOGRAPHIES
NOMOGRAPHY
NOMOLOGICAL
NOMOLOGIST
NOMOLOGY
NOMOPELMOUS
NOMOPHYLAX
NOMOPHYLLOUS
NOMOS
NOMOTHETE
NOMOTHETES
NOMOTHETIC
NOMOTHETICAL
NON
NONA
NONABILITY
NONABJURER
NONACCESS
NONACOSANE
NONACT
NONADDRESS
NONADDRESSER
NONADECANE
NONADJUSTIVE
NONAGE
NONAGENARIAN
NONAGENARIES
NONAGENARY
NONAGESIMAL
NONAGON
NONAGREEMENT
NONAHYDRATE
NONAMINO
NONAN
NONANE
NONAPPEARANCE
NONARCHING
NONARCKING
NONARY
NONASPIRATE
NONBEING
NONBELIEVER
NONBEVERAGE
NONCALLABLE
NONCASTE
NONCE
NONCERTAIN
NONCHALANCE
NONCHALANT
NONCHALANTLY
NONCHALANTNESS
NONCITIZEN
NONCLAIM
NONCLERICAL
NONCOMBATANT
NONCOMBUSTIBLE
NONCOME
NONCOMMISSIONED
NONCOMMITALLY
NONCOMMITTAL
NONCOMMITTALNESS
NONCOMMUNION
NONCOMMUTATIVE
NONCOMPEARANCE
NONCOMPLIANCE
NONCOMPOS
NONCOMPOSES
NONCOMPOUNDER
NONCON
NONCONDENSING
NONCONDUCTING
NONCONDUCTOR
NONCONFORM
NONCONFORMABLE
NONCONFORMABLY
NONCONFORMER
NONCONFORMING
NONCONFORMISM
NONCONFORMIST
NONCONFORMITY
NONCONTENT
NONCONTINUOUS
NONCONTRADICTION
NONCOOPERATION
NONCURANTIST
NONDA
NONDECIDUATE
NONDENUMERABLE
NONDEPENDENT
NONDESCRIPT
NONDETINET
NONDISCLOSURE
NONDISJUNCT
NONDISJUNCTION
NONDISTINCTIVE
NONDO
NONDUALISM
NONDUMPING
NONE
NONEFFECTIVE
NONEGO
NONELASTIC
NONENE
NONENT
NONENTITIES
NONENTITIVE
NONENTITIZE
NONENTITY
NONENTITYISM
NONENTRES
NONENTRESSE
NONENTRY
NONES
NONESSENTIAL
NONESUCH
NONET
NONETHELESS
NONETTO
NONEXISTENCE
NONEXISTENT
NONFEASANCE
NONFEASOR
NONFERROUS
NONFICTION
NONFICTIONALLY
NONFLAMMABLE
NONGYPSY
NONHARMONIC
NONHEARER
NONIC
NONILLION
NONINCREASING
NONINDUCTIVE
NONINDUCTIVELY
NONINDUCTIVITY
NONINJURY
NONINTRUSION
NONION
NONISOBARIC
NONISSUABLE
NONIUS
NONJOINDER
NONJURANCY
NONJURANT
NONJURANTISM
NONJURING
NONJUROR
NONLEGAL
NONLEGATO
NONLICET
NONMAGNETIC
NONMETAL
NONMETALLIC
NONMODAL
NONMORAL
NONMORALITY
NONNAT
NONNATURAL
NONNATURALISM
NONNATURALITY
NONNATURALS
NONNY
NONOBJECTIVE
NONOBJECTIVITY
NONOIC
NONOPENING
NONPAREIL
NONPAROUS
NONPARTICIPATING
NONPARTISAN
NONPARTIZAN
NONPASSERINE
NONPAYMENT
NONPERMANENT
NONPHENOMENAL
NONPLACET
NONPLANE
NONPLUS
NONPLUSATION
NONPLUSED
NONPLUSING
NONPLUSSATION
NONPLUSSED
NONPLUSSING
NONPOISONOUS
NONPOLAR
NONPOSITIVE
NONPRODUCTIVE
NONPRODUCTIVELY
NONPRODUCTIVENESS
NONPROFESSIONAL
NONPROFIT
NONPROTEIN
NONQUOTA
NONREACTIVE
NONREDUCING
NONREGENT
NONREGULATION
NONRESIDENCE
NONRESIDENCY
NONRESIDENT
NONRESIDENTER
NONRESIDENTIARY
NONRESIDENTOR
NONRESISTANCE
NONRESISTANT
NONRESTRAINT
NONRESTRICTIVE
NONRIGID
NONROTATING
NONSCRIPTURAL
NONSECTARIAN
NONSENSE
NONSENSICAL
NONSENSICALITY
NONSENSICALLY
NONSENSICALNESS
NONSENSIFICATION
NONSENSIFY
NONSENTENCE
NONSEPARATIST
NONSIPHONAGE
NONSKED
NONSKID
NONSKIDDING
NONSPORED
NONSTANDARD
NONSTELLAR
NONSTOP
NONSTRIATED
NONSUBSCRIBER
NONSUBSTANTIALISM
NONSUBSTANTIALIST
NONSUCH
NONSUGAR
NONSUIT
NONSUPPORT
NONSWEARER
NONSWEARING
NONSYLLABIC
NONSYLLABICNESS
NONSYMBIOTIC
NONSYMBIOTICALLY
NONSYNC
NONTENURE
NONTERM
NONTERMINATING
NONTHEMATIC
NONTRONITE
NONUMBILICATE
NONUNIFORM
NONUNIFORMIST
NONUNIFORMLY
NONUNION
NONUNIONISM
NONUNIONIST
NONUPLE
NONUPLET
NONUPLICATE
NONUSER
NONVALENT
NONVIBRATORY
NONVIOLENCE
NONVOLUNTARY
NONVORTICAL
NONVORTICALLY
NONWHITE
NONYA
NONYL
NONYLENE
NONYLIC
NOO
NOODLE
NOOK
NOOKED
NOOKERY
NOOKIER
NOOKIEST
NOOKING
NOOKY
NOOLOGICAL

NOOLOGIST
NOOLOGY
NOOMETRY
NOON
NOONDAY
NOONED
NOONFLOWER
NOONING
NOONLIGHT
NOONLIT
NOONMEAT
NOONSTEAD
NOONTIDE
NOONTIME
NOOP
NOOSCOPIC
NOOSE
NOOSED
NOOSER
NOOSING
NOOT
NOPAL
NOPALRY
NOPE
NOPINENE
NOR
NORATE
NORATION
NORBERGITE
NORCAMPHANE
NORDCAPER
NORDMARKITE
NORGINE
NORI
NORIA
NORICE
NORIE
NORIMON
NORIT
NORITE
NORITO
NORKYN
NORLAND
NORLANDER
NORLANDISM
NORLEUCINE
NORM
NORMA
NORMAL
NORMALCY
NORMALISM
NORMALIST
NORMALITY
NORMALIZATION
NORMALIZE
NORMALIZED
NORMALIZER
NORMALIZING
NORMALLY
NORMALNESS
NORMATED
NORMATIVE
NORMATIVENESS
NORMOCYTE
NORRY
NORSEL
NORSELED
NORSELING
NORSELLED
NORSELLING
NORSH
NORTELRY
NORTH
NORTHBOUND
NORTHEAST
NORTHEASTER
NORTHEASTERLY
NORTHEASTERN
NORTHEASTWARD
NORTHEASTWARDLY
NORTHEASTWARDS
NORTHEN
NORTHER
NORTHERED
NORTHERING
NORTHERLINESS
NORTHERLY
NORTHERN
NORTHERNER
NORTHERNLY
NORTHEST
NORTHING
NORTHLAND
NORTHLANDER
NORTHLIGHT
NORTHMOST
NORTHNESS
NORTHUPITE
NORTHWARD
NORTHWARDLY
NORTHWARDS
NORTHWEST
NORTHWESTER
NORTHWESTERLY
NORTHWESTERN
NORTHWESTWARD
NORTHWESTWARDLY
NORTHWESTWARDS
NORWARD
NORWARDS
NORWESTER
NOSARIAN
NOSE
NOSEAN
NOSEANITE
NOSEBAG
NOSEBAND
NOSEBLEED
NOSEBONE
NOSEBURN
NOSED
NOSEGAY
NOSEHOLE
NOSELITE
NOSEPIECE
NOSEPINCH
NOSER
NOSESMART
NOSETHIRL
NOSETIOLOGY
NOSEWING
NOSEWISE
NOSEWORT
NOSEY
NOSIER
NOSIEST
NOSILY
NOSINE
NOSINESS
NOSING
NOSISM
NOSITE
NOSOCOMIUM
NOSOGENESIS
NOSOGENETIC
NOSOGENIC
NOSOGENY
NOSOGRAPHER
NOSOGRAPHIC
NOSOGRAPHIES
NOSOGRAPHY
NOSOHAEMIA
NOSOHEMIA
NOSOLOGICAL
NOSOLOGICALLY
NOSOLOGIES
NOSOLOGIST
NOSOLOGY
NOSOMANIA
NOSOMYCOSIS
NOSONOMY
NOSOPHOBIA
NOSOPHYTE
NOSOPOETIC
NOSOPOIETIC
NOSOTAXY
NOSOTROPHY
NOSSEL
NOSTALGIA
NOSTALGIC
NOSTIC
NOSTOC
NOSTOCACEOUS
NOSTOLOGY
NOSTOMANIA
NOSTRIFICATE
NOSTRIFICATION
NOSTRIL
NOSTRILED
NOSTRILITY
NOSTRILLED
NOSTRUM
NOSTRUMS
NOSY
NOT
NOTA
NOTABILIA
NOTABILITIES
NOTABILITY
NOTABLE
NOTABLENESS
NOTABLY
NOTACANTHID
NOTACANTHOID
NOTACANTHOUS
NOTAEAL
NOTAEUM
NOTAL
NOTALGIA
NOTALGIC
NOTALIA
NOTAM
NOTAN
NOTANDUDA
NOTANDUM
NOTANDUMS
NOTAR
NOTARIAL
NOTARIALLY
NOTARIATE
NOTARIES
NOTARIKON
NOTARIZATION
NOTARIZE
NOTARIZED
NOTARIZING
NOTARY
NOTATE
NOTATION
NOTATIONAL
NOTATIVE
NOTATOR
NOTAULIX
NOTCH
NOTCHBOARD
NOTCHED
NOTCHEL
NOTCHER
NOTCHES
NOTCHING
NOTCHWEED
NOTCHWING
NOTCHWORT
NOTCHY
NOTE
NOTEBOOK
NOTECASE
NOTED
NOTEDLY
NOTEDNESS
NOTEHEAD
NOTEHOLDER
NOTELESS
NOTELESSLY
NOTELESSNESS
NOTEMAN
NOTEMIGGE
NOTEMUGGE
NOTER
NOTES
NOTEWORTHILY
NOTEWORTHY
NOTHAL
NOTHARCTID
NOTHER
NOTHING
NOTHINGARIAN
NOTHINGISM
NOTHINGIST
NOTHINGIZE
NOTHINGLESS
NOTHINGLY
NOTHINGNESS
NOTHOSAUR
NOTHOSAURIAN
NOTHOUS
NOTICE
NOTICEABILITY
NOTICEABLE
NOTICEABLY
NOTICED
NOTICER
NOTICING
NOTIDANIAN
NOTIFIABLE
NOTIFICATION
NOTIFIED
NOTIFIER
NOTIFY
NOTIFYING
NOTING
NOTION
NOTIONABLE
NOTIONAL
NOTIONALIST
NOTIONALITY
NOTIONALLY
NOTIONALNESS
NOTIONARY
NOTIONATE
NOTIONED
NOTIONIST
NOTIONS
NOTIST
NOTITIA
NOTITION
NOTOCENTRUM
NOTOCHORD
NOTODONTIAN
NOTODONTID
NOTODONTOID
NOTOIRE
NOTONECTID
NOTOPODIAL
NOTOPODIUM
NOTOPTERID
NOTOPTEROID
NOTORHIZAL
NOTORIETIES
NOTORIETY
NOTORIOUS
NOTORIOUSLY
NOTORIOUSNESS
NOTORNIS
NOTOTRIBE
NOTOUNGULATE
NOTOUR
NOTOURLY
NOTSELF
NOTT
NOTUM
NOTUNGULATE
NOTWITHSTANDING
NOUCH
NOUCHE
NOUE
NOUGAT
NOUGATINE
NOUGHT
NOUGHTILY
NOUGHTINESS
NOUGHTLY
NOUGHTY
NOUILLE
NOUILLES
NOUMEA
NOUMEAITE
NOUMEITE
NOUMENAL
NOUMENALISM
NOUMENALIST
NOUMENALITY
NOUMENALLY
NOUMENISM
NOUMENON
NOUMMOS
NOUN
NOUNAL
NOUNALLY
NOUNIZE
NOUNS
NOUP
NOURISH
NOURISHABLE
NOURISHED
NOURISHER
NOURISHING
NOURISHINGLY
NOURISHMENT
NOURITURE
NOUS
NOUTHER
NOUVEAU
NOUVEAUTE
NOUVELLE
NOUVELLES
NOVA
NOVACULITE
NOVAE
NOVALE
NOVALIA
NOVANTIQUE
NOVAS
NOVATE
NOVATIVE
NOVATOR
NOVATORY
NOVATRIX
NOVCIC
NOVEL
NOVELA
NOVELANT
NOVELCRAFT
NOVELET
NOVELETIST

NOVELETTE
NOVELETTER
NOVELISM
NOVELIST
NOVELISTIC
NOVELISTICALLY
NOVELIZATION
NOVELIZE
NOVELIZED
NOVELIZING
NOVELLA
NOVELLAE
NOVELLAS
NOVELLE
NOVELRY
NOVELTIES
NOVELTY
NOVELWRIGHT
NOVENA
NOVENAE
NOVENARY
NOVENDIAL
NOVENE
NOVENNIAL
NOVERCAL
NOVERINT
NOVICE
NOVICEHOOD
NOVICERY
NOVICIATE
NOVILLADA
NOVILLO
NOVILUNAR
NOVITIAL
NOVITIATE
NOVITIATION
NOVITY
NOVOCAIN
NOVOCAINE
NOVODAMUS
NOVUM
NOW
NOWADAYS
NOWANIGHTS
NOWAY
NOWAYS
NOWDER
NOWED
NOWEL
NOWHAT
NOWHEN
NOWHENCE
NOWHERE
NOWHERES
NOWHIT
NOWHITHER
NOWISE
NOWN
NOWNESS
NOWT
NOWTHE
NOWTHER
NOWTHERD
NOWY
NOXA
NOXAE
NOXAL
NOXIAL
NOXIOUS
NOXIOUSLY
NOXIOUSNESS
NOY
NOYADE
NOYADED
NOYADING
NOYANCE
NOYANT
NOYAU
NOYFUL
NOYOUS
NOZZLE
NOZZLER
NRITTA
NTH
NU
NUADU
NUANCE
NUANCED
NUANCES
NUANCING
NUB
NUBBIN
NUBBLE
NUBBLING
NUBBLY
NUBECULA
NUBECULAE
NUBIA
NUBILATE
NUBILATION
NUBILE
NUBILITY
NUBILOSE
NUBILOUS
NUBK
NUCAL
NUCAMENT
NUCELLAR
NUCELLI
NUCELLUS
NUCHA
NUCHAE
NUCHAL
NUCHALE
NUCHALGIA
NUCHE
NUCICULTURE
NUCIFEROUS
NUCIFORM
NUCIN
NUCIVOROUS
NUCK
NUCLEAL
NUCLEAR
NUCLEARY
NUCLEASE
NUCLEATE
NUCLEATED
NUCLEATING
NUCLEATION
NUCLEATOR
NUCLEI
NUCLEIFORM
NUCLEIN
NUCLEINASE
NUCLEOALBUMIN
NUCLEOFUGAL
NUCLEOHISTONE
NUCLEOID
NUCLEOLAR
NUCLEOLATE
NUCLEOLATED
NUCLEOLE
NUCLEOLI
NUCLEOLINI
NUCLEOLINUS
NUCLEOLOID
NUCLEOLUS
NUCLEOLYSIS
NUCLEON
NUCLEONE
NUCLEONIC
NUCLEONICS
NUCLEONS
NUCLEOPLASM
NUCLEOPLASMIC
NUCLEOPROTEIN
NUCLEOSID
NUCLEOSIDE
NUCLEOTIDE
NUCLEUS
NUCLEUSES
NUCULANE
NUCULANIA
NUCULANIUM
NUCULE
NUCULIFORM
NUCULOID
NUD
NUDATE
NUDDLE
NUDE
NUDELY
NUDENESS
NUDGE
NUDGED
NUDGING
NUDIBRANCH
NUDICAUDATE
NUDICAUL
NUDICAULOUS
NUDIFIER
NUDIFLOROUS
NUDIPED
NUDISM
NUDIST
NUDITARIAN
NUDITY
NUDNICK
NUE
NUGACIOUS
NUGACIOUSNESS
NUGACITIES
NUGACITY
NUGAE
NUGAMENT
NUGATOR
NUGATORILY
NUGATORINESS
NUGATORY
NUGGAR
NUGGET
NUGGETY
NUGIFY
NUGILOGUE
NUIK
NUISANCE
NUISANCER
NUISOME
NUIT
NUKE
NUL
NULL
NULLA
NULLABLE
NULLAH
NULLED
NULLIBICITY
NULLIBIETY
NULLIBILITY
NULLIBIQUITOUS
NULLIBIST
NULLIFICATION
NULLIFICATOR
NULLIFIDIAN
NULLIFIED
NULLIFIER
NULLIFY
NULLIFYING
NULLING
NULLIPARA
NULLIPARAE
NULLIPARITY
NULLIPAROUS
NULLIPENNATE
NULLIPLEX
NULLIPORE
NULLIPOROUS
NULLITIES
NULLITY
NULLIVERSE
NULLO
NUMB
NUMBAT
NUMBED
NUMBEDNESS
NUMBER
NUMBERED
NUMBERER
NUMBERFUL
NUMBERING
NUMBERLESS
NUMBEROUS
NUMBERS
NUMBERSOME
NUMBFISH
NUMBFISHES
NUMBING
NUMBINGLY
NUMBLE
NUMBLES
NUMBLY
NUMBNESS
NUMDA
NUMDAH
NUMEN
NUMERABLE
NUMERABLY
NUMERAL
NUMERALLY
NUMERALS
NUMERANT
NUMERARY
NUMERATE
NUMERATED
NUMERATING
NUMERATION
NUMERATIVE
NUMERATOR
NUMERIC
NUMERICAL
NUMERICALLY
NUMERICALNESS
NUMERIST
NUMERO
NUMEROLOGY
NUMEROS
NUMEROSITY
NUMEROUS
NUMEROUSLY
NUMEROUSNESS
NUMINA
NUMINISM
NUMINOUS
NUMINOUSLY
NUMISMATIC
NUMISMATICAL
NUMISMATICALLY
NUMISMATICS
NUMISMATIST
NUMMARY
NUMMIFORM
NUMMULAR
NUMMULARY
NUMMULATION
NUMMULINE
NUMMULITE
NUMMULITIC
NUMMULOIDAL
NUMMUS
NUMNAH
NUMPS
NUMSKULL
NUMSKULLED
NUMSKULLISM
NUN
NUNATAK
NUNATAKS
NUNBIRD
NUNCE
NUNCHEON
NUNCHION
NUNCIATE
NUNCIATIVE
NUNCIATORY
NUNCIATURE
NUNCIO
NUNCIOS
NUNCLE
NUNCUPATE
NUNCUPATION
NUNCUPATIVE
NUNCUPATIVELY
NUNDINAL
NUNDINATION
NUNDINE
NUNKY
NUNLET
NUNNARI
NUNNATION
NUNNED
NUNNERIES
NUNNERY
NUNNI
NUNNIFY
NUNNING
NUNNISH
NUNNISHNESS
NUNRY
NUNTING
NUNTIUS
NUPSON
NUPTIAL
NUPTIALITY
NUPTIALIZE
NUPTIALLY
NUQUE
NUR
NURAGH
NURAGHE
NURL
NURLY
NURRY
NURSE
NURSED
NURSEGIRL
NURSEHOUND
NURSEMAID
NURSER
NURSERIES
NURSERY
NURSERYMAID
NURSERYMAN
NURSERYMEN
NURSETENDER
NURSING
NURSINGLY
NURSLE
NURSLING
NURSY
NURTURAL
NURTURE
NURTURED
NURTURER
NURTURING

NUSFIAH
NUSS
NUSUB
NUT
NUTANT
NUTARIAN
NUTATE
NUTATED
NUTATING
NUTATION
NUTATIONAL
NUTBREAKER
NUTBROWN
NUTCAKE
NUTCRACK
NUTCRACKER
NUTCRACKERS
NUTCRACKERY
NUTGALL
NUTGRASS
NUTHATCH
NUTHOOK
NUTJOBBER
NUTLET
NUTLIKE
NUTMEG
NUTMEGGED
NUTMEGGY
NUTPECKER
NUTPICK
NUTRAMIN
NUTRIA
NUTRICE
NUTRICIAL
NUTRICISM
NUTRIENT
NUTRIFY
NUTRIMENT
NUTRIMENTAL
NUTRITION
NUTRITIONAL
NUTRITIONALLY
NUTRITIONARY
NUTRITIONIST
NUTRITIOUS
NUTRITIOUSLY
NUTRITIVE
NUTRITIVELY
NUTRITIVENESS
NUTRITORY
NUTS
NUTSHELL
NUTTED
NUTTER
NUTTERY
NUTTIER
NUTTIEST
NUTTILY
NUTTINESS
NUTTING
NUTTY
NUTWOOD
NUWAB
NUZZER
NUZZLE
NUZZLED
NUZZLING
NYALA
NYANZA
NYAS
NYASA
NYCE
NYCHTHEMERON
NYCTALOPE
NYCTALOPIA
NYCTALOPIC
NYCTALOPS
NYCTERIBIID
NYCTIPELAGIC
NYCTITROPIC
NYCTITROPISM
NYCTOPHOBIA
NYCTURIA
NYE
NYET
NYLAST
NYLGAU
NYLON
NYMIL
NYMPH
NYMPHA
NYMPHAE
NYMPHAEA
NYMPHAEUM
NYMPHAL
NYMPHALINE
NYMPHEAL
NYMPHEAN
NYMPHET
NYMPHEUM
NYMPHIC
NYMPHICAL
NYMPHID
NYMPHINE
NYMPHITIS
NYMPHLIN
NYMPHOLEPSIA
NYMPHOLEPSY
NYMPHOLEPT
NYMPHOLEPTIC
NYMPHOMANIA
NYMPHOMANIAC
NYMPHOSIS
NYMPHOTOMY
NYMSS
NYSTAGMIC
NYSTAGMUS
NYSTATIN
NYTRIL
NYXIS

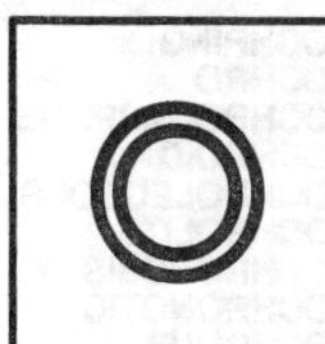

OADAL
OADE
OAF
OAFDOM
OAFISH
OAFISHLY
OAFISHNESS
OAFS
OAK
OAKBERRY
OAKEN
OAKENSHAW
OAKER
OAKMOSS
OAKS
OAKUM
OAKWEB
OAKWOOD
OAKY
OAM
OAR
OARAGE
OARCOCK
OARED
OARFISH
OARFISHES
OARIALGIA
OARING
OARIOCELE
OARIOPATHIC
OARIOPATHY
OARIOTOMY
OARITIC
OARITIS
OARIUM
OARLOCK
OARLOP
OARS
OARSMAN
OARSMANSHIP
OARSMEN
OARSWOMAN
OARSWOMEN
OARWEED
OARY
OASAL
OASEAN
OASES
OASIS
OASITIC
OAST
OASTHOUSE
OASY
OAT
OATCAKE
OATEAR
OATEN
OATENMEAL
OATFOWL
OATH
OATHAY
OATHED
OATHS
OATLAND
OATMEAL
OATS
OATSEED
OATY
OAVES
OB
OBA
OBAMBULATE
OBAMBULATION
OBAMBULATORY
OBAN
OBANG
OBARNE
OBARNI
OBBA
OBBLIGATI
OBBLIGATO
OBBLIGATOS
OBCLAVATE
OBCLUDE
OBCOMPRESSED
OBCONIC
OBCONICAL
OBCORDATE
OBCORDIFORM
OBCUNEATE
OBDELTOID
OBDORMITION
OBDUCTION
OBDURACY
OBDURATE
OBDURATELY
OBDURATENESS
OBDURATION
OBDURE
OBE
OBEAHISM
OBECHE
OBEDIENCE
OBEDIENCY
OBEDIENT
OBEDIENTIAL
OBEDIENTIALLY
OBEDIENTIAR
OBEDIENTIARIES
OBEDIENTIARY
OBEDIENTLY
OBEISANCE
OBEISANT
OBEISANTLY
OBEISH
OBEISM
OBELI
OBELIA
OBELIAC
OBELIAL
OBELION
OBELISCAL
OBELISCAR
OBELISK
OBELISKED
OBELISKING
OBELISKOID
OBELISM
OBELIZE
OBELIZED
OBELIZING
OBELUS
OBESE
OBESELY
OBESENESS
OBESITY
OBEX
OBEY
OBEYED
OBEYER
OBEYING
OBFUSCABLE
OBFUSCATE
OBFUSCATED
OBFUSCATING
OBFUSCATION
OBFUSCATOR
OBFUSCITY
OBFUSCOUS
OBFUSK
OBI
OBIA
OBIAH
OBIISM
OBIIT
OBISPO
OBIT
OBITAL
OBITER
OBITUAL
OBITUARIAN
OBITUARIES
OBITUARIST
OBITUARIZE
OBITUARY
OBJECT
OBJECTABLE
OBJECTATION
OBJECTATIVE
OBJECTED
OBJECTEE
OBJECTIFICATION
OBJECTIFIED
OBJECTIFY
OBJECTIFYING
OBJECTING
OBJECTION
OBJECTIONABILITY
OBJECTIONABLE
OBJECTIONABLY
OBJECTIONAL
OBJECTIONER
OBJECTIONIST
OBJECTIONS
OBJECTIVAL
OBJECTIVATE
OBJECTIVATED
OBJECTIVATING
OBJECTIVATION
OBJECTIVE
OBJECTIVELY
OBJECTIVENESS
OBJECTIVISM
OBJECTIVIST
OBJECTIVISTIC
OBJECTIVITY
OBJECTIVIZE
OBJECTIVIZED
OBJECTIVIZING
OBJECTIZATION
OBJECTIZE
OBJECTIZED
OBJECTIZING
OBJECTLESS
OBJECTOR
OBJECTS
OBJICIENT
OBJURATION
OBJURE
OBJURGATE
OBJURGATED
OBJURGATING
OBJURGATION
OBJURGATIVE
OBJURGATIVELY
OBJURGATOR
OBJURGATORILY
OBJURGATORY
OBJURGATRIX
OBLANCEOLATE
OBLAST
OBLAT
OBLATA
OBLATE
OBLATED
OBLATELY
OBLATENESS
OBLATING
OBLATIO
OBLATION
OBLATIONAL
OBLATIONARY
OBLATORY
OBLECTATE
OBLECTATION
OBLEY
OBLICQUE
OBLIGABLE
OBLIGANCY
OBLIGANT
OBLIGATE
OBLIGATED
OBLIGATING
OBLIGATION
OBLIGATIONAL
OBLIGATIONARY
OBLIGATIVE
OBLIGATIVENESS
OBLIGATO
OBLIGATOR
OBLIGATORILY
OBLIGATORINESS
OBLIGATORY
OBLIGATUM
OBLIGE
OBLIGED
OBLIGEDLY
OBLIGEDNESS
OBLIGEE
OBLIGEMENT
OBLIGER
OBLIGING
OBLIGINGLY
OBLIGINGNESS
OBLIGISTIC
OBLIGOR
OBLIQUATE
OBLIQUATION
OBLIQUE
OBLIQUED
OBLIQUELY
OBLIQUENESS
OBLIQUING
OBLIQUITIES
OBLIQUITOUS
OBLIQUITY
OBLIQUUS
OBLITERABLE
OBLITERATE
OBLITERATED
OBLITERATING
OBLITERATION
OBLITERATIVE
OBLITERATOR
OBLIVESCENCE
OBLIVIAL
OBLIVIALITY
OBLIVION
OBLIVIONATE
OBLIVIONIZE
OBLIVIOUS
OBLIVIOUSLY
OBLIVIOUSNESS
OBLIVISCENCE
OBLIVISCIBLE
OBLOCUTOR
OBLONG
OBLONGATA
OBLONGATAL
OBLONGATED
OBLONGITUDE
OBLONGITUDINAL
OBLONGLY
OBLONGNESS
OBLOQUIAL
OBLOQUIES
OBLOQUIOUS
OBLOQUY
OBMIT
OBMUTESCENCE
OBMUTESCENT
OBNEBULATE
OBNOUNCE
OBNOXIETY
OBNOXIOUS
OBNOXIOUSLY
OBNOXIOUSNESS
OBNUBILATE
OBNUBILATION
OBOE
OBOIST
OBOL
OBOLARY
OBOLE
OBOLI
OBOLOS
OBOLUS
OBOMEGOID
OBOVAL
OBOVATE
OBOVOID
OBPYRAMIDAL
OBPYRIFORM
OBREPTION
OBREPTITIOUS
OBREPTITIOUSLY
OBRIZE
OBROGATE
OBROGATION
OBROK
OBROTUND
OBSCENE
OBSCENELY
OBSCENENESS
OBSCENITIES
OBSCENITY
OBSCURANCY
OBSCURANT
OBSCURANTIC
OBSCURANTISM
OBSCURANTIST
OBSCURATION
OBSCURATIVE
OBSCURE
OBSCURED
OBSCURELY
OBSCUREMENT
OBSCURENESS
OBSCURER
OBSCUREST
OBSCURING
OBSCURITIES
OBSCURITY
OBSECRATE
OBSECRATED
OBSECRATING
OBSECRATION
OBSECRATIONARY
OBSECRATORY
OBSEDE
OBSEQUENCE
OBSEQUENT
OBSEQUIAL
OBSEQUIES
OBSEQUIOUS

OBSEQUIOUSLY
OBSEQUITY
OBSEQUY
OBSERVABILITY
OBSERVABLE
OBSERVABLENESS
OBSERVABLY
OBSERVANCE
OBSERVANDA
OBSERVANDUM
OBSERVANT
OBSERVANTLY
OBSERVANTNESS
OBSERVATION
OBSERVATIONAL
OBSERVATIONALLY
OBSERVATIVE
OBSERVATORIAL
OBSERVATORIES
OBSERVATORY
OBSERVE
OBSERVED
OBSERVER
OBSERVING
OBSERVINGLY
OBSESS
OBSESSED
OBSESSING
OBSESSION
OBSESSIONAL
OBSESSIVE
OBSESSOR
OBSIDE
OBSIDIAN
OBSIDIANITE
OBSIDIONAL
OBSIDIONARY
OBSIDIOUS
OBSIGN
OBSIGNATE
OBSIGNATION
OBSIGNATORY
OBSOLESCE
OBSOLESCED
OBSOLESCENCE
OBSOLESCENT
OBSOLESCENTLY
OBSOLESCING
OBSOLETE
OBSOLETELY
OBSOLETENESS
OBSOLETION
OBSOLETISM
OBSTACLE
OBSTANCY
OBSTANT
OBSTETRIC
OBSTETRICAL
OBSTETRICALLY
OBSTETRICATE
OBSTETRICATED
OBSTETRICATING
OBSTETRICIAN
OBSTETRICS
OBSTETRICY
OBSTETRIST
OBSTETRIX
OBSTINACIES
OBSTINACIOUS
OBSTINACY
OBSTINANCE
OBSTINANCY
OBSTINATE
OBSTINATELY
OBSTINATENESS
OBSTINATION
OBSTINATIVE
OBSTIPANT
OBSTIPATION
OBSTREPERATE
OBSTREPEROUS
OBSTREPEROUSLY
OBSTRICTION
OBSTRINGE
OBSTRUCT
OBSTRUCTANT
OBSTRUCTED
OBSTRUCTER
OBSTRUCTING
OBSTRUCTION
OBSTRUCTIONISM
OBSTRUCTIONIST
OBSTRUCTIVE
OBSTRUCTIVELY
OBSTRUCTIVENESS
OBSTRUCTIVITY
OBSTRUCTOR
OBSTRUENT
OBSTRUSE
OBTAIN
OBTAINABLE
OBTAINAL
OBTAINANCE
OBTAINED
OBTAINER
OBTAINING
OBTAINMENT
OBTECT
OBTECTED
OBTEMPER
OBTEND
OBTENEBRATE
OBTENEBRATION
OBTENT
OBTENTION
OBTEST
OBTESTATION
OBTESTED
OBTESTING
OBTRECT
OBTRIANGULAR
OBTRUDE
OBTRUDED
OBTRUDER
OBTRUDING
OBTRUNCATE
OBTRUNCATION
OBTRUNCATOR
OBTRUSION
OBTRUSIONIST
OBTRUSIVE
OBTRUSIVELY
OBTRUSIVENESS
OBTUND
OBTUNDED
OBTUNDENT
OBTUNDER
OBTUNDING
OBTUNDITY
OBTURATE
OBTURATED
OBTURATING
OBTURATION
OBTURATOR
OBTURATORY
OBTURBINATE
OBTUSE
OBTUSELY
OBTUSENESS
OBTUSER
OBTUSEST
OBTUSIFID
OBTUSILOBOUS
OBTUSION
OBTUSITY
OBUMBRANT
OBUMBRATE
OBUMBRATION
OBUS
OBVALLATE
OBVELATION
OBVENTION
OBVERSE
OBVERSELY
OBVERSION
OBVERT
OBVERTED
OBVERTEND
OBVERTING
OBVIABLE
OBVIATE
OBVIATED
OBVIATING
OBVIATION
OBVIATOR
OBVIOUS
OBVIOUSLY
OBVIOUSNESS
OBVOLUTE
OBVOLUTED
OBVOLUTION
OBVOLUTIVE
OBVOLVE
OBVOLVENT
OC
OCA
OCARINA
OCCAMY
OCCASION
OCCASIONAL
OCCASIONALISM
OCCASIONALIST
OCCASIONALISTIC
OCCASIONALITY
OCCASIONALLY
OCCASIONARY
OCCASIONED
OCCASIONER
OCCASIONING
OCCASIVE
OCCIDENT
OCCIDENTAL
OCCIDENTALITY
OCCIDENTALLY
OCCIPITA
OCCIPITAL
OCCIPITALIS
OCCIPITOOTIC
OCCIPUT
OCCISION
OCCITONE
OCCLUDE
OCCLUDED
OCCLUDENT
OCCLUDING
OCCLUSAL
OCCLUSE
OCCLUSION
OCCLUSIVE
OCCLUSOMETER
OCCLUSOR
OCCULT
OCCULTATE
OCCULTATION
OCCULTED
OCCULTER
OCCULTING
OCCULTISM
OCCULTIST
OCCULTLY
OCCULTNESS
OCCUPANCE
OCCUPANCIES
OCCUPANCY
OCCUPANT
OCCUPATION
OCCUPATIONAL
OCCUPATIONALIST
OCCUPATIONALLY
OCCUPATIVE
OCCUPIED
OCCUPIER
OCCUPY
OCCUPYING
OCCUR
OCCURRED
OCCURRENCE
OCCURRENT
OCCURRING
OCCURSE
OCEAN
OCEANED
OCEANET
OCEANIC
OCEANITY
OCEANOGRAPHER
OCEANOGRAPHIC
OCEANOGRAPHICAL
OCEANOGRAPHICALLY
OCEANOGRAPHIST
OCEANOGRAPHY
OCEANOUS
OCEANSIDE
OCELLANA
OCELLAR
OCELLATE
OCELLATED
OCELLATION
OCELLI
OCELLICYST
OCELLICYSTIC
OCELLIFEROUS
OCELLIFORM
OCELLIGEROUS
OCELLUS
OCELOID
OCELOT
OCELOTS
OCH
OCHAVA
OCHAVO
OCHE
OCHER
OCHERED
OCHERING
OCHERISH
OCHEROUS
OCHERY
OCHIDORE
OCHLESIS
OCHLESITIC
OCHLETIC
OCHLOCRACY
OCHLOCRAT
OCHLOCRATIC
OCHLOCRATICAL
OCHLOMANIA
OCHLOPHOBIA
OCHLOPHOBIST
OCHNACEOUS
OCHONE
OCHRA
OCHRACEOUS
OCHRE
OCHREA
OCHRED
OCHREISH
OCHREOUS
OCHRING
OCHRO
OCHROCARPOUS
OCHROID
OCHROLEUCOUS
OCHROLITE
OCHRONOSIS
OCHRONOTIC
OCHROUS
OCHRY
OCK
OCKER
OCKSTER
OCOTE
OCOTILLO
OCQUE
OCRACY
OCREA
OCREACEOUS
OCREAE
OCREATE
OCREATED
OCTACHLORIDE
OCTACHORD
OCTACHORDAL
OCTACOLIC
OCTACTINAL
OCTACTINE
OCTAD
OCTADECANE
OCTADECYL
OCTADIC
OCTADRACHM
OCTADRACHMA
OCTAECHOS
OCTAEMERA
OCTAEMERON
OCTAETERIC
OCTAETERID
OCTAETERIS
OCTAGON
OCTAGONAL
OCTAGONALLY
OCTAHEDRA
OCTAHEDRAL
OCTAHEDRIC
OCTAHEDRICAL
OCTAHEDRITE
OCTAHEDROID
OCTAHEDRON
OCTAHEDROUS
OCTAHYDRATE
OCTAHYDRATED
OCTAMERISM
OCTAMEROUS
OCTAMETER
OCTAN
OCTANDRIAN
OCTANDRIOUS
OCTANE
OCTANGLE
OCTANGULAR
OCTANGULARNESS
OCTANT
OCTANTAL
OCTAPLA
OCTAPLOID
OCTAPLOIDIC
OCTAPLOIDY
OCTAPODIC
OCTAPODY
OCTARCH
OCTARCHIES
OCTARCHY
OCTARIUS
OCTASEMIC
OCTASTICH

OCTASTICHON
OCTASTROPHIC
OCTASTYLOS
OCTATEUCH
OCTAVAL
OCTAVALENT
OCTAVARIA
OCTAVARIUM
OCTAVE
OCTAVIC
OCTAVINA
OCTAVO
OCTAVOS
OCTENE
OCTENNIAL
OCTENNIALLY
OCTET
OCTETTE
OCTIC
OCTILLION
OCTILLIONTH
OCTINE
OCTOAD
OCTOALLOY
OCTOATE
OCTOBASS
OCTOCOTYLOID
OCTODACTYL
OCTODACTYLE
OCTODE
OCTODECIMAL
OCTODECIMO
OCTODECIMOS
OCTODENTATE
OCTODIANOME
OCTODONT
OCTOECHOS
OCTOFID
OCTOFOIL
OCTOFOILED
OCTOGAMY
OCTOGENARIAN
OCTOGENARIES
OCTOGENARY
OCTOGILD
OCTOGLOT
OCTOGYNIAN
OCTOGYNIOUS
OCTOGYNOUS
OCTOHEDRAL
OCTOIC
OCTOID
OCTOLATERAL
OCTOLOCULAR
OCTOMERAL
OCTOMEROUS
OCTONAL
OCTONARE
OCTONARIAN
OCTONARIES
OCTONARIUS
OCTONARY
OCTONEMATOUS
OCTONION
OCTONOCULAR
OCTOON
OCTOPARTITE
OCTOPEAN
OCTOPED
OCTOPEDE
OCTOPETALOUS
OCTOPHYLLOUS
OCTOPI
OCTOPINE
OCTOPOD
OCTOPODAN
OCTOPODES
OCTOPODOUS
OCTOPOLAR
OCTOPUS
OCTOPUSES
OCTORADIAL
OCTORADIATE
OCTORADIATED
OCTOREME
OCTOROON
OCTOSE
OCTOSEPALOUS
OCTOSPERMOUS
OCTOSPORE
OCTOSPOROUS
OCTOSTICHOUS
OCTOSYLLABIC
OCTOSYLLABLE
OCTOVALENT
OCTOYL
OCTROI
OCTROY
OCTUOR
OCTUPLE
OCTUPLED
OCTUPLET
OCTUPLEX
OCTUPLICATE
OCTUPLICATION
OCTUPLING
OCTUPLY
OCTYL
OCTYLENE
OCTYNE
OCUBY
OCULAR
OCULARIST
OCULARLY
OCULARY
OCULATE
OCULATED
OCULAUDITORY
OCULI
OCULIFEROUS
OCULIFORM
OCULIGEROUS
OCULINID
OCULINOID
OCULIST
OCULISTIC
OCULOFACIAL
OCULOFRONTAL
OCULOMOTOR
OCULOMOTORY
OCULONASAL
OCULOSPINAL
OCULUS
OCYDROME
OCYDROMINE
OCYME
OCYPODAN
OCYPODIAN
OCYPODOID
OD
ODA
ODACOID
ODAL
ODALBORN
ODALISK
ODALISQUE
ODALLER
ODD
ODDBALL
ODDER
ODDEST
ODDITIES
ODDITY
ODDLEGS
ODDLY
ODDMAN
ODDMENT
ODDMENTS
ODDNESS
ODDS
ODDSMAN
ODE
ODEA
ODEL
ODELET
ODEON
ODEUM
ODHAL
ODIBLE
ODIC
ODICALLY
ODINISM
ODINITE
ODIOMETER
ODIOUS
ODIOUSLY
ODIOUSNESS
ODIST
ODIUM
ODLING
ODOGRAPH
ODOLOGY
ODOMETER
ODOMETRICAL
ODOMETRY
ODONTOTRIPSIS
ODONTAGRA
ODONTALGIA
ODONTALGIC
ODONTATROPHY
ODONTEXESIS
ODONTIASIS
ODONTIC
ODONTIST
ODONTITIS
ODONTOBLAST
ODONTOBLASTIC
ODONTOCELE
ODONTOCETE
ODONTOCETOUS
ODONTOCLASIS
ODONTOCLAST
ODONTODYNIA
ODONTOGEN
ODONTOGENESIS
ODONTOGENIC
ODONTOGENY
ODONTOGRAPH
ODONTOGRAPHIC
ODONTOGRAPHY
ODONTOID
ODONTOLCATE
ODONTOLCOUS
ODONTOLITE
ODONTOLITH
ODONTOLOGICAL
ODONTOLOGIST
ODONTOLOGY
ODONTOLOXIA
ODONTOMA
ODONTOMOUS
ODONTOPATHY
ODONTOPHORAL
ODONTOPHORE
ODONTOSCOPE
ODONTOTECHNY
ODOOM
ODOPHONE
ODOR
ODORABLE
ODORANT
ODORATE
ODORATOR
ODORED
ODORIFERANT
ODORIFEROUS
ODORIFEROUSLY
ODORIFIC
ODORIPHOR
ODORIPHORE
ODORIVECTOR
ODORIZE
ODORLESS
ODORLESSLY
ODORLESSNESS
ODOROMETER
ODOROSITY
ODOROUS
ODOROUSLY
ODOROUSNESS
ODORS
ODOUR
ODOURED
ODSO
ODUM
ODYL
ODYLE
ODYLIC
ODYLISM
ODYLIST
ODYLIZATION
ODYLIZE
ODYSSEYS
OE
OECIST
OECODOMIC
OECOID
OECONOMUS
OECOPARASITE
OECOPARASITISM
OECUMENIAN
OECUMENIC
OECUMENICAL
OECUMENICITY
OECUS
OEDEMA
OEDEMERID
OEDICNEMINE
OEILLADE
OEKIST
OELET
OENANTHATE
OENANTHIC
OENANTHYL
OENANTHYLATE
OENIN
OENOCHOAE
OENOCHOE
OENOCYTE
OENOCYTIC
OENOLIN
OENOLOGICAL
OENOLOGIES
OENOLOGIST
OENOLOGY
OENOMANCY
OENOMEL
OENOMETER
OENOPHILIST
OENOPHOBIST
OENOPOETIC
OERSTED
OESOPHAGAL
OESOPHAGEAL
OESOPHAGEAN
OESOPHAGISM
OESOPHAGITIS
OESOPHAGUS
OESTRIAN
OESTRIASIS
OESTRID
OESTRIN
OESTRIOL
OESTROGEN
OESTROID
OESTRONE
OESTROUS
OESTRUAL
OESTRUATE
OESTRUATION
OESTRUM
OESTRUS
OEUVRE
OEUVRES
OF
OFAY
OFF
OFFAL
OFFALING
OFFBEAT
OFFBREAK
OFFCAST
OFFCOME
OFFCUT
OFFED
OFFENCE
OFFENCELESS
OFFENCELESSLY
OFFEND
OFFENDANT
OFFENDED
OFFENDEDLY
OFFENDEDNESS
OFFENDER
OFFENDERS
OFFENDING
OFFENDRESS
OFFENSE
OFFENSELESS
OFFENSELESSLY
OFFENSIBLE
OFFENSIVE
OFFENSIVELY
OFFENSIVENESS
OFFER
OFFERED
OFFERER
OFFERING
OFFERINGS
OFFEROR
OFFERTORIAL
OFFERTORIES
OFFERTORY
OFFGOING
OFFGRADE
OFFHAND
OFFHANDED
OFFHANDEDLY
OFFHANDEDNESS
OFFICARIES
OFFICE
OFFICEHOLDER
OFFICER
OFFICERAGE
OFFICERED
OFFICERESS
OFFICERIAL
OFFICERING
OFFICERS
OFFICIAL
OFFICIALDOM
OFFICIALISM
OFFICIALITIES
OFFICIALITY
OFFICIALIZE

OFFICIALLY
OFFICIANT
OFFICIARY
OFFICIATE
OFFICIATED
OFFICIATING
OFFICIATION
OFFICIATOR
OFFICINA
OFFICINAL
OFFICINALLY
OFFICIOUS
OFFICIOUSLY
OFFICIOUSNESS
OFFING
OFFISH
OFFISHLY
OFFISHNESS
OFFLAP
OFFLET
OFFLOOK
OFFPRINT
OFFSADDLE
OFFSCAPE
OFFSCOUR
OFFSCOURER
OFFSCOURING
OFFSCOURINGS
OFFSCUM
OFFSET
OFFSHOOT
OFFSHORE
OFFSIDE
OFFSIDER
OFFSPRING
OFFTAKE
OFFTYPE
OFFUSCATE
OFFUSCATION
OFFWARD
OFFWARDS
OFICINA
OFLAG
OFLETE
OFT
OFTEN
OFTENNESS
OFTENS
OFTENTIME
OFTENTIMES
OFTHINK
OFTLY
OFTNESS
OFTTIME
OFTTIMES
OFTWHILES
OGAM
OGAMIC
OGDOAD
OGDOAS
OGEE
OGEED
OGGANITION
OGHAM
OGHAMIC
OGIVAL
OGIVE
OGIVED
OGLE
OGLED
OGLER
OGLING
OGLIO
OGRE
OGREISH
OGRESS
OGRISH
OGTIERN
OGUM
OH
OHED
OHELO
OHIA
OHING
OHM
OHMAGE
OHMIC
OHMMETER
OHNE
OHO
OHONE
OIDIA
OIDIOID
OIDIOMYCOSIS
OIDIOMYCOTIC
OII
OIKOLOGY
OIKOMANIA
OIKOPLAST
OIL
OILBERRIES
OILBERRY
OILBIRD
OILCAN
OILCASE
OILCLOTH
OILCOAT
OILDOM
OILED
OILER
OILERY
OILFISH
OILFISHES
OILHOLE
OILIER
OILIEST
OILILY
OILINESS
OILISH
OILLESS
OILLESSNESS
OILLET
OILMAN
OILMEN
OILMONGER
OILMONGERY
OILOMETER
OILPAPER
OILPROOF
OILPROOFING
OILSEED
OILSKIN
OILSKINNED
OILSTOCK
OILSTONE
OILSTONED
OILSTONING
OILSTOVE
OILTIGHT
OILTIGHTNESS
OILWAY
OILWELL
OILY
OIME
OIMEE
OINOCHOE
OINOLOGY
OINOMANCY
OINOMANIA
OINOMEL
OINT
OINTMENT
OISIVITY
OITA
OITAVA
OJO
OK
OKA
OKAPI
OKAPIS
OKAY
OKE
OKEE
OKEH
OKENITE
OKET
OKEYDOKE
OKI
OKIA
OKIE
OKIEH
OKOLEHAO
OKONITE
OKOUME
OKOW
OKRA
OKRO
OKROOG
OKRUG
OKRUZI
OKSHOOFD
OKTHABAH
OLA
OLACACEOUS
OLACAD
OLAM
OLAY
OLD
OLDEN
OLDENED
OLDENING
OLDER
OLDERMOST
OLDERS
OLDEST
OLDFANGLED
OLDFANGLEDNESS
OLDHAMITE
OLDHEARTED
OLDISH
OLDLAND
OLDNESS
OLDS
OLDSTER
OLDWENCH
OLDWIFE
OLDWIVES
OLE
OLEACEOUS
OLEAGINOUS
OLEAGINOUSLY
OLEANA
OLEANDER
OLEANDRIN
OLEASE
OLEASTER
OLEATE
OLECRANAL
OLECRANON
OLEFIANT
OLEFIN
OLEFINE
OLEFINIC
OLEIC
OLEIFEROUS
OLEIN
OLEINE
OLEN
OLENA
OLENELLIDIAN
OLENID
OLENIDIAN
OLENT
OLEO
OLEOCELLOSIS
OLEOCYST
OLEODUCT
OLEOGRAPH
OLEOGRAPHER
OLEOGRAPHIC
OLEOGRAPHY
OLEOMARGARIN
OLEOMARGARINE
OLEOMETER
OLEOPTENE
OLEORESIN
OLEORESINOUS
QLEOSE
OLEOSITY
OLEOSTEARATE
OLEOSTEARIN
OLEOSTEARINE
OLEOTHORAX
OLEOUS
OLEPI
OLEPY
OLER
OLERACEOUS
OLERICULTURE
OLETHREUTID
OLEUM
OLFACT
OLFACTABLE
OLFACTIBLE
OLFACTION
OLFACTOLOGY
OLFACTOMETER
OLFACTOMETRIC
OLFACTOMETRY
OLFACTOR
OLFACTORIES
OLFACTORILY
OLFACTORY
OLFACTY
OLIBAN
OLIBANUM
OLID
OLIGAEMIA
OLIGANDROUS
OLIGANTHOUS
OLIGARCH
OLIGARCHAL
OLIGARCHIC
OLIGARCHICAL
OLIGARCHIES
OLIGARCHISM
OLIGARCHIST
OLIGARCHIZE
OLIGARCHY
OLIGEMIA
OLIGIDRIA
OLIGIST
OLIGISTIC
OLIGISTICAL
OLIGOCARPOUS
OLIGOCHAETE
OLIGOCHETE
OLIGOCHOLIA
OLIGOCHROME
OLIGOCHYLIA
OLIGOCLASE
OLIGOCLASITE
OLIGOCYSTIC
OLIGODIPSIA
OLIGODONTOUS
OLIGODYNAMIC
OLIGOHEMIA
OLIGOLACTIA
OLIGOMEROUS
OLIGOMERY
OLIGOMYODIAN
OLIGOMYOID
OLIGONEPHRIC
OLIGONITE
OLIGOPEPSIA
OLIGOPHAGOUS
OLIGOPHRENIA
OLIGOPHRENIC
OLIGOPLASMIA
OLIGOPNEA
OLIGOPOLIST
OLIGOPOLY
OLIGOPSYCHIA
OLIGOPYRENE
OLIGORHIZOUS
OLIGOSIALIA
OLIGOSITE
OLIGOSPERMIA
OLIGOTOKEUS
OLIGOTRICHIA
OLIGOTROPHIC
OLIGOTROPHY
OLIGURESIA
OLIGURESIS
OLIGURETIC
OLIGURIA
OLIO
OLIOS
OLIPHANT
OLIPRANCE
OLITORY
OLIVA
OLIVACEOUS
OLIVARY
OLIVASTER
OLIVE
OLIVED
OLIVENESS
OLIVENITE
OLIVERMAN
OLIVERMEN
OLIVERSMITH
OLIVES
OLIVESCENT
OLIVET
OLIVETTE
OLIVEWOOD
OLIVIFEROUS
OLIVIFORM
OLIVIL
OLIVILE
OLIVILIN
OLIVINE
OLIVINEFELS
OLIVINIC
OLIVINITE
OLIVINITIC
OLLA
OLLAE
OLLAMH
OLLAPOD
OLLAV
OLLENITE
OLLOCK
OLLUCK
OLM
OLOGICAL
OLOGIST
OLOGISTIC
OLOGY
OLOMAO
OLONA
OLOROSO
OLP
OLPAE

OLPE
OLPH
OLTONDE
OLTUNNA
OLYCOOK
OLYKOEK
OM
OMADAWN
OMADHAUN
OMAGRA
OMALGIA
OMAO
OMARTHRITIS
OMASA
OMASUM
OMBER
OMBRE
OMBRETTE
OMBRIFUGE
OMBROGRAPH
OMBROLOGICAL
OMBROLOGY
OMBROMETER
OMBROPHIL
OMBROPHILE
OMBROPHILIC
OMBROPHILOUS
OMBROPHILY
OMBROPHOBE
OMBROPHOBOUS
OMBROPHOBY
OMBROPHYTE
OMBUDSMAN
OMBUDSMEN
OMDA
OMDEH
OMEGA
OMEGOID
OMEL
OMELET
OMELETTE
OMELIE
OMEN
OMENED
OMENOLOGY
OMENTA
OMENTAL
OMENTECTOMY
OMENTITIS
OMENTOCELE
OMENTOPEXY
OMENTOPLASTY
OMENTOTOMY
OMENTULUM
OMENTUM
OMER
OMICRON
OMIKRON
OMINATE
OMINOUS
OMINOUSLY
OMINOUSNESS
OMISSIBLE
OMISSION
OMISSIVE
OMISSIVELY
OMIT
OMITIS
OMITTED
OMITTER
OMITTING
OMLAH
OMMATEA
OMMATEAL
OMMATEUM
OMMATIDIA
OMMATIDIAL
OMMATIDIUM
OMMATOPHORE
OMNEITY
OMNES
OMNIACTIVE
OMNIANA
OMNIARCH
OMNIBUS
OMNIBUSES
OMNIBUSMAN
OMNIERUDITE
OMNIESSENCE
OMNIFACIAL
OMNIFARIOUS
OMNIFEROUS
OMNIFIC
OMNIFICENT
OMNIFIDEL
OMNIFIED
OMNIFORM
OMNIFORMAL
OMNIFORMITY
OMNIFY
OMNIFYING
OMNIGENOUS
OMNIGERENT
OMNIGRAPH
OMNIHUMAN
OMNIHUMANITY
OMNILEGENT
OMNILINGUAL
OMNILOQUENT
OMNILUCENT
OMNIMENTAL
OMNIMETER
OMNIMODE
OMNIMODOUS
OMNINESCIENT
OMNIPARENT
OMNIPARIENT
OMNIPARITY
OMNIPAROUS
OMNIPATIENT
OMNIPERFECT
OMNIPOTENCE
OMNIPOTENCY
OMNIPOTENT
OMNIPOTENTLY
OMNIPRESENCE
OMNIPRESENT
OMNIPRUDENCE
OMNIPRUDENT
OMNIRANGE
OMNIREGENCY
OMNIREGENT
OMNISCIENCE
OMNISCIENCY
OMNISCIENT
OMNISCIENTLY
OMNISCOPE
OMNISCRIBENT
OMNISENTIENT
OMNISPECTIVE
OMNIST
OMNITEMPORAL
OMNITENENT
OMNITOLERANT
OMNITONAL
OMNITONALITY
OMNITONIC
OMNITUDE
OMNIUM
OMNIVAGANT
OMNIVALENCE
OMNIVALENT
OMNIVALOUS
OMNIVARIOUS
OMNIVIDENCE
OMNIVIDENT
OMNIVISION
OMNIVOLENT
OMNIVORACITY
OMNIVORE
OMNIVOROUS
OMNIVOROUSLY
OMODYNIA
OMOHYOID
OMOIDEUM
OMOPHAGIA
OMOPHAGIC
OMOPHAGIST
OMOPHAGOUS
OMOPHAGY
OMOPHORIA
OMOPHORION
OMOPLATE
OMOSTEGITE
OMOSTERNAL
OMOSTERNUM
OMPHACINE
OMPHACITE
OMPHACY
OMPHALECTOMY
OMPHALI
OMPHALIC
OMPHALISM
OMPHALITIS
OMPHALOCELE
OMPHALODE
OMPHALODIA
OMPHALODIUM
OMPHALOID
OMPHALOMA
OMPHALONCUS
OMPHALORRHEA
OMPHALOS
OMPHALOSITE
OMPHALOTOMY
OMPHALUS
OMRAH
ON
ONA
ONAGER
ONAGERS
ONAGRA
ONAGRACEOUS
ONAGRI
ONANISM
ONANIST
ONANISTIC
ONCA
ONCE
ONCET
ONCETTA
ONCIA
ONCIN
ONCOGRAPH
ONCOGRAPHY
ONCOLOGIC
ONCOLOGICAL
ONCOLOGY
ONCOME
ONCOMETER
ONCOMETRIC
ONCOMETRY
ONCOMING
ONCOSIMETER
ONCOSIS
ONCOSPHERE
ONCOST
ONCOSTMAN
ONCOTOMY
ONDAGRAM
ONDAGRAPH
ONDAMETER
ONDASCOPE
ONDATRA
ONDE
ONDINE
ONDOGRAM
ONDOGRAPH
ONDOMETER
ONDOSCOPE
ONDOYANT
ONDULE
ONE
ONEBERRY
ONEFOLD
ONEFOLDNESS
ONEGITE
ONEHOOD
ONEHOW
ONEIRIC
ONEIROCRITIC
ONEIROCRITICS
ONEIRODYNIA
ONEIROLOGIST
ONEIROLOGY
ONEIROMANCER
ONEIROMANCY
ONEIROSCOPIC
ONEIROSCOPY
ONEIROTIC
ONEISM
ONEMENT
ONENESS
ONER
ONERARY
ONERATE
ONERATIVE
ONEROSE
ONEROSITY
ONEROUS
ONEROUSLY
ONEROUSNESS
ONERY
ONESELF
ONETHE
ONETIME
ONEWHERE
ONEYER
ONFALL
ONFLEMED
ONFLOW
ONFLOWING
ONGARO
ONGLE
ONGOING
ONHANGER
ONI
ONIOMANIA
ONIOMANIAC
ONION
ONIONET
ONIONIZED
ONIONPEEL
ONIONS
ONIONSKIN
ONIONY
ONIROTIC
ONISCIFORM
ONISCOID
ONISCOIDEAN
ONKILONITE
ONKOS
ONLAP
ONLAY
ONLEPY
ONLESS
ONLINESS
ONLOOK
ONLOOKER
ONLOOKING
ONLY
ONMARCH
ONOCENTAUR
ONOCROTAL
ONOFRITE
ONOLATRY
ONOMANCY
ONOMASTIC
ONOMASTICAL
ONOMASTICON
ONOMASTICS
ONOMATOLOGY
ONOMATOPE
ONOMATOPLASM
ONOMATOPOEIA
ONOMATOPOEIC
ONOMATOPOESY
ONOMATOPY
ONOMATOUS
ONON
ONOTOGENIC
ONRUSH
ONRUSHING
ONS
ONSET
ONSETTER
ONSHORE
ONSIDE
ONSIGHT
ONSLAUGHT
ONSTAND
ONSTANDING
ONSTEAD
ONSWEEP
ONSWEEPING
ONTAL
ONTIC
ONTO
ONTOCYCLE
ONTOCYCLIC
ONTOGENAL
ONTOGENESIS
ONTOGENETIC
ONTOGENIST
ONTOGENY
ONTOGRAPHY
ONTOLOGIC
ONTOLOGICAL
ONTOLOGICALLY
ONTOLOGIES
ONTOLOGISM
ONTOLOGIST
ONTOLOGISTIC
ONTOLOGIZE
ONTOLOGY
ONUS
ONWAITING
ONWARD
ONWARDLY
ONWARDNESS
ONWARDS
ONY
ONYCHA
ONYCHAUXIS
ONYCHIA
ONYCHIN
ONYCHITE
ONYCHITIS
ONYCHIUM
ONYCHOID
ONYCHOLYSIS
ONYCHOPATHIC
ONYCHOPATHY
ONYCHOPHAGIA
ONYCHOPHAGY

ONYCHOPHORAN
ONYCHOPHYMA
ONYCHOPTOSIS
ONYCHOSIS
ONYCHOTROPHY
ONYM
ONYMAL
ONYMATIC
ONYMITY
ONYMIZE
ONYMOUS
ONYMY
ONYX
ONYXES
ONYXIS
ONZA
OO
OOANGIUM
OOBLAST
OOBLASTIC
OOCYESIS
OOCYST
OOCYSTACEOUS
OOCYSTIC
OOCYTE
OODLES
OODLINS
OOECIA
OOECIAL
OOECIUM
OOF
OOFBIRD
OOFIER
OOFIEST
OOFTISH
OOFY
OOGAMETE
OOGAMOUS
OOGAMY
OOGENESIS
OOGENETIC
OOGENY
OOGLEA
OOGLOEA
OOGONE
OOGONIA
OOGONIAL
OOGONIOPHORE
OOGONIUM
OOGONIUMS
OOGRAPH
OOID
OOIDAL
OOK
OOKINESIS
OOKINETE
OOKINETIC
OOLACHAN
OOLAK
OOLEMMA
OOLITE
OOLITIC
OOLLIES
OOLLY
OOLOGIC
OOLOGICAL
OOLOGICALLY
OOLOGIST
OOLOGIZE
OOLOGY
OOLONG
OOM
OOMANCY
OOMANTIA
OOMETER
OOMETRIC
OOMETRY
OOMIAC
OOMIAK
OOMPAH
OOMPH
OOMYCETE
OOMYCETES
OOMYCETOUS
OON
OONS
OONT
OOP
OOPACK
OOPAK
OOPHORALGIA
OOPHORAUXE
OOPHORE
OOPHORECTOMY
OOPHORIC
OOPHORIDIA
OOPHORIDIUM
OOPHORIDIUMS
OOPHORITIS
OOPHOROCELE
OOPHOROMA
OOPHOROMANIA
OOPHORON
OOPHOROPEXY
OOPHOROSTOMY
OOPHOROTOMY
OOPHYTE
OOPHYTIC
OOPLASM
OOPLASMIC
OOPLAST
OOPOD
OOPODAL
OOPORPHYRIN
OOPUHUE
OORALI
OORD
OORIAL
OORIE
OOSCOPE
OOSCOPY
OOSPERM
OOSPHERE
OOSPORANGIA
OOSPORANGIUM
OOSPORE
OOSPORIC
OOSPOROUS
OOSTEGITE
OOSTEGITIC
OOT
OOTHECA
OOTHECAL
OOTID
OOTOCOID
OOTOCOIDEAN
OOTOCOUS
OOTWITH
OOTYPE
OOZE
OOZED
OOZEL
OOZIER
OOZIEST
OOZILY
OOZINESS
OOZING
OOZOID
OOZY
OPACATE
OPACIFIER
OPACIFY
OPACITE
OPACITIES
OPACITY
OPACOUS
OPACOUSNESS
OPAH
OPAL
OPALED
OPALESCE
OPALESCED
OPALESCENCE
OPALESCENT
OPALESCING
OPALEYE
OPALINE
OPALINID
OPALININE
OPALIZE
OPALIZED
OPALIZING
OPALOID
OPAQUE
OPAQUED
OPAQUELY
OPAQUENESS
OPAQUING
OPDALITE
OPE
OPED
OPEIDOSCOPE
OPELET
OPELU
OPEN
OPENBAND
OPENBEAK
OPENBILL
OPENCAST
OPENCUT
OPENED
OPENER
OPENEST
OPENHANDED
OPENHANDEDLY
OPENHEAD
OPENHEARTED
OPENHEARTEDLY
OPENING
OPENINGS
OPENLY
OPENMOUTHED
OPENNESS
OPENSIDE
OPENWORK
OPERA
OPERABILITY
OPERABLE
OPERABLY
OPERAGOER
OPERALOGUE
OPERAMETER
OPERANCE
OPERANCY
OPERAND
OPERANT
OPERARY
OPERAS
OPERATABLE
OPERATE
OPERATED
OPERATEE
OPERATIC
OPERATICAL
OPERATICALLY
OPERATING
OPERATION
OPERATIONAL
OPERATIONS
OPERATIVE
OPERATIVELY
OPERATIVENESS
OPERATIVITY
OPERATIZE
OPERATOR
OPERATORY
OPERATRICES
OPERATRIX
OPERCELE
OPERCLE
OPERCLED
OPERCULA
OPERCULAR
OPERCULATE
OPERCULATED
OPERCULE
OPERCULIFORM
OPERCULUM
OPERETTIST
OPERETTA
OPERETTAS
OPERETTE
OPEROSE
OPEROSELY
OPEROSENESS
OPHELIMITY
OPHIASIS
OPHIC
OPHICALCITE
OPHICHTHYOID
OPHICLEIDE
OPHICLEIDEAN
OPHICLEIDIST
OPHIDIAN
OPHIDIOID
OPHIDIOMANIA
OPHIDIOUS
OPHIOGRAPHY
OPHIOID
OPHIOLATER
OPHIOLATROUS
OPHIOLATRY
OPHIOLITE
OPHIOLITIC
OPHIOLOGIC
OPHIOLOGICAL
OPHIOLOGIST
OPHIOLOGY
OPHIOMANCY
OPHIOMORPHIC
OPHIONID
OPHIONINE
OPHIOPHAGOUS
OPHIOPHILISM
OPHIOPHILIST
OPHIOPHOBE
OPHIOPHOBIA
OPHIOPHOBY
OPHIOPLUTEUS
OPHIOURIDE
OPHITE
OPHITIC
OPHIURAN
OPHIURID
OPHIUROID
OPHIUROIDEAN
OPHRYON
OPHTHALMAGRA
OPHTHALMIA
OPHTHALMIAC
OPHTHALMIATER
OPHTHALMIC
OPHTHALMIOUS
OPHTHALMIST
OPHTHALMITE
OPHTHALMITIC
OPHTHALMITIS
OPHTHALMOPOD
OPHTHALMY
OPIANE
OPIANIC
OPIANYL
OPIATE
OPIATED
OPIATIC
OPIATING
OPIE
OPIFEX
OPIFICE
OPIFICER
OPIHI
OPIISM
OPILIACEOUS
OPIME
OPINABILITY
OPINABLE
OPINABLY
OPINANT
OPINATIVE
OPINATIVELY
OPINATOR
OPINE
OPINED
OPINER
OPING
OPINIATE
OPINIATED
OPINIATEDLY
OPINIATER
OPINIATIVE
OPINIATIVELY
OPINIATRE
OPINIATRETY
OPINICUS
OPINING
OPINION
OPINIONABLE
OPINIONAL
OPINIONATE
OPINIONATED
OPINIONATEDLY
OPINIONATELY
OPINIONATIVE
OPINIONED
OPINIONIST
OPINIONS
OPIOMANIA
OPIOMANIAC
OPIOPHAGISM
OPIOPHAGY
OPISOMETER
OPISTHENAR
OPISTHION
OPISTHOCOME
OPISTHODETIC
OPISTHODOME
OPISTHODONT
OPISTHOGRAPH
OPISTHOSOMAL
OPISTHOTIC
OPISTHOTONIC
OPISTHOTONOS
OPIUM
OPIUMISM
OPOBALSAM
OPOBALSAMUM
OPODELDOC
OPODIDYMUS
OPOPANAX
OPOSSUM
OPOSSUMS
OPPIDA
OPPIDAN
OPPIDUM
OPPIGNERATE

OPPIGNORATE
OPPILANT
OPPILATE
OPPILATED
OPPILATING
OPPILATION
OPPILATIVE
OPPLETE
OPPLETION
OPPO
OPPONENCY
OPPONENS
OPPONENT
OPPORTUNE
OPPORTUNELY
OPPORTUNISM
OPPORTUNIST
OPPORTUNISTIC
OPPORTUNITIES
OPPORTUNITY
OPPOSABILITY
OPPOSABLE
OPPOSAL
OPPOSE
OPPOSED
OPPOSELESS
OPPOSER
OPPOSING
OPPOSINGLY
OPPOSIT
OPPOSITE
OPPOSITELY
OPPOSITENESS
OPPOSITION
OPPOSITIONAL
OPPOSITIOUS
OPPOSITIVE
OPPOSITIVELY
OPPOSURE
OPPRESS
OPPRESSED
OPPRESSING
OPPRESSION
OPPRESSIVE
OPPRESSIVELY
OPPRESSIVENESS
OPPRESSOR
OPPROBRIATE
OPPROBRIOUS
OPPROBRIUM
OPPROBRY
OPPUGN
OPPUGNACY
OPPUGNANCE
OPPUGNANCY
OPPUGNANT
OPPUGNATE
OPPUGNATION
OPPUGNED
OPPUGNER
OPPUGNING
OPSIGAMY
OPSIMATH
OPSIMATHY
OPSISFORM
OPSISTYPE
OPSONIA
OPSONIC
OPSONIFEROUS
OPSONIFIED
OPSONIFY
OPSONIFYING
OPSONIN
OPSONIST
OPSONIUM
OPSONIZATION
OPSONIZE
OPSONOGEN
OPSONOID
OPSONOMETRY
OPSONOPHILIA
OPSONOPHILIC
OPSONOPHORIC
OPSONOTHERAPY
OPT
OPTABLE
OPTABLENESS
OPTABLY
OPTANT
OPTATE
OPTATION
OPTATIVE
OPTATIVELY
OPTED
OPTIC
OPTICAL
OPTICALLY
OPTICIAN
OPTICIST
OPTICITY
OPTICS
OPTIGRAPH
OPTIMA
OPTIMACY
OPTIMAL
OPTIMATE
OPTIMATES
OPTIME
OPTIMISM
OPTIMIST
OPTIMISTIC
OPTIMISTICAL
OPTIMISTICALLY
OPTIMITY
OPTIMIZATION
OPTIMIZE
OPTIMIZED
OPTIMIZING
OPTIMUM
OPTIMUMS
OPTING
OPTION
OPTIONAL
OPTIONALITY
OPTIONALIZE
OPTIONALLY
OPTIONARY
OPTIONEE
OPTIONOR
OPTIVE
OPTOBLAST
OPTOGRAM
OPTOGRAPHY
OPTOLOGICAL
OPTOLOGIST
OPTOLOGY
OPTOMENINX
OPTOMETER
OPTOMETRICAL
OPTOMETRIST
OPTOMETRY
OPTOPHONE
OPTOTYPE
OPULENCE
OPULENCY
OPULENT
OPULENTLY
OPULUS
OPUNTIA
OPUNTIOID
OPUS
OPUSCLE
OPUSCULAR
OPUSCULE
OPUSCULUM
OQUASSA
OQUE
OQUI
OR
ORA
ORABASSU
ORACH
ORACHE
ORACLE
ORACLER
ORACULA
ORACULAR
ORACULARITY
ORACULARLY
ORACULARNESS
ORACULATE
ORACULOUS
ORACULOUSLY
ORACULOUSNESS
ORACULUM
ORAD
ORAGE
ORAGIOUS
ORAL
ORALE
ORALER
ORALISM
ORALIST
ORALITY
ORALLY
ORALOGIST
ORALOGY
ORANG
ORANGE
ORANGEADE
ORANGEADO
ORANGEAT
ORANGEBERRIES
ORANGEBERRY
ORANGEBIRD
ORANGELEAF
ORANGER
ORANGEROOT
ORANGERY
ORANGEWOMAN
ORANGEWOOD
ORANGEY
ORANGIST
ORANGITE
ORANGIZE
ORANGOUTANG
ORANGUTAN
ORANS
ORANT
ORANTE
ORANTES
ORARIA
ORARIAN
ORARION
ORARY
ORAS
ORATE
ORATED
ORATING
ORATION
ORATIONAL
ORATIONER
ORATOR
ORATORIAL
ORATORIALLY
ORATORIAN
ORATORIC
ORATORICAL
ORATORICALLY
ORATORIES
ORATORIO
ORATORIOS
ORATORIZE
ORATORY
ORATRESS
ORATRICES
ORATRIX
ORB
ORBAL
ORBATE
ORBED
ORBELL
ORBIC
ORBICAL
ORBICLE
ORBICULAR
ORBICULARIS
ORBICULARITY
ORBICULARLY
ORBICULATE
ORBICULATED
ORBICULATELY
ORBICULATION
ORBIFIC
ORBING
ORBIT
ORBITAL
ORBITALE
ORBITAR
ORBITARY
ORBITE
ORBITELAR
ORBITELARIAN
ORBITELE
ORBITELOUS
ORBITER
ORBITOLITE
ORBITOMALAR
ORBITONASAL
ORBITOSTAT
ORBITOTOMY
ORBITUDE
ORBITY
ORBY
ORC
ORCANET
ORCANETTE
ORCEIN
ORCHAMUS
ORCHANET
ORCHARD
ORCHARDING
ORCHARDIST
ORCHARDMAN
ORCHARDMEN
ORCHEITIS
ORCHEN
ORCHESIS
ORCHESTIAN
ORCHESTIC
ORCHESTIID
ORCHESTRA
ORCHESTRAL
ORCHESTRALLY
ORCHESTRATE
ORCHESTRATED
ORCHESTRATER
ORCHESTRATING
ORCHESTRATION
ORCHESTRATOR
ORCHESTRIC
ORCHESTRION
ORCHIALGIA
ORCHIC
ORCHICHOREA
ORCHID
ORCHIDACEAN
ORCHIDACEOUS
ORCHIDALGIA
ORCHIDECTOMY
ORCHIDIST
ORCHIDITIS
ORCHIDOCELE
ORCHIDOLOGIST
ORCHIDOLOGY
ORCHIDOPEXY
ORCHIDOTOMY
ORCHIDS
ORCHIECTOMY
ORCHIL
ORCHILLA
ORCHILYTIC
ORCHIOCELE
ORCHIODYNIA
ORCHIONCUS
ORCHIOPEXY
ORCHIOPLASTY
ORCHIOTOMY
ORCHIS
ORCHISES
ORCHITIC
ORCHITIS
ORCHOTOMY
ORCIN
ORCINE
ORCINOL
ORDAIN
ORDAINABLE
ORDAINED
ORDAINER
ORDAINING
ORDAINMENT
ORDALIAN
ORDALIUM
ORDANCHITE
ORDEAL
ORDENE
ORDER
ORDERABLE
ORDERED
ORDEREDNESS
ORDERER
ORDERING
ORDERLESS
ORDERLIES
ORDERLINESS
ORDERLY
ORDERS
ORDINABILITY
ORDINABLE
ORDINAL
ORDINANCE
ORDINAND
ORDINANT
ORDINAR
ORDINARIES
ORDINARILY
ORDINARINESS
ORDINARY
ORDINATE
ORDINATED
ORDINATING
ORDINATION
ORDINATIVE
ORDINATOR
ORDINEE
ORDINES
ORDNANCE
ORDO
ORDONNANCE
ORDONNANT
ORDOS
ORDOSITE
ORDU
ORDURE

ORDUROUS
ORE
OREAD
ORECCHION
ORECTIC
ORECTIVE
OREGANO
OREIDE
OREILET
OREILLER
OREILLETTE
OREJON
ORELLIN
OREMUS
ORENDA
ORENDITE
OREOPHASINE
OREOPITHECUS
OREOTRAGINE
ORES
OREWEED
OREWOOD
OREXIS
ORF
ORFE
ORFEVRERIE
ORFGILD
ORFRAY
ORGAMENT
ORGAMY
ORGAN
ORGANA
ORGANAL
ORGANBIRD
ORGANDIE
ORGANDIES
ORGANDY
ORGANELLA
ORGANELLAE
ORGANELLE
ORGANER
ORGANETTE
ORGANIC
ORGANICAL
ORGANICALLY
ORGANICISM
ORGANICISMAL
ORGANICIST
ORGANICISTIC
ORGANICITY
ORGANIFIC
ORGANIFIER
ORGANIFY
ORGANING
ORGANISATION
ORGANISE
ORGANISM
ORGANISMAL
ORGANISMIC
ORGANISMS
ORGANIST
ORGANISTIC
ORGANISTRUM
ORGANITY
ORGANIZABLE
ORGANIZATION
ORGANIZATIONAL
ORGANIZATORY
ORGANIZE
ORGANIZED
ORGANIZER
ORGANIZING
ORGANOGEL
ORGANOGEN
ORGANOGENIC
ORGANOGENIST
ORGANOGENY
ORGANOGRAPHY
ORGANOID
ORGANOLEPTIC
ORGANOLOGIC
ORGANOLOGIST
ORGANOLOGY
ORGANON
ORGANONOMIC
ORGANONOMY
ORGANONS
ORGANONYMAL
ORGANONYMIC
ORGANONYMY
ORGANONYN
ORGANOPATHY
ORGANOPHONE
ORGANOPHONIC
ORGANOPHYLY
ORGANOSCOPY
ORGANOSOL
ORGANOTROPY
ORGANRY
ORGANULE
ORGANUM
ORGANUMS
ORGANY
ORGANZA
ORGANZINE
ORGANZINED
ORGANZINING
ORGASM
ORGASMIC
ORGASTIC
ORGEAT
ORGIA
ORGIAC
ORGIACS
ORGIASM
ORGIAST
ORGIASTIC
ORGIASTICAL
ORGIC
ORGIES
ORGONE
ORGUE
ORGUEIL
ORGUIL
ORGUINETTE
ORGUL
ORGULOUS
ORGULOUSLY
ORGY
ORGYIA
ORHAMWOOD
ORIBATID
ORIBI
ORIBIS
ORICHALC
ORICHALCEOUS
ORICHALCH
ORICHALCUM
ORIEL
ORIENCY
ORIENT
ORIENTAL
ORIENTALISM
ORIENTALIST
ORIENTALITY
ORIENTALIZE
ORIENTALIZED
ORIENTALIZING
ORIENTALLY
ORIENTATE
ORIENTATED
ORIENTATING
ORIENTATION
ORIENTATIVE
ORIENTATOR
ORIENTED
ORIENTING
ORIENTITE
ORIENTIZE
ORIENTNESS
ORIFACIAL
ORIFICE
ORIFICIAL
ORIFLAMB
ORIFLAMME
ORIFORM
ORIGAMI
ORIGAN
ORIGANIZED
ORIGIN
ORIGINABLE
ORIGINAL
ORIGINALIST
ORIGINALITIES
ORIGINALITY
ORIGINALLY
ORIGINANT
ORIGINARILY
ORIGINARY
ORIGINATE
ORIGINATED
ORIGINATING
ORIGINATION
ORIGINATIVE
ORIGINATIVELY
ORIGINATOR
ORIGINATRESS
ORIGINES
ORIGINIST
ORIGNAL
ORIHON
ORILLON
ORINASAL
ORINASALITY
ORIOLE
ORISHA
ORISMOLOGIC
ORISMOLOGY
ORISON
ORISTIC
ORKEY
ORKYN
ORLAGE
ORLE
ORLEAN
ORLET
ORLO
ORLOP
ORMER
ORMOLU
ORMUZINE
ORN
ORNA
ORNAMENT
ORNAMENTAL
ORNAMENTALLY
ORNAMENTARY
ORNAMENTATION
ORNAMENTED
ORNAMENTER
ORNAMENTING
ORNAMENTIST
ORNAMENTS
ORNARY
ORNATE
ORNATELY
ORNATENESS
ORNATION
ORNATURE
ORNE
ORNERINESS
ORNERY
ORNES
ORNIFY
ORNIS
ORNISCOPIC
ORNISCOPIST
ORNISCOPY
ORNITHIC
ORNITHICHNITE
ORNITHINE
ORNITHOGAL
ORNITHOID
ORNITHOLITE
ORNITHOLITIC
ORNITHOLOGIC
ORNITHOLOGIST
ORNITHOLOGY
ORNITHOMANCY
ORNITHOMANIA
ORNITHON
ORNITHOPHILE
ORNITHOPHILY
ORNITHOPOD
ORNITHOPTER
ORNITHOSCOPY
ORNITHOSIS
ORNITHOTOMY
ORNITHURIC
ORNITHUROUS
ORNOITE
ORO
OROANAL
OROBANCHEOUS
OROCRATIC
OROGEN
OROGENESIS
OROGENESY
OROGENETIC
OROGENIC
OROGENY
OROGRAPH
OROGRAPHIC
OROGRAPHICAL
OROGRAPHY
OROIDE
OROLOGICAL
OROLOGIST
OROLOGY
OROMETER
OROMETRIC
OROMETRY
ORONOCO
ORONOKO
ORONOOKO
OROPHARYNGES
OROPHARYNX
OROPHARYNXES
OROTUND
OROTUNDITY
ORP
ORPED
ORPHAN
ORPHANAGE
ORPHANED
ORPHANHOOD
ORPHANING
ORPHANRY
ORPHARION
ORPHEON
ORPHEONIST
ORPHEUM
ORPHIC
ORPHICAL
ORPHICALLY
ORPHREY
ORPHREYED
ORPHREYS
ORPIMENT
ORPIN
ORPINE
ORPIT
ORRA
ORRERIES
ORRERY
ORRHOID
ORRHOLOGY
ORRHOTHERAPY
ORRICE
ORRIS
ORRISROOT
ORROW
ORSEDE
ORSEDUE
ORSEILLE
ORSEILLINE
ORSEL
ORSELLER
ORSELLINATE
ORSELLINIC
ORT
ORTALID
ORTALIDIAN
ORTERDE
ORTHAL
ORTHIAN
ORTHICON
ORTHID
ORTHITE
ORTHITIC
ORTHO
ORTHOBIOSIS
ORTHOBORATE
ORTHOCARPOUS
ORTHOCENTER
ORTHOCENTRE
ORTHOCENTRIC
ORTHOCLASE
ORTHOCLASITE
ORTHOCLASTIC
ORTHOCYMENE
ORTHODIAGRAM
ORTHODONTIA
ORTHODONTIC
ORTHODONTICS
ORTHODONTIST
ORTHODOX
ORTHODOXAL
ORTHODOXALLY
ORTHODOXIAN
ORTHODOXICAL
ORTHODOXIES
ORTHODOXISM
ORTHODOXIST
ORTHODOXLY
ORTHODOXNESS
ORTHODOXY
ORTHODROMIC
ORTHODROMICS
ORTHODROMY
ORTHOEPIC
ORTHOEPICAL
ORTHOEPIST
ORTHOEPISTIC
ORTHOEPY
ORTHOGENESIS
ORTHOGENETIC
ORTHOGENIC
ORTHOGNATHIC
ORTHOGNATHUS
ORTHOGNATHY
ORTHOGONAL
ORTHOGONALLY
ORTHOGONIAL
ORTHOGRADE

ORTHOGRANITE
ORTHOGRAPH
ORTHOGRAPHER
ORTHOGRAPHIC
ORTHOGRAPHIES
ORTHOGRAPHY
ORTHOLOGER
ORTHOLOGIAN
ORTHOLOGICAL
ORTHOLOGY
ORTHOMETOPIC
ORTHOMETRIC
ORTHOMETRY
ORTHOPAEDIA
ORTHOPAEDIC
ORTHOPAEDICS
ORTHOPAEDIST
ORTHOPAEDY
ORTHOPATH
ORTHOPATHIC
ORTHOPATHY
ORTHOPEDIA
ORTHOPEDIC
ORTHOPEDICS
ORTHOPEDIST
ORTHOPEDY
ORTHOPHONIC
ORTHOPHONY
ORTHOPHORIA
ORTHOPHORIC
ORTHOPHYRE
ORTHOPHYRIC
ORTHOPLASTIC
ORTHOPLASY
ORTHOPNEA
ORTHOPNEIC
ORTHOPNOEA
ORTHOPNOEIC
ORTHOPRAXY
ORTHOPRISM
ORTHOPTER
ORTHOPTERAL
ORTHOPTERAN
ORTHOPTERIST
ORTHOPTEROID
ORTHOPTERON
ORTHOPTEROUS
ORTHOPTIC
ORTHOPTICS
ORTHORHOMBIC
ORTHORRHAPHY
ORTHOSCOPE
ORTHOSCOPIC
ORTHOSE
ORTHOSILICIC
ORTHOSIS
ORTHOSITE
ORTHOSOMATIC
ORTHOSTATIC
ORTHOSTICHIES
ORTHOSTICHY
ORTHOSTYLE
ORTHOTACTIC
ORTHOTECTIC
ORTHOTIC
ORTHOTOMIC
ORTHOTONE
ORTHOTONESIS
ORTHOTONIC
ORTHOTONUS
ORTHOTROPAL
ORTHOTROPIC
ORTHOTROPISM
ORTHOTROPOUS
ORTHOTROPY
ORTHOTYPE
ORTHOTYPOUS
ORTHRON
ORTHROS
ORTIGA
ORTIVE
ORTOLAN
ORTS
ORTSTALER
ORTSTEIN
ORTYGAN
ORTYGINE
ORVET
ORVIETAN
ORVIETITE
ORY
ORYCTICS
ORYCTOGNOSY
ORYCTOLOGIC
ORYCTOLOGIST
ORYCTOLOGY
ORYSSID
ORYX
ORYXES
ORYZANIN
ORYZANINE
ORYZENIN
ORYZIVOROUS
OS
OSAMINE
OSAR
OSAZONE
OSCELLA
OSCHEITIS
OSCHEOCELE
OSCHEOLITH
OSCHEOMA
OSCHEONCUS
OSCHEOPLASTY
OSCILLANCE
OSCILLANCY
OSCILLANT
OSCILLATE
OSCILLATED
OSCILLATING
OSCILLATION
OSCILLATIVE
OSCILLATOR
OSCILLATORY
OSCILLOGRAM
OSCILLOGRAPH
OSCILLOMETER
OSCILLOMETRY
OSCILLOSCOPE
OSCIN
OSCINE
OSCINIAN
OSCININE
OSCITANCE
OSCITANCIES
OSCITANCY
OSCITANT
OSCITANTLY
OSCITATE
OSCITATION
OSCNODE
OSCULA
OSCULABLE
OSCULANT
OSCULAR
OSCULARITY
OSCULATE
OSCULATED
OSCULATING
OSCULATION
OSCULATORIES
OSCULATORY
OSCULATRIX
OSCULATRIXES
OSCULE
OSCULIFEROUS
OSCULUM
OSCURANTIST
OSE
OSELA
OSELE
OSELLA
OSELLE
OSHAC
OSID
OSIDE
OSIER
OSIERED
OSIERIES
OSIERS
OSIERY
OSITE
OSKEN
OSMATE
OSMATIC
OSMATISM
OSMAZOMATIC
OSMAZOMATOUS
OSMAZOME
OSMESIS
OSMETERIA
OSMETERIUM
OSMIC
OSMICS
OSMIDROSIS
OSMIN
OSMIOUS
OSMIRIDIUM
OSMIUM
OSMOGENE
OSMOGRAPH
OSMOLAGNIA
OSMOLOGY
OSMOMETER
OSMOMETRIC
OSMOMETRY
OSMOND
OSMONDITE
OSMOSCOPE
OSMOSE
OSMOSED
OSMOSING
OSMOSIS
OSMOTACTIC
OSMOTAXIS
OSMOTHERAPY
OSMOTIC
OSMOTICALLY
OSMOUS
OSMUND
OSMUNDACEOUS
OSMUNDINE
OSNABURG
OSOBERRIES
OSOBERRY
OSONE
OSOPHIES
OSOPHY
OSPHRADIA
OSPHRADIAL
OSPHRADIUM
OSPHRESIS
OSPHRETIC
OSPHYALGIA
OSPHYALGIC
OSPHYITIS
OSPHYOCELE
OSPREY
OSPREYS
OSS
OSSA
OSSAL
OSSARIUM
OSSATURE
OSSE
OSSEIN
OSSELET
OSSEMENTS
OSSEOMUCOID
OSSEOUS
OSSEOUSLY
OSSIA
OSSICLE
OSSICULA
OSSICULAR
OSSICULATE
OSSICULATED
OSSICULE
OSSICULOTOMY
OSSICULUM
OSSIFEROUS
OSSIFIC
OSSIFICATION
OSSIFIED
OSSIFIER
OSSIFLUENCE
OSSIFLUENT
OSSIFORM
OSSIFRAGE
OSSIFRANGENT
OSSIFY
OSSIFYING
OSSIVOROUS
OSSUARIES
OSSUARIUM
OSSUARY
OSSYPITE
OSTALGIA
OSTARTHRITIS
OSTE
OSTEAL
OSTEALGIA
OSTECTOMY
OSTEECTOMY
OSTEECTOPIA
OSTEECTOPY
OSTEIN
OSTEITIC
OSTEITIS
OSTEMIA
OSTEMPYESIS
OSTEND
OSTENSIBLE
OSTENSIBLY
OSTENSION
OSTENSIVE
OSTENSIVELY
OSTENSORIA
OSTENSORIES
OSTENSORIUM
OSTENSORY
OSTENT
OSTENTATE
OSTENTATION
OSTENTATIOUS
OSTENTATIOUSLY
OSTEOBLAST
OSTEOBLASTIC
OSTEOCELE
OSTEOCLASIA
OSTEOCLASIS
OSTEOCLAST
OSTEOCLASTIC
OSTEOCLASTY
OSTEOCOLLA
OSTEOCOMMA
OSTEOCRANIUM
OSTEOCYSTOMA
OSTEODENTINE
OSTEODERM
OSTEODERMAL
OSTEODERMIA
OSTEODERMIS
OSTEODERMOUS
OSTEODYNIA
OSTEOFIBROUS
OSTEOGEN
OSTEOGENESIS
OSTEOGENETIC
OSTEOGENIC
OSTEOGENIST
OSTEOGENOUS
OSTEOGENY
OSTEOGLOSSID
OSTEOGRAPHER
OSTEOGRAPHY
OSTEOID
OSTEOLITE
OSTEOLOGIC
OSTEOLOGICAL
OSTEOLOGIST
OSTEOLOGY
OSTEOLYSIS
OSTEOLYTIC
OSTEOMA
OSTEOMALACIA
OSTEOMALACIC
OSTEOMANCY
OSTEOMANTY
OSTEOMAS
OSTEOMATA
OSTEOMATOID
OSTEOME
OSTEOMERE
OSTEOMETRIC
OSTEOMETRY
OSTEONCUS
OSTEOPATH
OSTEOPATHIC
OSTEOPATHIST
OSTEOPATHY
OSTEOPHAGIA
OSTEOPHONE
OSTEOPHONY
OSTEOPHORE
OSTEOPHYMA
OSTEOPHYTE
OSTEOPHYTIC
OSTEOPLAQUE
OSTEOPLAST
OSTEOPLASTIC
OSTEOPLASTIES
OSTEOPLASTY
OSTEOPOROSIS
OSTEOPOROTIC
OSTEORRHAPHY
OSTEOSARCOMA
OSTEOSCOPE
OSTEOSTIXIS
OSTEOSTOMOUS
OSTEOTOME
OSTEOTOMIES
OSTEOTOMIST
OSTEOTOMY
OSTEOTRIBE
OSTEOTRITE
OSTEOTROPHY
OSTERIA
OSTIA
OSTIAL
OSTIARIES
OSTIARY
OSTIATE
OSTINATO
OSTIOLAR

OSTIOLATE
OSTIOLE
OSTITIS
OSTIUM
OSTLER
OSTLERESS
OSTMARK
OSTOMATID
OSTOSIS
OSTRACA
OSTRACEAN
OSTRACEOUS
OSTRACINE
OSTRACIOID
OSTRACISE
OSTRACISM
OSTRACITE
OSTRACIZATION
OSTRACIZE
OSTRACIZED
OSTRACIZER
OSTRACIZING
OSTRACOD
OSTRACODE
OSTRACODERM
OSTRACODOUS
OSTRACON
OSTRACOPHORE
OSTRACUM
OSTRAITE
OSTREACEOUS
OSTREGER
OSTREIFORM
OSTREOID
OSTREOPHAGE
OSTRICH
OSTRICHES
OSTRICHLIKE
OTACOUSTIC
OTACOUSTICON
OTACUST
OTALGIA
OTALGIC
OTALGY
OTARIAN
OTARIES
OTARIINE
OTARINE
OTARIOID
OTARY
OTATE
OTECTOMY
OTELCOSIS
OTHAEMATOMA
OTHELCOSIS
OTHEMATOMA
OTHEMATOMATA
OTHEMORRHEA
OTHEOSCOPE
OTHER
OTHEREST
OTHERGATES
OTHERGUESS
OTHERGUISE
OTHERHOW
OTHERISM
OTHERIST
OTHERNESS
OTHERS
OTHERSOME
OTHERTIME
OTHERTIMES
OTHERWHENCE
OTHERWHERE
OTHERWHERES
OTHERWHILE
OTHERWHILES
OTHERWHITHER
OTHERWISE
OTHERWORLDLY
OTHMANY
OTHYGROMA
OTIANT
OTIATRIC
OTIATRICS
OTIATRY
OTIC
OTICODINIA
OTIDIA
OTIDIFORM
OTIDINE
OTIDIUM
OTIORHYNCHID
OTIOSE
OTIOSELY
OTIOSENESS
OTIOSITY
OTITIC
OTITIS
OTIUM
OTKON
OTOANTRITIS
OTOCARIASIS
OTOCLEISIS
OTOCONIA
OTOCONIAL
OTOCONITE
OTOCONIUM
OTOCRANIAL
OTOCRANIC
OTOCRANIUM
OTOCYST
OTOCYSTIC
OTODYNIA
OTODYNIC
OTOGENIC
OTOGENOUS
OTOGRAPHICAL
OTOGRAPHY
OTOLITE
OTOLITH
OTOLITIC
OTOLOGICAL
OTOLOGIST
OTOLOGY
OTOMASSAGE
OTOMYCES
OTOMYCOSIS
OTONEURALGIA
OTOPATHIC
OTOPATHY
OTOPHONE
OTOPIESIS
OTOPLASTIC
OTOPLASTY
OTOPOLYPUS
OTOPYORRHEA
OTOPYOSIS
OTORRHAGIA
OTORRHEA
OTORRHOEA
OTOSCLEROSIS
OTOSCOPE
OTOSCOPIC
OTOSCOPY
OTOSIS
OTOSTEAL
OTOSTEON
OTOTOI
OTOTOMY
OTTAJANITE
OTTAR
OTTAVA
OTTAVARIMA
OTTAVE
OTTAVINO
OTTER
OTTERER
OTTERHOUND
OTTETTO
OTTINGER
OTTO
OTTOMAN
OTTRELITE
OTTROYE
OU
OUABAIN
OUABAIO
OUABE
OUACHITITE
OUAKARI
OUANANICHE
OUANGA
OUBLIANCE
OUBLIET
OUBLIETTE
OUCH
OUD
OUDENARDE
OUED
OUENITE
OUF
OUGH
OUGHT
OUGHTLINGS
OUGHTLINS
OUGLE
OUIJA
OUISTITI
OUK
OUKIA
OULAP
OULK
OUNCE
OUNDING
OUNDY
OUPH
OUPHE
OUR
OURANG
OURARI
OURE
OUREBI
OURICURY
OURIE
OUROUB
OURS
OURSEL
OURSELF
OURSELS
OURSELVES
OUSEL
OUSIA
OUST
OUSTED
OUSTEE
OUSTER
OUSTING
OUT
OUTACT
OUTADMIRAL
OUTAGE
OUTAMBUSH
OUTARDE
OUTARGUE
OUTAS
OUTASK
OUTBABBLE
OUTBACK
OUTBACKER
OUTBADE
OUTBAKE
OUTBALANCE
OUTBANTER
OUTBARGAIN
OUTBARK
OUTBAWL
OUTBEAM
OUTBEAR
OUTBEARING
OUTBEG
OUTBEGGAR
OUTBELCH
OUTBELLOW
OUTBETTER
OUTBID
OUTBIDDEN
OUTBIDDER
OUTBIDDING
OUTBIRTH
OUTBLACKEN
OUTBLAZE
OUTBLEAT
OUTBLESS
OUTBLOOM
OUTBLOSSOM
OUTBLOWN
OUTBLUFF
OUTBLUNDER
OUTBLUSH
OUTBLUSTER
OUTBOARD
OUTBOAST
OUTBOND
OUTBOOK
OUTBORE
OUTBORN
OUTBORNE
OUTBOUND
OUTBOWL
OUTBOX
OUTBRAG
OUTBRAID
OUTBRAVE
OUTBRAVED
OUTBRAVING
OUTBRAZEN
OUTBREAK
OUTBREAKING
OUTBREATHE
OUTBREATHER
OUTBRED
OUTBREED
OUTBREEDING
OUTBRIBE
OUTBUILD
OUTBUILDING
OUTBULK
OUTBULLY
OUTBURN
OUTBURST
OUTBUY
OUTBUZZ
OUTBY
OUTBYE
OUTCAME
OUTCANT
OUTCAPER
OUTCAROL
OUTCARRY
OUTCASE
OUTCAST
OUTCASTE
OUTCASTED
OUTCASTING
OUTCASTS
OUTCAVIL
OUTCEPT
OUTCHAMBER
OUTCHARM
OUTCHATTER
OUTCHEAT
OUTCHIDE
OUTCLASS
OUTCLIMB
OUTCOME
OUTCOMER
OUTCOMING
OUTCOMPASS
OUTCOMPLETE
OUTCOUNTRY
OUTCRAWL
OUTCRICKET
OUTCRIED
OUTCRIER
OUTCRIES
OUTCROP
OUTCROPPED
OUTCROPPER
OUTCROPPING
OUTCROSS
OUTCROSSING
OUTCROW
OUTCRY
OUTCRYING
OUTCURE
OUTCURSE
OUTCURVE
OUTCURVED
OUTCURVING
OUTDANCE
OUTDARE
OUTDATE
OUTDATED
OUTDATING
OUTDAZZLE
OUTDEVIL
OUTDID
OUTDISPATCH
OUTDISTANCE
OUTDISTANCED
OUTDISTANCING
OUTDO
OUTDODGE
OUTDOER
OUTDOING
OUTDONE
OUTDOOR
OUTDOORS
OUTDOORSMAN
OUTDOORSMEN
OUTDRAFT
OUTDRAGON
OUTDRAUGHT
OUTDREAM
OUTDRESS
OUTDRINK
OUTDRIVE
OUTDURE
OUTDWELLER
OUTE
OUTEAT
OUTECHO
OUTED
OUTEN
OUTER
OUTERLY
OUTERMOST
OUTERWEAR
OUTFABLE
OUTFACE
OUTFACED
OUTFACING
OUTFALL
OUTFAME

OUTFAST
OUTFAWN
OUTFEAST
OUTFEAT
OUTFERRET
OUTFICTION
OUTFIELD
OUTFIELDER
OUTFIELDSMAN
OUTFIELDSMEN
OUTFIGHT
OUTFIGHTER
OUTFIGHTING
OUTFISH
OUTFIT
OUTFITTED
OUTFITTER
OUTFITTING
OUTFLANK
OUTFLANKER
OUTFLANKING
OUTFLATTER
OUTFLING
OUTFLOAT
OUTFLOW
OUTFLUNKY
OUTFLUSH
OUTFLUX
OUTFLY
OUTFOOL
OUTFOOT
OUTFORM
OUTFORT
OUTFORTH
OUTFOX
OUTFRONT
OUTFROWN
OUTGABBLE
OUTGAIN
OUTGALLOP
OUTGAMBLE
OUTGAME
OUTGANG
OUTGARTH
OUTGATE
OUTGAUGE
OUTGAZE
OUTGENERAL
OUTGENERALED
OUTGENERALING
OUTGENERALLED
OUTGENERALLING
OUTGIVE
OUTGIVING
OUTGLAD
OUTGLARE
OUTGLITTER
OUTGLOW
OUTGNAW
OUTGO
OUTGOER
OUTGOES
OUTGOING
OUTGONE
OUTGREEN
OUTGREW
OUTGRIN
OUTGROWING
OUTGROWN
OUTGROWTH
OUTGUARD
OUTGUESS
OUTGUN
OUTGUSH
OUTHAMMER
OUTHASTEN
OUTHAUL
OUTHAULER
OUTHEAR
OUTHECTOR
OUTHEEL
OUTHER
OUTHIT
OUTHOLD
OUTHORN
OUTHORROR
OUTHOUSE
OUTHOUSING
OUTHOWL
OUTHUE
OUTHUMOR
OUTHUNT
OUTHUT
OUTHYMN
OUTIMAGE
OUTING
OUTINVENT
OUTISH
OUTJAZZ
OUTJINX
OUTJOCKEY
OUTJOURNEY
OUTJUGGLE
OUTJUMP
OUTJUT
OUTKEEPER
OUTKICK
OUTKILL
OUTKING
OUTKISS
OUTKNAVE
OUTKNEE
OUTLABOR
OUTLAND
OUTLANDER
OUTLANDISH
OUTLANDISHLY
OUTLASH
OUTLAST
OUTLAUGH
OUTLAW
OUTLAWED
OUTLAWING
OUTLAWRIES
OUTLAWRY
OUTLAY
OUTLEAP
OUTLEARN
OUTLEGEND
OUTLER
OUTLET
OUTLIE
OUTLIER
OUTLIGHTEN
OUTLIMN
OUTLINE
OUTLINEAR
OUTLINED
OUTLINER
OUTLINGER
OUTLINING
OUTLIVE
OUTLIVED
OUTLIVER
OUTLIVING
OUTLODGING
OUTLOOK
OUTLOOKER
OUTLOPE
OUTLORD
OUTLOVE
OUTLUNG
OUTLUSTER
OUTLY
OUTLYING
OUTMAGIC
OUTMALAPROP
OUTMAN
OUTMANEUVER
OUTMANNED
OUTMANNING
OUTMANTLE
OUTMARCH
OUTMARRIAGE
OUTMARRY
OUTMASTER
OUTMATCH
OUTMATE
OUTMEASURE
OUTMIRACLE
OUTMODE
OUTMODED
OUTMOST
OUTMOUNT
OUTMOUTH
OUTMOVE
OUTNAME
OUTNESS
OUTNIGHT
OUTNOISE
OUTNUMBER
OUTPAGE
OUTPAINT
OUTPARAGON
OUTPARAMOUR
OUTPARISH
OUTPART
OUTPARTS
OUTPASS
OUTPASSION
OUTPATIENT
OUTPAYMENT
OUTPEER
OUTPENSION
OUTPENSIONER
OUTPERFORM
OUTPICK
OUTPICKET
OUTPIPE
OUTPITCH
OUTPITY
OUTPLACE
OUTPLAN
OUTPLAY
OUTPLAYED
OUTPLEASE
OUTPLOD
OUTPLOT
OUTPOCKETING
OUTPOINT
OUTPOISE
OUTPOISON
OUTPOLL
OUTPOMP
OUTPOPULATE
OUTPORT
OUTPORTER
OUTPORTION
OUTPOST
OUTPOUR
OUTPOURED
OUTPOURER
OUTPOURING
OUTPRACTICE
OUTPRAISE
OUTPRAY
OUTPREACH
OUTPREEN
OUTPRICE
OUTPRODIGY
OUTPRODUCE
OUTPROMISE
OUTPRY
OUTPULL
OUTPURL
OUTPURSE
OUTPUSH
OUTPUT
OUTPUTTER
OUTQUEEN
OUTQUESTION
OUTQUIBBLE
OUTQUOTE
OUTRACE
OUTRAGE
OUTRAGED
OUTRAGELY
OUTRAGEOUS
OUTRAGEOUSLY
OUTRAGER
OUTRAGING
OUTRAIL
OUTRAKE
OUTRAN
OUTRANCE
OUTRANGE
OUTRANK
OUTRANT
OUTRAP
OUTRATE
OUTRAVE
OUTRAY
OUTRAZE
OUTRE
OUTREACH
OUTREASON
OUTRECKON
OUTREDDEN
OUTREIGN
OUTRELIEF
OUTREMER
OUTRHYME
OUTRIDDEN
OUTRIDE
OUTRIDER
OUTRIDING
OUTRIG
OUTRIGGED
OUTRIGGER
OUTRIGGERED
OUTRIGGING
OUTRIGHT
OUTRIGHTLY
OUTRIGHTNESS
OUTRIVAL
OUTRIVE
OUTROAD
OUTROAR
OUTRODE
OUTROGUE
OUTROLL
OUTROMANCE
OUTROOP
OUTROOPER
OUTROOT
OUTROVE
OUTROW
OUTROYAL
OUTRUN
OUTRUNNER
OUTRUNNING
OUTRUSH
OUTS
OUTSAIL
OUTSAINT
OUTSAT
OUTSATISFY
OUTSAVOR
OUTSCAPE
OUTSCENT
OUTSCOLD
OUTSCORE
OUTSCORN
OUTSCOUR
OUTSCOURING
OUTSCOUT
OUTSCREAM
OUTSEA
OUTSEE
OUTSELL
OUTSELLING
OUTSEND
OUTSENTINEL
OUTSENTRY
OUTSERT
OUTSET
OUTSETTING
OUTSHADOW
OUTSHAKE
OUTSHAME
OUTSHARP
OUTSHARPEN
OUTSHEATHE
OUTSHIFTS
OUTSHINE
OUTSHINER
OUTSHINING
OUTSHONE
OUTSHOOT
OUTSHOOTING
OUTSHOT
OUTSHOUT
OUTSHOWER
OUTSHRIEK
OUTSHUT
OUTSIDE
OUTSIDED
OUTSIDER
OUTSIDES
OUTSIGHT
OUTSIN
OUTSING
OUTSIT
OUTSITTING
OUTSIZE
OUTSIZED
OUTSKILL
OUTSKIP
OUTSKIRMISH
OUTSKIRT
OUTSKIRTER
OUTSKIRTS
OUTSLANDER
OUTSLANG
OUTSLEEP
OUTSLING
OUTSLIP
OUTSMART
OUTSMILE
OUTSNORE
OUTSOAR
OUTSOLD
OUTSOLE
OUTSOLER
OUTSONNET
OUTSOUND
OUTSPAN
OUTSPANNED
OUTSPANNING
OUTSPARKLE
OUTSPEAK
OUTSPEAKER
OUTSPEAKING
OUTSPEECH
OUTSPEED

OUTSPEND
OUTSPENT
OUTSPIT
OUTSPLENDOR
OUTSPOKE
OUTSPOKEN
OUTSPOKENLY
OUTSPORT
OUTSPOUT
OUTSPREAD
OUTSPREADING
OUTSPRINT
OUTSTAGGER
OUTSTAID
OUTSTAND
OUTSTANDER
OUTSTANDING
OUTSTANDINGLY
OUTSTARE
OUTSTART
OUTSTARTER
OUTSTATE
OUTSTATION
OUTSTATURE
OUTSTAY
OUTSTAYED
OUTSTAYING
OUTSTEP
OUTSTING
OUTSTINK
OUTSTOOD
OUTSTORM
OUTSTRETCH
OUTSTRETCHED
OUTSTRETCHER
OUTSTRETCHING
OUTSTRIDE
OUTSTRIP
OUTSTRIPPED
OUTSTRIPPING
OUTSTRIVE
OUTSTROKE
OUTSTRUT
OUTSTUDY
OUTSTUNT
OUTSUBTLE
OUTSUCKEN
OUTSUFFER
OUTSUITOR
OUTSULK
OUTSUM
OUTSWAGGER
OUTSWEAR
OUTSWEEPING
OUTSWEETEN
OUTSWELL
OUTSWIFT
OUTSWIM
OUTSWINDLE
OUTTAKE
OUTTAKEN
OUTTALENT
OUTTALK
OUTTASK
OUTTASTE
OUTTEASE
OUTTELL
OUTTELLING
OUTTHIEVE
OUTTHINK
OUTTHREATEN
OUTTHROB
OUTTHROUGH
OUTTHROW
OUTTHRUST
OUTTHWACK
OUTTOIL
OUTTOLD
OUTTONGUE
OUTTOP
OUTTOPPED
OUTTOPPING
OUTTOWER
OUTTRADE
OUTTRAIL
OUTTRAVEL
OUTTRICK
OUTTROT
OUTTRUMP
OUTTURN
OUTTURNED
OUTTWINE
OUTTYRANNIZE
OUTUSURE
OUTVALUE
OUTVAUNT
OUTVELVET
OUTVENOM
OUTVICTOR
OUTVIE
OUTVILLAIN
OUTVOICE
OUTVOTE
OUTVOTER
OUTWAIT
OUTWAKE
OUTWALE
OUTWALK
OUTWALL
OUTWALLOP
OUTWAR
OUTWARBLE
OUTWARD
OUTWARDLY
OUTWARDS
OUTWASH
OUTWASTE
OUTWATCH
OUTWAY
OUTWEALTH
OUTWEAPON
OUTWEAR
OUTWEARING
OUTWEARY
OUTWEIGH
OUTWEIGHT
OUTWENT
OUTWHIRL
OUTWICK
OUTWILE
OUTWILL
OUTWIN
OUTWIND
OUTWING
OUTWISH
OUTWIT
OUTWITH
OUTWITTAL
OUTWITTED
OUTWITTER
OUTWITTING
OUTWOE
OUTWOMAN
OUTWORD
OUTWORE
OUTWORK
OUTWORKED
OUTWORKING
OUTWORLD
OUTWORN
OUTWORTH
OUTWRANGLE
OUTWREST
OUTWRESTLE
OUTWRIGGLE
OUTWRITE
OUTWRITING
OUTWRITTEN
OUTWROTE
OUTWROUGHT
OUTYELP
OUTYIELD
OUTZANY
OUVERT
OUVERTE
OUVRAGE
OUVRIER
OUVRIERE
OUYEZD
OUZEL
OUZO
OVA
OVAL
OVALBUMIN
OVALIFORM
OVALIZATION
OVALIZE
OVALNESS
OVALOID
OVALWISE
OVANT
OVARIA
OVARIAL
OVARIAN
OVARIECTOMY
OVARIES
OVARIN
OVARIOCELE
OVARIOCYESIS
OVARIOLE
OVARIOSTOMY
OVARIOTOMIES
OVARIOTOMIST
OVARIOTOMIZE
OVARIOTOMY
OVARIOUS
OVARITIS
OVARIUM
OVARY
OVATE
OVATECONICAL
OVATED
OVATELY
OVATION
OVATIONAL
OVATOCONICAL
OVATOCORDATE
OVATODELTOID
OVATOGLOBOSE
OVATOOBLONG
OVATOSERRATE
OVEN
OVENBIRD
OVENDRY
OVENED
OVENING
OVENLY
OVENMAN
OVENMEN
OVENPEEL
OVENS
OVENSMAN
OVENSTONE
OVENWARE
OVENWISE
OVER
OVERABUNDANCE
OVERABUNDANT
OVERACT
OVERAGE
OVERALL
OVERALLED
OVERALLS
OVERARCH
OVERARM
OVERATE
OVERAWE
OVERAWED
OVERAWING
OVERBADE
OVERBALANCE
OVERBANK
OVERBARISH
OVERBEAR
OVERBEARANCE
OVERBEARER
OVERBEARING
OVERBEARINGLY
OVERBEND
OVERBERG
OVERBID
OVERBIDDEN
OVERBIDDING
OVERBIDE
OVERBIT
OVERBITE
OVERBLEW
OVERBLOUSE
OVERBLOW
OVERBLOWING
OVERBLOWN
OVERBOARD
OVERBODY
OVERBOIL
OVERBOOK
OVERBORE
OVERBORNE
OVERBOUGHT
OVERBOWED
OVERBOWL
OVERBREATHE
OVERBRIBE
OVERBRIDGE
OVERBRIM
OVERBRIMMED
OVERBRIMMING
OVERBROOD
OVERBROW
OVERBUILD
OVERBUILDING
OVERBUILT
OVERBURDEN
OVERBURN
OVERBURST
OVERBUSY
OVERBUY
OVERBUYING
OVERBY
OVERCALL
OVERCAME
OVERCARRY
OVERCAST
OVERCASTING
OVERCATCH
OVERCERTIFY
OVERCHARGE
OVERCHARGED
OVERCHARGER
OVERCHARGING
OVERCHECK
OVERCLOTHES
OVERCLOUD
OVERCOAT
OVERCOATED
OVERCOATING
OVERCOIL
OVERCOME
OVERCOMER
OVERCOMING
OVERCOMPOUND
OVERCONFIDENT
OVERCOOK
OVERCORRECT
OVERCOUNT
OVERCOVER
OVERCROP
OVERCROW
OVERCROWD
OVERCURRENT
OVERCUT
OVERDARE
OVERDATED
OVERDECK
OVERDECORATED
OVERDEN
OVERDEVELOP
OVERDEVELOPED
OVERDID
OVERDO
OVERDOER
OVERDOING
OVERDONE
OVERDOOR
OVERDOSAGE
OVERDOSE
OVERDRAFT
OVERDRAPE
OVERDRAPERY
OVERDRAUGHT
OVERDRAW
OVERDRAWER
OVERDRAWING
OVERDRAWN
OVERDRESS
OVERDREW
OVERDRIED
OVERDRIVE
OVERDRIVEN
OVERDRIVING
OVERDROVE
OVERDUE
OVERDYE
OVERDYED
OVERDYEING
OVEREAGER
OVEREAT
OVEREATEN
OVEREATING
OVERED
OVEREDUCATED
OVERELABORATE
OVERENTER
OVERENTRY
OVEREST
OVERESTIMATE
OVERESTIMATED
OVERESTIMATING
OVEREXERT
OVEREXPOSE
OVEREXPOSED
OVEREXPOSING
OVEREXPOSURE
OVEREYE
OVERFACE
OVERFALL
OVERFALLEN
OVERFALLING
OVERFASTIDIOUS
OVERFED
OVERFEED
OVERFELL
OVERFINE
OVERFISH
OVERFLEW
OVERFLIGHT

OVERFLOAT
OVERFLOOD
OVERFLOURISH
OVERFLOW
OVERFLOWED
OVERFLOWER
OVERFLOWING
OVERFLOWN
OVERFLUSH
OVERFLUTTER
OVERFLY
OVERFLYING
OVERFOLD
OVERFOOT
OVERFREIGHT
OVERFRET
OVERFRIEZE
OVERFULL
OVERGANG
OVERGARMENT
OVERGAZE
OVERGET
OVERGETTING
OVERGILD
OVERGIVE
OVERGLANCE
OVERGLAZE
OVERGLAZED
OVERGLAZING
OVERGLIDE
OVERGLOOM
OVERGO
OVERGOING
OVERGONE
OVERGOT
OVERGOTTEN
OVERGOVERN
OVERGRAIN
OVERGRAINER
OVERGRAZE
OVERGREW
OVERGROUND
OVERGROW
OVERGROWING
OVERGROWN
OVERGROWTH
OVERHAIL
OVERHAIR
OVERHALE
OVERHAND
OVERHANDED
OVERHANG
OVERHANGING
OVERHAUL
OVERHAULED
OVERHAULER
OVERHAULING
OVERHEAD
OVERHEAP
OVERHEAR
OVERHEARD
OVERHEARER
OVERHEARING
OVERHEAT
OVERHEAVE
OVERHIE
OVERHIP
OVERHIT
OVERHUNG
OVERINFORM
OVERING
OVERINSURE
OVERISSUE
OVERISSUED
OVERISSUING
OVERJOY
OVERJUDGE
OVERJUMP
OVERKEEP
OVERKILL
OVERKING
OVERKNEE
OVERKNOW
OVERLABOR
OVERLABORED
OVERLABORING
OVERLABOUR
OVERLABOURED
OVERLABOURING
OVERLADE
OVERLADED
OVERLADEN
OVERLADING
OVERLAID
OVERLAIN
OVERLAND
OVERLANDER
OVERLAP
OVERLAPPED
OVERLAPPING
OVERLASH
OVERLAUNCH
OVERLAVE
OVERLAY
OVERLAYER
OVERLAYING
OVERLEAD
OVERLEAF
OVERLEAP
OVERLEAPED
OVERLEAPING
OVERLEAPT
OVERLEATHER
OVERLEAVE
OVERLEAVEN
OVERLICK
OVERLIE
OVERLIER
OVERLIFT
OVERLINE
OVERLING
OVERLIP
OVERLISTEN
OVERLIVE
OVERLIVER
OVERLOAD
OVERLOADED
OVERLOCK
OVERLOCKER
OVERLONG
OVERLOOK
OVERLOOKED
OVERLOOKER
OVERLOOKING
OVERLORD
OVERLOUP
OVERLOVE
OVERLOVER
OVERLY
OVERLYING
OVERMAN
OVERMANTLE
OVERMARCH
OVERMARK
OVERMARKING
OVERMASK
OVERMAST
OVERMASTER
OVERMATCH
OVERMATURITY
OVERMEASURE
OVERMEN
OVERMICKLE
OVERMIND
OVERMODEST
OVERMORE
OVERMOST
OVERMOUNT
OVERMOUNTS
OVERMUCH
OVERMUSE
OVERNAME
OVERNET
OVERNICE
OVERNICELY
OVERNICETY
OVERNIGHT
OVERNOISE
OVERNUMBER
OVERPAID
OVERPAINT
OVERPART
OVERPARTED
OVERPARTY
OVERPASS
OVERPASSED
OVERPASSING
OVERPAY
OVERPAYING
OVERPAYMENT
OVERPEER
OVERPENDING
OVERPEOPLE
OVERPERSUADE
OVERPERSUADED
OVERPERSUADING
OVERPICK
OVERPICTURE
OVERPITCH
OVERPITCHED
OVERPLAY
OVERPLIED
OVERPLUS
OVERPLY
OVERPLYING
OVERPOLE
OVERPOPULATE
OVERPOPULATED
OVERPOPULATING
OVERPOST
OVERPOT
OVERPOUR
OVERPOWER
OVERPOWERED
OVERPOWERING
OVERPREACH
OVERPRECISE
OVERPRESS
OVERPRICE
OVERPRICED
OVERPRICING
OVERPRINT
OVERPRIZE
OVERPRIZED
OVERPRIZER
OVERPRIZING
OVERPRODUCE
OVERPRODUCED
OVERPRODUCING
OVERPROOF
OVERPROTECT
OVERPURCHASE
OVERPUT
OVERQUELL
OVERRACK
OVERRAKE
OVERRAKED
OVERRAKING
OVERRAN
OVERRATE
OVERRATED
OVERRATING
OVERRAUGHT
OVERREACH
OVERREACHED
OVERREACHER
OVERREACHING
OVERREAD
OVERREADER
OVERREADING
OVERREADY
OVERRECKON
OVERREFINED
OVERREGISTER
OVERRENT
OVERRID
OVERRIDDEN
OVERRIDE
OVERRIDER
OVERRIDING
OVERRIGHT
OVERRIM
OVERRIOT
OVERRIPE
OVERRIPENESS
OVERRISE
OVERRISEN
OVERRISING
OVERRODE
OVERROLL
OVERROOF
OVERROSE
OVERRUFF
OVERRULE
OVERRULED
OVERRULER
OVERRULING
OVERRUN
OVERRUNNER
OVERRUNNING
OVERS
OVERSAID
OVERSAIL
OVERSANDED
OVERSAW
OVERSAY
OVERSCENTED
OVERSCORE
OVERSCORED
OVERSCORING
OVERSCURF
OVERSCUTCHED
OVERSEA
OVERSEAM
OVERSEAMER
OVERSEARCH
OVERSEAS
OVERSEE
OVERSEEING
OVERSEEN
OVERSEER
OVERSELL
OVERSELLING
OVERSENSITIVE
OVERSENTIMENTAL
OVERSET
OVERSETTER
OVERSETTING
OVERSEW
OVERSEWED
OVERSEWING
OVERSEWN
OVERSEXED
OVERSHADE
OVERSHADED
OVERSHADING
OVERSHADOW
OVERSHADOWED
OVERSHADOWER
OVERSHADOWING
OVERSHAVE
OVERSHINE
OVERSHINING
OVERSHIRT
OVERSHOE
OVERSHOES
OVERSHONE
OVERSHOOT
OVERSHOOTING
OVERSHOT
OVERSIDE
OVERSIGHT
OVERSIGNED
OVERSILE
OVERSIZE
OVERSIZED
OVERSKIP
OVERSKIPPER
OVERSKIRT
OVERSLAUGH
OVERSLAUGHED
OVERSLAUGHING
OVERSLEEP
OVERSLEEPING
OVERSLEPT
OVERSLID
OVERSLIDDEN
OVERSLIDE
OVERSLIDING
OVERSLIP
OVERSLIPPED
OVERSLIPPING
OVERSLOP
OVERSMOKE
OVERSNOW
OVERSOFT
OVERSOLD
OVERSOUL
OVERSOUND
OVERSOW
OVERSOWED
OVERSOWING
OVERSOWN
OVERSPAN
OVERSPANNED
OVERSPANNING
OVERSPARRED
OVERSPEAK
OVERSPEAKING
OVERSPEND
OVERSPENDING
OVERSPENT
OVERSPILL
OVERSPIN
OVERSPOKE
OVERSPOKEN
OVERSPREAD
OVERSPREADING
OVERSPRING
OVERSPRUNG
OVERSPUN
OVERSTAID
OVERSTAND
OVERSTANDING
OVERSTATE
OVERSTATED
OVERSTATEMENT
OVERSTATING
OVERSTAY
OVERSTAYAL
OVERSTAYED
OVERSTAYING
OVERSTEP
OVERSTEPPED
OVERSTEPPING

OVERSTITCH
OVERSTOCK
OVERSTOOD
OVERSTOPING
OVERSTORY
OVERSTRAIN
OVERSTRAINED
OVERSTRAINING
OVERSTRAITEN
OVERSTRETCH
OVERSTREW
OVERSTREWED
OVERSTREWING
OVERSTREWN
OVERSTRICKEN
OVERSTRIDDEN
OVERSTRIDE
OVERSTRIDING
OVERSTRIKE
OVERSTRIKING
OVERSTRING
OVERSTRINGING
OVERSTRODE
OVERSTRUCK
OVERSTRUNG
OVERSTUDIED
OVERSTUDY
OVERSTUFF
OVERSUM
OVERSUPPLIED
OVERSUPPLY
OVERSUPPLYING
OVERSWARM
OVERSWAY
OVERSWELL
OVERSWELLED
OVERSWELLING
OVERSWOLLEN
OVERT
OVERTAKE
OVERTAKEN
OVERTAKER
OVERTAKING
OVERTASK
OVERTAX
OVERTAXATION
OVERTAXED
OVERTAXING
OVERTEEM
OVERTELL
OVERTELLING
OVERTEST
OVERTHINK
OVERTHREW
OVERTHROW
OVERTHROWAL
OVERTHROWER
OVERTHROWING
OVERTHROWN
OVERTHRUST
OVERTHWART
OVERTHWARTLY
OVERTIDE
OVERTILT
OVERTIME
OVERTIMED
OVERTIMER
OVERTIMING
OVERTITLE
OVERTLY
OVERTOE
OVERTOIL
OVERTOISE
OVERTOLD
OVERTONE
OVERTOOK
OVERTOP
OVERTOWER
OVERTRACE
OVERTRACK
OVERTRADE
OVERTRADED
OVERTRADER
OVERTRADING
OVERTRAIN
OVERTRAINED
OVERTRAINING
OVERTRAVEL
OVERTREAD
OVERTREADING
OVERTRICK
OVERTROD
OVERTRODDEN
OVERTRUMP
OVERTUMBLE
OVERTURE
OVERTURED
OVERTURING
OVERTURN
OVERTURNED
OVERTURNING
OVERTYPE
OVERUSE
OVERVAULT
OVERVEIL
OVERVIEW
OVERVOLTAGE
OVERVOTE
OVERWADE
OVERWAGES
OVERWAKE
OVERWALK
OVERWART
OVERWASH
OVERWATCH
OVERWATCHER
OVERWEAR
OVERWEARIED
OVERWEARING
OVERWEARY
OVERWEARYING
OVERWEATHER
OVERWEEN
OVERWEENED
OVERWEENER
OVERWEENING
OVERWEEP
OVERWEIGH
OVERWEIGHT
OVERWELT
OVERWEND
OVERWENT
OVERWHELM
OVERWHELMER
OVERWHELMING
OVERWHELMINGLY
OVERWIN
OVERWIND
OVERWINDING
OVERWING
OVERWINNING
OVERWINTER
OVERWIPED
OVERWOMAN
OVERWON
OVERWOOD
OVERWORD
OVERWORE
OVERWORK
OVERWORKED
OVERWORKING
OVERWORN
OVERWOUND
OVERWREST
OVERWRITE
OVERWRITING
OVERWRITTEN
OVERWROTE
OVERWROUGHT
OVERYEAR
OVERZEALOUS
OVEST
OVEY
OVIBOS
OVIBOVINE
OVICAPSULAR
OVICAPSULE
OVICELL
OVICELLULAR
OVICIDAL
OVICIDE
OVICULAR
OVICULATED
OVICULUM
OVICYST
OVICYSTIC
OVIDUCAL
OVIDUCT
OVIDUCTAL
OVIFEROUS
OVIFICATION
OVIFORM
OVIGENESIS
OVIGENETIC
OVIGENIC
OVIGENOUS
OVIGER
OVIGERM
OVIGEROUS
OVILE
OVIN
OVINE
OVINIA
OVIPARA
OVIPARAL
OVIPARITY
OVIPAROUS
OVIPAROUSLY
OVIPOSIT
OVIPOSITED
OVIPOSITING
OVIPOSITION
OVIPOSITOR
OVISAC
OVISM
OVIST
OVISTIC
OVIVOROUS
OVOCYTE
OVOELLIPTIC
OVOGENESIS
OVOGENETIC
OVOGENOUS
OVOGONIUM
OVOID
OVOIDAL
OVOLI
OVOLO
OVOLOGICAL
OVOLOGIST
OVOLOGY
OVOLYTIC
OVOMUCOID
OVOPLASM
OVOPLASMIC
OVOPYRIFORM
OVORHOMBOID
OVOTESTIS
OVULA
OVULAR
OVULARIAN
OVULARY
OVULATE
OVULATED
OVULATING
OVULATION
OVULE
OVULIFEROUS
OVULIGEROUS
OVULITE
OVULUM
OVUM
OW
OWE
OWED
OWELTY
OWER
OWERANCE
OWHERE
OWING
OWL
OWLER
OWLERIES
OWLERY
OWLET
OWLHEAD
OWLING
OWLISH
OWLISHLY
OWLISHNESS
OWLLIGHT
OWLY
OWN
OWNABLE
OWNED
OWNER
OWNERLESS
OWNERSHIP
OWNHOOD
OWNING
OWNNESS
OWNWAYISH
OWRE
OWRECOME
OWREHIP
OWRELAY
OWSE
OWSEN
OWTCHAH
OWYHEEITE
OWZEL
OX
OXADIAZOLE
OXALACETIC
OXALAEMIA
OXALATE
OXALATO
OXALEMIA
OXALIC
OXALIS
OXALURAMID
OXALURAMIDE
OXALURATE
OXALURIA
OXALURIC
OXALYL
OXALYLUREA
OXAMATE
OXAMETHANE
OXAMIC
OXAMIDE
OXAMIDIN
OXAMIDINE
OXAMMITE
OXAN
OXANE
OXANILATE
OXANILIC
OXANILIDE
OXAZIN
OXAZINE
OXAZOLE
OXBANE
OXBERRIES
OXBERRY
OXBIRD
OXBITER
OXBLOOD
OXBOW
OXBOY
OXBRAKE
OXCART
OXCHEEK
OXDIAZOLE
OXEA
OXEATE
OXEN
OXEOTE
OXER
OXEYE
OXFLY
OXFORD
OXGALL
OXGANG
OXGATE
OXGOAD
OXHARROW
OXHEAD
OXHEAL
OXHEART
OXHIDE
OXHOFT
OXHORN
OXHOUSE
OXHUVUD
OXID
OXIDABILITY
OXIDABLE
OXIDANT
OXIDASE
OXIDASIC
OXIDATE
OXIDATED
OXIDATING
OXIDATION
OXIDATIONAL
OXIDATIVE
OXIDATOR
OXIDE
OXIDIMETRIC
OXIDIMETRY
OXIDISE
OXIDIZABLE
OXIDIZE
OXIDIZED
OXIDIZER
OXIDIZING
OXIDO
OXIDULATED
OXIM
OXIMATE
OXIMATION
OXIME
OXLAND
OXLIKE
OXLIP
OXMAN
OXMANSHIP
OXMEN
OXO
OXONIUM
OXOZONE
OXOZONIDES
OXPECKER
OXREIM

OXSHOE
OXSKIN
OXTAIL
OXTER
OXTONGUE
OXWORT
OXY
OXYACANTHIN
OXYACANTHINE
OXYACANTHOUS
OXYACETYLENE
OXYACID
OXYALDEHYDE
OXYAMINE
OXYAPHIA
OXYASTER
OXYAZO
OXYBAPHA
OXYBENZYL
OXYBERBERINE
OXYBLEPSIA
OXYBROMIDE
OXYBUTYRIA
OXYCALCIUM
OXYCAMPHOR
OXYCAPROIC
OXYCARBONATE
OXYCELLULOSE
OXYCEPHALIC
OXYCEPHALISM
OXYCEPHALOUS
OXYCEPHALY
OXYCHLORATE
OXYCHLORIC
OXYCHLORID
OXYCHLORIDE
OXYCHLORINE
OXYCHROMATIC
OXYCHROMATIN
OXYCINNAMIC
OXYCOPAIVIC
OXYCOUMARIN
OXYCRATE
OXYCYANIDE
OXYDACTYL
OXYDIACT
OXYESTHESIA
OXYETHER
OXYETHYL
OXYGEN
OXYGENANT
OXYGENATE
OXYGENATED
OXYGENATING
OXYGENATOR
OXYGENERATOR
OXYGENIC
OXYGENICITY
OXYGENIUM
OXYGENIZABLE
OXYGENIZE
OXYGENIZED
OXYGENIZER
OXYGENIZING
OXYGENOUS
OXYGEUSIA
OXYGNATHOUS
OXYGON
OXYGONAL
OXYGONIAL
OXYHAEMATIN
OXYHALIDE
OXYHALOID
OXYHEMATIN
OXYHEXACTINE
OXYHEXASTER
OXYHYDRATE
OXYHYDRIC
OXYHYDROGEN
OXYIODIDE
OXYKETONE
OXYL
OXYLUCIFERIN
OXYMEL
OXYMETHYLENE
OXYMORA
OXYMORON
OXYMURIATE
OXYMURIATIC
OXYNEURIN
OXYNEURINE
OXYNITRATE
OXYNTIC
OXYOPHITIC
OXYOPIA
OXYOPY
OXYOSPHRESIA
OXYPETALOUS
OXYPHENOL
OXYPHENYL
OXYPHIL
OXYPHILE
OXYPHILIC
OXYPHILOUS
OXYPHONIA
OXYPHONY
OXYPHOSPHATE
OXYPHTHALIC
OXYPHYLLOUS
OXYPHYTE
OXYPICRIC
OXYPROLINE
OXYPROPIONIC
OXYPURINE
OXYPYCNOS
OXYQUINOLINE
OXYQUINONE
OXYRHINE
OXYRHINOUS
OXYRHYNCH
OXYRHYNCHID
OXYRHYNCHOUS
OXYRRHYNCHID
OXYSALICYLIC
OXYSALT
OXYSTEARIC
OXYSTOMATOUS
OXYSTOME
OXYSULFID
OXYSULFIDE
OXYSULPHATE
OXYSULPHID
OXYSULPHIDE
OXYTERPENE
OXYTOCIA
OXYTOCIC
OXYTOCIN
OXYTOCOUS
OXYTOLUENE
OXYTOLUIC
OXYTONE
OXYTONESIS
OXYTONICAL
OXYTONIZE
OXYTYLOTATE
OXYTYLOTE
OXYURIASIS
OXYURICIDE
OXYURID
OXYUROUS
OXYWELDING
OY
OYAPOCK
OYE
OYER
OYES
OYEZ
OYSTER
OYSTERAGE
OYSTERBIRD
OYSTERER
OYSTERFISH
OYSTERFISHES
OYSTERGREEN
OYSTERHOUSE
OYSTERING
OYSTERLING
OYSTERMAN
OYSTERMEN
OYSTEROUS
OYSTERROOT
OYSTERS
OYSTERSEED
OYSTERSHELL
OYSTERWIFE
OYSTERWOMAN
OZAENA
OZARKITE
OZENA
OZOBROME
OZOCERITE
OZOENA
OZONATE
OZONATION
OZONE
OZONED
OZONER
OZONIC
OZONID
OZONIDE
OZONIFEROUS
OZONIFY
OZONIZATION
OZONIZE
OZONIZED
OZONIZER
OZONIZING
OZONOMETER
OZONOMETRY
OZONOSCOPE
OZONOSCOPIC
OZONOSPHERE
OZONOSPHERIC
OZONOUS
OZOSTOMIA
OZOTYPE

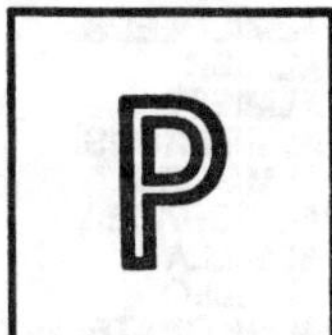

PA
PAAGE
PAAL
PAAR
PAAUW
PAB
PABBLE
PABLO
PABULAR
PABULARY
PABULATION
PABULATORY
PABULOUS
PABULUM
PAC
PACA
PACABLE
PACANE
PACATE
PACATELY
PACATION
PACATIVE
PACAY
PACAYA
PACCIOLI
PACE
PACEBOARD
PACED
PACEMAKER
PACEMAKING
PACER
PACHA
PACHAK
PACHALIC
PACHINKO
PACHISI
PACHNOLITE
PACHOULI
PACHUCO
PACHYDACTYL
PACHYDACTYLY
PACHYDERM
PACHYDERMA
PACHYDERMAL
PACHYDERMIA
PACHYDERMIAL
PACHYDERMIC
PACHYDERMOID
PACHYDERMOUS
PACHYGLOSSAL
PACHYLOSIS
PACHYMENIA
PACHYMENIC
PACHYMENINX
PACHYMETER
PACHYNEMA
PACHYNSIS
PACHYNTIC
PACHYSANDRA
PACHYTENE
PACIFIABLE
PACIFIC
PACIFICAL
PACIFICALLY
PACIFICATE
PACIFICATED
PACIFICATING
PACIFICATION
PACIFICATOR
PACIFICATORY
PACIFICITY
PACIFICO
PACIFICOS
PACIFIED
PACIFIER
PACIFISM
PACIFIST
PACIFISTIC
PACIFY
PACIFYING
PACING
PACK
PACKAGE
PACKAGED
PACKAGING
PACKALL
PACKBUILDER
PACKCLOTH
PACKED
PACKER
PACKERIES
PACKERY
PACKET
PACKETED
PACKETING
PACKHORSE
PACKHOUSE
PACKING
PACKINGHOUSE
PACKLESS
PACKLY
PACKMAN
PACKMEN
PACKNESS
PACKSACK
PACKSADDLE
PACKSTAFF
PACKSTAVES
PACKTHREAD
PACKTONG
PACKWARE
PACKWAX
PACKWAY
PACO
PACOS
PACOTA
PACOURYUVA
PACT
PACTA
PACTION
PACTIONAL
PACTIONALLY
PACTUM
PAD
PADANG
PADASHA
PADAUK
PADCLOTH
PADDED
PADDER
PADDING
PADDLE
PADDLED
PADDLEFISH
PADDLEFISHES
PADDLER
PADDLEWOOD
PADDLING
PADDO
PADDOCK
PADDOCKED
PADDOCKING
PADDOCKRIDE
PADDOCKSTONE
PADDOCKSTOOL
PADDY
PADDYBIRD
PADDYMELON
PADDYWACK
PADDYWATCH
PADDYWHACK
PADELION
PADELLA
PADEMELON
PADFOOT
PADGE
PADI
PADISHAH
PADLE
PADLOCK
PADLOCKED
PADLOCKING
PADMASANA
PADMELON
PADNAG
PADOU
PADRE
PADRES
PADRI
PADRINO
PADROADIST
PADROADO
PADRONA
PADRONE
PADRONES
PADRONI
PADRONISM
PADS
PADSHAH
PADSTONE
PADTREE
PADUASOY
PAEAN
PAEANISM
PAEANIZE
PAEANIZED
PAEANIZING
PAEDARCHY
PAEDATROPHIA
PAEDATROPHY
PAEDERAST
PAEDERASTIC
PAEDERASTY
PAEDIATRIC
PAEDIATRICS
PAEDOBAPTISM
PAEDOBAPTIST
PAEDOGENESIS
PAEDOGENETIC
PAEDOLOGICAL
PAEDOLOGIST
PAEDOLOGY
PAEDOMETER
PAEDOMORPHIC
PAEDONYMIC
PAEDONYMY
PAEDOTRIBE
PAEDOTROPHIC
PAEDOTROPHY
PAEGEL
PAEGL
PAEGLE
PAELLA
PAENULA
PAENULAE
PAEON
PAEONIC
PAEPAE
PAGA
PAGADOR
PAGAN
PAGANDOM
PAGANIC
PAGANICAL
PAGANICALLY
PAGANISH
PAGANISM
PAGANIST
PAGANISTIC
PAGANITY
PAGANIZATION
PAGANIZE
PAGANIZED
PAGANIZER
PAGANIZING
PAGANRY
PAGE
PAGEANT
PAGEANTED
PAGEANTEER
PAGEANTIC
PAGEANTRIES
PAGEANTRY
PAGEBOY
PAGED
PAGER
PAGES
PAGGLE
PAGINA
PAGINAE
PAGINAL
PAGINARY
PAGINATE
PAGINATED
PAGINATING
PAGINATION
PAGINE
PAGING
PAGLE
PAGNE
PAGODA
PAGODAS
PAGOSCOPE
PAGRUS
PAGURIAN
PAGURID
PAGURINE
PAGUROID
PAGUS
PAH
PAHA
PAHAUTEA
PAHI
PAHLAVI
PAHLEVI
PAHMI
PAHO
PAHOEHOE
PAHUA
PAHUTAN
PAI
PAICHE
PAID
PAIDEIA
PAIDEUTIC
PAIDEUTICS
PAIDLE
PAIDOLOGICAL
PAIDOLOGIST
PAIDOLOGY
PAIK
PAIL
PAILETTE
PAILFUL
PAILLASSE
PAILLES
PAILLETTE
PAILLETTED
PAILLETTES
PAILLON
PAILLONS
PAILOLO
PAILOO
PAILOU
PAILOW
PAIN
PAINCH
PAINDEMAINE
PAINED
PAINFUL
PAINFULLY
PAINFULNESS
PAINING
PAININGLY
PAINKILLER
PAINLESS
PAINLESSLY
PAINLESSNESS
PAINS
PAINSTAKER
PAINSTAKING
PAINSWORTHY
PAINT
PAINTBOX
PAINTBRUSH
PAINTED
PAINTER
PAINTERLY
PAINTIER
PAINTIEST
PAINTINESS
PAINTING
PAINTINGNESS
PAINTINGS
PAINTLESS
PAINTPOT
PAINTRESS
PAINTRY
PAINTS
PAINTURE
PAINTY
PAIOCK
PAIOCKE
PAIP
PAIR
PAIRED
PAIREDNESS
PAIRER
PAIRIAL
PAIRING
PAIRMENT
PAIRS
PAIRT
PAIS
PAISA
PAISANITE
PAISANO
PAISE
PAIWARI
PAJAHUELLO
PAJAK
PAJAMA
PAJAMAED
PAJAMAS
PAJAROELLO
PAJERO
PAJOCK
PAKCHOI
PAKE
PAKEHA
PAKKA
PAKTONG
PAL
PALA
PALABRA

PALACE
PALACED
PALACEOUS
PALACH
PALADIN
PALAEOBOTANY
PALAEOCYCLIC
PALAEOETHNIC
PALAEOGLYPH
PALAEOGRAPH
PALAEOGRAPHY
PALAEOLATRY
PALAEOLITH
PALAEOLITHIC
PALAEOLITHY
PALAEOLOGIST
PALAEOLOGY
PALAEOPHYTIC
PALAEOPLAIN
PALAEOSOPHY
PALAEOSTYLIC
PALAEOSTYLY
PALAEOTYPE
PALAESTRA
PALAESTRAE
PALAESTRAL
PALAESTRIAN
PALAESTRIC
PALAESTRICS
PALAETIOLOGY
PALAFITTE
PALAGONITE
PALAGONITIC
PALAIOTYPE
PALAIS
PALAISTE
PALAITE
PALAKA
PALAMA
PALAMAE
PALAMATE
PALAME
PALAMPORE
PALANDER
PALANKA
PALANKEEN
PALANKEENED
PALANKEENING
PALANQUIN
PALANQUINED
PALANQUINING
PALAPALA
PALAPALAI
PALAR
PALAS
PALATABILITY
PALATABLE
PALATABLY
PALATAL
PALATALISM
PALATALITY
PALATALIZE
PALATE
PALATED
PALATEFUL
PALATIAL
PALATIALLY
PALATIALNESS
PALATIAN
PALATIC
PALATINAL
PALATINATE
PALATINE
PALATINITE
PALATION
PALATIST
PALATITIS
PALATIVE
PALATIZATION
PALATIZE
PALATODENTAL
PALATOGRAM
PALATOGRAPH
PALATOGRAPHY
PALATOMETER
PALAVER
PALAVERED
PALAVERER
PALAVERING
PALAVERIST
PALAVERMENT
PALAVEROUS
PALAY
PALAYAN
PALAZZI
PALAZZO
PALBERRY
PALCH
PALE
PALEA
PALEACEOUS
PALEAE
PALEANTHROPIC
PALEATE
PALEBELLY
PALEBREAST
PALEBUCK
PALED
PALEDNESS
PALEFACE
PALEGOLD
PALEHEARTED
PALEIFORM
PALELY
PALENESS
PALEOATAVISM
PALEOBIOLOGY
PALEOBOTANIC
PALEOBOTANY
PALEOCOSMIC
PALEOCRYSTAL
PALEOCRYSTIC
PALEOCYCLIC
PALEOECOLOGY
PALEOETHNIC
PALEOFAUNA
PALEOGENETIC
PALEOGLYPH
PALEOGRAPH
PALEOGRAPHER
PALEOGRAPHY
PALEOKINETIC
PALEOLA
PALEOLATE
PALEOLATRY
PALEOLITH
PALEOLITHIC
PALEOLITHIST
PALEOLITHOID
PALEOLITHY
PALEOLOGIST
PALEOLOGY
PALEONTOLOGY
PALEOPHYTIC
PALEOPICRITE
PALEOPLAIN
PALEOPSYCHIC
PALEOSTYLIC
PALEOSTYLY
PALEOTECHNIC
PALEOTHERMAL
PALEOTHERMIC
PALEOZOOLOGY
PALER
PALERON
PALEST
PALESTRA
PALESTRAE
PALESTRAL
PALESTRIAN
PALESTRIC
PALET
PALETIOLOGY
PALETOT
PALETTE
PALETZ
PALEW
PALEWISE
PALFRENIER
PALFREY
PALFREYED
PALFREYS
PALFRY
PALGAT
PALI
PALIER
PALIEST
PALIFICATION
PALIFORM
PALIKAR
PALIKINESIA
PALILA
PALILALIA
PALILOGETIC
PALILOGY
PALIMBACCHIC
PALIMPSEST
PALINAL
PALINDROME
PALINDROMIC
PALINDROMIST
PALING
PALINGENESIS
PALINGENETIC
PALINGENIST
PALINGENY
PALINODE
PALINODED
PALINODIAL
PALINODIC
PALINODIST
PALINODY
PALIPHRASIA
PALIRRHEA
PALIS
PALISADE
PALISADED
PALISADING
PALISADO
PALISADOES
PALISADOING
PALISH
PALISANDER
PALISTROPHIA
PALKEE
PALKI
PALL
PALLA
PALLADAMMIN
PALLADAMMINE
PALLADIC
PALLADIUM
PALLADIUMIZE
PALLADIZE
PALLADOUS
PALLAE
PALLAH
PALLALL
PALLAR
PALLASITE
PALLBEARER
PALLE
PALLED
PALLESCENCE
PALLESCENT
PALLESTHESIA
PALLET
PALLETING
PALLETIZE
PALLETIZED
PALLETIZING
PALLETTE
PALLHOLDER
PALLI
PALLIA
PALLIAL
PALLIARD
PALLIASSE
PALLIATA
PALLIATE
PALLIATED
PALLIATING
PALLIATION
PALLIATIVE
PALLIATIVELY
PALLIATOR
PALLIATORY
PALLID
PALLIDITY
PALLIDLY
PALLIDNESS
PALLIER
PALLIES
PALLIEST
PALLINESS
PALLING
PALLION
PALLIOPEDAL
PALLISER
PALLIUM
PALLIUMS
PALLOGRAPH
PALLOGRAPHIC
PALLOMETRIC
PALLONE
PALLOR
PALLY
PALM
PALMA
PALMACEOUS
PALMAD
PALMAR
PALMARIAN
PALMARIS
PALMARY
PALMATE
PALMATED
PALMATELY
PALMATIFID
PALMATIFORM
PALMATILOBED
PALMATION
PALMATISECT
PALMATURE
PALMCRIST
PALMED
PALMELLOID
PALMER
PALMERIES
PALMERITE
PALMERY
PALMETTE
PALMETTO
PALMETTOES
PALMETTOS
PALMETUM
PALMFUL
PALMI
PALMICOLEUS
PALMIER
PALMIEST
PALMIFEROUS
PALMIFORM
PALMIGRADE
PALMILLA
PALMILLO
PALMILOBATE
PALMILOBATED
PALMILOBED
PALMINERVATE
PALMINERVED
PALMING
PALMIPED
PALMIRA
PALMIST
PALMISTRY
PALMITATE
PALMITE
PALMITIC
PALMITIN
PALMITINE
PALMITO
PALMITONE
PALMITOS
PALMIVEINED
PALMIVOROUS
PALMO
PALMODIC
PALMOSCOPY
PALMOSPASMUS
PALMS
PALMULA
PALMUS
PALMWISE
PALMWOOD
PALMY
PALMYRA
PALO
PALOLO
PALOMA
PALOMBINO
PALOMETA
PALOMINO
PALOMINOS
PALOOKA
PALOSAPIS
PALOUR
PALOUSER
PALOVERDE
PALP
PALPABILITY
PALPABLE
PALPABLENESS
PALPABLY
PALPACLE
PALPAL
PALPATE
PALPATED
PALPATING
PALPATION
PALPATORY
PALPEBRA
PALPEBRAE
PALPEBRAL
PALPEBRATE
PALPEBRATION
PALPEBRITIS
PALPED
PALPI
PALPIFER
PALPIFEROUS
PALPIFORM
PALPIGER
PALPIGEROUS
PALPITANT

PALPITATE
PALPITATED
PALPITATING
PALPITATION
PALPOCIL
PALPON
PALPULUS
PALPUS
PALSGRAVE
PALSGRAVINE
PALSIED
PALSIES
PALSIFY
PALSTAFF
PALSTAVE
PALSTER
PALSY
PALSYING
PALT
PALTER
PALTERED
PALTERER
PALTERING
PALTERLY
PALTOCK
PALTRIER
PALTRIEST
PALTRILY
PALTRINESS
PALTRY
PALU
PALUDAL
PALUDAMENT
PALUDE
PALUDIAL
PALUDIC
PALUDICOLE
PALUDICOLINE
PALUDICOLOUS
PALUDIFEROUS
PALUDINAL
PALUDINE
PALUDINOUS
PALUDISM
PALUDOSE
PALUDOUS
PALULE
PALULI
PALULUS
PALUS
PALUSTRAL
PALUSTRIAN
PALUSTRINE
PALY
PALYNOLOGY
PAM
PAMBANMANCHE
PAMBY
PAMENT
PAMMENT
PAMPA
PAMPANITO
PAMPAS
PAMPEAN
PAMPER
PAMPERED
PAMPEREDLY
PAMPEREDNESS
PAMPERER
PAMPERING
PAMPERIZE
PAMPERO
PAMPEROS
PAMPHAGOUS
PAMPHARMACON
PAMPHLET
PAMPHLETAGE
PAMPHLETARY
PAMPHLETEER
PAMPHLETER
PAMPHLETIC
PAMPHLETICAL
PAMPHLETIZE
PAMPHYSIC
PAMPHYSICAL
PAMPHYSICISM
PAMPILION
PAMPINIFORM
PAMPINOCELE
PAMPLEGIA
PAMPOOTEE
PAMPOOTIE
PAMPRE
PAMPRODACTYL
PAMPSYCHISM
PAMPSYCHIST
PAN
PANABASE
PANACE
PANACEA
PANACEAN
PANACEIST
PANACHE
PANACHED
PANACHURE
PANADA
PANADE
PANAESTHESIA
PANAESTHETIC
PANAGIARION
PANAMA
PANAPOSPORY
PANARCHIC
PANARCHY
PANARIS
PANARITIUM
PANARTERITIS
PANARTHRITIS
PANARY
PANATELA
PANATROPHY
PANAX
PANCAKE
PANCAKED
PANCAKING
PANCARDITIS
PANCHAMA
PANCHART
PANCHAX
PANCHAYAT
PANCHAYET
PANCHEON
PANCHION
PANCHRESTON
PANCHROMATIC
PANCHWAY
PANCOSMIC
PANCOSMISM
PANCOSMIST
PANCRATIAN
PANCRATIAST
PANCRATIC
PANCRATICAL
PANCRATISM
PANCRATIST
PANCRATIUM
PANCREAS
PANCREATIC
PANCREATIN
PANCREATISM
PANCREATITIC
PANCREATITIS
PANCREATIZE
PANCREATOID
PANCREATOMY
PAND
PANDA
PANDAL
PANDAN
PANDAR
PANDARAM
PANDAS
PANDATION
PANDAVA
PANDECT
PANDEMIA
PANDEMIC
PANDEMICITY
PANDEMONIAC
PANDEMONIC
PANDEMONISM
PANDEMONIUM
PANDEMY
PANDER
PANDERAGE
PANDERED
PANDERER
PANDERESS
PANDERING
PANDERISM
PANDERIZE
PANDERLY
PANDERMITE
PANDEROUS
PANDIED
PANDIES
PANDIT
PANDITA
PANDLE
PANDLEWHEW
PANDOOR
PANDORA
PANDORE
PANDOUR
PANDOWDY
PANDROP
PANDURA
PANDURATE
PANDURIFORM
PANDY
PANDYING
PANE
PANED
PANEE
PANEGOISM
PANEGOIST
PANEGYRE
PANEGYRIC
PANEGYRICA
PANEGYRICAL
PANEGYRICIZE
PANEGYRICON
PANEGYRICUM
PANEGYRIS
PANEGYRIST
PANEGYRIZE
PANEGYRIZED
PANEGYRIZER
PANEGYRIZING
PANEITY
PANEL
PANELA
PANELATION
PANELED
PANELER
PANELING
PANELIST
PANELLATION
PANELLING
PANELWORK
PANENTHEISM
PANESTHESIA
PANESTHETIC
PANETELA
PANETELLA
PANETIERE
PANFIL
PANFISH
PANFRY
PANG
PANGA
PANGAMIC
PANGAMOUS
PANGAMOUSLY
PANGAMY
PANGANE
PANGARA
PANGASI
PANGEN
PANGENE
PANGENESIS
PANGENETIC
PANGENIC
PANGENS
PANGERANG
PANGLESS
PANGLESSLY
PANGLIMA
PANGOLIN
PANGUINGUI
PANHANDLE
PANHANDLED
PANHANDLER
PANHANDLING
PANHARMONIC
PANHAS
PANHEAD
PANHEADED
PANHIDROSIS
PANHUMAN
PANHYGROUS
PANHYPEREMIA
PANIC
PANICKED
PANICKING
PANICKY
PANICLE
PANICLED
PANICMONGER
PANICULATE
PANICULATED
PANICULATELY
PANIDROSIS
PANIER
PANIFICATION
PANIME
PANIMMUNITY
PANINI
PANIOLO
PANION
PANISC
PANISCUS
PANISK
PANIVOROUS
PANJANDRUM
PANK
PANKIN
PANLOGICAL
PANLOGISM
PANMAN
PANMELODION
PANMERISM
PANMERISTIC
PANMIXIA
PANMIXY
PANMNESIA
PANMUG
PANNADE
PANNAG
PANNAGE
PANNAM
PANNE
PANNED
PANNEL
PANNER
PANNERY
PANNEURITIC
PANNEURITIS
PANNICLE
PANNICULAR
PANNICULITIS
PANNICULUS
PANNIER
PANNIERED
PANNIERMAN
PANNIKIN
PANNING
PANNOSE
PANNOSELY
PANNUM
PANNUS
PANOCHA
PANOCHE
PANOCOCO
PANOISTIC
PANOMPHAEAN
PANOMPHAIC
PANOMPHEAN
PANOMPHIC
PANOPLIED
PANOPLIES
PANOPLIST
PANOPLY
PANOPLYING
PANOPTIC
PANOPTICAL
PANOPTICON
PANORAM
PANORAMA
PANORAMIC
PANORAMICAL
PANORAMIST
PANORPID
PANOSTEITIS
PANOSTITIS
PANOTITIS
PANOWIE
PANPHARMACON
PANPLEGIA
PANPOLISM
PANPSYCHIC
PANPSYCHISM
PANPSYCHIST
PANS
PANSCIENTIST
PANSCLEROSIS
PANSCLEROTIC
PANSE
PANSEXUAL
PANSEXUALISM
PANSEXUALIST
PANSEXUALITY
PANSEXUALIZE
PANSHARD
PANSIDE
PANSIDEMAN
PANSIED
PANSIERE
PANSIES
PANSIL
PANSINUITIS
PANSINUSITIS
PANSIT
PANSMITH
PANSOPHIC

PANSOPHICAL
PANSOPHISM
PANSOPHIST
PANSOPHY
PANSPERMIA
PANSPERMY
PANSY
PANT
PANTACOSM
PANTAGAMY
PANTAGOGUE
PANTAGRAPH
PANTAGRAPHIC
PANTALAN
PANTALEON
PANTALET
PANTALETS
PANTALETTE
PANTALETTED
PANTALETTES
PANTALGIA
PANTALON
PANTALOON
PANTALOONED
PANTALOONERY
PANTALOONS
PANTAMETER
PANTAMORPH
PANTAMORPHIA
PANTAMORPHIC
PANTANEMONE
PANTAPHOBIA
PANTARBE
PANTARCHY
PANTAS
PANTASCOPE
PANTASCOPIC
PANTATROPHIA
PANTATROPHY
PANTATYPE
PANTECHNIC
PANTECHNICON
PANTED
PANTELEPHONE
PANTELLERITE
PANTER
PANTERER
PANTH
PANTHEA
PANTHEIC
PANTHEISM
PANTHEIST
PANTHEISTIC
PANTHELISM
PANTHEOLOGY
PANTHEON
PANTHEONIC
PANTHEONIZE
PANTHER
PANTHERESS
PANTHERINE
PANTHERS
PANTHERWOOD
PANTHEUM
PANTIES
PANTILE
PANTILED
PANTILING
PANTINE
PANTING
PANTINGLY
PANTISOCRACY
PANTISOCRAT
PANTLE
PANTLER
PANTO
PANTOCHROME
PANTOCHROMIC
PANTOFFLE
PANTOFLE
PANTOGLOT
PANTOGRAPH
PANTOGRAPHER
PANTOGRAPHIC
PANTOGRAPHY
PANTOLOGIC
PANTOLOGICAL
PANTOLOGIST
PANTOLOGY
PANTOMANCER
PANTOMANIA
PANTOMETER
PANTOMETRY
PANTOMIME
PANTOMIMIC
PANTOMIMICAL
PANTOMIMICRY
PANTOMIMIST
PANTOMNESIA
PANTOMNESIC
PANTOMORPH
PANTOMORPHIA
PANTOMORPHIC
PANTON
PANTOON
PANTOPHAGIC
PANTOPHAGIST
PANTOPHAGY
PANTOPHILE
PANTOPHOBIA
PANTOPHOBIC
PANTOPHOBOUS
PANTOPTEROUS
PANTOSCOPE
PANTOSCOPIC
PANTOTACTIC
PANTOTHENATE
PANTOTYPE
PANTOUM
PANTRIES
PANTRY
PANTRYMAN
PANTRYWOMAN
PANTS
PANTSUIT
PANTUN
PANTYWAIST
PANUELO
PANUELOS
PANUNG
PANURE
PANURGIC
PANURGY
PANYAR
PANZER
PANZOISM
PANZOOTIA
PANZOOTIC
PANZOOTY
PAOLI
PAOLO
PAON
PAOPAO
PAP
PAPA
PAPABILITY
PAPABLE
PAPABOT
PAPABOTE
PAPACIES
PAPACY
PAPAGALLO
PAPAGAYO
PAPAIN
PAPAIO
PAPAL
PAPALISM
PAPALIST
PAPALISTIC
PAPALIZATION
PAPALIZE
PAPALIZER
PAPALOI
PAPALTY
PAPANE
PAPAPHOBIA
PAPAPHOBIST
PAPARCHICAL
PAPARCHY
PAPAVERIN
PAPAVERINE
PAPAVEROUS
PAPAW
PAPAYA
PAPAYOTIN
PAPBOAT
PAPE
PAPELON
PAPELONNE
PAPER
PAPERBACK
PAPERBARK
PAPERBOARD
PAPERED
PAPERER
PAPERHANGER
PAPERHANGING
PAPERING
PAPERKNIFE
PAPERKNIVES
PAPERMAKER
PAPERMAKING
PAPERMOUTH
PAPERN
PAPERS
PAPERSHELL
PAPERWEIGHT
PAPERWORK
PAPERY
PAPETERIE
PAPEY
PAPICOLAR
PAPICOLIST
PAPIER
PAPILLA
PAPILLAE
PAPILLAR
PAPILLARY
PAPILLATE
PAPILLECTOMY
PAPILLEDEMA
PAPILLIFORM
PAPILLITIS
PAPILLOEDEMA
PAPILLOMA
PAPILLOMAS
PAPILLOMATA
PAPILLON
PAPILLOSE
PAPILLOSITY
PAPILLOTE
PAPILLOUS
PAPILLULATE
PAPILLULE
PAPINGO
PAPION
PAPIOPIO
PAPISH
PAPISHER
PAPISM
PAPIST
PAPISTIC
PAPISTICAL
PAPISTICALLY
PAPISTRY
PAPIZE
PAPLESS
PAPMEAT
PAPOLATER
PAPOLATROUS
PAPOLATRY
PAPOOSE
PAPOOSEROOT
PAPOULA
PAPPESCENT
PAPPI
PAPPIER
PAPPIES
PAPPIEST
PAPPIFEROUS
PAPPIFORM
PAPPOOSE
PAPPOSE
PAPPOUS
PAPPOX
PAPPUS
PAPPY
PAPREG
PAPRICA
PAPRIKA
PAPULA
PAPULAE
PAPULAN
PAPULAR
PAPULATE
PAPULATED
PAPULATION
PAPULE
PAPULIFEROUS
PAPULOSE
PAPULOUS
PAPYRACEOUS
PAPYRAL
PAPYRI
PAPYRIAN
PAPYRIN
PAPYRINE
PAPYRITIOUS
PAPYROCRACY
PAPYROGRAPH
PAPYROLOGIST
PAPYROLOGY
PAPYROPHOBIA
PAPYROTAMIA
PAPYROTINT
PAPYROTYPE
PAPYRUS
PAR
PARA
PARABANATE
PARABANIC
PARABAPTISM
PARABASIC
PARABASIS
PARABEMA
PARABEMATA
PARABEMATIC
PARABIEN
PARABIOSIS
PARABIOTIC
PARABLAST
PARABLASTIC
PARABLE
PARABLED
PARABLEPSIA
PARABLEPSIS
PARABLEPSY
PARABLEPTIC
PARABLING
PARABOLA
PARABOLANUS
PARABOLAS
PARABOLIC
PARABOLICAL
PARABOLIFORM
PARABOLIST
PARABOLIZE
PARABOLIZED
PARABOLIZER
PARABOLIZING
PARABOLOID
PARABOLOIDAL
PARABOTULISM
PARABRANCHIA
PARABULIA
PARABULIC
PARACARMINE
PARACENTESIS
PARACENTRAL
PARACENTRIC
PARACEPHALUS
PARACHOLIA
PARACHOR
PARACHORDAL
PARACHROMA
PARACHRONISM
PARACHROSE
PARACHUTE
PARACHUTED
PARACHUTIC
PARACHUTING
PARACHUTISM
PARACHUTIST
PARACHUTISTS
PARACLETE
PARACME
PARACOELE
PARACOELIAN
PARACOLPITIS
PARACOLPIUM
PARACONE
PARACONID
PARACOROLLA
PARACROSTIC
PARACUSIA
PARACUSIC
PARACUSIS
PARACYANOGEN
PARACYESIS
PARACYSTIC
PARACYSTITIS
PARACYSTIUM
PARADE
PARADED
PARADENTAL
PARADENTIUM
PARADER
PARADERM
PARADIASTOLE
PARADIDYMAL
PARADIDYMIS
PARADIGM
PARADIGMATIC
PARADING
PARADINGLY
PARADISAIC
PARADISAICAL
PARADISAL
PARADISE
PARADISEAN
PARADISIAC
PARADISIACAL
PARADISIAL
PARADISIAN
PARADISIC

PARADISICAL
PARADO
PARADOS
PARADOSES
PARADOX
PARADOXAL
PARADOXER
PARADOXIAL
PARADOXIC
PARADOXICAL
PARADOXICIAN
PARADOXIDIAN
PARADOXIST
PARADOXOLOGY
PARADOXURE
PARADOXY
PARADROMIC
PARADROP
PARAENESIS
PARAENESIZE
PARAENETIC
PARAENETICAL
PARAESTHESIA
PARAESTHETIC
PARAFFIN
PARAFFINE
PARAFFINED
PARAFFINER
PARAFFINIC
PARAFFINING
PARAFFINOID
PARAFFLE
PARAFLE
PARAFORM
PARAFRONT
PARAGANGLION
PARAGASTER
PARAGASTRAL
PARAGASTRIC
PARAGASTRULA
PARAGE
PARAGENESIA
PARAGENESIS
PARAGENETIC
PARAGENIC
PARAGERONTIC
PARAGEUSIA
PARAGEUSIC
PARAGEUSIS
PARAGLENAL
PARAGLOSSA
PARAGLOSSAE
PARAGLOSSAL
PARAGLOSSATE
PARAGLOSSIA
PARAGNATH
PARAGNATHISM
PARAGNATHOUS
PARAGNATHS
PARAGNATHUS
PARAGNOSIA
PARAGOGE
PARAGOGIC
PARAGOGICAL
PARAGOGIZE
PARAGON
PARAGONED
PARAGONING
PARAGONITE
PARAGONITIC
PARAGRAM
PARAGRAPH
PARAGRAPHED
PARAGRAPHER
PARAGRAPHIA
PARAGRAPHIC
PARAGRAPHING
PARAGRAPHIST
PARAH
PARAHEMATIN
PARAHEPATIC
PARAHOPEITE
PARAHORMONE
PARAHYPNOSIS
PARAIBA
PARAKEET
PARAKILYA
PARAKINESIA
PARAKINESIS
PARAKINETIC
PARALALIA
PARALDEHYDE
PARALEIPSIS
PARALEPSIS
PARALEXIA
PARALEXIC
PARALGESIA
PARALGESIC
PARALIAN
PARALININ
PARALIPOMENA
PARALIPSIS
PARALITICAL
PARALLACTIC
PARALLAX
PARALLEL
PARALLELED
PARALLELER
PARALLELING
PARALLELISM
PARALLELIST
PARALLELITH
PARALLELIZE
PARALLELIZED
PARALLELIZER
PARALLELLED
PARALLELLING
PARALLELLY
PARALLELOGRAM
PARALLELS
PARALOGIC
PARALOGICAL
PARALOGISM
PARALOGIST
PARALOGISTIC
PARALOGIZE
PARALOGY
PARALUMINITE
PARALYSES
PARALYSIS
PARALYTIC
PARALYTICAL
PARALYZANT
PARALYZATION
PARALYZE
PARALYZED
PARALYZER
PARALYZING
PARAMAGNET
PARAMAGNETIC
PARAMASTITIS
PARAMASTOID
PARAMATTA
PARAMECIUM
PARAMEDIAN
PARAMENIA
PARAMENT
PARAMERE
PARAMERIC
PARAMESE
PARAMESIAL
PARAMETER
PARAMETRAL
PARAMETRIC
PARAMETRICAL
PARAMETRITIC
PARAMETRITIS
PARAMID
PARAMIDE
PARAMILITARY
PARAMIMIA
PARAMITA
PARAMITOM
PARAMITOME
PARAMNESIA
PARAMO
PARAMORPH
PARAMORPHIC
PARAMORPHISM
PARAMORPHOUS
PARAMOS
PARAMOUNT
PARAMOUNTCY
PARAMOUNTLY
PARAMOUR
PARAMOURS
PARAMUTHETIC
PARAMYELIN
PARAMYOTONE
PARAMYOTONIA
PARANASAL
PARANATELLON
PARANEMA
PARANEMATIC
PARANEPHROS
PARANEPIONIC
PARANETE
PARANG
PARANGI
PARANJA
PARANOEAC
PARANOIA
PARANOIAC
PARANOID
PARANOIDAL
PARANOIDISM
PARANOMIA
PARANOSIC
PARANTHELION
PARANUCLEAR
PARANUCLEATE
PARANUCLEI
PARANUCLEIC
PARANUCLEIN
PARANUCLEUS
PARANYMPH
PARANYMPHAL
PARAO
PARAPARESIS
PARAPARETIC
PARAPEGM
PARAPEGMA
PARAPEGMATA
PARAPET
PARAPETALOUS
PARAPETED
PARAPH
PARAPHASIA
PARAPHASIC
PARAPHED
PARAPHEMIA
PARAPHERNA
PARAPHERNAL
PARAPHIA
PARAPHIMOSIS
PARAPHING
PARAPHONIA
PARAPHONIC
PARAPHRASE
PARAPHRASED
PARAPHRASER
PARAPHRASIA
PARAPHRASING
PARAPHRAST
PARAPHRASTIC
PARAPHRENIA
PARAPHRENIC
PARAPHYLLIA
PARAPHYLLIUM
PARAPHYSATE
PARAPHYSICAL
PARAPHYSIS
PARAPLASM
PARAPLASMIC
PARAPLASTIC
PARAPLASTIN
PARAPLECTIC
PARAPLEGIA
PARAPLEGIC
PARAPLEGY
PARAPLEURUM
PARAPOD
PARAPODIAL
PARAPODIUM
PARAPRAXES
PARAPRAXIA
PARAPRAXIS
PARAPROCTIUM
PARAPSIDAL
PARAPSIS
PARAPSYCHISM
PARAPTERA
PARAPTERAL
PARAPTERON
PARAPTERUM
PARAQUADRATE
PARAQUET
PARAREKA
PARARTHRIA
PARASANG
PARASCENIUM
PARASCEVE
PARASELENAE
PARASELENE
PARASELENIC
PARASHAH
PARASHIOTH
PARASHOTH
PARASITAL
PARASITARY
PARASITE
PARASITES
PARASITIC
PARASITICAL
PARASITICIDE
PARASITISM
PARASITIZE
PARASITOID
PARASITOLOGY
PARASITOSIS
PARASOL
PARASOLED
PARASOLETTE
PARASPECIFIC
PARASPHENOID
PARASTADES
PARASTAS
PARASTATIC
PARASTEMON
PARASTEMONAL
PARASTERNAL
PARASTERNUM
PARASTICHIES
PARASTICHY
PARASTYLE
PARASYNAPSIS
PARASYNAPTIC
PARASYNDESIS
PARASYNESIS
PARASYNETIC
PARASYPHILIS
PARASYSTOLE
PARATACTIC
PARATACTICAL
PARATAXIS
PARATE
PARATERMINAL
PARATHESIS
PARATHETIC
PARATHORMONE
PARATHYROID
PARATITLA
PARATITLES
PARATITLON
PARATOMIAL
PARATOMIUM
PARATONIC
PARATONNERRE
PARATORIUM
PARATORY
PARATRIPTIC
PARATROOPER
PARATROOPS
PARATROPHIC
PARATROPHY
PARATYPE
PARATYPHOID
PARATYPIC
PARATYPICAL
PARAVAIL
PARAVANE
PARAVANT
PARAVAUXITE
PARAVENT
PARAVESICAL
PARAXIAL
PARAXIALLY
PARAXON
PARAXONIC
PARAZONIUM
PARBAKE
PARBOIL
PARBOILED
PARBOILING
PARBREAK
PARBUCKLE
PARBUCKLED
PARBUCKLING
PARCEL
PARCELED
PARCELING
PARCELLED
PARCELLING
PARCELS
PARCENARY
PARCENER
PARCH
PARCHED
PARCHEESI
PARCHEMIN
PARCHER
PARCHESI
PARCHING
PARCHINGLY
PARCHISI
PARCHMENT
PARCHMENTIZE
PARCHY
PARCIDENTATE
PARCILOQUY
PARCITY
PARCLOSE
PARCOOK
PARD
PARDAL

PARDALE
PARDALOTE
PARDAO
PARDAOS
PARDE
PARDED
PARDEE
PARDESI
PARDHAN
PARDI
PARDIE
PARDIEU
PARDINE
PARDNER
PARDO
PARDON
PARDONABLE
PARDONABLY
PARDONED
PARDONEE
PARDONER
PARDONING
PARDONMONGER
PARDY
PARE
PAREA
PARECIOUS
PARED
PAREGAL
PAREGORIC
PAREGORICAL
PAREIRA
PAREJA
PAREL
PARELL
PARELLA
PARELLE
PAREN
PARENCHYM
PARENCHYMA
PARENCHYMAL
PARENCHYME
PARENCHYMOUS
PARENESIS
PARENESIZE
PARENETIC
PARENETICAL
PARENT
PARENTAGE
PARENTAL
PARENTALISM
PARENTALITY
PARENTALLY
PARENTATE
PARENTATION
PARENTELA
PARENTELIC
PARENTERAL
PARENTERALLY
PARENTHESES
PARENTHESIS
PARENTHESIZE
PARENTHETIC
PARENTHOOD
PARENTICIDE
PARER
PARERETHESIS
PARERGAL
PARERGIC
PARERGON
PARESES
PARESIS
PARESTHESIA
PARESTHETIC
PARETIC
PARETICALLY
PAREU
PAREUNIA
PAREVE
PARFAIT
PARFEY
PARFILAGE
PARFLECHE
PARFLESH
PARFOCAL
PARGANA
PARGANNA
PARGASITE
PARGE
PARGET
PARGETED
PARGETER
PARGETING
PARGETTED
PARGETTING
PARGO
PARGOS
PARHELIA
PARHELIACAL
PARHELIC
PARHELION
PARHELIUM
PARHOMOLOGY
PARHYPATE
PARI
PARIAH
PARIAL
PARIAN
PARICA
PARIDIGITATE
PARIDROSIS
PARIES
PARIET
PARIETAL
PARIETARY
PARIETES
PARIETOJUGAL
PARIFY
PARIGENIN
PARIGLIN
PARILLIN
PARIMUTUEL
PARINE
PARING
PARINGS
PARIPINNATE
PARISH
PARISHED
PARISHEN
PARISHIONAL
PARISHIONATE
PARISHIONER
PARISIA
PARISIS
PARISOLOGY
PARISON
PARISONIC
PARISTHMIC
PARISTHMION
PARISYLLABIC
PARITIES
PARITOR
PARITY
PARIVINCULAR
PARK
PARKA
PARKED
PARKEE
PARKER
PARKIN
PARKING
PARKLAND
PARKLEAVES
PARKWAY
PARKY
PARLANCE
PARLANDO
PARLATORY
PARLAY
PARLE
PARLEMENT
PARLESIE
PARLEY
PARLEYED
PARLEYER
PARLEYING
PARLEYS
PARLIAMENT
PARLIAMENTAL
PARLIAMENTARIAN
PARLIAMENTARY
PARLIAMENTER
PARLING
PARLISH
PARLOR
PARLORMAID
PARLOUR
PARLOUS
PARLOUSLY
PARLOUSNESS
PARLY
PARMA
PARMACETY
PARMACK
PARMAK
PARMENTIER
PARNAS
PARNEL
PARO
PAROARION
PAROARIUM
PAROCCIPITAL
PAROCH
PAROCHIAL
PAROCHIALISM
PAROCHIALIST
PAROCHIAN
PAROCHIN
PAROCHINE
PARODE
PARODI
PARODIABLE
PARODIAL
PARODIC
PARODICAL
PARODIED
PARODIES
PARODINIA
PARODIST
PARODISTIC
PARODONTITIS
PARODOS
PARODUS
PARODY
PARODYING
PAROECIOUS
PAROECIOUSLY
PAROECISM
PAROECY
PAROEMIA
PAROEMIAC
PAROEMIOLOGY
PAROICOUS
PAROL
PAROLABLE
PAROLE
PAROLED
PAROLEE
PAROLI
PAROLING
PAROLIST
PAROMOEON
PAROMOLOGIA
PAROMOLOGY
PARONOMASIA
PARONOMASIAN
PARONOMASTIC
PARONYCHIA
PARONYCHIAL
PARONYCHIUM
PARONYM
PARONYMIC
PARONYMIZE
PARONYMOUS
PARONYMY
PAROO
PAROOPHORON
PAROPSIS
PAROPTESIS
PAROPTIC
PAROQUET
PAROREXIA
PAROSMIA
PAROSMIC
PAROSTEAL
PAROSTEITIS
PAROSTEOSIS
PAROSTOSIS
PAROSTOTIC
PAROTIC
PAROTID
PAROTIDITIS
PAROTIS
PAROTITIC
PAROTITIS
PAROTOID
PAROUS
PAROUSIA
PAROVARIAN
PAROVARIUM
PAROXYSM
PAROXYSMAL
PAROXYSMALLY
PAROXYSMIC
PAROXYTONE
PAROXYTONIC
PARPAL
PARPEN
PARQUET
PARQUETED
PARQUETING
PARQUETRY
PARR
PARRAH
PARRAKEET
PARRAL
PARRALL
PARRAMATTA
PARRED
PARREL
PARRHESIA
PARRICIDAL
PARRICIDALLY
PARRICIDE
PARRICIDED
PARRICIDIAL
PARRIDGE
PARRIED
PARRIER
PARRIES
PARRING
PARRITCH
PARROCK
PARROKET
PARROQUET
PARROT
PARROTBEAK
PARROTBILL
PARROTED
PARROTER
PARROTING
PARROTLET
PARROTRY
PARROTY
PARRS
PARRY
PARRYING
PARS
PARSE
PARSEC
PARSED
PARSER
PARSIMONIOUS
PARSIMONY
PARSING
PARSLEY
PARSLEYWORT
PARSNIP
PARSON
PARSONAGE
PARSONARCHY
PARSONED
PARSONESE
PARSONESS
PARSONET
PARSONIC
PARSONICAL
PARSONICALLY
PARSONING
PARSONITY
PARSONLY
PARSONOLATRY
PARSONOLOGY
PARSONRY
PARSONS
PARSONSITE
PART
PARTABLE
PARTAGE
PARTAKE
PARTAKEN
PARTAKER
PARTAKING
PARTAN
PARTANFULL
PARTED
PARTEN
PARTER
PARTERRE
PARTERRED
PARTES
PARTHENIAD
PARTHENIAN
PARTHENIC
PARTHENOGENY
PARTHENOLOGY
PARTI
PARTIAL
PARTIALIST
PARTIALITIES
PARTIALITY
PARTIALLY
PARTIALNESS
PARTIARY
PARTIBILITY
PARTIBLE
PARTICIPABLE
PARTICIPANCE
PARTICIPANCY
PARTICIPANT
PARTICIPATE
PARTICIPATED
PARTICIPATOR
PARTICIPIAL
PARTICIPLE

PARTICLE
PARTICLES
PARTICULAR
PARTICULARLY
PARTICULATE
PARTICULE
PARTIES
PARTIGEN
PARTILE
PARTIM
PARTIMEN
PARTIMENTO
PARTING
PARTINIUM
PARTISAN
PARTISANSHIP
PARTITA
PARTITE
PARTITION
PARTITIONAL
PARTITIONARY
PARTITIONED
PARTITIONER
PARTITIONING
PARTITIONIST
PARTITIVE
PARTITURA
PARTIVERSAL
PARTIVITY
PARTIZAN
PARTLESS
PARTLET
PARTLY
PARTNER
PARTNERSHIP
PARTOOK
PARTRIDGE
PARTRIDGES
PARTRIDGING
PARTS
PARTSCHINITE
PARTURE
PARTURIATE
PARTURIENCE
PARTURIENCY
PARTURIENT
PARTURITION
PARTURITIVE
PARTY
PARTYISM
PARTYIST
PARTYMONGER
PARULIS
PARUMBILICAL
PARURA
PARURE
PARURIA
PARVANIMITY
PARVE
PARVENU
PARVENUISM
PARVIFLOROUS
PARVIFOLIATE
PARVIFOLIOUS
PARVIPOTENT
PARVIS
PARVISCIENT
PARVITUDE
PARVOLIN
PARVOLINE
PARVULE
PARYPHODROME
PAS
PASA
PASAN
PASANG
PASAR
PASCHAL
PASCHALIST
PASCHFLOWER
PASCOITE
PASCOLA
PASCUAGE
PASCUAL
PASCUOUS
PASEAR
PASENG
PASEO
PASEWA
PASH
PASHA
PASHALIC
PASHALIK
PASHED
PASHIM
PASHING
PASHM
PASHMINA
PASI
PASIG
PASIGRAPHIC
PASIGRAPHY
PASILALY
PASILLO
PASIN
PASIS
PASMO
PASO
PASQUEFLOWER
PASQUIL
PASQUILANT
PASQUILER
PASQUILIC
PASQUILLANT
PASQUILLER
PASQUILLIC
PASQUIN
PASQUINADE
PASQUINADED
PASQUINADER
PASQUINADING
PASS
PASSABLE
PASSABLENESS
PASSABLY
PASSACAGLIA
PASSACAGLIO
PASSADE
PASSADO
PASSADOES
PASSADOS
PASSAGE
PASSAGEABLE
PASSAGED
PASSAGER
PASSAGEWAY
PASSAGGI
PASSAGGIO
PASSAGING
PASSAGIO
PASSAMENT
PASSANGRAHAN
PASSANT
PASSAREE
PASSATA
PASSAY
PASSBACK
PASSBOOK
PASSE
PASSED
PASSEE
PASSEGARDE
PASSEL
PASSEMEASURE
PASSEMENT
PASSEMENTED
PASSEMENTING
PASSEMEZZO
PASSEN
PASSENGER
PASSEPIED
PASSER
PASSERBY
PASSERINE
PASSERS
PASSES
PASSEWA
PASSGANG
PASSIBILITY
PASSIBLE
PASSIBLENESS
PASSIM
PASSING
PASSINGLY
PASSION
PASSIONAL
PASSIONATE
PASSIONATELY
PASSIONATIVE
PASSIONATO
PASSIONED
PASSIONFLOWER
PASSIONLESS
PASSIONWORT
PASSIR
PASSIVAL
PASSIVATE
PASSIVATION
PASSIVE
PASSIVELY
PASSIVENESS
PASSIVISM
PASSIVIST
PASSIVITY
PASSKEY
PASSLESS
PASSMAN
PASSOMETER
PASSOUT
PASSOVER
PASSPENNY
PASSPORT
PASSULATE
PASSULATION
PASSUS
PASSWAY
PASSWORD
PAST
PASTA
PASTE
PASTEBOARD
PASTEBOARDY
PASTED
PASTEDOWN
PASTEL
PASTELIST
PASTELLIST
PASTER
PASTERER
PASTERN
PASTERNED
PASTEURELLA
PASTEURISE
PASTEURISM
PASTEURIZE
PASTEURIZED
PASTEURIZER
PASTEURIZING
PASTICCIO
PASTICHE
PASTICHEUR
PASTIER
PASTIES
PASTIEST
PASTIL
PASTILE
PASTILED
PASTILING
PASTILLE
PASTILLED
PASTILLING
PASTIME
PASTIMER
PASTINESS
PASTING
PASTLER
PASTNESS
PASTOPHOR
PASTOPHORION
PASTOPHORIUM
PASTOPHORUS
PASTOR
PASTORA
PASTORAL
PASTORALE
PASTORALES
PASTORALI
PASTORALIST
PASTORALITY
PASTORALIZE
PASTORALLY
PASTORALNESS
PASTORATE
PASTORITA
PASTORIUM
PASTORIUMS
PASTORIZE
PASTORLY
PASTORSHIP
PASTOSE
PASTOSITY
PASTOUR
PASTOURELLE
PASTRAMI
PASTRIES
PASTRY
PASTRYMAN
PASTURABLE
PASTURAGE
PASTURAL
PASTURE
PASTURED
PASTURELAND
PASTURER
PASTURES
PASTURING
PASTY
PASUL
PAT
PATA
PATACA
PATACAO
PATACHE
PATACO
PATACOON
PATAGIA
PATAGIAL
PATAGIATE
PATAGIUM
PATAGON
PATAGONIA
PATAKA
PATAMAR
PATANA
PATAND
PATAO
PATAPAT
PATAQUE
PATART
PATAS
PATASHTE
PATATA
PATAVINITY
PATBALL
PATBALLER
PATCH
PATCHABLE
PATCHCOCK
PATCHED
PATCHER
PATCHERIES
PATCHERY
PATCHES
PATCHHEAD
PATCHIER
PATCHIEST
PATCHILY
PATCHINESS
PATCHING
PATCHLEAF
PATCHOULI
PATCHOULY
PATCHWORD
PATCHWORK
PATCHY
PATE
PATEFY
PATEL
PATELLA
PATELLAE
PATELLAR
PATELLAROID
PATELLATE
PATELLIFORM
PATELLINE
PATELLOID
PATELLULA
PATELLULAE
PATELLULATE
PATEN
PATENCY
PATENER
PATENT
PATENTABLE
PATENTABLY
PATENTE
PATENTED
PATENTEE
PATENTING
PATENTLY
PATENTOR
PATER
PATERA
PATERAE
PATERERO
PATERIFORM
PATERISSA
PATERNAL
PATERNALISM
PATERNALIST
PATERNALITY
PATERNALIZE
PATERNALLY
PATERNITY
PATERNOSTER
PATESI
PATESIATE
PATETICO
PATH
PATHBREAKER
PATHED
PATHEMA
PATHEMATIC
PATHETIC
PATHETICAL

PATHETICALLY
PATHETICATE
PATHFARER
PATHFINDER
PATHFINDING
PATHIC
PATHLESS
PATHLESSNESS
PATHMENT
PATHOANATOMY
PATHOBIOLOGY
PATHOCHEMISTRY
PATHODONTIA
PATHOGEN
PATHOGENE
PATHOGENESIS
PATHOGENESY
PATHOGENETIC
PATHOGENIC
PATHOGENOUS
PATHOGENY
PATHOGERM
PATHOGERMIC
PATHOGNOMIC
PATHOGNOMY
PATHOGNOSTIC
PATHOGRAPHY
PATHOLOGIC
PATHOLOGICAL
PATHOLOGIST
PATHOLOGY
PATHOLYSIS
PATHOLYTIC
PATHOMANIA
PATHOMIMESIS
PATHOMIMICRY
PATHONOMIA
PATHONOMY
PATHOPHOBIA
PATHOPHORIC
PATHOPLASTIC
PATHOPOEIA
PATHOPOIESIS
PATHOPOIETIC
PATHOS
PATHOSOCIAL
PATHS
PATHWAY
PATHY
PATIBLE
PATIBULARY
PATIBULATE
PATIENCE
PATIENCY
PATIENT
PATIENTLY
PATIENTNESS
PATIN
PATINA
PATINAE
PATINATE
PATINATION
PATINE
PATINED
PATINIZE
PATINOUS
PATIO
PATIOS
PATISE
PATISSERIE
PATNIDAR
PATO
PATOIS
PATOLA
PATONCE
PATRIA
PATRIAL
PATRIARCH
PATRIARCHAL
PATRIARCHATE
PATRIARCHESS
PATRIARCHIC
PATRIARCHIST
PATRIARCHY
PATRICIAN
PATRICIANLY
PATRICIATE
PATRICIDAL
PATRICIDE
PATRICK
PATRICO
PATRIDGE
PATRILINEAL
PATRILINEAR
PATRILINY
PATRILOCAL
PATRIMONIAL
PATRIMONIES
PATRIMONY
PATRIN
PATRIOLATRY
PATRIOT
PATRIOTEER
PATRIOTIC
PATRIOTICAL
PATRIOTICS
PATRIOTISM
PATRIST
PATRISTIC
PATRISTICAL
PATRISTICISM
PATRISTICS
PATRIX
PATRIZATE
PATRIZATION
PATROCINIUM
PATROCLINIC
PATROCLINOUS
PATROCLINY
PATROGENESIS
PATROL
PATROLE
PATROLLED
PATROLLER
PATROLLING
PATROLMAN
PATROLOGIC
PATROLOGICAL
PATROLOGIST
PATROLOGY
PATRON
PATRONAGE
PATRONAL
PATRONATE
PATRONESS
PATRONITE
PATRONIZE
PATRONIZED
PATRONIZER
PATRONIZING
PATRONLY
PATRONNE
PATRONYM
PATRONYMIC
PATRONYMY
PATROON
PATROONRY
PATROULLART
PATRUITY
PATSY
PATT
PATTA
PATTAMAR
PATTARA
PATTE
PATTED
PATTEE
PATTEN
PATTENED
PATTENER
PATTER
PATTERED
PATTERER
PATTERING
PATTERIST
PATTERN
PATTERNED
PATTERNER
PATTERNING
PATTERNIZE
PATTERNMAKER
PATTERNS
PATTERNY
PATTI
PATTIDARI
PATTIE
PATTIES
PATTING
PATTOO
PATTU
PATTY
PATTYPAN
PATU
PATUCA
PATULENT
PATULIN
PATULOUS
PATULOUSLY
PATULOUSNESS
PATWARI
PATY
PAU
PAUA
PAUCIDENTATE
PAUCIFLOROUS
PAUCIFOLIATE
PAUCIFOLIOUS
PAUCIFY
PAUCIJUGATE
PAUCILOCULAR
PAUCILOQUENT
PAUCILOQUY
PAUCINERVATE
PAUCIPINNATE
PAUCIPLICATE
PAUCIRADIATE
PAUCISPIRAL
PAUCITIES
PAUCITY
PAUGHTY
PAUK
PAUKPAN
PAUKY
PAUL
PAULAR
PAULDRON
PAULIE
PAULIN
PAULOPAST
PAULOPOST
PAULOSPORE
PAUN
PAUNCH
PAUNCHE
PAUNCHED
PAUNCHFUL
PAUNCHILY
PAUNCHINESS
PAUNCHY
PAUNE
PAUP
PAUPER
PAUPERAGE
PAUPERATE
PAUPERED
PAUPERESS
PAUPERISM
PAUPERITIC
PAUPERIZE
PAUPERIZED
PAUPERIZING
PAURAQUE
PAUROPOD
PAUSABLY
PAUSAL
PAUSATION
PAUSE
PAUSED
PAUSEMENT
PAUSER
PAUSING
PAUSSID
PAUT
PAUXI
PAVADE
PAVAGE
PAVAN
PAVANE
PAVE
PAVED
PAVEED
PAVEMENT
PAVEMENTAL
PAVEN
PAVER
PAVESTONE
PAVID
PAVIDITY
PAVIE
PAVIES
PAVILION
PAVILLON
PAVING
PAVIOR
PAVIOUR
PAVIS
PAVISADE
PAVISADO
PAVISE
PAVISER
PAVISOR
PAVISSE
PAVOIS
PAVONATED
PAVONAZZO
PAVONE
PAVONIAN
PAVONINE
PAVONIZE
PAVY
PAW
PAWAW
PAWDITE
PAWED
PAWER
PAWING
PAWK
PAWKERY
PAWKIER
PAWKIEST
PAWKILY
PAWKINESS
PAWKRIE
PAWKY
PAWL
PAWN
PAWNABLE
PAWNAGE
PAWNBROKER
PAWNBROKERY
PAWNBROKING
PAWNE
PAWNED
PAWNEE
PAWNER
PAWNIE
PAWNING
PAWNOR
PAWNS
PAWNSHOP
PAWPAW
PAX
PAXILLA
PAXILLAE
PAXILLAR
PAXILLARY
PAXILLATE
PAXILLI
PAXILLIFORM
PAXILLOSE
PAXILLUS
PAXIUBA
PAXWAX
PAY
PAYABILITY
PAYABLE
PAYABLY
PAYBOX
PAYCHECK
PAYDAY
PAYED
PAYEE
PAYER
PAYING
PAYLOAD
PAYMASTER
PAYMENT
PAYMISTRESS
PAYNIM
PAYNIMHOOD
PAYNIMRIE
PAYNIMRY
PAYOFF
PAYOLA
PAYONG
PAYROLL
PAYSAGE
PAYSAGIST
PAYSANNE
PAYYETAN
PAZAREE
PE
PEA
PEABERRY
PEABIRD
PEABUSH
PEACE
PEACEABLE
PEACEABLY
PEACEBREAKER
PEACEFUL
PEACEFULLY
PEACEFULNESS
PEACELESS
PEACEMAKER
PEACEMAKING
PEACEMAN
PEACEMONGER
PEACETIME
PEACH
PEACHBERRY
PEACHBLOOM
PEACHBLOSSOM
PEACHBLOW
PEACHEN

PEACHER
PEACHERY
PEACHICK
PEACHIER
PEACHIEST
PEACHIFY
PEACHINESS
PEACHLET
PEACHWOOD
PEACHWORT
PEACHY
PEACK
PEACOAT
PEACOCK
PEACOCKERY
PEACOCKISH
PEACOCKISHLY
PEACOCKS
PEACOCKY
PEACOD
PEAFOWL
PEAFOWLS
PEAG
PEAGE
PEAGOOSE
PEAHEN
PEAI
PEAIISM
PEAK
PEAKED
PEAKEDLY
PEAKEDNESS
PEAKER
PEAKGOOSE
PEAKILY
PEAKINESS
PEAKING
PEAKISH
PEAKISHLY
PEAKISHNESS
PEAKY
PEAL
PEALED
PEALER
PEALIKE
PEALING
PEAN
PEANE
PEANUT
PEAPOD
PEAR
PEARCE
PEARCEITE
PEARCH
PEARL
PEARLASH
PEARLBERRY
PEARLBIRD
PEARLBUSH
PEARLED
PEARLER
PEARLET
PEARLFISH
PEARLIER
PEARLIEST
PEARLIN
PEARLING
PEARLINGS
PEARLISH
PEARLITE
PEARLITIC
PEARLSIDES
PEARLSPAR
PEARLWEED
PEARLWORT
PEARLY
PEARMAIN
PEARMONGER
PEARS
PEART
PEARTEN
PEARWOOD
PEAS
PEASANT
PEASANTIZE
PEASANTLIKE
PEASANTLY
PEASANTRY
PEASCOD
PEASE
PEASECOD
PEASEWEEP
PEASHOOTER
PEASOUPER
PEASTAKE
PEASTAKING
PEASTICK
PEASTICKING
PEASTONE
PEASY
PEAT
PEATERY
PEATHOUSE
PEATIER
PEATIEST
PEATMAN
PEATMEN
PEATSHIP
PEATSTACK
PEATWEED
PEATWOOD
PEATY
PEAU
PEAUDER
PEAVEY
PEAVIE
PEAVINE
PEAVY
PEBA
PEBBLE
PEBBLED
PEBBLES
PEBBLESTONE
PEBBLEWARE
PEBBLIER
PEBBLIEST
PEBBLING
PEBBLY
PEBRINE
PEBRINOUS
PECA
PECAN
PECCABILITY
PECCABLE
PECCADILLO
PECCADILLOES
PECCADILLOS
PECCANCIES
PECCANCY
PECCANT
PECCANTLY
PECCANTNESS
PECCARIES
PECCARY
PECCATION
PECCAVI
PECE
PECH
PECHAN
PECHAY
PECHILI
PECHT
PECHYS
PECIFY
PECITE
PECK
PECKAGE
PECKED
PECKER
PECKERWOOD
PECKET
PECKHAMITE
PECKIER
PECKIEST
PECKINESS
PECKING
PECKISH
PECKISHLY
PECKISHNESS
PECKLE
PECKLED
PECKLY
PECKY
PECORINO
PECTASE
PECTATE
PECTEN
PECTIC
PECTIN
PECTINACEOUS
PECTINAL
PECTINASE
PECTINATE
PECTINATED
PECTINATELY
PECTINATION
PECTINEAL
PECTINES
PECTINEUS
PECTINID
PECTINIFORM
PECTINITE
PECTINOUS
PECTIZABLE
PECTIZATION
PECTIZE
PECTIZED
PECTIZING
PECTOLITE
PECTORAL
PECTORALGIA
PECTORALIS
PECTORALIST
PECTORILOQUE
PECTORILOQUY
PECTOUS
PECTRON
PECTUNCULATE
PECTUS
PECUL
PECULATE
PECULATED
PECULATING
PECULATION
PECULATOR
PECULIAR
PECULIARISM
PECULIARITY
PECULIARIZE
PECULIARIZED
PECULIARLY
PECULIUM
PECUNIARY
PECUNIOSITY
PECUNIOUS
PED
PEDA
PEDAGE
PEDAGESE
PEDAGOG
PEDAGOGIC
PEDAGOGICAL
PEDAGOGICS
PEDAGOGISM
PEDAGOGIST
PEDAGOGUE
PEDAGOGUERY
PEDAGOGUISH
PEDAGOGY
PEDAL
PEDALED
PEDALER
PEDALFER
PEDALIAN
PEDALIER
PEDALING
PEDALIST
PEDALITER
PEDALITY
PEDALLED
PEDALLER
PEDANT
PEDANTESS
PEDANTIC
PEDANTICAL
PEDANTICALLY
PEDANTICISM
PEDANTISM
PEDANTIZE
PEDANTOCRACY
PEDANTOCRAT
PEDANTRY
PEDARY
PEDATE
PEDATED
PEDATELY
PEDATIFID
PEDATIFORM
PEDATILOBATE
PEDATILOBED
PEDATINERVED
PEDATISECT
PEDATISECTED
PEDATROPHIA
PEDATROPHY
PEDDER
PEDDLE
PEDDLED
PEDDLER
PEDDLERY
PEDDLING
PEDDLINGLY
PEDEE
PEDELION
PEDERAST
PEDERASTIC
PEDERASTY
PEDERERO
PEDES
PEDESIS
PEDESTAL
PEDESTALED
PEDESTALING
PEDESTALLED
PEDESTALLING
PEDESTRIAL
PEDESTRIALLY
PEDESTRIAN
PEDETENTOUS
PEDIAL
PEDIALGIA
PEDIATRIC
PEDIATRICIAN
PEDIATRICS
PEDIATRIST
PEDIATRY
PEDICAB
PEDICEL
PEDICELED
PEDICELLAR
PEDICELLARIA
PEDICELLATE
PEDICELLATED
PEDICELLED
PEDICLE
PEDICULAR
PEDICULATE
PEDICULATED
PEDICULE
PEDICULICIDE
PEDICULOSIS
PEDICULOUS
PEDICURE
PEDICURED
PEDICURING
PEDICURISM
PEDICURIST
PEDIFORM
PEDIGEROUS
PEDIGRAIC
PEDIGREE
PEDIGREED
PEDILUVIUM
PEDIMENT
PEDIMENTAL
PEDIMENTED
PEDIMENTUM
PEDION
PEDIONOMITE
PEDIPALP
PEDIPALPAL
PEDIPALPATE
PEDIPALPUS
PEDIPULATE
PEDIPULATION
PEDIPULATOR
PEDIWAK
PEDLAR
PEDLARY
PEDLER
PEDOBAPTISM
PEDOBAPTIST
PEDODONTIA
PEDODONTIC
PEDODONTIST
PEDOGRAPH
PEDOLOGICAL
PEDOLOGIST
PEDOLOGY
PEDOMANCY
PEDOMANIA
PEDOMETER
PEDOMETRICAL
PEDOMETRIST
PEDOMORPHIC
PEDOMORPHISM
PEDOMOTIVE
PEDOMOTOR
PEDOPHILIA
PEDOPHILIC
PEDOSPHERE
PEDOSPHERIC
PEDOTRIBE
PEDOTROPHIC
PEDOTROPHIST
PEDOTROPHY
PEDRAIL
PEDREGAL
PEDRERO
PEDRO
PEDROS
PEDULE
PEDUM
PEDUNCLE
PEDUNCLED

PEDUNCULAR
PEDUNCULATE
PEDUNCULATED
PEDUNCULI
PEDUNCULUS
PEE
PEEBEEN
PEEBLES
PEED
PEEING
PEEK
PEEKABOO
PEEKED
PEEKING
PEEL
PEELCROW
PEELE
PEELED
PEELEDNESS
PEELER
PEELHOUSE
PEELING
PEELMAN
PEELS
PEEN
PEENED
PEENGE
PEENING
PEEOY
PEEP
PEEPED
PEEPER
PEEPEYE
PEEPHOLE
PEEPING
PEEPUL
PEEPY
PEER
PEERAGE
PEERDOM
PEERED
PEERESS
PEERIE
PEERING
PEERLESS
PEERLESSLY
PEERLESSNESS
PEERLING
PEERLY
PEERT
PEERY
PEES
PEESASH
PEESEWEEP
PEESOREH
PEESWEEP
PEETWEET
PEEVE
PEEVED
PEEVEDLY
PEEVEDNESS
PEEVER
PEEVERS
PEEVING
PEEVISH
PEEVISHLY
PEEVISHNESS
PEEWEE
PEEWEEP
PEG
PEGA
PEGADOR
PEGALL
PEGANITE
PEGBOARD
PEGBOX
PEGGED
PEGGER
PEGGING
PEGGLE
PEGGY
PEGGYMAST
PEGH
PEGMA
PEGMAN
PEGMATITE
PEGMATITIC
PEGMATIZE
PEGMATOID
PEGMATOPHYRE
PEGME
PEGMEN
PEGOLOGY
PEGOMANCY
PEGROOTS
PEGWOOD
PEHO
PEIGNOIR
PEIKTHA
PEINE
PEIRAMETER
PEIRASTIC
PEIS
PEISAGE
PEISANT
PEISE
PEISER
PEIXERE
PEIXEREY
PEIZE
PEJERREY
PEJORATE
PEJORATION
PEJORATIVE
PEJORATIVELY
PEJORISM
PEJORIST
PEJORITY
PEKAN
PEKIN
PEKOE
PEKOK
PEL
PELA
PELADE
PELADIC
PELADO
PELADORE
PELAGE
PELAGIAL
PELAGIAN
PELAGIC
PELAGRA
PELAMYD
PELANOS
PELARGIC
PELARGONATE
PELARGONIC
PELARGONIDIN
PELARGONIN
PELARGONIUM
PELEAN
PELECAN
PELELITH
PELELIU
PELENG
PELERIN
PELERINE
PELETRE
PELF
PELICAN
PELICANRY
PELICK
PELICOMETER
PELIKE
PELIOM
PELIOMA
PELIOSIS
PELISSE
PELITE
PELITIC
PELL
PELLAGE
PELLAGRA
PELLAGRIN
PELLAGROSE
PELLAGROUS
PELLAR
PELLARD
PELLAS
PELLATE
PELLATION
PELLER
PELLET
PELLETED
PELLETIERINE
PELLETING
PELLETS
PELLETY
PELLICLE
PELLICULAR
PELLICULATE
PELLILE
PELLITORIES
PELLITORY
PELLMELL
PELLOCK
PELLOTIN
PELLOTINE
PELLUCID
PELLUCIDLY
PELLUCIDNESS
PELMA
PELMATA
PELMATIC
PELMATOGRAM
PELMET
PELOG
PELOID
PELOK
PELON
PELOPEA
PELORIA
PELORIAN
PELORIATE
PELORIC
PELORISM
PELORIZATION
PELORIZE
PELORUS
PELOTA
PELOTAS
PELOTHERAPY
PELOTON
PELT
PELTA
PELTAE
PELTAST
PELTATE
PELTATED
PELTATELY
PELTATION
PELTER
PELTERER
PELTIFEROUS
PELTIFOLIOUS
PELTIFORM
PELTIGERINE
PELTIGEROUS
PELTINERVATE
PELTINERVED
PELTING
PELTINGLY
PELTISH
PELTMONGER
PELTRIES
PELTRY
PELU
PELUDO
PELURE
PELVES
PELVIC
PELVIFORM
PELVIGRAPH
PELVIGRAPHY
PELVIMETER
PELVIMETRIC
PELVIMETRY
PELVIOPLASTY
PELVIOSCOPY
PELVIOTOMY
PELVIRECTAL
PELVIS
PELVISES
PELVISTERNAL
PELVISTERNUM
PELYCOGRAM
PELYCOGRAPHY
PELYCOLOGY
PELYCOMETER
PELYCOMETRY
PEMBINA
PEMBROKE
PEMICAN
PEMMICAN
PEMMICANIZE
PEMPHIGOID
PEMPHIGOUS
PEMPHIGUS
PEMPHIX
PEN
PENACUTE
PENAL
PENALISE
PENALIST
PENALITY
PENALIZATION
PENALIZE
PENALIZED
PENALIZING
PENALLY
PENALTIES
PENALTY
PENANCE
PENANCED
PENANCER
PENANCING
PENANCY
PENANG
PENANNULAR
PENATES
PENBARD
PENCATITE
PENCE
PENCEL
PENCEY
PENCH
PENCHANT
PENCHE
PENCHUTE
PENCIL
PENCILED
PENCILER
PENCILIFORM
PENCILING
PENCILLED
PENCILLER
PENCILLIKE
PENCILLING
PENCILRY
PENCILWOOD
PENCLERK
PENCRAFT
PEND
PENDA
PENDANT
PENDANTED
PENDANTING
PENDELOQUE
PENDENCY
PENDENT
PENDENTIVE
PENDENTLY
PENDICLE
PENDICLER
PENDING
PENDLE
PENDOM
PENDRAGON
PENDRAGONISH
PENDULANT
PENDULAR
PENDULATE
PENDULE
PENDULINE
PENDULOSITY
PENDULOUS
PENDULOUSLY
PENDULUM
PENDULUMS
PENE
PENEID
PENEPLAIN
PENEPLANE
PENES
PENESEISMIC
PENEST
PENETRABLE
PENETRABLY
PENETRAL
PENETRALIA
PENETRALIAN
PENETRANCE
PENETRANCY
PENETRANT
PENETRATE
PENETRATED
PENETRATING
PENETRATION
PENETRATIVE
PENETRATOR
PENETROLOGY
PENETROMETER
PENFIELDITE
PENFUL
PENGHULU
PENGO
PENGOS
PENGUIN
PENGUINERY
PENGUN
PENHEAD
PENHOLDER
PENIAL
PENIBLE
PENICILLATE
PENICILLATED
PENICILLIN
PENICILLIUM
PENIDE
PENILE
PENINSULA
PENINSULAR
PENINSULATE
PENINTIME

PENINVARIANT
PENIS
PENISES
PENISTONE
PENITENCE
PENITENCER
PENITENT
PENITENTIAL
PENITENTIARIES
PENITENTIARY
PENITENTLY
PENK
PENKEEPER
PENKNIFE
PENKNIVES
PENLITE
PENLOP
PENMAKER
PENMAKING
PENMAN
PENMANSHIP
PENMASTER
PENMEN
PENNA
PENNACEOUS
PENNAE
PENNAGE
PENNANT
PENNATE
PENNATED
PENNATULID
PENNATULOID
PENNED
PENNEECH
PENNEECK
PENNER
PENNI
PENNIA
PENNIED
PENNIES
PENNIFEROUS
PENNIFORM
PENNIGEROUS
PENNILESS
PENNILESSLY
PENNILL
PENNINE
PENNINERVATE
PENNINERVED
PENNING
PENNINITE
PENNIPOTENT
PENNIS
PENNIVEINED
PENNON
PENNONCEL
PENNONCELLE
PENNONED
PENNOPLUMA
PENNOPLUME
PENNORTH
PENNY
PENNYBIRD
PENNYCRESS
PENNYEARTH
PENNYFLOWER
PENNYHOLE
PENNYLAND
PENNYLEAF
PENNYROT
PENNYROYAL
PENNYSILLER
PENNYSTONE
PENNYWEIGHT
PENNYWINKLE
PENNYWORT
PENNYWORTH
PENOCHI
PENOLOGIC
PENOLOGICAL
PENOLOGIES
PENOLOGIST
PENOLOGY
PENONCEL
PENORCON
PENOUN
PENRACK
PENROSEITE
PENS
PENSCRIPT
PENSE
PENSEE
PENSEFUL
PENSEFULNESS
PENSEROSO
PENSHIP
PENSIL
PENSILE
PENSILENESS
PENSILITY
PENSION
PENSIONABLE
PENSIONARIES
PENSIONARY
PENSIONED
PENSIONER
PENSIONING
PENSIONNAIRE
PENSIONNAT
PENSIVE
PENSIVED
PENSIVELY
PENSIVENESS
PENSTEMON
PENSTER
PENSTICK
PENSTOCK
PENSUM
PENSY
PENT
PENTABASIC
PENTABROMIDE
PENTACAPSULAR
PENTACARBON
PENTACE
PENTACETATE
PENTACHENIUM
PENTACHLORIDE
PENTACHORD
PENTACHROMIC
PENTACID
PENTACLE
PENTACOCCOUS
PENTACONTANE
PENTACOSANE
PENTACRINITE
PENTACRINOID
PENTACRON
PENTACROSTIC
PENTACTINAL
PENTACTINE
PENTACULAR
PENTACYCLIC
PENTAD
PENTADACTYL
PENTADACTYLE
PENTADECAGON
PENTADECANE
PENTADECOIC
PENTADECYL
PENTADICITY
PENTADRACHM
PENTADRACHMA
PENTAFID
PENTAGAMIST
PENTAGLOSSAL
PENTAGLOT
PENTAGON
PENTAGONAL
PENTAGONALLY
PENTAGONOID
PENTAGONON
PENTAGRAM
PENTAGYN
PENTAGYNIAN
PENTAGYNOUS
PENTAHALIDE
PENTAHEDRA
PENTAHEDRAL
PENTAHEDROID
PENTAHEDRON
PENTAHEDROUS
PENTAHYDRATE
PENTAHYDRIC
PENTAIL
PENTAIODIDE
PENTALOBATE
PENTALOGUE
PENTALOGY
PENTALPHA
PENTAMERAL
PENTAMERAN
PENTAMERID
PENTAMERISM
PENTAMEROID
PENTAMEROUS
PENTAMERY
PENTAMETER
PENTAMETRIST
PENTAMETRIZE
PENTANDER
PENTANDRIAN
PENTANDROUS
PENTANE
PENTANGLE
PENTANGULAR
PENTANITRATE
PENTANOLIDE
PENTANONE
PENTAPLOID
PENTAPLOIDIC
PENTAPLOIDY
PENTAPODY
PENTAPOLIS
PENTAPOLITAN
PENTAPTEROUS
PENTAPTOTE
PENTAPTYCH
PENTARCH
PENTARCHICAL
PENTARCHIES
PENTARCHY
PENTASILICATE
PENTASPHERIC
PENTASTICH
PENTASTICHY
PENTASTYLE
PENTASTYLOS
PENTATEUCHAL
PENTATHIONIC
PENTATHLETE
PENTATHLON
PENTATHLOS
PENTATOMIC
PENTATOMID
PENTATONE
PENTATONIC
PENTAVALENCE
PENTAVALENCY
PENTAVALENT
PENTECONTER
PENTECOSTAL
PENTECOSTYS
PENTENE
PENTETERIC
PENTHEMIMER
PENTHIOPHENE
PENTHOUSE
PENTHOUSED
PENTHOUSING
PENTICLE
PENTILE
PENTIMENTO
PENTINE
PENTIT
PENTITOL
PENTLANDITE
PENTODE
PENTOIC
PENTOMIC
PENTOSAN
PENTOSANE
PENTOSE
PENTOSID
PENTOSIDE
PENTOSURIA
PENTOXIDE
PENTREMITAL
PENTREMITE
PENTROUGH
PENTSTEMON
PENTSTOCK
PENTYL
PENTYLENE
PENTYLIC
PENTYNE
PENUCHE
PENUCHI
PENUCHLE
PENUCKLE
PENULT
PENULTIMA
PENULTIMATE
PENUMBRA
PENUMBRAE
PENUMBRAL
PENUMBRAS
PENUMBROUS
PENURIOUS
PENURIOUSLY
PENURY
PENWIPER
PENWOMAN
PENWOMANSHIP
PENWOMEN
PENWORK
PENWORKER
PENWRIGHT
PEON
PEONAGE
PEONES
PEONIES
PEONISM
PEONY
PEOPLE
PEOPLED
PEOPLEIZE
PEOPLER
PEOPLES
PEOPLET
PEOPLING
PEOPLISH
PEOTOMY
PEP
PEPEREK
PEPERINE
PEPERINO
PEPERONI
PEPINELLA
PEPINO
PEPLOS
PEPLOSED
PEPLUM
PEPLUMS
PEPLUS
PEPO
PEPON
PEPONIDA
PEPONIUM
PEPOS
PEPPED
PEPPER
PEPPERBOX
PEPPERCORN
PEPPERED
PEPPERER
PEPPERGRASS
PEPPERIDGE
PEPPERING
PEPPERMINT
PEPPERONI
PEPPERROOT
PEPPERS
PEPPERWEED
PEPPERWOOD
PEPPERWORT
PEPPERY
PEPPILY
PEPPIN
PEPPINESS
PEPPING
PEPPY
PEPSIN
PEPSINATE
PEPSINATED
PEPSINATING
PEPSINE
PEPSINOGEN
PEPSIS
PEPTIC
PEPTICAL
PEPTICITY
PEPTIDASE
PEPTIDE
PEPTIZABLE
PEPTIZATION
PEPTIZE
PEPTIZED
PEPTIZER
PEPTIZING
PEPTOGASTER
PEPTONATE
PEPTONE
PEPTONIC
PEPTONIZE
PEPTONIZED
PEPTONIZER
PEPTONIZING
PEPTONOID
PEPTOTOXINE
PER
PERACEPHALUS
PERACID
PERACIDITE
PERACIDITY
PERACT
PERACUTE
PERADVENTURE
PERAGRATE
PERAGRATION
PERAMBLE
PERAMBULANT
PERAMBULATE
PERAMBULATED
PERAMBULATION

PERAMBULATOR
PERAMELINE
PERAMELOID
PERAU
PERBORATE
PERBROMIDE
PERCALE
PERCALINE
PERCARBONIC
PERCASE
PERCEANT
PERCEIVABLE
PERCEIVABLY
PERCEIVANCE
PERCEIVE
PERCEIVED
PERCEIVER
PERCEIVING
PERCENTABLE
PERCENTABLY
PERCENTAGE
PERCENTAGED
PERCENTAL
PERCENTILE
PERCENTS
PERCENTUAL
PERCENTUM
PERCEPT
PERCEPTIBLE
PERCEPTIBLY
PERCEPTION
PERCEPTIONAL
PERCEPTIVE
PERCEPTIVELY
PERCEPTIVITY
PERCEPTUAL
PERCEPTUALLY
PERCEPTUM
PERCESOCINE
PERCH
PERCHANCE
PERCHE
PERCHED
PERCHER
PERCHES
PERCHING
PERCHLORATE
PERCHLORIC
PERCHLORIDE
PERCHROMATE
PERCHROMIC
PERCID
PERCIFORM
PERCIPI
PERCIPIENCE
PERCIPIENCY
PERCIPIENT
PERCLOSE
PERCNOSOME
PERCOCT
PERCOID
PERCOIDEAN
PERCOLATE
PERCOLATION
PERCOLATIVE
PERCOLATOR
PERCOMORPH
PERCONTATION
PERCONTATORIAL
PERCRIBRATE
PERCRIBRATION
PERCULSION
PERCULSIVE
PERCUR
PERCURRATION
PERCURRENT
PERCURSORY
PERCUSS
PERCUSSION
PERCUSSIONAL
PERCUSSIONER
PERCUSSIVE
PERCUSSIVELY
PERCUSSOR
PERCUTANEOUS
PERCUTIENT
PERCYLITE
PERDENDO
PERDENDOSI
PERDIE
PERDILIGENCE
PERDILIGENT
PERDIT
PERDITION
PERDRICIDE
PERDRIGON
PERDU
PERDUE
PERDUELLION
PERDURABLE
PERDURABLY
PERDURANCE
PERDURANT
PERDURE
PERDURED
PERDURING
PERDURINGLY
PERDY
PERE
PEREGRIN
PEREGRINA
PEREGRINATE
PEREGRINATED
PEREGRINATOR
PEREGRINE
PEREGRINITY
PEREGRINOID
PEREGRINUS
PEREION
PEREIOPOD
PEREIRA
PEREIRINE
PEREJONET
PEREJONETTE
PEREMPT
PEREMPTION
PEREMPTORILY
PEREMPTORY
PERENDINANT
PERENDINATE
PERENDURE
PERENNATE
PERENNATION
PERENNIAL
PERENNIALITY
PERENNIALIZE
PERENNIALLY
PERENNIBRANCH
PEREQUITATE
PERES
PEREUNDEM
PEREZONE
PERFAY
PERFECT
PERFECTATION
PERFECTED
PERFECTER
PERFECTI
PERFECTIBLE
PERFECTING
PERFECTION
PERFECTIONER
PERFECTIONIST
PERFECTISM
PERFECTIST
PERFECTIVE
PERFECTIVELY
PERFECTIVIZE
PERFECTLY
PERFECTNESS
PERFECTO
PERFECTOR
PERFECTOS
PERFERVENT
PERFERVID
PERFERVIDLY
PERFICIENT
PERFIDIES
PERFIDIOUS
PERFIDIOUSLY
PERFIDY
PERFILOGRAPH
PERFINS
PERFIX
PERFLATE
PERFLATION
PERFLUENT
PERFOLIATE
PERFOLIATION
PERFORABLE
PERFORANT
PERFORATE
PERFORATED
PERFORATING
PERFORATION
PERFORATIONS
PERFORATIVE
PERFORATOR
PERFORATORY
PERFORCE
PERFORM
PERFORMABLE
PERFORMANCE
PERFORMANCES
PERFORMANT
PERFORMATIVE
PERFORMED
PERFORMER
PERFORMING
PERFRICATION
PERFUMATORY
PERFUME
PERFUMED
PERFUMER
PERFUMERY
PERFUMES
PERFUMING
PERFUMY
PERFUNCTORY
PERFUSATE
PERFUSE
PERFUSED
PERFUSING
PERFUSION
PERFUSIVE
PERGAMENEOUS
PERGAMYN
PERGE
PERGOLA
PERGOLAS
PERHALIDE
PERHALOGEN
PERHAPS
PERHAZARD
PERHORRESCE
PERI
PERIACINAL
PERIACTUS
PERIADENITIS
PERIANAL
PERIANGIOMA
PERIANGITIS
PERIANTH
PERIANTHIAL
PERIANTHIUM
PERIAORTIC
PERIAORTITIS
PERIAPICAL
PERIAPT
PERIAREUM
PERIARTERIAL
PERIARTERITIS
PERIARTHRIC
PERIARTHRITIS
PERIARTICULAR
PERIASTRAL
PERIASTRON
PERIASTRUM
PERIATRIAL
PERIAXIAL
PERIAXILLARY
PERIAXONAL
PERIBLASTIC
PERIBLASTULA
PERIBLEM
PERIBOLOS
PERIBOLUS
PERIBULBAR
PERIBURSAL
PERICAECAL
PERICAECITIS
PERICAPSULAR
PERICARDIA
PERICARDIAC
PERICARDIAL
PERICARDIAN
PERICARDITIS
PERICARDIUM
PERICARP
PERICARPIAL
PERICARPIC
PERICECAL
PERICECITIS
PERICELLULAR
PERICEMENTAL
PERICEMENTUM
PERICENTER
PERICENTRAL
PERICENTRE
PERICENTRIC
PERICEPHALIC
PERICEREBRAL
PERICHAETE
PERICHAETIAL
PERICHAETIUM
PERICHETE
PERICHONDRAL
PERICHORD
PERICHORDAL
PERICHORESIS
PERICHYLOUS
PERICLADIUM
PERICLASE
PERICLASITE
PERICLINAL
PERICLINALLY
PERICLINE
PERICLINIUM
PERICLITATE
PERICOLITIS
PERICOLPITIS
PERICONCHAL
PERICOPAL
PERICOPE
PERICOPE
PERICOPIC
PERICORNEAL
PERICOXITIS
PERICRANIA
PERICRANIAL
PERICRANITIS
PERICRANIUM
PERICRISTATE
PERICULANT
PERICULUM
PERICYCLE
PERICYCLIC
PERICYCLOID
PERICYCLONE
PERICYCLONIC
PERICYSTIC
PERICYSTITIS
PERICYSTIUM
PERICYTIAL
PERIDERM
PERIDERMAL
PERIDERMIC
PERIDESM
PERIDESMIC
PERIDESMITIS
PERIDESMIUM
PERIDIA
PERIDIAL
PERIDIASTOLE
PERIDIDYMIS
PERIDIIFORM
PERIDINIAL
PERIDINIAN
PERIDINID
PERIDIOLE
PERIDIOLUM
PERIDIUM
PERIDOT
PERIDOTIC
PERIDOTITE
PERIDOTITIC
PERIDUCTAL
PERIEGESIS
PERIEGETIC
PERIELESIS
PERIENTERIC
PERIENTERON
PERIERGY
PERIFISTULAR
PERIFOLIARY
PERIGASTRIC
PERIGASTRULA
PERIGEAL
PERIGEAN
PERIGEE
PERIGEMMAL
PERIGENESIS
PERIGENITAL
PERIGEUM
PERIGLIAL
PERIGLOEA
PERIGLOTTIC
PERIGLOTTIS
PERIGNATHIC
PERIGON
PERIGONADIAL
PERIGONE
PERIGONIAL
PERIGONIUM
PERIGRAPH
PERIGRAPHIC
PERIGYNIAL
PERIGYNIUM
PERIGYNOUS
PERIGYNY
PERIHELIA
PERIHELIAL
PERIHELIAN
PERIHELION
PERIHEPATIC

PERIHERNIAL
PERIHYSTERIC
PERIJOVE
PERIKARYA
PERIKARYON
PERIL
PERILED
PERILING
PERILLED
PERILLING
PERILOBAR
PERILOUS
PERILOUSLY
PERILOUSNESS
PERILUNE
PERILYMPH
PERIMASTITIS
PERIMETER
PERIMETRIC
PERIMETRICAL
PERIMETRITIC
PERIMETRITIS
PERIMETRIUM
PERIMETRY
PERIMORPH
PERIMORPHIC
PERIMORPHISM
PERIMORPHOUS
PERIMYELITIS
PERIMYSIAL
PERIMYSIUM
PERINAEUM
PERINE
PERINEAL
PERINEOCELE
PERINEOSTOMY
PERINEOTOMY
PERINEPHRAL
PERINEPHRIAL
PERINEPHRIC
PERINEPHRIUM
PERINEUM
PERINEURAL
PERINEURIA
PERINEURIAL
PERINEURITIS
PERINEURIUM
PERINIUM
PERINUCLEAR
PERIOCULAR
PERIOD
PERIODATE
PERIODIC
PERIODICAL
PERIODICALLY
PERIODICALNESS
PERIODICITY
PERIODID
PERIODIDE
PERIODOGRAM
PERIODOLOGY
PERIODONTAL
PERIODONTIA
PERIODONTIC
PERIODONTICS
PERIODONTIST
PERIODONTIUM
PERIODOSCOPE
PERIOECI
PERIOECIC
PERIOECID
PERIOMPHALIC
PERIONYCHIA
PERIONYCHIUM
PERIOPLE
PERIOPLIC
PERIOQUE
PERIORAL
PERIORBIT
PERIORBITA
PERIORBITAL
PERIORCHITIS
PERIOSTEAL
PERIOSTEOMA
PERIOSTEOUS
PERIOSTEUM
PERIOSTITIC
PERIOSTITIS
PERIOSTOSIS
PERIOSTRACAL
PERIOSTRACUM
PERIOTIC
PERIOVULAR
PERIPATETIC
PERIPATIZE
PERIPATOID
PERIPENIAL
PERIPETALOUS
PERIPETASMA
PERIPETEIA
PERIPETIA
PERIPETY
PERIPHACITIS
PERIPHERAD
PERIPHERAL
PERIPHERALLY
PERIPHERIAL
PERIPHERIC
PERIPHERICAL
PERIPHERIES
PERIPHERY
PERIPHRACTIC
PERIPHRASE
PERIPHRASED
PERIPHRASES
PERIPHRASING
PERIPHRASIS
PERIPHRASTIC
PERIPHRAXY
PERIPHYLLUM
PERIPHYSIS
PERIPLASM
PERIPLAST
PERIPLASTIC
PERIPLEURAL
PERIPLUS
PERIPNEUSTIC
PERIPOLAR
PERIPORTAL
PERIPROCT
PERIPROCTAL
PERIPROCTOUS
PERIPTER
PERIPTERAL
PERIPTEROI
PERIPTEROS
PERIPTEROUS
PERIPTERY
PERIPYLORIC
PERIQUE
PERIRECTAL
PERIRECTITIS
PERIRENAL
PERIRHINAL
PERIS
PERISARC
PERISARCAL
PERISARCOUS
PERISCIANS
PERISCII
PERISCOPAL
PERISCOPE
PERISCOPIC
PERISCOPICAL
PERISH
PERISHABLE
PERISHABLY
PERISHED
PERISHING
PERISHINGLY
PERISINUITIS
PERISINUOUS
PERISOMA
PERISOMAL
PERISOMATIC
PERISOME
PERISOMIAL
PERISPERM
PERISPERMAL
PERISPERMIC
PERISPHERE
PERISPHERIC
PERISPLENIC
PERISPOMENA
PERISPOMENON
PERISPORE
PERISSAD
PERISSOLOGIC
PERISSOLOGY
PERISTALITH
PERISTALSIS
PERISTALTIC
PERISTELE
PERISTERITE
PERISTERONIC
PERISTEROPOD
PERISTETHIUM
PERISTOLE
PERISTOMA
PERISTOMAL
PERISTOMATIC
PERISTOME
PERISTOMIAL
PERISTOMIUM
PERISTREPHIC
PERISTYLAR
PERISTYLE
PERISTYLOS
PERISYNOVIAL
PERISYSTOLE
PERISYSTOLIC
PERIT
PERITE
PERITECTIC
PERITHECE
PERITHECIAL
PERITHECIUM
PERITHELIAL
PERITHELIOMA
PERITHELIUM
PERITHORACIC
PERITOMIZE
PERITOMOUS
PERITOMY
PERITONAEA
PERITONAEAL
PERITONAEUM
PERITONEA
PERITONEAL
PERITONEALLY
PERITONEUM
PERITONISM
PERITONITAL
PERITONITIC
PERITONITIS
PERITRACHEAL
PERITREMA
PERITREME
PERITRICH
PERITRICHA
PERITRICHAN
PERITRICHIC
PERITRICHOUS
PERITROCH
PERITROCHAL
PERITROPAL
PERITROPHIC
PERITROPOUS
PERITYPHLIC
PERIUNGUAL
PERIURETERIC
PERIURETHRAL
PERIUTERINE
PERIUVULAR
PERIVAGINAL
PERIVASCULAR
PERIVENOUS
PERIVESICAL
PERIVISCERAL
PERIVITELLIN
PERIWIG
PERIWIGPATED
PERIWINKLE
PERIWINKLED
PERIWINKLER
PERIZONIUM
PERJINK
PERJINKETY
PERJINKITIES
PERJINKLY
PERJURE
PERJURED
PERJUREDLY
PERJUREDNESS
PERJURER
PERJURIES
PERJURING
PERJURIOUS
PERJURIOUSLY
PERJURY
PERK
PERKIER
PERKIEST
PERKILY
PERKIN
PERKINESS
PERKING
PERKISH
PERKNITE
PERKY
PERLACEOUS
PERLE
PERLECHE
PERLECTION
PERLID
PERLIGENOUS
PERLINGUAL
PERLINGUALLY
PERLITE
PERLITIC
PERLOIR
PERLUSTRATE
PERLUSTRATOR
PERMAFROST
PERMALLOY
PERMANENCE
PERMANENCY
PERMANENT
PERMANENTLY
PERMANGANATE
PERMANGANIC
PERMANSIVE
PERMEABILITY
PERMEABLE
PERMEABLY
PERMEAMETER
PERMEANCE
PERMEANT
PERMEATE
PERMEATED
PERMEATING
PERMEATION
PERMEATIVE
PERMEATOR
PERMILLAGE
PERMIRIFIC
PERMISS
PERMISSIBLE
PERMISSIBLY
PERMISSION
PERMISSIONED
PERMISSIVE
PERMISSIVELY
PERMISSORY
PERMIT
PERMITTABLE
PERMITTED
PERMITTEDLY
PERMITTEE
PERMITTER
PERMITTIVITY
PERMIX
PERMIXABLE
PERMIXTION
PERMIXTIVE
PERMIXTURE
PERMORALIZE
PERMUTABLE
PERMUTABLY
PERMUTATE
PERMUTATION
PERMUTATOR
PERMUTATORY
PERMUTE
PERMUTED
PERMUTER
PERMUTING
PERN
PERNANCY
PERNASAL
PERNAVIGATE
PERNICIOUS
PERNICIOUSLY
PERNICKETTY
PERNICKETY
PERNICKITY
PERNINE
PERNIO
PERNOCTATE
PERNOCTATION
PERNOR
PERO
PEROBA
PEROCHIRUS
PERODACTYLUS
PEROMELOUS
PEROMELUS
PERONATE
PERONEAL
PERONEUS
PERONIAL
PERONIUM
PEROPOD
PEROPODOUS
PEROPUS
PERORAL
PERORALLY
PERORATE
PERORATED
PERORATING
PERORATION
PERORATIONAL
PERORATIVE
PERORATOR
PERORATORY

PEROSMATE
PEROSOMUS
PEROVSKITE
PEROXIDASE
PEROXIDE
PEROXIDED
PEROXIDIC
PEROXIDING
PEROXIDIZE
PEROXY
PEROXYL
PERPEND
PERPENDICLE
PERPENDICULAR
PERPENDICULARITY
PERPENDICULARLY
PERPENSE
PERPENT
PERPERA
PERPET
PERPETRABLE
PERPETRATE
PERPETRATED
PERPETRATING
PERPETRATION
PERPETRATOR
PERPETUABLE
PERPETUAL
PERPETUALIST
PERPETUALLY
PERPETUANA
PERPETUANCE
PERPETUANT
PERPETUATE
PERPETUATED
PERPETUATING
PERPETUATION
PERPETUATOR
PERPETUITY
PERPLANTAR
PERPLEX
PERPLEXED
PERPLEXEDLY
PERPLEXER
PERPLEXING
PERPLEXINGLY
PERPLEXITIES
PERPLEXITY
PERPLICATION
PERQUADRAT
PERQUEER
PERQUEERLY
PERQUEIR
PERQUEST
PERQUISITE
PERQUISITION
PERQUISITOR
PERRADIAL
PERRADIALLY
PERRADIATE
PERRADIUS
PERRIE
PERRIER
PERRON
PERRUCHE
PERRUQUIER
PERRUTHENATE
PERRY
PERRYMAN
PERSALT
PERSCRIBE
PERSCRUTATE
PERSCRUTATOR
PERSE
PERSECUTE
PERSECUTED
PERSECUTEE
PERSECUTING
PERSECUTION
PERSECUTIVE
PERSECUTOR
PERSECUTORY
PERSEITE
PERSEITOL
PERSEITY
PERSEVERANCE
PERSEVERANT
PERSEVERATE
PERSEVERE
PERSEVERED
PERSEVERING
PERSICARIA
PERSICARY
PERSICO
PERSICOT
PERSIENNE
PERSIENNES
PERSIFLAGE
PERSIFLATE
PERSIFLEUR
PERSILICIC
PERSILLADE
PERSIMMON
PERSIO
PERSIS
PERSIST
PERSISTENCE
PERSISTENCY
PERSISTENT
PERSISTENTLY
PERSISTER
PERSISTINGLY
PERSISTIVE
PERSISTIVELY
PERSNICKETY
PERSOLVE
PERSON
PERSONA
PERSONABLE
PERSONABLY
PERSONAE
PERSONAGE
PERSONAL
PERSONALIA
PERSONALISM
PERSONALIST
PERSONALITY
PERSONALIZE
PERSONALIZED
PERSONALLY
PERSONALTIES
PERSONALTY
PERSONATE
PERSONATED
PERSONATING
PERSONATION
PERSONATIVE
PERSONATOR
PERSONED
PERSONEITY
PERSONIFIANT
PERSONIFICATION
PERSONIFY
PERSONIFYING
PERSONIZE
PERSONNEL
PERSONS
PERSPECTIVE
PERSPECTIVED
PERSPICACIOUS
PERSPICACITY
PERSPICUITY
PERSPICUOUS
PERSPIRABLE
PERSPIRANT
PERSPIRATION
PERSPIRATIVE
PERSPIRATORY
PERSPIRE
PERSPIRED
PERSPIRING
PERSPIRY
PERSTAND
PERSTRINGE
PERSTRINGED
PERSUADABLE
PERSUADABLY
PERSUADE
PERSUADED
PERSUADER
PERSUADING
PERSUASIBLE
PERSUASIBLY
PERSUASION
PERSUASIVE
PERSUASIVELY
PERSUASORY
PERSUE
PERSULFATE
PERSULPHATE
PERSULPHIDE
PERSULPHURIC
PERT
PERTAIN
PERTAINING
PERTEN
PERTENENCIA
PERTHITE
PERTHOSITE
PERTINACIOUS
PERTINACITY
PERTINENCE
PERTINENCY
PERTINENT
PERTINENTIA
PERTINENTLY
PERTLY
PERTNESS
PERTURB
PERTURBABLE
PERTURBANCE
PERTURBANCY
PERTURBANT
PERTURBATE
PERTURBATION
PERTURBATIVE
PERTURBATOR
PERTURBATORY
PERTURBED
PERTURBEDLY
PERTURBER
PERTURBING
PERTUSE
PERTUSED
PERTUSION
PERTUSSAL
PERTUSSIS
PERUKE
PERUKER
PERUKERY
PERUKIER
PERULA
PERULATE
PERULE
PERUSABLE
PERUSAL
PERUSE
PERUSED
PERUSER
PERUSING
PERVADE
PERVADED
PERVADENCE
PERVADER
PERVADING
PERVADINGLY
PERVAGATE
PERVAGATION
PERVALVAR
PERVASION
PERVASIVE
PERVASIVELY
PERVENCHE
PERVERSE
PERVERSELY
PERVERSENESS
PERVERSION
PERVERSITIES
PERVERSITY
PERVERSIVE
PERVERT
PERVERTED
PERVERTEDLY
PERVERTER
PERVERTIBLE
PERVERTIBLY
PERVERTING
PERVERTIVE
PERVIAL
PERVICACIOUS
PERVICACITY
PERVIGILIUM
PERVIOUS
PERVIOUSLY
PERVIOUSNESS
PERVULGATE
PERWICK
PERWITSKY
PERY
PES
PESA
PESADE
PESAGE
PESANTE
PESCOD
PESETA
PESHKAR
PESHKASH
PESHWA
PESKIER
PESKIEST
PESKILY
PESKINESS
PESKY
PESO
PESOS
PESS
PESSA
PESSARIES
PESSARY
PESSIMISM
PESSIMIST
PESSIMISTIC
PESSIMIZE
PESSONER
PESSULAR
PESSULUS
PEST
PESTE
PESTER
PESTERED
PESTERER
PESTERING
PESTEROUS
PESTFUL
PESTHOLE
PESTHOUSE
PESTICIDAL
PESTICIDE
PESTIDUCT
PESTIFEROUS
PESTIFUGOUS
PESTIFY
PESTILENCE
PESTILENT
PESTILENTIAL
PESTILENTLY
PESTIS
PESTLE
PESTLED
PESTLING
PESTO
PESTOLOGICAL
PESTOLOGIST
PESTOLOGY
PET
PETA
PETAL
PETALAGE
PETALED
PETALIFEROUS
PETALINE
PETALING
PETALISM
PETALITE
PETALLED
PETALLING
PETALOCEROUS
PETALODIC
PETALODONT
PETALODONTID
PETALODY
PETALOID
PETALOIDEOUS
PETALON
PETALOUS
PETALY
PETARA
PETARD
PETARDING
PETASMA
PETASOS
PETASUS
PETATE
PETAURINE
PETAURIST
PETCHARY
PETCOCK
PETE
PETECA
PETECHIA
PETECHIAE
PETECHIAL
PETECHIATE
PETEGREU
PETEMAN
PETER
PETERED
PETERERO
PETERING
PETERMAN
PETERMEN
PETERNET
PETERSHAM
PETFUL
PETHER
PETIOLAR
PETIOLATE
PETIOLATED
PETIOLE
PETIOLED
PETIOLI
PETIOLULAR
PETIOLULATE
PETIOLULE

PETIOLUS
PETIT
PETITE
PETITGRAIN
PETITION
PETITIONAL
PETITIONARY
PETITIONED
PETITIONEE
PETITIONER
PETITIONING
PETITIONIST
PETITOR
PETITORY
PETKIN
PETLING
PETO
PETRARY
PETRE
PETREAN
PETREITY
PETREL
PETRESCENCE
PETRESCENCY
PETRESCENT
PETRICOLOUS
PETRIE
PETRIFACTION
PETRIFACTIVE
PETRIFIABLE
PETRIFIC
PETRIFIED
PETRIFIER
PETRIFY
PETRIFYING
PETRISSAGE
PETROGENESIS
PETROGENIC
PETROGENY
PETROGLYPH
PETROGLYPHIC
PETROGLYPHY
PETROGRAPH
PETROGRAPHER
PETROGRAPHIC
PETROGRAPHY
PETROHYOID
PETROL
PETROLAGE
PETROLATUM
PETROLEAN
PETROLENE
PETROLEOUS
PETROLEUM
PETROLEUR
PETROLEUSE
PETROLIC
PETROLIFIC
PETROLIST
PETROLITHIC
PETROLIZE
PETROLIZED
PETROLIZING
PETROLOGIC
PETROLOGICAL
PETROLOGIST
PETROLOGY
PETROMASTOID
PETRONEL
PETRONELLA
PETRONELLIER
PETROSA
PETROSAL
PETROSILEX
PETROSTEARIN
PETROUS
PETROXOLIN
PETTABLE
PETTAH
PETTED
PETTEDLY
PETTEDNESS
PETTER
PETTI
PETTIAGUA
PETTICHAPS
PETTICOAT
PETTICOATED
PETTICOATERY
PETTICOATING
PETTICOATISM
PETTIER
PETTIEST
PETTIFOG
PETTIFOGGED
PETTIFOGGER
PETTIFOGGERY
PETTIFOGGING
PETTILY
PETTINESS
PETTING
PETTISH
PETTISHLY
PETTISHNESS
PETTITOES
PETTLE
PETTLED
PETTLING
PETTO
PETTY
PETTYFOG
PETTYGOD
PETULANCE
PETULANCY
PETULANT
PETULANTLY
PETUN
PETUNE
PETUNIA
PETUNSE
PETUNTZE
PETWOOD
PETZITE
PEUCITES
PEUGH
PEULVAN
PEVA
PEW
PEWAGE
PEWEE
PEWFELLOW
PEWHOLDER
PEWING
PEWIT
PEWKE
PEWMATE
PEWTER
PEWTERER
PEWTERWORT
PEWTERY
PEWY
PEY
PEYOTE
PEYOTISM
PEYOTL
PEYTON
PEZANTIC
PEZIZACEOUS
PEZIZAEFORM
PEZIZIFORM
PEZIZOID
PEZOGRAPH
PEZZO
PFEFFERNUSS
PFENNIG
PFENNIGE
PFENNIGS
PFIFF
PFUI
PFUND
PFUNDE
PHACELITE
PHACELLA
PHACELLITE
PHACELLUS
PHACITIS
PHACOCELE
PHACOCHERE
PHACOCHOERE
PHACOCYST
PHACOID
PHACOIDAL
PHACOLITE
PHACOLITH
PHACOLYSIS
PHACOMETER
PHACOPID
PHACOSCOPE
PHAEISM
PHAENANTHERY
PHAENOLOGY
PHAEOCHROUS
PHAEOPHORE
PHAEOPHYL
PHAEOPHYLL
PHAEOPHYTIN
PHAEOPLAST
PHAEOSPORE
PHAEOSPOROUS
PHAET
PHAETON
PHAGEDAENA
PHAGEDAENIC
PHAGEDAENICAL
PHAGEDAENOUS
PHAGEDENA
PHAGEDENIC
PHAGEDENICAL
PHAGEDENOUS
PHAGOCYTABLE
PHAGOCYTAL
PHAGOCYTE
PHAGOCYTER
PHAGOCYTIC
PHAGOCYTISM
PHAGOCYTIZE
PHAGOCYTOSE
PHAGOCYTOSED
PHAGOCYTOSIS
PHAGOLYSIS
PHAGOMANIA
PHALACROSIS
PHALAENOPSID
PHALANGAL
PHALANGE
PHALANGEAL
PHALANGEAN
PHALANGER
PHALANGES
PHALANGETTE
PHALANGIAN
PHALANGID
PHALANGIDAN
PHALANGIDEAN
PHALANGIFORM
PHALANGIST
PHALANGITE
PHALANSTERIC
PHALANSTERY
PHALANX
PHALANXED
PHALANXES
PHALARICA
PHALAROPE
PHALERA
PHALERAE
PHALERATE
PHALERATED
PHALLACEOUS
PHALLALGIA
PHALLEPHORIC
PHALLIC
PHALLICAL
PHALLICISM
PHALLICIST
PHALLIN
PHALLISM
PHALLIST
PHALLITIS
PHALLODYNIA
PHALLOID
PHALLONCUS
PHALLOPLASTY
PHALLUS
PHAN
PHANERIC
PHANERITE
PHANEROCRYST
PHANEROGAM
PHANEROGAMY
PHANEROGENIC
PHANEROMERE
PHANEROSCOPE
PHANEROSIS
PHANEROZOIC
PHANIC
PHANO
PHANSIGAR
PHANTASCOPE
PHANTASIA
PHANTASIES
PHANTASIZE
PHANTASM
PHANTASMA
PHANTASMAL
PHANTASMALLY
PHANTASMATA
PHANTASMATIC
PHANTASMIC
PHANTAST
PHANTASY
PHANTIC
PHANTOM
PHANTOMATIC
PHANTOMIC
PHANTOMIZE
PHANTOMIZER
PHANTOMRY
PHANTOMY
PHANTOSCOPE
PHARE
PHARISAICAL
PHARISAISM
PHARISEE
PHARMACAL
PHARMACEUTIC
PHARMACIC
PHARMACIES
PHARMACIST
PHARMACITE
PHARMACOLITE
PHARMACOLOGY
PHARMACON
PHARMACY
PHARMAKOI
PHARMAKOS
PHARMIC
PHARO
PHAROLOGY
PHAROS
PHARYNGAL
PHARYNGEAL
PHARYNGES
PHARYNGIC
PHARYNGISMUS
PHARYNGITIS
PHARYNGOCELE
PHARYNGOLITH
PHARYNGOLOGY
PHARYNGOTOME
PHARYNGOTOMY
PHARYNX
PHARYNXES
PHASCACEOUS
PHASCOLOME
PHASE
PHASEAL
PHASED
PHASELIN
PHASEMETER
PHASEMY
PHASEOLIN
PHASEOLOUS
PHASES
PHASIANIC
PHASIANID
PHASIANINE
PHASIANOID
PHASIC
PHASING
PHASIS
PHASM
PHASMA
PHASMATID
PHASMATOID
PHASMATROPE
PHASOGENEOUS
PHASOR
PHASOTROPY
PHAT
PHEAL
PHEALE
PHEARSE
PHEASANT
PHEASANTRY
PHEASANTS
PHEBE
PHEEAL
PHEER
PHELLANDRENE
PHELLEM
PHELLODERM
PHELLODERMAL
PHELLOGEN
PHELLOGENIC
PHELLOPLASTIC
PHEMIC
PHENACAINE
PHENACETIN
PHENACETINE
PHENACETURIC
PHENACITE
PHENACYL
PHENAKISM
PHENANTHRENE
PHENANTHROL
PHENARSINE
PHENAZIN
PHENAZINE
PHENAZONE
PHENE
PHENENE
PHENETHYL
PHENETIDINE
PHENETOL

PHENETOLE
PHENGITE
PHENGITICAL
PHENIC
PHENICATE
PHENICIOUS
PHENICOPTER
PHENIN
PHENINE
PHENIX
PHENMIAZINE
PHENOBARBITOL
PHENOCOLL
PHENOCOPY
PHENOCRYST
PHENOGENESIS
PHENOGENETIC
PHENOL
PHENOLATE
PHENOLIC
PHENOLIZE
PHENOLOGIC
PHENOLOGICAL
PHENOLOGIST
PHENOLOGY
PHENOMENA
PHENOMENAL
PHENOMENALLY
PHENOMENON
PHENOQUINONE
PHENOSAL
PHENOSOL
PHENOSPERMY
PHENOTYPE
PHENOTYPIC
PHENOTYPICAL
PHENOXAZINE
PHENOXIDE
PHENYL
PHENYLACETIC
PHENYLAMIDE
PHENYLAMINE
PHENYLATE
PHENYLATED
PHENYLATION
PHENYLENE
PHENYLIC
PHEON
PHEOPHYTIN
PHERETRER
PHEW
PHI
PHIAL
PHIALE
PHIALED
PHIALINE
PHIALING
PHIALLED
PHIALLING
PHILABEG
PHILADELPHITE
PHILADELPHY
PHILALETHIST
PHILAMOT
PHILANDER
PHILANDERED
PHILANDERER
PHILANDERING
PHILANTHID
PHILANTHROPE
PHILANTHROPIC
PHILANTHROPIST
PHILANTHROPY
PHILANTOMBA
PHILARCHAIST
PHILATELIC
PHILATELIST
PHILATELY
PHILATHLETIC
PHILAUTY
PHILHARMONIC
PHILHELLENE
PHILHELLENIC
PHILHIPPIC
PHILHYMNIC
PHILIA
PHILIATER
PHILIBEG
PHILINE
PHILIPPICIZE
PHILIPPIZE
PHILIPPIZER
PHILIPPUS
PHILLILEW
PHILLILOO
PHILLIPEENER
PHILLIPSINE
PHILLIPSITE
PHILLYRIN
PHILOBIBLIAN
PHILOBIBLIC
PHILOBIBLICAL
PHILOBIBLIST
PHILOBOTANIC
PHILOBRUTISH
PHILOCALIC
PHILOCALIST
PHILOCALY
PHILOCOMAL
PHILOCUBIST
PHILOCYNIC
PHILOCYNICAL
PHILOCYNY
PHILODEMIC
PHILODENDRON
PHILODESPOT
PHILODOX
PHILODOXER
PHILODOXICAL
PHILOFELIST
PHILOFELON
PHILOGARLIC
PHILOGASTRIC
PHILOGEANT
PHILOGRAPH
PHILOGRAPHIC
PHILOGYNIST
PHILOGYNOUS
PHILOGYNY
PHILOKLEPTIC
PHILOLOGER
PHILOLOGIC
PHILOLOGICAL
PHILOLOGIST
PHILOLOGIZE
PHILOLOGUE
PHILOLOGY
PHILOMATH
PHILOMATHIC
PHILOMATHY
PHILOME
PHILOMEL
PHILOMELIAN
PHILOMUSE
PHILOMUSICAL
PHILOMYSTIC
PHILOMYTHIA
PHILOMYTHIC
PHILONATURAL
PHILONEISM
PHILONIST
PHILONIUM
PHILONOIST
PHILOPAGAN
PHILOPATER
PHILOPATRIAN
PHILOPENA
PHILOPIG
PHILOPOET
PHILOPOGON
PHILOPOLEMIC
PHILOPORNIST
PHILORADICAL
PHILORNITHIC
PHILOSOPH
PHILOSOPHE
PHILOSOPHEME
PHILOSOPHER
PHILOSOPHERESS
PHILOSOPHESS
PHILOSOPHIC
PHILOSOPHICAL
PHILOSOPHIES
PHILOSOPHISM
PHILOSOPHIST
PHILOSOPHIZE
PHILOSOPHY
PHILOTADPOLE
PHILOTECHNIC
PHILOTHEISM
PHILOTHEIST
PHILOTHERIAN
PHILOZOIC
PHILOZOIST
PHILOZOONIST
PHILP
PHILTER
PHILTERED
PHILTERER
PHILTERING
PHILTRE
PHILTRED
PHILTRING
PHILTRUM
PHIMOSED
PHIMOSIS
PHIMOTIC
PHIP
PHIPPE
PHIT
PHITONES
PHIZ
PHIZOG
PHLEBALGIA
PHLEBECTASIA
PHLEBECTASIS
PHLEBECTASY
PHLEBECTOMY
PHLEBECTOPIA
PHLEBECTOPY
PHLEBENTERIC
PHLEBITIS
PHLEBOGRAM
PHLEBOGRAPH
PHLEBOGRAPHY
PHLEBOID
PHLEBOIDAL
PHLEBOLITE
PHLEBOLITH
PHLEBOLITHIC
PHLEBOLITIC
PHLEBOLOGY
PHLEBOPEXY
PHLEBOPLASTY
PHLEBORRHAGE
PHLEBORRHEXIS
PHLEBOSTASIA
PHLEBOSTASIS
PHLEBOTOME
PHLEBOTOMIC
PHLEBOTOMIST
PHLEBOTOMIZE
PHLEBOTOMY
PHLEGM
PHLEGMA
PHLEGMAGOGUE
PHLEGMASIA
PHLEGMATIC
PHLEGMATICAL
PHLEGMATICLY
PHLEGMATISM
PHLEGMATIST
PHLEGMATOUS
PHLEGMON
PHLEGMONIC
PHLEGMONOID
PHLEGMONOUS
PHLEGMY
PHLOBAPHENE
PHLOBATANNIN
PHLOEM
PHLOEOTERMA
PHLOEUM
PHLOGISTIAN
PHLOGISTIC
PHLOGISTON
PHLOGOGENIC
PHLOGOPITE
PHLOGOSED
PHLOGOSIN
PHLOGOSIS
PHLOGOTIC
PHLORETIN
PHLORHIZIN
PHLORIDZIN
PHLORINA
PHLORIZIN
PHLOROL
PHLYCTAENA
PHLYCTAENULA
PHLYCTENA
PHLYCTENAE
PHLYCTENOID
PHLYCTENULA
PHLYCTENULE
PHLYZACIOUS
PHLYZACIUM
PHO
PHOBIA
PHOBIAC
PHOBIC
PHOBIES
PHOBISM
PHOBIST
PHOBIST
PHOBY
PHOCA
PHOCACEAN
PHOCACEOUS
PHOCAENINE
PHOCAL
PHOCENIN
PHOCID
PHOCIFORM
PHOCINE
PHOCODONT
PHOCOID
PHOCOMELIA
PHOCOMELUS
PHOEBADS
PHOEBE
PHOENICEAN
PHOENICOPTER
PHOENICUROUS
PHOENIGM
PHOENIX
PHOENIXES
PHOENIXITY
PHOLAD
PHOLADIAN
PHOLADID
PHOLADOID
PHOLCID
PHOLCOID
PHOLIDOLITE
PHOLIDOTE
PHON
PHONAL
PHONATE
PHONATED
PHONATING
PHONATION
PHONATORY
PHONAUTOGRAM
PHONE
PHONED
PHONEME
PHONEMIC
PHONEMICALLY
PHONEMICS
PHONES
PHONESIS
PHONETIC
PHONETICAL
PHONETICALLY
PHONETICIAN
PHONETICISM
PHONETICIST
PHONETICIZE
PHONETICS
PHONETISM
PHONETIST
PHONETIZATION
PHONETIZE
PHONEY
PHONGHI
PHONIATRICS
PHONIATRY
PHONIC
PHONICS
PHONIER
PHONIES
PHONIEST
PHONIKON
PHONING
PHONO
PHONOCAMPTIC
PHONODEIK
PHONOGLYPH
PHONOGRAM
PHONOGRAMIC
PHONOGRAMMIC
PHONOGRAPH
PHONOGRAPHER
PHONOGRAPHIC
PHONOGRAPHY
PHONOLITE
PHONOLITIC
PHONOLOGER
PHONOLOGIC
PHONOLOGICAL
PHONOLOGIST
PHONOLOGY
PHONOMANIA
PHONOMETER
PHONOMETRY
PHONOMIMIC
PHONOMOTOR
PHONON
PHONOPATHY
PHONOPHONE
PHONOPHORE
PHONOPHORIC
PHONOPHOROUS
PHONOPHOTE

PHONOPLEX
PHONOSCOPE
PHONOTYPE
PHONOTYPER
PHONOTYPIC
PHONOTYPIST
PHONOTYPY
PHONY
PHOO
PHOOEY
PHOOKA
PHORANTHIUM
PHORBIN
PHORESIS
PHORESY
PHORIA
PHORID
PHORMINX
PHOROMETER
PHOROMETRIC
PHOROMETRY
PHORONE
PHORONID
PHORONOMIA
PHORONOMIC
PHORONOMICS
PHORONOMY
PHOROSCOPE
PHOROZOOID
PHORRHEA
PHOS
PHOSE
PHOSGENE
PHOSGENITE
PHOSIS
PHOSPHAGEN
PHOSPHAM
PHOSPHAMIDE
PHOSPHATASE
PHOSPHATE
PHOSPHATED
PHOSPHATEMIA
PHOSPHATESE
PHOSPHATIC
PHOSPHATIDE
PHOSPHATION
PHOSPHATIZE
PHOSPHATIZED
PHOSPHATIZING
PHOSPHATURIA
PHOSPHATURIC
PHOSPHENE
PHOSPHENYL
PHOSPHID
PHOSPHIDE
PHOSPHINATE
PHOSPHINE
PHOSPHINIC
PHOSPHITE
PHOSPHOLIPID
PHOSPHONATE
PHOSPHONIC
PHOSPHONIUM
PHOSPHOR
PHOSPHORATE
PHOSPHORE
PHOSPHOREAL
PHOSPHORENT
PHOSPHOREOUS
PHOSPHORESCE
PHOSPHORESCENCE
PHOSPHORESCENT
PHOSPHORETED
PHOSPHORI
PHOSPHORIC
PHOSPHORICAL
PHOSPHORISM
PHOSPHORITE
PHOSPHORITIC
PHOSPHORIZE
PHOSPHOROGEN
PHOSPHOROGENE
PHOSPHOROUS
PHOSPHORUS
PHOSPHORYL
PHOSPHURIA
PHOSPHYL
PHOSS
PHOSSY
PHOT
PHOTA
PHOTAL
PHOTALGIA
PHOTECHY
PHOTEOLIC
PHOTIC
PHOTICS
PHOTISM
PHOTISTIC
PHOTO
PHOTOACTINIC
PHOTOBATHIC
PHOTOBIOTIC
PHOTOBROMIDE
PHOTOCAMPSIS
PHOTOCATHODE
PHOTOCHEMIST
PHOTOCHLORIDE
PHOTOCHROME
PHOTOCHROMY
PHOTOCOMPOSE
PHOTOCOPIER
PHOTOCOPY
PHOTOCRAYON
PHOTOCURRENT
PHOTODRAMA
PHOTODROME
PHOTODROMY
PHOTODYNAMIC
PHOTOELECTRIC
PHOTOENGRAVE
PHOTOENGRAVED
PHOTOENGRAVER
PHOTOENGRAVING
PHOTOETCH
PHOTOETCHED
PHOTOETCHER
PHOTOETCHING
PHOTOGELATIN
PHOTOGEN
PHOTOGENE
PHOTOGENIC
PHOTOGENY
PHOTOGEOLOGY
PHOTOGLYPH
PHOTOGLYPHIC
PHOTOGLYPHY
PHOTOGRAM
PHOTOGRAPH
PHOTOGRAPHEE
PHOTOGRAPHER
PHOTOGRAPHIC
PHOTOGRAPHY
PHOTOGRAVURE
PHOTOGYRIC
PHOTOHALIDE
PHOTOKINESIS
PHOTOLITH
PHOTOLOGIC
PHOTOLOGICAL
PHOTOLOGIST
PHOTOLOGY
PHOTOLYSIS
PHOTOLYTIC
PHOTOMA
PHOTOMAP
PHOTOMAPPER
PHOTOMETEOR
PHOTOMETER
PHOTOMETRIC
PHOTOMETRY
PHOTOMONTAGE
PHOTOMURAL
PHOTON
PHOTONASTY
PHOTONIC
PHOTONOSUS
PHOTONUCLEAR
PHOTOPATHIC
PHOTOPATHY
PHOTOPERIOD
PHOTOPHANE
PHOTOPHILE
PHOTOPHILIC
PHOTOPHILOUS
PHOTOPHILY
PHOTOPHOBE
PHOTOPHOBIA
PHOTOPHOBIC
PHOTOPHOBOUS
PHOTOPHONE
PHOTOPHONIC
PHOTOPHONY
PHOTOPHORE
PHOTOPHYGOUS
PHOTOPIA
PHOTOPIC
PHOTOPILE
PHOTOPLAY
PHOTOPLAYER
PHOTOPRINT
PHOTOPRINTER
PHOTORADIO
PHOTORELIEF
PHOTOSALT
PHOTOSCOPE
PHOTOSCOPIC
PHOTOSCOPY
PHOTOSPHERE
PHOTOSPHERIC
PHOTOSTABLE
PHOTOSTAT
PHOTOSTATED
PHOTOSTATIC
PHOTOSTATING
PHOTOSTATTED
PHOTOSTATTING
PHOTOSYNTAX
PHOTOTACTIC
PHOTOTACTISM
PHOTOTAXIS
PHOTOTAXY
PHOTOTHERAPY
PHOTOTHERMIC
PHOTOTIMER
PHOTOTONIC
PHOTOTONUS
PHOTOTROPE
PHOTOTROPIC
PHOTOTROPISM
PHOTOTUBE
PHOTOTYPE
PHOTOTYPIC
PHOTOTYPY
PHOTOVISUAL
PHOTOVOLTAIC
PHOTURIA
PHOUSDAR
PHRAGMA
PHRAGMOID
PHRAGMOSIS
PHRAMPEL
PHRASABLE
PHRASAL
PHRASALLY
PHRASE
PHRASEABLE
PHRASED
PHRASELESS
PHRASEMAKER
PHRASEMAKING
PHRASEMAN
PHRASEMONGER
PHRASEOGRAM
PHRASEOGRAPH
PHRASEOLOGIES
PHRASEOLOGY
PHRASER
PHRASINESS
PHRASING
PHRASY
PHRATOR
PHRATRAL
PHRATRIAC
PHRATRIAL
PHRATRIC
PHRATRIES
PHRATRY
PHREATIC
PHREATOPHYTE
PHREN
PHRENESIA
PHRENESIAC
PHRENESIS
PHRENETIC
PHRENETICAL
PHRENIC
PHRENICOTOMY
PHRENICS
PHRENITIC
PHRENITIS
PHRENOCARDIA
PHRENOGRAM
PHRENOGRAPH
PHRENOGRAPHY
PHRENOLOGER
PHRENOLOGIST
PHRENOLOGIZE
PHRENOLOGY
PHRENOPATHIC
PHRENOPATHY
PHRENOPLEGIA
PHRENOSIN
PHRENOSINIC
PHRENOTROPIC
PHRENSY
PHRONESIS
PHRYGANEID
PHRYGANEOID
PHRYGIA
PHRYGIUM
PHRYNID
PHRYNIN
PHTHALACENE
PHTHALAN
PHTHALATE
PHTHALEIN
PHTHALEINE
PHTHALIC
PHTHALIDE
PHTHALIMIDE
PHTHALIN
PHTHALYL
PHTHANITE
PHTHINOID
PHTHIRIASIS
PHTHISIC
PHTHISICAL
PHTHISICKY
PHTHISIS
PHTHONGAL
PHTHOR
PHTHORIC
PHTOR
PHU
PHUGOID
PHUL
PHULKARI
PHULWARA
PHUT
PHYCITE
PHYCITID
PHYCITOL
PHYCOCHROM
PHYCOCHROME
PHYCOCYANIN
PHYCOGRAPHY
PHYCOLOGICAL
PHYCOLOGIST
PHYCOLOGY
PHYCOMYCETE
PHYCOMYCETES
PHYCOPHAEIN
PHYLA
PHYLACTERIC
PHYLACTERIED
PHYLACTERIES
PHYLACTERIZE
PHYLACTERY
PHYLACTIC
PHYLARCH
PHYLARCHIC
PHYLARCHICAL
PHYLARCHY
PHYLE
PHYLEPHEBIC
PHYLESIS
PHYLETIC
PHYLETICALLY
PHYLETISM
PHYLIC
PHYLLADE
PHYLLARY
PHYLLIFORM
PHYLLIN
PHYLLINE
PHYLLITE
PHYLLITIC
PHYLLOCARID
PHYLLOCERATE
PHYLLOCLAD
PHYLLOCLADE
PHYLLOCYST
PHYLLOCYSTIC
PHYLLODE
PHYLLODIA
PHYLLODIAL
PHYLLODINOUS
PHYLLODIUM
PHYLLODY
PHYLLOGENOUS
PHYLLOID
PHYLLOIDAL
PHYLLOMANCY
PHYLLOMANIA
PHYLLOME
PHYLLOMIC
PHYLLOMORPH
PHYLLOMORPHY
PHYLLOPHORE
PHYLLOPOD
PHYLLOPODAN
PHYLLOPODE
PHYLLOPODOUS
PHYLLOPTOSIS

PHYLLORHINE
PHYLLOSOMA
PHYLLOSOME
PHYLLOTACTIC
PHYLLOTAXIS
PHYLLOTAXY
PHYLLOUS
PHYLLOXERA
PHYLLOXERAN
PHYLLOXERIC
PHYLLOZOOID
PHYLOGENESIS
PHYLOGENETIC
PHYLOGENY
PHYLON
PHYLUM
PHYMA
PHYMATA
PHYMATIC
PHYMATOID
PHYMATOSIS
PHYSAGOGUE
PHYSALIAN
PHYSALITE
PHYSCIOID
PHYSETEROID
PHYSIATRIC
PHYSIATRICS
PHYSIC
PHYSICAL
PHYSICALIST
PHYSICALITY
PHYSICALLY
PHYSICALNESS
PHYSICIAN
PHYSICIANCY
PHYSICIANED
PHYSICIANER
PHYSICIANING
PHYSICIANLY
PHYSICISM
PHYSICIST
PHYSICKED
PHYSICKER
PHYSICKING
PHYSICKY
PHYSICOLOGIC
PHYSICOMORPH
PHYSICS
PHYSID
PHYSIFORM
PHYSIOCRACY
PHYSIOCRAT
PHYSIOCRATIC
PHYSIOGENIC
PHYSIOGENY
PHYSIOGNOMIC
PHYSIOGNOMY
PHYSIOGONY
PHYSIOGRAPHY
PHYSIOLATER
PHYSIOLATRY
PHYSIOLOGER
PHYSIOLOGIAN
PHYSIOLOGIC
PHYSIOLOGICAL
PHYSIOLOGIST
PHYSIOLOGIZE
PHYSIOLOGUE
PHYSIOLOGUS
PHYSIOLOGY
PHYSIOSOPHIC
PHYSIOSOPHY
PHYSIQUE
PHYSIQUED
PHYSIS
PHYSITHEISM
PHYSITISM
PHYSIURGIC
PHYSIURGY
PHYSOCARPOUS
PHYSOCELE
PHYSOCLIST
PHYSOCLISTIC
PHYSOGASTRIC
PHYSOGASTRY
PHYSOMETRA
PHYSONECTOUS
PHYSOPOD
PHYSOSTIGMINE
PHYSOSTOME
PHYSOSTOMOUS
PHYTASE
PHYTATE
PHYTIC
PHYTIN
PHYTIVOROUS
PHYTOBEZOAR
PHYTOCHLORE
PHYTOCHLORIN
PHYTOGAMY
PHYTOGENESIS
PHYTOGENETIC
PHYTOGENIC
PHYTOGENY
PHYTOGNOMY
PHYTOGRAPH
PHYTOGRAPHER
PHYTOGRAPHIC
PHYTOGRAPHY
PHYTOID
PHYTOKININ
PHYTOL
PHYTOLOGIC
PHYTOLOGICAL
PHYTOLOGIST
PHYTOLOGY
PHYTOMA
PHYTOME
PHYTOMER
PHYTOMERA
PHYTOMETER
PHYTOMONAD
PHYTON
PHYTONIC
PHYTOPHAGAN
PHYTOPHAGIC
PHYTOPHAGOUS
PHYTOPHAGY
PHYTOPHILOUS
PHYTOPSYCHE
PHYTOPTID
PHYTOPTOSE
PHYTOPTOSIS
PHYTORHODIN
PHYTOSAUR
PHYTOSAURIAN
PHYTOSIS
PHYTOSTEROL
PHYTOSTROTE
PHYTOTOMIST
PHYTOTOMY
PHYTOTOXIC
PHYTOTOXIN
PHYTOTRON
PHYTOZOAN
PHYTOZOON
PHYTYL
PI
PIA
PIABA
PIACABA
PIACEVOLE
PIACHE
PIACLE
PIACULA
PIACULAR
PIACULARITY
PIACULARLY
PIACULUM
PIAFFE
PIAFFED
PIAFFER
PIAFFING
PIALYN
PIAN
PIANET
PIANETA
PIANETTE
PIANGENDO
PIANI
PIANIC
PIANINO
PIANISM
PIANISSIMO
PIANISSIMOS
PIANIST
PIANISTE
PIANISTIC
PIANNET
PIANO
PIANOFORTE
PIANOGRAPH
PIANOLA
PIANOLIST
PIANOLOGUE
PIANOS
PIANOSA
PIARHAEMIC
PIARHEMIC
PIASABA
PIASAVA
PIASSABA
PIASSAVA
PIASTER
PIASTRE
PIAT
PIATION
PIATTI
PIAY
PIAZIN
PIAZZA
PIAZZAED
PIAZZETTA
PIAZZIAN
PIBCORN
PIBGORN
PIBLOCKTO
PIBLOKTO
PIBROCH
PIC
PICA
PICACHO
PICACHOS
PICADOR
PICADURA
PICAL
PICAMAR
PICARA
PICARD
PICAREL
PICARESQUE
PICARIAN
PICARO
PICAROON
PICAYUNE
PICAYUNISH
PICAYUNISHLY
PICCADILL
PICCADILLY
PICCAGE
PICCALILLI
PICCANINNY
PICCIOTTO
PICCOLO
PICCOLOIST
PICCOLOS
PICE
PICEIN
PICENE
PICEOUS
PICEWORTH
PICHI
PICHICIAGO
PICHICIAGOS
PICHICIEGO
PICHURIC
PICHURIM
PICIFORM
PICINE
PICK
PICKABACK
PICKADIL
PICKAGE
PICKANINNIES
PICKANINNY
PICKAROON
PICKAX
PICKAXE
PICKBACK
PICKED
PICKEDEVANT
PICKEDLY
PICKEDNESS
PICKEER
PICKEERED
PICKEERING
PICKEL
PICKER
PICKEREL
PICKERELS
PICKERELWEED
PICKERING
PICKERINGITE
PICKERY
PICKET
PICKETEER
PICKETER
PICKI
PICKING
PICKLE
PICKLED
PICKLEMAN
PICKLER
PICKLES
PICKLEWEED
PICKLEWORM
PICKLING
PICKLOCK
PICKMAN
PICKMAW
PICKMEN
PICKOFF
PICKOUT
PICKOVER
PICKPENNY
PICKPOCKET
PICKPOCKETRY
PICKPOLE
PICKPURSE
PICKSMAN
PICKSMITH
PICKSOME
PICKSOMENESS
PICKTHANK
PICKTHATCH
PICKTOOTH
PICKUP
PICKWICK
PICKY
PICNIC
PICNICKED
PICNICKER
PICNICKERY
PICNICKING
PICNICKY
PICO
PICOID
PICOLINE
PICOLINIC
PICORY
PICOT
PICOTAH
PICOTE
PICOTEE
PICOTITE
PICOTS
PICOTTAH
PICQUET
PICQUETER
PICRA
PICRASMIN
PICRATE
PICRATED
PICRIC
PICRITE
PICROCARMINE
PICROL
PICROLITE
PICROMERITE
PICRORHIZA
PICRORHIZIN
PICROTIN
PICROTOXIC
PICROTOXIN
PICRY
PICRYL
PICT
PICTARNIE
PICTOGRAM
PICTOGRAPH
PICTOGRAPHIC
PICTOGRAPHY
PICTORIAL
PICTORIALLY
PICTORIC
PICTORICAL
PICTORICALLY
PICTUN
PICTURABLE
PICTURABLY
PICTURAL
PICTURE
PICTURED
PICTUREDOM
PICTUREDROME
PICTURELY
PICTURER
PICTURESQUE
PICTURING
PICTURIZE
PICTURY
PICUCULE
PICUDA
PICUDILLA
PICUDO
PICUL
PICULE
PICULET
PICULS
PICULULE
PIDAN
PIDDLE
PIDDLED
PIDDLER

PIDDLING
PIDDOCK
PIDGIN
PIE
PIEBALD
PIEBALDLY
PIEBALDNESS
PIECE
PIECEABLE
PIECED
PIECEMEAL
PIECEN
PIECENER
PIECER
PIECES
PIECETTE
PIECEWORK
PIECEWORKER
PIECING
PIECRUST
PIED
PIEDE
PIEDFORT
PIEDLY
PIEDMONT
PIEDMONTITE
PIEDNESS
PIEDRA
PIEDROIT
PIEHOUSE
PIEING
PIEMAG
PIEMAN
PIEMARKER
PIEN
PIENA
PIENANNY
PIEND
PIENO
PIENTAO
PIEPAN
PIEPLANT
PIEPOUDRE
PIEPOWDER
PIEPRINT
PIER
PIERCE
PIERCED
PIERCEL
PIERCER
PIERCING
PIERCINGLY
PIERCINGNESS
PIERDROP
PIERHEAD
PIERID
PIERIDINE
PIERINE
PIERRETTE
PIERROT
PIERROTIC
PIERT
PIESHOP
PIET
PIETAS
PIETIC
PIETIES
PIETISM
PIETIST
PIETISTIC
PIETISTICAL
PIETON
PIETOSE
PIETOSO
PIETY
PIEWIFE
PIEWIPE
PIEWOMAN
PIEZO
PIEZOMETER
PIEZOMETRIC
PIEZOMETRY
PIFERO
PIFF
PIFFERO
PIFFLE
PIFFLED
PIFFLING
PIG
PIGBELLY
PIGBOAT
PIGDAN
PIGEON
PIGEONABLE
PIGEONBERRY
PIGEONEER
PIGEONER
PIGEONFOOT
PIGEONGRAM
PIGEONHOLE
PIGEONRY
PIGEONS
PIGEONTAIL
PIGEONWEED
PIGEONWING
PIGEONWOOD
PIGFACE
PIGFISH
PIGFISHES
PIGFLOWER
PIGFOOT
PIGGED
PIGGERIES
PIGGERY
PIGGIE
PIGGIN
PIGGING
PIGGISH
PIGGISHLY
PIGGISHNESS
PIGGLE
PIGGY
PIGGYBACK
PIGGYBACKING
PIGHEAD
PIGHEADED
PIGHEADEDLY
PIGHERD
PIGHTEL
PIGHTLE
PIGLET
PIGLIKE
PIGLING
PIGLY
PIGMAKER
PIGMAKING
PIGMAN
PIGMENT
PIGMENTARY
PIGMENTATION
PIGMENTIZE
PIGMENTOSE
PIGMEW
PIGMY
PIGNOLIA
PIGNON
PIGNORA
PIGNORATE
PIGNORATION
PIGNORATIVE
PIGNUS
PIGNUT
PIGPEN
PIGRITIA
PIGROOT
PIGROOTS
PIGS
PIGSKIN
PIGSNEY
PIGSNIES
PIGSTICK
PIGSTICKER
PIGSTICKING
PIGSTIES
PIGSTY
PIGTAIL
PIGTAILED
PIGWASH
PIGWEED
PIGWIDGEON
PIGWIDGIN
PIGWIGEON
PIGYARD
PIITIS
PIJA
PIK
PIKA
PIKAKE
PIKE
PIKED
PIKEL
PIKELET
PIKEMAN
PIKEMEN
PIKEMONGER
PIKER
PIKES
PIKESTAFF
PIKESTAVES
PIKETAIL
PIKEY
PIKI
PIKING
PIKLE
PIKOL
PIKY
PIL
PILA
PILAF
PILAFF
PILAGE
PILANDITE
PILAPIL
PILAR
PILARY
PILASTER
PILASTERED
PILASTERING
PILASTRADE
PILASTRADED
PILASTRIC
PILAU
PILAUED
PILAW
PILCH
PILCHARD
PILCHER
PILCHERD
PILCORN
PILCROW
PILE
PILEA
PILEATA
PILEATE
PILEATED
PILED
PILEIFORM
PILELESS
PILEOLATED
PILEOLI
PILEOLUS
PILEORHIZA
PILEORHIZE
PILEOUS
PILER
PILES
PILEUM
PILEUS
PILEWEED
PILEWORK
PILEWORM
PILEWORT
PILFER
PILFERAGE
PILFERER
PILFERING
PILFERY
PILFRE
PILGARLIC
PILGARLICKY
PILGER
PILGRIM
PILGRIMAGE
PILGRIMAGER
PILGRIMATIC
PILGRIMER
PILGRIMESS
PILGRIMIZE
PILI
PILIDIUM
PILIFER
PILIFEROUS
PILIFORM
PILIGAN
PILIGANIN
PILIGANINE
PILIKAI
PILIKIA
PILILLOO
PILIMICTION
PILINE
PILING
PILITICO
PILK
PILKINS
PILL
PILLAGE
PILLAGED
PILLAGER
PILLAGERS
PILLAGING
PILLAR
PILLARED
PILLARET
PILLARING
PILLARIST
PILLARLET
PILLARLIKE
PILLARY
PILLAS
PILLBOX
PILLED
PILLEDNESS
PILLER
PILLERY
PILLET
PILLEUS
PILLICOCK
PILLION
PILLIVER
PILLIWINKS
PILLMAKER
PILLMAKING
PILLMONGER
PILLORIED
PILLORIES
PILLORIZE
PILLORY
PILLORYING
PILLOW
PILLOWBEER
PILLOWBER
PILLOWBERE
PILLOWCASE
PILLOWING
PILLOWMADE
PILLOWWORK
PILLOWY
PILLS
PILLULE
PILLWORM
PILLWORT
PILM
PILMY
PILOCARPIN
PILOCARPINE
PILOCYSTIC
PILOERECTION
PILOMOTOR
PILON
PILONCILLO
PILONIDAL
PILORI
PILOSE
PILOSIN
PILOSINE
PILOSIS
PILOSISM
PILOSITY
PILOT
PILOTAGE
PILOTAXITIC
PILOTED
PILOTHOUSE
PILOTING
PILOTISM
PILOTMAN
PILOTRY
PILOTWEED
PILOUS
PILPUL
PILPULIST
PILPULISTIC
PILSENER
PILSNER
PILT
PILTOCK
PILULA
PILULAR
PILULE
PILULIST
PILULOUS
PILUM
PILUS
PILWILLET
PILY
PIMA
PIMBINA
PIMELATE
PIMELIC
PIMELITE
PIMELITIS
PIMENT
PIMENTO
PIMENTON
PIMENTOS
PIMGENET
PIMIENTA
PIMIENTO
PIMIENTOS
PIMLICO
PIMOLA
PIMP
PIMPED
PIMPERNEL

PIMPERY
PIMPING
PIMPLE
PIMPLEBACK
PIMPLED
PIMPLIER
PIMPLIEST
PIMPLINESS
PIMPLING
PIMPLO
PIMPLY
PIN
PINA
PINABETE
PINACEOUS
PINACHROME
PINACLE
PINACOCYTAL
PINACOCYTE
PINACOID
PINACOIDAL
PINACOL
PINACOLATE
PINACOLIN
PINACOLINE
PINACULUM
PINAFORE
PINAG
PINAKIOLITE
PINAKOID
PINAKOIDAL
PINAKOTHEKE
PINANG
PINAS
PINASTER
PINATA
PINAVERDOL
PINAX
PINAYUSA
PINBALL
PINBEFORE
PINBONE
PINBUSH
PINCASE
PINCEMENT
PINCER
PINCERLIKE
PINCERS
PINCETTE
PINCH
PINCHBACK
PINCHBECK
PINCHBUG
PINCHCOCK
PINCHE
PINCHED
PINCHEDLY
PINCHEDNESS
PINCHEM
PINCHER
PINCHFIST
PINCHFISTED
PINCHGUT
PINCHING
PINCHPENNY
PINCPINC
PINCUSHION
PINCUSHIONY
PIND
PINDA
PINDAL
PINDARICAL
PINDARICALLY
PINDARICS
PINDER
PINDJAJAP
PINDLING
PINDY
PINE
PINEAL
PINEALISM
PINEALOMA
PINEAPPLE
PINEBANK
PINECONE
PINED
PINEDROPS
PINELAND
PINENE
PINER
PINERIES
PINERY
PINES
PINESAP
PINETA
PINETUM
PINEWEED
PINEWOODS
PINEY
PINFALL
PINFEATHER
PINFEATHERED
PINFEATHERER
PINFEATHERY
PINFIRE
PINFISH
PINFISHES
PINFOLD
PING
PINGE
PINGED
PINGING
PINGLE
PINGLER
PINGO
PINGRASS
PINGSTER
PINGUE
PINGUECULA
PINGUEDINOUS
PINGUEFACTION
PINGUEFY
PINGUESCENCE
PINGUESCENT
PINGUICULA
PINGUID
PINGUIDITY
PINGUIN
PINGUITE
PINGUITUDE
PINHEAD
PINHEADED
PINHOLD
PINHOLE
PINHOOK
PINIC
PINIER
PINIEST
PINING
PININGLY
PININGS
PINION
PINIONED
PINIONING
PINIPICRIN
PINITE
PINITOL
PINJANE
PINJRA
PINK
PINKANY
PINKBERRY
PINKED
PINKEEN
PINKEN
PINKENY
PINKER
PINKEYE
PINKFISH
PINKFISHES
PINKIE
PINKIFIED
PINKIFY
PINKIFYING
PINKING
PINKISH
PINKROOT
PINKSOME
PINKWEED
PINKWOOD
PINKWORT
PINKY
PINLOCK
PINMAKER
PINMAKING
PINMAN
PINNA
PINNACE
PINNACLE
PINNACLED
PINNACLING
PINNAE
PINNAGE
PINNAGLOBIN
PINNAL
PINNAS
PINNATE
PINNATED
PINNATELY
PINNATIFID
PINNATIFIDLY
PINNATION
PINNATIPED
PINNATISECT
PINNATULATE
PINNED
PINNEL
PINNER
PINNET
PINNIGRADE
PINNING
PINNIPED
PINNIPEDIAN
PINNOCK
PINNOITE
PINNOTERE
PINNOTHERE
PINNOTHERIAN
PINNULA
PINNULAE
PINNULAR
PINNULATE
PINNULATED
PINNULE
PINNULET
PINNY
PINNYWINKLE
PINO
PINOCHLE
PINOCLE
PINOLE
PINOLEUM
PINOLIA
PINOLIN
PINON
PINOT
PINPATCH
PINPILLOW
PINPOINT
PINPRICK
PINPROOF
PINRAIL
PINROWED
PINS
PINSCHER
PINSETTER
PINSON
PINSONS
PINT
PINTA
PINTADERA
PINTADO
PINTADOES
PINTADOITE
PINTADOS
PINTAIL
PINTAILS
PINTANO
PINTANOS
PINTE
PINTID
PINTLE
PINTO
PINTURA
PINUELA
PINULUS
PINUP
PINWEED
PINWHEEL
PINWORK
PINWORM
PINXIT
PINY
PINYL
PINYON
PIOLET
PION
PIONED
PIONEER
PIONEERED
PIONEERING
PIONERY
PIONNOTES
PIOSCOPE
PIOTED
PIOTINE
PIOTTY
PIOUPIOU
PIOURY
PIOUS
PIOUSLY
PIOUSNESS
PIP
PIPA
PIPAGE
PIPAL
PIPE
PIPEAGE
PIPECOLIN
PIPECOLINE
PIPECOLINIC
PIPED
PIPEFISH
PIPEFISHES
PIPEFITTER
PIPEFITTING
PIPEFUL
PIPEFULS
PIPELAYER
PIPELAYING
PIPELESS
PIPELIKE
PIPELINE
PIPEMAN
PIPEMOUTH
PIPER
PIPERACEOUS
PIPERATE
PIPERAZINE
PIPERIDE
PIPERIDEINE
PIPERIDGE
PIPERIDID
PIPERIDIDE
PIPERIDIN
PIPERIDINE
PIPERINE
PIPERITIOUS
PIPERITONE
PIPERLY
PIPERONAL
PIPERONYL
PIPERY
PIPERYLENE
PIPES
PIPESTAPPLE
PIPESTEM
PIPESTONE
PIPET
PIPETTE
PIPEWALKER
PIPEWOOD
PIPEWORK
PIPEWORT
PIPEY
PIPI
PIPID
PIPIER
PIPIEST
PIPIKAULA
PIPING
PIPINGLY
PIPINGNESS
PIPIRI
PIPISTREL
PIPISTRELLE
PIPIT
PIPKIN
PIPPED
PIPPEN
PIPPER
PIPPIER
PIPPIEST
PIPPIN
PIPPINER
PIPPINFACE
PIPPING
PIPPLE
PIPPY
PIPRINE
PIPROID
PIPSISSEWA
PIPUNCULID
PIPY
PIQUABLE
PIQUANCY
PIQUANT
PIQUANTLY
PIQUANTNESS
PIQUE
PIQUED
PIQUERO
PIQUET
PIQUETTE
PIQUEUR
PIQUIA
PIQUIERE
PIQUING
PIQURE
PIR
PIRACIES
PIRACY
PIRAGUA
PIRAI
PIRANA

PIRANHA
PIRARUCU
PIRATE
PIRATED
PIRATERY
PIRATIC
PIRATICAL
PIRATICALLY
PIRATING
PIRATISM
PIRATRY
PIRATY
PIRAYA
PIRCA
PIRE
PIRIJIRI
PIRIPIRI
PIRIRIGUA
PIRL
PIRLIE
PIRN
PIRNED
PIRNER
PIRNIE
PIRNY
PIROGEN
PIROGUE
PIROJKI
PIROL
PIROOT
PIROPLASM
PIROPLASMOSIS
PIROSHKI
PIROT
PIROUETTE
PIROUETTED
PIROUETTER
PIROUETTIST
PIRR
PIRRAURA
PIRRAURU
PIRRMAW
PIRSSONITE
PIRY
PISACA
PISACHA
PISACHEE
PISACHI
PISANG
PISANITE
PISAY
PISCARIES
PISCARY
PISCATION
PISCATOLOGY
PISCATOR
PISCATORIAL
PISCATORIAN
PISCATORIOUS
PISCATORY
PISCIAN
PISCICAPTURE
PISCICOLOUS
PISCICULTURE
PISCIFAUNA
PISCIFEROUS
PISCIFORM
PISCINA
PISCINAL
PISCINE
PISCINITY
PISCIVOROUS
PISCO
PISE
PISH
PISHAUG
PISHOGUE
PISHPASH
PISHU
PISIFORM
PISK
PISKUN
PISKY
PISMIRE
PISMIRISM
PISO
PISOLITE
PISOLITIC
PISOTE
PISS
PISSABED
PISSANT
PISSED
PISSING
PIST
PISTACHE
PISTACHIO
PISTACHIOS
PISTACITE
PISTAREEN
PISTE
PISTEOLOGY
PISTIC
PISTICK
PISTIL
PISTILLAR
PISTILLARY
PISTILLATE
PISTILLID
PISTILLIDIUM
PISTILLINE
PISTILLODE
PISTILLODY
PISTILLOID
PISTILS
PISTIOLOGY
PISTLE
PISTLER
PISTOL
PISTOLADE
PISTOLE
PISTOLED
PISTOLEER
PISTOLET
PISTOLETER
PISTOLETIER
PISTOLGRAM
PISTOLGRAPH
PISTOLIER
PISTOLING
PISTOLLED
PISTOLLING
PISTOLOGY
PISTOLPROOF
PISTON
PISTONHEAD
PISTRICES
PISTRIX
PIT
PITA
PITAHAYA
PITANGA
PITANGUA
PITAPAT
PITAPATATION
PITARAH
PITAU
PITBIRD
PITCH
PITCHBLENDE
PITCHED
PITCHER
PITCHERED
PITCHERY
PITCHFIELD
PITCHFORK
PITCHHOLE
PITCHI
PITCHIER
PITCHIEST
PITCHILY
PITCHINESS
PITCHING
PITCHMAN
PITCHOMETER
PITCHPIKE
PITCHSTONE
PITCHWORK
PITCHY
PITE
PITEIRA
PITEOUS
PITEOUSLY
PITEOUSNESS
PITFALL
PITFOLD
PITH
PITHANOLOGY
PITHEAD
PITHECAN
PITHECIAN
PITHECIINE
PITHECISM
PITHECOID
PITHECOLOGY
PITHECUS
PITHED
PITHIER
PITHIEST
PITHILY
PITHINESS
PITHING
PITHLESS
PITHOI
PITHOLE
PITHOS
PITHSOME
PITHY
PITIABILITY
PITIABLE
PITIABLENESS
PITIABLY
PITIED
PITIER
PITIES
PITIFUL
PITIFULLY
PITIFULNESS
PITIKINS
PITILESS
PITILESSLY
PITILESSNESS
PITIRRI
PITMAN
PITMANS
PITMEN
PITMIRK
PITO
PITOMETER
PITOMIE
PITON
PITPAN
PITPIT
PITPROP
PITSAW
PITSIDE
PITTACAL
PITTANCE
PITTANCER
PITTARD
PITTED
PITTER
PITTICITE
PITTINE
PITTING
PITTITE
PITTO
PITTOID
PITTOSPORE
PITUITAL
PITUITARIES
PITUITARY
PITUITE
PITUITOUS
PITURI
PITWOOD
PITWORK
PITWRIGHT
PITY
PITYING
PITYINGLY
PITYOCAMPA
PITYOCAMPE
PITYRIASIC
PITYRIASIS
PITYROID
PIU
PIUI
PIUPIU
PIURA
PIURI
PIVA
PIVOT
PIVOTAL
PIVOTALLY
PIVOTED
PIVOTER
PIVOTING
PIX
PIXIE
PIXIES
PIXILATED
PIXY
PIYYUT
PIZE
PIZZA
PIZZERIA
PIZZICATO
PIZZLE
PLACABILITY
PLACABLE
PLACABLENESS
PLACABLY
PLACARD
PLACARDED
PLACARDER
PLACARDING
PLACATE
PLACATED
PLACATER
PLACATING
PLACATION
PLACATIVE
PLACATORY
PLACCATE
PLACE
PLACEBO
PLACEBOES
PLACEBOS
PLACED
PLACEHOLDER
PLACEMAKER
PLACEMAN
PLACEMEN
PLACEMENT
PLACEMONGER
PLACENT
PLACENTA
PLACENTAE
PLACENTAL
PLACENTALIAN
PLACENTARY
PLACENTAS
PLACENTATE
PLACENTATION
PLACENTIFORM
PLACENTITIS
PLACENTOID
PLACENTOMA
PLACER
PLACET
PLACID
PLACIDAMENTE
PLACIDITY
PLACIDLY
PLACIDNESS
PLACING
PLACIT
PLACITUM
PLACK
PLACKET
PLACKLESS
PLACODE
PLACODERM
PLACODERMAL
PLACODERMOID
PLACODONT
PLACOID
PLACOIDAL
PLACOIDEAN
PLACOPLAST
PLACULA
PLADAROMA
PLAFOND
PLAGA
PLAGAL
PLAGATE
PLAGE
PLAGIAPLITE
PLAGIARICAL
PLAGIARIES
PLAGIARISE
PLAGIARISM
PLAGIARIST
PLAGIARISTIC
PLAGIARIZE
PLAGIARIZED
PLAGIARIZER
PLAGIARIZING
PLAGIARY
PLAGIHEDRAL
PLAGIOCLASE
PLAGIOCLINAL
PLAGIODONT
PLAGIOGRAPH
PLAGIONITE
PLAGIOPHYRE
PLAGIOSTOME
PLAGIOTROPIC
PLAGIUM
PLAGOSE
PLAGOSITY
PLAGUE
PLAGUED
PLAGUER
PLAGUESOME
PLAGUEY
PLAGUILY
PLAGUING
PLAGULA
PLAGUY
PLAICE
PLAID
PLAIDED
PLAIDMAN

PLAIDOYER
PLAIK
PLAIN
PLAINBACK
PLAINBACKS
PLAINED
PLAINER
PLAINEST
PLAINFUL
PLAINING
PLAINLY
PLAINNESS
PLAINS
PLAINSCRAFT
PLAINSFOLK
PLAINSMAN
PLAINSMEN
PLAINSOLED
PLAINSONG
PLAINSTONES
PLAINSWOMAN
PLAINSWOMEN
PLAINT
PLAINTAIL
PLAINTEXT
PLAINTIFF
PLAINTILE
PLAINTIVE
PLAINTIVELY
PLAINWARD
PLAINY
PLAISTER
PLAIT
PLAITED
PLAITER
PLAITING
PLAITWORK
PLAKAT
PLAN
PLANAEA
PLANAR
PLANARIAN
PLANARIFORM
PLANARIOID
PLANARITY
PLANATE
PLANATION
PLANCH
PLANCHE
PLANCHEITE
PLANCHER
PLANCHET
PLANCHETTE
PLANCHING
PLANCIER
PLANDOK
PLANE
PLANED
PLANER
PLANES
PLANET
PLANETA
PLANETABLE
PLANETABLER
PLANETAL
PLANETARIA
PLANETARIAN
PLANETARIES
PLANETARIUM
PLANETARIUMS
PLANETARY
PLANETED
PLANETESIMAL
PLANETFALL
PLANETIC
PLANETICOSE
PLANETING
PLANETOGENY
PLANETOID
PLANETOIDAL
PLANETOLOGIC
PLANETOLOGY
PLANETS
PLANFORM
PLANFUL
PLANFULLY
PLANFULNESS
PLANG
PLANGENCY
PLANGENT
PLANGENTLY
PLANGI
PLANGOR
PLANGOROUS
PLANICIPITAL
PLANIFOLIOUS
PLANIFORM
PLANIGRAPH
PLANILLA
PLANIMETER
PLANIMETRIC
PLANIMETRY
PLANING
PLANIPENNATE
PLANIPENNINE
PLANIROSTAL
PLANISCOPE
PLANISCOPIC
PLANISH
PLANISHED
PLANISHER
PLANISHING
PLANISPHERAL
PLANISPHERE
PLANISPHERIC
PLANISPIRAL
PLANK
PLANKAGE
PLANKED
PLANKER
PLANKING
PLANKS
PLANKTER
PLANKTOLOGY
PLANKTON
PLANKTONIC
PLANKTONT
PLANKWAYS
PLANKWISE
PLANLESS
PLANLESSLY
PLANLESSNESS
PLANNED
PLANNER
PLANNING
PLANOBLAST
PLANOBLASTIC
PLANOFERRITE
PLANOGAMETE
PLANOGRAPH
PLANOGRAPHIC
PLANOGRAPHY
PLANOMETER
PLANOMETRY
PLANOMILLER
PLANONT
PLANORBIFORM
PLANORBINE
PLANORBOID
PLANOSOME
PLANOSPORE
PLANT
PLANTA
PLANTAD
PLANTAGE
PLANTAIN
PLANTAL
PLANTANO
PLANTAR
PLANTARIS
PLANTARIUM
PLANTATION
PLANTATOR
PLANTED
PLANTER
PLANTERLY
PLANTIGRADE
PLANTIGRADY
PLANTING
PLANTIVOROUS
PLANTLET
PLANTLING
PLANTOCRACY
PLANTS
PLANTSMAN
PLANTULAE
PLANTULAR
PLANTULE
PLANULA
PLANULAE
PLANULAN
PLANULAR
PLANULATE
PLANULIFORM
PLANULOID
PLANUM
PLANURIA
PLANXTY
PLAP
PLAPPERT
PLAQUE
PLAQUETTE
PLASH
PLASHED
PLASHER
PLASHET
PLASHING
PLASHY
PLASM
PLASMA
PLASMASE
PLASMATIC
PLASMATICAL
PLASMATION
PLASMIC
PLASMOCHIN
PLASMOCYTE
PLASMODESM
PLASMODESMUS
PLASMODIA
PLASMODIAL
PLASMODIATE
PLASMODIUM
PLASMOGEN
PLASMOID
PLASMOLYSIS
PLASMOLYTIC
PLASMOLYZE
PLASMOMA
PLASMOMATA
PLASMON
PLASMOPHAGY
PLASMOPTYSIS
PLASMOQUIN
PLASMOQUINE
PLASMOSOMA
PLASMOSOMATA
PLASMOSOME
PLASMOTOMY
PLASOME
PLASS
PLASSON
PLASTEIN
PLASTER
PLASTERBILL
PLASTERBOARD
PLASTERED
PLASTERER
PLASTERINESS
PLASTERING
PLASTERWORK
PLASTERY
PLASTIC
PLASTICALLY
PLASTICINE
PLASTICISM
PLASTICITY
PLASTICIZE
PLASTICIZED
PLASTICIZER
PLASTICIZING
PLASTICLY
PLASTICS
PLASTID
PLASTIDIUM
PLASTIDOME
PLASTIDULAR
PLASTIDULE
PLASTIFY
PLASTIN
PLASTINOID
PLASTIQUE
PLASTOGAMIC
PLASTOGAMY
PLASTOMERE
PLASTOMETER
PLASTOSOME
PLASTOTYPE
PLASTRAL
PLASTRON
PLASTRUM
PLAT
PLATALEIFORM
PLATALEINE
PLATAN
PLATANE
PLATANIST
PLATANNA
PLATANO
PLATBAND
PLATCH
PLATE
PLATEA
PLATEASM
PLATEAU
PLATEAUS
PLATEAUX
PLATED
PLATEFUL
PLATEFULS
PLATEHOLDER
PLATEIASMUS
PLATELAYER
PLATELET
PLATEMAKER
PLATEMAKING
PLATEMAN
PLATEMEN
PLATEN
PLATER
PLATERER
PLATERESQUE
PLATERY
PLATES
PLATEWAY
PLATEWORK
PLATFORM
PLATFORMALLY
PLATFORMIST
PLATIC
PLATICLY
PLATIE
PLATILLA
PLATINA
PLATINAMIN
PLATINAMINE
PLATINAMMIN
PLATINAMMINE
PLATINATE
PLATINE
PLATING
PLATINIC
PLATINIZE
PLATINIZED
PLATINIZING
PLATINOID
PLATINOTYPE
PLATINOUS
PLATINUM
PLATITUDE
PLATITUDINAL
PLATLY
PLATODE
PLATOID
PLATONICALLY
PLATOON
PLATOPIC
PLATTED
PLATTEN
PLATTER
PLATTERFACE
PLATTING
PLATTNERITE
PLATTY
PLATUROUS
PLATY
PLATYBASIC
PLATYCARPOUS
PLATYCELIAN
PLATYCELOUS
PLATYCEPHALY
PLATYCHEIRIA
PLATYCNEMIA
PLATYCNEMIC
PLATYCOELIAN
PLATYCOELOUS
PLATYCORIA
PLATYCRANIA
PLATYCRANIAL
PLATYDACTYL
PLATYDACTYLE
PLATYFISH
PLATYGLOSSAL
PLATYGLOSSIA
PLATYHIERIC
PLATYLOBATE
PLATYMERIA
PLATYMETER
PLATYMYOID
PLATYNITE
PLATYNOTAL
PLATYODONT
PLATYOPE
PLATYOPIA
PLATYOPIC
PLATYPELLIC
PLATYPOD
PLATYPODIA
PLATYPODOUS
PLATYPUS
PLATYPUSES
PLATYPYGOUS
PLATYRRHIN
PLATYRRHINE
PLATYRRHINY

PLATYSMA
PLATYSOMID
PLATYSTERNAL
PLATYTROPE
PLAUD
PLAUDATION
PLAUDIT
PLAUDITE
PLAUDITOR
PLAUDITORY
PLAUENITE
PLAUSIBILITY
PLAUSIBLE
PLAUSIBLY
PLAUSIVE
PLAUSTRAL
PLAY
PLAYA
PLAYABILITY
PLAYABLE
PLAYAS
PLAYBACK
PLAYBILL
PLAYBOOK
PLAYBOX
PLAYBOY
PLAYBROKER
PLAYDAY
PLAYDOWN
PLAYED
PLAYER
PLAYERESS
PLAYFELLOW
PLAYFERE
PLAYFIELD
PLAYFUL
PLAYFULLY
PLAYFULNESS
PLAYGOER
PLAYGOING
PLAYGROUND
PLAYHOUSE
PLAYING
PLAYINGLY
PLAYLET
PLAYMAKER
PLAYMAKING
PLAYMAN
PLAYMARE
PLAYMATE
PLAYMONGER
PLAYOCK
PLAYOFF
PLAYPEN
PLAYREADER
PLAYROOM
PLAYSCRIPT
PLAYSOME
PLAYSOMELY
PLAYSOMENESS
PLAYSTEAD
PLAYSTOW
PLAYTE
PLAYTHING
PLAYTIME
PLAYWARD
PLAYWOMAN
PLAYWOMEN
PLAYWORK
PLAYWRIGHT
PLAYWRITER
PLAYWRITING
PLAZA
PLAZOLITE
PLEA
PLEACH
PLEACHED
PLEACHER
PLEACHING
PLEAD
PLEADABLE
PLEADED
PLEADER
PLEADING
PLEADINGLY
PLEADINGNESS
PLEASANCE
PLEASANT
PLEASANTLY
PLEASANTNESS
PLEASANTRY
PLEASANTSOME
PLEASAUNCE
PLEASE
PLEASED
PLEASEDLY
PLEASEDNESS
PLEASEMAN
PLEASEMEN
PLEASER
PLEASHIP
PLEASING
PLEASINGLY
PLEASINGNESS
PLEASURABLE
PLEASURABLY
PLEASURE
PLEASURED
PLEASUREFUL
PLEASUREMAN
PLEASUREMENT
PLEASURER
PLEASURING
PLEASURIST
PLEASUROUS
PLEAT
PLEATED
PLEATER
PLEATS
PLEB
PLEBE
PLEBEIAN
PLEBEIANISM
PLEBEIANIZE
PLEBEIANIZED
PLEBEIANLY
PLEBEIANNESS
PLEBEITY
PLEBES
PLEBICOLAR
PLEBICOLIST
PLEBICOLOUS
PLEBIFY
PLEBISCITARY
PLEBISCITE
PLEBISCITIC
PLEBISCITUM
PLEBS
PLECK
PLECOPTERAN
PLECOPTERID
PLECOPTEROUS
PLECOTINE
PLECTOGNATH
PLECTRA
PLECTRE
PLECTRIDIAL
PLECTRIDIUM
PLECTRON
PLECTRUM
PLECTRUMS
PLED
PLEDGE
PLEDGED
PLEDGEE
PLEDGEOR
PLEDGER
PLEDGESHOP
PLEDGET
PLEDGING
PLEDGOR
PLEE
PLEGAPHONIA
PLEGOMETER
PLEIN
PLEIOBAR
PLEIOCHROMIA
PLEIOCHROMIC
PLEIOMEROUS
PLEIOMERY
PLEION
PLEIONIAN
PLEIOPHYLLY
PLEIOTAXIS
PLEISTOSEIST
PLEMOCHOE
PLENA
PLENAL
PLENARILY
PLENARINESS
PLENARIUM
PLENARTY
PLENARY
PLENICORN
PLENILUNAL
PLENILUNE
PLENIPO
PLENIPOTENCE
PLENIPOTENT
PLENISH
PLENISHING
PLENISHMENT
PLENISM
PLENIST
PLENITUDE
PLENITY
PLENTEOUS
PLENTEOUSLY
PLENTIES
PLENTIFUL
PLENTIFULLY
PLENTIFULNESS
PLENTY
PLENUM
PLENUMS
PLENY
PLEOCHROIC
PLEOCHROISM
PLEOCHROOUS
PLEODONT
PLEOMASTIA
PLEOMASTIC
PLEOMETROSIS
PLEOMETROTIC
PLEOMORPHIC
PLEOMORPHIST
PLEOMORPHY
PLEON
PLEONASM
PLEONAST
PLEONASTE
PLEONASTIC
PLEONASTICAL
PLEONECTIC
PLEONEXIA
PLEONIC
PLEOPOD
PLEOPODITE
PLERERGATE
PLEROCERCOID
PLEROMA
PLEROMATIC
PLEROME
PLEROMORPH
PLEROPHORIC
PLEROPHORY
PLEROSIS
PLEROTIC
PLESIOBIOSIS
PLESIOSAUR
PLESIOSAURUS
PLESIOTYPE
PLESSIGRAPH
PLESSOR
PLET
PLETE
PLETHORA
PLETHORIC
PLETHORICAL
PLETHOROUS
PLETHORY
PLETHRON
PLETHRUM
PLEURA
PLEURAE
PLEURAL
PLEURIC
PLEURISY
PLEURITIC
PLEURITIS
PLEUROBRANCH
PLEUROCARP
PLEUROCELE
PLEUROCEROID
PLEURODONT
PLEUROGENIC
PLEUROLITH
PLEURON
PLEURONECTID
PLEUROPEDAL
PLEUROPODIUM
PLEUROSTEAL
PLEUROSTICT
PLEUROTOMIES
PLEUROTOMY
PLEUROTRIBE
PLEURUM
PLEUSTON
PLEVIN
PLEW
PLEWCH
PLEWE
PLEWGH
PLEX
PLEXAL
PLEXICOSE
PLEXIFORM
PLEXIGLAS
PLEXIGLASS
PLEXIMETER
PLEXIMETRIC
PLEXIMETRY
PLEXIPPUS
PLEXODONT
PLEXOR
PLEXURE
PLEXUS
PLEXUSES
PLIABILITY
PLIABLE
PLIABLENESS
PLIABLY
PLIANCY
PLIANT
PLIANTLY
PLIANTNESS
PLICA
PLICABLE
PLICAE
PLICAL
PLICATE
PLICATED
PLICATELY
PLICATENESS
PLICATINE
PLICATION
PLICATOR
PLICATULATE
PLICATURE
PLICIFEROUS
PLICIFORM
PLIED
PLIER
PLIERS
PLIES
PLIGHT
PLIGHTED
PLIGHTER
PLIGHTING
PLIM
PLIMSOLL
PLINTH
PLINTHER
PLINTHIFORM
PLIOSAUR
PLIOSAURIAN
PLIOTHERMIC
PLISKIE
PLISKY
PLISSE
PLITCH
PLOAT
PLOCE
PLOCEIFORM
PLOCK
PLOD
PLODDED
PLODDER
PLODDERLY
PLODDING
PLODDINGLY
PLODDINGNESS
PLODGE
PLOESTI
PLOIMATE
PLOMB
PLONK
PLOOK
PLOP
PLOPPED
PLOPPING
PLORATION
PLORATORY
PLOSH
PLOSION
PLOSIVE
PLOT
PLOTCH
PLOTCOCK
PLOTFUL
PLOTOSID
PLOTPROOF
PLOTT
PLOTTAGE
PLOTTED
PLOTTER
PLOTTERY
PLOTTING
PLOTTINGLY
PLOTTON
PLOTTY
PLOUGH
PLOUGHBOY
PLOUGHED
PLOUGHFISH

PLOUGHFOOT
PLOUGHGANG
PLOUGHGATE
PLOUGHHEAD
PLOUGHING
PLOUGHJOGGER
PLOUGHLAND
PLOUGHLINE
PLOUGHMAN
PLOUGHMELL
PLOUGHPOINT
PLOUGHSHARE
PLOUGHSHOE
PLOUGHSTAFF
PLOUGHSTILT
PLOUGHTAIL
PLOUGHWISE
PLOUGHWRIGHT
PLOUK
PLOUNCE
PLOUSIOCRACY
PLOUT
PLOUTER
PLOVER
PLOVERS
PLOVERY
PLOW
PLOWABLE
PLOWBOTE
PLOWBOY
PLOWED
PLOWER
PLOWFISH
PLOWFOOT
PLOWGANG
PLOWGATE
PLOWGRAITH
PLOWHEAD
PLOWING
PLOWJOGGER
PLOWLAND
PLOWLIGHT
PLOWLINE
PLOWMAKER
PLOWMAKING
PLOWMAN
PLOWMELL
PLOWMEN
PLOWPOINT
PLOWSHARE
PLOWSHOE
PLOWSTAFF
PLOWSTILT
PLOWTAIL
PLOWTER
PLOWWISE
PLOWWOMAN
PLOWWRIGHT
PLOY
PLOYMENT
PLUCK
PLUCKED
PLUCKER
PLUCKIER
PLUCKIEST
PLUCKILY
PLUCKINESS
PLUCKING
PLUCKY
PLUD
PLUFF
PLUFFER
PLUFFY
PLUG
PLUGBOARD
PLUGDRAWER
PLUGGABLE
PLUGGED
PLUGGER
PLUGGING
PLUGGINGLY
PLUGGY
PLUGHOLE
PLUGMAN
PLUGMEN
PLUGS
PLUGTRAY
PLUKE
PLUM
PLUMA
PLUMACEOUS
PLUMACH
PLUMADE
PLUMAGE
PLUMAGED
PLUMAGERY
PLUMASITE
PLUMASSIER
PLUMATE
PLUMATELLID
PLUMATELLOID
PLUMB
PLUMBAGE
PLUMBAGINE
PLUMBAGINOUS
PLUMBAGO
PLUMBAGOS
PLUMBATE
PLUMBEAN
PLUMBED
PLUMBEOUS
PLUMBER
PLUMBERIES
PLUMBERY
PLUMBET
PLUMBIC
PLUMBING
PLUMBISM
PLUMBITE
PLUMBLESS
PLUMBNESS
PLUMBOG
PLUMBOUS
PLUMBUM
PLUMCOT
PLUME
PLUMED
PLUMELET
PLUMEMAKER
PLUMEMAKING
PLUMEOUS
PLUMER
PLUMERY
PLUMET
PLUMETE
PLUMETIS
PLUMETTE
PLUMICORN
PLUMIER
PLUMIERIDE
PLUMIEST
PLUMING
PLUMIPED
PLUMIPEDE
PLUMIST
PLUMLIKE
PLUMMER
PLUMMET
PLUMMETED
PLUMMETLESS
PLUMMIER
PLUMMIEST
PLUMMING
PLUMMY
PLUMOSE
PLUMOSELY
PLUMOSENESS
PLUMOSITY
PLUMOUS
PLUMP
PLUMPEN
PLUMPER
PLUMPEST
PLUMPING
PLUMPLY
PLUMPNESS
PLUMPS
PLUMPY
PLUMROCK
PLUMULA
PLUMULACEOUS
PLUMULAR
PLUMULARIAN
PLUMULATE
PLUMULE
PLUMULIFORM
PLUMULOSE
PLUMY
PLUNDER
PLUNDERAGE
PLUNDERBUND
PLUNDERED
PLUNDERER
PLUNDERESS
PLUNDERING
PLUNDERINGLY
PLUNDEROUS
PLUNDERPROOF
PLUNGE
PLUNGED
PLUNGEON
PLUNGER
PLUNGING
PLUNGY
PLUNK
PLUNKED
PLUNKING
PLUNTHER
PLUPATRIOTIC
PLUPERFECT
PLUPERFECTLY
PLURAL
PLURALISM
PLURALIST
PLURALISTIC
PLURALITIES
PLURALITY
PLURALIZE
PLURALIZED
PLURALIZER
PLURALIZING
PLURALLY
PLURATIVE
PLUREL
PLURENNIAL
PLURIAXIAL
PLURICIPITAL
PLURICUSPID
PLURIES
PLURIFACIAL
PLURIFOLIATE
PLURIFY
PLURILATERAL
PLURILINGUAL
PLURILOCULAR
PLURINOMINAL
PLURIPARA
PLURIPARITY
PLURIPAROUS
PLURIPARTITE
PLURIPOTENCE
PLURIPOTENT
PLURISEPTATE
PLURISERIAL
PLURISERIATE
PLURISETOSE
PLURISPIRAL
PLURISPOROUS
PLURISY
PLURIVALENT
PLURIVALVE
PLURIVOROUS
PLURIVORY
PLUS
PLUSES
PLUSH
PLUSHED
PLUSHETTE
PLUSHIER
PLUSHIEST
PLUSHILY
PLUSHINESS
PLUSHY
PLUSQUAM
PLUSSAGE
PLUTEAL
PLUTEAN
PLUTEI
PLUTEIFORM
PLUTEUS
PLUTEUSES
PLUTOCRACIES
PLUTOCRACY
PLUTOCRAT
PLUTOCRATIC
PLUTOCRATICAL
PLUTOLATRY
PLUTOLOGICAL
PLUTOLOGIST
PLUTOLOGY
PLUTOMANIA
PLUTONIAN
PLUTONIC
PLUTONISM
PLUTONIST
PLUTONITE
PLUTONIUM
PLUTONOMIC
PLUTONOMIST
PLUTONOMY
PLUTTER
PLUVIAL
PLUVIALINE
PLUVINE
PLUVIOGRAPH
PLUVIOGRAPHY
PLUVIOMETER
PLUVIOMETRIC
PLUVIOMETRY
PLUVIOSCOPE
PLUVIOSITY
PLUVIOUS
PLY
PLYER
PLYGAIN
PLYING
PLYWOOD
PNEOGRAPH
PNEOMETER
PNEOMETRY
PNEOSCOPE
PNEUMA
PNEUMATIC
PNEUMATICAL
PNEUMATICITY
PNEUMATICS
PNEUMATISM
PNEUMATIST
PNEUMATIZE
PNEUMATIZED
PNEUMATOCELE
PNEUMATOCYST
PNEUMATOGRAM
PNEUMATOLOGY
PNEUMATOSIS
PNEUMATURIA
PNEUME
PNEUMECTOMY
PNEUMOCELE
PNEUMOCOCCUS
PNEUMODERMA
PNEUMOGASTRIC
PNEUMOGRAM
PNEUMOGRAPH
PNEUMOLITH
PNEUMOLOGY
PNEUMOLYSIS
PNEUMONALGIA
PNEUMONIA
PNEUMONIC
PNEUMONITIC
PNEUMONOCACE
PNEUMONOCELE
PNEUMONOLITH
PNEUMONOPEXY
PNEUMONOSIS
PNEUMOPEXY
PNEUMOTHORAX
PNEUMOTOMY
PNEUMOTOXIN
PO
POACEOUS
POACH
POACHED
POACHER
POACHIER
POACHIEST
POACHINESS
POACHING
POACHY
POAK
POAKE
POALI
POALO
POAP
POB
POBBIES
POBBY
POBEDY
POBLACION
POBS
POCAN
POCHADE
POCHARD
POCHAY
POCHE
POCHETTE
POCHETTINO
POCHISMO
POCHOIR
POCHOTE
POCILLIFORM
POCK
POCKET
POCKETABLE
POCKETBOOK
POCKETED
POCKETER
POCKETFUL
POCKETFULS
POCKETING
POCKETKNIFE
POCKETKNIVES
POCKETS
POCKETY

POCKHOUSE
POCKIER
POCKIEST
POCKMANKY
POCKMARK
POCKWEED
POCKWOOD
POCKY
POCO
POCOCURANTE
POCOSIN
POCULARY
POCULATION
POCULENT
POCULIFORM
POD
PODAGRA
PODAGRAL
PODAGRIC
PODAGRICAL
PODAGROUS
PODAGRY
PODAL
PODALGIA
PODALIC
PODANGER
PODARGUE
PODARTHRITIS
PODARTHRUM
PODATUS
PODDED
PODDER
PODDIDGE
PODDIGE
PODDING
PODDISH
PODDLE
PODDOCK
PODDY
PODE
PODELCOMA
PODEON
PODESTA
PODESTERATE
PODETIIFORM
PODETIUM
PODEX
PODGE
PODGER
PODGIER
PODGIEST
PODGILY
PODGINESS
PODGY
PODIA
PODIAL
PODIATRIST
PODIATRY
PODICAL
PODILEGOUS
PODITE
PODITIC
PODITTI
PODIUM
PODLER
PODLEY
PODO
PODOBRANCH
PODOCARP
PODODERM
PODODYNIA
PODOGYN
PODOGYNE
PODOGYNIUM
PODOLITE
PODOLOGY
PODOMANCY
PODOMERE
PODOPHYLLIC
PODOPHYLLIN
PODOPHYLLOUS
PODOS
PODOSCAPH
PODOSCAPHER
PODOSCOPY
PODOSPERM
PODOTHECA
PODOTHECAL
PODS
PODSOL
PODURAN
PODURID
PODWARE
PODZOL
PODZOLIC
POE
POEBIRD
POECHORE
POECHORIC
POECILITIC
POECILOGONY
POECILOMERE
POECILONYM
POECILONYMIC
POECILONYMY
POECILOPOD
POEM
POEMATIC
POEMS
POENOLOGY
POEPHAGOUS
POESIS
POESY
POET
POETASTER
POETASTERING
POETASTERY
POETASTRIC
POETASTRICAL
POETASTRY
POETESQUE
POETESS
POETIC
POETICAL
POETICALITY
POETICALLY
POETICIZE
POETICS
POETICULE
POETITO
POETIZATION
POETIZE
POETIZED
POETIZER
POETIZING
POETLING
POETLY
POETOMACHIA
POETRY
POFFLE
POGAMOGGAN
POGEY
POGGE
POGGIES
POGGY
POGIE
POGIES
POGO
POGONIA
POGONIASIS
POGONIATE
POGONION
POGONIP
POGONITE
POGONOLOGIST
POGONOLOGY
POGONOTOMY
POGONOTROPHY
POGROM
POGROMIST
POGUE
POGY
POH
POHA
POHICKORY
POHUTUKAWA
POI
POIESIS
POIETIC
POIGNADO
POIGNANCE
POIGNANCIES
POIGNANCY
POIGNANT
POIGNANTLY
POIGNET
POIKILE
POIKILITIC
POIKILOBLAST
POIKILOCYTE
POIKILOTHERM
POIKILOTHERMAL
POIL
POILU
POIMENIC
POIMENICS
POINADO
POINARD
POINCIANA
POIND
POINDABLE
POINDER
POINDING
POING
POINT
POINTABLE
POINTAGE
POINTAL
POINTBLANK
POINTE
POINTED
POINTEDLY
POINTEDNESS
POINTEL
POINTER
POINTES
POINTIER
POINTIEST
POINTILLE
POINTILLISM
POINTILLIST
POINTING
POINTINGLY
POINTLESS
POINTLESSLY
POINTLET
POINTLETED
POINTMAKER
POINTMAKING
POINTMAN
POINTMEN
POINTMENT
POINTS
POINTSMAN
POINTURE
POINTWAYS
POINTWISE
POINTY
POIS
POISE
POISED
POISER
POISING
POISON
POISONABLE
POISONBERRY
POISONBUSH
POISONED
POISONER
POISONING
POISONMAKER
POISONOUS
POISONOUSLY
POISONWEED
POISONWOOD
POISSARDE
POISSON
POISTER
POISURE
POIT
POITRAIL
POITREL
POITRINAIRE
POIVRADE
POIZE
POKAL
POKE
POKEBERRY
POKED
POKEFUL
POKELOKEN
POKER
POKERISH
POKERISHLY
POKERISHNESS
POKEROOT
POKEWEED
POKEY
POKIES
POKING
POKKE
POKOMOO
POKUNT
POKY
POLACCA
POLACRE
POLAK
POLAR
POLARIC
POLARIMETER
POLARIMETRIC
POLARIMETRY
POLARISCOPE
POLARISCOPY
POLARISE
POLARISTIC
POLARITY
POLARIZABLE
POLARIZATION
POLARIZE
POLARIZED
POLARIZER
POLARIZING
POLARON
POLARY
POLATOUCHE
POLAXIS
POLDAVIS
POLDAVY
POLDER
POLDERBOY
POLDERLAND
POLDERMAN
POLDOODY
POLDRON
POLE
POLEARM
POLEAX
POLEAXE
POLEAXER
POLEBURN
POLECAT
POLECATS
POLED
POLEHEAD
POLEMAN
POLEMARCH
POLEMIC
POLEMICAL
POLEMICALLY
POLEMICIAN
POLEMICIST
POLEMICS
POLEMIST
POLEMIZE
POLEMOSCOPE
POLENTA
POLER
POLES
POLESAW
POLESETTER
POLESTAR
POLEWARD
POLEWARDS
POLEY
POLEYN
POLEYNE
POLI
POLIAD
POLIADIC
POLIANITE
POLICE
POLICED
POLICEMAN
POLICEMEN
POLICEWOMAN
POLICEWOMEN
POLICIAL
POLICIES
POLICING
POLICIZE
POLICIZER
POLICLINIC
POLICY
POLICYHOLDER
POLIES
POLIGAR
POLIGARSHIP
POLILLA
POLING
POLIO
POLIORCETIC
POLIOSIS
POLIS
POLISH
POLISHED
POLISHER
POLISHING
POLISHINGS
POLISHMENT
POLISSOIR
POLISTA
POLITARCH
POLITARCHIC
POLITE
POLITEFUL
POLITEIA
POLITELY
POLITENESS
POLITER
POLITESSE
POLITEST
POLITIC
POLITICAL
POLITICALISM

POLITICALIZE
POLITICALLY
POLITICIAN
POLITICIOUS
POLITICIST
POLITICIZE
POLITICIZED
POLITICIZER
POLITICIZING
POLITICK
POLITICLY
POLITICOS
POLITICS
POLITIED
POLITIES
POLITIST
POLITIZE
POLITURE
POLITY
POLITZERIZE
POLJE
POLK
POLKA
POLKAED
POLKAING
POLL
POLLABLE
POLLACK
POLLAGE
POLLAKIURIA
POLLAM
POLLAN
POLLARCHY
POLLARD
POLLARDED
POLLARDING
POLLBOOK
POLLE
POLLED
POLLEE
POLLEN
POLLENATE
POLLENATION
POLLENED
POLLENITE
POLLENT
POLLER
POLLERA
POLLET
POLLETEN
POLLETTE
POLLEX
POLLICAL
POLLICAR
POLLICES
POLLICITATION
POLLINAR
POLLINARIUM
POLLINATE
POLLINATED
POLLINATING
POLLINATION
POLLINATOR
POLLINCTOR
POLLINCTURE
POLLING
POLLINIC
POLLINIUM
POLLINIZE
POLLINIZER
POLLINODIAL
POLLINODIUM
POLLINOID
POLLINOSE
POLLINOSIS
POLLIWOG
POLLOCK
POLLSTER
POLLUCITE
POLLUTANT
POLLUTE
POLLUTED
POLLUTER
POLLUTING
POLLUTION
POLLYWOG
POLO
POLOCONIC
POLOIST
POLONAISE
POLONICK
POLONIUM
POLONY
POLOS
POLSKA
POLSTER
POLT
POLTERGEIST
POLTFOOT
POLTFOOTED
POLTINA
POLTINIK
POLTOPHAGIC
POLTOPHAGIST
POLTOPHAGY
POLTROON
POLTROONERY
POLTROONISH
POLTROONISM
POLVERINE
POLY
POLYACID
POLYACOUSTIC
POLYACT
POLYACTINAL
POLYACTINE
POLYAD
POLYADELPH
POLYADENIA
POLYADIC
POLYAEMIA
POLYAEMIC
POLYALCOHOL
POLYAMIDE
POLYAMYLOSE
POLYANDRIA
POLYANDRIAN
POLYANDRIC
POLYANDRISM
POLYANDRIST
POLYANDRIUM
POLYANDROUS
POLYANDRY
POLYANTHA
POLYANTHUS
POLYARCH
POLYARCHAL
POLYARCHICAL
POLYARCHIST
POLYARCHY
POLYAXON
POLYAXONE
POLYBASIC
POLYBASICITY
POLYBASITE
POLYBLAST
POLYBORINE
POLYBRID
POLYBUNOUS
POLYBUNY
POLYCARPIC
POLYCARPOUS
POLYCARPY
POLYCENTRISM
POLYCENTRIST
POLYCHAETAL
POLYCHAETAN
POLYCHAETE
POLYCHAETOUS
POLYCHASIAL
POLYCHASIUM
POLYCHLORIDE
POLYCHOERANY
POLYCHORD
POLYCHREST
POLYCHRESTIC
POLYCHRESTY
POLYCHROIC
POLYCHROMATE
POLYCHROME
POLYCHROMIA
POLYCHROMIC
POLYCHROMISM
POLYCHROMIZE
POLYCHROMOUS
POLYCHROMY
POLYCLAD
POLYCLADINE
POLYCLINIC
POLYCONIC
POLYCOTYL
POLYCRACY
POLYCRASE
POLYCRATIC
POLYCROTIC
POLYCROTISM
POLYCYCLIC
POLYCYESIS
POLYDACTYL
POLYDACTYLE
POLYDACTYLY
POLYDEMIC
POLYDIPSIA
POLYDISPERSE
POLYDOMOUS
POLYDYMITE
POLYDYNAMIC
POLYEIDIC
POLYEIDISM
POLYEMIA
POLYEMIC
POLYERGIC
POLYESTHESIA
POLYETHNIC
POLYETHYLENE
POLYGALIN
POLYGAM
POLYGAMIAN
POLYGAMIC
POLYGAMICAL
POLYGAMIST
POLYGAMIZE
POLYGAMOUS
POLYGAMY
POLYGAR
POLYGENE
POLYGENESIC
POLYGENESIS
POLYGENESIST
POLYGENETIC
POLYGENIC
POLYGENISM
POLYGENIST
POLYGENOUS
POLYGENY
POLYGLOSSARY
POLYGLOT
POLYGLOTRY
POLYGLOTTAL
POLYGLOTTED
POLYGLOTTER
POLYGLOTTERY
POLYGLOTTIC
POLYGLOTTING
POLYGLOTTISM
POLYGLOTTIST
POLYGLYCEROL
POLYGON
POLYGONAL
POLYGONALLY
POLYGONEUTIC
POLYGONIC
POLYGONOID
POLYGONOUS
POLYGONUM
POLYGONY
POLYGRAM
POLYGRAPH
POLYGRAPHER
POLYGRAPHIC
POLYGRAPHY
POLYGYN
POLYGYNAIKY
POLYGYNIAN
POLYGYNIST
POLYGYNOUS
POLYGYNY
POLYGYRAL
POLYGYRIA
POLYHAEMIA
POLYHAEMIC
POLYHALIDE
POLYHALITE
POLYHARMONIC
POLYHARMONY
POLYHEDRA
POLYHEDRAL
POLYHEDRIC
POLYHEDRICAL
POLYHEDROID
POLYHEDRON
POLYHEDRONS
POLYHEDROUS
POLYHEMIA
POLYHEMIC
POLYHIDROSIS
POLYHISTOR
POLYHISTORIC
POLYHISTORY
POLYHYBRID
POLYHYDRIC
POLYHYDROXY
POLYIDEIC
POLYIDEISM
POLYIDROSIS
POLYLEMMA
POLYLEPIDOUS
POLYLITH
POLYLITHIC
POLYLOGY
POLYLOQUENT
POLYMAGNET
POLYMANIA
POLYMASTIA
POLYMASTIC
POLYMASTISM
POLYMASTY
POLYMATH
POLYMATHIC
POLYMATHIST
POLYMATHY
POLYMAZIA
POLYMELIA
POLYMELIAN
POLYMELY
POLYMER
POLYMERE
POLYMERIA
POLYMERIC
POLYMERISE
POLYMERISM
POLYMERIZE
POLYMEROUS
POLYMETER
POLYMETOCHIC
POLYMICRIAN
POLYMICROBIC
POLYMIGNITE
POLYMIXIID
POLYMNITE
POLYMNY
POLYMORPH
POLYMORPHIC
POLYMORPHISM
POLYMORPHOUS
POLYMORPHY
POLYMYARIAN
POLYMYODIAN
POLYMYODOUS
POLYMYOID
POLYMYOSITIS
POLYMYTHIC
POLYMYTHY
POLYNEE
POLYNEMID
POLYNEMOID
POLYNESIC
POLYNEURITIC
POLYNEURITIS
POLYNICES
POLYNOID
POLYNOMIAL
POLYNOMIC
POLYNUCLEAR
POLYNUCLEATE
POLYNYA
POLYODON
POLYODONT
POLYODONTAL
POLYODONTIA
POLYODONTOID
POLYOECIOUS
POLYOECISM
POLYOICOUS
POLYOL
POLYONOMOUS
POLYONOMY
POLYONYCHIA
POLYONYM
POLYONYMAL
POLYONYMIC
POLYONYMIST
POLYONYMOUS
POLYONYMY
POLYOPIA
POLYORAMA
POLYORGANIC
POLYOSE
POLYOXIDE
POLYP
POLYPARIA
POLYPARIAN
POLYPARIES
POLYPARIUM
POLYPAROUS
POLYPARY
POLYPEAN
POLYPED
POLYPEPTIDE
POLYPETAL
POLYPETALOUS
POLYPETALY
POLYPHAGE
POLYPHAGIA
POLYPHAGIAN

POLYPHAGIC
POLYPHAGIST
POLYPHAGOUS
POLYPHAGY
POLYPHARMACY
POLYPHARMIC
POLYPHASAL
POLYPHASE
POLYPHASER
POLYPHEMIAN
POLYPHEMIC
POLYPHEMUS
POLYPHENOL
POLYPHOBIA
POLYPHONE
POLYPHONED
POLYPHONIC
POLYPHONICAL
POLYPHONIES
POLYPHONISM
POLYPHONIST
POLYPHONIUM
POLYPHONOUS
POLYPHONY
POLYPHORE
POLYPHOTAL
POLYPHOTE
POLYPHYLESIS
POLYPHYLETIC
POLYPHYLLINE
POLYPHYLY
POLYPHYODONT
POLYPIAN
POLYPIDE
POLYPIDOM
POLYPIFEROUS
POLYPIGEROUS
POLYPITE
POLYPLASTIC
POLYPLOID
POLYPLOIDIC
POLYPLOIDY
POLYPNOEA
POLYPOD
POLYPODIA
POLYPODIES
POLYPODY
POLYPOID
POLYPOIDAL
POLYPORE
POLYPORITE
POLYPOROID
POLYPOSE
POLYPOSIS
POLYPOTOME
POLYPOUS
POLYPRAGMACY
POLYPRAGMATY
POLYPRAGMON
POLYPRENE
POLYPRISM
POLYPSYCHIC
POLYPSYCHISM
POLYPTERID
POLYPTEROID
POLYPTOTE
POLYPTOTON
POLYPTYCH
POLYPUS
POLYRHYTHMIC
POLYSACCHARIDE
POLYSARCIA
POLYSARCOUS
POLYSCOPE
POLYSCOPIC
POLYSEMANT
POLYSEMANTIC
POLYSEMEIA
POLYSEMIA
POLYSEMY
POLYSENSUOUS
POLYSIPHONIC
POLYSOMIA
POLYSOMITIC
POLYSPAST
POLYSPASTON
POLYSPERMIA
POLYSPERMIC
POLYSPERMY
POLYSPONDYLY
POLYSPORE
POLYSPORED
POLYSPORIC
POLYSPOROUS
POLYSTAURION
POLYSTELE
POLYSTELLIC
POLYSTICHOID
POLYSTOME
POLYSTOMIUM
POLYSTYLE
POLYSTYLOUS
POLYSTYRENE
POLYSULFIDE
POLYSULPHID
POLYSULPHIDE
POLYSYLLABIC
POLYSYLLABLE
POLYSYNDETIC
POLYSYNDETON
POLYTECHNIC
POLYTECHNICS
POLYTECHNIST
POLYTHEISM
POLYTHEIST
POLYTHEISTIC
POLYTHEIZE
POLYTHELIA
POLYTHIONIC
POLYTOCOUS
POLYTOMOUS
POLYTOMY
POLYTONAL
POLYTONALISM
POLYTONALITY
POLYTONE
POLYTONIC
POLYTONY
POLYTOPE
POLYTOPIC
POLYTOPICAL
POLYTRICHIA
POLYTRICHOUS
POLYTROCHAL
POLYTROCHOUS
POLYTROPE
POLYTROPHIC
POLYTYPE
POLYTYPED
POLYTYPIC
POLYTYPICAL
POLYTYPING
POLYTYPY
POLYURESIS
POLYURETHANE
POLYURIA
POLYURIC
POLYVALENCE
POLYVALENT
POLYVE
POLYVINYL
POLYVIRULENT
POLYVOLTINE
POLYZOAN
POLYZOARIA
POLYZOARIAL
POLYZOARIUM
POLYZOARY
POLYZOIC
POLYZOISM
POLYZONAL
POLYZOOID
POLYZOON
POLZENITE
POM
POMACE
POMACENTRID
POMACENTROID
POMACEOUS
POMADA
POMADE
POMADED
POMADING
POMANDER
POMANE
POMARINE
POMARIUM
POMARY
POMATE
POMATO
POMATOES
POMATOMID
POMATORHINE
POMATUM
POMBE
POMBO
POME
POMEGRANATE
POMELO
POMELY
POMERIA
POMERIUM
POMEROY
POMESHCHIK
POMEWATER
POMEY
POMEYS
POMFRET
POMICULTURE
POMIFEROUS
POMIFORM
POMIVOROUS
POMMADO
POMMAGE
POMME
POMMEE
POMMEL
POMMELED
POMMELER
POMMELING
POMMELION
POMMELLED
POMMELLER
POMMELLING
POMMELO
POMMER
POMMIES
POMMY
POMOERIUM
POMOLO
POMOLOGICAL
POMOLOGIST
POMOLOGY
POMONAL
POMONIC
POMP
POMPA
POMPADOUR
POMPAL
POMPANO
POMPANOS
POMPELMOOSE
POMPELMOUS
POMPERKIN
POMPHOLIX
POMPHOLYX
POMPHUS
POMPIER
POMPILID
POMPILOID
POMPION
POMPIST
POMPLESS
POMPON
POMPOON
POMPOSITY
POMPOSO
POMPOUS
POMPOUSLY
POMPOUSNESS
POMSTER
PON
PONCE
PONCEAU
PONCELET
PONCHO
PONCHOED
PONCHOS
POND
PONDAGE
PONDBUSH
PONDER
PONDERABILITY
PONDERABLE
PONDERAL
PONDERANCE
PONDERANCY
PONDERANT
PONDERARY
PONDERATE
PONDERATION
PONDERATIVE
PONDERED
PONDERER
PONDERING
PONDERINGLY
PONDERLING
PONDEROSITY
PONDEROUS
PONDEROUSLY
PONDEROUSNESS
PONDFISH
PONDFISHES
PONDGRASS
PONDMAN
PONDOK
PONDOKKIE
PONDUS
PONDWEED
PONDWORT
PONDY
PONE
PONENT
PONERID
PONERINE
PONEROID
PONEROLOGY
PONEY
PONG
PONGA
PONGEE
PONGID
PONGO
PONHAWS
PONIARD
PONIARDED
PONIARDING
PONICA
PONIER
PONIES
PONJA
PONOR
PONS
PONT
PONTAGE
PONTAL
PONTEE
PONTES
PONTIC
PONTICELLO
PONTICULAR
PONTICULUS
PONTIFEX
PONTIFF
PONTIFIC
PONTIFICAL
PONTIFICALLY
PONTIFICATE
PONTIFICATED
PONTIFICES
PONTIFICIAL
PONTIFY
PONTIL
PONTILE
PONTIN
PONTINE
PONTIST
PONTLEVIS
PONTON
PONTONIER
PONTOON
PONTUS
PONTVOLANT
PONY
PONYTAIL
PONZITE
POO
POOA
POOAH
POOCH
POOD
POODLE
POODLER
POOGYE
POOH
POOJA
POOJAH
POOK
POOKA
POOKAUN
POOKAWN
POOKHAUN
POOKOO
POOL
POOLER
POOLI
POOLROOM
POOLROOT
POOLWORT
POOLY
POON
POONA
POONAC
POONGEE
POONGHEE
POONGHIE
POOP
POOPED
POOPHYTE
POOPHYTIC
POOR
POORER
POOREST
POORHOUSE
POORISH

POORLINESS
POORLING
POORLY
POORLYISH
POORMASTER
POORNESS
POORT
POORTITH
POORWILL
POOSE
POOT
POOTHER
POOTY
POP
POPADAM
POPAL
POPCORN
POPDOCK
POPE
POPEDOM
POPEHOLY
POPEHOOD
POPEISM
POPEL
POPELER
POPELINE
POPELING
POPELY
POPERY
POPEYE
POPEYED
POPGLOVE
POPGUN
POPGUNNER
POPGUNNERY
POPINAC
POPINJAY
POPISH
POPISHLY
POPISHNESS
POPJOY
POPLAR
POPLARED
POPLEMAN
POPLESIE
POPLET
POPLIN
POPLINETTE
POPLITAEAL
POPLITEAL
POPLITEUS
POPLITIC
POPLOLLY
POPOMASTIC
POPOVER
POPPA
POPPABILITY
POPPABLE
POPPEAN
POPPED
POPPER
POPPET
POPPETHEAD
POPPIED
POPPIES
POPPIN
POPPING
POPPLE
POPPLED
POPPLING
POPPLY
POPPY
POPPYCOCK
POPPYCOCKISH
POPPYFISH
POPPYFISHES
POPPYHEAD
POPPYWORT
POPSHOP
POPSICLE
POPSKULL
POPULACE
POPULACY
POPULAR
POPULARES
POPULARISE
POPULARISM
POPULARITY
POPULARIZE
POPULARIZED
POPULARIZER
POPULARIZING
POPULARLY
POPULARNESS
POPULATE
POPULATED
POPULATING
POPULATION
POPULATIONAL
POPULATOR
POPULEON
POPULICIDE
POPULIN
POPULOUS
POPULOUSLY
POPULOUSNESS
POPWEED
PORAIL
PORAL
PORBEAGLE
PORCATE
PORCATED
PORCELAIN
PORCELAINIZE
PORCELAINLIKE
PORCELAINOUS
PORCELANEOUS
PORCELANIC
PORCELANITE
PORCELANOUS
PORCELLANIAN
PORCELLANIC
PORCELLANID
PORCELLANITE
PORCELLANIZE
PORCELLANOUS
PORCH
PORCHED
PORCHING
PORCINE
PORCUPINE
PORCUPINISH
PORE
PORED
PORER
PORES
PORET
PORETT
PORGE
PORGER
PORGIES
PORGY
PORI
PORICIDAL
PORIFERAL
PORIFERAN
PORIFEROUS
PORIFORM
PORINA
PORINESS
PORING
PORION
PORISM
PORISMATIC
PORISTIC
PORISTICAL
PORITE
PORITOID
PORK
PORKEATER
PORKER
PORKERY
PORKET
PORKFISH
PORKFISHES
PORKIER
PORKIES
PORKIEST
PORKIN
PORKISH
PORKLING
PORKMAN
PORKPEN
PORKPIE
PORKWOOD
PORKY
PORNERASTIC
PORNO
PORNOCRACY
PORNOCRAT
PORNOGRAPHER
PORNOGRAPHIC
PORNOGRAPHIES
PORNOGRAPHY
PORNOLOGICAL
PORO
PORODINE
PORODITE
POROGAM
POROGAMIC
POROGAMOUS
POROGAMY
POROMA
POROMAS
POROMATA
POROMETER
POROPLASTIC
POROPORO
POROROCA
POROS
POROSCOPE
POROSCOPIC
POROSCOPY
POROSE
POROSENESS
POROSIMETER
POROSIS
POROSITIES
POROSITY
POROTIC
POROTYPE
POROUS
POROUSLY
POROUSNESS
PORPENTINE
PORPHYRATIN
PORPHYRIAN
PORPHYRIES
PORPHYRIN
PORPHYRINE
PORPHYRION
PORPHYRITE
PORPHYRITIC
PORPHYROID
PORPHYROUS
PORPHYRY
PORPITOID
PORPOISE
PORPOISES
PORPORATE
PORR
PORRACEOUS
PORRECT
PORRET
PORRIDGE
PORRIDGY
PORRIGINOUS
PORRIGO
PORRINGER
PORRY
PORT
PORTA
PORTABILITY
PORTABLE
PORTABLENESS
PORTABLY
PORTAGE
PORTAGUE
PORTAL
PORTALED
PORTALLED
PORTAMENTI
PORTAMENTO
PORTANCE
PORTAS
PORTASS
PORTATILE
PORTATIVE
PORTATO
PORTATOR
PORTCRAYON
PORTCULLIS
PORTCULLISED
PORTCULLISING
PORTEACID
PORTED
PORTEND
PORTENDANCE
PORTENDED
PORTENDING
PORTENSION
PORTENT
PORTENTION
PORTENTIVE
PORTENTOSITY
PORTENTOUS
PORTENTOUSLY
PORTEOUS
PORTER
PORTERAGE
PORTERESS
PORTERHOUSE
PORTERLY
PORTESSE
PORTFIRE
PORTFOLIO
PORTFOLIOS
PORTGLAIVE
PORTGLAVE
PORTGRAVE
PORTGREVE
PORTHOLE
PORTHOOK
PORTHORS
PORTHOUSE
PORTICO
PORTICOED
PORTICOES
PORTICOS
PORTICUS
PORTIERE
PORTIERED
PORTIFY
PORTING
PORTIO
PORTION
PORTIONAL
PORTIONALLY
PORTIONED
PORTIONER
PORTIONING
PORTIONIST
PORTIONLESS
PORTITOR
PORTLAST
PORTLET
PORTLIGATURE
PORTLIGHT
PORTLILY
PORTLINESS
PORTLY
PORTMAN
PORTMANMOTE
PORTMANTEAU
PORTMANTLE
PORTMENT
PORTMOOT
PORTMOTE
PORTO
PORTOISE
PORTOLANO
PORTPAYNE
PORTRAIT
PORTRAITIST
PORTRAITURE
PORTRAY
PORTRAYABLE
PORTRAYAL
PORTRAYED
PORTRAYER
PORTRAYING
PORTRAYIST
PORTRAYMENT
PORTREEVE
PORTRESS
PORTSALE
PORTSIDE
PORTSIDER
PORTSMAN
PORTSOKEN
PORTUGAIS
PORTULACA
PORTUNIAN
PORTUNID
PORTURE
PORTY
PORULE
PORULOSE
PORULOUS
PORUS
PORWIGLE
PORY
POS
POSADA
POSADAS
POSCA
POSCHAY
POSE
POSED
POSEMENT
POSER
POSEUR
POSEUSE
POSEY
POSH
POSIED
POSIES
POSING
POSIT
POSITED
POSITING
POSITION
POSITIONAL
POSITIONED
POSITIONER

POSITIONING
POSITIVAL
POSITIVE
POSITIVELY
POSITIVENESS
POSITIVISM
POSITIVIST
POSITIVISTIC
POSITIVITY
POSITIVIZE
POSITOR
POSITRINO
POSITRON
POSITRONIUM
POSITUM
POSITURE
POSNET
POSOL
POSOLE
POSOLOGIC
POSOLOGICAL
POSOLOGIST
POSOLOGY
POSOSTEMAD
POSPOLITE
POSS
POSSE
POSSEMAN
POSSEMEN
POSSESS
POSSESSED
POSSESSEDLY
POSSESSING
POSSESSION
POSSESSIONAL
POSSESSIONED
POSSESSIONER
POSSESSIONS
POSSESSIVE
POSSESSOR
POSSESSORIAL
POSSESSORY
POSSET
POSSIBILE
POSSIBILIST
POSSIBILITY
POSSIBLE
POSSIBLENESS
POSSIBLY
POSSIE
POSSODIE
POSSUM
POSSUMHAW
POST
POSTABDOMEN
POSTABLE
POSTADJUNCT
POSTAGE
POSTAL
POSTALVEOLAR
POSTAMENT
POSTANTENNAL
POSTASPIRATE
POSTAXIAD
POSTAXIAL
POSTAXIALLY
POSTBAG
POSTBOOK
POSTBOX
POSTBOY
POSTCARD
POSTCARDINAL
POSTCARNATE
POSTCART
POSTCAVA
POSTCAVAL
POSTCENAL
POSTCENTRAL
POSTCENTRUM
POSTCIBAL
POSTCLASSIC
POSTCLAVICLE
POSTCLIVAL
POSTCOENAL
POSTCOLONIAL
POSTCOMITIAL
POSTCONTACT
POSTCORNU
POSTCOSMIC
POSTCRIBRATE
POSTDATE
POSTDATED
POSTDATING
POSTDENTAL
POSTDICROTIC
POSTDILUVIAL
POSTDILUVIAN
POSTE
POSTEA
POSTED
POSTEEN
POSTEL
POSTENTRIES
POSTENTRY
POSTER
POSTERIAD
POSTERIAL
POSTERIOR
POSTERIORI
POSTERIORIC
POSTERIORITY
POSTERIORLY
POSTERIORS
POSTERIORUMS
POSTERIST
POSTERITY
POSTERIZE
POSTERN
POSTETERNITY
POSTEXILIAN
POSTEXILIC
POSTEXIST
POSTEXISTENT
POSTFACE
POSTFACT
POSTFIX
POSTFIXED
POSTFLECTION
POSTFLEXION
POSTFRONTAL
POSTFURCA
POSTFURCAL
POSTGEMINUM
POSTGENITURE
POSTGLACIAL
POSTGLENOID
POSTGRACILE
POSTGRADUATE
POSTHABIT
POSTHASTE
POSTHITIS
POSTHOLDER
POSTHOLE
POSTHOUSE
POSTHUMA
POSTHUME
POSTHUMOUS
POSTHUMOUSLY
POSTHYPNOTIC
POSTIC
POSTICAL
POSTICALLY
POSTICHE
POSTICOUS
POSTICUM
POSTICUS
POSTIL
POSTILER
POSTILION
POSTILIONED
POSTILLATE
POSTILLATION
POSTILLATOR
POSTILLER
POSTILLION
POSTILLIONED
POSTILS
POSTIN
POSTING
POSTINGLY
POSTIQUE
POSTJACENT
POSTLIMINARY
POSTLIMINIUM
POSTLIMINOUS
POSTLIMINY
POSTLUDE
POSTLUDIUM
POSTMAN
POSTMARITAL
POSTMARK
POSTMARRIAGE
POSTMASTER
POSTMATURITY
POSTMEDIA
POSTMEDIAL
POSTMEDIAN
POSTMEN
POSTMERIDIAN
POSTMINERAL
POSTMISTRESS
POSTMORTAL
POSTMORTEM
POSTMORTUARY
POSTMUNDANE
POSTMUTATIVE
POSTNARIAL
POSTNARIS
POSTNASAL
POSTNATAL
POSTNATE
POSTNATI
POSTNATUS
POSTNUPTIAL
POSTOCULAR
POSTORBITAL
POSTOTIC
POSTPAGAN
POSTPAID
POSTPALATAL
POSTPALATINE
POSTPARIETAL
POSTPARTUM
POSTPHRAGMA
POSTPLACE
POSTPONABLE
POSTPONE
POSTPONED
POSTPONEMENT
POSTPONENCE
POSTPONER
POSTPONING
POSTPOSE
POSTPOSITED
POSTPOSITION
POSTPOSITIVE
POSTPRANDIAL
POSTPROPHESY
POSTPUBIC
POSTPUBIS
POSTRAMUS
POSTREMOTE
POSTRIDER
POSTRORSE
POSTS
POSTSCAPULA
POSTSCAPULAR
POSTSCENIUM
POSTSCHOOL
POSTSCRIBE
POSTSCRIPT
POSTSCRIPTUM
POSTSPHENOID
POSTSYNAPTIC
POSTSYSTOLIC
POSTTEMPORAL
POSTTONIC
POSTTYMPANIC
POSTULANCY
POSTULANT
POSTULATE
POSTULATED
POSTULATING
POSTULATION
POSTULATOR
POSTULATORY
POSTULATUM
POSTURAL
POSTURE
POSTURED
POSTURER
POSTURING
POSTURIST
POSTURIZE
POSTURIZED
POSTURIZING
POSTVELAR
POSTVERBAL
POSTVIDE
POSTVOCALIC
POSTWAR
POSTWARD
POSTWISE
POSTWOMAN
POSTWOMEN
POSTYARD
POSY
POT
POTABILITY
POTABLE
POTABLENESS
POTAGE
POTAGER
POTAGERE
POTAGERIE
POTAGERY
POTAIL
POTAMIC
POTAMOLOGIST
POTAMOLOGY
POTAMOMETER
POTASH
POTASHERY
POTASS
POTASSA
POTASSAMIDE
POTASSIC
POTASSIUM
POTATE
POTATION
POTATIVE
POTATO
POTATOES
POTATOR
POTATORY
POTBANK
POTBELLIED
POTBELLY
POTBOIL
POTBOILER
POTBOY
POTBOYDOM
POTCH
POTCHER
POTCHERMAN
POTCHERMEN
POTDAR
POTE
POTECARY
POTEEN
POTENCE
POTENCIES
POTENCY
POTENT
POTENTACY
POTENTATE
POTENTIAL
POTENTIALITY
POTENTIALIZE
POTENTIALLY
POTENTIATE
POTENTIATION
POTENTILLA
POTENTIZE
POTENTLY
POTENTNESS
POTER
POTESTAL
POTESTAS
POTESTATE
POTESTATIVE
POTEYE
POTFUL
POTGUN
POTHANGER
POTHEAD
POTHECARIES
POTHECARY
POTHEEN
POTHER
POTHERB
POTHERED
POTHERING
POTHERMENT
POTHERY
POTHOLE
POTHOOK
POTHOOKERY
POTHOOKS
POTHOUSE
POTHOUSEY
POTHUNT
POTHUNTED
POTHUNTER
POTHUNTING
POTICHE
POTICHES
POTIFER
POTIN
POTION
POTLACH
POTLACHE
POTLATCH
POTLEG
POTLICKER
POTLID
POTLIKKER
POTLINE
POTLING
POTLUCK
POTMAN
POTMEN
POTOMANIA
POTOMATO
POTOMETER

POTONG
POTOO
POTOROO
POTPIE
POTPOURRI
POTRACK
POTRERO
POTRO
POTS
POTSHARD
POTSHAW
POTSHERD
POTSHOOT
POTSHOOTER
POTSHOT
POTSIE
POTSTICK
POTSTONE
POTSY
POTT
POTTAGE
POTTAH
POTTARO
POTTED
POTTER
POTTERED
POTTERER
POTTERIES
POTTERING
POTTERINGLY
POTTERN
POTTERY
POTTIES
POTTING
POTTINGER
POTTLE
POTTLED
POTTO
POTTOS
POTTUR
POTTY
POTWALLER
POTWALLING
POTWARE
POTWHISKY
POTWORK
POTWORT
POTYCARY
POU
POUAH
POUCE
POUCER
POUCEY
POUCH
POUCHED
POUCHING
POUCY
POUDRET
POUDRETTE
POUF
POUFFE
POUL
POULAINE
POULARD
POULARDIZE
POULDRON
POULE
POULET
POULETTE
POULP
POULPE
POULT
POULTER
POULTERER
POULTICE
POULTICED
POULTICING
POULTRY
POULTRYMAN
POUNAMU
POUNCE
POUNCED
POUNCER
POUNCET
POUNCING
POUNCY
POUND
POUNDAGE
POUNDAL
POUNDCAKE
POUNDER
POUNDING
POUNDKEEPER
POUNDMAN
POUNDMASTER
POUNDMEAL
POUNDS
POUNDSTONE
POUNDWORTH
POUNE
POUR
POURBOIRE
POURED
POURER
POURIE
POURING
POURPARLER
POURPARLEY
POURPOINT
POURPOINTER
POURPRISE
POURVETE
POUS
POUSE
POUSER
POUSSE
POUSSETTE
POUSSETTED
POUSSETTING
POUSSIE
POUSSIN
POUSTIE
POUSY
POUT
POUTED
POUTER
POUTFUL
POUTING
POUTINGLY
POUTY
POVERISH
POVERISHMENT
POVERTY
POVERTYWEED
POVIE
POW
POWAN
POWCAT
POWDER
POWDERED
POWDERER
POWDERING
POWDERIZE
POWDERIZER
POWDERMAN
POWDERY
POWDIKE
POWELLITE
POWER
POWERABLE
POWERABLY
POWERBOAT
POWERED
POWERFUL
POWERFULLY
POWERFULNESS
POWERHOUSE
POWERLESS
POWERLESSLY
POWERMONGER
POWERS
POWHEAD
POWITCH
POWLDOODY
POWNIE
POWNY
POWSODDY
POWSOWDY
POWT
POWWOW
POWWOWER
POWWOWISM
POX
POXY
POY
POYBIRD
POYOU
POZ
POZZOLANA
POZZOLANIC
POZZUOLANA
POZZUOLANIC
PRAAM
PRABBLE
PRABHU
PRACTIC
PRACTICABLE
PRACTICABLY
PRACTICAL
PRACTICALISM
PRACTICALIST
PRACTICALITY
PRACTICALIZE
PRACTICALIZED
PRACTICALLY
PRACTICALNESS
PRACTICANT
PRACTICE
PRACTICED
PRACTICER
PRACTICIAN
PRACTICING
PRACTICO
PRACTICUM
PRACTISANT
PRACTISE
PRACTISED
PRACTISER
PRACTISING
PRACTITIONAL
PRACTITIONER
PRACTIVE
PRAD
PRADHANA
PRAEABDOMEN
PRAEANAL
PRAECAVA
PRAECIPE
PRAECIPUUM
PRAECOCES
PRAECOCIAL
PRAECORACOID
PRAECORDIA
PRAECORDIAL
PRAECORDIUM
PRAECORNU
PRAECOX
PRAECUNEUS
PRAEDIAL
PRAEDIALIST
PRAEDIALITY
PRAEDIUM
PRAEFECT
PRAEFECTORIAL
PRAEFECTUS
PRAEFERVID
PRAEHALLUX
PRAELABRUM
PRAELECT
PRAELECTION
PRAELECTOR
PRAELECTRESS
PRAELUDIUM
PRAEMAXILLA
PRAEMOLAR
PRAEMUNIRE
PRAENARIAL
PRAENEURAL
PRAENOMEN
PRAENOMINA
PRAENOMINAL
PRAEPOSITOR
PRAEPOSITURE
PRAEPOSITUS
PRAEPOSTER
PRAEPUBIS
PRAEPUCE
PRAESCUTUM
PRAESERTIM
PRAESES
PRAESIDIUM
PRAESPHENOID
PRAESTERNAL
PRAESTERNUM
PRAESTOMIUM
PRAESYSTOLIC
PRAETAXATION
PRAETEXTA
PRAETOR
PRAETORIAL
PRAETORIAN
PRAETORIUM
PRAETORSHIP
PRAGMATIC
PRAGMATICA
PRAGMATICAL
PRAGMATICISM
PRAGMATISM
PRAGMATIST
PRAGMATISTIC
PRAGMATIZE
PRAGMATIZER
PRAHAM
PRAHU
PRAIRIE
PRAIRIED
PRAIRIEWEED
PRAIRILLON
PRAISABLE
PRAISABLY
PRAISE
PRAISED
PRAISEFUL
PRAISEFULLY
PRAISER
PRAISES
PRAISEWORTHY
PRAISING
PRAISINGLY
PRAISS
PRAJNA
PRAKRITI
PRALINE
PRALLTRILLER
PRAM
PRANA
PRANCE
PRANCED
PRANCER
PRANCING
PRANCINGLY
PRANCOME
PRANDIAL
PRANG
PRANK
PRANKED
PRANKER
PRANKIER
PRANKIEST
PRANKING
PRANKINGLY
PRANKISH
PRANKISHLY
PRANKISHNESS
PRANKLE
PRANKS
PRANKSOME
PRANKSTER
PRANKT
PRANKY
PRASE
PRASEOLITE
PRASINE
PRASKEEN
PRASOID
PRASOPHAGOUS
PRASOPHAGY
PRASTHA
PRAT
PRATAL
PRATE
PRATED
PRATEMENT
PRATENSIAN
PRATER
PRATEY
PRATFALL
PRATILOMA
PRATINCOLE
PRATINCOLINE
PRATINCOLOUS
PRATING
PRATINGLY
PRATIQUE
PRATTLE
PRATTLED
PRATTLEMENT
PRATTLER
PRATTLING
PRATTLINGLY
PRATTLY
PRATTY
PRAU
PRAVE
PRAVILEGE
PRAVITY
PRAVOUS
PRAWN
PRAWNER
PRAWNY
PRAXINOSCOPE
PRAXIOLOGY
PRAXIS
PRAXITHEA
PRAY
PRAYA
PRAYABLE
PRAYED
PRAYER
PRAYERFUL
PRAYERFULLY
PRAYERMAKER
PRAYERMAKING
PRAYERS
PRAYFUL

PRAYING
PREACE
PREACH
PREACHED
PREACHER
PREACHERESS
PREACHERIZE
PREACHIER
PREACHIEST
PREACHIFIED
PREACHIFY
PREACHIFYING
PREACHILY
PREACHING
PREACHMAN
PREACHMENT
PREACHY
PREADAMIC
PREADAMITE
PREADAMITIC
PREADAMITISM
PREADJUNCT
PREADMISSION
PREAGONAL
PREAGONY
PREALLABLE
PREALLABLY
PREALVEOLAR
PREAMBLE
PREAMBLED
PREAMBLING
PREAMBULARY
PREAMBULATE
PREAMP
PREAMPLIFIER
PREANIMISM
PREANTERIOR
PREARRANGE
PREARRANGED
PREASEPTIC
PREATAXIC
PREAUDIENCE
PREAXIAL
PREAXIALLY
PREBACILLARY
PREBELLUM
PREBEND
PREBENDAL
PREBENDARIES
PREBENDARY
PREBENDATE
PREBRACHIAL
PREBRACHIUM
PREBRONCHIAL
PRECANCEL
PRECANCELED
PRECANCELING
PRECANCELLED
PRECANCELLING
PRECANCEROUS
PRECANONICAL
PRECANT
PRECANTATION
PRECARIOUS
PRECARIOUSLY
PRECARIUM
PRECARTILAGE
PRECARY
PRECAST
PRECATION
PRECATIVE
PRECATIVELY
PRECATORY
PRECAUSATION
PRECAUTION
PRECAUTIONAL
PRECAUTIOUS
PRECAVA
PRECEDABLE
PRECEDANEOUS
PRECEDE
PRECEDED
PRECEDENCE
PRECEDENCIES
PRECEDENCY
PRECEDENT
PRECEDENTARY
PRECEDENTED
PRECEDENTIAL
PRECEDER
PRECEDING
PRECEL
PRECENT
PRECENTOR
PRECENTORIAL
PRECENTORY
PRECENTRAL
PRECENTRESS
PRECENTRUM
PRECEPT
PRECEPTION
PRECEPTIST
PRECEPTIVE
PRECEPTIVELY
PRECEPTOR
PRECEPTORAL
PRECEPTORATE
PRECEPTORIAL
PRECEPTORY
PRECEPTRESS
PRECEPTUAL
PRECEPTUALLY
PRECERAMIC
PRECES
PRECESS
PRECESSED
PRECESSING
PRECESSION
PRECESSIONAL
PRECHORDAL
PRECIATION
PRECIDE
PRECIEUSE
PRECIEUX
PRECINCT
PRECINCTION
PRECINCTIVE
PRECIOSITIES
PRECIOSITY
PRECIOUS
PRECIOUSLY
PRECIOUSNESS
PRECIPE
PRECIPICE
PRECIPICED
PRECIPITABLE
PRECIPITANCE
PRECIPITANCY
PRECIPITANT
PRECIPITATE
PRECIPITATED
PRECIPITATELY
PRECIPITATION
PRECIPITATOR
PRECIPITIN
PRECIPITOUS
PRECIPITOUSLY
PRECIS
PRECISE
PRECISELY
PRECISENESS
PRECISIAN
PRECISIANISM
PRECISIANIST
PRECISION
PRECISIONAL
PRECISIONER
PRECISIONIST
PRECISIVE
PRECISO
PRECLARE
PRECLINICAL
PRECLIVAL
PRECLUDE
PRECLUDED
PRECLUDING
PRECLUSION
PRECLUSIVE
PRECOCIAL
PRECOCIOUS
PRECOCIOUSLY
PRECOCITY
PRECOGITATE
PRECOGNITION
PRECOGNITIVE
PRECOGNIZE
PRECOGNOSCE
PRECOMPOSE
PRECONCEIVE
PRECONCEIVED
PRECONCEIVING
PRECONCEPT
PRECONCERT
PRECONCERTED
PRECONDITION
PRECONIZE
PRECONIZED
PRECONIZER
PRECONIZING
PRECONQUEST
PRECONSCIOUS
PRECONSIGN
PRECONTACT
PRECONY
PRECOOK
PRECOOL
PRECOOLER
PRECOOLING
PRECORACOID
PRECORDIA
PRECORDIAL
PRECORDIALLY
PRECORNU
PRECOSTAL
PRECOURSE
PRECOX
PRECRITICAL
PRECRURAL
PRECULE
PRECUNEATE
PRECUNEUS
PRECURRENT
PRECURRER
PRECURSAL
PRECURSE
PRECURSIVE
PRECURSOR
PRECURSORY
PREDABLE
PREDACEAN
PREDACEOUS
PREDACIOUS
PREDACITY
PREDATE
PREDATED
PREDATING
PREDATION
PREDATISM
PREDATIVE
PREDATOR
PREDATORILY
PREDATORY
PREDAZZITE
PREDE
PREDECAY
PREDECEASE
PREDECEASER
PREDECESS
PREDECESSOR
PREDEFINE
PREDEFINITE
PREDELLA
PREDENTARY
PREDENTATE
PREDESIGNATE
PREDESTINATE
PREDESTINATION
PREDESTINE
PREDESTINED
PREDESTINING
PREDESTINY
PREDETERMINE
PREDETERMINED
PREDEVOTE
PREDIAL
PREDIALIST
PREDIALITY
PREDIASTOLIC
PREDIATORY
PREDICABLE
PREDICABLY
PREDICAMENT
PREDICANT
PREDICATE
PREDICATED
PREDICATING
PREDICATION
PREDICATIVE
PREDICATOR
PREDICATORY
PREDICROTIC
PREDICT
PREDICTABLE
PREDICTABLY
PREDICTED
PREDICTING
PREDICTION
PREDICTIONAL
PREDICTIVE
PREDICTIVELY
PREDICTOR
PREDICTORY
PREDIGEST
PREDIGESTION
PREDIKANT
PREDILECT
PREDILECTED
PREDILECTION
PREDISPONENT
PREDISPOSE
PREDISPOSED
PREDISPOSITION
PREDOMINANCE
PREDOMINANT
PREDOMINATE
PREDOMINATING
PREDOMINATOR
PREDOOM
PREDY
PREDYNASTIC
PREE
PREED
PREEING
PREEMINENCE
PREEMINENT
PREEMINENTLY
PREEMPT
PREEMPTION
PREEMPTIVE
PREEMPTOR
PREEMPTORY
PREEN
PREENED
PREENER
PREENING
PREEXILIAN
PREEXILIC
PREEXIST
PREEXISTENCE
PREEXISTENT
PREFABRICATE
PREFABRICATED
PREFABRICATING
PREFACE
PREFACED
PREFACER
PREFACIAL
PREFACING
PREFACIST
PREFACTOR
PREFATOR
PREFATORIAL
PREFATORILY
PREFATORY
PREFECT
PREFECTLY
PREFECTORAL
PREFECTORIAL
PREFECTORIAN
PREFECTUAL
PREFECTURAL
PREFECTURE
PREFER
PREFERABLE
PREFERABLY
PREFERENCE
PREFERENT
PREFERENTIAL
PREFERMENT
PREFERRED
PREFERREDLY
PREFERRER
PREFERRING
PREFERVID
PREFET
PREFIGURATE
PREFIGURE
PREFIGURED
PREFIGURING
PREFILTER
PREFINAL
PREFINE
PREFIX
PREFIXAL
PREFIXALLY
PREFIXATION
PREFIXED
PREFIXEDLY
PREFIXION
PREFIXTURE
PREFLECTION
PREFLEXION
PREFLIGHT
PREFORM
PREFORMATION
PREFORMATIVE
PREFORMED
PREFORMISM
PREFORMIST
PREFORMISTIC
PREFORMULATE
PREFRACT
PREFRONTAL
PREFULGENCE
PREFULGENCY

PREFULGENT
PREGEMINUM
PREGENIAL
PREGENICULUM
PREGENITAL
PREGHIERA
PREGLACIAL
PREGLOBULIN
PREGNABILITY
PREGNABLE
PREGNANCE
PREGNANCIES
PREGNANCY
PREGNANT
PREGNANTLY
PREGNANTNESS
PREGRACILE
PREGUST
PREGUSTANT
PREGUSTATION
PREGUSTATOR
PREGUSTIC
PREHALLUX
PREHALTER
PREHALTERES
PREHEND
PREHENSIBLE
PREHENSILE
PREHENSILITY
PREHENSION
PREHENSIVE
PREHENSOR
PREHENSORIAL
PREHENSORY
PREHEPATIC
PREHEPATICUS
PREHISTORIAN
PREHISTORIC
PREHISTORICS
PREHISTORY
PREHNITE
PREHUMAN
PREHYDRATION
PREIGNITION
PREINCARNATE
PREINDICANT
PREINDICATE
PREINSTRUCT
PREINSULA
PREINSULAR
PREINTONE
PREIOTIZE
PREJACENT
PREJUDGE
PREJUDGED
PREJUDGEMENT
PREJUDGER
PREJUDGING
PREJUDGMENT
PREJUDICATE
PREJUDICATOR
PREJUDICE
PREJUDICED
PREJUDICEDLY
PREJUDICIAL
PREJUDICING
PREJUDICIOUS
PREKE
PRELABRUM
PRELACHRYMAL
PRELACIES
PRELACTEAL
PRELACY
PRELAPSARIAN
PRELATE
PRELATEITY
PRELATESHIP
PRELATESS
PRELATIAL
PRELATIC
PRELATICAL
PRELATICALLY
PRELATION
PRELATISH
PRELATISM
PRELATIST
PRELATIZE
PRELATRY
PRELATURE
PRELE
PRELECT
PRELECTION
PRELECTOR
PRELECTRESS
PRELEGACY
PRELEGATE
PRELEGATEE
PRELIBATION
PRELIM
PRELIMINARY
PRELIMIT
PRELIMITATE
PRELINGUAL
PRELITERATE
PRELITHIC
PRELOGIC
PRELOGICAL
PRELORAL
PRELOREAL
PRELUDE
PRELUDED
PRELUDER
PRELUDIAL
PRELUDING
PRELUDIO
PRELUDIOUS
PRELUDIOUSLY
PRELUDIUM
PRELUDIZE
PRELUMBAR
PRELUSION
PRELUSIVE
PRELUSIVELY
PRELUSORILY
PRELUSORY
PREMAN
PREMATERNITY
PREMATURE
PREMATURELY
PREMATURITY
PREMAXILLA
PREMAXILLARY
PREMED
PREMEDIA
PREMEDIAL
PREMEDIAN
PREMEDIC
PREMEDICAL
PREMEDITATE
PREMEDITATED
PREMEDITATOR
PREMENSTRUAL
PREMERIDIAN
PREMETALLIC
PREMIAL
PREMIANT
PREMIATED
PREMIATING
PREMIE
PREMIER
PREMIERAL
PREMIERE
PREMIERED
PREMIERESS
PREMIERING
PREMIERSHIP
PREMIO
PREMIOUS
PREMISAL
PREMISE
PREMISED
PREMISING
PREMISORY
PREMISS
PREMIUM
PREMIUMS
PREMIXED
PREMOLAR
PREMONISH
PREMONITION
PREMONITIVE
PREMONITOR
PREMONITORY
PREMORSE
PREMOTION
PREMOVE
PREMOVEMENT
PREMOVER
PREMULTIPLY
PREMUNDANE
PREMUNE
PREMUNITORY
PREMUTATIVE
PRENAME
PRENARIAL
PRENASAL
PRENATAL
PRENATALIST
PRENDER
PRENDRE
PRENEPHRITIC
PRENEURAL
PRENOBLE
PRENODAL
PRENOMEN
PRENOMINATE
PRENOMINATED
PRENOTATION
PRENOTE
PRENOTICE
PRENOTIFY
PRENOTION
PRENTICE
PRENTICESHIP
PRENUNCIAL
PRENUPTIAL
PRENZIE
PREOCCUPANCY
PREOCCUPATE
PREOCCUPATION
PREOCCUPIED
PREOCCUPIER
PREOCCUPY
PREOCCUPYING
PREOCULAR
PREOPERATIVE
PREOPERCLE
PREOPERCULAR
PREOPERCULUM
PREOPINION
PREOPTION
PREORAL
PREORBITAL
PREORDAIN
PREORDER
PREORGANIC
PREP
PREPACKAGE
PREPACKAGED
PREPACKAGING
PREPAID
PREPALATAL
PREPARATEUR
PREPARATION
PREPARATIVE
PREPARATOR
PREPARATORY
PREPARDON
PREPARE
PREPARED
PREPAREDLY
PREPAREDNESS
PREPAREMENT
PREPARENTAL
PREPARER
PREPARIETAL
PREPARING
PREPARINGLY
PREPATELLAR
PREPAY
PREPAYING
PREPAYMENT
PREPEND
PREPENIAL
PREPENSE
PREPENSELY
PREPERCEIVE
PREPERFECT
PREPHRAGMA
PREPLACENTAL
PREPOLLENCE
PREPOLLENCY
PREPOLLENT
PREPOLLEX
PREPONDER
PREPONDERANCE
PREPONDERANT
PREPONDERATE
PREPONDERATING
PREPONDEROUS
PREPONTINE
PREPOSE
PREPOSED
PREPOSING
PREPOSITION
PREPOSITIVE
PREPOSITOR
PREPOSITURE
PREPOSSESS
PREPOSSESSED
PREPOSSESSION
PREPOSTER
PREPOSTEROUS
PREPOSTOR
PREPOTENCE
PREPOTENCY
PREPOTENT
PREPOTENTIAL
PREPOTENTLY
PREPRINT
PREPUBERTAL
PREPUBERTY
PREPUBESCENT
PREPUBIC
PREPUBIS
PREPUCE
PREPUPA
PREPUPAL
PREPUTIAL
PREPUTIUM
PRERAMUS
PREREDUCTION
PREREGAL
PREREGNANT
PRERELEASE
PREREMOTE
PREREPTION
PREREQUISITE
PREROGATIVAL
PREROGATIVE
PREROGATIVED
PRERUPT
PRES
PRESA
PRESAGE
PRESAGED
PRESAGEFUL
PRESAGEFULLY
PRESAGEMENT
PRESAGER
PRESAGIENT
PRESAGING
PRESAID
PRESANCTIFY
PRESAY
PRESAYING
PRESBYOPE
PRESBYOPIA
PRESBYOPIC
PRESBYTE
PRESBYTER
PRESBYTERAL
PRESBYTERATE
PRESBYTERE
PRESBYTERESS
PRESBYTERIAL
PRESBYTERIAN
PRESBYTERY
PRESBYTIA
PRESBYTIC
PRESCAPULA
PRESCAPULAR
PRESCHOOL
PRESCIENCE
PRESCIENT
PRESCIENTLY
PRESCIND
PRESCINDENT
PRESCISSION
PRESCRIBE
PRESCRIBED
PRESCRIBER
PRESCRIBING
PRESCRIPT
PRESCRIPTION
PRESCRIPTIVE
PRESCUTAL
PRESCUTUM
PRESE
PRESEMINAL
PRESEMINARY
PRESENCE
PRESENCED
PRESENCELESS
PRESENILE
PRESENILITY
PRESENSION
PRESENT
PRESENTABLE
PRESENTABLY
PRESENTAL
PRESENTATION
PRESENTATIVE
PRESENTED
PRESENTEE
PRESENTER
PRESENTIAL
PRESENTIENT
PRESENTIMENT
PRESENTING
PRESENTIST
PRESENTIVE
PRESENTIVELY
PRESENTLY
PRESENTMENT

PRESERVABLE
PRESERVAL
PRESERVATION
PRESERVATIVE
PRESERVATIZE
PRESERVATORY
PRESERVE
PRESERVED
PRESERVER
PRESERVING
PRESES
PRESEXUAL
PRESHOW
PRESIDE
PRESIDED
PRESIDENCE
PRESIDENCIA
PRESIDENCY
PRESIDENT
PRESIDENTE
PRESIDENTES
PRESIDENTIAL
PRESIDENTS
PRESIDER
PRESIDIAL
PRESIDIARY
PRESIDING
PRESIDIO
PRESIDIOS
PRESIDIUM
PRESIDY
PRESIGNIFIED
PRESIGNIFY
PRESIGNIFYING
PRESIMIAN
PRESOCIAL
PRESPHENOID
PRESPHYGMIC
PRESS
PRESSBOARD
PRESSED
PRESSEL
PRESSER
PRESSFAT
PRESSGANG
PRESSING
PRESSINGLY
PRESSION
PRESSIROSTRAL
PRESSIVE
PRESSLY
PRESSMAN
PRESSMARK
PRESSMASTER
PRESSMEN
PRESSOR
PRESSPACK
PRESSROOM
PRESSURAGE
PRESSURAL
PRESSURE
PRESSURIZE
PRESSURIZED
PRESSURIZING
PRESSWOMAN
PRESSWOMEN
PRESSWORK
PRESSWORKER
PREST
PRESTABILISM
PRESTABLE
PRESTANT
PRESTATE
PRESTATED
PRESTATING
PRESTATION
PRESTER
PRESTERNAL
PRESTERNUM
PRESTEZZA
PRESTIDIGITATOR
PRESTIGE
PRESTIGIATE
PRESTIGIATOR
PRESTIGIOUS
PRESTISSIMO
PRESTLY
PRESTO
PRESTOMIAL
PRESTOMIUM
PRESUBICULUM
PRESUL
PRESUMABLE
PRESUMABLY
PRESUME
PRESUMED
PRESUMEDLY
PRESUMER
PRESUMING
PRESUMPTION
PRESUMPTIVE
PRESUMPTUOUS
PRESUMPTUOUSLY
PRESUPPOSAL
PRESUPPOSE
PRESURMISE
PRESYLVIAN
PRESYNAPSIS
PRESYNAPTIC
PRESYSTOLE
PRESYSTOLIC
PRET
PRETA
PRETAN
PRETANNAGE
PRETANNED
PRETANNING
PRETEMPORAL
PRETENCE
PRETEND
PRETENDANT
PRETENDED
PRETENDEDLY
PRETENDER
PRETENDING
PRETENSE
PRETENSES
PRETENSION
PRETENSIONAL
PRETENSIVE
PRETENSIVELY
PRETENTIOUS
PRETENTIOUSNESS
PRETER
PRETERCANINE
PRETEREQUINE
PRETERGRESS
PRETERHUMAN
PRETERIENCE
PRETERIENT
PRETERIST
PRETERIT
PRETERITE
PRETERITION
PRETERITIVE
PRETERLEGAL
PRETERLETHAL
PRETERMIT
PRETERMITTED
PRETERMITTER
PRETERMITTING
PRETERNATIVE
PRETERNATURAL
PRETERROYAL
PRETERVECTION
PRETEST
PRETEXT
PRETEXTED
PRETEXTUOUS
PRETHORACIC
PRETIL
PRETIUM
PRETONE
PRETONIC
PRETOR
PRETORIAL
PRETORIAN
PRETORIUM
PRETREAT
PRETREATMENT
PRETREATY
PRETREMATIC
PRETTIER
PRETTIES
PRETTIEST
PRETTIFIED
PRETTIFIER
PRETTIFY
PRETTIFYING
PRETTIKIN
PRETTILY
PRETTINESS
PRETTY
PRETTYFACE
PRETTYISM
PRETYMPANIC
PRETYPIFY
PRETZEL
PREU
PREUX
PREVAIL
PREVAILED
PREVAILING
PREVAILINGLY
PREVAILMENT
PREVALENCE
PREVALENCIES
PREVALENCY
PREVALENT
PREVALENTLY
PREVALESCENT
PREVARICATE
PREVARICATED
PREVARICATOR
PREVASCULAR
PREVE
PREVELAR
PREVENANCE
PREVENANT
PREVENE
PREVENED
PREVENIENCE
PREVENIENT
PREVENING
PREVENT
PREVENTABLE
PREVENTATIVE
PREVENTED
PREVENTER
PREVENTIBLE
PREVENTING
PREVENTION
PREVENTIVE
PREVENTIVELY
PREVENTORIUM
PREVERNAL
PREVESICAL
PREVIDE
PREVIDENCE
PREVIEW
PREVIOUS
PREVIOUSLY
PREVIOUSNESS
PREVISE
PREVISED
PREVISING
PREVISION
PREVISIONAL
PREVISIVE
PREVISOR
PREVOCALIC
PREVOMER
PREVOST
PREVOT
PREVOTAL
PREVOYANCE
PREVOYANT
PREVUE
PREWAR
PREWARN
PREWE
PREX
PREXIES
PREXY
PREY
PREYED
PREYER
PREYFUL
PREYING
PREYINGLY
PREZONAL
PREZONE
PRIACANTHID
PRIAPISM
PRIAPUS
PRIBBLE
PRICE
PRICED
PRICEITE
PRICELESS
PRICER
PRICES
PRICING
PRICK
PRICKADO
PRICKANT
PRICKED
PRICKER
PRICKET
PRICKFOOT
PRICKING
PRICKISH
PRICKLE
PRICKLED
PRICKLIER
PRICKLIEST
PRICKLING
PRICKLINGLY
PRICKLOUSE
PRICKLY
PRICKMADAM
PRICKSEAM
PRICKSHOT
PRICKSPUR
PRICKTIMBER
PRICKWOOD
PRICKY
PRIDE
PRIDED
PRIDEFUL
PRIDEFULLY
PRIDEFULNESS
PRIDELING
PRIDIAN
PRIDING
PRIDY
PRIE
PRIED
PRIER
PRIES
PRIEST
PRIESTAL
PRIESTCAP
PRIESTCRAFT
PRIESTEEN
PRIESTERY
PRIESTESS
PRIESTFISH
PRIESTHOOD
PRIESTIANITY
PRIESTISM
PRIESTLIER
PRIESTLIEST
PRIESTLIKE
PRIESTLINESS
PRIESTLING
PRIESTLY
PRIESTS
PRIESTSHIRE
PRIG
PRIGGED
PRIGGER
PRIGGERY
PRIGGING
PRIGGISH
PRIGGISHLY
PRIGGISHNESS
PRIGGISM
PRIGMAN
PRIGSTER
PRILL
PRILLION
PRIM
PRIMA
PRIMACY
PRIMAGE
PRIMAL
PRIMALITY
PRIMAR
PRIMARIAN
PRIMARIED
PRIMARIES
PRIMARILY
PRIMARY
PRIMATAL
PRIMATE
PRIMATESHIP
PRIMATIAL
PRIMATIC
PRIMATICAL
PRIMATOLOGY
PRIMAVERA
PRIMAVERAL
PRIME
PRIMED
PRIMELY
PRIMENESS
PRIMER
PRIMERO
PRIMEROLE
PRIMEUR
PRIMEVAL
PRIMEVALLY
PRIMEVERIN
PRIMEVEROSE
PRIMEVITY
PRIMEVOUS
PRIMI
PRIMICES
PRIMIGENE
PRIMIGENIAL
PRIMIGENIAN
PRIMIGRAVIDA
PRIMINE
PRIMING

PRIMIPARA
PRIMIPARAE
PRIMIPARITY
PRIMIPAROUS
PRIMIPILAR
PRIMITIAE
PRIMITIAL
PRIMITIVE
PRIMITIVELY
PRIMITIVENESS
PRIMITIVISM
PRIMITIVITY
PRIMITY
PRIMLY
PRIMMED
PRIMMER
PRIMMEST
PRIMMING
PRIMNESS
PRIMO
PRIMOGENIAL
PRIMOGENITOR
PRIMOGENOUS
PRIMOMO
PRIMOPRIME
PRIMORDIAL
PRIMORDIALLY
PRIMORDIATE
PRIMORDIUM
PRIMOSITY
PRIMOST
PRIMP
PRIMPED
PRIMPING
PRIMPRINT
PRIMROSE
PRIMROSED
PRIMROSETIDE
PRIMROSETIME
PRIMROSY
PRIMSIE
PRIMULACEOUS
PRIMULAVERIN
PRIMULINE
PRIMUS
PRIMWORT
PRIMY
PRIN
PRINCE
PRINCEAGE
PRINCECRAFT
PRINCEDOM
PRINCEHOOD
PRINCEKIN
PRINCELET
PRINCELIER
PRINCELIEST
PRINCELIKE
PRINCELINESS
PRINCELING
PRINCELY
PRINCEPS
PRINCES
PRINCESS
PRINCESSE
PRINCESSLY
PRINCEWOOD
PRINCIFIED
PRINCIFY
PRINCIPAL
PRINCIPALITY
PRINCIPALLY
PRINCIPATE
PRINCIPE
PRINCIPES
PRINCIPIA
PRINCIPIANT
PRINCIPIUM
PRINCIPLE
PRINCIPLED
PRINCIPLES
PRINCIPLING
PRINCOCK
PRINCOD
PRINCOX
PRINE
PRINGLE
PRINK
PRINKED
PRINKER
PRINKING
PRINKLE
PRINKY
PRINOS
PRINT
PRINTABILITY
PRINTABLE
PRINTED
PRINTER
PRINTERIES
PRINTERY
PRINTING
PRINTLESS
PRINTLINE
PRINTSCRIPT
PRINTWORKS
PRIODONT
PRION
PRIONID
PRIONINE
PRIONODONT
PRIONOPINE
PRIOR
PRIORACY
PRIORAL
PRIORATE
PRIORESS
PRIORIES
PRIORISTIC
PRIORITE
PRIORITIES
PRIORITY
PRIORLY
PRIORSHIP
PRIORY
PRISABLE
PRISAGE
PRISAL
PRISCAN
PRISE
PRISM
PRISMAL
PRISMATIC
PRISMATICAL
PRISMATIZE
PRISMATOID
PRISMATOIDAL
PRISMED
PRISMOID
PRISMOIDAL
PRISMY
PRISOMETER
PRISON
PRISONER
PRISONERS
PRISONMENT
PRISONOUS
PRISS
PRISSIER
PRISSIES
PRISSIEST
PRISSILY
PRISSINESS
PRISSY
PRISTANE
PRISTAV
PRISTAW
PRISTINE
PRITCH
PRITCHEL
PRITHEE
PRITTLE
PRIUS
PRIVACIES
PRIVACITY
PRIVACY
PRIVADO
PRIVANT
PRIVATE
PRIVATEER
PRIVATEERED
PRIVATEERING
PRIVATELY
PRIVATENESS
PRIVATION
PRIVATIVE
PRIVATIVELY
PRIVE
PRIVET
PRIVIES
PRIVILEGE
PRIVILEGED
PRIVILEGER
PRIVILEGING
PRIVILY
PRIVITIES
PRIVITY
PRIVY
PRIX
PRIZABLE
PRIZE
PRIZEABLE
PRIZED
PRIZEFIGHT
PRIZEFIGHTER
PRIZEHOLDER
PRIZEMAN
PRIZEMEN
PRIZER
PRIZERY
PRIZES
PRIZETAKER
PRIZING
PRO
PROA
PROACH
PROAERESIS
PROAIRESIS
PROAL
PROAMBIENT
PROAMNION
PROAMNIOTIC
PROANAPHORA
PROANAPHORAL
PROANTHROPOS
PROATLAS
PROAULION
PROAVIAN
PROB
PROBABILISM
PROBABILIST
PROBABILITY
PROBABILIZE
PROBABLE
PROBABLY
PROBAL
PROBANG
PROBANT
PROBATE
PROBATED
PROBATING
PROBATION
PROBATIONAL
PROBATIONARY
PROBATIONER
PROBATIONISM
PROBATIONIST
PROBATIVE
PROBATOR
PROBATORY
PROBE
PROBEABLE
PROBED
PROBER
PROBING
PROBITY
PROBLEM
PROBLEMATIC
PROBLEMATICAL
PROBLEMATIST
PROBLEMATIZE
PROBLEMIST
PROBLEMISTIC
PROBLEMIZE
PROBOSCIDAL
PROBOSCIDATE
PROBOSCIDEAN
PROBOSCIDES
PROBOSCIDIAL
PROBOSCIDIAN
PROBOSCIFORM
PROBOSCIS
PROBOSCISES
PROBOULEUTIC
PROCACCIA
PROCACCIO
PROCACIOUS
PROCACIOUSLY
PROCACITY
PROCAINE
PROCAMBIAL
PROCAMBIUM
PROCARP
PROCARPIUM
PROCATARCTIC
PROCATARXIS
PROCATHEDRAL
PROCEDENDO
PROCEDURAL
PROCEDURE
PROCEED
PROCEEDED
PROCEEDER
PROCEEDING
PROCEEDINGS
PROCEEDS
PROCELLAS
PROCELLOSE
PROCELLOUS
PROCEPHALIC
PROCERCOID
PROCERE
PROCEREBRAL
PROCEREBRUM
PROCERES
PROCERITE
PROCERITY
PROCERUS
PROCESS
PROCESSAL
PROCESSED
PROCESSER
PROCESSING
PROCESSION
PROCESSIONAL
PROCESSIONER
PROCESSIVE
PROCESSOR
PROCESSUAL
PROCESSUS
PROCHAIN
PROCHEIN
PROCHLORITE
PROCHONDRAL
PROCHOOS
PROCHORDAL
PROCHORION
PROCHRONIC
PROCHRONISM
PROCHRONIZE
PROCIDENCE
PROCIDENT
PROCINCT
PROCK
PROCLAIM
PROCLAIMANT
PROCLAIMED
PROCLAIMER
PROCLAIMING
PROCLAMATION
PROCLAMATOR
PROCLINE
PROCLISIS
PROCLITIC
PROCLIVE
PROCLIVITIES
PROCLIVITOUS
PROCLIVITY
PROCLIVOUS
PROCNEMIAL
PROCOELIA
PROCOELIAN
PROCOELOUS
PROCONSUL
PROCONSULAR
PROCONSULATE
PROCRASTINATE
PROCRASTINATION
PROCREANT
PROCREATE
PROCREATED
PROCREATING
PROCREATION
PROCREATIVE
PROCREATOR
PROCREATORY
PROCTALGIA
PROCTALGY
PROCTATRESIA
PROCTATRESY
PROCTECTASIA
PROCTECTOMY
PROCTITIS
PROCTOCELE
PROCTOCLYSIS
PROCTOCOLITIS
PROCTODAEAL
PROCTODAEUM
PROCTODYNIA
PROCTOLOGIC
PROCTOLOGICAL
PROCTOLOGIST
PROCTOLOGY
PROCTOPLASTY
PROCTOPLEGIA
PROCTOPTOSIS
PROCTOR
PROCTORAGE
PROCTORAL
PROCTORIAL
PROCTORIALLY
PROCTORICAL
PROCTORIZE
PROCTORRHEA
PROCTORSHIP

PROCTOSCOPE
PROCTOSCOPIC
PROCTOSCOPY
PROCTOSPASM
PROCTOSTOMY
PROCTOTOME
PROCTOTOMY
PROCTOTRESIA
PROCULCATE
PROCULCATION
PROCUMBENT
PROCURABLE
PROCURACIES
PROCURACY
PROCURAL
PROCURANCE
PROCURATE
PROCURATION
PROCURATIVE
PROCURATOR
PROCURATORY
PROCURATRIX
PROCURE
PROCURED
PROCUREMENT
PROCURER
PROCURESS
PROCUREUR
PROCURING
PROCURRENT
PROCURSIVE
PROCURVATION
PROCURVED
PROCYONINE
PROD
PRODATARY
PRODD
PRODDED
PRODDER
PRODDING
PRODDLE
PRODELISION
PRODENTINE
PRODIALOGUE
PRODIGAL
PRODIGALISH
PRODIGALISM
PRODIGALITY
PRODIGALIZE
PRODIGALLY
PRODIGIOSITY
PRODIGIOUS
PRODIGIOUSLY
PRODIGUS
PRODIGY
PRODITION
PRODITOR
PRODITORIOUS
PRODROMAL
PRODROME
PRODROMOUS
PRODROMUS
PRODUCE
PRODUCEABLE
PRODUCED
PRODUCEMENT
PRODUCENT
PRODUCER
PRODUCIBLE
PRODUCING
PRODUCT
PRODUCTED
PRODUCTIBLE
PRODUCTID
PRODUCTILE
PRODUCTION
PRODUCTIONAL
PRODUCTIVE
PRODUCTIVELY
PRODUCTIVITY
PRODUCTOID
PRODUCTOR
PRODUCTORY
PRODUCTS
PROEGUMENAL
PROEM
PROEMBRYO
PROEMBRYONIC
PROEMIAL
PROEMIUM
PROEMPTOSIS
PROEPIMERON
PROETHICAL
PROETHNIC
PROETID
PROETTE
PROF
PROFACE
PROFANATION
PROFANATORY
PROFANE
PROFANED
PROFANELY
PROFANEMENT
PROFANENESS
PROFANER
PROFANING
PROFANISM
PROFANITIES
PROFANITY
PROFANIZE
PROFECTION
PROFECTIONAL
PROFER
PROFERMENT
PROFERT
PROFESS
PROFESSED
PROFESSEDLY
PROFESSION
PROFESSIONAL
PROFESSIONALLY
PROFESSIVE
PROFESSIVELY
PROFESSOR
PROFESSORATE
PROFESSORIAL
PROFESSORSHIP
PROFESSORY
PROFFER
PROFFERED
PROFFERER
PROFFERING
PROFICHI
PROFICIENCE
PROFICIENCY
PROFICIENT
PROFICIENTLY
PROFICUOUS
PROFICUOUSLY
PROFILE
PROFILED
PROFILER
PROFILING
PROFILIST
PROFILOGRAPH
PROFIT
PROFITABLE
PROFITABLY
PROFITED
PROFITEER
PROFITEERING
PROFITER
PROFITING
PROFITLESS
PROFITMONGER
PROFITS
PROFLATED
PROFLAVINE
PROFLIGACIES
PROFLIGACY
PROFLIGATE
PROFLIGATED
PROFLIGATELY
PROFLUENCE
PROFLUENT
PROFLUVIOUS
PROFLUVIUM
PROFONDE
PROFOUND
PROFOUNDLY
PROFOUNDNESS
PROFRE
PROFUGATE
PROFULGENT
PROFUNDA
PROFUNDITY
PROFUSE
PROFUSELY
PROFUSENESS
PROFUSER
PROFUSION
PROFUSIVELY
PROG
PROGAMETE
PROGAMIC
PROGANOSAUR
PROGENERATE
PROGENIES
PROGENITAL
PROGENITIVE
PROGENITOR
PROGENITRIX
PROGENITURE
PROGENITY
PROGENY
PROGERIA
PROGESTIN
PROGG
PROGGED
PROGGER
PROGGING
PROGLOTTIC
PROGLOTTID
PROGLOTTIDES
PROGLOTTIS
PROGNATHI
PROGNATHIC
PROGNATHISM
PROGNATHOUS
PROGNATHY
PROGNE
PROGNOSE
PROGNOSIS
PROGNOSTIC
PROGNOSTICAL
PROGNOSTICATE
PROGNOSTICATION
PROGNOSTICATOR
PROGONEATE
PROGRAM
PROGRAMATIC
PROGRAMED
PROGRAMER
PROGRAMING
PROGRAMIST
PROGRAMISTIC
PROGRAMMA
PROGRAMMATIC
PROGRAMMED
PROGRAMMER
PROGRAMMING
PROGRAMMIST
PROGREDE
PROGREDIENCY
PROGREDIENT
PROGRESS
PROGRESSED
PROGRESSER
PROGRESSING
PROGRESSION
PROGRESSISM
PROGRESSIST
PROGRESSIVE
PROGRESSIVELY
PROGRESSOR
PROHEIM
PROHIBIT
PROHIBITED
PROHIBITER
PROHIBITING
PROHIBITION
PROHIBITIONIST
PROHIBITIVE
PROHIBITOR
PROHIBITORY
PROJACIENT
PROJECT
PROJECTEDLY
PROJECTILE
PROJECTING
PROJECTINGLY
PROJECTION
PROJECTIONAL
PROJECTIVE
PROJECTIVITY
PROJECTOR
PROJECTRIX
PROJECTURE
PROJET
PROJICIENCE
PROJICIENT
PROJICIENTLY
PROKE
PROKEIMENON
PROKER
PROLABIUM
PROLACTIN
PROLAMIN
PROLAMINE
PROLAPSE
PROLAPSED
PROLAPSING
PROLAPSION
PROLAPSUS
PROLATE
PROLATELY
PROLATENESS
PROLATION
PROLATIVE
PROLEAGUE
PROLEAGUER
PROLEG
PROLEGATE
PROLEGOMENAL
PROLEGOMENON
PROLEPSES
PROLEPSIS
PROLEPTIC
PROLEPTICAL
PROLEPTICS
PROLES
PROLETAIRE
PROLETAIRISM
PROLETARIAN
PROLETARIAT
PROLETARIATE
PROLETARIZE
PROLETARY
PROLETCULT
PROLETKULT
PROLICIDAL
PROLICIDE
PROLIFERANT
PROLIFERATE
PROLIFEROUS
PROLIFIC
PROLIFICACY
PROLIFICAL
PROLIFICALLY
PROLIFICATE
PROLIFICATED
PROLIFICATING
PROLIFICITY
PROLIFICNESS
PROLIFY
PROLIGEROUS
PROLIN
PROLINE
PROLIX
PROLIXITY
PROLIXLY
PROLIXNESS
PROLLER
PROLOCUTION
PROLOCUTOR
PROLOCUTRIX
PROLOG
PROLOGIST
PROLOGIZE
PROLOGIZER
PROLOGUE
PROLOGUIST
PROLOGUIZE
PROLOGUIZER
PROLONG
PROLONGATE
PROLONGATION
PROLONGE
PROLONGED
PROLONGER
PROLONGING
PROLONGMENT
PROLUSION
PROLUSIONIZE
PROLUSORY
PROLYL
PROM
PROMACHOS
PROMENADE
PROMENADED
PROMENADER
PROMENADING
PROMERISTEM
PROMERIT
PROMETHIUM
PROMIC
PROMINENCE
PROMINENCY
PROMINENT
PROMINENTLY
PROMISCUITY
PROMISCUOUS
PROMISCUOUSLY
PROMISE
PROMISED
PROMISEE
PROMISER
PROMISING
PROMISINGLY
PROMISOR
PROMISS
PROMISSIVE
PROMISSOR
PROMISSORY

PROMIT
PROMITOSIS
PROMITTOR
PROMNESIA
PROMONTORIES
PROMONTORY
PROMORPH
PROMOTE
PROMOTED
PROMOTER
PROMOTING
PROMOTION
PROMOTIONAL
PROMOTIVE
PROMOTORIAL
PROMOVAL
PROMOVE
PROMOVENT
PROMPT
PROMPTBOOK
PROMPTER
PROMPTING
PROMPTITUDE
PROMPTIVE
PROMPTLY
PROMPTNESS
PROMPTUARY
PROMPTURE
PROMULGATE
PROMULGATED
PROMULGATING
PROMULGATION
PROMULGE
PROMULGED
PROMULGER
PROMULGING
PROMUSCIDATE
PROMUSCIS
PROMYCELIAL
PROMYCELIUM
PRONAOS
PRONATE
PRONATED
PRONATING
PRONATION
PRONATOR
PRONE
PRONELY
PRONENESS
PRONEPHRIC
PRONEPHROS
PRONEUR
PRONG
PRONGBUCK
PRONGED
PRONGER
PRONGHORN
PRONGHORNS
PRONGY
PRONIC
PRONITY
PRONOGRADE
PRONOMINAL
PRONOMINALLY
PRONONCE
PRONOTUM
PRONOUN
PRONOUNAL
PRONOUNCE
PRONOUNCEABLE
PRONOUNCED
PRONOUNCEDLY
PRONOUNCEMENT
PRONOUNCER
PRONOUNCING
PRONTO
PRONUBA
PRONUBIAL
PRONUCLEAR
PRONUCLEI
PRONUCLEUS
PRONUNCIABLE
PRONUNCIAL
PRONUNCIATION
PRONUNCIATOR
PRONYMPH
PRONYMPHAL
PROO
PROODE
PROOEMIAC
PROOEMION
PROOEMIUM
PROOF
PROOFER
PROOFFUL
PROOFING
PROOFLESS
PROOFLESSLY
PROOFREAD
PROOFREADER
PROOFREADING
PROOFROOM
PROOFY
PROP
PROPAEDEUTIC
PROPAGABLE
PROPAGANDA
PROPAGANDIC
PROPAGANDISM
PROPAGANDIST
PROPAGANDIZE
PROPAGATE
PROPAGATED
PROPAGATING
PROPAGATION
PROPAGATIVE
PROPAGATOR
PROPAGATORY
PROPAGINES
PROPAGO
PROPAGULE
PROPAGULUM
PROPALE
PROPALINAL
PROPANE
PROPANEDIOL
PROPARENT
PROPARGYL
PROPARGYLIC
PROPARIAN
PROPASSION
PROPATAGIAL
PROPATAGIAN
PROPATAGIUM
PROPEL
PROPELLANT
PROPELLED
PROPELLENT
PROPELLER
PROPELLING
PROPELMENT
PROPEND
PROPENDENT
PROPENE
PROPENSE
PROPENSELY
PROPENSENESS
PROPENSION
PROPENSITIES
PROPENSITY
PROPENYL
PROPENYLIC
PROPER
PROPERISPOME
PROPERLY
PROPERNESS
PROPERTIED
PROPERTIES
PROPERTY
PROPERTYSHIP
PROPHASE
PROPHASIS
PROPHECIES
PROPHECY
PROPHESIED
PROPHESIER
PROPHESY
PROPHESYING
PROPHET
PROPHETESS
PROPHETHOOD
PROPHETIC
PROPHETICAL
PROPHETICISM
PROPHETICLY
PROPHETISM
PROPHETIZE
PROPHETRY
PROPHLOEM
PROPHORIC
PROPHYLACTIC
PROPHYLAXIS
PROPHYLL
PROPHYLLUM
PROPINATION
PROPINE
PROPINED
PROPINING
PROPINQUANT
PROPINQUE
PROPINQUITY
PROPINQUOUS
PROPIO
PROPIOLATE
PROPIOLIC
PROPIONATE
PROPIONE
PROPIONIC
PROPIONYL
PROPITIABLE
PROPITIAL
PROPITIATE
PROPITIATED
PROPITIATING
PROPITIATION
PROPITIATIVE
PROPITIATOR
PROPITIATORY
PROPITIOUS
PROPITIOUSLY
PROPJET
PROPLASM
PROPLASTIC
PROPLEURON
PROPLEX
PROPLEXUS
PROPODEAL
PROPODEUM
PROPODIAL
PROPODIALE
PROPODITE
PROPODITIC
PROPODIUM
PROPOLIS
PROPOLIZE
PROPOMA
PROPOMATA
PROPONE
PROPONED
PROPONEMENT
PROPONENT
PROPONER
PROPONING
PROPONS
PROPORT
PROPORTION
PROPORTIONAL
PROPORTIONATENESS
PROPORTIONED
PROPORTIONER
PROPOSAL
PROPOSANT
PROPOSE
PROPOSED
PROPOSEDLY
PROPOSER
PROPOSING
PROPOSITIO
PROPOSITION
PROPOSITUS
PROPOUND
PROPOUNDED
PROPOUNDER
PROPOUNDING
PROPOUNDMENT
PROPOXY
PROPPAGE
PROPPED
PROPPER
PROPPING
PROPRAETOR
PROPRETOR
PROPRIATION
PROPRIATORY
PROPRIETAGE
PROPRIETARY
PROPRIETIES
PROPRIETOR
PROPRIETORY
PROPRIETOUS
PROPRIETRESS
PROPRIETY
PROPRIUM
PROPROCTOR
PROPS
PROPTERYGIAL
PROPTERYGIUM
PROPTOSED
PROPTOSES
PROPTOSIS
PROPUGN
PROPUGNACLED
PROPUGNATION
PROPUGNATOR
PROPULSATION
PROPULSATORY
PROPULSE
PROPULSION
PROPULSITY
PROPULSIVE
PROPULSOR
PROPULSORY
PROPUPA
PROPUPAL
PROPWOOD
PROPYGIDIUM
PROPYL
PROPYLAEA
PROPYLAEUM
PROPYLAMINE
PROPYLATION
PROPYLENE
PROPYLIC
PROPYLIDENE
PROPYLITE
PROPYLON
PROPYNE
PROQUAESTOR
PRORATA
PRORATABLE
PRORATE
PRORATED
PRORATING
PRORATION
PRORE
PROREAN
PRORECTOR
PRORECTORATE
PROREPTION
PROREX
PRORHINAL
PROROGATE
PROROGATION
PROROGATOR
PROROGUE
PROROGUED
PROROGUER
PROROGUING
PRORRHESIS
PRORSA
PRORSAL
PRORUMP
PRORUPTION
PROS
PROSAIC
PROSAICAL
PROSAICALLY
PROSAICISM
PROSAICNESS
PROSAISM
PROSAIST
PROSAL
PROSAPY
PROSAR
PROSCAPULA
PROSCAPULAR
PROSCENIA
PROSCENIUM
PROSCIND
PROSCIUTTO
PROSCOLECINE
PROSCOLEX
PROSCOLICES
PROSCRIBE
PROSCRIBED
PROSCRIBER
PROSCRIBING
PROSCRIPT
PROSCRIPTION
PROSCRIPTIVE
PROSE
PROSECT
PROSECTION
PROSECTOR
PROSECUTE
PROSECUTED
PROSECUTING
PROSECUTION
PROSECUTOR
PROSED
PROSELENIC
PROSELYTE
PROSELYTED
PROSELYTER
PROSELYTICAL
PROSELYTING
PROSELYTISM
PROSELYTIST
PROSELYTIZE
PROSELYTIZED
PROSELYTIZER
PROSEMAN
PROSEMINAR
PROSEMINARY
PROSEMINATE

PROSENCHYMA
PROSER
PROSETHMOID
PROSEUCHA
PROSEUCHE
PROSIER
PROSIEST
PROSIFY
PROSILIENCY
PROSILIENT
PROSILIENTLY
PROSILY
PROSIMIAN
PROSINESS
PROSING
PROSIPHON
PROSIPHONAL
PROSIPHONATE
PROSISH
PROSIT
PROSLAVER
PROSLAVERY
PROSNEUSIS
PROSO
PROSOBRANCH
PROSOCELE
PROSOCOELE
PROSODE
PROSODEMIC
PROSODETIC
PROSODIAC
PROSODIAL
PROSODIAN
PROSODIC
PROSODICAL
PROSODICALLY
PROSODION
PROSODIST
PROSODUS
PROSODY
PROSOGASTER
PROSOGYRATE
PROSOMA
PROSOMAL
PROSOMATIC
PROSONOMASIA
PROSOPIC
PROSOPICALLY
PROSOPITE
PROSOPLASIA
PROSOPOLEPSY
PROSOPON
PROSOPYLE
PROSORUS
PROSPECT
PROSPECTED
PROSPECTING
PROSPECTIVE
PROSPECTOR
PROSPECTUS
PROSPER
PROSPERED
PROSPERER
PROSPERING
PROSPERITY
PROSPEROUS
PROSPEROUSLY
PROSPICE
PROSPICIENCE
PROSS
PROSSY
PROSTATE
PROSTATIC
PROSTATISM
PROSTATOLITH
PROSTATOTOMY
PROSTERN
PROSTERNAL
PROSTERNUM
PROSTHECA
PROSTHENIC
PROSTHESES
PROSTHESIS
PROSTHETIC
PROSTHETICS
PROSTHETIST
PROSTHION
PROSTHIONIC
PROSTITUTE
PROSTITUTED
PROSTITUTING
PROSTITUTION
PROSTITUTOR
PROSTOMIAL
PROSTOMIATE
PROSTOMIUM
PROSTRATE
PROSTRATED
PROSTRATING
PROSTRATION
PROSTRATIVE
PROSTRATOR
PROSTYLE
PROSTYLOS
PROSY
PROSYLLOGISM
PROTACTIC
PROTACTINIUM
PROTAGON
PROTAGONISM
PROTAGONIST
PROTAMIN
PROTAMINE
PROTANDRIC
PROTANDRISM
PROTANDROUS
PROTANDRY
PROTANOMAL
PROTANOPE
PROTANOPIA
PROTANOPIC
PROTARSAL
PROTARSUS
PROTASIS
PROTASPIS
PROTATIC
PROTATICALLY
PROTAXIAL
PROTAXIS
PROTE
PROTEAD
PROTEAN
PROTEASE
PROTECT
PROTECTED
PROTECTIBLE
PROTECTING
PROTECTINGLY
PROTECTION
PROTECTIONAL
PROTECTIVE
PROTECTIVELY
PROTECTOR
PROTECTORAL
PROTECTORATE
PROTECTORIAN
PROTECTORIES
PROTECTORY
PROTECTRESS
PROTEGE
PROTEGEE
PROTEGULUM
PROTEIC
PROTEID
PROTEIDE
PROTEIFORM
PROTEIN
PROTEINASE
PROTEINOUS
PROTEINS
PROTEINURIA
PROTEND
PROTENDED
PROTENDING
PROTENSE
PROTENSION
PROTENSITY
PROTENSIVE
PROTENSIVELY
PROTEOLYSIS
PROTEOLYTIC
PROTEOPECTIC
PROTEOPEXIC
PROTEOPEXIS
PROTEOPEXY
PROTEOSE
PROTEOSOMAL
PROTEOSOME
PROTEOSURIA
PROTERANDRY
PROTEROBASE
PROTEROGLYPH
PROTEROGYNY
PROTEROTYPE
PROTERVE
PROTERVITY
PROTEST
PROTESTANCY
PROTESTANT
PROTESTATION
PROTESTATOR
PROTESTATORY
PROTESTED
PROTESTER
PROTESTING
PROTESTINGLY
PROTESTIVE
PROTEXT
PROTHALAMION
PROTHALAMIUM
PROTHALLIAL
PROTHALLINE
PROTHALLIUM
PROTHALLOID
PROTHALLUS
PROTHECA
PROTHESES
PROTHESIS
PROTHETIC
PROTHETICAL
PROTHONOTARY
PROTHORACES
PROTHORACIC
PROTHORAX
PROTHORAXES
PROTHROMBIN
PROTHYSTERON
PROTID
PROTIDE
PROTIST
PROTISTAN
PROTISTIC
PROTISTOLOGY
PROTISTON
PROTOBLAST
PROTOBLASTIC
PROTOCITIZEN
PROTOCLASTIC
PROTOCNEME
PROTOCOCCOID
PROTOCOL
PROTOCOLAR
PROTOCOLARY
PROTOCOLED
PROTOCOLING
PROTOCOLIST
PROTOCOLIZE
PROTOCOLLED
PROTOCOLLING
PROTOCONCH
PROTOCONCHAL
PROTOCONE
PROTOCONID
PROTOCONULE
PROTOCORM
PROTODEACON
PROTODERM
PROTODEVIL
PROTODONATAN
PROTODONATE
PROTODONT
PROTOGENAL
PROTOGENES
PROTOGENESIS
PROTOGENETIC
PROTOGENIC
PROTOGENIST
PROTOGINE
PROTOGOD
PROTOGONOUS
PROTOGRAPH
PROTOGYNOUS
PROTOGYNY
PROTOHOMO
PROTOHUMAN
PROTOLITHIC
PROTOLOG
PROTOLOGIST
PROTOMA
PROTOMALA
PROTOMALAL
PROTOMALAR
PROTOMARTYR
PROTOME
PROTOMERITE
PROTOMERITIC
PROTOMETALS
PROTOMORPH
PROTOMORPHIC
PROTON
PROTONE
PROTONEGROID
PROTONEMA
PROTONEMAL
PROTONEMATA
PROTONEMATAL
PROTONEME
PROTONEPHROS
PROTONEUTRON
PROTONIC
PROTONOTARY
PROTONOTATER
PROTONYM
PROTONYMPH
PROTONYMPHAL
PROTOPAPAS
PROTOPARENT
PROTOPATHIC
PROTOPATHY
PROTOPECTIN
PROTOPEPSIA
PROTOPHLOEM
PROTOPHYTE
PROTOPHYTIC
PROTOPINE
PROTOPLASM
PROTOPLASMAL
PROTOPLASMIC
PROTOPLAST
PROTOPLASTIC
PROTOPOD
PROTOPODIAL
PROTOPODITE
PROTOPODITIC
PROTOPOPE
PROTOPRISM
PROTORE
PROTOREBEL
PROTOSALT
PROTOSINNER
PROTOSOCIAL
PROTOSPASM
PROTOSPORE
PROTOSTELE
PROTOSTELIC
PROTOSTOME
PROTOTHECA
PROTOTHECAL
PROTOTHEME
PROTOTHERE
PROTOTRAITOR
PROTOTROCH
PROTOTROPHIC
PROTOTYPAL
PROTOTYPE
PROTOTYPIC
PROTOTYPICAL
PROTOVILLAIN
PROTOVUM
PROTOXID
PROTOXIDE
PROTOXIDIZE
PROTOXIDIZED
PROTOXYLEM
PROTOZOAL
PROTOZOAN
PROTOZOEA
PROTOZOEAN
PROTOZOIASIS
PROTOZOIC
PROTOZOON
PROTOZOONAL
PROTRACT
PROTRACTED
PROTRACTEDLY
PROTRACTER
PROTRACTILE
PROTRACTING
PROTRACTION
PROTRACTIVE
PROTRACTOR
PROTREPTIC
PROTREPTICAL
PROTRIAENE
PROTRUDE
PROTRUDED
PROTRUDENT
PROTRUDING
PROTRUSIBLE
PROTRUSILE
PROTRUSION
PROTRUSIVE
PROTRUSIVELY
PROTUBERANCE
PROTUBERANCES
PROTUBERANT
PROTUBERATE
PROTUBERATED
PROTUBEROUS
PROTURAN
PROTUTOR
PROTUTORY
PROTYL
PROTYLE
PROTYPE

PROUD
PROUDER
PROUDEST
PROUDFUL
PROUDHEARTED
PROUDISH
PROUDISHLY
PROUDLING
PROUDLY
PROUSTITE
PROVABILITY
PROVABLE
PROVABLENESS
PROVABLY
PROVAND
PROVANT
PROVE
PROVECT
PROVECTION
PROVED
PROVEDITOR
PROVEDOR
PROVEDORE
PROVEN
PROVENANCE
PROVEND
PROVENDER
PROVENE
PROVENIENCE
PROVENIENT
PROVENLY
PROVENT
PROVER
PROVERB
PROVERBIAL
PROVERBIALLY
PROVERBIC
PROVERBIZE
PROVES
PROVIANT
PROVICAR
PROVICARIATE
PROVIDANCE
PROVIDE
PROVIDED
PROVIDENCE
PROVIDENT
PROVIDENTIAL
PROVIDENTLY
PROVIDER
PROVIDING
PROVIDORE
PROVINCE
PROVINCES
PROVINCIAL
PROVINCIALLY
PROVINCIATE
PROVINCULUM
PROVINE
PROVING
PROVINGLY
PROVISION
PROVISIONAL
PROVISIONARY
PROVISIONER
PROVISIONS
PROVISIVE
PROVISO
PROVISOES
PROVISOR
PROVISORILY
PROVISORY
PROVISOS
PROVITAMIN
PROVO
PROVOCANT
PROVOCATION
PROVOCATIVE
PROVOCATOR
PROVOCATORY
PROVOKE
PROVOKED
PROVOKEE
PROVOKER
PROVOKING
PROVOKINGLY
PROVOLA
PROVOST
PROVOSTAL
PROVOSTRY
PROVOSTSHIP
PROW
PROWED
PROWER
PROWERSITE
PROWESS
PROWESSED
PROWL
PROWLED
PROWLER
PROWLING
PROWLINGLY
PROX
PROXENET
PROXENETE
PROXENETISM
PROXENOS
PROXENUS
PROXENY
PROXICALLY
PROXIED
PROXIES
PROXIMAD
PROXIMAL
PROXIMATE
PROXIMATELY
PROXIMATION
PROXIME
PROXIMITY
PROXIMO
PROXY
PROXYING
PROXYSM
PROZYMITE
PRUDE
PRUDELY
PRUDENCE
PRUDENT
PRUDENTIAL
PRUDENTIALLY
PRUDENTLY
PRUDERIES
PRUDERY
PRUDISH
PRUDISHLY
PRUDISHNESS
PRUDIST
PRUDITY
PRUINESCENCE
PRUINOSE
PRUINOUS
PRULAURASIN
PRUNABLE
PRUNABLENESS
PRUNABLY
PRUNASE
PRUNASIN
PRUNE
PRUNED
PRUNELL
PRUNELLA
PRUNELLE
PRUNELLO
PRUNER
PRUNING
PRUNITRIN
PRUNT
PRUNTED
PRURIENCE
PRURIENCY
PRURIENT
PRURIENTLY
PRURIGINOUS
PRURIGO
PRURIOUSNESS
PRURITIC
PRURITUS
PRUSIANO
PRUSSIATE
PRUSSIC
PRUSSIN
PRUSSINE
PRUT
PRY
PRYER
PRYING
PRYINGLY
PRYINGNESS
PRYLER
PRYS
PRYSE
PRYTANEUM
PRYTANIS
PRYTANIZE
PRYTANY
PSALIS
PSALLOID
PSALM
PSALMIC
PSALMIST
PSALMISTRY
PSALMODIAL
PSALMODIC
PSALMODICAL
PSALMODIES
PSALMODIST
PSALMODIZE
PSALMODY
PSALMOGRAPH
PSALMY
PSALOID
PSALTER
PSALTERER
PSALTERIA
PSALTERIAL
PSALTERIAN
PSALTERIST
PSALTERIUM
PSALTERY
PSAMMITE
PSAMMITIC
PSAMMOLITHIC
PSAMMOLOGY
PSAMMOMA
PSAMMOPHILE
PSAMMOUS
PSCHENT
PSELLISM
PSELLISMUS
PSEPHISM
PSEPHISMA
PSEPHITE
PSEPHITIC
PSEPHOLOGIST
PSEPHOLOGY
PSEPHOMANCY
PSEUDACONIN
PSEUDACONINE
PSEUDACUSIS
PSEUDANDRY
PSEUDAPHIA
PSEUDAPOSTLE
PSEUDATOLL
PSEUDAXIS
PSEUDHAEMAL
PSEUDHEMAL
PSEUDIMAGO
PSEUDO
PSEUDOACACIA
PSEUDOALUM
PSEUDOANGINA
PSEUDOAQUATIC
PSEUDOBRANCH
PSEUDOBULB
PSEUDOBULBAR
PSEUDOBULBIL
PSEUDOCARP
PSEUDOCHINA
PSEUDOCLASSIC
PSEUDOCONE
PSEUDOCORTEX
PSEUDOCUMYL
PSEUDOCYST
PSEUDODERM
PSEUDODONT
PSEUDODOX
PSEUDODOXAL
PSEUDOFARCY
PSEUDOGALENA
PSEUDOGLIOMA
PSEUDOGRAPH
PSEUDOGRAPHY
PSEUDOGYNE
PSEUDOGYNY
PSEUDOISM
PSEUDOLALIA
PSEUDOLATRY
PSEUDOLICHEN
PSEUDOLOGICAL
PSEUDOLOGIST
PSEUDOLOGUE
PSEUDOLOGY
PSEUDOMANCY
PSEUDOMANIA
PSEUDOMANTIC
PSEUDOMITOTIC
PSEUDOMORPH
PSEUDOMUCIN
PSEUDONITROL
PSEUDONYM
PSEUDONYMAL
PSEUDONYMIC
PSEUDONYMITY
PSEUDONYMOUS
PSEUDOPLASM
PSEUDOPOD
PSEUDOPODAL
PSEUDOPODE
PSEUDOPODIAL
PSEUDOPODIUM
PSEUDOPORE
PSEUDOPSIA
PSEUDOPTICS
PSEUDOPTOSIS
PSEUDOPUPA
PSEUDOPUPAL
PSEUDORABIES
PSEUDORAMOSE
PSEUDOSALT
PSEUDOSCININE
PSEUDOSCOPE
PSEUDOSCOPIC
PSEUDOSCOPY
PSEUDOSMIA
PSEUDOSOPH
PSEUDOSOPHER
PSEUDOSPERM
PSEUDOSPHERE
PSEUDOSPORE
PSEUDOSTOMA
PSEUDOSUCHIAN
PSEUDOTABES
PSEUDOVUM
PSHA
PSHAW
PSHAWED
PSHAWING
PSHEM
PSI
PSILANTHROPIC
PSILANTHROPY
PSILATRO
PSILOCERAN
PSILOCERATAN
PSILOCERATID
PSILOI
PSILOLOGY
PSILOMELANE
PSILOMELANIC
PSILOPHYTE
PSILOSIS
PSILOSOPHER
PSILOSOPHY
PSILOTACEOUS
PSILOTHRUM
PSILOTIC
PSITHURISM
PSITTACEOUS
PSITTACINE
PSITTACINITE
PSITTACISM
PSITTACISTIC
PSITTACOSIS
PSOAS
PSOATIC
PSOCID
PSOCINE
PSOITIS
PSOMOPHAGIST
PSOMOPHAGY
PSORA
PSORIASIFORM
PSORIASIS
PSORIATIC
PSOROID
PSOROPTIC
PSOROSIS
PSOROSPERM
PSOROSPERMIC
PSOROUS
PSOVIE
PST
PSYCHAGOGIC
PSYCHAGOGOS
PSYCHAGOGUE
PSYCHAGOGY
PSYCHAL
PSYCHALGIA
PSYCHE
PSYCHEDELIC
PSYCHEOMETRY
PSYCHIASIS
PSYCHIATER
PSYCHIATRIC
PSYCHIATRIST
PSYCHIATRIZE
PSYCHIATRY
PSYCHIC
PSYCHICAL
PSYCHICALLY
PSYCHICISM
PSYCHICIST
PSYCHICS
PSYCHID
PSYCHISM

PSYCHO
PSYCHOANALYST
PSYCHOCLINIC
PSYCHODRAMA
PSYCHOFUGAL
PSYCHOGENESIS
PSYCHOGENETIC
PSYCHOGENIC
PSYCHOGENY
PSYCHOGNOSIS
PSYCHOGNOSY
PSYCHOGRAM
PSYCHOGRAPH
PSYCHOGRAPHY
PSYCHOID
PSYCHOKINESIA
PSYCHOKYME
PSYCHOLEPSY
PSYCHOLEPTIC
PSYCHOLOGER
PSYCHOLOGIC
PSYCHOLOGICAL
PSYCHOLOGICS
PSYCHOLOGISM
PSYCHOLOGIST
PSYCHOLOGIZE
PSYCHOLOGUE
PSYCHOLOGY
PSYCHOMACHY
PSYCHOMANCY
PSYCHOMETER
PSYCHOMETRIC
PSYCHOMETRY
PSYCHOMOTOR
PSYCHON
PSYCHONOMIC
PSYCHONOMICS
PSYCHOPATH
PSYCHOPATHIC
PSYCHOPATHY
PSYCHOPETAL
PSYCHOPHOBIA
PSYCHOPLASM
PSYCHOPOMP
PSYCHOPOMPOS
PSYCHOREFLEX
PSYCHOSES
PSYCHOSEXUAL
PSYCHOSIS
PSYCHOSOCIAL
PSYCHOSOME
PSYCHOSOPHY
PSYCHOSTATIC
PSYCHOTAXIS
PSYCHOTHEISM
PSYCHOTIC
PSYCHOTRINE
PSYCHOTROPIC
PSYCHROGRAPH
PSYCHROMETER
PSYCHROMETRY
PSYCHROPHILE
PSYCHROPHOBIA
PSYCHROPHORE
PSYCHROPHYTE
PSYCHURGY
PSYKTER
PSYLLID
PSYLLIUM
PSYWAR
PTARMIC
PTARMICAL
PTARMIGAN
PTARMIGANS
PTERANODONT
PTERASPID
PTERERGATE
PTERIC
PTERIDEOUS
PTERIDIUM
PTERIDOID
PTERIDOLOGY
PTERIDOPHYTE
PTERIDOSPERM
PTERIN
PTERION
PTERNA
PTEROCARPOUS
PTERODACTYL
PTEROGRAPHY
PTEROID
PTEROMA
PTEROMALID
PTERON
PTEROPAEDES
PTEROPEGAL
PTEROPEGOUS
PTEROPEGUM
PTEROPID
PTEROPINE
PTEROPOD
PTEROPODAL
PTEROPODAN
PTEROPODIAL
PTEROPODIUM
PTEROPODOUS
PTEROSAUR
PTEROSAURIAN
PTEROSTIGMA
PTEROSTIGMAL
PTEROTHECA
PTEROTHORAX
PTEROTIC
PTERYGIAL
PTERYGIUM
PTERYGIUMS
PTERYGODE
PTERYGODUM
PTERYGOID
PTERYGOIDAL
PTERYGOIDEAN
PTERYGOPHORE
PTERYGOTE
PTERYGOTOUS
PTERYLA
PTERYLAE
PTERYLOGRAPHY
PTERYLOLOGY
PTERYLOSIS
PTILINAL
PTILINUM
PTILOPAEDES
PTILOPAEDIC
PTILOSIS
PTINID
PTINOID
PTISAN
PTOCHOCRACY
PTOCHOGONY
PTOCHOLOGY
PTOMAIN
PTOMAINE
PTOMAINIC
PTOMATROPINE
PTOSIS
PTOTIC
PTYALAGOGUE
PTYALIN
PTYALISM
PTYALIZE
PTYALIZED
PTYALIZING
PTYALOCELE
PTYALOGENIC
PTYALOLITH
PTYALORRHEA
PTYXIS
PU
PUAN
PUB
PUBAL
PUBBLE
PUBERAL
PUBERTAL
PUBERTIC
PUBERTY
PUBERULENT
PUBES
PUBESCENCE
PUBESCENCY
PUBESCENT
PUBIAN
PUBIGEROUS
PUBIOTOMY
PUBIS
PUBLIC
PUBLICAN
PUBLICANISM
PUBLICATE
PUBLICATION
PUBLICE
PUBLICISM
PUBLICIST
PUBLICITY
PUBLICIZE
PUBLICIZED
PUBLICIZING
PUBLICLY
PUBLICNESS
PUBLISH
PUBLISHABLE
PUBLISHED
PUBLISHER
PUBLISHING
PUBLISHMENT
PUBOFEMORAL
PUBOILIAC
PUBOISCHIAC
PUBOISCHIAL
PUBORECTALIS
PUBOTIBIAL
PUCCA
PUCCOON
PUCE
PUCELAGE
PUCELLAGE
PUCELLE
PUCERON
PUCHERA
PUCHERITE
PUCHERO
PUCK
PUCKA
PUCKBALL
PUCKER
PUCKERBUSH
PUCKERED
PUCKEREL
PUCKERER
PUCKERIER
PUCKERIEST
PUCKERING
PUCKERMOUTH
PUCKERY
PUCKFIST
PUCKFOIST
PUCKISH
PUCKISHLY
PUCKISHNESS
PUCKNEEDLE
PUCKREL
PUCKSEY
PUCKSTER
PUD
PUDDEE
PUDDENING
PUDDER
PUDDING
PUDDINGBERRY
PUDDINGHEAD
PUDDINGHEADED
PUDDINGHOUSE
PUDDINGWIFE
PUDDINGWIVES
PUDDINGY
PUDDLE
PUDDLEBALL
PUDDLEBAR
PUDDLED
PUDDLER
PUDDLING
PUDDLY
PUDDOCK
PUDDY
PUDENCY
PUDENDAL
PUDENDOUS
PUDENDUM
PUDENT
PUDER
PUDGE
PUDGIER
PUDGIEST
PUDGILY
PUDGINESS
PUDGY
PUDIANO
PUDIBUND
PUDIBUNDITY
PUDIC
PUDICAL
PUDICITIA
PUDICITY
PUDOR
PUDU
PUE
PUEBLITO
PUEBLO
PUEBLOS
PUER
PUERARIA
PUERICULTURE
PUERILE
PUERILELY
PUERILENESS
PUERILISM
PUERILITIES
PUERILITY
PUERPERA
PUERPERAL
PUERPERALISM
PUERPERANT
PUERPERIUM
PUERPEROUS
PUFF
PUFFBACK
PUFFBALL
PUFFBIRD
PUFFED
PUFFER
PUFFERIES
PUFFERY
PUFFIER
PUFFIEST
PUFFIN
PUFFINESS
PUFFINET
PUFFING
PUFFS
PUFFWIG
PUFFY
PUG
PUGENELLO
PUGGAREE
PUGGED
PUGGER
PUGGI
PUGGING
PUGGISH
PUGGLE
PUGGREE
PUGGRY
PUGGY
PUGH
PUGIL
PUGILANT
PUGILISM
PUGILIST
PUGILISTIC
PUGILISTICAL
PUGLIANITE
PUGMARK
PUGMILL
PUGMILLER
PUGNACIOUS
PUGNACIOUSLY
PUGNACITY
PUGREE
PUGUA
PUHA
PUIRTITH
PUISNE
PUISNY
PUISSANCE
PUISSANT
PUISSANTLY
PUISSANTNESS
PUIST
PUIT
PUJA
PUKA
PUKATEA
PUKATEINE
PUKE
PUKED
PUKEKA
PUKEKO
PUKER
PUKEWEED
PUKING
PUKISH
PUKISHNESS
PUKKA
PUKRAS
PUKU
PUKY
PUL
PULAHAN
PULAHANES
PULAHANISM
PULAJAN
PULAS
PULASAN
PULASKITE
PULCHRIFY
PULCHRITUDE
PULE
PULED
PULEGOL
PULEGONE
PULER
PULEYN
PULGADA
PULI
PULICARIOUS

PULICAT
PULICATE
PULICENE
PULICID
PULICIDAL
PULICIDE
PULICINE
PULICOID
PULICOSE
PULICOSITY
PULICOUS
PULIJAN
PULING
PULINGLY
PULIOL
PULISH
PULK
PULKA
PULL
PULLABLE
PULLAILE
PULLALUE
PULLBACK
PULLBOAT
PULLDEVIL
PULLDOO
PULLDOWN
PULLED
PULLEN
PULLER
PULLERIES
PULLERY
PULLET
PULLEY
PULLEYS
PULLICAT
PULLING
PULLISEE
PULLOCK
PULLOUT
PULLOVER
PULLSHOVEL
PULLULANT
PULLULATE
PULLULATED
PULLULATING
PULLULATION
PULLULATIVE
PULLUS
PULMENT
PULMOGASTRIC
PULMOMETER
PULMOMETRY
PULMONAR
PULMONARIAN
PULMONARY
PULMONATE
PULMONIC
PULMONICAL
PULMONITIS
PULMOTOR
PULP
PULPACEOUS
PULPAL
PULPALGIA
PULPATONE
PULPATOON
PULPBOARD
PULPECTOMY
PULPED
PULPEFACTION
PULPER
PULPERIA
PULPIER
PULPIEST
PULPIFIED
PULPIFIER
PULPIFY
PULPIFYING
PULPILY
PULPINESS
PULPING
PULPIT
PULPITAL
PULPITARIAN
PULPITEER
PULPITER
PULPITIC
PULPITICAL
PULPITICALLY
PULPITIS
PULPITLESS
PULPITLY
PULPITRY
PULPOTOMY
PULPOUS
PULPOUSNESS
PULPSTONE
PULPWOOD
PULPY
PULQUE
PULSANT
PULSAR
PULSATE
PULSATED
PULSATILE
PULSATING
PULSATION
PULSATIONAL
PULSATIVE
PULSATIVELY
PULSATOR
PULSATORY
PULSE
PULSED
PULSEJET
PULSELESS
PULSELESSLY
PULSELLUM
PULSIDGE
PULSIFIC
PULSIMETER
PULSING
PULSION
PULSIVE
PULSOMETER
PULSUS
PULTACEOUS
PULTON
PULTUN
PULTURE
PULU
PULVERABLE
PULVERACEOUS
PULVERANT
PULVERATE
PULVERATED
PULVERATING
PULVEREOUS
PULVERIN
PULVERINE
PULVERIZATE
PULVERIZATOR
PULVERIZE
PULVERIZED
PULVERIZER
PULVERIZING
PULVEROUS
PULVERULENCE
PULVERULENT
PULVIL
PULVILLAR
PULVILLI
PULVILLIFORM
PULVILLUS
PULVINAR
PULVINARIAN
PULVINATE
PULVINATED
PULVINATION
PULVINIFORM
PULVINO
PULVINULUS
PULVINUS
PULVIPLUME
PULWAR
PULY
PUMA
PUMEX
PUMICATE
PUMICATED
PUMICATING
PUMICE
PUMICED
PUMICEOUS
PUMICER
PUMICIFORM
PUMICITE
PUMICOSE
PUMIE
PUMMEL
PUMMELED
PUMMELING
PUMMELLED
PUMMELLING
PUMMICE
PUMP
PUMPAGE
PUMPELLYITE
PUMPER
PUMPERNICKEL
PUMPET
PUMPHANDLE
PUMPING
PUMPKIN
PUMPKINIFY
PUMPKINITY
PUMPKINSEED
PUMPKNOT
PUMPMAN
PUMPS
PUMPWRIGHT
PUN
PUNA
PUNAISE
PUNALUA
PUNALUAN
PUNAMU
PUNATOO
PUNCH
PUNCHABLE
PUNCHAYET
PUNCHBOARD
PUNCHED
PUNCHEON
PUNCHER
PUNCHINELLO
PUNCHINESS
PUNCHING
PUNCHY
PUNCT
PUNCTAL
PUNCTATE
PUNCTATED
PUNCTATIM
PUNCTATION
PUNCTATOR
PUNCTICULAR
PUNCTICULOSE
PUNCTIFORM
PUNCTILIAR
PUNCTILIO
PUNCTILIOS
PUNCTILIOUS
PUNCTION
PUNCTIST
PUNCTUAL
PUNCTUALIST
PUNCTUALITY
PUNCTUALLY
PUNCTUATE
PUNCTUATED
PUNCTUATING
PUNCTUATION
PUNCTUATIVE
PUNCTUATOR
PUNCTUIST
PUNCTULATE
PUNCTULATED
PUNCTULATION
PUNCTULE
PUNCTULUM
PUNCTUM
PUNCTURATION
PUNCTURE
PUNCTURER
PUNCTURING
PUNCTUS
PUND
PUNDIGRION
PUNDIT
PUNDITA
PUNDITIC
PUNDITICALLY
PUNDITRY
PUNDONOR
PUNDUM
PUNECA
PUNEE
PUNESE
PUNG
PUNGAPUNG
PUNGAR
PUNGE
PUNGENCE
PUNGENCY
PUNGENT
PUNGENTLY
PUNGER
PUNGEY
PUNGI
PUNGLE
PUNGLED
PUNGY
PUNGYI
PUNICACEOUS
PUNICEOUS
PUNICIAL
PUNICIN
PUNIER
PUNIEST
PUNILY
PUNINESS
PUNISH
PUNISHABLE
PUNISHED
PUNISHER
PUNISHING
PUNISHMENT
PUNITION
PUNITIONAL
PUNITIONALLY
PUNITIVE
PUNITIVELY
PUNITIVENESS
PUNITORY
PUNJUM
PUNK
PUNKA
PUNKAH
PUNKER
PUNKETTO
PUNKIE
PUNKIES
PUNKISH
PUNKLING
PUNKT
PUNKWOOD
PUNKY
PUNNABLE
PUNNAGE
PUNNED
PUNNER
PUNNET
PUNNIC
PUNNICAL
PUNNIGRAM
PUNNING
PUNNINGLY
PUNNOLOGY
PUNSTER
PUNT
PUNTA
PUNTABOUT
PUNTAL
PUNTELLO
PUNTER
PUNTI
PUNTIES
PUNTILLA
PUNTIST
PUNTO
PUNTOUT
PUNTSMAN
PUNTY
PUNY
PUNYISM
PUNYSHIP
PUP
PUPA
PUPAE
PUPAL
PUPARIAL
PUPARIUM
PUPAS
PUPATE
PUPATED
PUPATING
PUPATION
PUPELO
PUPIFEROUS
PUPIFORM
PUPIGENOUS
PUPIL
PUPILABILITY
PUPILAGE
PUPILAR
PUPILARITY
PUPILARY
PUPILATE
PUPILED
PUPILIZE
PUPILLAGE
PUPILLAR
PUPILLARITY
PUPILLARY
PUPILLATE
PUPILLED
PUPILLIZE
PUPILLONIAN
PUPILMONGER
PUPIPAROUS
PUPIVORE
PUPIVOROUS
PUPPED

PUPPET
PUPPETEER
PUPPETHEAD
PUPPETISM
PUPPETIZE
PUPPETMAN
PUPPETMASTER
PUPPETRY
PUPPIED
PUPPIES
PUPPIFY
PUPPILY
PUPPING
PUPPY
PUPPYDOM
PUPPYFISH
PUPPYFOOT
PUPPYHOOD
PUPPYING
PUPPYISM
PUPULO
PUPUNHA
PUR
PURAQUE
PURAU
PURBLIND
PURBLINDLY
PURBLINDNESS
PURCHASABLE
PURCHASE
PURCHASED
PURCHASER
PURCHASERY
PURCHASING
PURDAH
PURDY
PURE
PUREAYN
PUREBLOOD
PUREBRED
PURED
PUREDEE
PUREE
PURELY
PURENESS
PURER
PUREST
PUREY
PURFLE
PURFLED
PURFLER
PURFLING
PURFLY
PURGA
PURGAMENT
PURGATION
PURGATIVE
PURGATORIAL
PURGATORIAN
PURGATORY
PURGE
PURGED
PURGER
PURGERY
PURGING
PURIFICANT
PURIFICATION
PURIFICATOR
PURIFICATORY
PURIFIED
PURIFIER
PURIFORM
PURIFY
PURIFYING
PURIN
PURINE
PURIRI
PURISM
PURIST
PURISTIC
PURISTICAL
PURITAN
PURITANIC
PURITANICAL
PURITANISM
PURITANO
PURITY
PURL
PURLED
PURLER
PURLHOUSE
PURLICUE
PURLICUES
PURLIEU
PURLIEUMAN
PURLIEUMEN
PURLIEUS
PURLIN
PURLINE
PURLING
PURLMAN
PURLOIN
PURLOINER
PURO
PURPARTY
PURPENSE
PURPIE
PURPLE
PURPLED
PURPLEHEART
PURPLELY
PURPLES
PURPLESCENT
PURPLEWORT
PURPLING
PURPLISH
PURPLISHNESS
PURPLY
PURPORT
PURPORTED
PURPORTEDLY
PURPORTING
PURPOSE
PURPOSED
PURPOSEDLY
PURPOSEFUL
PURPOSEFULLY
PURPOSELESS
PURPOSELIKE
PURPOSELY
PURPOSER
PURPOSES
PURPOSING
PURPOSIVE
PURPOSIVELY
PURPOSIVISM
PURPRESTURE
PURPRISE
PURPRISION
PURPURA
PURPURACEOUS
PURPURATE
PURPURE
PURPUREAL
PURPUREAN
PURPURESCENT
PURPURIC
PURPURIN
PURPURINE
PURPURITE
PURPURIZE
PURPUROID
PURR
PURRAH
PURRE
PURRED
PURREE
PURREL
PURRER
PURRING
PURRONE
PURRY
PURSE
PURSED
PURSEFUL
PURSELIKE
PURSER
PURSES
PURSET
PURSIER
PURSIEST
PURSINESS
PURSING
PURSIVE
PURSLANE
PURSLEY
PURSUABLE
PURSUAL
PURSUANCE
PURSUANT
PURSUANTLY
PURSUE
PURSUED
PURSUER
PURSUING
PURSUIT
PURSUITMETER
PURSUIVANT
PURSY
PURTENANCE
PURTY
PURULENCE
PURULENCY
PURULENT
PURULENTLY
PURULOID
PURUSHA
PURUSHARTHA
PURVEY
PURVEYABLE
PURVEYAL
PURVEYANCE
PURVEYANCER
PURVEYED
PURVEYING
PURVEYOR
PURVIEW
PURVOE
PURWANNAH
PUS
PUSH
PUSHBALL
PUSHCARD
PUSHCART
PUSHED
PUSHER
PUSHFUL
PUSHFULLY
PUSHFULNESS
PUSHIER
PUSHIEST
PUSHILY
PUSHINESS
PUSHING
PUSHINGLY
PUSHINGNESS
PUSHMOBILE
PUSHOVER
PUSHPIN
PUSHUM
PUSHWAINLING
PUSHY
PUSIL
PUSILL
PUSILLANIMOUS
PUSS
PUSSCAT
PUSSIER
PUSSIES
PUSSIEST
PUSSLEY
PUSSLY
PUSSY
PUSSYCAT
PUSSYFOOT
PUSSYFOOTED
PUSSYFOOTER
PUSSYFOOTING
PUSSYFOOTISM
PUSSYTOE
PUSTULANT
PUSTULAR
PUSTULATE
PUSTULATED
PUSTULATING
PUSTULATION
PUSTULATOUS
PUSTULE
PUSTULED
PUSTULIFORM
PUSTULOSE
PUSTULOUS
PUSZTA
PUT
PUTAGE
PUTAIN
PUTAMEN
PUTAMINOUS
PUTANISM
PUTATION
PUTATIONARY
PUTATIVE
PUTATIVELY
PUTBACK
PUTCHEN
PUTCHER
PUTE
PUTEAL
PUTELEE
PUTELI
PUTHERY
PUTID
PUTIDLY
PUTIDNESS
PUTING
PUTLOCK
PUTLOG
PUTOIS
PUTREDINOUS
PUTREFACIENT
PUTREFACTION
PUTREFACTIVE
PUTREFIED
PUTREFIER
PUTREFY
PUTREFYING
PUTRESCE
PUTRESCENCE
PUTRESCENCY
PUTRESCENT
PUTRESCIBLE
PUTRESCINE
PUTRICIDE
PUTRID
PUTRIDITY
PUTRIDLY
PUTRIDNESS
PUTRIFACTED
PUTRIFORM
PUTRILAGE
PUTSCHISM
PUTSCHIST
PUTT
PUTTAN
PUTTEE
PUTTER
PUTTERER
PUTTERINGLY
PUTTI
PUTTIED
PUTTIER
PUTTING
PUTTO
PUTTOCK
PUTTOO
PUTTY
PUTTYBLOWER
PUTTYHEARTED
PUTTYING
PUTTYROOT
PUTURE
PUTZ
PUUD
PUXY
PUY
PUZZLE
PUZZLEATION
PUZZLED
PUZZLEDLY
PUZZLEDNESS
PUZZLEHEAD
PUZZLEHEADED
PUZZLEMAN
PUZZLEMENT
PUZZLEPATE
PUZZLEPATED
PUZZLER
PUZZLING
PUZZLINGLY
PUZZLINGNESS
PYAEMIA
PYAEMIC
PYAL
PYARTHROSIS
PYAT
PYCHE
PYCNIAL
PYCNIC
PYCNID
PYCNIDIOSPORE
PYCNIDIUM
PYCNIOSPORE
PYCNITE
PYCNIUM
PYCNODONT
PYCNOGONID
PYCNOGONOID
PYCNOMETER
PYCNOSIS
PYCNOSPORE
PYCNOSPORIC
PYCNOSTYLE
PYCNOTIC
PYE
PYELECTASIS
PYELIC
PYELITIC
PYELITIS
PYELOGRAM
PYELOGRAPHIC
PYELOGRAPHY
PYEMESIS
PYEMIA
PYEMIC
PYENGADU

PYGAL
PYGARG
PYGARGUS
PYGIDID
PYGIDIUM
PYGMAEAN
PYGMEAN
PYGMIES
PYGMOID
PYGMY
PYGMYWEED
PYGOFER
PYGON
PYGOPAGUS
PYGOPOD
PYGOPODINE
PYGOPODOUS
PYGOSTYLE
PYGOSTYLED
PYGOSTYLOUS
PYIC
PYIN
PYJAMA
PYJAMAED
PYJAMAS
PYKAR
PYKE
PYKNATOM
PYKNIC
PYLA
PYLAGORE
PYLANGIAL
PYLANGIUM
PYLAR
PYLIC
PYLON
PYLORALGIA
PYLORIC
PYLORITIS
PYLOROPLASTY
PYLOROPTOSIS
PYLOROSCOPY
PYLOROSPASM
PYLORUS
PYNE
PYNOT
PYNUNG
PYOCELE
PYOCTANIN
PYOCTANINE
PYOCYANASE
PYOCYANIN
PYOCYST
PYOCYTE
PYODERMIA
PYODERMIC
PYOGENESIS
PYOGENETIC
PYOGENIC
PYOGENIN
PYOGENOUS
PYOID
PYOLYMPH
PYOMETRA
PYOMETRITIS
PYONEPHRITIS
PYONEPHROTIC
PYOPHAGIA
PYOPHTHALMIA
PYOPLANIA
PYOPOIESIS
PYOPOIETIC
PYOPTYSIS
PYORRHEAL
PYORRHOEAL
PYOSALPINX
PYOSIS
PYOSPERMIA
PYOT
PYOTHERAPY
PYOTHORAX
PYOURETER
PYOXANTHOSE
PYR
PYRACANTH
PYRACANTHA
PYRACENE
PYRAL
PYRALIDAN
PYRALIDID
PYRALIDIFORM
PYRALIS
PYRALOID
PYRAMID
PYRAMIDAIRE
PYRAMIDAL
PYRAMIDALE
PYRAMIDALIS
PYRAMIDALLY
PYRAMIDATE
PYRAMIDED
PYRAMIDELLID
PYRAMIDER
PYRAMIDIA
PYRAMIDIC
PYRAMIDICAL
PYRAMIDING
PYRAMIDION
PYRAMIDOIDAL
PYRAMIDS
PYRAMOIDAL
PYRAN
PYRANOMETER
PYRANOSE
PYRANYL
PYRARGYRITE
PYRAZIN
PYRAZINE
PYRAZOLE
PYRAZOLINE
PYRAZOLONE
PYRAZOLYL
PYRE
PYRECTIC
PYRENA
PYRENE
PYRENIN
PYRENOCARP
PYRENODEAN
PYRENODEOUS
PYRENOID
PYRENOLICHEN
PYRETHRIN
PYRETHRUM
PYRETIC
PYRETICOSIS
PYRETOGENIC
PYRETOGENOUS
PYRETOGRAPHY
PYRETOLOGY
PYRETOLYSIS
PYREX
PYREXIA
PYREXIAL
PYREXIC
PYREXICAL
PYRGEOMETER
PYRGOIDAL
PYRGOLOGIST
PYRGOM
PYRIBOLE
PYRIDAZINE
PYRIDIC
PYRIDINE
PYRIDINIUM
PYRIDINIZE
PYRIDONE
PYRIDOXINE
PYRIDYL
PYRIFORM
PYRIFORMIS
PYRIMIDIN
PYRIMIDINE
PYRIMIDYL
PYRITACEOUS
PYRITE
PYRITES
PYRITIC
PYRITICAL
PYRITIFEROUS
PYRITIZE
PYRITOHEDRAL
PYRITOHEDRON
PYRITOID
PYRITOLOGY
PYRITOUS
PYROACETIC
PYROARSENATE
PYROARSENIC
PYROARSENITE
PYROBALLOGY
PYROBELONITE
PYROBORATE
PYROBORIC
PYROCATECHIN
PYROCATECHOL
PYROCHEMICAL
PYROCHLORE
PYROCITRIC
PYROCLASTIC
PYROCOLL
PYROCOTTON
PYROELECTRIC
PYROGALLATE
PYROGALLIC
PYROGALLOL
PYROGEN
PYROGENATION
PYROGENESIA
PYROGENESIS
PYROGENIC
PYROGENOUS
PYROGNOMIC
PYROGNOSTIC
PYROGNOSTICS
PYROGRAPH
PYROGRAPHER
PYROGRAPHIC
PYROGRAPHY
PYROGRAVURE
PYROGUAIACIN
PYROID
PYROLACEOUS
PYROLATER
PYROLATRY
PYROLIGNEOUS
PYROLIGNIC
PYROLIGNITE
PYROLIGNOUS
PYROLITE
PYROLOGICAL
PYROLOGIST
PYROLOGY
PYROLUSITE
PYROLYSIS
PYROLYTIC
PYROMACHY
PYROMAGNETIC
PYROMANCER
PYROMANCY
PYROMANIA
PYROMANIACAL
PYROMANTIC
PYROMELLITIC
PYROMETER
PYROMETRIC
PYROMETRICAL
PYROMETRY
PYROMORPHITE
PYROMORPHOUS
PYROMOTOR
PYROMUCATE
PYROMUCIC
PYROMUCYL
PYRONAPHTHA
PYRONE
PYRONOMICS
PYRONYXIS
PYROPE
PYROPEN
PYROPHANITE
PYROPHANOUS
PYROPHILE
PYROPHILOUS
PYROPHOBIA
PYROPHONE
PYROPHORIC
PYROPHOROUS
PYROPHORUS
PYROPHYLLITE
PYROPUNCTURE
PYROPUS
PYROSCOPE
PYROSCOPY
PYROSIS
PYROSMALITE
PYROSPHERE
PYROSTAT
PYROSTILPNITE
PYROSULPHATE
PYROSULPHITE
PYROTARTARIC
PYROTARTRATE
PYROTECHNIAN
PYROTECHNIC
PYROTECHNICS
PYROTECHNIST
PYROTECHNY
PYROTEREBIC
PYROTIC
PYROTOXIN
PYROTRITARIC
PYROURIC
PYROVANADIC
PYROXANTHIN
PYROXENE
PYROXENIC
PYROXENITE
PYROXMANGITE
PYROXYLIC
PYROXYLIN
PYROXYLINE
PYRRHIC
PYRRHICHIAN
PYRRHICHIUS
PYRRHICIST
PYRRHOTINE
PYRRHOTISM
PYRRHOTITE
PYRRHOUS
PYRRHULOXIA
PYRRHUS
PYRRODIAZOLE
PYRROL
PYRROLE
PYRROLIC
PYRROLIDINE
PYRROLIDONE
PYRROLIDYL
PYRROLINE
PYRROPHYLLIN
PYRROYL
PYRRYL
PYRRYLENE
PYRUVATE
PYRUVIC
PYRUVYL
PYRYLIUM
PYSE
PYTHOGENIC
PYTHON
PYTHONESS
PYTHONIC
PYTHONICAL
PYTHONID
PYTHONIFORM
PYTHONINE
PYTHONISM
PYTHONIST
PYTHONIZE
PYTHONOID
PYTHONOMORPH
PYURIA
PYX
PYXIDATE
PYXIDES
PYXIDIUM
PYXIE
PYXIS

QABBALA
QABBALAH
QADARITE
QADI
QAID
QAIMAQAM
QANEH
QANTAR
QASAB
QAT
QAZAQ
QERI
QIBLA
QINAH
QIYAS
QOBAR
QRI
QU
QUA
QUAA
QUAB
QUABIRD
QUACHIL
QUACK
QUACKED
QUACKERIES
QUACKERY
QUACKHOOD
QUACKING
QUACKISH
QUACKISHLY
QUACKISHNESS
QUACKISM
QUACKLE
QUACKSALVER
QUACKSTER
QUACKY
QUAD
QUADDED
QUADDLE
QUADE
QUADER
QUADLE
QUADRA
QUADRABLE
QUADRAE
QUADRAGESIMAL
QUADRAL
QUADRANGLE
QUADRANGLED
QUADRANGULAR
QUADRANGULED
QUADRANS
QUADRANT
QUADRANTAL
QUADRANTILE
QUADRAPHONIC
QUADRAT
QUADRATE
QUADRATED
QUADRATIC
QUADRATICAL
QUADRATICS
QUADRATING
QUADRATRIX
QUADRATUM
QUADRATURE
QUADRATUS
QUADREL
QUADRENNIA
QUADRENNIAL
QUADRENNIUM
QUADRENNIUMS
QUADRIAD
QUADRIC
QUADRICEPS
QUADRICINIUM
QUADRICIPITAL
QUADRICONE
QUADRICYCLE
QUADRICYCLER
QUADRIENNIUM
QUADRIFID
QUADRIFILAR
QUADRIFOCAL
QUADRIFOLIUM
QUADRIFORM
QUADRIFRONS
QUADRIGA
QUADRIGAE
QUADRIGAMIST
QUADRIGATE
QUADRIGATUS
QUADRIHYBRID
QUADRIJUGAL
QUADRILATERAL
QUADRILLE
QUADRILLED
QUADRILLES
QUADRILLING
QUADRILLION
QUADRILOGY
QUADRIMUM
QUADRIN
QUADRINE
QUADRINOMIAL
QUADRIPAROUS
QUADRIPLANAR
QUADRISECT
QUADRIURATE
QUADRIVALENT
QUADRIVIA
QUADRIVIAL
QUADRIVIOUS
QUADRIVIUM
QUADROON
QUADRUAL
QUADRUM
QUADRUMANAL
QUADRUMANE
QUADRUMANOUS
QUADRUPED
QUADRUPEDAL
QUADRUPEDAN
QUADRUPEDANT
QUADRUPEDATE
QUADRUPEDOUS
QUADRUPLANE
QUADRUPLATE
QUADRUPLATOR
QUADRUPLE
QUADRUPLED
QUADRUPLET
QUADRUPLEX
QUADRUPLING
QUAEDAM
QUAERE
QUAESITA
QUAESITUM
QUAESTIO
QUAESTIONES
QUAESTOR
QUAESTORIAL
QUAESTORIAN
QUAESTORSHIP
QUAESTUARY
QUAFF
QUAFFED
QUAFFER
QUAFFING
QUAG
QUAGGA
QUAGGAS
QUAGGIER
QUAGGIEST
QUAGGLE
QUAGGY
QUAGMIRE
QUAGMIRED
QUAGMIRY
QUAHAUG
QUAHOG
QUAI
QUAICH
QUAIFE
QUAIGH
QUAIL
QUAILED
QUAILERIES
QUAILERY
QUAILHEAD
QUAILING
QUAILY
QUAINT
QUAINTANCE
QUAINTER
QUAINTEST
QUAINTISE
QUAINTLY
QUAINTNESS
QUAIR
QUAIS
QUAKE
QUAKED
QUAKER
QUAKERBIRD
QUAKETAIL
QUAKIER
QUAKIEST
QUAKILY
QUAKINESS
QUAKING
QUAKINGLY
QUAKY
QUALE
QUALIA
QUALIFIABLE
QUALIFICATION
QUALIFICATOR
QUALIFIED
QUALIFIEDLY
QUALIFIER
QUALIFY
QUALIFYING
QUALIMETER
QUALITATIVE
QUALITIED
QUALITIES
QUALITY
QUALLY
QUALM
QUALMISH
QUALMISHLY
QUALMISHNESS
QUALMY
QUALTAGH
QUAMASH
QUAN
QUANDANG
QUANDARIES
QUANDARY
QUANDONG
QUANDY
QUANNET
QUANT
QUANTA
QUANTIC
QUANTICAL
QUANTIFIED
QUANTIFIER
QUANTIFY
QUANTIFYING
QUANTIMETER
QUANTITATE
QUANTITATIVE
QUANTITIED
QUANTITIES
QUANTITIVE
QUANTITIVELY
QUANTITY
QUANTIVALENT
QUANTIZATION
QUANTIZE
QUANTIZED
QUANTIZING
QUANTOMETER
QUANTONG
QUANTULUM
QUANTUM
QUAP
QUAQUAVERSAL
QUAR
QUARANTINE
QUARANTINED
QUARANTINER
QUARANTINING
QUARANTY
QUARDEEL
QUARE
QUARENDEN
QUARENDER
QUARENTENE
QUARESMA
QUARION
QUARK
QUARL
QUARLE
QUARLES
QUARRED
QUARREL
QUARRELED
QUARRELING
QUARRELLED
QUARRELLING
QUARRELLOUS
QUARRELOUS
QUARRELOUSLY
QUARRELSOME
QUARRELSOMENESS
QUARRIED
QUARRIER
QUARRIES
QUARRION
QUARROME
QUARRY
QUARRYING
QUARRYMAN
QUARRYMEN
QUARRYSTONE
QUART
QUARTA
QUARTAN
QUARTANE
QUARTANO
QUARTATION
QUARTAUT
QUARTE
QUARTER
QUARTERAGE
QUARTERBACK
QUARTERED
QUARTERER
QUARTERFOIL
QUARTERING
QUARTERLAND
QUARTERLIES
QUARTERLY
QUARTERMAN
QUARTERMASTER
QUARTERMEN
QUARTERN
QUARTERNIGHT
QUARTERNION
QUARTERON
QUARTERPACE
QUARTERS
QUARTERSAW
QUARTERSAWED
QUARTERSAWING
QUARTERSAWN
QUARTERSTAFF
QUARTERSTAVES
QUARTET
QUARTETTE
QUARTIC
QUARTILE
QUARTIN
QUARTINE
QUARTINHO
QUARTIPAROUS
QUARTO
QUARTOLE
QUARTOS
QUARTZ
QUARTZIC
QUARTZITE
QUARTZITIC
QUARTZOID
QUARTZOSE
QUARTZOUS
QUARTZY
QUAS
QUASAR
QUASH
QUASHED
QUASHEY
QUASHING
QUASHY
QUASI
QUASKIES
QUASKY
QUASS
QUASSATION
QUASSATIVE
QUASSIA
QUASSIIN
QUASSIN
QUAT
QUATCH
QUATE
QUATENUS
QUATERN
QUATERNARIES
QUATERNARIUS
QUATERNARY
QUATERNATE
QUATERNION
QUATERNIONIC
QUATERNITIES
QUATERNITY
QUATERON
QUATERS
QUATERTENSES
QUATORZAIN
QUATORZE

QUATRAIN
QUATRAL
QUATRAYLE
QUATRE
QUATREBLE
QUATREFOIL
QUATREFOILED
QUATRIBLE
QUATRIN
QUATTIE
QUATTRINI
QUATTRINO
QUATTROCENTO
QUATTY
QUATUOR
QUAVER
QUAVERED
QUAVERER
QUAVERING
QUAVERINGLY
QUAVEROUS
QUAVERY
QUAVIVER
QUAW
QUAWK
QUAX
QUAY
QUAYAGE
QUAYED
QUAYING
QUAYSIDE
QUAYSIDER
QUEACH
QUEACHIER
QUEACHIEST
QUEACHY
QUEAK
QUEAL
QUEAN
QUEANISH
QUEASE
QUEASIER
QUEASIEST
QUEASILY
QUEASINESS
QUEASOM
QUEASY
QUEAZEN
QUEBRACHITE
QUEBRACHITOL
QUEBRACHO
QUEBRADA
QUEBRADILLA
QUEBRITH
QUECH
QUED
QUEDE
QUEDLY
QUEDNESS
QUEDSHIP
QUEE
QUEECHY
QUEED
QUEEL
QUEEN
QUEENCAKE
QUEENCRAFT
QUEENCUP
QUEENFISH
QUEENFISHES
QUEENING
QUEENITE
QUEENLET
QUEENLIER
QUEENLIEST
QUEENLIKE
QUEENLINESS
QUEENLY
QUEENRIGHT
QUEENROOT
QUEENS
QUEENSBERRIES
QUEENSBERRY
QUEENWEED
QUEENWOOD
QUEER
QUEERER
QUEEREST
QUEERITY
QUEERLY
QUEERNESS
QUEERSOME
QUEERY
QUEEST
QUEET
QUEEVE
QUEI
QUEINTISE
QUELCH
QUELITE
QUELL
QUELLED
QUELLER
QUELLING
QUELLIO
QUELLUNG
QUELME
QUELT
QUEMADO
QUEME
QUEMEFUL
QUEMELY
QUENA
QUENCH
QUENCHABLE
QUENCHED
QUENCHER
QUENCHING
QUENCHLESS
QUENCHLESSLY
QUENDA
QUENELLE
QUENSELITE
QUENT
QUENTISE
QUERCETIC
QUERCETIN
QUERCETUM
QUERCIC
QUERCIN
QUERCINE
QUERCITANNIN
QUERCITE
QUERCITOL
QUERCITRIN
QUERCITRON
QUERCIVOROUS
QUERELA
QUERELAE
QUERELE
QUERENCIA
QUERENT
QUERIDA
QUERIDAS
QUERIDO
QUERIDOS
QUERIED
QUERIER
QUERIES
QUERIMAN
QUERIMANS
QUERIMONIES
QUERIMONIOUS
QUERIMONY
QUERIST
QUERKEN
QUERL
QUERN
QUERNAL
QUERNSTONE
QUERRE
QUERULENT
QUERULENTIAL
QUERULIST
QUERULITY
QUERULOSITY
QUERULOUS
QUERULOUSLY
QUERY
QUERYING
QUERYINGLY
QUESAL
QUESITED
QUESITIVE
QUEST
QUESTED
QUESTER
QUESTEUR
QUESTHOUSE
QUESTING
QUESTION
QUESTIONABLE
QUESTIONABLY
QUESTIONARIES
QUESTIONARY
QUESTIONED
QUESTIONEE
QUESTIONER
QUESTIONING
QUESTIONIST
QUESTIONLESS
QUESTIONNAIRE
QUESTIONS
QUESTMAN
QUESTMEN
QUESTMONGER
QUESTOR
QUESTORIAL
QUESTRIST
QUET
QUETCH
QUETENITE
QUETHE
QUETSCH
QUETZAL
QUEUE
QUEY
QUEZAL
QUEZALES
QUI
QUIAPO
QUIAQUIA
QUIB
QUIBBLE
QUIBBLED
QUIBBLER
QUIBBLING
QUIBLET
QUICA
QUICK
QUICKBEAM
QUICKBORN
QUICKED
QUICKEN
QUICKENANCE
QUICKENBEAM
QUICKENED
QUICKENER
QUICKENING
QUICKER
QUICKEST
QUICKFOOT
QUICKHATCH
QUICKIE
QUICKING
QUICKLIME
QUICKLY
QUICKNESS
QUICKSAND
QUICKSANDY
QUICKSET
QUICKSIDE
QUICKSILVER
QUICKSILVERY
QUICKSTEP
QUICKTHORN
QUICKWATER
QUICKWORK
QUID
QUIDAM
QUIDDANY
QUIDDATIVE
QUIDDER
QUIDDIT
QUIDDITATIVE
QUIDDITIES
QUIDDITY
QUIDDLE
QUIDDLED
QUIDDLER
QUIDDLING
QUIDNUNC
QUIENAL
QUIESCE
QUIESCED
QUIESCENCE
QUIESCENCY
QUIESCENT
QUIESCENTLY
QUIESCING
QUIET
QUIETAGE
QUIETED
QUIETEN
QUIETENER
QUIETER
QUIETEST
QUIETING
QUIETISM
QUIETIST
QUIETISTIC
QUIETIVE
QUIETLIKE
QUIETLY
QUIETNESS
QUIETSOME
QUIETUDE
QUIETUS
QUIFF
QUIINACEOUS
QUILA
QUILATE
QUILE
QUILECES
QUILES
QUILESES
QUILEZ
QUILISMA
QUILK
QUILKIN
QUILL
QUILLAI
QUILLAIC
QUILLAJIC
QUILLBACK
QUILLED
QUILLER
QUILLET
QUILLETED
QUILLFISH
QUILLFISHES
QUILLING
QUILLITY
QUILLON
QUILLTAIL
QUILLWORK
QUILLWORT
QUILLY
QUILT
QUILTED
QUILTER
QUILTING
QUIM
QUIN
QUINA
QUINACRINE
QUINALDIC
QUINALDIN
QUINALDINE
QUINALDINIC
QUINALDINIUM
QUINALDYL
QUINAMICIN
QUINAMICINE
QUINAMIDIN
QUINAMIDINE
QUINAMIN
QUINAMINE
QUINANISOLE
QUINAQUINA
QUINARIAN
QUINARIES
QUINARIUS
QUINARY
QUINAS
QUINATE
QUINATOXIN
QUINATOXINE
QUINAZOLIN
QUINAZOLINE
QUINAZOLYL
QUINCE
QUINCEWORT
QUINCH
QUINCUNCIAL
QUINCUNX
QUINCUNXES
QUINCUNXIAL
QUINDECAD
QUINDECAGON
QUINDECEMVIR
QUINDECEMVIRI
QUINDECIM
QUINDECIMA
QUINDECIMVIR
QUINDENE
QUINE
QUINELLA
QUINET
QUINETUM
QUINHYDRONE
QUINIA
QUINIBLE
QUINIC
QUINICIN
QUINICINE
QUINIDIN
QUINIDINE
QUINIELA
QUININ
QUININA
QUININE
QUININISM
QUININIZE
QUINIRETIN

QUINISEXT
QUINISEXTINE
QUINITE
QUINITOL
QUINIZARIN
QUINK
QUINNAT
QUINNET
QUINOA
QUINOFORM
QUINOGEN
QUINOID
QUINOIDAL
QUINOIDATION
QUINOIDIN
QUINOIDINE
QUINOL
QUINOLAS
QUINOLIN
QUINOLINE
QUINOLINIUM
QUINOLINYL
QUINOLOGIST
QUINOLOGY
QUINOLYL
QUINOMETRY
QUINON
QUINONE
QUINONIC
QUINONIMIN
QUINONIMINE
QUINONIZE
QUINONOID
QUINONYL
QUINOPYRIN
QUINOVATE
QUINOVIN
QUINOVOSE
QUINOXALIN
QUINOXALINE
QUINOXALYL
QUINOYL
QUINQUENNIA
QUINQUENNIAD
QUINQUENNIAL
QUINQUENNIUM
QUINQUENNIUMS
QUINQUERTIUM
QUINQUEVIR
QUINQUEVIRS
QUINQUINA
QUINQUINO
QUINSE
QUINSIED
QUINSY
QUINSYBERRIES
QUINSYBERRY
QUINSYWORT
QUINT
QUINTA
QUINTAD
QUINTADENA
QUINTADENE
QUINTAIN
QUINTAL
QUINTAN
QUINTANT
QUINTARY
QUINTE
QUINTELEMENT
QUINTERNION
QUINTESSENCE
QUINTET
QUINTETTE
QUINTETTO
QUINTFOIL
QUINTIC
QUINTILE
QUINTILLION
QUINTIN
QUINTIPED
QUINTO
QUINTOLE
QUINTON
QUINTROON
QUINTUPLE
QUINTUPLED
QUINTUPLET
QUINTUPLING
QUINTUS
QUINUCLIDINE
QUINYIE
QUINYL
QUINZAINE
QUINZE
QUINZIEME
QUIP
QUIPO
QUIPPE
QUIPPED
QUIPPER
QUIPPING
QUIPPISH
QUIPPISHNESS
QUIPPU
QUIPPY
QUIPSOME
QUIPSTER
QUIPU
QUIPUS
QUIRA
QUIRCAL
QUIRE
QUIRED
QUIREWISE
QUIRING
QUIRITARIAN
QUIRK
QUIRKED
QUIRKIER
QUIRKIEST
QUIRKING
QUIRKSEY
QUIRKSOME
QUIRKY
QUIRL
QUIRQUINCHO
QUIRT
QUIS
QUISBY
QUISCOS
QUISLING
QUISLINGISM
QUISQUEITE
QUISQUILIAN
QUISQUILIARY
QUISQUILIOUS
QUISQUOUS
QUIST
QUISTRON
QUISUTSCH
QUIT
QUITANTIE
QUITCH
QUITCLAIM
QUITCLAIMED
QUITCLAIMING
QUITE
QUITELY
QUITEVE
QUITRENT
QUITS
QUITTANCE
QUITTED
QUITTER
QUITTERBONE
QUITTING
QUITTOR
QUIVER
QUIVERED
QUIVERER
QUIVERFUL
QUIVERING
QUIVERLEAF
QUIVERY
QUIXOTIC
QUIXOTICAL
QUIXOTISM
QUIXOTIZE
QUIXOTRY
QUIZ
QUIZZACIOUS
QUIZZATORIAL
QUIZZED
QUIZZEE
QUIZZER
QUIZZERY
QUIZZICAL
QUIZZICALITY
QUIZZICALLY
QUIZZIFY
QUIZZING
QUIZZISH
QUIZZISM
QUIZZITY
QUIZZY
QUO
QUOAD
QUOCK
QUOD
QUODDED
QUODDIES
QUODDING
QUODDITY
QUODLIBET
QUODLIBETARY
QUODLIBETIC
QUODLING
QUOG
QUOILERS
QUOIN
QUOINED
QUOINING
QUOIT
QUOITER
QUOITS
QUOKKA
QUOMINUS
QUOMODO
QUONDAM
QUONIAM
QUONK
QUONKING
QUOP
QUORUM
QUORUMS
QUOT
QUOTA
QUOTABILITY
QUOTABLE
QUOTABLENESS
QUOTABLY
QUOTAS
QUOTATION
QUOTATIONAL
QUOTATIONIST
QUOTATIVE
QUOTE
QUOTED
QUOTEE
QUOTELESS
QUOTENNIAL
QUOTER
QUOTEWORTHY
QUOTH
QUOTHA
QUOTIDIAN
QUOTIDIANLY
QUOTIENT
QUOTIETIES
QUOTIETY
QUOTING
QUOTINGLY
QUOTITY
QUOTT
QUOTUM
QUOY
QUOZ
QUYTE

RA
RAAD
RAADZAAL
RAAN
RAASCH
RAASH
RAB
RABAND
RABANNA
RABAT
RABATINE
RABATO
RABATTE
RABATTED
RABATTEMENT
RABATTING
RABBAN
RABBET
RABBETED
RABBETING
RABBI
RABBIES
RABBIN
RABBINATE
RABBINIC
RABBINICAL
RABBINICALLY
RABBINISM
RABBINIST
RABBINISTIC
RABBINISTICAL
RABBINITE
RABBINITIC
RABBINIZE
RABBIS
RABBISH
RABBIT
RABBITBERRIES
RABBITBERRY
RABBITER
RABBITEYE
RABBITFISH
RABBITMOUTH
RABBITRIES
RABBITROOT
RABBITRY
RABBITS
RABBITSKIN
RABBITWEED
RABBITWOOD
RABBITY
RABBLE
RABBLED
RABBLEMENT
RABBLEPROOF
RABBLER
RABBLESOME
RABBLING
RABBONI
RABDOMANCY
RABFAK
RABI
RABIATOR
RABIC
RABID
RABIDITY
RABIDLY
RABIDNESS
RABIES
RABIETIC
RABIFIC
RABIFORM
RABIGENIC
RABINET
RABIOUS
RABIRUBIA
RABITIC
RABLIN
RABULISTIC
RABULOUS
RACA
RACAHOUT
RACALLABLE
RACCHE
RACCOON
RACCOONBERRY
RACCOONS
RACE
RACEABOUT
RACECOURSE
RACED
RACEGOER
RACEGOING
RACEHORSE
RACEHORSES
RACELIKE
RACELINE
RACEMASE
RACEMATE
RACEMATION
RACEME
RACEMED
RACEMIC
RACEMIFEROUS
RACEMIFORM
RACEMISM
RACEMIZATION
RACEMIZE
RACEMIZED
RACEMIZING
RACEMOID
RACEMOSE
RACEMOSELY
RACEMOUS
RACEMULE
RACEMULOSE
RACER
RACES
RACETRACK
RACETTE
RACEWAY
RACH
RACHE
RACHES
RACHIAL
RACHIALGIA
RACHIALGIC
RACHICENTESIS
RACHIDES
RACHIDIAN
RACHIFORM
RACHIGRAPH
RACHILLA
RACHILLAE
RACHIODONT
RACHIODYNIA
RACHIOMETER
RACHIOPLEGIA
RACHIOTOME
RACHIOTOMY
RACHIPAGUS
RACHIS
RACHISCHISIS
RACHISES
RACHITIC
RACHITIS
RACHITISM
RACHITOGENIC
RACHITOME
RACHITOMOUS
RACHITOMY
RACIAL
RACIALISM
RACIALIST
RACIALITY
RACIALIZATION
RACIALIZE
RACIALLY
RACILY
RACINESS
RACING
RACION
RACISM
RACIST
RACK
RACKABONES
RACKAN
RACKAPEE
RACKBONE
RACKED
RACKER
RACKET
RACKETEER
RACKETEERING
RACKETER
RACKETRY
RACKETT
RACKETY
RACKING
RACKLE
RACKMAN
RACKWAY
RACKWORK
RACLOIR
RACON
RACONTEUR
RACOON
RACQUET
RACY
RAD
RADA
RADAR
RADARSCOPE
RADDLE
RADDLED
RADDLEMAN
RADDLEMEN
RADDLING
RADDLINGS
RADE
RADEAU
RADECTOMY
RADEUR
RADEVORE
RADFORD
RADIABILITY
RADIABLE
RADIAL
RADIALE
RADIALITY
RADIALIZATION
RADIALIZE
RADIALLY
RADIAN
RADIANCE
RADIANCY
RADIANT
RADIANTLY
RADIANTNESS
RADIATE
RADIATED
RADIATIFORM
RADIATING
RADIATION
RADIATIONAL
RADIATIVE
RADIATOR
RADIATORS
RADIATORY
RADIATURE
RADICAL
RADICALISM
RADICALITY
RADICALIZATION
RADICALIZE
RADICALLY
RADICALNESS
RADICAND
RADICANT
RADICATE
RADICATED
RADICATING
RADICATION
RADICEL
RADICES
RADICICOLA
RADICLE
RADICOLOUS
RADICOSE
RADICULA
RADICULAR
RADICULE
RADICULECTOMY
RADICULITIS
RADICULOSE
RADIENT
RADIESCENT
RADIFEROUS
RADII
RADIO
RADIOACOUSTICS
RADIOACTINIUM
RADIOACTIVATE
RADIOACTIVE
RADIOACTIVITY
RADIOBIOLOGY
RADIOBSERVER
RADIOCARBON
RADIOCARPAL
RADIOCHEMICAL
RADIOCHEMISTRY
RADIOCONDUCTOR
RADIODATING
RADIODE
RADIODETECTOR
RADIODIGITAL
RADIODONTIA
RADIODONTIC
RADIODONTIST
RADIODYNAMIC
RADIODYNAMICS
RADIOED
RADIOELEMENT
RADIOGRAM
RADIOGRAPH
RADIOGRAPHER
RADIOGRAPHIC
RADIOGRAPHICAL
RADIOGRAPHICALLY
RADIOGRAPHY
RADIOHUMERAL
RADIOING
RADIOISOTOPE
RADIOLARIAN
RADIOLEAD
RADIOLITE
RADIOLITIC
RADIOLOCATION
RADIOLOGIC
RADIOLOGICAL
RADIOLOGIST
RADIOLOGY
RADIOLUCENCY
RADIOLUCENT
RADIOMAN
RADIOMEN
RADIOMETER
RADIOMETRIC
RADIOMETRICALLY
RADIOMETRY
RADIOMICROMETER
RADIOMOVIES
RADIONIC
RADIOPACITY
RADIOPALMAR
RADIOPAQUE
RADIOPHARE
RADIOPHONE
RADIOPHONIC
RADIOPHONY
RADIOPHOTOGRAPH
RADIOPHOTOGRAPHY
RADIOPRAXIS
RADIOS
RADIOSCOPE
RADIOSCOPIC
RADIOSCOPICAL
RADIOSCOPY
RADIOSENSIBILITY
RADIOSENSITIVE
RADIOSENSITIVITY
RADIOSONDE
RADIOSONIC
RADIOSYMMETRICAL
RADIOTECHNOLOGY
RADIOTELEGRAM
RADIOTELEGRAPH
RADIOTELEGRAPHY
RADIOTELEPHONE
RADIOTELEPHONIC
RADIOTELEPHONY
RADIOTHALLIUM
RADIOTHERAPEUTIC
RADIOTHERAPEUTICS
RADIOTHERAPEUTIST
RADIOTHERAPIST
RADIOTHERAPY
RADIOTHERMY
RADIOTHORIUM
RADIOTOXIC
RADIOTRANSPARENCY
RADIOTRANSPARENT
RADIOTRICIAN
RADIOTROPIC
RADIOTROPISM
RADIOUS
RADIOVISION
RADISH
RADIUM
RADIUMIZATION
RADIUMIZE
RADIUS
RADIUSES
RADIX
RADKNIGHT
RADLY
RADMAN
RADOME
RADON
RADULA
RADULAE
RADULAR
RADULATE
RADULIFEROUS
RADULIFORM

RADZIMIR
RAE
RAFALE
RAFF
RAFFE
RAFFEE
RAFFIA
RAFFINASE
RAFFING
RAFFINOSE
RAFFISH
RAFFISHLY
RAFFISHNESS
RAFFLE
RAFFLED
RAFFLER
RAFFLESIA
RAFFLESIACEOUS
RAFFLING
RAFFMAN
RAFT
RAFTAGE
RAFTER
RAFTINESS
RAFTMAN
RAFTSMAN
RAFTSMEN
RAFTY
RAG
RAGA
RAGABASH
RAGABRASH
RAGAMUFFIN
RAGAMUFFINLY
RAGBAG
RAGE
RAGED
RAGEOUS
RAGEOUSLY
RAGEOUSNESS
RAGERY
RAGFISH
RAGGED
RAGGEDLY
RAGGEDNESS
RAGGEE
RAGGER
RAGGERY
RAGGETY
RAGGI
RAGGIL
RAGGILY
RAGGING
RAGGLE
RAGGLED
RAGGY
RAGHOUSE
RAGI
RAGING
RAGINGLY
RAGLAN
RAGLANITE
RAGLET
RAGLIN
RAGMAN
RAGMEN
RAGONDIN
RAGOUT
RAGOUTED
RAGOUTING
RAGPICKER
RAGS
RAGSELLER
RAGSHAG
RAGSORTER
RAGSTONE
RAGTAG
RAGTIME
RAGTIMER
RAGTIMEY
RAGULE
RAGULY
RAGUSYE
RAGWEED
RAGWORT
RAH
RAHDAR
RAHDAREE
RAHDARI
RAIA
RAID
RAIDER
RAIK
RAIL
RAILAGE
RAILBIRD
RAILED
RAILER
RAILHEAD
RAILING
RAILLERY
RAILLEUR
RAILLY
RAILMAN
RAILMEN
RAILROAD
RAILROADER
RAILROADING
RAILWAY
RAIM
RAIMENT
RAIN
RAINBAND
RAINBIRD
RAINBOUND
RAINBOW
RAINBOWY
RAINBURST
RAINCOAT
RAINDROP
RAINER
RAINES
RAINFALL
RAINFOWL
RAINIER
RAINIEST
RAINILY
RAININESS
RAINLESS
RAINLIGHT
RAINMAKER
RAINMAKING
RAINOUT
RAINPROOF
RAINPROOFER
RAINSPOUT
RAINSTORM
RAINTIGHT
RAINWASH
RAINWATER
RAINWORM
RAINY
RAIOID
RAIR
RAIS
RAISE
RAISED
RAISER
RAISIN
RAISINE
RAISING
RAISINS
RAISINY
RAISONNE
RAIT
RAITH
RAIYAT
RAJ
RAJA
RAJAH
RAJAS
RAJBANSI
RAJOGUNA
RAK
RAKA
RAKAH
RAKAN
RAKE
RAKEAGE
RAKED
RAKEE
RAKEHELL
RAKEHELLISH
RAKEHELLY
RAKELY
RAKEOFF
RAKER
RAKERY
RAKESTEEL
RAKESTELE
RAKH
RAKI
RAKIA
RAKIJA
RAKILY
RAKING
RAKING
RAKISH
RAKISHLY
RAKISHNESS
RAKIT
RAKSHASA
RALE
RALISH
RALLENTANDO
RALLERY
RALLIANCE
RALLIER
RALLIES
RALLIFORM
RALLINE
RALLY
RALLYING
RALO
RALPH
RALSTONITE
RAM
RAMACK
RAMADA
RAMAGE
RAMARAMA
RAMARK
RAMASS
RAMATE
RAMBARRE
RAMBEH
RAMBERGE
RAMBLA
RAMBLE
RAMBLED
RAMBLER
RAMBLING
RAMBLINGLY
RAMBONG
RAMBOOZE
RAMBUNCTIOUS
RAMBURE
RAMBUTAN
RAME
RAMEAL
RAMEE
RAMEKIN
RAMELLOSE
RAMENT
RAMENTA
RAMENTACEOUS
RAMENTAL
RAMENTUM
RAMEOUS
RAMEQUIN
RAMEX
RAMFEEZLED
RAMFORCE
RAMGUNSHOCH
RAMHEAD
RAMI
RAMICORN
RAMIE
RAMIFICATE
RAMIFICATION
RAMIFIED
RAMIFORM
RAMIFY
RAMIFYING
RAMILLIE
RAMISECTION
RAMISECTOMY
RAMLINE
RAMMACK
RAMMAGE
RAMMASS
RAMMED
RAMMEL
RAMMELSBERGITE
RAMMER
RAMMERMAN
RAMMERMEN
RAMMING
RAMMISH
RAMMISHNESS
RAMMY
RAMON
RAMONEUR
RAMOSE
RAMOUS
RAMP
RAMPACIOUS
RAMPACIOUSLY
RAMPAGE
RAMPAGED
RAMPAGEOUS
RAMPAGEOUSLY
RAMPAGEOUSNESS
RAMPAGER
RAMPAGING
RAMPAGIOUS
RAMPANCY
RAMPANT
RAMPANTLY
RAMPART
RAMPARTED
RAMPARTING
RAMPER
RAMPICK
RAMPIER
RAMPIKE
RAMPION
RAMPIRE
RAMPISH
RAMPLER
RAMPLOR
RAMPOLE
RAMRACE
RAMROD
RAMRODDY
RAMSCALLION
RAMSCH
RAMSHACKLE
RAMSHACKLENESS
RAMSON
RAMSTAM
RAMSTEAD
RAMTIL
RAMULAR
RAMULIFEROUS
RAMULOSE
RAMULOUS
RAMULUS
RAMUS
RAMVERSE
RAN
RANA
RANAL
RANARIA
RANARIAN
RANARIUM
RANCE
RANCEL
RANCELLOR
RANCELMAN
RANCELMEN
RANCER
RANCESCENT
RANCH
RANCHE
RANCHER
RANCHERIA
RANCHERO
RANCHEROS
RANCHMAN
RANCHMEN
RANCHO
RANCHOS
RANCHWOMAN
RANCID
RANCIDIFICATION
RANCIDIFY
RANCIDITY
RANCIDLY
RANCIDNESS
RANCIO
RANCOR
RANCOROUS
RANCOROUSLY
RANCOUR
RAND
RANDALL
RANDAN
RANDANNITE
RANDEM
RANDER
RANDERS
RANDIE
RANDING
RANDIR
RANDOM
RANDOMIZE
RANDOMIZED
RANDOMIZING
RANDOMLY
RANDOMNESS
RANDOMWISE
RANDON
RANDORI
RANDY
RANE
RANEE
RANFORCE
RANG
RANGALE
RANGDOODLES
RANGE
RANGED
RANGEHEADS
RANGEMAN

RANGEMEN
RANGER
RANGERSHIP
RANGEWORK
RANGIER
RANGIEST
RANGING
RANGLE
RANGY
RANI
RANINE
RANINIAN
RANK
RANKER
RANKET
RANKING
RANKISH
RANKLE
RANKLED
RANKLING
RANKLY
RANKNESS
RANKS
RANKSMAN
RANKSMEN
RANN
RANNEL
RANNIGAL
RANNY
RANPIKE
RANSACK
RANSACKER
RANSEL
RANSELMEN
RANSES
RANSOM
RANSOMER
RANSOMLESS
RANSTEAD
RANT
RANTAN
RANTANKEROUS
RANTEPOLE
RANTER
RANTING
RANTIPOLE
RANTISM
RANTIZE
RANTOCK
RANTOON
RANTREE
RANTY
RANULA
RANUNCULI
RANUNCULUS
RANUNCULUSES
RAOB
RAP
RAPACEUS
RAPACIOUS
RAPACIOUSLY
RAPACITY
RAPAKIVI
RAPATEACEOUS
RAPE
RAPED
RAPEFUL
RAPELY
RAPER
RAPESEED
RAPEYE
RAPHAE
RAPHANIA
RAPHANUS
RAPHANY
RAPHE
RAPHIA
RAPHIDE
RAPHIDES
RAPHIDIFEROUS
RAPHIS
RAPHUS
RAPIC
RAPID
RAPIDAMENTE
RAPIDE
RAPIDITY
RAPIDLY
RAPIDNESS
RAPIDO
RAPIDS
RAPIER
RAPIERED
RAPILLO
RAPIN
RAPINE
RAPING
RAPINIC
RAPIST
RAPLOCH
RAPORT
RAPPAGE
RAPPAREE
RAPPE
RAPPED
RAPPEE
RAPPEL
RAPPELLED
RAPPELLING
RAPPEN
RAPPER
RAPPING
RAPPINI
RAPPIST
RAPPORT
RAPSCALLION
RAPSCALLIONISM
RAPSCALLIONLY
RAPSCALLIONRY
RAPT
RAPTATORIAL
RAPTER
RAPTLY
RAPTNESS
RAPTOR
RAPTORIAL
RAPTORIOUS
RAPTRIL
RAPTURE
RAPTURED
RAPTURIST
RAPTURIZE
RAPTUROUS
RAPTUROUSLY
RAPTUROUSNESS
RAPTUS
RAQUET
RARE
RAREBIT
RAREFACTION
RAREFACTIONAL
RAREFACTIVE
RAREFIABLE
RAREFICATION
RAREFIED
RAREFIER
RAREFY
RAREFYING
RARELY
RARENESS
RARER
RARERIPE
RAREST
RARICONSTANT
RARIETY
RARING
RARIORA
RARISH
RARITIES
RARITY
RAS
RASA
RASAMALA
RASANT
RASBORA
RASCACIO
RASCAL
RASCALITIES
RASCALITY
RASCALLY
RASCALRY
RASCETA
RASE
RASED
RASEE
RASEN
RASER
RASGADO
RASH
RASHBUSS
RASHER
RASHFUL
RASHING
RASHLY
RASHNESS
RASING
RASION
RASOIR
RASON
RASOR
RASORIAL
RASOUR
RASP
RASPATORY
RASPBERRY
RASPED
RASPER
RASPIER
RASPIEST
RASPING
RASPINGLY
RASPINGNESS
RASPIS
RASPISH
RASPITE
RASPY
RASSASY
RASSE
RASSLE
RASTIK
RASTY
RASURE
RAT
RATA
RATABLE
RATABLENESS
RATABLY
RATAFEE
RATAFIA
RATAL
RATAN
RATANY
RATAPLAN
RATAPLANNED
RATAPLANNING
RATBAG
RATBITE
RATCATCHER
RATCH
RATCHEL
RATCHER
RATCHET
RATCHETY
RATE
RATEABILITY
RATEABLE
RATED
RATEL
RATEPAYER
RATEPAYING
RATER
RATERO
RATES
RATFISH
RATH
RATHA
RATHE
RATHELY
RATHENESS
RATHER
RATHERIPE
RATHERISH
RATHERLY
RATHEST
RATHITE
RATHOLE
RATHRIPE
RATHSKELLER
RATI
RATIFIA
RATIFICATION
RATIFICATIONIST
RATIFIED
RATIFY
RATIFYING
RATIHABITION
RATINE
RATING
RATIO
RATIOCINANT
RATIOCINATE
RATIOCINATED
RATIOCINATING
RATIOCINATION
RATIOCINATIVE
RATIOCINATOR
RATIOCINATORY
RATIOMETER
RATION
RATIONABLE
RATIONAL
RATIONALE
RATIONALISM
RATIONALIST
RATIONALISTIC
RATIONALITIES
RATIONALITY
RATIONALIZE
RATIONALIZED
RATIONALIZER
RATIONALLY
RATIONALNESS
RATIONATE
RATIONING
RATIONS
RATIOS
RATITE
RATIUNCLE
RATLINE
RATLINER
RATO
RATON
RATOON
RATS
RATSBANE
RATTAIL
RATTAN
RATTAREE
RATTATTOO
RATTED
RATTEEN
RATTEL
RATTEN
RATTENED
RATTENER
RATTENING
RATTER
RATTERY
RATTI
RATTINET
RATTING
RATTINGLY
RATTISH
RATTLE
RATTLEBAG
RATTLEBONES
RATTLEBOX
RATTLEBRAIN
RATTLEBRAINED
RATTLEBUSH
RATTLED
RATTLEHEAD
RATTLEHEADED
RATTLEJACK
RATTLEMOUSE
RATTLENUT
RATTLEPATE
RATTLEPATED
RATTLER
RATTLERAN
RATTLEROOT
RATTLERTREE
RATTLES
RATTLESKULL
RATTLESKULLED
RATTLESNAKE
RATTLESOME
RATTLETRAP
RATTLEWEED
RATTLEWORT
RATTLING
RATTLINGNESS
RATTLY
RATTON
RATTONER
RATTOON
RATTRAP
RATTY
RATWA
RATWOOD
RAUCID
RAUCIDITY
RAUCITY
RAUCOUS
RAUCOUSLY
RAUCOUSNESS
RAUGRAVE
RAUK
RAULI
RAUN
RAUNCHY
RAUNGE
RAUNPICK
RAUPO
RAURACI
RAURIKI
RAVAGE
RAVAGED
RAVAGEMENT
RAVAGER
RAVAGING
RAVE
RAVED
RAVEHOOK
RAVEL

RAVELED
RAVELER
RAVELIN
RAVELING
RAVELLED
RAVELLER
RAVELLING
RAVELLY
RAVELMENT
RAVEN
RAVENER
RAVENING
RAVENINGLY
RAVENLING
RAVENOUS
RAVENOUSLY
RAVENOUSNESS
RAVENRY
RAVENSTONE
RAVER
RAVERY
RAVIGOTE
RAVIN
RAVINATE
RAVINE
RAVINED
RAVINEMENT
RAVINEY
RAVING
RAVIOLI
RAVISH
RAVISHED
RAVISHER
RAVISHING
RAVISHINGLY
RAVISHMENT
RAVISON
RAVISSANT
RAW
RAWBONE
RAWBONED
RAWBONES
RAWED
RAWHEAD
RAWHIDE
RAWHIDER
RAWIN
RAWING
RAWISH
RAWISHNESS
RAWKY
RAWLY
RAWNESS
RAWNIE
RAX
RAY
RAYA
RAYAGE
RAYAH
RAYAT
RAYED
RAYGRASS
RAYING
RAYLESS
RAYLESSLY
RAYLESSNESS
RAYNE
RAYON
RAYONNANCE
RAYONNANT
RAYS
RAZE
RAZED
RAZEE
RAZEED
RAZEEING
RAZING
RAZON
RAZOO
RAZOR
RAZORBACK
RAZORBILL
RAZOREDGE
RAZORMAKER
RAZORMAKING
RAZORMAN
RAZORSTROP
RAZOUR
RAZZ
RAZZBERRIES
RAZZBERRY
RAZZIA
RAZZING
RAZZLY
RE
REA
REAAL
REABLE
REACCESS
REACH
REACHED
REACHER
REACHING
REACHLESS
REACHY
REACQUIRE
REACT
REACTANCE
REACTANT
REACTION
REACTIONAL
REACTIONALLY
REACTIONARIES
REACTIONARINESS
REACTIONARISM
REACTIONARIST
REACTIONARY
REACTIONARYISM
REACTIONISM
REACTIONIST
REACTIVATE
REACTIVATED
REACTIVATING
REACTIVATION
REACTIVATOR
REACTIVE
REACTIVELY
REACTIVENESS
REACTIVITY
REACTOLOGICAL
REACTOLOGY
REACTOR
REACTUALIZATION
REACTUALIZE
REACTUATE
READ
READABILITY
READABLE
READABLENESS
READABLY
READDRESS
READEPT
READER
READERSHIP
READIED
READIER
READIEST
READILY
READINESS
READING
READINGDOM
READJUST
READJUSTABLE
READJUSTER
READJUSTMENT
READMISSION
READMIT
READMITTANCE
READMITTED
READMITTING
READS
READVERTENCY
READY
READYING
REAFFIRM
REAFFIRMANCE
REAFFIRMER
REAGENCY
REAGENT
REAGGRAVATE
REAGGRAVATION
REAGIN
REAK
REAKS
REAL
REALES
REALEST
REALGAR
REALIA
REALIGN
REALIGNMENT
REALISM
REALIST
REALISTIC
REALISTICALLY
REALISTICIZE
REALITIES
REALITY
REALIZABLE
REALIZATION
REALIZE
REALIZED
REALIZER
REALIZING
REALLY
REALM
REALNESS
REALS
REALTIES
REALTOR
REALTY
REAM
REAMAGE
REAME
REAMER
REAMERER
REAMY
REAN
REANIMATE
REANIMATED
REANIMATING
REANIMATION
REANSWER
REAP
REAPABLE
REAPDOLE
REAPER
REAPERS
REAPING
REAPPEAR
REAPPEARANCE
REAR
REARDOSS
REARED
REARER
REARHORSE
REARING
REARLING
REARLY
REARM
REARMAMENT
REARMED
REARMOST
REARMOUSE
REARRANGE
REARRANGED
REARRANGEMENT
REARRANGING
REARWARD
REARWARDS
REASINESS
REASON
REASONABILITY
REASONABLE
REASONABLENESS
REASONABLY
REASONAL
REASONED
REASONER
REASONING
REASONLESS
REASONLESSLY
REASONLESSNESS
REASONS
REASSEMBLE
REASSERT
REASSERTION
REASSERTOR
REASSIGN
REASSOCIATION
REASSUME
REASSUMPTION
REASSURANCE
REASSURE
REASSURED
REASSUREDLY
REASSUREMENT
REASSURER
REASSURING
REASSURINGLY
REASTINESS
REASTY
REASY
REATUS
REAUTE
REAVE
REAVED
REAVER
REAVERY
REAVING
REB
REBAB
REBACK
REBAIT
REBAN
REBAPTISM
REBAPTISMAL
REBAPTIZATION
REBAPTIZE
REBAPTIZER
REBAR
REBARBATIVE
REBATE
REBATED
REBATEMENT
REBATER
REBATING
REBATO
REBBE
REBEAT
REBEC
REBECK
REBEL
REBELDOM
REBELLED
REBELLING
REBELLION
REBELLIOUS
REBELLIOUSLY
REBELLIOUSNESS
REBELLY
REBIA
REBID
REBILLING
REBIND
REBIRTH
REBOANT
REBOANTIC
REBOATION
REBOIL
REBOISE
REBOISEMENT
REBOKE
REBOLERA
REBOLT
REBORN
REBOTE
REBOUND
REBOUNDER
REBOUNDING
REBOZO
REBROADCAST
REBUFF
REBUILD
REBUILDER
REBUILT
REBUKABLE
REBUKE
REBUKED
REBUKER
REBUKING
REBUN
REBURSE
REBUS
REBUSED
REBUSES
REBUSING
REBUT
REBUTE
REBUTTAL
REBUTTED
REBUTTER
REBUTTING
RECADENCY
RECADO
RECALCITRANCE
RECALCITRANCY
RECALCITRANT
RECALCITRATE
RECALCITRATION
RECALESCE
RECALESCED
RECALESCENCE
RECALESCENT
RECALESCING
RECALL
RECALLED
RECALLING
RECALLIST
RECALLMENT
RECAMERA
RECANT
RECANTATION
RECANTED
RECANTER
RECANTING
RECAP
RECAPITALIZATION
RECAPITALIZE
RECAPITALIZED
RECAPITALIZING
RECAPITULATE
RECAPITULATED
RECAPITULATING
RECAPITULATION

RECAPPED
RECAPPER
RECAPPING
RECAPTION
RECAPTOR
RECAPTURE
RECAPTURED
RECAPTURING
RECARBON
RECARBONIZE
RECARBONIZER
RECARBURIZATION
RECARBURIZE
RECARBURIZER
RECAST
RECASTER
RECASTING
RECAULESCENCE
RECCE
RECCHE
RECCO
RECCY
RECEDE
RECEDED
RECEDENCE
RECEDENT
RECEDER
RECEDING
RECEIPT
RECEIPTED
RECEIPTER
RECEIPTING
RECEIPTMENT
RECEIPTOR
RECEIVABILITY
RECEIVABLE
RECEIVABLENESS
RECEIVABLES
RECEIVAL
RECEIVE
RECEIVED
RECEIVEDNESS
RECEIVER
RECEIVERSHIP
RECEIVING
RECENCY
RECENSE
RECENSION
RECENSURE
RECENT
RECENTLY
RECENTNESS
RECEPT
RECEPTACLE
RECEPTACULAR
RECEPTANT
RECEPTIBILITY
RECEPTIBLE
RECEPTION
RECEPTIONISM
RECEPTIONIST
RECEPTITIOUS
RECEPTIVE
RECEPTIVELY
RECEPTIVENESS
RECEPTIVITY
RECEPTOR
RECEPTORAL
RECEPTORIAL
RECEPTUAL
RECEPTUALLY
RECERCELEE
RECESS
RECESSED
RECESSER
RECESSION
RECESSIONAL
RECESSIONARY
RECESSIVE
RECESSIVELY
RECHANGE
RECHARGE
RECHARTER
RECHASE
RECHASER
RECHATE
RECHAUFFE
RECHE
RECHEAT
RECHERCHE
RECIDE
RECIDIVATE
RECIDIVATION
RECIDIVE
RECIDIVISM
RECIDIVIST
RECIDIVISTIC
RECIDIVITY
RECIDIVOUS
RECIPE
RECIPIANGLE
RECIPIENCE
RECIPIENCY
RECIPIEND
RECIPIENDARY
RECIPIENT
RECIPIOMOTOR
RECIPROCABLE
RECIPROCAL
RECIPROCALITY
RECIPROCALIZE
RECIPROCALLY
RECIPROCANT
RECIPROCANTIVE
RECIPROCATE
RECIPROCATED
RECIPROCATING
RECIPROCATION
RECIPROCATIVE
RECIPROCATOR
RECIPROCATORY
RECIPROCITY
RECISION
RECIT
RECITAL
RECITALIST
RECITANDO
RECITATION
RECITATIONIST
RECITATIVE
RECITE
RECITED
RECITEMENT
RECITER
RECITING
RECK
RECKLA
RECKLESS
RECKLESSLY
RECKLESSNESS
RECKLING
RECKON
RECKONED
RECKONER
RECKONING
RECLAIM
RECLAIMABLE
RECLAIMABLENES
RECLAIMABLY
RECLAIMANT
RECLAIMED
RECLAIMER
RECLAIMLESS
RECLAIMMENT
RECLAMA
RECLAMATION
RECLAME
RECLINABLE
RECLINATE
RECLINATED
RECLINATION
RECLINE
RECLINED
RECLINER
RECLINING
RECLOSE
RECLUDE
RECLUSE
RECLUSELY
RECLUSENESS
RECLUSERY
RECLUSION
RECLUSIVE
RECLUSIVENESS
RECOCT
RECOCTION
RECOGITATE
RECOGITATION
RECOGNITA
RECOGNITION
RECOGNITIVE
RECOGNITOR
RECOGNITORY
RECOGNIZABLE
RECOGNIZABLY
RECOGNIZANCE
RECOGNIZANT
RECOGNIZE
RECOGNIZED
RECOGNIZEE
RECOGNIZER
RECOGNIZING
RECOGNIZOR
RECOGNOSCE
RECOIL
RECOILED
RECOILING
RECOILLESS
RECOILMENT
RECOIN
RECOINAGE
RECOLLECT
RECOLLECTED
RECOLLECTEDLY
RECOLLECTEDNESS
RECOLLECTION
RECOLLECTIVE
RECOLLECTIVELY
RECOLLECTIVENESS
RECOLLET
RECOMBINATION
RECOMEMBER
RECOMFORT
RECOMMAND
RECOMMENCE
RECOMMENCEMENT
RECOMMENCER
RECOMMEND
RECOMMENDABILITY
RECOMMENDABLE
RECOMMENDABLENESS
RECOMMENDABLY
RECOMMENDATION
RECOMMENDATORY
RECOMMENDEE
RECOMMENDER
RECOMMIT
RECOMMITING
RECOMMITMENT
RECOMMITTAL
RECOMMITTED
RECOMPENSABLE
RECOMPENSATION
RECOMPENSE
RECOMPENSED
RECOMPENSER
RECOMPENSING
RECOMPENSIVE
RECOMPOSE
RECOMPOSED
RECOMPOSER
RECOMPOSING
RECOMPOSITION
RECOMPRESS
RECOMPRESSION
RECONCENTRADO
RECONCENTRATE
RECONCENTRATION
RECONCILABILITY
RECONCILABLE
RECONCILABLENESS
RECONCILABLY
RECONCILE
RECONCILED
RECONCILEE
RECONCILELESS
RECONCILEMENT
RECONCILER
RECONCILIABILITY
RECONCILIABLE
RECONCILIATE
RECONCILIATION
RECONCILIATIVE
RECONCILIATOR
RECONCILIATORY
RECONCILING
RECONCILINGLY
RECOND
RECONDITE
RECONDITELY
RECONDITENESS
RECONDITION
RECONDUCT
RECONDUCTION
RECONNAISSANCE
RECONNOITER
RECONNOITERED
RECONNOITERER
RECONNOITERING
RECONSIDER
RECONSIDERATIO
RECONSIGN
RECONSIGNMENT
RECONSTITUENT
RECONSTITUTE
RECONSTITUTION
RECONSTRUCT
RECONSTRUCTED
RECONSTRUCTION
RECONSTRUCTIONAL
RECONSTRUCTIONARY
RECONSTRUCTIONIST
RECONSTRUCTIVE
RECONSTRUCTIVENESS
RECONSTRUCTOR
RECONTER
RECONVENTION
RECONVENTIONAL
RECONVERT
RECONVERTIBLE
RECONVEY
RECONVEYANCE
RECOPILATION
RECORD
RECORDANT
RECORDATION
RECORDATIVE
RECORDATIVELY
RECORDATORY
RECORDED
RECORDER
RECORDING
RECORDIST
RECORDS
RECOUNT
RECOUNTAL
RECOUNTED
RECOUNTER
RECOUNTING
RECOUNTMENT
RECOUP
RECOUPABLE
RECOUPE
RECOUPED
RECOUPER
RECOUPING
RECOUPLING
RECOUPMENT
RECOUR
RECOURSE
RECOVER
RECOVERABILITY
RECOVERABLE
RECOVERABLENES
RECOVERANCE
RECOVERED
RECOVEREE
RECOVERER
RECOVERIES
RECOVERY
RECRAYED
RECREANCE
RECREANCY
RECREANT
RECREANTLY
RECREANTNESS
RECREATE
RECREATED
RECREATING
RECREATION
RECREATIONAL
RECREATIONIST
RECREATIVE
RECREATIVELY
RECREATIVENESS
RECREATOR
RECREDENTIAL
RECREMENT
RECREMENTAL
RECREMENTITIAL
RECREMENTITIOUS
RECRESCENCE
RECREW
RECRIMINATE
RECRIMINATOR
RECRUDENCY
RECRUDESCE
RECRUDESCED
RECRUDESCENCE
RECRUDESCENCY
RECRUDESCENT
RECRUDESCING
RECRUIT
RECRUITAGE
RECRUITAL
RECRUITEE
RECRUITER
RECRUITING
RECRUITMENT
RECRUSHER
RECRYSTALLIZE
RECT
RECTAL
RECTANGLE
RECTANGLED

RECTANGULAR
RECTANGULARLY
RECTANGULARNESS
RECTANGULATE
RECTIFIABLE
RECTIFICATION
RECTIFICATIVE
RECTIFICATOR
RECTIFIED
RECTIFIER
RECTIFY
RECTIFYING
RECTIGRADE
RECTILINEAL
RECTILINEALLY
RECTILINEAR
RECTILINEAR
RECTILINEARITY
RECTILINEARNESS
RECTINERVED
RECTION
RECTIROSTRAL
RECTISERIAL
RECTITUDE
RECTITUDINOUS
RECTO
RECTOCELE
RECTOCLYSIS
RECTOCOLITIC
RECTOCOLONIC
RECTOGENITAL
RECTOPEXY
RECTOPLASTY
RECTOR
RECTORAL
RECTORATE
RECTORIAL
RECTORRHAPHY
RECTORY
RECTOS
RECTOSCOPE
RECTOSCOPY
RECTOSIGMOID
RECTOSTOMY
RECTOTOME
RECTOTOMY
RECTOVESICAL
RECTRESS
RECTRICES
RECTRICIAL
RECTRIX
RECTUM
RECTUS
RECU
RECUBANT
RECUBATE
RECUBATION
RECUEIL
RECUEILLEMENT
RECULADE
RECULE
RECUMB
RECUMBENCE
RECUMBENCY
RECUMBENT
RECUMBENTLY
RECUPERANCE
RECUPERATE
RECUPERATED
RECUPERATING
RECUPERATION
RECUPERATIVE
RECUPERATOR
RECUPERATORY
RECUR
RECURE
RECURRED
RECURRENCE
RECURRENCY
RECURRENT
RECURRENTLY
RECURRER
RECURRING
RECURRINGLY
RECURSE
RECURSION
RECURSIVE
RECURVANT
RECURVATE
RECURVATION
RECURVATURE
RECURVE
RECURVED
RECURVING
RECURVOUS
RECUSANCE
RECUSANCY
RECUSANT
RECUSATION
RECUSATIVE
RECUSATOR
RECUSE
RECUSED
RECUSING
RECUSSION
RECUTTING
RECYCLE
RED
REDACT
REDACTED
REDACTEUR
REDACTING
REDACTION
REDACTIONAL
REDACTOR
REDACTORIAL
REDAMATION
REDAME
REDAN
REDARGUE
REDARGUED
REDARGUING
REDARGUTION
REDARGUTIVE
REDARGUTORY
REDBACK
REDBAITING
REDBAY
REDBEARD
REDBELLY
REDBERRY
REDBILL
REDBIRD
REDBONE
REDBREAST
REDBRUSH
REDBUCK
REDBUD
REDCAP
REDCOAT
REDCOLL
REDD
REDDE
REDDED
REDDEN
REDDENDA
REDDENDO
REDDENDUM
REDDER
REDDEST
REDDING
REDDINGITE
REDDISH
REDDISHLY
REDDISHNESS
REDDITION
REDDITIVE
REDDLE
REDDLED
REDDLEMEN
REDDLING
REDDOCK
REDDSMAN
REDDY
REDE
REDEAR
REDECORATE
REDECORATED
REDECORATING
REDECORATION
REDECUSSATE
REDEEM
REDEEMABLE
REDEEMABLY
REDEEMER
REDEEMING
REDEEMLESS
REDELESS
REDELIVER
REDELIVERANCE
REDELIVERER
REDELIVERY
REDELY
REDEMAND
REDEMANDABLE
REDEMPTIBLE
REDEMPTION
REDEMPTIONAL
REDEMPTIONER
REDEMPTIVE
REDEMPTIVELY
REDEMPTOR
REDEMPTORIAL
REDEMPTORY
REDEMPTRESS
REDEMPTRICE
REDESMAN
REDETERMINE
REDEVELOP
REDEVELOPER
REDEYE
REDFIN
REDFINCH
REDFISH
REDHEAD
REDHEADEDLY
REDHEARTED
REDHIBITION
REDHIBITORY
REDHOOP
REDHORSE
REDIA
REDIENT
REDIF
REDINGOTE
REDINTEGRATE
REDINTEGRATED
REDINTEGRATION
REDINTEGRATIVE
REDINTEGRATOR
REDIRECT
REDIRECTION
REDISCOUNT
REDISSEIZE
REDISTILL
REDISTRIBUTE
REDISTRICT
REDITION
REDIVIVE
REDIVIVOUS
REDIVIVUS
REDJACKET
REDKNEES
REDLEG
REDLEGS
REDLINE
REDLY
REDMOUTH
REDNECK
REDNESS
REDO
REDOLENCE
REDOLENCY
REDOLENT
REDOLENTLY
REDONDILLA
REDOUBLE
REDOUBLED
REDOUBLEMENT
REDOUBLER
REDOUBLING
REDOUBT
REDOUBTABLE
REDOUBTABLENESS
REDOUBTABLY
REDOUBTED
REDOUBTING
REDOUND
REDOUNDED
REDOUNDING
REDOUTE
REDOWA
REDPOLL
REDRAFT
REDRAW
REDRAWER
REDRESS
REDRESSAL
REDRESSED
REDRESSER
REDRESSING
REDRESSIVE
REDRESSOR
REDROOT
REDSEAR
REDSHANK
REDSHIRT
REDSKIN
REDSTART
REDSTREAK
REDTAB
REDTAIL
REDTOP
REDUB
REDUBBER
REDUCCION
REDUCE
REDUCED
REDUCED
REDUCEMENT
REDUCENT
REDUCER
REDUCIBILITY
REDUCIBLE
REDUCIBLENESS
REDUCIBLY
REDUCING
REDUCT
REDUCTANT
REDUCTASE
REDUCTIBILITY
REDUCTIO
REDUCTION
REDUCTIONAL
REDUCTIONIST
REDUCTIVE
REDUCTIVELY
REDUCTOR
REDUCTORIAL
REDUE
REDUIT
REDUNDANCE
REDUNDANCIES
REDUNDANCY
REDUNDANT
REDUNDANTLY
REDUPLICATE
REDUPLICATED
REDUPLICATING
REDUPLICATION
REDUPLICATIVE
REDUPLICATIVELY
REDUPLICATORY
REDUPLICATURE
REDUX
REDWARD
REDWARE
REDWEED
REDWING
REDWITHE
REDWOOD
REDYE
REE
REECH
REECHO
REECHY
REED
REEDBIRD
REEDBUCK
REEDBUSH
REEDED
REEDEN
REEDER
REEDIER
REEDIEST
REEDINESS
REEDING
REEDISH
REEDLESS
REEDLIKE
REEDLING
REEDMAKER
REEDMAKING
REEDPLOT
REEDS
REEDWORK
REEDY
REEF
REEFABLE
REEFED
REEFER
REEFING
REEFY
REEK
REEKED
REEKER
REEKIER
REEKIEST
REEKING
REEKY
REEL
REELABLE
REELED
REELER
REELING
REELRALL
REEM
REEMISH
REENFORCE
REENFORCEMENT
REENLISTMENT
REENTER
REENTERING
REENTRANT
REENTRY

REEPER
REERE
REESE
REESHIE
REESHLE
REESK
REESLE
REEST
REESTER
REESTLE
REESTY
REET
REEVALUATE
REEVALUATED
REEVALUATING
REEVALUATION
REEVE
REEVED
REEVELAND
REEVING
REEVOKE
REEXAMINE
REEXPORT
REF
REFACE
REFAIT
REFATHERED
REFECT
REFECTION
REFECTIONARY
REFECTIONER
REFECTIVE
REFECTORER
REFECTORIAL
REFECTORIAN
REFECTORY
REFEL
REFER
REFERABLE
REFEREE
REFEREED
REFEREEING
REFERENCE
REFERENDAL
REFERENDARIES
REFERENDARY
REFERENDUM
REFERENT
REFERENTIAL
REFERENTLY
REFERRABLE
REFERRAL
REFERRED
REFERRER
REFERRIBLE
REFERRING
REFETE
REFFO
REFIGURE
REFILL
REFILTER
REFINAGE
REFINANCE
REFINE
REFINED
REFINEDLY
REFINEDNESS
REFINEMENT
REFINER
REFINERIES
REFINERY
REFINING
REFININGLY
REFINISH
REFIT
REFITMENT
REFITTED
REFITTING
REFLAIR
REFLATE
REFLATED
REFLATING
REFLATION
REFLECT
REFLECTANCE
REFLECTED
REFLECTEDLY
REFLECTENT
REFLECTER
REFLECTING
REFLECTINGLY
REFLECTION
REFLECTIONAL
REFLECTIONING
REFLECTIVE
REFLECTIVELY
REFLECTIVITY
REFLECTOR
REFLET
REFLEX
REFLEXED
REFLEXIBLE
REFLEXIONAL
REFLEXISM
REFLEXIVE
REFLEXIVELY
REFLEXIVITY
REFLEXOLOGY
REFLORESCENT
REFLOURISH
REFLOW
REFLUENCE
REFLUENCY
REFLUENT
REFLUOUS
REFLUX
REFLUXED
REFOCILLATE
REFONT
REFOREST
REFORESTIZE
REFORGE
REFORGER
REFORM
REFORMADO
REFORMANDA
REFORMANDUM
REFORMATION
REFORMATIVE
REFORMATORY
REFORMED
REFORMER
REFORMING
REFORMISM
REFORMIST
REFORMISTIC
REFOUND
REFOUNDER
REFRACT
REFRACTED
REFRACTEDLY
REFRACTILE
REFRACTILITY
REFRACTING
REFRACTION
REFRACTIONAL
REFRACTIVE
REFRACTIVELY
REFRACTIVITY
REFRACTOR
REFRACTORIES
REFRACTORILY
REFRACTORY
REFRACTURE
REFRAGABLE
REFRAIN
REFRAINER
REFRAINMENT
REFRANGENT
REFRANGIBLE
REFREID
REFREIT
REFRENATION
REFRESCO
REFRESH
REFRESHANT
REFRESHED
REFRESHER
REFRESHFUL
REFRESHFULLY
REFRESHING
REFRESHINGLY
REFRESHMENT
REFRIGERANT
REFRIGERATE
REFRIGERATED
REFRIGERATION
REFRIGERATOR
REFRINGE
REFRINGENCE
REFRINGENCY
REFRINGENT
REFROID
REFT
REFUEL
REFUELED
REFUELING
REFUELLED
REFUELLING
REFUGE
REFUGED
REFUGEE
REFUGEEISM
REFUGING
REFULGE
REFULGENCE
REFULGENCY
REFULGENT
REFULGENTLY
REFULGENTNESS
REFUND
REFUNDED
REFUNDER
REFUNDING
REFURBISH
REFURBISHMENT
REFUSABLE
REFUSAL
REFUSE
REFUSED
REFUSER
REFUSING
REFUSION
REFUSIVE
REFUTABILITY
REFUTABLE
REFUTABLY
REFUTAL
REFUTATION
REFUTATIVE
REFUTATORY
REFUTE
REFUTED
REFUTER
REFUTING
REG
REGAIN
REGAINER
REGAL
REGALADO
REGALD
REGALE
REGALED
REGALEMENT
REGALER
REGALIA
REGALIAN
REGALING
REGALIO
REGALISM
REGALIST
REGALITIES
REGALITY
REGALIZE
REGALLY
REGALO
REGARD
REGARDANCE
REGARDANCY
REGARDANT
REGARDED
REGARDER
REGARDFUL
REGARDFULLY
REGARDING
REGARDLESS
REGARDLESSLY
REGATTA
REGELATE
REGELATED
REGELATING
REGELATION
REGENCE
REGENCIES
REGENCY
REGENERABLE
REGENERACY
REGENERANCE
REGENERANT
REGENERATE
REGENERATED
REGENERATING
REGENERATION
REGENERATIVE
REGENERATOR
REGENESIS
REGENT
REGENTAL
REGES
REGEST
REGIA
REGIAN
REGICIDAL
REGICIDE
REGICIDISM
REGIDOR
REGIE
REGIFUGE
REGIME
REGIMEN
REGIMENAL
REGIMENT
REGIMENTAL
REGIMENTALED
REGIMENTALLED
REGIMENTALS
REGIMENTARY
REGIMENTATION
REGIMENTED
REGIMENTING
REGIMINAL
REGIN
REGINA
REGINAL
REGION
REGIONAL
REGIONALISM
REGIONALIST
REGIONALISTIC
REGIONALIZE
REGIONALLY
REGIONARY
REGIONED
REGIONS
REGISSEUR
REGISTER
REGISTERED
REGISTERER
REGISTERING
REGISTRABILITY
REGISTRABLE
REGISTRAL
REGISTRANT
REGISTRAR
REGISTRARSHIP
REGISTRARY
REGISTRATE
REGISTRATION
REGISTRATOR
REGISTRER
REGISTRY
REGITIVE
REGIUS
REGLE
REGLEMENTARY
REGLEMENTIST
REGLET
REGLOW
REGMA
REGMACARP
REGMATA
REGNAL
REGNANCY
REGNANT
REGNUM
REGOLITH
REGORGE
REGORGED
REGORGING
REGOSOL
REGRACY
REGRADATION
REGRADE
REGRADED
REGRADING
REGRANT
REGRASS
REGRATE
REGRATED
REGRATER
REGRATING
REGREDE
REGREET
REGRESS
REGRESSED
REGRESSING
REGRESSION
REGRESSIVE
REGRESSIVELY
REGRESSIVITY
REGRESSOR
REGRET
REGRETFUL
REGRETFULLY
REGRETTABLE
REGRETTABLY
REGRETTED
REGRETTER
REGRETTING
REGULA
REGULABLE
REGULAR
REGULARISE
REGULARITIES
REGULARITY

REGULARIZATION
REGULARIZE
REGULARIZED
REGULARIZER
REGULARLY
REGULARNESS
REGULATE
REGULATED
REGULATES
REGULATING
REGULATION
REGULATIVE
REGULATOR
REGULATORY
REGULI
REGULINE
REGULIZE
REGULUS
REGUR
REGURGITANT
REGURGITATE
REGURGITATED
REH
REHABILITATE
REHABILITATION
REHAIR
REHANDLING
REHARMONIZE
REHASH
REHAYTE
REHBOC
REHEARD
REHEARING
REHEARSAL
REHEARSE
REHEARSED
REHEARSER
REHEARSING
REHEAT
REHEATED
REHEATER
REHETE
REHOUSE
REI
REICHSGULDEN
REICHSMARK
REICHSPFENNIG
REICHSTALER
REIF
REIFICATION
REIFIED
REIFIER
REIFY
REIFYING
REIGN
REIGNED
REIGNER
REIGNING
REIK
REIMBURSABLE
REIMBURSE
REIMBURSED
REIMBURSEMENT
REIMBURSER
REIMBURSING
REIMBUSH
REIMBUSHMENT
REIMKENNAR
REIMMIGRANT
REIMPEL
REIMPLANT
REIMPORT
REIMPOSE
REIMPOSITION
REIMPOSURE
REIMPRESSION
REIN
REINA
REINCARNATE
REINCARNATED
REINCENSE
REINCIDENCE
REINCIDENCY
REINCRUDATE
REINDEER
REINDICTMENT
REINETTE
REINFECT
REINFECTION
REINFECTIOUS
REINFORCE
REINFORCED
REINFORCEMENT
REINFORCER
REINLESS
REINS
REINSMAN
REINSTALL
REINSTALMENT
REINSTATE
REINSTATED
REINSTATING
REINSTATION
REINSTATOR
REINSURANCE
REINSURE
REINSURED
REINSURER
REINSURING
REINTEGRATE
REINTHRONE
REINVERSION
REINVEST
REINVESTMENT
REINVIGORATE
REIS
REISE
REISSUE
REISSUING
REISTER
REIT
REITBOK
REITER
REITERABLE
REITERANCE
REITERANT
REITERATE
REITERATED
REITERATING
REITERATION
REITERATIVE
REIVE
REIVER
REJA
REJECT
REJECTAGE
REJECTAMENTA
REJECTED
REJECTER
REJECTING
REJECTION
REJECTIVE
REJECTOR
REJOICE
REJOICED
REJOICEFUL
REJOICEMENT
REJOICER
REJOICING
REJOIN
REJOINDER
REJOINED
REJOINING
REJOLT
REJON
REJONEADOR
REJONEO
REJOUNCE
REJOURN
REJUDGE
REJUNCTION
REJUVENANT
REJUVENATE
REJUVENATED
REJUVENATING
REJUVENATION
REJUVENATIVE
REJUVENATOR
REJUVENESCE
REJUVENIZE
REKE
REKHTI
REKINDLE
REKINDLER
REL
RELACHE
RELAIS
RELAPSE
RELAPSED
RELAPSER
RELAPSING
RELAST
RELASTER
RELATA
RELATABILITY
RELATABLE
RELATE
RELATED
RELATEDNESS
RELATER
RELATING
RELATION
RELATIONAL
RELATIONALLY
RELATIONARY
RELATIONISM
RELATIONIST
RELATIONS
RELATIONSHIP
RELATIONSHIPS
RELATIVAL
RELATIVE
RELATIVELY
RELATIVENESS
RELATIVES
RELATIVISM
RELATIVIST
RELATIVISTIC
RELATIVITY
RELATOR
RELATRIX
RELATUM
RELAX
RELAXABLE
RELAXANT
RELAXATION
RELAXATIVE
RELAXATORY
RELAXED
RELAXEDLY
RELAXEDNESS
RELAXER
RELAXIN
RELAXING
RELAY
RELAYER
RELAYMAN
RELBUN
RELEARN
RELEASE
RELEASED
RELEASEE
RELEASEMENT
RELEASER
RELEASING
RELEASOR
RELECTION
RELEGABLE
RELEGATE
RELEGATED
RELEGATING
RELEGATION
RELENT
RELENTED
RELENTING
RELENTINGLY
RELENTLESS
RELENTLESSLY
RELENTMENT
RELES
RELESSEE
RELESSOR
RELEVANCE
RELEVANCY
RELEVANT
RELEVANTLY
RELEVATE
RELEVATION
RELEVATOR
RELEVE
RELIABILITY
RELIABLE
RELIABLENESS
RELIABLY
RELIANCE
RELIANT
RELIANTLY
RELIC
RELICARY
RELICMONGER
RELICS
RELICT
RELICTED
RELICTION
RELIDE
RELIED
RELIEF
RELIER
RELIEVABLE
RELIEVE
RELIEVED
RELIEVEDLY
RELIEVER
RELIEVING
RELIEVINGLY
RELIEVO
RELIGATE
RELIGATION
RELIGIEUSE
RELIGIEUSES
RELIGIO
RELIGION
RELIGIONARY
RELIGIONATE
RELIGIONER
RELIGIONISM
RELIGIONIST
RELIGIONIZE
RELIGIOSE
RELIGIOSITY
RELIGIOSO
RELIGIOUS
RELIGIOUSLY
RELINQUENT
RELINQUISH
RELINQUISHED
RELINQUISHER
RELIQUAIRE
RELIQUARIES
RELIQUARY
RELIQUE
RELIQUIAE
RELIQUIAN
RELIQUISM
RELISH
RELISHABLE
RELISHED
RELISHER
RELISHING
RELISHINGLY
RELISHY
RELIVE
RELIVED
RELIVING
RELOCABLE
RELOCATE
RELOCATION
RELOCATOR
RELONG
RELUCE
RELUCENT
RELUCT
RELUCTANCE
RELUCTANCY
RELUCTANT
RELUCTANTLY
RELUCTATE
RELUCTATION
RELUCTIVITY
RELUME
RELUMED
RELUMINE
RELUMING
RELY
RELYING
REM
REMAIN
REMAINDER
REMAINDERMAN
REMAINDERMEN
REMAINED
REMAINER
REMAINING
REMAINS
REMAN
REMANATION
REMANCIPATE
REMAND
REMANDMENT
REMANENCE
REMANENCY
REMANENT
REMANET
REMANIE
REMANNED
REMANNING
REMARGIN
REMARK
REMARKABILITY
REMARKABLE
REMARKABLENESS
REMARKABLY
REMARKED
REMARKER
REMARKING
REMARQUE
REMARRIAGE
REMARRIED
REMARRY
REMARRYING
REMATCH
REMBLAI
REMBLE
REMBLERE
REME

REMEANT
REMEDE
REMEDIABLE
REMEDIABLENESS
REMEDIABLY
REMEDIAL
REMEDIALLY
REMEDIATION
REMEDIED
REMEDIES
REMEDILESS
REMEDILESSLY
REMEDILESSNESS
REMEDY
REMEDYING
REMEMBER
REMEMBERABLE
REMEMBERED
REMEMBERER
REMEMBERING
REMEMBRANCE
REMEMBRANCER
REMEMORATE
REMEMORATION
REMEMORATIVE
REMENE
REMERCY
REMEX
REMICLE
REMIGATE
REMIGES
REMIGIAL
REMIGRANT
REMIGRATE
REMIGRATION
REMIND
REMINDAL
REMINDER
REMINDFUL
REMINISCE
REMINISCED
REMINISCENCE
REMINISCENT
REMINISCENTLY
REMINISCING
REMIPED
REMISE
REMISED
REMISING
REMISS
REMISSFUL
REMISSIBLE
REMISSION
REMISSIVE
REMISSIVELY
REMISSNESS
REMISSORY
REMIT
REMITMENT
REMITTABLE
REMITTAL
REMITTANCE
REMITTANCER
REMITTED
REMITTEE
REMITTENCE
REMITTENCY
REMITTENT
REMITTENTLY
REMITTER
REMITTING
REMITTITUR
REMITTOR
REMNANT
REMNANTAL
REMNANTS
REMODEL
REMODELED
REMODELER
REMODELING
REMODELLED
REMODELLER
REMODELLING
REMODELMENT
REMOLADE
REMONETIZATION
REMONETIZE
REMONSTRANCE
REMONSTRANT
REMONSTRATE
REMONSTRATED
REMONSTRATING
REMONSTRATOR
REMONTADO
REMONTANT
REMONTOIR
REMORA
REMORD
REMORE
REMORSE
REMORSEFUL
REMORSEFULLY
REMORSEFULNESS
REMORSELESS
REMOTE
REMOTELY
REMOTENESS
REMOTER
REMOTEST
REMOTION
REMOTIVE
REMOULADE
REMOUNT
REMOVABILITY
REMOVABLE
REMOVABLY
REMOVAL
REMOVE
REMOVED
REMOVEDLY
REMOVEDNESS
REMOVELESS
REMOVEMENT
REMOVER
REMOVES
REMOVING
REMUABLE
REMUDA
REMUE
REMUNERABLE
REMUNERABLY
REMUNERATE
REMUNERATED
REMUNERATING
REMUNERATION
REMUNERATIVE
REMUNERATOR
REMUNERATORY
REMURMUR
REMUTATION
RENA
RENABLE
RENABLY
RENAIL
RENAISSANCE
RENAL
RENAME
RENASCENCE
RENASCENCY
RENASCENT
RENASCIBLE
RENATURE
RENAY
RENCH
RENCONTRE
RENCOUNTER
RENCOUNTERED
RENCOUNTERING
REND
RENDEMENT
RENDER
RENDERABLE
RENDERED
RENDERER
RENDERING
RENDERSET
RENDEZVOUS
RENDING
RENDITION
RENDLEWOOD
RENDOUN
RENDROCK
RENDU
RENDZINA
RENEGADE
RENEGADO
RENEGATION
RENEGE
RENEGED
RENEGER
RENEGING
RENERVE
RENES
RENETTE
RENEW
RENEWABLE
RENEWAL
RENEWED
RENEWING
RENEWMENT
RENGE
RENGUE
RENGUERA
RENICULUS
RENIFORM
RENIG
RENIN
RENIPORTAL
RENISH
RENISHLY
RENITENCE
RENITENCY
RENITENT
RENK
RENKY
RENNE
RENNER
RENNET
RENNIN
RENNINOGEN
RENOGASTRIC
RENOGRAPHY
RENOMEE
RENOMINATE
RENOMME
RENOMMEE
RENONE
RENOUNCE
RENOUNCED
RENOUNCEMENT
RENOUNCER
RENOUNCING
RENOVATE
RENOVATED
RENOVATER
RENOVATING
RENOVATION
RENOVATIVE
RENOVATOR
RENOVATORY
RENOVE
RENOVIZE
RENOWN
RENOWNED
RENOWNEDLY
RENOWNEDNESS
RENOWNER
RENOWNFUL
RENSH
RENT
RENTABLE
RENTAGE
RENTAL
RENTE
RENTED
RENTEE
RENTER
RENTIER
RENTING
RENTLESS
RENTRANT
RENTREE
RENUMERATE
RENUMERATION
RENUNCIABLE
RENUNCIANCE
RENUNCIANT
RENUNCIATE
RENUNCIATION
RENUNCIATIVE
RENUNCIATOR
RENUNCIATORY
RENVERSE
RENVERSEMENT
RENVOI
RENVOY
REOCCUPY
REOCCUR
REOIL
REOMETER
REOPEN
REOPHORE
REORDER
REORDINATION
REORGANISE
REORGANIZATION
REORGANIZE
REORGANIZED
REORGANIZER
REORGANIZING
REORIENT
REP
REPACE
REPAID
REPAINT
REPAIR
REPAIRABLE
REPAIRED
REPAIRER
REPAIRING
REPAIRMAN
REPAIRMEN
REPAIRS
REPAND
REPANDLY
REPANDOUS
REPARABILITY
REPARABLE
REPARABLY
REPARATE
REPARATION
REPARATIVE
REPARATORY
REPAREL
REPART
REPARTABLE
REPARTEE
REPARTITION
REPASS
REPASSAGE
REPASSER
REPAST
REPASTURE
REPATENCY
REPATRIATE
REPATRIATED
REPATRIATING
REPATRIATION
REPAY
REPAYABLE
REPAYAL
REPAYING
REPAYMENT
REPEAL
REPEALABLE
REPEALED
REPEALER
REPEALING
REPEALIST
REPEAT
REPEATABLE
REPEATAL
REPEATED
REPEATEDLY
REPEATER
REPEATING
REPEL
REPELLED
REPELLENCE
REPELLENCY
REPELLENT
REPELLER
REPELLING
REPENT
REPENTANCE
REPENTANT
REPENTANTLY
REPENTED
REPENTER
REPENTING
REPEOPLE
REPERCEPT
REPERCUSS
REPERCUSSION
REPERCUSSIVE
REPERCUSSOR
REPERCUTIENT
REPERIBLE
REPERTOIRE
REPERTORIAL
REPERTORILY
REPERTORIUM
REPERTORY
REPETEND
REPETITION
REPETITIONAL
REPETITIOUS
REPETITIOUSLY
REPETITIVE
REPETITIVELY
REPETITORY
REPHRASE
REPHRASED
REPHRASING
REPINE
REPINED
REPINEMENT
REPINER
REPINING
REPIQUE
REPIQUED
REPIQUING
REPKIE
REPLACE
REPLACEABLE

REPLACED
REPLACEMENT
REPLACER
REPLACING
REPLANT
REPLANTATION
REPLANTER
REPLEADER
REPLEDGE
REPLEDGER
REPLENISH
REPLENISHED
REPLENISHER
REPLENISHING
REPLETE
REPLETION
REPLETIVE
REPLETIVELY
REPLETORY
REPLEVIABLE
REPLEVIED
REPLEVIN
REPLEVISABLE
REPLEVISOR
REPLEVY
REPLEVYING
REPLIAL
REPLIANT
REPLICA
REPLICATE
REPLICATED
REPLICATILE
REPLICATION
REPLICATIVE
REPLICATIVELY
REPLICATORY
REPLIED
REPLIER
REPLIES
REPLIQUE
REPLOT
REPLOTMENT
REPLOTTER
REPLUM
REPLUME
REPLY
REPLYING
REPOLON
REPONE
REPOPE
REPORT
REPORTABLE
REPORTAGE
REPORTED
REPORTEDLY
REPORTER
REPORTING
REPORTINGLY
REPORTORIAL
REPORTORIALLY
REPORTS
REPOSAL
REPOSE
REPOSED
REPOSEDLY
REPOSEDNESS
REPOSEFUL
REPOSEFULLY
REPOSER
REPOSING
REPOSIT
REPOSITION
REPOSITOR
REPOSITORY
REPOSOIR
REPOSSESS
REPOSSESSION
REPOSSESSOR
REPOST
REPOSTPONE
REPOSURE
REPOUSSAGE
REPOUSSE
REPP
REPPED
REPREHEND
REPREHENDED
REPREHENDER
REPREHENDING
REPREHENSIBLE
REPREHENSION
REPREHENSORY
REPRESENT
REPRESENTAMEN
REPRESENTANT
REPRESENTATION
REPRESENTATIVE
REPRESENTED
REPRESENTER
REPRESENTING
REPRESENTMENT
REPRESENTS
REPRESS
REPRESSED
REPRESSEDLY
REPRESSER
REPRESSIBLE
REPRESSIBLY
REPRESSING
REPRESSION
REPRESSIVE
REPRESSIVELY
REPRESSOR
REPRESSORY
REPRESSURE
REPRIEVABLE
REPRIEVAL
REPRIEVE
REPRIEVED
REPRIEVER
REPRIEVING
REPRIMAND
REPRIMANDED
REPRIMANDER
REPRIMANDING
REPRIME
REPRIMER
REPRINT
REPRINTER
REPRISAL
REPRISE
REPRISTINATE
REPROACH
REPROACHABLE
REPROACHABLY
REPROACHED
REPROACHER
REPROACHES
REPROACHFUL
REPROACHING
REPROBACY
REPROBANCE
REPROBATE
REPROBATED
REPROBATER
REPROBATING
REPROBATION
REPROBATIVE
REPROBATOR
REPROBATORY
REPRODUCE
REPRODUCEABLE
REPRODUCED
REPRODUCER
REPRODUCIBLE
REPRODUCING
REPRODUCTION
REPRODUCTIVE
REPRODUCTORY
REPROFFER
REPROOF
REPROVABLE
REPROVABLY
REPROVAL
REPROVE
REPROVED
REPROVER
REPROVING
REPROVINGLY
REPRY
REPTANT
REPTATION
REPTATORIAL
REPTATORY
REPTILE
REPTILIAN
REPTILIARY
REPTILIOUS
REPTILISM
REPTILITY
REPTILOID
REPUBLIC
REPUBLICAL
REPUBLICAN
REPUBLISH
REPUBLISHER
REPUDIABLE
REPUDIATE
REPUDIATED
REPUDIATING
REPUDIATION
REPUDIATIVE
REPUDIATOR
REPUDIATORY
REPUGN
REPUGNABLE
REPUGNANCE
REPUGNANCY
REPUGNANT
REPUGNATE
REPUGNER
REPULLULATE
REPULPIT
REPULSE
REPULSED
REPULSELESS
REPULSER
REPULSING
REPULSION
REPULSIVE
REPULSIVELY
REPULSORY
REPURCHASE
REPURCHASER
REPUTABILITY
REPUTABLE
REPUTABLY
REPUTATION
REPUTATIVE
REPUTATIVELY
REPUTE
REPUTED
REPUTEDLY
REPUTELESS
REPUTING
REQUEEN
REQUEST
REQUESTER
REQUIEM
REQUIESCAT
REQUIESCENCE
REQUIN
REQUINS
REQUIRABLE
REQUIRE
REQUIRED
REQUIREMENT
REQUIRER
REQUIRING
REQUISITE
REQUISITELY
REQUISITION
REQUISITOR
REQUISITORY
REQUITABLE
REQUITAL
REQUITATIVE
REQUITE
REQUITED
REQUITELESS
REQUITEMENT
REQUITER
REQUITING
RERADIATION
RERAILER
RERD
RERDE
REREAD
REREBRACE
RERECORD
REREDOS
REREE
REREFIEF
REREMOUSE
RERESUPPER
REROLL
RERUN
RERUNNING
RES
RESACA
RESAI
RESAIL
RESAK
RESALABLE
RESALE
RESAW
RESAWER
RESAWYER
RESAY
RESCIND
RESCINDABLE
RESCINDED
RESCINDER
RESCINDING
RESCISSIBLE
RESCISSION
RESCISSORY
RESCORE
RESCRIBE
RESCRIPT
RESCRIPTION
RESCRIPTIVE
RESCUABLE
RESCUE
RESCUED
RESCUER
RESCUING
RESE
RESEAL
RESEARCH
RESEARCHER
RESEARCHFUL
RESEARCHIST
RESEAT
RESEAU
RESEAUX
RESECATE
RESECT
RESECTION
RESECTIONAL
RESEDA
RESEDACEOUS
RESEISER
RESEIZE
RESEIZER
RESEIZURE
RESELL
RESELLING
RESEMBLANCE
RESEMBLANT
RESEMBLE
RESEMBLED
RESEMBLER
RESEMBLING
RESEMINATE
RESEND
RESENDING
RESENE
RESENT
RESENTED
RESENTER
RESENTFUL
RESENTFULLY
RESENTIENCE
RESENTING
RESENTIVE
RESENTLESS
RESENTMENT
RESERATE
RESERPINE
RESERVABLE
RESERVAL
RESERVATION
RESERVATIVE
RESERVATORY
RESERVE
RESERVED
RESERVEDLY
RESERVEDNESS
RESERVEE
RESERVER
RESERVERY
RESERVING
RESERVIST
RESERVOIR
RESERVOIRED
RESET
RESETTER
RESETTING
RESGAT
RESH
RESHIP
RESHIPMENT
RESHIPPED
RESHIPPER
RESHIPPING
RESIANCE
RESIANCY
RESIANT
RESICCATE
RESIDE
RESIDENCE
RESIDENCER
RESIDENCIA
RESIDENCIES
RESIDENCY
RESIDENT
RESIDENTAL
RESIDENTER
RESIDENTIAL
RESIDENTIARY
RESIDER
RESIDING
RESIDUA
RESIDUAL

RESIDUARY
RESIDUATION
RESIDUE
RESIDUENT
RESIDUOUS
RESIDUUM
RESIGN
RESIGNATARY
RESIGNATION
RESIGNED
RESIGNEDLY
RESIGNEDNESS
RESIGNEE
RESIGNER
RESIGNFUL
RESIGNMENT
RESILE
RESILED
RESILEMENT
RESILIA
RESILIAL
RESILIATE
RESILIENCE
RESILIENCY
RESILIENT
RESILIENTLY
RESILIFER
RESILING
RESILIOMETER
RESILITION
RESILIUM
RESILVER
RESIN
RESINA
RESINACEOUS
RESINATE
RESINATED
RESINATING
RESINBUSH
RESINER
RESINIC
RESINIFEROUS
RESINIFLUOUS
RESINIFORM
RESINIFY
RESINIZE
RESINOGENOUS
RESINOID
RESINOL
RESINOPHORE
RESINOSIS
RESINOUS
RESINOUSLY
RESINOUSNESS
RESINY
RESIPISCENCE
RESIPISCENT
RESIST
RESISTABLE
RESISTANCE
RESISTANT
RESISTED
RESISTER
RESISTFUL
RESISTIBLE
RESISTIBLY
RESISTING
RESISTINGLY
RESISTIVE
RESISTIVELY
RESISTIVITY
RESISTLESS
RESISTLESSLY
RESISTOR
RESITTING
RESIZE
RESIZED
RESIZER
RESIZING
RESKEW
RESNATRON
RESOJET
RESOLE
RESOLED
RESOLING
RESOLUBILITY
RESOLUBLE
RESOLUTE
RESOLUTELY
RESOLUTENESS
RESOLUTION
RESOLUTIONER
RESOLUTIVE
RESOLUTORY
RESOLVABLE
RESOLVANCY
RESOLVE
RESOLVED
RESOLVEDLY
RESOLVEDNESS
RESOLVENT
RESOLVER
RESOLVIBLE
RESOLVING
RESON
RESONANCE
RESONANCIES
RESONANCY
RESONANT
RESONANTLY
RESONATE
RESONATED
RESONATING
RESONATOR
RESONATORY
RESORB
RESORBENCE
RESORBENT
RESORCIN
RESORCINAL
RESORCINISM
RESORCINOL
RESORCINUM
RESORCYLIC
RESORPTION
RESORPTIVE
RESORT
RESORTED
RESORTER
RESORUFIN
RESOUND
RESOUNDER
RESOUNDING
RESOURCE
RESOURCEFUL
RESOURCEFULLY
RESOURCEFULNESS
RESOURCES
RESOWN
RESP
RESPASSE
RESPEAK
RESPECT
RESPECTABILITY
RESPECTABLE
RESPECTABLY
RESPECTANT
RESPECTED
RESPECTER
RESPECTFUL
RESPECTFULLY
RESPECTING
RESPECTIVE
RESPECTIVELY
RESPECTLESS
RESPECTUOUS
RESPELL
RESPERSIVE
RESPIRABLE
RESPIRATION
RESPIRATIVE
RESPIRATOR
RESPIRATORY
RESPIRE
RESPIRED
RESPIRING
RESPIRIT
RESPIROMETER
RESPITE
RESPITED
RESPITING
RESPLEND
RESPLENDENCE
RESPLENDENCY
RESPLENDENT
RESPOND
RESPONDE
RESPONDENCE
RESPONDENCY
RESPONDENT
RESPONDENTIA
RESPONDER
RESPONSABLE
RESPONSAL
RESPONSARY
RESPONSE
RESPONSER
RESPONSIBILITY
RESPONSIBLE
RESPONSIBLY
RESPONSION
RESPONSIVE
RESPONSIVELY
RESPONSIVENESS
RESPONSIVITY
RESPONSORIAL
RESPONSORY
RESPUE
RESSAIDAR
RESSALA
RESSAUT
RESSORT
REST
RESTANT
RESTATE
RESTATEMENT
RESTAUR
RESTAURANT
RESTAURATE
RESTAURATEUR
RESTAURATION
RESTBALK
RESTED
RESTER
RESTERILIZE
RESTES
RESTFUL
RESTFULLY
RESTFULNESS
RESTHARROW
RESTHOUSE
RESTIAD
RESTIFORM
RESTING
RESTIS
RESTITUE
RESTITUTE
RESTITUTION
RESTITUTIVE
RESTITUTOR
RESTITUTORY
RESTIVE
RESTIVELY
RESTIVENESS
RESTLESS
RESTLESSLY
RESTLESSNESS
RESTOCK
RESTORAL
RESTORATION
RESTORATIVE
RESTORATOR
RESTORATORY
RESTORE
RESTORED
RESTORER
RESTORING
RESTRAIN
RESTRAINABLE
RESTRAINED
RESTRAINEDLY
RESTRAINER
RESTRAINING
RESTRAINT
RESTRESS
RESTRICT
RESTRICTED
RESTRICTING
RESTRICTION
RESTRICTIVE
RESTRICTIVELY
RESTRIKE
RESTRINGE
RESTRINGENCY
RESTRINGENT
RESTY
RESTYLE
RESUDATION
RESUE
RESUING
RESULT
RESULTANCE
RESULTANCY
RESULTANT
RESULTATIVE
RESULTED
RESULTING
RESULTIVE
RESUMABLE
RESUME
RESUMED
RESUMEING
RESUMER
RESUMING
RESUMMON
RESUMMONS
RESUMPTION
RESUMPTIVE
RESUMPTIVELY
RESUPINATE
RESUPINATED
RESUPINATION
RESUPINE
RESURFACE
RESURFACED
RESURFACING
RESURGAM
RESURGE
RESURGED
RESURGENCE
RESURGENCY
RESURGENT
RESURGING
RESURRECT
RESURRECTION
RESURRECTIVE
RESURRECTOR
RESURVEY
RESUSCITABLE
RESUSCITANT
RESUSCITATE
RESUSCITATED
RESUSCITATION
RESUSCITATOR
RESYNTHESIS
RET
RETABLE
RETABLO
RETAIL
RETAILER
RETAIN
RETAINABLE
RETAINAL
RETAINED
RETAINER
RETAINING
RETAKE
RETAKEN
RETAKER
RETAKING
RETALIATE
RETALIATED
RETALIATING
RETALIATION
RETALIATIVE
RETALIATOR
RETALIATORY
RETAMA
RETAN
RETARD
RETARDANCE
RETARDANT
RETARDATE
RETARDATION
RETARDATIVE
RETARDED
RETARDER
RETARDING
RETARDIVE
RETARDMENT
RETARDURE
RETCH
RETE
RETECIOUS
RETELL
RETELLING
RETEM
RETENE
RETENT
RETENTION
RETENTIVE
RETENTIVELY
RETENTIVITIES
RETENTIVITY
RETENTOR
RETENUE
RETEPORE
RETEXTURE
RETHE
RETHENESS
RETHER
RETIA
RETIARIAN
RETIARII
RETIARIUS
RETIARY
RETICELLA
RETICENCE
RETICENCIES
RETICENCY
RETICENT
RETICENTLY
RETICLE
RETICULA
RETICULAR

RETICULARIAN
RETICULARY
RETICULATE
RETICULATED
RETICULATING
RETICULATION
RETICULE
RETICULED
RETICULIN
RETICULITIS
RETICULOCYTE
RETICULOSE
RETICULUM
RETIFORM
RETINA
RETINACULA
RETINACULAR
RETINACULATE
RETINACULUM
RETINAL
RETINASPHALT
RETINENE
RETINERVED
RETINIAN
RETINISPORA
RETINITE
RETINITIS
RETINIZE
RETINOID
RETINOL
RETINOPHORAL
RETINOPHORE
RETINOSCOPE
RETINOSCOPIC
RETINOSCOPIST
RETINOSCOPY
RETINUE
RETINULA
RETINULAE
RETINULE
RETIP
RETIRACIED
RETIRACY
RETIRADE
RETIRAL
RETIRE
RETIRED
RETIREMENT
RETIRING
RETIRINGLY
RETIRINGNESS
RETOLD
RETOLERATE
RETOLERATION
RETOMB
RETONATION
RETOOK
RETORSION
RETORT
RETORTED
RETORTER
RETORTING
RETORTION
RETORTIVE
RETORTS
RETOUCH
RETOUCHER
RETOUCHING
RETOUCHMENT
RETOUR
RETRACE
RETRACEABLE
RETRACED
RETRACEMENT
RETRACT
RETRACTABLE
RETRACTATION
RETRACTED
RETRACTIBLE
RETRACTILE
RETRACTILITY
RETRACTING
RETRACTION
RETRACTIVE
RETRACTIVELY
RETRACTOR
RETRAD
RETRADITION
RETRAHENT
RETRAIT
RETRAL
RETRALLY
RETRAXIT
RETREAD
RETREADED
RETREADING
RETREAT
RETREATED
RETREATER
RETREATFUL
RETREATING
RETREATIVE
RETREATMENT
RETREE
RETRENCH
RETRENCHED
RETRENCHER
RETRENCHING
RETRENCHMENT
RETRIAL
RETRIBUTE
RETRIBUTION
RETRIBUTIVE
RETRIBUTOR
RETRIBUTORY
RETRICKED
RETRIED
RETRIEVABLE
RETRIEVABLY
RETRIEVAL
RETRIEVE
RETRIEVED
RETRIEVELESS
RETRIEVEMENT
RETRIEVER
RETRIEVING
RETRIM
RETRIMMER
RETROACT
RETROACTION
RETROACTIVE
RETROBUCCAL
RETROBULBAR
RETROCAECAL
RETROCEDE
RETROCEDENCE
RETROCEDENT
RETROCESSION
RETROCESSIVE
RETROCHOIR
RETROCLUSION
RETROCOLIC
RETROCOSTAL
RETROCURVED
RETRODATE
RETRODUCTION
RETRODURAL
RETROFIRE
RETROFLECTED
RETROFLEX
RETROFLEXED
RETROFLEXION
RETROFRACT
RETROFRACTED
RETROFRONTAL
RETROGASTRIC
RETROGRADE
RETROGRADED
RETROGRADELY
RETROGRADING
RETROGRADISM
RETROGRADIST
RETROGRESS
RETROGRESSION
RETROHEPATIC
RETROINSULAR
RETROIRIDIAN
RETROJECT
RETROJECTION
RETROJUGULAR
RETROLENTAL
RETROLINGUAL
RETROMINGENT
RETRONASAL
RETROPOSED
RETROPUBIC
RETROPULSION
RETROPULSIVE
RETRORECTAL
RETRORENAL
RETROROCKET
RETRORSE
RETRORSELY
RETROSERRATE
RETROSPECT
RETROSPLENIC
RETROSTALSIS
RETROSTALTIC
RETROSTERNAL
RETROTARSAL
RETROTHYROID
RETROUSSAGE
RETROUSSE
RETROVACCINE
RETROVERSE
RETROVERSION
RETROVERT
RETROXIPHOID
RETRUDE
RETRUSIBLE
RETRUSION
RETRY
RETRYING
RETTE
RETTED
RETTER
RETTERIES
RETTERY
RETTI
RETTING
RETTORY
RETUND
RETUNDED
RETUNDING
RETURN
RETURNABLE
RETURNED
RETURNER
RETURNING
RETURNLESS
RETURNLESSLY
RETURNS
RETUSE
RETZIAN
REUNE
REUNIFY
REUNION
REUNIONISM
REUNIONIST
REUNIONISTIC
REUNITE
REUNITED
REUNITER
REUNITING
REUNITION
REUNITIVE
REUS
REUT
REUTE
REV
REVACCINATE
REVALENTA
REVALESCENCE
REVALESCENT
REVALIDATE
REVALIDATION
REVALORIZE
REVALUATE
REVALUATED
REVALUATING
REVALUATION
REVALUE
REVALUED
REVALUING
REVAMP
REVAMPER
REVAMPMENT
REVANCHE
REVANCHISM
REVANCHIST
REVAY
REVE
REVEAL
REVEALABLE
REVEALED
REVEALER
REVEALING
REVEALMENT
REVEILLE
REVEL
REVELABILITY
REVELANT
REVELATION
REVELATIONAL
REVELATIONER
REVELATIVE
REVELATOR
REVELATORY
REVELED
REVELER
REVELING
REVELLED
REVELLENT
REVELLER
REVELLER
REVELLING
REVELLY
REVELMENT
REVELOUS
REVELROUS
REVELROUT
REVELRY
REVELS
REVENANT
REVENDICATE
REVENEER
REVENGE
REVENGEABLE
REVENGED
REVENGEFUL
REVENGEFULLY
REVENGEMENT
REVENGER
REVENGING
REVENUAL
REVENUE
REVENUED
REVENUER
REVENUES
REVERB
REVERBATORY
REVERBERANT
REVERBERATE
REVERBERATING
REVERBERATION
REVERBERATIONS
REVERBERATIVE
REVERBERATOR
REVERBRATE
REVERDI
REVERDURE
REVERE
REVERED
REVEREE
REVERENCE
REVERENCED
REVERENCER
REVERENCING
REVEREND
REVERENDLY
REVERENT
REVERENTIAL
REVERENTLY
REVERER
REVERIE
REVERIES
REVERIFY
REVERING
REVERIST
REVERS
REVERSAL
REVERSE
REVERSED
REVERSEDLY
REVERSEFUL
REVERSELESS
REVERSELY
REVERSEMENT
REVERSER
REVERSI
REVERSIBLE
REVERSIBLY
REVERSING
REVERSINGLY
REVERSION
REVERSIONABLE
REVERSIONAL
REVERSIONARY
REVERSIONER
REVERSIONIST
REVERSIST
REVERSIVE
REVERSO
REVERT
REVERTAL
REVERTED
REVERTER
REVERTIBLE
REVERTING
REVERTIVE
REVERTIVELY
REVERY
REVEST
REVESTIARY
REVESTRY
REVET
REVETMENT
REVETTED
REVETTING
REVICTUAL
REVICTUALED
REVICTUALING
REVICTUALLED
REVICTUALLING
REVIE

REVIEW
REVIEWAGE
REVIEWAL
REVIEWED
REVIEWER
REVIEWING
REVIGOR
REVIGORATE
REVIGORATION
REVIGOUR
REVILE
REVILED
REVILEMENT
REVILER
REVILING
REVILING
REVILINGLY
REVINCE
REVINDICATE
REVIRADO
REVIRESCENCE
REVIRESCENT
REVISAL
REVISE
REVISED
REVISER
REVISING
REVISION
REVISIONAL
REVISIONARY
REVISIONISM
REVISIONIST
REVISIT
REVISITANT
REVISITATION
REVITALIZE
REVITALIZED
REVITALIZER
REVITALIZING
REVIVAL
REVIVALISM
REVIVALIST
REVIVALISTIC
REVIVATORY
REVIVE
REVIVED
REVIVEMENT
REVIVER
REVIVIFIED
REVIVIFIER
REVIVIFY
REVIVIFYING
REVIVING
REVIVINGLY
REVIVISCENCE
REVIVISCENCY
REVIVISCENT
REVIVISCIBLE
REVIVOR
REVOCABILITY
REVOCABLE
REVOCABLY
REVOCATE
REVOCATION
REVOCATIVE
REVOCATORY
REVOICE
REVOICED
REVOICING
REVOKABLE
REVOKE
REVOKED
REVOKEMENT
REVOKER
REVOKING
REVOLANT
REVOLT
REVOLTED
REVOLTER
REVOLTING
REVOLTINGLY
REVOLUBILITY
REVOLUBLE
REVOLUBLY
REVOLUTE
REVOLUTION
REVOLUTIONAL
REVOLUTIONARY
REVOLUTIONER
REVOLUTIONIST
REVOLVABLE
REVOLVE
REVOLVED
REVOLVENCY
REVOLVER
REVOLVES
REVOLVING
REVOLVINGLY
REVS
REVUE
REVUETTE
REVUIST
REVULSANT
REVULSE
REVULSED
REVULSION
REVULSIONARY
REVULSIVE
REVULSIVELY
REVVED
REVVING
REW
REWARD
REWARDED
REWARDER
REWARDING
REWARDINGLY
REWCH
REWE
REWED
REWEIGHT
REWET
REWIND
REWINDER
REWIRE
REWIRED
REWIRING
REWME
REWORD
REWORKED
REWRITE
REWRITER
REWRITTEN
REWROTE
REX
REXEN
REXINE
REY
REYE
REYLE
REYOUTH
REYSON
REZAI
REZBANYITE
RH
RHABDITE
RHABDITIFORM
RHABDIUM
RHABDOID
RHABDOLITH
RHABDOM
RHABDOMAL
RHABDOMANCER
RHABDOMANCY
RHABDOMANTIC
RHABDOME
RHABDOMYOMA
RHABDOPHANE
RHABDOPOD
RHABDOS
RHABDOSOME
RHABDOSOPHY
RHABDOSPHERE
RHABDUS
RHACHIS
RHAEBOSIS
RHAGADES
RHAGADIFORM
RHAGIONID
RHAGITE
RHAGON
RHAGONATE
RHAGOSE
RHAMN
RHAMNACEOUS
RHAMNAL
RHAMNETIN
RHAMNINASE
RHAMNINOSE
RHAMNITE
RHAMNITOL
RHAMNOHEXITE
RHAMNOHEXOSE
RHAMNONIC
RHAMNOSE
RHAMNOSIDE
RHAMPHOID
RHAMPHOTHECA
RHAPHE
RHAPONTIC
RHAPONTICIN
RHAPONTIN
RHAPSODE
RHAPSODIC
RHAPSODICAL
RHAPSODIES
RHAPSODISM
RHAPSODIST
RHAPSODISTIC
RHAPSODIZE
RHAPSODIZED
RHAPSODIZING
RHAPSODY
RHASON
RHASOPHORE
RHATANIA
RHATANY
RHATIKON
RHE
RHEA
RHEADINE
RHEBOK
RHEBOSIS
RHEEBOK
RHEEN
RHEGMATYPE
RHEGMATYPY
RHEIM
RHEINBERRY
RHEINGOLD
RHEMA
RHEMATIC
RHEMATOLOGY
RHEME
RHENEA
RHENIUM
RHEOBASE
RHEOCRAT
RHEOLOGIST
RHEOLOGY
RHEOMETER
RHEOMETRIC
RHEOMETRY
RHEOPHILE
RHEOPHORE
RHEOPHORIC
RHEOPLANKTON
RHEOSCOPE
RHEOSCOPIC
RHEOSTAT
RHEOSTATIC
RHEOSTATICS
RHEOTACTIC
RHEOTAN
RHEOTAXIS
RHEOTOME
RHEOTROPE
RHEOTROPIC
RHEOTROPISM
RHESIAN
RHESIS
RHESUS
RHETOR
RHETORIC
RHETORICAL
RHETORICALLY
RHETORICALS
RHETORICIAN
RHETORIZE
RHEUM
RHEUMATALGIA
RHEUMATIC
RHEUMATICAL
RHEUMATICKY
RHEUMATISM
RHEUMATISMAL
RHEUMATIVE
RHEUMATIZ
RHEUMATIZE
RHEUMATOID
RHEUMATOIDAL
RHEUMED
RHEUMIC
RHEUMILY
RHEUMINESS
RHEUMY
RHEXIS
RHIGOLENE
RHIGOSIS
RHIGOTIC
RHINAL
RHINALGIA
RHINARIUM
RHINCOSPASM
RHIND
RHINESTONE
RHINEURYNTER
RHINION
RHINITIS
RHINO
RHINOBYON
RHINOCAUL
RHINOCELE
RHINOCELIAN
RHINOCERINE
RHINOCEROID
RHINOCEROS
RHINOCEROSES
RHINOCEROTIC
RHINOCOELE
RHINOCOELIAN
RHINODYNIA
RHINOGENOUS
RHINOLALIA
RHINOLITH
RHINOLITHIC
RHINOLOGIST
RHINOLOGY
RHINOPHARYNX
RHINOPHORE
RHINOPHYMA
RHINOPLASTIC
RHINOPLASTY
RHINOPOLYPUS
RHINORRHAGIA
RHINORRHEA
RHINORRHEAL
RHINORRHOEA
RHINOS
RHINOSCOPE
RHINOSCOPIC
RHINOSCOPY
RHINOTHECA
RHINOTHECAL
RHIPIDATE
RHIPIDION
RHIPIDISTIAN
RHIPIDIUM
RHIPIPHORID
RHIZANTHOUS
RHIZINE
RHIZINOUS
RHIZOBIA
RHIZOBIUM
RHIZOCARP
RHIZOCARPIC
RHIZOCARPOUS
RHIZOCAUL
RHIZOCAULUS
RHIZOCORM
RHIZODERMIS
RHIZOGEN
RHIZOGENETIC
RHIZOGENIC
RHIZOGENOUS
RHIZOID
RHIZOIDAL
RHIZOMA
RHIZOMATIC
RHIZOMATOUS
RHIZOME
RHIZOMELIC
RHIZOMIC
RHIZOMORPH
RHIZOMORPHIC
RHIZONEURE
RHIZOPHAGOUS
RHIZOPHILOUS
RHIZOPHORE
RHIZOPHYTE
RHIZOPLAST
RHIZOPOD
RHIZOPODAL
RHIZOPODAN
RHIZOPODIST
RHIZOPODOUS
RHIZOSTOME
RHIZOSTOMOUS
RHIZOTAXIS
RHIZOTAXY
RHIZOTE
RHIZOTIC
RHIZOTOMI
RHIZOTOMY
RHO
RHODA
RHODAMIN
RHODAMINE
RHODANATE
RHODANINE
RHODANTHE
RHODEOSE
RHODESWOOD
RHODIC
RHODING

RHODINOL
RHODITE
RHODIUM
RHODIZITE
RHODIZONIC
RHODOCYTE
RHODODAPHNE
RHODODENDRON
RHODOLITE
RHODONITE
RHODOPHANE
RHODOPHYLL
RHODOPLAST
RHODOPSIN
RHODORA
RHODOSPERM
RHODOSPERMIN
RHOMB
RHOMBI
RHOMBIC
RHOMBICAL
RHOMBIFORM
RHOMBOCLASE
RHOMBOGANOID
RHOMBOGENE
RHOMBOGENIC
RHOMBOGENOUS
RHOMBOHEDRA
RHOMBOHEDRAL
RHOMBOHEDRIC
RHOMBOHEDRON
RHOMBOID
RHOMBOIDAL
RHOMBOIDALLY
RHOMBOIDES
RHOMBOIDEUS
RHOMBOIDLY
RHOMBOS
RHOMBOVATE
RHOMBUS
RHOMBUSES
RHONCHAL
RHONCHIAL
RHONCHUS
RHOPALIC
RHOPALISM
RHOPALIUM
RHOTACISM
RHOTACISMUS
RHOTACIST
RHUBARB
RHUBARBY
RHUM
RHUMB
RHUMBA
RHYACOLITE
RHYME
RHYMED
RHYMEMAKER
RHYMEMAKING
RHYMER
RHYMERY
RHYMESTER
RHYMIC
RHYMING
RHYMY
RHYNCHODONT
RHYNCHOLITE
RHYNIA
RHYOBASALT
RHYODACITE
RHYOLITE
RHYOLITIC
RHYOTAXITIC
RHYPOGRAPHY
RHYPTIC
RHYPTICAL
RHYSIMETER
RHYTHM
RHYTHMAL
RHYTHMIC
RHYTHMICAL
RHYTHMICALLY
RHYTHMICITY
RHYTHMICIZE
RHYTHMICS
RHYTHMIST
RHYTHMIZABLE
RHYTHMIZE
RHYTHMOMETER
RHYTHMUS
RHYTIDOME
RHYTINA
RHYTON
RI
RIA
RIAL
RIALTY
RIANT
RIANTLY
RIATA
RIB
RIBALD
RIBALDISH
RIBALDRIES
RIBALDROUS
RIBALDRY
RIBAND
RIBANDMAKER
RIBANDRY
RIBAT
RIBAUDEQUIN
RIBAUDRED
RIBAZUBA
RIBBAND
RIBBED
RIBBER
RIBBET
RIBBING
RIBBLE
RIBBON
RIBBONBACK
RIBBONER
RIBBONFISH
RIBBONFISHES
RIBBONLIKE
RIBBONMAKER
RIBBONS
RIBBONWOOD
RIBBONY
RIBBY
RIBE
RIBGRASS
RIBIBE
RIBLESS
RIBOFLAVIN
RIBONIC
RIBONUCLEASE
RIBOSE
RIBOSOMAL
RIBOSOME
RIBROAST
RIBROASTER
RIBROASTING
RIBS
RIBSKIN
RIBWORT
RIBZUBA
RICASSO
RICE
RICEBIRD
RICEGRASS
RICER
RICERCARE
RICERCATA
RICEY
RICH
RICHARD
RICHDOM
RICHE
RICHELLITE
RICHEN
RICHER
RICHES
RICHESSE
RICHEST
RICHLING
RICHLY
RICHNESS
RICHT
RICHTERITE
RICHWEED
RICIN
RICINELAIDIC
RICININE
RICINIUM
RICINOLEATE
RICINOLEIC
RICINOLEIN
RICK
RICKARDITE
RICKER
RICKETIER
RICKETIEST
RICKETILY
RICKETINESS
RICKETISH
RICKETS
RICKETTSIA
RICKETTSIAE
RICKETTSIAL
RICKETY
RICKEYS
RICKLE
RICKMATIC
RICKRACK
RICKSHAW
RICKSTADDLE
RICKSTAND
RICKSTICK
RICKYARD
RICO
RICOCHET
RICOCHETED
RICOCHETING
RICOCHETTED
RICOLETTAITE
RICOTTA
RICRAC
RICTAL
RICTUS
RID
RIDABLE
RIDDAM
RIDDANCE
RIDDED
RIDDEL
RIDDEN
RIDDER
RIDDING
RIDDLE
RIDDLED
RIDDLEMEREE
RIDDLER
RIDDLING
RIDDLINGLY
RIDDLINGS
RIDE
RIDEN
RIDENT
RIDER
RIDERED
RIDGE
RIDGEBAND
RIDGEBONE
RIDGED
RIDGELING
RIDGEPOLE
RIDGEPOLED
RIDGER
RIDGEROPE
RIDGEROPE
RIDGES
RIDGIER
RIDGIEST
RIDGIL
RIDGING
RIDGLING
RIDGY
RIDIBUND
RIDICULE
RIDICULED
RIDICULER
RIDICULING
RIDICULOSITY
RIDICULOUS
RIDICULOUSLY
RIDING
RIDINGMAN
RIDINGMEN
RIDOTTO
RIDOTTOS
RIE
RIEBECKITE
RIEL
RIEM
RIEMPIE
RIER
RIEVER
RIFACIMENTO
RIFART
RIFE
RIFELY
RIFENESS
RIFER
RIFEST
RIFF
RIFFLE
RIFFLED
RIFFLER
RIFFRAFF
RIFLE
RIFLEBIRD
RIFLED
RIFLEMAN
RIFLEMANSHIP
RIFLEMEN
RIFLEPROOF
RIFLER
RIFLERY
RIFLESHOT
RIFLING
RIFT
RIFTER
RIFTY
RIG
RIGADIG
RIGADON
RIGADOON
RIGAMAJIG
RIGAMAROLE
RIGAUDON
RIGBANE
RIGESCENCE
RIGESCENT
RIGGAL
RIGGED
RIGGER
RIGGING
RIGGISH
RIGGOT
RIGHT
RIGHTABOUT
RIGHTEN
RIGHTEOUS
RIGHTEOUSLY
RIGHTEOUSNESS
RIGHTER
RIGHTEST
RIGHTFORTH
RIGHTFUL
RIGHTFULLY
RIGHTFULNESS
RIGHTHAND
RIGHTHEADED
RIGHTHEARTED
RIGHTIST
RIGHTLE
RIGHTLESS
RIGHTLY
RIGHTMOST
RIGHTNESS
RIGHTO
RIGHTS
RIGHTSHIP
RIGHTWARD
RIGHTWARDLY
RIGHTWARDS
RIGHTY
RIGID
RIGIDIFIED
RIGIDIFY
RIGIDIFYING
RIGIDIST
RIGIDITIES
RIGIDITY
RIGIDLY
RIGIDNESS
RIGIDULOUS
RIGINAL
RIGLET
RIGLING
RIGMAREE
RIGMAROLE
RIGMAROLERY
RIGNUM
RIGO
RIGODON
RIGOL
RIGOLE
RIGOLETTE
RIGOR
RIGORISM
RIGORIST
RIGORISTIC
RIGOROUS
RIGOROUSLY
RIGOROUSNESS
RIGOUR
RIGOURISM
RIGOURISTIC
RIGSBY
RIGSDALER
RIGWIDDIE
RIGWIDDY
RIGWOODIE
RIKK
RIKSDAALDER
RILAWA
RILE
RILED
RILEY
RILIEVO
RILING
RILL

RILLE
RILLET
RILLETT
RILLETTE
RILLOCK
RILLOW
RILLS
RILLSTONE
RILY
RIM
RIMA
RIMAL
RIMAS
RIMATE
RIMBASE
RIME
RIMED
RIMER
RIMERY
RIMESTER
RIMFIRE
RIMIC
RIMIER
RIMIEST
RIMIFORM
RIMING
RIMLESS
RIMMAKER
RIMMAKING
RIMMED
RIMMER
RIMOSE
RIMOSELY
RIMOSITY
RIMOUS
RIMPI
RIMPLE
RIMPLED
RIMPLING
RIMPTION
RIMROCK
RIMU
RIMULA
RIMULOSE
RIMUR
RIMY
RIN
RINCEAU
RINCON
RIND
RINDED
RINDERPEST
RINDLE
RINDS
RINDY
RINE
RINFORZANDO
RING
RINGBILL
RINGBIRD
RINGBOLT
RINGBONE
RINGBONED
RINGCRAFT
RINGDOVE
RINGE
RINGED
RINGENT
RINGER
RINGEYE
RINGGIVER
RINGGIVING
RINGGOER
RINGHALS
RINGHALSES
RINGHEAD
RINGINESS
RINGING
RINGINGLY
RINGITE
RINGLE
RINGLEAD
RINGLEADER
RINGLET
RINGLETED
RINGLETS
RINGLETY
RINGLIKE
RINGMAKER
RINGMAKING
RINGMAN
RINGMASTER
RINGNECK
RINGS
RINGSAIL
RINGSIDE
RINGSIDER
RINGSTER
RINGSTICK
RINGSTRAKED
RINGTAIL
RINGTAW
RINGTIME
RINGTOSS
RINGWALK
RINGWALL
RINGWISE
RINGWORM
RINGY
RINK
RINKA
RINKER
RINKITE
RINN
RINNEITE
RINNER
RINNING
RINSE
RINSED
RINSER
RINSING
RINTHEREOUT
RIO
RIOT
RIOTED
RIOTER
RIOTING
RIOTINGLY
RIOTISE
RIOTIST
RIOTISTIC
RIOTOCRACY
RIOTOUS
RIOTOUSLY
RIOTOUSNESS
RIOTRY
RIP
RIPA
RIPAL
RIPARIAL
RIPARIAN
RIPARIOUS
RIPCORD
RIPE
RIPED
RIPELY
RIPEN
RIPENED
RIPENER
RIPENESS
RIPENING
RIPENINGLY
RIPER
RIPEST
RIPGUT
RIPICOLOUS
RIPIDOLITE
RIPIENIST
RIPIENO
RIPIER
RIPON
RIPOST
RIPOSTE
RIPOSTED
RIPOSTING
RIPPABLE
RIPPED
RIPPER
RIPPERMAN
RIPPERMEN
RIPPET
RIPPIER
RIPPING
RIPPINGLY
RIPPINGNESS
RIPPIT
RIPPLE
RIPPLED
RIPPLER
RIPPLES
RIPPLET
RIPPLING
RIPPLINGLY
RIPPLY
RIPPON
RIPRAP
RIPRAPPED
RIPRAPPING
RIPSACK
RIPSAW
RIPSNORTER
RIPSNORTING
RIPTIDE
RIPUP
RIRORIRO
RISALA
RISALDAR
RISBERM
RISCO
RISDALER
RISE
RISEN
RISER
RISH
RISHI
RISHTADAR
RISIBILITIES
RISIBILITY
RISIBLE
RISIBLENESS
RISIBLES
RISIBLY
RISING
RISK
RISKED
RISKER
RISKFUL
RISKFULNESS
RISKIER
RISKIEST
RISKILY
RISKINESS
RISKING
RISKISH
RISKLESS
RISKY
RISOM
RISORGIMENTO
RISORIAL
RISORIUS
RISORSE
RISOTTO
RISP
RISPER
RISPETTO
RISPOSTA
RISQUE
RISSER
RISSLE
RISSOID
RISSOLE
RISSOM
RIST
RISTORI
RISUS
RIT
RITARD
RITARDANDO
RITARDANDOS
RITE
RITELY
RITENUTO
RITES
RITHE
RITMASTER
RITORNEL
RITORNELLE
RITORNELLO
RITRATTO
RITSU
RITTINGERITE
RITTOCK
RITUAL
RITUALISM
RITUALIST
RITUALISTIC
RITUALITIES
RITUALITY
RITUALLY
RITUS
RITZ
RITZIER
RITZIEST
RITZY
RIVA
RIVAGE
RIVAL
RIVALED
RIVALING
RIVALISM
RIVALITY
RIVALIZE
RIVALLED
RIVALLING
RIVALRIES
RIVALROUS
RIVALRY
RIVE
RIVED
RIVEL
RIVELED
RIVELING
RIVELL
RIVEN
RIVER
RIVERAIN
RIVERBANK
RIVERBED
RIVERBOAT
RIVERDAMP
RIVERED
RIVERET
RIVERHEAD
RIVERINE
RIVERISH
RIVERLET
RIVERLING
RIVERLY
RIVERMAN
RIVERMEN
RIVERS
RIVERSIDE
RIVERSIDER
RIVERWASH
RIVERWAY
RIVERWEED
RIVERY
RIVET
RIVETED
RIVETER
RIVETING
RIVETS
RIVIERE
RIVING
RIVO
RIVOSE
RIVULATION
RIVULET
RIVULETS
RIVULOSE
RIX
RIXATRIX
RIXDALER
RIXY
RIYAL
RIZIFORM
RIZZAR
RIZZER
RIZZLE
RIZZOM
RIZZOMED
RO
ROACH
ROACHBACK
ROACHED
ROACHING
ROAD
ROADABILITY
ROADBED
ROADBLOCK
ROADBOOK
ROADCRAFT
ROADED
ROADER
ROADFELLOW
ROADHEAD
ROADHOUSE
ROADING
ROADITE
ROADMAN
ROADMASTER
ROADRUNNER
ROADS
ROADSIDE
ROADSIDER
ROADSTEAD
ROADSTER
ROADSTONE
ROADWAY
ROADWEED
ROADWISE
ROADWORK
ROADWORTHY
ROAG
ROAM
ROAMAGE
ROAMED
ROAMER
ROAMING
ROAMINGLY
ROAN
ROAR
ROARED
ROARER
ROARING

ROARINGLY
ROAST
ROASTABLE
ROASTED
ROASTER
ROASTING
ROASTINGLY
ROB
ROBALITO
ROBALO
ROBAND
ROBBED
ROBBER
ROBBERY
ROBBIN
ROBBING
ROBE
ROBED
ROBER
ROBERD
ROBERT
ROBHAH
ROBIN
ROBINET
ROBING
ROBININ
ROBLE
ROBORANT
ROBORATE
ROBORATION
ROBORATIVE
ROBOREAN
ROBOREOUS
ROBOT
ROBOTESQUE
ROBOTIAN
ROBOTISM
ROBOTISTIC
ROBOTIZATION
ROBOTIZE
ROBOTRY
ROBUR
ROBURITE
ROBUST
ROBUSTFUL
ROBUSTFULLY
ROBUSTIC
ROBUSTICITY
ROBUSTIOUS
ROBUSTIOUSLY
ROBUSTITY
ROBUSTLY
ROBUSTNESS
ROC
ROCAILLE
ROCAMBOLE
ROCCA
ROCCELLIN
ROCCELLINE
ROCHE
ROCHELIME
ROCHER
ROCHET
ROCK
ROCKABLE
ROCKABLY
ROCKABY
ROCKABYE
ROCKALLITE
ROCKAT
ROCKBELL
ROCKBIRD
ROCKBORN
ROCKBRUSH
ROCKCIST
ROCKCRAFT
ROCKELAY
ROCKER
ROCKERTHON
ROCKERY
ROCKET
ROCKETED
ROCKETER
ROCKETING
ROCKETRY
ROCKETS
ROCKETSONDE
ROCKETY
ROCKFALL
ROCKFISH
ROCKFISHES
ROCKFOIL
ROCKHAIR
ROCKHEARTED
ROCKIER
ROCKIEST
ROCKINESS
ROCKING
ROCKINGLY
ROCKISH
ROCKLAY
ROCKLING
ROCKLINGS
ROCKMAN
ROCKOON
ROCKRIBBED
ROCKROSE
ROCKS
ROCKSHAFT
ROCKSLIDE
ROCKSTAFF
ROCKTREE
ROCKWEED
ROCKWOOD
ROCKWORK
ROCKY
ROCOCO
ROCOLO
ROCTA
ROD
RODD
RODDEN
RODDIKIN
RODDIN
RODDING
RODE
RODENT
RODENTIAL
RODENTIALLY
RODENTIAN
RODEO
RODGE
RODHAM
RODING
RODINGITE
RODLESS
RODLIKE
RODMAKER
RODMAN
RODNEY
RODOMONTADE
RODOMONTADOR
RODS
RODSMAN
RODSTER
RODWOOD
ROEBLINGITE
ROEBUCK
ROED
ROEDE
ROENENG
ROENTGEN
ROENTGENISM
ROENTGENIZE
ROER
ROESTONE
ROEY
ROG
ROGAN
ROGATION
ROGATIVE
ROGATORY
ROGER
ROGERIAN
ROGERSITE
ROGGLE
ROGNON
ROGNONS
ROGUE
ROGUED
ROGUERIES
ROGUERY
ROGUING
ROGUISH
ROGUISHLY
ROGUISHNESS
ROGUY
ROHAN
ROHOB
ROHU
ROHUN
ROHUNA
ROI
ROID
ROIL
ROILED
ROILIER
ROILIEST
ROILING
ROILY
ROIN
ROINISH
ROIS
ROIST
ROISTER
ROISTERER
ROISTERING
ROISTERLY
ROISTEROUS
ROISTEROUSLY
ROIT
ROITELET
ROJO
ROKA
ROKE
ROKEAGE
ROKEE
ROKELAY
ROKER
ROKEY
ROKY
ROLA
ROLE
ROLEO
ROLL
ROLLABLE
ROLLAWAY
ROLLBACK
ROLLED
ROLLEJEE
ROLLER
ROLLERMAKER
ROLLERMAKING
ROLLERMAN
ROLLEY
ROLLEYWAY
ROLLEYWAYMAN
ROLLICHE
ROLLICHIE
ROLLICK
ROLLICKED
ROLLICKER
ROLLICKING
ROLLICKINGLY
ROLLICKSOME
ROLLICKY
ROLLING
ROLLIX
ROLLMOP
ROLLTOP
ROLLWAY
ROLOWAY
ROLP
ROLPENS
ROM
ROMAIKA
ROMAINE
ROMAL
ROMAN
ROMANCE
ROMANCEALIST
ROMANCEAN
ROMANCED
ROMANCER
ROMANCES
ROMANCICAL
ROMANCING
ROMANCIST
ROMANCY
ROMANESQUE
ROMANIUM
ROMANTIC
ROMANTICAL
ROMANTICALLY
ROMANTICISM
ROMANTICIST
ROMANTICITY
ROMANTICIZE
ROMANTICLY
ROMANTICNESS
ROMANTISM
ROMANTIST
ROMANZA
ROMAUNT
ROMBLE
ROMBOS
ROMBOWLINE
ROMEITE
ROMERILLO
ROMERO
ROMI
ROMMACK
ROMNI
ROMP
ROMPED
ROMPER
ROMPERS
ROMPING
ROMPINGLY
ROMPISH
ROMPISHLY
ROMPISHNESS
ROMPU
ROMPY
RON
RONCADOR
RONCET
RONCHO
RONCO
ROND
RONDACHE
RONDACHER
RONDAWEL
RONDE
RONDEAU
RONDEAUX
RONDEL
RONDELET
RONDELIER
RONDELLE
RONDELLIER
RONDINO
RONDLE
RONDO
RONDOLETTO
RONDOS
RONDURE
RONE
RONEO
RONG
RONGEUR
RONIER
RONIN
RONION
RONQUIL
RONTGENISM
RONYON
ROO
ROOD
ROODEBOK
ROODLES
ROODSTONE
ROOF
ROOFAGE
ROOFED
ROOFER
ROOFING
ROOFLESS
ROOFLET
ROOFMAN
ROOFMEN
ROOFTREE
ROOFWARD
ROOFY
ROOIBOK
ROOINEK
ROOK
ROOKED
ROOKER
ROOKERIED
ROOKERY
ROOKIE
ROOKING
ROOKS
ROOKUS
ROOKY
ROOL
ROOM
ROOMAGE
ROOMER
ROOMETTE
ROOMFUL
ROOMIE
ROOMIER
ROOMIEST
ROOMILY
ROOMINESS
ROOMING
ROOMKEEPER
ROOMMATE
ROOMS
ROOMSOME
ROOMSTEAD
ROOMTH
ROOMTHILY
ROOMTHINESS
ROOMTHY
ROOMWARD
ROOMY
ROON
ROOP
ROORBACK
ROOSA
ROOSE
ROOSEVELT

ROOST
ROOSTED
ROOSTER
ROOSTERFISH
ROOSTERS
ROOSTY
ROOT
ROOTAGE
ROOTCAP
ROOTED
ROOTEDLY
ROOTEDNESS
ROOTER
ROOTERY
ROOTFAST
ROOTFASTNESS
ROOTHOLD
ROOTIER
ROOTIEST
ROOTINESS
ROOTLE
ROOTLESS
ROOTLESSNESS
ROOTLET
ROOTLIKE
ROOTLING
ROOTS
ROOTSTALK
ROOTSTOCK
ROOTWALT
ROOTWORM
ROOTY
ROOVE
ROOYEBOK
ROPABLE
ROPAND
ROPANI
ROPE
ROPEBAND
ROPEBARK
ROPED
ROPEDANCE
ROPEDANCER
ROPEDANCING
ROPELAYER
ROPELAYING
ROPEMAKER
ROPEMAKING
ROPEMAN
ROPEMEN
ROPER
ROPERIPE
ROPERY
ROPES
ROPESMITH
ROPEWALK
ROPEWALKER
ROPEWAY
ROPEWORK
ROPEY
ROPIER
ROPIEST
ROPILY
ROPINESS
ROPING
ROPISH
ROPISHNESS
ROPLOCH
ROPY
ROQUE
ROQUELAURE
ROQUET
ROQUETED
ROQUETING
ROQUETTE
ROQUILLE
ROQUIST
RORAL
RORATORIO
RORIC
RORID
RORIFEROUS
RORIFLUENT
RORITORIOUS
RORQUAL
RORT
RORTY
RORULENT
ROSACE
ROSACEAN
ROSACEOUS
ROSAKER
ROSANILINE
ROSARIAN
ROSARIES
ROSARIUM
ROSARUBY
ROSARY
ROSATED
ROSCHERITE
ROSCID
ROSCOELITE
ROSE
ROSEAL
ROSEATE
ROSEATELY
ROSEBAY
ROSEBUD
ROSEBUSH
ROSED
ROSEDROP
ROSEFISH
ROSEFISHES
ROSEHEAD
ROSEHILL
ROSEHILLER
ROSEI
ROSEINE
ROSEL
ROSELET
ROSELITE
ROSELLA
ROSELLATE
ROSELLE
ROSEMARIES
ROSEMARY
ROSEN
ROSENBUSCHITE
ROSEOLA
ROSEOLAR
ROSEOLIFORM
ROSEOLOUS
ROSEOUS
ROSER
ROSEROOT
ROSES
ROSET
ROSETAN
ROSETANGLE
ROSETIME
ROSETTE
ROSETTED
ROSETTY
ROSETTY
ROSETUM
ROSETY
ROSEWAYS
ROSEWISE
ROSEWOOD
ROSEWORT
ROSIED
ROSIER
ROSIERESITE
ROSIEST
ROSILLA
ROSILLO
ROSILY
ROSIN
ROSINESS
ROSING
ROSINOUS
ROSINWEED
ROSINY
ROSLAND
ROSMARINE
ROSOLIC
ROSOLIO
ROSOLITE
ROSORIAL
ROSSER
ROSSITE
ROSTEL
ROSTELLA
ROSTELLAR
ROSTELLATE
ROSTELLIFORM
ROSTELLUM
ROSTER
ROSTRA
ROSTRAL
ROSTRALLY
ROSTRATE
ROSTRATED
ROSTRIFEROUS
ROSTRIFORM
ROSTROID
ROSTRULAR
ROSTRULATE
ROSTRULUM
ROSTRUM
ROSTRUMS
ROSULAR
ROSULATE
ROSY
ROT
ROTA
ROTACISM
ROTAL
ROTALIAN
ROTALIFORM
ROTAMAN
ROTAMEN
ROTAMETER
ROTAN
ROTANG
ROTARIANIZE
ROTARY
ROTATABLE
ROTATE
ROTATED
ROTATING
ROTATION
ROTATIONAL
ROTATIVE
ROTATIVELY
ROTATIVISM
ROTATOPLANE
ROTATOR
ROTATORES
ROTATORY
ROTCH
ROTCHE
ROTE
ROTELLA
ROTENONE
ROTGE
ROTGUT
ROTHER
ROTHERMUCK
ROTI
ROTIFER
ROTIFERAL
ROTIFEROUS
ROTIFORM
ROTISSERIE
ROTL
ROTN
ROTO
ROTOGRAPH
ROTOGRAVURE
ROTONDE
ROTOR
ROTTA
ROTTAN
ROTTE
ROTTED
ROTTEN
ROTTENLY
ROTTENNESS
ROTTENSTONE
ROTTER
ROTTING
ROTTLE
ROTTLERA
ROTTLERIN
ROTTOCK
ROTTOLO
ROTULA
ROTULAD
ROTULAR
ROTULET
ROTULIAN
ROTULIFORM
ROTULUS
ROTUND
ROTUNDA
ROTUNDATE
ROTUNDITIES
ROTUNDITY
ROTUNDLY
ROTUNDNESS
ROTURIER
ROTURIERS
ROUB
ROUBLE
ROUBOUH
ROUCH
ROUCHE
ROUCOU
ROUDAS
ROUE
ROUERIE
ROUGE
ROUGEAU
ROUGED
ROUGEMONTITE
ROUGEOT
ROUGH
ROUGHAGE
ROUGHCAST
ROUGHCASTER
ROUGHCASTING
ROUGHDRAFT
ROUGHDRAW
ROUGHDRESS
ROUGHDRIED
ROUGHDRY
ROUGHDRYING
ROUGHEN
ROUGHENED
ROUGHENER
ROUGHER
ROUGHET
ROUGHHEW
ROUGHHEWED
ROUGHHEWER
ROUGHHEWING
ROUGHHEWN
ROUGHHOUSE
ROUGHHOUSER
ROUGHHOUSING
ROUGHHOUSY
ROUGHIE
ROUGHINGS
ROUGHISH
ROUGHISHLY
ROUGHISHNESS
ROUGHLEG
ROUGHLY
ROUGHNECK
ROUGHNESS
ROUGHOMETER
ROUGHRIDE
ROUGHRIDER
ROUGHROOT
ROUGHSCUFF
ROUGHSETTER
ROUGHSHOD
ROUGHSLANT
ROUGHSOME
ROUGHSTRING
ROUGHSTUFF
ROUGHT
ROUGHTAILED
ROUGHWORK
ROUGHWROUGHT
ROUGHY
ROUGING
ROUKY
ROULADE
ROULEAU
ROULEAUS
ROULEAUX
ROULETTE
ROUN
ROUNCE
ROUNCEVAL
ROUNCY
ROUND
ROUNDABOUT
ROUNDABOUTLY
ROUNDED
ROUNDEL
ROUNDELAY
ROUNDELEER
ROUNDER
ROUNDERS
ROUNDHEADED
ROUNDHOUSE
ROUNDING
ROUNDISH
ROUNDISHNESS
ROUNDLET
ROUNDLINE
ROUNDLY
ROUNDNESS
ROUNDNOSE
ROUNDNOSED
ROUNDS
ROUNDSMAN
ROUNDTAIL
ROUNDTOP
ROUNDUP
ROUNDWORM
ROUNDY
ROUNGE
ROUNSPIK
ROUNTREE
ROUP
ROUPET
ROUPIE
ROUPIT
ROUPY
ROUSE
ROUSEABOUT

ROUSED
ROUSEMENT
ROUSER
ROUSETTE
ROUSING
ROUSINGLY
ROUSSEAU
ROUST
ROUSTABOUT
ROUSTING
ROUT
ROUTE
ROUTED
ROUTER
ROUTH
ROUTHERCOCK
ROUTHY
ROUTIER
ROUTINARY
ROUTINE
ROUTINEER
ROUTINELY
ROUTING
ROUTINISH
ROUTINISM
ROUTINIST
ROUTINIZE
ROUTINIZED
ROUTINIZING
ROUTIVARITE
ROUTOUS
ROUTOUSLY
ROUVILLITE
ROUX
ROVE
ROVED
ROVER
ROVESCIO
ROVET
ROVETTO
ROVING
ROVINGLY
ROVINGNESS
ROW
ROWABLE
ROWAN
ROWANBERRIES
ROWANBERRY
ROWBOAT
ROWDILY
ROWDINESS
ROWDY
ROWDYDOW
ROWDYISH
ROWDYISHLY
ROWDYISM
ROWED
ROWEL
ROWELED
ROWELHEAD
ROWELING
ROWELLED
ROWELLING
ROWEN
ROWER
ROWET
ROWINESS
ROWING
ROWK
ROWLANDITE
ROWLET
ROWLOCK
ROWN
ROWP
ROWPORT
ROWS
ROWTH
ROWTY
ROWY
ROX
ROXY
ROY
ROYAL
ROYALE
ROYALET
ROYALISM
ROYALIST
ROYALISTIC
ROYALIZATION
ROYALIZE
ROYALLY
ROYALMAST
ROYALME
ROYALTIES
ROYALTY
ROYD
ROYET
ROYETNESS
ROYETOUS
ROYETOUSLY
ROYLE
ROYNOUS
ROYT
ROZUM
RSI
RUACH
RUADE
RUANA
RUAY
RUB
RUBABOO
RUBACE
RUBAIYAT
RUBAN
RUBASSE
RUBATO
RUBBABOO
RUBBED
RUBBEE
RUBBER
RUBBERIZE
RUBBERIZED
RUBBERIZING
RUBBERNECK
RUBBERNOSE
RUBBERS
RUBBERSTONE
RUBBERY
RUBBING
RUBBIO
RUBBISHING
RUBBISHINGLY
RUBBISHLY
RUBBISHRY
RUBBISHY
RUBBLE
RUBBLER
RUBBLES
RUBBLESTONE
RUBBLEWORK
RUBBLY
RUBDOWN
RUBEDINOUS
RUBEDITY
RUBEFACIENCE
RUBEFACIENT
RUBEFACTION
RUBELET
RUBELLA
RUBELLE
RUBELLITE
RUBEOLA
RUBEOLAR
RUBEOLOID
RUBERYTHRIC
RUBESCENCE
RUBESCENT
RUBIACEOUS
RUBIANIC
RUBIATE
RUBIATOR
RUBIBLE
RUBICAN
RUBICUND
RUBICUNDITY
RUBIDIC
RUBIDINE
RUBIDIUM
RUBIED
RUBIES
RUBIFIC
RUBIFICATION
RUBIFICATIVE
RUBIFY
RUBIGINOUS
RUBIGO
RUBIJERVINE
RUBIN
RUBINE
RUBINEOUS
RUBIOUS
RUBLE
RUBLIS
RUBOR
RUBRIC
RUBRICAL
RUBRICALITY
RUBRICALLY
RUBRICATE
RUBRICATED
RUBRICATING
RUBRICATION
RUBRICATOR
RUBRICIAN
RUBRICISM
RUBRICIST
RUBRICITY
RUBRICIZE
RUBRICOSE
RUBRIFIC
RUBRIFY
RUBROSPINAL
RUBSTONE
RUBY
RUBYING
RUBYTAIL
RUCERVINE
RUCERVUS
RUCHE
RUCHING
RUCK
RUCKLE
RUCKSACK
RUCKSEY
RUCKUS
RUCKY
RUCTION
RUCTIOUS
RUD
RUDAS
RUDBECKIA
RUDD
RUDDER
RUDDERFISH
RUDDERHEAD
RUDDERHOLE
RUDDERLESS
RUDDERPOST
RUDDERSTOCK
RUDDIED
RUDDIER
RUDDIEST
RUDDINESS
RUDDISH
RUDDLE
RUDDLED
RUDDLEMAN
RUDDLEMEN
RUDDLING
RUDDOCK
RUDDY
RUDE
RUDELY
RUDENESS
RUDENTED
RUDER
RUDERA
RUDERAL
RUDERATE
RUDESBY
RUDEST
RUDGE
RUDIMENT
RUDIMENTAL
RUDIMENTARY
RUDISH
RUDITY
RUDLOFF
RUDOUS
RUE
RUED
RUEFUL
RUEFULLY
RUEFULNESS
RUELLE
RUELY
RUEN
RUER
RUESOME
RUESOMENESS
RUEWORT
RUF
RUFESCENCE
RUFESCENT
RUFF
RUFFE
RUFFED
RUFFER
RUFFIAN
RUFFIANAGE
RUFFIANISH
RUFFIANISM
RUFFIANIZE
RUFFIANLY
RUFFING
RUFFLE
RUFFLED
RUFFLER
RUFFLINESS
RUFFLING
RUFFLY
RUFFMANS
RUFOUS
RUFULOUS
RUFUS
RUG
RUGA
RUGAE
RUGATE
RUGG
RUGGED
RUGGEDLY
RUGGEDNESS
RUGGING
RUGGLE
RUGGY
RUGINE
RUGOSE
RUGOSITY
RUGOUS
RUIN
RUINABLE
RUINATE
RUINATED
RUINATING
RUINATION
RUINATIOUS
RUINATOR
RUINED
RUINER
RUING
RUINIFORM
RUINOUS
RUINOUSLY
RUINOUSNESS
RUINPROOF
RUINS
RUKH
RULE
RULED
RULEMONGER
RULER
RULERS
RULERSHIP
RULES
RULING
RULINGLY
RULL
RULLER
RULLION
RULLOCK
RUM
RUMAL
RUMBA
RUMBARGE
RUMBELOW
RUMBLE
RUMBLED
RUMBLEGARIE
RUMBLEGUMPTION
RUMBLEMENT
RUMBLER
RUMBLING
RUMBLINGLY
RUMBLY
RUMBO
RUMBOOZE
RUMBOWLINE
RUMBOWLING
RUMBULLION
RUMBUMPTIOUS
RUMBUSTICAL
RUMBUSTIOUS
RUMCHUNDER
RUMEN
RUMENITIS
RUMENOTOMY
RUMFUSTIAN
RUMGUMPTION
RUMGUMPTIOUS
RUMINA
RUMINAL
RUMINANT
RUMINANTLY
RUMINANTS
RUMINATE
RUMINATED
RUMINATING
RUMINATINGLY
RUMINATION
RUMINATIVE
RUMINATIVELY
RUMINATOR
RUMKIN
RUMMAGE

RUMMAGED
RUMMAGER
RUMMAGING
RUMMAGY
RUMMER
RUMMES
RUMMIER
RUMMIEST
RUMMILY
RUMMINESS
RUMMLE
RUMMY
RUMNESS
RUMNEY
RUMOR
RUMORED
RUMORER
RUMORING
RUMORMONGER
RUMOROUS
RUMOUR
RUMOURED
RUMOURER
RUMOURING
RUMP
RUMPAD
RUMPADE
RUMPLE
RUMPLED
RUMPLING
RUMPUS
RUMPY
RUMRUNNER
RUMSHOP
RUMTYTOO
RUN
RUNABOUT
RUNAGADO
RUNAGATE
RUNAROUND
RUNAWAY
RUNBACK
RUNBY
RUNCH
RUNCHWEED
RUNCINATE
RUND
RUNDALE
RUNDEL
RUNDLE
RUNDLET
RUNDOWN
RUNE
RUNECRAFT
RUNEFOLK
RUNER
RUNES
RUNESMITH
RUNESTAFF
RUNEWORD
RUNFISH
RUNG
RUNGHEAD
RUNHOLDER
RUNIC
RUNIFORM
RUNITE
RUNKEEPER
RUNKLE
RUNLET
RUNMAN
RUNN
RUNNEL
RUNNER
RUNNERS
RUNNET
RUNNING
RUNNY
RUNOFF
RUNOLOGIST
RUNOLOGY
RUNOUT
RUNOVER
RUNRIG
RUNROUND
RUNS
RUNSY
RUNT
RUNTED
RUNTEE
RUNTIER
RUNTIEST
RUNTINESS
RUNTISH
RUNTISHLY
RUNTISHNESS
RUNTY
RUNWAY
RUPA
RUPEE
RUPELLARY
RUPESTRAL
RUPESTRIAN
RUPESTRINE
RUPIA
RUPIAH
RUPICOLINE
RUPICOLOUS
RUPIE
RUPITIC
RUPTILE
RUPTION
RUPTIVE
RUPTUARY
RUPTURABLE
RUPTURE
RUPTURED
RUPTUREWORT
RUPTURING
RURAL
RURALISM
RURALIST
RURALITE
RURALITIES
RURALITY
RURALIZATION
RURALIZE
RURALIZED
RURALIZING
RURALLY
RURIC
RURIDECANAL
RURIGENOUS
RURU
RUSE
RUSH
RUSHBUSH
RUSHED
RUSHEN
RUSHER
RUSHES
RUSHIER
RUSHIEST
RUSHINESS
RUSHING
RUSHLAND
RUSHLIGHT
RUSHLIGHTED
RUSHLIKE
RUSHY
RUSINE
RUSK
RUSKY
RUSMA
RUSOT
RUSPONE
RUSSEL
RUSSELET
RUSSET
RUSSETING
RUSSETISH
RUSSUD
RUST
RUSTIC
RUSTICAL
RUSTICALLY
RUSTICALNESS
RUSTICATE
RUSTICATED
RUSTICATING
RUSTICATION
RUSTICATOR
RUSTICIAL
RUSTICISM
RUSTICITIES
RUSTICITY
RUSTICIZE
RUSTICOAT
RUSTICWORK
RUSTIER
RUSTIEST
RUSTINESS
RUSTLE
RUSTLED
RUSTLER
RUSTLING
RUSTLINGLY
RUSTLY
RUSTRE
RUSTRED
RUSTY
RUSTYISH
RUSWUT
RUT
RUTAB
RUTABAGA
RUTACEOUS
RUTE
RUTELIAN
RUTH
RUTHE
RUTHENATE
RUTHENIC
RUTHENIOUS
RUTHENIUM
RUTHENOUS
RUTHER
RUTHERFORD
RUTHFUL
RUTHFULLY
RUTHFULNESS
RUTHLESS
RUTHLESSLY
RUTHLESSNESS
RUTIC
RUTIDOSIS
RUTILANT
RUTILATE
RUTILATED
RUTILATION
RUTILE
RUTILOUS
RUTIN
RUTINOSE
RUTTEE
RUTTER
RUTTIER
RUTTIEST
RUTTINESS
RUTTING
RUTTISH
RUTTISHNESS
RUTTLE
RUTTY
RUTYL
RUTYLENE
RUVID
RUX
RYAL
RYBAT
RYDER
RYE
RYEGRASS
RYEL
RYEN
RYFT
RYG
RYKE
RYKED
RYKING
RYME
RYND
RYNT
RYOT
RYOTWAR
RYOTWARI
RYPE
RYPECK
RYTIDOSIS

SA
SAA
SAAH
SAAME
SAB
SABA
SABADILLA
SABADIN
SABADINE
SABAKHA
SABALO
SABALOTE
SABANA
SABATON
SABAYON
SABBAT
SABBATICAL
SABBATINE
SABBATISM
SABBATON
SABBEKA
SABBITHA
SABBY
SABDARIFFA
SABE
SABECA
SABED
SABEING
SABELLAN
SABELLID
SABELLOID
SABER
SABERBILL
SABERED
SABERING
SABERTOOTH
SABHA
SABIACEOUS
SABICU
SABIN
SABINA
SABINE
SABINO
SABIO
SABLA
SABLE
SABLEFISH
SABLEFISHES
SABLENESS
SABLES
SABLY
SABORA
SABORAIM
SABOT
SABOTAGE
SABOTAGED
SABOTAGING
SABOTED
SABOTEUR
SABOTIER
SABOTINE
SABRE
SABREBILL
SABRETACHE
SABRETOOTH
SABREUR
SABRING
SABULINE
SABULITE
SABULOSE
SABULOSITY
SABULOUS
SABULUM
SABURRA
SABURRAL
SABURRATE
SABURRATION
SABUTAN
SABZI
SAC
SACALAIT
SACALINE
SACATE
SACATON
SACATRA
SACBROOD
SACCADE
SACCADGE
SACCADIC
SACCAGE
SACCATE
SACCATED
SACCHARATE
SACCHARATED
SACCHARIC
SACCHARIDE
SACCHARIFIED
SACCHARIFIER
SACCHARIFY
SACCHARIFYING
SACCHARILLA
SACCHARIN
SACCHARINATE
SACCHARINE
SACCHARINELY
SACCHARINIC
SACCHARINITY
SACCHARIZE
SACCHARIZED
SACCHARIZING
SACCHAROID
SACCHAROIDAL
SACCHARONATE
SACCHARONE
SACCHARONIC
SACCHAROSE
SACCHAROSURIA
SACCODERM
SACCOON
SACCOS
SACCULAR
SACCULATE
SACCULATED
SACCULATION
SACCULE
SACCULUS
SACCUS
SACE
SACELLA
SACELLUM
SACER
SACERDOCY
SACERDOS
SACERDOTAGE
SACERDOTAL
SACERDOTALLY
SACERDOTICAL
SACERDOTISM
SACERDOTIUM
SACHEM
SACHEMDOM
SACHEMIC
SACHET
SACK
SACKAGE
SACKBAG
SACKBUT
SACKBUTT
SACKCLOTH
SACKCLOTHED
SACKDOUDLE
SACKED
SACKEN
SACKER
SACKET
SACKFUL
SACKING
SACKLESS
SACKMAKER
SACKMAKING
SACKS
SACO
SACOPE
SACQUE
SACRA
SACRAD
SACRAL
SACRALGIA
SACRAMENT
SACRAMENTAL
SACRAMENTALISM
SACRAMENTALIST
SACRAMENTALITY
SACRAMENTALLY
SACRAMENTARIAN
SACRAMENTARY
SACRAMENTER
SACRAMENTIZE
SACRAMENTUM
SACRARIA
SACRARIAL
SACRARIUM
SACRARY
SACRATE
SACRE
SACRECTOMY
SACRED
SACREDLY
SACREDNESS
SACRI
SACRIFICATION
SACRIFICATOR
SACRIFICATORY
SACRIFICATURE
SACRIFICE
SACRIFICED
SACRIFICER
SACRIFICES
SACRIFICIAL
SACRIFICIALLY
SACRIFICING
SACRIFICINGLY
SACRILEGE
SACRILEGER
SACRILEGIOUS
SACRILEGIOUSLY
SACRILEGIST
SACRING
SACRIST
SACRISTAN
SACRISTIES
SACRISTY
SACRO
SACROCOCCYX
SACROCOXITIS
SACRODORSAL
SACRODYNIA
SACROILIAC
SACROSANCT
SACROSCIATIC
SACROSPINOUS
SACROTUBEROUS
SACRUM
SACRY
SAD
SADD
SADDEN
SADDENED
SADDENING
SADDER
SADDEST
SADDHU
SADDIK
SADDISH
SADDLE
SADDLEBACK
SADDLEBAG
SADDLEBOW
SADDLECLOTH
SADDLED
SADDLELEAF
SADDLELESS
SADDLELIKE
SADDLEMAKER
SADDLENOSE
SADDLER
SADDLERIES
SADDLERY
SADDLES
SADDLESICK
SADDLESORE
SADDLETREE
SADDLETREES
SADDLING
SADE
SADH
SADHANA
SADHE
SADHEARTED
SADHU
SADIC
SADIRON
SADISM
SADIST
SADISTIC
SADISTICALLY
SADLY
SADNESS
SADO
SADOO
SADR
SADWARE
SAE
SAEBEINS
SAECULAR
SAECULUM
SAER
SAERNAITE
SAETER
SAEX
SAFARI
SAFE
SAFEBLOWER
SAFEBLOWING
SAFEBREAKER
SAFEBREAKING
SAFECRACKER
SAFECRACKING
SAFEGUARD
SAFEGUARDER
SAFEHOLD
SAFEKEEPER
SAFEKEEPING
SAFELIGHT
SAFELY
SAFEMAKER
SAFENER
SAFENESS
SAFER
SAFEST
SAFETIES
SAFETY
SAFFI
SAFFIAN
SAFFIOR
SAFFLOR
SAFFLORITE
SAFFLOW
SAFFLOWER
SAFFO
SAFFRON
SAFFRONED
SAFFRONWOOD
SAFFRONY
SAFIE
SAFIR
SAFRANIN
SAFRANINE
SAFRANOPHIL
SAFRANOPHILE
SAFROL
SAFROLE
SAFTLY
SAG
SAGA
SAGACIATE
SAGACIOUS
SAGACIOUSLY
SAGACIOUSNESS
SAGACITY
SAGAIE
SAGAMAN
SAGAMITE
SAGAMORE
SAGANASH
SAGAPEN
SAGAPENUM
SAGATHY
SAGE
SAGEBRUSH
SAGEBRUSHER
SAGEER
SAGELEAF
SAGELY
SAGENE
SAGENESS
SAGENITE
SAGENITIC
SAGER
SAGEROSE
SAGESHIP
SAGESSE
SAGEST
SAGEWOOD
SAGGAR
SAGGARD
SAGGED
SAGGER
SAGGING
SAGGON
SAGGY
SAGHAVART
SAGIER
SAGIEST
SAGINATE
SAGINATION
SAGING
SAGITTA
SAGITTAE
SAGITTAL
SAGITTALLY
SAGITTARII
SAGITTARIUS
SAGITTARY
SAGITTATE

SAGITTIFORM
SAGITTOCYST
SAGITTOID
SAGO
SAGOIN
SAGOS
SAGOWEER
SAGUARO
SAGUAROS
SAGUING
SAGUM
SAGURAN
SAGURANES
SAGVANDITE
SAGWIRE
SAGY
SAH
SAHEB
SAHH
SAHIB
SAHLITE
SAHME
SAHRAS
SAHU
SAI
SAIBLING
SAIC
SAICE
SAID
SAIDE
SAIF
SAIGA
SAIL
SAILABLE
SAILAGE
SAILBOAT
SAILCLOTH
SAILED
SAILER
SAILFIN
SAILFISH
SAILFISHES
SAILING
SAILMAKER
SAILMAKING
SAILOR
SAILORING
SAILORIZING
SAILORLY
SAILORMAN
SAILOUR
SAILPLANE
SAILS
SAILSHIP
SAILSMAN
SAILY
SAILYE
SAIM
SAIMIRI
SAIMY
SAIN
SAINDOUX
SAINFOIN
SAINT
SAINTE
SAINTED
SAINTHOOD
SAINTING
SAINTISH
SAINTISM
SAINTLIER
SAINTLIEST
SAINTLIKE
SAINTLINESS
SAINTLY
SAINTS
SAINTSHIP
SAIR
SAIRVE
SAIS
SAITHE
SAIYID
SAJ
SAJOU
SAKE
SAKEBER
SAKEEN
SAKER
SAKHA
SAKI
SAKIA
SAKIEH
SAKIYEH
SAKKOS
SAKULYA
SAL
SALA
SALAAM
SALABILITY
SALABLE
SALABLENESS
SALABLY
SALACIOUS
SALACIOUSLY
SALACIOUSNESS
SALACITY
SALACOT
SALAD
SALADA
SALADANG
SALADE
SALADERO
SALADIN
SALADING
SALAGO
SALAGRAMA
SALAL
SALAM
SALAMANDARIN
SALAMANDER
SALAMANDRA
SALAMANDRINE
SALAMANDROID
SALAMAT
SALAMBAO
SALAME
SALAMI
SALAMO
SALAMPORE
SALANGANE
SALANGID
SALAR
SALARIAT
SALARIED
SALARIEGO
SALARIES
SALARY
SALARYING
SALAT
SALAY
SALBAND
SALCHOW
SALDID
SALE
SALEABLE
SALEB
SALEEITE
SALEGOER
SALELE
SALEM
SALEMA
SALEP
SALERATUS
SALEROOM
SALES
SALESCLERK
SALESGIRL
SALESITE
SALESLADIES
SALESLADY
SALESMAN
SALESMANSHIP
SALESMEN
SALESPEOPLE
SALESPERSON
SALESROOM
SALESWOMAN
SALESWOMEN
SALEW
SALEWARE
SALEWORK
SALEYARD
SALFERN
SALIANT
SALIC
SALICACEOUS
SALICETUM
SALICIN
SALICIONAL
SALICORN
SALICYL
SALICYLAL
SALICYLATE
SALICYLIC
SALICYLIDE
SALICYLISM
SALICYLIZE
SALICYLURIC
SALICYLYL
SALIENCE
SALIENCY
SALIENT
SALIENTIAN
SALIENTLY
SALIENTNESS
SALIFEROUS
SALIFIABLE
SALIFICATION
SALIFIED
SALIFY
SALIFYING
SALIGENIN
SALIGENOL
SALIGOT
SALIGRAM
SALINA
SALINAS
SALINATION
SALINE
SALINELLE
SALINIFORM
SALINITY
SALINIZE
SALINOMETER
SALINOMETRY
SALITE
SALITED
SALIVA
SALIVANT
SALIVARY
SALIVATE
SALIVATED
SALIVATING
SALIVATION
SALIVATOR
SALIVATORY
SALIVOUS
SALL
SALLE
SALLEE
SALLEEMAN
SALLEEMEN
SALLENDERS
SALLET
SALLIED
SALLIER
SALLIES
SALLO
SALLOO
SALLOW
SALLOWED
SALLOWER
SALLOWING
SALLOWISH
SALLOWNESS
SALLOWY
SALLY
SALLYING
SALLYMAN
SALLYMEN
SALLYWOOD
SALM
SALMA
SALMAGUNDI
SALMARY
SALMI
SALMIAC
SALMIN
SALMINE
SALMIS
SALMON
SALMONBERRIES
SALMONBERRY
SALMONELLOSIS
SALMONET
SALMONID
SALMONIFORM
SALMONOID
SALMONSITE
SALMWOOD
SALNATRON
SALOL
SALOMETER
SALOMETRY
SALOMON
SALON
SALONIKA
SALONS
SALOON
SALOONIST
SALOONKEEPER
SALOOP
SALOP
SALOPIAN
SALP
SALPACEAN
SALPIAN
SALPICON
SALPID
SALPIFORM
SALPINGES
SALPINGIAN
SALPINGION
SALPINGITIS
SALPINGOCELE
SALPINX
SALPOID
SALSE
SALSIFIES
SALSIFY
SALSILLA
SALSO
SALSODA
SALSUGINOSE
SALSUGINOUS
SALT
SALTA
SALTANDO
SALTANT
SALTARELLO
SALTARY
SALTATE
SALTATION
SALTATIVENESS
SALTATO
SALTATORIAL
SALTATORIC
SALTATORY
SALTATRAS
SALTBOX
SALTBRUSH
SALTBUSH
SALTCAT
SALTCATCH
SALTCELLAR
SALTEAUX
SALTED
SALTEE
SALTEN
SALTER
SALTERETTO
SALTERN
SALTERY
SALTEST
SALTFAT
SALTFOOT
SALTHOUSE
SALTICID
SALTIE
SALTIER
SALTIERRA
SALTIERWISE
SALTIEST
SALTIGRADE
SALTILY
SALTIMBANCO
SALTINE
SALTINESS
SALTING
SALTIRE
SALTIREWISE
SALTISH
SALTMAKING
SALTMAN
SALTMOUTH
SALTNESS
SALTO
SALTOMETER
SALTOREL
SALTPAN
SALTPANS
SALTPETER
SALTPETRE
SALTS
SALTSHAKER
SALTSPOONFUL
SALTSPRINKLER
SALTUS
SALTWEED
SALTWORK
SALTWORKER
SALTWORKS
SALTWORT
SALTY
SALUBRIFY
SALUBRIOUS
SALUBRIOUSLY
SALUBRITY
SALUDA
SALUE
SALUKI
SALUNG
SALUS
SALUTARILY
SALUTARINESS

SALUTARY
SALUTATION
SALUTATIONAL
SALUTATIOUS
SALUTATORIAN
SALUTATORIES
SALUTATORY
SALUTE
SALUTER
SALUTES
SALVABILITY
SALVABLE
SALVABLY
SALVAGE
SALVAGEABLE
SALVAGED
SALVAGEE
SALVAGER
SALVAGING
SALVARSAN
SALVATELLA
SALVATION
SALVATIONAL
SALVATIONISM
SALVATIONIST
SALVATOR
SALVATORY
SALVE
SALVED
SALVER
SALVERFORM
SALVIA
SALVIANIN
SALVIFIC
SALVIFICAL
SALVING
SALVIOL
SALVO
SALVOES
SALVOR
SALVOS
SALVY
SALWE
SALWIN
SAM
SAMA
SAMADH
SAMADHI
SAMAJ
SAMAN
SAMARA
SAMARIA
SAMARIFORM
SAMARIUM
SAMAROID
SAMARSKITE
SAMBA
SAMBAL
SAMBAQUI
SAMBAQUIS
SAMBAR
SAMBARS
SAMBAS
SAMBEL
SAMBHAR
SAMBHUR
SAMBO
SAMBOS
SAMBOUK
SAMBOUSE
SAMBUCA
SAMBUK
SAMBUKE
SAMBUL
SAMBUNIGRIN
SAMBUR
SAME
SAMECH
SAMEK
SAMEKH
SAMEL
SAMELY
SAMEN
SAMENESS
SAMESOME
SAMGHA
SAMH
SAMHITA
SAMIEL
SAMIRESITE
SAMIRI
SAMISEN
SAMITE
SAMKARA
SAMKHYA
SAMLET
SAMM
SAMMEL
SAMMER
SAMMIER
SAMMY
SAMNANI
SAMOGON
SAMOGONKA
SAMOHU
SAMORY
SAMOTHERE
SAMOVAR
SAMP
SAMPAGUITA
SAMPALOC
SAMPAN
SAMPHIRE
SAMPI
SAMPLE
SAMPLED
SAMPLEMAN
SAMPLEMEN
SAMPLER
SAMPLERY
SAMPLES
SAMPLING
SAMSARA
SAMSHU
SAMSKARA
SAMSONITE
SAMUIN
SAMUM
SAMURAI
SAMVAT
SAN
SANA
SANABILITY
SANABLE
SANAD
SANAI
SANATION
SANATIVE
SANATIVENESS
SANATORIUM
SANATORIUMS
SANATORY
SANBENITO
SANCHO
SANCORD
SANCT
SANCTA
SANCTANIMITY
SANCTIFICATE
SANCTIFICATION
SANCTIFIED
SANCTIFIEDLY
SANCTIFIER
SANCTIFY
SANCTIFYING
SANCTILOGY
SANCTILOQUENT
SANCTIMONIAL
SANCTIMONIOUS
SANCTIMONIOUSLY
SANCTIMONIOUSNESS
SANCTIMONY
SANCTION
SANCTIONARY
SANCTIONATIVE
SANCTIONED
SANCTIONER
SANCTITIES
SANCTITUDE
SANCTITY
SANCTOLOGIST
SANCTORIUM
SANCTUARIED
SANCTUARIES
SANCTUARIZE
SANCTUARY
SANCTUM
SANCTUMS
SANCYITE
SAND
SANDAK
SANDAL
SANDALED
SANDALIFORM
SANDALING
SANDALLED
SANDALLING
SANDALWOOD
SANDALWORT
SANDAN
SANDARAC
SANDARACIN
SANDASTRA
SANDASTROS
SANDBAG
SANDBAGGED
SANDBAGGER
SANDBAGGING
SANDBANK
SANDBAR
SANDBLAST
SANDBLASTER
SANDBLIND
SANDBOARD
SANDBOX
SANDBOY
SANDBUR
SANDBURR
SANDCLUB
SANDED
SANDER
SANDERLING
SANDERS
SANDERSWOOD
SANDFISH
SANDGOBY
SANDHEAT
SANDHI
SANDHOG
SANDIA
SANDIER
SANDIES
SANDIEST
SANDING
SANDIVER
SANDIX
SANDKEY
SANDLAPPER
SANDLING
SANDLOT
SANDMAN
SANDMITE
SANDNATTER
SANDPAPER
SANDPAPERER
SANDPEEP
SANDPILE
SANDPIPER
SANDPIPERS
SANDRA
SANDROCK
SANDSHOE
SANDSOAP
SANDSPIT
SANDSPUR
SANDSTAY
SANDSTONE
SANDSTORM
SANDUNGA
SANDUST
SANDWEED
SANDWICH
SANDWICHED
SANDWICHING
SANDWOOD
SANDWORM
SANDWORT
SANDY
SANDYISH
SANDYX
SANE
SANELY
SANENESS
SANER
SANEST
SANG
SANGA
SANGAH
SANGAMON
SANGAR
SANGAREE
SANGFROID
SANGGAU
SANGH
SANGHA
SANGIL
SANGLANT
SANGLEY
SANGLIER
SANGREEROOT
SANGREL
SANGU
SANGUICOLOUS
SANGUIFEROUS
SANGUIFIER
SANGUIMOTOR
SANGUIMOTORY
SANGUINARY
SANGUINE
SANGUINELESS
SANGUINELY
SANGUINENESS
SANGUINEOUS
SANGUINITY
SANGUINOLENT
SANGUINOUS
SANGUISUGE
SANGUISUGENT
SANGUISUGOUS
SANICLE
SANIDINE
SANIDINITE
SANIES
SANIFICATION
SANIFY
SANIOUS
SANITARIA
SANITARIAN
SANITARIES
SANITARIST
SANITARIUM
SANITARIUMS
SANITARY
SANITATE
SANITATED
SANITATING
SANITATION
SANITIZE
SANITIZED
SANITY
SANJAK
SANJAKBEG
SANK
SANKH
SANKHA
SANN
SANNA
SANNAITE
SANNHEMP
SANNUP
SANNYASI
SANNYASIN
SANS
SANSAR
SANSARA
SANSCULOT
SANSERIF
SANSHACH
SANSI
SANT
SANTA
SANTAL
SANTALACEOUS
SANTALIN
SANTALOL
SANTAPEE
SANTAR
SANTENE
SANTIMS
SANTIR
SANTO
SANTOL
SANTON
SANTONICA
SANTONIN
SANTONINE
SANTORINITE
SANTOS
SANTOUR
SANTY
SANUKITE
SAO
SAORA
SAP
SAPA
SAPAJOU
SAPAN
SAPANWOOD
SAPBUSH
SAPE
SAPEC
SAPEK
SAPFUL
SAPHEAD
SAPHEADED
SAPHEADEDNESS
SAPHENA
SAPHENAE
SAPHENAL
SAPHENOUS
SAPHIE
SAPIAO
SAPID
SAPIDITY
SAPIDNESS

SAPIENCE
SAPIENCY
SAPIENT
SAPIENTIAL
SAPIENTIALLY
SAPIENTIZE
SAPIENTLY
SAPIN
SAPINDA
SAPINDACEOUS
SAPINDASHIP
SAPINDUS
SAPIT
SAPIUTAN
SAPLE
SAPLESS
SAPLESSNESS
SAPLING
SAPO
SAPODILLA
SAPODILLO
SAPOGENIN
SAPONACEOUS
SAPONACITY
SAPONARIN
SAPONARY
SAPONIFIABLE
SAPONIFIED
SAPONIFIER
SAPONIFY
SAPONIFYING
SAPONIN
SAPONINE
SAPONITE
SAPONUL
SAPONULE
SAPOPHORIC
SAPOR
SAPORIFIC
SAPOROSITY
SAPOROUS
SAPOTACEOUS
SAPOTE
SAPOTOXIN
SAPPANWOOD
SAPPARE
SAPPED
SAPPER
SAPPHIRE
SAPPHIRED
SAPPHIRINE
SAPPIER
SAPPIEST
SAPPILY
SAPPING
SAPPLES
SAPPY
SAPRAEMIA
SAPREMIA
SAPREMIC
SAPRIN
SAPRINE
SAPROCOLL
SAPRODIL
SAPRODONTIA
SAPROGEN
SAPROGENIC
SAPROGENOUS
SAPROLITE
SAPROLITIC
SAPROPEL
SAPROPELIC
SAPROPELITE
SAPROPHAGAN
SAPROPHAGOUS
SAPROPHILOUS
SAPROPHYTE
SAPROPHYTIC
SAPROPHYTISM
SAPROPLANKTON
SAPROSTOMOUS
SAPROZOIC
SAPS
SAPSAGO
SAPSAP
SAPSUCK
SAPSUCKER
SAPUCAIA
SAPUCAINHA
SAPWOOD
SAPWORT
SARAAD
SARABAND
SARAF
SARAFAN
SARAN
SARANGI
SARANGOUSTY
SARAPE
SARAVAN
SARAWAKITE
SARBACANE
SARCASM
SARCAST
SARCASTIC
SARCASTICAL
SARCASTICALLY
SARCASTICNESS
SARCEL
SARCELLE
SARCELLY
SARCENET
SARCILIS
SARCITIS
SARCLE
SARCLER
SARCOBLAST
SARCOCARP
SARCOCELE
SARCOCOL
SARCOCOLLIN
SARCOCYTE
SARCODE
SARCODERM
SARCODERMA
SARCODES
SARCODIC
SARCOGENIC
SARCOGENOUS
SARCOGLIA
SARCOID
SARCOLEMMA
SARCOLEMMIC
SARCOLEMMOUS
SARCOLINE
SARCOLITE
SARCOLOGIC
SARCOLOGICAL
SARCOLOGIST
SARCOLOGY
SARCOLYSIS
SARCOLYTE
SARCOLYTIC
SARCOMA
SARCOMATA
SARCOMATOID
SARCOMATOSIS
SARCOMATOUS
SARCOMERE
SARCOPHAGAL
SARCOPHAGI
SARCOPHAGIC
SARCOPHAGID
SARCOPHAGIZE
SARCOPHAGOUS
SARCOPHAGUS
SARCOPHAGY
SARCOPHILE
SARCOPHILOUS
SARCOPLASM
SARCOPLASMA
SARCOPLASMIC
SARCOPLAST
SARCOPLASTIC
SARCOPTIC
SARCOPTID
SARCOSEPSIS
SARCOSINE
SARCOSIS
SARCOSOMA
SARCOSOME
SARCOSPERM
SARCOSPORID
SARCOSTOSIS
SARCOSTYLE
SARCOTHECA
SARCOTIC
SARCOUS
SARD
SARDACHATE
SARDANA
SARDAR
SARDEL
SARDELLE
SARDINE
SARDINES
SARDIUS
SARDONIC
SARDONICALLY
SARDONICISM
SARDONYX
SAREE
SARGASSO
SARGASSUM
SARGE
SARGO
SARGOS
SARGUS
SARI
SARIGUE
SARIN
SARINDA
SARIP
SARIS
SARK
SARKFUL
SARKICAL
SARKING
SARKINITE
SARKIT
SARKLESS
SARLAK
SARLYK
SARMATIER
SARMENT
SARMENTA
SARMENTOSE
SARMENTOUS
SARMENTUM
SARNA
SAROD
SARON
SARONG
SARONIC
SARONIDE
SAROS
SAROTHRUM
SARPE
SARPLER
SARPO
SARRA
SARRAZIN
SARRE
SARROW
SARRUSOPHONE
SARSA
SARSAPARILLA
SARSAR
SARSEN
SARSENET
SARSNET
SARSON
SARTOR
SARTORIAD
SARTORIAL
SARTORIALLY
SARTORIAN
SARTORITE
SARTORIUS
SARUS
SARWAN
SASAN
SASANI
SASANQUA
SASARARA
SASH
SASHAY
SASHED
SASHERIES
SASHERY
SASHES
SASHIMI
SASHING
SASHOON
SASIN
SASINE
SASKATOON
SASS
SASSABIES
SASSABY
SASSAFRAS
SASSAGUM
SASSANDRA
SASSE
SASSIER
SASSIEST
SASSOLIN
SASSOLINE
SASSWOOD
SASSY
SASSYBARK
SASSYWOOD
SASTRA
SASTRUGA
SASTRUGI
SAT
SATANG
SATANIC
SATANICAL
SATANICALLY
SATANIST
SATANIZE
SATARA
SATCHEL
SATCHELED
SATE
SATED
SATEEN
SATEENWOOD
SATELLES
SATELLITE
SATELLITED
SATELLITIAN
SATELLITIC
SATELLITIOUS
SATELLITIUM
SATELLITOID
SATELLITORY
SATELLOID
SATI
SATIABILITY
SATIABLE
SATIABLENESS
SATIABLY
SATIATE
SATIATED
SATIATING
SATIATION
SATIENT
SATIETIES
SATIETY
SATIN
SATINAY
SATINBUSH
SATINE
SATINED
SATINET
SATINETTE
SATINFIN
SATINFLOWER
SATING
SATINING
SATINITE
SATINITY
SATINIZE
SATINLEAF
SATINPOD
SATINWOOD
SATINY
SATION
SATIRE
SATIRIC
SATIRICAL
SATIRICALLY
SATIRICALNESS
SATIRIST
SATIRIZABLE
SATIRIZE
SATIRIZED
SATIRIZER
SATIRIZING
SATISDATION
SATISDICTION
SATISFACTION
SATISFACTIONAL
SATISFACTIVE
SATISFACTORILY
SATISFACTORY
SATISFIED
SATISFIEDLY
SATISFIEDNESS
SATISFIER
SATISFY
SATISFYING
SATISFYINGLY
SATISPASSION
SATIVE
SATLIJK
SATORI
SATRAP
SATRAPATE
SATRAPESS
SATRAPIC
SATRAPICAL
SATRAPIES
SATRAPY
SATRON
SATSOP
SATTAR
SATTIE
SATTVA
SATURA
SATURABILITY
SATURABLE
SATURANT

SATURATE
SATURATED
SATURATER
SATURATING
SATURATION
SATURATOR
SATURITY
SATURNIID
SATURNINE
SATURNINELY
SATURNINITY
SATURNISM
SATURNIST
SATURNIZE
SATURY
SATYAGRAHA
SATYASHODAK
SATYR
SATYRESQUE
SATYRESS
SATYRIASIS
SATYRIC
SATYRICAL
SATYRID
SATYRINE
SATYRION
SATYRISM
SATYROMANIAC
SAUCE
SAUCEBOAT
SAUCEBOX
SAUCEDISH
SAUCEMAN
SAUCEMEN
SAUCEPAN
SAUCEPOT
SAUCER
SAUCERLEAF
SAUCERLIKE
SAUCERY
SAUCH
SAUCIER
SAUCIEST
SAUCILY
SAUCINESS
SAUCISSE
SAUCY
SAUERBRATEN
SAUERKRAUT
SAUGER
SAUGH
SAUGHEN
SAUGHT
SAUK
SAUL
SAULGE
SAULIE
SAULT
SAUM
SAUMON
SAUMONT
SAUNA
SAUNDERS
SAUNT
SAUNTER
SAUNTERED
SAUNTERER
SAUNTERING
SAUQUI
SAUR
SAUREL
SAURIAN
SAURIOSIS
SAURISCHIAN
SAURLESS
SAURODONT
SAUROID
SAUROPOD
SAUROPSID
SAUROPSIDAN
SAURY
SAUSAGE
SAUSINGER
SAUSSURITE
SAUTE
SAUTEED
SAUTEING
SAUTER
SAUTEREAU
SAUTERELLE
SAUTERNE
SAUTERNES
SAUTEUR
SAUTOIR
SAUTREE
SAUVE
SAVABLE
SAVABLENESS
SAVAGE
SAVAGED
SAVAGEDOM
SAVAGELY
SAVAGENESS
SAVAGER
SAVAGERIES
SAVAGEROUS
SAVAGERY
SAVAGESS
SAVAGEST
SAVAGING
SAVAGISM
SAVAGIZE
SAVANILLA
SAVANNA
SAVANNAH
SAVANT
SAVARIN
SAVATE
SAVATION
SAVE
SAVED
SAVELHA
SAVELOY
SAVEMENT
SAVER
SAVEY
SAVILE
SAVIN
SAVINE
SAVING
SAVINGLY
SAVINGNESS
SAVINGS
SAVIOR
SAVIORESS
SAVIOUR
SAVIOURESS
SAVOLA
SAVOR
SAVORED
SAVORER
SAVORILY
SAVORINESS
SAVORING
SAVORLESS
SAVORLY
SAVOROUS
SAVORY
SAVOUR
SAVOURIER
SAVOURIEST
SAVOURY
SAVOY
SAVOYED
SAVOYING
SAVSSAT
SAVVIED
SAVVY
SAVVYING
SAW
SAWAH
SAWALI
SAWBACK
SAWBELLY
SAWBILL
SAWBONES
SAWBUCK
SAWBWA
SAWDER
SAWDUST
SAWDUSTISH
SAWDUSTY
SAWED
SAWER
SAWFISH
SAWFISHES
SAWFLIES
SAWFLOM
SAWFLY
SAWHORSE
SAWING
SAWINGS
SAWLIKE
SAWLOG
SAWLSHOT
SAWMAN
SAWMILL
SAWMONT
SAWN
SAWNEB
SAWNEY
SAWNIE
SAWNY
SAWSETTER
SAWSMITH
SAWT
SAWTOOTH
SAWWAY
SAWWORT
SAWYER
SAX
SAXATILE
SAXAUL
SAXBOARD
SAXCORNET
SAXHORN
SAXICOLE
SAXICOLINE
SAXICOLOUS
SAXIFRAGANT
SAXIFRAGOUS
SAXIFRAX
SAXIGENOUS
SAXON
SAXONITE
SAXOPHONE
SAXOPHONIC
SAXOPHONIST
SAXOTROMBA
SAXTUBA
SAY
SAYA
SAYER
SAYETTE
SAYID
SAYING
SAYINGS
SAYNAY
SAYNETE
SAYON
SAYONARA
SAYYID
SAZEN
SAZERAC
SBIRRO
SCAB
SCABBADO
SCABBARD
SCABBED
SCABBEDNESS
SCABBERY
SCABBIER
SCABBIEST
SCABBILY
SCABBINESS
SCABBING
SCABBLE
SCABBLED
SCABBLER
SCABBLING
SCABBY
SCABELLUM
SCABERULOUS
SCABETIC
SCABIA
SCABIES
SCABIETIC
SCABINE
SCABINUS
SCABIOSA
SCABIOSITY
SCABIOUS
SCABISH
SCABLAND
SCABRATE
SCABRESCENT
SCABRID
SCABRIDITY
SCABRIDULOUS
SCABRIN
SCABRITIES
SCABROCK
SCABROUS
SCABROUSLY
SCABROUSNESS
SCABWORT
SCACCHIC
SCAD
SCADDLE
SCADS
SCAENA
SCAFF
SCAFFER
SCAFFERY
SCAFFIE
SCAFFLE
SCAFFOLD
SCAFFOLDAGE
SCAFFOLDED
SCAFFOLDER
SCAFFOLDING
SCAFFY
SCAGLIA
SCAGLIOLA
SCAGLIOLIST
SCAIFE
SCALA
SCALABLE
SCALADE
SCALADO
SCALAE
SCALAGE
SCALAR
SCALARE
SCALARIFORM
SCALARWISE
SCALARY
SCALAWAG
SCALAWAGGERY
SCALAWAGGY
SCALD
SCALDBERRY
SCALDED
SCALDER
SCALDFISH
SCALDIC
SCALDING
SCALDINI
SCALDINO
SCALDWEED
SCALDY
SCALE
SCALEBACK
SCALEBARK
SCALEBOARD
SCALED
SCALEDRAKE
SCALEFISH
SCALEFUL
SCALEMAN
SCALEMEN
SCALENE
SCALENON
SCALENOUS
SCALENUM
SCALENUS
SCALEPAN
SCALER
SCALES
SCALESMITH
SCALET
SCALETAIL
SCALEWING
SCALEWORK
SCALFE
SCALIER
SCALIEST
SCALIGER
SCALINESS
SCALING
SCALL
SCALLAGE
SCALLAWAG
SCALLED
SCALLION
SCALLOM
SCALLOP
SCALLOPED
SCALLOPER
SCALLOPING
SCALLYWAG
SCALMA
SCALOPPINE
SCALP
SCALPED
SCALPEEN
SCALPEL
SCALPELLAR
SCALPELLIC
SCALPELLUM
SCALPER
SCALPING
SCALPLESS
SCALPRA
SCALPRIFORM
SCALPRUM
SCALPTURE
SCALY
SCAM
SCAMBLE
SCAMBLED
SCAMBLER
SCAMBLING
SCAMILLUS
SCAMMEL

SCAMMONIATE
SCAMMONY
SCAMP
SCAMPAVIA
SCAMPER
SCAMPERED
SCAMPERER
SCAMPERING
SCAMPI
SCAMPING
SCAMPISH
SCAMPISHLY
SCAMPISHNESS
SCAN
SCANCE
SCANDAL
SCANDALED
SCANDALING
SCANDALIZATION
SCANDALIZE
SCANDALIZED
SCANDALIZING
SCANDALLED
SCANDALLING
SCANDALMONGER
SCANDALOUS
SCANDALOUSLY
SCANDALOUSNESS
SCANDAROON
SCANDENT
SCANDIA
SCANDIC
SCANDICUS
SCANDIUM
SCANMAG
SCANNABLE
SCANNED
SCANNER
SCANNING
SCANNINGLY
SCANSION
SCANSIONIST
SCANSORIAL
SCANSORIOUS
SCANSORY
SCANT
SCANTED
SCANTER
SCANTEST
SCANTIER
SCANTIES
SCANTIEST
SCANTILY
SCANTINESS
SCANTING
SCANTITY
SCANTLE
SCANTLET
SCANTLING
SCANTLINGED
SCANTLY
SCANTNESS
SCANTY
SCAPE
SCAPEGOAT
SCAPEGRACE
SCAPEL
SCAPELESS
SCAPETHRIFT
SCAPHA
SCAPHE
SCAPHION
SCAPHISM
SCAPHITE
SCAPHITOID
SCAPHOCERITE
SCAPHOCERITIC
SCAPHOID
SCAPHOLUNAR
SCAPHOPOD
SCAPHOPODOUS
SCAPI
SCAPIFORM
SCAPIGEROUS
SCAPOID
SCAPOLITE
SCAPOSE
SCAPPLE
SCAPPLER
SCAPULA
SCAPULAR
SCAPULARE
SCAPULARY
SCAPULATED
SCAPULET
SCAPULETTE
SCAPULIMANCY
SCAPULOPEXY
SCAPUS
SCAR
SCARAB
SCARABAEAN
SCARABAEI
SCARABAEID
SCARABAEOID
SCARABAEUS
SCARABAEUSES
SCARABEE
SCARABOID
SCARCE
SCARCELINS
SCARCELY
SCARCEMENT
SCARCEN
SCARCENESS
SCARCER
SCARCEST
SCARCITY
SCARCY
SCARE
SCAREBABE
SCAREBUG
SCARECROW
SCARECROWISH
SCARECROWY
SCARED
SCAREFUL
SCAREHEAD
SCAREMONGER
SCAREMONGERING
SCARER
SCAREY
SCARF
SCARFE
SCARFED
SCARFER
SCARFING
SCARFPIN
SCARFS
SCARFSKIN
SCARID
SCARIER
SCARIEST
SCARIFICATION
SCARIFICATOR
SCARIFIED
SCARIFIER
SCARIFY
SCARIFYING
SCARING
SCARINGLY
SCARIOLE
SCARIOSE
SCARIOUS
SCARLATINA
SCARLATINAL
SCARLATINOID
SCARLET
SCARLETBERRY
SCARLETSEED
SCARLETY
SCARN
SCAROID
SCAROLA
SCARP
SCARPA
SCARPE
SCARPED
SCARPER
SCARPETTI
SCARPH
SCARPINES
SCARPING
SCARPLET
SCARR
SCARRED
SCARRER
SCARRING
SCARROW
SCARRY
SCARS
SCART
SCARTH
SCARUS
SCARVED
SCARVES
SCARY
SCAT
SCATBACK
SCATCH
SCATH
SCATHE
SCATHED
SCATHEFUL
SCATHELESS
SCATHELESSLY
SCATHFUL
SCATHING
SCATHINGLY
SCATHY
SCATLAND
SCATOLOGIA
SCATOLOGIC
SCATOLOGICAL
SCATOLOGIST
SCATOLOGY
SCATOPHAGOUS
SCATOPHAGY
SCATOSCOPY
SCATT
SCATTED
SCATTER
SCATTERATION
SCATTERAWAY
SCATTERBRAIN
SCATTERBRAINED
SCATTERBRAINS
SCATTERED
SCATTERER
SCATTERGOOD
SCATTERING
SCATTERINGLY
SCATTERLING
SCATTERMOUCH
SCATTERY
SCATTIER
SCATTIEST
SCATTING
SCATTY
SCATULA
SCATURIENT
SCAUD
SCAUM
SCAUP
SCAUPER
SCAUPS
SCAUR
SCAURIE
SCAUT
SCAVAGE
SCAVAGER
SCAVAGERY
SCAVENAGE
SCAVENGE
SCAVENGED
SCAVENGER
SCAVENGERY
SCAVENGING
SCAW
SCAWTITE
SCAZON
SCAZONTIC
SCEAR
SCEAT
SCEGGER
SCELERAT
SCELOTYRBE
SCENA
SCENARIO
SCENARIOS
SCENARIST
SCENARIZE
SCENARIZING
SCENARY
SCEND
SCENE
SCENECRAFT
SCENERY
SCENES
SCENESHIFTER
SCENEWRIGHT
SCENIC
SCENICAL
SCENIST
SCENITE
SCENOGRAPH
SCENOGRAPHER
SCENOGRAPHIC
SCENOGRAPHY
SCENSION
SCENT
SCENTED
SCENTER
SCENTFUL
SCENTING
SCENTLESS
SCENTWOOD
SCEPSIS
SCEPTER
SCEPTERDOM
SCEPTERED
SCEPTERING
SCEPTERLESS
SCEPTIC
SCEPTICAL
SCEPTICISM
SCEPTICIZE
SCEPTICIZED
SCEPTICIZING
SCEPTRAL
SCEPTRE
SCEPTRED
SCEPTREDOM
SCEPTRELESS
SCEPTRING
SCEPTROSOPHY
SCEPTRY
SCERNE
SCETE
SCEUOPHYLAX
SCEWING
SCHADCHAN
SCHAIRERITE
SCHAL
SCHALMEI
SCHALMEY
SCHALSTEIN
SCHANZ
SCHAPPE
SCHAPPING
SCHAPSKA
SCHARF
SCHATCHEN
SCHEAT
SCHEDIASM
SCHEDULAR
SCHEDULATE
SCHEDULE
SCHEDULED
SCHEDULING
SCHEDULIZE
SCHEELIN
SCHEELITE
SCHEFFEL
SCHEFFERITE
SCHEL
SCHELLING
SCHELLY
SCHELM
SCHELTOPUSIK
SCHEMA
SCHEMATA
SCHEMATIC
SCHEMATICAL
SCHEMATICALLY
SCHEMATISM
SCHEMATIST
SCHEMATIZE
SCHEMATOGRAM
SCHEMATOGRAPH
SCHEMATONICS
SCHEME
SCHEMED
SCHEMER
SCHEMERY
SCHEMING
SCHEMIST
SCHEMOZZLE
SCHEMY
SCHENE
SCHEPEL
SCHEPEN
SCHERM
SCHERZANDO
SCHERZI
SCHERZO
SCHERZOS
SCHESIS
SCHIAVONE
SCHIFFLI
SCHIH
SCHILLER
SCHILLERFELS
SCHILLERIZE
SCHILLERIZED
SCHILLERIZING
SCHILLING
SCHILLU
SCHIMMEL
SCHIPPERKE
SCHISM
SCHISMA
SCHISMATIC
SCHISMATICAL
SCHISMATICALLY

SCHISMATISM
SCHISMATIST
SCHISMATIZE
SCHISMATIZED
SCHISMATIZING
SCHISMIC
SCHIST
SCHISTACEOUS
SCHISTIC
SCHISTOCYTE
SCHISTOID
SCHISTOSCOPE
SCHISTOSE
SCHISTOSITY
SCHISTOSOME
SCHISTOUS
SCHIZAXON
SCHIZOCARP
SCHIZOCARPIC
SCHIZOCHROAL
SCHIZOCOELE
SCHIZODINIC
SCHIZOGAMY
SCHIZOGENESIS
SCHIZOGENETIC
SCHIZOGENIC
SCHIZOGENOUS
SCHIZOGNATH
SCHIZOGONIC
SCHIZOGONY
SCHIZOID
SCHIZOIDISM
SCHIZOLITE
SCHIZOMYCETE
SCHIZOMYCETES
SCHIZONT
SCHIZOPELMOUS
SCHIZOPHASIA
SCHIZOPHRENE
SCHIZOPHRENIA
SCHIZOPHYTE
SCHIZOPOD
SCHIZOPODAL
SCHIZOPODOUS
SCHIZORHINAL
SCHIZOSPORE
SCHIZOSTELE
SCHIZOSTELIC
SCHIZOSTELY
SCHIZOTHECAL
SCHIZOTHYME
SCHIZOTHYMIA
SCHIZOTHYMIC
SCHIZOTRICHIA
SCHIZTIC
SCHIZZO
SCHLEMIEL
SCHLENTER
SCHLEPP
SCHLIEREN
SCHLOCK
SCHLOOP
SCHMALTZ
SCHMALZ
SCHMALZY
SCHMEISS
SCHMELZ
SCHMO
SCHMOOSE
SCHMOOZE
SCHMUCK
SCHNAPPER
SCHNAPPS
SCHNAUZER
SCHNEIDER
SCHNELL
SCHNITZ
SCHNITZEL
SCHNOOK
SCHNORRER
SCHNOZZLE
SCHO
SCHOCHE
SCHOENANTH
SCHOENOBATIC
SCHOKKER
SCHOLA
SCHOLAPTITUDE
SCHOLAR
SCHOLARCH
SCHOLARIAN
SCHOLARISM
SCHOLARLIKE
SCHOLARLY
SCHOLARS
SCHOLARSHIP
SCHOLASM
SCHOLASTIC
SCHOLASTICAL
SCHOLASTICALLY
SCHOLASTICATE
SCHOLASTICISM
SCHOLASTICLY
SCHOLASTICUS
SCHOLIA
SCHOLIAST
SCHOLIASTIC
SCHOLION
SCHOLIUM
SCHOLIUMS
SCHONE
SCHONFELSITE
SCHOOL
SCHOOLABLE
SCHOOLAGE
SCHOOLBOOK
SCHOOLBOOKISH
SCHOOLBOY
SCHOOLBOYDOM
SCHOOLBOYISH
SCHOOLBOYISHLY
SCHOOLBOYISM
SCHOOLCRAFT
SCHOOLDAME
SCHOOLED
SCHOOLER
SCHOOLERY
SCHOOLFELLOW
SCHOOLGIRL
SCHOOLGIRLHOOD
SCHOOLGIRLISH
SCHOOLGIRLISHLY
SCHOOLGIRLISM
SCHOOLGIRLY
SCHOOLHOUSE
SCHOOLING
SCHOOLINGLY
SCHOOLISH
SCHOOLKEEPER
SCHOOLMAN
SCHOOLMARM
SCHOOLMASTER
SCHOOLMASTERING
SCHOOLMASTERISM
SCHOOLMASTERLY
SCHOOLMASTERY
SCHOOLMATE
SCHOOLMEN
SCHOOLMISTRESS
SCHOOLMISTRESSY
SCHOOLROOM
SCHOOLTEACHER
SCHOOLTIME
SCHOOLWARD
SCHOOLWARDS
SCHOOLWORK
SCHOOLYARD
SCHOON
SCHOONER
SCHOPPEN
SCHORL
SCHORLACEOUS
SCHORLOMITE
SCHORLOUS
SCHORLY
SCHOTTISCHE
SCHOUT
SCHOUW
SCHRADAN
SCHREINER
SCHRIK
SCHROTHER
SCHRUND
SCHTICK
SCHUH
SCHUIT
SCHUL
SCHULE
SCHULTENITE
SCHUNGITE
SCHUSS
SCHUYT
SCHWA
SCHWABACHER
SCHWANPAN
SCHWARZ
SCHYL
SCIAENID
SCIAENIFORM
SCIAENOID
SCIAGRAPH
SCIAGRAPHED
SCIAGRAPHIC
SCIAGRAPHING
SCIALYTIC
SCIAMACHIES
SCIAMACHY
SCIAMETRY
SCIAPOD
SCIAPODOUS
SCIARID
SCIASCOPE
SCIASCOPY
SCIATH
SCIATHERIC
SCIATHERICAL
SCIATIC
SCIATICA
SCIATICAL
SCIATICALLY
SCIATICKY
SCIBILE
SCIENCE
SCIENCED
SCIENT
SCIENTER
SCIENTIA
SCIENTIAL
SCIENTIARUM
SCIENTIFIC
SCIENTIFICAL
SCIENTIFICALLY
SCIENTISM
SCIENTIST
SCIENTISTIC
SCIENTIZE
SCIENTOLISM
SCILICET
SCILLAIN
SCILLIPICRIN
SCILLITIN
SCILLITINE
SCILLITOXIN
SCIMETAR
SCIMITAR
SCIMITARED
SCIMITARPOD
SCIMITER
SCIMITERED
SCIMITERPOD
SCINCID
SCINCIDOID
SCINCIFORM
SCINCOID
SCINCOIDIAN
SCIND
SCINIPH
SCINK
SCINTIL
SCINTILLA
SCINTILLANT
SCINTILLANTLY
SCINTILLATE
SCINTILLATED
SCINTILLATING
SCINTILLATINGLY
SCINTILLATION
SCINTILLATOR
SCINTILLESCENT
SCINTILLOMETER
SCINTILLOSCOPE
SCINTILLOSE
SCINTILLOUS
SCINTILLOUSLY
SCINTLE
SCINTLED
SCINTLER
SCINTLING
SCIOLISM
SCIOLIST
SCIOLISTIC
SCIOLOUS
SCIOLTO
SCIOMACHY
SCIOMANCY
SCION
SCIOPHILOUS
SCIOPHYTE
SCIOPTIC
SCIOPTICON
SCIOPTICS
SCIOPTRIC
SCIOSOPHIST
SCIOSOPHY
SCIOTHEISM
SCIOUS
SCIRENGA
SCIRRHI
SCIRRHOID
SCIRRHOSIS
SCIRRHOSITIES
SCIRRHOSITY
SCIRRHOUS
SCIRRHUS
SCIRRHUSES
SCIRTOPOD
SCIRTOPODOUS
SCISCITATION
SCISSEL
SCISSIBLE
SCISSIL
SCISSILE
SCISSION
SCISSOR
SCISSORBILL
SCISSORBIRD
SCISSORED
SCISSORER
SCISSORIA
SCISSORING
SCISSORIUM
SCISSORS
SCISSORTAIL
SCISSURA
SCISSURE
SCITUATE
SCIURID
SCIURINE
SCIUROID
SCLAFF
SCLAFFED
SCLAFFER
SCLAFFERT
SCLAFFING
SCLAT
SCLATCH
SCLAW
SCLERA
SCLERAL
SCLERANTH
SCLERE
SCLEREDEMA
SCLEREID
SCLEREMA
SCLERENCHYMA
SCLERENCHYME
SCLERERYTHRIN
SCLERETINITE
SCLERIASIS
SCLERIFY
SCLERITE
SCLERITIC
SCLERITIS
SCLERIZED
SCLEROBASE
SCLEROBASIC
SCLEROBLAST
SCLEROBLASTIC
SCLEROCAULY
SCLERODERM
SCLERODERMA
SCLERODERMIA
SCLERODERMIC
SCLERODERMITE
SCLEROGEN
SCLEROGENIC
SCLEROGENOUS
SCLEROID
SCLEROMA
SCLEROMATA
SCLEROMERE
SCLEROMETER
SCLERONYCHIA
SCLERONYXIS
SCLEROPHYLL
SCLEROPHYLLY
SCLEROPROTEIN
SCLEROSAL
SCLEROSE
SCLEROSED
SCLEROSEPTUM
SCLEROSES
SCLEROSIS
SCLEROTAL
SCLEROTE
SCLEROTIA
SCLEROTIAL
SCLEROTIC
SCLEROTICA
SCLEROTICAL
SCLEROTINIAL
SCLEROTIOID
SCLEROTITIC
SCLEROTITIS
SCLEROTIUM

SCLEROTIZED
SCLEROTOID
SCLEROTOME
SCLEROTOMIC
SCLEROTOMIES
SCLEROTOMY
SCLEROUS
SCLIFF
SCLIMB
SCLUM
SCLY
SCOAD
SCOB
SCOBBY
SCOBE
SCOBICULAR
SCOBIFORM
SCOBS
SCODGY
SCOFF
SCOFFED
SCOFFER
SCOFFERY
SCOFFING
SCOFFLAW
SCOG
SCOGGAN
SCOGGER
SCOGGIN
SCOGIE
SCOKE
SCOLD
SCOLDED
SCOLDENORE
SCOLDER
SCOLDING
SCOLDINGLY
SCOLECES
SCOLECIASIS
SCOLECID
SCOLECIFORM
SCOLECITE
SCOLECOID
SCOLERYNG
SCOLEX
SCOLEY
SCOLIA
SCOLICES
SCOLIID
SCOLIOGRAPTIC
SCOLIOMETER
SCOLION
SCOLIOSIS
SCOLIOTIC
SCOLIOTONE
SCOLITE
SCOLLOP
SCOLLOPER
SCOLOC
SCOLOG
SCOLOPENDRID
SCOLOPHORE
SCOLYTID
SCOLYTOID
SCOLYTUS
SCOMBRID
SCOMBRIFORM
SCOMBRINE
SCOMBROID
SCOMBRONE
SCOMFIT
SCOMM
SCON
SCONCE
SCONCED
SCONCER
SCONCHEON
SCONCIBLE
SCONCING
SCONE
SCOOCH
SCOON
SCOOP
SCOOPED
SCOOPER
SCOOPFUL
SCOOPING
SCOOR
SCOOT
SCOOTER
SCOOTERS
SCOOTS
SCOP
SCOPA
SCOPARIN
SCOPARIUS
SCOPATE
SCOPE
SCOPELISM
SCOPHONY
SCOPIC
SCOPINE
SCOPIOUS
SCOPIPED
SCOPOLA
SCOPOLAMIN
SCOPOLAMINE
SCOPOLEINE
SCOPOLETIN
SCOPOLINE
SCOPONE
SCOPPERIL
SCOPS
SCOPTICAL
SCOPULA
SCOPULARIAN
SCOPULATE
SCOPULIPED
SCOPULITE
SCORBUCH
SCORBUTE
SCORBUTIC
SCORBUTICAL
SCORBUTIZE
SCORBUTUS
SCORCE
SCORCH
SCORCHED
SCORCHER
SCORCHING
SCORCHINGLY
SCORCHINGNESS
SCORDATO
SCORDATURA
SCORDIUM
SCORE
SCORED
SCOREKEEPER
SCORELESS
SCORER
SCORES
SCORIA
SCORIAC
SCORIACEOUS
SCORIAE
SCORIFICATION
SCORIFIED
SCORIFIER
SCORIFORM
SCORIFY
SCORIFYING
SCORING
SCORIOUS
SCORKLE
SCORN
SCORNED
SCORNER
SCORNFUL
SCORNFULLY
SCORNFULNESS
SCORNING
SCORNY
SCORODITE
SCORPAENID
SCORPAENOID
SCORPENE
SCORPER
SCORPIOID
SCORPIOIDAL
SCORPION
SCORPIONIC
SCORPIONID
SCORPIONWORT
SCORSE
SCORSER
SCORTATION
SCORTATORY
SCORZA
SCOT
SCOTAL
SCOTALE
SCOTCH
SCOTCHED
SCOTCHER
SCOTCHING
SCOTCHMAN
SCOTE
SCOTER
SCOTERS
SCOTIA
SCOTINO
SCOTODINIA
SCOTOGRAM
SCOTOGRAPH
SCOTOGRAPHIC
SCOTOGRAPHY
SCOTOMA
SCOTOMATOUS
SCOTOMIA
SCOTOMIC
SCOTOMY
SCOTOPHOBIA
SCOTOPIA
SCOTOPIC
SCOTOSCOPE
SCOTOSIS
SCOTT
SCOUCH
SCOUNDREL
SCOUNDRELISH
SCOUNDRELLY
SCOUP
SCOUR
SCOURAGE
SCOURED
SCOURER
SCOURFISH
SCOURFISHES
SCOURGE
SCOURGED
SCOURGER
SCOURGING
SCOURGINGLY
SCOURING
SCOURINGS
SCOURWAY
SCOURWEED
SCOURWORT
SCOURY
SCOUSE
SCOUT
SCOUTCRAFT
SCOUTED
SCOUTER
SCOUTH
SCOUTHER
SCOUTHOOD
SCOUTING
SCOUTMASTER
SCOUTS
SCOUTWATCH
SCOVE
SCOVEL
SCOVY
SCOW
SCOWBANK
SCOWBANKER
SCOWDER
SCOWL
SCOWLED
SCOWLER
SCOWLING
SCOWLINGLY
SCOWMAN
SCOWMEN
SCOWTHER
SCRAB
SCRABBLE
SCRABBLED
SCRABBLER
SCRABBLING
SCRABBLY
SCRABE
SCRABER
SCRAE
SCRAFFLE
SCRAG
SCRAGGED
SCRAGGEDLY
SCRAGGEDNESS
SCRAGGER
SCRAGGIER
SCRAGGIEST
SCRAGGINESS
SCRAGGING
SCRAGGLE
SCRAGGLED
SCRAGGLING
SCRAGGLY
SCRAGGY
SCRAICH
SCRAIGH
SCRAILY
SCRAM
SCRAMASAX
SCRAMBLE
SCRAMBLED
SCRAMBLER
SCRAMBLING
SCRAMBLINGLY
SCRAMBLY
SCRAMMED
SCRAMMING
SCRAMPUM
SCRAN
SCRANCH
SCRANK
SCRANKY
SCRANNEL
SCRANNIER
SCRANNIEST
SCRANNING
SCRANNY
SCRAP
SCRAPABLE
SCRAPBOOK
SCRAPE
SCRAPED
SCRAPEPENNY
SCRAPER
SCRAPIE
SCRAPING
SCRAPINGLY
SCRAPMAN
SCRAPMONGER
SCRAPPAGE
SCRAPPER
SCRAPPET
SCRAPPIER
SCRAPPIEST
SCRAPPILY
SCRAPPINESS
SCRAPPLE
SCRAPPY
SCRAPS
SCRAPY
SCRAT
SCRATCH
SCRATCHBOARD
SCRATCHBRUSH
SCRATCHCARDING
SCRATCHCAT
SCRATCHED
SCRATCHER
SCRATCHES
SCRATCHIER
SCRATCHIEST
SCRATCHING
SCRATCHWEED
SCRATCHY
SCRATTER
SCRATTLE
SCRATTLING
SCRAUCHLE
SCRAW
SCRAWK
SCRAWL
SCRAWLED
SCRAWLER
SCRAWLIER
SCRAWLIEST
SCRAWLINESS
SCRAWLING
SCRAWLY
SCRAWM
SCRAWNIER
SCRAWNIEST
SCRAWNILY
SCRAWNINESS
SCRAWNY
SCRAY
SCRAYE
SCRAZE
SCREAK
SCREAKED
SCREAKING
SCREAKY
SCREAM
SCREAMED
SCREAMER
SCREAMINESS
SCREAMING
SCREAMINGLY
SCREAMY
SCREAR
SCREE
SCREECH
SCREECHBIRD
SCREECHED
SCREECHER
SCREECHIER
SCREECHIEST
SCREECHING
SCREECHY
SCREED

SCREEK
SCREEL
SCREEMAN
SCREEN
SCREENABLE
SCREENAGE
SCREENED
SCREENER
SCREENING
SCREENINGS
SCREENMAN
SCREENO
SCREENPLAY
SCREENSMAN
SCREENY
SCREEVE
SCREEVED
SCREEVER
SCREEVING
SCREW
SCREWBALL
SCREWBARREL
SCREWDRIVER
SCREWED
SCREWER
SCREWING
SCREWLESS
SCREWMAN
SCREWPILE
SCREWPOD
SCREWSMAN
SCREWSTOCK
SCREWWORM
SCREWY
SCRIB
SCRIBABLE
SCRIBACIOUS
SCRIBAL
SCRIBATIOUS
SCRIBBET
SCRIBBLAGE
SCRIBBLATIVE
SCRIBBLATORY
SCRIBBLE
SCRIBBLED
SCRIBBLEMENT
SCRIBBLER
SCRIBBLING
SCRIBBLINGLY
SCRIBBLY
SCRIBE
SCRIBED
SCRIBER
SCRIBING
SCRIBISM
SCRIDE
SCRIEVE
SCRIEVED
SCRIEVER
SCRIEVING
SCRIGGLE
SCRIGGLY
SCRIKE
SCRIM
SCRIME
SCRIMER
SCRIMMAGE
SCRIMMAGED
SCRIMMAGER
SCRIMMAGING
SCRIMP
SCRIMPED
SCRIMPER
SCRIMPIER
SCRIMPIEST
SCRIMPINESS
SCRIMPING
SCRIMPIT
SCRIMPTION
SCRIMPY
SCRIMSHANK
SCRIMSHAW
SCRIMY
SCRIN
SCRINCH
SCRINE
SCRINGE
SCRINIARY
SCRIP
SCRIPEE
SCRIPPAGE
SCRIPSIT
SCRIPT
SCRIPTER
SCRIPTION
SCRIPTITIOUS
SCRIPTITORY
SCRIPTIVE
SCRIPTOR
SCRIPTORIAL
SCRIPTORIUM
SCRIPTORY
SCRIPTURAL
SCRIPTURALLY
SCRIPTURE
SCRIPTURIENT
SCRIPTWRITER
SCRIPULUM
SCRIT
SCRITCH
SCRITE
SCRITHE
SCRIVAN
SCRIVANO
SCRIVE
SCRIVED
SCRIVELLO
SCRIVELLOES
SCRIVELLOS
SCRIVEN
SCRIVENER
SCRIVENERY
SCRIVENING
SCRIVER
SCRIVING
SCROB
SCROBBLE
SCROBE
SCROBICULA
SCROBICULAR
SCROBICULATE
SCROBICULE
SCROBICULUS
SCROBIS
SCROD
SCRODGILL
SCROFF
SCROFULA
SCROFULAROOT
SCROFULAWEED
SCROFULISM
SCROFULITIC
SCROFULODERM
SCROFULOSIS
SCROFULOUS
SCROFULOUSLY
SCROG
SCROGGED
SCROGGIE
SCROGGY
SCROGIE
SCROGS
SCROINOCH
SCROINOGH
SCROLAR
SCROLL
SCROLLED
SCROLLERY
SCROLLHEAD
SCROLLING
SCROLLWORK
SCROLLY
SCRONACH
SCROO
SCROOCH
SCROOP
SCROTAL
SCROTIFORM
SCROTUM
SCROUGE
SCROUGER
SCROUNGE
SCROUNGED
SCROUNGING
SCROUT
SCROW
SCROYLE
SCRUB
SCRUBBED
SCRUBBER
SCRUBBING
SCRUBBIRD
SCRUBBLY
SCRUBBOARD
SCRUBBY
SCRUBGRASS
SCRUBLAND
SCRUFF
SCRUFFLE
SCRUFFMAN
SCRUFFY
SCRUM
SCRUMMAGE
SCRUMMAGED
SCRUMMAGER
SCRUMMAGING
SCRUMP
SCRUMPLE
SCRUMPTIOUS
SCRUMPTIOUSLY
SCRUNCH
SCRUNCHY
SCRUNGE
SCRUNT
SCRUNTY
SCRUPLE
SCRUPLED
SCRUPLER
SCRUPLING
SCRUPULAR
SCRUPULIST
SCRUPULOSITY
SCRUPULOUS
SCRUPULOUSLY
SCRUSH
SCRUTABILITY
SCRUTABLE
SCRUTATE
SCRUTATION
SCRUTATOR
SCRUTATORY
SCRUTINANT
SCRUTINATE
SCRUTINEER
SCRUTINIZE
SCRUTINIZED
SCRUTINIZER
SCRUTINIZING
SCRUTINOUS
SCRUTINOUSLY
SCRUTINY
SCRUTO
SCRUTOIRE
SCRUZE
SCRY
SCRYER
SCRYING
SCUBA
SCUD
SCUDDALER
SCUDDAWN
SCUDDED
SCUDDER
SCUDDICK
SCUDDING
SCUDDLE
SCUDDY
SCUDI
SCUDO
SCUDS
SCUFE
SCUFF
SCUFFED
SCUFFER
SCUFFING
SCUFFLE
SCUFFLED
SCUFFLER
SCUFFLING
SCUFFY
SCUFT
SCUFTER
SCUG
SCUGGERY
SCULCH
SCULDUDDERIES
SCULDUDDERY
SCULL
SCULLED
SCULLER
SCULLERIES
SCULLERY
SCULLING
SCULLION
SCULLOG
SCULLOGUE
SCULLS
SCULP
SCULPIN
SCULPINS
SCULPSIT
SCULPT
SCULPTILE
SCULPTITORY
SCULPTOGRAPH
SCULPTOR
SCULPTRESS
SCULPTURAL
SCULPTURE
SCULPTURED
SCULPTURER
SCULPTURESQUE
SCULPTURING
SCULT
SCUM
SCUMBER
SCUMBLE
SCUMBLED
SCUMBLING
SCUMBOARD
SCUMFISH
SCUMMED
SCUMMER
SCUMMIER
SCUMMIEST
SCUMMING
SCUMMY
SCUN
SCUNDER
SCUNGILI
SCUNGILLI
SCUNNER
SCUP
SCUPPAUG
SCUPPER
SCUPPERNONG
SCUPPERS
SCUPPET
SCUPPIT
SCUPPLER
SCUR
SCURDY
SCURF
SCURFER
SCURFIER
SCURFIEST
SCURFINESS
SCURFY
SCURLING
SCURRIED
SCURRIER
SCURRIL
SCURRILE
SCURRILITY
SCURRILOUS
SCURRILOUSLY
SCURRY
SCURRYING
SCURVIED
SCURVILY
SCURVINESS
SCURVISH
SCURVY
SCUSE
SCUSIN
SCUT
SCUTA
SCUTAGE
SCUTAL
SCUTATE
SCUTATED
SCUTATIFORM
SCUTATION
SCUTCH
SCUTCHEON
SCUTCHER
SCUTCHING
SCUTE
SCUTELLA
SCUTELLAE
SCUTELLAR
SCUTELLARIN
SCUTELLATE
SCUTELLATED
SCUTELLATION
SCUTELLIFORM
SCUTELLUM
SCUTIFER
SCUTIFEROUS
SCUTIFORM
SCUTIGER
SCUTIGERAL
SCUTIGEROUS
SCUTIPED
SCUTTER
SCUTTLE
SCUTTLEBUTT
SCUTTLED
SCUTTLEMAN
SCUTTLER
SCUTTLING
SCUTTOCK
SCUTTY
SCUTULA
SCUTULAR

SCUTULATE
SCUTULUM
SCUTUM
SCYBALUM
SCYE
SCYELITE
SCYLD
SCYLLITE
SCYLLITOL
SCYPHA
SCYPHATE
SCYPHIFORM
SCYPHISTOMA
SCYPHOPHORE
SCYPHOSE
SCYPHOZOAN
SCYPHULA
SCYPHULUS
SCYPHUS
SCYTALE
SCYTHE
SCYTHED
SCYTHEMAN
SCYTHESMITH
SCYTHESTONE
SCYTHING
SDAIN
SDEIGN
SDRUCCIOLA
SE
SEA
SEABAG
SEABEACH
SEABEARD
SEABED
SEABERRY
SEABIRD
SEABOARD
SEABOOT
SEABORDERER
SEACANNIE
SEACATCH
SEACOAST
SEACONNY
SEACRAFT
SEACRAFTY
SEACROSS
SEACUNNY
SEADOG
SEADROME
SEAFARE
SEAFARER
SEAFARING
SEAFLOOD
SEAFLOWER
SEAFOAM
SEAFOLK
SEAFOOD
SEAFOWL
SEAGIRT
SEAGOER
SEAGOING
SEAH
SEAHOUND
SEAK
SEAL
SEALABLE
SEALCH
SEALED
SEALER
SEALERIES
SEALERY
SEALET
SEALIKE
SEALINE
SEALING
SEALKIE
SEALLESS
SEALS
SEALSKIN
SEALSKINS
SEALWORT
SEAM
SEAMAN
SEAMANITE
SEAMANLIKE
SEAMANLY
SEAMANSHIP
SEAMARK
SEAMBITER
SEAMED
SEAMEN
SEAMER
SEAMIER
SEAMIEST
SEAMINESS
SEAMING
SEAMLESS
SEAMLET
SEAMLIKE
SEAMOST
SEAMOUNT
SEAMREND
SEAMROG
SEAMS
SEAMSTER
SEAMSTRESS
SEAMY
SEANCE
SEAPIECE
SEAPLANE
SEAPOOSE
SEAPORT
SEAPOST
SEAQUAKE
SEAR
SEARCE
SEARCER
SEARCH
SEARCHABLE
SEARCHANT
SEARCHER
SEARCHFUL
SEARCHING
SEARCHINGLY
SEARCHINGNESS
SEARCHLESS
SEARCHLIGHT
SEARED
SEARER
SEARING
SEARY
SEAS
SEASCAPE
SEASCOUTING
SEASHELL
SEASHINE
SEASHORE
SEASICK
SEASICKNESS
SEASIDE
SEASIDER
SEASON
SEASONABLE
SEASONABLY
SEASONAL
SEASONALITY
SEASONALLY
SEASONED
SEASONER
SEASONING
SEAT
SEATANG
SEATED
SEATER
SEATING
SEATRAIN
SEATRON
SEATS
SEATSTONE
SEAVE
SEAVY
SEAWALL
SEAWAN
SEAWARD
SEAWARDLY
SEAWARDS
SEAWARE
SEAWATER
SEAWAY
SEAWEED
SEAWIFE
SEAWORN
SEAWORTHINESS
SEAWORTHY
SEAX
SEBACATE
SEBACEOUS
SEBACIC
SEBAGO
SEBAIT
SEBASTIANITE
SEBAT
SEBEL
SEBESTEN
SEBIC
SEBIFEROUS
SEBIFIC
SEBILLA
SEBKA
SEBKHA
SEBOLITH
SEBORRHAGIA
SEBORRHEA
SEBORRHEAL
SEBORRHOEA
SEBUM
SEBUNDY
SEC
SECABLE
SECALIN
SECALINE
SECALOSE
SECANCY
SECANT
SECANTLY
SECATEUR
SECCHIO
SECCO
SECEDE
SECEDED
SECEDER
SECEDING
SECERN
SECERNED
SECERNING
SECERNMENT
SECESH
SECESHER
SECESS
SECESSION
SECESSIONAL
SECESSIONALIST
SECESSIONISM
SECESSIONIST
SECK
SECLE
SECLUDE
SECLUDED
SECLUDEDLY
SECLUDEDNESS
SECLUDING
SECLUSE
SECLUSION
SECLUSIONIST
SECLUSIVE
SECLUSIVELY
SECODONT
SECOHM
SECOND
SECONDAR
SECONDARILY
SECONDARY
SECONDE
SECONDER
SECONDHAND
SECONDINE
SECONDLY
SECONDO
SECONDS
SECOURS
SECQUE
SECRECY
SECRET
SECRETA
SECRETAGE
SECRETAIRE
SECRETAR
SECRETARIAL
SECRETARIAN
SECRETARIAT
SECRETARIES
SECRETARY
SECRETE
SECRETED
SECRETIN
SECRETING
SECRETION
SECRETIONAL
SECRETIONARY
SECRETITIOUS
SECRETIVE
SECRETIVELY
SECRETIVENESS
SECRETLY
SECRETOR
SECRETORY
SECRETS
SECRETUM
SECT
SECTA
SECTARIAL
SECTARIAN
SECTARIANISM
SECTARIANIZE
SECTARIANIZED
SECTARIANIZING
SECTARIANLY
SECTARIES
SECTARISM
SECTARIST
SECTARY
SECTATOR
SECTILE
SECTILITY
SECTION
SECTIONAL
SECTIONALISM
SECTIONALIST
SECTIONALIZE
SECTIONALIZED
SECTIONALIZING
SECTIONALLY
SECTIONARY
SECTIONIZE
SECTISM
SECTIST
SECTOR
SECTORAL
SECTORIAL
SECTUARY
SECULAR
SECULARISM
SECULARIST
SECULARISTIC
SECULARITIES
SECULARITY
SECULARIZE
SECULARIZED
SECULARIZING
SECULUM
SECUND
SECUNDINE
SECUNDIPARA
SECUNDLY
SECUNDUM
SECURABLE
SECURE
SECURED
SECUREFUL
SECURELY
SECUREMENT
SECURENESS
SECURER
SECURING
SECURITIES
SECURITY
SECUS
SECUTOR
SEDAN
SEDANIER
SEDATE
SEDATELY
SEDATENESS
SEDATION
SEDATIVE
SEDENT
SEDENTARILY
SEDENTARINESS
SEDENTARY
SEDENTATION
SEDERUNT
SEDGE
SEDGELIKE
SEDGY
SEDILE
SEDILIA
SEDILIUM
SEDIMENT
SEDIMENTAL
SEDIMENTARIES
SEDIMENTARY
SEDIMENTATE
SEDIMENTATION
SEDIMENTOUS
SEDIMETRIC
SEDITION
SEDITIONARY
SEDITIONIST
SEDITIOUS
SEDITIOUSLY
SEDITIOUSNESS
SEDJADEH
SEDUCE
SEDUCEABLE
SEDUCED
SEDUCEE
SEDUCEMENT
SEDUCER
SEDUCIBLE
SEDUCING
SEDUCIVE
SEDUCT
SEDUCTION
SEDUCTIONIST

SEDUCTIVE
SEDUCTIVELY
SEDUCTIVENESS
SEDUCTRESS
SEDULITY
SEDULOUS
SEDULOUSLY
SEDULOUSNESS
SEDUM
SEE
SEECATCH
SEECATCHIE
SEECAWK
SEECHELT
SEED
SEEDAGE
SEEDBALL
SEEDBED
SEEDBIRD
SEEDBOX
SEEDCAKE
SEEDCASE
SEEDEATER
SEEDED
SEEDER
SEEDFUL
SEEDGALL
SEEDIER
SEEDIEST
SEEDILY
SEEDINESS
SEEDING
SEEDKIN
SEEDLEAF
SEEDLESS
SEEDLET
SEEDLING
SEEDLINGS
SEEDLIP
SEEDMAN
SEEDNESS
SEEDS
SEEDSMAN
SEEDSMEN
SEEDSTALK
SEEDSTER
SEEDTIME
SEEDY
SEEGE
SEEING
SEEINGLY
SEEINGNESS
SEEK
SEEKER
SEEKING
SEEL
SEELED
SEELFUL
SEELILY
SEELINESS
SEELING
SEELY
SEEM
SEEMABLE
SEEMER
SEEMING
SEEMINGLY
SEEMINGNESS
SEEMLESS
SEEMLIER
SEEMLIEST
SEEMLIHEAD
SEEMLILY
SEEMLINESS
SEEMLY
SEEN
SEENIL
SEEP
SEEPAGE
SEEPED
SEEPWEED
SEEPY
SEER
SEERBAND
SEERESS
SEERFISH
SEERHAND
SEERPAW
SEERSUCKER
SEESAW
SEESAWINESS
SEESEE
SEET
SEETHE
SEETHED
SEETHER
SEETHING
SEETHINGLY
SEEWEE
SEG
SEGA
SEGAR
SEGATHY
SEGE
SEGETAL
SEGG
SEGGE
SEGGED
SEGGIO
SEGGIOLA
SEGGROM
SEGGY
SEGHOL
SEGHOLATE
SEGMENT
SEGMENTAL
SEGMENTALLY
SEGMENTARY
SEGMENTATE
SEGMENTATION
SEGMENTED
SEGMENTS
SEGNI
SEGNO
SEGO
SEGOL
SEGOLATE
SEGOS
SEGOU
SEGRA
SEGREANT
SEGREGABLE
SEGREGATE
SEGREGATED
SEGREGATING
SEGREGATION
SEGREGATIONAL
SEGREGATIONIST
SEGREGATIVE
SEGREGATOR
SEGUE
SEGUENDO
SEGUIDILLA
SEI
SEICENTO
SEICHE
SEID
SEIDEL
SEIF
SEIGNEUR
SEIGNEURESS
SEIGNEURIAL
SEIGNEURY
SEIGNIOR
SEIGNIORAGE
SEIGNIORAL
SEIGNIORALTY
SEIGNIORIES
SEIGNIORY
SEIGNORAGE
SEIGNORAL
SEIGNORIAL
SEIGNORIZE
SEIGNORY
SEIL
SEIMAS
SEIN
SEINE
SEINED
SEINER
SEINING
SEIROSPORE
SEIROSPORIC
SEISE
SEISM
SEISMAL
SEISMATICAL
SEISMETIC
SEISMIC
SEISMICAL
SEISMICALLY
SEISMICITY
SEISMISM
SEISMOGRAM
SEISMOGRAPH
SEISMOGRAPHER
SEISMOGRAPHY
SEISMOLOGIC
SEISMOLOGICAL
SEISMOLOGIST
SEISMOLOGUE
SEISMOLOGY
SEISMOMETER
SEISMOMETRIC
SEISMOMETRY
SEISMOSCOPE
SEISMOTECTONIC
SEISMOTHERAPY
SEISMOTIC
SEISOR
SEIT
SEITH
SEITY
SEIZABLE
SEIZE
SEIZED
SEIZER
SEIZIN
SEIZING
SEIZOR
SEIZURE
SEJANT
SEJEANT
SEJERO
SEJOIN
SEJOINED
SEJOUR
SEJUGATE
SEJUGOUS
SEJUNCT
SEJUNCTION
SEJUNCTIVE
SEJUNCTIVELY
SEJUNCTLY
SEKERE
SEL
SELACHIAN
SELACHOID
SELACHOSTOME
SELADANG
SELAGINELLA
SELAGITE
SELAH
SELAMIN
SELAMLIK
SELBERGITE
SELCOUTH
SELD
SELDEN
SELDOM
SELDOMCY
SELDOMLY
SELDSEEN
SELE
SELECT
SELECTED
SELECTEDLY
SELECTEE
SELECTING
SELECTION
SELECTIONISM
SELECTIONIST
SELECTIVE
SELECTIVITY
SELECTMAN
SELECTMEN
SELECTNESS
SELECTOR
SELENATE
SELENIAN
SELENIATE
SELENIC
SELENIDE
SELENIFEROUS
SELENION
SELENIOUS
SELENITE
SELENITIC
SELENITICAL
SELENIUM
SELENODONT
SELENODONTY
SELENOGRAPH
SELENOGRAPHER
SELENOGRAPHIC
SELENOGRAPHY
SELENOLOGICAL
SELENOLOGIST
SELENOLOGY
SELENOMANCY
SELENOSCOPE
SELENOTROPISM
SELENOTROPY
SELENSILVER
SELENSULPHUR
SELETAR
SELETY
SELEUCIA
SELF
SELFDOM
SELFFUL
SELFHEAL
SELFHOOD
SELFISH
SELFISHLY
SELFISHNESS
SELFISM
SELFIST
SELFLESS
SELFLESSLY
SELFLESSNESS
SELFLIKE
SELFLY
SELFNESS
SELFSAID
SELFSAME
SELFSAMENESS
SELI
SELICTAR
SELIGMANNITE
SELIHOTH
SELING
SELION
SELL
SELLA
SELLABLE
SELLAITE
SELLAR
SELLARY
SELLATE
SELLE
SELLER
SELLING
SELLOUT
SELLY
SELSOVIET
SELT
SELTZER
SELTZOGENE
SELVA
SELVAGE
SELVAGED
SELVAGEE
SELVEDGE
SELVEDGED
SELVES
SELY
SEMANG
SEMANTEME
SEMANTIC
SEMANTICALLY
SEMANTICIST
SEMANTICS
SEMANTOLOGY
SEMANTRON
SEMAPHORE
SEMAPHORIST
SEMAR
SEMARUM
SEMASIOLOGIST
SEMASIOLOGY
SEMATEME
SEMATOGRAPHY
SEMATOLOGY
SEMATROPE
SEMBE
SEMBLABLE
SEMBLABLY
SEMBLANCE
SEMBLANT
SEMBLATIVE
SEMBLE
SEME
SEMEE
SEMEED
SEMEIA
SEMEIOGRAPHY
SEMEIOLOGY
SEMEION
SEMEIOTIC
SEMEIOTICS
SEMELFACTIVE
SEMEME
SEMEN
SEMENCE
SEMENCINAE
SEMENCONTRA
SEMENTERA
SEMESE
SEMESTER
SEMESTRAL
SEMESTRIAL
SEMI
SEMIAN
SEMIANNA

SEMIANTHRACITE
SEMIANTIQUE
SEMIAPE
SEMIAQUATIC
SEMIARCH
SEMIBASTION
SEMIBEAM
SEMIBEJAN
SEMIBREVE
SEMIBULL
SEMIC
SEMICADENCE
SEMICELL
SEMICENTENNIAL
SEMICHA
SEMICHORIC
SEMICHORUS
SEMICIRCLE
SEMICIRCLED
SEMICIRCULAR
SEMICIRQUE
SEMICIVILIZED
SEMICLASSIC
SEMICLIMBING
SEMICOKE
SEMICOLON
SEMICOLUMN
SEMICOMA
SEMICONDUCTOR
SEMICONSCIOUS
SEMICOPE
SEMICUBICAL
SEMICUPE
SEMICURSIVE
SEMICYCLIC
SEMIDARKNESS
SEMIDEPONENT
SEMIDETACHED
SEMIDIAMETER
SEMIDIAPASON
SEMIDIAPENTE
SEMIDINE
SEMIDITONE
SEMIDIURNAL
SEMIDIVINE
SEMIDOLE
SEMIDOME
SEMIDOMED
SEMIDOUBLE
SEMIDRESS
SEMIDRYING
SEMIEDUCATED
SEMIEFFIGY
SEMIELISION
SEMIFIGURE
SEMIFINAL
SEMIFINALIST
SEMIFINISHED
SEMIFLEXIBLE
SEMIFLORET
SEMIFLOSCULE
SEMIFLUID
SEMIFLUIDIC
SEMIFORM
SEMIFORMAL
SEMIFRATER
SEMIFY
SEMIGIRDER
SEMIGLOSS
SEMIHIATUS
SEMIHORAL
SEMIJUBILEE
SEMIKAH
SEMILIQUID
SEMILOCULAR
SEMILOR
SEMILUNAR
SEMILUNATE
SEMILUNE
SEMIMACHINE
SEMIMEMBER
SEMIMETAL
SEMIMETALLIC
SEMIMINIM
SEMIMONTHLY
SEMIMUTE
SEMINAL
SEMINALITY
SEMINALLY
SEMINAR
SEMINARIAL
SEMINARIAN
SEMINARIST
SEMINARISTIC
SEMINARIZE
SEMINARY
SEMINASE
SEMINATE
SEMINATED
SEMINATING
SEMINATION
SEMINATIVE
SEMINIFERAL
SEMINIFEROUS
SEMINIFIC
SEMINIFICAL
SEMINIST
SEMINIUM
SEMINIVOROUS
SEMINOMA
SEMINOMAS
SEMINOMATA
SEMINOSE
SEMINULE
SEMINURIA
SEMINVARIANT
SEMIOFFICIAL
SEMIOFFICIALLY
SEMIOGRAPHY
SEMIOLOGIST
SEMIOLOGY
SEMIOPAL
SEMIOPAQUE
SEMIOTIC
SEMIOTICAL
SEMIOTICS
SEMIOVIPAROUS
SEMIPALMATE
SEMIPALMATION
SEMIPED
SEMIPEDAL
SEMIPERMEABLE
SEMIPLUME
SEMIPORCELAIN
SEMIPORTABLE
SEMIPOSTAL
SEMIPRECIOUS
SEMIPRIVATE
SEMIPRO
SEMIPROOF
SEMIPUPA
SEMIQUARTILE
SEMIQUAVER
SEMIQUIETIST
SEMIQUOTE
SEMIREGULAR
SEMIRIGID
SEMIRING
SEMIROTARY
SEMIROTATING
SEMIROUND
SEMIS
SEMISAGITTATE
SEMISERIOUS
SEMISERVILE
SEMISEVERE
SEMISEVERELY
SEMISEXTILE
SEMISHRUB
SEMISHRUBBY
SEMISKILLED
SEMISOFT
SEMISOLEMN
SEMISOLID
SEMISOUN
SEMISPINALIS
SEMISQUARE
SEMISTEEL
SEMISTOCK
SEMISUCCESSFUL
SEMITA
SEMITAL
SEMITANDEM
SEMITANGENT
SEMITAUR
SEMITERTIAN
SEMITONAL
SEMITONE
SEMITONIC
SEMITRAILER
SEMIUNCIAL
SEMIVOCAL
SEMIVOCALIC
SEMIVOWEL
SEMIWEEKLY
SEMIYEARLY
SEMMEL
SEMMET
SEMMIT
SEMOIS
SEMOLA
SEMOLELLA
SEMOLINA
SEMOLOGY
SEMOTED
SEMOULE
SEMPER
SEMPERIDEM
SEMPERVIRENT
SEMPERVIRID
SEMPITERN
SEMPITERNAL
SEMPITERNITY
SEMPITERNIZE
SEMPITERNOUS
SEMPLE
SEMPLICE
SEMPRE
SEMPSTER
SEMPSTRESS
SEMPSTRY
SEMSEM
SEMUL
SEMUNCIA
SEMUNCIAL
SEMY
SEN
SENACHIE
SENAGE
SENAITE
SENAL
SENAM
SENARIAN
SENARIUS
SENARMONTITE
SENARY
SENATE
SENATOR
SENATORIAL
SENATORIAN
SENATORSHIP
SENATORY
SENATRESS
SENATRIX
SENATUS
SENCIO
SENCION
SEND
SENDA
SENDAL
SENDER
SENDING
SENDLE
SENDOFF
SENE
SENECIOID
SENECIONINE
SENECTITUDE
SENECTUDE
SENECTUOUS
SENEGA
SENEGIN
SENESCE
SENESCENCE
SENESCENCY
SENESCENT
SENESCHAL
SENGE
SENGREEN
SENHOR
SENHORA
SENHORITA
SENICIDE
SENILE
SENILISM
SENILITY
SENIOR
SENIORITY
SENIORY
SENIT
SENIUM
SENN
SENNA
SENNE
SENNET
SENNETT
SENNIGHT
SENNIT
SENNITE
SENOCULAR
SENOR
SENORA
SENORES
SENORITA
SENOUFO
SENS
SENSABLE
SENSAL
SENSATE
SENSATED
SENSATING
SENSATION
SENSATIONAL
SENSATIONALISM
SENSATIONALIST
SENSATIONALISTIC
SENSATIONARY
SENSATIONISM
SENSATIONIST
SENSATIONISTIC
SENSATORIAL
SENSATORY
SENSE
SENSED
SENSEFUL
SENSELESS
SENSELESSLY
SENSELESSNESS
SENSES
SENSIBILITIES
SENSIBILITIST
SENSIBILITOUS
SENSIBILITY
SENSIBILIZATION
SENSIBILIZE
SENSIBLE
SENSIBLENESS
SENSIBLY
SENSICAL
SENSIFACIENT
SENSIFIC
SENSIFICATORY
SENSIFICS
SENSIFY
SENSILE
SENSILLA
SENSILLAE
SENSING
SENSION
SENSISM
SENSIST
SENSISTIC
SENSITIVE
SENSITIVELY
SENSITIVENESS
SENSITIVITY
SENSITIZATION
SENSITIZE
SENSITIZED
SENSITIZER
SENSITIZING
SENSITOMETER
SENSITORY
SENSIVE
SENSO
SENSOR
SENSORIA
SENSORIAL
SENSORIES
SENSORIMOTOR
SENSORIUM
SENSORIUMS
SENSORY
SENSUAL
SENSUALISE
SENSUALISM
SENSUALIST
SENSUALISTIC
SENSUALITIES
SENSUALITY
SENSUALIZE
SENSUALIZED
SENSUALIZING
SENSUALLY
SENSUALNESS
SENSUISM
SENSUIST
SENSUM
SENSUOSITY
SENSUOUS
SENSUOUSLY
SENSUOUSNESS
SENSUS
SENT
SENTENCE
SENTENCED
SENTENCER
SENTENCING
SENTENTIAL
SENTENTIALLY
SENTENTIARIST
SENTENTIARY
SENTENTIOSITY
SENTENTIOUS
SENTENTIOUSLY

SENTIENCE
SENTIENCY
SENTIENDUM
SENTIENT
SENTIMENT
SENTIMENTAL
SENTIMENTALISM
SENTIMENTALIST
SENTIMENTALITIES
SENTIMENTALITY
SENTIMENTALIZE
SENTIMENTALIZED
SENTIMENTALIZER
SENTIMENTALIZING
SENTIMENTALLY
SENTIMENTER
SENTIMENTO
SENTINE
SENTINEL
SENTINELED
SENTINELING
SENTINELLED
SENTINELLING
SENTISECTION
SENTITION
SENTRIES
SENTRY
SENUFO
SENVY
SENYE
SEPAD
SEPAL
SEPALED
SEPALINE
SEPALODY
SEPALOID
SEPALOUS
SEPARABILITY
SEPARABLE
SEPARABLENESS
SEPARABLY
SEPARATE
SEPARATED
SEPARATELY
SEPARATENESS
SEPARATICAL
SEPARATING
SEPARATION
SEPARATISM
SEPARATIST
SEPARATISTIC
SEPARATIVE
SEPARATIVELY
SEPARATIVENESS
SEPARATOR
SEPARATORY
SEPARATRIX
SEPARTE
SEPAWN
SEPHEN
SEPHIRA
SEPHIRAH
SEPIA
SEPIACEOUS
SEPIAE
SEPIAN
SEPIARIAN
SEPIARY
SEPIAS
SEPICOLOUS
SEPIMENT
SEPIOLITE
SEPION
SEPIOSTAIRE
SEPIUM
SEPON
SEPONE
SEPOSE
SEPOY
SEPPUKU
SEPS
SEPSID
SEPSIN
SEPSINE
SEPSIS
SEPT
SEPTA
SEPTAL
SEPTAN
SEPTANE
SEPTANGLE
SEPTANGLED
SEPTARIA
SEPTARIAN
SEPTARIATE
SEPTARIUM
SEPTATE
SEPTATED
SEPTATION
SEPTAVE
SEPTECTOMY
SEPTEMVIOUS
SEPTEMVIR
SEPTENAR
SEPTENARIES
SEPTENARIUS
SEPTENARY
SEPTENATE
SEPTENNATE
SEPTENNIAL
SEPTENNIUM
SEPTENTRION
SEPTET
SEPTETTE
SEPTFOIL
SEPTIC
SEPTICAL
SEPTICALLY
SEPTICEMIA
SEPTICEMIC
SEPTICIDAL
SEPTICIDE
SEPTICITY
SEPTICIZATION
SEPTIER
SEPTIFOLIOUS
SEPTIFRAGAL
SEPTILATERAL
SEPTILE
SEPTILLION
SEPTILLIONTH
SEPTIMAL
SEPTIME
SEPTIMOLE
SEPTINSULAR
SEPTIVALENT
SEPTLEVA
SEPTOCOSTA
SEPTOIC
SEPTONASAL
SEPTOTOMY
SEPTUAGENARY
SEPTULA
SEPTULATE
SEPTULUM
SEPTUM
SEPTUNCIAL
SEPTUOR
SEPTUPLE
SEPTUPLET
SEPTUPLICATE
SEPULCHER
SEPULCHERED
SEPULCHERING
SEPULCHRAL
SEPULCHRALLY
SEPULCHRE
SEPULCHRED
SEPULCHRING
SEPULCHROUS
SEPULT
SEPULTURAL
SEPULTURE
SEQUA
SEQUACES
SEQUACIOUS
SEQUACIOUSLY
SEQUACITY
SEQUEL
SEQUELA
SEQUELAE
SEQUELANT
SEQUENCE
SEQUENCER
SEQUENT
SEQUENTIAL
SEQUENTIALITY
SEQUEST
SEQUESTER
SEQUESTERED
SEQUESTERING
SEQUESTERMENT
SEQUESTRA
SEQUESTRABLE
SEQUESTRAL
SEQUESTRANT
SEQUESTRATE
SEQUESTRATED
SEQUESTRATING
SEQUESTRATION
SEQUESTRATOR
SEQUESTRUM
SEQUIN
SEQUITUR
SEQUOIA
SER
SERA
SERAB
SERAC
SERAGLI
SERAGLIO
SERAHULI
SERAI
SERAIL
SERAING
SERAL
SERAPE
SERAPH
SERAPHIC
SERAPHICAL
SERAPHICALLY
SERAPHICISM
SERAPHICNESS
SERAPHIM
SERAPHINE
SERAPHISM
SERAPHS
SERAPHTIDE
SERASKER
SERASKIER
SERASKIERAT
SERAU
SERAYA
SERCIAL
SERDAB
SERE
SEREH
SEREIN
SEREMENT
SERENA
SERENADE
SERENADED
SERENADER
SERENADING
SERENATA
SERENATAS
SERENATE
SERENDIBITE
SERENDIPITY
SERENDITE
SERENE
SERENED
SERENELY
SERENENESS
SERENIFY
SERENISSIMO
SERENITIES
SERENITY
SERENIZE
SERENO
SERF
SERFAGE
SERFDOM
SERFHOOD
SERFISM
SERFS
SERFSHIP
SERGE
SERGEANCY
SERGEANT
SERGEANTRY
SERGEANTSHIP
SERGEANTY
SERGEDESOY
SERGEDUSOY
SERGELIM
SERGER
SERGETTE
SERGING
SERGIPE
SERGLOBULIN
SERIAL
SERIALISM
SERIALITY
SERIALIZATION
SERIALIZE
SERIALIZED
SERIALIZING
SERIALLY
SERIARY
SERIATE
SERIATELY
SERIATIM
SERIATION
SERIAUNT
SERICATE
SERICATED
SERICEA
SERICEOUS
SERICICULTURE
SERICIN
SERICON
SERICTERIES
SERICTERY
SERICULTURE
SERIEMA
SERIES
SERIF
SERIFIC
SERIFORM
SERIGRAPH
SERIGRAPHER
SERIGRAPHIC
SERIGRAPHY
SERIMETER
SERIMPI
SERIN
SERINE
SERINETTE
SERINGA
SERINGAL
SERINGHI
SERIO
SERIOCOMIC
SERIOLINE
SERIOSITIES
SERIOSITY
SERIOSO
SERIOUS
SERIOUSLY
SERIOUSNESS
SERIPOSITOR
SERIR
SERJEANCY
SERJEANT
SERJEANTRY
SERJEANTY
SERMENT
SERMO
SERMON
SERMONEER
SERMONER
SERMONET
SERMONIC
SERMONICAL
SERMONICALLY
SERMONICS
SERMONISH
SERMONISM
SERMONIST
SERMONIZE
SERMONIZED
SERMONIZER
SERMONIZING
SERMONOID
SERMONOLOGY
SERMUNCLE
SERNAMBY
SERO
SEROLEMMA
SEROLIN
SEROLOGIC
SEROLOGICAL
SEROLOGIST
SEROLOGY
SERON
SERONEGATIVE
SEROON
SEROOT
SEROPOSITIVE
SEROPURULENT
SEROSA
SEROSE
SEROSITIES
SEROSITIS
SEROSITY
SEROTINAL
SEROTINE
SEROTINOUS
SEROTONIN
SEROTYPE
SEROUS
SEROUSNESS
SEROVACCINE
SEROW
SEROZEM
SERPEDINOUS
SERPENT
SERPENTARIA
SERPENTARIUM
SERPENTARY
SERPENTEAU
SERPENTESS
SERPENTILE
SERPENTIN

SERPENTINE
SERPENTINIC
SERPENTINIZE
SERPENTINOID
SERPENTINOUS
SERPENTIZE
SERPENTLIKE
SERPENTLY
SERPENTOID
SERPENTRY
SERPENTWOOD
SERPETTE
SERPHID
SERPHOID
SERPIERITE
SERPIGINOUS
SERPIGO
SERPIVOLANT
SERPOLET
SERPULAN
SERPULID
SERPULIDAN
SERPULINE
SERPULITE
SERPULOID
SERR
SERRA
SERRADELLA
SERRAE
SERRAGE
SERRAI
SERRAN
SERRANA
SERRANID
SERRANO
SERRANOID
SERRANOS
SERRATE
SERRATED
SERRATIA
SERRATIC
SERRATILE
SERRATION
SERRATURE
SERRATUS
SERRICORN
SERRIED
SERRIEDLY
SERRIEDNESS
SERRIFEROUS
SERRIFORM
SERRING
SERRIPED
SERRULA
SERRULATE
SERRULATED
SERRULATION
SERRURERIE
SERRY
SERRYING
SERT
SERTA
SERTO
SERTULARIAN
SERTULARIOID
SERTULAROID
SERTULE
SERTULUM
SERTUM
SERULE
SERUM
SERUMAL
SERUMS
SERVABLE
SERVAGE
SERVAL
SERVALINE
SERVANT
SERVANTS
SERVATION
SERVE
SERVED
SERVENTE
SERVER
SERVERY
SERVES
SERVET
SERVETTE
SERVIABLE
SERVICE
SERVICEABLE
SERVICEABLY
SERVICEBERRIES
SERVICEBERRY
SERVICED
SERVICELESS
SERVICEMAN
SERVICEMEN
SERVICING
SERVIENT
SERVIETTE
SERVILE
SERVILELY
SERVILENESS
SERVILISM
SERVILITIES
SERVILITY
SERVING
SERVINGMAN
SERVIST
SERVITEUR
SERVITIAL
SERVITIUM
SERVITOR
SERVITORIAL
SERVITRIX
SERVITUDE
SERVITURE
SERVO
SERVOMECHANISM
SERVOMOTOR
SERVOS
SERVOTAB
SERVULATE
SERVUS
SERWAMBY
SESAME
SESAMIN
SESAMINE
SESAMOID
SESAMOIDAL
SESAMOIDITIS
SESAMOL
SESCUPLE
SESI
SESKIN
SESMA
SESPERAL
SESQUI
SESQUIALTER
SESQUIALTERA
SESQUIALTERAL
SESQUICENTENNIAL
SESQUINONA
SESQUINONAL
SESQUIOCTAVA
SESQUIPEDAL
SESQUIPLICATE
SESQUIQUARTA
SESQUIQUINTA
SESQUISEXTAL
SESQUITERPENE
SESQUITERTIA
SESS
SESSA
SESSILE
SESSILITY
SESSION
SESSIONAL
SESSIONALLY
SESSIONARY
SESSIONS
SESSPOOL
SESTERCE
SESTERCES
SESTERTIA
SESTERTIUM
SESTERTIUS
SESTET
SESTETTO
SESTI
SESTIAD
SESTINA
SESTINE
SESTOLE
SESTOLET
SESTON
SESTUOR
SET
SETA
SETACEOUS
SETACEOUSLY
SETAE
SETAL
SETARID
SETARIOUS
SETATION
SETBACK
SETBOLT
SETDOWN
SETE
SETER
SETH
SETHEAD
SETIER
SETIFEROUS
SETIFORM
SETIGER
SETLINE
SETLING
SETNESS
SETNET
SETOFF
SETON
SETOSE
SETOUS
SETOUT
SETOVER
SETSCREW
SETSMAN
SETT
SETTAINE
SETTE
SETTECENTO
SETTEE
SETTER
SETTERGRASS
SETTERS
SETTERWORT
SETTIMA
SETTIMO
SETTING
SETTLE
SETTLED
SETTLEMENT
SETTLEMENTS
SETTLER
SETTLERS
SETTLING
SETTLOR
SETTSMAN
SETULA
SETULE
SETULIFORM
SETULOSE
SETULOUS
SETUP
SETWALL
SETWISE
SETWORK
SETWORKS
SEUCH
SEUDAH
SEUGH
SEVE
SEVEN
SEVENBARK
SEVENER
SEVENFOLD
SEVENFOLDED
SEVENSCORE
SEVENTEEN
SEVENTEENTH
SEVENTH
SEVENTHLY
SEVENTIES
SEVENTIETH
SEVENTY
SEVER
SEVERABLE
SEVERAL
SEVERALITY
SEVERALIZE
SEVERALLY
SEVERALTY
SEVERANCE
SEVERATE
SEVERATION
SEVERE
SEVERED
SEVERELY
SEVERENESS
SEVERER
SEVEREST
SEVERING
SEVERISH
SEVERITY
SEVERIZE
SEVERY
SEVIER
SEVILLANAS
SEVUM
SEW
SEWAGE
SEWAN
SEWED
SEWELLEL
SEWEN
SEWER
SEWERAGE
SEWERED
SEWERMAN
SEWERY
SEWIN
SEWING
SEWLESS
SEWN
SEWROUND
SEWSTER
SEX
SEXADECIMAL
SEXAGENARIAN
SEXAGENARY
SEXAGESIMAL
SEXANGLE
SEXANGLED
SEXANGULAR
SEXANGULARLY
SEXCENTENARY
SEXDIGITAL
SEXDIGITATE
SEXDIGITATED
SEXDIGITISM
SEXED
SEXENARY
SEXENNIAL
SEXENNIUM
SEXERN
SEXIER
SEXIEST
SEXISM
SEXIST
SEXISYLLABLE
SEXLESS
SEXLESSLY
SEXLESSNESS
SEXLIKE
SEXLY
SEXOLOGIC
SEXOLOGICAL
SEXOLOGIST
SEXOLOGY
SEXPARTITE
SEXPLOITATION
SEXT
SEXTACTIC
SEXTAIN
SEXTAN
SEXTANS
SEXTANT
SEXTANTAL
SEXTARIUS
SEXTENNIAL
SEXTERN
SEXTET
SEXTETTE
SEXTIC
SEXTILE
SEXTILLION
SEXTILLIONTH
SEXTIPARA
SEXTIPARTITE
SEXTIPLY
SEXTIPOLAR
SEXTO
SEXTOLE
SEXTOLET
SEXTON
SEXTRY
SEXTUOR
SEXTUPLE
SEXTUPLED
SEXTUPLET
SEXTUPLICATE
SEXTUPLICATED
SEXTUPLICATING
SEXTUPLING
SEXTUPLY
SEXTUR
SEXUAL
SEXUALE
SEXUALISM
SEXUALIST
SEXUALITY
SEXUALIZE
SEXUALLY
SEXUOUS
SEXUPARA
SEXUPAROUS
SEXY
SEY
SEYBERTITE
SEYID
SFERICS
SFOGATO

SFORZANDO
SFORZANDOS
SFORZATO
SFUMATO
SGABELLO
SGRAFFIATO
SGRAFFITO
SHA
SHAATNEZ
SHAB
SHABANDAR
SHABASH
SHABBAT
SHABBED
SHABBIER
SHABBIEST
SHABBIFY
SHABBILY
SHABBINESS
SHABBLE
SHABBOS
SHABBY
SHABEQUE
SHABRACK
SHABROON
SHABUNDER
SHACHLE
SHACK
SHACKANITE
SHACKATORY
SHACKBOLT
SHACKLE
SHACKLEBONE
SHACKLED
SHACKLER
SHACKLING
SHACKLY
SHACKY
SHAD
SHADBELLY
SHADBERRIES
SHADBERRY
SHADBIRD
SHADBLOW
SHADBUSH
SHADCHAN
SHADDOCK
SHADE
SHADED
SHADER
SHADES
SHADETAIL
SHADFLOWER
SHADIER
SHADIEST
SHADILY
SHADINE
SHADINESS
SHADING
SHADKAN
SHADOOF
SHADOW
SHADOWBOX
SHADOWED
SHADOWER
SHADOWGRAM
SHADOWGRAPH
SHADOWINESS
SHADOWING
SHADOWIST
SHADOWLAND
SHADOWLESS
SHADOWLY
SHADOWS
SHADOWY
SHADRACH
SHADS
SHADUF
SHADY
SHAFFLE
SHAFII
SHAFT
SHAFTED
SHAFTER
SHAFTING
SHAFTMAN
SHAFTMENT
SHAFTSMAN
SHAFTWAY
SHAFTY
SHAG
SHAGANAPPI
SHAGANAPPY
SHAGBARK
SHAGBUSH
SHAGGED
SHAGGEDNESS
SHAGGIER
SHAGGIEST
SHAGGILY
SHAGGINESS
SHAGGING
SHAGGY
SHAGLET
SHAGRAG
SHAGREEN
SHAGREENED
SHAGROON
SHAGTAIL
SHAH
SHAHARIT
SHAHARITH
SHAHDOM
SHAHEE
SHAHEEN
SHAHI
SHAHIDI
SHAHIN
SHAHZADA
SHAHZADAH
SHAIKH
SHAIKHI
SHAIRD
SHAIRN
SHAITAN
SHAKABLE
SHAKE
SHAKEABLE
SHAKEDOWN
SHAKEFORK
SHAKEN
SHAKEOUT
SHAKEPROOF
SHAKER
SHAKES
SHAKESCENE
SHAKEUP
SHAKHA
SHAKIER
SHAKIEST
SHAKILY
SHAKINESS
SHAKING
SHAKINGS
SHAKO
SHAKOS
SHAKSHEER
SHAKTIS
SHAKU
SHAKY
SHAL
SHALDER
SHALE
SHALED
SHALEE
SHALEMAN
SHALL
SHALLAL
SHALLON
SHALLOON
SHALLOP
SHALLOT
SHALLOW
SHALLOWER
SHALLOWEST
SHALLOWLY
SHALLOWNESS
SHALLOWPATE
SHALLOWPATED
SHALLU
SHALLY
SHALM
SHALOM
SHALWAR
SHALY
SHAM
SHAMA
SHAMAL
SHAMAN
SHAMANESS
SHAMANIC
SHAMANISM
SHAMANIST
SHAMANISTIC
SHAMATEUR
SHAMATEURISM
SHAMBA
SHAMBLE
SHAMBLED
SHAMBLES
SHAMBLING
SHAMBRIER
SHAME
SHAMED
SHAMEFACE
SHAMEFACED
SHAMEFACEDLY
SHAMEFACEDNESS
SHAMEFAST
SHAMEFASTLY
SHAMEFASTNESS
SHAMEFUL
SHAMEFULLY
SHAMEFULNESS
SHAMELESS
SHAMELESSLY
SHAMELESSNESS
SHAMER
SHAMES
SHAMIANAH
SHAMING
SHAMMAS
SHAMMASH
SHAMMED
SHAMMER
SHAMMING
SHAMMISH
SHAMMOCK
SHAMMOCKING
SHAMMOS
SHAMMY
SHAMPOO
SHAMPOOED
SHAMPOOER
SHAMPOOING
SHAMROCK
SHAMROOT
SHAMSHEER
SHAMUS
SHANACHAS
SHANACHIE
SHANACHUS
SHAND
SHANDITE
SHANDRY
SHANDRYDAN
SHANDY
SHANDYGAFF
SHANGAN
SHANGHAI
SHANGHAIED
SHANGHAIING
SHANGY
SHANK
SHANKED
SHANKER
SHANKING
SHANKINGS
SHANKPIECE
SHANKS
SHANNA
SHANNY
SHANT
SHANTEY
SHANTIES
SHANTUNG
SHANTY
SHANTYMAN
SHANTYMEN
SHANTYTOWN
SHAPABLE
SHAPE
SHAPED
SHAPEFUL
SHAPELESS
SHAPELESSLY
SHAPELESSNESS
SHAPELIER
SHAPELIEST
SHAPELINESS
SHAPELY
SHAPEN
SHAPER
SHAPEUP
SHAPIER
SHAPIEST
SHAPING
SHAPINGLY
SHAPOMETER
SHAPOO
SHAPY
SHAR
SHARD
SHARDY
SHARE
SHAREBONE
SHAREBROKER
SHARECROPPER
SHARED
SHAREEF
SHAREHOLDER
SHAREMAN
SHAREPENNY
SHARER
SHARES
SHAREWORT
SHARGAR
SHARGER
SHARGOSS
SHARIAT
SHARING
SHARK
SHARKED
SHARKER
SHARKI
SHARKING
SHARKISH
SHARKLET
SHARKSKIN
SHARKY
SHARN
SHARNBUD
SHARNBUG
SHARNY
SHARON
SHARP
SHARPED
SHARPEN
SHARPENED
SHARPENER
SHARPENING
SHARPER
SHARPERS
SHARPEST
SHARPIE
SHARPING
SHARPISH
SHARPITE
SHARPLING
SHARPLY
SHARPNESS
SHARPS
SHARPSAW
SHARPSHOD
SHARPSHOOTER
SHARPTAIL
SHARPWARE
SHARPY
SHARRY
SHASLIK
SHASTAITE
SHASTRA
SHASTRAIK
SHASTRAS
SHASTRI
SHASTRIK
SHAT
SHATHMONT
SHATTER
SHATTERBRAIN
SHATTERED
SHATTERER
SHATTERING
SHATTERPATED
SHATTERPROOF
SHATTERWIT
SHATTERY
SHATTUCKITE
SHAUCHLE
SHAUGH
SHAUL
SHAUP
SHAURI
SHAVE
SHAVED
SHAVEE
SHAVELING
SHAVEN
SHAVER
SHAVERY
SHAVESTER
SHAVETAIL
SHAVIE
SHAVING
SHAVINGS
SHAW
SHAWABTI
SHAWFOWL
SHAWL
SHAWLED
SHAWLING
SHAWM
SHAWNEEWOOD
SHAWNY
SHAY

SHAYED
SHAYKH
SHCHI
SHE
SHEA
SHEADING
SHEAF
SHEAFAGE
SHEAFY
SHEAL
SHEALING
SHEAR
SHEARBILL
SHEARED
SHEARER
SHEARERS
SHEARGRASS
SHEARHOG
SHEARING
SHEARLING
SHEARMAN
SHEARMOUSE
SHEARS
SHEARTAIL
SHEARWATER
SHEARWATERS
SHEATFISH
SHEATFISHES
SHEATH
SHEATHBILL
SHEATHE
SHEATHED
SHEATHER
SHEATHERY
SHEATHING
SHEATHS
SHEAVE
SHEAVED
SHEAVEMAN
SHEAVES
SHEAVING
SHEBANG
SHEBAR
SHEBEEN
SHEBEENER
SHECHITA
SHED
SHEDDED
SHEDDER
SHEDDING
SHEDER
SHEDHAND
SHEDIM
SHEDMAN
SHEDU
SHEE
SHEEFISH
SHEELING
SHEEN
SHEENLY
SHEENY
SHEEP
SHEEPBACK
SHEEPBACKS
SHEEPBERRY
SHEEPBINE
SHEEPBITER
SHEEPBITING
SHEEPCOT
SHEEPCOTE
SHEEPCROOK
SHEEPFACED
SHEEPFOLD
SHEEPFOOT
SHEEPFOOTS
SHEEPGATE
SHEEPHEADED
SHEEPHERDER
SHEEPHERDING
SHEEPHOOK
SHEEPIFIED
SHEEPIFY
SHEEPIFYING
SHEEPISH
SHEEPISHLY
SHEEPISHNESS
SHEEPKILL
SHEEPLIKE
SHEEPMAN
SHEEPMASTER
SHEEPMEN
SHEEPMINT
SHEEPNOSE
SHEEPNUT
SHEEPPEN
SHEEPSHEAD
SHEEPSHEADS
SHEEPSHEAR
SHEEPSHEARER
SHEEPSHEARING
SHEEPSKIN
SHEEPSKINS
SHEEPSPLIT
SHEEPSTEAL
SHEEPWALK
SHEEPWALKER
SHEEPWEED
SHEEPY
SHEER
SHEERING
SHEERLY
SHEERNESS
SHEERS
SHEET
SHEETAGE
SHEETED
SHEETER
SHEETFLOOD
SHEETING
SHEETLET
SHEETS
SHEETWASH
SHEETWAYS
SHEETWISE
SHEETWORK
SHEETY
SHEEVE
SHEGETZ
SHEHITA
SHEIK
SHEIKDOM
SHEIKH
SHEIKHDOM
SHEIKHLY
SHEIKLY
SHEILING
SHEITAN
SHEITEL
SHEKEL
SHELA
SHELAH
SHELD
SHELDER
SHELDFOWL
SHELDRAKE
SHELDRAKES
SHELDUCK
SHELF
SHELL
SHELLAC
SHELLACK
SHELLACKED
SHELLACKING
SHELLAK
SHELLAPPLE
SHELLBACK
SHELLBARK
SHELLBLOW
SHELLBOUND
SHELLBURST
SHELLEATER
SHELLED
SHELLER
SHELLFIRE
SHELLFISH
SHELLFISHERIES
SHELLFISHERY
SHELLFISHES
SHELLFLOWER
SHELLHEAD
SHELLIER
SHELLING
SHELLMAN
SHELLMEN
SHELLMONGER
SHELLPAD
SHELLPOT
SHELLPROOF
SHELLS
SHELLUM
SHELLWORK
SHELLY
SHELLYCOAT
SHELM
SHELTA
SHELTER
SHELTERAGE
SHELTERED
SHELTERER
SHELTERING
SHELTERLESS
SHELTERWOOD
SHELTERY
SHELTIE
SHELTIES
SHELTRON
SHELTY
SHELVE
SHELVED
SHELVER
SHELVES
SHELVING
SHELVY
SHENANIGAN
SHEND
SHENDFUL
SHENDING
SHENG
SHENT
SHEOGUE
SHEOL
SHEOLIC
SHEP
SHEPE
SHEPHERD
SHEPHERDESS
SHEPHERDISM
SHEPHERDS
SHEPHERDY
SHEPPECK
SHEPPERDING
SHEPPEY
SHEPPHERDED
SHEPPICK
SHEPSTARE
SHEPSTER
SHER
SHERARDIZE
SHERARDIZED
SHERARDIZING
SHERBACHA
SHERBET
SHERBETLEE
SHERBETZIDE
SHERD
SHERE
SHEREEF
SHERIAT
SHERIF
SHERIFATE
SHERIFF
SHERIFFDOM
SHERIFFESS
SHERIFFRY
SHERIFFWICK
SHERIFIAN
SHERISTADAR
SHERLOCK
SHEROOT
SHERRIES
SHERRIS
SHERRY
SHERRYVALLIES
SHERWANI
SHETH
SHEUCH
SHEUGH
SHEVEL
SHEVELED
SHEVRI
SHEW
SHEWBREAD
SHEWEL
SHEWER
SHEYLE
SHI
SHIBAH
SHIBAR
SHIBBOLETH
SHIBUICHI
SHICE
SHICER
SHICK
SHICKER
SHICKERED
SHICKSA
SHIDE
SHIED
SHIEL
SHIELD
SHIELDED
SHIELDER
SHIELDFERN
SHIELDFLOWER
SHIELDING
SHIELDLESS
SHIELDLESSLY
SHIELDLESSNESS
SHIELDMAY
SHIELDS
SHIELDTAIL
SHIELING
SHIER
SHIEST
SHIFT
SHIFTED
SHIFTER
SHIFTFUL
SHIFTFULNESS
SHIFTIER
SHIFTIEST
SHIFTINESS
SHIFTING
SHIFTINGLY
SHIFTLESS
SHIFTLESSLY
SHIFTLESSNESS
SHIFTMAN
SHIFTS
SHIFTY
SHIGGAION
SHIGIONOTH
SHIGRAM
SHIH
SHIKAR
SHIKARA
SHIKAREE
SHIKARGAH
SHIKARI
SHIKASTA
SHIKII
SHIKIMI
SHIKIMOL
SHIKIMOTOXIN
SHIKKEN
SHIKO
SHIKRA
SHIKSE
SHILF
SHILFA
SHILL
SHILLA
SHILLABER
SHILLALA
SHILLALAH
SHILLELAGH
SHILLER
SHILLET
SHILLETY
SHILLIBEER
SHILLING
SHILLOO
SHILLY
SHILP
SHILPIT
SHIM
SHIMAL
SHIMMED
SHIMMER
SHIMMERED
SHIMMERING
SHIMMERY
SHIMMEY
SHIMMIED
SHIMMING
SHIMMY
SHIMMYING
SHIMOSE
SHIMPER
SHIN
SHINARUMP
SHINBONE
SHINDIG
SHINDLE
SHINDY
SHINE
SHINED
SHINER
SHING
SHINGLE
SHINGLED
SHINGLER
SHINGLES
SHINGLEWOOD
SHINGLING
SHINGLY
SHINGON
SHINIER
SHINIEST
SHININESS
SHINING
SHININGLY
SHININGNESS
SHINLEAF
SHINNER

SHINNERIES
SHINNERY
SHINNIED
SHINNY
SHINNYING
SHINPLASTER
SHINS
SHINTAI
SHINTIYAN
SHINTY
SHINTYAN
SHINWOOD
SHINY
SHINZA
SHIP
SHIPBOARD
SHIPBOY
SHIPBUILDER
SHIPBUILDING
SHIPFERD
SHIPFITTER
SHIPFUL
SHIPFULS
SHIPHIRE
SHIPHOLDER
SHIPKEEPER
SHIPLAP
SHIPLET
SHIPLOAD
SHIPMAN
SHIPMANSHIP
SHIPMAST
SHIPMASTER
SHIPMATE
SHIPMEN
SHIPMENT
SHIPOWNER
SHIPPABLE
SHIPPAGE
SHIPPED
SHIPPEN
SHIPPER
SHIPPING
SHIPPLANE
SHIPPO
SHIPPON
SHIPPY
SHIPRADE
SHIPS
SHIPSHAPE
SHIPSIDE
SHIPWAY
SHIPWORM
SHIPWRECK
SHIPWRECKY
SHIPWRIGHT
SHIPYARD
SHIR
SHIRALEE
SHIRE
SHIREHOUSE
SHIREMAN
SHIREMEN
SHIRK
SHIRKER
SHIRL
SHIRPIT
SHIRR
SHIRRA
SHIRRED
SHIRREL
SHIRRER
SHIRRING
SHIRT
SHIRTBAND
SHIRTING
SHIRTLESS
SHIRTLESSNESS
SHIRTMAKER
SHIRTMAKING
SHIRTMAN
SHIRTMEN
SHIRTS
SHIRTTAIL
SHIRTWAIST
SHIRTY
SHISH
SHISHAM
SHISN
SHIST
SHITA
SHITHER
SHITTAH
SHITTEN
SHITTIMWOOD
SHITTLE
SHIV
SHIVA
SHIVAREE
SHIVE
SHIVER
SHIVERED
SHIVEREENS
SHIVERING
SHIVERINGLY
SHIVERS
SHIVERWEED
SHIVERY
SHIVEY
SHIVOO
SHIVVY
SHIZOKU
SHLEMIEL
SHO
SHOADER
SHOAL
SHOALBRAIN
SHOALER
SHOALIER
SHOALIEST
SHOALINESS
SHOALNESS
SHOALY
SHOAR
SHOAT
SHOCHET
SHOCK
SHOCKABLE
SHOCKED
SHOCKER
SHOCKHEAD
SHOCKHEADED
SHOCKING
SHOCKINGLY
SHOCKINGNESS
SHOCKS
SHOD
SHODDIED
SHODDIER
SHODDIES
SHODDIEST
SHODDY
SHODDYING
SHODE
SHODER
SHOE
SHOEBILL
SHOEBINDER
SHOEBINDERY
SHOEBINDING
SHOEBIRD
SHOEBLACK
SHOEBOY
SHOECRAFT
SHOEFLOWER
SHOEHORN
SHOEING
SHOEINGSMITH
SHOELACE
SHOEMAKE
SHOEMAKER
SHOEMAKING
SHOEMAN
SHOEPAC
SHOEPACK
SHOER
SHOES
SHOESHINE
SHOESTRING
SHOETREE
SHOFAR
SHOFUL
SHOG
SHOGGIE
SHOGGLE
SHOGGLY
SHOGI
SHOGUN
SHOHET
SHOJI
SHOLA
SHOLE
SHOMA
SHONDE
SHONE
SHONEEN
SHONEENS
SHONKINITE
SHOO
SHOOD
SHOOFA
SHOOFLIES
SHOOFLY
SHOOGLE
SHOOH
SHOOI
SHOOK
SHOOL
SHOON
SHOOP
SHOOT
SHOOTER
SHOOTING
SHOOTIST
SHOOTMAN
SHOP
SHOPBOARD
SHOPBOOK
SHOPBOY
SHOPBREAKER
SHOPBREAKING
SHOPGIRL
SHOPHAR
SHOPKEEPER
SHOPKEEPERY
SHOPKEEPING
SHOPLIFT
SHOPLIFTER
SHOPLIFTING
SHOPLIKE
SHOPMAID
SHOPMAN
SHOPMARK
SHOPMATE
SHOPOCRACY
SHOPOCRAT
SHOPPE
SHOPPED
SHOPPER
SHOPPIER
SHOPPIEST
SHOPPING
SHOPPINI
SHOPPISH
SHOPPY
SHOPSTER
SHOPTALK
SHOPWALKER
SHOPWEAR
SHOPWINDOW
SHOPWORK
SHOPWORKER
SHOPWORN
SHOQ
SHOR
SHORAN
SHORE
SHOREBERRY
SHOREBIRD
SHORED
SHOREFISH
SHORELAND
SHORELESS
SHORELINE
SHOREMAN
SHORER
SHORESMAN
SHOREWARD
SHOREWARDS
SHOREYER
SHORING
SHORL
SHORN
SHORT
SHORTAGE
SHORTBREAD
SHORTCAKE
SHORTCHANGE
SHORTCHANGED
SHORTCHANGER
SHORTCHANGING
SHORTCOAT
SHORTCOMER
SHORTCOMING
SHORTCUT
SHORTEN
SHORTENED
SHORTENER
SHORTENING
SHORTER
SHORTEST
SHORTFALL
SHORTHAND
SHORTHANDED
SHORTHEAD
SHORTHEELS
SHORTHORN
SHORTIA
SHORTIE
SHORTISH
SHORTITE
SHORTLY
SHORTNESS
SHORTS
SHORTSIGHTED
SHORTSIGHTEDLY
SHORTSOME
SHORTSTAFF
SHORTSTOP
SHORTY
SHOSHONITE
SHOT
SHOTBUSH
SHOTCRETE
SHOTE
SHOTGUN
SHOTMAKER
SHOTMAN
SHOTS
SHOTSHELL
SHOTSTAR
SHOTT
SHOTTED
SHOTTEN
SHOTTY
SHOU
SHOUGH
SHOULD
SHOULDER
SHOULDERED
SHOULDERER
SHOULDERETTE
SHOULDERING
SHOULDERS
SHOULDEST
SHOULDNA
SHOULDST
SHOULERD
SHOUT
SHOUTED
SHOUTER
SHOUTHER
SHOUTING
SHOUTS
SHOVAL
SHOVE
SHOVED
SHOVEL
SHOVELBILL
SHOVELBOARD
SHOVELED
SHOVELER
SHOVELFISH
SHOVELHEAD
SHOVELLED
SHOVELLING
SHOVELNOSE
SHOVELWEED
SHOVER
SHOVING
SHOW
SHOWABLE
SHOWANCE
SHOWBIRD
SHOWBOARD
SHOWBOAT
SHOWBREAD
SHOWCASE
SHOWD
SHOWDOWN
SHOWED
SHOWER
SHOWERED
SHOWERER
SHOWERIER
SHOWERIEST
SHOWERING
SHOWERY
SHOWFUL
SHOWIER
SHOWIEST
SHOWILY
SHOWINESS
SHOWING
SHOWISH
SHOWMAN
SHOWMANSHIP
SHOWN
SHOWOFF
SHOWPIECE
SHOWROOM
SHOWSHOP
SHOWUP
SHOWY
SHOYA

SHOYU
SHRAB
SHRADD
SHRADDHA
SHRAG
SHRAM
SHRAME
SHRAMMED
SHRANK
SHRAP
SHRAPE
SHRAPNEL
SHRAVE
SHRAVEY
SHRED
SHREDCOCK
SHREDDED
SHREDDER
SHREDDING
SHREDDY
SHREDS
SHREE
SHREEVE
SHREND
SHREW
SHREWD
SHREWDER
SHREWDEST
SHREWDLY
SHREWDNESS
SHREWDY
SHREWISH
SHREWISHLY
SHREWISHNESS
SHREWMOUSE
SHREWSTRUCK
SHRI
SHRIDE
SHRIEK
SHRIEKED
SHRIEKER
SHRIEKERY
SHRIEKING
SHRIEKY
SHRIEVAL
SHRIEVALTIES
SHRIEVALTY
SHRIEVE
SHRIFT
SHRIKE
SHRILL
SHRILLED
SHRILLER
SHRILLEST
SHRILLING
SHRILLY
SHRIMP
SHRIMPER
SHRIMPFISH
SHRIMPI
SHRIMPISH
SHRIMPISHNESS
SHRIMPY
SHRINAL
SHRINE
SHRINED
SHRINING
SHRINK
SHRINKABLE
SHRINKAGE
SHRINKER
SHRINKING
SHRINKINGLY
SHRIP
SHRITE
SHRIVE
SHRIVED
SHRIVEL
SHRIVELED
SHRIVELING
SHRIVELLED
SHRIVELLING
SHRIVEN
SHRIVER
SHRIVING
SHROFF
SHROG
SHROGS
SHROUD
SHROUDED
SHROUDING
SHROUDS
SHROUDY
SHROVE
SHROVED
SHROVER
SHROVING
SHROVY
SHRUB
SHRUBBED
SHRUBBERIES
SHRUBBERY
SHRUBBIER
SHRUBBIEST
SHRUBBINESS
SHRUBBY
SHRUBLET
SHRUBS
SHRUBWOOD
SHRUFF
SHRUG
SHRUGGED
SHRUGGING
SHRUNK
SHRUNKEN
SHRUPS
SHRUTI
SHTCHEE
SHTETEL
SHTETL
SHTICK
SHUBA
SHUBUNKIN
SHUCK
SHUCKED
SHUCKER
SHUCKING
SHUCKS
SHUD
SHUDDER
SHUDDERED
SHUDDERING
SHUDDERSOME
SHUDDERY
SHUDE
SHUDNA
SHUFF
SHUFFLE
SHUFFLEBOARD
SHUFFLECAP
SHUFFLED
SHUFFLER
SHUFFLEWING
SHUFFLING
SHUG
SHUILER
SHUL
SHULER
SHULWAURS
SHUMAN
SHUN
SHUNE
SHUNLESS
SHUNNABLE
SHUNNED
SHUNNER
SHUNNING
SHUNPIKE
SHUNT
SHUNTED
SHUNTER
SHUNTING
SHURE
SHURF
SHURGEE
SHUSH
SHUT
SHUTDOWN
SHUTE
SHUTEYE
SHUTOFF
SHUTOUT
SHUTTER
SHUTTERBUG
SHUTTERING
SHUTTING
SHUTTLE
SHUTTLECOCK
SHUTTLECOCKED
SHUTTLECOCKING
SHUTTLER
SHUTTLEWISE
SHWA
SHWANPAN
SHWEBO
SHY
SHYER
SHYING
SHYISH
SHYLY
SHYNESS
SHYSTER
SI
SIACALLE
SIAFU
SIAK
SIAL
SIALAGOGIC
SIALAGOGUE
SIALIC
SIALID
SIALIDAN
SIALOID
SIAMANG
SIAMESE
SIAMOISE
SIAPO
SIAULIAI
SIB
SIBBED
SIBBENDY
SIBBENS
SIBBING
SIBERITE
SIBILANCE
SIBILANCY
SIBILANT
SIBILANTLY
SIBILATE
SIBILATOR
SIBILATORY
SIBILI
SIBILOUS
SIBILUS
SIBLING
SIBNESS
SIBREDE
SIBRIT
SIBSHIP
SIBUCAO
SIBYL
SIBYLIC
SIBYLLA
SIBYLLAE
SIBYLLIC
SIBYLLINE
SIBYLLISM
SIBYLLIST
SIC
SICARIAN
SICARII
SICARIOUS
SICARIUS
SICCA
SICCANEOUS
SICCANT
SICCAR
SICCATE
SICCATED
SICCATING
SICCATION
SICCATIVE
SICCIMETER
SICCITY
SICE
SICER
SICHT
SICILIENNE
SICINNIAN
SICK
SICKBAY
SICKBED
SICKED
SICKEN
SICKENED
SICKENER
SICKENING
SICKENINGLY
SICKER
SICKEST
SICKET
SICKING
SICKISH
SICKISHLY
SICKISHNESS
SICKLE
SICKLEBILL
SICKLED
SICKLEMAN
SICKLEMEN
SICKLEMIA
SICKLEPOD
SICKLER
SICKLERITE
SICKLEWORT
SICKLIED
SICKLIER
SICKLIEST
SICKLILY
SICKLING
SICKLY
SICKLYING
SICKNESS
SICKROOM
SICLIKE
SICSAC
SICU
SICULA
SICULAR
SIDDER
SIDDOW
SIDDUR
SIDE
SIDEAGE
SIDEARM
SIDEBAND
SIDEBAR
SIDEBOARD
SIDEBONE
SIDEBONES
SIDEBOX
SIDEBURNS
SIDECAR
SIDECHECK
SIDED
SIDEFLASH
SIDEHEAD
SIDEHILL
SIDEHOLD
SIDEKICK
SIDELANG
SIDELIGHT
SIDELINE
SIDELINED
SIDELING
SIDELINGS
SIDELINING
SIDELINS
SIDELOCK
SIDELONG
SIDEMAN
SIDENESS
SIDENOTE
SIDEPIECE
SIDER
SIDERAL
SIDERATE
SIDERATED
SIDERATION
SIDEREAL
SIDEREALIZE
SIDEREALLY
SIDEREAN
SIDERISM
SIDERITE
SIDERITIC
SIDEROGNOST
SIDEROGRAPHY
SIDEROLITE
SIDEROLOGY
SIDEROMANCY
SIDEROMELANE
SIDERONATRITE
SIDERONYM
SIDEROSCOPE
SIDEROSE
SIDEROSIS
SIDEROSTAT
SIDEROSTATIC
SIDEROUS
SIDES
SIDESADDLE
SIDESHAKE
SIDESHOW
SIDESLIP
SIDESMAN
SIDESMEN
SIDESPIN
SIDESPLITTER
SIDESPLITTING
SIDESTEP
SIDESTEPPED
SIDESTEPPER
SIDESTEPPING
SIDESWAY
SIDESWIPE
SIDESWIPED
SIDESWIPER
SIDESWIPING
SIDETONE
SIDETRACK
SIDETRACKED
SIDETRACKING
SIDEWALK
SIDEWALL

SIDEWARD
SIDEWARDS
SIDEWASH
SIDEWAY
SIDEWAYS
SIDEWINDER
SIDEWISE
SIDHE
SIDI
SIDING
SIDLE
SIDLED
SIDLER
SIDLING
SIDLINGLY
SIDLINS
SIDTH
SIDY
SIE
SIECLE
SIEGE
SIEGED
SIEGENITE
SIEGER
SIEGEWORK
SIEGING
SIENITE
SIENITIC
SIENNA
SIER
SIEROZEM
SIERRA
SIERRAN
SIESTA
SIEUR
SIEVE
SIEVED
SIEVEFUL
SIEVELIKE
SIEVER
SIEVING
SIEVINGS
SIEVY
SIFAC
SIFAKA
SIFE
SIFF
SIFFILATE
SIFFLE
SIFFLEMENT
SIFFLET
SIFFLEUR
SIFFLEURS
SIFFLEUSE
SIFFLEUSES
SIFFLOT
SIFT
SIFTAGE
SIFTED
SIFTER
SIFTING
SIG
SIGATOKA
SIGGER
SIGH
SIGHED
SIGHER
SIGHFUL
SIGHING
SIGHINGLY
SIGHINGNESS
SIGHT
SIGHTED
SIGHTEN
SIGHTENING
SIGHTER
SIGHTFUL
SIGHTFULNESS
SIGHTHOLE
SIGHTING
SIGHTLESS
SIGHTLESSLY
SIGHTLESSNESS
SIGHTLIER
SIGHTLY
SIGHTPROOF
SIGHTS
SIGHTSEEING
SIGHTSMAN
SIGHTY
SIGIL
SIGILLARIAN
SIGILLARID
SIGILLARIOID
SIGILLARIST
SIGILLARY
SIGILLATE
SIGILLATED
SIGILLATION
SIGILLATIVE
SIGILLISTIC
SIGILLOGRAPHY
SIGILLUM
SIGLA
SIGLARIAN
SIGLOS
SIGLUM
SIGMA
SIGMASPIRE
SIGMATE
SIGMATIC
SIGMATION
SIGMODONT
SIGMOID
SIGMOIDAL
SIGMOIDALLY
SIGMOIDITIS
SIGN
SIGNABLE
SIGNACLE
SIGNAL
SIGNALED
SIGNALER
SIGNALETIC
SIGNALETICS
SIGNALING
SIGNALIST
SIGNALITIES
SIGNALITY
SIGNALIZE
SIGNALIZED
SIGNALIZING
SIGNALLER
SIGNALLING
SIGNALLY
SIGNALMAN
SIGNALMENT
SIGNANCE
SIGNARY
SIGNATE
SIGNATION
SIGNATOR
SIGNATORY
SIGNATURAL
SIGNATURE
SIGNATURIST
SIGNBOARD
SIGNED
SIGNEE
SIGNER
SIGNET
SIGNEURY
SIGNIFER
SIGNIFIABLE
SIGNIFICAL
SIGNIFICANCE
SIGNIFICANCY
SIGNIFICANT
SIGNIFICANTLY
SIGNIFICATE
SIGNIFICATION
SIGNIFICATIVE
SIGNIFICATOR
SIGNIFICATORY
SIGNIFICATURE
SIGNIFICAVIT
SIGNIFICIAN
SIGNIFICS
SIGNIFIE
SIGNIFIED
SIGNIFIER
SIGNIFY
SIGNIFYING
SIGNING
SIGNIOR
SIGNIST
SIGNITOR
SIGNLESS
SIGNMAN
SIGNOR
SIGNORA
SIGNORE
SIGNORIA
SIGNORIAL
SIGNORINA
SIGNORINE
SIGNORINO
SIGNORY
SIGNPOST
SIGNS
SIGNUM
SIGNWRITER
SIGRIM
SIJIL
SIJILL
SIKA
SIKAR
SIKARA
SIKE
SIKER
SIKERLY
SIKHARA
SIKIMI
SIKSIKA
SIKU
SIL
SILAGE
SILANE
SILANGA
SILCRETE
SILD
SILE
SILEN
SILENACEOUS
SILENCE
SILENCED
SILENCER
SILENCING
SILENIC
SILENT
SILENTIAL
SILENTIARY
SILENTIOUS
SILENTIUM
SILENTLY
SILENTNESS
SILENTS
SILENUS
SILESIA
SILEX
SILEXITE
SILGREEN
SILHOUETTE
SILHOUETTED
SILHOUETTING
SILHOUETTIST
SILICA
SILICAM
SILICATE
SILICATION
SILICATIZATION
SILICEAN
SILICEOUS
SILICIC
SILICIDE
SILICIDIZE
SILICIFEROUS
SILICIFIED
SILICIFY
SILICIFYING
SILICIOPHITE
SILICIOUS
SILICIUM
SILICIZE
SILICLE
SILICON
SILICONE
SILICONIZE
SILICOSIS
SILICOTIC
SILICULA
SILICULAR
SILICULE
SILICULOSE
SILICULOUS
SILICYL
SILIQUA
SILIQUE
SILIQUOSE
SILK
SILKALENE
SILKALINE
SILKED
SILKEN
SILKER
SILKFLOWER
SILKGROWER
SILKIE
SILKIER
SILKIEST
SILKILY
SILKINESS
SILKMAN
SILKMEN
SILKNESS
SILKSMAN
SILKTAIL
SILKWEED
SILKWOMAN
SILKWOOD
SILKWORK
SILKWORKER
SILKWORKS
SILKWORM
SILKY
SILL
SILLABUB
SILLADAR
SILLANDAR
SILLAR
SILLER
SILLIER
SILLIES
SILLIEST
SILLILY
SILLINESS
SILLOCK
SILLOGRAPH
SILLOGRAPHER
SILLOMETER
SILLON
SILLY
SILLYHOW
SILLYTON
SILO
SILOED
SILOING
SILOS
SILOXANE
SILPHID
SILPHIUM
SILT
SILTAGE
SILTATION
SILTED
SILTING
SILTY
SILUNDUM
SILURID
SILUROID
SILVA
SILVAN
SILVANITY
SILVANRY
SILVENDY
SILVER
SILVERBACK
SILVERBELLY
SILVERBERRIES
SILVERBERRY
SILVERBIDDY
SILVERBILL
SILVERBUSH
SILVERED
SILVERER
SILVERFIN
SILVERFISH
SILVERFISHES
SILVERIER
SILVERIEST
SILVERINESS
SILVERING
SILVERITE
SILVERIZE
SILVERLEAF
SILVERLING
SILVERLY
SILVERN
SILVERROD
SILVERSIDE
SILVERSIDES
SILVERSKIN
SILVERSMITH
SILVERSMITHING
SILVERSMITHS
SILVERSPOT
SILVERTAIL
SILVERTIP
SILVERTOP
SILVERVINE
SILVERWARE
SILVERWEED
SILVERWING
SILVERWOOD
SILVERWORK
SILVERY
SILVICAL
SILVICOLOUS
SILVICS
SILVICULTURE
SIM
SIMA
SIMAGRE
SIMAL
SIMAR

SIMARA
SIMARRE
SIMARUBA
SIMBA
SIMBALL
SIMBIL
SIMBLIN
SIMBLING
SIMBLOT
SIME
SIMIAD
SIMIAL
SIMIAN
SIMIANITY
SIMIESQUE
SIMIID
SIMILAR
SIMILARITY
SIMILARLY
SIMILATE
SIMILATIVE
SIMILE
SIMILIMUM
SIMILITER
SIMILITIVE
SIMILITUDE
SIMILITUDINIZE
SIMILIZE
SIMILOR
SIMIOID
SIMIOUS
SIMIOUSNESS
SIMIR
SIMITAR
SIMITY
SIMKIN
SIMLIN
SIMLING
SIMMER
SIMMERED
SIMMERING
SIMMON
SIMMONS
SIMNEL
SIMOLEON
SIMONIAC
SIMONIACAL
SIMONIOUS
SIMONISM
SIMONIST
SIMONIZE
SIMONY
SIMOOM
SIMOON
SIMOUS
SIMP
SIMPAI
SIMPATICO
SIMPER
SIMPERED
SIMPERER
SIMPERING
SIMPERINGLY
SIMPLE
SIMPLED
SIMPLER
SIMPLES
SIMPLEST
SIMPLETON
SIMPLETONIAN
SIMPLETONIC
SIMPLEX
SIMPLEXED
SIMPLEXITY
SIMPLICIST
SIMPLICITER
SIMPLICITIES
SIMPLICITY
SIMPLICIZE
SIMPLIFICATION
SIMPLIFICATIVE
SIMPLIFICATOR
SIMPLIFIED
SIMPLIFIEDLY
SIMPLIFIER
SIMPLIFY
SIMPLIFYING
SIMPLING
SIMPLISM
SIMPLIST
SIMPLISTIC
SIMPLUM
SIMPLY
SIMPSON
SIMRI
SIMSON
SIMULACRA
SIMULACRAL
SIMULACRE
SIMULACRIZE
SIMULACRUM
SIMULANCE
SIMULANT
SIMULAR
SIMULATE
SIMULATED
SIMULATING
SIMULATION
SIMULATIVE
SIMULATIVELY
SIMULATOR
SIMULATORY
SIMULCAST
SIMULE
SIMULIID
SIMULIZE
SIMULTANEOUS
SIMULTANEOUSLY
SIMULTY
SIMURG
SIMURGH
SIN
SINA
SINAITE
SINAL
SINALBIN
SINAMAY
SINAMIN
SINAMINE
SINAPATE
SINAPIC
SINAPIN
SINAPINE
SINAPISM
SINAPIZE
SINAPOLINE
SINAWA
SINCALINE
SINCAMAS
SINCE
SINCERE
SINCERELY
SINCERENESS
SINCERER
SINCEREST
SINCERITY
SINCIPITAL
SINCIPUT
SINDER
SINDLE
SINDON
SINE
SINEBADA
SINECURAL
SINECURE
SINECURED
SINECURING
SINECURISM
SINECURIST
SINEW
SINEWED
SINEWING
SINEWLESS
SINEWOUS
SINEWY
SINFONIA
SINFUL
SINFULLY
SINFULNESS
SING
SINGABLE
SINGALLY
SINGARIP
SINGE
SINGED
SINGEING
SINGEINGLY
SINGER
SINGERESS
SINGERIE
SINGERS
SINGH
SINGILLATIM
SINGING
SINGKAMAS
SINGLE
SINGLEBAR
SINGLED
SINGLEHANDED
SINGLEHANDEDLY
SINGLEHANDEDNESS
SINGLEHEARTED
SINGLEHEARTEDLY
SINGLEHEARTEDNESS
SINGLEHOOD
SINGLENESS
SINGLER
SINGLES
SINGLESTICK
SINGLET
SINGLETON
SINGLETREE
SINGLING
SINGLY
SINGSONG
SINGSPIEL
SINGSTRESS
SINGULAR
SINGULARISM
SINGULARIST
SINGULARITIES
SINGULARITY
SINGULARIZATION
SINGULARIZE
SINGULARIZED
SINGULARIZING
SINGULARLY
SINGULARNESS
SINGULT
SINGULTOUS
SINGULTUS
SINHASAN
SINIGRIN
SINISTER
SINISTERLY
SINISTERNESS
SINISTRA
SINISTRAD
SINISTRAL
SINISTRALITY
SINISTRALLY
SINISTRATION
SINISTRIN
SINISTRORSAL
SINISTRORSE
SINISTROUS
SINISTROUSLY
SINJER
SINK
SINKAGE
SINKBOAT
SINKBOX
SINKER
SINKHEAD
SINKHOLE
SINKING
SINKLESS
SINKROOM
SINKSTONE
SINKY
SINLESS
SINLESSLY
SINLESSNESS
SINNED
SINNER
SINNET
SINNING
SINNOWED
SINOMENINE
SINOPIA
SINOPITE
SINOPLE
SINSRING
SINSYNE
SINTER
SINTOC
SINUATE
SINUATED
SINUATEDENTATE
SINUATELY
SINUATING
SINUATION
SINUITIS
SINUOSE
SINUOSITIES
SINUOSITY
SINUOUS
SINUOUSLY
SINUOUSNESS
SINUPALLIAL
SINUPALLIATE
SINUS
SINUSAL
SINUSITIS
SINUSOID
SINUSOIDAL
SINUSOIDALLY
SINZER
SIOL
SION
SIP
SIPAGE
SIPAPU
SIPE
SIPER
SIPERS
SIPHAC
SIPHON
SIPHONACEOUS
SIPHONAGE
SIPHONAL
SIPHONATED
SIPHONEOUS
SIPHONET
SIPHONIA
SIPHONIC
SIPHONIFORM
SIPHONIUM
SIPHONOGAM
SIPHONOGAMIC
SIPHONOGLYPH
SIPHONOPHORAN
SIPHONOPHORE
SIPHONOPLAX
SIPHONOSOME
SIPHONOSTELE
SIPHONOSTELIC
SIPHONOSTELY
SIPHONOSTOME
SIPHONOZOOID
SIPHONULA
SIPHORHINAL
SIPHUNCLE
SIPHUNCLED
SIPHUNCULAR
SIPID
SIPIDITY
SIPING
SIPLING
SIPO
SIPPED
SIPPER
SIPPET
SIPPING
SIPPIO
SIPPLE
SIPUNCULID
SIPUNCULOID
SIPYLITE
SIR
SIRCAR
SIRDAR
SIRE
SIRED
SIRELESS
SIREN
SIRENE
SIRENIAN
SIRENIC
SIRENICAL
SIRENICALLY
SIRENING
SIRENIZE
SIRENOID
SIRENOMELUS
SIRENY
SIREX
SIRGANG
SIRI
SIRIAN
SIRICID
SIRIH
SIRING
SIRIOMETER
SIRKAR
SIRKEER
SIRKI
SIRKY
SIRLOIN
SIRLOINY
SIRMARK
SIROCCO
SIROS
SIRPEA
SIRPLE
SIRPOON
SIRRAH
SIRREE
SIRS
SIRSE
SIRUABALLI
SIRUELAS
SIRUP
SIRUPED
SIRUPER

SIRUPY
SIRVENT
SIS
SISAL
SISALANA
SISCOWET
SISE
SISEL
SISERARA
SISERARY
SISH
SISI
SISITH
SISKIN
SISS
SISSIES
SISSIFICATION
SISSIFIED
SISSONE
SISSONNE
SISSOO
SISSU
SISSY
SIST
SISTEN
SISTER
SISTERHOOD
SISTERING
SISTERIZE
SISTERLINESS
SISTERLY
SISTERN
SISTERS
SISTERSHIP
SISTLE
SISTOMENSIN
SISTREN
SISTROID
SISTRUM
SIT
SITAO
SITAR
SITATUNGA
SITATUNGAS
SITE
SITFAST
SITH
SITHE
SITHENCE
SITHENS
SITHES
SITIENT
SITIO
SITOLOGY
SITOMANIA
SITOSTERIN
SITOSTEROL
SITOTOXISM
SITREP
SITTER
SITTINE
SITTING
SITTRINGY
SITU
SITUAL
SITUATE
SITUATED
SITUATION
SITUATIONAL
SITULA
SITUS
SITZ
SITZMARK
SIVE
SIVER
SIVVENS
SIWASH
SIWASHED
SIWASHING
SIX
SIXAIN
SIXER
SIXFOLD
SIXMO
SIXPENCE
SIXPENCES
SIXPENNY
SIXPENNYWORTH
SIXSCORE
SIXSOME
SIXTE
SIXTEEN
SIXTEENER
SIXTEENMO
SIXTEENTH
SIXTH
SIXTIES
SIXTIETH
SIXTY
SIZABLE
SIZABLENESS
SIZABLY
SIZAR
SIZARSHIP
SIZE
SIZEABLE
SIZED
SIZEINE
SIZEMAN
SIZER
SIZES
SIZIER
SIZIEST
SIZINESS
SIZING
SIZINGS
SIZY
SIZYGIUM
SIZZ
SIZZARD
SIZZING
SIZZLE
SIZZLED
SIZZLER
SIZZLING
SIZZLINGLY
SJAMBOK
SJOMIL
SJOMILA
SKAALPUND
SKAAMOOG
SKADDLE
SKAFF
SKAFFIE
SKAG
SKAIF
SKAIL
SKAILLIE
SKAINSMATE
SKAIR
SKAITBIRD
SKAITHY
SKALAWAG
SKALD
SKALDIC
SKALPUND
SKANDHAS
SKARN
SKAT
SKATE
SKATED
SKATER
SKATES
SKATIKAS
SKATING
SKATIST
SKATOL
SKATOLE
SKATOLOGY
SKATOSINE
SKATOXYL
SKEAN
SKEANOCKLE
SKEAT
SKED
SKEDADDLE
SKEDADDLED
SKEDADDLER
SKEDADDLING
SKEDGE
SKEDLOCK
SKEE
SKEED
SKEEG
SKEEING
SKEEL
SKEELING
SKEENYIE
SKEER
SKEERED
SKEERY
SKEES
SKEESICKS
SKEET
SKEETER
SKEEZIX
SKEG
SKEGGER
SKEICH
SKEIF
SKEIGH
SKEIN
SKEINER
SKELB
SKELDER
SKELDOCK
SKELDRAKE
SKELET
SKELETAL
SKELETIN
SKELETON
SKELETONIAN
SKELETONIC
SKELETONIZATION
SKELETONIZE
SKELETONIZED
SKELETONIZER
SKELETONIZING
SKELETONY
SKELF
SKELGOOSE
SKELL
SKELLAT
SKELLER
SKELLOCH
SKELLUM
SKELLY
SKELP
SKELPED
SKELPER
SKELPIN
SKELPING
SKELTER
SKELVY
SKEMMEL
SKEMP
SKEN
SKENAI
SKENE
SKEO
SKEOUGH
SKEP
SKEPFUL
SKEPPE
SKEPPIST
SKEPPUND
SKEPSIS
SKEPTIC
SKEPTICAL
SKEPTICALLY
SKEPTICALNESS
SKEPTICISM
SKEPTICIZE
SKEPTICIZED
SKEPTICIZING
SKERM
SKERRICK
SKERRIES
SKERRY
SKETCH
SKETCHABLE
SKETCHBOOK
SKETCHED
SKETCHER
SKETCHIER
SKETCHIEST
SKETCHILY
SKETCHINESS
SKETCHING
SKETCHIST
SKETCHY
SKETE
SKETIOTAI
SKEUOMORPH
SKEVISH
SKEW
SKEWBACK
SKEWBACKED
SKEWBALD
SKEWED
SKEWER
SKEWERED
SKEWERER
SKEWERING
SKEWERWOOD
SKEWING
SKEWINGS
SKEWL
SKEWNESS
SKEWWISE
SKEWY
SKEY
SKEYTING
SKHIAN
SKI
SKIAGRAM
SKIAGRAPH
SKIAGRAPHED
SKIAGRAPHIC
SKIAGRAPHING
SKIAMETER
SKIAMETRY
SKIAPOD
SKIAPODOUS
SKIASCOPE
SKIASCOPY
SKIBBET
SKIBBY
SKICE
SKID
SKIDDED
SKIDDER
SKIDDING
SKIDDOO
SKIDDY
SKIDDYCOCK
SKIDOO
SKIDPAN
SKIDPROOF
SKIDS
SKIDWAY
SKIED
SKIEGH
SKIEPPE
SKIER
SKIES
SKIEUR
SKIFF
SKIFFLE
SKIFFLED
SKIFFLING
SKIFT
SKIING
SKIJORE
SKIJORER
SKIJORING
SKIL
SKILDER
SKILDFEL
SKILFISH
SKILFUL
SKILFULLY
SKILL
SKILLAGALEE
SKILLED
SKILLET
SKILLFUL
SKILLFULLY
SKILLFULNESS
SKILLING
SKILLION
SKILLO
SKILLS
SKILLY
SKILPOT
SKILTS
SKILTY
SKIM
SKIMBACK
SKIME
SKIMMED
SKIMMER
SKIMMING
SKIMMINGS
SKIMMINGTON
SKIMMITY
SKIMP
SKIMPIER
SKIMPIEST
SKIMPILY
SKIMPINESS
SKIMPY
SKIN
SKINBALL
SKINBOUND
SKINCH
SKINFLICK
SKINFLINT
SKINFLINTILY
SKINFLINTINESS
SKINFLINTY
SKINFUL
SKINFULS
SKINHEAD
SKINK
SKINKED
SKINKER
SKINKING
SKINKLE
SKINLESS
SKINNED
SKINNER
SKINNERS
SKINNERY
SKINNIER

SKINNIEST
SKINNING
SKINNY
SKINS
SKINTIGHT
SKINWORM
SKIOGRAM
SKIOGRAPH
SKIP
SKIPBRAIN
SKIPDENT
SKIPJACK
SKIPJACKLY
SKIPJACKS
SKIPKENNEL
SKIPMAN
SKIPPED
SKIPPER
SKIPPERED
SKIPPERSHIP
SKIPPERY
SKIPPET
SKIPPING
SKIPPLE
SKIPPUND
SKIPPY
SKIPS
SKIPTAIL
SKIRL
SKIRLCOCK
SKIRLING
SKIRM
SKIRMISH
SKIRMISHED
SKIRMISHER
SKIRMISHING
SKIRP
SKIRR
SKIRREH
SKIRRET
SKIRT
SKIRTBOARD
SKIRTED
SKIRTER
SKIRTING
SKIRTS
SKIRTY
SKIS
SKISE
SKISH
SKIT
SKITE
SKITER
SKITHER
SKITTER
SKITTERY
SKITTISH
SKITTISHLY
SKITTISHNESS
SKITTLE
SKITTLED
SKITTLES
SKITTLING
SKITTY
SKITTYBOOT
SKIV
SKIVE
SKIVED
SKIVER
SKIVERWOOD
SKIVIE
SKIVING
SKIVVIES
SKIVVY
SKLENT
SKLEROPELITE
SKLIM
SKLINTER
SKOAL
SKOGBOLITE
SKOKIAAN
SKOLLY
SKOMERITE
SKOOKUM
SKOOT
SKOUT
SKRAELLING
SKREEL
SKREIGH
SKRIKE
SKRUPUL
SKRYER
SKUA
SKUG
SKULDUGGERY
SKULK
SKULKED
SKULKER
SKULKING
SKULL
SKULLBANKER
SKULLCAP
SKULLERY
SKULLFISH
SKULLY
SKUNK
SKUNKBILL
SKUNKBUSH
SKUNKERY
SKUNKISH
SKUNKTOP
SKUNKWEED
SKUNKY
SKURRY
SKUTTERUDITE
SKY
SKYBAL
SKYBALD
SKYCOACH
SKYCRAFT
SKYED
SKYER
SKYEY
SKYFTE
SKYHOOK
SKYHOOT
SKYING
SKYISH
SKYJACK
SKYJACKING
SKYLARK
SKYLARKED
SKYLARKER
SKYLARKING
SKYLESS
SKYLIGHT
SKYLINE
SKYLOOK
SKYMAN
SKYME
SKYPHOS
SKYPORT
SKYR
SKYRE
SKYRGALIARD
SKYRIN
SKYROCKET
SKYROCKETY
SKYSAIL
SKYSCAPE
SKYSCRAPER
SKYSCRAPING
SKYSHINE
SKYSTONE
SKYT
SKYUGLE
SKYWARD
SKYWARDS
SKYWAY
SKYWRITE
SKYWRITER
SKYWRITING
SLA
SLAB
SLABBED
SLABBER
SLABBERED
SLABBERER
SLABBERING
SLABBERY
SLABBINESS
SLABBING
SLABBY
SLABMAN
SLABS
SLABSTONE
SLABWOOD
SLACK
SLACKAGE
SLACKED
SLACKEN
SLACKENED
SLACKENING
SLACKER
SLACKEST
SLACKIE
SLACKING
SLACKLY
SLACKNESS
SLACKS
SLAD
SLADE
SLAG
SLAGGED
SLAGGING
SLAGGY
SLAIN
SLAINTE
SLAISTER
SLAISTERY
SLAIT
SLAKE
SLAKED
SLAKELESS
SLAKER
SLAKIER
SLAKIEST
SLAKIN
SLAKING
SLAKY
SLALOM
SLAM
SLAMBANG
SLAMMED
SLAMMING
SLAMMOCK
SLAMMOCKING
SLAMMOCKY
SLAMP
SLAMPAMP
SLAMPANT
SLANDER
SLANDERER
SLANDERING
SLANDEROUS
SLANDEROUSLY
SLANDEROUSNESS
SLANE
SLANG
SLANGED
SLANGIER
SLANGIEST
SLANGILY
SLANGINESS
SLANGING
SLANGISH
SLANGISHLY
SLANGISM
SLANGKOP
SLANGOUS
SLANGRELL
SLANGSTER
SLANGUAGE
SLANGULAR
SLANGY
SLANK
SLANT
SLANTED
SLANTER
SLANTING
SLANTINGLY
SLANTLY
SLANTWAYS
SLANTWISE
SLAP
SLAPDAB
SLAPDASH
SLAPDASHERIES
SLAPDASHERY
SLAPE
SLAPHAPPIER
SLAPHAPPIEST
SLAPHAPPY
SLAPJACK
SLAPPED
SLAPPER
SLAPPING
SLAPPY
SLAPSTICK
SLARE
SLART
SLARTH
SLASH
SLASHED
SLASHER
SLASHERS
SLASHING
SLASHINGLY
SLASHY
SLAT
SLATCH
SLATE
SLATED
SLATELIKE
SLATER
SLATES
SLATH
SLATHER
SLATIER
SLATIEST
SLATIFIED
SLATIFY
SLATIFYING
SLATING
SLATISH
SLATS
SLATTED
SLATTER
SLATTERED
SLATTERING
SLATTERN
SLATTERNISH
SLATTERNLINESS
SLATTERNLY
SLATTERY
SLATTING
SLATY
SLAUGHTER
SLAUGHTERDOM
SLAUGHTERED
SLAUGHTERER
SLAUGHTERHOUSE
SLAUGHTERING
SLAUGHTERMAN
SLAUGHTEROUS
SLAUGHTEROUSLY
SLAUM
SLAVE
SLAVED
SLAVEHOLDER
SLAVEHOLDING
SLAVELET
SLAVELING
SLAVER
SLAVERED
SLAVERER
SLAVERING
SLAVERY
SLAVES
SLAVEY
SLAVIKITE
SLAVIN
SLAVING
SLAVISH
SLAVOCRACY
SLAVOCRAT
SLAVOCRATIC
SLAW
SLAWBANK
SLAY
SLAYER
SLEATHY
SLEAVE
SLEAVED
SLEAVING
SLEAZINESS
SLEAZY
SLED
SLEDDED
SLEDDER
SLEDDING
SLEDGE
SLEDGED
SLEDGEHAMMER
SLEDGEMETER
SLEDGER
SLEDGING
SLEE
SLEECH
SLEECHY
SLEEK
SLEEKED
SLEEKEN
SLEEKENED
SLEEKENING
SLEEKER
SLEEKIER
SLEEKING
SLEEKIT
SLEEKLY
SLEEKNESS
SLEEKY
SLEEP
SLEEPER
SLEEPERED
SLEEPIER
SLEEPIEST
SLEEPIFY
SLEEPING
SLEEPISH
SLEEPLESS
SLEEPLESSLY
SLEEPLESSNESS
SLEEPMARKEN
SLEEPRY

SLEEPWALK
SLEEPWALKER
SLEEPWALKING
SLEEPWORT
SLEEPY
SLEEPYHEAD
SLEER
SLEET
SLEETED
SLEETIER
SLEETIEST
SLEETING
SLEETY
SLEEVE
SLEEVED
SLEEVEEN
SLEEVEFISH
SLEEVELESS
SLEEVELET
SLEEVER
SLEEVES
SLEEVING
SLEEZY
SLEIDED
SLEIGH
SLEIGHER
SLEIGHING
SLEIGHT
SLEIGHTNESS
SLEIGHTY
SLENDANG
SLENDER
SLENDERER
SLENDEREST
SLENDERISH
SLENDERIZE
SLENDERIZED
SLENDERIZING
SLENDERLY
SLENDERNESS
SLENT
SLEPEZ
SLEUTH
SLEUTHED
SLEUTHHOUND
SLEUTHING
SLEW
SLEWED
SLEWER
SLEWING
SLEWTH
SLEY
SLEYED
SLEYING
SLIBBERSAUCE
SLICE
SLICED
SLICER
SLICES
SLICING
SLICINGLY
SLICK
SLICKED
SLICKENS
SLICKENSIDE
SLICKENSIDED
SLICKER
SLICKERED
SLICKERY
SLICKEST
SLICKING
SLICKLY
SLID
SLIDAGE
SLIDDEN
SLIDDER
SLIDDERNESS
SLIDDERY
SLIDDRY
SLIDE
SLIDEGROAT
SLIDEHEAD
SLIDEKNOT
SLIDEMAN
SLIDER
SLIDEWAY
SLIDING
SLIDOMETER
SLIER
SLIEST
SLIFTER
SLIGGEEN
SLIGHT
SLIGHTED
SLIGHTER
SLIGHTEST
SLIGHTIER
SLIGHTIEST
SLIGHTING
SLIGHTINGLY
SLIGHTLY
SLIGHTNESS
SLIGHTY
SLIKE
SLILY
SLIM
SLIME
SLIMED
SLIMEMAN
SLIMEMEN
SLIMER
SLIMIER
SLIMIEST
SLIMILY
SLIMINESS
SLIMING
SLIMISH
SLIMISHNESS
SLIMLY
SLIMMED
SLIMMER
SLIMMEST
SLIMMING
SLIMMISH
SLIMNESS
SLIMPSY
SLIMSIER
SLIMSIEST
SLIMSY
SLIMY
SLINE
SLING
SLINGE
SLINGER
SLINGING
SLINGSHOT
SLINGSMAN
SLINGSMEN
SLINGSTONE
SLINK
SLINKER
SLINKIER
SLINKIEST
SLINKING
SLINKINGLY
SLINKSKIN
SLINKWEED
SLINKY
SLIP
SLIPBACK
SLIPBAND
SLIPBOARD
SLIPBODIES
SLIPBODY
SLIPCASE
SLIPCOAT
SLIPCOTE
SLIPCOVER
SLIPE
SLIPES
SLIPHALTER
SLIPHORN
SLIPHOUSE
SLIPKNOT
SLIPMAN
SLIPOVER
SLIPPAGE
SLIPPED
SLIPPER
SLIPPERED
SLIPPERFLOWER
SLIPPERIER
SLIPPERIEST
SLIPPERILY
SLIPPERINESS
SLIPPERWEED
SLIPPERWORT
SLIPPERY
SLIPPERYBACK
SLIPPERYROOT
SLIPPIER
SLIPPIEST
SLIPPINESS
SLIPPING
SLIPPINGLY
SLIPPROOF
SLIPPY
SLIPRAIL
SLIPS
SLIPSHEET
SLIPSHOD
SLIPSHOE
SLIPSKIN
SLIPSLAP
SLIPSLOP
SLIPSLOPPISH
SLIPSLOPPISM
SLIPSOLE
SLIPSTICK
SLIPSTREAM
SLIPSTRING
SLIPT
SLIPTOPPED
SLIPUP
SLIPWARE
SLIPWAY
SLIRT
SLISH
SLIT
SLITE
SLITHER
SLITHERING
SLITHEROO
SLITHERS
SLITHERY
SLITING
SLITSHELL
SLITTED
SLITTER
SLITTING
SLITTY
SLITWORK
SLIVE
SLIVER
SLIVERED
SLIVERER
SLIVERING
SLIVERS
SLIVERY
SLIVING
SLIVOVIC
SLIVOVITZ
SLIVVER
SLO
SLOAK
SLOAN
SLOAT
SLOB
SLOBBER
SLOBBERCHOPS
SLOBBERER
SLOBBERS
SLOBBERY
SLOBBY
SLOCK
SLOCKEN
SLOCKER
SLOCKINGSTONE
SLOCKSTER
SLOD
SLODDER
SLODGE
SLODGER
SLOE
SLOEBERRIES
SLOEBERRY
SLOEBUSH
SLOETREE
SLOG
SLOGAN
SLOGANEER
SLOGGED
SLOGGER
SLOGGING
SLOGWOOD
SLOID
SLOJD
SLOKA
SLOKE
SLOKED
SLOKEN
SLOKING
SLOMMACK
SLON
SLONE
SLONK
SLOO
SLOOM
SLOOMY
SLOOP
SLOOPMAN
SLOOPMEN
SLOOSH
SLOOT
SLOP
SLOPE
SLOPED
SLOPER
SLOPEWAYS
SLOPING
SLOPINGLY
SLOPINGNESS
SLOPMAKER
SLOPMAKING
SLOPPAGE
SLOPPED
SLOPPERIES
SLOPPERY
SLOPPIER
SLOPPIEST
SLOPPILY
SLOPPINESS
SLOPPING
SLOPPY
SLOPS
SLOPSELLER
SLOPSELLING
SLOPSHOP
SLOPSTONE
SLOPWORK
SLOPWORKER
SLOPY
SLORP
SLOSH
SLOSHED
SLOSHER
SLOSHILY
SLOSHINESS
SLOSHING
SLOSHY
SLOT
SLOTE
SLOTH
SLOTHFUL
SLOTHFULLY
SLOTHFULNESS
SLOTTED
SLOTTEN
SLOTTER
SLOTTERY
SLOTTING
SLOUBBIE
SLOUCH
SLOUCHED
SLOUCHER
SLOUCHIER
SLOUCHIEST
SLOUCHILY
SLOUCHINESS
SLOUCHING
SLOUCHINGLY
SLOUCHY
SLOUGH
SLOUGHED
SLOUGHING
SLOUGHY
SLOUM
SLOUNGE
SLOUNGER
SLOUR
SLOVEN
SLOVENLIER
SLOVENLIEST
SLOVENLINESS
SLOVENLY
SLOW
SLOWBACK
SLOWBELLIED
SLOWBELLIES
SLOWBELLY
SLOWDOWN
SLOWED
SLOWER
SLOWEST
SLOWFUL
SLOWGOING
SLOWHEADED
SLOWHEARTED
SLOWING
SLOWISH
SLOWLY
SLOWMOUTHED
SLOWNESS
SLOWPOKE
SLOWRIE
SLOWS
SLOWWITTED
SLOWWITTEDLY
SLOWWORM
SLOYD
SLUB
SLUBBED
SLUBBER
SLUBBERED
SLUBBERER

SLUBBERING
SLUBBERINGLY
SLUBBERY
SLUBBING
SLUBBY
SLUD
SLUDDER
SLUDDERY
SLUDE
SLUDGE
SLUDGED
SLUDGER
SLUDGING
SLUDGY
SLUE
SLUED
SLUER
SLUFF
SLUG
SLUGABED
SLUGFEST
SLUGGARD
SLUGGARDING
SLUGGARDIZE
SLUGGARDLY
SLUGGED
SLUGGER
SLUGGING
SLUGGINGLY
SLUGGISH
SLUGGISHLY
SLUGGISHNESS
SLUGGY
SLUGHORN
SLUICE
SLUICED
SLUICER
SLUICEWAY
SLUICING
SLUICY
SLUIG
SLUING
SLUIT
SLUM
SLUMBER
SLUMBERED
SLUMBERER
SLUMBERING
SLUMBERINGLY
SLUMBERLAND
SLUMBERLESS
SLUMBEROUS
SLUMBEROUSLY
SLUMBERY
SLUMBROUS
SLUMDOM
SLUMGULLION
SLUMGUM
SLUMLAND
SLUMLORD
SLUMMAGE
SLUMMED
SLUMMER
SLUMMIER
SLUMMIEST
SLUMMING
SLUMMOCK
SLUMMOCKY
SLUMMY
SLUMP
SLUMPED
SLUMPING
SLUMPWORK
SLUMPY
SLUMS
SLUNG
SLUNGBODIES
SLUNGBODY
SLUNGE
SLUNGSHOT
SLUNK
SLUNKEN
SLUP
SLUR
SLURBOW
SLURP
SLURRED
SLURRIED
SLURRIES
SLURRING
SLURRY
SLURRYING
SLUSH
SLUSHED
SLUSHER
SLUSHIER
SLUSHIEST
SLUSHING
SLUSHPIT
SLUSHY
SLUT
SLUTCH
SLUTCHY
SLUTE
SLUTHER
SLUTTED
SLUTTER
SLUTTERED
SLUTTERING
SLUTTERY
SLUTTING
SLUTTISH
SLUTTISHLY
SLUTTISHNESS
SLUTTY
SLY
SLYBOOTS
SLYER
SLYEST
SLYISH
SLYLY
SLYNESS
SLYPE
SMA
SMACH
SMACHRIE
SMACK
SMACKED
SMACKEE
SMACKER
SMACKING
SMACKINGLY
SMACKSMAN
SMACKSMEN
SMAD
SMAIK
SMAIL
SMAK
SMALL
SMALLAGE
SMALLCLOTHES
SMALLCOAL
SMALLEN
SMALLER
SMALLEST
SMALLHEARTED
SMALLHOLDER
SMALLING
SMALLISH
SMALLMOUTH
SMALLMOUTHED
SMALLNESS
SMALLNESSES
SMALLPOX
SMALLS
SMALLSWORD
SMALLTIME
SMALLWARE
SMALLY
SMALM
SMALMED
SMALMING
SMALT
SMALTER
SMALTI
SMALTINE
SMALTITE
SMALTO
SMALTZ
SMARAGD
SMARAGDE
SMARAGDINE
SMARAGDITE
SMARM
SMARMIER
SMARMIEST
SMARMY
SMART
SMARTED
SMARTEN
SMARTER
SMARTEST
SMARTIES
SMARTING
SMARTINGLY
SMARTISM
SMARTLESS
SMARTLY
SMARTNESS
SMARTWEED
SMARTY
SMASH
SMASHAGE
SMASHED
SMASHER
SMASHERY
SMASHING
SMASHINGLY
SMASHUP
SMATCH
SMATCHET
SMATTER
SMATTERED
SMATTERER
SMATTERING
SMATTERINGLY
SMATTERY
SMAZE
SMEAR
SMEARCASE
SMEARED
SMEARER
SMEARIER
SMEARIEST
SMEARINESS
SMEARING
SMEARLESS
SMEARY
SMECTIC
SMECTITE
SMEDDUM
SMEE
SMEECH
SMEEK
SMEEKY
SMEER
SMEETH
SMEGMA
SMEGMATIC
SMEIR
SMELL
SMELLAGE
SMELLED
SMELLER
SMELLFUL
SMELLIE
SMELLIER
SMELLIEST
SMELLING
SMELLY
SMELT
SMELTED
SMELTER
SMELTERIES
SMELTERY
SMELTING
SMELTS
SMERK
SMERVY
SMETHE
SMEU
SMEUSE
SMEUTH
SMEW
SMICH
SMICKER
SMICKET
SMICKLY
SMIDDY
SMIDGE
SMIDGEN
SMIDGEON
SMIDGIN
SMIFT
SMIGGINS
SMILACACEOUS
SMILAX
SMILE
SMILED
SMILEFUL
SMILEFULNESS
SMILEMAKER
SMILEMAKING
SMILER
SMILEY
SMILING
SMILINGLY
SMILINGNESS
SMILO
SMILY
SMINTHURID
SMIRCH
SMIRCHED
SMIRCHER
SMIRCHING
SMIRCHY
SMIRIS
SMIRK
SMIRKED
SMIRKER
SMIRKING
SMIRKINGLY
SMIRKISH
SMIRKLE
SMIRKY
SMIRR
SMIRTLE
SMIT
SMITABLE
SMITCH
SMITE
SMITER
SMITH
SMITHCRAFT
SMITHER
SMITHEREENS
SMITHERIES
SMITHERS
SMITHERY
SMITHIED
SMITHIER
SMITHIES
SMITHING
SMITHITE
SMITHSONITE
SMITHUM
SMITHWORK
SMITHY
SMITHYDANDER
SMITHYING
SMITING
SMITTEN
SMITTER
SMITTING
SMITTLE
SMITTLEISH
SMITTLISH
SMOCK
SMOCKED
SMOCKER
SMOCKFACE
SMOCKING
SMOCKLESS
SMOG
SMOKABLES
SMOKE
SMOKEBOX
SMOKEBUSH
SMOKED
SMOKEHOUSE
SMOKEJACK
SMOKEJUMPER
SMOKELESS
SMOKELESSLY
SMOKELESSNESS
SMOKEPOT
SMOKEPROOF
SMOKER
SMOKERY
SMOKES
SMOKESTACK
SMOKESTONE
SMOKETIGHT
SMOKEWOOD
SMOKEY
SMOKIER
SMOKIEST
SMOKILY
SMOKINESS
SMOKING
SMOKISH
SMOKO
SMOKY
SMOKYSEEMING
SMOLDER
SMOLDERED
SMOLDERING
SMOLT
SMOOCH
SMOOCHY
SMOODGE
SMOODGER
SMOOGE
SMOOR
SMOORICH
SMOOT
SMOOTH
SMOOTHBOOTS
SMOOTHBORE
SMOOTHBORED
SMOOTHCOAT
SMOOTHED
SMOOTHEN
SMOOTHER
SMOOTHEST

SMOOTHIE
SMOOTHIFY
SMOOTHING
SMOOTHINGLY
SMOOTHLY
SMOOTHNESS
SMOOTHPATE
SMOOTHY
SMOPPLE
SMORE
SMORGASBORD
SMORZANDO
SMORZATO
SMOT
SMOTE
SMOTHER
SMOTHERATION
SMOTHERED
SMOTHERER
SMOTHERINESS
SMOTHERING
SMOTHERINGLY
SMOTHERY
SMOTTER
SMOUCH
SMOUCHER
SMOULDER
SMOULDERED
SMOULDERING
SMOUS
SMOUSE
SMOUSER
SMOUT
SMRITI
SMRTI
SMUDDER
SMUDGE
SMUDGED
SMUDGEDLY
SMUDGER
SMUDGIER
SMUDGIEST
SMUDGILY
SMUDGINESS
SMUDGING
SMUDGY
SMUG
SMUGGER
SMUGGERY
SMUGGEST
SMUGGISH
SMUGGISHLY
SMUGGISHNESS
SMUGGLE
SMUGGLED
SMUGGLER
SMUGGLERY
SMUGGLING
SMUGLY
SMUGNESS
SMUISTY
SMUR
SMURR
SMURRY
SMURTLE
SMUSE
SMUSH
SMUT
SMUTCH
SMUTCHED
SMUTCHIN
SMUTCHING
SMUTCHY
SMUTTED
SMUTTER
SMUTTIER
SMUTTIEST
SMUTTILY
SMUTTINESS
SMUTTING
SMUTTY
SMY
SMYTH
SMYTRIE
SNA
SNAB
SNABBIE
SNABBLE
SNABBY
SNACK
SNACKLE
SNACKY
SNAFF
SNAFFLE
SNAFFLEBIT
SNAFFLED
SNAFFLES
SNAFFLING
SNAFU
SNAFUED
SNAFUING
SNAFUS
SNAG
SNAGBUSH
SNAGGED
SNAGGER
SNAGGIER
SNAGGIEST
SNAGGING
SNAGGLE
SNAGGLED
SNAGGLETEETH
SNAGGLETOOTH
SNAGGLETOOTHED
SNAGGY
SNAGLINE
SNAGREL
SNAIL
SNAILEATER
SNAILERY
SNAILFLOWER
SNAILISH
SNAILISHLY
SNAILY
SNAKE
SNAKEBARK
SNAKEBERRY
SNAKEBIRD
SNAKEBITE
SNAKED
SNAKEFISH
SNAKEFISHES
SNAKEFLOWER
SNAKEHEAD
SNAKEHOLING
SNAKELET
SNAKELIKE
SNAKEMOUTH
SNAKENECK
SNAKEOLOGY
SNAKEPIECE
SNAKEPIPE
SNAKER
SNAKEROOT
SNAKERY
SNAKES
SNAKESKIN
SNAKESTONE
SNAKEWEED
SNAKEWOOD
SNAKEWORM
SNAKEWORT
SNAKEY
SNAKIER
SNAKIEST
SNAKILY
SNAKINESS
SNAKING
SNAKISH
SNAKY
SNAP
SNAPBACK
SNAPBAG
SNAPBERRY
SNAPDRAGON
SNAPE
SNAPER
SNAPHAAN
SNAPHANCE
SNAPHEAD
SNAPHOLDER
SNAPJACK
SNAPLESS
SNAPPAGE
SNAPPED
SNAPPER
SNAPPIER
SNAPPIEST
SNAPPILY
SNAPPINESS
SNAPPING
SNAPPINGLY
SNAPPISH
SNAPPISHLY
SNAPPISHNESS
SNAPPY
SNAPS
SNAPSACK
SNAPSHARE
SNAPSHOT
SNAPSHOTTED
SNAPSHOTTER
SNAPSHOTTING
SNAPWEED
SNAPWOOD
SNAPWORT
SNAPY
SNARE
SNARED
SNARER
SNARING
SNARK
SNARL
SNARLED
SNARLER
SNARLEYOW
SNARLEYYOW
SNARLING
SNARLINGLY
SNARLISH
SNARLY
SNARY
SNASH
SNAST
SNASTE
SNASTY
SNATCH
SNATCHED
SNATCHER
SNATCHIER
SNATCHIEST
SNATCHING
SNATCHINGLY
SNATCHY
SNATH
SNATHE
SNATTOCK
SNAVEL
SNAVVLE
SNAW
SNAZZY
SNEAD
SNEAK
SNEAKED
SNEAKER
SNEAKIER
SNEAKIEST
SNEAKILY
SNEAKINESS
SNEAKING
SNEAKINGLY
SNEAKINGNESS
SNEAKISH
SNEAKISHLY
SNEAKISHNESS
SNEAKSBY
SNEAKY
SNEAP
SNEATH
SNEB
SNECK
SNECKDRAW
SNECKDRAWING
SNECKDRAWN
SNECKED
SNECKER
SNECKET
SNECKING
SNED
SNEDDED
SNEDDING
SNEE
SNEER
SNEERED
SNEERER
SNEERFUL
SNEERFULNESS
SNEERING
SNEERINGLY
SNEERY
SNEESH
SNEESHIN
SNEESHING
SNEEST
SNEESTY
SNEEZE
SNEEZED
SNEEZER
SNEEZEWEED
SNEEZEWOOD
SNEEZEWORT
SNEEZING
SNEEZY
SNEG
SNELL
SNELLY
SNERP
SNEW
SNIB
SNIBBLE
SNIBBLED
SNIBBLER
SNIBEL
SNICK
SNICKDRAW
SNICKED
SNICKER
SNICKERED
SNICKERING
SNICKERINGLY
SNICKERSNEE
SNICKET
SNICKEY
SNICKING
SNICKLE
SNIDDLE
SNIDE
SNIDENESS
SNIDERY
SNIFF
SNIFFED
SNIFFER
SNIFFIER
SNIFFIEST
SNIFFILY
SNIFFINESS
SNIFFING
SNIFFINGLY
SNIFFISH
SNIFFISHNESS
SNIFFLE
SNIFFLED
SNIFFLER
SNIFFLES
SNIFFLING
SNIFFY
SNIFT
SNIFTED
SNIFTER
SNIFTERS
SNIFTING
SNIFTY
SNIG
SNIGGER
SNIGGERER
SNIGGERING
SNIGGERS
SNIGGLE
SNIGGLED
SNIGGLER
SNIGGLING
SNIGGORINGLY
SNIGHT
SNIGS
SNIP
SNIPE
SNIPEBILL
SNIPED
SNIPEFISH
SNIPEFISHES
SNIPER
SNIPERSCOPE
SNIPES
SNIPING
SNIPISH
SNIPJACK
SNIPOCRACY
SNIPPED
SNIPPER
SNIPPERADO
SNIPPERTY
SNIPPET
SNIPPETY
SNIPPIER
SNIPPIEST
SNIPPING
SNIPPY
SNIPS
SNIPTIOUS
SNIPY
SNIRL
SNIRT
SNIRTLE
SNIT
SNITCH
SNITCHER
SNITE
SNITHE
SNITHY
SNITS
SNITTLE
SNITZ
SNIVEL
SNIVELED
SNIVELER

SNIVELING
SNIVELLED
SNIVELLER
SNIVELLING
SNIVELLY
SNIVELS
SNIVELY
SNIVEY
SNIVY
SNOB
SNOBBER
SNOBBERY
SNOBBING
SNOBBISH
SNOBBISHLY
SNOBBISHNESS
SNOBBISM
SNOBBY
SNOBISM
SNOBOCRACY
SNOBOCRAT
SNOBOGRAPHER
SNOBOGRAPHY
SNOBOLOGIST
SNOBONOMER
SNOBS
SNOBSCAT
SNOCAT
SNOCHER
SNOCK
SNOCKER
SNOD
SNODE
SNODLY
SNOEK
SNOEKING
SNOGA
SNOOD
SNOODED
SNOODING
SNOOK
SNOOKER
SNOOKERED
SNOOKS
SNOOL
SNOOP
SNOOPER
SNOOPIER
SNOOPIEST
SNOOPY
SNOOT
SNOOTFUL
SNOOTIER
SNOOTIEST
SNOOTY
SNOOVE
SNOOZE
SNOOZED
SNOOZER
SNOOZING
SNOOZLE
SNOOZY
SNOP
SNORE
SNORED
SNORER
SNORING
SNORINGLY
SNORK
SNORKEL
SNORKELED
SNORKELING
SNORKER
SNORT
SNORTED
SNORTER
SNORTING
SNORTINGLY
SNORTLE
SNORTY
SNOT
SNOTTER
SNOTTERY
SNOTTIE
SNOTTIER
SNOTTIEST
SNOTTY
SNOUCH
SNOUT
SNOUTED
SNOUTER
SNOUTFAIR
SNOUTISH
SNOUTY
SNOVE
SNOW
SNOWBALL
SNOWBALLED
SNOWBALLING
SNOWBANK
SNOWBELL
SNOWBERG
SNOWBERRIES
SNOWBERRY
SNOWBIRD
SNOWBLINK
SNOWBLOWER
SNOWBOUND
SNOWBREAK
SNOWBROTH
SNOWBUSH
SNOWCAP
SNOWCRAFT
SNOWDRIFT
SNOWDROP
SNOWED
SNOWFALL
SNOWFLAKE
SNOWFLIGHT
SNOWFLOWER
SNOWFOWL
SNOWHAMMER
SNOWHOUSE
SNOWIER
SNOWIEST
SNOWILY
SNOWINESS
SNOWING
SNOWK
SNOWL
SNOWLAND
SNOWLESS
SNOWLIKE
SNOWMAN
SNOWMELT
SNOWMEN
SNOWMOBILE
SNOWPACK
SNOWPLOUGH
SNOWPLOW
SNOWS
SNOWSCAPE
SNOWSHADE
SNOWSHED
SNOWSHINE
SNOWSHOE
SNOWSHOED
SNOWSHOEING
SNOWSHOER
SNOWSLIDE
SNOWSLIP
SNOWSTORM
SNOWSUIT
SNOWTHROWER
SNOWWORM
SNOWY
SNOZZLE
SNUB
SNUBBED
SNUBBEE
SNUBBER
SNUBBING
SNUBBINGLY
SNUBBISH
SNUBBISHLY
SNUBBISHNESS
SNUBBY
SNUCK
SNUDGE
SNUDGERY
SNUFF
SNUFFBOX
SNUFFBOXER
SNUFFCOLORED
SNUFFED
SNUFFER
SNUFFERS
SNUFFIER
SNUFFIEST
SNUFFILY
SNUFFINESS
SNUFFING
SNUFFINGLY
SNUFFISH
SNUFFKIN
SNUFFLE
SNUFFLED
SNUFFLER
SNUFFLES
SNUFFLESS
SNUFFLINESS
SNUFFLING
SNUFFLINGLY
SNUFFLY
SNUFFMAN
SNUFFY
SNUG
SNUGGED
SNUGGER
SNUGGERIES
SNUGGERY
SNUGGEST
SNUGGIES
SNUGGING
SNUGGISH
SNUGGLE
SNUGGLED
SNUGGLING
SNUGIFY
SNUGLY
SNUGNESS
SNUM
SNUP
SNUPPER
SNUR
SNURL
SNURLY
SNURP
SNURT
SNUSH
SNUZZLE
SNY
SNYE
SNYED
SNYING
SO
SOA
SOAK
SOAKAGE
SOAKAWAY
SOAKED
SOAKEN
SOAKER
SOAKERS
SOAKING
SOAKINGLY
SOAKY
SOAL
SOALLIES
SOALLY
SOAM
SOAP
SOAPBARK
SOAPBERRIES
SOAPBERRY
SOAPBOX
SOAPBOXER
SOAPBUBBLY
SOAPBUSH
SOAPED
SOAPER
SOAPERIES
SOAPERY
SOAPFISH
SOAPFISHES
SOAPIER
SOAPIEST
SOAPING
SOAPLEES
SOAPLESS
SOAPMAKER
SOAPMAKING
SOAPROCK
SOAPROOT
SOAPSTONE
SOAPSTONER
SOAPSUDDY
SOAPSUDS
SOAPSUDSY
SOAPWEED
SOAPWOOD
SOAPWORT
SOAPY
SOAR
SOARABILITY
SOARABLE
SOARED
SOARER
SOARING
SOARINGLY
SOARY
SOAVE
SOAVEMENTE
SOB
SOBBED
SOBBER
SOBBING
SOBBINGLY
SOBBY
SOBEIT
SOBER
SOBERED
SOBERER
SOBEREST
SOBERING
SOBERINGLY
SOBERIZE
SOBERLY
SOBERNESS
SOBERSIDED
SOBERSIDES
SOBFUL
SOBOL
SOBOLE
SOBOLES
SOBOLIFEROUS
SOBOR
SOBPROOF
SOBRALITE
SOBREVEST
SOBRIETIES
SOBRIETY
SOBRIQUET
SOC
SOCAGE
SOCAGER
SOCCAGE
SOCCER
SOCCERIST
SOCCERITE
SOCE
SOCIABILITIES
SOCIABILITY
SOCIABLE
SOCIABLENESS
SOCIABLY
SOCIAL
SOCIALISM
SOCIALIST
SOCIALISTIC
SOCIALITE
SOCIALITIES
SOCIALITY
SOCIALIZATION
SOCIALIZE
SOCIALIZED
SOCIALIZER
SOCIALIZING
SOCIALLY
SOCIATE
SOCIATION
SOCIATIVE
SOCIES
SOCIETAL
SOCIETALLY
SOCIETARIAN
SOCIETARY
SOCIETAS
SOCIETE
SOCIETEIT
SOCIETIES
SOCIETIFIED
SOCIETISM
SOCIETIST
SOCIETOLOGIST
SOCIETOLOGY
SOCIETY
SOCIETYISH
SOCII
SOCIOCENTRIC
SOCIOCRACY
SOCIOCRAT
SOCIOCRATIC
SOCIOCULTURAL
SOCIOECONOMIC
SOCIOECONOMICALLY
SOCIOEDUCATIONAL
SOCIOGENESIS
SOCIOGENETIC
SOCIOGENY
SOCIOGRAPHY
SOCIOLATRY
SOCIOLEGAL
SOCIOLOGIAN
SOCIOLOGIC
SOCIOLOGICAL
SOCIOLOGICALLY
SOCIOLOGIST
SOCIOLOGISTIC
SOCIOLOGY
SOCIOMEDICAL
SOCIOMETRIC
SOCIOMETRY
SOCIONOMIC
SOCIONOMY

SOCIOPHAGOUS
SOCIOPOLITICAL
SOCIORELIGIOUS
SOCIOROMANTIC
SOCIOSTATIC
SOCIOTECHNICAL
SOCIUS
SOCK
SOCKDOLAGER
SOCKDOLOGER
SOCKER
SOCKEROO
SOCKET
SOCKETED
SOCKETING
SOCKEYE
SOCKHEAD
SOCKMAKER
SOCKMAKING
SOCKMAN
SOCKO
SOCKS
SOCKY
SOCLE
SOCMAN
SOCMANRY
SOCMEN
SOCO
SOD
SODA
SODACLASE
SODAIC
SODALIST
SODALITE
SODALITHITE
SODALITIES
SODALITY
SODAMID
SODAMIDE
SODAR
SODBUSTER
SODDED
SODDEN
SODDENLY
SODDENNESS
SODDIER
SODDIES
SODDIEST
SODDING
SODDITE
SODDY
SODIC
SODIOAUROUS
SODIOCITRATE
SODIOHYDRIC
SODIUM
SODOKU
SODOMITE
SODOMITIC
SODOMITICAL
SODOMITICALLY
SODOMY
SODS
SODWORK
SOE
SOEVER
SOFA
SOFANE
SOFAR
SOFFARID
SOFFIONE
SOFFIONI
SOFFIT
SOFI
SOFKEE
SOFT
SOFTA
SOFTBALL
SOFTCOAL
SOFTEN
SOFTENED
SOFTENER
SOFTENING
SOFTER
SOFTEST
SOFTHEAD
SOFTHEARTED
SOFTHEARTEDLY
SOFTHEARTEDNESS
SOFTHORN
SOFTIE
SOFTIES
SOFTISH
SOFTLING
SOFTLY
SOFTNESS
SOFTS
SOFTTACK
SOFTWARE
SOFTWOOD
SOFTY
SOG
SOGA
SOGGARTH
SOGGED
SOGGENDALITE
SOGGIER
SOGGIEST
SOGGILY
SOGGINESS
SOGGING
SOGGY
SOH
SOHO
SOIGNE
SOIGNEE
SOIL
SOILAGE
SOILED
SOILIER
SOILIEST
SOILING
SOILS
SOILURE
SOILY
SOIREE
SOIXANTINE
SOJA
SOJOURN
SOJOURNED
SOJOURNER
SOJOURNING
SOJOURNMENT
SOK
SOKA
SOKE
SOKEMAN
SOKEMANEMOT
SOKEMANRIES
SOKEMANRY
SOKEN
SOL
SOLA
SOLACE
SOLACED
SOLACEMENT
SOLACER
SOLACH
SOLACING
SOLAH
SOLAK
SOLAN
SOLANACEOUS
SOLANAL
SOLAND
SOLANDER
SOLANDRA
SOLANEIN
SOLANEINE
SOLANEOUS
SOLANIDIN
SOLANIDINE
SOLANIN
SOLANINE
SOLANO
SOLANOS
SOLANUM
SOLAR
SOLARIA
SOLARIEGO
SOLARIMETER
SOLARISM
SOLARIST
SOLARISTIC
SOLARISTICALLY
SOLARISTICS
SOLARIUM
SOLARIUMS
SOLARIZATION
SOLARIZE
SOLARIZED
SOLARIZING
SOLAROMETER
SOLARY
SOLATE
SOLATIA
SOLATION
SOLATIUM
SOLAY
SOLD
SOLDADO
SOLDADOES
SOLDADOS
SOLDAN
SOLDANEL
SOLDANELLE
SOLDANRIE
SOLDAT
SOLDATESQUE
SOLDER
SOLDERED
SOLDERER
SOLDERING
SOLDI
SOLDIER
SOLDIERBIRD
SOLDIERBUSH
SOLDIERED
SOLDIERFARE
SOLDIERFISH
SOLDIERFISHES
SOLDIERHEARTED
SOLDIERIES
SOLDIERING
SOLDIERLIKE
SOLDIERLINESS
SOLDIERLY
SOLDIERPROOF
SOLDIERS
SOLDIERWOOD
SOLDIERY
SOLDO
SOLE
SOLEA
SOLECISE
SOLECISM
SOLECIST
SOLECISTIC
SOLECISTICAL
SOLECISTICALLY
SOLECIZE
SOLECIZED
SOLECIZER
SOLECIZING
SOLED
SOLEIFORM
SOLEIL
SOLEIN
SOLELESS
SOLELY
SOLEMN
SOLEMNCHOLY
SOLEMNESS
SOLEMNIFIED
SOLEMNIFY
SOLEMNIFYING
SOLEMNISE
SOLEMNITIES
SOLEMNITUDE
SOLEMNITY
SOLEMNIZATION
SOLEMNIZE
SOLEMNIZED
SOLEMNIZER
SOLEMNIZING
SOLEMNLY
SOLEMNNESS
SOLENACEAN
SOLENACEOUS
SOLENETTE
SOLENIAL
SOLENITE
SOLENITIS
SOLENIUM
SOLENNE
SOLENNEMENTE
SOLENOCYTE
SOLENODONT
SOLENOGASTER
SOLENOGLYPH
SOLENOID
SOLENOIDAL
SOLENOIDALLY
SOLENOSTELE
SOLENOSTELIC
SOLENOSTOMID
SOLENTINE
SOLEPIECE
SOLEPLATE
SOLEPRINT
SOLER
SOLERET
SOLERT
SOLES
SOLEUS
SOLEYN
SOLEYNE
SOLFATARA
SOLFATARIC
SOLFEGE
SOLFEGGI
SOLFEGGIARE
SOLFEGGIO
SOLFEGGIOS
SOLFERINO
SOLI
SOLICIT
SOLICITANT
SOLICITATION
SOLICITED
SOLICITEE
SOLICITER
SOLICITING
SOLICITOR
SOLICITOUS
SOLICITOUSLY
SOLICITOUSNESS
SOLICITUDE
SOLID
SOLIDAGO
SOLIDAGOS
SOLIDARE
SOLIDARIC
SOLIDARISM
SOLIDARIST
SOLIDARISTIC
SOLIDARITIES
SOLIDARITY
SOLIDARIZE
SOLIDARIZED
SOLIDARIZING
SOLIDARY
SOLIDATE
SOLIDATED
SOLIDATING
SOLIDEO
SOLIDER
SOLIDEST
SOLIDI
SOLIDIFICATION
SOLIDIFIED
SOLIDIFIER
SOLIDIFORM
SOLIDIFY
SOLIDIFYING
SOLIDISM
SOLIDIST
SOLIDISTIC
SOLIDITIES
SOLIDITY
SOLIDLY
SOLIDNESS
SOLIDUM
SOLIDUNGULAR
SOLIDUS
SOLIFIDIAN
SOLIFIDIANISM
SOLIFLUCTION
SOLIFORM
SOLIFUGE
SOLILOQUACIOUS
SOLILOQUIES
SOLILOQUISE
SOLILOQUIST
SOLILOQUIZE
SOLILOQUIZED
SOLILOQUIZER
SOLILOQUIZING
SOLILOQUIZINGLY
SOLILOQUY
SOLILUNAR
SOLING
SOLION
SOLIPED
SOLIPEDAL
SOLIPEDOUS
SOLIPSISM
SOLIPSISMAL
SOLIPSIST
SOLIPSISTIC
SOLIQUID
SOLISTE
SOLITAIRE
SOLITARIAN
SOLITARIES
SOLITARILY
SOLITARINESS
SOLITARY
SOLITIDAL
SOLITUDE
SOLITUDINIZE
SOLITUDINIZED
SOLITUDINIZING
SOLITUDINOUS
SOLIVAGANT

SOLIVAGOUS
SOLLAR
SOLLER
SOLLERET
SOLMIZATE
SOLMIZATION
SOLO
SOLOED
SOLOING
SOLOIST
SOLONETZ
SOLONIST
SOLOS
SOLOTH
SOLPUGID
SOLS
SOLSTICE
SOLSTICION
SOLSTITIAL
SOLSTITIALLY
SOLUBILITIES
SOLUBILITY
SOLUBILIZE
SOLUBLE
SOLUBLENESS
SOLUBLY
SOLUM
SOLUS
SOLUTE
SOLUTIO
SOLUTION
SOLUTIONAL
SOLUTIONER
SOLUTIONIST
SOLUTIONS
SOLUTIVE
SOLUTORY
SOLVABILITY
SOLVABLE
SOLVABLENESS
SOLVATE
SOLVATION
SOLVE
SOLVED
SOLVENCIES
SOLVENCY
SOLVEND
SOLVENT
SOLVENTLY
SOLVER
SOLVING
SOLVOLYSIS
SOLVOLYTIC
SOLVOLYZE
SOLVOLYZED
SOLVOLYZING
SOLVSBERGITE
SOLVUS
SOMA
SOMACULE
SOMAL
SOMALO
SOMAPLASM
SOMATA
SOMATEN
SOMATENES
SOMATIC
SOMATICAL
SOMATICALLY
SOMATISM
SOMATIST
SOMATOCHROME
SOMATOCYST
SOMATOCYSTIC
SOMATODERM
SOMATOGENIC
SOMATOGNOSIS
SOMATOLOGIC
SOMATOLOGIST
SOMATOLOGY
SOMATOME
SOMATOMIC
SOMATOPHYTE
SOMATOPHYTIC
SOMATOPLASM
SOMATOPLEURE
SOMATOTROPIC
SOMBER
SOMBERISH
SOMBERLY
SOMBERNESS
SOMBRE
SOMBREISH
SOMBREITE
SOMBRELY
SOMBRENESS
SOMBRERO
SOMBREROED
SOMBREROS
SOMBROUS
SOMBROUSLY
SOMBROUSNESS
SOMDEL
SOMDIEL
SOME
SOMEBODIES
SOMEBODY
SOMEDAY
SOMEDEAL
SOMEGATE
SOMEHOW
SOMEONE
SOMEPART
SOMEPLACE
SOMER
SOMERS
SOMERSAULT
SOMERSET
SOMERVILLITE
SOMESTHESIA
SOMESTHESIS
SOMESTHETIC
SOMETHING
SOMETIME
SOMETIMES
SOMEWAY
SOMEWAYS
SOMEWHAT
SOMEWHATLY
SOMEWHATNESS
SOMEWHEN
SOMEWHENCE
SOMEWHERE
SOMEWHERES
SOMEWHILE
SOMEWHILES
SOMEWHITHER
SOMEWHY
SOMEWISE
SOMITAL
SOMITE
SOMITIC
SOMLER
SOMMA
SOMMAITE
SOMME
SOMMELIER
SOMMITE
SOMNAMBULANCE
SOMNAMBULANCY
SOMNAMBULANT
SOMNAMBULAR
SOMNAMBULARY
SOMNAMBULATE
SOMNAMBULATED
SOMNAMBULATING
SOMNAMBULATION
SOMNAMBULATOR
SOMNAMBULE
SOMNAMBULENCY
SOMNAMBULIC
SOMNAMBULICALLY
SOMNAMBULISM
SOMNAMBULIST
SOMNAMBULISTIC
SOMNAMBULIZE
SOMNAMBULOUS
SOMNIAL
SOMNIATE
SOMNIATIVE
SOMNIFACIENT
SOMNIFEROUS
SOMNIFIC
SOMNIFUGE
SOMNIFUGOUS
SOMNIFY
SOMNILOQUENCE
SOMNILOQUENT
SOMNILOQUISM
SOMNILOQUIST
SOMNILOQUOUS
SOMNILOQUY
SOMNIPATHIST
SOMNIPATHY
SOMNIVOLENCY
SOMNIVOLENT
SOMNO
SOMNOLENCE
SOMNOLENCY
SOMNOLENT
SOMNOLENTLY
SOMNOLESCENT
SOMNOLISM
SOMNORIFIC
SOMNUS
SOMPAY
SOMPNE
SOMPNER
SON
SONABLE
SONANCE
SONANT
SONANTAL
SONANTIC
SONAR
SONARMAN
SONATA
SONATINA
SONATINAS
SONATINE
SONATION
SONCY
SONDAGE
SONDATION
SONDE
SONDELI
SONDER
SONDERCLASS
SONE
SONED
SONERI
SONG
SONGBIRD
SONGBOOK
SONGCRAFT
SONGER
SONGFUL
SONGFULLY
SONGFULNESS
SONGISH
SONGLAND
SONGLE
SONGLESS
SONGLET
SONGMAN
SONGS
SONGSTER
SONGSTRESS
SONGWRIGHT
SONGWRITER
SONGY
SONIC
SONICA
SONICS
SONIFEROUS
SONIFICATION
SONING
SONIOU
SONK
SONLY
SONNET
SONNETARY
SONNETED
SONNETEER
SONNETIC
SONNETING
SONNETIST
SONNETIZE
SONNETRY
SONNETTED
SONNETTING
SONNY
SONOBUOY
SONORANT
SONORESCENCE
SONORESCENT
SONORIC
SONORIFEROUS
SONORIFIC
SONORITIES
SONORITY
SONORIZE
SONOROPHONE
SONOROUS
SONOROUSLY
SONOROUSNESS
SONOVOX
SONS
SONSE
SONSHIP
SONSIE
SONSY
SONTAG
SOO
SOOCHONG
SOODLE
SOODLED
SOODLING
SOODLY
SOOEY
SOOGAN
SOOGEE
SOOK
SOOKIE
SOOKY
SOOL
SOOLOOS
SOOM
SOON
SOOND
SOONER
SOONEST
SOONISH
SOOP
SOOPER
SOOR
SOORAWN
SOOREYN
SOORKEE
SOORKI
SOORKY
SOORMA
SOOSOO
SOOT
SOOTED
SOOTER
SOOTERKIN
SOOTH
SOOTHE
SOOTHED
SOOTHER
SOOTHERER
SOOTHEST
SOOTHFAST
SOOTHFASTLY
SOOTHFUL
SOOTHING
SOOTHINGLY
SOOTHINGNESS
SOOTHLY
SOOTHSAID
SOOTHSAW
SOOTHSAY
SOOTHSAYER
SOOTHSAYING
SOOTIED
SOOTIER
SOOTIEST
SOOTILY
SOOTINESS
SOOTING
SOOTISH
SOOTY
SOOTYING
SOP
SOPE
SOPH
SOPHEME
SOPHENE
SOPHER
SOPHIC
SOPHICAL
SOPHICALLY
SOPHIOLOGIC
SOPHIOLOGY
SOPHISM
SOPHIST
SOPHISTER
SOPHISTIC
SOPHISTICAL
SOPHISTICALLY
SOPHISTICALNESS
SOPHISTICANT
SOPHISTICATE
SOPHISTICATED
SOPHISTICATING
SOPHISTICATION
SOPHISTICATIVE
SOPHISTICATOR
SOPHISTICISM
SOPHISTRIES
SOPHISTRY
SOPHOMORE
SOPHOMORIC
SOPHOMORICAL
SOPHOMORICALLY
SOPHORIA
SOPHRONIZE
SOPHRONIZED
SOPHRONIZING
SOPHTA
SOPHY
SOPIE
SOPITE
SOPITED

SOPITING
SOPITION
SOPOR
SOPORATE
SOPORIFEROUS
SOPORIFIC
SOPORIFICAL
SOPOROSE
SOPPED
SOPPER
SOPPIER
SOPPIEST
SOPPING
SOPPY
SOPRA
SOPRANI
SOPRANINO
SOPRANIST
SOPRANO
SOPRANOS
SOPT
SORA
SORAGE
SORAL
SORANCE
SORB
SORBATE
SORBEFACIENT
SORBENT
SORBET
SORBIC
SORBILE
SORBITAN
SORBITE
SORBITIC
SORBITIZE
SORBITOL
SORBOSE
SORBOSID
SORBOSIDE
SORCER
SORCERER
SORCERESS
SORCERIES
SORCERING
SORCEROUS
SORCEROUSLY
SORCERY
SORD
SORDA
SORDAVALITE
SORDAWALITE
SORDELLINA
SORDES
SORDID
SORDIDITY
SORDIDLY
SORDIDNESS
SORDINE
SORDINO
SORDO
SORDOR
SORE
SOREDIA
SOREDIAL
SOREDIATE
SOREDIFEROUS
SOREDIFORM
SOREDIOID
SOREDIUM
SOREFALCON
SOREFOOT
SOREHAWK
SOREHEAD
SOREHEADED
SOREHEADEDLY
SOREHEADEDNESS
SOREHEARTED
SOREHON
SOREL
SORELY
SOREMA
SORENESS
SORER
SOREST
SORGE
SORGHE
SORGHO
SORGHUM
SORGO
SORGOS
SORI
SORICID
SORICIDENT
SORICINE
SORICOID
SORIFEROUS
SORITE
SORITES
SORITIC
SORITICAL
SORN
SORNARI
SORNER
SOROBAN
SOROCHE
SORORAL
SORORATE
SORORIAL
SORORIALLY
SORORICIDAL
SORORICIDE
SORORITIES
SORORITY
SORORIZE
SOROSE
SOROSES
SOROSIS
SOROSPHERE
SORPTION
SORRA
SORRANCE
SORREL
SORREN
SORRENTO
SORRIER
SORRIEST
SORRILY
SORRINESS
SORROW
SORROWED
SORROWER
SORROWFUL
SORROWFULLY
SORROWFULNESS
SORROWING
SORROWINGLY
SORRY
SORRYHEARTED
SORRYISH
SORS
SORT
SORTABLE
SORTABLY
SORTAL
SORTANCE
SORTATION
SORTED
SORTER
SORTES
SORTIARY
SORTIE
SORTILEGE
SORTILEGER
SORTILEGI
SORTILEGIC
SORTILEGIOUS
SORTILEGUS
SORTIMENT
SORTING
SORTITA
SORTITION
SORTLY
SORTMENT
SORTS
SORTY
SORUS
SORVA
SORY
SOSH
SOSHED
SOSIE
SOSO
SOSOISH
SOSPIRO
SOSQUIL
SOSS
SOSSIEGO
SOSSLE
SOSTENENDO
SOSTENENTE
SOSTENUTI
SOSTENUTO
SOSTENUTOS
SOSTINENTE
SOSTINENTO
SOT
SOTERIOLOGIC
SOTERIOLOGY
SOTH
SOTIE
SOTNIA
SOTNIK
SOTOL
SOTS
SOTTAGE
SOTTED
SOTTER
SOTTERY
SOTTING
SOTTISE
SOTTISH
SOTTISHLY
SOTTISHNESS
SOTTO
SOTWEED
SOU
SOUARI
SOUBISE
SOUBRETTE
SOUBRETTISH
SOUBRIQUET
SOUCAR
SOUCE
SOUCH
SOUCHIE
SOUCHONG
SOUD
SOUDAGUR
SOUDAN
SOUFFLE
SOUFFLEED
SOUFFLEUR
SOUGAN
SOUGH
SOUGHED
SOUGHER
SOUGHING
SOUGHT
SOUK
SOUL
SOULACK
SOULCAKE
SOULDIE
SOULE
SOULED
SOULFUL
SOULFULLY
SOULFULNESS
SOULHEAL
SOULHEALTH
SOULICAL
SOULISH
SOULLESS
SOULLESSLY
SOULLESSNESS
SOULPENCE
SOULPENNY
SOULS
SOULTER
SOULTRE
SOULX
SOULY
SOULZ
SOUM
SOUMAK
SOUMANSITE
SOUND
SOUNDABLE
SOUNDAGE
SOUNDBOARD
SOUNDED
SOUNDER
SOUNDFUL
SOUNDHEADED
SOUNDHEADEDNESS
SOUNDHEARTED
SOUNDHEARTEDNESS
SOUNDING
SOUNDINGLY
SOUNDINGNESS
SOUNDLESS
SOUNDLESSLY
SOUNDLESSNESS
SOUNDLY
SOUNDNESS
SOUNDPROOF
SOUNDPROOFING
SOUNDS
SOUNE
SOUP
SOUPBONE
SOUPCON
SOUPER
SOUPFIN
SOUPIER
SOUPIEST
SOUPLE
SOUPLED
SOUPLESS
SOUPLIKE
SOUPLING
SOUPSPOON
SOUPY
SOUR
SOURBALL
SOURBELLIES
SOURBELLY
SOURBERRIES
SOURBERRY
SOURBREAD
SOURBUSH
SOURCE
SOURCROUT
SOURD
SOURDINE
SOURDOOK
SOURDOUGH
SOURDRE
SOURED
SOUREDNESS
SOUREN
SOURER
SOUREST
SOURING
SOURJACK
SOURLING
SOURLY
SOURNESS
SOUROCK
SOURPUSS
SOURSOP
SOURTOP
SOURVELD
SOURWEED
SOURWOOD
SOURY
SOUS
SOUSAPHONE
SOUSAPHONIST
SOUSE
SOUSED
SOUSER
SOUSEWIFE
SOUSING
SOUSLIK
SOUTACHE
SOUTAGE
SOUTANE
SOUTAR
SOUTENU
SOUTER
SOUTERLY
SOUTERRAIN
SOUTH
SOUTHARD
SOUTHBOUND
SOUTHEAST
SOUTHEASTER
SOUTHEASTERLY
SOUTHEASTERN
SOUTHEASTERNMOST
SOUTHEASTWARD
SOUTHEASTWARDLY
SOUTHEASTWARDS
SOUTHED
SOUTHER
SOUTHERLAND
SOUTHERLIES
SOUTHERLINESS
SOUTHERLY
SOUTHERMOST
SOUTHERN
SOUTHERNER
SOUTHERNEST
SOUTHERNISM
SOUTHERNIZE
SOUTHERNLINESS
SOUTHERNLY
SOUTHERNMOST
SOUTHERNWOOD
SOUTHING
SOUTHLAND
SOUTHLANDER
SOUTHMOST
SOUTHNESS
SOUTHPAW
SOUTHRON
SOUTHWARD
SOUTHWARDLY
SOUTHWARDS
SOUTHWEST
SOUTHWESTER
SOUTHWESTERLIES
SOUTHWESTERLY

SOUTHWESTERN
SOUTHWESTERNMOST
SOUTHWESTWARD
SOUTHWESTWARDLY
SOUTHWESTWARDS
SOUVENIR
SOUVERAIN
SOV
SOVENEZ
SOVEREIGN
SOVEREIGNESS
SOVEREIGNIZE
SOVEREIGNLY
SOVEREIGNNESS
SOVEREIGNTIES
SOVEREIGNTY
SOVERTY
SOVIET
SOVIETIC
SOVIETISM
SOVIETIST
SOVIETISTIC
SOVIETIZATION
SOVIETIZE
SOVIETIZED
SOVIETIZING
SOVIK
SOVITE
SOVKHOS
SOVKHOSE
SOVKHOZ
SOVPRENE
SOVRAN
SOVRANLY
SOVRANTY
SOW
SOWAN
SOWAR
SOWARREE
SOWARRY
SOWBACK
SOWBACKED
SOWBANE
SOWBELLY
SOWBREAD
SOWCAR
SOWCE
SOWD
SOWDER
SOWDONES
SOWED
SOWEL
SOWENS
SOWER
SOWF
SOWFF
SOWFOOT
SOWING
SOWISH
SOWL
SOWLE
SOWLTH
SOWN
SOWP
SOWSE
SOWTH
SOX
SOY
SOYA
SOYATE
SOYBEAN
SOYL
SOYLE
SOYLED
SOZIN
SOZOLIC
SOZZLE
SOZZLED
SOZZLY
SPA
SPAAD
SPACE
SPACEBAND
SPACECRAFT
SPACED
SPACEFUL
SPACELESS
SPACEMAN
SPACEMANSHIP
SPACEMEN
SPACEPORT
SPACER
SPACES
SPACESHIP
SPACEWALK
SPACIAL
SPACINESS
SPACING
SPACIOSITY
SPACIOUS
SPACIOUSLY
SPACIOUSNESS
SPACK
SPACKLE
SPACKLED
SPACKLING
SPACY
SPAD
SPADAITE
SPADASSIN
SPADDLE
SPADE
SPADEBONE
SPADED
SPADEFISH
SPADEFOOT
SPADEFUL
SPADEMAN
SPADEMEN
SPADER
SPADES
SPADESMAN
SPADEWORK
SPADGER
SPADIARD
SPADICEOUS
SPADICES
SPADICIFORM
SPADICOSE
SPADILLA
SPADILLE
SPADILLO
SPADING
SPADISH
SPADIX
SPADO
SPADONES
SPADONIC
SPADONISM
SPADROON
SPAE
SPAEBOOK
SPAECRAFT
SPAED
SPAEDOM
SPAEING
SPAEMAN
SPAER
SPAEWIFE
SPAEWOMAN
SPAEWORK
SPAEWRIGHT
SPAGHETTI
SPAGNUOLO
SPAGYRIC
SPAGYRICAL
SPAGYRIST
SPAHEE
SPAHI
SPAHIS
SPAIL
SPAIN
SPAIR
SPAIRGE
SPAIT
SPAK
SPAKE
SPAKED
SPALACID
SPALACINE
SPALD
SPALDER
SPALDING
SPALE
SPALL
SPALLATION
SPALLED
SPALLER
SPALLING
SPALPEEN
SPALT
SPAN
SPANAEMIA
SPANAEMIC
SPANCEL
SPANCELED
SPANCELING
SPANCELLED
SPANCELLING
SPANDEX
SPANDLE
SPANDREL
SPANDRIL
SPANDY
SPANE
SPANED
SPANEMIA
SPANEMIC
SPANEMY
SPANG
SPANGED
SPANGHEW
SPANGING
SPANGLE
SPANGLED
SPANGLER
SPANGLET
SPANGLIER
SPANGLIEST
SPANGLING
SPANGLY
SPANGOLITE
SPANIEL
SPANING
SPANIPELAGIC
SPANK
SPANKED
SPANKER
SPANKILY
SPANKING
SPANKINGLY
SPANKLED
SPANKY
SPANLESS
SPANN
SPANNED
SPANNER
SPANNERMAN
SPANNERMEN
SPANNING
SPANOPNEA
SPANOPNOEA
SPANPIECE
SPANSPEK
SPANULE
SPANWORM
SPAR
SPARABLE
SPARADA
SPARADRAP
SPARAGE
SPARASSODONT
SPARCH
SPARE
SPARED
SPAREFUL
SPARELESS
SPARELY
SPARENESS
SPARER
SPARERIB
SPARESOME
SPAREST
SPARGANUM
SPARGE
SPARGED
SPARGER
SPARGING
SPARGOSIS
SPARHAWK
SPARID
SPARILY
SPARING
SPARINGLY
SPARINGNESS
SPARK
SPARKBACK
SPARKED
SPARKER
SPARKIER
SPARKIEST
SPARKINESS
SPARKING
SPARKINGLY
SPARKISH
SPARKISHLY
SPARKISHNESS
SPARKLE
SPARKLEBERRY
SPARKLED
SPARKLER
SPARKLET
SPARKLINESS
SPARKLING
SPARKLINGNESS
SPARKLY
SPARKPLUG
SPARKPLUGGED
SPARKPLUGGING
SPARKS
SPARKY
SPARLING
SPAROID
SPARPLE
SPARPLED
SPARPLING
SPARRED
SPARRER
SPARRIER
SPARRIEST
SPARRING
SPARRINGLY
SPARROW
SPARROWCIDE
SPARROWGRASS
SPARROWISH
SPARROWWORT
SPARROWY
SPARRY
SPARRYGRASS
SPARSE
SPARSEDLY
SPARSELY
SPARSENESS
SPARSER
SPARSEST
SPARSILE
SPARSIM
SPARSIOPLAST
SPARSITY
SPART
SPARTACIST
SPARTEIN
SPARTEINE
SPARTERIE
SPARTH
SPARTLE
SPARTLED
SPARTLING
SPARVER
SPARY
SPASM
SPASMATIC
SPASMATICAL
SPASMED
SPASMIC
SPASMODIC
SPASMODICAL
SPASMODICALLY
SPASMODICALNESS
SPASMODISM
SPASMODIST
SPASMOPHILIA
SPASMOPHILIC
SPASMOTIN
SPASMOTOXIN
SPASMOTOXINE
SPASMOUS
SPASMUS
SPASTIC
SPASTICALLY
SPASTICITY
SPAT
SPATALAMANCY
SPATANGOID
SPATCHCOCK
SPATE
SPATED
SPATH
SPATHA
SPATHACEOUS
SPATHAE
SPATHAL
SPATHE
SPATHED
SPATHIC
SPATHILLA
SPATHILLAE
SPATHOSE
SPATHOUS
SPATHULATE
SPATIAL
SPATIALITY
SPATIALIZATION
SPATIALIZE
SPATIALLY
SPATIATE
SPATIATION
SPATILOMANCY
SPATING
SPATIUM
SPATTANIA
SPATTED
SPATTER
SPATTERDASH

SPATTERDOCK
SPATTERED
SPATTERING
SPATTERINGLY
SPATTERWORK
SPATTING
SPATTLE
SPATTLED
SPATTLEHOE
SPATTLING
SPATULA
SPATULAMANCY
SPATULAR
SPATULATE
SPATULATION
SPATULE
SPATULIFORM
SPATULOSE
SPATULOUS
SPATZLE
SPAUGHT
SPAUL
SPAULD
SPAULDROCHY
SPAVER
SPAVIE
SPAVIED
SPAVIET
SPAVIN
SPAVINE
SPAVINED
SPAVIT
SPAWL
SPAWLER
SPAWN
SPAWNEATER
SPAWNED
SPAWNER
SPAWNING
SPAWNY
SPAY
SPAYAD
SPAYARD
SPAYED
SPAYING
SPEAK
SPEAKABLE
SPEAKABLENESS
SPEAKABLY
SPEAKEASIES
SPEAKEASY
SPEAKER
SPEAKERESS
SPEAKERSHIP
SPEAKHOUSE
SPEAKIES
SPEAKING
SPEAKINGLY
SPEAKINGNESS
SPEAKLESS
SPEAKLESSLY
SPEAL
SPEALBONE
SPEAN
SPEAR
SPEARED
SPEARER
SPEAREYE
SPEARFISH
SPEARFISHES
SPEARFLOWER
SPEARHEAD
SPEARING
SPEARMAN
SPEARMANSHIP
SPEARMEN
SPEARMINT
SPEARPROOF
SPEARSMAN
SPEARSMEN
SPEARWOOD
SPEARWORT
SPEARY
SPEAVE
SPEC
SPECCHIE
SPECE
SPECH
SPECIAL
SPECIALISE
SPECIALISM
SPECIALIST
SPECIALISTIC
SPECIALITIES
SPECIALITY
SPECIALIZATION
SPECIALIZE
SPECIALIZED
SPECIALIZER
SPECIALIZING
SPECIALLY
SPECIALNESS
SPECIALTIES
SPECIALTY
SPECIATE
SPECIATION
SPECIE
SPECIES
SPECIFIABLE
SPECIFIC
SPECIFICAL
SPECIFICALITY
SPECIFICALLY
SPECIFICATE
SPECIFICATION
SPECIFICATIVE
SPECIFICATIVELY
SPECIFICITY
SPECIFICIZE
SPECIFICLY
SPECIFIED
SPECIFIER
SPECIFIST
SPECIFY
SPECIFYING
SPECIMEN
SPECIMENIZE
SPECIMENIZED
SPECIMENS
SPECIOLOGY
SPECIOSITIES
SPECIOSITY
SPECIOUS
SPECIOUSLY
SPECIOUSNESS
SPECK
SPECKED
SPECKEDNESS
SPECKFALL
SPECKIER
SPECKIEST
SPECKING
SPECKLE
SPECKLEBELLY
SPECKLEBREAST
SPECKLED
SPECKLEDBILL
SPECKLEDY
SPECKLEHEAD
SPECKLESS
SPECKLESSLY
SPECKLESSNESS
SPECKLING
SPECKLY
SPECKS
SPECKSIONEER
SPECKY
SPECS
SPECTACLE
SPECTACLED
SPECTACLES
SPECTACULAR
SPECTACULARISM
SPECTACULARITY
SPECTACULARLY
SPECTATE
SPECTATOR
SPECTATORIAL
SPECTATORY
SPECTATRESS
SPECTATRIX
SPECTER
SPECTERED
SPECTERLIKE
SPECTRA
SPECTRAL
SPECTRALISM
SPECTRALITY
SPECTRALLY
SPECTRALNESS
SPECTRE
SPECTRED
SPECTROGRAM
SPECTROGRAPH
SPECTROLOGY
SPECTROMETER
SPECTROMETRIC
SPECTROMETRY
SPECTROPHOBY
SPECTROPHONE
SPECTROSCOPE
SPECTROSCOPY
SPECTRUM
SPECTRUMS
SPECTRY
SPECULA
SPECULAR
SPECULARLY
SPECULATE
SPECULATED
SPECULATING
SPECULATION
SPECULATIST
SPECULATIVE
SPECULATIVELY
SPECULATIVENESS
SPECULATOR
SPECULATORY
SPECULATRICES
SPECULATRIX
SPECULIST
SPECULUM
SPECULUMS
SPECUS
SPED
SPEECE
SPEECH
SPEECHCRAFT
SPEECHER
SPEECHFUL
SPEECHFULNESS
SPEECHIFICATION
SPEECHIFIED
SPEECHIFIER
SPEECHIFY
SPEECHIFYING
SPEECHING
SPEECHLESS
SPEECHLESSLY
SPEECHLESSNESS
SPEECHLORE
SPEECHMAKER
SPEECHMAKING
SPEECHMENT
SPEED
SPEEDBALL
SPEEDBOAT
SPEEDBOATING
SPEEDBOATMAN
SPEEDED
SPEEDER
SPEEDFUL
SPEEDFULLY
SPEEDFULNESS
SPEEDGUN
SPEEDIER
SPEEDIEST
SPEEDILY
SPEEDINESS
SPEEDING
SPEEDINGLY
SPEEDLY
SPEEDOMETER
SPEEDSTER
SPEEDUP
SPEEDWAY
SPEEDWELL
SPEEDY
SPEEL
SPEELLESS
SPEER
SPEERED
SPEERING
SPEERINGS
SPEIGHT
SPEIR
SPEISE
SPEISKOBALT
SPEISS
SPEISSCOBALT
SPEKBOOM
SPEKT
SPELAEAN
SPELD
SPELDER
SPELDING
SPELDRIN
SPELDRING
SPELDRON
SPELE
SPELEAN
SPELEOLOGIST
SPELEOLOGY
SPELK
SPELL
SPELLBIND
SPELLBINDER
SPELLBINDING
SPELLBOUND
SPELLCRAFT
SPELLDOWN
SPELLED
SPELLER
SPELLFUL
SPELLING
SPELLINGDOWN
SPELLINGLY
SPELLKEN
SPELLMONGER
SPELLPROOF
SPELLWORD
SPELLWORK
SPELMAN
SPELT
SPELTER
SPELTERMAN
SPELTERMEN
SPELTOID
SPELTZ
SPELUNCAR
SPELUNCEAN
SPELUNK
SPELUNKER
SPELUNKING
SPENCE
SPENCER
SPENCERITE
SPENCIE
SPENCY
SPEND
SPENDER
SPENDFUL
SPENDIBLE
SPENDING
SPENDLESS
SPENDTHRIFT
SPENDTHRIFTY
SPENSE
SPENT
SPEOS
SPERAGE
SPERATE
SPERE
SPERK
SPERKET
SPERLING
SPERM
SPERMA
SPERMACETI
SPERMADUCT
SPERMALIST
SPERMAPHYTE
SPERMAPHYTIC
SPERMARIES
SPERMARIUM
SPERMARY
SPERMATA
SPERMATHECA
SPERMATHECAE
SPERMATHECAL
SPERMATIA
SPERMATIC
SPERMATID
SPERMATIN
SPERMATISM
SPERMATIST
SPERMATITIS
SPERMATIUM
SPERMATIZE
SPERMATOCELE
SPERMATOCYST
SPERMATOCYTE
SPERMATOGENY
SPERMATOID
SPERMATOVA
SPERMATOVUM
SPERMATOZOA
SPERMATOZOAL
SPERMATOZOAN
SPERMATOZOIC
SPERMATOZOID
SPERMATOZOON
SPERMATURIA
SPERMIC
SPERMIDIN
SPERMIDINE
SPERMIDUCAL
SPERMIDUCT
SPERMIGEROUS
SPERMIN
SPERMINE
SPERMISM
SPERMIST
SPERMOBLAST
SPERMOCARP

SPERMODERM
SPERMODUCT
SPERMOGENOUS
SPERMOGONE
SPERMOGONIA
SPERMOGONIUM
SPERMOGONOUS
SPERMOLOGER
SPERMOLOGIST
SPERMOLOGY
SPERMOPHILE
SPERMOPHORE
SPERMOSPHERE
SPERMOTHECA
SPERMOTOXIN
SPERMOUS
SPERMULE
SPERMY
SPERON
SPERONARA
SPERONARAS
SPERONARES
SPERONARO
SPERONAROES
SPERONAROS
SPERONE
SPERPLE
SPERRYLITE
SPERSE
SPES
SPESSARTINE
SPESSARTITE
SPET
SPETCH
SPETCHES
SPEUCHAN
SPEW
SPEWED
SPEWER
SPEWIER
SPEWIEST
SPEWINESS
SPEWING
SPEWY
SPEX
SPEY
SPEYERIA
SPHACEL
SPHACELATE
SPHACELATED
SPHACELATING
SPHACELATION
SPHACELIA
SPHACELIAL
SPHACELISM
SPHACELOUS
SPHACELUS
SPHAERIDIA
SPHAERIDIAL
SPHAERIDIUM
SPHAERITE
SPHAEROBLAST
SPHAEROSOME
SPHAEROSPORE
SPHAGIA
SPHAGION
SPHAGNACEOUS
SPHAGNOLOGY
SPHAGNOUS
SPHAGNUM
SPHALERITE
SPHALM
SPHALMA
SPHECID
SPHECIUS
SPHECOID
SPHENDONE
SPHENE
SPHENETHMOID
SPHENIC
SPHENION
SPHENISCINE
SPHENODON
SPHENODONT
SPHENOGRAM
SPHENOGRAPHY
SPHENOID
SPHENOIDAL
SPHENOIDITIS
SPHENOLITH
SPHENOMALAR
SPHENOTIC
SPHENOTRIBE
SPHENOTRIPSY
SPHERABLE
SPHERADIAN
SPHERAL
SPHERALITY
SPHERASTER
SPHERATION
SPHERE
SPHERED
SPHERELESS
SPHERIC
SPHERICAL
SPHERICALITY
SPHERICALLY
SPHERICALNESS
SPHERICIST
SPHERICITIES
SPHERICITY
SPHERICLE
SPHERICS
SPHERIER
SPHERIEST
SPHERIFORM
SPHERIFY
SPHERING
SPHEROGRAPH
SPHEROID
SPHEROIDAL
SPHEROIDALLY
SPHEROIDIC
SPHEROIDICAL
SPHEROIDISM
SPHEROIDITY
SPHEROIDIZE
SPHEROME
SPHEROMERE
SPHEROMETER
SPHERULA
SPHERULAR
SPHERULATE
SPHERULE
SPHERULITE
SPHERULITIC
SPHERULITIZE
SPHERY
SPHETERIZE
SPHEXIDE
SPHINCTER
SPHINCTERAL
SPHINCTERATE
SPHINCTERIAL
SPHINCTERIC
SPHINDID
SPHINGAL
SPHINGES
SPHINGID
SPHINGIFORM
SPHINGINE
SPHINGOMETER
SPHINGOSIN
SPHINGOSINE
SPHINX
SPHINXES
SPHINXIAN
SPHINXINE
SPHINXLIKE
SPHRAGIDE
SPHRAGISTIC
SPHRAGISTICS
SPHYGMIA
SPHYGMIC
SPHYGMODIC
SPHYGMOGRAM
SPHYGMOGRAPH
SPHYGMOID
SPHYGMOLOGY
SPHYGMOMETER
SPHYGMOPHONE
SPHYGMUS
SPIAL
SPICA
SPICAE
SPICANT
SPICATE
SPICATED
SPICCATO
SPICE
SPICEBERRIES
SPICEBERRY
SPICEBUSH
SPICECAKE
SPICED
SPICEFUL
SPICEHOUSE
SPICELAND
SPICER
SPICERIES
SPICERY
SPICES
SPICEWOOD
SPICIER
SPICIEST
SPICIFEROUS
SPICIFORM
SPICIGEROUS
SPICILEGE
SPICILY
SPICINESS
SPICING
SPICK
SPICKET
SPICKLE
SPICKNEL
SPICOSE
SPICOSITY
SPICOUS
SPICOUSNESS
SPICULA
SPICULAR
SPICULATE
SPICULATED
SPICULATION
SPICULE
SPICULIFORM
SPICULOFIBER
SPICULOSE
SPICULOUS
SPICULUM
SPICY
SPIDER
SPIDERED
SPIDERFLOWER
SPIDERISH
SPIDERLING
SPIDERLY
SPIDERWEB
SPIDERWORK
SPIDERWORT
SPIDERY
SPIDGER
SPIED
SPIEGEL
SPIEGELEISEN
SPIEL
SPIELER
SPIER
SPIES
SPIFF
SPIFFED
SPIFFIER
SPIFFIEST
SPIFFILY
SPIFFINESS
SPIFFING
SPIFFLICATE
SPIFFLICATED
SPIFFLICATION
SPIFFY
SPIFLICATE
SPIFLICATED
SPIFLICATION
SPIG
SPIGGOTY
SPIGNEL
SPIGNET
SPIGNUT
SPIGOT
SPIKE
SPIKEBILL
SPIKED
SPIKEDNESS
SPIKEFISH
SPIKEFISHES
SPIKEHOLE
SPIKEHORN
SPIKELET
SPIKELIKE
SPIKENARD
SPIKER
SPIKES
SPIKETAIL
SPIKETOP
SPIKEWEED
SPIKIER
SPIKIEST
SPIKILY
SPIKINESS
SPIKING
SPIKY
SPILE
SPILED
SPILEHOLE
SPILER
SPILEWORM
SPILI
SPILIKIN
SPILING
SPILITE
SPILITIC
SPILL
SPILLAGE
SPILLED
SPILLER
SPILLET
SPILLIKIN
SPILLING
SPILLOVER
SPILLWAY
SPILLY
SPILOMA
SPILOMAS
SPILOSITE
SPILT
SPILTH
SPILUS
SPIN
SPINA
SPINACEOUS
SPINACH
SPINACHLIKE
SPINAE
SPINAGE
SPINAL
SPINALES
SPINALIS
SPINALLY
SPINATE
SPINDER
SPINDLAGE
SPINDLE
SPINDLEAGE
SPINDLED
SPINDLEHEAD
SPINDLELEGS
SPINDLER
SPINDLETAIL
SPINDLEWOOD
SPINDLIER
SPINDLIEST
SPINDLINESS
SPINDLING
SPINDLY
SPINDRIFT
SPINE
SPINEBILL
SPINEBONE
SPINED
SPINEFINNED
SPINEL
SPINELESS
SPINELESSLY
SPINELESSNESS
SPINELET
SPINELLE
SPINES
SPINESCENCE
SPINESCENT
SPINET
SPINETAIL
SPINGEL
SPINIBULBAR
SPINICARPOUS
SPINIDENTATE
SPINIER
SPINIEST
SPINIFEROUS
SPINIFEX
SPINIFORM
SPINIFUGAL
SPINIGEROUS
SPINIGRADE
SPININESS
SPINIPETAL
SPINITIS
SPINK
SPINNABLE
SPINNAKER
SPINNEL
SPINNER
SPINNERET
SPINNERETTE
SPINNERIES
SPINNERS
SPINNERULAR
SPINNERULE
SPINNERY
SPINNEY
SPINNEYS
SPINNIES
SPINNING
SPINNINGLY
SPINNY

SPINOBULBAR
SPINODE
SPINOGLENOID
SPINOID
SPINONEURAL
SPINOR
SPINOSE
SPINOSELY
SPINOSENESS
SPINOSITY
SPINOTECTAL
SPINOUS
SPINSTER
SPINSTERHOOD
SPINSTERIAL
SPINSTERISH
SPINSTERISHLY
SPINSTERLY
SPINSTEROUS
SPINSTRESS
SPINSTRY
SPINTEXT
SPINTHERISM
SPINTRY
SPINTURNIX
SPINULA
SPINULATE
SPINULATED
SPINULATION
SPINULE
SPINULESCENT
SPINULIFORM
SPINULOSE
SPINULOSELY
SPINULOUS
SPINY
SPION
SPIONID
SPIRABLE
SPIRACLE
SPIRACULA
SPIRACULAR
SPIRACULATE
SPIRACULUM
SPIRAEA
SPIRAL
SPIRALE
SPIRALED
SPIRALIFORM
SPIRALING
SPIRALISM
SPIRALITY
SPIRALIZATION
SPIRALIZE
SPIRALLED
SPIRALLING
SPIRALLY
SPIRALOID
SPIRALTAIL
SPIRAN
SPIRANE
SPIRANT
SPIRANTHIC
SPIRANTHY
SPIRANTIZE
SPIRASTER
SPIRATE
SPIRATED
SPIRATION
SPIRE
SPIREA
SPIRED
SPIREGRASS
SPIRELET
SPIREM
SPIREME
SPIRICLE
SPIRIFERID
SPIRIFEROID
SPIRIFEROUS
SPIRIFORM
SPIRILLA
SPIRILLAR
SPIRILLOSIS
SPIRILLUM
SPIRING
SPIRIT
SPIRITALLY
SPIRITED
SPIRITEDLY
SPIRITEDNESS
SPIRITER
SPIRITFUL
SPIRITFULLY
SPIRITFULNESS
SPIRITING
SPIRITISM
SPIRITIST
SPIRITISTIC
SPIRITIZE
SPIRITLAND
SPIRITLEAF
SPIRITLESS
SPIRITLESSLY
SPIRITLESSNESS
SPIRITLIKE
SPIRITOSO
SPIRITOUS
SPIRITS
SPIRITSOME
SPIRITUAL
SPIRITUALISE
SPIRITUALISM
SPIRITUALIST
SPIRITUALISTIC
SPIRITUALISTICALLY
SPIRITUALITIES
SPIRITUALITY
SPIRITUALIZATION
SPIRITUALIZE
SPIRITUALIZED
SPIRITUALIZER
SPIRITUALIZING
SPIRITUALLY
SPIRITUALNESS
SPIRITUALTY
SPIRITUEL
SPIRITUELLE
SPIRITUOSITY
SPIRITUOUS
SPIRITUOUSLY
SPIRITUOUSNESS
SPIRITUS
SPIRITWEED
SPIRITY
SPIRIVALVE
SPIRKET
SPIRKETING
SPIRLIE
SPIRO
SPIROCHAETAL
SPIROCHAETE
SPIROCHETAL
SPIROCHETE
SPIROCHETIC
SPIROGRAM
SPIROGRAPH
SPIROGRAPHIC
SPIROGRAPHIN
SPIROGRAPHY
SPIROGYRA
SPIROID
SPIROIDAL
SPIROILIC
SPIROL
SPIROLE
SPIROMETER
SPIROMETRIC
SPIROMETRY
SPIROSCOPE
SPIROUS
SPIRT
SPIRTLE
SPIRULA
SPIRULAE
SPIRULATE
SPIRY
SPISE
SPISS
SPISSATED
SPISSITUDE
SPISSY
SPIT
SPITAL
SPITBALL
SPITBALLER
SPITBOX
SPITCHCOCK
SPITCHCOCKED
SPITCHCOCKING
SPITE
SPITED
SPITEFUL
SPITEFULLY
SPITEFULNESS
SPITFIRE
SPITFROG
SPITFUL
SPITHAME
SPITING
SPITISH
SPITKID
SPITKIT
SPITOUS
SPITPOISON
SPITSCOCKED
SPITSTICK
SPITSTICKER
SPITTED
SPITTER
SPITTING
SPITTLE
SPITTLEFORK
SPITTLEMAN
SPITTLEMEN
SPITTLESTAFF
SPITTOON
SPITZ
SPITZENBERG
SPITZENBURG
SPITZER
SPITZFLUTE
SPITZKOP
SPIV
SPLACHNOID
SPLACKNUCK
SPLAIRGE
SPLAKE
SPLANCHNIC
SPLASH
SPLASHBOARD
SPLASHDOWN
SPLASHED
SPLASHER
SPLASHIER
SPLASHIEST
SPLASHING
SPLASHPROOF
SPLASHWING
SPLASHY
SPLAT
SPLATCH
SPLATCHER
SPLATHER
SPLATHERING
SPLATTER
SPLATTERDASH
SPLATTERER
SPLATTERFACED
SPLATTERWORK
SPLAY
SPLAYED
SPLAYER
SPLAYFEET
SPLAYFOOT
SPLAYFOOTED
SPLAYMOUTH
SPLAYMOUTHED
SPLAYMOUTHS
SPLEEN
SPLEENED
SPLEENFUL
SPLEENFULLY
SPLEENIER
SPLEENIEST
SPLEENING
SPLEENISH
SPLEENISHLY
SPLEENISHNESS
SPLEENLESS
SPLEENWORT
SPLEENY
SPLEET
SPLENADENOMA
SPLENALGIA
SPLENALGIC
SPLENALGY
SPLENATROPHY
SPLENAUXE
SPLENCULI
SPLENCULUS
SPLENDACEOUS
SPLENDACIOUS
SPLENDACIOUSLY
SPLENDATIOUS
SPLENDENT
SPLENDENTLY
SPLENDESCENT
SPLENDID
SPLENDIDER
SPLENDIDEST
SPLENDIDLY
SPLENDIDNESS
SPLENDIFEROUS
SPLENDOR
SPLENDOROUS
SPLENDOUR
SPLENDROUS
SPLENECTAMA
SPLENECTASIS
SPLENECTOMIES
SPLENECTOMY
SPLENECTOPIA
SPLENECTOPY
SPLENELCOSIS
SPLENEMIA
SPLENEOLUS
SPLENETIC
SPLENETICAL
SPLENETIVE
SPLENIA
SPLENIAL
SPLENIC
SPLENICAL
SPLENICTERUS
SPLENIFORM
SPLENII
SPLENITIS
SPLENITIVE
SPLENIUM
SPLENIUS
SPLENIZATION
SPLENOBLAST
SPLENOCELE
SPLENOCLEISIS
SPLENOCOLIC
SPLENOCYTE
SPLENODYNIA
SPLENOGRAPHY
SPLENOHEMIA
SPLENOID
SPLENOLOGY
SPLENOLYMPH
SPLENOLYSIN
SPLENOLYSIS
SPLENOMA
SPLENOMEGALY
SPLENONCUS
SPLENOPATHY
SPLENOPEXIA
SPLENOPEXIS
SPLENOPEXY
SPLENOPTOSIA
SPLENOPTOSIS
SPLENOTOMY
SPLENOTOXIN
SPLENT
SPLENULUS
SPLEUCHAN
SPLICE
SPLICED
SPLICER
SPLICING
SPLINE
SPLINED
SPLINING
SPLINT
SPLINTAGE
SPLINTED
SPLINTER
SPLINTERED
SPLINTERING
SPLINTERNEW
SPLINTERPROOF
SPLINTERY
SPLINTING
SPLINTS
SPLINTWOOD
SPLINTY
SPLIT
SPLITBEAK
SPLITE
SPLITFINGER
SPLITFRUIT
SPLITMOUTH
SPLITNEW
SPLITNUT
SPLITSAW
SPLITTAIL
SPLITTED
SPLITTER
SPLITTERMAN
SPLITTING
SPLITWORM
SPLODGE
SPLOIT
SPLORE
SPLOSH
SPLOSHY
SPLOTCH
SPLOTCHED
SPLOTCHIER
SPLOTCHIEST
SPLOTCHILY
SPLOTCHINESS

SPLOTCHING
SPLOTCHY
SPLOTHER
SPLUNGE
SPLUNT
SPLURGE
SPLURGED
SPLURGILY
SPLURGING
SPLURGY
SPLURT
SPLUTHER
SPLUTTER
SPLUTTERED
SPLUTTERER
SPLUTTERING
SPOACH
SPODE
SPODIOSITE
SPODIUM
SPODOGENIC
SPODOGENOUS
SPODOMANCY
SPODOMANTIC
SPODUMENE
SPOFFISH
SPOFFLE
SPOFFY
SPOGEL
SPOIL
SPOILAGE
SPOILATION
SPOILED
SPOILER
SPOILFIVE
SPOILFUL
SPOILING
SPOILMENT
SPOILS
SPOILSMAN
SPOILSMEN
SPOILSMONGER
SPOILSPORT
SPOILT
SPOKE
SPOKED
SPOKEN
SPOKES
SPOKESHAVE
SPOKESMAN
SPOKESMEN
SPOKESTER
SPOKESWOMAN
SPOKESWOMEN
SPOKING
SPOKY
SPOLIA
SPOLIARIA
SPOLIARIUM
SPOLIARY
SPOLIATE
SPOLIATED
SPOLIATING
SPOLIATION
SPOLIATIVE
SPOLIATOR
SPOLIATORY
SPOLIUM
SPONDAIC
SPONDAICAL
SPONDAIZE
SPONDEAN
SPONDEE
SPONDIL
SPONDULICKS
SPONDULICS
SPONDULIX
SPONDYL
SPONDYLE
SPONDYLIC
SPONDYLIOID
SPONDYLITIC
SPONDYLITIS
SPONDYLIUM
SPONDYLIZEMA
SPONDYLOCACE
SPONDYLOID
SPONDYLOSIS
SPONDYLOTOMY
SPONDYLOUS
SPONDYLUS
SPONE
SPONG
SPONGE
SPONGECAKE
SPONGED
SPONGEOUS
SPONGER
SPONGEWOOD
SPONGIAN
SPONGICOLOUS
SPONGIER
SPONGIEST
SPONGIFEROUS
SPONGIFORM
SPONGILLID
SPONGILLINE
SPONGILY
SPONGIN
SPONGINBLAST
SPONGINESS
SPONGING
SPONGIOBLAST
SPONGIOCYTE
SPONGIOLE
SPONGIOLIN
SPONGIOPILIN
SPONGIOSE
SPONGIOSITY
SPONGIOUS
SPONGIOUSNESS
SPONGOBLAST
SPONGOID
SPONGOLOGY
SPONGOPHORE
SPONGY
SPONK
SPONSAL
SPONSALIA
SPONSION
SPONSIONAL
SPONSON
SPONSOR
SPONSORIAL
SPONSORSHIP
SPONSPECK
SPONTANEITIES
SPONTANEITY
SPONTANEOUS
SPONTANEOUSLY
SPONTANEOUSNESS
SPONTON
SPONTOON
SPOOF
SPOOFED
SPOOFER
SPOOFERIES
SPOOFERY
SPOOFING
SPOOFISH
SPOOK
SPOOKERIES
SPOOKERY
SPOOKIER
SPOOKIES
SPOOKIEST
SPOOKILY
SPOOKINESS
SPOOKISH
SPOOKISM
SPOOKIST
SPOOKOLOGIST
SPOOKOLOGY
SPOOKY
SPOOL
SPOOLED
SPOOLER
SPOOLING
SPOOLWOOD
SPOON
SPOONBILL
SPOONBREAD
SPOONDRIFT
SPOONED
SPOONER
SPOONERISM
SPOONEY
SPOONEYISM
SPOONEYLY
SPOONEYNESS
SPOONEYS
SPOONFUL
SPOONFULS
SPOONHUTCH
SPOONIER
SPOONIES
SPOONIEST
SPOONILY
SPOONINESS
SPOONING
SPOONISM
SPOONMAKER
SPOONMAKING
SPOONWAYS
SPOONWISE
SPOONWOOD
SPOONY
SPOONYISM
SPOOR
SPOORED
SPOORER
SPOORING
SPOORN
SPORABOLA
SPORACEOUS
SPORADES
SPORADIAL
SPORADIC
SPORADICAL
SPORADICALLY
SPORADICALNESS
SPORADICITY
SPORADIN
SPORADISM
SPORAL
SPORANGE
SPORANGIA
SPORANGIAL
SPORANGIFORM
SPORANGIOID
SPORANGIOLA
SPORANGIOLE
SPORANGIOLUM
SPORANGITE
SPORANGIUM
SPORATION
SPORE
SPORED
SPOREFORMER
SPOREFORMING
SPORELING
SPORES
SPORICIDE
SPORID
SPORIDESM
SPORIDIA
SPORIDIAL
SPORIDIOLE
SPORIDIOLUM
SPORIDIUM
SPORIFEROUS
SPORING
SPORIPARITY
SPORIPAROUS
SPOROBLAST
SPOROCARP
SPOROCARPIA
SPOROCARPIUM
SPOROCYST
SPOROCYSTIC
SPOROCYSTID
SPOROCYTE
SPORODERM
SPORODOCHIA
SPORODOCHIUM
SPORODUCT
SPOROGEN
SPOROGENESIS
SPOROGENIC
SPOROGENOUS
SPOROGENY
SPOROGONE
SPOROGONIA
SPOROGONIAL
SPOROGONIC
SPOROGONIUM
SPOROGONY
SPOROID
SPOROLOGIST
SPOROMYCOSIS
SPORONT
SPOROPHORE
SPOROPHORIC
SPOROPHOROUS
SPOROPHYDIUM
SPOROPHYL
SPOROPHYLL
SPOROPHYLLUM
SPOROPHYTE
SPOROPHYTIC
SPOROPLASM
SPOROSAC
SPOROSTEGIUM
SPOROSTROTE
SPOROUS
SPOROZOAL
SPOROZOAN
SPOROZOIC
SPOROZOID
SPOROZOITE
SPOROZOOID
SPOROZOON
SPORRAN
SPORT
SPORTABILITY
SPORTABLE
SPORTANCE
SPORTED
SPORTER
SPORTFUL
SPORTFULLY
SPORTFULNESS
SPORTIER
SPORTIEST
SPORTILY
SPORTINESS
SPORTING
SPORTIVE
SPORTIVELY
SPORTIVENESS
SPORTLING
SPORTS
SPORTSCAST
SPORTSCASTER
SPORTSMAN
SPORTSMANLIKE
SPORTSMANLY
SPORTSMANSHIP
SPORTSMEN
SPORTSOME
SPORTSWEAR
SPORTSWOMAN
SPORTULA
SPORTULAE
SPORTY
SPORULAR
SPORULATE
SPORULATED
SPORULATING
SPORULATION
SPORULE
SPORULOID
SPOSH
SPOSHY
SPOT
SPOTLESS
SPOTLESSLY
SPOTLESSNESS
SPOTLIGHT
SPOTLIGHTER
SPOTRUMP
SPOTS
SPOTSMAN
SPOTSMEN
SPOTTABLE
SPOTTAIL
SPOTTED
SPOTTELDY
SPOTTER
SPOTTIER
SPOTTIEST
SPOTTILY
SPOTTINESS
SPOTTING
SPOTTLE
SPOTTY
SPOTWELDER
SPOUCHER
SPOUSAGE
SPOUSAL
SPOUSALLY
SPOUSE
SPOUSED
SPOUSEHOOD
SPOUSING
SPOUT
SPOUTED
SPOUTER
SPOUTINESS
SPOUTING
SPOUTLESS
SPOUTY
SPOW
SPOWE
SPRACHLE
SPRACK
SPRACKLY
SPRACKNESS
SPRADDLE
SPRAG
SPRAGGED
SPRAGGER
SPRAGGING
SPRAGGLY
SPRAGMAN

SPRAICH
SPRAIN
SPRAINED
SPRAING
SPRAINING
SPRAINTS
SPRAITH
SPRANG
SPRANGLE
SPRANGLY
SPRANK
SPRAT
SPRATTED
SPRATTER
SPRATTING
SPRATTLE
SPRATTLED
SPRATTLING
SPRATTY
SPRAUCHLE
SPRAWL
SPRAWLED
SPRAWLER
SPRAWLIER
SPRAWLIEST
SPRAWLING
SPRAWLINGLY
SPRAWLY
SPRAY
SPRAYBOARD
SPRAYED
SPRAYER
SPRAYEY
SPRAYING
SPRAYS
SPREAD
SPREADATION
SPREADBOARD
SPREADER
SPREADHEAD
SPREADING
SPREADINGLY
SPREADINGNESS
SPREADOVER
SPREADY
SPREAGH
SPREAGHERY
SPREATH
SPRECKLE
SPREE
SPREED
SPREEING
SPREEUW
SPRENG
SPRENGE
SPRENGING
SPRENT
SPRET
SPRETTY
SPREW
SPRIDHOGUE
SPRIER
SPRIEST
SPRIG
SPRIGGED
SPRIGGER
SPRIGGIER
SPRIGGIEST
SPRIGGING
SPRIGGY
SPRIGHT
SPRIGHTED
SPRIGHTFUL
SPRIGHTFULLY
SPRIGHTFULNESS
SPRIGHTLIER
SPRIGHTLIEST
SPRIGHTLILY
SPRIGHTLINESS
SPRIGHTLY
SPRIGHTY
SPRIGTAIL
SPRINDGE
SPRING
SPRINGAL
SPRINGALD
SPRINGBOARD
SPRINGBOK
SPRINGBOKS
SPRINGBUCK
SPRINGE
SPRINGED
SPRINGEING
SPRINGER
SPRINGERLE
SPRINGFINGER
SPRINGFISH
SPRINGFISHES
SPRINGFUL
SPRINGHAAS
SPRINGHALT
SPRINGHEAD
SPRINGHOUSE
SPRINGIER
SPRINGIEST
SPRINGILY
SPRINGINESS
SPRINGING
SPRINGINGLY
SPRINGLE
SPRINGLED
SPRINGLESS
SPRINGLET
SPRINGLIKE
SPRINGLING
SPRINGLY
SPRINGMAKER
SPRINGMAKING
SPRINGS
SPRINGTAIL
SPRINGTIDE
SPRINGTIME
SPRINGTRAP
SPRINGWOOD
SPRINGWORM
SPRINGWORT
SPRINGY
SPRINK
SPRINKLE
SPRINKLED
SPRINKLER
SPRINKLERED
SPRINKLING
SPRINT
SPRINTED
SPRINTER
SPRINTING
SPRIT
SPRITE
SPRITELY
SPRITISH
SPRITSAIL
SPRITTAIL
SPRITTED
SPRITTING
SPRITTY
SPRITZ
SPRITZER
SPROAT
SPROCKET
SPROD
SPROGUE
SPROIL
SPRONG
SPROSE
SPROT
SPROTTLE
SPROTY
SPROUT
SPROUTAGE
SPROUTED
SPROUTER
SPROUTING
SPROUTLAND
SPROUTLING
SPROUTS
SPROWSY
SPRUCE
SPRUCED
SPRUCELY
SPRUCENESS
SPRUCER
SPRUCERY
SPRUCEST
SPRUCIFICATION
SPRUCIFY
SPRUCING
SPRUE
SPRUER
SPRUG
SPRUIKER
SPRUIT
SPRUNG
SPRUNK
SPRUNNY
SPRUNT
SPRUNTLY
SPRUSADO
SPRUSH
SPRY
SPRYER
SPRYEST
SPRYLY
SPRYNESS
SPUD
SPUDDED
SPUDDER
SPUDDING
SPUDDLE
SPUDDY
SPUDS
SPUE
SPUFFLE
SPUG
SPUILZIE
SPULE
SPULYIEMENT
SPULZIE
SPUME
SPUMED
SPUMESCENCE
SPUMESCENT
SPUMIER
SPUMIEST
SPUMIFEROUS
SPUMIFORM
SPUMING
SPUMOID
SPUMONE
SPUMONI
SPUMOSE
SPUMOUS
SPUMY
SPUN
SPUNG
SPUNGE
SPUNK
SPUNKIE
SPUNKIER
SPUNKIEST
SPUNKILY
SPUNKINESS
SPUNKY
SPUNNIES
SPUNNY
SPUR
SPURDIE
SPURDOG
SPURFLOWER
SPURGALL
SPURGE
SPURIA
SPURIAE
SPURIOUS
SPURIOUSLY
SPURIOUSNESS
SPURL
SPURLESS
SPURLET
SPURLIKE
SPURMAKER
SPURMONEY
SPURN
SPURNED
SPURNER
SPURNING
SPURNPOINT
SPURNWATER
SPURRED
SPURRER
SPURREY
SPURRIER
SPURRIES
SPURRING
SPURRINGS
SPURRITE
SPURRY
SPURS
SPURT
SPURTED
SPURTER
SPURTING
SPURTIVE
SPURTIVELY
SPURTLE
SPURTLEBLADE
SPURTS
SPURWAY
SPURWING
SPURWORT
SPUT
SPUTA
SPUTATIVE
SPUTE
SPUTNIK
SPUTTER
SPUTTERED
SPUTTERER
SPUTTERING
SPUTTERINGLY
SPUTTERY
SPUTUM
SPUTUMARY
SPUTUMOSE
SPUTUMOUS
SPY
SPYBOAT
SPYER
SPYGLASS
SPYING
SQUAB
SQUABASH
SQUABASHER
SQUABBED
SQUABBER
SQUABBIER
SQUABBIEST
SQUABBING
SQUABBISH
SQUABBLE
SQUABBLED
SQUABBLER
SQUABBLING
SQUABBLINGLY
SQUABBLY
SQUABBY
SQUACCO
SQUACCOS
SQUAD
SQUADDED
SQUADDING
SQUADDY
SQUADER
SQUADRATE
SQUADRISM
SQUADROL
SQUADRON
SQUADRONE
SQUADRONED
SQUADRONING
SQUAGGA
SQUAIL
SQUAILER
SQUAILS
SQUALENE
SQUALID
SQUALIDITY
SQUALIDLY
SQUALIDNESS
SQUALIFORM
SQUALL
SQUALLED
SQUALLER
SQUALLERY
SQUALLIER
SQUALLIEST
SQUALLING
SQUALLY
SQUALODONT
SQUALOID
SQUALOR
SQUAM
SQUAMA
SQUAMACEOUS
SQUAMAE
SQUAMATE
SQUAMATED
SQUAMATINE
SQUAMATION
SQUAME
SQUAMELLA
SQUAMELLAE
SQUAMELLATE
SQUAMEOUS
SQUAMIFEROUS
SQUAMIFORM
SQUAMIFY
SQUAMIGEROUS
SQUAMISH
SQUAMOID
SQUAMOSA
SQUAMOSAL
SQUAMOSE
SQUAMOSELY
SQUAMOSENESS
SQUAMOSITY
SQUAMOUS
SQUAMOUSLY
SQUAMOUSNESS
SQUAMULA
SQUAMULAE
SQUAMULATE
SQUAMULATION
SQUAMULE
SQUAMULOSE

SQUAMY
SQUANDER
SQUANDERED
SQUANDERER
SQUANDERING
SQUANDERINGLY
SQUANTUM
SQUAP
SQUARE
SQUAREAGE
SQUARECAP
SQUARED
SQUAREFACE
SQUAREHEAD
SQUARELY
SQUAREMAN
SQUAREMEN
SQUARENESS
SQUARER
SQUARES
SQUARETAIL
SQUARIER
SQUARING
SQUARISH
SQUARISHLY
SQUARK
SQUARROSE
SQUARROSELY
SQUARROUS
SQUARRULOSE
SQUARSON
SQUARSONRY
SQUARY
SQUASH
SQUASHBERRY
SQUASHED
SQUASHER
SQUASHIER
SQUASHIEST
SQUASHILY
SQUASHINESS
SQUASHING
SQUASHY
SQUAT
SQUATAROLE
SQUATEROLE
SQUATINID
SQUATINOID
SQUATLY
SQUATMORE
SQUATNESS
SQUATTAGE
SQUATTED
SQUATTER
SQUATTIER
SQUATTIEST
SQUATTILY
SQUATTINESS
SQUATTING
SQUATTISH
SQUATTLE
SQUATTOCRACY
SQUATTY
SQUAW
SQUAWBERRIES
SQUAWBERRY
SQUAWBUSH
SQUAWFISH
SQUAWFISHES
SQUAWFLOWER
SQUAWK
SQUAWKED
SQUAWKER
SQUAWKIE
SQUAWKIER
SQUAWKIEST
SQUAWKING
SQUAWKINGLY
SQUAWKY
SQUAWL
SQUAWROOT
SQUAWWEED
SQUDGE
SQUDGY
SQUEAK
SQUEAKED
SQUEAKER
SQUEAKERY
SQUEAKILY
SQUEAKINESS
SQUEAKING
SQUEAKINGLY
SQUEAKY
SQUEAL
SQUEALED
SQUEALER
SQUEALING
SQUEAM
SQUEAMISH
SQUEAMISHLY
SQUEAMISHNESS
SQUEEF
SQUEEGE
SQUEEGEE
SQUEEGEED
SQUEEGEEING
SQUEEL
SQUEEZABLE
SQUEEZE
SQUEEZED
SQUEEZEMAN
SQUEEZER
SQUEEZING
SQUEEZINGLY
SQUEEZY
SQUEG
SQUELCH
SQUELCHED
SQUELCHER
SQUELCHIER
SQUELCHIEST
SQUELCHILY
SQUELCHINESS
SQUELCHING
SQUELCHINGLY
SQUELCHINGNESS
SQUELCHY
SQUELETTE
SQUET
SQUETEAGUE
SQUETEE
SQUIB
SQUIBBED
SQUIBBER
SQUIBBERY
SQUIBBING
SQUIBBISH
SQUIBCRACK
SQUIBSTER
SQUID
SQUIDDED
SQUIDDER
SQUIDDING
SQUIDDLE
SQUIDGE
SQUIDGEREEN
SQUIDGIER
SQUIDGIEST
SQUIDGY
SQUIDS
SQUIFFED
SQUIFFER
SQUIFFIER
SQUIFFIEST
SQUIFFY
SQUIGGLE
SQUIGGLIER
SQUIGGLIEST
SQUIGGLY
SQUILGEE
SQUILGEED
SQUILGEEING
SQUILGEER
SQUILL
SQUILLA
SQUILLAGEE
SQUILLGEE
SQUILLIAN
SQUILLID
SQUILLITIC
SQUIN
SQUINACY
SQUINANCE
SQUINANT
SQUINCH
SQUINNY
SQUINT
SQUINTED
SQUINTER
SQUINTING
SQUINTINGLY
SQUINTINGNESS
SQUINTY
SQUIR
SQUIRAGE
SQUIRALTY
SQUIRARCH
SQUIRARCHAL
SQUIRARCHY
SQUIRE
SQUIREARCH
SQUIREARCHAL
SQUIREARCHIES
SQUIREARCHY
SQUIRED
SQUIREEN
SQUIRELING
SQUIRELY
SQUIRESS
SQUIRET
SQUIRING
SQUIRISH
SQUIRK
SQUIRL
SQUIRM
SQUIRMED
SQUIRMER
SQUIRMIER
SQUIRMIEST
SQUIRMINESS
SQUIRMING
SQUIRMINGLY
SQUIRR
SQUIRREL
SQUIRRELFISH
SQUIRRELFISHES
SQUIRRELTAIL
SQUIRRELY
SQUIRT
SQUIRTED
SQUIRTER
SQUIRTINESS
SQUIRTING
SQUIRTINGLY
SQUIRTISH
SQUIRTS
SQUIRTY
SQUISH
SQUISHED
SQUISHING
SQUISHY
SQUISS
SQUIT
SQUITCH
SQUITTER
SQUIZ
SQUSH
SQUSHY
SQUUSH
SQUUSHY
SRADDHA
SRADH
SRADHA
SRAMANA
SRAVAKA
SRI
SRUTI
SSU
STAAB
STAATSRAAD
STAB
STABBED
STABBER
STABBING
STABBINGLY
STABILATE
STABILE
STABILIFY
STABILISE
STABILIST
STABILITATE
STABILITIES
STABILITY
STABILIZATION
STABILIZATOR
STABILIZE
STABILIZED
STABILIZER
STABILIZING
STABLE
STABLEBOY
STABLED
STABLEKEEPER
STABLEMAN
STABLEMEAL
STABLEMEN
STABLENESS
STABLER
STABLES
STABLESTAND
STABLING
STABLISH
STABLY
STABOY
STABWORT
STACCATO
STACCATOS
STACHER
STACHYDRIN
STACHYDRINE
STACHYOSE
STACK
STACKAGE
STACKED
STACKENCLOUD
STACKER
STACKET
STACKFREED
STACKGARTH
STACKING
STACKMAN
STACKMEN
STACKS
STACKSTAND
STACKYARD
STACTE
STACTOMETER
STAD
STADDA
STADDLE
STADDLING
STADE
STADHOLDER
STADHOUSE
STADIA
STADIAL
STADIC
STADIE
STADIMETER
STADIOMETER
STADION
STADIUM
STADTHOLDER
STAFETTE
STAFF
STAFFAGE
STAFFED
STAFFELITE
STAFFER
STAFFIER
STAFFING
STAFFISH
STAFFMAN
STAFFMEN
STAFFS
STAFFSTRIKER
STAG
STAGBUSH
STAGE
STAGECOACH
STAGECOACHING
STAGECRAFT
STAGED
STAGEHAND
STAGEHOUSE
STAGELAND
STAGELIKE
STAGEMAN
STAGEMEN
STAGER
STAGERY
STAGES
STAGEWORTHY
STAGEY
STAGGARD
STAGGART
STAGGED
STAGGER
STAGGERBUSH
STAGGERED
STAGGERER
STAGGERING
STAGGERINGLY
STAGGERS
STAGGERWEED
STAGGERWORT
STAGGERY
STAGGIE
STAGGING
STAGGY
STAGHEAD
STAGHORN
STAGHOUND
STAGHUNT
STAGHUNTER
STAGHUNTING
STAGIARY
STAGIER
STAGIEST
STAGILY
STAGINESS
STAGING
STAGION
STAGMOMETER
STAGNANCY

STAGNANT
STAGNANTLY
STAGNANTNESS
STAGNATE
STAGNATED
STAGNATING
STAGNATION
STAGNATORY
STAGNE
STAGNICOLOUS
STAGNUM
STAGS
STAGSKIN
STAGWORM
STAGY
STAID
STAIDLY
STAIDNESS
STAIG
STAIL
STAIN
STAINABLE
STAINED
STAINER
STAINIERITE
STAINING
STAINLESS
STAINLESSLY
STAIO
STAIR
STAIRBEAK
STAIRBUILDER
STAIRBUILDING
STAIRCASE
STAIRHEAD
STAIRS
STAIRSTEP
STAIRWAY
STAIRWELL
STAIRWORK
STAITH
STAITHMAN
STAITHMEN
STAIVER
STAKE
STAKED
STAKEHEAD
STAKEHOLDER
STAKEMASTER
STAKEOUT
STAKER
STAKING
STALACE
STALACTIC
STALACTICAL
STALACTIFORM
STALACTITAL
STALACTITE
STALACTITES
STALACTITIC
STALACTITIED
STALAG
STALAGMITE
STALAGMITIC
STALDER
STALE
STALED
STALELY
STALEMATE
STALEMATED
STALEMATING
STALENESS
STALER
STALEST
STALING
STALK
STALKED
STALKER
STALKIER
STALKIEST
STALKING
STALKINGLY
STALKLESS
STALKLET
STALKLIKE
STALKO
STALKOES
STALKS
STALKY
STALL
STALLAGE
STALLAND
STALLAR
STALLARY
STALLBOARD
STALLBOAT
STALLED
STALLENGER
STALLER
STALLING
STALLINGER
STALLINGKEN
STALLION
STALLIONIZE
STALLKEEPER
STALLMAN
STALLMEN
STALLMENT
STALLON
STALLS
STALWART
STALWARTISM
STALWARTIZE
STALWARTLY
STALWARTNESS
STALWORTH
STALWORTHLY
STALWORTHNESS
STAM
STAMBHA
STAMBOULINE
STAMEN
STAMENED
STAMENS
STAMIN
STAMINA
STAMINAL
STAMINATE
STAMINEAL
STAMINEOUS
STAMINODE
STAMINODIA
STAMINODIUM
STAMINODY
STAMMEL
STAMMER
STAMMERER
STAMMERING
STAMMERINGLY
STAMMERINGNESS
STAMMERWORT
STAMNOS
STAMP
STAMPAGE
STAMPED
STAMPEDE
STAMPEDED
STAMPEDER
STAMPEDING
STAMPEDO
STAMPEE
STAMPER
STAMPERY
STAMPHEAD
STAMPING
STAMPLE
STAMPMAN
STAMPMEN
STAMPS
STAMPSMAN
STAMPSMEN
STAMPWEED
STANCE
STANCH
STANCHED
STANCHEL
STANCHELED
STANCHER
STANCHEST
STANCHING
STANCHION
STAND
STANDAGE
STANDARD
STANDARDBRED
STANDARDIZABLE
STANDARDIZATION
STANDARDIZE
STANDARDIZED
STANDARDIZER
STANDARDIZING
STANDBY
STANDBYS
STANDEE
STANDEL
STANDELWELKS
STANDELWORT
STANDER
STANDERGRASS
STANDERWORT
STANDFAST
STANDING
STANDISH
STANDOFF
STANDOFFISH
STANDOFFISHNESS
STANDOUT
STANDPAT
STANDPATISM
STANDPATTER
STANDPATTISM
STANDPIPE
STANDPOINT
STANDPOST
STANDSTILL
STANDUP
STANE
STANG
STANHOPE
STANINE
STANITSA
STANITZA
STANJEN
STANK
STANKIE
STANN
STANNANE
STANNARIES
STANNARY
STANNATE
STANNATOR
STANNEL
STANNER
STANNERS
STANNERY
STANNIC
STANNID
STANNIDE
STANNIFEROUS
STANNITE
STANNO
STANNOTYPE
STANNOUS
STANNUM
STANNYL
STANZA
STANZAED
STANZAIC
STANZAICAL
STANZAICALLY
STANZAS
STANZE
STANZO
STAP
STAPEDECTOMY
STAPEDES
STAPEDIAL
STAPEDIFORM
STAPEDIUS
STAPELIA
STAPES
STAPH
STAPHISAGRIA
STAPHYLE
STAPHYLEDEMA
STAPHYLIC
STAPHYLINE
STAPHYLINIC
STAPHYLINID
STAPHYLION
STAPHYLITIS
STAPHYLOMA
STAPHYLONCUS
STAPHYLOSIS
STAPHYLOTOME
STAPHYLOTOMY
STAPLE
STAPLED
STAPLER
STAPLING
STAPP
STAPPLE
STAR
STARBLIND
STARBLOOM
STARBOARD
STARBOLINS
STARBOWLINES
STARBRIGHT
STARCH
STARCHBOARD
STARCHED
STARCHER
STARCHFLOWER
STARCHIER
STARCHIEST
STARCHILY
STARCHINESS
STARCHING
STARCHLY
STARCHMAKER
STARCHMAKING
STARCHMAN
STARCHMEN
STARCHROOT
STARCHWORKS
STARCHWORT
STARCHY
STARCRAFT
STARDOM
STARDUST
STARE
STARED
STAREE
STARER
STARETS
STARFISH
STARFISHES
STARFLOWER
STARFRUIT
STARGAZE
STARGAZED
STARGAZER
STARGAZING
STARIK
STARING
STARK
STARKEN
STARKER
STARKEST
STARKLE
STARKY
STARLESS
STARLESSLY
STARLESSNESS
STARLET
STARLIGHT
STARLIGHTED
STARLIGHTS
STARLIKE
STARLING
STARLIT
STARLITE
STARLITTEN
STARMONGER
STARN
STARNEL
STARNIE
STARNOSE
STARNY
STAROST
STAROSTA
STAROSTI
STAROSTY
STARR
STARRED
STARRIER
STARRIEST
STARRIFY
STARRILY
STARRINESS
STARRING
STARRINGLY
STARRY
STARS
STARSHAKE
STARSHINE
STARSHIP
STARSHOOT
STARSHOT
STARSTONE
STARSTROKE
START
STARTED
STARTER
STARTFUL
STARTFULNESS
STARTHROAT
STARTING
STARTINGLY
STARTISH
STARTLE
STARTLED
STARTLER
STARTLING
STARTLINGLY
STARTLINGNESS
STARTLISH
STARTLISHNESS
STARTLY
STARTS
STARTY
STARVATION
STARVE
STARVEACRE

STARVED
STARVEDLY
STARVELING
STARVEN
STARVER
STARVING
STARVY
STARWISE
STARWORM
STARWORT
STARY
STASES
STASH
STASHIE
STASIDIA
STASIDION
STASIMA
STASIMETRIC
STASIMON
STASIMORPHY
STASIPHOBIA
STASIS
STASSFURTITE
STATABLE
STATANT
STATARY
STATCOULOMB
STATE
STATECRAFT
STATED
STATEDLY
STATEFUL
STATEFULLY
STATEFULNESS
STATELESS
STATELET
STATELIER
STATELIEST
STATELINESS
STATELY
STATEMENT
STATEMENTS
STATEMONGER
STATEQUAKE
STATER
STATERA
STATEROOM
STATESBOY
STATESIDE
STATESMAN
STATESMANLIKE
STATESMANLY
STATESMANSHIP
STATESMEN
STATESMONGER
STATESWOMAN
STATESWOMEN
STATEWAY
STATFARAD
STATHMOS
STATIC
STATICAL
STATICALLY
STATICS
STATING
STATION
STATIONAL
STATIONARIES
STATIONARILY
STATIONARINESS
STATIONARY
STATIONED
STATIONER
STATIONERY
STATIONING
STATIONMAN
STATIONMASTER
STATISM
STATIST
STATISTIC
STATISTICAL
STATISTICALLY
STATISTICIAN
STATISTICIZE
STATISTICS
STATISTOLOGY
STATIVE
STATIZE
STATOBLAST
STATOCRACY
STATOCYST
STATOHM
STATOLATRY
STATOLITH
STATOLITHIC
STATOMETER
STATOR
STATORHAB
STATOSCOPE
STATOSPORE
STATUA
STATUARIES
STATUARISM
STATUARIST
STATUARY
STATUE
STATUECRAFT
STATUED
STATUELIKE
STATUES
STATUESQUE
STATUESQUELY
STATUESQUENESS
STATUETTE
STATUING
STATURE
STATURED
STATUS
STATUSES
STATUTABLE
STATUTABLY
STATUTE
STATUTORILY
STATUTORY
STATUTUM
STATVOLT
STAUMREL
STAUNCH
STAUNCHED
STAUNCHER
STAUNCHEST
STAUNCHING
STAUNCHLY
STAUNCHNESS
STAUP
STAURACIN
STAURAXONIA
STAURAXONIAL
STAURION
STAUROLATRIES
STAUROLATRY
STAUROLITE
STAUROLITIC
STAUROPEGIAL
STAUROPEGION
STAUROSCOPE
STAUROSCOPIC
STAUROTIDE
STAVE
STAVED
STAVER
STAVERS
STAVERWORT
STAVES
STAVESACRE
STAVEWOOD
STAVING
STAVRITE
STAW
STAWSOME
STAXIS
STAY
STAYED
STAYER
STAYING
STAYLACE
STAYLESS
STAYLESSNESS
STAYMAKER
STAYMAKING
STAYNIL
STAYPAK
STAYS
STAYSAIL
STAYSHIP
STCHI
STEAD
STEADABLE
STEADFAST
STEADFASTLY
STEADFASTNESS
STEADIED
STEADIER
STEADIEST
STEADILY
STEADIMENT
STEADINESS
STEADING
STEADITE
STEADMAN
STEADY
STEADYING
STEADYINGLY
STEAK
STEAKHOUSE
STEAL
STEALAGE
STEALER
STEALING
STEALINGLY
STEALTH
STEALTHIER
STEALTHIEST
STEALTHILY
STEALTHINESS
STEALTHLIKE
STEALTHY
STEALY
STEAM
STEAMBOAT
STEAMBOATING
STEAMBOATMAN
STEAMBOATMEN
STEAMCAR
STEAMED
STEAMER
STEAMERLOAD
STEAMFITTER
STEAMFITTING
STEAMIER
STEAMIEST
STEAMILY
STEAMINESS
STEAMING
STEAMPIPE
STEAMROLLER
STEAMSHIP
STEAMTIGHT
STEAMY
STEAN
STEANING
STEAPSIN
STEARATE
STEARIC
STEARIFORM
STEARIN
STEARINE
STEARONE
STEAROPTENE
STEARRHEA
STEARRHOEA
STEARYL
STEATIN
STEATITE
STEATITIC
STEATOCELE
STEATOGENOUS
STEATOLYSIS
STEATOLYTIC
STEATOMA
STEATOMAS
STEATOMATA
STEATOMATOUS
STEATOPATHIC
STEATOPYGA
STEATOPYGIA
STEATOPYGIC
STEATOPYGOUS
STEATOPYGY
STEATORRHEA
STEATORRHOEA
STEATOSES
STEATOSIS
STECH
STECHADOS
STECHLING
STECKLING
STEDFAST
STEDFASTLY
STEDFASTNESS
STEE
STEED
STEEK
STEEKKAN
STEEL
STEELBOW
STEELE
STEELED
STEELEN
STEELER
STEELHEAD
STEELHEADS
STEELHEARTED
STEELIER
STEELIEST
STEELIFICATION
STEELIFIED
STEELIFY
STEELIFYING
STEELINESS
STEELING
STEELMAKER
STEELMAKING
STEELPROOF
STEELWARE
STEELWORK
STEELWORKER
STEELWORKING
STEELWORKS
STEELY
STEELYARD
STEELYARDS
STEEM
STEEN
STEENBOK
STEENBRAS
STEENBRASS
STEENING
STEENKIRK
STEEP
STEEPDOWN
STEEPED
STEEPEN
STEEPER
STEEPEST
STEEPGRASS
STEEPING
STEEPISH
STEEPLE
STEEPLEBUSH
STEEPLECHASE
STEEPLECHASER
STEEPLECHASING
STEEPLED
STEEPLEJACK
STEEPLETOP
STEEPLY
STEEPNESS
STEEPWEED
STEEPWORT
STEEPY
STEER
STEERABLE
STEERAGE
STEERAGEWAY
STEERED
STEERER
STEERING
STEERLING
STEERSMAN
STEERSMATE
STEERSMEN
STEERY
STEEVE
STEEVED
STEEVELY
STEEVER
STEEVING
STEFLY
STEG
STEGANOGRAM
STEGH
STEGNOSIS
STEGNOTIC
STEGOCARPOUS
STEGODON
STEGODONS
STEGODONT
STEGODONTINE
STEGOMYIA
STEGOSAUR
STEGOSAURI
STEGOSAURIAN
STEGOSAUROID
STEGOSAURUS
STEIN
STEINBOK
STEINBUCK
STEINKIRK
STELA
STELAE
STELAR
STELE
STELENE
STELES
STELIC
STELL
STELLAR
STELLARATOR
STELLARY
STELLATE
STELLATED
STELLATELY
STELLATION
STELLATURE

STELLED
STELLERINE
STELLIFEROUS
STELLIFORM
STELLIFY
STELLING
STELLIONATE
STELLISCRIPT
STELLULAR
STELLULARLY
STELLULATE
STELOGRAPHY
STEM
STEMBOK
STEMFORM
STEMHEAD
STEMLESS
STEMLET
STEMMA
STEMMAS
STEMMATA
STEMMATOUS
STEMMED
STEMMER
STEMMERIES
STEMMERY
STEMMIER
STEMMIEST
STEMMING
STEMMY
STEMONACEOUS
STEMPEL
STEMPLE
STEMPOST
STEMSON
STEMWARE
STEN
STENCH
STENCHIER
STENCHIEST
STENCHING
STENCHY
STENCIL
STENCILED
STENCILER
STENCILING
STENCILLED
STENCILLER
STENCILLING
STENCILMAKER
STENCILMAKING
STEND
STENGAH
STENIA
STENION
STENO
STENOBENTHIC
STENOBREGMA
STENOCARDIA
STENOCARDIAC
STENOCEPHALY
STENOCHORIA
STENOCHROME
STENOCHROMY
STENOCRANIAL
STENOGASTRIC
STENOGASTRY
STENOGRAPH
STENOGRAPHED
STENOGRAPHER
STENOGRAPHIC
STENOGRAPHING
STENOGRAPHIST
STENOGRAPHY
STENOHALINE
STENOMETER
STENOPAEIC
STENOPAIC
STENOPEIC
STENOSED
STENOSIS
STENOSPHERE
STENOSTOMIA
STENOTHERMAL
STENOTHORAX
STENOTIC
STENOTROPIC
STENOTYPE
STENOTYPIC
STENOTYPIST
STENOTYPY
STENT
STENTER
STENTERER
STENTING
STENTMASTER
STENTON
STENTOR
STENTORIAN
STENTORIANLY
STENTORINE
STENTORIOUS
STENTORONIC
STENTREL
STEP
STEPAUNT
STEPBAIRN
STEPBROTHER
STEPCHILD
STEPDAME
STEPDAUGHTER
STEPFATHER
STEPFATHERLY
STEPGRANDCHILD
STEPGRANDFATHER
STEPGRANDMOTHER
STEPGRANDSON
STEPHANE
STEPHANIAL
STEPHANIC
STEPHANION
STEPHANITE
STEPHANOME
STEPHANOS
STEPLADDER
STEPMINNIE
STEPMOTHER
STEPMOTHERLINESS
STEPMOTHERLY
STEPNEPHEW
STEPNIECE
STEPONY
STEPPARENT
STEPPE
STEPPED
STEPPER
STEPPING
STEPPINGSTONE
STEPRELATION
STEPS
STEPSIRE
STEPSISTER
STEPSON
STEPSTONE
STEPT
STEPUNCLE
STEPWAY
STEPWISE
STERACLE
STERAD
STERADIAN
STERCOLIN
STERCORAEMIA
STERCORAL
STERCORARIES
STERCORARY
STERCORATE
STERCORATION
STERCOREMIA
STERCORITE
STERCOROL
STERCOROUS
STERCOVOROUS
STERCULIAD
STERE
STEREAGNOSIS
STEREID
STEREO
STEREOBATE
STEREOBATIC
STEREOCAMERA
STEREOCHEMIC
STEREOCHROME
STEREOCHROMY
STEREOED
STEREOGNOSIS
STEREOGRAM
STEREOGRAPH
STEREOGRAPHY
STEREOING
STEREOISOMER
STEREOM
STEREOMATRIX
STEREOME
STEREOMERIC
STEREOMETER
STEREOMETRIC
STEREOMETRY
STEREONEURAL
STEREOPHONE
STEREOPHONIC
STEREOPHONY
STEREOPHYSICS
STEREOPICTURE
STEREOPLASM
STEREOPSIS
STEREOPTICON
STEREOS
STEREOSCOPE
STEREOSCOPIC
STEREOSCOPY
STEREOSTATIC
STEREOSTATICS
STEREOTACTIC
STEREOTAXIS
STEREOTAXY
STEREOTOMIC
STEREOTOMIST
STEREOTOMY
STEREOTROPIC
STEREOTYPE
STEREOTYPED
STEREOTYPER
STEREOTYPERY
STEREOTYPIC
STEREOTYPICAL
STEREOTYPING
STEREOTYPIST
STEREOTYPY
STEREOVISION
STERIC
STERICAL
STERICALLY
STERID
STERIDE
STERIGMA
STERIGMATA
STERIGMATIC
STERILANT
STERILE
STERILELY
STERILENESS
STERILISE
STERILITIES
STERILITY
STERILIZATION
STERILIZE
STERILIZED
STERILIZER
STERILIZING
STERIN
STERLET
STERLING
STERLINGLY
STERLINGNESS
STERN
STERNA
STERNAD
STERNAGE
STERNAL
STERNALIS
STERNBERGITE
STERNCASTLE
STERNEBER
STERNEBRA
STERNEBRAL
STERNER
STERNEST
STERNFOREMOST
STERNFUL
STERNFULLY
STERNITE
STERNKNEE
STERNLY
STERNMAN
STERNMEN
STERNMOST
STERNNESS
STERNOCOSTAL
STERNOFACIAL
STERNOHYOID
STERNOMANCY
STERNONUCHAL
STERNOTHERE
STERNOTRIBE
STERNPOST
STERNSON
STERNUM
STERNUMS
STERNUTATION
STERNUTATIVE
STERNUTATOR
STERNUTATORY
STERNWARD
STERNWARDS
STERNWAY
STERNWAYS
STERNWORKS
STERO
STEROID
STEROL
STERRINCK
STERTOR
STERTORIOUS
STERTOROUS
STERTOROUSLY
STET
STETHAL
STETHOMETER
STETHOMETRIC
STETHOMETRY
STETHOPHONE
STETHOSCOPE
STETHOSCOPIC
STETHOSCOPY
STETHOSPASM
STETHY
STETTED
STETTING
STEVE
STEVEDORAGE
STEVEDORE
STEVEDORED
STEVEDORING
STEVEL
STEVEN
STEW
STEWARD
STEWARDESS
STEWARDLY
STEWARDRY
STEWARDSHIP
STEWART
STEWARTRY
STEWBUM
STEWED
STEWHOUSE
STEWING
STEWISH
STEWPAN
STEWPOND
STEWPOT
STEWY
STEY
STEYN
STEYNING
STHENE
STHENIA
STHENIC
STHENOCHIRE
STIACCIATO
STIB
STIBBLE
STIBBLER
STIBBLERIG
STIBIAL
STIBIALISM
STIBIATE
STIBIATED
STIBICONITE
STIBINE
STIBIUM
STIBNITE
STIBONIUM
STIBOPHEN
STICCADO
STICH
STICHADO
STICHARION
STICHEL
STICHERON
STICHIC
STICHICALLY
STICHID
STICHIDIA
STICHIDIUM
STICHOI
STICHOMANCY
STICHOMETRIC
STICHOMETRY
STICHOMYTHIC
STICHOMYTHY
STICHOS
STICHWORT
STICK
STICKAGE
STICKBALL
STICKED
STICKER
STICKERS
STICKERY
STICKFAST
STICKFUL
STICKFULS
STICKIER

STICKIEST
STICKILY
STICKINESS
STICKING
STICKIT
STICKJAW
STICKLE
STICKLEAF
STICKLEBACK
STICKLED
STICKLER
STICKLING
STICKLY
STICKMAN
STICKPIN
STICKS
STICKSEED
STICKTAIL
STICKTIGHT
STICKUM
STICKUP
STICKWEED
STICKWORK
STICKY
STICTIFORM
STIDDY
STIED
STIFE
STIFF
STIFFEN
STIFFENED
STIFFENER
STIFFENING
STIFFER
STIFFEST
STIFFHEARTED
STIFFISH
STIFFLEG
STIFFLER
STIFFLY
STIFFNECK
STIFFNESS
STIFFRUMP
STIFFTAIL
STIFLE
STIFLED
STIFLEDLY
STIFLER
STIFLING
STIFLINGLY
STIGMA
STIGMAI
STIGMAL
STIGMARIA
STIGMARIAE
STIGMARIAN
STIGMARIOID
STIGMAS
STIGMASTEROL
STIGMATA
STIGMATAL
STIGMATIC
STIGMATICAL
STIGMATICALLY
STIGMATICALNESS
STIGMATIFORM
STIGMATISE
STIGMATISM
STIGMATIST
STIGMATIZATION
STIGMATIZE
STIGMATIZED
STIGMATIZER
STIGMATIZING
STIGMATOID
STIGMATOSE
STIGME
STIGMEOLOGY
STIGMES
STIGMONOSE
STIGONOMANCY
STILB
STILBENE
STILBESTROL
STILBITE
STILE
STILEMAN
STILEMEN
STILET
STILETTE
STILETTO
STILETTOED
STILETTOES
STILETTOING
STILETTOS
STILL
STILLAGE
STILLATORY
STILLBIRTH
STILLBORN
STILLED
STILLER
STILLERY
STILLEST
STILLHOUSE
STILLICIDE
STILLICIDIUM
STILLIER
STILLIEST
STILLIFORM
STILLING
STILLION
STILLISH
STILLMAN
STILLMEN
STILLNESS
STILLROOM
STILLSTAND
STILLY
STILO
STILT
STILTED
STILTEDLY
STILTEDNESS
STILTER
STILTIER
STILTIEST
STILTIFIED
STILTIFY
STILTIFYING
STILTINESS
STILTING
STILTISH
STILTY
STIM
STIME
STIMPART
STIMULABILITY
STIMULABLE
STIMULANCE
STIMULANCY
STIMULANT
STIMULATE
STIMULATED
STIMULATER
STIMULATING
STIMULATION
STIMULATIVE
STIMULATOR
STIMULATORY
STIMULATRESS
STIMULATRIX
STIMULI
STIMULUS
STIMY
STING
STINGAREE
STINGAREEING
STINGBULL
STINGE
STINGER
STINGFISH
STINGFISHES
STINGIER
STINGIEST
STINGILY
STINGINESS
STINGING
STINGINGLY
STINGINGNESS
STINGLESS
STINGO
STINGRAY
STINGTAIL
STINGY
STINK
STINKARD
STINKARDLY
STINKBALL
STINKBERRIES
STINKBERRY
STINKBIRD
STINKBUG
STINKBUSH
STINKDAMP
STINKER
STINKHORN
STINKING
STINKINGLY
STINKINGNESS
STINKO
STINKPOT
STINKS
STINKSTONE
STINKWEED
STINKWOOD
STINKWORT
STINKY
STINT
STINTED
STINTEDLY
STINTEDNESS
STINTER
STINTING
STINTS
STINTY
STIPATE
STIPE
STIPED
STIPEL
STIPELLATE
STIPEND
STIPENDIA
STIPENDIAL
STIPENDIARIES
STIPENDIARY
STIPENDIATE
STIPENDIUM
STIPENDIUMS
STIPES
STIPIFORM
STIPITATE
STIPITES
STIPITIFORM
STIPITURE
STIPPEN
STIPPLE
STIPPLED
STIPPLER
STIPPLING
STIPPLY
STIPULA
STIPULABLE
STIPULACEOUS
STIPULAR
STIPULARY
STIPULATE
STIPULATED
STIPULATING
STIPULATIO
STIPULATION
STIPULATOR
STIPULATORY
STIPULE
STIPULED
STIPULIFORM
STIR
STIRABOUT
STIRIA
STIRK
STIRLESS
STIRLESSLY
STIRLESSNESS
STIRLING
STIRP
STIRPES
STIRPS
STIRRA
STIRRAGE
STIRRED
STIRRER
STIRRING
STIRRINGLY
STIRRUP
STITCH
STITCHBIRD
STITCHDOWN
STITCHED
STITCHER
STITCHERY
STITCHES
STITCHING
STITCHWHILE
STITCHWORK
STITCHWORT
STITE
STITH
STITHE
STITHIED
STITHIES
STITHLY
STITHY
STITHYING
STIVE
STIVER
STIVY
STOA
STOACH
STOAE
STOAK
STOAS
STOAT
STOATER
STOATING
STOATS
STOB
STOBBALL
STOBBED
STOBBING
STOCAH
STOCCADO
STOCCATA
STOCHASTIC
STOCHASTICAL
STOCK
STOCKADE
STOCKADED
STOCKADING
STOCKADO
STOCKAGE
STOCKANNET
STOCKBOW
STOCKBREEDER
STOCKBREEDING
STOCKBROKER
STOCKBROKERAGE
STOCKBROKING
STOCKCAR
STOCKED
STOCKER
STOCKFATHER
STOCKFISH
STOCKFISHES
STOCKHOLDER
STOCKHOLDING
STOCKHOUSE
STOCKIER
STOCKIEST
STOCKILY
STOCKINESS
STOCKINET
STOCKINETTE
STOCKING
STOCKINGED
STOCKINGER
STOCKINGING
STOCKINGLESS
STOCKINGS
STOCKISH
STOCKISHLY
STOCKISHNESS
STOCKJOBBER
STOCKJOBBERY
STOCKJOBBING
STOCKJUDGING
STOCKKEEPER
STOCKKEEPING
STOCKMAKER
STOCKMAKING
STOCKMAN
STOCKMEN
STOCKOWNER
STOCKPILE
STOCKPILED
STOCKPILING
STOCKPOT
STOCKPROOF
STOCKRIDER
STOCKRIDING
STOCKROOM
STOCKS
STOCKSTONE
STOCKTAKER
STOCKTAKING
STOCKWORK
STOCKWRIGHT
STOCKY
STOCKYARD
STOD
STODE
STODGE
STODGED
STODGER
STODGERY
STODGIER
STODGIEST
STODGILY
STODGINESS
STODGING
STODGY
STODTONE
STOECHIOLOGY
STOEP
STOF
STOFF

STOG
STOGA
STOGIE
STOGIES
STOGY
STOIC
STOICAL
STOICALLY
STOICALNESS
STOICHIOLOGY
STOICISM
STOIT
STOITER
STOKE
STOKED
STOKEHOLD
STOKEHOLE
STOKER
STOKES
STOKESITE
STOKING
STOKROOS
STOKVIS
STOLA
STOLAE
STOLE
STOLED
STOLEN
STOLENLY
STOLENNESS
STOLENWISE
STOLID
STOLIDITY
STOLIDLY
STOLIDNESS
STOLIST
STOLKJAERRE
STOLLEN
STOLO
STOLON
STOLONATE
STOLZITE
STOMA
STOMACACE
STOMACH
STOMACHABLE
STOMACHACHE
STOMACHAL
STOMACHED
STOMACHER
STOMACHFUL
STOMACHFULLY
STOMACHFULNESS
STOMACHIC
STOMACHICAL
STOMACHICALLY
STOMACHING
STOMACHLESS
STOMACHLESSNESS
STOMACHY
STOMATA
STOMATAL
STOMATE
STOMATIC
STOMATITIC
STOMATITIS
STOMATOCACE
STOMATODE
STOMATOGRAPH
STOMATOLOGIC
STOMATOLOGY
STOMATOMENIA
STOMATOMY
STOMATOPATHY
STOMATOPOD
STOMATOSCOPE
STOMATOSCOPY
STOMATOSE
STOMATOTOMY
STOMATOUS
STOMION
STOMIUM
STOMODAEA
STOMODAEAL
STOMODAEUM
STOMODEAL
STOMODEUM
STOMOXYS
STOMP
STOMPER
STONAGE
STONE
STONEBASS
STONEBIRD
STONEBITER
STONEBOAT
STONEBOW
STONEBRASH
STONEBREAK
STONEBROOD
STONECAST
STONECAT
STONECHAT
STONECROP
STONECUTTER
STONECUTTING
STONED
STONEFISH
STONEGALE
STONEGALL
STONEHAND
STONEHATCH
STONEHEAD
STONEHEARTED
STONEITE
STONELAYER
STONELAYING
STONELIKE
STONEMAN
STONEMASON
STONEMASONRY
STONEMEN
STONEMINT
STONEN
STONEPECKER
STONEPUT
STONER
STONEROOT
STONES
STONESHOT
STONESMATCH
STONESMITCH
STONESMITH
STONEWALL
STONEWALLED
STONEWALLER
STONEWALLING
STONEWALLY
STONEWARE
STONEWEED
STONEWISE
STONEWOOD
STONEWORK
STONEWORKER
STONEWORT
STONEY
STONEYARD
STONIER
STONIEST
STONIFIABLE
STONIFY
STONILY
STONINESS
STONING
STONISH
STONISHMENT
STONK
STONKER
STONY
STONYHEARTED
STOOD
STOODED
STOOF
STOOGE
STOOGED
STOOGING
STOOK
STOOKER
STOOKIE
STOOL
STOOLBALL
STOOLED
STOOLIE
STOOLING
STOOP
STOOPED
STOOPER
STOOPGALLANT
STOOPING
STOOPINGLY
STOOR
STOOREY
STOORY
STOOTER
STOOTH
STOOTHING
STOP
STOPA
STOPBACK
STOPBLOCK
STOPBOARD
STOPCOCK
STOPDICE
STOPE
STOPED
STOPEN
STOPER
STOPGAP
STOPHOUND
STOPING
STOPLESS
STOPLESSNESS
STOPLIGHT
STOPOVER
STOPPABILITY
STOPPABLE
STOPPABLY
STOPPAGE
STOPPED
STOPPEL
STOPPER
STOPPERED
STOPPERING
STOPPING
STOPPLE
STOPPLED
STOPPLING
STOPS
STOPSHIP
STOPT
STOPWATCH
STOPWATER
STOPWORK
STOR
STORABLE
STORAGE
STORAX
STORE
STORED
STOREEN
STOREHOUSE
STOREKEEP
STOREKEEPER
STOREKEEPING
STOREMAN
STOREMASTER
STOREMEN
STORER
STOREROOM
STORES
STORESHIP
STOREY
STOREYED
STOREYS
STORGE
STORIAL
STORIATE
STORIATION
STORIED
STORIER
STORIES
STORIETTE
STORIFIED
STORIFY
STORIFYING
STORING
STORIOLOGIST
STORIOLOGY
STORK
STORKEN
STORKLIKE
STORKS
STORKSBILL
STORM
STORMABLE
STORMBELT
STORMBIRD
STORMBOUND
STORMCOCK
STORMED
STORMER
STORMFUL
STORMFULLY
STORMFULNESS
STORMIER
STORMIEST
STORMILY
STORMINESS
STORMING
STORMINGLY
STORMISH
STORMPROOF
STORMS
STORMWIND
STORMY
STORNELLI
STORNELLO
STORY
STORYBOOK
STORYING
STORYMAKER
STORYMONGER
STORYTELLER
STORYTELLING
STORYWORK
STOSH
STOSS
STOSSTON
STOT
STOTER
STOTINKA
STOTINKI
STOTT
STOTTER
STOUN
STOUND
STOUNDMEAL
STOUP
STOUR
STOURE
STOURIE
STOURING
STOURLINESS
STOURLY
STOURNESS
STOURY
STOUSH
STOUT
STOUTEN
STOUTER
STOUTEST
STOUTH
STOUTHEARTED
STOUTHEARTEDLY
STOUTHEARTEDNESS
STOUTHRIEF
STOUTLY
STOUTNESS
STOUTWOOD
STOUTY
STOVE
STOVEBRUSH
STOVED
STOVEHOUSE
STOVEMAKER
STOVEMAKING
STOVEMAN
STOVEMEN
STOVEN
STOVEPIPE
STOVER
STOVEWOOD
STOVIES
STOVING
STOW
STOWAGE
STOWAWAY
STOWBALL
STOWBOARD
STOWBORD
STOWBORDMAN
STOWBORDMEN
STOWCE
STOWDOWN
STOWED
STOWER
STOWING
STOWL
STOWLINS
STOWNET
STOWP
STOWSE
STOWTH
STOWWOOD
STRABISM
STRABISMAL
STRABISMALLY
STRABISMIC
STRABISMICAL
STRABISMUS
STRABOMETER
STRABOMETRY
STRABOTOME
STRABOTOMIES
STRABOTOMY
STRACKLING
STRACT
STRAD
STRADDLE
STRADDLEBACK
STRADDLEBUG
STRADDLED
STRADDLER
STRADDLING
STRADDLINGLY

STRADICO
STRADINE
STRADIOT
STRADLINGS
STRAFE
STRAFED
STRAFER
STRAFING
STRAG
STRAGE
STRAGGLE
STRAGGLED
STRAGGLER
STRAGGLIER
STRAGGLIEST
STRAGGLING
STRAGGLINGLY
STRAGGLY
STRAGULAR
STRAGULUM
STRAIGHT
STRAIGHTAWAY
STRAIGHTEDGE
STRAIGHTEDGED
STRAIGHTEDGING
STRAIGHTEN
STRAIGHTENED
STRAIGHTENER
STRAIGHTENING
STRAIGHTER
STRAIGHTEST
STRAIGHTFORWARD
STRAIGHTFORWARDLY
STRAIGHTFORWARDNESS
STRAIGHTFORWARDS
STRAIGHTHEAD
STRAIGHTLY
STRAIGHTNESS
STRAIGHTWAY
STRAIGHTWAYS
STRAIGHTWISE
STRAIK
STRAIKE
STRAIL
STRAIN
STRAINABLE
STRAINABLY
STRAINED
STRAINEDLY
STRAINEDNESS
STRAINER
STRAINERMAN
STRAINERMEN
STRAINING
STRAININGLY
STRAINSLIP
STRAINT
STRAIT
STRAITEN
STRAITENED
STRAITENING
STRAITER
STRAITEST
STRAITJACKET
STRAITLACED
STRAITLACING
STRAITLY
STRAITNESS
STRAITSMAN
STRAITSMEN
STRAITWORK
STRAKE
STRAKED
STRAKES
STRAKY
STRALET
STRAM
STRAMASH
STRAMAZON
STRAMINEOUS
STRAMMEL
STRAMMER
STRAMONIUM
STRAMONY
STRAMP
STRAN
STRAND
STRANDAGE
STRANDED
STRANDER
STRANDING
STRANDLOOPER
STRANDS
STRANG
STRANGE
STRANGELING
STRANGELY
STRANGENESS
STRANGER
STRANGEST
STRANGLE
STRANGLEABLE
STRANGLED
STRANGLEHOLD
STRANGLEMENT
STRANGLER
STRANGLES
STRANGLETARE
STRANGLEWEED
STRANGLING
STRANGULATE
STRANGULATED
STRANGULATING
STRANGULATION
STRANGULATIVE
STRANGULLION
STRANGURIOUS
STRANGURY
STRANNER
STRANY
STRAP
STRAPHANG
STRAPHANGER
STRAPHEAD
STRAPLESS
STRAPPABLE
STRAPPADO
STRAPPADOES
STRAPPED
STRAPPER
STRAPPING
STRAPPLE
STRAPS
STRAPWORK
STRAPWORT
STRASS
STRATA
STRATAGEM
STRATAGEMS
STRATAL
STRATAMETER
STRATEGE
STRATEGETIC
STRATEGETICAL
STRATEGETICS
STRATEGI
STRATEGIAN
STRATEGIC
STRATEGICAL
STRATEGICALLY
STRATEGICS
STRATEGIES
STRATEGIST
STRATEGIZE
STRATEGOI
STRATEGOS
STRATEGUS
STRATEGY
STRATH
STRATHSPEY
STRATI
STRATIC
STRATICULATE
STRATIFICATION
STRATIFIED
STRATIFORM
STRATIFY
STRATIFYING
STRATIGRAPHER
STRATIGRAPHIC
STRATIGRAPHY
STRATLIN
STRATOCRACIES
STRATOCRACY
STRATOCRAT
STRATOCRATIC
STRATOGRAPHIC
STRATOGRAPHY
STRATONIC
STRATOPAUSE
STRATOSE
STRATOSPHERE
STRATOSPHERIC
STRATOUS
STRATUM
STRATUMS
STRATUS
STRAUGHT
STRAVAGANT
STRAVAGE
STRAVAGED
STRAVAGING
STRAVAGUE
STRAVAIG
STRAVAIGER
STRAW
STRAWBERRIES
STRAWBERRY
STRAWBILL
STRAWBOARD
STRAWBREADTH
STRAWEN
STRAWER
STRAWFLOWER
STRAWFORK
STRAWHAT
STRAWIER
STRAWIEST
STRAWMOTE
STRAWSMEAR
STRAWSTACK
STRAWSTACKER
STRAWWALKER
STRAWWORK
STRAWWORM
STRAWY
STRAWYARD
STRAY
STRAYAWAY
STRAYED
STRAYER
STRAYING
STREAK
STREAKED
STREAKEDLY
STREAKEDNESS
STREAKER
STREAKIER
STREAKIEST
STREAKILY
STREAKINESS
STREAKING
STREAKS
STREAKY
STREAM
STREAMED
STREAMER
STREAMIER
STREAMIEST
STREAMING
STREAMINGLY
STREAMLET
STREAMLINE
STREAMLINED
STREAMLING
STREAMLINING
STREAMS
STREAMWAY
STREAMWORT
STREAMY
STRECK
STRECKLY
STREEK
STREEL
STREELER
STREEN
STREEP
STREET
STREETAGE
STREETCAR
STREETS
STREETWALKER
STREETWALKING
STREETWARD
STREETWAY
STREIT
STREITE
STREMMA
STREMMAS
STRENGITE
STRENGTH
STRENGTHEN
STRENGTHENED
STRENGTHENER
STRENGTHENING
STRENGTHENINGLY
STRENGTHILY
STRENGTHLESS
STRENGTHLESSLY
STRENGTHLESSNESS
STRENGTHY
STRENT
STRENUITY
STRENUOSITY
STRENUOUS
STRENUOUSLY
STRENUOUSNESS
STREPENT
STREPERA
STREPEROUS
STREPHONADE
STREPITANT
STREPITANTLY
STREPITATION
STREPITOSO
STREPITOUS
STREPOR
STREPSINEMA
STREPSIPTERAL
STREPSIPTERON
STREPSIS
STREPSITENE
STREPTASTER
STREPTOCOCCI
STREPTOLYSIN
STREPTOMYCIN
STRESS
STRESSED
STRESSER
STRESSFUL
STRESSING
STRESSLESS
STRETCH
STRETCHABLE
STRETCHBERRY
STRETCHED
STRETCHER
STRETCHERMAN
STRETCHINESS
STRETCHING
STRETCHNECK
STRETCHPANTS
STRETCHY
STRETMAN
STRETMEN
STRETTA
STRETTAS
STRETTE
STRETTI
STRETTO
STRETTOS
STREUSEL
STREW
STREWED
STREWER
STREWING
STREWMENT
STREWN
STRIA
STRIAE
STRIAL
STRIATE
STRIATED
STRIATING
STRIATION
STRIATURE
STRICH
STRICK
STRICKEN
STRICKENLY
STRICKENNESS
STRICKER
STRICKLE
STRICKLED
STRICKLER
STRICKLING
STRICT
STRICTER
STRICTEST
STRICTION
STRICTLY
STRICTNESS
STRICTURE
STRICTURED
STRID
STRIDDEN
STRIDDLE
STRIDE
STRIDELEG
STRIDELEGS
STRIDENCE
STRIDENCY
STRIDENT
STRIDENTLY
STRIDER
STRIDES
STRIDEWAYS
STRIDHAN
STRIDHANA
STRIDHANUM
STRIDING
STRIDLING
STRIDLINS
STRIDOR
STRIDULANT

STRIDULATE
STRIDULATED
STRIDULATING
STRIDULATION
STRIDULATOR
STRIDULATORY
STRIDULENT
STRIDULOUS
STRIDULOUSLY
STRIE
STRIFE
STRIFFEN
STRIFT
STRIG
STRIGA
STRIGAE
STRIGAL
STRIGATE
STRIGGLE
STRIGIL
STRIGILATE
STRIGILATION
STRIGILATOR
STRIGILES
STRIGILIS
STRIGILLOSE
STRIGINE
STRIGOSE
STRIGOUS
STRIGOVITE
STRIKE
STRIKEBOUND
STRIKEBREAKER
STRIKEBREAKING
STRIKEOUT
STRIKER
STRIKES
STRIKING
STRIKINGLY
STRIKINGNESS
STRIND
STRING
STRINGBOARD
STRINGCOURSE
STRINGED
STRINGENCIES
STRINGENCY
STRINGENDO
STRINGENDOS
STRINGENT
STRINGENTLY
STRINGENTNESS
STRINGER
STRINGHALT
STRINGHALTED
STRINGHALTY
STRINGIER
STRINGIEST
STRINGILY
STRINGINESS
STRINGING
STRINGMAKER
STRINGMAKING
STRINGMAN
STRINGMEN
STRINGPIECE
STRINGS
STRINGSMAN
STRINGSMEN
STRINGWAYS
STRINGWOOD
STRINGY
STRINGYBARK
STRINKLE
STRIOLA
STRIOLAE
STRIOLATE
STRIOLATED
STRIOLET
STRIP
STRIPE
STRIPED
STRIPER
STRIPES
STRIPIER
STRIPIEST
STRIPING
STRIPLIGHT
STRIPLING
STRIPPAGE
STRIPPED
STRIPPER
STRIPPING
STRIPPLER
STRIPS
STRIPT
STRIPTEASE
STRIPTEASER
STRIPY
STRIT
STRIVE
STRIVED
STRIVEN
STRIVER
STRIVING
STRIX
STROAM
STROBE
STROBIC
STROBIL
STROBILA
STROBILAE
STROBILATE
STROBILATION
STROBILE
STROBILI
STROBILIFORM
STROBILINE
STROBILOID
STROBILUS
STROBOSCOPE
STROBOSCOPIC
STROBOSCOPY
STROCKLE
STROIL
STROKE
STROKED
STROKER
STROKES
STROKESMAN
STROKING
STROKINGS
STROKY
STROLL
STROLLED
STROLLER
STROLLING
STROM
STROMA
STROMAL
STROMATA
STROMATEOID
STROMATIC
STROMATIFORM
STROMATOLOGY
STROMATOUS
STROMB
STROMBIFORM
STROMBITE
STROMBOID
STROMBOLIAN
STROME
STROMEYERITE
STROMMING
STROMUHR
STROND
STRONE
STRONG
STRONGBACK
STRONGBARK
STRONGBOX
STRONGER
STRONGEST
STRONGFULLY
STRONGHAND
STRONGHANDED
STRONGHEADED
STRONGHEARTED
STRONGHOLD
STRONGISH
STRONGLY
STRONGMAN
STRONGMEN
STRONGNESS
STRONGPOINT
STRONGROOM
STRONGYL
STRONGYLATE
STRONGYLE
STRONGYLID
STRONGYLOID
STRONGYLON
STRONGYLOSIS
STRONTIA
STRONTIAN
STRONTIANITE
STRONTIC
STRONTION
STRONTITIC
STRONTIUM
STROOT
STROP
STROPHAIC
STROPHANTHIN
STROPHE
STROPHES
STROPHIC
STROPHICAL
STROPHICALLY
STROPHIOLATE
STROPHIOLE
STROPHOID
STROPHOMENID
STROPHOSIS
STROPHOTAXIS
STROPHULUS
STROPPED
STROPPER
STROPPING
STROPPINGS
STROSSER
STROTH
STROTHER
STROUD
STROUDING
STROUNGE
STROUP
STROUT
STROVE
STROW
STROWD
STROWED
STROWING
STROWN
STROY
STROYER
STROYGOOD
STRUB
STRUBBLY
STRUCION
STRUCK
STRUCKEN
STRUCTURAL
STRUCTURALISM
STRUCTURALIST
STRUCTURALIZATION
STRUCTURALIZE
STRUCTURALLY
STRUCTURATION
STRUCTURE
STRUCTURED
STRUCTURELESS
STRUCTURELESSNESS
STRUCTURELY
STRUCTURES
STRUCTURIST
STRUDE
STRUDEL
STRUE
STRUGGLE
STRUGGLED
STRUGGLER
STRUGGLING
STRUGGLINGLY
STRUIS
STRUISSLE
STRUM
STRUMA
STRUMAE
STRUMATIC
STRUMECTOMY
STRUMIFEROUS
STRUMIFORM
STRUMIPRIVIC
STRUMITIS
STRUMMED
STRUMMER
STRUMMING
STRUMOSE
STRUMOUS
STRUMOUSNESS
STRUMPET
STRUMPETRY
STRUMSTRUM
STRUMULOSE
STRUNG
STRUNT
STRUSE
STRUT
STRUTHIAN
STRUTHIFORM
STRUTHIIFORM
STRUTHIIN
STRUTHIN
STRUTHIOID
STRUTHIONINE
STRUTHIOUS
STRUTTED
STRUTTER
STRUTTING
STRUTTINGLY
STRUVITE
STRY
STRYCH
STRYCHNIA
STRYCHNIC
STRYCHNIN
STRYCHNINE
STRYCHNINISM
STRYCHNINIZE
STRYPE
STUB
STUBACHITE
STUBB
STUBBED
STUBBER
STUBBIER
STUBBIEST
STUBBILY
STUBBINESS
STUBBING
STUBBLE
STUBBLEBERRY
STUBBLED
STUBBLES
STUBBLIER
STUBBLIEST
STUBBLING
STUBBLY
STUBBORN
STUBBORNLY
STUBBORNNESS
STUBBY
STUBCHEN
STUBE
STUBRUNNER
STUCCO
STUCCOED
STUCCOER
STUCCOES
STUCCOING
STUCCOS
STUCCOWORK
STUCCOWORKER
STUCK
STUCKEN
STUCKING
STUCKLING
STUD
STUDBOOK
STUDDED
STUDDER
STUDDERY
STUDDIE
STUDDING
STUDDINGSAIL
STUDDLE
STUDDY
STUDENT
STUDENTRY
STUDENTS
STUDENTSHIP
STUDERITE
STUDFISH
STUDFISHES
STUDHORSE
STUDIA
STUDIED
STUDIEDLY
STUDIEDNESS
STUDIER
STUDIES
STUDIO
STUDIOS
STUDIOUS
STUDIOUSLY
STUDIOUSNESS
STUDIUM
STUDWORK
STUDY
STUDYING
STUE
STUFA
STUFE
STUFF
STUFFAGE
STUFFATA
STUFFED
STUFFENDER
STUFFER
STUFFIER
STUFFIEST
STUFFILY
STUFFINESS
STUFFING

STUFFY
STUG
STUGGY
STUIVER
STULL
STULLER
STULM
STULP
STULTIFIED
STULTIFIER
STULTIFY
STULTIFYING
STULTILOQUY
STULTY
STUM
STUMBLE
STUMBLEBUM
STUMBLED
STUMBLER
STUMBLING
STUMBLINGLY
STUMBLY
STUMER
STUMMED
STUMMEL
STUMMER
STUMMING
STUMMY
STUMOR
STUMOUR
STUMP
STUMPAGE
STUMPED
STUMPER
STUMPIER
STUMPIEST
STUMPINESS
STUMPING
STUMPISH
STUMPLING
STUMPNOSE
STUMPS
STUMPSUCKER
STUMPY
STUN
STUNG
STUNK
STUNKARD
STUNNED
STUNNER
STUNNING
STUNNINGLY
STUNPOLL
STUNSAIL
STUNT
STUNTED
STUNTEDLY
STUNTEDNESS
STUNTER
STUNTINESS
STUNTING
STUNTIST
STUNTNESS
STUNTY
STUP
STUPA
STUPE
STUPED
STUPEFACIENT
STUPEFACTION
STUPEFACTIVE
STUPEFIED
STUPEFIEDNESS
STUPEFIER
STUPEFY
STUPEFYING
STUPEND
STUPENDLY
STUPENDOUS
STUPENDOUSLY
STUPENDOUSNESS
STUPENT
STUPEOUS
STUPEX
STUPHE
STUPID
STUPIDHEAD
STUPIDITIES
STUPIDITY
STUPIDLY
STUPIDNESS
STUPING
STUPOR
STUPORIFIC
STUPOROSE
STUPOROUS
STUPOSE
STUPP
STUPRATE
STUPRATED
STUPRATING
STUPRATION
STUPRUM
STUPULOSE
STURBLE
STURDIED
STURDIER
STURDIEST
STURDILY
STURDINESS
STURDY
STURGEON
STURGEONS
STURIN
STURINE
STURNIFORM
STURNINE
STURNOID
STUROCH
STURSHUM
STURT
STURTAN
STURTE
STURTIN
STURTION
STURTITE
STUSS
STUT
STUTTER
STUTTERER
STUTTERING
STUTTERINGLY
STY
STYAN
STYANY
STYCA
STYCERIN
STYCERINOL
STYCHOMYTHIA
STYE
STYFZIEKTE
STYGIAN
STYING
STYKE
STYLAR
STYLATE
STYLE
STYLEBOOK
STYLED
STYLEDOM
STYLER
STYLET
STYLEWORT
STYLI
STYLIFEROUS
STYLIFORM
STYLINE
STYLING
STYLION
STYLISH
STYLISHLY
STYLISHNESS
STYLIST
STYLISTIC
STYLISTICAL
STYLISTICALLY
STYLISTICS
STYLITE
STYLITISM
STYLIZATION
STYLIZE
STYLIZED
STYLIZER
STYLIZING
STYLO
STYLOBATE
STYLOGLOSSAL
STYLOGLOSSUS
STYLOGRAPH
STYLOGRAPHIC
STYLOGRAPHY
STYLOHYAL
STYLOHYOID
STYLOID
STYLOLITE
STYLOLITIC
STYLOMASTOID
STYLOMETER
STYLOPID
STYLOPIZED
STYLOPOD
STYLOPODIA
STYLOPODIUM
STYLOSPORE
STYLOSPOROUS
STYLOSTEGIUM
STYLOSTEMON
STYLOTYPITE
STYLUS
STYLUSES
STYME
STYMIE
STYMIED
STYMYING
STYPHNATE
STYPHNIC
STYPSIS
STYPTIC
STYPTICAL
STYPTICITY
STYPTICNESS
STYRACACEOUS
STYRACIN
STYRENE
STYROFOAM
STYROGALLOL
STYROL
STYRONE
STYRYL
STYRYLIC
STYTH
STYTHE
SUABILITY
SUABLE
SUABLY
SUADE
SUAHARO
SUANT
SUANTLY
SUASIBLE
SUASION
SUASIONIST
SUASIVE
SUASIVELY
SUASIVENESS
SUASORIA
SUASORY
SUAVE
SUAVELY
SUAVENESS
SUAVEOLENT
SUAVIFY
SUAVILOQUENT
SUAVITIES
SUAVITY
SUB
SUBABDOMINAL
SUBACID
SUBACIDITY
SUBACIDLY
SUBACIDNESS
SUBACT
SUBACTION
SUBACUTE
SUBACUTELY
SUBADAR
SUBADULT
SUBAERIAL
SUBAERIALLY
SUBAGE
SUBAGENCY
SUBAGENT
SUBAH
SUBAHDAR
SUBAHDARY
SUBAHSHIP
SUBAID
SUBALARY
SUBALBID
SUBALKALINE
SUBALMONER
SUBALPINE
SUBALTERN
SUBALTERNANT
SUBALTERNATE
SUBALTERNITY
SUBAMARE
SUBANGLED
SUBANGULAR
SUBANGULATE
SUBANGULATED
SUBANTARCTIC
SUBAPICAL
SUBAPOSTOLIC
SUBAPTEROUS
SUBAQUATIC
SUBAQUEAN
SUBAQUEOUS
SUBARACHNOID
SUBARCH
SUBARCTIC
SUBARCUATE
SUBARCUATED
SUBARCUATION
SUBAREA
SUBAREOLAR
SUBARID
SUBARMALE
SUBARMOR
SUBARRATION
SUBARRHATION
SUBASHI
SUBASSEMBLY
SUBASTRAL
SUBATOM
SUBATOMIC
SUBAUD
SUBAUDIBLE
SUBAUDITION
SUBAUDITUR
SUBAURAL
SUBAURICULAR
SUBAXILLAR
SUBAXILLARY
SUBBASAL
SUBBASE
SUBBASEMENT
SUBBASS
SUBBASSA
SUBBIFID
SUBBING
SUBBOREAL
SUBBOURDON
SUBBRACHIAL
SUBBRACHIAN
SUBBRACHIATE
SUBBRANCH
SUBBRANCHED
SUBBREED
SUBBRIGADIER
SUBCALCARINE
SUBCALIBER
SUBCALIBRE
SUBCALLOSAL
SUBCANTOR
SUBCAPSULAR
SUBCAPTION
SUBCARBIDE
SUBCARBONATE
SUBCARDINAL
SUBCAST
SUBCASTE
SUBCAUDAL
SUBCAUDATE
SUBCELESTIAL
SUBCELLAR
SUBCENTER
SUBCENTRAL
SUBCENTRALLY
SUBCENTRE
SUBCHAIRMAN
SUBCHANTER
SUBCHASER
SUBCHELA
SUBCHELAE
SUBCHELATE
SUBCHIEF
SUBCHLORIDE
SUBCHONDRAL
SUBCHORDAL
SUBCHORIOID
SUBCHORIONIC
SUBCINCTORIUM
SUBCLAIM
SUBCLASS
SUBCLAUSE
SUBCLAVIAN
SUBCLAVIUS
SUBCLIMACTIC
SUBCLIMAX
SUBCLINICAL
SUBCLONE
SUBCOASTAL
SUBCOAT
SUBCOLUMNAR
SUBCOMMIT
SUBCOMMITTEE
SUBCONSCIOUS
SUBCONSCIOUSLY
SUBCONSCIOUSNESS
SUBCONSTABLE
SUBCONTINENT
SUBCONTRACT
SUBCONTRACTED
SUBCONTRACTOR

SUBCONTRARIES
SUBCONTRARY
SUBCOOL
SUBCORNEOUS
SUBCORTEX
SUBCORTICAL
SUBCORTICES
SUBCOSTA
SUBCOSTAL
SUBCOSTALIS
SUBCREPITANT
SUBCRITICAL
SUBCRUREAL
SUBCRUREUS
SUBCRUST
SUBCRUSTAL
SUBCULTURE
SUBCULTURED
SUBCULTURING
SUBCUTANEOUS
SUBCUTIS
SUBDEACON
SUBDEACONATE
SUBDEACONESS
SUBDEACONRY
SUBDEAN
SUBDEANERY
SUBDEB
SUBDEBUTANTE
SUBDECANAL
SUBDECIMAL
SUBDECUPLE
SUBDELEGATE
SUBDELEGATED
SUBDELIRIUM
SUBDENTED
SUBDERMAL
SUBDIACONAL
SUBDIACONATE
SUBDIAL
SUBDICHOTOMY
SUBDIT
SUBDITITIOUS
SUBDIVERSIFY
SUBDIVIDE
SUBDIVIDED
SUBDIVIDER
SUBDIVIDING
SUBDIVISIBLE
SUBDIVISION
SUBDIVISIVE
SUBDOLOUS
SUBDOLOUSLY
SUBDOMINANT
SUBDORSAL
SUBDORSALLY
SUBDOUBLE
SUBDRAIN
SUBDRAINAGE
SUBDRILL
SUBDUABLE
SUBDUABLY
SUBDUAL
SUBDUCE
SUBDUCED
SUBDUCING
SUBDUCT
SUBDUCTION
SUBDUE
SUBDUED
SUBDUEDLY
SUBDUEDNESS
SUBDUEMENT
SUBDUER
SUBDUING
SUBDUINGLY
SUBDUPLE
SUBDUPLICATE
SUBDURAL
SUBDURALLY
SUBDURE
SUBDWARF
SUBEDIT
SUBEDITOR
SUBEDITORIAL
SUBELAPHINE
SUBELECTRON
SUBENFEOFF
SUBENTITLE
SUBER
SUBERATE
SUBERECT
SUBEREOUS
SUBERIC
SUBERIFEROUS
SUBERIFORM
SUBERIN
SUBERINE
SUBERINIZE
SUBERITE
SUBERIZATION
SUBERIZE
SUBERIZED
SUBERIZING
SUBEROSE
SUBEROUS
SUBETH
SUBEXCITE
SUBFACTORIAL
SUBFAMILIES
SUBFAMILY
SUBFEBRILE
SUBFEU
SUBFEUDATION
SUBFEUDATORY
SUBFIEF
SUBFIX
SUBFLAVOR
SUBFLAVOUR
SUBFLOOR
SUBFLOORING
SUBFLORA
SUBFLUVIAL
SUBFOCAL
SUBFRESHMAN
SUBFUNCTIONAL
SUBFUSC
SUBFUSCOUS
SUBFUSK
SUBGALEA
SUBGALLATE
SUBGENERA
SUBGENERIC
SUBGENERICAL
SUBGENITAL
SUBGENUAL
SUBGENUS
SUBGENUSES
SUBGIANT
SUBGLACIAL
SUBGLACIALLY
SUBGLENOID
SUBGLOSSITIS
SUBGOVERNOR
SUBGRADE
SUBGROUP
SUBHARMONIC
SUBHASTATION
SUBHEAD
SUBHEADING
SUBHEDRAL
SUBHUMAN
SUBHYMENIAL
SUBHYMENIUM
SUBICTERIC
SUBICULAR
SUBICULUM
SUBIMAGINAL
SUBIMAGO
SUBINCIDENT
SUBINCISE
SUBINCISION
SUBINDEX
SUBINDICATE
SUBINDICATED
SUBINDICATING
SUBINDICATION
SUBINDICATIVE
SUBINDICES
SUBINDIVIDUAL
SUBINDUCE
SUBINFEUD
SUBINFEUDATE
SUBINGUINAL
SUBINSPECTOR
SUBINTENT
SUBINVOLUTED
SUBIRRIGATE
SUBIRRIGATED
SUBIRRIGATING
SUBIRRIGATION
SUBITANE
SUBITANEOUS
SUBITANY
SUBITO
SUBITOUS
SUBJACENCY
SUBJACENT
SUBJECT
SUBJECTED
SUBJECTEDLY
SUBJECTEDNESS
SUBJECTIFY
SUBJECTILE
SUBJECTING
SUBJECTION
SUBJECTIONAL
SUBJECTIVE
SUBJECTIVELY
SUBJECTIVENESS
SUBJECTIVISM
SUBJECTIVIST
SUBJECTIVITY
SUBJICIBLE
SUBJOIN
SUBJOINDER
SUBJOINED
SUBJOINING
SUBJOINT
SUBJUGABLE
SUBJUGAL
SUBJUGATE
SUBJUGATED
SUBJUGATING
SUBJUGATION
SUBJUGATOR
SUBJUGULAR
SUBJUNCT
SUBJUNCTION
SUBJUNCTIVE
SUBJUNCTIVELY
SUBKINGDOM
SUBLABIAL
SUBLANGUAGE
SUBLAPSARIAN
SUBLAPSARY
SUBLATE
SUBLATED
SUBLATERAL
SUBLATING
SUBLATION
SUBLATIVE
SUBLEADER
SUBLEASE
SUBLEASED
SUBLEASING
SUBLESSEE
SUBLESSOR
SUBLET
SUBLETHAL
SUBLETTABLE
SUBLETTER
SUBLETTING
SUBLEVATE
SUBLEVATION
SUBLICENSEE
SUBLIEUTENANT
SUBLIGATION
SUBLIMANT
SUBLIMATE
SUBLIMATED
SUBLIMATING
SUBLIMATION
SUBLIMATIONAL
SUBLIMATIONIST
SUBLIMATOR
SUBLIMATORY
SUBLIME
SUBLIMED
SUBLIMELY
SUBLIMENESS
SUBLIMER
SUBLIMEST
SUBLIMIFICATION
SUBLIMINAL
SUBLIMINALLY
SUBLIMING
SUBLIMITIES
SUBLIMITY
SUBLINE
SUBLINEATION
SUBLINGUA
SUBLINGUAE
SUBLINGUAL
SUBLITTORAL
SUBLOBULAR
SUBLUNAR
SUBLUNARY
SUBLUXATE
SUBLUXATION
SUBMAIN
SUBMAN
SUBMARGINAL
SUBMARGINALLY
SUBMARGINATE
SUBMARGINED
SUBMARINE
SUBMARINED
SUBMARINER
SUBMARINING
SUBMARINISM
SUBMARINIST
SUBMAXILLA
SUBMAXILLAE
SUBMAXILLARY
SUBMAXIMAL
SUBMEDIAL
SUBMEDIAN
SUBMEDIANT
SUBMEN
SUBMENTA
SUBMENTAL
SUBMENTUM
SUBMERGE
SUBMERGED
SUBMERGEMENT
SUBMERGENCE
SUBMERGIBILITY
SUBMERGIBLE
SUBMERGING
SUBMERSE
SUBMERSED
SUBMERSIBILITY
SUBMERSIBLE
SUBMERSION
SUBMETER
SUBMETERING
SUBMICRON
SUBMILIARY
SUBMINIATURE
SUBMINIMAL
SUBMINISTER
SUBMISS
SUBMISSIBLE
SUBMISSION
SUBMISSIONIST
SUBMISSIVE
SUBMISSIVELY
SUBMISSIVENESS
SUBMIT
SUBMITTAL
SUBMITTED
SUBMITTER
SUBMITTING
SUBMONTAGNE
SUBMONTANE
SUBMONTANELY
SUBMORPHOUS
SUBMOTIVE
SUBMUCOSA
SUBMUCOSAE
SUBMUCOSAL
SUBMUCOUS
SUBMULTIPLE
SUBNASAL
SUBNASCENT
SUBNATURAL
SUBNECT
SUBNEURAL
SUBNITRATE
SUBNIVEAL
SUBNIVEAN
SUBNORMAL
SUBNORMALITY
SUBNUBILAR
SUBNUCLEUS
SUBNUVOLAR
SUBOCCIPITAL
SUBOCEANIC
SUBOCTAVE
SUBOCTILE
SUBOCTUPLE
SUBOCULAR
SUBOFFICER
SUBOPERCLE
SUBOPERCULAR
SUBOPERCULUM
SUBOPPOSITE
SUBOPTIMAL
SUBORBITAL
SUBORBITAR
SUBORBITARY
SUBORDAIN
SUBORDER
SUBORDINACY
SUBORDINAL
SUBORDINARY
SUBORDINATE
SUBORDINATED
SUBORDINATELY
SUBORDINATENESS
SUBORDINATING
SUBORDINATION
SUBORDINATIVE
SUBORN

SUBORNATION
SUBORNATIVE
SUBORNED
SUBORNER
SUBORNING
SUBOVAL
SUBOXID
SUBOXIDATION
SUBOXIDE
SUBPASSAGE
SUBPENA
SUBPERMANENT
SUBPETIOLAR
SUBPHRENIC
SUBPHYLAR
SUBPHYLUM
SUBPIAL
SUBPLAT
SUBPLATE
SUBPLEURAL
SUBPLINTH
SUBPLOT
SUBPOENA
SUBPOENAED
SUBPOENAING
SUBPOENAL
SUBPOTENCIES
SUBPOTENCY
SUBPOTENT
SUBPRESS
SUBPRINCIPAL
SUBPRIOR
SUBPUNCH
SUBPURCHASER
SUBPURLIN
SUBQUINTUPLE
SUBRACE
SUBRADIAL
SUBRADIUS
SUBRATIONAL
SUBREADER
SUBREGION
SUBREGIONAL
SUBREGULI
SUBREGULUS
SUBRENT
SUBREPTARY
SUBREPTION
SUBRESIN
SUBRIDENT
SUBRIDENTLY
SUBRISION
SUBRISIVE
SUBRISORY
SUBROGATE
SUBROGATED
SUBROGATING
SUBROGATION
SUBROUND
SUBSARTORIAL
SUBSCALE
SUBSCAPULAR
SUBSCAPULARY
SUBSCLERAL
SUBSCLEROTIC
SUBSCRIBE
SUBSCRIBED
SUBSCRIBER
SUBSCRIBING
SUBSCRIPT
SUBSCRIPTION
SUBSCRIPTIONIST
SUBSCRIPTIVE
SUBSCRIVE
SUBSCRIVER
SUBSEA
SUBSECIVE
SUBSECT
SUBSECTION
SUBSECUTE
SUBSECUTIVE
SUBSEGMENT
SUBSELLA
SUBSELLIA
SUBSELLIUM
SUBSEMIFUSA
SUBSEMITONE
SUBSENSIBLE
SUBSEPTUPLE
SUBSEQUENCE
SUBSEQUENCY
SUBSEQUENT
SUBSEQUENTIAL
SUBSEQUENTIALLY
SUBSEQUENTLY
SUBSEQUENTNESS
SUBSEROSA
SUBSEROUS
SUBSERVE
SUBSERVED
SUBSERVIATE
SUBSERVIENCE
SUBSERVIENCY
SUBSERVIENT
SUBSERVIENTLY
SUBSERVIENTNESS
SUBSERVING
SUBSESQUI
SUBSESSILE
SUBSET
SUBSEXTUPLE
SUBSHRUB
SUBSHRUBBY
SUBSICIVE
SUBSIDE
SUBSIDED
SUBSIDENCE
SUBSIDENCY
SUBSIDENT
SUBSIDER
SUBSIDIARIE
SUBSIDIARIES
SUBSIDIARILY
SUBSIDIARINESS
SUBSIDIARY
SUBSIDIES
SUBSIDING
SUBSIDISE
SUBSIDIST
SUBSIDIUM
SUBSIDIZATION
SUBSIDIZE
SUBSIDIZED
SUBSIDIZER
SUBSIDIZING
SUBSIDY
SUBSIGN
SUBSILICIC
SUBSILL
SUBSIMILATION
SUBSIMPLE
SUBSIST
SUBSISTED
SUBSISTENCE
SUBSISTENCY
SUBSISTENT
SUBSISTER
SUBSISTING
SUBSIZAR
SUBSOIL
SUBSOILER
SUBSOLAR
SUBSONIC
SUBSPACE
SUBSPECIES
SUBSPECIFIC
SUBSPECIFICALLY
SUBSPINOUS
SUBSTAGE
SUBSTANCE
SUBSTANCH
SUBSTANDARD
SUBSTANT
SUBSTANTIA
SUBSTANTIAL
SUBSTANTIALISM
SUBSTANTIALIST
SUBSTANTIALITY
SUBSTANTIALIZE
SUBSTANTIALLY
SUBSTANTIALNESS
SUBSTANTIATE
SUBSTANTIATED
SUBSTANTIATING
SUBSTANTIATION
SUBSTANTIATIVE
SUBSTANTIATOR
SUBSTANTIFY
SUBSTANTIOUS
SUBSTANTIVAL
SUBSTANTIVALLY
SUBSTANTIVE
SUBSTANTIVELY
SUBSTANTIVENESS
SUBSTANTIVITY
SUBSTANTIVIZE
SUBSTANTIVIZED
SUBSTANTIVIZING
SUBSTANTIZE
SUBSTATION
SUBSTILE
SUBSTITUENT
SUBSTITUTE
SUBSTITUTED
SUBSTITUTER
SUBSTITUTING
SUBSTITUTION
SUBSTITUTIONAL
SUBSTITUTIONALLY
SUBSTITUTIVE
SUBSTITUTIVELY
SUBSTORY
SUBSTRAT
SUBSTRATA
SUBSTRATAL
SUBSTRATE
SUBSTRATIVE
SUBSTRATOSE
SUBSTRATUM
SUBSTRATUMS
SUBSTREAM
SUBSTRUCT
SUBSTRUCTION
SUBSTRUCTIONAL
SUBSTRUCTURAL
SUBSTRUCTURE
SUBSTYLAR
SUBSTYLE
SUBSULPHATE
SUBSULT
SUBSULTORILY
SUBSULTORY
SUBSULTUS
SUBSUMABLE
SUBSUME
SUBSUMED
SUBSUMING
SUBSUMPTION
SUBSUMPTIVE
SUBSURFACE
SUBTACK
SUBTACKSMAN
SUBTACKSMEN
SUBTANGENT
SUBTARGET
SUBTARTAREAN
SUBTECTACLE
SUBTECTAL
SUBTEEN
SUBTEGMINAL
SUBTEMPERATE
SUBTENANCY
SUBTENANT
SUBTEND
SUBTENDED
SUBTENDING
SUBTENSE
SUBTENURE
SUBTERFLUENT
SUBTERFLUOUS
SUBTERFUGE
SUBTERHUMAN
SUBTERJACENT
SUBTERMARINE
SUBTERPOSE
SUBTERRANE
SUBTERRANEAL
SUBTERRANEAN
SUBTERRENE
SUBTERRESTRIAL
SUBTHALAMIC
SUBTHALAMUS
SUBTHORACIC
SUBTILE
SUBTILELY
SUBTILENESS
SUBTILIATE
SUBTILIATION
SUBTILIN
SUBTILISM
SUBTILIST
SUBTILITIES
SUBTILITY
SUBTILIZATION
SUBTILIZED
SUBTILIZER
SUBTILIZING
SUBTILTIES
SUBTILTY
SUBTITLE
SUBTITULAR
SUBTLE
SUBTLENESS
SUBTLER
SUBTLEST
SUBTLETIES
SUBTLETY
SUBTLIST
SUBTLY
SUBTONE
SUBTONIC
SUBTORRID
SUBTOTAL
SUBTRACT
SUBTRACTED
SUBTRACTER
SUBTRACTING
SUBTRACTION
SUBTRACTIVE
SUBTRAHEND
SUBTRAY
SUBTREASURER
SUBTREASURIES
SUBTREASURY
SUBTRIBE
SUBTRIST
SUBTROPIC
SUBTROPICAL
SUBTROPICS
SUBTRUDE
SUBTUBERANT
SUBTUNIC
SUBTURBARY
SUBTYPE
SUBTYPICAL
SUBUCULA
SUBULATE
SUBULATED
SUBULICORN
SUBULIFORM
SUBUMBONAL
SUBUMBRAL
SUBUMBRELLA
SUBUMBRELLAR
SUBUNGUAL
SUBUNGUIAL
SUBUNGULATE
SUBURB
SUBURBAN
SUBURBANITE
SUBURBANITIES
SUBURBANITY
SUBURBANIZATION
SUBURBANIZE
SUBURBED
SUBURBIA
SUBURBICAN
SUBURBS
SUBVAGINAL
SUBVALUATION
SUBVARIETAL
SUBVARIETY
SUBVENDEE
SUBVENE
SUBVENED
SUBVENING
SUBVENTION
SUBVENTIONED
SUBVENTIVE
SUBVERSAL
SUBVERSION
SUBVERSIONARY
SUBVERSIVE
SUBVERSIVELY
SUBVERT
SUBVERTED
SUBVERTER
SUBVERTIBLE
SUBVERTING
SUBVIRATE
SUBVIRILE
SUBVISIBLE
SUBVITALIZED
SUBVITREOUS
SUBVOCAL
SUBVOLA
SUBWATER
SUBWAY
SUBWEIGHT
SUBZONAL
SUBZONE
SUCCADE
SUCCAH
SUCCEDANEA
SUCCEDANEOUS
SUCCEDANEUM
SUCCEDANEUMS
SUCCEDENT
SUCCEED
SUCCEEDED
SUCCEEDER
SUCCEEDING
SUCCEEDINGLY
SUCCENT
SUCCENTOR

SUCCESS
SUCCESSFUL
SUCCESSFULLY
SUCCESSFULNESS
SUCCESSION
SUCCESSIONAL
SUCCESSIONALLY
SUCCESSIONIST
SUCCESSIVE
SUCCESSIVELY
SUCCESSIVENESS
SUCCESSIVITY
SUCCESSOR
SUCCESSORAL
SUCCIN
SUCCINAMATE
SUCCINAMIC
SUCCINAMIDE
SUCCINANIL
SUCCINATE
SUCCINCT
SUCCINCTLY
SUCCINCTNESS
SUCCINCTORIA
SUCCINCTURE
SUCCINIC
SUCCINIMID
SUCCINIMIDE
SUCCINITE
SUCCINOUS
SUCCINUM
SUCCINYL
SUCCISE
SUCCOR
SUCCORABLE
SUCCORED
SUCCORER
SUCCORING
SUCCORRHEA
SUCCORRHOEA
SUCCORY
SUCCOSE
SUCCOTASH
SUCCOUR
SUCCOURABLE
SUCCOURED
SUCCOURER
SUCCOURING
SUCCOUS
SUCCUBA
SUCCUBAE
SUCCUBI
SUCCUBINE
SUCCUBOUS
SUCCUBUS
SUCCUBUSES
SUCCUDRY
SUCCULA
SUCCULENCE
SUCCULENCIES
SUCCULENCY
SUCCULENT
SUCCULENTLY
SUCCULENTNESS
SUCCULOUS
SUCCUMB
SUCCUMBED
SUCCUMBENCE
SUCCUMBENCY
SUCCUMBENT
SUCCUMBER
SUCCUMBING
SUCCURSAL
SUCCURSALE
SUCCUS
SUCCUSS
SUCCUSSATION
SUCCUSSATORY
SUCCUSSION
SUCCUSSIVE
SUCH
SUCHLIKE
SUCHNESS
SUCHWISE
SUCK
SUCKABOB
SUCKAUHOCK
SUCKED
SUCKEN
SUCKENER
SUCKER
SUCKERED
SUCKEREL
SUCKERFISH
SUCKERFISHES
SUCKERING
SUCKFISH
SUCKFISHES
SUCKHOLE
SUCKING
SUCKLE
SUCKLEBUSH
SUCKLED
SUCKLER
SUCKLING
SUCKSTONE
SUCLAT
SUCRAMIN
SUCRAMINE
SUCRASE
SUCRATE
SUCRE
SUCRIER
SUCROACID
SUCROSE
SUCTION
SUCTIONAL
SUCTORIAL
SUCTORIAN
SUCTORIOUS
SUCUPIRA
SUCURI
SUCURIU
SUCURUJU
SUCURY
SUD
SUDADERO
SUDAMEN
SUDAMINA
SUDAMINAL
SUDARIA
SUDARIUM
SUDARY
SUDATE
SUDATION
SUDATORIA
SUDATORIES
SUDATORIUM
SUDATORY
SUDBURITE
SUDD
SUDDEN
SUDDENLY
SUDDENNESS
SUDDENTY
SUDDER
SUDDLE
SUDIFORM
SUDOR
SUDORAL
SUDORESIS
SUDORIC
SUDORIFEROUS
SUDORIFIC
SUDORIPAROUS
SUDOROUS
SUDS
SUDSIER
SUDSIEST
SUDSMAN
SUDSMEN
SUDSY
SUE
SUED
SUEDE
SUEDINE
SUENT
SUER
SUERTE
SUET
SUETY
SUFF
SUFFARI
SUFFECT
SUFFECTION
SUFFER
SUFFERABLE
SUFFERABLENESS
SUFFERABLY
SUFFERANCE
SUFFERANT
SUFFERED
SUFFERER
SUFFERING
SUFFERINGLY
SUFFETE
SUFFETES
SUFFICE
SUFFICED
SUFFICER
SUFFICIENCIES
SUFFICIENCY
SUFFICIENT
SUFFICIENTLY
SUFFICIENTNESS
SUFFICING
SUFFICINGLY
SUFFICINGNESS
SUFFICTION
SUFFIX
SUFFIXAL
SUFFIXATION
SUFFIXED
SUFFIXING
SUFFIXION
SUFFIXMENT
SUFFLATE
SUFFLATED
SUFFLATING
SUFFLATION
SUFFLUE
SUFFOCATE
SUFFOCATED
SUFFOCATING
SUFFOCATINGLY
SUFFOCATION
SUFFOCATIVE
SUFFRAGAN
SUFFRAGANAL
SUFFRAGANATE
SUFFRAGANCY
SUFFRAGATORY
SUFFRAGE
SUFFRAGETTE
SUFFRAGIAL
SUFFRAGISM
SUFFRAGIST
SUFFRAGISTIC
SUFFRAGO
SUFFRAIN
SUFFRONT
SUFFRUTEX
SUFFRUTICES
SUFFRUTICOSE
SUFFRUTICOUS
SUFFUMIGATE
SUFFUMIGATED
SUFFUSE
SUFFUSED
SUFFUSEDLY
SUFFUSING
SUFFUSION
SUFFUSIVE
SUG
SUGAMO
SUGAN
SUGANN
SUGAR
SUGARBERRIES
SUGARBERRY
SUGARBIRD
SUGARBUSH
SUGARED
SUGARELLY
SUGARER
SUGARHOUSE
SUGARIES
SUGARINESS
SUGARING
SUGARLESS
SUGARPLATE
SUGARPLUM
SUGARSOP
SUGARSWEET
SUGARWORKS
SUGARY
SUGAT
SUGENT
SUGESCENT
SUGGAN
SUGGEST
SUGGESTA
SUGGESTED
SUGGESTER
SUGGESTIBILITY
SUGGESTIBLE
SUGGESTIBLENESS
SUGGESTIBLY
SUGGESTING
SUGGESTINGLY
SUGGESTION
SUGGESTIVE
SUGGESTIVELY
SUGGESTIVENESS
SUGGESTIVITY
SUGGESTUM
SUGGIL
SUGGILLATE
SUGGILLATION
SUGH
SUGI
SUGSLOOT
SUHA
SUICIDAL
SUICIDALLY
SUICIDE
SUICIDED
SUICIDING
SUICIDISM
SUICISM
SUID
SUIDIAN
SUIFORM
SUIKERBOSCH
SUILINE
SUIMATE
SUING
SUINGLY
SUINT
SUISIMILAR
SUISSE
SUIST
SUIT
SUITABILITY
SUITABLE
SUITABLENESS
SUITABLY
SUITCASE
SUITE
SUITED
SUITHOLD
SUITING
SUITLY
SUITOR
SUITORESS
SUITY
SUIVANTE
SUIVEZ
SUJEE
SUJI
SUK
SUKIYAKI
SUKKAH
SUKKENYE
SUL
SULBASUTRA
SULCAL
SULCALIZATION
SULCALIZE
SULCATE
SULCATED
SULCATION
SULCI
SULCIFORM
SULCULAR
SULCULATE
SULCULUS
SULCUS
SULD
SULEA
SULFA
SULFACID
SULFADIAZINE
SULFAMATE
SULFAMIC
SULFAMIDATE
SULFAMIDE
SULFAMIDIC
SULFAMINE
SULFAMINIC
SULFAMYL
SULFANILIC
SULFARSENIDE
SULFARSENITE
SULFATASE
SULFATE
SULFATED
SULFATIC
SULFATING
SULFATIZE
SULFATIZED
SULFATIZING
SULFATO
SULFAZIDE
SULFHYDRATE
SULFHYDRIC
SULFHYDRYL
SULFID
SULFIDE
SULFINATE
SULFINDYLIC
SULFINE
SULFINIC
SULFINIDE
SULFINYL

SULFION
SULFIONIDE
SULFITE
SULFITIC
SULFITO
SULFOACID
SULFOAMIDE
SULFOBENZIDE
SULFOBENZOIC
SULFOBORITE
SULFOCYAN
SULFOCYANIDE
SULFOHALITE
SULFOHYDRATE
SULFOLEIC
SULFOLYSIS
SULFONAL
SULFONAMIC
SULFONAMIDE
SULFONATE
SULFONATED
SULFONATING
SULFONATION
SULFONATOR
SULFONE
SULFONIC
SULFONIUM
SULFONYL
SULFORICINIC
SULFOUREA
SULFOVINATE
SULFOVINIC
SULFOXIDE
SULFOXISM
SULFOXYLATE
SULFOXYLIC
SULFUR
SULFURAGE
SULFURAN
SULFURATE
SULFURATION
SULFURATOR
SULFUREA
SULFURED
SULFUREOUS
SULFUREOUSLY
SULFURET
SULFURET
SULFURETED
SULFURETING
SULFURETTED
SULFURETTING
SULFURIC
SULFURING
SULFURIZE
SULFURIZED
SULFURIZING
SULFUROSYL
SULFUROUS
SULFURY
SULFURYL
SULK
SULKA
SULKED
SULKER
SULKIER
SULKIES
SULKIEST
SULKILY
SULKINESS
SULKING
SULKS
SULKY
SULL
SULLA
SULLAGE
SULLEN
SULLENLY
SULLENNESS
SULLENS
SULLIED
SULLIES
SULLOW
SULLY
SULLYING
SULPHA
SULPHACID
SULPHAMATE
SULPHAMIC
SULPHAMID
SULPHAMIDATE
SULPHAMIDE
SULPHAMIDIC
SULPHAMIN
SULPHAMINE
SULPHAMINIC
SULPHAMINO
SULPHAMYL
SULPHANILIC
SULPHARSENIC
SULPHARSENID
SULPHATASE
SULPHATE
SULPHATED
SULPHATIC
SULPHATING
SULPHATION
SULPHATIZE
SULPHATIZED
SULPHATIZING
SULPHATO
SULPHAZID
SULPHAZIDE
SULPHAZOTIZE
SULPHETHYLIC
SULPHID
SULPHIDATION
SULPHIDE
SULPHIDIC
SULPHIDIZE
SULPHIMIDE
SULPHIN
SULPHINATE
SULPHINE
SULPHINIC
SULPHINIDE
SULPHINYL
SULPHITATION
SULPHITE
SULPHITIC
SULPHITO
SULPHO
SULPHOBENZID
SULPHOBORITE
SULPHOCYAN
SULPHOCYANIC
SULPHOFY
SULPHOGALLIC
SULPHOGEL
SULPHOHALITE
SULPHOHALOID
SULPHOLEATE
SULPHOLIPIN
SULPHOLYSIS
SULPHONAL
SULPHONALISM
SULPHONAMID
SULPHONAMIDE
SULPHONAMIDO
SULPHONAMINE
SULPHONATE
SULPHONATED
SULPHONATING
SULPHONATION
SULPHONATOR
SULPHONE
SULPHONIC
SULPHONIUM
SULPHONYL
SULPHOPHENYL
SULPHOSOL
SULPHOTANNIC
SULPHOTOLUIC
SULPHOUREA
SULPHOVINATE
SULPHOVINIC
SULPHOXID
SULPHOXIDE
SULPHOXISM
SULPHOXYLIC
SULPHUR
SULPHURAGE
SULPHURAN
SULPHURATE
SULPHURATED
SULPHURATING
SULPHURATION
SULPHURATOR
SULPHUREA
SULPHURED
SULPHUREITY
SULPHUREOUS
SULPHURET
SULPHURETED
SULPHURETING
SULPHURETTED
SULPHURETTING
SULPHURIC
SULPHURING
SULPHURIZE
SULPHURIZED
SULPHURIZING
SULPHUROSYL
SULPHUROUS
SULPHUROUSLY
SULPHURWEED
SULPHURWORT
SULPHURY
SULPHURYL
SULPHYDRATE
SULPHYDRYL
SULTAM
SULTAN
SULTANA
SULTANATE
SULTANE
SULTANESS
SULTANIC
SULTANIN
SULTANISM
SULTANIST
SULTANIZE
SULTANSHIP
SULTANY
SULTONE
SULTRIER
SULTRIEST
SULTRILY
SULTRINESS
SULTRY
SULUNG
SULVANITE
SULVASUTRA
SUM
SUMAC
SUMACH
SUMAGE
SUMBAL
SUMBUL
SUMBULIC
SUMEN
SUMI
SUMLESS
SUMLESSNESS
SUMMA
SUMMABILITY
SUMMABLE
SUMMAE
SUMMAGE
SUMMAND
SUMMAR
SUMMARIES
SUMMARILY
SUMMARINESS
SUMMARISE
SUMMARIST
SUMMARIZATION
SUMMARIZE
SUMMARIZED
SUMMARIZER
SUMMARIZING
SUMMARY
SUMMAT
SUMMATE
SUMMATED
SUMMATING
SUMMATION
SUMMATIONAL
SUMMATIVE
SUMMATORY
SUMMED
SUMMER
SUMMERBIRD
SUMMERCASTLE
SUMMERED
SUMMERER
SUMMERGAME
SUMMERHEAD
SUMMERHOUSE
SUMMERING
SUMMERINGS
SUMMERLAND
SUMMERLAY
SUMMERLINESS
SUMMERLING
SUMMERLY
SUMMERROOM
SUMMERSAULT
SUMMERSET
SUMMERTIDE
SUMMERTIME
SUMMERWARD
SUMMERWOOD
SUMMERY
SUMMING
SUMMIST
SUMMIT
SUMMITAL
SUMMITLESS
SUMMITRY
SUMMITY
SUMMON
SUMMONED
SUMMONER
SUMMONING
SUMMONS
SUMMONSED
SUMMONSES
SUMMONSING
SUMMULA
SUMMULAE
SUMMULIST
SUMNER
SUMP
SUMPAGE
SUMPER
SUMPH
SUMPHISH
SUMPHISHLY
SUMPHISHNESS
SUMPHY
SUMPIT
SUMPITAN
SUMPLE
SUMPMAN
SUMPSIMUS
SUMPT
SUMPTER
SUMPTION
SUMPTUARY
SUMPTUOSITY
SUMPTUOUS
SUMPTUOUSLY
SUMPTUOUSNESS
SUMPTURE
SUMPWEED
SUN
SUNBATHER
SUNBATHING
SUNBEAM
SUNBEAMED
SUNBEAMY
SUNBERRY
SUNBIRD
SUNBLIND
SUNBLINK
SUNBONNET
SUNBOW
SUNBREAK
SUNBURN
SUNBURNED
SUNBURNING
SUNBURNT
SUNBURNTNESS
SUNBURST
SUNCHERCHOR
SUNCK
SUNCKE
SUNCUP
SUNDAE
SUNDANG
SUNDARI
SUNDER
SUNDERANCE
SUNDERED
SUNDERER
SUNDERING
SUNDERLY
SUNDERMENT
SUNDEW
SUNDIAL
SUNDIK
SUNDOG
SUNDOWN
SUNDOWNER
SUNDOWNING
SUNDRESS
SUNDRI
SUNDRIES
SUNDRILY
SUNDRINESS
SUNDROPS
SUNDRY
SUNDRYMAN
SUNDRYMEN
SUNFALL
SUNFAST
SUNFISH
SUNFISHER
SUNFISHERY
SUNFISHES
SUNFLOWER
SUNFOIL
SUNG
SUNGAR

SUNGLADE
SUNGLASS
SUNGLASSES
SUNGLO
SUNGLOW
SUNK
SUNKE
SUNKEN
SUNKET
SUNKIE
SUNKLAND
SUNLAMP
SUNLAND
SUNLESS
SUNLESSNESS
SUNLET
SUNLIGHT
SUNLIGHTED
SUNLIT
SUNN
SUNNA
SUNNED
SUNNIER
SUNNIEST
SUNNILY
SUNNINESS
SUNNING
SUNNUD
SUNNY
SUNNYASEE
SUNNYHEARTED
SUNPROOF
SUNQUAKE
SUNRAY
SUNRISE
SUNRISING
SUNROOM
SUNROSE
SUNSCALD
SUNSCORCH
SUNSET
SUNSETTING
SUNSETTY
SUNSHADE
SUNSHINE
SUNSHINY
SUNSMIT
SUNSMITTEN
SUNSPOT
SUNSPOTTED
SUNSPOTTERY
SUNSPOTTY
SUNSQUALL
SUNSTAY
SUNSTEAD
SUNSTONE
SUNSTRICKEN
SUNSTROKE
SUNSTRUCK
SUNT
SUNTAN
SUNTANS
SUNUP
SUNWARD
SUNWARDS
SUNWAYS
SUNWEED
SUNWISE
SUNYATA
SUNYIE
SUP
SUPA
SUPARI
SUPAWN
SUPE
SUPELLECTILE
SUPELLEX
SUPER
SUPERABILITY
SUPERABLE
SUPERABLY
SUPERABOUND
SUPERABUNDANCE
SUPERABUNDANT
SUPERABUNDANTLY
SUPERACID
SUPERADD
SUPERALBAL
SUPERALTAR
SUPERANAL
SUPERANNATE
SUPERANNUATE
SUPERANNUATED
SUPERANNUATING
SUPERARCTIC
SUPERATE
SUPERAURAL
SUPERAVIT
SUPERB
SUPERBIOUS
SUPERBITY
SUPERBLY
SUPERBNESS
SUPERBOMB
SUPERCARGO
SUPERCARGOES
SUPERCARGOS
SUPERCARPAL
SUPERCARRIER
SUPERCENTRAL
SUPERCHARGE
SUPERCHARGED
SUPERCHARGER
SUPERCHARGING
SUPERCILIA
SUPERCILIARY
SUPERCILIOUS
SUPERCILIOUSLY
SUPERCILIOUSNESS
SUPERCILIUM
SUPERCLASS
SUPERCOMBING
SUPERCONSCIOUS
SUPERCONSCIOUSNESS
SUPERCOOL
SUPERCRUST
SUPERDUPER
SUPERDURAL
SUPEREDIFY
SUPEREGO
SUPEREMINENT
SUPEREROGANT
SUPEREROGATE
SUPEREXIST
SUPERFAMILY
SUPERFAT
SUPERFECTA
SUPERFEMALE
SUPERFETATE
SUPERFETATED
SUPERFICIAL
SUPERFICIALISM
SUPERFICIALIST
SUPERFICIALITIES
SUPERFICIALITY
SUPERFICIALIZE
SUPERFICIALLY
SUPERFICIALNESS
SUPERFICIARIES
SUPERFICIARY
SUPERFICIES
SUPERFINE
SUPERFINISH
SUPERFIX
SUPERFLEXION
SUPERFLUENT
SUPERFLUID
SUPERFLUITIES
SUPERFLUITY
SUPERFLUOUS
SUPERFLUOUSLY
SUPERFLUOUSNESS
SUPERFLUX
SUPERFRONTAL
SUPERFUSE
SUPERFUSED
SUPERFUSING
SUPERFUSION
SUPERGENE
SUPERGENERIC
SUPERGENUAL
SUPERGLACIAL
SUPERGLOTTAL
SUPERHEAT
SUPERHEATED
SUPERHEATER
SUPERHEATING
SUPERHIGHWAY
SUPERHUMAN
SUPERHUMANLY
SUPERHUMERAL
SUPERI
SUPERIAL
SUPERIMPOSE
SUPERIMPOSED
SUPERIMPOSING
SUPERIMPOSITION
SUPERIMPOSURE
SUPERINDUCE
SUPERINDUCED
SUPERINDUCING
SUPERINDUCT
SUPERINDUE
SUPERINFUSE
SUPERINTEND
SUPERINTENDED
SUPERINTENDENCE
SUPERINTENDENCY
SUPERINTENDENT
SUPERINTENDING
SUPERIOR
SUPERIORESS
SUPERIORITY
SUPERIORLY
SUPERIUS
SUPERJACENT
SUPERLABIAL
SUPERLATION
SUPERLATIVE
SUPERLATIVELY
SUPERLATIVENESS
SUPERLUNAR
SUPERLUNARY
SUPERMALE
SUPERMAN
SUPERMANLY
SUPERMARINE
SUPERMARKET
SUPERMAXILLA
SUPERMEDIAL
SUPERMEN
SUPERMUSCAN
SUPERNACULAR
SUPERNACULUM
SUPERNAL
SUPERNALLY
SUPERNATANT
SUPERNATURAL
SUPERNATURALIST
SUPERNATURALIZE
SUPERNATURALLY
SUPERNATURALNESS
SUPERNATURE
SUPERNORMAL
SUPERNOVA
SUPERNOVAE
SUPERNOVAS
SUPEROCTAVE
SUPEROCULAR
SUPERODORSAL
SUPERORBITAL
SUPERORDER
SUPERORDINAL
SUPERORDINATE
SUPERORDINATION
SUPERORGANIC
SUPERPARTICULAR
SUPERPHYSICAL
SUPERPLANT
SUPERPLUS
SUPERPOSABLE
SUPERPOSE
SUPERPOSED
SUPERPOSING
SUPERPOSITION
SUPERPOWER
SUPERPOWERED
SUPERRENAL
SUPERROYAL
SUPERSACRAL
SUPERSALIENCY
SUPERSALIENT
SUPERSALT
SUPERSATURATE
SUPERSATURATED
SUPERSATURATING
SUPERSATURATION
SUPERSCRIBE
SUPERSCRIBED
SUPERSCRIBING
SUPERSCRIPT
SUPERSCRIPTION
SUPERSEDE
SUPERSEDEAS
SUPERSEDED
SUPERSEDENCE
SUPERSEDER
SUPERSEDERE
SUPERSEDING
SUPERSEDURE
SUPERSENSIBLE
SUPERSENSIBLY
SUPERSENSORY
SUPERSENSUAL
SUPERSEPTAL
SUPERSESSION
SUPERSESSIVE
SUPERSEX
SUPERSEXUAL
SUPERSISTENT
SUPERSOCIAL
SUPERSOLID
SUPERSONANT
SUPERSONIC
SUPERSONICS
SUPERSTATE
SUPERSTITION
SUPERSTITIONIST
SUPERSTITIOUS
SUPERSTITIOUSLY
SUPERSTITIOUSNESS
SUPERSTRATA
SUPERSTRATUM
SUPERSTRUCT
SUPERSTRUCTED
SUPERSTRUCTING
SUPERSTRUCTION
SUPERSTRUCTIVE
SUPERSTRUCTOR
SUPERSTRUCTORY
SUPERSTRUCTRAL
SUPERSTRUCTURE
SUPERSUBTLE
SUPERTAX
SUPERTERRENE
SUPERTONIC
SUPERTUNIC
SUPERVENE
SUPERVENED
SUPERVENIENT
SUPERVENING
SUPERVENTION
SUPERVISAL
SUPERVISANCE
SUPERVISE
SUPERVISED
SUPERVISING
SUPERVISION
SUPERVISIONARY
SUPERVISIVE
SUPERVISOR
SUPERVISORY
SUPERVISURE
SUPERVOLUTE
SUPERWEENING
SUPINATE
SUPINATED
SUPINATING
SUPINATION
SUPINATOR
SUPINE
SUPINELY
SUPINENESS
SUPPABLE
SUPPAGE
SUPPED
SUPPEDANEA
SUPPEDANEOUS
SUPPEDANEUM
SUPPEDIT
SUPPER
SUPPERING
SUPPERLESS
SUPPERTIME
SUPPERWARD
SUPPERWARDS
SUPPING
SUPPLACE
SUPPLANT
SUPPLANTED
SUPPLANTER
SUPPLANTING
SUPPLE
SUPPLED
SUPPLEJACK
SUPPLELY
SUPPLEMENT
SUPPLEMENTAL
SUPPLEMENTARY
SUPPLEMENTATION
SUPPLEMENTED
SUPPLEMENTER
SUPPLEMENTING
SUPPLENESS
SUPPLER
SUPPLETORIES
SUPPLETORILY
SUPPLETORY
SUPPLIAL
SUPPLIANCE
SUPPLIANCY
SUPPLIANT
SUPPLIANTLY
SUPPLIANTNESS
SUPPLICANCY

SUPPLICANT
SUPPLICANTLY
SUPPLICAT
SUPPLICATE
SUPPLICATED
SUPPLICATING
SUPPLICATION
SUPPLICATOR
SUPPLICATORY
SUPPLICAVIT
SUPPLICE
SUPPLIED
SUPPLIER
SUPPLIES
SUPPLING
SUPPLY
SUPPLYING
SUPPONE
SUPPORT
SUPPORTABILITY
SUPPORTABLE
SUPPORTABLENES
SUPPORTABLY
SUPPORTANCE
SUPPORTASSE
SUPPORTED
SUPPORTER
SUPPORTING
SUPPORTINGLY
SUPPORTIVE
SUPPOSABLE
SUPPOSABLENESS
SUPPOSABLY
SUPPOSAL
SUPPOSE
SUPPOSED
SUPPOSEDLY
SUPPOSER
SUPPOSING
SUPPOSITAL
SUPPOSITION
SUPPOSITIONAL
SUPPOSITITIOUS
SUPPOSITIVE
SUPPOSITIVELY
SUPPOSITORIES
SUPPOSITORY
SUPPOSITUM
SUPPOST
SUPPRESS
SUPPRESSAL
SUPPRESSED
SUPPRESSEDLY
SUPPRESSER
SUPPRESSIBLE
SUPPRESSING
SUPPRESSION
SUPPRESSIVE
SUPPRESSIVELY
SUPPRESSOR
SUPPRIME
SUPPRISE
SUPPURANT
SUPPURATE
SUPPURATED
SUPPURATING
SUPPURATION
SUPPURATIVE
SUPPUTE
SUPRA
SUPRABUCCAL
SUPRACAECAL
SUPRACAUDAL
SUPRACILIARY
SUPRACLAVICLE
SUPRACLUSION
SUPRACOSTAL
SUPRACOXAL
SUPRACRANIAL
SUPRADENTAL
SUPRADORSAL
SUPRADURAL
SUPRAFINE
SUPRAFOLIAR
SUPRAGLACIAL
SUPRAGLENOID
SUPRAGLOTTIC
SUPRAHEPATIC
SUPRAHUMAN
SUPRAHUMANITY
SUPRAILIAC
SUPRAILIUM
SUPRAJURAL
SUPRALABIAL
SUPRALATERAL
SUPRALEGAL
SUPRALIMINAL
SUPRALINEAL
SUPRALINEAR
SUPRALOCAL
SUPRALOCALLY
SUPRALORAL
SUPRALUNAR
SUPRALUNARY
SUPRAMAMMARY
SUPRAMARINE
SUPRAMASTOID
SUPRAMAXILLA
SUPRAMAXIMAL
SUPRAMEATAL
SUPRAMEDIAL
SUPRAMENTAL
SUPRAMORAL
SUPRAMORTAL
SUPRAMUNDANE
SUPRANASAL
SUPRANATIONAL
SUPRANATURAL
SUPRANATURE
SUPRANERVIAN
SUPRANEURAL
SUPRANORMAL
SUPRANUCLEAR
SUPRAOCULAR
SUPRAOPTIMAL
SUPRAOPTIONAL
SUPRAORAL
SUPRAORBITAL
SUPRAORBITAR
SUPRAORDINARY
SUPRAPEDAL
SUPRAPROTEST
SUPRAPUBIAN
SUPRAPUBIC
SUPRAPYGAL
SUPRARATIONAL
SUPRARENAL
SUPRARENALIN
SUPRARENIN
SUPRARENINE
SUPRARIMAL
SUPRASCAPULA
SUPRASCRIPT
SUPRASENSUAL
SUPRASEPTAL
SUPRASOLAR
SUPRASPINAL
SUPRASPINATE
SUPRASPINOUS
SUPRASTATE
SUPRASTERNAL
SUPRASTIGMAL
SUPRASUBTLE
SUPRAVAGINAL
SUPRAVERSION
SUPRAVITAL
SUPRAWORLD
SUPREMACIES
SUPREMACY
SUPREME
SUPREMELY
SUPREMENESS
SUPREMITY
SUPTION
SUQ
SUR
SURA
SURADDITION
SURAH
SURAHEE
SURAHI
SURAL
SURAMIN
SURANAL
SURANGULAR
SURAT
SURBASE
SURBASED
SURBASEMENT
SURBATE
SURBATER
SURBED
SURBEDDED
SURBEDDING
SURCEASE
SURCEASED
SURCEASING
SURCHARGE
SURCHARGED
SURCHARGER
SURCHARGING
SURCINGLE
SURCINGLED
SURCINGLING
SURCLE
SURCLOY
SURCOAT
SURCRUE
SURCULI
SURCULOSE
SURCULOUS
SURCULUS
SURD
SURDATION
SURDENT
SURDIMUTISM
SURDITY
SURDOMUTE
SURE
SUREFIRE
SURELY
SUREMENT
SURENESS
SURER
SURES
SURESBY
SUREST
SURETIES
SURETTE
SURETY
SURETYSHIP
SURF
SURFACE
SURFACED
SURFACEDLY
SURFACELESS
SURFACELY
SURFACEMAN
SURFACEMEN
SURFACER
SURFACING
SURFACTANT
SURFACY
SURFBIRD
SURFBOARD
SURFBOARDING
SURFBOAT
SURFBOATMAN
SURFCASTER
SURFCASTING
SURFEIT
SURFEITED
SURFEITER
SURFEITING
SURFER
SURFICIAL
SURFING
SURFLE
SURFMAN
SURFMANSHIP
SURFMEN
SURFRAPPE
SURFRIDING
SURFUSE
SURFUSION
SURFY
SURGE
SURGED
SURGENCY
SURGENT
SURGEON
SURGEONCIES
SURGEONCY
SURGEONFISH
SURGEONFISHES
SURGER
SURGERIES
SURGERIZE
SURGERY
SURGICAL
SURGICALLY
SURGIER
SURGIEST
SURGING
SURGY
SURHAI
SURICAT
SURICATE
SURIGA
SURINAMINE
SURIQUE
SURLIER
SURLIEST
SURLILY
SURLINESS
SURLY
SURMA
SURMARK
SURMASTER
SURMENAGE
SURMISAL
SURMISANT
SURMISE
SURMISED
SURMISEDLY
SURMISER
SURMISING
SURMIT
SURMOUNT
SURMOUNTABLE
SURMOUNTAL
SURMOUNTED
SURMOUNTER
SURMOUNTING
SURMULLET
SURMULLETS
SURN
SURNAI
SURNAME
SURNAMED
SURNAMER
SURNAMING
SURNAP
SURNAPE
SURNAY
SURNOMINAL
SURNOUN
SURPASS
SURPASSABLE
SURPASSED
SURPASSER
SURPASSING
SURPASSINGLY
SURPASSINGNESS
SURPHUL
SURPLICE
SURPLICED
SURPLICIAN
SURPLUS
SURPLUSAGE
SURPLUSES
SURPOOSE
SURPRINT
SURPRISABLE
SURPRISAL
SURPRISE
SURPRISED
SURPRISEDLY
SURPRISEMENT
SURPRISER
SURPRISING
SURPRISINGLY
SURPRISINGNESS
SURPRIZAL
SURQUEDRY
SURQUIDRY
SURQUIDY
SURRA
SURRAH
SURREALISM
SURREALIST
SURREALISTIC
SURREALISTICALLY
SURREBOUND
SURREBUT
SURREBUTTAL
SURREBUTTER
SURRECTION
SURREIN
SURREJOIN
SURREJOINDER
SURRENDER
SURRENDERED
SURRENDEREE
SURRENDERER
SURRENDERING
SURRENDEROR
SURREPT
SURREPTION
SURREPTITIOUS
SURREPTITIOUSLY
SURREPTITIOUSNESS
SURREVERENCE
SURREY
SURROGATE
SURROGATED
SURROGATING
SURROGATION
SURROSION
SURROUND
SURROUNDED
SURROUNDEDLY
SURROUNDER
SURROUNDING
SURROYAL

SURSISE
SURSIZE
SURSOLID
SURSTYLE
SURTAX
SURTAXED
SURTAXING
SURTOUT
SURTURBRAND
SURUCUCU
SURVEILLANCE
SURVEILLANT
SURVEY
SURVEYAGE
SURVEYAL
SURVEYANCE
SURVEYED
SURVEYING
SURVEYOR
SURVEYORSHIP
SURVIEW
SURVIGROUS
SURVISE
SURVIVAL
SURVIVALISM
SURVIVALIST
SURVIVANCE
SURVIVANCY
SURVIVE
SURVIVED
SURVIVER
SURVIVING
SURVIVOR
SURVIVORSHIP
SUSANEE
SUSCEPT
SUSCEPTANCE
SUSCEPTIBILITY
SUSCEPTIBLE
SUSCEPTIBLENESS
SUSCEPTIBLY
SUSCEPTION
SUSCEPTIVE
SUSCEPTIVENESS
SUSCEPTIVITY
SUSCEPTOR
SUSCITATE
SUSCITATION
SUSCITE
SUSI
SUSLIK
SUSOTOXIN
SUSPECT
SUSPECTED
SUSPECTEDNESS
SUSPECTER
SUSPECTFUL
SUSPECTFULNESS
SUSPECTING
SUSPECTOR
SUSPEND
SUSPENDED
SUSPENDER
SUSPENDIBILITY
SUSPENDIBLE
SUSPENDING
SUSPENSATION
SUSPENSE
SUSPENSION
SUSPENSIVE
SUSPENSIVELY
SUSPENSIVENESS
SUSPENSOID
SUSPENSOR
SUSPENSORIA
SUSPENSORIAL
SUSPENSORIUM
SUSPENSORY
SUSPICION
SUSPICIONAL
SUSPICIOUS
SUSPICIOUSLY
SUSPICIOUSNESS
SUSPIRAL
SUSPIRATION
SUSPIRATIOUS
SUSPIRATIVE
SUSPIRE
SUSPIRED
SUSPIRING
SUSPIRIOUS
SUSS
SUSSEXITE
SUSSULTATORY
SUSSULTORIAL
SUSSY
SUSTAIN
SUSTAINABLE
SUSTAINED
SUSTAINEDLY
SUSTAINER
SUSTAINING
SUSTAININGLY
SUSTAINMENT
SUSTENANCE
SUSTENANT
SUSTENTATE
SUSTENTATION
SUSTENTATIVE
SUSTENTATOR
SUSTENTION
SUSTENTIVE
SUSTENTOR
SUSTINENT
SUSU
SUSURR
SUSURRANT
SUSURRATE
SUSURRATED
SUSURRATING
SUSURRATION
SUSURRINGLY
SUSURROUS
SUSURRUS
SUTE
SUTEL
SUTERBERRIES
SUTERBERRY
SUTHER
SUTILE
SUTLER
SUTLERAGE
SUTLERSHIP
SUTLERY
SUTOR
SUTORIAL
SUTORIAN
SUTORIOUS
SUTRA
SUTRAS
SUTTA
SUTTEE
SUTTEEISM
SUTTER
SUTTLE
SUTURAL
SUTURALLY
SUTURATION
SUTURE
SUTURED
SUTURING
SUUM
SUWAR
SUWARRO
SUZ
SUZERAIN
SUZERAINTY
SUZU
SVABITE
SVAMI
SVAMIN
SVARABHAKTI
SVARABHAKTIC
SVARAJ
SVASTIKA
SVEDBERG
SVELT
SVELTE
SVIATONOSITE
SWAB
SWABBED
SWABBER
SWABBERLY
SWABBING
SWABBLE
SWABBY
SWACK
SWACKED
SWACKEN
SWACKING
SWAD
SWADDER
SWADDISH
SWADDLE
SWADDLEBILL
SWADDLED
SWADDLER
SWADDLING
SWADDY
SWADE
SWAG
SWAGBELLIED
SWAGBELLIES
SWAGBELLY
SWAGE
SWAGED
SWAGER
SWAGGED
SWAGGER
SWAGGERED
SWAGGERER
SWAGGERING
SWAGGERINGLY
SWAGGIE
SWAGGING
SWAGGY
SWAGING
SWAGMAN
SWAGMEN
SWAGSMAN
SWAGSMEN
SWAIL
SWAIMOUS
SWAIN
SWAINISH
SWAINISHNESS
SWAINMOTE
SWAIRD
SWAK
SWALE
SWALER
SWALING
SWALINGLY
SWALLET
SWALLO
SWALLOW
SWALLOWABLE
SWALLOWED
SWALLOWER
SWALLOWING
SWALLOWPIPE
SWALLOWS
SWALLOWTAIL
SWALLOWWORT
SWAM
SWAMI
SWAMIS
SWAMP
SWAMPABLE
SWAMPBERRIES
SWAMPBERRY
SWAMPED
SWAMPER
SWAMPHEN
SWAMPIER
SWAMPIEST
SWAMPINE
SWAMPING
SWAMPISH
SWAMPISHNESS
SWAMPLAND
SWAMPWEED
SWAMPWOOD
SWAMPY
SWAMY
SWAN
SWANFLOWER
SWANG
SWANGY
SWANHERD
SWANIMOTE
SWANK
SWANKER
SWANKEY
SWANKIE
SWANKIER
SWANKIEST
SWANKILY
SWANKINESS
SWANKING
SWANKY
SWANLIKE
SWANMARK
SWANMARKER
SWANMARKING
SWANMOTE
SWANNECK
SWANNECKED
SWANNERIES
SWANNERY
SWANNET
SWANNISH
SWANNY
SWANPAN
SWANS
SWANSDOWN
SWANSKIN
SWANWEED
SWANWORT
SWAP
SWAPE
SWAPPED
SWAPPER
SWAPPING
SWARAJ
SWARAJISM
SWARAJIST
SWARBIE
SWARD
SWARDED
SWARDING
SWARDY
SWARE
SWARF
SWARGA
SWARM
SWARMED
SWARMER
SWARMING
SWARMY
SWART
SWARTBACK
SWARTH
SWARTHIER
SWARTHIEST
SWARTHILY
SWARTHINESS
SWARTHNESS
SWARTHY
SWARTISH
SWARTNESS
SWARTRUTTER
SWARTRUTTING
SWARTY
SWARVE
SWASH
SWASHBUCKLE
SWASHBUCKLER
SWASHBUCKLING
SWASHED
SWASHER
SWASHING
SWASHINGLY
SWASHWAY
SWASHWORK
SWASHY
SWASTICA
SWASTIKA
SWAT
SWATCH
SWATCHER
SWATH
SWATHE
SWATHED
SWATHER
SWATHING
SWATHY
SWATS
SWATTED
SWATTER
SWATTING
SWATTLE
SWAVER
SWAY
SWAYBACK
SWAYED
SWAYER
SWAYING
SWAYINGLY
SWAYLESS
SWEAL
SWEAM
SWEAR
SWEARER
SWEARING
SWEARINGLY
SWEARWORD
SWEAT
SWEATBAND
SWEATBOX
SWEATED
SWEATER
SWEATFUL
SWEATH
SWEATHOUSE
SWEATIER
SWEATIEST
SWEATILY
SWEATINESS
SWEATING
SWEATS
SWEATSHOP
SWEATWEED
SWEATY
SWEB

SWEDE
SWEDGE
SWEDGER
SWEDRU
SWEE
SWEEK
SWEEL
SWEENS
SWEENY
SWEEP
SWEEPAGE
SWEEPBACK
SWEEPBOARD
SWEEPDOM
SWEEPER
SWEEPING
SWEEPINGLY
SWEEPINGNESS
SWEEPSTAKE
SWEEPSTAKES
SWEEPUP
SWEEPWASHER
SWEEPY
SWEER
SWEERT
SWEESWEE
SWEET
SWEETBERRY
SWEETBREAD
SWEETBRIAR
SWEETBRIER
SWEETBRIERY
SWEETCLOVER
SWEETEN
SWEETENED
SWEETENER
SWEETENING
SWEETER
SWEETEST
SWEETFISH
SWEETFUL
SWEETHEART
SWEETHEARTING
SWEETIE
SWEETING
SWEETISH
SWEETISHLY
SWEETISHNESS
SWEETLEAF
SWEETLY
SWEETMAKER
SWEETMEAT
SWEETNESS
SWEETROOT
SWEETS
SWEETSHOP
SWEETSOP
SWEETWATER
SWEETWEED
SWEETWOOD
SWEETWORT
SWEETY
SWEGO
SWELCHIE
SWELL
SWELLAGE
SWELLDOM
SWELLDOODLE
SWELLED
SWELLER
SWELLFISH
SWELLFISHES
SWELLING
SWELLISH
SWELLISHNESS
SWELLMOBSMAN
SWELLNESS
SWELLTOAD
SWELLY
SWELP
SWELT
SWELTER
SWELTERED
SWELTERING
SWELTERINGLY
SWELTH
SWELTRY
SWELTY
SWEPE
SWEPT
SWEPTBACK
SWEPTWING
SWERVE
SWERVED
SWERVER
SWERVILY
SWERVING
SWEVEN
SWEYN
SWICH
SWICK
SWIDDEN
SWIDGE
SWIFT
SWIFTEN
SWIFTER
SWIFTEST
SWIFTFOOT
SWIFTLET
SWIFTLIER
SWIFTLIEST
SWIFTLY
SWIFTNESS
SWIFTY
SWIG
SWIGGED
SWIGGER
SWIGGING
SWIGGLE
SWIKE
SWILE
SWILK
SWILKIE
SWILL
SWILLBOWL
SWILLED
SWILLER
SWILLING
SWILLTUB
SWIM
SWIMBEL
SWIMMER
SWIMMERET
SWIMMING
SWIMMINGLY
SWIMMIST
SWIMMY
SWIMSUIT
SWIMY
SWINDLE
SWINDLED
SWINDLER
SWINDLERS
SWINDLERY
SWINDLING
SWINE
SWINEBREAD
SWINECOTE
SWINEHEAD
SWINEHERD
SWINEHERDSHIP
SWINEHULL
SWINELY
SWINEPIPE
SWINEPOX
SWINERY
SWINESTONE
SWINESTY
SWINEY
SWING
SWINGBACK
SWINGDEVIL
SWINGDINGLE
SWINGE
SWINGED
SWINGEING
SWINGEINGLY
SWINGEL
SWINGEOUR
SWINGER
SWINGING
SWINGINGLY
SWINGKNIFE
SWINGLE
SWINGLEBAR
SWINGLED
SWINGLETAIL
SWINGLETREE
SWINGLING
SWINGMAN
SWINGSTOCK
SWINGTREE
SWINGY
SWINISH
SWINISHLY
SWINISHNESS
SWINK
SWINKER
SWINKING
SWINNEY
SWIP
SWIPE
SWIPED
SWIPES
SWIPING
SWIPLE
SWIPPER
SWIPPLE
SWIPY
SWIRE
SWIRL
SWIRLED
SWIRLING
SWIRLY
SWIRRING
SWISH
SWISHED
SWISHER
SWISHING
SWISHINGLY
SWISHY
SWISS
SWISSING
SWITCH
SWITCHBACK
SWITCHBACKER
SWITCHBOARD
SWITCHED
SWITCHEL
SWITCHER
SWITCHGEAR
SWITCHING
SWITCHKEEPER
SWITCHLIKE
SWITCHMAN
SWITCHMEN
SWITCHTAIL
SWITCHY
SWITCHYARD
SWITH
SWITHE
SWITHEN
SWITHER
SWITHLY
SWIVE
SWIVEL
SWIVELED
SWIVELEYE
SWIVELEYED
SWIVELING
SWIVELLED
SWIVELLIKE
SWIVELLING
SWIVER
SWIVET
SWIVETTY
SWIVVET
SWIZ
SWIZZ
SWIZZLE
SWIZZLER
SWOB
SWOBBER
SWOLLEN
SWONK
SWOON
SWOONED
SWOONING
SWOONINGLY
SWOONY
SWOOP
SWOOPED
SWOOPER
SWOOPING
SWOOSH
SWOP
SWOPE
SWORD
SWORDBILL
SWORDCRAFT
SWORDER
SWORDFISH
SWORDFISHERMAN
SWORDFISHERY
SWORDFISHES
SWORDFISHING
SWORDICK
SWORDING
SWORDKNOT
SWORDMAKER
SWORDMAKING
SWORDMAN
SWORDMANSHIP
SWORDPLAY
SWORDPLAYER
SWORDPROOF
SWORDSLIPPER
SWORDSMAN
SWORDSMANSHIP
SWORDSMEN
SWORDSMITH
SWORDSTICK
SWORDSWOMAN
SWORDTAIL
SWORDWEED
SWORE
SWORL
SWORN
SWOSH
SWOT
SWOTTER
SWOUGH
SWOUN
SWOUND
SWOUNDS
SWOUNS
SWOW
SWUM
SWUNG
SWY
SWYTHE
SY
SYAGUSH
SYBARITICAL
SYBIL
SYBO
SYBOES
SYBOTIC
SYBOTISM
SYBOW
SYCAMINE
SYCAMORE
SYCE
SYCEE
SYCHEE
SYCITE
SYCOCK
SYCOMA
SYCOMANCY
SYCONARIAN
SYCONATE
SYCONES
SYCONIA
SYCONID
SYCONIUM
SYCONOID
SYCONUS
SYCOPHANCIES
SYCOPHANCY
SYCOPHANT
SYCOPHANTIC
SYCOPHANTISH
SYCOPHANTISM
SYCOPHANTIZE
SYCOPHANTRY
SYCOSIFORM
SYCOSIS
SYDDIR
SYE
SYENITE
SYENITIC
SYENODIORITE
SYENOGABBRO
SYKE
SYKER
SYKERLY
SYLE
SYLENE
SYLIB
SYLING
SYLLAB
SYLLABARIES
SYLLABARIUM
SYLLABARY
SYLLABATIM
SYLLABATION
SYLLABE
SYLLABI
SYLLABIC
SYLLABICAL
SYLLABICALLY
SYLLABICATE
SYLLABICATED
SYLLABICATING
SYLLABICNESS
SYLLABIFIED
SYLLABIFY
SYLLABIFYING
SYLLABISM
SYLLABIZE
SYLLABIZED
SYLLABIZING
SYLLABLE
SYLLABLED
SYLLABLES

SYLLABLING
SYLLABUB
SYLLABUS
SYLLABUSES
SYLLEPSES
SYLLEPSIS
SYLLEPTIC
SYLLEPTICAL
SYLLID
SYLLIDIAN
SYLLOGE
SYLLOGISM
SYLLOGIST
SYLLOGISTIC
SYLLOGISTICAL
SYLLOGISTICALL
SYLLOGISTICS
SYLLOGIZE
SYLLOGIZED
SYLLOGIZER
SYLLOGIZING
SYLPH
SYLPHID
SYLPHIDINE
SYLPHISH
SYLPHLIKE
SYLPHY
SYLVA
SYLVAE
SYLVAGE
SYLVAN
SYLVANITE
SYLVANITIC
SYLVANITY
SYLVANRY
SYLVAS
SYLVATE
SYLVATIC
SYLVATICAL
SYLVESTER
SYLVESTRAL
SYLVESTRENE
SYLVESTRIAN
SYLVIID
SYLVIINE
SYLVIN
SYLVINE
SYLVINITE
SYLVITE
SYMAR
SYMBASIC
SYMBASICAL
SYMBASICALLY
SYMBASIS
SYMBION
SYMBIONT
SYMBIONTIC
SYMBIOSIS
SYMBIOT
SYMBIOTE
SYMBIOTIC
SYMBIOTICAL
SYMBIOTICALLY
SYMBIOTICS
SYMBIOTISM
SYMBLEPHARON
SYMBOL
SYMBOLATER
SYMBOLIC
SYMBOLICAL
SYMBOLICALLY
SYMBOLICALNESS
SYMBOLICS
SYMBOLISE
SYMBOLISM
SYMBOLIST
SYMBOLISTIC
SYMBOLISTICAL
SYMBOLISTICALLY
SYMBOLIZATION
SYMBOLIZE
SYMBOLIZED
SYMBOLIZER
SYMBOLIZING
SYMBOLOGICAL
SYMBOLOGIST
SYMBOLOGY
SYMBOLOLATRY
SYMBOLOLOGY
SYMBOLRY
SYMBOLS
SYMBOLUM
SYMBOULEUTIC
SYMBRANCH
SYMBRANCHOID
SYMBRANCHOUS
SYMMACHY
SYMMEDIAN
SYMMELUS
SYMMETALLISM
SYMMETRAL
SYMMETRIAN
SYMMETRIC
SYMMETRICAL
SYMMETRICALITY
SYMMETRICALLY
SYMMETRICALNESS
SYMMETRIES
SYMMETRIST
SYMMETRIZE
SYMMETRIZED
SYMMETRIZING
SYMMETROID
SYMMETRY
SYMMIST
SYMPATHETIC
SYMPATHETICAL
SYMPATHETICALLY
SYMPATHIES
SYMPATHIN
SYMPATHIQUE
SYMPATHISE
SYMPATHISM
SYMPATHIST
SYMPATHIZE
SYMPATHIZED
SYMPATHIZER
SYMPATHIZING
SYMPATHIZINGLY
SYMPATHY
SYMPATRIC
SYMPATRY
SYMPETALOUS
SYMPHILE
SYMPHILIC
SYMPHILOUS
SYMPHILY
SYMPHOGENOUS
SYMPHONETIC
SYMPHONIA
SYMPHONIC
SYMPHONICALLY
SYMPHONIES
SYMPHONION
SYMPHONIOUS
SYMPHONIOUSLY
SYMPHONIST
SYMPHONIZE
SYMPHONIZED
SYMPHONIZING
SYMPHONOUS
SYMPHONY
SYMPHRASE
SYMPHYLAN
SYMPHYLLOUS
SYMPHYLOUS
SYMPHYNOTE
SYMPHYSEAL
SYMPHYSES
SYMPHYSION
SYMPHYSIS
SYMPHYSY
SYMPHYTIC
SYMPHYTISM
SYMPHYTIZE
SYMPLASM
SYMPLAST
SYMPLECTIC
SYMPLESITE
SYMPLOCE
SYMPLOCIUM
SYMPODE
SYMPODIA
SYMPODIAL
SYMPODIALLY
SYMPODIUM
SYMPOSIA
SYMPOSIAC
SYMPOSIACAL
SYMPOSIAL
SYMPOSIARCH
SYMPOSIAST
SYMPOSION
SYMPOSIUM
SYMPOSIUMS
SYMPTOM
SYMPTOMATIC
SYMPTOMATICAL
SYMPTOMATICALLY
SYMPTOMATICS
SYMPTOMATIZE
SYMPTOMS
SYMPTOSIS
SYMPUS
SYN
SYNACME
SYNACMIC
SYNACMY
SYNACTIC
SYNADELPHITE
SYNAERESIS
SYNAESTHESIA
SYNAGOG
SYNAGOGAL
SYNAGOGICAL
SYNAGOGUE
SYNALEPHA
SYNALEPHE
SYNALLACTIC
SYNALOEPHA
SYNALOEPHE
SYNANGE
SYNANGIA
SYNANGIAL
SYNANGIC
SYNANGIUM
SYNANTHEMA
SYNANTHEROUS
SYNANTHESIS
SYNANTHETIC
SYNANTHIC
SYNANTHOUS
SYNANTHROSE
SYNANTHY
SYNAPHEA
SYNAPHEIA
SYNAPSE
SYNAPSES
SYNAPSID
SYNAPSIDAN
SYNAPSIS
SYNAPTAI
SYNAPTASE
SYNAPTE
SYNAPTEROUS
SYNAPTIC
SYNAPTICAL
SYNAPTICALLY
SYNAPTICULA
SYNAPTICULAR
SYNAPTICULUM
SYNAPTID
SYNAPTYCHUS
SYNARCHICAL
SYNARCHY
SYNARMOGOID
SYNARTESIS
SYNARTETE
SYNARTETIC
SYNARTHRODIA
SYNARTHROSES
SYNARTHROSIS
SYNASTRY
SYNAXAR
SYNAXARION
SYNAXARIST
SYNAXARY
SYNAXIS
SYNCARP
SYNCARPIA
SYNCARPIUM
SYNCARPOUS
SYNCARPY
SYNCARYON
SYNCEPHALIC
SYNCEPHALUS
SYNCEREBRAL
SYNCEREBRUM
SYNCHITIC
SYNCHORESIS
SYNCHRO
SYNCHROMESH
SYNCHRONAL
SYNCHRONE
SYNCHRONIC
SYNCHRONICAL
SYNCHRONISM
SYNCHRONIZATION
SYNCHRONIZE
SYNCHRONIZED
SYNCHRONIZER
SYNCHRONIZING
SYNCHRONOUS
SYNCHRONOUSLY
SYNCHRONY
SYNCHROSCOPE
SYNCHROTRON
SYNCHYSIS
SYNCLADOUS
SYNCLASTIC
SYNCLINAL
SYNCLINALLY
SYNCLINE
SYNCLINICAL
SYNCLINORIAL
SYNCLINORIAN
SYNCLINORIUM
SYNCLITIC
SYNCLITICISM
SYNCLITISM
SYNCOELOM
SYNCOPAL
SYNCOPATE
SYNCOPATED
SYNCOPATING
SYNCOPATION
SYNCOPATOR
SYNCOPE
SYNCOPES
SYNCOPIC
SYNCOPISM
SYNCOPIST
SYNCOPIZE
SYNCRANIATE
SYNCRANTERIC
SYNCRASY
SYNCRETIC
SYNCRETICAL
SYNCRETICISM
SYNCRETION
SYNCRETISM
SYNCRETIST
SYNCRETISTIC
SYNCRETIZE
SYNCRETIZED
SYNCRETIZING
SYNCRISIS
SYNCRYPTIC
SYNCYTIA
SYNCYTIAL
SYNCYTIOMA
SYNCYTIOMAS
SYNCYTIOMATA
SYNCYTIUM
SYNDACTYL
SYNDACTYLE
SYNDACTYLIA
SYNDACTYLIC
SYNDACTYLISM
SYNDACTYLOUS
SYNDACTYLY
SYNDERESIS
SYNDESIS
SYNDESMITIS
SYNDESMOLOGY
SYNDESMOMA
SYNDESMOSES
SYNDESMOSIS
SYNDESMOTIC
SYNDESMOTOMY
SYNDET
SYNDETIC
SYNDETICAL
SYNDETICALLY
SYNDIC
SYNDICAL
SYNDICALISM
SYNDICALIST
SYNDICALIZE
SYNDICAT
SYNDICATE
SYNDICATED
SYNDICATEER
SYNDICATING
SYNDICATION
SYNDICATOR
SYNDROME
SYNDROMIC
SYNDYASMIAN
SYNE
SYNECDOCHE
SYNECDOCHIC
SYNECDOCHISM
SYNECHIA
SYNECHIAE
SYNECHIOLOGY
SYNECHOLOGY
SYNECHOTOMY
SYNECHTHRAN
SYNECHTHRY
SYNECIOUS
SYNECOLOGY
SYNECTIC
SYNECTICITY
SYNEDRAL

SYNEDRIAL
SYNEDRIAN
SYNEIDESIS
SYNEMA
SYNEMATA
SYNEMMENON
SYNENTOGNATH
SYNERESIS
SYNERGASTIC
SYNERGETIC
SYNERGIA
SYNERGIC
SYNERGID
SYNERGIDAE
SYNERGIDAL
SYNERGISM
SYNERGIST
SYNERGISTIC
SYNERGIZE
SYNERGY
SYNERIZE
SYNESIS
SYNESTHESIA
SYNESTHETIC
SYNETHNIC
SYNEZISIS
SYNGAMIC
SYNGAMOUS
SYNGAMY
SYNGENESIAN
SYNGENESIOUS
SYNGENESIS
SYNGENETIC
SYNGENISM
SYNGENITE
SYNGNATHID
SYNGNATHOID
SYNGNATHOUS
SYNGRAPH
SYNIZESIS
SYNKARYON
SYNKINESIS
SYNKINETIC
SYNNEMA
SYNNEUROSIS
SYNOCHAL
SYNOCHOUS
SYNOCHUS
SYNOCREATE
SYNOD
SYNODAL
SYNODALIST
SYNODALLY
SYNODIAN
SYNODIC
SYNODICAL
SYNODICALLY
SYNODICON
SYNODIST
SYNODITE
SYNODONTID
SYNODONTOID
SYNODSMAN
SYNODSMEN
SYNOECETE
SYNOECIOSIS
SYNOECIOUS
SYNOECIOUSLY
SYNOECISM
SYNOECIZE
SYNOECY
SYNOEKY
SYNOICOUS
SYNOMOSY
SYNONYM
SYNONYMATIC
SYNONYME
SYNONYMIC
SYNONYMICAL
SYNONYMICON
SYNONYMICS
SYNONYMIES
SYNONYMIST
SYNONYMITY
SYNONYMIZE
SYNONYMIZED
SYNONYMIZING
SYNONYMOUS
SYNONYMOUSLY
SYNONYMY
SYNOPSES
SYNOPSIS
SYNOPSIZE
SYNOPSY
SYNOPTIC
SYNOPTICAL
SYNOPTICALLY
SYNORCHIDISM
SYNORCHISM
SYNOSTEOLOGY
SYNOSTEOSES
SYNOSTEOSIS
SYNOSTOSE
SYNOSTOSES
SYNOSTOSIS
SYNOSTOTIC
SYNOSTOTICAL
SYNOUSIACS
SYNOVECTOMY
SYNOVIA
SYNOVIAL
SYNOVIALLY
SYNOVIPAROUS
SYNOVITIC
SYNOVITIS
SYNPELMOUS
SYNSACRAL
SYNSACRUM
SYNSEPALOUS
SYNSPERMOUS
SYNSPOROUS
SYNTACTIC
SYNTACTICAL
SYNTACTICALLY
SYNTACTICIAN
SYNTAGMA
SYNTAN
SYNTAX
SYNTAXIS
SYNTAXIST
SYNTECHNIC
SYNTECTIC
SYNTECTICAL
SYNTENOSIS
SYNTERESIS
SYNTEXIS
SYNTHEME
SYNTHERMAL
SYNTHESES
SYNTHESIS
SYNTHESISE
SYNTHESISM
SYNTHESIST
SYNTHESIZE
SYNTHESIZED
SYNTHESIZER
SYNTHESIZING
SYNTHETE
SYNTHETIC
SYNTHETICAL
SYNTHETICALLY
SYNTHETICISM
SYNTHETIST
SYNTHETIZATION
SYNTHETIZE
SYNTHETIZER
SYNTHOL
SYNTHRONI
SYNTHRONOI
SYNTHRONOS
SYNTHRONUS
SYNTOMIA
SYNTOMY
SYNTONE
SYNTONIC
SYNTONICAL
SYNTONICALLY
SYNTONIN
SYNTONIZE
SYNTONIZED
SYNTONIZER
SYNTONIZING
SYNTONOUS
SYNTONY
SYNTROPE
SYNTROPHIC
SYNTROPICAL
SYNTROPY
SYNTYPE
SYNTYPIC
SYNTYPICISM
SYNURA
SYNURAE
SYNUSIAST
SYPH
SYPHER
SYPHERED
SYPHERING
SYPHILID
SYPHILIDE
SYPHILIS
SYPHILITIC
SYPHILIZE
SYPHILIZED
SYPHILIZING
SYPHILODERM
SYPHILOGENY
SYPHILOID
SYPHILOLOGY
SYPHILOMA
SYPHILOPHOBE
SYPHILOSIS
SYPHON
SYRETTE
SYRINGA
SYRINGE
SYRINGEAL
SYRINGED
SYRINGES
SYRINGIN
SYRINGING
SYRINGITIS
SYRINGIUM
SYRINGOCELE
SYRINGOCOELE
SYRINGOTOME
SYRINGOTOMY
SYRINX
SYRINXES
SYRMA
SYRPHID
SYRT
SYRTIC
SYRUP
SYRUPED
SYRUPER
SYRUPY
SYRUS
SYSE
SYSSARCOSIC
SYSSARCOSIS
SYSSARCOTIC
SYSSEL
SYSSELMAN
SYSSITIA
SYSSITION
SYSTALTIC
SYSTASIS
SYSTATIC
SYSTEM
SYSTEMATIC
SYSTEMATICAL
SYSTEMATICALITY
SYSTEMATICALLY
SYSTEMATICIAN
SYSTEMATICS
SYSTEMATISE
SYSTEMATISM
SYSTEMATIST
SYSTEMATIZATION
SYSTEMATIZE
SYSTEMATIZED
SYSTEMATIZER
SYSTEMATIZING
SYSTEMIC
SYSTEMICALLY
SYSTEMIZATION
SYSTEMIZE
SYSTEMIZED
SYSTEMIZER
SYSTEMIZING
SYSTILIUS
SYSTOLATED
SYSTOLE
SYSTOLIC
SYSTYLE
SYSTYLOUS
SYZYGAL
SYZYGETIC
SYZYGIA
SYZYGIAL
SYZYGIES
SYZYGIUM
SYZYGY
SZAIBELYITE
SZLACHTA
SZOPELKA

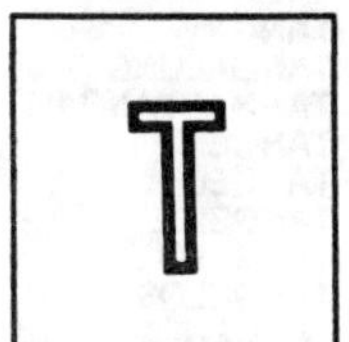

TA
TAA
TAAR
TAB
TABAC
TABACIN
TABACOSIS
TABACUM
TABAGIE
TABANID
TABANUCO
TABARD
TABARDED
TABARDILLO
TABARET
TABASHEER
TABASHIR
TABATIERE
TABBER
TABBIES
TABBINET
TABBY
TABEFACTION
TABEFY
TABELLA
TABELLION
TABER
TABERDAR
TABERNA
TABERNACLE
TABERNACLED
TABERNACLER
TABERNACLING
TABERNACULAR
TABERNAE
TABES
TABESCENCE
TABESCENT
TABET
TABETIC
TABETIFORM
TABETLESS
TABI
TABIA
TABID
TABIDLY
TABIDNESS
TABIFIC
TABIFICAL
TABINET
TABITUDE
TABLA
TABLAS
TABLATURE
TABLE
TABLEAU
TABLEAUS
TABLEAUX
TABLECLOTH
TABLECLOTHY
TABLED
TABLEITY
TABLELAND
TABLEMAID
TABLEMAKER
TABLEMAKING
TABLEMAN
TABLEMATE
TABLER
TABLES
TABLESPOON
TABLESPOONFUL
TABLESPOONFULS
TABLET
TABLETARY
TABLETOP
TABLEWARE
TABLEWISE
TABLIER
TABLINA
TABLING
TABLINUM
TABLITA
TABLOID
TABOG
TABOO
TABOOS
TABOPARALYSIS
TABOPARESIS
TABOPARETIC
TABOPHOBIA
TABOR
TABORED
TABORER
TABORET
TABORIN
TABORINE
TABORING
TABOUR
TABOURED
TABOURER
TABOURET
TABOURINE
TABOURING
TABRET
TABS
TABU
TABULA
TABULABLE
TABULAE
TABULAR
TABULARE
TABULARIA
TABULARIUM
TABULARIZE
TABULARIZED
TABULARIZING
TABULARLY
TABULARY
TABULATE
TABULATED
TABULATING
TABULATION
TABULATOR
TABULATORY
TABULE
TABUN
TABUS
TABUT
TACAHOUT
TACAMAHAC
TACAMAHACA
TACAMAHACK
TACCACEOUS
TACCADA
TACE
TACET
TACH
TACHE
TACHEOGRAPHY
TACHEOMETER
TACHEOMETRIC
TACHEOMETRY
TACHETURE
TACHHYDRITE
TACHIBANA
TACHINA
TACHINARIAN
TACHINID
TACHIOL
TACHOGRAM
TACHOGRAPH
TACHOMETER
TACHOMETRIC
TACHOMETRY
TACHOSCOPE
TACHYCARDIA
TACHYCARDIAC
TACHYGEN
TACHYGENESIS
TACHYGENETIC
TACHYGLOSSAL
TACHYGRAPH
TACHYGRAPHER
TACHYGRAPHIC
TACHYGRAPHY
TACHYLITE
TACHYLYTE
TACHYLYTIC
TACHYMETER
TACHYMETRIC
TACHYMETRY
TACHYSCOPE
TACHYTYPE
TACIT
TACITLY
TACITNESS
TACITURN
TACITURNIST
TACITURNITY
TACITURNLY
TACK
TACKED
TACKER
TACKET
TACKETY
TACKEY
TACKIER
TACKIEST
TACKING
TACKINGLY
TACKLE
TACKLED
TACKLEMAN
TACKLER
TACKLES
TACKLESS
TACKLING
TACKSMAN
TACKSMEN
TACKY
TACLOCUS
TACMAHACK
TACNODE
TACON
TACONITE
TACSO
TACT
TACTFUL
TACTFULLY
TACTFULNESS
TACTIC
TACTICAL
TACTICALLY
TACTICIAN
TACTICS
TACTILE
TACTILIST
TACTILITIES
TACTILITY
TACTION
TACTITE
TACTLESS
TACTLESSLY
TACTLESSNESS
TACTOMETER
TACTOR
TACTUAL
TACTUALITY
TACTUALLY
TACTUS
TACUACINE
TAD
TADBHAVA
TADPOLE
TAE
TAEL
TAENIA
TAENIACIDAL
TAENIACIDE
TAENIAE
TAENIAFUGE
TAENIAL
TAENIAN
TAENIASIS
TAENIATE
TAENICIDE
TAENIDIA
TAENIDIUM
TAENIFORM
TAENIFUGE
TAENIIFORM
TAENIOID
TAENIOSOME
TAENIOSOMOUS
TAENITE
TAENNIN
TAEPO
TAFFAREL
TAFFEREL
TAFFETA
TAFFETY
TAFFIA
TAFFLE
TAFFRAIL
TAFFY
TAFIA
TAFT
TAFWIZ
TAG
TAGASASTE
TAGATOSE
TAGBOARD
TAGETOL
TAGETONE
TAGGE
TAGGED
TAGGER
TAGGERS
TAGGING
TAGGLE
TAGGY
TAGHAIRM
TAGILITE
TAGLIA
TAGLIONI
TAGLOCK
TAGMEME
TAGRAG
TAGRAGGERY
TAGSORE
TAGSTER
TAGTAIL
TAGUA
TAGUAN
TAGWERK
TAHA
TAHALI
TAHANUN
TAHARAH
TAHEEN
TAHGOOK
TAHIN
TAHKHANA
TAHLI
TAHONA
TAHR
TAHSEELDAR
TAHSIL
TAHSILDAR
TAHUA
TAI
TAIAHA
TAIGA
TAIGLE
TAIGLESOME
TAIHOA
TAIKIH
TAIKUN
TAIL
TAILAGE
TAILBAND
TAILBOARD
TAILED
TAILENDER
TAILER
TAILET
TAILFIRST
TAILFLOWER
TAILFOREMOST
TAILGATE
TAILGATED
TAILGATING
TAILGUNNER
TAILHEAD
TAILING
TAILINGS
TAILLE
TAILLESS
TAILLEUR
TAILLIGHT
TAILLOIR
TAILOR
TAILORAGE
TAILORBIRD
TAILORED
TAILORING
TAILORISM
TAILORLY
TAILORS
TAILORY
TAILPIECE
TAILPIN
TAILPIPE
TAILRACE
TAILSKID
TAILSPIN
TAILSTOCK
TAILWISE
TAILY
TAILYE
TAILZEE
TAILZIE
TAILZIED
TAIMEN
TAIMYRITE
TAIN
TAINT
TAINTE
TAINTED
TAINTING
TAINTMENT
TAINTOR
TAINTURE
TAINTWORM

TAIPAN
TAIPO
TAIRA
TAIRGE
TAIS
TAISCH
TAISSLE
TAISTREL
TAISTRIL
TAIT
TAIVER
TAIVERS
TAIVERT
TAJ
TAJO
TAKABLE
TAKAHE
TAKAR
TAKE
TAKEDOWN
TAKEFUL
TAKEN
TAKEOFF
TAKEOUT
TAKER
TAKIN
TAKING
TAKINGLY
TAKINGNESS
TAKKANAH
TAKOSIS
TAKROURI
TAKT
TAKY
TAKYR
TAL
TALA
TALABON
TALAJE
TALAK
TALALGIA
TALANTON
TALAO
TALAPOIN
TALAR
TALARI
TALARIA
TALARIC
TALAYOT
TALAYOTI
TALBOT
TALC
TALCED
TALCER
TALCING
TALCKED
TALCKING
TALCKY
TALCOID
TALCOSE
TALCOUS
TALCUM
TALE
TALEBEARER
TALEBEARING
TALEBOOK
TALECARRIER
TALECARRYING
TALEMASTER
TALEMONGER
TALENT
TALENTED
TALENTER
TALENTING
TALEPYET
TALER
TALES
TALESMAN
TALESMEN
TALETELLER
TALETELLING
TALEWISE
TALI
TALIATION
TALIERA
TALIGRADE
TALION
TALIONIC
TALIPED
TALIPEDIC
TALIPES
TALIPOMANUS
TALIPOT
TALISAY
TALISMAN
TALISMANIC
TALISMANICAL
TALISMANNI
TALISMANS
TALITE
TALITOL
TALK
TALKABILITY
TALKABLE
TALKATHON
TALKATIVE
TALKATIVELY
TALKATIVENESS
TALKED
TALKER
TALKFEST
TALKIE
TALKIER
TALKIEST
TALKING
TALKWORTHY
TALKY
TALL
TALLAGE
TALLAGEABLE
TALLAGED
TALLAGING
TALLAPOI
TALLATE
TALLBOY
TALLEGALANE
TALLER
TALLERO
TALLEST
TALLET
TALLIABLE
TALLIAR
TALLIATE
TALLIATED
TALLIATING
TALLIED
TALLIER
TALLIES
TALLIS
TALLISH
TALLIT
TALLITH
TALLNESS
TALLOL
TALLOTE
TALLOW
TALLOWBERRIES
TALLOWBERRY
TALLOWED
TALLOWER
TALLOWINESS
TALLOWING
TALLOWMAKER
TALLOWMAKING
TALLOWMAN
TALLOWROOT
TALLOWWEED
TALLOWWOOD
TALLOWY
TALLWOOD
TALLY
TALLYHO
TALLYHOS
TALLYING
TALLYMAN
TALLYMEN
TALLYWAG
TALLYWALKA
TALLYWOMAN
TALLYWOMEN
TALMA
TALMAS
TALMOUSE
TALO
TALOFIBULAR
TALON
TALONED
TALONID
TALOSE
TALOTIBIAL
TALPACOTI
TALPATATE
TALPETATE
TALPICIDE
TALPID
TALPIFORM
TALPIFY
TALPINE
TALPOID
TALSHIDE
TALTER
TALTHIB
TALUK
TALUKA
TALUKDAR
TALUKDARI
TALUS
TALUTO
TALWOOD
TAM
TAMABLE
TAMALE
TAMANDU
TAMANDUA
TAMANOAS
TAMANOIR
TAMANOWUS
TAMANU
TAMARA
TAMARACK
TAMARAITE
TAMARAO
TAMARAU
TAMARIN
TAMARIND
TAMARISK
TAMAS
TAMASHA
TAMBAC
TAMBAROORA
TAMBER
TAMBO
TAMBOOKIE
TAMBOR
TAMBOUR
TAMBOURA
TAMBOURED
TAMBOURER
TAMBOURET
TAMBOURGI
TAMBOURIN
TAMBOURINE
TAMBOURING
TAMBOURIST
TAMBREET
TAMBURA
TAMBURAN
TAMBURELLO
TAMBURONE
TAME
TAMEABLE
TAMED
TAMEHEARTED
TAMEIN
TAMELESS
TAMELESSNESS
TAMELY
TAMEN
TAMENES
TAMER
TAMEST
TAMIDINE
TAMIN
TAMINE
TAMING
TAMINY
TAMIS
TAMISE
TAMLUNG
TAMMAR
TAMMIE
TAMMIES
TAMMY
TAMP
TAMPALA
TAMPAN
TAMPANG
TAMPED
TAMPER
TAMPERED
TAMPERER
TAMPERING
TAMPING
TAMPION
TAMPIONED
TAMPOE
TAMPON
TAMPONADE
TAMPONAGE
TAMPONMENT
TAMPOON
TAMPOY
TAMURE
TAN
TANA
TANACETIN
TANACETYL
TANACH
TANADAR
TANAGER
TANAGRINE
TANAK
TANAN
TANBARK
TANBUR
TANCEL
TANDAN
TANDAVA
TANDEM
TANDEMER
TANDEMIST
TANDEMIZE
TANDEMWISE
TANDLE
TANDSTICKA
TANEGA
TANEKAHA
TANG
TANGA
TANGALUNG
TANGANTANGAN
TANGE
TANGED
TANGEITE
TANGELO
TANGELOS
TANGENCE
TANGENCIES
TANGENCY
TANGENT
TANGENTAL
TANGENTALLY
TANGENTIAL
TANGENTIALLY
TANGENTLY
TANGERINE
TANGFISH
TANGFISHES
TANGHAN
TANGHIN
TANGHININ
TANGI
TANGIBILITY
TANGIBLE
TANGIBLENESS
TANGIBLY
TANGIE
TANGIER
TANGIEST
TANGILIN
TANGING
TANGKA
TANGLAD
TANGLE
TANGLEBERRIES
TANGLEBERRY
TANGLED
TANGLEFISH
TANGLEFISHES
TANGLEFOOT
TANGLEHEAD
TANGLER
TANGLEROOT
TANGLING
TANGLY
TANGO
TANGOS
TANGRAM
TANGUE
TANGUILE
TANGUIN
TANGUM
TANGUN
TANGY
TANHA
TANIA
TANICA
TANIER
TANIKO
TANIST
TANISTIC
TANISTRY
TANISTSHIP
TANJIB
TANJONG
TANK
TANKA
TANKAGE
TANKAH
TANKARD
TANKED
TANKER
TANKERABOGUS
TANKETTE
TANKFUL

TANKIE
TANKING
TANKLE
TANKODROME
TANKS
TANLING
TANNA
TANNADAR
TANNAGE
TANNAIC
TANNAIM
TANNAITIC
TANNAKIN
TANNASE
TANNATE
TANNED
TANNER
TANNERIES
TANNERY
TANNIC
TANNID
TANNIDE
TANNIFEROUS
TANNIGEN
TANNIN
TANNINED
TANNING
TANNOGEN
TANNOID
TANNOMETER
TANNY
TANNYL
TANOA
TANQUAM
TANQUEN
TANREC
TANSEL
TANSEY
TANSIES
TANSY
TANTA
TANTADLIN
TANTALATE
TANTALIC
TANTALISE
TANTALITE
TANTALIZE
TANTALIZED
TANTALIZER
TANTALIZING
TANTALUM
TANTAMOUNT
TANTARA
TANTARARA
TANTI
TANTIEME
TANTIVIES
TANTIVY
TANTLE
TANTO
TANTRA
TANTRIC
TANTRIK
TANTRISM
TANTRIST
TANTRUM
TANTUM
TANWOOD
TANYA
TANYSTOME
TAO
TAOS
TAOTAI
TAOYIN
TAP
TAPA
TAPACULO
TAPADERA
TAPADERO
TAPALO
TAPALOS
TAPAMAKER
TAPAMAKING
TAPAS
TAPASVI
TAPE
TAPED
TAPELESS
TAPELINE
TAPEMAN
TAPEMEN
TAPEN
TAPER
TAPERED
TAPERER
TAPERING
TAPERINGLY
TAPERY
TAPESIUM
TAPESTER
TAPESTRIED
TAPESTRIES
TAPESTRY
TAPESTRYING
TAPET
TAPETA
TAPETAL
TAPETI
TAPETIS
TAPETUM
TAPEWORM
TAPHEPHOBIA
TAPHOLE
TAPHOUSE
TAPIA
TAPIDERO
TAPING
TAPINOSIS
TAPIOCA
TAPIR
TAPIRIDIAN
TAPIRINE
TAPIROID
TAPIRS
TAPIS
TAPISER
TAPISM
TAPISSERIE
TAPISSIER
TAPIST
TAPIT
TAPLASH
TAPLET
TAPLING
TAPNET
TAPOA
TAPOTEMENT
TAPOUN
TAPPA
TAPPABLE
TAPPABLENESS
TAPPALL
TAPPAUL
TAPPED
TAPPEN
TAPPER
TAPPET
TAPPING
TAPPISH
TAPPIT
TAPPOON
TAPROOM
TAPROOT
TAPROOTED
TAPS
TAPSALTEERIE
TAPSMAN
TAPSTER
TAPSTRESS
TAPT
TAPU
TAPUL
TAPWORT
TAQIYA
TAQLID
TAR
TARA
TARABOOKA
TARADIDDLE
TARAF
TARAFDAR
TARAGE
TARAIRI
TARAKIHI
TARAMELLITE
TARAN
TARAND
TARANTARIZE
TARANTAS
TARANTASS
TARANTELLA
TARANTELLE
TARANTISM
TARANTIST
TARANTULA
TARANTULAE
TARANTULAR
TARANTULAS
TARANTULATED
TARANTULID
TARANTULITE
TARANTULOUS
TARASSIS
TARATA
TARATAH
TARATANTARA
TARAU
TARAXACUM
TARBAGAN
TARBET
TARBLE
TARBOARD
TARBOOSH
TARBOX
TARBOY
TARBRUSH
TARBUSH
TARBUTTITE
TARCEL
TARCHON
TARDAMENTE
TARDANDO
TARDANT
TARDE
TARDIER
TARDIEST
TARDIGRADE
TARDILOQUENT
TARDILOQUOUS
TARDILOQUY
TARDILY
TARDINESS
TARDITY
TARDIVE
TARDLE
TARDO
TARDY
TARE
TAREA
TARED
TAREFA
TAREFITCH
TARENTE
TARENTISM
TARES
TARFA
TARFE
TARFLOWER
TARGE
TARGED
TARGEMAN
TARGER
TARGET
TARGETED
TARGETEER
TARGETIER
TARGETING
TARGING
TARHOOD
TARI
TARIE
TARIFF
TARIFFED
TARIFFING
TARIFFIST
TARIFFITE
TARIFFIZE
TARIN
TARING
TARIQA
TARIQAT
TARIRIC
TARIRINIC
TARISH
TARKASHI
TARKEEAN
TARKHAN
TARLATAN
TARLATANED
TARLEATHER
TARLETAN
TARLIES
TARLTONIZE
TARMAC
TARMOSINED
TARN
TARNAL
TARNALLY
TARNATION
TARNISH
TARNISHABLE
TARNISHED
TARNISHER
TARNISHING
TARO
TAROCCO
TAROGATO
TAROPATCH
TAROS
TAROT
TARP
TARPAN
TARPAPER
TARPAULIAN
TARPAULIN
TARPON
TARPONS
TARPOT
TARR
TARRABA
TARRACK
TARRADIDDLE
TARRADIDDLER
TARRAGON
TARRAGONA
TARRASS
TARRED
TARRER
TARRI
TARRIANCE
TARRIED
TARRIER
TARRIEST
TARRILY
TARRINESS
TARRING
TARRISH
TARROCK
TARROW
TARRY
TARRYING
TARRYINGLY
TARRYINGNESS
TARS
TARSAL
TARSALE
TARSALIA
TARSE
TARSECTOMY
TARSI
TARSIA
TARSIER
TARSIOID
TARSO
TARSOME
TARSOMETATARSUS
TARSONEMID
TARSOTARSAL
TARSUS
TART
TARTAGO
TARTAN
TARTANA
TARTAR
TARTAREOUS
TARTARET
TARTARIC
TARTARIN
TARTARINE
TARTARISH
TARTARIZE
TARTARIZED
TARTARIZING
TARTARLY
TARTAROUS
TARTARUM
TARTE
TARTEN
TARTINE
TARTISH
TARTISHLY
TARTLE
TARTLET
TARTLY
TARTNESS
TARTRAMATE
TARTRAMID
TARTRAMIDE
TARTRATE
TARTRATED
TARTRAZIN
TARTRAZINE
TARTRAZINIC
TARTRO
TARTRONATE
TARTRONIC
TARTRONYL
TARTROUS
TARTRYL
TARTRYLIC
TARTUFE
TARTUFERY
TARTUFFE
TARTUFFERY
TARTUFFIAN

TARTUFFISH
TARTUFFISHLY
TARTUFFISM
TARTUFIAN
TARTUFISH
TARTUFISHLY
TARTUFISM
TARTWOMAN
TARTWOMEN
TARVE
TARWEED
TARWHINE
TARWOOD
TARZAN
TASAJILLO
TASAJO
TASBIH
TASCAL
TASCO
TASH
TASHERIFF
TASHIE
TASHLIK
TASHREEF
TASHRIF
TASIMETER
TASIMETRIC
TASIMETRY
TASK
TASKAGE
TASKED
TASKER
TASKING
TASKIT
TASKMASTER
TASKMISTRESS
TASKSETTER
TASKSETTING
TASKWORK
TASMANITE
TASS
TASSARD
TASSE
TASSEL
TASSELED
TASSELER
TASSELFISH
TASSELING
TASSELLED
TASSELLUS
TASSELS
TASSELY
TASSES
TASSET
TASSIE
TASSOO
TASTABLE
TASTE
TASTED
TASTEFUL
TASTEFULLY
TASTEFULNESS
TASTELESS
TASTELESSLY
TASTEN
TASTER
TASTIER
TASTIEST
TASTILY
TASTINESS
TASTING
TASTINGLY
TASTO
TASTY
TASU
TAT
TATA
TATAMI
TATAUPA
TATBEB
TATCH
TATCHY
TATE
TATER
TATH
TATHATA
TATINEK
TATLER
TATMJOLK
TATOU
TATOUAY
TATPURUSHA
TATS
TATSMAN
TATT
TATTED
TATTER
TATTERED
TATTEREDLY
TATTEREDNESS
TATTERING
TATTERLY
TATTERSALL
TATTERWAG
TATTERWALLOP
TATTERY
TATTIED
TATTIES
TATTING
TATTLE
TATTLED
TATTLER
TATTLERY
TATTLETALE
TATTLING
TATTLINGLY
TATTOO
TATTOOAGE
TATTOOED
TATTOOER
TATTOOING
TATTOOIST
TATTOOMENT
TATTOOS
TATTVA
TATTY
TATU
TATUASU
TATUKIRA
TAU
TAUGA
TAUGHT
TAULA
TAULCH
TAUM
TAUN
TAUNT
TAUNTED
TAUNTER
TAUNTING
TAUNTINGLY
TAUNTINGNESS
TAUNTRESS
TAUPE
TAUPO
TAUPOU
TAURANGA
TAUREAN
TAURIAN
TAURIC
TAURICIDE
TAURICORNOUS
TAURIFEROUS
TAURIFORM
TAURIN
TAURINE
TAURITE
TAUROBOLIA
TAUROBOLIUM
TAUROCHOLATE
TAUROCHOLIC
TAUROCOL
TAUROCOLLA
TAURODONT
TAUROESQUE
TAUROLATRY
TAUROMACHIA
TAUROMACHIAN
TAUROMACHIC
TAUROMACHY
TAUROMORPHIC
TAUROPHILE
TAUROPHOBE
TAURYL
TAUT
TAUTAUG
TAUTED
TAUTEGORICAL
TAUTEGORY
TAUTEN
TAUTIRITE
TAUTLY
TAUTNESS
TAUTOCHRONE
TAUTOCHRONISM
TAUTOCHRONOUS
TAUTOG
TAUTOLOGIC
TAUTOLOGIES
TAUTOLOGISM
TAUTOLOGIST
TAUTOLOGIZE
TAUTOLOGIZED
TAUTOLOGIZER
TAUTOLOGIZING
TAUTOLOGY
TAUTOMER
TAUTOMERAL
TAUTOMERIC
TAUTOMERISM
TAUTOMERIZE
TAUTOMERS
TAUTOMETER
TAUTOMETRIC
TAUTONYM
TAUTONYMIC
TAUTONYMIES
TAUTONYMY
TAUTOOUSIAN
TAUTOPHONIC
TAUTOPHONY
TAUTOPODIC
TAUTOPODY
TAUTOTYPE
TAUTOZONAL
TAV
TAVE
TAVELL
TAVER
TAVERN
TAVERNER
TAVERNIZE
TAVERNLY
TAVERNOUS
TAVERNRY
TAVERS
TAVERT
TAVESTOCK
TAVISTOCKITE
TAVOLA
TAVOLATITE
TAVOY
TAW
TAWA
TAWDERED
TAWDRIER
TAWDRIES
TAWDRIEST
TAWDRILY
TAWDRINESS
TAWDRY
TAWED
TAWER
TAWERY
TAWHAI
TAWHID
TAWIE
TAWING
TAWITE
TAWKEE
TAWKIN
TAWN
TAWNEY
TAWNIE
TAWNIER
TAWNIEST
TAWNINESS
TAWNY
TAWPIE
TAWPY
TAWS
TAWSE
TAX
TAXABILITY
TAXABLE
TAXABLENESS
TAXABLY
TAXACEOUS
TAXAMETER
TAXASPIDEAN
TAXATION
TAXATIONAL
TAXATIVE
TAXATIVELY
TAXATOR
TAXEATER
TAXEATING
TAXED
TAXEL
TAXEME
TAXEOPOD
TAXEOPODOUS
TAXEOPODY
TAXER
TAXES
TAXGATHERER
TAXGATHERING
TAXI
TAXIARCH
TAXIAUTO
TAXIBUS
TAXICAB
TAXIDERMAL
TAXIDERMIC
TAXIDERMIST
TAXIDERMIZE
TAXIDERMY
TAXIED
TAXIMAN
TAXIMETER
TAXIMETERED
TAXINE
TAXING
TAXINGLY
TAXIPLANE
TAXIS
TAXITE
TAXITIC
TAXMAN
TAXODONT
TAXOLOGY
TAXOMETER
TAXON
TAXONOMER
TAXONOMIC
TAXONOMICAL
TAXONOMIST
TAXONOMY
TAXOR
TAXPAID
TAXPAYER
TAXPAYING
TAXY
TAXYING
TAY
TAYASSUID
TAYER
TAYIR
TAYLORITE
TAYRA
TAYSAAM
TAZEEA
TAZIA
TAZZA
TCH
TCHA
TCHAI
TCHAPAN
TCHAST
TCHE
TCHEIREK
TCHERVONETS
TCHERVONETZ
TCHI
TCHICK
TCHIN
TCHINCOU
TCHU
TCK
TE
TEA
TEABERRIES
TEABERRY
TEABOARD
TEABOX
TEABOY
TEACAKE
TEACART
TEACH
TEACHABILITY
TEACHABLE
TEACHABLENESS
TEACHABLY
TEACHE
TEACHED
TEACHER
TEACHERAGE
TEACHERESS
TEACHERLY
TEACHERY
TEACHES
TEACHING
TEACHINGLY
TEACHLESS
TEACHY
TEACUP
TEACUPFUL
TEACUPFULS
TEADISH
TEAED
TEAER
TEAEY
TEAGARDENY
TEAGLE
TEAHOUSE

TEAING
TEAK
TEAKETTLE
TEAKWOOD
TEAL
TEALEAFY
TEALLITE
TEALS
TEAM
TEAMAKER
TEAMAKING
TEAMAN
TEAMED
TEAMEO
TEAMING
TEAMLAND
TEAMMAN
TEAMMATE
TEAMSTER
TEAMWORK
TEAN
TEANAL
TEAP
TEAPOT
TEAPOY
TEAR
TEARAGE
TEARCAT
TEARDOWN
TEARDROP
TEARER
TEARFUL
TEARFULLY
TEARFULNESS
TEARIER
TEARIEST
TEARING
TEARLESS
TEARLESSLY
TEARLESSNESS
TEAROOM
TEARPIT
TEARS
TEARSTAIN
TEART
TEARTHUMB
TEARY
TEASE
TEASED
TEASEHOLE
TEASEL
TEASELED
TEASELER
TEASELING
TEASELLED
TEASELLER
TEASELLING
TEASELS
TEASELWORT
TEASER
TEASHOP
TEASING
TEASINGLY
TEASLE
TEASPOON
TEASPOONFUL
TEASPOONFULS
TEASY
TEAT
TEATASTER
TEATED
TEATFISH
TEATIME
TEATLING
TEATMAN
TEATY
TEAVE
TEAZE
TEAZEL
TEAZLE
TEBBAD
TEBELDI
TEC
TECA
TECALI
TECH
TECHIER
TECHIEST
TECHNE
TECHNETIUM
TECHNIC
TECHNICA
TECHNICAL
TECHNICALISM
TECHNICALIST
TECHNICALITIES
TECHNICALITY
TECHNICALIZE
TECHNICALLY
TECHNICIAN
TECHNICISM
TECHNICIST
TECHNICOLOGY
TECHNICOLOR
TECHNICON
TECHNICS
TECHNIPHONE
TECHNIQUE
TECHNISM
TECHNOCAUSIS
TECHNOCRACIES
TECHNOCRACY
TECHNOCRAT
TECHNOCRATIC
TECHNOGRAPHY
TECHNOLITHIC
TECHNOLOGIC
TECHNOLOGICAL
TECHNOLOGIES
TECHNOLOGIST
TECHNOLOGY
TECHNONOMY
TECHOUS
TECHY
TECK
TECOMIN
TECON
TECT
TECTAL
TECTIBRANCH
TECTIFORM
TECTOCEPHALY
TECTOLOGY
TECTONIC
TECTONICS
TECTORIAL
TECTORIUM
TECTOSPHERE
TECTOSPINAL
TECTRICES
TECTRICIAL
TECTRIX
TECTUM
TECTURE
TECUM
TED
TEDDED
TEDDER
TEDDIES
TEDDING
TEDDY
TEDESCA
TEDESCHE
TEDESCHI
TEDESCO
TEDGE
TEDIOSITY
TEDIOUS
TEDIOUSLY
TEDIOUSNESS
TEDIOUSOME
TEDISOME
TEDIUM
TEE
TEECALL
TEED
TEEDLE
TEEING
TEEKA
TEEL
TEEM
TEEMED
TEEMER
TEEMFUL
TEEMFULNESS
TEEMING
TEEMINGLY
TEEMINGNESS
TEEMLESS
TEEMS
TEEN
TEENAGER
TEENET
TEENFUL
TEENFULLY
TEENIER
TEENIEST
TEENS
TEENSY
TEENY
TEENYBOPPER
TEEPEE
TEER
TEES
TEEST
TEET
TEETAN
TEETEE
TEETER
TEETERBOARD
TEETERER
TEETERTAIL
TEETH
TEETHE
TEETHED
TEETHIER
TEETHIEST
TEETHING
TEETHLESS
TEETHRIDGE
TEETHY
TEETING
TEETOTAL
TEETOTALED
TEETOTALER
TEETOTALING
TEETOTALISM
TEETOTALIST
TEETOTALLED
TEETOTALLER
TEETOTALLING
TEETOTALLY
TEETOTUM
TEETOTUMISM
TEETOTUMIZE
TEETSOOK
TEEWHAAP
TEFF
TEFILLIN
TEG
TEGG
TEGMEN
TEGMENT
TEGMENTA
TEGMENTAL
TEGMENTUM
TEGMINA
TEGMINAL
TEGS
TEGU
TEGUA
TEGUEXIN
TEGULA
TEGULAE
TEGULAR
TEGULARLY
TEGULATED
TEGUMEN
TEGUMENT
TEGUMENTAL
TEGUMENTARY
TEGURIA
TEGURIUM
TEHOO
TEHSIL
TEICHER
TEIGLACH
TEIGLECH
TEIHTE
TEIID
TEIL
TEIND
TEINDABLE
TEINDER
TEINLAND
TEINOSCOPE
TEIOID
TEJANO
TEJON
TEJU
TEK
TEKE
TEKIAH
TEKKE
TEKNONYMOUS
TEKNONYMY
TEKTITE
TEKYA
TEL
TELA
TELACOUSTIC
TELAE
TELAESTHESIA
TELAKUCHA
TELAMON
TELAMONES
TELANGIOSIS
TELAR
TELARIAN
TELARLY
TELAUTOGRAM
TELAUTOGRAPH
TELD
TELEBLEM
TELECAST
TELECASTED
TELECASTING
TELECHEMIC
TELECODE
TELEDU
TELEGA
TELEGNOSIS
TELEGNOSTIC
TELEGONIC
TELEGONOUS
TELEGONY
TELEGRAF
TELEGRAM
TELEGRAMMIC
TELEGRAPH
TELEGRAPHED
TELEGRAPHEME
TELEGRAPHER
TELEGRAPHESE
TELEGRAPHIC
TELEGRAPHING
TELEGRAPHIST
TELEGRAPHONE
TELEGRAPHY
TELEIANTHOUS
TELEIOSIS
TELEKINESIS
TELEKINETIC
TELELECTRIC
TELEMARK
TELEMECHANIC
TELEMETER
TELEMETERING
TELEMETRIC
TELEMETRICAL
TELEMETRIST
TELEMETRY
TELEMOTOR
TELENCEPHALON
TELENERGIC
TELENERGY
TELENEURITE
TELENEURON
TELENGISCOPE
TELEODONT
TELEOLOGIC
TELEOLOGICAL
TELEOLOGIES
TELEOLOGISM
TELEOLOGIST
TELEOLOGY
TELEOPHOBIA
TELEOPHORE
TELEOPHYTE
TELEOPTILE
TELEORGANIC
TELEOSAUR
TELEOST
TELEOSTEAN
TELEOSTEOUS
TELEOSTOME
TELEOSTOMOUS
TELEOZOIC
TELEOZOON
TELEPATH
TELEPATHIC
TELEPATHIST
TELEPATHIZE
TELEPATHY
TELEPHEME
TELEPHONE
TELEPHONED
TELEPHONER
TELEPHONIC
TELEPHONING
TELEPHONIST
TELEPHONY
TELEPHOTE
TELEPHOTO
TELEPLASM
TELEPLASMIC
TELEPLASTIC
TELEPOST
TELEPRINTER
TELEPROMPTER
TELERAN
TELERGIC
TELERGICAL
TELERGICALLY
TELERGY

TELESCOPE
TELESCOPED
TELESCOPIC
TELESCOPICAL
TELESCOPING
TELESCOPIST
TELESCOPY
TELESCRIBE
TELESCRIPT
TELESCRIPTOR
TELESEISM
TELESEISMIC
TELESEME
TELESIA
TELESIS
TELESIURGIC
TELESM
TELESMATIC
TELESMATICAL
TELESMETER
TELESOMATIC
TELESTERION
TELESTHESIA
TELESTHETIC
TELESTIC
TELESTICH
TELETACTILE
TELETACTOR
TELETAPE
TELETHERAPY
TELETHON
TELETYPE
TELETYPED
TELETYPER
TELETYPING
TELEUTO
TELEUTOSORUS
TELEUTOSPORE
TELEVIEW
TELEVIEWER
TELEVISE
TELEVISED
TELEVISING
TELEVISION
TELEVISIONAL
TELEVISOR
TELEVISUAL
TELEVOCAL
TELEVOX
TELEX
TELFER
TELFERAGE
TELFORD
TELFORDIZE
TELFORDIZED
TELFORDIZING
TELHARMONIC
TELHARMONIUM
TELHARMONY
TELI
TELIA
TELIAL
TELIC
TELICAL
TELICALLY
TELIFEROUS
TELIOSPORE
TELIOSPORIC
TELIOSTAGE
TELIUM
TELL
TELLABLE
TELLACH
TELLE
TELLER
TELLERSHIP
TELLIES
TELLIGRAPH
TELLINACEAN
TELLINACEOUS
TELLING
TELLINGLY
TELLINOID
TELLSOME
TELLTALE
TELLTALELY
TELLTRUTH
TELLURAL
TELLURATE
TELLURETED
TELLURETHYL
TELLURETTED
TELLURIAN
TELLURIC
TELLURIDE
TELLURION
TELLURISM
TELLURIST
TELLURITE
TELLURIUM
TELLURIZE
TELLURIZED
TELLURIZING
TELLURONIUM
TELLUROUS
TELLY
TELMATOLOGY
TELOBLAST
TELOBLASTIC
TELODENDRIA
TELODENDRION
TELODYNAMIC
TELOKINESIS
TELOLECITHAL
TELOLEMMA
TELOLEMMATA
TELOMITIC
TELONISM
TELOPHASE
TELOPSIS
TELOPTIC
TELOS
TELOSYNAPSIS
TELOSYNAPTIC
TELOTROCH
TELOTROCHA
TELOTROCHAL
TELOTROCHOUS
TELOTYPE
TELPHER
TELPHERAGE
TELPHERIC
TELPHERMAN
TELPHERMEN
TELPHERWAY
TELSON
TELSONIC
TELURGY
TELYN
TEMA
TEMACHA
TEMADAU
TEMALACATL
TEMAN
TEMBE
TEMBEITERA
TEMBETA
TEMBETARA
TEMBLOR
TEMBLORES
TEMBLORS
TEME
TEMENE
TEMENOS
TEMERARIOUS
TEMERATE
TEMERITOUS
TEMERITY
TEMEROUS
TEMEROUSLY
TEMEROUSNESS
TEMESCAL
TEMIAK
TEMIN
TEMP
TEMPER
TEMPERA
TEMPERABLE
TEMPERABLY
TEMPERALITY
TEMPERAMENT
TEMPERAMENTAL
TEMPERANCE
TEMPERATE
TEMPERATELY
TEMPERATIVE
TEMPERATURE
TEMPERED
TEMPEREDLY
TEMPEREDNESS
TEMPERER
TEMPERING
TEMPERSOME
TEMPERY
TEMPEST
TEMPESTICAL
TEMPESTIVE
TEMPESTIVELY
TEMPESTIVITY
TEMPESTUOUS
TEMPESTY
TEMPETE
TEMPI
TEMPLAR
TEMPLARDOM
TEMPLARISM
TEMPLARY
TEMPLATE
TEMPLATER
TEMPLE
TEMPLED
TEMPLES
TEMPLET
TEMPLIZE
TEMPLUM
TEMPO
TEMPORAL
TEMPORALE
TEMPORALIS
TEMPORALISM
TEMPORALIST
TEMPORALITIES
TEMPORALITY
TEMPORALIZE
TEMPORALLY
TEMPORALTIES
TEMPORALTY
TEMPORANEOUS
TEMPORARIES
TEMPORARILY
TEMPORARY
TEMPORATOR
TEMPORE
TEMPORISE
TEMPORIZE
TEMPORIZED
TEMPORIZER
TEMPORIZING
TEMPOS
TEMPRE
TEMPS
TEMPT
TEMPTABLE
TEMPTATION
TEMPTATIONAL
TEMPTATIOUS
TEMPTATORY
TEMPTED
TEMPTER
TEMPTING
TEMPTINGLY
TEMPTINGNESS
TEMPTRESS
TEMPTSOME
TEMPURA
TEMPUS
TEMS
TEMSE
TEMSEBREAD
TEMSELOAF
TEMULENCE
TEMULENCY
TEMULENT
TEMULENTIVE
TEMULENTLY
TEN
TENA
TENABILITY
TENABLE
TENABLENESS
TENABLY
TENACE
TENACIOUS
TENACIOUSLY
TENACIOUSNESS
TENACITY
TENACLE
TENACULA
TENACULUM
TENACY
TENAI
TENAIL
TENAILLE
TENAILLON
TENALGIA
TENANCIES
TENANCY
TENANT
TENANTABLE
TENANTED
TENANTER
TENANTING
TENANTLESS
TENANTLIKE
TENANTRIES
TENANTRY
TENANTS
TENANTSHIP
TENCH
TENCHES
TENCHWEED
TEND
TENDANCE
TENDED
TENDEJON
TENDENCE
TENDENCIES
TENDENCIOUS
TENDENCY
TENDENT
TENDENTIAL
TENDENTIOUS
TENDER
TENDEREE
TENDERER
TENDEREST
TENDERFEET
TENDERFOOT
TENDERFUL
TENDERFULLY
TENDERHEART
TENDERHEARTED
TENDERIZE
TENDERIZED
TENDERIZER
TENDERIZING
TENDERLING
TENDERLOIN
TENDERLY
TENDERNESS
TENDERSOME
TENDICLE
TENDIDO
TENDINAL
TENDINEAL
TENDING
TENDINGLY
TENDINOUS
TENDMENT
TENDO
TENDOMUCOID
TENDON
TENDONOUS
TENDONS
TENDOOR
TENDOPLASTY
TENDOTOME
TENDOTOMY
TENDOUR
TENDRAC
TENDRE
TENDREL
TENDRESSE
TENDRIL
TENDRILED
TENDRILLAR
TENDRILLED
TENDRILOUS
TENDRON
TENDRY
TENEBRA
TENEBRES
TENEBRIFIC
TENEBRION
TENEBRIONID
TENEBRIOUS
TENEBRIOUSLY
TENEBRITY
TENEBROSE
TENEBROSI
TENEBROSITY
TENEBROUS
TENEBROUSLY
TENEMENT
TENEMENTAL
TENEMENTARY
TENEMENTER
TENEMENTIZE
TENENDA
TENENDAS
TENENDUM
TENENT
TENER
TENERAL
TENERAMENTE
TENERITY
TENESMIC
TENESMUS
TENET
TENEZ
TENFOLD
TENFOLDNESS
TENG
TENGERE
TENGERITE

TENGU
TENIA
TENIACIDAL
TENIACIDE
TENIAFUGE
TENIASIS
TENIENTE
TENIO
TENMANTALE
TENNANTITE
TENNE
TENNER
TENNIS
TENNISY
TENNU
TENON
TENONECTOMY
TENONED
TENONER
TENONING
TENONITIS
TENONTOLOGY
TENONTOTOMY
TENOR
TENORE
TENORINO
TENORIST
TENORITE
TENOROON
TENORRHAPHIES
TENORRHAPHY
TENOSITIS
TENOTOMIES
TENOTOMIST
TENOTOMIZE
TENOTOMY
TENPENCE
TENPENNY
TENPIN
TENPINS
TENPOUNDER
TENREC
TENS
TENSAS
TENSAW
TENSE
TENSED
TENSELY
TENSENESS
TENSER
TENSES
TENSEST
TENSIBILITY
TENSIBLE
TENSIBLENESS
TENSIBLY
TENSIFY
TENSILE
TENSILELY
TENSILENESS
TENSILITY
TENSIMETER
TENSING
TENSIOMETER
TENSION
TENSIONAL
TENSIONED
TENSIONING
TENSITY
TENSIVE
TENSOME
TENSON
TENSOR
TENSORSHIP
TENSURE
TENT
TENTABILITY
TENTACLE
TENTACLED
TENTACULA
TENTACULAR
TENTACULATE
TENTACULATED
TENTACULITE
TENTACULOID
TENTACULUM
TENTAGE
TENTAMEN
TENTATION
TENTATIVE
TENTATIVELY
TENTED
TENTER
TENTERBELLY
TENTERER
TENTERHOOK
TENTFUL
TENTH
TENTHLY
TENTHMETER
TENTHMETRE
TENTHREDINID
TENTICLE
TENTIE
TENTIFORM
TENTIGO
TENTILLA
TENTILLUM
TENTILY
TENTLESS
TENTLET
TENTMAKER
TENTMAKING
TENTMATE
TENTOR
TENTORIAL
TENTORIUM
TENTORY
TENTS
TENTURE
TENTWORK
TENTWORT
TENTY
TENUATE
TENUE
TENUES
TENUIFLOROUS
TENUIFOLIOUS
TENUIROSTER
TENUIROSTRAL
TENUIS
TENUISTRIATE
TENUITY
TENUOUS
TENUOUSLY
TENUOUSNESS
TENURE
TENURIAL
TENURIALLY
TENURY
TENUTO
TENZON
TEOCALLI
TEOCALLIS
TEOPAN
TEOSINTE
TEPACHE
TEPAL
TEPARIES
TEPARY
TEPEE
TEPEFACTION
TEPEFIED
TEPEFY
TEPEFYING
TEPETATE
TEPHILLIN
TEPHRAMANCY
TEPHRITE
TEPHRITIC
TEPHROITE
TEPHROSIS
TEPID
TEPIDARIA
TEPIDARIUM
TEPIDITY
TEPIDLY
TEPIDNESS
TEPONAZTLI
TEPOR
TEQUILA
TEQUILLA
TER
TERA
TERAGLIN
TERAKIHI
TERAMORPHOUS
TERAP
TERAPH
TERAPHIM
TERAS
TERATA
TERATICAL
TERATISM
TERATOGENIC
TERATOGENY
TERATOID
TERATOLOGIC
TERATOLOGIST
TERATOLOGY
TERATOMA
TERATOMAS
TERATOMATA
TERATOMATOUS
TERATOSCOPY
TERATOSIS
TERBIA
TERBIC
TERBIUM
TERCE
TERCEL
TERCELET
TERCENTENARIES
TERCENTENARY
TERCER
TERCERON
TERCET
TERCHLORIDE
TERCIA
TERCINE
TERCIO
TERDIURNAL
TEREBATE
TEREBELLA
TEREBELLID
TEREBELLOID
TEREBELLUM
TEREBENE
TEREBENTHENE
TEREBIC
TEREBINTH
TEREBINTHIC
TEREBINTHINA
TEREBINTHINE
TEREBRA
TEREBRAE
TEREBRAL
TEREBRANT
TEREBRAS
TEREBRATE
TEREBRATION
TEREBRATULAR
TEREBRATULID
TEREDINES
TEREDO
TEREDOS
TEREK
TEREPHAH
TEREPHTHALLIC
TERETE
TERETIAL
TERETISM
TEREU
TERFA
TERFEZ
TERGA
TERGAL
TERGANT
TERGEMINAL
TERGEMINATE
TERGIFEROUS
TERGITE
TERGITIC
TERGIVERSANT
TERGIVERSATE
TERGIVERSATED
TERGIVERSATING
TERGIVERSATION
TERGIVERSE
TERGOLATERAL
TERGUM
TERIN
TERLINGUAITE
TERM
TERMA
TERMAGANCY
TERMAGANT
TERMAGANTISH
TERMAGANTISM
TERMAGANTLY
TERMAGE
TERMAL
TERMATIC
TERMED
TERMEN
TERMER
TERMIN
TERMINABLE
TERMINABLY
TERMINAL
TERMINALLY
TERMINANT
TERMINATE
TERMINATED
TERMINATING
TERMINATION
TERMINATIVE
TERMINATOR
TERMINATORY
TERMINE
TERMINER
TERMING
TERMINI
TERMININE
TERMINISM
TERMINIST
TERMINISTIC
TERMINIZE
TERMINO
TERMINOLOGIES
TERMINOLOGY
TERMINUS
TERMINUSES
TERMITAL
TERMITARIA
TERMITARIUM
TERMITARY
TERMITE
TERMITIC
TERMITOPHILE
TERMLESS
TERMLY
TERMON
TERMOR
TERMS
TERMTIME
TERN
TERNA
TERNAL
TERNAR
TERNARIANT
TERNARIES
TERNARIOUS
TERNARY
TERNATE
TERNATELY
TERNE
TERNED
TERNEPLATE
TERNER
TERNERY
TERNING
TERNION
TERNLET
TERNO
TERP
TERPADIENE
TERPANE
TERPEN
TERPENE
TERPHENYL
TERPILENE
TERPINENE
TERPINEOL
TERPINOL
TERPINOLENE
TERPODION
TERRA
TERRACE
TERRACED
TERRACEOUS
TERRACER
TERRACETTE
TERRACEWORK
TERRACIFORM
TERRACING
TERRAEFILIAL
TERRAEFILIAN
TERRAGE
TERRAIN
TERRAL
TERRAMARA
TERRAMARE
TERRAMYCIN
TERRANE
TERRANEAN
TERRANEOUS
TERRAPIN
TERRAQUEAN
TERRAQUEOUS
TERRAR
TERRARIA
TERRARIUM
TERRARIUMS
TERRAS
TERRASSE
TERRAZZO
TERRE
TERREEN
TERREITY
TERRELLA
TERREMOTIVE
TERRENE
TERRENELY
TERRENENESS

TERRENO
TERREOUS
TERREPLEIN
TERRESTRIAL
TERRESTRIALLY
TERRESTRIFY
TERRET
TERRIBLE
TERRIBLENESS
TERRIBLY
TERRICOLINE
TERRICOLIST
TERRICOLOUS
TERRIE
TERRIER
TERRIES
TERRIFIC
TERRIFICALLY
TERRIFICLY
TERRIFICNESS
TERRIFIED
TERRIFIER
TERRIFY
TERRIFYING
TERRIFYINGLY
TERRIGENE
TERRIGENOUS
TERRINE
TERRITORIAL
TERRITORIALISM
TERRITORIAN
TERRITORIED
TERRITORIES
TERRITORY
TERRON
TERROR
TERRORFUL
TERRORIFIC
TERRORISE
TERRORISM
TERRORIST
TERRORISTIC
TERRORIZE
TERRORIZED
TERRORIZER
TERRORIZING
TERRORSOME
TERRY
TERSE
TERSELY
TERSENESS
TERSER
TERSEST
TERSION
TERSULFID
TERSULFIDE
TERSULPHATE
TERSULPHID
TERSULPHIDE
TERSULPHURET
TERTIA
TERTIAL
TERTIAN
TERTIANA
TERTIANSHIP
TERTIARIES
TERTIARY
TERTIATE
TERTIO
TERTON
TERTULIA
TERUAH
TERUNCIUS
TERUTERO
TERUTERU
TERVALENCE
TERVALENCY
TERVALENT
TERVARIANT
TERVE
TERVEE
TERZET
TERZETTO
TERZETTOS
TERZINA
TERZIO
TERZO
TESACK
TESCARIA
TESCHENITE
TESKERIA
TESSARA
TESSARACE
TESSARADECAD
TESSARAGLOT
TESSEL
TESSELLA
TESSELLAE
TESSELLAR
TESSELLATE
TESSELLATED
TESSELLATING
TESSELLATION
TESSERA
TESSERACT
TESSERAE
TESSERAL
TESSERARIAN
TESSERATOMIC
TESSERATOMY
TESSITURA
TESSULAR
TEST
TESTA
TESTABLE
TESTACEAN
TESTACEOLOGY
TESTACEOUS
TESTACY
TESTAE
TESTAMENT
TESTAMENTA
TESTAMENTAL
TESTAMENTARY
TESTAMENTATE
TESTAMENTUM
TESTAMUR
TESTAO
TESTAR
TESTATA
TESTATE
TESTATION
TESTATOR
TESTATORY
TESTATRICES
TESTATRIX
TESTATUM
TESTE
TESTED
TESTEE
TESTER
TESTES
TESTICLE
TESTICOND
TESTICULAR
TESTICULATE
TESTICULATED
TESTIER
TESTIERE
TESTIEST
TESTIFICATE
TESTIFICATOR
TESTIFIED
TESTIFIER
TESTIFY
TESTIFYING
TESTIMONIA
TESTIMONIAL
TESTIMONIES
TESTIMONIUM
TESTIMONY
TESTINESS
TESTING
TESTIS
TESTO
TESTON
TESTONE
TESTOON
TESTOR
TESTOSTERONE
TESTRIL
TESTS
TESTUDINAL
TESTUDINATE
TESTUDINEAL
TESTUDINEOUS
TESTUDINES
TESTUDINOUS
TESTUDO
TESTULE
TESTY
TESVINO
TETANIA
TETANIC
TETANICAL
TETANICALLY
TETANIFORM
TETANIGENOUS
TETANILLA
TETANINE
TETANISM
TETANIZATION
TETANIZE
TETANIZED
TETANIZING
TETANOID
TETANOLYSIN
TETANOMOTOR
TETANUS
TETANY
TETARD
TETARTOCONE
TETARTOCONID
TETARTOID
TETCH
TETCHIER
TETCHIEST
TETCHILY
TETCHINESS
TETCHY
TETE
TETEL
TETH
TETHELIN
TETHER
TETHERBALL
TETHERED
TETHERING
TETHERY
TETHYDAN
TETOTUM
TETRA
TETRAAMYLOSE
TETRABASIC
TETRABIBLOS
TETRABORATE
TETRABORIC
TETRABRACH
TETRABROMID
TETRABROMIDE
TETRACHLORID
TETRACHLORIDE
TETRACHLORO
TETRACHORD
TETRACHORDAL
TETRACHORDON
TETRACHORIC
TETRACID
TETRACOCCUS
TETRACOLIC
TETRACOLON
TETRACORAL
TETRACOSANE
TETRACT
TETRACTINAL
TETRACTINOSE
TETRACTYS
TETRACYCLIC
TETRACYCLINE
TETRAD
TETRADACTYL
TETRADACTYLE
TETRADACTYLY
TETRADARCHY
TETRADECANE
TETRADECYL
TETRADIC
TETRADRACHM
TETRADRACHMA
TETRADYMITE
TETRAETHYL
TETRAGAMY
TETRAGENOUS
TETRAGLOT
TETRAGLOTTIC
TETRAGON
TETRAGONAL
TETRAGONALLY
TETRAGONOUS
TETRAGRAM
TETRAGYN
TETRAGYNIAN
TETRAGYNOUS
TETRAHEDRA
TETRAHEDRAL
TETRAHEDRIC
TETRAHEDRITE
TETRAHEDROID
TETRAHEDRON
TETRAHEDRONS
TETRAHEXAHEDRON
TETRAHYDRATE
TETRAHYDRIC
TETRAHYDRID
TETRAHYDRIDE
TETRAHYDRO
TETRAHYDROXY
TETRAIODO
TETRAKETONE
TETRAKIS
TETRAKISAZO
TETRALEMMA
TETRALOGIC
TETRALOGIES
TETRALOGUE
TETRALOGY
TETRAMASTIA
TETRAMERAL
TETRAMERIC
TETRAMERISM
TETRAMEROUS
TETRAMETER
TETRAMETHYL
TETRAMINE
TETRAMORPH
TETRAMORPHIC
TETRANDER
TETRANDROUS
TETRANE
TETRANITRATE
TETRANITRO
TETRANT
TETRAODONT
TETRAONID
TETRAONINE
TETRAPHENOL
TETRAPHONY
TETRAPLA
TETRAPLEGIA
TETRAPLEURON
TETRAPLOID
TETRAPLOIDIC
TETRAPLOIDY
TETRAPLOUS
TETRAPOD
TETRAPODIC
TETRAPODOUS
TETRAPODY
TETRAPOLAR
TETRAPOLIS
TETRAPOLITAN
TETRAPOUS
TETRAPTERAN
TETRAPTERON
TETRAPTEROUS
TETRAPTOTE
TETRAPTYCH
TETRAPYLON
TETRAPYRAMID
TETRARCH
TETRARCHATE
TETRARCHIC
TETRARCHICAL
TETRARCHIES
TETRARCHY
TETRASACCHARIDE
TETRASEME
TETRASEMIC
TETRASKELE
TETRASKELION
TETRASPHERIC
TETRASPORE
TETRASPORIC
TETRASPOROUS
TETRASTER
TETRASTICH
TETRASTICHAL
TETRASTICHIC
TETRASTOON
TETRASTYLE
TETRASTYLIC
TETRASTYLOS
TETRASTYLOUS
TETRASULFID
TETRASULFIDE
TETRASULPHID
TETRATHEISM
TETRATHEITE
TETRATHIONIC
TETRATOMIC
TETRATONE
TETRAVALENCE
TETRAVALENCY
TETRAVALENT
TETRAXIAL
TETRAXILE
TETRAXON
TETRAZANE
TETRAZENE
TETRAZIN
TETRAZINE
TETRAZO
TETRAZOLE
TETRAZOLIUM
TETRAZOLYL

TETRAZONE
TETRAZOTIZE
TETREMIMERAL
TETRIC
TETRICAL
TETRICALNESS
TETRICITY
TETRICOUS
TETRIFOL
TETRIGID
TETRIODIDE
TETROBOL
TETROBOLON
TETRODE
TETROL
TETROLE
TETROLIC
TETRONIC
TETRONYMAL
TETROSE
TETROUS
TETROXALATE
TETROXID
TETROXIDE
TETRYL
TETTER
TETTERED
TETTERING
TETTEROUS
TETTERWORT
TETTERY
TETTISH
TETTIX
TETTY
TETUR
TEU
TEUCH
TEUCHIT
TEUCRIN
TEUGH
TEUGHLY
TEUGHNESS
TEUK
TEVEL
TEVISS
TEW
TEWART
TEWED
TEWEL
TEWER
TEWING
TEWIT
TEWKE
TEWLY
TEWSOME
TEWTAW
TEWTER
TEXAS
TEXGUINO
TEXT
TEXTARIAN
TEXTBOOK
TEXTIFEROUS
TEXTILE
TEXTILES
TEXTILIST
TEXTLET
TEXTMAN
TEXTORIAL
TEXTRINE
TEXTUAL
TEXTUALISM
TEXTUALIST
TEXTUALLY
TEXTUARIES
TEXTUARIST
TEXTUARY
TEXTURAL
TEXTURALLY
TEXTURE
TEXTURED
TEXTUS
TEYNE
TEZ
TEZKIRAH
THA
THACK
THACKER
THACKLESS
THACKOOR
THAE
THAG
THAIL
THAIRM
THAKUR
THAKURATE
THALAMI
THALAMIA
THALAMIC
THALAMITE
THALAMIUM
THALAMOCELE
THALAMOCOELE
THALAMUS
THALASSA
THALASSAL
THALASSIAN
THALASSIARCH
THALASSIC
THALASSICAL
THALASSINID
THALASSINOID
THALATTA
THALENITE
THALER
THALIACEAN
THALIDOMIDE
THALLI
THALLIC
THALLIFEROUS
THALLIFORM
THALLIN
THALLINE
THALLIOUS
THALLIUM
THALLOCHLORE
THALLODAL
THALLODIC
THALLOGEN
THALLOGENOUS
THALLOID
THALLOIDAL
THALLOME
THALLOPHYTE
THALLOPHYTIC
THALLOSE
THALLOUS
THALLUS
THALLUSES
THALPOSIS
THALPOTIC
THALTHAN
THALWEG
THAM
THAMAKAU
THAMENG
THAMIN
THAMNIUM
THAMNOPHILE
THAMNOPHILINE
THAMURIA
THAN
THANA
THANADAR
THANAGE
THANAH
THANATISM
THANATIST
THANATOID
THANATOLOGY
THANATOMETER
THANATOPSIS
THANATOSIS
THANATOTIC
THANATOUSIA
THANE
THANELAND
THANESS
THANK
THANKED
THANKEE
THANKER
THANKFUL
THANKFULLY
THANKFULNESS
THANKING
THANKLESS
THANKLESSLY
THANKS
THANKSGIVER
THANKSGIVING
THANKWORTHY
THANNADAR
THAPES
THAR
THARF
THARFCAKE
THARGINYAH
THARM
THAT
THATCH
THATCHED
THATCHER
THATCHING
THATCHWOOD
THATCHY
THATNESS
THAUGHT
THAUMASITE
THAUMATOGENY
THAUMATOLOGIES
THAUMATOLOGY
THAUMATROPE
THAUMATURGE
THAUMATURGI
THAUMATURGIA
THAUMATURGIC
THAUMATURGUS
THAUMATURGY
THAUMOSCOPIC
THAW
THAWED
THAWER
THAWIER
THAWIEST
THAWING
THAWY
THE
THEACEOUS
THEAK
THEAL
THEAM
THEANDRIC
THEANTHROPIC
THEANTHROPOS
THEANTHROPY
THEARCHIC
THEARCHIES
THEARCHY
THEASUM
THEAT
THEATER
THEATERGOER
THEATERGOING
THEATERS
THEATRAL
THEATRE
THEATREGOER
THEATREGOING
THEATRIC
THEATRICABLE
THEATRICAL
THEATRICALITY
THEATRICALS
THEATRICIAN
THEATRICISM
THEATRICIZE
THEATRICS
THEATRIZE
THEATROCRACY
THEATRON
THEAVE
THEB
THEBAIN
THEBAINE
THEBAISM
THECA
THECAE
THECAL
THECAPHORE
THECASPORAL
THECASPORE
THECASPORED
THECASPOROUS
THECATE
THECIA
THECITIS
THECIUM
THECLAN
THECODONT
THEDE
THEE
THEEDOM
THEEK
THEEKED
THEEKER
THEEKING
THEELIN
THEELOL
THEET
THEETSEE
THEEZAN
THEFT
THEFTBOTE
THEFTDOM
THEFTUOUS
THEFTUOUSLY
THEGETHER
THEGIDDER
THEGITHER
THEGN
THEGNDOM
THEGNHOOD
THEGNLAND
THEGNLIKE
THEGNLY
THEGNSHIP
THEGNWORTHY
THEI
THEIC
THEIFORM
THEIN
THEINE
THEIR
THEIRN
THEIRS
THEIRSELVES
THEISM
THEIST
THEISTIC
THEISTICAL
THELION
THELITIS
THELIUM
THELORRHAGIA
THELPHUSIAN
THELYBLAST
THELYBLASTIC
THELYOTOKOUS
THELYOTOKY
THEM
THEMA
THEMATA
THEMATIC
THEMATICAL
THEMATICALLY
THEMATIST
THEME
THEMED
THEMER
THEMING
THEMSELVES
THEN
THENABOUTS
THENADAYS
THENAGE
THENAL
THENAR
THENARDITE
THENCE
THENCEAFTER
THENCEFORTH
THENCEFROM
THENCEWARD
THENNESS
THEOBROMIN
THEOBROMINE
THEOCENTRIC
THEOCHRISTIC
THEOCRACIES
THEOCRACY
THEOCRASICAL
THEOCRASIES
THEOCRASY
THEOCRAT
THEOCRATIC
THEOCRATICAL
THEOCRATIST
THEODICEAN
THEODICIES
THEODICY
THEODIDACT
THEODOLITE
THEODOLITIC
THEODY
THEOGAMY
THEOGONAL
THEOGONIC
THEOGONICAL
THEOGONIES
THEOGONISM
THEOGONIST
THEOGONY
THEOKRASIA
THEOKTONIC
THEOKTONY
THEOLATROUS
THEOLATRY
THEOLOG
THEOLOGASTER
THEOLOGATE
THEOLOGEION
THEOLOGER
THEOLOGI
THEOLOGIAN

THEOLOGIC
THEOLOGICAL
THEOLOGICIAN
THEOLOGICS
THEOLOGIES
THEOLOGISE
THEOLOGISM
THEOLOGIST
THEOLOGIUM
THEOLOGIZE
THEOLOGIZED
THEOLOGIZER
THEOLOGIZING
THEOLOGUE
THEOLOGUS
THEOLOGY
THEOMACHIES
THEOMACHIST
THEOMACHY
THEOMAGIC
THEOMAGICAL
THEOMAGICS
THEOMAGY
THEOMANCY
THEOMANIA
THEOMANIAC
THEOMANTIC
THEOMASTIX
THEOMICRIST
THEOMORPHIC
THEOMORPHISM
THEOMORPHIZE
THEONOMY
THEOPANTISM
THEOPATHETIC
THEOPATHIC
THEOPATHIES
THEOPATHY
THEOPHAGIC
THEOPHAGITE
THEOPHAGOUS
THEOPHAGY
THEOPHANIA
THEOPHANIC
THEOPHANIES
THEOPHANISM
THEOPHANOUS
THEOPHANY
THEOPHILE
THEOPHOBIA
THEOPHORIC
THEOPHOROUS
THEOPHYLLIN
THEOPHYLLINE
THEOPNEUST
THEOPNEUSTED
THEOPNEUSTIC
THEOPNEUSTY
THEORBIST
THEORBO
THEORBOS
THEOREM
THEOREMATIC
THEOREMATIST
THEOREMIC
THEORETIC
THEORETICAL
THEORETICIAN
THEORETICS
THEORIA
THEORIAI
THEORIC
THEORICA
THEORICAL
THEORICALLY
THEORICIAN
THEORICON
THEORICS
THEORIES
THEORISE
THEORISM
THEORIST
THEORIZATION
THEORIZE
THEORIZED
THEORIZER
THEORIZING
THEORUM
THEORY
THEORYLESS
THEOSOPH
THEOSOPHEME
THEOSOPHER
THEOSOPHIC
THEOSOPHICAL
THEOSOPHIES
THEOSOPHISM
THEOSOPHIST
THEOSOPHY
THEOTECHNIC
THEOTECHNIST
THEOTECHNY
THEOTHERAPY
THEOW
THEOWDOM
THEOWMAN
THEOWMEN
THERALITE
THERAPEUSIS
THERAPEUTIC
THERAPEUTICS
THERAPEUTIST
THERAPIA
THERAPIES
THERAPIST
THERAPSID
THERAPY
THERAVADA
THERBLIG
THERE
THEREABOUT
THEREABOUTS
THEREABOVE
THEREACROSS
THEREAFTER
THEREAGAINST
THEREAMONG
THEREAMONGST
THEREANENT
THEREANENTS
THEREAROUND
THEREAS
THEREAT
THEREAWAY
THEREAWAYS
THEREBEFORE
THEREBEN
THEREBESIDE
THEREBIFORN
THEREBY
THEREFOR
THEREFORE
THEREFRO
THEREFROM
THEREIN
THEREINAFTER
THEREINTO
THERENESS
THEREOF
THEREOID
THEREOLOGIST
THEREOLOGY
THEREON
THEREONTO
THEREOUT
THEREOVER
THERERIGHT
THERESE
THERETHROUGH
THERETIL
THERETILL
THERETO
THERETOFORE
THERETOWARD
THEREUNDER
THEREUNTIL
THEREUNTO
THEREUP
THEREUPON
THEREVID
THEREWHILE
THEREWHILES
THEREWHILST
THEREWITH
THEREWITHAL
THEREWITHIN
THERF
THERIAC
THERIACA
THERIACAL
THERIAL
THERIATRICS
THERIDIID
THERIODONT
THERIOMANCY
THERIOMORPH
THERM
THERMAE
THERMAIC
THERMAL
THERMALGESIA
THERMALITY
THERMALLY
THERMANTIC
THERMATOLOGY
THERME
THERMEL
THERMIC
THERMICAL
THERMICALLY
THERMION
THERMIONIC
THERMIONICS
THERMISTOR
THERMIT
THERMITE
THERMOCHROIC
THERMOCHROSY
THERMOCLINE
THERMOCOUPLE
THERMOGEN
THERMOGENIC
THERMOGENOUS
THERMOGRAM
THERMOGRAPH
THERMOGRAPHY
THERMOLABILE
THERMOLOGY
THERMOLYSIS
THERMOLYTIC
THERMOLYZE
THERMOLYZED
THERMOLYZING
THERMOMETER
THERMOMETRIC
THERMOMETRY
THERMOMOTIVE
THERMOMOTOR
THERMONASTIC
THERMONASTY
THERMONOUS
THERMOPAIR
THERMOPHIL
THERMOPHILE
THERMOPHILIC
THERMOPHONE
THERMOPHORE
THERMOPILE
THERMOPLASTIC
THERMOPLEION
THERMOSCOPE
THERMOSCOPIC
THERMOSIPHON
THERMOSPHERE
THERMOSTABLE
THERMOSTAT
THERMOSTATIC
THERMOTACTIC
THERMOTANK
THERMOTAXIC
THERMOTAXIS
THERMOTIC
THERMOTICAL
THERMOTICS
THERMOTROPIC
THERMOTROPY
THERMOTYPE
THERMOTYPIC
THERMOTYPY
THERODONT
THEROID
THEROLOGIC
THEROLOGICAL
THEROLOGIST
THEROLOGY
THEROMORPH
THEROMORPHIA
THEROMORPHIC
THEROPOD
THEROPODAN
THEROPODOUS
THERSITEAN
THERSITICAL
THESAUR
THESAURI
THESAURUS
THESAURY
THESE
THESIAL
THESICLE
THESIS
THESMOTHETE
THESMOTHETES
THESOCYTE
THESTER
THESTREEN
THETA
THETCH
THETIC
THETICAL
THETICALLY
THETICS
THETIN
THETINE
THEURGIC
THEURGICAL
THEURGICALLY
THEURGIES
THEURGIST
THEURGY
THEVETIN
THEW
THEWED
THEWIER
THEWIEST
THEWLESS
THEWLIKE
THEWS
THEWY
THEY
THEYAOU
THIADIAZOLE
THIALDIN
THIALDINE
THIAMID
THIAMIDE
THIAMIN
THIAMINE
THIANTHRENE
THIASI
THIASITE
THIASOI
THIASOS
THIASOTE
THIASUS
THIAZIN
THIAZINE
THIAZOL
THIAZOLE
THIAZOLINE
THIBET
THIBLE
THICK
THICKE
THICKEN
THICKENED
THICKENER
THICKENING
THICKER
THICKEST
THICKET
THICKETED
THICKETY
THICKHEAD
THICKHEADED
THICKISH
THICKLEAF
THICKLIPS
THICKLY
THICKNESS
THICKSET
THICKSKIN
THICKSKULL
THICKSKULLED
THICKWIND
THICKWIT
THICKY
THIEF
THIEFCRAFT
THIEFDOM
THIEFLAND
THIEFLY
THIEFMAKER
THIEFMAKING
THIEFPROOF
THIEFTAKER
THIENONE
THIENYL
THIEVE
THIEVED
THIEVELESS
THIEVER
THIEVERIES
THIEVERY
THIEVES
THIEVING
THIEVISH
THIEVISHLY
THIEVISHNESS
THIG
THIGGER
THIGGING
THIGH
THIGHBONE
THIGHED

THIGHS
THIGHT
THIGHTNESS
THIGMOTACTIC
THIGMOTAXIS
THIGMOTROPIC
THIK
THILK
THILL
THILLER
THILLY
THIMBLE
THIMBLEBERRIES
THIMBLEBERRY
THIMBLED
THIMBLEFUL
THIMBLEFULS
THIMBLEMAKER
THIMBLEMAKING
THIMBLEMAN
THIMBLERIG
THIMBLERIGGED
THIMBLERIGGING
THIMBLES
THIMBLEWEED
THIN
THINDOWN
THINE
THING
THINGAL
THINGAMABOB
THINGAMAJIG
THINGISH
THINGLET
THINGMAN
THINGS
THINGUM
THINGUMABOB
THINGUMAJIG
THINGUMBOB
THINGUT
THINGY
THINK
THINKABLE
THINKABLY
THINKER
THINKING
THINKINGLY
THINLY
THINNED
THINNER
THINNESS
THINNEST
THINNING
THIO
THIOACETIC
THIOALDEHYDE
THIOAMID
THIOAMIDE
THIOARSENATE
THIOARSENIATE
THIOARSENITE
THIOCARBAMIC
THIOCARBONYL
THIOCRESOL
THIOCYANATE
THIOCYANIC
THIOCYANIDE
THIOCYANO
THIOCYANOGEN
THIOHYDRATE
THIOKETONE
THIOL
THIOLACETIC
THIONATE
THIONATION
THIONEINE
THIONIC
THIONIN
THIONINE
THIONITRITE
THIONYL
THIONYLAMINE
THIOPHEN
THIOPHENE
THIOPHENIC
THIOPHENOL
THIOPHOSGENE
THIOPHTHENE
THIOPYRAN
THIOSINAMINE
THIOSTANNIC
THIOSTANNITE
THIOSULFATE
THIOSULPHATE
THIOTOLENE
THIOTUNGSTIC
THIOUREA
THIOURETHAN
THIOXENE
THIOZONE
THIOZONID
THIOZONIDE
THIR
THIRD
THIRDBOROUGH
THIRDENDEAL
THIRDINGS
THIRDLING
THIRDLY
THIRDNESS
THIRDS
THIRDSMAN
THIRL
THIRLAGE
THIRLED
THIRLING
THIRST
THIRSTED
THIRSTER
THIRSTIER
THIRSTIEST
THIRSTILY
THIRSTINESS
THIRSTING
THIRSTINGLY
THIRSTLE
THIRSTY
THIRTEEN
THIRTEENER
THIRTEENTH
THIRTEENTHLY
THIRTIES
THIRTIETH
THIRTY
THIS
THISHOW
THISLIKE
THISNESS
THISSEN
THISTLE
THISTLEBIRD
THISTLED
THISTLEDOWN
THISTLY
THISWISE
THITHER
THITHERTO
THITHERWARD
THITHERWARDS
THITKA
THITSIOL
THIURAM
THIVEL
THIXLE
THIXOLABILE
THIXOTROPIC
THIXOTROPY
THLIPSIS
THO
THOA
THOB
THODE
THOFT
THOFTFELLOW
THOGHT
THOKE
THOKISH
THOLANCE
THOLE
THOLED
THOLEITE
THOLEMOD
THOLING
THOLOI
THOLOS
THOLUS
THOMAN
THOMASING
THOMISID
THOMIST
THOMSENOLITE
THOMSONITE
THON
THONDER
THONE
THONG
THONGED
THONGMAN
THONGS
THONGY
THOOID
THORACECTOMY
THORACES
THORACIC
THORACICAL
THORACIFORM
THORACOGRAPH
THORACOLYSIS
THORACOPAGUS
THORACOSCOPE
THORACOSCOPY
THORAL
THORAX
THORAXES
THORE
THORIA
THORIANITE
THORIATE
THORIC
THORIFEROUS
THORITE
THORIUM
THORN
THORNBACK
THORNBILL
THORNBUSH
THORNED
THORNEN
THORNIER
THORNIEST
THORNING
THORNLESS
THORNLET
THORNTAIL
THORNY
THORO
THOROGUMMITE
THORON
THOROUGH
THOROUGHBRED
THOROUGHFARE
THOROUGHFOOT
THOROUGHFOOTED
THOROUGHFOOTING
THOROUGHGOING
THOROUGHLY
THOROUGHNESS
THOROUGHPIN
THOROUGHSPED
THOROUGHSTEM
THOROUGHWAX
THOROUGHWORT
THORP
THORPE
THORTER
THORTVEITITE
THOSE
THOU
THOUGH
THOUGHT
THOUGHTED
THOUGHTFUL
THOUGHTFULLY
THOUGHTFULNESS
THOUGHTLESS
THOUGHTLESSLY
THOUGHTNESS
THOUGHTS
THOUGHTSICK
THOUGHTY
THOUSAND
THOUSANDFOLD
THOUSANDTH
THOWLESS
THRACK
THRAIL
THRAIN
THRALDOM
THRALL
THRALLBORN
THRALLDOM
THRAM
THRAMMLE
THRANG
THRANGITY
THRANITE
THRAP
THRAPPLE
THRASH
THRASHED
THRASHEL
THRASHER
THRASHERMAN
THRASHING
THRASONIC
THRASONICAL
THRAST
THRATCH
THRAVE
THRAVER
THRAW
THRAWART
THRAWARTLIKE
THRAWARTNESS
THRAWN
THRAWNLY
THRAWNNESS
THREAD
THREADBARE
THREADED
THREADEN
THREADER
THREADFIN
THREADFISH
THREADFISHES
THREADFLOWER
THREADFOOT
THREADIER
THREADIEST
THREADING
THREADLE
THREADLIKE
THREADMAKER
THREADMAKING
THREADS
THREADWAY
THREADWEED
THREADWORM
THREADY
THREAP
THREAPED
THREAPEN
THREAPER
THREAPING
THREAT
THREATEN
THREATENED
THREATENER
THREATENING
THREATENINGLY
THREAVE
THREE
THREEFOLD
THREELING
THREENESS
THREEP
THREEPED
THREEPENCE
THREEPENNY
THREEPING
THREES
THREESCORE
THREESOME
THREIP
THRENE
THRENETIC
THRENETICAL
THRENODE
THRENODIAL
THRENODIAN
THRENODIC
THRENODIES
THRENODIST
THRENODY
THRENOS
THREONINE
THREOSE
THREP
THREPE
THREPSOLOGY
THRESH
THRESHAL
THRESHED
THRESHEL
THRESHER
THRESHERMAN
THRESHING
THRESHOLD
THRESTLE
THREW
THRIBBLE
THRICE
THRICECOCK
THRID
THRIDACE
THRIDACIUM
THRIE
THRIFT
THRIFTBOX
THRIFTIER
THRIFTIEST
THRIFTILY
THRIFTINESS
THRIFTLESS

THRIFTY
THRILL
THRILLED
THRILLER
THRILLIER
THRILLIEST
THRILLING
THRILLINGLY
THRILLY
THRIMBLE
THRIMP
THRING
THRINGING
THRINTER
THRIOBOLY
THRIP
THRIPEL
THRIPID
THRIPPLE
THRIPS
THRIST
THRIVE
THRIVED
THRIVELESS
THRIVEN
THRIVER
THRIVING
THRIVINGLY
THRIVINGNESS
THRO
THROAT
THROATAL
THROATBAND
THROATBOLL
THROATED
THROATFUL
THROATIER
THROATIEST
THROATILY
THROATINESS
THROATING
THROATLASH
THROATLATCH
THROATLET
THROATROOT
THROATSTRAP
THROATWORT
THROATY
THROB
THROBBED
THROBBER
THROBBING
THROBBINGLY
THROBLESS
THROCK
THRODDEN
THRODDY
THROE
THROED
THROEING
THROM
THROMBI
THROMBIN
THROMBOCYST
THROMBOCYTE
THROMBOGEN
THROMBOGENIC
THROMBOID
THROMBOPENIA
THROMBOSE
THROMBOSED
THROMBOSES
THROMBOSING
THROMBOSIS
THROMBOTIC
THROMBUS
THRONAL
THRONE
THRONED
THRONELET
THRONES
THRONG
THRONGED
THRONGER
THRONGING
THRONING
THRONIZE
THROPE
THROPPLE
THROSTLE
THROTTLE
THROTTLED
THROTTLER
THROTTLING
THROTTLINGLY
THROUGH
THROUGHBEAR
THROUGHGANG
THROUGHGOING
THROUGHGROW
THROUGHLY
THROUGHOUT
THROUGHPUT
THROUGHWAY
THROVE
THROW
THROWAWAY
THROWBACK
THROWDOWN
THROWER
THROWING
THROWN
THROWOFF
THROWOUT
THROWST
THROWSTER
THRU
THRUM
THRUMBLE
THRUMMED
THRUMMER
THRUMMING
THRUMMY
THRUMWORT
THRUOUT
THRUSH
THRUSHEL
THRUSHER
THRUSHLIKE
THRUSHY
THRUST
THRUSTER
THRUSTING
THRUSTLE
THRUTCH
THRUTCHINGS
THRUWAY
THRYMSA
THUD
THUDDED
THUDDING
THUDDINGLY
THUG
THUGA
THUGGED
THUGGEE
THUGGERIES
THUGGERY
THUGGESS
THUGGING
THUGGISH
THUGGISM
THUJA
THUJENE
THUJONE
THUJYL
THULIA
THULIR
THULITE
THULIUM
THULUTH
THUMB
THUMBED
THUMBER
THUMBING
THUMBKIN
THUMBLE
THUMBLESS
THUMBLING
THUMBMARK
THUMBNAIL
THUMBNUT
THUMBPIECE
THUMBPRINT
THUMBROPE
THUMBSCREW
THUMBSTALL
THUMBSTRING
THUMBTACK
THUMBY
THUMP
THUMPED
THUMPER
THUMPING
THUMPINGLY
THUNBERGILENE
THUNDER
THUNDERBIRD
THUNDERBLAST
THUNDERBOLT
THUNDERBURST
THUNDERCLAP
THUNDERCLOUD
THUNDERCRACK
THUNDERED
THUNDERER
THUNDERFISH
THUNDERFISHES
THUNDERHEAD
THUNDERING
THUNDERINGLY
THUNDERLIGHT
THUNDEROUS
THUNDEROUSLY
THUNDERPEAL
THUNDERPLUMP
THUNDERPUMP
THUNDERSMITE
THUNDERSMITING
THUNDERSMOTE
THUNDERSQUALL
THUNDERSTONE
THUNDERSTORM
THUNDERSTROKE
THUNDERWOOD
THUNDERWORM
THUNDERWORT
THUNDERY
THUNDROUS
THUNGE
THUNK
THUOC
THUR
THURGI
THURIBLE
THURIBULER
THURIBULUM
THURIFER
THURIFEROUS
THURIFICATE
THURIFICATI
THURIFY
THURINGITE
THURL
THURLE
THURM
THURMUS
THURROCK
THURSE
THURST
THURT
THUS
THUSGATE
THUSLY
THUSWISE
THUTTER
THUYA
THWACK
THWACKED
THWACKER
THWACKING
THWACKINGLY
THWACKSTAVE
THWAITE
THWART
THWARTED
THWARTEOUS
THWARTER
THWARTING
THWARTINGLY
THWARTMAN
THWARTMEN
THWARTOVER
THWARTSAW
THWARTSHIP
THWARTSHIPS
THWITE
THWITTLE
THWORL
THY
THYINE
THYLACINE
THYLACITIS
THYMACETIN
THYME
THYMECTOMY
THYMELCOSIS
THYMELE
THYMELIC
THYMELICAL
THYMELICI
THYMENE
THYMETIC
THYMIAMA
THYMIC
THYMIER
THYMIEST
THYMIN
THYMINE
THYMIOSIS
THYMITIS
THYMOCYTE
THYMOGENIC
THYMOL
THYMOLATE
THYMOLIZE
THYMOMA
THYMOMATA
THYMOPATHY
THYMOPRIVIC
THYMOPSYCHE
THYMOQUINONE
THYMOTACTIC
THYMOTIC
THYMOTINIC
THYMS
THYMUS
THYMY
THYMYL
THYMYLIC
THYNNID
THYRATRON
THYREOID
THYRIDIA
THYRIDIAL
THYRIDIUM
THYROCARDIAC
THYROCELE
THYROCOLLOID
THYROGENIC
THYROGENOUS
THYROGLOSSAL
THYROHYAL
THYROHYOID
THYROID
THYROIDEA
THYROIDISM
THYROIDITIS
THYROIDLESS
THYROIDOTOMY
THYROLINGUAL
THYRONIN
THYRONINE
THYROPRIVAL
THYROPRIVIA
THYROPRIVIC
THYROPROTEIN
THYROSTRACAN
THYROTHERAPY
THYROTOMY
THYROTOXIC
THYROXIN
THYROXINE
THYROXINIC
THYRSE
THYRSI
THYRSOID
THYRSOIDAL
THYRSUS
THYSANOPTER
THYSANURAN
THYSANUROUS
THYSELF
THYSEN
TI
TIA
TIAL
TIANG
TIANGUE
TIAO
TIAR
TIARA
TIARELLA
TIB
TIBBIT
TIBBY
TIBERT
TIBET
TIBEY
TIBIA
TIBIAE
TIBIAL
TIBIALE
TIBIALIA
TIBIALIS
TIBIAS
TIBICEN
TIBIOFIBULA
TIBIOTARSAL
TIBIOTARSI
TIBIOTARSUS
TIBOURBOU
TIBURON
TIC
TICAL

TICCA
TICCHEN
TICE
TICEMENT
TICER
TICHEL
TICHODROME
TICHORRHINE
TICK
TICKBEAN
TICKBIRD
TICKED
TICKEN
TICKER
TICKET
TICKETED
TICKETER
TICKETING
TICKETMONGER
TICKEY
TICKIE
TICKING
TICKLE
TICKLEBACK
TICKLEBRAIN
TICKLED
TICKLELY
TICKLENBURG
TICKLENESS
TICKLER
TICKLESOME
TICKLEWEED
TICKLING
TICKLINGLY
TICKLISH
TICKLISHLY
TICKLISHNESS
TICKLY
TICKNEY
TICKSEED
TICKSEEDED
TICKTACK
TICKTACKER
TICKTACKTOE
TICKTACKTOO
TICKTICK
TICKTOCK
TICKWEED
TICKY
TICTACTOE
TICTIC
TICUL
TID
TIDAL
TIDBIT
TIDBITS
TIDDER
TIDDLE
TIDDLEDYWINKS
TIDDLER
TIDDLEY
TIDDLEYWINK
TIDDLING
TIDDLY
TIDDLYWINK
TIDDLYWINKER
TIDDLYWINKING
TIDDLYWINKS
TIDDY
TIDE
TIDECOACH
TIDED
TIDEFUL
TIDEHEAD
TIDELAND
TIDELESS
TIDELY
TIDEMAKER
TIDEMAKING
TIDEMARK
TIDERACE
TIDERIP
TIDES
TIDESMAN
TIDESURVEYOR
TIDEWAITER
TIDEWATER
TIDEWAY
TIDIED
TIDIER
TIDIES
TIDIEST
TIDIFE
TIDILY
TIDINESS
TIDING
TIDINGS
TIDIOSE
TIDLEY
TIDLING
TIDOLOGICAL
TIDOLOGY
TIDY
TIDYING
TIDYTIPS
TIE
TIEBACK
TIEBOY
TIED
TIEDOG
TIEGO
TIEING
TIEMANNITE
TIEN
TIENDA
TIENS
TIENTA
TIENTO
TIEPIN
TIER
TIERCE
TIERCERON
TIERED
TIERER
TIERRAS
TIERSMAN
TIES
TIETICK
TIEVINE
TIEWIG
TIFF
TIFFANIES
TIFFANY
TIFFANYITE
TIFFED
TIFFIE
TIFFIN
TIFFING
TIFFISH
TIFFLE
TIFFY
TIFINAGH
TIFLE
TIFT
TIFTER
TIG
TIGE
TIGELLA
TIGELLATE
TIGELLE
TIGELLUM
TIGELLUS
TIGER
TIGERBIRD
TIGEREYE
TIGERFLOWER
TIGERFOOT
TIGERISH
TIGERISHLY
TIGERISHNESS
TIGERISM
TIGERKIN
TIGERLY
TIGERNUT
TIGERS
TIGERWOOD
TIGGER
TIGH
TIGHT
TIGHTEN
TIGHTENED
TIGHTENER
TIGHTENING
TIGHTER
TIGHTEST
TIGHTFISTED
TIGHTISH
TIGHTLIER
TIGHTLIEST
TIGHTLIPPED
TIGHTLY
TIGHTNESS
TIGHTROPE
TIGHTS
TIGHTWAD
TIGHTWIRE
TIGLALDEHYDE
TIGLIC
TIGLINIC
TIGNON
TIGNUM
TIGRESS
TIGRINE
TIGRISH
TIGROID
TIGROLYSIS
TIGROLYTIC
TIGRONE
TIGTAG
TIKAL
TIKE
TIKI
TIKITIKI
TIKKA
TIKKER
TIKKUN
TIKLIN
TIKOLOSH
TIKOOR
TIKOR
TIKUG
TIKUR
TIL
TILAITE
TILAK
TILAKA
TILASITE
TILBURIES
TILBURY
TILDE
TILE
TILED
TILEFISH
TILEFISHES
TILER
TILERIES
TILEROOT
TILERY
TILES
TILESEED
TILESHERD
TILESTONE
TILETTE
TILIACEOUS
TILICETUM
TILIKUM
TILING
TILL
TILLABLE
TILLAGE
TILLANDSIA
TILLED
TILLER
TILLERED
TILLERING
TILLERMAN
TILLET
TILLEY
TILLICUM
TILLING
TILLITE
TILLMAN
TILLODONT
TILLOT
TILLY
TILMA
TILMUS
TILPAH
TILT
TILTBOARD
TILTED
TILTER
TILTH
TILTING
TILTUP
TILTURE
TILTY
TILTYARD
TILYER
TIMALIINE
TIMALINE
TIMAR
TIMARAU
TIMARIOT
TIMARRI
TIMAUA
TIMAWA
TIMAZITE
TIMBAL
TIMBALE
TIMBANG
TIMBE
TIMBER
TIMBERED
TIMBERER
TIMBERHEAD
TIMBERING
TIMBERJACK
TIMBERLAND
TIMBERLESS
TIMBERLIKE
TIMBERLING
TIMBERMAN
TIMBERMEN
TIMBERN
TIMBERS
TIMBERSOME
TIMBERTUNED
TIMBERWOOD
TIMBERWORK
TIMBERY
TIMBESTERE
TIMBO
TIMBRE
TIMBREL
TIMBRELED
TIMBRELER
TIMBRELLED
TIMBRELLER
TIME
TIMECARD
TIMED
TIMEFUL
TIMEKEEP
TIMEKEEPER
TIMEKEEPING
TIMELESS
TIMELESSLY
TIMELESSNESS
TIMELIER
TIMELIEST
TIMELILY
TIMELINESS
TIMELY
TIMENOGUY
TIMEOUS
TIMEOUSLY
TIMEPIECE
TIMEPLEASER
TIMER
TIMERAU
TIMERITY
TIMES
TIMESAVER
TIMESAVING
TIMESERVER
TIMESERVING
TIMETABLE
TIMETAKER
TIMETAKING
TIMEWORK
TIMEWORKER
TIMEWORN
TIMID
TIMIDER
TIMIDEST
TIMIDITY
TIMIDLY
TIMIDNESS
TIMIDOUS
TIMING
TIMISH
TIMIST
TIMMER
TIMOCRACIES
TIMOCRACY
TIMOCRATIC
TIMOCRATICAL
TIMON
TIMONEER
TIMOR
TIMOROSO
TIMOROUS
TIMOROUSLY
TIMOROUSNESS
TIMOTHY
TIMPANI
TIMPANIST
TIMPANO
TIMPANUM
TIN
TINA
TINAGE
TINAJA
TINAMINE
TINAMOU
TINAMPIPI
TINCAL
TINCHEL
TINCHILL
TINCLAD
TINCT
TINCTED
TINCTING
TINCTION

TINCTORIAL
TINCTORIALLY
TINCTURE
TINCTURED
TINCTURING
TIND
TINDAL
TINDALO
TINDER
TINDERBOX
TINDERED
TINDERISH
TINDERY
TINE
TINEA
TINEAL
TINEAN
TINED
TINEGRASS
TINEID
TINEINE
TINEMAN
TINEMEN
TINEOID
TINEOLA
TINES
TINETARE
TINETY
TINEWEED
TINFOIL
TING
TINGE
TINGED
TINGEING
TINGENT
TINGER
TINGI
TINGID
TINGING
TINGITID
TINGLASS
TINGLE
TINGLED
TINGLER
TINGLING
TINGLINGLY
TINGLISH
TINGLY
TINGTANG
TINGUAITE
TINGUAITIC
TINGUY
TINHORN
TINHOUSE
TINIER
TINIEST
TINING
TINK
TINKER
TINKERBIRD
TINKERED
TINKERER
TINKERING
TINKERLY
TINKERSHIRE
TINKERSHUE
TINKLE
TINKLED
TINKLER
TINKLING
TINKLINGLY
TINKLY
TINLET
TINMAN
TINMEN
TINNED
TINNEN
TINNER
TINNERY
TINNET
TINNIENT
TINNIER
TINNIEST
TINNIFIED
TINNILY
TINNINESS
TINNING
TINNITUS
TINNOCK
TINNY
TINOSA
TINSEL
TINSELED
TINSELING
TINSELLED
TINSELLING
TINSELLY
TINSELRY
TINSMAN
TINSMEN
TINSMITH
TINSMITHING
TINSMITHY
TINSTONE
TINSTUFF
TINSY
TINT
TINTA
TINTAGE
TINTAMAR
TINTAMARRE
TINTARRON
TINTED
TINTER
TINTERNELL
TINTIE
TINTING
TINTIST
TINTO
TINTOMETER
TINTOMETRIC
TINTOMETRY
TINTY
TINTYPE
TINTYPER
TINWALD
TINWARE
TINWORK
TINWORKER
TINWORKING
TINWORKS
TINY
TINZENITE
TIP
TIPBURN
TIPCART
TIPCAT
TIPE
TIPFUL
TIPHEAD
TIPI
TIPITI
TIPLE
TIPLET
TIPMAN
TIPMEN
TIPMOST
TIPOFF
TIPONI
TIPPABLE
TIPPED
TIPPEE
TIPPER
TIPPET
TIPPIER
TIPPIEST
TIPPING
TIPPLE
TIPPLED
TIPPLER
TIPPLING
TIPPY
TIPREE
TIPSIER
TIPSIEST
TIPSIFIER
TIPSIFY
TIPSILY
TIPSINESS
TIPSTAFF
TIPSTAFFS
TIPSTAVES
TIPSTER
TIPSTOCK
TIPSY
TIPTAIL
TIPTEERER
TIPTILT
TIPTOE
TIPTOED
TIPTOEING
TIPTOEINGLY
TIPTOES
TIPTOP
TIPTOPPER
TIPULID
TIPULOID
TIPUP
TIQUEUR
TIR
TIRADE
TIRAGE
TIRAILLEUR
TIRALEE
TIRASSE
TIRAZ
TIRE
TIRED
TIREDER
TIREDEST
TIREDLY
TIREDNESS
TIREHOUSE
TIRELESS
TIRELESSLY
TIRELESSNESS
TIREMAID
TIREMAN
TIREMEN
TIREMENT
TIRER
TIRES
TIRESMITH
TIRESOL
TIRESOME
TIRESOMELY
TIRESOMENESS
TIREWOMAN
TIREWOMEN
TIRIBA
TIRING
TIRL
TIRLING
TIRMA
TIRO
TIROCINIA
TIROCINIUM
TIROS
TIRR
TIRRACKE
TIRRALIRRA
TIRRET
TIRRIT
TIRRIVEE
TIRRIVIE
TIRRLIE
TIRRWIRR
TIRTHANKARA
TIRVE
TIRWIT
TIRY
TIS
TISANE
TISAR
TISSUAL
TISSUE
TISSUED
TISSUES
TISSUEY
TISSUING
TISSWOOD
TISWIN
TIT
TITANATE
TITANAUGITE
TITANIA
TITANIC
TITANIFEROUS
TITANITE
TITANITIC
TITANIUM
TITANOSAUR
TITANOTHERE
TITANOUS
TITANYL
TITAR
TITBIT
TITBITTY
TITE
TITER
TITFISH
TITHABLE
TITHAL
TITHE
TITHED
TITHER
TITHES
TITHING
TITHINGMAN
TITHINGMEN
TITHINGPENNY
TITHONIC
TITHONICITY
TITHONOMETER
TITHYMAL
TITI
TITIAN
TITIEN
TITILLABILITY
TITILLANT
TITILLATE
TITILLATED
TITILLATER
TITILLATING
TITILLATINGLY
TITILLATION
TITILLATIVE
TITILLATOR
TITILLATORY
TITIVATE
TITIVATION
TITIVATOR
TITIVIL
TITIVILLER
TITLARK
TITLE
TITLEBOARD
TITLED
TITLEHOLDER
TITLENE
TITLER
TITLING
TITLIST
TITMAL
TITMALL
TITMAN
TITMEN
TITMICE
TITMOUSE
TITOKI
TITRANT
TITRATABLE
TITRATE
TITRATED
TITRATING
TITRATION
TITRE
TITTER
TITTERATION
TITTERED
TITTEREL
TITTERER
TITTERING
TITTERINGLY
TITTERY
TITTIE
TITTIVATE
TITTIVATED
TITTIVATING
TITTIVATION
TITTIVATOR
TITTLE
TITTLEBAT
TITTLER
TITTLIN
TITTUP
TITTUPED
TITTUPING
TITTUPPED
TITTUPPING
TITTUPPY
TITTUPY
TITTY
TITTYMOUSE
TITUBANCY
TITUBANT
TITUBANTLY
TITUBATE
TITUBATION
TITULADO
TITULAR
TITULARIES
TITULARITY
TITULARLY
TITULARY
TITULE
TITULI
TITULUS
TIVER
TIVOLI
TIVY
TIZA
TIZEUR
TIZZIES
TIZZY
TJAELE
TJALK
TJANDI
TJANTING
TJENKAL
TJI
TJOSITE
TJURUNGA
TLAC
TLACO

TMEMA
TMEMATA
TMESIS
TO
TOA
TOAD
TOADBACK
TOADEAT
TOADEATER
TOADFISH
TOADFISHES
TOADFLAX
TOADFLOWER
TOADHEAD
TOADIED
TOADIER
TOADIES
TOADISH
TOADO
TOADPIPE
TOADPIPES
TOADROOT
TOADSTONE
TOADSTOOL
TOADY
TOADYING
TOADYISH
TOADYISM
TOAST
TOASTED
TOASTEE
TOASTER
TOASTINESS
TOASTING
TOASTMASTER
TOASTMASTERY
TOASTY
TOAT
TOATOA
TOBACCO
TOBACCOES
TOBACCOFIED
TOBACCOITE
TOBACCOMAN
TOBACCOMEN
TOBACCONING
TOBACCONIZE
TOBACCOROOT
TOBACCOS
TOBACCOSIM
TOBACCOY
TOBE
TOBER
TOBIES
TOBINE
TOBIRA
TOBOGGAN
TOBOGGANED
TOBOGGANER
TOBOGGANING
TOBOGGANIST
TOBY
TOBYMAN
TOBYMEN
TOCALOTE
TOCCATA
TOCCATINA
TOCHER
TOCK
TOCO
TOCOGENETIC
TOCOGONY
TOCOKININ
TOCOLOGICAL
TOCOLOGIST
TOCOLOGY
TOCOME
TOCOPHEROL
TOCORORO
TOCSIN
TOCUSSO
TOD
TODAY
TODAYISH
TODDER
TODDICK
TODDIES
TODDITE
TODDLE
TODDLED
TODDLER
TODDLING
TODDY
TODDYIZE
TODDYMAN
TODDYMEN
TODE
TODIES
TODLOWRIE
TODY
TOE
TOEBOARD
TOECAP
TOED
TOEHOLD
TOEING
TOELLITE
TOENAIL
TOEPLATE
TOETOE
TOEY
TOFF
TOFFEE
TOFFEEMAN
TOFFISH
TOFFY
TOFFYMAN
TOFFYMEN
TOFORE
TOFORN
TOFT
TOFTER
TOFTMAN
TOFTMEN
TOFU
TOG
TOGA
TOGAE
TOGAED
TOGAS
TOGATE
TOGATED
TOGE
TOGEMAN
TOGETHER
TOGETHERNESS
TOGGED
TOGGEL
TOGGERIES
TOGGERY
TOGGING
TOGGLE
TOGGLED
TOGGLER
TOGGLING
TOGLESS
TOGS
TOGT
TOGUE
TOHEROA
TOHI
TOHO
TOHUBOHU
TOHUNGA
TOI
TOIL
TOILE
TOILED
TOILER
TOILET
TOILETED
TOILETRIES
TOILETRY
TOILETTE
TOILETWARE
TOILFUL
TOILFULLY
TOILINET
TOILINETTE
TOILING
TOILINGLY
TOILSOME
TOILSOMELY
TOILSOMENESS
TOISE
TOISECH
TOISED
TOISING
TOISON
TOIST
TOIT
TOITISH
TOITOI
TOITY
TOKAY
TOKE
TOKEN
TOKENED
TOKENWORTH
TOKO
TOKOLOGY
TOKONOMA
TOKOPAT
TOKTOKJE
TOL
TOLA
TOLAN
TOLANE
TOLBOOTH
TOLD
TOLDERIA
TOLDO
TOLE
TOLED
TOLEDO
TOLERABILITY
TOLERABLE
TOLERABLY
TOLERANCE
TOLERANCY
TOLERANT
TOLERANTLY
TOLERATE
TOLERATED
TOLERATING
TOLERATION
TOLERATIVE
TOLERATOR
TOLERISM
TOLFRAEDIC
TOLGUACHA
TOLIDIN
TOLIDINE
TOLING
TOLIPANE
TOLITE
TOLKE
TOLL
TOLLABLE
TOLLAGE
TOLLBAR
TOLLBOOK
TOLLBOOTH
TOLLED
TOLLER
TOLLERY
TOLLGATE
TOLLGATHERER
TOLLHALL
TOLLHOUSE
TOLLHOUSES
TOLLIKER
TOLLING
TOLLKEEPER
TOLLMAN
TOLLMEN
TOLLON
TOLLS
TOLLWAY
TOLLY
TOLMEN
TOLPATCH
TOLPATCHERY
TOLSEL
TOLSESTER
TOLSEY
TOLT
TOLTER
TOLU
TOLUALDEHYDE
TOLUATE
TOLUENE
TOLUIC
TOLUID
TOLUIDE
TOLUIDIN
TOLUIDINE
TOLUIDO
TOLUNITRILE
TOLUOL
TOLUOLE
TOLUTATION
TOLUYL
TOLUYLENE
TOLYL
TOLYLENE
TOLYPEUTINE
TOLZEY
TOM
TOMAHAWK
TOMAHAWKED
TOMAHAWKER
TOMAHAWKING
TOMALLEY
TOMAN
TOMAND
TOMATILLO
TOMATO
TOMATOES
TOMB
TOMBAC
TOMBACK
TOMBAK
TOMBAL
TOMBE
TOMBED
TOMBIC
TOMBING
TOMBLET
TOMBOLA
TOMBOLO
TOMBOY
TOMBOYFUL
TOMBOYISH
TOMBOYISHLY
TOMBS
TOMBSTONE
TOMCAT
TOMCOD
TOME
TOMENT
TOMENTA
TOMENTOSE
TOMENTULOSE
TOMENTUM
TOMFOOL
TOMFOOLERIES
TOMFOOLERY
TOMFOOLISH
TOMIA
TOMIAL
TOMIN
TOMINES
TOMISH
TOMIUM
TOMJOHN
TOMJON
TOMKIN
TOMME
TOMMED
TOMMIES
TOMMING
TOMMY
TOMMYBAG
TOMMYCOD
TOMMYROT
TOMNODDY
TOMNORRY
TOMNOUP
TOMOGRAPHY
TOMOLO
TOMORN
TOMORROW
TOMORROWER
TOMORROWING
TOMORROWNESS
TOMOSIS
TOMPION
TOMPIPER
TOMRIG
TOMTATE
TOMTIT
TON
TONADA
TONAL
TONALAMATL
TONALIST
TONALITE
TONALITIES
TONALITIVE
TONALITY
TONALLY
TONALMATL
TONANT
TONDE
TONDI
TONDINO
TONDO
TONE
TONED
TONEDEAFNESS
TONEE
TONEL
TONELADA
TONELESS
TONELESSLY
TONELESSNESS
TONEME
TONER
TONES
TONETIC
TONETICALLY
TONETICIAN
TONETICS
TONETTE

TONG
TONGA
TONGED
TONGING
TONGKANG
TONGS
TONGSMAN
TONGSMEN
TONGUE
TONGUEBIRD
TONGUED
TONGUEFENCE
TONGUEFENCER
TONGUEFISH
TONGUEFISHES
TONGUEFUL
TONGUEFULS
TONGUELESS
TONGUELET
TONGUEMAN
TONGUEMEN
TONGUER
TONGUEY
TONGUING
TONGUY
TONIC
TONICAL
TONICALLY
TONICITY
TONICIZE
TONICKED
TONICKING
TONIER
TONIES
TONIEST
TONIFY
TONIGHT
TONING
TONISH
TONISHLY
TONISHNESS
TONITE
TONITRUONE
TONITRUOUS
TONJON
TONK
TONKA
TONLET
TONNAGE
TONNE
TONNEAU
TONNEAUS
TONNEAUX
TONNELLE
TONNER
TONNISH
TONNISHLY
TONNISHNESS
TONNLAND
TONOGRAM
TONOGRAPH
TONOLOGICAL
TONOLOGY
TONOMETRIC
TONOMETRY
TONOPHANT
TONOPLAST
TONOSCOPE
TONOTACTIC
TONOTAXIS
TONOUS
TONSBERGITE
TONSIL
TONSILAR
TONSILE
TONSILITIS
TONSILLAR
TONSILLARY
TONSILLITIC
TONSILLOLITH
TONSILLOTOMIES
TONSILLOTOMY
TONSOR
TONSORIAL
TONSURATE
TONSURE
TONSURED
TONSURING
TONTINE
TONTINER
TONUS
TONY
TONYHOOP
TOO
TOOART
TOODLE
TOOK
TOOL
TOOLACH
TOOLBOX
TOOLBUILDER
TOOLBUILDING
TOOLED
TOOLER
TOOLHOLDER
TOOLING
TOOLMAKER
TOOLMAKING
TOOLMAN
TOOLMARK
TOOLMARKING
TOOLMEN
TOOLPLATE
TOOLROOM
TOOLS
TOOLSI
TOOLSLIDE
TOOLSMITH
TOOLSTOCK
TOOLSTONE
TOOLSY
TOOM
TOOMLY
TOON
TOONWOOD
TOOP
TOORIE
TOOROCK
TOOROO
TOOSE
TOOSH
TOOSIE
TOOT
TOOTED
TOOTER
TOOTH
TOOTHACHE
TOOTHACHING
TOOTHACHY
TOOTHBILL
TOOTHBRUSH
TOOTHBRUSHY
TOOTHDRAWER
TOOTHDRAWING
TOOTHED
TOOTHER
TOOTHFLOWER
TOOTHFUL
TOOTHIER
TOOTHIEST
TOOTHILL
TOOTHING
TOOTHLESS
TOOTHLESSLY
TOOTHLET
TOOTHLETED
TOOTHPASTE
TOOTHPICK
TOOTHPLATE
TOOTHPOWDER
TOOTHPROOF
TOOTHSHELL
TOOTHSOME
TOOTHSOMELY
TOOTHSTICK
TOOTHWASH
TOOTHWORK
TOOTHWORT
TOOTHY
TOOTING
TOOTINGHOLE
TOOTLE
TOOTLED
TOOTLER
TOOTLING
TOOTLISH
TOOTMOOT
TOOTS
TOOTSIE
TOOTSIES
TOOTSY
TOOZLE
TOOZOO
TOP
TOPAESTHESIA
TOPARCH
TOPARCHIA
TOPARCHIAE
TOPARCHICAL
TOPARCHIES
TOPARCHY
TOPAS
TOPASS
TOPATO
TOPAU
TOPAZ
TOPAZES
TOPAZFELS
TOPAZINE
TOPAZITE
TOPAZOLITE
TOPAZY
TOPCAP
TOPCAST
TOPCOAT
TOPCOATING
TOPE
TOPECHEE
TOPECTOMIES
TOPECTOMY
TOPED
TOPEE
TOPEEWALLAH
TOPEK
TOPENG
TOPEPO
TOPER
TOPESTHESIA
TOPFILLED
TOPFLIGHT
TOPFUL
TOPFULL
TOPGALLANT
TOPH
TOPHACEOUS
TOPHAIKE
TOPHE
TOPHETIC
TOPHETICAL
TOPHI
TOPHUS
TOPI
TOPIA
TOPIARIA
TOPIARIAN
TOPIARIES
TOPIARIST
TOPIARY
TOPIC
TOPICAL
TOPICALITY
TOPICALLY
TOPINAMBOU
TOPING
TOPIS
TOPIWALA
TOPKICK
TOPKNOT
TOPKNOTTED
TOPLESS
TOPLESSNESS
TOPLIGHTED
TOPLINE
TOPLOFTICAL
TOPLOFTIER
TOPLOFTIEST
TOPLOFTILY
TOPLOFTINESS
TOPLOFTY
TOPMAKER
TOPMAN
TOPMAST
TOPMEN
TOPMINNOW
TOPMOST
TOPMOSTLY
TOPNET
TOPNOTCH
TOPNOTCHER
TOPO
TOPOALGIA
TOPODEME
TOPOGNOSIA
TOPOGNOSIS
TOPOGRAPH
TOPOGRAPHER
TOPOGRAPHIC
TOPOGRAPHICAL
TOPOGRAPHICS
TOPOGRAPHIES
TOPOGRAPHIST
TOPOGRAPHY
TOPOLATRY
TOPOLOGIC
TOPOLOGICAL
TOPOLOGY
TOPONARCOSIS
TOPONEURAL
TOPONEUROSIS
TOPONYM
TOPONYMAL
TOPONYMIC
TOPONYMICAL
TOPONYMICS
TOPONYMIES
TOPONYMY
TOPOPHOBIA
TOPOPHONE
TOPOPOLITAN
TOPOTACTIC
TOPOTAXIS
TOPOTYPE
TOPOTYPIC
TOPOTYPICAL
TOPPED
TOPPER
TOPPIECE
TOPPING
TOPPINGLY
TOPPINGNESS
TOPPLE
TOPPLED
TOPPLER
TOPPLING
TOPPLY
TOPPO
TOPPY
TOPRAIL
TOPROPE
TOPS
TOPSAIL
TOPSAILITE
TOPSIDE
TOPSMAN
TOPSMEN
TOPSOIL
TOPSTONE
TOPSWARM
TOPSYTURN
TOPT
TOPTAIL
TOPWORK
TOQUE
TOQUET
TOQUILLA
TOR
TORA
TORAH
TORAN
TORANA
TORBANITE
TORBANITIC
TORBERNITE
TORC
TORCEL
TORCH
TORCHBEARER
TORCHBEARING
TORCHER
TORCHERE
TORCHET
TORCHLIGHT
TORCHLIGHTED
TORCHLIKE
TORCHLIT
TORCHMAN
TORCHON
TORCHWOOD
TORCHWORT
TORCULAR
TORCULUS
TORDION
TORDRILLITE
TORE
TOREADOR
TORERO
TOREROS
TORET
TOREUTIC
TOREUTICS
TORFACEOUS
TORFEL
TORFLE
TORGOCH
TORI
TORIC
TORIES
TORII
TORIL
TORMA
TORMAE
TORMENT
TORMENTA
TORMENTATIVE
TORMENTED

TORMENTEDLY
TORMENTER
TORMENTIL
TORMENTILLA
TORMENTING
TORMENTINGLY
TORMENTIVE
TORMENTOR
TORMENTOUS
TORMENTRY
TORMENTUM
TORMINA
TORMINAL
TORMINOUS
TORMODONT
TORN
TORNADA
TORNADE
TORNADIC
TORNADO
TORNADOES
TORNADOS
TORNARIA
TORNARIAE
TORNARIAN
TORNESE
TORNESI
TORNILLA
TORNILLO
TORNOTE
TORNUS
TORO
TOROID
TOROIDAL
TOROLILLO
TORONJA
TOROROKOMBU
TOROS
TOROSE
TOROSITY
TOROTH
TOROTORO
TOROUS
TORP
TORPEDINEER
TORPEDINOUS
TORPEDO
TORPEDOED
TORPEDOER
TORPEDOES
TORPEDOING
TORPEDOIST
TORPEDOPLANE
TORPEDOS
TORPENT
TORPESCENCE
TORPESCENT
TORPEX
TORPID
TORPIDITIES
TORPIDITY
TORPIDLY
TORPIDNESS
TORPIDS
TORPIFIED
TORPIFY
TORPIFYING
TORPITUDE
TORPOR
TORPORIFIC
TORQUATE
TORQUATED
TORQUE
TORQUED
TORQUES
TORR
TORREFACTION
TORREFIED
TORREFY
TORREFYING
TORRENT
TORRENTFUL
TORRENTIAL
TORRENTIALLY
TORRENTINE
TORRENTUOUS
TORRET
TORRID
TORRIDITY
TORRIDLY
TORRIDNESS
TORRIFY
TORRONE
TORSADE
TORSALO
TORSE
TORSEL
TORSI
TORSIGRAPH
TORSILE
TORSIOGRAM
TORSIOGRAPH
TORSION
TORSIONAL
TORSIONALLY
TORSIONING
TORSIVE
TORSK
TORSKS
TORSO
TORSOCLUSION
TORSOS
TORT
TORTA
TORTAYS
TORTE
TORTEAU
TORTEAUS
TORTEAUX
TORTEN
TORTICOLLAR
TORTICOLLIS
TORTICONE
TORTIE
TORTIL
TORTILE
TORTILITY
TORTILLA
TORTILLAS
TORTILLE
TORTILLON
TORTIOUS
TORTIS
TORTIVE
TORTOISE
TORTOISES
TORTOISESHELL
TORTONI
TORTOR
TORTRICES
TORTRICID
TORTRICINE
TORTRICOID
TORTRIX
TORTUE
TORTULA
TORTULACEOUS
TORTUOSITIES
TORTUOSITY
TORTUOUS
TORTUOUSLY
TORTUOUSNESS
TORTURABLE
TORTURE
TORTURED
TORTUREDLY
TORTURER
TORTURING
TORTURINGLY
TORTUROUS
TORTUROUSLY
TORU
TORULA
TORULACEOUS
TORULAE
TORULI
TORULIFORM
TORULOID
TORULOSE
TORULOSIS
TORULOUS
TORULUS
TORUS
TORVID
TORVITY
TORVOUS
TORY
TORYHILLITE
TORYWEED
TOSAPHIST
TOSAPHOTH
TOSCA
TOSE
TOSH
TOSHAKHANA
TOSHER
TOSHERY
TOSHLY
TOSHNAIL
TOSHY
TOSIE
TOSS
TOSSED
TOSSER
TOSSICATED
TOSSING
TOSSINGLY
TOSSMENT
TOSSPOT
TOSSUP
TOSSUT
TOSSY
TOST
TOSTADO
TOSTAMENTE
TOSTAO
TOSTICATE
TOSTICATED
TOSTICATING
TOSTICATION
TOSTO
TOSTON
TOSY
TOSYL
TOT
TOTA
TOTAL
TOTALED
TOTALING
TOTALISATOR
TOTALITARIAN
TOTALITIES
TOTALITY
TOTALIZATION
TOTALIZATOR
TOTALIZE
TOTALIZED
TOTALIZER
TOTALIZING
TOTALLED
TOTALLING
TOTALLY
TOTANINE
TOTAQUINE
TOTARA
TOTE
TOTED
TOTELOAD
TOTEM
TOTEMIC
TOTEMICALLY
TOTEMISM
TOTEMIST
TOTEMISTIC
TOTEMIZATION
TOTER
TOTHER
TOTIENT
TOTING
TOTIPALMATE
TOTIPOTENCE
TOTIPOTENCY
TOTIPOTENT
TOTITIVE
TOTO
TOTOABA
TOTORA
TOTQUOT
TOTTED
TOTTER
TOTTERED
TOTTERER
TOTTERGRASS
TOTTERING
TOTTERINGLY
TOTTERISH
TOTTERY
TOTTING
TOTTLE
TOTTLISH
TOTTUM
TOTTY
TOTTYHEAD
TOTUAVA
TOTUM
TOTY
TOTYMAN
TOU
TOUART
TOUCAN
TOUCH
TOUCHABLE
TOUCHBACK
TOUCHBELL
TOUCHBOX
TOUCHDOWN
TOUCHE
TOUCHED
TOUCHEDNESS
TOUCHER
TOUCHHOLE
TOUCHIER
TOUCHIEST
TOUCHILY
TOUCHINESS
TOUCHING
TOUCHINGLY
TOUCHINGNESS
TOUCHLINE
TOUCHMARK
TOUCHOUS
TOUCHPAN
TOUCHPIECE
TOUCHSTONE
TOUCHUP
TOUCHWOOD
TOUCHY
TOUG
TOUGH
TOUGHEN
TOUGHENED
TOUGHENER
TOUGHENING
TOUGHER
TOUGHEST
TOUGHHEAD
TOUGHLY
TOUGHNESS
TOUGHRA
TOUGHT
TOUMNAH
TOUN
TOUP
TOUPEE
TOUPEED
TOUPET
TOUR
TOURACO
TOURBE
TOURBILLON
TOURED
TOURELLE
TOURER
TOURET
TOURETTE
TOURING
TOURISM
TOURIST
TOURISTIC
TOURISTICAL
TOURISTRY
TOURISTY
TOURMALIN
TOURMALINE
TOURMALINIC
TOURMALINIZE
TOURMALITE
TOURN
TOURNAI
TOURNAMENT
TOURNAMENTAL
TOURNASIN
TOURNAY
TOURNE
TOURNEE
TOURNEL
TOURNETTE
TOURNEUR
TOURNEY
TOURNEYED
TOURNEYER
TOURNEYING
TOURNEYS
TOURNIQUET
TOURNOIS
TOURNURE
TOURS
TOURT
TOURTE
TOUSCHE
TOUSE
TOUSEL
TOUSER
TOUSLE
TOUSLED
TOUSLING
TOUSLY
TOUST
TOUSTIE
TOUSY
TOUT
TOUTE
TOUTER
TOUZLE
TOVAR

TOVARIACEOUS
TOVARICH
TOVARISCH
TOVARISH
TOVE
TOVET
TOW
TOWAGE
TOWAI
TOWAN
TOWARD
TOWARDLINESS
TOWARDLY
TOWARDNESS
TOWARDS
TOWAWAY
TOWBOAT
TOWCOCK
TOWDIE
TOWED
TOWEL
TOWELED
TOWELETTE
TOWELING
TOWELLED
TOWELLING
TOWELRY
TOWER
TOWERED
TOWERING
TOWERINGLY
TOWERLET
TOWERLIKE
TOWERMAN
TOWERMEN
TOWERWORT
TOWERY
TOWGHT
TOWHEAD
TOWHEADED
TOWHEE
TOWING
TOWKAY
TOWLINE
TOWMAST
TOWMOND
TOWMONT
TOWN
TOWNED
TOWNEE
TOWNER
TOWNET
TOWNFARING
TOWNFOLK
TOWNFOLKS
TOWNGATE
TOWNHOUSE
TOWNIE
TOWNIES
TOWNIFIED
TOWNIFY
TOWNIFYING
TOWNINESS
TOWNISH
TOWNISHLY
TOWNISHNESS
TOWNIST
TOWNLAND
TOWNLET
TOWNLIKE
TOWNLING
TOWNLY
TOWNMAN
TOWNMEN
TOWNSBOY
TOWNSFELLOW
TOWNSHIP
TOWNSITE
TOWNSMAN
TOWNSMEN
TOWNSPEOPLE
TOWNSWOMAN
TOWNSWOMEN
TOWNWEAR
TOWNY
TOWPATH
TOWROPE
TOWSE
TOWSER
TOWSON
TOWSY
TOWT
TOWY
TOWZIE
TOX
TOXA
TOXAEMIA
TOXAEMIAS
TOXAEMIC
TOXALBUMIC
TOXALBUMIN
TOXALBUMOSE
TOXAMIN
TOXANAEMIA
TOXANEMIA
TOXEMIA
TOXEMIC
TOXIC
TOXICAL
TOXICALLY
TOXICANT
TOXICAROL
TOXICATE
TOXICATION
TOXICITIES
TOXICITY
TOXICOGENIC
TOXICOGNATH
TOXICOID
TOXICOLOGIC
TOXICOLOGIST
TOXICOLOGY
TOXICOMANIA
TOXICON
TOXICOPATHIC
TOXICOPATHY
TOXICOPHAGY
TOXICOPHIDIA
TOXICOSES
TOXICOSIS
TOXICUM
TOXIDERMIC
TOXIFER
TOXIFEROUS
TOXIFY
TOXIGENIC
TOXIN
TOXINAEMIA
TOXINE
TOXINEMIA
TOXINFECTION
TOXINOSIS
TOXIPHAGI
TOXIPHAGUS
TOXIPHOBIA
TOXIPHOBIAC
TOXIPHORIC
TOXITABELLAE
TOXITY
TOXODONT
TOXOGENESIS
TOXOGLOSSATE
TOXOID
TOXOLOGY
TOXOLYSIS
TOXON
TOXONE
TOXOPHIL
TOXOPHILE
TOXOPHILISM
TOXOPHILITE
TOXOPHILITIC
TOXOPHILOUS
TOXOPHILY
TOXOTAE
TOY
TOYED
TOYER
TOYFUL
TOYFULNESS
TOYING
TOYISH
TOYISHLY
TOYISHNESS
TOYLE
TOYMAN
TOYMEN
TOYO
TOYON
TOYOS
TOYSHOP
TOYSOME
TOYWORT
TOZE
TOZEE
TOZER
TOZIE
TRA
TRABACOLI
TRABACOLO
TRABACOLOS
TRABAL
TRABANT
TRABASCOLO
TRABEA
TRABEAE
TRABEATE
TRABEATED
TRABEATION
TRABECULA
TRABECULAE
TRABECULAR
TRABECULATE
TRABECULATED
TRABECULE
TRABES
TRABU
TRABUCH
TRABUCHO
TRABUCO
TRABUCOS
TRACASSERIE
TRACASSERIES
TRACE
TRACEABILITY
TRACEABLE
TRACEABLY
TRACED
TRACER
TRACERIED
TRACERIES
TRACERY
TRACHEA
TRACHEAE
TRACHEAL
TRACHEALGIA
TRACHEALIS
TRACHEAN
TRACHEARIAN
TRACHEARY
TRACHEAS
TRACHEATE
TRACHEATION
TRACHEID
TRACHEIDAL
TRACHEITIS
TRACHELAGRA
TRACHELATE
TRACHELISMUS
TRACHELITIS
TRACHELIUM
TRACHELOTOMY
TRACHENCHYMA
TRACHEOCELE
TRACHEOLAR
TRACHEOLE
TRACHEOPHONE
TRACHEOPHYTE
TRACHEOSCOPY
TRACHEOTOMIES
TRACHEOTOMY
TRACHINOID
TRACHITIS
TRACHLE
TRACHLED
TRACHLING
TRACHODONT
TRACHODONTID
TRACHOMA
TRACHOMATOUS
TRACHYANDESITE
TRACHYBASALT
TRACHYLINE
TRACHYPHONIA
TRACHYTE
TRACHYTIC
TRACHYTOID
TRACING
TRACK
TRACKABLE
TRACKAGE
TRACKBARROW
TRACKED
TRACKER
TRACKHOUND
TRACKING
TRACKLAYER
TRACKLESS
TRACKLESSLY
TRACKMAN
TRACKMASTER
TRACKMEN
TRACKPOT
TRACKSHIFTER
TRACKSICK
TRACKSIDE
TRACKWALKER
TRACKWAY
TRACT
TRACTABILITIES
TRACTABILITY
TRACTABLE
TRACTABLY
TRACTARIAN
TRACTATE
TRACTATION
TRACTATOR
TRACTELLATE
TRACTELLUM
TRACTIFEROUS
TRACTILE
TRACTILITY
TRACTION
TRACTIONAL
TRACTITIAN
TRACTIVE
TRACTOR
TRACTORATION
TRACTORISM
TRACTORIST
TRACTORIZE
TRACTRICES
TRACTRIX
TRACTUS
TRADAL
TRADE
TRADECRAFT
TRADED
TRADEFUL
TRADEMARK
TRADEMASTER
TRADER
TRADES
TRADESCANTIA
TRADESFOLK
TRADESMAN
TRADESMEN
TRADESPEOPLE
TRADESPERSON
TRADESWOMAN
TRADIMENT
TRADING
TRADITE
TRADITION
TRADITIONAL
TRADITIONARIES
TRADITIONARY
TRADITIONATE
TRADITIONER
TRADITIONIST
TRADITIONS
TRADITIVE
TRADITOR
TRADITORES
TRADUCE
TRADUCED
TRADUCENT
TRADUCER
TRADUCIAN
TRADUCIANISM
TRADUCIANIST
TRADUCIBLE
TRADUCING
TRADUCINGLY
TRADUCT
TRADUCTION
TRADY
TRAFFIC
TRAFFICABLE
TRAFFICKED
TRAFFICKER
TRAFFICKING
TRAFFICS
TRAFFICWAY
TRAG
TRAGACANTH
TRAGACANTHA
TRAGACANTHIN
TRAGICOLORED
TRAGICOMEDY
TRAGICOMIC
TRAGICOMICAL
TRAGION
TRAGOEDIA
TRAGOPAN
TRAGULE
TRAGUS
TRAH
TRAHEEN
TRAHISON
TRAIK
TRAIKY
TRAIL
TRAILBASTON
TRAILBLAZER

TRAILBLAZING
TRAILED
TRAILER
TRAILERY
TRAILING
TRAILINGLY
TRAILMAN
TRAILSMAN
TRAILSMEN
TRAILWAY
TRAILY
TRAIN
TRAINABLE
TRAINAGE
TRAINAGRAPH
TRAINANT
TRAINANTE
TRAINBAND
TRAINBEARER
TRAINBOLT
TRAINBOY
TRAINEAU
TRAINED
TRAINEE
TRAINEL
TRAINER
TRAINFUL
TRAINING
TRAINLOAD
TRAINMAN
TRAINMASTER
TRAINMEN
TRAINS
TRAINSTER
TRAINWAY
TRAINY
TRAIPSE
TRAIPSED
TRAIPSING
TRAIST
TRAIT
TRAITEUR
TRAITEURS
TRAITOR
TRAITOROUS
TRAITOROUSLY
TRAITORY
TRAITRESS
TRAITS
TRAJECT
TRAJECTED
TRAJECTILE
TRAJECTING
TRAJECTION
TRAJECTORIES
TRAJECTORY
TRAJET
TRALATITION
TRALATITIOUS
TRALIRA
TRAM
TRAMA
TRAMAL
TRAMCAR
TRAME
TRAMFUL
TRAMLINE
TRAMMED
TRAMMEL
TRAMMELED
TRAMMELER
TRAMMELHEAD
TRAMMELING
TRAMMELINGLY
TRAMMELLED
TRAMMELLER
TRAMMELLING
TRAMMER
TRAMMING
TRAMMON
TRAMONTANA
TRAMONTANE
TRAMP
TRAMPCOCK
TRAMPED
TRAMPER
TRAMPING
TRAMPLE
TRAMPLED
TRAMPLER
TRAMPLING
TRAMPOLIN
TRAMPOLINE
TRAMPOOSE
TRAMPOSO
TRAMPOT
TRAMPS
TRAMROAD
TRAMS
TRAMWAY
TRAMWAYMAN
TRAMWAYMEN
TRANCE
TRANCED
TRANCEDLY
TRANCHANT
TRANCHANTE
TRANCHE
TRANCHEFER
TRANCHET
TRANCHOIR
TRANCING
TRANEEN
TRANGAM
TRANI
TRANK
TRANKA
TRANKER
TRANKUM
TRANKY
TRANQUIL
TRANQUILER
TRANQUILEST
TRANQUILITY
TRANQUILIZE
TRANQUILIZER
TRANQUILIZING
TRANQUILLER
TRANQUILLEST
TRANQUILLISE
TRANQUILLITY
TRANQUILLIZE
TRANQUILLIZED
TRANQUILLO
TRANQUILLY
TRANQUILNESS
TRANS
TRANSACT
TRANSACTED
TRANSACTING
TRANSACTION
TRANSACTOR
TRANSALPINE
TRANSANNULAR
TRANSAPICAL
TRANSAUDIENT
TRANSBAIKAL
TRANSBOARD
TRANSBORDER
TRANSCALENCY
TRANSCALENT
TRANSCEIVER
TRANSCEND
TRANSCENDED
TRANSCENDENT
TRANSCENDENTAL
TRANSCENDING
TRANSCENSION
TRANSCOLOR
TRANSCREATE
TRANSCRIBBLE
TRANSCRIBE
TRANSCRIBED
TRANSCRIBER
TRANSCRIBING
TRANSCRIPT
TRANSCUR
TRANSCURRENT
TRANSDIALECT
TRANSDIURNAL
TRANSDUCER
TRANSDUCTION
TRANSECT
TRANSECTED
TRANSECTING
TRANSECTION
TRANSELEMENT
TRANSENNA
TRANSENNAE
TRANSEPT
TRANSEPTAL
TRANSEPTALLY
TRANSEUNT
TRANSFER
TRANSFERABLE
TRANSFERAL
TRANSFEREE
TRANSFERENCE
TRANSFERENT
TRANSFEROR
TRANSFERRAL
TRANSFERRED
TRANSFERRER
TRANSFERRING
TRANSFIGURE
TRANSFIGURED
TRANSFIGURING
TRANSFINITE
TRANSFIX
TRANSFIXED
TRANSFIXING
TRANSFIXION
TRANSFIXTURE
TRANSFLUENT
TRANSFLUX
TRANSFORM
TRANSFORMATION
TRANSFORMED
TRANSFORMER
TRANSFORMING
TRANSFORMISM
TRANSFORMIST
TRANSFUGE
TRANSFUSE
TRANSFUSED
TRANSFUSER
TRANSFUSING
TRANSFUSION
TRANSFUSIVE
TRANSGRESS
TRANSGRESSED
TRANSGRESSING
TRANSGRESSION
TRANSGRESSOR
TRANSHAPE
TRANSHIP
TRANSHIPMENT
TRANSHUMAN
TRANSHUMANCE
TRANSHUMANT
TRANSIENCE
TRANSIENCY
TRANSIENT
TRANSIENTLY
TRANSIGENCE
TRANSIGENT
TRANSILIAC
TRANSILIENCE
TRANSILIENCY
TRANSILIENT
TRANSIRE
TRANSISCHIAC
TRANSISTOR
TRANSIT
TRANSITABLE
TRANSITER
TRANSITION
TRANSITIONAL
TRANSITIVE
TRANSITIVELY
TRANSITIVISM
TRANSITIVITIES
TRANSITIVITY
TRANSITMAN
TRANSITMEN
TRANSITORILY
TRANSITORINESS
TRANSITORY
TRANSITUS
TRANSLADE
TRANSLATABLE
TRANSLATE
TRANSLATED
TRANSLATING
TRANSLATION
TRANSLATIVE
TRANSLATOR
TRANSLATORY
TRANSLAY
TRANSLEITHAN
TRANSLOCATE
TRANSLOCATED
TRANSLOCATING
TRANSLUCE
TRANSLUCENCE
TRANSLUCENCY
TRANSLUCENT
TRANSLUCID
TRANSLUNAR
TRANSLUNARY
TRANSMAKE
TRANSMARINE
TRANSMEDIAN
TRANSMEW
TRANSMIGRANT
TRANSMIGRATE
TRANSMIGRATED
TRANSMIGRATING
TRANSMIGRATION
TRANSMISSION
TRANSMISSIVE
TRANSMISSORY
TRANSMIT
TRANSMITTAL
TRANSMITTED
TRANSMITTER
TRANSMITTING
TRANSMOGRIFIED
TRANSMOGRIFY
TRANSMOGRIFYING
TRANSMONTANE
TRANSMUE
TRANSMUTATE
TRANSMUTATION
TRANSMUTE
TRANSMUTED
TRANSMUTER
TRANSMUTING
TRANSMUTUAL
TRANSNATURAL
TRANSNORMAL
TRANSOCEANIC
TRANSOM
TRANSOMED
TRANSONIC
TRANSPACIFIC
TRANSPADANE
TRANSPARENCE
TRANSPARENCIES
TRANSPARENCY
TRANSPARENT
TRANSPASS
TRANSPECIATE
TRANSPICUITY
TRANSPICUOUS
TRANSPIERCE
TRANSPIERCED
TRANSPIERCING
TRANSPIRE
TRANSPIRED
TRANSPIRING
TRANSPLACE
TRANSPLANT
TRANSPLANTED
TRANSPLANTER
TRANSPLANTING
TRANSPONDER
TRANSPONIBLE
TRANSPONTINE
TRANSPORT
TRANSPORTAL
TRANSPORTATION
TRANSPORTED
TRANSPORTER
TRANSPORTING
TRANSPORTIVE
TRANSPOSABLE
TRANSPOSE
TRANSPOSED
TRANSPOSER
TRANSPOSING
TRANSPOSITION
TRANSPOSITOR
TRANSPRINT
TRANSPROSE
TRANSPROSER
TRANSPYLORIC
TRANSRHENANE
TRANSSHAPE
TRANSSHAPED
TRANSSHAPING
TRANSSHIP
TRANSSHIPPED
TRANSSHIPPING
TRANSUBSTANTIATION
TRANSUDATE
TRANSUDATION
TRANSUDATIVE
TRANSUDATORY
TRANSUDE
TRANSUDED
TRANSUDING
TRANSUME
TRANSUMED
TRANSUMING
TRANSUMPT
TRANSUMPTION
TRANSUMPTIVE
TRANSURANIAN
TRANSURANIC
TRANSVAAL
TRANSVALUE
TRANSVALUED
TRANSVALUING
TRANSVASE

TRANSVECTANT
TRANSVECTION
TRANSVENOM
TRANSVERBATE
TRANSVERSAL
TRANSVERSALE
TRANSVERSAN
TRANSVERSARY
TRANSVERSE
TRANSVERSELY
TRANSVERSER
TRANSVERSION
TRANSVERSIVE
TRANSVERSUM
TRANSVERSUS
TRANSVERT
TRANSVERTER
TRANSVEST
TRANSVESTISM
TRANSVESTITE
TRANSWRITTEN
TRANT
TRANTER
TRANTLUM
TRANVIA
TRAP
TRAPAN
TRAPANNER
TRAPBALL
TRAPDOOR
TRAPES
TRAPEZE
TRAPEZIA
TRAPEZIAL
TRAPEZIAN
TRAPEZIFORM
TRAPEZING
TRAPEZIST
TRAPEZIUM
TRAPEZIUMS
TRAPEZIUS
TRAPEZOID
TRAPEZOIDAL
TRAPFALL
TRAPHOLE
TRAPICHE
TRAPIFEROUS
TRAPISH
TRAPLIGHT
TRAPPEAN
TRAPPED
TRAPPER
TRAPPING
TRAPPINGLY
TRAPPINGS
TRAPPIST
TRAPPOID
TRAPPOSE
TRAPPOUS
TRAPPY
TRAPROCK
TRAPS
TRAPSHOOT
TRAPSHOOTER
TRAPSHOOTING
TRAPSTICK
TRAPT
TRASH
TRASHED
TRASHERY
TRASHIER
TRASHIEST
TRASHIFY
TRASHILY
TRASHINESS
TRASHING
TRASHTRIE
TRASHY
TRASS
TRASY
TRATLER
TRATTLE
TRATTORIA
TRAUCHLE
TRAULISM
TRAUMA
TRAUMAS
TRAUMATA
TRAUMATIC
TRAUMATICIN
TRAUMATICINE
TRAUMATISM
TRAUMATIZE
TRAUMATOLOGY
TRAUMATOPNEA
TRAUMATOSIS
TRAUMATROPIC
TRAVADO
TRAVAIL
TRAVAILED
TRAVAILER
TRAVAILING
TRAVAILS
TRAVALE
TRAVALLY
TRAVATED
TRAVE
TRAVEL
TRAVELED
TRAVELER
TRAVELERS
TRAVELING
TRAVELLED
TRAVELLER
TRAVELLING
TRAVELOG
TRAVELOGUE
TRAVELOGUER
TRAVELS
TRAVERSABLE
TRAVERSAL
TRAVERSARY
TRAVERSE
TRAVERSED
TRAVERSER
TRAVERSING
TRAVERSION
TRAVERTIN
TRAVERTINE
TRAVEST
TRAVESTIED
TRAVESTIER
TRAVESTIES
TRAVESTY
TRAVESTYING
TRAVIS
TRAVISS
TRAVOIS
TRAVOISE
TRAVOISES
TRAVOY
TRAWL
TRAWLBOAT
TRAWLED
TRAWLER
TRAWLERMAN
TRAWLERMEN
TRAWLEY
TRAWLING
TRAWLNET
TRAY
TRAYNE
TREACHER
TREACHERIES
TREACHEROUS
TREACHERY
TREACLE
TREACLEWORT
TREACLINESS
TREACLY
TREAD
TREADBOARD
TREADER
TREADING
TREADLE
TREADLED
TREADLER
TREADLING
TREADMILL
TREADWHEEL
TREAGUE
TREASON
TREASONABLE
TREASONABLY
TREASONIST
TREASONOUS
TREASURABLE
TREASURE
TREASURED
TREASURER
TREASURIES
TREASURING
TREASUROUS
TREASURY
TREASURYSHIP
TREAT
TREATABLE
TREATABLY
TREATED
TREATEE
TREATER
TREATIES
TREATING
TREATISE
TREATISER
TREATMENT
TREATOR
TREATY
TREATYIST
TREATYITE
TREBLE
TREBLED
TREBLENESS
TREBLET
TREBLETREE
TREBLING
TREBLY
TREBUCHET
TREBUCKET
TRECENTIST
TRECENTO
TRECHMANNITE
TRECK
TRECKPOT
TRECKSCHUYT
TREDDLE
TREDECILE
TREDEFOWEL
TREDILLE
TREDRILLE
TREE
TREEBEARD
TREEBINE
TREED
TREEFISH
TREEFISHES
TREEHAIR
TREEING
TREELESS
TREELET
TREELIKE
TREELING
TREEMAKER
TREEMAKING
TREEMAN
TREEN
TREENAIL
TREES
TREESPEELER
TREETISE
TREETOP
TREEY
TREF
TREFA
TREFGORDD
TREFLE
TREFLEE
TREFOIL
TREFOILED
TREGET
TREGETOUR
TREHALA
TREHALASE
TREHALOSE
TREILLAGE
TREITOUR
TREITRE
TREK
TREKBOER
TREKKED
TREKKER
TREKKING
TREKOMETER
TREKPATH
TRELLIS
TRELLISED
TRELLISES
TRELLISING
TRELLISWORK
TREMATODE
TREMATOID
TREMBLE
TREMBLED
TREMBLEMENT
TREMBLER
TREMBLING
TREMBLINGLY
TREMBLY
TREMELINE
TREMELLIFORM
TREMELLOID
TREMELLOSE
TREMENDOUS
TREMENDOUSLY
TREMETOL
TREMEX
TREMIE
TREMOLANDO
TREMOLANT
TREMOLIST
TREMOLITE
TREMOLITIC
TREMOLO
TREMOLOS
TREMOLOSO
TREMOR
TREMPLIN
TREMULANDO
TREMULANT
TREMULATE
TREMULATION
TREMULENT
TREMULOUS
TREMULOUSLY
TREN
TRENAIL
TRENCH
TRENCHANCY
TRENCHANT
TRENCHANTLY
TRENCHED
TRENCHER
TRENCHERING
TRENCHERMAN
TRENCHERMEN
TRENCHES
TRENCHING
TRENCHLIKE
TRENCHMASTER
TRENCHMORE
TREND
TRENDED
TRENDEL
TRENDING
TRENDLE
TRENDY
TRENE
TRENTAL
TREPAN
TREPANATION
TREPANG
TREPANNED
TREPANNER
TREPANNING
TREPANNINGLY
TREPHINATION
TREPHINE
TREPHINED
TREPHINER
TREPHINING
TREPHONE
TREPID
TREPIDANCY
TREPIDANT
TREPIDATE
TREPIDATION
TREPIDATORY
TREPIDITY
TREPIDLY
TREPIDNESS
TREPONEME
TREPPE
TRES
TRESAIEL
TRESANCE
TRESCHE
TRESILLO
TRESIS
TRESPASS
TRESPASSAGE
TRESPASSED
TRESPASSER
TRESPASSING
TRESPASSORY
TRESS
TRESSED
TRESSILATE
TRESSILATION
TRESSON
TRESSOUR
TRESSURE
TRESSURED
TRESSY
TREST
TRESTLE
TRESTLETREE
TRESTLEWORK
TRESTLING
TRET
TRETIS
TREVALLY
TREVET
TREVIS
TREW
TREWAGE

TREWEL
TREWS
TREWSMAN
TREWSMEN
TREY
TRIABLE
TRIABLENESS
TRIACETATE
TRIACHENIUM
TRIACID
TRIACONTANE
TRIACONTER
TRIACT
TRIACTINAL
TRIACTINE
TRIAD
TRIADELPHOUS
TRIADIC
TRIADICAL
TRIADICALLY
TRIADISM
TRIADIST
TRIAENE
TRIAENOSE
TRIAGE
TRIAGONAL
TRIAKID
TRIAL
TRIALATE
TRIALISM
TRIALIST
TRIALITY
TRIALOGUE
TRIAMID
TRIAMIDE
TRIAMIN
TRIAMINE
TRIAMINO
TRIAMMONIUM
TRIAMORPH
TRIAMORPHOUS
TRIAMYLOSE
TRIANDER
TRIANDRIAN
TRIANDROUS
TRIANGLE
TRIANGLED
TRIANGLER
TRIANGULAR
TRIANGULARIS
TRIANGULARLY
TRIANGULATE
TRIANGULATED
TRIANGULATING
TRIANGULATOR
TRIANGULOID
TRIANNUAL
TRIANNULATE
TRIANON
TRIANTHOUS
TRIAPSIDAL
TRIARCH
TRIARCHATE
TRIARCHIES
TRIARCHY
TRIARIAN
TRIARII
TRIARY
TRIASTER
TRIATIC
TRIATOMIC
TRIATOMICITY
TRIAXAL
TRIAXIAL
TRIAXON
TRIAXONIAN
TRIAZANE
TRIAZIN
TRIAZINE
TRIAZO
TRIAZOLE
TRIBADE
TRIBADISM
TRIBADY
TRIBAL
TRIBALISM
TRIBALIST
TRIBALLY
TRIBASE
TRIBASIC
TRIBBLE
TRIBE
TRIBELESS
TRIBESMAN
TRIBESMEN
TRIBESPEOPLE
TRIBLET
TRIBOMETER
TRIBOROUGH
TRIBRACH
TRIBRACHIAL
TRIBRACHIC
TRIBRACTEATE
TRIBROMID
TRIBROMIDE
TRIBROMOETHANOL
TRIBUAL
TRIBUALLY
TRIBULAR
TRIBULATE
TRIBULATION
TRIBULOID
TRIBUNA
TRIBUNAL
TRIBUNARY
TRIBUNATE
TRIBUNE
TRIBUNESHIP
TRIBUNICIAL
TRIBUNICIAN
TRIBUNITIAL
TRIBUNITIAN
TRIBUNITIVE
TRIBUTABLE
TRIBUTARIES
TRIBUTARILY
TRIBUTARY
TRIBUTE
TRIBUTED
TRIBUTER
TRIBUTING
TRIBUTORIAN
TRICA
TRICAE
TRICALCIUM
TRICAR
TRICARBIMIDE
TRICARBON
TRICE
TRICED
TRICENARIES
TRICENARIUM
TRICENARY
TRICENNIAL
TRICEPHAL
TRICEPHALOUS
TRICEPHALUS
TRICEPS
TRICEPSES
TRICERATOPS
TRICERIA
TRICERION
TRICHAUXIS
TRICHECHINE
TRICHEVRON
TRICHI
TRICHIA
TRICHIASIS
TRICHINA
TRICHINAE
TRICHINAL
TRICHINIZE
TRICHINIZED
TRICHINIZING
TRICHINOPOLY
TRICHINOSIS
TRICHINOTIC
TRICHINOUS
TRICHION
TRICHITE
TRICHITIC
TRICHITIS
TRICHIURID
TRICHIUROID
TRICHLORID
TRICHLORIDE
TRICHLORO
TRICHOBLAST
TRICHOCLASIS
TRICHOCYST
TRICHOCYSTIC
TRICHODE
TRICHOGEN
TRICHOGENOUS
TRICHOGYNE
TRICHOGYNIAL
TRICHOGYNIC
TRICHOID
TRICHOLOGIST
TRICHOLOGY
TRICHOMA
TRICHOMATOSE
TRICHOME
TRICHOMIC
TRICHOMONAD
TRICHOMONIASIS
TRICHONOSIS
TRICHONOSUS
TRICHOPATHIC
TRICHOPATHY
TRICHOPHORE
TRICHOPHORIC
TRICHOPHYTE
TRICHOPHYTIC
TRICHOPORE
TRICHOPTER
TRICHOPTERA
TRICHOPTERAN
TRICHOPTERON
TRICHORD
TRICHOSIS
TRICHOTOMIC
TRICHOTOMIES
TRICHOTOMIST
TRICHOTOMIZE
TRICHOTOMOUS
TRICHROIC
TRICHROISM
TRICHROMAT
TRICHROMATE
TRICHROMATIC
TRICHROME
TRICHROMIC
TRICHRONOUS
TRICHURIASIS
TRICHY
TRICING
TRICINIUM
TRICIPITAL
TRICIRCULAR
TRICK
TRICKED
TRICKER
TRICKERIES
TRICKERY
TRICKIER
TRICKIEST
TRICKILY
TRICKINESS
TRICKING
TRICKINGLY
TRICKISH
TRICKISHLY
TRICKISHNESS
TRICKLE
TRICKLED
TRICKLESS
TRICKLET
TRICKLING
TRICKLINGLY
TRICKLY
TRICKMENT
TRICKS
TRICKSIER
TRICKSIEST
TRICKSINESS
TRICKSOME
TRICKSTER
TRICKSTERING
TRICKSY
TRICKTRACK
TRICKY
TRICLAD
TRICLINATE
TRICLINIA
TRICLINIARCH
TRICLINIARY
TRICLINIC
TRICLINIUM
TRICOCCOUS
TRICOLETTE
TRICOLIC
TRICOLON
TRICOLOR
TRICOLORED
TRICOLOUR
TRICON
TRICONCH
TRICONODONT
TRICONODONTY
TRICORN
TRICORNE
TRICORNERED
TRICORNUTE
TRICORPORAL
TRICORPORATE
TRICORYPHEAN
TRICOSANE
TRICOSANONE
TRICOSTATE
TRICOSYLIC
TRICOT
TRICOTEE
TRICOTINE
TRICOUNI
TRICRESOL
TRICROTIC
TRICROTISM
TRICROTOUS
TRICURVATE
TRICUSPID
TRICUSPIDAL
TRICUSPIDATE
TRICUSSATE
TRICYANIDE
TRICYCLE
TRICYCLED
TRICYCLENE
TRICYCLER
TRICYCLIC
TRICYCLING
TRICYCLIST
TRIDACTYL
TRIDAILY
TRIDDLER
TRIDECANE
TRIDECENE
TRIDECOIC
TRIDECYL
TRIDECYLENE
TRIDENT
TRIDENTAL
TRIDENTATE
TRIDENTATED
TRIDERMIC
TRIDIAPASON
TRIDIGITATE
TRIDIURNAL
TRIDOMINIUM
TRIDRACHM
TRIDUAN
TRIDUUM
TRIDYMITE
TRIDYNAMOUS
TRIECIOUS
TRIECIOUSLY
TRIED
TRIELAIDIN
TRIENE
TRIENNIA
TRIENNIAL
TRIENNIALITY
TRIENNIALLY
TRIENNIUM
TRIENNIUMS
TRIENS
TRIENTAL
TRIENTES
TRIER
TRIERARCH
TRIERARCHAL
TRIERARCHIES
TRIERARCHY
TRIES
TRIETERIC
TRIETERICS
TRIETHYL
TRIFACIAL
TRIFARIOUS
TRIFEROUS
TRIFID
TRIFISTULARY
TRIFLE
TRIFLED
TRIFLER
TRIFLES
TRIFLET
TRIFLING
TRIFLINGLY
TRIFLINGNESS
TRIFLORAL
TRIFLORATE
TRIFLOROUS
TRIFLUORIDE
TRIFOCAL
TRIFOIL
TRIFOLD
TRIFOLIATE
TRIFOLIATED
TRIFOLIOLATE
TRIFOLIOSIS
TRIFOLIUM
TRIFOLY
TRIFORIA
TRIFORIAL

TRIFORIUM
TRIFORM
TRIFORMED
TRIFORMITY
TRIFURCATE
TRIFURCATED
TRIFURCATION
TRIG
TRIGA
TRIGAMIST
TRIGAMOUS
TRIGAMY
TRIGEMINAL
TRIGEMINI
TRIGEMINOUS
TRIGEMINUS
TRIGENERIC
TRIGESIMAL
TRIGGED
TRIGGER
TRIGGERED
TRIGGERFISH
TRIGGERFISHES
TRIGGING
TRIGINTAL
TRIGLANDULAR
TRIGLID
TRIGLOT
TRIGLYPH
TRIGLYPHAL
TRIGLYPHED
TRIGLYPHIC
TRIGLYPHICAL
TRIGNESS
TRIGO
TRIGON
TRIGONAL
TRIGONALLY
TRIGONE
TRIGONELLIN
TRIGONELLINE
TRIGONEUTIC
TRIGONEUTISM
TRIGONIACEAN
TRIGONIC
TRIGONID
TRIGONITE
TRIGONITIS
TRIGONOID
TRIGONOMETER
TRIGONOMETRIES
TRIGONOMETRY
TRIGONON
TRIGONOTYPE
TRIGONOUS
TRIGRAM
TRIGRAMMATIC
TRIGRAPH
TRIGRAPHIC
TRIGYN
TRIGYNIAN
TRIGYNOUS
TRIHALID
TRIHALIDE
TRIHEDRA
TRIHEDRAL
TRIHEDRON
TRIHEDRONS
TRIHEMERAL
TRIHEMIMER
TRIHEMIMERAL
TRIHEMIMERIS
TRIHORAL
TRIHOURLY
TRIHYBRID
TRIHYDRATE
TRIHYDRATED
TRIHYDRIC
TRIHYDRIDE
TRIHYDROXY
TRIJUGATE
TRIJUGOUS
TRIKAYA
TRIKE
TRIKER
TRIKERIA
TRIKERION
TRIKETO
TRIKETONE
TRIKIR
TRILABE
TRILABIATE
TRILAMINAR
TRILATERAL
TRILATERALLY
TRILBIES
TRILEMMA
TRILINEAR
TRILINGUAL
TRILINGUAR
TRILINOLENIN
TRILITERAL
TRILITH
TRILITHIC
TRILITHON
TRILL
TRILLACHAN
TRILLADO
TRILLANDO
TRILLED
TRILLET
TRILLETTO
TRILLI
TRILLIACEOUS
TRILLIBUB
TRILLIIN
TRILLIL
TRILLING
TRILLION
TRILLIONAIRE
TRILLIONIZE
TRILLIONTH
TRILLIUM
TRILLO
TRILLOES
TRILOBAL
TRILOBATE
TRILOBATED
TRILOBATION
TRILOBE
TRILOBED
TRILOBITE
TRILOBITIC
TRILOCULAR
TRILOCULATE
TRILOGIC
TRILOGICAL
TRILOGIES
TRILOGIST
TRILOGY
TRILOPHODONT
TRILUMINAR
TRILUMINOUS
TRIM
TRIMACER
TRIMACULAR
TRIMACULATE
TRIMACULATED
TRIMASTIGATE
TRIME
TRIMELLIC
TRIMELLITIC
TRIMEMBRAL
TRIMENSUAL
TRIMER
TRIMERIC
TRIMERITE
TRIMEROUS
TRIMESIC
TRIMESITIC
TRIMESTER
TRIMESTRAL
TRIMESTRIAL
TRIMESYL
TRIMETALLIC
TRIMETALLISM
TRIMETER
TRIMETHOXY
TRIMETHYL
TRIMETHYLENE
TRIMETRIC
TRIMETRICAL
TRIMETROGON
TRIMLY
TRIMMED
TRIMMER
TRIMMERS
TRIMMEST
TRIMMING
TRIMNESS
TRIMOLECULAR
TRIMONTHLY
TRIMORIC
TRIMORPH
TRIMORPHIC
TRIMORPHISM
TRIMORPHOUS
TRIMSTONE
TRIMTRAM
TRIN
TRINAL
TRINALITY
TRINALIZE
TRINARY
TRINCHERA
TRINDLE
TRINE
TRINED
TRINELY
TRINEURAL
TRINGINE
TRINGLE
TRINGOID
TRINIDADO
TRINING
TRINITIES
TRINITRATE
TRINITRATION
TRINITRID
TRINITRIDE
TRINITRO
TRINITROTOLUENE
TRINITY
TRINK
TRINKERMAN
TRINKERMEN
TRINKET
TRINKETRIES
TRINKETRY
TRINKETY
TRINKLE
TRINKLET
TRINKUMS
TRINOCTIAL
TRINOCTILE
TRINODAL
TRINODE
TRINODINE
TRINOMIAL
TRINOMIALISM
TRINOMIALIST
TRINOMIALITY
TRINOMIALLY
TRINOPTICON
TRINQ
TRINTLE
TRINUCLEATE
TRINUNITY
TRIO
TRIOBOL
TRIOBOLON
TRIOCTILE
TRIODE
TRIODIA
TRIODION
TRIODONTOID
TRIOECIOUS
TRIOECIOUSLY
TRIOECISM
TRIOICOUS
TRIOLE
TRIOLEFIN
TRIOLEFINE
TRIOLET
TRIONFI
TRIONFO
TRIONYCHID
TRIONYCHOID
TRIONYM
TRIONYMAL
TRIOR
TRIORCHIS
TRIOS
TRIOSE
TRIOVULATE
TRIOXID
TRIOXIDE
TRIOZONID
TRIOZONIDE
TRIP
TRIPAL
TRIPALEOLATE
TRIPALMITATE
TRIPALMITIN
TRIPARA
TRIPART
TRIPARTED
TRIPARTEDLY
TRIPARTIBLE
TRIPARTIENT
TRIPARTITE
TRIPARTITELY
TRIPARTITION
TRIPASCHAL
TRIPE
TRIPEDAL
TRIPEL
TRIPEMAN
TRIPEMONGER
TRIPENNATE
TRIPENNY
TRIPERIES
TRIPERSONAL
TRIPERY
TRIPESHOP
TRIPESTONE
TRIPETALOID
TRIPETALOUS
TRIPEWIFE
TRIPEWOMAN
TRIPHAMMER
TRIPHANE
TRIPHASE
TRIPHENYL
TRIPHONY
TRIPHTHONG
TRIPHTHONGAL
TRIPHYLINE
TRIPHYLITE
TRIPHYLLOUS
TRIPINNATE
TRIPINNATED
TRIPINNATELY
TRIPLA
TRIPLANE
TRIPLASIAN
TRIPLASIC
TRIPLE
TRIPLEBACK
TRIPLED
TRIPLEFOLD
TRIPLEGIA
TRIPLET
TRIPLETAIL
TRIPLETREE
TRIPLEX
TRIPLEXITY
TRIPLICATE
TRIPLICATED
TRIPLICATELY
TRIPLICATING
TRIPLICATION
TRIPLICATIVE
TRIPLICATURE
TRIPLICE
TRIPLICITIES
TRIPLICITY
TRIPLING
TRIPLITE
TRIPLOID
TRIPLOIDIC
TRIPLOIDITE
TRIPLOIDY
TRIPLOPIA
TRIPLUM
TRIPLUMBIC
TRIPLY
TRIPOD
TRIPODAL
TRIPODIAL
TRIPODIAN
TRIPODIC
TRIPODIES
TRIPODY
TRIPOINTED
TRIPOLAR
TRIPOLI
TRIPOS
TRIPOSES
TRIPOT
TRIPOTAGE
TRIPOTER
TRIPPANT
TRIPPED
TRIPPER
TRIPPET
TRIPPING
TRIPPINGLY
TRIPPINGNESS
TRIPPLE
TRIPPLER
TRIPSILL
TRIPSIS
TRIPSOME
TRIPSOMELY
TRIPT
TRIPTANE
TRIPTEROUS
TRIPTOTE
TRIPTYCA
TRIPTYCH
TRIPTYQUE
TRIPUDIA
TRIPUDIAL
TRIPUDIANT

TRIPUDIARY
TRIPUDIATE
TRIPUDIATION
TRIPUDIST
TRIPUDIUM
TRIPY
TRIPYLAEAN
TRIPYLARIAN
TRIPYLEAN
TRIPYRENOUS
TRIQUET
TRIQUETRA
TRIQUETRAL
TRIQUETRIC
TRIQUETROUS
TRIQUETRUM
TRIQUINATE
TRIQUINOYL
TRIRADIAL
TRIRADIALLY
TRIRADIATE
TRIRADIATELY
TRIRADIATION
TRIREGNUM
TRIREME
TRISALT
TRISAZO
TRISECT
TRISECTED
TRISECTING
TRISECTION
TRISECTOR
TRISECTRIX
TRISEME
TRISEMIC
TRISEPALOUS
TRISEPTATE
TRISERIAL
TRISERIALLY
TRISERIATE
TRISERIATIM
TRISETOSE
TRISHA
TRISHNA
TRISKELE
TRISKELIA
TRISKELION
TRISMEGIST
TRISMEGISTIC
TRISMIC
TRISMUS
TRISOME
TRISPAST
TRISPASTON
TRISPERMOUS
TRISPORIC
TRISPOROUS
TRIST
TRISTACHYOUS
TRISTE
TRISTEARATE
TRISTESSE
TRISTEZA
TRISTFUL
TRISTFULLY
TRISTFULNESS
TRISTICH
TRISTICHIC
TRISTICHOUS
TRISTIGMATIC
TRISTILOQUY
TRISTISONOUS
TRISTIVE
TRISTYLOUS
TRISUL
TRISULA
TRISULC
TRISULCATE
TRISULCATED
TRISULFATE
TRISULFID
TRISULFIDE
TRISULFONE
TRISULFOXID
TRISULFOXIDE
TRISULPHATE
TRISULPHID
TRISULPHIDE
TRISULPHONE
TRISULPHONIC
TRISULPHOXID
TRISYLLABIC
TRISYLLABISM
TRISYLLABLE
TRITACTIC
TRITAGONIST
TRITANGENT
TRITANOPIA
TRITANOPSIA
TRITANOPTIC
TRITAPH
TRITE
TRITELY
TRITENESS
TRITERNATE
TRITERNATELY
TRITERPENE
TRITERPENOID
TRITHEISM
TRITHEIST
TRITHEISTIC
TRITHEITE
TRITHING
TRITHIONATES
TRITICAL
TRITICALITY
TRITICALLY
TRITICALNESS
TRITICEUM
TRITICIN
TRITICISM
TRITICOID
TRITICUM
TRITISH
TRITIUM
TRITOCONE
TRITOCONID
TRITOMITE
TRITON
TRITONE
TRITONOID
TRITONYMPH
TRITONYMPHAL
TRITOPATORES
TRITOR
TRITORAL
TRITOZOOID
TRITTICHAN
TRITUBERCULY
TRITURABLE
TRITURAL
TRITURATE
TRITURATED
TRITURATING
TRITURATION
TRITURATOR
TRITURATURE
TRITURIUM
TRIUMPH
TRIUMPHAL
TRIUMPHANCE
TRIUMPHANCY
TRIUMPHANT
TRIUMPHANTLY
TRIUMPHATOR
TRIUMPHED
TRIUMPHER
TRIUMPHING
TRIUMVIR
TRIUMVIRAL
TRIUMVIRATE
TRIUMVIRI
TRIUMVIRS
TRIUMVIRSHIP
TRIUNE
TRIUNGULIN
TRIUNITARIAN
TRIUNITIES
TRIUNITY
TRIURID
TRIVALENCE
TRIVALENCY
TRIVALENT
TRIVALVE
TRIVALVULAR
TRIVANT
TRIVARIANT
TRIVAT
TRIVERBIAL
TRIVET
TRIVIA
TRIVIAL
TRIVIALISM
TRIVIALIST
TRIVIALITIES
TRIVIALITY
TRIVIALIZE
TRIVIALLY
TRIVIALNESS
TRIVIRGA
TRIVIRGATE
TRIVIUM
TRIVOLTINE
TRIVVET
TRIWEEKLY
TRIZOIC
TRIZOMAL
TROAK
TROAT
TROBADOR
TROCA
TROCAR
TROCHA
TROCHAIC
TROCHAL
TROCHALOPOD
TROCHANTER
TROCHANTERIC
TROCHANTIN
TROCHANTINE
TROCHAR
TROCHATE
TROCHE
TROCHEAMETER
TROCHED
TROCHEE
TROCHEEIZE
TROCHEUS
TROCHID
TROCHIFEROUS
TROCHIFORM
TROCHIL
TROCHILI
TROCHILIC
TROCHILICS
TROCHILIDINE
TROCHILIDIST
TROCHILINE
TROCHILOS
TROCHILUS
TROCHING
TROCHISCI
TROCHISCUS
TROCHITE
TROCHITIC
TROCHLEA
TROCHLEAE
TROCHLEAR
TROCHLEARIS
TROCHLEARY
TROCHLEATE
TROCHLEIFORM
TROCHOID
TROCHOIDAL
TROCHOIDALLY
TROCHOIDES
TROCHOMETER
TROCHOPHORE
TROCHOSPHERE
TROCHOZOIC
TROCHOZOON
TROCK
TROCKERY
TROCO
TROCTOLITE
TROD
TRODDEN
TRODE
TROEGERITE
TROFFER
TROFT
TROG
TROGERITE
TROGGER
TROGGIN
TROGGS
TROGLODYTAL
TROGLODYTE
TROGLODYTIC
TROGON
TROGONOID
TROGS
TROGUE
TROIKA
TROIL
TROILITE
TROILUS
TROKE
TROKED
TROKER
TROKING
TROLAND
TROLL
TROLLED
TROLLEITE
TROLLER
TROLLEY
TROLLEYMAN
TROLLEYMEN
TROLLEYS
TROLLFLOWER
TROLLIES
TROLLIMOG
TROLLING
TROLLMAN
TROLLMEN
TROLLOL
TROLLOP
TROLLOPING
TROLLOPISH
TROLLOPS
TROLLOPY
TROLLY
TROLLYMAN
TROLLYMEN
TROMBA
TROMBASH
TROMBE
TROMBIDIASIS
TROMBONE
TROMBONIST
TROMBONY
TROMMEL
TROMOMETER
TROMOMETRIC
TROMOMETRY
TROMP
TROMPE
TROMPIL
TROMPILLO
TRON
TRONA
TRONADOR
TRONAGE
TRONC
TRONDHJEMITE
TRONE
TRONER
TRONK
TROODONT
TROOLIE
TROOLY
TROOP
TROOPED
TROOPER
TROOPFOWL
TROOPIAL
TROOPING
TROOPS
TROOPSHIP
TROOSHLACH
TROOSTITE
TROOZ
TROP
TROPACOCAINE
TROPAEOLA
TROPAEOLIN
TROPAEOLUM
TROPAEOLUMS
TROPAION
TROPAL
TROPARIA
TROPARION
TROPARY
TROPATE
TROPE
TROPEIC
TROPEIN
TROPEINE
TROPEOLIN
TROPER
TROPESIS
TROPHAEA
TROPHAEUM
TROPHALLAXIS
TROPHEDEMA
TROPHEMA
TROPHESIAL
TROPHESY
TROPHI
TROPHIC
TROPHICAL
TROPHICALLY
TROPHICITY
TROPHIED
TROPHIES
TROPHISM
TROPHOBIONT
TROPHOBIOSIS
TROPHOBIOTIC
TROPHOBLAST
TROPHOCYTE
TROPHODERM
TROPHODISC
TROPHOGENIC

TROPHOGENY
TROPHOLOGY
TROPHON
TROPHONEMA
TROPHOPATHY
TROPHOPHORE
TROPHOPHYTE
TROPHOPLASM
TROPHOPLAST
TROPHOSOMAL
TROPHOSOME
TROPHOSPERM
TROPHOSPHERE
TROPHOSPORE
TROPHOTAXIS
TROPHOTHYLAX
TROPHOTROPIC
TROPHOZOITE
TROPHOZOOID
TROPHY
TROPIC
TROPICAL
TROPICALITY
TROPICALIZE
TROPICALIZED
TROPICALIZING
TROPICALLY
TROPIDINE
TROPIN
TROPINE
TROPISM
TROPISMATIC
TROPIST
TROPISTIC
TROPOLOGIC
TROPOLOGICAL
TROPOLOGIES
TROPOLOGIZE
TROPOLOGIZED
TROPOLOGIZING
TROPOLOGY
TROPOMETER
TROPOPAUSE
TROPOPHIL
TROPOPHILOUS
TROPOPHYTE
TROPOPHYTIC
TROPOSPHERE
TROPOSPHERIC
TROPOYL
TROPPO
TROPTOMETER
TROPYL
TROSTERA
TROT
TROTCOZY
TROTH
TROTHED
TROTHING
TROTHLESS
TROTHPLIGHT
TROTLINE
TROTTED
TROTTER
TROTTERS
TROTTEUR
TROTTIE
TROTTING
TROTTLES
TROTTOIR
TROTTOIRED
TROTTY
TROTYL
TROUBADOR
TROUBADOUR
TROUBLE
TROUBLED
TROUBLEDLY
TROUBLEDNESS
TROUBLEMAKER
TROUBLER
TROUBLESHOOTER
TROUBLESOME
TROUBLESOMENESS
TROUBLING
TROUBLINGLY
TROUBLOUS
TROUBLOUSLY
TROUBLY
TROUGH
TROUGHING
TROUGHSTER
TROUGHWAY
TROUGHY
TROUNCE
TROUNCED
TROUNCER
TROUNCING
TROUPAND
TROUPE
TROUPED
TROUPER
TROUPIAL
TROUPING
TROUSE
TROUSER
TROUSERED
TROUSERETTES
TROUSERIAN
TROUSERING
TROUSERS
TROUSS
TROUSSE
TROUSSEAU
TROUSSEAUS
TROUSSEAUX
TROUT
TROUTER
TROUTLET
TROUTLING
TROUTY
TROUVAILLE
TROUVERE
TROUVEUR
TROVATORE
TROVE
TROVER
TROW
TROWABLE
TROWANE
TROWEL
TROWELBEAK
TROWELED
TROWELER
TROWELING
TROWELLED
TROWELLING
TROWELMAN
TROWIE
TROWING
TROWMAN
TROWSERS
TROWTH
TROY
TRUANCIES
TRUANCY
TRUANDISE
TRUANT
TRUANTISM
TRUANTLY
TRUANTNESS
TRUANTRY
TRUB
TRUBU
TRUCE
TRUCHA
TRUCHMAN
TRUCIAL
TRUCIDATION
TRUCK
TRUCKAGE
TRUCKED
TRUCKER
TRUCKING
TRUCKLE
TRUCKLED
TRUCKLER
TRUCKLING
TRUCKLINGLY
TRUCKMAN
TRUCKMASTER
TRUCKMEN
TRUCKS
TRUCKSTER
TRUCKWAY
TRUCULENCE
TRUCULENCY
TRUCULENT
TRUCULENTLY
TRUDDO
TRUDELLITE
TRUDGE
TRUDGED
TRUDGEN
TRUDGEON
TRUDGER
TRUDGING
TRUE
TRUEBORN
TRUEBRED
TRUED
TRUELOVE
TRUEMAN
TRUENESS
TRUEPENNY
TRUER
TRUEST
TRUEWOOD
TRUFF
TRUFFES
TRUFFLE
TRUFFLED
TRUFFLER
TRUG
TRUGMALLION
TRUING
TRUISM
TRUISMATIC
TRUISTIC
TRUISTICAL
TRULL
TRULLER
TRULLI
TRULLIZATION
TRULLO
TRULY
TRUMBASH
TRUMEAU
TRUMMEL
TRUMP
TRUMPED
TRUMPER
TRUMPERIES
TRUMPERINESS
TRUMPERY
TRUMPET
TRUMPETBUSH
TRUMPETED
TRUMPETER
TRUMPETING
TRUMPETRY
TRUMPETS
TRUMPETWEED
TRUMPETWOOD
TRUMPETY
TRUMPIE
TRUMPING
TRUMPS
TRUNCAGE
TRUNCAL
TRUNCATE
TRUNCATED
TRUNCATING
TRUNCATION
TRUNCATOR
TRUNCH
TRUNCHED
TRUNCHEON
TRUNCHEONED
TRUNCHEONER
TRUNCUS
TRUNDLE
TRUNDLED
TRUNDLEHEAD
TRUNDLER
TRUNDLESHOT
TRUNDLETAIL
TRUNDLING
TRUNK
TRUNKBACK
TRUNKED
TRUNKFISH
TRUNKFISHES
TRUNKING
TRUNKS
TRUNKWORK
TRUNNEL
TRUNNION
TRUNNIONED
TRUONG
TRUSH
TRUSION
TRUSS
TRUSSED
TRUSSELL
TRUSSER
TRUSSERY
TRUSSING
TRUSSWORK
TRUST
TRUSTBUSTER
TRUSTBUSTING
TRUSTED
TRUSTEE
TRUSTEED
TRUSTEEING
TRUSTEEISM
TRUSTEESHIP
TRUSTER
TRUSTFUL
TRUSTFULLY
TRUSTFULNESS
TRUSTIER
TRUSTIEST
TRUSTIFIED
TRUSTIFY
TRUSTIFYING
TRUSTING
TRUSTINGLY
TRUSTINGNESS
TRUSTLESS
TRUSTLESSLY
TRUSTMAN
TRUSTMEN
TRUSTWOMAN
TRUSTWORTHINESS
TRUSTWORTHY
TRUSTY
TRUTH
TRUTHABLE
TRUTHFUL
TRUTHFULLY
TRUTHFULNESS
TRUTHS
TRUTHSMAN
TRUTHTELLER
TRUTHTELLING
TRUTHY
TRUTINATE
TRUTINATION
TRUTINE
TRUTTACEOUS
TRUXILLIC
TRUXILLIN
TRUXILLINE
TRY
TRYE
TRYGON
TRYHOUSE
TRYING
TRYINGLY
TRYINGNESS
TRYMA
TRYMATA
TRYMS
TRYNE
TRYOUT
TRYP
TRYPA
TRYPANOLYSIN
TRYPANOSOMA
TRYPANOSOME
TRYPETID
TRYPIATE
TRYPOGRAPH
TRYPOGRAPHIC
TRYPSIN
TRYPSINIZE
TRYPSINOGEN
TRYPTASE
TRYPTIC
TRYPTONE
TRYPTONIZE
TRYPTOPHAN
TRYPTOPHANE
TRYSAIL
TRYST
TRYSTE
TRYSTED
TRYSTER
TRYSTING
TRYWORKS
TSADE
TSAMA
TSAMBA
TSANTSA
TSAR
TSARISM
TSARIST
TSATLEE
TSESSEBE
TSETSE
TSIA
TSINE
TSINGTAUITE
TSIOLOGY
TSITSITH
TSUBA
TSUBO
TSUKUPIN
TSUMEBITE
TSUN
TSUNAMI
TSUNGTU
TSWANA

TU
TUA
TUAN
TUANT
TUARN
TUART
TUATARA
TUATERA
TUATH
TUB
TUBA
TUBAE
TUBAGE
TUBAL
TUBAPHONE
TUBAR
TUBARON
TUBAS
TUBATE
TUBBA
TUBBABLE
TUBBAL
TUBBECK
TUBBED
TUBBER
TUBBIE
TUBBIER
TUBBIEST
TUBBING
TUBBISH
TUBBIST
TUBBOE
TUBBY
TUBE
TUBED
TUBEFORM
TUBEHEAD
TUBEHEARTED
TUBELET
TUBEMAN
TUBEMEN
TUBER
TUBERACEOUS
TUBERATION
TUBERCLE
TUBERCLED
TUBERCULA
TUBERCULAR
TUBERCULARLY
TUBERCULATE
TUBERCULATED
TUBERCULE
TUBERCULID
TUBERCULIDE
TUBERCULIN
TUBERCULINE
TUBERCULIZE
TUBERCULOID
TUBERCULOMA
TUBERCULOMAS
TUBERCULOMATA
TUBERCULOSED
TUBERCULOSIS
TUBERCULOUS
TUBERCULUM
TUBERIFEROUS
TUBERIFORM
TUBERIN
TUBERIZATION
TUBERIZE
TUBEROID
TUBEROSE
TUBEROSITIES
TUBEROSITY
TUBEROUS
TUBEROUSLY
TUBEROUSNESS
TUBFISH
TUBFISHES
TUBHUNTER
TUBICEN
TUBICINATE
TUBICINATION
TUBICOLAR
TUBICOLOUS
TUBICORN
TUBICORNOUS
TUBIFACIENT
TUBIFER
TUBIFEROUS
TUBIFEX
TUBIFLOROUS
TUBIFORM
TUBIG
TUBIK
TUBILINGUAL
TUBINARIAL
TUBINARINE
TUBING
TUBIPAROUS
TUBIPORE
TUBIPORID
TUBIPOROID
TUBIPOROUS
TUBMAN
TUBMEN
TUBOCURARINE
TUBORRHEA
TUBOTYMPANAL
TUBS
TUBSTER
TUBTAIL
TUBULAR
TUBULARITY
TUBULATE
TUBULATED
TUBULATING
TUBULATION
TUBULATOR
TUBULATURE
TUBULE
TUBULET
TUBULI
TUBULIFERAN
TUBULIFLORAL
TUBULIFORM
TUBULIPORE
TUBULIPORID
TUBULIPOROID
TUBULIZATION
TUBULOSE
TUBULOUS
TUBULOUSLY
TUBULOUSNESS
TUBULURE
TUBULUS
TUCAN
TUCANDERA
TUCHUN
TUCHUNATE
TUCHUNISM
TUCHUNIZE
TUCK
TUCKAHOE
TUCKED
TUCKER
TUCKERED
TUCKERING
TUCKET
TUCKING
TUCKNER
TUCKSHOP
TUCKTOO
TUCKY
TUCUM
TUCUMA
TUCUMAN
TUEBOR
TUEIRON
TUFA
TUFACEOUS
TUFAN
TUFF
TUFFACEOUS
TUFFET
TUFFING
TUFFOON
TUFT
TUFTAFFETA
TUFTED
TUFTER
TUFTHUNTER
TUFTHUNTING
TUFTING
TUFTS
TUFTY
TUG
TUGBOAT
TUGBOATMAN
TUGBOATMEN
TUGGED
TUGGER
TUGGERY
TUGGING
TUGGINGLY
TUGHRA
TUGUI
TUGURIA
TUGURIUM
TUI
TUILLE
TUILLETTE
TUILYIE
TUILZIE
TUINGA
TUISM
TUITION
TUITIONAL
TUITIONARY
TUITIVE
TUKE
TUKRA
TUKUTUKU
TULADI
TULARAEMIA
TULARE
TULAREMIA
TULASI
TULCAN
TULCE
TULCHAN
TULCHIN
TULE
TULIAC
TULIP
TULIPANT
TULIPFLOWER
TULIPI
TULIPIFEROUS
TULIPIST
TULIPOMANIA
TULIPOMANIAC
TULIPS
TULIPWOOD
TULIPY
TULISAN
TULISANES
TULK
TULLE
TULLIBEE
TULNIC
TULSI
TULWAR
TULWAUR
TULY
TUM
TUMAIN
TUMATAKURU
TUMB
TUMBAK
TUMBAKI
TUMBEK
TUMBEKI
TUMBLE
TUMBLEBUG
TUMBLED
TUMBLER
TUMBLEWEED
TUMBLING
TUMBLINGLY
TUMBLY
TUMBREL
TUMBRIL
TUMEFACIENT
TUMEFACTION
TUMEFIED
TUMEFY
TUMEFYING
TUMESCENCE
TUMESCENT
TUMFIE
TUMID
TUMIDITY
TUMIDLY
TUMIDNESS
TUMMALS
TUMMED
TUMMEL
TUMMELS
TUMMER
TUMMING
TUMMOCK
TUMMY
TUMOR
TUMORED
TUMORLIKE
TUMOROUS
TUMORS
TUMOUR
TUMOURED
TUMP
TUMPHY
TUMPLINE
TUMTUM
TUMULAR
TUMULARY
TUMULATE
TUMULATION
TUMULI
TUMULOSE
TUMULOSITY
TUMULOUS
TUMULT
TUMULTER
TUMULTUARIES
TUMULTUARILY
TUMULTUARY
TUMULTUOSO
TUMULTUOUS
TUMULTUOUSLY
TUMULUS
TUN
TUNA
TUNABLE
TUNABLENESS
TUNABLY
TUNAS
TUNBELLIED
TUNBELLY
TUNCA
TUND
TUNDATION
TUNDISH
TUNDRA
TUNDUN
TUNE
TUNED
TUNEFUL
TUNEFULLY
TUNEFULNESS
TUNELESS
TUNELESSLY
TUNELESSNESS
TUNER
TUNESMITH
TUNESOME
TUNG
TUNGAH
TUNGATE
TUNGO
TUNGSTATE
TUNGSTEN
TUNGSTENIC
TUNGSTENITE
TUNGSTIC
TUNGSTITE
TUNHOOF
TUNIC
TUNICA
TUNICAE
TUNICARY
TUNICATE
TUNICIN
TUNICKED
TUNICLE
TUNING
TUNK
TUNKET
TUNLAND
TUNMOOT
TUNNA
TUNNAGE
TUNNED
TUNNEL
TUNNELED
TUNNELER
TUNNELING
TUNNELITE
TUNNELLED
TUNNELLER
TUNNELLING
TUNNELLITE
TUNNELMAN
TUNNELMEN
TUNNER
TUNNERIES
TUNNERY
TUNNIES
TUNNING
TUNNLAND
TUNNY
TUNO
TUNS
TUNU
TUNY
TUP
TUPAIID
TUPAKIHI
TUPAN
TUPARA
TUPEK
TUPELO
TUPELOS
TUPIK
TUPMAN

TUPMEN
TUPPED
TUPPENCE
TUPPENY
TUPPING
TUPUNA
TUQUE
TUR
TURACIN
TURACOU
TURAKOO
TURANITE
TURANOSE
TURB
TURBAN
TURBANED
TURBANTO
TURBANTOP
TURBARIES
TURBARY
TURBEH
TURBELLARIAN
TURBESCENCY
TURBETH
TURBID
TURBIDIMETER
TURBIDIMETRY
TURBIDITY
TURBIDLY
TURBIDNESS
TURBINACEOUS
TURBINAGE
TURBINAL
TURBINATE
TURBINATED
TURBINATION
TURBINE
TURBINECTOMY
TURBINED
TURBINELLOID
TURBINER
TURBINIFORM
TURBINOID
TURBINOTOME
TURBINOTOMY
TURBIT
TURBITH
TURBITTEEN
TURBLE
TURBOCAR
TURBOFAN
TURBOJET
TURBOPROP
TURBOT
TURBOTS
TURBULENCE
TURBULENCY
TURBULENT
TURBULENTLY
TURCO
TURCOIS
TURCOPOLE
TURCOPOLIER
TURD
TURDIFORM
TURDINE
TURDOID
TUREEN
TURF
TURFED
TURFEN
TURFIER
TURFIEST
TURFINESS
TURFING
TURFITE
TURFMAN
TURFMEN
TURFS
TURFY
TURGENT
TURGENTLY
TURGESCE
TURGESCED
TURGESCENCE
TURGESCENCY
TURGESCENT
TURGESCENTLY
TURGESCING
TURGID
TURGIDITY
TURGIDLY
TURGIDNESS
TURGITE
TURGOID
TURGOR
TURGY
TURICATA
TURIO
TURION
TURJAITE
TURJITE
TURKEN
TURKESS
TURKEY
TURKEYBACK
TURKEYBERRY
TURKEYBUSH
TURKEYFOOT
TURKEYS
TURKIS
TURKLE
TURKOIS
TURLOUGH
TURM
TURMA
TURMALINE
TURMERIC
TURMET
TURMIT
TURMOIL
TURMOILER
TURMUT
TURN
TURNABLE
TURNABOUT
TURNAGAIN
TURNAROUND
TURNAWAY
TURNBACK
TURNBOUT
TURNBROACH
TURNBUCKLE
TURNCAP
TURNCOAT
TURNCOATISM
TURNCOCK
TURNDOWN
TURNDUN
TURNED
TURNEL
TURNER
TURNERACEOUS
TURNERIES
TURNERITE
TURNERY
TURNEY
TURNGATE
TURNHALL
TURNICINE
TURNING
TURNIP
TURNIPWEED
TURNIPWOOD
TURNIPY
TURNKEY
TURNKEYS
TURNOFF
TURNOR
TURNOUT
TURNOVER
TURNPIKE
TURNPIKER
TURNPIN
TURNPLATE
TURNPLOUGH
TURNPLOW
TURNPOKE
TURNROW
TURNS
TURNSCREW
TURNSHEET
TURNSKIN
TURNSOLE
TURNSPIT
TURNSTILE
TURNSTONE
TURNTABLE
TURNTAIL
TURNTALE
TURNUP
TURNVEREIN
TURNWAY
TURNWREST
TURNWRIST
TUROPHILE
TURP
TURPENTINE
TURPENTINED
TURPENTINIC
TURPENTINING
TURPENTINOUS
TURPENTINY
TURPETH
TURPETHIN
TURPID
TURPIDLY
TURPIFY
TURPITUDE
TURPS
TURQUET
TURQUOIS
TURQUOISE
TURQUOISES
TURR
TURREL
TURRELL
TURRET
TURRETED
TURRETING
TURRICAL
TURRICLE
TURRICULA
TURRICULAE
TURRICULAR
TURRICULATE
TURRICULATED
TURRIFEROUS
TURRIFORM
TURRIGEROUS
TURRILITE
TURRION
TURRITELLID
TURRITELLOID
TURRUM
TURSE
TURSIO
TURTLE
TURTLEBACK
TURTLEBLOOM
TURTLED
TURTLEDOM
TURTLEDOVE
TURTLEDOVED
TURTLEDOVING
TURTLEHEAD
TURTLEIZE
TURTLEPEG
TURTLER
TURTLES
TURTLESTONE
TURTLET
TURTLING
TURTOSA
TURTUR
TURURI
TURUS
TURVES
TURWAR
TUSCH
TUSCHE
TUSHE
TUSHED
TUSHER
TUSHERY
TUSHING
TUSK
TUSKAR
TUSKED
TUSKER
TUSKIER
TUSKIEST
TUSKING
TUSKLESS
TUSKY
TUSSAH
TUSSAL
TUSSAR
TUSSEH
TUSSER
TUSSICULAR
TUSSIS
TUSSIVE
TUSSLE
TUSSLED
TUSSLING
TUSSOCK
TUSSOCKED
TUSSOCKER
TUSSOCKY
TUSSORE
TUSSUCK
TUSSUR
TUT
TUTAMENT
TUTANIA
TUTBALL
TUTE
TUTEE
TUTEL
TUTELA
TUTELAE
TUTELAGE
TUTELAR
TUTELARIES
TUTELARY
TUTELE
TUTENAG
TUTENAGUE
TUTIN
TUTLER
TUTLY
TUTMAN
TUTMEN
TUTOIEMENT
TUTOR
TUTORAGE
TUTORED
TUTORER
TUTORESS
TUTORHOOD
TUTORIAL
TUTORIALLY
TUTORIATE
TUTORING
TUTORISM
TUTORIZATION
TUTORIZE
TUTORLY
TUTORSHIP
TUTORY
TUTOYER
TUTSAN
TUTSTER
TUTTA
TUTTE
TUTTED
TUTTI
TUTTIMAN
TUTTING
TUTTIS
TUTTO
TUTTY
TUTTYMAN
TUTU
TUTUH
TUTULUS
TUTWORK
TUUM
TUWI
TUX
TUXEDO
TUXEDOES
TUXEDOS
TUYERE
TUZ
TUZA
TUZZ
TWA
TWADDLE
TWADDLED
TWADDLEMENT
TWADDLER
TWADDLIER
TWADDLIEST
TWADDLING
TWADDLY
TWADDY
TWAG
TWAGGER
TWAIN
TWAITE
TWAL
TWALE
TWALPENNY
TWALT
TWANG
TWANGED
TWANGER
TWANGING
TWANGLE
TWANGLED
TWANGLER
TWANGLING
TWANGY
TWANK
TWANKER
TWANKING
TWANKINGLY
TWANKLE
TWANKY
TWARLY
TWASOME
TWAT
TWATCHEL

TWATTERLIGHT
TWATTLE
TWATTLED
TWATTLER
TWATTLING
TWAY
TWAYBLADE
TWAZZY
TWEAK
TWEAKED
TWEAKER
TWEAKING
TWEAKY
TWEE
TWEED
TWEEDED
TWEEDLE
TWEEDLED
TWEEDLEDEE
TWEEDLEDUM
TWEEDLING
TWEEDY
TWEEG
TWEEL
TWEEN
TWEENY
TWEER
TWEESE
TWEESH
TWEESHT
TWEEST
TWEET
TWEETER
TWEEZE
TWEEZED
TWEEZER
TWEEZERED
TWEEZERING
TWEEZERS
TWEEZING
TWEIL
TWELFTH
TWELL
TWELVE
TWELVEFOLD
TWELVEMO
TWELVEMONTH
TWELVEPENCE
TWELVEPENNY
TWELVESCORE
TWENTIES
TWENTIETH
TWENTY
TWENTYFOLD
TWENTYMO
TWERP
TWEYFOLD
TWIBIL
TWIBILL
TWIBILLED
TWICE
TWICER
TWICH
TWICHILD
TWICK
TWIDDLE
TWIDDLED
TWIDDLER
TWIDDLING
TWIDDLY
TWIER
TWIFALLOW
TWIFOIL
TWIFOLD
TWIG
TWIGGED
TWIGGEN
TWIGGER
TWIGGIER
TWIGGIEST
TWIGGING
TWIGGY
TWIGLESS
TWIGLET
TWIGS
TWIGWITHY
TWILIGHT
TWILIGHTY
TWILIT
TWILL
TWILLED
TWILLER
TWILLING
TWILLY
TWIN
TWINBERRIES
TWINBERRY
TWINBORN
TWIND
TWINDLE
TWINE
TWINEBUSH
TWINED
TWINER
TWINFLOWER
TWINFOLD
TWINGE
TWINGED
TWINGING
TWINGLE
TWINIGHT
TWINING
TWINK
TWINKLE
TWINKLED
TWINKLEDUM
TWINKLER
TWINKLES
TWINKLING
TWINKLINGLY
TWINKLY
TWINLEAF
TWINLING
TWINLY
TWINNED
TWINNER
TWINNING
TWINS
TWINSHIP
TWINSOMENESS
TWINT
TWINTER
TWINY
TWIRE
TWIRK
TWIRL
TWIRLED
TWIRLER
TWIRLIGIG
TWIRLING
TWIRLY
TWIRP
TWISCAR
TWISEL
TWIST
TWISTED
TWISTEDLY
TWISTER
TWISTHAND
TWISTICAL
TWISTING
TWISTINGLY
TWISTIWAYS
TWISTIWISE
TWISTLE
TWISTY
TWIT
TWITCH
TWITCHED
TWITCHEL
TWITCHELING
TWITCHER
TWITCHET
TWITCHETY
TWITCHFIRE
TWITCHING
TWITCHINGLY
TWITCHY
TWITE
TWITLARK
TWITTED
TWITTEN
TWITTER
TWITTERATION
TWITTERER
TWITTERING
TWITTERINGLY
TWITTERLY
TWITTERY
TWITTING
TWITTINGLY
TWITTLE
TWITTY
TWIXT
TWIZZLE
TWO
TWOES
TWOFER
TWOFOLD
TWOFOLDLY
TWOFOLDNESS
TWOLING
TWONESS
TWOPENCE
TWOPENNY
TWOS
TWOSOME
TWYER
TY
TYALL
TYAUVE
TYCHISM
TYCHITE
TYCHOPOTAMIC
TYCOON
TYCOONATE
TYDDEN
TYDDYN
TYDIE
TYE
TYEE
TYER
TYG
TYING
TYKE
TYKEN
TYKING
TYLARI
TYLARUS
TYLASTER
TYLE
TYLER
TYLI
TYLION
TYLOMA
TYLOPOD
TYLOPODOUS
TYLOSE
TYLOSES
TYLOSIS
TYLOSOID
TYLOSTERESIS
TYLOSTYLAR
TYLOSTYLE
TYLOSTYLOTE
TYLOSTYLUS
TYLOTATE
TYLOTE
TYLOTIC
TYLOTOXEA
TYLOTOXEATE
TYLUS
TYMBAL
TYMBALON
TYMP
TYMPAN
TYMPANA
TYMPANAL
TYMPANI
TYMPANIC
TYMPANIES
TYMPANING
TYMPANISM
TYMPANIST
TYMPANITES
TYMPANITIC
TYMPANITIS
TYMPANIZE
TYMPANO
TYMPANOHYAL
TYMPANOSIS
TYMPANOTOMY
TYMPANUM
TYMPANUMS
TYMPANY
TYND
TYPAL
TYPARCHICAL
TYPE
TYPECAST
TYPECASTING
TYPED
TYPEFACE
TYPEFACES
TYPEHOLDER
TYPER
TYPES
TYPESCRIPT
TYPESET
TYPESETTER
TYPESETTING
TYPEWRITE
TYPEWRITER
TYPEWRITING
TYPEWRITTEN
TYPEWROTE
TYPHAEMIA
TYPHEMIA
TYPHIA
TYPHIC
TYPHINIA
TYPHIZATION
TYPHLITIC
TYPHLITIS
TYPHLOLOGIES
TYPHLOLOGY
TYPHLON
TYPHLOPHILE
TYPHLOPID
TYPHLOSIS
TYPHLOSOLAR
TYPHLOSOLE
TYPHOAEMIA
TYPHOEMIA
TYPHOGENIC
TYPHOID
TYPHOIDAL
TYPHOIDIN
TYPHOIDLIKE
TYPHOLYSIN
TYPHOMALARIA
TYPHOMANIA
TYPHONIC
TYPHOON
TYPHOSE
TYPHOSIS
TYPHOTOXINE
TYPHOUS
TYPHUS
TYPIC
TYPICA
TYPICAL
TYPICALITY
TYPICALLY
TYPICALNESS
TYPICON
TYPICUM
TYPIFICATION
TYPIFIED
TYPIFIER
TYPIFY
TYPIFYING
TYPING
TYPIST
TYPO
TYPOBAR
TYPOCOSMY
TYPOGRAPHER
TYPOGRAPHIA
TYPOGRAPHIC
TYPOGRAPHIES
TYPOGRAPHIST
TYPOGRAPHY
TYPOLOGICAL
TYPOLOGIES
TYPOLOGIST
TYPOLOGY
TYPOMANIA
TYPOMETRY
TYPONYM
TYPONYMAL
TYPONYMIC
TYPONYMOUS
TYPOPHILE
TYPORAMA
TYPOS
TYPOTHETAE
TYPP
TYPTOLOGICAL
TYPTOLOGIST
TYPTOLOGY
TYPY
TYRAMIN
TYRAMINE
TYRANNESS
TYRANNIAL
TYRANNIC
TYRANNICAL
TYRANNICALLY
TYRANNICIDAL
TYRANNICIDE
TYRANNICLY
TYRANNIES
TYRANNINE
TYRANNIS
TYRANNISM
TYRANNIZE
TYRANNIZED
TYRANNIZER
TYRANNIZING
TYRANNOSAUR
TYRANNOUS
TYRANNOUSLY
TYRANNY
TYRANT

TYRASOLE
TYRE
TYREMESIS
TYRIASIS
TYRO
TYROGLYPHID
TYROLITE
TYROLOGY
TYROMA
TYROMANCY
TYROMAS
TYROMATA
TYROMATOUS
TYRONE
TYRONIC
TYRONISM
TYROS
TYROSINASE
TYROSINE
TYROSINURIA
TYROSYL
TYROTHRICIN
TYROTOXICON
TYROTOXINE
TYSONITE
TYSTE
TYSTIE
TYT
TYTE
TZAR
TZARDOM
TZARINA
TZEDAKAH
TZETZE
TZIGANE
TZIMMES
TZIRID
TZOLKIN
TZONTLE
TZUT
TZUTE

UAKARI
UALIS
UANG
UAYED
UBE
UBERANT
UBEROUS
UBEROUSLY
UBEROUSNESS
UBERTY
UBI
UBICATION
UBIETY
UBIQUARIAN
UBIQUE
UBIQUIOUS
UBIQUIT
UBIQUITARIAN
UBIQUITARIES
UBIQUITARY
UBIQUITOUS
UBIQUITOUSLY
UBIQUITY
UBUSSU
UCH
UCHE
UCKERS
UCKIA
UCUUBA
UDAD
UDAL
UDALER
UDALLER
UDALMAN
UDASI
UDDER
UDDERED
UDDERFUL
UDDERLESS
UDELL
UDGE
UDO
UDOMETER
UDOMETRIC
UDOMETRY
UDOMOGRAPH
UEBA
UFER
UG
UGGE
UGGLESOME
UGH
UGHTEN
UGLIER
UGLIEST
UGLIFICATION
UGLIFIED
UGLIFIER
UGLIFY
UGLIFYING
UGLILY
UGLINESS
UGLISOME
UGLY
UGRIANIZE
UGRUG
UGSOME
UHLAN
UHLLO
UHTENSANG
UHTSONG
UINAL
UINTAHITE
UINTAITE
UINTATHERE
UINTJIE
UIT
UITLANDER
UITSPAN
UJI
UKASE
UKE
UKIYO
UKIYOYE
UKU
UKULELE
ULA
ULAE
ULAMA
ULAN
ULATROPHIA
ULATROPHY
ULAULA
ULCER
ULCERATE
ULCERATED
ULCERATING
ULCERATION
ULCERATIVE
ULCERED
ULCEROUS
ULCEROUSLY
ULCEROUSNESS
ULCUS
ULCUSCLE
ULCUSCULE
ULE
ULEMA
ULERYTHEMA
ULETIC
ULEXINE
ULEXITE
ULIGINOSE
ULIGINOUS
ULITIS
ULL
ULLAGE
ULLAGED
ULLAGONE
ULLER
ULLING
ULLMANNITE
ULLUCO
ULLUCU
ULMACEOUS
ULME
ULMIC
ULMIN
ULMINIC
ULMO
ULNA
ULNAD
ULNAE
ULNAR
ULNARE
ULNARIA
ULNAS
ULNOCARPAL
ULNOCONDYLAR
ULNORADIAL
ULOBORID
ULOID
ULONCUS
ULOTRICHAN
ULOTRICHOUS
ULOTRICHY
ULPAN
ULRICHITE
ULSTER
ULSTERED
ULSTERETTE
ULSTERING
ULTERIOR
ULTERIORLY
ULTIMA
ULTIMACY
ULTIMATA
ULTIMATE
ULTIMATED
ULTIMATELY
ULTIMATENESS
ULTIMATING
ULTIMATION
ULTIMATUM
ULTIMATUMS
ULTIME
ULTIMITY
ULTIMO
ULTIMUM
ULTION
ULTRA
ULTRABASIC
ULTRABASITE
ULTRACIVIL
ULTRACOMPLEX
ULTRACONSERVATISM
ULTRACONSERVATIVE
ULTRACORDIAL
ULTRAFASHIONABLE
ULTRAFIDIAN
ULTRAFILTER
ULTRAGASEOUS
ULTRAGENTEEL
ULTRAGOOD
ULTRAGRAVE
ULTRAHEROIC
ULTRAISM
ULTRAIST
ULTRAISTIC
ULTRALENIENT
ULTRALIBERAL
ULTRALOGICAL
ULTRALOYAL
ULTRAMARINE
ULTRAMAXIMAL
ULTRAMINUTE
ULTRAMODERN
ULTRAMODEST
ULTRAMONTANE
ULTRAMONTANISM
ULTRAMOROSE
ULTRAMULISH
ULTRAMUNDANE
ULTRANICE
ULTRAOBSCURE
ULTRAORNATE
ULTRAPAPIST
ULTRAPERFECT
ULTRAPIOUS
ULTRAPOPISH
ULTRAPROUD
ULTRAPRUDENT
ULTRARADICAL
ULTRARAPID
ULTRARED
ULTRAREFINED
ULTRASELECT
ULTRASERVILE
ULTRASEVERE
ULTRASHREWD
ULTRASOLEMN
ULTRASONIC
ULTRASONICS
ULTRASPARTAN
ULTRASTELLAR
ULTRASTERILE
ULTRASTRICT
ULTRASUBTLE
ULTRATENSE
ULTRATRIVIAL
ULTRAUGLY
ULTRAURGENT
ULTRAVICIOUS
ULTRAVIOLENT
ULTRAVIOLET
ULTRAVIRUS
ULTRAVISIBLE
ULTRAWEALTHY
ULTRAWISE
ULTRAYOUNG
ULTRAZEALOUS
ULTRONEOUS
ULTRONEOUSLY
ULU
ULUA
ULUHI
ULULANT
ULULATE
ULULATED
ULULATING
ULULATION
ULULATIVE
ULULATORY
ULULU
ULUS
ULVACEOUS
ULYIE
ULZIE
UM
UMANGITE
UMBE
UMBECAST
UMBEL
UMBELAP
UMBELED
UMBELLA
UMBELLAR
UMBELLATE
UMBELLATED
UMBELLATELY
UMBELLED
UMBELLET
UMBELLIC
UMBELLIFER
UMBELLIFERONE
UMBELLIFORM
UMBELLOID
UMBELLULATE
UMBELLULE
UMBELWORT
UMBER
UMBERED
UMBERING
UMBERTY
UMBESET
UMBETHINK
UMBILIC
UMBILICAL
UMBILICALLY
UMBILICAR
UMBILICATE
UMBILICATED
UMBILICATION
UMBILICI
UMBILICIFORM
UMBILICUS
UMBILIFORM
UMBILROOT
UMBLES
UMBO
UMBOLATERAL
UMBONAL
UMBONATE
UMBONATED
UMBONATION
UMBONE
UMBONES
UMBONIAL
UMBONIC
UMBONULATE
UMBONULE
UMBRA
UMBRACLE
UMBRACULATE
UMBRACULUM
UMBRAE
UMBRAGE
UMBRAGEOUS
UMBRAGEOUSLY
UMBRAID
UMBRAL
UMBRALLY
UMBRANA
UMBRATE
UMBRATIC
UMBRATILE
UMBRE
UMBREL
UMBRELLA
UMBRELLAED
UMBRELLAWORT
UMBRET
UMBRETTE
UMBRIFEROUS
UMBRIL
UMBRINE
UMBROSE
UMBROSITY
UMBROUS
UME
UMEST
UMFAAN
UMGANG
UMIACK
UMIAK
UMIRI
UMLAND
UMLAUT
UMMAN
UMP
UMPIRAGE
UMPIRE
UMPIRED
UMPIRESHIP
UMPIRESS
UMPIRING
UMPLE
UMPTEEN
UMPTEENTH
UMPTEKITE
UMPTIETH
UMPTY
UMQUHILE
UMSET
UMSTROKE
UMU
UN
UNABASHED
UNABBREVIATED
UNABLE
UNABLENESS
UNABLY
UNABRIDGED
UNABSOLVABLE
UNACCENTED
UNACCEPTABLE
UNACCEPTED
UNACCOMPANIED
UNACCOUNTABLE

UNACCUSTOMED
UNACQUAINTED
UNACTION
UNACTIVE
UNACTIVELY
UNACTIVITY
UNACTUAL
UNACTUALITY
UNACTUALLY
UNADAPTABLE
UNADAPTABLY
UNADDITIONED
UNADDRESS
UNADEQUATE
UNADEQUATELY
UNADHERENCE
UNADHERENT
UNADHERENTLY
UNADORNED
UNADULTERATED
UNADVANCED
UNADVANCEDLY
UNADVANTAGEOUSLY
UNADVERTENCY
UNADVISABLE
UNADVISABLY
UNADVISED
UNADVISEDLY
UNAFFECTED
UNAFFECTEDLY
UNAFFIED
UNAFRAID
UNAGGRESSIVE
UNAGING
UNAGREEABLE
UNAIDED
UNAIMED
UNAKIN
UNAKITE
UNAL
UNALERT
UNALIENABLE
UNALIENABLY
UNALIKE
UNALIST
UNALLIED
UNALLIEDLY
UNALLOYED
UNALMSED
UNALTERABLE
UNALTERABLY
UNALTERED
UNAMBIGUOUS
UNAMBITION
UNAMBITIOUS
UNAMENABLE
UNAMENABLY
UNAMIABILITY
UNAMIABLE
UNAMIABLY
UNAMO
UNAMUSIVE
UNANCESTORED
UNANCESTRIED
UNANCHOR
UNANELED
UNANIMATE
UNANIMATED
UNANIMATEDLY
UNANIMATELY
UNANIME
UNANIMISM
UNANIMIST
UNANIMISTIC
UNANIMITER
UNANIMITY
UNANIMOUS
UNANIMOUSLY
UNANSWERABLE
UNANSWERABLY
UNANSWERED
UNAPPEALABLE
UNAPPEALABLY
UNAPPROACHABLE
UNAPPROVED
UNAPT
UNAPTLY
UNAPTNESS
UNARGUED
UNARK
UNARM
UNARMED
UNARMEDLY
UNARMEDNESS
UNARMORED
UNARMOURED
UNARRAY
UNARTED
UNARTFUL
UNARTFULLY
UNARTFULNESS
UNARTIFICIAL
UNARTISTIC
UNARTISTICAL
UNARY
UNASINOUS
UNASSAILABLE
UNASSAILABLY
UNASSENTED
UNASSISTED
UNASSOILED
UNASSUETUDE
UNASSUMED
UNASSUMING
UNASSUMINGLY
UNASSURED
UNASSUREDLY
UNATONABLE
UNATTACHED
UNATTAINABLE
UNATTAINTED
UNATTAINTEDLY
UNATTENDED
UNATTIRE
UNATTRACTIVE
UNAU
UNAUDIBLE
UNAUDIBLY
UNAUDIENCED
UNAUSPICIOUS
UNAUTHORIZE
UNAUTHORIZED
UNAUTORITIED
UNAVAILING
UNAVAILINGLY
UNAVOIDABLE
UNAVOIDABLY
UNAVOIDED
UNAVOWED
UNAWARE
UNAWARED
UNAWAREDLY
UNAWARENESS
UNAWARES
UNBACKED
UNBAG
UNBAIN
UNBAITED
UNBAIZED
UNBAKED
UNBALANCE
UNBALANCED
UNBALANCING
UNBALLAST
UNBALLASTED
UNBALLASTING
UNBANE
UNBANK
UNBANKED
UNBAPTIZED
UNBAR
UNBARBED
UNBARE
UNBARK
UNBARRED
UNBARREL
UNBARRING
UNBATED
UNBE
UNBEAR
UNBEARABLE
UNBEARABLY
UNBEARDED
UNBEARED
UNBEARING
UNBEAST
UNBEATEN
UNBEAVERED
UNBECOME
UNBECOMING
UNBECOMINGLY
UNBED
UNBEDDED
UNBEFIT
UNBEFITTING
UNBEFOOL
UNBEFRIEND
UNBEGET
UNBEGILT
UNBEGINNING
UNBEGOT
UNBEGOTTEN
UNBEGOTTENLY
UNBEGUILE
UNBEGUN
UNBEHOVING
UNBEING
UNBEJUGGLED
UNBEKNOWN
UNBEKNOWNST
UNBELIEF
UNBELIEFFUL
UNBELIEVABLE
UNBELIEVABLY
UNBELIEVE
UNBELIEVED
UNBELIEVER
UNBELIEVERS
UNBELIEVING
UNBELT
UNBEND
UNBENDED
UNBENDER
UNBENDING
UNBENDINGLY
UNBENT
UNBEREAVEN
UNBEREFT
UNBERUFEN
UNBESEEM
UNBESEEMING
UNBETHINK
UNBETHOUGHT
UNBETIDE
UNBEWARE
UNBEWILLED
UNBEWITCH
UNBIAS
UNBIASABLE
UNBIASED
UNBIASEDLY
UNBIASEDNESS
UNBIASING
UNBIASSABLE
UNBIASSED
UNBIASSEDLY
UNBIASSING
UNBID
UNBIDABLE
UNBIDDEN
UNBIGGED
UNBIND
UNBINDING
UNBIRDLY
UNBISHOP
UNBITTED
UNBITTING
UNBLAMABLE
UNBLAMABLY
UNBLEACHED
UNBLEMISHED
UNBLENCHED
UNBLESS
UNBLESSED
UNBLEST
UNBLISS
UNBLITHE
UNBLOCK
UNBLOCKED
UNBLOODED
UNBLOODILY
UNBLOODINESS
UNBLOODY
UNBLOOM
UNBLOWN
UNBLUSHING
UNBLUSHINGLY
UNBOAT
UNBODIED
UNBODILINESS
UNBODILY
UNBODKINED
UNBODY
UNBOLD
UNBOLDLY
UNBOLDNESS
UNBOLT
UNBOLTED
UNBOLTING
UNBONE
UNBONED
UNBONNET
UNBONNETED
UNBONNY
UNBOOKED
UNBOOT
UNBORN
UNBOSOM
UNBOSOMED
UNBOSOMER
UNBOSOMING
UNBOTTOMED
UNBOUGHT
UNBOUND
UNBOUNDED
UNBOUNDEDLY
UNBOUNDLESS
UNBOW
UNBOWABLE
UNBOWED
UNBOWEL
UNBOWELED
UNBOWELLED
UNBOWERED
UNBOWSOME
UNBOY
UNBRACE
UNBRACED
UNBRACING
UNBRAID
UNBRAINED
UNBRANDED
UNBREAKABLE
UNBREAST
UNBREATH
UNBREATHED
UNBRED
UNBREECH
UNBRENT
UNBREWED
UNBRICK
UNBRIDLE
UNBRIDLED
UNBRIDLEDLY
UNBROID
UNBROKE
UNBROKEN
UNBROKENLY
UNBROKENNESS
UNBRUTALIZE
UNBRUTE
UNBRUTIFY
UNBRUTIZE
UNBUCKLE
UNBUCKRAMED
UNBUDGEABLE
UNBUDGEABLY
UNBUILD
UNBUILDED
UNBUILDING
UNBUILT
UNBUNDLE
UNBUNG
UNBURDEN
UNBURDENMENT
UNBURIABLE
UNBURIAL
UNBURN
UNBURNISHED
UNBURNT
UNBURROW
UNBURTHEN
UNBURY
UNBUSH
UNBUSIED
UNBUSK
UNBUTTON
UNBUTTONED
UNBUXOM
UNBUXOMLY
UNC
UNCA
UNCAGE
UNCAGED
UNCALLED
UNCALLOW
UNCALLOWER
UNCALM
UNCAMP
UNCANDOR
UNCANDOUR
UNCANNILY
UNCANNINESS
UNCANNY
UNCANONIZE
UNCANONIZED
UNCANONIZING
UNCAP
UNCAPABLE
UNCAPABLY
UNCAPACITATE
UNCAPPED
UNCAPPER
UNCAPPING
UNCAREFUL

UNCAREFULLY
UNCARNATE
UNCART
UNCASE
UNCASTE
UNCASTLE
UNCASTRATED
UNCATE
UNCATHEDRALED
UNCAUGHT
UNCAUSED
UNCAUTELOUS
UNCAUTIOUS
UNCAUTIOUSLY
UNCE
UNCEASABLE
UNCEASING
UNCEASINGLY
UNCELLAR
UNCENTER
UNCENTRE
UNCENTURY
UNCEREMONIOUS
UNCEREMONIOUSLY
UNCERTAIN
UNCERTAINLY
UNCERTAINNESS
UNCERTAINTIES
UNCERTAINTY
UNCERTITUDE
UNCESSANT
UNCESSANTLY
UNCH
UNCHAIN
UNCHALLENGED
UNCHANCE
UNCHANCY
UNCHANGEABLE
UNCHANGEABLENESS
UNCHANGEABLY
UNCHANGING
UNCHARGE
UNCHARGED
UNCHARILY
UNCHARINESS
UNCHARITABLE
UNCHARITABLY
UNCHARITY
UNCHARM
UNCHARNEL
UNCHARTERED
UNCHARY
UNCHASTE
UNCHASTELY
UNCHASTENESS
UNCHASTITY
UNCHECK
UNCHECKED
UNCHEERFUL
UNCHEERFULLY
UNCHILD
UNCHILDISH
UNCHILDISHLY
UNCHRISOM
UNCHRIST
UNCHRISTEN
UNCHRISTENED
UNCHRISTIAN
UNCHURCH
UNCHURCHED
UNCI
UNCIA
UNCIAE
UNCIAL
UNCIALIZE
UNCIALLY
UNCIATIM
UNCIFORM
UNCINAL
UNCINARIASIS
UNCINARIATIC
UNCINATE
UNCINATED
UNCINI
UNCINUS
UNCIPHER
UNCIROSTRATE
UNCITY
UNCIVIL
UNCIVILIZED
UNCIVILLY
UNCLAD
UNCLAMP
UNCLASP
UNCLASSIFY
UNCLE
UNCLEAD
UNCLEAN
UNCLEANLILY
UNCLEANLY
UNCLEANNESS
UNCLEANSE
UNCLEAR
UNCLEARED
UNCLEARLY
UNCLEAVE
UNCLEMENT
UNCLEMENTLY
UNCLENCH
UNCLEVER
UNCLEVERLY
UNCLEW
UNCLIFY
UNCLINCH
UNCLING
UNCLOAK
UNCLOG
UNCLOISTER
UNCLOSE
UNCLOSED
UNCLOSING
UNCLOTHE
UNCLOTHED
UNCLOTHING
UNCLOUD
UNCLOUDED
UNCLUBABLE
UNCLUBBABLE
UNCLUBBY
UNCLUTCH
UNCO
UNCOACH
UNCOACTED
UNCOCK
UNCOFFER
UNCOFFLE
UNCOFT
UNCOGITABLE
UNCOGUIDISM
UNCOHERENT
UNCOHERENTLY
UNCOIF
UNCOIL
UNCOIN
UNCOINED
UNCOLIKE
UNCOLLECTED
UNCOLORED
UNCOLT
UNCOLY
UNCOMBED
UNCOMBINABLE
UNCOMBINABLY
UNCOMBINE
UNCOMBINED
UNCOME
UNCOMELIER
UNCOMELIEST
UNCOMELILY
UNCOMELY
UNCOMFORTABLE
UNCOMFORTABLY
UNCOMMERCIAL
UNCOMMITTED
UNCOMMIXED
UNCOMMODIOUS
UNCOMMON
UNCOMMONER
UNCOMMONEST
UNCOMMONLY
UNCOMMONNESS
UNCOMMUNICATIVE
UNCOMPACT
UNCOMPANIED
UNCOMPASSED
UNCOMPATIBLE
UNCOMPATIBLY
UNCOMPLIABLE
UNCOMPLICATED
UNCOMPLIMENTARY
UNCOMPOSED
UNCOMPOUND
UNCOMPOUNDED
UNCOMPREHEND
UNCOMPROMISING
UNCOMPT
UNCONCEALED
UNCONCEIVING
UNCONCERN
UNCONCERNED
UNCONCERNEDLY
UNCONCERNING
UNCONCLUDENT
UNCONCLUDING
UNCONCLUSIVE
UNCONCOCTED
UNCONDITED
UNCONDITIONAL
UNCONDITIONED
UNCONFINE
UNCONFINED
UNCONFIRMED
UNCONFORMIST
UNCONFORMITIES
UNCONFORMITY
UNCONGENIAL
UNCONNECTED
UNCONQUERED
UNCONQUEST
UNCONSCIOUS
UNCONSCIOUSLY
UNCONSECRATE
UNCONSENT
UNCONSIDERED
UNCONSISTENT
UNCONSONANCY
UNCONSONANT
UNCONSTANCY
UNCONSTANT
UNCONSTANTLY
UNCONSTRAINED
UNCONSTRAINT
UNCONSULT
UNCONTENT
UNCONTENTED
UNCONTROL
UNCONTROLLABLE
UNCONTROLLABLY
UNCONTROLLED
UNCONVENIENT
UNCONVENTIONAL
UNCONVERSING
UNCONVERSION
UNCONVERTED
UNCONVINCING
UNCOOKED
UNCORD
UNCORDED
UNCORDING
UNCORK
UNCORKER
UNCORKING
UNCORPORAL
UNCORRECTED
UNCORRIGIBLE
UNCORRUPT
UNCORRUPTION
UNCORVEN
UNCOS
UNCOST
UNCOUCH
UNCOUCHED
UNCOUCHING
UNCOUNTABLE
UNCOUNTABLY
UNCOUNTED
UNCOUPLE
UNCOUPLED
UNCOUPLER
UNCOUPLING
UNCOURSED
UNCOURTEOUS
UNCOUS
UNCOUTH
UNCOUTHLY
UNCOUTHNESS
UNCOUTHSOME
UNCOVENABLE
UNCOVER
UNCOVERABLE
UNCOVERED
UNCOVEREDLY
UNCOVERING
UNCOW
UNCOWL
UNCRAFTILY
UNCRAFTINESS
UNCRAFTY
UNCRAZED
UNCREATE
UNCREATED
UNCREATING
UNCREATION
UNCREDIBLE
UNCREDIT
UNCREDITABLE
UNCREDITABLY
UNCRINKLE
UNCRINKLED
UNCRINKLING
UNCRITICALLY
UNCRITICISM
UNCROOK
UNCROOKING
UNCROSS
UNCROWN
UNCROWNED
UNCROWNING
UNCRUDDED
UNCRUMPLE
UNCTION
UNCTIONAL
UNCTIONEER
UNCTIONLESS
UNCTIOUS
UNCTIOUSNESS
UNCTORIAN
UNCTUOSITY
UNCTUOUS
UNCTUOUSLY
UNCTUOUSNESS
UNCUBBED
UNCULAR
UNCULTED
UNCULTIVATED
UNCULTURE
UNCULTURED
UNCUMBER
UNCUMBERED
UNCUNNING
UNCUNNINGLY
UNCURABLE
UNCURABLY
UNCURB
UNCURBED
UNCURBING
UNCURED
UNCURL
UNCURLING
UNCURRENT
UNCURRENTLY
UNCURSE
UNCURTAIN
UNCURTAINED
UNCUS
UNCUSTOMED
UNCUT
UNCYA
UNDAMAGED
UNDAMPED
UNDANGERED
UNDARK
UNDARKENED
UNDASHED
UNDATE
UNDATED
UNDATEDNESS
UNDAUGHTERLY
UNDAUNTABLE
UNDAUNTED
UNDAUNTEDLY
UNDAZZLE
UNDE
UNDEADLY
UNDEAF
UNDEAN
UNDEAR
UNDECAGON
UNDECAYED
UNDECEIVABLE
UNDECEIVABLY
UNDECEIVE
UNDECEIVED
UNDECEIVER
UNDECEIVING
UNDECENCY
UNDECENNIAL
UNDECENT
UNDECENTLY
UNDECEPTION
UNDECIDE
UNDECIDED
UNDECIDEDLY
UNDECIDING
UNDECIMAL
UNDECIMAN
UNDECIMOLE
UNDECIPHER
UNDECIPHERED
UNDECISIVE
UNDECISIVELY
UNDECK
UNDECKED
UNDECLARE
UNDECLARED

UNDECLINABLE
UNDECOYED
UNDECREE
UNDECYL
UNDECYLENE
UNDECYLENIC
UNDECYLIC
UNDEE
UNDEEDED
UNDEEMED
UNDEEMOUS
UNDEEMOUSLY
UNDEEP
UNDEFEASIBLE
UNDEFECATED
UNDEFENDED
UNDEFENSIBLE
UNDEFILED
UNDEFINABLE
UNDEFINABLY
UNDEFINE
UNDEFINED
UNDEIFIED
UNDEIFY
UNDEIFYING
UNDELAYEDLY
UNDELIGHT
UNDELIVERABLE
UNDELIVERY
UNDELUDABLE
UNDEMONSTRATIVE
UNDENIABLE
UNDENIABLY
UNDEPENDABLE
UNDEPENDING
UNDEPRIVABLE
UNDER
UNDERACT
UNDERACTED
UNDERACTING
UNDERACTION
UNDERACTOR
UNDERAGE
UNDERAID
UNDERAIR
UNDERARM
UNDERARMING
UNDERBACK
UNDERBARRING
UNDERBEAR
UNDERBEARER
UNDERBEARING
UNDERBEING
UNDERBELLIES
UNDERBELLY
UNDERBID
UNDERBIDDER
UNDERBIDDING
UNDERBILL
UNDERBIND
UNDERBIT
UNDERBITTED
UNDERBITTEN
UNDERBOARD
UNDERBODICE
UNDERBODY
UNDERBORN
UNDERBOUGHT
UNDERBOWED
UNDERBOY
UNDERBRACED
UNDERBRED
UNDERBRIGHT
UNDERBRIM
UNDERBRUSH
UNDERBUILD
UNDERBURN
UNDERBURNED
UNDERBURNT
UNDERBURY
UNDERBUSH
UNDERBUTLER
UNDERBUY
UNDERBUYING
UNDERCANOPY
UNDERCARRIAGE
UNDERCARVED
UNDERCAST
UNDERCHARGE
UNDERCHARGED
UNDERCHARGING
UNDERCLASS
UNDERCLASSMAN
UNDERCLASSMEN
UNDERCLAY
UNDERCLIFF
UNDERCLOTHE
UNDERCLOTHES
UNDERCLUB
UNDERCOAT
UNDERCOATED
UNDERCOATING
UNDERCOLOR
UNDERCOLORED
UNDERCOOL
UNDERCOVER
UNDERCOVERT
UNDERCRAFT
UNDERCREEP
UNDERCREST
UNDERCROFT
UNDERCROP
UNDERCRUST
UNDERCURRENT
UNDERCUT
UNDERCUTTER
UNDERCUTTING
UNDERDEALER
UNDERDEALING
UNDERDECK
UNDERDEVELOPED
UNDERDID
UNDERDITCH
UNDERDO
UNDERDOER
UNDERDOG
UNDERDOING
UNDERDONE
UNDERDOSE
UNDERDRAG
UNDERDRAIN
UNDERDRAINER
UNDERDRAW
UNDERDRAWERS
UNDERDRAWN
UNDERDRESS
UNDERDRIVE
UNDEREARTH
UNDEREATEN
UNDEREDUCATED
UNDERENTER
UNDERER
UNDERESTIMATE
UNDERESTIMATED
UNDERESTIMATING
UNDEREXPOSE
UNDEREXPOSED
UNDEREXPOSING
UNDERFALL
UNDERFED
UNDERFEED
UNDERFEEDING
UNDERFEEL
UNDERFEET
UNDERFELLOW
UNDERFILL
UNDERFILLING
UNDERFIND
UNDERFIRE
UNDERFLEECE
UNDERFLOW
UNDERFO
UNDERFOLD
UNDERFONG
UNDERFOOT
UNDERFRAME
UNDERFRAMING
UNDERFREIGHT
UNDERFUR
UNDERFURROW
UNDERGAGE
UNDERGARMENT
UNDERGAUGE
UNDERGEAR
UNDERGIRD
UNDERGIRDED
UNDERGIRDER
UNDERGIRDING
UNDERGIRDLE
UNDERGIRT
UNDERGIRTH
UNDERGLAZE
UNDERGO
UNDERGOER
UNDERGOES
UNDERGOING
UNDERGONE
UNDERGOWN
UNDERGRADE
UNDERGRADUATE
UNDERGRADUETTE
UNDERGREEN
UNDERGROAN
UNDERGROPE
UNDERGROUND
UNDERGROVE
UNDERGROW
UNDERGROWN
UNDERGROWTH
UNDERHAND
UNDERHANDED
UNDERHANGING
UNDERHEAD
UNDERHEW
UNDERHIVE
UNDERHOLD
UNDERHOLE
UNDERHUNG
UNDERIVED
UNDERJAWED
UNDERKEEP
UNDERLAID
UNDERLAIN
UNDERLAP
UNDERLAY
UNDERLAYER
UNDERLAYING
UNDERLEAF
UNDERLEASE
UNDERLESSEE
UNDERLET
UNDERLETTER
UNDERLETTING
UNDERLEVEL
UNDERLEVER
UNDERLIE
UNDERLIER
UNDERLIFE
UNDERLINE
UNDERLINED
UNDERLINEN
UNDERLINER
UNDERLING
UNDERLINING
UNDERLIP
UNDERLIVE
UNDERLOAD
UNDERLOCK
UNDERLOOK
UNDERLOOKER
UNDERLOUT
UNDERLY
UNDERLYING
UNDERMAN
UNDERMANNED
UNDERMANNING
UNDERMASTED
UNDERMATCH
UNDERMATCHED
UNDERMEAL
UNDERMINE
UNDERMINED
UNDERMINER
UNDERMINING
UNDERMIRTH
UNDERMONEY
UNDERMOST
UNDERMUSLIN
UNDERN
UNDERNAM
UNDERNATURAL
UNDERNEATH
UNDERNESS
UNDERNIM
UNDERNOME
UNDERNOMEN
UNDERNOURISH
UNDERNSONG
UNDERNTIDE
UNDERNTIME
UNDERNUMEN
UNDERPAID
UNDERPAN
UNDERPANTS
UNDERPART
UNDERPASS
UNDERPASSION
UNDERPAY
UNDERPAYING
UNDERPICK
UNDERPICKED
UNDERPIN
UNDERPINNED
UNDERPINNER
UNDERPINNING
UNDERPITCH
UNDERPLANT
UNDERPLANTED
UNDERPLANTING
UNDERPLAY
UNDERPLOT
UNDERPLOTTER
UNDERPOLE
UNDERPOSE
UNDERPOWER
UNDERPRICE
UNDERPRINT
UNDERPROOF
UNDERPROP
UNDERPROPPED
UNDERPROPPER
UNDERPROPPING
UNDERPULL
UNDERPULLER
UNDERPUT
UNDERQUOTE
UNDERQUOTED
UNDERQUOTING
UNDERRAN
UNDERRATE
UNDERRATED
UNDERRATING
UNDERREACH
UNDERREAD
UNDERREAM
UNDERREAMER
UNDERRENT
UNDERRENTED
UNDERRIVER
UNDERROLL
UNDERROOF
UNDERROOT
UNDERRUN
UNDERRUNNING
UNDERSACRISTAN
UNDERSAIL
UNDERSAILED
UNDERSALLY
UNDERSAY
UNDERSCALE
UNDERSCORE
UNDERSCORED
UNDERSCORING
UNDERSCRIBER
UNDERSCRUB
UNDERSEA
UNDERSEAMAN
UNDERSEAS
UNDERSELL
UNDERSELLER
UNDERSELLING
UNDERSENSE
UNDERSERVE
UNDERSET
UNDERSETTER
UNDERSETTING
UNDERSETTLE
UNDERSEXED
UNDERSHAPEN
UNDERSHARP
UNDERSHERIFF
UNDERSHINING
UNDERSHIRT
UNDERSHOOT
UNDERSHOOTING
UNDERSHORE
UNDERSHOT
UNDERSHRUB
UNDERSHRUBBY
UNDERSHUT
UNDERSIDE
UNDERSIGN
UNDERSIGNED
UNDERSIGNER
UNDERSINGING
UNDERSIZE
UNDERSIZED
UNDERSKIRT
UNDERSLEEVE
UNDERSLOPE
UNDERSLUICE
UNDERSLUNG
UNDERSOIL
UNDERSOLD
UNDERSONG
UNDERSPARRED
UNDERSPEND
UNDERSPHERE
UNDERSPIN
UNDERSPORE
UNDERSPREAD
UNDERSPRING
UNDERSTAIRS
UNDERSTAND
UNDERSTANDED

UNDERSTANDER
UNDERSTANDING
UNDERSTATE
UNDERSTATED
UNDERSTATEMENT
UNDERSTATING
UNDERSTOCK
UNDERSTOOD
UNDERSTORY
UNDERSTRATA
UNDERSTRATUM
UNDERSTRATUMS
UNDERSTRIDE
UNDERSTRING
UNDERSTROKE
UNDERSTRUNG
UNDERSTUDIED
UNDERSTUDIES
UNDERSTUDY
UNDERSTUDYING
UNDERSURFACE
UNDERSWEAT
UNDERTAKE
UNDERTAKEN
UNDERTAKER
UNDERTAKING
UNDERTEACHER
UNDERTEAMED
UNDERTENANT
UNDERTHING
UNDERTHINK
UNDERTHRUST
UNDERTIME
UNDERTIMED
UNDERTINT
UNDERTONE
UNDERTONED
UNDERTOOK
UNDERTOW
UNDERTREAD
UNDERTREAT
UNDERTRICK
UNDERTRODDEN
UNDERTRUMP
UNDERTURF
UNDERTURN
UNDERTYPE
UNDERVALUE
UNDERVALUED
UNDERVALUER
UNDERVALUING
UNDERVEST
UNDERVOLTAGE
UNDERWAIST
UNDERWALK
UNDERWARD
UNDERWARP
UNDERWATCH
UNDERWATER
UNDERWAY
UNDERWEAR
UNDERWEIGH
UNDERWEIGHT
UNDERWENT
UNDERWING
UNDERWIT
UNDERWITTED
UNDERWOOD
UNDERWORK
UNDERWORKED
UNDERWORKER
UNDERWORKING
UNDERWORLD
UNDERWRIT
UNDERWRITE
UNDERWRITER
UNDERWRITING
UNDERWRITTEN
UNDERWROTE
UNDERWROUGHT
UNDESCRIPT
UNDESERT
UNDESERVE
UNDESERVED
UNDESERVER
UNDESIGNED
UNDESIGNING
UNDESIRABLE
UNDESIRABLY
UNDESIRE
UNDESIREDLY
UNDETERMINED
UNDEVELOPED
UNDEVIATING
UNDEVIATINGLY
UNDEVIL
UNDEVOTION
UNDID
UNDIES
UNDIFFERENCED
UNDIFFERENTIATED
UNDIG
UNDIGENOUS
UNDIGESTABLE
UNDIGESTED
UNDIGESTIBLE
UNDIGESTION
UNDIGHT
UNDIGHTED
UNDIGNE
UNDIGNIFIED
UNDIGNIFY
UNDILUTED
UNDIMINISHED
UNDIMMED
UNDINE
UNDINED
UNDIOCESED
UNDIRECT
UNDIRECTED
UNDIRECTLY
UNDISCERNING
UNDISCIPLINED
UNDISCLOSE
UNDISCLOSED
UNDISCOURSED
UNDISCREET
UNDISCREETLY
UNDISCRETION
UNDISCRIMINATING
UNDISGUISE
UNDISGUISED
UNDISMAY
UNDISMAYED
UNDISPENSED
UNDISPENSING
UNDISPLAY
UNDISPOSE
UNDISPOSED
UNDISPUTABLE
UNDISPUTABLY
UNDISPUTED
UNDISTINCT
UNDISTINCTLY
UNDISTINGUISHED
UNDISTORTED
UNDISTRESS
UNDISTURBED
UNDIVIDABLE
UNDIVIDABLY
UNDIVIDED
UNDIVIDEDLY
UNDIVIDUAL
UNDIVORCING
UNDO
UNDOCIBLE
UNDOCK
UNDOCTOR
UNDOER
UNDOG
UNDOGMATIC
UNDOING
UNDOMESTICATED
UNDONE
UNDOSE
UNDOUBLE
UNDOUBLED
UNDOUBLING
UNDOUBTABLE
UNDOUBTABLY
UNDOUBTED
UNDOUBTEDLY
UNDRAPE
UNDRAPED
UNDRAW
UNDRAWING
UNDRAWN
UNDREAMED
UNDREAMT
UNDRESS
UNDRESSED
UNDREST
UNDREW
UNDUE
UNDUKE
UNDULANT
UNDULAR
UNDULATANCE
UNDULATE
UNDULATED
UNDULATELY
UNDULATING
UNDULATION
UNDULATIVE
UNDULATORY
UNDULOID
UNDULOSE
UNDULOUS
UNDULY
UNDURE
UNDUST
UNDUSTED
UNDUTIFULNESS
UNDUTY
UNDWELT
UNDY
UNDYED
UNDYING
UNDYINGLY
UNDYINGNESS
UNE
UNEARED
UNEARNED
UNEARTH
UNEARTHED
UNEARTHING
UNEARTHLY
UNEASE
UNEASEFUL
UNEASEFULNESS
UNEASIER
UNEASIEST
UNEASILY
UNEASINESS
UNEASY
UNEATH
UNEATHS
UNEBRIATE
UNEDIBLE
UNEDIBLENESS
UNEDIBLY
UNEDITED
UNEDUCABLE
UNEDUCABLY
UNEDUCATE
UNEDUCATED
UNEFFABLE
UNEFFECTUAL
UNEGAL
UNEGALLY
UNEGALNESS
UNELEGANT
UNELEGANTLY
UNELIGIBLE
UNELIGIBLY
UNEMBELLISHED
UNEMBODIED
UNEMOTIONAL
UNEMOTIONALLY
UNEMOTIONED
UNEMPHATIC
UNEMPLOY
UNEMPLOYABLE
UNEMPLOYED
UNEMPLOYMENT
UNEMPT
UNENCUMBER
UNENCUMBERED
UNENDED
UNENDING
UNENDINGLY
UNENDLY
UNENGAGED
UNENGLISH
UNENJOYABLE
UNENLIGHTENED
UNENTANGLE
UNENTANGLER
UNENTERING
UNENTHUSIASTIC
UNENTRANCE
UNEPISCOPAL
UNEQUABLE
UNEQUABLY
UNEQUAL
UNEQUALED
UNEQUALITY
UNEQUALLED
UNEQUALLY
UNEQUIAXED
UNEQUITABLE
UNEQUITABLY
UNEQUIVOCAL
UNEQUIVOCALLY
UNERECT
UNERRABLE
UNERRABLY
UNERRING
UNERRINGLY
UNESCAPABLE
UNESCAPABLY
UNESSENCE
UNESSENTIAL
UNESTABLISH
UNESTIMABLE
UNETHIC
UNETHICAL
UNETHICALLY
UNEVEN
UNEVENLY
UNEVENNESS
UNEVENTFUL
UNEVENTFULLY
UNEVIDENT
UNEVITABLE
UNEVITABLY
UNEXACT
UNEXACTLY
UNEXACTNESS
UNEXAMPLED
UNEXCEPTIVE
UNEXCITED
UNEXCITING
UNEXCLUSIVE
UNEXCUSABLE
UNEXCUSABLY
UNEXPECT
UNEXPECTED
UNEXPECTEDLY
UNEXPEDIENT
UNEXPENDED
UNEXPENSIVE
UNEXPERIENCE
UNEXPERIENT
UNEXPERT
UNEXPERTLY
UNEXPIRED
UNEXPLAINED
UNEXPLICABLE
UNEXPLOITED
UNEXPOSED
UNEXPRESS
UNEXPRESSIVE
UNEXPURGATED
UNEXTRICABLE
UNEYED
UNFACE
UNFACT
UNFADABLE
UNFADED
UNFADING
UNFADINGLY
UNFAILABLE
UNFAILABLY
UNFAILING
UNFAILINGLY
UNFAIN
UNFAIR
UNFAIRLY
UNFAIRNESS
UNFAITH
UNFAITHFUL
UNFAITHFULLY
UNFALCATED
UNFALLIBLE
UNFALLIBLY
UNFALTERING
UNFAMILIAR
UNFAMILIARLY
UNFAMOUS
UNFARDLE
UNFASHION
UNFASHIONED
UNFAST
UNFASTEN
UNFATHERED
UNFATHOMABLE
UNFATHOMED
UNFAVORABLE
UNFAVORABLY
UNFAVOURABLE
UNFAVOURABLY
UNFEARY
UNFEASABLE
UNFEASABLY
UNFEASIBLE
UNFEASIBLY
UNFEASTLY
UNFEATHER
UNFEATURED
UNFEATY
UNFEEL
UNFEELABLE
UNFEELING
UNFEELINGLY

UNFEELINGNESS
UNFEIGNABLE
UNFEIGNABLY
UNFEIGNED
UNFEIGNEDLY
UNFEIGNING
UNFEIGNINGLY
UNFELE
UNFELICITOUS
UNFELLOWED
UNFERMENTED
UNFERTILE
UNFERTILITY
UNFESTIVAL
UNFETTER
UNFETTERED
UNFEUDALIZE
UNFEUED
UNFIGURED
UNFILIAL
UNFILIALLY
UNFILIALNESS
UNFILLABLE
UNFILLED
UNFILLETED
UNFINANCIAL
UNFINE
UNFINGERED
UNFINISH
UNFINISHED
UNFINISHEDLY
UNFIRED
UNFIRM
UNFIRMLY
UNFIRMNESS
UNFIT
UNFITLY
UNFITNESS
UNFITTED
UNFITTEN
UNFITTING
UNFITTY
UNFIX
UNFIXED
UNFLAG
UNFLAGGING
UNFLAGGINGLY
UNFLAME
UNFLAPPABLE
UNFLEDGED
UNFLEECE
UNFLESH
UNFLESHED
UNFLESHLY
UNFLESHY
UNFLEXIBLE
UNFLEXIBLY
UNFLINCHING
UNFLOWER
UNFLUSH
UNFOLD
UNFOLDED
UNFOLDEN
UNFOLDER
UNFOLDING
UNFOLDMENT
UNFOOL
UNFOOTED
UNFORBADE
UNFORCED
UNFORCEDLY
UNFORCEDNESS
UNFORESEE
UNFORESEEN
UNFORGIVER
UNFORGIVING
UNFORMAL
UNFORMALITY
UNFORMALLY
UNFORMALNESS
UNFORMED
UNFORTIFIED
UNFORTUNATE
UNFORTUNE
UNFOUND
UNFOUNDED
UNFOUNDEDLY
UNFOXED
UNFRAME
UNFRANGIBLE
UNFRANK
UNFRAUGHT
UNFREE
UNFREEDOM
UNFREELY
UNFREEMAN
UNFREENESS
UNFREQUENCY
UNFREQUENT
UNFREQUENTED
UNFREQUENTLY
UNFRET
UNFRIEND
UNFRIENDED
UNFRIENDING
UNFRIENDLY
UNFRIGHTED
UNFROCK
UNFROZEN
UNFRUCTIFY
UNFRUCTUOUS
UNFRUITFUL
UNFRUITFULLY
UNFULFIL
UNFULFILL
UNFULFILLMENT
UNFULFILMENT
UNFUMED
UNFUNDED
UNFUR
UNFURL
UNFURNISH
UNFURNISHED
UNFUSIBLE
UNFUSIBLY
UNGAIN
UNGAINLIKE
UNGAINLINESS
UNGAINLY
UNGAINNESS
UNGAITE
UNGALLANT
UNGALLANTLY
UNGARO
UNGEAR
UNGENDERED
UNGENEROUS
UNGENEROUSLY
UNGENIAL
UNGENIALITY
UNGENIALLY
UNGENIALNESS
UNGENITURED
UNGENTEEL
UNGENTEELY
UNGENTLE
UNGENTLEMAN
UNGENTLENESS
UNGENTLY
UNGET
UNGIFTED
UNGILD
UNGILL
UNGIRD
UNGIRDED
UNGIRT
UNGIRTH
UNGIVE
UNGKA
UNGLAZE
UNGLAZED
UNGLE
UNGLEE
UNGLORIOUS
UNGLORIOUSLY
UNGLORY
UNGLOSSY
UNGLOVE
UNGLUE
UNGNAW
UNGOD
UNGODLILY
UNGODLINESS
UNGODLY
UNGONE
UNGOOD
UNGOT
UNGOTTEN
UNGOVERNABLE
UNGOVERNABLY
UNGOWN
UNGRACE
UNGRACEFUL
UNGRACEFULLY
UNGRACIOUS
UNGRACIOUSLY
UNGRADED
UNGRAMMATIC
UNGRATEFUL
UNGRATEFULLY
UNGRAVE
UNGRAVELY
UNGREEABLE
UNGREEN
UNGRIPE
UNGROOMED
UNGROUNDED
UNGROUNDEDLY
UNGUAL
UNGUARD
UNGUARDED
UNGUARDEDLY
UNGUEAL
UNGUENT
UNGUENTARIA
UNGUENTARIAN
UNGUENTARIUM
UNGUENTARY
UNGUENTO
UNGUENTOUS
UNGUENTUM
UNGUES
UNGUICORN
UNGUICULATE
UNGUICULE
UNGUIFEROUS
UNGUIFORM
UNGUILED
UNGUILEFUL
UNGUILEFULLY
UNGUILTILY
UNGUILTINESS
UNGUILTLESS
UNGUILTY
UNGUINOUS
UNGUIROSTRAL
UNGUIS
UNGULA
UNGULAE
UNGULAR
UNGULATE
UNGULED
UNGULIGRADE
UNGULOUS
UNGUM
UNGUMMED
UNGYVE
UNGYVED
UNHABILE
UNHABIT
UNHAD
UNHAIR
UNHAIRER
UNHAIRING
UNHALE
UNHALLOW
UNHALLOWED
UNHALSED
UNHALTER
UNHAMPERED
UNHAND
UNHANDILY
UNHANDINESS
UNHANDSOME
UNHANDSOMELY
UNHANDY
UNHANG
UNHAP
UNHAPPIER
UNHAPPIEST
UNHAPPILY
UNHAPPINESS
UNHAPPY
UNHARBOR
UNHARBORED
UNHARBOUR
UNHARBOURED
UNHARD
UNHARDILY
UNHARDINESS
UNHARDY
UNHARMED
UNHARMONIOUS
UNHARNESS
UNHASP
UNHASTE
UNHAT
UNHATTED
UNHATTING
UNHEAD
UNHEADER
UNHEAL
UNHEALED
UNHEALTH
UNHEALTHFUL
UNHEALTHIER
UNHEALTHIEST
UNHEALTHILY
UNHEALTHSOME
UNHEALTHY
UNHEARD
UNHEARSE
UNHEART
UNHEARTEN
UNHEARTSOME
UNHEARTY
UNHEATED
UNHEAVEN
UNHEED
UNHEEDED
UNHEEDING
UNHEEDY
UNHEIRED
UNHELE
UNHELER
UNHELM
UNHELMET
UNHELP
UNHENDE
UNHENT
UNHEPPEN
UNHERD
UNHEROISM
UNHESITATING
UNHIDABLE
UNHIDABLY
UNHIDE
UNHIDEABLE
UNHIDEABLY
UNHINGE
UNHINGED
UNHINGING
UNHITCH
UNHIVE
UNHOARD
UNHOLD
UNHOLIER
UNHOLIEST
UNHOLILY
UNHOLINESS
UNHOLPEN
UNHOLY
UNHOME
UNHONEST
UNHONESTLY
UNHONESTY
UNHONORABLE
UNHONORABLY
UNHONOURABLE
UNHONOURABLY
UNHOOD
UNHOOK
UNHOOP
UNHOOPABLE
UNHOOPER
UNHOPE
UNHOPED
UNHOPEDLY
UNHOPEDNESS
UNHOPEFUL
UNHOPEFULLY
UNHOPPED
UNHORSE
UNHORSED
UNHORSING
UNHOSPITABLE
UNHOSPITABLY
UNHOSPITAL
UNHOUSE
UNHOUSED
UNHOUSELED
UNHUMAN
UNHURRIED
UNHURRIEDLY
UNHURT
UNHUSK
UNHUSKED
UNIAT
UNIATE
UNIAXIAL
UNIBIVALENT
UNIBLE
UNIC
UNICAMERAL
UNICELL
UNICELLATE
UNICELLED
UNICELLULAR
UNICHORD
UNICISM
UNICIST
UNICITY
UNICOLOR
UNICONSTANT
UNICORN

UNICORNIC
UNICOSTATE
UNICUM
UNICURSAL
UNICURSALITY
UNICURSALLY
UNICYCLE
UNICYCLIST
UNIDEAED
UNIDEAL
UNIDENTIFIED
UNIDEXTRAL
UNIDIRECT
UNIDLE
UNIDLENESS
UNIDLY
UNIE
UNIFACE
UNIFACED
UNIFACTORIAL
UNIFARIOUS
UNIFIABLE
UNIFIC
UNIFICATION
UNIFIED
UNIFIEDLY
UNIFIEDNESS
UNIFIER
UNIFILAR
UNIFLOROUS
UNIFLOW
UNIFOLIATE
UNIFOLIOLATE
UNIFORM
UNIFORMALIZE
UNIFORMALIZED
UNIFORMALIZING
UNIFORMED
UNIFORMIST
UNIFORMITIES
UNIFORMITY
UNIFORMIZE
UNIFORMLY
UNIFORMNESS
UNIFY
UNIFYING
UNIGENESIS
UNIGENETIC
UNIGENITAL
UNIGENITURE
UNIGENOUS
UNIGRAVIDA
UNIJUGATE
UNILATERAL
UNILATERALLY
UNILINGUAL
UNILITERAL
UNILOBE
UNILOCULAR
UNIMAGINABLE
UNIMAGINATIVE
UNIMANUAL
UNIMBATTLED
UNIMEDIAL
UNIMITABLE
UNIMITABLY
UNIMMERGIBLE
UNIMODAL
UNIMODALITY
UNIMPAIRED
UNIMPASSIONED
UNIMPEDED
UNIMPEDEDLY
UNIMPLICATE
UNIMPORTANCE
UNIMPORTANT
UNIMPRESSED
UNIMPRESSIVE
UNIMPROVABLE
UNIMPROVED
UNIMPROVEDLY
UNINCULCATED
UNINDEBTED
UNINDEBTEDLY
UNINDENTED
UNINFORMED
UNINGENIOUS
UNINGENUOUS
UNINGENUOUSLY
UNINHABITED
UNINHIBITED
UNINJURED
UNINOMINAL
UNINSPIRED
UNINSTRUCTED
UNINTELLIGENT
UNINTELLIGIBLE
UNINTENTIONAL
UNINTENTIONALLY
UNINTERESTED
UNINTERESTING
UNINTERMITTED
UNINTERMITTENT
UNINTERRUPTED
UNINTERRUPTEDLY
UNINTROITIVE
UNINVENTIVE
UNINVITE
UNINVITED
UNIOID
UNION
UNIONED
UNIONIC
UNIONID
UNIONIFORM
UNIONISM
UNIONIST
UNIONISTIC
UNIONIZATION
UNIONIZE
UNIONIZED
UNIONIZING
UNIONOID
UNIOVAL
UNIPARA
UNIPARENTAL
UNIPARIENT
UNIPAROUS
UNIPARTITE
UNIPED
UNIPERIODIC
UNIPERSONAL
UNIPETALOUS
UNIPLANAR
UNIPOLAR
UNIPOLARITY
UNIPOROUS
UNIPOTENCE
UNIPOTENT
UNIPULSE
UNIQUANTIC
UNIQUE
UNIQUELY
UNIQUENESS
UNIQUITY
UNIREME
UNISEPTATE
UNISEX
UNISEXED
UNISEXUAL
UNISEXUALITY
UNISEXUALLY
UNISON
UNISONAL
UNISONANT
UNISONO
UNISONOUS
UNISPARKER
UNISPIRAL
UNISTYLIST
UNIT
UNITABILITY
UNITABLE
UNITABLY
UNITAL
UNITARIAN
UNITARILY
UNITARINESS
UNITARISM
UNITARIST
UNITARY
UNITATION
UNITE
UNITEABLE
UNITEABLY
UNITED
UNITEDLY
UNITEDNESS
UNITELY
UNITEMIZED
UNITENESS
UNITER
UNITIES
UNITING
UNITION
UNITISM
UNITISTIC
UNITIVE
UNITIVELY
UNITIVENESS
UNITIZE
UNITRIVALENT
UNITROPE
UNITS
UNITUDE
UNITY
UNIVALENCE
UNIVALENCY
UNIVALENT
UNIVALID
UNIVALVE
UNIVALVED
UNIVALVULAR
UNIVARIANT
UNIVERSAL
UNIVERSALIA
UNIVERSALITIES
UNIVERSALITY
UNIVERSALIZE
UNIVERSALIZED
UNIVERSALIZING
UNIVERSALLY
UNIVERSE
UNIVERSEFUL
UNIVERSITAS
UNIVERSITIES
UNIVERSITIZE
UNIVERSITY
UNIVERSOLOGY
UNIVOCACY
UNIVOCAL
UNIVOCALLY
UNIVOCATION
UNIVOCITY
UNIVOLTINE
UNIVOROUS
UNJUDICIOUS
UNJUST
UNJUSTIFIED
UNJUSTLY
UNJUSTNESS
UNKAMED
UNKED
UNKEELED
UNKEMBED
UNKEMPT
UNKEMPTLY
UNKEMPTNESS
UNKEN
UNKEND
UNKENNED
UNKENNEL
UNKENNELED
UNKENNELING
UNKENNELLED
UNKENNELLING
UNKENNING
UNKENSOME
UNKENT
UNKEPT
UNKET
UNKID
UNKIND
UNKINDLILY
UNKINDLY
UNKINDNESS
UNKINDRED
UNKINDREDLY
UNKING
UNKINGER
UNKINGSHIP
UNKINK
UNKISS
UNKNIT
UNKNITTED
UNKNITTING
UNKNOW
UNKNOWABLE
UNKNOWABLY
UNKNOWING
UNKNOWINGLY
UNKNOWLEDGED
UNKNOWN
UNKNOWNLY
UNKNOWNNESS
UNKNOWNST
UNKO
UNLABORED
UNLABOURED
UNLACE
UNLACED
UNLACING
UNLADE
UNLADED
UNLADEN
UNLADIFIED
UNLADING
UNLADYFIED
UNLAID
UNLAND
UNLAP
UNLASH
UNLASHER
UNLATCH
UNLATINED
UNLAW
UNLAWED
UNLAWFUL
UNLAWFULLY
UNLAWFULNESS
UNLAY
UNLAYED
UNLAYING
UNLEAD
UNLEADED
UNLEARED
UNLEARN
UNLEARNED
UNLEARNEDLY
UNLEARNING
UNLEARNT
UNLEASH
UNLEAVE
UNLEAVENED
UNLEDE
UNLEEFUL
UNLEESOME
UNLEGITIMATE
UNLEISUM
UNLEISURED
UNLENGTH
UNLERED
UNLESS
UNLETTED
UNLETTERED
UNLETTEREDLY
UNLEVEL
UNLEWTY
UNLICKED
UNLID
UNLIEF
UNLIGHT
UNLIGHTED
UNLIGHTEDLY
UNLIGHTSOME
UNLIKE
UNLIKELIER
UNLIKELIEST
UNLIKELIHOOD
UNLIKELINESS
UNLIKELY
UNLIKEN
UNLIKENESS
UNLIKING
UNLIMB
UNLIMBER
UNLIME
UNLIMITABLE
UNLIMITABLY
UNLIMITED
UNLIMITEDLY
UNLINE
UNLINED
UNLINK
UNLINKED
UNLINKING
UNLIQUIDATED
UNLIQUORED
UNLIST
UNLISTED
UNLISTENED
UNLISTY
UNLIT
UNLITERAL
UNLITERALLY
UNLITTLE
UNLITURGICAL
UNLITURGIZE
UNLIVE
UNLIVED
UNLIVERY
UNLIVING
UNLOAD
UNLOADEN
UNLOADER
UNLOCATED
UNLOCK
UNLOCKER
UNLODGE
UNLOGIC
UNLOGICAL
UNLOGICALLY
UNLOOK
UNLOOKED
UNLOOSE

UNLOOSEN
UNLORD
UNLORDED
UNLORDLY
UNLOUKEN
UNLOUSY
UNLOVE
UNLOVED
UNLOVELIER
UNLOVELIEST
UNLOVELILY
UNLOVELINESS
UNLOVELY
UNLOVERLIKE
UNLOVERLY
UNLOVESOME
UNLOVING
UNLOVINGLY
UNLOVINGNESS
UNLUCK
UNLUCKFUL
UNLUCKIER
UNLUCKIEST
UNLUCKILY
UNLUCKINESS
UNLUCKLY
UNLUCKY
UNLUST
UNLUSTIE
UNLUSTIER
UNLUSTIEST
UNLUSTILY
UNLUSTINESS
UNLUSTY
UNLUTE
UNMACKLY
UNMADE
UNMAGISTRATE
UNMAIDEN
UNMAIL
UNMAILABLE
UNMAKE
UNMAKER
UNMAKING
UNMAN
UNMANACLE
UNMANAGEABLE
UNMANHOOD
UNMANIABLE
UNMANLIER
UNMANLIEST
UNMANLILY
UNMANLINESS
UNMANLY
UNMANNED
UNMANNERED
UNMANNEREDLY
UNMANNERLY
UNMANNING
UNMANTLE
UNMARKED
UNMARRIED
UNMARRY
UNMASK
UNMASKER
UNMASKING
UNMATCHED
UNMATURE
UNMATURELY
UNMATURENESS
UNMATURITY
UNMAZE
UNMEANING
UNMEANINGLY
UNMEANT
UNMEASURABLE
UNMEASURABLY
UNMEASURED
UNMEASUREDLY
UNMEASURELY
UNMECHANIC
UNMECHANICAL
UNMECHANIZE
UNMEDDLE
UNMEDULLATED
UNMEEDFUL
UNMEEDY
UNMEEK
UNMEEKLY
UNMEEKNESS
UNMEET
UNMEETLY
UNMEETNESS
UNMELODIOUS
UNMELT
UNMEMBER
UNMERCHANTABLE
UNMERCIABLE
UNMERCIABLY
UNMERCIED
UNMERCIFUL
UNMERCIFULLY
UNMERCILESS
UNMERITABLE
UNMESH
UNMETE
UNMETH
UNMETHODICAL
UNMEW
UNMIGHT
UNMIGHTY
UNMILD
UNMILDNESS
UNMILITARILY
UNMILITARY
UNMILLED
UNMIND
UNMINDED
UNMINDFUL
UNMINDFULLY
UNMINDING
UNMINGLE
UNMINGLEABLE
UNMINGLED
UNMIST
UNMISTAKABLE
UNMISTAKABLY
UNMITER
UNMITIGATED
UNMITRE
UNMIX
UNMIXED
UNMOBLE
UNMODERATE
UNMODERATELY
UNMODERNIZE
UNMODIFIED
UNMODULATED
UNMOLD
UNMOLEST
UNMOLESTED
UNMONEYED
UNMONOPOLIZE
UNMOOR
UNMOORED
UNMORAL
UNMORALIST
UNMORALITY
UNMORALIZED
UNMORALIZING
UNMORALLY
UNMORALNESS
UNMORRISED
UNMORTALIZE
UNMORTISE
UNMORTISED
UNMORTISING
UNMOTHERED
UNMOTIVED
UNMOULD
UNMOUNT
UNMOUNTED
UNMOVABILITY
UNMOVABLE
UNMOVABLETY
UNMOVABLY
UNMOVED
UNMOVEDLY
UNMOVING
UNMUDDLE
UNMUFFLE
UNMUFFLED
UNMUFFLING
UNMUSICAL
UNMUTABLE
UNMUZZLE
UNMYSTERY
UNNAIL
UNNAPKINED
UNNAPPED
UNNAPT
UNNATURAL
UNNATURALISM
UNNATURALIST
UNNATURALITY
UNNATURALIZE
UNNATURALLY
UNNATURE
UNNEALED
UNNEAR
UNNEATH
UNNECESSARY
UNNEEDED
UNNEIGHBORED
UNNEIGHBORLY
UNNERVE
UNNERVED
UNNERVING
UNNEST
UNNET
UNNETH
UNNETHE
UNNEWSED
UNNIMBED
UNNOBILITY
UNNOBLE
UNNOBLENESS
UNNOBLY
UNNOOKED
UNNOSE
UNNOTED
UNNOTICEABLE
UNNOTICEABLY
UNNOTICED
UNNOTIFY
UNNUMBERABLE
UNNUMBERABLY
UNNUMBERED
UNNUMERABLE
UNNUN
UNOBEDIENCE
UNOBEDIENT
UNOBEDIENTLY
UNOBJECTIONABLE
UNOBLIGING
UNOBLIGINGLY
UNOBSERVANCE
UNOBSERVANT
UNOBSERVED
UNOBSERVEDLY
UNOBSERVING
UNOBSTRUCTED
UNOBTAINABLE
UNOBTAINABLY
UNOBTRUSIVE
UNOCCUPIED
UNOCCUPIEDLY
UNODE
UNOFFENDED
UNOFFENDEDLY
UNOFFENDING
UNOFFENSIVE
UNOFFICIAL
UNOFFICIALLY
UNOFFICINAL
UNOFTEN
UNOIL
UNOLD
UNOPED
UNOPEN
UNOPENED
UNOPENLY
UNOPENNESS
UNOPERATIVE
UNOPERCULATE
UNOPPORTUNE
UNORDAINED
UNORDER
UNORDERED
UNORDERLY
UNORDINARILY
UNORDINARY
UNORDINATE
UNORDINATELY
UNORGANED
UNORGANIC
UNORGANICAL
UNORGANISED
UNORGANIZED
UNORIENTED
UNORIGINAL
UNORIGINATE
UNORIGINATED
UNORN
UNORTHODOX
UNORTHODOXLY
UNORTHODOXY
UNOSTENTATIOUS
UNOWED
UNOWN
UNOWNED
UNPACIFIED
UNPACIFIEDLY
UNPACK
UNPACKER
UNPAGED
UNPAID
UNPAINT
UNPAINTABLE
UNPAINTED
UNPAINTEDLY
UNPAIRED
UNPAISED
UNPALATABLE
UNPALE
UNPALPED
UNPANEL
UNPANNEL
UNPAPER
UNPARADISE
UNPARAGONED
UNPARALLELED
UNPARCH
UNPARDONABLE
UNPARDONABLY
UNPAREGAL
UNPARENTED
UNPARREL
UNPARROTED
UNPARTED
UNPARTIAL
UNPARTIALITY
UNPARTIALLY
UNPASSABLE
UNPASSABLY
UNPASSIONATE
UNPASTOR
UNPATHED
UNPATHWAYED
UNPATIENCE
UNPATIENT
UNPATIENTLY
UNPATRIOTIC
UNPATROLLED
UNPATRONIZED
UNPAVE
UNPAVED
UNPAWN
UNPAY
UNPEACE
UNPEDIGREED
UNPEEL
UNPEELED
UNPEERABLE
UNPEERED
UNPEG
UNPEN
UNPENITENT
UNPENITENTLY
UNPEOPLE
UNPEOPLED
UNPEOPLING
UNPERCEIVED
UNPERCH
UNPERFECT
UNPERFECTED
UNPERFECTION
UNPERFECTLY
UNPERFORATED
UNPERFORMING
UNPERISHABLE
UNPERISHABLY
UNPERMANENCY
UNPERMANENT
UNPERPLEX
UNPERSUASION
UNPERTURBED
UNPERVERT
UNPHRASABLE
UNPHRASED
UNPICK
UNPIECE
UNPIERCED
UNPILE
UNPILLED
UNPIN
UNPINION
UNPINKED
UNPINNED
UNPINNING
UNPITEOUS
UNPITEOUSLY
UNPITIED
UNPITIEDLY
UNPITIEDNESS
UNPITY
UNPITYING
UNPITYINGLY
UNPLACABLE
UNPLACABLY
UNPLACE
UNPLACED
UNPLAID
UNPLAIN
UNPLAINED

UNPLAINLY
UNPLAINNESS
UNPLAIT
UNPLANK
UNPLANNED
UNPLANNEDLY
UNPLANT
UNPLANTED
UNPLAT
UNPLAUSIVE
UNPLAYABLE
UNPLEASANT
UNPLEASANTLY
UNPLEASANTNESS
UNPLEASANTRIES
UNPLEASANTRY
UNPLEASED
UNPLEASING
UNPLEASINGLY
UNPLEASIVE
UNPLEASURE
UNPLEAT
UNPLEDGED
UNPLIGHT
UNPLOWED
UNPLUG
UNPLUMB
UNPLUMBED
UNPLUME
UNPOETIC
UNPOETICAL
UNPOETICALLY
UNPOISED
UNPOISON
UNPOLICED
UNPOLICIED
UNPOLISH
UNPOLISHED
UNPOLITE
UNPOLITELY
UNPOLITENESS
UNPOLITIC
UNPOLITICLY
UNPOLLED
UNPOLLUTED
UNPOLLUTEDLY
UNPOPE
UNPOPULAR
UNPOPULARITY
UNPOPULARIZE
UNPOPULARLY
UNPOPULATE
UNPOPULATED
UNPORTABLE
UNPORTUNATE
UNPORTUOUS
UNPOSSESS
UNPOSSIBLE
UNPOSSIBLY
UNPOWER
UNPOWERFUL
UNPRACTICAL
UNPRACTICED
UNPRACTISED
UNPRAISABLE
UNPRAISE
UNPRAY
UNPRAYABLE
UNPRAYED
UNPREACH
UNPREACHING
UNPREDICT
UNPREDICTABLE
UNPREGNABLE
UNPREJUDICE
UNPREJUDICED
UNPREMEDITATED
UNPREPARE
UNPREPARED
UNPREPAREDLY
UNPREPOSSESSING
UNPREST
UNPRETENDING
UNPRETENTIOUS
UNPREVENTED
UNPRICED
UNPRIEST
UNPRIME
UNPRINCE
UNPRINCIPLE
UNPRINCIPLED
UNPRINTABLE
UNPRINTABLY
UNPRISON
UNPRIVILEGED
UNPRIZABLE
UNPROBABLE
UNPROBABLY
UNPROCLAIMED
UNPROCREATE
UNPRODUCIBLE
UNPRODUCIBLY
UNPRODUCTIVE
UNPRODUCTIVENESS
UNPROFESSIONAL
UNPROFICIENT
UNPROFIT
UNPROFITABLE
UNPROFITABLY
UNPROFITED
UNPROGRESSIVE
UNPROMISE
UNPROMISING
UNPRONOUNCED
UNPROP
UNPROPER
UNPROPERLY
UNPROPERNESS
UNPROPERTIED
UNPROPICE
UNPROPITIOUS
UNPROPORTION
UNPROPRIETY
UNPROSELYTE
UNPROSPERITY
UNPROSPEROUS
UNPROTECTED
UNPROVABLE
UNPROVABLY
UNPROVIDE
UNPROVIDED
UNPROVIDEDLY
UNPROVIDENT
UNPROVISED
UNPROVISEDLY
UNPROVISION
UNPRUDENCE
UNPRUDENT
UNPRUDENTLY
UNPUBLISHED
UNPUCKER
UNPUFF
UNPULLED
UNPUNISHED
UNPUNISHEDLY
UNPUNISHING
UNPURE
UNPURED
UNPURELY
UNPURENESS
UNPURSE
UNPURVEYED
UNPUZZLE
UNQUAILED
UNQUALIFIED
UNQUALIFY
UNQUALITIED
UNQUALITY
UNQUANTIFIED
UNQUEEN
UNQUEME
UNQUEMELY
UNQUERT
UNQUESTIONABLE
UNQUESTIONED
UNQUESTIONING
UNQUICK
UNQUIESCENCE
UNQUIESCENT
UNQUIET
UNQUIETLY
UNQUIETNESS
UNQUIETOUS
UNQUIETUDE
UNQUIT
UNQUOD
UNQUOTE
UNRACED
UNRAKE
UNRAM
UNRANK
UNRATED
UNRATIFIED
UNRATTLED
UNRAVAGED
UNRAVEL
UNRAVELABLE
UNRAVELED
UNRAVELER
UNRAVELING
UNRAVELLABLE
UNRAVELLED
UNRAVELLER
UNRAVELLING
UNRAVELMENT
UNRAY
UNREAD
UNREADABLE
UNREADABLY
UNREADIER
UNREADIEST
UNREADILY
UNREADINESS
UNREADY
UNREAL
UNREALISM
UNREALIST
UNREALISTIC
UNREALITIES
UNREALITY
UNREALIZE
UNREALIZED
UNREALLY
UNREALNESS
UNREASON
UNREASONABLE
UNREASONABLENESS
UNREASONABLY
UNREASONED
UNREASONING
UNREAVE
UNREBUKABLE
UNREBUKABLY
UNREBUKEABLE
UNRECALLING
UNRECKLESS
UNRECOGNIZED
UNRECORDED
UNRECOVERABLE
UNRECOVERED
UNRECTIFIED
UNRECURING
UNRED
UNREDEEMED
UNREDUCT
UNREEL
UNREEVE
UNREEVED
UNREEVING
UNREFINE
UNREFINED
UNREFINEDLY
UNREFINEMENT
UNREFLECTING
UNREFLECTIVE
UNREGARD
UNREGENERACY
UNREGENERATE
UNREGENERATELY
UNREGISTERED
UNREGULAR
UNREGULATED
UNREHEARSED
UNREIN
UNRELATED
UNRELAXED
UNRELENTABLE
UNRELENTANCE
UNRELENTING
UNRELENTLESS
UNRELENTOR
UNRELEVANT
UNRELIABLE
UNRELIABLY
UNRELIANCE
UNRELIEVED
UNRELIGION
UNRELIGIOUS
UNREMEDIABLE
UNREMEMBER
UNREMITTING
UNREMOVED
UNREMUNERATIVE
UNRENOWNED
UNRENOWNEDLY
UNREPAIR
UNREPAIRABLE
UNREPENTABLE
UNREPENTANCE
UNREPLIABLE
UNREPLIABLY
UNREPORTED
UNREPORTEDLY
UNREPROVED
UNREPROVEDLY
UNREPUGNABLE
UNREPUTABLE
UNREQUEST
UNREQUITER
UNRESERVE
UNRESERVED
UNRESERVEDLY
UNRESERVEDNESS
UNRESISTABLE
UNRESISTABLY
UNRESISTANT
UNRESISTED
UNRESISTEDLY
UNRESISTIBLE
UNRESISTIBLY
UNRESISTING
UNRESOLUTE
UNRESOLVE
UNRESPECT
UNRESPECTIVE
UNRESPONSAL
UNRESPONSIVE
UNREST
UNRESTED
UNRESTING
UNRESTRAINED
UNRESTRAINT
UNRESTRICTED
UNRESTY
UNRETURNED
UNREVEALED
UNREVENUED
UNREVERENCE
UNREVEREND
UNREVERENDLY
UNREVERENT
UNREVERENTLY
UNREVOCABLE
UNREVOCABLY
UNREWARDED
UNRICHT
UNRID
UNRIDDLE
UNRIDDLED
UNRIDDLER
UNRIDDLING
UNRIDE
UNRIFLED
UNRIG
UNRIGGED
UNRIGGING
UNRIGHT
UNRIGHTEOUS
UNRIGHTEOUSNESS
UNRIGHTFUL
UNRIGHTFULLY
UNRIGHTLY
UNRIGHTWISE
UNRIND
UNRING
UNRINGED
UNRIP
UNRIPE
UNRIPELY
UNRIPENED
UNRIPENESS
UNRIPPED
UNRIPPING
UNRIVALED
UNRIVALEDLY
UNRIVALLED
UNRIVALLEDLY
UNRIVET
UNRO
UNROADED
UNROAST
UNROBE
UNROLL
UNROLLER
UNROLLMENT
UNROMANTIC
UNROMANTICAL
UNROOF
UNROOST
UNROOT
UNROPE
UNROUGH
UNROUND
UNROUT
UNROVE
UNROW
UNROYAL
UNROYALIST
UNROYALLY
UNROYALNESS
UNRUDE
UNRUEFULLY
UNRUFE
UNRUFFLE
UNRUFFLED

UNRULE
UNRULED
UNRULEDLY
UNRULEDNESS
UNRULEFUL
UNRULIER
UNRULIEST
UNRULILY
UNRULIMENT
UNRULINESS
UNRULY
UNRUMPLE
UNRUTH
UNSACK
UNSACRAMENT
UNSAD
UNSADDEN
UNSADDLE
UNSADDLED
UNSADDLING
UNSADNESS
UNSAFE
UNSAFELY
UNSAFENESS
UNSAFER
UNSAFEST
UNSAFETY
UNSAID
UNSAINT
UNSAINTLY
UNSAKED
UNSALABILITY
UNSALABLE
UNSALABLY
UNSALEABLE
UNSALEABLY
UNSAME
UNSAMPLED
UNSANCTIFIED
UNSANCTIFY
UNSANCTION
UNSANE
UNSANITARY
UNSANITATION
UNSASH
UNSATIABLE
UNSATIABLY
UNSATIATE
UNSATISFACTORY
UNSATISFY
UNSATISFYING
UNSATURABLE
UNSATURATED
UNSATURATION
UNSAUGHT
UNSAVOR
UNSAVORED
UNSAVORILY
UNSAVORINESS
UNSAVORLY
UNSAVORY
UNSAVOURED
UNSAVOURILY
UNSAVOURY
UNSAY
UNSAYING
UNSCALE
UNSCALED
UNSCALEDNESS
UNSCAPABLE
UNSCATHED
UNSCATHEDLY
UNSCENT
UNSCENTED
UNSCHOLAR
UNSCHOLARLY
UNSCHOOLED
UNSCHOOLEDLY
UNSCIENCE
UNSCIENCED
UNSCIENTIFIC
UNSCOTCH
UNSCOTTIFY
UNSCRAMBLE
UNSCRAMBLED
UNSCRAMBLING
UNSCRAPED
UNSCREEN
UNSCREW
UNSCRUPULOUS
UNSCRUTABLE
UNSEAL
UNSEALER
UNSEAM
UNSEARCHABLE
UNSEARCHABLY
UNSEASON
UNSEASONABLE
UNSEASONABLY
UNSEASONED
UNSEAT
UNSEATED
UNSEAWORTHY
UNSECONDED
UNSECRECY
UNSECRET
UNSECTARIAN
UNSECULARIZE
UNSECURE
UNSECURED
UNSECUREDLY
UNSECURELY
UNSECURENESS
UNSECURITY
UNSEE
UNSEEING
UNSEEL
UNSEELINESS
UNSEELY
UNSEEMING
UNSEEMINGLY
UNSEEMLIER
UNSEEMLIEST
UNSEEMLILY
UNSEEMLINESS
UNSEEMLY
UNSEEN
UNSEIZE
UNSEL
UNSELDOM
UNSELF
UNSELFISH
UNSELFISHLY
UNSELFNESS
UNSELINESS
UNSELTH
UNSELY
UNSEMINARED
UNSENSE
UNSENSED
UNSENSIBLE
UNSENSIBLY
UNSENSUALIZE
UNSENTENCED
UNSEPARABLE
UNSEPARABLY
UNSEPTATE
UNSEPTATED
UNSERRIED
UNSERVED
UNSERVICE
UNSET
UNSETTING
UNSETTLE
UNSETTLED
UNSEVEN
UNSEW
UNSEWERED
UNSEX
UNSEXED
UNSEXING
UNSHACKLE
UNSHACKLED
UNSHACKLING
UNSHADOW
UNSHAKABLE
UNSHAKABLY
UNSHAKEABLE
UNSHAKED
UNSHAKEN
UNSHAKENLY
UNSHAKENNESS
UNSHALE
UNSHAMEFUL
UNSHAMEFULLY
UNSHAPE
UNSHAPED
UNSHAPELY
UNSHAPEN
UNSHAPENLY
UNSHAPENNESS
UNSHARED
UNSHARPEN
UNSHAVE
UNSHAVED
UNSHAVEDLY
UNSHAVEDNESS
UNSHAVEN
UNSHAVENLY
UNSHAVENNESS
UNSHAWL
UNSHEAF
UNSHEATHE
UNSHEATHED
UNSHEATHING
UNSHED
UNSHEET
UNSHELL
UNSHELVE
UNSHENT
UNSHERIFF
UNSHEWED
UNSHIFTABLE
UNSHIFTINESS
UNSHIP
UNSHIPMENT
UNSHIPPED
UNSHIPPING
UNSHOD
UNSHOE
UNSHOOK
UNSHOP
UNSHORN
UNSHOT
UNSHOULDER
UNSHOUT
UNSHRINE
UNSHRINEMENT
UNSHRINK
UNSHROUD
UNSHRUBBED
UNSHUNNING
UNSHUT
UNSHUTTER
UNSIB
UNSICKER
UNSICKERLY
UNSICKERNESS
UNSICKLED
UNSIDED
UNSIEGE
UNSIGHT
UNSIGHTABLE
UNSIGHTED
UNSIGHTEDLY
UNSIGHTING
UNSIGHTLIER
UNSIGHTLIEST
UNSIGHTLY
UNSIGNABLE
UNSIGNED
UNSILENCED
UNSIMILAR
UNSIMILARLY
UNSIMPLICITY
UNSIN
UNSINCERE
UNSINCERELY
UNSINCERITY
UNSINEW
UNSING
UNSINGABLE
UNSISTER
UNSISTERLY
UNSISTING
UNSITTING
UNSITTINGLY
UNSIZED
UNSKAITHED
UNSKILFUL
UNSKILFULLY
UNSKILL
UNSKILLED
UNSKILLEDLY
UNSKILLFUL
UNSKILLFULLY
UNSKIMMED
UNSKIN
UNSKIRMISHED
UNSLAKED
UNSLATE
UNSLAVE
UNSLEEVE
UNSLEPT
UNSLING
UNSLINGING
UNSLIP
UNSLIT
UNSLOCKENED
UNSLOGH
UNSLOT
UNSLOTHFUL
UNSLOTHFULLY
UNSLUICE
UNSLUNG
UNSMART
UNSMARTLY
UNSMARTNESS
UNSMILING
UNSMOOTH
UNSMOTE
UNSNAP
UNSNAPPED
UNSNAPPING
UNSNARE
UNSNARL
UNSNECK
UNSOBER
UNSOBERLY
UNSOBERNESS
UNSOBRIETY
UNSOCIABLE
UNSOCIABLY
UNSOCIAL
UNSOCIALLY
UNSOCIALNESS
UNSOCKET
UNSODDEN
UNSOFT
UNSOIL
UNSOILED
UNSOLDER
UNSOLDIER
UNSOLDIERED
UNSOLDIERLY
UNSOLDIERY
UNSOLEMN
UNSOLEMNESS
UNSOLEMNIZE
UNSOLEMNLY
UNSOLICITED
UNSOLUBILITY
UNSOLUBLE
UNSOLVABLE
UNSOLVABLY
UNSOLVE
UNSOLVED
UNSOME
UNSON
UNSONCY
UNSONSIE
UNSONSY
UNSOOT
UNSOPHISTICATE
UNSOPHISTICATED
UNSORROWED
UNSORTED
UNSOUGHT
UNSOUL
UNSOUND
UNSOUNDLY
UNSOUNDNESS
UNSPAR
UNSPARABLE
UNSPARING
UNSPARINGLY
UNSPEAK
UNSPEAKABLE
UNSPEAKABLY
UNSPEAKING
UNSPECIFIED
UNSPED
UNSPEED
UNSPEEDFUL
UNSPELL
UNSPHERE
UNSPHERED
UNSPHERING
UNSPIABLE
UNSPIKE
UNSPILLABLE
UNSPIN
UNSPIRIT
UNSPIRITUAL
UNSPIT
UNSPLEENED
UNSPOIL
UNSPOILED
UNSPOILT
UNSPOKE
UNSPOKEN
UNSPOKENLY
UNSPORTSMANLIKE
UNSPOT
UNSPOTTED
UNSPOTTEDLY
UNSPOTTEN
UNSPREAD
UNSPRIGHTLY
UNSPRING
UNSPRUNG
UNSQUARE
UNSQUARED
UNSQUIRE
UNSTABILITY

UNSTABLE
UNSTABLED
UNSTABLENESS
UNSTABLY
UNSTACK
UNSTACKER
UNSTAID
UNSTAIDLY
UNSTAIDNESS
UNSTAIN
UNSTAINED
UNSTALKED
UNSTAR
UNSTARCH
UNSTATE
UNSTAYED
UNSTEADFAST
UNSTEADIER
UNSTEADIEST
UNSTEADILY
UNSTEADINESS
UNSTEADY
UNSTECK
UNSTEEK
UNSTEEL
UNSTEP
UNSTEPPED
UNSTEPPING
UNSTERILIZED
UNSTICK
UNSTIFFEN
UNSTILL
UNSTILLNESS
UNSTING
UNSTINTED
UNSTITCH
UNSTOCK
UNSTOIC
UNSTOICIZE
UNSTOKEN
UNSTONE
UNSTOP
UNSTOPPED
UNSTOPPER
UNSTOPPING
UNSTOPPLE
UNSTORE
UNSTORED
UNSTORIED
UNSTOW
UNSTOWED
UNSTRAIN
UNSTRAINED
UNSTRAND
UNSTRAP
UNSTRAPPED
UNSTRAPPING
UNSTRATIFIED
UNSTRENG
UNSTRENGTH
UNSTRENGTHEN
UNSTRESS
UNSTRESSED
UNSTRESSEDLY
UNSTRETCH
UNSTRIATED
UNSTRIDE
UNSTRIKE
UNSTRING
UNSTRINGING
UNSTRIP
UNSTRIPED
UNSTRONG
UNSTRUNG
UNSTUDIED
UNSTUFF
UNSTY
UNSTYLISH
UNSTYLISHLY
UNSUBDUED
UNSUBMISSION
UNSUBSTANTIAL
UNSUBTLE
UNSUBTLENESS
UNSUBTLETY
UNSUBTLY
UNSUCCESS
UNSUCCESSFUL
UNSUCCESSIVE
UNSUFFERABLE
UNSUFFERABLY
UNSUFFERED
UNSUFFICIENT
UNSUIT
UNSUITABLE
UNSUITABLENESS
UNSUITABLY
UNSUITED
UNSULLIED
UNSULLIEDLY
UNSUMMED
UNSUMMERED
UNSUNG
UNSUNNED
UNSUPERABLE
UNSUPERVISED
UNSUPPED
UNSUPPLIED
UNSUPPORTED
UNSURE
UNSURETY
UNSURMISED
UNSURPASSED
UNSUSPECT
UNSUSPECTED
UNSUSPECTING
UNSUSPICION
UNSUSPICIOUS
UNSWADDLE
UNSWATHE
UNSWATHED
UNSWATHING
UNSWEAR
UNSWEARING
UNSWEAT
UNSWEET
UNSWEETEN
UNSWEETLY
UNSWEETNESS
UNSWELL
UNSWERVING
UNSWERVINGLY
UNSWORE
UNSWORN
UNSYLLABIC
UNSYMMETRICAL
UNSYMMETRY
UNSYMPATHETIC
UNSYMPATHY
UNSYSTEMATIC
UNT
UNTACK
UNTACKLE
UNTACTFUL
UNTACTFULLY
UNTAINTED
UNTAKEN
UNTALENTED
UNTAMED
UNTAMEDLY
UNTAMEDNESS
UNTANGIBLE
UNTANGIBLY
UNTANGLE
UNTANGLED
UNTANGLING
UNTAP
UNTAPPICE
UNTAR
UNTASTE
UNTAUGHT
UNTAX
UNTEACH
UNTEACHABLE
UNTEACHABLY
UNTEACHING
UNTEAM
UNTECHNICAL
UNTEEM
UNTELL
UNTELLING
UNTEMPER
UNTEMPERANCE
UNTEMPERATE
UNTENABLE
UNTENABLY
UNTENANT
UNTENANTED
UNTENDED
UNTENDER
UNTENDERLY
UNTENIBLE
UNTENIBLY
UNTENT
UNTENTED
UNTENTY
UNTERMED
UNTERMINABLE
UNTERMINABLY
UNTERRED
UNTESTATE
UNTETHER
UNTEWED
UNTHANK
UNTHANKFUL
UNTHANKFULLY
UNTHATCH
UNTHAW
UNTHENDE
UNTHEWED
UNTHINK
UNTHINKABLE
UNTHINKABLY
UNTHINKER
UNTHINKING
UNTHINKINGLY
UNTHOLEABLE
UNTHOLEABLY
UNTHOUGHT
UNTHOUGHTED
UNTHOUGHTFUL
UNTHRALL
UNTHRASHED
UNTHREAD
UNTHRID
UNTHRIDDEN
UNTHRIFT
UNTHRIFTIER
UNTHRIFTIEST
UNTHRIFTILY
UNTHRIFTY
UNTHRIVE
UNTHRIVEN
UNTHRIVING
UNTHRIVINGLY
UNTHRONE
UNTIDIER
UNTIDIEST
UNTIDILY
UNTIDINESS
UNTIDY
UNTIE
UNTIED
UNTIGHT
UNTIGHTEN
UNTIGHTENED
UNTIGHTENING
UNTIGHTNESS
UNTIL
UNTILE
UNTILED
UNTILLED
UNTIME
UNTIMELESS
UNTIMELIER
UNTIMELIEST
UNTIMELINESS
UNTIMELY
UNTIMEOUS
UNTIMEOUSLY
UNTIMOUS
UNTIN
UNTINCT
UNTINE
UNTIRE
UNTIRING
UNTITLED
UNTO
UNTOGGLE
UNTOGGLER
UNTOILED
UNTOLD
UNTOLERABLE
UNTOLERABLY
UNTOLERATED
UNTOLLED
UNTOMB
UNTONALITY
UNTONE
UNTONGUE
UNTOOTH
UNTOP
UNTOPPED
UNTOUCH
UNTOUCHABLE
UNTOUCHABLY
UNTOUCHED
UNTOWARD
UNTOWARDLY
UNTOWARDNESS
UNTOWN
UNTRACE
UNTRACEABLE
UNTRACEABLY
UNTRACTABLE
UNTRACTABLY
UNTRACTED
UNTRADED
UNTRAINED
UNTRAINEDLY
UNTRAMMELED
UNTRAMMELLED
UNTRANCE
UNTRAVELED
UNTRAVELLED
UNTREAD
UNTREADING
UNTREASURE
UNTREATABLE
UNTREATABLY
UNTRENCHED
UNTREND
UNTRESSED
UNTRIED
UNTRIM
UNTRIMMED
UNTRIPE
UNTRIST
UNTRIUMPHED
UNTROD
UNTRODDEN
UNTROTH
UNTROUBLE
UNTROUBLED
UNTROUBLEDLY
UNTROWABLE
UNTROWED
UNTRUCED
UNTRUE
UNTRUENESS
UNTRUISM
UNTRULY
UNTRUNKED
UNTRUSS
UNTRUSSER
UNTRUST
UNTRUSTFUL
UNTRUSTWORTHINESS
UNTRUSTWORTHY
UNTRUSTY
UNTRUTH
UNTRUTHER
UNTRUTHFUL
UNTRUTHFULLY
UNTRUTHS
UNTUCK
UNTUCKERED
UNTUNE
UNTURF
UNTURN
UNTUTORED
UNTUTOREDLY
UNTWILLED
UNTWIND
UNTWINE
UNTWINED
UNTWINING
UNTWIRL
UNTWIST
UNTWISTED
UNTWITTEN
UNTYING
UNTZ
UNUNANIMITY
UNUNANIMOUS
UNUNIFORM
UNUNIFORMITY
UNUNIFORMLY
UNUNITABLE
UNUNITABLY
UNUNITED
UNUNIVERSITY
UNUPRIGHT
UNUPRIGHTLY
UNURED
UNUSABLE
UNUSABLY
UNUSAGE
UNUSE
UNUSED
UNUSEDNESS
UNUSUAL
UNUSUALITY
UNUSUALLY
UNUSUALNESS
UNUTTERABLE
UNUTTERABLY
UNUTTERED
UNVACCINATED
UNVALID
UNVALIDITY
UNVALIDLY
UNVALIDNESS
UNVALUABLE
UNVALUABLY

UNVALUE
UNVALUED
UNVARIABLE
UNVARIABLY
UNVARIED
UNVARIEDLY
UNVARNISHED
UNVARYING
UNVARYINGLY
UNVASSAL
UNVEIL
UNVEILED
UNVEILEDLY
UNVEILEDNESS
UNVEILER
UNVEILMENT
UNVENGED
UNVENOM
UNVENUED
UNVERACITY
UNVERBALIZED
UNVERIFIABLE
UNVERIFIABLY
UNVERIFIED
UNVERITY
UNVERSED
UNVERSEDLY
UNVERSEDNESS
UNVEST
UNVICAR
UNVINCIBLE
UNVINDICTIVE
UNVIOLATE
UNVIRGIN
UNVIRILITY
UNVIRTUE
UNVIRTUOUS
UNVIRTUOUSLY
UNVISIBLE
UNVISIBLY
UNVISOR
UNVITIATED
UNVITIATEDLY
UNVIZARD
UNVOCAL
UNVOICE
UNVOICED
UNVOICING
UNVOLUNTARY
UNVOTE
UNVOUCHED
UNVOUCHEDLY
UNVOWELED
UNVOWELLED
UNVULGARIZE
UNWAGED
UNWALKABLE
UNWALKING
UNWALLET
UNWALLOWED
UNWAN
UNWANDERED
UNWANTED
UNWARDED
UNWARE
UNWARELY
UNWARENESS
UNWARES
UNWARILY
UNWARINESS
UNWARLIKE
UNWARM
UNWARNED
UNWARNEDLY
UNWARNEDNESS
UNWARNING
UNWARNISHED
UNWARP
UNWARRANT
UNWARRANTED
UNWARRAYED
UNWARRED
UNWARREN
UNWARY
UNWASHED
UNWASHEN
UNWASTEFUL
UNWATER
UNWATERED
UNWAVERING
UNWAVERINGLY
UNWAX
UNWAYED
UNWEAKENED
UNWEAL
UNWEANED
UNWEAPON
UNWEARIABLE
UNWEARIABLY
UNWEARIED
UNWEARIEDLY
UNWEARILY
UNWEARINESS
UNWEARY
UNWEARYING
UNWEARYINGLY
UNWEATHERED
UNWEAVE
UNWEB
UNWED
UNWEDDED
UNWEDDEDLY
UNWEDDEDNESS
UNWEDGEABLE
UNWEEL
UNWEELNESS
UNWEETING
UNWEETINGLY
UNWEFT
UNWELCOME
UNWELCOMELY
UNWELDE
UNWELL
UNWELLNESS
UNWELTH
UNWEMMED
UNWEPT
UNWHETTED
UNWHIG
UNWHOLE
UNWHOLESOME
UNWIELD
UNWIELDIER
UNWIELDIEST
UNWIELDILY
UNWIELDINESS
UNWIELDLY
UNWIELDSOME
UNWIELDY
UNWIFED
UNWILD
UNWILIER
UNWILILY
UNWILINESS
UNWILL
UNWILLE
UNWILLED
UNWILLFUL
UNWILLFULLY
UNWILLING
UNWILLINGLY
UNWILLINGNESS
UNWILY
UNWIMPLE
UNWIN
UNWINCING
UNWINCINGLY
UNWIND
UNWINDING
UNWINDINGLY
UNWINK
UNWINKING
UNWINKINGLY
UNWINLY
UNWINTER
UNWIRE
UNWIRED
UNWISDOM
UNWISE
UNWISELY
UNWISENESS
UNWISH
UNWIST
UNWIT
UNWITCH
UNWITHHOLDEN
UNWITNESSED
UNWITTED
UNWITTILY
UNWITTING
UNWITTINGLY
UNWITTY
UNWIVED
UNWOMAN
UNWOMANLY
UNWONDER
UNWONT
UNWONTED
UNWONTEDLY
UNWONTEDNESS
UNWOODED
UNWOOF
UNWORDED
UNWORDY
UNWORK
UNWORKABLE
UNWORKABLY
UNWORKER
UNWORKMANLY
UNWORLD
UNWORLDLY
UNWORMED
UNWORN
UNWORRIED
UNWORRIEDLY
UNWORSHIP
UNWORTH
UNWORTHIER
UNWORTHIEST
UNWORTHILY
UNWORTHINESS
UNWORTHY
UNWOUND
UNWOUNDED
UNWRAP
UNWRAPPED
UNWRAPPER
UNWRAPPERED
UNWRAPPING
UNWREAKED
UNWREAKEN
UNWREATHE
UNWRENCH
UNWREST
UNWRINKLE
UNWRINKLED
UNWRINKLING
UNWRIT
UNWRITE
UNWRITTEN
UNWROKEN
UNWROUGHT
UNWRY
UNY
UNYEANED
UNYIELDING
UNYIELDINGLY
UNYOKE
UNYOKED
UNYOKING
UNYOLDEN
UNZE
UNZEN
UNZONED
UP
UPAITHRIC
UPALONG
UPANAYA
UPANAYANA
UPANISHADIC
UPAPURANA
UPARCHING
UPARNA
UPAS
UPBAND
UPBANK
UPBAR
UPBEAT
UPBRAID
UPBRAIDED
UPBRAIDER
UPBRAIDING
UPBRAIDINGLY
UPBRAST
UPBRAY
UPBREAK
UPBREATHE
UPBRING
UPBRINGING
UPBROUGHT
UPBROW
UPBUILD
UPBUILDER
UPBY
UPBYE
UPCARD
UPCAST
UPCHAMBER
UPCHAUNCE
UPCHEER
UPCHUCK
UPCLIMB
UPCLOSE
UPCLOSER
UPCOAST
UPCOME
UPCOMING
UPCOUNTRY
UPCUT
UPDATE
UPDATED
UPDATING
UPDIVE
UPDRAFT
UPDRAUGHT
UPDRESS
UPEND
UPERIZE
UPEYGAN
UPFEED
UPFINGERED
UPFOLD
UPGANG
UPGIVE
UPGO
UPGRADE
UPGRADED
UPGRADING
UPGRAVE
UPGROWTH
UPHALE
UPHAND
UPHEARTED
UPHEAVAL
UPHEAVALIST
UPHEAVE
UPHEAVED
UPHEAVING
UPHELD
UPHELYA
UPHER
UPHILL
UPHOLD
UPHOLDEN
UPHOLDER
UPHOLDING
UPHOLSTER
UPHOLSTERED
UPHOLSTERER
UPHOLSTERIES
UPHOLSTEROUS
UPHOLSTERY
UPHOVE
UPHROE
UPKEEP
UPLA
UPLAND
UPLANDER
UPLANDISH
UPLAY
UPLEAN
UPLEAP
UPLIFT
UPLIFTED
UPLIFTEDLY
UPLIFTEDNESS
UPLIFTER
UPLIFTING
UPLIFTINGLY
UPLIMBER
UPLONG
UPLOOK
UPLOOKER
UPLYING
UPMAKING
UPMOST
UPON
UPPBAD
UPPER
UPPERCLASSMAN
UPPERCLASSMEN
UPPERCUT
UPPERCUTTING
UPPERER
UPPERMORE
UPPERMOST
UPPERS
UPPERSTOCKS
UPPING
UPPISH
UPPISHLY
UPPISHNESS
UPPITY
UPPOWOC
UPRAISAL
UPRAISE
UPRAISED
UPRAISER
UPRAISING
UPRAUGHT
UPREAR
UPREARED
UPREARING
UPREST
UPRIGHT

UPRIGHTEOUS
UPRIGHTING
UPRIGHTLY
UPRIGHTMAN
UPRIGHTNESS
UPRISAL
UPRISE
UPRISEN
UPRISER
UPRISING
UPRIST
UPRIVER
UPROAR
UPROARER
UPROARIOUS
UPROARIOUSLY
UPROOT
UPROOTAL
UPROOTED
UPROOTER
UPROOTING
UPROSE
UPROUSE
UPROUSED
UPROUSING
UPSADDLE
UPSCUDDLE
UPSEDOUN
UPSEE
UPSEEK
UPSET
UPSETTAL
UPSETTED
UPSETTER
UPSETTING
UPSETTINGLY
UPSHOOT
UPSHOT
UPSIDE
UPSIDES
UPSIGHTED
UPSILON
UPSILONISM
UPSITTEN
UPSITTING
UPSKIP
UPSLIP
UPSPEAR
UPSPIN
UPSPRANG
UPSPRING
UPSPRINGING
UPSPRUNG
UPSTAGE
UPSTAGED
UPSTAGING
UPSTAIRS
UPSTAND
UPSTANDER
UPSTANDING
UPSTARE
UPSTART
UPSTATE
UPSTATER
UPSTAY
UPSTIR
UPSTRAIGHT
UPSTREAM
UPSTREET
UPSTRETCHED
UPSTROKE
UPSUN
UPSURGE
UPSURGED
UPSURGENCE
UPSURGING
UPSWARM
UPSWEEP
UPSWEEPING
UPSWELL
UPSWELLED
UPSWELLING
UPSWEPT
UPSWING
UPSWINGING
UPSWOLLEN
UPSWUNG
UPSY
UPTAKE
UPTAKER
UPTEAR
UPTHROW
UPTHRUST
UPTIGHT
UPTILL
UPTOWN
UPTOWNER
UPTRAIN
UPTREND
UPTRILL
UPTURN
UPTURNED
UPTURNING
UPUPOID
UPWARD
UPWARDLY
UPWARDS
UPWAY
UPWAYS
UPWIND
UPWITH
UR
URACHAL
URACHUS
URACIL
URAEMIA
URAEMIC
URAEUS
URAL
URALI
URALITE
URALITIC
URALITIZE
URALITIZED
URALITIZING
URAMIDO
URAMIL
URAMINO
URAN
URANALYSIS
URANATE
URANIC
URANIDIN
URANIDINE
URANIFEROUS
URANIN
URANINITE
URANION
URANISCUS
URANISM
URANIST
URANITE
URANITIC
URANIUM
URANOCIRCITE
URANOGRAPHER
URANOGRAPHIC
URANOGRAPHY
URANOLATRY
URANOLITE
URANOLOGICAL
URANOLOGY
URANOMETRIA
URANOMETRY
URANOPHANE
URANOPLASTIC
URANOPLASTY
URANOPLEGIA
URANORRHAPHY
URANOSCHISIS
URANOSCHISM
URANOSCOPE
URANOSCOPIA
URANOSCOPIC
URANOSCOPY
URANOSPINITE
URANOTHORITE
URANOTIL
URANOUS
URANYL
URANYLIC
URAO
URARE
URARI
URASE
URATAEMIA
URATE
URATEMIA
URATIC
URATOMA
URATOSIS
URATURIA
URAZIN
URAZINE
URAZOLE
URBACITY
URBAINITE
URBAN
URBANE
URBANELY
URBANENESS
URBANISM
URBANIST
URBANITE
URBANITIES
URBANITY
URBANIZATION
URBANIZE
URBANIZED
URBANIZING
URBARIAL
URBIC
URBICOLOUS
URBINATE
URBS
URCEI
URCEIFORM
URCEOLAR
URCEOLATE
URCEOLE
URCEOLI
URCEOLUS
URCEUS
URCHIN
URCHINESS
URCHINLY
URD
URDE
URDEE
URDY
URE
UREA
UREAL
UREAMETER
UREAMETRY
UREASE
URECHITIN
URECHITOXIN
UREDEMA
UREDINEAL
UREDINEOUS
UREDINIA
UREDINIAL
UREDINIUM
UREDINOID
UREDINOLOGY
UREDINOUS
UREDIUM
UREDO
UREDOSORUS
UREDOSPORE
UREDOSPORIC
UREDOSTAGE
UREIC
UREIDE
UREIDO
UREMIA
UREMIC
URENT
UREOMETER
UREOMETRY
URESIS
URETAL
URETER
URETERAL
URETERECTOMIES
URETERECTOMY
URETERIC
URETEROCELE
URETEROGRAM
URETEROGRAPH
URETEROLITH
URETEROLYSIS
URETEROSTOMA
URETEROSTOMY
URETEROTOMY
URETHAN
URETHANE
URETHRA
URETHRAE
URETHRAL
URETHRALGIA
URETHRAS
URETHRISM
URETHRITIC
URETHRITIS
URETHROCELE
URETHROGRAM
URETHROGRAPH
URETHROMETER
URETHROPHYMA
URETHROPLASTY
URETHRORRHEA
URETHROSCOPE
URETHROSCOPY
URETHROSPASM
URETHROSTOMY
URETHROTOME
URETHROTOMIC
URETHROTOMY
URETHYLAN
URETHYLANE
URETIC
UREYLENE
URF
URFIRNIS
URGE
URGED
URGEFUL
URGENCE
URGENCIES
URGENCY
URGENT
URGENTLY
URGER
URGING
URGINGLY
URHEEN
URIAL
URIC
URICOLYSIS
URICOLYTIC
URIDROSIS
URIN
URINAEMIA
URINAEMIC
URINAL
URINALIST
URINALYSIS
URINANT
URINARIES
URINARIUM
URINARY
URINATE
URINATED
URINATING
URINATION
URINATIVE
URINATOR
URINE
URINEMIA
URINEMIC
URINIFEROUS
URINIPAROUS
URINOGENITAL
URINOGENOUS
URINOLOGIST
URINOLOGY
URINOMANCY
URINOMETER
URINOMETRIC
URINOMETRY
URINOSCOPIC
URINOSCOPIES
URINOSCOPIST
URINOSCOPY
URINOSE
URINOUS
URINOUSNESS
URITE
URLAR
URLED
URLING
URLUCH
URMAN
URN
URNA
URNAL
URNFIELD
URNFLOWER
URNFUL
URNFULS
URNING
URNINGISM
UROBILIN
UROBILINEMIA
UROBILINOGEN
UROBILINURIA
UROCELE
UROCHLORALIC
UROCHORD
UROCHORDAL
UROCHORDATE
UROCHROME
UROCHROMOGEN
UROCHS
UROCYANOGEN
UROCYST
UROCYSTIC
UROCYSTITIS
URODAEUM
URODELAN
URODELE
URODELOUS
URODIALYSIS

URODYNIA
UROEDEMA
UROERYTHRIN
UROGASTER
UROGASTRIC
UROGENIC
UROGENITAL
UROGENOUS
UROGLAUCIN
UROGRAM
UROGRAPHY
UROHAEMATIN
UROHEMATIN
UROHYAL
UROLAGNIA
UROLITH
UROLITHIASIS
UROLITHIC
UROLITHOLOGY
UROLOGIC
UROLOGICAL
UROLOGIST
UROLOGY
UROLUTEIN
UROMANCY
UROMANTIA
UROMANTIST
UROMELANIN
UROMELUS
UROMERE
URONEPHROSIS
URONIC
UROPATAGIUM
UROPHAEIN
UROPHANIC
UROPHANOUS
UROPHEIN
UROPHTHISIS
UROPLANIA
UROPOD
UROPODAL
UROPODOUS
UROPOETIC
UROPOIESIS
UROPOIETIC
UROPORPHYRIN
UROPSILE
UROPTYSIS
UROPYGIAL
UROPYGIUM
UROPYLORIC
UROROSEIN
URORRHAGIA
URORRHEA
URORUBIN
UROSACRAL
UROSCHESIS
UROSCOPIC
UROSCOPIES
UROSCOPIST
UROSCOPY
UROSEPSIS
UROSIS
UROSOMATIC
UROSOME
UROSOMITE
UROSOMITIC
UROSTEALITH
UROSTEGAL
UROSTEGE
UROSTEGITE
UROSTEON
UROSTERNITE
UROSTHENE
UROSTHENIC
UROSTYLAR
UROSTYLE
UROTOXIC
UROTOXICITY
UROTOXIES
UROTOXIN
UROTOXY
UROX
UROXANATE
UROXANTHIN
UROXIN
URRHODIN
URRHODINIC
URSICIDAL
URSICIDE
URSIFORM
URSIGRAM
URSINE
URSOID
URSON
URSONE
URSUK
URTICACEOUS
URTICAL
URTICANT
URTICARIA
URTICARIAL
URTICARIOUS
URTICATE
URTICATED
URTICATING
URTICATION
URTICOSE
URTITE
URUBU
URUCA
URUCU
URUCUM
URUCURI
URUCURY
URUISG
URUNDAY
URUS
URUSHI
URUSHIOL
URUSHIYE
URVA
URVED
US
USABILITY
USABLE
USABLENESS
USABLY
USAGE
USAGER
USANCE
USANT
USAR
USARON
USATION
USAUNCE
USE
USEABLE
USED
USEDLY
USEDNESS
USEE
USEFUL
USEFULLISH
USEFULLY
USEFULNESS
USEHOLD
USELESS
USELESSLY
USELESSNESS
USER
USES
USHABTI
USHABTIU
USHER
USHERANCE
USHERED
USHERER
USHERETTE
USHERIAN
USHERING
USING
USINGS
USITATE
USITATIVE
USNEACEOUS
USNEOID
USQUABAE
USQUE
USQUEBAE
USQUEBAUGH
USSELF
USSELS
USSELVEN
USSINGITE
USTION
USTORIOUS
USTULATE
USTULATION
USUAL
USUALISM
USUALLY
USUALNESS
USUARY
USUCAPIENT
USUCAPION
USUCAPIONARY
USUCAPT
USUCAPTABLE
USUCAPTIBLE
USUFRUCT
USUFRUCTUARIES
USUFRUCTUARY
USURA
USURE
USURER
USURIES
USURIOUS
USURIOUSLY
USURIOUSNESS
USURP
USURPATION
USURPATIVE
USURPATIVELY
USURPATORY
USURPATURE
USURPED
USURPER
USURPING
USURPINGLY
USURY
USUS
UT
UTAC
UTAHITE
UTAI
UTAS
UTCH
UTCHY
UTENSIL
UTENSILE
UTENSILS
UTERALGIA
UTERECTOMY
UTERI
UTERINE
UTEROCELE
UTEROGRAM
UTEROGRAPHY
UTEROLITH
UTEROLOGY
UTEROMETER
UTEROPELVIC
UTEROPLASTY
UTEROSACRAL
UTEROSCOPE
UTEROTOMY
UTEROTONIC
UTEROTUBAL
UTEROVAGINAL
UTEROVENTRAL
UTEROVESICAL
UTERUS
UTIA
UTIBLE
UTICK
UTILE
UTILIDOR
UTILITARIAN
UTILITIES
UTILITY
UTILIZABLE
UTILIZATION
UTILIZE
UTILIZED
UTILIZER
UTILIZING
UTINAM
UTIS
UTLAGARY
UTMOST
UTOPIA
UTOPIAN
UTOPIANISM
UTOPIANIST
UTOPIAST
UTOPISM
UTOPIST
UTOPISTIC
UTOPOGRAPHER
UTRAQUIST
UTRAQUISTIC
UTRECHT
UTRICLE
UTRICULAR
UTRICULATE
UTRICULIFORM
UTRICULITIS
UTRICULOID
UTRICULOSE
UTRICULUS
UTRIFORM
UTRUBI
UTRUM
UTTER
UTTERABILITY
UTTERABLE
UTTERANCE
UTTERED
UTTERER
UTTEREST
UTTERING
UTTERLESS
UTTERLY
UTTERMOST
UTTERNESS
UTU
UTUM
UTURUNCU
UVA
UVAL
UVALA
UVALHA
UVANITE
UVAROVITE
UVATE
UVEA
UVEAL
UVEITIC
UVEITIS
UVEOUS
UVID
UVITIC
UVITO
UVULA
UVULAE
UVULAR
UVULARLY
UVULAS
UVULE
UVULITIS
UVULOPTOSIS
UVULOTOME
UVULOTOMIES
UVULOTOMY
UXORIAL
UXORIALITY
UXORIALLY
UXORICIDAL
UXORICIDE
UXORIOUS
UXORIOUSLY
UYEZD
UZAN
UZARIN
UZARON

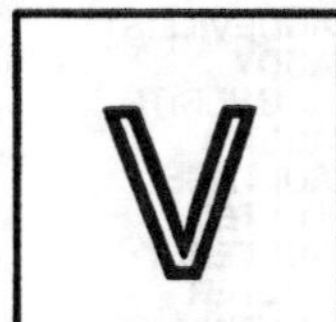

VA
VAAD
VAAGMAER
VAAGMAR
VAALITE
VACANCE
VACANCIES
VACANCY
VACANT
VACANTIA
VACANTLY
VACATE
VACATED
VACATING
VACATION
VACATIONAL
VACATIONER
VACATIONIST
VACATUR
VACCARY
VACCICIDE
VACCIGENOUS
VACCINA
VACCINABLE
VACCINAL
VACCINATE
VACCINATED
VACCINATING
VACCINATION
VACCINATOR
VACCINATORY
VACCINE
VACCINEE
VACCINELLA
VACCINIA
VACCINIAL
VACCINIFER
VACCINIFORM
VACCINIOLA
VACCINIST
VACCINIZATION
VACHE
VACILLANCY
VACILLANT
VACILLATE
VACILLATED
VACILLATING
VACILLATION
VACILLATOR
VACILLATORY
VACOA
VACONA
VACOUA
VACOUF
VACUA
VACUAL
VACUATE
VACUATION
VACUEFY
VACUIST
VACUIT
VACUITIES
VACUITY
VACUO
VACUOLAR
VACUOLATED
VACUOLATION
VACUOLE
VACUOME
VACUOMETER
VACUOUS
VACUOUSLY
VACUUM
VACUUMIZE
VACUUMS
VADE
VADELECT
VADER
VADIMONIUM
VADIMONY
VADIUM
VADOSE
VADY
VAE
VAFROUS
VAG
VAGABOND
VAGABONDAGE
VAGABONDIA
VAGABONDISM
VAGABONDIZE
VAGABONDIZED
VAGABONDIZER
VAGABONDIZING
VAGABONDRY
VAGAL
VAGANCY
VAGANT
VAGARIAN
VAGARIES
VAGARIOUS
VAGARISH
VAGARISOME
VAGARIST
VAGARITY
VAGARY
VAGAS
VAGATION
VAGI
VAGIENT
VAGIFORM
VAGILE
VAGINA
VAGINAL
VAGINALITIS
VAGINANT
VAGINATE
VAGINECTOMY
VAGINERVOSE
VAGINICOLOUS
VAGINIFEROUS
VAGINISMUS
VAGINITIS
VAGINULA
VAGINULATE
VAGINULE
VAGITUS
VAGOGRAM
VAGOLYSIS
VAGOTOMIZE
VAGOTOMY
VAGOTONIA
VAGOTONIC
VAGOTONY
VAGOTROPIC
VAGOTROPISM
VAGOUS
VAGRANCE
VAGRANCY
VAGRANT
VAGRANTISM
VAGRANTIZE
VAGRANTLY
VAGRANTNESS
VAGRATE
VAGROM
VAGUE
VAGUELY
VAGUENESS
VAGUER
VAGUEST
VAGUITY
VAGULOUS
VAGUS
VAH
VAHINE
VAIL
VAILABLE
VAILE
VAIN
VAINER
VAINEST
VAINFUL
VAINGLORIOUS
VAINGLORY
VAINLY
VAIR
VAIRAGI
VAIRE
VAIREE
VAIVODE
VAJRA
VAJRASANA
VAKASS
VAKEEL
VAKIA
VAKIL
VAKKALIGA
VAKUF
VALANCE
VALANCED
VALANCHE
VALBELLITE
VALE
VALEDICTION
VALEDICTORIES
VALEDICTORY
VALENCE
VALENCIA
VALENCIANITE
VALENCIES
VALENCY
VALENT
VALENTINE
VALERAMID
VALERAMIDE
VALERATE
VALERIAN
VALERIANATE
VALERIANIC
VALERIC
VALERIN
VALERONE
VALERYL
VALERYLENE
VALET
VALETA
VALETED
VALETING
VALETRY
VALETUDE
VALETUDINARY
VALEUR
VALEW
VALEWE
VALGOID
VALGUS
VALI
VALIANCE
VALIANCY
VALIANT
VALIANTLY
VALIANTNESS
VALID
VALIDATE
VALIDATED
VALIDATING
VALIDATION
VALIDATORY
VALIDITY
VALIDOUS
VALINCH
VALINE
VALISE
VALISES
VALLA
VALLANCY
VALLAR
VALLARY
VALLATE
VALLATED
VALLATION
VALLECULA
VALLECULAR
VALLECULATE
VALLEVARITE
VALLEY
VALLEYS
VALLICULA
VALLICULAE
VALLICULAR
VALLIDOM
VALLIES
VALLIS
VALLUM
VALLUMS
VALONIA
VALONIACEOUS
VALOP
VALOR
VALORIZATION
VALORIZE
VALOROUS
VALOROUSLY
VALOROUSNESS
VALOUR
VALOUWE
VALSE
VALSOID
VALUABLE
VALUABLY
VALUATE
VALUATION
VALUATIONAL
VALUATOR
VALUE
VALUED
VALUELESS
VALUER
VALUES
VALUING
VALURE
VALUTA
VALVA
VALVAE
VALVAL
VALVAR
VALVATE
VALVE
VALVELESS
VALVELET
VALVEMAN
VALVEMEN
VALVIFEROUS
VALVIFORM
VALVOTOMY
VALVULA
VALVULAE
VALVULAR
VALVULATE
VALVULE
VALVULITIS
VALVULOTOME
VALVULOTOMY
VALYL
VALYLENE
VAMBRACE
VAMBRACED
VAMBRASH
VAMFONT
VAMMAZSA
VAMOOSE
VAMOS
VAMOSE
VAMP
VAMPED
VAMPER
VAMPEY
VAMPHORN
VAMPING
VAMPIRE
VAMPIRIC
VAMPIRISH
VAMPIRISM
VAMPIRIZE
VAMPLATE
VAMPYRE
VAMURE
VAN
VANADATE
VANADIATE
VANADIC
VANADINITE
VANADIOUS
VANADIUM
VANADOUS
VANADYL
VANCOURIER
VANDAL
VANDALISH
VANDALISM
VANDALISTIC
VANDALIZE
VANDELAS
VANE
VANED
VANESSIAN
VANFOSS
VANG
VANGEE
VANGELI
VANGLO
VANGLOE
VANGUARD
VANILLA
VANILLAL
VANILLAS
VANILLATE
VANILLE
VANILLERY
VANILLIC
VANILLIN
VANILLINE
VANILLISM
VANILLON
VANILLOYL
VANILLYL
VANISH
VANISHED
VANISHER
VANISHING
VANISHINGLY
VANISHMENT
VANITARIANISM
VANITIED

VANITIES
VANITORY
VANITOUS
VANITY
VANLAY
VANMAN
VANMEN
VANMOST
VANNED
VANNER
VANNERMAN
VANNERMEN
VANNET
VANNING
VANNUS
VANQUISH
VANQUISHED
VANQUISHER
VANQUISHING
VANS
VANSIRE
VANT
VANTAGE
VANTERIE
VANWARD
VAPID
VAPIDISM
VAPIDITY
VAPIDLY
VAPIDNESS
VAPOGRAPHY
VAPOR
VAPORABILITY
VAPORABLE
VAPORARIUM
VAPORATE
VAPORED
VAPORER
VAPORETTI
VAPORETTO
VAPORIFORM
VAPORIMETER
VAPORING
VAPORINGLY
VAPORISH
VAPORIZATION
VAPORIZE
VAPORIZER
VAPOROGRAPH
VAPOROSE
VAPOROSITY
VAPOROUS
VAPOROUSLY
VAPORS
VAPORY
VAPOUR
VAPOURABILITY
VAPOURABLE
VAPOURED
VAPOURER
VAPOURING
VAPOURINGLY
VAPOURISH
VAPOURIZE
VAPOURIZED
VAPOURIZER
VAPOURIZING
VAPOUROSE
VAPOUROUS
VAPOUROUSLY
VAPOURS
VAPOURY
VAPULATE
VAPULATION
VAPULATORY
VAQUERO
VAQUEROS
VAR
VARA
VARAN
VARAS
VARDAPET
VARDI
VARDY
VARE
VAREC
VARECH
VAREHEADED
VARELLA
VAREUSE
VARGE
VARGUENO
VARI
VARIA
VARIABILITY
VARIABLE
VARIABLENESS
VARIANCE
VARIANCY
VARIANT
VARIATE
VARIATED
VARIATING
VARIATION
VARIATIONAL
VARIATIONIST
VARIATIONS
VARIATIVE
VARIATIVELY
VARIATOR
VARICATED
VARICATION
VARICELLA
VARICELLAR
VARICELLATE
VARICELLATION
VARICELLOID
VARICELLOUS
VARICES
VARICIFORM
VARICOCELE
VARICOID
VARICOLORED
VARICOLOROUS
VARICOLOURED
VARICOSE
VARICOSED
VARICOSIS
VARICOSITIES
VARICOSITY
VARICOTOMY
VARICULA
VARIED
VARIEGATE
VARIEGATED
VARIEGATING
VARIEGATION
VARIEGATOR
VARIER
VARIETAL
VARIETAS
VARIETIES
VARIETIST
VARIETY
VARIFORM
VARIFORMED
VARIFORMITY
VARIFORMLY
VARIFY
VARIGRADATION
VARIOCOUPLER
VARIOLA
VARIOLAR
VARIOLATE
VARIOLATE
VARIOLATED
VARIOLATING
VARIOLATION
VARIOLE
VARIOLIC
VARIOLIFORM
VARIOLITE
VARIOLITIC
VARIOLOID
VARIOLOUS
VARIOMETER
VARIORUM
VARIOTINTED
VARIOUS
VARIOUSLY
VARIOUSNESS
VARISCITE
VARISSE
VARITYPE
VARITYPED
VARITYPING
VARITYPIST
VARIX
VARKAS
VARLET
VARLETAILLE
VARLETESS
VARLETRY
VARLETTO
VARMENT
VARMINT
VARNA
VARNASHRAMA
VARNISH
VARNISHED
VARNISHER
VARNISHING
VARNISHMENT
VARNISHY
VARNPLIKTIGE
VARNSINGITE
VARSHA
VARSITY
VARSOVIANA
VARSOVIENNE
VARTABED
VARUS
VARVE
VARVED
VARY
VARYING
VAS
VASA
VASAL
VASALLED
VASCON
VASCULA
VASCULAR
VASCULARITIES
VASCULARITY
VASCULARIZE
VASCULARIZED
VASCULARIZING
VASCULARLY
VASCULATED
VASCULATURE
VASCULIFEROUS
VASCULIFORM
VASCULITIS
VASCULOMOTOR
VASCULOSE
VASCULUM
VASE
VASECTOMIES
VASECTOMIZE
VASECTOMY
VASEFUL
VASHEGYITE
VASICENTRIC
VASICINE
VASIFEROUS
VASIFORM
VASO
VASOCORONA
VASODENTINE
VASODILATIN
VASODILATING
VASODILATION
VASODILATOR
VASOFACTIVE
VASOGANGLION
VASOLIGATION
VASOMOTION
VASOMOTOR
VASOPARESIS
VASOREFLEX
VASOSPASM
VASOTONIC
VASOTROPHIC
VASQUINE
VASSAL
VASSALAGE
VASSALED
VASSALESS
VASSALIC
VASSALING
VASSALISM
VASSALITY
VASSALIZE
VASSALIZED
VASSALIZING
VASSALLING
VASSALRY
VASSALS
VAST
VASTATE
VASTATION
VASTIDITY
VASTITIES
VASTITUDE
VASTITY
VASTLY
VASTNESS
VASTY
VASU
VAT
VATES
VATFUL
VATFULS
VATIC
VATICAL
VATICANAL
VATICANIC
VATICANICAL
VATICIDE
VATICINAL
VATICINANT
VATICINATE
VATICINATED
VATICINATING
VATICINATION
VATICINATOR
VATICINE
VATMAKER
VATMAKING
VATMAN
VATS
VATTED
VATTER
VATTING
VAU
VAUDEVILLE
VAUDEVILLIAN
VAUDEVILLIST
VAUDY
VAUGNERITE
VAULT
VAULTAGE
VAULTED
VAULTEDLY
VAULTER
VAULTING
VAULTY
VAUMURE
VAUNCE
VAUNT
VAUNTAGE
VAUNTED
VAUNTER
VAUNTERY
VAUNTFUL
VAUNTIE
VAUNTINESS
VAUNTING
VAUNTINGLY
VAUNTLAY
VAUNTMURE
VAUNTY
VAURIEN
VAUXITE
VAVASOR
VAVASORY
VAVASOUR
VAWARD
VAY
VAZA
VEADORE
VEAL
VEALER
VEALINESS
VEALSKIN
VEALY
VEAU
VECKE
VECTIGAL
VECTION
VECTIS
VECTOR
VECTORIAL
VECTORIALLY
VECTURE
VEDANA
VEDET
VEDETTE
VEDIKA
VEDRO
VEE
VEEN
VEER
VEERABLE
VEERIES
VEERING
VEERY
VEGA
VEGASITE
VEGECULTURE
VEGETABILITY
VEGETABLE
VEGETABLES
VEGETABLIZE
VEGETABLY
VEGETAL
VEGETALCULE
VEGETALITY
VEGETANT
VEGETARIAN
VEGETATE
VEGETATED
VEGETATING
VEGETATION

VEGETATIVE
VEGETE
VEGETENESS
VEGETISM
VEGETIVE
VEGETOUS
VEHEMENCE
VEHEMENCY
VEHEMENT
VEHEMENTLY
VEHICLE
VEHICLES
VEHICULAR
VEHICULARY
VEHICULATE
VEHICULATION
VEI
VEIGLE
VEIL
VEILED
VEILEDLY
VEILEDNESS
VEILER
VEILING
VEILLESS
VEILLEUSE
VEILY
VEIN
VEINAGE
VEINAL
VEINED
VEINER
VEINERY
VEINING
VEINLET
VEINOUS
VEINS
VEINSTONE
VEINULE
VEINULET
VEINY
VELA
VELAMEN
VELAMENTOUS
VELAMENTUM
VELAMINA
VELAR
VELARIC
VELARIUM
VELARIZE
VELARY
VELATE
VELATED
VELATION
VELATURA
VELD
VELDE
VELDMAN
VELDSCHOEN
VELDSCHOENEN
VELDSCHOENS
VELDT
VELDTSCHOEN
VELDTSMAN
VELIC
VELIFEROUS
VELIFORM
VELIGER
VELITATION
VELITES
VELL
VELLALA
VELLEITIES
VELLEITY
VELLICATE
VELLICATED
VELLICATING
VELLICATION
VELLICATIVE
VELLINCH
VELLINCHER
VELLON
VELLOSIN
VELLOSINE
VELLUM
VELLUMY
VELLUTE
VELO
VELOCE
VELOCIMAN
VELOCIMETER
VELOCIOUS
VELOCIOUSLY
VELOCIPEDAL
VELOCIPEDE
VELOCIPEDED
VELOCIPEDIC
VELOCIPEDING
VELOCITIES
VELOCITOUS
VELOCITY
VELODROME
VELOMETER
VELOUR
VELOURS
VELOUTE
VELOUTINE
VELT
VELTE
VELTFARE
VELUM
VELUMEN
VELUMINA
VELUNGE
VELURE
VELURED
VELURING
VELUTINOUS
VELVERET
VELVET
VELVETBREAST
VELVETED
VELVETEEN
VELVETEENED
VELVETINESS
VELVETING
VELVETLEAF
VELVETMAKER
VELVETMAKING
VELVETRY
VELVETSEED
VELVETWEED
VELVETWORK
VELVETY
VELYARDE
VENA
VENADA
VENAE
VENAL
VENALITIES
VENALITY
VENALIZATION
VENALIZE
VENANZITE
VENATIC
VENATICAL
VENATICALLY
VENATION
VENATIONAL
VENATOR
VENATORIAL
VENATORIOUS
VENATORY
VENCOLA
VEND
VENDACE
VENDAGE
VENDAVAL
VENDED
VENDEE
VENDER
VENDETTA
VENDETTAS
VENDETTIST
VENDEUSE
VENDIBILITIES
VENDIBILITY
VENDIBLE
VENDIBLENESS
VENDIBLY
VENDICATE
VENDING
VENDIS
VENDITATE
VENDITION
VENDITOR
VENDOR
VENDUE
VENE
VENEER
VENEERED
VENEERER
VENEERING
VENEERS
VENEFIC
VENEFICAL
VENEFICIOUS
VENENATE
VENENATION
VENENE
VENENIFEROUS
VENENIFIC
VENENOSE
VENENOSITY
VENENOUS
VENEPUNCTURE
VENERABILITY
VENERABLE
VENERABLY
VENERAL
VENERANCE
VENERANT
VENERATE
VENERATED
VENERATING
VENERATION
VENERATIVE
VENERATIVELY
VENERATOR
VENERE
VENEREAL
VENEREAN
VENERER
VENERIAL
VENERIAN
VENERIFORM
VENERO
VENEROS
VENERY
VENESECT
VENESECTION
VENESECTOR
VENESIA
VENEUR
VENEZOLANO
VENGEABLE
VENGEANCE
VENGEANCELY
VENGEANT
VENGEFUL
VENGEFULLY
VENGEOUSLY
VENGER
VENIABLE
VENIAL
VENIALITIES
VENIALITY
VENIALLY
VENIALNESS
VENIE
VENIN
VENIPLEX
VENIPUNCTURE
VENIRE
VENIREMAN
VENIREMEN
VENISE
VENISON
VENKISEN
VENLIN
VENNEL
VENNER
VENOM
VENOMED
VENOMER
VENOMIZE
VENOMOUS
VENOMOUSLY
VENOMSOME
VENOMY
VENOSAL
VENOSE
VENOSITY
VENOSTASIS
VENOUS
VENOUSLY
VENOUSNESS
VENT
VENTA
VENTAGE
VENTAIL
VENTANA
VENTED
VENTER
VENTHOLE
VENTIDUCT
VENTIFACT
VENTIL
VENTILABLE
VENTILAGIN
VENTILATE
VENTILATED
VENTILATING
VENTILATION
VENTILATIVE
VENTILATOR
VENTILATORY
VENTIN
VENTING
VENTOMETER
VENTOSE
VENTOSENESS
VENTOSITY
VENTOY
VENTPIECE
VENTRAD
VENTRAL
VENTRALLY
VENTRIC
VENTRICLE
VENTRICOSE
VENTRICOSITY
VENTRICULAR
VENTRICULI
VENTRICULUS
VENTRIDUCT
VENTRILOQUAL
VENTRILOQUE
VENTRILOQUIST
VENTRILOQUY
VENTRIMESAL
VENTRIMESON
VENTRINE
VENTRIPOTENT
VENTROMYEL
VENTROSITY
VENTS
VENTURE
VENTURED
VENTURER
VENTURESOME
VENTURESOMELY
VENTURI
VENTURINE
VENTURING
VENTUROUS
VENTUROUSLY
VENUE
VENULA
VENULAE
VENULAR
VENULE
VENULOSE
VENULOUS
VENUST
VENUSTY
VENVILLE
VENY
VER
VERA
VERACIOUS
VERACIOUSLY
VERACITIES
VERACITY
VERAMENT
VERANDA
VERANDAED
VERANDAH
VERANDAHED
VERASCOPE
VERATRAL
VERATRALBIN
VERATRALBINE
VERATRATE
VERATRIA
VERATRIC
VERATRIDIN
VERATRIDINE
VERATRIN
VERATRINA
VERATRINE
VERATRINIZE
VERATRINIZED
VERATRINIZING
VERATRIZED
VERATRIZING
VERATROL
VERATROLE
VERATROYL
VERATRYL
VERAY
VERB
VERBAL
VERBALISM
VERBALIST
VERBALITY
VERBALIZE
VERBALIZED
VERBALIZER
VERBALIZING
VERBARIAN
VERBARIUM
VERBASCO
VERBASCOSE
VERBATE

VERBATIM
VERBENA
VERBENACEOUS
VERBENALIKE
VERBENALIN
VERBENATE
VERBENATED
VERBENATING
VERBENE
VERBENONE
VERBERATE
VERBERATION
VERBERATIVE
VERBIAGE
VERBICIDE
VERBICULTURE
VERBID
VERBIFIED
VERBIFYING
VERBIGERATE
VERBIGERATED
VERBIGERATING
VERBILE
VERBOMANIAC
VERBOMOTOR
VERBOSE
VERBOSELY
VERBOSENESS
VERBOSITIES
VERBOSITY
VERBOTEN
VERBY
VERCHOC
VERD
VERDANCIES
VERDANCY
VERDANT
VERDEA
VERDELHO
VERDERER
VERDEROR
VERDET
VERDETTO
VERDICT
VERDIGRIS
VERDIGRISY
VERDIN
VERDITER
VERDOY
VERDUGO
VERDUN
VERDURE
VERDURED
VERDURER
VERDUROUS
VERECUND
VERECUNDITY
VERECUNDNESS
VEREDICT
VEREK
VERENDA
VERGE
VERGED
VERGENCE
VERGENCY
VERGENT
VERGENTNESS
VERGER
VERGERISM
VERGERY
VERGI
VERGIFORM
VERGING
VERGLAS
VERGOBRET
VERGOYNE
VERGUNNING
VERI
VERIDIC
VERIDICAL
VERIDICALITIES
VERIDICALITY
VERIDICALLY
VERIDICOUS
VERIDITY
VERIER
VERIEST
VERIFIABLE
VERIFIABLY
VERIFICATE
VERIFICATION
VERIFICATIVE
VERIFIED
VERIFIER
VERIFY
VERIFYING
VERILY
VERIMENT
VERIN
VERINE
VERISCOPE
VERISIMILAR
VERISIMILITY
VERISM
VERISMO
VERIST
VERISTIC
VERITABLE
VERITABLY
VERITAS
VERITE
VERITIES
VERITISM
VERITIST
VERITISTIC
VERITY
VERJUICE
VERMEIL
VERMENGING
VERMEOLOGIST
VERMEOLOGY
VERMETID
VERMIAN
VERMICELLI
VERMICEOUS
VERMICIDAL
VERMICIDE
VERMICIOUS
VERMICLE
VERMICULAR
VERMICULARLY
VERMICULATE
VERMICULATED
VERMICULATING
VERMICULATION
VERMICULE
VERMICULITE
VERMICULOSE
VERMICULOUS
VERMIFORM
VERMIFORMITY
VERMIFUGAL
VERMIFUGE
VERMIFUGOUS
VERMIGEROUS
VERMIGRADE
VERMIL
VERMILION
VERMILIONETTE
VERMILIONIZE
VERMILY
VERMIN
VERMINAL
VERMINATE
VERMINATION
VERMINER
VERMINLY
VERMINOSIS
VERMINOUS
VERMINOUSLY
VERMINY
VERMIPAROUS
VERMIS
VERMIVOROUS
VERMIX
VERMOREL
VERMOULU
VERMOULUE
VERMOUTH
VERNACCIA
VERNACLE
VERNACULAR
VERNACULARLY
VERNACULATE
VERNAGE
VERNAL
VERNALITY
VERNALIZE
VERNANT
VERNATION
VERNEUK
VERNEUKER
VERNEUKERY
VERNICLE
VERNICOSE
VERNIER
VERNILE
VERNILITY
VERNISSAGE
VERNITION
VERNIX
VERNONIN
VERONALISM
VERQUERE
VERRA
VERRAY
VERRE
VERREL
VERRELL
VERRICULATE
VERRICULATED
VERRICULE
VERRUCA
VERRUCAE
VERRUCANO
VERRUCATED
VERRUCOSE
VERRUCOSIS
VERRUCOSITIES
VERRUCOSITY
VERRUCOUS
VERRUCULOSE
VERRUGA
VERRUGAS
VERS
VERSABILITY
VERSABLE
VERSABLENESS
VERSAL
VERSANT
VERSATE
VERSATILE
VERSATILITIES
VERSATILITY
VERSATION
VERSATIVE
VERSE
VERSED
VERSEMAN
VERSEMANSHIP
VERSEMEN
VERSEMONGER
VERSER
VERSES
VERSET
VERSETTE
VERSEWRIGHT
VERSICLE
VERSICLER
VERSICOLOR
VERSICOLOUR
VERSICULAR
VERSICULE
VERSICULI
VERSICULUS
VERSIERA
VERSIFIABLE
VERSIFIASTER
VERSIFICATION
VERSIFICATOR
VERSIFIED
VERSIFIER
VERSIFORM
VERSIFY
VERSIFYING
VERSILOQUY
VERSION
VERSIONAL
VERSIONER
VERSIONIST
VERSIONIZE
VERSIPEL
VERSO
VERSOR
VERST
VERSTA
VERSTE
VERSUAL
VERSUS
VERSUTE
VERTEBRA
VERTEBRAE
VERTEBRAL
VERTEBRALESS
VERTEBRALLY
VERTEBRAS
VERTEBRATE
VERTEBRATED
VERTEBRATION
VERTEBRIFORM
VERTEP
VERTEX
VERTEXES
VERTIBILITY
VERTIBLE
VERTIBLENESS
VERTICAL
VERTICALED
VERTICALING
VERTICALISM
VERTICALITY
VERTICALLED
VERTICALLING
VERTICALLY
VERTICES
VERTICIL
VERTICILLARY
VERTICILLATE
VERTICILLI
VERTICILLUS
VERTICITY
VERTICOMENTAL
VERTIGINATE
VERTIGINES
VERTIGINOUS
VERTIGO
VERTIGOES
VERTILINEAR
VERTIMETER
VERTU
VERTUGAL
VERTY
VERULED
VERUMONTANUM
VERUTA
VERUTUM
VERVAIN
VERVE
VERVECEAN
VERVECINE
VERVEL
VERVELED
VERVELLE
VERVELLED
VERVENIA
VERVER
VERVET
VERVINE
VERY
VERZINI
VERZINO
VES
VESANIA
VESANIC
VESBITE
VESI
VESICA
VESICAE
VESICAL
VESICANT
VESICATE
VESICATED
VESICATING
VESICATION
VESICATORY
VESICLE
VESICOCELE
VESICOCLYSIS
VESICOTOMY
VESICULA
VESICULAE
VESICULAR
VESICULARLY
VESICULASE
VESICULATE
VESICULATED
VESICULATING
VESICULATION
VESICULE
VESICULOSE
VESICULOUS
VESICULUS
VESKIT
VESPACIDE
VESPAL
VESPER
VESPERAL
VESPERIAN
VESPERING
VESPERS
VESPERTIDE
VESPERTILIAN
VESPERTINAL
VESPERTINE
VESPETRO
VESPIARIES
VESPIARY
VESPID
VESPIFORM
VESPINE
VESPOID
VESSEL
VESSELED
VESSELLED
VESSELS

VESSES
VESSETS
VESSICNON
VESSIGNON
VEST
VESTAL
VESTED
VESTEE
VESTER
VESTIARIAN
VESTIARIES
VESTIARIUM
VESTIARY
VESTIBLE
VESTIBULA
VESTIBULAR
VESTIBULATE
VESTIBULE
VESTIBULED
VESTIBULING
VESTIBULUM
VESTIGE
VESTIGIA
VESTIGIAL
VESTIGIALLY
VESTIGIARY
VESTIGIUM
VESTIMENT
VESTIMENTAL
VESTING
VESTITURE
VESTLET
VESTMENT
VESTMENTAL
VESTMENTED
VESTRAL
VESTRICAL
VESTRIES
VESTRIFY
VESTRY
VESTRYMAN
VESTRYMANLY
VESTRYMEN
VESTUARY
VESTURAL
VESTURE
VESTURED
VESTURER
VESTURING
VESUVIAN
VESUVIANITE
VESUVIATE
VESUVIN
VESUVITE
VESZELYITE
VET
VETA
VETANDA
VETCH
VETCHIER
VETCHIEST
VETCHLING
VETCHY
VETERAN
VETERANIZE
VETERANS
VETERINARIAN
VETERINARIES
VETERINARY
VETITIVE
VETIVENE
VETIVENOL
VETIVER
VETO
VETOED
VETOER
VETOES
VETOING
VETOISM
VETOIST
VETOISTIC
VETOISTICAL
VETTED
VETTING
VETTURA
VETTURE
VETTURINO
VETUST
VETUSTY
VEUGLAIRE
VEUVE
VEX
VEXATION
VEXATIOUS
VEXATIOUSLY
VEXATORY
VEXED
VEXEDLY
VEXEDNESS
VEXER
VEXFUL
VEXIL
VEXILLA
VEXILLARIOUS
VEXILLARY
VEXILLATE
VEXILLATION
VEXILLUM
VEXING
VEYN
VIA
VIABILITY
VIABLE
VIADUCT
VIAE
VIAGE
VIAGGIATORY
VIAGRAM
VIAGRAPH
VIAJACA
VIAL
VIALED
VIALING
VIALLED
VIALLING
VIAMETER
VIAND
VIANDEN
VIANDER
VIANDRY
VIANDS
VIATIC
VIATICA
VIATICAL
VIATICALS
VIATICUM
VIATOR
VIATORES
VIATORIAL
VIATORIALLY
VIBES
VIBETOITE
VIBEX
VIBGYOR
VIBICES
VIBRACULA
VIBRACULAR
VIBRACULOID
VIBRACULUM
VIBRANCIES
VIBRANCY
VIBRANT
VIBRANTLY
VIBRAPHONE
VIBRATE
VIBRATED
VIBRATILE
VIBRATILITY
VIBRATING
VIBRATION
VIBRATIONAL
VIBRATIUNCLE
VIBRATIVE
VIBRATO
VIBRATOR
VIBRATORY
VIBRIOID
VIBRION
VIBRIONIC
VIBRISSA
VIBRISSAE
VIBRISSAL
VIBROGRAPH
VIBROMETER
VIBROMOTIVE
VIBROPHONE
VIBROSCOPE
VIBURNIC
VIBURNIN
VIC
VICAIRE
VICAR
VICARAGE
VICARATE
VICARESS
VICARIAL
VICARIAN
VICARIANISM
VICARIATE
VICARII
VICARIOUS
VICARIOUSLY
VICARIUS
VICARLY
VICARSHIP
VICE
VICECOMES
VICECOMITAL
VICECOMITES
VICED
VICEGERAL
VICEGERENCY
VICEGERENT
VICENARY
VICENNIAL
VICEREGAL
VICEREGALLY
VICEREINE
VICEROY
VICEROYAL
VICEROYALTY
VICETY
VICHY
VICHYSSOISE
VICI
VICIANIN
VICIANOSE
VICILIN
VICIN
VICINAGE
VICINAL
VICINE
VICING
VICINITIES
VICINITY
VICIOUS
VICIOUSLY
VICIOUSNESS
VICISSITOUS
VICISSITUDE
VICOITE
VICONTIEL
VICONTIELS
VICTIM
VICTIMIZABLE
VICTIMIZATION
VICTIMIZE
VICTIMIZED
VICTIMIZER
VICTIMIZING
VICTLESS
VICTOR
VICTORDOM
VICTORESS
VICTORFISH
VICTORFISHES
VICTORIATE
VICTORIATUS
VICTORIES
VICTORINE
VICTORIOUS
VICTORIOUSLY
VICTORIUM
VICTORY
VICTRESS
VICTRIX
VICTUAL
VICTUALAGE
VICTUALED
VICTUALER
VICTUALING
VICTUALLED
VICTUALLER
VICTUALLING
VICTUALS
VICTUS
VICUDA
VICUNA
VICUNAS
VICUS
VID
VIDAME
VIDAN
VIDDUI
VIDDUY
VIDE
VIDELICET
VIDENDA
VIDENDUM
VIDEO
VIDERUFF
VIDETTE
VIDETUR
VIDICON
VIDIMUS
VIDONIA
VIDRY
VIDUAGE
VIDUAL
VIDUALLY
VIDUATE
VIDUATED
VIDUATION
VIDUITY
VIDUOUS
VIDYA
VIE
VIED
VIEJA
VIELLE
VIER
VIERKLEUR
VIERLING
VIERTEL
VIEW
VIEWED
VIEWER
VIEWING
VIEWLESS
VIEWLESSLY
VIEWLY
VIEWPOINT
VIEWSTER
VIEWY
VIF
VIFDA
VIGA
VIGAS
VIGENTENNIAL
VIGESIMAL
VIGESIMATION
VIGGLE
VIGIA
VIGIL
VIGILANCE
VIGILANCY
VIGILANT
VIGILANTE
VIGILANTLY
VIGILATE
VIGILATION
VIGNERON
VIGNERONS
VIGNETTE
VIGNETTED
VIGNETTER
VIGNETTING
VIGNETTIST
VIGNIN
VIGOGNE
VIGONE
VIGONIA
VIGOR
VIGORISH
VIGORIST
VIGOROSO
VIGOROUS
VIGOROUSLY
VIGOROUSNESS
VIGOUR
VIHARA
VIHUELA
VIJAO
VIKING
VIKINGISM
VILA
VILAYET
VILD
VILDLY
VILDNESS
VILE
VILELY
VILENESS
VILER
VILEST
VILEYNS
VILIACO
VILIFICATION
VILIFIED
VILIFIER
VILIFY
VILIFYING
VILIPEND
VILIPENDED
VILIPENDER
VILIPENDING
VILIPENDIOUS
VILITIES
VILITY
VILL
VILLA
VILLACHE
VILLADOM
VILLAETTE
VILLAGE

VILLAGELET
VILLAGEOUS
VILLAGER
VILLAGERY
VILLAGET
VILLAGEY
VILLAGISM
VILLAIN
VILLAINESS
VILLAINIES
VILLAINIST
VILLAINOUS
VILLAINOUSLY
VILLAINY
VILLAKIN
VILLANAGE
VILLANCICO
VILLANELLA
VILLANELLE
VILLANETTE
VILLAR
VILLATE
VILLATIC
VILLAYET
VILLE
VILLEGIATURE
VILLEIN
VILLEINAGE
VILLEINHOLD
VILLENAGE
VILLI
VILLIAUMITE
VILLICUS
VILLIFORM
VILLITIS
VILLOID
VILLOSE
VILLOSITY
VILLOTA
VILLOTE
VILLOUS
VILLUS
VILY
VIM
VIMANA
VIMEN
VIMINA
VIMINAL
VIMINEOUS
VIMPA
VIN
VINA
VINACEOUS
VINAGE
VINAGRON
VINAIGRE
VINAIGRETTE
VINAIGRETTED
VINAIGRIER
VINAIGROUS
VINAL
VINASSE
VINATA
VINCENT
VINCETOXIN
VINCHUCA
VINCIBILITY
VINCIBLE
VINCIBLENESS
VINCIBLY
VINCULA
VINCULAR
VINCULATE
VINCULATION
VINCULUM
VINDEMIAL
VINDEMIATE
VINDEMIATION
VINDEMIATORY
VINDEX
VINDICABLE
VINDICABLY
VINDICATE
VINDICATED
VINDICATING
VINDICATION
VINDICATIVE
VINDICATOR
VINDICATORY
VINDICATRESS
VINDICES
VINDICT
VINDICTA
VINDICTIVE
VINDICTIVELY
VINE
VINEA
VINEAE
VINEAL
VINEATIC
VINED
VINEDRESSER
VINEGAR
VINEGARER
VINEGARETTE
VINEGARIST
VINEGARROON
VINEGARWEED
VINEGARY
VINEGROWER
VINEITY
VINELAND
VINELET
VINER
VINERIES
VINERY
VINESTALK
VINETTA
VINEW
VINEYARD
VINEYARDING
VINEYARDIST
VINEYARDS
VINGT
VINGTIEME
VINGTUN
VINHATICO
VINIA
VINIC
VINICULTURAL
VINICULTURE
VINIFERA
VINIFEROUS
VINIFICATION
VINIFICATOR
VINING
VINITOR
VINNY
VINO
VINOLENT
VINOLOGIST
VINOLOGY
VINOMETER
VINOSE
VINOSITY
VINOUS
VINOUSLY
VINOUSNESS
VINT
VINTA
VINTAGE
VINTAGER
VINTAGING
VINTEM
VINTENER
VINTLITE
VINTNER
VINTNERESS
VINTNERY
VINTRESS
VINTRY
VINUM
VINY
VINYL
VINYLENE
VINYLIC
VINYLIDENE
VINYON
VIOL
VIOLA
VIOLABILITY
VIOLABLE
VIOLABLENESS
VIOLABLY
VIOLACEOUS
VIOLACEOUSLY
VIOLAL
VIOLAN
VIOLAND
VIOLANIN
VIOLATE
VIOLATED
VIOLATER
VIOLATING
VIOLATION
VIOLATIONAL
VIOLATIVE
VIOLATOR
VIOLATURE
VIOLE
VIOLENCE
VIOLENT
VIOLENTLY
VIOLENTNESS
VIOLER
VIOLESCENT
VIOLET
VIOLETTE
VIOLETY
VIOLIN
VIOLINA
VIOLINE
VIOLINED
VIOLINETTE
VIOLINING
VIOLINIST
VIOLINISTIC
VIOLINO
VIOLIST
VIOLON
VIOLONCELLIST
VIOLONCELLO
VIOLONCELLOS
VIOLONE
VIOLOTTA
VIOLOUS
VIOLURIC
VIOSTEROL
VIPER
VIPERESS
VIPERFISH
VIPERFISHES
VIPERID
VIPERIFORM
VIPERINE
VIPEROID
VIPEROUS
VIPEROUSLY
VIPEROUSNESS
VIPERY
VIR
VIRAGIN
VIRAGINIAN
VIRAGINITY
VIRAGO
VIRAGOES
VIRAL
VIRASON
VIRE
VIRELAI
VIRELAY
VIREMENT
VIRENT
VIREO
VIREONINE
VIREOS
VIRES
VIRESCENCE
VIRESCENT
VIRGA
VIRGAL
VIRGATE
VIRGATER
VIRGATION
VIRGE
VIRGIN
VIRGINAL
VIRGINALIST
VIRGINALITY
VIRGINALLY
VIRGINEOUS
VIRGINHEAD
VIRGINITY
VIRGINIUM
VIRGINLY
VIRGULA
VIRGULAR
VIRGULATE
VIRGULE
VIRGULTUM
VIRIAL
VIRICIDE
VIRID
VIRIDARIA
VIRIDARIUM
VIRIDESCENCE
VIRIDESCENT
VIRIDIAN
VIRIDIGENOUS
VIRIDIN
VIRIDINE
VIRIDITE
VIRIDITY
VIRIFIC
VIRIFY
VIRILE
VIRILELY
VIRILENESS
VIRILESCENCE
VIRILIA
VIRILIFY
VIRILIOUSLY
VIRILISM
VIRILIST
VIRILITIES
VIRILITY
VIRIPOTENT
VIRITOOT
VIRITRATE
VIRL
VIROLE
VIROLED
VIROLOGIST
VIROLOGY
VIRON
VIROSE
VIROSES
VIROSIS
VIROUS
VIRTU
VIRTUAL
VIRTUALISM
VIRTUALIST
VIRTUALITY
VIRTUALLY
VIRTUE
VIRTUED
VIRTUEFY
VIRTUOSA
VIRTUOSE
VIRTUOSI
VIRTUOSIC
VIRTUOSITY
VIRTUOSO
VIRTUOSOS
VIRTUOUS
VIRTUOUSLY
VIRTUS
VIRTUTI
VIRTUTIS
VIRUCIDAL
VIRUCIDE
VIRUELA
VIRULENCE
VIRULENCY
VIRULENT
VIRULENTED
VIRULENTLY
VIRUS
VIS
VISA
VISAED
VISAGE
VISAGED
VISAGRAPH
VISAING
VISAMMIN
VISARD
VISARGA
VISCACHA
VISCERA
VISCERAL
VISCERATE
VISCERATED
VISCERATING
VISCERATION
VISCEROUS
VISCID
VISCIDITY
VISCIDIZE
VISCIDLY
VISCIDNESS
VISCIDULOUS
VISCIN
VISCOID
VISCOIDAL
VISCOMETER
VISCOMETRY
VISCONTAL
VISCONTIAL
VISCOSCOPE
VISCOSE
VISCOSIMETER
VISCOSITIES
VISCOSITY
VISCOUNT
VISCOUNTCIES
VISCOUNTCY
VISCOUNTESS
VISCOUNTY
VISCOUS
VISCOUSLY
VISCOUSNESS
VISCUS
VISE

VISED
VISEED
VISEING
VISEMENT
VISENOMY
VISIBILITIES
VISIBILITY
VISIBILIZE
VISIBLE
VISIBLENESS
VISIBLY
VISIE
VISIER
VISILE
VISING
VISION
VISIONAL
VISIONALLY
VISIONARILY
VISIONARY
VISIONED
VISIONER
VISIONIZE
VISIONS
VISIT
VISITA
VISITABLE
VISITADOR
VISITANT
VISITATION
VISITATIONAL
VISITATIVE
VISITATOR
VISITATORIAL
VISITE
VISITED
VISITING
VISITOR
VISITORIAL
VISITRESS
VISITS
VISIVE
VISNE
VISNEY
VISON
VISOR
VISORED
VISORING
VISORY
VISS
VISTA
VISTAED
VISTAL
VISTAMENTE
VISTO
VISUAL
VISUALIST
VISUALITIES
VISUALITY
VISUALIZE
VISUALIZED
VISUALIZER
VISUALIZING
VISUOMETER
VITA
VITAE
VITAGRAPH
VITAL
VITALISM
VITALIST
VITALISTIC
VITALITY
VITALIZATION
VITALIZE
VITALIZED
VITALIZER
VITALIZING
VITALIZINGLY
VITALLY
VITALNESS
VITALS
VITAMIN
VITAMINE
VITAMINIC
VITAMINIZE
VITAMINOLOGY
VITAMINS
VITAPATH
VITAPATHY
VITAPHONE
VITASCOPE
VITASCOPIC
VITASTI
VITATIVENESS
VITE
VITELLARIUM
VITELLARY
VITELLIN
VITELLINE
VITELLOSE
VITELLUS
VITERBITE
VITESSE
VITIABLE
VITIAL
VITIATE
VITIATED
VITIATING
VITIATION
VITIATOR
VITICETUM
VITICULTURE
VITICULTURIST
VITIFEROUS
VITILIGINOUS
VITILIGO
VITILITIGATE
VITIOSITIES
VITIOSITY
VITIUM
VITRAGE
VITRAIL
VITRAILED
VITRAILLIST
VITRAIN
VITRAUX
VITRE
VITREAL
VITREAN
VITRELLA
VITREMYTE
VITREOSITY
VITREOUS
VITREOUSLY
VITREOUSNESS
VITRESCENCE
VITRESCENCY
VITRESCENT
VITRESCIBLE
VITREUM
VITRIAL
VITRIC
VITRICS
VITRIFACTION
VITRIFACTURE
VITRIFIABLE
VITRIFICATE
VITRIFICATION
VITRIFIED
VITRIFORM
VITRIFY
VITRIFYING
VITRINE
VITRINOID
VITRIOL
VITRIOLATE
VITRIOLATED
VITRIOLATING
VITRIOLATION
VITRIOLED
VITRIOLIC
VITRIOLINE
VITRIOLING
VITRIOLIZE
VITRIOLIZED
VITRIOLIZING
VITRIOLLED
VITRIOLLING
VITRITE
VITRO
VITROBASALT
VITROPHYRE
VITROPHYRIC
VITROTYPE
VITROUS
VITRUM
VITRY
VITTA
VITTAE
VITTATE
VITTLE
VITTLES
VITULAR
VITULARY
VITULINE
VITUPER
VITUPERABLE
VITUPERATE
VITUPERATED
VITUPERATING
VITUPERATION
VITUPERATIVE
VITUPERATOR
VITUPERATORY
VITUPERY
VIUVA
VIVA
VIVACE
VIVACIOUS
VIVACIOUSLY
VIVACISSIMO
VIVACITIES
VIVACITY
VIVAMENTE
VIVANDIER
VIVANDIERE
VIVANT
VIVARIA
VIVARIES
VIVARIUM
VIVARIUMS
VIVARY
VIVAT
VIVAX
VIVDA
VIVE
VIVELY
VIVENCY
VIVER
VIVERRIFORM
VIVERRINE
VIVERS
VIVES
VIVEUR
VIVIANITE
VIVID
VIVIDER
VIVIDEST
VIVIDITY
VIVIDLY
VIVIDNESS
VIVIFIC
VIVIFICAL
VIVIFICANT
VIVIFICATE
VIVIFICATED
VIVIFICATING
VIVIFICATION
VIVIFICATIVE
VIVIFICATOR
VIVIFIED
VIVIFIER
VIVIFY
VIVIFYING
VIVIPARISM
VIVIPARITY
VIVIPAROUS
VIVIPARY
VIVIPERFUSE
VIVISECT
VIVISECTED
VIVISECTING
VIVISECTION
VIVISECTIVE
VIVISECTOR
VIVO
VIVRE
VIVRES
VIX
VIXEN
VIXENISH
VIXENISHLY
VIXENLY
VIZARD
VIZARDED
VIZARDING
VIZCACHA
VIZIER
VIZIERATE
VIZIERIAL
VIZIR
VIZIRATE
VIZIRIAL
VIZNOMY
VIZOR
VIZORED
VIZORING
VIZSLA
VIZY
VIZZY
VLEI
VLEY
VLOKA
VLY
VOAR
VOCABILITY
VOCABLE
VOCABLY
VOCABULAR
VOCABULARIAN
VOCABULARIED
VOCABULARIES
VOCABULARY
VOCABULATION
VOCABULIST
VOCAL
VOCALIC
VOCALION
VOCALISATION
VOCALISE
VOCALISM
VOCALIST
VOCALITY
VOCALIZATION
VOCALIZE
VOCALIZED
VOCALIZER
VOCALIZING
VOCALLER
VOCALLY
VOCALNESS
VOCATE
VOCATION
VOCATIONAL
VOCATIONALLY
VOCATIVE
VOCATIVELY
VOCE
VOCES
VOCI
VOCICULTURAL
VOCIFERANCE
VOCIFERANT
VOCIFERATE
VOCIFERATED
VOCIFERATING
VOCIFERATION
VOCIFERATIVE
VOCIFERATOR
VOCIFERIZE
VOCIFEROSITY
VOCIFEROUS
VOCIFEROUSLY
VOCIFICATION
VOCIMOTOR
VOCODER
VOCOID
VOCULAR
VOCULE
VODKA
VODUN
VOE
VOET
VOETGANGER
VOETSAK
VOEU
VOG
VOGER
VOGESITE
VOGIE
VOGLITE
VOGUE
VOGUISH
VOICE
VOICED
VOICEFUL
VOICEFULNESS
VOICELESS
VOICELESSLY
VOICER
VOICES
VOICING
VOID
VOIDABLE
VOIDANCE
VOIDED
VOIDEE
VOIDER
VOIDING
VOIDLY
VOIDNESS
VOIDS
VOILA
VOILE
VOILIER
VOISINAGE
VOITURE
VOITURETTE
VOITURIER
VOIVOD
VOIVODE
VOKIE
VOL
VOLA
VOLABLE

VOLACIOUS
VOLADOR
VOLAGE
VOLAILLE
VOLANT
VOLANTE
VOLANTLY
VOLAPIE
VOLAR
VOLARY
VOLATA
VOLATIC
VOLATILE
VOLATILELY
VOLATILENESS
VOLATILITIES
VOLATILITY
VOLATILIZATION
VOLATILIZE
VOLATILIZED
VOLATILIZER
VOLATILIZING
VOLATION
VOLATIONAL
VOLBORTHITE
VOLCANIAN
VOLCANIC
VOLCANICALLY
VOLCANICITY
VOLCANIST
VOLCANITE
VOLCANITY
VOLCANIZE
VOLCANIZED
VOLCANIZING
VOLCANO
VOLCANOES
VOLCANOLOGY
VOLCANOS
VOLE
VOLEE
VOLEMITE
VOLEMITOL
VOLENCY
VOLENT
VOLENTLY
VOLERIES
VOLERY
VOLET
VOLGE
VOLHYNITE
VOLITANT
VOLITATE
VOLITATION
VOLITATIONAL
VOLITIENCY
VOLITIENT
VOLITION
VOLITIONAL
VOLITIONARY
VOLITIONATE
VOLITIVE
VOLITORIAL
VOLK
VOLKSRAAD
VOLLENGE
VOLLEY
VOLLEYBALL
VOLLEYED
VOLLEYER
VOLLEYING
VOLLEYINGLY
VOLLEYS
VOLOST
VOLOW
VOLPLANE
VOLPLANIST
VOLSELLA
VOLT
VOLTA
VOLTAGE
VOLTAGRAPHY
VOLTAIC
VOLTAISM
VOLTAITE
VOLTAMETER
VOLTAMETRIC
VOLTAMMETER
VOLTAPLAST
VOLTATYPE
VOLTE
VOLTEADOR
VOLTEADORES
VOLTI
VOLTIGEUR
VOLTINISM
VOLTIVITY
VOLTIZE
VOLTMETER
VOLTO
VOLTZINE
VOLTZITE
VOLUBILITY
VOLUBLE
VOLUBLENESS
VOLUBLY
VOLUCRINE
VOLUME
VOLUMED
VOLUMEN
VOLUMETER
VOLUMETRIC
VOLUMETRY
VOLUMINA
VOLUMINAL
VOLUMINOSITY
VOLUMINOUS
VOLUMINOUSLY
VOLUMIST
VOLUMOMETER
VOLUNTARIATE
VOLUNTARIES
VOLUNTARILY
VOLUNTARIOUS
VOLUNTARISM
VOLUNTARIST
VOLUNTARITY
VOLUNTARY
VOLUNTARYISM
VOLUNTARYIST
VOLUNTATIVE
VOLUNTEER
VOLUNTEERED
VOLUNTEERING
VOLUNTEERLY
VOLUNTY
VOLUPER
VOLUPT
VOLUPTAS
VOLUPTUARIES
VOLUPTUARY
VOLUPTUATE
VOLUPTUOSITY
VOLUPTUOUS
VOLUPTUOUSNESS
VOLUPTY
VOLUTA
VOLUTAE
VOLUTATE
VOLUTATION
VOLUTE
VOLUTED
VOLUTIFORM
VOLUTIN
VOLUTION
VOLUTOID
VOLVA
VOLVATE
VOLVE
VOLVELL
VOLVELLE
VOLVENT
VOLVOCACEOUS
VOLVULUS
VOLYER
VOMBATID
VOME
VOMER
VOMERINE
VOMICA
VOMICIN
VOMICINE
VOMIT
VOMITED
VOMITER
VOMITING
VOMITINGLY
VOMITION
VOMITIVE
VOMITO
VOMITORIES
VOMITORY
VOMITURE
VOMITUS
VON
VONSENITE
VOODOO
VOODOOED
VOODOOING
VOODOOISM
VOODOOIST
VOODOOISTIC
VOOG
VOORHUIS
VOORTREKKER
VORACIOUS
VORACIOUSLY
VORACITY
VORAGE
VORAGINOUS
VORAGO
VORANT
VORAZ
VORHAND
VORLAGE
VORONDREO
VORPAL
VORTEX
VORTEXES
VORTICAL
VORTICALLY
VORTICEL
VORTICELLID
VORTICES
VORTICIFORM
VORTICISM
VORTICIST
VORTICITY
VORTICOSE
VORTICOSELY
VORTICULAR
VORTICULARLY
VORTIGINOUS
VOTA
VOTABLE
VOTAL
VOTALLY
VOTARESS
VOTARIES
VOTARIST
VOTARY
VOTATION
VOTE
VOTEABLE
VOTED
VOTEEN
VOTER
VOTES
VOTING
VOTIST
VOTIVE
VOTIVELY
VOTIVENESS
VOTOMETER
VOTRESS
VOUCH
VOUCHABLE
VOUCHED
VOUCHEE
VOUCHER
VOUCHING
VOUCHMENT
VOUCHSAFE
VOUCHSAFED
VOUCHSAFING
VOUGE
VOULGE
VOUR
VOUSSOIR
VOUST
VOUSTER
VOUSTY
VOW
VOWED
VOWEL
VOWELISM
VOWELIST
VOWELIZE
VOWELLIKE
VOWELLY
VOWELS
VOWELY
VOWER
VOWESS
VOWING
VOX
VOYAGE
VOYAGEABLE
VOYAGED
VOYAGER
VOYAGEUR
VOYAGING
VOYAL
VOYANCE
VOYEUR
VOYEURISM
VOYEUSE
VOYOL
VRAI
VRAIC
VRAICKER
VRAICKING
VRBAITE
VRIDDHI
VRILLE
VROCHT
VROTHER
VROUW
VUE
VUG
VUGG
VUGGY
VUGH
VUIDE
VULCANICITY
VULCANISM
VULCANIST
VULCANITE
VULCANIZATE
VULCANIZATION
VULCANIZE
VULCANIZED
VULCANIZER
VULCANIZING
VULCANO
VULCANOLOGY
VULGAR
VULGARE
VULGARER
VULGAREST
VULGARIAN
VULGARISM
VULGARIST
VULGARITIES
VULGARITY
VULGARIZATION
VULGARIZE
VULGARIZED
VULGARIZER
VULGARIZING
VULGARLY
VULGARNESS
VULGO
VULGUS
VULGUSES
VULN
VULNED
VULNERABILITY
VULNERABLE
VULNERABLY
VULNERAL
VULNERARY
VULNERATE
VULNERATIVE
VULNIFIC
VULNIFICAL
VULNOSE
VULPECULAR
VULPIC
VULPICIDAL
VULPICIDE
VULPICIDISM
VULPINE
VULPINIC
VULPINISM
VULPINITE
VULSELLA
VULSELLUM
VULSINITE
VULT
VULTURE
VULTURINE
VULTURISH
VULTURISM
VULTURN
VULTUROUS
VULVA
VULVAL
VULVAR
VULVATE
VULVIFORM
VULVITIS
VULVOCRURAL
VULVOUTERINE
VULVOVAGINAL
VULVOVAGINITIS
VUM
VYINGLY
VYT

WA
WAAG
WAAPA
WAB
WABAYO
WABBER
WABBLE
WABBLED
WABBLER
WABBLINESS
WABBLING
WABBLINGLY
WABBLY
WABBY
WABE
WABENO
WABI
WABRON
WABUR
WACADASH
WACAPOU
WACE
WACHNA
WACK
WACKE
WACKER
WACKIER
WACKIEST
WACKY
WAD
WADCUTTER
WADD
WADDED
WADDENT
WADDER
WADDIE
WADDIED
WADDIES
WADDING
WADDLE
WADDLED
WADDLER
WADDLESOME
WADDLING
WADDLY
WADDY
WADDYING
WADDYWOOD
WADE
WADED
WADER
WADGE
WADI
WADIES
WADING
WADINGLY
WADMAAL
WADMAKER
WADMAKING
WADMAL
WADMOL
WADMOLL
WADNA
WADSET
WADSETTED
WADSETTING
WADY
WAEFU
WAEFUL
WAEG
WAENESS
WAESUCK
WAESUCKS
WAF
WAFER
WAFERED
WAFERER
WAFERING
WAFERMAKER
WAFERWOMAN
WAFERWORK
WAFERY
WAFF
WAFFIE
WAFFLE
WAFFLIKE
WAFFLY
WAFFNESS
WAFT
WAFTAGE
WAFTED
WAFTER
WAFTING
WAFTURE
WAFTY
WAG
WAGANG
WAGATI
WAGBEARD
WAGE
WAGED
WAGELESS
WAGELING
WAGER
WAGERED
WAGERER
WAGERING
WAGES
WAGET
WAGEWORK
WAGEWORKER
WAGEWORKING
WAGGED
WAGGEL
WAGGER
WAGGERIES
WAGGERY
WAGGIE
WAGGING
WAGGISH
WAGGISHLY
WAGGISHNESS
WAGGLE
WAGGLED
WAGGLING
WAGGLINGLY
WAGGLY
WAGGON
WAGGONABLE
WAGGONAGE
WAGGONED
WAGGONER
WAGGONETTE
WAGGONING
WAGGONLOAD
WAGGONRY
WAGGONSMITH
WAGGONWAY
WAGGONWAYMAN
WAGGONWRIGHT
WAGGY
WAGH
WAGING
WAGNERITE
WAGON
WAGONABLE
WAGONAGE
WAGONED
WAGONER
WAGONETTE
WAGONING
WAGONLOAD
WAGONMAKER
WAGONMAKING
WAGONMAN
WAGONRY
WAGONSMITH
WAGONWAY
WAGONWAYMAN
WAGONWRIGHT
WAGSOME
WAGTAIL
WAGWAG
WAGWANTS
WAGWIT
WAH
WAHAHE
WAHCONDA
WAHINE
WAHOO
WAHWAH
WAIATA
WAIF
WAIK
WAIKLY
WAIKNESS
WAIL
WAILED
WAILER
WAILFUL
WAILFULLY
WAILING
WAILMENT
WAILSOME
WAILY
WAIN
WAINAGE
WAINBOTE
WAINER
WAINMAN
WAINMEN
WAINROPE
WAINSCOT
WAINSCOTED
WAINSCOTING
WAINSCOTTED
WAINSCOTTING
WAINWRIGHT
WAIPIRO
WAIR
WAIRCH
WAIRD
WAIREPO
WAIRSH
WAISE
WAIST
WAISTBAND
WAISTCLOTH
WAISTCOAT
WAISTCOATED
WAISTCOATEER
WAISTED
WAISTER
WAISTING
WAISTLESS
WAISTLINE
WAIT
WAITED
WAITER
WAITERAGE
WAITERING
WAITING
WAITINGLY
WAITRESS
WAITSMEN
WAIVATUA
WAIVE
WAIVED
WAIVER
WAIVERY
WAIVING
WAJANG
WAK
WAKA
WAKAN
WAKANDA
WAKE
WAKEA
WAKED
WAKEFUL
WAKEFULLY
WAKEFULNESS
WAKELESS
WAKEMAN
WAKEMEN
WAKEN
WAKENED
WAKENER
WAKENING
WAKER
WAKERIFE
WAKERIFENESS
WAKES
WAKETIME
WAKF
WAKIF
WAKIKI
WAKING
WAKINGLY
WAKIUP
WAKON
WAKONDA
WAKY
WAL
WALAHEE
WALD
WALDFLUTE
WALDGRAVE
WALDGRAVINE
WALDHORN
WALDMEISTER
WALE
WALED
WALEPIECE
WALER
WALI
WALING
WALK
WALKAWAY
WALKED
WALKENE
WALKER
WALKERS
WALKING
WALKIST
WALKMILL
WALKMILLER
WALKOUT
WALKOVER
WALKRIFE
WALKSMAN
WALKSMEN
WALKUP
WALKWAY
WALKYRIE
WALL
WALLA
WALLABA
WALLABIES
WALLABY
WALLAGO
WALLAH
WALLAROO
WALLBIRD
WALLBOARD
WALLED
WALLER
WALLET
WALLEYE
WALLEYED
WALLFLOWER
WALLHICK
WALLIE
WALLING
WALLOCH
WALLOON
WALLOP
WALLOPER
WALLOPING
WALLOW
WALLOWED
WALLOWER
WALLOWING
WALLOWISH
WALLOWISHLY
WALLPAPER
WALLPAPERING
WALLPIECE
WALLS
WALLWORT
WALLY
WALLYDRAG
WALLYDRAIGLE
WALM
WALNUT
WALPURGITE
WALRUS
WALRUSES
WALSH
WALSPERE
WALT
WALTER
WALTRON
WALTROT
WALTY
WALTZ
WALTZED
WALTZER
WALTZING
WALWE
WALY
WALYCOAT
WAMARA
WAMB
WAMBAIS
WAMBLE
WAMBLED
WAMBLINESS
WAMBLING
WAMBLINGLY
WAMBLY
WAME
WAMED
WAMEFOU
WAMEFU
WAMEFUL
WAMEL
WAMFLE
WAMMUS
WAMP
WAMPEE
WAMPISH
WAMPLE
WAMPUM
WAMPUMPEAG

WAMPUS
WAMUS
WAN
WANA
WANCHANCY
WAND
WANDE
WANDER
WANDERER
WANDERING
WANDERINGLY
WANDERLUST
WANDERLUSTER
WANDEROO
WANDERY
WANDERYEAR
WANDFLOWER
WANDLE
WANDOO
WANDOUGHT
WANDRETH
WANDSMAN
WANDY
WANE
WANED
WANELESS
WANEY
WANG
WANGA
WANGALA
WANGAN
WANGATEUR
WANGER
WANGHEE
WANGLE
WANGLED
WANGLER
WANGLING
WANGO
WANGRACE
WANGTOOTH
WANGUN
WANHAP
WANHAPPY
WANHOPE
WANHORN
WANIAND
WANIGAN
WANING
WANION
WANKAPIN
WANKLE
WANKLINESS
WANKLY
WANKY
WANLAS
WANLE
WANLY
WANMOL
WANNED
WANNER
WANNESS
WANNEST
WANNIGAN
WANNING
WANNY
WANREST
WANRESTFUL
WANRUFE
WANRULY
WANSHAPE
WANSITH
WANSOME
WANSONSY
WANT
WANTAGE
WANTED
WANTER
WANTFUL
WANTHILL
WANTHRIFT
WANTHRIVEN
WANTING
WANTINGLY
WANTINGNESS
WANTON
WANTONED
WANTONER
WANTONING
WANTONIZE
WANTONLY
WANTONNESS
WANTROKE
WANTRUST
WANTWIT
WANTY
WANWEIRD
WANWIT
WANWORDY
WANWORTH
WANY
WANZE
WAP
WAPACUT
WAPATA
WAPATOO
WAPED
WAPENTAKE
WAPIN
WAPITI
WAPITIS
WAPP
WAPPED
WAPPENED
WAPPENSCHAW
WAPPER
WAPPET
WAPPING
WAQF
WAR
WARABI
WARAL
WARATAH
WARBIRD
WARBITE
WARBLE
WARBLED
WARBLELIKE
WARBLER
WARBLERLIKE
WARBLET
WARBLING
WARBLINGLY
WARBLY
WARCH
WARCRAFT
WARD
WARDABLE
WARDAGE
WARDATOUR
WARDAY
WARDCORS
WARDED
WARDEN
WARDENCY
WARDENRIES
WARDENRY
WARDENSHIP
WARDER
WARDHOLDING
WARDIAN
WARDING
WARDITE
WARDMAID
WARDMAN
WARDMEN
WARDMOTE
WARDRESS
WARDROBE
WARDROBER
WARDROOM
WARDSHIP
WARDSMAID
WARDSMAN
WARDSWOMAN
WARDWITE
WARDWOMAN
WARDWOMEN
WARDWORD
WARE
WARED
WAREFUL
WAREHOU
WAREHOUSE
WAREHOUSED
WAREHOUSEMAN
WAREHOUSEMEN
WAREHOUSING
WARELESS
WARELY
WARENTMENT
WAREROOM
WARES
WARESHIP
WARF
WARFA
WARFARE
WARFARED
WARFARER
WARFARING
WARFUL
WARGUS
WARHEAD
WARI
WARIANCE
WARIANGLE
WARIED
WARIER
WARIEST
WARILY
WARIMENT
WARINE
WARINESS
WARINGIN
WARISH
WARISON
WARK
WARKAMOOWEE
WARKLOOM
WARKLUME
WARLIKE
WARLIKELY
WARLIKENESS
WARLING
WARLOCK
WARLOCKRY
WARLORD
WARLOW
WARLUCK
WARLY
WARM
WARMAKER
WARMAKING
WARMAN
WARMED
WARMEDLY
WARMEN
WARMER
WARMEST
WARMFUL
WARMHEARTED
WARMHOUSE
WARMING
WARMLY
WARMMESS
WARMONGER
WARMONGERING
WARMOUTH
WARMTH
WARMUP
WARMUS
WARN
WARNAGE
WARND
WARNED
WARNEL
WARNER
WARNING
WARNINGLY
WARNISH
WARNISON
WARNISS
WARNOTH
WARP
WARPAGE
WARPATH
WARPED
WARPER
WARPING
WARPLANE
WARPLE
WARPOWER
WARPROOF
WARRAGAL
WARRAMBOOL
WARRANDICE
WARRANT
WARRANTABLE
WARRANTABLY
WARRANTED
WARRANTEE
WARRANTER
WARRANTIES
WARRANTING
WARRANTISE
WARRANTIZE
WARRANTOR
WARRANTY
WARRAY
WARRE
WARRED
WARREE
WARREN
WARRENER
WARRER
WARRIGAL
WARRIN
WARRING
WARRIOR
WARRISH
WARROK
WARRYN
WARSAW
WARSHIP
WARSLE
WARSLED
WARSLER
WARSLING
WARSTLE
WARSTLER
WART
WARTED
WARTFLOWER
WARTH
WARTIER
WARTIEST
WARTIME
WARTLIKE
WARTWEED
WARTWORT
WARTY
WARTYBACK
WARVE
WARWARDS
WARWICKITE
WARWOLF
WARWORK
WARWORKER
WARWORN
WARY
WARYTREE
WAS
WASABI
WASE
WASEL
WASH
WASHABILITY
WASHABLE
WASHBASIN
WASHBASKET
WASHBOARD
WASHBOWL
WASHBREW
WASHCLOTH
WASHDAY
WASHDISH
WASHDOWN
WASHED
WASHER
WASHERIES
WASHERLESS
WASHERMAN
WASHERMEN
WASHERWIFE
WASHERWOMAN
WASHERWOMEN
WASHERY
WASHERYMAN
WASHERYMEN
WASHHAND
WASHHOUSE
WASHIER
WASHIEST
WASHIN
WASHINESS
WASHING
WASHINGS
WASHLAND
WASHLEATHER
WASHMAID
WASHMAN
WASHMEN
WASHOFF
WASHOUT
WASHPOT
WASHRAG
WASHROOM
WASHSHED
WASHSTAND
WASHTAIL
WASHTRAY
WASHTROUGH
WASHTUB
WASHWAY
WASHWOMAN
WASHWOMEN
WASHWORK
WASHY
WASP
WASPEN
WASPIER
WASPIEST
WASPISH
WASPISHLY
WASPISHNESS

WASPLING
WASPNESTING
WASPS
WASPY
WASSAIL
WASSAILED
WASSAILER
WASSAILING
WASSAILOUS
WASSIE
WAST
WASTABLE
WASTAGE
WASTE
WASTEBASKET
WASTED
WASTEFUL
WASTEFULLY
WASTEFULNESS
WASTEL
WASTELAND
WASTELBREAD
WASTELESS
WASTELOT
WASTELY
WASTEMAN
WASTEMEN
WASTEMENT
WASTENESS
WASTEPAPER
WASTER
WASTERFUL
WASTERIE
WASTERN
WASTERY
WASTETHRIFT
WASTEWAY
WASTEWEIR
WASTEWORD
WASTEYARD
WASTIER
WASTIEST
WASTINE
WASTING
WASTINGLY
WASTINGNESS
WASTME
WASTREL
WASTRIE
WASTRIFE
WASTRY
WASTY
WAT
WATAP
WATAPE
WATAPEH
WATCH
WATCHBAND
WATCHBILL
WATCHBOAT
WATCHCASE
WATCHCRY
WATCHDOG
WATCHED
WATCHER
WATCHERS
WATCHES
WATCHET
WATCHEYE
WATCHFREE
WATCHFUL
WATCHFULLY
WATCHFULNESS
WATCHGLASS
WATCHHOUSE
WATCHING
WATCHINGLY
WATCHKEEPER
WATCHLESS
WATCHMAKER
WATCHMAKING
WATCHMAN
WATCHMANLY
WATCHMATE
WATCHMEN
WATCHMENT
WATCHOUT
WATCHTOWER
WATCHWORD
WATCHWORK
WATE
WATER
WATERAGE
WATERBAILAGE
WATERBANK
WATERBEAR
WATERBELLY
WATERBLINK
WATERBLOOM
WATERBOARD
WATERBOK
WATERBORNE
WATERBOSH
WATERBOUND
WATERBRAIN
WATERBROO
WATERBROSE
WATERBUCK
WATERBUCKS
WATERBUSH
WATERCASTER
WATERCHAT
WATERCOLOR
WATERCOURSE
WATERCRAFT
WATERCRESS
WATERCUP
WATERDOE
WATERDROP
WATERED
WATERER
WATERFALL
WATERFINDER
WATERFLOOD
WATERFOWL
WATERFOWLS
WATERFREE
WATERFRONT
WATERGLASS
WATERHEAD
WATERHEAP
WATERHORSE
WATERIE
WATERILY
WATERINESS
WATERING
WATERINGLY
WATERINGMAN
WATERISH
WATERISHLY
WATERISHNESS
WATERLEAF
WATERLEAVE
WATERLESS
WATERLESSLY
WATERLINE
WATERLOG
WATERLOGGED
WATERLOGGER
WATERMAN
WATERMANSHIP
WATERMARK
WATERMARKED
WATERMASTER
WATERMELON
WATERMEN
WATERMONGER
WATERPIT
WATERPLANE
WATERPOT
WATERPOWER
WATERPROOF
WATERPROOFED
WATERPROOFER
WATERRUG
WATERSCAPE
WATERSHAKE
WATERSHED
WATERSHOOT
WATERSHUT
WATERSIDE
WATERSIDER
WATERSKIN
WATERSMEET
WATERSPOUT
WATERSTOUP
WATERTIGHT
WATERTIGHTAL
WATERWALL
WATERWAY
WATERWEED
WATERWHEEL
WATERWISE
WATERWOOD
WATERWORK
WATERWORKER
WATERWORKS
WATERWORM
WATERWORN
WATERWORT
WATERY
WATH
WATHE
WATHER
WATHSTEAD
WATO
WATT
WATTAGE
WATTAPE
WATTER
WATTEST
WATTIS
WATTLE
WATTLEBIRD
WATTLEBOY
WATTLED
WATTLES
WATTLESS
WATTLEWORK
WATTLING
WATTMAN
WATTMEN
WATTMETER
WAUBEEN
WAUBLE
WAUCH
WAUCHLE
WAUCHT
WAUF
WAUFF
WAUGH
WAUGHT
WAUGHY
WAUK
WAUKE
WAUKIT
WAUKRIFE
WAUL
WAUNS
WAUR
WAUREGAN
WAUVE
WAVABLE
WAVABLY
WAVE
WAVED
WAVELENGTH
WAVELESS
WAVELET
WAVELLITE
WAVEMARK
WAVEMENT
WAVEMETER
WAVEOFF
WAVER
WAVERED
WAVERER
WAVERING
WAVERINGLY
WAVERINGNESS
WAVEROUS
WAVERY
WAVESON
WAVEY
WAVEYS
WAVIER
WAVIES
WAVIEST
WAVILY
WAVINESS
WAVING
WAVINGLY
WAVY
WAW
WAWA
WAWAH
WAWASKEESH
WAWE
WAWL
WAX
WAXAND
WAXBERRIES
WAXBERRY
WAXBILL
WAXBIRD
WAXBUSH
WAXCHANDLER
WAXCHANDLERY
WAXCOMB
WAXED
WAXEN
WAXER
WAXES
WAXFLOWER
WAXHEARTED
WAXIER
WAXIEST
WAXINESS
WAXING
WAXINGLY
WAXMAKER
WAXMAKING
WAXMAN
WAXWEED
WAXWING
WAXWORK
WAXWORKER
WAXWORKING
WAXWORM
WAXY
WAY
WAYAKA
WAYANG
WAYBACK
WAYBERRY
WAYBILL
WAYBIRD
WAYBOOK
WAYBREAD
WAYBUNG
WAYER
WAYFARE
WAYFARER
WAYFARING
WAYFARINGLY
WAYFELLOW
WAYGANG
WAYGATE
WAYGOER
WAYGOING
WAYGONE
WAYGOOSE
WAYHOUSE
WAYING
WAYLAID
WAYLAY
WAYLAYER
WAYLAYING
WAYLEAVE
WAYMAKER
WAYMAN
WAYMARK
WAYMATE
WAYMEN
WAYMENT
WAYNE
WAYPOST
WAYS
WAYSIDE
WAYSIDER
WAYSLIDING
WAYTE
WAYTHORN
WAYWARD
WAYWARDEN
WAYWARDLY
WAYWARDNESS
WAYWISER
WAYWORN
WAYWORT
WAYZGOOSE
WAZIR
WAZIRATE
WAZIRSHIP
WE
WEA
WEAK
WEAKBRAINED
WEAKEN
WEAKENED
WEAKENER
WEAKENING
WEAKER
WEAKEST
WEAKFISH
WEAKFISHES
WEAKHANDED
WEAKHEARTED
WEAKISH
WEAKISHLY
WEAKISHNESS
WEAKLIER
WEAKLIEST
WEAKLINESS
WEAKLING
WEAKLY
WEAKMOUTHED
WEAKNESS
WEAKY
WEAL
WEALD
WEALDISH
WEALDSMAN
WEALDSMEN
WEALFUL

WEALSMAN
WEALSOME
WEALTH
WEALTHFUL
WEALTHFULLY
WEALTHIER
WEALTHIEST
WEALTHILY
WEALTHINESS
WEALTHMAKER
WEALTHMAKING
WEALTHMONGER
WEALTHY
WEAM
WEAN
WEANED
WEANEDNESS
WEANEL
WEANER
WEANIE
WEANING
WEANLING
WEANLY
WEANYER
WEAPON
WEAPONED
WEAPONEER
WEAPONLESS
WEAPONMAKER
WEAPONMAKING
WEAPONPROOF
WEAPONRY
WEAPONS
WEAR
WEARABILITY
WEARABLE
WEARED
WEARER
WEARIED
WEARIEDLY
WEARIEDNESS
WEARIER
WEARIEST
WEARIFUL
WEARIFULLY
WEARIFULNESS
WEARILESS
WEARILESSLY
WEARILY
WEARINESS
WEARING
WEARINGLY
WEARISH
WEARISHLY
WEARISHNESS
WEARISOME
WEARISOMELY
WEARISOMENESS
WEARY
WEARYING
WEARYINGLY
WEASAND
WEASEL
WEASELED
WEASELING
WEASELLY
WEASELS
WEASELSKIN
WEASELSNOUT
WEASER
WEASON
WEATHER
WEATHERBEATEN
WEATHERBOARD
WEATHERBREAK
WEATHERCAST
WEATHERCOCK
WEATHERCOCKY
WEATHERED
WEATHERER
WEATHERGLASS
WEATHERGLEAM
WEATHERHEAD
WEATHERING
WEATHERLY
WEATHERMAKER
WEATHERMAN
WEATHERMEN
WEATHERMOST
WEATHEROLOGY
WEATHERPROOF
WEATHERSICK
WEATHERTIGHT
WEATHERWORN
WEATHERY
WEATINGS
WEAVE
WEAVED
WEAVER
WEAVERBIRD
WEAVERESS
WEAVING
WEAZEN
WEAZENED
WEAZENY
WEB
WEBB
WEBBE
WEBBED
WEBBER
WEBBING
WEBBY
WEBELOS
WEBER
WEBEYE
WEBFEET
WEBFOOT
WEBMAKER
WEBMAKING
WEBSTER
WEBSTERITE
WEBWORK
WEBWORM
WECCHE
WECHT
WED
WEDANA
WEDBED
WEDBEDRIP
WEDDED
WEDDEDLY
WEDDEDNESS
WEDDEED
WEDDER
WEDDING
WEDDINGER
WEDE
WEDFEE
WEDGE
WEDGEBILL
WEDGED
WEDGER
WEDGIE
WEDGIER
WEDGIEST
WEDGING
WEDGWOOD
WEDGY
WEDLOCK
WEE
WEEBLE
WEED
WEEDA
WEEDAGE
WEEDED
WEEDER
WEEDERY
WEEDHOOK
WEEDIER
WEEDIEST
WEEDILY
WEEDINESS
WEEDING
WEEDLESS
WEEDS
WEEDY
WEEK
WEEKDAY
WEEKEND
WEEKENDER
WEEKLIES
WEEKLONG
WEEKLY
WEEKS
WEEKWAM
WEEL
WEELFARD
WEEM
WEEN
WEENIE
WEENIER
WEENIEST
WEENING
WEENONG
WEENSY
WEENT
WEENTY
WEENY
WEEP
WEEPER
WEEPERED
WEEPIER
WEEPIEST
WEEPING
WEEPLY
WEEPS
WEEPY
WEER
WEERISH
WEESHEE
WEESHY
WEEST
WEET
WEETBIRD
WEETLESS
WEETY
WEEVER
WEEVIL
WEEVILED
WEEVILLED
WEEVILLY
WEEVILY
WEEWAW
WEEWOW
WEEZE
WEEZLE
WEFT
WEFTAGE
WEFTED
WEFTWISE
WEFTY
WEGENERIAN
WEGOTISM
WEHRLITE
WEIBYEITE
WEICHSELWOOD
WEID
WEIGELA
WEIGELITE
WEIGH
WEIGHAGE
WEIGHBAR
WEIGHBAUK
WEIGHBRIDGE
WEIGHED
WEIGHER
WEIGHHOUSE
WEIGHIN
WEIGHING
WEIGHLOCK
WEIGHMAN
WEIGHMASTER
WEIGHMEN
WEIGHSHAFT
WEIGHT
WEIGHTCHASER
WEIGHTED
WEIGHTEDLY
WEIGHTEDNESS
WEIGHTER
WEIGHTIER
WEIGHTIEST
WEIGHTILY
WEIGHTINESS
WEIGHTING
WEIGHTLESS
WEIGHTLESSLY
WEIGHTOMETER
WEIGHTS
WEIGHTY
WEIHE
WEILANG
WEIN
WEIR
WEIRD
WEIRDFUL
WEIRDIE
WEIRDIES
WEIRDLESS
WEIRDLINESS
WEIRDLY
WEIRDNESS
WEIRDSOME
WEIRDWOMAN
WEIRDWOMEN
WEIRING
WEISBACHITE
WEISE
WEISSITE
WEIZE
WEJACK
WEKA
WEKAU
WEKEEN
WEKI
WEL
WELCH
WELCHER
WELCOME
WELCOMED
WELCOMELY
WELCOMENESS
WELCOMER
WELCOMING
WELCOMINGLY
WELD
WELDABILITY
WELDABLE
WELDED
WELDER
WELDING
WELE
WELFARE
WELFARING
WELI
WELK
WELKIN
WELL
WELLADAY
WELLAT
WELLAWAY
WELLBORN
WELLCURB
WELLED
WELLER
WELLHEAD
WELLHOLE
WELLING
WELLINGTON
WELLISH
WELLMAKER
WELLMAKING
WELLMAN
WELLMEN
WELLMOST
WELLNEAR
WELLQUEME
WELLRING
WELLS
WELLSIDE
WELLSITE
WELLSPRING
WELLSTEAD
WELLSTRAND
WELLY
WELLYARD
WELME
WELOO
WELS
WELSH
WELSHED
WELSHER
WELSHING
WELSIUM
WELSOM
WELT
WELTED
WELTER
WELTERED
WELTERING
WELTERWEIGHT
WELTING
WELY
WEM
WEME
WEMLESS
WEMMY
WEMOD
WEMODNESS
WEN
WENCH
WENCHED
WENCHEL
WENCHER
WENCHING
WEND
WENDE
WENDED
WENDIGO
WENDIGOS
WENDING
WENE
WENETH
WENLICHE
WENNEBERGITE
WENNISH
WENNY
WENRO
WENT
WENTLE
WENTLETRAP
WENZEL
WEPMAN
WEPMANKIN
WEPT

WER
WERD
WERE
WEREBEAR
WERECALF
WERED
WEREFOLK
WEREFOX
WEREGILD
WEREHYENA
WEREJAGUAR
WERELEOPARD
WERETIGER
WEREWALL
WEREWOLF
WEREWOLFISH
WEREWOLFISM
WEREWOLVES
WERF
WERGELD
WERGELT
WERGILD
WERI
WERING
WERK
WERMETHE
WERN
WERNARD
WERNE
WERNERITE
WEROOLE
WEROWANCE
WERP
WERSE
WERSH
WERSLETE
WERT
WERTE
WESKIT
WESSEL
WESSELTON
WEST
WESTAWAY
WESTBOUND
WESTE
WESTEN
WESTER
WESTERING
WESTERLIES
WESTERLINESS
WESTERLING
WESTERLY
WESTERN
WESTERNER
WESTERNISM
WESTERNIZE
WESTERNIZED
WESTERNIZING
WESTERNMOST
WESTERWARDS
WESTFALITE
WESTING
WESTLAN
WESTLAND
WESTLANDWAYS
WESTLINS
WESTME
WESTMELESS
WESTMOST
WESTNESS
WESTWARD
WESTWARDLY
WESTWARDS
WESTY
WET
WETA
WETBACK
WETBIRD
WETE
WETHE
WETHER
WETHERHOG
WETHERTEG
WETLANDS
WETLY
WETNESS
WETTABILITY
WETTABLE
WETTED
WETTER
WETTEST
WETTING
WETTISH
WEVE
WEVED
WEVET
WEY
WEYNE
WHA
WHAAP
WHABBY
WHACK
WHACKED
WHACKER
WHACKING
WHACKY
WHADDIE
WHALE
WHALEBACK
WHALEBIRD
WHALEBOAT
WHALEBONE
WHALEBONED
WHALED
WHALEHEAD
WHALELIKE
WHALEMAN
WHALEMEN
WHALER
WHALERIES
WHALEROAD
WHALERS
WHALERY
WHALES
WHALESHIP
WHALING
WHALISH
WHALL
WHALLY
WHALM
WHALY
WHAM
WHAMBLE
WHAME
WHAMMED
WHAMMIES
WHAMMING
WHAMMY
WHAMP
WHAMPLE
WHANG
WHANGAM
WHANGDOODLE
WHANGEE
WHANK
WHAP
WHAPPER
WHAPPET
WHAPPING
WHAPUKA
WHAPUKEE
WHAPUKU
WHAR
WHARE
WHARF
WHARFAGE
WHARFED
WHARFHEAD
WHARFHOLDER
WHARFIE
WHARFING
WHARFINGER
WHARFLAND
WHARFMAN
WHARFMASTER
WHARFMEN
WHARFRAE
WHARFS
WHARFSIDE
WHARL
WHARP
WHARROW
WHART
WHARVE
WHARVES
WHAT
WHATA
WHATABOUTS
WHATE
WHATEVER
WHATKIN
WHATLIKE
WHATMAN
WHATNESS
WHATNOT
WHATRECK
WHATSO
WHATSOEVER
WHATTEN
WHAU
WHAUP
WHAUVE
WHAWL
WHEAL
WHEALED
WHEALING
WHEALWORM
WHEAM
WHEAT
WHEATBIRD
WHEATEAR
WHEATEARED
WHEATEN
WHEATGRASS
WHEATGROWER
WHEATLAND
WHEATLIKE
WHEATWORM
WHEATY
WHEE
WHEEDLE
WHEEDLED
WHEEDLER
WHEEDLING
WHEEDLINGLY
WHEEL
WHEELAGE
WHEELBAND
WHEELBARROW
WHEELBASE
WHEELBIRD
WHEELBOX
WHEELCHAIR
WHEELED
WHEELER
WHEELERY
WHEELHOUSE
WHEELING
WHEELINGLY
WHEELLESS
WHEELMAKER
WHEELMAKING
WHEELMAN
WHEELMEN
WHEELRACE
WHEELROAD
WHEELS
WHEELSMAN
WHEELSMEN
WHEELSMITH
WHEELSPIN
WHEELWAY
WHEELWORK
WHEELWRIGHT
WHEELY
WHEEN
WHEENCAT
WHEEP
WHEEPLE
WHEEPLED
WHEEPLING
WHEERIKINS
WHEESHT
WHEETLE
WHEEZE
WHEEZED
WHEEZER
WHEEZIER
WHEEZIEST
WHEEZILY
WHEEZINESS
WHEEZING
WHEEZINGLY
WHEEZLE
WHEEZY
WHEFT
WHEKAU
WHEKI
WHELK
WHELKED
WHELKER
WHELKIER
WHELKIEST
WHELKY
WHELM
WHELMED
WHELMING
WHELP
WHELPED
WHELPING
WHELPLESS
WHELPLING
WHELVE
WHEMMEL
WHEMMLE
WHEN
WHENABOUTS
WHENAS
WHENCE
WHENCEFORTH
WHENCESOEVER
WHENCEVER
WHENEVER
WHENNESS
WHENSO
WHENSOEVER
WHENSOMEVER
WHERE
WHEREABOUT
WHEREABOUTS
WHEREAFTER
WHEREANENT
WHEREAS
WHEREASES
WHEREAT
WHEREAWAY
WHEREBY
WHEREFOR
WHEREFORE
WHEREFORTH
WHEREFROM
WHEREHENCE
WHEREIN
WHEREINTO
WHERENESS
WHEREOF
WHEREON
WHEREOUT
WHEREOVER
WHERESO
WHERESOEVER
WHERESOMEVER
WHERETHROUGH
WHERETILL
WHERETO
WHERETOEVER
WHEREUNDER
WHEREUNTIL
WHEREUNTO
WHEREUP
WHEREUPON
WHEREVER
WHEREWITH
WHEREWITHAL
WHERRET
WHERRIED
WHERRIES
WHERRIT
WHERRY
WHERRYING
WHERRYMAN
WHERVE
WHET
WHETHER
WHETILE
WHETROCK
WHETSTONE
WHETTED
WHETTER
WHETTING
WHEW
WHEWELLITE
WHEWER
WHEWL
WHEWT
WHEY
WHEYBEARD
WHEYBIRD
WHEYEY
WHEYEYNESS
WHEYFACE
WHEYFACED
WHEYISH
WHEYISNESS
WHEYNESS
WHEYWORM
WHEYWORMED
WHI
WHIBA
WHICH
WHICHEVER
WHICHSOEVER
WHICHWAY
WHICHWAYS
WHICK
WHICKER
WHID
WHIDAH
WHIFF
WHIFFED
WHIFFER
WHIFFET
WHIFFING
WHIFFLE
WHIFFLED

WHIFFLER
WHIFFLERIES
WHIFFLERY
WHIFFLETREE
WHIFFLING
WHIFFLINGLY
WHIFFY
WHIFT
WHIG
WHIGMALEERIE
WHIGMALEERY
WHIGMELEERIE
WHILE
WHILEAS
WHILEEN
WHILEND
WHILES
WHILEY
WHILIE
WHILK
WHILLABALLOO
WHILLALOO
WHILLILEW
WHILLY
WHILLYWHA
WHILOCK
WHILOM
WHILST
WHILTER
WHIM
WHIMBREL
WHIMLING
WHIMMED
WHIMMIER
WHIMMIEST
WHIMMING
WHIMMY
WHIMPER
WHIMPERED
WHIMPERER
WHIMPERING
WHIMPERINGLY
WHIMSEY
WHIMSEYS
WHIMSIC
WHIMSICAL
WHIMSICALITY
WHIMSICALLY
WHIMSIED
WHIMSIES
WHIMSY
WHIMWHAM
WHIN
WHINBERRIES
WHINBERRY
WHINCHACKER
WHINCHAT
WHINCHECK
WHINCOW
WHINDLE
WHINE
WHINED
WHINER
WHINESTONE
WHING
WHINGE
WHINGER
WHINING
WHININGLY
WHINNEL
WHINNER
WHINNIED
WHINNIES
WHINNOCK
WHINNY
WHINNYING
WHINSTONE
WHINY
WHINYARD
WHIP
WHIPBELLY
WHIPBIRD
WHIPCAT
WHIPCORD
WHIPCORDY
WHIPCRACK
WHIPCRACKER
WHIPCRAFT
WHIPGRAFT
WHIPJACK
WHIPKING
WHIPLASH
WHIPMAKER
WHIPMAKING
WHIPMAN
WHIPMANSHIP
WHIPMASTER
WHIPPA
WHIPPABLE
WHIPPAREE
WHIPPED
WHIPPER
WHIPPERGINNY
WHIPPERSNAPPER
WHIPPERTAIL
WHIPPET
WHIPPETER
WHIPPING
WHIPPINGLY
WHIPPLETREE
WHIPPOORWILL
WHIPPOST
WHIPPY
WHIPS
WHIPSAW
WHIPSAWED
WHIPSAWING
WHIPSAWN
WHIPSAWYER
WHIPSOCKET
WHIPSTAFF
WHIPSTALK
WHIPSTALL
WHIPSTER
WHIPSTICK
WHIPSTITCH
WHIPSTOCK
WHIPT
WHIPTAIL
WHIPTREE
WHIPWORM
WHIR
WHIRL
WHIRLABOUT
WHIRLBAT
WHIRLBLAST
WHIRLBONE
WHIRLBRAIN
WHIRLED
WHIRLER
WHIRLGIG
WHIRLICANE
WHIRLICOTE
WHIRLIGIG
WHIRLING
WHIRLPOOL
WHIRLPUFF
WHIRLS
WHIRLWIG
WHIRLWIND
WHIRLWINDISH
WHIRLWINDY
WHIRLY
WHIRLYBIRD
WHIRR
WHIRRED
WHIRREY
WHIRRICK
WHIRRIED
WHIRRING
WHIRRY
WHIRRYING
WHIRTLE
WHISH
WHISHT
WHISK
WHISKBROOM
WHISKED
WHISKER
WHISKERAGE
WHISKERANDO
WHISKERANDOS
WHISKERED
WHISKERER
WHISKERS
WHISKERY
WHISKET
WHISKEY
WHISKEYS
WHISKIED
WHISKIES
WHISKIFIED
WHISKIN
WHISKING
WHISKINGLY
WHISKY
WHISP
WHISPER
WHISPERATION
WHISPERED
WHISPERER
WHISPERING
WHISPERINGLY
WHISPEROUS
WHISPEROUSLY
WHISPERY
WHISS
WHIST
WHISTER
WHISTERPOOP
WHISTLE
WHISTLEBELLY
WHISTLED
WHISTLEFISH
WHISTLEFISHES
WHISTLER
WHISTLERISM
WHISTLEWING
WHISTLEWOOD
WHISTLING
WHISTLINGLY
WHIT
WHITBLOW
WHITE
WHITEBAIT
WHITEBARK
WHITEBEAM
WHITEBEARD
WHITEBELLY
WHITEBERRY
WHITEBILL
WHITEBLAZE
WHITEBLOW
WHITEBOY
WHITECAP
WHITECAPPER
WHITECOAT
WHITECOMB
WHITECORN
WHITECUP
WHITED
WHITEFACE
WHITEFEET
WHITEFISH
WHITEFISHER
WHITEFISHERY
WHITEFISHES
WHITEFLY
WHITEFOOT
WHITEFOOTISM
WHITEHANDED
WHITEHASS
WHITEHAWSE
WHITEHEAD
WHITEHEARTED
WHITELIKE
WHITELY
WHITEN
WHITENED
WHITENER
WHITENESS
WHITENING
WHITENOSE
WHITEOUT
WHITEPOT
WHITER
WHITEROOT
WHITERUMP
WHITES
WHITESARK
WHITESHANK
WHITESIDE
WHITESMITH
WHITEST
WHITESTONE
WHITESTRAITS
WHITETAIL
WHITETHORN
WHITETHROAT
WHITETIP
WHITETOP
WHITEVEIN
WHITEVEINS
WHITEWALL
WHITEWARE
WHITEWASH
WHITEWASHED
WHITEWASHER
WHITEWASHING
WHITEWEED
WHITEWING
WHITEWOOD
WHITEWORT
WHITEY
WHITHER
WHITHERWARD
WHITHERWARDS
WHITING
WHITINGS
WHITISH
WHITISHNESS
WHITLEATHER
WHITLING
WHITLOW
WHITLOWWORT
WHITNEY
WHITNEYITE
WHITRACK
WHITS
WHITSTER
WHITTAW
WHITTAWER
WHITTEN
WHITTER
WHITTERICK
WHITTLE
WHITTLED
WHITTLER
WHITTLING
WHITTLINGS
WHITTRET
WHITY
WHIZ
WHIZBANG
WHIZGIG
WHIZZ
WHIZZED
WHIZZER
WHIZZERMAN
WHIZZES
WHIZZING
WHIZZINGLY
WHIZZLE
WHO
WHOA
WHODUNIT
WHOEVER
WHOLE
WHOLEHEARTED
WHOLENESS
WHOLESALE
WHOLESALED
WHOLESALER
WHOLESALING
WHOLESOME
WHOLESOMELY
WHOLESOMER
WHOLESOMEST
WHOLEWISE
WHOLLY
WHOM
WHOMP
WHOMSO
WHOMSOEVER
WHON
WHONE
WHOO
WHOOF
WHOOP
WHOOPE
WHOOPED
WHOOPEE
WHOOPER
WHOOPING
WHOOPINGLY
WHOOSH
WHOOT
WHOP
WHOPPED
WHOPPER
WHOPPING
WHORAGE
WHORE
WHORED
WHOREDOM
WHOREHOUSE
WHOREMASTER
WHOREMASTERY
WHOREMONGER
WHOREMONGING
WHORESON
WHORING
WHORISH
WHORISHLY
WHORISHNESS
WHORL
WHORLE
WHORLED
WHORLFLOWER
WHORLY
WHORLYWORT
WHORRY
WHORT
WHORTLE
WHORTLEBERRY

WHOSE
WHOSESOEVER
WHOSO
WHOSOEVER
WHUD
WHUFF
WHUFFLE
WHULE
WHULTER
WHUMP
WHUP
WHURL
WHUSH
WHUTE
WHUTTER
WHUTTERING
WHY
WHYDAH
WHYEVER
WHYFOR
WHYO
WIBBLE
WICH
WICHTISITE
WICHTJE
WICK
WICKAWEE
WICKED
WICKEDLY
WICKEDNESS
WICKEN
WICKER
WICKERWARE
WICKERWORK
WICKERWORKED
WICKERWORKER
WICKET
WICKETKEEPER
WICKETS
WICKING
WICKIUP
WICKY
WICOPIES
WICOPY
WID
WIDBIN
WIDDERSHINS
WIDDIES
WIDDIFOW
WIDDLE
WIDDLED
WIDDLING
WIDDRIM
WIDDY
WIDE
WIDEGAB
WIDEGAP
WIDEHEARTED
WIDELY
WIDEMOUTHED
WIDEN
WIDENED
WIDENER
WIDENESS
WIDENING
WIDER
WIDERSHINS
WIDESPREAD
WIDESPREADLY
WIDEST
WIDEWHERE
WIDEWORK
WIDGE
WIDGEON
WIDGEONS
WIDGET
WIDOW
WIDOWED
WIDOWER
WIDOWERED
WIDOWERY
WIDOWHOOD
WIDOWLY
WIDOWMAN
WIDOWMEN
WIDOWY
WIDTH
WIDTHLESS
WIDTHWAY
WIDTHWAYS
WIDTHWISE
WIDU
WIEL
WIELARE
WIELD
WIELDED
WIELDER
WIELDING
WIELDY
WIENER
WIENERWURST
WIENIE
WIES
WIFE
WIFECARL
WIFED
WIFEHOOD
WIFELESS
WIFELESSNESS
WIFELIER
WIFELIEST
WIFELY
WIFETHING
WIFEWARD
WIFING
WIFLE
WIFT
WIG
WIGAN
WIGELING
WIGEON
WIGG
WIGGED
WIGGEN
WIGGER
WIGGERIES
WIGGERY
WIGGING
WIGGISM
WIGGLE
WIGGLER
WIGGLY
WIGGY
WIGHER
WIGHT
WIGHTLY
WIGHTNESS
WIGMAKER
WIGMAKING
WIGTAIL
WIGWAG
WIGWAGGED
WIGWAGGER
WIGWAGGING
WIGWAM
WIIKITE
WIKE
WIKEN
WIKING
WIKIUP
WIKIWIKI
WILCWEME
WILD
WILDBORE
WILDCAT
WILDCATS
WILDCATTED
WILDCATTER
WILDCATTING
WILDE
WILDEBEEST
WILDED
WILDER
WILDERED
WILDERING
WILDERMENT
WILDERN
WILDERNESS
WILDEST
WILDFIRE
WILDFLOWER
WILDFOWL
WILDFOWLS
WILDGRAVE
WILDING
WILDISH
WILDISHLY
WILDISHNESS
WILDLIFE
WILDLING
WILDLY
WILDNESS
WILDWIND
WILDWOOD
WILE
WILED
WILFUL
WILFULLY
WILFULNESS
WILGA
WILGERS
WILIER
WILIEST
WILILY
WILINESS
WILING
WILIWILI
WILK
WILKEITE
WILL
WILLABLE
WILLAWA
WILLE
WILLED
WILLEDNESS
WILLEMITE
WILLER
WILLES
WILLET
WILLETS
WILLEY
WILLFUL
WILLFULLY
WILLFULNESS
WILLIAMSITE
WILLICHE
WILLIED
WILLIER
WILLIES
WILLIEWAUCHT
WILLING
WILLINGHOOD
WILLINGLY
WILLINGNESS
WILLIWAW
WILLMAKER
WILLMAKING
WILLNESS
WILLOCK
WILLOW
WILLOWBITER
WILLOWED
WILLOWER
WILLOWISH
WILLOWLIKE
WILLOWWARE
WILLOWWEED
WILLOWWORM
WILLOWWORT
WILLOWY
WILLY
WILLYARD
WILLYART
WILLYER
WILLYING
WILN
WILNE
WILNING
WILRONE
WILROUN
WILSOME
WILSOMELY
WILSOMENESS
WILT
WILTED
WILTER
WILTING
WILY
WILYCOAT
WIM
WIMBLE
WIMBLED
WIMBLING
WIMICK
WIMLUNGE
WIMPLE
WIMPLED
WIMPLER
WIMPLING
WIN
WINARE
WINBROW
WINCE
WINCED
WINCER
WINCEY
WINCH
WINCHER
WINCHMAN
WINCHMEN
WINCING
WINCOPIPE
WIND
WINDABLE
WINDAGE
WINDAS
WINDBAG
WINDBAGGED
WINDBAGGERY
WINDBALL
WINDBERRY
WINDBIBBER
WINDBRACING
WINDBREAK
WINDBREAKER
WINDBROACH
WINDBURN
WINDBURNED
WINDBURNT
WINDCLOTHES
WINDCUFFER
WINDDOG
WINDED
WINDEDLY
WINDEDNESS
WINDEL
WINDER
WINDFALL
WINDFALLEN
WINDFANNER
WINDFIRM
WINDFISH
WINDFISHES
WINDFLAW
WINDFLOWER
WINDGALL
WINDGALLED
WINDHOLE
WINDHOVER
WINDIER
WINDIEST
WINDIGO
WINDIGOS
WINDILL
WINDILY
WINDINESS
WINDING
WINDINGLY
WINDINGNESS
WINDJAM
WINDJAMMER
WINDJAMMING
WINDLASS
WINDLASSED
WINDLASSER
WINDLASSING
WINDLE
WINDLES
WINDLESS
WINDLESTRAE
WINDLESTRAW
WINDLIN
WINDLING
WINDMILL
WINDMILLY
WINDORE
WINDOW
WINDOWED
WINDOWING
WINDOWLIKE
WINDOWMAKER
WINDOWMAKING
WINDOWMAN
WINDOWPANE
WINDOWPEEPER
WINDOWS
WINDOWSILL
WINDOWY
WINDPIPE
WINDPROOF
WINDRING
WINDROAD
WINDROOT
WINDROW
WINDROWED
WINDROWER
WINDROWING
WINDS
WINDSAIL
WINDSCREEN
WINDSHAKE
WINDSHIELD
WINDSHOCK
WINDSLAB
WINDSOCK
WINDSORITE
WINDSTORM
WINDSUCKER
WINDTIGHT
WINDUP
WINDWARD
WINDWARDLY
WINDWARDNESS
WINDWAY
WINDWAYWARD

WINDY
WINE
WINEBALL
WINEBERRIES
WINEBERRY
WINEBIBBER
WINEBIBBERY
WINEBIBBING
WINECONNER
WINED
WINEDRAF
WINEGLASS
WINEGLASSFUL
WINEGLASSFULS
WINEGROWER
WINEGROWING
WINEHOUSE
WINELIKE
WINEMAY
WINEPOT
WINEPRESS
WINEPRESSER
WINER
WINERIES
WINERY
WINES
WINESHOP
WINESKIN
WINESOP
WINETASTER
WINETREE
WINEVAT
WINEYARD
WINFREE
WING
WINGBACK
WINGBEAT
WINGBOW
WINGCUT
WINGDING
WINGED
WINGER
WINGFISH
WINGFISHES
WINGHANDED
WINGIER
WINGIEST
WINGING
WINGLE
WINGLESS
WINGLESSNESS
WINGLET
WINGLIKE
WINGMAN
WINGMANSHIP
WINGOVER
WINGPIECE
WINGPOST
WINGS
WINGSEED
WINGSPREAD
WINGSTEM
WINGY
WINIER
WINIEST
WINISH
WINK
WINKED
WINKEL
WINKELMAN
WINKER
WINKERED
WINKERS
WINKING
WINKINGLY
WINKLE
WINKLEHAWK
WINKLEHOLE
WINKLOT
WINLY
WINNA
WINNABLE
WINNARD
WINNEL
WINNER
WINNING
WINNINGLY
WINNINGNESS
WINNINISH
WINNLE
WINNOCK
WINNONISH
WINNOW
WINNOWED
WINNOWER
WINNOWING
WINOES
WINOS
WINSOME
WINSOMELY
WINSOMENESS
WINSOMER
WINSOMEST
WINSTER
WINTER
WINTERBERRY
WINTERBLOOM
WINTERBOURNE
WINTERDYKES
WINTERED
WINTERER
WINTERFEED
WINTERGREEN
WINTERHAIN
WINTERING
WINTERIZE
WINTERIZED
WINTERIZING
WINTERKILL
WINTERKILLED
WINTERLESS
WINTERLIKE
WINTERLINESS
WINTERLY
WINTERTIDE
WINTERTIME
WINTERWEED
WINTERY
WINTLE
WINTRIER
WINTRIEST
WINTRIFY
WINTRILY
WINTRINESS
WINTRY
WINY
WINZE
WINZEMAN
WINZEMEN
WIO
WIP
WIPE
WIPED
WIPER
WIPING
WIPPEN
WIR
WIRABLE
WIRBLE
WIRE
WIREBAR
WIREBIRD
WIRED
WIREDANCER
WIREDANCING
WIREDRAW
WIREDRAWER
WIREDRAWING
WIREDRAWN
WIREDREW
WIREGRASS
WIREHAIR
WIRELESS
WIRELESSLY
WIRELESSNESS
WIREMAKER
WIREMAKING
WIREMAN
WIREMEN
WIREMONGER
WIREPHOTO
WIREPULL
WIREPULLER
WIREPULLING
WIRER
WIRES
WIRESMITH
WIRESPUN
WIRESTITCHED
WIRETAIL
WIRETAP
WIRETAPPED
WIRETAPPER
WIRETAPPING
WIREWALKER
WIREWAY
WIREWEED
WIREWORK
WIREWORKER
WIREWORKING
WIREWORKS
WIREWORM
WIRIER
WIRIEST
WIRILY
WIRINESS
WIRING
WIRL
WIRLING
WIRR
WIRRA
WIRRAH
WIRRASTHRU
WIRTH
WIRY
WIS
WISDOM
WISE
WISEACRE
WISEACRED
WISECRACK
WISECRACKER
WISECRACKERY
WISEHEAD
WISEHEARTED
WISEHEIMER
WISELIER
WISELIEST
WISELIKE
WISELING
WISELY
WISEMAN
WISEN
WISENESS
WISENHEIMER
WISENT
WISER
WISEST
WISEWEED
WISEWOMAN
WISEWOMEN
WISH
WISHA
WISHBONE
WISHED
WISHEDLY
WISHER
WISHFUL
WISHFULLY
WISHFULNESS
WISHING
WISHINGLY
WISHLY
WISHMAY
WISHNESS
WISHT
WISHTONWISH
WISKET
WISKINKIE
WISKINKY
WISMUTH
WISP
WISPED
WISPIER
WISPIEST
WISPING
WISPISH
WISPY
WISS
WISSE
WISSEL
WISSHE
WISSING
WISSLE
WIST
WISTED
WISTENED
WISTER
WISTERIA
WISTFUL
WISTFULLY
WISTFULNESS
WISTING
WISTIT
WISTITI
WISTLESS
WISTLESSNESS
WISURE
WIT
WITAN
WITCH
WITCHBELLS
WITCHBROOM
WITCHCRAFT
WITCHED
WITCHEDLY
WITCHEN
WITCHERCULLY
WITCHERIES
WITCHERING
WITCHERY
WITCHET
WITCHETTY
WITCHGRASS
WITCHING
WITCHINGLY
WITCHLEAF
WITCHMAN
WITCHMONGER
WITCHUCK
WITCHWEED
WITCHWIFE
WITCHWOMAN
WITCHWOOD
WITCHWORK
WITCHY
WITCRAFT
WITE
WITELESS
WITENAGEMOT
WITENAGEMOTE
WITEPENNY
WITESS
WITFUL
WITH
WITHAL
WITHAM
WITHAMITE
WITHBEG
WITHCALL
WITHDRAUGHT
WITHDRAW
WITHDRAWAL
WITHDRAWER
WITHDRAWING
WITHDRAWMENT
WITHDRAWN
WITHDREW
WITHE
WITHED
WITHEN
WITHER
WITHERBAND
WITHERBLENCH
WITHERCRAFT
WITHERDEED
WITHERED
WITHEREDLY
WITHEREDNESS
WITHERER
WITHERING
WITHERINGLY
WITHERITE
WITHERLING
WITHERLY
WITHERNAM
WITHERS
WITHERSHINS
WITHERTIP
WITHERWEIGHT
WITHERY
WITHGANG
WITHGATE
WITHHELD
WITHHELE
WITHHIE
WITHHOLD
WITHHOLDAL
WITHHOLDEN
WITHHOLDER
WITHHOLDING
WITHHOLDMENT
WITHIES
WITHIN
WITHINDOORS
WITHINFORTH
WITHING
WITHINWARD
WITHINWARDS
WITHNAY
WITHNESS
WITHNIM
WITHOUT
WITHOUTDOORS
WITHOUTEN
WITHOUTFORTH
WITHOUTSIDE
WITHOUTWARDS
WITHSAVE
WITHSAW
WITHSAY
WITHSAYER
WITHSET
WITHSLIP
WITHSPAR

WITHSTAND
WITHSTANDER
WITHSTANDING
WITHSTAY
WITHSTOOD
WITHSTRAIN
WITHTAKE
WITHTEE
WITHTURN
WITHVINE
WITHY
WITHYPOT
WITHYWIND
WITIE
WITJAR
WITLESS
WITLESSLY
WITLESSNESS
WITLET
WITLING
WITLOOF
WITLOSEN
WITMONGER
WITNESS
WITNESSED
WITNESSER
WITNESSING
WITNEY
WITNEYER
WITS
WITSAFE
WITSHIP
WITTALL
WITTED
WITTEN
WITTER
WITTERING
WITTERLY
WITTERNESS
WITTICASTER
WITTICHENITE
WITTICISM
WITTICIZE
WITTIER
WITTIEST
WITTIFIED
WITTILY
WITTINESS
WITTING
WITTINGLY
WITTOL
WITTOME
WITTY
WITWALL
WITWANTON
WITWORD
WITWORM
WITZCHOURA
WIVE
WIVED
WIVER
WIVERN
WIVES
WIVING
WIWI
WIZ
WIZARD
WIZARDLY
WIZARDRY
WIZEN
WIZENED
WIZENEDNESS
WIZZEN
WLACH
WLAFF
WLANK
WLATE
WLATFUL
WLATSOME
WLECCHE
WLECH
WLENCH
WLITE
WLITY
WLO
WLOKA
WLONK
WLONKHEDE
WO
WOAD
WOADED
WOADER
WOADMAN
WOADWAXEN
WOALD
WOB
WOBBEGONG
WOBBLE
WOBBLED
WOBBLER
WOBBLIES
WOBBLINESS
WOBBLING
WOBBLINGLY
WOBBLY
WOBEGONE
WOBEGONENESS
WOBEGONISH
WOBSTER
WOCAS
WOCHEINITE
WOD
WODE
WODELEIE
WODGE
WODGY
WOE
WOEBEGONE
WOEBEGONISH
WOEFARE
WOEFUL
WOEFULLY
WOEFULNESS
WOEHLERITE
WOESOME
WOEVINE
WOEWORN
WOFFLER
WOFUL
WOFULLY
WOFULNESS
WOG
WOGE
WOGGLE
WOGH
WOGHE
WOGHNESS
WOGIET
WOHLAC
WOHLERITE
WOIBE
WOID
WOIDRE
WOIK
WOILIE
WOK
WOKAS
WOKE
WOKEN
WOKIE
WOKOWI
WOLD
WOLDES
WOLDSMAN
WOLDY
WOLE
WOLEAI
WOLF
WOLFACHITE
WOLFBERRIES
WOLFBERRY
WOLFED
WOLFEN
WOLFER
WOLFFISH
WOLFHOUND
WOLFING
WOLFISH
WOLFISHLY
WOLFISHNESS
WOLFKIN
WOLFLIKE
WOLFLING
WOLFRAM
WOLFRAMITE
WOLFRAMIUM
WOLFSBANE
WOLFSBERGITE
WOLFSKIN
WOLLASTONITE
WOLLOCK
WOLLOMAI
WOLVE
WOLVEBOON
WOLVER
WOLVERENE
WOLVERINE
WOLVERINES
WOLVES
WOMAN
WOMANBODIES
WOMANBODY
WOMANED
WOMANFOLK
WOMANFULLY
WOMANHEAD
WOMANHEARTED
WOMANHOOD
WOMANHOUSE
WOMANING
WOMANISH
WOMANISHLY
WOMANISM
WOMANIST
WOMANITY
WOMANIZE
WOMANIZED
WOMANIZER
WOMANIZING
WOMANKIND
WOMANLIER
WOMANLIEST
WOMANLIKE
WOMANLINESS
WOMANLY
WOMANMUCKLE
WOMANPOST
WOMB
WOMBAT
WOMBED
WOMBSIDE
WOMBSTONE
WOMBY
WOMEN
WOMENFOLK
WOMENFOLKS
WOMERA
WOMERAH
WOMMALA
WOMMERA
WOMMERAH
WOMP
WOMPLIT
WON
WOND
WONDE
WONDER
WONDERBERRY
WONDERDEED
WONDERED
WONDERER
WONDERFUL
WONDERFULLER
WONDERFULLY
WONDERING
WONDERINGLY
WONDERLAND
WONDERMENT
WONDERSMITH
WONDERSOME
WONDERWORK
WONDERWORTHY
WONDIE
WONDROUS
WONDROUSLY
WONDROUSNESS
WONE
WONG
WONGA
WONGAH
WONGSHY
WONGSKY
WONING
WONKIER
WONKIEST
WONKY
WONNA
WONNED
WONNER
WONNING
WONNOT
WONT
WONTED
WONTEDLY
WONTEDNESS
WONTING
WONTLESS
WOO
WOOABLE
WOOD
WOODBARK
WOODBIN
WOODBIND
WOODBINE
WOODBINED
WOODBLOCK
WOODBORER
WOODBOUND
WOODBUSH
WOODCARVER
WOODCARVING
WOODCHAT
WOODCHUCK
WOODCOCK
WOODCOCKIZE
WOODCOCKS
WOODCRACKER
WOODCRAFT
WOODCRAFTER
WOODCRAFTY
WOODCUT
WOODCUTTER
WOODCUTTING
WOODED
WOODEN
WOODENDITE
WOODENHEAD
WOODENHEADED
WOODENLY
WOODENNESS
WOODENWARE
WOODENWEARY
WOODFALL
WOODFISH
WOODGELD
WOODGRUB
WOODHACK
WOODHACKER
WOODHEN
WOODHEWER
WOODHOLE
WOODHORSE
WOODHOUSE
WOODHUNG
WOODIE
WOODIER
WOODIEST
WOODINE
WOODINESS
WOODING
WOODISH
WOODJOBBER
WOODKERN
WOODKNACKER
WOODLAND
WOODLANDER
WOODLARK
WOODLESS
WOODLIND
WOODLOCKED
WOODMAID
WOODMAN
WOODMANCRAFT
WOODMANSHIP
WOODMEN
WOODMONGER
WOODMOTE
WOODNESS
WOODNOTE
WOODPECK
WOODPECKER
WOODPECKERS
WOODPENNY
WOODPILE
WOODPRINT
WOODREED
WOODREEVE
WOODRICK
WOODRIME
WOODRIS
WOODROCK
WOODROW
WOODRUFF
WOODS
WOODSCREW
WOODSERE
WOODSHED
WOODSHIP
WOODSHOP
WOODSIDE
WOODSIER
WOODSIEST
WOODSILVER
WOODSKIN
WOODSMAN
WOODSMEN
WOODSPITE
WOODSTONE
WOODSY
WOODTURNER
WOODTURNING
WOODWALE
WOODWALL
WOODWARD
WOODWAX

WOODWAXEN
WOODWIND
WOODWINDS
WOODWISE
WOODWORK
WOODWORKER
WOODWORKING
WOODWORM
WOODWOSE
WOODY
WOODYARD
WOOED
WOOER
WOOF
WOOFED
WOOFELL
WOOFER
WOOFY
WOOHOO
WOOING
WOOINGLY
WOOL
WOOLD
WOOLDED
WOOLDER
WOOLDING
WOOLED
WOOLEN
WOOLENET
WOOLENETTE
WOOLENIZE
WOOLER
WOOLERT
WOOLFELL
WOOLGATHERER
WOOLGROWER
WOOLGROWING
WOOLHEAD
WOOLIE
WOOLLED
WOOLLEN
WOOLLENIZE
WOOLLENS
WOOLLIER
WOOLLIES
WOOLLIEST
WOOLLINESS
WOOLLY
WOOLLYHEAD
WOOLLYISH
WOOLMAN
WOOLMEN
WOOLPACK
WOOLPRESS
WOOLSACK
WOOLSEY
WOOLSHEARER
WOOLSHEARING
WOOLSHEARS
WOOLSHED
WOOLSKIN
WOOLSORTER
WOOLSORTING
WOOLSOWER
WOOLSTOCK
WOOLULOSE
WOOLWASHER
WOOLWEED
WOOLWHEEL
WOOLWINDER
WOOLWORK
WOOLWORKER
WOOLWORKING
WOOLY
WOOM
WOOMERA
WOOMERAH
WOOMERANG
WOON
WOONE
WOONS
WOORALI
WOORARI
WOOSH
WOOSTER
WOOT
WOOTZ
WOOZIER
WOOZIEST
WOOZILY
WOOZINESS
WOOZLE
WOOZY
WOP
WOPPISH
WOPS
WOPSE
WOPSY
WOPY
WORBLE
WORCESTER
WORD
WORDABLE
WORDABLY
WORDAGE
WORDBOOK
WORDBUILDING
WORDCRAFT
WORDED
WORDER
WORDIER
WORDIEST
WORDILY
WORDINESS
WORDING
WORDISH
WORDISHLY
WORDISHNESS
WORDLE
WORDLESS
WORDLESSLY
WORDLESSNESS
WORDLIER
WORDLORIST
WORDMAKER
WORDMAKING
WORDMAN
WORDMANSHIP
WORDMEN
WORDMONGER
WORDMONGERY
WORDNESS
WORDPLAY
WORDS
WORDSMAN
WORDSMANSHIP
WORDSMEN
WORDSMITH
WORDSPITE
WORDSTER
WORDY
WORE
WORK
WORKABILITY
WORKABLE
WORKABLENESS
WORKADAY
WORKAWAY
WORKBAG
WORKBASKET
WORKBENCH
WORKBOOK
WORKBOX
WORKBRITTLE
WORKDAY
WORKED
WORKER
WORKFELLOW
WORKFOLK
WORKFOLKS
WORKFUL
WORKGIRL
WORKHAND
WORKHORSE
WORKHOUSE
WORKHOUSED
WORKING
WORKINGLY
WORKINGMAN
WORKINGMEN
WORKINGWOMAN
WORKLESS
WORKLESSNESS
WORKLOAD
WORKLOOM
WORKMAN
WORKMANLIKE
WORKMANLY
WORKMANSHIP
WORKMASTER
WORKMEN
WORKOUT
WORKPEOPLE
WORKPIECE
WORKPLACE
WORKROOM
WORKS
WORKSHEET
WORKSHIP
WORKSHOP
WORKSOME
WORKSTAND
WORKTABLE
WORKTIME
WORKWAYS
WORKWISE
WORKWOMAN
WORKWOMANLY
WORKWOMEN
WORKY
WORKYARD
WORLD
WORLDAUGHT
WORLDED
WORLDISH
WORLDLIEST
WORLDLINESS
WORLDLING
WORLDLY
WORLDMAKER
WORLDMAKING
WORLDMAN
WORLDPROOF
WORLDQUAKE
WORLDS
WORLDWAY
WORLDWIDE
WORM
WORMED
WORMER
WORMHOLE
WORMHOLED
WORMIER
WORMIEST
WORMIL
WORMINESS
WORMING
WORMLIKE
WORMLING
WORMROOT
WORMS
WORMSEED
WORMWEED
WORMWOOD
WORMY
WORN
WORNNESS
WORRAL
WORREL
WORRIABLE
WORRICOW
WORRIECOW
WORRIED
WORRIEDLY
WORRIEDNESS
WORRIER
WORRIES
WORRIMENT
WORRISOME
WORRISOMELY
WORRIT
WORRITER
WORRY
WORRYING
WORRYINGLY
WORRYWART
WORSE
WORSEMENT
WORSEN
WORSENED
WORSENESS
WORSENING
WORSER
WORSET
WORSHIP
WORSHIPED
WORSHIPER
WORSHIPERS
WORSHIPFUL
WORSHIPFULLY
WORSHIPING
WORSHIPPED
WORSHIPPER
WORSHIPPING
WORST
WORSTED
WORSTING
WORSUM
WORT
WORTH
WORTHFUL
WORTHIER
WORTHIES
WORTHIEST
WORTHILY
WORTHINESS
WORTHING
WORTHLESS
WORTHLESSLY
WORTHLESSNESS
WORTHWHILE
WORTHY
WORTS
WORTWORM
WORY
WOSBIRD
WOSITH
WOSOME
WOST
WOT
WOTH
WOTLINK
WOTTE
WOU
WOUBIT
WOUGH
WOUHLECHE
WOULD
WOULDEST
WOULDING
WOULDST
WOUND
WOUNDED
WOUNDEDLY
WOUNDER
WOUNDILY
WOUNDING
WOUNDINGLY
WOUNDLESS
WOUNDLY
WOUNDS
WOUNDWORT
WOUNDWORTH
WOUNDY
WOURNIL
WOUSTOUR
WOVE
WOVEN
WOW
WOWENING
WOWER
WOWF
WOWL
WOWSER
WOWSERIAN
WOWSERISH
WOWSERISM
WOWSERY
WOWT
WOX
WOXE
WRABBE
WRABILL
WRACK
WRACKFUL
WRAGER
WRAGGLE
WRAIST
WRAITH
WRAITHE
WRAITHY
WRAKE
WRAKER
WRALL
WRAMP
WRANG
WRANGLE
WRANGLED
WRANGLER
WRANGLESOME
WRANGLING
WRANNOCK
WRANNY
WRAP
WRAPAROUND
WRAPLE
WRAPPAGE
WRAPPED
WRAPPER
WRAPPERER
WRAPPERING
WRAPPING
WRAPRASCAL
WRAPS
WRAPT
WRASE
WRASSE
WRAST
WRASTLE
WRASTLER
WRAT
WRATACK
WRATE
WRATH
WRATHFUL

WRATHFULLY
WRATHFULNESS
WRATHIER
WRATHIEST
WRATHILY
WRATHINESS
WRATHY
WRAW
WRAWL
WRAWLER
WRAXLE
WRAXLED
WRAXLING
WRAY
WRAYFUL
WREAK
WREAKED
WREAKER
WREAKFUL
WREAKING
WREAKLESS
WREATH
WREATHAGE
WREATHE
WREATHED
WREATHEN
WREATHER
WREATHING
WREATHMAKER
WREATHMAKING
WREATHS
WREATHWORK
WREATHWORT
WREATHY
WRECK
WRECKAGE
WRECKED
WRECKER
WRECKFISH
WRECKFISHES
WRECKFUL
WRECKING
WRECKY
WREIL
WRELE
WREN
WRENCH
WRENCHED
WRENCHER
WRENCHING
WRENCHINGLY
WRENLET
WRENTAIL
WREST
WRESTED
WRESTER
WRESTING
WRESTINGLY
WRESTLE
WRESTLED
WRESTLER
WRESTLING
WRETCH
WRETCHED
WRETCHEDLY
WRETCHEDNESS
WRETCHLESS
WRETCHLESSLY
WRETCHOCK
WRIBLE
WRICK
WRIDE
WRIED
WRIEL
WRIER
WRIEST
WRIG
WRIGGLE
WRIGGLED
WRIGGLER
WRIGGLESOME
WRIGGLING
WRIGGLY
WRIGHT
WRIGHTRY
WRIHTE
WRIMPLE
WRINE
WRING
WRINGBOLT
WRINGED
WRINGER
WRINGING
WRINGLE
WRINGSTAFF
WRINGSTAVES
WRINK
WRINKLE
WRINKLED
WRINKLEDY
WRINKLEFUL
WRINKLES
WRINKLET
WRINKLIER
WRINKLIEST
WRINKLING
WRINKLY
WRIST
WRISTBAND
WRISTBONE
WRISTED
WRISTER
WRISTFALL
WRISTIKIN
WRISTLET
WRISTLOCK
WRISTS
WRISTWATCH
WRISTWORK
WRIT
WRITABILITY
WRITABLE
WRITATION
WRITATIVE
WRITE
WRITEABLE
WRITEE
WRITER
WRITHE
WRITHED
WRITHEDLY
WRITHEDNESS
WRITHEN
WRITHENECK
WRITHER
WRITHING
WRITHINGLY
WRITHLED
WRITHY
WRITING
WRITINGER
WRITINGS
WRITTEN
WRITTER
WRIXLE
WRIZZLED
WRO
WROIK
WRONG
WRONGDOER
WRONGDOING
WRONGED
WRONGER
WRONGFUL
WRONGFULLY
WRONGFULNESS
WRONGHEAD
WRONGHEADED
WRONGHEARTED
WRONGING
WRONGLESS
WRONGLESSLY
WRONGLY
WRONGNESS
WRONGOUS
WRONGOUSLY
WRONGOUSNESS
WROOT
WROT
WROTE
WROTH
WROTHE
WROTHFUL
WROTHLY
WROTHSOME
WROUGHT
WROX
WRUNG
WRUNGNESS
WRY
WRYBILL
WRYER
WRYEST
WRYING
WRYLY
WRYMOUTH
WRYNECK
WRYNECKED
WRYNESS
WUD
WUDDIE
WUDGE
WUDU
WUGG
WULDER
WULFENITE
WUMMEL
WUN
WUND
WUNGEE
WUNNA
WUNTEE
WURD
WURLEY
WURLEYS
WURLIES
WURLY
WURP
WURRALUH
WURRUNG
WURRUP
WURRUS
WURST
WURTH
WURTZITE
WUSP
WUTHER
WUTHERING
WUYEN
WUZ
WUZU
WUZZER
WUZZLE
WUZZLED
WUZZLING
WY
WYCH
WYDE
WYE
WYES
WYF
WYLE
WYLED
WYLIECOAT
WYLING
WYLW
WYME
WYMOTE
WYN
WYND
WYNE
WYNKERNEL
WYNN
WYNRIS
WYPE
WYRE
WYROCK
WYROK
WYS
WYSTY
WYTHE

XALLE
XANTHALINE
XANTHAMID
XANTHAMIDE
XANTHANE
XANTHATE
XANTHATION
XANTHEIN
XANTHELASMA
XANTHENE
XANTHIC
XANTHID
XANTHIDE
XANTHIN
XANTHINE
XANTHINURIA
XANTHIONE
XANTHITE
XANTHIURIA
XANTHOCHROIA
XANTHOCHROID
XANTHOCONE
XANTHOCONITE
XANTHODERM
XANTHODERMA
XANTHOGEN
XANTHOGENATE
XANTHOGENIC
XANTHOMA
XANTHOMAS
XANTHOMATA
XANTHOMATOUS
XANTHOMETER
XANTHONE
XANTHOPHANE
XANTHOPHORE
XANTHOPHYL
XANTHOPHYLL
XANTHOPIA
XANTHOPSIA
XANTHOPSIN
XANTHOPTERIN
XANTHOSIS
XANTHOUS
XANTHOXENITE
XANTHOXYLIN
XANTHURIA
XANTHYDROL
XANTHYL
XARQUE
XAT
XEBEC
XEME
XENACANTHINE
XENAGOGUE
XENAGOGY
XENARTHRAL
XENARTHROUS
XENELASIA
XENELASY
XENIA
XENIAL
XENIAN
XENIUM
XENOBIOSIS
XENOBLAST
XENOCYST
XENODERM
XENODOCHIUM
XENODOCHY
XENOGAMOUS
XENOGAMY
XENOGENESIS
XENOGENOUS
XENOLITE
XENOLITH
XENOMANIA
XENOMORPHIC
XENON
XENOPARASITE
XENOPELTID
XENOPHOBE
XENOPHOBIA
XENOPHOBIC
XENOPHYA
XENOPODID
XENOPODOID
XENOPTERAN
XENOSAURID
XENOSAUROID
XENOTIME
XENYL
XENYLAMINE
XERAFIN
XERANSIS
XERANTIC
XERAPHIN
XERARCH
XERASIA
XERIC
XERIF
XERIFF
XERODERMA
XEROGRAPHER
XEROGRAPHIC
XEROGRAPHY
XEROMA
XEROMORPH
XEROMORPHIC
XEROMORPHOUS
XEROMORPHY
XEROMYRON
XERONATE
XERONIC
XEROPHAGY
XEROPHIL
XEROPHILE
XEROPHILOUS
XEROPHILY
XEROPHOBOUS
XEROPHYTE
XEROPHYTIC
XEROPHYTISM
XEROSERE
XEROSIS
XEROSTOMA
XEROTES
XEROTHERM
XEROTIC
XEROTRIPSIS
XEROX
XIBALBA
XIFOID
XIPHIIFORM
XIPHIOID
XIPHISTERNAL
XIPHISTERNUM
XIPHOCOSTAL
XIPHODYNIA
XIPHOID
XIPHOIDAL
XIPHOIDIAN
XIPHOPAGIC
XIPHOPAGOUS
XIPHOPAGUS
XIPHOSURAN
XIPHOSURE
XIPHOSUROUS
XIPHYDRIID
XOANA
XOANON
XUREL
XYLAN
XYLANTHRAX
XYLATE
XYLEM
XYLENE
XYLENOL
XYLENYL
XYLIC
XYLIDIN
XYLIDINE
XYLINDEIN
XYLITE
XYLITOL
XYLITONE
XYLOCARP
XYLOCARPOUS
XYLOCOPID
XYLOGEN
XYLOGLYPHY
XYLOGRAPH
XYLOGRAPHER
XYLOGRAPHIC
XYLOGRAPHY
XYLOID
XYLOIDIN
XYLOIDINE
XYLOL
XYLOLOGY
XYLOMA
XYLOMANCY
XYLOMAS
XYLOMATA
XYLOMETER
XYLON
XYLOPHAGAN
XYLOPHAGE
XYLOPHAGID
XYLOPHAGOUS
XYLOPHILOUS
XYLOPHONE
XYLOPHONIC
XYLOPHONIST
XYLOPLASTIC
XYLOPOLIST
XYLOQUINONE
XYLORCIN
XYLORCINOL
XYLOSE
XYLOSID
XYLOSIDE
XYLOSTROMA
XYLOSTROMATA
XYLOTILE
XYLOTOMIST
XYLOTOMOUS
XYLOTOMY
XYLOYL
XYLYL
XYLYLENE
XYRID
XYRIDACEOUS
XYST
XYSTA
XYSTER
XYSTUS

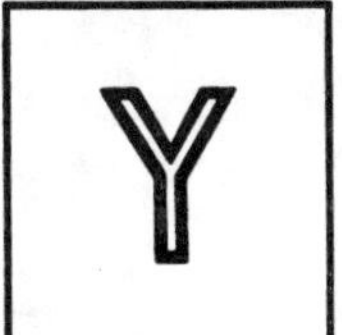

YA
YABBER
YABBI
YABBIE
YABBLE
YABBY
YABOA
YABOO
YABU
YACAL
YACARE
YACATA
YACCA
YACH
YACHAN
YACHT
YACHTER
YACHTING
YACHTIST
YACHTMAN
YACHTSMAN
YACHTSMEN
YACHTY
YAD
YADAYIM
YADE
YAE
YAF
YAFE
YAFF
YAFFIL
YAFFLE
YAFFLER
YAGER
YAGUA
YAGUARUNDI
YAGUAS
YAGUAZA
YAH
YAHAN
YAHOO
YAHRZEIT
YAIR
YAIRD
YAJE
YAJEIN
YAJEINE
YAJENIN
YAJENINE
YAJNOPAVITA
YAK
YAKALO
YAKAMIK
YAKATTALO
YAKIN
YAKKA
YAKMAK
YAKS
YAKSA
YAKSHA
YAKSHI
YAL
YALD
YALI
YALLOCK
YAM
YAMAMAI
YAMASKITE
YAMEN
YAMILKE
YAMMADJI
YAMMER
YAMMERLY
YAMP
YAMPEE
YAMPH
YAMSHIK
YAMSTCHIK
YAN
YANACONA
YANCE
YANE
YANG
YANGGONA
YANGTAO
YANK
YANKED
YANKER
YANKING
YANKY
YANNAM
YANOLITE
YANQUI
YANTRA
YAP
YAPA
YAPNESS
YAPOCK
YAPOK
YAPON
YAPP
YAPPED
YAPPER
YAPPINESS
YAPPING
YAPPINGLY
YAPPISH
YAPPY
YAPSTER
YAQONA
YAR
YARAGE
YARAK
YARAY
YARB
YARD
YARDAGE
YARDANG
YARDARM
YARDBIRD
YARDED
YARDER
YARDGRASS
YARDING
YARDKEEP
YARDLAND
YARDMAN
YARDMASTER
YARDMEN
YARDS
YARDSMAN
YARDSTICK
YARDWAND
YARE
YARELY
YARETA
YARIYARI
YARK
YARKE
YARKEE
YARM
YARMULKE
YARN
YARNEN
YARNER
YARNS
YARNWINDLE
YAROVIZE
YARPHA
YARR
YARRAMAN
YARRAN
YARROW
YARRY
YARTHEN
YARWHELP
YARWHIP
YAS
YASHIRO
YASHMAC
YASHMAK
YAT
YATAGAN
YATAGHAN
YATALITE
YATCH
YATE
YATI
YATTER
YAUD
YAULD
YAUP
YAUPER
YAUPON
YAUTIA
YAVA
YAW
YAWD
YAWED
YAWING
YAWL
YAWLER
YAWMETER
YAWN
YAWNED
YAWNER
YAWNILY
YAWNINESS
YAWNING
YAWNINGLY
YAWNY
YAWP
YAWPER
YAWROOT
YAWS
YAWSHRUB
YAWWEED
YAWY
YAXCHE
YAY
YAYA
YCIE
YCLEPED
YCLEPT
YDRIADES
YE
YEA
YEAD
YEAGHE
YEAH
YEALING
YEAN
YEANED
YEANING
YEANLING
YEAR
YEARA
YEARBIRD
YEARBOOK
YEARDAY
YEARED
YEARLING
YEARLONG
YEARLY
YEARN
YEARNED
YEARNFUL
YEARNFULLY
YEARNFULNESS
YEARNING
YEARNINGLY
YEARNINGS
YEARNLING
YEAROCK
YEARS
YEAST
YEASTIER
YEASTIEST
YEASTING
YEASTY
YEAT
YED
YEDDA
YEDDE
YEDDING
YEDE
YEDER
YEDERLY
YEELIN
YEGG
YEGGMAN
YEGUITA
YEILD
YEKE
YELD
YELDE
YELDRIN
YELDRINE
YELDRING
YELDROCK
YELK
YELL
YELLED
YELLER
YELLING
YELLOCH
YELLOW
YELLOWBACK
YELLOWBARK
YELLOWBELLY
YELLOWBERRIES
YELLOWBERRY
YELLOWBILL
YELLOWBIRD
YELLOWER
YELLOWEST
YELLOWFIN
YELLOWFISH
YELLOWHAMMER
YELLOWHEAD
YELLOWISH
YELLOWLEGS
YELLOWLY
YELLOWMAN
YELLOWNESS
YELLOWROOT
YELLOWS
YELLOWSEED
YELLOWSHANK
YELLOWSHANKS
YELLOWSHINS
YELLOWTAIL
YELLOWTAILS
YELLOWTHROAT
YELLOWTOP
YELLOWWARE
YELLOWWEED
YELLOWWOOD
YELLOWWORT
YELLOWY
YELM
YELMER
YELP
YELPED
YELPER
YELPING
YELVER
YELWE
YEME
YEMELESS
YEMER
YEMING
YEMSCHIK
YEMSEL
YEN
YEND
YENI
YENITE
YENNED
YENNING
YENTNITE
YEOMAN
YEOMANLY
YEOMANRY
YEOMEN
YEORLING
YEOWOMAN
YEOWOMEN
YEP
YEPE
YEPELEIC
YEPELY
YEPHEDE
YEPLY
YER
YERBA
YERBAL
YERBALES
YERCUM
YERGA
YERK
YERN
YERNE
YERRA
YERTCHUK
YES
YESES
YESO
YESSO
YESTER
YESTERDAY
YESTEREVE
YESTEREVEN
YESTERMORN
YESTERN
YESTERNIGHT
YESTERNOON
YESTERWEEK
YESTERYEAR
YESTREEN
YET
YETAPA
YETER
YETH
YETHHOUNDS
YETI
YETLIN
YETLING
YETT
YETTE
YETTER
YETZER
YEUK
YEUKIENESS
YEUKY

YEW
YEWEN
YEWK
YEX
YEZ
YEZZY
YFACKS
YFERRE
YGOE
YGONE
YHTE
YIELD
YIELDANCE
YIELDED
YIELDER
YIELDING
YIELDINGLY
YIGH
YILL
YILT
YIN
YINCE
YIP
YIPE
YIPPIE
YIRD
YIRM
YIRMILIK
YIRN
YIRR
YIS
YISSE
YISSER
YISSING
YIT
YITE
YIVER
YIVERLY
YIVERNESS
YIZKOR
YLAHAYLL
YLE
YLEM
YLESPIL
YLICHE
YMAGE
YMMOTE
YMPET
YMPNE
YMUR
YNAMBU
YNGOODLY
YNKELL
YNPRIDID
YO
YOB
YOBI
YOCCO
YOCKEL
YOCKERNUT
YOD
YODEL
YODELED
YODELER
YODELING
YODELIST
YODELLED
YODELLER
YODELLING
YODH
YODLE
YODLED
YODLER
YOE
YOGA
YOGH
YOGHOURT
YOGHURT
YOGI
YOGIN
YOGISM
YOGIST
YOGOITE
YOGURT
YOHIMBI
YOHIMBIN
YOHIMBINE
YOHO
YOHOURT
YOICK
YOICKS
YOJAN
YOJANA
YOK
YOKAGE
YOKE
YOKEAGE
YOKED
YOKEFELLOW
YOKEL
YOKELESS
YOKELISH
YOKELRY
YOKEMATE
YOKEMATING
YOKER
YOKEWOOD
YOKING
YOKY
YOLDRING
YOLE
YOLK
YOLKED
YOLKIER
YOLKIEST
YOLKY
YOLL
YOLPE
YOM
YOMER
YON
YONCOPIN
YOND
YONDER
YONDWARD
YONGE
YONI
YONKER
YONSIDE
YOOP
YORA
YORE
YORETIME
YORK
YORKER
YORLIN
YOT
YOTACISM
YOTACIZE
YOTE
YOU
YOUDITH
YOUFF
YOUNG
YOUNGBERRIES
YOUNGBERRY
YOUNGER
YOUNGEST
YOUNGISH
YOUNGLET
YOUNGLING
YOUNGLY
YOUNGSTER
YOUNGTH
YOUNKER
YOUPON
YOUR
YOURN
YOURS
YOURSELF
YOURSELVES
YOURT
YOUSE
YOUSTIR
YOUT
YOUTH
YOUTHEN
YOUTHFUL
YOUTHFULLY
YOUTHFULNESS
YOUTHILY
YOUTHINESS
YOUTHLESS
YOUTHLIKE
YOUTHS
YOUTHSOME
YOUTHWORT
YOUTHY
YOUWARD
YOUWARDS
YOUZE
YOW
YOWDEN
YOWE
YOWIE
YOWL
YOWLED
YOWLER
YOWLEY
YOWLING
YOWT
YOX
YOY
YPERITE
YPSILIFORM
YPSILOID
YSOWNDIR
YTHE
YTTERBIA
YTTERBIC
YTTERBIUM
YTTRIA
YTTRIALITE
YTTRIC
YTTRIFEROUS
YTTRIUM
YTTROCERITE
YTTROCRASITE
YTTROGUMMITE
YTWYN
YUCA
YUCCA
YUCK
YUCKER
YUCKLE
YUFT
YUGADA
YUH
YUK
YUKKEL
YULAN
YULE
YULETIDE
YULOH
YUMMY
YUNGAN
YUNKER
YUPON
YURT
YURTA
YUS
YUSDRUM
YUTU
YUZLIK
YUZLUK
YWIS

Z

ZA
ZABAGLIONE
ZABETA
ZABRA
ZABTI
ZABURRO
ZAC
ZACATE
ZACATON
ZACHUN
ZAD
ZADDIK
ZADRUGA
ZAFFAR
ZAFFER
ZAFFIR
ZAFFRE
ZAFFREE
ZAG
ZAGGED
ZAGGING
ZAGUAN
ZAIBATSU
ZAIN
ZAK
ZAKAH
ZAKAT
ZAKUSKA
ZALAMBDODONT
ZAMAN
ZAMANG
ZAMARRA
ZAMARRO
ZAMBO
ZAMBOMBA
ZAMINDAR
ZAMINDARI
ZAMINDARY
ZAMORIN
ZAMORINE
ZAMOUSE
ZAMPOGNA
ZANANA
ZANDER
ZANDMOLE
ZANELLA
ZANIES
ZANJA
ZANJERO
ZANJON
ZANJONA
ZANT
ZANTE
ZANTHOXYLUM
ZANY
ZANYISH
ZANYISM
ZANZE
ZAPAS
ZAPATEADO
ZAPATERO
ZAPHARA
ZAPHRENTID
ZAPHRENTOID
ZAPOTE
ZAPTIAH
ZAPTIEH
ZAPUPE
ZAR
ZARAH
ZARATITE
ZAREBA
ZAREEBA
ZARF
ZARNEC
ZARNICH
ZARP
ZART
ZARZUELA
ZASTRUGA
ZASTRUGI
ZATI
ZATTARE
ZAX
ZAYAT
ZAYIN
ZEAL
ZEALED
ZEALOT
ZEALOTIC
ZEALOTICAL
ZEALOTISM
ZEALOTIST
ZEALOTRY
ZEALOUS
ZEALOUSLY
ZEALOUSNESS
ZEALOUSY
ZEAXANTHIN
ZEBEC
ZEBECK
ZEBRA
ZEBRAIC
ZEBRALIKE
ZEBRAS
ZEBRASS
ZEBRAWOOD
ZEBRINE
ZEBRINNIES
ZEBRINNY
ZEBROID
ZEBRULA
ZEBRULE
ZEBU
ZEBUB
ZEBURRO
ZEBUS
ZECCHINO
ZECHIN
ZED
ZEDOARY
ZEDS
ZEE
ZEEKOE
ZEES
ZEHNER
ZEIN
ZEINE
ZEISM
ZEIST
ZEL
ZELANT
ZELATOR
ZELATRICE
ZELATRIX
ZELOTYPIA
ZELOTYPIE
ZEME
ZEMEISM
ZEMI
ZEMIISM
ZEMINDAR
ZEMINDARI
ZEMMI
ZEMNI
ZEMSTVO
ZEMSTVOS
ZENANA
ZENDICIAN
ZENDIK
ZENDIKITE
ZENICK
ZENIK
ZENITH
ZENITHAL
ZENOCENTRIC
ZENOGRAPHIC
ZENOGRAPHY
ZENTNER
ZENU
ZENZIC
ZEOLITE
ZEOLITIC
ZEOLITIZE
ZEOLITIZED
ZEOLITIZING
ZEOSCOPE
ZEPHYR
ZEPHYREAN
ZEPHYRIAN
ZEPHYROUS
ZEPHYRUS
ZEPHYRY
ZEPP
ZEPPELIN
ZEQUIN
ZER
ZERDA
ZEREBA
ZERMAHBUB
ZERO
ZEROAXIAL
ZEROES
ZEROIZE
ZEROS
ZERUMBET
ZEST
ZESTED
ZESTFUL
ZESTING
ZESTY
ZETA
ZETACISM
ZETETIC
ZEUGITE
ZEUGLODONT
ZEUGMA
ZEUGMATIC
ZEUNERITE
ZHO
ZIAMET
ZIARA
ZIARAT
ZIBEB
ZIBELINE
ZIBELLINE
ZIBETH
ZIBETUM
ZIEGA
ZIEGER
ZIFFS
ZIG
ZIGANKA
ZIGGER
ZIGGURAT
ZIGZAG
ZIGZAGGEDLY
ZIGZAGGER
ZIGZAGGERY
ZIGZAGGY
ZIHAR
ZIIM
ZIKURAT
ZILLAH
ZIMARRA
ZIMB
ZIMBABWE
ZIMBALON
ZIMBI
ZIMENTWATER
ZIMME
ZIMMI
ZIMMIS
ZIMMY
ZIMOCCA
ZINC
ZINCALISM
ZINCATE
ZINCED
ZINCIC
ZINCID
ZINCIDE
ZINCIFEROUS
ZINCIFIED
ZINCIFY
ZINCIFYING
ZINCING
ZINCITE
ZINCKE
ZINCKED
ZINCKING
ZINCKY
ZINCO
ZINCOGRAPH
ZINCOGRAPHER
ZINCOGRAPHIC
ZINCOGRAPHY
ZINCOID
ZINCOLYSIS
ZINCOUS
ZINCUM
ZINCURET
ZINCY
ZINDIQ
ZINEB
ZINFANDEL
ZING
ZINGANA
ZINGANO
ZINGARA
ZINGARESCA
ZINGARI
ZINGARO
ZINGEL
ZINGERONE
ZINGIBERENE
ZINGIBEROL
ZINK
ZINKE
ZINKENITE
ZINKY
ZINNIA
ZINNWALDITE
ZINOBER
ZINSANG
ZIP
ZIPHIAN
ZIPHIOID
ZIPPER
ZIPPIER
ZIPPIEST
ZIPPING
ZIPPINGLY
ZIPPY
ZIRA
ZIRAI
ZIRAM
ZIRCITE
ZIRCON
ZIRCONATE
ZIRCONIA
ZIRCONIC
ZIRCONIUM
ZIRCONOID
ZIRCONYL
ZIRKELITE
ZIRKITE
ZITHER
ZITHERIST
ZITTERN
ZIZANY
ZIZEL
ZIZITH
ZIZZ
ZIZZLE
ZIZZLED
ZIZZLING
ZLOTY
ZLOTYS
ZNAK
ZO
ZOA
ZOACUM
ZOANTHID
ZOANTHODEME
ZOANTHODEMIC
ZOANTHOID
ZOANTHROPY
ZOARIA
ZOARIAL
ZOARIUM
ZOBO
ZOBTENITE
ZOBU
ZOCALO
ZOCCO
ZOCCOLO
ZODIAC
ZODIACAL
ZODIOPHILOUS
ZOEA
ZOEAFORM
ZOEAL
ZOEHEMERA
ZOETIC
ZOETROPE
ZOETROPIC
ZOGAN
ZOGO
ZOH
ZOIATRIA
ZOIC
ZOID
ZOIDOGAMOUS
ZOILUS
ZOISITE
ZOISITIZATION
ZOISM
ZOIST
ZOISTIC
ZOKOR
ZOLL
ZOLOTNIK
ZOMBI
ZOMBIE
ZOMBIES
ZOMBIISM
ZOMBIS
ZOMOTHERAPY
ZONA
ZONAE
ZONAESTHESIA
ZONAL
ZONALITY
ZONALLY

ZONAR
ZONARY
ZONATE
ZONATED
ZONATION
ZONDA
ZONE
ZONED
ZONELESS
ZONELET
ZONESTHESIA
ZONIC
ZONIFEROUS
ZONING
ZONITE
ZONITID
ZONNAR
ZONOCHLORITE
ZONOCILIATE
ZONOID
ZONOLIMNETIC
ZONOSKELETON
ZONULA
ZONULAR
ZONULE
ZONULET
ZONURE
ZONURID
ZONUROID
ZOO
ZOOBENTHOS
ZOOBLAST
ZOOCARP
ZOOCECIDIUM
ZOOCHEMY
ZOOCHORE
ZOOCULTURAL
ZOOCULTURE
ZOOCURRENT
ZOOCYST
ZOOCYTIAL
ZOOCYTIUM
ZOODENDRIUM
ZOODYNAMICS
ZOOECIA
ZOOECIAL
ZOOECIUM
ZOOERYTHRIN
ZOOFULVIN
ZOOGAMETE
ZOOGAMOUS
ZOOGAMY
ZOOGENE
ZOOGENOUS
ZOOGEOGRAPHY
ZOOGLER
ZOOGLOEA
ZOOGLOEAL
ZOOGLOEIC
ZOOGONIDIUM
ZOOGONOUS
ZOOGRAFT
ZOOGRAFTING
ZOOGRAPHER
ZOOGRAPHIC
ZOOGRAPHY
ZOOID
ZOOIDAL
ZOOLATER
ZOOLATRIES
ZOOLATROUS
ZOOLATRY
ZOOLITE
ZOOLITH
ZOOLITHIC
ZOOLITIC
ZOOLOGIC
ZOOLOGICAL
ZOOLOGIES
ZOOLOGIST
ZOOLOGIZE
ZOOLOGIZED
ZOOLOGIZING
ZOOLOGY
ZOOM
ZOOMAGNETIC
ZOOMAGNETISM
ZOOMANIA
ZOOMELANIN
ZOOMETRIC
ZOOMETRY
ZOOMIMETIC
ZOOMIMIC
ZOOMORPH
ZOOMORPHIC
ZOOMORPHISM
ZOOMORPHIZE
ZOOMORPHY
ZOON
ZOONAL
ZOONIC
ZOONIST
ZOONITE
ZOONITIC
ZOONOMY
ZOONOSES
ZOONOSIS
ZOONOSOLOGY
ZOONOTIC
ZOONS
ZOONULE
ZOOPANTHEON
ZOOPARASITE
ZOOPATHOLOGY
ZOOPERAL
ZOOPERIST
ZOOPERY
ZOOPHAGAN
ZOOPHAGOUS
ZOOPHARMACY
ZOOPHILE
ZOOPHILIA
ZOOPHILIC
ZOOPHILISM
ZOOPHILIST
ZOOPHILITE
ZOOPHILOUS
ZOOPHILY
ZOOPHOBIA
ZOOPHOBOUS
ZOOPHORI
ZOOPHORIC
ZOOPHORUS
ZOOPHYSICAL
ZOOPHYSICS
ZOOPHYTAL
ZOOPHYTE
ZOOPHYTIC
ZOOPHYTICAL
ZOOPHYTISH
ZOOPHYTOID
ZOOPHYTOLOGY
ZOOPLANKTON
ZOOPLASTIC
ZOOPLASTY
ZOOPRAXISCOPE
ZOOSCOPIC
ZOOSCOPY
ZOOSIS
ZOOSPERM
ZOOSPHERE
ZOOSPORANGE
ZOOSPORE
ZOOSPORIC
ZOOSPOROUS
ZOOTAXY
ZOOTECHNIC
ZOOTECHNY
ZOOTHECIA
ZOOTHECIAL
ZOOTHECIUM
ZOOTHEISM
ZOOTHEIST
ZOOTHEISTIC
ZOOTHERAPY
ZOOTHOME
ZOOTIC
ZOOTOMIC
ZOOTOMICAL
ZOOTOMIST
ZOOTOXIN
ZOOTROPHIC
ZOOTROPHY
ZOOTYPE
ZOOXANTHELLA
ZOOXANTHIN
ZOOZOO
ZOPE
ZOPILOTE
ZOPPA
ZOPPO
ZORGITE
ZORIL
ZORILLA
ZORILLE
ZORRA
ZORRILLO
ZORRO
ZORTZICO
ZOSTER
ZOSTERIFORM
ZOUNDS
ZOWIE
ZOYSIA
ZUCCARINO
ZUCCHETTO
ZUCCHINI
ZUCHE
ZUDDA
ZUFFOLO
ZUFOLO
ZUGZWANG
ZUISIN
ZULU
ZUMATIC
ZUMBOORUK
ZUNYITE
ZUPA
ZUPAN
ZUPANATE
ZUURVELDT
ZUZA
ZWANZIGER
ZWIEBACK
ZWITTER
ZWITTERION
ZYGA
ZYGADENIN
ZYGADENINE
ZYGAENID
ZYGAL
ZYGANTRUM
ZYGAPOPHYSIS
ZYGENID
ZYGION
ZYGITE
ZYGOBRANCH
ZYGODACTYL
ZYGODACTYLE
ZYGODACTYLIC
ZYGODONT
ZYGOLABIALIS
ZYGOMA
ZYGOMATA
ZYGOMATIC
ZYGOMATICUM
ZYGOMATICUS
ZYGOMORPHIC
ZYGOMORPHOUS
ZYGOMYCETE
ZYGOMYCETES
ZYGOMYCETOUS
ZYGON
ZYGONEURE
ZYGOPHORE
ZYGOPHORIC
ZYGOPHYCEOUS
ZYGOPHYTE
ZYGOPLEURAL
ZYGOPTERAN
ZYGOPTERID
ZYGOPTEROUS
ZYGOSE
ZYGOSIS
ZYGOSPERM
ZYGOSPHENAL
ZYGOSPHENE
ZYGOSPHERE
ZYGOSPORE
ZYGOSPORIC
ZYGOSTYLE
ZYGOTACTIC
ZYGOTAXIS
ZYGOTE
ZYGOTENE
ZYGOTOID
ZYGOUS
ZYGOZOOSPORE
ZYMASE
ZYME
ZYMIC
ZYMIN
ZYMITE
ZYMOGEN
ZYMOGENE
ZYMOGENESIS
ZYMOGENIC
ZYMOGENOUS
ZYMOID
ZYMOLOGIC
ZYMOLOGICAL
ZYMOLOGIST
ZYMOLOGY
ZYMOLYSIS
ZYMOLYTIC
ZYMOME
ZYMOMETER
ZYMOMIN
ZYMOPHORE
ZYMOPHORIC
ZYMOPLASTIC
ZYMOSCOPE
ZYMOSIMETER
ZYMOSIS
ZYMOSTEROL
ZYMOSTHENIC
ZYMOTECHNIC
ZYMOTECHNICS
ZYMOTIC
ZYMOTICALLY
ZYMURGY
ZYTHUM

PART II

High-Scoring Word Lists

Words Containing

High-Point Letters

J, Q, X and Z

High-Scoring Words Containing J

2-3 LETTER WORDS

ALPHABETICAL ORDER

AJI
AJO
DJO
HAJ
JA
JAB
JAD
JAG
JAK
JAM
JAN
JAP
JAR
JAW
JAY
JED
JEE
JEN
JES
JET
JEU
JEW
JIB
JIG
JIZ
JO
JOB
JOD
JOE
JOG
JOT
JOW
JOY
JUB
JUD
JUG
JUM
JUR
JUS
JUT
OJO
RAJ
SAJ
TAJ
TJI
UJI

POSITIONAL ORDER

JA
JAB
JAD
JAG
JAK
JAM
JAN
JAP
JAR
JAW
JAY
JED
JEE
JEN
JES
JET
JEU
JEW
JIB
JIG
JIZ
JO
JOB
JOD
JOE
JOG
JOT
JOW
JOY
JUB
JUD
JUG
JUM
JUR
JUS
JUT

AJI
AJO
DJO
OJO
TJI
UJI

HAJ
RAJ
SAJ
TAJ

SCORING ORDER

19
JIZ

14
JAK

13
HAJ
JAW
JAY
JEW
JOW
JOY

12
JAB
JAM
JAP
JIB
JOB
JUB
JUM

11
DJO
JAD
JAG
JED
JIG
JOD
JOG
JUD
JUG

10
AJI
AJO
JAN
JAR
JEE
JEN
JES
JET
JEU
JOE
JOT
JUR
JUS
JUT
OJO
RAJ
SAJ
TAJ
TJI

9
JA
JO

ALPHABETICAL LIST OF 4-LETTER WORDS

AJAR
AJAX
AJEE
AJOG
BAJU
BENJ
BIJA
CAJA
CAJI
CAJU
DJIN
DOJO
EJOO
FAJA
GAJO
GUNJ
HADJ
HAJE
HAJI
HAJJ
HOJA
IJMA
JACA
JACK
JACU
JADE
JADU
JADY
JAGG
JAGS
JAIL
JAKE
JAKO
JAMA

JAMB
JAMI
JANE
JANG
JANK
JANN
JAOB
JAPE
JARA
JARG
JARK
JARL
JASK
JASM
JASS
JATI
JATO
JAUD
JAUG
JAUK
JAUN
JAUP
JAVA
JAWS
JAWY
JAZZ
JEAN
JEEL
JEEP
JEER
JEEZ
JEFE
JEFF
JELL

JERK
JERL
JERM
JERT
JESS
JEST
JETE
JEUX
JHIL
JHOW
JHUM
JIBE
JIBI
JIFF
JILL
JILT
JIMP
JINA
JING
JINK
JINN
JINX
JIRD
JIRT
JITI
JIVA
JIVE
JOBE
JOBO
JOBS
JOCH
JOCK
JOCO

JOCU
JOES
JOEY
JOGI
JOHN
JOIN
JOKE
JOKY
JOLE
JOLI
JOLL
JOLT
JONG
JONK
JOOM
JOPY
JOSH
JOSS
JOTA
JOTI
JOUG
JOUK
JOVY
JOWL
JUBA
JUBE
JUBO
JUCK
JUDD
JUDO
JUEY
JUEZ
JUGA

JUJU
JUKE
JUMP
JUNE
JUNK
JUNT
JUPE
JURA
JURE
JURM
JURR
JURT
JURY
JUSI
JUST
JUTE
JYNX
KOJI
LIJA
LOJA
MAJA
MAJO
MOJO
MUNJ
PUJA
RAJA
REJA
ROJO
SOJA
SUJI
TAJO
TEJU
YAJE

POSITIONAL ORDER LIST OF 4-LETTER WORDS

JACA
JACK
JACU
JADE
JADU
JADY
JAGG
JAGS
JAIL
JAKE
JAKO
JAMA
JAMB
JAMI
JANE
JANG
JANK
JANN
JAOB
JAPE
JARA
JARG
JARK
JARL
JASK
JASM
JASS
JATI
JATO
JAUD
JAUG
JAUK
JAUN
JAUP
JAVA

JAWS
JAWY
JAZZ
JEAN
JEEL
JEEP
JEER
JEEZ
JEFE
JEFF
JELL
JERK
JERL
JERM
JERT
JESS
JEST
JETE
JEUX
JHIL
JHOW
JHUM
JIBE
JIBI
JIFF
JILL
JILT
JIMP
JINA
JING
JINK
JINN
JINX
JIRD

JIRT
JITI
JIVA
JIVE
JOBE
JOBO
JOBS
JOCH
JOCK
JOCO
JOCU
JOES
JOEY
JOGI
JOHN
JOIN
JOKE
JOKY
JOLE
JOLI
JOLL
JOLT
JONG
JONK
JOOM
JOPY
JOSH
JOSS
JOTA
JOTI
JOUG
JOUK
JOVY
JOWL

JUBA
JUBE
JUBO
JUCK
JUDD
JUDO
JUEY
JUEZ
JUGA
JUJU
JUKE
JUMP
JUNE
JUNK
JUNT
JUPE
JURA
JURE
JURM
JURR
JURT
JURY
JUSI
JUST
JUTE
JYNX

AJAR
AJAX
AJEE
AJOG
DJIN
EJOO
IJMA

BAJU
BIJA
CAJA
CAJI
CAJU
DOJO
FAJA
GAJO
HAJE
HAJI
HAJJ
HOJA
JUJU
KOJI
LIJA
LOJA
MAJA
MAJO
MOJO
PUJA
RAJA
REJA
ROJO
SOJA
SUJI
TAJO
TEJU
YAJE

BENJ
GUNJ
HADJ
HAJJ
MUNJ

SCORING ORDER LIST OF 4-LETTER WORDS

21
JYNX

20
JEEZ
JUEZ

19
JAZZ

18
AJAX
JEUX
JINX
JOKY

17
JACK
JAWY
JEFF
JHOW
JIFF
JOCK
JOVY
JUCK

16
JHUM
JOCH
JOPY

15
HADJ
JADY
JAKE
JAKO
JAMB
JANK
JARK
JASK
JAUK
JERK
JIMP
JINK
JOKE
JONK
JOUK
JUKE
JUMP
JUNK
KOJI

14
FAJA
HAJE
HAJI
HOJA
JAVA
JAWS
JEFE
JHIL
JIVA
JIVE
JOEY
JOHN
JOSH
JOWL
JUEY
JURY
YAJE

13
BAJU
BENJ
BIJA
CAJA
CAJI
CAJU
HAJJ
IJMA
JACA
JACU
JAGG
JAMA
JAMI
JAOB
JAPE
JASM
JAUP
JEEP
JERM
JIBE
JIBI
JOBE
JOBO
JOBS
JOCO
JOCU
JOOM
JUBA
JUBE
JUBO
JUDD
JUPE
JURM
MAJA
MAJO
MOJO
MUNJ
PUJA

12
AJOG
DJIN
DOJO
GAJO
GUNJ
JADE
JADU
JAGS
JANG
JARG
JAUD
JAUG
JING
JIRD
JOGI
JONG
JOUG
JUDO
JUGA

11
AJAR
AJEE
EJOO
JAIL
JANE
JANN
JARA
JARL
JASS
JATI
JATO
JAUN
JEAN
JEEL
JEER
JELL
JERL
JERT
JESS
JEST
JETE
JILL
JILT
JINA
JINN
JIRT
JITI
JOES
JOIN
JOLE
JOLI
JOLL
JOLT
JOSS
JOTA
JOTI
JUNE
JUNT
JURA
JURE
JURR
JURT
JUSI
JUST
JUTE
LIJA
LOJA
RAJA
REJA
ROJO
SOJA
SUJI
TAJO
TEJU

10
JUJU

ALPHABETICAL LIST OF 5-LETTER WORDS

ADJAB
ADJAG
AGUJA
AJAJA
AJARI
AJAVA
AJHAR
AJIVA
AJOUR
ANJAN
ARJAN
ARJUN
ATAJO
BADJU
BAJRA
BANJO
BEJAN
BEJEL
BENJY
BIJOU
BRUJO
CAJON
CAJOU
CAJUN
CHAJA
COOJA
DJATI
DJINN
DORJE
DUJAN
EJECT
EJIDO
ENJOY
FJALL
FJELD
FJORD
GANJA
GJOLL
GUIJO
GUNJA
HADJI
HAJIB
HAJJI
HODJA
IJMAA
INAJA
JABIA
JABOT
JACAL
JACKO
JACKS
JACKY
JADED
JADOO
JAELA
JAGAT
JAGER
JAGGY
JAGIR
JAGLA
JAGRA
JAGUA
JAKES
JAKEY
JAKOS
JALAP
JALEO
JALET
JALOP
JAMAH
JAMAN
JAMBA
JAMBE
JAMBO
JAMMY
JAMON
JANTU
JANTY
JANUA
JAOUR
JAPAN
JAPED
JAPER
JARDE
JARRA
JARRY
JASEY
JASPE
JATHA
JAUNE
JAUNT
JAUPS
JAVEL
JAVER
JAWAB
JAWED
JAZEL
JAZZY
JEANS
JEBAT
JEBEL
JEDGE
JEERS
JEERY
JEHAD
JEHUP
JELAB
JELLO
JELLY
JEMMY
JENNA
JENNY
JEREZ
JERIB
JERKS
JERKY
JERRY
JETEE
JETON
JETTO
JETTY
JEWEL
JEZIA
JHANA
JHEEL

JHOOL
JHOOM
JIBBA
JIBED
JIBER
JIBOA
JIFFY
JIGGY
JIGUA
JIHAD
JIMMY
JIMPY
JINGO
JINJA
JINKS
JINNI
JINNY
JIPPO
JIQUE
JIQUI
JIRGA
JIXIE
JIZYA
JNANA
JNANI
JOCKO
JOCKS
JOCUM
JODEL
JOINT
JOISE
JOIST
JOKED
JOKER
JOKEY
JOKUL
JOLIE
JOLLY
JOLTY
JOOLA
JORAM
JOREE
JORUM
JOSEF
JOSEY
JOSHI
JOSIE
JOSSA
JOSUP
JOTTY
JOUGH
JOUGS
JOULE
JOURS
JOUST
JOWAR
JOWEL
JOWER
JOWLY
JOWPY
JOYED
JUBBE
JUBUS
JUDEX
JUDGE
JUDKA
JUFTI
JUFTS
JUGAL
JUGER
JUGUM
JUICE
JUICY
JUISE
JUKES
JULEP
JULID
JULIO
JULOL
JUMBA
JUMBO
JUMBY
JUMMA
JUMPS
JUMPY
JUNCO
JUNDY
JUNKY
JUNTA
JUNTO
JUPES
JUPON
JURAL
JURAT
JUREL
JUROR
JUSTO
JUTES
JUTIA
JUTKA
JUTTY
JUVIA
JUXTA
KALIJ
KHAJA
KHOJA
KOPJE
LINJA
LINJE
MAJAS
MAJID
MAJOE
MAJOR
MAJOS
MOJOS
MUJER
MUJIK
NJAVE
OUIJA
PAJAK
POLJE
PONJA
POOJA
RAJAH
RAJAS
REJON
SAJOU
SAMAJ
SHOJI
SIJIL
SLOJD
SUJEE
TEJON
THUJA
TJALK
VAJRA
VIEJA
VIJAO
YOJAN
ZANJA

POSITIONAL ORDER LIST OF 5-LETTER WORDS

JABIA
JABOT
JACAL
JACKO
JACKS
JACKY
JADED
JADOO
JAELA
JAGAT
JAGER
JAGGY
JAGIR
JAGLA
JAGRA
JAGUA
JAKES
JAKEY
JAKOS
JALAP
JALEO
JALET
JALOP
JAMAH
JAMAN
JAMBA
JAMBE
JAMBO
JAMMY
JAMON
JANTU
JANTY
JANUA
JAOUR
JAPAN
JAPED
JAPER
JARDE
JARRA
JARRY
JASEY
JASPE
JATHA
JAUNE
JAUNT
JAUPS
JAVEL
JAVER
JAWAB
JAWED
JAZEL
JAZZY
JEANS
JEBAT
JEBEL
JEDGE
JEERS
JEERY
JEHAD
JEHUP
JELAB
JELLO
JELLY
JEMMY
JENNA
JENNY
JEREZ
JERIB
JERKS
JERKY
JERRY
JETEE
JETON
JETTO
JETTY
JEWEL
JEZIA
JHANA
JHEEL
JHOOL
JHOOM
JIBBA
JIBED
JIBER
JIBOA
JIFFY
JIGGY
JIGUA
JIHAD
JIMMY
JIMPY
JINGO
JINJA
JINKS
JINNI
JINNY
JIPPO
JIQUE
JIQUI
JIRGA
JIXIE
JIZYA
JNANA
JNANI
JOCKO
JOCKS
JOCUM
JODEL
JOINT
JOISE
JOIST
JOKED
JOKER
JOKEY
JOKUL
JOLIE
JOLLY
JOLTY
JOOLA
JORAM
JOREE
JORUM
JOSEF
JOSEY
JOSHI
JOSIE
JOSSA
JOSUP
JOTTY
JOUGH
JOUGS
JOULE
JOURS
JOUST
JOWAR
JOWEL
JOWER
JOWLY
JOWPY
JOYED
JUBBE
JUBUS
JUDEX
JUDGE
JUDKA
JUFTI
JUFTS
JUGAL
JUGER
JUGUM
JUICE
JUICY
JUISE
JUKES
JULEP
JULID
JULIO
JULOL
JUMBA
JUMBO
JUMBY
JUMMA
JUMPS
JUMPY
JUNCO
JUNDY
JUNKY
JUNTA
JUNTO
JUPES
JUPON
JURAL
JURAT
JUREL
JUROR
JUSTO
JUTES
JUTIA
JUTKA
JUTTY
JUVIA
JUXTA

AJAJA
AJARI
AJAVA
AJHAR
AJIVA
AJOUR
DJATI
DJINN
EJECT
EJIDO
FJALL
FJELD
FJORD
GJOLL
IJMAA
NJAVE
TJALK

ADJAB
ADJAG
ANJAN
ARJAN
ARJUN
BAJRA
BEJAN
BEJEL
BIJOU
CAJON
CAJOU
CAJUN
DUJAN
ENJOY

HAJIB
HAJJI
MAJAS
MAJID
MAJOE
MAJOR
MAJOS
MOJOS
MUJER
MUJIK
PAJAK
RAJAH
RAJAS
REJON
SAJOU
SIJIL
SUJEE
TEJON
VAJRA
VIJAO
YOJAN

AGUJA
AJAJA
ATAJO
BADJU
BANJO
BENJY
BRUJO
CHAJA
COOJA
DORJE
GANJA
GUIJO
GUNJA
HADJI
HAJJI
HODJA
INAJA
JINJA
KHAJA
KHOJA
KOPJE
LINJA
LINJE
OUIJA
POLJE
PONJA
POOJA
SHOJI
SLOJD
THUJA
VIEJA
ZANJA

KALIJ
SAMAJ

SCORING ORDER LIST OF 5-LETTER WORDS

24
JIZYA

23
JAZZY

21
JACKY
JAZEL
JEREZ
JEZIA
JIFFY
JIQUE
JIQUI
ZANJA

20
JOWPY
JUDEX

19
JAKEY
JAMMY
JEMMY
JERKY
JIMMY
JIMPY
JIXIE
JOKEY
JUMBY
JUMPY
JUNKY
JUXTA
KHAJA
KHOJA

18
JACKO
JACKS
JOCKO
JOCKS
JOWLY
KOPJE
MUJIK
PAJAK

17
BENJY
CHAJA
HAJIB
JAGGY
JAMAH
JAWAB
JEHUP
JHOOM
JIGGY
JOKED
JUDKA
JUICY

16
FJELD
FJORD
HADJI
HODJA
JAKES
JAKOS
JAMBA
JAMBE
JAMBO
JAWED
JEHAD
JERKS
JIBBA
JIHAD
JINKS
JIPPO
JOCUM
JOKER
JOKUL
JOUGH
JOYED
JUBBE
JUKES
JUMBA
JUMBO
JUMMA
JUMPS
JUNDY
JUTKA
KALIJ
TJALK

15
ADJAB
AJAVA
AJHAR
AJIVA
BADJU
ENJOY
FJALL
JANTY
JAPED
JARRY
JASEY
JATHA
JAVEL
JAVER
JEERY
JELLY
JENNY
JERRY
JETTY
JEWEL
JHANA
JHEEL
JHOOL
JIBED
JINNY
JOLLY
JOLTY
JOSEF
JOSEY
JOSHI
JOTTY
JOWAR
JOWEL
JOWER
JUFTI
JUFTS
JUGUM
JUTTY
JUVIA
MAJID
NJAVE
RAJAH
SHOJI
THUJA
VAJRA
VIEJA
VIJAO
YOJAN

14
ADJAG
BAJRA
BANJO
BEJAN
BEJEL
BIJOU
BRUJO
CAJON
CAJOU
CAJUN
COOJA
EJECT
HAJJI
IJMAA
JABIA
JABOT
JACAL
JADED
JALAP
JALOP
JAMAN
JAMON
JAPAN
JAPER
JASPE
JAUPS
JEBAT
JEBEL
JEDGE
JELAB
JERIB
JIBER
JIBOA
JORAM
JORUM
JOSUP
JUBUS
JUDGE
JUICE
JULEP
JUNCO
JUPES
JUPON
MAJAS
MAJOE
MAJOR
MAJOS
MOJOS
MUJER
POLJE
PONJA
POOJA
SAMAJ

13
AGUJA
DJATI
DJINN
DORJE
DUJAN
EJIDO
GANJA
GJOLL
GUIJO
GUNJA
JADOO
JAGAT
JAGER
JAGIR
JAGLA
JAGRA
JAGUA
JARDE
JIGUA
JINGO
JIRGA
JODEL
JOUGS
JUGAL
JUGER
JULID
SLOJD

12
AJARI
AJOUR
ANJAN
ARJAN
ARJUN
ATAJO
INAJA
JAELA
JALEO
JALET
JANTU
JANUA
JAOUR
JARRA
JAUNE
JAUNT
JEANS
JEERS
JELLO
JENNA
JETEE
JETON
JETTO
JINNI
JNANA
JNANI
JOINT
JOISE
JOIST
JOLIE
JOOLA
JOREE
JOSIE
JOSSA
JOULE
JOURS
JOUST
JUISE
JULIO
JULOL
JUNTA
JUNTO
JURAL
JURAT
JUREL
JUROR
JUSTO
JUTES
JUTIA
LINJA
LINJE
OUIJA
RAJAS
REJON
SAJOU
SIJIL
SUJEE
TEJON

11
AJAJA
JINJA

ALPHABETICAL LIST OF 6-LETTER WORDS

ABJECT
ABJURE
ACAJOU
ADJECT
ADJIGA
ADJOIN
ADJURE
ADJUST
AGUAJI
AGUJON
AJENJO
AJIMEZ
AJOINT
AJOURE
AJOWAN
ALFAJE
ALJAMA
ANTJAR
AVIJJA
BAJADA
BAJREE
BANJAK
BANJOS
BEJADE
BEJANT
BEJAPE
BEJUCO
BIJOUX
BOJITE
BOOJUM
CABUJA
CADJAN
CAJAVA
CAJETA
CAJOLE
CARAJO
CONJEE
CONJON
COROJO
CROJIK
CUNJAH
CUNJER
DEEJAY
DEJECT
DJEBEL
DJELFA
DJERIB
DJERSA
DJINNI
DONJON
EJECTA
EJIDAL
ELCAJA
ENJAIL
ENJAMB
ENJOIN
EVEJAR
FANJET
FINJAN
FREIJO
FYLGJA
GIDJEE
GOUJAT
GOUJON
GUNJAH
GURJAN
GURJUN
GYTTJA
HEJIRA
HIJACK
INJECT
INJURE
INJURY
INJUST
JABBED
JABBER
JABBLE
JABERS
JABIRU
JABOTS
JABULS
JACANA
JACARE
JACATE
JACENT
JACKAL
JACKED
JACKER
JACKET
JACOBY
JADDED
JADDER
JADERY
JADING
JADISH
JAEGER
JAGEER
JAGGAR
JAGGED
JAGGER
JAGHIR
JAGONG
JAGUAR
JAGUEY
JAILED
JAILER
JAILOR
JALAPA
JALKAR
JALOPY
JAMBEE
JAMBER
JAMBON
JAMBUL
JAMMED
JAMMER
JAMNUT
JAMOKE
JAMPAN
JANAPA
JANGAR
JANGLE
JANGLY
JANKER
JANNER
JANTEE
JAPERY
JAPING
JAPISH
JARABE
JARANA
JARBLE
JARBOT
JAREED
JARFLY
JARFUL
JARGON
JARINA
JARNUT
JAROOL
JARRAH
JARRED
JARRET
JARVEY
JASEYS
JASMIN
JASPER
JASPIS
JASSID
JATACO
JATOBA
JAUDIE
JAUNCE
JAUNER
JAUNTY
JAVALI
JAVVER
JAWING
JAYGEE
JAYPIE
JAYVEE
JAZZER
JEERED
JEERER
JEETEE
JEJUNA
JEJUNE
JELICK
JELLAB
JEMBLE
JENKIN
JENNET
JENOAR
JERBOA
JEREED
JERKED
JERKER
JERKIN
JERNIE
JERQUE
JERRID
JERSEY
JERVIA
JERVIN
JESSED
JESSUR
JESTED
JESTEE
JESTER
JETSAM
JETTED
JETTER
JETTON
JETTRU
JEWELS
JEWELY
JEWING
JEZAIL
JEZIAH
JHARAL
JIBBAH
JIBBED
JIBBEH
JIBBER
JIBING
JIBMAN
JIBMEN
JIBOYA
JICAMA
JICARA
JIFFLE
JIGGED
JIGGER
JIGGET
JIGGIT
JIGGLE
JIGGLY
JIGMAN
JIGMEN
JIGOTE
JIGSAW
JILLET
JILTED
JILTEE
JILTER
JIMJAM
JIMMER
JIMPLY
JIMSON
JINETE
JINGAL
JINGLE
JINGLY
JINKED
JINKER
JINKET
JINKLE
JINNEE
JINSHA
JIPPER
JIRBLE
JIRGAH
JITNEY
JITTER
JIZYAH
JIZZEN
JOBADE
JOBBED
JOBBER
JOBBLE
JOBMAN
JOBMEN
JOBSON
JOCANT
JOCKER
JOCKEY
JOCKOS
JOCOSE
JOCOTE
JOCUMA
JOCUND
JOGGED
JOGGER
JOGGLE
JOGGLY
JOHNIN
JOINED
JOINER
JOINTS
JOINTY
JOJOBA
JOKIER
JOKING
JOKISH
JOKIST
JOLLOP
JOLTED
JOLTER
JONDLA
JORDAN
JORDEN
JOROPO
JORRAM
JOSEPH
JOSHER
JOSKIN
JOSSER
JOSTLE
JOTISI
JOTTED
JOTTER
JOUNCE
JOUSTS
JOUTES
JOVIAL
JOWARI
JOWERY
JOWLER
JOWLOP
JOWSER
JOWTER
JOYANT
JOYFUL
JOYHOP
JOYING
JOYOUS
JUBARB
JUBATE
JUBBAH
JUBHAH
JUBILE
JUDDER
JUDGED
JUDGER
JUECES
JUFFER
JUGALE
JUGATE
JUGFUL
JUGGED
JUGGER
JUGGLE
JUGLAR
JUGULA
JUGUMS
JUICER
JUJUBE
JULOID
JULOLE
JUMART
JUMBIE
JUMBLE
JUMBLY
JUMBOS
JUMENT
JUMFRU
JUMPED
JUMPER
JUNCOS
JUNCUS
JUNDIE
JUNGLE
JUNGLI
JUNGLY
JUNIOR
JUNKER
JUNKET
JUNKIE
JUNTAS
JUNTOS
JUPATI
JURANT
JURARA
JURATA
JURIES
JURING
JURIST
JURORS
JUSLIK
JUSSAL
JUSSEL
JUSTEN
JUSTER
JUSTLE
JUSTLY
JUTTED
JUVENT
JUVITE
JUWISE
JUZAIL

KHAJUR
KHARAJ
KHOJAH
KONJAK
KURUNJ
LOGJAM
LUJULA
MAATJE
MAJOON
MANJAK
MANJEL
MASJID
MEISJE
MILJEE
MOONJA
MOUJIK
MUSJID
MUTSJE
MUZJIK
OBJECT
OBJURE
OREJON
OUTJUT
PAJAMA
PAJERO
PAJOCK
PAREJA
PINJRA
POOJAH
POPJOY
PRAJNA
PUNJUM
PYJAMA
RAKIJA
REJECT
REJOIN
REJOLT
SANJAK
SEJANT
SEJERO
SEJOIN
SEJOUR
SIJILL
SINJER
SJOMIL
SVARAJ
SWARAJ
TALAJE
TANJIB
TASAJO
TEJANO
THUJYL
TINAJA
TJAELE
TJANDI
TOMJON
TONJON
TRAJET
UNJUST
WAJANG
WEJACK
WITJAR
YAJEIN
YOJANA
ZANJON

POSITIONAL ORDER LIST OF 6-LETTER WORDS

JABBED
JABBER
JABBLE
JABERS
JABIRU
JABOTS
JABULS
JACANA
JACARE
JACATE
JACENT
JACKAL
JACKED
JACKER
JACKET
JACOBY
JADDED
JADDER
JADERY
JADING
JADISH
JAEGER
JAGEER
JAGGAR
JAGGED
JAGGER
JAGHIR
JAGONG
JAGUAR
JAGUEY
JAILED
JAILER
JAILOR
JALAPA
JALKAR
JALOPY
JAMBEE
JAMBER
JAMBON
JAMBUL
JAMMED
JAMMER
JAMNUT
JAMOKE
JAMPAN
JANAPA
JANGAR
JANGLE
JANGLY
JANKER
JANNER
JANTEE
JAPERY
JAPING
JAPISH
JARABE
JARANA
JARBLE
JARBOT
JAREED
JARFLY
JARFUL
JARGON
JARINA
JARNUT
JAROOL
JARRAH
JARRED
JARRET
JARVEY
JASEYS
JASMIN
JASPER
JASPIS
JASSID
JATACO
JATOBA
JAUDIE
JAUNCE
JAUNER
JAUNTY
JAVALI
JAVVER
JAWING
JAYGEE
JAYPIE
JAYVEE
JAZZER
JEERED
JEERER
JEETEE
JEJUNA
JEJUNE
JELICK
JELLAB
JEMBLE
JENKIN
JENNET
JENOAR
JERBOA
JEREED
JERKED
JERKER
JERKIN
JERNIE
JERQUE
JERRID
JERSEY
JERVIA
JERVIN
JESSED
JESSUR
JESTED
JESTEE
JESTER
JETSAM
JETTED
JETTER
JETTON
JETTRU
JEWELS
JEWELY
JEWING
JEZAIL
JEZIAH
JHARAL
JIBBAH
JIBBED
JIBBEH
JIBBER
JIBING
JIBMAN
JIBMEN
JIBOYA
JICAMA
JICARA
JIFFLE
JIGGED
JIGGER
JIGGET
JIGGIT
JIGGLE
JIGGLY
JIGMAN
JIGMEN
JIGOTE
JIGSAW
JILLET
JILTED
JILTEE
JILTER
JIMJAM
JIMJAM
JIMMER
JIMPLY
JIMSON
JINETE
JINGAL
JINGLE
JINGLY
JINKED
JINKER
JINKET
JINKLE
JINNEE
JINSHA
JIPPER
JIRBLE
JIRGAH
JITNEY
JITTER
JIZYAH
JIZZEN
JOBADE
JOBBED
JOBBER
JOBBLE
JOBMAN
JOBMEN
JOBSON
JOCANT
JOCKER
JOCKEY
JOCKOS
JOCOSE
JOCOTE
JOCUMA
JOCUND
JOGGED
JOGGER
JOGGLE
JOGGLY
JOHNIN
JOINED
JOINER
JOINTS
JOINTY
JOKIER
JOKING
JOKISH
JOKIST
JOLLOP
JOLTED
JOLTER
JONDLA
JORDAN
JORDEN
JOROPO
JORRAM
JOSEPH
JOSHER
JOSKIN
JOSSER
JOSTLE
JOTISI
JOTTED
JOTTER
JOUNCE
JOUSTS
JOUTES
JOVIAL
JOWARI
JOWERY
JOWLER
JOWLOP
JOWSER
JOWTER
JOYANT
JOYFUL
JOYHOP
JOYING
JOYOUS
JUBARB
JUBATE
JUBBAH
JUBHAH
JUBILE
JUDDER
JUDGED
JUDGER
JUECES
JUFFER
JUGALE
JUGATE
JUGFUL
JUGGED
JUGGER
JUGGLE
JUGLAR
JUGULA
JUGUMS
JUICER
JUJUBE
JULOID
JULOLE
JUMART
JUMBIE
JUMBLE
JUMBLY
JUMBOS
JUMENT
JUMFRU
JUMPED
JUMPER
JUNCOS
JUNCUS
JUNDIE
JUNGLE
JUNGLI
JUNGLY
JUNIOR
JUNKER
JUNKET
JUNKIE
JUNTAS
JUNTOS
JUPATI
JURANT
JURARA
JURATA
JURIES
JURING
JURIST
JURORS
JUSLIK

JUSSAL
JUSSEL
JUSTEN
JUSTER
JUSTLE
JUSTLY
JUTTED
JUVENT
JUVITE
JUWISE
JUZAIL

AJENJO
AJIMEZ
AJOINT
AJOURE
AJOWAN
DJEBEL
DJELFA
DJERIB
DJERSA
DJINNI
EJECTA
EJIDAL
SJOMIL
TJAELE
TJANDI

ABJECT
ABJURE
ADJECT
ADJIGA

ADJOIN
ADJURE
ADJUST
ALJAMA
BAJADA
BAJREE
BEJADE
BEJANT
BEJAPE
BEJUCO
BIJOUX
BOJITE
CAJAVA
CAJETA
CAJOLE
DEJECT
ENJAIL
ENJAMB
ENJOIN
HEJIRA
HIJACK
INJECT
INJURE
INJURY
INJUST
JEJUNA
JEJUNE
JUJUBE
LUJULA
MAJOON
OBJECT
OBJURE

PAJAMA
PAJERO
PAJOCK
PYJAMA
REJECT
REJOIN
REJOLT
SEJANT
SEJERO
SEJOIN
SEJOUR
SIJILL
TEJANO
UNJUST
WAJANG
WEJACK
YAJEIN
YOJANA

ACAJOU
AGUJON
ANTJAR
AVIJJA
BANJAK
BANJOS
BOOJUM
CROJIK
CADJAN
CONJEE
CONJON
CUNJAH
CUNJER

DEEJAY
DONJON
EVEJAR
FANJET
FINJAN
GIDJEE
GOUJAT
GOUJON
GUNJAH
GURJAN
GURJUN
KHAJUR
KHOJAH
KONJAK
LOGJAM
MANJAK
MANJEL
MASJID
MILJEE
MOUJIK
MUSJID
MUZJIK
OREJON
OUTJUT
PINJRA
POOJAH
POPJOY
PRAJNA
PUNJUM
SANJAK
SINJER
TANJIB

THUJYL
TOMJON
TONJON
TRAJET
WITJAR
ZANJON

AGUAJI
AJENJO
ALFAJE
AVIJJA
CABUJA
CARAJO
COROJO
ELCAJA
FREIJO
FYLGJA
GYTTJA
MAATJE
MEISJE
MOONJA
MUTSJE
PAREJA
RAKIJA
TALAJE
TASAJO
TINAJA

KHARAJ
KURUNJ
SVARAJ
SWARAJ

SCORING ORDER LIST OF 6-LETTER WORDS

28
JIZYAH
MUZJIK

25
JEZIAH

24
AJIMEZ

23
KHOJAH

22
BIJOUX
HIJACK
JERQUE
JEZAIL
JOCKEY
JUZAIL
WEJACK
ZANJON

21
JAZZER
JIZZEN
JOYHOP
JUBHAH
PAJOCK

20
FYLGJA
JACKED
JACOBY
JIBBAH
JIBBEH
JIMPLY
JOKISH
JUBBAH
JUMBLY
KHAJUR
KHARAJ
POPJOY
PYJAMA

19
BANJAK
CROJIK
JACKAL
JACKER
JACKET
JAMOKE
JARFLY
JARVEY
JAVVER
JAYVEE
JELICK
JEWELY
JIFFLE
JOCKER
JOCKOS
JOWERY
JOYFUL
JUFFER
MANJAK
MOUJIK
THUJYL

18
CAJAVA
CUNJAH
JABBED
JALOPY
JAMMED
JAPERY
JAPISH
JAYPIE
JERKED
JIBBED
JIBOYA
JIGGLY
JINKED
JOBBED
JOGGLY
JOKING
JOSEPH
JOWLOP
JUMFRU
JUMPED
POOJAH

17
ABJECT
BEJAPE
BEJUCO
BOOJUM
CABUJA
DEEJAY
DJELFA
ENJAMB
GUNJAH
GYTTJA
JABBER
JABBLE
JADERY
JADISH
JAGHIR
JAGUEY
JALKAR
JAMBEE
JAMBER
JAMBON
JAMBUL
JAMMER
JAMPAN
JANGLY
JANKER
JAWING
JAYGEE
JEMBLE
JENKIN
JERKER
JERKIN
JEWING
JIBBER
JIBMAN
JIBMEN
JICAMA
JIGSAW
JIMMER
JINGLY
JINKER
JINKET
JINKLE
JIPPER
JIRGAH
JOBBER
JOBBLE
JOBMAN
JOBMEN
JOCUMA
JOKIER
JOKIST
JOSKIN
JOYING
JUBARB
JUGFUL
JUMBIE
JUMBLE
JUMBOS
JUMPER
JUNGLY
JUNKER
JUNKET
JUNKIE
JUSLIK
KURUNJ
OBJECT
PAJAMA
PUNJUM
RAKIJA
SANJAK
WAJANG

16
ADJECT
AJOWAN
ALFAJE
BAJADA
BEJADE
CADJAN
DEJECT
DJEBEL
DJERIB
EVEJAR
FANJET
FINJAN
FREIJO
HEJIRA
INJURY
JADDED
JAGGED
JAPING
JARFUL
JARRAH
JASEYS
JAUNTY
JAVALI
JERSEY
JERVIA

JERVIN
JEWELS
JHARAL
JIBING
JIGGED
JIGMAN
JIGMEN
JIMJAM
JINSHA
JITNEY
JOBADE
JOCUND
JOGGED
JOINTY
JOSHER
JOVIAL
JOWARI
JOWLER
JOWSER
JOWTER
JOYANT
JOYOUS
JUDGED
JUGGED
JUGUMS
JUSTLY
JUVENT
JUVITE
JUWISE
KONJAK
LOGJAM
MASJID
MUSJID
SVARAJ
SWARAJ
WITJAR
YAJEIN
YOJANA

15

ABJURE
ACAJOU
ADJIGA
ALJAMA
AVIJJA
BAJREE
BANJOS
BEJANT
BOJITE
CAJETA
CAJOLE
CARAJO
CONJEE
CONJON
COROJO
CUNJER
EJECTA
ELCAJA
GIDJEE
INJECT
JABERS
JABIRU
JABOTS
JABULS
JACANA
JACARE
JACATE
JACENT
JADDER
JADING
JAGGAR
JAGGER
JAGONG
JALAPA
JAMNUT
JANAPA
JARABE
JARBLE
JARBOT
JASMIN
JASPER
JASPIS
JATACO
JATOBA
JAUNCE
JELLAB
JERBOA
JETSAM
JICARA
JIGGER
JIGGET
JIGGIT
JIGGLE
JIMSON
JIRBLE
JOBSON
JOCANT
JOCOSE
JOCOTE
JOGGER
JOGGLE
JOLLOP
JOROPO
JORRAM
JOUNCE
JUBATE
JUBILE
JUDDER
JUDGER
JUECES
JUGGER
JUGGLE
JUICER
JUMART
JUMENT
JUNCOS
JUNCUS
JUPATI
MAATJE
MAJOON
MANJEL
MEISJE
MILJEE
MOONJA
MUTSJE
OBJURE
PAJERO
PAREJA
PINJRA
PRAJNA
REJECT
SJOMIL
TANJIB
TOMJON

14

ADJOIN
ADJURE
ADJUST
AGUAJI
AGUJON
DJERSA
DJINNI
DONJON
EJIDAL
GOUJAT
GOUJON
GURJAN
GURJUN
JAEGER
JAGEER
JAGUAR
JAILED
JANGAR
JANGLE
JAREED
JARGON
JARRED
JASSID
JAUDIE
JEERED
JEREED
JERRID
JESSED
JESTED
JETTED
JIGOTE
JILTED
JINGAL
JINGLE
JOINED
JOJOBA
JOLTED
JONDLA
JORDAN
JORDEN
JOTTED
JUGALE
JUGATE
JUGLAR
JUGULA
JUJUBE
JULOID
JUNDIE
JUNGLE
JUNGLI
JURING
JUTTED
TJANDI

13

AJOINT
AJOURE
ANTJAR
ENJAIL
ENJOIN
INJURE
INJUST
JAILER
JAILOR
JANNER
JANTEE
JARANA
JARINA
JARNUT
JAROOL
JARRET
JAUNER
JEERER
JEETEE
JENNET
JENOAR
JERNIE
JESSUR
JESTEE
JESTER
JETTER
JETTON
JETTRU
JILLET
JILTEE
JILTER
JINETE
JINNEE
JITTER
JOINER
JOINTS
JOLTER
JOSSER
JOSTLE
JOTISI
JOTTER
JOUSTS
JOUTES
JULOLE
JUNIOR
JUNTAS
JUNTOS
JURANT
JURARA
JURATA
JURIES
JURIST
JURORS
JUSSAL
JUSSEL
JUSTEN
JUSTER
JUSTLE
LUJULA
OREJON
OUTJUT
REJOIN
REJOLT
SEJANT
SEJERO
SEJOIN
SEJOUR
SIJILL
SINJER
TALAJE
TASAJO
TEJANO
TINAJA
TJAELE
TONJON
TRAJET
UNJUST

12

AJENJO
JEJUNA
JEJUNE

ALPHABETICAL LIST OF 7-LETTER WORDS

ABADEJO
ABJOINT
ABJUDGE
ABJURED
ABJURER
ADJIGER
ADJOINT
ADJOURN
ADJOUST
ADJUDGE
ADJUNCT
ADJURED
ADJURER
ADJUROR
ADJUTOR
AJANGLE
AJITTER
AJIVIKA
ALFORJA
ALJAMIA
APAREJO
APOJOVE
ARVEJON
AZUELJO
BACKJAW
BAJOCCO
BAJOCHI
BAJOIRE
BANJARA
BANJOES
BANJORE
BASENJI
BEJESUS
BEJEWEL
BENJOIN
BIJASAL
BLIJVER
BRINJAL
CAJAPUT
CAJEPUT
CAJOLED
CAJOLER
CAJUELA
CAJUPUT
CATJANG
COJUROR
COMITJE
CONJECT
CONJOIN
CONJURE
CONJURY
DEJECTA
DEJEUNE
DISJECT
DISJOIN

DISJUNE
DJIBBAH
EJECTED
EJECTOR
EJULATE
EJURATE
ENJEWEL
ENJOYED
ENJOYER
FAUJDAR
FERIDJI
FERIJEE
FINDJAN
FJORDED
FOUJDAR
GALJOEN
GEITJIE
GIOJOSO
GJEDOST
GOTRAJA
GUAJIRA
HAJILIJ
HANDJAR
HIJINKS
IJOLITE
INJELLY
INJOINT
INJUNCT
INJURED
INJURER
INJURIA
JABBING
JABORIN
JABULES
JACALES
JACAMAR
JACAMIN
JACATOO
JACCHUS
JACINTH
JACKALS
JACKASH
JACKASS
JACKBOX
JACKBOY
JACKDAW
JACKEEN
JACKETY
JACKING
JACKLEG
JACKMAN
JACKMEN
JACKPOT
JACKROD
JACKSAW
JACKTAN
JACOBIN
JACOBUS
JACONET
JACTANT
JACTURE
JACUARU
JADDING
JADEDLY
JADEITE
JAGGARY
JAGGERY
JAGGIER
JAGGING
JAGHEER
JAGHIRE
JAGRATA
JAGUARS
JAILAGE
JALAPIC
JALAPIN
JALOPPY
JALOUSE
JAMBEAU
JAMBONE
JAMBOOL
JAMBOSA
JAMDANI
JAMMING
JAMPANI
JAMWOOD
JANAPAN
JANAPUM
JANDERS
JANGADA
JANGKAR
JANGLED
JANGLER
JANITOR
JANKERS
JANNOCK
JAPYGID
JAQUIMA
JARAGUA
JARBIRD
JARGOON
JARHEAD
JARKMAN
JARLESS
JARLITE
JARRING
JARVEYS
JASEYED
JASMINE
JASMONE
JASPERY
JASPOID
JAUNDER
JAUNTED
JAUNTIE
JAVELIN
JAVELOT
JAWBONE
JAWFALL
JAWFEET
JAWFISH
JAWFOOT
JAWHOLE
JAYHAWK
JAYPIET
JAYWALK
JAZERAN
JAZZBOW
JAZZIER
JAZZILY
JEALOUS
JECORAL
JECORIN
JEDCOCK
JEDDOCK
JEEPERS
JEEPNEY
JEERING
JEJUNAL
JEJUNUM
JELLICA
JELLICO
JELLIED
JELLIES
JELLIFY
JELLILY
JELLOID
JEMADAR
JEMIDAR
JEMMIES
JEMMILY
JENNIER
JENNIES
JEOFAIL
JEOPARD
JERICAN
JERKIER
JERKILY
JERKING
JERKISH
JERQUED
JERQUER
JERRIES
JERSEYS
JERVINA
JERVINE
JESSAMY
JESSANT
JESSING
JESTING
JETBEAD
JETPORT
JETTAGE
JETTEAU
JETTIED
JETTIES
JETTING
JETWARE
JEWBIRD
JEWBUSH
JEWELED
JEWELER
JEWELLY
JEWELRY
JEWFISH
JIBBING
JIBBOOM
JIBHEAD
JIBSTAY
JIFFIES
JIGGERS
JIGGETY
JIGGING
JIGGISH
JIGGLED
JIKUNGU
JILLING
JILLION
JILTING
JIMBANG
JIMJAMS
JIMMIED
JIMMIES
JINGALL
JINGLED
JINGLER
JINGLET
JINGOED
JINGOES
JINJILI
JINKING
JINNIES
JINRIKI
JINSING
JITNEUR
JITNEYS
JITTERS
JITTERY
JIVATMA
JOANNES
JOBARBE
JOBBERY
JOBBING
JOBBISH
JOBLESS
JOBSITE
JOCKEYS
JOCOQUE
JOCOQUI
JOCULAR
JOEBUSH
JOEWOOD
JOGGING
JOGGLED
JOGGLER
JOINANT
JOINDER
JOINERY
JOINING
JOINTED
JOINTER
JOINTLY
JOISTED
JOKELET
JOKIEST
JOLLIED
JOLLIER
JOLLIES
JOLLIFY
JOLLILY
JOLLITY
JOLTING
JONQUIL
JORNADA
JOSEITE
JOSTLED
JOSTLER
JOTTING
JOUBARB
JOUKERY
JOULEAN
JOUNCED
JOURNAL
JOURNEY
JOUSTER
JOYANCE
JOYANCY
JOYLEAF
JOYLESS
JOYRIDE
JOYSOME
JOYWEED
JUAMAVE
JUBILEE
JUBILUS
JUCHART
JUCKIES
JUDCOCK
JUDDOCK
JUDGING
JUDICES
JUGATED
JUGGING
JUGGINS
JUGGLED
JUGGLER
JUGHEAD
JUGLONE
JUGULAR
JUGULUM
JUICIER
JUICILY
JUJUIST
JUJITSU
JUJUISM
JUJUTSU
JUKEBOX
JULIDAN
JULIETT
JULOLIN
JUMBLED
JUMBLER
JUMBUCK
JUMELLE
JUMPERS
JUMPIER
JUMPING
JUMPOFF
JUNCITE
JUNCOUS
JUNCTLY
JUNGLED
JUNIATA
JUNIPER
JUNKING
JUNKMAN
JUNKMEN
JURALLY
JURATOR
JURIDIC
JURYMAN
JURYMEN
JUSSION
JUSSIVE
JUSSORY
JUSTICE
JUSTICO
JUSTIFY
JUSTLER
JUTTIES
JUTTING
JUVENAL
JYNGINE
KAJAWAH
KAJEPUT
KANDJAR
KANKREJ
KEDJAVE
KHANJAR
KHANJEE
KILADJA
KILLJOY
KORADJI
LOCKJAW
LONGJAW
MAHAJAN
MAHAJUN
MAHJONG
MAJAGUA
MAJESTY
MAJORAT
MANJACK
MANJEET
MOJARRA
MONTJOY
MUJERES
MUMJUMA
MUNJEET
MUNTJAC
MUNTJAK
NAARTJE
OBJECTS
OUTJAZZ
OUTJINX
OUTJUMP
OVERJOY
PAJAMAS
PARANJA
PERJINK
PERJURE
PERJURY
PINJANE
PIROJKI
PROJECT
PROPJET
PULAJAN
PULIJAN
PYJAMAS
REJOICE
REJONEO
REJOURN
REJUDGE
SAPAJOU
SATLIJK
SEJEANT

SEJUNCT
SJAMBOK
SJOMILA
SKIJORE
SKYJACK
SOJOURN
STANJEN
SUBJECT
SUBJOIN
TANJONG
THUJENE
THUJONE
TJENKAL
TJOSITE
TOMJOHN
TORONJA
TRAJECT
TURJITE
UINTJIE
VANJOHN
VIAJACA
WICHTJE
WINDJAM
YAJEINE
YAJENIN
ZANJERO
ZANJONA

POSITIONAL ORDER LIST OF 7-LETTER WORDS

JABBING
JABORIN
JABULES
JACALES
JACAMAR
JACAMIN
JACATOO
JACCHUS
JACINTH
JACKALS
JACKASH
JACKASS
JACKBOX
JACKBOY
JACKDAW
JACKEEN
JACKETY
JACKING
JACKLEG
JACKMAN
JACKMEN
JACKPOT
JACKROD
JACKSAW
JACKTAN
JACOBIN
JACOBUS
JACONET
JACTANT
JACTURE
JACUARU
JADDING
JADEDLY
JADEITE
JAGGARY
JAGGERY
JAGGIER
JAGGING
JAGHEER
JAGHIRE
JAGRATA
JAGUARS
JAILAGE
JALAPIC
JALAPIN
JALOPPY
JALOUSE
JAMBEAU
JAMBONE
JAMBOOL
JAMBOSA
JAMDANI
JAMMING
JAMPANI
JAMWOOD
JANAPAN
JANAPUM
JANDERS
JANGADA
JANGKAR
JANGLED
JANGLER
JANITOR
JANKERS
JANNOCK
JAPYGID
JAQUIMA
JARAGUA
JARBIRD
JARGOON
JARHEAD
JARKMAN
JARLESS
JARLITE
JARRING
JARVEYS
JASEYED
JASMINE
JASMONE
JASPERY
JASPOID
JAUNDER
JAUNTED
JAUNTIE
JAVELIN
JAVELOT
JAWBONE
JAWFALL
JAWFEET
JAWFISH
JAWFOOT
JAWHOLE
JAYHAWK
JAYPIET
JAYWALK
JAZERAN
JAZZBOW
JAZZIER
JAZZILY
JEALOUS
JECORAL
JECORIN
JEDCOCK
JEDDOCK
JEEPERS
JEEPNEY
JEERING
JEJUNAL
JEJUNUM
JELLICA
JELLICO
JELLIED
JELLIES
JELLIFY
JELLILY
JELLOID
JEMADAR
JEMIDAR
JEMMIES
JEMMILY
JENNIER
JENNIES
JEOFAIL
JEOPARD
JERICAN
JERKIER
JERKILY
JERKING
JERKISH
JERQUED
JERQUER
JERRIES
JERSEYS
JERVINA
JERVINE
JESSAMY
JESSANT
JESSING
JESTING
JETBEAD
JETPORT
JETTAGE
JETTEAU
JETTIED
JETTIES
JETTING
JETWARE
JEWBIRD
JEWBUSH
JEWELED
JEWELER
JEWELLY
JEWELRY
JEWFISH
JIBBING
JIBBOOM
JIBHEAD
JIBSTAY
JIFFIES
JIGGERS
JIGGETY
JIGGING
JIGGISH
JIGGLED
JIKUNGU
JILLING
JILLION
JILTING
JIMBANG
JIMJAMS
JIMMIED
JIMMIES
JINGALL
JINGLED
JINGLER
JINGLET
JINGOED
JINGOES
JINJILI
JINKING
JINNIES
JINRIKI
JINSING
JITNEUR
JITNEYS
JITTERS
JITTERY
JIVATMA
JOANNES
JOBARBE
JOBBERY
JOBBING
JOBBISH
JOBLESS
JOBSITE
JOCKEYS
JOCOQUE
JOCOQUI
JOCULAR
JOEBUSH
JOEWOOD
JOGGING
JOGGLED
JOGGLER
JOINANT
JOINDER
JOINERY
JOINING
JOINTED
JOINTER
JOINTLY
JOISTED
JOKELET
JOKIEST
JOLLIED
JOLLIER
JOLLIES
JOLLIFY
JOLLILY
JOLLITY
JOLTING
JONQUIL
JORNADA
JOSEITE
JOSTLED
JOSTLER
JOTTING
JOUBARB
JOUKERY
JOULEAN
JOUNCED
JOURNAL
JOURNEY
JOUSTER
JOYANCE
JOYANCY
JOYLEAF
JOYLESS
JOYRIDE
JOYSOME
JOYWEED
JUAMAVE
JUBILEE
JUBILUS
JUCHART
JUCKIES
JUDCOCK
JUDDOCK
JUDGING
JUDICES
JUGATED
JUGGING
JUGGINS
JUGGLED
JUGGLER
JUGHEAD
JUGLONE
JUGULAR
JUGULUM
JUICIER
JUICILY
JUJUIST
JUJITSU
JUJUISM
JUJUTSU
JUKEBOX
JULIDAN
JULIETT
JULOLIN
JUMBLED
JUMBLER
JUMBUCK
JUMELLE
JUMPERS
JUMPIER
JUMPING
JUMPOFF
JUNCITE
JUNCOUS
JUNCTLY
JUNGLED
JUNIATA
JUNIPER
JUNKING
JUNKMAN
JUNKMEN
JURALLY
JURATOR
JURIDIC
JURYMAN
JURYMEN
JUSSION
JUSSIVE
JUSSORY
JUSTICE
JUSTICO
JUSTIFY
JUSTLER
JUTTIES
JUTTING
JUVENAL
JYNGINE

AJANGLE
AJITTER
AJIVIKA
DJIBBAH
EJECTED
EJECTOR
EJULATE
EJURATE
FJORDED
GJEDOST
IJOLITE
SJAMBOK
SJOMILA
TJENKAL
TJOSITE

ABJOINT
ABJUDGE
ABJURED
ABJURER
ADJIGER
ADJOINT

ADJOURN
ADJOUST
ADJUDGE
ADJUNCT
ADJURED
ADJURER
ADJUROR
ADJUTOR
ALJAMIA
BAJOCCO
BAJOCHI
BAJOIRE
BEJESUS
BEJEWEL
BIJASAL
CAJAPUT
CAJEPUT
CAJOLED
CAJOLER
CAJUELA
CAJUPUT
COJUROR
DEJECTA
DEJEUNE
ENJEWEL
ENJOYED
ENJOYER
HAJILIJ
HIJINKS
INJELLY
INJOINT
INJUNCT

INJURED
INJURER
INJURIA
JEJUNAL
JEJUNUM
JUJUIST
JUJITSU
JUJUISM
JUJUTSU
KAJAWAH
KAJEPUT
MAJAGUA
MAJESTY
MAJORAT
MOJARRA
MUJERES
OBJECTS
PAJAMAS
PYJAMAS
REJOICE
REJONEO
REJOURN
REJUDGE
SEJEANT
SEJUNCT
SOJOURN
YAJEINE
YAJENIN

APOJOVE
BANJARA
BANJOES

BANJORE
BENJOIN
BLIJVER
CATJANG
CONJECT
CONJOIN
CONJURE
CONJURY
DISJECT
DISJOIN
DISJUNE
FAUJDAR
FOUJDAR
GALJOEN
GIOJOSO
GUAJIRA
JIMJAMS
JINJILI
KEDJAVE
MAHJONG
MANJACK
MANJEET
MUMJUMA
MUNJEET
OUTJAZZ
OUTJINX
OUTJUMP
PERJINK
PERJURE
PERJURY
PINJANE

PROJECT
SKIJORE
SKYJACK
SUBJECT
SUBJOIN
TANJONG
THUJENE
THUJONE
TOMJOHN
TRAJECT
TURJITE
VANJOHN
VIAJACA
ZANJERO
ZANJONA

ARVEJON
BACKJAW
BRINJAL
FERIJEE
FINDJAN
GEITJIE
HANDJAR
KANDJAR
KHANJAR
KHANJEE
KILLJOY
LOCKJAW
LONGJAW
MAHAJAN
MAHAJUN

MONTJOY
MUNTJAC
MUNTJAK
OVERJOY
PIROJKI
PROPJET
PULAJAN
PULIJAN
SAPAJOU
STANJEN
UINTJIE
WINDJAM

ABADEJO
ALFORJA
APAREJO
AZUELJO
BASENJI
COMITJE
FERIDJI
GOTRAJA
KILADJA
KORADJI
NAARTJE
PARANJA
SATLIJK
TORONJA
WICHTJE

HAJILIJ
KANKREJ

SCORING ORDER LIST OF 7-LETTER WORDS

29
JACKBOX

27
JAYHAWK
JAZZBOW
JUKEBOX

25
BACKJAW
JACKBOY
JAQUIMA
JAZZILY
JOCOQUE
JOCOQUI

24
JACKDAW
JAYWALK
JERQUED
JUMBUCK
JUMPOFF
KAJAWAH

23
AZUELJO
JACKASH
JACKETY
JACKSAW
JAWFISH
JAZERAN
JEDCOCK
JERQUER
JEWFISH
JOCKEYS
JONQUIL
JUDCOCK
LOCKJAW

ZANJERO
ZANJONA

22
DJIBBAH
JACKMAN
JACKMEN
JACKPOT
JAZZIER
JEDDOCK
JEWBUSH
JOYANCY
JUDDOCK
KEDJAVE
MANJACK
OUTJAZZ
SJAMBOK
SKYJACK
WICHTJE

21
AJIVIKA
BAJOCHI
HIJINKS
JACCHUS
JACKING
JACKLEG
JACKROD
JALOPPY
JAPYGID
JEMMILY
JERKILY
JERKISH
JOBBERY
JOBBISH
JOUKERY
JOYWEED
KHANJAR
KHANJEE

KILLJOY
OUTJINX
PYJAMAS

20
BAJOCCO
JACKALS
JACKASS
JACKEEN
JACKTAN
JAMWOOD
JANNOCK
JARKMAN
JARVEYS
JAWFALL
JAWFEET
JAWFOOT
JAWHOLE
JELLIFY
JEWBIRD
JEWELLY
JEWELRY
JIBBOOM
JIBHEAD
JIFFIES
JOLLIFY
JOYLEAF
JUCKIES
JUNKMAN
JUNKMEN
JUSTIFY
KAJEPUT
MAHJONG
MUNTJAK
OVERJOY
PERJINK
PIROJKI
VANJOHN
WINDJAM

19
APOJOVE
BEJEWEL
BLIJVER
CONJURY
FJORDED
JABBING
JACINTH
JADEDLY
JAGGARY
JAGGERY
JAMMING
JANGKAR
JASPERY
JAWBONE
JAYPIET
JEEPNEY
JERKING
JESSAMY
JIBBING
JIBSTAY
JIGGETY
JIGGISH
JIKUNGU
JIMBANG
JIMMIED
JINKING
JIVATMA
JOBBING
JOEBUSH
JOYANCE
JOYSOME
JUAMAVE
JUCHART
JUGHEAD
JUICILY
JUMBLED
JUMPING
JUNCTLY

JUNKING
JURYMAN
JURYMEN
KANDJAR
KILADJA
KORADJI
MAHAJAN
MAHAJUN
MAJESTY
MONTJOY
PERJURY
TOMJOHN
VIAJACA

18
ABJUDGE
CAJAPUT
CAJEPUT
CAJUPUT
COMITJE
CONJECT
ENJOYED
FAUJDAR
FERIDJI
FINDJAN
FOUJDAR
HANDJAR
JACAMAR
JACAMIN
JACOBIN
JACOBUS
JAGHEER
JAGHIRE
JALAPIC
JAMBEAU
JAMBONE
JAMBOOL
JAMBOSA
JAMPANI

JANAPUM
JANKERS
JARHEAD
JASEYED
JEMMIES
JERKIER
JEWELED
JIMMIES
JINRIKI
JOBARBE
JOEWOOD
JOKELET
JOKIEST
JOUBARB
JOYRIDE
JUMBLER
JUMPERS
JUMPIER
JYNGINE
LONGJAW
MUNTJAC
OBJECTS
OUTJUMP
PAJAMAS
PROJECT
PROPJET
SATLIJK
SKIJORE
SUBJECT
TJENKAL

17
ABADEJO
ABJURED
ADJUDGE
ADJUNCT
ALFORJA
ARVEJON
CAJOLED
CATJANG
DEJECTA
DISJECT
EJECTED
ENJEWEL
ENJOYER
FERIJEE
INJELLY
JADDING
JAGGING
JAMDANI
JARBIRD
JASPOID
JAVELIN
JAVELOT
JELLILY
JEMADAR
JEMIDAR
JEOFAIL
JEOPARD
JERSEYS
JERVINA
JERVINE
JETBEAD
JETWARE
JEWELER
JIGGING
JIGGLED
JIMJAMS
JITNEYS
JITTERY
JOGGING
JOGGLED
JOINERY
JOINTLY
JOLLILY
JOLLITY
JOUNCED
JOURNEY
JOYLESS
JUDGING
JUDICES
JUGGING
JUGGLED
JUGULUM
JURALLY
JURIDIC
JUSSIVE
JUSSORY
JUVENAL
KANKREJ
MAJAGUA
MUMJUMA
THUJENE
THUJONE
YAJEINE
YAJENIN

16
ABJOINT
ABJURER
ADJIGER
ADJURED
ALJAMIA
APAREJO
BAJOIRE
BANJARA
BANJOES
BANJORE
BASENJI
BEJESUS
BENJOIN
BIJASAL
BRINJAL
CAJOLER
CAJUELA
COJUROR
CONJOIN
CONJURE
EJECTOR
GJEDOST
HAJILIJ
INJUNCT
JABORIN
JABULES
JACALES
JACATOO
JACONET
JACTANT
JACTURE
JACUARU
JAGGIER
JALAPIN
JANAPAN
JANGADA
JANGLED
JASMINE
JASMONE
JECORAL
JECORIN
JEEPERS
JELLICA
JELLICO
JERICAN
JETPORT
JIGGERS
JINGLED
JINGOED
JOBLESS
JOBSITE
JOCULAR
JOGGLER
JUBILEE
JUBILUS
JUGATED
JUGGINS
JUGGLER
JUICIER
JUMELLE
JUNCITE
JUNCOUS
JUNGLED
JUNIPER
JUSTICE
JUSTICO
MAJORAT
MANJEET
MOJARRA
MUJERES
MUNJEET
PARANJA
PERJURE
PINJANE
PULAJAN
PULIJAN
REJOICE
REJUDGE
SAPAJOU
SEJUNCT
SJOMILA
SUBJOIN
TRAJECT

15
ADJOINT
ADJOURN
ADJOUST
ADJURER
ADJUROR
ADJUTOR
AJANGLE
DEJEUNE
DISJOIN
DISJUNE
GALJOEN
GEITJIE
GIOJOSO
GOTRAJA
GUAJIRA
INJURED
JADEITE
JAGRATA
JAGUARS
JAILAGE
JANDERS
JANGLER
JARAGUA
JARGOON
JARRING
JAUNDER
JAUNTED
JEERING
JEJUNUM
JELLIED
JELLOID
JESSING
JESTING
JETTAGE
JETTIED
JETTING
JILLING
JILTING
JINGALL
JINGLER
JINGLET
JINGOES
JINSING
JOINDER
JOINING
JOINTED
JOISTED
JOLLIED
JOLTING
JORNADA
JOSTLED
JOTTING
JUGLONE
JUGULAR
JUJUISM
JULIDAN
JUTTING
TANJONG

14
AJITTER
EJULATE
EJURATE
IJOLITE
INJOINT
INJURER
INJURIA
JALOUSE
JANITOR
JARLESS
JARLITE
JAUNTIE
JEALOUS
JELLIES
JENNIER
JENNIES
JERRIES
JESSANT
JETTEAU
JETTIES
JILLION
JINNIES
JITNEUR
JITTERS
JOANNES
JOINANT
JOINTER
JOLLIER
JOLLIES
JOSEITE
JOSTLER
JOULEAN
JOURNAL
JOUSTER
JULIETT
JULOLIN
JUNIATA
JURATOR
JUSSION
JUSTLER
JUTTIES
NAARTJE
REJONEO
REJOURN
SEJEANT
SOJOURN
STANJEN
TJOSITE
TORONJA
TURJITE
UINTJIE

13
JEJUNAL
JINJILI
JUJUIST
JUJITSU
JUJUTSU

ALPHABETICAL LIST OF 8-LETTER WORDS

ABJECTLY
ABJURING
ADJACENT
ADJOINED
ADJUDGED
ADJUDGER
ADJUGATE
ADJUMENT
ADJURING
ADJUSTED
ADJUSTER
ADJUSTOR
ADJUTAGE
ADJUTANT
ADJUTORY
ADJUTRIX
ADJUVANT
ADJUVATE
AJONJOLI
AJOURISE
AJUTMENT
ALJAMADO
ALJAMIAH
ALLELUJA
APAREJOS

BABAJAGA
BAJONADO
BAJULATE
BEJABERS
BEJUGGLE
BENJAMIN
BIAJAIBA
BIJUGATE
BIJUGOUS
BIJWONER
BLATJANG
BLUEJACK
BOBJEROM
BOOTJACK
BOSTANJI
BRINJAUL
BRUJERIA
BUCKJUMP
CAJOLERY
CAJOLING
CANAJONG
CARAJURA
CARCAJOU
COADJUST
COADJUTE
CONJOINT
CONJUGAL
CONJUNCT
CONJURED
CONJURER
CONJUROR
CRACKJAW
CUNJEVOI
DEJECTED
DEJERATE
DEJEUNER
DEMIJOHN
DEVARAJA
DISJEUNE
DISJOINT
DISJUNCT
DJAGOONG
DOORJAMB
EARJEWEL
EJECTING
EJECTION
EJECTIVE
EJICIENT
EMAJAGUA
ENJAMBED
ENJOINED
ENJOINER
ENJOYING
FERIDJEE
FLAPJACK
FLIPJACK
FORJUDGE
FOUJDARY
FRABJOUS
GALIONJI
GRANJENO
GUAJILLO
HAMINGJA
HIGHJACK
HIJACKER
HUAJILLO
IJUSSITE
INJECTED
INJECTOR
INJURIES
INJURING
INJUSTLY
JABBERED
JABBERER
JABORINE
JACCONET
JACCONOT
JACINTHE
JACITARA
JACKAROO
JACKBIRD
JACKBOOT
JACKEROO
JACKETED
JACKFISH
JACKHEAD
JACKPOTS
JACKROLL
JACKSHAY
JACKSHEA
JACKSTAY
JACKWEED
JACKWOOD
JACOBAEA
JACOLATT
JACOUNCE
JACQUARD
JACTANCE
JACTANCY
JACULATE
JADISHLY
JAGGEDLY
JAGGHERY
JAGGIEST
JAGIRDAR
JAILBIRD
JAILMATE
JAILYARD
JAKFRUIT
JALAPENO
JALLOPED
JALOPIES
JALOUSED
JALOUSIE
JALPAITE
JAMBEAUX
JAMBOLAN
JAMBOREE
JAMDANEE
JAMPANEE
JAMTLAND
JANGLING
JANICEPS
JANISARY
JANITRIX
JANIZARY
JAPANNED
JAPANNER
JAPERIES
JAPISHLY
JAPONICA
JAPYGOID
JAQUETTE
JARARACA
JARGONAL
JARGONED
JARGONEL
JARGONER
JARGONIC
JAROSITE
JAROVIZE
JASMINED
JASPERED
JASPONYX
JASPOPAL
JAUNDERS
JAUNDICE
JAUNTIER
JAUNTILY
JAUNTING
JAVELINA
JAWSMITH
JAZERANT
JAZZIEST
JEALOUSE
JEALOUSY
JECORIZE
JEJUNELY
JEJUNITY
JELERANG
JELLYING
JELOTONG
JELUTONG
JEOPARDY
JEREMIAD
JERKIEST
JERKINED
JERKSOME
JERMONAL
JEROBOAM
JERQUING
JERRICAN
JERRYISM
JERSEYED
JESTBOOK
JESTWORD
JETLINER
JETTISON
JEUNESSE
JEWELING
JEWELLED
JEWELLER
JEZEKITE
JIBBINGS
JIGGERED
JIGGERER
JIGGLING
JIMCRACK
JIMMYING
JIMPNESS
JIMSEDGE
JINGBANG
JINGLING
JINGOISH
JINGOISM
JINGOIST
JINNIYEH
JINSHANG
JIPIJAPA
JIRKINET
JITNEUSE
JIUJITSU
JIUJUTSU
JOBATION
JOBSMITH
JOCATORY
JOCKEYED
JOCOSELY
JOCOSITY
JOCTELEG
JOCUNDLY
JOCUNDRY
JODHPURS
JOGGLETY
JOGGLING
JOHANNES
JOHNBOAT
JOINERED
JOINHAND
JOINTAGE
JOINTING
JOINTIST
JOINTURE
JOISTING
JOKESOME
JOKESTER
JOKINGLY
JOLLIEST
JOLLITRY
JOLLOPED
JOLLYING
JOLTHEAD
JONGLERY
JONGLEUR
JOOKERIE
JORDANON
JOSEFITE
JOSTLING
JOTATION
JOTISARU
JOUNCING
JOURNEYS
JOUSTING
JOVIALLY
JOVIALTY
JOVILABE
JOYFULLY
JOYHOUSE
JOYOUSLY
JUBARTAS
JUBARTES
JUBEROUS
JUBILANT
JUBILATE
JUBILEAN
JUBILIST
JUBILIZE
JUDAIZER
JUDGMENT
JUDICATE
JUDICIAL
JUDICIUM
JUGATION
JUGGLERY
JUGGLING
JUGULATE
JUICIEST
JULIENNE
JULOLINE
JUMBLING
JUMBOISM
JUMPIEST
JUMPROCK
JUMPSEED
JUMPSOME
JUNCTION
JUNCTIVE
JUNCTURE
JUNEFISH
JUNGLIER
JUNKETED
JUNKETER
JUNKYARD
JURAMENT
JURATION
JURATIVE
JURATORY
JURISTIC
JUSSHELL
JUSTICED
JUSTICER
JUSTITIA
JUSTMENT
JUSTNESS
JUVENATE
JUVENILE
KABELJOU
KAJUGARU
KINKAJOU
KOMITAJI
KOMMETJE
KUJAWIAK
LONGJAWS
LUTJANID
MAHARAJA
MAHJONGG
MAJESTIC
MAJIDIEH
MAJOLICA
MAJOLIST
MAJORATE
MAJORITY
MAJORIZE
MARJORAM
MEDJIDIE
MEJORANA
MIJAKITE
MIJNHEER
MISJUDGE
MONTJOYE
MUJTAHID
NAUJAITE
NIGHTJAR
NONJUROR
OBJECTED
OBJECTEE
OBJECTOR
OVERJUMP
PAJAMAED
PEJERREY
PEJORATE
PEJORISM
PEJORIST
PEJORITY
PEJORITY
PERIJOVE
PERJURED
PERJURER
POPINJAY
PREJUDGE
PULSEJET
PYJAMAED
RAJBANSI
RAJOGUNA
READJUST
REJECTED
REJECTER
REJECTOR
REJOICED
REJOICER
REJOINED
REJOUNCE
SEDJADEH
SEJOINED
SEJUGATE
SEJUGOUS
SERJEANT
SKIJORER
SKIPJACK
SLAPJACK
SNAPJACK
SNIPJACK
SOURJACK
STICKJAW
SUBJOINT
SUBJUGAL
SUBJUNCT
SUCURUJU
TATMJOLK
TENDEJON
TJANTING
TJURUNGA
TOKTOKJE
TURBOJET
TURJAITE
UNJUSTLY
VERJUICE
YAJENINE
YAMMADJI

POSITIONAL ORDER LIST OF 8-LETTER WORDS

JABBERED
JABBERER
JABORINE
JACCONET
JACCONOT
JACINTHE
JACITARA
JACKAROO
JACKBIRD
JACKBOOT
JACKEROO
JACKETED
JACKFISH
JACKHEAD
JACKPOTS
JACKROLL
JACKSHAY
JACKSHEA
JACKSTAY
JACKWEED
JACKWOOD
JACOBAEA
JACOLATT
JACOUNCE
JACQUARD
JACTANCE
JACTANCY
JACULATE
JADISHLY
JAGGEDLY
JAGGHERY
JAGGIEST
JAGIRDAR
JAILBIRD
JAILMATE
JAILYARD
JAKFRUIT
JALAPENO
JALLOPED
JALOPIES
JALOUSED
JALOUSIE
JALPAITE
JAMBEAUX
JAMBOLAN
JAMBOREE
JAMDANEE
JAMPANEE
JAMTLAND
JANGLING
JANICEPS
JANISARY
JANITRIX
JANIZARY
JAPANNED
JAPANNER
JAPERIES
JAPISHLY
JAPONICA
JAPYGOID
JAQUETTE
JARARACA
JARGONAL
JARGONED
JARGONEL
JARGONER
JARGONIC
JAROSITE
JAROVIZE
JASMINED
JASPERED
JASPONYX
JASPOPAL
JAUNDERS
JAUNDICE
JAUNTIER
JAUNTILY
JAUNTING
JAVELINA
JAWSMITH
JAZERANT
JAZZIEST
JEALOUSE
JEALOUSY
JECORIZE
JEJUNELY
JEJUNITY
JELERANG
JELLYING
JELOTONG
JELUTONG
JEOPARDY
JEREMIAD
JERKIEST
JERKINED
JERKSOME
JERMONAL
JEROBOAM
JERQUING
JERRICAN
JERRYISM
JERSEYED
JESTBOOK
JESTWORD
JETLINER
JETTISON
JEUNESSE
JEWELING
JEWELLED
JEWELLER
JEZEKITE
JIBBINGS
JIGGERED
JIGGERER
JIGGLING
JIMCRACK
JIMMYING
JIMPNESS
JIMSEDGE
JINGBANG
JINGLING
JINGOISH
JINGOISM
JINGOIST
JINNIYEH
JINSHANG
JIPIJAPA
JIRKINET
JITNEUSE
JIUJITSU
JIUJUTSU
JOBATION
JOBSMITH
JOCATORY
JOCKEYED
JOCOSELY
JOCOSITY
JOCTELEG
JOCUNDLY
JOCUNDRY
JODHPURS
JOGGLETY
JOGGLING
JOHANNES
JOHNBOAT
JOINERED
JOINHAND
JOINTAGE
JOINTING
JOINTIST
JOINTURE
JOISTING
JOKESOME
JOKESTER
JOKINGLY
JOLLIEST
JOLLITRY
JOLLOPED
JOLLYING
JOLTHEAD
JONGLERY
JONGLEUR
JOOKERIE
JORDANON
JOSEFITE
JOSTLING
JOTATION
JOTISARU
JOUNCING
JOURNEYS
JOUSTING
JOVIALLY
JOVIALTY
JOVILABE
JOYFULLY
JOYHOUSE
JOYOUSLY
JUBARTAS
JUBARTES
JUBEROUS
JUBILANT
JUBILATE
JUBILEAN
JUBILIST
JUBILIZE
JUDAIZER
JUDGMENT
JUDICATE
JUDICIAL
JUDICIUM
JUGATION
JUGGLERY
JUGGLING
JUGULATE
JUICIEST
JULIENNE
JULOLINE
JUMBLING
JUMBOISM
JUMPIEST
JUMPROCK
JUMPSEED
JUMPSOME
JUNCTION
JUNCTIVE
JUNCTURE
JUNEFISH
JUNGLIER
JUNKETED
JUNKETER
JUNKYARD
JURAMENT
JURATION
JURATIVE
JURATORY
JURISTIC
JUSSHELL
JUSTICED
JUSTICER
JUSTITIA
JUSTMENT
JUSTNESS
JUVENATE
JUVENILE

AJONJOLI
AJONJOLI
AJOURISE
AJUTMENT
DJAGOONG
EJECTING
EJECTION
EJECTIVE
EJICIENT
IJUSSITE
TJANTING
TJURUNGA

ABJECTLY
ABJURING
ADJACENT
ADJOINED
ADJUDGED
ADJUDGER
ADJUGATE
ADJUMENT
ADJURING
ADJUSTED
ADJUSTER
ADJUSTOR
ADJUTAGE
ADJUTANT
ADJUTORY
ADJUTRIX
ADJUVANT
ADJUVATE
ALJAMADO
ALJAMIAH
BAJONADO
BAJULATE
BEJABERS
BEJUGGLE
BIJUGATE
BIJUGOUS
BIJWONER
CAJOLERY
CAJOLING
DEJECTED
DEJERATE
DEJEUNER
ENJAMBED
ENJOINED
ENJOINER
ENJOYING
HIJACKER
INJECTED
INJECTOR
INJURIES
INJURING
INJUSTLY
JEJUNELY
JEJUNITY
KAJUGARU
KUJAWIAK
MAJESTIC
MAJIDIEH
MAJOLICA
MAJOLIST
MAJORATE
MAJORITY
MAJORIZE
MEJORANA
MIJAKITE
MIJNHEER
MUJTAHID
OBJECTED
OBJECTEE
OBJECTOR
PAJAMAED
PEJERREY
PEJORATE
PEJORISM
PEJORIST
PEJORITY
PYJAMAED
RAJBANSI
RAJOGUNA
REJECTED
REJECTER
REJECTOR
REJOICED
REJOICER
REJOINED
REJOUNCE
SEJOINED
SEJUGATE
SEJUGOUS
UNJUSTLY
YAJENINE

BENJAMIN
BIAJAIBA
BOBJEROM
BRUJERIA
CONJOINT
CONJUGAL
CONJUNCT
CONJURED
CONJURER
CONJUROR
CUNJEVOI
DISJEUNE
DISJOINT
DISJUNCT
EARJEWEL
EMAJAGUA
FORJUDGE
FOUJDARY
GUAJILLO
HUAJILLO
JIUJITSU
JIUJUTSU
LUTJANID
MAHJONGG
MARJORAM
MEDJIDIE
MISJUDGE
NAUJAITE
NONJUROR
PERJURED
PERJURER
PREJUDGE
SEDJADEH
SERJEANT
SKIJORER
SUBJOINT
SUBJUGAL
SUBJUNCT
TURJAITE
VERJUICE

BABAJAGA
BLATJANG
BLUEJACK
BOOTJACK
BRINJAUL
BUCKJUMP
CANAJONG
CARAJURA
COADJUST

COADJUTE
DEMIJOHN
DOORJAMB
FLAPJACK
FLIPJACK
FRABJOUS
GRANJENO
HIGHJACK
JIPIJAPA
LONGJAWS
MONTJOYE
OVERJUMP
PERIJOVE
READJUST
SKIPJACK
SLAPJACK
SNAPJACK
SNIPJACK
SOURJACK
TATMJOLK

APAREJOS
CARCAJOU
CRACKJAW
FERIDJEE
KABELJOU
KINKAJOU
NIGHTJAR
POPINJAY
PULSEJET
STICKJAW
TENDEJON
TURBOJET

ALLELUJA
BOSTANJI
DEVARAJA
GALIONJI
HAMINGJA
KOMITAJI
KOMMETJE
MAHARAJA
SUCURUJU
TOKTOKJE
YAMMADJI

SCORING ORDER LIST OF 8-LETTER WORDS

28
HIGHJACK
JEZEKITE

27
BUCKJUMP
JACKFISH
JACKSHAY
JACQUARD
JANIZARY
JAROVIZE
JASPONYX

26
CRACKJAW
FLAPJACK
FLIPJACK
JAMBEAUX
JECORIZE
JUBILIZE
MAJORIZE

25
JACKHEAD
JACKWEED
JACKWOOD
JERQUING
JIMCRACK
JOCKEYED
JUDAIZER
JUMPROCK

24
HIJACKER
JACKBIRD
JACKSHEA
JACKSTAY
JAQUETTE
JAZERANT
JOYFULLY
STICKJAW

23
ADJUTRIX
BLUEJACK
BOOTJACK
JACKBOOT
JACKPOTS
JAGGHERY
JAPISHLY
JAWSMITH
JAZZIEST
JIMMYING
JOKINGLY
JUNKYARD
KOMMETJE
PYJAMAED
SLAPJACK
SNAPJACK
SNIPJACK
YAMMADJI

22
ABJECTLY
FOUJDARY
JACKETED
JACTANCY
JADISHLY
JAKFRUIT
JANITRIX
JAPYGOID
JOBSMITH
MAHJONGG
OVERJUMP
POPINJAY
SKIPJACK

21
BOBJEROM
DEMIJOHN
HAMINGJA
JACKAROO
JACKEROO
JACKROLL
JAGGEDLY
JEOPARDY
JERKSOME
JESTBOOK
JINNIYEH
JOCUNDLY
JOCUNDRY
JODHPURS
JOKESOME
JOVIALLY
JOVIALTY
JOYHOUSE
JOYOUSLY
JUMBOISM
JUMPSOME
JUNEFISH
KABELJOU
KOMITAJI
KUJAWIAK
MAJIDIEH
MIJAKITE
MUJTAHID
SOURJACK
TATMJOLK

20
ALJAMIAH
BABAJAGA
BIJWONER
CAJOLERY
CUNJEVOI
DOORJAMB
EJECTIVE
ENJAMBED
FORJUDGE
FRABJOUS
JABBERED
JACINTHE
JERKINED
JERRYISM
JIBBINGS
JOCATORY
JOCOSELY
JOCOSITY
JOGGLETY
JOHNBOAT
JOVILABE
JUDICIUM
JUGGLERY
JUMBLING
JUMPSEED
JUNCTIVE
JUNKETED
KAJUGARU
MAHARAJA
MAJORITY
MIJNHEER
MONTJOYE
OBJECTED
PAJAMAED
PEJERREY
PERIJOVE
SEDJADEH
VERJUICE

19
ADJUDGED
ADJUTORY
ADJUVANT
ADJUVATE
BEJABERS
BEJUGGLE
BENJAMIN
BIAJAIBA
CARCAJOU
CONJUNCT
DEJECTED
DEVARAJA
ENJOYING
FERIDJEE
JABBERER
JACCONET
JACCONOT
JACOBAEA
JACOUNCE
JACTANCE
JAILYARD
JAMBOLAN
JAMBOREE
JAMPANEE
JANICEPS
JAPONICA
JASPOPAL
JELLYING
JERKIEST
JEROBOAM
JERSEYED
JESTWORD
JEWELING
JEWELLED
JIMPNESS
JIMSEDGE
JINGBANG
JINGOISH
JINSHANG
JIRKINET
JOINHAND
JOKESTER
JOLLYING
JOLTHEAD
JONGLERY
JOOKERIE
JUDGMENT
JUMPIEST
JUNKETER
LONGJAWS
MAJESTIC
MAJOLICA
MARJORAM
MEDJIDIE
MISJUDGE
NIGHTJAR
OBJECTEE
OBJECTOR
PEJORISM
PREJUDGE
SKIJORER
SUBJUNCT

18
ABJURING
ADJACENT
ADJUDGER
ADJUMENT
ALJAMADO
BAJONADO
BIJUGATE
BIJUGOUS
BLATJANG
CAJOLING
CANAJONG
COADJUST
COADJUTE
CONJUGAL
CONJURED
DISJUNCT
DJAGOONG
EARJEWEL
EJECTING
EMAJAGUA
HUAJILLO
INJECTED
INJUSTLY
JAILBIRD
JALLOPED
JAMDANEE
JAMTLAND
JANISARY
JAPANNED
JARGONIC
JASMINED
JASPERED
JAUNDICE
JAUNTILY
JAVELINA
JEALOUSY
JEREMIAD
JEWELLER
JIGGERED
JIGGLING
JINGOISM
JIPIJAPA
JOCTELEG
JOGGLING
JOHANNES
JOLLITRY
JOLLOPED
JOSEFITE
JOUNCING
JOURNEYS
JUDICATE
JUDICIAL
JUGGLING
JURATIVE
JURATORY
JUSSHELL
JUSTICED
JUVENATE
JUVENILE
KINKAJOU
PERJURED
REJECTED
REJOICED
SUBJUGAL
TOKTOKJE
UNJUSTLY
YAJENINE

17
ADJOINED
ADJUGATE
ADJURING
ADJUSTED
ADJUTAGE
AJUTMENT
APAREJOS
BAJULATE
BOSTANJI
BRINJAUL
BRUJERIA
CARAJURA
CONJOINT
CONJURER
CONJUROR
EJECTION
EJICIENT
INJECTOR
JABORINE
JACITARA
JACOLATT
JACULATE
JAGGIEST
JAGIRDAR
JAILMATE
JALAPENO
JALOPIES

JALPAITE
JANGLING
JAPANNER
JAPERIES
JARARACA
JARGONED
JEJUNELY
JEJUNITY
JERMONAL
JERRICAN
JIGGERER
JINGLING
JOBATION
JUBARTAS
JUBARTES
JUBEROUS
JUBILANT
JUBILATE
JUBILEAN
JUBILIST
JUICIEST
JUNCTION
JUNCTURE
JURAMENT
JURISTIC

JUSTICER
JUSTMENT
MAJOLIST
MAJORATE
MEJORANA
PEJORATE
PEJORIST
PERJURER
PULSEJET
RAJBANSI
REJECTER
REJECTOR
REJOICER
REJOUNCE
SUBJOINT
SUCURUJU
TURBOJET

16
ADJUSTER
ADJUSTOR
ADJUTANT
DEJERATE
DEJEUNER
DISJEUNE

DISJOINT
ENJOINED
GALIONJI
GRANJENO
GUAJILLO
INJURING
JALOUSED
JARGONAL
JARGONEL
JARGONER
JAUNDERS
JAUNTING
JELERANG
JELOTONG
JELUTONG
JINGOIST
JOINERED
JOINTAGE
JOINTING
JOISTING
JONGLEUR
JORDANON
JOSTLING
JOUSTING

JUGATION
JUGULATE
JUNGLIER
LUTJANID
RAJOGUNA
READJUST
REJOINED
SEJOINED
SEJUGATE
SEJUGOUS
TENDEJON
TJANTING
TJURUNGA

15
AJOURISE
ALLELUJA
ENJOINER
IJUSSITE
INJURIES
JALOUSIE
JAROSITE
JAUNTIER
JEALOUSE

JETLINER
JETTISON
JEUNESSE
JITNEUSE
JOINTIST
JOINTURE
JOLLIEST
JOTATION
JOTISARU
JULIENNE
JULOLINE
JURATION
JUSTITIA
JUSTNESS
NAUJAITE
NONJUROR
SERJEANT
TURJAITE

14
AJONJOLI
JIUJITSU
JIUJUTSU

ALPHABETICAL LIST OF 9-LETTER WORDS

ABJECTION
ABJECTIVE
ADJACENCY
ADJECTION
ADJECTIVE
ADJOINING
ADJOURNAL
ADJUDGING
ADJUNCTLY
ADJUSTAGE
ADJUSTIVE
ADJUTANCY
ADJUTRICE
ALJAMIADO
ALJOFAINA
AMBERJACK
ANKLEJACK
APJOHNITE
APPLEJACK
APPLEJOHN
BACKJOINT
BANJORINE
BARAJILLO
BEJABBERS
BEJEWELED
BIJUGULAR
BLACKJACK
BLUEJOINT
BOOTJACKS
BRINJAREE
BRINJARRY
CAJUPUTOL
CISJURANE
COADJUTOR
CONJOINED
CONJOINER
CONJOBBLE
CONJUGACY

CONJUGANT
CONJUGATA
CONJUGATE
CONJUGIAL
CONJUGIUM
CONJURING
CROSSJACK
DEJECTILE
DEJECTION
DEJECTORY
DEJECTURE
DEMIJAMBE
DISJASKED
DISJASKIT
DISJECTED
DISJOINED
DJALMAITE
EJACULATE
EJECTMENT
ENJEOPARD
ENJOINDER
ENJOINING
ENJOYABLE
ENJOYABLY
ENJOYMENT
FAUJASITE
FOREJUDGE
FORJASKIT
FORJESKET
FORJUDGED
FORJUDGER
FOUJDARRY
FRAILEJON
GUEJARITE
INJECTING
INJECTION
INJUREDLY
INJURIOUS

INJUSTICE
INTERJECT
INTERJOIN
JABBERING
JABORANDI
JACARANDA
JACKEROOS
JACKETING
JACKFRUIT
JACKKNIFE
JACKLIGHT
JACKPLANE
JACKSCREW
JACKSHAFT
JACKSLAVE
JACKSMELT
JACKSMITH
JACKSNIPE
JACKSTOCK
JACKSTONE
JACKSTRAW
JACOBSITE
JACQUERIE
JACTATION
JACTITATE
JACULATED
JACULATOR
JACUTINGA
JADEDNESS
JAGHIRDAR
JAGUARETE
JAILERESS
JAILERING
JAILHOUSE
JAILORING
JALOUSIED
JALOUSING
JAMBALAYA

JAMBOLANA
JAMBSTONE
JAMROSADE
JANISSARY
JANITRESS
JAPACONIN
JAPANNERY
JAPANNING
JARGONING
JARGONISH
JARGONIST
JARGONIUM
JARGONIZE
JAROVIZED
JASPAGATE
JASPERITE
JASPERIZE
JASPEROID
JASPIDEAN
JASPILITE
JASPILYTE
JATAMANSI
JATROPHIC
JAUNDICED
JAUNTIEST
JAWBATION
JAWFALLEN
JAWFISHES
JAWFOOTED
JAYHAWKER
JAYWALKER
JAZZINESS
JEALOUSLY
JEERINGLY
JEJUNATOR
JEJUNITIS
JELLIFIED
JELLYBEAN

JELLYFISH
JELLYLEAF
JELLYLIKE
JEMMINESS
JENNERIZE
JENNETING
JEOPARDED
JEOPARDER
JEQUERITY
JEQUIRITY
JERKINESS
JERKWATER
JERMOONAL
JESSAKEED
JESSAMIES
JESSAMINE
JESTINGLY
JETTATORE
JETTATURA
JETTINESS
JETTYHEAD
JEWELLERY
JEWELLING
JEWELWEED
JEWFISHES
JIGAMAREE
JIGGERMAN
JIGGINESS
JIGGUMBOB
JILLFLIRT
JIMBERJAW
JIMMYWEED
JINGLEBOB
JINNESTAN
JINNIWINK
JINNYWINK
JITNEYMAN
JITTERBUG

JNANAYOGA
JOBBERIES
JOBHOLDER
JOBMASTER
JOBMONGER
JOCKEYING
JOCKEYISM
JOCKSTRAP
JOCKTELEG
JOCULARLY
JOCULATOR
JOCUNDITY
JOHANNITE
JOINERING
JOININGLY
JOINTEDLY
JOINTRESS
JOINTURED
JOINTWEED
JOINTWOOD
JOINTWORM
JOKESMITH
JOLLIFIED
JOLLIMENT
JOLLINESS
JOLLITIES
JOLLYHEAD
JOLTINESS
JONQUILLE
JORDANITE
JOURNALED
JOURNEYED
JOURNEYER
JOVIALIST
JOVIALITY
JOVIALIZE
JOYLESSLY
JOYPOPPER
JUBILANCE
JUBILANCY
JUBILATED
JUBILATIO
JUCUNDITY
JUDGEMENT
JUDGMATIC
JUDGMENTS
JUDICABLE
JUDICATOR
JUDICIARY
JUDICIOUS
JUGLANDIN
JUGULATED
JUICINESS
JULIENITE
JULOIDIAN
JULOLIDIN
JUMENTOUS
JUMILLITE
JUMPINESS
JUMPROCKS
JUNCIFORM
JUNECTOMY
JUNGLIEST
JUNIORATE
JUNIORITY
JUNKBOARD
JUNKERDOM
JUNKERISM
JUNKETING
JURAMENTA
JURIDICAL
JURUPAITE
JURYWOMAN
JUSTICIAL
JUSTICIAR
JUSTICIER
JUSTICIES
JUSTICING
JUSTIFIED
JUSTIFIER
JUSTMENTS
JUTTINGLY
JUVENILIA
JUVENTUDE
JUXTAPOSE
KILOJOULE
KOMITADJI
KOORAJONG
KURRAJONG
LUJAURITE
LUJAVRITE
MAHARAJAH
MAJESTIES
MAJORDOMO
MAJORETTE
MAJUSCULE
MARIJUANA
MATAJUELO
MEDJIDIEH
MISJUDGED
MISJUDGER
MUNJISTIN
NONINJURY
NONJURANT
NONJURING
NUTJOBBER
OBJECTIFY
OBJECTING
OBJECTION
OBJECTIVE
OBJECTIZE
OBJICIENT
OBJURGATE
OUTJOCKEY
OUTJUGGLE
OVERJUDGE
PEREJONET
PERJINKLY
PERJURIES
PERJURING
PREJACENT
PREJUDGED
PREJUDGER
PREJUDICE
PROJECTOR
QUILLAJIC
REDJACKET
REJECTAGE
REJECTING
REJECTION
REJECTIVE
REJOICING
REJOINDER
REJOINING
RETROJECT
SANJAKBEG
SEJUNCTLY
SEMIBEJAN
SERJEANCY
SERJEANTY
SKIJORING
SKIPJACKS
SMOKEJACK
SOJOURNED
SOJOURNER
SUBJACENT
SUBJECTED
SUBJOINED
SUBJUGATE
SURREJOIN
SWARAJISM
SWARAJIST
TASAJILLO
TRAJECTED
TRIJUGATE
TRIJUGOUS
UNIJUGATE
UNINJURED
VAJRASANA

POSITIONAL ORDER LIST OF 9-LETTER WORDS

JABBERING
JABORANDI
JACARANDA
JACKEROOS
JACKETING
JACKFRUIT
JACKKNIFE
JACKLIGHT
JACKPLANE
JACKSCREW
JACKSHAFT
JACKSLAVE
JACKSMELT
JACKSMITH
JACKSNIPE
JACKSTOCK
JACKSTONE
JACKSTRAW
JACOBSITE
JACQUERIE
JACTATION
JACTITATE
JACULATED
JACULATOR
JACUTINGA
JADEDNESS
JAGHIRDAR
JAGUARETE
JAILERESS
JAILERING
JAILHOUSE
JAILORING
JALOUSIED
JALOUSING
JAMBALAYA
JAMBOLANA
JAMBSTONE
JAMROSADE
JANISSARY
JANITRESS
JAPACONIN
JAPANNERY
JAPANNING
JARGONING
JARGONISH
JARGONIST
JARGONIUM
JARGONIZE
JAROVIZED
JASPAGATE
JASPERITE
JASPERIZE
JASPEROID
JASPIDEAN
JASPILITE
JASPILYTE
JATAMANSI
JATROPHIC
JAUNDICED
JAUNTIEST
JAWBATION
JAWFALLEN
JAWFISHES
JAWFOOTED
JAYHAWKER
JAYWALKER
JAZZINESS
JEALOUSLY
JEERINGLY
JEJUNATOR
JEJUNITIS
JELLIFIED
JELLYBEAN
JELLYFISH
JELLYLEAF
JELLYLIKE
JEMMINESS
JENNERIZE
JENNETING
JEOPARDED
JEOPARDER
JEQUERITY
JEQUIRITY
JERKINESS
JERKWATER
JERMOONAL
JESSAKEED
JESSAMIES
JESSAMINE
JESTINGLY
JETTATORE
JETTATURA
JETTINESS
JETTYHEAD
JEWELLERY
JEWELLING
JEWELWEED
JEWFISHES
JIGAMAREE
JIGGERMAN
JIGGINESS
JIGGUMBOB
JILLFLIRT
JIMBERJAW
JIMMYWEED
JINGLEBOB
JINNESTAN
JINNIWINK
JINNYWINK
JITNEYMAN
JITTERBUG
JNANAYOGA
JOBBERIES
JOBHOLDER
JOBMASTER
JOBMONGER
JOCKEYING
JOCKEYISM
JOCKSTRAP
JOCKTELEG
JOCULARLY
JOCULATOR
JOCUNDITY
JOHANNITE
JOINERING
JOININGLY
JOINTEDLY
JOINTRESS
JOINTURED
JOINTWEED
JOINTWOOD
JOINTWORM
JOKESMITH
JOLLIFIED
JOLLIMENT
JOLLINESS
JOLLITIES
JOLLYHEAD
JOLTINESS
JONQUILLE
JORDANITE
JOURNALED
JOURNEYED
JOURNEYER
JOVIALIST
JOVIALITY
JOVIALIZE
JOYLESSLY
JOYPOPPER
JUBILANCE
JUBILANCY
JUBILATED
JUBILATIO
JUCUNDITY
JUDGEMENT
JUDGMATIC
JUDGMENTS
JUDICABLE
JUDICATOR
JUDICIARY
JUDICIOUS
JUGLANDIN
JUGULATED
JUICINESS
JULIENITE
JULOIDIAN
JULOLIDIN
JUMENTOUS
JUMILLITE
JUMPINESS
JUMPROCKS
JUNCIFORM
JUNECTOMY
JUNGLIEST
JUNIORATE
JUNIORITY
JUNKBOARD
JUNKERDOM
JUNKERISM
JUNKETING
JURAMENTA
JURIDICAL
JURUPAITE
JURYWOMAN
JUSTICIAL
JUSTICIAR
JUSTICIER
JUSTICIES
JUSTICING
JUSTIFIED
JUSTIFIER
JUSTMENTS
JUTTINGLY
JUVENILIA
JUVENTUDE

JUXTAPOSE

DJALMAITE
EJACULATE
EJECTMENT

ABJECTION
ABJECTIVE
ADJACENCY
ADJECTION
ADJECTIVE
ADJOINING
ADJOURNAL
ADJUDGING
ADJUNCTLY
ADJUSTAGE
ADJUSTIVE
ADJUTANCY
ADJUTRICE
ALJAMIADO
ALJOFAINA
APJOHNITE
BEJABBERS
BEJEWELED
BIJUGULAR
CAJUPUTOL
DEJECTILE
DEJECTION
DEJECTORY
DEJECTURE
ENJEOPARD
ENJOINDER
ENJOINING
ENJOYABLE
ENJOYABLY
ENJOYMENT
INJECTING
INJECTION
INJUREDLY
INJURIOUS
INJUSTICE
JEJUNATOR
JEJUNITIS
LUJAURITE
LUJAVRITE
MAJESTIES
MAJORDOMO
MAJORETTE
MAJUSCULE
OBJECTIFY
OBJECTING
OBJECTION
OBJECTIVE
OBJECTIZE
OBJICIENT
OBJURGATE
REJECTAGE
REJECTING
REJECTION
REJECTIVE
REJOICING
REJOINDER
REJOINING
SEJUNCTLY
SOJOURNED
SOJOURNER

VAJRASANA

BANJORINE
CISJURANE
CONJOINED
CONJOINER
CONJOBBLE
CONJUGACY
CONJUGANT
CONJUGATA
CONJUGATE
CONJUGIAL
CONJUGIUM
CONJURING
DISJASKED
DISJASKIT
DISJECTED
DISJOINED
FAUJASITE
FORJASKIT
FORJESKET
FORJUDGED
FORJUDGER
FOUJDARRY
GUEJARITE
MEDJIDIEH
MISJUDGED
MISJUDGER
MUNJISTIN
NONJURANT
NONJURING
NUTJOBBER
OUTJOCKEY
OUTJUGGLE
PERJINKLY
PERJURIES
PERJURING
PREJACENT
PREJUDGED
PREJUDGER
PREJUDICE
PROJECTOR
REDJACKET
SANJAKBEG
SERJEANCY
SERJEANTY
SKIJORING
SUBJACENT
SUBJECTED
SUBJOINED
SUBJUGATE
TRAJECTED
TRIJUGATE
TRIJUGOUS
UNIJUGATE

BACKJOINT
BARAJILLO
BLUEJOINT
BOOTJACKS
BRINJAREE
BRINJARRY
COADJUTANT
COADJUTOR
DEMIJAMBE
FOREJUDGE

KILOJOULE
MARIJUANA
MATAJUELO
OVERJUDGE
PEREJONET
SKIPJACKS
TASAJILLO
UNINJURED

AMBERJACK
ANKLEJACK
APPLEJACK
APPLEJOHN
BLACKJACK
CROSSJACK
INTERJECT
INTERJOIN
KOORAJONG
KURRAJONG
NONINJURY
RETROJECT
SMOKEJACK
SURREJOIN
SWARAJISM
SWARAJIST

FRAILEJON
JIMBERJAW
MAHARAJAH
QUILLAJIC
SEMIBEJAN

KOMITADJI

SCORING ORDER LIST OF 9-LETTER WORDS

29
JAROVIZED
JAYHAWKER
OBJECTIZE

28
JACKSHAFT
JEQUERITY
JEQUIRITY
JOVIALIZE

27
JACKSCREW
JACKSMITH
JACQUERIE
JASPERIZE
JIMMYWEED
JOCKEYISM
QUILLAJIC

26
AMBERJACK
APPLEJACK
JACKLIGHT
JARGONIZE
JAYWALKER
JINNYWINK
JOCKEYING
JUMPROCKS
OBJECTIFY

25
BLACKJACK
JACKFRUIT
JACKSLAVE
JACKSTRAW
JAWFISHES
JELLYFISH
JENNERIZE
JEWFISHES
JOKESMITH
JONQUILLE
JUXTAPOSE
OUTJOCKEY
PERJINKLY

24
ADJACENCY
BACKJOINT
BOOTJACKS
CONJUGACY
CROSSJACK
ENJOYABLY
JACKKNIFE
JACKPLANE
JACKSMELT
JACKSNIPE
JAZZINESS
JIGGUMBOB
JOCKSTRAP
JURYWOMAN
MAHARAJAH

23
ABJECTIVE
APPLEJOHN
DEMIJAMBE
FORJASKIT
FORJESKET
FOUJDARRY
JACKETING
JACKSTOCK
JAMBALAYA
JATROPHIC
JAWFOOTED
JELLYLIKE
JERKWATER
JETTYHEAD
JEWELWEED
JINNIWINK
JOCKTELEG
JOLLYHEAD
JUBILANCY
JUNCIFORM
JUNECTOMY
JUNKBOARD
JUNKERDOM
KOMITADJI
MEDJIDIEH
OBJECTIVE
REDJACKET
SANJAKBEG
SKIPJACKS
SMOKEJACK

22
ADJECTIVE
ADJUNCTLY
ADJUTANCY
BEJEWELED
CONJOBBLE
DEJECTORY
DISJASKED
FORJUDGED
JACKEROOS
JACKSTONE
JAWFALLEN
JELLYLEAF
JEWELLERY
JIMBERJAW
JOBHOLDER
JOCUNDITY
JOVIALITY
JOYLESSLY
JOYPOPPER
JUCUNDITY
JUDGMATIC
JUDICIARY
JUNKERISM

21
ANKLEJACK
APJOHNITE
BRINJARRY
CONJUGIUM
DISJASKIT
ENJOYABLE
ENJOYMENT
FOREJUDGE
FORJUDGER
JABBERING
JAGHIRDAR
JAPANNERY
JASPILYTE
JAWBATION
JELLYBEAN
JESSAKEED
JINGLEBOB
JITNEYMAN
JOBMONGER
JOCULARLY
JOINTWORM
JUDICABLE
JUNKETING
KOORAJONG
KURRAJONG
MAJORDOMO
MISJUDGED
OBJECTING
OVERJUDGE
PREJUDGED
PREJUDICE
REJECTIVE
SEJUNCTLY
SERJEANCY
SKIJORING
SUBJECTED
SWARAJISM

20
ABJECTION
ADJUDGING
ADJUSTIVE
CAJUPUTOL
DISJECTED
EJECTMENT
INJUREDLY
JACOBSITE
JAMBOLANA
JAMBSTONE
JAPACONIN
JARGONISH
JAUNDICED
JEERINGLY
JELLIFIED
JEMMINESS
JEOPARDED
JERKINESS
JESTINGLY
JEWELLING
JIGGERMAN
JNANAYOGA
JOBBERIES
JOBMASTER
JOININGLY
JOINTEDLY
JOINTWEED
JOINTWOOD
JOLLIFIED
JOURNEYED

JUBILANCE
JUDGEMENT
JUDGMENTS
JUMPINESS
JUSTIFIED
JUTTINGLY
JUVENTUDE
KILOJOULE
MAJUSCULE
MISJUDGER
NUTJOBBER
OBJECTION
OBJICIENT
PREJACENT
PREJUDGER
PROJECTOR
SEMIBEJAN
SUBJACENT

19
ADJECTION
ADJUTRICE
ALJAMIADO
ALJOFAINA
BEJABBERS
BIJUGULAR
COADJUTOR
CONJOINED
CONJUGANT
CONJUGATA
CONJUGATE
CONJUGIAL
CONJURING
DEJECTILE
DEJECTION
DEJECTURE
DJALMAITE
ENJEOPARD
FAUJASITE
FRAILEJON
INJECTING
JABORANDI
JACARANDA
JACULATED
JACUTINGA
JAILHOUSE
JAMROSADE
JANISSARY
JAPANNING
JARGONIUM
JASPAGATE
JASPEROID
JASPIDEAN
JEALOUSLY
JEOPARDER
JIGAMAREE
JILLFLIRT
JITTERBUG
JOHANNITE
JOURNEYER
JOVIALIST
JUBILATED
JUDICATOR
JUDICIOUS
JUNIORITY
JURIDICAL
JUSTICING
JUSTIFIER
JUVENILIA
LUJAVRITE
NONINJURY
OBJURGATE
PERJURING
REJECTAGE
REJECTING
REJOICING
SERJEANTY
SUBJOINED
SUBJUGATE
SWARAJIST
TRAJECTED
VAJRASANA

18
ADJOINING
ADJUSTAGE
BANJORINE
BARAJILLO
BLUEJOINT
BRINJAREE
CISJURANE
CONJOINER
DISJOINED
EJACULATE
INJECTION
INJUSTICE
INTERJECT
JACTATION
JACTITATE
JACULATOR
JADEDNESS
JARGONING
JASPERITE
JASPILITE
JATAMANSI
JERMOONAL
JESSAMIES
JESSAMINE
JIGGINESS
JOCULATOR
JOLLIMENT
JUBILATIO
JUGLANDIN
JUGULATED
JUICINESS
JUMENTOUS
JUMILLITE
JURAMENTA
JURUPAITE
JUSTICIAL
JUSTICIAR
JUSTICIER
JUSTICIES
JUSTMENTS
MAJESTIES
MAJORETTE
MARIJUANA
MATAJUELO
MUNJISTIN
OUTJUGGLE
PEREJONET
PERJURIES
REJECTION
RETROJECT

17
ADJOURNAL
ENJOINDER
ENJOINING
GUEJARITE
JAGUARETE
JAILERING
JAILORING
JALOUSIED
JALOUSING
JARGONIST
JENNETING
JOINERING
JOINTURED
JORDANITE
JOURNALED
JULOIDIAN
JULOLIDIN
JUNGLIEST
NONJURING
REJOINDER
REJOINING
SOJOURNED
TRIJUGATE
TRIJUGOUS
UNIJUGATE
UNINJURED

16
INJURIOUS
INTERJOIN
JAILERESS
JANITRESS
JAUNTIEST
JETTATORE
JETTATURA
JETTINESS
JINNESTAN
JOINTRESS
JOLLINESS
JOLLITIES
JOLTINESS
JULIENITE
JUNIORATE
LUJAURITE
NONJURANT
SOJOURNER
SURREJOIN
TASAJILLO

15
JEJUNATOR
JEJUNITIS

ALPHABETICAL LIST OF 10-LETTER WORDS

ABJECTNESS
ABJUDICATE
ABJUNCTIVE
ABJURATION
ABJURATORY
ABJUREMENT
ADJACENTLY
ADJECTIVAL
ADJOINEDLY
ADJUDICATE
ADJUNCTION
ADJUNCTIVE
ADJURATION
ADJURATORY
ADJUSTABLE
ADJUSTMENT
ARROJADITE
BEJEWELING
BEJEWELLED
BIJOUTERIE
BLUEJACKET
BUTTERJAGS
CAJOLEMENT
CAJOLERIES
CAJOLINGLY
CAJUPUTENE
CAODJACENCY
CHAPARAJOS
CHAPAREJOS
CLAMJAMFRY
COADJACENT
COADJUMENT
COADJUTANT
COADJUTIVE
COADJUTRIX
COADJUVANT
CONJECTIVE
CONJECTURE
CONJOINING
CONJOINTLY
CONJUGABLE
CONJUGALLY
CONJUGATED
CONJUGATOR
CONJUNCTLY
CONJUNCTUR
CONJURATOR
CRACKAJACK
DEJECTEDLY
DIJUDICATE
DISJECTING
DISJECTION
DISJOINING
DISJOINTED
DISJOINTLY
DISJUNCTOR
EJACULATED
EJACULATOR
EJECTIVELY
EJECTIVITY
ENJAMBMENT
ENJEOPARDY
ENJOINMENT
EQUIJACENT
FIDEJUSSOR
FOREJUDGED
FOREJUDGER
FORJUDGING
FRABJOUSLY
HIGHJACKER
INCONJUNCT
INJUDICIAL
INJUNCTION
INJUNCTIVE
INTERJOIST
JABBERMENT
JABOTICABA
JACKANAPES
JACKASSERY
JACKFISHES
JACKHAMMER
JACKKNIVES
JACKSNIPES
JACTITATED
JACULATING
JACULATION
JACULATIVE
JACULATORY
JADISHNESS
JAGGEDNESS
JAGHEERDAR
JAGHIREDAR
JAGUARONDI
JAGUARUNDI
JAILKEEPER
JAMESONITE
JANITORIAL
JANIZARIES
JAPACONINE
JAPISHNESS
JARDINIERE
JARGONELLE
JARGONIZED
JAROVIZING
JASPACHATE
JASPERATED
JASPERIZED
JASPIDEOUS
JAUNDICING
JAUNTINESS
JAVELINEER
JAWBREAKER
JAWCRUSHER
JAYWALKING
JEALOUSIES
JEJUNENESS
JEJUNOTOMY
JELLIFYING
JENTACULAR
JEOPARDIED
JEOPARDING
JEOPARDIZE
JEOPARDOUS
JERRYBUILD
JERRYBUILT
JEWELHOUSE
JEWELSMITH
JIMPRICUTE
JINGLINGLY
JINGOISTIC
JINRICKSHA
JINRIKIMAN
JINRIKIMEN
JINRIKISHA
JNANAMARGA
JOAQUINITE
JOBBERNOWL
JOCOSENESS
JOCOSITIES
JOCULARITY

JOCULATORY
JOCUNDNESS
JOGGLEWORK
JOHNNYCAKE
JOINTURESS
JOINTURING
JOLLIFYING
JOLTERHEAD
JOLTHEADED
JOSTLEMENT
JOUISSANCE
JOULEMETER
JOURNALESE
JOURNALING
JOURNALISE
JOURNALISM
JOURNALIST
JOURNALIZE
JOURNALLED
JOURNEYING
JOURNEYMAN
JOURNEYMEN
JOVIALIZED
JOYFULNESS
JOYOUSNESS
JUBILANTLY
JUBILARIAN
JUBILATING
JUBILATION
JUBILATORY
JUDICATION
JUDICATIVE
JUDICATORY
JUDICATURE
JUDICIABLE
JUDICIALLY
JUDOPHOBIA
JUGGERNAUT
JUGGLEMENT
JUGGLERIES
JUGGLINGLY
JUGULATING
JUGULATION
JULOLIDINE
JUMBLEMENT
JUMPSCRAPE
JUNCACEOUS
JUNCTIONAL
JUNGLESIDE
JUNGLEWOOD
JUNKDEALER
JURAMENTAL
JURAMENTUM
JURATORIAL
JURIDICIAL
JURISTICAL
JUSTICIARY
JUSTIFYING
JUVENILELY
JUVENILIFY
JUVENILISM
JUVENILITY
JUXTAPOSED
JUXTAPOSIT
LUMBERJACK
MAJESTICAL
MAJESTIOUS
MAJORATION
MAJORITIES
MAJUSCULAE
MAJUSCULAR
MISJOINDER
MISJUDGING
NATTERJACK
NONABJURER
NONJOINDER
NONJURANCY
OBJECTABLE
OBJECTIONS
OBJECTIVAL
OBJECTIZED
OBJECTLESS
OBJURATION
OBJURGATED
OBJURGATOR
OTTAJANITE
OUTJOURNEY
PAJAHUELLO
PAJAROELLO
PANJANDRUM
PEJORATION
PEJORATIVE
PERJINKETY
PERJUREDLY
PERJURIOUS
POSTJACENT
PREADJUNCT
PREJUDGING
PREJUDICED
PROJACIENT
PROJECTILE
PROJECTING
PROJECTION
PROJECTIVE
PROJECTRIX
PROJECTURE
PROJICIENT
RATTLEJACK
READJUSTER
REJOICEFUL
REJONEADOR
REJUNCTION
REJUVENANT
REJUVENATE
REJUVENIZE
SEJUNCTION
SEJUNCTIVE
SERJEANTRY
SKIPJACKLY
SKYJACKING
SOJOURNING
SUBJACENCY
SUBJECTIFY
SUBJECTILE
SUBJECTING
SUBJECTION
SUBJECTIVE
SUBJICIBLE
SUBJOINDER
SUBJOINING
SUBJUGABLE
SUBJUGATED
SUBJUGATOR
SUBJUGULAR
SUPPLEJACK
SUPRAJURAL
TIMBERJACK
TRAJECTILE
TRAJECTING
TRAJECTION
TRAJECTORY
UNDERJAWED
UNJUSTNESS
WEREJAGUAR
WINDJAMMER
WOODJOBBER

POSITIONAL ORDER LIST OF 10-LETTER WORDS

JABBERMENT
JABOTICABA
JACKANAPES
JACKASSERY
JACKFISHES
JACKHAMMER
JACKKNIVES
JACKSNIPES
JACTITATED
JACULATING
JACULATION
JACULATIVE
JACULATORY
JADISHNESS
JAGGEDNESS
JAGHEERDAR
JAGHIREDAR
JAGUARONDI
JAGUARUNDI
JAILKEEPER
JAMESONITE
JANITORIAL
JANIZARIES
JAPACONINE
JAPISHNESS
JARDINIERE
JARGONELLE
JARGONIZED
JAROVIZING
JASPACHATE
JASPERATED
JASPERIZED
JASPIDEOUS
JAUNDICING
JAUNTINESS
JAVELINEER
JAWBREAKER
JAWCRUSHER
JAYWALKING
JEALOUSIES
JEJUNENESS
JEJUNOTOMY
JELLIFYING
JENTACULAR
JEOPARDIED
JEOPARDING
JEOPARDIZE
JEOPARDOUS
JERRYBUILD
JERRYBUILT
JEWELHOUSE
JEWELSMITH
JIMPRICUTE
JINGLINGLY
JINGOISTIC
JINRICKSHA
JINRIKIMAN
JINRIKIMEN
JINRIKISHA
JNANAMARGA
JOAQUINITE
JOBBERNOWL
JOCOSENESS
JOCOSITIES
JOCULARITY
JOCULATORY
JOCUNDNESS
JOGGLEWORK
JOHNNYCAKE
JOINTURESS
JOINTURING
JOLLIFYING
JOLTERHEAD
JOLTHEADED
JOSTLEMENT
JOUISSANCE
JOULEMETER
JOURNALESE
JOURNALING
JOURNALISE
JOURNALISM
JOURNALIST
JOURNALIZE
JOURNALLED
JOURNEYING
JOURNEYMAN
JOURNEYMEN
JOVIALIZED
JOYFULNESS
JOYOUSNESS
JUBILANTLY
JUBILARIAN
JUBILATING
JUBILATION
JUBILATORY
JUDICATION
JUDICATIVE
JUDICATORY
JUDICATURE
JUDICIABLE
JUDICIALLY
JUDOPHOBIA
JUGGERNAUT
JUGGLEMENT
JUGGLERIES
JUGGLINGLY
JUGULATING
JUGULATION
JULOLIDINE
JUMBLEMENT
JUMPSCRAPE
JUNCACEOUS
JUNCTIONAL
JUNGLESIDE
JUNGLEWOOD
JUNKDEALER
JURAMENTAL
JURAMENTUM
JURATORIAL
JURIDICIAL
JURISTICAL
JUSTICIARY
JUSTIFYING
JUVENILELY
JUVENILIFY
JUVENILISM
JUVENILITY
JUXTAPOSED
JUXTAPOSIT

EJACULATED
EJACULATOR
EJECTIVELY
EJECTIVITY

ABJECTNESS
ABJUDICATE
ABJUNCTIVE
ABJURATION
ABJURATORY
ABJUREMENT
ADJACENTLY
ADJECTIVAL
ADJOINEDLY
ADJUDICATE
ADJUNCTION
ADJUNCTIVE
ADJURATION
ADJURATORY
ADJUSTABLE
ADJUSTMENT
BEJEWELING
BEJEWELLED
BIJOUTERIE
CAJOLEMENT
CAJOLERIES
CAJOLINGLY
CAJUPUTENE
DEJECTEDLY
DIJUDICATE
ENJAMBMENT
ENJEOPARDY
ENJOINMENT
INJUDICIAL
INJUNCTION
INJUNCTIVE
JEJUNENESS
JEJUNOTOMY
MAJESTICAL
MAJESTIOUS
MAJORATION
MAJORITIES
MAJUSCULAE
MAJUSCULAR
OBJECTABLE
OBJECTIONS
OBJECTIVAL
OBJECTIZED
OBJECTLESS
OBJURATION
OBJURGATED
OBJURGATOR
PAJAHUELLO
PAJAROELLO
PEJORATION
PEJORATIVE
REJOICEFUL
REJONEADOR
REJUNCTION
REJUVENANT
REJUVENATE
REJUVENIZE
SEJUNCTION
SEJUNCTIVE
SOJOURNING
UNJUSTNESS

CONJECTIVE
CONJOINING
CONJOINTLY
CONJUGABLE
CONJUGALLY
CONJUGATED
CONJUGATOR
CONJUNCTLY

CONJUNCTUR
CONJURATOR
DISJECTING
DISJECTION
DISJOINING
DISJOINTED
DISJOINTLY
DISJUNCTOR
FORJUDGING
MISJOINDER
MISJUDGING
NONJOINDER
NONJURANCY
OUTJOURNEY
PANJANDRUM
PERJUREDLY
PERJURIOUS
PREJUDGING
PREJUDICED
PROJACIENT
PROJECTILE
PROJECTING
PROJECTION
PROJECTIVE
PROJECTRIX
PROJECTURE
PROJICIENT
SERJEANTRY
SKYJACKING
SUBJACENCY
SUBJECTIFY
SUBJECTILE
SUBJECTING
SUBJECTION
SUBJECTIVE
SUBJICIBLE
SUBJOINDER
SUBJOINING
SUBJUGABLE
SUBJUGATED
SUBJUGATOR
SUBJUGULAR
TRAJECTILE
TRAJECTING
TRAJECTION
TRAJECTORY

ARROJADITE
BLUEJACKET
CLAMJAMFRY
COADJACENT
COADJUMENT
COADJUTIVE
COADJUTRIX
COADJUVANT
EQUIJACENT
FIDEJUSSOR
FOREJUDGED
FOREJUDGER
FRABJOUSLY
HIGHJACKER
OTTAJANITE
POSTJACENT
READJUSTER
SKIPJACKLY
WEREJAGUAR
WINDJAMMER
WOODJOBBER
INCONJUNCT
INTERJOIST
NONABJURER
PREADJUNCT
SUPRAJURAL
UNDERJAWED

BUTTERJAGS
CRACKAJACK
LUMBERJACK
NATTERJACK
RATTLEJACK
SUPPLEJACK
TIMBERJACK

CHAPARAJOS
CHAPAREJOS

SCORING ORDER LIST OF 10-LETTER WORDS

31
OBJECTIZED

30
HIGHJACKER
JACKHAMMER
JAROVIZING
JOVIALIZED

29
CLAMJAMFRY
JACKFISHES
JASPERIZED
JEOPARDIZE
JOHNNYCAKE
REJUVENIZE

28
EQUIJACENT
JARGONIZED
JAYWALKING
PROJECTRIX

27
JUXTAPOSED
LUMBERJACK
SKIPJACKLY
SUBJECTIFY
SUPPLEJACK
TIMBERJACK

26
JACKASSERY
JANIZARIES
JAWBREAKER
JINRICKSHA
JOAQUINITE
JOGGLEWORK
JOURNALIZE
JUVENILIFY
JUXTAPOSIT
PERJINKETY
SKYJACKING
SUBJACENCY

25
BLUEJACKET
EJECTIVELY
EJECTIVITY
FRABJOUSLY
JACKANAPES
JACKKNIVES
JACKSNIPES
JAWCRUSHER
JEWELSMITH
JUDOPHOBIA
JUMPSCRAPE
WINDJAMMER
WOODJOBBER

24
ABJUNCTIVE
CHAPARAJOS
CHAPAREJOS
CONJECTIVE
CONJUNCTLY
DEJECTEDLY
JASPACHATE
JELLIFYING
JINRIKISHA
JOBBERNOWL
JOLLIFYING
JUSTIFYING
OBJECTIVAL
PROJECTIVE
SUBJECTIVE

23
ADJACENTLY
ADJECTIVAL
ADJUNCTIVE
BEJEWELING
BEJEWELLED
CAJOLINGLY
COADJUTIVE
COADJUVANT
CONJUGALLY
CRACKAJACK
ENJAMBMENT
ENJEOPARDY
FOREJUDGED
FORJUDGING
JABBERMENT
JABOTICABA
JAILKEEPER
JERRYBUILD
JEWELHOUSE
JIMPRICUTE
JINRIKIMAN
JINRIKIMEN
JOYFULNESS
JUDICATIVE
JUDICATORY
JUDICIALLY
JUGGLINGLY
JUMBLEMENT
JUVENILELY
JUVENILITY
NATTERJACK
OBJECTABLE
PERJUREDLY
PREJUDICED
RATTLEJACK
SUBJICIBLE

22
ABJUDICATE
ABJURATORY
ADJOINEDLY
COADJACENT
COADJUMENT
CONJOINTLY
CONJUGABLE
FOREJUDGER
INJUNCTIVE
JACULATIVE
JACULATORY
JAGHEERDAR
JAGHIREDAR
JAPISHNESS
JERRYBUILT
JINGLINGLY
JOCULARITY
JOCULATORY
JOLTHEADED
JOURNEYMAN
JOURNEYMEN
JUBILANTLY
JUBILATORY
JUDICIABLE
JUNGLEWOOD
JUNKDEALER
JUSTICIARY
JUVENILISM
MISJUDGING
NONJURANCY
PAJAHUELLO
PANJANDRUM
PEJORATIVE
PREADJUNCT
PREJUDGING
PROJECTING
REJOICEFUL
SEJUNCTIVE
SUBJECTING
SUBJUGABLE
TRAJECTORY
UNDERJAWED

21
ABJECTNESS
ABJUREMENT
ADJUDICATE
ADJURATORY
CAJOLEMENT
CAJUPUTENE
CONJECTURE
CONJUGATED
CONJUNCTUR
DIJUDICATE
DISJECTING
DISJOINTLY
FIDEJUSSOR
INCONJUNCT
JADISHNESS
JAPACONINE
JAUNDICING
JEJUNOTOMY
JEOPARDIED
JEOPARDING
JOLTERHEAD
JOURNEYING
JUGGLEMENT
JUNCACEOUS
JURAMENTUM
MAJESTICAL
MAJUSCULAE
MAJUSCULAR
OBJECTIONS
OBJECTLESS
OBJURGATED
POSTJACENT
PROJACIENT
PROJECTILE
PROJECTION
PROJECTURE
PROJICIENT
SUBJECTILE
SUBJECTION
SUBJUGATED
WEREJAGUAR

20
ADJUNCTION
ADJUSTABLE
ADJUSTMENT
BUTTERJAGS
COADJUTANT
CONJOINING
CONJUGATOR
DISJECTION
DISJUNCTOR
EJACULATED
INJUDICIAL
JACTITATED
JACULATING
JAGGEDNESS
JASPERATED
JASPIDEOUS
JAVELINEER
JEOPARDOUS
JINGOISTIC
JNANAMARGA
JOCUNDNESS
JOYOUSNESS
JUBILATING
JUDICATION
JUDICATURE
JURIDICIAL
MISJOINDER
OBJURGATOR
OUTJOURNEY
REJUVENANT
REJUVENATE
SERJEANTRY
SUBJOINDER
SUBJOINING
SUBJUGATOR
SUBJUGULAR
TRAJECTING

19
ABJURATION
BIJOUTERIE
CAJOLERIES
CONJURATOR
DISJOINING
DISJOINTED
EJACULATOR
ENJOINMENT
INJUNCTION
JACULATION
JAGUARONDI
JAGUARUNDI
JAMESONITE
JENTACULAR
JOCOSENESS
JOCOSITIES
JOSTLEMENT
JOUISSANCE

JOULEMETER
JOURNALISM
JUBILARIAN
JUBILATION
JUGGERNAUT
JUGGLERIES
JUGULATING
JUNCTIONAL
JUNGLESIDE
JURAMENTAL
JURISTICAL
MAJESTIOUS
MAJORATION
MAJORITIES
NONABJURER
OBJURATION
PAJAROELLO
PEJORATION
PERJURIOUS
REJUNCTION
SEJUNCTION
SUPRAJURAL
TRAJECTILE
TRAJECTION

18

ADJURATION
ARROJADITE
JARDINIERE
JARGONELLE
JOINTURING
JOURNALING
JOURNALLED
JUGULATION
JULOLIDINE
NONJOINDER
READJUSTER
REJONEADOR
SOJOURNING

17

INTERJOIST
JANITORIAL
JAUNTINESS
JEALOUSIES
JOINTURESS
JOURNALESE
JOURNALISE
JOURNALIST
JURATORIAL
OTTAJANITE
UNJUSTNESS

16

JEJUNENESS

ALPHABETICAL LIST OF WORDS OVER 10 LETTERS

ABJECTEDNESS
ABJUDICATION
ABJUDICATOR
ADJECTIONAL
ADJECTIVALLY
ADJECTIVELY
ADJOURNMENT
ADJUDICATED
ADJUDICATING
ADJUDICATION
ADJUDICATIVE
ADJUDICATOR
ADJUDICATURE
ADJUNCTIVELY
ADJUTANCIES
ADJUTANTSHIP
ADJUTORIOUS
BEJEWELLING
BENJAMINITE
BICONJUGATE
BRINJARRIES
CIRCUMJACENT
CLAMJAMFERY
CLAMJAMPHRIE
COADDJUVANCY
COADJACENCE
COADJACENTLY
COADJUTATOR
COADJUTEMENT
COADJUTRESS
COADJUTRICE
COADJUTRICES
CONJECTURAL
CONJECTURALLY
CONJECTURED
CONJECTURER
CONJECTURING
CONJOINTNESS
CONJUBILANT
CONJUGALITY
CONJUGATING
CONJUGATION
CONJUGATIVE
CONJUNCTION
CONJUNCTIVAE
CONJUNCTIVAL
CONJUNCTIVAS
CONJUNCTIVE
CONJUNCTIVELY
CONJUNCTURAL
CONJUNCTURE
CONJURATION
COPALJOCOTE
DEJECTEDNESS
DEJUNKERIZE
DIJUDICATION
DISJOINTEDLY
DISJOINTING
DISJOINTURE
DISJUNCTION
DISJUNCTIVE
DISJUNCTIVELY
DISJUNCTURE
EJACULATING
EJACULATION
EJACULATIVE
EJACULATORY
EJECTAMENTA
ENJAMBEMENT
ENJOYABLENESS
EXCONJUGANT
EXTRAJUDICIAL
FIDEJUSSION
FIDEJUSSORY
FOREJUDGING
GIMBALJAWED
GIMBERJAWED
GUANAJUATITE
IMPREJUDICE
INCONJOINABLE
INJUDICIALLY
INJUDICIOUS
INJUDICIOUSLY
INJUNCTIVELY
INJUREDNESS
INJURIOUSLY
INSUBJECTION
INTERJACENCE
INTERJACENT
INTERJECTED
INTERJECTING
INTERJECTION
INTERJECTOR
INTERJECTORY
INTERJUNCTION
INTROJECTION
JABBERINGLY
JACAMEROPINE
JACKPUDDING
JACTITATING
JACTITATION
JACULATORIAL
JACULIFEROUS
JAPACONITIN
JAPACONITINE
JARARACUSSU
JARGONIZING
JARGONNELLE
JAROVIZATION
JASMINEWOOD
JASPERIZING
JATEORHIZIN
JATEORHIZINE
JAUNDICEROOT
JAWBREAKING
JAWBREAKINGLY
JEALOUSNESS
JEFFERISITE
JEFFERSONITE
JEJUNOSTOMY
JELLIEDNESS
JELLIFICATION
JELLYFISHES
JEOPARDIOUS
JEOPARDIZED
JEOPARDIZING
JEOPARDOUSLY
JEOPARDYING
JEQUIRITIES
JERRYBUILDING
JESTINGSTOCK
JIMBERJAWED
JINGLEJANGLE
JNANASHAKTI
JNANENDRIYA
JOBLESSNESS
JOBMISTRESS
JOCOSERIOUS
JOCULARNESS
JOCUNDITIES
JOGTROTTISM
JOHNSTRUPITE
JOINTEDNESS
JOKESOMENESS
JOLLIFICATION
JOLTERHEADED
JOSEPHINITE
JOURNALISTIC
JOURNALIZED
JOURNALIZER
JOURNALIZING
JOURNALLING
JOURNEYCAKE
JOURNEYWOMAN
JOURNEYWOMEN
JOURNEYWORK
JOVIALISTIC
JOVIALIZING
JOVIALNESS
JOYLESSNESS
JUBILIZATION
JUDGMATICAL
JUDICATORIAL
JUDICATORIES
JUDICIALITY
JUDICIALIZE
JUDICIARIES
JUDICIARILY
JUDICIOUSLY
JUDICIOUSNESS
JURAMENTADO
JURAMENTALLY
JURIDICALLY
JURISCONSULT
JURISDICTION
JURISDICTIVE
JURISPRUDENCE
JURISPRUDENT
JURISTICALLY
JUSTAUCORPS
JUSTICEHOOD
JUSTICESHIP
JUSTICEWEED
JUSTICIABLE
JUSTIFIABLE
JUSTIFIABLY
JUSTIFICATION
JUSTIFICATIVE
JUSTIFICATOR
JUSTIFYINGLY
JUVENESCENCE
JUVENESCENT
JUVENILENESS
JUVENILITIES
JUXTAMARINE
JUXTAPOSING
JUXTAPOSITION
JUXTAPYLORIC
JUXTASPINAL
KATJEPIERING
KATZENJAMMER
KJELDAHLIZE
LEATHERJACKET
LUMBERJACKET
MAHARAJRANA
MAJESTICALLY
MALADJUSTED
MALADJUSTMENT
MISJUDGEMENT
MISJUDGINGLY
MISJUDGMENT
NATROJAROSITE
NONADJUSTIVE
NONDISJUNCT
NONJURANTISM
NONOBJECTIVE
OBJECTATION
OBJECTATIVE
OBJECTIFIED
OBJECTIFYING
OBJECTIONABLE
OBJECTIONABLY
OBJECTIONAL
OBJECTIONER
OBJECTIONIST
OBJECTIVATE
OBJECTIVATED
OBJECTIVATING
OBJECTIVATION
OBJECTIVELY
OBJECTIVENESS
OBJECTIVISM
OBJECTIVIST
OBJECTIVISTIC
OBJECTIVITY
OBJECTIVIZE
OBJECTIVIZED
OBJECTIVIZING
OBJECTIZATION
OBJECTIZING
OBJURGATING
OBJURGATION
OBJURGATIVE
OBJURGATIVELY
OBJURGATORILY
OBJURGATORY
OBJURGATRIX
PARIETOJUGAL
PAUCIJUGATE
PEJORATIVELY
PEREJONETTE
PERJINKITIES
PERJUREDNESS
PERJURIOUSLY
POSTADJUNCT
PREJUDGEMENT
PREJUDGMENT
PREJUDICATE
PREJUDICATOR
PREJUDICEDLY
PREJUDICIAL
PREJUDICING
PREJUDICIOUS
PROJECTEDLY
PROJECTINGLY
PROJECTIONAL
PROJECTIVITY
PROJICIENCE
PROJICIENTLY
READJUSTABLE
READJUSTMENT
REJECTAMENTA
REJOICEMENT
REJUVENATED
REJUVENATING
REJUVENATION
REJUVENATIVE
REJUVENATOR
REJUVENESCE
RETROJECTION
RETROJUGULAR
RUBIJERVINE
SEJUNCTIVELY
SEMIJUBILEE
SMOKEJUMPER
SOJOURNMENT
STEEPLEJACK
STOCKJOBBER
STOCKJOBBERY
STOCKJOBBING
STOCKJUDGING
STOLKJAERRE
STRAITJACKET
SUBJECTEDLY
SUBJECTEDNESS

SUBJECTIONAL
SUBJECTIVELY
SUBJECTIVISM
SUBJECTIVIST
SUBJECTIVITY
SUBJUGATING
SUBJUGATION
SUBJUNCTION
SUBJUNCTIVE
SUBJUNCTIVELY
SUBTERJACENT
SUPERJACENT
SURREJOINDER
THINGAMAJIG
THINGUMAJIG
TRAJECTORIES
TRONDHJEMITE
UNBEJUGGLED
UNJUDICIOUS
UNJUSTIFIED
UNPREJUDICE
UNPREJUDICED
WINDJAMMING
YAJNOPAVITA

POSITIONAL ORDER LIST OF WORDS OVER 10 LETTERS

JABBERINGLY
JACAMEROPINE
JACKPUDDING
JACTITATING
JACTITATION
JACULATORIAL
JACULIFEROUS
JAPACONITIN
JAPACONITINE
JARARACUSSU
JARGONIZING
JARGONNELLE
JAROVIZATION
JASMINEWOOD
JASPERIZING
JATEORHIZIN
JATEORHIZINE
JAUNDICEROOT
JAWBREAKING
JAWBREAKINGLY
JEALOUSNESS
JEFFERISITE
JEFFERSONITE
JEJUNOSTOMY
JELLIEDNESS
JELLIFICATION
JELLYFISHES
JEOPARDIOUS
JEOPARDIZED
JEOPARDIZING
JEOPARDOUSLY
JEOPARDYING
JEQUIRITIES
JERRYBUILDING
JESTINGSTOCK
JIMBERJAWED
JINGLEJANGLE
JNANASHAKTI
JNANENDRIYA
JOBLESSNESS
JOBMISTRESS
JOCOSERIOUS
JOCULARNESS
JOCUNDITIES
JOGTROTTISM
JOHNSTRUPITE
JOINTEDNESS
JOKESOMENESS
JOLLIFICATION
JOLTERHEADED
JOSEPHINITE
JOURNALISTIC
JOURNALIZED
JOURNALIZER
JOURNALIZING
JOURNALLING
JOURNEYCAKE
JOURNEYWOMAN
JOURNEYWOMEN
JOURNEYWORK
JOVIALISTIC
JOVIALIZING
JOVIALNESS
JOYLESSNESS
JUBILIZATION
JUDGMATICAL
JUDICATORIAL
JUDICATORIES
JUDICIALITY
JUDICIALIZE
JUDICIARIES
JUDICIARILY
JUDICIOUSLY
JUDICIOUSNESS
JURAMENTADO
JURAMENTALLY
JURIDICALLY
JURISCONSULT
JURISDICTION
JURISDICTIVE
JURISPRUDENCE
JURISPRUDENT
JURISTICALLY
JUSTAUCORPS
JUSTICEHOOD
JUSTICESHIP
JUSTICEWEED
JUSTICIABLE
JUSTIFIABLE
JUSTIFIABLY
JUSTIFICATION
JUSTIFICATIVE
JUSTIFICATOR
JUSTIFYINGLY
JUVENESCENCE
JUVENESCENT
JUVENILENESS
JUVENILITIES
JUXTAMARINE
JUXTAPOSING
JUXTAPOSITION
JUXTAPYLORIC
JUXTASPINAL

EJACULATING
EJACULATION
EJACULATIVE
EJACULATORY
EJECTAMENTA
JEJUNOSTOMY
KJELDAHLIZE

ABJECTEDNESS
ABJUDICATION
ABJUDICATOR
ADJECTIONAL
ADJECTIVALLY
ADJECTIVELY
ADJOURNMENT
ADJUDICATED
ADJUDICATING
ADJUDICATION
ADJUDICATIVE
ADJUDICATOR
ADJUDICATURE
ADJUNCTIVELY
ADJUTANCIES
ADJUTANTSHIP
ADJUTORIUS
BEJEWELLING
DEJECTEDNESS
DEJUNKERIZE
DIJUDICATION
ENJAMBEMENT
ENJOYABLENESS
INJUDICIALLY
INJUDICIOUS
INJUDICIOUSLY
INJUNCTIVELY
INJUREDNESS
INJURIOUSLY
MAJESTICALLY
OBJECTATION
OBJECTATIVE
OBJECTIFIED
OBJECTIFYING
OBJECTIONABLE
OBJECTIONABLY
OBJECTIONAL
OBJECTIONER
OBJECTIONIST
OBJECTIVATE
OBJECTIVATED
OBJECTIVATING
OBJECTIVATION
OBJECTIVELY
OBJECTIVENESS
OBJECTIVISM
OBJECTIVIST
OBJECTIVISTIC
OBJECTIVITY
OBJECTIVIZE
OBJECTIVIZED
OBJECTIVIZING
OBJECTIZATION
OBJECTIZING
OBJURGATING
OBJURGATION
OBJURGATIVE
OBJURGATIVELY
OBJURGATORILY
OBJURGATORY
OBJURGATRIX
PEJORATIVELY
REJECTAMENTA
REJOICEMENT
REJUVENATED
REJUVENATING
REJUVENATION
REJUVENATIVE
REJUVENATOR
REJUVENESCE
SEJUNCTIVELY
SOJOURNMENT
UNJUDICIOUS
UNJUSTIFIED
YAJNOPAVITA

BENJAMINITE
CAODJACENCY
CONJECTURAL
CONJECTURALLY
CONJECTURE
CONJECTURED
CONJECTURER
CONJECTURING
CONJOINTNESS
CONJUBILANT
CONJUGALITY
CONJUGATING
CONJUGATION
CONJUGATIVE
CONJUNCTION
CONJUNCTIVAE
CONJUNCTIVAL
CONJUNCTIVAS
CONJUNCTIVE
CONJUNCTIVELY
CONJUNCTURAL
CONJUNCTURE
CONJURATION
DISJOINTEDLY
DISJOINTING
DISJOINTURE
DISJUNCTION
DISJUNCTIVE
DISJUNCTIVELY
DISJUNCTURE
KATJEPIERING
MISJUDGEMENT
MISJUDGINGLY
MISJUDGMENT
NONJURANTISM
PERJINKITIES
PERJUREDNESS
PERJURIOUSLY
PREJUDGEMENT
PREJUDGMENT
PREJUDICATE
PREJUDICATOR
PREJUDICEDLY
PREJUDICIAL
PREJUDICING
PREJUDICIOUS
PROJECTEDLY
PROJECTINGLY
PROJECTIONAL
PROJECTIVITY
PROJICIENCE
PROJICIENTLY
SUBJECTEDLY
SUBJECTEDNESS
SUBJECTIONAL
SUBJECTIVELY
SUBJECTIVISM
SUBJECTIVIST
SUBJECTIVITY
SUBJUGATING
SUBJUGATION
SUBJUNCTION
SUBJUNCTIVE
SUBJUNCTIVELY
TRAJECTORIES

BRINJARRIES
CLAMJAMFERY
CLAMJAMPHRIE
COADJACENCE
COADJACENTLY
COADJUTATOR
COADJUTEMENT
COADJUTRESS
COADJUTRICE
COADJUTRICES
FIDEJUSSION
FIDEJUSSORY
FOREJUDGING
PEREJONETTE
READJUSTABLE
READJUSTMENT
SEMIJUBILEE
UNBEJUGGLED

WINDJAMMING

BICONJUGATE
COADDJUVANCY
COPALJOCOTE
EXCONJUGANT
EXTRAJUDICIAL
GUANAJUATITE
IMPREJUDICE
INCONJOINABLE
INSUBJECTION
INTERJACENCE
INTERJACENT
INTERJECTED
INTERJECTING
INTERJECTION
INTERJECTOR
INTERJECTORY
INTERJUNCTION
INTROJECTION
MALADJUSTED
MALADJUSTMENT
NATROJAROSITE
NONADJUSTIVE
NONOBJECTIVE
PAUCIJUGATE
RETROJECTION
RETROJUGULAR
RUBIJERVINE
SMOKEJUMPER
STOCKJOBBER
STOCKJOBBERY
STOCKJOBBING
STOCKJUDGING
STOLKJAERRE
SUPERJACENT
SURREJOINDER
UNPREJUDICE
UNPREJUDICED

CIRCUMJACENT
GIMBALJAWED
GIMBERJAWED
JIMBERJAWED
JINGLEJANGLE
KATZENJAMMER
LUMBERJACKET
MAHARAJRANA
NONDISJUNCT
POSTADJUNCT
STRAITJACKET
SUBTERJACENT
TRONDHJEMITE

LEATHERJACKET
PARIETOJUGAL
STEEPLEJACK

THINGAMAJIG
THINGUMAJIG

SCORING ORDER LIST OF WORDS OVER 10 LETTERS

37
OBJECTIVIZING

36
KATZENJAMMER
OBJECTIVIZED

35
KJELDAHLIZE

34
OBJECTIVIZE

33
JAWBREAKINGLY
JUXTAPYLORIC
OBJECTIZATION

32
DEJUNKERIZE
JEOPARDIZING
OBJECTIZING
STOCKJOBBERY

31
COADDJUVANCY
JAROVIZATION
JATEORHIZINE
JEOPARDIZED
JOVIALIZING

30
CLAMJAMFERY
CLAMJAMPHRIE
CONJUNCTIVELY
EXTRAJUDICIAL
JASPERIZING
JATEORHIZIN
JUBILIZATION
JUDICIALIZE
OBJECTIFYING
STOCKJOBBING
SUBJUNCTIVELY

29
DISJUNCTIVELY
JACKPUDDING
JARGONIZING
JOURNALIZING
JUSTIFYINGLY
JUXTAPOSITION
LEATHERJACKET
LUMBERJACKET
OBJECTIONABLY
OBJECTIVISTIC
OBJURGATIVELY
PROJECTIVITY
SUBJECTIVELY
SUBJECTIVITY

28
ADJECTIVALLY
ADJUNCTIVELY
EXCONJUGANT
JAWBREAKING
JOURNALIZED
JOURNEYWORK
JUSTIFICATIVE
JUXTAPOSING
OBJECTIVATING
OBJECTIVELY
OBJECTIVITY
OBJURGATRIX
PREJUDICEDLY
SMOKEJUMPER
STOCKJOBBER
STOCKJUDGING
SUBJECTIVISM

27
ADJECTIVELY
COADJACENTLY
CONJECTURALLY
GIMBALJAWED
GIMBERJAWED
INJUNCTIVELY
JELLYFISHES
JEQUIRITIES
JERRYBUILDING
JOURNALIZER
JOURNEYCAKE
JOURNEYWOMAN
JOURNEYWOMEN
JUXTASPINAL
MISJUDGINGLY
OBJECTIVATED
OBJECTIVATION
OBJECTIVENESS
OBJECTIVISM
PEJORATIVELY
PROJECTINGLY
SEJUNCTIVELY
WINDJAMMING

26
ADJUDICATIVE
CONJUNCTIVAE
CONJUNCTIVAL
CONJUNCTIVAS
INJUDICIOUSLY
JABBERINGLY
JESTINGSTOCK
JUSTIFIABLY
JUVENESCENCE
KATJEPIERING
MAJESTICALLY
NONOBJECTIVE
OBJECTIFIED
OBJECTIONABLE
OBJURGATORILY
PROJECTEDLY
PROJICIENTLY
STEEPLEJACK
SUBJECTEDLY
SUBJECTIVIST
YAJNOPAVITA

25
ADJUTANTSHIP
CAODJACENCY
CONJUNCTIVE
ENJOYABLENESS
FIDEJUSSORY
IMPREJUDICE
INJUDICIALLY
JACAMEROPINE
JEFFERSONITE
JELLIFICATION
JEOPARDOUSLY
JEOPARDYING
JIMBERJAWED
JNANASHAKTI
JOKESOMENESS
JOLLIFICATION
JURISDICTIVE
JURISPRUDENCE
JUSTICESHIP
JUSTIFICATION
MALADJUSTMENT
MISJUDGEMENT
OBJECTATIVE
OBJECTIVATE
OBJECTIVIST
PERJINKITIES
PREJUDGEMENT
REJUVENATIVE
STRAITJACKET
SUBJECTEDNESS
SUBJUNCTIVE
THINGAMAJIG
THINGUMAJIG
TRONDHJEMITE
UNPREJUDICED

24
ABJECTEDNESS
ABJUDICATION
ADJUDICATING
BEJEWELLING
CIRCUMJACENT
COADJUTEMENT
COADJUTRICES
CONJECTURING
CONJUGALITY
CONJUGATIVE
COPALJOCOTE
DISJOINTEDLY
DISJUNCTIVE
ENJAMBEMENT
FOREJUDGING
INCONJOINABLE
INTERJECTORY
JACULIFEROUS
JASMINEWOOD
JEFFERISITE
JOHNSTRUPITE
JOLTERHEADED
JUDGMATICAL
JUDICIALITY
JUDICIARILY
JUDICIOUSLY
JURAMENTALLY
JURIDICALLY
JURISTICALLY
JUSTICEHOOD
JUSTICEWEED
JUSTIFICATOR
MISJUDGMENT
OBJURGATIVE
OBJURGATORY
PERJURIOUSLY
PREJUDGMENT
PREJUDICATOR
PREJUDICING
PREJUDICIOUS
PROJICIENCE

23
ABJUDICATOR
ADJUDICATED
ADJUDICATION
ADJUDICATURE
BICONJUGATE
COADJUTRICE
CONJECTURED
CONJUNCTURAL
DEJECTEDNESS
DIJUDICATION
EJACULATIVE
EJACULATORY
INSUBJECTION
INTERJACENCE
JAPACONITINE
JOSEPHINITE
JOVIALISTIC
JUDICIOUSNESS
JUSTIFIABLE
JUVENESCENT
MAHARAJRANA
NONADJUSTIVE
OBJECTIONIST
PAUCIJUGATE
POSTADJUNCT
PREJUDICATE
PREJUDICIAL
PROJECTIONAL
REJECTAMENTA
REJUVENATING
REJUVENESCE
RUBIJERVINE
SUBJECTIONAL
SUBTERJACENT
UNBEJUGGLED
UNPREJUDICE

22
ADJUDICATOR
BENJAMINITE
COADJACENCE
CONJECTURAL
CONJECTURER
CONJUBILANT
CONJUGATING
CONJUNCTION
CONJUNCTURE
EJECTAMENTA
FIDEJUSSION
INTERJECTING
INTERJUNCTION
JAPACONITIN
JAUNDICEROOT
JEJUNOSTOMY
JNANENDRIYA
JOBMISTRESS
JUDICATORIAL
JUDICATORIES
JURISDICTION
JURISPRUDENT
JUSTAUCORPS
JUSTICIABLE
JUVENILENESS
JUVENILITIES
MALADJUSTED
OBJECTATION
OBJECTIONAL
OBJECTIONER
OBJURGATING
PARIETOJUGAL
PERJUREDNESS
READJUSTABLE
READJUSTMENT
REJOICEMENT
REJUVENATED
REJUVENATION
SEMIJUBILEE
STOLKJAERRE
SUBJUGATING
SUBJUNCTION
SUPERJACENT
UNJUSTIFIED

21
ADJECTIONAL
ADJOURNMENT
ADJUTANCIES
COADJUTATOR
COADJUTRESS
CONJOINTNESS
CONJUGATION
DISJUNCTION
DISJUNCTURE
EJACULATING
INJUDICIOUS
INJURIOUSLY
INTERJECTED
INTERJECTION
INTROJECTION
JACTITATING
JACULATORIAL
JEOPARDIOUS
JOCUNDITIES
JOGTROTTISM
JOURNALISTIC
JOYLESSNESS
JUDICIARIES
JURAMENTADO
JURISCONSULT
NONDISJUNCT
NONJURANTISM
OBJURGATION
REJUVENATOR
RETROJECTION
SUBJUGATION
TRAJECTORIES
UNJUDICIOUS

20
BRINJARRIES
CONJURATION
DISJOINTING
EJACULATION
GUANAJUATITE
INTERJACENT
INTERJECTOR
JACTITATION
JARARACUSSU
JINGLEJANGLE
JOBLESSNESS
JOCOSERIOUS
JOCULARNESS
JOVIALNESS
NATROJAROSITE
PEREJONETTE
RETROJUGULAR
SOJOURNMENT
SURREJOINDER

19
ADJUTORIOUS
DISJOINTURE
INJUREDNESS
JARGONNELLE
JELLIEDNESS
JOINTEDNESS
JOURNALLING

18
JEALOUSNESS

High-Scoring Words Containing

2-3 LETTER WORDS

ALPHABETICAL ORDER

QAT
QRI
QU
QUA
QUI
QUO
SUQ

POSITIONAL ORDER

QAT
QRI
QU
QUA
QUI
QUO

SUQ

SCORING ORDER

12

QAT
QRI
QUA
QUI
QUO
SUQ

11

QU

ALPHABETICAL LIST OF 4-LETTER WORDS

AQUA
AQUO
CINQ
OQUE
OQUI
QADI
QAID
QERI
QUAA
QUAB
QUAD
QUAG
QUAI
QUAN
QUAP
QUAR
QUAS
QUAT
QUAW
QUAX
QUAY
QUED
QUEE
QUEI
QUET
QUEY
QUIB
QUID
QUIM
QUIN
QUIP
QUIS
QUIT
QUIZ
QUOD
QUOG
QUOP
QUOT
QUOY
QUOZ
SHOQ
WAQF

POSITIONAL ORDER LIST OF 4-LETTER WORDS

QADI
QAID
QERI
QUAA
QUAB
QUAD
QUAG
QUAI
QUAN
QUAP
QUAR
QUAS
QUAT
QUAW
QUAX
QUAY
QUED
QUEE
QUEI
QUET
QUEY
QUIB
QUID
QUIM
QUIN
QUIP
QUIS
QUIT
QUIZ
QUOD
QUOG
QUOP
QUOT
QUOY
QUOZ

AQUA
AQUO
OQUE
OQUI

WAQF

CINQ
SHOQ

SCORING ORDER LIST OF 4-LETTER WORDS

22
QUIZ
QUOZ

20
QUAX

19
WAQF

16
QUAW
QUAY
QUEY
QUOY
SHOQ

15
CINQ
QUAB
QUAP
QUIB
QUIM
QUIP
QUOP

14
QADI
QAID
QUAD
QUAG
QUED
QUID
QUOD
QUOG

13
AQUA
AQUO
OQUE
OQUI
QERI
QUAA
QUAI
QUAN
QUAR
QUAS
QUAT
QUEE
QUEI
QUET
QUIN
QUIS
QUIT
QUOT

ALPHABETICAL LIST OF 5-LETTER WORDS

AQUAE
AQUAS
BEQAA
BULAQ
CEQUI
COQUE
EQUAL
EQUES
EQUID
EQUIP
FAQIH
JIQUE
JIQUI
MAQUI
MIQRA
NUQUE
OCQUE
PIQUE
QANEH
QASAB
QAZAQ
QIBLA
QINAH
QIYAS
QOBAR
QUACK
QUADE
QUAFF
QUAIL
QUAIR
QUAIS
QUAKE
QUAKY
QUALE
QUALM
QUANT
QUARE
QUARK
QUARL
QUART
QUASH
QUASI
QUASS
QUATE
QUAWK
QUEAK
QUEAL
QUEAN
QUECH
QUEDE
QUEED
QUEEL
QUEEN
QUEER
QUEET
QUELL
QUELT
QUEME
QUENA
QUENT
QUERL
QUERN
QUERY
QUEST
QUEUE
QUICA
QUICK
QUIET
QUIFF
QUILA
QUILE
QUILK
QUILL
QUILT
QUINA
QUINE
QUINK
QUINT
QUIPO
QUIPU
QUIRA
QUIRE
QUIRK
QUIRL
QUIRT
QUIST
QUITE
QUITS
QUOAD
QUOCK
QUOIN
QUOIT
QUONK
QUOTA
QUOTE
QUOTH
QUOTT
QUYTE
ROQUE
SEQUA
SQUAB
SQUAD
SQUAM
SQUAP
SQUAT

SQUAW
SQUEG
SQUET
SQUIB
SQUID
SQUIN
SQUIR
SQUIT
SQUIZ
SQUSH
TOQUE
TRINQ
TUQUE
USQUE

POSITIONAL ORDER LIST OF 5-LETTER WORDS

QANEH
QASAB
QAZAQ
QIBLA
QINAH
QIYAS
QOBAR
QUACK
QUADE
QUAFF
QUAIL
QUAIR
QUAIS
QUAKE
QUAKY
QUALE
QUALM
QUANT
QUARE
QUARK
QUARL
QUART
QUASH
QUASI
QUASS
QUATE
QUAWK
QUEAK
QUEAL
QUEAN
QUECH
QUEDE
QUEED
QUEEL
QUEEN
QUEER
QUEET
QUELL
QUELT
QUEME
QUENA
QUENT
QUERL
QUERN
QUERY
QUEST
QUEUE
QUICA
QUICK
QUIET
QUIFF
QUILA
QUILE
QUILK
QUILL
QUILT
QUINA
QUINE
QUINK
QUINT
QUIPO
QUIPU
QUIRA
QUIRE
QUIRK
QUIRL
QUIRT
QUIST
QUITE
QUITS
QUOAD
QUOCK
QUOIN
QUOIT
QUONK
QUOTA
QUOTE
QUOTH
QUOTT
QUYTE

AQUAE
AQUAS
EQUAL
EQUES
EQUID
EQUIP
SQUAB
SQUAD
SQUAM
SQUAP
SQUAT
SQUAW
SQUEG
SQUET
SQUIB
SQUID
SQUIN
SQUIR
SQUIT
SQUIZ
SQUSH

BEQAA
CEQUI
COQUE
FAQIH
JIQUE
JIQUI
MAQUI
MIQRA
NUQUE
OCQUE
PIQUE
ROQUE
SEQUA
TOQUE
TUQUE
USQUE

BULAQ
QAZAQ
TRINQ

SCORING ORDER LIST OF 5-LETTER WORDS

23
SQUIZ

22
QAZAQ

21
JIQUE
JIQUI
QUAKY
QUAWK

20
FAQIH
QUACK
QUAFF
QUICK
QUIFF
QUOCK

19
QUECH

18
QUAKE
QUARK
QUEAK
QUILK
QUINK
QUIRK
QUONK

17
QANEH
QINAH
QIYAS
QUASH
QUERY
QUOTH
QUYTE
SQUAW
SQUSH

16
BEQAA
BULAQ
CEQUI
COQUE
EQUIP
MAQUI
MIQRA
OCQUE
PIQUE
QASAB
QIBLA
QOBAR
QUALM
QUEME
QUICA
QUIPO
QUIPU
SQUAB
SQUAM
SQUAP
SQUIB

15
EQUID
QUADE
QUEDE
QUEED
QUOAD
SQUAD
SQUEG
SQUID

14
AQUAE
AQUAS
EQUAL
EQUES
NUQUE
QUAIL
QUAIR
QUAIS
QUALE
QUANT
QUARE
QUARL
QUART
QUASI
QUASS
QUATE
QUEAL
QUEAN
QUEEL
QUEEN
QUEER
QUEET
QUELL
QUELT
QUENA
QUENT
QUERL
QUERN
QUEST
QUEUE
QUIET
QUILA
QUILE
QUILL
QUILT
QUINA
QUINE
QUINT
QUIRA
QUIRE
QUIRL
QUIRT
QUIST
QUITE
QUITS
QUOIN
QUOIT
QUOTA
QUOTE
QUOTT
ROQUE
SEQUA
SQUAT
SQUET
SQUIN
SQUIR
SQUIT
TOQUE
TRINQ
TUQUE
USQUE

ALPHABETICAL LIST OF 6-LETTER WORDS

ACQUIT
AEQUOR
ANAQUA
AQUAGE
AQUATE
AQUILA
AQUOSE
ASQUAT
BANQUE
BARQUE
BASQUE
BISQUE
BOSQUE
BRIQUE
CAIQUE
CALQUE
CASQUE
CHEQUE
CINQUE
CIRQUE
CLAQUE
CLIQUE
CLIQUY
COQUET
COQUIN
EQUANT
EQUATE
EQUINE
EQUIPT
EQUITY
EQUOID
EVEQUE
EXEQUY
FAQUIR
JERQUE
LASQUE
LIQUET
LIQUID
LIQUOR
LOQUAT
MANQUE
MAQUIS
MARQUE
MASQUE
MOSQUE
NAIQUE
OPAQUE
PIQUED
PIQUET
PIQUIA
PIQURE
PLAQUE
PULQUE
QANTAR
QUACKY
QUADER
QUADLE
QUADRA
QUAERE
QUAGGA
QUAGGY
QUAHOG
QUAICH
QUAIFE
QUAIGH
QUAILY
QUAINT
QUAKED
QUAKER
QUALIA
QUALLY
QUALMY
QUANDY
QUANTA
QUARLE
QUARRY
QUARTA
QUARTE
QUARTO
QUARTZ
QUASAR
QUASHY
QUASKY
QUATCH
QUATRE
QUATTY
QUAVER
QUAYED
QUEACH
QUEASE
QUEASY
QUEDLY
QUEENS
QUEERY
QUEEST
QUEEVE
QUELCH
QUELME
QUENCH
QUENDA
QUERRE
QUESAL
QUETCH
QUETHE
QUEZAL
QUIAPO
QUIDAM
QUILES
QUILEZ
QUILLY
QUINAS
QUINCE
QUINCH
QUINET
QUINIA
QUINIC
QUININ
QUINOA
QUINOL
QUINON
QUINSE
QUINSY
QUINTA
QUINTE
QUINTO
QUINYL
QUINZE
QUIPPE
QUIPPU
QUIPPY
QUIPUS
QUIRED
QUIRKY
QUISBY
QUITCH
QUIVER
QUIZZY
QUOITS
QUOKKA
QUORUM
QUOTAS
QUOTED
QUOTEE
QUOTER
QUOTHA
QUOTUM
RAQUET
REQUIN
RISQUE
ROQUET
SACQUE
SAUQUI
SECQUE
SEQUEL
SEQUIN
SESQUI
SQUAIL
SQUALL
SQUAMA
SQUAME
SQUAMY
SQUARE
SQUARK
SQUARY
SQUASH
SQUAWK
SQUAWL
SQUDGE
SQUDGY
SQUEAK
SQUEAL
SQUEAM
SQUEEF
SQUEEL
SQUIDS
SQUILL
SQUINT
SQUIRE
SQUIRK
SQUIRL
SQUIRM
SQUIRR
SQUIRT
SQUISH
SQUISS
SQUSHY
SQUUSH
TAQIYA
TAQLID
TARIQA
TOQUET
TORQUE
UBIQUE
UNIQUE
UNQUIT
UNQUOD
XARQUE
YANQUI
YAQONA
ZEQUIN
ZINDIQ

POSITIONAL ORDER LIST OF 6-LETTER WORDS

QANTAR
QUACKY
QUADER
QUADLE
QUADRA
QUAERE
QUAGGA
QUAGGY
QUAHOG
QUAICH
QUAIFE
QUAIGH
QUAILY
QUAINT
QUAKED
QUAKER
QUALIA
QUALLY
QUALMY
QUANDY
QUANTA
QUARLE
QUARRY
QUARTA
QUARTE
QUARTO
QUARTZ
QUASAR
QUASHY
QUASKY
QUATCH
QUATRE
QUATTY
QUAVER
QUAYED
QUEACH
QUEASE
QUEASY
QUEDLY
QUEENS
QUEERY
QUEEST
QUEEVE
QUELCH
QUELME
QUENCH
QUENDA
QUERRE
QUESAL
QUETCH
QUETHE
QUEZAL
QUIAPO
QUIDAM
QUILES
QUILEZ
QUILLY
QUINAS
QUINCE
QUINCH
QUINET
QUINIA
QUINIC
QUININ
QUINOA
QUINOL
QUINON
QUINSE
QUINSY
QUINTA
QUINTE
QUINTO
QUINYL
QUINZE
QUIPPE
QUIPPU
QUIPPY
QUIPUS
QUIRED
QUIRKY
QUISBY
QUITCH
QUIZZY
QUIVER
QUOITS
QUOKKA
QUORUM
QUOTAS
QUOTED
QUOTEE
QUOTER
QUOTHA
QUOTUM

AQUAGE
AQUATE
AQUILA
AQUOSE
EQUANT
EQUATE
EQUINE
EQUIPT
EQUITY
EQUOID
SQUAIL
SQUALL
SQUAMA
SQUAME
SQUAMY
SQUARE
SQUARK
SQUARY
SQUASH
SQUAWK
SQUAWL
SQUDGE
SQUDGY
SQUEAK
SQUEAL
SQUEAM
SQUEEF
SQUEEL
SQUIDS
SQUILL
SQUINT
SQUIRE
SQUIRK
SQUIRL
SQUIRM
SQUIRR
SQUIRT
SQUISH
SQUISS
SQUSHY
SQUUSH

ACQUIT
AEQUOR
ASQUAT
COQUET
COQUIN
FAQUIR
LIQUET
LIQUID
LIQUOR
LOQUAT
MAQUIS
PIQUED
PIQUET
PIQUIA

PIQURE
RAQUET
REQUIN
ROQUET
SEQUEL
SEQUIN
TAQIYA
TAQLID
TOQUET
UNQUIT
UNQUOD
YAQONA
ZEQUIN

ANAQUA
BANQUE
BARQUE
BASQUE
BISQUE
BOSQUE
BRIQUE
CAIQUE
CALQUE
CASQUE
CHEQUE
CINQUE
CIRQUE
CLAQUE

CLIQUE
CLIQUY
EVEQUE
EXEQUY
JERQUE
LASQUE
MANQUE
MARQUE
MASQUE
MOSQUE
NAIQUE
OPAQUE
PLAQUE
PULQUE

RISQUE
SACQUE
SAUQUI
SECQUE
SESQUI
TORQUE
UBIQUE
UNIQUE
XARQUE
YANQUI

TARIQA

ZINDIQ

SCORING ORDER LIST OF 6-LETTER WORDS

26
QUIZZY

25
EXEQUY
ZINDIQ

24
QUACKY
QUARTZ
QUEZAL
QUILEZ
QUINZE
ZEQUIN

22
JERQUE
QUASKY
QUIPPY
QUIRKY
SQUAWK
XARQUE

21
QUASHY
SQUSHY

20
CHEQUE
CLIQUY
QUAGGY
QUAICH
QUAKED
QUALMY
QUATCH
QUEACH
QUELCH
QUENCH
QUETCH
QUINCH
QUISBY
QUITCH
SQUAMY
SQUDGY

19
QUAHOG
QUAIGH
QUAKER
QUANDY
QUAYED
QUEDLY
QUIPPE
QUIPPU
SQUARK
SQUEAK
SQUIRK

18
EQUITY
EVEQUE
FAQUIR
PIQUED
QUAIFE
QUAILY
QUALLY
QUARRY
QUATTY
QUAVER
QUEASY
QUEERY
QUEEVE
QUETHE
QUIDAM
QUILLY
QUINSY
QUINYL
QUIVER
QUOKKA
QUOTHA
SQUARY
SQUASH
SQUAWL
SQUEEF
SQUISH
SQUUSH
TAQIYA
YANQUI
YAQONA

17
ACQUIT
BANQUE
BARQUE
BASQUE
BISQUE
BOSQUE
BRIQUE
CAIQUE
CALQUE
CASQUE
CINQUE
CIRQUE
CLAQUE
CLIQUE
COQUET
COQUIN
EQUIPT
MANQUE
MAQUIS
MARQUE
MASQUE
MOSQUE
OPAQUE
PIQUET
PIQUIA
PIQURE
PLAQUE
PULQUE
QUAGGA
QUELME
QUIAPO
QUINCE
QUINIC
QUIPUS
QUORUM
QUOTUM
SACQUE
SECQUE
SQUAMA
SQUAME
SQUDGE
SQUEAM
SQUIRM

UBIQUE

16
AQUAGE
EQUOID
LIQUID
QUADER
QUADLE
QUADRA
QUENDA
QUIRED
QUOTED
SQUIDS
TAQLID
UNQUOD

15
AEQUOR
ANAQUA
AQUATE
AQUILA
AQUOSE
ASQUAT
EQUANT
EQUATE
EQUINE
LASQUE
LIQUET
LIQUOR
LOQUAT
NAIQUE
QANTAR
QUAERE
QUAINT
QUALIA
QUANTA
QUARLE
QUARTA
QUARTE
QUARTO
QUASAR
QUATRE
QUEASE
QUEENS

QUEEST
QUERRE
QUESAL
QUILES
QUINAS
QUINET
QUINIA
QUININ
QUINOA
QUINOL
QUINON
QUINSE
QUINTA
QUINTE
QUINTO
QUOITS
QUOTAS
QUOTEE
QUOTER
RAQUET
REQUIN
RISQUE
ROQUET
SAUQUI
SEQUEL
SEQUIN
SESQUI
SQUAIL
SQUALL
SQUARE
SQUEAL
SQUEEL
SQUILL
SQUINT
SQUIRE
SQUIRL
SQUIRR
SQUIRT
SQUISS
TARIQA
TOQUET
TORQUE
UNIQUE
UNQUIT

ALPHABETICAL LIST OF 7-LETTER WORDS

ACEQUIA
ACQUENT
ACQUEST

ACQUIRE
ACQUIST
ALFAQUI

ALIQUID
ALIQUOT
ALQUIER

ANQUERA
ANTIQUA
ANTIQUE

AQUABIB
AQUAFER
AQUARIA

AQUATIC
AQUAVIT
AQUEITY
AQUEOUS
AQUIFER
AQUIVER
ASQUARE
ASQUEAL
ASQUINT
ASQUIRM
BANQUET
BAROQUE
BASQUED
BATUQUE
BEQUEST
BEZIQUE
BOSQUET
BOUQUET
BRASQUE
BRIQUET
BRISQUE
BRUSQUE
CACIQUE
CASAQUE
CASQUED
CASQUET
CAWQUAW
CAZIQUE
CHALQUE
CHARQUI
CHEQUER
CLIQUED
COEQUAL
COMIQUE
CONQUER
COQUINA
COQUITA
COQUITO
COSAQUE
CROQUET
CROQUIS
CUMQUAT
DEQUEEN
ENQUIRE
ENQUIRY
EQUABLE
EQUABLY
EQUALED
EQUALLY
EQUATED
EQUATOR
EQUERRY
EQUILIN
EQUINAL
EQUINIA
EQUINOX
EQUINUS
EQUISON
EQUITES
EQUULEI
ESQUIRE
ESTOQUE
ETIQUET
EXQUIRE
FLASQUE
GRECQUE
INEQUAL
INQUEST
INQUIET
INQUIRE
INQUIRY
JAQUIMA
JERQUED
JERQUER
JOCOQUE
JOCOQUI
JONQUIL
KUMQUAT
LACQUER
LACQUEY
LAQUEAR
LAQUEUS
LIQUATE
LIQUEFY
LIQUEUR
LIQUIDS
LIQUIDY
LIQUIFY
LIQUORS
LIQUORY
LOQUENT
MACAQUE
MADOQUA
MANQUEE
MARQUEE
MARQUIS
MASQUER
MESQUIN
MEZQUIT
MUSQUAW
NAMAQUA
OBLIQUE
OBLOQUY
OBSEQUY
OPAQUED
OQUASSA
PARQUET
PASQUIL
PASQUIN
PATAQUE
PERIQUE
PICQUET
PIQUANT
PIQUERO
PIQUEUR
PIQUING
PURAQUE
QABBALA
QUABIRD
QUACHIL
QUACKED
QUACKLE
QUADDED
QUADDLE
QUADRAE
QUADRAL
QUADRAT
QUADREL
QUADRIC
QUADRIN
QUADRUM
QUAEDAM
QUAFFED
QUAFFER
QUAGGAS
QUAGGLE
QUAHAUG
QUAILED
QUAKIER
QUAKILY
QUAKING
QUALIFY
QUALITY
QUAMASH
QUANNET
QUANTIC
QUANTUM
QUARION
QUARLES
QUARRED
QUARREL
QUARTAN
QUARTER
QUARTET
QUARTIC
QUARTIN
QUARTOS
QUARTZY
QUASHED
QUASHEY
QUASSIA
QUASSIN
QUATERN
QUATERS
QUATRAL
QUATRIN
QUATTIE
QUATUOR
QUAVERY
QUAYAGE
QUAYING
QUEACHY
QUEASOM
QUEAZEN
QUEECHY
QUEENLY
QUEERER
QUEERLY
QUELITE
QUELLED
QUELLER
QUELLIO
QUEMADO
QUEMELY
QUERCIC
QUERCIN
QUERELA
QUERELE
QUERENT
QUERIDA
QUERIDO
QUERIED
QUERIER
QUERIES
QUERIST
QUERKEN
QUERNAL
QUESTED
QUESTER
QUESTOR
QUETSCH
QUETZAL
QUIBBLE
QUIBLET
QUICKED
QUICKEN
QUICKER
QUICKIE
QUICKLY
QUIDDER
QUIDDIT
QUIDDLE
QUIENAL
QUIESCE
QUIETED
QUIETEN
QUIETER
QUIETLY
QUIETUS
QUILATE
QUILKIN
QUILLAI
QUILLED
QUILLER
QUILLET
QUILLON
QUILTED
QUILTER
QUINARY
QUINATE
QUININA
QUININE
QUINITE
QUINNAT
QUINNET
QUINOID
QUINONE
QUINOYL
QUINTAD
QUINTAL
QUINTAN
QUINTET
QUINTIC
QUINTIN
QUINTON
QUINTUS
QUINYIE
QUIPPED
QUIPPER
QUIRCAL
QUIRING
QUIRKED
QUISCOS
QUITELY
QUITEVE
QUITTED
QUITTER
QUITTOR
QUIVERY
QUIZZED
QUIZZEE
QUIZZER
QUODDED
QUOINED
QUOITER
QUOMODO
QUONDAM
QUONIAM
QUORUMS
QUOTING
QUOTITY
RACQUET
RELIQUE
REQUEEN
REQUEST
REQUIEM
REQUINS
REQUIRE
REQUITE
RONQUIL
ROQUIST
RORQUAL
SEQUELA
SEQUENT
SEQUEST
SEQUOIA
SILIQUA
SILIQUE
SOSQUIL
SQUABBY
SQUACCO
SQUADDY
SQUADER
SQUAGGA
SQUAILS
SQUALID
SQUALLY
SQUALOR
SQUAMAE
SQUARED
SQUARER
SQUARES
SQUASHY
SQUATLY
SQUATTY
SQUAWKY
SQUEAKY
SQUEEGE
SQUEEZE
SQUEEZY
SQUELCH
SQUETEE
SQUIDGE
SQUIDGY
SQUIFFY
SQUILLA
SQUINCH
SQUINNY
SQUINTY
SQUIRED
SQUIRET
SQUIRTS
SQUIRTY
SQUISHY
SQUITCH
SQUUSHY
SURIQUE
TANQUAM
TANQUEN
TARIQAT
TEQUILA
TORQUED
TORQUES
TOTQUOT
TRIQUET
TURQUET
UBIQUIT
UNEQUAL
UNQUEEN
UNQUEME
UNQUERT
UNQUICK
UNQUIET
UNQUOTE
VAQUERO
VAQUITA

POSITIONAL ORDER LIST OF 7-LETTER WORDS

QABBALA
QUABIRD
QUACHIL
QUACKED
QUACKLE
QUADDED
QUADDLE
QUADRAE
QUADRAL
QUADRAT
QUADREL
QUADRIC
QUADRIN
QUADRUM
QUAEDAM

QUAFFED
QUAFFER
QUAGGAS
QUAGGLE
QUAHAUG
QUAILED
QUAKIER
QUAKILY
QUAKING
QUALIFY
QUALITY
QUAMASH
QUANNET
QUANTIC
QUANTUM
QUARION
QUARLES
QUARRED
QUARREL
QUARTAN
QUARTER
QUARTET
QUARTIC
QUARTIN
QUARTOS
QUARTZY
QUASHED
QUASHEY
QUASSIA
QUASSIN
QUATERN
QUATERS
QUATRAL
QUATRIN
QUATTIE
QUATUOR
QUAVERY
QUAYAGE
QUAYING
QUEACHY
QUEASOM
QUEAZEN
QUEECHY
QUEENLY
QUEERER
QUEERLY
QUELITE
QUELLED
QUELLER
QUELLIO
QUEMADO
QUEMELY
QUERCIC
QUERCIN
QUERELA
QUERELE
QUERENT
QUERIDA
QUERIDO
QUERIED
QUERIER
QUERIES
QUERIST
QUERKEN
QUERNAL
QUESTED
QUESTER
QUESTOR
QUETSCH
QUETZAL
QUIBBLE

QUIBLET
QUICKED
QUICKEN
QUICKER
QUICKIE
QUICKLY
QUIDDER
QUIDDIT
QUIDDLE
QUIENAL
QUIESCE
QUIETED
QUIETEN
QUIETER
QUIETLY
QUIETUS
QUILATE
QUILKIN
QUILLAI
QUILLED
QUILLER
QUILLET
QUILLON
QUILTED
QUILTER
QUINARY
QUINATE
QUININA
QUININE
QUINITE
QUINNAT
QUINNET
QUINOID
QUINONE
QUINOYL
QUINTAD
QUINTAL
QUINTAN
QUINTET
QUINTIC
QUINTIN
QUINTON
QUINTUS
QUINYIE
QUIPPED
QUIPPER
QUIRCAL
QUIRING
QUIRKED
QUISCOS
QUITELY
QUITEVE
QUITTED
QUITTER
QUITTOR
QUIVERY
QUIZZED
QUIZZEE
QUIZZER
QUODDED
QUOINED
QUOITER
QUOMODO
QUONDAM
QUONIAM
QUORUMS
QUOTING
QUOTITY

AQUABIB
AQUAFER
AQUARIA
AQUATIC
AQUAVIT
AQUEITY
AQUEOUS
AQUIFER
AQUIVER
EQUABLE
EQUABLY
EQUALED
EQUALLY
EQUATED
EQUATOR
EQUERRY
EQUILIN
EQUINAL
EQUINIA
EQUINOX
EQUINUS
EQUISON
EQUITES
EQUULEI
OQUASSA
SQUABBY
SQUACCO
SQUADDY
SQUADER
SQUAGGA
SQUAILS
SQUALID
SQUALLY
SQUALOR
SQUAMAE
SQUARED
SQUARER
SQUARES
SQUASHY
SQUATLY
SQUATTY
SQUAWKY
SQUEAKY
SQUEEGE
SQUEEZE
SQUEEZY
SQUELCH
SQUETEE
SQUIDGE
SQUIDGY
SQUIFFY
SQUILLA
SQUINCH
SQUINNY
SQUINTY
SQUIRED
SQUIRET
SQUIRTS
SQUIRTY
SQUISHY
SQUITCH
SQUUSHY

ACQUENT
ACQUEST
ACQUIRE
ACQUIST
ALQUIER
ANQUERA
ASQUARE
ASQUEAL
ASQUINT
ASQUIRM
BEQUEST
COQUINA
COQUITA
COQUITO
DEQUEEN
ENQUIRE
ENQUIRY
ESQUIRE
EXQUIRE
INQUEST
INQUIET
INQUIRE
INQUIRY
JAQUIMA
LAQUEAR
LAQUEUS
LIQUATE
LIQUEFY
LIQUEUR
LIQUIDS
LIQUIDY
LIQUIFY
LIQUORS
LIQUORY
LOQUENT
PIQUANT
PIQUERO
PIQUEUR
PIQUING
REQUEEN
REQUEST
REQUIEM
REQUINS
REQUIRE
REQUITE
ROQUIST
SEQUELA
SEQUENT
SEQUEST
SEQUOIA
TEQUILA
UNQUEEN
UNQUEME
UNQUERT
UNQUICK
UNQUIET
UNQUOTE
VAQUERO
VAQUITA

ACEQUIA
ALIQUID
ALIQUOT
BANQUET
BASQUED
BOSQUET
BOUQUET
BRIQUET
CASQUED
CASQUET
CAWQUAW
CHEQUER
CLIQUED
COEQUAL
CONQUER
CROQUET
CROQUIS
CUMQUAT
ETIQUET
INEQUAL
JERQUED
JERQUER
JONQUIL
KUMQUAT
LACQUER
LACQUEY
MANQUEE
MARQUEE
MARQUIS
MASQUER
MESQUIN
MEZQUIT
MUSQUAW
OPAQUED
PARQUET
PASQUIL
PASQUIN
PICQUET
RACQUET
RONQUIL
RORQUAL
SOSQUIL
TANQUAM
TANQUEN
TORQUED
TORQUES
TOTQUOT
TRIQUET
TURQUET
UBIQUIT
UNEQUAL

ALFAQUI
ANTIQUA
ANTIQUE
BAROQUE
BATUQUE
BEZIQUE
BRASQUE
BRISQUE
BRUSQUE
CACIQUE
CASAQUE
CAZIQUE
CHALQUE
CHARQUI
COMIQUE
COSAQUE
ESTOQUE
FLASQUE
GRECQUE
JOCOQUE
JOCOQUI
MACAQUE
MADOQUA
NAMAQUA
OBLIQUE
OBLOQUY
OBSEQUY
PATAQUE
PERIQUE
PURAQUE
RELIQUE
SILIQUA
SILIQUE
SURIQUE
TARIQAT

SCORING ORDER LIST OF 7-LETTER WORDS

28
QUARTZY
SQUEEZY

27
BEZIQUE
MEZQUIT

26
SQUAWKY

25
JAQUIMA
JOCOQUE
JOCOQUI
QUEAZEN
QUETZAL
QUICKLY
QUIZZED
SQUEEZE
SQUIFFY

24
CAWQUAW
JERQUED
QUEACHY
QUEECHY
QUIZZEE
QUIZZER

23
EQUINOX
EXQUIRE
JERQUER
JONQUIL
QUACKED
QUAFFED
QUAKILY
QUICKED
SQUABBY
SQUEAKY

22
KUMQUAT
LIQUEFY
LIQUIFY
QUACKLE
QUAFFER
QUALIFY
QUASHEY
QUAVERY
QUICKEN
QUICKER
QUICKIE
QUIVERY
SQUASHY
SQUISHY
SQUUSHY
UNQUICK

21
CHALQUE
CHARQUI
CHEQUER
EQUABLY
LACQUEY
MUSQUAW
OBLOQUY
OBSEQUY
QUACHIL
QUAKING
QUAMASH
QUEMELY
QUETSCH
QUIPPED
QUIRKED
SQUADDY
SQUELCH
SQUIDGY
SQUINCH
SQUITCH

20
AQUABIB
CACIQUE
COMIQUE
CUMQUAT
LIQUIDY
MACAQUE
PICQUET
QABBALA
QUAHAUG
QUAKIER
QUASHED
QUAYAGE
QUAYING
QUERCIC
QUERKEN
QUIBBLE
QUILKIN
QUIPPER
SQUACCO

19
ALFAQUI
AQUAFER
AQUAVIT
AQUEITY
AQUIFER
AQUIVER
BASQUED
CASQUED
CLIQUED
ENQUIRY
EQUALLY
EQUERRY
FLASQUE
GRECQUE
INQUIRY
LIQUORY
MADOQUA
OPAQUED
PIQUING
QUABIRD
QUADDED
QUADRIC
QUADRUM
QUAEDAM
QUALITY
QUEENLY
QUEERLY
QUEMADO
QUIETLY
QUINARY
QUINOYL
QUINYIE
QUITELY
QUITEVE
QUODDED
QUOMODO
QUONDAM
QUOTITY
SQUALLY
SQUATLY
SQUATTY
SQUINNY
SQUINTY
SQUIRTY
VAQUERO
VAQUITA

18
ACEQUIA
ACQUENT
ACQUEST
ACQUIRE
ACQUIST
AQUATIC
ASQUIRM
BANQUET
BAROQUE
BATUQUE
BEQUEST
BOSQUET
BOUQUET
BRASQUE
BRIQUET
BRISQUE
BRUSQUE
CASAQUE
CASQUET
COEQUAL
CONQUER
COQUINA
COQUITA
COQUITO
COSAQUE
CROQUET
CROQUIS
EQUABLE
LACQUER
MANQUEE
MARQUEE
MARQUIS
MASQUER
MESQUIN
NAMAQUA
OBLIQUE
PARQUET
PASQUIL
PASQUIN
PATAQUE
PERIQUE
PIQUANT
PIQUERO
PIQUEUR
PURAQUE
QUADDLE
QUAGGAS
QUAGGLE
QUANTIC
QUANTUM
QUARTIC
QUEASOM
QUERCIN
QUIBLET
QUIDDER
QUIDDIT
QUIDDLE
QUIESCE
QUINTIC
QUIRCAL
QUISCOS
QUONIAM
QUORUMS
RACQUET
REQUIEM
SQUAGGA
SQUAMAE
SQUIDGE
TANQUAM
UBIQUIT
UNQUEME

17
ALIQUID
DEQUEEN
EQUALED
EQUATED
LIQUIDS
QUADRAE
QUADRAL
QUADRAT
QUADREL
QUADRIN
QUAILED
QUARRED
QUELLED
QUERIDA
QUERIDO
QUERIED
QUESTED
QUIETED
QUILLED
QUILTED
QUINOID
QUINTAD
QUIRING
QUITTED
QUOINED
QUOTING
SQUADER
SQUALID
SQUARED
SQUEEGE
SQUIRED
TORQUED

16
ALIQUOT
ALQUIER
ANQUERA
ANTIQUA
ANTIQUE
AQUARIA
AQUEOUS
ASQUARE
ASQUEAL
ASQUINT
ENQUIRE
EQUATOR
EQUILIN
EQUINAL
EQUINIA
EQUINUS
EQUISON
EQUITES
EQUULEI
ESQUIRE
ESTOQUE
ETIQUET
INEQUAL
INQUEST
INQUIET
INQUIRE
LAQUEAR
LAQUEUS
LIQUATE
LIQUEUR
LIQUORS
LOQUENT
OQUASSA
QUANNET
QUARION
QUARLES
QUARREL
QUARTAN
QUARTER
QUARTET
QUARTIN
QUARTOS
QUASSIA
QUASSIN
QUATERN
QUATERS
QUATRAL
QUATRIN
QUATTIE
QUATUOR
QUEERER
QUELITE
QUELLER
QUELLIO
QUERELA
QUERELE
QUERENT
QUERIER
QUERIES
QUERIST
QUERNAL
QUESTER
QUESTOR
QUIENAL
QUIETEN
QUIETER
QUIETUS
QUILATE
QUILLAI
QUILLER
QUILLET
QUILLON
QUILTER
QUINATE
QUININA
QUININE
QUINITE
QUINNAT
QUINNET
QUINONE
QUINTAL
QUINTAN
QUINTET
QUINTIN
QUINTON
QUINTUS
QUITTER
QUITTOR
QUOITER
RELIQUE
REQUEEN
REQUEST
REQUINS
REQUIRE
REQUITE
RONQUIL
ROQUIST
RORQUAL
SEQUELA
SEQUENT
SEQUEST
SEQUOIA
SILIQUA
SILIQUE
SOSQUIL
SQUAILS
SQUALOR
SQUARER
SQUARES
SQUETEE
SQUILLA

SQUIRET
SQUIRTS
SURIQUE
TANQUEN
TARIQAT
TEQUILA
TORQUES
TOTQUOT
TRIQUET
TURQUET
UNEQUAL
UNQUEEN
UNQUERT
UNQUIET
UNQUOTE

ALPHABETICAL LIST OF 8-LETTER WORDS

ACQUAINT
ACQUIRED
ACQUIRER
ACQUITAL
ADEQUACY
ADEQUATE
ALAMIQUI
ALFAQUIN
ALIQUANT
ALQUEIRE
ALQUIFOU
ANTIQUED
ANTIQUER
APPLIQUE
AQUACADE
AQUALUNG
AQUANAUT
AQUARIAL
AQUARIAN
AQUARIST
AQUARIUM
AQUARTER
AQUATICS
AQUATILE
AQUATINT
AQUATION
AQUATONE
AQUEDUCT
AQUIFORM
AQUIFUGE
AQUILEGE
AQUILINE
AQUILINO
AQUOSITY
AQUOTIZE
ARQUEBUS
ASPIQUEE
BARBEQUE
BARQUEST
BASQUINE
BEDQUILT
BELDUQUE
BEQUEATH
BERLOQUE
BIQUARTZ
BORASQUE
BOUTIQUE
BRASQUED
BRELOQUE
BROQUERY
CALANQUE
CASAQUIN
CHAQUETA
CHEQUEEN
CHEQUERS
CHICQUED
CHICQUER
CHIQUEST
CINQFOIL
CINQUAIN
CLAQUEUR
CLINIQUE
CLIQUIER
CLIQUING
CLIQUISH
CLIQUISM
COEQUATE
COLLOQUE
COLLOQUY
CONQUEST
CONQUIAN
COQUETRY
COQUETTE
COQUILLE
CORSEQUE
COTQUEAN
CRITIQUE
DAIQUIRI
DETRAQUE
DISQUIET
ELIQUATE
ELOQUENT
EMBUSQUE
ENQUIRER
EQUACITY
EQUAEVAL
EQUALING
EQUALISE
EQUALIST
EQUALITY
EQUALIZE
EQUALLED
EQUATING
EQUATION
EQUATIVE
EQUAIXED
EQUIFORM
EQUINATE
EQUINITY
EQUIPAGA
EQUIPAGE
EQUIPPED
EQUIPPER
EQUISETA
EQUITANT
EQUITIES
EQUITIST
EQUIVOKE
EQUULEUS
ESQUIRED
ESQUISSE
EXEQUIES
FABRIQUE
FILIOQUE
FREQUENT
HAQUETON
HENEQUEN
HUISQUIL
ICEQUAKE
ILLIQUID
INEQUITY
INIQUITY
INQUIRED
INQUIRER
INQUISIT
JACQUARD
JAQUETTE
JERQUING
LIMEQUAT
LINQUISH
LIQUABLE
LIQUAMEN
LIQUATED
LIQUESCE
LIQUIDLY
LIQUIDUS
LIQUORED
LIQUORER
LOQUENCE
LOQUENCY
LOQUITUR
MAQUETTE
MAROQUIN
MARQUESS
MARQUISE
MARQUITO
MESQUITA
MESQUITE
MEZQUITE
MIQUELET
MISQUOTE
MOQUETTE
MOSQUITO
MUSQUASH
MYSTIQUE
NASTALIQ
NONQUOTA
OBLICQUE
OBLIQUED
OBLIQUUS
OPAQUELY
OPAQUING
OUTQUEEN
OUTQUOTE
PARAQUET
PAROQUET
PAURAQUE
PERIOQUE
PERQUEER
PERQUEIR
PERQUEST
PHYSIQUE
PIQUABLE
PIQUANCY
PIQUETTE
PIQUIERE
QABBALAH
QADARITE
QAIMAQAM
QUACKERY
QUACKING
QUACKISH
QUACKISM
QUADRANS
QUADRANT
QUADRATE
QUADRIAD
QUADRIGA
QUADRINE
QUADROON
QUADRUAL
QUAESITA
QUAESTIO
QUAESTOR
QUAFFING
QUAGGIER
QUAGMIRE
QUAGMIRY
QUAILERY
QUAILING
QUAINTER
QUAINTLY
QUAKIEST
QUALMISH
QUALTAGH
QUANDANG
QUANDARY
QUANDONG
QUANTIFY
QUANTITY
QUANTIZE
QUANTONG
QUARANTY
QUARDEEL
QUARESMA
QUARRIED
QUARRIER
QUARRIES
QUARRION
QUARROME
QUARTANE
QUARTANO
QUARTAUT
QUARTERN
QUARTERS
QUARTILE
QUARTINE
QUARTOLE
QUARTZIC
QUASHING
QUASKIES
QUASSIIN
QUATENUS
QUATERON
QUATORZE
QUATRAIN
QUAVERED
QUAVERER
QUAVIVER
QUAYSIDE
QUEANISH
QUEASIER
QUEASILY
QUEBRADA
QUEBRITH
QUEDNESS
QUEDSHIP
QUEENCUP
QUEENING
QUEENITE
QUEENLET
QUEEREST
QUEERITY
QUELLING
QUELLUNG
QUEMEFUL
QUENCHED
QUENCHER
QUENELLE
QUENTISE
QUERCINE
QUERCITE
QUERELAE
QUERIDAS
QUERIDOS
QUERIMAN
QUERYING
QUESITED
QUESTEUR
QUESTING
QUESTION
QUESTMAN
QUESTMEN
QUEZALES
QUIAQUIA
QUIBBLED
QUIBBLER
QUICKEST
QUICKING
QUICKSET
QUIDDANY
QUIDDITY
QUIDDLED
QUIDDLER
QUIDNUNC
QUIESCED
QUIETAGE
QUIETEST
QUIETING
QUIETISM
QUIETIST
QUIETIVE
QUIETUDE
QUILECES
QUILESES
QUILISMA
QUILLAIC
QUILLING
QUILLITY
QUILTING
QUINAMIN
QUINCUNX
QUINDENE
QUINELLA
QUINETUM
QUINIBLE
QUINICIN
QUINIDIN
QUINIELA
QUINITOL
QUINOGEN
QUINOLAS
QUINOLIN
QUINOLYL
QUINONIC

QUINONYL
QUINOVIN
QUINSIED
QUINTAIN
QUINTANT
QUINTARY
QUINTILE
QUINTOLE
QUIPPING
QUIPPISH
QUIPSOME
QUIPSTER
QUIRKIER
QUIRKING
QUIRKSEY
QUISLING
QUISTRON
QUITRENT
QUITTING
QUIVERED
QUIVERER
QUIXOTIC
QUIXOTRY
QUIZZERY
QUIZZIFY
QUIZZING
QUIZZISH
QUIZZISM
QUIZZITY
QUODDIES
QUODDING

QUODDITY
QUODLING
QUOILERS
QUOINING
QUOMINUS
QUONKING
QUOTABLE
QUOTABLY
QUOTIENT
QUOTIETY
RAMEQUIN
REMARQUE
REPIQUED
REPLIQUE
REQUIRED
REQUIRER
REQUITAL
REQUITED
REQUITER
ROQUETED
ROQUETTE
ROQUILLE
SAMBAQUI
SASANQUA
SEAQUAKE
SEQUACES
SEQUELAE
SEQUENCE
SEQUITUR
SHABEQUE
SOLIQUID

SQUABBED
SQUABBER
SQUABBLE
SQUABBLY
SQUACCOS
SQUADDED
SQUADROL
SQUADRON
SQUAILER
SQUALENE
SQUALLED
SQUALLER
SQUALOID
SQUAMATE
SQUAMIFY
SQUAMISH
SQUAMOID
SQUAMOSA
SQUAMOSE
SQUAMOUS
SQUAMULA
SQUAMULE
SQUANDER
SQUANTUM
SQUARELY
SQUARIER
SQUARING
SQUARISH
SQUARSON
SQUASHED
SQUASHER

SQUATTED
SQUATTER
SQUATTLE
SQUAWKED
SQUAWKER
SQUAWKIE
SQUEAKED
SQUEAKER
SQUEALED
SQUEALER
SQUEEGEE
SQUEEZED
SQUEEZER
SQUELCHY
SQUIBBED
SQUIBBER
SQUIDDED
SQUIDDER
SQUIDDLE
SQUIFFED
SQUIFFER
SQUIGGLE
SQUIGGLY
SQUILGEE
SQUILLID
SQUINACY
SQUINANT
SQUINTED
SQUINTER
SQUIRAGE

SQUIREEN
SQUIRELY
SQUIRESS
SQUIRING
SQUIRISH
SQUIRMED
SQUIRMER
SQUIRREL
SQUIRTED
SQUIRTER
SQUISHED
SQUITTER
SUNQUAKE
SURQUIDY
TEQUILLA
TORQUATE
TRANQUIL
TURQUOIS
UBIQUITY
UMQUHILE
UNIQUELY
UNIQUITY
UNSQUARE
UNSQUIRE
USQUABAE
USQUEBAE
VANQUISH
VAQUEROS
VASQUINE
VERQUERE

POSITIONAL ORDER LIST OF 8-LETTER WORDS

QABBALAH
QADARITE
QAIMAQAM
QUACKERY
QUACKING
QUACKISH
QUACKISM
QUADRANS
QUADRANT
QUADRATE
QUADRIAD
QUADRIGA
QUADRINE
QUADROON
QUADRUAL
QUAESITA
QUAESTIO
QUAESTOR
QUAFFING
QUAGGIER
QUAGMIRE
QUAGMIRY
QUAILERY
QUAILING
QUAINTER
QUAINTLY
QUAKIEST
QUALMISH
QUALTAGH
QUANDANG
QUANDARY
QUANDONG
QUANTIFY
QUANTITY
QUANTIZE
QUANTONG
QUARANTY
QUARDEEL
QUARESMA
QUARRIED

QUARRIER
QUARRIES
QUARRION
QUARROME
QUARTANE
QUARTANO
QUARTAUT
QUARTERN
QUARTERS
QUARTILE
QUARTINE
QUARTOLE
QUARTZIC
QUASHING
QUASKIES
QUASSIIN
QUATENUS
QUATERON
QUATORZE
QUATRAIN
QUAVERED
QUAVERER
QUAVIVER
QUAYSIDE
QUEANISH
QUEASIER
QUEASILY
QUEBRADA
QUEBRITH
QUEDNESS
QUEDSHIP
QUEENCUP
QUEENING
QUEENITE
QUEENLET
QUEEREST
QUEERITY
QUELLING
QUELLUNG
QUEMEFUL

QUENCHED
QUENCHER
QUENELLE
QUENTISE
QUERCINE
QUERCITE
QUERELAE
QUERIDAS
QUERIDOS
QUERIMAN
QUERYING
QUESITED
QUESTEUR
QUESTING
QUESTION
QUESTMAN
QUESTMEN
QUEZALES
QUIAQUIA
QUIBBLED
QUIBBLER
QUICKEST
QUICKING
QUICKSET
QUIDDANY
QUIDDITY
QUIDDLED
QUIDDLER
QUIDNUNC
QUIESCED
QUIETAGE
QUIETEST
QUIETING
QUIETISM
QUIETIST
QUIETIVE
QUIETUDE
QUILECES
QUILESES
QUILISMA

QUILLAIC
QUILLING
QUILLITY
QUILTING
QUINAMIN
QUINCUNX
QUINDENE
QUINELLA
QUINETUM
QUINIBLE
QUINICIN
QUINIDIN
QUINIELA
QUINITOL
QUINOGEN
QUINOLAS
QUINOLIN
QUINOLYL
QUINONIC
QUINONYL
QUINOVIN
QUINSIED
QUINTAIN
QUINTANT
QUINTARY
QUINTILE
QUINTOLE
QUIPPING
QUIPPISH
QUIPSOME
QUIPSTER
QUIRKIER
QUIRKING
QUIRKSEY
QUISLING
QUISTRON
QUITRENT
QUITTING
QUIVERED
QUIVERER

QUIXOTIC
QUIXOTRY
QUODDIES
QUIZZERY
QUIZZIFY
QUIZZING
QUIZZISH
QUIZZISM
QUIZZITY
QUODDING
QUODDITY
QUODLING
QUOILERS
QUOINING
QUOMINUS
QUONKING
QUOTABLE
QUOTABLY
QUOTIENT
QUOTIETY

AQUACADE
AQUALUNG
AQUANAUT
AQUARIAL
AQUARIAN
AQUARIST
AQUARIUM
AQUARTER
AQUATICS
AQUATILE
AQUATINT
AQUATION
AQUATONE
AQUEDUCT
AQUIFORM
AQUIFUGE
AQUILEGE
AQUILINE
AQUILINO

AQUOSITY
AQUOTIZE
EQUACITY
EQUAEVAL
EQUALING
EQUALISE
EQUALIST
EQUALITY
EQUALIZE
EQUALLED
EQUATING
EQUATION
EQUATIVE
EQUAIXED
EQUIFORM
EQUINATE
EQUINITY
EQUIPAGA
EQUIPAGE
EQUIPPED
EQUIPPER
EQUISETA
EQUITANT
EQUITIES
EQUITIST
EQUIVOKE
EQUULEUS
SQUABBED
SQUABBER
SQUABBLE
SQUABBLY
SQUACCOS
SQUADDED
SQUADROL
SQUADRON
SQUAILER
SQUALENE
SQUALLED
SQUALLER
SQUALOID
SQUAMATE
SQUAMIFY
SQUAMISH
SQUAMOID
SQUAMOSA
SQUAMOSE
SQUAMOUS
SQUAMULA
SQUAMULE
SQUANDER
SQUANTUM
SQUARELY
SQUARIER
SQUARING
SQUARISH
SQUARSON

SQUASHED
SQUASHER
SQUATTED
SQUATTER
SQUATTLE
SQUAWKED
SQUAWKER
SQUAWKIE
SQUEAKED
SQUEAKER
SQUEALED
SQUEALER
SQUEEGEE
SQUEEZED
SQUEEZER
SQUELCHY
SQUIBBED
SQUIBBER
SQUIDDED
SQUIDDER
SQUIDDLE
SQUIFFED
SQUIFFER
SQUIGGLE
SQUIGGLY
SQUILGEE
SQUILLID
SQUINACY
SQUINANT
SQUINTED
SQUINTER
SQUIRAGE
SQUIREEN
SQUIRELY
SQUIRESS
SQUIRING
SQUIRISH
SQUIRMED
SQUIRMER
SQUIRREL
SQUIRTED
SQUIRTER
SQUISHED
SQUITTER

ACQUAINT
ACQUIRED
ACQUIRER
ACQUITAL
ALQUEIRE
ALQUIFOU
ARQUEBUS
BEQUEATH
BIQUARTZ
COQUETRY

COQUETTE
COQUILLE
ENQUIRER
ESQUIRED
ESQUISSE
HAQUETON
INQUIRED
INQUIRER
INQUISIT
JAQUETTE
LIQUABLE
LIQUAMEN
LIQUATED
LIQUESCE
LIQUIDLY
LIQUIDUS
LIQUORED
LIQUORER
LOQUENCE
LOQUENCY
LOQUITUR
MAQUETTE
MIQUELET
MOQUETTE
PIQUABLE
PIQUANCY
PIQUETTE
PIQUIERE
REQUIRED
REQUIRER
REQUITAL
REQUITED
REQUITER
ROQUETED
ROQUETTE
ROQUILLE
SEQUACES
SEQUELAE
SEQUENCE
SEQUITUR
TEQUILLA
UMQUHILE
USQUABAE
USQUEBAE
VAQUEROS

ADEQUACY
ADEQUATE
ALIQUANT
BARQUEST
BASQUINE
BEDQUILT
BROQUERY
CHAQUETA
CHEQUEEN

CHEQUERS
CHIQUEST
CINQFOIL
CINQUAIN
CLAQUEUR
CLIQUIER
CLIQUING
CLIQUISH
CLIQUISM
COEQUATE
CONQUEST
CONQUIAN
COTQUEAN
DAIQUIRI
DISQUIET
ELIQUATE
ELOQUENT
EXEQUIES
FREQUENT
ICEQUAKE
INEQUITY
INIQUITY
JACQUARD
JERQUING
LINQUISH
MARQUESS
MARQUISE
MARQUITO
MESQUITA
MESQUITE
MEZQUITE
MISQUOTE
MOSQUITO
MUSQUASH
NONQUOTA
OPAQUELY
OPAQUING
OUTQUEEN
OUTQUOTE
PERQUEER
PERQUEIR
PERQUEST
SEAQUAKE
SUNQUAKE
SURQUIDY
TORQUATE
TURQUOIS
UBIQUITY
UNIQUELY
UNIQUITY
UNSQUARE
UNSQUIRE
VANQUISH
VASQUINE
VERQUERE

ALFAQUIN
ANTIQUED
ANTIQUER
ASPIQUEE
BRASQUED
CASAQUIN
CHICQUED
CHICQUER
HENEQUEN
HUISQUIL
ILLIQUID
LIMEQUAT
MAROQUIN
OBLIQUED
OBLIQUUS
PARAQUET
PAROQUET
QUIAQUIA
RAMEQUIN
REPIQUED
SOLIQUID
TRANQUIL

ALAMIQUI
APPLIQUE
BARBEQUE
BELDUQUE
BERLOQUE
BORASQUE
BOUTIQUE
BRELOQUE
CALANQUE
CLINIQUE
COLLOQUE
COLLOQUY
CORSEQUE
CRITIQUE
DETRAQUE
EMBUSQUE
FABRIQUE
FILIOQUE
MYSTIQUE
OBLICQUE
PAURAQUE
PERIOQUE
PHYSIQUE
QAIMAQAM
REMARQUE
REPLIQUE
SAMBAQUI
SASANQUA
SHABEQUE

NASTALIQ

SCORING ORDER LIST OF 8-LETTER WORDS

31
QUIZZIFY

28
BIQUARTZ
MEZQUITE
QUARTZIC
QUIZZERY
QUIZZISH
QUIZZITY

27
JACQUARD
QUIXOTRY
QUIZZISM

SQUEEZED

26
AQUOTIZE
EQUALIZE
QUACKERY
QUACKISH
QUANTIZE
QUATORZE
QUEZALES
QUINCUNX
QUIXOTIC
QUIZZING
SQUEEZER

25
CHICQUED
EQUAIXED
JERQUING
PHYSIQUE
QUACKISM
SQUAMIFY
SQUAWKED
SQUELCHY

24
CHICQUER
EQUIVOKE
EXEQUIES
JAQUETTE

PIQUANCY
QABBALAH
QUACKING
QUAFFING
QUICKING
QUIPPISH
QUIRKSEY
SQUABBLY
SQUAWKER
SQUAWKIE
SQUIFFED

23
ADEQUACY
ICEQUAKE

QUAGMIRY
QUANTIFY
QUAVIVER
QUEDSHIP
QUENCHED
QUICKEST
QUICKSET
SQUIFFER
VANQUISH

22
AQUIFORM
BEQUEATH
BROQUERY
CHAQUETA

CHEQUEEN
CHEQUERS
CHIQUEST
CINQFOIL
CLIQUISH
COLLOQUY
COQUETRY
EQUACITY
EQUIFORM
EQUIPPED
FABRIQUE
LOQUENCY
MUSQUASH
MYSTIQUE
OPAQUELY
QUALMISH
QUEBRITH
QUEMEFUL
QUENCHER
QUIBBLED
QUIDDANY
QUIDDITY
QUIPPING
QUIRKING
QUODDITY
QUONKING
QUOTABLY
SHABEQUE
SQUABBED
SQUAMISH
SQUEAKED
SQUIBBED
SQUIGGLY
SQUINACY
UBIQUITY
UMQUHILE

21

APPLIQUE
AQUIFUGE
BARBEQUE
CLIQUISM
EMBUSQUE
EQUIPPER
LIQUIDLY
OBLICQUE
PIQUABLE
QUAKIEST
QUALTAGH
QUANDARY
QUASHING
QUASKIES
QUAVERED
QUAYSIDE
QUEENCUP
QUERYING
QUIBBLER
QUIPSOME
QUIRKIER
QUIVERED
SAMBAQUI
SEAQUAKE
SQUABBER
SQUABBLE
SQUACCOS
SQUASHED
SQUEAKER
SQUIBBER
SQUISHED
SUNQUAKE
SURQUIDY

20

ACQUIRED
ALFAQUIN
ALQUIFOU
AQUACADE
AQUEDUCT
AQUOSITY
BEDQUILT
BELDUQUE
BRASQUED
CLIQUING
EQUAEVAL
EQUALITY
EQUATIVE
EQUINITY
EQUIPAGA
EQUIPAGE
FILIOQUE
FREQUENT
HAQUETON
HENEQUEN
HUISQUIL
INEQUITY
INIQUITY
LINQUISH
OBLIQUED
OPAQUING
QAIMAQAM
QUAGMIRE
QUAILERY
QUAINTLY
QUANTITY
QUARANTY
QUAVERER
QUEANISH
QUEASILY
QUEBRADA
QUEERITY
QUIDDLED
QUIDNUNC
QUIESCED
QUIETIVE
QUILLITY
QUINOLYL
QUINONYL
QUINOVIN
QUINTARY
QUIVERER
QUODDING
QUOTIETY
REPIQUED
SQUADDED
SQUAMOID
SQUARELY
SQUARISH
SQUASHER
SQUIDDED
SQUIRELY
SQUIRISH
SQUIRMED
UNIQUELY
UNIQUITY
VAQUEROS
VASQUINE
VERQUERE

19

ACQUAINT
ACQUIRER
ACQUITAL
ALAMIQUI
AQUARIUM
AQUATICS
ARQUEBUS
ASPIQUEE
BARQUEST
BASQUINE
BERLOQUE
BORASQUE
BOUTIQUE
BRELOQUE
CALANQUE
CASAQUIN
CINQUAIN
CLAQUEUR
CLINIQUE
CLIQUIER
COEQUATE
COLLOQUE
CONQUEST
CONQUIAN
COQUETTE
COQUILLE
CORSEQUE
COTQUEAN
CRITIQUE
LIMEQUAT
LIQUABLE
LIQUAMEN
LIQUESCE
LOQUENCE
MAQUETTE
MAROQUIN
MARQUESS
MARQUISE
MARQUITO
MESQUITA
MESQUITE
MIQUELET
MISQUOTE
MOQUETTE
MOSQUITO
OBLIQUUS
PARAQUET
PAROQUET
PAURAQUE
PERIOQUE
PERQUEER
PERQUEIR
PERQUEST
PIQUETTE
PIQUIERE
QUADRIAD
QUADRIGA
QUAGGIER
QUANDANG
QUANDONG
QUARESMA
QUARROME
QUERCINE
QUERCITE
QUERIMAN
QUESTMAN
QUESTMEN
QUIDDLER
QUIETISM
QUILECES
QUILISMA
QUILLAIC
QUINAMIN
QUINETUM
QUINIBLE
QUINICIN
QUINONIC
QUIPSTER
QUODDIES
QUODLING
QUOMINUS
QUOTABLE
RAMEQUIN
REMARQUE
REPLIQUE
SEQUACES
SEQUENCE
SQUAMATE
SQUAMOSA
SQUAMOSE
SQUAMOUS
SQUAMULA
SQUAMULE
SQUANTUM
SQUIDDER
SQUIDDLE
SQUIGGLE
SQUIRMER
USQUABAE

18

ADEQUATE
ANTIQUED
AQUALUNG
AQUILEGE
DAIQUIRI
DETRAQUE
DISQUIET
EQUALING
EQUALLED
EQUATING
ESQUIRED
ILLIQUID
INQUIRED
LIQUATED
LIQUIDUS
LIQUORED
QUADRANS
QUADRANT
QUADRATE
QUADRINE
QUADROON
QUADRUAL
QUAILING
QUANTONG
QUARDEEL
QUARRIED
QUEDNESS
QUEENING
QUELLING
QUELLUNG
QUERIDAS
QUERIDOS
QUESITED
QUESTING
QUIETAGE
QUIETING
QUIETUDE
QUILLING
QUILTING
QUINDENE
QUINIDIN
QUINOGEN
QUINSIED
QUISLING
QUITTING
QUOINING
REQUIRED
REQUITED
ROQUETED
SOLIQUID
SQUADROL
SQUADRON
SQUALLED
SQUALOID
SQUANDER
SQUARING
SQUATTED
SQUEALED
SQUEEGEE
SQUILGEE
SQUILLID
SQUINTED
SQUIRAGE
SQUIRING
SQUIRTED

17

ALIQUANT
ALQUEIRE
ANTIQUER
AQUANAUT
AQUARIAL
AQUARIAN
AQUARIST
AQUARTER
AQUATILE
AQUATINT
AQUATION
AQUATONE
AQUILINE
AQUILINO
ELIQUATE
ELOQUENT
ENQUIRER
EQUALISE
EQUALIST
EQUATION
EQUINATE
EQUISETA
EQUITANT
EQUITIES
EQUITIST
EQUULEUS
ESQUISSE
INQUIRER
INQUISIT
LIQUORER
LOQUITUR
NASTALIQ
NONQUOTA
OUTQUEEN
OUTQUOTE
QUAESITA
QUAESTIO
QUAESTOR
QUAINTER
QUARRIER
QUARRIES
QUARRION
QUARTANE
QUARTANO
QUARTAUT
QUARTERN
QUARTERS
QUARTILE
QUARTINE
QUARTOLE
QUASSIIN
QUATENUS
QUATERON
QUATRAIN
QUEASIER
QUEENITE
QUEENLET
QUEEREST
QUENELLE
QUENTISE
QUERELAE
QUESTEUR
QUESTION
QUIETEST
QUIETIST
QUILESES
QUINELLA
QUINIELA
QUINITOL
QUINOLAS
QUINOLIN
QUINTAIN
QUINTANT
QUINTILE
QUINTOLE
QUISTRON
QUITRENT
QUOILERS

QUOTIENT
REQUIRER
REQUITAL
REQUITER
ROQUETTE
ROQUILLE
SASANQUA
SEQUELAE
SEQUITUR
SQUAILER
SQUALENE
SQUALLER
SQUARIER
SQUARSON
SQUATTER
SQUATTLE
SQUEALER
SQUINANT
SQUINTER
SQUIREEN
SQUIRESS
SQUIRREL
SQUIRTER
SQUITTER
TEQUILLA
TORQUATE
TRANQUIL
TURQUOIS
UNSQUARE
UNSQUIRE

16

QUIAQUIA

ALPHABETICAL LIST OF 9-LETTER WORDS

ACQUEREUR
ACQUIESCE
ACQUIRING
ACQUISITA
ACQUISITE
ACQUITTAL
ACQUITTED
ACQUITTER
AEQUOREAL
ALAMBIQUE
ANGELIQUE
ANTILOQUY
ANTIQUARY
ANTIQUATE
ANTIQUELY
ANTIQUING
ANTIQUIST
ANTIQUITY
APPLIQUED
AQUAGREEN
AQUAMETER
AQUAPLANE
AQUARELLE
AQUARIIST
AQUARIUMS
AQUATICAL
AQUEOUSLY
AQUILEGIA
ARABESQUE
ARQUERITE
BALDAQUIN
BANQUETED
BANQUETER
BANQUETTE
BEQUIRTLE
BILBOQUET
BISQUETTE
BOURASQUE
BRASQUING
BRIQUETTE
BRODEQUIN
BRUSQUELY
BURLESQUE
CACIQUISM
CAIQUEJEE
CANNEQUIN
CARQUAISE
CASQUETEL
CASQUETTE
CHIBOUQUE
CHICQUING
CLINQUANT
CLIQUIEST
COEQUALLY
COEQUATED
COLOQUIES
CONQUEDLE
CONQUERED
CONQUEROR
COQUETOON
COQUETTED
CROQUETED
CROQUETTE
CUCKQUEAN
DELIQUIUM
DEMIPIQUE
DISQUISIT
DURAQUARA
ELIQUATED
ELOQUENCE
ENCHEQUER
EQUALIZED
EQUALIZER
EQUALLING
EQUALNESS
EQUERRIES
EQUIMODAL
EQUIMOLAR
EQUIPEDAL
EQUIPLUVE
EQUIPMENT
EQUIPOISE
EQUIPPING
EQUISETIC
EQUISETUM
EQUITABLE
EQUITABLY
EQUIVALVE
EQUIVOCAL
EQUIVOQUE
ESQUAMATE
ESQUIRING
ETIQUETTE
EXCHEQUER
EXEQUATUR
EXQUISITE
FANTASQUE
FOURQUINE
FREQUENCE
FREQUENCY
GRASSQUIT
GRIQUAITE
GROTESQUE
HALOESQUE
HARLEQUIN
HARQUEBUS
INEQUALLY
INQUIETLY
INQUILINE
INQUINATE
INQUIRENT
INQUIRIES
INQUIRING
INQUISITE
INSEQUENT
JACQUERIE
JEQUERITY
JEQUIRITY
JONQUILLE
LACQUERED
LACQUERER
LAQUEARIA
LIQUATING
LIQUATION
LIQUEFIED
LIQUEFIER
LIQUEURED
LIQUIDATE
LIQUIDITY
LIQUIDIZE
LIQUIFORM
LIQUORICE
LIQUORING
LIQUORISH
LIQUORIST
LONQUHARD
LOQUACITY
LOQUENTLY
MANNEQUIN
MARQUETRY
MARQUISAL
MISQUOTED
MISQUOTER
MONOCOQUE
MOSQUITAL
MOSQUITOS
OBLIQUATE
OBLIQUELY
OBLIQUING
OBLIQUITY
OBLOQUIAL
OBLOQUIES
OBSEQUENT
OBSEQUIAL
OBSEQUIES
OBSEQUITY
ODALISQUE
OVERQUELL
PALANQUIN
PARQUETED
PARQUETRY
PARROQUET
PASQUILER
PASQUILIC
PHYSIQUED
PICQUETER
PIQUANTLY
PLAQUETTE
PLASTIQUE
PROPINQUE
QUACKHOOD
QUACKSTER
QUADRABLE
QUADRATED
QUADRATIC
QUADRATUM
QUADRATUS
QUADRIFID
QUADRIGAE
QUADRILLE
QUADRIMUM
QUADRIVIA
QUADRUPED
QUADRUPLE
QUAESITUM
QUAGGIEST
QUAGMIRED
QUAILHEAD
QUAINTEST
QUAINTISE
QUAKETAIL
QUAKINESS
QUAKINGLY
QUALIFIED
QUALIFIER
QUALITIED
QUALITIES
QUANTICAL
QUANTIZED
QUANTULUM
QUARENDEN
QUARENDER
QUARRELED
QUARRYING
QUARRYMAN
QUARRYMEN
QUARTERED
QUARTERER
QUARTERLY
QUARTERON
QUARTETTE
QUARTINHO
QUARTZITE
QUARTZOID
QUARTZOSE
QUARTZOUS
QUATRAYLE
QUATREBLE
QUATRIBLE
QUATTRINI
QUATTRINO
QUAVERING
QUAVEROUS
QUAYSIDER
QUEACHIER
QUEASIEST
QUEBRACHO
QUEENCAKE
QUEENFISH
QUEENLIER
QUEENLIKE
QUEENROOT
QUEENWEED
QUEENWOOD
QUEERNESS
QUEERSOME
QUEINTISE
QUENCHING
QUERCETIC
QUERCETIN
QUERCETUM
QUERCITOL
QUERENCIA
QUERIMANS
QUERIMONY
QUERULENT
QUERULIST
QUERULITY
QUERULOUS
QUESITIVE
QUESTIONS
QUESTRIST
QUETENITE
QUIBBLING
QUICKBEAM
QUICKBORN
QUICKENED
QUICKENER
QUICKFOOT
QUICKLIME
QUICKNESS
QUICKSAND
QUICKSIDE
QUICKSTEP
QUICKWORK
QUIDDLING
QUIESCENT
QUIESCING
QUIETENER
QUIETLIKE
QUIETNESS
QUIETSOME
QUILLAJIC
QUILLBACK
QUILLETED
QUILLFISH
QUILLTAIL
QUILLWORK
QUILLWORT
QUINALDIC
QUINALDIN
QUINALDYL
QUINAMINE
QUINARIAN
QUINARIES
QUINARIUS
QUINDECAD
QUINDECIM
QUINICINE
QUINIDINE
QUININISM
QUININIZE
QUINISEXT
QUINOFORM
QUINOIDAL

QUINOIDIN
QUINOLINE
QUINOLOGY
QUINONIZE
QUINONOID
QUINOVATE
QUINOVOSE
QUINQUINA
QUINQUINO
QUINTETTE
QUINTETTO
QUINTFOIL
QUINTIPED
QUINTROON
QUINTUPLE
QUINZAINE
QUINZIEME
QUIREWISE
QUIRKIEST
QUIRKSOME
QUISQUOUS
QUISUTSCH
QUITANTIE
QUITCLAIM
QUITTANCE
QUIVERFUL
QUIVERING
QUIXOTISM
QUIXOTIZE
QUIZZICAL
QUODLIBET

QUOTATION
QUOTATIVE
QUOTELESS
QUOTIDIAN
QUOTINGLY
REACQUIRE
RELIQUARY
RELIQUIAE
RELIQUIAN
RELIQUISM
REPIQUING
REQUESTER
REQUIRING
REQUISITE
REQUITING
ROQUETING
SAMBAQUIS
SEMIQUOTE
SEQUACITY
SEQUELANT
SEQUENCER
SEQUESTER
SEQUESTRA
SILIQUOSE
SIMIESQUE
SOBRIQUET
SOLILOQUY
SQUABBASH
SQUABBIER
SQUABBING
SQUABBISH

SQUABBLED
SQUABBLER
SQUADDING
SQUADRATE
SQUADRISM
SQUADRONE
SQUALIDLY
SQUALLERY
SQUALLIER
SQUALLING
SQUAMATED
SQUAMELLA
SQUAMEOUS
SQUAMOSAL
SQUAMULAE
SQUAREAGE
SQUARECAP
SQUAREMAN
SQUAREMEN
SQUARROSE
SQUARROUS
SQUASHIER
SQUASHILY
SQUASHING
SQUATINID
SQUATMORE
SQUATNESS
SQUATTAGE
SQUATTIER
SQUATTILY
SQUATTING

SQUATTISH
SQUAWBUSH
SQUAWFISH
SQUAWKIER
SQUAWKING
SQUAWROOT
SQUAWWEED
SQUEAKERY
SQUEAKILY
SQUEAKING
SQUEALING
SQUEAMISH
SQUEEGEED
SQUEEZING
SQUELCHED
SQUELCHER
SQUELETTE
SQUIBBERY
SQUIBBING
SQUIBBISH
SQUIBSTER
SQUIDDING
SQUIDGIER
SQUIFFIER
SQUILGEED
SQUILGEER
SQUILLGEE
SQUILLIAN
SQUINANCE
SQUINTING
SQUIRALTY

SQUIRARCH
SQUIRMIER
SQUIRMING
SQUIRRELY
SQUIRTING
SQUIRTISH
SQUISHING
SUBAQUEAN
SUBSESQUI
SURQUEDRY
SURQUIDRY
TECHNIQUE
TORQUATED
TOTAQUINE
TRIPTYQUE
TRIQUETRA
TURQUOISE
UBIQUIOUS
UNEQUABLE
UNEQUABLY
UNEQUALED
UNEQUALLY
UNQUAILED
UNQUALIFY
UNQUALITY
UNQUEMELY
UNQUIETLY
UNREQUEST
UNSQUARED
UTRAQUIST
WELLQUEME

POSITIONAL ORDER LIST OF 9-LETTER WORDS

QUACKHOOD
QUACKSTER
QUADRABLE
QUADRATED
QUADRATIC
QUADRATUM
QUADRATUS
QUADRIFID
QUADRIGAE
QUADRILLE
QUADRIMUM
QUADRIVIA
QUADRUPED
QUADRUPLE
QUAESITUM
QUAGGIEST
QUAGMIRED
QUAILHEAD
QUAINTEST
QUAINTISE
QUAKETAIL
QUAKINESS
QUAKINGLY
QUALIFIED
QUALIFIER
QUALITIED
QUALITIES
QUANTICAL
QUANTIZED
QUANTULUM
QUARENDEN
QUARENDER
QUARRELED
QUARRYING
QUARRYMAN
QUARRYMEN
QUARTERED
QUARTERER
QUARTERLY
QUARTERON

QUARTETTE
QUARTINHO
QUARTZITE
QUARTZOID
QUARTZOSE
QUARTZOUS
QUATRAYLE
QUATREBLE
QUATRIBLE
QUATTRINI
QUATTRINO
QUAVERING
QUAVEROUS
QUAYSIDER
QUEACHIER
QUEASIEST
QUEBRACHO
QUEENCAKE
QUEENFISH
QUEENLIER
QUEENLIKE
QUEENROOT
QUEENWEED
QUEENWOOD
QUEERNESS
QUEERSOME
QUEINTISE
QUENCHING
QUERCETIC
QUERCETIN
QUERCETUM
QUERCITOL
QUERENCIA
QUERIMANS
QUERIMONY
QUERULENT
QUERULIST
QUERULITY
QUERULOUS
QUESITIVE

QUESTIONS
QUESTRIST
QUETENITE
QUIBBLING
QUICKBEAM
QUICKBORN
QUICKENED
QUICKENER
QUICKFOOT
QUICKLIME
QUICKNESS
QUICKSAND
QUICKSIDE
QUICKSTEP
QUICKWORK
QUIDDLING
QUIESCENT
QUIESCING
QUIETENER
QUIETLIKE
QUIETNESS
QUIETSOME
QUILLAJIC
QUILLBACK
QUILLETED
QUILLFISH
QUILLTAIL
QUILLWORK
QUILLWORT
QUINALDIC
QUINALDIN
QUINALDYL
QUINAMINE
QUINARIAN
QUINARIES
QUINARIUS
QUINDECAD
QUINDECIM
QUINICINE
QUINIDINE

QUININISM
QUININIZE
QUINISEXT
QUINOFORM
QUINOIDAL
QUINOIDIN
QUINOLINE
QUINOLOGY
QUINONIZE
QUINONOID
QUINOVATE
QUINOVOSE
QUINQUINA
QUINQUINO
QUINTETTE
QUINTETTO
QUINTFOIL
QUINTIPED
QUINTROON
QUINTUPLE
QUINZAINE
QUINZIEME
QUIREWISE
QUIRKIEST
QUIRKSOME
QUISQUOUS
QUISUTSCH
QUITANTIE
QUITCLAIM
QUITTANCE
QUIVERFUL
QUIVERING
QUIXOTISM
QUIXOTIZE
QUIZZICAL
QUODLIBET
QUOTATION
QUOTATIVE
QUOTELESS
QUOTIDIAN

QUOTINGLY

AQUAGREEN
AQUAMETER
AQUAPLANE
AQUARELLE
AQUARIIST
AQUARIUMS
AQUATICAL
AQUEOUSLY
AQUILEGIA
EQUALIZED
EQUALIZER
EQUALLING
EQUALNESS
EQUERRIES
EQUIMODAL
EQUIMOLAR
EQUIPEDAL
EQUIPLUVE
EQUIPMENT
EQUIPOISE
EQUIPPING
EQUISETIC
EQUISETUM
EQUITABLE
EQUITABLY
EQUIVALVE
EQUIVOCAL
EQUIVOQUE
SQUABBASH
SQUABBIER
SQUABBING
SQUABBISH
SQUABBLED
SQUABBLER
SQUADDING
SQUADRATE
SQUADRISM
SQUADRONE

SQUALIDLY
SQUALLERY
SQUALLIER
SQUALLING
SQUAMATED
SQUAMELLA
SQUAMEOUS
SQUAMOSAL
SQUAMULAE
SQUAREAGE
SQUARECAP
SQUAREMAN
SQUAREMEN
SQUARROSE
SQUARROUS
SQUASHIER
SQUASHILY
SQUASHING
SQUATINID
SQUATMORE
SQUATNESS
SQUATTAGE
SQUATTIER
SQUATTILY
SQUATTING
SQUATTISH
SQUAWBUSH
SQUAWFISH
SQUAWKIER
SQUAWKING
SQUAWROOT
SQUAWWEED
SQUEAKERY
SQUEAKILY
SQUEAKING
SQUEALING
SQUEAMISH
SQUEEGEED
SQUEEZING
SQUELCHED
SQUELCHER
SQUELETTE
SQUIBBERY
SQUIBBING
SQUIBBISH
SQUIBSTER
SQUIDDING
SQUIDGIER
SQUIFFIER
SQUILGEED
SQUILGEER
SQUILLGEE
SQUILLIAN

SQUINANCE
SQUINTING
SQUIRALTY
SQUIRARCH
SQUIRMIER
SQUIRMING
SQUIRRELY
SQUIRTING
SQUIRTISH

ACQUEREUR
ACQUIESCE
ACQUIRING
ACQUISITA
ACQUISITE
ACQUITTAL
ACQUITTED
ACQUITTER
AEQUOREAL
ARQUERITE
BEQUIRTLE
COQUETOON
COQUETTED
ESQUAMATE
ESQUIRING
EXQUISITE
INQUIETLY
INQUILINE
INQUINATE
INQUIRENT
INQUIRIES
INQUIRING
INQUISITE
JEQUERITY
JEQUIRITY
LAQUEARIA
LIQUATING
LIQUATION
LIQUEFIED
LIQUEFIER
LIQUEURED
LIQUIDATE
LIQUIDITY
LIQUIDIZE
LIQUIFORM
LIQUORICE
LIQUORING
LIQUORISH
LIQUORIST
LOQUACITY
LOQUENTLY
PIQUANTLY
REQUESTER

REQUIRING
REQUISITE
REQUITING
ROQUETING
SEQUACITY
SEQUELANT
SEQUENCER
SEQUESTER
SEQUESTRA
UNQUAILED
UNQUALIFY
UNQUALITY
UNQUEMELY
UNQUIETLY

BANQUETED
BANQUETER
BANQUETTE
BISQUETTE
BRIQUETTE
CAIQUEJEE
CARQUAISE
CASQUETEL
CASQUETTE
CLIQUIEST
COEQUALLY
COEQUATED
CONQUEDLE
CONQUERED
CONQUEROR
CROQUETED
CROQUETTE
DISQUISIT
ELIQUATED
ELOQUENCE
ETIQUETTE
EXEQUATUR
FREQUENCE
FREQUENCY
GRIQUAITE
HARQUEBUS
INEQUALLY
JACQUERIE
JONQUILLE
LACQUERED
LACQUERER
LONQUHARD
MARQUETRY
MARQUISAL
MISQUOTED
MISQUOTER
MOSQUITAL
MOSQUITOS

PARQUETED
PARQUETRY
PASQUILER
PASQUILIC
PICQUETER
PLAQUETTE
SURQUEDRY
SURQUIDRY
TORQUATED
TRIQUETRA
TURQUOISE
UBIQUIOUS
UNEQUABLE
UNEQUABLY
UNEQUALED
UNEQUALLY
UNSQUARED
VANQUISHER
VANQUISHED

ANTIQUARY
ANTIQUATE
ANTIQUELY
ANTIQUING
ANTIQUIST
ANTIQUITY
BRASQUING
BRUSQUELY
CACIQUISM
CHICQUING
CLINQUANT
COLOQUIES
CUCKQUEAN
DELIQUIUM
DURAQUARA
FOURQUINE
INSEQUENT
OBLIQUATE
OBLIQUELY
OBLIQUING
OBLIQUITY
OBLOQUIAL
OBLOQUIES
OBSEQUENT
OBSEQUIAL
OBSEQUIES
OBSEQUITY
OVERQUELL
QUINQUINA
QUINQUINO
QUISQUOUS
REACQUIRE

RELIQUARY
RELIQUIAE
RELIQUIAN
RELIQUISM
REPIQUING
SEMIQUOTE
SILIQUOSE
SUBAQUEAN
TOTAQUINE
UNREQUEST
UTRAQUIST
WELLQUEME

APPLIQUED
BALDAQUIN
BILBOQUET
BRODEQUIN
CANNEQUIN
ENCHEQUER
EXCHEQUER
GRASSQUIT
HARLEQUIN
MANNEQUIN
PALANQUIN
PARROQUET
PHYSIQUED
SAMBAQUIS
SOBRIQUET

ALAMBIQUE
ANGELIQUE
ANTILOQUY
ARABESQUE
BOURASQUE
BURLESQUE
CHIBOUQUE
DEMIPIQUE
EQUIVOQUE
FANTASQUE
GROTESQUE
HALOESQUE
MONOCOQUE
ODALISQUE
PLASTIQUE
PROPINQUE
SIMIESQUE
SOLILOQUY
SUBSESQUI
TECHNIQUE
TRIPTYQUE

SCORING ORDER LIST OF 9-LETTER WORDS

34
QUIXOTIZE

30
EXCHEQUER

29
QUINZIEME

28
EQUALIZED
JEQUERITY
JEQUIRITY
LIQUIDIZE
QUACKHOOD
QUANTIZED
QUARTZOID
QUICKBEAM
QUIZZICAL
SQUEEZING

27
CAIQUEJEE
EQUALIZER
JACQUERIE
PHYSIQUED
QUARTZITE
QUARTZOSE
QUARTZOUS
QUICKFOOT
QUILLAJIC
QUININIZE
QUINONIZE
QUINZAINE
QUIXOTISM
SQUAWFISH

26
CHICQUING
CUCKQUEAN
FREQUENCY
QUAKINGLY
QUICKBORN
QUICKLIME
QUICKSTEP
QUICKWORK
QUILLBACK
SQUAWBUSH
SQUAWKING
QUEBRACHO
QUICKENED
QUICKSAND
QUICKSIDE
QUILLWORK
QUINISEXT
SQUABBASH
SQUABBISH
SQUAWKIER
SQUAWWEED
SQUEAKERY
SQUEAKILY
SQUIBBERY
SQUIBBISH
QUACKSTER
QUEENCAKE
QUEENFISH
QUENCHING
QUICKENER
QUICKNESS
QUILLFISH
QUIRKSOME
QUIVERFUL
SQUASHILY
SQUELCHED
SQUIFFIER
UNQUALIFY

25
CHIBOUQUE
EXEQUATUR
EXQUISITE
JONQUILLE

24
CACIQUISM
EQUIVALVE

23
APPLIQUED
BRUSQUELY
COEQUALLY

DEMIPIQUE
ENCHEQUER
EQUIPLUVE
EQUIPPING
EQUITABLY
EQUIVOCAL
FREQUENCE
HARQUEBUS
LIQUIFORM
LOQUACITY
MARQUETRY
OBLIQUELY
OBLIQUITY
OBSEQUITY
PARQUETRY
PIQUANTLY
QUADRIFID
QUADRIMUM
QUARRYMAN
QUARRYMEN
QUEACHIER
QUERIMONY
QUIBBLING
QUINDECIM
QUINOFORM
QUISUTSCH
SEQUACITY
SQUABBING
SQUABBLED
SQUEAKING
SQUEAMISH
SQUELCHER
SQUIBBING
SQUIRARCH
TECHNIQUE
TRIPTYQUE
UNEQUABLY
UNQUEMELY
WELLQUEME

22

ACQUIESCE
ALAMBIQUE
BILBOQUET
EQUIPMENT
LIQUEFIED
LIQUIDITY
LONQUHARD
MONOCOQUE
PASQUILIC
PICQUETER
PROPINQUE
QUADRIVIA
QUADRUPED
QUAGMIRED
QUAILHEAD
QUAKETAIL
QUAKINESS
QUALIFIED
QUARRYING
QUAVERING
QUAYSIDER
QUEENLIKE
QUEENWEED
QUEENWOOD
QUERCETIC
QUERCETUM
QUIETLIKE
QUINALDYL
QUINDECAD
QUINOLOGY
QUIRKIEST
QUITCLAIM
QUIVERING
QUOTINGLY
SAMBAQUIS
SQUABBIER
SQUABBLER

SQUALIDLY
SQUARECAP
SQUASHING
SQUISHING
SURQUEDRY
SURQUIDRY

21

ACQUIRING
ACQUITTED
ANTILOQUY
ANTIQUARY
ANTIQUELY
ANTIQUITY
AQUEOUSLY
BALDAQUIN
BANQUETED
BRASQUING
BRODEQUIN
COEQUATED
CONQUEDLE
CONQUERED
COQUETTED
CROQUETED
DELIQUIUM
EQUIMODAL
EQUIPEDAL
FANTASQUE
FOURQUINE
HALOESQUE
HARLEQUIN
INEQUALLY
INQUIETLY
LACQUERED
LIQUEFIER
LIQUORISH
LOQUENTLY
MISQUOTED
OBLIQUING
OVERQUELL
PARQUETED
QUADRABLE
QUADRATIC
QUADRATUM
QUADRUPLE
QUALIFIER
QUARTERLY
QUARTINHO
QUATRAYLE
QUAVEROUS
QUERULITY
QUESITIVE
QUIDDLING
QUIESCING
QUILLWORT
QUINALDIC
QUINOVATE
QUINOVOSE
QUINTFOIL
QUINTIPED
QUIREWISE
QUODLIBET
QUOTATIVE
RELIQUARY
REPIQUING
SOLILOQUY
SQUADDING
SQUADRISM
SQUALLERY
SQUAMATED
SQUASHIER
SQUATTILY
SQUATTISH
SQUAWROOT
SQUIDDING
SQUIRALTY
SQUIRMING
SQUIRRELY

SQUIRTISH
UNEQUALLY
UNQUALITY
UNQUIETLY

20

ACQUEREUR
ACQUISITA
ACQUISITE
ACQUITTAL
ACQUITTER
AQUAMETER
AQUAPLANE
AQUARIUMS
AQUATICAL
ARABESQUE
BANQUETER
BANQUETTE
BEQUIRTLE
BISQUETTE
BOURASQUE
BRIQUETTE
BURLESQUE
CANNEQUIN
CARQUAISE
CASQUETEL
CASQUETTE
CLINQUANT
CLIQUIEST
COLOQUIES
CONQUEROR
COQUETOON
CROQUETTE
ELOQUENCE
EQUIMOLAR
EQUIPOISE
EQUISETIC
EQUISETUM
EQUITABLE
EQUIVOQUE
ESQUAMATE
LACQUERER
LIQUORICE
MANNEQUIN
MARQUISAL
MISQUOTER
MOSQUITAL
MOSQUITOS
OBLIQUATE
OBLOQUIAL
OBLOQUIES
OBSEQUENT
OBSEQUIAL
OBSEQUIES
PALANQUIN
PARROQUET
PASQUILER
PLAQUETTE
PLASTIQUE
QUADRATED
QUADRIGAE
QUAESITUM
QUAGGIEST
QUANTICAL
QUANTULUM
QUATREBLE
QUATRIBLE
QUEERSOME
QUERCETIN
QUERCITOL
QUERENCIA
QUERIMANS
QUIESCENT
QUIETSOME
QUINAMINE
QUINICINE
QUININISM
QUINTUPLE

QUITTANCE
REACQUIRE
RELIQUISM
SEMIQUOTE
SEQUENCER
SIMIESQUE
SOBRIQUET
SQUAMELLA
SQUAMEOUS
SQUAMOSAL
SQUAMULAE
SQUAREMAN
SQUAREMEN
SQUATMORE
SQUEEGEED
SQUIBSTER
SQUIDGIER
SQUILGEED
SQUINANCE
SQUIRMIER
SUBAQUEAN
SUBSESQUI
UBIQUIOUS
UNEQUABLE

19

ANGELIQUE
ANTIQUING
AQUAGREEN
AQUILEGIA
DISQUISIT
DURAQUARA
ELIQUATED
EQUALLING
ESQUIRING
GRASSQUIT
GRIQUAITE
GROTESQUE
INQUIRING
LIQUATING
LIQUEURED
LIQUIDATE
LIQUORING
ODALISQUE
QUADRATUS
QUADRILLE
QUALITIED
QUARENDEN
QUARENDER
QUARRELED
QUARTERED
QUILLETED
QUINALDIN
QUINIDINE
QUINOIDAL
QUINOIDIN
QUINONOID
QUOTIDIAN
REQUIRING
REQUITING
ROQUETING
SQUADRATE
SQUADRONE
SQUALLING
SQUAREAGE
SQUATINID
SQUATTAGE
SQUATTING
SQUEALING
SQUILGEER
SQUILLGEE
SQUINTING
SQUIRTING
TORQUATED
UNEQUALED
UNQUAILED
UNSQUARED

18

AEQUOREAL
ANTIQUATE
ANTIQUIST
AQUARELLE
AQUARIIST
ARQUERITE
EQUALNESS
EQUERRIES
ETIQUETTE
INQUILINE
INQUINATE
INQUIRENT
INQUIRIES
INQUISITE
INSEQUENT
LAQUEARIA
LIQUATION
LIQUORIST
QUAINTEST
QUAINTISE
QUALITIES
QUARTERER
QUARTERON
QUARTETTE
QUATTRINI
QUATTRINO
QUEASIEST
QUEENLIER
QUEENROOT
QUEERNESS
QUEINTISE
QUERULENT
QUERULIST
QUERULOUS
QUESTIONS
QUESTRIST
QUETENITE
QUIETENER
QUIETNESS
QUILLTAIL
QUINARIAN
QUINARIES
QUINARIUS
QUINOLINE
QUINTETTE
QUINTETTO
QUINTROON
QUITANTIE
QUOTATION
QUOTELESS
RELIQUIAE
RELIQUIAN
REQUESTER
REQUISITE
SEQUELANT
SEQUESTER
SEQUESTRA
SILIQUOSE
SQUALLIER
SQUARROSE
SQUARROUS
SQUATNESS
SQUATTIER
SQUELETTE
SQUILLIAN
TOTAQUINE
TRIQUETRA
TURQUOISE
UNREQUEST
UTRAQUIST

17

QUINQUINA
QUINQUINO
QUISQUOUS

ALPHABETICAL LIST OF 10-LETTER WORDS

ACEQUIADOR
ACQUAINTED
ACQUIESCED
ACQUIESCER
ACQUIRABLE
ACQUIRENDA
ACQUISIBLE
ACQUISITED
ACQUISITOR
ACQUISITUM
ACQUITMENT
ACQUITTING
ADEQUATELY
ADEQUATION
ADEQUATIVE
ALCORNOQUE
ANTIMASQUE
ANTIQUATED
ANTISQUAMA
APOQUININE
AQUAFORTIS
AQUAMARINE
AQUAPLANED
AQUASCUTUM
AQUATINTER
AQUAVALENT
AQUICOLOUS
AQUIFEROUS
AQUILAWOOD
AQUIPAROUS
ARBORESQUE
BANQUETEER
BANQUETING
BEQUEATHAL
BEQUEATHER
BIQUADRATE
BIQUINTILE
BLANQUETTE
BLANQUILLO
BLOTTESQUE
BROQUINEER
BRUSQUERIE
BURLESQUED
BURLESQUER
CATAFALQUE
CHAUTAUQUA
CHEQUERING
CHERQUERED
CHINQUAPIN
CHOUQUETTE
CIGARESQUE
CINQUEFOIL
CINQUEPACE
CLIQUISHLY
COEQUALITY
COEQUATION
COLLIQUATE
COLLOQUIAL
COLLOQUIST
COLLOQUIUM
COLLOQUIZE
CONQUERING
CONQUININE
CONSEQUENT
COQUELICOT
COQUELUCHE
COQUETRIES
COQUETTING
COQUETTISH
COQUIMBITE
CRAQUELURE
CROQUETING
DELINQUENT
DELIQUESCE
DEMIQUAVER
DESQUAMATE
DISQUALIFY
DISQUIETED
DISQUIETER
DISQUIETLY
DISQUISITE
DISQUIXOTE
DULCILOQUY
EARTHQUAKE
EARTHQUAVE
ELIQUATING
ELIQUATION
EQUABILITY
EQUALITIES
EQUALIZING
EQUANGULAR
EQUANIMITY
EQUANIMOUS
EQUATIONAL
EQUATOREAL
EQUATORIAL
EQUESTRIAN
EQUIFORMAL
EQUIJACENT
EQUILIBRIA
EQUIPARANT
EQUIPARATE
EQUIPOISED
EQUISETUMS
EQUISIGNAL
EQUISONANT
EQUITATION
EQUITATIVE
EQUIVALENT
EQUIVOCACY
EQUIVOCATE
EQUIVOROUS
EUMOLPIQUE
FOURSQUARE
FREQUENTED
FREQUENTER
FREQUENTLY
GRANDESQUE
HARLEQUINA
HARQUEBUSS
HEARTQUAKE
HUMORESQUE
ILLAQUEATE
ILLIQUIDLY
INADEQUACY
INADEQUATE
INELOQUENT
INEQUALITY
INEQUATION
INEQUITIES
INFREQUENT
INIQUITIES
INIQUITOUS
INQUESTUAL
INQUIETUDE
INQUINATED
INQUIRABLE
INQUIRENDO
INQUISITOR
JOAQUINITE
LACQUERING
LACQUERIST
LAMBREQUIN
LANSQUENET
LAQUEARIAN
LIQUEFYING
LIQUESCENT
LIQUEURING
LIQUIDABLE
LIQUIDATED
LIQUIDATOR
LIQUIDIZED
LIQUIDNESS
LOQUACIOUS
MAGNIFIQUE
MAQUAHUITL
MARQUISATE
MARQUISDOM
MARQUISESS
MARQUISINA
MASQUERADE
MEDRINAQUE
MISQUOTING
MOSQUITOES
MOSQUITOEY
MULTILOQUY
MUSQUASPEN
NOVANTIQUE
OBLOQUIOUS
OBSEQUENCE
OBSEQUIOUS
OPAQUENESS
OUTQUIBBLE
OXYQUINONE
PARCILOQUY
PARQUETING
PASQUILANT
PASQUILLER
PASQUILLIC
PASQUINADE
PAUCILOQUY
PENDELOQUE
PERQUADRAT
PERQUEERLY
PERQUISITE
PERRUQUIER
PLASMOQUIN
QUACKERIES
QUACKISHLY
QUADRANGLE
QUADRANTAL
QUADRATICS
QUADRATING
QUADRATRIX
QUADRATURE
QUADRENNIA
QUADRICEPS
QUADRICONE
QUADRIFORM
QUADRIGATE
QUADRILLED
QUADRILLES
QUADRILOGY
QUADRISECT
QUADRIVIAL
QUADRIVIUM
QUADRUMANE
QUADRUPLED
QUADRUPLET
QUADRUPLEX
QUAESTUARY
QUAILERIES
QUAINTANCE
QUAINTNESS
QUAKERBIRD
QUALIFYING
QUALIMETER
QUALMISHLY
QUANDARIES
QUANTIFIED
QUANTIFIER
QUANTITATE
QUANTITIED
QUANTITIES
QUANTITIVE
QUARANTINE
QUARENTENE
QUARRELING
QUARRELLED
QUARRELOUS
QUARTATION
QUARTERAGE
QUARTERING
QUARTERMAN
QUARTERMEN
QUARTERSAW
QUARTZITIC
QUASSATION
QUASSATIVE
QUATERNARY
QUATERNATE
QUATERNION
QUATERNITY
QUATORZAIN
QUATREFOIL
QUEACHIEST
QUEASINESS
QUEENCRAFT
QUEENLIEST
QUEENRIGHT
QUENCHABLE
QUENCHLESS
QUENSELITE
QUERCITRIN
QUERCITRON
QUERNSTONE
QUERYINGLY
QUESTHOUSE
QUESTIONED
QUESTIONEE
QUESTIONER
QUESTORIAL
QUICKENING
QUICKHATCH
QUICKSANDY
QUICKTHORN
QUICKWATER
QUIDDATIVE
QUIDDITIES
QUIESCENCE
QUIESCENCY
QUIETISTIC
QUINACRINE
QUINALDINE
QUINAMICIN
QUINAMIDIN
QUINAQUINA
QUINATOXIN
QUINAZOLIN
QUINAZOLYL
QUINCEWORT
QUINCUNXES
QUINDECIMA
QUINIRETIN
QUINIZARIN
QUINOIDINE
QUINOLINYL
QUINOMETRY
QUINONIMIN
QUINOPYRIN
QUINOXALIN
QUINOXALYL
QUINQUEVIR
QUINSYWORT
QUINTADENA
QUINTADENE
QUINTUPLED
QUINTUPLET
QUISQUEITE
QUIVERLEAF
QUIXOTICAL
QUOTENNIAL
QUOTIETIES
RADIOPAQUE
RELINQUENT
RELINQUISH
RELIQUAIRE
REQUIESCAT
REQUIRABLE
REQUISITOR
REQUITABLE
ROBOTESQUE
ROQUELAURE
SATYRESQUE
SEMICIRQUE
SEMIQUAVER
SEMISQUARE
SEQUACIOUS
SEQUENTIAL
SEQUESTRAL
SEQUESTRUM
SESQUINONA
SOMNILOQUY
SOUBRIQUET
SQUABASHER
SQUABBIEST
SQUABBLING
SQUADRONED
SQUALIDITY
SQUALIFORM
SQUALLIEST
SQUALODONT
SQUAMATINE
SQUAMATION
SQUAMELLAE
SQUAMIFORM
SQUAMOSELY
SQUAMOSITY
SQUAMOUSLY
SQUAMULATE
SQUAMULOSE
SQUANDERED
SQUANDERER
SQUAREFACE
SQUAREHEAD
SQUARENESS
SQUARETAIL
SQUARISHLY
SQUARSONRY
SQUASHIEST
SQUATAROLE
SQUATEROLE
SQUATINOID
SQUATTIEST
SQUAWBERRY
SQUAWKIEST
SQUEEZABLE
SQUEEZEMAN
SQUELCHIER
SQUELCHILY
SQUELCHING
SQUETEAGUE
SQUIBCRACK
SQUIDGIEST
SQUIFFIEST
SQUIGGLIER
SQUILLAGEE
SQUILLITIC
SQUIRARCHY
SQUIREARCH

SQUIRELING
SQUIRMIEST
STATEQUAKE
STATUESQUE
SUBAQUATIC
SUBAQUEOUS
SUBSEQUENT
TAUROESQUE
TERRAQUEAN
TOURNIQUET
TRANQUILER
TRANQUILLO
TRANQUILLY
TRIQUETRAL
TRIQUETRIC
TRIQUETRUM
TRIQUINATE
TRIQUINOYL
TURQUOISES
UBIQUARIAN
UBIQUITARY
UBIQUITOUS
UNADEQUATE
UNCONQUEST
UNDERQUOTE
UNEQUALITY
UNEQUALLED
UNEQUIAXED
UNFREQUENT
UNIQUANTIC
UNIQUENESS
UNLIQUORED
UNQUIETOUS
UNQUIETUDE
UNREQUITER
USQUEBAUGH
VANQUISHED
VANQUISHER
VERSILOQUY
WORLDQUAKE

POSITIONAL ORDER LIST OF 10-LETTER WORDS

QUACKERIES
QUACKISHLY
QUADRANGLE
QUADRANTAL
QUADRATICS
QUADRATING
QUADRATRIX
QUADRATURE
QUADRENNIA
QUADRICEPS
QUADRICONE
QUADRIFORM
QUADRIGATE
QUADRILLED
QUADRILLES
QUADRILOGY
QUADRISECT
QUADRIVIAL
QUADRIVIUM
QUADRUMANE
QUADRUPLED
QUADRUPLET
QUADRUPLEX
QUAESTUARY
QUAILERIES
QUAINTANCE
QUAINTNESS
QUAKERBIRD
QUALIFYING
QUALIMETER
QUALMISHLY
QUANDARIES
QUANTIFIED
QUANTIFIER
QUANTITATE
QUANTITIED
QUANTITIES
QUANTITIVE
QUARANTINE
QUARENTENE
QUARRELING
QUARRELLED
QUARRELOUS
QUARTATION
QUARTERAGE
QUARTERING
QUARTERMAN
QUARTERMEN
QUARTERSAW
QUARTZITIC
QUASSATION
QUASSATIVE
QUATERNARY
QUATERNATE
QUATERNION
QUATERNITY
QUATORZAIN
QUATREFOIL
QUEACHIEST
QUEASINESS
QUEENCRAFT
QUEENLIEST
QUEENRIGHT
QUENCHABLE
QUENCHLESS
QUENSELITE
QUERCITRIN
QUERCITRON
QUERNSTONE
QUERYINGLY
QUESTHOUSE
QUESTIONED
QUESTIONEE
QUESTIONER
QUESTORIAL
QUICKENING
QUICKHATCH
QUICKSANDY
QUICKTHORN
QUICKWATER
QUIDDATIVE
QUIDDITIES
QUIESCENCE
QUIESCENCY
QUIETISTIC
QUINACRINE
QUINALDINE
QUINAMICIN
QUINAMIDIN
QUINAQUINA
QUINATOXIN
QUINAZOLIN
QUINAZOLYL
QUINCEWORT
QUINCUNXES
QUINDECIMA
QUINIRETIN
QUINIZARIN
QUINOIDINE
QUINOLINYL
QUINOMETRY
QUINONIMIN
QUINOPYRIN
QUINOXALIN
QUINOXALYL
QUINQUEVIR
QUINSYWORT
QUINTADENA
QUINTADENE
QUINTUPLED
QUINTUPLET
QUISQUEITE
QUIVERLEAF
QUIXOTICAL
QUOTENNIAL
QUOTIETIES

AQUAFORTIS
AQUAMARINE
AQUAPLANED
AQUASCUTUM
AQUATINTER
AQUAVALENT
AQUICOLOUS
AQUIFEROUS
AQUILAWOOD
AQUIPAROUS
EQUABILITY
EQUALITIES
EQUALIZING
EQUANGULAR
EQUANIMITY
EQUANIMOUS
EQUATIONAL
EQUATOREAL
EQUATORIAL
EQUESTRIAN
EQUIFORMAL
EQUIJACENT
EQUILIBRIA
EQUIPARANT
EQUIPARATE
EQUIPOISED
EQUISETUMS
EQUISIGNAL
EQUISONANT
EQUITATION
EQUITATIVE
EQUIVALENT
EQUIVOCACY
EQUIVOCATE
EQUIVOROUS
SQUABASHER
SQUABBIEST
SQUABBLING
SQUADRONED
SQUALIDITY
SQUALIFORM
SQUALLIEST
SQUALODONT
SQUAMATINE
SQUAMATION
SQUAMELLAE
SQUAMIFORM
SQUAMOSELY
SQUAMOSITY
SQUAMOUSLY
SQUAMULATE
SQUAMULOSE
SQUANDERED
SQUANDERER
SQUAREFACE
SQUAREHEAD
SQUARENESS
SQUARETAIL
SQUARISHLY
SQUARSONRY
SQUASHIEST
SQUATAROLE
SQUATEROLE
SQUATINOID
SQUATTIEST
SQUAWBERRY
SQUAWKIEST
SQUEEZABLE
SQUEEZEMAN
SQUELCHIER
SQUELCHILY
SQUELCHING
SQUETEAGUE
SQUIBCRACK
SQUIDGIEST
SQUIFFIEST
SQUIGGLIER
SQUILLAGEE
SQUILLITIC
SQUIRARCHY
SQUIREARCH
SQUIRELING
SQUIRMIEST

ACQUAINTED
ACQUIESCED
ACQUIESCER
ACQUIRABLE
ACQUIRENDA
ACQUISIBLE
ACQUISITED
ACQUISITOR
ACQUISITUM
ACQUITMENT
ACQUITTING
BEQUEATHAL
BEQUEATHER
BIQUADRATE
BIQUINTILE
COQUELICOT
COQUELUCHE
COQUETRIES
COQUETTING
COQUETTISH
COQUIMBITE
INQUESTUAL
INQUIETUDE
INQUINATED
INQUIRABLE
INQUIRENDO
INQUISITOR
LAQUEARIAN
LIQUEFYING
LIQUESCENT
LIQUEURING
LIQUIDABLE
LIQUIDATED
LIQUIDATOR
LIQUIDIZED
LIQUIDNESS
LOQUACIOUS
MAQUAHUITL
REQUIESCAT
REQUIRABLE
REQUISITOR
REQUITABLE
ROQUELAURE
SEQUACIOUS
SEQUENTIAL
SEQUESTRAL
SEQUESTRUM
UNQUIETOUS
UNQUIETUDE
USQUEBAUGH
ACEQUIADOR
ADEQUATELY
ADEQUATION
ADEQUATIVE
APOQUININE
BANQUETEER
BANQUETING
BROQUINEER
CHEQUERING
CINQUEFOIL
CINQUEPACE
CLIQUISHLY
COEQUALITY
COEQUATION
CONQUERING
CONQUININE
CRAQUELURE
CROQUETING
DESQUAMATE
DISQUALIFY
DISQUIETED
DISQUIETER
DISQUIETLY
DISQUISITE
DISQUIXOTE
ELIQUATING
ELIQUATION
FREQUENTED
FREQUENTER
FREQUENTLY
HARQUEBUSS
INEQUALITY
INEQUATION
INEQUITIES
INIQUITIES
INIQUITOUS
JOAQUINITE
LACQUERING
LACQUERIST
MARQUISATE
MARQUISDOM
MARQUISESS
MARQUISINA
MASQUERADE
MISQUOTING
MOSQUITOES
MOSQUITOEY
MUSQUASPEN
OPAQUENESS
OUTQUIBBLE
OXYQUINONE
PARQUETING
PASQUILANT
PASQUILLER
PASQUILLIC
PASQUINADE
PERQUADRAT
PERQUEERLY
PERQUISITE
SESQUINONA
TRIQUETRAL
TRIQUETRIC
TRIQUETRUM

TRIQUINATE
TRIQUINOYL
TURQUOISES
UBIQUARIAN
UBIQUITARY
UBIQUITOUS
UNEQUALITY
UNEQUALLED
UNEQUIAXED
UNIQUANTIC
UNIQUENESS

ANTIQUATED
BLANQUETTE
BLANQUILLO
BRUSQUERIE
CHERQUERED
CHINQUAPIN
CHOUQUETTE
DELIQUESCE
DEMIQUAVER

ILLAQUEATE
ILLIQUIDLY
LANSQUENET
OBLOQUIOUS
OBSEQUENCE
OBSEQUIOUS
QUINQUEVIR
QUISQUEITE
RELIQUAIRE
SEMIQUAVER
SUBAQUATIC
SUBAQUEOUS
TRANQUILER
TRANQUILLO
TRANQUILLY
UNLIQUORED
UNREQUITER

ANTISQUAMA
COLLIQUATE
COLLOQUIAL

COLLOQUIST
COLLOQUIUM
COLLOQUIZE
CONSEQUENT
DELINQUENT
EARTHQUAKE
EARTHQUAVE
FOURSQUARE
HARLEQUINA
HEARTQUAKE
INADEQUACY
INADEQUATE
INELOQUENT
INFREQUENT
PERRUQUIER
QUINAQUINA
RELINQUENT
RELINQUISH
SEMISQUARE
STATEQUAKE

SUBSEQUENT
TERRAQUEAN
UNADEQUATE
UNCONQUEST
UNDERQUOTE
UNFREQUENT
WORLDQUAKE

BURLESQUED
BURLESQUER
LAMBREQUIN
PLASMOQUIN
SOUBRIQUET
TOURNIQUET

ALCORNOQUE
ANTIMASQUE
ARBORESQUE
BLOTTESQUE
CATAFALQUE

CHAUTAUQUA
CIGARESQUE
DULCILOQUY
EUMOLPIQUE
GRANDESQUE
HUMORESQUE
MAGNIFIQUE
MEDRINAQUE
MULTILOQUY
NOVANTIQUE
PARCILOQUY
PAUCILOQUY
PENDELOQUE
RADIOPAQUE
ROBOTESQUE
SATYRESQUE
SEMICIRQUE
SOMNILOQUY
STATUESQUE
TAUROESQUE

SCORING ORDER LIST OF 10-LETTER WORDS

33
QUICKHATCH

31
QUACKISHLY
QUINAZOLYL

30
LIQUIDIZED
QUARTZITIC
SQUEEZABLE
SQUEEZEMAN

29
EQUALIZING
EQUIVOCACY
OXYQUINONE
QUADRUPLEX
QUICKSANDY
QUINOXALYL
SQUIBCRACK

28
EQUIJACENT
QUATORZAIN
QUICKTHORN
QUICKWATER
QUINAZOLIN
QUINCUNXES
QUINIZARIN
QUIXOTICAL

27
CLIQUISHLY
DISQUIXOTE
QUADRATRIX
QUALMISHLY
SQUAWBERRY
SQUELCHILY
SQUILLAGEE
SQUIRARCHY
UNEQUIAXED
WORLDQUAKE

26
CHINQUAPIN
COQUELUCHE
DISQUALIFY
EARTHQUAKE
ELIQUATING

HEARTQUAKE
JOAQUINITE
LIQUEFYING
PARCILOQUY
PAUCILOQUY
QUAKERBIRD
QUALIFYING
QUENCHABLE
QUERYINGLY
QUICKENING
QUIESCENCY
QUINATOXIN
QUINOXALIN
SQUAMIFORM
SQUAWKIEST
VANQUISHED

25
CHEQUERING
CHERQUERED
CINQUEPACE
COQUIMBITE
DULCILOQUY
EARTHQUAVE
FREQUENTLY
INADEQUACY
MAGNIFIQUE
QUACKERIES
QUADRIFORM
QUADRIVIUM
QUINSYWORT
QUIVERLEAF
SQUARISHLY
SQUELCHING
SQUIFFIEST
USQUEBAUGH
VANQUISHER
VERSILOQUY

24
ACQUIESCED
BEQUEATHAL
BEQUEATHER
CATAFALQUE
CHAUTAUQUA
CHOUQUETTE
CINQUEFOIL
COEQUALITY
COQUETTISH
EQUABILITY

EQUANIMITY
EQUIFORMAL
EQUIVOCATE
HARQUEBUSS
HUMORESQUE
MAQUAHUITL
MARQUISDOM
MOSQUITOEY
MULTILOQUY
PERQUEERLY
QUADRICEPS
QUADRILOGY
QUEACHIEST
QUEENCRAFT
QUENCHLESS
QUIDDATIVE
QUINCEWORT
QUINDECIMA
QUINOMETRY
QUINOPYRIN
SEMIQUAVER
SOMNILOQUY
SQUABASHER
SQUABBLING
SQUALIFORM
SQUAMOSELY
SQUAMOSITY
SQUAMOUSLY
SQUAREFACE
SQUELCHIER
SQUIREARCH
UBIQUITARY

23
ACQUIESCER
ACQUIRABLE
ACQUISIBLE
ACQUISITUM
ACQUITMENT
ADEQUATELY
ADEQUATIVE
AQUASCUTUM
AQUILAWOOD
COLLOQUIUM
COQUELICOT
DISQUIETLY
EUMOLPIQUE
FREQUENTED
ILLIQUIDLY
LAMBREQUIN

MUSQUASPEN
OBSEQUENCE
OUTQUIBBLE
PASQUILLIC
PLASMOQUIN
QUADRIVIAL
QUADRUPLED
QUANTIFIED
QUEENRIGHT
QUIESCENCE
QUINAMICIN
SEMICIRQUE
SQUABBIEST
SQUALIDITY
SQUAREHEAD
STATEQUAKE
SUBAQUATIC
SUBSEQUENT

22
ACEQUIADOR
ACQUAINTED
ACQUIRENDA
ACQUISITED
ACQUITTING
AQUAFORTIS
AQUAPLANED
AQUAVALENT
AQUIFEROUS
BANQUETING
BIQUADRATE
BURLESQUED
CIGARESQUE
CONQUERING
COQUETTING
CROQUETING
DELIQUESCE
EQUIPOISED
EQUITATIVE
EQUIVALENT
EQUIVOROUS
FOURSQUARE
FREQUENTER
HARLEQUINA
INEQUALITY
INFREQUENT
LACQUERING
LIQUIDABLE
MASQUERADE
MEDRINAQUE

MISQUOTING
NOVANTIQUE
PARQUETING
PASQUINADE
PENDELOQUE
PERQUADRAT
QUADRATICS
QUADRICONE
QUADRISECT
QUADRUMANE
QUADRUPLET
QUAESTUARY
QUANTIFIER
QUANTITIVE
QUARTERSAW
QUASSATIVE
QUATERNARY
QUATERNITY
QUATREFOIL
QUESTHOUSE
QUINAMIDIN
QUINOLINYL
QUINTUPLED
RADIOPAQUE
SATYRESQUE
SQUARSONRY
SQUASHIEST
TRANQUILLY
TRIQUINOYL
UNEQUALITY
UNFREQUENT

21
ACQUISITOR
ALCORNOQUE
ANTIMASQUE
ANTISQUAMA
APOQUININE
AQUAMARINE
AQUICOLOUS
AQUIPAROUS
ARBORESQUE
BANQUETEER
BIQUINTILE
BLANQUETTE
BLANQUILLO
BLOTTESQUE
BROQUINEER
BRUSQUERIE
BURLESQUER

COEQUATION
COLLIQUATE
COLLOQUIAL
COLLOQUIST
CONQUININE
CONSEQUENT
COQUETRIES
CRAQUELURE
DISQUIETED
EQUANIMOUS
EQUIPARANT
EQUIPARATE
EQUISETUMS
GRANDESQUE
INQUIRABLE
LACQUERIST
LIQUESCENT
LIQUIDATED
LOQUACIOUS
MARQUISATE
MARQUISESS
MARQUISINA
MOSQUITOES
OBLOQUIOUS
OBSEQUIOUS
OPAQUENESS
PASQUILANT
PASQUILLER
PERQUISITE
PERRUQUIER
QUADRANGLE
QUADRATING
QUADRIGATE
QUADRILLED
QUAINTANCE
QUALIMETER
QUARTERMAN

QUARTERMEN
QUERCITRIN
QUERCITRON
QUIDDITIES
QUIETISTIC
QUINACRINE
QUINONIMIN
QUINQUEVIR
QUINTUPLET
REQUIESCAT
REQUIRABLE
REQUITABLE
ROBOTESQUE
SEMISQUARE
SEQUACIOUS
SEQUESTRUM
SOUBRIQUET
SQUADRONED
SQUAMATINE
SQUAMATION
SQUAMELLAE
SQUAMULATE
SQUAMULOSE
SQUANDERED
SQUIGGLIER
SQUILLITIC
SQUIRMIEST
TRIQUETRIC
TRIQUETRUM
UBIQUARIAN
UBIQUITOUS
UNCONQUEST
UNIQUANTIC

20

ADEQUATION

ANTIQUATED
DELINQUENT
DISQUIETER
DISQUISITE
EQUISIGNAL
INADEQUATE
INQUIETUDE
INQUINATED
INQUIRENDO
LIQUEURING
LIQUIDATOR
LIQUIDNESS
QUADRANTAL
QUADRATURE
QUADRENNIA
QUADRILLES
QUANDARIES
QUANTITIED
QUARRELING
QUARTERAGE
QUARTERING
QUESTIONED
QUINALDINE
QUINOIDINE
QUINTADENA
QUINTADENE
SQUALODONT
SQUANDERER
SQUATINOID
SQUETEAGUE
UNADEQUATE
UNDERQUOTE
UNEQUALLED
UNLIQUORED
UNQUIETUDE

19

AQUATINTER
ELIQUATION
EQUALITIES
EQUANGULAR
EQUATIONAL
EQUATOREAL
EQUATORIAL
EQUESTRIAN
EQUILIBRIA
EQUISONANT
EQUITATION
ILLAQUEATE
INELOQUENT
INEQUATION
INEQUITIES
INIQUITIES
INIQUITOUS
INQUESTUAL
INQUISITOR
LANSQUENET
LAQUEARIAN
QUAILERIES
QUAINTNESS
QUANTITATE
QUANTITIES
QUARANTINE
QUARENTENE
QUARRELOUS
QUARTATION
QUASSATION
QUATERNATE
QUATERNION
QUEASINESS
QUEENLIEST
QUENSELITE

QUERNSTONE
QUESTIONEE
QUESTIONER
QUESTORIAL
QUINIRETIN
QUOTENNIAL
QUOTIETIES
RELINQUENT
RELIQUAIRE
REQUISITOR
ROQUELAURE
SEQUENTIAL
SEQUESTRAL
SESQUINONA
SQUALLIEST
SQUARENESS
SQUARETAIL
SQUATAROLE
SQUATEROLE
SQUATTIEST
STATUESQUE
TAUROESQUE
TERRAQUEAN
TOURNIQUET
TRANQUILER
TRANQUILLO
TRIQUETRAL
TRIQUINATE
TURQUOISES
UNIQUENESS
UNQUIETOUS
UNREQUITER

18

QUINAQUINA
QUISQUEITE

ALPHABETICAL LIST OF WORDS OVER 10 LETTERS

ABSQUATULATE
ACQUAINTANCE
ACQUAINTANT
ACQUIESCENCE
ACQUIESCENT
ACQUIESCING
ACQUIREMENT
ACQUISITION
ACQUISITIVE
ACQUISITIVELY
ACQUITTANCE
ADEQUATENESS
ALTILOQUENCE
ALTILOQUENT
AMPHORILOQUY
ANTHRAQUINOL
ANTIMASQUER
ANTIQUARIAN
ANTIQUARIES
ANTIQUARISM
ANTIQUATING
ANTIQUATION
ANTIQUENESS
ANTIQUITIES
APPLIQUEING
AQUACULTURAL
AQUACULTURE
AQUAEMANALE
AQUAEMANALIA

AQUAFORTIST
AQUAPLANING
AQUAPUNCTURE
AQUARELLIST
AQUATICALLY
AQUATIVENESS
AQUEOGLACIAL
AQUEOIGNEOUS
AQUEOUSNESS
AQUICULTURAL
AQUICULTURE
AQUOTIZATION
ARABESQUELY
ARABESQUERIE
BANQUETEERING
BARBARESQUE
BARQUENTINE
BECQUERELITE
BIQUADRANTAL
BIQUADRATIC
BIQUARTERLY
BLOTTESQUELY
BOUDOIRESQUE
BOUQUETIERE
BOUQUINISTE
BREVILOQUENT
BRONCHILOQUY
BRUSQUENESS
BURLESQUELY

BURLESQUING
CHEQUERBOARD
CHEQUERWISE
CHEQUERWORK
CHIVALRESQUE
CHYMAQUEOUS
CINQUECENTO
CLIQUISHNESS
COEQUALNESS
COLLIQUATION
COLLIQUATIVE
COLLOQUIALLY
COLLOQUIZED
COLLOQUIZING
COLOQUINTIDA
CONQUERABLE
CONQUERINGLY
CONQUINAMINE
CONQUISTADOR
CONSEQUENCE
CONSEQUENTIAL
CONSEQUENTLY
CONTRAMARQUE
COQUECIGRUE
COQUETTISHLY
CROQUIGNOLE
DELINQUENCIES
DELINQUENCY
DELINQUENTLY

DELIQUESCED
DELIQUESCENT
DELIQUESCING
DENTILOQUIST
DESQUAMATED
DESQUAMATING
DESQUAMATION
DESQUAMATIVE
DESQUAMATORY
DISACQUAINT
DISCOTHEQUE
DISEQUALIZE
DISQUALIFIED
DISQUIETEDLY
DISQUIETING
DISQUIETUDE
DISQUIPARANT
DISQUISITED
DISQUISITING
DISQUISITION
DISQUISITIVE
DISQUISITOR
DISQUISITORY
DULCILOQUENT
DUROQUINONE
EARTHQUAKED
EARTHQUAKEN
EARTHQUAKING
ELOQUENTIAL

EQUABLENESS
EQUALITARIAN
EQUALIZATION
EQUANIMOUSLY
EQUATIONALLY
EQUATIONISM
EQUATIONIST
EQUATORIALLY
EQUESTRIENNE
EQUIDISTANCE
EQUIDISTANT
EQUIDISTANTLY
EQUIDIURNAL
EQUIFORMITY
EQUIGRANULAR
EQUILATERAL
EQUILIBRANT
EQUILIBRATE
EQUILIBRATED
EQUILIBRATING
EQUILIBRATING
EQUILIBRATION
EQUILIBRATIVE
EQUILIBRATOR
EQUILIBRATORY
EQUILIBRIAL
EQUILIBRIATE
EQUILIBRIOUS
EQUILIBRIST

EQUILIBRISTAT
EQUILIBRISTIC
EQUILIBRITY
EQUILIBRIUM
EQUILIBRIUMS
EQUILIBRIZE
EQUIMOLECULAR
EQUIMOMENTAL
EQUIMULTIPLE
EQUINANGULAR
EQUINOCTIAL
EQUINOCTIAL
EQUINOCTIALLY
EQUINOVARUS
EQUIPARATION
EQUIPARTILE
EQUIPARTITION
EQUIPOISING
EQUIPOISING
EQUIPOLLENCE
EQUIPOLLENCY
EQUIPOLLENT
EQUIPOLLENTLY
EQUIPONDERANT
EQUIPONDERATE
EQUIPOSTILE
EQUIPOTENTIAL
EQUIPROBABLE
EQUISETACEOUS
EQUISONANCE
EQUIVALENCE
EQUIVALENCED
EQUIVALENCY
EQUIVALENTLY
EQUIVOCALITY
EQUIVOCATED
EQUIVOCATING
EQUIVOCATION
EQUIVOCATOR
EQUIVOCATORY
EQUIVOLUMINAL
ESQUAMULOSE
ETIQUETTICAL
EXQUISITELY
EXQUISITENESS
EXQUISITISM
EXQUISITIVELY
FATILOQUENT
FOREQUARTER
FORMALESQUE
FOURSQUARELY
FREQUENCIES
FREQUENTABLE
FREQUENTAGE
FREQUENTATION
FREQUENTATIVE
FREQUENTING
FREQUENTNESS
GIGANTESQUE
GORGONESQUE
GRANDILOQUENT
GROTESQUELY
GROTESQUERIE
GROTESQUERY
HARLEQUINADE
HARLEQUINIC
HARLEQUINIZE
HEADQUARTER
HEADQUARTERS
HINDQUARTER
HINDQUARTERS
HYDROQUININE
HYDROQUINONE
ILLIQUATION
INADEQUATELY
INADEQUATION
INCONSEQUENCE
INCONSEQUENT
INELOQUENCE
INEQUALITIES
INEQUALNESS
INEQUITABLE
INEQUITABLY
INEQUIVALVE
INFREQUENCE
INFREQUENCY
INIQUITABLE
INIQUITOUSLY
INQUAINTANCE
INQUARTATION
INQUIETNESS
INQUILINISM
INQUILINITY
INQUILINOUS
INQUINATING
INQUINATION
INQUIRATION
INQUIRINGLY
INQUISITION
INQUISITIONAL
INQUISITIVE
INQUISITORIAL
INQUISITORY
ISOQUINOLINE
JEQUIRITIES
LACQUERWORK
LIQUEFACIENT
LIQUEFACTION
LIQUEFACTIVE
LIQUEFIABLE
LIQUESCENCE
LIQUESCENCY
LIQUIDAMBAR
LIQUIDAMBER
LIQUIDATING
LIQUIDATION
LIQUIDIZING
LIQUIDOGENIC
LIQUORISHLY
LIQUORISHNESS
LONGINQUITY
LOQUACIOUSLY
MAGNILOQUENT
MARQUETERIE
MARQUISETTE
MARQUISOTTE
MASQUERADED
MASQUERADER
MASQUERADING
MERIQUINONE
MERIQUINONIC
MILQUETOAST
MISQUOTATION
MONCHIQUITE
MOSQUITOBILL
MOUSQUETAIRE
MULTILOQUENT
MULTILOQUOUS
MUSQUASHROOT
MUSQUASHWEED
NATURALESQUE
NESQUEHONITE
OBLIQUATION
OBLIQUENESS
OBLIQUITIES
OBLIQUITOUS
OBSEQUIOUSLY
OMNILOQUENT
OSTEOPLAQUE
OUTQUESTION
OXYQUINOLINE
PALANQUINED
PALANQUINING
PARAQUADRATE
PASQUEFLOWER
PASQUILLANT
PASQUINADED
PASQUINADER
PASQUINADING
PAUCILOQUENT
PECTORILOQUE
PECTORILOQUY
PEREQUITATE
PERQUISITION
PERQUISITOR
PHENOQUINONE
PICTURESQUE
PIQUANTNESS
PLASMOQUINE
PLATERESQUE
POLYLOQUENT
PRECONQUEST
PREREQUISITE
PRETEREQUINE
PROPINQUANT
PROPINQUITY
PROPINQUOUS
PROQUAESTOR
PSEUDOAQUATIC
QUACKISHNESS
QUACKSALVER
QUADRAGESIMAL
QUADRANGLED
QUADRANGULAR
QUADRANGULED
QUADRANTILE
QUADRAPHONIC
QUADRATICAL
QUADRENNIAL
QUADRENNIUM
QUADRENNIUMS
QUADRICINIUM
QUADRICIPITAL
QUADRICYCLE
QUADRICYCLER
QUADRIENNIUM
QUADRIFILAR
QUADRIFOCAL
QUADRIFOLIUM
QUADRIFRONS
QUADRIGAMIST
QUADRIGATUS
QUADRIHYBRID
QUADRIJUGAL
QUADRILATERAL
QUADRILLING
QUADRILLION
QUADRINOMIAL
QUADRIPAROUS
QUADRIPLANAR
QUADRIURATE
QUADRIVALENT
QUADRIVIOUS
QUADRUMANAL
QUADRUMANOUS
QUADRUPEDAL
QUADRUPEDAN
QUADRUPEDANT
QUADRUPEDATE
QUADRUPEDOUS
QUADRUPLANE
QUADRUPLATE
QUADRUPLATOR
QUADRUPLING
QUAESTIONES
QUAESTORIAL
QUAESTORIAN
QUAESTORSHIP
QUALIFIABLE
QUALIFICATION
QUALIFICATOR
QUALIFIEDLY
QUALITATIVE
QUALMISHNESS
QUANTIFYING
QUANTIMETER
QUANTITATIVE
QUANTITIVELY
QUANTIVALENT
QUANTIZATION
QUANTIZING
QUANTOMETER
QUAQUAVERSAL
QUARANTINED
QUARANTINER
QUARANTINING
QUARRELLING
QUARRELLOUS
QUARRELOUSLY
QUARRELSOME
QUARRYSTONE
QUARTERBACK
QUARTERFOIL
QUARTERLAND
QUARTERLIES
QUARTERMASTER
QUARTERNIGHT
QUARTERNION
QUARTERPACE
QUARTERSAWED
QUARTERSAWING
QUARTERSAWN
QUARTERSTAFF
QUARTERSTAVES
QUARTIPAROUS
QUATERNARIES
QUATERNARIUS
QUATERNIONIC
QUATERNITIES
QUATERTENSES
QUATREFOILED
QUATTROCENTO
QUAVERINGLY
QUEBRACHITE
QUEBRACHITOL
QUEBRADILLA
QUEENFISHES
QUEENLINESS
QUEENSBERRIES
QUEENSBERRY
QUENCHLESSLY
QUERCITANNIN
QUERCIVOROUS
QUERIMONIES
QUERIMONIOUS
QUERULENTIAL
QUERULOSITY
QUERULOUSLY
QUESTIONABLE
QUESTIONABLY
QUESTIONARIES
QUESTIONARY
QUESTIONING
QUESTIONIST
QUESTIONLESS
QUESTIONNAIRE
QUESTMONGER
QUICKENANCE
QUICKENBEAM
QUICKSILVER
QUICKSILVERY
QUIDDITATIVE
QUIESCENTLY
QUIINACEOUS
QUILLFISHES
QUINALDINIC
QUINALDINIUM
QUINAMICINE
QUINAMIDINE
QUINANISOLE
QUINATOXINE
QUINAZOLINE
QUINCUNCIAL
QUINCUNXIAL
QUINDECAGON
QUINDECEMVIR
QUINDECEMVIRI
QUINDECIMVIR
QUINHYDRONE
QUINISEXTINE
QUINOIDATION
QUINOLINIUM
QUINOLOGIST
QUINONIMINE
QUINOXALINE
QUINQUENNIAD
QUINQUENNIA
QUINQUENNIAL
QUINQUENNIUM
QUINQUENNIUMS
QUINQUERTIUM
QUINQUEVIRS
QUINSYBERRIES
QUINSYBERRY
QUINTELEMENT
QUINTERNION
QUINTESSENCE
QUINTILLION
QUINTUPLING
QUINUCLIDINE
QUIPPISHNESS
QUIRITARIAN
QUIRQUINCHO
QUISLINGISM
QUISQUILIAN
QUISQUILIARY
QUISQUILIOUS
QUITCLAIMED
QUITCLAIMING
QUITTERBONE
QUIZZACIOUS
QUIZZATORIAL
QUIZZICALITY
QUIZZICALLY
QUODLIBETARY
QUODLIBETIC
QUOTABILITY
QUOTABLENESS
QUOTATIONAL
QUOTATIONIST
QUOTEWORTHY
QUOTIDIANLY
RELINQUISHED
RELINQUISHER
RELIQUARIES
REQUIESCENCE
REQUIREMENT
REQUISITELY
REQUISITION
REQUISITORY
REQUITATIVE
REQUITELESS
REQUITEMENT
RIBAUDEQUIN
SANCTILOQUENT
SCULPTURESQUE
SEMIANTIQUE
SEMIAQUATIC
SEMIQUARTILE
SEMIQUIETIST
SEQUACIOUSLY
SEQUENTIALITY
SEQUESTERED
SEQUESTERING
SEQUESTERMENT

SEQUESTRABLE
SEQUESTRANT
SEQUESTRATE
SEQUESTRATED
SEQUESTRATING
SEQUESTRATION
SEQUESTRATOR
SESQUIALTER
SESQUIALTERA
SESQUIALTERAL
SESQUINONAL
SESQUIOCTAVA
SESQUIPEDAL
SESQUIPLICATE
SESQUIQUARTA
SESQUIQUINTA
SESQUISEXTAL
SESQUITERPENE
SESQUITERTIA
SOLDATESQUE
SOLILOQUIES
SOLILOQUISE
SOLILOQUIST
SOLILOQUIZE
SOLILOQUIZED
SOLILOQUIZER
SOLILOQUIZING
SOMNILOQUENCE
SOMNILOQUENT
SOMNILOQUISM
SOMNILOQUIST
SOMNILOQUOUS
SQUABBLINGLY
SQUADRONING
SQUALIDNESS
SQUAMACEOUS
SQUAMELLATE
SQUAMIFEROUS
SQUAMIGEROUS
SQUAMOSENESS
SQUAMOUSNESS
SQUAMULATION
SQUANDERING
SQUANDERINGLY
SQUARROSELY
SQUARRULOSE
SQUASHBERRY
SQUASHINESS
SQUATTINESS
SQUATTOCRACY
SQUAWBERRIES
SQUAWFISHES
SQUAWFLOWER
SQUAWKINGLY
SQUEAKINESS
SQUEAKINGLY
SQUEAMISHLY
SQUEAMISHNESS
SQUEEGEEING
SQUEEZINGLY
SQUELCHIEST
SQUELCHINESS
SQUELCHINGLY
SQUIDGEREEN
SQUIGGLIEST
SQUILGEEING
SQUINTINGLY
SQUINTINGNESS
SQUIRARCHAL
SQUIREARCHAL
SQUIREARCHIES
SQUIREARCHY
SQUIRMINESS
SQUIRMINGLY
SQUIRRELFISH
SQUIRRELTAIL
SQUIRTINESS
SQUIRTINGLY
STATUESQUELY
STULTILOQUY
SUAVILOQUENT
SUBQUINTUPLE
SUBSEQUENCE
SUBSEQUENCY
SUBSEQUENTIAL
SUBSEQUENTLY
SYMPATHIQUE
TERLINQUAITE
TERRAQUEOUS
THUNDERSQUALL
THYMOQUINONE
TRANQUILEST
TRANQUILITY
TRANQUILIZE
TRANQUILIZER
TRANQUILIZING
TRANQUILLER
TRANQUILLEST
TRANQUILLISE
TRANQUILLITY
TRANQUILLIZE
TRANQUILLIZED
TRANQUILNESS
TRIQUETROUS
TRISTILOQUY
UBIQUITARIAN
UBIQUITARIES
UBIQUITOUSLY
UNACQUAINTED
UNADEQUATELY
UNCONQUERED
UNDERQUOTED
UNDERQUOTING
UNEQUITABLE
UNEQUITABLY
UNEQUIVOCAL
UNEQUIVOCALLY
UNFREQUENCY
UNFREQUENTED
UNFREQUENTLY
UNLIQUIDATED
UNQUALIFIED
UNQUALITIED
UNQUANTIFIED
UNQUESTIONED
UNQUESTIONING
UNQUIESCENCE
UNQUIESCENT
UNQUIETNESS
UTRAQUISTIC
VANQUISHING
VENTRILOQUAL
VENTRILOQUE
VENTRILOQUIST
VENTRILOQUY
XYLOQUINONE

POSITIONAL ORDER LIST OF WORDS OVER 10 LETTERS

QUACKISHNESS
QUACKSALVER
QUADRAGESIMAL
QUADRANGLED
QUADRANGULAR
QUADRANGULED
QUADRANTILE
QUADRAPHONIC
QUADRATICAL
QUADRENNIAL
QUADRENNIUM
QUADRENNIUMS
QUADRICINIUM
QUADRICIPITAL
QUADRICYCLE
QUADRICYCLER
QUADRIENNIUM
QUADRIFILAR
QUADRIFOCAL
QUADRIFOLIUM
QUADRIFRONS
QUADRIGAMIST
QUADRIGATUS
QUADRIHYBRID
QUADRIJUGAL
QUADRILATERAL
QUADRILLING
QUADRILLION
QUADRINOMIAL
QUADRIPAROUS
QUADRIPLANAR
QUADRIURATE
QUADRIVALENT
QUADRIVIOUS
QUADRUMANAL
QUADRUMANOUS
QUADRUPEDAL
QUADRUPEDAN
QUADRUPEDANT
QUADRUPEDATE
QUADRUPEDOUS
QUADRUPLANE
QUADRUPLATE
QUADRUPLATOR
QUADRUPLING
QUAESTIONES
QUAESTORIAL
QUAESTORIAN
QUAESTORSHIP
QUALIFIABLE
QUALIFICATION
QUALIFICATOR
QUALIFIEDLY
QUALITATIVE
QUALMISHNESS
QUANTIFYING
QUANTIMETER
QUANTITATIVE
QUANTITIVELY
QUANTIVALENT
QUANTIZATION
QUANTIZING
QUANTOMETER
QUAQUAVERSAL
QUARANTINED
QUARANTINER
QUARANTINING
QUARRELLING
QUARRELLOUS
QUARRELOUSLY
QUARRELSOME
QUARRYSTONE
QUARTERBACK
QUARTERFOIL
QUARTERLAND
QUARTERLIES
QUARTERMASTER
QUARTERNIGHT
QUARTERNION
QUARTERPACE
QUARTERSAWED
QUARTERSAWING
QUARTERSAWN
QUARTERSTAFF
QUARTERSTAVES
QUARTIPAROUS
QUATERNARIES
QUATERNARIUS
QUATERNIONIC
QUATERNITIES
QUATERTENSES
QUATREFOILED
QUATTROCENTO
QUAVERINGLY
QUEBRACHITE
QUEBRACHITOL
QUEBRADILLA
QUEENFISHES
QUEENLINESS
QUEENSBERRIES
QUEENSBERRY
QUENCHLESSLY
QUERCITANNIN
QUERCIVOROUS
QUERIMONIES
QUERIMONIOUS
QUERULENTIAL
QUERULOSITY
QUERULOUSLY
QUESTIONABLE
QUESTIONABLY
QUESTIONARIES
QUESTIONARY
QUESTIONING
QUESTIONIST
QUESTIONLESS
QUESTIONNAIRE
QUESTMONGER
QUICKENANCE
QUICKENBEAM
QUICKSILVER
QUICKSILVERY
QUIDDITATIVE
QUIESCENTLY
QUIINACEOUS
QUILLFISHES
QUINALDINIC
QUINALDINIUM
QUINAMICINE
QUINAMIDINE
QUINANISOLE
QUINATOXINE
QUINAZOLINE
QUINCUNCIAL
QUINCUNXIAL
QUINDECAGON
QUINDECEMVIR
QUINDECEMVIRI
QUINDECIMVIR
QUINHYDRONE
QUINISEXTINE
QUINOIDATION
QUINOLINIUM
QUINOLOGIST
QUINONIMINE
QUINOXALINE
QUINQUENNIA
QUINQUENNIAD
QUINQUENNIAL
QUINQUENNIUM
QUINQUENNIUMS
QUINQUERTIUM
QUINQUEVIRS
QUINSYBERRIES
QUINSYBERRY
QUINTELEMENT
QUINTERNION
QUINTESSENCE
QUINTILLION
QUINTUPLING
QUINUCLIDINE
QUIPPISHNESS
QUIRITARIAN
QUIRQUINCHO
QUISLINGISM
QUISQUILIAN
QUISQUILIARY
QUISQUILIOUS
QUITCLAIMED
QUITCLAIMING
QUITTERBONE
QUIZZACIOUS
QUIZZATORIAL
QUIZZICALITY
QUIZZICALLY
QUODLIBETARY
QUODLIBETIC
QUOTABILITY
QUOTABLENESS
QUOTATIONAL
QUOTATIONIST
QUOTEWORTHY
QUOTIDIANLY

AQUACULTURAL
AQUACULTURE
AQUAEMANALE
AQUAEMANALIA
AQUAFORTIST
AQUAPLANING
AQUAPUNCTURE
AQUARELLIST
AQUATICALLY
AQUATIVENESS
AQUEOGLACIAL
AQUEOIGNEOUS
AQUEOUSNESS
AQUICULTURAL
AQUICULTURE
AQUOTIZATION
EQUABLENESS
EQUALITARIAN
EQUALIZATION
EQUANIMOUSLY
EQUATIONALLY
EQUATIONISM
EQUATIONIST
EQUATORIALLY
EQUESTRIENNE
EQUIDISTANCE
EQUIDISTANT
EQUIDISTANTLY
EQUIDIURNAL
EQUIFORMITY
EQUIGRANULAR

EQUILATERAL
EQUILIBRANT
EQUILIBRATE
EQUILIBRATED
EQUILIBRATING
EQUILIBRATION
EQUILIBRATIVE
EQUILIBRATOR
EQUILIBRATORY
EQUILIBRIAL
EQUILIBRIATE
EQUILIBRIOUS
EQUILIBRIST
EQUILIBRISTAT
EQUILIBRISTIC
EQUILIBRITY
EQUILIBRIUM
EQUILIBRIUMS
EQUILIBRIZE
EQUIMOLECULAR
EQUIMOMENTAL
EQUIMULTIPLE
EQUINANGULAR
EQUINOCTIAL
EQUINOCTIAL
EQUINOCTIALLY
EQUINOVARUS
EQUIPARATION
EQUIPARTILE
EQUIPARTITION
EQUIPOISING
EQUIPOLLENCE
EQUIPOLLENCY
EQUIPOLLENT
EQUIPOLLENTLY
EQUIPONDERANT
EQUIPONDERAT
EQUIPOSTILE
EQUIPOTENTIAL
EQUIPROBABLE
EQUISETACEOUS
EQUISONANCE
EQUIVALENCE
EQUIVALENCED
EQUIVALENCY
EQUIVALENTLY
EQUIVOCALITY
EQUIVOCATED
EQUIVOCATING
EQUIVOCATION
EQUIVOCATOR
EQUIVOCATORY
EQUIVOLUMINAL
SQUABBLINGLY
SQUADRONING
SQUALIDNESS
SQUAMACEOUS
SQUAMELLATE
SQUAMIFEROUS
SQUAMIGEROUS
SQUAMOSENESS
SQUAMOUSNESS
SQUAMULATION
SQUANDERING
SQUANDERINGLY
SQUARROSELY
SQUARRULOSE
SQUASHBERRY
SQUASHINESS
SQUATTINESS
SQUATTOCRACY
SQUAWBERRIES
SQUAWFISHES
SQUAWFLOWER
SQUAWKINGLY
SQUEAKINESS
SQUEAKINGLY

SQUEAMISHLY
SQUEAMISHNESS
SQUEEGEEING
SQUEEZINGLY
SQUELCHIEST
SQUELCHINESS
SQUELCHINGLY
SQUIDGEREEN
SQUIGGLIEST
SQUILGEEING
SQUINTINGLY
SQUINTINGNESS
SQUIRARCHAL
SQUIREARCHAL
SQUIREARCHIES
SQUIREARCHY
SQUIRMINESS
SQUIRMINGLY
SQUIRRELFISH
SQUIRRELTAIL
SQUIRTINESS
SQUIRTINGLY

ACQUAINTANCE
ACQUAINTANT
ACQUIESCENCE
ACQUIESCENT
ACQUIESCING
ACQUIREMENT
ACQUISITION
ACQUISITIVE
ACQUISITIVELY
ACQUITTANCE
BIQUADRANTAL
BIQUADRATIC
BIQUARTERLY
COQUECIGRUE
COQUETTISHLY
ESQUAMULOSE
EXQUISITELY
EXQUISITENESS
EXQUISITISM
EXQUISITIVELY
INQUAINTANCE
INQUARTATION
INQUIETNESS
INQUILINISM
INQUILINITY
INQUILINOUS
INQUINATING
INQUINATION
INQUIRATION
INQUIRINGLY
INQUISITION
INQUISITIONAL
INQUISITIVE
INQUISITORIAL
INQUISITORY
JEQUIRITIES
LIQUEFACIENT
LIQUEFACTION
LIQUEFACTIVE
LIQUEFIABLE
LIQUESCENCE
LIQUESCENCY
LIQUIDAMBAR
LIQUIDAMBER
LIQUIDATING
LIQUIDATION
LIQUIDIZING
LIQUIDOGENIC
LIQUORISHLY
LIQUORISHNESS
LOQUACIOUSLY
PIQUANTNESS
REQUIESCENCE
REQUIREMENT

REQUISITELY
REQUISITION
REQUISITORY
REQUITATIVE
REQUITELESS
REQUITEMENT
SEQUACIOUSLY
SEQUENTIALITY
SEQUESTERED
SEQUESTERING
SEQUESTERMENT
SEQUESTRABLE
SEQUESTRANT
SEQUESTRATE
SEQUESTRATED
SEQUESTRATING
SEQUESTRATION
SEQUESTRATOR
UNQUALIFIED
UNQUALITIED
UNQUANTIFIED
UNQUESTIONED
UNQUESTIONING
UNQUIESCENCE
UNQUIESCENT
UNQUIETNESS

ABSQUATULATE
ADEQUATENESS
BANQUETEERING
BARQUENTINE
BECQUERELITE
BOUQUETIERE
BOUQUINISTE
CHEQUERBOARD
CHEQUERWISE
CHEQUERWORK
CINQUECENTO
CLIQUISHNESS
COEQUALNESS
CONQUERABLE
CONQUERINGLY
CONQUINAMINE
CONQUISTADOR
CONQUISTADORES
CROQUIGNOLE
DESQUAMATED
DESQUAMATING
DESQUAMATION
DESQUAMATIVE
DESQUAMATORY
DISQUALIFIED
DISQUIETEDLY
DISQUIETING
DISQUIETUDE
DISQUIPARANT
DISQUISITED
DISQUISITING
DISQUISITION
DISQUISITIVE
DISQUISITOR
DISQUISITORY
ELOQUENTIAL
ETIQUETTICAL
FREQUENCIES
FREQUENTABLE
FREQUENTAGE
FREQUENTATION
FREQUENTATIVE
FREQUENTING
FREQUENTNESS
INEQUALITIES
INEQUALNESS
INEQUITABLE
INEQUITABLY
INEQUIVALVE
INIQUITABLE

INIQUITOUSLY
ISOQUINOLINE
LACQUERWORK
MARQUETERIE
MARQUISETTE
MARQUISOTTE
MASQUERADED
MASQUERADER
MASQUERADING
MILQUETOAST
MISQUOTATION
MOSQUITOBILL
MUSQUASHROOT
MUSQUASHWEED
NESQUEHONITE
OUTQUESTION
OXYQUINOLINE
PASQUEFLOWER
PASQUILLANT
PASQUINADED
PASQUINADER
PASQUINADING
PERQUISITION
PERQUISITOR
PROQUAESTOR
QUAQUAVERSAL
SESQUIALTER
SESQUIALTERA
SESQUIALTERAL
SESQUINONAL
SESQUIOCTAVA
SESQUIPEDAL
SESQUIPLICATE
SESQUIQUARTA
SESQUIQUINTA
SESQUISEXTAL
SESQUITERPENE
SESQUITERTIA
SUBQUINTUPLE
TRIQUETROUS
UBIQUITARIAN
UBIQUITARIES
UBIQUITOUSLY
UNEQUITABLE
UNEQUITABLY
UNEQUIVOCAL
UNEQUIVOCALLY
VANQUISHING

ANTIQUARIAN
ANTIQUARIES
ANTIQUARISM
ANTIQUATING
ANTIQUATION
ANTIQUENESS
ANTIQUITIES
BRUSQUENESS
COLOQUINTIDA
DELIQUESCED
DELIQUESCENT
DELIQUESCING
DISEQUALIZE
DUROQUINONE
FOREQUARTER
HEADQUARTER
HEADQUARTERS
HINDQUARTER
HINDQUARTERS
ILLIQUATION
MERIQUINONE
MERIQUINONIC
MOUSQUETAIRE
OBLIQUATION
OBLIQUENESS
OBLIQUITIES
OBLIQUITOUS
OBSEQUIOUSLY

PARAQUADRATE
PEREQUITATE
QUINQUENNIA
QUINQUENNIAD
QUINQUENNIAL
QUINQUENNIUM
QUINQUENNIUMS
QUINQUERTIUM
QUINQUEVIRS
QUIRQUINCHO
QUISQUILIAN
QUISQUILIARY
QUISQUILIOUS
RELIQUARIES
SEMIQUARTILE
SEMIQUIETIST
TRANQUILEST
TRANQUILITY
TRANQUILIZE
TRANQUILIZER
TRANQUILIZING
TRANQUILLER
TRANQUILLEST
TRANQUILLISE
TRANQUILLITY
TRANQUILLIZE
TRANQUILLIZED
TRANQUILNESS
UNACQUAINTED
UNLIQUIDATED
UTRAQUISTIC
XYLOQUINONE

APPLIQUEING
CHYMAQUEOUS
COLLIQUATION
COLLIQUATIVE
COLLOQUIALLY
COLLOQUIZED
COLLOQUIZING
CONSEQUENCE
CONSEQUENTIAL
CONSEQUENTLY
DELINQUENCIES
DELINQUENCY
DELINQUENTLY
DISACQUAINT
EARTHQUAKED
EARTHQUAKEN
EARTHQUAKING
FOURSQUARELY
HARLEQUINADE
HARLEQUINIC
HARLEQUINIZE
HYDROQUININE
HYDROQUINONE
INADEQUATELY
INADEQUATION
INELOQUENCE
INFREQUENCE
INFREQUENCY
PALANQUINED
PALANQUINING
PHENOQUINONE
PREREQUISITE
RELINQUISHED
RELINQUISHER
SEMIAQUATIC
SUBSEQUENCE
SUBSEQUENCY
SUBSEQUENTIAL
SUBSEQUENTLY
TERRAQUEOUS
THYMOQUINONE
UNADEQUATELY
UNCONQUERED
UNDERQUOTED

UNDERQUOTING
UNFREQUENCY
UNFREQUENTED
UNFREQUENTLY

ALTILOQUENCE
ALTILOQUENT
ANTHRAQUINOL
ARABESQUELY
ARABESQUERIE
BURLESQUELY
BURLESQUING
FATILOQUENT
GROTESQUELY
GROTESQUERIE
GROTESQUERY
LONGINQUITY
MONCHIQUITE
OMNILOQUENT
PLASMOQUINE
POLYLOQUENT
PRECONQUEST
PROPINQUANT
PROPINQUITY
PROPINQUOUS
SESQUIQUARTA
SESQUIQUINTA
SOLILOQUIES
SOLILOQUISE
SOLILOQUIST
SOLILOQUIZE
SOLILOQUIZED
SOLILOQUIZER
SOLILOQUIZING
TERLINQUAITE
ANTIMASQUER
BLOTTESQUELY
BREVILOQUENT
DENTILOQUIST
DULCILOQUENT
INCONSEQUENCE
INCONSEQUENT
MAGNILOQUENT
MULTILOQUENT
MULTILOQUOUS
PAUCILOQUENT
PRETEREQUINE
PSEUDOAQUATIC
RIBAUDEQUIN
SOMNILOQUENCE
SOMNILOQUENT
SOMNILOQUISM
SOMNILOQUIST
SOMNILOQUOUS
STATUESQUELY
SUAVILOQUENT

BARBARESQUE
DISCOTHEQUE
FORMALESQUE
GIGANTESQUE
GORGONESQUE
GRANDILOQUENT
OSTEOPLAQUE
PICTURESQUE
PLATERESQUE
SANCTILOQUENT
SEMIANTIQUE
SOLDATESQUE
STULTILOQUY
SYMPATHIQUE
THUNDERSQUALL
TRISTILOQUY
VENTRILOQUAL
VENTRILOQUE
VENTRILOQUIST
VENTRILOQUY

AMPHORILOQUY
BOUDOIRESQUE
BRONCHILOQUY
CHIVALRESQUE
CONTRAMARQUE
NATURALESQUE
PECTORILOQUE
PECTORILOQUY

SCULPTURESQUE

SCORING ORDER LIST OF WORDS OVER 10 LETTERS

35
EXQUISITIVELY

34
QUIZZICALITY

33
HARLEQUINIZE
QUICKSILVERY
QUIZZICALLY
SQUEEZINGLY

32
CHEQUERWORK
SOLILOQUIZING
TRANQUILIZING

31
AMPHORILOQUY
BRONCHILOQUY
LIQUIDIZING
SOLILOQUIZED
SQUAWKINGLY

30
ACQUISITIVELY
AQUOTIZATION
CHYMAQUEOUS
DISEQUALIZE
EQUALIZATION
EXQUISITELY
MUSQUASHWEED
QUACKISHNESS
QUANTIZATION
QUICKENBEAM
QUINDECEMVIRI
QUIZZACIOUS
SOLILOQUIZER
SQUELCHINGLY
SYMPATHIQUE
TRANQUILIZER
TRANQUILLIZE
UNEQUIVOCALLY
XYLOQUINONE

29
CHEQUERBOARD
CHIVALRESQUE
COQUETTISHLY
EARTHQUAKING
EQUIVOCATORY
EXQUISITENESS
EXQUISITISM
LACQUERWORK
LIQUEFACTIVE
PASQUEFLOWER
QUACKSALVER
QUADRAPHONIC
QUADRICYCLER
QUADRIJUGAL
QUANTIZING
QUENCHLESSLY
QUICKSILVER
QUINAZOLINE
QUINCUNXIAL
QUINDECEMVIR
QUINDECIMVIR
QUIZZATORIAL
QUOTEWORTHY
SOLILOQUIZE
SQUABBLINGLY
SQUAWFISHES
SQUAWFLOWER
THYMOQUINONE
TRANQUILIZE

28
CHEQUERWISE
EARTHQUAKED
EQUIFORMITY
EQUIPOLLENCY
FREQUENTATIVE
HYDROQUININE
HYDROQUINONE
PECTORILOQUY
QUADRICYCLE
QUARTERBACK
QUEBRACHITOL
QUICKENANCE
QUINISEXTINE
QUINSYBERRY
QUIPPISHNESS
SESQUISEXTAL
SQUASHBERRY
SQUATTOCRACY
SQUEAKINGLY
SQUEAMISHLY
SQUIREARCHY
UNFREQUENCY

27
CONQUERINGLY
DESQUAMATIVE
DESQUAMATORY
EARTHQUAKEN
EQUILIBRATIVE
EQUILIBRATORY
EQUINOCTIALLY
EQUIPOLLENTLY
EQUIPROBABLE
EQUIVALENCED
EQUIVOCATING
EQUIVOLUMINAL
FOURSQUARELY
JEQUIRITIES
LIQUESCENCY
MONCHIQUITE
PROPINQUITY
PSEUDOAQUATIC
QUADRICIPITAL
QUADRIFOLIUM
QUALIFICATION
QUALIFIEDLY
QUANTIFYING
QUANTITIVELY
QUARTERSTAFF
QUAVERINGLY
QUEBRACHITE
QUINATOXINE
QUINHYDRONE
QUINOXALINE
QUINSYBERRIES
QUODLIBETARY
SQUANDERINGLY
SQUEAMISHNESS
SQUIREARCHIES
SQUIRRELFISH
SUBSEQUENCY
UNFREQUENTLY
VANQUISHING
LIQUEFACIENT
LIQUEFACTION
LIQUORISHLY
LOQUACIOUSLY
MUSQUASHROOT
OBSEQUIOUSLY
PHENOQUINONE
QUADRAGESIMAL
QUADRICINIUM
QUADRIFOCAL
QUAESTORSHIP
QUALIFICATOR
QUALMISHNESS
QUARTERSAWING
QUEENFISHES
QUERCIVOROUS
QUESTIONABLY
QUIDDITATIVE
QUILLFISHES
QUITCLAIMING
SCULPTURESQUE
SEQUACIOUSLY
SESQUIOCTAVA
SESQUIPLICATE
SOMNILOQUENCE
SQUAMIFEROUS
SQUAWBERRIES
SQUELCHINESS
SQUIREARCHAL
SQUIRMINGLY
SUBSEQUENTLY
THUNDERSQUALL
UBIQUITOUSLY
VENTRILOQUY

26
BLOTTESQUELY
BREVILOQUENT
CLIQUISHNESS
COLLIQUATIVE
COLLOQUIALLY
CONSEQUENTLY
DELINQUENCY
DISCOTHEQUE
DISQUALIFIED
DISQUIETEDLY
EQUANIMOUSLY
EQUIDISTANTLY
EQUILIBRISTIC
EQUIMOLECULAR
EQUIVOCATED
EQUIVOCATION
FREQUENTABLE

25
ACQUAINTANCE
ACQUIESCING
ACQUISITIVE
APPLIQUEING
AQUAPUNCTURE
AQUATICALLY
ARABESQUELY
BANQUETEERING
BECQUERELITE
BIQUADRATIC
BIQUARTERLY
BURLESQUELY
CONQUINAMINE
CONTRAMARQUE
COQUECIGRUE
DELINQUENCIES
DELINQUENTLY
DELIQUESCING
DESQUAMATING
DISQUISITIVE
DISQUISITORY
EQUILIBRITY
EQUILIBRIUMS
EQUIMOMENTAL
EQUIMULTIPLE
EQUIPOLLENCE
EQUIPONDERANT
EQUIVALENCE
EQUIVOCATOR
FORMALESQUE
FREQUENCIES
FREQUENTATION
HARLEQUINADE
HARLEQUINIC
HEADQUARTERS
HINDQUARTERS
LIQUEFIABLE
LIQUIDAMBAR
LIQUIDAMBER
LIQUIDOGENIC
LIQUORISHNESS
MASQUERADING
MERIQUINONIC
MOSQUITOBILL
PASQUINADING
PAUCILOQUENT
PECTORILOQUE
POLYLOQUENT
QUADRIGAMIST
QUADRIVALENT
QUADRUPEDANT
QUADRUPEDATE
QUADRUPEDOUS
QUALIFIABLE
QUARTERNIGHT
QUARTERSAWED
QUARTERSTAVES
QUATREFOILED
QUEENSBERRY
QUIESCENTLY
QUITCLAIMED
QUODLIBETIC
QUOTABILITY
RELINQUISHED
REQUIESCENCE
SEQUENTIALITY
SOMNILOQUISM
SQUELCHIEST
SQUIRARCHAL
SUBQUINTUPLE

UNADEQUATELY
UNEQUITABLY
UNEQUIVOCAL
UNFREQUENTED
UNQUANTIFIED
UNQUIESCENCE
VENTRILOQUIST

24

ACQUIESCENCE
ACQUIESCENT
ACQUIREMENT
ACQUITTANCE
ANTHRAQUINOL
AQUATIVENESS
AQUEOGLACIAL
BARBARESQUE
BIQUADRANTAL
BOUDOIRESQUE
CINQUECENTO
COLOQUINTIDA
CONQUERABLE
CONQUISTADOR
CONSEQUENCE
CONSEQUENTIAL
DELIQUESCED
DELIQUESCENT
DESQUAMATED
DESQUAMATION
DISQUIPARANT
DULCILOQUENT
EQUATIONALLY
EQUATORIALLY
EQUIDISTANCE
EQUILIBRATED
EQUILIBRATION
EQUILIBRISTAT
EQUILIBRIUM
EQUIPARTITION
EQUIPONDERAT
EQUIPOTENTIAL
EQUISETACEOUS
FREQUENTAGE
FREQUENTING
FREQUENTNESS
GRANDILOQUENT
GROTESQUELY
GROTESQUERY
HEADQUARTER
HINDQUARTER
INQUIRINGLY
LIQUESCENCE
LONGINQUITY
MAGNILOQUENT
MASQUERADED
NESQUEHONITE
PALANQUINING
PARAQUADRATE
PASQUINADED
PICTURESQUE
PLASMOQUINE
PRECONQUEST
PROPINQUANT
PROPINQUOUS
QUADRANGULED
QUADRENNIUMS
QUADRIENNIUM
QUADRIFILAR
QUADRIFRONS
QUADRINOMIAL
QUADRIPAROUS
QUADRIPLANAR
QUADRIVIOUS
QUADRUMANOUS
QUADRUPEDAL
QUADRUPEDAN
QUADRUPLATOR
QUADRUPLING
QUANTITATIVE
QUANTIVALENT
QUARRELOUSLY
QUARTERMASTER
QUARTERPACE
QUEENSBERRIES
QUINALDINIUM
QUINAMICINE
QUINCUNCIAL
QUINDECAGON
QUINUCLIDINE
QUIRQUINCHO
QUOTIDIANLY
RELINQUISHER
SANCTILOQUENT
SEMIAQUATIC
SEQUESTERMENT
SESQUITERPENE
SQUAMACEOUS
SQUAMIGEROUS
SQUEAKINESS
SQUINTINGLY
SQUIRTINGLY
STATUESQUELY
SUAVILOQUENT
SUBSEQUENCE
SUBSEQUENTIAL
TRANQUILLITY
UNACQUAINTED
UNQUALIFIED
VENTRILOQUAL

23

ABSQUATULATE
ALTILOQUENCE
AQUACULTURAL
AQUAEMANALIA
AQUAFORTIST
AQUAPLANING
AQUICULTURAL
ARABESQUERIE
BURLESQUING
COLLIQUATION
CROQUIGNOLE
DISACQUAINT
DISQUISITING
EQUILIBRATOR
EQUILIBRIATE
EQUILIBRIOUS
EQUINOVARUS
EQUIPARATION
ETIQUETTICAL
FATILOQUENT
FOREQUARTER
INELOQUENCE
INQUISITIVE
INQUISITORY
MASQUERADER
MISQUOTATION
MOUSQUETAIRE
MULTILOQUENT
MULTILOQUOUS
PALANQUINED
PASQUINADER
PERQUISITION
PREREQUISITE
PRETEREQUINE
QUADRANGLED
QUADRANGULAR
QUADRATICAL
QUADRENNIUM
QUADRILATERAL
QUADRUMANAL
QUADRUPLANE
QUADRUPLATE
QUALITATIVE
QUAQUAVERSAL
QUARRYSTONE
QUARTERFOIL
QUARTERSAWN
QUARTIPAROUS
QUATERNIONIC
QUATTROCENTO
QUEBRADILLA
QUERCITANNIN
QUERIMONIOUS
QUERULOSITY
QUERULOUSLY
QUESTIONABLE
QUESTIONARY
QUESTMONGER
QUINALDINIC
QUINAMIDINE
QUINQUENNIUMS
QUINTELEMENT
QUINTESSENCE
QUINTUPLING
QUISLINGISM
QUISQUILIARY
QUOTABLENESS
REQUISITELY
REQUISITORY
REQUITATIVE
RIBAUDEQUIN
SEMIQUARTILE
SEMIQUIETIST
SEQUESTRABLE
SEQUESTRATING
SESQUIPEDAL
SOMNILOQUENT
SOMNILOQUIST
SOMNILOQUOUS
SQUAMOSENESS
SQUAMOUSNESS
SQUAMULATION
SQUARROSELY
SQUASHINESS
SQUINTINGNESS
STULTILOQUY
TRANQUILITY
TRISTILOQUY
UBIQUITARIAN
UBIQUITARIES
UNCONQUERED
UNDERQUOTING
UNLIQUIDATED
UNQUESTIONING
VENTRILOQUE

22

ACQUAINTANT
ACQUISITION
ADEQUATENESS
ANTIMASQUER
ANTIQUARISM
AQUACULTURE
AQUAEMANALE
AQUEOIGNEOUS
AQUICULTURE
BARQUENTINE
BOUQUETIERE
BOUQUINISTE
BRUSQUENESS
COEQUALNESS
DENTILOQUIST
DISQUIETING
DISQUIETUDE
DISQUISITED
DISQUISITION
EQUABLENESS
EQUATIONISM
EQUINANGULAR
EQUIGRANULAR
EQUILIBRANT
EQUILIBRATE
EQUILIBRIAL
EQUILIBRIST
EQUINOCTIAL
EQUINOCTIAL
EQUIPARTILE
EQUIPOLLENT
EQUIPOSTILE
EQUISONANCE
ESQUAMULOSE
GIGANTESQUE
GORGONESQUE
GROTESQUERIE
LIQUIDATING
MARQUETERIE
MARQUISETTE
MARQUISOTTE
MERIQUINONE
MILQUETOAST
OBLIQUATION
OBLIQUENESS
OBLIQUITIES
OBLIQUITOUS
OMNILOQUENT
OSTEOPLAQUE
PASQUILLANT
PEREQUITATE
PERQUISITOR
PIQUANTNESS
PLATERESQUE
PROQUAESTOR
QUADRIGATUS
QUADRILLING
QUANTIMETER
QUANTOMETER
QUARANTINING
QUARRELSOME
QUERIMONIES
QUESTIONARIES
QUESTIONNAIRE
QUIINACEOUS
QUINOIDATION
QUINOLINIUM
QUINONIMINE
QUINQUENNIUM
QUINQUERTIUM
QUINQUEVIRS
QUITTERBONE
REQUIREMENT
REQUITEMENT
SEMIANTIQUE
SEQUESTERING
SEQUESTRATED
SEQUESTRATION
SESQUIALTERAL
SQUADRONING
SQUAMELLATE
SQUANDERING
SQUEEGEEING
SQUIDGEREEN
SQUIGGLIEST
SQUILGEEING
SQUIRMINESS
UNDERQUOTED
UNEQUITABLE
UNQUESTIONED
UNQUIESCENT
UTRAQUISTIC

21

ANTIQUATING
DISQUISITOR
DUROQUINONE
EQUALITARIAN
EQUESTRIENNE
EQUIDISTANT
EQUIDIURNAL
ISOQUINOLINE
LIQUIDATION
NATURALESQUE
QUADRANTILE
QUADRENNIAL
QUADRILLION
QUADRIURATE
QUARANTINED
QUARRELLING
QUARTERLAND
QUATERNARIES
QUATERNARIUS
QUATERNITIES
QUATERTENSES
QUERULENTIAL
QUESTIONING
QUESTIONLESS
QUINOLOGIST
QUINQUENNIAD
QUOTATIONIST
SEQUESTERED
SEQUESTRATOR
SESQUIALTERA
SOLDATESQUE
SESQUITERTIA
SQUALIDNESS
SQUIRRELTAIL
TERLINQUAITE
TRANQUILLEST
TRANQUILLISE
TRANQUILNESS
UNQUALITIED

20

ALTILOQUENT
ANTIQUARIAN
ANTIQUARIES
ANTIQUATION
ANTIQUENESS
ANTIQUITIES
AQUARELLIST
AQUEOUSNESS
ELOQUENTIAL
EQUATIONIST
EQUILATERAL
ILLIQUATION
INQUIRATION
OUTQUESTION
QUAESTIONES
QUAESTORIAL
QUAESTORIAN
QUARANTINER
QUARRELLOUS
QUARTERLIES
QUARTERNION
QUEENLINESS
QUESTIONIST
QUINANISOLE
QUINQUENNIAL
QUINTERNION
QUINTILLION
QUIRITARIAN
QUISQUILIOUS
QUOTATIONAL
RELIQUARIES
REQUISITION
REQUITELESS
SEQUESTRANT
SEQUESTRATE
SESQUIALTER
SESQUIQUARTA
SESQUIQUINTA
SESQUINONAL
SOLILOQUIES
SOLILOQUISE
SOLILOQUIST
SQUATTINESS
SQUIRTINESS
TERRAQUEOUS
TRANQUILEST
TRANQUILLER
TRIQUETROUS
UNQUIETNESS

19

QUINQUENNIA
QUISQUILIAN

High-Scoring Words Containing

2-3 LETTER WORDS

ALPHABETICAL ORDER

ARX
AUX
AX
AXE
BOX
COX
DIX
DUX
EX
FAX
FIX
FOX
HEX
HOX
KEX
LAX
LEX
LOX
LUX
MAX
MIX
MUX
NIX
OX
OXO
OXY
PAX
PIX
POX
PYX
RAX
REX
RIX
ROX
RUX
SAX
SEX
SIX
SOX
TAX
TOX
TUX
VEX
VIX
VOX
WAX
WOX
XAT
YEX
YOX
ZAX

POSITIONAL ORDER

XAT

AX
AXE
EX
EXUL
OX
OXO
OXY

ARX
AUX
BOX
DIX
DUX
COX
FAX
FIX
FOX
HEX
HOX
KEX
LAX
LEX
LOX
LUX
MAX
MIX
MUX
NIX
PAX
PIX
POX
PYX
RAX
REX
RIX
ROX
RUX
SAX
SEX
SIX
SOX
TAX
TOX
TUX
VEX
VIX
VOX
WAX
WOX
YEX
YOX
ZAX

SCORING ORDER

19
ZAX

15
PYX

14
KEX

13
FAX
FIX
FOX
HEX
HOX
OXY
VEX
VIX
VOX
WAX
WOX
YEX
YOX

12
BOX
COX
MAX
MIX
MUX
PAX
PIX
POX

11
DIX
DUX

10
ARX
AUX
AXE
LAX
LEX
LOX
LUX
NIX
OXO
RAX
REX
RIX
ROX
RUX
SAX
SEX
SIX
SOX
TAX
TOX
TUX
XAT

9
AX
EX
OX

ALPHABETICAL LIST OF 4-LETTER WORDS

ABOX
APEX
AXAL
AXAN
AXED
AXEL
AXES
AXIL
AXIS
AXLE
AXON
BAXA
BOXY
CALX
CAXI
COAX
COIX
COXA
COXY
CRUX
DIXI
DIXY
DOUX
DOXY
EAUX
ELIX
ESOX
EXAM
EXEC
EXES
EXIT
EXON
EXUL
FAEX
FALX
FAUX
FIXT
FIXY
FLAX
FLEX
FLIX
FLUX
FOXY
GREX
HEXT
HOAX
IBEX
ILEX
JEUX
JINX
JYNX
KEXY
KREX
LANX
LUXE
LYNX
MAUX
MINX
MIXT
MIXY
MOXA
MYXA
MYXO
NEXT
NIXE
NIXY
NOIX
NOXA
OBEX
ONYX
ORYX
OXAN
OXEA
OXEN
OXER
OXID
OXIM
OXYL
PIXY
PLEX
POXY
PREX
PRIX
PROX
PUXY
QUAX
RIXY
ROUX
ROXY
SAEX
SEAX
SEXT
SEXY
SPEX
TAXI
TAXY
TEXT
TOXA
UROX
WAXY
WOXE
WROX
XEME
XYST

POSITIONAL ORDER LIST OF 4-LETTER WORDS

XEME
XYST

AXAL
AXAN
AXED
AXEL
AXES
AXIL
AXIS
AXLE
AXON
EXAM
EXEC
EXES
EXIT
EXON
OXAN
OXEA
OXEN
OXER
OXID
OXIM
OXYL

BAXA
BOXY
CAXI
COXA
COXY
DIXI
DIXY
DOXY
FIXT
FIXY
FOXY
HEXT
KEXY
LUXE
MIXT
MIXY
MOXA
MYXA
MYXO
NEXT
NIXE
NIXY
NOXA
PIXY
POXY
PUXY
RIXY
ROXY
SEXT
SEXY
TAXI
TAXY
TEXT
TOXA
WAXY
WOXE

ABOX
APEX
CALX
COAX
COIX
CRUX
DOUX
EAUX
ELIX
ESOX
FAEX
FALX
FAUX
FLAX
FLEX
FLIX
FLUX
GREX
HOAX
IBEX
ILEX
JEUX
JINX
JYNX
KREX
LANX
LYNX
MAUX
MINX
NOIX
OBEX
ONYX
ORYX
PLEX
PREX
PRIX
PROX
QUAX
ROUX
SAEX
SEAX
SPEX
UROX
WROX

SCORING ORDER LIST OF 4-LETTER WORDS

21
JYNX

20
QUAX

18
JEUX
JINX
KEXY

17
FIXY
FOXY
WAXY

16
BOXY
COXY
MIXY
MYXA
MYXO
PIXY
POXY
PUXY

15
DIXY
DOXY
KREX

14
FAEX
FALX
FAUX
FIXT
FLAX
FLEX
FLIX
FLUX
HEXT
HOAX
LYNX
NIXY
ONYX
ORYX
OXYL
RIXY
ROXY
SEXY
TAXY
WOXE
WROX
XYST

13
ABOX
APEX
BAXA
CALX
CAXI
COAX
COIX
COXA
CRUX
EXAM
EXEC
IBEX
MAUX
MINX
MIXT
MOXA
OBEX
OXIM
PLEX
PREX
PRIX
PROX
SPEX
XEME

12
AXED
DIXI
DOUX
GREX
OXID

11
AXAL
AXAN
AXEL
AXES
AXIL
AXIS

AXLE
AXON
EAUX
ELIX
ESOX
EXES
EXIT
EXON
EXUL
ILEX
LANX
LUXE
NEXT
NIXE
NOIX
NOXA
OXAN
OXEA
OXEN
OXER
ROUX
SAEX
SEAX
SEXT
TAXI
TEXT
TOXA
UROX

ALPHABETICAL LIST OF 5-LETTER WORDS

ADDAX
ADFIX
ADMIX
ADNEX
ADOXY
AFFIX
ALPAX
AMPYX
ANNEX
ATAXY
AUXIN
AXIAL
AXILE
AXINE
AXIOM
AXION
AXITE
AXLED
AXMAN
AXMEN
AXOID
AXONE
AZOXY
BERYX
BIXIN
BORAX
BOXEN
BOXER
BOXES
BOXTY
BRAXY
BUXOM
CAPAX
CAREX
CAXON
CHOUX
CIMEX
COAXY
CODEX
COXAE
COXAL
CYLIX
DEFIX
DESEX
DEVEX
DEWAX
DIOXY
DIXIE
DIXIT
DONAX
DOXIE
DRUXY
DURAX
DUXES
EMBOX
EPOXY
EXACT
EXALT
EXCEL
EXCUR
EXEAT
EXEDE
EXEEM
EXEME
EXERT
EXIDO
EXIES
EXILE
EXINE
EXIST
EXITE
EXLEX
EXODE
EXODY
EXORN
EXPEL
EXTER
EXTOL
EXTRA
EXTRE
EXUDE
EXULT
EXURB
EXUST
EXUTE
FAULX
FAXED
FIXED
FIXER
FLAXY
FOXED
FOXER
FOXES
GULIX
HELIX
HEXAD
HEXER
HEXIS
HEXYL
HUXEN
HYRAX
IMMIX
INDEX
INFIX
IXTLE
JIXIE
JUDEX
JUXTA
KYLIX
LARIX
LATEX
LAXER
LAXLY
LEXIA
LEXIC
LOXIA
LUXES
LUXUR
LUXUS
MALAX
MATAX
MAXIM
MIXED
MIXEN
MIXER
MIXUP
MONAX
MOXIE
MUREX
NEXAL
NEXUM
NEXUS
NIXEN
NIXES
NIXIE
NOXAE
NOXAL
NYXIS
OXANE
OXBOW
OXBOY
OXEYE
OXFLY
OXIDE
OXIDO
OXIME
OXLIP
OXMAN
OXMEN
OXTER
PANAX
PAUXI
PINAX
PIXIE
PODEX
PREXY
PROXY
PUMEX
PYREX
PYXIE
PYXIS
RADIX
RAMEX
REDUX
RELAX
REMEX
REXEN
SAXON
SEXED
SEXLY
SEXTO
SILEX
SIREX
SIXER
SIXMO
SIXTE
SIXTH
SIXTY
SOULX
STRIX
TAXED
TAXEL
TAXER
TAXES
TAXIS
TAXON
TAXOR
TELEX
TEXAS
TOXIC
TOXIN
TOXON
TWIXT
UNFIX
UNMIX
UNSEX
UNTAX
UNWAX
VARIX
VEXED
VEXER
VEXIL
VIBEX
VIVAX
VIXEN
WAXED
WAXEN
WAXER
WAXES
XALLE
XEBEC
XENIA
XENON
XENYL
XERIC
XERIF
XEROX
XOANA
XUREL
XYLAN
XYLEM
XYLIC
XYLON
XYLYL
XYRID
XYSTA

POSITIONAL ORDER LIST OF 5-LETTER WORDS

XALLE
XEBEC
XENIA
XENON
XENYL
XERIC
XERIF
XEROX
XOANA
XUREL
XYLAN
XYLEM
XYLIC
XYLON
XYLYL
XYRID
XYSTA

AXIAL
AXILE
AXINE
AXIOM
AXION
AXITE
AXLED
AXMAN
AXMEN
AXOID
AXONE
EXACT
EXALT
EXCEL
EXCUR
EXEAT
EXEDE
EXEEM
EXEME
EXERT
EXIDO
EXIES

EXILE
EXINE
EXIST
EXITE
EXLEX
EXODE
EXODY
EXORN
EXPEL
EXTER
EXTOL
EXTRA
EXTRE
EXUDE
EXULT
EXURB
EXUST
EXUTE
IXTLE
OXANE
OXBOW
OXBOY
OXEYE
OXFLY
OXIDE
OXIDO
OXIME
OXLIP
OXMAN
OXMEN
OXTER

AUXIN
BIXIN
BOXEN
BOXER
BOXES
BOXTY

BUXOM
CAXON
COXAE
COXAL
DIXIE
DIXIT
DOXIE
DUXES
FAXED
FIXED
FIXER
FOXED
FOXER
FOXES
HEXAD
HEXER
HEXIS
HEXYL
HUXEN
JIXIE
JUXTA
LAXER
LAXLY
LEXIA
LEXIC
LOXIA
LUXES
LUXUR
LUXUS
MAXIM
MIXED
MIXEN
MIXER
MIXUP
MOXIE
NEXAL
NEXUM
NEXUS

NIXEN
NIXES
NIXIE
NOXAE
NOXAL
NYXIS
PIXIE
PYXIE
PYXIS
REXEN
SAXON
SEXED
SEXLY
SEXTO
SIXER
SIXMO
SIXTE
SIXTH
SIXTY
TAXED
TAXEL
TAXER
TAXES
TAXIS
TAXON
TAXOR
TEXAS
TOXIC
TOXIN
TOXON
VEXED
VEXER
VEXIL
VIXEN
WAXED
WAXEN
WAXER
WAXES

ADOXY
ATAXY
AZOXY
BRAXY
COAXY
DIOXY
DRUXY
EPOXY
FLAXY
PAUXI
PREXY
PROXY
TWIXT

ADDAX
ADFIX
ADMIX
ADNEX
AFFIX
ALPAX
AMPYX
ANNEX
BERYX
BORAX
CAPAX
CAREX
CHOUX
CIMEX
CODEX
CYLIX
DEFIX
DESEX
DEVEX
DEWAX
DONAX
DURAX
EMBOX
FAULX

GULIX
HELIX
HYRAX
IMMIX
INDEX
INFIX
JUDEX
KYLIX
LARIX
LATEX
MALAX
MATAX
MONAX
MUREX
PANAX
PINAX
PODEX
PUMEX
PYREX
RADIX
RAMEX
REDUX
RELAX
REMEX
SILEX
SIREX
SOULX
STRIX
TELEX
UNFIX
UNMIX
UNSEX
UNTAX
UNWAX
VARIX
VIBEX
VIVAX
XEROX

SCORING ORDER LIST OF 5-LETTER WORDS

24
AZOXY

20
JUDEX

19
AMPYX
JIXIE
JUXTA
KYLIX

18
AFFIX
FLAXY
HEXYL
HYRAX
OXFLY
VIVAX
XYLYL

17
BERYX
BOXTY
BRAXY
CHOUX
COAXY
CYLIX
EPOXY
OXBOW
OXBOY
PREXY
PROXY
PYREX
PYXIE
PYXIS
VIBEX
XYLEM
XYLIC

16
ADFIX
ADOXY
BUXOM
CAPAX
CIMEX
DEFIX
DEVEX
DEWAX
DIOXY
DRUXY
EMBOX
EXODY
FAXED
FIXED
FOXED
HEXAD
IMMIX
MAXIM
MIXUP
PUMEX
VEXED
WAXED
XEBEC

XYRID

15
ADMIX
ATAXY
CODEX
FAULX
FIXER
FOXER
FOXES
HELIX
HEXER
HEXIS
HUXEN
INFIX
LAXLY
MIXED
NYXIS
OXEYE
PODEX
SEXLY
SIXTH
SIXTY
TWIXT
UNFIX
UNWAX
VARIX
VEXER
VEXIL
VIXEN
WAXEN
WAXER

WAXES
XENYL
XERIF
XYLAN
XYLON
XYSTA

14
ADDAX
ALPAX
AXIOM
AXMAN
AXMEN
BIXIN
BORAX
BOXEN
BOXER
BOXES
CAREX
CAXON
COXAE
COXAL
EXACT
EXCEL
EXCUR
EXEEM
EXEME
EXPEL
EXURB
LEXIC
MALAX
MATAX

MIXEN
MIXER
MONAX
MOXIE
MUREX
NEXUM
OXIME
OXLIP
OXMAN
OXMEN
PANAX
PAUXI
PINAX
PIXIE
RAMEX
REMEX
SIXMO
TOXIC
UNMIX
XERIC

13
ADNEX
AXLED
AXOID
DESEX
DIXIE
DIXIT
DONAX
DOXIE
DURAX
DUXES

EXEDE
EXIDO
EXODE
EXUDE
GULIX
INDEX
OXIDE
OXIDO
RADIX
REDUX
SEXED
TAXED

12
ANNEX
AUXIN
AXIAL
AXILE
AXINE
AXION
AXITE
AXONE
EXALT
EXEAT
EXERT
EXIES
EXILE
EXINE
EXIST
EXITE
EXORN
EXTER
EXTOL
EXTRA
EXTRE
EXULT
EXUST
EXUTE
IXTLE
LARIX
LATEX
LAXER
LEXIA
LOXIA
LUXES
LUXUR
LUXUS
NEXAL
NEXUS
NIXEN
NIXES
NIXIE
NOXAE
NOXAL
OXANE
OXTER
RELAX
REXEN
SAXON
SEXTO
SILEX
SIREX
SIXER
SIXTE
SOULX
STRIX
TAXEL
TAXER
TAXES
TAXIS
TAXON
TAXOR
TELEX
TEXAS
TOXIN
TOXON
UNSEX
UNTAX
XALLE
XENIA
XENON
XOANA
XUREL

11
EXLEX
XEROX

ALPHABETICAL LIST OF 6-LETTER WORDS

ADIEUX
ADMIXT
ADNEXA
AFFIXT
AFFLUX
ALEXIA
ALEXIN
ALKOXY
ALLOXY
AMIXIA
AMPLEX
ANAXON
ANNEXA
ANNEXE
ANOXIA
ANOXIC
APEXED
APEXES
AROXYL
ATAXIA
ATAXIC
ATWIXT
AUSPEX
AXEMAN
AXENIC
AXIATE
AXILLA
AXLIKE
AXONAL
AXSEED
AXTREE
AXUNGE
AXWEED
BADAXE
BAXTER
BIAXAL
BIFLEX
BIJOUX
BISEXT
BOLLIX
BOMBYX
BONXIE
BOXCAR
BOXING
BOXMAN
BOYAUX
BUTOXY
CALXES
CARANX
CARFAX
CAUDEX
CAXIRI
CERVIX
CIXIID
CLIMAX
COAXAL
COAXED
COAXER
COCCYX
COMMIX
CONFIX
CONNEX
CONVEX
CORDAX
CORTEX
COUXIA
COUXIO
COXIER
COXITE
CRUXES
DARNEX
DEFLEX
DEFLUX
DELUXE
DENTEX
DEXTER
DEXTRO
DIAXON
DIOXAN
DIPLEX
DIXAIN
DOXIES
DRUXEY
DUPLEX
EARWAX
EFFLUX
ELIXIR
EMPEXA
EUTAXY
EXACTA
EXALTE
EXAMEN
EXARCH
EXCAMB
EXCAVE
EXCEED
EXCELS
EXCEPT
EXCERN
EXCESS
EXCIDE
EXCISE
EXCITE
EXCOCT
EXCUSE
EXCUSS
EXCYST
EXEDRA
EXEMPT
EXEQUY
EXERCE
EXEUNT
EXHALE
EXHORT
EXHUME
EXILED
EXILER
EXILIC
EXITUS
EXODIC
EXODUS
EXOGEN
EXOLVE
EXOMIS
EXONER
EXOPOD
EXOTIC
EXPAND
EXPECT
EXPEDE
EXPEND
EXPERT
EXPIRE
EXPIRY
EXPLAT
EXPONE
EXPORT
EXPOSE
EXPUGN
EXSECT
EXSERT
EXTANT
EXTEND
EXTENT
EXTERN
EXTILL
EXTIMA
EXTIME
EXTINE
EXTIRP
EXTOLL
EXTORT
EXTUND
EXTURB
EXUDED
FIXAGE
FIXATE
FIXING
FIXITY
FIXURE
FLAXEN
FLEXED
FLEXOR
FLUXED
FLUXER
FORFEX
FORNIX
FOXERY
FOXIER
FOXILY
FOXING
FOXISH
FRAXIN
FRUTEX
GALAXY
HALLUX
HATBOX
HEXADE
HEXANE
HEXENE
HEXINE
HEXODE
HEXOIC
HEXONE
HEXOSE
HEXYNE
HOAXEE
HOAXER
HOTBOX
IBEXES
ICEBOX
ILEXES
IMBREX
IMMIXT
IMPLEX
INAXON
INFLEX
INFLUX
INTEXT
IODOXY
IXODIC
IXODID
KLAXON
KORDAX
LARNAX
LARYNX
LASTEX
LAXATE
LAXEST
LAXISM
LAXIST
LAXITY
LUMMOX
LUXATE
LUXIVE
LUXURY
LYNXES
LYXOSE
MASTAX
MATRIX
MAXIMA
MAXIXE
MENINX
MINXES
MIXING
MIXITE
MYSTAX
MYXOID
MYXOMA
NEXTLY
NOXIAL
ONYXES
ONYXIS
OPIFEX
OREXIS

OUTBOX
OUTFOX
OXALIC
OXALIS
OXALYL
OXAMIC
OXAZIN
OXBANE
OXBIRD
OXCART
OXEATE
OXEOTE
OXFORD
OXGALL
OXGANG
OXGATE
OXGOAD
OXHEAD
OXHEAL
OXHIDE
OXHOFT
OXHORN
OXLAND
OXLIKE
OXREIM
OXSHOE
OXSKIN
OXTAIL
OXWORT

OXYAZO
OXYGEN
OXYGON
OXYMEL
OXYOPY
PAPPOX
PATRIX
PAXWAX
PEGBOX
PERFIX
PERMIX
PEROXY
PHENIX
PICKAX
PINXIT
PIXIES
PLEXAL
PLEXOR
PLEXUS
POLEAX
POLLEX
PRAXIS
PRECOX
PREFIX
PROLIX
PROREX
PTYXIS
REFLEX

REFLUX
REXINE
RHEXIS
ROLLIX
SANDIX
SANDYX
SAXAUL
SCOLEX
SEXERN
SEXIER
SEXISM
SEXIST
SEXTAN
SEXTET
SEXTIC
SEXTON
SEXTRY
SEXTUR
SEXUAL
SIXAIN
SMILAX
SPADIX
SPHINX
STAXIS
STORAX
STUPEX
SUBFIX
SUFFIX

SURTAX
SYNTAX
SYRINX
TARBOX
TAXEME
TAXIED
TAXINE
TAXING
TAXITE
TAXMAN
TEABOX
TETTIX
TEXTUS
THIXLE
THORAX
TORPEX
TOXIFY
TOXINE
TOXITY
TOXOID
TOXONE
TREMEX
TUXEDO
UNISEX
UROXIN
VERMIX
VERNIX
VERTEX

VEXFUL
VEXING
VINDEX
VORTEX
WAXAND
WAXIER
WAXING
WAXMAN
WRAXLE
WRIXLE
XARQUE
XENIAL
XENIAN
XENIUM
XERIFF
XEROMA
XIFOID
XOANON
XYLATE
XYLENE
XYLITE
XYLOID
XYLOMA
XYLOSE
XYLOYL
XYSTER
XYSTUS
YAXCHE

POSITIONAL ORDER LIST OF 6-LETTER WORDS

XARQUE
XENIAL
XENIAN
XENIUM
XERIFF
XEROMA
XIFOID
XOANON
XYLATE
XYLENE
XYLITE
XYLOID
XYLOMA
XYLOSE
XYLOYL
XYSTER
XYSTUS

AXEMAN
AXENIC
AXIATE
AXILLA
AXLIKE
AXONAL
AXSEED
AXTREE
AXUNGE
AXWEED
EXACTA
EXALTE
EXAMEN
EXARCH
EXCAMB
EXCAVE
EXCEED
EXCELS
EXCEPT
EXCERN
EXCESS
EXCIDE
EXCISE

EXCITE
EXCOCT
EXCUSE
EXCUSS
EXCYST
EXEDRA
EXEMPT
EXEQUY
EXERCE
EXEUNT
EXHALE
EXHORT
EXHUME
EXILED
EXILER
EXILIC
EXITUS
EXODIC
EXODUS
EXOGEN
EXOLVE
EXOMIS
EXONER
EXOPOD
EXOTIC
EXPAND
EXPECT
EXPEDE
EXPEND
EXPERT
EXPIRE
EXPIRY
EXPLAT
EXPONE
EXPORT
EXPOSE
EXPUGN
EXSECT
EXSERT
EXTANT
EXTEND

EXTENT
EXTERN
EXTILL
EXTIMA
EXTIME
EXTINE
EXTIRP
EXTOLL
EXTORT
EXTUND
EXTURB
EXUDED
IXODIC
IXODID
OXALIC
OXALIS
OXALYL
OXAMIC
OXAZIN
OXBANE
OXBIRD
OXCART
OXEATE
OXEOTE
OXFORD
OXGALL
OXGANG
OXGATE
OXGOAD
OXHEAD
OXHEAL
OXHIDE
OXHOFT
OXHORN
OXLAND
OXLIKE
OXREIM
OXSHOE
OXSKIN
OXTAIL
OXWORT

OXYAZO
OXYGEN
OXYGON
OXYMEL
OXYOPY

BAXTER
BOXCAR
BOXING
BOXMAN
CAXIRI
CIXIID
COXIER
COXITE
DEXTER
DEXTRO
DIXAIN
DOXIES
FIXAGE
FIXATE
FIXING
FIXITY
FIXURE
FOXERY
FOXIER
FOXILY
FOXING
FOXISH
HEXADE
HEXANE
HEXENE
HEXINE
HEXODE
HEXOIC
HEXONE
HEXOSE
HEXYNE
LAXATE
LAXEST
LAXISM
LAXIST

LAXITY
LUXATE
LUXIVE
LUXURY
LYXOSE
MAXIMA
MAXIXE
MIXING
MIXITE
MYXOID
MYXOMA
NEXTLY
NOXIAL
PAXWAX
PIXIES
REXINE
SAXAUL
SEXERN
SEXIER
SEXISM
SEXIST
SEXTAN
SEXTET
SEXTIC
SEXTON
SEXTRY
SEXTUR
SEXUAL
SIXAIN
TAXEME
TAXIED
TAXINE
TAXING
TAXITE
TAXMAN
TEXTUS
TOXIFY
TOXINE
TOXITY
TOXOID
TOXONE

TUXEDO
VEXFUL
VEXING
WAXAND
WAXIER
WAXING
WAXMAN
YAXCHE

ALEXIA
ALEXIN
AMIXIA
ANAXON
ANOXIA
ANOXIC
APEXED
APEXES
AROXYL
ATAXIA
ATAXIC
BIAXAL
BONXIE
CALXES
COAXAL
COAXED
COAXER
COUXIA
COUXIO
CRUXES
DIAXON
DIOXAN
DRUXEY
ELIXIR
FLAXEN
FLEXED
FLEXOR

FLUXED
FLUXER
FRAXIN
HOAXEE
HOAXER
IBEXES
ILEXES
INAXON
KLAXON
LYNXES
MINXES
ONYXES
ONYXIS
OREXIS
PINXIT
PLEXAL
PLEXOR
PLEXUS
PRAXIS
PTYXIS
RHEXIS
STAXIS
THIXLE
UROXIN
WRAXLE
WRIXLE

ADMIXT
ADNEXA
AFFIXT
ALKOXY
ALLOXY
ANNEXA
ANNEXE
ATWIXT
BADAXE

BISEXT
BUTOXY
DELUXE
EMPEXA
EUTAXY
GALAXY
IMMIXT
INTEXT
IODOXY
MAXIXE
PEROXY

ADIEUX
AFFLUX
AMPLEX
AUSPEX
BIFLEX
BIJOUX
BOLLIX
BOMBYX
BOYAUX
CARANX
CARFAX
CAUDEX
CERVIX
CLIMAX
COCCYX
COMMIX
CONFIX
CONNEX
CONVEX
CORDAX
CORTEX
DARNEX
DEFLEX
DEFLUX

DENTEX
DIPLEX
DUPLEX
EARWAX
EFFLUX
FORFEX
FORNIX
FRUTEX
HALLUX
HATBOX
HOTBOX
ICEBOX
IMBREX
IMPLEX
INFLEX
INFLUX
KORDAX
LARNAX
LARYNX
LASTEX
LUMMOX
MASTAX
MATRIX
MENINX
MYSTAX
OPIFEX
OUTBOX
OUTFOX
PAPPOX
PATRIX
PAXWAX
PEGBOX
PERFIX
PERMIX
PHENIX

PICKAX
POLEAX
POLLEX
PRECOX
PREFIX
PROLIX
PROREX
REFLEX
REFLUX
ROLLIX
SANDIX
SANDYX
SCOLEX
SMILAX
SPADIX
SPHINX
STORAX
STUPEX
SUBFIX
SUFFIX
SURTAX
SYNTAX
SYRINX
TARBOX
TEABOX
TETTIX
THORAX
TORPEX
TREMEX
UNISEX
VERMIX
VERNIX
VERTEX
VINDEX
VORTEX

SCORING ORDER LIST OF 6-LETTER WORDS

25
EXEQUY
OXYAZO

22
BIJOUX
BOMBYX
OXAZIN
XARQUE

21
OXYOPY
PICKAX
YAXCHE

20
ALKOXY
MYXOMA

19
AFFIXT
AFFLUX
COCCYX
COMMIX
EFFLUX
EXCAMB
FIXITY
FORFEX
FOXERY
FOXILY
FOXISH
HEXYNE
MYXOID
OXHOFT
SUFFIX

TOXIFY
VEXFUL
XERIFF
XYLOYL

18
BIFLEX
BOYAUX
BUTOXY
CARFAX
CERVIX
CONFIX
CONVEX
EXARCH
EXCAVE
EXCYST
EXHUME
EXPIRY
HATBOX
HEXOIC
HOTBOX
KORDAX
MYSTAX
OPIFEX
OXYMEL
PEGBOX
PERFIX
PEROXY
PHENIX
PREFIX
PTYXIS
SPHINX
SUBFIX
VERMIX
WAXMAN

XYLOMA

17
AMPLEX
AXLIKE
AXWEED
BOXCAR
BOXMAN
CLIMAX
DEFLEX
DEFLUX
DRUXEY
EMPEXA
EXCEPT
EXCOCT
EXEMPT
EXPECT
FIXAGE
FIXING
FLEXED
FLUXED
FOXING
GALAXY
HEXADE
HEXODE
ICEBOX
IMBREX
IMMIXT
IMPLEX
IODOXY
KLAXON
LUMMOX
MAXIMA
OXAMIC
OXFORD

OXHEAD
OXHIDE
OXLIKE
OXSKIN
OXYGEN
OXYGON
PAXWAX
PERMIX
PRECOX
SANDYX
VEXING
VINDEX
WAXAND
WAXING
XIFOID
XYLOID

16
ADMIXT
ALLOXY
APEXED
AROXYL
ATWIXT
BADAXE
BOXING
CAUDEX
CIXIID
COAXED
CORDAX
DIPLEX
DUPLEX
EARWAX
EUTAXY
EXCEED
EXCIDE

EXHALE
EXHORT
EXODIC
EXOLVE
EXOPOD
EXPAND
EXPEDE
EXPEND
EXPUGN
FIXATE
FIXURE
FLAXEN
FLEXOR
FLUXER
FORNIX
FOXIER
FRAXIN
FRUTEX
HALLUX
HEXANE
HEXENE
HEXINE
HEXONE
HEXOSE
HOAXEE
HOAXER
INFLEX
INFLUX
IXODIC
LARYNX
LAXITY
LUXIVE
LUXURY
LYNXES
LYXOSE

MIXING
NEXTLY
ONYXES
ONYXIS
OUTFOX
OXALYL
OXBIRD
OXHEAL
OXHORN
OXSHOE
OXWORT
PAPPOX
REFLEX
REFLUX
RHEXIS
SEXTRY
SPADIX
SYNTAX
SYRINX
THIXLE
THORAX
TOXITY
VERNIX
VERTEX
VORTEX
WAXIER
WRAXLE
WRIXLE
XYLATE
XYLENE
XYLITE
XYLOSE
XYSTER
XYSTUS

15

AMIXIA
ANOXIC
APEXES
ATAXIC
AUSPEX
AXEMAN
AXENIC
BAXTER
BIAXAL

BISEXT
BOLLIX
BONXIE
CALXES
CARANX
CAXIRI
COAXAL
COAXER
CONNEX
CORTEX
COUXIA
COUXIO
COXIER
COXITE
CRUXES
EXACTA
EXAMEN
EXCELS
EXCERN
EXCESS
EXCISE
EXCITE
EXCUSE
EXCUSS
EXERCE
EXILIC
EXOMIS
EXOTIC
EXPERT
EXPIRE
EXPLAT
EXPONE
EXPORT
EXPOSE
EXSECT
EXTIMA
EXTIME
EXTIRP
EXTURB
EXUDED
IBEXES
IXODID
LAXISM
MASTAX
MATRIX

MENINX
MINXES
MIXITE
OUTBOX
OXALIC
OXBANE
OXCART
OXGANG
OXGOAD
OXREIM
PATRIX
PINXIT
PIXIES
PLEXAL
PLEXOR
PLEXUS
POLEAX
POLLEX
PRAXIS
PROLIX
PROREX
SCOLEX
SEXISM
SEXTIC
SMILAX
STUPEX
TARBOX
TAXEME
TAXMAN
TEABOX
TORPEX
TREMEX
XENIUM
XEROMA

14

ADIEUX
ADNEXA
AXSEED
AXUNGE
DARNEX
DELUXE
DENTEX
DEXTER

DEXTRO
DIAXON
DIOXAN
DIXAIN
DOXIES
EXEDRA
EXILED
EXODUS
EXOGEN
EXTEND
EXTUND
MAXIXE
OXGALL
OXGATE
OXLAND
SANDIX
TAXIED
TAXING
TOXOID
TUXEDO

13

ALEXIA
ALEXIN
ANAXON
ANNEXA
ANNEXE
ANOXIA
ATAXIA
AXIATE
AXILLA
AXONAL
AXTREE
ELIXIR
EXALTE
EXEUNT
EXILER
EXITUS
EXONER
EXSERT
EXTANT
EXTENT
EXTERN
EXTILL

EXTINE
EXTOLL
EXTORT
ILEXES
INAXON
INTEXT
LARNAX
LASTEX
LAXATE
LAXEST
LAXIST
LUXATE
NOXIAL
OREXIS
OXALIS
OXEATE
OXEOTE
OXTAIL
REXINE
ROLLIX
SAXAUL
SEXERN
SEXIER
SEXIST
SEXTAN
SEXTET
SEXTON
SEXTUR
SEXUAL
SIXAIN
STAXIS
STORAX
SURTAX
TAXINE
TAXITE
TETTIX
TEXTUS
TOXINE
TOXONE
UNISEX
UROXIN
XENIAL
XENIAN
XOANON

ALPHABETICAL LIST OF 7-LETTER WORDS

ABACAXI
ABAXIAL
ABAXILE
ABRASAX
ABRAXAS
ACRONYX
ADAXIAL
ADMIXED
ADNEXAL
ADNEXED
ADOXIES
AFFIXAL
AFFIXED
AFFIXER
AFFREUX
AGALAXY
AGNEAUX
ALEXINE
ALKOXID
ALKOXYL

ALLOXAN
AMPYXES
ANAXIAL
ANAXONE
ANNEXED
ANNEXER
ANOREXY
ANTAPEX
ANTEFIX
ANTHRAX
ANXIETY
ANXIOUS
APEXING
APOPLEX
APRAXIA
APTERYX
APYREXY
ARTIFEX
ARUSPEX
ASEXUAL

ASPHYXY
ATARAXY
ATAXITE
AURIFEX
AUXESIS
AUXETIC
AUXOTOX
AXIALLY
AXIFORM
AXILLAE
AXILLAR
AXINITE
AXMAKER
AXOGAMY
AXOLOTL
AXONEME
AXONOST
AXSTONE
AZOXINE
BANDBOX

BATEAUX
BAUXITE
BEESWAX
BENZOXY
BETWIXT
BIAXIAL
BIOTAXY
BISEXED
BISSEXT
BOSTRYX
BOXBUSH
BOXCARS
BOXFISH
BOXHAUL
BOXHEAD
BOXINGS
BOXLIKE
BOXROOM
BOXTREE
BOXWOOD

BOXWORK
BRAXIES
BREAKAX
BROADAX
BRUXISM
BUREAUX
BUTOXYL
BUXERRY
BUXOMLY
CACHEXY
CAKEBOX
CARAPAX
CAREFOX
CASEBOX
CASHBOX
CHOENIX
COALBOX
COAXIAL
COAXING
COEXIST

COLAUXE
COMMIXT
COMPLEX
CONFLUX
CONTEXT
COXALGY
COXCOMB
COXIEST
COXITIS
CURTAXE
CURTLAX
DEEDBOX
DEXTRAD
DEXTRAL
DEXTRAN
DEXTRIN
DIAXIAL
DIAXONE
DICEBOX
DIGOXIN
DIOXANE
DIOXIDE
DIOXIME
DUSTBOX
ELIXATE
EPAXIAL
EPOXIDE
EQUINOX
ESEXUAL
ETHOXYL
EUTAXIC
EUTAXIE
EUTEXIA
EXACTED
EXACTER
EXACTLY
EXACTOR
EXALATE
EXALTED
EXALTEE
EXALTER
EXAMINE
EXAMPLE
EXARATE
EXARCHY
EXASPER
EXCELSE
EXCERPT
EXCHEAT
EXCIDED
EXCIPLE
EXCISED
EXCISOR
EXCITED
EXCITER
EXCITON
EXCITOR
EXCLAIM
EXCLAVE
EXCLUDE
EXCRETA
EXCRETE
EXCUDIT
EXCURSE
EXCUSAL
EXCUSED
EXCUSER
EXECUTE
EXEDENT
EXEGETE
EXEMPLA
EXERGUE
EXERTED
EXESION
EXFLECT
EXHALED
EXHANCE
EXHAUST
EXHEDRA
EXHIBIT
EXHUMED
EXHUMER
EXIGENT
EXILIAN
EXILING
EXILITY
EXINITE
EXISTED
EXISTER
EXITIAL
EXITION
EXITURE
EXOCARP
EXOCONE
EXODERM
EXODIST
EXODIUM
EXOGAMY
EXOLETE
EXOMION
EXORATE
EXORMIA
EXOSMIC
EXOSTRA
EXOTISM
EXPANSE
EXPEDED
EXPENSE
EXPIATE
EXPIRED
EXPIREE
EXPIRER
EXPLAIN
EXPLANT
EXPLETE
EXPLODE
EXPLOIT
EXPLORE
EXPOSAL
EXPOSED
EXPOSER
EXPOSIT
EXPOUND
EXPREME
EXPRESS
EXPULSE
EXPUNGE
EXPURGE
EXQUIRE
EXRADIO
EXSCIND
EXSOLVE
EXSURGE
EXTANCY
EXTENSE
EXTERNA
EXTERNE
EXTINCT
EXTRACT
EXTREAT
EXTREME
EXTRUCT
EXTRUDE
EXUDATE
EXUDING
EXULATE
EXULTED
EXULTET
EXURBIA
EXUVIAE
EXUVIAL
FACTRIX
FEEDBOX
FIREBOX
FIXABLE
FIXATED
FIXATIF
FIXATOR
FIXEDLY
FIXINGS
FIXTURE
FLAXIER
FLAXMAN
FLEXILE
FLEXING
FLEXION
FLEXIVE
FLEXURA
FLEXURE
FLUMMOX
FLUXILE
FLUXING
FLUXION
FLUXIVE
FLUXURE
FOXBANE
FOXCHOP
FOXFEET
FOXFIRE
FOXFISH
FOXHOLE
FOXIEST
FOXLIKE
FOXSKIN
FOXTAIL
FOXTROT
GEARBOX
GEOTAXY
GITOXIN
GLOMMOX
GLYOXAL
GLYOXYL
GUAXIMA
HEADBOX
HELIXIN
HELLBOX
HEMIXIS
HEXACID
HEXADIC
HEXAGON
HEXAGYN
HEXAMER
HEXANAL
HEXAPED
HEXAPLA
HEXAPOD
HEXAXON
HEXEREI
HEXERIS
HEXITOL
HEXONIC
HEXOSAN
HEXYLIC
HOMODOX
INDEXED
INDEXER
INDEXES
INDOXYL
INEXACT
INEXIST
INFIXED
INFIXES
IXODIAN
JACKBOX
JUKEBOX
KICKXIA
KINEPOX
KLEENEX
LARIXIN
LATEXES
LAXNESS
LEXICAL
LEXICON
LOCKBOX
LOXOTIC
LUXATED
MAILBOX
MALAXED
MARTEXT
MARTRIX
MAXILLA
MAXIMAL
MAXIMED
MAXIMUM
MAXIMUS
MAXWELL
METHOXY
MEXICAL
MIXABLE
MIXHILL
MIXIBLE
MIXTION
MIXTURE
MONAXON
MUREXAN
MUREXES
MUREXID
MYOXINE
MYXEMIA
MYXOMAS
NARTHEX
NEXUSES
NOXIOUS
ORATRIX
OUTFLUX
OUTJINX
OVERTAX
OXALATE
OXALATO
OXAMATE
OXAMIDE
OXAZINE
OXAZOLE
OXBERRY
OXBITER
OXBLOOD
OXBRAKE
OXCHEEK
OXHEART
OXHOUSE
OXHUVUD
OXIDANT
OXIDASE
OXIDATE
OXIDISE
OXIDIZE
OXIMATE
OXONIUM
OXOZONE
OXYACID
OXYMORA
OXYNTIC
OXYOPIA
OXYPHIL
OXYTONE
OXYURID
PACKWAX
PANCHAX
PANMIXY
PARADOX
PARAXON
PAXILLA
PAXILLI
PAXIUBA
PEIXERE
PEMPHIX
PEROXYL
PERPLEX
PHALANX
PHARYNX
PHOENIX
PICKAXE
PILLBOX
PISTRIX
PLANXTY
PLAYBOX
PLEXURE
POLAXIS
POLEAXE
POSTBOX
POSTFIX
PRAECOX
PRETEXT
PREXIES
PRINCOX
PROPLEX
PROPOXY
PROTEXT
PROXENY
PROXIED
PROXIES
PROXIME
PROXIMO
PROXYSM
PYREXIA
PYREXIC
PYXIDES
RECTRIX
RELAXED
RELAXER
RELAXIN
RESEAUX
SALPINX
SALTBOX
SANDBOX
SAXHORN
SAXTUBA
SEEDBOX
SEXIEST
SEXLESS
SEXLIKE
SEXTAIN
SEXTANS
SEXTANT
SEXTERN
SEXTILE
SEXTOLE
SEXTUOR
SEXUALE
SEXUOUS
SIDEBOX
SIMPLEX
SINKBOX
SIXFOLD
SIXSOME
SIXTEEN
SIXTIES
SKEEZIX
SOAPBOX
SONOVOX
SPANDEX
SPITBOX
SUBOXID
SYNAXAR
SYNAXIS
TAXABLE
TAXABLY
TAXATOR
TAXIBUS
TAXICAB
TAXIMAN
TAXITIC
TAXPAID
TAXYING
TECTRIX

TELEVOX
TEXTILE
TEXTLET
TEXTMAN
TEXTUAL
TEXTURE
TOOLBOX
TORTRIX
TOXAMIN
TOXEMIA
TOXEMIC
TOXICAL
TOXICON
TOXICUM
TOXIFER
TOXOTAE
TRIAXAL
TRIAXON
TRIOXID
TRIPLEX
TUBIFEX
TUXEDOS
ULEXINE
ULEXITE
UNBUXOM
UNEXACT
UNFIXED
UNFOXED
UNSEXED
UROTOXY
UXORIAL
VAUXITE
VEXEDLY
VEXILLA
VICTRIX
VITRAUX
VIXENLY
WAXBILL
WAXBIRD
WAXBUSH
WAXCOMB
WAXIEST
WAXWEED
WAXWING
WAXWORK
WAXWORM
WEREFOX
WOODWAX
WORKBOX
WRAXLED
XANTHIC
XANTHID
XANTHIN
XANTHYL
XERAFIN
XERARCH
XERASIA
XERONIC
XEROSIS
XEROTES
XEROTIC
XIBALBA
XIPHOID
XYLENOL
XYLENYL
XYLIDIN
XYLITOL
XYLOGEN
XYLOMAS
XYLOSID
ZOOTAXY

POSITIONAL ORDER LIST OF 7-LETTER WORDS

XANTHIC
XANTHID
XANTHIN
XANTHYL
XERAFIN
XERARCH
XERASIA
XERONIC
XEROSIS
XEROTES
XEROTIC
XIBALBA
XIPHOID
XYLENOL
XYLENYL
XYLIDIN
XYLITOL
XYLOGEN
XYLOMAS
XYLOSID

AXIALLY
AXIFORM
AXILLAE
AXILLAR
AXINITE
AXMAKER
AXOGAMY
AXOLOTL
AXONEME
AXONOST
AXSTONE
EXACTED
EXACTER
EXACTLY
EXACTOR
EXALATE
EXALTED
EXALTEE
EXALTER
EXAMINE
EXAMPLE
EXARATE
EXARCHY
EXASPER
EXCELSE
EXCERPT
EXCHEAT
EXCIDED
EXCIPLE
EXCISED
EXCISOR
EXCITED
EXCITER
EXCITON
EXCITOR
EXCLAIM
EXCLAVE
EXCLUDE
EXCRETA
EXCRETE
EXCUDIT
EXCURSE
EXCUSAL
EXCUSED
EXCUSER
EXECUTE
EXEDENT
EXEGETE
EXEMPLA
EXERGUE
EXERTED
EXESION
EXFLECT
EXHALED
EXHANCE
EXHAUST
EXHEDRA
EXHIBIT
EXHUMED
EXHUMER
EXIGENT
EXILIAN
EXILING
EXILITY
EXINITE
EXISTED
EXISTER
EXITIAL
EXITION
EXITURE
EXOCARP
EXOCONE
EXODERM
EXODIST
EXODIUM
EXOGAMY
EXOLETE
EXOMION
EXORATE
EXORMIA
EXOSMIC
EXOSTRA
EXOTISM
EXPANSE
EXPEDED
EXPENSE
EXPIATE
EXPIRED
EXPIREE
EXPIRER
EXPLAIN
EXPLANT
EXPLETE
EXPLODE
EXPLOIT
EXPLORE
EXPOSAL
EXPOSED
EXPOSER
EXPOSIT
EXPOUND
EXPREME
EXPRESS
EXPULSE
EXPUNGE
EXPURGE
EXQUIRE
EXRADIO
EXSCIND
EXSOLVE
EXSURGE
EXTANCY
EXTENSE
EXTERNA
EXTERNE
EXTINCT
EXTRACT
EXTREAT
EXTREME
EXTRUCT
EXTRUDE
EXUDATE
EXUDING
EXULATE
EXULTED
EXULTET
EXURBIA
EXUVIAE
EXUVIAL
IXODIAN
OXALATE
OXALATO
OXAMATE
OXAMIDE
OXAZINE
OXAZOLE
OXBERRY
OXBITER
OXBLOOD
OXBRAKE
OXCHEEK
OXHEART
OXHOUSE
OXHUVUD
OXIDANT
OXIDASE
OXIDATE
OXIDISE
OXIDIZE
OXIMATE
OXONIUM
OXOZONE
OXYACID
OXYMORA
OXYNTIC
OXYOPIA
OXYPHIL
OXYSALT
OXYTONE
OXYURID
UXORIAL

ANXIETY
ANXIOUS
AUXESIS
AUXETIC
AUXOTOX
AUXOTOX
BOXBUSH
BOXCARS
BOXFISH
BOXHAUL
BOXHEAD
BOXINGS
BOXLIKE
BOXROOM
BOXTREE
BOXWOOD
BOXWORK
BUXERRY
BUXOMLY
COXALGY
COXCOMB
COXIEST
COXITIS
DEXTRAD
DEXTRAL
DEXTRAN
DEXTRIN
FIXABLE
FIXATED
FIXATIF
FIXATOR
FIXEDLY
FIXINGS
FIXTURE
FOXBANE
FOXCHOP
FOXFEET
FOXFIRE
FOXFISH
FOXHOLE
FOXIEST
FOXLIKE
FOXSKIN
FOXTAIL
FOXTROT
HEXACID
HEXADIC
HEXAGON
HEXAGYN
HEXAMER
HEXANAL
HEXAPED
HEXAPLA
HEXAPOD
HEXAXON
HEXEREI
HEXERIS
HEXITOL
HEXONIC
HEXOSAN
HEXYLIC
LAXNESS
LEXICAL
LEXICON
LOXOTIC
LUXATED
MAXILLA
MAXIMAL
MAXIMED
MAXIMUM
MAXIMUS
MAXWELL
MEXICAL
MIXABLE
MIXHILL
MIXIBLE
MIXTION
MIXTURE
MYXEMIA
MYXOMAS
NEXUSES
NOXIOUS
PAXILLA
PAXILLI
PAXIUBA
PYXIDES
SAXHORN
SAXTUBA
SEXIEST
SEXLESS
SEXLIKE
SEXTAIN
SEXTANS
SEXTANT
SEXTERN
SEXTILE
SEXTOLE

SEXTUOR
SEXUALE
SEXUOUS
SIXFOLD
SIXSOME
SIXTEEN
SIXTIES
TAXABLE
TAXABLY
TAXATOR
TAXIBUS
TAXICAB
TAXIMAN
TAXITIC
TAXPAID
TAXYING
TEXTILE
TEXTLET
TEXTMAN
TEXTUAL
TEXTURE
TOXAMIN
TOXEMIA
TOXEMIC
TOXICAL
TOXICON
TOXICUM
TOXIFER
TOXOTAE
TUXEDOS
VEXEDLY
VEXILLA
VIXENLY
WAXBILL
WAXBIRD
WAXBUSH
WAXCOMB
WAXIEST
WAXWEED
WAXWING
WAXWORK
WAXWORM

ABAXIAL
ABAXILE
ADAXIAL
ADOXIES
ALEXINE
ANAXIAL
ANAXONE
APEXING
ASEXUAL
ATAXITE
AZOXINE
BAUXITE
BIAXIAL
BRAXIES

BRUXISM
COAXIAL
COAXING
COEXIST
DIAXIAL
DIAXONE
DIOXANE
DIOXIDE
DIOXIME
ELIXATE
EPAXIAL
EPOXIDE
ESEXUAL
FLAXIER
FLAXMAN
FLEXILE
FLEXING
FLEXION
FLEXIVE
FLEXURA
FLEXURE
FLUXILE
FLUXING
FLUXION
FLUXIVE
FLUXURE
GUAXIMA
INEXACT
INEXIST
MYOXINE
PEIXERE
PLEXURE
PREXIES
PROXENY
PROXIED
PROXIES
PROXIME
PROXIMO
PROXYSM
ULEXINE
ULEXITE
UNEXACT
VAUXITE
WRAXLED

ABRAXAS
ADMIXED
ADNEXAL
ADNEXED
AFFIXAL
AFFIXED
AFFIXER
ALKOXID
ALKOXYL
ALLOXAN
AMPYXES
ANNEXED

ANNEXER
APRAXIA
BISEXED
BUTOXYL
DIGOXIN
ETHOXYL
EUTAXIC
EUTAXIE
EUTEXIA
GITOXIN
GLYOXAL
GLYOXYL
HELIXIN
HEMIXIS
HEXAXON
INDEXED
INDEXER
INDEXES
INDOXYL
INFIXED
INFIXES
KICKXIA
LARIXIN
LATEXES
MALAXED
MONAXON
MUREXAN
MUREXES
MUREXID
PARAXON
PEROXYL
PLANXTY
POLAXIS
PYREXIA
PYREXIC
RELAXED
RELAXER
RELAXIN
SUBOXID
SYNAXAR
SYNAXIS
TRIAXAL
TRIAXON
TRIOXID
UNBUXOM
UNFIXED
UNFOXED
UNSEXED

ABACAXI
AGALAXY
ANOREXY
APYREXY
ASPHYXY
ATARAXY
BENZOXY
BETWIXT

BIOTAXY
BISSEXT
CACHEXY
COLAUXE
COMMIXT
CONTEXT
CURTAXE
GEOTAXY
MARTEXT
METHOXY
PANMIXY
PICKAXE
POLEAXE
PRETEXT
PROPOXY
PROTEXT
UROTOXY
ZOOTAXY

ABRASAX
ACRONYX
AFFREUX
AGNEAUX
ANTAPEX
ANTEFIX
ANTHRAX
APOPLEX
APTERYX
ARTIFEX
ARUSPEX
AURIFEX
BANDBOX
BATEAUX
BEESWAX
BOSTRYX
BREAKAX
BROADAX
BUREAUX
CAKEBOX
CARAPAX
CAREFOX
CASEBOX
CASHBOX
CHOENIX
COALBOX
COMPLEX
CONFLUX
CURTLAX
DEEDBOX
DICEBOX
DUSTBOX
EQUINOX
FACTRIX
FEEDBOX
FIREBOX
FLUMMOX
GEARBOX

GLOMMOX
HEADBOX
HELLBOX
HOMODOX
JACKBOX
JUKEBOX
KINEPOX
KLEENEX
LOCKBOX
MAILBOX
MARTRIX
NARTHEX
ORATRIX
OUTFLUX
OUTJINX
OVERTAX
PACKWAX
PANCHAX
PARADOX
PEMPHIX
PERPLEX
PHALANX
PHARYNX
PHOENIX
PILLBOX
PISTRIX
PLAYBOX
POSTBOX
POSTFIX
PRAECOX
PRINCOX
PROPLEX
RECTRIX
RESEAUX
SALPINX
SALTBOX
SANDBOX
SEEDBOX
SIDEBOX
SIMPLEX
SINKBOX
SKEEZIX
SOAPBOX
SONOVOX
SPANDEX
SPITBOX
TECTRIX
TELEVOX
TOOLBOX
TORTRIX
TRIPLEX
TUBIFEX
VICTRIX
VITRAUX
WEREFOX
WOODWAX
WORKBOX

SCORING ORDER LIST OF 7-LETTER WORDS

29
JACKBOX

28
BENZOXY

27
JUKEBOX
SKEEZIX

26
ZOOTAXY

25
ASPHYXY
PACKWAX

24
CACHEXY
FOXCHOP
OXIDIZE
WAXWORK

23
AZOXINE
BOXWORK
EQUINOX
EXQUIRE
FOXFISH
OXAZINE
OXAZOLE
OXCHEEK
OXOZONE
PEMPHIX
WAXCOMB
WORKBOX

22
APYREXY
BOXFISH
CAKEBOX
COXCOMB
EXARCHY
HEXYLIC
LOCKBOX
METHOXY
OXYPHIL
PHARYNX
PICKAXE
WAXBUSH
WAXWORM

21
AFFIXED
ALKOXYL
AMPYXES
BOXBUSH
BUXOMLY
CASHBOX
FIXEDLY
FLUMMOX
FOXLIKE
FOXSKIN
GLYOXYL

HEXAGYN
MYXEMIA
MYXOMAS
OUTJINX
OXHUVUD
PANCHAX
PANMIXY
PLAYBOX
PROPOXY
PROXYSM
PYREXIC
VEXEDLY
WAXWEED
WAXWING
WOODWAX

20
AFFIXAL
AFFIXER
AFFREUX
AXMAKER
AXOGAMY
BOXHEAD
BOXLIKE
BOXWOOD
BREAKAX
COMMIXT
COMPLEX
COXALGY
ETHOXYL
EXHUMED
EXOGAMY
FEEDBOX
FIXATIF
FLEXIVE
FLUXIVE
FOXFEET
FOXFIRE
FOXHOLE
HEADBOX
HEXACID
HEXADIC
HEXAPED
HEXAPOD
HOMODOX
KINEPOX
OXBRAKE
OXYACID
PYXIDES
SINKBOX
VIXENLY
WAXBIRD
WEREFOX
XANTHYL
XIPHOID
XYLENYL

19
ACRONYX
ALKOXID
APTERYX
AXIFORM
BANDBOX
BEESWAX
BETWIXT
BIOTAXY
BOSTRYX
BOXHAUL
BUTOXYL
BUXERRY
CAREFOX
CHOENIX
CONFLUX
DICEBOX
EXACTLY
EXCHEAT
EXCLAVE
EXFLECT
EXHANCE
EXHIBIT
EXHUMER
EXTANCY
FACTRIX
FIREBOX
FIXABLE
FLAXMAN
FOXBANE
GLOMMOX
HELLBOX
HEMIXIS
HEXAMER
HEXAPLA
HEXONIC
KICKXIA
MAXIMED
MAXWELL
MIXHILL
MYOXINE
OXBERRY
OXYMORA
OXYNTIC
OXYOPIA
PEROXYL
PHALANX
PHOENIX
PLANXTY
POSTFIX
PROXENY
PYREXIA
TAXABLY
TUBIFEX
VICTRIX
WAXBILL
XANTHIC
XERARCH
XYLOMAS

18
ABACAXI
ADMIXED
AGALAXY
APOPLEX
BOXCARS
BOXROOM
BRUXISM
CARAPAX
CASEBOX
COALBOX
DEEDBOX
EXAMPLE
EXCERPT
EXCIDED
EXCIPLE
EXCLAIM
EXEMPLA
EXHALED
EXHEDRA
EXOCARP
EXOSMIC
EXPEDED
EXPREME
FIXATED
FIXINGS
FLEXING
FLUXING
GEOTAXY
GLYOXAL
HEXAGON
INDOXYL
INFIXED
KLEENEX
MAILBOX
MAXIMAL
MAXIMUS
MEXICAL
MIXABLE
MIXIBLE
OXYURID
PAXIUBA
PERPLEX
PILLBOX
POSTBOX
PRAECOX
PRINCOX
PROPLEX
PROXIME
PROXIMO
SEXLIKE
SIMPLEX
SIXFOLD
SOAPBOX
SPITBOX
TAXICAB
TAXYING
TOXEMIC
TOXICUM
UNBUXOM
UNFIXED
UNFOXED
WRAXLED
XANTHID
XIBALBA
XYLIDIN
XYLOGEN
XYLOSID

17
ANOREXY
ANTEFIX
ANTHRAX
ANXIETY
APEXING
ARTIFEX
ATARAXY
AURIFEX
AXIALLY
BISEXED
BOXINGS
BROADAX
COAXING
DIOXIME
DUSTBOX
EPOXIDE
EXACTED
EXCISED
EXCITED
EXCLUDE
EXCUDIT
EXCUSED
EXHAUST
EXILITY
EXODERM
EXODIUM
EXPIRED
EXPLODE
EXPOSED
EXPOUND
EXPUNGE
EXPURGE
EXSCIND
EXSOLVE
EXUVIAE
EXUVIAL
FIXATOR
FIXTURE
FLAXIER
FLEXILE
FLEXION
FLEXURA
FLEXURE
FLUXILE
FLUXION
FLUXURE
FOXIEST
FOXTAIL
FOXTROT
GEARBOX
GUAXIMA
HELIXIN
HEXANAL
HEXEREI
HEXERIS
HEXITOL
HEXOSAN
INFIXES
MALAXED
MAXIMUM
MUREXID
NARTHEX
OUTFLUX
OVERTAX
OXAMIDE
OXBLOOD
OXHEART
OXHOUSE
OXYTONE
PARADOX
PROXIED
SANDBOX
SAXHORN
SEEDBOX
SIDEBOX
SONOVOX
SPANDEX
SUBOXID
SYNAXAR
SYNAXIS
TAXPAID
TELEVOX
TOXIFER
UROTOXY
VAUXITE
VEXILLA
VITRAUX
WAXIEST
XANTHIN
XERAFIN
XYLENOL
XYLITOL

16
ABAXIAL
ABAXILE
ABRASAX
ABRAXAS
ADNEXED
ANTAPEX
APRAXIA
ARUSPEX
AUXETIC
AXONEME
BATEAUX
BAUXITE
BIAXIAL
BISSEXT
BOXTREE
BRAXIES
BUREAUX
COAXIAL
COEXIST
COLAUXE
CONTEXT
COXIEST
COXITIS
CURTAXE
CURTLAX
DEXTRAD
DIGOXIN
DIOXIDE
EPAXIAL
EUTAXIC
EXACTER
EXACTOR
EXAMINE
EXASPER
EXCELSE
EXCISOR
EXCITER
EXCITON
EXCITOR
EXCRETA
EXCRETE
EXCURSE
EXCUSAL
EXCUSER
EXECUTE
EXOCONE
EXOMION
EXORMIA
EXOTISM
EXPANSE
EXPENSE
EXPIATE
EXPIREE
EXPIRER
EXPLAIN
EXPLANT
EXPLETE
EXPLOIT
EXPLORE
EXPOSAL
EXPOSER
EXPOSIT
EXPRESS
EXPULSE
EXTINCT
EXTRACT
EXTREME
EXTRUCT
EXUDING
EXURBIA
HEXAXON
INDEXED
INEXACT
LEXICAL
LEXICON
LOXOTIC
MARTEXT
MARTRIX
MAXILLA
MIXTION
MIXTURE
MONAXON
MUREXAN
MUREXES
OXAMATE
OXBITER
OXIMATE
OXONIUM
PARAXON
PAXILLA
PAXILLI
PEIXERE
PISTRIX
PLEXURE
POLAXIS
POLEAXE
PRETEXT
PREXIES
PROTEXT
PROXIES
RECTRIX
SALPINX
SALTBOX
SAXTUBA

SIXSOME
TAXABLE
TAXIBUS
TAXIMAN
TAXITIC
TECTRIX
TEXTMAN
TOOLBOX
TOXAMIN
TOXEMIA
TOXICAL
TOXICON
TRIPLEX
UNEXACT
XERONIC
XEROTIC

15
ADAXIAL
ADNEXAL
ADOXIES
AGNEAUX
ANNEXED
DEXTRAL
DEXTRAN
DEXTRIN
DIAXIAL
DIAXONE
DIOXANE
EXALTED
EXEDENT
EXEGETE
EXERGUE
EXERTED
EXIGENT
EXILING
EXISTED
EXODIST
EXRADIO
EXSURGE
EXTRUDE
EXUDATE
EXULTED
GITOXIN
INDEXER
INDEXES
IXODIAN
LUXATED
OXIDANT
OXIDASE
OXIDATE
OXIDISE
RELAXED
TRIOXID
TUXEDOS
UNSEXED

14
ALEXINE
ALLOXAN
ANAXIAL
ANAXONE
ANNEXER
ANXIOUS
ASEXUAL
ATAXITE
AUXESIS
AXILLAE
AXILLAR
AXINITE
AXOLOTL
AXONOST
AXSTONE
ELIXATE
ESEXUAL
EUTAXIE
EUTEXIA
EXALATE
EXALTEE
EXALTER
EXARATE
EXESION
EXILIAN
EXINITE
EXISTER
EXITIAL
EXITION
EXITURE
EXOLETE
EXORATE
EXOSTRA
EXTENSE
EXTERNA
EXTERNE
EXTREAT
EXULATE
EXULTET
INEXIST
LARIXIN
LATEXES
LAXNESS
NEXUSES
NOXIOUS
ORATRIX
OXALATE
OXALATO
RELAXER
RELAXIN
RESEAUX
SEXIEST
SEXLESS
SEXTAIN
SEXTANS
SEXTANT
SEXTERN
SEXTILE
SEXTOLE
SEXTUOR
SEXUALE
SEXUOUS
SIXTEEN
SIXTIES
TAXATOR
TEXTILE
TEXTLET
TEXTUAL
TEXTURE
TORTRIX
TOXOTAE
TRIAXAL
TRIAXON
ULEXINE
ULEXITE
UXORIAL
XERASIA
XEROSIS
XEROTES

13
AUXOTOX

ALPHABETICAL LIST OF 8-LETTER WORDS

ACETOXIM
ACETOXYL
ACXOYATL
ADJUTRIX
ADMIXING
AFFIXING
AFFIXION
AGALAXIA
ALDOXIME
ALEXINIC
ALKOXIDE
AMIDOXYL
AMPLEXUS
ANATEXIS
ANATOXIN
ANAUXITE
ANNEXING
ANNEXION
ANNEXIVE
ANNEXURE
ANOREXIA
ANOXEMIA
ANOXEMIC
ANTEFIXA
ANTHELIX
APODIXIS
APOMIXIS
APOPLEXY
APOXESIS
APPENDIX
APPRAXIC
APYREXIA
ASPHYXIA
ATARAXIA
ATARAXIC
AUXILIAR
AUXILIUM
AUXIMONE
AUXOBODY
AUXOCYTE
AUXOLOGY
AVIATRIX
AXHAMMER
AXIALITY
AXIFUGAL
AXILEMMA
AXILLANT
AXILLARY
AXIOLITE
AXIOLOGY
AXLETREE
AXMAKING
AXMASTER
AXOFUGAL
AXOIDEAN
AXOLYSIS
AXOMETER
AXONEURE
AXOPETAL
AXOPHYTE
AXOPLASM
AXOSTYLE
BANDBOXY
BANDEAUX
BAROTAXY
BETWIXEN
BICONVEX
BILLYWIX
BINOXIDE
BISEXUAL
BIXBYITE
BOLLIXED
BOXBERRY
BOXBOARD
BOXTHORN
BREADBOX
BREAKAXE
BROADAXE
CACHEXIA
CACHEXIC
CACODOXY
CACOMIXL
CARBOXYL
CARNIFEX
CATHEXIS
CAUDEXES
CEROXYLE
CERVIXES
CHAFEWAX
CHAFFWAX
CHAPEAUX
CHATEAUX
CHRONAXY
CICATRIX
CLAVILUX
CLIMAXED
COEXTEND
COLOPEXY
COLTPIXY
COMMIXED
CONFIXED
CONNEXES
CONNEXUS
CONTUMAX
CONVEXED
CONVEXLY
COUTEAUX
COXALGIA
COXALGIC
COXBONES
COXCOMBY
COXSWAIN
CRESOXID
CRUCIFIX
DEFLEXED
DETOXIFY
DEXTRANE
DEXTRINE
DEXTROSE
DEXTROUS
DIAXONIC
DIPLEXER
DISANNEX
DIXENITE
DOXASTIC
DOXOLOGY
DUPLEXED
DUPLEXER
DUPLEXES
DUXELLES
DYSOREXY
DYSTAXIA
EFFLUXES
EPICALYX
EQUAIXED
ESSEXITE
ETHOXIDE
EUPRAXIA
EUTAXITE
EUXENITE
EXACTING
EXACTION
EXACTIVE
EXACUATE
EXALTATE
EXALTING
EXAMINED
EXAMINEE
EXAMINER
EXAMPLED
EXANTHEM
EXARCHAL
EXCALATE
EXCAMBER
EXCAVATE
EXCECATE
EXCEDENT
EXCEEDED
EXCELLED
EXCELSIN
EXCEPTED
EXCEPTER
EXCEPTIO
EXCERPTA
EXCHANGE
EXCIDING
EXCIPULE
EXCIRCLE
EXCISING
EXCISION
EXCITANT
EXCITATE
EXCITING
EXCITIVE
EXCITORY
EXCITRON
EXCLUDED
EXCLUDER
EXCRESCE
EXCRETAL
EXCRETED
EXCRETER
EXCRETES
EXCUBANT
EXCUDATE
EXCURSED
EXCURSUS
EXCURVED
EXCUSING
EXCUSIVE

EXCUSSED
EXCYSTED
EXECRATE
EXECUTED
EXECUTER
EXECUTOR
EXECUTRY
EXEGESES
EXEGESIS
EXEGETIC
EXEMPLAR
EXEMPLUM
EXEQUIAL
EXEQUIES
EXERCENT
EXERCISE
EXERESIS
EXERGUAL
EXERTING
EXERTION
EXERTIVE
EXFIGURE
EXHALANT
EXHALATE
EXHALING
EXHIBITS
EXHORTED
EXHORTER
EXHUMATE
EXHUMING
EXIGEANT
EXIGENCE
EXIGENCY
EXIGIBLE
EXIGUITY
EXIGUOUS
EXILARCH
EXIMIOUS
EXISTENT
EXISTING
EXITIOUS
EXOCLINE
EXOCOELE
EXODROMY
EXOGAMIC
EXOGENIC
EXOGRAPH
EXOLEMMA
EXOPHAGY
EXORABLE
EXORCISE
EXORCISM
EXORCIST
EXORCIZE
EXORDIAL
EXORDIUM
EXORDIZE
EXOSPERM
EXOSPORE
EXOSTOME
EXOSTRAE
EXOTERIC
EXOTHECA
EXOTOXIC
EXOTOXIN
EXPANDED
EXPANDER
EXPANSUM
EXPECTED
EXPECTER
EXPEDING
EXPEDITE
EXPELLED
EXPELLEE
EXPELLER
EXPENDED
EXPENDER
EXPENSES
EXPERTLY
EXPIABLE
EXPIATED
EXPIATOR
EXPILATE
EXPIRANT
EXPIRATE
EXPIRIES
EXPIRING
EXPLICIT
EXPLODED
EXPLODER
EXPLORED
EXPLORER
EXPONENT
EXPORTED
EXPORTER
EXPOSING
EXPOSURE
EXPULSER
EXPUNGED
EXPUNGER
EXRADIUS
EXRUPEAL
EXSCRIBE
EXSCRIPT
EXSECANT
EXSECTOR
EXSERTED
EXSHEATH
EXTENDED
EXTENDER
EXTENSOR
EXTENSUM
EXTERIOR
EXTERNAL
EXTERNAT
EXTERNUM
EXTISPEX
EXTOLLED
EXTOLLER
EXTORTED
EXTORTER
EXTRACTS
EXTRADOS
EXTRARED
EXTREMER
EXTREMES
EXTREMUM
EXTRORSE
EXTRUDED
EXTRUDER
EXTUBATE
EXTUSION
EXUDENCE
EXULTANT
EXULTING
EXUMBRAL
EXUNDATE
EXUVIATE
FABLIAUX
FIXATING
FIXATION
FIXATIVE
FIXATURE
FIXIDITY
FIXITIES
FLAXBIRD
FLAXBUSH
FLAXDROP
FLAXIEST
FLAXSEED
FLAXTAIL
FLAXWEED
FLAXWIFE
FLAXWORT
FLEXIBLE
FLEXIBLY
FLEXUOSE
FLEXUOUS
FLEXURAL
FLEXURED
FLUXIBLE
FLUXIBLY
FLUXROOT
FLUXWEED
FORNAXID
FOXBERRY
FOXGLOVE
FOXHOUND
FOXINESS
FRAXETIN
GALAXIAN
GALAXIAS
GENETRIX
GEOTAXIS
GLYOXIME
GREENWAX
HARUSPEX
HERITRIX
HEXAFOIL
HEXAFOOS
HEXAGLOT
HEXAGRAM
HEXAMINE
HEXAMMIN
HEXANDRY
HEXAPLAR
HEXAPODY
HEXARCHY
HEXASEME
HEXASTER
HEXYLENE
HOMAXIAL
HOMOTAXY
HORSEPOX
HYPAXIAL
INDEXING
INEXPERT
INFIXING
INFIXION
INFLEXED
INTERMIX
INTERREX
INTERSEX
INTERTEX
INTEXINE
JAMBEAUX
JANITRIX
JASPONYX
KETOXIME
LARYNXES
LAXATION
LAXATIVE
LEUCORYX
LIPOXENY
LITHOXYL
LIXIVIAL
LIXIVIUM
LOXOCOSM
LOXODONT
LOXOSOMA
LOXOTOMY
LUXATING
LUXATION
LUXURIES
LUXURIST
LUXURITY
MALAXAGE
MALAXATE
MALAXING
MANTEAUX
MASTAUXE
MATCHBOX
MATRIXES
MAXILLAE
MAXIMATE
MAXIMIST
MAXIMITE
MAXIMIZE
MAXIMUMS
MAZOPEXY
MEIOTAXY
MELAXUMA
MERETRIX
MEROXENE
METAXITE
METHOXYL
MILLILUX
MIREPOIX
MISOXENE
MISOXENY
MIXBLOOD
MIXERESS
MONAXIAL
MONOXIDE
MONOXYLA
MONOXYLE
MORCEAUX
MOROXITE
MORTREUX
MOUSSEUX
MUREXIDE
MYELAUXE
MYXAEMIA
MYXEDEMA
MYXINOID
MYXOCYTE
MYXOMATA
NEURAXIS
NEURAXON
NEXTNESS
NITROXYL
NIXTAMAL
NOSOTAXY
NOTAULIX
NOVATRIX
OCTUPLEX
OPOPANAX
ORTHODOX
OXALEMIA
OXALURIA
OXALURIC
OXAMIDIN
OXAMMITE
OXANILIC
OXHARROW
OXIDABLE
OXIDASIC
OXIDATED
OXIDATOR
OXIDIZED
OXIDIZER
OXPECKER
OXTONGUE
OXYAMINE
OXYAPHIA
OXYASTER
OXYBAPHA
OXYCRATE
OXYDIACT
OXYETHER
OXYETHYL
OXYGENIC
OXYGONAL
OXYMORON
OXYPHILE
OXYPHONY
OXYPHYTE
OXYRHINE
OXYSALT
OXYSTOME
OXYTOCIA
OXYTOCIC
OXYTOCIN
OXYUROUS
PAINTBOX
PANMIXIA
PARADOXY
PARALLAX
PARAXIAL
PAROXYSM
PAXILLAE
PAXILLAR
PAXILLUS
PEIXEREY
PEROXIDE
PHILODOX
PHORMINX
PLATEAUX
PLEXUSES
POLEAXER
POLYAXON
PONTIFEX
PREAXIAL
PRECIEUX
PREEXIST
PREFIXAL
PREFIXED
PREMIXED
PROLIXLY
PROTAXIS
PROTOXID
PROXENET
PROXENOS
PROXENUS
PROXIMAD
PROXIMAL
PROXYING
PYREXIAL
PYXIDATE
PYXIDIUM
QUINCUNX
QUIXOTIC
QUIXOTRY
REEXPORT
REFLEXED
REFLUXED
RELATRIX
RELAXANT
RELAXING
RETRAXIT
RIXATRIX
RIXDALER
RONDEAUX
ROULEAUX
SARDONYX
SAXATILE
SAXBOARD
SAXICOLE
SAXIFRAX
SAXONITE
SENATRIX
SEXANGLE
SEXENARY
SEXOLOGY
SEXTETTE
SEXTIPLY
SEXTOLET
SEXTUPLE
SEXTUPLY
SEXUALLY
SEXUPARA
SILEXITE
SILOXANE
SIXPENCE
SIXPENNY

SIXSCORE
SIXTIETH
SKATOXYL
SMALLPOX
SMOKEBOX
SNUFFBOX
SPHEXIDE
SPHINXES
SPINIFEX
SPINTEXT
SUBINDEX
SUBOXIDE
SUFFIXAL
SUFFIXED
SUPELLEX
SUPERFIX
SUPERSEX
SUPERTAX
SURTAXED
SWEATBOX
SWINEPOX
SYNAXARY
SYNTAXIS
SYNTEXIS
SYRINXES
TABLEAUX
TAXATION
TAXATIVE
TAXEATER
TAXEOPOD
TAXIARCH
TAXIAUTO
TAXINGLY
TAXODONT
TAXOLOGY
TAXONOMY
TAXPAYER
TEGUEXIN
TETRAXON
TETROXID
TEXGUINO
TEXTBOOK
TEXTILES
TEXTRINE
TEXTUARY
TEXTURAL
TEXTURED
THIOXENE
THORAXES
THYROXIN
TOADFLAX
TONNEAUX
TORTEAUX
TOUCHBOX
TOXAEMIA
TOXAEMIC
TOXICANT
TOXICATE
TOXICITY
TOXICOID
TOXODONT
TOXOLOGY
TOXOPHIL
TRACTRIX
TRANSFIX
TRIAXIAL
TRIOXIDE
TUXEDOES
UNEXPECT
UNEXPERT
UNIAXIAL
UNISEXED
UNSEXING
UROTOXIC
UROTOXIN
UXORIOUS
VENIPLEX
VERTEXES
VEXATION
VEXATORY
VEXILLUM
VIXENISH
VORTEXES
WAXBERRY
WAXINESS
WAXINGLY
WAXMAKER
WHEELBOX
WRAXLING
XANTHANE
XANTHATE
XANTHEIN
XANTHENE
XANTHIDE
XANTHINE
XANTHITE
XANTHOMA
XANTHONE
XANTHOUS
XENAGOGY
XENELASY
XENOCYST
XENODERM
XENOGAMY
XENOLITE
XENOLITH
XENOPHYA
XENOTIME
XERANSIS
XERANTIC
XERAPHIN
XERONATE
XEROPHIL
XEROSERE
XIPHIOID
XYLIDINE
XYLITONE
XYLOCARP
XYLOIDIN
XYLOLOGY
XYLOMATA
XYLORCIN
XYLOSIDE
XYLOTILE
XYLOTOMY
XYLYLENE
ZELATRIX
ZOOTOXIN

POSITIONAL ORDER LIST OF 8-LETTER WORDS

XANTHANE
XANTHATE
XANTHEIN
XANTHENE
XANTHIDE
XANTHINE
XANTHITE
XANTHOMA
XANTHONE
XANTHOUS
XENAGOGY
XENELASY
XENOCYST
XENODERM
XENOGAMY
XENOLITE
XENOLITH
XENOPHYA
XENOTIME
XERANSIS
XERANTIC
XERAPHIN
XERONATE
XEROPHIL
XEROSERE
XIPHIOID
XYLIDINE
XYLITONE
XYLOCARP
XYLOIDIN
XYLOLOGY
XYLOMATA
XYLORCIN
XYLOSIDE
XYLOTILE
XYLOTOMY
XYLYLENE

AXHAMMER
AXIALITY
AXIFUGAL
AXILEMMA
AXILLANT
AXILLARY
AXIOLITE
AXIOLOGY
AXLETREE
AXMAKING
AXMASTER
AXOFUGAL
AXOIDEAN
AXOLYSIS
AXOMETER
AXONEURE
AXOPETAL
AXOPHYTE
AXOPLASM
AXOSTYLE
EXACTING
EXACTION
EXACTIVE
EXACUATE
EXALTATE
EXALTING
EXAMINED
EXAMINEE
EXAMINER
EXAMPLED
EXANTHEM
EXARCHAL
EXCALATE
EXCAMBER
EXCAVATE
EXCECATE
EXCEDENT
EXCEEDED
EXCELLED
EXCELSIN
EXCEPTED
EXCEPTER
EXCEPTIO
EXCERPTA
EXCHANGE
EXCIDING
EXCIPULE
EXCIRCLE
EXCISING
EXCISION
EXCITANT
EXCITATE
EXCITING
EXCITIVE
EXCITORY
EXCITRON
EXCLUDED
EXCLUDER
EXCRESCE
EXCRETAL
EXCRETED
EXCRETER
EXCRETES
EXCUBANT
EXCUDATE
EXCURSED
EXCURSUS
EXCURVED
EXCUSING
EXCUSIVE
EXCUSSED
EXCYSTED
EXECRATE
EXECUTED
EXECUTER
EXECUTOR
EXECUTRY
EXEGESES
EXEGESIS
EXEGETIC
EXEMPLAR
EXEMPLUM
EXEQUIAL
EXEQUIES
EXERCENT
EXERCISE
EXERESIS
EXERGUAL
EXERTING
EXERTION
EXERTIVE
EXFIGURE
EXHALANT
EXHALATE
EXHALING
EXHIBITS
EXHORTED
EXHORTER
EXHUMATE
EXHUMING
EXIGEANT
EXIGENCE
EXIGENCY
EXIGIBLE
EXIGUITY
EXIGUOUS
EXILARCH
EXIMIOUS
EXISTENT
EXISTING
EXITIOUS
EXOCLINE
EXOCOELE
EXODROMY
EXOGAMIC
EXOGENIC
EXOGRAPH
EXOLEMMA
EXOPHAGY
EXORABLE
EXORCISE
EXORCISM
EXORCIST
EXORCIZE
EXORDIAL
EXORDIUM
EXORDIZE
EXOSPERM
EXOSPORE
EXOSTOME
EXOSTRAE
EXOTERIC
EXOTHECA
EXOTOXIC
EXOTOXIN
EXPANDED
EXPANDER
EXPANSUM
EXPECTED
EXPECTER
EXPEDING
EXPEDITE
EXPELLED
EXPELLEE
EXPELLER
EXPENDED
EXPENDER
EXPENSES
EXPERTLY
EXPIABLE
EXPIATED
EXPIATOR
EXPILATE
EXPIRANT
EXPIRATE
EXPIRIES
EXPIRING
EXPLICIT
EXPLODED
EXPLODER
EXPLORED
EXPLORER
EXPONENT
EXPORTED
EXPORTER
EXPOSING
EXPOSURE
EXPULSER
EXPUNGED
EXPUNGER
EXRADIUS
EXRUPEAL
EXSCRIBE
EXSCRIPT
EXSECANT
EXSECTOR
EXSERTED
EXSHEATH
EXTENDED
EXTENDER
EXTENSOR
EXTENSUM
EXTERIOR
EXTERNAL
EXTERNAT
EXTERNUM
EXTISPEX

EXTOLLED
EXTOLLER
EXTORTED
EXTORTER
EXTRACTS
EXTRADOS
EXTRARED
EXTREMER
EXTREMES
EXTREMUM
EXTRORSE
EXTRUDED
EXTRUDER
EXTUBATE
EXTUSION
EXUDENCE
EXULTANT
EXULTING
EXUMBRAL
EXUNDATE
EXUVIATE
OXALEMIA
OXALURIA
OXALURIC
OXAMIDIN
OXAMMITE
OXANILIC
OXHARROW
OXIDABLE
OXIDASIC
OXIDATED
OXIDATOR
OXIDIZED
OXIDIZER
OXPECKER
OXTONGUE
OXYAMINE
OXYAPHIA
OXYASTER
OXYBAPHA
OXYCRATE
OXYDIACT
OXYETHER
OXYETHYL
OXYGENIC
OXYGONAL
OXYMORON
OXYPHILE
OXYPHONY
OXYPHYTE
OXYRHINE
OXYSALT
OXYSTOME
OXYTOCIA
OXYTOCIC
OXYTOCIN
OXYUROUS
UXORIOUS

ACXOYATL
AUXILIAR
AUXILIUM
AUXIMONE
AUXOBODY
AUXOCYTE
AUXOLOGY
BIXBYITE
BOXBERRY
BOXBOARD
BOXTHORN
COXALGIA
COXALGIC
COXBONES
COXCOMBY
COXSWAIN
DEXTRANE
DEXTRINE
DEXTROSE
DEXTROUS
DIXENITE
DOXASTIC
DOXOLOGY
DUXELLES
EUXENITE
FIXATING
FIXATION
FIXATIVE
FIXATURE
FIXIDITY
FIXITIES
FOXBERRY
FOXGLOVE
FOXHOUND
FOXINESS
HEXAFOIL
HEXAFOOS
HEXAGLOT
HEXAGRAM
HEXAMINE
HEXAMMIN
HEXANDRY
HEXAPLAR
HEXAPODY
HEXARCHY
HEXASEME
HEXASTER
HEXYLENE
LAXATION
LAXATIVE
LIXIVIAL
LIXIVIUM
LOXOCOSM
LOXODONT
LOXOSOMA
LOXOTOMY
LUXATING
LUXATION
LUXURIES
LUXURIST
LUXURITY
MAXILLAE
MAXIMATE
MAXIMIST
MAXIMITE
MAXIMIZE
MAXIMUMS
MIXBLOOD
MIXERESS
MYXAEMIA
MYXEDEMA
MYXINOID
MYXOCYTE
MYXOMATA
NEXTNESS
NIXTAMAL
PAXILLAE
PAXILLAR
PAXILLUS
PYXIDATE
PYXIDIUM
RIXATRIX
RIXDALER
SAXATILE
SAXBOARD
SAXICOLE
SAXIFRAX
SAXONITE
SEXANGLE
SEXENARY
SEXOLOGY
SEXTETTE
SEXTIPLY
SEXTOLET
SEXTUPLE
SEXTUPLY
SEXUALLY
SEXUPARA
SIXPENCE
SIXPENNY
SIXSCORE
SIXTIETH
TAXATION
TAXATIVE
TAXEATER
TAXEOPOD
TAXIARCH
TAXIAUTO
TAXINGLY
TAXODONT
TAXOLOGY
TAXONOMY
TAXPAYER
TEXGUINO
TEXTBOOK
TEXTILES
TEXTRINE
TEXTUARY
TEXTURAL
TEXTURED
TOXAEMIA
TOXAEMIC
TOXICANT
TOXICATE
TOXICITY
TOXICOID
TOXODONT
TOXOLOGY
TOXOPHIL
TUXEDOES
VEXATION
VEXATORY
VEXILLUM
VIXENISH
WAXBERRY
WAXINESS
WAXINGLY
WAXMAKER

ALEXINIC
ANOXEMIA
ANOXEMIC
APOXESIS
COEXTEND
DIAXONIC
FLAXBIRD
FLAXBUSH
FLAXDROP
FLAXIEST
FLAXSEED
FLAXTAIL
FLAXWEED
FLAXWIFE
FLAXWORT
FLEXIBLE
FLEXIBLY
FLEXUOSE
FLEXUOUS
FLEXURAL
FLEXURED
FLUXIBLE
FLUXIBLY
FLUXROOT
FLUXWEED
FRAXETIN
INEXPERT
PEIXEREY
PLEXUSES
PROXENET
PROXENOS
PROXENUS
PROXIMAD
PROXIMAL
PROXYING
QUIXOTIC
QUIXOTRY
REEXPORT
UNEXPECT
UNEXPERT
WRAXLING

ADMIXING
AFFIXING
AFFIXION
ALDOXIME
ALKOXIDE
ANAUXITE
ANNEXING
ANNEXION
ANNEXIVE
ANNEXURE
BINOXIDE
BISEXUAL
CACOXENE
CEROXYLE
DETOXIFY
ESSEXITE
ETHOXIDE
EUTAXITE
GALAXIAN
GALAXIAS
GLYOXIME
HOMAXIAL
HYPAXIAL
INDEXING
INFIXING
INFIXION
INTEXINE
KETOXIME
LIPOXENY
MALAXAGE
MALAXATE
MALAXING
MELAXUMA
MEROXENE
METAXITE
MISOXENE
MISOXENY
MONAXIAL
MONOXIDE
MONOXYLA
MONOXYLE
MOROXITE
MUREXIDE
PARAXIAL
PAROXYSM
PEROXIDE
PREAXIAL
PREEXIST
PYREXIAL
RELAXANT
RELAXING
SILEXITE
SILOXANE
SPHEXIDE
SUBOXIDE
SYNAXARY
THIOXENE
TRIAXIAL
TRIOXIDE
UNIAXIAL
UNSEXING

ACETOXIM
ACETOXYL
AGALAXIA
AMIDOXYL
AMPLEXUS
ANATEXIS
ANATOXIN
ANOREXIA
APODIXIS
APOMIXIS
APPRAXIC
APYREXIA
ASPHYXIA
ATARAXIA
ATARAXIC
BETWIXEN
BOLLIXED
CACHEXIA
CACHEXIC
CARBOXYL
CATHEXIS
CAUDEXES
CERVIXES
CLIMAXED
COMMIXED
CONFIXED
CONNEXES
CONNEXUS
CONVEXED
CONVEXLY
CRESOXID
DEFLEXED
DIPLEXER
DUPLEXED
DUPLEXER
DUPLEXES
DYSTAXIA
EFFLUXES
EQUAIXED
EUPRAXIA
EXOTOXIC
EXOTOXIN
FORNAXID
GEOTAXIS
INFLEXED
LARYNXES
LITHOXYL
MATRIXES
METHOXYL
NEURAXIS
NEURAXON
NITROXYL
PANMIXIA
POLEAXER
POLYAXON
PREFIXAL
PREFIXED
PREMIXED
PROLIXLY
PROTAXIS
PROTOXID
REFLEXED
REFLUXED
RETRAXIT
SKATOXYL
SPHINXES
SUFFIXAL
SUFFIXED
SURTAXED
SYNTAXIS
SYNTEXIS
SYRINXES
TEGUEXIN
TETRAXON
TETROXID
THORAXES
THYROXIN
UNISEXED
UROTOXIC
UROTOXIN
VERTEXES
VORTEXES
ZOOTOXIN

ANTEFIXA
APOPLEXY
BANDBOXY
BAROTAXY
BREAKAXE
BROADAXE
CACODOXY
CACOMIXL
CHRONAXY
COLOPEXY
COLTPIXY
DYSOREXY
HOMOTAXY
MASTAUXE
MAZOPEXY
MEIOTAXY
MYELAUXE
NOSOTAXY
PARADOXY
SPINTEXT
ADJUTRIX
ANTHELIX
APPENDIX
AVIATRIX
BANDEAUX
BICONVEX
BILLYWIX
BREADBOX
CARNIFEX
CHAFEWAX
CHAFFWAX
CHAPEAUX
CHATEAUX
CICATRIX
CLAVILUX
CONTUMAX
COUTEAUX
CRUCIFIX
DISANNEX
EPICALYX
EXTISPEX
FABLIAUX
GENETRIX
GREENWAX
HARUSPEX
HERITRIX
HORSEPOX
INTERMIX
INTERREX
INTERSEX
INTERTEX
JAMBEAUX
JANITRIX
JASPONYX
LEUCORYX
MANTEAUX
MATCHBOX
MERETRIX
MILLILUX
MIREPOIX
MORCEAUX
MORTREUX
MOUSSEUX
NOTAULIX
NOVATRIX
OCTUPLEX
OPOPANAX
ORTHODOX
PAINTBOX
PARALLAX
PHILODOX
PHORMINX
PLATEAUX
PONTIFEX
PRECIEUX
QUINCUNX
RELATRIX
RIXATRIX
RONDEAUX
ROULEAUX
SARDONYX
SAXIFRAX
SENATRIX
SMALLPOX
SMOKEBOX
SNUFFBOX
SPINIFEX
SUBINDEX
SUPELLEX
SUPERFIX
SUPERSEX
SUPERTAX
SWEATBOX
SWINEPOX
TABLEAUX
TOADFLAX
TONNEAUX
TORTEAUX
TOUCHBOX
TRACTRIX
TRANSFIX
VENIPLEX
WHEELBOX
ZELATRIX

SCORING ORDER LIST OF 8-LETTER WORDS

31
MAZOPEXY

29
CHAFFWAX

28
MAXIMIZE

27
JASPONYX
QUIXOTRY

26
CHAFEWAX
COXCOMBY
EXORCIZE
HEXARCHY
JAMBEAUX
OXIDIZED
OXYPHONY
OXYPHYTE
QUINCUNX
QUIXOTIC

25
EQUAIXED
EXORDIZE
MYXOCYTE
OXIDIZER
OXYBAPHA

24
EXEQUIAL
EXEQUIES
EXOPHAGY
FLAXWIFE
HEXAPODY
MATCHBOX
OXYETHYL
WAXMAKER
ZELATRIX
ZOOTOXIN

23
ADJUTRIX
ASPHYXIA
AXOPHYTE
BANDBOXY
BILLYWIX
CACODOXY
CHRONAXY
CONVEXLY
FLAXBUSH
FLEXIBLY
FLUXIBLY
FOXBERRY
HOMOTAXY
HYPAXIAL
METHOXYL
MYXEDEMA
OXPECKER
OXYAPHIA
OXYPHILE
PYXIDIUM
SMOKEBOX
SNUFFBOX
WAXBERRY
WHEELBOX
XENOPHYA
XYLOTOMY

22
AFFIXING
APOPLEXY
AXHAMMER
AXMAKING
BICONVEX
BIXBYITE
BOXBERRY
CACHEXIA
CARBOXYL
CHAPEAUX
COLOPEXY
COLTPIXY
COMMIXED
CRUCIFIX
DETOXIFY
DYSOREXY
EPICALYX
FIXIDITY
FLAXWEED
FLUXWEED
FOXGLOVE
FOXHOUND
HEXAMMIN
HEXANDRY
JANITRIX
MYXAEMIA
MYXOMATA
OXYTOCIC
PAROXYSM
PHORMINX
SKATOXYL
SUFFIXED
TOUCHBOX
WAXINGLY
XYLOCARP
XYLOLOGY

21
AFFIXION
AMIDOXYL
APPRAXIC
AUXOBODY
BREAKAXE
CACHEXIC
CACOMIXL
CONFIXED
CONVEXED
EFFLUXES
EXCAMBER
EXCHANGE
EXCURVED
EXCYSTED
EXEMPLUM
EXHUMING
EXIGENCY
EXODROMY
EXOGRAPH
EXSHEATH
FIXATIVE
FLAXBIRD
FLAXDROP
FLAXWORT
GLYOXIME
HEXAFOIL
HEXAFOOS
HEXAGRAM
HEXYLENE
KETOXIME
LITHOXYL
MYXINOID
OXHARROW
OXYDIACT
OXYETHER
OXYGENIC
OXYRHINE
PARADOXY
PHILODOX
PREFIXED
PROXYING
PYXIDATE
SPHEXIDE
SUFFIXAL
SYNAXARY
TEXTBOOK
THYROXIN
VEXATORY
VIXENISH
XENOGAMY
XIPHIOID
XYLYLENE

20
ACETOXYL
ACXOYATL
ALKOXIDE
APPENDIX
APYREXIA
AUXOCYTE
BAROTAXY
BETWIXEN
BOXBOARD
BOXTHORN
BREADBOX
CARNIFEX
CATHEXIS
CEROXYLE
CERVIXES
CHATEAUX
CLAVILUX
CLIMAXED
COXALGIC
COXSWAIN
DEFLEXED
DOXOLOGY
EXACTIVE
EXAMPLED
EXANTHEM
EXARCHAL
EXCAVATE
EXCEPTED
EXCITIVE
EXCITORY
EXCUSIVE
EXECUTRY
EXHIBITS
EXHUMATE
EXILARCH
EXOGAMIC
EXOTHECA
EXPECTED
EXPERTLY
FABLIAUX
FLEXIBLE
FLUXIBLE
HARUSPEX
HEXAMINE
HEXAPLAR
HEXASEME
HOMAXIAL
HORSEPOX
LEUCORYX
LIPOXENY
LIXIVIUM
LOXOTOMY
MEIOTAXY
MISOXENY
MIXBLOOD
MONOXYLA
MONOXYLE
MYELAUXE
OXYAMINE
OXYCRATE
OXYMORON
OXYSTOME
OXYTOCIA
OXYTOCIN
PEIXEREY
POLYAXON
PONTIFEX
PREFIXAL
PREMIXED
PROLIXLY
PROXIMAD
PYREXIAL
SEXTIPLY
SEXTUPLY
SIXPENNY
SPHINXES
SPINIFEX
SUPERFIX
SWEATBOX
SWINEPOX
TAXIARCH
TAXONOMY
TAXPAYER
TOXICITY
TOXOPHIL

VENIPLEX
VEXILLUM
XANTHOMA
XENAGOGY
XENOCYST
XERAPHIN
XEROPHIL
XYLOMATA
XYLORCIN

19
ACETOXIM
ADMIXING
AMPLEXUS
ANOXEMIC
APOMIXIS
AUXOLOGY
AXIFUGAL
AXILEMMA
AXIOLOGY
AXOFUGAL
AXOPLASM
CACOXENE
CICATRIX
CONTUMAX
COXBONES
DUPLEXED
DYSTAXIA
ETHOXIDE
EXCECATE
EXCEEDED
EXCEPTER
EXCEPTIO
EXCERPTA
EXCIDING
EXCIPULE
EXCIRCLE
EXCLUDED
EXCRESCE
EXCUBANT
EXEMPLAR
EXFIGURE
EXHALING
EXHORTED
EXIGUITY
EXOLEMMA
EXORCISM
EXOSPERM
EXPANDED
EXPANSUM
EXPECTER
EXPEDING
EXPENDED
EXPIABLE
EXPLICIT
EXPLODED
EXPUNGED
EXSCRIBE
EXSCRIPT
EXTREMUM
EXUMBRAL
FIXATING
FLAXSEED
FLEXURED
FORNAXID
GREENWAX
HEXAGLOT
INFIXING
INFLEXED
LOXOCOSM
MAXIMATE
MAXIMIST
MAXIMITE
MELAXUMA
MIREPOIX
MORCEAUX

OCTUPLEX
OPOPANAX
ORTHODOX
OXAMMITE
OXYGONAL
PAINTBOX
PANMIXIA
PRECIEUX
PROXIMAL
REFLEXED
REFLUXED
SARDONYX
SEXOLOGY
SIXPENCE
SMALLPOX
TAXINGLY
TAXOLOGY
TOADFLAX
TOXAEMIC
TOXOLOGY
UNEXPECT
WRAXLING
XANTHIDE
XYLIDINE
XYLOIDIN
XYLOSIDE

18
ALDOXIME
ANNEXIVE
ANTEFIXA
ANTHELIX
APODIXIS
AVIATRIX
AXIALITY
AXILLARY
AXOLYSIS
AXOSTYLE
BANDEAUX
BINOXIDE
BOLLIXED
BROADAXE
CAUDEXES
COEXTEND
COXALGIA
CRESOXID
DIAXONIC
DIPLEXER
DOXASTIC
DUPLEXER
DUPLEXES
EXACTING
EXAMINED
EXCEDENT
EXCELLED
EXCISING
EXCITING
EXCLUDER
EXCRETED
EXCUDATE
EXCURSED
EXCUSING
EXCUSSED
EXECUTED
EXEGETIC
EXERTIVE
EXHALANT
EXHALATE
EXHORTER
EXIGENCE
EXIGIBLE
EXOGENIC
EXORDIUM
EXPANDER
EXPEDITE
EXPELLED

EXPENDER
EXPIATED
EXPIRING
EXPLODER
EXPLORED
EXPORTED
EXPOSING
EXPUNGER
EXUDENCE
EXUVIATE
FIXATION
FIXATURE
FIXITIES
FLAXIEST
FLAXTAIL
FLEXUOSE
FLEXUOUS
FLEXURAL
FLUXROOT
FOXINESS
FRAXETIN
HERITRIX
HEXASTER
INFIXION
LARYNXES
LAXATIVE
LIXIVIAL
LUXURITY
MALAXAGE
MALAXING
MAXIMUMS
MONOXIDE
MUREXIDE
NITROXYL
NOSOTAXY
NOVATRIX
OXAMIDIN
OXIDABLE
OXIDASIC
OXYASTER
OXYUROUS
PEROXIDE
PROTOXID
SAXBOARD
SEXENARY
SEXUALLY
SIXTIETH
SUBINDEX
SUBOXIDE
SYNTAXIS
SYNTEXIS
SYRINXES
TAXATIVE
TAXEOPOD
TEXTUARY
THIOXENE
THORAXES
TOXICOID
TRANSFIX
VERTEXES
VEXATION
VORTEXES
WAXINESS
XANTHANE
XANTHATE
XANTHEIN
XANTHENE
XANTHINE
XANTHITE
XANTHONE
XANTHOUS
XENELASY
XENODERM
XENOLITH
XYLITONE
XYLOTILE

17
ALEXINIC
ANOXEMIA
APOXESIS
ATARAXIC
AUXILIUM
AUXIMONE
AXMASTER
AXOMETER
AXOPETAL
BISEXUAL
CONNEXES
CONNEXUS
COUTEAUX
EUPRAXIA
EXACTION
EXACUATE
EXAMINEE
EXAMINER
EXCALATE
EXCELSIN
EXCISION
EXCITANT
EXCITATE
EXCITRON
EXCRETAL
EXCRETER
EXCRETES
EXCURSUS
EXECRATE
EXECUTER
EXECUTOR
EXERCENT
EXERCISE
EXIMIOUS
EXOCLINE
EXOCOELE
EXORABLE
EXORCISE
EXORCIST
EXOSPORE
EXOSTOME
EXOTERIC
EXPELLEE
EXPELLER
EXPENSES
EXPIATOR
EXPILATE
EXPIRANT
EXPIRATE
EXPIRIES
EXPLORER
EXPONENT
EXPORTER
EXPOSURE
EXPULSER
EXRUPEAL
EXSECANT
EXSECTOR
EXTENDED
EXTENSUM
EXTERNUM
EXTRACTS
EXTREMER
EXTREMES
EXTRUDED
EXTUBATE
INDEXING
INEXPERT
INTERMIX
LOXOSOMA
MALAXATE
MANTEAUX
MASTAUXE
MATRIXES
MAXILLAE

MERETRIX
MEROXENE
METAXITE
MILLILUX
MISOXENE
MIXERESS
MONAXIAL
MOROXITE
MORTREUX
MOUSSEUX
NIXTAMAL
OXALEMIA
OXALURIC
OXANILIC
OXIDATED
OXYSALT
PARALLAX
PARAXIAL
PAXILLAE
PAXILLAR
PAXILLUS
PLATEAUX
PLEXUSES
POLEAXER
PREAXIAL
PREEXIST
PROTAXIS
PROXENET
PROXENOS
PROXENUS
REEXPORT
SAXICOLE
SAXIFRAX
SEXTUPLE
SEXUPARA
SIXSCORE
SPINTEXT
SUPELLEX
SUPERSEX
SUPERTAX
TABLEAUX
TOXAEMIA
TOXICANT
TOXICATE
TRACTRIX
UNEXPERT
UROTOXIC
XENOTIME
XERANTIC

16
AGALAXIA
ANNEXING
AXOIDEAN
DEXTRANE
DEXTRINE
DEXTROSE
DEXTROUS
DISANNEX
DIXENITE
DUXELLES
EXALTING
EXEGESES
EXEGESIS
EXERGUAL
EXERTING
EXIGEANT
EXIGUOUS
EXISTING
EXORDIAL
EXOTOXIC
EXRADIUS
EXSERTED
EXTENDER
EXTISPEX
EXTOLLED

EXTORTED
EXTRADOS
EXTRARED
EXTRUDER
EXULTING
EXUNDATE
GALAXIAN
GALAXIAS
GENETRIX
GEOTAXIS
LOXODONT
LUXATING
OXIDATOR
OXTONGUE
RELAXING
RIXDALER
RONDEAUX
SEXANGLE
SURTAXED
TAXODONT
TEGUEXIN
TETROXID
TEXGUINO
TEXTURED
TOXODONT
TRIOXIDE
TUXEDOES
UNISEXED
UNSEXING

15

ANATEXIS
ANATOXIN
ANAUXITE
ANNEXION
ANNEXURE
ANOREXIA
ATARAXIA
AUXILIAR
AXILLANT
AXIOLITE
AXLETREE
AXONEURE
ESSEXITE
EUTAXITE
EUXENITE
EXALTATE
EXERESIS
EXERTION
EXISTENT
EXITIOUS
EXOSTRAE
EXTENSOR
EXTERIOR
EXTERNAL
EXTERNAT
EXTOLLER
EXTORTER
EXTRORSE
EXTUSION
EXULTANT
INTERREX
INTERSEX
INTERTEX
INTEXINE
LAXATION
LUXATION
LUXURIES
LUXURIST
NEURAXIS
NEURAXON
NEXTNESS
NOTAULIX
OXALURIA
RELATRIX
RELAXANT
RETRAXIT
RIXATRIX
ROULEAUX
SAXATILE
SAXONITE
SENATRIX
SEXTETTE
SEXTOLET
SILEXITE
SILOXANE
TAXATION
TAXEATER
TAXIAUTO
TETRAXON
TEXTILES
TEXTRINE
TEXTURAL
TONNEAUX
TORTEAUX
TRIAXIAL
UNIAXIAL
UROTOXIN
UXORIOUS
XENOLITE
XERANSIS
XERONATE
XEROSERE

14

EXOTOXIN

ALPHABETICAL LIST OF 9-LETTER WORDS

ABOIDEAUX
ACETOXIME
ADMIXTION
ADMIXTURE
ADNEXITIS
AEROTAXIS
AFFIXTURE
AFFLUXION
AGITATRIX
ALLOXANIC
ALLOXURIC
AMIDOXIME
AMPHIOXUS
AMYOTAXIA
ANAPTYXIS
ANNEXABLE
ANNEXMENT
ANOXAEMIA
ANOXAEMIC
ANTECOXAL
ANTEFIXAL
ANTEFIXES
ANTHOTAXY
ANTHROXAN
ANTIHELIX
ANXIETIES
ANXIETUDE
ANXIOUSLY
APOSTAXIS
APROSEXIA
APYREXIAL
ASEXUALLY
ASPHYXIAL
ASPHYXIED
ASSERTRIX
ATLOAXOID
AUTOTOXIC
AUTOTOXIN
AUXETICAL
AUXILIARY
AUXILIATE
AUXOBLAST
AUXOFLORE
AUXOFLUOR
AUXOGRAPH
AUXOMETER
AUXOSPORE
AUXOTONIC
AXBREAKER
AXEMASTER
AXILEMMAS
AXIOLITIC
AXIOMATIC
AXIOPISTY
AXLESMITH
AXMANSHIP
AXONEURON
AXOPODIUM
AZOXONIUM
BAROTAXIS
BAROXYTON
BASIFIXED
BAUXITITE
BIAXIALLY
BISECTRIX
BISEXUOUS
BIXACEOUS
BOISSEAUX
BOLLIXING
BOXHOLDER
BOXKEEPER
BOXWALLAH
BUTTERBOX
BUXACEOUS
BUXERRIES
BUXOMNESS
CACOMIXLE
CALCIPEXY
CANDLEBOX
CARBOXIDE
CARDIAUXE
CATALEXIS
CATAPLEXY
CAULOTAXY
CHEMOTAXY
CHRONAXIA
CHRONAXIE
CICUTOXIN
CLIMAXING
COAXATION
COAXIALLY
COAXINGLY
COLOPEXIA
COMMIXING
COMPLEXLY
COMPLEXUS
CONFIXING
CONNEXION
CONNEXITY
CONNEXIVA
CONNEXIVE
CONVEXITY
COXCOMBRY
COXODYNIA
CRESOXIDE
CYTOTAXIS
CYTOTOXIC
CYTOTOXIN
DECOMPLEX
DEFLEXING
DEFLEXION
DEFLEXURE
DEFLUXION
DENDRAXON
DEOXIDIZE
DEXTERITY
DEXTEROUS
DEXTRALLY
DEXTRORSE
DIAPLEXUS
DIAZEUXIS
DICTATRIX
DIGITOXIN
DIHYDROXY
DIMETHOXY
DIRECTRIX
DORSIFLEX
DRUXINESS
DUPLEXING
DUPLEXITY
ELIXATION
EMPHRAXIS
ENDOMIXIS
ENDOTOXIC
ENDOTOXIN
ENTERAUXE
ENTREDEUX
EPAXIALLY
EPIPLEXIS
EPISTAXIS
EPITOXOID
EPIZEUXIS
EUTAXITIC
EXACTABLE
EXACTMENT
EXACTNESS
EXADVERSO
EXAGITATE
EXAIRESIS
EXALTEDLY
EXAMINANT
EXAMINATE
EXAMINING
EXAMPLING
EXANIMATE
EXANTHEMA
EXANTLATE
EXARATION
EXARCHATE
EXARCHIST
EXCAMBION
EXCARNATE
EXCAUDATE
EXCAVATED
EXCAVATOR
EXCEEDING
EXCELENTE
EXCELLENT
EXCELLING
EXCELSIOR
EXCENTRAL
EXCENTRIC
EXCEPTANT
EXCEPTING
EXCEPTION
EXCEPTIVE
EXCERPTED
EXCERPTOR
EXCESSIVE
EXCESSMAN
EXCESSMEN
EXCHANGED
EXCHANGER
EXCHEQUER
EXCIPIENT
EXCIPULAR
EXCIPULUM
EXCISABLE
EXCISEMAN
EXCISEMEN
EXCITABLE
EXCITABLY
EXCITANCY
EXCITATOR
EXCITEDLY
EXCLAIMED
EXCLAIMER
EXCLUDING
EXCLUSION
EXCLUSIVE
EXCLUSORY
EXCOCTION
EXCORIATE
EXCREMENT
EXCRETING
EXCRETION
EXCRETIVE
EXCRETORY
EXCULPATE
EXCURRENT
EXCURSING
EXCURSION
EXCURSIVE
EXCURVATE
EXCUSABLE

EXCUSABLY
EXCUSATOR
EXCUSSING
EXECRABLE
EXECRABLY
EXECRATED
EXECRATOR
EXECUTANT
EXECUTING
EXECUTION
EXECUTIVE
EXECUTORY
EXECUTRIX
EXEGETICS
EXEGETIST
EXEMPLARY
EXEMPLIFY
EXEMPTILE
EXEMPTION
EXEMPTIVE
EXEQUATUR
EXERCISED
EXERCISER
EXERCISES
EXERCITOR
EXFODIATE
EXFOLIATE
EXHALABLE
EXHAUSTED
EXHAUSTER
EXHIBITED
EXHIBITOR
EXHORTING
EXHUMATED
EXHUMATOR
EXIGEANTE
EXIGENTER
EXIGENTLY
EXINANITE
EXISTENCE
EXOCARDIA
EXOCLINAL
EXOCOELAR
EXOCOELIC
EXOCOELOM
EXOCOELUM
EXOCULATE
EXOCYCLIC
EXODERMIS
EXODONTIA
EXODROMIC
EXOENZYME
EXOGAMOUS
EXOGENOUS
EXONERATE
EXONEURAL
EXOPATHIC
EXOPHORIA
EXOPHORIA
EXOPHORIC
EXOPODITE
EXORBITAL
EXORCISED
EXORCISER
EXORCIZED
EXORCIZER
EXORDIUMS
EXORGANIC
EXOSEPSIS
EXOSMOSIS
EXOSMOTIC
EXOSPHERE
EXOSPORAL
EXOSTOSED
EXOSTOSES
EXOSTOSIS
EXOSTOTIC

EXOTERICS
EXOTHECAL
EXOTICISM
EXOTICIST
EXOTICITY
EXOTROPIA
EXPALPATE
EXPANDING
EXPANSILE
EXPANSION
EXPANSIVE
EXPANSURE
EXPATIATE
EXPECTANT
EXPECTING
EXPECTIVE
EXPEDIATE
EXPEDIENT
EXPEDITED
EXPEDITER
EXPEDITOR
EXPELLANT
EXPELLENT
EXPELLING
EXPENDING
EXPENSIVE
EXPERIENT
EXPERTISE
EXPIATING
EXPIATION
EXPIATIST
EXPIATIVE
EXPIATORY
EXPILATOR
EXPIRATOR
EXPISCATE
EXPLAINED
EXPLAINER
EXPLANATE
EXPLEMENT
EXPLETIVE
EXPLETORY
EXPLICATE
EXPLODENT
EXPLODING
EXPLOITED
EXPLOITER
EXPLORING
EXPLOSION
EXPLOSIVE
EXPONENCE
EXPONENTS
EXPONIBLE
EXPORTING
EXPOSITOR
EXPOUNDED
EXPOUNDER
EXPRESSED
EXPRESSER
EXPRESSLY
EXPROBATE
EXPUITION
EXPULSION
EXPULSIVE
EXPULSORY
EXPUNGING
EXPURGATE
EXQUISITE
EXSCINDED
EXSECTILE
EXSECTION
EXSERTILE
EXSERTING
EXSERTION
EXSICCATE
EXSOMATIC
EXSPUTORY

EXSTROPHY
EXSUCCOUS
EXSUCTION
EXSURGENT
EXTEMPORE
EXTENDING
EXTENSILE
EXTENSION
EXTENSITY
EXTENSIVE
EXTENUATE
EXTERMINE
EXTERNATE
EXTERNIZE
EXTERNIZE
EXTINCTOR
EXTIRPATE
EXTISPICY
EXTOLLING
EXTOLMENT
EXTORSIVE
EXTORTING
EXTORTION
EXTORTIVE
EXTRABOLD
EXTRACTED
EXTRACTOR
EXTRADITE
EXTRALITE
EXTRALITY
EXTRANEAN
EXTRAVERT
EXTREMELY
EXTREMEST
EXTREMISM
EXTREMIST
EXTREMITY
EXTRICATE
EXTRINSIC
EXTRORSAL
EXTROVERT
EXTRUDING
EXTRUSILE
EXTRUSION
EXTRUSIVE
EXTRUSORY
EXUBERANT
EXUBERATE
EXUDATION
EXUDATIVE
EXUDATORY
EXULTANCY
EXULULATE
EXUVIABLE
EXUVIATED
FIXEDNESS
FLAMBEAUX
FLAXBOARD
FLAXWENCH
FLAXWOMAN
FLEXILITY
FLEXIONAL
FLUMMOXED
FLUXATION
FLUXILITY
FLUXIONAL
FLUXMETER
FOXTAILED
FUNDATRIX
GLYOXALIC
GLYOXYLIC
GONOCALYX
HEMIAUXIN
HEMOTOXIC
HEMOTOXIN
HEPTOXIDE
HETERODOX

HEXABASIC
HEXABIOSE
HEXACHORD
HEXACOLIC
HEXADECYL
HEXADIENE
HEXADIINE
HEXADIYNE
HEXAGONAL
HEXAHEDRA
HEXAMERAL
HEXAMERON
HEXAMETER
HEXAMMINE
HEXANDRIC
HEXAPLOID
HEXASEMIC
HEXASTICH
HEXASTIGM
HEXATHLON
HEXATOMIC
HOAXPROOF
HOMOTAXIS
HYDROXIDE
HYPOTAXIA
HYPOTAXIC
HYPOTAXIS
IMMIXTURE
IMPERMIXT
IMPOSTRIX
INCOMPLEX
INDEXICAL
INDOXYLIC
INEXACTLY
INEXPIATE
INEXPRESS
INFLEXION
INFLEXIVE
INFLUXION
INFLUXIVE
INMIXTURE
INNOXIOUS
INOXIDIZE
INTERAXAL
INTERAXIS
INTERMIXT
INTEXTINE
INTEXTURE
INTROFLEX
ISOXAZOLE
JUXTAPOSE
KATAPLEXY
KENOTOXIN
KOSOTOXIN
LATEXOSIS
LEPOTHRIX
LEUCOXENE
LEXICALIC
LIPOPEXIA
LITHOXYLE
LIXIVIATE
LIXIVIOUS
LOOMFIXER
LOXOCLASE
LOXODROME
LOXODROMY
LUXURIANT
LUXURIATE
LUXURIOUS
MALAXABLE
MALAXATOR
MALPRAXIS
MASTOPEXY
MAXILLARY
MAXIMALLY
MAXIMIZED
MAXIMIZER

MEDIATRIX
MEDIFIXED
MENOXENIA
MESAXONIC
MESOXALIC
MESOXALYL
METATAXIC
METATAXIS
METAXYLEM
MIXTIFORM
MONAXONIC
MONOXYLIC
MONOXYLON
MULTIPLEX
MYELOPLAX
MYXAMOEBA
MYXEDEMIC
MYXOEDEMA
MYXOINOMA
MYXOMYOMA
MYXOPODIA
MYXORRHEA
MYXOSPORE
MYXOTHECA
NEPHRAUXE
NEURATAXY
NEURAXONE
NOXIOUSLY
NULLIPLEX
OBNOXIETY
OBNOXIOUS
OBSTETRIX
OPERATRIX
ORTHODOXY
OVEREXERT
OVERSEXED
OVERTAXED
OXALAEMIA
OXALURATE
OXAMIDINE
OXANILATE
OXANILIDE
OXBERRIES
OXDIAZOLE
OXIDATING
OXIDATION
OXIDATIVE
OXIDIZING
OXIMATION
OXMANSHIP
OXYBENZYL
OXYDACTYL
OXYGENANT
OXYGENATE
OXYGENIUM
OXYGENIZE
OXYGENOUS
OXYGEUSIA
OXYGONIAL
OXYHALIDE
OXYHALOID
OXYHYDRIC
OXYIODIDE
OXYKETONE
OXYNEURIN
OXYPHENOL
OXYPHENYL
OXYPHILIC
OXYPHONIA
OXYPICRIC
OXYPURINE
OXYPYCNOS
OXYRHYNCH
OXYSULFID
OXYTOCOUS
OXYTOLUIC
OXYTONIZE

OXYTYLOTE
PANSEXUAL
PARADOXAL
PARADOXER
PARADOXIC
PARALEXIA
PARALEXIC
PARATAXIS
PARAXONIC
PAROREXIA
PAXILLARY
PAXILLATE
PAXILLOSE
PENTOXIDE
PEPPERBOX
PERIAXIAL
PEROXIDED
PEROXIDIC
PERPLEXED
PERPLEXER
PHALANXED
PHALANXES
PHARYNXES
PHENOXIDE
PHOENIXES
PHONOPLEX
PHOTOTAXY
PIXILATED
PLAINTEXT
PLEONEXIA
PLEXICOSE
PLEXIFORM
PLEXIGLAS
PLEXIPPUS
PLEXODONT
POLYAXONE
POLYOXIDE
POMPHOLIX
POMPHOLYX
POSTAXIAD
POSTAXIAL
POSTEXIST
POSTFIXED
PRAETEXTA
PRAXITHEA
PREATAXIC
PREEXILIC
PREFIXION
PREHALLUX
PREPOLLEX
PRESEXUAL
PRETEXTED
PROLIXITY
PROPLEXUS
PROSCOLEX
PROTAXIAL
PROTHORAX
PROTOXIDE
PROXENETE
PROXIMATE
PROXIMITY
PSEUDAXIS
PSEUDODOX
PYOTHORAX
PYREXICAL
PYRONYXIS
PYROTOXIN
PYROXENIC
PYROXYLIC
PYROXYLIN
QUINISEXT
QUIXOTISM
QUIXOTIZE
RATTLEBOX
RECTOPEXY
REEXAMINE
REFLEXISM
REFLEXIVE
RELAXABLE
RELAXEDLY
RETEXTURE
RETROFLEX
RHEOTAXIS
RHIZOTAXY
SAPOTOXIN
SAXCORNET
SAXOPHONE
SCHIZAXON
SCRAMASAX
SERVITRIX
SEXANGLED
SEXENNIAL
SEXENNIUM
SEXLESSLY
SEXOLOGIC
SEXTACTIC
SEXTANTAL
SEXTARIUS
SEXTIPARA
SEXTUPLED
SEXTUPLET
SEXUALISM
SEXUALIST
SEXUALITY
SEXUALIZE
SHADOWBOX
SIMPLEXED
SIXPENCES
SIXTEENER
SIXTEENMO
SIXTEENTH
SOAPBOXER
SPHINXIAN
SPHINXINE
SPLENAUXE
SPONDULIX
STRONGBOX
SUBCLIMAX
SUBCORTEX
SUBEXCITE
SUBLUXATE
SUFFIXING
SUFFIXION
SUFFRUTEX
SULFOXIDE
SULFOXISM
SULPHOXID
SUPERFLUX
SURTAXING
SUSOTOXIN
SUSSEXITE
SYNTAXIST
TARAXACUM
TAXACEOUS
TAXAMETER
TAXEATING
TAXEOPODY
TAXIDERMY
TAXIMETER
TAXIPLANE
TAXOMETER
TAXONOMER
TAXONOMIC
TAXPAYING
TESTATRIX
TETRAXILE
TETROXIDE
TEXTARIAN
TEXTILIST
TEXTORIAL
TEXTUALLY
THRIFTBOX
THYROXINE
TINDERBOX
TONOTAXIS
TOPOTAXIS
TOXAEMIAS
TOXANEMIA
TOXICALLY
TOXICAROL
TOXICOSES
TOXICOSIS
TOXIGENIC
TOXINEMIA
TOXINOSIS
TOXIPHAGI
TOXOLYSIS
TOXOPHILE
TOXOPHILY
TRANSFLUX
TRUXILLIC
TRUXILLIN
TYLOTOXEA
UNBUXOMLY
UNEXACTLY
UNEXCITED
UNEXPIRED
UNEXPOSED
UNEXPRESS
UNISEXUAL
UNPERPLEX
UNRELAXED
UROTOXIES
UROXANATE
UXORIALLY
UXORICIDE
VEXATIOUS
VEXEDNESS
VEXILLARY
VEXILLATE
WAXFLOWER
WAXMAKING
WAXWORKER
WOADWAXEN
WOODWAXEN
XANTHAMID
XANTHIONE
XANTHOGEN
XANTHOMAS
XANTHOPIA
XANTHOSIS
XANTHURIA
XENAGOGUE
XENELASIA
XENOBLAST
XENODOCHY
XENOMANIA
XENOPODID
XERODERMA
XEROMORPH
XEROMYRON
XEROPHAGY
XEROPHILE
XEROPHILY
XEROPHYTE
XEROSTOMA
XEROTHERM
XIPHOIDAL
XIPHOSURE
XYLINDEIN
XYLOCOPID
XYLOGRAPH
XYLOIDINE
XYLOMANCY
XYLOMETER
XYLOPHAGE
XYLOPHONE
ZEROAXIAL
ZYGOTAXIS

POSITIONAL ORDER LIST OF 9-LETTER WORDS

XANTHAMID
XANTHIONE
XANTHOGEN
XANTHOMAS
XANTHOPIA
XANTHOSIS
XANTHURIA
XENAGOGUE
XENELASIA
XENOBLAST
XENODOCHY
XENOMANIA
XENOPODID
XERODERMA
XEROMORPH
XEROMYRON
XEROPHAGY
XEROPHILE
XEROPHILY
XEROPHYTE
XEROSTOMA
XEROTHERM
XIPHOIDAL
XIPHOSURE
XYLINDEIN
XYLOCOPID
XYLOGRAPH
XYLOIDINE
XYLOMANCY
XYLOMETER
XYLOPHAGE
XYLOPHONE

AXBREAKER
AXEMASTER
AXILEMMAS
AXIOLITIC
AXIOMATIC
AXIOPISTY
AXLESMITH
AXMANSHIP
AXONEURON
AXOPODIUM
EXACTABLE
EXACTMENT
EXACTNESS
EXADVERSO
EXAGITATE
EXAIRESIS
EXALTEDLY
EXAMINANT
EXAMINATE
EXAMINING
EXAMPLING
EXANIMATE
EXANTHEMA
EXANTLATE
EXARATION
EXARCHATE
EXARCHIST
EXCAMBION
EXCARNATE
EXCAUDATE
EXCAVATED
EXCAVATOR
EXCEEDING
EXCELENTE
EXCELLENT
EXCELLING
EXCELSIOR
EXCENTRAL
EXCENTRIC
EXCEPTANT
EXCEPTING
EXCEPTION
EXCEPTIVE
EXCERPTED
EXCERPTOR
EXCESSIVE
EXCESSMAN
EXCESSMEN
EXCHANGED
EXCHANGER
EXCHEQUER
EXCIPIENT
EXCIPULAR
EXCIPULUM
EXCISABLE
EXCISEMAN
EXCISEMEN
EXCITABLE
EXCITABLY
EXCITANCY
EXCITATOR
EXCITEDLY
EXCLAIMED
EXCLAIMER
EXCLUDING
EXCLUSION
EXCLUSIVE
EXCLUSORY
EXCULPATE
EXCOCTION
EXCORIATE
EXCREMENT
EXCRETING
EXCRETION
EXCRETIVE
EXCRETORY
EXCURRENT
EXCURSING
EXCURSION
EXCURSIVE
EXCURVATE
EXCUSABLE
EXCUSABLY
EXCUSATOR
EXCUSSING
EXECRABLE
EXECRABLY
EXECRATED
EXECRATOR
EXECUTANT
EXECUTING
EXECUTION

EXECUTIVE
EXECUTORY
EXECUTRIX
EXEGETICS
EXEGETIST
EXEMPLARY
EXEMPLIFY
EXEMPTILE
EXEMPTION
EXEMPTIVE
EXEQUATUR
EXERCISED
EXERCISER
EXERCISES
EXERCITOR
EXFODIATE
EXFOLIATE
EXHALABLE
EXHAUSTED
EXHAUSTER
EXHIBITED
EXHIBITOR
EXHORTING
EXHUMATED
EXHUMATOR
EXIGEANTE
EXIGENTER
EXIGENTLY
EXINANITE
EXISTENCE
EXOCARDIA
EXOCLINAL
EXOCOELAR
EXOCOELIC
EXOCOELOM
EXOCOELUM
EXOCULATE
EXOCYCLIC
EXODERMIS
EXODONTIA
EXODROMIC
EXOENZYME
EXOGAMOUS
EXOGENOUS
EXONERATE
EXONEURAL
EXOPATHIC
EXOPHORIA
EXOPHORIC
EXOPODITE
EXORBITAL
EXORCISED
EXORCISER
EXORCIZED
EXORCIZER
EXORDIUMS
EXORGANIC
EXOSEPSIS
EXOSMOSIS
EXOSMOTIC
EXOSPHERE
EXOSPORAL
EXOSTOSED
EXOSTOSES
EXOSTOSIS
EXOSTOTIC
EXOTERICS
EXOTHECAL
EXOTICISM
EXOTICIST
EXOTICITY
EXOTROPIA
EXPALPATE
EXPANDING
EXPANSILE
EXPANSION
EXPANSIVE
EXPANSURE
EXPATIATE
EXPECTANT
EXPECTING
EXPECTIVE
EXPEDIATE
EXPEDIENT
EXPEDITED
EXPEDITER
EXPEDITOR
EXPELLANT
EXPELLENT
EXPELLING
EXPENDING
EXPENSIVE
EXPERIENT
EXPERTISE
EXPIATING
EXPIATION
EXPIATIST
EXPIATIVE
EXPIATORY
EXPILATOR
EXPIRATOR
EXPISCATE
EXPLAINED
EXPLAINER
EXPLANATE
EXPLEMENT
EXPLETIVE
EXPLETORY
EXPLICATE
EXPLODENT
EXPLODING
EXPLOITED
EXPLOITER
EXPLORING
EXPLOSION
EXPLOSIVE
EXPONENCE
EXPONENTS
EXPONIBLE
EXPORTING
EXPOSITOR
EXPOUNDED
EXPOUNDER
EXPRESSED
EXPRESSER
EXPRESSLY
EXPROBATE
EXPUITION
EXPULSION
EXPULSIVE
EXPULSORY
EXPUNGING
EXPURGATE
EXQUISITE
EXSCINDED
EXSECTILE
EXSECTION
EXSERTILE
EXSERTING
EXSERTION
EXSICCATE
EXSOMATIC
EXSPUTORY
EXSTROPHY
EXSUCCOUS
EXSUCTION
EXSURGENT
EXTEMPORE
EXTENDING
EXTENSILE
EXTENSION
EXTENSITY
EXTENSIVE
EXTENUATE
EXTERMINE
EXTERNATE
EXTERNIZE
EXTERNIZE
EXTINCTOR
EXTIRPATE
EXTISPICY
EXTOLLING
EXTOLMENT
EXTORSIVE
EXTORTING
EXTORTION
EXTORTIVE
EXTRABOLD
EXTRACTED
EXTRACTOR
EXTRADITE
EXTRALITE
EXTRALITY
EXTRANEAN
EXTRAVERT
EXTREMELY
EXTREMEST
EXTREMISM
EXTREMIST
EXTREMITY
EXTRICATE
EXTRINSIC
EXTRORSAL
EXTROVERT
EXTRUDING
EXTRUSILE
EXTRUSION
EXTRUSIVE
EXTRUSORY
EXUBERANT
EXUBERATE
EXUDATION
EXUDATIVE
EXUDATORY
EXULTANCY
EXULULATE
EXUVIABLE
EXUVIATED
OXALAEMIA
OXALURATE
OXAMIDINE
OXANILATE
OXANILIDE
OXBERRIES
OXDIAZOLE
OXIDATING
OXIDATION
OXIDATIVE
OXIDIZING
OXIMATION
OXMANSHIP
OXYBENZYL
OXYDACTYL
OXYGENANT
OXYGENATE
OXYGENIUM
OXYGENIZE
OXYGENOUS
OXYGEUSIA
OXYGONIAL
OXYHALIDE
OXYHALOID
OXYHYDRIC
OXYIODIDE
OXYKETONE
OXYNEURIN
OXYPHENOL
OXYPHENYL
OXYPHILIC
OXYPHONIA
OXYPICRIC
OXYPURINE
OXYPYCNOS
OXYRHYNCH
OXYSULFID
OXYTOCOUS
OXYTOLUIC
OXYTONIZE
OXYTYLOTE
UXORIALLY
UXORICIDE

ANXIETIES
ANXIETUDE
ANXIOUSLY
AUXETICAL
AUXILIARY
AUXILIATE
AUXOBLAST
AUXOFLORE
AUXOFLUOR
AUXOGRAPH
AUXOMETER
AUXOSPORE
AUXOTONIC
BIXACEOUS
BOXHOLDER
BOXKEEPER
BOXWALLAH
BUXACEOUS
BUXERRIES
BUXOMNESS
COXCOMBRY
COXODYNIA
DEXTERITY
DEXTEROUS
DEXTRALLY
DEXTRORSE
FIXEDNESS
FOXTAILED
HEXABASIC
HEXABIOSE
HEXACHORD
HEXACOLIC
HEXADECYL
HEXADIENE
HEXADIINE
HEXADIYNE
HEXAGONAL
HEXAHEDRA
HEXAMERAL
HEXAMERON
HEXAMETER
HEXAMMINE
HEXANDRIC
HEXAPLOID
HEXASEMIC
HEXASTICH
HEXASTIGM
HEXATHLON
HEXATOMIC
JUXTAPOSE
LEXICALIC
LIXIVIATE
LIXIVIOUS
LOXOCLASE
LOXODROME
LOXODROMY
LUXURIANT
LUXURIATE
LUXURIOUS
MAXILLARY
MAXIMALLY
MAXIMIZED
MAXIMIZER
MIXTIFORM
MYXAMOEBA
MYXEDEMIC
MYXOEDEMA
MYXOINOMA
MYXOMYOMA
MYXOPODIA
MYXORRHEA
MYXOSPORE
MYXOTHECA
NOXIOUSLY
PAXILLARY
PAXILLATE
PAXILLOSE
PIXILATED
SAXCORNET
SAXOPHONE
SEXANGLED
SEXENNIAL
SEXENNIUM
SEXLESSLY
SEXOLOGIC
SEXTACTIC
SEXTANTAL
SEXTARIUS
SEXTIPARA
SEXTUPLED
SEXTUPLET
SEXUALISM
SEXUALIST
SEXUALITY
SEXUALIZE
SIXPENCES
SIXTEENER
SIXTEENMO
SIXTEENTH
TAXACEOUS
TAXAMETER
TAXEATING
TAXEOPODY
TAXIDERMY
TAXIMETER
TAXIPLANE
TAXOMETER
TAXONOMER
TAXONOMIC
TAXPAYING
TEXTARIAN
TEXTILIST
TEXTORIAL
TEXTUALLY
TOXAEMIAS
TOXANEMIA
TOXICALLY
TOXICAROL
TOXICOSES
TOXICOSIS
TOXIGENIC
TOXINEMIA
TOXINOSIS
TOXIPHAGI
TOXOLYSIS
TOXOPHILE
TOXOPHILY
VEXATIOUS
VEXEDNESS
VEXILLARY
VEXILLATE
WAXFLOWER
WAXMAKING
WAXWORKER

ANOXAEMIA
ANOXAEMIC
ASEXUALLY
AZOXONIUM
BAUXITITE
BIAXIALLY
COAXATION
COAXIALLY

COAXINGLY
DEOXIDIZE
DRUXINESS
ELIXATION
EPAXIALLY
FLAXBOARD
FLAXWENCH
FLAXWOMAN
FLEXILITY
FLEXIONAL
FLUXATION
FLUXILITY
FLUXIONAL
FLUXMETER
HOAXPROOF
INEXACTLY
INEXPIATE
INEXPRESS
INOXIDIZE
ISOXAZOLE
PLEXICOSE
PLEXIFORM
PLEXIGLAS
PLEXIPPUS
PLEXODONT
PRAXITHEA
PROXENETE
PROXIMATE
PROXIMITY
QUIXOTISM
QUIXOTIZE
REEXAMINE
TRUXILLIC
TRUXILLIN
UNEXACTLY
UNEXCITED
UNEXPIRED
UNEXPOSED
UNEXPRESS
UROXANATE

ADMIXTION
ADMIXTURE
ADNEXITIS
AFFIXTURE
ALLOXANIC
ALLOXURIC
ANNEXABLE
ANNEXMENT
BAROXYTON
BISEXUOUS
EUTAXITIC
GLYOXALIC
GLYOXYLIC
IMMIXTURE
INDEXICAL
INDOXYLIC
INMIXTURE
INNOXIOUS
INTEXTINE
INTEXTURE
LATEXOSIS
MALAXABLE
MALAXATOR
MENOXENIA
MESAXONIC

MESOXALIC
MESOXALYL
METAXYLEM
MONAXONIC
MONOXYLIC
MONOXYLON
OBNOXIETY
OBNOXIOUS
PARAXONIC
PEROXIDED
PEROXIDIC
PREEXILIC
PYREXICAL
PYROXENIC
PYROXYLIC
PYROXYLIN
RELAXABLE
RELAXEDLY
RETEXTURE
SUBEXCITE
TARAXACUM
UNBUXOMLY

ACETOXIME
AFFLUXION
AMIDOXIME
APYREXIAL
ASPHYXIAL
ASPHYXIED
ATLOAXOID
BOLLIXING
CARBOXIDE
CLIMAXING
COMMIXING
CONFIXING
CONNEXION
CONNEXITY
CONNEXIVA
CONNEXIVE
CONVEXITY
CRESOXIDE
DEFLEXING
DEFLEXION
DEFLEXURE
DEFLUXION
DUPLEXING
DUPLEXITY
EPITOXOID
HEPTOXIDE
HYDROXIDE
INFLEXION
INFLEXIVE
INFLUXION
INFLUXIVE
LEUCOXENE
LITHOXYLE
NEURAXONE
OVEREXERT
PANSEXUAL
PENTOXIDE
PERIAXIAL
PHENOXIDE
POLYAXONE
POLYOXIDE
POSTAXIAD
POSTAXIAL

POSTEXIST
PREFIXION
PRESEXUAL
PRETEXTED
PROLIXITY
PROTAXIAL
PROTOXIDE
REFLEXISM
REFLEXIVE
SPHINXIAN
SPHINXINE
SUBLUXATE
SUFFIXING
SUFFIXION
SULFOXIDE
SULFOXISM
SURTAXING
SUSSEXITE
SYNTAXIST
TETRAXILE
TETROXIDE
THYROXINE
UNISEXUAL
UROTOXIES
ZEROAXIAL

AEROTAXIS
AMPHIOXUS
AMYOTAXIA
ANAPTYXIS
ANTECOXAL
ANTEFIXAL
ANTEFIXES
ANTHROXAN
APOSTAXIS
APROSEXIA
AUTOTOXIC
AUTOTOXIN
BAROTAXIS
BASIFIXED
CACOMIXLE
CATALEXIS
CHRONAXIA
CHRONAXIE
CICUTOXIN
COLOPEXIA
COMPLEXLY
COMPLEXUS
CYTOTAXIS
CYTOTOXIC
CYTOTOXIN
DENDRAXON
DIAPLEXUS
DIAZEUXIS
DIGITOXIN
EMPHRAXIS
ENDOMIXIS
ENDOTOXIC
ENDOTOXIN
EPIPLEXIS
EPISTAXIS
EPIZEUXIS
FLUMMOXED
HEMIAUXIN
HEMOTOXIC

HEMOTOXIN
HOMOTAXIS
HYPOTAXIA
HYPOTAXIC
HYPOTAXIS
INTERAXAL
INTERAXIS
KENOTOXIN
KOSOTOXIN
LIPOPEXIA
LOOMFIXER
MALPRAXIS
MEDIFIXED
METATAXIC
METATAXIS
OVERSEXED
OVERTAXED
PARADOXAL
PARADOXER
PARADOXIC
PARALEXIA
PARALEXIC
PARATAXIS
PAROREXIA
PERPLEXED
PERPLEXER
PHALANXED
PHALANXES
PHARYNXES
PHOENIXES
PLEONEXIA
POSTFIXED
PRAETEXTA
PREATAXIC
PROPLEXUS
PSEUDAXIS
PYRONYXIS
PYROTOXIN
RHEOTAXIS
SAPOTOXIN
SCHIZAXON
SIMPLEXED
SOAPBOXER
SULPHOXID
SUSOTOXIN
TONOTAXIS
TOPOTAXIS
TYLOTOXEA
UNRELAXED
WOADWAXEN
WOODWAXEN
ZYGOTAXIS

ANTHOTAXY
CALCIPEXY
CARDIAUXE
CATAPLEXY
CAULOTAXY
CHEMOTAXY
DIHYDROXY
DIMETHOXY
ENTERAUXE
IMPERMIXT
INTERMIXT
KATAPLEXY

MASTOPEXY
NEPHRAUXE
NEURATAXY
ORTHODOXY
PHOTOTAXY
PLAINTEXT
QUINISEXT
RECTOPEXY
RHIZOTAXY
SPLENAUXE

ABOIDEAUX
AGITATRIX
ANTIHELIX
ASSERTRIX
BISECTRIX
BOISSEAUX
BUTTERBOX
CANDLEBOX
DECOMPLEX
DICTATRIX
DIRECTRIX
DORSIFLEX
ENTREDEUX
EXECUTRIX
FLAMBEAUX
FUNDATRIX
GONOCALYX
HETERODOX
IMPOSTRIX
INCOMPLEX
INTROFLEX
LEPOTHRIX
MEDIATRIX
MULTIPLEX
MYELOPLAX
NULLIPLEX
OBSTETRIX
OPERATRIX
PEPPERBOX
PHONOPLEX
POMPHOLIX
POMPHOLYX
PREHALLUX
PREPOLLEX
PROSCOLEX
PROTHORAX
PSEUDODOX
PYOTHORAX
RATTLEBOX
RETROFLEX
SCRAMASAX
SERVITRIX
SHADOWBOX
SPONDULIX
STRONGBOX
SUBCLIMAX
SUBCORTEX
SUFFRUTEX
SUPERFLUX
TESTATRIX
THRIFTBOX
TINDERBOX
TRANSFLUX
UNPERPLEX

SCORING ORDER LIST OF 9-LETTER WORDS

34
QUIXOTIZE

33
OXYBENZYL

31
RHIZOTAXY

30
EXCHEQUER
EXOENZYME
MAXIMIZED
OXYRHYNCH
SCHIZAXON

29
MAXIMIZER
OXYGENIZE
ZYGOTAXIS

28
EXORCIZED
OXYHYDRIC
OXYTONIZE
POMPHOLYX

27
AZOXONIUM
COXCOMBRY
DEOXIDIZE
DIHYDROXY
DUPLEXITY
EPIZEUXIS
EXORCIZER
FLAXWENCH
OXIDIZING
OXYPHENYL
QUIXOTISM

26
CHEMOTAXY
DIAZEUXIS
EXEMPLIFY
HYPOTAXIC
INOXIDIZE
MYXEDEMIC
MYXOTHECA
OXDIAZOLE
OXYPHILIC
OXYPYCNOS
PYROXYLIC
WAXMAKING
WAXWORKER
XYLOMANCY

25
ASPHYXIED
CALCIPEXY
COMPLEXLY
DIMETHOXY
EXEQUATUR
EXQUISITE
EXTERNIZE
GLYOXYLIC
HEXACHORD
HEXADECYL
ISOXAZOLE
JUXTAPOSE
KATAPLEXY
MYXAMOEBA
MYXOMYOMA
OXYDACTYL
OXYPICRIC
POMPHOLIX
QUINISEXT
SEXUALIZE
SHADOWBOX
WAXFLOWER
XENODOCHY
XEROPHAGY
XYLOGRAPH
XYLOPHAGE
ZEROAXIAL

24
ASPHYXIAL
BOXKEEPER
BOXWALLAH
CONVEXITY
EXSTROPHY
FLAXWOMAN
FLUMMOXED
HEXASTICH
HOAXPROOF
HYDROXIDE
HYPOTAXIA
HYPOTAXIS
MYXOEDEMA
MYXOPODIA
MYXORRHEA
OXYPHENOL
OXYPHONIA
PHARYNXES
PHOTOTAXY
PYOTHORAX
PYRONYXIS
PYROXYLIN
THRIFTBOX
TOXOPHILY
XEROPHILY
XEROPHYTE
XYLOCOPID
XYLOPHONE

23
AMPHIOXUS
AXMANSHIP
CATAPLEXY
COMMIXING
CYTOTOXIC
DECOMPLEX
EMPHRAXIS
EXCEPTIVE
EXCHANGED
EXCITABLY
EXCITANCY
EXCUSABLY
EXECRABLY
EXEMPLARY
EXEMPTIVE
EXOPATHIC
EXOPHORIC
EXPECTIVE
EXTISPICY
FLAMBEAUX
HEMOTOXIC
HEXABASIC
HEXACOLIC
HEXADIYNE
HEXAHEDRA
HEXAMMINE
HEXASEMIC
HEXATOMIC
MASTOPEXY
MAXIMALLY
MEDIFIXED
METAXYLEM
MIXTIFORM
MONOXYLIC
MYELOPLAX
MYXOINOMA
MYXOSPORE
ORTHODOXY
OXMANSHIP
OXYHALIDE
OXYHALOID
OXYKETONE
OXYSULFID
PHONOPLEX
PLEXIFORM
PROXIMITY
PYREXICAL
PYROXENIC
RECTOPEXY
SUFFIXING
UNBUXOMLY
WOADWAXEN
WOODWAXEN
XEROMORPH

22
AFFIXTURE
AFFLUXION
ANTHOTAXY
AUXOGRAPH
AXBREAKER
BASIFIXED
BOXHOLDER
CACOMIXLE
COAXINGLY
COMPLEXUS
CONFIXING
COXODYNIA
EXCAMBION
EXCAVATED
EXCHANGER
EXCIPULUM
EXCITEDLY
EXHIBITED
EXHUMATED
EXOCYCLIC
FLAXBOARD
FLEXILITY
FLUXILITY
GLYOXALIC
GONOCALYX
HEPTOXIDE
HEXANDRIC
HEXAPLOID
HEXASTIGM
HEXATHLON
IMPERMIXT
INCOMPLEX
INDOXYLIC
INFLEXIVE
INFLUXIVE
LITHOXYLE
LOXODROMY
OXYGENIUM
OXYTYLOTE
PHALANXED
PHENOXIDE
POLYOXIDE
POSTFIXED
REFLEXIVE
SUBCLIMAX
SUFFIXION
SUFFRUTEX
SULPHOXID
TAXEOPODY
TAXIDERMY
TAXPAYING
THYROXINE
TOXIPHAGI
VEXILLARY
XANTHAMID
XIPHOIDAL

21
AMIDOXIME
AMYOTAXIA
ANAPTYXIS
APYREXIAL
AXIOPISTY
AXLESMITH
AXOPODIUM
BAROXYTON
BIAXIALLY
CANDLEBOX
CARBOXIDE
CAULOTAXY
CHRONAXIA
CHRONAXIE
CLIMAXING
COAXIALLY
CONNEXITY
CONNEXIVA
CONNEXIVE
CYTOTAXIS
CYTOTOXIN
DEFLEXING
EPAXIALLY
EXAMPLING
EXANTHEMA
EXARCHATE
EXARCHIST
EXCAVATOR
EXCEPTING
EXCERPTED
EXCESSIVE
EXCLAIMED
EXCLUSIVE
EXCLUSORY
EXCRETIVE
EXCRETORY
EXCURSIVE
EXCURVATE
EXECUTIVE
EXECUTORY
EXHALABLE
EXHIBITOR
EXHUMATOR
EXODROMIC
EXOSPHERE
EXOTHECAL
EXOTICITY
EXPANSIVE
EXPECTING
EXPENSIVE
EXPIATIVE
EXPIATORY
EXPLETIVE
EXPLETORY
EXPLOSIVE
EXPRESSLY
EXPULSIVE
EXPULSORY
EXSPUTORY
EXTREMELY
EXTREMITY
EXULTANCY
EXUVIABLE
FLUXMETER
HEMIAUXIN
HEMOTOXIN
HEXABIOSE
HEXAMERAL
HEXAMERON
HEXAMETER
HOMOTAXIS
INEXACTLY
LEPOTHRIX
LOOMFIXER
MAXILLARY
MESOXALYL
MONOXYLON
NEPHRAUXE
OBNOXIETY
OXYIODIDE
OXYPURINE
OXYTOCOUS
OXYTOLUIC
PARADOXIC
PAXILLARY
PEPPERBOX
PEROXIDIC
PERPLEXED
PHALANXES
PHOENIXES
POLYAXONE
PRAXITHEA
PREFIXION
PREHALLUX
PROLIXITY
PROTHORAX
PYROTOXIN
REFLEXISM
SAXOPHONE
SIMPLEXED
SPHINXIAN
SPHINXINE
SULFOXISM
SUPERFLUX
TOXICALLY
TOXOPHILE
UNEXACTLY
XANTHOMAS
XANTHOPIA
XEROMYRON
XEROPHILE
XEROTHERM
XIPHOSURE
XYLOMETER

20
ACETOXIME
ANOXAEMIC
AXILEMMAS
AXIOMATIC
BISECTRIX
BIXACEOUS
BUTTERBOX
BUXACEOUS
BUXOMNESS
CICUTOXIN
COLOPEXIA
DEFLEXION
DEFLEXURE
DEFLUXION
DEXTERITY
DEXTRALLY
DORSIFLEX
DUPLEXING
EPIPLEXIS
EXACTABLE
EXACTMENT
EXADVERSO
EXALTEDLY
EXCEEDING
EXCENTRIC
EXCEPTANT
EXCEPTION
EXCERPTOR
EXCESSMAN
EXCESSMEN
EXCIPIENT
EXCIPULAR
EXCISABLE
EXCISEMAN
EXCISEMEN
EXCITABLE
EXCLAIMER
EXCLUDING
EXCOCTION
EXCREMENT
EXCULPATE
EXCUSABLE
EXECRABLE
EXEMPTILE
EXEMPTION
EXFODIATE
EXHAUSTED
EXHORTING
EXIGENTLY
EXOCOELIC
EXOCOELOM
EXOCOELUM
EXOSMOTIC
EXOTICISM
EXPALPATE
EXPANDING
EXPECTANT
EXPEDITED
EXPENDING
EXPISCATE
EXPLEMENT
EXPLICATE
EXPLODING
EXPONENCE
EXPONIBLE
EXPOUNDED

EXPROBATE
EXPUNGING
EXSCINDED
EXSICCATE
EXSOMATIC
EXSUCCOUS
EXTEMPORE
EXTREMISM
EXUDATIVE
EXUDATORY
EXUVIATED
FIXEDNESS
FOXTAILED
FUNDATRIX
HETERODOX
HEXADIENE
HEXADIINE
HEXAGONAL
IMMIXTURE
IMPOSTRIX
KENOTOXIN
KOSOTOXIN
LEXICALIC
LIPOPEXIA
MALAXABLE
MALPRAXIS
MESAXONIC
MESOXALIC
METATAXIC
MONAXONIC
MULTIPLEX
OVERSEXED
OVERTAXED
OXIDATIVE
OXYGENANT
OXYGENATE
OXYGENOUS
OXYGEUSIA
OXYGONIAL
PARALEXIC
PARAXONIC
PEROXIDED
PERPLEXER
PLEXICOSE
PREATAXIC
PREEXILIC
PREPOLLEX
PROPLEXUS
PROSCOLEX
PROXIMATE
PSEUDODOX
RELAXEDLY
SCRAMASAX
SEXTACTIC
SIXPENCES
SOAPBOXER
SUBCORTEX
SUBEXCITE
SULFOXIDE
TARAXACUM
TAXONOMIC
UNPERPLEX
VEXEDNESS
XANTHOGEN
XENOPODID
XYLINDEIN
XYLOIDINE

19

ABOIDEAUX
ADMIXTION
ADMIXTURE
ANTEFIXAL
ANTEFIXES
ANTHROXAN
ANTIHELIX
ANXIOUSLY
ASEXUALLY
AUXILIARY
AUXOFLORE
AUXOFLUOR
BOLLIXING
CARDIAUXE
CRESOXIDE
DIAPLEXUS
DICTATRIX
DIRECTRIX
ENDOMIXIS
EPITOXOID
EXAMINING
EXCAUDATE
EXCELLING
EXCRETING
EXCURSING
EXCUSSING
EXECRATED
EXECUTING
EXEGETICS
EXERCISED
EXFOLIATE
EXHAUSTER
EXOCARDIA
EXODERMIS
EXOGAMOUS
EXOPODITE
EXORCISED
EXORDIUMS
EXORGANIC
EXPEDIATE
EXPEDIENT
EXPEDITER
EXPEDITOR
EXPELLING
EXPIATING
EXPLAINED
EXPLODENT
EXPLOITED
EXPLORING
EXPORTING
EXPOUNDER
EXPRESSED
EXPURGATE
EXTENSITY
EXTENSIVE
EXTORSIVE
EXTORTIVE
EXTRABOLD
EXTRACTED
EXTRALITY
EXTRAVERT
EXTROVERT
EXTRUSIVE
EXTRUSORY
FLEXIONAL
FLUXATION
FLUXIONAL
INDEXICAL
INFLEXION
INFLUXION
INTROFLEX
LIXIVIATE
LIXIVIOUS
LOXODROME
MEDIATRIX
NEURATAXY
NOXIOUSLY
OVEREXERT
OXAMIDINE
OXYNEURIN
PARADOXAL
PARADOXER
PENTOXIDE
PIXILATED
PLEXIGLAS
PLEXIPPUS
PLEXODONT
POSTAXIAD
PRETEXTED
PROTOXIDE
PSEUDAXIS
RETROFLEX
RHEOTAXIS
SERVITRIX
SEXLESSLY
SEXOLOGIC
SEXTUPLED
SEXUALITY
SIXTEENTH
SPONDULIX
STRONGBOX
SYNTAXIST
TEXTUALLY
TINDERBOX
TOXIGENIC
TOXOLYSIS
TRANSFLUX
TYLOTOXEA
UNEXCITED
UNEXPIRED
UNEXPOSED
UXORIALLY
UXORICIDE
VEXATIOUS
VEXILLATE
XANTHIONE
XANTHOSIS
XANTHURIA
XERODERMA

18

ALLOXANIC
ALLOXURIC
ANNEXABLE
ANNEXMENT
ANOXAEMIA
ANTECOXAL
APOSTAXIS
APROSEXIA
AUTOTOXIC
AUXETICAL
AUXOBLAST
AUXOMETER
AUXOSPORE
AUXOTONIC
AXEMASTER
AXIOLITIC
BAROTAXIS
BAUXITITE
BISEXUOUS
BOISSEAUX
BUXERRIES
CATALEXIS
COAXATION
CONNEXION
DENDRAXON
DIGITOXIN
EPISTAXIS
EUTAXITIC
EXACTNESS
EXAMINANT
EXAMINATE
EXANIMATE
EXCARNATE
EXCELENTE
EXCELLENT
EXCELSIOR
EXCENTRAL
EXCITATOR
EXCLUSION
EXCORIATE
EXCRETION
EXCURRENT
EXCURSION
EXCUSATOR
EXECRATOR
EXECUTANT
EXECUTION
EXERCISER
EXERCISES
EXERCITOR
EXISTENCE
EXOCLINAL
EXOCOELAR
EXOCULATE
EXORBITAL
EXORCISER
EXOSEPSIS
EXOSMOSIS
EXOSPORAL
EXOSTOTIC
EXOTERICS
EXOTICIST
EXOTROPIA
EXPANSILE
EXPANSION
EXPANSURE
EXPATIATE
EXPELLANT
EXPELLENT
EXPERIENT
EXPERTISE
EXPIATION
EXPIATIST
EXPILATOR
EXPIRATOR
EXPLAINER
EXPLANATE
EXPLOITER
EXPLOSION
EXPONENTS
EXPOSITOR
EXPRESSER
EXPUITION
EXPULSION
EXSECTILE
EXSECTION
EXSUCTION
EXTENDING
EXTERMINE
EXTINCTOR
EXTIRPATE
EXTOLMENT
EXTRACTOR
EXTREMEST
EXTREMIST
EXTRICATE
EXTRINSIC
EXTRUDING
EXUBERANT
EXUBERATE
INEXPIATE
INEXPRESS
INMIXTURE
INTERMIXT
LEUCOXENE
LOXOCLASE
MALAXATOR
MENOXENIA
METATAXIS
NULLIPLEX
OBNOXIOUS
OBSTETRIX
OPERATRIX
OXALAEMIA
OXBERRIES
OXIDATING
OXIMATION
PANSEXUAL
PARALEXIA
PARATAXIS
PAROREXIA
PAXILLATE
PAXILLOSE
PERIAXIAL
PLAINTEXT
PLEONEXIA
POSTAXIAL
POSTEXIST
PRAETEXTA
PRESEXUAL
PROTAXIAL
PROXENETE
RATTLEBOX
REEXAMINE
RELAXABLE
SAPOTOXIN
SAXCORNET
SEXANGLED
SEXENNIUM
SEXTIPARA
SEXTUPLET
SEXUALISM
SIXTEENMO
SPLENAUXE
SUBLUXATE
TAXACEOUS
TAXAMETER
TAXIMETER
TAXIPLANE
TAXOMETER
TAXONOMER
TOPOTAXIS
TOXAEMIAS
TOXANEMIA
TOXICAROL
TOXICOSES
TOXICOSIS
TOXINEMIA
TRUXILLIC
UNEXPRESS
XENAGOGUE
XENOBLAST
XENOMANIA
XEROSTOMA

17

ADNEXITIS
AGITATRIX
ANXIETUDE
ATLOAXOID
DEXTEROUS
DEXTRORSE
DRUXINESS
ENDOTOXIN
ENTREDEUX
EXAGITATE
EXECUTRIX
EXEGETIST
EXIGEANTE
EXIGENTER
EXODONTIA
EXOGENOUS
EXOSTOSED
EXSERTING
EXSURGENT
EXTOLLING
EXTORTING
EXTRADITE
EXUDATION
OXANILIDE
OXIDATION
SURTAXING
TAXEATING
TETROXIDE
UNRELAXED

16
AEROTAXIS
ANXIETIES
ASSERTRIX
AUTOTOXIN
AUXILIATE
AXONEURON
ELIXATION
ENTERAUXE
EXAIRESIS
EXARATION
EXINANITE
EXONERATE
EXONEURAL
EXOSTOSES
EXOSTOSIS
EXSERTILE
EXSERTION
EXTENSILE
EXTENSION
EXTENUATE
EXTERNATE
EXTORTION
EXTRALITE
EXTRANEAN
EXTRORSAL
EXTRUSILE
EXTRUSION
EXULULATE
INNOXIOUS
INTERAXAL
INTERAXIS
INTEXTINE
INTEXTURE
LATEXOSIS
LUXURIANT
LUXURIATE
LUXURIOUS
NEURAXONE
OXALURATE
OXANILATE
RETEXTURE
SEXENNIAL
SEXTANTAL
SEXTARIUS
SEXUALIST
SIXTEENER
SUSOTOXIN
SUSSEXITE
TESTATRIX
TETRAXILE
TEXTARIAN
TEXTILIST
TEXTORIAL
TONOTAXIS
TOXINOSIS
TRUXILLIN
UNISEXUAL
UROTOXIES
UROXANATE
XENELASIA

ALPHABETICAL LIST OF 10-LETTER WORDS

ACAROTOXIC
ACCUSATRIX
ACROATAXIA
ADIPOPEXIA
ADIPOPEXIS
ADNEXOPEXY
ADOXACEOUS
AFFIXATION
ALEXANDERS
ALEXITERIC
ALLOXANATE
ALLOXANTIN
AMAXOMANIA
AMBIDEXTER
AMBOSEXOUS
AMINOXYLOL
AMPHIMIXIS
ANEMOTAXIS
ANNEXATION
ANOXYSCOPE
ANTEFLEXED
ANTHOTAXIS
ANTICLIMAX
ANTIOXYGEN
ANTISPADIX
ANTITOXINE
APICIFIXED
APLOTAXENE
APPENDIXED
APPENDIXES
APPROXIMAL
ARSENOXIDE
ASEXUALITY
ASEXUALIZE
ASPHYXIANT
ASPHYXIATE
ATAXIAGRAM
ATAXINOMIC
ATAXONOMIC
AUTOXIDIZE
AUXANOGRAM
AUXANOLOGY
AUXILIARLY
AUXILIATOR
AUXOACTION
AUXOCARDIA
AUXOCHROME
AXEBREAKER
AXHAMMERED
AXILEMMATA
AXILLARIES
AXINOMANCY
AXIOLOGIST
AXIOMATIZE
AXONOMETRY
BIAXIALITY
BINOXALATE
BISEXUALLY
BISSEXTILE
BOBBYSOXER
BORDEREAUX
BOXBERRIES
BRACHYAXIS
CACODOXIAN
CACOXENITE
CARBOXYLIC
CARNIFEXES
CHAETOTAXY
CHALUMEAUX
CHATTERBOX
CHEMOTAXIS
CHRONAXIES
CICATRIXES
CIRCUMFLEX
COADJUTRIX
COEXISTENT
COLLOXYLIN
COLONOPEXY
COMMIXTION
COMMIXTURE
COMPLEXIFY
COMPLEXION
COMPLEXITY
CONNEXIVUM
CONTEXTUAL
CONTEXTURE
CONTRAPLEX
CONVEXEDLY
CONVEXNESS
COXCOMBESS
COXCOMICAL
COXOCERITE
COXOPODITE
CRIOSPHINX
CYCLOHEXYL
DEOXIDIZED
DEOXIDIZER
DERMATAUXE
DESOXALATE
DETOXICANT
DETOXICATE
DEXIOTROPE
DEXTERICAL
DEXTRALITY
DEXTRAURAL
DEXTRINASE
DEXTRINATE
DEXTRINIZE
DEXTRINOUS
DEXTROGYRE
DEXTRORSAL
DEXTROUSLY
DIASTATAXY
DIETOTOXIC
DIGITOXOSE
DISQUIXOTE
DISULFOXID
DORSIFIXED
DOXASTICON
DOXOGRAPHY
DOXOLOGIES
DOXOLOGIZE
DYSOXIDIZE
ECHOPRAXIA
ENDOTHORAX
ENTOMOTAXY
EPEXEGESIS
EPEXEGETIC
EPICALYXES
EPIPHARYNX
EPIPLOPEXY
ERGOTOXINE
ESONARTHEX
EUXANTHATE
EUXANTHONE
EXACERBATE
EXACTINGLY
EXACTITUDE
EXADVERSUM
EXAGGERATE
EXALTATION
EXALTATIVE
EXAMINABLE
EXAMINATOR
EXANTHEMAS
EXASPERATE
EXASPIDEAN
EXAUGURATE
EXCALATION
EXCALCEATE
EXCAVATING
EXCAVATION
EXCECATION
EXCELLENCE
EXCELLENCY
EXCEPTIOUS
EXCERPTING
EXCERPTION
EXCERPTIVE
EXCHANGING
EXCITATION
EXCITATIVE
EXCITATORY
EXCITEMENT
EXCITINGLY
EXCLAIMING
EXCOGITATE
EXCORIABLE
EXCORIATED
EXCORIATOR
EXCRESCENT
EXCRUCIATE
EXCUDERUNT
EXCULPABLE
EXCULPATED
EXCURVATED
EXCUSATIVE
EXCUSATORY
EXCYSTMENT
EXECRATING
EXECRATION
EXECRATIVE
EXECRATORY
EXECUTABLE
EXECUTANCY
EXECUTIONS
EXECUTRESS
EXEGETICAL
EXEMPLARIC
EXEMPTIBLE
EXENTERATE
EXERCISING
EXERCITANT
EXFOLIATED
EXHALATION
EXHALATORY
EXHAUSTING
EXHAUSTION
EXHAUSTIVE
EXHIBITANT
EXHIBITING
EXHIBITION
EXHIBITIVE
EXHIBITORY
EXHILARANT
EXHILARATE
EXHUMATING
EXHUMATION
EXHUMATORY
EXIGENCIES
EXIGUOUSLY
EXIMIOUSLY
EXINGUINAL
EXISTENTLY
EXOCARDIAC
EXOCARDIAL
EXOCENTRIC
EXOCHORION
EXOCOLITIS
EXOCULATED
EXOGASTRIC
EXOGENETIC
EXOMORPHIC
EXOMPHALOS
EXOMPHALUS
EXONARTHEX
EXONERATED
EXONERATOR
EXONERETUR
EXOPHAGOUS
EXOPODITIC
EXORBITANT
EXORBITATE
EXORCISING
EXORCISMAL
EXORCISORY
EXORCISTIC
EXORCIZING
EXORNATION
EXOSPHERIC
EXOSPORIUM
EXOSPOROUS
EXOTERICAL
EXOTHECATE
EXOTHECIUM
EXOTHERMAL
EXOTHERMIC
EXOTICALLY
EXOTICNESS
EXOTOSPORE
EXOTROPISM
EXPANDEDLY
EXPANSIBLE
EXPANSIBLY
EXPATIATED
EXPATIATER
EXPATIATOR
EXPATRIATE
EXPECTABLE
EXPECTANCE
EXPECTANCY
EXPEDIENCE
EXPEDIENCY
EXPEDIENTE
EXPEDITATE

EXPEDITELY
EXPEDITING
EXPEDITION
EXPELLABLE
EXPENDABLE
EXPENDITOR
EXPENSEFUL
EXPERIENCE
EXPERIMENT
EXPERTNESS
EXPILATION
EXPIRATION
EXPIRATORY
EXPISCATED
EXPISCATOR
EXPLAINING
EXPLANATOR
EXPLICABLE
EXPLICATED
EXPLICATOR
EXPLICITLY
EXPLOITAGE
EXPLOITING
EXPLOITIVE
EXPLOITURE
EXPLORATOR
EXPLOSIBLE
EXPLOSIVES
EXPORTABLE
EXPOSITION
EXPOSITIVE
EXPOSITORY
EXPOUNDING
EXPRESSAGE
EXPRESSING
EXPRESSIVE
EXPRESSMAN
EXPRESSWAY
EXPUGNABLE
EXPUNCTION
EXPURGATED
EXPURGATOR
EXSANGUINE
EXSCINDING
EXSIBILATE
EXSICCATAE
EXSICCATED
EXSILIENCY
EXSPUITION
EXSUFFLATE
EXTEMPORAL
EXTENDEDLY
EXTENDIBLE
EXTENSIBLE
EXTENUATED
EXTENUATOR
EXTERIORLY
EXTERNALLY
EXTINCTEUR
EXTINCTION
EXTINCTIVE
EXTINGUISH
EXTIRPATED
EXTIRPATOR
EXTISPICES
EXTOGENOUS
EXTOLLMENT
EXTOOLITIC
EXTRACTING
EXTRACTION
EXTRACTIVE
EXTRADITED
EXTRADOSED
EXTRADOTAL
EXTRAMURAL
EXTRANEITY
EXTRANEOUS
EXTRAPOLAR
EXTRASOLAR
EXTRATUBAL
EXTREMITAL
EXTRICABLE
EXTRICABLY
EXTRICATED
EXTROITIVE
EXTROPICAL
EXTRORSELY
EXTROSPECT
EXTUBATION
EXUBERANCE
EXUBERANCY
EXUBERATED
EXULCERATE
EXULTANTLY
EXULTATION
EXULTINGLY
EXUMBRELLA
EXUNDATION
EXURBANITE
EXUVIATING
EXUVIATION
EXZODIACAL
FLEXUOSITY
FLEXUOUSLY
FLUMMOXING
FLUXIONARY
FLUXIONIST
FOXBERRIES
FRAXINELLA
GASTROPEXY
GENERATRIX
GERONTOXON
GLYOXALASE
GLYOXALINE
GOOGOLPLEX
HELIOTAXIS
HEMOTHORAX
HETERODOXY
HEXABROMID
HEXACOSANE
HEXACTINAL
HEXACYCLIC
HEXADECANE
HEXAEMERIC
HEXAEMERON
HEXAGYNOUS
HEXAHEDRAL
HEXAHEDRON
HEXAHYDRIC
HEXAMERISM
HEXAMEROUS
HEXAMETRAL
HEXAMETRIC
HEXANDROUS
HEXANGULAR
HEXAPLARIC
HEXAPODIES
HEXARADIAL
HEXARCHIES
HEXASTICHY
HEXASTYLOS
HEXATRIOSE
HEXAVALENT
HEXPARTITE
HOLOPLEXIA
HOMOSEXUAL
HYDROTAXIS
HYPEROXIDE
HYPOPRAXIA
HYPOZEUXIS
IMPERATRIX
INDICATRIX
INEXERTION
INEXISTENT
INEXORABLE
INEXORABLY
INEXPECTED
INEXPERTLY
INEXPIABLE
INEXPIABLY
INEXPLICIT
INFLEXIBLE
INFLEXIBLY
INOXIDIZED
INSPECTRIX
INSPEXIMUS
INTERAXIAL
INTERMIXED
INTOXATION
INTOXICANT
INTOXICATE
JUXTAPOSED
JUXTAPOSIT
KERFLUMMOX
LACROIXITE
LACTOTOXIN
LAXATIVELY
LEUCOTOXIC
LEXICALITY
LEXICOLOGY
LEXICONIST
LEXICONIZE
LEXIGRAPHY
LEXIPHANIC
LIBERATRIX
LIENOTOXIN
LIPOMYXOMA
LIPOXENOUS
LIXIVIATED
LIXIVIATOR
LOXODROMIC
LUXURIANCE
LUXURIANCY
LUXURIATED
MALAXATION
MALAXERMAN
MALAXERMEN
MAXILLIPED
MAXIMATION
MAXIMISTIC
MAXIMIZING
MEDITHORAX
MENOSTAXIS
MESOTHORAX
MESOXALATE
METAGALAXY
METATHORAX
MIXILINEAL
MONAXONIAL
MONOXENOUS
MONOXYLOUS
MOXIEBERRY
MYDATOXINE
MYORRHEXIS
MYXADENOMA
MYXANGITIS
MYXOEDEMIC
MYXOGASTER
MYXOGLIOMA
MYXOLIPOMA
MYXOMATOUS
MYXOMYCETE
MYXOPODIUM
NECTOCALYX
NEPHROPEXY
NEURATAXIA
NEUROTOXIA
NEUROTOXIC
NEUROTOXIN
NOMINATRIX
NOMOPHYLAX
OXIDIZABLE
OLEOTHORAX
OMENTOPEXY
ONYCHAUXIS
OOPHORAUXE
OPTOMENINX
ORCHIOPEXY
OROPHARYNX
ORTHODOXAL
ORTHODOXLY
ORTHOPRAXY
OSCULATRIX
OVEREXPOSE
OVERTAXING
OXADIAZOLE
OXALACETIC
OXALURAMID
OXALYLUREA
OXAMETHANE
OXIDIMETRY
OXIDIZABLE
OXIDULATED
OXOZONIDES
OXYBLEPSIA
OXYBROMIDE
OXYBUTYRIA
OXYCALCIUM
OXYCAMPHOR
OXYCAPROIC
OXYCEPHALY
OXYCHLORIC
OXYCHLORID
OXYCYANIDE
OXYGENATED
OXYGENATOR
OXYGENIZED
OXYGENIZER
OXYHEMATIN
OXYHYDRATE
OXYMURIATE
OXYNEURINE
OXYNITRATE
OXYOPHITIC
OXYPHILOUS
OXYPROLINE
OXYQUINONE
OXYRHINOUS
OXYSTEARIC
OXYSULFIDE
OXYSULPHID
OXYTERPENE
OXYTOLUENE
OXYTONESIS
OXYTONICAL
OXYURIASIS
OXYURICIDE
OXYWELDING
PARADOXIAL
PARADOXIST
PARADOXURE
PARAPRAXIA
PARAPRAXES
PARAPRAXIS
PARAXIALLY
PAROXYSMAL
PAROXYSMIC
PAROXYTONE
PERIAXONAL
PERIPHRAXY
PERMIXABLE
PERMIXTION
PERMIXTIVE
PERMIXTURE
PEROXIDASE
PEROXIDING
PEROXIDIZE
PERPLEXING
PERPLEXITY
PETROSILEX
PETROXOLIN
PHILODOXER
PHLEBOPEXY
PHOENIXITY
PHOTOTAXIS
PHYLLOTAXY
PHYLLOXERA
PHYTOTOXIC
PHYTOTOXIN
PICROTOXIC
PICROTOXIN
PLEIOTAXIS
PLEXIGLASS
PLEXIMETER
PLEXIMETRY
PLURIAXIAL
PNEUMOPEXY
POLYMIXIID
POSTEXILIC
PRAEHALLUX
PRAXIOLOGY
PREAXIALLY
PREEXILIAN
PREFIXALLY
PREFIXEDLY
PREFIXTURE
PREFLEXION
PREMAXILLA
PROJECTRIX
PROLIXNESS
PROTEOPEXY
PROTOXYLEM
PROXICALLY
PYOSALPINX
PYRIDOXINE
PYROXENITE
PYROXYLINE
QUADRATRIX
QUADRUPLEX
QUINATOXIN
QUINCUNXES
QUINOXALIN
QUINOXALYL
QUIXOTICAL
RADIOTOXIC
REFLEXIBLE
RELAXATION
RELAXATIVE
RELAXATORY
RHIZOTAXIS
SAXICOLINE
SAXICOLOUS
SAXIGENOUS
SAXOPHONIC
SAXOTROMBA
SEPARATRIX
SEXAGENARY
SEXANGULAR
SEXDIGITAL
SEXOLOGIST
SEXPARTITE
SEXTENNIAL
SEXTILLION
SEXTIPOLAR
SEXTUPLING
SEXUPAROUS
SIMPLEXITY
SITOTOXISM
SNUFFBOXER
SOIXANTINE
SPECTATRIX
SPHINXLIKE
SPINTURNIX
SPLENOPEXY
STEREOTAXY

SUBAXILLAR
SUBMAXILLA
SUBMAXIMAL
SUFFIXMENT
SULFOXYLIC
SULPHOXIDE
SULPHOXISM
SUPEREXIST
SUPRACOXAL
SYNAXARION
SYNAXARIST
TAXABILITY
TAXATIONAL
TAXATIVELY
TAXIDERMAL
TAXIDERMIC
TAXONOMIST
TEXTUALISM
TEXTUALIST
TEXTUARIES
TEXTUARIST
TEXTURALLY
THEOMASTIX
THIXOTROPY
THYROTOXIC
TOXALBUMIC
TOXALBUMIN
TOXANAEMIA
TOXICATION
TOXICITIES
TOXICOLOGY
TOXIDERMIC
TOXIFEROUS
TOXINAEMIA
TOXIPHAGUS
TOXIPHOBIA
TOXIPHORIC
TRANSFIXED
TRIAXONIAN
TRICHAUXIS
TRIHYDROXY
TRIMETHOXY
TRIPLEXITY
TRISECTRIX
TROUSSEAUX
TRUXILLINE
TYROTOXINE
UNCOMMIXED
UNDERSEXED
UNEQUIAXED
UNEXAMPLED
UNEXCITING
UNEXPECTED
UNEXPENDED
UNEXPERTLY
UNFLEXIBLE
UNFLEXIBLY
UNIDEXTRAL
UNORTHODOX
UROXANTHIN
UXORIALITY
UXORICIDAL
UXORIOUSLY
VINCETOXIN
VIXENISHLY
WAXBERRIES
WAXHEARTED
WAXWORKING
XANTHALINE
XANTHAMIDE
XANTHATION
XANTHIURIA
XANTHOCONE
XANTHODERM
XANTHOMATA
XANTHOPHYL
XANTHOPSIA
XANTHOPSIN
XANTHYDROL
XENARTHRAL
XENOBIOSIS
XENOGAMOUS
XENOGENOUS
XENOPELTID
XENOPHOBIA
XENOPHOBIC
XENOPODOID
XENOPTERAN
XENOSAURID
XEROGRAPHY
XEROMORPHY
XEROPHYTIC
XIPHIIFORM
XIPHODYNIA
XIPHOIDIAN
XIPHOPAGIC
XIPHOPAGUS
XIPHOSURAN
XIPHYDRIID
XYLANTHRAX
XYLOGLYPHY
XYLOGRAPHY
XYLOPHAGAN
XYLOPHAGID
XYLOPHONIC
XYLOPOLIST
XYLORCINOL
XYLOSTROMA
XYLOTOMIST
XYLOTOMOUS
ZOOXANTHIN

POSITIONAL ORDER LIST OF 10-LETTER WORDS

XANTHALINE
XANTHAMIDE
XANTHATION
XANTHIURIA
XANTHOCONE
XANTHODERM
XANTHOMATA
XANTHOPHYL
XANTHOPSIA
XANTHOPSIN
XANTHYDROL
XENARTHRAL
XENOBIOSIS
XENOGAMOUS
XENOGENOUS
XENOPELTID
XENOPHOBIA
XENOPHOBIC
XENOPODOID
XENOPTERAN
XENOSAURID
XEROGRAPHY
XEROMORPHY
XEROPHYTIC
XIPHIIFORM
XIPHODYNIA
XIPHOIDIAN
XIPHOPAGIC
XIPHOPAGUS
XIPHOSURAN
XIPHYDRIID
XYLANTHRAX
XYLOGLYPHY
XYLOGRAPHY
XYLOPHAGAN
XYLOPHAGID
XYLOPHONIC
XYLOPOLIST
XYLORCINOL
XYLOSTROMA
XYLOTOMIST
XYLOTOMOUS

AXEBREAKER
AXHAMMERED
AXILEMMATA
AXILLARIES
AXINOMANCY
AXIOLOGIST
AXIOMATIZE
AXONOMETRY
EXACERBATE
EXACTINGLY
EXACTITUDE
EXADVERSUM
EXAGGERATE
EXALTATION
EXALTATIVE
EXAMINABLE
EXAMINATOR
EXANTHEMAS
EXASPERATE
EXASPIDEAN
EXAUGURATE
EXCALATION
EXCALCEATE
EXCAVATING
EXCAVATION
EXCECATION
EXCELLENCE
EXCELLENCY
EXCEPTIOUS
EXCERPTING
EXCERPTION
EXCERPTIVE
EXCHANGING
EXCITATION
EXCITATIVE
EXCITATORY
EXCITEMENT
EXCITINGLY
EXCLAIMING
EXCOGITATE
EXCORIABLE
EXCORIATED
EXCORIATOR
EXCRESCENT
EXCRUCIATE
EXCUDERUNT
EXCULPABLE
EXCULPATED
EXCURVATED
EXCUSATIVE
EXCUSATORY
EXCYSTMENT
EXECRATING
EXECRATION
EXECRATIVE
EXECRATORY
EXECUTABLE
EXECUTANCY
EXECUTIONS
EXECUTRESS
EXEGETICAL
EXEMPLARIC
EXEMPTIBLE
EXENTERATE
EXERCISING
EXERCITANT
EXFOLIATED
EXHALATION
EXHALATORY
EXHAUSTING
EXHAUSTION
EXHAUSTIVE
EXHIBITANT
EXHIBITING
EXHIBITION
EXHIBITIVE
EXHIBITORY
EXHILARANT
EXHILARATE
EXHUMATING
EXHUMATION
EXHUMATORY
EXIGENCIES
EXIGUOUSLY
EXIMIOUSLY
EXINGUINAL
EXISTENTLY
EXOCARDIAC
EXOCARDIAL
EXOCENTRIC
EXOCHORION
EXOCOLITIS
EXOCULATED
EXOGASTRIC
EXOGENETIC
EXOMORPHIC
EXOMPHALOS
EXOMPHALUS
EXONARTHEX
EXONERATED
EXONERATOR
EXONERETUR
EXOPHAGOUS
EXOPODITIC
EXORBITANT
EXORBITATE
EXORCISING
EXORCISMAL
EXORCISORY
EXORCISTIC
EXORCIZING
EXORNATION
EXOSPHERIC
EXOSPORIUM
EXOSPOROUS
EXOTERICAL
EXOTHECATE
EXOTHECIUM
EXOTHERMAL
EXOTHERMIC
EXOTICALLY
EXOTICNESS
EXOTOSPORE
EXOTROPISM
EXPANDEDLY
EXPANSIBLE
EXPANSIBLY
EXPATIATED
EXPATIATER
EXPATIATOR
EXPATRIATE
EXPECTABLE
EXPECTANCE
EXPECTANCY
EXPEDIENCE
EXPEDIENCY
EXPEDIENTE
EXPEDITATE
EXPEDITELY
EXPEDITING
EXPEDITION
EXPELLABLE
EXPENDABLE
EXPENDITOR
EXPENSEFUL
EXPERIENCE
EXPERIMENT
EXPERTNESS
EXPILATION
EXPIRATION
EXPIRATORY
EXPISCATED
EXPISCATOR
EXPLAINING
EXPLANATOR
EXPLICABLE
EXPLICATED
EXPLICATOR
EXPLICITLY
EXPLOITAGE
EXPLOITING
EXPLOITIVE
EXPLOITURE
EXPLORATOR
EXPLOSIBLE
EXPLOSIVES
EXPORTABLE
EXPOSITION
EXPOSITIVE
EXPOSITORY
EXPOUNDING
EXPRESSAGE
EXPRESSING
EXPRESSIVE
EXPRESSMAN
EXPRESSWAY
EXPUGNABLE
EXPUNCTION
EXPURGATED
EXPURGATOR
EXSANGUINE
EXSCINDING
EXSIBILATE
EXSICCATAE
EXSICCATED
EXSILIENCY
EXSPUITION
EXSUFFLATE
EXTEMPORAL
EXTENDEDLY
EXTENDIBLE
EXTENSIBLE
EXTENUATED
EXTENUATOR
EXTERIORLY
EXTERNALLY
EXTINCTEUR

EXTINCTION
EXTINCTIVE
EXTINGUISH
EXTIRPATED
EXTIRPATOR
EXTISPICES
EXTOGENOUS
EXTOLLMENT
EXTOOLITIC
EXTRACTING
EXTRACTION
EXTRACTIVE
EXTRADITED
EXTRADOSED
EXTRADOTAL
EXTRAMURAL
EXTRANEITY
EXTRANEOUS
EXTRAPOLAR
EXTRASOLAR
EXTRATUBAL
EXTREMITAL
EXTRICABLE
EXTRICABLY
EXTRICATED
EXTROITIVE
EXTROPICAL
EXTRORSELY
EXTROSPECT
EXTUBATION
EXUBERANCE
EXUBERANCY
EXUBERATED
EXULCERATE
EXULTANTLY
EXULTATION
EXULTINGLY
EXUMBRELLA
EXUNDATION
EXURBANITE
EXUVIATING
EXUVIATION
EXZODIACAL
OXIDIZABLE
OXADIAZOLE
OXALACETIC
OXALURAMID
OXALYLUREA
OXAMETHANE
OXIDIMETRY
OXIDIZABLE
OXIDULATED
OXOZONIDES
OXYBLEPSIA
OXYBROMIDE
OXYBUTYRIA
OXYCALCIUM
OXYCAMPHOR
OXYCAPROIC
OXYCEPHALY
OXYCHLORIC
OXYCHLORID
OXYCYANIDE
OXYGENATED
OXYGENATOR
OXYGENIZED
OXYGENIZER
OXYHEMATIN
OXYHYDRATE
OXYMURIATE
OXYNEURINE
OXYNITRATE
OXYOPHITIC
OXYPHILOUS
OXYPROLINE
OXYQUINONE
OXYRHINOUS

OXYSTEARIC
OXYSULFIDE
OXYSULPHID
OXYTERPENE
OXYTOLUENE
OXYTONESIS
OXYTONICAL
OXYURIASIS
OXYURICIDE
OXYWELDING
UXORIALITY
UXORICIDAL
UXORIOUSLY

AUXANOGRAM
AUXANOLOGY
AUXILIARLY
AUXILIATOR
AUXOACTION
AUXOCARDIA
AUXOCHROME
BOXBERRIES
COXCOMBESS
COXCOMICAL
COXOCERITE
COXOPODITE
DEXIOTROPE
DEXTERICAL
DEXTRALITY
DEXTRAURAL
DEXTRINASE
DEXTRINATE
DEXTRINIZE
DEXTRINOUS
DEXTROGYRE
DEXTRORSAL
DEXTROUSLY
DOXASTICON
DOXOGRAPHY
DOXOLOGIES
DOXOLOGIZE
EUXANTHATE
EUXANTHONE
FOXBERRIES
HEXABROMID
HEXACOSANE
HEXACTINAL
HEXACYCLIC
HEXADECANE
HEXAEMERIC
HEXAEMERON
HEXAGYNOUS
HEXAHEDRAL
HEXAHEDRON
HEXAHYDRIC
HEXAMERISM
HEXAMEROUS
HEXAMETRAL
HEXAMETRIC
HEXANDROUS
HEXANGULAR
HEXAPLARIC
HEXAPODIES
HEXARADIAL
HEXARCHIES
HEXASTICHY
HEXASTYLOS
HEXATRIOSE
HEXAVALENT
HEXPARTITE
JUXTAPOSED
JUXTAPOSIT
LAXATIVELY
LEXICALITY
LEXICOLOGY
LEXICONIST
LEXICONIZE

LEXIGRAPHY
LEXIPHANIC
LIXIVIATED
LIXIVIATOR
LOXODROMIC
LUXURIANCE
LUXURIANCY
LUXURIATED
MAXILLIPED
MAXIMATION
MAXIMISTIC
MAXIMIZING
MIXILINEAL
MOXIEBERRY
MYXADENOMA
MYXANGITIS
MYXOEDEMIC
MYXOGASTER
MYXOGLIOMA
MYXOLIPOMA
MYXOMATOUS
MYXOMYCETE
MYXOPODIUM
SAXICOLINE
SAXICOLOUS
SAXIGENOUS
SAXOPHONIC
SAXOTROMBA
SEXAGENARY
SEXANGULAR
SEXDIGITAL
SEXOLOGIST
SEXPARTITE
SEXTENNIAL
SEXTILLION
SEXTIPOLAR
SEXTUPLING
SEXUPAROUS
TAXABILITY
TAXATIONAL
TAXATIVELY
TAXIDERMAL
TAXIDERMIC
TAXONOMIST
TEXTUALISM
TEXTUALIST
TEXTUARIES
TEXTUARIST
TEXTURALLY
TOXALBUMIC
TOXALBUMIN
TOXANAEMIA
TOXICATION
TOXICITIES
TOXICOLOGY
TOXIDERMIC
TOXIFEROUS
TOXINAEMIA
TOXIPHAGUS
TOXIPHOBIA
TOXIPHORIC
VIXENISHLY
WAXBERRIES
WAXHEARTED
WAXWORKING

ADOXACEOUS
ALEXANDERS
ALEXITERIC
AMAXOMANIA
ANOXYSCOPE
ASEXUALITY
ASEXUALIZE
ATAXIAGRAM
ATAXINOMIC
ATAXONOMIC
BIAXIALITY

COEXISTENT
DEOXIDIZED
DEOXIDIZER
EPEXEGESIS
EPEXEGETIC
FLEXUOSITY
FLEXUOUSLY
FLUXIONARY
FLUXIONIST
FRAXINELLA
INEXERTION
INEXISTENT
INEXORABLE
INEXORABLY
INEXPECTED
INEXPERTLY
INEXPIABLE
INEXPIABLY
INEXPLICIT
INOXIDIZED
PLEXIGLASS
PLEXIMETER
PLEXIMETRY
PRAXIOLOGY
PROXICALLY
QUIXOTICAL
SOIXANTINE
THIXOTROPY
TRUXILLINE
UNEXAMPLED
UNEXCITING
UNEXPECTED
UNEXPENDED
UNEXPERTLY
UROXANTHIN
ZOOXANTHIN

AFFIXATION
ALLOXANATE
ALLOXANTIN
ANNEXATION
AUTOXIDIZE
BINOXALATE
BISEXUALLY
CACOXENITE
DESOXALATE
DETOXICANT
DETOXICATE
DYSOXIDIZE
GLYOXALASE
GLYOXALINE
INTOXATION
INTOXICANT
INTOXICATE
LIPOXENOUS
MALAXATION
MALAXERMAN
MALAXERMEN
MESOXALATE
MONAXONIAL
MONOXENOUS
MONOXYLOUS
PARAXIALLY
PAROXYSMAL
PAROXYSMIC
PAROXYTONE
PEROXIDASE
PEROXIDING
PEROXIDIZE
PREAXIALLY
PREEXILIAN
PYROXENITE
PYROXYLINE
RELAXATION
RELAXATIVE
RELAXATORY
SUBAXILLAR

SYNAXARION
SYNAXARIST
TRIAXONIAN

AMINOXYLOL
ANTIOXYGEN
APPROXIMAL
ASPHYXIANT
ASPHYXIATE
BISSEXTILE
CARBOXYLIC
COLLOXYLIN
COMMIXTION
COMMIXTURE
CONNEXIVUM
CONTEXTUAL
CONTEXTURE
CONVEXEDLY
CONVEXNESS
INFLEXIBLE
INFLEXIBLY
INSPEXIMUS
OVEREXPOSE
PERIAXONAL
PERMIXABLE
PERMIXTION
PERMIXTIVE
PERMIXTURE
PETROXOLIN
POSTEXILIC
PREFIXALLY
PREFIXEDLY
PREFIXTURE
PREMAXILLA
PROLIXNESS
PROTOXYLEM
QUINOXALIN
QUINOXALYL
REFLEXIBLE
SPHINXLIKE
SUBMAXILLA
SUBMAXIMAL
SUFFIXMENT
SULFOXYLIC
UNFLEXIBLE
UNFLEXIBLY
UNIDEXTRAL

AMBIDEXTER
AMBOSEXOUS
ANTITOXINE
APLOTAXENE
ARSENOXIDE
CACODOXIAN
CHRONAXIES
COMPLEXIFY
COMPLEXION
COMPLEXITY
DIGITOXOSE
DISQUIXOTE
ERGOTOXINE
FLUMMOXING
HOMOSEXUAL
HYPEROXIDE
INTERAXIAL
LACROIXITE
LIPOMYXOMA
MYDATOXINE
OVERTAXING
PARADOXIAL
PARADOXIST
PARADOXURE
PERPLEXING
PERPLEXITY
PHOENIXITY
PHYLLOXERA
PLURIAXIAL

POLYMIXIID
PREFLEXION
PYRIDOXINE
SIMPLEXITY
SITOTOXISM
SULPHOXIDE
SULPHOXISM
SUPEREXIST
TRIPLEXITY
TYROTOXINE

ACAROTOXIC
ACROATAXIA
ADIPOPEXIA
ADIPOPEXIS
AMPHIMIXIS
ANEMOTAXIS
ANTEFLEXED
ANTHOTAXIS
APICIFIXED
APPENDIXED
APPENDIXES
BOBBYSOXER
BRACHYAXIS
CARNIFEXES
CHEMOTAXIS
CICATRIXES
CYCLOHEXYL
DIETOTOXIC
DISULFOXID

DORSIFIXED
ECHOPRAXIA
EPICALYXES
GERONTOXON
HELIOTAXIS
HOLOPLEXIA
HYDROTAXIS
HYPOPRAXIA
HYPOZEUXIS
INTERMIXED
LACTOTOXIN
LEUCOTOXIC
LIENOTOXIN
MENOSTAXIS
MYORRHEXIS
NEURATAXIA
NEUROTOXIA
NEUROTOXIC
NEUROTOXIN
ONYCHAUXIS
ORTHODOXAL
ORTHODOXLY
PARAPRAXIA
PARAPRAXES
PARAPRAXIS
PHILODOXER
PHOTOTAXIS
PHYTOTOXIC
PHYTOTOXIN

PICROTOXIC
PICROTOXIN
PLEIOTAXIS
QUINATOXIN
QUINCUNXES
RADIOTOXIC
RHIZOTAXIS
SNUFFBOXER
SUPRACOXAL
THYROTOXIC
TRANSFIXED
TRICHAUXIS
UNCOMMIXED
UNDERSEXED
UNEQUIAXED
VINCETOXIN

ADNEXOPEXY
CHAETOTAXY
DERMATAUXE
DIASTATAXY
ENTOMOTAXY
EPIPLOPEXY
GASTROPEXY
HETERODOXY
METAGALAXY
NEPHROPEXY
OMENTOPEXY
OOPHORAUXE

ORCHIOPEXY
ORTHOPRAXY
PERIPHRAXY
PHLEBOPEXY
PHYLLOTAXY
PNEUMOPEXY
PROTEOPEXY
SPLENOPEXY
STEREOTAXY
TRIHYDROXY
TRIMETHOXY

ACCUSATRIX
ANTICLIMAX
ANTISPADIX
BORDEREAUX
CHALUMEAUX
CHATTERBOX
CIRCUMFLEX
COADJUTRIX
CONTRAPLEX
CRIOSPHINX
ENDOTHORAX
EPIPHARYNX
ESONARTHEX
EXONARTHEX
GENERATRIX
GOOGOLPLEX
HEMOTHORAX

IMPERATRIX
INDICATRIX
INSPECTRIX
KERFLUMMOX
LIBERATRIX
MEDITHORAX
MESOTHORAX
METATHORAX
NECTOCALYX
NOMINATRIX
NOMOPHYLAX
OLEOTHORAX
OPTOMENINX
OROPHARYNX
OSCULATRIX
PETROSILEX
PRAEHALLUX
PROJECTRIX
PYOSALPINX
QUADRATRIX
QUADRUPLEX
SEPARATRIX
SPECTATRIX
SPINTURNIX
THEOMASTIX
TRISECTRIX
TROUSSEAUX
UNORTHODOX
XYLANTHRAX

SCORING ORDER LIST OF 10-LETTER WORDS

34
HYPOZEUXIS

31
DYSOXIDIZE
MAXIMIZING
OXYGENIZED

30
CYCLOHEXYL
OXYCEPHALY
OXYGENIZER

29
COMPLEXIFY
DEOXIDIZED
EXORCIZING
EXZODIACAL
HEXAHYDRIC
MYXOMYCETE
OXIDIZABLE
OXYCAMPHOR
OXYQUINONE
PEROXIDIZE
PHLEBOPEXY
QUADRUPLEX
QUINOXALYL
RHIZOTAXIS
XYLOGRAPHY
ZOOXANTHIN

28
AXIOMATIZE
DEOXIDIZER
DOXOLOGIZE
HEXASTICHY
INOXIDIZED
KERFLUMMOX
LEXICONIZE
PHYLLOTAXY
PROJECTRIX
QUINCUNXES
QUIXOTICAL
WAXWORKING
XANTHOPHYL
XYLOGLYPHY

27
AUTOXIDIZE
BRACHYAXIS
DEXTRINIZE
DISQUIXOTE
DOXOGRAPHY
EPIPHARYNX
HYPOPRAXIA
JUXTAPOSED
MYXOEDEMIC
MYXOPODIUM
NEPHROPEXY
NOMOPHYLAX
ORCHIOPEXY
OXADIAZOLE
OXOZONIDES
OXYCHLORIC
OXYHYDRATE
OXYOPHITIC
PERIPHRAXY
PHYTOTOXIC
QUADRATRIX
TRIHYDROXY
UNEQUIAXED
XEROMORPHY
XEROPHYTIC
XIPHIIFORM
XIPHOPAGIC
XIPHYDRIID
XYLOPHAGID
XYLOPHONIC

26
AMPHIMIXIS
ASEXUALIZE
CARBOXYLIC
CIRCUMFLEX
COMPLEXITY
CONVEXEDLY
EXOMORPHIC
EXPECTANCY
HEXACYCLIC
HYPEROXIDE
JUXTAPOSIT
LEXIGRAPHY
LIPOMYXOMA
MYXOLIPOMA
OXYCALCIUM
OXYCAPROIC
OXYCHLORID
OXYCYANIDE
OXYSULPHID
PAROXYSMIC
PNEUMOPEXY
PREFIXEDLY
QUINATOXIN
QUINOXALIN
SPHINXLIKE
VIXENISHLY
XENOPHOBIC
XEROGRAPHY
XIPHODYNIA
XYLOPHAGAN

25
APICIFIXED
ASPHYXIANT
ASPHYXIATE
AXHAMMERED
CHAETOTAXY
COXCOMBESS
EXHIBITIVE
EXHIBITORY
EXHUMATORY
EXPEDIENCY
EXPRESSWAY
FLUMMOXING
HEMOTHORAX
HEXABROMID
HEXARCHIES
INFLEXIBLY
MYORRHEXIS
MYXADENOMA
MYXOGLIOMA
ONYCHAUXIS
OROPHARYNX
ORTHOPRAXY
OXYBROMIDE
OXYBUTYRIA
OXYHEMATIN
OXYPHILOUS
OXYWELDING
PHOENIXITY
PHYLLOXERA
PHYTOTOXIN
POLYMIXIID
PREFIXALLY
PYROXYLINE
SNUFFBOXER
SUFFIXMENT
SULFOXYLIC
THIXOTROPY
THYROTOXIC
TRIMETHOXY
UNFLEXIBLY
XIPHOPAGUS

24
ANOXYSCOPE
AUXOCHROME
AXINOMANCY
CHALUMEAUX
CHATTERBOX
CHEMOTAXIS
COLONOPEXY
CONNEXIVUM
CRIOSPHINX
ECHOPRAXIA
EPICALYXES
EXCELLENCY
EXCERPTIVE
EXCHANGING
EXCYSTMENT
EXECUTANCY
EXOMPHALOS
EXOMPHALUS
EXOSPHERIC
EXOTHECIUM
EXOTHERMIC
EXPANDEDLY
EXPANSIBLY
EXPLICITLY
EXTRICABLY
EXUBERANCY
HETERODOXY
HEXAEMERIC
HEXAGYNOUS
HEXAHEDRAL
HEXAHEDRON
HEXAMERISM
HEXAMETRIC
HEXAPLARIC
HYDROTAXIS
INEXPIABLY
LEXIPHANIC
MOXIEBERRY
MYXOMATOUS
NECTOCALYX
OMENTOPEXY
ORTHODOXLY
OXYBLEPSIA
OXYSULFIDE
PAROXYSMAL
PERMIXTIVE
PERPLEXITY
PLEXIMETRY
PROTEOPEXY
PROTOXYLEM

PROXICALLY
PYOSALPINX
SAXOPHONIC
SIMPLEXITY
SPLENOPEXY
SULPHOXISM
TOXIPHOBIA
TOXIPHORIC
UNCOMMIXED
WAXHEARTED
XANTHYDROL
XENOPHOBIA

23
AFFIXATION
APPENDIXED
APPROXIMAL
AXEBREAKER
BOBBYSOXER
COMMIXTION
COMMIXTURE
COMPLEXION
EPIPLOPEXY
EXACTINGLY
EXADVERSUM
EXCAVATING
EXCITINGLY
EXCULPABLE
EXCURVATED
EXEMPLARIC
EXEMPTIBLE
EXHALATORY
EXHAUSTIVE
EXHIBITING
EXHUMATING
EXOPHAGOUS
EXPECTABLE
EXPECTANCE
EXPEDITELY
EXPLICABLE
EXSUFFLATE
FLEXUOSITY
FLEXUOUSLY
FLUXIONARY
GASTROPEXY
HEXADECANE
HEXAPODIES
HEXASTYLOS
HEXAVALENT
LAXATIVELY
LEXICOLOGY
MAXIMISTIC
MEDITHORAX
METAGALAXY
MYDATOXINE
MYXANGITIS
MYXOGASTER
OXIDIMETRY
OXYRHINOUS
OXYURICIDE
PERMIXABLE
PHILODOXER
PICROTOXIC
PRAXIOLOGY
PYRIDOXINE
SUBMAXIMAL
SULPHOXIDE
TAXATIVELY
TOXALBUMIC
TOXICOLOGY
TOXIPHAGUS
XANTHAMIDE
XANTHODERM
XIPHOIDIAN

22
ADIPOPEXIA
ADIPOPEXIS
ADNEXOPEXY
AMBIDEXTER
AMINOXYLOL
APPENDIXES
AXONOMETRY
BIAXIALITY
BISEXUALLY
CACODOXIAN
CARNIFEXES
CHRONAXIES
COLLOXYLIN
CONVEXNESS
COXCOMICAL
COXOPODITE
DEXTROGYRE
DISULFOXID
DORSIFIXED
ENTOMOTAXY
EPEXEGETIC
EXANTHEMAS
EXCAVATION
EXCERPTING
EXCITATIVE
EXCITATORY
EXCLAIMING
EXCULPATED
EXCUSATIVE
EXCUSATORY
EXECRATIVE
EXECRATORY
EXHIBITANT
EXHIBITION
EXHUMATION
EXIMIOUSLY
EXOCARDIAC
EXOCHORION
EXOPODITIC
EXORCISORY
EXOTHECATE
EXOTHERMAL
EXOTICALLY
EXPEDIENCE
EXPENDABLE
EXPENSEFUL
EXPIRATORY
EXPISCATED
EXPLICATED
EXPLOITIVE
EXPLOSIVES
EXPOSITIVE
EXPOSITORY
EXPRESSIVE
EXPUGNABLE
EXSICCATED
EXSILIENCY
EXTENDEDLY
EXTINCTIVE
EXTRACTIVE
FOXBERRIES
HEXACOSANE
HEXACTINAL
HEXAEMERON
HEXAMEROUS
HEXAMETRAL
HEXPARTITE
HOLOPLEXIA
HOMOSEXUAL
INEXORABLY
INEXPECTED
INEXPERTLY
INFLEXIBLE
LEXICALITY
LOXODROMIC
LUXURIANCY
MAXILLIPED
MESOTHORAX
METATHORAX
MONOXYLOUS
OOPHORAUXE
OVEREXPOSE
OXAMETHANE
OXYGENATED
OXYMURIATE
OXYPROLINE
OXYSTEARIC
OXYTERPENE
OXYTONICAL
PARAXIALLY
PAROXYTONE
PERPLEXING
PHOTOTAXIS
PRAEHALLUX
PREAXIALLY
PREFIXTURE
PREFLEXION
PYROXENITE
REFLEXIBLE
TAXABILITY
TAXIDERMIC
THEOMASTIX
TOXIDERMIC
TRICHAUXIS
TRIPLEXITY
UNEXAMPLED
UNEXPECTED
UNEXPERTLY
UNFLEXIBLE
VINCETOXIN
WAXBERRIES
XANTHOCONE
XANTHOMATA
XANTHOPSIA
XANTHOPSIN
XIPHOSURAN
XYLANTHRAX
XYLOPOLIST
XYLORCINOL
XYLOSTROMA
XYLOTOMIST
XYLOTOMOUS

21
ACAROTOXIC
ACCUSATRIX
AMAXOMANIA
AMBOSEXOUS
ANTEFLEXED
ANTICLIMAX
ANTIOXYGEN
ATAXINOMIC
ATAXONOMIC
AUXANOLOGY
AXILEMMATA
BOXBERRIES
CACOXENITE
CICATRIXES
CONTRAPLEX
COXOCERITE
DEXTRALITY
DEXTROUSLY
DIASTATAXY
ENDOTHORAX
EXACERBATE
EXAMINABLE
EXCALCEATE
EXCECATION
EXCELLENCE
EXCEPTIOUS
EXCERPTION
EXCITEMENT
EXECUTABLE
EXFOLIATED
EXHAUSTING
EXIGUOUSLY
EXOCENTRIC
EXORCISMAL
EXORCISTIC
EXOSPORIUM
EXOTROPISM
EXPANSIBLE
EXPEDITING
EXPELLABLE
EXPERIENCE
EXPERIMENT
EXPISCATOR
EXPLICATOR
EXPLOSIBLE
EXPORTABLE
EXPOUNDING
EXPRESSMAN
EXPUNCTION
EXPURGATED
EXSCINDING
EXSICCATAE
EXTEMPORAL
EXTINGUISH
EXTISPICES
EXTRICABLE
EXTROPICAL
EXTROSPECT
EXUBERANCE
EXULTINGLY
EXUMBRELLA
EXUVIATING
GLYOXALASE
GLYOXALINE
GOOGOLPLEX
HEXANDROUS
HEXANGULAR
HEXARADIAL
IMPERATRIX
INEXPIABLE
INEXPLICIT
INSPECTRIX
INSPEXIMUS
LEUCOTOXIC
LIXIVIATED
MALAXERMAN
MALAXERMEN
MAXIMATION
OPTOMENINX
ORTHODOXAL
OVERTAXING
OXALACETIC
OXYGENATOR
PARAPRAXIA
PARAPRAXES
PARAPRAXIS
PERMIXTION
PERMIXTURE
PEROXIDING
PICROTOXIN
PLEXIMETER
POSTEXILIC
PREMAXILLA
SAXOTROMBA
SEXAGENARY
SPECTATRIX
SUBMAXILLA
SUPRACOXAL
TOXALBUMIN
TRANSFIXED
UNEXPENDED
UNORTHODOX
XENOPODOID

20
ADOXACEOUS
ANTHOTAXIS
ANTISPADIX
ASEXUALITY
ATAXIAGRAM
AUXANOGRAM
AUXILIARLY
AUXOCARDIA
BORDEREAUX
DERMATAUXE
DETOXICANT
DETOXICATE
DEXIOTROPE
DEXTERICAL
DIETOTOXIC
DOXASTICON
EPEXEGESIS
ESONARTHEX
EUXANTHATE
EUXANTHONE
EXACTITUDE
EXALTATIVE
EXASPIDEAN
EXCUDERUNT
EXECRATING
EXEGETICAL
EXERCISING
EXHALATION
EXHAUSTION
EXHILARANT
EXHILARATE
EXIGENCIES
EXISTENTLY
EXOCARDIAL
EXOCULATED
EXOGASTRIC
EXOGENETIC
EXORCISING
EXPATIATED
EXPEDIENTE
EXPEDITATE
EXPEDITION
EXPENDITOR
EXPLAINING
EXPLOITAGE
EXPLOITING
EXPRESSAGE
EXPRESSING
EXPURGATOR
EXTENDIBLE
EXTERIORLY
EXTERNALLY
EXTIRPATED
EXTRACTING
EXTRANEITY
EXTRICATED
EXTROITIVE
EXTRORSELY
EXUBERATED
EXULTANTLY
EXUVIATION
FLUXIONIST
FRAXINELLA
HELIOTAXIS
HEXATRIOSE
INDICATRIX
INTERMIXED
LIXIVIATOR
OLEOTHORAX
OXALURAMID
OXALYLUREA
OXYNEURINE
OXYNITRATE
OXYTOLUENE
OXYTONESIS
OXYURIASIS
PARADOXIAL
PARADOXIST
PARADOXURE
PEROXIDASE

PLEXIGLASS
RADIOTOXIC
RELAXATIVE
RELAXATORY
SEXTUPLING
STEREOTAXY
SYNAXARION
SYNAXARIST
TAXIDERMAL
TEXTURALLY
TOXIFEROUS
TYROTOXINE
UNEXCITING
UROXANTHIN
UXORIALITY
UXORICIDAL
UXORIOUSLY
XANTHALINE
XANTHATION
XANTHIURIA
XENARTHRAL
XENOGAMOUS
XENOPELTID

19
ACROATAXIA
ALEXITERIC
ANEMOTAXIS
APLOTAXENE
AUXOACTION
BINOXALATE
BISSEXTILE
COEXISTENT
CONTEXTUAL
CONTEXTURE
DIGITOXOSE
DOXOLOGIES
EXAGGERATE
EXAMINATOR
EXASPERATE
EXCALATION
EXCITATION
EXECRATION
EXECUTIONS
EXECUTRESS
EXERCITANT
EXOCOLITIS
EXONARTHEX
EXORBITANT
EXORBITATE
EXOSPOROUS
EXOTERICAL
EXOTICNESS
EXOTOSPORE
EXPATIATER
EXPATIATOR
EXPATRIATE
EXPERTNESS
EXPILATION
EXPIRATION
EXPLANATOR
EXPLOITURE
EXPLORATOR
EXPOSITION
EXSIBILATE
EXSPUITION
EXTENSIBLE
EXTINCTEUR
EXTINCTION
EXTIRPATOR
EXTOLLMENT
EXTOOLITIC
EXTRACTION
EXTRADITED
EXTRADOSED
EXTRAMURAL
EXTRAPOLAR
EXTRATUBAL
EXTREMITAL
EXTUBATION
EXULCERATE
EXURBANITE
INEXORABLE
INTOXICANT
INTOXICATE
LACROIXITE
LACTOTOXIN
LEXICONIST
LIBERATRIX
LIPOXENOUS
LUXURIANCE
MALAXATION
MENOSTAXIS
MESOXALATE
MIXILINEAL
MONAXONIAL
MONOXENOUS
NEUROTOXIC
NOMINATRIX
OSCULATRIX
OXIDULATED
PERIAXONAL
PETROSILEX
PETROXOLIN
PLEIOTAXIS
PLURIAXIAL
PREEXILIAN
PROLIXNESS
SAXICOLINE
SAXICOLOUS
SEPARATRIX
SEXDIGITAL
SEXPARTITE
SEXTIPOLAR
SEXUPAROUS
SITOTOXISM
SPINTURNIX
SUBAXILLAR
SUPEREXIST
TAXONOMIST
TEXTUALISM
TOXANAEMIA
TOXICATION
TOXICITIES
TOXINAEMIA
TRISECTRIX
UNDERSEXED
XENOBIOSIS
XENOPTERAN

18
ALEXANDERS
ARSENOXIDE
AXIOLOGIST
DESOXALATE
DEXTRAURAL
DEXTRINASE
DEXTRINATE
DEXTRINOUS
DEXTRORSAL
ERGOTOXINE
EXAUGURATE
EXINGUINAL
EXONERATED
EXSANGUINE
EXTENUATED
EXTOGENOUS
EXTRADOTAL
EXUNDATION
GENERATRIX
GERONTOXON
LUXURIATED
SAXIGENOUS
SEXANGULAR
SEXOLOGIST
UNIDEXTRAL
XENOGENOUS
XENOSAURID

17
ALLOXANATE
ALLOXANTIN
ANNEXATION
ANTITOXINE
AUXILIATOR
AXILLARIES
EXALTATION
EXENTERATE
EXONERATOR
EXONERETUR
EXORNATION
EXTENUATOR
EXTRANEOUS
EXTRASOLAR
EXULTATION
INEXERTION
INEXISTENT
INTERAXIAL
INTOXATION
LIENOTOXIN
NEURATAXIA
NEUROTOXIA
NEUROTOXIN
RELAXATION
SEXTENNIAL
SEXTILLION
SOIXANTINE
TAXATIONAL
TEXTUALIST
TEXTUARIES
TEXTUARIST
TRIAXONIAN
TROUSSEAUX
TRUXILLINE

ALPHABETICAL LIST OF WORDS OVER 10 LETTERS

ACROASPHYXIA
ACTINOPRAXIS
ADENOMYXOMA
ADMAXILLARY
ADOXOGRAPHY
ALEXANDRITE
ALEXIPHARMIC
ALEXIPYRETIC
AMBIDEXTERITY
AMBIDEXTRAL
AMBIDEXTROUS
AMIDOHEXOSE
AMPLEXATION
AMPLEXICAUL
AMYLODEXTRIN
ANAPHYLAXIS
ANDROSPHINX
ANGIOATAXIA
ANGIORRHEXIS
ANHYDROXIME
ANILIDOXIME
ANISALDOXIME
ANNEXATIONAL
ANNEXATIONIST
ANNEXIONIST
ANOXIDATIVE
ANOXYBIOSIS
ANOXYBIOTIC
ANTEFLEXION
ANTHEXIMETER
ANTHOXANTHIN
ANTHRAXOLITE
ANTHRAXYLON
ANTHROXANIC
ANTIOXIDANT
ANTIOXYGENIC
ANXIOUSNESS
AORTOMALAXIS
APHOTOTAXIS
APOPHYLAXIS
APOPLEXIOUS
APPENDIXING
APPROXIMATE
APPROXIMATED
APPROXIMATELY
APPROXIMATING
APPROXIMATION
APPROXIMATIVE
APPROXIMATOR
ARCHEOPTERYX
ARCHOSYRINX
ARTHROSYRINX
ASEXUALIZED
ASEXUALIZING
ASPHYXIATED
ASPHYXIATING
ASPHYXIATION
ASPHYXIATOR
ATAXAPHASIA
ATAXIAGRAPH
ATAXIAMETER
ATAXIAPHASIA
ATAXOPHEMIA
ATLANTOAXIAL
ATLOIDOAXOID
AUTOCRATRIX
AUTOTOXAEMIA
AUTOTOXEMIA
AUTOXIDATION
AUTOXIDATOR
AUXANOMETER
AUXETICALLY
AUXILIARIES
AUXILIATION
AUXILIATORY
AUXOAMYLASE
AUXOCHROMIC
AUXOCHROMISM
AUXOCHROMOUS
AUXOGRAPHIC
AUXOHORMONE
AXIOLOGICAL
AXIOMATICAL
AXISYMMETRIC
AXODENDRITE
AXONOLIPOUS
AXONOMETRIC
AXONOPHOROUS
AXOSPERMOUS
BACTERIOTOXIC
BANDBOXICAL
BENZALDOXIME
BIMAXILLARY
BISAXILLARY
BISEXUALISM
BISEXUALITY
CARBETHOXYL
CARBOLXYLOL
CARBOXYLASE
CARBOXYLATE
CARBOXYLATED
CARDIATAXIA
CARDIOTOXIC
CHALCEDONYX
CHARTOPHYLAX
CHEMIOTAXIC
CHEMIOTAXIS
CHEMOREFLEX
CHIROPRAXIS
CHYLOTHORAX
CIRCUMAXIAL
CIRCUMAXILE
CLITORIDAUXE
COEXISTENCE
COEXISTENCY
COEXTENSION
COEXTENSIVE
COLOPEXOTOMY
COLPORRHEXIS
COMPETITRIX
COMPLEXIONAL
COMPLEXIONARY
COMPLEXIONED
COMPLEXITIES
COMPLEXNESS
CONFLUXIBLE
CONNEXITIES
CONSOLATRIX
CONTEXTUALLY
CONTEXTURAL
CONTEXTURED
CONVEXEDNESS
CONVEXITIES
COSTOXIPHOID
COXARTHRITIS

COXCOMBICAL
COXOCERITIC
COXOFEMORAL
CREATOTOXISM
CRUCIFIXION
CYCLOHEXANE
CYCLOHEXANOL
CYCLOHEXENE
CYSTOMYXOMA
CYSTOSYRINX
CYTOPHARYNX
DECIMOSEXTO
DEOXIDIZING
DEOXYGENATE
DEOXYGENATED
DEOXYGENIZE
DESEXUALIZE
DESEXUALIZED
DETOXICATED
DETOXICATING
DETOXICATION
DETOXICATOR
DEXIOTROPIC
DEXIOTROPISM
DEXIOTROPOUS
DEXTEROUSLY
DEXTROCARDIA
DEXTROCULAR
DEXTROGYRATE
DEXTROSAZONE
DEXTROSURIA
DEXTROUSNESS
DIASTATAXIC
DICARBOXYLIC
DICATALEXIS
DIHEXAHEDRAL
DIHEXAHEDRON
DIRECTRIXES
DISOXYGENATE
DISPENSATRIX
DISULPHOXID
DISULPHOXIDE
DOPAOXIDASE
DORSIFLEXION
DORSIFLEXOR
DOXOGRAPHER
DOXOLOGICAL
DOXOLOGIZED
DOXOLOGIZING
DYSOXIDATION
ELECTROTAXIS
ENTEROPEXIA
ENTEROTOXEMIA
EPEXEGETICAL
ESOTHYROPEXY
EXACERBATED
EXACERBATING
EXACERBATION
EXACTINGNESS
EXACTIVENESS
EXAGGERATED
EXAGGERATING
EXAGGERATION
EXAGGERATIVE
EXAGGERATOR
EXAGGERATORY
EXALBUMINOSE
EXALBUMINOUS
EXALLOTRIOTE
EXALTEDNESS
EXAMINATION
EXAMINATIONAL
EXAMINATIVE
EXAMINATORY
EXANIMATION
EXANTHEMATIC
EXANTLATION
EXARTERITIS
EXARTICULATE
EXASPERATED
EXASPERATING
EXASPERATION
EXASPERATER
EXASPERATIVE
EXAUCTORATE
EXAUGURATION
EXAUTHORIZE
EXCALCARATE
EXCANDESCENT
EXCANTATION
EXCARNATION
EXCATHEDRAL
EXCAVATIONS
EXCEEDINGLY
EXCELLENCIES
EXCELLENTLY
EXCEPTIONAL
EXCEPTIONALLY
EXCEPTIONARY
EXCEPTIONER
EXCEPTIVELY
EXCERPTIBLE
EXCESSIVELY
EXCESSIVENESS
EXCHANGEABLE
EXCHANGEABLY
EXCIPULIFORM
EXCITABILITY
EXCITABLENESS
EXCITEDNESS
EXCITOMOTOR
EXCITOMOTORY
EXCLAMATION
EXCLAMATIONAL
EXCLAMATIVE
EXCLAMATIVELY
EXCLAMATORILY
EXCLAMATORY
EXCLUSIONARY
EXCLUSIONER
EXCLUSIONISM
EXCLUSIONIST
EXCLUSIVELY
EXCLUSIVENESS
EXCLUSIVISM
EXCLUSIVITY
EXCOGITABLE
EXCOGITATED
EXCOGITATING
EXCOGITATION
EXCOGITATIVE
EXCOGITATOR
EXCOMMUNICANT
EXCOMMUNICATE
EXCOMMUNION
EXCONJUGANT
EXCORIATING
EXCORIATION
EXCORTICATE
EXCORTICATED
EXCORTICATING
EXCORTICATION
EXCREMENTAL
EXCREMENTARY
EXCREMENTIVE
EXCRESCENCE
EXCRESCENCES
EXCRESCENCIES
EXCRESCENCY
EXCRESCENTIAL
EXCRETIONARY
EXCRIMINATE
EXCRUCIABLE
EXCRUCIATED
EXCRUCIATING
EXCRUCIATION
EXCRUCIATOR
EXCULPATING
EXCULPATION
EXCULPATIVE
EXCULPATORY
EXCURSIONAL
EXCURSIONARY
EXCURSIONER
EXCURSIONISM
EXCURSIONIST
EXCURSIONIZE
EXCURSIVELY
EXCURVATURE
EXCUSABILITY
EXCUSABLENESS
EXCYSTATION
EXECRABLENESS
EXECUTIONAL
EXECUTIONER
EXECUTIVELY
EXECUTIVENESS
EXECUTORIAL
EXECUTRICES
EXECUTRIXES
EXEGETICALLY
EXEMPLARILY
EXEMPLARINESS
EXEMPLARISM
EXEMPLARITY
EXEMPLIFIED
EXEMPLIFIER
EXEMPLIFYING
EXENCEPHALIA
EXENCEPHALIC
EXENCEPHALUS
EXENTERATED
EXENTERATING
EXENTERATION
EXERCISABLE
EXERCITATION
EXERCITORIAL
EXFIGURATION
EXFILTRATION
EXFLAGELLATE
EXFODIATION
EXFOLIATING
EXFOLIATION
EXFOLIATIVE
EXFOLIATORY
EXHAUSTEDLY
EXHAUSTEDNESS
EXHAUSTIBLE
EXHAUSTINGLY
EXHAUSTIVELY
EXHAUSTLESS
EXHAUSTLESSLY
EXHIBITIONAL
EXHIBITIONER
EXHIBITIONISM
EXHIBITIONIST
EXHIBITIVELY
EXHIBITORSHIP
EXHILARATED
EXHILARATING
EXHILARATION
EXHILARATIVE
EXHILARATOR
EXHILARATORY
EXHORTATIVE
EXHORTATIVELY
EXHORTATORY
EXIGUOUSNESS
EXILARCHATE
EXIMIOUSNESS
EXINANITION
EXISTENTIAL
EXISTENTIALLY
EXISTLESSNESS
EXOARTERITIS
EXOCCIPITAL
EXOCULATING
EXOGASTRITIS
EXOGENOUSLY
EXOGNATHION
EXOGNATHITE
EXOMETRITIS
EXOMOLOGESIS
EXOMORPHISM
EXOMPHALOUS
EXONERATING
EXONERATION
EXONERATIVE
EXOPERIDIUM
EXOPHTHALMIA
EXOPHTHALMIC
EXOPHTHALMOS
EXOPHTHALMUS
EXORABILITY
EXORABLENESS
EXORBITANCE
EXORBITANCY
EXORBITANTLY
EXORBITATION
EXORCISATION
EXORCISEMENT
EXORCISTICAL
EXORCIZATION
EXORCIZEMENT
EXOSKELETAL
EXOSKELETON
EXOSTRACISM
EXOSTRACIZE
EXOTERICALLY
EXOTERICISM
EXOTHERMOUS
EXOTICALNESS
EXPANDEDNESS
EXPANDINGLY
EXPANSIBILITY
EXPANSIONAL
EXPANSIONISM
EXPANSIONIST
EXPANSIVELY
EXPANSIVENESS
EXPANSIVITY
EXPATIATING
EXPATIATION
EXPATIATIVE
EXPATIATORY
EXPATRIATED
EXPATRIATING
EXPATRIATION
EXPECTANCIES
EXPECTANTLY
EXPECTATION
EXPECTATIVE
EXPECTORANT
EXPECTORATE
EXPECTORATED
EXPECTORATING
EXPECTORATION
EXPECTORATOR
EXPEDIENCIES
EXPEDIENTIAL
EXPEDIENTIST
EXPEDIENTLY
EXPEDITATED
EXPEDITATING
EXPEDITATION
EXPEDITENESS
EXPEDITIONARY
EXPEDITIONIST
EXPEDITIOUS
EXPEDITIOUSLY
EXPENDABILITY
EXPENDITRIX
EXPENDITURE
EXPENSILATION
EXPENSIVELY
EXPENSIVENESS
EXPENTHESIS
EXPERIENCED
EXPERIENCER
EXPERIENCES
EXPERIENCING
EXPERIENTIAL
EXPERIMENTAL
EXPERIMENTED
EXPERIMENTEE
EXPERIMENTER
EXPERIMENTING
EXPERIMENTIST
EXPERIMENTIZE
EXPERMENTIZED
EXPERIMENTLY
EXPIATIONAL
EXPIATORINESS
EXPISCATING
EXPISCATION
EXPISCATORY
EXPLAINABLE
EXPLANATION
EXPLANATIVE
EXPLANATIVELY
EXPLANATORILY
EXPLANATORY
EXPLANTATION
EXPLEMENTAL
EXPLETIVELY
EXPLETIVENESS
EXPLICATING
EXPLICATION
EXPLICATIVE
EXPLICATORY
EXPLICITNESS
EXPLOITABLE
EXPLOITATION
EXPLOITATIVE
EXPLORATION
EXPLORATIONAL
EXPLORATIVE
EXPLORATIVELY
EXPLORATORY
EXPLOREMENT
EXPLOSIBILITY
EXPLOSIONIST
EXPLOSIVELY
EXPLOSIVENESS
EXPONENTIAL
EXPONENTIALLY
EXPORTABILITY
EXPORTATION
EXPOSITIONAL
EXPOSITIONARY
EXPOSITIVELY
EXPOSITORIAL
EXPOSITORILY
EXPOSTULATE
EXPOSTULATED
EXPOSTULATING
EXPOSTULATION
EXPOSTULATIVE
EXPOSTULATOR
EXPOSTULATORY
EXPRESSIBLE
EXPRESSION
EXPRESSIONAL
EXPRESSIONISM
EXPRESSIONIST

EXPRESSIVELY
EXPRESSLESS
EXPROBRATORY
EXPROMISSION
EXPROPRIATE
EXPROPRIATED
EXPROPRIATING
EXPROPRIATION
EXPROPRIATOR
EXPULSATORY
EXPURGATING
EXPURGATION
EXPURGATIVE
EXPURGATORIAL
EXPURGATORY
EXQUISITELY
EXQUISITENESS
EXQUISITISM
EXQUISITIVELY
EXSANGUINATE
EXSANGUINOUS
EXSANGUIOUS
EXSCRIPTURAL
EXSCULPTATE
EXSCUTELLATE
EXSICCATING
EXSICCATION
EXSICCATIVE
EXSTIPULATE
EXSUFFLATION
EXSUFFLICATE
EXTEMPORALLY
EXTEMPORARY
EXTEMPORARILY
EXTEMPORIZE
EXTEMPORIZED
EXTEMPORIZER
EXTEMPORIZING
EXTENDEDNESS
EXTENDIBILITY
EXTENSIBILITY
EXTENSIMETER
EXTENSIONAL
EXTENSIONIST
EXTENSIVELY
EXTENSIVENESS
EXTENSOMETER
EXTENUATING
EXTENUATINGLY
EXTENUATION
EXTENUATIVE
EXTENUATORY
EXTERIORATE
EXTERIORATION
EXTERIORITY
EXTERIORIZE
EXTERIORIZED
EXTERIORIZING
EXTERIORNESS
EXTERMINATE
EXTERMINATED
EXTERMINATING
EXTERMINATION
EXTERMINATIVE
EXTERMINATOR
EXTERMINATORY
EXTERNALISM
EXTERNALIST
EXTERNALISTIC
EXTERNALITIES
EXTERNALITY
EXTERNALIZE
EXTERNATION
EXTERNIZATION
EXTEROCEPTIST
EXTEROCEPTIVE
EXTEROCEPTOR
EXTERRANEOUS
EXTERRESTRIAL
EXTERRITORIAL
EXTINGUISHED
EXTINGUISHER
EXTIRPATING
EXTIRPATION
EXTIRPATIVE
EXTIRPATORY
EXTISPICIOUS
EXTOLLATION
EXTORSIVELY
EXTORTIONARY
EXTORTIONATE
EXTORTIONER
EXTORTIONIST
EXTRABULBAR
EXTRACAPSULAR
EXTRACARPAL
EXTRACOSTAL
EXTRACTABLE
EXTRACTIBLE
EXTRACTIFORM
EXTRACYSTIC
EXTRADITABLE
EXTRADITING
EXTRADITION
EXTRADUCTION
EXTRAENTERIC
EXTRAFORMAL
EXTRAGALACTIC
EXTRAJUDICIAL
EXTRALATERAL
EXTRAMUNDANE
EXTRAMURALLY
EXTRANEOUSLY
EXTRAORDINARY
EXTRAPHYSICAL
EXTRAPOLATE
EXTRAPOLATED
EXTRAPOLATING
EXTRAPOLATION
EXTRAPOLATIVE
EXTRAPOLATOR
EXTRAREGULAR
EXTRARETINAL
EXTRASENSORY
EXTRASEROUS
EXTRASYSTOLE
EXTRATARSAL
EXTRATRIBAL
EXTRAUTERINE
EXTRAVAGANCE
EXTRAVAGANCY
EXTRAVAGANT
EXTRAVAGANTLY
EXTRAVAGANZA
EXTRAVAGATE
EXTRAVAGATED
EXTRAVAGATING
EXTRAVAGATION
EXTRAVAGINAL
EXTRAVASATE
EXTRAVASATED
EXTRAVASATING
EXTRAVASATION
EXTRAVASCULAR
EXTRAVERSION
EXTRAVIOLET
EXTREMENESS
EXTREMISTIC
EXTREMITIES
EXTRICATING
EXTRICATION
EXTRINSICAL
EXTRINSICALLY
EXTRINSICATE
EXTROSPECTION
EXTROSPECTIVE
EXTROVERSION
EXTROVERSIVE
EXTUMESCENCE
EXUBERANTLY
EXUBERANTNESS
EXUBERATING
EXUBERATION
EXULCERATED
EXULCERATING
EXULCERATION
EXULCERATIVE
EXULCERATORY
EXUMBRELLAR
EXUVIABILITY
FIBROMYXOMA
FLEXANIMOUS
FLEXIBILITY
FLEXIBLENESS
FLEXUOSITIES
FLEXUOUSNESS
FLUXIBILITY
FLUXIBLENESS
FLUXIONALLY
FORMALDOXIME
FORNICATRIX
FRICANDEAUX
FUCOXANTHIN
GALVANOTAXIS
GASTROTAXIS
GASTROXYNSIS
GENUFLEXION
GENUFLEXUOUS
GITOXIGENIN
GRIPPOTOXIN
GUBERNATRIX
HETERODOXIES
HETEROSEXUAL
HETEROTAXIA
HETEROTAXIC
HETEROTAXIS
HETEROXENOUS
HEXABROMIDE
HEXAGONALLY
HEXASTICHIC
HEXOBARBITAL
HOMOSEXUALITY
HYDROEXTRACT
HYDROTHORAX
HYPOPHARYNX
HYPOTOXICITY
HYPOXANTHINE
ICHTHYOTOXIN
IDEOPRAXIST
IMMUNOTOXIN
IMPROPRIATRIX
INDEXICALLY
INDEXTERITY
INEXACTITUDE
INEXACTNESS
INEXCUSABLE
INEXCUSABLY
INEXECUTION
INEXHAUSTIBLE
INEXHAUSTIVE
INEXISTENCE
INEXISTENCY
INEXPECTEDLY
INEXPEDIENCY
INEXPEDIENT
INEXPENSIVE
INEXPERIENCE
INEXPERIENCED
INEXPERTNESS
INEXPLICABLE
INEXPLICABLES
INEXPLICABLY
INEXPLICITLY
INEXPRESSIBLE
INEXPRESSIVE
INEXTENSIVE
INEXTIRPABLE
INEXTRICABLE
INEXTRICABLY
INFLEXIBILITY
INFLUXIONISM
INNOXIOUSLY
INOBNOXIOUS
INOXIDIZING
INTERMIXEDLY
INTERMIXING
INTERMIXTLY
INTERMIXTURE
INTERSEXUAL
INTERTEXTURE
INTERXYLARY
INTOXICABLE
INTOXICATED
INTOXICATING
INTOXICATION
INTOXICATIVE
INTOXICATOR
INTRAXYLARY
INTROFLEXION
IRREFLEXIVE
JUXTAMARINE
JUXTAPOSING
JUXTAPOSITION
JUXTAPYLORIC
JUXTASPINAL
KARYORRHEXIS
KERATONYXIS
LAURINOXYLON
LAXATIVENESS
LAXIFLOROUS
LAXIFOLIATE
LAXIFOLIOUS
LEGISLATRIX
LEXICOGRAPHY
LEXICOLOGIC
LEXICOLOGICAL
LEXICOLOGIST
LEXIGRAPHIC
LEXIGRAPHICAL
LIFERENTRIX
LITHANTHRAX
LITHOLAPAXY
LITHOXYLITE
LIXIVIATING
LIXIVIATION
LOXODOGRAPH
LOXODROMICS
LOXODROMISM
LUXULLIANITE
LUXURIANTLY
LUXURIANTNESS
LUXURIATING
LUXURIATION
LUXURIOUSLY
LUXURIOUSNESS
LYMPHOTOXIN
MAXILLARIES
MAXILLIFORM
MAXILLIPEDARY
MAXILLIPEDE
MAXILLOJUGAL
MAXILLOLABIAL
MAXIMIZATION
MERVEILLEUX
MESOAPPENDIX
MESOSALPINX
METAGALAXIES
METAVAUXITE
MICROTHORAX
MIXOBARBARIC
MIXOTROPHIC
MIXTILINEAR
MONILETHRIX
MORPHALLAXIS
MYELAPOPLEXY
MYELOPLAXES
MYTILOTOXINE
MYXADENITIS
MYXASTHENIA
MYXEDEMATOUS
MYXOBLASTOMA
MYXOCYSTOMA
MYXOFIBROMA
MYXOMATOSIS
MYXOMYCETOUS
MYXONEUROMA
MYXOSARCOMA
MYXOSPOROUS
NASOPHARYNX
NEGOTIATRIX
NEOORTHODOXY
NEPHROTOXIC
NEPHROTOXIN
NEUROPLEXUS
NONEXISTENCE
NONEXISTENT
NOXIOUSNESS
OBJURGATRIX
OBNOXIOUSLY
OBNOXIOUSNESS
ODONTEXESIS
ODONTOLOXIA
OOPHOROPEXY
ORCHIDOPEXY
OROPHARYNXES
ORTHODOXALLY
ORTHODOXIAN
ORTHODOXICAL
ORTHODOXIES
ORTHODOXISM
ORTHODOXIST
ORTHODOXNESS
OSCULATRIXES
OSTEOSTIXIS
OVEREXPOSED
OVEREXPOSING
OVEREXPOSURE
OVERTAXATION
OXALURAMIDE
OXIDABILITY
OXIDATIONAL
OXIDIMETRIC
OXYACANTHIN
OXYACANTHINE
OXYACANTHOUS
OXYACETYLENE
OXYALDEHYDE
OXYBERBERINE
OXYCARBONATE
OXYCELLULOSE
OXYCEPHALIC
OXYCEPHALISM
OXYCEPHALOUS
OXYCHLORATE
OXYCHLORIDE
OXYCHLORINE
OXYCHROMATIC
OXYCHROMATIN
OXYCINNAMIC
OXYCOPAIVIC
OXYCOUMARIN
OXYESTHESIA
OXYGENATING
OXYGENERATOR
OXYGENICITY

OXYGENIZABLE
OXYGENIZING
OXYGNATHOUS
OXYHAEMATIN
OXYHEXACTINE
OXYHEXASTER
OXYHYDROGEN
OXYLUCIFERIN
OXYMETHYLENE
OXYMURIATIC
OXYOSPHRESIA
OXYPETALOUS
OXYPHOSPHATE
OXYPHTHALIC
OXYPHYLLOUS
OXYPROPIONIC
OXYQUINOLINE
OXYRHYNCHID
OXYRHYNCHOUS
OXYRRHYNCHID
OXYSALICYLIC
OXYSTOMATOUS
OXYSULPHATE
OXYSULPHIDE
OXYTYLOTATE
PACHYMENINX
PANSEXUALISM
PANSEXUALIST
PANSEXUALITY
PANSEXUALIZE
PARADOXICAL
PARADOXICIAN
PARADOXIDIAN
PARADOXOLOGY
PARAVAUXITE
PAROXYSMALLY
PAROXYTONIC
PAXILLIFORM
PEPTOTOXINE
PERIAXILLARY
PERICOXITIS
PERPLEXEDLY
PERPLEXINGLY
PERPLEXITIES
PHENOXAZINE
PHILODOXICAL
PHLEBORRHEXIS
PHOTOSYNTAX
PHYLLOTAXIS
PHYLLOXERAN
PHYLLOXERIC
PILOTAXITIC
PLEXIMETRIC
PNEUMONOPEXY
PNEUMOTHORAX
PNEUMOTOXIN
POLYHYDROXY
POSTAXIALLY
POSTEXILIAN
POSTEXISTENT

POSTFLEXION
PRAEMAXILLA
PRAETAXATION
PRAXINOSCOPE
PREEXISTENCE
PREEXISTENT
PREFIXATION
PREMAXILLARY
PRETEXTUOUS
PROCATARXIS
PROCURATRIX
PROGENITRIX
PROLOCUTRIX
PROPHYLAXIS
PROTEOPEXIC
PROTEOPEXIS
PROTHORAXES
PROTOXIDIZE
PROTOXIDIZED
PROXENETISM
PROXIMATELY
PROXIMATION
PSEUDOCORTEX
PSEUDODOXAL
PSYCHOREFLEX
PSYCHOSEXUAL
PSYCHOTAXIS
PTEROTHORAX
PYOXANTHOSE
PYROXMANGITE
PYRRHULOXIA
QUINATOXINE
QUINCUNXIAL
QUINISEXTINE
QUINOXALINE
RADIOPRAXIS
REFLEXIONAL
REFLEXIVELY
REFLEXIVITY
REFLEXOLOGY
RELAXEDNESS
RETROFLEXED
RETROFLEXION
RETROXIPHOID
RHAMNOHEXOSE
RHAMNOHEXITE
RHINOPHARYNX
RHYOTAXITIC
SACROCOCCYX
SACROCOXITIS
SAXIFRAGANT
SAXIFRAGOUS
SAXOPHONIST
SCAPULOPEXY
SCEUOPHYLAX
SCILLITOXIN
SCLERONYXIS
SEMIFLEXIBLE
SEMISEXTILE

SESQUISEXTAL
SEXADECIMAL
SEXAGENARIAN
SEXAGESIMAL
SEXANGULARLY
SEXCENTENARY
SEXDIGITATE
SEXDIGITATED
SEXDIGITISM
SEXISYLLABLE
SEXLESSNESS
SEXOLOGICAL
SEXPLOITATION
SEXTILLIONTH
SEXTIPARTITE
SEXTUPLICATE
SEXTUPLICATED
SHIKIMOTOXIN
SIPHONOPLAX
SPASMOTOXIN
SPASMOTOXINE
SPECULATRIX
SPERMOTOXIN
SPLENOPEXIA
SPLENOPEXIS
SPLENOTOXIN
STAURAXONIA
STAURAXONIAL
STENOTHORAX
STEREOMATRIX
STEREOTAXIS
STIMULATRIX
STROPHOTAXIS
SUBAXILLARY
SUBLUXATION
SUBMAXILLAE
SUBMAXILLARY
SUBOXIDATION
SUBSEXTUPLE
SUFFIXATION
SULFOXYLATE
SULPHOXYLIC
SUPERFLEXION
SUPERMAXILLA
SUPERSEXUAL
SUPRAMAXILLA
SUPRAMAXIMAL
TAXABLENESS
TAXASPIDEAN
TAXEOPODOUS
TAXGATHERER
TAXGATHERING
TAXIDERMIST
TAXIDERMIZE
TAXIMETERED
TAXONOMICAL
TETRAHYDROXY
TETROXALATE
TEXTIFEROUS

THERMOTAXIC
THERMOTAXIS
THIGMOTAXIS
THIXOLABILE
THIXOTROPIC
THOROUGHWAX
TOXALBUMOSE
TOXICOGENIC
TOXICOGNATH
TOXICOLOGIC
TOXICOLOGIST
TOXICOMANIA
TOXICOPATHIC
TOXICOPATHY
TOXICOPHAGY
TOXICOPHIDIA
TOXINFECTION
TOXIPHOBIAC
TOXITABELLAE
TOXOGENESIS
TOXOGLOSSATE
TOXOPHILISM
TOXOPHILITIC
TOXOPHILOUS
TRANSFIXING
TRANSFIXION
TRANSFIXTURE
TRISULFOXID
TRISULPHOXID
TROPHALLAXIS
TROPHOTAXIS
TROPHOTHYLAX
TYLOTOXEATE
TYPHOTOXINE
TYROTOXICON
ULTRACOMPLEX
ULTRAMAXIMAL
UNDEREXPOSE
UNDEREXPOSED
UNDEREXPOSING
UNEXACTNESS
UNEXCEPTIVE
UNEXCLUSIVE
UNEXCUSABLE
UNEXCUSABLY
UNEXPECTEDLY
UNEXPEDIENT
UNEXPENSIVE
UNEXPERIENCE
UNEXPERIENT
UNEXPLAINED
UNEXPLICABLE
UNEXPLOITED
UNEXPRESSIVE
UNEXPURGATED
UNEXTRICABLE
UNISEXUALITY
UNISEXUALLY
UNORTHODOXLY

UNORTHODOXY
URECHITOXIN
UROTOXICITY
VASOREFLEX
VEXATIOUSLY
VEXILLARIOUS
VEXILLATION
WAXCHANDLER
WAXCHANDLERY
XANTHELASMA
XANTHINURIA
XANTHOCHROIA
XANTHOCHROID
XANTHOCONITE
XANTHODERMA
XANTHOGENATE
XANTHOGENIC
XANTHOMATOUS
XANTHOMETER
XANTHOPHANE
XANTHOPHORE
XANTHOPHYLL
XANTHOPTERIN
XANTHOXENITE
XANTHOXYLIN
XENACANTHINE
XENARTHROUS
XENODOCHIUM
XENOGENESIS
XENOMORPHIC
XENOPARASITE
XENOSAUROID
XENYLAMINE
XEROGRAPHER
XEROGRAPHIC
XEROMORPHIC
XEROMORPHOUS
XEROPHILOUS
XEROPHOBOUS
XEROPHYTISM
XEROTRIPSIS
XIPHISTERNAL
XIPHISTERNUM
XIPHOCOSTAL
XIPHOPAGOUS
XIPHOSUROUS
XYLOCARPOUS
XYLOGRAPHER
XYLOGRAPHIC
XYLOPHAGOUS
XYLOPHILOUS
XYLOPHONIST
XYLOPLASTIC
XYLOQUINONE
XYLOSTROMATA
XYRIDACEOUS
ZANTHOXYLUM
ZOOPRAXISCOPE
ZOOXANTHELLA

POSITIONAL ORDER LIST OF WORDS OVER 10 LETTERS

XANTHELASMA
XANTHINURIA
XANTHOCHROIA
XANTHOCHROID
XANTHOCONITE
XANTHODERMA
XANTHOGENATE
XANTHOGENIC
XANTHOMATOUS
XANTHOMETER
XANTHOPHANE

XANTHOPHORE
XANTHOPHYLL
XANTHOPTERIN
XANTHOXENITE
XANTHOXYLIN
XENACANTHINE
XENARTHROUS
XENODOCHIUM
XENOGENESIS
XENOMORPHIC
XENOPARASITE

XENOSAUROID
XENYLAMINE
XEROGRAPHER
XEROGRAPHIC
XEROMORPHIC
XEROMORPHOUS
XEROPHILOUS
XEROPHOBOUS
XEROPHYTISM
XEROTRIPSIS
XIPHISTERNAL

XIPHISTERNUM
XIPHOCOSTAL
XIPHOPAGOUS
XIPHOSUROUS
XYLOCARPOUS
XYLOGRAPHER
XYLOGRAPHIC
XYLOPHAGOUS
XYLOPHILOUS
XYLOPHONIST
XYLOPLASTIC

XYLOQUINONE
XYLOSTROMATA
XYRIDACEOUS

AXIOLOGICAL
AXIOMATICAL
AXISYMMETRIC
AXODENDRITE
AXONOLIPOUS
AXONOMETRIC
AXONOPHOROUS

AXOSPERMOUS
EXACERBATED
EXACERBATING
EXACERBATION
EXACTINGNESS
EXACTIVENESS
EXAGGERATED
EXAGGERATING
EXAGGERATION
EXAGGERATIVE
EXAGGERATOR
EXAGGERATORY
EXALBUMINOSE
EXALBUMINOUS
EXALLOTRIOTE
EXALTEDNESS
EXAMINATION
EXAMINATIONAL
EXAMINATIVE
EXAMINATORY
EXANIMATION
EXANTHEMATIC
EXARTERITIS
EXARTICULATE
EXASPERATED
EXASPERATER
EXASPERATING
EXASPERATION
EXASPERATIVE
EXAUCTORATE
EXAUGURATION
EXAUTHORIZE
EXCALCARATE
EXCANDESCENT
EXCANTATION
EXCARNATION
EXCATHEDRAL
EXCAVATIONS
EXCEEDINGLY
EXCELLENCIES
EXCELLENTLY
EXCEPTIONAL
EXCEPTIONALLY
EXCEPTIONARY
EXCEPTIONER
EXCEPTIVELY
EXCERPTIBLE
EXCESSIVELY
EXCESSIVENESS
EXCHANGEABLE
EXCHANGEABLY
EXCIPULIFORM
EXCITABILITY
EXCITABLENESS
EXCITEDNESS
EXCITOMOTOR
EXCITOMOTORY
EXCLAMATION
EXCLAMATIONAL
EXCLAMATIVE
EXCLAMATIVELY
EXCLAMATORILY
EXCLAMATORY
EXCLUSIONARY
EXCLUSIONER
EXCLUSIONISM
EXCLUSIONIST
EXCLUSIVELY
EXCLUSIVENESS
EXCLUSIVISM
EXCLUSIVITY
EXCOGITABLE
EXCOGITATED
EXCOGITATING
EXCOGITATION
EXCOGITATIVE
EXCOGITATOR
EXCOMMUNICANT
EXCOMMUNICATE
EXCOMMUNION
EXCONJUGANT
EXCORIATING
EXCORIATION
EXCORTICATE
EXCORTICATED
EXCORTICATING
EXCORTICATION
EXCREMENTAL
EXCREMENTARY
EXCREMENTIVE
EXCRESCENCE
EXCRESCENCES
EXCRESCENCIES
EXCRESCENCY
EXCRESCENTIAL
EXCRETIONARY
EXCRIMINATE
EXCRUCIABLE
EXCRUCIATED
EXCRUCIATING
EXCRUCIATION
EXCRUCIATOR
EXCULPATING
EXCULPATION
EXCULPATIVE
EXCULPATORY
EXCURSIONAL
EXCURSIONARY
EXCURSIONER
EXCURSIONISM
EXCURSIONIST
EXCURSIONIZE
EXCURSIVELY
EXCURVATURE
EXCUSABILITY
EXCUSABLENESS
EXCYSTATION
EXECRABLENESS
EXECUTIONAL
EXECUTIONER
EXECUTIVELY
EXECUTIVENESS
EXECUTORIAL
EXECUTRICES
EXECUTRIXES
EXEGETICALLY
EXEMPLARILY
EXEMPLARINESS
EXEMPLARISM
EXEMPLARITY
EXEMPLIFIED
EXEMPLIFIER
EXEMPLIFYING
EXENCEPHALIA
EXENCEPHALIC
EXENCEPHALUS
EXENTERATED
EXENTERATING
EXENTERATION
EXERCISABLE
EXERCITATION
EXERCITORIAL
EXFIGURATION
EXFILTRATION
EXFLAGELLATE
EXFODIATION
EXFOLIATING
EXFOLIATION
EXFOLIATIVE
EXFOLIATORY
EXHAUSTEDLY
EXHAUSTEDNESS
EXHAUSTIBLE
EXHAUSTINGLY
EXHAUSTIVELY
EXHAUSTLESS
EXHAUSTLESSLY
EXHIBITIONAL
EXHIBITIONER
EXHIBITIONISM
EXHIBITIONIST
EXHIBITIVELY
EXHIBITORSHIP
EXHILARATED
EXHILARATING
EXHILARATION
EXHILARATIVE
EXHILARATOR
EXHILARATORY
EXHORTATIVE
EXHORTATIVELY
EXHORTATORY
EXIGUOUSNESS
EXILARCHATE
EXIMIOUSNESS
EXINANITION
EXISTENTIAL
EXISTENTIALLY
EXISTLESSNESS
EXOARTERITIS
EXOCCIPITAL
EXOCULATING
EXOGASTRITIS
EXOGENOUSLY
EXOGNATHION
EXOGNATHITE
EXOMETRITIS
EXOMOLOGESIS
EXOMORPHISM
EXOMPHALOUS
EXONERATING
EXONERATION
EXONERATIVE
EXOPERIDIUM
EXOPHTHALMIA
EXOPHTHALMIC
EXOPHTHALMOS
EXOPHTHALMUS
EXORABILITY
EXORABLENESS
EXORBITANCE
EXORBITANCY
EXORBITANTLY
EXORBITATION
EXORCISATION
EXORCISEMENT
EXORCISTICAL
EXORCIZATION
EXORCIZEMENT
EXOSKELETAL
EXOSKELETON
EXOSTRACISM
EXOSTRACIZE
EXOTERICALLY
EXOTERICISM
EXOTHERMOUS
EXOTICALNESS
EXPANDEDNESS
EXPANDINGLY
EXPANSIBILITY
EXPANSIONAL
EXPANSIONISM
EXPANSIONIST
EXPANSIVELY
EXPANSIVENESS
EXPANSIVITY
EXPATIATING
EXPATIATION
EXPATIATIVE
EXPATIATORY
EXPATRIATED
EXPATRIATING
EXPATRIATION
EXPECTANCIES
EXPECTANTLY
EXPECTATION
EXPECTATIVE
EXPECTORANT
EXPECTORATE
EXPECTORATED
EXPECTORATING
EXPECTORATION
EXPECTORATOR
EXPEDIENCIES
EXPEDIENTIAL
EXPEDIENTIST
EXPEDIENTLY
EXPEDITATED
EXPEDITATING
EXPEDITATION
EXPEDITENESS
EXPEDITIONARY
EXPEDITIONIST
EXPEDITIOUS
EXPEDITIOUSLY
EXPENDABILITY
EXPENDITRIX
EXPENDITURE
EXPENSILATION
EXPENSIVELY
EXPENSIVENESS
EXPENTHESIS
EXPERIENCED
EXPERIENCER
EXPERIENCES
EXPERIENCING
EXPERIENTIAL
EXPERIMENTAL
EXPERIMENTED
EXPERIMENTEE
EXPERIMENTER
EXPERIMENTING
EXPERIMENTIST
EXPERIMENTIZE
EXPERMENTIZED
EXPERIMENTLY
EXPIATIONAL
EXPIATORINESS
EXPISCATING
EXPISCATION
EXPISCATORY
EXPLAINABLE
EXPLANATION
EXPLANATIVE
EXPLANATIVELY
EXPLANATORILY
EXPLANATORY
EXPLANTATION
EXPLEMENTAL
EXPLETIVELY
EXPLETIVENESS
EXPLICATING
EXPLICATION
EXPLICATIVE
EXPLICATORY
EXPLICITNESS
EXPLOITABLE
EXPLOITATION
EXPLOITATIVE
EXPLORATION
EXPLORATIONAL
EXPLORATIVE
EXPLORATIVELY
EXPLORATORY
EXPLOREMENT
EXPLOSIBILITY
EXPLOSIONIST
EXPLOSIVELY
EXPLOSIVENESS
EXPONENTIAL
EXPONENTIALLY
EXPORTABILITY
EXPORTATION
EXPOSITIONAL
EXPOSITIONARY
EXPOSITIVELY
EXPOSITORIAL
EXPOSITORILY
EXPOSTULATE
EXPOSTULATED
EXPOSTULATING
EXPOSTULATION
EXPOSTULATIVE
EXPOSTULATOR
EXPOSTULATORY
EXPRESSIBLE
EXPRESSION
EXPRESSIONAL
EXPRESSIONISM
EXPRESSIONIST
EXPRESSIVELY
EXPRESSLESS
EXPROBRATORY
EXPROMISSION
EXPROPRIATE
EXPROPRIATED
EXPROPRIATING
EXPROPRIATION
EXPROPRIATOR
EXPULSATORY
EXPURGATING
EXPURGATION
EXPURGATIVE
EXPURGATORIAL
EXPURGATORY
EXQUISITELY
EXQUISITENESS
EXQUISITISM
EXQUISITIVELY
EXSANGUINATE
EXSANGUINOUS
EXSANGUIOUS
EXSCRIPTURAL
EXSCULPTATE
EXSCUTELLATE
EXSICCATING
EXSICCATION
EXSICCATIVE
EXSTIPULATE
EXSUFFLATION
EXSUFFLICATE
EXTEMPORALLY
EXTEMPORARY
EXTEMPORARILY
EXTEMPORIZE
EXTEMPORIZED
EXTEMPORIZER
EXTEMPORIZING
EXTENDEDNESS
EXTENDIBILITY
EXTENSIBILITY
EXTENSIMETER
EXTENSIONAL
EXTENSIONIST
EXTENSIVELY
EXTENSIVENESS
EXTENSOMETER
EXTENUATING
EXTENUATINGLY
EXTENUATION
EXTENUATIVE
EXTENUATORY
EXTERIORATE
EXTERIORATION
EXTERIORITY

EXTERIORIZE
EXTERIORIZED
EXTERIORIZING
EXTERIORNESS
EXTERMINATE
EXTERMINATED
EXTERMINATING
EXTERMINATION
EXTERMINATIVE
EXTERMINATOR
EXTERMINATORY
EXTERNALISM
EXTERNALIST
EXTERNALISTIC
EXTERNALITIES
EXTERNALITY
EXTERNALIZE
EXTERNATION
EXTERNIZATION
EXTEROCEPTIST
EXTEROCEPTIVE
EXTEROCEPTOR
EXTERRANEOUS
EXTERRESTRIAL
EXTERRITORIAL
EXTINGUISHED
EXTINGUISHER
EXTIRPATING
EXTIRPATION
EXTIRPATIVE
EXTIRPATORY
EXTISPICIOUS
EXTOLLATION
EXTORSIVELY
EXTORTIONARY
EXTORTIONATE
EXTORTIONER
EXTORTIONIST
EXTRABULBAR
EXTRACAPSULAR
EXTRACARPAL
EXTRACOSTAL
EXTRACTABLE
EXTRACTIBLE
EXTRACTIFORM
EXTRACYSTIC
EXTRADITABLE
EXTRADITING
EXTRADITION
EXTRADUCTION
EXTRAENTERIC
EXTRAFORMAL
EXTRAGALACTIC
EXTRAJUDICIAL
EXTRALATERAL
EXTRAMUNDANE
EXTRAMURALLY
EXTRANEOUSLY
EXTRAORDINARY
EXTRAPHYSICAL
EXTRAPOLATE
EXTRAPOLATED
EXTRAPOLATING
EXTRAPOLATION
EXTRAPOLATIVE
EXTRAPOLATOR
EXTRAREGULAR
EXTRARETINAL
EXTRASENSORY
EXTRASEROUS
EXTRASYSTOLE
EXTRATARSAL
EXTRATRIBAL
EXTRAUTERINE
EXTRAVAGANCE
EXTRAVAGANCY
EXTRAVAGANT
EXTRAVAGANTLY
EXTRAVAGANZA
EXTRAVAGATE
EXTRAVAGATED
EXTRAVAGATING
EXTRAVAGATION
EXTRAVAGINAL
EXTRAVASATE
EXTRAVASATED
EXTRAVASATING
EXTRAVASATION
EXTRAVASCULAR
EXTRAVERSION
EXTRAVIOLET
EXTREMENESS
EXTREMISTIC
EXTREMITIES
EXTRICATING
EXTRICATION
EXTRINSICAL
EXTRINSICALLY
EXTRINSICATE
EXTROSPECTION
EXTROSPECTIVE
EXTROVERSION
EXTROVERSIVE
EXTUMESCENCE
EXUBERANTLY
EXUBERANTNESS
EXUBERATING
EXUBERATION
EXULCERATED
EXULCERATING
EXULCERATION
EXULCERATIVE
EXULCERATORY
EXUMBRELLAR
EXUVIABILITY
OXALURAMIDE
OXIDABILITY
OXIDATIONAL
OXIDIMETRIC
OXYACANTHIN
OXYACANTHINE
OXYACANTHOUS
OXYACETYLENE
OXYALDEHYDE
OXYBERBERINE
OXYCARBONATE
OXYCELLULOSE
OXYCEPHALIC
OXYCEPHALISM
OXYCEPHALOUS
OXYCHLORATE
OXYCHLORIDE
OXYCHLORINE
OXYCHROMATIC
OXYCHROMATIN
OXYCINNAMIC
OXYCOPAIVIC
OXYCOUMARIN
OXYESTHESIA
OXYGENATING
OXYGENERATOR
OXYGENICITY
OXYGENIZABLE
OXYGENIZING
OXYGNATHOUS
OXYHAEMATIN
OXYHEXACTINE
OXYHEXASTER
OXYHYDROGEN
OXYLUCIFERIN
OXYMETHYLENE
OXYMURIATIC
OXYOSPHRESIA
OXYPETALOUS
OXYPHOSPHATE
OXYPHTHALIC
OXYPHYLLOUS
OXYPROPIONIC
OXYQUINOLINE
OXYRHYNCHID
OXYRHYNCHOUS
OXYRRHYNCHID
OXYSALICYLIC
OXYSTOMATOUS
OXYSULPHATE
OXYSULPHIDE
OXYTYLOTATE

ANXIOUSNESS
AUXANOMETER
AUXETICALLY
AUXILIARIES
AUXILIATION
AUXILIATORY
AUXOAMYLASE
AUXOCHROMIC
AUXOCHROMISM
AUXOCHROMOUS
AUXOGRAPHIC
AUXOHORMONE
COXARTHRITIS
COXCOMBICAL
COXOCERITIC
COXOFEMORAL
DEXIOTROPIC
DEXIOTROPISM
DEXIOTROPOUS
DEXTEROUSLY
DEXTROCARDIA
DEXTROCULAR
DEXTROGYRATE
DEXTROSAZONE
DEXTROSURIA
DEXTROUSNESS
DOXOGRAPHER
DOXOLOGICAL
DOXOLOGIZED
DOXOLOGIZING
HEXABROMIDE
HEXAGONALLY
HEXASTICHIC
HEXOBARBITAL
JUXTAMARINE
JUXTAPOSING
JUXTAPOSITION
JUXTAPYLORIC
JUXTASPINAL
LAXATIVENESS
LAXIFLOROUS
LAXIFOLIATE
LAXIFOLIOUS
LEXICOGRAPHY
LEXICOLOGIC
LEXICOLOGICAL
LEXICOLOGIST
LEXIGRAPHIC
LEXIGRAPHICAL
LIXIVIATING
LIXIVIATION
LOXODOGRAPH
LOXODROMICS
LOXODROMISM
LUXULLIANITE
LUXURIANTLY
LUXURIANTNESS
LUXURIATING
LUXURIATION
LUXURIOUSLY
LUXURIOUSNESS
MAXILLARIES
MAXILLIFORM
MAXILLIPEDARY
MAXILLIPEDE
MAXILLOJUGAL
MAXILLOLABIAL
MAXIMIZATION
MIXOBARBARIC
MIXOTROPHIC
MIXTILINEAR
MYXADENITIS
MYXASTHENIA
MYXEDEMATOUS
MYXOBLASTOMA
MYXOCYSTOMA
MYXOFIBROMA
MYXOMATOSIS
MYXOMYCETOUS
MYXONEUROMA
MYXOSARCOMA
MYXOSPOROUS
NOXIOUSNESS
PAXILLIFORM
SAXIFRAGANT
SAXIFRAGOUS
SAXOPHONIST
SEXADECIMAL
SEXAGENARIAN
SEXAGESIMAL
SEXANGULARLY
SEXCENTENARY
SEXDIGITATE
SEXDIGITATED
SEXDIGITISM
SEXISYLLABLE
SEXLESSNESS
SEXOLOGICAL
SEXPLOITATION
SEXTILLIONTH
SEXTIPARTITE
SEXTUPLICATE
SEXTUPLICATED
TAXABLENESS
TAXASPIDEAN
TAXEOPODOUS
TAXGATHERER
TAXGATHERING
TAXIDERMIST
TAXIDERMIZE
TAXIMETERED
TAXONOMICAL
TEXTIFEROUS
TOXALBUMOSE
TOXICOGENIC
TOXICOGNATH
TOXICOLOGIC
TOXICOLOGIST
TOXICOMANIA
TOXICOPATHIC
TOXICOPATHY
TOXICOPHAGY
TOXICOPHIDIA
TOXINFECTION
TOXIPHOBIAC
TOXITABELLAE
TOXOGENESIS
TOXOGLOSSATE
TOXOPHILISM
TOXOPHILITIC
TOXOPHILOUS
VEXATIOUSLY
VEXILLARIOUS
VEXILLATION
WAXCHANDLER
WAXCHANDLERY

ADOXOGRAPHY
ALEXANDRITE
ALEXIPHARMIC
ALEXIPYRETIC
ANOXIDATIVE
ANOXYBIOSIS
ANOXYBIOTIC
ASEXUALIZED
ASEXUALIZING
ATAXAPHASIA
ATAXIAGRAPH
ATAXIAMETER
ATAXIAPHASIA
ATAXOPHEMIA
COEXISTENCE
COEXISTENCY
COEXTENSION
COEXTENSIVE
DEOXIDIZING
DEOXYGENATE
DEOXYGENATED
DEOXYGENIZE
EPEXEGETICAL
FLEXANIMOUS
FLEXIBILITY
FLEXIBLENESS
FLEXUOSITIES
FLEXUOUSNESS
FLUXIBILITY
FLUXIBLENESS
FLUXIONALLY
INEXACTITUDE
INEXACTNESS
INEXCUSABLE
INEXCUSABLY
INEXECUTION
INEXHAUSTIBLE
INEXHAUSTIVE
INEXISTENCE
INEXISTENCY
INEXPECTEDLY
INEXPEDIENCY
INEXPEDIENT
INEXPENSIVE
INEXPERIENCE
INEXPERIENCED
INEXPERTNESS
INEXPLICABLE
INEXPLICABLES
INEXPLICABLY
INEXPLICITLY
INEXPRESSIBLE
INEXPRESSIVE
INEXTENSIVE
INEXTIRPABLE
INEXTRICABLE
INEXTRICABLY
INOXIDIZING
PLEXIMETRIC
PRAXINOSCOPE
PROXENETISM
PROXIMATELY
PROXIMATION
PYOXANTHOSE
THIXOLABILE
THIXOTROPIC
UNEXACTNESS
UNEXCEPTIVE
UNEXCLUSIVE
UNEXCUSABLE
UNEXCUSABLY
UNEXPECTEDLY
UNEXPEDIENT
UNEXPENSIVE
UNEXPERIENCE
UNEXPERIENT
UNEXPLAINED
UNEXPLICABLE
UNEXPLOITED
UNEXPRESSIVE

UNEXPURGATED
UNEXTRICABLE
ZOOXANTHELLA

ADMAXILLARY
ANNEXATIONAL
ANNEXATIONIST
ANNEXIONIST
AUTOXIDATION
AUTOXIDATOR
BIMAXILLARY
BISAXILLARY
BISEXUALISM
BISEXUALITY
DESEXUALIZE
DESEXUALIZED
DETOXICATED
DETOXICATING
DETOXICATION
DETOXICATOR
DIHEXAHEDRAL
DIHEXAHEDRON
DISOXYGENATE
DYSOXIDATION
FUCOXANTHIN
GITOXIGENIN
HYPOXANTHINE
INDEXICALLY
INDEXTERITY
INNOXIOUSLY
INTOXICABLE
INTOXICATED
INTOXICATING
INTOXICATION
INTOXICATIVE
INTOXICATOR
NONEXISTENCE
NONEXISTENT
OBNOXIOUSLY
OBNOXIOUSNESS
PAROXYSMALLY
PAROXYTONIC
PREEXISTENCE
PREEXISTENT
PYROXMANGITE
RELAXEDNESS
SUBAXILLARY
SUBOXIDATION

AMPLEXATION
AMPLEXICAUL
ANTHEXIMETER
ANTHOXANTHIN
ANTIOXIDANT
ANTIOXYGENIC
APPROXIMATE
APPROXIMATED
APPROXIMATELY
APPROXIMATING
APPROXIMATION
APPROXIMATIVE
APPROXIMATOR
ASPHYXIATED
ASPHYXIATING
ASPHYXIATION
ASPHYXIATOR
CARBOXYLASE
CARBOXYLATE
CARBOXYLATED
CONNEXITIES
CONTEXTUALLY
CONTEXTURAL
CONTEXTURED
CONVEXEDNESS
CONVEXITIES
COSTOXIPHOID

DOPAOXIDASE
INFLEXIBILITY
INFLUXIONISM
INTERXYLARY
INTRAXYLARY
LITHOXYLITE
OVEREXPOSED
OVEREXPOSING
OVEREXPOSURE
OXYHEXACTINE
OXYHEXASTER
PANSEXUALISM
PANSEXUALIST
PANSEXUALITY
PANSEXUALIZE
PERIAXILLARY
PHENOXAZINE
POSTAXIALLY
POSTEXILIAN
POSTEXISTENT
PREFIXATION
PREMAXILLARY
PRETEXTUOUS
PROTOXIDIZE
PROTOXIDIZED
QUINOXALINE
REFLEXIONAL
REFLEXIVELY
REFLEXIVITY
REFLEXOLOGY
RETROXIPHOID
SUBLUXATION
SUBMAXILLAE
SUBMAXILLARY
SUBSEXTUPLE
SUFFIXATION
SULFOXYLATE
TETROXALATE
UNISEXUALITY
UNISEXUALLY
UROTOXICITY

AMBIDEXTERITY
AMBIDEXTRAL
AMBIDEXTROUS
ANTHRAXOLITE
ANTHRAXYLON
ANTHROXANIC
APOPLEXIOUS
AUTOTOXAEMIA
AUTOTOXEMIA
BANDBOXICAL
CARBOLXYLOL
COLOPEXOTOMY
COMPLEXIONAL
COMPLEXIONARY
COMPLEXIONED
COMPLEXITIES
COMPLEXNESS
CONFLUXIBLE
GASTROXYNSIS
HETEROXENOUS
HOMOSEXUALITY
HYDROEXTRACT
HYPOTOXICITY
INOBNOXIOUS
ODONTEXESIS
OVERTAXATION
PARADOXICAL
PARADOXICIAN
PARADOXIDIAN
PARADOXOLOGY
PERICOXITIS
PERPLEXEDLY
PERPLEXINGLY
PERPLEXITIES

PHYLLOXERAN
PHYLLOXERIC
PILOTAXITIC
PRAEMAXILLA
PRAETAXATION
RHYOTAXITIC
SEMISEXTILE
STAURAXONIA
STAURAXONIAL
SULPHOXYLIC
TYLOTOXEATE
TYROTOXICON
UNDEREXPOSE
UNDEREXPOSED
UNDEREXPOSING
XANTHOXENITE
XANTHOXYLIN
ZANTHOXYLUM
ZOOPRAXISCOPE

ADENOMYXOMA
AMIDOHEXOSE
AMYLODEXTRIN
ANHYDROXIME
ANILIDOXIME
ANTEFLEXION
APPENDIXING
CIRCUMAXIAL
CIRCUMAXILE
CRUCIFIXION
CYCLOHEXANE
CYCLOHEXANOL
CYCLOHEXENE
CYSTOMYXOMA
DICARBOXYLIC
FIBROMYXOMA
GENUFLEXION
GENUFLEXUOUS
IDEOPRAXIST
INTERMIXEDLY
INTERMIXING
INTERMIXTLY
INTERMIXTURE
INTERSEXUAL
INTERTEXTURE
IRREFLEXIVE
LAURINOXYLON
METAVAUXITE
ORTHODOXALLY
ORTHODOXIAN
ORTHODOXICAL
ORTHODOXIES
ORTHODOXISM
ORTHODOXIST
ORTHODOXNESS
PARAVAUXITE
PEPTOTOXINE
PHILODOXICAL
POSTFLEXION
QUINATOXINE
QUINCUNXIAL
QUINISEXTINE
SACROCOXITIS
SEMIFLEXIBLE
SUPERMAXILLA
SUPERSEXUAL
SUPRAMAXILLA
SUPRAMAXIMAL
TRANSFIXING
TRANSFIXION
TRANSFIXTURE
TYPHOTOXINE
ULTRAMAXIMAL

ANAPHYLAXIS
ANGIOATAXIA

ANISALDOXIME
APHOTOTAXIS
APOPHYLAXIS
ATLANTOAXIAL
ATLOIDOAXOID
BENZALDOXIME
CARBETHOXYL
CARDIATAXIA
CARDIOTOXIC
CHEMIOTAXIC
CHEMIOTAXIS
CHIROPRAXIS
COLONOPEXY
CREATOTOXISM
DECIMOSEXTO
DIASTATAXIC
DICATALEXIS
DIRECTRIXES
DISULPHOXID
DISULPHOXIDE
DORSIFLEXION
DORSIFLEXOR
ENTEROPEXIA
ENTEROTOXEMIA
EXECUTRIXES
FORMALDOXIME
GASTROTAXIS
GRIPPOTOXIN
HETERODOXIES
HETEROSEXUAL
HETEROTAXIA
HETEROTAXIC
HETEROTAXIS
IMMUNOTOXIN
INTROFLEXION
KERATONYXIS
LYMPHOTOXIN
METAGALAXIES
MYELOPLAXES
MYTILOTOXINE
NEPHROTOXIC
NEPHROTOXIN
NEUROPLEXUS
ODONTOLOXIA
OSTEOSTIXIS
PHYLLOTAXIS
PNEUMOTOXIN
PROCATARXIS
PROPHYLAXIS
PROTEOPEXIC
PROTEOPEXIS
PROTHORAXES
PSEUDODOXAL
PSYCHOSEXUAL
PSYCHOTAXIS
PYRRHULOXIA
RADIOPRAXIS
RETROFLEXED
RETROFLEXION
RHAMNOHEXOSE
RHAMNOHEXITE
SCILLITOXIN
SCLERONYXIS
SESQUISEXTAL
SPASMOTOXIN
SPASMOTOXINE
SPERMOTOXIN
SPLENOPEXIA
SPLENOPEXIS
SPLENOTOXIN
STEREOTAXIS
SUPERFLEXION
THERMOTAXIC
THERMOTAXIS
THIGMOTAXIS
TRISULFOXID

TROPHOTAXIS
URECHITOXIN

ACROASPHYXIA
ACTINOPRAXIS
ANGIORRHEXIS
AORTOMALAXIS
COLPORRHEXIS
ELECTROTAXIS
GALVANOTAXIS
ICHTHYOTOXIN
KARYORRHEXIS
LITHOLAPAXY
MORPHALLAXIS
OOPHOROPEXY
ORCHIDOPEXY
OROPHARYNXES
OSCULATRIXES
POLYHYDROXY
SCAPULOPEXY
SHIKIMOTOXIN
STROPHOTAXIS
TRISULPHOXID
TROPHALLAXIS
UNORTHODOXLY
UNORTHODOXY
VASOREFLEX

ANDROSPHINX
ARCHOSYRINX
AUTOCRATRIX
BACTERIOTOXIC
CHALCEDONYX
CHEMOREFLEX
CHYLOTHORAX
CLITORIDAUXE
COMPETITRIX
CONSOLATRIX
CYSTOSYRINX
CYTOPHARYNX
ESOTHYROPEXY
EXPENDITRIX
FORNICATRIX
FRICANDEAUX
GUBERNATRIX
HYDROTHORAX
HYPOPHARYNX
LEGISLATRIX
LIFERENTRIX
LITHANTHRAX
MERVEILLEUX
MESOSALPINX
MICROTHORAX
MONILETHRIX
MYELAPOPLEXY
NASOPHARYNX
NEGOTIATRIX
NEOORTHODOXY
OBJURGATRIX
PACHYMENINX
PHLEBORRHEXIS
PHOTOSYNTAX
PNEUMONOPEXY
PROCURATRIX
PROGENITRIX
PROLOCUTRIX
PTEROTHORAX
SACROCOCCYX
SCEUOPHYLAX
SIPHONOPLAX
SPECULATRIX
STENOTHORAX
STIMULATRIX
TETRAHYDROXY
THOROUGHWAX

ARCHEOPTERYX
ARTHROSYRINX
CHARTOPHYLAX
DISPENSATRIX
MESOAPPENDIX
PNEUMOTHORAX
PSEUDOCORTEX
PSYCHOREFLEX
RHINOPHARYNX
STEREOMATRIX
TROPHOTHYLAX
ULTRACOMPLEX
IMPROPRIATRIX

SCORING ORDER LIST OF WORDS OVER 10 LETTERS

35
EXQUISITIVELY
ZANTHOXYLUM
ZOOPRAXISCOPE

34
EXPERMENTIZED
EXTEMPORIZING
HYPOPHARYNX
OXYGENIZABLE
OXYRRHYNCHID

33
BENZALDOXIME
EXPERIMENTIZE
EXTEMPORIZED
JUXTAPYLORIC
OXYRHYNCHID
OXYRHYNCHOUS

32
CHARTOPHYLAX
DEOXYGENIZE
EXORCIZEMENT
EXTEMPORIZER
EXTRAVAGANZA
HYPOTOXICITY
MAXIMIZATION
OXYGENIZING
OXYPHOSPHATE
PHENOXAZINE
PROTOXIDIZED
PSYCHOREFLEX

31
CYTOPHARYNX
DOXOLOGIZING
EXOPHTHALMIC
EXTEMPORIZE
MYELAPOPLEXY
MYXOMYCETOUS
OXYCEPHALISM
OXYCHROMATIC
OXYPHTHALIC
OXYQUINOLINE
WAXCHANDLERY
ZOOXANTHELLA

30
CYSTOMYXOMA
DEOXIDIZING
DESEXUALIZED
DOXOLOGIZED
ESOTHYROPEXY
EXAUTHORIZE
EXCHANGEABLY
EXCLAMATIVELY
EXCURSIONIZE
EXEMPLIFYING
EXHIBITIVELY
EXHIBITORSHIP
EXORCIZATION
EXQUISITELY
EXTERIORIZING
EXTRAPHYSICAL
HYPOXANTHINE
ICHTHYOTOXIN
LEXICOGRAPHY
MYXOCYSTOMA
MYXOFIBROMA
OXYCEPHALIC
OXYCOPAIVIC
OXYMETHYLENE
PACHYMENINX
PANSEXUALIZE
PHLEBORRHEXIS
PROTOXIDIZE
RHINOPHARYNX
TAXIDERMIZE
TROPHOTHYLAX
XYLOQUINONE

29
ACROASPHYXIA
APPROXIMATELY
APPROXIMATIVE
ARCHEOPTERYX
ASEXUALIZING
CHALCEDONYX
CHYLOTHORAX
COMPLEXIONARY
CYCLOHEXANOL
DEXTROSAZONE
DICARBOXYLIC
EXHORTATIVELY
EXOPHTHALMIA
EXOPHTHALMOS
EXOPHTHALMUS
EXOSTRACIZE
EXQUISITENESS
EXQUISITISM
EXTERIORIZED
EXTERNIZATION
INOXIDIZING
JUXTAPOSITION
KARYORRHEXIS
MAXILLOJUGAL
ORCHIDOPEXY
OXYALDEHYDE
OXYCEPHALOUS
OXYCHROMATIN
OXYHYDROGEN
OXYPHYLLOUS
OXYSALICYLIC
PAROXYSMALLY
POLYHYDROXY
PSYCHOSEXUAL
QUINCUNXIAL
TETRAHYDROXY
TOXICOPHAGY
XANTHOPHYLL
XYLOGRAPHIC

28
ADOXOGRAPHY
ALEXIPHARMIC
AMBIDEXTERITY
APOPHYLAXIS
ASEXUALIZED
ASPHYXIATING
AUXOCHROMISM
AXISYMMETRIC
CARBETHOXYL
CHEMOREFLEX
COLOPEXOTOMY
CYCLOHEXANE
CYCLOHEXENE
DESEXUALIZE
EXCEPTIVELY
EXCIPULIFORM
EXCOMMUNICANT
EXCOMMUNICATE
EXCONJUGANT
EXENCEPHALIC
EXHAUSTIVELY
EXPENDABILITY
EXPLANATIVELY
EXPLORATIVELY
EXTRAVAGANCY
HEXASTICHIC
HOMOSEXUALITY
HYDROEXTRACT
HYDROTHORAX
INEXPLICABLY
INFLEXIBILITY
JUXTAPOSING
LEXIGRAPHICAL
LYMPHOTOXIN
MAXILLIPEDARY
MYXOBLASTOMA
OBJURGATRIX
OOPHOROPEXY
OXYPROPIONIC
PHYLLOXERIC
PNEUMONOPEXY
PROPHYLAXIS
PSYCHOTAXIS
QUINISEXTINE
SCEUOPHYLAX
SESQUISEXTAL
SHIKIMOTOXIN
SULPHOXYLIC
THOROUGHWAX
TOXICOPATHIC
TOXICOPATHY
XANTHOCHROID
XEROPHYTISM

27
ANHYDROXIME
APPROXIMATING
ASPHYXIATED
ASPHYXIATION
AUXOCHROMIC
CARBOXYLATED
CHEMIOTAXIC
COSTOXIPHOID
DIHEXAHEDRAL
DIHEXAHEDRON
EXCEPTIONALLY
EXCHANGEABLE
EXCLAMATORILY
EXHIBITIONISM
EXOMORPHISM
EXPANSIBILITY
EXPLOSIBILITY
EXPORTABILITY
EXPOSITIVELY
EXPRESSIVELY
EXSUFFLICATE
EXTEMPORARILY
EXTERIORIZE
EXTERNALIZE
EXTEROCEPTIVE
EXTRAVAGANTLY
EXTROSPECTIVE
EXUVIABILITY
FORMALDOXIME
INEXPECTEDLY
INEXPEDIENCY
JUXTASPINAL
MIXOBARBARIC
MIXOTROPHIC
MYXEDEMATOUS
MYXOSARCOMA
OROPHARYNXES
OXYACANTHINE
OXYACANTHOUS
OXYACETYLENE
OXYCHLORIDE
OXYCINNAMIC
OXYGENICITY
OXYLUCIFERIN
OXYOSPHRESIA
OXYSULPHIDE
PERPLEXINGLY
PHILODOXICAL
PYROXMANGITE
QUINATOXINE
QUINOXALINE
REFLEXIVELY
REFLEXIVITY
RHAMNOHEXOSE
RHAMNOHEXITE
SCAPULOPEXY
TOXICOPHIDIA
TOXIPHOBIAC
UNEXPECTEDLY
WAXCHANDLER
XANTHOCHROIA
XENOMORPHIC
XEROMORPHIC
XYLOGRAPHER
XYLOPHAGOUS

26
ADENOMYXOMA
ALEXIPYRETIC
ANAPHYLAXIS
APPROXIMATED
APPROXIMATION
ARCHOSYRINX
ASPHYXIATOR
AUXOCHROMOUS
AUXOGRAPHIC
BACTERIOTOXIC
COLPORRHEXIS
COMPLEXIONED
CYSTOSYRINX
DISULPHOXIDE
EXANTHEMATIC
EXCEPTIONARY
EXCESSIVELY
EXCITABILITY
EXCITOMOTORY
EXCLUSIVELY
EXCLUSIVITY
EXCREMENTARY
EXCREMENTIVE
EXCURSIVELY
EXCUSABILITY
EXECUTIVELY
EXEMPLIFIED
EXENCEPHALIA
EXENCEPHALUS
EXHAUSTINGLY
EXHAUSTLESSLY
EXPANSIVELY
EXPANSIVITY
EXPEDITIONARY
EXPEDITIOUSLY
EXPENSIVELY
EXPERIMENTLY
EXPLETIVELY
EXPLOSIVELY
EXPROBRATORY
EXTEMPORALLY
EXTENDIBILITY
EXTRACTIFORM
FLEXIBILITY
FLUXIBILITY
FUCOXANTHIN
HEXABROMIDE
HEXOBARBITAL
IMPROPRIATRIX
INEXPLICABLES
INEXPLICITLY
INEXTRICABLY
LEXIGRAPHIC
LITHOLAPAXY
MESOAPPENDIX
MORPHALLAXIS
MYXASTHENIA
NASOPHARYNX
NEOORTHODOXY
ORTHODOXALLY
OXYACANTHIN
OXYBERBERINE
OXYCARBONATE
OXYCHLORATE
OXYCHLORINE
OXYHAEMATIN
OXYHEXACTINE
OXYSULPHATE
PARADOXOLOGY
PERPLEXEDLY
PHOTOSYNTAX
PHYLLOTAXIS
PHYLLOXERAN
PNEUMOTHORAX
PREMAXILLARY
PYOXANTHOSE
PYRRHULOXIA
RHYOTAXITIC
SEMIFLEXIBLE
SUBMAXILLARY
TOXOPHILITIC
TYPHOTOXINE
UNORTHODOXLY
XANTHOPHANE
XANTHOPHORE
XENODOCHIUM
XEROGRAPHIC
XEROMORPHOUS
XIPHISTERNUM

XIPHOPAGOUS
XYLOPHILOUS
XYLOPHONIST

25
AMYLODEXTRIN
ANOXYBIOTIC
ANTHOXANTHIN
ANTIOXYGENIC
APPROXIMATOR
ARTHROSYRINX
ATAXOPHEMIA
BANDBOXICAL
BIMAXILLARY
CARBOLXYLOL
CARBOXYLASE
CARBOXYLATE
CHEMIOTAXIS
CHIROPRAXIS
COEXISTENCY
COMPLEXIONAL
COMPLEXITIES
CONFLUXIBLE
CONVEXEDNESS
COXCOMBICAL
COXOFEMORAL
CRUCIFIXION
DEOXYGENATED
DISULPHOXID
DOXOGRAPHER
EXCEEDINGLY
EXCESSIVENESS
EXCLAMATIVE
EXCLAMATORY
EXCLUSIVENESS
EXCLUSIVISM
EXCOGITATIVE
EXCORTICATING
EXCULPATIVE
EXCULPATORY
EXECUTIVENESS
EXEGETICALLY
EXEMPLARILY
EXEMPLARITY
EXEMPLIFIER
EXHAUSTEDLY
EXHIBITIONIST
EXHILARATIVE
EXHILARATORY
EXOMPHALOUS
EXORBITANCY
EXPANDINGLY
EXPANSIVENESS
EXPECTANCIES
EXPECTANTLY
EXPECTATIVE
EXPECTORATING
EXPENSIVENESS
EXPERIMENTING
EXPISCATORY
EXPLANATORILY
EXPLETIVENESS
EXPLICATIVE
EXPLICATORY
EXPLOSIVENESS
EXPONENTIALLY
EXPOSITIONARY
EXPOSTULATIVE
EXPOSTULATORY
EXPROPRIATING
EXSICCATIVE
EXSUFFLATION
EXTEMPORARY
EXTENSIBILITY
EXTERMINATIVE
EXTERMINATORY
EXTRACYSTIC
EXTRAGALACTIC
EXTRAPOLATIVE
EXTRAVAGANCE
EXTRAVAGATING
EXTRAVASCULAR
EXTRINSICALLY
EXTROVERSIVE
EXTUMESCENCE
HEXAGONALLY
INEXCUSABLY
INEXHAUSTIBLE
INEXHAUSTIVE
INEXPERIENCED
INEXPLICABLE
INTERMIXEDLY
KERATONYXIS
LEXICOLOGICAL
LOXODOGRAPH
MAXILLIFORM
MICROTHORAX
MYELOPLAXES
MYXOMATOSIS
MYXONEUROMA
MYXOSPOROUS
NEPHROTOXIC
ORTHODOXICAL
OVEREXPOSING
OXYCOUMARIN
OXYGNATHOUS
OXYMURIATIC
PAROXYTONIC
PAXILLIFORM
PRAXINOSCOPE
PROXIMATELY
REFLEXOLOGY
RETROXIPHOID
SEXTUPLICATED
SIPHONOPLAX
SUPRAMAXIMAL
THERMOTAXIC
THIXOTROPIC
TOXOPHILISM
TRISULPHOXID
ULTRACOMPLEX
UNEXCEPTIVE
UNEXCUSABLY
UNEXPLICABLE
UNORTHODOXY
XEROPHOBOUS
XIPHOCOSTAL
XYLOCARPOUS
XYLOPLASTIC

24
ADMAXILLARY
AMBIDEXTROUS
AMIDOHEXOSE
AMPLEXICAUL
ANDROSPHINX
ANTHEXIMETER
ANTHRAXYLON
APPENDIXING
APPROXIMATE
ATAXIAGRAPH
ATAXIAPHASIA
AXONOPHOROUS
CIRCUMAXIAL
CIRCUMAXILE
COMPETITRIX
COMPLEXNESS
CONTEXTUALLY
COXARTHRITIS
DEXIOTROPISM
DEXTROGYRATE
DISOXYGENATE
DYSOXIDATION
EPEXEGETICAL
EXACERBATING
EXACTIVENESS
EXAGGERATIVE
EXAGGERATORY
EXASPERATIVE
EXCANDESCENT
EXCATHEDRAL
EXCERPTIBLE
EXCITABLENESS
EXCLAMATIONAL
EXCLUSIONARY
EXCOMMUNION
EXCORTICATED
EXCORTICATION
EXCRESCENCY
EXCRESCENTIAL
EXCRETIONARY
EXCRUCIABLE
EXCRUCIATING
EXCURSIONARY
EXCUSABLENESS
EXECRABLENESS
EXEMPLARINESS
EXEMPLARISM
EXFOLIATIVE
EXFOLIATORY
EXHAUSTEDNESS
EXHIBITIONAL
EXHIBITIONER
EXHORTATIVE
EXHORTATORY
EXOCCIPITAL
EXORBITANTLY
EXOTERICALLY
EXPECTORATED
EXPECTORATION
EXPEDIENCIES
EXPEDIENTLY
EXPERIENCING
EXPERIMENTED
EXPERIMENTIST
EXPLOITATIVE
EXPOSITORILY
EXPRESSIONISM
EXPROPRIATED
EXPROPRIATION
EXPURGATIVE
EXPURGATORY
EXTENSIVELY
EXTENUATINGLY
EXTEROCEPTIST
EXTINGUISHED
EXTORSIVELY
EXTRACAPSULAR
EXTRAMURALLY
EXTRAORDINARY
EXTRAVAGATED
EXTRAVAGATION
EXTRAVASATING
EXTROSPECTION
EXULCERATIVE
EXULCERATORY
FLEXIBLENESS
FLUXIBLENESS
FLUXIONALLY
FRICANDEAUX
INDEXICALLY
INEXPRESSIBLE
INEXPRESSIVE
INFLUXIONISM
INTERXYLARY
INTOXICATIVE
INTRAXYLARY
IRREFLEXIVE
LITHANTHRAX
LITHOXYLITE
MAXILLOLABIAL
MYTILOTOXINE
MYXADENITIS
ORTHODOXISM
OVEREXPOSED
OVEREXPOSURE
OXIDABILITY
OXYCELLULOSE
OXYESTHESIA
OXYSTOMATOUS
OXYTYLOTATE
PANSEXUALITY
PARADOXICIAN
PERIAXILLARY
PLEXIMETRIC
PROTEOPEXIC
PSEUDOCORTEX
SEXCENTENARY
SEXISYLLABLE
STROPHOTAXIS
SUFFIXATION
SULFOXYLATE
SUPERFLEXION
TAXGATHERING
THIGMOTAXIS
TOXICOGNATH
TOXINFECTION
TROPHALLAXIS
UNDEREXPOSING
UNEXPRESSIVE
VEXATIOUSLY
XANTHOCONITE
XANTHODERMA
XANTHOGENIC
XANTHOMATOUS
XANTHOPTERIN
XENACANTHINE
XEROGRAPHER
XIPHISTERNAL
XYLOSTROMATA
XYRIDACEOUS

23
ACTINOPRAXIS
AMBIDEXTRAL
ANGIORRHEXIS
ANOXYBIOSIS
ANTHROXANIC
APHOTOTAXIS
ATAXAPHASIA
AUXETICALLY
AUXOAMYLASE
AUXOHORMONE
BISAXILLARY
BISEXUALITY
CARDIOTOXIC
COEXTENSIVE
CONVEXITIES
CREATOTOXISM
DECIMOSEXTO
DEOXYGENATE
DETOXICATING
DEXIOTROPIC
DEXTROCARDIA
DORSIFLEXION
EXACERBATED
EXACERBATION
EXALBUMINOSE
EXALBUMINOUS
EXAMINATIVE
EXAMINATORY
EXCAVATIONS
EXCELLENCIES
EXCELLENTLY
EXCLUSIONISM
EXCOGITABLE
EXCOGITATING
EXCRESCENCIES
EXCRUCIATED
EXCRUCIATION
EXCULPATING
EXCURSIONISM
EXCURVATURE
EXCYSTATION
EXFIGURATION
EXFLAGELLATE
EXHAUSTIBLE
EXHILARATING
EXILARCHATE
EXISTENTIALLY
EXOPERIDIUM
EXORABILITY
EXORCISEMENT
EXORCISTICAL
EXOTHERMOUS
EXPANDEDNESS
EXPANSIONISM
EXPATIATIVE
EXPATIATORY
EXPECTORATOR
EXPEDITATING
EXPEDITIONIST
EXPENTHESIS
EXPERIENCED
EXPERIMENTAL
EXPERIMENTEE
EXPERIMENTER
EXPISCATING
EXPLANATIVE
EXPLANATORY
EXPLICATING
EXPLICITNESS
EXPLORATIVE
EXPLORATORY
EXPOSTULATING
EXPROMISSION
EXPROPRIATOR
EXPULSATORY
EXPURGATORIAL
EXSCRIPTURAL
EXSICCATING
EXTENSIVENESS
EXTERMINATING
EXTEROCEPTOR
EXTINGUISHER
EXTIRPATIVE
EXTIRPATORY
EXTISPICIOUS
EXTRAFORMAL
EXTRAPOLATING
EXTRAVAGINAL
EXTRAVASATED
EXTRAVASATION
EXUBERANTLY
FLEXANIMOUS
FORNICATRIX
GALVANOTAXIS
GASTROXYNSIS
GENUFLEXUOUS
GRIPPOTOXIN
HETERODOXIES
HETEROTAXIC
INEXISTENCY
INEXPENSIVE
INEXPERIENCE
INEXTIRPABLE
INEXTRICABLE
INTERMIXTLY
LEXICOLOGIC
LOXODROMICS
LOXODROMISM
MAXILLIPEDE
MERVEILLEUX
METAVAUXITE
MONILETHRIX

NEPHROTOXIN
OBNOXIOUSLY
ORTHODOXNESS
OXIDIMETRIC
OXYGENATING
OXYGENERATOR
OXYHEXASTER
OXYPETALOUS
PANSEXUALISM
PARADOXICAL
PARADOXIDIAN
PARAVAUXITE
PERPLEXITIES
POSTAXIALLY
POSTFLEXION
PREEXISTENCE
PREFIXATION
PROTHORAXES
PTEROTHORAX
SACROCOCCYX
SACROCOXITIS
SAXOPHONIST
SCLERONYXIS
SEXADECIMAL
SEXANGULARLY
SEXTUPLICATE
SPASMOTOXINE
SUBAXILLARY
SUPERMAXILLA
SUPRAMAXILLA
THERMOTAXIS
THIXOLABILE
TOXICOGENIC
TOXICOLOGIC
TOXOPHILOUS
TROPHOTAXIS
TYROTOXICON
ULTRAMAXIMAL
UNDEREXPOSED
UNEXCLUSIVE
UNEXPENSIVE
UNEXPERIENCE
UNEXPURGATED
UNEXTRICABLE
URECHITOXIN
UROTOXICITY
VASOREFLEX
XANTHELASMA
XANTHOGENATE
XANTHOMETER
XANTHOXYLIN
XEROPHILOUS
XIPHOSUROUS

22
AMPLEXATION
ANISALDOXIME
ANOXIDATIVE
ANTHRAXOLITE
APOPLEXIOUS
AXIOMATICAL
AXONOMETRIC
AXOSPERMOUS
BISEXUALISM
CLITORIDAUXE
COEXISTENCE
DETOXICATED
DETOXICATION
DEXIOTROPOUS
DEXTEROUSLY
DISPENSATRIX
DOPAOXIDASE
DORSIFLEXOR
DOXOLOGICAL
EXACTINGNESS
EXAGGERATING
EXAMINATIONAL
EXASPERATING
EXCALCARATE
EXCEPTIONAL
EXCEPTIONER
EXCITOMOTOR
EXCLAMATION
EXCOGITATED
EXCOGITATION
EXCORTICATE
EXCREMENTAL
EXCRESCENCES
EXCRUCIATOR
EXCULPATION
EXECUTRICES
EXERCISABLE
EXFILTRATION
EXFODIATION
EXFOLIATING
EXHILARATED
EXHILARATION
EXOGENOUSLY
EXOGNATHION
EXOGNATHITE
EXOMOLOGESIS
EXORBITANCE
EXOSKELETAL
EXOSKELETON
EXOSTRACISM
EXOTERICISM
EXPATRIATING
EXPECTATION
EXPECTORANT
EXPECTORATE
EXPEDIENTIAL
EXPEDIENTIST
EXPEDITATED
EXPEDITATION
EXPEDITENESS
EXPENSILATION
EXPERIENCER
EXPERIENCES
EXPIATORINESS
EXPISCATION
EXPLAINABLE
EXPLEMENTAL
EXPLICATION
EXPLOITABLE
EXPLORATIONAL
EXPLOREMENT
EXPOSTULATED
EXPOSTULATION
EXPRESSIBLE
EXPRESSIONIST
EXPROPRIATE
EXPURGATING
EXSCULPTATE
EXSICCATION
EXTERMINATED
EXTERMINATION
EXTERNALISTIC
EXTORTIONARY
EXTRABULBAR
EXTRACARPAL
EXTRACTABLE
EXTRACTIBLE
EXTRADITABLE
EXTRADUCTION
EXTRAMUNDANE
EXTRANEOUSLY
EXTRAPOLATED
EXTRAPOLATION
EXTRASENSORY
EXTRASYSTOLE
EXTRAVAGANT
EXTRAVAGATE
EXTRAVERSION
EXTREMISTIC
EXTROVERSION
EXUBERANTNESS
EXULCERATING
EXUMBRELLAR
FLEXUOSITIES
FLEXUOUSNESS
GENUFLEXION
HETEROSEXUAL
HETEROXENOUS
INDEXTERITY
INEXACTITUDE
INEXCUSABLE
INTOXICABLE
INTOXICATING
INTROFLEXION
LAURINOXYLON
LAXATIVENESS
LEXICOLOGIST
LIXIVIATING
MESOSALPINX
METAGALAXIES
OBNOXIOUSNESS
ORTHODOXIAN
ORTHODOXIES
ORTHODOXIST
OVERTAXATION
PEPTOTOXINE
PERICOXITIS
PILOTAXITIC
PNEUMOTOXIN
PRAEMAXILLA
PROCATARXIS
PROCURATRIX
PROLOCUTRIX
PROTEOPEXIS
PROXENETISM
PROXIMATION
PSEUDODOXAL
RETROFLEXED
RETROFLEXION
SAXIFRAGANT
SAXIFRAGOUS
SEXDIGITATED
SEXDIGITISM
SEXPLOITATION
SEXTILLIONTH
SPASMOTOXIN
SPECULATRIX
SPERMOTOXIN
SPLENOPEXIA
SPLENOPEXIS
SUBMAXILLAE
SUBOXIDATION
SUBSEXTUPLE
TAXGATHERER
TAXONOMICAL
TOXALBUMOSE
TOXICOLOGIST
TOXICOMANIA
TRANSFIXING
TRANSFIXTURE
TRISULFOXID
UNEXCUSABLE
UNISEXUALITY
VEXILLARIOUS
XENYLAMINE

21
ANILIDOXIME
ANTEFLEXION
AORTOMALAXIS
ATLOIDOAXOID
AUTOTOXAEMIA
AUXILIATORY
AXIOLOGICAL
CARDIATAXIA
CONTEXTURED
COXOCERITIC
DETOXICATOR
DEXTROCULAR
DIASTATAXIC
DICATALEXIS
DIRECTRIXES
ELECTROTAXIS
EXAGGERATED
EXAGGERATION
EXARTICULATE
EXASPERATED
EXASPERATION
EXCITEDNESS
EXCLUSIONIST
EXCOGITATOR
EXCORIATING
EXCRESCENCE
EXCURSIONIST
EXERCITATION
EXERCITORIAL
EXFOLIATION
EXHAUSTLESS
EXHILARATOR
EXIMIOUSNESS
EXOCULATING
EXONERATIVE
EXORABLENESS
EXORBITATION
EXORCISATION
EXOTICALNESS
EXPANSIONIST
EXPATIATING
EXPATRIATED
EXPATRIATION
EXPEDITIOUS
EXPENDITURE
EXPERIENTIAL
EXPLANTATION
EXPLOITATION
EXPLOSIONIST
EXPOSITIONAL
EXPOSITORIAL
EXPOSTULATOR
EXPRESSIONAL
EXPURGATION
EXSCUTELLATE
EXTENDEDNESS
EXTENSIMETER
EXTENSOMETER
EXTENUATIVE
EXTENUATORY
EXTERIORITY
EXTERMINATOR
EXTERNALITY
EXTIRPATING
EXTRAENTERIC
EXTRAPOLATOR
EXTRAVASATE
EXTRAVIOLET
EXTRICATING
EXTRINSICATE
EXUBERATING
EXULCERATED
EXULCERATION
GUBERNATRIX
HETEROTAXIA
HETEROTAXIS
IDEOPRAXIST
INEXPEDIENT
INEXPERTNESS
INEXTENSIVE
INNOXIOUSLY
INTERMIXING
INTERMIXTURE
INTOXICATED
INTOXICATION
LAXIFLOROUS
LAXIFOLIATE
LAXIFOLIOUS
LIFERENTRIX
LIXIVIATION
LUXURIANTLY
LUXURIOUSLY
NONEXISTENCE
OSCULATRIXES
OXALURAMIDE
PANSEXUALIST
POSTEXISTENT
PRAETAXATION
PROGENITRIX
RADIOPRAXIS
REFLEXIONAL
SEXAGESIMAL
SEXOLOGICAL
SEXTIPARTITE
STENOTHORAX
STEREOMATRIX
TAXASPIDEAN
TAXEOPODOUS
TAXIDERMIST
TAXIMETERED
TEXTIFEROUS
TOXITABELLAE
TRANSFIXION
TYLOTOXEATE
UNDEREXPOSE
UNEXPEDIENT
UNEXPLAINED
UNEXPLOITED
UNISEXUALLY
VEXILLATION
XANTHINURIA
XANTHOXENITE
XENARTHROUS
XENOPARASITE

20
ANNEXATIONIST
ATAXIAMETER
AUTOCRATRIX
AUTOTOXEMIA
AUTOXIDATION
AUXANOMETER
AXODENDRITE
AXONOLIPOUS
COEXTENSION
CONNEXITIES
CONSOLATRIX
CONTEXTURAL
DEXTROUSNESS
ENTEROPEXIA
EXAGGERATOR
EXAMINATION
EXANIMATION
EXASPERATER
EXAUCTORATE
EXAUGURATION
EXCANTATION
EXCARNATION
EXCLUSIONER
EXCORIATION
EXCURSIONAL
EXCURSIONER
EXECUTIONAL
EXECUTIONER
EXECUTORIAL
EXENTERATING
EXIGUOUSNESS
EXISTLESSNESS
EXOGASTRITIS
EXOMETRITIS
EXPANSIONAL
EXPATIATION
EXPENDITRIX

EXPLANATION
EXPLORATION
EXPONENTIAL
EXPORTATION
EXPOSTULATE
EXPRESSLESS
EXSANGUINATE
EXSANGUINOUS
EXSTIPULATE
EXTERIORATION
EXTERMINATE
EXTERNALISM
EXTERNALITIES
EXTERRESTRIAL
EXTERRITORIAL
EXTIRPATION
EXTRACOSTAL
EXTRADITING
EXTRAPOLATE
EXTRAREGULAR
EXTRATRIBAL
EXTREMENESS
EXTREMITIES
EXTRICATION
EXTRINSICAL
EXUBERATION
GITOXIGENIN
INEXACTNESS
INEXECUTION
INEXISTENCE
INOBNOXIOUS
INTOXICATOR
LUXURIANTNESS
LUXURIOUSNESS
MAXILLARIES
MIXTILINEAR
NEUROPLEXUS
POSTEXILIAN
PREEXISTENT
PRETEXTUOUS
SCILLITOXIN
SEMISEXTILE
SEXAGENARIAN
SEXDIGITATE
SPLENOTOXIN
STIMULATRIX
SUBLUXATION
SUPERSEXUAL
TAXABLENESS
TOXOGLOSSATE
UNEXACTNESS
UNEXPERIENT
XEROTRIPSIS

19

ALEXANDRITE
ANGIOATAXIA
ANNEXATIONAL
ANTIOXIDANT
ATLANTOAXIAL
AUTOXIDATOR
DEXTROSURIA
EXALLOTRIOTE
EXALTEDNESS
EXECUTRIXES
EXENTERATED
EXENTERATION
EXOARTERITIS
EXONERATING
EXPIATIONA
EXPRESSION
EXSANGUIOUS
EXTENSIONIST
EXTENUATING
EXTERIORNESS
EXTERRANEOUS
EXTORTIONATE
EXTORTIONIST
EXTRADITION
EXTRALATERAL
EXTRARETINAL
EXTRAUTERINE
GASTROTAXIS
INTERTEXTURE
LEGISLATRIX
LUXULLIANITE
LUXURIATING
NEGOTIATRIX
ODONTEXESIS
ODONTOLOXIA
OXIDATIONAL
RELAXEDNESS
STAURAXONIAL
TOXOGENESIS
XENOGENESIS
XENOSAUROID

18

ANNEXIONIST
ANXIOUSNESS
AUXILIARIES
AUXILIATION
EXANTLATION
EXARTERITIS
EXINANITION
EXISTENTIAL
EXONERATION
EXTENSIONAL
EXTENUATION
EXTERIORATE
EXTERNALIST
EXTERNATION
EXTOLLATION
EXTORTIONER
EXTRASEROUS
EXTRATARSAL
INTERSEXUAL
LUXURIATION
NONEXISTENT
NOXIOUSNESS
OSTEOSTIXIS
SEXLESSNESS
STAURAXONIA
STEREOTAXIS
TETROXALATE

High-Scoring Words Containing

Z

2–3 LETTER WORDS

ALPHABETICAL ORDER

ADZ
AZO
BIZ
DZO
FEZ
FIZ
GAZ
GEZ
GUZ
HIZ
HUZ
JIZ
NIZ
POZ
SUZ
TEZ
TUZ
VIZ
WIZ
WUZ
YEZ
ZA
ZAC
ZAD
ZAG
ZAK
ZAR
ZAX
ZED
ZEE
ZEL
ZER
ZHO
ZIG
ZIP
ZO
ZOA
ZOH
ZOO

POSITIONAL ORDER

ZA
ZAC
ZAD
ZAG
ZAK
ZAR
ZAX
ZED
ZEE
ZEL
ZER
ZHO
ZIG
ZIP
ZO
ZOA
ZOH
ZOO

AZO
DZO

ADZ
BIZ
FEZ
FIZ
GAZ
GEZ
GUZ
HIZ
HUZ
JIZ
NIZ
POZ
SUZ
TEZ
TUZ
VIZ
WIZ
WUZ
YEZ

SCORING ORDER

19
JIZ
ZAX

16
ZAK

15
FEZ
FIZ
HIZ
HUZ
VIZ
WIZ
WUZ
YEZ
ZHO
ZOH

14
BIZ
POZ
ZAC
ZIP

13
ADZ
DZO
GAZ
GEZ
GUZ
ZAD
ZAG
ZED
ZIG

12
AZO
NIZ
SUZ
TEZ
TUZ
ZAR
ZEE
ZEL
ZER
ZOA
ZOO

11
ZA
ZO

ALPHABETICAL LIST OF 4-LETTER WORDS

ADZE
AZAM
AZAN
AZEW
AZON
AZYM
BATZ
BAZE
BIZE
BOZA
BOZO
BUZZ
CAZA
CAZY
CHEZ
COZE
COZY
CZAR
DAZE
DAZY
DOZE
DOZY
EZBA
FAZE
FIZZ
FOZE
FOZY
FRIZ
FUZE
FUZZ
GAZE
GAZI
GAZY
GIZZ
GUZE
HAYZ
HAZE
HAZY
HIZZ
HUZZ
IZAR
IZBA
IZLE
JAZZ
JEEZ
JUEZ
KAZI
KAZY
KNEZ
KOZO
LAZE
LAZO
LAZY
LEZA
LITZ
LIZA
LUTZ
MAZA
MAZE
MAZY
MOZO
MUZZ
NAZE
NAZI
NIZY
ONZA
OOZE
OOZY
OUZO
OYEZ
PIZE
PUTZ
QUIZ
QUOZ
RAZE
RAZZ
RITZ
SITZ
SIZE
SIZY
SIZZ
SUZU
SWIZ
TIZA
TOZE
TUZA
TUZZ
TZAR
TZUT
UNTZ
UNZE
UZAN
VAZA
VIZY
WHIZ
WUZU
ZAIN
ZANT
ZANY
ZARF
ZARP
ZART
ZATI
ZEAL
ZEBU
ZEDS
ZEES
ZEIN
ZEME
ZEMI
ZENU
ZEPP
ZERO
ZEST
ZETA
ZIIM
ZIMB
ZINC
ZING
ZINK
ZIRA
ZIZZ
ZNAK
ZOBO
ZOBU
ZOEA
ZOGO
ZOIC
ZOID
ZOLL
ZONA
ZONE
ZOOM
ZOON
ZOPE
ZULU
ZUPA
ZUZA
ZYME

POSITIONAL ORDER LIST OF 4-LETTER WORDS

ZAIN
ZANT
ZANY
ZARF
ZARP
ZART
ZATI
ZEAL
ZEBU
ZEDS
ZEES
ZEIN
ZEME
ZEMI
ZENU
ZEPP
ZERO
ZEST
ZETA
ZIIM
ZIMB
ZINC
ZING
ZINK
ZIRA
ZIZZ
ZNAK
ZOBO
ZOBU
ZOEA
ZOGO
ZOIC
ZOID
ZOLL
ZONA
ZONE
ZOOM
ZOON
ZOPE
ZULU
ZUPA
ZUZA
ZYGA
ZYME

AZAM
AZAN
AZEW
AZON
AZYM
CZAR
EZBA
IZAR
IZBA
IZLE
TZAR
TZUT
UZAN

ADZE
BAZE
BIZE
BOZA
BOZO
BUZZ
CAZA
CAZY
COZE
COZY
DAZE
DAZY
DOZE
DOZY
FAZE
FIZZ
FOZE
FOZY
FUZE
FUZZ
GAZE
GAZY
GIZZ
GUZE
HAZE
HAZY
HIZZ
HUZZ
JAZZ
KAZI
KAZY
KOZO
LAZE
LAZO
LAZY
LEZA
LIZA
MAZA
MAZE
MAZY
MOZO
MUZZ
NAZE
NAZI
NIZY
ONZA
OOZE
OOZY
OUZO
PIZE
RAZE
RAZZ
SIZE
SIZY
SIZZ
SUZU
TIZA
TOZE
TUZA
TUZZ
UNZE
VAZA
VIZY
WUZU
ZIZZ
ZUZA

BATZ
BUZZ
CHEZ
FIZZ
FRIZ
FUZZ
GIZZ
HAYZ
HIZZ
HUZZ
JAZZ
JEEZ
JUEZ
KNEZ
LITZ
LUTZ
MUZZ
OYEZ
PUTZ
QUIZ
QUOZ
RAZZ
RITZ
SITZ
SIZZ
SWIZ
TUZZ
UNTZ
WHIZ
ZIZZ

SCORING ORDER LIST OF 4-LETTER WORDS

22
QUIZ
QUOZ

20
JEEZ
JUEZ
KAZY

19
FOZY
HAYZ
HAZY
JAZZ
VIZY
WHIZ

18
AZYM
CAZY
CHEZ

COZY
MAZY
ZYME

17
DAZY
DOZY
GAZY
KAZI
KNEZ
KOZO
ZEPP
ZIMB
ZINK
ZNAK

16
AZEW
FAZE
FOZE
FRIZ
FUZE
HAZE
LAZY
NIZY
OOZY
OYEZ
SIZY

SWIZ
VAZA
WUZU
ZANY
ZARF

15
AZAM
BATZ
BAZE
BIZE
BOZA
BOZO
CAZA
COZE
CZAR
EZBA
FIZZ
FUZZ
HIZZ
HUZZ
IZBA
MAZA
MAZE
MOZO
PIZE
PUTZ

ZARP
ZEBU
ZEME
ZEMI
ZIIM
ZINC
ZOBO
ZOBU
ZOIC
ZOOM
ZOPE
ZUPA

14
ADZE
BUZZ
DAZE
DOZE
GAZE
GAZI
GUZE
MUZZ
ZEDS
ZING
ZOGO
ZOID

13
AZAN
AZON
GIZZ
IZAR
IZLE
LAZE
LAZO
LEZA
LITZ
LIZA
LUTZ
NAZE
NAZI
ONZA
OOZE
OUZO
RAZE
RITZ
SITZ
SIZE
SUZU
TIZA
TOZE
TUZA
TZAR
TZUT
UNTZ
UNZE

UZAN
ZAIN
ZANT
ZART
ZATI
ZEAL
ZEES
ZEIN
ZENU
ZERO
ZEST
ZETA
ZIRA
ZOEA
ZOLL
ZONA
ZONE
ZOON
ZULU

12
RAZZ
SIZZ
TUZZ
ZUZA

11
ZIZZ

ALPHABETICAL LIST OF 5-LETTER WORDS

ABAZE
ABUZZ
ADOZE
ADZER
ADZES
AGAZE
AIZLE
ALEZE
AMAZE
AMUZE
ARROZ
ARZUN
AZIDE
AZINE
AZLON
AZOCH
AZOFY
AZOIC
AZOLE
AZOTE
AZOTH
AZOXY
AZURE
AZURY
AZYME
BAIZA
BAIZE
BAZAR
BAZOO
BEZEL
BEZIL
BEZZO
BIZLE
BLAZE
BLAZY
BLITZ

BLIZZ
BONZA
BONZE
BORTZ
BOZAH
BOZAL
BOZZE
BRAZA
BRAZE
BRIZE
BRIZZ
BRUZZ
BUAZE
BUZZY
BWAZI
BYZEN
CAFIZ
CAHIZ
CHOZA
CLIZA
COLZA
COZED
COZEN
COZEY
COZIE
CRAZE
CRAZY
CROZE
DANZA
DARZI
DAZED
DIAZO
DIZEN
DIZZY
DOOZY
DOZED

DOZEN
DOZER
DROZE
ECIZE
ENZYM
ERIZO
FAIZE
FAZED
FEAZE
FEEZE
FELZE
FEZZY
FIZZY
FRAZE
FRIZE
FRIZZ
FROZE
FURZE
FURZY
FUZEE
FUZIL
FUZZY
GAIZE
GANZA
GAUZE
GAUZY
GAZED
GAZEL
GAZER
GAZET
GAZON
GAZOO
GAZOZ
GEYZE
GHAZI
GIZMO

GLAZE
GLAZY
GLOZE
GRAZE
GROSZ
GUAZA
HAFIZ
HAMZA
HAZAN
HAZEL
HAZEN
HAZER
HAZLE
HEAZY
HEEZE
HERTZ
HOOZE
HUZZA
HUZZY
IZARD
IZOTE
IZTLE
IZTLI
IZZAT
JAZEL
JAZZY
JEREZ
JEZIA
JIZYA
KAFIZ
KANZU
KAREZ
KAZAK
KAZOO
KNEZI
KNIAZ

KNYAZ
KONZE
KOUZA
KUDZU
LANAZ
LAZAR
LAZED
LAZZO
LEAZE
LOZEN
MAINZ
MAIZE
MATZO
MAZAR
MAZED
MAZER
MAZIC
MAZUT
METZE
MEZZA
MEZZO
MIMZY
MIRZA
MIZZY
MURZA
MUZZY
NAMAZ
NAZIM
NAZIR
NAZIS
NEEZE
NIZEY
OOZED
OOZEL
OUZEL
OWZEL

OZENA
OZONE
PEIZE
PEZZO
PIEZO
PIZZA
PLAZA
POIZE
PRIZE
QAZAQ
RAZEE
RAZED
RAZON
RAZOO
RAZOR
REZAI
RITZY
ROZUM
SABZI
SAZEN
SEIZE
SIZAR
SIZED
SIZER
SIZES
SMAZE
SNITZ
SOULZ
SOZIN
SPITZ
SQUIZ
SWIZZ
TAZIA
TAZZA
TEAZE
TENEZ
TERZO
TIRAZ
TIZZY
TOPAZ
TOZEE
TOZER
TOZIE
TROOZ
TZUTE
ULZIE
UNZEN
UYEZD
VIZIR
VIZOR
VIZZY
VORAZ
WALTZ
WANZE
WAZIR
WEEZE
WEIZE
WHIZZ
WINZE
WIZEN
WOOTZ
WOOZY
YEZZY
YOUZE
ZABRA
ZABTI
ZAKAH
ZAKAT
ZAMAN
ZAMBO
ZANJA
ZANTE
ZANZE
ZAPAS
ZARAH
ZAYAT
ZAYIN
ZEBEC
ZEBRA
ZEBUB
ZEBUS
ZEINE
ZEISM
ZEIST
ZEMMI
ZEMNI
ZENIK
ZERDA
ZEROS
ZESTY
ZIARA
ZIBEB
ZIEGA
ZIFFS
ZIHAR
ZIMBI
ZIMME
ZIMMI
ZIMMY
ZINCO
ZINCY
ZINEB
ZINKE
ZINKY
ZIPPY
ZIRAI
ZIRAM
ZIZEL
ZLOTY
ZOCCO
ZOEAL
ZOGAN
ZOISM
ZOIST
ZOKOR
ZOMBI
ZONAE
ZONAL
ZONAR
ZONDA
ZONED
ZONIC
ZOOID
ZOONS
ZOPPA
ZOPPO
ZORIL
ZORRA
ZORRO
ZOWIE
ZUCHE
ZUDDA
ZUPAN
ZYGAL
ZYGON
ZYMIC
ZYMIN

POSITIONAL ORDER LIST OF 5-LETTER WORDS

ZABRA
ZABTI
ZAKAH
ZAKAT
ZAMAN
ZAMBO
ZANJA
ZANTE
ZANZE
ZAPAS
ZARAH
ZAYAT
ZAYIN
ZEBEC
ZEBRA
ZEBUB
ZEBUS
ZEINE
ZEISM
ZEIST
ZEMMI
ZEMNI
ZENIK
ZERDA
ZEROS
ZESTY
ZIARA
ZIBEB
ZIEGA
ZIFFS
ZIHAR
ZIMBI
ZIMME
ZIMMI
ZIMMY
ZINCO
ZINCY
ZINEB
ZINKE
ZINKY
ZIPPY
ZIRAI
ZIRAM
ZIZEL
ZLOTY
ZOCCO
ZOEAL
ZOGAN
ZOISM
ZOIST
ZOKOR
ZOMBI
ZONAE
ZONAL
ZONAR
ZONDA
ZONED
ZONIC
ZOOID
ZOONS
ZOPPA
ZOPPO
ZORIL
ZORRA
ZORRO
ZOWIE
ZUCHE
ZUDDA
ZUPAN
ZYGAL
ZYGON
ZYMIC
ZYMIN

AZIDE
AZINE
AZLON
AZOCH
AZOFY
AZOIC
AZOLE
AZOTE
AZOTH
AZOXY
AZURE
AZURY
AZYME
IZARD
IZOTE
IZTLE
IZTLI
IZZAT
OZENA
OZONE
TZUTE

ADZER
ADZES
AIZLE
ARZUN
BAZAR
BAZOO
BEZEL
BEZIL
BEZZO
BIZLE
BOZAH
BOZAL
BOZZE
BUZZY
BYZEN
COZED
COZEN
COZEY
COZIE
DAZED
DIZEN
DIZZY
DOZED
DOZEN
DOZER
ENZYM
FAZED
FEZZY
FIZZY
FUZEE
FUZIL
FUZZY
GAZED
GAZEL
GAZER
GAZET
GAZI
GAZON
GAZOO
GAZOZ
GIZMO
HAZAN
HAZEL
HAZEN
HAZER
HAZLE
HUZZA
HUZZY
IZZAT
JAZEL
JAZZY
JEZIA
JIZYA
KAZAK
KAZOO
LAZAR
LAZED
LAZZO
LOZEN
MAZAR
MAZED
MAZER
MAZIC
MAZUT
MEZZA
MEZZO
MIZZY
MUZZY
NAZIM
NAZIR
NAZIS
NIZEY
OOZED
OOZEL
OUZEL
OWZEL
PEZZO
PIZZA
QAZAQ
RAZEE
RAZED
RAZON
RAZOO
RAZOR
REZAI
ROZUM
SAZEN
SIZAR
SIZED
SIZER
SIZES
SOZIN
TAZIA
TAZZA
TIZZY
TOZEE
TOZER
TOZIE
ULZIE
UNZEN
VIZIR
VIZOR
VIZZY
WAZIR
WIZEN
YEZZY
ZIZEL
ABAZE
ABUZZ
ADOZE
AGAZE
ALEZE
AMAZE
AMUZE
BAIZA
BAIZE
BEZZO
BLAZE
BLAZY

BLIZZ
BONZA
BONZE
BOZZE
BRAZA
BRAZE
BRIZE
BRIZZ
BRUZZ
BUAZE
BUZZY
BWAZI
CHOZA
CLIZA
COLZA
CRAZE
CRAZY
CROZE
DANZA
DARZI
DIAZO
DIZZY
DOOZY
DROZE
ECIZE
ERIZO
FAIZE
FEAZE
FEEZE
FELZE
FEZZY
FIZZY
FRAZE
FRIZE
FRIZZ
FROZE
FURZE
FURZY
FUZZY
GAIZE
GANZA
GAUZE
GAUZY
GEYZE
GHAZI
GLAZE
GLAZY
GLOZE
GRAZE
GUAZA
HAMZA
HEAZY
HEEZE
HOOZE
HUZZA
HUZZY
JAZZY
KANZU
KNEZI
KONZE
KOUZA
KUDZU
LAZZO
LEAZE
MAIZE
MATZO
METZE
MEZZA
MEZZO
MIMZY
MIRZA
MIZZY
MURZA
MUZZY
NEEZE
PEIZE
PEZZO
PIEZO
PIZZA
PLAZA
POIZE
PRIZE
RITZY
SABZI
SEIZE
SMAZE
SWIZZ
TAZZA
TEAZE
TERZO
TIZZY
UYEZD
VIZZY
WANZE
WEEZE
WEIZE
WHIZZ
WINZE
WOOZY
YEZZY
YOUZE
ZANZE

ABUZZ
ARROZ
BLITZ
BLIZZ
BORTZ
BRIZZ
BRUZZ
CAFIZ
CAHIZ
FRIZZ
GAZOZ
GROSZ
HAFIZ
HERTZ
JEREZ
KAFIZ
KAREZ
KNIAZ
KNYAZ
LANAZ
MAINZ
NAMAZ
SNITZ
SOULZ
SPITZ
SQUIZ
SWIZZ
TENEZ
TIRAZ
TOPAZ
TROOZ
VORAZ
WALTZ
WHIZZ
WOOTZ

SCORING ORDER LIST OF 5-LETTER WORDS

24
AZOXY
JIZYA

23
JAZZY
SQUIZ

22
QAZAQ

21
JAZEL
JEREZ
JEZIA
KAFIZ
KNYAZ
MIMZY
ZAKAH
ZANJA
ZIMMY
ZINKY
ZIPPY
ZYMIC

20
AZOFY
FURZY
HAFIZ
HEAZY
WOOZY
ZIFFS

19
AZOCH
AZYME
BLAZY
BOZAH
BWAZI
BYZEN
CAFIZ
CAHIZ
CHOZA
COZEY
CRAZY
ENZYM
FEZZY
FIZZY
FUZZY
HAMZA
HUZZY
KUDZU
VIZZY
WHIZZ
YEZZY
ZINCY
ZUCHE
ZYMIN

18
BUZZY
DOOZY
FAZED
GAUZY
GEYZE
GHAZI
GLAZY
KANZU
KAREZ
KAZOO
KNEZI
KNIAZ
KONZE
KOUZA
MAZIC
MIZZY
MUZZY
UYEZD
ZAKAT
ZAMBO
ZEBEC
ZEBUB
ZEMMI
ZENIK
ZIBEB
ZIMBI
ZIMME
ZIMMI
ZINKE
ZOCCO
ZOKOR
ZOMBI
ZOPPA
ZOPPO
ZYGAL
ZYGON

17
AZOTH
AZURY
COZED
DIZZY
FAIZE
FEAZE
FEEZE
FELZE
FRAZE
FRIZE
FROZE
FURZE
FUZEE
FUZIL
GIZMO
HAZAN
HAZEL
HAZEN
HAZER
HAZLE
HEEZE
HERTZ
HOOZE
KAZAK
MAZED
NIZEY
OWZEL
RITZY
VIZIR
VIZOR
VORAZ
WALTZ
WANZE
WAZIR
WEEZE
WEIZE
WINZE
WIZEN
WOOTZ
YOUZE
ZARAH
ZAYAT
ZAYIN
ZESTY
ZIHAR
ZLOTY
ZOWIE

16
ABAZE
AMAZE
AMUZE
AZOIC
BAIZA
BAIZE
BAZAR
BAZOO
BEZEL
BEZIL
BIZLE
BLAZE
BLITZ
BONZA
BONZE
BORTZ
BOZAL
BRAZA
BRAZE
BRIZE
BUAZE
CLIZA
COLZA
COZEN
COZIE
CRAZE
CROZE
DAZED
DOZED
ECIZE
FRIZZ
GAZED
HUZZA
MAINZ
MAIZE
MATZO
MAZAR
MAZER
MAZUT
METZE
MIRZA
MURZA
NAMAZ
NAZIM
PEIZE
PIEZO
PLAZA
POIZE
PRIZE
ROZUM
SABZI
SMAZE
SPITZ
SWIZZ
TIZZY
TOPAZ
ZABRA
ZABTI
ZAMAN
ZAPAS
ZEBRA
ZEBUS
ZEISM
ZEMNI
ZINCO
ZINEB
ZIRAM
ZOISM

ZONIC
ZUDDA
ZUPAN

15
ABUZZ
ADOZE
ADZER
ADZES
AGAZE
AZIDE
BEZZO
BLIZZ
BOZZE
BRIZZ
BRUZZ
DANZA
DARZI
DIAZO
DIZEN
DOZEN
DOZER
DROZE
GAIZE
GANZA
GAUZE
GAZEL
GAZER
GAZET
GAZON
GAZOO
GLAZE
GLOZE
GRAZE
GROSZ
GUAZA
IZARD
LAZED
MEZZA
MEZZO
OOZED
PEZZO
PIZZA
RAZED
SIZED
ZERDA
ZIEGA
ZOGAN
ZONDA
ZONED
ZOOID

14
AIZLE
ALEZE
ARROZ
ARZUN
AZINE
AZLON
AZOLE
AZOTE
AZURE
ERIZO
GAZOZ
IZOTE
IZTLE
IZTLI
LANAZ
LAZAR
LEAZE
LOZEN
NAZIR
NAZIS
NEEZE
OOZEL
OUZEL
OZENA
OZONE
RAZEE
RAZON
RAZOO
RAZOR
REZAI
SAZEN
SEIZE
SIZAR
SIZER
SIZES
SNITZ
SOULZ
SOZIN
TAZIA
TEAZE
TENEZ
TERZO
TIRAZ
TOZEE
TOZER
TOZIE
TROOZ
TZUTE
ULZIE
UNZEN
ZANTE
ZEINE
ZEIST
ZEROS
ZIARA
ZIRAI
ZOEAL
ZOIST
ZONAE
ZONAL
ZONAR
ZOONS
ZORIL
ZORRA
ZORRO

13
IZZAT
LAZZO
TAZZA
ZANZE

ALPHABETICAL LIST OF 6-LETTER WORDS

ABLAZE
ABRAZO
ACRAZE
AGAZED
AGNIZE
AJIMEZ
AKAZGA
ALAZOR
ALEZAN
ALTEZA
AMAZED
AMAZON
APOZEM
ASSIZE
ATAZIR
AVELOZ
AZALEA
AZILUT
AZIMIN
AZIOLA
AZONAL
AZONIC
AZOTEA
AZOTED
AZOTIC
AZOTIN
AZTECA
AZURED
AZYGOS
BAIZED
BANZAI
BATZEN
BAZAAR
BEDAZE
BEEZER
BENZAL
BENZIL
BENZIN
BENZOL
BENZYL
BEZANT
BEZOAR
BEZZLE
BLAZED
BLAZER
BLAZES
BLAZON
BLEEZE
BLEEZY
BLINTZ
BLOWZE
BLOWZY
BONNAZ
BONZER
BORIZE
BORZOI
BOZINE
BRAIZE
BRAZED
BRAZEN
BRAZER
BRAZIL
BREEZE
BREEZY
BRONZE
BRONZY
BROUZE
BRYNZA
BUDZAT
BUZANE
BUZZED
BUZZER
BUZZLE
BYZANT
CABEZA
CANZON
CAZIBI
CAZIMI
CENIZO
CEREZA
CHAZAN
CHINTZ
COROZO
CORYZA
COZIER
COZILY
COZING
CRAZED
CROZED
CROZER
CROZLE
CUNZIE
DANZON
DARZEE
DAZING
DAZZLE
DENIZE
DESIZE
DEUZAN
DEZINC
DIAZID
DIAZIN
DIZAIN
DIZDAR
DIZZEN
DONZEL
DOZENS
DOZENT
DOZIER
DOZILY
DOZING
DOZZLE
DRAZEL
DRAZIL
DURZEE
DZEREN
DZERIN
DZERON
ECZEMA
EGOIZE
ENDAZE
ENGAZE
ENTREZ
ENZYME
EOZOON
EPIZOA
ERSATZ
ETHIZE
FAZING
FEAZED
FEZZED
FEZZES
FIZGIG
FIZZED
FIZZER
FIZZLE
FLOOZY
FOOZLE
FRAZER
FRAZIL
FREEZE
FREEZY
FRENZY
FRIEZE
FRIEZY
FRIZEL
FRIZER
FRIZZY
FROUZE
FROUZY
FROWZE
FROWZY
FROZEN
FURZED
FUZZLE
GANZIE
GAZABO
GAZEBO
GAZING
GAZOOK
GEEZER
GHAZAL
GHAZEL
GIZZEN
GLAZED
GLAZEN
GLAZER
GLOZED
GLOZER
GOOZLE
GOZELL
GOZILL
GOZZAN
GRANZA
GRAZED
GROSZY
GROUZE
GROWZE
GROZER
GUZZLE
HALERZ
HALUTZ
HAMETZ
HAMZAH
HAZARD
HAZIER
HAZILY
HAZING
HAZZAN
HELZEL
HIZZIE
HOWITZ
HUZOOR
HUZZAH
IODIZE
IONIZE
IOTIZE
ITZEBU
IZAFAT
IZZARD

JAZZER
JEZAIL
JEZIAH
JIZYAH
JUZAIL
KHAZEN
KIBITZ
KOLKOZ
KORZEC
KRANTZ
KUDIZE
KUVASZ
KVUTZA
LANZON
LAZARY
LAZIER
LAZILY
LAZING
LAZULE
LAZULI
LIZARD
LIZARY
MAHZOR
MAIZER
MAMZER
MANZIL
MARKAZ
MATZOH
MATZOS
MATZOT
MAZAME
MAZARD
MAZIER
MAZILY
MAZING
MAZUCA
MAZUMA
MEZCAL
MEZUZA
MEZZOS
MIZZEN
MIZZLE
MIZZLY
MOUZAH
MOZING
MUZHIK
MUZJIK
MUZZLE
MYZONT
NAZARD
NAZIFY
NOZZLE
NUZZER
NUZZLE
OBRIZE
OKRUZI
OOZIER
OOZILY
OOZING
OOZOID
OUYEZD
OXAZIN
OZAENA
OZOENA
OZONED
OZONER
OZONIC
OZONID
PALETZ
PANZER
PAPIZE
PHIZOG
PIAZIN
PIAZZA
PIZZLE
PRIZED
PRIZER
PRIZES
PUSZTA
PUZZLE
QUARTZ
QUEZAL
QUILEZ
QUINZE
QUIZZY
RAZEED
RAZING
RAZOUR
RAZZIA
RAZZLY
REBOZO
RESIZE
RIZZAR
RIZZER
RIZZLE
RIZZOM
SCAZON
SCHANZ
SCORZA
SCRAZE
SCRUZE
SEIZED
SEIZER
SEIZIN
SEIZOR
SHINZA
SINZER
SIZIER
SIZING
SIZZLE
SLEAZY
SLEEZY
SLEPEZ
SMALTZ
SNAZZY
SNEEZE
SNEEZY
SNOOZE
SNOOZY
SOZZLE
SOZZLY
SPELTZ
SPRITZ
STANZA
STANZE
STANZO
SUIVEZ
SYZYGY
TAFWIZ
TARZAN
TAZEEA
TEAZEL
TEAZLE
TENZON
TERFEZ
TERZET
TERZIO
TIZEUR
TOLZEY
TOOZLE
TOOZOO
TOPAZY
TOUZLE
TOWZIE
TRIAZO
TWAZZY
TWEEZE
TZETZE
TZIRID
UNMAZE
URAZIN
UZARIN
UZARON
VIZARD
VIZIER
VIZSLA
WEAZEN
WEEZLE
WENZEL
WHEEZE
WHEEZY
WIZARD
WIZZEN
WOOZLE
WUZZER
WUZZLE
YETZER
YIZKOR
YUZLIK
YUZLUK
ZABETA
ZACATE
ZACHUN
ZADDIK
ZAFFAR
ZAFFER
ZAFFIR
ZAFFRE
ZAGGED
ZAGUAN
ZAMANG
ZANANA
ZANDER
ZANIES
ZANJON
ZAPOTE
ZAPUPE
ZAREBA
ZARNEC
ZEALED
ZEALOT
ZEBECK
ZEBRAS
ZECHIN
ZEEKOE
ZEHNER
ZELANT
ZENANA
ZENDIK
ZENICK
ZENITH
ZENZIC
ZEPHYR
ZEQUIN
ZEREBA
ZEROES
ZESTED
ZEUGMA
ZIAMET
ZIARAT
ZIBETH
ZIEGER
ZIGGER
ZIGZAG
ZILLAH
ZIMMIS
ZINCED
ZINCIC
ZINCID
ZINCKE
ZINCKY
ZINCUM
ZINDIQ
ZINGEL
ZINNIA
ZIPPER
ZIRCON
ZITHER
ZIZANY
ZIZITH
ZIZZLE
ZLOTYS
ZOACUM
ZOARIA
ZOCALO
ZODIAC
ZOETIC
ZOILUS
ZOMBIE
ZOMBIS
ZONARY
ZONATE
ZONING
ZONITE
ZONNAR
ZONOID
ZONULA
ZONULE
ZONURE
ZOONAL
ZOONIC
ZOOSIS
ZOOTIC
ZOOZOO
ZOSTER
ZOUNDS
ZOYSIA
ZUFOLO
ZUISIN
ZYGION
ZYGITE
ZYGOMA
ZYGOSE
ZYGOTE
ZYGOUS
ZYMASE
ZYMITE
ZYMOID
ZYMOME
ZYTHUM

POSITIONAL ORDER LIST OF 6-LETTER WORDS

ZABETA
ZACATE
ZACHUN
ZADDIK
ZAFFAR
ZAFFER
ZAFFIR
ZAFFRE
ZAGGED
ZAGUAN
ZAMANG
ZANANA
ZANDER
ZANIES
ZANJON
ZAPOTE
ZAPUPE
ZAREBA
ZARNEC
ZEALED
ZEALOT
ZEBECK
ZEBRAS
ZECHIN
ZEEKOE
ZEHNER
ZELANT
ZENANA
ZENDIK
ZENICK
ZENITH
ZENZIC
ZEPHYR
ZEQUIN
ZEREBA
ZEROES
ZESTED
ZEUGMA
ZIAMET
ZIARAT
ZIBETH
ZIEGER
ZIGGER
ZIGZAG
ZILLAH
ZIMMIS
ZINCED
ZINCIC
ZINCID
ZINCKE
ZINCKY
ZINCUM
ZINDIQ
ZINGEL
ZINNIA
ZIPPER
ZIRCON
ZITHER
ZIZANY
ZIZITH
ZIZZLE
ZLOTYS
ZOACUM
ZOARIA
ZOCALO
ZODIAC
ZOETIC
ZOILUS
ZOMBIE
ZOMBIS
ZONARY
ZONATE
ZONING
ZONITE
ZONNAR
ZONOID
ZONULA
ZONULE
ZONURE
ZOONAL

ZOONIC
ZOOSIS
ZOOTIC
ZOOZOO
ZOSTER
ZOUNDS
ZOYSIA
ZUFOLO
ZUISIN
ZYGION
ZYGITE
ZYGOMA
ZYGOSE
ZYGOTE
ZYGOUS
ZYMASE
ZYMITE
ZYMOID
ZYMOME
ZYTHUM

AZALEA
AZILUT
AZIMIN
AZIOLA
AZONAL
AZONIC
AZOTEA
AZOTED
AZOTIC
AZOTIN
AZTECA
AZURED
AZYGOS
DZEREN
DZERIN
DZERON
IZAFAT
IZZARD
OZAENA
OZOENA
OZONED
OZONER
OZONIC
OZONID
TZETZE
TZIRID
UZARIN
UZARON

BAZAAR
BEZANT
BEZOAR
BEZZLE
BOZINE
BUZANE
BUZZED
BUZZER
BUZZLE
BYZANT
CAZIBI
CAZIMI
COZIER
COZILY
COZING
DAZING
DAZZLE
DEZINC
DIZAIN
DIZDAR
DIZZEN
DOZENS
DOZENT
DOZIER
DOZILY
DOZING
DOZZLE

ECZEMA
ENZYME
EOZOON
FAZING
FEZZED
FEZZES
FIZGIG
FIZZED
FIZZER
FIZZLE
FUZZLE
GAZABO
GAZEBO
GAZING
GAZOOK
GIZZEN
GOZELL
GOZILL
GOZZAN
GUZZLE
HAZARD
HAZIER
HAZILY
HAZING
HAZZAN
HIZZIE
HUZOOR
HUZZAH
ITZEBU
IZZARD
JAZZER
JEZAIL
JEZIAH
JIZYAH
JUZAIL
LAZARY
LAZIER
LAZILY
LAZING
LAZULE
LAZULI
LIZARD
LIZARY
MAZAME
MAZARD
MAZIER
MAZILY
MAZING
MAZUCA
MAZUMA
MEZCAL
MEZUZA
MEZZOS
MIZZEN
MIZZLE
MIZZLY
MOZING
MUZHIK
MUZJIK
MUZZLE
MYZONT
NAZARD
NAZIFY
NOZZLE
NUZZER
NUZZLE
OOZIER
OOZILY
OOZING
OOZOID
PIZZLE
PUZZLE
RAZEED
RAZING
RAZOUR
RAZZIA
RAZZLY

RIZZAR
RIZZER
RIZZLE
RIZZOM
SIZIER
SIZING
SIZZLE
SOZZLE
SOZZLY
SYZYGY
TAZEEA
TIZEUR
VIZARD
VIZIER
VIZSLA
WIZARD
WIZZEN
WUZZER
WUZZLE
YIZKOR
YUZLIK
YUZLUK
ZIZANY
ZIZITH
ZIZZLE

AGAZED
AKAZGA
ALAZOR
ALEZAN
AMAZED
AMAZON
APOZEM
ATAZIR
BAIZED
BANZAI
BATZEN
BEEZER
BENZAL
BENZIL
BENZIN
BENZOL
BENZYL
BEZZLE
BLAZED
BLAZER
BLAZES
BLAZON
BONZER
BORZOI
BRAZED
BRAZEN
BRAZER
BRAZIL
BUDZAT
BUZZED
BUZZER
BUZZLE
CANZON
CHAZAN
CRAZED
CROZED
CROZER
CROZLE
CUNZIE
DANZON
DARZEE
DAZZLE
DEUZAN
DIAZID
DIAZIN
DIZZEN
DONZEL
DOZZLE
DRAZEL
DRAZIL
DURZEE

EPIZOA
FEAZED
FEZZED
FEZZES
FIZZED
FIZZER
FIZZLE
FOOZLE
FRAZER
FRAZIL
FRIZEL
FRIZER
FRIZZY
FROZEN
FURZED
FUZZLE
GANZIE
GEEZER
GHAZAL
GHAZEL
GIZZEN
GLAZED
GLAZEN
GLAZER
GLOZED
GLOZER
GOOZLE
GOZZAN
GRAZED
GROZER
GUZZLE
HAMZAH
HAZZAN
HELZEL
HIZZIE
HUZZAH
JAZZER
KHAZEN
KORZEC
LANZON
MAHZOR
MAIZER
MAMZER
MANZIL
MATZOH
MATZOS
MATZOT
MEZZOS
MIZZEN
MIZZLE
MIZZLY
MOUZAH
MUZZLE
NOZZLE
NUZZER
NUZZLE
OXAZIN
PANZER
PHIZOG
PIAZIN
PIAZZA
PIZZLE
PRIZED
PRIZER
PRIZES
PUSZTA
PUZZLE
QUEZAL
QUIZZY
RAZZIA
RAZZLY
RIZZAR
RIZZER
RIZZLE
RIZZOM
SCAZON
SEIZED

SEIZER
SEIZIN
SEIZOR
SINZER
SIZZLE
SNAZZY
SOZZLE
SOZZLY
TARZAN
TEAZEL
TEAZLE
TENZON
TERZET
TERZIO
TOLZEY
TOOZLE
TOOZOO
TOUZLE
TOWZIE
TWAZZY
URAZIN
WEAZEN
WEEZLE
WENZEL
WIZZEN
WOOZLE
WUZZER
WUZZLE
YETZER
ZENZIC
ZIGZAG
ZIZZLE
ZOOZOO

ABLAZE
ABRAZO
ACRAZE
AGNIZE
ALTEZA
ASSIZE
BEDAZE
BLEEZE
BLEEZY
BLOWZE
BLOWZY
BORIZE
BRAIZE
BREEZE
BREEZY
BRONZE
BRONZY
BROUZE
BRYNZA
CABEZA
CENIZO
CEREZA
COROZO
CORYZA
DENIZE
DESIZE
EGOIZE
ENDAZE
ENGAZE
ETHIZE
FLOOZY
FREEZE
FREEZY
FRENZY
FRIEZE
FRIEZY
FRIZZY
FROUZE
FROUZY
FROWZE
FROWZY
GRANZA
GROSZY

GROUZE
GROWZE
IODIZE
IONIZE
IOTIZE
KUDIZE
KVUTZA
MEZUZA
OBRIZE
OKRUZI
OUYEZD
PAPIZE
PIAZZA
QUINZE

QUIZZY
REBOZO
RESIZE
SCORZA
SCRAZE
SCRUZE
SHINZA
SLEAZY
SLEEZY
SNAZZY
SNEEZE
SNEEZY
SNOOZE
SNOOZY

STANZA
STANZE
STANZO
TOPAZY
TRIAZO
TWAZZY
TWEEZE
TZETZE
UNMAZE
WHEEZE
WHEEZY

AJIMEZ

AVELOZ
BLINTZ
BONNAZ
CHINTZ
ENTREZ
ERSATZ
HALERZ
HALUTZ
HAMETZ
HOWITZ
KIBITZ
KOLKOZ
KRANTZ

KUVASZ
MARKAZ
PALETZ
QUARTZ
QUILEZ
SCHANZ
SLEPEZ
SMALTZ
SPELTZ
SPRITZ
SUIVEZ
TAFWIZ
TERFEZ

SCORING ORDER LIST OF 6-LETTER WORDS

28
JIZYAH
MUZJIK

26
QUIZZY

25
JEZIAH
ZINDIQ

24
AJIMEZ
FROWZY
MUZHIK
QUARTZ
QUEZAL
QUILEZ
QUINZE
WHEEZY
ZEQUIN
ZINCKY

23
BLOWZY
HAMZAH
ZEBECK
ZEPHYR
ZYTHUM

22
JEZAIL
JUZAIL
KHAZEN
KUVASZ
KVUTZA
OXAZIN
YIZKOR
YUZLIK
YUZLUK
ZANJON
ZYMOME

21
FLOOZY
FREEZY
FRENZY
FRIEZY
FROUZY
FROWZE
HAZILY
HOWITZ
JAZZER
KIBITZ
KORZEC
MARKAZ
NAZIFY
PHIZOG
SYZYGY
TAFWIZ
WHEEZE
ZADDIK
ZAFFAR
ZAFFER
ZAFFIR
ZAFFRE
ZENICK
ZINCKE
ZYGOMA
ZYMOID

20
AKAZGA
BENZYL
BLEEZY
BLOWZE
BREEZY
BRONZY
BRYNZA
BYZANT
CHAZAN
CHINTZ
CORYZA
COZILY
ENZYME
FIZGIG
FRIZZY
GAZOOK
HAMETZ
HUZZAH
KUDIZE
MAHZOR
MATZOH
MAZILY
MOUZAH
MYZONT
SCHANZ
TOPAZY
TWAZZY
ZACHUN
ZECHIN
ZENDIK
ZIBETH
ZYMASE
ZYMITE

19
APOZEM
AZYGOS
CABEZA
CAZIBI
CAZIMI
DOZILY
ECZEMA
FAZING
FEAZED
FURZED
GHAZAL
GHAZEL
GROSZY
GROWZE
HAZARD
HAZING
KRANTZ
MAMZER
MAZAME
MAZUCA
MAZUMA
MEZCAL
MIZZLY
OKRUZI
OUYEZD
PAPIZE
VIZARD
WIZARD
ZAPUPE
ZEEKOE
ZIMMIS
ZINCIC
ZINCUM
ZIPPER
ZOACUM
ZOMBIE
ZOMBIS
ZYGION
ZYGITE
ZYGOSE
ZYGOTE
ZYGOUS

18
AMAZED
AVELOZ
BAIZED
BEDAZE
BLAZED
BRAZED
BUDZAT
COZING
CRAZED
CROZED
DEZINC
ETHIZE
FEZZED
FIZZED
FOOZLE
FRAZER
FRAZIL
FREEZE
FRIEZE
FRIZEL
FRIZER
FROZEN
GAZABO
GAZEBO
HALERZ
HALUTZ
HAZIER
HELZEL
HUZOOR
IZAFAT
KOLKOZ
LAZARY
LAZILY
LIZARY
MAZARD
MAZING
MOZING
OOZILY
OOZING
PRIZED
SHINZA
SLEAZY
SLEEZY
SNEEZY
SNOOZY
SUIVEZ
TERFEZ
TOLZEY
TOWZIE
TWEEZE
VIZIER
VIZSLA
WEAZEN
WEEZLE
WENZEL
WOOZLE
YETZER
ZAGGED
ZAMANG
ZEHNER
ZENITH
ZEUGMA
ZILLAH
ZINCED
ZINCID
ZITHER
ZLOTYS
ZODIAC
ZONARY
ZOYSIA
ZUFOLO

17
ABLAZE
ABRAZO
ACRAZE
AGAZED
AMAZON
AZIMIN
AZONIC
AZOTIC
AZTECA
BANZAI
BATZEN
BAZAAR
BEEZER
BENZAL
BENZIL
BENZIN
BENZOL
BEZANT
BEZOAR
BLAZER
BLAZES
BLAZON
BLEEZE
BLINTZ
BONNAZ
BONZER
BORIZE
BORZOI
BOZINE
BRAIZE
BRAZEN
BRAZER
BRAZIL
BREEZE
BRONZE
BROUZE
BUZANE
BUZZED
CANZON
CENIZO
CEREZA
COROZO
COZIER
CROZER
CROZLE
CUNZIE
DAZING
DIAZID
DIZDAR
DOZING
EPIZOA
FEZZES
FIZZER
FIZZLE
FUZZLE
GAZING
GLAZED
GLOZED
GRAZED
HAZZAN
HIZZIE
ITZEBU
MAIZER
MANZIL
MATZOS
MATZOT

MAZIER
OBRIZE
OZONIC
PALETZ
PANZER
PIAZIN
PRIZER
PRIZES
PUSZTA
RAZZLY
REBOZO
SCAZON
SCORZA
SCRAZE
SCRUZE
SLEPEZ
SMALTZ
SNAZZY
SOZZLY
SPELTZ
SPRITZ
UNMAZE
WIZZEN
WUZZER
WUZZLE
ZABETA
ZACATE
ZAPOTE
ZAREBA
ZARNEC
ZEBRAS
ZEREBA
ZIAMET
ZIGGER
ZIRCON
ZIZANY
ZIZITH
ZOCALO
ZOETIC
ZOONIC
ZOOTIC

16
AGNIZE
AZOTED
AZURED
BEZZLE
BUZZER
BUZZLE
DANZON
DARZEE
DENIZE
DESIZE
DEUZAN
DIAZIN
DIZAIN
DONZEL
DOZENS
DOZENT
DOZIER
DRAZEL
DRAZIL
DURZEE
DZEREN
DZERIN
DZERON
EGOIZE
ENDAZE
ENGAZE
GANZIE
GEEZER
GLAZEN
GLAZER
GLOZER
GOOZLE
GOZELL
GOZILL
GRANZA
GROUZE
GROZER
IODIZE
LAZING
LIZARD

MEZUZA
MEZZOS
MIZZEN
MIZZLE
MUZZLE
NAZARD
OOZOID
OZONED
OZONID
PIAZZA
PIZZLE
PUZZLE
RAZEED
RAZING
RIZZOM
SEIZED
SIZING
TZIRID
ZAGUAN
ZANDER
ZEALED
ZENZIC
ZESTED
ZIEGER
ZIGZAG
ZINGEL
ZONING
ZONOID
ZOUNDS

15
ALAZOR
ALEZAN
ALTEZA
ASSIZE
ATAZIR
AZALEA
AZILUT
AZIOLA
AZONAL
AZOTEA
AZOTIN

DAZZLE
DIZZEN
DOZZLE
ENTREZ
EOZOON
ERSATZ
GIZZEN
GOZZAN
GUZZLE
IONIZE
IOTIZE
IZZARD
LANZON
LAZIER
LAZULE
LAZULI
OOZIER
OZAENA
OZOENA
OZONER
RAZOUR
RESIZE
SEIZER
SEIZIN
SEIZOR
SINZER
SIZIER
SNEEZE
SNOOZE
STANZA
STANZE
STANZO
TARZAN
TAZEEA
TEAZEL
TEAZLE
TENZON
TERZET
TERZIO
TIZEUR
TOOZLE
TOOZOO

TOUZLE
TRIAZO
URAZIN
UZARIN
UZARON
ZANANA
ZANIES
ZEALOT
ZELANT
ZENANA
ZEROES
ZIARAT
ZINNIA
ZOARIA
ZOILUS
ZONATE
ZONITE
ZONNAR
ZONULA
ZONULE
ZONURE
ZOONAL
ZOOSIS
ZOSTER
ZUISIN

14
NOZZLE
NUZZER
NUZZLE
RAZZIA
RIZZAR
RIZZER
RIZZLE
SIZZLE
SOZZLE
TZETZE
ZOOZOO

13
ZIZZLE

ALPHABETICAL LIST OF 7-LETTER WORDS

ABBOZZO
ABLEEZE
ACIDIZE
ADAZZLE
ADONIZE
AGATIZE
AGENIZE
AGNIZED
AGONIZE
AKAZGIN
ALCAZAR
ALECIZE
ALFEREZ
ALGAZEL
ALIZARI
ALTEZZA
ALVELOZ
AMAZING
ANALYZE
ANIMIZE
ANODIZE
APOZEMA
APPRIZE

ARIENZO
ARMSIZE
ASSEIZE
ASSIZED
ASSIZER
ASSIZES
ATHEIZE
ATOMIZE
AZAFRAN
AZAFRIN
AZAROLE
AZELAIC
AZELATE
AZIMENE
AZIMINE
AZIMINO
AZIMUTH
AZOFIER
AZONIUM
AZOPHEN
AZORITE
AZOTATE
AZOTINE

AZOTITE
AZOTOUS
AZOXINE
AZUELJO
AZULENE
AZULITE
AZUMBRE
AZUREAN
AZURINE
AZURITE
AZUROUS
AZYGOTE
AZYGOUS
AZYMITE
AZYMOUS
BAIZING
BAPTIZE
BAZOOKA
BAZZITE
BEDIZEN
BEMAZED
BENZEIN
BENZENE

BENZINE
BENZOIC
BENZOIN
BENZOLE
BENZOXY
BENZOYL
BEZANTE
BEZANTY
BEZETTA
BEZETTE
BEZIQUE
BEZZANT
BEZZLED
BIOZONE
BIZARRE
BLAZING
BLINTZE
BLOWZED
BONANZA
BONZERY
BONZIAN
BOOZING
BORAZON

BRAZERA
BRAZIER
BRAZING
BREEZED
BRITZKA
BROMIZE
BRONZED
BRONZEN
BRONZER
BROWZER
BRULZIE
BUDZART
BUMBAZE
BUZZARD
BUZZIER
BUZZIES
BUZZING
BUZZWIG
CABEZON
CACHAZA
CADENZA
CALZADA
CANEZOU

CANZONA
CANZONE
CANZONI
CAPATAZ
CAPSIZE
CARRIZO
CAZIQUE
CHALAZA
CHALAZE
CHAZZAN
CHEMIZO
CHINTZE
CHINTZY
CHIZZEL
CITIZEN
COALIZE
COCUIZA
COGNIZE
COROZOS
COZENER
COZIEST
CRAZIER
CRAZIES
CRAZILY
CRAZING
CRITIZE
CRIZZLE
CRIZZEL
CROZIER
CROZING
CROZZLE
CROZZLY
CRUZADO
CYANIZE
CYCLIZE
CZARDOM
CZARINA
CZARISH
CZARISM
CZARIST
CZIGANY
DAMOZEL
DAZEDLY
DAZZLED
DAZZLED
DAZZLER
DEGLAZE
DENIZEN
DIALYZE
DIARIZE
DIAZIDE
DIAZINE
DIAZOIC
DIAZOLE
DIAZOMA
DIZAINE
DIZENED
DIZZARD
DIZZIED
DIZZIER
DIZZILY
DOCKIZE
DOZENED
DOZENER
DOZENTH
DOZIEST
DOZZLED
DRIZZLE
DRIZZLY
DUALIZE
DUREZZA
EBONIZE
ECHOIZE
ECTOZOA
EGOTIZE
ELEGIZE

EMBLAZE
EMERIZE
EMPRIZE
ENOLIZE
ENTOZOA
EPIZOAL
EPIZOAN
EPIZOIC
EPIZOON
FAHLERZ
FANZINE
FAZENDA
FEAZING
FILAZER
FILMIZE
FIZZIER
FIZZING
FIZZLED
FOOZLED
FOOZLER
FRAZZLE
FREEZER
FRIEZED
FRIEZER
FRISZKA
FRIZADO
FRIZZES
FRIZZED
FRIZZEN
FRIZZER
FRIZZLE
FRIZZLY
FURZERY
FUZZIER
FUZZILY
GALLIZE
GARNETZ
GAUZIER
GAUZILY
GAZABOS
GAZEBOS
GAZELLE
GAZETTE
GENIZAH
GEZERAH
GHAWAZI
GHAZIES
GHIZITE
GIZZARD
GIZZERN
GLAIZIE
GLAZIER
GLAZILY
GLAZING
GLOZING
GODDIZE
GONZALO
GOZZARD
GRAZIER
GRAZING
GRIZARD
GRIZZLE
GRIZZLY
GROTZEN
GROZART
GRUNZIE
GUANIZE
GUAZUTI
GUEREZA
GUZERAT
GUZZLED
GUZZLER
HAMOTZI
HAZANUT
HAZELED
HAZELLY

HAZIEST
HOATZIN
HORIZON
HUARIZO
HUMBUZZ
HUTZPAH
HUZZARD
IAMBIZE
IDOLIZE
IMBLAZE
INDAZOL
IODIZED
IODIZER
IONIZER
IOTIZED
IRIDIZE
IRONIZE
ITEMIZE
JAZERAN
JAZZBOW
JAZZIER
JAZZILY
KIBBUTZ
KLEZMER
KOLKHOZ
KREUZER
KUNZITE
KVUTZAH
KWAZOKU
KYANIZE
LAICIZE
LAZARET
LAZARLY
LAZIEST
LAZYBED
LIONIZE
LOZENGE
LOZENGY
MAGHZEN
MAKHZAN
MAKHZEN
MANZANA
MATANZA
MATZOON
MATZOTH
MAZDOOR
MAZEDLY
MAZEFUL
MAZIEST
MAZURKA
MAZZARD
MESTIZA
MESTIZO
METREZA
MEZQUIT
MEZUZAH
MINOIZE
MISMAZE
MITZVAH
MIZMAZE
MIZRACH
MIZZLED
MONOAZO
MOZETTA
MUZOONA
MUZZIER
MUZZLED
MUZZLER
NIZAMAT
NIZAMUT
NOUNIZE
NOZZLER
NUZZLED
OBELIZE
ODORIZE
ODYLIZE

ONYMIZE
OOZIEST
OPALIZE
ORGANZA
OSAZONE
OUTBUZZ
OUTGAZE
OUTJAZZ
OUTRAZE
OUTSIZE
OUTZANY
OVALIZE
OXAZINE
OXAZOLE
OXIDIZE
OXOZONE
OZONATE
OZONIDE
OZONIFY
OZONIZE
OZONOUS
OZOTYPE
PALAZZI
PALAZZO
PAZAREE
PECTIZE
PEPTIZE
PETZITE
POETIZE
PONZITE
PRENZIE
PRETZEL
PREZONE
PRIZERY
PRIZING
PUZZLED
PUZZLER
PYRAZIN
QUARTZY
QUEAZEN
QUETZAL
QUIZZED
QUIZZEE
QUIZZER
RANTIZE
RAZZING
REALIZE
RESEIZE
RESIZED
RESIZER
RETZIAN
RHIZINE
RHIZOID
RHIZOMA
RHIZOME
RHIZOTE
RIBZUBA
RITZIER
ROMANZA
SAZERAC
SCHERZI
SCHERZO
SCHIZZO
SCHMALZ
SCHMELZ
SCHNITZ
SCHWARZ
SEIZING
SEIZURE
SELTZER
SEROZEM
SHEGETZ
SHIZOKU
SIZABLE
SIZABLY
SIZEINE

SIZEMAN
SIZIEST
SIZINGS
SIZZARD
SIZZING
SIZZLED
SIZZLER
SKEEZIX
SNEEZED
SNEEZER
SNOOZED
SNOOZER
SNOOZLE
SNOZZLE
SNUZZLE
SOVENEZ
SOVKHOZ
SOZOLIC
SOZZLED
SPATZLE
SPITZER
SPULZIE
SQUEEZE
SQUEEZY
STANZAS
STATIZE
STYLIZE
SUBZONE
SURSIZE
SWIZZLE
SYZYGAL
SYZYGIA
TAILZEE
TAILZIE
TERZINA
TETRAZO
THEEZAN
THIAZIN
THIAZOL
TIZZIES
TOPAZES
TRAPEZE
TRIAZIN
TRISAZO
TRIZOIC
TUILZIE
TWEEZED
TWEEZER
TWIZZLE
TZARDOM
TZARINA
TZIGANE
TZIMMES
TZOLKIN
TZONTLE
UNGLAZE
UNITIZE
UNSEIZE
UNSIZED
UNZONED
UPERIZE
URAZINE
URAZOLE
UTILIZE
VERZINI
VERZINO
VIZNOMY
VIZORED
VOLTIZE
WALTZED
WALTZER
WEAZENY
WHEEZED
WHEEZER
WHEEZLE
WHIZGIG

WHIZZED
WHIZZER
WHIZZES
WHIZZLE
WIZENED
WOOZIER
WOOZILY
WUZZLED
YAGUAZA
ZABURRO
ZACATON
ZADRUGA
ZAFFREE
ZAGGING
ZAKUSKA
ZAMARRA
ZAMARRO
ZAMORIN
ZAMOUSE
ZANELLA
ZANJERO
ZANJONA
ZANYISH
ZANYISM

ZAPHARA
ZAPTIAH
ZAPTIEH
ZAREEBA
ZARNICH
ZATTARE
ZEALOUS
ZEBRAIC
ZEBRINE
ZEBROID
ZEBRULE
ZEBURRO
ZEDOARY
ZELATOR
ZEMEISM
ZEMIISM
ZEMSTVO
ZENTNER
ZEOLITE
ZEPHYRY
ZEROIZE
ZESTFUL
ZESTING
ZETETIC

ZEUGITE
ZIBETUM
ZIGANKA
ZIKURAT
ZIMARRA
ZIMOCCA
ZINCATE
ZINCIDE
ZINCIFY
ZINCING
ZINCITE
ZINCKED
ZINCOID
ZINCOUS
ZINGANA
ZINGANO
ZINGARA
ZINGARI
ZINGARO
ZINOBER
ZINSANG
ZIPHIAN
ZIPPIER
ZIPPING

ZIRCITE
ZIRKITE
ZITTERN
ZIZZLED
ZOARIAL
ZOARIUM
ZOCCOLO
ZOISITE
ZOISTIC
ZOMBIES
ZONALLY
ZONATED
ZONELET
ZONITID
ZONULAR
ZONULET
ZONURID
ZOOCARP
ZOOCYST
ZOOECIA
ZOOGAMY
ZOOGENE
ZOOGLER
ZOOIDAL

ZOOLITE
ZOOLITH
ZOOLOGY
ZOONIST
ZOONITE
ZOONOMY
ZOONULE
ZOOPERY
ZOOTAXY
ZOOTYPE
ZORGITE
ZORILLA
ZORILLE
ZUFFOLO
ZUMATIC
ZUNYITE
ZWITTER
ZYGENID
ZYGOSIS
ZYMOGEN
ZYMOMIN
ZYMOSIS
ZYMOTIC
ZYMURGY

POSITIONAL ORDER LIST OF 7-LETTER WORDS

ZABURRO
ZACATON
ZADRUGA
ZAFFREE
ZAGGING
ZAKUSKA
ZAMARRA
ZAMARRO
ZAMORIN
ZAMOUSE
ZANELLA
ZANJERO
ZANJONA
ZANYISH
ZANYISM
ZAPHARA
ZAPTIAH
ZAPTIEH
ZAREEBA
ZARNICH
ZATTARE
ZEALOUS
ZEBRAIC
ZEBRINE
ZEBROID
ZEBRULE
ZEBURRO
ZEDOARY
ZELATOR
ZEMEISM
ZEMIISM
ZEMSTVO
ZENTNER
ZEOLITE
ZEPHYRY
ZEROIZE
ZESTFUL
ZESTING
ZETETIC
ZEUGITE
ZIBETUM
ZIGANKA
ZIKURAT
ZIMARRA
ZIMOCCA
ZINCATE

ZINCIDE
ZINCIFY
ZINCING
ZINCITE
ZINCKED
ZINCOID
ZINCOUS
ZINGANA
ZINGANO
ZINGARA
ZINGARI
ZINGARO
ZINOBER
ZINSANG
ZIPHIAN
ZIPPIER
ZIPPING
ZIRCITE
ZIRKITE
ZITTERN
ZIZZLED
ZOARIAL
ZOARIUM
ZOCCOLO
ZOISITE
ZOISTIC
ZOMBIES
ZONALLY
ZONATED
ZONELET
ZONITID
ZONULAR
ZONULET
ZONURID
ZOOCARP
ZOOCYST
ZOOECIA
ZOOGAMY
ZOOGENE
ZOOGLER
ZOOIDAL
ZOOLITE
ZOOLITH
ZOOLOGY
ZOONIST
ZOONITE

ZOONOMY
ZOONULE
ZOOPERY
ZOOTAXY
ZOOTYPE
ZORGITE
ZORILLA
ZORILLE
ZUFFOLO
ZUMATIC
ZUNYITE
ZWITTER
ZYGENID
ZYGOSIS
ZYMOGEN
ZYMOMIN
ZYMOSIS
ZYMOTIC
ZYMURGY

AZAFRAN
AZAFRIN
AZAROLE
AZELAIC
AZELATE
AZIMENE
AZIMINE
AZIMINO
AZIMUTH
AZOFIER
AZONIUM
AZOPHEN
AZORITE
AZOTATE
AZOTINE
AZOTITE
AZOTOUS
AZOXINE
AZUELJO
AZULENE
AZULITE
AZUMBRE
AZUREAN
AZURINE
AZURITE
AZUROUS

AZYGOTE
AZYGOUS
AZYMITE
AZYMOUS
CZARDOM
CZARINA
CZARISH
CZARISM
CZARIST
CZIGANY
OZONATE
OZONIDE
OZONIFY
OZONIZE
OZONOUS
OZOTYPE
TZARDOM
TZARINA
TZIGANE
TZIMMES
TZOLKIN
TZONTLE

BAZOOKA
BAZZITE
BEZANTE
BEZANTY
BEZETTA
BEZETTE
BEZIQUE
BEZZANT
BEZZLED
BIZARRE
BUZZARD
BUZZIER
BUZZIES
BUZZING
BUZZWIG
COZENER
COZIEST
DAZEDLY
DAZZLED
DAZZLER
DIZAINE
DIZENED
DIZZARD

DIZZIED
DIZZIER
DIZZILY
DOZENED
DOZENER
DOZENTH
DOZIEST
DOZZLED
FAZENDA
FIZZIER
FIZZING
FIZZLED
FUZZIER
FUZZILY
GAZABOS
GAZEBOS
GAZELLE
GAZETTE
GEZERAH
GIZZARD
GIZZERN
GOZZARD
GUZERAT
GUZZLED
GUZZLER
HAZANUT
HAZELED
HAZELLY
HAZIEST
HUZZARD
JAZERAN
JAZZBOW
JAZZIER
JAZZILY
LAZARET
LAZARLY
LAZIEST
LAZYBED
LOZENGE
LOZENGY
MAZDOOR
MAZEDLY
MAZEFUL
MAZIEST
MAZURKA
MAZZARD

MEZQUIT
MEZUZAH
MIZMAZE
MIZRACH
MIZZLED
MOZETTA
MUZOONA
MUZZIER
MUZZLED
MUZZLER
NIZAMAT
NIZAMUT
NOZZLER
NUZZLED
OOZIEST
PAZAREE
PUZZLED
PUZZLER
RAZZING
SAZERAC
SIZABLE
SIZABLY
SIZEINE
SIZEMAN
SIZIEST
SIZINGS
SIZZARD
SIZZING
SIZZLED
SIZZLER
SOZOLIC
SOZZLED
SYZYGAL
SYZYGIA
TIZZIES
UNZONED
VIZNOMY
VIZORED
WIZENED
WUZZLED
ZIZZLED

ADAZZLE
AKAZGIN
ALIZARI
AMAZING
APOZEMA
BAIZING
BAZZITE
BENZEIN
BENZENE
BENZINE
BENZOIC
BENZOIN
BENZOLE
BENZOXY
BENZOYL
BEZZANT
BEZZLED
BIOZONE
BLAZING
BONZERY
BONZIAN
BOOZING
BRAZERA
BRAZIER
BRAZING
BUDZART
BUZZARD
BUZZIER
BUZZIES
BUZZING
BUZZWIG
CALZADA
CANZONA
CANZONE
CANZONI

CHAZZAN
CHIZZEL
CRAZIER
CRAZIES
CRAZILY
CRAZING
CRIZZLE
CRIZZEL
CROZIER
CROZING
CROZZLE
CROZZLY
CRUZADO
DAZZLED
DAZZLER
DIAZIDE
DIAZINE
DIAZOIC
DIAZOLE
DIAZOMA
DIZZARD
DIZZIED
DIZZIER
DIZZILY
DOZZLED
DRIZZLE
DRIZZLY
EPIZOAL
EPIZOAN
EPIZOIC
EPIZOON
FANZINE
FEAZING
FIZZIER
FIZZING
FIZZLED
FOOZLED
FOOZLER
FRAZZLE
FRIZADO
FRIZZES
FRIZZED
FRIZZEN
FRIZZER
FRIZZLE
FRIZZLY
FURZERY
FUZZIER
FUZZILY
GAUZIER
GAUZILY
GHAZIES
GHIZITE
GIZZARD
GIZZERN
GLAZIER
GLAZILY
GLAZING
GLOZING
GONZALO
GOZZARD
GRAZIER
GRAZING
GRIZARD
GRIZZLE
GRIZZLY
GROZART
GUAZUTI
GUZZLED
GUZZLER
HUTZPAH
HUZZARD
JAZZBOW
JAZZIER
JAZZILY
KLEZMER
KUNZITE

KWAZOKU
MANZANA
MATZOON
MATZOTH
MAZZARD
MITZVAH
MIZZLED
MUZZIER
MUZZLED
MUZZLER
NOZZLER
NUZZLED
OSAZONE
OUTZANY
OXAZINE
OXAZOLE
OXOZONE
PETZITE
PONZITE
PREZONE
PRIZERY
PRIZING
PUZZLED
PUZZLER
QUIZZED
QUIZZEE
QUIZZER
RAZZING
RETZIAN
RHIZINE
RHIZOID
RHIZOMA
RHIZOME
RHIZOTE
RIBZUBA
RITZIER
SEIZURE
SHIZOKU
SIZZARD
SIZZING
SIZZLED
SIZZLER
SNOZZLE
SNUZZLE
SOZZLED
SUBZONE
SWIZZLE
TERZINA
TIZZIES
TRIZOIC
TWIZZLE
URAZINE
URAZOLE
VERZINI
VERZINO
WEAZENY
WHIZGIG
WHIZZED
WHIZZER
WHIZZES
WHIZZLE
WOOZIER
WOOZILY
WUZZLED
ZIZZLED

ABBOZZO
ADAZZLE
AGNIZED
ALCAZAR
ALGAZEL
ALTEZZA
ASSIZED
ASSIZER
ASSIZES
BEDIZEN
BEMAZED

BLOWZED
BORAZON
BREEZED
BRITZKA
BRONZED
BRONZEN
BRONZER
BROWZER
BRULZIE
CABEZON
CANEZOU
CHAZZAN
CHIZZEL
CITIZEN
COROZOS
CRIZZLE
CRIZZEL
CROZZLE
CROZZLY
DAMOZEL
DENIZEN
DRIZZLE
DRIZZLY
DUREZZA
ECTOZOA
ENTOZOA
FILAZER
FRAZZLE
FREEZER
FRIEZED
FRIEZER
FRISZKA
FRIZZES
FRIZZED
FRIZZEN
FRIZZER
FRIZZLE
FRIZZLY
GENIZAH
GLAIZIE
GRIZZLE
GRIZZLY
GROTZEN
GRUNZIE
HOATZIN
HORIZON
INDAZOL
IODIZED
IODIZER
IONIZER
IOTIZED
KREUZER
KVUTZAH
MAGHZEN
MAKHZAN
MAKHZEN
MEZUZAH
PALAZZI
PALAZZO
PRENZIE
PRETZEL
PYRAZIN
QUEAZEN
QUETZAL
QUIZZED
QUIZZEE
QUIZZER
RESIZED
RESIZER
SCHIZZO
SELTZER
SEROZEM
SKEEZIX
SNEEZED
SNEEZER
SNOOZED
SNOOZER

SNOOZLE
SNOZZLE
SNUZZLE
SPATZLE
SPITZER
SPULZIE
STANZAS
SWIZZLE
TAILZEE
TAILZIE
THEEZAN
THIAZIN
THIAZOL
TOPAZES
TRIAZIN
TUILZIE
TWEEZED
TWEEZER
TWIZZLE
UNSIZED
WALTZED
WALTZER
WHEEZED
WHEEZER
WHEEZLE
WHIZZED
WHIZZER
WHIZZES
WHIZZLE

ABBOZZO
ABLEEZE
ACIDIZE
ADONIZE
AGATIZE
AGENIZE
AGONIZE
ALECIZE
ALTEZZA
ANALYZE
ANIMIZE
ANODIZE
APPRIZE
ARIENZO
ARMSIZE
ASSEIZE
ATHEIZE
ATOMIZE
BAPTIZE
BLINTZE
BONANZA
BROMIZE
BUMBAZE
CACHAZA
CAPSIZE
CARRIZO
CHALAZA
CHALAZE
CHEMIZO
CHINTZE
CHINTZY
COALIZE
COCUIZA
COGNIZE
CRITIZE
CYANIZE
CYCLIZE
DEGLAZE
DIALYZE
DIARIZE
DOCKIZE
DUALIZE
DUREZZA
EBONIZE
ECHOIZE
EGOTIZE
ELEGIZE

EMBLAZE
EMERIZE
EMPRIZE
ENOLIZE
FILMIZE
GALLIZE
GHAWAZI
GODDIZE
GUANIZE
GUEREZA
HAMOTZI
HUARIZO
HUMBUZZ
IAMBIZE
IDOLIZE
IMBLAZE
IRIDIZE
IRONIZE
ITEMIZE
KYANIZE
LAICIZE
LIONIZE
MATANZA
MESTIZA
MESTIZO
METREZA
MINOIZE
MISMAZE
MIZMAZE
MONOAZO
NOUNIZE
OBELIZE
ODORIZE
ODYLIZE
ONYMIZE
OPALIZE
ORGANZA
OUTBUZZ
OUTGAZE
OUTJAZZ
OUTRAZE
OUTSIZE
OVALIZE
OXIDIZE
OZONIZE
PALAZZI
PALAZZO
PECTIZE
PEPTIZE
POETIZE
QUARTZY
RANTIZE
REALIZE
RESEIZE
ROMANZA
SCHERZI
SCHERZO
SCHIZZO
SQUEEZE
SQUEEZY
STATIZE
STYLIZE
SURSIZE
TETRAZO
TRAPEZE
TRISAZO
UNGLAZE
UNITIZE
UNSEIZE
UPERIZE
UTILIZE
VOLTIZE
YAGUAZA
ZEROIZE
ALFEREZ
ALVELOZ
CAPATAZ
FAHLERZ
GARNETZ
HUMBUZZ
KIBBUTZ
KOLKHOZ
OUTBUZZ
OUTJAZZ
SCHMALZ
SCHMELZ
SCHNITZ
SCHWARZ
SHEGETZ
SOVENEZ
SOVKHOZ

SCORING ORDER LIST OF 7-LETTER WORDS

28
BENZOXY
QUARTZY
SQUEEZY

27
BEZIQUE
JAZZBOW
MEZQUIT
SKEEZIX
ZEPHYRY

26
KVUTZAH
SOVKHOZ
ZOOTAXY

25
JAZZILY
MAKHZAN
MAKHZEN
QUEAZEN
QUETZAL
QUIZZED
SQUEEZE
ZYMURGY

24
CHINTZY
HUTZPAH
KIBBUTZ
MITZVAH
OXIDIZE
QUIZZEE
QUIZZER
SCHWARZ
VIZNOMY
WHIZGIG
ZINCIFY

23
AZOXINE
AZUELJO
CACHAZA
CHEMIZO
CYCLIZE
DOCKIZE
FRISZKA
GHAWAZI
JAZERAN
KYANIZE
MIZRACH
OXAZINE
OXAZOLE
OXOZONE
SCHMALZ
SCHMELZ
SHIZOKU
SYZYGAL
SYZYGIA
WHEEZED
ZANJERO
ZANJONA
ZINCKED
ZYMOMIN
ZYMOTIC

22
BAZOOKA
BLOWZED
BRITZKA
BUMBAZE
CZIGANY
FAHLERZ
FURZERY
HAZELLY
HUMBUZZ
JAZZIER
KLEZMER
KOLKHOZ
KWAZOKU
LAZYBED
MAGHZEN
MAZEDLY
MAZURKA
OUTJAZZ
OZONIFY
WEAZENY
WHEEZER
WHEEZLE
WHIZZED
WOOZILY
ZAFFREE
ZANYISH
ZIMOCCA
ZOOGAMY
ZUFFOLO
ZYMOGEN

21
AKAZGIN
AZIMUTH
AZOPHEN
AZYMITE
AZYMOUS
BEMAZED
BENZOYL
BEZANTY
BONZERY
BROWZER
BUZZWIG
CHALAZA
CHALAZE
CHINTZE
CRAZILY
CYANIZE
CZARDOM
CZARISH
DAZEDLY
ECHOIZE
FILMIZE
FRIZZLY
FUZZILY
HAMOTZI
MATZOTH
MAZEFUL
ONYMIZE
OZOTYPE
PRIZERY
PYRAZIN
RHIZOMA
RHIZOME
SCHERZI
SCHERZO
SCHNITZ
SIZABLY
WHIZZER
WHIZZES
WHIZZLE
ZANYISM
ZAPHARA
ZAPTIAH
ZAPTIEH
ZARNICH
ZEMSTVO
ZIGANKA
ZIPHIAN
ZIPPING
ZOOCYST
ZOONOMY
ZOOPERY
ZOOTYPE
ZYGENID
ZYMOSIS

20
APOZEMA
APPRIZE
AZUMBRE
AZYGOTE
AZYGOUS
BAPTIZE
BENZOIC
BROMIZE
CABEZON
CAPATAZ
CAPSIZE
COCUIZA
COZENAGE
CROZZLY
CZARISM
DIALYZE
DOZENTH
EMBLAZE
EMPRIZE
EPIZOIC
FAZENDA
FEAZING
FOOZLED
FRIEZED
FRIZADO
GAUZILY
GENIZAH
GEZERAH
GHAZIES
GHIZITE
GLAZILY
HAZELED
IAMBIZE
IMBLAZE
KREUZER
KUNZITE
LOZENGY
MEZUZAH
MISMAZE
ODYLIZE
PECTIZE
PEPTIZE
RHIZOID
RIBZUBA
SCHIZZO
SHEGETZ
TWEEZED
TZIMMES
TZOLKIN
VIZORED
WALTZED
WIZENED
YAGUAZA
ZEBRAIC
ZEDOARY
ZEMEISM
ZEMIISM
ZIBETUM
ZIKURAT
ZIPPIER
ZIRKITE
ZOCCOLO
ZOMBIES
ZOOCARP
ZOOLOGY
ZUMATIC
ZYGOSIS

19
ABBOZZO
ACIDIZE
ALFEREZ
ALVELOZ
AMAZING
ANALYZE
ATHEIZE
AZAFRAN
AZAFRIN
AZOFIER
BAIZING
BEDIZEN
BLAZING
BOOZING
BRAZING
BREEZED
BRONZED
BUDZART
CADENZA
CALZADA
COGNIZE
CRAZING
CROZING
CRUZADO
DAMOZEL
DIAZOIC
DIAZOMA
DIZZILY
DRIZZLY
FANZINE
FILAZER
FIZZING
FIZZLED
FOOZLER
FREEZER
FRIEZER
FRIZZED
GAZABOS
GAZEBOS
GODDIZE

GRIZZLY
HAZANUT
HAZIEST
HOATZIN
HORIZON
HUARIZO
HUZZARD
LAZARLY
MAZDOOR
MIZMAZE
OUTZANY
OVALIZE
PRIZING
RHIZINE
RHIZOTE
SOVENEZ
STYLIZE
THEEZAN
THIAZIN
THIAZOL
TWEEZER
TZARDOM
VERZINI
VERZINO
VOLTIZE
WALTZER
WOOZIER
WUZZLED
ZAGGING
ZAKUSKA
ZEBROID
ZESTFUL
ZINCIDE
ZINCING
ZINCOID
ZONALLY
ZOOLITH
ZUNYITE
ZWITTER

18

ABLEEZE
AGNIZED
ALCAZAR
ALECIZE
ANIMIZE
ARMSIZE
ATOMIZE
AZELAIC
AZIMENE
AZIMINE
AZIMINO
AZONIUM
BENZEIN
BENZENE
BENZINE
BENZOIN
BENZOLE
BEZANTE
BEZETTA
BEZETTE
BEZZLED
BIOZONE
BIZARRE
BLINTZE
BONANZA
BONZIAN
BORAZON
BRAZERA
BRAZIER
BRONZEN
BRONZER
BRULZIE
BUZZARD
BUZZING
CANEZOU
CANZONA
CANZONE
CANZONI
CARRIZO
CITIZEN
COALIZE
COROZOS
COZENER
COZIEST
CRAZIER
CRAZIES
CRITIZE
CROZIER
CZARINA
CZARIST
DEGLAZE
DIAZIDE
DIZENED
DOZENED
EBONIZE
ECTOZOA
EMERIZE
EPIZOAL
EPIZOAN
EPIZOON
FIZZIER
FRAZZLE
FRIZZES
FRIZZEN
FRIZZER
FRIZZLE
FUZZIER
GLAZING
GLOZING
GRAZING
GRIZARD
IODIZED
ITEMIZE
LAICIZE
MANZANA
MATANZA
MATZOON
MAZIEST
MAZZARD
MESTIZA
MESTIZO
METREZA
MINOIZE
MIZZLED
MONOAZO
MOZETTA
MUZOONA
MUZZLED
NIZAMAT
NIZAMUT
OBELIZE
OPALIZE
PAZAREE
PETZITE
POETIZE
PONZITE
PRENZIE
PRETZEL
PREZONE
PUZZLED
ROMANZA
SAZERAC
SEROZEM
SIZABLE
SIZEMAN
SOZOLIC
SPATZLE
SPITZER
SPULZIE
SUBZONE
SWIZZLE
TOPAZES
TRAPEZE
TRIZOIC
TWIZZLE
UPERIZE
ZABURRO
ZACATON
ZADRUGA
ZAMARRA
ZAMARRO
ZAMORIN
ZAMOUSE
ZAREEBA
ZEBRINE
ZEBRULE
ZEBURRO
ZETETIC
ZIMARRA
ZINCATE
ZINCITE
ZINCOUS
ZINOBER
ZIRCITE
ZOARIUM
ZOISTIC
ZOOECIA

17

ADONIZE
AGATIZE
AGENIZE
AGONIZE
ALGAZEL
ANODIZE
ASSIZED
BAZZITE
BEZZANT
BUZZIER
BUZZIES
CRIZZLE
CRIZZEL
CROZZLE
DAZZLED
DENIZEN
DIARIZE
DIAZINE
DIAZOLE
DIZAINE
DIZZARD
DIZZIED
DOZENER
DOZIEST
DOZZLED
DUALIZE
EGOTIZE
ELEGIZE
GALLIZE
GARNETZ
GAUZIER
GAZELLE
GAZETTE
GIZZARD
GLAIZIE
GLAZIER
GONZALO
GOZZARD
GRAZIER
GROTZEN
GROZART
GRUNZIE
GUANIZE
GUAZUTI
GUEREZA
GUZERAT
GUZZLED
IDOLIZE
INDAZOL
IODIZER
IOTIZED
IRIDIZE
LOZENGE
MUZZIER
MUZZLER
ODORIZE
ORGANZA
OUTBUZZ
OUTGAZE
OZONIDE
PALAZZI
PALAZZO
PUZZLER
RESIZED
SEIZING
SIZINGS
SNEEZED
SNOOZED
TZIGANE
UNGLAZE
UNSIZED
UNZONED
ZESTING
ZEUGITE
ZINGANA
ZINGANO
ZINGARA
ZINGARI
ZINGARO
ZINSANG
ZONATED
ZONITID
ZONURID
ZOOGENE
ZOOGLER
ZOOIDAL
ZORGITE

16

ADAZZLE
ALIZARI
ARIENZO
ASSEIZE
ASSIZER
ASSIZES
AZAROLE
AZELATE
AZORITE
AZOTATE
AZOTINE
AZOTITE
AZOTOUS
AZULENE
AZULITE
AZUREAN
AZURINE
AZURITE
AZUROUS
DAZZLER
DIZZIER
DRIZZLE
DUREZZA
ENOLIZE
ENTOZOA
GIZZERN
GRIZZLE
GUZZLER
IONIZER
IRONIZE
LAZARET
LAZIEST
LIONIZE
NOUNIZE
NUZZLED
OOZIEST
OSAZONE
OUTRAZE
OUTSIZE
OZONATE
OZONOUS
RANTIZE
RAZZING
REALIZE
RESEIZE
RESIZER
RETZIAN
RITZIER
SEIZURE
SELTZER
SIZEINE
SIZIEST
SIZZARD
SIZZING
SIZZLED
SNEEZER
SNOOZER
SNOOZLE
SOZZLED
STANZAS
STATIZE
SURSIZE
TAILZEE
TAILZIE
TERZINA
TETRAZO
TRIAZIN
TRISAZO
TUILZIE
TZARINA
TZONTLE
UNITIZE
UNSEIZE
URAZINE
URAZOLE
UTILIZE
ZANELLA
ZATTARE
ZEALOUS
ZELATOR
ZENTNER
ZEOLITE
ZITTERN
ZOARIAL
ZOISITE
ZONELET
ZONULAR
ZONULET
ZOOLITE
ZOONIST
ZOONITE
ZOONULE
ZORILLA
ZORILLE

15

ALTEZZA
NOZZLER
OZONIZE
SIZZLER
SNOZZLE
SNUZZLE
TIZZIES
ZEROIZE
ZIZZLED

ALPHABETICAL LIST OF 8-LETTER WORDS

ACTIVIZE
ADONIZED
AGATIZED
AGNIZING
AGONIZED
AGONIZER
AKAZGINE
ALBIZZIA
ALBRONZE
ALCAZABA
ALCAZAVA
ALDOLIZE
ALGUAZIL
ALIZARIN
ALKALIZE
ALKYLIZE
ALMUERZO
AMAZEFUL
AMINOAZO
AMORTIZE
ANALGIZE
ANALYZED
ANALYZER
ANGELIZE
ANNALIZE
ANODIZED
ANTICIZE
ANTIZOEA
APHETIZE
APHORIZE
APPETIZE
APPRIZAL
APPRIZER
APRENDIZ
ARANZADA
ARBORIZE
ARCHAIZE
ARMOZEEN
ARMOZINE
ARRHIZAL
ASSIZING
ASTATIZE
ATHEIZER
ATHETIZE
ATMOLYZE
ATOMIZED
ATOMIZER
ATTICIZE
AUTOLYZE
AVESTRUZ
AVIANIZE
AZOBLACK
AZOGREEN
AZOHUMIC
AZOIMIDE
AZOTEMIA
AZOTIZED
AZOTURIA
BACONIZE
BAETZNER
BAKELIZE
BAPTIZED
BAPTIZEE
BAPTIZER
BAROMETZ
BARTIZAN
BARUKHZY
BEDAZZLE
BENZENYL
BENZIDIN
BENZILIC
BENZOATE
BENZOBIS
BENZYLIC
BEZANTEE
BEZONIAN
BEZZLING
BIBENZYL
BIGAMIZE
BIQUARTZ
BIZZARRO
BLAZONED
BLAZONER
BLAZONRY
BLIZZARD
BLOWZIER
BLOWZING
BOMBAZET
BOTANIZE
BRACOZZO
BRAGOZZO
BOZZETTO
BRAZENED
BRAZENLY
BRAZIERY
BREEZIER
BREEZING
BREEZILY
BRITZSKA
BROMIZER
BRONZIFY
BRONZING
BRONZINE
BRONZITE
BROOZLED
BRUNIZEM
BRYOZOAN
BRYOZOON
BRYOZOUM
BULLDOZE
BUZZIEST
CACOZEAL
CACOZYME
CALABAZA
CALABOZO
CALORIZE
CALZOONS
CANALIZE
CANONIZE
CANZONET
CAPONIZE
CAPSIZAL
CAPSIZED
CARBAZIC
CARBAZIN
CARROZZA
CATALYZE
CATZERIE
CHALAZAE
CHALAZAL
CHALAZAS
CHINTZES
CHUTZPAH
CINEMIZE
CIVILIZE
COALIZED
COENZYME
COGNIZED
COGNIZEE
COGNIZER
COGNIZOR
COLONIZE
COMPRIZE
CORONIZE
COZENAGE
COZENING
COZINESS
CRAZEDLY
CRAZIEST
CRAZYCAT
CREOLIZE
CRUELIZE
CRUZEIRO
CURARIZE
CUTINIZE
CYANIZED
CYTOZOIC
CYTOZOON
CYTOZYME
CZAREVNA
CZARITZA
DANDYIZE
DAZZLING
DECATIZE
DEGLAZED
DEIONIZE
DEMONIZE
DENAZIFY
DENIZATE
DEPUTIZE
DETONIZE
DEVILIZE
DIALYZED
DIALYZER
DIAZOATE
DIAZOTIC
DIBENZYL
DIGITIZE
DISDIAZO
DISPRIZE
DISSEIZE
DIVINIZE
DIZENING
DIZZIEST
DIZZYING
DONZELLA
DOUZAINE
DOUZEPER
DOZINESS
DRIZZLED
DUALIZED
DUELLIZE
DYNAMIZE
EBONIZED
ECHOIZED
ECTOZOAN
ECTOZOIC
EGOTIZED
ELEGIZED
EMBEZZLE
EMBLAZED
EMBLAZER
EMBLAZON
EMBOLIZE
EMBRONZE
ENERGIZE
ENFRENZY
ENTOZOAL
ENTOZOAN
ENTOZOIC
ENTOZOON
ENZOOTIC
EOZOONAL
EPIZOOTY
EQUALIZE
ERGOTIZE
ERZAHLER
ESTERIZE
ETERNIZE
ETHERIZE
ETHICIZE
ETIOLIZE
EULOGIZE
EUPHUIZE
EXORCIZE
EXORDIZE
FABULIZE
FARADIZE
FATALIZE
FEAZINGS
FEMINIZE
FIBERIZE
FIGURIZE
FILMIZED
FINALIZE
FIZZIEST
FIZZLING
FLOOZIES
FLUIDIZE
FOCALIZE
FOOZLING
FORMAZAN
FORMAZYL
FORUMIZE
FOZINESS
FRAZZLED
FREEZING
FRENZIED
FRENZIES
FRENZILY
FRIEZING
FRIZETTE
FRIZZIER
FRIZZILY
FRIZZING
FRIZZLED
FRIZZLER
FROWZIER
FROWZILY
FROWZLED
FROZENLY
FUELIZER
FURZETOP
FUZZBALL
FUZZIEST
FUZZTAIL
GARBANZO
GARVANZO
GAUZIEST
GAZABOES
GAZEBOES
GAZELESS
GAZELLES
GAZEMENT
GAZETTAL
GAZETTED
GAZINGLY
GAZOGENE
GAZPACHO
GAZZETTA
GHAWAZEE
GIANTIZE
GIZZENED
GLAZIERS
GLAZIERY
GLAZIEST
GOYAZITE
GRANDEZA
GRAZIERY
GRAZIOSO
GRIZZLED
GRIZZLER
GUZZLING
GWERZIOU
HALAZONE
HALUTZIM
HAZARDER
HAZARDRY
HAZELNUT
HAZINESS
HAZNADAR
HAZZANUT
HEMOZOON
HEPATIZE
HEREZELD
HERTZIAN
HETERIZE
HOACTZIN
HOLOZOIC
HOMILIZE
HOWITZER
HUMANIZE
HUMORIZE
HYDRAZIN
HYLOZOIC
HYPOZOAN
HYPOZOIC
IDEALIZE
IDIOZOME
IDOLIZED
IDOLIZER
IMIDAZOL
IMMUNIZE
INDAZOLE
INDENIZE
INFAMIZE
INSULIZE
IODIZING
IOTIZING
IRIDIZED
ISOZOOID
ITEMIZED
ITEMIZER
JANIZARY
JAROVIZE
JAZERANT
JAZZIEST
JECORIZE
JEZEKITE
JUBILIZE
JUDAIZER
KAMIKAZE
KATALYZE
KETONIZE
KEVUTZAH
KIBITZER
KREUTZER
LABILIZE
LACONIZE
LAICIZED
LAICIZER
LATINIZE
LAZAROLE
LAZARONE
LAZAROUS
LAZINESS
LAZULITE
LAZURITE
LAZYBACK
LAZYBIRD
LAZYBONE
LAZYLEGS
LEGALIZE
LHERZITE
LINENIZE
LIONIZED
LIONIZER
LOCALIZE
LOGICIZE
LOZENGED

LOZENGER
LUNATIZE
MACARIZE
MAGADIZE
MAGAZINE
MAGAZINY
MAJORIZE
MALGUZAR
MARKAZES
MARZIPAN
MATEZITE
MAXIMIZE
MAZAGRAN
MAZALGIA
MAZARINE
MAZINESS
MAZOPEXY
MAZOURKA
MEDALIZE
MELANIZE
MELODIZE
MEMORIZE
MESOZOAN
MESTIZOS
METALIZE
METAZOAL
METAZOAN
METAZOEA
METAZOIC
METAZOON
METRAZOL
MEZEREON
MEZEREUM
MEZQUITE
MEZUZAHS
MEZUZOTH
MICASIZE
MICROZOA
MINIMIZE
MISPRIZE
MITZVAHS
MITZVOTH
MIZZLING
MOBILIZE
MODALIZE
MODELIZE
MODULIZE
MONAZITE
MONETIZE
MONODIZE
MONOZOAN
MONOZOIC
MORALIZE
MOTORIZE
MOUZOUNA
MOZEMIZE
MUSTAFUZ
MUZZIEST
MUZZLING
NAKEDIZE
NAMAZLIK
NASALIZE
NATURIZE
NAZIFIED
NEBULIZE
NICOTIZE
NIZAMATE
NODULIZE
NOTARIZE
NOVELIZE
NUZZLING
OBELIZED
OOLOGIZE
OOZINESS
OPALIZED
OPSONIZE
OPTIMIZE

ORANGIZE
ORGANIZE
ORMUZINE
ORYZANIN
ORYZENIN
OSMAZOME
OUTBLAZE
OUTSIZED
OVERGAZE
OVERSIZE
OXIDIZED
OXIDIZER
OZARKITE
OZOBROME
OZONIZED
OZONIZER
PAEANIZE
PAGANIZE
PALATIZE
PANZOISM
PANZOOTY
PAPALIZE
PARALYZE
PARTIZAN
PATINIZE
PAVONIZE
PECTIZED
PELORIZE
PENALIZE
PEPTIZED
PEPTIZER
PEREZONE
PETUNTZE
PEZANTIC
PEZIZOID
PHENAZIN
PIAZZAED
PIAZZIAN
PIZZERIA
POETIZED
POETIZER
POLARIZE
POLEMIZE
POLICIZE
POLITIZE
POLYZOAN
POLYZOIC
POLYZOON
PREZONAL
PRIZABLE
PRIZEMAN
PRIZEMEN
PROTOZOA
PTYALIZE
PUPILIZE
PUZZLING
PYRAZINE
PYRAZOLE
PYRITIZE
QUANTIZE
QUARTZIC
QUATORZE
QUEZALES
QUIZZERY
QUIZZIFY
QUIZZING
QUIZZISH
QUIZZISM
QUIZZITY
RAADZAAL
RACEMIZE
RADZIMIR
RAMBOOZE
RAZBOOCH
RAZEEING
RAZORMAN
REALIZED

REALIZER
REGALIZE
REGULIZE
RENDZINA
RENOVIZE
RESEIZER
RESINIZE
RESIZING
RETINIZE
RHIZOBIA
RHIZOGEN
RHIZOIDAL
RHIZOMIC
RHIZOPOD
RHIZOTIC
RIBAZUBA
RITZIEST
RIVALIZE
RIZIFORM
RIZZOMED
ROBOTIZE
ROYALIZE
RUMBOOZE
RURALIZE
SALINIZE
SANITIZE
SARRAZIN
SATANIZE
SATINIZE
SATIRIZE
SAVAGIZE
SCHERZOS
SCHIZOID
SCHIZONT
SCHIZTIC
SCHMALTZ
SCHMALZY
SCHMOOZE
SEIZABLE
SERENIZE
SEVERIZE
SFORZATO
SHAATNEZ
SHAHZADA
SIEROZEM
SILICIZE
SIMILIZE
SIMONIZE
SIMULIZE
SINAPIZE
SIRENIZE
SITZMARK
SIZEABLE
SIZINESS
SIZYGIUM
SIZZLING
SMORZATO
SNEEZING
SNOOZING
SOBERIZE
SOLARIZE
SOLECIZE
SOLONETZ
SONORIZE
SORORIZE
SPITZKOP
SPRITZER
SPUILZIE
SQUEEZED
SQUEEZER
STANITZA
STANZAED
STANZAIC
STARGAZE
STOLZITE
STYLIZED
STYLIZER

SUBERIZE
SUBSIZAR
SUBZONAL
SUZERAIN
SWIZZLER
SYNERIZE
SYZYGIAL
SYZYGIES
SYZYGIUM
SZLACHTA
SZOPELKA
TAILZIED
TEMPLIZE
TERRAZZO
TERZETTO
TETANIZE
TETRAZIN
TEZKIRAH
THEORIZE
THIAZINE
THIAZOLE
THIOZONE
THRONIZE
TIMAZITE
TODDYIZE
TONICIZE
TOPAZINE
TOPAZITE
TOTALIZE
TRAPEZIA
TRIAZANE
TRIAZINE
TRIAZOLE
TRISTEZA
TRIZOMAL
TROTCOZY
TUBERIZE
TUTORIZE
TWEEZERS
TWEEZING
TZEDAKAH
UNBAIZED
UNCRAZED
UNDAZZLE
UNFROZEN
UNGLAZED
UNIONIZE
UNMUZZLE
UNPUZZLE
UNVIZARD
URBANIZE
VALORIZE
VAMMAZSA
VAPORIZE
VELARIZE
VENALIZE
VENOMIZE
VITALIZE
VIZARDED
VIZCACHA
VIZIRATE
VIZIRIAL
VIZORING
VOCALIZE
VOLTZINE
VOLTZITE
VOWELIZE
UTILIZED
UTILIZER
WALTZING
WAZIRATE
WEAZENED
WHEEZIER
WHEEZILY
WHEEZING
WHIZBANG
WHIZZING

WINZEMAN
WINZEMEN
WIZARDLY
WIZARDRY
WOOZIEST
WRIZZLED
WOMANIZE
WURTZITE
WUZZLING
YAHRZEIT
YAROVIZE
YOTACIZE
ZAIBATSU
ZAMBOMBA
ZAMINDAR
ZAMORINE
ZAMPOGNA
ZANDMOLE
ZAPATERO
ZARATITE
ZARZUELA
ZASTRUGA
ZASTRUGI
ZEALOTIC
ZEALOTRY
ZEALOUSY
ZEBRINNY
ZECCHINO
ZELATRIX
ZEMINDAR
ZEMSTVOS
ZENITHAL
ZEOLITIC
ZEOSCOPE
ZEPHYRUS
ZEPPELIN
ZERUMBET
ZETACISM
ZIBELINE
ZIGGURAT
ZIGZAGGY
ZIMBABWE
ZIMBALON
ZINCKING
ZINCURET
ZIPHIOID
ZIPPIEST
ZIRCONIA
ZIRCONIC
ZIRCONYL
ZIZZLING
ZOANTHID
ZODIACAL
ZOEAFORM
ZOETROPE
ZOIATRIA
ZOLOTNIK
ZOMBIISM
ZONALITY
ZONATION
ZONELESS
ZONUROID
ZOOBLAST
ZOOCHEMY
ZOOCHORE
ZOOECIAL
ZOOECIUM
ZOOGLOEA
ZOOGRAFT
ZOOLATER
ZOOLATRY
ZOOLITIC
ZOOLOGIC
ZOOMANIA
ZOOMETRY
ZOOMIMIC
ZOOMORPH

ZOONITIC
ZOONOSES
ZOONOSIS
ZOONOTIC
ZOOPERAL
ZOOPHILE
ZOOPHILY
ZOOPHORI
ZOOPHYTE
ZOOSCOPY
ZOOSPORE
ZOOTHOME
ZOOTOMIC
ZOOTOXIN
ZOPILOTE
ZORRILLO
ZORTZICO
ZUCCHINI
ZUGZWANG
ZUPANATE
ZWIEBACK
ZYGAENID
ZYGODONT
ZYGOMATA
ZYGOTENE
ZYGOTOID
ZYMOGENE
ZYMOLOGY

POSITIONAL ORDER LIST OF 8-LETTER WORDS

ZAIBATSU
ZAMBOMBA
ZAMINDAR
ZAMORINE
ZAMPOGNA
ZANDMOLE
ZAPATERO
ZARATITE
ZARZUELA
ZASTRUGA
ZASTRUGI
ZEALOTIC
ZEALOTRY
ZEALOUSY
ZEBRINNY
ZECCHINO
ZELATRIX
ZEMINDAR
ZEMSTVOS
ZENITHAL
ZEOLITIC
ZEOSCOPE
ZEPHYRUS
ZEPPELIN
ZERUMBET
ZETACISM
ZIBELINE
ZIGGURAT
ZIGZAGGY
ZIMBABWE
ZIMBALON
ZINCKING
ZINCURET
ZIPHIOID
ZIPPIEST
ZIRCONIA
ZIRCONIC
ZIRCONYL
ZIZZLING
ZOANTHID
ZODIACAL
ZOEAFORM
ZOETROPE
ZOIATRIA
ZOLOTNIK
ZOMBIISM
ZONALITY
ZONATION
ZONELESS
ZONUROID
ZOOBLAST
ZOOCHEMY
ZOOCHORE
ZOOECIAL
ZOOECIUM
ZOOGLOEA
ZOOGRAFT
ZOOLATER
ZOOLATRY
ZOOLITIC
ZOOLOGIC
ZOOMANIA
ZOOMETRY
ZOOMIMIC
ZOOMORPH

ZOONITIC
ZOONOSES
ZOONOSIS
ZOONOTIC
ZOOPERAL
ZOOPHILE
ZOOPHILY
ZOOPHORI
ZOOPHYTE
ZOOSCOPY
ZOOSPERM
ZOOSPORE
ZOOTHOME
ZOOTOMIC
ZOOTOXIN
ZOPILOTE
ZORRILLO
ZORTZICO
ZUCCHINI
ZUGZWANG
ZUPANATE
ZWIEBACK
ZYGAENID
ZYGODONT
ZYGOMATA
ZYGOTENE
ZYGOTOID
ZYMOGENE
ZYMOLOGY

AZOBLACK
AZOGREEN
AZOHUMIC
AZOIMIDE
AZOTEMIA
AZOTIZED
AZOTURIA
CZAREVNA
CZARITZA
OZARKITE
OZOBROME
OZONIZED
OZONIZER
SZLACHTA
SZOPELKA
TZEDAKAH

BEZANTEE
BEZONIAN
BEZZLING
BIZZARRO
BOZZETTO
BUZZIEST
CAZIQUE
COZENAGE
COZENING
COZINESS
DAZZLING
DIZENING
DIZZIEST
DIZZYING
DOZINESS
ENZOOTIC
EOZOONAL
ERZAHLER

FIZZIEST
FIZZLING
FOZINESS
FUZZBALL
FUZZIEST
FUZZTAIL
GAZABOES
GAZEBOES
GAZELESS
GAZELLES
GAZEMENT
GAZETTAL
GAZETTED
GAZINGLY
GAZOGENE
GAZPACHO
GAZZETTA
GIZZENED
GUZZLING
HAZARDER
HAZARDRY
HAZELNUT
HAZINESS
HAZNADAR
HAZZANUT
JAZERANT
JAZZIEST
JEZEKITE
LAZAROLE
LAZARONE
LAZAROUS
LAZINESS
LAZULITE
LAZURITE
LAZYBACK
LAZYBIRD
LAZYBONE
LAZYLEGS
LOZENGED
LOZENGER
MAZAGRAN
MAZALGIA
MAZARINE
MAZINESS
MAZOPEXY
MAZOURKA
MEZEREON
MEZEREUM
MEZQUITE
MEZUZAHS
MEZUZOTH
MIZZLING
MOZEMIZE
MOZEMIZE
MUZZIEST
MUZZLING
NAZIFIED
NIZAMATE
NUZZLING
OOZINESS
PEZANTIC
PEZIZOID
PIZZERIA
PUZZLING
RAZBOOCH

RAZEEING
RAZORMAN
RIZIFORM
RIZZOMED
SIZEABLE
SIZINESS
SIZYGIUM
SIZZLING
SUZERAIN
SYZYGIAL
SYZYGIES
SYZYGIUM
TEZKIRAH
VIZARDED
VIZCACHA
VIZIRATE
VIZIRIAL
VIZORING
WAZIRATE
WIZARDLY
WIZARDRY
WUZZLING
ZIZZLING
ZYZYPHUS

AKAZGINE
ALIZARIN
AMAZEFUL
BENZENYL
BENZIDIN
BENZILIC
BENZOATE
BENZOBIS
BENZYLIC
BEZZLING
BIZZARRO
BLAZONED
BLAZONER
BLAZONRY
BLIZZARD
BOZZETTO
BRAZENED
BRAZENLY
BRAZIERY
BUZZIEST
CALZOONS
CANZONET
CATZERIE
CRAZEDLY
CRAZIEST
CRAZYCAT
CRUZEIRO
DAZZLING
DIAZOATE
DIAZOTIC
DIZZIEST
DIZZYING
DONZELLA
DOUZAINE
DOUZEPER
DRIZZLED
EPIZOOTY
FEAZINGS
FIZZIEST
FIZZLING

FOOZLING
FRAZZLED
FRIZETTE
FRIZZIER
FRIZZILY
FRIZZING
FRIZZLED
FRIZZLER
FROZENLY
FURZETOP
FUZZBALL
FUZZIEST
FUZZTAIL
GAUZIEST
GAZZETTA
GIZZENED
GLAZIERS
GLAZIERY
GLAZIEST
GRAZIERY
GRAZIOSO
GRIZZLED
GRIZZLER
GUZZLING
HAZZANUT
ISOZOOID
JAZZIEST
MARZIPAN
MITZVAHS
MITZVOTH
MIZZLING
MOUZOUNA
MUZZIEST
MUZZLING
NUZZLING
ORYZANIN
ORYZENIN
PANZOISM
PANZOOTY
PIAZZAED
PIAZZIAN
PIZZERIA
PREZONAL
PRIZABLE
PRIZEMAN
PRIZEMEN
PUZZLING
QUEZALES
QUIZZERY
QUIZZIFY
QUIZZING
QUIZZISH
QUIZZISM
QUIZZITY
RADZIMIR
RHIZOBIA
RHIZOGEN
RHIZOIDAL
RHIZOMIC
RHIZOPOD
RHIZOTIC
RITZIEST
RIZZOMED
SEIZABLE
SITZMARK

SIZZLING
SUBZONAL
SWIZZLER
TERZETTO
TRIZOMAL
WEAZENED
WHIZBANG
WHIZZING
WINZEMAN
WINZEMEN
WOOZIEST
WRIZZLED
WUZZLING
ZARZUELA
ZIGZAGGY
ZIZZLING
ZUGZWANG

AGNIZING
ALBIZZIA
ALCAZABA
ALCAZAVA
ANTIZOEA
ARANZADA
ARMOZEEN
ARMOZINE
ASSIZING
BAETZNER
BEDAZZLE
BLIZZARD
BLOWZIER
BLOWZING
BREEZIER
BREEZING
BREEZILY
BRITZSKA
BRONZIFY
BRONZING
BRONZINE
BRONZITE
BROOZLED
BRYOZOAN
BRYOZOON
BRYOZOUM
CACOZEAL
CACOZYME
CHUTZPAH
COENZYME
CYTOZOIC
CYTOZOON
CYTOZYME
DENAZIFY
DENIZATE
DRIZZLED
ECTOZOAN
ECTOZOIC
EMBEZZLE
ENTOZOAL
ENTOZOAN
ENTOZOIC
ENTOZOON
FLOOZIES
FRAZZLED
FREEZING
FRENZIED
FRENZIES
FRENZILY
FRIEZING
FRIZZIER
FRIZZILY
FRIZZING
FRIZZLED
FRIZZLER
FROWZIER
FROWZILY
FROWZLED
GOYAZITE

GRIZZLED
GRIZZLER
GWERZIOU
HALAZONE
HEMOZOON
HEREZELD
HERTZIAN
HOLOZOIC
HYLOZOIC
HYPOZOAN
HYPOZOIC
IDIOZOME
INDAZOLE
IODIZING
IOTIZING
JANIZARY
LHERZITE
MAGAZINE
MAGAZINY
MATEZITE
MESOZOAN
METAZOAL
METAZOAN
METAZOEA
METAZOIC
METAZOON
MEZUZAHS
MEZUZOTH
MONAZITE
MONOZOAN
MONOZOIC
NAMAZLIK
ORMUZINE
OSMAZOME
PEREZONE
PEZIZOID
PIAZZAED
PIAZZIAN
POLYZOAN
POLYZOIC
POLYZOON
PYRAZINE
PYRAZOLE
QUIZZERY
QUIZZIFY
QUIZZING
QUIZZISH
QUIZZISM
QUIZZITY
RAADZAAL
RENDZINA
RESIZING
RIBAZUBA
SCHIZOID
SCHIZONT
SCHIZTIC
SFORZATO
SHAHZADA
SMORZATO
SNEEZING
SNOOZING
SPITZKOP
STANZAED
STANZAIC
STOLZITE
SWIZZLER
TAILZIED
THIAZINE
THIAZOLE
THIOZONE
TIMAZITE
TOPAZINE
TOPAZITE
TRIAZANE
TRIAZINE
TRIAZOLE
TWEEZERS

TWEEZING
UNDAZZLE
UNMUZZLE
UNPUZZLE
UNVIZARD
VOLTZINE
VOLTZITE
WALTZING
WHEEZIER
WHEEZILY
WHEEZING
WHIZZING
WRIZZLED
WURTZITE
YAHRZEIT
ZORTZICO

ADONIZED
AGATIZED
AGONIZED
AGONIZER
ALBIZZIA
ALGUAZIL
ANALYZED
ANALYZER
ANODIZED
APPRIZAL
APPRIZER
ARRHIZAL
ATHEIZER
ATOMIZED
ATOMIZER
AZOTIZED
BAPTIZED
BAPTIZEE
BAPTIZER
BARTIZAN
BEDAZZLE
BIBENZYL
BOMBAZET
BRACOZZO
BRAGOZZO
BROMIZER
BRUNIZEM
CADENZA
CAPSIZAL
CARBAZIC
CARBAZIN
CARROZZA
CHALAZAE
CHALAZAL
CHALAZAS
CHINTZES
COALIZED
COGNIZED
COGNIZEE
COGNIZER
COGNIZOR
CYANIZED
DEGLAZED
DIALYZED
DIALYZER
DIBENZYL
DUALIZED
EBONIZED
ECHOIZED
EGOTIZED
ELEGIZED
EMBEZZLE
EMBLAZED
EMBLAZER
EMBLAZON
FILMIZED
FORMAZAN
FORMAZYL
FUELIZER
GHAWAZEE

HALUTZIM
HOACTZIN
HOWITZER
HYDRAZIN
IDOLIZED
IDOLIZER
IMIDAZOL
IRIDIZED
ITEMIZED
ITEMIZER
JUDAIZER
KEVUTZAH
KIBITZER
KREUTZER
LAICIZED
LAICIZER
LIONIZED
LIONIZER
MALGUZAR
MARKAZES
MESTIZOS
METRAZOL
MICROZOA
OBELIZED
OPALIZED
OUTSIZED
OXIDIZED
OXIDIZER
OZONIZED
OZONIZER
PARTIZAN
PECTIZED
PEPTIZED
PEPTIZER
PHENAZIN
POETIZED
POETIZER
PROTOZOA
QUARTZIC
REALIZED
REALIZER
RESEIZER
SARRAZIN
SCHERZOS
SIEROZEM
SPRITZER
SPUILZIE
SQUEEZED
SQUEEZER
STYLIZED
STYLIZER
SUBSIZAR
TERRAZZO
TETRAZIN
TRAPEZIA
UNBAIZED
UNCRAZED
UNDAZZLE
UNFROZEN
UNGLAZED
UNMUZZLE
UNPUZZLE
UTILIZED
UTILIZER
VAMMAZSA

ACTIVIZE
ALBRONZE
ALDOLIZE
ALKALIZE
ALKYLIZE
ALMUERZO
AMINOAZO
AMORTIZE
ANALGIZE
ANGELIZE
ANNALIZE

ANTICIZE
APHETIZE
APHORIZE
APPETIZE
ARBORIZE
ARCHAIZE
ASTATIZE
ATHETIZE
ATMOLYZE
ATTICIZE
AUTOLYZE
AVIANIZE
BACONIZE
BAKELIZE
BARUKHZY
BIGAMIZE
BOTANIZE
BRACOZZO
BRAGOZZO
BULLDOZE
CALABAZA
CALABOZO
CALORIZE
CANALIZE
CANONIZE
CAPONIZE
CARROZZA
CATALYZE
CINEMIZE
CIVILIZE
COLONIZE
COMPRIZE
CORONIZE
CREOLIZE
CRUELIZE
CURARIZE
CUTINIZE
CZARITZA
DANDYIZE
DECATIZE
DEIONIZE
DEMONIZE
DEPUTIZE
DETONIZE
DEVILIZE
DIGITIZE
DISDIAZO
DISPRIZE
DISSEIZE
DIVINIZE
DUELLIZE
DYNAMIZE
EMBOLIZE
EMBRONZE
ENERGIZE
ENFRENZY
EQUALIZE
ERGOTIZE
ESTERIZE
ETERNIZE
ETHERIZE
ETHICIZE
ETIOLIZE
EULOGIZE
EUPHUIZE
EXORCIZE
EXORDIZE
FABULIZE
FARADIZE
FATALIZE
FEMINIZE
FIBERIZE
FIGURIZE
FINALIZE
FLUIDIZE
FOCALIZE
FORUMIZE

GARBANZO
GARVANZO
GIANTIZE
GRANDEZA
HEPATIZE
HETERIZE
HOMILIZE
HUMANIZE
HUMORIZE
IDEALIZE
IMMUNIZE
INDENIZE
INFAMIZE
INSULIZE
JAROVIZE
JECORIZE
JUBILIZE
KAMIKAZE
KATALYZE
KETONIZE
LABILIZE
LACONIZE
LATINIZE
LEGALIZE
LINENIZE
LOCALIZE
LOGICIZE
LUNATIZE
MACARIZE
MAGADIZE
MAJORIZE

MAXIMIZE
MEDALIZE
MELANIZE
MELODIZE
MEMORIZE
METALIZE
MICASIZE
MINIMIZE
MISPRIZE
MOBILIZE
MODALIZE
MODELIZE
MODULIZE
MONETIZE
MONODIZE
MORALIZE
MOTORIZE
NAKEDIZE
NASALIZE
NATURIZE
NEBULIZE
NICOTIZE
NODULIZE
NOTARIZE
NOVELIZE
OOLOGIZE
OPSONIZE
OPTIMIZE
ORANGIZE
ORGANIZE
OUTBLAZE

OVERGAZE
OVERSIZE
PAEANIZE
PAGANIZE
PALATIZE
PAPALIZE
PARALYZE
PATINIZE
PAVONIZE
PELORIZE
PENALIZE
PETUNTZE
POLARIZE
POLEMIZE
POLICIZE
POLITIZE
PTYALIZE
PUPILIZE
PYRITIZE
QUANTIZE
QUATORZE
RACEMIZE
RAMBOOZE
REGALIZE
REGULIZE
RENOVIZE
RESINIZE
RETINIZE
RIVALIZE
ROBOTIZE
ROYALIZE

RUMBOOZE
RURALIZE
SALINIZE
SANITIZE
SATANIZE
SATINIZE
SATIRIZE
SAVAGIZE
SCHMALZY
SCHMOOZE
SERENIZE
SEVERIZE
SILICIZE
SIMILIZE
SIMONIZE
SIMULIZE
SINAPIZE
SIRENIZE
SOBERIZE
SOLARIZE
SOLECIZE
SONORIZE
SORORIZE
STANITZA
STARGAZE
SUBERIZE
SYNERIZE
TEMPLIZE
TERRAZZO
TETANIZE
THEORIZE

THRONIZE
TODDYIZE
TONICIZE
TOTALIZE
TRISTEZA
TROTCOZY
TUBERIZE
TUTORIZE
UNIONIZE
URBANIZE
VALORIZE
VAPORIZE
VELARIZE
VENALIZE
VENOMIZE
VITALIZE
VOCALIZE
VOWELIZE
WOMANIZE
YAROVIZE
YOTACIZE

APRENDIZ
AVESTRUZ
BAROMETZ
BIQUARTZ
MUSTAFUZ
SCHMALTZ
SHAATNEZ
SOLONETZ

SCORING ORDER LIST OF 8-LETTER WORDS

31
MAZOPEXY
QUIZZIFY

29
BARUKHZY

28
BIQUARTZ
JEZEKITE
LAZYBACK
MAXIMIZE
MEZQUITE
QUARTZIC
QUIZZERY
QUIZZISH
QUIZZITY
ZWIEBACK

27
CHUTZPAH
CYTOZYME
HYPOZOIC
JANIZARY
JAROVIZE
KEVUTZAH
QUIZZISM
SCHMALZY
SQUEEZED
VIZCACHA
ZOOCHEMY

26
CACOZYME
EQUALIZE
EXORCIZE
FROWZILY
JECORIZE
JUBILIZE
MAJORIZE
OXIDIZED
QUANTIZE
QUATORZE
QUEZALES
QUIZZING
SQUEEZER
SYZYGIUM
WHEEZILY
WHIZBANG
ZIMBABWE
ZYMOLOGY

25
AZOBLACK
BRONZIFY
EXORDIZE
FORMAZYL
GAZPACHO
HYLOZOIC
HYPOZOAN
JUDAIZER
MITZVAHS
MITZVOTH
OXIDIZER
SPITZKOP
TZEDAKAH
ZAMBOMBA
ZEPHYRUS
ZOOPHILY
ZOOPHYTE

24
ALKYLIZE
AZOHUMIC
BENZYLIC
BIBENZYL
BRYOZOUM
COENZYME
CRAZYCAT
CYTOZOIC
DENAZIFY
FROWZLED
GHAWAZEE
HAZARDRY
HYDRAZIN
JAZERANT
KATALYZE
POLYZOIC
RAZBOOCH
RHIZOMIC
SCHIZTIC
SCHMALTZ
SCHMOOZE
SHAHZADA
SYZYGIAL
SYZYGIES
TEZKIRAH
VAMMAZSA
WHEEZING
WIZARDLY
WIZARDRY
ZECCHINO
ZELATRIX
ZINCKING
ZOOMORPH
ZOOSCOPY
ZOOTOXIN
ZUCCHINI

23
BAKELIZE
BLOWZING
BOMBAZET
BRITZSKA
CARBAZIC
CARBAZIDE
COMPRIZE
CRAZEDLY
CYANIZED
DIBENZYL
DYNAMIZE
ECHOIZED
ENFRENZY
FILMIZED
FRENZILY
FROWZIER
FROZENLY
HOWITZER
JAZZIEST
KIBITZER
LAZYBIRD
MAGAZINY
MARKAZES
MAZOURKA
NAMAZLIK
RHIZOPOD
SCHIZOID
SITZMARK
SIZYGIUM
SZOPELKA
VOWELZED
WHEEZIER
WHIZZING
YAHRZEIT
YAROVIZE
ZIPHIOID
ZOMBIISM
ZOOMIMIC
ZYGOMATA
ZYMOGENE

22
ACTIVIZE
AKAZGINE
ALCAZAVA
AMAZEFUL
APHETIZE
APHORIZE
ARCHAIZE
ATMOLYZE
BAPTIZED
BENZENYL
BIGAMIZE
BLAZONRY
BLOWZIER
BRAZENLY
BRAZIERY
BREEZILY
BRYOZOAN
BRYOZOON
CAPSIZED
CATALYZE
CHALAZAE
CHALAZAL
CHALAZAS
CHINTZES
CIVILIZE
CYTOZOON
CZAREVNA
DANDYIZE
DIALYZED
EMBLAZED
EPIZOOTY
ETHICIZE
EUPHUIZE
FABULIZE
FEMINIZE
FIBERIZE
FOCALIZE
FORMAZAN
FORUMIZE
FRIZZILY
FURZETOP
GAZINGLY
HALUTZIM
HEMOZOON
HEPATIZE
HOACTZIN
HOLOZOIC
HOMILIZE

HUMANIZE
HUMORIZE
INFAMIZE
KAMIKAZE
LAZYBONE
MUSTAFUZ
NAKEDIZE
PANZOOTY
PARALYZE
PAVONIZE
PECTIZED
PEPTIZED
PHENAZIN
POLYZOAN
POLYZOON
PTYALIZE
PYRAZINE
PYRAZOLE
PYRITIZE
RHIZOBIA
RHIZOIDAL
RHIZOTIC
RIZIFORM
SCHERZOS
SCHIZONT
SZLACHTA
TODDYIZE
TROTCOZY
VAPORIZE
VENOMIZE
VIZARDED
VOCALIZE
WINZEMAN
WINZEMEN
WOMANIZE
YOTACIZE
ZAMPOGNA
ZEBRINNY
ZEMSTVOS
ZIGZAGGY
ZIRCONYL
ZOEAFORM
ZOOCHORE
ZOOMETRY
ZOOPHILE
ZOOPHORI
ZOOTHOME
ZYGAENID
ZYGODONT
ZYGOTOID

21

ALCAZABA
ALKALIZE
ANALYZED
APPETIZE
APPRIZAL
APPRIZER
BACONIZE
BAPTIZEE
BAPTIZER
BAROMETZ
BENZILIC
BENZOBIS
BROMIZER
BRUNIZEM
CACOZEAL
CALABAZA
CALABOZO
CAPONIZE
CAPSIZAL
CARBAZIN
CINEMIZE
COGNIZED
DEVILIZE
DIALYZER
DIVINIZE
DIZZYING
ECTOZOIC
EMBLAZER
EMBLAZON
EMBOLIZE
EMBRONZE
FARADIZE
FEAZINGS
FIGURIZE
FLUIDIZE
FOOZLING
FREEZING
FRENZIED
FRIEZING
FUZZBALL
GARVANZO
GLAZIERY
GOYAZITE
GRAZIERY
GWERZIOU
HAZARDER
HAZNADAR
HEREZELD
IMMUNIZE
KETONIZE
KREUTZER
LAZYLEGS
MACARIZE
MAGADIZE
MARZIPAN
MEMORIZE
METAZOIC
MEZEREUM
MEZUZAHS
MEZUZOTH
MICASIZE
MICROZOA
MINIMIZE
MISPRIZE
MOBILIZE
MONOZOIC
NAZIFIED
OPTIMIZE
OSMAZOME
OVERGAZE
OZARKITE
OZOBROME
PANZOISM
PAPALIZE
PEPTIZER
PEZANTIC
POLEMIZE
POLICIZE
PRIZABLE
PRIZEMAN
PRIZEMEN
PUPILIZE
RACEMIZE
RAMBOOZE
RHIZOGEN
RIBAZUBA
RUMBOOZE
SAVAGIZE
STYLIZED
TEMPLIZE
TWEEZING
UNVIZARD
VIZORING
WALTZING
WEAZENED
ZEOSCOPE
ZEPPELIN
ZERUMBET
ZETACISM
ZIMBALON
ZIPPIEST
ZIRCONIC
ZOANTHID
ZOLOTNIK
ZOOECIUM
ZOOGRAFT
ZOOTOMIC
ZUGZWANG
ZYGOTENE

20

ANALYZER
APRENDIZ
ARRHIZAL
ATHEIZER
ATHETIZE
ATOMIZED
AUTOLYZE
AVESTRUZ
AVIANIZE
AZOIMIDE
BENZIDIN
BLAZONED
BRACOZZO
BRAZENED
BREEZING
BRONZING
BROOZLED
BULLDOZE
COALIZED
COGNIZEE
COGNIZER
COGNIZOR
COZENING
DECATIZE
DEGLAZED
DEMONIZE
DEPUTIZE
DIAZOTIC
DISPRIZE
DOUZEPER
EBONIZED
EMBEZZLE
ERZAHLER
ETHERIZE
FATALIZE
FINALIZE
FIZZLING
FLOOZIES
FOZINESS
FRAZZLED
FRENZIES
FRIZETTE
FRIZZING
FRIZZLED
FUELIZER
GARBANZO
GAZABOES
GAZEBOES
GAZEMENT
HALAZONE
HAZELNUT
HAZINESS
HERTZIAN
HETERIZE
IDIOZOME
IMIDAZOL
ITEMIZED
LAICIZED
LHERZITE
LOGICIZE
MAGAZINE
MALGUZAR
MAZAGRAN
MAZALGIA
MEDALIZE
MELODIZE
MODALIZE
MODELIZE
MODULIZE
MONODIZE
MOZEMIZE
NOVELIZE
OBELIZED
OPALIZED
ORYZANIN
ORYZENIN
OVERSIZE
PAGANIZE
POETIZED
RADZIMIR
RENOVIZE
RIVALIZE
ROYALIZE
SEVERIZE
SFORZATO
SHAATNEZ
STYLIZER
SYNERIZE
THEORIZE
THIAZINE
THIAZOLE
THIOZONE
THRONIZE
TWEEZERS
UNBAIZED
UNCRAZED
UNFROZEN
VALORIZE
VELARIZE
VENALIZE
VITALIZE
VIZIRATE
VIZIRIAL
VOLTZINE
VOLTZITE
WAZIRATE
WOOZIEST
WRIZZLED
WURTZITE
WUZZLING
ZAMINDAR
ZANDMOLE
ZEALOTRY
ZEALOUSY
ZEMINDAR
ZENITHAL
ZODIACAL
ZONALITY
ZOOLATRY
ZOOLOGIC

19

ADONIZED
AGATIZED
AGNIZING
AGONIZED
ALBRONZE
ALMUERZO
AMINOAZO
AMORTIZE
ANODIZED
ANTICIZE
ARBORIZE
ARMOZEEN
ARMOZINE
ATOMIZER
ATTICIZE
AZOTEMIA
BAETZNER
BARTIZAN
BEDAZZLE
BENZOATE
BEZANTEE
BEZONIAN
BEZZLING
BLAZONER
BLIZZARD
BOTANIZE
BRAGOZZO
BREEZIER
BRONZINE
BRONZITE
CALORIZE
CALZOONS
CANALIZE
CANONIZE
CANZONET
CATZERIE
COLONIZE
CORONIZE
COZINESS
CRAZIEST
CREOLIZE
CRUELIZE
CRUZEIRO
CURARIZE
CUTINIZE
DIGITIZE
DISDIAZO
DIZENING
DUALIZED
ECTOZOAN
EGOTIZED
ELEGIZED
ENTOZOIC
ENZOOTIC
FIZZIEST
FRIZZIER
FRIZZLER
FUZZIEST
FUZZTAIL
GAZETTED
GAZOGENE
GRANDEZA
HAZZANUT
IDOLIZED
IODIZING
IRIDIZED
ITEMIZER
LABILIZE
LACONIZE
LAICIZER
LOCALIZE
LOZENGED
MATEZITE
MAZARINE
MAZINESS
MELANIZE
MESOZOAN
MESTIZOS
METALIZE
METAZOAL
METAZOAN
METAZOEA
METAZOON
METRAZOL
MEZEREON
MIZZLING
MONAZITE
MONETIZE
MONOZOAN
MORALIZE
MOTORIZE
MOUZOUNA
MUZZLING
NEBULIZE
NICOTIZE
NIZAMATE
OPSONIZE
ORMUZINE
OUTBLAZE
PAEANIZE

PALATIZE
PARTIZAN
PATINIZE
PELORIZE
PENALIZE
PEREZONE
PETUNTZE
PEZIZOID
PIAZZAED
POETIZER
POLARIZE
POLITIZE
PREZONAL
PROTOZOA
PUZZLING
RAZORMAN
RIZZOMED
ROBOTIZE
SEIZABLE
SIEROZEM
SILICIZE
SIMILIZE
SIMONIZE
SIMULIZE
SINAPIZE
SIZEABLE
SMORZATO
SOBERIZE
SOLECIZE
SPRITZER
SPUILZIE
STANZAIC
SUBERIZE
SUBSIZAR
SUBZONAL
SWIZZLER
TIMAZITE
TONICIZE
TOPAZINE
TOPAZITE
TRAPEZIA
TRIZOMAL
TUBERIZE
UNGLAZED
URBANIZE
ZAIBATSU
ZAMORINE
ZAPATERO
ZEALOTIC
ZEOLITIC
ZIBELINE
ZIGGURAT
ZINCURET
ZIRCONIA
ZOETROPE
ZOOBLAST
ZOOECIAL
ZOOLITIC
ZOOMANIA
ZOONITIC
ZOONOTIC
ZOOPERAL
ZOOSPORE
ZOPILOTE
ZUPANATE

18
AGONIZER
ALBIZZIA
ALDOLIZE
ALGUAZIL
ANALGIZE
ANGELIZE
ARANZADA
ASSIZING
AZOGREEN
BIZZARRO
BUZZIEST
CZARITZA
DAZZLING
DEIONIZE
DENIZATE
DETONIZE
DIAZOATE
DISSEIZE
DONZELLA
DOUZAINE
DOZINESS
DRIZZLED
DUELLIZE
ENERGIZE
ERGOTIZE
EULOGIZE
GAUZIEST
GAZELESS
GAZELLES
GAZETTAL
GIANTIZE
GIZZENED
GLAZIERS
GLAZIEST
GRAZIOSO
GRIZZLED
GUZZLING
IDEALIZE
IDOLIZER
INDAZOLE
INDENIZE
IOTIZING
ISOZOOID
LEGALIZE
LIONIZED
LOZENGER
MUZZIEST
NODULIZE
OOLOGIZE
ORANGIZE
ORGANIZE
OUTSIZED
PIAZZIAN
PIZZERIA
RAADZAAL
RAZEEING
REALIZED
REALIZER
REGALIZE
REGULIZE
RENDZINA
RESIZING
SNEEZING
SNOOZING
STANZAED
STARGAZE
TAILZIED
UNMUZZLE
UNPUZZLE
UTILIZED
ZASTRUGA
ZASTRUGI
ZONUROID
ZOOGLOEA
ZORTZICO

17
ALIZARIN
ANNALIZE
ANTIZOEA
ASTATIZE
AZOTIZED
AZOTURIA
DIZZIEST
ENTOZOAL
ENTOZOAN
ENTOZOON
EOZOONAL
ESTERIZE
ETERNIZE
ETIOLIZE
GAZZETTA
GRIZZLER
INSULIZE
LATINIZE
LAZAROLE
LAZARONE
LAZAROUS
LAZINESS
LAZULITE
LAZURITE
LINENIZE
LIONIZER
LUNATIZE
NASALIZE
NATURIZE
NOTARIZE
NUZZLING
OOZINESS
OZONIZED
RESEIZER
RESINIZE
RETINIZE
RITZIEST
RURALIZE
SALINIZE
SANITIZE
SARRAZIN
SATANIZE
SATINIZE
SATIRIZE
SERENIZE
SIRENIZE
SIZINESS
SIZZLING
SOLARIZE
SOLONETZ
SONORIZE
SORORIZE
STANITZA
STOLZITE
SUZERAIN
TERZETTO
TETANIZE
TETRAZIN
TOTALIZE
TRIAZANE
TRIAZINE
TRIAZOLE
TRISTEZA
TUTORIZE
UNDAZZLE
UNIONIZE
UTILIZER
ZARATITE
ZOIATRIA
ZONATION
ZONELESS
ZOOLATER
ZOONOSES
ZOONOSIS
ZORRILLO

16
OZONIZER
TERRAZZO
ZARZUELA
ZIZZLING

ALPHABETICAL LIST OF 9-LETTER WORDS

ABURABOZU
ACADEMIZE
ACETALIZE
ACETONIZE
ACETYLIZE
ACTIONIZE
ACTUALIZE
ADONIZING
ADVERTIZE
AGATIZING
AGONIZING
AGROMYZID
ALCARRAZA
ALCHEMIZE
ALDOLIZED
ALIZARATE
ALIZARINE
ALKALIZER
ALLOZOOID
ALTERNIZE
ALUMETIZE
ALUMINIZE
AMAZEMENT
AMAZONITE
AMORTIZED
ANABOLIZE
ANALOGIZE
ANALYZING
ANARCHIZE
ANATOMIZE
ANGELIZED
ANGLICIZE
ANHYDRIZE
ANIMALIZE
ANNUALIZE
ANODIZING
ANTHOZOAN
ANTHOZOIC
ANTHOZOON
APHIDOZER
APHORIZED
APHORIZER
APHRIZITE
APOLOGIZE
APPETIZED
APPETIZER
APPRIZING
ARBORIZED
ARCHAIZED
ARCHAIZER
ARCHIZOIC
ARCTICIZE
ARIZONITE
AROMATIZE
ARRHIZOUS
ARZRUNITE
ASSOILZIE
ASTATIZED
ASTATIZER
ATHETIZED
ATMOLYZER
ATOMIZING
ATTICIZED
AUTHORIZE
AUTOZOOID
AVIZANDUM
AZALEAMUM
AZEDARACH
AZEOTROPE
AZEOTROPY
AZIETHANE
AZIMUTHAL
AZLACTONE
AZOBENZIL
AZOBENZOL
AZOCYCLIC
AZOFORMIC
AZOLITMIN
AZOPHENOL
AZOPHENYL
AZOTIZING
AZOXONIUM
BACTERIZE
BALKANIZE
BALSAMIZE
BALZARINE
BAMBOOZLE
BANTAMIZE
BAPTIZING
BARBARIZE
BEAVERIZE
BEDAZZLED
BEDIZENED
BEDLAMIZE
BENZAMIDE
BENZAMIDO
BENZENOID
BENZIDINE
BENZIDINO
BENZOATED
BENZOLATE
BENZOLINE
BENZOLIZE
BERGINIZE
BEZESTEEN

BEZOARDIC
BILHARZIC
BIOLOGIZE
BIZARDITE
BIZARRELY
BLAZONING
BLIZZARDY
BLOWZIEST
BOMBAZINE
BOOZINESS
BOTANIZED
BOTANIZER
BRAZENING
BRAZILEIN
BRAZILITE
BREEZEWAY
BREEZIEST
BRUTALIZE
BULLDOZED
BULLDOZER
BURKUNDAZ
BURTONIZE
BUZZARDLY
BUZZGLOAK
CALORIZER
CANALIZED
CANONIZED
CANONIZER
CAPONIZER
CAPRIZANT
CAPSIZING
CARBAZIDE
CARBAZINE
CARBAZOLE
CARBOLIZE
CARBONIZE
CARBURIZE
CARNALIZE
CARTELIZE
CATALYZED
CATALYZER
CATECHIZE
CATHARIZE
CAUPONIZE
CAUTERIZE
CEREBRIZE
CHABAZITE
CHALAZIAN
CHALAZION
CHALAZIUM
CHEMOLYZE
CHERNOZEM
CHINTZIER
CHORIZONT
CHRYSAZIN
CHRYSAZOL
CICATRIZE
CITIZENLY
CITIZENRY
CITRONIZE
CIVILIZEE
CIVILIZED
CIVILIZER
CLAVELIZE
CLIMATIZE
COALIZING
COCAINIZE
COELOZOIC
COGNIZANT
COGNIZING
COLAZIONE
COLONIZED
COLONIZER
COMMUNIZE
COMPRIZAL
COMPRIZED
COPPERIZE

COPROZOIC
COSMOZOIC
COTTONIZE
COURTEZAN
CRAZINESS
CRAZYWEED
CREOLEIZE
CREOLIZED
CRITICIZE
CURARIZED
CUTINIZED
CYANIZING
CZARINIAN
CZARISTIC
DAZEDNESS
DECADENZA
DECATIZER
DEEPFROZE
DEFERRIZE
DEGLAZING
DEMONIZED
DENITRIZE
DENTALIZE
DEODORIZE
DEOXIDIZE
DEOZONIZE
DEPUTIZED
DESPOTIZE
DEVILIZED
DEZINCIFY
DEZINKIFY
DIABOLIZE
DIALOGIZE
DIALYZATE
DIALYZING
DIAZEUTIC
DIAZEUXIS
DIAZOAMIN
DIAZONIUM
DIAZOTATE
DIAZOTIZE
DIAZOTYPE
DIBENZOYL
DIESELIZE
DIETZEITE
DIGITIZED
DIGITIZER
DISPRIZED
DISSEIZED
DISSEIZEE
DISSEIZOR
DIVINIZED
DIZENMENT
DIZYGOTIC
DIZZARDLY
DIZZINESS
DOCTORIZE
DOGMATIZE
DOUZEPERS
DRAGONIZE
DRAMATIZE
DRIZZLING
DUALIZING
DUCTILIZE
DUNZIEKTE
DZIGGETAI
EBONIZING
ECHOIZING
ECONOMIZE
ECPHORIZE
ECTOENZYM
EGOTIZING
EKPHORIZE
ELECTRIZE
ELEGIZING
ELENCHIZE
EMBEZZLED

EMBEZZLER
EMBLAZING
EMBLEMIZE
EMPHASIZE
ENDENIZEN
ENERGIZED
ENERGIZER
ENZYMATIC
ENZYMOSIS
ENZYMOTIC
EPILOGIZE
EPIPOLIZE
EPITOMIZE
EPIZEUXIS
EPIZOOTIC
EQUALIZED
EQUALIZER
ERGOTIZED
ESOTERIZE
ETERNIZED
ETHERIZED
ETHERIZER
ETHICIZED
EULOGIZED
EULOGIZER
EUPHEMIZE
EUPHONIZE
EUPHUIZED
EVAPORIZE
EXOENZYME
EXORCIZED
EXORCIZER
FACTORIZE
FACULTIZE
FANTASIZE
FARADIZED
FARADIZER
FAUCALIZE
FECUNDIZE
FERTILIZE
FETICHIZE
FEUDALIZE
FIBERIZER
FILMIZING
FINALIZED
FISCALIZE
FISTULIZE
FIZELYITE
FLORIZINE
FLUIDIZED
FOCALIZED
FOREPRIZE
FORMALIZE
FORMULIZE
FORTHGAZE
FOSSILIZE
FRAZZLING
FREEZABLE
FRENZYING
FRIVOLIZE
FRIZZIEST
FRIZZLING
FROWZIEST
FURZECHAT
FUZZINESS
GALLINAZO
GALVANIZE
GARDENIZE
GAUZELIKE
GAUZEWING
GAUZINESS
GAZEHOUND
GAZETTEER
GAZETTING
GENIALIZE
GENTILIZE
GEOLOGIZE

GERMANIZE
GIGANTIZE
GLAMORIZE
GLAZEWORK
GLAZINESS
GLUTINIZE
GLYCERIZE
GONOZOOID
GORGONIZE
GOSPELIZE
GRANITIZE
GRANULIZE
GRAZINGLY
GRIZZLIER
GRIZZLIES
GRIZZLING
GUACONIZE
HAMLETIZE
HAPHAZARD
HARMONIZE
HAZARDOUS
HELIOZOAN
HERALDIZE
HERBALIZE
HERBARIZE
HERBORIZE
HISTORIZE
HUMANIZER
HUMOURIZE
HYALINIZE
HYBRIDIZE
HYDRAZINE
HYDRAZOIC
HYDRAZONE
HYDROLYZE
HYDROZOAL
HYDROZOAN
HYDROZOIC
HYDROZOON
HYGIENIZE
HYLOZOISM
HYLOZOIST
HYPNOTIZE
HYPOCRIZE
IDEALIZED
IDEALIZER
IDOLIZING
IMIDAZOLE
IMMUNIZED
INFAMIZED
INFLUENZA
INOXIDIZE
IONIZABLE
IRIDIZING
ISOMERIZE
ISONIAZID
ISOXAZOLE
ITALICIZE
ITEMIZING
IZVOZCHIK
JARGONIZE
JAROVIZED
JASPERIZE
JAZZINESS
JENNERIZE
JOVIALIZE
KAOLINIZE
KEVAZINGO
KEVUTZOTH
KIBBUTZIM
KRANTZITE
LABIALIZE
LACONIZED
LACONIZER
LACTONIZE
LADRONIZE
LAICIZING

LAMZIEKTE
LAZARETTE
LAZARETTO
LAZULITIC
LAZYBONES
LAZYBOOTS
LAZZARONE
LAZZARONI
LEGALIZED
LICHENIZE
LIGNITIZE
LINEARIZE
LINENIZER
LIONIZING
LIQUIDIZE
LITURGIZE
LOCALIZED
LOCALIZER
MACARIZED
MAGAZINED
MAGAZINER
MAGNETIZE
MAINPRIZE
MAIZEBIRD
MALGUZARI
MAMMONIZE
MANGANIZE
MANGONIZE
MANNERIZE
MANZANITA
MARBELIZE
MARBLEIZE
MARMARIZE
MARRANIZE
MARTYRIZE
MATRONIZE
MAXIMIZED
MAXIMIZER
MAZEDNESS
MAZODYNIA
MAZOLYSIS
MAZOLYTIC
MECHANIZE
MEDIALIZE
MEDIATIZE
MEDIUMIZE
MEGAZOOID
MELODIZED
MELODIZER
MEMORIZED
MEMORIZER
MENDOZITE
MENSALIZE
MERCERIZE
MERCURIZE
MESMERIZE
MESTIZOES
METALIZED
METALLIZE
METEORIZE
METHODIZE
METRICIZE
MEZCALINE
MEZZANINE
MEZZOTINT
MICROZOAL
MICROZOAN
MICROZOIC
MICROZONE
MICROZOON
MICROZYMA
MICROZYME
MINIMIZED
MINIMIZER
MISPRIZED
MISPRIZER
MIZENMAST

MIZZONITE
MNEMONIZE
MOBILIZED
MODERNIZE
MONACHIZE
MONETIZED
MONZONITE
MORALIZED
MORALIZER
MORGANIZE
MORSELIZE
MORTALIZE
MOTORIZED
MULLENIZE
MUTUALIZE
MYCORHIZA
MYSTERIZE
MYTHICIZE
NARCOTIZE
NASALIZED
NAZIFYING
NEBULIZED
NEBULIZER
NECROTIZE
NECTARIZE
NEOLOGIZE
NEOTERIZE
NEUMATIZE
NICKELIZE
NITRIDIZE
NODULIZED
NORMALIZE
NOTARIZED
NOVELIZED
OBELIZING
OBJECTIZE
ONIONIZED
OPALIZING
OPERATIZE
OPTIMIZED
ORATORIZE
ORGANIZED
ORGANIZER
ORGANZINE
ORIENTIZE
ORYZANINE
OSTRACIZE
OUTBRAZEN
OUTDAZZLE
OVERGLAZE
OVERGRAZE
OVERPRIZE
OVERSIZED
OXDIAZOLE
OXIDIZING
OXYBENZYL
OXYGENIZE
OXYTONIZE
OZOCERITE
OZONATION
OZONIZING
OZOSTOMIA
PAEANIZED
PAGANIZED
PAGANIZER
PALLADIZE
PALLETIZE
PAMPERIZE
PANDERIZE
PANZOOTIA
PANZOOTIC
PAPALIZER
PARALYZED
PARALYZER
PASTORIZE
PATRIZATE
PATRONIZE
PAUPERIZE
PAVONAZZO
PECTIZING
PEDANTIZE
PEGMATIZE
PENALIZED
PEOPLEIZE
PEPTIZING
PEPTONIZE
PERHAZARD
PERSONIZE
PESSIMIZE
PETROLIZE
PEZOGRAPH
PHENAZINE
PHENAZONE
PHENOLIZE
PHILOZOIC
PHLORIZIN
PHONETIZE
PHYTOZOAN
PHYTOZOON
PIAZZETTA
PICTURIZE
PILLORIZE
PIZZICATO
PLATINIZE
PLURALIZE
POETICIZE
POETIZING
POLARIZED
POLARIZER
POLICIZER
POLYZOARY
POLYZOISM
POLYZONAL
POLYZOOID
POLZENITE
POSTERIZE
POSTURIZE
POTENTIZE
POWDERIZE
POZZOLANA
PRECONIZE
PREIOTIZE
PRELATIZE
PRELUDIZE
PRESTEZZA
PRIZEABLE
PROFANIZE
PROLOGIZE
PROPOLIZE
PROTOZOAL
PROTOZOAN
PROTOZOEA
PROTOZOIC
PROTOZOON
PROZYMITE
PRYTANIZE
PTYALIZED
PUBLICIZE
PULVERIZE
PUPILLIZE
PUPPETIZE
PURPURIZE
PUZZLEDLY
PUZZLEMAN
PYRAZOLYL
PYTHONIZE
QUANTIZED
QUARTZITE
QUARTZOID
QUARTZOSE
QUARTZOUS
QUININIZE
QUINONIZE
QUINZAINE
QUINZIEME
QUIZZICAL
RABBINIZE
RACEMIZED
RACIALIZE
RADIALIZE
RADIUMIZE
RANDOMIZE
RAPTURIZE
RAZORBACK
RAZORBILL
RAZOREDGE
RAZZBERRY
REALIZING
REBAPTIZE
RECOGNIZE
RESEIZURE
RHETORIZE
RHEUMATIZ
RHIZINOUS
RHIZOBIUM
RHIZOCARP
RHIZOCAUL
RHIZOCORM
RHIZOTAXY
RHIZOTOMI
RHIZOTOMY
RHODIZITE
RHYTHMIZE
ROUTINIZE
RUBBERIZE
RUBRICIZE
RURALIZED
RUSTICIZE
SANITIZED
SAPROZOIC
SATIRIZED
SATIRIZER
SATURNIZE
SCAZONTIC
SCENARIZE
SCHIZAXON
SCHIZOPOD
SCHNAUZER
SCHNITZEL
SCHNOZZLE
SCIENTIZE
SCLERIZED
SENSITIZE
SERIALIZE
SERMONIZE
SEXUALIZE
SFORZANDO
SHAHZADAH
SIGNALIZE
SILVERIZE
SISTERIZE
SIZARSHIP
SLIVOVITZ
SMORZANDO
SOCIALIZE
SOLARIZED
SOLECIZED
SOLECIZER
SOLEMNIZE
SOLMIZATE
SOLVOLYZE
SONNETIZE
SORBITIZE
SOVIETIZE
SPIRALIZE
SPIRITIZE
SPONDAIZE
SPOROZOAL
SPOROZOAN
SPOROZOIC
SPOROZOID
SPOROZOON
SQUEEZING
STABILIZE
STARGAZED
STARGAZER
STERILIZE
STRAMAZON
STYLIZING
SUBERIZED
SUBSIDIZE
SULCALIZE
SULFATIZE
SULFAZIDE
SULFURIZE
SULPHAZID
SULTANIZE
SUMMARIZE
SURGERIZE
SURPRIZAL
SYLLABIZE
SYLLOGIZE
SYMBOLIZE
SYNCOPIZE
SYNERGIZE
SYNEZISIS
SYNIZESIS
SYNOECIZE
SYNOPSIZE
SYNTONIZE
SYPHILIZE
SYSTEMIZE
SYZYGETIC
TANDEMIZE
TANTALIZE
TARIFFIZE
TARTARIZE
TARTRAZIN
TAVERNIZE
TELEOZOIC
TELEOZOON
TELLURIZE
TEMPORIZE
TENDERIZE
TERMINIZE
TERRORIZE
TERZETTOS
TETANIZED
TETRAZANE
TETRAZENE
TETRAZINE
TETRAZOLE
TETRAZONE
THEATRIZE
THEORIZED
THEORIZER
THIOZONID
THYMOLIZE
TINZENITE
TOPAZFELS
TOTALIZED
TOTALIZER
TRAPEZIAL
TRAPEZIAN
TRAPEZING
TRAPEZIST
TRAPEZIUM
TRAPEZIUS
TRAPEZOID
TRINALIZE
TRIOZONID
TUCHUNIZE
TURTLEIZE
TWEEZERED
TYMPANIZE
TYRANNIZE
UGRIANIZE
UNBRUTIZE
UNCIALIZE
UNDERSIZE
UNIONIZED
UNREALIZE
URALITIZE
URBANIZED
UTILIZING
VACUUMIZE
VAMPIRIZE
VANDALIZE
VAPORIZER
VAPOURIZE
VASSALIZE
VERBALIZE
VERNALIZE
VICTIMIZE
VISCIDIZE
VISIONIZE
VISUALIZE
VITALIZED
VITALIZER
VIZARDING
VIZIERATE
VIZIERIAL
VOCALIZED
VOCALIZER
VOLCANIZE
VULCANIZE
VULGARIZE
WANTONIZE
WAYZGOOSE
WAZIRSHIP
WHEEZIEST
WINTERIZE
WITTICIZE
WOMANIZED
WOMANIZER
WOOLENIZE
WOOZINESS
ZAMINDARI
ZAMINDARY
ZAPATEADO
ZEALOTISM
ZEALOTIST
ZEALOUSLY
ZEBRALIKE
ZEBRAWOOD
ZELATRICE
ZELOTYPIA
ZELOTYPIE
ZEMINDARI
ZENDICIAN
ZENDIKITE
ZEOLITIZE
ZEPHYREAN
ZEPHYRIAN
ZEPHYROUS
ZERMAHBUB
ZEROAXIAL
ZEUGMATIC
ZEUNERITE
ZIBELLINE
ZINCALISM
ZINCIFIED
ZINFANDEL
ZINGERONE
ZINKENITE
ZIPPINGLY
ZIRCONATE
ZIRCONIUM
ZIRCONOID
ZIRKELITE
ZITHERIST
ZOANTHOID
ZOBTENITE
ZOEHEMERA
ZOETROPIC

ZOOCYTIAL
ZOOCYTIUM
ZOOFULVIN
ZOOGAMETE
ZOOGAMOUS
ZOOGENOUS
ZOOGLOEAL
ZOOGLOEIC
ZOOGONOUS
ZOOGRAPHY
ZOOLITHIC
ZOOLOGIES
ZOOLOGIST
ZOOLOGIZE
ZOOMETRIC
ZOOMORPHY
ZOOPERIST
ZOOPHAGAN
ZOOPHILIA
ZOOPHILIC
ZOOPHOBIA
ZOOPHORIC
ZOOPHORUS
ZOOPHYTAL
ZOOPHYTIC
ZOOPLASTY
ZOOSCOPIC
ZOOSPHERE
ZOOSPORIC
ZOOTECHNY
ZOOTHECIA
ZOOTHEISM
ZOOTHEIST
ZOOTOMIST
ZOOTROPHY
ZUCCARINO
ZUCCHETTO
ZUMBOORUK
ZUURVELDT
ZWANZIGER
ZYGADENIN
ZYGANTRUM
ZYGOMATIC
ZYGONEURE
ZYGOPHORE
ZYGOPHYTE
ZYGOSPERM
ZYGOSPORE
ZYGOSTYLE
ZYGOTAXIS
ZYMOGENIC
ZYMOLOGIC
ZYMOLYSIS
ZYMOLYTIC
ZYMOMETER
ZYMOPHORE
ZYMOSCOPE

POSITIONAL ORDER LIST OF 9-LETTER WORDS

ZAMINDARI
ZAMINDARY
ZAPATEADO
ZEALOTISM
ZEALOTIST
ZEALOUSLY
ZEBRALIKE
ZEBRAWOOD
ZELATRICE
ZELOTYPIA
ZELOTYPIE
ZEMINDARI
ZENDICIAN
ZENDIKITE
ZEOLITIZE
ZEPHYREAN
ZEPHYRIAN
ZEPHYROUS
ZERMAHBUB
ZEROAXIAL
ZEUGMATIC
ZEUNERITE
ZIBELLINE
ZINCALISM
ZINCIFIED
ZINFANDEL
ZINGERONE
ZINKENITE
ZIPPINGLY
ZIRCONATE
ZIRCONIUM
ZIRCONOID
ZIRKELITE
ZITHERIST
ZOANTHOID
ZOBTENITE
ZOEHEMERA
ZOETROPIC
ZOOCYTIAL
ZOOCYTIUM
ZOOFULVIN
ZOOGAMETE
ZOOGAMOUS
ZOOGENOUS
ZOOGLOEAL
ZOOGLOEIC
ZOOGONOUS
ZOOGRAPHY
ZOOLITHIC
ZOOLOGIES
ZOOLOGIST
ZOOLOGIZE
ZOOMETRIC
ZOOMORPHY
ZOOPERIST
ZOOPHAGAN
ZOOPHILIA
ZOOPHILIC
ZOOPHOBIA
ZOOPHORIC
ZOOPHORUS
ZOOPHYTAL
ZOOPHYTIC
ZOOPLASTY
ZOOSCOPIC
ZOOSPHERE
ZOOSPORIC
ZOOTECHNY
ZOOTHECIA
ZOOTHEISM
ZOOTHEIST
ZOOTOMIST
ZOOTROPHY
ZUCCARINO
ZUCCHETTO
ZUMBOORUK
ZUURVELDT
ZWANZIGER
ZYGADENIN
ZYGANTRUM
ZYGOMATIC
ZYGONEURE
ZYGOPHORE
ZYGOPHYTE
ZYGOSPERM
ZYGOSPORE
ZYGOSTYLE
ZYGOTAXIS
ZYMOGENIC
ZYMOLOGIC
ZYMOLYSIS
ZYMOLYTIC
ZYMOMETER
ZYMOPHORE
ZYMOSCOPE

AZALEAMUM
AZEDARACH
AZEOTROPE
AZEOTROPY
AZIETHANE
AZIMUTHAL
AZLACTONE
AZOBENZIL
AZOBENZOL
AZOCYCLIC
AZOFORMIC
AZOLITMIN
AZOPHENOL
AZOPHENYL
AZOTIZING
AZOXONIUM
CZARINIAN
CZARISTIC
DZIGGETAI
IZVOZCHIK
OZOCERITE
OZONATION
OZONIZING
OZOSTOMIA

ARZRUNITE
BEZESTEEN
BEZOARDIC
BIZARDITE
BIZARRELY
BUZZARDLY
BUZZGLOAK
DAZEDNESS
DEZINCIFY
DEZINKIFY
DIZENMENT
DIZYGOTIC
DIZZARDLY
DIZZINESS
ENZYMATIC
ENZYMOSIS
ENZYMOTIC
FIZELYITE
FUZZINESS
GAZEHOUND
GAZETTEER
GAZETTING
HAZARDOUS
JAZZINESS
LAZARETTE
LAZARETTO
LAZULITIC
LAZYBONES
LAZYBOOTS
LAZZARONE
LAZZARONI
MAZEDNESS
MAZODYNIA
MAZOLYSIS
MAZOLYTIC
MEZCALINE
MEZZANINE
MEZZOTINT
MIZENMAST
MIZZONITE
NAZIFYING
PEZOGRAPH
PIZZICATO
POZZOLANA
PUZZLEDLY
PUZZLEMAN
RAZORBACK
RAZORBILL
RAZOREDGE
RAZZBERRY
SIZARSHIP
SYZYGETIC
VIZARDING
VIZIERATE
VIZIERIAL
WAZIRSHIP

ALIZARATE
ALIZARINE
AMAZEMENT
AMAZONITE
ARIZONITE
AVIZANDUM
BALZARINE
BENZAMIDE
BENZAMIDO
BENZENOID
BENZIDINE
BENZIDINO
BENZOATED
BENZOLATE
BENZOLINE
BENZOLIZE
BLAZONING
BLIZZARDY
BOOZINESS
BRAZENING
BRAZILEIN
BRAZILITE
BUZZARDLY
BUZZGLOAK
CRAZINESS
CRAZYWEED
DIAZEUTIC
DIAZEUXIS
DIAZOAMIN
DIAZONIUM
DIAZOTATE
DIAZOTIZE
DIAZOTYPE
DIZZARDLY
DIZZINESS
DOUZEPERS
DRIZZLING
DUNZIEKTE
EPIZEUXIS
EPIZOOTIC
FRAZZLING
FRIZZIEST
FRIZZLING
FURZECHAT
FUZZINESS
GAUZELIKE
GAUZEWING
GAUZINESS
GLAZEWORK
GLAZINESS
GRAZINGLY
GRIZZLIER
GRIZZLIES
GRIZZLING
JAZZINESS
LAMZIEKTE
LAZZARONE
LAZZARONI
MAIZEBIRD
MANZANITA
MEZZANINE
MEZZOTINT
MIZZONITE
MONZONITE
ORYZANINE
PANZOOTIA
PANZOOTIC
PIAZZETTA
PIZZICATO
POLZENITE
POZZOLANA
PRIZEABLE
PROZYMITE
PUZZLEDLY
PUZZLEMAN
QUIZZICAL
RAZZBERRY
RHIZINOUS
RHIZOBIUM
RHIZOCARP
RHIZOCAUL
RHIZOCORM
RHIZOTAXY
RHIZOTOMI
RHIZOTOMY
SCAZONTIC
TERZETTOS
TINZENITE
WAYZGOOSE
WOOZINESS

ALLOZOOID
AUTOZOOID
BEDAZZLED
BEDIZENED
BLIZZARDY
BLOWZIEST
BREEZEWAY
BREEZIEST
CITIZENLY
CITIZENRY
COLAZIONE
DIETZEITE
DRIZZLING
EMBEZZLED
EMBEZZLER
FRAZZLING
FREEZABLE
FRENZYING
FRIZZIEST
FRIZZLING
FROWZIEST
GONOZOOID
GRIZZLIER
GRIZZLIES
GRIZZLING
HYLOZOISM
HYLOZOIST

IONIZABLE
IZVOZCHIK
KEVAZINGO
MAGAZINED
MAGAZINER
MEGAZOOID
PIAZZETTA
POLYZOARY
POLYZOISM
POLYZONAL
POLYZOOID
PYRAZOLYL
QUINZAINE
QUINZIEME
QUIZZICAL
SCHIZAXON
SCHIZOPOD
SFORZANDO
SHAHZADAH
SMORZANDO
SYNEZISIS
SYNIZESIS
THIOZONID
TOPAZFELS
TRIOZONID
TWEEZERED
WHEEZIEST
ZWANZIGER

ADONIZING
AGATIZING
AGONIZING
ANALYZING
ANODIZING
ANTHOZOAN
ANTHOZOIC
ANTHOZOON
APHRIZITE
APPRIZING
ARCHIZOIC
ARRHIZOUS
ATOMIZING
AZOTIZING
BAPTIZING
BEDAZZLED
BOMBAZINE
CAPRIZANT
CAPSIZED
CAPSIZING
CARBAZIDE
CARBAZINE
CARBAZOLE
CHABAZITE
CHALAZIAN
CHALAZION
CHALAZIUM
CHINTZIER
CHORIZONT
COALIZING
COELOZOIC
COGNIZANT
COGNIZING
COPROZOIC
COSMOZOIC
CYANIZING
DEGLAZING
DIALYZATE
DIALYZING
DIBENZOYL
DUALIZING
EBONIZING
ECHOIZING
EGOTIZING
ELEGIZING
EMBEZZLED
EMBEZZLER
EMBLAZING

EXOENZYME
FILMIZING
FLORIZINE
HAPHAZARD
HELIOZOAN
HYDRAZINE
HYDRAZOIC
HYDRAZONE
HYDROZOAL
HYDROZOAN
HYDROZOIC
HYDROZOON
IDOLIZING
IMIDAZOLE
IRIDIZING
ISOXAZOLE
ITEMIZING
KEVUTZOTH
KRANTZITE
LAICIZING
LIONIZING
MALGUZARI
MENDOZITE
MESTIZOES
MICROZOAL
MICROZOAN
MICROZOIC
MICROZONE
MICROZOON
MICROZYMA
MICROZYME
OBELIZING
OPALIZING
ORGANZINE
OUTDAZZLE
OXDIAZOLE
OXIDIZING
OZONIZING
PATRIZATE
PECTIZING
PEPTIZING
PERHAZARD
PHENAZINE
PHENAZONE
PHILOZOIC
PHYTOZOAN
PHYTOZOON
POETIZING
PROTOZOAL
PROTOZOAN
PROTOZOEA
PROTOZOIC
PROTOZOON
QUARTZITE
QUARTZOID
QUARTZOSE
QUARTZOUS
REALIZING
RESEIZURE
RHODIZITE
SAPROZOIC
SCHNOZZLE
SOLMIZATE
SPOROZOAL
SPOROZOAN
SPOROZOIC
SPOROZOID
SPOROZOON
SQUEEZING
STYLIZING
SULFAZIDE
TELEOZOIC
TELEOZOON
TETRAZANE
TETRAZENE
TETRAZINE
TETRAZOLE

TETRAZONE
TRAPEZIAL
TRAPEZIAN
TRAPEZING
TRAPEZIST
TRAPEZIUM
TRAPEZIUS
TRAPEZOID
UTILIZING

AGROMYZID
ALDOLIZED
ALKALIZER
AMORTIZED
ANGELIZED
APHIDOZER
APHORIZED
APHORIZER
APPETIZED
APPETIZER
ARBORIZED
ARCHAIZED
ARCHAIZER
ASSOILZIE
ASTATIZED
ASTATIZER
ATHETIZED
ATMOLYZER
ATTICIZED
AZOBENZIL
AZOBENZOL
BAMBOOZLE
BILHARZIC
BOTANIZED
BOTANIZER
BULLDOZED
BULLDOZER
CALORIZER
CANALIZED
CANONIZED
CANONIZER
CAPONIZER
CATALYZED
CATALYZER
CHERNOZEM
CHRYSAZIN
CHRYSAZOL
CIVILIZEE
CIVILIZED
CIVILIZER
COLONIZED
COLONIZER
COMPRIZAL
COMPRIZED
COURTEZAN
CREOLIZED
CURARIZED
CUTINIZED
DECATIZER
DEMONIZED
DEPUTIZED
DEVILIZED
DIGITIZED
DIGITIZER
DISPRIZED
DISSEIZED
DISSEIZEE
DISSEIZOR
DIVINIZED
ECTOENZYM
ENDENIZEN
ENERGIZED
ENERGIZER
EQUALIZED
EQUALIZER
ERGOTIZED
ETERNIZED

ETHERIZED
ETHERIZER
ETHICIZED
EULOGIZED
EULOGIZER
EUPHUIZED
EXORCIZED
EXORCIZER
FARADIZED
FARADIZER
FIBERIZER
FINALIZED
FLUIDIZED
FOCALIZED
HUMANIZER
IDEALIZED
IDEALIZER
IMMUNIZED
INFAMIZED
ISONIAZID
JAROVIZED
KIBBUTZIM
LACONIZED
LACONIZER
LEGALIZED
LINENIZER
LOCALIZED
LOCALIZER
MACARIZED
MAXIMIZED
MAXIMIZER
MELODIZED
MELODIZER
MEMORIZER
METALIZED
MINIMIZED
MINIMIZER
MISPRIZED
MISPRIZER
MOBILIZED
MONETIZED
MORALIZED
MORALIZER
MOTORIZED
NASALIZED
NEBULIZED
NEBULIZER
NODULIZED
NOTARIZED
NOVELIZED
ONIONIZED
OPTIMIZED
ORGANIZED
ORGANIZER
OUTBRAZEN
OUTDAZZLE
OVERSIZED
OXYBENZYL
PAEANIZED
PAGANIZED
PAGANIZER
PAPALIZER
PARALYZED
PARALYZER
PAVONAZZO
PENALIZED
PHLORIZIN
POLARIZED
POLARIZER
POLICIZER
PRESTEZZA
PTYALIZED
QUANTIZED
RACEMIZED
RURALIZED
SANITIZED
SATIRIZED

SATIRIZER
SCHNAUZER
SCHNITZEL
SCHNOZZLE
SCLERIZED
SOLARIZED
SOLECIZED
SOLECIZER
STARGAZED
STARGAZER
STRAMAZON
SUBERIZED
SULPHAZID
SURPRIZAL
TARTRAZIN
TETANIZED
THEORIZED
THEORIZER
TOTALIZED
TOTALIZER
UNIONIZED
URBANIZED
VAPORIZER
VITALIZED
VITALIZER
VOCALIZED
VOCALIZER
WOMANIZED
WOMANIZER

ABURABOZU
ACADEMIZE
ACETALIZE
ACETONIZE
ACETYLIZE
ACTIONIZE
ACTUALIZE
ADVERTIZE
ALCARRAZA
ALCHEMIZE
ALTERNIZE
ALUMETIZE
ALUMINIZE
ANABOLIZE
ANALOGIZE
ANARCHIZE
ANATOMIZE
ANGLICIZE
ANHYDRIZE
ANIMALIZE
ANNUALIZE
APOLOGIZE
ARCTICIZE
AROMATIZE
AUTHORIZE
BACTERIZE
BALKANIZE
BALSAMIZE
BANTAMIZE
BARBARIZE
BEAVERIZE
BEDLAMIZE
BERGINIZE
BIOLOGIZE
BRUTALIZE
BURTONIZE
CARBOLIZE
CARBONIZE
CARBURIZE
CARNALIZE
CARTELIZE
CATECHIZE
CATHARIZE
CAUPONIZE
CAUTERIZE
CEREBRIZE
CHEMOLYZE

CICATRIZE
CITRONIZE
CLAVELIZE
CLIMATIZE
COCAINIZE
COMMUNIZE
COPPERIZE
COTTONIZE
CREOLEIZE
CRITICIZE
DECADENZA
DEEPFROZE
DEFERRIZE
DENITRIZE
DENTALIZE
DEODORIZE
DEOXIDIZE
DEOZONIZE
DESPOTIZE
DIABOLIZE
DIALOGIZE
DIAZOTIZE
DIESELIZE
DOCTORIZE
DOGMATIZE
DRAGONIZE
DRAMATIZE
DUCTILIZE
ECONOMIZE
ECPHORIZE
EKPHORIZE
ELECTRIZE
ELENCHIZE
EMBLEMIZE
EMPHASIZE
EPILOGIZE
EPIPOLIZE
EPITOMIZE
ESOTERIZE
EUPHEMIZE
EUPHONIZE
EVAPORIZE
FACTORIZE
FACULTIZE
FANTASIZE
FAUCALIZE
FECUNDIZE
FERTILIZE
FETICHIZE
FEUDALIZE
FISCALIZE
FISTULIZE
FOREPRIZE
FORMALIZE
FORMULIZE
FORTHGAZE
FOSSILIZE
FRIVOLIZE
GALLINAZO
GALVANIZE
GARDENIZE
GENIALIZE
GENTILIZE
GEOLOGIZE
GERMANIZE
GIGANTIZE
GLAMORIZE
GLUTINIZE
GLYCERIZE
GORGONIZE
GOSPELIZE
GRANITIZE
GRANULIZE
GUACONIZE
HAMLETIZE
HARMONIZE
HERALDIZE
HERBALIZE
HERBARIZE
HERBORIZE
HISTORIZE
HUMOURIZE
HYALINIZE
HYBRIDIZE
HYDROLYZE
HYGIENIZE
HYPNOTIZE
HYPOCRIZE
INFLUENZA
INOXIDIZE
ISOMERIZE
ITALICIZE
JARGONIZE
JASPERIZE
JENNERIZE
JOVIALIZE
KAOLINIZE
LABIALIZE
LACTONIZE
LADRONIZE
LICHENIZE
LIGNITIZE
LINEARIZE
LIQUIDIZE
LITURGIZE
MAGNETIZE
MAINPRIZE
MAMMONIZE
MANGANIZE
MANGONIZE
MANNERIZE
MARBELIZE
MARBLEIZE
MARMARIZE
MARRANIZE
MARTYRIZE
MATRONIZE
MECHANIZE
MEDIALIZE
MEDIATIZE
MEDIUMIZE
MEMORIZED
MENSALIZE
MERCERIZE
MERCURIZE
MESMERIZE
METALLIZE
METEORIZE
METHODIZE
METRICIZE
MNEMONIZE
MODERNIZE
MONACHIZE
MORGANIZE
MORSELIZE
MORTALIZE
MULLENIZE
MUTUALIZE
MYCORHIZA
MYSTERIZE
MYTHICIZE
NARCOTIZE
NECROTIZE
NECTARIZE
NEOLOGIZE
NEOTERIZE
NEUMATIZE
NICKELIZE
NITRIDIZE
NORMALIZE
OBJECTIZE
OPERATIZE
ORATORIZE
ORIENTIZE
OSTRACIZE
OVERGLAZE
OVERGRAZE
OVERPRIZE
OXYGENIZE
OXYTONIZE
PALLADIZE
PALLETIZE
PAMPERIZE
PANDERIZE
PASTORIZE
PATRONIZE
PAUPERIZE
PAVONAZZO
PEDANTIZE
PEGMATIZE
PEOPLEIZE
PEPTONIZE
PERSONIZE
PESSIMIZE
PETROLIZE
PHENOLIZE
PHONETIZE
PICTURIZE
PILLORIZE
PLATINIZE
PLURALIZE
POETICIZE
POSTERIZE
POSTURIZE
POTENTIZE
POWDERIZE
PRECONIZE
PREIOTIZE
PRELATIZE
PRELUDIZE
PRESTEZZA
PROFANIZE
PROLOGIZE
PROPOLIZE
PRYTANIZE
PUBLICIZE
PULVERIZE
PUPILLIZE
PUPPETIZE
PURPURIZE
PYTHONIZE
QUININIZE
QUINONIZE
RABBINIZE
RACIALIZE
RADIALIZE
RADIUMIZE
RANDOMIZE
RAPTURIZE
REBAPTIZE
RECOGNIZE
RHETORIZE
RHYTHMIZE
ROUTINIZE
RUBBERIZE
RUBRICIZE
RUSTICIZE
SATURNIZE
SCENARIZE
SCIENTIZE
SENSITIZE
SERIALIZE
SERMONIZE
SEXUALIZE
SIGNALIZE
SILVERIZE
SISTERIZE
SOCIALIZE
SOLEMNIZE
SOLVOLYZE
SONNETIZE
SORBITIZE
SOVIETIZE
SPIRALIZE
SPIRITIZE
SPONDAIZE
STABILIZE
STERILIZE
SUBSIDIZE
SULCALIZE
SULFATIZE
SULFURIZE
SULTANIZE
SUMMARIZE
SURGERIZE
SYLLABIZE
SYLLOGIZE
SYMBOLIZE
SYNCOPIZE
SYNERGIZE
SYNOECIZE
SYNOPSIZE
SYNTONIZE
SYPHILIZE
SYSTEMIZE
TANDEMIZE
TANTALIZE
TARIFFIZE
TARTARIZE
TAVERNIZE
TELLURIZE
TEMPORIZE
TENDERIZE
TERMINIZE
TERRORIZE
THEATRIZE
THYMOLIZE
TRINALIZE
TUCHUNIZE
TURTLEIZE
TYMPANIZE
TYRANNIZE
UGRIANIZE
UNBRUTIZE
UNCIALIZE
UNDERSIZE
UNREALIZE
URALITIZE
VACUUMIZE
VAMPIRIZE
VANDALIZE
VAPOURIZE
VASSALIZE
VERBALIZE
VERNALIZE
VICTIMIZE
VISCIDIZE
VISIONIZE
VISUALIZE
VOLCANIZE
VULCANIZE
VULGARIZE
WANTONIZE
WINTERIZE
WITTICIZE
WOOLENIZE
ZOOLOGIZE

BURKUNDAZ
RHEUMATIZ
SLIVOVITZ

SCORING ORDER LIST OF 9-LETTER WORDS

33
OXYBENZYL

31
RHIZOTAXY

30
EXOENZYME
MAXIMIZED
SCHIZAXON
ZYGOPHYTE

29
DEZINKIFY
IZVOZCHIK
JAROVIZED
MAXIMIZER
OBJECTIZE
OXYGENIZE
QUINZIEME
ZYGOTAXIS

28
CHEMOLYZE
EQUALIZED
EXORCIZED
HYDROLYZE
HYPOCRIZE
JOVIALIZE
KEVUTZOTH
KIBBUTZIM
LIQUIDIZE
MYCORHIZA
MYTHICIZE
OXYTONIZE
QUANTIZED
QUARTZOID
QUIZZICAL
SQUEEZING
ZOOMORPHY
ZOOPHYTIC
ZYMOLYTIC
ZYMOPHORE

27
AZOXONIUM
CRAZYWEED
DEOXIDIZE
DEZINCIFY
EKPHORIZE

EPIZEUXIS
EQUALIZER
EXORCIZER
HAPHAZARD
HYBRIDIZE
HYDRAZOIC
HYDROZOIC
JASPERIZE
MICROZYMA
MICROZYME
OXIDIZING
QUARTZITE
QUARTZOSE
QUARTZOUS
QUININIZE
QUINONIZE
QUINZAINE
SYZYGETIC
ZERMAHBUB
ZOOGRAPHY
ZYGOPHORE
ZYMOSCOPE

26

AZOPHENYL
BREEZEWAY
CHRYSAZIN
CHRYSAZOL
DIAZEUXIS
FETICHIZE
FURZECHAT
GLAZEWORK
HYLOZOISM
HYPNOTIZE
INOXIDIZE
JARGONIZE
KEVAZINGO
OXDIAZOLE
PEZOGRAPH
PHYTOZOAN
PHYTOZOON
POLYZOARY
PYRAZOLYL
PYTHONIZE
RAZORBACK
RHIZOTOMY
SCHIZOPOD
SYPHILIZE
THYMOLIZE
WAZIRSHIP
ZEPHYREAN
ZEPHYRIAN
ZEPHYROUS
ZIPPINGLY
ZOOPHYTAL
ZOOTECHNY
ZOOTROPHY
ZUMBOORUK
ZYGOMATIC
ZYGOSPERM
ZYMOGENIC
ZYMOLOGIC
ZYMOLYSIS

25

AGROMYZID
ALCHEMIZE
ANHYDRIZE
ARCHIZOIC
AZOFORMIC
BILHARZIC
BURKUNDAZ
CATECHIZE
CHABAZITE
CHALAZIUM
CHERNOZEM
COMPRIZED
DIZYGOTIC
ECPHORIZE
ECTOENZYM
EMPHASIZE
ENZYMATIC
ENZYMOTIC
EUPHEMIZE
FORTHGAZE
FRENZYING
HYDRAZINE
HYDRAZONE
HYDROZOAL
HYDROZOAN
HYDROZOON
HYGIENIZE
ISOXAZOLE
JENNERIZE
MAZOLYTIC
MECHANIZE
MONACHIZE
NAZIFYING
PHILOZOIC
POLYZOISM
PROZYMITE
RHIZOBIUM
RHIZOCARP
RHIZOCORM
SEXUALIZE
SYMBOLIZE
SYNCOPIZE
TYMPANIZE
VACUUMIZE
VAMPIRIZE
VICTIMIZE
WAYZGOOSE
ZEROAXIAL
ZOOCYTIUM
ZOOPHILIC
ZOOPHOBIA
ZOOPHORIC
ZUCCHETTO
ZYGOSTYLE
ZYMOMETER

24

APHIDOZER
APHORIZED
ARCHAIZED
AVIZANDUM
AZEDARACH
AZOCYCLIC
BALKANIZE
BAMBOOZLE
BOMBAZINE
BUZZGLOAK
CATALYZED
CIVILIZED
COMMUNIZE
COMPRIZAL
COPPERIZE
COPROZOIC
COSMOZOIC
CYANIZING
DEEPFROZE
DIAZOTYPE
DIBENZOYL
ECHOIZING
EMBLEMIZE
ETHICIZED
EUPHUIZED
FECUNDIZE
FILMIZING
FIZELYITE
FOCALIZED
FRIVOLIZE
FROWZIEST
GLYCERIZE
HYALINIZE
HYLOZOIST
INFAMIZED
JAZZINESS
LAMZIEKTE
MAZODYNIA
METHODIZE
MICROZOIC
NICKELIZE
PAMPERIZE
PARALYZED
PERHAZARD
POLYZOOID
POWDERIZE
PTYALIZED
PUBLICIZE
SHAHZADAH
SLIVOVITZ
SOLVOLYZE
SULPHAZID
TARIFFIZE
VISCIDIZE
VOCALIZED
WHEEZIEST
WOMANIZED
ZAMINDARY
ZEBRALIKE
ZEBRAWOOD
ZINCIFIED
ZOOFULVIN
ZOOPHAGAN
ZOOSCOPIC
ZYGANTRUM
ZYGOSPORE

23

ACADEMIZE
ACETYLIZE
ANARCHIZE
ANTHOZOIC
APHORIZER
APHRIZITE
APPETIZED
APPRIZING
ARCHAIZER
ATMOLYZER
AZEOTROPY
AZIMUTHAL
AZOPHENOL
BAPTIZING
BEAVERIZE
BEDLAMIZE
BENZAMIDE
BENZAMIDO
BEZOARDIC
BIZARRELY
BLIZZARDY
BLOWZIEST
BUZZARDLY
CAPSIZING
CATALYZER
CATHARIZE
CHALAZIAN
CHALAZION
CHINTZIER
CHORIZONT
CITIZENLY
CITIZENRY
CIVILIZEE
CIVILIZER
CLAVELIZE
FACTORIZE
DEVILIZED
DIALYZING
DIVINIZED
DUNZIEKTE
ELENCHIZE
EMBLAZING
ENZYMOSIS
EUPHONIZE
EVAPORIZE
FACULTIZE
FARADIZED
FAUCALIZE
FIBERIZER
FISCALIZE
FLUIDIZED
FOREPRIZE
FORMALIZE
FORMULIZE
FREEZABLE
GAUZELIKE
GAUZEWING
GAZEHOUND
GRAZINGLY
GRIZZLIER
HAMLETIZE
HARMONIZE
HERBALIZE
HERBARIZE
HERBORIZE
HUMANIZER
HUMOURIZE
IMMUNIZED
LAZYBONES
LAZYBOOTS
LICHENIZE
MACARIZED
MAIZEBIRD
MARTYRIZE
MAZOLYSIS
MEDIUMIZE
MEMORIZED
MINIMIZED
MISPRIZED
MOBILIZED
MYSTERIZE
OPTIMIZED
OVERPRIZE
PARALYZER
PECTIZING
PEGMATIZE
PEPTIZING
PHENAZINE
PHENAZONE
PHENOLIZE
PHLORIZIN
PHONETIZE
POLYZONAL
PROFANIZE
PRYTANIZE
PULVERIZE
PUZZLEDLY
RACEMIZED
RHEUMATIZ
RHIZOCAUL
RHIZOTOMI
SCHNAUZER
SCHNITZEL
SIZARSHIP
SYLLABIZE
SYNOECIZE
SYNOPSIZE
SYSTEMIZE
TOPAZFELS
TUCHUNIZE
VAPORIZER
VAPOURIZE
VERBALIZE
VIZARDING
VOCALIZER
VOLCANIZE
VULCANIZE
WITTICIZE
WOMANIZER
ZELOTYPIA
ZELOTYPIE
ZENDIKITE
ZEUGMATIC
ZOEHEMERA
ZOOCYTIAL
ZOOLITHIC
ZOOPHILIA
ZOOPHORUS
ZOOPLASTY
ZOOSPHERE
ZOOTHECIA
ZOOTHEISM
ZYGADENIN

22

ABURABOZU
ADVERTIZE
ALKALIZER
AMAZEMENT
ANALYZING
APPETIZER
ARCTICIZE
ATHETIZED
AZALEAMUM
BACTERIZE
BALSAMIZE
BANTAMIZE
BARBARIZE
BEDIZENED
BULLDOZED
CAPONIZER
CAPRIZANT
CARBAZINE
CARBAZOLE
CARBOLIZE
CARBONIZE
CARBURIZE
CAUPONIZE
CEREBRIZE
CICATRIZE
CLIMATIZE
COCAINIZE
COELOZOIC
COGNIZING
CRITICIZE
CZARISTIC
DECADENZA
DEFERRIZE
DEMONIZED
DEPUTIZED
DIALYZATE
DISPRIZED
DIZZARDLY
DOGMATIZE
ECONOMIZE
EMBEZZLED
EPIPOLIZE
EPITOMIZE
EPIZOOTIC
ETHERIZED
FARADIZER
FEUDALIZE
FINALIZED
GALVANIZE
HAZARDOUS
HERALDIZE
KAOLINIZE
KRANTZITE
MAGAZINED
MAINPRIZE
MARBELIZE
MARBLEIZE
MARMARIZE
MEGAZOOID
MELODIZED

MEMORIZER
MERCERIZE
MERCURIZE
MESMERIZE
METRICIZE
MEZCALINE
MICROZOAL
MICROZOAN
MICROZONE
MICROZOON
MINIMIZER
MISPRIZER
MIZENMAST
MNEMONIZE
NOVELIZED
OVERGLAZE
OVERGRAZE
OVERSIZED
PAGANIZED
PANZOOTIC
PAPALIZER
PAUPERIZE
PAVONAZZO
PEOPLEIZE
PEPTONIZE
PESSIMIZE
POETICIZE
POLICIZER
PRECONIZE
PRIZEABLE
PROPOLIZE
PROTOZOIC
PUPILLIZE
PURPURIZE
RABBINIZE
RAZZBERRY
REBAPTIZE
RHODIZITE
RUBBERIZE
RUBRICIZE
SAPROZOIC
SCAZONTIC
SCHNOZZLE
SFORZANDO
SPOROZOIC
STYLIZING
SULFAZIDE
SUMMARIZE
SYLLOGIZE
SYNERGIZE
TEMPORIZE
THEORIZED
THIOZONID
TRAPEZIUM
TWEEZERED
VANDALIZE
VITALIZED
VULGARIZE
ZINCALISM
ZINFANDEL
ZINKENITE
ZIRCONIUM
ZIRKELITE
ZOANTHOID
ZOETROPIC
ZOOMETRIC
ZOOSPORIC
ZUCCARINO
ZUURVELDT
ZYGONEURE

21

AMORTIZED
ANGLICIZE
ANTHOZOAN
ANTHOZOON
APOLOGIZE
ARBORIZED
ARRHIZOUS
ATOMIZING
ATTICIZED
AUTHORIZE
AZIETHANE
BEDAZZLED
BENZENOID
BENZIDINE
BENZIDINO
BENZOATED
BERGINIZE
BIOLOGIZE
BIZARDITE
BLAZONING
BOTANIZED
BRAZENING
BULLDOZER
CANALIZED
CANONIZED
COALIZING
COGNIZANT
COLONIZED
CREOLIZED
CURARIZED
CUTINIZED
DECATIZER
DEGLAZING
DESPOTIZE
DIABOLIZE
DIAZEUTIC
DIAZOAMIN
DIÀZONIUM
DIGITIZED
DIZENMENT
DOCTORIZE
DOUZEPERS
DRAMATIZE
DUCTILIZE
DZIGGETAI
EBONIZING
EMBEZZLER
EPILOGIZE
ETHERIZER
FANTASIZE
FERTILIZE
FISTULIZE
FLORIZINE
FOSSILIZE
FRAZZLING
FRIZZLING
GERMANIZE
GLAMORIZE
GOSPELIZE
GUACONIZE
HELIOZOAN
HISTORIZE
IMIDAZOLE
INFLUENZA
ITEMIZING
LACONIZED
LAICIZING
LOCALIZED
MAGAZINER
MAGNETIZE
MALGUZARI
MAMMONIZE
MANGANIZE
MANGONIZE
MAZEDNESS
MEDIALIZE
MEDIATIZE
MELODIZER
MENDOZITE
METALIZED
MODERNIZE
MONETIZED
MORALIZED
MORGANIZE
MOTORIZED
NEBULIZED
OBELIZING
OPALIZING
ORYZANINE
PAEANIZED
PAGANIZER
PALLADIZE
PANDERIZE
PEDANTIZE
PENALIZED
PIZZICATO
POETIZING
POLARIZED
PRELUDIZE
PROLOGIZE
PUPPETIZE
PUZZLEMAN
RADIUMIZE
RANDOMIZE
RECOGNIZE
RHETORIZE
RHIZINOUS
SCLERIZED
SILVERIZE
SMORZANDO
SOLECIZED
SOVIETIZE
SPONDAIZE
SPOROZOID
SUBERIZED
SUBSIDIZE
SULFATIZE
SULFURIZE
SYNEZISIS
SYNIZESIS
SYNTONIZE
TANDEMIZE
TAVERNIZE
THEATRIZE
THEORIZER
TRAPEZING
TRAPEZOID
TYRANNIZE
URBANIZED
VASSALIZE
VERNALIZE
VISIONIZE
VISUALIZE
VITALIZER
VIZIERATE
VIZIERIAL
WANTONIZE
WINTERIZE
WOOLENIZE
WOOZINESS
ZAMINDARI
ZAPATEADO
ZEALOUSLY
ZEMINDARI
ZENDICIAN
ZIRCONOID
ZITHERIST
ZOOGAMETE
ZOOGAMOUS
ZOOGLOEIC
ZOOTHEIST
ZWANZIGER

20

ACETALIZE
ACETONIZE
ACTIONIZE
ACTUALIZE
ADONIZING
AGATIZING
AGONIZING
ALCARRAZA
ALDOLIZED
ALUMETIZE
ALUMINIZE
AMAZONITE
ANABOLIZE
ANATOMIZE
ANGELIZED
ANIMALIZE
ANODIZING
AROMATIZE
AZEOTROPE
AZLACTONE
AZOLITMIN
BALZARINE
BENZOLATE
BENZOLINE
BEZESTEEN
BOOZINESS
BOTANIZER
BRAZILEIN
BRAZILITE
BRUTALIZE
BURTONIZE
CALORIZER
CANONIZER
CARNALIZE
CARTELIZE
CAUTERIZE
CITRONIZE
COLAZIONE
COLONIZER
COTTONIZE
COURTEZAN
CRAZINESS
CREOLEIZE
CZARINIAN
DAZEDNESS
DEODORIZE
DIALOGIZE
DIGITIZER
DISSEIZED
DRAGONIZE
DUALIZING
EGOTIZING
ELECTRIZE
ELEGIZING
ENERGIZED
ERGOTIZED
EULOGIZED
FRIZZIEST
FUZZINESS
GARDENIZE
GAZETTING
GEOLOGIZE
GIGANTIZE
GONOZOOID
GORGONIZE
IDEALIZED
IDOLIZING
IONIZABLE
IRIDIZING
ISOMERIZE
ITALICIZE
LABIALIZE
LACONIZER
LACTONIZE
LAZULITIC
LEGALIZED
LOCALIZER
MANNERIZE
MANZANITA
MARRANIZE
MATRONIZE
MENSALIZE
MESTIZOES
METALLIZE
METEORIZE
MONZONITE
MORALIZER
MORSELIZE
MORTALIZE
MULLENIZE
MUTUALIZE
NARCOTIZE
NEBULIZER
NECROTIZE
NECTARIZE
NEUMATIZE
NODULIZED
NORMALIZE
OPERATIZE
ORGANIZED
OSTRACIZE
OUTBRAZEN
OZOCERITE
OZOSTOMIA
PALLETIZE
PANZOOTIA
PASTORIZE
PATRIZATE
PATRONIZE
PERSONIZE
PETROLIZE
PILLORIZE
PLATINIZE
PLURALIZE
POLARIZER
POLZENITE
POSTERIZE
POSTURIZE
POTENTIZE
PREIOTIZE
PRELATIZE
PROTOZOAL
PROTOZOAN
PROTOZOEA
PROTOZOON
RACIALIZE
RAPTURIZE
RAZORBILL
RAZOREDGE
RUSTICIZE
SCENARIZE
SCIENTIZE
SERMONIZE
SOCIALIZE
SOLECIZER
SOLEMNIZE
SOLMIZATE
SORBITIZE
SPIRALIZE
SPIRITIZE
SPOROZOAL
SPOROZOAN
SPOROZOON
STABILIZE
STARGAZED
STRAMAZON
SULCALIZE
SURPRIZAL
TELEOZOIC
TERMINIZE
TRAPEZIAL
TRAPEZIAN
TRAPEZIST
TRAPEZIUS
UNBRUTIZE
UNCIALIZE
ZEALOTISM
ZELATRICE
ZIBELLINE

ZIRLONATE
ZOOPERIST
ZOOTOMIST

19
ALLOZOOID
ANALOGIZE
ASTATIZED
AUTOZOOID
AZOBENZIL
AZOBENZOL
BENZOLIZE
DENITRIZE
DENTALIZE
DIAZOTATE
DIESELIZE
DIETZEITE
DISSEIZOR
DRIZZLING
ENDENIZEN
ENERGIZER
ETERNIZED
EULOGIZER
GALLINAZO
GAUZINESS
GAZETTEER
GENIALIZE
GENTILIZE
GLAZINESS
GLUTINIZE
GRANITIZE
GRANULIZE
GRIZZLING
IDEALIZER
ISONIAZID
LADRONIZE
LIGNITIZE
LIONIZING
LITURGIZE
MEZZANINE
MEZZOTINT
MIZZONITE
NASALIZED
NEOLOGIZE
NITRIDIZE
NOTARIZED
ONIONIZED
ORGANIZER
ORGANZINE
PIAZZETTA
POZZOLANA
PRESTEZZA
RADIALIZE
REALIZING
RURALIZED
SANITIZED
SATIRIZED
SIGNALIZE
SOLARIZED
STARGAZER
SURGERIZE
TENDERIZE
TETANIZED
TOTALIZED
TRIOZONID
UNDERSIZE
UNIONIZED
UTILIZING
ZINGERONE
ZOOGENOUS
ZOOGLOEAL
ZOOGONOUS
ZOOLOGIES
ZOOLOGIST

18
ALIZARATE
ALIZARINE
ALTERNIZE
ANNUALIZE
ARIZONITE
ARZRUNITE
ASSOILZIE
ASTATIZER
AZOTIZING
DEOZONIZE
DIAZOTIZE
DIZZINESS
ESOTERIZE
GRIZZLIES
LAZARETTE
LAZARETTO
LINEARIZE
LINENIZER
NEOTERIZE
ORATORIZE
ORIENTIZE
OUTDAZZLE
OZONATION
OZONIZING
RESEIZURE
ROUTINIZE
SATIRIZER
SATURNIZE
SENSITIZE
SERIALIZE
SISTERIZE
SONNETIZE
STERILIZE
SULTANIZE
TANTALIZE
TARTARIZE
TARTRAZIN
TELEOZOON
TELLURIZE
TERRORIZE
TERZETTOS
TETRAZANE
TETRAZENE
TETRAZINE
TETRAZOLE
TETRAZONE
TINZENITE
TOTALIZER
TRINALIZE
TURTLEIZE
UNREALIZE
URALITIZE
ZEALOTIST
ZEUNERITE
ZOOLOGIZE

17
LAZZARONE
LAZZARONI
ZEOLITIZE

ALPHABETICAL LIST OF 10-LETTER WORDS

ACADEMIZED
ACETYLIZER
ACTINOZOAL
ACTINOZOAN
ACTIONIZED
ACTUALIZED
ADRENALIZE
ADULTERIZE
AGGRANDIZE
AGLAOZONIA
AIZOACEOUS
AKHUNDZADA
ALBUMENIZE
ALBUMINIZE
ALCALIZATE
ALCHEMIZED
ALCOHOLIZE
ALDOLIZING
ALGEBRAIZE
ALKALINIZE
ALKALIZATE
ALLEGORIZE
ALLOCHEZIA
ALTAZIMUTH
ALUMINIZED
AMALGAMIZE
AMIDRAZONE
AMMONOLYZE
AMORTIZING
ANABIBAZON
ANALOGIZED
ANALYZABLE
ANATHEMIZE
ANATOMIZED
ANATOMIZER
ANAZOTURIA
ANGELICIZE
ANGELIZING
ANGLICIZED
ANGULARIZE
ANIMALIZED
ANTAGONIZE
ANTHOZOOID
ANTIFREEZE
APHORIZING
APOLOGIZED
APOLOGIZER
APOSTATIZE
APOSTOLIZE
APOZEMICAL
APPETIZING
ARBORIZING
ARCHAIZING
ARCTICIZED
AROMATIZED
AROMATIZER
ARSENICIZE
ARTHROZOAN
ARTHROZOIC
ASEPTICIZE
ASEXUALIZE
ASSIZEMENT
ASTATIZING
ASYZYGETIC
ATHETIZING
ATROPINIZE
ATTICIZING
AUTHORIZED
AUTHORIZER
AUTOLYZATE
AUTOMATIZE
AUTONOMIZE
AUTOTOMIZE
AUTOXIDIZE
AXIOMATIZE
AZEOTROPIC
AZOBENZENE
AZOBENZOIC
AZOCORINTH
AZOCYANIDE
AZOGALLEIN
AZOMETHINE
AZOPHENINE
AZOPROTEIN
AZOTENESIS
AZOTOLUENE
AZOTOMETER
AZOTORRHEA
AZOVERNINE
AZTHIONIUM
AZYGOSPERM
AZYGOSPORE
BACTERIZED
BALKANIZED
BAMBOOZLED
BAMBOOZLER
BANTINGIZE
BARBARIZED
BARTIZANED
BASTARDIZE
BEBIZATION
BEDAZZLING
BEDIZENING
BENZEDRINE
BENZOCAINE
BENZOPYRAN
BENZOYLATE
BERZELIITE
BESTIALIZE
BILHARZIAL
BITUMINIZE
BIZARRERIE
BLAZONMENT
BLIZZARDLY
BOBIZATION
BOLSHEVIZE
BOMBAZETTE
BOTANIZING
BOUCHERIZE
BOURBONIZE
BOWDLERIZE
BRAZENFACE
BRAZENNESS
BRAZILETTE
BRAZILWOOD
BREEZINESS
BRONZEWING
BRONZITITE
BRUTALIZED
BULLDOZING
BURGLARIZE
BURNETTIZE
CALZONERAS
CAÑALIZING
CANONIZANT
CANONIZING
CAPITALIZE
CARAMELIZE
CARBAZYLIC
CARBOLIZED
CARBONIZED
CARBONIZER
CARBURIZED
CARBURIZER
CARNALIZED
CASTORIZED
CATABOLIZE
CATALYZING
CATECHIZED
CATECHIZER
CATEGORIZE
CATHARIZED
CAUSTICIZE
CAUTERIZED
CENTRALIZE
CHALAZOGAM
CHANNELIZE
CHATTELIZE
CHERVONETZ
CHIMPANZEE
CHINTZIEST
CHITINIZED
CHLORALIZE
CHLORAZIDE
CHLORIDIZE
CHLORITIZE
CHLORODIZE
CHRIZONTAL
CHROMATIZE
CHROMICIZE
CICATRIZED
CICATRIZER
CICERONIZE
CINCHONIZE
CITIZENESS
CITIZENISM
CITIZENIZE
CIVILIZING
CLASSICIZE
COAZERVATE
COCAINIZED
COCKNEYIZE
COGNIZABLE
COGNIZABLY
COGNIZANCE
COLEORHIZA
COLLOQUIZE
COLONIZING
COMMUNIZED
COMPRIZING

CONCERTIZE
CONCRETIZE
COSMOZOANS
COSMOZOISM
COZENINGLY
CRAZEDNESS
CREOLIZING
CRITICIZED
CRITICIZER
CROFTERIZE
CRYPTOZOIC
CUCKOLDIZE
CURARIZING
CUTINIZING
CUTIZATION
CYTOZYMASE
CZAREVITCH
DANDIZETTE
DASTARDIZE
DAZZLINGLY
DEALKALIZE
DECIMALIZE
DECIVILIZE
DECOLORIZE
DEEPFREEZE
DEEPFROZEN
DEFEMINIZE
DEFERRIZED
DEFINITIZE
DEHEMATIZE
DEHEPATIZE
DEHUMANIZE
DELEGALIZE
DELIMITIZE
DELOCALIZE
DELUMINIZE
DEMOBILIZE
DEMONIZING
DEMORALIZE
DENATURIZE
DENAZIFIED
DENIZATION
DENIZENIZE
DEODORIZED
DEODORIZER
DEOXIDIZED
DEOXIDIZER
DEOZONIZER
DEPETALIZE
DEPOLARIZE
DEPRIORIZE
DEPUTIZING
DERESINIZE
DEVILIZING
DEVIRILIZE
DEVITALIZE
DEVOCALIZE
DEXTRINIZE
DEZYMOTIZE
DIABOLIZED
DIALOGIZED
DIALYZABLE
DIALYZATOR
DIAMONDIZE
DIAZOAMINE
DIAZOIMIDE
DIAZOTIZED
DIGITALIZE
DIGITIZING
DIPLOIDIZE
DIPOLARIZE
DISASINIZE
DISPRIZING
DISREALIZE
DISSEIZURE
DIVINIZING
DOCTRINIZE
DOGGRELIZE
DOGMATIZED
DOGMATIZER
DOLOMITIZE
DOUZAINIER
DOXOLOGIZE
DRAMATIZED
DRAMATIZER
DUCTILIZED
DYSOXIDIZE
ECONOMIZED
ECONOMIZER
ECTOENZYME
ECZEMATOID
ECZEMATOUS
EFFEMINIZE
ELASTICIZE
ELECTRIZED
ELECTRIZER
EMBEZZLING
EMBLAZONED
EMBLAZONER
EMBLAZONRY
EMBLEMIZED
EMOTIONIZE
EMPATHIZED
EMPHASIZED
EMPHATHIZE
ENDOENZYME
ENERGIZING
ENGRANDIZE
ENIGMATIZE
ENOLIZABLE
ENTHRONIZE
ENZYMOLOGY
EPILOGIZED
EPIRHIZOUS
EPISCOPIZE
EPISTOLIZE
EPITAPHIZE
EPITHELIZE
EPITOMIZED
EPITOMIZER
EQUALIZING
ERGOTIZING
ESTERIZING
ETERNALIZE
ETERNIZING
ETHERIZING
ETHICIZING
EUHEMERIZE
EULOGIZING
EUPHEMIZED
EUPHEMIZER
EUPHONIZED
EUPHUIZING
EUPOLYZOAN
EURYZYGOUS
EVANGELIZE
EXORCIZING
EXZODIACAL
FACKELTANZ
FACTORIZED
FANATICIZE
FANTASIZED
FARCIALIZE
FASCISTIZE
FASHIONIZE
FAZENDEIRO
FEDERALIZE
FERTILIZED
FERTILIZER
FERTILIZIN
FEUDALIZED
FICTIONIZE
FINALIZING
FISCALIZED
FLUIDIZING
FOCALIZING
FORMALIZED
FORMULIZED
FORMULIZER
FOSSILIZED
FRATERNIZE
FRENZIEDLY
FRIVOLIZED
FRIZZINESS
FROWZINESS
FROZENNESS
GALLICIZER
GALVANIZED
GALVANIZER
GAZANGABIN
GELATINIZE
GENERALIZE
GEOLOGIZED
GEOMETRIZE
GLAMORIZED
GLOTTALIZE
GLUTTONIZE
GNATHONIZE
GOLANDAUZE
GOLUNDAUZE
GORGONIZED
GRANGERIZE
GRAPHITIZE
GRIZZLIEST
GRIZZLYMAN
HARMONIZER
HEMATOZOON
HERETICIZE
HOMOGENIZE
HOMOLOGIZE
HOMOZYGOTE
HOMOZYGOUS
HORIZONTAL
HYBRIDIZER
HYDRAZOATE
HYDRORHIZA
HYPNOIDIZE
HYPOZEUGMA
HYPOZEUXIS
ICHTHYIZED
IDEALIZING
IDOLATRIZE
ILLEGALIZE
IMIDAZOLYL
IMMOBILIZE
INFAMIZING
INFAMONIZE
INFLUENZAL
INFLUENZIC
INGRANDIZE
INKHORNIZE
INOXIDIZED
INTERMEZZI
INTERMEZZO
INTERZONAL
INTHRONIZE
IODIZATION
IONIZATION
IOTIZATION
ITALICIZED
JANIZARIES
JARGONIZED
JAROVIZING
JASPERIZED
JEOPARDIZE
JOURNALIZE
JOVIALIZED
KAMAREZITE
KATABOLIZE
KERATINIZE
LABIALIZED
LACONIZING
LATERALIZE
LATIBULIZE
LAZARETTOS
LEGALIZING
LEGITIMIZE
LETHARGIZE
LEXICONIZE
LIBERALIZE
LINGUALIZE
LIONIZABLE
LIQUIDIZED
LITERALIZE
LIZARDTAIL
LOCALIZING
LOGICALIZE
MACADAMIZE
MACARIZING
MAGAZINAGE
MAGAZINING
MAGAZINISM
MAGAZINIST
MAGNETIZED
MAGNETIZER
MAHOGANIZE
MAINPRIZER
MALLEINIZE
MANZANILLA
MANZANILLO
MARBLEIZED
MARBLEIZER
MARMARIZED
MARTIALIZE
MARTYRIZED
MARTYRIZER
MATRONIZED
MAXIMIZING
MAZAPILITE
MAZOPATHIA
MAZOPATHIC
MECHANIZER
MEDIATIZED
MELEZITASE
MELEZITOSE
MELODIZING
MEMORIZING
MERCERIZED
MERCERIZER
MERCURIZED
MEROTOMIZE
MESMERIZED
MESMERIZEE
MESMERIZER
METABOLIZE
METALIZING
METHODIZED
METHODIZER
MEZZOGRAPH
MEZZOTINTO
MICROZOARY
MICROZOOID
MILITARIZE
MILLIONIZE
MINERALIZE
MINIMIZING
MIRACULIZE
MISBAPTIZE
MISPRIZING
MIZZENMAST
MNEMONIZED
MOBILIZING
MODERNIZED
MODERNIZER
MONARCHIZE
MONETIZING
MONGRELIZE
MONOLOGIZE
MONONYMIZE
MONOPOLIZE
MONOTONIZE
MONZONITIC
MORALIZING
MORPHINIZE
MORTALIZED
MOTORIZING
MOZZARELLA
MUSICALIZE
MUTUALIZED
MUZZLEWOOD
MYCETOZOAN
MYCETOZOON
MYCOLOGIZE
MYCORHIZAL
MYCORRHIZA
MYECTOMIZE
MYTHICIZED
MYTHICIZER
MYZOSTOMID
NANIZATION
NARCOTIZED
NASALIZING
NATURALIZE
NEBULARIZE
NEBULIZING
NEOLOGIZED
NESSLERIZE
NEUTRALIZE
NICOTINIZE
NONCITIZEN
NORMALIZED
NORMALIZER
NOTARIZING
NOTHINGIZE
NOTORHIZAL
NOVELIZING
OBITUARIZE
OBJECTIZED
ONTOLOGIZE
ORGANIZING
ORGANZINED
ORIGANIZED
OSTRACIZED
OSTRACIZER
OVERFRIEZE
OVERGLAZED
OVERPRIZED
OVERPRIZER
OXADIAZOLE
OXIDIZABLE
OXOZONIDES
OXYGENIZED
OXYGENIZER
OZONOMETER
OZONOMETRY
OZONOSCOPE
PAEANIZING
PAGANIZING
PALATALIZE
PALLETIZED
PANEGYRIZE
PARABOLIZE
PARAGOGIZE
PARALOGIZE
PARALYZANT
PARALYZING
PARASITIZE
PARAZONIUM
PARENESIZE
PARONYMIZE
PASSEMEZZO
PASTEURIZE
PATRONIZED
PATRONIZER
PATTERNIZE

PAUPERIZED
PEASANTIZE
PECTIZABLE
PENALIZING
PEPTIZABLE
PEPTONIZED
PEPTONIZER
PERIPATIZE
PERITOMIZE
PERIZONIUM
PEROXIDIZE
PETROLIZED
PEZIZIFORM
PHANTASIZE
PHANTOMIZE
PHILIPPIZE
PHILOZOIST
PHLORHIZIN
PHLORIDZIN
PHLYZACIUM
PICRORHIZA
PIEZOMETER
PIEZOMETRY
PIGMENTIZE
PILEORHIZA
PILEORHIZE
PILGRIMIZE
PIPERAZINE
PLAGIARIZE
PLASMOLYZE
PLASTICIZE
PLATINIZED
PLURALIZED
PLURALIZER
PNEUMATIZE
POLARIZING
POLITICIZE
POLYGAMIZE
POLYMERIZE
POLYTHEIZE
POLYZOARIA
POPULARIZE
POSITIVIZE
POSTURIZED
POULARDIZE
POWDERIZER
POZZOLANIC
POZZUOLANA
PRAGMATIZE
PRECOGNIZE
PRECONIZED
PRECONIZER
PREDAZZITE
PRESSURIZE
PRISMATIZE
PRIZEFIGHT
PRIZETAKER
PROBLEMIZE
PROCTORIZE
PROLOGUIZE
PROPHETIZE
PROVERBIZE
PSALMODIZE
PTYALIZING
PUBLICIZED
PULVERIZED
PULVERIZER
PUZZLEHEAD
PUZZLEMENT
PUZZLEPATE
PUZZLINGLY
PYRAZOLINE
PYRAZOLONE
PYRIDAZINE
PYRIDINIZE
QUINAZOLIN
QUINAZOLYL
QUINIZARIN
QUARTZITIC
QUATORZAIN
RACEMIZING
RADICALIZE
RAMFEEZLED
RANDOMIZED
RAZORMAKER
RAZORSTROP
REALIZABLE
REBAPTIZER
RECOGNIZEE
RECOGNIZED
RECOGNIZER
RECOGNIZOR
REDISSEIZE
REGULARIZE
REJUVENIZE
REMONETIZE
RENDEZVOUS
REORGANIZE
REVALORIZE
REVITALIZE
REZBANYITE
RHAPSODIZE
RHEUMATIZE
RHIZOGENIC
RHIZOMATIC
RHIZOMELIC
RHIZOMORPH
RHIZONEURE
RHIZOPHORE
RHIZOPHYTE
RHIZOPLAST
RHIZOPODAL
RHIZOPODAN
RHIZOSTOME
RHIZOTAXIS
RHODIZONIC
ROUTINIZED
RUBBERIZED
RUFFIANIZE
RURALIZING
SACCHARIZE
SALICYLIZE
SAPIENTIZE
SATIRIZING
SCANDALIZE
SCEPTICIZE
SCHEDULIZE
SCHEMATIZE
SCHEMOZZLE
SCHERZANDO
SCHIZOCARP
SCHIZOGAMY
SCHIZOGONY
SCHIZOLITE
SCORBUTIZE
SCRUTINIZE
SCYPHOZOAN
SECTIONIZE
SECULARIZE
SELTZOGENE
SEMINARIZE
SENSITIZED
SENSITIZER
SENSUALIZE
SERIALIZED
SERMONIZED
SERMONIZER
SERPENTIZE
SEVERALIZE
SFORZANDOS
SHERARDIZE
SIGNALIZED
SILICIDIZE
SILICONIZE
SIMPLICIZE
SIZZLINGLY
SKEPTICIZE
SLEAZINESS
SLENDERIZE
SNEEZEWEED
SNEEZEWOOD
SNEEZEWORT
SOCIALIZED
SOCIALIZER
SOLARIZING
SOLECIZING
SOLEMNIZED
SOLEMNIZER
SOLIDARIZE
SOLUBILIZE
SOLVOLYZED
SOPHRONIZE
SOVIETIZED
SPATIALIZE
SPECIALIZE
SPERMATIZE
SPHETERIZE
SPIRANTIZE
SPITZFLUTE
SPOROZOITE
SPOROZOOID
SQUEEZABLE
SQUEEZEMAN
STABILIZED
STABILIZER
STANZAICAL
STARGAZING
STERILIZED
STERILIZER
STIGMATIZE
STRATEGIZE
STYFZIEKTE
STYLOPIZED
SUBERINIZE
SUBERIZING
SUBSIDIZED
SUBSIDIZER
SUBTILIZED
SUBTILIZER
SULFATIZED
SULFURIZED
SULPHATIZE
SULPHAZIDE
SULPHIDIZE
SULPHURIZE
SUMMARIZED
SUMMARIZER
SUZERAINTY
SYLLABIZED
SYLLOGIZED
SYLLOGIZER
SYMBOLIZED
SYMBOLIZER
SYMMETRIZE
SYMPATHIZE
SYMPHONIZE
SYMPHYTIZE
SYNCRETIZE
SYNONYMIZE
SYNTHESIZE
SYNTHETIZE
SYNTONIZED
SYNTONIZER
SYPHILIZED
SYSTEMIZED
SYSTEMIZER
TABULARIZE
TANTALIZED
TANTALIZER
TARLTONIZE
TARTARIZED
TARTRAZINE
TAUTOZONAL
TELFORDIZE
TELLURIZED
TEMPORIZED
TEMPORIZER
TENDERIZED
TENDERIZER
TENOTOMIZE
TEPONAZTLI
TERRORIZED
TERRORIZER
TETANIZING
TETRAZOLYL
THEOLOGIZE
THEORIZING
THERMOLYZE
THIAZOLINE
THIOZONIDE
TOPAZOLITE
TOTALIZING
TRACTORIZE
TRAPEZIUMS
TRAUMATIZE
TRICHINIZE
TRIOZONIDE
TRITOZOOID
TRIVIALIZE
TROCHEEIZE
TROCHOZOIC
TROCHOZOON
TRYPSINIZE
TRYPTONIZE
TWEEZERING
TYRANNIZED
TYRANNIZER
WARRANTIZE
UNBAPTIZED
UNCANONIZE
UNDERGLAZE
UNDERSIZED
UNIFORMIZE
UNIONIZING
UNITEMIZED
UNPRIZABLE
UNREALIZED
UNSTOICIZE
URALITIZED
URBANIZING
UTILIZABLE
VAGOTOMIZE
VAGRANTIZE
VAPOURIZED
VAPOURIZER
VASSALIZED
VENEZOLANO
VERATRIZED
VERBALIZED
VERBALIZER
VERSIONIZE
VESZELYITE
VETERANIZE
VICTIMIZED
VICTIMIZER
VISIBILIZE
VISUALIZED
VISUALIZER
VITALIZING
VITAMINIZE
VITRIOLIZE
VOCALIZING
VOCIFERIZE
VOLATILIZE
VOLCANIZED
VULCANIZED
VULCANIZER
VULGARIZED
VULGARIZER
WESTERNIZE
WHEEZINESS
WHEEZINGLY
WHITEBLAZE
WHIZZERMAN
WHIZZINGLY
WINTERIZED
WITZCHOURA
WOMANIZING
WOOLLENIZE
ZABAGLIONE
ZAPHRENTID
ZEALOTICAL
ZEBRINNIES
ZENOGRAPHY
ZEOLITIZED
ZEUGLODONT
ZIGZAGGERY
ZINCIFYING
ZINCOGRAPH
ZINCOLYSIS
ZINGARESCA
ZINGIBEROL
ZOANTHROPY
ZONIFEROUS
ZOOBENTHOS
ZOOCULTURE
ZOOCURRENT
ZOOGRAPHER
ZOOGRAPHIC
ZOOLATRIES
ZOOLATROUS
ZOOLOGICAL
ZOOLOGIZED
ZOOMELANIN
ZOOMIMETIC
ZOOMORPHIC
ZOOPHAGOUS
ZOOPHILISM
ZOOPHILIST
ZOOPHILITE
ZOOPHILOUS
ZOOPHOBOUS
ZOOPHYSICS
ZOOPHYTISH
ZOOPHYTOID
ZOOPLASTIC
ZOOSPOROUS
ZOOTECHNIC
ZOOTHECIAL
ZOOTHECIUM
ZOOTHERAPY
ZOOTOMICAL
ZOOTROPHIC
ZOOXANTHIN
ZWITTERION
ZYGADENINE
ZYGOBRANCH
ZYGODACTYL
ZYGOMYCETE
ZYGOPHORIC
ZYGOSPHENE
ZYGOSPHERE
ZYGOSPORIC
ZYGOTACTIC
ZYMOGENOUS
ZYMOLOGIST
ZYMOPHORIC
ZYMOSTEROL

POSITIONAL ORDER LIST OF 10-LETTER WORDS

ZABAGLIONE
ZAPHRENTID
ZEALOTICAL
ZEBRINNIES
ZENOGRAPHY
ZEOLITIZED
ZEUGLODONT
ZIGZAGGERY
ZINCIFYING
ZINCOGRAPH
ZINCOLYSIS
ZINGARESCA
ZINGIBEROL
ZOANTHROPY
ZONIFEROUS
ZOOBENTHOS
ZOOCULTURE
ZOOCURRENT
ZOOGRAPHER
ZOOGRAPHIC
ZOOLATRIES
ZOOLATROUS
ZOOLOGICAL
ZOOLOGIZED
ZOOMELANIN
ZOOMIMETIC
ZOOMORPHIC
ZOOPHAGOUS
ZOOPHILISM
ZOOPHILIST
ZOOPHILITE
ZOOPHILOUS
ZOOPHOBOUS
ZOOPHYSICS
ZOOPHYTISH
ZOOPHYTOID
ZOOPLASTIC
ZOOSPOROUS
ZOOTECHNIC
ZOOTHECIAL
ZOOTHECIUM
ZOOTHERAPY
ZOOTOMICAL
ZOOTROPHIC
ZOOXANTHIN
ZWITTERION
ZYGADENINE
ZYGOBRANCH
ZYGODACTYL
ZYGOMYCETE
ZYGOPHORIC
ZYGOSPHENE
ZYGOSPHERE
ZYGOSPORIC
ZYGOTACTIC
ZYMOGENOUS
ZYMOLOGIST
ZYMOPHORIC
ZYMOSTEROL

AZEOTROPIC
AZOBENZENE
AZOBENZOIC
AZOCORINTH
AZOCYANIDE
AZOGALLEIN
AZOMETHINE
AZOPHENINE
AZOPROTEIN
AZOTENESIS
AZOTOLUENE
AZOTOMETER
AZOTORRHEA
AZOVERNINE
AZTHIONIUM
AZYGOSPERM
AZYGOSPORE
CZAREVITCH
OZONOMETER
OZONOMETRY
OZONOSCOPE

AIZOACEOUS
BIZARRERIE
COZENINGLY
DAZZLINGLY
DEZYMOTIZE
ECZEMATOID
ECZEMATOUS
ENZYMOLOGY
EXZODIACAL
FAZENDEIRO
GAZANGABIN
LAZARETTOS
LIZARDTAIL
MAZAPILITE
MAZOPATHIA
MAZOPATHIC
MEZZOGRAPH
MEZZOTINTO
MIZZENMAST
MOZZARELLA
MUZZLEWOOD
MYZOSTOMID
PEZIZIFORM
POZZOLANIC
POZZUOLANA
PUZZLEHEAD
PUZZLEMENT
PUZZLEPATE
PUZZLINGLY
RAZORMAKER
RAZORSTROP
REZBANYITE
SIZZLINGLY
SUZERAINTY

ANAZOTURIA
APOZEMICAL
ASYZYGETIC
BENZEDRINE
BENZOCAINE
BENZOPYRAN
BENZOYLATE
BERZELIITE
BLAZONMENT
BLIZZARDLY
BRAZENFACE
BRAZENNESS
BRAZILETTE
BRAZILWOOD
CALZONERAS
COAZERVATE
CRAZEDNESS
DAZZLINGLY
DEOZONIZER
DIAZOAMINE
DIAZOIMIDE
DIAZOTIZED
DOUZAINIER
FRIZZINESS
FROZENNESS
GRIZZLIEST
GRIZZLYMAN
MANZANILLA
MANZANILLO
MEZZOGRAPH
MEZZOTINTO
MIZZENMAST
MONZONITIC
MOZZARELLA
MUZZLEWOOD
OXOZONIDES
PIEZOMETER
PIEZOMETRY
POZZOLANIC
POZZUOLANA
PRIZEFIGHT
PRIZETAKER
PUZZLEHEAD
PUZZLEMENT
PUZZLEPATE
PUZZLINGLY
RHIZOGENIC
RHIZOMATIC
RHIZOMELIC
RHIZOMORPH
RHIZONEURE
RHIZOPHORE
RHIZOPHYTE
RHIZOPLAST
RHIZOPODAL
RHIZOPODAN
RHIZOSTOME
RHIZOTAXIS
SIZZLINGLY
VESZELYITE
WHIZZERMAN
WHIZZINGLY
WITZCHOURA
ZIGZAGGERY

ALTAZIMUTH
ASSIZEMENT
BEBIZATION
BEDAZZLING
BEDIZENING
BLIZZARDLY
BOBIZATION
BREEZINESS
BRONZEWING
BRONZITITE
CHRIZONTAL
CITIZENESS
CITIZENISM
CITIZENIZE
CUTIZATION
CYTOZYMASE
DENAZIFIED
DENIZATION
DENIZENIZE
EMBEZZLING
EURYZYGOUS
FRENZIEDLY
FRIZZINESS
FROWZINESS
GRIZZLIEST
GRIZZLYMAN
HOMOZYGOTE
HOMOZYGOUS
HORIZONTAL
HYPOZEUGMA
HYPOZEUXIS
IODIZATION
IONIZATION
IOTIZATION
JANIZARIES
MAGAZINAGE
MAGAZINING
MAGAZINISM
MAGAZINIST
MELEZITASE
MELEZITOSE
NANIZATION
PARAZONIUM
PERIZONIUM
PEZIZIFORM
PHLYZACIUM
POLYZOARIA
PYRAZOLINE
PYRAZOLONE
SCHIZOCARP
SCHIZOGAMY
SCHIZOGONY
SCHIZOLITE
SELTZOGENE
SFORZANDOS
SLEAZINESS
SNEEZEWEED
SNEEZEWOOD
SNEEZEWORT
SPITZFLUTE
STANZAICAL
STYFZIEKTE
THIAZOLINE
THIOZONIDE
TOPAZOLITE
TRIOZONIDE
TWEEZERING
VENEZOLANO
WHEEZINESS
WHEEZINGLY
WHIZZERMAN
WHIZZINGLY

AGLAOZONIA
ANALYZABLE
ANTHOZOOID
BARTIZANED
BEDAZZLING
BOMBAZETTE
CARBAZYLIC
CHALAZOGAM
CHINTZIEST
COGNIZABLE
COGNIZABLY
COGNIZANCE
COSMOZOANS
COSMOZOISM
DANDIZETTE
DIALYZABLE
DIALYZATOR
EMBEZZLING
EMBLAZONED
EMBLAZONER
EMBLAZONRY
ENOLIZABLE
HYDRAZOATE
IMIDAZOLYL
INTERZONAL
LIONIZABLE
MICROZOARY
MICROZOOID
ORGANZINED
OXIDIZABLE
PECTIZABLE
PEPTIZABLE
PHILOZOIST
PREDAZZITE
QUARTZITIC
QUINAZOLIN
QUINAZOLYL
QUINIZARIN
REALIZABLE
RENDEZVOUS
RHODIZONIC
SCHERZANDO
SPOROZOITE
SPOROZOOID
SQUEEZABLE
SQUEEZEMAN
TAUTOZONAL
TETRAZOLYL
TRAPEZIUMS
TRITOZOOID
UNPRIZABLE
UTILIZABLE

ACTINOZOAL
ACTINOZOAN
AKHUNDZADA
ALCALIZATE
ALDOLIZING
ALKALIZATE
AMIDRAZONE
AMORTIZING
ANGELIZING
APHORIZING
APPETIZING
ARBORIZING
ARCHAIZING
ARTHROZOAN
ARTHROZOIC
ASTATIZING
ATHETIZING
ATTICIZING
AUTOLYZATE
AZOBENZENE
AZOBENZOIC
BAMBOOZLED
BAMBOOZLER
BILHARZIAL
BOTANIZING
BULLDOZING
CANALIZING
CANONIZANT
CANONIZING
CATALYZING
CHLORAZIDE
CIVILIZING
COLONIZING
COMPRIZING
CREOLIZING
CRYPTOZOIC
CURARIZING
CUTINIZING
DEMONIZING
DEPUTIZING
DEVILIZING
DIGITIZING
DISPRIZING
DISSEIZURE
DIVINIZING
ECTOENZYME
ENDOENZYME
ENERGIZING
EPIRHIZOUS
EQUALIZING
ERGOTIZING
ESTERIZING
ETERNIZING
ETHERIZING
ETHICIZING
EULOGIZING
EUPHUIZING
EUPOLYZOAN
EXORCIZING
FINALIZING
FLUIDIZING
FOCALIZING

HEMATOZOON
IDEALIZING
INFAMIZING
JAROVIZING
KAMAREZITE
LACONIZING
LEGALIZING
LOCALIZING
MACARIZING
MAXIMIZING
MELODIZING
MEMORIZING
METALIZING
MINIMIZING
MISPRIZING
MOBILIZING
MONETIZING
MORALIZING
MOTORIZING
MYCETOZOAN
MYCETOZOON
NASALIZING
NEBULIZING
NOTARIZING
NOVELIZING
ORGANIZING
OXADIAZOLE
PAEANIZING
PAGANIZING
PARALYZANT
PARALYZING
PENALIZING
PIPERAZINE
POLARIZING
PREDAZZITE
PTYALIZING
PYRIDAZINE
QUATORZAIN
RACEMIZING
RAMFEEZLED
RURALIZING
SATIRIZING
SCHEMOZZLE
SCYPHOZOAN
SOLARIZING
SOLECIZING
STARGAZING
SUBERIZING
SULPHAZIDE
TARTRAZINE
TEPONAZTLI
TETANIZING
THEORIZING
TOTALIZING
TROCHOZOIC
TROCHOZOON
UNIONIZING
URBANIZING
VITALIZING
VOCALIZING

ACADEMIZED
ACETYLIZER
ACTIONIZED
ACTUALIZED
ALCHEMIZED
ALLOCHEZIA
ALUMINIZED
ANABIBAZON
ANALOGIZED
ANGLICIZED
ANIMALIZED
APOLOGIZED
APOLOGIZER
ARCTICIZED
AROMATIZED
AROMATIZER
AUTHORIZED
AUTHORIZER
BACTERIZED
BALKANIZED
BARBARIZED
BRUTALIZED
CARBOLIZED
CARBONIZED
CARBONIZER
CARBURIZED
CARBURIZER
CARNALIZED
CASTORIZED
CATECHIZED
CATECHIZER
CATHARIZED
CAUTERIZED
CHIMPANZEE
CHITINIZED
CICATRIZED
CICATRIZER
COCAINIZED
COMMUNIZED
CRITICIZED
CRITICIZER
DEEPFROZEN
DEFERRIZED
DEODORIZED
DEODORIZER
DEOXIDIZED
DEOXIDIZER
DEOZONIZER
DIABOLIZED
DIALOGIZED
DIAZOTIZED
DOGMATIZED
DOGMATIZER
DRAMATIZED
DRAMATIZER
DUCTILIZED
ECONOMIZED
ECONOMIZER
ELECTRIZED
ELECTRIZER
EMBLEMIZED
EMPATHIZED
EMPHASIZED
EPILOGIZED
EPITOMIZED
EPITOMIZER
EUPHEMIZED
EUPHEMIZER
EUPHONIZED
FACTORIZING
FANTASIZED
FERTILIZED
FERTILIZER
FERTILIZIN
FEUDALIZED
FISCALIZED
FORMALIZED
FORMULIZED
FORMULIZER
FOSSILIZED
FRIVOLIZED
GALLICIZER
GALVANIZED
GALVANIZER
GEOLOGIZED
GLAMORIZED
GORGONIZED
HARMONIZER
HYBRIDIZER
ICHTHYIZED
INFLUENZAL
INFLUENZIC
INOXIDIZED
INTERMEZZI
INTERMEZZO
ITALICIZED
JARGONIZED
JASPERIZED
JOVIALIZED
LABIALIZED
LIQUIDIZED
MAGNETIZED
MAGNETIZER
MAINPRIZER
MARBLEIZED
MARBLEIZER
MARMARIZED
MARTYRIZED
MARTYRIZER
MATRONIZED
MECHANIZER
MEDIATIZED
MERCERIZED
MERCERIZER
MERCURIZED
MESMERIZED
MESMERIZEE
MESMERIZER
METHODIZED
METHODIZER
MNEMONIZED
MODERNIZED
MODERNIZER
MORTALIZED
MUTUALIZED
MYCORHIZAL
MYTHICIZED
MYTHICIZER
NARCOTIZED
NEOLOGIZED
NONCITIZEN
NORMALIZED
NORMALIZER
NOTORHIZAL
OBJECTIZED
ORIGANIZED
OSTRACIZED
OSTRACIZER
OVERGLAZED
OVERPRIZED
OVERPRIZER
OXYGENIZED
OXYGENIZER
PALLETIZED
PASSEMEZZO
PATRONIZED
PATRONIZER
PAUPERIZED
PEPTONIZED
PEPTONIZER
PETROLIZED
PHLORHIZIN
PHLORIDZIN
PLATINIZED
PLURALIZED
PLURALIZER
POSTURIZED
POWDERIZER
PRECONIZED
PRECONIZER
PUBLICIZED
PULVERIZED
PULVERIZER
RANDOMIZED
REBAPTIZER
RECOGNIZEE
RECOGNIZED
RECOGNIZER
RECOGNIZOR
ROUTINIZED
RUBBERIZED
SCHEMOZZLE
SENSITIZED
SENSITIZER
SERIALIZED
SERMONIZED
SERMONIZER
SIGNALIZED
SOCIALIZED
SOCIALIZER
SOLEMNIZED
SOLEMNIZER
SOLVOLYZED
SOVIETIZED
STABILIZED
STABILIZER
STERILIZED
STERILIZER
STYLOPIZED
SUBSIDIZED
SUBSIDIZER
SUBTILIZED
SUBTILIZER
SULFATIZED
SULFURIZED
SUMMARIZED
SUMMARIZER
SYLLABIZED
SYLLOGIZED
SYLLOGIZER
SYMBOLIZED
SYMBOLIZER
SYNTONIZED
SYNTONIZER
SYPHILIZED
SYSTEMIZED
SYSTEMIZER
TANTALIZED
TANTALIZER
TARTARIZED
TELLURIZED
TEMPORIZED
TEMPORIZER
TENDERIZED
TENDERIZER
TERRORIZED
TERRORIZER
TYRANNIZED
TYRANNIZER
UNBAPTIZED
UNDERSIZED
UNITEMIZED
UNREALIZED
URALITIZED
VAPOURIZED
VAPOURIZER
VASSALIZED
VERATRIZED
VERBALIZED
VERBALIZER
VICTIMIZED
VICTIMIZER
VISUALIZED
VISUALIZER
VOLCANIZED
VULCANIZED
VULCANIZER
VULGARIZED
VULGARIZER
WINTERIZED
ZOOLOGIZED

ADRENALIZE
ADULTERIZE
AGGRANDIZE
ALBUMENIZE
ALBUMINIZE
ALCOHOLIZE
ALGEBRAIZE
ALKALINIZE
ALLEGORIZE
AMALGAMIZE
AMMONOLYZE
ANATHEMIZE
ANGELICIZE
ANGULARIZE
ANTAGONIZE
ANTIFREEZE
APOSTATIZE
APOSTOLIZE
ARSENICIZE
ASEPTICIZE
ASEXUALIZE
ATROPINIZE
AUTOMATIZE
AUTONOMIZE
AUTOTOMIZE
AUTOXIDIZE
AXIOMATIZE
BANTINGIZE
BASTARDIZE
BESTIALIZE
BITUMINIZE
BOLSHEVIZE
BOUCHERIZE
BOURBONIZE
BOWDLERIZE
BURGLARIZE
BURNETTIZE
CAPITALIZE
CARAMELIZE
CATABOLIZE
CATEGORIZE
CAUSTICIZE
CENTRALIZE
CHANNELIZE
CHATTELIZE
CHLORALIZE
CHLORIDIZE
CHLORITIZE
CHLORODIZE
CHROMATIZE
CHROMICIZE
CICERONIZE
CINCHONIZE
CITIZENIZE
CLASSICIZE
COCKNEYIZE
COLEORHIZA
COLLOQUIZE
CONCERTIZE
CROFTERIZE
CUCKOLDIZE
DASTARDIZE
DEALKALIZE
DECIMALIZE
DECIVILIZE
DECOLORIZE
DEEPFREEZE
DEFEMINIZE
DEFINITIZE
DEHEMATIZE
DEHEPATIZE
DEHUMANIZE
DELEGALIZE
DELIMITIZE
DELOCALIZE
DELUMINIZE
DEMOBILIZE
DEMORALIZE
DENATURIZE
DENIZENIZE
DEPETALIZE
DEPOLARIZE

DEPRIORIZE
DERESINIZE
DEVIRILIZE
DEVITALIZE
DEVOCALIZE
DEXTRINIZE
DEZYMOTIZE
DIAMONDIZE
DIGITALIZE
DIPLOIDIZE
DIPOLARIZE
DISASINIZE
DISREALIZE
DOCTRINIZE
DOGGRELIZE
DOLOMITIZE
DOXOLOGIZE
DYSOXIDIZE
EFFEMINIZE
ELASTICIZE
EMOTIONIZE
EMPHATHIZE
ENGRANDIZE
ENIGMATIZE
ENTHRONIZE
EPISCOPIZE
EPISTOLIZE
EPITAPHIZE
EPITHELIZE
ETERNALIZE
EUHEMERIZE
EVANGELIZE
FANATICIZE
FARCIALIZE
FASCISTIZE
FASHIONIZE
FEDERALIZE
FICTIONIZE
FRATERNIZE
GELATINIZE
GENERALIZE
GEOMETRIZE
GLOTTALIZE
GLUTTONIZE
GNATHONIZE
GOLANDAUZE
GOLUNDAUZE
GORMANDIZE

GRANGERIZE
GRAPHITIZE
HERETICIZE
HOMOGENIZE
HOMOLOGIZE
HYDRORHIZA
HYPNOIDIZE
IDOLATRIZE
ILLEGALIZE
IMMOBILIZE
INFAMONIZE
INGRANDIZE
INKHORNIZE
INTERMEZZI
INTERMEZZO
INTHRONIZE
JEOPARDIZE
JOURNALIZE
KATABOLIZE
KERATINIZE
LATERALIZE
LATIBULIZE
LEGITIMIZE
LETHARGIZE
LEXICONIZE
LIBERALIZE
LINGUALIZE
LITERALIZE
LOGICALIZE
MACADAMIZE
MAHOGANIZE
MALLEINIZE
MARTIALIZE
MEROTOMIZE
METABOLIZE
MILITARIZE
MILLIONIZE
MINERALIZE
MIRACULIZE
MISBAPTIZE
MONARCHIZE
MONGRELIZE
MONOLOGIZE
MONONYMIZE
MONOPOLIZE
MONOTONIZE
MORPHINIZE
MUSICALIZE

MYCOLOGIZE
MYCORRHIZA
MYECTOMIZE
NATURALIZE
NEBULARIZE
NESSLERIZE
NEUTRALIZE
NICOTINIZE
NOTHINGIZE
OBITUARIZE
ONTOLOGIZE
OVERFRIEZE
PALATALIZE
PANEGYRIZE
PARABOLIZE
PARAGOGIZE
PARALOGIZE
PARASITIZE
PARENESIZE
PARONYMIZE
PASSEMEZZO
PASTEURIZE
PATTERNIZE
PEASANTIZE
PERIPATIZE
PERITOMIZE
PEROXIDIZE
PHANTASIZE
PHANTOMIZE
PHILIPPIZE
PICRORHIZA
PIGMENTIZE
PILEORHIZA
PILEORHIZE
PILGRIMIZE
PLAGIARIZE
PLASMOLYZE
PLASTICIZE
PNEUMATIZE
POLITICIZE
POLYGAMIZE
POLYMERIZE
POLYTHEIZE
POPULARIZE
POSITIVIZE
POULARDIZE
PRAGMATIZE
PRECOGNIZE

PRESSURIZE
PRISMATIZE
PROBLEMIZE
PROCTORIZE
PROLOGUIZE
PROPHETIZE
PROVERBIZE
PSALMODIZE
PYRIDINIZE
RADICALIZE
REDISSEIZE
REGULARIZE
REJUVENIZE
REMONETIZE
REORGANIZE
REVALORIZE
REVITALIZE
RHAPSODIZE
RHEUMATIZE
RUFFIANIZE
SACCHARIZE
SALICYLIZE
SAPIENTIZE
SCANDALIZE
SCEPTICIZE
SCHEDULIZE
SCHEMATIZE
SCORBUTIZE
SCRUTINIZE
SECTIONIZE
SECULARIZE
SEMINARIZE
SENSUALIZE
SERPENTIZE
SEVERALIZE
SHERARDIZE
SILICIDIZE
SILICONIZE
SIMPLICIZE
SKEPTICIZE
SLENDERIZE
SOLIDARIZE
SOLUBILIZE
SOPHRONIZE
SPATIALIZE
SPECIALIZE
SPERMATIZE
SPHETERIZE

SPIRANTIZE
STIGMATIZE
STRATEGIZE
SUBERINIZE
SULPHATIZE
SULPHIDIZE
SULPHURIZE
SYMMETRIZE
SYMPATHIZE
SYMPHONIZE
SYMPHYTIZE
SYNCRETIZE
SYNONYMIZE
SYNTHESIZE
SYNTHETIZE
TABULARIZE
TARLTONIZE
TELFORDIZE
TENOTOMIZE
THEOLOGIZE
THERMOLYZE
TRACTORIZE
TRAUMATIZE
TRICHINIZE
TRIVIALIZE
TROCHEEIZE
TRYPSINIZE
TRYPTONIZE
UNCANONIZE
UNDERGLAZE
UNIFORMIZE
UNSTOICIZE
VAGOTOMIZE
VAGRANTIZE
VERSIONIZE
VETERANIZE
VISIBILIZE
VITAMINIZE
VITRIOLIZE
VOCIFERIZE
VOLATILIZE
WARRANTIZE
WESTERNIZE
WHITEBLAZE
WOOLLENIZE

CHERVONETZ
FACKELTANZ

SCORING ORDER LIST OF 10-LETTER WORDS

34
HYPOZEUXIS

32
SYMPHYTIZE

31
DYSOXIDIZE
ICHTHYIZED
MAXIMIZING
OBJECTIZED
OXYGENIZED
PHLYZACIUM
QUINAZOLYL
ZYMOPHORIC

30
COCKNEYIZE
HYPOZEUGMA
JAROVIZING
JOVIALIZED
LIQUIDIZED
MYTHICIZED
OXYGENIZER
QUARTZITIC
RHIZOPHYTE
SCHIZOGAMY
SQUEEZABLE
SQUEEZEMAN
ZOOPHYTISH
ZYGOBRANCH
ZYGOMYCETE
ZYGOPHORIC

29
CYTOZYMASE
CZAREVITCH
DEOXIDIZED
EMPHATHIZE
EQUALIZING
EXORCIZING
EXZODIACAL
HYDRORHIZA
JASPERIZED
JEOPARDIZE
MYCORHIZAL
MYCORRHIZA
MYTHICIZER
OXIDIZABLE
PEROXIDIZE
REJUVENIZE
RHIZOMORPH
RHIZOTAXIS
SCYPHOZOAN
STYFZIEKTE
SYMPATHIZE
SYMPHONIZE
WHEEZINGLY
ZOOPHYSICS
ZOOXANTHIN
ZYGODACTYL

28
AKHUNDZADA
ASYZYGETIC
AXIOMATIZE
CARBAZYLIC
CHIMPANZEE
CHROMICIZE
CRYPTOZOIC
CUCKOLDIZE
DEOXIDIZER
DOXOLOGIZE
ENZYMOLOGY
FACKELTANZ
HOMOZYGOTE
HOMOZYGOUS
HYBRIDIZER
HYPNOIDIZE
INOXIDIZED
JARGONIZED
LEXICONIZE
MAZOPATHIC
MYECTOMIZE
PRIZEFIGHT
QUATORZAIN
QUINAZOLIN
QUINIZARIN
SCHIZOCARP
SCHIZOGONY
SYPHILIZED
WHIZZINGLY
ZENOGRAPHY
ZINCIFYING
ZOOMORPHIC
ZOOPHYTOID
ZYGOSPHENE
ZYGOSPHERE

27
ALCHEMIZED
AUTOXIDIZE
AZYGOSPERM
BOLSHEVIZE
CATECHIZED
CHALAZOGAM
CHERVONETZ
COGNIZABLY
DEXTRINIZE
EFFEMINIZE
EMPATHIZED
EMPHASIZED
EUPHEMIZED
MYCOLOGIZE
MYZOSTOMID

OXADIAZOLE
OXOZONIDES
PHLORHIZIN
POLYGAMIZE
POLYTHEIZE
RHIZOPHORE
SKEPTICIZE
SYMBOLIZED
SYNONYMIZE
THERMOLYZE
VICTIMIZED
VOCIFERIZE
WHITEBLAZE
WITZCHOURA
ZINCOGRAPH
ZOANTHROPY
ZOOGRAPHIC
ZOOTHERAPY
ZYGOSPORIC
ZYGOTACTIC

26

AMMONOLYZE
ASEXUALIZE
BALKANIZED
BAMBOOZLED
BENZOPYRAN
BOUCHERIZE
BRAZENFACE
CATECHIZER
CHROMATIZE
CINCHONIZE
COMMUNIZED
COMPRIZING
ECTOENZYME
EMBLAZONRY
EMBLEMIZED
EPITAPHIZE
EUPHEMIZER
EURYZYGOUS
FRENZIEDLY
FRIVOLIZED
HYDRAZOATE
INKHORNIZE
JANIZARIES
JOURNALIZE
MACADAMIZE
MAZOPATHIA
MECHANIZER
METHODIZED
MEZZOGRAPH
MICROZOARY
MONARCHIZE
MONONYMIZE
MORPHINIZE
MYCETOZOAN
MYCETOZOON
PARONYMIZE
PHANTOMIZE
PICRORHIZA
PIEZOMETRY
PLASMOLYZE
POLYMERIZE
PROPHETIZE
PROVERBIZE
PUBLICIZED
RHIZOMATIC
RHIZOMELIC
SACCHARIZE
SCHEMATIZE
SOLVOLYZED
SYMBOLIZER
SYMMETRIZE
TANTALIZED
TROCHOZOIC
VICTIMIZER
WHIZZERMAN

ZOOPHILISM
ZOOPHOBOUS
ZOOTECHNIC
ZOOTHECIUM
ZOOTROPHIC

25

ACADEMIZED
APHORIZING
APOZEMICAL
ARCHAIZING
AZOCYANIDE
AZYGOSPORE
BAMBOOZLER
BOMBAZETTE
BOWDLERIZE
BRAZILWOOD
BRONZEWING
CATALYZING
CATHARIZED
CHITINIZED
CHLORAZIDE
CHLORIDIZE
CHLORODIZE
CIVILIZING
COSMOZOISM
COZENINGLY
DECIVILIZE
DEEPFREEZE
DEEPFROZEN
DEFEMINIZE
DEHEMATIZE
DEHEPATIZE
DEHUMANIZE
DEVOCALIZE
DIALYZABLE
ENDOENZYME
EPISCOPIZE
ETHICIZING
EUPHONIZED
EUPHUIZING
FACTORIZED
FASHIONIZE
FISCALIZED
FOCALIZING
FORMALIZED
FORMULIZED
FROWZINESS
GRAPHITIZE
HOMOGENIZE
HOMOLOGIZE
IMIDAZOLYL
IMMOBILIZE
INFAMIZING
KAMAREZITE
KATABOLIZE
MAHOGANIZE
MARTYRIZED
METHODIZER
MISBAPTIZE
OVERFRIEZE
OVERPRIZED
PANEGYRIZE
PARALYZING
PECTIZABLE
PEPTIZABLE
PEZIZIFORM
PHILIPPIZE
PHLORIDZIN
POWDERIZER
PRIZETAKER
PROBLEMIZE
PTYALIZING
PULVERIZED
PYRIDAZINE
PYRIDINIZE
RAMFEEZLED

RAZORMAKER
RHAPSODIZE
RHIZOGENIC
RHIZOPODAL
RHIZOPODAN
RHODIZONIC
RUFFIANIZE
SCEPTICIZE
SCHEDULIZE
SCHEMOZZLE
SCHERZANDO
SIMPLICIZE
STYLOPIZED
SULPHAZIDE
SULPHIDIZE
SYLLABIZED
SYNTHESIZE
SYNTHETIZE
SYSTEMIZED
VAGOTOMIZE
VAPOURIZED
VERBALIZED
VESZELYITE
VOCALIZING
VOLCANIZED
VULCANIZED
WHEEZINESS
WOMANIZING
ZAPHRENTID
ZOOGRAPHER
ZOOMIMETIC
ZOOPHAGOUS
ZYMOGENOUS
ZYMOLOGIST

24

ACETYLIZER
ALCOHOLIZE
ALLOCHEZIA
ALTAZIMUTH
AMALGAMIZE
ANALYZABLE
ANATHEMIZE
APPETIZING
ARCTICIZED
ARTHROZOIC
AZOCORINTH
AZOMETHINE
AZOPHENINE
AZTHIONIUM
BACTERIZED
BARBARIZED
BENZOYLATE
BILHARZIAL
BLIZZARDLY
CARBOLIZED
CARBONIZED
CARBURIZED
CHANNELIZE
CHATTELIZE
CHINTZIEST
CHLORALIZE
CHLORITIZE
CHRIZONTAL
CICATRIZED
COAZERVATE
COCAINIZED
COGNIZABLE
COGNIZANCE
COLEORHIZA
CRITICIZED
CROFTERIZE
DEALKALIZE
DECIMALIZE
DEFERRIZED
DEMOBILIZE
DENAZIFIED

DEVILIZING
DEZYMOTIZE
DIVINIZING
DOGMATIZED
ECONOMIZED
ECZEMATOID
EMBLAZONED
EPIRHIZOUS
EPITHELIZE
EPITOMIZED
EUHEMERIZE
EUPOLYZOAN
FANATICIZE
FARCIALIZE
FASCISTIZE
FEUDALIZED
FICTIONIZE
FLUIDIZING
FORMULIZER
GALVANIZED
GRIZZLYMAN
HARMONIZER
HEMATOZOON
HERETICIZE
INFAMONIZE
INFLUENZIC
MACARIZING
MAGAZINISM
MARBLEIZED
MARMARIZED
MARTYRIZER
MEMORIZING
MERCERIZED
MERCURIZED
MESMERIZED
MICROZOOID
MINIMIZING
MISPRIZING
MNEMONIZED
MOBILIZING
MUZZLEWOOD
OVERGLAZED
OVERPRIZER
OZONOMETRY
PARALYZANT
PAUPERIZED
PEPTONIZED
PHANTASIZE
PHILOZOIST
PIGMENTIZE
PILEORHIZA
PILEORHIZE
PILGRIMIZE
POLYZOARIA
POSITIVIZE
PRAGMATIZE
PRECOGNIZE
PRECONIZED
PSALMODIZE
PULVERIZER
PUZZLEHEAD
PUZZLINGLY
PYRAZOLINE
PYRAZOLONE
RACEMIZING
REZBANYITE
RHEUMATIZE
RHIZOPLAST
RHIZOSTOME
RUBBERIZED
SALICYLIZE
SCHIZOLITE
SOPHRONIZE
SPHETERIZE
SPITZFLUTE
SULPHATIZE
SULPHURIZE

SUMMARIZED
SYLLOGIZED
SYNCRETIZE
SYSTEMIZER
TEMPORIZED
TRICHINIZE
TROCHEEIZE
TROCHOZOON
TRYPSINIZE
TRYPTONIZE
UNBAPTIZED
UNIFORMIZE
VAPOURIZER
VERBALIZER
VISIBILIZE
VITAMINIZE
VULCANIZER
VULGARIZED
ZIGZAGGERY
ZINCOLYSIS
ZOOBENTHOS
ZOOPHILIST
ZOOPHILITE
ZOOPHILOUS
ZOOTHECIAL
ZYGADENINE
ZYMOSTEROL

23

ALBUMENIZE
ALBUMINIZE
ALKALINIZE
ALKALIZATE
ANABIBAZON
ANGLICIZED
ANTHOZOOID
APOLOGIZED
ASEPTICIZE
ATHETIZING
AUTHORIZED
AZEOTROPIC
BEBIZATION
BEDIZENING
BENZOCAINE
BITUMINIZE
BLAZONMENT
BOBIZATION
BOURBONIZE
BULLDOZING
CAPITALIZE
CARAMELIZE
CARBONIZER
CARBURIZER
CATABOLIZE
CAUSTICIZE
CICATRIZER
CICERONIZE
CITIZENISM
CLASSICIZE
CONCERTIZE
CONCRETIZE
COSMOZOANS
CRITICIZER
DAZZLINGLY
DEFINITIZE
DEMONIZING
DEPUTIZING
DEVIRILIZE
DEVITALIZE
DIABOLIZED
DIALYZATOR
DIAMONDIZE
DIAZOIMIDE
DIPLOIDIZE
DISPRIZING
DOGMATIZER
DRAMATIZED

DUCTILIZED
ECONOMIZER
ECZEMATOUS
EMBEZZLING
EMBLAZONER
EPILOGIZED
EPITOMIZER
ETHERIZING
EVANGELIZE
FANTASIZED
FAZENDEIRO
FEDERALIZE
FERTILIZED
FINALIZING
FOSSILIZED
GALVANIZER
GAZANGABIN
GLAMORIZED
GNATHONIZE
GORMANDIZE
KERATINIZE
LETHARGIZE
MAGAZINAGE
MAGAZINING
MAGNETIZED
MAINPRIZER
MARBLEIZER
MAZAPILITE
MEDIATIZED
MELODIZING
MERCERIZER
MEROTOMIZE
MESMERIZEE
MESMERIZER
METABOLIZE
MIRACULIZE
MODERNIZED
MONOPOLIZE
MONZONITIC
MUSICALIZE
NOTHINGIZE
NOVELIZING
OZONOSCOPE
PAGANIZING
PARABOLIZE
PARAGOGIZE
PARAZONIUM
PEPTONIZER
PERIPATIZE
PERITOMIZE
PERIZONIUM
PIEZOMETER
PIPERAZINE
PLASTICIZE
PNEUMATIZE
POLITICIZE
POPULARIZE
PRECONIZER
PRISMATIZE
PROCTORIZE
RANDOMIZED
REBAPTIZER
RECOGNIZED
RENDEZVOUS
SCORBUTIZE
SFORZANDOS
SHERARDIZE
SNEEZEWEED
SNEEZEWOOD
SOVIETIZED
SPECIALIZE
SPERMATIZE
SUBSIDIZED
SULFATIZED
SULFURIZED
SUMMARIZER
SYLLOGIZER
SYNTONIZED
TELFORDIZE
TEMPORIZER
THEOLOGIZE
THEORIZING
THIOZONIDE
TRAPEZIUMS
TWEEZERING
TYRANNIZED
UNPRIZABLE
VAGRANTIZE
VASSALIZED
VERATRIZED
VISUALIZED
VITALIZING
VULGARIZER
WINTERIZED
ZOOPLASTIC
ZOOTOMICAL

22

ACTIONIZED
ACTUALIZED
AGGRANDIZE
ALGEBRAIZE
ALUMINIZED
AMIDRAZONE
AMORTIZING
ANATOMIZED
ANGELICIZE
ANIMALIZED
ANTIFREEZE
APOLOGIZER
ARBORIZING
AROMATIZED
ARTHROZOAN
ATTICIZING
AUTHORIZER
AUTOLYZATE
AZOBENZOIC
AZOTORRHEA
AZOVERNINE
BANTINGIZE
BARTIZANED
BASTARDIZE
BEDAZZLING
BENZEDRINE
BOTANIZING
BRUTALIZED
BURGLARIZE
CANALIZING
CANONIZING
CARNALIZED
CASTORIZED
CATEGORIZE
CAUTERIZED
COLONIZING
CRAZEDNESS
CREOLIZING
CURARIZING
CUTINIZING
DECOLORIZE
DELIMITIZE
DELOCALIZE
DELUMINIZE
DEMORALIZE
DEODORIZED
DEPETALIZE
DEPOLARIZE
DEPRIORIZE
DIALOGIZED
DIAZOAMINE
DIGITIZING
DIPOLARIZE
DOCTRINIZE
DOGGRELIZE
DOLOMITIZE
DRAMATIZER
ELECTRIZED
ENIGMATIZE
ENTHRONIZE
FERTILIZER
FERTILIZIN
FRATERNIZE
FROZENNESS
GALLICIZER
GEOLOGIZED
GEOMETRIZE
GORGONIZED
HORIZONTAL
INFLUENZAL
INTHRONIZE
ITALICIZED
LABIALIZED
LACONIZING
LEGITIMIZE
LOCALIZING
LOGICALIZE
MAGAZINIST
MAGNETIZER
MATRONIZED
METALIZING
MIZZÈNMAST
MODERNIZER
MONETIZING
MONGRELIZE
MONOLOGIZE
MORALIZING
MORTALIZED
MOTORIZING
MUTUALIZED
NARCOTIZED
NEBULIZING
NORMALIZED
NOTORHIZAL
OSTRACIZED
PAEANIZING
PALLETIZED
PARALOGIZE
PASSEMEZZO
PATRONIZED
PENALIZING
PETROLIZED
PLAGIARIZE
PLATINIZED
PLURALIZED
POLARIZING
POSTURIZED
POULARDIZE
POZZOLANIC
PROLOGUIZE
PUZZLEMENT
PUZZLEPATE
RADICALIZE
RECOGNIZEE
RECOGNIZER
RECOGNIZOR
REVALORIZE
REVITALIZE
RHIZONEURE
SCANDALIZE
SERMONIZED
SEVERALIZE
SILICIDIZE
SIZZLINGLY
SNEEZEWORT
SOCIALIZED
SOLECIZING
SOLEMNIZED
SPOROZOOID
STABILIZED
STIGMATIZE
SUBERIZING
SUBSIDIZER
SUBTILIZED
SUZERAINTY
SYNTONIZER
TETRAZOLYL
THIAZOLINE
TRIVIALIZE
TYRANNIZER
UNITEMIZED
URBANIZING
VENEZOLANO
VERSIONIZE
VETERANIZE
VISUALIZER
VITRIOLIZE
VOLATILIZE
WARRANTIZE
WESTERNIZE
WOOLLENIZE
ZABAGLIONE
ZINGARESCA
ZINGIBEROL
ZONIFEROUS
ZOOLOGICAL
ZWITTERION

21

ACTINOZOAL
ACTINOZOAN
AIZOACEOUS
ALCALIZATE
ALDOLIZING
ANALOGIZED
ANATOMIZER
ANGELIZING
APOSTATIZE
APOSTOLIZE
AROMATIZER
ARSENICIZE
ASSIZEMENT
ATROPINIZE
AUTOMATIZE
AUTONOMIZE
AUTOTOMIZE
AZOPROTEIN
AZOTOMETER
BERZELIITE
BESTIALIZE
BIZARRERIE
BRAZENNESS
BRAZILETTE
BREEZINESS
BRONZITITE
BURNETTIZE
CALZONERAS
CANONIZANT
CENTRALIZE
CITIZENESS
CUTIZATION
DASTARDIZE
DELEGALIZE
DEODORIZER
DIGITALIZE
ELASTICIZE
ELECTRIZER
EMOTIONIZE
ENERGIZING
ENGRANDIZE
ENOLIZABLE
EPISTOLIZE
ERGOTIZING
EULOGIZING
FRIZZINESS
GOLANDAUZE
GOLUNDAUZE
GRANGERIZE
IDEALIZING
INGRANDIZE
LATIBULIZE
LEGALIZING
LIBERALIZE
LIONIZABLE
MALLEINIZE
MANZANILLA
MANZANILLO
MARTIALIZE
MELEZITASE
MELEZITOSE
MILITARIZE
MILLIONIZE
MINERALIZE
MONOTONIZE
NEBULARIZE
NEOLOGIZED
NICOTINIZE
NONCITIZEN
NORMALIZER
OBITUARIZE
ORGANIZING
ORGANZINED
ORIGANIZED
OSTRACIZER
OZONOMETER
PALATALIZE
PARASITIZE
PARENESIZE
PASTEURIZE
PATRONIZER
PATTERNIZE
PEASANTIZE
PLURALIZER
PREDAZZITE
PRESSURIZE
RAZORSTROP
REALIZABLE
REMONETIZE
SAPIENTIZE
SCRUTINIZE
SECTIONIZE
SECULARIZE
SEMINARIZE
SERMONIZER
SERPENTIZE
SIGNALIZED
SILICONIZE
SOCIALIZER
SOLEMNIZER
SOLUBILIZE
SPATIALIZE
SPIRANTIZE
SPOROZOITE
STABILIZER
STANZAICAL
STARGAZING
SUBERINIZE
SUBTILIZER
TABULARIZE
TENDERIZED
TENOTOMIZE
TEPONAZTLI
TOPAZOLITE
TRACTORIZE
TRAUMATIZE
UNCANONIZE
UNDERGLAZE
UNDERSIZED
UTILIZABLE
ZEALOTICAL
ZEBRINNIES
ZEUGLODONT
ZOOCULTURE
ZOOCURRENT
ZOOMELANIN
ZOOSPOROUS

20
ADRENALIZE
ADULTERIZE
AGLAOZONIA
ALLEGORIZE
ANGULARIZE
ANTAGONIZE
ASTATIZING
AZOBENZENE
AZOGALLEIN
CITIZENIZE
DENATURIZE
DENIZATION
DERESINIZE
DIAZOTIZED
DISASINIZE
DISREALIZE
DISSEIZURE
DOUZAINIER
ESTERIZING
ETERNIZING
GELATINIZE
GENERALIZE
GLOTTALIZE
GLUTTONIZE
IDOLATRIZE
ILLEGALIZE
INTERMEZZI
INTERMEZZO
IODIZATION
LINGUALIZE
LIZARDTAIL
MEZZOTINTO
MOZZARELLA
NASALIZING
NOTARIZING
ONTOLOGIZE
POZZUOLANA
REDISSEIZE
REGULARIZE
REORGANIZE
ROUTINIZED
RURALIZING
SATIRIZING
SELTZOGENE
SENSITIZED
SERIALIZED
SLENDERIZE
SOLARIZING
SOLIDARIZE
STERILIZED
STRATEGIZE
TARTARIZED
TELLURIZED
TENDERIZER
TERRORIZED
TETANIZING
TOTALIZING
TRIOZONIDE
TRITOZOOID
UNIONIZING
UNREALIZED
URALITIZED
ZOOLOGIZED

19
ANAZOTURIA
AZOTENESIS
AZOTOLUENE
DENIZENIZE
DEOZONIZER
ETERNALIZE
GRIZZLIEST
INTERZONAL
IONIZATION
IOTIZATION
LATERALIZE
LAZARETTOS
LITERALIZE
NANIZATION
NATURALIZE
NESSLERIZE
NEUTRALIZE
SENSITIZER
SENSUALIZE
SLEAZINESS
STERILIZER
TANTALIZER
TARLTONIZE
TARTRAZINE
TAUTOZONAL
TERRORIZER
UGRIANIZE
ZEOLITIZED
ZOOLATRIES
ZOOLATROUS

ALPHABETICAL LIST OF WORDS OVER 10 LETTERS

ABASTARDIZE
ABNORMALIZE
ABOLITIONIZE
ACADEMIZING
ACCLIMATIZE
ACCLIMATIZED
ACCLIMATIZER
ACCLIMATIZING
ACCULTURIZE
ACCUSTOMIZE
ACCUSTOMIZED
ACCUSTOMIZING
ACETOBENZOIC
ACETONIZATION
ACETYLIZABLE
ACETYLIZATION
ACHROMATIZE
ACHROMATIZED
ACTIONIZING
ACTUALIZATION
ACTUALIZING
ADENIZATION
ADVERBIALIZE
ADVERTIZEMENT
ADVERTIZING
AESTHETICIZE
AGGUTINIZE
AGGRANDIZED
AGGRANDIZER
AGGRANDIZING
AGRARIANIZE
ALBITIZATION
ALBUMENIZED
ALBUMENIZER
ALBUMENIZING
ALBUMINIZED
ALBUMINIZING
ALCHEMIZING
ALCOHOLIZED
ALCOHOLIZING
ALDOLIZATION
ALGEBRAIZED
ALGEBRIZATION
ALGEBRAIZING
ALKALINIZED
ALKALINIZING
ALKALIZABLE
ALKALIZATION
ALLEGORIZED
ALLEGORIZER
ALLEGORIZING
ALLOTROPIZE
ALPHABETIZE
ALPHABETIZED
ALPHABETIZER
ALPHABETIZING
ALUMINIZING
AMMONIZATION
AMORTIZABLE
AMORTIZATION
AMORTIZEMENT
ANABAPTIZED
ANABAPTIZING
ANACEPHALIZE
ANACHRONIZE
ANAESTHETIZE
ANAESTHETIZED
ANAESTHETIZER
ANALOGIZING
ANALYZATION
ANATHEMATIZE
ANATOMIZING
ANESTHETIZE
ANESTHETIZER
ANGIOSTOMIZE
ANGLICIZING
ANHYDRIDIZE
ANIMALIZATION
ANIMALIZING
ANTAGONIZED
ANTAGONIZER
ANTAGONIZING
ANTHEROZOID
ANTHEROZOOID
ANTHOLOGIZE
ANTHOLOGIZED
ANTHOLOGIZING
ANTHROPOZOIC
ANTIFREEZING
ANTIPATHIZE
ANTISEPTICIZE
ANTITHESIZE
APAESTHETIZE
APESTHETIZE
APOLOGIZING
APOSTATIZED
APOSTATIZING
APOSTROPHIZE
APOTHEOSIZE
APOTHEOSIZED
APPETIZINGLY
APPRIZEMENT
ARBORIZATION
ARCTICIZING
ARITHMETIZE
AROMATIZING
ARSENIZATION
ARTERIALIZE
ARTERIALIZED
ASBESTINIZE
ASCIDIOZOOID
ASEPTICIZED
ASEPTICIZING
ASEXUALIZED
ASEXUALIZING
ASPHETERIZE
ASTIGMATIZER
ASTROLOGIZE
ASTRONOMIZE
ATMOLYZATION
ATOMIZATION
ATTITUDINIZE
AUTHORIZATION
AUTHORIZING
AUTOCATALYZE
AZADIRACHTA
AZEOTROPISM
AZIMETHYLENE
AZIMUTHALLY
AZOCOCHINEAL
AZOCORALLINE
AZODIPHENYL
AZOERYTHRIN
AZOFICATION
AZOOSPERMIA
AZOPARAFFIN
AZOPHENETOLE
AZOPHENYLENE
AZOPHOSPHIN
AZOPHOSPHORE
AZOSULPHINE
AZOSULPHONIC
AZOTETRAZOLE
AZOTHIONIUM
AZOTOBACTER
AZOTORRHOEA
AZYGOMATOUS
BACCHANALIZE
BACHELORIZE
BACTERIOLYZE
BACTERIZING
BALKANIZING
BAMBOOZLEMENT
BAMBOOZLING
BAPTIZEMENT
BARBARIZING
BASTARDIZED
BASTARDIZING
BATTOLOGIZE
BEDAZZLINGLY
BEDIZENMENT
BENZALDEHYDE
BENZALDOXIME
BENZINDULINE
BENZOHYDROL
BENZOINATED
BENZONITRILE
BENZONITROL
BENZOPHENONE
BENZOYLATION
BENZYLAMINE
BERGINIZATION
BERZELIANITE
BESSEMERIZE
BESSEMERIZED
BESSEMERIZING
BESTIALIZED
BESTIALIZING
BILHARZIASIS
BILHARZIOSIS
BIOGRAPHIZE
BISTETRAZOLE
BISTRIAZOLE
BITUMINIZED
BIVOCALIZED
BIZARRENESS
BIZYGOMATIC
BLIZZARDOUS
BOLSHEVIZED
BOLSHEVIZING
BOWDLERIZED
BOWDLERIZING
BRAZENFACED
BROMIZATION
BROMOBENZENE
BROMOIODIZED
BRONZESMITH
BRUTALIZING
BURGLARIZED
BURGLARIZING
BURKUNDAUZE
BURNETTIZED
BURNETTIZING
BURTONIZATION
BUZZERPHONE
CACOPHONIZE
CACOZEALOUS
CALABAZILLA
CANALIZATION
CANNIBALIZE
CANNIBALIZED
CANNIBALIZING
CANONIZATION
CANTHARIDIZE
CAPERCAILZIE
CAPITALIZED
CAPITALIZING
CARAMELIZED
CARAMELIZING
CARBOAZOTINE
CARBOLIZING
CARBONIZING
CARBURIZING
CARNALIZING
CATABIBAZON
CATABOLIZED
CATABOLIZING
CATALEPTIZE
CATALOGUIZE
CATALYZATOR

CATECHIZATION
CATECHIZING
CATEGORIZED
CATEGORIZING
CATHARIZING
CATHETERIZE
CATHETERIZED
CATHOLICIZE
CATHOLICIZED
CATHOLICIZING
CAUSTICIZED
CAUSTICIZER
CAUSTICIZING
CAUTERIZATION
CAUTERIZING
CELESTIALIZE
CELESTIALIZED
CENOZOOLOGY
CENTRALIZED
CENTRALIZER
CENTRALIZING
CHALAZOGAMIC
CHALAZOGAMY
CHALAZOIDITE
CHAMELEONIZE
CHAMPAGNIZE
CHAMPAGNIZED
CHAMPAGNIZING
CHANNELIZED
CHANNELIZING
CHARACTERIZE
CHARACTERIZED
CHARACTERIZER
CHEERFULIZE
CHEMICALIZE
CHITINIZATION
CHLAMYDOZOAN
CHLORALIZED
CHLORALIZING
CHLORIDIZED
CHLORIDIZING
CHLORODIZED
CHLORODIZING
CHORIAMBIZE
CHORIZATION
CHORIZONTES
CHORIZONTIC
CHORIZONTIST
CHROMICIZING
CHRONOLOGIZE
CHRONOLOGIZED
CICATRIZANT
CICATRIZATE
CICATRIZING
CINCHONIZED
CINCHONIZING
CIRCULARIZE
CIRCULARIZED
CIRCULARIZING
CITIZENIZED
CITIZENIZING
CITIZENRIES
CITIZENSHIP
CIVILIZABLE
CIVILIZATION
CIVILIZATORY
CLASSICIZED
CLASSICIZING
COAZERVATION
COCAINIZING
COLLECTIVIZE
COLLECTIVIZED
COLLODIONIZE
COLLOQUIZED
COLLOQUIZING
COLONIZATION
COMMEMORIZE
COMMEMORIZED
COMMEMORIZING
COMMERCIALIZE
COMMUNALIZE
COMMUNALIZED
COMMUNALIZER
COMMUNIZATION
COMMUNIZING
COMPANIONIZE
COMPANIONIZED
CONCERTIZED
CONCERTIZER
CONCERTIZING
CONCRETIZED
CONCRETIZING
CONSERVATIZE
CONSONANTIZE
CONTEMPORIZE
CONTEMPORIZED
COPOLYMERIZE
COPOLYMERIZED
COPPERIZATION
CORPOREALIZE
COSMOGONIZE
CREOLIZATION
CRITICIZABLE
CRITICIZING
CRYPTOZONATE
CRYPTOZYGOUS
CRYSTALLIZE
CRYSTALLIZED
CRYSTALLIZER
CRYSTALLIZING
CURARIZATION
CUTICULARIZE
CUTINIZATION
CYCLIZATION
DACTYLOZOOID
DAMENIZATION
DEBENZOLIZE
DECAFFEINIZE
DECARBONIZE
DECARBONIZED
DECARBONIZER
DECARBURIZE
DECARBURIZED
DECENTRALIZE
DECEREBRIZE
DECHORALIZE
DECICERONIZE
DECIMALIZED
DECIMALIZING
DECOLORIZED
DECOLORIZER
DECOLORIZING
DECOLOURIZE
DEEPFREEZED
DEEPFREEZING
DEFERRIZING
DEFIBRINIZE
DEFINITIZED
DEFINITIZING
DEHUMANIZED
DEHUMANIZING
DEHYPNOTIZE
DEHYPNOTIZED
DEJUNKERIZE
DELIMITIZED
DELIMITIZING
DELOCALIZED
DELOCALIZING
DEMAGNETIZE
DEMAGNETIZED
DEMAGNETIZER
DEMANGANIZE
DEMENTHOLIZE
DEMEPHITIZE
DEMICIVILIZED
DEMILITARIZE
DEMILITARIZED
DEMINERALIZE
DEMOBILIZED
DEMOBILIZING
DEMOCRATIZE
DEMOCRATIZED
DEMONETIZED
DEMONETIZING
DEMORALIZED
DEMORALIZER
DEMORALIZING
DEMUTIZATION
DENATURALIZE
DENATURIZER
DENAZIFYING
DENICOTINIZE
DENIZENATION
DEODORIZING
DEOXIDIZING
DEOXYGENIZE
DEPAUPERIZE
DEPAUPERIZED
DEPERSONIZE
DEPIGMENTIZE
DEPOLARIZED
DEPOLARIZER
DEPOLARIZING
DEPOLYMERIZE
DERACIALIZE
DERATIZATION
DERMATOZOON
DESACRALIZE
DESCLOIZITE
DESENSITIZE
DESENSITIZER
DESEXUALIZE
DESEXUALIZED
DESILICONIZE
DESILVERIZE
DESILVERIZER
DESTERILIZE
DESTINEZITE
DESULFURIZE
DESULFURIZED
DESULFURIZER
DESULPHURIZE
DESYNONYMIZE
DETRIBALIZE
DEUTEROZOOID
DEVITALIZED
DEVITALIZING
DEVITAMINIZE
DEVOCALIZED
DEVOCALIZING
DEVULGARIZE
DEXTROSAZONE
DEZINCATION
DEZINCIFIED
DEZINCIFYING
DIABOLIZING
DIAGONALIZE
DIALECTALIZE
DIALECTICIZE
DIALOGIZING
DIALYZATION
DIAMONDIZED
DIAMONDIZING
DIAZENTITHAL
DIAZOBENZENE
DIAZOMETHANE
DIAZOTIZING
DICHOTOMIZE
DICHOTOMIZED
DIEZEUGMENON
DIMERIZATION
DIPHTHONGIZE
DIPHTHONGIZED
DIPHYOZOOID
DIPLOMATIZE
DIPLOMATIZED
DISCANONIZE
DISCANONIZED
DISEQUALIZE
DISGOSPELIZE
DISHARMONIZE
DISORGANIZE
DISORGANIZED
DISORGANIZER
DISPAUPERIZE
DISSEIZORESS
DISSOCIALIZE
DISSYLLABIZE
DIVINIZATION
DOCKIZATION
DOCTRINIZED
DOCTRINIZING
DOCUMENTIZE
DOGGERELIZE
DOGGERELIZER
DOGGERELIZING
DOGMATIZING
DOMESTICIZE
DOMESTICIZED
DOXOLOGIZED
DOXOLOGIZING
DRAMATIZATION
DRAMATIZING
DUALIZATION
DUCTILIZING
DYNAMIZATION
ECONOMIZATION
ECONOMIZING
ECZEMATOSIS
EDITORIALIZE
EDITORIALIZED
EFFECTUALIZE
EFFEMINATIZE
EFFEMINIZED
EFFEMINIZING
ELASTICIZER
ELECTRALIZE
ELECTRICALIZE
ELECTRICIZE
ELECTRIZING
ELECTROLYZE
ELECTROLYZED
ELECTROLYZER
ELECTROLYZING
ELECTROTONIZE
EMBEZZLEMENT
EMBLEMATICIZE
EMBLEMATIZE
EMBLEMATIZED
EMBLEMATIZING
EMBLEMIZING
EMOTIONALIZE
EMOTIONALIZED
EMPATHIZING
EMPHASIZING
EMULSIONIZE
ENCARNALIZE
ENCARNALIZED
ENCARNALIZING
ENCYCLOPEDIZE
ENHYPOSTATIZE
ENIGMATIZED
ENIGMATIZING
ENOLIZATION
ENSORCELIZE
ENSORCERIZE
ENTHRONIZED
ENTHRONIZING
ENTOMOLOGIZE
ENTOMOLOGIZED
ENTOZOOLOGY
ENZYMICALLY
ENZYMOLYSIS
ENZYMOLYTIC
EPENTHESIZE
EPIDOTIZATION
EPIGRAMMATIZE
EPILOGIZING
EPISCOPIZED
EPISCOPIZING
EPISTOLIZABLE
EPITHALAMIZE
EPITOMIZATION
EPITOMIZING
EPIZOOTIOLOGY
EQUALIZATION
EQUILIBRIZE
ERGOTIZATION
ERYTHROZYME
ESTERIZATION
ETERNIZATION
ETHEREALIZE
ETHEREALIZED
ETHEREALIZING
ETHERIZATION
ETHNOZOOLOGY
ETYMOLOGIZE
ETYMOLOGIZED
ETYMOLOGIZING
EUCHARISTIZE
EUCHARISTIZED
EUDAEMONIZE
EUHEMERIZED
EUHEMERIZING
EULOGIZATION
EUPHEMIZING
EUPHONIZING
EVANGELIZED
EVANGELIZER
EVANGELIZING
EVENTUALIZE
EVOLUTIONIZE
EXAUTHORIZE
EXCURSIONIZE
EXORCIZATION
EXORCIZEMENT
EXOSTRACIZE
EXPERIMENTIZE
EXPERMENTIZED
EXTEMPORIZE
EXTEMPORIZED
EXTEMPORIZER
EXTEMPORIZING
EXTERIORIZE
EXTERIORIZED
EXTERIORIZING
EXTERNALIZE
EXTERNIZATION
EXTRAVAGANZA
FACSIMILIZE
FACTORIZATION
FACTORIZING
FAMILIARIZE
FAMILIARIZED
FAMILIARIZER
FAMILIARIZING
FANATICIZED
FANATICIZING
FANTASIZING
FARADIZATION
FASCISTICIZE
FEDERALIZED
FEDERALIZING
FEMINIZATION
FERTILIZABLE

FERTILIZATION
FERTILIZING
FEUDALIZATION
FEUDALIZING
FICTIONALIZED
FICTIONIZED
FICTIONIZING
FISCALIZATION
FISCALIZING
FLAMBOYANTIZE
FLUIDIZATION
FOCALIZATION
FORMALIZATION
FORMALIZING
FORMULARIZE
FORMULARIZED
FORMULARIZING
FORMULIZATION
FORMULIZING
FOSSILIZATION
FOSSILIZING
FRACTIONALIZE
FRACTIONIZE
FRACTIONIZING
FRATERNIZED
FRATERNIZER
FRATERNIZING
FRICTIONIZE
FRICTIONIZED
FRICTIONIZING
FRIVOLIZING
FUNCTIONIZE
FUROMONAZOLE
GABERLUNZIE
GALVANIZATION
GALVANIZING
GASTEROZOOID
GASTROZOOID
GAZETTEERAGE
GAZINGSTOCK
GELATINIZED
GELATINIZER
GELATINIZING
GENEALOGIZE
GENEALOGIZER
GENERALIZABLE
GENERALIZED
GENERALIZER
GEOGRAPHIZE
GEOGRAPHIZED
GEOLOGIZING
GEOMETRICIZE
GEOMETRIZED
GEOMETRIZING
GLAMORIZING
GLUCOSAZONE
GLUTTONIZED
GLUTTONIZING
GLYCERINIZE
GLYCYRRHIZIN
GORMANDIZER
GRAMMATICIZE
GRANULITIZE
GRAPHITIZED
GUTTURALIZE
GUTTURALIZING
GYNECOMAZIA
GYROHORIZON
HAPHAZARDLY
HAPHAZARDNESS
HARLEQUINIZE
HARMONIZING
HARZBURGITE
HAZARDOUSLY
HAZARDOUSNESS
HETEROZYGOTE
HETEROZYGOUS
HIERARCHIZE
HOMOGENIZER
HOPPERDOZER
HORIZOMETER
HORIZONTALITY
HORIZONTALIZE
HORIZONTALLY
HORIZONTICAL
HOSPITALIZE
HURRICANIZE
HYBRIDIZABLE
HYBRIDIZATION
HYDROBENZOIN
HYDROGENIZE
HYDROLYZATE
HYDRORHIZAL
HYDROZINCITE
HYPERBOLIZE
HYPERBOLIZED
HYPOSTATIZE
ICHTHYIZATION
IDEALIZATION
IDOLATRIZED
IDOLATRIZER
IDOLATRIZING
IDOLIZATION
ILLEGALIZED
ILLEGALIZING
IMBASTARDIZE
IMMATERIALIZE
IMMETHODIZE
IMMOBILIZED
IMMOBILIZING
IMMORTALIZE
IMMORTALIZED
IMMORTALIZER
IMMORTALIZING
IMPACTIONIZE
IMPATRONIZE
IMPERIALIZE
IMPERIALIZED
IMPERIALIZING
IMPERSONALIZE
IMPROBABILIZE
INDIVIDUALIZE
INDOCTRINIZE
INFORMALIZE
INOXIDIZING
INTELLIGIZE
INTERMEZZOS
INTERNALIZE
INTHRONIZATE
IODOBENZENE
IRIDIZATION
IRREALIZABLE
IRREGULARIZE
ISOCHRONIZE
ISOCHRONIZED
ISOCHRONIZING
ITALICIZING
ITEMIZATION
JARGONIZING
JAROVIZATION
JASPERIZING
JATEORHIZIN
JATEORHIZINE
JEOPARDIZED
JEOPARDIZING
JOURNALIZED
JOURNALIZER
JOURNALIZING
JOVIALIZING
JUBILIZATION
JUDICIALIZE
KATZENJAMMER
KETONIZATION
KJELDAHLIZE
KYANIZATION
LABIALIZING
LABILIZATION
LAICIZATION
LALAPALOOZA
LALLAPALOOZA
LAPAROTOMIZE
LATERALIZED
LATERALIZING
LATERIZATION
LEGALIZATION
LEGITIMATIZE
LEGITIMATIZED
LEGITIMIZED
LEGITIMIZING
LETHARGIZED
LETHARGIZING
LIBERALIZED
LIBERALIZER
LIBERALIZING
LICHENIZATION
LIEDERKRANZ
LINEARIZATION
LIONIZATION
LIQUIDIZING
LITERALIZED
LITERALIZER
LITERALIZING
LITHOTOMIZE
LOCALIZABLE
LOCALIZATION
LOGOMACHIZE
LORENZENITE
MACADAMIZED
MACADAMIZER
MACADAMIZING
MAGAZINABLE
MAGNETIZABLE
MAGNETIZATION
MAGNETIZING
MALLEABLEIZE
MALLEABLEIZED
MALLEABLIZE
MAMMONIZATION
MANORIALIZE
MARBLEIZING
MARGINALIZE
MARMARIZING
MARSUPIALIZE
MARTYRIZING
MATERIALIZE
MATERIALIZED
MATERIALIZER
MATERIALIZING
MATERNALIZE
MATHEMATIZE
MATRONIZING
MAXIMIZATION
MECHANALIZE
MECHANIZATION
MEDIATIZING
MEGAZOOSPORE
MEIZOSEISMAL
MEIZOSEISMIC
MELANCHOLIZE
MELODRAMATIZE
MEMORANDIZE
MEMORIALIZE
MEMORIALIZED
MEMORIALIZER
MEMORIALIZING
MEMORIZATION
MERCERIZING
MERCHANDIZE
MERCURIALIZE
MERCURIZING
MERMITHIZED
MERORGANIZE
MESMERIZATION
MESMERIZING
METABOLIZED
METABOLIZING
METALIZATION
METALLIZATION
METAMERIZED
METAMORPHIZE
METAPHONIZE
METASTASIZE
METASTASIZED
METHODIZING
MEZZOTINTED
MEZZOTINTER
MEZZOTINTING
MICASIZATION
MICROSCOPIZE
MICROZOARIA
MICROZOARIAN
MICROZYMIAN
MIGNIARDIZE
MILITARIZED
MILITARIZING
MINERALIZED
MINERALIZER
MINERALIZING
MINERALOGIZE
MINIATURIZE
MINIATURIZED
MINIMIZATION
MISCOGNIZANT
MISEMPHASIZE
MISSIONARIZE
MISSIONIZER
MITHRIDATIZE
MIZZENTOPMAN
MIZZENTOPMEN
MNEMONIZING
MOBILIZATION
MODERNIZATION
MODERNIZING
MONARCHIZED
MONARCHIZER
MONARCHIZING
MONETIZATION
MONOCHORDIZE
MONOLOGIZED
MONOLOGIZING
MONOPOLIZED
MONOPOLIZER
MONOPOLIZING
MONOZYGOTIC
MONZODIORITE
MONZOGABBRO
MORALIZATION
MORTALIZING
MOTORIZATION
MUNICIPALIZE
MUNICIPALIZED
MUSCOVITIZE
MUSCOVITIZED
MUSCULARIZE
MUTUALIZING
MUZZLELOADER
MUZZLELOADING
MYCORRHIZAL
MYCORRHIZIC
MYOSYNIZESIS
MYTHICIZING
MYTHOLOGIZE
MYTHOLOGIZED
MYTHOLOGIZER
MYTHOLOGIZING
MYTHOPOETIZE
MYZOSTOMIDAN
MYZOSTOMOUS
NAPHTHALIZE
NARCOTIZING
NASALIZATION
NATIONALIZE
NATIONALIZED
NATIONALIZER
NATIONALIZING
NATURALIZED
NATURALIZER
NATURALIZING
NAZIFICATION
NEBULIZATION
NEMATOZOOID
NEOLOGIZING
NEOPAGANIZE
NESSLERIZED
NEUROLOGIZE
NEUROTOMIZE
NEUTRALIZED
NEUTRALIZER
NEUTRALIZING
NEWSMAGAZINE
NIGHTINGALIZE
NITRIDIZATION
NITROBENZENE
NITROGENIZE
NITROGENIZED
NITROGENIZING
NIVELLIZATION
NODULIZING
NONENTITIZE
NONPARTIZAN
NORMALIZATION
NORMALIZING
NOTARIZATION
NOVELIZATION
NUPTIALIZE
OBJECTIVIZE
OBJECTIVIZED
OBJECTIVIZING
OBJECTIZATION
OBJECTIZING
OBLIVIONIZE
ODYLIZATION
OFFICIALIZE
OLIGARCHIZE
OLIGORHIZOUS
OPSONIZATION
OPTIMIZATION
OPTIMIZING
OPTIONALIZE
ORGANIZABLE
ORGANIZATION
ORGANIZATORY
ORGANZINING
ORIENTALIZE
ORIENTALIZED
ORIENTALIZING
ORYZIVOROUS
OSMAZOMATIC
OSMAZOMATOUS
OSTRACIZATION
OSTRACIZING
OUTTYRANNIZE
OVALIZATION
OVARIOTOMIZE
OVERGLAZING
OVERPRIZING
OVERZEALOUS
OXYGENIZABLE
OXYGENIZING
OZONIFEROUS
OZONIZATION
OZONOSCOPIC
OZONOSPHERE
OZONOSPHERIC
PAGANIZATION

PALATIZATION
PALEOZOOLOGY
PALLADIUMIZE
PALLETIZING
PAMPHLETIZE
PANCREATIZE
PANEGYRICIZE
PANEGYRIZED
PANEGYRIZER
PANEGYRIZING
PANSEXUALIZE
PANTHEONIZE
PAPALIZATION
PARABOLIZED
PARABOLIZER
PARABOLIZING
PARAENESIZE
PARALYZATION
PARCHMENTIZE
PARENTHESIZE
PASTEURIZED
PASTEURIZER
PASTEURIZING
PASTORALIZE
PATERNALIZE
PATRIZATION
PATRONIZING
PAUPERIZING
PECTIZATION
PECULIARIZE
PECULIARIZED
PELORIZATION
PEMMICANIZE
PENALIZATION
PENTAMETRIZE
PEPTIZATION
PEPTONIZING
PERFECTIVIZE
PERMORALIZE
PERSONALIZE
PERSONALIZED
PETROLIZING
PEZIZACEOUS
PEZIZAEFORM
PHAGOCYTIZE
PHANEROZOIC
PHANTOMIZER
PHENMIAZINE
PHENOXAZINE
PHILIPPICIZE
PHILIPPIZER
PHILOLOGIZE
PHILOSOPHIZE
PHILOZOONIST
PHLEBOTOMIZE
PHLYZACIOUS
PHONETICIZE
PHONETIZATION
PHOSPHATIZE
PHOSPHATIZED
PHOSPHORIZE
PHRENOLOGIZE
PHYLACTERIZE
PHYLLOZOOID
PHYSIOLOGIZE
PHYTOBEZOAR
PICRORHIZIN
PIEZOMETRIC
PLAGIARIZED
PLAGIARIZER
PLAGIARIZING
PLASTICIZED
PLASTICIZER
PLASTICIZING
PLATINIZING
PLEBEIANIZE
PLEBEIANIZED
PLURALIZING
PNEUMATIZED
POETIZATION
POLARIZABLE
POLARIZATION
POLITICALIZE
POLITICIZED
POLITICIZER
POLITICIZING
POLITZERIZE
POLYCHROMIZE
POLYZOARIAL
POLYZOARIUM
POPULARIZED
POPULARIZER
POPULARIZING
PORCELAINIZE
PORCELLANIZE
POSTURIZING
POTENTIALIZE
POZZUOLANIC
PRACTICALIZE
PRACTICALIZED
PRAGMATIZER
PREACHERIZE
PRESERVATIZE
PRESSURIZED
PRESSURIZING
PRIZEFIGHTER
PRIZEHOLDER
PROBABILIZE
PROBLEMATIZE
PRODIGALIZE
PROLETARIZE
PROLOGUIZER
PROPAGANDIZE
PROSELYTIZE
PROSELYTIZED
PROSELYTIZER
PROTOCITIZEN
PROTOCOLIZE
PROTOXIDIZE
PROTOXIDIZED
PROTOZOEAN
PROTOZOIASIS
PROTOZOONAL
PSYCHIATRIZE
PSYCHOLOGIZE
PUBLICIZING
PULVERIZATE
PULVERIZATOR
PULVERIZING
PUZZLEATION
PUZZLEDNESS
PUZZLEHEADED
PUZZLEPATED
PUZZLINGNESS
PYRRODIAZOLE
QUANTIZATION
QUIZZICALITY
QUIZZICALLY
QUIZZACIOUS
QUIZZATORIAL
RACEMIZATION
RACIALIZATION
RADIALIZATION
RADIUMIZATION
RANDOMIZING
RATIONALIZE
RATIONALIZED
RATIONALIZER
RAZORMAKING
RAZZBERRIES
REACTUALIZE
REALISTICIZE
REALIZATION
REBAPTIZATION
RECAPITALIZE
RECAPITALIZED
RECARBONIZE
RECARBONIZER
RECARBURIZE
RECARBURIZER
RECIPROCALIZE
RECOGNIZABLE
RECOGNIZABLY
RECOGNIZANCE
RECOGNIZANT
RECOGNIZING
RECRYSTALLIZE
REFORESTIZE
REGIONALIZE
REGULARIZED
REGULARIZER
REHARMONIZE
RELIGIONIZE
REORGANIZED
REORGANIZER
REORGANIZING
RESTERILIZE
REVITALIZED
REVITALIZER
REVITALIZING
RHAPSODIZED
RHAPSODIZING
RHIZANTHOUS
RHIZOCARPIC
RHIZOCARPOUS
RHIZOCAULUS
RHIZODERMIS
RHIZOGENETIC
RHIZOGENOUS
RHIZOMATOUS
RHIZOMORPHIC
RHIZOPHAGOUS
RHIZOPHILOUS
RHIZOPODIST
RHIZOPODOUS
RHIZOSTOMOUS
RHYTHMICIZE
RHYTHMIZABLE
RINFORZANDO
ROBOTIZATION
ROENTGENIZE
ROMANTICIZE
ROTARIANIZE
ROUTINIZING
ROYALIZATION
RUBBERIZING
RURALIZATION
SACCHARIZED
SACCHARIZING
SACRAMENTIZE
SAILORIZING
SANCTUARIZE
SARCOPHAGIZE
SATIRIZABLE
SCANDALIZED
SCANDALIZING
SCENARIZING
SCEPTICIZED
SCEPTICIZING
SCHILLERIZE
SCHILLERIZED
SCHILLERIZING
SCHISMATIZE
SCHISMATIZED
SCHISMATIZING
SCHIZOCARPIC
SCHIZOCHROAL
SCHIZOCOELE
SCHIZODINIC
SCHIZOGENESIS
SCHIZOGENETIC
SCHIZOGENIC
SCHIZOGENOUS
SCHIZOGNATH
SCHIZOGONIC
SCHIZOIDISM
SCHIZOMYCETE
SCHIZOMYCETES
SCHIZOPELMOUS
SCHIZOPHASIA
SCHIZOPHRENE
SCHIZOPHRENIA
SCHIZOPHYTE
SCHIZOPODAL
SCHIZOPODOUS
SCHIZORHINAL
SCHIZOSPORE
SCHIZOSTELE
SCHIZOSTELIC
SCHIZOSTELY
SCHIZOTHECAL
SCHIZOTHYME
SCHIZOTHYMIA
SCHIZOTHYMIC
SCHIZOTRICHIA
SCLEROTIZED
SCRUTINIZED
SCRUTINIZER
SCRUTINIZING
SECTARIANIZE
SECTARIANIZED
SECTIONALIZE
SECTIONALIZED
SECULARIZED
SECULARIZING
SEMICIVILIZED
SEMPITERNIZE
SENSIBILIZE
SENSITIZATION
SENSITIZING
SENSUALIZED
SENSUALIZING
SEPTICIZATION
SERIALIZATION
SERIALIZING
SERMONIZING
SERPENTINIZE
SHERARDIZED
SHERARDIZING
SHERBETZIDE
SIDEREALIZE
SIGNALIZING
SIMULACRIZE
SINGULARIZE
SINGULARIZED
SINGULARIZING
SIPHONOZOOID
SIZABLENESS
SKELETONIZE
SKELETONIZED
SKELETONIZER
SKELETONIZING
SKEPTICIZED
SKEPTICIZING
SLENDERIZED
SLENDERIZING
SLUGGARDIZE
SOCIALIZATION
SOCIALIZING
SOLARIZATION
SOLEMNIZATION
SOLEMNIZING
SOLIDARIZED
SOLIDARIZING
SOLILOQUIZE
SOLILOQUIZED
SOLILOQUIZER
SOLILOQUIZING
SOLITUDINIZE
SOLITUDINIZED
SOLMIZATION
SOLVOLYZING
SOMNAMBULIZE
SOPHRONIZED
SOPHRONIZING
SOUTHERNIZE
SOVEREIGNIZE
SOVIETIZATION
SOVIETIZING
SPECIALIZED
SPECIALIZER
SPECIALIZING
SPECIFICIZE
SPECIMENIZE
SPECIMENIZED
SPERMATOZOA
SPERMATOZOAL
SPERMATOZOAN
SPERMATOZOIC
SPERMATOZOID
SPERMATOZOON
SPHEROIDIZE
SPHERULITIZE
SPIRALIZATION
SPIRITUALIZE
SPIRITUALIZED
SPIRITUALIZER
SPITZENBERG
SPITZENBURG
SPLENIZATION
SPONDYLIZEMA
SQUEEZINGLY
STABILIZATION
STABILIZATOR
STABILIZING
STALLIONIZE
STALWARTIZE
STANDARDIZE
STANDARDIZED
STANDARDIZER
STANDARDIZING
STANZAICALLY
STATISTICIZE
STERILIZATION
STERILIZING
STIGMATIZED
STIGMATIZER
STIGMATIZING
STRUCTURALIZE
STRYCHNINIZE
STYLIZATION
SUBERIZATION
SUBSIDIZATION
SUBSIDIZING
SUBSTANTIVIZE
SUBSTANTIZE
SUBTILIZATION
SUBTILIZING
SUBURBANIZE
SUBVITALIZED
SULCALIZATION
SULFADIAZINE
SULFATIZING
SULFOBENZIDE
SULFOBENZOIC
SULFURIZING
SULPHATIZED
SULPHATIZING
SULPHAZOTIZE
SULPHOBENZID
SULPHURIZED
SULPHURIZING
SUMMARIZATION
SUMMARIZING
SYCOPHANTIZE

SYLLABIZING
SYLLOGIZING
SYMBOLIZATION
SYMBOLIZING
SYMMETRIZED
SYMMETRIZING
SYMPATHIZED
SYMPATHIZER
SYMPATHIZING
SYMPHONIZED
SYMPHONIZING
SYMPTOMATIZE
SYNCHRONIZE
SYNCHRONIZED
SYNCHRONIZER
SYNCHRONIZING
SYNCRETIZED
SYNCRETIZING
SYNDICALIZE
SYNONYMIZED
SYNONYMIZING
SYNTHESIZED
SYNTHESIZER
SYNTHESIZING
SYNTHETIZER
SYNTONIZING
SYPHILIZING
SYSTEMATIZE
SYSTEMATIZED
SYSTEMATIZER
SYSTEMATIZING
SYSTEMIZATION
SYSTEMIZING
SZAIBELYITE
TABULARIZED
TABULARIZING
TANTALIZING
TARANTARIZE
TARTARIZING
TARTRAZINIC
TAUTOLOGIZE
TAUTOLOGIZED
TAUTOLOGIZER
TAXIDERMIZE
TCHERVONETZ
TECHNICALIZE
TEETOTUMIZE
TELEPATHIZE
TELFORDIZED
TELFORDIZING
TELLURIZING
TEMPORALIZE
TEMPORIZING
TENDERIZING
TENEMENTIZE
TERRORIZING
TETANIZATION
TETRAKISAZO
TETRAZOLIUM
TETRAZOTIZE
THEATRICIZE
THEOLOGIZED
THEOLOGIZER
THEOLOGIZING
THEOMORPHIZE
THEORIZATION
THERMOLYZED
THERMOLYZING
THIADIAZOLE
TOBACCONIZE
TOTALIZATION
TOTALIZATOR
TOTEMIZATION
TOURMALINIZE
TRAILBLAZER
TRAILBLAZING
TRANQUILIZE
TRANQUILIZER
TRANQUILIZING
TRANQUILLIZE
TRANQUILLIZED
TRAPEZIFORM
TRAPEZOIDAL
TRICHINIZED
TRICHINIZING
TRICHOTOMIZE
TRILLIONIZE
TROPHOZOITE
TROPHOZOOID
TROPICALIZE
TROPICALIZED
TROPICALIZING
TROPOLOGIZE
TROPOLOGIZED
TROPOLOGIZING
TRULLIZATION
TUBERCULIZE
TUBERIZATION
TUBULIZATION
TUTORIZATION
TYPHIZATION
TYRANNIZING
ULTRAZEALOUS
UNAUTHORIZE
UNAUTHORIZED
UNBRUTALIZE
UNCANONIZED
UNCANONIZING
UNCIVILIZED
UNFEUDALIZE
UNIFORMALIZE
UNIFORMALIZED
UNIONIZATION
UNIVERSALIZED
UNIVERSITIZE
UNLITURGIZE
UNMECHANIZE
UNMODERNIZE
UNMORALIZED
UNMORALIZING
UNMORTALIZE
UNNATURALIZE
UNORGANIZED
UNPATRONIZED
UNPOPULARIZE
UNRECOGNIZED
UNSECULARIZE
UNSOLEMNIZE
UNSTERILIZED
UNVERBALIZED
UNVULGARIZE
URALITIZING
URBANIZATION
UTILIZATION
VACCINIZATION
VAGABONDIZE
VAGABONDIZED
VAGABONDIZER
VAGABONDIZING
VALORIZATION
VAPORIZATION
VAPOURIZING
VASCULARIZE
VASCULARIZED
VASCULARIZING
VASECTOMIZE
VASSALIZING
VEGETABLIZE
VENALIZATION
VERATRINIZE
VERATRINIZED
VERATRINIZING
VERATRIZING
VERBALIZING
VERMILIONIZE
VICTIMIZABLE
VICTIMIZATION
VICTIMIZING
VISUALIZING
VITALIZATION
VITALIZINGLY
VITRIOLIZED
VITRIOLIZING
VOCALIZATION
VOLATILIZED
VOLATILIZER
VOLATILIZING
VOLCANIZING
VULCANIZATE
VULCANIZATION
VULCANIZING
VULGARIZATION
VULGARIZING
WESTERNIZED
WESTERNIZING
WINTERIZING
WIZENEDNESS
WOODCOCKIZE
ZANTHOXYLUM
ZAPHRENTOID
ZEALOUSNESS
ZENOCENTRIC
ZENOGRAPHIC
ZEOLITIZING
ZIGZAGGEDLY
ZIMENTWATER
ZINCIFEROUS
ZINCOGRAPHER
ZINCOGRAPHIC
ZINCOGRAPHY
ZINGIBERENE
ZINNWALDITE
ZOANTHODEME
ZOANTHODEMIC
ZODIOPHILOUS
ZOIDOGAMOUS
ZOISITIZATION
ZOMOTHERAPY
ZONAESTHESIA
ZONESTHESIA
ZONOCHLORITE
ZONOCILIATE
ZONOLIMNETIC
ZONOSKELETON
ZOOCECIDIUM
ZOOCULTURAL
ZOODENDRIUM
ZOODYNAMICS
ZOOERYTHRIN
ZOOGEOGRAPHY
ZOOGONIDIUM
ZOOGRAFTING
ZOOLOGIZING
ZOOMAGNETIC
ZOOMAGNETISM
ZOOMORPHISM
ZOOMORPHIZE
ZOONOSOLOGY
ZOOPANTHEON
ZOOPARASITE
ZOOPATHOLOGY
ZOOPHARMACY
ZOOPHYSICAL
ZOOPHYTICAL
ZOOPHYTOLOGY
ZOOPLANKTON
ZOOPRAXISCOPE
ZOOSPORANGE
ZOOTHEISTIC
ZOOXANTHELLA
ZOSTERIFORM
ZYGAPOPHYSIS
ZYGODACTYLE
ZYGODACTYLIC
ZYGOLABIALIS
ZYGOMATICUM
ZYGOMATICUS
ZYGOMORPHIC
ZYGOMORPHOUS
ZYGOMYCETES
ZYGOMYCETOUS
ZYGOPHYCEOUS
ZYGOPLEURAL
ZYGOPTERAN
ZYGOPTERID
ZYGOPTEROUS
ZYGOSPHENAL
ZYMOGENESIS
ZYMOLOGICAL
ZYMOPLASTIC
ZYMOSIMETER
ZYMOSTHENIC
ZYMOTECHNIC
ZYMOTECHNICS
ZYMOTICALLY

POSITIONAL ORDER LIST OF WORDS OVER 10 LETTERS

ZANTHOXYLUM
ZAPHRENTOID
ZEALOUSNESS
ZENOCENTRIC
ZENOGRAPHIC
ZEOLITIZING
ZIGZAGGEDLY
ZIMENTWATER
ZINCIFEROUS
ZINCOGRAPHER
ZINCOGRAPHIC
ZINCOGRAPHY
ZINGIBERENE
ZINNWALDITE
ZOANTHODEME
ZOANTHODEMIC
ZODIOPHILOUS
ZOIDOGAMOUS
ZOISITIZATION
ZOMOTHERAPY
ZONAESTHESIA
ZONESTHESIA
ZONOCHLORITE
ZONOCILIATE
ZONOLIMNETIC
ZONOSKELETON
ZOOCECIDIUM
ZOOCULTURAL
ZOODENDRIUM
ZOODYNAMICS
ZOOERYTHRIN
ZOOGEOGRAPHY
ZOOGONIDIUM
ZOOGRAFTING
ZOOLOGIZING
ZOOMAGNETIC
ZOOMAGNETISM
ZOOMORPHISM
ZOOMORPHIZE
ZOONOSOLOGY
ZOOPANTHEON
ZOOPARASITE
ZOOPATHOLOGY
ZOOPHARMACY
ZOOPHYSICAL
ZOOPHYTICAL
ZOOPHYTOLOGY
ZOOPLANKTON
ZOOPRAXISCOPE
ZOOSPORANGE
ZOOTHEISTIC
ZOOXANTHELLA
ZOSTERIFORM
ZYGAPOPHYSIS
ZYGODACTYLE
ZYGODACTYLIC
ZYGOLABIALIS
ZYGOMATICUM
ZYGOMATICUS
ZYGOMORPHIC
ZYGOMORPHOUS
ZYGOMYCETES
ZYGOMYCETOUS
ZYGOPHYCEOUS
ZYGOPLEURAL
ZYGOPTERAN
ZYGOPTERID
ZYGOPTEROUS
ZYGOSPHENAL
ZYMOGENESIS
ZYMOLOGICAL
ZYMOPLASTIC
ZYMOSIMETER
ZYMOSTHENIC
ZYMOTECHNIC
ZYMOTECHNICS
ZYMOTICALLY

AZADIRACHTA
AZEOTROPISM
AZIMETHYLENE
AZIMUTHALLY
AZOCOCHINEAL
AZOCORALLINE
AZODIPHENYL
AZOERYTHRIN
AZOFICATION
AZOOSPERMIA
AZOPARAFFIN
AZOPHENETOLE
AZOPHENYLENE
AZOPHOSPHIN
AZOPHOSPHORE
AZOSULPHINE
AZOSULPHONIC
AZOTETRAZOLE
AZOTHIONIUM
AZOTOBACTER
AZOTORRHOEA
AZYGOMATOUS

OZONIFEROUS
OZONIZATION
OZONOSCOPIC
OZONOSPHERE
OZONOSPHERIC
SZAIBELYITE

BIZARRENESS
BIZYGOMATIC
BUZZERPHONE
DEZINCATION
DEZINCIFIED
DEZINCIFYING
ECZEMATOSIS
ENZYMICALLY
ENZYMOLYSIS
ENZYMOLYTIC
GAZETTEERAGE
GAZINGSTOCK
HAZARDOUSLY
HAZARDOUSNESS
MEZZOTINTED
MEZZOTINTER
MEZZOTINTING
MIZZENTOPMAN
MIZZENTOPMEN
MUZZLELOADER
MUZZLELOADING
MYZOSTOMIDAN
MYZOSTOMOUS
NAZIFICATION
PEZIZACEOUS
PEZIZAEFORM
POZZUOLANIC
PUZZLEATION
PUZZLEDNESS
PUZZLEHEADED
PUZZLEPATED
PUZZLINGNESS
RAZORMAKING
RAZZBERRIES
SIZABLENESS
WIZENEDNESS

BENZALDEHYDE
BENZALDOXIME
BENZINDULINE
BENZOHYDROL
BENZOINATED
BENZONITRILE
BENZONITROL
BENZOPHENONE
BENZOYLATION
BENZYLAMINE
BERZELIANITE
BLIZZARDOUS
BRAZENFACED
BUZZERPHONE
COAZERVATION
DIAZENTITHAL
DIAZOBENZENE
DIAZOMETHANE
DIAZOTIZING
DIEZEUGMENON
EPIZOOTIOLOGY
HARZBURGITE
KATZENJAMMER
MEIZOSEISMAL
MEIZOSEISMIC
MEZZOTINTED
MEZZOTINTER
MEZZOTINTING
MIZZENTOPMAN
MIZZENTOPMEN
MONZODIORITE
MONZOGABBRO
MUZZLELOADER

MUZZLELOADING
ORYZIVOROUS
PIEZOMETRIC
POZZUOLANIC
PRIZEFIGHTER
PRIZEHOLDER
PUZZLEATION
PUZZLEDNESS
PUZZLEHEADED
PUZZLEPATED
PUZZLINGNESS
QUIZZACIOUS
QUIZZATORIAL
QUIZZICALITY
QUIZZICALLY
RAZZBERRIES
RHIZANTHOUS
RHIZOCARPIC
RHIZOCARPOUS
RHIZOCAULUS
RHIZODERMIS
RHIZOGENETIC
RHIZOGENOUS
RHIZOMATOUS
RHIZOMORPHIC
RHIZOPHAGOUS
RHIZOPHILOUS
RHIZOPODIST
RHIZOPODOUS
RHIZOSTOMOUS
ZIGZAGGEDLY

BEDAZZLINGLY
BEDIZENMENT
BLIZZARDOUS
BRONZESMITH
CACOZEALOUS
CENOZOOLOGY
CITIZENIZED
CITIZENIZING
CITIZENRIES
CITIZENSHIP
DENAZIFYING
DENIZENATION
EMBEZZLEMENT
ENTOZOOLOGY
HORIZOMETER
HORIZONTALITY
HORIZONTALIZE
HORIZONTALLY
HORIZONTICAL
MAGAZINABLE
MEGAZOOSPORE
MONOZYGOTIC
OSMAZOMATIC
OSMAZOMATOUS
OVERZEALOUS
PEZIZACEOUS
PEZIZAEFORM
PHLYZACIOUS
POLYZOARIAL
POLYZOARIUM
QUIZZACIOUS
QUIZZATORIAL
QUIZZICALITY
QUIZZICALLY
SCHIZOCARPIC
SCHIZOCHROAL
SCHIZOCOELE
SCHIZODINIC
SCHIZOGENESIS
SCHIZOGENETIC
SCHIZOGENIC
SCHIZOGENOUS
SCHIZOGNATH
SCHIZOGONIC
SCHIZOIDISM

SCHIZOMYCETE
SCHIZOMYCETES
SCHIZOPELMOUS
SCHIZOPHASIA
SCHIZOPHRENE
SCHIZOPHRENIA
SCHIZOPHYTE
SCHIZOPODAL
SCHIZOPODOUS
SCHIZORHINAL
SCHIZOSPORE
SCHIZOSTELE
SCHIZOSTELIC
SCHIZOSTELY
SCHIZOTHECAL
SCHIZOTHYME
SCHIZOTHYMIA
SCHIZOTHYMIC
SCHIZOTRICHIA
SPITZENBERG
SPITZENBURG
STANZAICALLY

ADENIZATION
ANALYZATION
APPRIZEMENT
ATOMIZATION
BAPTIZEMENT
BEDAZZLINGLY
BROMIZATION
CHALAZOGAMIC
CHALAZOGAMY
CHALAZOIDITE
CHORIZATION
CHORIZONTES
CHORIZONTIC
CHORIZONTIST
CYCLIZATION
DEBENZOLIZE
DIALYZATION
DOCKIZATION
DUALIZATION
EMBEZZLEMENT
ENOLIZATION
ETHNOZOOLOGY
HAPHAZARDLY
HAPHAZARDNESS
HYDROZINCITE
IDOLIZATION
IRIDIZATION
ITEMIZATION
KYANIZATION
LAICIZATION
LIONIZATION
LORENZENITE
MICROZOARIA
MICROZOARIAN
MICROZYMIAN
ODYLIZATION
ORGANZINING
OVALIZATION
OZONIZATION
PALEOZOOLOGY
PATRIZATION
PECTIZATION
PEPTIZATION
PHILOZOONIST
POETIZATION
PROTOZOEAN
PROTOZOIASIS
PROTOZOONAL
QUINAZOLINE
QUINAZOLINE
REALIZATION
SOLMIZATION
SQUEEZINGLY
STYLIZATION

TETRAZOLIUM
TETRAZOTIZE
TRAPEZIFORM
TRAPEZOIDAL
TYPHIZATION
ULTRAZEALOUS
UTILIZATION

ALBITIZATION
ALDOLIZATION
ALKALIZABLE
ALKALIZATION
AMMONIZATION
AMORTIZABLE
AMORTIZATION
AMORTIZEMENT
APPETIZINGLY
ARBORIZATION
ARSENIZATION
ATMOLYZATION
BAMBOOZLEMENT
BAMBOOZLING
BILHARZIASIS
BILHARZIOSIS
CALABAZILLA
CANALIZATION
CANONIZATION
CARBOAZOTINE
CATALYZATOR
CIVILIZABLE
CIVILIZATION
CIVILIZATORY
COLONIZATION
CREOLIZATION
CRYPTOZONATE
CRYPTOZYGOUS
CURARIZATION
CUTINIZATION
DAMENIZATION
DEMUTIZATION
DERATIZATION
DIMERIZATION
DIPHYOZOOID
DISSEIZORESS
DIVINIZATION
DYNAMIZATION
EQUALIZATION
ERGOTIZATION
ESTERIZATION
ETERNIZATION
ETHERIZATION
EULOGIZATION
EXORCIZATION
EXORCIZEMENT
FARADIZATION
FEMINIZATION
FLUIDIZATION
FOCALIZATION
GASTROZOOID
HETEROZYGOTE
HETEROZYGOUS
IDEALIZATION
JAROVIZATION
JUBILIZATION
KETONIZATION
LABILIZATION
LATERIZATION
LEGALIZATION
LOCALIZABLE
LOCALIZATION
MAXIMIZATION
MEMORIZATION
METALIZATION
MICASIZATION
MINIMIZATION
MOBILIZATION
MONETIZATION

MORALIZATION
MOTORIZATION
NASALIZATION
NEBULIZATION
NEMATOZOOID
NODULIZING
NOTARIZATION
NOVELIZATION
OPSONIZATION
OPTIMIZATION
OPTIMIZING
ORGANIZABLE
ORGANIZATION
ORGANIZATORY
PAGANIZATION
PALATIZATION
PAPALIZATION
PARALYZATION
PELORIZATION
PENALIZATION
PHYLLOZOOID
POLARIZABLE
POLARIZATION
QUANTIZATION
QUANTIZING
QUANTIZING
RACEMIZATION
RINFORZANDO
ROBOTIZATION
ROYALIZATION
RURALIZATION
SATIRIZABLE
SOLARIZATION
SPLENIZATION
SUBERIZATION
TARTRAZINIC
TETANIZATION
THEORIZATION
TOTALIZATION
TOTALIZATOR
TOTEMIZATION
TROPHOZOITE
TROPHOZOOID
TRULLIZATION
TUBERIZATION
TUBULIZATION
TUTORIZATION
UNIONIZATION
URBANIZATION
VALORIZATION
VAPORIZATION
VENALIZATION
VITALIZATION
VITALIZINGLY
VOCALIZATION

ACADEMIZING
ACETONIZATION
ACETYLIZABLE
ACETYLIZATION
ACTIONIZING
ACTUALIZATION
ACTUALIZING
ADVERTIZEMENT
ADVERTIZING
ALCHEMIZING
ALGEBRIZATION
ALUMINIZING
ANALOGIZING
ANATOMIZING
ANGLICIZING
ANIMALIZATION
ANIMALIZING
ANTHEROZOID
ANTHEROZOOID
APOLOGIZING
ARCTICIZING

AROMATIZING
ASCIDIOZOOID
AUTHORIZATION
AUTHORIZING
BACTERIZING
BALKANIZING
BARBARIZING
BERGINIZATION
BISTRIAZOLE
BRUTALIZING
BURTONIZATION
CARBOLIZING
CARBONIZING
CARBURIZING
CARNALIZING
CATECHIZATION
CATECHIZING
CATHARIZING
CAUTERIZATION
CAUTERIZING
CHITINIZATION
CICATRIZANT
CICATRIZATE
CICATRIZING
COCAINIZING
COMMUNIZATION
COMMUNIZING
COPPERIZATION
CRITICIZABLE
CRITICIZING
DACTYLOZOOID
DEFERRIZING
DEODORIZING
DEOXIDIZING
DERMATOZOON
DESCLOIZITE
DESTINEZITE
DEUTEROZOOID
DIABOLIZING
DIALOGIZING
DIAZOTIZING
DOGMATIZING
DRAMATIZATION
DRAMATIZING
DUCTILIZING
ECONOMIZATION
ECONOMIZING
ELECTRIZING
EMBLEMIZING
EMPATHIZING
EMPHASIZING
EPIDOTIZATION
EPILOGIZING
EPITOMIZATION
EPITOMIZING
ERYTHROZYME
EUPHEMIZING
EUPHONIZING
EXTERNIZATION
FACTORIZATION
FANTASIZING
FERTILIZABLE
FERTILIZATION
FERTILIZING
FEUDALIZATION
FEUDALIZING
FISCALIZATION
FISCALIZING
FORMALIZATION
FORMALIZING
FORMULIZATION
FORMULIZING
FOSSILIZATION
FOSSILIZING
FRIVOLIZING
GALVANIZATION
GALVANIZING
GASTEROZOOID
GEOLOGIZING
GLAMORIZING
GLUCOSAZONE
HARMONIZING
HYBRIDIZABLE
HYBRIDIZATION
HYDROLYZATE
ICHTHYIZATION
INOXIDIZING
INTERMEZZOS
IODOBENZENE
IRREALIZABLE
ITALICIZING
JARGONIZING
JASPERIZING
JOVIALIZING
LABIALIZING
LICHENIZATION
LINEARIZATION
LIQUIDIZING
MAGNETIZABLE
MAGNETIZATION
MAGNETIZING
MAMMONIZATION
MARBLEIZING
MARMARIZING
MARTYRIZING
MATRONIZING
MECHANIZATION
MEDIATIZING
MERCERIZING
MERCURIZING
MESMERIZATION
MESMERIZING
METALLIZATION
METHODIZING
MNEMONIZING
MODERNIZATION
MODERNIZING
MORTALIZING
MUTUALIZING
MYOSYNIZESIS
MYTHICIZING
NARCOTIZING
NEOLOGIZING
NITRIDIZATION
NIVELLIZATION
NORMALIZATION
NORMALIZING
OBJECTIZATION
OBJECTIZING
OSTRACIZATION
OSTRACIZING
OVERGLAZING
OVERPRIZING
OXYGENIZABLE
OXYGENIZING
PALLETIZING
PATRONIZING
PAUPERIZING
PEPTONIZING
PETROLIZING
PHANEROZOIC
PHENMIAZINE
PHENOXAZINE
PHONETIZATION
PHYTOBEZOAR
PLATINIZING
PLURALIZING
POSTURIZING
PUBLICIZING
PULVERIZATE
PULVERIZATOR
PULVERIZING
RACIALIZATION
RADIALIZATION
RADIUMIZATION
RANDOMIZING
REBAPTIZATION
RECOGNIZABLE
RECOGNIZABLY
RECOGNIZANCE
RECOGNIZANT
RECOGNIZING
RHYTHMIZABLE
ROUTINIZING
RUBBERIZING
SAILORIZING
SCENARIZING
SENSITIZATION
SENSITIZING
SEPTICIZATION
SERIALIZATION
SERIALIZING
SERMONIZING
SHERBETZIDE
SIGNALIZING
SIPHONOZOOID
SOCIALIZATION
SOCIALIZING
SOLEMNIZATION
SOLEMNIZING
SOLVOLYZING
SOVIETIZATION
SOVIETIZING
SPIRALIZATION
STABILIZATION
STABILIZATOR
STABILIZING
STERILIZATION
STERILIZING
SUBSIDIZATION
SUBSIDIZING
SUBTILIZATION
SUBTILIZING
SULCALIZATION
SULFATIZING
SULFURIZING
SUMMARIZATION
SUMMARIZING
SYLLABIZING
SYLLOGIZING
SYMBOLIZATION
SYMBOLIZING
SYNTONIZING
SYPHILIZING
SYSTEMIZATION
SYSTEMIZING
TANTALIZING
TARTARIZING
TELLURIZING
TEMPORIZING
TENDERIZING
TERRORIZING
THIADIAZOLE
TYRANNIZING
URALITIZING
VACCINIZATION
VAPOURIZING
VASSALIZING
VERATRIZING
VERBALIZING
VICTIMIZABLE
VICTIMIZATION
VICTIMIZING
VISUALIZING
VOLCANIZING
VULCANIZATE
VULCANIZATION
VULCANIZING
VULGARIZATION
VULGARIZING
WINTERIZING
ZEOLITIZING
ZOISITIZATION
ZOOLOGIZING

ACETOBENZOIC
AGGUTINIZE
AGGRANDIZED
AGGRANDIZER
AGGRANDIZING
ALBUMENIZED
ALBUMENIZER
ALBUMENIZING
ALBUMINIZED
ALBUMINIZING
ALCOHOLIZED
ALCOHOLIZING
ALGEBRAIZED
ALKALINIZED
ALKALINIZING
ALLEGORIZED
ALLEGORIZER
ALLEGORIZING
ANABAPTIZED
ANABAPTIZING
ANTAGONIZED
ANTAGONIZER
ANTAGONIZING
ANTHROPOZOIC
ANTIFREEZING
APOSTATIZED
APOSTATIZING
ASEPTICIZED
ASEPTICIZING
ASEXUALIZED
ASEXUALIZING
AZOTETRAZOLE
BASTARDIZED
BASTARDIZING
BESTIALIZED
BESTIALIZING
BISTETRAZOLE
BITUMINIZED
BIVOCALIZED
BOLSHEVIZED
BOLSHEVIZING
BOWDLERIZED
BOWDLERIZING
BROMOBENZENE
BURGLARIZED
BURGLARIZING
BURNETTIZED
BURNETTIZING
CAPITALIZED
CAPITALIZING
CARAMELIZED
CARAMELIZING
CATABIBAZON
CATABOLIZED
CATABOLIZING
CATEGORIZED
CATEGORIZING
CAUSTICIZED
CAUSTICIZER
CAUSTICIZING
CENTRALIZED
CENTRALIZER
CENTRALIZING
CHANNELIZED
CHANNELIZING
CHLAMYDOZOAN
CHLORALIZED
CHLORALIZING
CHLORIDIZED
CHLORIDIZING
CHLORODIZED
CHLORODIZING
CHROMICIZING
CINCHONIZED
CINCHONIZING
CITIZENIZED
CITIZENIZING
CLASSICIZED
CLASSICIZING
COLLOQUIZED
COLLOQUIZING
CONCERTIZED
CONCERTIZER
CONCERTIZING
CONCRETIZE
CONCRETIZED
CONCRETIZING
DECIMALIZED
DECIMALIZING
DECOLORIZED
DECOLORIZER
DECOLORIZING
DEEPFREEZED
DEEPFREEZING
DEFINITIZED
DEFINITIZING
DEHUMANIZED
DEHUMANIZING
DELIMITIZED
DELIMITIZING
DELOCALIZED
DELOCALIZING
DEMOBILIZED
DEMOBILIZING
DEMONETIZED
DEMONETIZING
DEMORALIZED
DEMORALIZER
DEMORALIZING
DENATURIZER
DEPOLARIZED
DEPOLARIZER
DEPOLARIZING
DEVITALIZED
DEVITALIZING
DEVOCALIZED
DEVOCALIZING
DEXTROSAZONE
DIAMONDIZED
DIAMONDIZING
DIAZOBENZENE
DOCTRINIZED
DOCTRINIZING
DOXOLOGIZED
DOXOLOGIZING
EFFEMINIZED
EFFEMINIZING
ELASTICIZER
ENIGMATIZED
ENIGMATIZING
ENTHRONIZED
ENTHRONIZING
EPISCOPIZED
EPISCOPIZING
EPISTOLIZABLE
EUHEMERIZED
EUHEMERIZING
EVANGELIZED
EVANGELIZER
EVANGELIZING
FANATICIZED
FANATICIZING
FEDERALIZED
FEDERALIZING
FICTIONIZED
FICTIONIZING
FRATERNIZED
FRATERNIZER
FRATERNIZING
FUROMONAZOLE

GABERLUNZIE
GELATINIZED
GELATINIZER
GELATINIZING
GENERALIZABLE
GENERALIZED
GENERALIZER
GEOMETRIZED
GEOMETRIZING
GLUTTONIZED
GLUTTONIZING
GORMANDIZER
GRAPHITIZED
GYNECOMAZIA
GYROHORIZON
HOMOGENIZER
HOPPERDOZER
HYDROBENZOIN
HYDRORHIZAL
IDOLATRIZED
IDOLATRIZER
IDOLATRIZING
ILLEGALIZED
ILLEGALIZING
IMMOBILIZED
IMMOBILIZING
INTERMEZZOS
INTHRONIZATE
JATEORHIZIN
JATEORHIZINE
JEOPARDIZED
JEOPARDIZING
JOURNALIZED
JOURNALIZER
JOURNALIZING
LATERALIZED
LATERALIZING
LEGITIMIZED
LEGITIMIZING
LETHARGIZED
LETHARGIZING
LIBERALIZED
LIBERALIZER
LIBERALIZING
LITERALIZED
LITERALIZER
LITERALIZING
MACADAMIZED
MACADAMIZER
MACADAMIZING
MERMITHIZED
METABOLIZED
METABOLIZING
METAMERIZED
MILITARIZED
MILITARIZING
MINERALIZED
MINERALIZER
MINERALIZING
MISCOGNIZANT
MISSIONIZER
MONARCHIZED
MONARCHIZER
MONARCHIZING
MONOLOGIZED
MONOLOGIZING
MONOPOLIZED
MONOPOLIZER
MONOPOLIZING
MYCORRHIZAL
MYCORRHIZIC
NATURALIZED
NATURALIZER
NATURALIZING
NESSLERIZED
NEUTRALIZED
NEUTRALIZER

NEUTRALIZING
NEWSMAGAZINE
NITROBENZENE
NONPARTIZAN
NUPTIALIZE
OLIGORHIZOUS
PANEGYRIZED
PANEGYRIZER
PANEGYRIZING
PARABOLIZED
PARABOLIZER
PARABOLIZING
PASTEURIZED
PASTEURIZER
PASTEURIZING
PHANTOMIZER
PHILIPPIZER
PICRORHIZIN
PLAGIARIZED
PLAGIARIZER
PLAGIARIZING
PLASTICIZED
PLASTICIZER
PLASTICIZING
PNEUMATIZED
POLITICIZED
POLITICIZER
POLITICIZING
POPULARIZED
POPULARIZER
POPULARIZING
PRAGMATIZER
PRESSURIZED
PRESSURIZING
PROLOGUIZER
PYRRODIAZOLE
REGULARIZED
REGULARIZER
REORGANIZED
REORGANIZER
REORGANIZING
REVITALIZED
REVITALIZER
REVITALIZING
RHAPSODIZED
RHAPSODIZING
SACCHARIZED
SACCHARIZING
SCANDALIZED
SCANDALIZING
SCEPTICIZED
SCEPTICIZING
SCLEROTIZED
SCRUTINIZED
SCRUTINIZER
SCRUTINIZING
SECULARIZED
SECULARIZING
SENSUALIZED
SENSUALIZING
SHERARDIZED
SHERARDIZING
SKEPTICIZED
SKEPTICIZING
SLENDERIZED
SLENDERIZING
SOLIDARIZED
SOLIDARIZING
SOPHRONIZED
SOPHRONIZING
SPECIALIZED
SPECIALIZER
SPECIALIZING
SPERMATOZOA
SPERMATOZOAL
SPERMATOZOAN
SPERMATOZOIC

SPERMATOZOID
SPERMATOZOON
SPONDYLIZEMA
STIGMATIZED
STIGMATIZER
STIGMATIZING
SULFADIAZINE
SULFOBENZIDE
SULFOBENZOIC
SULPHATIZED
SULPHATIZING
SULPHURIZED
SULPHURIZING
SYMMETRIZED
SYMMETRIZING
SYMPATHIZED
SYMPATHIZER
SYMPATHIZING
SYMPHONIZED
SYMPHONIZING
SYNCRETIZED
SYNCRETIZING
SYNONYMIZED
SYNONYMIZING
SYNTHESIZED
SYNTHESIZER
SYNTHESIZING
SYNTHETIZER
TABULARIZED
TABULARIZING
TELFORDIZED
TELFORDIZING
THEOLOGIZED
THEOLOGIZER
THEOLOGIZING
THERMOLYZED
THERMOLYZING
TRAILBLAZER
TRAILBLAZING
TRICHINIZED
TRICHINIZING
UNCANONIZED
UNCANONIZING
UNCIVILIZED
UNMORALIZED
UNMORALIZING
UNORGANIZED
VITRIOLIZED
VITRIOLIZING
VOLATILIZED
VOLATILIZER
VOLATILIZING
WESTERNIZED
WESTERNIZING

ABASTARDIZE
ABNORMALIZE
ACCLIMATIZE
ACCLIMATIZED
ACCLIMATIZER
ACCLIMATIZING
ACCULTURIZE
ACCUSTOMIZE
ACCUSTOMIZED
ACCUSTOMIZING
ACHROMATIZE
ACHROMATIZED
AGRARIANIZE
ALGEBRAIZING
ALLOTROPIZE
ALPHABETIZE
ALPHABETIZED
ALPHABETIZER
ALPHABETIZING
ANACHRONIZE
ANESTHETIZE
ANESTHETIZER

ANHYDRIDIZE
ANTHOLOGIZE
ANTHOLOGIZED
ANTHOLOGIZING
ANTIPATHIZE
ANTITHESIZE
APESTHETIZE
APOTHEOSIZE
APOTHEOSIZED
ARITHMETIZE
ARTERIALIZE
ARTERIALIZED
ASBESTINIZE
ASPHETERIZE
ASTIGMATIZER
ASTROLOGIZE
ASTRONOMIZE
BACHELORIZE
BATTOLOGIZE
BESSEMERIZE
BESSEMERIZED
BESSEMERIZING
BIOGRAPHIZE
BROMOIODIZED
BURKUNDAUZE
CACOPHONIZE
CANNIBALIZE
CANNIBALIZED
CANNIBALIZING
CAPERCAILZIE
CATALEPTIZE
CATALOGUIZE
CATHETERIZE
CATHETERIZED
CATHOLICIZE
CATHOLICIZED
CATHOLICIZING
CHAMPAGNIZE
CHAMPAGNIZED
CHAMPAGNIZING
CHEERFULIZE
CHEMICALIZE
CHORIAMBIZE
CIRCULARIZE
CIRCULARIZED
CIRCULARIZING
COMMEMORIZE
COMMEMORIZED
COMMEMORIZING
COMMUNALIZE
COMMUNALIZED
COMMUNALIZER
COSMOGONIZE
CRYSTALLIZE
CRYSTALLIZED
CRYSTALLIZER
CRYSTALLIZING
DEBENZOLIZE
DECARBONIZE
DECARBONIZED
DECARBONIZER
DECARBURIZE
DECARBURIZED
DECEREBRIZE
DECHORALIZE
DECOLOURIZE
DEFIBRINIZE
DEHYPNOTIZE
DEHYPNOTIZED
DEJUNKERIZE
DEMAGNETIZE
DEMAGNETIZED
DEMAGNETIZER
DEMANGANIZE
DEMEPHITIZE
DEMOCRATIZE
DEMOCRATIZED

DEOXYGENIZE
DEPAUPERIZE
DEPAUPERIZED
DEPERSONIZE
DERACIALIZE
DESACRALIZE
DESENSITIZE
DESENSITIZER
DESEXUALIZE
DESEXUALIZED
DESILVERIZE
DESILVERIZER
DESTERILIZE
DESULFURIZE
DESULFURIZED
DESULFURIZER
DETRIBALIZE
DEVULGARIZE
DIAGONALIZE
DICHOTOMIZE
DICHOTOMIZED
DIPLOMATIZE
DIPLOMATIZED
DISCANONIZE
DISCANONIZED
DISEQUALIZE
DISORGANIZE
DISORGANIZED
DISORGANIZER
DOCUMENTIZE
DOGGERELIZE
DOGGERELIZER
DOGGERELIZING
DOMESTICIZE
DOMESTICIZED
ELECTRALIZE
ELECTRICIZE
ELECTROLYZE
ELECTROLYZED
ELECTROLYZER
ELECTROLYZING
EMBLEMATIZE
EMBLEMATIZED
EMBLEMATIZING
EMULSIONIZE
ENCARNALIZE
ENCARNALIZED
ENCARNALIZING
ENSORCELIZE
ENSORCERIZE
EPENTHESIZE
EQUILIBRIZE
ETHEREALIZE
ETHEREALIZED
ETHEREALIZING
ETYMOLOGIZE
ETYMOLOGIZED
ETYMOLOGIZING
EUDAEMONIZE
EVENTUALIZE
EXAUTHORIZE
EXOSTRACIZE
EXTEMPORIZE
EXTEMPORIZED
EXTEMPORIZER
EXTEMPORIZING
EXTERIORIZE
EXTERIORIZED
EXTERIORIZING
EXTERNALIZE
FACSIMILIZE
FAMILIARIZE
FAMILIARIZED
FAMILIARIZER
FAMILIARIZING
FORMULARIZE
FORMULARIZED

FORMULARIZING
FRACTIONIZATIO
FRACTIONIZE
FRACTIONIZING
FRICTIONIZE
FRICTIONIZED
FRICTIONIZING
FUNCTIONIZE
GENEALOGIZE
GENEALOGIZER
GEOGRAPHIZE
GEOGRAPHIZED
GLYCERINIZE
GLYCYRRHIZIN
GRANULITIZE
GUTTURALIZE
GUTTURALIZING
HIERARCHIZE
HOSPITALIZE
HURRICANIZE
HYDROGENIZE
HYPERBOLIZE
HYPERBOLIZED
HYPOSTATIZE
IMMETHODIZE
IMMORTALIZE
IMMORTALIZED
IMMORTALIZER
IMMORTALIZING
IMPATRONIZE
IMPERIALIZE
IMPERIALIZED
IMPERIALIZING
INFORMALIZE
INTELLIGIZE
INTERNALIZE
ISOCHRONIZE
ISOCHRONIZED
ISOCHRONIZING
JUDICIALIZE
KJELDAHLIZE
LALAPALOOZA
LITHOTOMIZE
LOGOMACHIZE
MALLEABLIZE
MANORIALIZE
MARGINALIZE
MATERIALIZE
MATERIALIZED
MATERIALIZER
MATERIALIZING
MATERNALIZE
MATHEMATIZE
MECHANALIZE
MEMORANDIZE
MEMORIALIZE
MEMORIALIZED
MEMORIALIZER
MEMORIALIZING
MERCHANDIZE
MERORGANIZE
METAPHONIZE
METASTASIZE
METASTASIZED
MIGNIARDIZE
MINIATURIZE
MINIATURIZED
MUSCOVITIZE
MUSCOVITIZED
MUSCULARIZE
MYTHOLOGIZE
MYTHOLOGIZED
MYTHOLOGIZER
MYTHOLOGIZING
NAPHTHALIZE
NATIONALIZE
NATIONALIZED

NATIONALIZER
NATIONALIZING
NEOPAGANIZE
NEUROLOGIZE
NEUROTOMIZE
NITROGENIZE
NITROGENIZED
NITROGENIZING
NONENTITIZE
OBJECTIVIZE
OBJECTIVIZED
OBJECTIVIZING
OBLIVIONIZE
OFFICIALIZE
OLIGARCHIZE
OPTIONALIZE
ORIENTALIZE
ORIENTALIZED
ORIENTALIZING
PAMPHLETIZE
PANCREATIZE
PANTHEONIZE
PARAENESIZE
PASTORALIZE
PATERNALIZE
PECULIARIZE
PECULIARIZED
PEMMICANIZE
PERMORALIZE
PERSONALIZE
PERSONALIZED
PHAGOCYTIZE
PHILOLOGIZE
PHONETICIZE
PHOSPHATIZE
PHOSPHATIZED
PHOSPHORIZE
PLEBEIANIZE
PLEBEIANIZED
POLITZERIZE
PREACHERIZE
PROBABILIZE
PRODIGALIZE
PROLETARIZE
PROSELYTIZE
PROSELYTIZED
PROSELYTIZER
PROTOCITIZEN
PROTOCOLIZE
PROTOXIDIZE
PROTOXIDIZED
RATIONALIZE
RATIONALIZED
RATIONALIZER
REACTUALIZE
RECARBONIZE
RECARBONIZER
RECARBURIZE
RECARBURIZER
REFORESTIZE
REGIONALIZE
REHARMONIZE
RELIGIONIZE
RESTERILIZE
RHYTHMICIZE
ROENTGENIZE
ROMANTICIZE
ROTARIANIZE
SANCTUARIZE
SCHILLERIZE
SCHILLERIZED
SCHILLERIZING
SCHISMATIZE
SCHISMATIZED
SCHISMATIZING
SENSIBILIZE
SIDEREALIZE

SIMULACRIZE
SINGULARIZE
SINGULARIZED
SINGULARIZING
SKELETONIZE
SKELETONIZED
SKELETONIZER
SKELETONIZING
SLUGGARDIZE
SOLILOQUIZE
SOLILOQUIZED
SOLILOQUIZER
SOLILOQUIZING
SOUTHERNIZE
SPECIFICIZE
SPECIMENIZE
SPECIMENIZED
SPHEROIDIZE
STALLIONIZE
STALWARTIZE
STANDARDIZE
STANDARDIZED
STANDARDIZER
STANDARDIZING
SUBSTANTIZE
SUBURBANIZE
SUBVITALIZED
SULPHOBENZID
SYNCHRONIZE
SYNCHRONIZED
SYNCHRONIZER
SYNCHRONIZING
SYNDICALIZE
SYSTEMATIZE
SYSTEMATIZED
SYSTEMATIZER
SYSTEMATIZING
TARANTARIZE
TAUTOLOGIZE
TAUTOLOGIZED
TAUTOLOGIZER
TAXIDERMIZE
TEETOTUMIZE
TELEPATHIZE
TEMPORALIZE
TENEMENTIZE
TETRAKISAZO
TETRAZOTIZE
THEATRICIZE
TOBACCONIZE
TRANQUILIZE
TRANQUILIZER
TRANQUILIZING
TRILLIONIZE
TROPICALIZE
TROPICALIZED
TROPICALIZING
TROPOLOGIZE
TROPOLOGIZED
TROPOLOGIZING
TUBERCULIZE
UNAUTHORIZE
UNAUTHORIZED
UNBRUTALIZE
UNFEUDALIZE
UNLITURGIZE
UNMECHANIZE
UNMODERNIZE
UNMORTALIZE
UNPATRONIZED
UNRECOGNIZED
UNSOLEMNIZE
UNSTERILIZED
UNVERBALIZED
UNVULGARIZE
VAGABONDIZE
VAGABONDIZED

VAGABONDIZER
VAGABONDIZING
VASCULARIZE
VASCULARIZED
VASCULARIZING
VASECTOMIZE
VEGETABLIZE
VERATRINIZE
VERATRINIZED
VERATRINIZING
WOODCOCKIZE
ZOOMORPHIZE

ABOLITIONIZE
ADVERBIALIZE
AESTHETICIZE
ANACEPHALIZE
ANAESTHETIZE
ANAESTHETIZED
ANAESTHETIZER
ANATHEMATIZE
ANGIOSTOMIZE
APAESTHETIZE
APOSTROPHIZE
ATTITUDINIZE
AUTOCATALYZE
BACCHANALIZE
BACTERIOLYZE
CANTHARIDIZE
CELESTIALIZE
CELESTIALIZED
CHAMELEONIZE
CHARACTERIZE
CHARACTERIZED
CHARACTERIZER
CHRONOLOGIZE
CHRONOLOGIZED
COLLECTIVIZE
COLLECTIVIZED
COLLODIONIZE
COMPANIONIZE
COMPANIONIZED
CONSERVATIZE
CONSONANTIZE
CONTEMPORIZE
CONTEMPORIZED
COPOLYMERIZE
COPOLYMERIZED
CORPOREALIZE
CUTICULARIZE
DECAFFEINIZE
DECENTRALIZE
DECICERONIZE
DEMENTHOLIZE
DEMICIVILIZED
DEMILITARIZE
DEMILITARIZED
DEMINERALIZE
DENATURALIZE
DENICOTINIZE
DEPIGMENTIZE
DEPOLYMERIZE
DESILICONIZE
DESULPHURIZE
DESYNONYMIZE
DEVITAMINIZE
DIALECTALIZE
DIALECTICIZE
DIPHTHONGIZE
DIPHTHONGIZED
DISGOSPELIZE
DISHARMONIZE
DISPAUPERIZE
DISSOCIALIZE
DISSYLLABIZE
EDITORIALIZE
EDITORIALIZED

EFFECTUALIZE
EFFEMINATIZE
EMOTIONALIZE
EMOTIONALIZED
ENTOMOLOGIZE
ENTOMOLOGIZED
EPITHALAMIZE
EUCHARISTIZE
EUCHARISTIZED
EVOLUTIONIZE
EXCURSIONIZE
EXPERMENTIZED
EXTRAVAGANZA
FASCISTICIZE
FICTIONALIZED
GEOMETRICIZE
GRAMMATICIZE
HARLEQUINIZE
IMBASTARDIZE
IMPACTIONIZE
INDOCTRINIZE
IRREGULARIZE
LALLAPALOOZA
LAPAROTOMIZE
LEGITIMATIZE
LEGITIMATIZED
LIEDERKRANZ
MALLEABLEIZE
MALLEABLEIZED
MARSUPIALIZE
MELANCHOLIZE
MERCURIALIZE
METAMORPHIZE
MICROSCOPIZE
MINERALOGIZE
MISEMPHASIZE
MISSIONARIZE
MITHRIDATIZE
MONOCHORDIZE
MUNICIPALIZE
MUNICIPALIZED
MYTHOPOETIZE
OUTTYRANNIZE
OVARIOTOMIZE
PALLADIUMIZE
PANEGYRICIZE
PANSEXUALIZE
PARCHMENTIZE
PARENTHESIZE
PENTAMETRIZE
PERFECTIVIZE
PHILIPPICIZE
PHILOSOPHIZE
PHLEBOTOMIZE
PHRENOLOGIZE
PHYLACTERIZE
PHYSIOLOGIZE
POLITICALIZE
POLYCHROMIZE
PORCELAINIZE
PORCELLANIZE
POTENTIALIZE
PRACTICALIZE
PRACTICALIZED
PRESERVATIZE
PROBLEMATIZE
PROPAGANDIZE
PSYCHIATRIZE
PSYCHOLOGIZE
REALISTICIZE
RECAPITALIZE
RECAPITALIZED
SACRAMENTIZE
SARCOPHAGIZE
SECTARIANIZE
SECTARIANIZED
SECTIONALIZE

SECTIONALIZED
SEMICIVILIZED
SEMPITERNIZE
SERPENTINIZE
SOLITUDINIZE
SOLITUDINIZED
SOMNAMBULIZE
SOVEREIGNIZE
SPHERULITIZE
SPIRITUALIZE
SPIRITUALIZED
SPIRITUALIZER
STATISTICIZE
STRYCHNINIZE
SULPHAZOTIZE
SULPHAZOTIZE
SYCOPHANTIZE
SYMPTOMATIZE
TCHERVONETZ
TECHNICALIZE
THEOMORPHIZE
TOURMALINIZE
TRANQUILLIZE
TRANQUILLIZED
TRICHOTOMIZE
UNIFORMALIZE
UNIFORMALIZED
UNIVERSALIZED
UNIVERSITIZE
UNNATURALIZE
UNPOPULARIZE
UNSECULARIZE
VERMILIONIZE
ANTISEPTICIZE
COMMERCIALIZE.
ELECTRICALIZE
ELECTROTONIZE
EMBLEMATICIZE
ENCYCLOPEDIZE
ENHYPOSTATIZE
EPIGRAMMATIZE
EXPERIMENTIZE
FLAMBOYANTIZE
FRACTIONALIZE
HORIZONTALIZE
IMMATERIALIZE
IMPERSONALIZE
IMPROBABILIZE
INDIVIDUALIZE
MELODRAMATIZE
NIGHTINGALIZE
RECIPROCALIZE
RECRYSTALLIZE
STRUCTURALIZE
SUBSTANTIVIZE

SCORING ORDER LIST OF WORDS OVER 10 LETTERS

37
OBJECTIVIZING

36
KATZENJAMMER
OBJECTIVIZED
SCHIZOTHYMIC

35
KJELDAHLIZE
ZANTHOXYLUM
ZOOPRAXISCOPE
ZYGAPOPHYSIS
ZYGOPHYCEOUS

34
EXPERMENTIZED
EXTEMPORIZING
OBJECTIVIZE
OXYGENIZABLE
QUIZZICALITY
RHYTHMIZABLE
SCHIZOMYCETES
SCHIZOTHYMIA

33
BENZALDOXIME
CHAMPAGNIZING
DIPHTHONGIZED
EXPERIMENTIZE
EXTEMPORIZED
GLYCYRRHIZIN
HARLEQUINIZE
ICHTHYIZATION
OBJECTIZATION
POLYCHROMIZE
QUIZZICALLY
RHIZOMORPHIC
SCHIZOMYCETE
SCHIZOPHYTE
SCHIZOTHYME
SQUEEZINGLY
ZOOPHYTOLOGY
ZYGODACTYLIC
ZYGOMORPHIC
ZYMOTECHNICS

32
CHAMPAGNIZED
CHLAMYDOZOAN
COPOLYMERIZED
CRYPTOZYGOUS
DEJUNKERIZE
DEOXYGENIZE
ENCYCLOPEDIZE
EXORCIZEMENT
EXTEMPORIZER
EXTRAVAGANZA
FLAMBOYANTIZE
HAPHAZARDLY
HYBRIDIZABLE
HYPERBOLIZED
JEOPARDIZING
MAXIMIZATION
MYCORRHIZIC
MYTHOLOGIZING
OBJECTIZING
OXYGENIZING
PHENOXAZINE
PHOSPHATIZED
PROTOXIDIZED
PSYCHOLOGIZE
SCHIZOPHRENIA
SCHIZOTRICHIA
SOLILOQUIZING
SYMPATHIZING
SYMPHONIZING
TRANQUILIZING
TRANQUILLIZED
WOODCOCKIZE
ZOOPHARMACY
ZYGOMORPHOUS
ZYGOMYCETOUS
ZYMOTECHNIC

31
AZOPHOSPHORE
BENZALDEHYDE
CHALAZOGAMIC
CHALAZOGAMY
CHROMICIZING
DEHYPNOTIZED
DEMICIVILIZED
DEZINCIFYING
DIPHTHONGIZE
DOXOLOGIZING
EQUILIBRIZE
ERYTHROZYME
EXTEMPORIZE
HAPHAZARDNESS
HYBRIDIZATION
JAROVIZATION
JATEORHIZINE
JEOPARDIZED
JOVIALIZING
LIQUIDIZING
MYTHICIZING
MYTHOLOGIZED
MYTHOPOETIZE
PERFECTIVIZE
PHAGOCYTIZE
PHILOSOPHIZE
PHYLACTERIZE
PSYCHIATRIZE
SCHIZOCHROAL
SCHIZOPELMOUS
SCHIZOPHASIA
SCHIZOPHRENE
SCHIZOTHECAL
SOLILOQUIZED
SYCOPHANTIZE
SYMPATHIZED
SYMPHONIZED
SYNCHRONIZING
THEOMORPHIZE
ZINCOGRAPHIC
ZINCOGRAPHY
ZOOGEOGRAPHY
ZOOXANTHELLA
ZYGOMYCETES

30
ALPHABETIZING
AZOPHOSPHIN
BACCHANALIZE
BAMBOOZLEMENT
BIZYGOMATIC
BOLSHEVIZING
CATHOLICIZING
CHAMPAGNIZE
CHARACTERIZED
COLLECTIVIZED
COMMERCIALIZE
COPOLYMERIZE
DECAFFEINIZE
DEOXIDIZING
DESEXUALIZED
DESYNONYMIZE
DICHOTOMIZED
DIPHYOZOOID
DISEQUALIZE
DOXOLOGIZED
EFFEMINIZING
EMBLEMATICIZE
ENHYPOSTATIZE
ENZYMICALLY
ENZYMOLYTIC
EQUALIZATION
EXAUTHORIZE
EXCURSIONIZE
EXORCIZATION
EXTERIORIZING
HYDROBENZOIN
HYDROLYZATE
HYDRORHIZAL
HYDROZINCITE
HYPERBOLIZE
IMPROBABILIZE
JASPERIZING
JATEORHIZIN
JUBILIZATION
JUDICIALIZE
METAMORPHIZE
MISEMPHASIZE
MYCORRHIZAL
MYTHOLOGIZER
PANSEXUALIZE
PARCHMENTIZE
PHLEBOTOMIZE
PHLYZACIOUS
PHOSPHATIZE
PHOSPHORIZE
PHYSIOLOGIZE
PHYTOBEZOAR
PRIZEFIGHTER
PROTOXIDIZE
QUANTIZATION
QUIZZACIOUS
RHIZOPHAGOUS
SCHISMATIZING
SCHIZOGENETIC
SEMICIVILIZED
SKEPTICIZING
SOLILOQUIZER
SYMPATHIZER
SYMPTOMATIZE
SYNCHRONIZED
SYNONYMIZING
TAXIDERMIZE
THERMOLYZING
TRANQUILIZER
TRANQUILLIZE
VAGABONDIZING
VICTIMIZABLE
ZOMOTHERAPY
ZOOPATHOLOGY
ZOOPHYSICAL
ZOOPHYTICAL
ZYGODACTYLE
ZYGOMATICUM
ZYMOSTHENIC
ZYMOTICALLY

29
ACCLIMATIZING
ACCUSTOMIZING
ACHROMATIZED
ALPHABETIZED
APPETIZINGLY
ASEXUALIZING
AZIMETHYLENE
AZODIPHENYL
AZOPHENYLENE
BENZOHYDROL
BOLSHEVIZED
CACOPHONIZE
CATECHIZATION
CATHOLICIZED
CHARACTERIZER
CHEMICALIZE
CHORIAMBIZE
CHRONOLOGIZED
CINCHONIZING
CIVILIZATORY
COMPANIONIZED
CONTEMPORIZED
DEHYPNOTIZE
DEPOLYMERIZE
DEXTROSAZONE
EFFECTUALIZE
EFFEMINATIZE
EFFEMINIZED
EMBLEMATIZING
EPIGRAMMATIZE
ETYMOLOGIZING
EXOSTRACIZE
EXTERIORIZED
EXTERNIZATION
GEOGRAPHIZED
INOXIDIZING
JARGONIZING
JOURNALIZING
MACADAMIZING
MECHANIZATION
MICROSCOPIZE
MICROZYMIAN
MONARCHIZING
MONOCHORDIZE
MUNICIPALIZED
MUSCOVITIZED
MYOSYNIZESIS
MYTHOLOGIZE
MYZOSTOMIDAN
PAMPHLETIZE
PANEGYRICIZE
PHILIPPICIZE
PHYLLOZOOID
PRACTICALIZED
QUANTIZING
QUINAZOLINE
QUIZZATORIAL
RECOGNIZABLY
RHIZOCARPIC
RHIZOPHILOUS
SACCHARIZING
SARCOPHAGIZE
SCHISMATIZED
SCHIZOCARPIC
SCHIZOGNATH
SCHIZOPODOUS
SCHIZORHINAL
SKEPTICIZED
SOLILOQUIZE
SPECIFICIZE
SPONDYLIZEMA
STRYCHNINIZE
SULPHOBENZID
SYMBOLIZATION
SYMMETRIZING
SYNCHRONIZER
SYNONYMIZED
SYPHILIZING
THERMOLYZED
TRANQUILIZE
VACCINIZATION
VAGABONDIZED
VICTIMIZATION
ZINCOGRAPHER
ZOANTHODEMIC
ZOOMORPHISM

ZYGOSPHENAL
ZYMOPLASTIC

28
ACCLIMATIZED
ACCUSTOMIZED
ACETYLIZABLE
ADVERTIZEMENT
ALCHEMIZING
ALPHABETIZER
ANACEPHALIZE
ANHYDRIDIZE
ANTHROPOZOIC
APOSTROPHIZE
ASEXUALIZED
AZIMUTHALLY
AZOCOCHINEAL
AZOPARAFFIN
AZOSULPHONIC
BACTERIOLYZE
BENZOPHENONE
BIOGRAPHIZE
BIVOCALIZED
BOWDLERIZING
BRAZENFACED
CATECHIZING
CHAMELEONIZE
CHARACTERIZE
CHEERFULIZE
CHLORIDIZING
CHLORODIZING
CINCHONIZED
COLLECTIVIZE
COMMEMORIZING
COMMUNALIZED
COMMUNIZATION
COPPERIZATION
CRYPTOZONATE
CRYSTALLIZING
DACTYLOZOOID
DEEPFREEZING
DEHUMANIZING
DEMEPHITIZE
DESEXUALIZE
DEVOCALIZING
DICHOTOMIZE
ELECTROLYZING
EMBLEMATIZED
EMPATHIZING
EMPHASIZING
ENZYMOLYSIS
EPISCOPIZING
EPITHALAMIZE
EPIZOOTIOLOGY
ETHNOZOOLOGY
ETYMOLOGIZED
EUCHARISTIZED
EUPHEMIZING
FAMILIARIZING
FASCISTICIZE
FICTIONALIZED
FORMULARIZING
FRACTIONIZING
FRICTIONIZING
GAZINGSTOCK
GRAMMATICIZE
GYNECOMAZIA
HETEROZYGOTE
HETEROZYGOUS
HIERARCHIZE
HOPPERDOZER
HORIZONTALITY
HYDROGENIZE
HYPOSTATIZE
IMMETHODIZE
IMMOBILIZING
ISOCHRONIZING
JOURNALIZED
LOGOMACHIZE
MACADAMIZED
MELANCHOLIZE
MERCHANDIZE
MERMITHIZED
MONARCHIZED
MONOZYGOTIC
NAPHTHALIZE
OFFICIALIZE
OZONOSPHERIC
PANEGYRIZING
PEMMICANIZE
RECIPROCALIZE
RHAPSODIZING
RHIZOCARPOUS
SACCHARIZED
SCEPTICIZING
SCHILLERIZING
SCHIZODINIC
SCHIZOGENESIS
SCHIZOGENIC
SCHIZOGONIC
SCHIZOIDISM
SCHIZOPODAL
SCHIZOSTELIC
SCHIZOSTELY
SPECIMENIZED
SULFOBENZOIC
SYMBOLIZING
SYMMETRIZED
SYNCHRONIZE
SYNTHESIZING
SYSTEMATIZING
TCHERVONETZ
TECHNICALIZE
TRICHOTOMIZE
TYPHIZATION
UNIFORMALIZED
VAGABONDIZER
VASCULARIZING
VICTIMIZING
VITALIZINGLY
ZENOGRAPHIC
ZOODYNAMICS
ZYGOMATICUS
ZYMOLOGICAL

27
ACCLIMATIZER
ACETOBENZOIC
ACETYLIZATION
ACHROMATIZE
ADVERBIALIZE
ALCOHOLIZING
ALPHABETIZE
ANTHOLOGIZING
APOTHEOSIZED
BACHELORIZE
BALKANIZING
BAMBOOZLING
BEDAZZLINGLY
BENZYLAMINE
BESSEMERIZING
BOWDLERIZED
BROMOBENZENE
BROMOIODIZED
BRONZESMITH
BURKUNDAUZE
CANNIBALIZING
CANTHARIDIZE
CAPERCAILZIE
CATHETERIZED
CATHOLICIZE
CHALAZOIDITE
CHANNELIZING
CHITINIZATION
CHLORALIZING
CHLORIDIZED
CHLORODIZED
CHORIZONTIC
CHRONOLOGIZE
CIRCULARIZING
CITIZENSHIP
CIVILIZABLE
COMMEMORIZED
COMMUNALIZER
COMMUNIZING
COMPANIONIZE
CONTEMPORIZE
CRITICIZABLE
CRYSTALLIZED
CYCLIZATION
DECARBONIZED
DECARBURIZED
DECIMALIZING
DEEPFREEZED
DEHUMANIZED
DEMENTHOLIZE
DEMOBILIZING
DEMOCRATIZED
DEPAUPERIZED
DEPIGMENTIZE
DESULPHURIZE
DEVITAMINIZE
DEVOCALIZED
DEZINCIFIED
DIAZOMETHANE
DIPLOMATIZED
DISHARMONIZE
DISSYLLABIZE
DOCKIZATION
DOMESTICIZED
DYNAMIZATION
ELECTROLYZED
EMBLEMIZING
EPISCOPIZED
EUHEMERIZING
EXTERIORIZE
EXTERNALIZE
FACSIMILIZE
FACTORIZATION
FAMILIARIZED
FANATICIZING
FICTIONIZING
FISCALIZATION
FORMALIZATION
FORMULARIZED
FORMULIZATION
FRACTIONALIZE
FRICTIONIZED
FRIVOLIZING
GEOGRAPHIZE
GRAPHITIZED
GYROHORIZON
HAZARDOUSLY
HORIZONTALLY
IMMOBILIZED
IMMORTALIZING
IMPACTIONIZE
IMPERIALIZING
INDIVIDUALIZE
ISOCHRONIZED
JOURNALIZER
KYANIZATION
LICHENIZATION
MACADAMIZER
MALLEABLEIZED
MATHEMATIZE
MECHANALIZE
MEIZOSEISMIC
MELODRAMATIZE
MEMORIALIZING
METAPHONIZE
METHODIZING
MITHRIDATIZE
MONARCHIZER
MONZOGABBRO
MUNICIPALIZE
MUSCOVITIZE
MYZOSTOMOUS
NEWSMAGAZINE
NIGHTINGALIZE
PALEOZOOLOGY
PANEGYRIZED
PHANEROZOIC
PHANTOMIZER
PHENMIAZINE
PHONETICIZE
PHONETIZATION
PHRENOLOGIZE
PICRORHIZIN
POLYZOARIUM
PRACTICALIZE
PREACHERIZE
PROBLEMATIZE
PROPAGANDIZE
PROSELYTIZED
PUBLICIZING
PUZZLEHEADED
PYRRODIAZOLE
RAZORMAKING
RECAPITALIZED
RECRYSTALLIZE
RHAPSODIZED
RHIZOGENETIC
SCEPTICIZED
SCHILLERIZED
SCHISMATIZE
SCHIZOCOELE
SCHIZOGENOUS
SCHIZOSPORE
SIPHONOZOOID
SKELETONIZING
SOLVOLYZING
SOMNAMBULIZE
SOPHRONIZING
SPERMATOZOIC
SUBSTANTIVIZE
SUBVITALIZED
SULFOBENZIDE
SULPHATIZING
SULPHURIZING
SYNCRETIZING
SYNTHESIZED
SYSTEMATIZED
SYSTEMIZATION
TRAPEZIFORM
TRICHINIZING
TROPICALIZING
UNMECHANIZE
UNVERBALIZED
VAGABONDIZE
VASCULARIZED
VASECTOMIZE
VULCANIZATION
ZODIOPHILOUS
ZOOCECIDIUM
ZYGOLABIALIS
ZYMOSIMETER

26
ACADEMIZING
ACCLIMATIZE
ACCUSTOMIZE
AESTHETICIZE
ALBUMENIZING
ALBUMINIZING
ALCOHOLIZED
ALKALINIZING
ALKALIZABLE
ANABAPTIZING
ANAESTHETIZED
ANATHEMATIZE
ANTHOLOGIZED
ANTISEPTICIZE
APAESTHETIZE
APPRIZEMENT
ASEPTICIZING
ATMOLYZATION
AUTOCATALYZE
AZADIRACHTA
AZOERYTHRIN
AZOPHENETOLE
AZYGOMATOUS
BAPTIZEMENT
BENZOYLATION
BESSEMERIZED
BILHARZIASIS
BILHARZIOSIS
BUZZERPHONE
CANNIBALIZED
CAPITALIZING
CARAMELIZING
CATABIBAZON
CATABOLIZING
CATHARIZING
CAUSTICIZING
CENOZOOLOGY
CHANNELIZED
CHLORALIZED
CHORIZONTIST
CIRCULARIZED
CIVILIZATION
CLASSICIZING
COAZERVATION
COMMUNALIZE
CONCERTIZING
CONCRETIZING
CONSERVATIZE
CRYSTALLIZER
DECARBONIZER
DECHORALIZE
DECICERONIZE
DECIMALIZED
DEFIBRINIZE
DEFINITIZING
DEMAGNETIZED
DEMILITARIZED
DEMOBILIZED
DESULFURIZED
DEVITALIZING
DIALECTICIZE
DIAMONDIZING
DISPAUPERIZE
DOGGERELIZING
ECONOMIZATION
ELECTROLYZER
EMBEZZLEMENT
EMBLEMATIZE
ENTOMOLOGIZED
EPISTOLIZABLE
EPITOMIZATION
ETHEREALIZING
ETYMOLOGIZE
EUCHARISTIZE
EUHEMERIZED
EUPHONIZING
EVANGELIZING
FACTORIZING
FAMILIARIZER
FANATICIZED
FEDERALIZING
FEMINIZATION
FERTILIZABLE
FEUDALIZATION
FICTIONIZED
FISCALIZING

FOCALIZATION
FORMALIZING
FORMULIZING
FUROMONAZOLE
GALVANIZATION
GEOMETRICIZE
GLYCERINIZE
HARMONIZING
HARZBURGITE
HAZARDOUSNESS
HOMOGENIZER
HORIZONTICAL
IMBASTARDIZE
IMMATERIALIZE
IMMORTALIZED
IMPERIALIZED
IMPERSONALIZE
LEGITIMATIZED
LETHARGIZING
MAGNETIZABLE
MARTYRIZING
MEGAZOOSPORE
MEMORIALIZED
MESMERIZATION
METABOLIZING
MISCOGNIZANT
MIZZENTOPMAN
MIZZENTOPMEN
MONOPOLIZING
NAZIFICATION
OLIGARCHIZE
ORYZIVOROUS
OSMAZOMATIC
OVARIOTOMIZE
OVERPRIZING
OZONOSCOPIC
PALLADIUMIZE
PANEGYRIZER
PARABOLIZING
PARALYZATION
PARENTHESIZE
PECULIARIZED
PEZIZAEFORM
PHILIPPIZER
PHILOLOGIZE
PHILOZOONIST
PIEZOMETRIC
PLASTICIZING
PLEBEIANIZED
POLITICIZING
POPULARIZING
PRESERVATIZE
PRIZEHOLDER
PROBABILIZE
PROSELYTIZER
PULVERIZATOR
PULVERIZING
REBAPTIZATION
RECOGNIZABLE
RECOGNIZANCE
RHIZANTHOUS
RHIZODERMIS
RHIZOPODIST
RHIZOPODOUS
RHIZOSTOMOUS
SEPTICIZATION
SHERARDIZING
SHERBETZIDE
SKELETONIZED
SOPHRONIZED
SPECIALIZING
SPECIMENIZE
SPERMATOZOID
SPHEROIDIZE
SPHERULITIZE
STANZAICALLY
SULPHATIZED
SULPHURIZED
SUMMARIZATION
SYLLABIZING
SYNCRETIZED
SYNDICALIZE
SYNTHESIZER
SYNTHETIZER
SYSTEMATIZER
SYSTEMIZING
TELFORDIZING
THEOLOGIZING
TOBACCONIZE
TRICHINIZED
TROPHOZOOID
TROPICALIZED
TROPOLOGIZING
UNCIVILIZED
UNIFORMALIZE
UNIVERSALIZED
VAPORIZATION
VAPOURIZING
VEGETABLIZE
VERATRINIZING
VERBALIZING
VERMILIONIZE
VOCALIZATION
VOLCANIZING
VULCANIZING
VULGARIZATION
ZAPHRENTOID
ZIGZAGGEDLY
ZOANTHODEME
ZONOCHLORITE
ZOOERYTHRIN
ZOOMAGNETISM
ZOOMORPHIZE
ZOOPLANKTON
ZYGOPLEURAL
ZYGOPTERID
ZYGOPTEROUS
ZYMOGENESIS

25

ADVERTIZING
AGGRANDIZING
ALBUMENIZED
ALBUMINIZED
ALGEBRIZATION
ALKALINIZED
ALKALIZATION
AMMONIZATION
AMORTIZEMENT
ANABAPTIZED
ANACHRONIZE
ANAESTHETIZER
ANTHEROZOOID
ANTIFREEZING
ANTIPATHIZE
APESTHETIZE
APOTHEOSIZE
ARCTICIZING
ARITHMETIZE
ASCIDIOZOOID
ASEPTICIZED
ASPHETERIZE
AUTHORIZATION
AZOFICATION
AZOSULPHINE
AZOTHIONIUM
BACTERIZING
BARBARIZING
BASTARDIZING
BEDIZENMENT
BERGINIZATION
BITUMINIZED
BURGLARIZING
CAPITALIZED
CARAMELIZED
CARBOAZOTINE
CARBOLIZING
CARBONIZING
CARBURIZING
CATABOLIZED
CATALYZATOR
CATEGORIZING
CATHETERIZE
CAUSTICIZED
CELESTIALIZED
CHORIZATION
CHORIZONTES
CICATRIZING
CLASSICIZED
COCAINIZING
COMMEMORIZE
CONCERTIZED
CONCRETIZED
CORPOREALIZE
COSMOGONIZE
CRITICIZING
CRYSTALLIZE
CUTICULARIZE
DECARBONIZE
DECARBURIZE
DECEREBRIZE
DECOLORIZING
DEFERRIZING
DEFINITIZED
DELIMITIZING
DELOCALIZING
DEMAGNETIZER
DEMOCRATIZE
DEMORALIZING
DEPAUPERIZE
DEPOLARIZING
DESILVERIZER
DESULFURIZER
DEVITALIZED
DEVULGARIZE
DIAMONDIZED
DIAZENTITHAL
DIEZEUGMENON
DIPLOMATIZE
DISCANONIZED
DISGOSPELIZE
DIVINIZATION
DOCTRINIZING
DOCUMENTIZE
DOGMATIZING
DOMESTICIZE
DRAMATIZATION
ECONOMIZING
ELECTROLYZE
EMOTIONALIZED
ENCARNALIZING
ENIGMATIZING
ENTHRONIZING
EPENTHESIZE
EPIDOTIZATION
EPITOMIZING
ETHEREALIZED
EVANGELIZED
FAMILIARIZE
FARADIZATION
FEDERALIZED
FERTILIZATION
FEUDALIZING
FLUIDIZATION
FORMULARIZE
FOSSILIZATION
FRACTIONIZE
FRATERNIZING
FRICTIONIZE
FUNCTIONIZE
GALVANIZING
GENERALIZABLE
GEOMETRIZING
HORIZOMETER
HOSPITALIZE
HURRICANIZE
IMMORTALIZER
INFORMALIZE
ISOCHRONIZE
KETONIZATION
LAPAROTOMIZE
LEGITIMIZING
LETHARGIZED
LIEDERKRANZ
LITHOTOMIZE
MAGAZINABLE
MAGNETIZATION
MALLEABLEIZE
MAMMONIZATION
MARBLEIZING
MARMARIZING
MARSUPIALIZE
MATERIALIZING
MEIZOSEISMAL
MEMORANDIZE
MEMORIALIZER
MEMORIZATION
MERCERIZING
MERCURIALIZE
MERCURIZING
MESMERIZING
METABOLIZED
METAMERIZED
MICASIZATION
MICROZOARIAN
MINIMIZATION
MNEMONIZING
MOBILIZATION
MODERNIZATION
MONOLOGIZING
MONOPOLIZED
MUZZLELOADING
NIVELLIZATION
OBLIVIONIZE
OLIGORHIZOUS
OPTIMIZATION
ORGANIZATORY
OSMAZOMATOUS
OVERGLAZING
OZONOSPHERE
PANTHEONIZE
PAPALIZATION
PARABOLIZED
PAUPERIZING
PENTAMETRIZE
PEPTONIZING
PLAGIARIZING
PLASTICIZED
PNEUMATIZED
POLITICALIZE
POLITICIZED
POLYZOARIAL
POPULARIZED
PORCELAINIZE
PORCELLANIZE
PRAGMATIZER
PROSELYTIZE
PROTOCITIZEN
PULVERIZATE
RACEMIZATION
RADIUMIZATION
RECAPITALIZE
RECARBONIZER
RECARBURIZER
REHARMONIZE
REVITALIZING
RHIZOCAULUS
RHIZOMATOUS
RUBBERIZING
SACRAMENTIZE
SCANDALIZING
SCHILLERIZE
SCHIZOSTELE
SECTARIANIZED
SECTIONALIZED
SEMPITERNIZE
SHERARDIZED
SKELETONIZER
SOVEREIGNIZE
SOVIETIZATION
SPECIALIZED
SPERMATOZOAL
SPERMATOZOAN
SPERMATOZOON
SPIRITUALIZED
SPITZENBERG
SPITZENBURG
STANDARDIZING
STIGMATIZING
SUBSIDIZATION
SULFADIAZINE
SULPHAZOTIZE
SUMMARIZING
SYLLOGIZING
SYSTEMATIZE
SZAIBELYITE
TELEPATHIZE
TELFORDIZED
TEMPORIZING
THEATRICIZE
THEOLOGIZED
TROPHOZOITE
TROPOLOGIZED
UNAUTHORIZED
UNPOPULARIZE
UNRECOGNIZED
VASCULARIZE
VERATRINIZED
VITRIOLIZING
VOLATILIZING
VULCANIZATE
VULGARIZING
WESTERNIZING
ZIMENTWATER
ZINCIFEROUS
ZONOLIMNETIC
ZONOSKELETON
ZOOGRAFTING
ZOOMAGNETIC
ZOOPANTHEON
ZOOTHEISTIC
ZOSTERIFORM
ZYGOPTERAN

24

ABNORMALIZE
ACCULTURIZE
ACETONIZATION
ACTUALIZATION
AGGRANDIZED
ALBUMENIZER
ALGEBRAIZED
AMORTIZABLE
ANAESTHETIZE
ANESTHETIZER
ANGIOSTOMIZE
ANGLICIZING
ANIMALIZATION
ANTHEROZOID
ANTHOLOGIZE
APOLOGIZING
APOSTATIZING
ASTIGMATIZER
AUTHORIZING
AZEOTROPISM

AZOOSPERMIA
AZOTOBACTER
BASTARDIZED
BENZINDULINE
BESSEMERIZE
BESTIALIZING
BROMIZATION
BURGLARIZED
BURNETTIZING
BURTONIZATION
CACOZEALOUS
CALABAZILLA
CANNIBALIZE
CATALEPTIZE
CATEGORIZED
CAUSTICIZER
CAUTERIZATION
CENTRALIZING
CICATRIZANT
CICATRIZATE
CIRCULARIZE
COLLODIONIZE
CONCERTIZER
DAMENIZATION
DECENTRALIZE
DECOLORIZED
DELIMITIZED
DELOCALIZED
DEMAGNETIZE
DEMANGANIZE
DEMILITARIZE
DEMINERALIZE
DEMONETIZED
DEMORALIZED
DENICOTINIZE
DEPOLARIZED
DESILICONIZE
DESILVERIZE
DESULFURIZE
DIABOLIZING
DIALECTALIZE
DIALYZATION
DIMERIZATION
DISORGANIZED
DISSOCIALIZE
DOCTRINIZED
DOGGERELIZER
DRAMATIZING
DUCTILIZING
ECZEMATOSIS
EDITORIALIZED
ELECTRICIZE
ELECTROTONIZE
ENCARNALIZED
ENIGMATIZED
ENTHRONIZED
ENTOMOLOGIZE
ENTOZOOLOGY
EPILOGIZING
ETHERIZATION
EVANGELIZER
EVOLUTIONIZE
FANTASIZING
FERTILIZING
FOSSILIZING
FRATERNIZED
GEOMETRIZED
GLAMORIZING
GORMANDIZER
GUTTURALIZING
HORIZONTALIZE
IMMORTALIZE
IMPATRONIZE
IMPERIALIZE
INDOCTRINIZE
INTHRONIZATE
LEGITIMATIZE

LEGITIMIZED
LIBERALIZING
LOCALIZABLE
MAGNETIZING
MALLEABLIZE
MATERIALIZED
MEDIATIZING
MEMORIALIZE
METALLIZATION
METASTASIZED
MICROZOARIA
MIGNIARDIZE
MILITARIZING
MINERALIZING
MINERALOGIZE
MINIATURIZED
MODERNIZING
MONOLOGIZED
MONOPOLIZER
MONZODIORITE
MUSCULARIZE
NITROGENIZING
NORMALIZATION
NOVELIZATION
ODYLIZATION
OPTIMIZING
OSTRACIZATION
OUTTYRANNIZE
PAGANIZATION
PANCREATIZE
PARABOLIZER
PASTEURIZING
PECTIZATION
PECULIARIZE
PEPTIZATION
PERMORALIZE
PERSONALIZED
PLAGIARIZED
PLASTICIZER
PLEBEIANIZE
POLARIZABLE
POLITICIZER
POPULARIZER
PRESSURIZING
PRODIGALIZE
PROTOCOLIZE
PUZZLEPATED
RACIALIZATION
RANDOMIZING
RECARBONIZE
RECARBURIZE
RECOGNIZING
REVITALIZED
RHIZOGENOUS
RINFORZANDO
ROMANTICIZE
ROYALIZATION
SCANDALIZED
SCRUTINIZING
SECULARIZING
SIMULACRIZE
SINGULARIZING
SKELETONIZE
SOCIALIZATION
SOLEMNIZATION
SOLITUDINIZED
SOVIETIZING
SPECIALIZER
SPERMATOZOA
SPIRALIZATION
SPIRITUALIZER
STABILIZATION
STANDARDIZED
STIGMATIZED
STRUCTURALIZE
SUBSIDIZING
SUBTILIZATION

SUBURBANIZE
SULCALIZATION
SULFATIZING
SULFURIZING
SYNTONIZING
TABULARIZING
TEMPORALIZE
TETRAKISAZO
THEOLOGIZER
THEORIZATION
THIADIAZOLE
TRAILBLAZING
TROPICALIZE
TUBERCULIZE
TYRANNIZING
UNCANONIZING
UNFEUDALIZE
UNIVERSITIZE
UNMORALIZING
UNPATRONIZED
UNVULGARIZE
VALORIZATION
VASSALIZING
VENALIZATION
VERATRIZING
VISUALIZING
VITALIZATION
VITRIOLIZED
VOLATILIZED
WESTERNIZED
WINTERIZING
WIZENEDNESS
ZENOCENTRIC
ZINNWALDITE
ZOIDOGAMOUS
ZONAESTHESIA
ZOODENDRIUM
ZOOGONIDIUM

23

ABASTARDIZE
ABOLITIONIZE
ACTIONIZING
ACTUALIZING
AGGRANDIZER
ALBITIZATION
ALLEGORIZING
ALUMINIZING
AMORTIZATION
ANALYZATION
ANATOMIZING
ANESTHETIZE
ANIMALIZING
ANTAGONIZING
ANTITHESIZE
APOSTATIZED
ARBORIZATION
AROMATIZING
AZOCORALLINE
AZOTORRHOEA
BATTOLOGIZE
BENZOINATED
BENZONITRILE
BERZELIANITE
BESTIALIZED
BISTETRAZOLE
BRUTALIZING
BURNETTIZED
CANALIZATION
CANONIZATION
CARNALIZING
CATALOGUIZE
CAUTERIZING
CELESTIALIZE
CENTRALIZED
CITIZENIZING
COLONIZATION

CONSONANTIZE
CREOLIZATION
CURARIZATION
CUTINIZATION
DECOLORIZER
DECOLOURIZE
DEMONTETIZE
DEMORALIZER
DENAZIFYING
DEODORIZING
DEPERSONIZE
DEPOLARIZER
DERACIALIZE
DERMATOZOON
DESACRALIZE
DESCLOIZITE
DETRIBALIZE
DEUTEROZOOID
DEZINCATION
DIALOGIZING
DIAZOBENZENE
DISCANONIZE
DISORGANIZER
DOGGERELIZE
ELECTRIZING
EMOTIONALIZE
ETHEREALIZE
EUDAEMONIZE
EVENTUALIZE
FRATERNIZER
GABERLUNZIE
GASTEROZOOID
GAZETTEERAGE
GELATINIZING
GENEALOGIZER
GEOLOGIZING
GLUCOSAZONE
GLUTTONIZING
IDOLATRIZING
ILLEGALIZING
IODOBENZENE
IRREALIZABLE
ITALICIZING
LABIALIZING
LABILIZATION
LALLAPALOOZA
LIBERALIZED
LOCALIZATION
MARGINALIZE
MATERIALIZER
MATRONIZING
MERORGANIZE
METALIZATION
MEZZOTINTING
MILITARIZED
MINERALIZED
MISSIONARIZE
MONETIZATION
MORALIZATION
MORTALIZING
MOTORIZATION
MUTUALIZING
MUZZLELOADER
NARCOTIZING
NATIONALIZING
NEBULIZATION
NEMATOZOOID
NEOPAGANIZE
NITRIDIZATION
NITROBENZENE
NITROGENIZED
NORMALIZING
OPSONIZATION
ORGANIZABLE
ORIENTALIZING
OSTRACIZING
OVALIZATION

OVERZEALOUS
OZONIFEROUS
PALATIZATION
PALLETIZING
PASTEURIZED
PATRONIZING
PELORIZATION
PENALIZATION
PETROLIZING
PEZIZACEOUS
PLAGIARIZER
PLATINIZING
PLURALIZING
POLARIZATION
POSTURIZING
POTENTIALIZE
POZZUOLANIC
PRESSURIZED
PROLOGUIZER
PROTOZOIASIS
PUZZLINGNESS
RADIALIZATION
REALISTICIZE
RECOGNIZANT
REFORESTIZE
REORGANIZING
REVITALIZER
RHYTHMICIZE
ROBOTIZATION
SCENARIZING
SCLEROTIZED
SCRUTINIZED
SECTARIANIZE
SECTIONALIZE
SECULARIZED
SERMONIZING
SERPENTINIZE
SINGULARIZED
SLENDERIZING
SLUGGARDIZE
SOCIALIZING
SOLEMNIZING
SOLIDARIZING
SOUTHERNIZE
SPIRITUALIZE
SPLENIZATION
STABILIZATOR
STABILIZING
STALWARTIZE
STANDARDIZER
STATISTICIZE
STIGMATIZER
STYLIZATION
SUBERIZATION
SUBTILIZING
TABULARIZED
TAUTOLOGIZED
TOTEMIZATION
TOURMALINIZE
TRAPEZOIDAL
TROPOLOGIZE
TUBERIZATION
TUBULIZATION
UNAUTHORIZE
UNCANONIZED
UNMODERNIZE
UNMORALIZED
UNSECULARIZE
URBANIZATION
VERATRINIZE
VOLATILIZER
ZINGIBERENE
ZONESTHESIA
ZOOSPORANGE

22

ALDOLIZATION

ALLEGORIZED
ALLOTROPIZE
ANALOGIZING
ANTAGONIZED
ARTERIALIZED
ASBESTINIZE
ASTRONOMIZE
ATOMIZATION
ATTITUDINIZE
BENZONITROL
BISTRIAZOLE
BIZARRENESS
BLIZZARDOUS
CENTRALIZER
CITIZENIZED
CITIZENRIES
DEBENZOLIZE
DENATURALIZE
DENIZENATION
DERATIZATION
DESENSITIZER
DIAGONALIZE
DISORGANIZE
DISSEIZORESS
EDITORIALIZE
ELASTICIZER
ELECTRALIZE
ELECTRICALIZE
EMULSIONIZE
ENCARNALIZE
ENSORCELIZE
ENSORCERIZE
ERGOTIZATION
EULOGIZATION
GASTROZOOID
GELATINIZED
GENEALOGIZE
GENERALIZED
GLUTTONIZED
IDEALIZATION
IDOLATRIZED
ILLEGALIZED
IRREGULARIZE
ITEMIZATION
LAICIZATION
LALAPALOOZA
LATERALIZING
LEGALIZATION
LIBERALIZER
LINEARIZATION
LITERALIZING
MANORIALIZE
MATERIALIZE
MATERNALIZE
METASTASIZE
MEZZOTINTED
MINERALIZER
MINIATURIZE
MISSIONIZER
NATIONALIZED
NATURALIZING
NEOLOGIZING
NEUROTOMIZE
NEUTRALIZING
NONPARTIZAN
OPTIONALIZE
ORGANIZATION
ORGANZINING
ORIENTALIZED
PARAENESIZE
PASTEURIZER
PASTORALIZE
PATERNALIZE
PATRIZATION
PERSONALIZE
POETIZATION
PROLETARIZE
PROTOZOONAL
PUZZLEDNESS
RATIONALIZED
REACTUALIZE
REGULARIZED
REORGANIZED
SANCTUARIZE
SATIRIZABLE
SCRUTINIZER
SENSIBILIZE
SENSITIZATION
SENSUALIZING
SERIALIZATION
SIGNALIZING
SIZABLENESS
SLENDERIZED
SOLIDARIZED
SOLITUDINIZE
SOLMIZATION
STANDARDIZE
STERILIZATION
SUBSTANTIZE
TARTRAZINIC
TAUTOLOGIZER
TEETOTUMIZE
TENDERIZING
TENEMENTIZE
TETRAZOLIUM
TRAILBLAZER
UNBRUTALIZE
UNMORTALIZE
UNORGANIZED
UNSOLEMNIZE
UNSTERILIZED
ZONOCILIATE
ZOOCULTURAL
ZOOPARASITE

21

ADENIZATION
AGGUTINIZE
AGRARIANIZE
ALLEGORIZER
ANTAGONIZER
ARSENIZATION
ASTROLOGIZE
DENATURIZER
DESENSITIZE
DESTERILIZE
DESTINEZITE
DIAZOTIZING
DUALIZATION
ESTERIZATION
ETERNIZATION
GELATINIZER
GENERALIZER
GRANULITIZE
GUTTURALIZE
IDOLATRIZER
IDOLIZATION
INTELLIGIZE
INTERMEZZOS
IRIDIZATION
LATERALIZED
LATERIZATION
LITERALIZED
MEZZOTINTER
NASALIZATION
NATIONALIZER
NATURALIZED
NESSLERIZED
NEUROLOGIZE
NEUTRALIZED
NITROGENIZE
NODULIZING
NOTARIZATION
NUPTIALIZE
POLITZERIZE
PROTOZOEAN
PUZZLEATION
RATIONALIZER
RAZZBERRIES
REGIONALIZE
REGULARIZER
RELIGIONIZE
REORGANIZER
ROENTGENIZE
ROUTINIZING
RURALIZATION
SAILORIZING
SENSITIZING
SENSUALIZED
SERIALIZING
SIDEREALIZE
SINGULARIZE
SOLARIZATION
STERILIZING
TANTALIZING
TARTARIZING
TAUTOLOGIZE
TELLURIZING
TERRORIZING
TETANIZATION
TOTALIZATION
TRULLIZATION
TUTORIZATION
ULTRAZEALOUS
UNIONIZATION
UNLITURGIZE
UNNATURALIZE
URALITIZING
ZOISITIZATION
ZOOLOGIZING

20

ARTERIALIZE
AZOTETRAZOLE
ENOLIZATION
INTERNALIZE
LIONIZATION
LITERALIZER
LORENZENITE
NATIONALIZE
NATURALIZER
NEUTRALIZER
NONENTITIZE
ORIENTALIZE
RATIONALIZE
REALIZATION
RESTERILIZE
ROTARIANIZE
STALLIONIZE
TARANTARIZE
TOTALIZATOR
TRILLIONIZE
UTILIZATION
ZEALOUSNESS
ZEOLITIZING

19

OZONIZATION
TETRAZOTIZE

The Newnes Reference Series includes:

English Language:

Newnes Pocket English Dictionary
Newnes Pocket Thesaurus of English Words
Newnes Guide to English Usage
Newnes Pocket Dictionary of Quotations
Newnes Pocket Crossword Dictionary

Foreign Language Dictionaries and Phrasebooks:

Newnes French Dictionary
Newnes German Dictionary
Newnes Italian Dictionary
Newnes Spanish Dictionary
Newnes Arabic Phrase Book
Newnes French Phrase Book
Newnes German Phrase Book
Newnes Greek Phrase Book
Newnes Italian Phrase Book
Newnes Portuguese Phrase Book
Newnes Russian Phrase Book
Newnes Spanish Phrase Book

Other subjects:

Newnes Concise Dictionary of Greek and Roman Mythology
Newnes Pocket Dictionary of Business Terms
Newnes Pocket Dictionary of Wines
Newnes Pocket Gazetteer of the World
Newnes Pocket Medical Dictionary